MACMILLAN
COMPENDIUM

THE
CONFEDERACY

**SELECTIONS FROM THE
FOUR-VOLUME**

Macmillan *Encyclopedia of the Confederacy*

MACMILLAN LIBRARY REFERENCE USA

Simon & Schuster Macmillan
New York

Prentice Hall International
London Mexico City New Delhi Singapore Sydney Toronto

Produced and Designed by Miller Williams Design Associates, Mundelein, IL USA

Cartography by Donald S. Frazier, Abilene, TX USA

Macmillan Library Reference USA
Simon & Schuster Macmillan
1633 Broadway, 5th Floor
New York, NY 10019

Manufactured in the United States of America.

printing number
1 2 3 4 5 6 7 8 9 10

Library of Congress Cataloging-in-Publication Data

The Confederacy
          p.   cm. — (Macmillan compendium)
Includes index.
ISBN 0-02-864920-6 (alk. paper)
1. Confederate States of America—History—Dictionaries. 2. United States—History—Civil War, 1861-1865—Dictionaries. I. Series.
E487.C723   1997
973.7 ' 13—dc21   97-23462
                                                                            CIP

This paper meets the requirements of ANSI/NISO Z39.48-1992 (Permanence of Paper).

THE
CONFEDERACY

The Confederacy
Table of Contents

CONTENTS

CONTENTS

Preface

This single-volume is the one reference book on the Confederacy. It is garnered and assembled from the award-winning heritage of the four-volume Macmillan *Encyclopedia of the Confederacy*.

The legacy of the multivolume encyclopedia set goes almost unmatched in honors and awards for its outstanding contribution to Confederate studies. Foremost among the encyclopedia's accolades is the honor of winning the prestigious Douglas Southall Freeman History Award in recognition for outstanding scholarship in the field of Southern history.

Originally edited by Richard N. Current, the text in the multivolume encyclopedia, and in these pages, reflects his distinguished professorship at the University of North Carolina. Current's distinction came from his past presidency of the Southern Historical Association, and his authorship of 17 books and numerous articles.

Many other noted historians, experts, and professors contributed to the original multivolume Confederacy encyclopedia, and selected efforts are presented in this volume. For complete author information, please consult the multivolume set.

From such peerage comes this single-volume encyclopedia of a nation called the Confederate States of America. The *Macmillan Compendium*, like its parent set, treats the Confederacy as a working nation unto itself and reflects that view throughout the text.

It is no simple editorial task to take the 2,200 pages of the multivolume work and publish a 1,200-page version; our editors, therefore, selected the most relevant articles with complete bibliographies and cross-references, and presented them for the most part as whole, uncut selections (rather than trying to edit down each of the multivolume's articles into pieces that would fit into 1,200 pages). Thus, this volume is an overview of the Confederacy.

The *Macmillan Compendium: The Confederacy* is the concise, one source reference for discussion, clarification, definition, research, and elucidation for the reader on Confederate history and issues.

— Macmillan Library Reference

Abbreviations and Symbols

A.D. *anno Domini*, in the year of the (our) Lord
Adj. Gen. adjutant general
Adm. admiral
Ala. Alabama
A.M. *ante meridiem*, before noon
Ariz. Arizona
Ark. Arkansas
b. born; beam (interior measurement of width of a ship)
B.C. before Christ
brig. brigade
Brig. Gen. brigadier general
c. *circa*, about, approximately
Calif. California
Capt. captain
cf. *confer*, compare
chap. chapter (pl., chaps.)
cm centimeters
Col. colonel
Colo. Colorado
Comdr. commander
Como. commodore
Conn. Connecticut
Cpl. corporal
C.S. Confederate States
C.S.A. Confederate States of America, Confederate States Army
CSS Confederate States ship
cwt. hundredweight (equals 772 lbs.)
d. died
D.C. District of Columbia
Del. Delaware
diss. dissertation

div. division
dph. depth of hold
ed. editor (pl., eds.); edition; edited by
e.g. *exempli gratia*, for example
Eng. England
enl. enlarged
Ens. ensign
esp. especially
et al. *et alii*, and others
etc. *et cetera*, and so forth
exp. expanded
f. and following (pl., ff.)
1st Lt. first lieutenant
fl. *floruit*, flourished
Fla. Florida
frag. fragment
ft. feet
Ga. Georgia
Gen. general
Gov. governor
HMS Her Majesty's ship
ibid. *ibidem*, in the same place (as the one immediately preceding)
i.e. *id est*, that is
Ill. Illinois
Ind. Indiana
Kans. Kansas
km kilometers
Ky. Kentucky
l. length
La. Louisiana
lb. pound (pl., lbs.)
Lt. lieutenant
Lt. Col. lieutenant colonel

Lt. Comdr. lieutenant commander
Lt. Gen. lieutenant general
m meters
M.A. Master of Arts
Maj. Major
Maj. Gen. major general
Mass. Massachusetts
mi. miles
Mich. Michigan
Minn. Minnesota
Miss. Mississippi
Mo. Missouri
Mont. Montana
n. note
N.C. North Carolina
n.d. no date
N.Dak. North Dakota
Neb. Nebraska
Nev. Nevada
N.H. New Hampshire
N.J. New Jersey
N.Mex. New Mexico
no. number (pl., nos.)
n.p. no place
n.s. new series
N.Y. New York
Okla. Oklahoma
Oreg. Oregon
p. page (pl., pp.)
Pa. Pennsylvania
pdr. pounder (weight of projectile in pounds; pl., pdrs.)
pl. plural, plate (pl., pls.)
P.M. *post meridiem*, after noon
Pres. president
pt. part (pl., pts.)

Pvt. private
r. reigned; ruled; river
Rear Adm. rear admiral
regt. regiment
Rep. representative
rev. revised
R.I. Rhode Island
S.C. South Carolina
S.Dak. South Dakota
sec. section (pl., secs.)
2d Lt. second lieutenant
Sen. senator
ser. series
Sgt. sergeant
sing. singular
sq. square
supp. supplement; supplementary
Tenn. Tennessee
Tex. Texas
trans. translator, translators; translated by; translation
U.S. United States
USS United States ship
Va. Virginia
var. variant; variation
vol. volume (pl., vols.)
Vt. Vermont
Wash. Washington
Wis. Wisconsin
W.Va. West Virginia
Wyo. Wyoming
° degress
′ feet; minutes
″ inches; seconds
£ pounds
? uncertain; possibly; perhaps

Key to Map Symbols

	Troops, Confederate		Elevation
	Troops, Union		River
	Cavalry, Confederate		Railroad
	Cavalry, Union		Unfinished Railroad
	Tactical Movement, Confederate		Road
	Tactical Movement, Union		State Boundary
	Strategic Movement, Confedederate		
	Strategic Movement, Union		
	Retreat		
	Engagement		
	Artillery		
	Encampment		
	Headquarters		
	Fortifications		Building
	Entrenchments		Church
			Village
	Casemate Ironclad		Town, Strategic
	Gunboat		Town, Tactical
	Monitor		Pontoon Bridge
	Warship		Bridge

AFRICAN AMERICAN FORGEWORKERS

Critically important to the Confederate war effort, African Americans often comprised half or more of the labor force of a given foundry. Furnaces were located in Virginia, eastern Tennessee, central Alabama, and northern Georgia. Principal manufacturers were located in Norfolk, Richmond, Charlotte, Fayetteville, Charleston, Columbia, Macon, Atlanta, Columbus, Selma, New Orleans, and Memphis. Available records and research permit no comprehensive statements for all establishments, but known situations in a number of specific firms provide representative pictures.

When the Civil War began, the Tredegar Iron Works of Richmond, Virginia, the South's preeminent iron manufacturer, employed 900 workers, of whom about 100 were slaves. As Northern and immigrant laborers left and native white workers enlisted for military service, the number of slaves in the work force increased. By 1864, blacks held over half of all Tredegar's 2,500 jobs. Many were laborers in mines and charcoal pits, but many also held more skilled positions in the rolling mill and blacksmith shops.

The Shelby Iron Company in central Alabama employed 350 to 400 slaves throughout the war, some three-fourths of their total force. They performed service in all aspects of work, with 70 to 100 employed in skilled positions.

Near the end of the war, Secretary of the Navy Stephen R. Mallory reported to Jefferson Davis that he needed 677 black workers and 675 white workers in his ordnance and machinery works at Richmond, Augusta, Charlotte, and Selma. This ratio of black to white workers appears in the records of other firms as well.

BIBLIOGRAPHY

Dew, Charles B. *Iron Maker to the Confederacy: Joseph R. Anderson and the Tredegar Iron Works.* New Haven, 1966.
Starobin, Robert S. *Industrial Slavery in the Old South.* New York, 1970.

ROBERT H. MCKENZIE

AFRICAN AMERICANS IN THE CONFEDERACY

More than a third of the population of the Confederate States of America was African American. The 9.1 million people living in the eleven future Confederate states as of 1860 consisted of 5.5 million whites and 3.6 million blacks. Of the latter, approximately 3.5 million were slaves. During the Civil War, these blacks played an important role in keeping the Confederate war machine functioning. The Confederacy was dealt a heavy blow, therefore, when President Abraham Lincoln's Emancipation Proclamation impelled at least half a million and perhaps as many as a million of the Confederate blacks to flee their posts in order to follow or serve with the Union forces.

Following the firing on Fort Sumter and Lincoln's call to arms in April 1861, some Southern free blacks rallied to the cause of their region. Historian Emory Thomas has written that "during 1861 several groups of free black Southerners offered themselves as soldiers to the Confederate War Department, and although the War Office rejected each of these applications, some blacks did serve in the Southern armies." In Louisiana, some well-to-do African Americans

> *. . . it seems strange that some southern blacks volunteered to aid the bastion of slavery.*

from New Orleans were allowed to form regiments of free blacks who served as home guards. Their function was to protect their state against invaders. In the light of subsequent developments—emancipation and the antislavery crusade into which the war turned—it seems strange that some Southern blacks volunteered to aid the bastion of slavery. Most were caught up, however, in the general Southern view of Northerners as aggressively bent on imposing their materialistic way of life on the South. Moreover, the president, the U.S. Congress, and the Republican party declared vigorously at the beginning of the war that the North's sole aim was to preserve the Union and that there was no intention to disrupt slavery where it existed.

Although the Union had twice as many states and people as the South and far more naval, financial, and industrial resources, the Confederacy had better generals at the outset and was fighting a defensive war on home ground with soldiers accustomed to hunting, riding, and outdoor life. Alongside these strong points of the Confederacy should be placed the value of its black population, only 3 percent of which was free. (In contrast, in the five border slave states on the Union side—Delaware, Maryland, Kentucky, Missouri, and later West Virginia—the 150,000 free blacks constituted 25 percent of the black population of 591,000. Baltimore alone had nearly 26,000 free blacks, more than any other city North or South.) In the North, all 238,000 blacks listed in the 1860 census were free persons, since slavery had ceased north of the Mason-Dixon line and the Ohio River. Often overlooked is the importance to the Confederacy of having 3.4 million persons who could be forcibly mobilized for the war effort. They were used in two ways: first, as military laborers, freeing white males to fight, and second, as workers on the home front.

Blacks as Military Laborers. The Confederate armies were greatly aided by the use of blacks, especially slaves, as military laborers. The historian Bell I. Wiley has written that

> much of the hard work entailed by military activities of the Confederacy was performed by Negroes. The aversion of the white soldier to menial tasks was one reason for this, but it was not the only one. Conservation of white man-power for fighting purposes was an appreciable factor. Every [black] wielding a shovel released a [white] for the ranks.

Southern blacks loaded, transported, and unloaded supplies. They dug trenches, built roads, erected barricades, constructed fortifications, repaired and built railroads, bridges, trestles, and tunnels, and cooked and served food. Some troops raised money to hire black cooks, and in 1862 the Confederate Congress enacted a law authorizing four black cooks per company, to be paid fifteen dollars a month if free and used with their master's permission if slave. Blacks washed uniforms, shined boots, mended clothes and tents, moved ordnance, and generally did much of the drudgery for the armed forces. Wiley points to the use of blacks "as teamsters, many of whom were expert from prior plantation experience," and adds that "slaves and free Negroes were employed as hospital attendants, ambulance drivers, and stretcher bearers." In contrast, far more Union army soldiers were tied down in such tasks, since the Union did not have a large pool of free black labor to take over these noncombat duties.

Blacks' Work on the Home Front. African Americans in the Confederacy were also essential as workers throughout the economy. Plantations continued to function under the supervision of the mistress of the house when masters, sons, overseers, and neighbors enlisted. Even though overseers supervising twenty or more slaves were exempted from the draft in 1862, many plantations and smaller farms functioned without the presence of any white males to supervise the slaves' labor.

Blacks manned the factories of the Confederacy, too, such as the Tredegar Iron Works in Richmond, the South's leading manufacturer and a crucial cog in turning out Confederate war goods. Historian James H. Brewer says that this firm "at the peak of its productivity . . . employed over 1,200 Negroes, free and slave, and 1,200 whites. Negro manpower enabled this plant to fulfill vital contracts with the various bureaus of the War Department." As the war continued, the plant became increasingly dependent on blacks, who were "engaged in highly skilled tasks previously performed almost exclusively by white technicians."

Slave-Master Relations. These wartime experiences affected the relationships of slaves and masters. When large numbers of slaves were pulled from plantations and urban households to work as military laborers or in arms production, subtle changes developed in how they viewed themselves. Their sense of self-esteem and relative freedom inevitably increased as they fulfilled important duties under new circumstances. Their newfound attitude of self-confidence did not escape the notice of whites, who worried about the consequences. According to historian Joseph Reidy, slavemasters objected to slaves being employed in ways other than as field hands and house servants. To have them taken over by governmental and military authorities for other uses in the war effort tended, they thought, to undermine the institution of slavery.

Objections were made to use of slaves as mechanics in work outside of the plantation. The trouble, according to one observer, was that slaves were brought "into habitual contact with white men, beyond those to whom they owe obedience. It is at the hazard of themselves and of society when this occurs." Others nevertheless saw the need to utilize slaves in any fashion necessary to save the Confederacy, since President Lincoln seemed increasingly determined to free them and use them against the South.

The dislocations caused by the war also had an impact on slave-master relations. For example, the flight of coastal plantation owners inland with their entire plantations temporarily saved them from the invading Union armies, but the uprooting of the plantation made it almost impossible physically and psychologically to retain the traditional patterns. As historian Clarence Mohr has written, "the entire refugee process served to undermine the traditional authority structure of previously autonomous and self-contained plantation units."

Blacks as Soldiers. As in the Confederacy, free blacks in the Union volunteered to serve at the start of the war, hoping to strike a blow at slavery. But since the Lincoln administration had five border slave states on the Union's side (Virginia's western counties seceded from that state in 1861 and became West Virginia in 1863), it could not initially make the conflict an antislavery war, nor did it especially want to. Hence, free blacks were turned away. But pressures by abolitionists, Congress, and generals, coupled with Union losses in the East, caused Lincoln to conclude, as he later recalled, that "things had gone on from bad to worse, until I felt that we must change our tactics, or lose the game. I now determined upon the emancipation policy." In a preliminary proclamation on September 22, 1862, and the final proclamation in 1863, he declared slaves in areas still in rebellion on January 1, 1863, to be free. He also urged slaves to flee their masters and serve in the Union armies.

The first unit of free Southern blacks accepted by the Union was the First Louisiana Native Guards, which entered the army on September 27, 1862, five days after the preliminary proclamation. Confederate defenders had fled when Union forces seized New Orleans on April 26, 1862, but the home guard regiments that had been formed by free blacks remained. Union Gen. Benjamin Butler was puzzled as to why they were fighting for the Confederacy, and their leaders explained that they volunteered so they could serve on their own terms in a dignified role rather than being impressed as military laborers and that they hoped to improve the standing of blacks and increase their chances for equality by serving alongside whites. With Federal forces occupying the city, they were willing to switch to the side more likely to end slavery.

As soon as he received word of Lincoln's proclamation, Butler enrolled this unit officially. Two other regiments entered in October and November 1862 as the Second and Third Louisiana Native Guards. These men were the first of what would become a torrent of Southern blacks, mostly former slaves, joining the Union army. Nearly 200,000 soldiers and sailors of African descent served in all, about 140,000 of them former slaves and the rest free blacks, mostly from the North. The first regiment of former slaves to enlist was the First South Carolina Volunteers. This regiment had been organized in April 1862 by Union Gen. David Hunter. He had done so contrary to the policy at that time of the Lincoln administration. Hunter commanded the Port Royal and Sea Islands area of the South Carolina and Georgia coast, which had been taken by Union forces in November 1861. Lacking authority and funds to pay or provision this regiment, Hunter had had to disband it in August, keeping together only Company A (about one hundred men) as a nucleus around which to rebuild the regiment when policy changed and authorization was forthcoming. During November 1862, Company A participated in a coastal raid in which they freed 155 slaves and killed or captured a dozen Confederate

defenders. With Company A as a nucleus, the First South Carolina Volunteer Regiment was rebuilt and taken into the Union army in January 1863. Also joining that month was the First Kansas Colored Volunteers, a regiment made up primarily of runaway slaves congregated in Kansas.

Emancipation Policy. President Lincoln became increasingly convinced that emancipation was the key to victory. In August 1864, he noted that emancipation was "inducing the colored people to come bodily over from the rebel side to ours." Answering a suggestion that the emancipation policy should be abandoned as soon as the Union was victorious,

> **". . . no human power can subdue this rebellion without using the Emancipation lever as I have done."**

Lincoln replied that blacks would desert the Union ranks and return to the Confederate side in the face of such betrayal. He pointed out: "Drive back to the support of the rebellion the physical force which the colored people now give and promise us, and neither the present nor any coming administration can save the Union. Take from us and give to the enemy the hundred and thirty, forty, or fifty thousand colored persons now serving us as soldiers, seamen, and laborers, and we can not longer maintain the contest." He told Judge Joseph Mills of Wisconsin that "no human power can subdue this rebellion without using the Emancipation lever as I have done. Freedom has given us the control of 200,000 able bodied men, born and raised on southern soil. It will give us more yet. Just so much has it subtracted from the strength of our enemies." And in September 1864 he wrote in a letter of the physical force represented by the African American soldiers: "Keep it and you can save the Union. Throw it away and the Union goes with it."

Lincoln's enthusiasm was not shared universally in the North. Some Union commanders were very pleased with the African American troops, but others had less regard for them. Early in the war, before the Emancipation Proclamation was issued, some Union generals—such as William S. Harney in Missouri, Don Carlos Buell in Tennessee, and George B. McClellan in Virginia—had enforced the Fugitive Slave Law and restored to their owners those slaves who escaped and made their way to the Union lines.

A different stance was taken by Gen. Benjamin Butler. When three runaway slaves came to Fort Monroe, along Virginia's southeastern coast at Hampton, on May 23, 1861, Butler questioned them closely and learned that they were field hands who were being employed along with other slaves to build fortifications for the Confederates. When a Southern major came on behalf of Col. Charles Mallory to reclaim the three runaways, Butler labeled them "contrabands of war," saying they were being used by the Confederate States as part of the war effort. Hence, he confiscated them and claimed them as property of the United States.

In August 1861 the U.S. Congress, seeing the value of drawing black labor from the Confederates, passed a law confiscating any property, including slaves, used in the Confederate war effort. In July 1862 Congress enacted another law freeing the slaves of masters who were "disloyal or treasonous" or bore arms against the United States. Lincoln's Emancipation Proclamation, issued by the commander in chief, struck yet another blow at slavery. Finally, the Thirteenth Amendment ending slavery was proposed by Congress early in 1865 and ratified by the states in December.

Treatment of Black Soldiers. Confederate reaction initially caused much hardship for black soldiers in the Union army. Authorities announced two somewhat contradictory policies concerning Union soldiers of African descent: first, that none would be allowed to surrender, meaning they would be killed on the field of combat; and second, that any free blacks captured would be sold into slavery in the Deep South. Both policies were abandoned before long, however, because of the consequences. Black soldiers, with no chance to surrender, fought to the death, even in hopeless situations, adding to Confederate casualties. And the Lincoln administration pledged to impose "hard labor" on one Confederate prisoner of war for every Union soldier sold into slavery.

Black soldiers in the Union army suffered other discrimination, also. They were paid less than their white counterparts until Congress equalized their pay in 1864, and they did not receive the bonuses, pensions, and support for dependents other troops did. Moreover, black soldiers served in segregated units under white officers; only one hundred African Americans were officers, mostly in the Louisiana Native Guard regiments or as chaplains or physicians. Nonetheless, they fought valiantly. Some 37,000 died in combat, a mortality rate 40 percent higher than for white Union soldiers.

Desertions by Southern Blacks. Naval forces, Union and Confederate, had integrated crews (not until World War I did the U.S. Navy become segregated). In the famous encounter between USS *Monitor* and CSS *Virginia* in March 1862, about one-third of the *Monitor*'s crew was black. African Americans, usually slaves, served on Confederate ships, too, both merchant and naval. Robert Smalls and his fellow slave crewmates on the Confederate vessel *Planter* took that steamship out of Charleston Harbor early one morning in May 1862 when its three white officers were ashore. In a well-planned escape, the crew members were joined by seven women and children, including two wives, one sister, and four youngsters. They steamed past the

Confederate guns with Smalls wearing the captain's hat and waving as if he were the captain. Then they hastily ran up a flag of truce to keep the Union blockading ships from firing on them. *Planter,* which was an armed steamer used for dispatch and transportation purposes, was taken over by the U.S. Navy, along with its six guns.

Smalls's escape was spectacular, but many other slaves abandoned their masters in less dramatic ways. Most were inspired by the Emancipation Proclamation, but some fled to the Union lines before the proclamation was issued. Partly they were driven by Confederate actions, state and national, to force slaves and free blacks to contribute to the South's war effort. In Virginia, for example, the state legislature passed laws, such as those in October 1862 and February 1863, that required slave owners to furnish their bondsmen for military labor with compensation to the owners and also required free blacks to pay, along with whites, a poll tax to support the war. The tax on free blacks was set at sixty cents in February 1863 and then was increased to two dollars two months later, with slave owners required to pay ninety cents for every slave twelve years of age and older. Many free blacks resented having to pay a tax to support a war intended to keep their people in slavery.

Fears of slave uprisings and conspiracies permeated the South's white population, although later, it became a staple of Southern belief that the slaves had been loyal. True, most remained at their stations and worked as before, and there were only a few isolated cases of slaves attacking their masters. But about a million deserted to the Union side at the first opportune moment, usually when Northern troops reached their vicinity. This steady erosion, which began before the Emancipation Proclamation and swelled thereafter, played a large role in weakening the Confederate side. The twin impact of drawing African Americans away from the Confederate side and of adding nearly 180,000 fresh troops to the war-weary Union ranks during the last two and a half years of the war helped tip the scales. At one point there were more black soldiers on the Union side than the total number of men able to engage actively in combat on the Confederate side. In addition, the emancipation policy persuaded England, France, and other European nations not to come to the aid of the Confederacy. This turn of events caused the Confederates to consider enlisting black soldiers and inaugurating a diplomatic approach based on ending slavery.

Arming Slaves as Soldiers in the South. As early as the summer of 1863, a council of Confederate officers had considered the question of arming slaves and enlisting them in the military but rejected the idea. During 1864, more talk of developing black soldiers to fight in the Confederate ranks was heard. President Jefferson Davis opposed the plan in November 1864, but by March of the next year, he was converted to the proposal. While still believing that slavery was the best way for the two races to coexist in the South, Gen. Robert E. Lee said in January that if military necessity made it imperative to use black soldiers he would do so, though on the basis that any such troops would be set free and that slavery in time would have to be abandoned. Writing on February 18, Lee indicated his support of a bill in the Confederate House to arm and free 200,000 slaves: "I think the measure not only expedient but necessary. The enemy will certainly use them against us if he can get possession of them. . . I think those who are employed should be freed. It would be neither just nor wise, in my opinion, to require them to serve as slaves."

Opposition to enlisting the slaves was strong. Gen. Howell Cobb, an ardent secessionist from Georgia, said that the proposal

to make soldiers of our slaves is the most pernicious idea that has been suggested since the war began. . . . Use all the Negroes you can get for all purposes for which you need them but don't arm them. The day you make soldiers of them is the beginning of the end of the revolution. If slaves make good soldiers, our whole theory of slavery is wrong.

The Confederate Congress, after considerable debate, enacted a modified law on March 13, 1865, permitting the arming of 300,000 slaves as soldiers. The measure came too late. Lee surrendered to Ulysses S. Grant less than a month later at Appomattox on April 9. Meanwhile, a number of black units were formed and began drilling, but the war ended before they could be mustered in.

The decision to arm slaves virtually sounded the Southern death knell for slavery. The Confederate States had been founded on the idea that the institution was to be preserved forever, as Vice President Alexander H. Stephens had asserted at his inauguration. Now the Confederacy in 1865 was moving to abandon the practice. Confederate envoys James Mason and John Slidell made approaches to the British and French governments, respectively, in early 1865 indicating the South's readiness to abandon slavery in exchange for help. The Confederacy's last desperate moves—arming the bondsmen and offering to end slavery—are indicative of the importance of blacks in the Southern nation.

[See also African American Forgeworkers; African American Troops in the Union Army; Army, article on African Americans in the Confederate Army; Contraband; Emancipation Proclamation; Free People of Color; Labor; Miscegenation; Navy, article on African Americans in the Confederate Navy; Slavery.]

BIBLIOGRAPHY

Brewer, James H. The Confederate Negro: Virginia's Craftsmen and Military Laborers, 1861–1865. Durham, N.C., 1969.

Mohr, Clarence L. On the Threshold of Freedom: Masters and Slaves in Civil War Georgia. Athens, Ga., 1986.

Quarles, Benjamin. The Negro in the Civil War. Boston, 1953.

Reidy, Joseph. From Slavery to Agrarian Capitalism in the Cotton Plantation South: Central Georgia, 1800–1880. Chapel Hill, N.C., 1992.

Spraggins, Tinsley Lee. "Mobilization of Negro Labor for the Department of Virginia and North Carolina, 1861–1865." North Carolina Historical Review 24 (April 1947): 160–197.

Stephenson, Nathaniel W. "The Question of Arming the Slaves." American Historical Review 18 (January 1913): 295–308.

Thomas, Emory M. The Confederate Nation, 1861–1865. New York, 1979.

Toppin, Edgar. The Black American in United States History. Boston, 1973.

Wesley, Charles H. "The Employment of Negroes as Soldiers in the Confederate Army." Journal of Negro History 4 (July 1919): 239–253.

Wiley, Bell I. Southern Negroes, 1861–1865. New Haven, 1938.

Wish, Harvey. "Slave Disloyalty under the Confederacy." Journal of Negro History 23 (October 1938): 435–450.

EDGAR A. TOPPIN

AFRICAN AMERICAN TROOPS IN THE UNION ARMY

Jefferson Davis condemned Abraham Lincoln's Emancipation Proclamation as "the most execrable measure recorded in the history of guilty man." In that proclamation Lincoln had finally authorized the use of black soldiers by the Union. This, "the enlistment of black soldiers to fight and kill their former masters," concludes historian James M. McPherson, "was by far the most revolutionary dimension of the emancipation policy." That revolution had been a long time coming.

Lincoln's primary war aim was the preservation of the Union; his War Department had consistently rejected black offers of military service, and commanders of the first blue columns marching south in 1861 were careful to offer civil authorities aid in putting down slave insurrections "with an iron hand" and in returning fugitive slaves to their masters. This stirred Northern indignation with the result that the U.S. Congress, in March 1862, enacted a new article of war prohibiting the return of fugitives by army officers. Increasingly antislavery in disposition, the Congress in April provided compensated emancipation for slaves in the District of Columbia and in May prohibited slavery in all U.S. territories. Two months later, on July 17, the Second Confiscation Act authorized the president to enlist black men. Lincoln, still wedded to colonization and compensated emancipation, was not yet persuaded of the necessity for that move, although some subordinates pressed forward, with or without War Department approval or authority. Gradually, inevitably, the conflict slipped from political to social revolution.

The spring and summer of 1862 saw unprecedented activity in three widely separated sections of the country: South Carolina, Louisiana, and Kansas. These shared common characteristics: military manpower shortages, safe distances from War Department interference, and ambitious, imaginative, and radical leadership. In all three locations, experimental organizations of black troops attracted national attention and stirred spirited discussion, North and South.

Maj. Gen. David Hunter, commanding the Department of the South, began recruiting among the thousands of former slaves on the Sea Islands along the Atlantic coast. Privates

> **President Davis's . . . promise [was] to hand over captured officers of black units to state governments for punishment as "criminals engaged in servile insurrection."**

in the first company of what was to become the First South Carolina Colored Volunteer Infantry were enlisted on May 8, 1862. The War Department declined to support the experiment beyond forwarding a supply of red Zouave trousers. Hunter could secure neither pay for his troops nor commissions for their officers. He did, however, set one precedent that lasted throughout the war: he chose officers for his black companies from among experienced noncommissioned officers in the white regiments around him. Sgt. Charles Trowbridge, First New York Engineers, became the captain commanding Company A; the end of war found him a lieutenant colonel commanding the regiment.

Bitterly disappointed by lack of War Department support, Hunter disbanded his "red-trowsered" regiment on August 10—but two weeks later, the same War Department authorized Brig. Gen. Rufus Saxton to raise five thousand black troops. Saxton invited Thomas Wentworth Higginson of Massachusetts to command the regiment. The result was a unique combination of Boston Brahmin and Sea Island ex-slaves. Their story, as Higginson told it in his classic *Army Life in a Black Regiment,* is a monument to both officer and men, as well as a sensitive and revealing eyewitness account of a revolutionary experiment, social as well as military.

Meanwhile, Maj. Gen. Benjamin F. Butler of Massachusetts found himself commanding the Department of the Gulf after the U.S. Navy had captured New Orleans in late April. Butler needed men, but the demands of George B. McClellan's Peninsular campaign took precedence over all

else. Then Butler discovered a military bonanza—thousands of "free men of color," many of whom had earlier belonged to Confederate militia units. Applying his authority to enroll former Confederate personnel (after they had taken a loyalty oath), Butler mustered into Federal service the First, Second, and Third Louisiana Native Guards in September, October, and November 1862. Eventually Louisiana furnished 24,000 black troops for the Union, more than any other state.

Out in the Trans-Mississippi West, on the Kansas-Missouri border, other Union leaders were also in dire need of troops. Kansas had joined the Union in January 1861, only three months before the firing on Fort Sumter. The new state faced twin challenges: organizing itself politically and defending itself militarily. Among the political giants of the time none stood taller than Senator (and erstwhile general) James Henry Lane, a genuine, charismatic radical with a brutally practical turn of mind. He began to enroll fugitives from Missouri in early August 1862, just as Hunter was disbanding his South Carolina levies. For officers, Lane turned to abolitionists who had learned border warfare in the bitter struggles between Kansas jayhawkers and Missouri bushwhackers. Capt. James Williams began the work in Leavenworth, eventually becoming the commanding colonel. Lane encouraged enlistments with such blandishments as "We have been saying that you would fight, and if you won't we will make you." By whatever means—and ignoring War Department orders—Lane and Williams had raised a battalion by early October and started it down the border to augment the garrison of Fort Scott, pivotal Union post in southeastern Kansas.

En route the new troops ran into a sizable force of bushwhackers at Island Mound, Missouri, thus earning the plaudits of the Northern press and the distinction of seeing action in the first recorded engagement between Confederate forces and Union blacks. Continuing to Fort Scott, the battalion was mustered into Federal service on January 13, 1863. The First Kansas Colored was the first black regiment raised by a Northern state, although by virtue of the Trowbridge company's record of unbroken service from May 8, 1862, Higginson's First South Carolina Colored Volunteer Infantry deserves the distinction of being the very first black regiment in the Union army.

President Davis's denunciation of Lincoln's proclamation was hardly surprising, nor was his promise to hand over captured officers of black units to state governments for punishment as "criminals engaged in servile insurrection." Generals Butler and Hunter had already been outlawed for their activities. By the end of May 1863, Confederate policy set by Davis and Congress had been refined to these points: former slaves "taken in arms" were to be delivered to state authorities for trial; their officers were to be tried and punished by military courts. "Wartime atrocities against the USCT [black troops]," writes historian Joseph Glatthaar, "were commonplace." Hardly surprising. As historian Bell I. Wiley explains it: "if the wishes of the private soldiers who fought them [black troops] had prevailed, no quarter would have been granted." One private soldier from Mississippi wrote his mother, "I hope I may never see a Negro Soldier or I cannot be . . . a Christian soldier."

The effects on black soldiers of these grimmer realities of combat seem to have run counter to Confederate anticipation. After the Fort Pillow massacre of April 12, 1864, Union blacks went into action shouting "Remember Fort Pillow." West of the Mississippi, a similar result followed the massacre of a foraging party of the First Kansas Colored near Camden, Arkansas. Its sister regiment, the Second Kansas Colored (recruited from Missouri and Arkansas ex-slaves) vowed to take no prisoners and thereafter sprang into action shouting "Remember Poison Spring." The men of the Second Kansas forgot themselves in combat and brought in a prisoner. Col. Samuel J. Crawford sent him back to Confederate lines under a flag of truce with a warning note pinned to his chest. Retaliation as a Union countermove to Confederate practices worked in limited circumstances only, serving in the main to magnify the horrors of war. Col. James Williams won no discernible military advantage by ordering the execution of a member of Maj. T. R. Livingston's guerrilla band in southwest Missouri because Livingston had killed a captured private of the First Kansas Colored. Whatever the actions of field commanders, whether in Arkansas, Missouri, Tennessee, or Virginia, the official positions of North and South on the treatment of black troops created an insoluble deadlock, one result of which was a breakdown in the cartel for prisoner exchange. In evident frustration, Gen. Ethan Allen Hitchcock, Federal commissioner for prisoner exchange, concluded in August 1863 that a solution could "only be effectually reached by a successful prosecution of the war." Lincoln, after hearing about Fort Pillow, put it this way: "The difficulty is not in stating the principle, but in practically applying it."

Thus, when Lincoln authorized black recruitment on January 1, 1863, between three and four thousand blacks were already in uniform in those first five regiments, all raised on a catch-as-catch-can basis with little or no control from Washington. In the first weeks of 1863 the same pattern, or lack thereof, continued: on January 13, the day the First Kansas Colored was mustered in at Fort Scott, the War Department authorized Col. Daniel Ullman of New York to recruit an officer cadre and lead it to Louisiana to raise a brigade there. On the same day, the department ordered Col. James Montgomery, an old Kansas colleague of abolitionist John Brown, to South Carolina to recruit the Second South Carolina Colored Volunteer Infantry. On January 26, 1863, Secretary of War Edwin Stanton gave Governor John Andrew authority to raise a regiment in Massachusetts. Here was the inception of that most famous of all black regiments, the Fifty-fourth Massachusetts Infantry.

Obviously, piecemeal organization by individuals and states was hardly the way to build an effective army, and Stanton's War Department moved, quickly and effectively, to bring the enterprise under centralized control. The result was the Bureau for Colored Troops established in May. The first major stride forward, however, had come a few weeks earlier when Stanton had ordered Adj. Gen. Lorenzo Thomas out to the Mississippi Valley to announce the new policy and stimulate the organization of new regiments. By the end of the year Thomas had initiated organization of twenty regiments in the valley; by the end of the war he could take credit for having started fifty.

While the adjutant general labored in the field, drawing on the great numbers of fugitive slaves engulfing every Union post, the Bureau for Colored Troops in Washington developed an effective office to advise, direct, and supervise. It encouraged recruitment in Northern cities as well as the occupied sections of the South and established a fairly efficient mechanism for selecting officers for the new regiments. The bureau meticulously supervised examining boards for officer candidates in Northern cities and in Union army divisions in the field. The result was a selection of generally better officers than those in the white volunteer regiments. The vast majority of white officers serving in black regiments had been junior or noncommissioned officers in white regiments, with invaluable troop and combat experience. Over one hundred black officers also served, the majority in Butler's Louisiana regiments.

Another important decision by the bureau was to federalize all black regiments by designating them United States Colored Troops. Higginson's First South Carolina became the Thirty-third USCT, for example; Butler's Native Guards became the Seventy-third, Seventy-fourth, and Seventy-fifth, and the First Kansas Colored served out the war as the new Seventy-ninth USCT. This put the black regiments in a national army rather than in state units. The symbolism was good, and the Federal umbrella covered all black regiments—aside from a handful permitted to retain their initial state designations, like the Fifty-fourth and Fifty-fifth Massachusetts and the Twenty-ninth Connecticut.

Organizing, recruiting, selecting officers, and training the troops went ahead steadily through 1863; at least 50,000 blacks were in the Union army by the end of that year. During 1864 the number tripled. Altogether, black troops in the Federal army numbered 180,000. Of these approximately 37,000 were listed as fatalities. Some 2,800 were killed in action or died of wounds; most of the others were victims of disease. It is impossible to give precise figures on the sick and wounded who survived. Possibly the worst case was that of the Fifty-Sixth USCT. They served for two years, chiefly on post and garrison duty around Helena, Arkansas, and participated in three minor engagements with combat losses of 4 officers and 21 enlisted men. But the regiment lost 6 officers and 647 men from disease. Substandard medical facilities and personnel and inadequate diet contributed largely to that sorry record. Here was one problem the Bureau for Colored Troops found insoluble. Another was the continuing, nagging struggle for equality of pay, solved finally in the spring of 1865 by which time thousands of black soldiers had given their lives for the Union at cut-rate prices: seven dollars per month plus a three-dollar clothing allowance (retained by the company) for the black soldier, whatever his rank, against thirteen dollars for white privates (including the clothing allowance in cash).

Although it was expected at first that blacks would serve largely in garrison duty, thus releasing white men for active service, by mid-1863 several engagements involving blacks had attracted startled and favorable attention. These first important tests of black fighting qualities came in May, June, and July, at Port Hudson and Milliken's Bend in Louisiana and Fort Wagner guarding Charleston, where the Fifty-fourth Massachusetts fought its way to permanent glory. In addition, the First Kansas Colored won praise for two engagements in June and July, at Cabin Creek and Honey Springs in present-day Oklahoma. A Wisconsin cavalry officer exclaimed after Cabin Creek: "I was never much for niggers, but, be Jasus, they are hell for fighting."

Black regiments served in every theater of war from Virginia to Texas. They fought in 449 engagements, 38 of them major, from Florida to Tennessee and well beyond the Big River in Nathaniel P. Banks's Red River campaign and Frederick Steele's equally ill-fated Camden expedition. What did these 160-plus underpaid and overworked black regiments do? Everything their white commanders asked or permitted them to do, from garrison duty up and down the Mississippi to escort duty for miles of wagon trains, from excessive fatigue duty (always and forever) to guarding confiscated plantations—and prisoners—as well as actual combat from the Petersburg Crater to Nashville, to Hatcher's Run, to Palmetto Ranch on the Rio Grande.

And what rewards did they win for this service to a republic that cheated them of half their wages? Slow, grudging acceptance in the white army around them—and fourteen Medals of Honor. But far more important was their active participation in a prodigious revolution. They had been more than spectators. Whether drafted in the North as substitutes for white men, free volunteers, or impressed fugitives, African Americans had won the right to fight. In so doing they gave emphatic affirmation of Howell Cobb's presentiment. Arguing against arming slaves to fight for the Confederacy, Cobb wrote in January 1865: "The day you make soldiers of them is the beginning of the end of the revolution. If slaves will make good soldiers, our whole theory of slavery is wrong."

Lt. Col. Charles F. Adams, Jr., commenting on the Petersburg Crater, said of the black troops caught in that fiasco: "They seem to have behaved just as well and as badly as the rest and to have suffered more severely." That cool judgment applies as well to the record of all African American troops in the Union army.

[*See also*; Emancipation Proclamation; Fort Pillow Massacre; Fort Wagner, South Carolina; Petersburg Campaign; Port Hudson, Louisiana; Prisoners of War; Red River Campaigns.]

BIBLIOGRAPHY

Cornish, Dudley Taylor. *The Sable Arm: Black Troops in the Union Army, 1861–1865.* New York, 1956. Reprint, Lawrence, Kans., 1987.

Durden, Robert F. *The Gray and the Black: The Confederate Debate on Emancipation.* Baton Rouge, La., 1972.

Glatthaar, Joseph T. *Forged in Battle: The Civil War Alliance of Black Soldiers and White Officers.* New York, 1990.

Gooding, James Henry. *On the Altar of Freedom: A Black Soldier's Civil War Letters from the Front.* Edited by Virginia Matzke Adams. Amherst, Mass., 1991.

Higginson, Thomas Wentworth. *Army Life in a Black Regiment.* Boston, 1870. Reprint, New York, 1984.

McPherson, James M. *Abraham Lincoln and the Second American Revolution.* New York, 1990.

Thomas, Emory M. *The Confederate Nation, 1861–1865.* New York, 1979.

DUDLEY T. CORNISH

ALABAMA

In the presidential election of 1860, Southern Democrat John C. Breckinridge carried Alabama, receiving support in all regions of the state: northern Alabama and the Tennessee valley, the black belt in southern Alabama, and the southeastern Wiregrass. Alabama seceded from the Union on January 11, 1861. Less than a month later, the Confederate States of America was launched at a convention in Montgomery, the state capital. Alabama's population consisted of 437,930 black people (of whom 2,850 were free) and 526,271 whites. Of the latter, approximately 75,000 served in the Confederate army, while about 3,000 joined the Union forces; in addition, 10,000 black Alabamians would fight for the Union.

Secession and Early Confederate Politics

By the late 1850s, slavery and other sectional issues had long been important in Alabama politics, but it was possible to make a case that Alabama was secure in the Union. In 1857, moderate Democrat Andrew Barry Moore was nominated for governor and elected without opposition. Two years later he was reelected, defeating his opponent, a fire-eater, by a huge margin. Most Democrats still looked to the national Democratic party for protection of the Southern way of life. Yet a series of events drove Alabamians toward the radical Southern rights stance of William Lowndes Yancey.

John Brown's raid in Virginia in October 1859 touched off a wave of fear and anger in the state. With Governor Moore's blessing the legislature authorized the formation of volunteer units, appropriated $200,000 for defense, and took steps to establish direct trade with Europe. On February 24, 1860, the legislature called for a state convention in the event of a Republican presidential victory.

Within a year the dynamics of presidential politics had made secession a certainty. Alabama delegates walked out of the Democratic National Convention at Charleston when supporters of Illinois senator Stephen A. Douglas would not approve a platform protecting slavery in the territories. A subsequent convention at Baltimore produced similar results. Breakaway Southerners nominated Kentuckian John C. Breckinridge for president.

Yancey campaigned for Breckinridge, who captured the state with 48,000 votes. Union-minded Democrats supported Douglas, who received 13,000 votes. Whigs cast 27,000 votes for Constitutional Union candidate John Bell of Tennessee. For backers of Douglas and Bell, the election had been one last chance to prove that political compromise could save the Union.

With no support in the state, Abraham Lincoln had been only a frightening abstraction during the campaign. After his election, Governor Moore—now a thoroughgoing secessionist—called for election of delegates to a January 7, 1861, state convention. Anticipating the arguments of "cooperationists" (who favored pan-Southern action), Moore sent commissioners to other slave states to arrange for coordinated action. Early in January he used Alabama troops to seize the Federal forts guarding Mobile Bay and the arsenal at Mount Vernon.

Moore had a firm grasp of sentiment in Alabama. Debates prior to the delegate elections had concerned only the method of secession. The voters elected a clear majority of "immediate secessionists" (fifty-four) over cooperationists (forty-six). Even some of the state's leading Whigs, including such previous moderates as Thomas Hill Watts, had gone over to the secessionist side. The cooperationists, for their part, were largely from northern Alabama—vulnerable to invasion in event of war and the closest thing the state had to a center of Unionist sentiment.

At the state convention, secession leaders claimed simply that Alabama, as a sovereign state, had the right to secede. The cooperationists were divided, though some favored using a Southern convention to demand constitutional amendments. Yancey, Watts, and other secessionist leaders

allowed four days for debate; then on January 11, amid scenes of wild rejoicing, they voted Alabama out of the Union and issued a call inviting other Southern states to send delegates to a February 4 convention in Montgomery.

For all the firing of cannon and unfurling of flags, the convention was far from unified. The vote on the secession ordinance was sixty-nine to thirty-one. Subsequently, thirty-three cooperationists refused to sign the official copy, though most of them recognized secession as legal and binding. Before and after the January 11 vote, cooperationists urged sub-

> **The vote on the secession ordinance was sixty-nine to thirty-one.**

mission of the ordinance to the people. The majority refused to comply, and cooperationist bitterness probably contributed to a movement to deny Yancey and other fire-eaters seats in the Confederate convention. In this the cooperationists were successful, and the delegation was of a markedly Whiggish cast.

Yet secession was apparently popular, and the high tide of Confederate political support in Alabama came with the state elections of 1861. The Democrats were the dominant party, but there was a feeling that patriotism demanded a suspension of partisanship. Gubernatorial candidates were nominated by newspapers and as a rule did not campaign. By August 8, election day, only two candidates remained: John Gill Shorter, a black belt fire-eater who was a member of the Provisional Congress, and Watts, the Whig secessionist leader.

Despite the avoidance of politics as usual, voting seemed to follow traditional lines. Shorter won 37,000 to 28,000, carrying northern Alabama and the southeastern Wiregrass counties like any good Democrat. The legislature also was staunchly secessionist, and it was in an atmosphere of hopeful determination that Shorter turned to the task of governing a state at war.

Military Affairs

In the meantime, preparations for war had been ongoing. Numerous volunteer regiments were raised in 1861, most of which were mustered into Confederate service. After the first year of war, enlistments tapered off; however, the passage of the Conscription Act of 1862 stimulated another wave of volunteering. Alabamians served in sixty-three infantry regiments, eleven cavalry regiments, and a number of artillery and naval units.

State officials worked hard to arm and equip many of Alabama's units, but arms procurement was an intractable problem. Governor Moore had sent agents out to scour the nation for weapons. Governor Shorter promoted local weapons production, contracting with small shops in Mobile, Selma, Talladega, and other towns and giving $250,000 in subsidies to the Alabama Arms Manufacturing Company in Montgomery. None of these ventures produced the hoped-for results, and the state was sometimes reduced to giving its fighters pikes or bowie knives.

As to military operations, Shorter gave much of his attention in 1862 to the defense of the Gulf coast. He understood the importance of Pensacola (where Moore had already sent state troops) and was instrumental in delaying evacuation of that city until May, thus saving guns and stores for the defense of Mobile. When that city was threatened by Federal forces in the spring of 1862, he arranged for recently formed regiments to be sent there and armed them with militia weapons.

At the same time a more pressing situation was developing in northern Alabama. The Shorter administration had helped commanders in Tennessee and Kentucky obtain troops and had impressed slaves to work on fortifications. Nonetheless, after the fall of Forts Henry and Donelson (February 1862), northern Alabama was open to invasion. By April the mixed plantation and hill lands of the Tennessee valley were occupied by Union forces under Gen. O. M. Mitchell. In the course of occupation, towns like Huntsville, Florence, Decatur, and especially Athens suffered violence and property damage. Shorter arranged for the continued defense of the area by securing Confederate cavalry under John Tyler Morgan and authorizing volunteer cavalry to serve under Philip Dale Roddy—but in fact the governor had few options. Except for brief intervals, the Tennessee valley and large areas of hill country to the south would be in Union hands for the duration.

Occupation brought disastrous consequences for northern Alabamians, aside from deaths and damage inflicted by Northern troops. Violent feuds broke out between Unionists and Confederate sympathizers. By the latter stages of the war the woods throughout the state were full of "Mossbacks" who sought to avoid Confederate service, deserters who sometimes traveled together to resist capture, and bands of outlaws. These groups often stole food and supplies, as did Federal and Confederate cavalry—though the soldiers used such terms as *foraging* or *impressment* to cover their depredations. Since large numbers of men were away in service, there was little protection for isolated farm families, and food was increasingly scarce.

Citizens might have been more secure had the state possessed a usable militia. At the time of secession the militia existed mostly on the statute books. Late in 1862, when the need for a state defense and peacekeeping force had become all too apparent to Governor Shorter, the legislature refused to cooperate. Evidently they reasoned that military affairs were the responsibility of the central government.

Besides, they supposed that any troops raised by the state would be absorbed into the Confederate army, as had been the case with the Alabama volunteers of 1861. The state government appeared indifferent, and public opinion was increasingly skeptical.

After the fall of Vicksburg in July 1863, deserters and paroled soldiers flooded into the state. Called into special session, a new legislature finally revised the militia law, but in so doing they created a cumbersome two-class system. One class consisted of sixteen-year-olds and men aged forty-five

> By the latter stages of the war the woods throughout the state were full of . . . deserters who sometimes traveled together to resist capture, and bands of outlaws.

to sixty, who by law could not be used outside their home counties. The system never really worked. Moreover the efforts of Shorter's successor, Thomas H. Watts, to obtain an effective militia met with failure in the legislature, which had become a refractory and virtually anti-Confederate body.

Thus it was that northern Alabama and the north-central border counties were left to the protection of cavalry commanders such as Morgan, Roddy, and Nathan Bedford Forrest. These were resourceful men, but their main purpose was to harass the Federals, not defend the local population. Skirmishes and small battles were common in 1863 and 1864, though there were no decisive fights. The most celebrated Confederate victory of this period came in May 1863, when Forrest pursued a Union raiding force commanded by Col. A. D. Streight. Sweeping through several northern Alabama counties with about 1,500 men, Streight intended to cut Chattanooga-to-Atlanta railroad lines and to destroy supplies stored in Rome, Georgia. Forrest pursued with a much smaller force, and after a chase of more than one hundred miles, Streight turned at bay. Some of his men were too tired to fight; and Forrest's placement of his 600 troops convinced the exhausted Federals that the Confederates had superior numbers. Persuaded by his officers, Streight surrendered.

Until the summer of 1864, central and southern Alabama had been spared the worst rigors of war. In July 1864, however, Gen. Lovell H. Rousseau launched a raid with some 2,300 men from Decatur in northern Alabama to Opelika in the southeast. His object was to destroy the railroad depots, track, and equipment of the Montgomery and West Point Railroad, thereby cutting off an important source of supplies for Confederate forces before Atlanta. Rousseau burned and wrecked as he went, accomplishing his mission without effective opposition and spreading insecurity among people in the interior of the state.

Residents of Mobile, on the other hand, had often felt insecure. Yet even the outer defenses of the city were not truly tested until August 1864—when Adm. David Farragut attacked Fort Gaines, Fort Morgan, and other posts that defended the entrances to Mobile Bay with 1,500 infantry, artillery, and a fleet of more than eighteen vessels. After a fierce naval battle on August 5 in which the Union warship *Tecumseh* was sunk by a mine and the Confederate ironclad *Tennessee* was captured after a heroic resistance, Farragut besieged the forts. Though Fort Morgan held out through a terrific bombardment, the outlying positions had been surrendered by August 23. For the time being the city itself—its fortifications built up by the labor of thousands of impressed slaves—was left to wither. Its downfall was delayed for eight months until more than 40,000 Federal troops converged upon a much smaller Confederate force. After prolonged fighting, Confederate Gen. D. H. Maury evacuated the town from April 10 through 12, 1865.

By the time Mobile fell, Gen. J. H. Wilson's brigade of 13,500 cavalry had carried its own brand of hell from northwestern Alabama into the black belt. Wilson's chief target was Selma, where important arms manufactories, powderworks, and a naval yard had been assembled at the behest of Confederate Quartermaster General Josiah Gorgas. Traveling in three columns through a countryside already stripped bare of foodstuffs, Wilson's men reached Elyton (near present-day Birmingham) on March 29 and burned the ironworks there. Wilson then detached a portion of his command under Gen. John Croxton to Tuscaloosa, where—after a brief fight with university cadets—they burned the University of Alabama and other facilities.

Nine thousand strong, Wilson's main force arrived at Selma on April 2 and soon defeated Forrest's force of five thousand. Over the course of several days the Union troops proceeded to destroy the legitimate prizes of their conquest. But the blue-coated soldiers also carried out one of the most complete devastations of a town during the war. When Wilson left Selma on April 10, the town was a smoking ruin, its streets filled with the carcasses of the hundreds of mules and horses that he had ordered shot. Terrified by Selma's fate, Montgomery surrendered without resistance on April 12 upon the approach of Union troops. After burning and confiscation of a more restrained sort, Wilson took his command farther east, into Georgia, taking the war with him.

Civil and Political Affairs

For decades before the war, Alabama Whigs and Democrats had debated the merits of state support for banks, schools, prisons, and business enterprises. Democratic leaders who had been reluctant to turn government to economic purposes reversed themselves after

1861. Their use of economic power began at the most basic levels, even before fighting broke out. In the winter of 1860–1861, the state persuaded banks to suspend specie payments. Subsequently these banks purchased quotas of state bonds with specie, thereby giving the state control of the supply of hard money. In 1861, the legislature gave Governor Moore power to issue paper money, a power that became the single most important means of state funding. The amount of state issues (some $7.5 million) was small in comparison to the massive Confederate output, but it contributed to inflation.

State taxes remained comparatively low for at least a year. Prewar property taxes were largely retained; apparently many citizens were exempt from these. By December 1862, however, the legislature needed money and was in a mood to raise it from persons who were too prosperous or who flaunted wealth. At that time, in addition to a poll tax, the state imposed taxes on luxury goods, "vices" (packs of cards, billiard tables), and some occupations. A more revolutionary tax passed at that session levied 5 percent of "legacies, profits and sales, [and] incomes."

A year later the state's needs were more pressing still, and the legislature taxed speculators in Confederate bonds while increasing taxes on profits. In December 1864, with inflation running away and government on the point of collapse, all taxes were increased by one-third. Radical as it seems, this measure was mild compared to the Confederate taxes-in-kind of 1863 and 1864. Since the latter often took food from families already in danger of starvation, the legislature asked the Confederate government to exempt white yeoman families from the tax-in-kind—evidently to little purpose.

State officials often subordinated their own goals to Confederate war aims; yet they did carry out sweeping policies aimed at helping ordinary citizens. By 1862, for example, the price of salt had risen by more than 2,000 percent. Determined to protect the people from speculators and to ensure an adequate supply of this vital substance, Governor Shorter bought salt from abroad and leased state salt reservation lands to private companies. Soon the state began to produce its own salt; and in the summer of 1862, Shorter opened other reservation lands to all Alabamians. Eventually he contracted with Virginia salt producers to obtain yet more. Much of the state-controlled salt was to be distributed to indigent families.

The state likewise tried to cope with the larger issues of hunger and deprivation raised by the war. Enlistments and conscription drained manpower from the whole state, but especially from the small-farm districts of northern Alabama and the Wiregrass. In 1861 legislators had set aside tax moneys for poor relief. In 1862, at Shorter's urging, they set aside $2 million for indigent families, adding $4 million the following year for soldiers' families.

Even so, food supplies dwindled in the troubled areas. Surveys by probate judges indicated that in 1863 three families out of ten needed help. "Corn women" from northern Alabama, who walked for days begging for food with sacks on their backs, were commonly seen in the black belt by 1863. The problem was not confined to rural areas: Mobile was troubled by shortages, food riots, and marching women in the same year.

As the story of the corn women indicates, not every part of the state was destitute. The black belt especially produced a surplus of food, which state officials sometimes tried to purchase directly for distribution to the poor. Yet the state's wretched (or nonexistent) roads and the Confederate control of rail transport frustrated most of their efforts. The food problem was accompanied by a shortage of medicines caused by the blockade of Mobile and by the scarcity of wool cards used in the home manufacture of cloth. These and other hardships could not be kept secret from soldiers in the field, and many men deserted to look after their families. Of course, such deserters were likely to have trouble with the authorities, thus increasing the cycle of violence in the state. Add to the above the resentment over increasingly demanding taxes and regulations and fears touched off by the likelihood of Union invasions, and it is easy to see why many Alabamians came to lose their enthusiasm for the Confederacy and for secessionist politicians.

In the state elections of 1863, Governor Shorter and his allies were caught in a wave of popular anger. Shorter hoped to be reelected but did not campaign. He was opposed once again by Watts, who had served as attorney general of the Confederacy since 1862. Watts was a committed Confederate; yet his Whiggish past history and his own refusal to campaign misled the people, thousands of whom thought that he would favor peace. The elections of 1863 were marked by the activities of a shadowy peace party whose activities were centered in (though not confined to) northern Alabama. In the event, Watts defeated Shorter by a vote to 28,000 to 9,000, winning all but four persistently Democratic northern Alabama counties. The state legislators chosen in 1863 included many little-known men whose sentiment may be gauged by their election of cooperationists Robert Jemmison and Richard Wilde Walker to the Confederate Senate. Likewise, the electorate sent several antiadministration politicians to the Confederate House of Representatives. Jabez L. M. Curry, one of the state's ablest young secessionists, was defeated for reelection.

During his term of office, Watts struggled with impossible conditions. The state continued to appropriate millions of dollars for poor relief and attempted to supply salt, wool cards, and other goods to its citizens. Despite his loyalty to the Confederacy, Watts quarreled so frequently with national officials over impressment and conscription policies that he is remembered as a state rights governor. On the other hand, in September 1864, Watts opposed peace resolutions introduced in the legislature by Lewis Parsons (future provisional governor). These resolutions were defeated by a vote of forty-five to thirty-two, which may indicate how strong the peace party had become. Indeed, peace party men expected to carry the state in 1865, and some scholars think they would have if the Confederacy had endured.

As it was, though, Watts with many others fled Montgomery in April 1865 at the approach of Wilson's raiders. After staying briefly in Eufaula on the Georgia border he returned to Montgomery. There was little for him to do, so he joined other Confederates who were assembling at the nearby town of Union Springs. He was captured by Union forces on May 1. The rebellion in Alabama—in reality an attempted revolution—was over.

[For further discussion of battles fought in Alabama, see Mobile, Alabama, articles on Battle of Mobile Bay and Mobile Campaign; Selma, Alabama, article on Wilson's Raid on Selma; Shiloh Campaign. For further discussion of Alabama cities, see Mobile, Alabama, article on City of Mobile; Montgomery, Alabama; Selma, Alabama, article on City of Selma. See also biographies of numerous figures mentioned herein.]

BIBLIOGRAPHY

Barney, William L. The Secessionist Impulse: Alabama and Mississippi in 1860. Princeton, 1974.

Bergeron, Arthur W., Jr. Confederate Mobile. Jackson, Miss., 1991.

Brewer, Willis. Alabama: Her History, Resources, War Record, and Public Men. Montgomery, Ala., 1872. Reprint, Spartanburg, S.C., 1975.

Fleming, Walter L. Civil War and Reconstruction in Alabama. New York, 1905. Reprint, Spartanburg, S.C., 1978.

Jones, James Pickett. Yankee Blitzkrieg: Wilson's Raid through Alabama and Georgia. Athens, Ga., 1976.

McMillan, Malcolm C. The Alabama Confederate Reader. University, Ala., 1963. Reprint with intro. by C. Peter Ripley. Tuscaloosa, Ala. 1992.

McMillan, Malcolm C. The Disintegration of a Confederate State: Three Governors and Alabama's Wartime Home Front, 1861–1865. Macon, Ga., 1986.

Rogers, William Warren. "Alabama." In The Encyclopedia of Southern History. Edited by David C. Roller and Robert Twyman. Baton Rouge, La., 1979.

Smith, William R. The History and Debates of the Convention of the People of Alabama, Begun and Held in the City of Montgomery, on the Seventh Day of January, 1861. Montgomery, Ala., 1861. Reprint, Spartanburg, S.C., 1975.

Thornton, J. Mills. Politics and Power in a Slave Society: Alabama, 1800–1860. Baton Rouge, La., 1978.

Wheeler, Joseph. Alabama. Vol. 7 of Confederate Military History. Edited by Clement A. Evans. Atlanta, 1899. Vol. 8 of extended ed. Wilmington, N.C., 1987.

PAUL M. PRUITT, JR.

CSS *ALABAMA*. Wash drawing by Clary Ray, November 1894.

ALABAMA

In June 1861, Comdr. James Dunwoody Bulloch of the Confederate navy arrived in England to purchase ships, guns, and ammunition for the Navy Department. The following month Bulloch contracted with Laird's Shipyard in Birkenhead, across the Mersey from Liverpool, for a wooden barkentine. According to the contract for vessel number *290*, the ship was to be 220 feet in length and 32 feet in beam and have a 15-foot draft. Although designed and built along the lines of a fast merchant ship, the *290* was to be unusually well equipped for extended cruising. In addition to being rigged for sail, the ship was equipped with a 300-horsepower steam engine that powered a patented screw propeller system. To reduce drag under sail, the propeller could be raised into a specially designed well in the stern.

In spite of protests by Charles Francis Adams, American minister to London, British authorities determined that the *290* did not violate Queen Victoria's May 1861 proclamation of neutrality, which prevented the sale of warships to either the United States or the Confederacy. After the *290* had been launched and christened *Enrica,* Bulloch took the ship down the Mersey on a trial and never returned. Later in the Azores *Enrica* rendezvoused with the bark *Agrippina* and transferred ordnance, ammunition, provisions, and coal that Bulloch had previously purchased in England. Four days later the vessel had been fitted out for war and, under the command of Raphael Semmes, *Enrica* was rechristened CSS *Alabama*. Captain Semmes assembled the crew and informed them of his orders from President Jefferson Davis to use the ship against the U.S. Merchant Marine.

Semmes initiated an unparalleled campaign with an attack on U.S. whaling ships in the vicinity of the Azores and merchant vessels off Newfoundland. After moving operations into the Gulf of Mexico *Alabama* encountered and sank in only thirteen minutes USS *Hatteras* off Galveston, Texas. After putting the rescued crew of *Hatteras* ashore at Port Royal, Jamaica, Semmes took the Confederate warship south to the coast of Brazil. With supplies from more than a dozen captured vessels, Semmes headed *Alabama* across the South Atlantic. En route to the Cape of Good Hope, Semmes captured the bark *Conrad.* Instead of destroying it, Semmes armed the vessel, put a small crew aboard, rechristened it CSS *Tuscaloosa,* and sent that vessel commerce raiding as well. Following a visit to Cape Town and a moderately successful cruise across the Indian Ocean, *Alabama* returned to Cape Town before recrossing the South Atlantic. It was apparent to Semmes that the ship was badly in need of repairs after nineteen months at sea, and he headed the raider for Cherbourg, France.

At Cherbourg USS *Kearsarge,* one of more than a dozen U.S. warships in pursuit of the Confederate raider, finally caught up with Captain Semmes. He considered his vessel a close match for *Kearsarge* and informed its captain, John A. Winslow, of his intention to fight. On June 19, 1864, *Alabama* steamed out of the French port and opened fire on *Kearsarge* at 10:57 A.M. Although one of *Alabama*'s initial shots lodged in the sternpost of *Kearsarge*, the shell failed to explode. As the engagement intensified, shots from

Kearsarge began to take effect, while those of *Alabama* hit the Union warship only twenty-eight times. In seventy minutes *Alabama* began sinking, and Semmes struck his colors to avoid continued loss of life. The U.S. Navy had destroyed *Alabama,* but Semmes and forty members of the crew escaped capture when the British yacht *Deerhound* came to their rescue.

In 1984 the wreck of the Confederate ship was discovered by a French navy mine hunter. Expeditions to the site carried out by divers and archaeologists of the CSS *Alabama* Association have documented the wreck and uncovered a unique collection of artifacts that illuminate life aboard the commerce raider.

During *Alabama*'s cruise Semmes had captured and burned fifty-five Union merchant vessels valued at more than $4.5 million. Ten other vessels were bonded at $562,000 and released. The impact of commerce raiding by *Alabama* and other Confederate warships was disastrous for the U.S. Merchant Marine. In what has been described as an unparalleled "flight from the flag," hundreds of U.S. vessels were sold or shifted to foreign registration in an effort to avoid capture and destruction. That impact on the Merchant Marine was felt until the end of the century.

[*See also* Alabama Claims.]

BIBLIOGRAPHY

Adams, Ephram Douglass. *Great Britain and the Civil War.* 2 vols. New York, 1958.

Merli, Frank J. *Great Britain and the Confederate Navy, 1861–1865.* Bloomington, Ind., 1970.

Merli, Frank J., ed. *Special Commemorative Naval Issue: CSS Alabama, 1864–1989.* Vol. 4 of *Journal of Confederate History.* Brentwood, Tenn., 1989.

Scharf, J. Thomas. *History of the Confederate States Navy.* New York, 1887. Reprint, New York, 1977.

Semmes, Raphael. *Service Afloat; or, the Remarkable Career of the Confederate Cruisers* Sumter *and* Alabama *during the War between the States.* New York, 1869.

Summersell, Charles G. *The C.S.S.* Alabama: *Builder, Captain, and Plans.* University, Ala., 1985.

GORDON WATTS

ALABAMA CLAIMS

During the Civil War commerce raiders fitted out by the Confederate navy carried out a series of successful campaigns against the U.S. Merchant Marine. Vessels like *Alabama, Georgia, Florida,* and *Shenandoah* cruised the routes of Union commerce and captured, destroyed, or released on bond millions of dollars worth of ships and cargoes. *Alabama* alone was credited with losses totaling $5 million. The success of Confederate commerce raiders caused a "flight from the flag" that forced 750 U.S. merchant ship owners to sell or shift their vessels to foreign registration in an effort to avoid capture or destruction. Whereas 65 percent of New York's maritime commerce was carried in American bottoms in 1860, U.S. ships carried only 25 percent three years later. Although the decline of U.S. maritime commerce was not entirely the result of Confederate attacks, they were a major factor.

Because many of the Confederacy's most effective commerce raiders were built in Great Britain, the United States maintained that Britain should be held responsible for their destructive activities. The U.S. government asserted that Great Britain had violated its May 1861 neutrality proclamation by permitting Confederate agents to obtain vessels for purposes of war with virtual impunity. When the Confederacy collapsed in 1865, the United States moved to press its claims against Great Britain. Both countries prepared arguments to support their position, and Charles F. Adams, U.S. minister to Great Britain, relayed that "nothing remains but arbitration." But in spite of Adams's optimism, the issue of reparations was far from arbitration or resolution.

Neither Great Britain nor the United States was willing to make significant concessions. The United States expected Britain to recognize the validity of U.S. claims before any negotiations could begin. Britain, to the contrary, refused to admit culpability for the commerce raiders' actions and adamantly refused to have a third power involved in deciding if it had been right or wrong in the matter. Negotiations reached an impasse and were suspended. When Lord Russell's government collapsed in June 1866, William H. Seward ordered Adams to reopen the issue. Though the attitude of both nations was more conciliatory and each informally offered to make concessions, both Seward and Lord Stanley, Lord Russell's successor, refused to compromise on the issue of British violation of the neutrality proclamation. Again the negotiations collapsed.

In 1868 the status of the negotiations was complicated by Adams's resignation and the need to resolve other issues that arose, but in November, President Andrew Johnson redirected attention to the *Alabama* claims. By January 1869 he and British Foreign Secretary George W. F. Clarendon had developed an agreement that both parties signed concerning the method of resolving the dispute.

A commission of two Britons and two Americans would hear the claims and decide on resolution. Wherever they could not come to an agreement, an arbitrator would be mutually approved and those matters submitted to his consideration. In the event that the commission could not agree on an arbitrator, two would be selected and lots cast to determine which would rule on the matter at hand. Heads of state could be selected as arbitrators by any two members of the commission. The agreement was anything but satisfactory, and the U.S. Senate voted against it in April 1869.

After the vote Senator Charles Sumner of Massachusetts voiced such vehement opposition to the agreement that it created a wave of renewed public resentment against Great Britain. In his speech Sumner reiterated U.S. grievances and

> **Senator Zachariah Chandler demanded that Canada be ceded to the United States. . . .**

condemned the Johnson-Clarendon agreement because there was no admission of British responsibility, no provisions for future policy on the matter, and no reparations for the United States. Sumner also claimed that Great Britain's violation of Queen Victoria's neutrality proclamation had prolonged the war by several years and resulted in over $100 million in damages to the American Merchant Marine. His accusations not only increased public antagonism against Britain but raised expectations for reparations to unrealistic levels. In Congress Michigan Senator Zachariah Chandler demanded that Canada be ceded to the United States to compensate for fully half of the expense of the Civil War.

The atmosphere made resolution of the issue seem unlikely, but when President Ulysses S. Grant came into office in 1869, his secretary of state, Hamilton Fish, moved to reopen negotiations. Although Great Britain and the United States appeared as polarized as ever, Grant was receptive to compromise within the bounds of political expediency, and the British appeared to be similarly disposed. After a year of delicate negotiations that were complicated by peripheral issues of British dominion in Canada, Canadian-American fishing and trading agreements, and the San Juan Island water boundary, both countries agreed on the formation of a joint high commission to resolve all issues between the United States, Great Britain, and Canada. The commission met in Washington, D.C., in March, and after considerable deliberation a treaty was drafted that included the *Alabama* claims articles. The United States and Great Britain signed the Treaty of Washington on May 8, 1871, and on May 24 Congress ratified it over last-minute objections. Parliament followed suit several weeks later, and ratifications were exchanged on June 17, 1871.

In addition to addressing the matter of future responsibilities of neutral governments toward the fitting out, arming, and equipping of vessels by belligerents, the articles of the treaty included an agreement to settle direct claims by arbitration. Accordingly an international commission of jurists was assembled in Geneva in December 1871. After the United States and Great Britain presented their arguments, the process of arbitration almost collapsed owing to the

intensity of disagreement over the issue of indirect claims. After heated exchanges the tribunal was charged with consideration of the direct claims and retired to reach a decision. On July 22 the members voted to dismiss outright the claims associated with CSS *Georgia,* but Britain was held responsible for damage done by CSS *Florida,* CSS *Alabama,* and CSS *Shenandoah* after that vessel was permitted to refit and resupply in Melbourne, Australia. A total of $15.5 million was determined to be the amount of damages for which Britain was responsible to the United States. Although the decision met with some dissatisfaction, both sides decided it was acceptable. The precedent set by two nations settling their differences by arbitration rather than war was lost in the power politics of the twentieth century, but the exercise contributed to a strengthening of Anglo-American relations that helped shape world history.

[*See also entries on the ships* Alabama; Florida; Georgia; Shenandoah.]

BIBLIOGRAPHY

Adams, Ephram Douglass. *Great Britain and the Civil War.* 2 vols. New York, 1958.

Beaman, Charles C., Jr. *The National and Private "Alabama Claims" and Their "Final and Amicable Settlement."* Washington, D.C., 1871.

Callahan, James Morton. *Diplomatic History of the Southern Confederacy.* Baltimore, 1901. Reprint, New York, 1964.

Cook, Adrian. *The* Alabama *Claims: American Politics and Anglo-American Relations, 1865–1872.* Ithaca, N.Y., 1975.

Lambert, C. S. "The CSS *Alabama* Lost and Found." *American History Illustrated* 23 (October 1988).

GORDON WATTS

ALEXANDER, EDWARD PORTER

ALEXANDER, EDWARD PORTER (1835–1910), brigadier general. Born on May 26, 1835, in Washington, Georgia, Alexander graduated from West Point in 1857, standing third out of thirty-eight cadets. He received a brevet second lieutenant's commission in the Engineer Corps and remained at the academy as an instructor. Expeditions to Utah and the Washington Territory interrupted his teaching routine. Promotion came slow for Alexander, but on October 10, 1858, he became a full second lieutenant. With his native state out of the Union, followed by Abraham Lincoln's call for troops, Alexander reluctantly tendered his resignation on May 1, 1861. "My people are going to war," he wrote. "If I don't come and bear my part, they will believe me to be a coward."

EDWARD PORTER ALEXANDER. NATIONAL ARCHIVES

A captain's commission, dated March 16, 1861, waited for Alexander when he arrived in Richmond the following month. Jefferson Davis placed the Georgian in charge of the Signal Corps in Richmond, and on June 29, he was instructed to perform the same service with the Confederate army at Manassas. From an observation tower that Alexander constructed near the Van Pelt house, he alerted officers to a Federal flanking movement on July 21. In the aftermath of the victory at Manassas, Gen. P. G. T. Beauregard complimented Alexander and his Signal Corps.

Alexander's superiors quickly recognized his wide talents. He consequently shouldered a number of diverse assignments. Not only was he chief of ordnance for Beauregard after Manassas, but he also handled similar duties for Gen. Joseph E. Johnston that fall; William N. Pendleton remained in control of Johnston's Ordnance Department but in name only. Besides his engineering and reconnoitering responsibilities, Alexander found time to create a more efficient supply system and experimented with new weapons ranging from rockets to flaming spears. For his efforts, he received a major's commission on April 18, 1862. After Robert E. Lee took command in May 1862, he instructed Alexander to oversee the operation of an observation balloon during the Seven Days' campaign (June 25–July 1). Alexander earned the confidence of his new superior who promoted him to lieutenant colonel on July 17, to date from December 31, 1861.

After the Army of the Potomac had been repelled outside Richmond, Alexander maintained his varied duties, plus the new chore of training the reserve artillery batteries. Pendleton had proved woefully inadequate as chief of artillery, but Lee could not find a delicate way of dismissing him. Alexander, as a result, consistently handled many of Pendleton's assignments throughout the war. While the fighting raged at Second Manassas (August 29–30) and Sharpsburg (September 17), Alexander busied himself behind the lines with the Ordnance Department. Supported by Lee's recommendation, Alexander received command of Stephen D. Lee's famous artillery battalion on November 7, although he did not relinquish control of the Ordnance Department until December 4. At Fredericksburg on December 13, Alexander insisted that Confederate batteries unlimber on the brow of Marye's Heights so that the guns could blast the infantry, a decision that sealed the fate of the attacking Union soldiers. On March 3, 1863, he was boosted in rank to full colonel.

Alexander constantly strove to enhance the artillery's effectiveness on the battlefield. During the winter of 1862–1863, he helped implement a battalion system that took tactical control of the artillery away from infantry commanders and restored it to ordnance officers. It also corralled batteries into groups of sixteen guns, which made it possible for Lee's artillery to concentrate its firepower. Alexander revealed the potency of this new system at Chancellorsville on May 3, when he massed over thirty guns at Hazel Grove. His skillful direction of Confederate artillery broke the Union defense at Fairview.

After the reorganization of the army following Thomas J. ("Stonewall") Jackson's death, Gen. James Longstreet and Lee wanted Alexander as chief of artillery of the First Corps. Because they did not wish to offend the senior officer, Col. James B. Walton, Longstreet decided on an awkward arrangement that allowed Walton to maintain his post while Alexander directed the tactical operations of the battalions. At Gettysburg on July 3, Alexander not only organized the massive cannonade that preceded Pickett's Charge but was also given the responsibility of determining when the infantry should advance toward Cemetery Ridge. "It was no longer Gen. Lee's inspiration" that would decide the battle, Alexander recalled, "but my cold judgment." Though his missiles proved indecisive, Alexander overall expertly managed the logistical problems that plagued his command during the entire Gettysburg campaign.

Alexander accompanied Longstreet's corps to the West in the fall of 1863 but arrived too late to participate in the fighting at Chickamauga (September 19–20). From October to December, Alexander's battalion saw limited action during the Chattanooga and Knoxville campaigns. The following winter, Johnston asked for Alexander's promotion to brigadier general and his transfer to the Army of Tennessee as chief of artillery. Jefferson Davis refused Johnston's application, confiding to a friend that Alexander was "one of a very few whom Gen Lee wd [sic] not give to anybody." Davis, however, promised Alexander a brigadier generalship, which he received on February 26, 1864. With the promotion—one of three such commissions awarded to a Confederate artillery officer during the war—came official control of artillery in the First Corps.

The spring of 1864 found Alexander and the rest of Longstreet's troops reunited with the Army of Northern Virginia. When the overland campaign opened in the Wilderness on May 5, Alexander had ninety-one guns under his command. He had little opportunity to use them until June 3 at Cold Harbor where the disposition of his ordnance produced a withering cross fire that doomed the Federal assault. During the siege of Petersburg, Alexander commanded the guns that guarded a twenty-four-mile line between the Appomattox and Chickahominy rivers. Because of Alexander's engineering expertise, Lee relied on him to perfect the mazelike fortifications of the Richmond defenses.

When Lee surrendered at Appomattox on April 9, Alexander had established himself as the army's most prominent artillerist. He recounted his war experiences in *Military Memoirs of a Confederate* (1907). A more revealing look at the Army of Northern Virginia is contained in Alexander's personal recollections, *Fighting for the Confederacy* (1989). This work stands as one of the richest firsthand accounts of Confederate operations in Virginia. Alexander also enjoyed a distinguished postwar career as a railroad president and professor of engineering while serving in a number of appointed government positions. He died on April 28, 1910.

BIBLIOGRAPHY

Alexander, Edward P. *Fighting for the Confederacy: The Personal Recollections of General Edward Porter Alexander.* Edited by Gary W. Gallagher. Chapel Hill, N.C., 1989.

Alexander, Edward P. *Military Memoirs of a Confederate: A Critical Narrative.* New York, 1907. Reprint, Dayton, Ohio, 1977.

Klein, Maury. *Edward Porter Alexander.* Athens, Ga., 1971.

PETER S. CARMICHAEL

ALLEN, HENRY W.

ALLEN, HENRY W. (1820–1866), brigadier general and governor of Confederate Louisiana. Allen's energy and initiative kept resources available to fuel the war effort after the Union army severed the Trans-Mississippi from the Confederacy. Historian E. Merton Coulter judged that "it was Henry W. Allen who showed the rest of the Confederate governors how good a Confederate a state governor could be."

Born April 29, 1820, in Farmville, Virginia, Allen moved with his family to Missouri when he was thirteen. He attended Marion College and left for Grand Gulf, Mississippi, where he worked as a tutor and set up his own law practice in 1841. On a six-month tour in Texas in 1842, he saw minor action with the militia against the Mexicans. Allen became a prosperous sugar planter in West Baton Rouge, Louisiana, attended law classes at Harvard, and showed promise as a politician.

As a soldier, Allen demonstrated considerable bravery under fire—a trait that also cut short his military career. Late in July 1861, he assumed command of the Fourth Louisiana, which was ordered to Tennessee to serve with the Second Corps of the Army of the Mississippi under Braxton Bragg. At Shiloh (April 6–7, 1862) the recently commissioned colonel led his men in a number of assaults on what became known as the Hornet's Nest. Despite wounds in both cheeks, Allen would not leave the field and even assisted in rallying stragglers to resist the successful Federal counterattack of April 7. At Baton Rouge on August 5, 1862, he sustained a crippling wound to his right leg while charging a Federal battery. Allen refused amputation, but the shattered leg caused great pain and prevented his return to active duty. Jefferson Davis recognized his contribution by promoting Allen to brigadier general on August 19, 1863.

The war hero returned home to Louisiana and on November 21, 1863, was elected governor of the Confederate government sitting at Shreveport. Rejecting any talk of peace, he vigorously pursued the Confederate cause, instituting a number of progressive actions to sustain the war effort. Allen placed a priority on regulating currency to reduce rampaging inflation, traded cotton with Mexico to secure supplies and medicines, instituted programs for relief of disabled veterans and their families, and imposed governmental direction on mining and manufacturing. Though he collided now and then with the Davis government over irregularities in impressment procedures, Allen time and again favored continued resistance: he called for arming slaves to fight and at first supported Gen. E. Kirby Smith's desire to battle on after the Army of Northern Virginia surrendered in April 1865. Only in the next month—when he realized the war was lost—did Allen meet with other governors to discuss acceptable terms for peace.

Fearing for his safety, Allen with a number of other Confederates fled to Mexico where he began publishing an English-language newspaper, *Mexican Times.* His wounds, however, continued to plague him, contributing to a general breakdown in his health. The former governor died in Mexico on April 22, 1866.

BIBLIOGRAPHY

Cassidy, Vincent H., and Amos E. Simpson. *Henry Watkins Allen of Louisiana.* Baton Rouge, La., 1964.

Dorsey, Sarah A. *Recollections of Henry Watkins Allen, Brigadier-General, Confederate States Army, Ex-Governor of Louisiana.* New York, 1866.

Kerby, Robert L. *Kirby Smith's Confederacy: The Trans-Mississippi South, 1863–1865.* New York, 1972.

WILLIAM ALAN BLAIR

ALLEN, WILLIAM WIRT

ALLEN, WILLIAM WIRT (1835–1894), brigadier general. Born in New York City, Allen moved to Montgomery, Alabama, as a child. After graduating from the College of New Jersey (now Princeton) in 1854, he studied law but left that profession in 1861 to farm in Alabama. Although unenthusiastic about the war, Allen entered the Confederate army as first lieutenant in the Montgomery Mounted Rifles. On March 18, 1862, he was elected major of the First Alabama Cavalry.

After his first serious action at Shiloh, Allen was promoted to colonel, leading his regiment in Gen. Braxton Bragg's invasion of Kentucky. He gained distinction at Bear Wallow, Horse Cave, and Green River and was wounded at Perryville. Allen commanded Brig. Gen. Joseph Wheeler's brigade during Wheeler's tenure as Bragg's chief of cavalry. He led this brigade on a raid near Murfreesboro, Tennessee, on November 27, 1862, earning praise from Bragg and Wheeler. Allen lost part of his right hand to a gunshot wound at Overall's Creek on December 31.

After recovering, Allen was commissioned brigadier general as of February 26, 1864, and commanded the only remaining full-strength cavalry brigade in the Army of Tennessee, stationed at Dalton, Georgia. He probed Maj. Gen. William Tecumseh Sherman's front and guarded against movements toward Atlanta. After the Army of Tennessee retreated into Georgia, Allen commanded an all-Alabama brigade during the Atlanta campaign. On a raid through Tennessee in August 1864, he succeeded Maj. Gen. William Thompson Martin as commander of the division containing his own and Col. Charles C. Crew's brigades. Allen further distinguished himself at Cassville, Pickett's Mill, and Decatur, and in the July 29 capture of Maj. Gen. George Stoneman's raiding column near Macon.

Allen's original brigade, now commanded by Brig. Gen. Robert Anderson, was added to his division in late 1864. When Allen fought at Waynesboro, Georgia, he remained on the field even though he was wounded and had two horses shot from under him. He then entered South Carolina, continually harassing Sherman's March to the Sea. His division prevented the enemy occupation of Aiken, drawing praise from Governor Andrew G. Magrath. The ladies of Aiken gave Allen a silk flag with the inscription: "Your valor cheers our hearts."

On March 4, 1865, Allen was appointed temporary major general, the last such promotion made by President Jefferson Davis. The Confederate Senate, however, failed to confirm the promotion before its final adjournment on March 18. Allen surrendered at Salisbury, North Carolina, on May 3, 1865, and was paroled as a brigadier general before the end of the year. He had a distinguished war record, suffering three wounds and having ten horses shot from under him.

After the war, Allen returned to his plantation and became involved in the railroad business. He served as federal marshal during President Grover Cleveland's first term. Allen died in Sheffield, Alabama, on November 21, 1894.

BIBLIOGRAPHY

Barrett, John G. *Sherman's March through the Carolinas.* Chapel Hill, N.C., 1956.

Derry, Joseph T. *Georgia.* Vol. 6 of *Confederate Military History.* Edited by Clement A. Evans. Atlanta, 1899. Vol. 7 of extended ed. Wilmington, N.C., 1987.

Wheeler, Joseph. *Alabama.* Vol. 7 of *Confederate Military History.* Edited by Clement A. Evans. Atlanta, 1899. Vol. 8 of extended ed. Wilmington, N.C., 1987.

ROBERT F. PACE

AMERICAN PARTY

The American party was a secret nativist organization that enjoyed momentary success in the South in the mid-1850s. Growing out of the Secret Order of the Star-Spangled Banner, the party capitalized on hostility to immigrants and Catholics and quickly became a power in the border states and Louisiana where there were significant immigrant populations. Throughout the South, it also attracted a number of ex-Whigs looking for a national conservative alternative to the Democratic party. When questioned, members pretended to know nothing about the party; hence, they became known as Know-Nothings.

A number of prominent Southern political leaders, including John J. Crittenden of Kentucky, Kenneth Rayner of North Carolina, John Bell of Tennessee, and Sam Houston of Texas, joined the party, and by 1855 it was the major rival to the Democrats in the South. The party's defeat that year in the Virginia gubernatorial election, however, coupled with deepening sectional divisions in the national organization over the slavery issue, severely weakened it in the region. In

1856 the Southern-controlled national convention nominated Millard Fillmore for president. Running as a Union candidate, Fillmore made a strong race in the South, polling almost 45 percent of the popular vote; he carried Maryland and only narrowly lost several other Southern states. But Northern desertions left Fillmore a distant third nationally and sealed the fate of the party.

The American party retained a separate organization in some parts of the South until 1860 (New Orleans elected a Know-Nothing mayor that year), but ultimately the bulk of its southern members joined various opposition coalitions and voted for Bell in 1860. The significance of Southern Know-Nothingism lay in its role in opposition to the Democratic party and in sectionalism before the war.

BIBLIOGRAPHY

Holt, Michael F. *The Political Crisis of the 1850s.* New York, 1978.
Overdyke, W. Darrell. *The Know-Nothing Party in the South.* Baton Rouge, La., 1950.

WILLIAM E. GIENAPP

ANDERSON, GEORGE B.

ANDERSON, GEORGE B. (1831–1862), brigadier general. A native of North Carolina, George Burgwyn Anderson was born April 12, 1831 (thirty years to the day before the firing on Fort Sumter). He attended West Point and performed so brilliantly a contemporary called him "the *very superior* mind" in the class of 1852. But nine years later, when he left the U.S. Army, he had advanced only to the rank of first lieutenant.

Anderson was commissioned commanding colonel of the Fourth North Carolina Infantry on May 16, 1861. He impressed his troops as "a splendid specimen." The regiment arrived at Manassas in July just after the battle there. Colonel Anderson served for months as post commandant at Manassas Junction. He led the Fourth during the Confederate retreat in March 1862 and on to the peninsula in April. Anderson and the Fourth fought their first battle at Seven Pines, where the colonel commanded Featherston's Brigade in the absence of its brigadier. In bitter fighting, the brigade lost nearly half of its strength.

Anderson won promotion to brigadier general soon after Seven Pines. His brigade included his old Fourth North Carolina and three other regiments from the state. He led his new command with real distinction during the Seven Days' fighting and was wounded in the hand at Malvern Hill. The brigade missed the Battle of Second Manassas, but played an important role at South Mountain. At Sharpsburg on September 17, 1862, Anderson posted his brigade in a sunken lane that his men immortalized as the Bloody Lane. A bullet wound in the ankle knocked the general out of the fight. Although the injury appeared to be more painful than serious, infection forced amputation of the limb and Anderson died of complications on October 16. His intellect, training, and early war performance all suggest that Anderson's premature death halted a career that might well have been spectacular.

BIBLIOGRAPHY

Gales, Seaton. "Gen. George Burgwyn Anderson." *Land We Love* 3 (1867): 93–100.
Waddell, A. M. "General George Burgwyn Anderson." *Southern Historical Society Papers* 14 (1890): 387–397.

ROBERT K. KRICK

ANDERSON, GEORGE THOMAS "TIGE"

ANDERSON, GEORGE THOMAS "TIGE" (1824–1901), brigadier general. George Thomas Anderson, more often called "Tige" by his soldiers, was one of eight colonels promoted to brigadier general in the Army of Northern Virginia on November 1, 1862. Of those eight, four—including Anderson—commanded their brigades, except when absent due to wounds, until the surrender at Appomattox in April 1865. They were among the most efficient brigadiers in the Confederate army.

Anderson was born in Covington, Georgia, on February 3, 1824, and left his studies at Emory College to enlist as a cavalryman in the Mexican War. He was later commissioned in the regular army and served as a captain in the First U.S. Cavalry from 1855 to 1858.

When the Eleventh Georgia Infantry was organized in July 1861, Anderson became its first colonel. He commanded his regiment until the summer of 1862, after the Seven Days' campaign, when he succeeded to brigade command. Anderson, though still a colonel, led the brigade through the Second Manassas and Sharpsburg campaigns and won the praise of his superiors.

Anderson's first battle as a brigadier general was in December 1862 at Fredericksburg. For the rest of the war his brigade of Georgians served in James Longstreet's First Corps in the division commanded by John Bell Hood and later by Charles W. Field. Anderson's brigade, with almost all of Longstreet's corps, did not participate in the Chancellorsville campaign. It rejoined Robert E. Lee for the

Gettysburg campaign, however, and engaged in the fierce fighting in the Wheatfield on July 2, 1863, where Anderson was severely wounded in the thigh. He recovered in time to lead his brigade in the Knoxville campaign of November 1863 and later commanded it in the final campaigns from the Wilderness to Appomattox, from May 1864 to April 1865.

Though not truly a brilliant officer in the mold of Robert Rodes, John B. Gordon, or William Mahone, Anderson was an able administrator, a fine combat leader, and one of the most dependable brigadiers under Lee. "Brave Old Tige, how his boys loved him!" a veteran who served in Anderson's brigade remembered years later. "With such officers as we had in the Army of Northern Virginia, how could the boys help fighting as we did?"

After the war Anderson lived in Georgia and Alabama and held several local government positions, most notably as a chief of police. He died in Anniston, Alabama, on April 4, 1901.

BIBLIOGRAPHY

Compiled Military Service Records. George T. Anderson. Microcopy M331, Roll 6. Record Group 109. National Archives, Washington, D.C.

Derry, Joseph T. *Georgia.* Vol. 6 of *Confederate Military History.* Edited by Clement A. Evans. Atlanta, 1899. Vol. 7 of extended ed. Wilmington, N.C., 1987.

J. TRACY POWER

ANDERSON, JAMES PATTON

ANDERSON, JAMES PATTON (1822–1872), congressman from Florida and major general. Born on February 16, 1822, in Winchester, Franklin County, Tennessee, James Patton Anderson was raised on the family farm, known as Craggy Hope, until after his father, William Preston Anderson, a former U.S. Army officer and Federal district attorney, died in April 1831. Following his father's death, Anderson's mother, Margaret Adair Anderson, took him and his five siblings to live at her parents' home in Mercer County, Kentucky. There he received his early education in country schools and from private tutors. In October 1836, Anderson was enrolled at Jefferson College in Cannonsburg, Pennsylvania, but because of family financial misfortunes, his education there was curtailed after one year. Moving to Hernando, DeSoto County, Mississippi, Anderson, known to his friends as Patton, spent part of the years 1838 and 1839 working with his mother's new husband, Dr. J. N. Bybee, in constructing a new family home. There, he also began the study and prac-

tice of medicine, presumably under Dr. Bybee's tutelage. Resuming his studies at Jefferson College early in 1839, Anderson was graduated from that school in the fall of 1840.

After graduation, Patton Anderson returned to DeSoto County and studied the practice of law with the firm of Buckner and Delafield, and in 1843 he was admitted to the bar. But, finding the legal profession overcrowded in that section of Mississippi, Anderson accepted a position as deputy sheriff of DeSoto County offered by his brother-in-law, the sheriff there. He held the position until 1846. During the years 1844 and 1845, Anderson spent his summers furthering his law studies at Montrose in Frankfort, Kentucky. Following his term as deputy sheriff, he formed a law partnership and began practicing law full-time.

Complying with a request of the governor of Mississippi, in October 1847, Anderson organized a company of volunteer troops from a local militia regiment and was quickly elected its captain. With the addition of four more companies, the First Battalion of Mississippi Rifles was formed, and, after being supplied in New Orleans, the battalion was sent to Tampico, Mexico, in January 1848. There the battalion performed garrison duty during the Mexican War, and on February 22 Anderson was elected lieutenant colonel of the unit at the age of twenty-six. Contracting malaria in Mexico, he suffered from the disease for the rest of his life. When the war ended, Anderson and his men were mustered out of service at Vicksburg, Mississippi, and he arrived back in DeSoto County on July 4, 1848.

Anderson continued his law practice after returning home, until the fall of 1849, when he was elected to the Mississippi legislature. During his term of office, Anderson closely supported the views of U.S. Senator Jefferson Davis and Governor John Quitman—both of Mississippi—regarding the Compromise of 1850, which they opposed. As a result of this stance, he lost his bid for reelection in 1851.

Once more reentering the field of law, Anderson remained in that profession until he left for Washington in 1853 in an attempt to secure a commission in a new regular infantry regiment. But when the bill responsible for creating the regiment failed to become law, Anderson instead accepted the position of U.S. marshal for the Territory of Washington. In obtaining this position in the administration of President Franklin Pierce, he was indebted to Jefferson Davis, then serving as secretary of state.

Before leaving for the Pacific coast, Anderson traveled to Memphis, Tennessee, where he married his cousin, Henrietta Buford Adair, on April 30, 1853, and within an hour of the ceremony he and his new bride were en route by steamer to Washington Territory. Traveling via New Orleans through Nicaragua and San Francisco, they finally reached Astoria, Oregon, in late June. Leaving his wife with relatives in Astoria, Anderson traveled overland to Olympia, Washington Territory, arriving on July 4. The next day, he began a months-long foot and canoe journey through the territory taking the census.

Upon completion of the census, Patton and Henrietta Anderson set out in a canoe up the Cowlitz River and then on foot overland to settle in Olympia. There the Andersons soon bought a house in which they lived for the rest of their stay in Washington Territory. During that time Anderson discharged his duties as marshal and practiced law when time and circumstances allowed.

Running as a Democrat, Anderson was elected in June 1855 as a delegate from the Territory to the Thirty-fourth U.S. Congress. In October of that year, he and his wife left for the District of Columbia, reaching the city several days before the first session of Congress began in December. Also in 1855, the Andersons spent the Christmas holidays with their aunt, Ellen Adair Beatty, at her plantation, Casa Bianca, in Monticello, Jefferson County, Florida, a few miles east of Tallahassee. During that time he agreed to manage his aunt's quite extensive holdings, which, among other property, consisted of at least 130 slaves.

When his term in Congress expired on March 4, 1857, Anderson was offered the position of governor and superintendant of Indian affairs of Washington Territory by newly elected President James Buchanan. Fearing the dissolution of the Union, however, he declined to leave the South. Wanting to be on hand for any eventuality, he then returned to manage Casa Bianca as his sole occupation.

In December 1860, nearly four years later, Anderson was elected as a delegate from Jefferson County to the Florida secession convention, which convened in Tallahassee on January 1, 1861. There he endorsed wholeheartedly the state's ordinance of secession, which was passed on January 10. While this convention was still in session, it chose Anderson and three others as delegates to the Provisional Congress in Montgomery, Alabama. There he served on the committees of Public Affairs and Public Lands and offered the unusual proposal that slaves serve the Confederate military as nurses, cooks, pioneers, and teamsters. After adopting the Provisional Constitution and electing Jefferson Davis provisional president, Congress adjourned, and Patton Anderson returned to Casa Bianca.

Late in March 1861, at the request of Florida Governor Madison S. Perry, Anderson organized a company of infantry (the Jefferson Rifles), which he took to the Chattahoochee Arsenal to become part of the First Florida Infantry (the Magnolia Regiment). While at Chattahoochee, Anderson was elected the regiment's colonel on April 5, and later that night the command left for Pensacola to join Confederate Gen. Braxton Bragg's army. Arriving at Pensacola on April 11—the day before the Civil War began—Anderson and his troops spent the next eight months in that vicinity drilling and organizing. During much of that time, Anderson served as a brigade commander, but the only action seen was a small but apparently successful amphibious raid on October 8 and 9, 1861, against Union defenders—the Sixth New York Infantry—on Santa Rosa Island, a mile and a half offshore.

On February 10, 1862, Anderson was commissioned brigadier general, and from March 29 until June 1862, he commanded the Second Brigade in Gen. Daniel Ruggle's First Division, Bragg's Second Corps, of Gen. Albert Sidney Johnston's Army of the Mississippi. On the first day of the Battle of Shiloh, April 6, 1862, he led his brigade of green troops credibly, helping to capture a Federal battery and

> ## Anderson bravely rode along his line, trying desperately to rally his men. . . .

overrunning the camps belonging to the Union troops of Gen. William Tecumseh Sherman's division. Later that day Anderson and his men battled successfully in the horror known as the "Hornet's Nest," where the brigade suffered heavy casualties. The next day, his troops covered the Confederate retreat after Gen. Ulysses S. Grant secured a decisive Union victory.

Following Shiloh, Anderson took divisional command in June without being formally promoted. At Perryville, Kentucky, on October 8, 1862, during Bragg's ill-fated Kentucky campaign, Anderson led his division satisfactorily, although as a result of the drawn battle, Bragg withdrew his army to Chattanooga, Tennessee, thereby signaling the failure of the campaign.

On November 20, 1862, Anderson was put in command of a division in Gen. William J. Hardee's First Corps, Army of Tennessee, until December 27, when he was assigned command of the Third Brigade in Gen. Jones M. Withers's Second Division of Gen. Leonidas Polk's Corps. From December 31, 1862, until January 2, 1863, at the Battle of Murfreesboro, Tennessee, Anderson gained in his military prominence by leading this brigade bravely. On the morning of the first day of the battle, in a series of bloody charges made against Gen. James S. Negley's division of the Federal Fourteenth Corps, Anderson's Mississippi and Alabama infantrymen were cut to pieces but eventually routed the Northerners and captured nine artillery pieces and many prisoners. Nevertheless, the result of this battle on January 2 was the resounding defeat of Bragg's army by Gen. William Rosecrans's Union forces.

From that point until the second day of the Battle of Chickamauga (September 19–20, 1863), Anderson, for the most part, continued commanding at brigade level. But when Gen. Thomas C. Hindman, who had replaced Withers, was wounded during the battle, Anderson again rose to division-level command when he replaced Hindman late on the night of September 20. During the Confederate breakthrough earlier that day, Anderson's men had helped defeat the Federal army's right, taking eight fieldpieces, a number of flags, and many prisoners. Sent to another part of the battlefield later, Anderson's brigade continued its efficient service, helping to secure the Confederacy's greatest victory in the western theater.

Remaining in command of Hindman's division after the battle, he led it all through the siege of Chattanooga in October and November 1863. On November 25, however, Anderson's men were routed at the Battle of Missionary Ridge. This disaster was Anderson's greatest humiliation of the war.

On February 17, 1864, Patton Anderson finally was appointed to the rank of major general in the Confederate army, a rank more in keeping with his military position. But with this promotion came his transfer from the Army of Tennessee on March 4 to the command of the relatively small District of Florida, where he held sway over some twelve thousand soldiers. His sojourn in Florida provided no great battles, and his duties there were comparatively pedestrian.

After Sherman began his campaign for Atlanta in May 1864, Anderson was recalled in July to again take over Hindman's division in the Army of Tennessee, now commanded by Gen. Joseph E. Johnston, who had succeeded Bragg after that general's defeat at Chattanooga. The division, at that time, belonged to Gen. Stephen D. Lee's corps, and Anderson took command on July 30, just after the Battle of Ezra Church near Atlanta.

During the Battle of Jonesboro, south of Atlanta, on August 31, 1864, Anderson was in charge of Lee's right division. The Confederate plan of attack against the Federal forces that day was to be a coordinated assault by Lee and Gen. William J. Hardee's corps, under the command of Gen. Patrick Cleburne, which was to begin at 3:00 in the afternoon. Lee, for some reason, advanced too early, however, stepping his men off at 2:20 against Union Gen. John Logan's Fifteenth Corps. Anderson pushed his troops hard over open ground until he reached a spot about eighty yards from Logan's entrenched Federals, who then rose to give the Southerners a brutal, killing fire that mowed them down in rows. With his soldiers pinned to the ground and waiting for reinforcements that never came, Anderson bravely rode along his line, trying desperately to rally his men to continue the charge. But, during this attempt, he received a wound which tore through the lower part of his face, fracturing his jawbone on both sides and slicing his tongue. So serious was the injury that he was nearly mustered out of service by military doctors for disability. After about an hour Lee withdrew his corps from the field and early the next morning marched off to the north. The Confederates lost the Battle of Jonesboro later that day after continued Federal pressure forced them to retreat to Lovejoy's Station.

While recuperating in Monticello, Anderson followed, as well as he could, the continuing defeat of the Confederate armies. Finally, feeling obliged for patriotic reasons to rejoin the Southern cause in the field—and against the better judgment of his physicians—he took command, on April 9, 1865—the day that Gen. Robert E. Lee surrendered his Army of Northern Virginia to Gen. Ulysses S. Grant—of a division of Georgia and South Carolina troops formerly under the command of Gen. William B. Taliaferro, Gen. Alexander P. Stewart's corps, Army of Tennessee. Fighting through some of the last battles of the Civil War in the Carolinas, James Patton Anderson finally surrendered with General Johnston and the Army of Tennessee at Durham Station, North Carolina, on April 26, 1865, thereby ending the Civil War in the East. Anderson and his men were paroled—under the same terms given General Lee at Appomattox—at Greensboro, North Carolina, shortly after the surrender.

With the war over, Anderson moved his family to Memphis, Tennessee, but his wound received at Jonesboro was too debilitating for a physically active occupation. To support himself, he served as a tax official, sold insurance, and edited a small journal devoted to agricultural topics until he died on September 20, 1872.

As a soldier, Anderson was considered to be quite capable and brave, although he certainly is not one of the Confederacy's better-known general officers. While serving under Braxton Bragg, who was extremely unpopular with his lieutenants because of his abrasive, erratic personality and his overall military incompetence, Anderson is said never to have participated in the verbal attacks and undermining tactics engaged in by those other officers. Later, though still ill from the effects of his gunshot wound, he felt it his duty to return to field command. He obviously was a man of high principals, abilities, and loyalties.

BIBLIOGRAPHY

Anderson, General James Patton. "Autobiography of General James Patton Anderson." *Southern Historical Society Papers* 24 (1896): 52–72. Reprint, Wilmington, N.C., 1991.

Bailey, Ronald H. *Battles for Atlanta: Sherman Moves East.* Alexandria, Va., 1985.

Cozzens, Peter. *No Better Place to Die: The Battle of Stones River.* Urbana, Ill., 1990.

Davis, William C., ed. *The Confederate General.* Vol. 1. Harrisburg, Pa., 1991.

McMurry, Richard M. "Patton Anderson: Major General, C.S.A." *Blue and Gray Magazine,* 1, no. 2, October–November, 1983.

U.S. War Department. *War of the Rebellion: A Compilation of the Official Records of the Union and Confederate Armies.* Washington, D.C., 1880–1901. Ser. 1: Vol. 10, pts. 1–2; vol. 16, pts. 1–2; vol. 20, pts. 1–2; vol. 30, pts. 1–4; vol. 38, pts. 1–5; vol. 47, pts. 1–3.

WARREN WILKINSON

ANDERSON, RICHARD HERON

ANDERSON, RICHARD HERON (1821–1879), lieutenant general. The grandson of Col. Richard Anderson, who commanded the Maryland Line in the Revolutionary War, was born on October 7, 1821, near Statesburg, Sumter County, South Carolina. Following his education at Edge Hill Academy, Anderson entered the United States Military Academy. He graduated in 1842, ranking fortieth of fifty-five in a class that also included future Confederate generals James Longstreet, Lafayette McLaws, and D. H. Hill. As brevet second lieutenant of Dragoons, Anderson saw extensive service on the western frontier and was with the troops occupying Texas in 1845 and 1846. During the war with Mexico, Anderson accompanied Gen. Winfield Scott's expedition from Vera Cruz and was breveted first lieutenant for gallant and meritorious conduct in the engagement at San Augustín. Ten years after the war the young officer was presented a sword by his native state inscribed: "South Carolina to Capt. Richard Heron Anderson, a memorial of gallant conduct in service at Vera Cruz, Cherubusco, Molino del Rey, Mexico."

On the secession of South Carolina in December 1860, Anderson resigned his commission and became colonel of the First South Carolina Infantry Regiment. He was present at the firing on Fort Sumter, and when P. G. T. Beauregard went north to take charge of forces in Virginia, Anderson was placed in command of the defenses of Charleston. He was promoted to brigadier general on July 18, 1861, and a month later was ordered to Pensacola as the top assistant to Gen. Braxton Bragg. In this capacity, Anderson directed the only engagement in the territory, a night attack against the Wilson Zouaves of New York.

Increased activity in Virginia caused the removal of Anderson to that state in early 1862. There he was given command of a brigade in the division of his old West Point classmate, James Longstreet. Anderson's conduct in the Battle of Williamsburg elicited high praise from Longstreet, who reported that the attack "of the two brigades under Gen. R. H. Anderson . . . was made with such spirit and regularity as to have driven back the most determined foe. This decided the day in our favor."

On July 14, following the repulse of the Federals in the Seven Days' Battles around Richmond, Anderson was promoted to major general and given command of a division formerly led by Benjamin Huger. When Longstreet's other units moved northward to combat a new Northern army under John Pope, Anderson remained behind to cover Richmond until it could be determined that the capital was safe from further attack. He rejoined the Army of Northern Virginia in time to participate in the final day's action at the Battle of Second Manassas. In the ensuing Maryland campaign, Anderson's division reinforced D. H. Hill at the Bloody Lane in the Battle of Sharpsburg. Anderson suffered a thigh wound early in the fighting but remained on the field until the victory was no longer in doubt; then, according to a contemporary, he "fell fainting from loss of blood."

Anderson returned to duty before the Battle of Fredericksburg in December. He saw little action in that contest, however, as his division held the left of the Confederate position and was not attacked in the Federals' assault on Robert E. Lee's lines.

In the Battle of Chancellorsville in May 1863, the divisions of Anderson and McLaws held the Federals in check while Thomas J. ("Stonewall") Jackson made his famous flank march and attack on the right of the Union line. Later Anderson and McLaws rushed to the assistance of Jubal Early, whose division was under attack by the Union Sixth Corps. Their vigorous action forced the enemy back across the Rappahannock River and closed another Northern "On to Richmond" campaign. For his conduct in this action, Anderson was cited by Lee: "Maj. Gen. R. H. Anderson was also distinguished for the promptness, courage, and skill with which he and his division executed every order."

When Lee reorganized the army in the wake of Jackson's death, Richard S. Ewell and A. P. Hill joined Longstreet as corps commanders. That Anderson was considered for such a post was implied in Lee's message to President Jefferson Davis that "R. H. Anderson and J. B. Hood are also capital officers. They are improving too and will make good corps commanders if necessary."

Anderson's division, one of three in Hill's corps, was at the rear of the column on the first day of the Battle of Gettysburg and saw no action. The next day, in conjunction with two of Longstreet's divisions, Anderson's troops participated in the

> **Anderson suffered a thigh wound early in the fighting but remained on the field until the victory was no longer in doubt.**

attack on the Union left. In this maneuver one of Anderson's brigades reached enemy batteries on Cemetery Ridge before they were surrounded and forced back. On July 3 Anderson supported Pickett's ill-starred attack on the Union center.

When Longstreet was wounded seriously in the Battle of the Wilderness, Anderson was placed in charge of the First Corps until "Old Pete" returned. Anderson's most notable achievement during his chief's absence occurred on the night of May 7–8, 1864. Ordered by Lee to begin his march to Spotsylvania Court House at 3:00 A.M. on the second day, Anderson left four hours earlier. Marching through smoke and searing heat caused by burning woodlands on both sides of the road, Anderson attained the strategic road junction ahead of the Federals. Had he failed in his objective, and enemy forces arrived there first, the Federals would have interposed between Lee and Richmond and enjoyed a shorter route to the capital. Commissioned a lieutenant general on May 31, 1864, Anderson led the corps creditably until Longstreet returned in October, at which time the South Carolinian was given command of the divisions of Robert Hoke and Bushrod Johnson.

On the retreat from Petersburg, Anderson's and Ewell's commands were routed at Sayler's Creek on April 6, 1865. Anderson's shattered divisions were subsequently divided between Longstreet and John B. Gordon. As a general without a command appropriate to his rank, Anderson was authorized to return home. His name, therefore, does not appear on the surrender rolls of Appomattox.

Trained in the profession of arms, Anderson found no demand for his talents in the postwar era. He tried to make a livelihood as a planter and failed. Ultimately, he went to Charleston and became a day laborer in the yards of the South Carolina Railroad. When his plight was called to the attention of authorities, Anderson was appointed state inspector of phosphates, a position he held until June 26, 1879, when he died of apoplexy in Beaufort, South Carolina. He was buried there in St. Helena's graveyard.

BIBLIOGRAPHY

Elliott, Joseph C. *Lieutenant General Richard Heron Anderson: Lee's Noble Soldier.* Dayton, Ohio, 1985.
Thurston, Edmund M. "Memoir of Richard H. Anderson." *Southern Historical Society Papers* 39 (1914): 146. Reprint, Wilmington, N.C., 1991.
Walker, C. Irvine. *The Life of Lieutenant General Richard Heron Anderson.* Charleston, S.C., 1917.
Warner, Ezra J. *Generals in Gray: Lives of the Confederate Commanders.* Baton Rouge, La., 1959.

LOWELL REIDENBAUGH

ANDERSONVILLE PRISON

In November 1863, the Confederate War Department ordered Capt. William Sidney Winder, son of Gen. John H. Winder (the most prominent official in charge of prisons), to locate a site for a new prison in southern Georgia. The Confederates wanted to reduce the problems caused by the accumulation of prisoners of war at Richmond. The younger Winder chose land close to the railroad station at

Andersonville, which gave its name to what its creators formally called Camp Sumter (after the county in which it was then located).

The supervisor of the prison's construction was Winder's cousin, Capt. Richard B. Winder, a quartermaster. From the beginning, local opposition and shortage of materials slowed the work. Nonetheless, in January 1864, Richard Winder put impressed slaves and free blacks to work cutting pine trees

> The dead were buried in trenches in which locations were marked for 12,912 bodies during the prison's existence.

and trimming the trunks into twenty-foot posts. The laborers buried the butts of these in a trench and thus formed a stockade surrounding about sixteen and a half acres. There were two gates with enclosures outside. Sentry boxes were spotted along the stockade's top.

Deficient planning paved the way for disaster. On February 18, 1864, before the prison was ready, the Confederates at Richmond shipped the first trainload of prisoners who arrived seven days later at a stockade whose unfinished end was closed only by threatening cannon. Far from providing shelter, the jailors had not even laid out streets or any other organization to facilitate the future cleansing of a camp intended to hold ten thousand men. While the Confederates finished the stockade, the prisoners used bits of scrap wood and pieces of cloth to cover burrows in the ground that served as shelter.

The Confederates at first issued uncooked rations to prisoners who often lacked utensils. By May the bakery and cookhouse were providing a below-standard version of army rations. Meat was often lacking in quantity and quality, and the cornmeal contained so much husk it caused bowel problems. Richard Winder exacerbated the problems by locating the cooking facilities upstream on the brook running through the stockade, so that the waste together with that of the latrines of the guards' camps polluted the already inadequate water supply. Prisoners dug wells from which to drink, but lacking soap in any case they were unable to keep themselves clean. Since from the start no discipline had been enforced in the disposal of human waste, a sewage-filled swamp along the stream rapidly expanded.

On March 27, 1864, Captain Henry Wirz was ordered to Andersonville to take charge of the prison's interior. Although he made efforts to impose some order, he had only limited authority over the quartermaster, commissary, and guard forces. The latter, who at first were line units of the Confederate army, were soon replaced by Georgia reserve troops composed of youths and older men whose inefficiency concerned everyone except their own commanders. Nonetheless, they manned the guard posts, called the roll within the stockade, and supervised the paroled prisoners who did an increasing amount of the work outside the walls. In the eyes of the inmates, Wirz was seen as responsible for whatever the others did and for all the deteriorating conditions; he became an object of hatred. One of his few popular actions was his support of a prisoner attempt to stop the robbing and murder of fellow captives by so-called raiders and his facilitating the hanging of six of them on July 11, 1864.

The ultimate responsibility for the executions as well as for all else at Andersonville by then lay with General Winder, who had taken command of the post on June 17, 1864. As in other aspects of his service with prisoners, Winder devoted his primary attention to matters of security. He repeatedly expressed concern about inmates' attempts to tunnel out or otherwise escape, and his warnings to the guards to be more vigilant may well have encouraged some to shoot prisoners who crossed the "deadline," which paralleled the stockade about fifteen feet inside, reducing the land available for prisoners.

Under Winder's command the Confederates enlarged the stockade on the north end in late June to take in an additional ten acres. To forestall Union raids on the prison, Winder recruited slaves to build earthworks and surround the enlarged stockade with a second wall and part of a third. He used this work force to repair the damage done to the stockade by an August flood, which also opened a new source of drinking water that prisoners dubbed the "Providence Spring." The spring's name represented an appeal to God—one of the prisoners' responses to the growing horror of conditions at Andersonville.

By July 1, Richmond authorities had sent 26,367 captives to a prison intended for 10,000. With rare exceptions these were enlisted men, and the bulk lived within the enlarged stockade where—even counting the uninhabitable swamp—they had only a bit more than four square yards per man. About 1,355 were in a hospital consisting of a few tents covering five acres. There they received scant treatment for diarrhea, dysentery, and scurvy (the leading killers) and such conditions as typhoid fever, smallpox, and gangrene. The dead were buried in trenches in which locations were marked for 12,912 bodies during the prison's existence.

The prison's population reached a maximum in August 1864 of some 33,000 men. A month later the Confederates began to remove prisoners to camps at Millen, Georgia, and elsewhere. At about the same time, responding to complaints about conditions at Andersonville, the Confederates erected sheds called "barracks." These later were used by the sick as the site became more a hospital than a prison.

When Union invading armies penetrated deeper into the Confederacy, many of the prisoners originally moved from Andersonville were returned, and the prison continued in use until the Confederacy's collapse. Captain Wirz was there paroling prisoners until May 1865, when Union troops arrested him.

After the war, the United States designated the Andersonville graveyard a national cemetery. Union veterans' groups also purchased and preserved the site of the prison yard, where several states erected monuments to their dead. Meanwhile Andersonville's sheer size, high mortality rate, and terrible conditions made it notorious as one of the Civil War's unique atrocities. It became a leading feature in attacks on the memory of the Confederacy, to which Southerners responded defensively. In the twentieth century, Andersonville became a national historic site whose interpreters point out its significance as a memorial to all American prisoners of war.

[*See also* Wirz, Henry.]

BIBLIOGRAPHY

Blakey, Arch Fredric. *General John H. Winder, C.S.A.* Gainesville, Fla., 1990.
Futch, Ovid. *History of Andersonville Prison.* Gainesville, Fla., 1968.
Hesseltine, William B. *Civil War Prisons: A Study in War Psychology.* Columbus, Ohio, 1930. Reprint, New York, 1964.

FRANK L. BYRNE

ANDREWS RAID

On April 12, 1862, the General, a northbound locomotive on the Western and Atlantic Railroad, pulled into Big Shanty, Georgia (present-day Kennesaw), twenty-five miles north of Atlanta. The crew and most of the passengers ambled to the nearby Lacy House for breakfast, but James J. Andrews lingered near the cars.

Andrews, another civilian, and twenty-two Union volunteers had left Shelbyville, Tennessee, on April 7 with orders from Brig. Gen. Ormsby M. Mitchel to steal a train and burn the bridges south of Chattanooga while Mitchel moved against Huntsville, Alabama. After rendezvousing in Marietta, Georgia, Andrews and nineteen of his men were aboard the train when it stopped at Big Shanty. While a dazed Confederate sentry looked on, they uncoupled the General, its tender, and three boxcars and sped northward.

Conductor William A. Fuller, engineer Jeff Cain, and shop foreman Anthony Murphy immediately gave chase on foot. Two miles north of Big Shanty, the winded trio borrowed a handcar and, with the help of some section hands, poled northward until the speeding car was derailed by a break Andrews's men had made in the tracks. Righting the car, the railroad men continued to Etowah, where they found the engine Yonah sitting on a siding.

Andrews had stopped several times to cut the telegraph wires, but for fear of arousing suspicion he had failed to disable the Yonah. Keeping to the railroad's timetable, he sidetracked the General upon reaching Kingston to allow a southbound freight to pass. But a second train followed, and a third. Claiming he had imperative orders to deliver a trainload of gunpowder to Confederate Gen. P. G. T. Beauregard, Andrews demanded an explanation for the delay and learned the increased traffic resulted from Mitchel's capture of Huntsville. Sixty-five minutes passed before the General left Kingston.

Five minutes later, the pursuing Yonah encountered the three southbound trains parked on the main line. Abandoning the little engine, Fuller, Murphy, and Cain sprinted to a junction two miles north of Kingston and commandeered the William L. Smith. A broken rail soon stopped the Smith, but Fuller and Murphy, setting out on foot again, flagged down the Texas just after it left the siding at Adairsville. Engineer Peter J. Bracken promptly backed his cars into the station and took up the chase, still in reverse.

Hampered by a lack of tools that made it difficult to pry up rails, the raiders cut loose two boxcars and dropped crossties across the tracks, desperately trying to gain enough time to burn the rain-soaked bridges north of Adairsville. The Texas pushed both cars onto the nearest siding and, avoiding all obstacles, pursued the fleeing General at speeds exceeding sixty miles per hour. Unable to stop for wood or water, the General ran out of steam two miles north of Ringgold.

> ### Captured and tried, Andrews and seven of his men were hanged. Eight others . . . later escaped from an Atlanta jail.

The relentless Confederate pursuit, bad weather, and just plain bad luck prevented the raiders from doing any lasting damage to the railroad. Captured and tried, Andrews and seven of his men were hanged. Eight others, including two who had missed the train when it left Marietta, later escaped from an Atlanta jail. The six remaining raiders, exchanged as prisoners of war, were the first recipients of the U.S. Medal of Honor.

BIBLIOGRAPHY

"The Battle of the Locomotives." *Atlanta Journal Magazine,* September 29, 1935.

Grose, Parlee C. *The Case of Private Smith and the Remaining Mysteries of the Andrews Raid.* McComb, Ohio, 1963.

McBryde, Randell W. *The Historic "General": A Thrilling Episode of the Civil War.* Chattanooga, [1904].

O'Neill, Charles. *Wild Train: The Story of the Andrews' Raiders.* New York, 1956.

Pittenger, William. *The Great Locomotive Chase: A History of the Andrews Railroad Raid into Georgia in 1862.* New York, [1893].

DAVID EVANS

ANGLO-CONFEDERATE PURCHASING

[*This entry is composed of two articles that discuss Confederate trade and purchasing with Great Britain during the Civil War:* An Overview *and* Anglo-Confederate Trading Company. *See also* Alabama Claims; Enchantress Affair; Erlanger Loan; Laird Rams; New Plan.]

An Overview

In 1861, the wealth of the South consisted chiefly of land and slaves. An agricultural society, it was poor in industrial and manufacturing resources, and its means of transportation were far behind those of the North. Its cities, with the exception of Charleston, Richmond, and New Orleans, were of little importance as trade centers. The states against which the Confederates waged war held roughly two-thirds of the country's population, and their financial and industrial resources were far superior to those of the South.

Despite these circumstances, however, the Confederacy was able to sustain a war lasting four years, largely because of the energetic activities of its commercial agents in Great Britain, who labored steadily to supply the needs of the Southern military forces. Confederate troops were valiant fighters and, in the main, were well led. But they could not fight without arms or supplies, and Southern arsenals and manufacturers could not possibly meet all their needs. The Confederate government, rapidly organized, was quick to appreciate the situation, and very early in the war, before the North had been thoroughly aroused, it dispatched its financial agents and purchasing emissaries to Great Britain.

From the outset, the Confederates were faced with a delicate commercial task. Great Britain, then the leading industrial power in the world, was obviously the most likely source of supplies and finance, and it was also the champion of free trade. But the majority of English people were opposed to slavery, so it was necessary to avoid discussions on the slavery issue and to concentrate on free trade. Of all the European powers, the Confederates looked to Great Britain first for sympathy and assistance. Thus, the primary need was to establish good relations between Great Britain and the Confederate States. In this the South succeeded, quickly laying the foundations of an entente, which, although subject to fluctuations, served admirably as a basis for four years of trade and financial cooperation.

The Confederate government, however, committed an error by using its available sterling exchange and coin at the outset of the war for procurement purposes. As later events showed, these valuable assets should have been held in reserve and cotton sent to Britain to purchase essential war supplies. The weakness of Confederate purchasing in Great Britain was its reliance on fiat money and its futile funding operation by means of unsecured bonds. These errors of policy eventually destroyed Confederate finance abroad and weakened its purchasing power.

The Civil War stimulated the shipbuilding industry in Great Britain. Altogether about four hundred steamers, many of them iron, and eight hundred sailing vessels were sold to the South, including the cruisers *Alabama, Florida,* and *Shenandoah.* English lawyers advised Confederate agents that ships might be built for the South in British yards, providing three conditions were observed: the Confederate government concealed its ownership; the ship's destination was concealed; and the South adhered to a prohibition against the shipping of war equipment and the enlisting of a crew in British waters. Capt. James D. Bulloch, C.S.N., who expertly planned, coordinated, and controlled Confederate naval activity in Britain, consistently observed these requirements. He always tried to dispatch ships as ordinary sailing vessels.

The difficulties encountered by Confederate officials in Great Britain, however, revealed that the U.S. consular agents had a well-organized and highly developed espionage system, the function of which was to prevent the shipment of goods and materials to the Confederacy. It says a great deal for the tact, diplomacy, and energies of Bulloch and the other agents that so many ships got away and so much equipment and materials were shipped. Although Confederate ships bought and constructed in Great Britain were too few in number to act with effective aggressive power against the U.S. Navy, the commanders of the Confederate ships were able to inflict great injuries upon the merchant vessels of the North and thus drive up insurance rates to a prohibitive degree.

Although the Confederate Congress appropriated large sums for the navy (to be spent in Great Britain), the rate of exchange in the money market always worked against the Confederates, and the Southern navy was always smaller than Congress might have hoped. Jefferson Davis was fairly consistent in his naval policy and clearly understood and strongly supported the need for ship construction in Great Britain.

In the area of ordnance, the Confederate government was never able to equip its forces adequately. The original stock of arms consisted almost wholly of smoothbore muskets, altered from flint to percussion. These disappeared almost entirely during the first two years of the war and were replaced by English rifled and percussion arms of high quality. No official account was kept of the value of the

> The difficulties encountered by Confederate officials in Great Britain, however, revealed that the U.S. consular agents had a well-organized and highly developed espionage system. . . .

Confederate government's purchases in Great Britain, and records are discouragingly fragmentary. Some statistical data has been collected in an attempt to record the quantity and value of articles that passed through the blockade, but it is difficult, in some instances, to give more than a reasoned estimate. About 1,350,000 bales of cotton were sent to Great Britain during the war, and approximately 600,000 items of equipment were shipped to the Confederacy through the blockade (the majority of blockade runners were English vessels). These included small arms, cannons, munitions of all kinds, clothing, hospital stores, manufactured goods, and some luxuries. Goods entering the Confederate States from British ports can be valued at almost $200 million. Agents of the Southern War Department alone spent more than $12,250,000 in Great Britain. Throughout the war, munitions and supplies of all kinds also poured into the North from Europe. In comparison, the South was isolated and had great difficulty equipping and supplying its armed forces. Without these essential imports, the Civil War could have ended possibly in eighteen months.

A careful analysis of the Confederate purchasing agents and their mission in Great Britain reveals that they did nothing that was not justified by the rule of fair and honorable warfare, nothing contrary to English law as construed by English jurists and confirmed by the judgment of English courts. These agents—poorly organized and badly instructed by their superiors (especially during the first thirty months of the war), inexperienced, sometimes guilty of serious errors of judgment, prone to disputes caused by vague orders from senior officers who knew little of the circumstances under which they were working, almost always short of funds, harried by Federal spies, and working for a government unrecognized by Great Britain—made it possible in spite of all their handicaps for the Confederates to sustain a war lasting over four years. Given the crippling difficulties, it is a tribute to their initiative, skill, and energy that they accomplished so much with so little.

BIBLIOGRAPHY

Bulloch, James D. *The Secret Service of the Confederate States in Europe.* 2 vols. New York, 1883.

Lester, Richard I. *Confederate Finance and Purchasing in Great Britain.* Charlottesville, Va., 1975.

Owsley, Frank L. *King Cotton Diplomacy.* 2d ed. Revised by Harriet Chappel Owsley. Chicago, 1959.

RICHARD I. LESTER

Anglo-Confederate Trading Company

The Anglo-Confederate Trading Company was a British shareholding blockade-running venture that was formed in early 1862 in Liverpool by members of the shipping firm Edward Lawrence and Company. The supercargo for the company was Thomas E. Taylor, whose zeal and attention to detail was instrumental in establishing a highly successful line of blockade runners that operated primarily between Nassau and Wilmington, North Carolina.

The company also took the lead in the technical development of blockade runners by constructing the steel-hulled sidewheeler *Banshee.* This was the first vessel built from the keel up as a blockade runner. In April 1863, she became the first steel-hulled vessel to cross the Atlantic. *Banshee* and her following consorts were hired by the Confederacy to carry in munitions. The contracts were so lucrative that a successful round trip paid the construction cost of a blockade runner and the salary of the crew. Besides the inbound cargo, the company also carried out over ten thousand bales of cotton.

The Anglo-Confederate Trading Company was one of the war's most successful blockade-running firms. Although its total fleet numbered only nine vessels, with no more than four operating at one time, its ships completed forty-nine runs out of fifty-eight attempts. Unlike its competitors, the company did not invest heavily in Confederate bonds and additional steamers. Instead, profits were returned to shareholders. In the fall of 1864, the firm paid dividends that amounted to 2,500 percent over the original cost of a share of stock. Even though at the war's end the company sold off its blockade runners at a substantial loss, these transactions were more than covered by the firm's profits.

BIBLIOGRAPHY

Bradlee, Francis B. C. *Blockade Running during the Civil War and the Effect of Land and Water Transportation on the Confederacy.* Salem, Mass., 1925.

Taylor, Thomas E. *Running the Blockade.* London, 1897.

Wise, Stephen R. *Lifeline of the Confederacy: Blockade Running during the Civil War.* Columbia, S.C., 1988.

STEPHEN R. WISE

ANTISLAVERY

Opposition to the practice of slavery was a long-range movement that began in colonial America. To understand the broad and complicated parameters of antislavery, however, one must distinguish between and among a variety of impulses causing Americans and others in the Western world to oppose the institution of slavery.

Among the first to do so were those who objected to the practice on religious grounds. The Society of Friends, or Quakers, in both England and America began to grieve the practice during the eighteenth century, especially in and around the Quaker-owned colony of Pennsylvania. By the time of the American Revolution, Anthony Benezet, a Philadelphia Quaker, was issuing strenuous condemnations of slaveholding and urging Quakers to set an example by ridding themselves of their slaves in works like *A Serious Address to the Rulers of America, on the Inconsistency of Their Conduct Respecting Slavery* (1783).

Close on the heels of Quaker antislavery testimony came the libertarian influences of the American Revolution and other subsequent democratic revolutions in France, Haiti, and eventually Latin America. As each of these focused on the rights of man and produced various declarations concerning "inalienable" rights to life, liberty, and property, the practice of slaveholding was sharply questioned. In each of these areas and in England there arose an antislavery tide that led first to the abolition of the African slave trade in 1808 in both Britain and America, and then to the emancipation of slaves in Northern American states and in 1833 in the British West Indies.

Religious and political scruples about slaveholding had its effect as well in Southern states. Prior to the 1830s thousands of slaveholders ranging from George Washington to ultraconservative John Randolph of Roanoke voluntarily manumitted their slaves. Viewing slavery as morally wrong or inconsistent with American republicanism, or at best as a "necessary evil," these Southerners were impelled to end slavery—usually through their last wills and testaments.

Southern qualms about slavery and frequently also about the role of African Americans in American society led after the War of 1812 to a spate of efforts to rid the nation both of slavery and of its African population. Manumission societies were formed throughout much of the South, especially in North Carolina and Tennessee, beginning in 1816. By 1827 forty-one organizations devoted to the ending of slavery existed in North Carolina alone. The American Colonization Society, founded in 1817 and headed by such men as James Madison, James Monroe, and John Marshall, also generated antislavery interest throughout the South as it sought to eliminate both slaveholding and Africans from the United States.

With the rise of radical abolitionism in the 1830s, however, the moderate antislavery position of many Southerners became untenable, at least publicly. Indeed, the emergence of American abolitionism, usually identified with William Lloyd Garrison and the founding of his Boston newspaper, the *Liberator,* on January 1, 1831, tended to undermine many moderate antislavery positions in the North and South. Given

> ## Quakers throughout the South grew quiet on the subject. . . .

the view of abolitionists that slavery was a moral evil and that it should be abolished immediately without compensation for slaveholders, abolitionism attacked virtually every other antislavery position. Northern opponents of abolitionist radicalism were quickly labeled "anti-abolitionists," and Southerners found it increasingly difficult to maintain any witness against slavery. Quakers throughout the South grew quiet on the subject, and manumission societies disappeared. Colonization efforts, largely discredited by abolitionists, continued until the Civil War but at a less significant pace. Laws regulating the manumission of slaves were enacted in the South. Other laws forbidding the migration of blacks into Northern states virtually halted voluntary acts of emancipation. The rise of a militant and sophisticated defense of slavery on religious, philosophical, ethical, scientific, and economic grounds during the 1830s and 1840s eliminated public expressions of antislavery opinion.

Southerners who had strong qualms about slavery found it expedient to move to the North. James Birney moved from Alabama to Kentucky and finally Ohio as he changed from slaveholder to abolitionist. William Henry Brisbane of South Carolina followed the same route until he settled in Wisconsin. North Carolina Quakers such as Levi Coffin followed suit and later helped establish the famous Underground Railroad that aided runaway slaves. Sarah and Angelina Grimke, sisters from a distinguished Charleston family, played key roles in propelling abolitionism in the North after 1835. Angelina's *Appeal to the Christian Women of the South* (1836) and Sarah's *Epistle to the Clergy of the Southern States* (1836) placed them at the forefront of abolitionism and in defining a reformist role for women.

By 1850 abolitionists from the North were no longer welcome or safe to proclaim their message in the South. Two Wesleyan Methodists sent from New York, Adam Crooks and Jesse McBride, were arrested and convicted that year of distributing "incendiary literature" in western North Carolina. Before their appeal could be heard, they were hounded out of the state by a mob. A decade later not even a native Southerner could operate openly as an abolitionist. In 1859 Daniel Worth, former Quaker from Guilford County, North

Carolina, and kinsman of governor Jonathan Worth, was arrested and convicted of the same crime as Crooks and McBride.

Interestingly, however, Worth was convicted of distributing a book written by another North Carolinian containing yet another antislavery position. Hinton Rowan Helper, in his sensational *Impending Crisis of the South* (1857), held that slavery was a curse on the South that hampered its economic development. Indeed, he argued, the costs of sustaining slavery had to be borne directly by nonslaveholding whites throughout the South. Though Helper's book was held publicly to be incendiary and was banned in much of the South, it is clear that many Southerners shared his views. Calvin Wiley, North Carolina's first public school administrator, said as much in a pamphlet he titled *A Sober View of the Slavery Question* in 1849. Frederick Law Olmsted encountered the same viewpoint as he traveled throughout the South in the 1850s.

A similar refrain appeared in the extensive writings of Daniel Reaves Goodloe, a native North Carolinian who published the moderate antislavery newspaper *National Era* in Washington, D.C. The title of his 1846 tract reveals his perspective: *Inquiry into the Causes Which Have Retarded the Accumulation of Wealth and Increase of Population in the Southern States: In Which the Question of Slavery is Considered in a Politico-Economical Point of View.* A similar economic comparison of South and North appeared a year later in *Address to the People of West Virginia,* written by Henry Ruffner, clergyman and president of Washington College (present-day Washington and Lee). Such strenuous arguments that were both antislavery and anti-Negro gave a new boost to large-scale colonization schemes in the 1850s.

With the publication of Harriet Beecher Stowe's *Uncle Tom's Cabin* in 1852 and of Helper's *Impending Crisis* in 1857, and with John Brown's raid on Harpers Ferry in 1859, the South became so embattled on the subject of slavery that it was no longer possible for strong antislavery views to be expressed publicly. Nevertheless, private doubts persisted. When the Civil War began, concerns about fighting a war to maintain slavery were expressed in a variety of ways. Antislavery opinion must have been part of the strong anti-secessionist vote taken in North Carolina on February 28, 1861, even after seven other states had left the Union. It was probably also a factor in the decision of a hundred thousand men from Confederate states to join and fight in the Union army during the Civil War.

Incipient antislavery opinion loomed in discussions about making use of slaves as Confederate soldiers. In 1864 various proposals were floated by Confederate generals to arm part of the slave population, and in November of that year the matter came before the Confederate Congress. By January of 1865 even Gen. Robert E. Lee was proposing that the Confederacy should consider abolishing slavery. Finally, in

March 1865, the policy of arming slaves and giving them emancipation for their service became the law of the Confederacy. By that time, of course, the Confederacy was already doomed, and the question of the fate of antislavery and abolitionism was settled.

[See also Harpers Ferry, West Virginia, article on John Brown's Raid; Helper, Hinton Rowan; Tubman, Harriet.]

BIBLIOGRAPHY

Degler, Carl N. *The Other South: Southern Dissenters in the Nineteenth Century.* New York, 1974.

Dillon, Merton L. *Slavery Attacked: Southern Slaves and Their Allies.* Baton Rouge, La., 1990.

Dumond, Dwight L. *Antislavery: The Crusade for Freedom in America.* Ann Arbor, Mich., 1961. Reprint, New York, 1966.

Filler, Louis. *Crusade against Slavery: Friends, Foes, and Reforms, 1820–1860.* New York, 1960. Rev. ed., Algonac, Mich., 1986.

Kraditor, Aileen S. *Means and Ends in American Abolitionism: Garrison and His Critics on Strategy and Tactics, 1834–1850.* New York, 1969.

Perry, Lewis, and Michael Fellman, eds. *Antislavery Reconsidered: New Perspectives on the Abolitionists.* Baton Rouge, La., 1979.

Stewart, James Brewer. *Holy Warriors: The Abolitionists and American Slavery.* New York, 1976.

Walters, Ronald G. *American Reformers, 1815–1860.* New York, 1978.

LARRY E. TISE

APPOMATTOX CAMPAIGN

Beginning on March 29, 1865, and lasting until April 9, this campaign in the concluding days of the Civil War is commonly referred to as Lee's Retreat. Lasting only twelve days,

> **With the Federals in his rear and cavalry across his line of march, Lee decided to attempt a breakthrough. . . .**

it culminated in the surrender of the largest and most powerful Confederate army.

The movement began on the twenty-ninth when Gen. Ulysses S. Grant sent a force of about 50,000 troops—the Second Corps under Gen. Andrew A. Humphreys, the Fifth Corps under Gen. Gouverneur K. Warren, and cavalry commanded by Gen. Philip Sheridan—to move around the Confederate right flank west of Petersburg and gain the South Side Railroad. This was Gen. Robert E. Lee's last major supply line into the city, and if captured, he would be forced to withdraw from the defenses of both Richmond, the Confederate capital, and Petersburg.

Lee, realizing the importance of protecting the railroad, dispatched a force under Gen. George E. Pickett to hold a strategic crossroads known as Five Forks. A preliminary series of battles (Quaker Road, March 29; White Oak Road and Dinwiddie Courthouse, March 31) allowed the Union army to maneuver into position to attack Pickett on April 1. Pickett, whose force numbered about 10,000 infantry and cavalry, confronted a similar force of 22,000 men led by General Sheridan at Five Forks. Pickett was defeated with the loss of over 2,000 prisoners, assuring the capture of the South Side Railroad. Federal casualties amounted to 633.

At dawn on the second, Grant issued orders for numerous assaults on the Petersburg lines, and the Sixth Corps under Gen. Horatio G. Wright broke through at one point. There was more fighting at Confederate Forts Mahone and Gregg and at Sutherland Station where the railroad was seized. Confederate Gen. A. P. Hill was killed in these battles. That night Lee issued orders for his troops to withdraw from both Petersburg and Richmond.

When General Lee left the two cities, his intention was for the scattered contingents of the Army of Northern Virginia, numbering about 58,000 men, to rendezvous at Amelia Court House, located on the Richmond and Danville Railroad. At this point he could replenish his army with needed supplies. The army would then continue into North Carolina and join with Gen. Joseph E. Johnston's force. Successfully bringing his army together at this county seat, Lee found to his dismay that, because of a mix-up in communications, no supplies had been sent. Deciding to remain in the area while his army foraged, Lee allowed General Grant with his force of about 76,000 men (the Army of the Potomac and Army of the James) to begin a pursuit that eliminated the one-day lead Lee held. Consequently, hard riding by Sheridan's cavalry, along with an occasional skirmish such as one at Namozine Church on April 3, enabled the Federals to move around and in front of the Confederate army. They then cut the path of Lee's retreat along the railroad at the next station, Jetersville.

The following day, the fifth, when the Southerners pulled out of Amelia Court House, they found not only Federal cavalry blocking their way but fast-marching Union infantry arriving in support. Lee, deciding not to engage in battle at this point, changed his plans and ordered a night march around the entrenched enemy left flank. His destination was the town of Farmville, where he could find rations for his men at the South Side Railroad station.

The Confederate army was able to carry out this plan until dawn on the sixth. Then the Federals spotted the rear of their column near Amelia Springs, north of Jetersville, and immediately gave chase. Traveling along roads parallel to the one

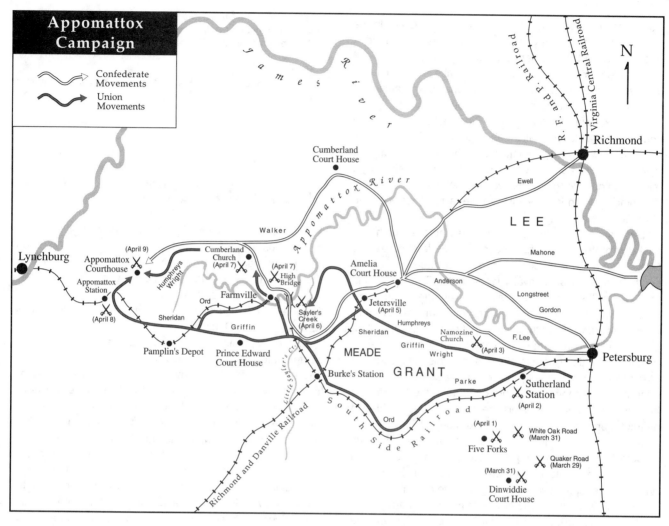

Appomattox Campaign

Confederate Movements

Union Movements

Lee's column was moving on, Sheridan's cavalry intercepted his line of march near Sayler's Creek. With the Second and Sixth Corps also close behind, the Confederates had to make a stand to save themselves. In three separate engagements, at the Hillsman farm, Lockett's farm, and Marshall's crossroads (or Harper's farm), the Federal infantry and cavalry put 7,700 men, almost a quarter of Lee's army, out of combat, mainly as prisoners. Those who survived continued on another night march to Farmville, situated on the southern bank of the Appomattox River.

It was also on this day that General E. O. C. Ord, commander of the Army of the James, sent a body of infantry and cavalry to destroy High Bridge so the Confederates could not use it in their retreat. High Bridge was a large trestle by which the South Side Railroad crossed the Appomattox River. Confederate cavalry learned of the raid and overtook the enemy force near the bridge. In the fight that ensued, most of the Federals were either killed or captured. Union Gen. Theodore Read and Confederate Gen. James Dearing were also mortally wounded.

When Lee's men arrived at Farmville at daylight on the seventh, they found some 40,000 rations of bread and 80,000 of meal in trains at the depot. As allotments were being issued to the troops, word came that Federal cavalrymen were coming into the town from the east. Lee had no alternative but to send the trains off toward Lynchburg. (These were captured the next day at Pamplin's Depot.)

Realizing that the Federals were also moving south of Farmville through Prince Edward Court House to cut off that avenue of escape, the Confederate commander decided to move his army to the north bank of the generally unfordable Appomattox River. If he could get his army safely over and burn all the bridge crossings behind him, including High Bridge to the east, he might delay Grant's men in their relentless chase. Unfortunately for Lee, the plan failed. One of the four bridges spanning the river (the wagon bridge under High Bridge) was not destroyed in time, which allowed the Union Second Corps to cross.

Lee then entrenched his army around Cumberland Church, about three miles north of Farmville, to protect his wagon train. Federal attempts to break the Confederate defense line that afternoon were unsuccessful but held a good portion of the Southern army at bay until darkness fell. The Confederates once again had to make a night march. That evening Grant sent the first of a series of dispatches to Lee requesting the surrender of his army.

The next point along the South Side Railroad where Lee could hope to obtain supplies was Appomattox Station, about three miles west of Appomattox Courthouse. To reach that point, the Confederates would have to march thirty-eight miles. A thirty-mile route was available south of the river, but this route, which generally followed the railroad, was open to Grant and his troops.

Lee's army was relatively unmolested on the eighth, the final day of the campaign, although two Federal corps, the Second and Sixth, pursued him north of the river. To the south, with Sheridan's cavalry leading, the Fifth Corps and the Army of the James were taking advantage of the situation. Arriving at Appomattox Station before the van of Lee's column, the cavalry captured the supply trains and, later that evening, a portion of the Confederate artillery and wagon train in the Battle of Appomattox Station. This put a segment of the Union forces directly in front of Lee's force now gathering around Appomattox Courthouse. With the Federals in his rear and cavalry across his line of march, Lee decided to attempt a breakthrough early the next morning.

At daybreak on the ninth, assuming that only Federal horsemen were confronting him, Lee pushed his combined force of infantry and cavalry under Gen. John B. Gordon against the enemy position, forcing them to give ground. But as they fell back, the Army of the James began arriving on the field in support, and it became apparent to Lee that he was about to be surrounded, especially when the Fifth Corps appeared on his flank. The Southerners sent out white flags of truce to suspend hostilities. That afternoon Lee met with Grant at Appomattox Courthouse in the home of Wilmer McLean to discuss terms of surrender. After four years of bloodshed, the fighting in Virginia was over.

The casualties for the Appomattox campaign totaled approximately 9,000 for the Federal army and 28,000, including desertions, for the Confederates. Lee surrendered close to 30,000 men at Appomattox. All were paroled and allowed to go home.

BIBLIOGRAPHY

Calkins, Christopher. *Thirty-Six Hours before Appomattox, April 6–7, 1865.* Farmville, Va., 1980.
Calkins, Christopher. *The Battles of Appomattox.* Lynchburg, Va., 1987.
Calkins, Christopher. *The Final Bivouac.* Lynchburg, Va., 1988.
Davis, Burke. *To Appomattox: Nine April Days.* New York, 1959.
Newhall, Colonel F. C. *With General Sheridan in Lee's Last Campaign.* Philadelphia, 1866.
Schaff, Morris. *The Sunset of the Confederacy.* Boston, 1912.
The Shenandoah Campaigns of 1862 and 1864, and the Appomattox Campaign. Papers of the Military Historical Society of Massachusetts, no. 6. Boston, 1906. Reprint, Wilmington, N.C., 1989.
Tremain, Henry Edwin. *Last Hours of Sheridan's Cavalry.* New York, 1904.

CHRIS CALKINS

ARCHAEOLOGY

Archaeology is the study of past societies through the material remains that have been left behind. A form of archaeological investigation of the Confederacy began immediately after the war, as people collected souvenirs and materials from veterans and battlefields. Veterans' groups and the Daughters of the Confederacy, in particular, tried to preserve items of the Lost Cause.

In the twentieth century, the initial excavation of most Confederate sites was conducted by relic hunters searching for salable or collectible items. The most common excavators today are still relic hunters using sophisticated electronic and research techniques to identify sites and then exploit them. For most sites undergoing this type of disturbance, little written documentation about what was found and its context exists.

Since about 1950, professional archaeologists have tried to discover patterns of material remains related to the Confederacy. Initially, their excavations focused on sites associated with important people and events. More recently, professional archaeology in the South has been funded by government agencies or by developers wishing to obtain government permits. Such permits require archaeologists to explore nontraditional sites like small farms and minor industrial sites as well as the better known locations. This work has opened the wide expanse of unwritten Confederate history to public view. The newly recovered materials encouraged a reevaluation of public and private documents to interpret atypical sites located during the surveys.

Battlefield archaeology originally tended to concentrate on studying people within forts, investigating extant structures on the battlefield, or trying to determine where houses once stood. This approach changed as archaeologists grew more sophisticated in developing research questions about battlefields. Important federal work has been done on battlefields such as Chancellorsville, Vicksburg, Shiloh, and Petersburg in conjunction with restoring the sites to their original ground conditions. More innovative work has tried to trace battle lines by examining artifact distributions, especially along now-buried trench lines.

Only within the last decade have archaeologists studied the major Confederate fortification type—the earthwork—as an artifact. Most earthwork research has been funded through government-mandated permit requirements on inland battlefields in Georgia and Tennessee, defense systems like those around Harpers Ferry, and coastal cities such as Wilmington, Savannah, Charleston, and Mobile. In Savannah and Wilmington, massive sand mounds have been found to contain enough remnants of the wooden frames and walls to allow schematic reconstructions of the interior chambers. Underwater obstructions and related defenses have been studied in Mobile Bay and the Cape Fear and Savannah rivers, revealing distinct differences between contemporary drawings and the actual barriers.

A growing number of excavations are concerned with the home front, especially urban and plantation life, including the slaves who made up more than a third of the Confederacy's population. Plantation archaeology originally concentrated on the "big house" because the occupants were famous, but more recent work has examined the slave rows and overseer cabins as well. Urban archaeology is common, but small farms have been receiving attention owing to highway, power, and pipe line surveys since the early 1970s. One unusual pattern relating to slave cabins on the southeastern coast is the large number of weapons found there. In one cabin in McIntosh County, Georgia, at least four weapons—a flintlock and a percussion pistol, a musket, and a shotgun—were represented by artifacts recovered during excavations in 1987 and 1988.

Industrial sites such as the Harpers Ferry and Fayetteville arsenals and Tredegar Iron Works have long been known, but archaeologists have done little work on these sites. Amateurs have reported on the lesser known sites such as the Mendenhall, Jones, and Gardner Machine Shop in North Carolina. Grapeshot recovered from the Savannah defenses was stacked in two tiers, rather than the more usual three and five tiers, indicating iron shortages late in the war. A 24-pounder flank howitzer recovered from CSS *Georgia* was not bored straight, nor were the molding seams removed.

Mundane operations such as salt extraction are even less well known, although some documentation does exist and abandoned sites have been encountered during coastal surveys in Georgia and Florida. Train yards have not been investigated in the South to the same extent as in the North, although Chattanooga and Savannah have been examined.

Along coastal and inland river systems, underwater archaeology has provided a wealth of information about the Confederacy. Sunken vessels are time capsules containing materials representative of those who sailed them. Among these vessels are the ironclads CSS *Neuse* and CSS *Georgia,* and the Richmond flotilla. Artillerymen in Fort Branch on the Roanoke River threw their entire complement of artillery into the river, and divers recovered it in the 1970s. The Fort Branch artillery revealed that iron field carriages were used for Blakely rifled cannon rather than Whitworths, and that Blakely cannon shipped to the Confederacy apparently had serial numbers that were separated by one number from other guns in the series. A cannon from *Georgia* had been marked on the barrel band to indicate elevation of the tube without recourse to sighting implements. This same gun was disabled by breaking off the sights and putting a live, percussion-fused shell down the barrel backwards as a booby trap.

Blockade runners such as *Modern Greece, Georgiana,* and *Minho* have yielded substantial information about Confederate imports ranging from cannons to straight pins. What has been found tends to confirm speculation about nonessential Confederate imports in many cases as well as attempts to obtain the latest ordnance such as Whitworth and Blakely rifled artillery. Confederate newspaper editorials often railed against blockade runners bringing luxury goods at the expense of war matériel. Finding both military goods (rifles, cannons, bowie knives, canteens, lead, tin) and civilian luxury goods (whiskey, fine china, pins) in wrecked vessels tends to confirm newspaper allegations. Outside the Confederacy, the ruptured hulk of CSS *Alabama* was recently found off the coast of France.

Although archaeology of the Confederacy as a separate field of endeavor does not exist, excavations have provided information about previously unsuspected aspects of Confederate life or have confirmed well-known facts such as the shortage of iron. No consolidation of Confederate-related material culture has been attempted from an archaeological standpoint. Such an effort would prove useful in confirming patterns of material culture already noted by collectors of items such as Confederate uniform coats, the boton ée cross pins worn by Maryland Confederates, and frame buckles. Additional recovery and analysis of artifacts might show projectile, sword, and leather goods' affiliations with certain arsenals and time periods.

Archaeological publications relating to the Confederacy are not numerous or readily available. But military sites owned by state and federal governments usually have research material regarding the particular site on hand, and the reports required by government agencies for construction projects on private sites are filed with the historic preservation officer of the state. The long interest in Confederate material culture that spawned relic hunting also resulted in artifact documentation.

[*See also* Museums and Archives.]

BIBLIOGRAPHY

Camp Chase Gazette. Lancaster, Ohio, 1979–.

Crouch, Daniel R. *Relic Hunter.* Falls Church, Va., 1978. Privately printed.

Lord, Francis. *The Civil War Collector's Encyclopedia.* Secaucus, N.J., 1982.

Military Collector and Historian, Journal of the Company of Military Historians. Westbrook, Conn., 1949–.

North-South Trader. Orange, Va., 1973–.

L. E. BABITS

ARKANSAS

On the eve of the Civil War, Arkansas was a microcosm of the American South, its people immersed in a stratified society characterized by class and race. Their ways of life varied widely: a few resided on comfortable plantations, most subsisted on piney-woods or mountain plots, and many labored on other people's land as white tenants or black slaves. The vast majority of its 324,191 whites and 111,269 blacks lived in the countryside, though a lesser number dwelt in the small, but important towns of Little Rock, Fort Smith, Camden, Pine Bluff, and Helena. Foreign-born whites constituted just over 1 percent of the population, and the free inhabitants included only 144 blacks.

The state's geographic features shaped its antebellum culture and its political and military dynamics in the Confederate era. Poised on the western fringe of Southern civilization, Arkansas encompassed a diverse landscape sculpted into low mountains, fertile alluvial plains, and mosquito-infested swamps. Mountains dominated Arkansas's northwestern half, and river bottoms, swamps, and bayous marked its eastern and southern regions. Although frequently inundated by floods, the latter sector had fecund soils suitable for plantation agriculture. The rivers that traversed the state had only marginal commercial worth, for in dry seasons shallows hindered steamboat traffic.

A plantation culture dominated the area southeast of an imaginary line drawn from the Missouri boot heel to the Texas boundary. Committed to cotton and slavery, that region's aristocrats campaigned for internal improvements: levees to prevent floods and railroads to tap markets at Memphis and New Orleans. Political bickering and difficult topography delayed the construction of the latter so that by 1860 the state's major project, a rail line from Memphis to Little Rock, was only two-thirds completed. Mountain citizens with little investment in slavery found themselves politically at odds with their aristocratic neighbors to the southeast.

Although disheartened by Abraham Lincoln's election in November 1860, few Arkansans advocated the Union's immediate demise. South Carolina's secession on December 20, however, galvanized powerful political voices. Recently inaugurated Governor Henry M. Rector pledged that should "any of the Southern states . . . deem it necessary to declare independence" Arkansas must give its "active support." Even though Senator Robert Ward Johnson, Congressman

Thomas C. Hindman, and Little Rock attorney Albert Pike added their endorsements, the state legislature demurred until mid-January before authorizing an election for convention delegates on February 18.

This crisis highlighted Arkansas's sectional dichotomy. Fearing domination by the slavocracy, Arkansas mountaineers firmly supported the Union, and emboldened by Tennessee's rejection of secession, they sent a solid pro-Union majority to the convention. At the same time, the cotton counties overwhelmingly backed secession. The convention assembled in Little Rock (March 3–18), fended off proposals for immediate dissolution, and in the end submitted the issue to a statewide plebiscite scheduled for August.

While politicians bickered, pro-Confederates in the southeast finessed Arkansas out of the Union. In February, Helena militia units marched on Little Rock, besieging its Federal arsenal and forcing its surrender; a Pine Bluff mob seized military supplies destined for Fort Smith; and regional leaders threatened to secede from the state should Arkansas fail in its duty to the South. Following the bombardment of Fort Sumter and Lincoln's subsequent call for volunteers, momentum shifted to the secessionists. Rector ordered Fort Smith seized on April 23, and the convention reconvened in Little Rock's volatile atmosphere. Cowed by secessionist mobs, even the mountain delegates, with one exception, declared for the Confederacy on May 6. Even though threatened by a lynch party, Isaac Murphy cast the dissenting vote. In 1864, he became the state's Union governor.

As the Civil War developed, crises in the Virginia and Trans-Appalachian theaters overwhelmed Jefferson Davis and his advisers, and they largely ignored Arkansas, forcing its leaders to plan their own campaigns. In the summer of 1861, they focused upon their own borders—the Indian Territory to the west and Missouri to the north. Commissioned to negotiate treaties with the Indians, Albert Pike bound several tribes—especially the Cherokees—to the Confederacy and thus ensured Arkansas's safety from that quarter. Missouri proved more troublesome. In July, Arkansas troops commanded by Gen. Ben McCulloch rushed to the aid of Gen. Sterling Price encamped near Springfield. Together they defeated Nathaniel Lyon at Oak Hills (August 10, 1861), but unfortunately for the Southern cause, personal conflicts led McCulloch to withdraw, leaving Price a force inadequate to hold Missouri.

Arkansas's Confederate leaders also faced difficult internal problems. Although the cotton counties enthusiastically fulfilled their quota of soldiers, mountain districts rarely supplied more than one-third of their allotments. Throughout the regions north and west of Little Rock, citizens fled Confederate recruiters, formed peace societies, and volunteered for the Union army. As civilian government collapsed, the military only partially replaced its functions. Threatened by Union forces in September 1863, Governor Harris

Flanagin, Rector's successor, fled Little Rock and established a new capital in the southwestern village of Washington, but he exercised little control over the state's weal. In this atmosphere of anarchy, Confederate guerrillas, Union partisans, and common bandits wreaked havoc upon the civilian population.

Cursed with inept and uncongenial military leaders, Arkansas's Confederate cause faltered. Arkansans Thomas C. Hindman and Albert Pike played major roles along with the North Carolinian Theophilus H. Holmes and the Missourian Sterling Price. The initial Trans-Mississippi commander, Hindman, proved incompetent as both an administrator and a strategist. Relieved of theater command in October 1862, he marched to defeat at the Battle of Prairie Grove (December 7) and thereafter transferred to the Army of Tennessee. Hindman's replacement, Holmes, was considered "a splendid example of a North Carolina patriot and gentleman," but he too floundered until March 1863 when E. Kirby Smith superseded him and moved the theater command to Louisiana. Holmes remained in Arkansas as an ineffectual field general. Pike and Price also commanded troops. Following his successful Indian negotiations, Pike assumed command of Indian soldiers, led them in the Battle of Elkhorn Tavern (March 7–8, 1862), and then resigned his commission in a jurisdictional dispute with Hindman. Price proved a competent leader, but his quarrels with Arkansas authorities diminished his effectiveness. Late in the war he executed a

> **Cursed with inept and uncongenial military leaders, Arkansas's Confederate cause faltered.**

spectacular, but strategically inconsequential, cavalry raid thrusting out of Arkansas to strike across half of Missouri.

Under this flaccid command structure, Arkansas's martial course developed in three phases: the shoring up of Federal control north of the Arkansas River; actions associated with the siege of Vicksburg; and operations in conjunction with the Red River campaign of 1864. The Confederate defeat at Elkhorn Tavern in 1862 allowed Federal forces to consolidate their hold on pro-Union mountain counties. Only the national government's more pressing commitments to the east and difficulties of campaigning in Arkansas's swamps prevented greater Union advances. Hindman's check at Prairie Grove ended the one Confederate effort at regaining its lost territory.

As Gen. Ulysses S. Grant marched on Vicksburg, he exposed his western flank to attack. To remedy this he sent a flotilla up the Arkansas River to invest the Confederate citadel at Arkansas Post; it fell after a brief siege (January 8–11, 1863). Although numbers of Confederate troops

ranged across Arkansas, command incompetence prevented serious threats to Grant before Holmes and Price attacked Helena on July 4. Repulsed in a sharp engagement, their defeat opened the state to further Federal incursions. But the Arkansas River's low water slowed the Union advance, and not until September 10 did Little Rock fall to Frederick Steele's Federals; the city thereafter served as the headquarters for Union military activities in the state.

The Red River campaign drew Steele south in March 1864. His command of thirteen thousand effectives, including two black regiments, trooped out of Little Rock intent on joining forces with Nathaniel Banks's army moving up the Red River to Shreveport. But Banks's defeats at Mansfield and Pleasant Hill, Louisiana (April 8, 9, 1864), stranded Steele deep in Arkansas's Confederate territory. Following an initial reverse at Okolona (April 2), he suffered further defeats at Poison Springs (April 17), Mark Mills (April 25), and Jenkins's Ferry (April 28). Harassed by Confederate cavalry, Steele abandoned his wounded and nonessential supplies; and his black troops suffered severe casualties. The Confederate commander at Poison Springs attacked a Union force he estimated at 1,500 blacks and 1,000 whites. Refusing to accept the surrender of African Americans, he boasted that his men killed 430 blacks and only 30 whites. The First Kansas Colored Volunteers' colonel raged that his men were "murdered on the spot." Having lost the confidence of Arkansas's Union leaders and the Lincoln government, Steele left his command in December 1864, effectively ending Union military movement in the state.

In the fall of 1863, Arkansas's Confederate government exercised suzerainty over little more than the state's southwestern third, a region roughly bounded by the Saline River to the east and the Ouachita River to the north. By necessity the military eclipsed civil authority, rendering the governor and his bureaucracy virtually impotent. Civilians—small farmers and planters alike—despaired of their personal fortunes. Typical of the South as a whole, antebellum Arkansans had depended upon small farmers for corn, pigs, and other foodstuffs, and they had allowed planters to concentrate upon the profitable production of cotton. With husbands and older sons marching in the Confederate army, small farmsteads declined in their output, fields became fallow, and hungry families consumed seed corn, draft animals, and breeding stock. Impoverished, many non-slave owners sold their land and other property to wealthy neighbors. As a result, by 1865 Arkansas experienced a net decline in noncommercial farms. Planters confronted their own difficulties. Burdened by antebellum debts, they resisted government orders to switch from cotton to less remunerative grain crops, and whenever possible they smuggled their cotton bales to Mexican and Northern speculators.

Confederate and Union armies further exasperated civilian problems. Southern commanders impounded draft animals, purchased foodstuffs with inflated Confederate currency, and conscripted slaves to labor as construction workers, teamsters, and hospital stewards. In the summer of 1864, Gen. E. Kirby Smith ordered the drafting of one-fifth of all male slaves aged 18 to 45—a move that enraged planters, many of whom had rushed their human chattel away from Union dominated areas. Federal General Steele's campaign through southwest Arkansas in the spring of 1864 strained a population already desperate for life's necessities.

In vain, Lincoln hoped that Arkansas would prove a model for the restoration of Federal rule. Appointed provisional governor, Isaac Murphy organized Union sympathizers who elected him to a four-year term in April 1864, but his administration could not control the countryside. Unionist citizens suffered attacks by Confederate sympathizers, robbery by bandits, and persecution by Federal soldiers who made no distinction between loyal and disloyal Arkansans. Along with former slaves, desperate Unionists fled to Little Rock and other Federal-controlled towns. Overwhelmed by resulting social problems, Union commanders transported some of them to the North and settled others on agricultural colonies established on land confiscated from Confederate supporters.

Murphy and his allies appealed to class hostilities in their attempt to construct a viable postwar Republican party. President Andrew Johnson unwittingly undermined the Republican cause with his liberal pardon policy, which enabled the former elites quickly to reestablish their control over local governments and then to engage in a campaign of anti-Republican violence—often under the rubric of the

> ## In vain, Lincoln hoped that Arkansas would prove a model for the restoration of Federal rule.

Ku Klux Klan. In 1874, the Republican party acknowledged defeat when it failed to nominate candidates for state office and thus conceded the government to prewar leaders.

Ironically, Arkansas's elites emerged from the Civil War in better financial shape than its other citizens. Although their affluence had been considerably diminished by the loss of slave property and the decline of real estate values, they retained a larger percentage of wealth than other Arkansans. By the century's end, many of the state's less affluent inhabitants—white as well as black—found themselves trapped in peonage, toiling as sharecroppers in debt to a comfortable few. As late as the civil rights movement of the 1960s, Arkansas retained social values and economic practices rooted in the antebellum epoch.

[For further discussion of battles fought in Arkansas, see Elkhorn Tavern, Arkansas. See also Price's Missouri Raid; Red River Campaigns; Wilson's Creek Campaign; and biographies of numerous figures mentioned herein.]

BIBLIOGRAPHY

Dougan, Michael Bruce. "Confederate Arkansas: The People and Politics of a Frontier State in Wartime." Ph.D. diss., Emory University, 1970.

Ellenburg, Martha A. "Reconstruction in Arkansas." Ph.D. diss., University of Missouri, 1967.

Moneyhon, Carl H. *The Impact of the Civil War and Reconstruction in Arkansas, 1850–1874.* Baton Rouge, La., forthcoming.

Staples, Thomas S. *Reconstruction in Arkansas, 1862–1874.* New York, 1923.

Thomas, David Y. *Arkansas in War and Reconstruction, 1861–1874.* Little Rock, Ark., 1926.

Thompson, George H. *Arkansas and Reconstruction: The Influence of Geography, Economics, and Personality.* Port Washington, N.Y., 1976.

Woods, James M. *Rebellion and Realignment: Arkansas's Road to Secession.* Fayetteville, Ark., 1987.

Worley, Ted R. "The Arkansas Peace Society of 1861: A Study of Mountain Unionism." *Southern Historical Quarterly* 24 (1958): 445–456.

FRED ARTHUR BAILEY

ARKANSAS

CSS *Arkansas* was laid down at Memphis, Tennessee, in October 1861, built by John Shirley. Before she could be completed, Memphis was threatened by Union forces descending the Mississippi River. The incomplete ironclad was towed down the Mississippi and up the Yazoo River. At Yazoo City, Mississippi, she was completed and commissioned in July 1862.

Arkansas was a twin-screw-propeller ram, 165 feet in length, 35 feet in width, with a draft of 11 to 12 feet. In contrast to the other Confederate armored vessels, the sides of her casemate were perpendicular, although the two ends were slanted. The casemate was covered with railway T-rails. The ship carried a crew of approximately two hundred officers and men and a battery of ten guns: two 9-inch smoothbores, two 9-inch shell guns, two 64-pounders, two 6-inch rifles, and two 32-pounder smoothbores.

On July 15, 1862, as the ironclad descended the Yazoo River, she encountered three Union vessels—*Carondelet, Tyler,* and *Queen of the West.* In the engagement that followed, *Carondelet* was disabled and the other two Union vessels retired downstream with *Arkansas* in pursuit. The chase continued into the Mississippi River where the Confederate ironclad found at anchor the combined naval forces of flag officers Charles Davis and David Farragut, some thirty warships in all. *Arkansas* steamed slowly through the Union

CSS ARKANSAS. Sepia wash drawing by R.G. Skerrett, 1904.

force, hit repeatedly by shot and shell. Several of the Union vessels were hit by *Arkansas*'s guns, but only *Lancaster* was seriously damaged.

Arkansas reached Vicksburg and that night came under attack a second time by Farragut's vessels as they ran the Confederate batteries and headed back downstream. The Confederate ironclad, already damaged from the early morning engagement, was hit several times again.

On August 3, *Arkansas,* repairs completed, left Vicksburg to cooperate in an attack on Baton Rouge, Louisiana. Twenty-four hours after leaving Vicksburg, the ironclad's engines began giving trouble, and the ship was anchored while engineers worked on them. The crew got the ship underway again the following morning, but when she was within sight of Baton Rouge, the engines broke down completely. With a Union naval force led by the ironclad *Essex* approaching, the Confederates abandoned *Arkansas* after setting her on fire. She drifted downstream before sinking.

BIBLIOGRAPHY

Milligan, John D. *Gunboats down the Mississippi.* Annapolis, Md., 1965.

Still, William N., Jr. *Iron Afloat: The Story of the Confederate Armorclads.* Columbia, S.C., 1986.

WILLIAM N. STILL, JR.

ARLINGTON HOUSE

Situated on a knoll overlooking the Potomac River and the city of Washington, Arlington was the Virginia home of Robert E. Lee. The mansion now lies in the heart of Arlington National Cemetery. Composed of a two-story center with flanking one-story wings, Arlington was set on an eleven-hundred-acre tract of land, most of which was wooded. Construction began in 1803 on the north wing, but the entire house was not completed until about 1817 or 1818. It was planned and built by George Washington Parke Custis, step-grandson of George Washington. George Hadfield, second architect of the U.S. Capitol, designed Arlington's portico, which is fronted by six massive Doric columns and modeled on the Greek temple at Paestum. The building is constructed of brick, but its exterior is stuccoed and patterned to simulate cut stone. It is considered one of the finest and earliest examples of the Greek Revival style in the United States.

Lt. Robert E. Lee married Mary Ann Randolph Custis at Arlington in 1831, and there the family raised seven children. With the outbreak of war in 1861, Lee left Arlington, never to return. The estate was occupied by Federal troops, and it became a training camp. The army felled the forests and ransacked or impounded the family's Washington memorabilia. In 1862 Congress levied a direct tax on all properties in insurrectionary territory and required that the owners personally appear to make payment. The Lees proved unable to cross Federal lines to pay the $92.07 tax. Pursuant to an amendment of the direct tax in 1863, the government purchased the plantation at a public auction.

In May 1864 Secretary of War Edwin Stanton ordered that a national cemetery be created on two hundred acres of the grounds at Arlington. The first burials began that year, and Quartermaster General Montgomery Meigs directed that the lawn and gardens be ringed with burial sites. Shattered by the loss of her family home, Mary Lee mourned that those officials had desecrated Arlington. More than seventeen thousand casualties or veterans of the Civil War were eventually buried there. Emancipated slaves also established Freedman's Village on the grounds. Over a twenty-year period, some two thousand residents lived in the settlement.

Remorseful over losing his wife's estate, Lee attempted to regain Arlington after the war, but failed. President Andrew Johnson proposed returning the Washington relics to the Lee family, but Congress balked. After Lee's death in 1870, his son George Washington Custis Lee pursued the matter, and the Supreme Court finally ruled in 1882 that the government had acted illegally in seizing the house. The Lee family settled the case with the government for $150,000. Arlington still served as headquarters for the cemetery until the late 1920s.

The fate of the mansion changed considerably with the cultural politics of the Southern Renaissance. Thousands of visitors annually paid homage to Lee at Arlington, and proposals were aired to restore the mansion to its earlier appearance. In 1921 author Frances Parkinson Keyes urged the formation of a private preservation society to shepherd the project, but Republican Congressman Louis C. Cramton of Michigan proposed instead that the government establish a national shrine at Arlington. In 1925 Congress unanimously passed legislation that directed the secretary of war to restore the building as "Arlington House, The Robert E. Lee Memorial." Arlington was transferred to the National Park Service in 1933. Today Arlington House displays the history of the Custis-Lee family, as well as upper-class Virginia life.

BIBLIOGRAPHY

Connelly, Thomas L. *The Marble Man: Robert E. Lee and His Image in American Society.* New York, 1977.

Lindgren, James M. *Preserving the Old Dominion: Historic Preservation and Virginia Traditionalism.* Charlottesville, Va., 1993.

Nelligan, Murray H. *"Old Arlington": The Story of the Lee Mansion National Memorial.* Washington, D.C., 1953.

U.S. National Park Service. *Arlington House: A Guide to Arlington House, The Robert E. Lee Memorial, Virginia.* Washington, D.C., 1985.

JAMES M. LINDGREN

LEWIS A. ARMISTEAD. LIBRARY OF CONGRESS.

ARMISTEAD, LEWIS A.

ARMISTEAD, LEWIS A. (1817–1863), brigadier general. Son of an army general, Lewis Addison Armistead was born February 18, 1817, in Newbern, North Carolina. He entered West Point in 1834 but left the academy two years later following an altercation with Cadet Jubal Early of Virginia. In 1839 Armistead joined the army as a lieutenant in the Sixth Infantry. Following active service in the Seminole War, Armistead fought in the Mexican War and received brevet promotion to major for heroism at Chapultepec. He spent the next fourteen years on frontier duty. One of his closest friends was fellow officer Winfield Scott Hancock of Pennsylvania.

With the advent of the Civil War, Armistead resigned his army commission and rushed from Texas to Virginia to offer his sword to the Confederacy. Older than most of his compatriots and thoroughly imbued with army ways, Armistead served the first year of the war as colonel of the Fifty-seventh Virginia. On April 1, 1862, he was promoted to brigadier general. His new command (Ninth, Fourteenth, Thirty-eighth, Fifty-third, and Fifty-seventh Virginia) became one of the most celebrated and battle-hardened brigades in the Army of Northern Virginia. One reason for its success was Armistead's leadership. He regarded obedience to duty, a superior noted, "as the first qualification of a soldier. For straggling on the march or neglect of duty on the part of his men, he held the officer in immediate command strictly responsible. The private must answer to the officer, but the officer to him."

From Seven Pines through Second Manassas, a colleague observed, Armistead increased his reputation—"displaying everywhere conspicuous gallantry, and winning by his coolness under fire, by his stern perseverance and his indomitable pluck, the applause of his superiors and the entire confidence of his men."

Armistead served as provost marshal for Robert E. Lee's army during the Sharpsburg campaign. His brigade then became part of Gen. George E. Pickett's division. Armistead played only a minor role at Fredericksburg and was with James Longstreet's command at Suffolk during the Chancellorsville campaign. He gained immortality at Gettysburg, however.

> "Men! Remember what you are fighting for—your homes, your friends, and your sweethearts! Follow me!"

On July 3, 1863, his brigade was part of the climactic Pickett-Pettigrew assault against the Union center. Armistead received the order to advance and then turned to his drawn-up columns and shouted: "Men! Remember what you are fighting for—your homes, your friends, and your sweethearts! Follow me!"

With his hat on the point of his sword, Armistead led his men forward. Barely 150 of them were left when they reached the Federal lines. Armistead jumped over the enemy obstruction on Cemetery Ridge and fell mortally wounded among the Federal cannon. He died July 5 in a Federal hospital, after requesting that his watch and other valuables be given to his old friend, Winfield Hancock—whose troops, unknown to Armistead, were the ones who had repulsed the Virginians.

The general is buried in the family plot at St. Paul's Church, Baltimore. Of Armistead and three other brigadiers slain at Gettysburg, Lee wrote that they "died as they had lived, discharging the highest duty of patriots with devotion that never faltered and courage that shrank from no danger."

BIBLIOGRAPHY

Dowdey, Clifford. *The Seven Days.* Boston, 1964.
Poindexter, James E. "Address on the Life and Services of Gen. Lewis A. Armistead." *Southern Historical Society Papers* 37 (1909): 144–151. Reprint, Wilmington, N.C., 1991.
Stewart, George R. *Pickett's Charge.* Boston, 1959.

JAMES I. ROBERTSON, JR.

ARMS, WEAPONS, AND AMMUNITION

[*This entry is composed of two articles,* Army Ordnance *and* Naval Ordnance, *which serve as an introduction to the discussion of ordnance used by the Confederacy. For more detailed discussions of weaponry used during the Civil War, see* Artillery; Edged Weapons; Naval Guns; Small Arms; Torpedoes and Mines. *For discussion of the production and acquisition of ordnance by the Confederacy, see* Niter and Mining Bureau; Ordnance Bureau; Powder Works. *For discussion of the changes in military tactics brought about by developments in weaponry, see* Civil War, *article on* Strategy and Tactics.]

Army Ordnance

The small arms of the Confederate soldier were of diverse type, quality, and source. The primary weapons of infantry and mounted soldiers were long arms, which fell into four basic categories. Muskets and rifle-muskets were arms with long, thin barrels, the former smoothbore, the latter rifled, both of which ranged in length from 37 to 42 inches. Rifles were arms with rifled, thick-walled, 33-to-34-inch barrels. Musketoons were generally muzzle-loading smoothbore arms with 24-to-30-inch barrels, favored by cavalry and mounted artillery for their ease of loading and use on horseback. Finally, there were carbines, similar to musketoons but generally breech-loading and often rifled, with 21-to-24-inch barrels, favored by cavalry. Of more limited value were handguns—revolvers and obsolete single-shot pistols—carried by officers and by cavalry for close mounted combat.

Many soldiers, especially officers and cavalrymen, also carried edged weapons. Sabers were used by cavalry and mounted artillery for hand-to-hand combat. Bayonets, used by infantry, inflicted very few documentable casualties. They were of two types: socket bayonets, which slid over the muzzle of muskets and rifle-musket, and saber bayonets, which locked to a lug on the side of a barrel. Long swords were carried by officers as a symbol of their rank. Short swords were carried by siege or garrison artillery to defend their artillery pieces at close quarters. At the beginning of the war, many Confederate enlisted men also brought crudely wrought bowie knives in anticipation of fighting at close quarters; they were soon discarded.

Prior to 1862, the majority of small arms had been secured through purchase in the North or through the seizure of Northern-made arms from Federal arsenals in the South. Early in the war, Confederates also attempted to increase the quantity, if not the quality, of their store of small arms by altering to a percussion ignition system those obsolete flintlock arms stored in Southern state arsenals (either as a result of earlier attempts at state production or from receipts of Northern-made arms allotted under the 1808 Militia Act).

This initial supply of arms would be supplemented through mid-1862 with the captured and repaired arms gleaned from the battlefields controlled by the dominant Army of Northern Virginia. At the same time, nascent Southern domestic production began contributing to the arms pool available to the Confederate Ordnance Bureau.

> **The diverse nature of Confederate small arms would have a subtle impact on Southern tactics.**

Plagued by inadequate resources in machinery, skilled mechanics, and eventually raw materials, this home production would, however, never prove a significant factor in equipping the Confederacy. Providently, in early 1861 both the Confederate government and the state governors had realized the probable inadequacy of domestic production and had sent agents abroad to secure arms. As a result, by mid-1862, importations of European (primarily English) weapons formed the backbone of the Confederate ordnance effort, stymied only by the lack of ready funds and the relatively ineffectual Union blockade. As a result of the massive importations, the Confederate armies were able to re-equip those army units that had received inferior arms in 1861 with the more technologically advanced rifled arms then available. Logistical problems, however, prevented the completion of this effort until the winter of 1863–1864.

The diverse nature of Confederate small arms would have a subtle impact on Southern tactics. The vast majority of the arms initially secured from the North or seized in Southern arsenals, with a few exceptions, were smoothbore, muzzle-loading, single-shot muskets. The maximum effective range of these arms was essentially one hundred yards, and only the employment of massed volley fire could compensate for their lack of accuracy. The smoothbore musket had been supplanted technologically in 1855 by the rifle-musket. This arm, though still muzzle-loading and single-shot, was rifled. Rifling itself was not new, but the muzzle-loading procedure of rifled weapons prior to 1855 had been a slow and tedious process. With the adoption of a hollow-base, conical projectile (known as the "minié ball") developed by the French Ordnance Bureau, however, the rifle-musket could be loaded and fired as fast as the old smoothbore musket. The new projectile in conjunction with the rifle-musket was theoretically capable of accurate fire up to nine hundred yards. The high trajectory of the rifle-musket and its minié ball projectile, how-ever, in combination with the inability of most field commanders to accurately judge the distance to an opposing force, reduced the practical range of the new weapon to three hundred yards.

Had the Northern forces been fully armed with this weapon at the outset of the conflict, the South would have been at a severe tactical disadvantage. But the production of the rifle-musket had been so limited that the North was forced to rely on the same inferior smoothbore arms as the South until mid-1862. In the interim, the doctrine of tactical offensive with massed volley fire still ruled the battlefield, an advantage the Southern armies, with their superior leadership and élan, exploited throughout 1862 (though often with dreadful consequences in terms of casualties). Additions of improved arms, either through import, capture, or limited domestic production, kept Southern forces at a par with their Northern counterparts through 1862 and 1863, so that neither side possessed a tactical advantage based solely upon weaponry. The tactical defensive advantage evolved in 1864, when the superior range of the rifle-musket was combined with defensive earthworks that severely reduced the ability of an attacker to inflict casualties on his opponent. Having finally completed the re-equipping of its forces with the rifle-musket during the winter of 1863–1864, the South was fully able to exploit this combination during the spring campaigns of 1864, probably adding an extra year to the short life of the Confederate States of America.

The same problems that the South encountered in equipping its military forces with small arms also applied to artillery. Like the small arms, the artillery of the Confederacy came from diverse sources: pre–Civil War acquisition of light artillery under the 1808 Militia Act, seizure of heavy ordnance at seacoast fortifications, capture of Union light artillery on the battlefield, importation, and domestic manufacture.

The light artillery in the South at the commencement of hostilities consisted of Mexican War–vintage guns. Prior to 1857, the standard six-gun field (also called "light") battery had consisted of four 6-pound guns and two 12-pound howitzers, both of whose tubes (barrels) were cast in bronze. The prime difference between a gun and a howitzer was the interior of the bore. Howitzers had a chamber of lesser diameter than the actual bore of the gun and so accepted a small amount of propellant charge; the small charge caused the projectile to travel in a relatively high arc to its target. Guns, on the other hand, had a chamber that was the same diameter as the bore; this permitted the projectile to travel a relatively low arc to its target. Until the introduction of rifled guns, light or field artillery was designated in terms of the weight of a solid round shot: 6-pound solid shot was 3.67 inches in diameter; 12-pound solid shot was 4.62 inches in diameter. Only the larger guns and mortars were designated by the true diameter of their bores.

The 6-pound gun, model 1841, formed the backbone of Confederate field artillery in 1861. Many were rifled during the early months of the conflict for increased accuracy and range (the latter increased from 1,523 to 1,700 yards). Rifling made the 6-pounder equivalent in range and striking power to the 12-pound smoothbore light gun introduced in 1857 and commonly known as the "Napoleon" (after Napoleon III of France, whose army pioneered its development). The "Napoleon" was the standard smoothbore gun of the U.S. Army in 1861 and continued in service throughout the war. At 1,227 pounds its tube was 530 pounds less than the old model 1841 12-pound gun, making it much more maneuverable on the field of battle. In addition to capturing Union Napoleons, the Confederacy widely copied the gun in its cannon foundries, and by 1863 many of the older 6-pound guns and 12-pound howitzers had been turned over to Ordnance Bureau authorities to be recast into the Napoleons.

At the beginning of the conflict, rifled muzzle-loading cannon were just beginning to be widely accepted by artillery tacticians. Two rifled field guns predominated in the Confederacy: the Parrott rifle with its shrunken band of reinforcing steel at its breech, and the light, sleek, evenly tapered "Ordnance" rifle. Both were made of iron. Although Virginia had acquired a few Parrott rifles just before secession, nearly all of the rifled iron guns in the Confederacy had been captured in combat. The Ordnance rifle was generally manufactured with a 3-inch diameter rifled bore that threw a 9.5-pound elongated projectile up to 1,830 yards. The Parrott came in three field grades: the 10-pound, 3-inch (actually 2.9-inch) Parrott threw a solid shot of 9.5 pounds 1,900 yards; the 20-pound, 3.67-inch threw a solid shot of 20 pounds the same distance; and the 30-pound, 4.5-inch threw a solid shot of 30 pounds 1,670 yards. (The last was usually considered a siege rather than a field gun, but numerous guns of this size were used by the Union and a few were captured by Confederate forces and pressed into service.)

The weight of the projectile that designated the type of gun was for a solid elongated shot, also called a "bolt." Such projectiles were primarily used for battering fortifications or for firing at long range at relatively fast-moving targets. When the target was not moving fast, the artillerist's preference was for shrapnel or case shot. These projectiles consisted of a sphere or bolt with a hollow cavity. The cavity was filled with a bursting charge and a number of musket balls. A fuze plugged or screwed into a hole in the nose of the projectile was supposed to catch fire upon the explosion of the propellent charge and spray the target with fragments. Shell, a similar projectile but lacking the musket balls, was intended primarily to burn structures. The standard fuze for the U.S. Army prior to the Civil War was the Bormann fuze, consisting of a zinc cylinder and a circular powder train within, all of which screwed into the nose of a projectile. Its exterior was marked

at intervals with explosion times; a cut across the mark exposed the proper timed detonation. The Confederacy attempted to copy this fuze at its laboratories, but its failure was so common that Southern gunners resorted to the old prewar wooden tapered fuze, a portion of which was cut off for timed explosions before being pounded into the hole at the nose of the projectile.

Because fuzes so often failed to ignite (the expanding bases of rifled projectiles often prevented the hot gasses of the cartridge's explosion from reaching the fuze at the nose of the projectile), percussion fuzes that detonated on impact were experimented with by both sides. But because these fuzes often buried into the ground before detonating or failed to detonate at all due to the low angle of the trajectory, they were not generally favored for field use.

The final antipersonnel projectile used during the war was called "canister." Sometimes erroneously referred to as "grape," the canister projectile gained its name from the shape of its exterior, a sheet-iron cylinder. The cylinder was filled with sawdust intermingled with small iron balls. Upon leaving the bore of a gun or howitzer, the momentum of the iron balls burst the cylinder, showering the area within three hundred yards of the muzzle with a shotgun-like blast of iron balls that was particularly destructive against advancing infantry or cavalry. At close range (one hundred yards or less), double and sometimes even triple loads of canister were used against oncoming forces.

All of these same type of projectiles were available not only to field batteries but also to the larger cannons for the defense of coastal or river fortifications. For the most part, these larger guns were captured or seized at Federal fortifications or naval stations in the South. The most common types captured consisted of 24-, 32-, and 42-pound iron guns. Many of these were subsequently rifled and fired elongated projectiles weighing respectively 48, 64, and 84 pounds. Smoothbore guns with diameters of 8 and 10 inches, throwing a ball of 68 and 128 pounds, respectively, were also captured and used by the Confederacy. By shifting these guns to vulnerable coastal and river defenses, the Confederacy was able to stall invasions at several critical places, though at the forts below New Orleans and at Forts Donelson and Henry they would not prove effective against superior Union naval power.

BIBLIOGRAPHY

Coates, Earl J. *Arms and Equipment of the Confederacy.* Vol. 2 of *Echoes of Glory.* Alexandria, Va., 1991.

Coggins, Jack. *Arms and Equipment of the Civil War.* New York, 1962.

Hazlett, James E., Edwin Olmstead, and Hume M. Parks. *Field Artillery Weapons of the Civil War.* Newark, N.J., 1983.

Ripley, Warren. *Artillery and Ammunition of the Civil War.* New York, 1970.

Todd, Frederick P. *American Military Equipage, 1851–1872.* Providence, R.I., 1974.

HOWARD MICHAEL MADAUS

Naval Ordnance

The beginning of the Civil War found the world's navies in a period of transition. In ordnance, there had been little change in the centuries-old smoothbore muzzle-loading guns firing solid shot. Extensive experiments were being conducted, however, with rifled breech-loading guns. Explosive shell had found favor at sea, and shell guns (as opposed to the old shot guns) were designed specifically for their use. Although rifled guns came into their own during the war, breechloaders continued to be plagued with problems; as a result, virtually all heavy pieces aboard ships during the Civil War were muzzleloaders. Cast iron had no serious rivals as a material for heavy ordnance, but there were numerous experiments with heavy wrought-iron guns despite the disastrous 1844 "Peacemaker" explosion aboard USS *Princeton.* Some guns were even being made of steel.

In composition of ship batteries, broadside batteries made up of many smaller guns were giving way to fewer guns of larger caliber and longer range mounted in pivot on the spar deck. This was particularly true aboard the new steamers. Civil War ironclad vessels were generally armed with a few heavy guns, usually a mix of rifled and smoothbore pieces. The largest gun in common broadside use during the war was the 9-inch shell gun. Pivot-mounted guns might be of any size, but were generally up to 11-inch.

Explosive shell fired at low velocity rendered wooden vessels extremely vulnerable. Ironically, shells proved largely ineffective against the new ironclad vessels during the war, and it was shot fired with higher charges of powder that did the most damage.

The U.S. Navy conducted important gunnery experiments in 1839, but the first experimental ordnance vessel was *Plymouth,* launched in 1857. The 1850s also saw the beginnings of scientific application to casting techniques (the Rodman process) and the design of guns (the Dahlgren design, which put the weight of metal at the breech, the point of greatest strain).

Improvements in gunpowder had led to reductions in the weight of charges. The Civil War saw continued improvements in cannon powder and the introduction of larger-grained powder.

Some new gun carriages had been introduced. The most prominent of these was the Marsilly, or two-truck (wheel) wooden carriage, which was much easier to train (aim) than the old four-truck carriage. It was adopted for the new 11-inch shell guns in broadside mounts.

The Confederacy secured a substantial quantity of cannons in the seizure of the Norfolk (Gosport) Navy Yard in April 1861 and also purchased some abroad. A limited number of guns were manufactured at home.

Confederate naval ordnance, including small arms and ammunition, was remarkably similar to that of the U.S. Navy, and ordnance practices were the same. This may be seen in a comparison of the U.S. Navy and Confederate States Navy ordnance manuals.

The Confederacy obtained small arms, too, by capture, purchase from abroad, and local manufacture. Most Federal arsenals within Confederate territory yielded many smoothbore muskets and some rifles, virtually all of which went to arm land forces. But the Confederacy failed to secure a substantial quantity of small arms from the Norfolk Navy Yard. The 1,329 carbines, 274 rifle-muskets, 950 naval pistols, and 337 Colt revolvers in the yard were either carried off in the frigate *Cumberland* or broken and thrown overboard by the Federals. Works were also established throughout the Confederacy for the manufacture of small arms and powder. Nonstandardization in small arms remained the rule in the South during the Civil War, and this applied to the navy.

Besides standard U.S. .58-caliber Springfield rifled muskets and local production of similar arms, Confederate agents purchased a variety of British carbines and muskets ranging from .44- to .75-caliber, Austrian .54-caliber rifles, and French .42-caliber carbines and Le Mat revolvers. Some may have found their way to the navy. The 1864 *Ordnance Instructions of the Confederate Navy* makes specific reference to Colt revolvers. The Model 1851 Navy .36-caliber pistol, weighing 2 pounds 10 ounces, was very popular in the South and the prototype of virtually all Southern-made revolvers.

Small arms were utilized by seamen and Confederate Marines. Afloat, Marines either augmented sailor crews or acted as sharpshooters and formed boarding parties. Their maximum number was only 540 officers and men, with many of these not available for service afloat. Their place was often taken by volunteers from cavalry and infantry units. As a result, Enfield .577-caliber rifles and shotguns were popular small arms on Confederate vessels. Boarding parties found shotguns particularly useful, as in the capture of USS *Harriet Lane* at Galveston, January 1, 1863.

The *Ordnance Instructions* called for regular exercise with the musket, carbine, pistol, and sword, and target practice with small arms. Captains of vessels determined when they were to be distributed and loaded and were also responsible for seeing that they were properly cleaned and stored. Small arms were to be inspected regularly and stored in unlined chests, if no proper armory was available.

Men armed with muskets afloat or on shore duty were to wear musket cartridge boxes, fitted with shoulder belt, and frog and scabbard for bayonet on their waist belt. Those armed with carbines on shore duty were to wear cartridge boxes with shoulder belts. For boat duty, or when armed with pistols and swords, they were to wear a waist belt with proper frog and boxes.

Allowance tables of the 1864 *Ordnance Instructions* specified quantities of small arms authorized for each class of ship. These included edged weapons such as battle axes, pikes, cutlasses, and swords, and muskets, carbines, revolvers, and pistols. The tables also provided ammunition allowances for each class of vessel.

BIBLIOGRAPHY

Albaugh, William A., III, and Edward N. Simmons. *Confederate Arms.* Harrisburg, Pa., 1957.
Ordnance Instructions for the Confederate States Navy. London, 1864.
Scharf, J. Thomas. *History of the Confederate States Navy.* New York, 1887. Reprint, New York, 1977.
Tucker, Spencer C. *Arming the Fleet: U.S. Navy Ordnance in the Muzzle-Loading Era.* Annapolis, Md., 1989.

SPENCER C. TUCKER

ARMY

[*This entry is composed of four articles:* Confederate Army, *which overviews the organization of the Confederate army and profiles several of its more prominent departments and special units;* Manpower, *which discusses the demographic makeup of the Confederate army;* Army Departments, *which discusses the location, command, and organization of the army departments; and* African Americans in the Confederate Army, *which examines the role of African Americans in the defense of the Confederacy. For further discussion of the organization and leadership of the cabinet-level department overseeing the Confederate war effort, see* War Department.]

Confederate Army

At the commencement of the secession crisis, hundreds of volunteer companies flocked to Montgomery, and then Richmond, to muster into the Confederate service. Specific field armies did not emerge at first, as companies were simply sent where needed without reference to organization. Jefferson Davis determined to pattern his new nation's forces after the armed forces of the old Union during the Mexican War of 1846 through 1848. He would have a small standing Regular Army, a cadre of professional soldiers, envisioned as lasting long after the conclusion of a peace and, presumably, the establishment of Confederate independence. But for meeting the urgent manpower needs of the current crisis, there would also be a Provisional Army of the Confederate States, comprising these volunteer outfits enlisted for specific terms of service, whether ninety days, twelve months, or eventually three years or the duration of the war.

The Regular Army

The Confederate Regular Army never really got off the ground. Authorized by Congress on March 6, 1861, it was to contain a corps of engineers, a corps of artillery, one cavalry regiment, and six infantry. But Regular enlistments were not attractive to would-be soldiers, since volunteers would do most of the fighting and win most of the glory and promotion. Moreover, volunteers would muster out as soon as the conflict was finished; Regulars were indentured for full terms of service regardless of when the war ceased. Thus, even though the enabling legislation called for 15,003 Regulars—roughly the size of the U.S. Regular service in 1860—only about 1,000 enlisted men and 750 officers and cadets eventually took their oaths. Not a single regiment was raised, and the few companies that did enlist were parceled out among other volunteer commands. Most of the officers took commands in the Provisional forces, achieving substantially higher rank there than their Regular commissions. Later in the war, a number of so-called Confederate regiments did appear, but they were not actually Regulars. Depleted companies from volunteer regiments from several states were consolidated to form full-strength units. Unable to decide what state designation to give such polyglot units, the War Department finally just called such outfits—twelve regiments and battalions of cavalry, nine regiments and battalions of infantry, five regiments and battalions of artillery—Confederate.

Most of the Regular companies served in the western theater of the war, but their histories—as distinct from the volunteers with whom they were grouped—are shadowy and difficult to extract. Indeed, even the War Department did not always keep track of them, and in 1864 Adjutant and Inspector General Samuel Cooper (the senior officer in the Regular service) seems to have forgotten that they even existed, telling a would-be appointee that "there have been no appointments in the regular army for several years, there being no regular army." In fact, recruiting stations for the Regular service had been closed as early as July 1861, never to open again.

The Regulars were hampered from the outset by the fact that the Confederacy needed men quickly. Accepting locally and privately raised companies and regiments furnished by the governors of the states met those needs much more rapidly and at less expense than recruiting Regulars. In the early days of the war, the volunteers arrived often already uniformed and armed and sometimes even trained, especially those companies that had existed as local home guard and privately maintained drill units before the war. With the ever-present strains on the Confederate Treasury, the government naturally had to channel all of its resources toward maintaining and equipping this instant army, leaving little or nothing for the fledgling Regulars. Thus, though it may have had much potential, the Regular Army died aborning, all but forgotten even by the men who served it.

The Provisional Army

Symbolic of the negligible role destined for the Regulars, Congress created them a week after addressing the immediate manpower needs by authorizing, on February 28, 1861, the Provisional Army of the Confederate States (PACS). Two days previously it had created the several staff departments of the new army, and the same day that it created the Regulars, Congress authorized the president to raise up to 100,000 volunteers for periods of no more than twelve months' service. In subsequent months, more recruitment bills were passed as manpower needs quickly expanded following the secession of Virginia. In May Congress authorized an additional 400,000, this time for three years' service or the duration of the war. These issues of numbers of men and terms of service were continuing vexations for Davis, as some state governors persisted in dangling regiments before him, but for less than the mandated terms of service.

Recruitment and Organization. In return for being furnished the roughly 1,000 men in ten companies that formed an ideal regiment, the government agreed to feed, clothe, train, arm, and equip the men, and pay them on a regular basis the eleven dollars per month mandated for private soldiers, with higher rankings receiving more. But before the war was very old, payment became a haphazard thing at best, its chronic absence hardly ameliorated by a subsequent increase in the soldiers' monthly allowance.

Eventually, somewhere between 650,000 and 750,000 Southern men enlisted in the PACS (authorities differ on the exact number). Virtually all of the men, exclusive of Regulars and militia and home guardsmen, served in PACS units, whose numbers have been estimated at from 750 to 1,009. As with so many other Confederate statistics, the numbers of regiments, battalions, companies, and batteries are disputed, thanks to incomplete records and duplication of the same unit at times under more than one designation. In 1861, for instance, two Fifth Kentucky Infantries were raised. One later became the Ninth Kentucky, yet it often shows up as separate from the original Fifth.

The PACS units were to consist of ten companies of from 64 to 100 men for infantry regiments, and up to twelve companies of no fewer than 64 men for the cavalry and no fewer than 70 men in an artillery battery. In actual practice, companies averaged between 81 and 93 men in 1862, but they

rapidly dwindled thereafter as casualties, disease, and desertions took their toll. By 1865, some regiments could muster fewer than 200, and many even smaller remnants were consolidated in 1864 and 1865 in order to create new regiments by combining those no longer large enough to perform effectively as battlefield units.

The dispersal of these volunteer regiments to the growing field armies of the Confederacy lay entirely with Davis and the War Department. From the outset efforts were made to combine units—from 3 to 5—from the same state into

> **. . . the the greatest discontent in the Southern forces arose when regiments were sent too far from their native states. . . .**

brigades, to serve under a brigadier from that state appointed by Davis; although there were many departures from this policy as the war ground on, it was honored more often than not. Further, the government did attempt to put such brigades into service more or less in their native region. Thus the major field army of the East, the Army of Northern Virginia, was composed chiefly of Virginia, North Carolina, South Carolina, Georgia, and Florida units, all of them raised east of the Appalachians. There were only smatterings of western regiments in Lee's army, just one regiment from Arkansas, and none at all from Kentucky and Missouri. The principal field army west of the mountains, the Army of Tennessee, was composed in its entirety of western units and those from the Deep South, with but a single brigade of Virginians and North Carolinians. Far to the west, across the Mississippi, E. Kirby Smith's Army of the Trans-Mississippi was similarly composed. It was a sound policy on the part of the War Department, for men could be expected to maintain their morale and élan more if they felt they were fighting for their own hearths. Moreover, it made recruiting to fill gaps, and the granting of occasional furloughs to visit home, that much more practicable. Some of the greatest discontent in the Southern forces arose when regiments were sent too far from their native states, often resulting in a commensurate rise in desertion.

Almost from the outset, the manpower available to the PACS lagged far behind needs. Only at the very outset did Davis have at his disposal more troops than he could arm and equip, forcing him reluctantly to turn away some proffered regiments that years later he would sorely miss. The largest field army, Robert E. Lee's in Virginia, never mustered more than about 85,000 men at its highest, while the Federal army opposing it rose at times as high as 130,000. The Army of Tennessee consistently hovered between 40,000 and 70,000, its numbers far less stable thanks to the much larger territory it had to defend and Richmond's frequent tampering with its organization.

At the beginning of the war, Congress authorized no organization larger than the brigade. Soon divisions composed of two or more brigades appeared, and then in 1862 Lee divided his army into "wings" that were finally formalized as corps in September. In the Army of Tennessee they began as "Grand Divisions" and were also called corps in the Shiloh campaign, but not until November 1862 did official corps organization appear.

Theoretically, at least, the military forces of the Confederacy assigned within a military department and commanded by the department officer in charge constituted its "army." By this definition, the Confederacy fielded at least forty "armies," though the number could be far higher thanks to departments changing names, being split or consolidated with others, and the commands themselves adopting designations other than those of the departments they served. (Ordinarily an army took its name from its department.) Most such armies were that in name only, being too small to merit the appellation. In 1864 the Army of Southwest Virginia was barely of brigade strength, for instance.

Army of Northern Virginia. The largest of the field armies of the Confederacy was also its best known and most storied, the Army of Northern Virginia, commanded by General Lee. It began, in fact, as the Army of the Potomac, and its origins lay in the first volunteers sent to the Department of Alexandria in April and May 1861. In June they were organized as the Army of the Potomac by Gen. P. G. T. Beauregard and fought as such at First Manassas. Even when forces from the Departments of Norfolk and the Peninsula were subsequently added, the combined organization continued to be the Army of the Potomac until June 1, 1862, when Lee assumed command. Informally he had taken to calling it the Army of Northern Virginia as far back as March. Now he made the change in fact, and the government quickly followed suit.

Certainly Lee and the government both took that designation literally to heart, for no other major field army of the Confederacy would operate through its entire career in so restricted an area. Although major portions of the First Corps did go to eastern Tennessee in the fall of 1863, and much of the Second Corps joined with other forces to form the Army of the (Shenandoah) Valley for a summer 1864 raid into Maryland, the Army of Northern Virginia as a whole set foot outside its department only three times. In September 1862 it crossed the Potomac into Maryland for the Sharpsburg campaign. In June and July 1863 it did so again, moving into Pennsylvania to Gettysburg. And in the summer of 1864 it withdrew to the defenses of Richmond and Petersburg, later to race toward Appomattox. With these exceptions, virtually all of its operations were conducted in an area sixty miles long, north of Richmond, and

about sixty miles wide, from the Rappahannock River to Gordonsville.

As with all the field armies of the Confederacy, manpower for the Army of Northern Virginia always lagged behind needs. At its largest, Lee's command numbered about 85,000, first when he took command just prior to the Seven Days' Battles of June and July 1862, and again at Gettysburg in July 1863. Thus Lee was consistently outnumbered on virtually every battlefield of the war—by a minimum of about 10,000 at Gettysburg and by as much as 70,000 during the Chancellorsville campaign two months earlier. Of all the Confederate field armies, it was the one hardest hit by a heavy attrition of battlefield losses among senior commanders at corps, division, and brigade levels. Gettysburg almost crippled its high command, which never recovered thereafter. Men who started the war as captains could finish it as major generals commanding a corps, as did John B. Gordon.

Strategically the army operated with the freest rein of any major field command, chiefly because of the excellent relationship between Lee and President Davis. Moreover, it remained almost untroubled by the command squabbles that so crippled the Army of Tennessee and others. This was chiefly due to the pacific influence of Lee, and the fact that for much of its career it was a winning army, with outstanding morale. Although unsteadily and somewhat timorously led by Joseph E. Johnston from First Manassas through Seven Pines, it enjoyed answering to the premier field commander of the war when Lee took charge, and he in turn was able, before the carnage of Gettysburg, to build an infrastructure of subordinates at every level whom he knew and understood, and with whom he could mold victories. After Gettysburg, the army, its officers, and Lee himself were simply too worn down to attempt ever again a major offensive.

Army of Tennessee. "The Confederacy, its government, its territory, its every thing is concentrated in these two armies," a Union officer said in March 1865. One was the Army of Northern Virginia; the other was the Army of Tennessee, a command as troubled and ill-starred as its counterpart was favored by fortune.

It had its origins in Department No. 2, created by Davis in July 1861 with Leonidas Polk in command, soon to be superseded by Albert Sidney Johnston. On March 5, 1862, the troops of the department were redesignated the Army of Mississippi, though the department did not change its name, and as such Johnston led them at Shiloh. After Johnston's death, P. G. T. Beauregard took command, and he was in turn replaced by Gen. Braxton Bragg on June 27. Five months later the Army of Tennessee was joined with the small Army of Kentucky, and on November 20, 1862, Bragg assumed command of the whole under the new designation Army of Tennessee, the name it would bear to the end.

Unlike Lee's army, this western command ranged in its career over the entire length of Tennessee, northern

Mississippi, and Alabama, and across Georgia and both of the Carolinas; it also launched a major offensive into Kentucky almost to the Ohio River. In all, the army campaigned over a vastness of nearly 200,000 square miles. Its manpower also ran consistently lower than Lee's. In most of its battles—Shiloh, Murfreesboro, Chickamauga—it numbered between 40,000 and 60,000. At its largest, commencing the Atlanta campaign in May 1864, it counted perhaps as many as 60,000 to 65,000 men.

Also unlike Lee's army, it was cursed with a command chaos almost from the start. The Virginia army benefited from a substantial percentage of professionally trained graduates

> **Nearly a third of the men, however, were poorly armed or lacking arms entirely, a condition common to the Trans-Mississippi.**

of West Point and private military academies; the Army of Tennessee had far more amateurs in positions of responsibility. And again unlike Lee, Bragg and his successors from the start faced more able enemies in the likes of Ulysses S. Grant and William Tecumseh Sherman. Bragg himself was the most discordant element of all. Hesitating and indecisive, he blamed his defeats on his subordinates, engaging in blatant scapegoatism, and thereby fomented virtual rebellion among his corps and division commanders. From November 1862 on, the high command fought among themselves. When Bragg was replaced by Joseph E. Johnston on December 27, 1863, the squabbling did not cease but did abate somewhat, only to return with renewed vigor when John Bell Hood—one of the anti-Bragg faction—replaced Johnston on July 18, 1864. Following Hood's disasters at Franklin and Nashville in the fall, Richard Taylor succeeded him briefly on January 23, 1865, only to be himself replaced by Johnston once more on February 25. Twice during the war President Davis had to visit the army headquarters to try to put down the infighting, but to no avail. Consistently outnumbered by its foes, sometimes by two to one, and crippled by an inept commander in 1863 and by internal strife throughout, it was an ill-starred command from the outset. Except for the one shining moment at Chickamauga, when almost by chance it inflicted one of the most demoralizing losses ever suffered by a Union army, its whole career was one long tale of sacrifice and defeat.

Army of Vicksburg. Substantially smaller, though still important, secondary field armies operated east of the Mississippi. Best known is the one surrendered by Gen. John C. Pemberton at Vicksburg, Mississippi, July 4, 1863. Officially the army of the Department of Mississippi and East

Louisiana, it was more generally referred to as the Army of Vicksburg. Constituted almost exclusively for the defense of that river city, it never saw open field campaigning except for the May 1863 operations east and south of the city when futile attempts were made to impede the approach of Grant's Federal army. Its manpower was always woefully inadequate, made worse by Richmond's failure to appreciate the magnitude of Grant's threat and the foot dragging of Joseph E. Johnston when ordered to come to its relief with additional forces. Commencing the campaign with about 30,000 to 35,000 men, Pemberton at last had to surrender about 29,000, the only instance in the war of a complete field army yielding prior to the 1865 collapse.

Army of Alabama, Mississippi, and East Louisiana. Richard Taylor, briefly the commander of the Army of Tennessee, also led another major field command, the Army of East Louisiana, Mississippi, and Alabama—later redesignated the Army of Alabama, Mississippi, and East Louisiana. This was the last army east of the Mississippi to surrender, accepting terms on May 4, 1865, and paroling some 12,000 men, mute testimony to the pitiable manpower available to army commanders at war's end. This army saw action in 1864 in cooperation with Johnston's forces during the Atlanta campaign, but otherwise spent its entire career in Alabama resisting Federal thrusts at Mobile and Selma.

Army of the Trans-Mississippi. The last major Confederate army to surrender was also the only principal force west of the great river, the Army of the Trans-Mississippi. It began as the Army of the West, organized in the winter of 1861–1862 by Gen. Earl Van Dorn as a subcommand of Department No. 2. It served briefly in Arkansas, including the defeat at Elkhorn Tavern in March, and was then reconstituted as the Army of the Trans-Mississippi in May under Gen. Thomas C. Hindman and shortly thereafter under Gen. Theophilus H. Holmes. Then in February 1863 this subdistrict was incorporated into a larger command including virtually all of Texas, Arkansas, and Louisiana west of the river. The new Trans-Mississippi Department and army were commanded thereafter by Gen. E. Kirby Smith until the close of the war.

Its activities were widespread, at least geographically, for the army had the task of defending fully one-third of all the territory of the Confederacy. Consequently, Smith's army was usually dispersed in detachments covering posts in Arkansas, chiefly along rivers and overlooking the Mississippi during the Vicksburg campaign, and along the Rio Grande and the Texas Gulf to repel Federal seaborne raids. The army saw major action in only two campaigns: the Red River campaign of March to May 1864, and the raid into Missouri led by Gen. Sterling Price in September and October of the same year.

Unlike the armies east of the river, the Trans-Mississippi—given its large territory and the ways of life of the men who filled its ranks—showed a heavy imbalance in favor of cavalry. Indeed, Price's raid was made by an army of cavalry, at least 12,000 of them, and their subsequent defeat at Westport, Missouri, involved the largest number of cavalry in any battle of the war. Nearly a third of the men, however, were poorly armed or lacking arms entirely, a condition common to the Trans-Mississippi. In 1863 and 1864 Smith's whole command numbered in the low 30,000s, though at times it rose higher, but so many were unarmed and so many were cavalry that were costly and troublesome to maintain that Smith actually tried to reduce his ranks occasionally in the name of improving efficiency. When he finally surrendered on May 26, 1865, there were over 40,000 men on his rolls, though it is doubtful that they could all have been mustered for battle in any one spot. Like the Army of Tennessee, the Trans-Mississippi also had its command problems, for the War Department made a habit of banishing inept or disgraced commanders to the region. Smith himself was alternately ambitious and timid, and operated in an imperious manner that alienated many subordinates, including Richard Taylor before that officer got his own army. Several of the cavalry generals were high-strung, one killing another in a quarrel, and another killing a fellow general in a duel. It was fortunate for the department that major Federal efforts at penetration were so few, for concert of action and cooperation were nearly impossible to achieve among such officers. The repulse of the Red River thrust owed as much to Federal ineptitude as it did to Confederate performance.

Guerrilla Units and Home Guards

Besides the Regular Army and the PACS, the Confederacy had a third organized force in its several state militia. In addition, there was an army of sorts in the less formally organized and maintained county and local home guards scattered about the country, and in those irregular and guerrilla commands that abounded in the less accessible mountain reaches and west of the Mississippi in Missouri, Arkansas, and Texas. Few records exist for such units because their members were often never formally enrolled or sworn in, nor were their officers officially commissioned. Instead, men often just appeared from their homes when a call went out, engaged in an operation, and then melted back into the shadows or returned to homes and hideouts until needed again. Their officers were little more than natural leaders informally selected because of community standing or their ability to maintain order over irregulars.

Most famous of all, probably, was William Clarke Quantrill and the band of raiders that he led in Missouri and the West. Rarely numbering more than 30 to 100 at a time, his raiders preyed on outposts, trains, and civilians, and obeyed Confederate army orders only as it suited them, making them eventually anathema to Southern as well as Northern military authorities. Moreover, such commands were often composed of several lesser bands, with their own leaders who might, at

any time, challenge an overall commander to seize his power, as happened with Quantrill. Estimates of the number of such organizations are haphazard at best, and as to their strengths one can only guess. During the whole course of the war, perhaps 5,000 or more men served intermittently.

The home guards and local citizenry militia—as distinct from the organized state militia—present a similar conundrum for historians, and for much the same reasons. They appeared when Northern raiders or armies threatened their locality, and they rarely if ever set foot outside their home county. Occasionally they were appended to a major army and acted under military orders, but as soon as the emergency was past or the army moved on, they returned to their civilian pursuits. Most of those so engaged were under eighteen or over forty-five, the legal ages for conscription and enlistment. Estimates of home guardsmen have ranged as high as 98,720, but this is certainly an exaggeration. Moreover, they were frequently incorporated later into PACS regiments, especially as manpower needs became more critical in 1864 and after. Especially in the Trans-Mississippi they emerged—often at the same time as the irregulars—as well as in the Deep South.

Although the irregulars—as distinct from *enlisted* home guards—were almost to a man mounted, the reserves served almost exclusively as foot soldiers, their chief service being the provision of information about local roads, bridges, and landscape. As for the numbers engaged in this army throughout the Confederacy, again only guesswork can suggest an answer. Perhaps as many as 300,000 were eligible for such service. Probably no more than 100,000 actually considered themselves members of such organizations, and barely 20,000 likely ever saw more than momentary service.

All of the myriad forms of organizations, whether Regulars, PACS, militia, home guards, or irregulars, faced the same insurmountable problem. Their task was to try to do too much with too little, over too large a territory. Complicating their task immeasurably was the nature and diversity of their several organizations. Command divisions were indistinct, authority clouded or overlapped, and vital manpower and attention were wasted on duplicated efforts. The Regulars were unnecessary; most of the home guards and militia were needed in the field armies; the irregulars were so ill-controlled and disorganized as to be sometimes as dangerous to friend as to foe. That these various components of the Confederate service achieved so much is testimony to the commitment of the men in the ranks to their cause.

[*For further discussion of the various branches of the army, see* Artillery, *overview article;* Cavalry; Engineer Bureau; Infantry; Medical Department; Signal Corps. *For further discussion of particular armies and special units, see* Army of Northern Virginia; Army of Tennessee; Special Units; Trans-Mississippi Department. *See also* Conscription;

Desertion; File Closers; Morale; *and entries on particular battles and biographies of numerous figures mentioned herein.*]

BIBLIOGRAPHY

Connelly, Thomas L. *Army of the Heartland: The Army of Tennessee, 1861–1862.* Baton Rouge, La., 1967.

Connelly, Thomas L. *Autumn of Glory: The Army of Tennessee, 1862–1865.* Baton Rouge, La., 1971.

Davis, William C. *Jefferson Davis: The Man and His Hour.* New York, 1991.

Freeman, Douglas S. *Lee's Lieutenants: A Study in Command.* 3 vols. New York, 1942–1944. Reprint, New York, 1986.

Kerby, Robert L. *Kirby Smith's Confederacy: The Trans-Mississippi South, 1863–1865.* New York, 1972.

Livermore, Thomas. *Numbers and Losses of the Civil War in America.* Boston, 1901.

McMurry, Richard M. *Two Great Rebel Armies.* Chapel Hill, N.C., 1989.

Weinert, Richard P. "The Confederate Regular Army." *Military Affairs* 25 (1962): 97–107.

Weinert, Richard P. *The Confederate Regular Army.* Shippensburg, Pa., 1991.

WILLIAM C. DAVIS

Manpower

Most of the men who fought in the armies of the Confederacy came from the eleven states that had seceded from the Union in 1861. At the outbreak of the war, the population of the Confederate States of America totaled just over 9 million people. Of these, 1.8 million were young men aged fifteen to thirty-nine—the likely age of men serving in the armed forces. About 700,000 of these, however, were black slaves, rejected by the South as prospective soldiers. This means that the Confederacy had just over 1 million young men of fighting age for service in its army. Allowing for the facts that some men over the age of forty might serve in the military and that additional youths would become old enough to fight during the course of the war, a reasonable estimate of the pool of available soldiers from within the Confederacy itself would be about 1.75 million men.

Some additional manpower was available from the slaveholding border states (Delaware, Maryland, Kentucky, and Missouri). A reasonable guess would be that perhaps one-third of the half million young men (or about 185,000) in the border states would choose to serve in the South rather than remain loyal to the Union. (The fraction would be somewhat higher in the western states such as Kentucky and Missouri, somewhat lower in Delaware and Maryland.) Thus, a generous estimate of the total manpower upon which the Confederacy could draw for soldiers would be somewhere in the neighborhood of 2 million men.

In contrast, the North, with a population of 18.9 million people, had a far larger pool of young men from which to obtain soldiers. If we construct an estimate of the number of men available to fight for the Union comparable to that just presented for the South it would be more than 6 million men. To this we must add a final source of manpower: freed blacks who left the South to fight for the Union. Although we do not have an accurate estimate of the number of freed slaves who served in the Union forces, we do know that as many as 200,000 blacks served in the Union army and navy during the Civil War.

If we look, then, simply at the number of *potential* soldiers, the South was at a disadvantage of at least three or four to one in terms of military manpower. Fortunately for the Confederates, this disadvantage was partially offset by the fact that the South was relatively more successful in actually getting men to serve in its army than the Union was. Over the course of the war, the Confederate armies enlisted a total of just under 900,000 men, while the Union, with more than three times as many young men, managed to get about 2.1 million in its armed forces. Because they recruited a higher fraction of young men into the army, the Confederate commanders faced a disadvantage of about 2.3 to 1 in favor of the North.

The success in mobilizing men for its armed forces left the Confederacy with fewer men to fill the needs of production on the home front. Some of this work could be done by the slaves who stayed behind on the farms and plantations of the South. And slaves could perform such military tasks as transporting goods to the front, ditching, and constructing fortifications, and a variety of other tasks behind the lines. In many instances their efforts were a crucial element in the Confederate military effort. A few slaves even accompanied their owners to the front lines.

But the contribution of slaves to both the Confederate military effort and production for the home front was limited by several factors. One was the problem posed by the presence of a population whose loyalty to the Southern cause was obviously questionable. White Southerners were understandably reluctant to use slaves as soldiers in the front lines. Not until February 1865, when the Southern cause was lost, did the Confederate Congress finally approve the enlistment of black slaves as soldiers. Another factor was that even when military tasks could be entrusted to slaves, many of their owners were reluctant to lease them to the army, where mistreatment by their overseers or capture by the Federals was all too likely. Moreover, throughout the war, there was a steady flow of blacks fleeing to the Union lines and offering their services to the South's enemy. At the time of Robert E. Lee's surrender, approximately 110,000 blacks were serving in the Union armed forces, many of them ex-slaves who had fled with their families to the protection of Union lines. Their presence in the enemy's army served as a constant reminder to Southerners of the danger inherent in an excessive reliance on slave labor. Of even greater concern to many whites was the threat of slave uprisings. Responding to this fear, state governments in the Confederacy sought to keep troops within their own borders despite pleas for more men from the government in Richmond. Fears of black rebellion spurred the Confederate Congress to pass an act exempting all whites who owned twenty or more slaves from military duty. In addition to reducing the number of men available for service in the army, this act had a very negative effect on the morale of nonslaveholders who were called up. All in all, it could be argued that the *Northern* military effort had been served as well by the labor of the former slaves who fled the Confederacy as were the interests of the South by those slaves who stayed behind.

The armies that campaigned in 1861 and early 1862 were manned by volunteers answering either Abraham Lincoln's or Jefferson Davis's call for soldiers at the outbreak of hostilities. By 1862, however, it had become clear that reliance on volunteers alone would not provide the manpower necessary to win the war. On March 29, 1862, the Confederate Congress enacted a Conscription Law that made every white male aged eighteen to thirty-five liable for service in the army and extended the length of service of those already in the army to the duration of the war. A subsequent act in 1864 set the age range at seventeen to fifty years. The Union also passed a draft law in March 1862, calling for all able-bodied males between the ages of twenty and forty to register for military service. Because of generous exemptions, however, neither draft law produced huge numbers of men for military service. About 82,000 were actually drafted into the Confederate army. Over 200,000 men were called up for service in the Union army, but only about half of them either served or purchased a substitute. It should be noted that these numbers do not reflect the full effect of the conscription laws. In both the North and the South, the threat of being drafted was often sufficient reason for young men to accept the bonuses offered by state governments to induce men to volunteer for military service.

The total number of men serving in Southern armies reached a peak at about the time of the Battle of Gettysburg; thereafter it declined steadily. The reasons for this were clear enough. First was the enormous casualties sustained by the Confederates during four years of heavy fighting. Over 250,000 Confederate soldiers died, and another 200,000 men were listed as wounded in the course of the war. As the fighting dragged on and morale deteriorated both at the front and at home, desertions increased steadily. At least 100,000 Southern men abandoned their units during the course of the war, and desertions reached epic proportions in the final year. The effect can be seen by the fact that at the end of the war, the Confederate army rolls listed 359,000 soldiers, but only 160,000 were on active duty and only 126,000 were

actually present on the front lines. In the North, by contrast, mobilization efforts produced an ever-increasing flow of men that was able to offset the even higher numbers of Northern soldiers who deserted or were killed or wounded. At the time of Appomattox, there were nearly a million men in the U.S. armed forces.

[*See also* African American Troops in the Union Army; Civil War, *article on* Losses and Numbers; Conscription; Contraband.]

BIBLIOGRAPHY

Livermore, Thomas L. *Numbers and Losses in the Civil War in America, 1861–1865.* Boston and New York, 1901.

McPherson, James M. *Battle Cry of Freedom: The Civil War Era.* New York, 1988.

Mohr, Clarence. *On the Threshold of Freedom: Masters and Slaves in Civil War Georgia.* Athens, Ga., 1986.

Ransom, Roger L. *Conflict and Compromise: The Political Economy of Slavery, Emancipation, and the American Civil War.* Cambridge, Mass., 1989.

ROGER L. RANSOM

Army Departments

To defend the borders of a new nation whose land area approximated that of western Europe, President Jefferson Davis in 1861 organized the Confederacy's territory and military resources into administrative entities called departments. Occasionally, specific tasks within departments were assigned to smaller entities called districts, but these districts were normally subordinate to their respective departments. Before the war ended in 1865 at least forty-six named departments and independent districts had been created, although not all existed at any one time.

Under Davis's scheme a general officer commanded each department, with responsibility for both defensive and offensive movements within its confines. Normally the department commander controlled all forces within his department, which, in the larger departments, were usually named armies. Well aware of the vastness of the South and the vagaries of communication, Davis generally allowed department commanders wide latitude in the conduct of business within their respective commands. In addition, the opinions of department commanders carried great weight whenever questions arose about the transfer of assets between departments.

Criticized by historians as indicative of Davis's rigidity of mind, this departmental system initially seemed to be a useful mechanism to control military activity over such a large area. In theory several advantages were apparent. Militarily, a department commander would be much more responsive to local conditions and enemy threats than would the central government, positioned on the edge of the Confederacy in Richmond, Virginia. Logistically, department commanders could both defend resource centers more effectively and organize distribution more efficiently than the bureaus in the War Department. Politically, the department system guaranteed that every section of the Confederacy had a military structure devoted to its specific protection. Diplomatically, organization of the new nation's territory into a coherent structure for military defense projected abroad an air of stability without being aggressive. Thus Davis's departmental system seemed at first to be an intelligent response to military problems of immense proportions.

Major geographical features divided the eleven states of the Confederacy into three large regions. In the East, a flat coastal strip gave way initially to rolling hills and then to the first great barrier, the Appalachian Mountains. In this region was the Confederacy's capital and much of its population. Beyond the Appalachians lay a rich agricultural domain of plains and hills stretching all the way to the Mississippi River. West of the river an even vaster region began in the Mississippi's flooded lowlands and ended somewhere in the arid high plains of Texas.

Davis paid little heed to these large regions when he established the first series of military departments. Virginia alone was divided into at least seven commands. Similarly, three departments covered Alabama. As 1861 ended, however, a gradual consolidation of small departments had begun to take place. In Virginia, departments north of Richmond merged into the Department of Northern Virginia, creating a unified command from the Shenandoah Valley to Chesapeake Bay. West of the Appalachians, an even greater consolidation formed the massive Department No. 2. This department stretched from Cumberland Gap to the Mississippi River and beyond into Arkansas and Missouri.

In theory Department No. 2, commanded by Gen. Albert Sidney Johnston, exemplified the principle of unity of command in the face of the multiple Union departments facing it. In practice, however, Johnston's resources permitted him to do no more than create a weak cordon defense along the northern boundary of his department. When that cordon was pierced at Forts Henry and Donelson in February 1862, Johnston withdrew precipitately, losing Nashville and central Tennessee in the process. Confederate fortunes were only partially retrieved by the first great concentration of military units from adjacent departments into Department No. 2. Orchestrated by Gen. P. G. T. Beauregard, this concentration gathered troops from all parts of Johnston's command as well as from Department No. 1 (the lower Mississippi) and the Department of Alabama and West Florida. Although the offensive mounted by Johnston's enlarged army came to grief at Shiloh in April 1862, the principle of interdepartmental transfers was established. Meanwhile, in the East, the

Department of Northern Virginia continued to expand at the expense of smaller departments as a large Federal army menaced Richmond from the southeast.

Federal threats from both the east and the west caused a reorganization of Davis's departmental system by the summer of 1862. The earlier consolidation of several small departments within the Department of Northern Virginia became permanent, giving that department primary responsibility for defending Virginia from the north. The territory below Richmond fell under a new Department of North Carolina and Southern Virginia, which faced Federal enclaves around Norfolk and the North Carolina sounds. Farther south still, the defense of the Confederacy's remaining Atlantic coast was entrusted to an expanded Department of South Carolina, Georgia, and Florida.

West of the Appalachians Davis acted even more vigorously. In late May he removed the vast area beyond the Mississippi River from Department No. 2 and gave it independent existence as the Trans-Mississippi Department. This new superdepartment now included Texas, Indian Territory, Arkansas, Missouri, and western Louisiana. Not long afterward, Department No. 2 was expanded to include the territory formerly belonging to Department No. 1 and the Department of Alabama and West Florida, both of which passed out of existence. Department No. 2 and its Army of Tennessee thus joined the Department of Northern Virginia and its army as the Confederacy's primary defenders.

For the next few months the departmental structure in the East remained intact as Gen. Robert E. Lee either defeated Federal thrusts toward Richmond or raided into Northern territory. Affairs in Department No. 2 were in flux, however, because of Gen. Braxton Bragg's decision to strike northward into Kentucky. Leaving a relatively small force in northern Mississippi, Bragg transferred the bulk of his army to Chattanooga, Tennessee, for an advance northward. Chattanooga lay within the boundaries of the Department of East Tennessee, one of two minor departments that provided a physical link between Bragg's and Lee's forces. Commanded by Maj. Gen. E. Kirby Smith, this department now became the host for Bragg's Army of Tennessee. The ensuing invasion of Kentucky was thus conducted by two semi-independent armies whose attempts at cooperation failed miserably. After the invasion ended in defeat, the two departments merged briefly, but this seemingly logical step was revoked by the end of 1862. Meanwhile, the forces Bragg had left behind in Mississippi had come under threat from Federal troops operating in the Mississippi River valley.

The deteriorating situation in Mississippi led Jefferson Davis in October 1862 to create a new department from within Department No. 2. Commanded by Lt. Gen. John C. Pemberton, the new Department of Mississippi and East Louisiana focused almost entirely upon the defense of the Mississippi River around Vicksburg, Mississippi. As the

Federal threat to Vicksburg grew and Bragg's invasion of Kentucky receded, Davis recognized that coordination would be required between Bragg's and Pemberton's departments. In response he created the Department of the West in November 1862 and assigned Gen. Joseph E. Johnston to its command.

Envisioned by Davis as another superdepartment, Johnston's actual command was ill defined at best. Although Johnston apparently had supreme powers within his domain, Bragg and Pemberton continued to exercise the prerogatives of department commanders, including the right to correspond directly with the Confederate War Department. If nothing else, Johnston's position should have enabled him to see the area between the Appalachians and the Mississippi River as a whole. In turn, this unified vision should have permitted the allocation of scarce resources to counter the most dangerous of several Federal threats. Unfortunately, Johnston did little to produce such a vision.

The year 1863 saw little change in the Virginia and coastal theaters, where the enemy was easily contained. West of the Appalachians, Federal forces in central Tennessee remained quiescent for six months, permitting Bragg to reinforce Johnston's weak attempt to lift the siege of Vicksburg. In July reverses struck all major Confederate field armies as Pemberton surrendered Vicksburg, Johnston withdrew to eastern Mississippi, Bragg evacuated central Tennessee, and Lee's invasion of the North was repulsed at Gettysburg. In response to these disasters, Davis again reorganized some of his western departments. Renamed the Department of Tennessee, Bragg's command by the end of the summer had absorbed the Department of East Tennessee once more. Johnston nominally retained both his title and his coordinat-

> **With the heartland either under Federal occupation or devastated, only the . . . periphery continued to hold out.**

ing function, but in reality he commanded only the forces in eastern Mississippi. Aided by an infusion of units from the Department of Northern Virginia, Bragg won a Pyrrhic victory at Chickamauga in September but was driven into northern Georgia after his resounding defeat at Missionary Ridge in November.

The disastrous events of the second half of 1863 in the western Confederacy caused still another change in departmental boundaries. Now severed from the remainder of the Confederacy, the Trans-Mississippi Department became virtually independent of central government control. Upon Bragg's removal from the Department of Tennessee in December 1863, Johnston assumed command in his stead.

Johnston's Department of the West was abolished and the Department of Tennessee expanded to include eastern Alabama and part of western Florida. The remnants of Pemberton's old Department of Mississippi and East Louisiana in early 1864 became first the Department of the Southwest and then the Department of Alabama, Mississippi, and East Louisiana. Elsewhere, the Virginia and coastal fronts remained stable as the Department of Northern Virginia, the Department of North Carolina and Southern Virginia, and the Department of South Carolina, Georgia, and Florida.

The year 1864 brought further Confederate reverses in both the East and the West. By midsummer, Lee's army was pinned to its fortifications around Petersburg, which straddled the boundary between the Department of Northern Virginia and the Department of North Carolina and Southern Virginia. In Georgia, Johnston gradually retreated to Atlanta's defenses, where Davis replaced him with Gen. John Bell Hood. After several bloody battles Hood was forced to relinquish the city. In September, he began an advance that would eventually take him into central Tennessee and would at the same time call forth the last major reorganization of Davis's departmental system. On October 17, 1864, Hood's Department of Tennessee became the Department of Tennessee and Georgia. Unlike the old, the new department excluded Alabama but in a bit of wishful thinking included western Tennessee. At the same time Johnston's old superdepartment, the Department of the West, reappeared as the Military Division of the West. Commanded by General Beauregard, the new organization was created to coordinate activity in both Hood's department and Lt. Gen. Richard Taylor's Department of Alabama, Mississippi, and East Louisiana.

The destruction of Hood's army at Nashville at the end of 1864 signaled the approaching end of the Confederacy and its departmental system. With the heartland either under Federal occupation or devastated, only the departments on the Confederacy's periphery continued to hold out. First to go was Lee's Department of Northern Virginia in April 1865. Next to collapse were the forces collected from the Department of Tennessee and Georgia; the Department of South Carolina, Georgia, and Florida; and the Department of North Carolina and Southern Virginia, all of which surrendered under Beauregard, Johnston, and Bragg in North Carolina later that same month. Taylor's Department of Alabama, Mississippi, and East Louisiana followed the others into oblivion in early May, and on May 26, 1865, Smith's Trans-Mississippi Department negotiated the capitulation of the final remnant of Confederate territory.

Created in 1861 to meet a variety of valid needs, Jefferson Davis's departmental system served to the end as a necessary administrative mechanism to command and control the Confederacy's scarce military assets. Where a brilliant commander like Lee was present or a major Federal threat was absent, as in the coastal departments and the Trans-Mississippi, the departmental system worked well. Where both brilliant commanders and resources were lacking and the Federal threat was great, as in Department No. 2 and its successors, no organizational system could have produced success. As events proved, neither fragmentation nor consolidation could succeed without adequate resources in the vast heartland of the Confederacy, and it was there that the war was lost.

BIBLIOGRAPHY

Connelly, Thomas L. *Army of the Heartland: The Army of Tennessee, 1861–1862.* Baton Rouge, La., 1967.

Connelly, Thomas L. *Autumn of Glory: The Army of Tennessee, 1862–1865.* Baton Rouge, La., 1971.

Connelly, Thomas Lawrence, and Archer Jones. *The Politics of Command: Factions and Ideas in Confederate Strategy.* Baton Rouge, La., 1973.

Jones, Archer. *Confederate Strategy from Shiloh to Vicksburg.* Baton Rouge, La., 1961.

Kerby, Robert L. *Kirby Smith's Confederacy: The Trans-Mississippi South, 1863–1865.* New York, 1972.

Vandiver, Frank E. *Rebel Brass: The Confederate Command System.* Baton Rouge, La., 1956. Reprint, Westport, Conn., 1971.

Woodworth, Steven E. *Jefferson Davis and His Generals: The Failure of Confederate Command in the West.* Lawrence, Kans., 1990.

WILLIAM GLENN ROBERTSON

African Americans in the Confederate Army

African American Southerners played a wide range of roles in support of the Confederate war effort. The war brought all kinds of new tasks at the same time that it gave new significance to customary work. On the home front, slaves grew the corn that fed Confederate soldiers, and they produced the cotton that clothed them. Emphasizing the battlefront, historian Bell Wiley employed a military metaphor: "Together they worked, white and black, . . . an army of soldiers and an army of laborers." Even in microcosm the metaphor worked, as, especially in the summer of 1861, slave men accompanied many masters to war and carried out various camp chores.

Throughout the Confederacy and the war, by the tens of thousands, black men, free and slave alike, contributed directly to the Confederate war effort. They worked in war industries—for example, at Tredegar Iron Works in Richmond, Virginia. They manufactured salt, vital to the preservation of meat. Supporting the South's transportation system, they worked on railroads, repaired bridges, and manufac-

tured and replaced or moved rails. As teamsters and stevedores, they moved Confederate supplies. As cooks, they prepared soldiers' meals, and as medical attendants, they bore stretchers, drove ambulances, and worked in hospitals. In each of their tasks, black workers released white men for combat duty.

Still more closely associated with the battlefront, black Confederates dug ditches, obstructed rivers, and erected batteries. A general impressment law, enacted in March 1863, followed the example of many states and made impressment universal. It authorized the secretary of war to impress free black men and, when their numbers proved insufficient, as many as twenty thousand male slaves between the ages of eighteen and forty-five. Impressment produced too few workers, however, and in late 1864, President Jefferson Davis proposed that the government purchase forty thousand slaves as military laborers. The winter of 1864–1865 brought urgent requests from Gen. Robert E. Lee for thousands of black laborers to support his efforts at Richmond and Petersburg.

By the autumn of 1864, white Confederates were widely discussing plans to go beyond black Confederates' combat support roles and arm slaves as part of the South's combat forces. As early as 1861, some state leaders had displayed a readiness to accept free black men into state service; the Tennessee legislature authorized the recruitment of free black men, either as volunteers or as conscripts, and a regiment of free men of color in Louisiana, the "Native Guards," entered state service. Meanwhile, the Confederate army proved unprepared to recruit free blacks; recruiting slaves had even less support. Howell Cobb, politician and general from Georgia, objected as late as January 1865 that "if slaves make good soldiers our whole theory of slavery is wrong." Yet such plans gained increasing acceptance. By the winter of 1864–1865, tens of thousands of black Unionists were fighting against the Confederacy and demonstrating that black men could indeed make good soldiers. Confederate Secretary of State Judah P. Benjamin was one who asked, in December 1864, "Is it better for the negro to fight for us or against us?" Proponents of the plan argued that it would provide manpower for the Confederacy's depleted army, counter nonslaveholding whites' jibes about "a poor man's fight," and attract diplomatic support in Europe. Those proponents differed, however, over significant details regarding the emancipation of black soldiers and their families.

By February 1865, General Lee's support for enrolling black troops became public knowledge. Still the Confederate Congress hesitated to adopt any version of such a plan. Only on March 13, 1865, did a Confederate measure to recruit black soldiers become law. Rather than promise anyone emancipation, the act barred freedom "except by consent of the owners and of the States" where slave soldiers resided. Lee then asked Virginia Governor William Smith for onefourth of the able-bodied slave men of military age in that state. Davis, having come to support the policy, still sought to avoid conscription and rely on owners' volunteering their slaves. In any case, the law came too late for companies of black soldiers to fight in large numbers for the Confederacy. But the image of slaves and free blacks drilling together in Richmond gave evidence that both slavery and the Confederacy were unraveling.

Having grown the corn to feed white soldiers, black Confederates worked on the railroads and drove the wagons that carried that food to the soldiers, and then cooked and served it to them. Moreover, they constructed Confederate defensive works. By the closing weeks of the war, they were forming companies to join forces with the white soldiers whom their labor had done so much to support.

BIBLIOGRAPHY

Berlin, Ira, Barbara J. Fields, Steven Miller, Joseph P. Reidy, and Leslie S. Rowland, eds. *Free at Last: A Documentary History of Slavery, Freedom, and the Civil War*. New York, 1992.

Brewer, James H. *The Confederate Negro: Virginia's Craftsmen and Military Laborers, 1861–1865*. Durham, N.C., 1969.

Durden, Robert F. *The Gray and the Black: The Confederate Debate on Emancipation*. Baton Rouge, La., 1972.

Mohr, Clarence L. *On the Threshold of Freedom: Masters and Slaves in Civil War Georgia*. Athens, Ga., 1986.

Wesley, Charles H. *The Collapse of the Confederacy*. Washington, D.C., 1937. Reprint, New York, 1968.

Wiley, Bell Irvin. *Southern Negroes, 1861–1865*. New Haven, Conn., 1938.

PETER WALLENSTEIN

ARMY OF NORTHERN VIRGINIA

The principal eastern army (1862–1865) of the Confederate States fought under the direction of Gen. Robert E. Lee with steady and sometimes spectacular success against the Federal Army of the Potomac. With a strength ranging between 35,000 and 85,000 men, the army opened its career by driving away an early threat to Richmond and then defending the capital across a broad arc of northern Virginia through the middle years of the Civil War. In 1864 and 1865 the Army of Northern Virginia was obliged to assume a limited defensive posture in siege lines surrounding Richmond and Petersburg. It surrendered at Appomattox Courthouse on April 9, 1865.

Early Operations in Virginia. During the war's first year Confederate detachments positioned around Virginia's northern perimeter resisted Federal threats on several fronts. The largest of these Confederate forces fought the First Battle of Manassas (or Bull Run) on July 21, 1861, when Gen. Joseph E. Johnston's command hurried eastward from the Shenandoah Valley to join with troops under Gen. P. G. T. Beauregard in repulsing an enemy advance southward from Washington, D.C. The unified Southern force, commanded by Johnston, became known as the Confederate Army of the Potomac—a label fraught with confusion because the premier eastern army of the Union became famous under precisely that name.

While Johnston maintained a line near Manassas and along the Potomac below Washington during 1861 and early 1862, Confederate forces concentrated at three other points on the state's military frontier. Gen. John B. Magruder commanded a modest army on Virginia's peninsula; a smaller detachment defended the important naval facilities around Norfolk; and Gen. Thomas J. ("Stonewall") Jackson led a small but aggressive command in the Shenandoah Valley. Pressure from Union forces brought action on all four fronts by the spring of 1862. Johnston felt obliged to abandon northern Virginia—and huge quantities of ordnance and other war matériel—in an awkward movement during March. A mighty Federal army under Gen. George B. McClellan successfully completed a waterborne movement to the peninsula opposite Magruder. Confederates near Norfolk witnessed the revolutionary first duel between ironclad warships as Northern strength became manifest in that area. In the Shenandoah Valley, Jackson launched in March the remarkable campaign that would win him lasting fame.

During the three months beginning with the dramatic events of March 1862, the components of what would become the Army of Northern Virginia played out their roles in the defense of Richmond. Most of Johnston's command moved east of Richmond to the peninsula, where it absorbed Magruder's men into a unified force facing McClellan's slow but massive advance. Johnston fought McClellan on May 5 at Williamsburg and then fell steadily back to the outskirts of the Southern capital. Confederates south of the James River who had been centered on Norfolk eventually moved toward Richmond and by June had augmented the strength of the main army directly defending the capital. Stonewall Jackson retained his independent command as a diversionary force in the Shenandoah Valley and exploited every opportunity he found there to attract the attention of Northern leaders away from the main prize at Richmond. From March 23 to June 9 Jackson fought six battles and marched hundreds of miles, occupying many times his own numbers in fruitless reaction to his daring thrusts.

While Jackson bedazzled a succession of foes in the Valley, Johnston committed his combined forces to battle under promising circumstances on May 31 and June 1, 1862, at Seven Pines (or Fair Oaks). Poor planning and an almost unbelievable degree of confusion among his ranking subordinates, particularly Gen. James Longstreet, dissipated Johnston's golden opportunity. Johnston also lost command of the army when he fell wounded late on May 31. The next day President Jefferson Davis designated Robert E. Lee as Johnston's replacement. Lee never relinquished command, to the intense disgust of Johnston and Longstreet but of almost no one else in the Confederate States.

Lee at once began to sculpt the army into his image of an effective field force. Although the Department of Northern Virginia had existed formally for months, Johnston had continued to call his command the Army of the Potomac. From his post as a nearly powerless military adviser in Richmond, Lee had referred to Johnston's force in March as the Army in Northern Virginia. By the end of that month he had begun, evidently on his own volition, to call the army he soon would make famous "The Army of Northern Virginia."

With Federals in great strength at the very gates of Richmond, Lee had little leisure in which to organize and prepare for the contest that he knew must come almost at once. The general did his best to organize the disparate elements that made up his new command, but his first priority was to entrench the lines it held in order to neutralize to some degree his enemy's preponderance in numbers. Southern soldiers still afflicted with naive notions of chivalry grumbled bitterly about wielding shovels instead of weapons. This stodgy new commander, they muttered, deserved the derisive title "King of Spades," and he might well blunt their offensive élan by turning them into laborers rather than warriors.

The Seven Days' Battles. A key element in Lee's planned combination was the triumphant army of Stonewall Jackson in the Shenandoah Valley. Jackson's men rested in the upper valley after dual victories at Cross Keys and Port Republic on June 8 and 9, 1862, and then moved eastward across the Blue Ridge toward Richmond. Confederate cavalry under the daring young Gen. J. E. B. Stuart had ridden all the way around McClellan's ponderous army during mid-June, so Lee knew that the Federal right flank north of Richmond dangled precariously. Jackson's men would approach from that direction and might be able to fall on that point with deadly effect. Lee's new fortifications dramatically increased his ability to secure the approaches to Richmond south of the Chickahominy. He concentrated his strength north of that river and during the last week of June hurled the Army of Northern Virginia against the Federals there.

The opening battles of the new army came to be known as the Seven Days' Battles because they covered a full week from June 25 to July 1, 1862. Stonewall Jackson repeatedly failed during the week in his important role as both the threat to the Federals' flank and the bludgeon to be applied there when necessary. At Mechanicsville on June 26, Gen. A. P. Hill launched a premature attack when Jackson's column arrived tardily and behaved without the wonted aggression once it reached the vicinity. The next day Jackson again failed to perform well as the army's maneuver element, and the result was a ghastly, grinding frontal assault at Gaines' Mill. Despite savage losses, Lee's infantry supplied him with his first major victory when they surged over the enemy line near sunset.

Pursuit of the beaten foe proceeded sluggishly and awkwardly on June 28 to 30, with missed opportunities at White Oak Swamp and another poorly coordinated bloodbath at Frayser's Farm. The week's crowning tactical disaster came at Malvern Hill on July 1, after which McClellan pulled his Federals back under shelter of Northern naval might well downstream from Richmond. Lee had struggled to apply his army to its opportunities and had been failed egregiously by many of his high-ranking subordinates as they all came to grips with the new organization. In the process of its tactical groping, however, the new army had won a great strategic victory by driving McClellan from the edge of Richmond. Jackson never again disappointed Lee and the lessons of the Seven Days' Battles served the army commander well as he prepared to reorganize and move forward. On the basis of his observations during the Seven Days', Lee sent away officers who had displayed incapacity and promoted promising candidates to fill their places.

Through July and into early August, McClellan's Federals continued to menace Richmond from the new base to which Lee had driven them. Meanwhile another Northern force moved into northern Virginia under the leadership of Gen. John Pope. To counter Pope's threat Lee divided his army and sent Stonewall Jackson toward Gordonsville and Culpeper with a sizable detachment of Confederate troops. A series of draconian anticivilian orders issued by Pope made him a particularly urgent target. With uncharacteristic choler Lee ordered Jackson "to suppress" this belligerent enemy, whom he called "the miscreant Pope." Jackson did just that in a campaign climaxed by a victory at Cedar Mountain on August 9. Soon thereafter Lee began moving the rest of the Army of Northern Virginia away from Richmond, where McClellan's threat had lapsed, to join Jackson.

Second Manassas. The campaign that ensued represented the first great battlefield collaboration between Lee and Jackson. Although Confederate law did not provide for any military organization larger than a division, nor for any rank higher than major general, Lee readily grasped the truth that his army must have direction at that higher level. Accordingly he assigned Jackson and Longstreet to the leadership of two wings into which the army's infantry was distributed. Stuart commanded all the cavalry and reported directly to Lee. Jackson's wing had been facing Pope for some time when Lee arrived with the vanguard of the remainder of the army. The rest of Longstreet's men reached the front in northern Virginia only in piecemeal fashion during the campaign; some arrived too late to participate in the Battle of Second Manassas. Because his wing was on the scene intact—and because it must have been already apparent that he was infinitely more aggressive than Longstreet—Jackson executed the bold initiatives that marked Lee's late August operations.

After failing to trap Pope between the Rapidan and Rappahannock rivers, Lee slipped Jackson up the right bank of the latter stream looking for an opening. On August 25 and 26 Jackson dashed far behind the Federal army on a march that covered more than fifty miles. Jackson's tattered "Foot Cavalry," as his hard-marching infantry came to be called, captured a vast Federal supply base at Manassas Junction and reveled in the unaccustomed bounty they found there. Jackson's march made Pope's line on the Rappahannock untenable and forced the Federals to fall back hurriedly. When Pope retired toward Manassas, Jackson grappled with him near Groveton on August 28 and then held tenaciously to a position behind an unfinished railroad until Lee and Longstreet arrived in support on August 29.

The Second Battle of Manassas reached its climax on August 30 when Jackson blunted renewed enemy attacks and Longstreet unleashed his wing of the army onto Pope's vulnerable left flank. The resultant rout swept the Federals from the field. Two days later Jackson tangled with an enemy force north of Manassas at Ox Hill (or Chantilly) in a blinding thunderstorm, killing two capable Union generals and compelling Pope's complete withdrawal into the defenses of Washington.

Maryland Campaign. In barely more than one month from its first battle, the Army of Northern Virginia had reoriented the war from the outskirts of the Confederate capital to the vicinity of the Union's capital. Lee eagerly pressed his advantage by ordering his divisions across the Potomac and into Maryland. He was riding the crest of a military tide of impressive proportions and of his own making. Any other strategic decision in the circumstances would have been utterly foolish. Circumstances conspired against Lee once he reached Maryland, however, and he eventually chose to offer battle when his chances had become so slender as to suggest that a return to Virginia without fighting was the only prudent alternative.

By September 10 the Army of Northern Virginia was centered on Frederick, Maryland, well situated to threaten Washington and other points to the north and east; but more than 12,000 Federals menaced the army's flank and rear from their bypassed positions around Harpers Ferry. Lee determined to remove that irritant by capturing the Federals and the bonanza of supplies, armaments, and equipment they held. Jackson's confident veterans received the mission and set out on another of the long marches designed to expend their sweat but not their blood. The operation worked reasonably well, if not as rapidly as Lee had hoped. Jackson captured Harpers Ferry and its garrison with its rich stores on September 15.

Unfortunately for Lee, a copy of his detailed operational order (Special Orders No. 191) fell into enemy hands. General McClellan, who had assumed command of his old army augmented by the troops of the disgraced Pope, knew how thoroughly Lee had dispersed the elements of his army. The eternally cautious Union general frittered away much of the dazzling advantage presented to him, however. Even so, he was able to penetrate westward through the gaps of Maryland's South Mountain, pushing aside the Confederate rear guard and forcing Lee back toward the Potomac.

Late on September 15 Lee took up a position near the village of Sharpsburg, behind Antietam Creek, with the

> **Lee eagerly pressed his advantage by ordering his divisions across the Potomac and into Maryland.**

Potomac River at his back. Resisting McClellan there, with an army shrunken by straggling and other causes to the smallest size it would ever number until the end of the war, offered Lee no prospect for a great success and posed the real danger of disaster. Lee nevertheless stayed to fight.

The Army of Northern Virginia staged one of its most impressive performances on the banks of Antietam Creek on September 17, 1862, when it contrived to win a costly draw. Federal dispersion and irresolution served Lee's army well, but even so the Confederates repeatedly stood at the brink of catastrophe. Lee had infected his army with his own sturdy spirit, and the men redeemed their general's poor strategic decision with their personal valor. The army returned to Virginia on the night of September 18, having stood through the day after the battle on its hard-won line.

A Renewed Army. In the aftermath of the Maryland campaign, Lee found time to rebuild carefully the army he had inherited at a moment of crisis. The army enjoyed a halcyon period in the beautiful and bountiful Shenandoah Valley that fall while its commander planned and organized. More than a dozen general officers had fought with the army in Maryland for the last time. In addition to replacing those men with the best available talent, Lee finally was able to formalize his wing system when the Confederate Congress authorized corps units and created the rank of lieutenant general. Jackson and Longstreet received promotions to the new rank that were confirmed on October 11. The new lieutenant generals took command of the Second Corps and the First Corps, which contained all of the army's infantry.

Lee also streamlined the army's support functions that fall as part of perfecting its organization. The acute straggling and near-starvation that had bedeviled the 1862 Maryland campaign never again plagued Lee until the Confederacy verged on collapse late in the war. When the army moved through the same territory during the succeeding summer, en route to Gettysburg, the severe problems that had marked its 1862 operations did not recur.

In mid-November 1862, the Federal Army of the Potomac, now commanded by Gen. Ambrose E. Burnside, moved southeastward toward Fredericksburg, in the process drawing the Army of Northern Virginia away from the Shenandoah Valley and Piedmont Virginia. For three weeks beginning November 20, the Confederates concentrated near Fredericksburg as Burnside's army gathered across the Rappahannock from the city. On the morning of December 11 the Federals opened the Battle of Fredericksburg by bombarding the city and building pontoon bridges across the river against stiff resistance.

Two days later the Northerners marched steadily westward from town against imposing positions held by the Army of Northern Virginia. The result was the easiest major victory won by Lee's army during the war. Confederate riflemen slaughtered enemy infantry, and Confederate artillery found ample targets from elevated positions rising above a shelterless plain. Federal casualties mounted all out of proportion to Southern losses, but Lee was unable to reap any substantial additional fruits of his victory.

The Army of Northern Virginia went into winter camps secure in the knowledge that it had achieved enormous success during its first six months of existence. Within sixty days the army had, almost unaided, relocated the war from its own capital to the environs of the enemy's capital. It had won a startling succession of victories for a nation that had known few. The brilliantly creative collaboration of Lee and Jackson at the army's head, augmented by Longstreet's stalwart defensive aptitude, boded well for the future of the army and of the country it recently had saved. For nearly five months the army sprawled across central Virginia from northwest at Germanna Ford to southeast around Carmel Church, with the Rappahannock and Rapidan as a front-line moat. Stuart's cavalrymen rode daring and exciting raids behind enemy lines, building élan and providing grist for campfire talk if not actually accomplishing much substantive good.

During the winter Lee approved an important reorganization of the army's artillery. Conventional dogma had assigned most batteries to infantry brigades, often turning the artillary, Lee's "long arm," into little more than larger-caliber infantry weapons. Henceforth batteries would be grouped into battalions of sixteen or more guns and directed by artillery officers with enough rank to determine the appropriate employment of their powerful weapons. As campaigning weather approached in the spring of 1863, the Army of Northern Virginia stood at the height of its power and potential.

Chancellorsville. Gen. Joseph Hooker commanded the army's familiar foe as it advanced across the Rappahannock and Rapidan west of Fredericksburg in late April 1863.

Hooker skillfully stole a march on Lee and concentrated behind the Confederates on April 30 at a country crossroads called Chancellorsville. Lee and Jackson hurried to meet this serious threat (Longstreet was away on a feckless mission in southern Virginia). On May 1 the two leaders blunted Hooker's drive near the edge of a seventy-square-mile body of densely thicketed woodland known as the Wilderness of Spotsylvania. Scrubby undergrowth in the region made maneuver, movement, and fighting difficult except in the clearings and along the roads. That negated much of Hooker's enormous advantage in numbers. Facing a disadvantage of more than two-to-one, Lee fought against the heaviest odds he encountered until the wars' closing weeks. On May 2 Lee and Jackson collaborated on their boldest and most successful—and last—tactical initiative. Lee calmly faced Hooker's legions with a handful of troops while Jackson carefully and secretly led nearly 30,000 men across the front of the Northern army. When Stonewall's troops thundered out

> **Lee considered the victory at Chancellorsville a springboard for his army to use in taking the war back into enemy country.**

of the Wilderness behind Hooker's right, screaming the Rebel yell and driving everything before them, the Army of Northern Virginia stood at its highest tide.

Jackson's mighty flank attack did much to win the battle, but its aftermath cost the Confederacy one of its few absolutely irreplaceable military commodities. Mistaken fire from the muskets of North Carolinians in Gen. James H. Lane's brigade struck Jackson down, mortally wounding him in the darkness of that confused night. When he died eight days later at Guiney Station, Jackson took with him much of the army's and the Confederacy's best hope for success. Back at Chancellorsville the Army of Northern Virginia had put the seal on Jackson's masterful movement by fighting its way stubbornly through the Wilderness on May 3 to sweep the field.

Lee considered the victory at Chancellorsville a springboard for his army to use in taking the war back into enemy country. Before he could use the army in an advance, however, the general faced the necessity of reorganizing it extensively in the absence of Stonewall Jackson. Lee had already considered splitting his infantry into three corps as a means of controlling it more effectively. In the weeks after Chancellorsville he followed that premise when he established a new corps and gave command of it to Gen. A. P. Hill. For Jackson's old Second Corps, somewhat truncated by the creation of the new corps, Lee selected Gen. Richard S.

Ewell. Neither officer would begin to fill the enormous gap left by Jackson's death, nor would either of them satisfy even the reduced expectations that their commanding general had for them.

Gettysburg and its Aftermath. The army shifted north-westward from the vicinity of Fredericksburg in early June 1863. Stuart's cavalry won a stern test at Brandy Station on the ninth, but for the first time their mounted foe had fought on approximately equal terms. That boded ill for a Confederate future that would be affected by declining horse-flesh and armaments. Ewell accomplished as much as Jackson could have done around Winchester on June 14 and 15, clearing the way for an advance into Pennsylvania and raising hopes that the Second Corps might continue its invincible record.

The meeting engagement that developed on July 1 through 3 at Gettysburg, however, revealed shortcomings in the high command as well as in the new organization. Stuart led his cavalry on another daring adventure en route to Pennsylvania, but this time it left Lee without the screening and reconnaissance support that he badly needed. Ewell equivocated when Lee gave him typically discretionary orders. Longstreet sulked, to the detriment of tactical arrangements on the field, when Lee disregarded his advice. The army commander himself was driven to a desperate and ill-advised attack when better opportunities had evaporated. Stout defense by the old adversary the Army of the Potomac, now led by the eminently competent Gen. George G. Meade, also must be credited in generous measure for the outcome.

The Army of Northern Virginia actually won a signal victory on July 1 north and west of Gettysburg and then swept into town on the heels of two routed Federal corps, gathering prisoners by the thousands. Bitter fighting on July 2 led to the brink of success, but never beyond. The dramatic and dreadful assault on July 3 directed by Gens. George E. Pickett and J. Johnston Pettigrew is one of the most famous episodes in all of American military history under the familiar—if unfair to Pettigrew—name of Pickett's Charge. The defeated army fell back through Pennsylvania and Maryland to the Potomac in a muddy, bloody, and painful retreat.

Once back in Virginia the Confederates regrouped and soon were ready for further action, but they simply could not replace the skilled officers and brave men buried in Pennsylvania. Lee realigned his cavalry command during this interval, leaving Stuart at its head but for the first time authorizing subordinate divisions under that general's control. Before fighting began anew against Meade's Federals, Longstreet had taken the First Corps to the western theater, where it remained in Georgia and Tennessee until the following spring.

The two remaining corps of the Army of Northern Virginia fought intermittently against Meade's army through the late summer and fall of 1863 in the Piedmont region of northern Virginia. Lee maneuvered the army northward in October and forced the enemy back with considerable success before a grotesque tactical fiasco under A. P. Hill's direction at Bristoe Station blunted the movement. The embarrassment at Bristoe was compounded on November 7 when a Federal storming party captured Lee's fortified bridgehead at Rappahannock Station.

At the end of November Meade crossed the Rapidan west of the Wilderness and attempted to find a means to close with the Army of Northern Virginia. For several days the armies jousted near Mine Run before Meade recognized that he faced checkmate. The Northern general fell back without launching a major assault because he recognized that it would fail, thus earning the gratitude of his troops but calumny from the Unionist press.

Grant's Offensives. The Army of Northern Virginia wintered in 1863–1864 in Orange County and prepared for the stern test that it knew spring would bring. Gen. Ulysses S. Grant, of western theater prominence, assumed command of all Federal armies in March 1864 and made his headquarters with Meade's Army of the Potomac opposite Lee. At the beginning of May, Grant and Meade put their troops across the Rapidan River into the same Wilderness that had foiled Hooker precisely one year earlier. As the Federal column attempted to slice through the thickets in the direction of Richmond, the Army of Northern Virginia surged into its flanks from the west on two parallel roads about two miles apart. The confusing woods fighting that resulted on May 5 and 6 inflicted enormous casualties on the Federal army but also pushed Lee's army to the verge of destruction. Longstreet's First Corps arrived on May 6 to fight with the army for the first time since Gettysburg, too late to prevent a major Federal success but just in time to avoid complete disaster. In the crisis Lee attempted to lead the famous shock troops of the Texas Brigade in a desperate assault. The men turned Lee back and hurled themselves into the breach, suffering terrible losses in the process.

Although his army had suffered appreciably more than had Hooker's in May 1863 and had hurt Lee appreciably less, Grant calmly pushed south from the Wilderness to continue with a war of bloody attrition. His route took him to Spotsylvania Court House—or nearly there, for the Army of Northern Virginia managed to block the Federals' path outside the village with moments to spare. For fourteen days the armies locked in incessant combat, often fighting over imposing lines of breastworks in a first precursor of the trench warfare of later conflicts.

Three more times Lee attempted to lead men personally as his army faced crisis after crisis. On May 10 a Federal frontal assault broke temporarily into the entrenched projection in the Confederate line known as the Mule Shoe Salient because of its shape. Two days later an enormous Northern assault crushed the nose of the salient and came close to breaking the Army of Northern Virginia in half. Lee crafted a new line near the base of the bulge as two brigades of his army sacrificed themselves in hand-to-hand fighting in a delaying action that lasted twenty hours. Their blood christened the curving line of earthworks where they fought as the Bloody Angle. Grant hammered brutally against other earthworks without success, one major attack on May 18 being repulsed by the Confederates so easily that most contemporary writers did not even mention it.

Meanwhile the Army of Northern Virginia suffered a tremendous loss on May 12 when its cavalry chief, J. E. B. Stuart, died in Richmond, victim of a wound suffered in resisting a passing raid on the capital. For the rest of the war, Wade Hampton and Fitzhugh Lee would try to fill Stuart's place.

When the Federal army side-slipped to the southeast again on May 21, leaving the vicinity of Spotsylvania Court House, the history of the Army of Northern Virginia entered a new phase. For nearly eleven months the army would remain locked in steady contact with its foe in a war featuring fortification and attrition rather than the meeting engagements and maneuver at which Lee had excelled since assuming command. The contending forces wrestled their way steadily across Virginia from May 21 to June 10, fighting regularly and sometimes fiercely. The Army of Northern Virginia missed a golden opportunity on the North Anna River May 23 through 27 because all three corps commanders were absent and Lee was ill. The troops next fought with their accustomed tenacity and skill at Totopotomoy Creek and Bethesda Church and then almost effortlessly butchered a mindless frontal assault ordered by Grant at Cold Harbor on June 3. The deterioration in command by this time was affecting the army almost as much as shortages of manpower and matériel. Longstreet had been hit hard in the Wilderness and would not return for five months; Ewell had collapsed and been removed from his corps command, replaced by Jubal Early; and A. P. Hill remained so regularly incapacitated by sickness as to require frequent relief.

With the army high command in disarray, Lee faced alone the tremendous burden of protecting Richmond. Operations in Virginia took a new and ominous turn when the Federal army succeeded in crossing the James River and attacking Petersburg before Lee had divined their intention. Fortunately for the Confederates, Grant had left the heart and brains of his army dead or bleeding in central Virginia when he destroyed its midlevel command in frontal assaults during May and early June. The Army of Northern Virginia managed to lunge across the James and into the Federals' path just outside Petersburg. Barred from Richmond and foiled at Petersburg, Grant settled into the siege operations that were the next logical extension of the intense but mobile trench war of May.

Lee's Army at Low Tide. The final chapters in the life of the Army of Northern Virginia were written in ten months of often colorless and always deadly trench warfare. Lee endeavored to inject maneuver back into the military equation by sending Jubal Early with the veteran Second Corps back into the Valley where it had won so many laurels in past years. Early used his fragment of the army to good effect in a campaign that swept the Valley from Lynchburg to Harpers Ferry and beyond, reaching in July to the suburbs of Washington, D.C. After a surprising series of successes, however, Early finally fell victim to Federals in overwhelming force during September and October.

Lee's other attempts at movement and fresh initiatives covered less ground and usually met with less dramatic results. Soon after Grant reached the doorsteps of Richmond and Petersburg two immutable strategic verities became apparent: the Confederates could not protect both cities against concentrated forces, so Grant repeatedly sought to concentrate on one or the other; and the railroad lifelines of the Army of Northern Virginia that approached from the south and southwest were vulnerable. In response to the first of those unavoidable issues, Lee deftly moved his dwindling resources back and forth between the two fronts on either side of the James River during the last half of 1864. Bitter battles at such places as Fort Harrison, Fort Gilmer, Darbytown Road, and Deep Bottom captured occasional small tracts of ground for the Federals; more than that, they killed and wounded irreplaceable Southern soldiers. Fighting over the railroads flared at Weldon Railroad, Globe Tavern, and Reams's Station.

None of these affairs accumulated casualties on the scale of the army's great meeting engagements from 1862 through the spring of 1864, but each further enervated the army. The most famous of the battles around Petersburg erupted on July 30 when some soldiers from Pennsylvania mining country blew up several tons of black powder in a tunnel under the Confederate lines. The Battle of the Crater resulted in no change in the military situation—just more casualties.

Lee commanded the Army of Northern Virginia in these closing scenes with the assistance of a new generation of young generals. Some five dozen of the general officers who played a role in the closing months were either new to their ranks or new to the army. Men like John B. Gordon and William Mahone proved to be capable replacements for the famous officers who had fallen, but others could not accomplish what was required of them for lack of ability or lack of experience. Using the dwindling resources in men and officers and supplies available to him, Lee directed the army's operations in early 1865 across a steadily expanding front. The deep reservoir of manpower in the Army of the Potomac allowed Grant to extend around Lee to the southwest and then press westward toward the last roads and railroads.

Fighting at Hatcher's Run in February killed Confederate Gen. John Pegram and brought the end closer.

The last offensive gasp of the Army of Northern Virginia came on March 25, 1865, against Fort Stedman near Petersburg. Gen. John B. Gordon led the forlorn hope whose initial success soon disappeared in the face of a horde of Northern reinforcements. A week later the army's tautly stretched lines finally snapped. Federals swarmed into Petersburg and Richmond, and Confederates hurried westward seeking refuge in the direction of Lynchburg, or junction with friendly troops coming up from North Carolina, or at least food near Farmville. All of those goals proved chimerical. Battered and fragmented at Five Forks and Sayler's Creek, and then hemmed in near Appomattox Courthouse on Palm Sunday, the Army of Northern Virginia ceased to exist when Robert E. Lee put on his best uniform and went to see Ulysses S. Grant in the village about terms of surrender.

Lee wrote a famous epitaph for the army in his General Orders No. 9, reviewing in moving terms the soldiers' "four years of arduous service marked by unsurpassed courage and fortitude," and expressing his "unceasing admiration of your constancy and devotion to your Country." William Swinton, a dedicated foe of the army and the early chronicler of the opposing Army of the Potomac, delivered an equally fitting tribute from across the lines:

Who that ever looked upon it can forget that body of tattered uniforms and bright muskets—that body of incomparable infantry which for four years carried the revolt on its bayonets . . . which, receiving terrible blows, did not fail to give the like; and which, vital in all its parts, died only with its annihilation?

[See also Appomattox Campaign; Beefsteak Raid; Bristoe Station, Virginia; Buckland Mills, Virginia; Cedar Mountain, Virginia; Chancellorsville Campaign; Cold Harbor, Virginia; Early's Washington Raid; Fredericksburg Campaign; Gettysburg Campaign; Kelly's Ford, Virginia; Lynchburg, Virginia; Manassas, First; Manassas, Second; Mine Run Campaign; Peninsular Campaign; Petersburg Campaign; Seven Days' Battles; Sharpsburg Campaign; Shenandoah Valley; Spotsylvania Campaign; Stuart's Raids; West Virginia Operations; Wilderness Campaign; and biographies of numerous figures mentioned herein.]

BIBLIOGRAPHY

Alexander, Edward Porter. Military Memoirs of a Confederate. New York, 1907. Reprint, Dayton, Ohio, 1977.

Allan, William. The Army of Northern Virginia in 1862. Boston, 1892. Reprint, Dayton, Ohio, 1984.

Dowdey, Clifford. Lee's Last Campaign. Boston, 1960. Reprint, Wilmington, N.C., 1988.

Evans, Clement A., ed. Confederate Military History. 12 vols. Atlanta, 1899. Extended ed. in 19 vols. Wilmington, N.C., 1987–1989.

Freeman, Douglas S. Lee's Lieutenants: A Study in Command. 3 vols. New York, 1942–1944. Reprint, New York, 1986.

Freeman, Douglas S. R. E. Lee. 4 vols. New York, 1934–1935.

McClelland, Henry B. The Life and Campaigns of Maj-Gen. J. E. B. Stuart. Richmond, Va., 1885.

Wise, Jennings Cropper. The Long Arm of Lee. 2 vols. Lynchburg, Va., 1915. Reprint, Richmond, Va., 1988.

ROBERT K. KRICK

ARMY OF TENNESSEE

This army was the major Confederate military force in the area between the Appalachian Mountains and the Mississippi River—a vast region known in the 1860s as the West. The Army of Tennessee was one of some two dozen independent field armies organized by the Confederates. It and the Army of Northern Virginia were the largest and longest-lived of those armies. In a very real sense, they were the Confederacy. They embodied its hope for national independence.

Although the Army of Tennessee was not formally so named until November 1862, its history dates from the first days of the Confederacy when its predecessor units came into being. Upon leaving the Union, each seceding state created its own army, and eventually these state-organized military forces were absorbed into Confederate service. The Army of Tennessee evolved from the forces of the western states of the Confederacy.

Organized by Governor Isham G. Harris in the spring and summer of 1861, the state army of Tennessee—although not the first predecessor unit—was the nucleus of what became the Confederate Army of Tennessee. Harris inadvertently created several problems that haunted the Army of Tennessee throughout the conflict. He overcommitted his force to protect the Mississippi River, for example, which left the northern border of Tennessee relatively vulnerable. Harris also appointed to positions of command several officers who displayed pettiness and questionable competence. Maj. Gen. Gideon Pillow, commander of the state army, was disgruntled at being commissioned only a brigadier general in the Confederate army, and he became a thorn in the side of the officers assigned to command him. He displayed incompetence and moral cowardice at Fort Donelson in early 1862 when he fled, leaving his men to be captured. He also exhibited physical cowardice at Murfreesboro almost a year later when he hid behind a tree rather than go into battle with his troops.

Formation under Albert Sidney Johnston

By late summer 1861 there were important concentrations of Confederate troops in northern Arkansas and southern Missouri, south central and southeastern Kentucky, western Tennessee, and at Columbus, Kentucky, New Orleans, Mobile, and Pensacola. Realizing the need for centralized control in the West, President Jefferson Davis sent Gen. Albert Sidney Johnston to command all Confederate forces between the Appalachian Mountains on the east and the Ozark Mountains on the west except the troops on the Gulf coast.

Johnston's assignment was the first of three attempts Davis made to establish a centralized military structure in the West. All three efforts failed because the president could never find a general willing or able to exercise such a command. In Johnston's case, the failure came when he established himself at Bowling Green, Kentucky, where he became

> **The western army usually got . . . those [units] raised after most of the state's trained personnel had gone.**

so bogged down in local matters that he largely neglected other parts of his far-flung command.

To be sure, Johnston's task was difficult. He had far too few men—about forty thousand—to hold the extended frontier line for which he was responsible. Many of his soldiers were untrained and poorly armed and equipped. Johnston was also hampered because his line was pierced by three great rivers—the Mississippi, the Tennessee, and the Cumberland—that provided avenues of invasion for Northern armies. To complicate matters, local political pressure to defend the Mississippi River was so great that nothing could be done about Harris's overcommitment of forces to western Tennessee. Worst of all, Maj. Gen. Leonidas Polk, commanding Southern forces on the Mississippi River, had violated the neutrality of Kentucky by occupying Columbus. Polk's action helped drive the Bluegrass State into the arms of the Federal government and enormously complicated the Confederates' military problems in the West.

In early 1862 Johnston's forces were scattered unevenly along a thin east-west line roughly matching the southern borders of Kentucky and Missouri. The line was vulnerable, and it was menaced by Federal armies at several points. The position lacked both naturally defensible terrain and good means for the east-west movement of troops. Despite its manifest drawbacks, Johnston's line had to be held. To abandon it and fall back to a better, more defensible position to the south would have given up much of the more valuable, most productive parts of Tennessee as well as all practical hope of having Kentucky and Missouri adhere to the Confederacy.

In January Johnston's line began to unravel. On the nineteenth at Mill Springs in southeastern Kentucky, a Federal force smashed the right of his line, and the Confederates fled

back into Tennessee. In the following month Union forces pushed the Confederates out of Missouri and then on March 7 and 8 at Elkhorn Tavern, Arkansas, defeated the Southerners' effort to regain their old position. Meanwhile, another Federal column began the conquest of Tennessee itself by thrusting up the Tennessee and Cumberland rivers to capture Forts Henry and Donelson near the points where those streams crossed the Tennessee-Kentucky border. Possession of the river forts opened those waterways to the Union navy, enabled the Federals to outflank the massive Confederate fortifications in western Tennessee, and put the Northerners in position to cut off Johnston's force at Bowling Green.

Realizing the magnitude of these defeats, Johnston evacuated Bowling Green, abandoned Nashville and most of western Tennessee, and retreated to Corinth, Mississippi. There he brought together fragments of his command and united them with reinforcements rushed from New Orleans, Mobile, Pensacola, and other points. The force that resulted from this Corinth concentration was known at its March birth as the Army of Mississippi (sometimes the Army of the Mississippi).

Gen. P. G. T. Beauregard was second in command of Johnston's new army, which was organized into four corps. The commanders of these units were men who played leading roles in the war in the West. Polk commanded the First Corps; Maj. Gen. Braxton Bragg, fresh from the Gulf coast, the Second; Maj. Gen. William J. Hardee, who had been with Johnston at Bowling Green, the Third; and Brig. Gen. John C. Breckinridge, a former vice president of the United States, the Reserve Corps. (Although called "corps," these units were, in fact, large "grand divisions.")

The army that Johnston assembled at Corinth was—and would remain—overwhelmingly a western army. Most of its troops hailed from Alabama, Georgia, Mississippi, and Tennessee. Almost all the others were from Texas, Louisiana, Arkansas, Kentucky, and Missouri. Unfortunately for this army, the great majority of Southerners with prewar military education and training came from the eastern states. Virginia, for example, had 104 living graduates of the U.S. Military Academy in 1860; the other ten Confederate states together had only 184. By one 1860 count, more than 70 percent of the U.S. Army officers who came from the soon-to-secede states were from the eastern Confederacy. To make matters worse, the few trained, experienced men available in the West usually joined the first units their states organized in 1861, and most of those units were rushed to Virginia early in the war. The western army usually got the later-organized regiments—those raised after most of the state's trained personnel had gone.

Owing in large part to this maldistribution of militarily knowledgeable Confederates, the Army of Tennessee never had the strength of command that the Army of Northern

Virginia enjoyed. The western officers were brave and intelligent enough, but they lacked—especially at the beginning of their service—the familiarity with military weapons and equipment and the knowledge of small-unit drill, tactics, and administration possessed by many of their counterparts in the East.

In early April 1862 Johnston moved his newly organized army out from Corinth to strike a Federal force that had advanced up the Tennessee River to Pittsburgh Landing just north of the Mississippi-Tennessee border. Johnston hoped to destroy that army and regain much of what he had lost in the preceding three months. He had about forty thousand men, and he was hopeful that the Confederate force that had fought at Elkhorn Tavern a month earlier and was now on the way east would join him before the battle.

On April 6 Johnston caught the Federals by surprise. His men overran their camps near Shiloh Church and drove them back to the Tennessee River. That afternoon, however, Johnston was killed. Beauregard, taking command, halted the attack, hoping to regroup and finish the victory on the seventh. That night thirty-five thousand Northern reinforcements arrived, and on the following day the combined Union forces drove Beauregard's men away. The Confederates pulled back to Corinth where they were joined by the men from the Trans-Mississippi. The Federals followed slowly, and at the end of May Beauregard was forced out of Corinth and back to Tupelo, some fifty miles to the south. The Confederate counteroffensive had failed.

The Army under Braxton Bragg

Soon after reaching Tupelo, Beauregard went on sick leave. Davis, who had been displeased by his behavior in Virginia in 1861 as well as by his conduct at Shiloh and his evacuation of Corinth, removed him from command and promoted Bragg to full general to replace him. Davis also reorganized the western command structure, separating eastern Tennessee and the area west of the Mississippi from Bragg's authority. Internally, too, the army was reorganized. Bragg created two wings of two divisions each. One wing was commanded by Polk; the other by Hardee.

Hoping to strike before the Federals in northern Mississippi could resume their advance, Bragg left about thirty thousand men and swung the rest of his army around to Chattanooga. (Most of the men remaining in Mississippi were the New Orleans garrison and the Trans-Mississippi troops who reached the army after Shiloh.) From Chattanooga, the Confederates moved into Kentucky to reestablish their claim to that state. Confident that thousands of Kentuckians would flock to their ranks, the Southerners advanced in two columns, one consisting of Bragg's army, the other the eastern Tennessee forces under Maj. Gen. E. Kirby Smith.

This second Confederate counteroffensive quickly ran into three major problems. For one thing, Davis—as was his habit—had not created clear lines of command. Assuming that officers of goodwill would cheerfully cooperate, Davis did not give Bragg authority over Smith until such time as their columns were united, when Bragg's higher grade would automatically put him in command of the combined force. Smith wanted to retain independent command, however, and refused to cooperate with Bragg. A second problem arose when the Southerners discovered that very few Kentuckians were sympathetic to the Confederacy or wished to join its army. Most pro-secession Kentuckians had long since left the state. The final problem developed because the two chief subordinates in the army—Polk and Hardee—personally disliked Bragg, resented his authority, often disobeyed his orders, and began what became a campaign to undermine his position and bring about his removal from command. For his part Bragg realized that several of his high-ranking generals—especially Polk—were major liabilities whose presence blocked the promotion of more able men. He urged that he be permitted to rid the army of its "deadwood."

After some early successes—which came mostly from the hard marching and fighting of his troops—Bragg found his campaign dissolving into confusion. Smith was off on his own in eastern Kentucky, and when Bragg left to attend the inauguration of the Confederate governor of Kentucky, Polk, who assumed command, disregarded Bragg's orders to attack the Federals and move on to Harrodsburg.

In the midst of this confusion, the Confederates blundered into the Federals at Perryville on October 8. The outnumbered Southerners won a tactical victory in the battle, but Bragg realized he could not remain in the state without more popular support than he had. He therefore fell back into middle Tennessee and took up a position at Murfreesboro. Bragg's counteroffensive had failed in its major objective, but it did transfer the Confederates' main western operations from Mississippi to Tennessee.

During the lull after Perryville the army acquired its new name—the Army of Tennessee—and was formally divided into two infantry corps. Polk and Hardee were promoted to the newly created grade of lieutenant general and assigned to command them. Smith, also named a lieutenant general, was transferred to the Trans-Mississippi. The army's cavalry, which had previously operated in small units, was consolidated under Brig. Gen. Joseph Wheeler.

Strains caused by the unsuccessful Perryville campaign brought into the open the rift in the army's high command. Bragg, bitter at the failure in Kentucky, sought scapegoats and blamed Polk for most of the army's troubles. Polk and Hardee—joined by Smith—renewed and intensified their campaign against Bragg. They sent criticisms of their commander to the president and to members of Congress. Hardee, who had great influence within the army, managed to turn many subordinate officers against Bragg and to undermine his support. Polk urged his old friend President

Davis to get rid of Bragg. The army soon divided into pro-Bragg and anti-Bragg factions. Much of Bragg's support came from the Pensacola-Mobile units he had brought north to the Corinth concentration. The Polk-Hardee bloc found its strongest adherents among the Tennessee-Kentucky officers. In one form or another this civil war within the army raged until Bragg left in December 1863, and vestiges of it lingered to the end of the war.

Two other post-Perryville developments affected the army. In November Davis again attempted to provide coordination for military efforts in the West, appointing Gen. Joseph E. Johnston to oversee Confederate activities in the area. Davis expected Johnston to provide guidance for both Bragg's army and the Southern forces in Mississippi. Specifically, Johnston was to transfer troops between the two areas to meet a threat to either. This second attempt at coordinated western command eventually failed because of intelligence, logistical, and transportation problems and because Johnston, lacking faith in the scheme, proved unwilling to assume responsibility for deciding when troops should be sent from one area to the other.

Bragg's army also received a visit from Davis himself. The president was pleased with the condition and morale of the troops when he visited their camps in December, but he was unable to curtail the bitter feuding among the generals. He ordered a division of nine thousand men transferred from the army to Mississippi, in effect taking over the command he had assigned to Johnston.

Not long after Davis departed, the Federals ventured out from their base at Nashville against Bragg at Murfreesboro. The two armies met along Stones River on December 31. Bragg attacked and, despite bungling by several of his subordinates, drove back the Federals. The Southerners, however, were too weak to complete the victory, and both armies settled down for the night. New Year's Day was quiet, but on January 2 Bragg launched a foolish attack that was repulsed with great loss of lives. On January 3 and 4, Bragg fell back to Tullahoma. Once again the Confederate troops had fought well and had won a tactical success. The army lacked the strength to complete the victory, however, and the generals were unable to provide the leadership their men deserved.

The army rested at Tullahoma for more than five months. Meanwhile, the Federals were threatening Vicksburg, Mississippi, and the Confederate government urged Johnston to coordinate an effort to save the town. When Johnston proved unwilling to do so, Davis ordered him to take personal command of the forces in Mississippi. Believing that this order ended his responsibility as overall commander in the West, Johnston ceased even to go through the motions of that office. Davis's second attempt at a western command structure had evaporated.

While the Army of Tennessee was at Tullahoma, the sniping between Bragg and the Polk-Hardee coterie intensified.

Murfreesboro joined Perryville as a subject of controversy. Bragg proved especially clumsy in the internecine squabbling, exposing himself first to one criticism and then to another. Davis, in fact, seems to have lost confidence in Bragg and desired to replace him with Johnston. The president, however, was unwilling to give a direct order on the subject, and his subtle maneuverings to that end were frustrated by Johnston's refusal to act on presidential hints. In May Johnston went to Mississippi, and the army faced its next crisis with its high command even more weakened than it had been earlier.

The Federal troops did not strike again at the Army of Tennessee until mid-June. When they did, Bragg's position quickly collapsed. Advancing in five columns, the Union forces deceived Bragg and outflanked his position. By the end of the month Bragg realized his predicament and retreated to the south side of the Tennessee River near Chattanooga.

While the army was being maneuvered out of middle Tennessee, it underwent another reorganization. Hardee, sent off to Mississippi, was replaced by Lt. Gen. D. H. Hill. Substitution of Hill for Hardee, however, did nothing to cool the anti-Bragg furor in the army's high echelons. The East Tennessee Department was reunited with Bragg's command, and the troops there under Maj. Gen. Simon Bolivar Buckner were designated a third corps in the Army of Tennessee.

In August and September the Federals crossed the Tennessee River below Chattanooga. By so doing, they threatened Bragg's supply line and forced him back into North Georgia. Meanwhile, an alarmed Confederate government rushed reinforcements to Bragg from Mississippi and Virginia. The troops from Mississippi arrived first, and their presence led Bragg to create another corps. Thus, in early September the army consisted of four corps, each of two divisions, under Polk, Hill, Buckner, and Maj. Gen. W. H. T. Walker.

After some confused maneuvering in North Georgia during which several of Bragg's subordinates refused to obey his orders, the Army of Tennessee met the Federals along Chickamauga Creek late on September 18. Heavy but indecisive fighting went on all the following day. That night reinforcements from Virginia under Lt. Gen. James Longstreet reached the field, and Bragg reorganized his army yet again. He now created two wings—the left under Longstreet; the right under Polk. Longstreet's wing contained some of the troops of Polk's old corps, Buckner's Corps, and the troops from Virginia. Polk's wing contained part of his old corps, Hill's Corps, and Walker's Corps.

On September 20 the Confederates were lucky enough to attack at a time and place where a misunderstanding had created a gap in the Northerners' line. The Southerners broke through and chased about half of the Federals from the field. The remaining Union forces held on until dark and then withdrew to Chattanooga. Bragg followed and occupied the heights east and southwest of the town. He hoped to cut the routes by which food reached Chattanooga and force his enemy to surrender or abandon the area.

Once the army settled down to besiege Chattanooga, the generals renewed their squabbling. Bragg sought to discover why his orders had not been obeyed on so many recent occasions. Polk, Longstreet, Hill, and Buckner all emerged as anti-Bragg critics, joined by several of their subordinates. Bragg sought to deal with the trouble by relieving Polk from command and sending him away to await orders. Far from quieting matters, however, his action only intensified the clamor of his critics who circulated a petition denouncing their commander.

President Davis himself traveled west to intervene in the dispute. At an incredible meeting, Davis and Bragg listened as, one by one, the senior generals of the army declared that Bragg should be removed from command. Davis decided to sustain Bragg, but he made several changes in the army's organization. Polk was sent to Mississippi to replace Hardee who returned to the army to command Polk's Corps. Hill was simply sent away to await orders. Buckner was given command of a division. Many of the units commanded by anti-Bragg generals were broken up and scattered through the army. Bragg also acted to get rid of Longstreet by sending him off to eastern Tennessee to operate against Knoxville. Unfortunately for Bragg, he also sent Longstreet's troops off with him. As a result of these changes, the army now consisted of Hardee's Corps and what had been Hill's Corps under the command of its senior officer, Maj. Gen. John C. Breckinridge.

This turmoil helped to destroy the unity of the army and demoralize the troops. All through October and November they sat on the hills around Chattanooga, watching the North pour reinforcements and supplies into the city. At the Battle of Missionary Ridge, November 23 through 25, the Federals attacked Bragg's army. When the Confederates' position collapsed, they fled south to Dalton, Georgia. Bragg asked to be relieved from command, and Davis granted his request.

The Command of Joseph E. Johnston

The Confederate government now faced the daunting task of rebuilding its main western army. The first problem—selecting a new commander—presented a dilemma. Davis had only one army commander of demonstrated ability—Robert E. Lee—and he commanded the main army in Virginia. The Army of Tennessee's new commander had to be selected from the Confederacy's other high-ranking generals, all of whom were political enemies of Davis, or of limited ability, or both. Finally Davis resurrected Joseph E. Johnston as the least undesirable choice and ordered him to Dalton. Lt. Gen. John Bell Hood came to take command of the second corps.

Over the next four months Johnston did a creditable job restoring the army's morale and preparing it for the next campaign. As was his wont, however, he also spent a great deal of time bickering with the government and explaining why he would not be able to accomplish very much. He and the government authorities were unable to reach any agreement about what strategy they should adopt, and when the 1864 campaign opened, the Confederates were working at cross purposes. The government wanted Johnston to launch an offensive; Johnston believed that he was too weak for aggressive action and that he should fall back into Georgia,

> **[The Army of Tennessee's] greatest handicap . . . was the absence of a strong, confident, stable hand at the helm.**

hoping the Federals would make a mistake that would give the Southerners a chance to strike.

When the Federals advanced in May 1864, the Southern government rushed reinforcements, building Johnston's strength up to about seventy-five thousand men. The largest single element of these reinforcements came from Mississippi and was commanded by Polk. Although technically a separate army operating with Johnston, Polk's command evolved into a third corps in the Army of Tennessee. Thus, in the Atlanta campaign, the army consisted of infantry corps under Hardee, Hood, and Polk and a cavalry corps under Wheeler. When Polk was killed on June 14, Alexander P. Stewart, a division commander, was promoted to lieutenant general to replace him.

All through May and June, Johnston sought a position in which he could block the Federal advance into Georgia. Unable to find one and constantly outmaneuvered by his adversary, he fell back toward Atlanta, abandoning valuable territory, exposing the heartland of the Confederacy, and demoralizing many soldiers and civilians. By mid-July Johnston had retreated to the outskirts of Atlanta and had lost some twenty-two thousand men.

The Final Offensive under Hood. Johnston's retreat created great alarm in both Georgia and Richmond, but when queried about his plans, Johnston gave only vague replies. Faced with these facts, Davis decided to replace Johnston with Hood who, on July 17, was promoted to the temporary grade of full general and named the Army of Tennessee's fifth commander. Lt. Gen. Stephen D. Lee was ordered from Mississippi to command what had been Hood's Corps.

Hood soon launched three attacks around Atlanta (Peachtree Creek, July 20; Atlanta, July 22; and Ezra Church, July 28). In all three the Confederates suffered tactical defeats, but they managed temporarily to check the Federals' progress. For a while, it seemed, Hood had thwarted the Federal advance and would hold the city.

In early August Hood tried to force the Northerners out of Georgia by cutting their railroad supply line from Chattanooga. He sent Wheeler with much of the army's cavalry north to wreck the railroad. Wheeler made a few half-hearted attempts to rip up the track. He soon abandoned efforts to wreck the railroad and rode off into northeastern Tennessee where, for several weeks, he was effectively out of the war.

With Wheeler gone, Hood was without his best means of gathering intelligence. In late August the Federals swung around southwest of Atlanta and cut the Confederates' rail line. Hood sent Hardee with two corps to drive them away. In a two-day battle at Jonesboro (August 31 and September 1) the Confederates failed to force back the Northerners. With his supply line cut, Hood had to surrender Atlanta. He evacuated the city and shifted to Palmetto. Both armies were exhausted, and both rested for several weeks.

Once again President Davis came west to visit the army. He removed Hardee from command of his corps and sent him to the south Atlantic coast. Maj. Gen. B. Franklin

> There, Hood threw the army into a headlong assault against a very strong position. In a battle that lasted long into the darkness, the army lost some five thousand men.

Cheatham, a division commander, took Hardee's place. Davis and Hood agreed that Hood should move the army into North Georgia and threaten the Union line of supply. Such a maneuver, they hoped, would force the Federals to leave Atlanta in order to preserve their connection with the North. The president also created a new command structure in the West, appointing Beauregard to oversee both Hood's army and the Confederates in Mississippi.

The new effort began auspiciously, with Hood slashing at the rail line as he moved north. The Federals followed and even pursued Hood into northern Alabama. Soon, however, they sent part of their army to defend Tennessee while the remainder abandoned its connection with the North and marched off across Georgia to the sea.

This development convinced Hood that he should move into Tennessee—a decision he reached without consulting either Davis or Beauregard. Indeed, Hood had come to resent Beauregard, and he ignored him as much as possible. Beauregard, for his part, decided not to do more than try to keep Hood's army supplied. Hood wandered west along the south bank of the Tennessee River to Tuscumbia.

There he was delayed for about three weeks by high water in the river and by his preparations for the Tennessee campaign.

In late November Hood marched north to the Duck River where he found the Federals near Columbia. On November 29 he sent most of his army around to the east, crossed the river, and marched for Spring Hill. If he reached the road there, he would be north of the Federals and in position either to dash on to Nashville or to try to destroy them as they attempted to escape northward.

In one last fiasco, the Army of Tennessee approached Spring Hill and then halted. All night the Southerners sat around their campfires while a few yards to the west the Federals raced past. There have been allegations that some of the Confederate generals were drunk, or using drugs, or spending time with ladies in the area. Certainly, Hood was exhausted from a long day in the saddle and went to bed, leaving no orders to block the road. This collapse of command has never been satisfactorily explained.

The next morning the Confederates followed the Federals north to Franklin. There, Hood threw the army into a headlong assault against a very strong position. In a battle that lasted long into the darkness, the army lost some five thousand men. During the night, the Northerners pulled back to Nashville.

On December 1 Hood followed the Federals northward. For two weeks he kept the army sitting near Nashville while the Unionists brought in reinforcements and built up a mighty force. When the Federals struck (December 15–16) Hood's army collapsed and fled south to Corinth, Mississippi—where it had been born almost three years before—and then on to Tupelo. There, on January 23, Hood turned the battered Army of Tennessee (now only eighteen thousand officers and men) over to Lt. Gen. Richard Taylor.

Taylor soon sent parts of the army to other areas. Some went to Mobile to help defend that city. Others left to join the meager force being assembled in North Carolina in an effort to block the Federals who had crossed Georgia and turned north toward Virginia. Still others remained in Mississippi. Many units were en route to one of these points when the end came in April and May 1865.

Throughout its existence, then, the Army of Tennessee struggled with numerous handicaps. It was defending an area where geography aided the enemy. It did not share equitably in the Confederacy's supply of trained officers. Often the army was neglected by its government, receiving short shrift with regard to supplies and weapons. It was hampered by internal feuds among its generals—by what historian Steven Woodworth has called "the ugly world of Army of Tennessee politics." Its greatest handicap, however, was the absence of a strong, confident, stable hand at the helm. Because of these weaknesses, the Army of Tennessee, in the end, could not hold the West.

[*See also* Atlanta, Georgia; Chattanooga, Tennessee; Corinth, Mississippi; Elkhorn Tavern, Arkansas; Franklin and Nashville Campaign; Henry and Donelson Campaign; Kentucky Campaign of Bragg; Mill Springs, Kentucky; Murfreesboro, Tennessee; Shiloh Campaign; *and biographies of numerous figures mentioned herein.*]

BIBLIOGRAPHY

Connelly, Thomas L. *Army of the Heartland: The Army of Tennessee, 1861–1862.* Baton Rouge, La., 1967.

Connelly, Thomas L. *Autumn of Glory: The Army of Tennessee, 1862–1865.* Baton Rouge, La., 1971.

Connelly, Thomas L., and Archer Jones. *The Politics of Command: Factions and Ideas in Confederate Strategy.* Baton Rouge, La., 1973.

Daniel, Larry J. *Cannoneers in Gray: The Field Artillery of the Army of Tennessee, 1861–1865.* Tuscaloosa, Ala., 1984.

Daniel, Larry J. *Soldiering in the Army of Tennessee: A Portrait of Life in a Confederate Army.* Chapel Hill, N.C., 1991.

Horn, Stanley F. *The Army of Tennessee: A Military History.* Indianapolis, 1941.

McMurry, Richard M. *Two Great Rebel Armies: An Essay in Confederate Military History.* Chapel Hill, N.C., 1989.

Woodworth, Steven E. *Jefferson Davis and His Generals: The Failure of Confederate Command in the West.* Lawrence, Kans., 1990.

RICHARD M. MCMURRY

ARTILLERY

[*This entry is composed of four articles:* An Overview,*which discusses the organization and role of artillery in the Confederate Army;* Confederate Artillery, *which discusses artillery produced within the Confederacy;* Captured U.S. Artillery, *which discusses U.S.-made artillery used in the Confederate Army;* and Imported English Artillery, *which discusses English-made artillery produced for or used by the Confederates. See also* Naval Guns.]

An Overview

The Confederate artillery was created around a number of militia companies formed in the years before the war by men who had a serious interest in military matters, inspired by Napoleon's campaigns and the exploits of the U.S. artillery in the Mexican War. Most of their officers and men were well educated and of considerable social standing. In 1861 these elite units attracted a better than usual type of volunteer and were able to organize and train additional companies. Organizations such as the Richmond Howitzers, the Rockbridge Artillery, and the Washington and Palmetto battalions were noted all through the war for their efficiency and morale.

Major weaknesses were the shortage of trained officers and the total lack of veteran noncommissioned officers to match the regular army artillerymen of the Federal armies. Though continued service gave the South excellent company and battalion officers and some competent corps artillery commanders, none of its army chiefs of artillery was really capable.

Another major weakness in 1861 was the almost total lack of modern field guns. Captures, imports, and domestic manufacture gradually provided enough weapons, but none of these sources was reliable, and the Confederate gunners were never as well armed as their opponents. For all their courage and increasing skill, Confederate artillerymen were continually overmatched—their successes at Second Manassas and Fredericksburg canceled by their losses in the "artillery hell" of Sharpsburg and their failure at Gettysburg.

Organization

Artillery of this period was classified as field, horse, pack, or heavy. Of these, field (sometimes called "light") artillery was the most common, being armed and equipped for service with infantry. In theory, during marches and maneuvers its cannoneers were mounted on their battery's caissons and limbers; in vulgar practice they walked—or when necessary, ran—beside their guns. Horse artillery (also called "flying artillery") served with the cavalry; its cannoneers all had individual mounts. Pack (or "jackass") artillery was used only briefly and unsuccessfully by the Confederates. Heavy artillery (also called "foot artillery") handled siege, seacoast, and fortress guns; they were usually armed and equipped as infantry.

The basic artillery unit was the company. (The modern term *battery*—which previously had meant only an indefinite number of guns emplaced together in the same position—came into general use during this war.) An ideal Confederate company consisted of a captain; four lieutenants (three serving as section chiefs, one in charge of the caissons); eight sergeants, including an orderly (first) sergeant and a quartermaster (supply) sergeant; twelve corporals; two artificers (blacksmith and saddler); two buglers; a guidon bearer; and approximately ninety drivers and cannoneers. (Confederate regulations set the number of privates at 64 to 125.) Horse artillery needed two extra privates per section to serve as horse holders while their company was in action.

This company would have four guns and two howitzers, each with its accompanying caisson, loaded with ammunition. Gun and caisson together formed a platoon, commanded by a sergeant "chief-of-piece" assisted by two corporals—one the gunner, the other in charge of the limbers and caisson. Two platoons made up a section. In addition, the company was to have a battery wagon for supplies, spare parts, and tools and a traveling forge, which was a mobile blacksmith's shop. (Artillery theory held that each 12-pounder or heavier gun should have two caissons, but this seems to have been followed only rarely in the Federal forces and very rarely, if ever, in the Confederate.) Officers, sergeants, buglers, and guidon bearers were to have individual mounts, and there would be seven to a dozen spare horses to replace casualties.

In fact, however, the existing Confederate artillery companies very seldom attained such a state of perfection and those that did could not long maintain it. The average company had four cannon (often of different types and caliber) and sometimes only two or three. It frequently was hampered by a shortage of horses and a lack of proper feed for those it had. Competent soldier-mechanics were scarce throughout the South. By late 1864, satisfactory recruits were increasingly hard to procure, most of the replacements furnished by the now-omnivorous Confederate conscription being too young, too old, or men who had been evading service for years and still had no appetite for soldiering.

During the 1862 campaigns most Confederate artillery companies were attached to infantry brigades; any remaining (and those companies still completing their organization) were lumped into temporary battalions as part of a haphazardly managed artillery reserve. This made it practically impossible to mass artillery at a critical point, with the result (as at Malvern Hill) that individual Confederate batteries were hurried into action against larger numbers of Federal guns and so were smashed piecemeal.

Consequently, during late 1862 and early 1863, the Army of Northern Virginia reorganized its artillery into battalions of four to six companies. Normally one of these was attached to each infantry division, and two additional ones to each corps, under the direct control of a corps chief of artillery. This flexible system never achieved its full possibilities because of the deficiencies of Confederate weapons, ammunition, and training. Nevertheless, for a time, Confederate artillery organization above company level was considerably superior to that of the Federals. Its effectiveness forced the Army of the Potomac to institute similar improvements in its artillery organization during 1863.

Other Confederate armies also initially attached artillery companies to infantry brigades. At Chickamauga in September 1863 the Army of Tennessee still had part of its artillery assigned in this fashion, but several divisions had grouped their artillery under division control, and there was a five-company army reserve. By the following November, however, it had adopted the Army of Northern Virginia's system.

In addition to the artillery serving with its field armies, the Confederacy had a large number of independent artillery companies assigned to seacoast and river defenses.

Clothing and Equipment

The uniforms of the Confederate artillery were practically identical with those of the infantry, with the exception that collars, cuffs, braid, and caps might be scarlet, that being the artillery's distinctive color. Exact patterns varied from company to company; generally they became plainer as the war went on. Some "dandy" organizations, such as the Washington Artillery, began the war in smart blue-and-scarlet uniforms, with short white gaiters. As in the infantry, there was considerable use of captured Union light blue trousers and overcoats. Final clothing issues included dark blue trousers and brown coats with black collars as the Confederate quartermasters used whatever materials they could get. Most companies must have made a variegated appearance by 1865, especially as many of the last replacements were not issued uniforms on enlistment and so arrived wearing citizens' clothes.

An artilleryman's individual equipment also resembled the infantryman's. By 1863 it seems usually to have consisted of a horseshoe blanket roll, haversack, and canteen, though—being able to pack some of their belongings on their limbers and caissons—the cannoneers seem to have been more inclined to keep their overcoats.

Weapons

Initially, enlisted men of the field and horse artillery were armed with sabers and revolvers when such weapons were available. The first quickly proved a nuisance and were either "lost" or turned in. Proving both a source of accidental shootings and too handy in personal quarrels, the pistols soon were collected, only officers being permitted to retain them. Consequently, when a battery was overrun by enemy troops, the cannoneers were defenseless except for their rammer staffs and handspikes. During the last months of the siege of Petersburg, field artillery units serving entrenched batteries were issued muskets so that those men not actually manning the guns might help the overextended infantry. Heavy artillery, as previously noted, was normally armed as infantry, often with older models of muskets.

The artillery's real weapon was its cannon, and here the Confederates remained at a disadvantage throughout the war. At first many companies had the old bronze (usually termed "brass") 6- and 12-pounder guns and 12-pounder howitzers. Even some of the light 12-pounder mountain howitzers were used for lack of better ones. The Virginia Rockbridge company had to improvise its caissons from the running gear of farm wagons and homemade ammunition chests; undoubtedly a good many other companies had the same experience.

Howitzers were shorter and more lightly built than guns. They had shorter ranges, but higher trajectories that were useful in shelling an enemy partially sheltered behind buildings or rough terrain. Since they weighed less, a 24-pounder howitzer could be mounted on a 12-pounder gun's carriage. This mix of weapons gave the battery commander greater flexibility in dealing with different targets; also the howitzers were very effective firing canister. But the need for two different calibers of ammunition and different types of equipment was always a problem; both armies came to favor only one type and caliber of cannon in each company.

The cannon that became the Confederate field artillery's major weapons were the smoothbore 12-pounder bronze gun-howitzer (the Napoleon gun), the wrought-iron 3-inch Ordnance rifled gun, and the 10-pounder Parrott rifle, made of cast iron with a distinctive wrought-iron reinforcing tube around its breech. A few James, Brooke (a Southern invention resembling the Parrott), and Blakely (a short, light English import with a vicious recoil) rifles also were in service. Some four-gun Confederate companies had three different types of cannon, each requiring its own particular ammunition. Heavier guns included the 20-pounder and 30-pounder Parrotts, the latter being much disliked because of its tendency to blow up while in action. (The Confederates had two at Fredericksburg; both exploded, one showering fragments around Robert E. Lee and James Longstreet.)

All of these cannon were muzzle-loaders. The rifled guns had a longer range and were more accurate, but the Napoleon had a higher rate of fire and was much more effective for short-range fighting since its smooth bore gave its canister a wider spread than rifled guns produced—the effect being like that of a 4.6-inch shotgun, making it an excellent infantry-killer.

The Confederates also imported newly developed breech-loading guns such as the Armstrong and Whitworth. The latter had a hexagonal bore and was extremely accurate, with a range of almost six miles, but its projectiles were too light to do appreciable damage. Also it took longer to load from the breech than the Napoleon did from the muzzle. (Federal artillerymen tested it, but found it too heavy, long, and cumbersome for active campaigning.)

> ## The Virginia Rockbridge company had to improvise its caissons from the running gear of farm wagons. . . .

Artillery ammunition consisted of solid shot, explosive shell, shrapnel (usually called "case"), and canister. Solid shot was effective against buildings and masses of troops; explosive shell against field fortifications, buildings (it had an incendiary effect), and hostile batteries; shrapnel against troops at over 400 yards range. Canister was for close-range fighting at 350 yards or less; as the range shortened, artillery would use double canister (two cans of shot with a single propelling charge), producing a blast of some fifty-four 7-ounce balls. The effectiveness of explosive shell and shrapnel was limited by the low power of their black-powder bursting charge and the unreliability of their fuzes; a round might explode anywhere between the muzzle of the gun and the target, to the hurt and anger of any friendly infantry in front of the battery. The Confederates were especially unfortunate in this respect, their fuzes being so unreliable that a high percentage of their shells and shrapnel rounds would not explode and so were no more effective than solid shot. Also many of these projectiles were so poorly made that they tumbled in flight, landing anywhere but near the target. After damning the ammunition regularly issued to them, those artillery units of the Army of Northern Virginia that were sent west with Longstreet in late 1863 found the Army of Tennessee's munitions were even more unreliable. Finally, the Confederate-manufactured versions of the Ordnance rifle and the Napoleon were inferior to the Federal originals in accuracy and general serviceability.

Taken as a whole, these matériel deficiencies not only put Confederate cannoneers at a serious disadvantage in their duels with Federal artillery but greatly complicated the problem of supporting their own infantry. Because of the tendency of their shrapnel and shell to explode short of the target, it was unwise for them to attempt to fire over their infantry. On more than one occasion Southern soldiers suffering from such friendly fire reportedly threatened to call the war off while they went back and cleaned out the offending batteries!

During the trench warfare around Petersburg in 1864 and 1865, some batteries were rearmed with 12-pounder iron mortars, newly manufactured by the Confederate Ordnance Department. These were supplemented by 12- or 24-pounder howitzers mounted on inclined skids and fired with reduced charges to give their shells the higher trajectory needed to drop them into the Federal earthworks.

As for seacoast and fortress artillery, the Confederacy had secured large numbers of excellent heavy guns by its seizure of lightly guarded U.S. coastal fortifications and naval bases during the first days of hostilities. The Norfolk naval yard alone provided over one thousand cannon, including some three hundred of the new Dahlgren 9- and 11-inch guns. These were soon distributed throughout the Confederacy, where they were used largely as fortress artillery. They were supplemented by a small number of British-made Armstrong guns (both breech- and muzzleloaders) and Blakely rifles. Seacoast batteries might employ grapeshot, a heavier form of canister, for short-range action against warships and attacking infantry. (Despite frequent mention, grapeshot apparently never actually was used by field artillery simply because the greater number of balls in a canister round provided a more effective spread of shot.)

Confederate artillerymen also experimented with rocket batteries and various novel types of ordnance, including double-barreled cannon; revolving cannon, which were described as looking like a huge revolver on wheels; and steam-guns, which were to employ compressed steam as a propellant. None was successful.

Tactics

Artillery employment during the Civil War tended to be clumsy. To begin with, few generals on either side—even veterans of the Mexican War—had much experience with combined infantry-artillery tactics. Though artillery had contributed substantially to the American victories in Mexico, it had usually fought as individual companies, driving recklessly forward, often in advance of their own infantry, into canister range of the Mexicans. The latter, being armed with often-indifferent smoothbore muskets, could not reply effectively to their devastating fire. Also, these had been small-scale battles; the largest American army, including a half-dozen companies of artillery, had numbered less than fifteen thousand, little more than half the strength of a single Confederate corps at Gettysburg.

This dashing use of artillery became too costly once the majority of the infantry were armed with rifle-muskets, accurate at roughly twice canister's range. Field artillery therefore was increasingly relegated to a supporting mission, especially during attacks, firing from commanding positions behind its infantry. In this role its effectiveness was sharply limited, especially at long range, by the unreliability of its ammunition and limited explosive power of its shells. Though it could destroy buildings, it could not significantly damage earthworks or cause serious casualties among dug-in troops. Similarly, in a defensive situation shrapnel and explosive shell were usually too inaccurate to stop a determined charge. If the enemy were advancing through a wooded area, solid shot could inflict heavy casualties at long range, ricocheting through the timber and bringing down branches and whole trees on the troops. At short range, however, the artillery would shift to canister, taking the same deadly part that machine guns play in modern defensive fighting.

These weaknesses were intensified by the general topography of the United States during the mid-nineteenth century—a rugged country of few roads (and those often bad) and extensive forests. Few battlefields offered large areas of open ground—as at Antietam and Gettysburg—where guns could be emplaced and employed in mass. And even under such favorable conditions, inexperienced generals and artillery officers alike might fail to take full advantage of their opportunity. (An excellent example is the third day of Gettysburg, where the Confederate preparatory bombardment before Pickett's charge was poorly planned, failing both to enfilade the Federal "fishhook" position from the north and to properly concentrate its fire against the Confederate objective on Cemetery Ridge.) Elsewhere, the artillery usually faced short-range engagements in terrain where maneuvering was difficult and only companies or battalions could get into position. Later, the increasing use of field fortifications sharply reduced the effectiveness of artillery fire, making it mostly a defensive arm against enemy attacks and counterattacks.

Whenever possible artillery commanders looked for positions from which they could deliver enfilade fire against the flank of attacking enemy troops or enemy defensive positions, thus sweeping the length of their lines. If the ground were hard, ricochet fire could be used—solid shot or explosive shell fired so as to strike the ground at a shallow angle just short of the enemy and then go bouncing and rolling through their lines. Such rounds retained a killing velocity even when apparently barely moving; only a fool or a greenhorn got in their way.

Throughout the war in sudden emergencies—an enemy breakthrough of the front, an unexpected flank attack—artillery might still drive forward in the old style through their broken infantry into canister range of the advancing enemy for a stand-up fight in the open. This usually meant heavy losses in men and horses, if not the sacrifice of the units involved, but the application—even if casualties made it brief—of artillery's superior fire power often was successful in checking or even stopping the enemy. In the same spirit, batteries in position might continue firing until overrun by hostile infantry, their last point-blank blasts of double canister being the most destructive, to give their infantry time to rally.

> **Confederate officers like Lt. Col. John Pelham of J. E. B. Stuart's horse artillery soon became legends in both armies and mostly died young.**

Horse artillery had a particular reputation for dash and daring. Confederate officers like Lt. Col. John Pelham of J. E. B. Stuart's horse artillery soon became legends in both armies and mostly died young. Their guns were pushed recklessly forward into the cavalry skirmish lines; some companies had the reputation of joining in cavalry charges, employing the superior weight of their formation to shatter the Federal cavalry formations.

In spite of its handicaps, the Confederate artillery achieved an honorable reputation. Even through the war's disastrous last months in 1865, while desertion was gutting the Army of Northern Virginia's famous infantry regiments, few artillerymen "went over the hill." In part, this can be attributed to the good quality of the original artillery personnel. In greater part it probably was due to the fact that the artillery had very seldom suffered casualties comparable to those the infantry took in action after action; consequently it still had many of its first volunteers, both officers and men. At Appomattox, a much higher proportion of artillerymen than infantry remained with Lee's dwindling army, standing by their guns, ready for another battle they knew they could not win.

BIBLIOGRAPHY

Alexander, Edward P. *Fighting for the Confederacy.* Chapel Hill, N.C., 1989.

Coggins, Jack. *Arms and Equipment of the Civil War.* Garden City, N.Y., 1962.

Department of Military Art and Engineering, U.S. Military Academy.*Supplemental Material: Weapons of the Civil War and Organization and Tactics.* West Point, N.Y., 1959–1960.

Elting, John R., and Michael J. McAfee. *Long Endure: The Civil War Period.* Vol. 2 of *Military Uniforms in America.* Novato, Calif., 1982.

Freeman, Douglas S. *Lee's Lieutenants.* 3 vols. New York, 1942–1944. Reprint, New York, 1986.

Krick, Robert K. *Parker's Virginia Battery, C.S.A.* Berryville, Va., 1975.

Todd, Frederick P., ed. *American Military Equipage.* Vol. 3. Providence, R.I., 1977.

Wise, Jennings C. *The Long Arm of Lee.* Richmond, Va., 1915.

JOHN R. ELTING

Confederate Artillery

The seizure of Federal installations in the South provided the Confederacy with sufficient heavy artillery to arm coastal and inland fortifications. The need for field artillery for the armies was partially filled by cannons received under the Militia Act of 1808, initial seizures, and early battlefield captures, but there remained a considerable deficiency. What little industry existed in the South set about to fill this need.

The Tredegar Iron Works in Richmond, operated by Joseph R. Anderson, had been casting cannons since 1842. Anderson, a West Point graduate, was the driving force at Tredegar and greatly expanded the capacity of the foundry in the two decades before the war. On the eve of conflict Tredegar was fully operational with proven leadership.

Most of the production at Tredegar in the prewar years had been large cannons. Anderson had to realign production to meet the requirement for field artillery. From April through December 1861 Tredegar delivered at least 33 field guns including 5 brass 12-pound howitzers in December, the first such guns from the foundry, and 8 iron Parrott rifles of current pattern. At least 98 were heavy guns of 8-, 9-, and 10-inch bore. In all, 214 guns of all types were delivered during 1861.

The next year proved to be the most productive at Tredegar with delivery of 351 guns of various calibers. Only about 85 were heavy guns. Of these, 11 were 6.4-inch (32-pound) Brooke rifles and 14 were 7-inch Brooke rifles, all of an advanced design by John M. Brooke, head of the Naval Ordnance and Hydrography Department. The Brooke gun, like the Federal Parrott, was cast iron with a wrought-iron reinforcing band or bands around the breech of the gun. Tredegar furnished two 6.4-inch and two 7-inch Brooke rifles as well as the armor plate for CSS *Virginia.* The bulk of production was made up of brass 12-pounders and iron 3-inch Parrott rifles together with 6-pounders and 24-pound howitzers.

In 1863, production of 12-pound Napoleons became the priority, with at least 111 delivered out of a total production of 286 guns. Only some 22 were heavy 6.4-inch, 7-inch, and 10-inch Brooke pieces. Output again declined in 1864 to 213 guns, the primary problem being the lack of high-grade iron. Bursting guns had become a major problem. Production centered on Napoleons and 10-, 20-, and 30-pound Parrott rifles with 104 of the former and 36 of the latter being delivered. At least another eighteen 6.4-inch, 7-inch, and 8-inch Brooke rifles were also furnished.

Cannon production continued to be hampered by lack of raw materials. Loss of the Cloverdale furnace in Botetourt County, Virginia, to Federal units was a major blow, for Cloverdale was the primary source of high-grade iron in the South. Skilled labor at the foundry also decreased as more workmen were called into the army and replaced by slave labor. Only thirty-five guns were fabricated before production ceased about March 1, 1865. Twenty of these were Napoleons and five were heavy pieces.

During the course of the war Tredegar cast guns as small as the Williams breech-loading iron rifle and the 2.25-inch bronze mountain rifle, and as large as an 11-inch naval smoothbore, for a total of 1,099 guns of all types, over half the guns made in the Confederacy. Only one other foundry, that of R. P. Parrott, Cold Spring, New York, boasted higher production.

The Bellona Foundry, thirteen miles above Richmond on the James River, had also been involved in the manufacture of cannons since the 1840s. The operation was run by Dr. Junius L. Archer. Providentially, Bellona was casting guns for the Federal government under an 1857 contract when the war began. The state of Virginia confiscated the twenty-three completed guns of various calibers and reimbursed the Federal government.

Tredegar expansion plans included the leasing of Bellona in 1861, but this was soon given up in favor of enlarging the facility in Richmond. The two foundries cooperated, however. Large guns cast at Bellona were floated downriver to Tredegar for finishing, sighting, and testing. Bellona manufactured only 8-inch, 9-inch, and 10-inch guns, of which an estimated 135 were produced.

The central government tried to manufacture cannons also at arsenals in Augusta, Columbus, and Macon, Georgia; Charleston, South Carolina; and Selma, Alabama. The importance of this effort was magnified by the loss, owing to Federal occupation of parts of Louisiana and Tennessee, of small private manufactories that had furnished cannons early in the war.

The Federal arsenal at Augusta was seized by the South at the beginning of the war, and cannon production began there late in 1862. A circular issued by the Ordnance Department in November stipulated that production be restricted to 12-pound Napoleons and Parrott rifles. This arsenal turned out about 130 guns, probably all Napoleons.

Columbus became the site of an arsenal when the Confederates moved a facility at Baton Rouge to a safer location after the Federal occupation of New Orleans. Authorities acquired the Columbus Iron Works and set about making cannons, with deliveries beginning in March 1863. Production at this facility, destined for western armies, was limited to the 4.62-inch, 12-pound Napoleon, although a small number of brass 9-pounders were also cast, raising total production to about eighty pieces.

> **The estimated output of all the New Orleans makers was about two hundred guns at best, and none was of the latest pattern.**

The Macon arsenal began in April 1862 with the purchase of the Findlay Iron Works. Production here was restricted to Napoleons and Parrott rifles in accordance with the Ordnance Department circular of November 1862. Fifty-six Napoleons and eighteen Parrotts, 10- and 20-pounders, were cast at Macon.

Charleston arsenal produced a considerable amount of artillery and small arms ammunition. Production of guns was quite small, about twenty to thirty at best, and only Napoleons are known to have been made there.

The Selma foundry was a different matter. The facility began as a private enterprise and was taken over by army and navy authorities on a joint basis. Initial construction proved problematic, and the Navy Department took control on June 1, 1863. Casting of cannons finally began that summer. The name of the installation was changed to the Selma Naval Gun Foundry, but no guns had been accepted by the fall of 1863, all having been condemned. January 1864 found the facility nearly complete and 7-inch Brooke rifles being finished for armament of the ironclad CSS *Tennessee*. In early 1864 a number of 6.4-inch and 7-inch Brooke rifles were finished, but bursting guns proved troublesome. Production at the factory was continually hampered by poor materials and a lack of skilled labor. Of the 450 men employed, at least 300 were unskilled slaves. Nevertheless, the factory managed to produce some guns before the place was captured April 2, 1865. It would appear that at least 102

Brooke guns (6.4-inch, 7-inch, 10-inch, and 11-inch), twelve 30-pound Parrott rifles, nineteen mortars, and twenty experimental 6-pounders were made during the fifteen months of operation. At least a third of the Brooke guns were for the navy.

Private gun makers contributed to cannon production during the early months of the war. Most were small foundries with limited skills and facilities. Federal occupation terminated much of this production.

During 1861 and until the occupation of New Orleans by Federal troops on April 26, 1862, much ordnance activity took place in that city. The firms of Bennett and Lurges, Bujac and Bennett, John Clark & Company, Leeds and Company, and S. Wolff & Company produced some types of artillery. Bennett and Lurges, also known as the New Orleans Foundry and Ornamental Works, manufactured twelve or thirteen guns, five 8-inch Columbiads, and eight 6-pound guns before the city fell. Bujac and Bennett products were known for their poor quality, with the twenty Parrott rifles and six 32-pounders the firm turned out being prone to burst. Clark was very active the summer of 1861, manufacturing brass 6-pounders and 12-pound howitzers of excellent quality. The company had delivered over one hundred guns by March 1862.

Leeds was the largest foundry in New Orleans. The company delivered forty-nine guns, variously 6-pounders, 6-pound rifles, 12-pounders, and 12-pound Napoleons. Wolff set up his foundry at a personal cost of $100,000. The foundry never really got started and finished only six fieldpieces and one 10-inch mortar. The estimated output of all the New Orleans makers was about two hundred guns at best, and none was of the latest pattern. These early guns had been replaced by Napoleons and Parrott rifles by late 1863.

The firm of T. M. Brennan & Company of Nashville, Tennessee, was an active source of ordnance until that city was occupied by Federal troops February 25, 1862. Also known as the Claiborne Machine Works, the firm manufactured iron guns of excellent quality. A total of seventy-one 6- and 12-pounders were delivered to western armies.

Quinby & Robinson of Memphis, Tennessee, produced some of the best guns made in the western Confederacy. A total of seventy-seven were delivered before Federal troops occupied this city June 6, 1862. During the preceding weeks, the firm had sent much of its material down to Columbus, Mississippi, but production was never resumed. Quinby & Robinson products were primarily 6-pounders, 12-pound Napoleons, 12- and 24-pound howitzers, and some 24-pound iron guns. Also in Memphis was the foundry of Street, Hungerford & Company. Its guns were of poor quality, and many burst during use. Some 32- and 64-pound heavy guns were made along with ten small Hughes breechloading 1-pound guns. Three Parrott rifles of unknown caliber were also delivered. Production was limited to about twenty guns in all.

Noble Brothers & Company of Rome, Georgia, produced fifty-eight fieldpieces and six 8-inch siege howitzers before problems with ordnance inspectors and the Union sympathies of one of the principals impelled the government to confiscate the plant and move most of the machinery to Augusta. From April 1861 until October 1862 the company delivered a variety of iron ordnance including 3-inch rifles, 6-pound rifles, and 12-pound howitzers.

A. B. Reading & Brother of Vicksburg, Mississippi, delivered forty-five brass guns between December 1861 and April 1862. Most were 6-pounders and 3-inch bronze rifles. It appears that production terminated over a year before Federal troops took the town. The firm of J. R. Young & Company of Huntsville, Alabama, also produced some guns before that city fell to Northern troops on April 11, 1862. Total production may have reached ten pieces. Examples of guns made at the Briarfield Arsenal, Cameron & Company, the Congaree Foundry, A. T. Patterson Company, A. M. Paxton Company, and Skates & Company exist, but production was very limited.

Combined production of the smaller private foundries may have approached 300 guns of all types, and government arsenals fabricated about 475 pieces. Add to these figures the output of Tredegar and Bellona, and Confederate production of artillery totals about 2,100 pieces. By comparison, Federal production was over 6,000 guns, which were consistently superior in quality. Lack of materials and a shortage of skilled labor were the major hampering circumstances in the South.

Ammunition of various types and calibers was manufactured at most of the same establishments. Fabrication of projectiles for smoothbores followed those patterns already in service with production of solid shot, case shot, common shell, and canister. The Mallet polygonal cavity shell was developed in an effort to achieve better fragment dispersion.

Confederate conical projectiles show considerable innovation. Various systems were developed that had no Federal counterpart, such as the Archer, Burton, Mullane, New Orleans, and Selma patterns found in various calibers, although the first three proved ineffective and were discontinued during the war. There were also adaptations of the Federal Hotchkiss, James, Parrott, and Schenkl projectiles. Most used a variation of the expansion cup or forcing cone principle to allow the projectile to "take" the rifling of the gun. Confederate conical projectiles exhibit characteristics such as lathe finishing of bearing surfaces known as bourrelets and copper fuze plugs never seen in Federal service. In the case of larger projectiles a number of heavy armor-punching or crunching bolts were developed along the Brooke, Reed-Parrott, and Selma patterns for naval use against ironclads at point-blank range.

A lack of reliable fuzes was a problem that was never resolved. The Girardy percussion fuze was developed, but it came too late and never received wide distribution. The McEvoy fuze ignitor was used to ignite the fuze in conical projectiles independently rather than relying on ignition from flame from the propellant charge. Because of this deficiency, Confederate artillery did not function effectively.

[*See also* Selma, Alabama, *article on* Selma Naval Iron Works; Tredegar Iron Works.]

BIBLIOGRAPHY

Daniel, Larry J., and Riley W. Gunter. *Confederate Cannon Foundries.* Union City, Tenn., 1977.

Dew, Charles B. *Ironmaker to the Confederacy: Joseph R. Anderson and the Tredegar Iron Works.* New Haven, 1966.

Hazlett, James C., Edwin Olmstead, and M. Hume Parks. *Field Artillery Weapons of the Civil War.* Newark, Del., 1983.

Kerksis, Sydney C., and Thomas S. Dickey. *Field Artillery Projectiles of the Civil War, 1861–1865.* Atlanta, Ga., 1968.

Kerksis, Sydney C., and Thomas S. Dickey. *Heavy Artillery Projectiles of the Civil War, 1861–1865.* Kennesaw, Ga., 1972.

Mallet, J. W. "Work of the Ordnance Bureau." *Southern Historical Society Papers* 37 (1909):1–20. Reprint, Wilmington, N.C., 1991.

Ripley, Warren. *Artillery and Ammunition in the Civil War.* New York, 1985.

Wise, Jennings Cropper. *The Long Arm of Lee: The History of the Artillery of the Army of Northern Virginia.* 2 vols. Lynchburg, Va., 1915.

RUSS A. PRITCHARD

Captured U.S. Artillery

In the post–Civil War years, former president Jefferson Davis wrote that "the South had gone to war without counting the cost. Our chief difficulty was want of arms and munitions." That may not have been entirely the case, however.

Under the Militia Act of 1808, substantial numbers of all types of arms including artillery had been transferred to the states and were in the hands of their militias. Besides guns received in this manner, the Confederacy acquired artillery through the seizure of Federal installations in the South, early battlefield recoveries, imports from abroad, and manufacture within the Confederacy.

The guns available to the state militias and those stored at various military academies had been secured primarily through the 1808 act, although there were some private purchases such as Virginia's acquisition of thirteen modern Parrott 3-inch rifles from Northern foundries. The best of the guns transferred under the act were the model 1841 6-pound bronze smoothbore field gun and the model 1841 12-pound bronze howitzer, both veterans of the Mexican War but still in service.

Actually, the seizure of Federal installations in the South netted the Confederacy a wealth of artillery, primarily heavy seacoast models but also a few batteries of field artillery. The guns acquired were four basic types: field artillery consisting of iron and bronze 6- and 12-pound guns; siege and garrison models consisting of iron 12-, 18-, and 24-pound guns; seacoast artillery, big iron 32- and 42-pound guns; and iron navy 32- and 64-pound guns, all smoothbore. Seized installations from Virginia to Texas furnished critical munitions, but it was the capture of the Gosport Navy Yard that proved the most fortuitous.

On April 21, 1861, barely a week after the fall of Fort Sumter at Charleston, Virginia troops occupied the U.S. Navy Yard at Gosport near Portsmouth. There they secured for the South 1,202 gun barrels (tubes) of large caliber, which were either in storage or aboard ships anchored in the yard. The bulk of this lot, 959 tubes, were various models of iron 32-pound smoothbore guns, which became the backbone of Confederate heavy artillery throughout the war. Substantial numbers of 8- and 9-inch guns were also seized plus a variety of other armaments. Such was the impact of this windfall that the Confederate need for siege, garrison, and coastal artillery was temporarily satisfied, and initial efforts to manufacture artillery could focus on the fabrication of field guns.

Southern troops also seized 1,750 cannons to add to an estimated 400 guns of smaller caliber already in state hands, 296 of them in Virginia alone. The same seizures secured some 282,149 pounds of old but usable cannon powder at Gosport, another 50,000 pounds at other sites, sufficient ammunition for 60 field guns at Baton Rouge, and literally tons of projectiles. It appears that the Confederate artillery began the war with over 2,000 guns, most of them not of current pattern but certainly serviceable and of the same type with which Northern forces were then armed.

Early battlefield recoveries proved to be the best source of current-pattern artillery for Confederate forces. Sites of the Seven Days' Battles around Richmond were carefully gleaned. Later, after the Battle of First Manassas, officers reported capturing twenty-seven guns—one Parrott 30-pound rifle with 300 rounds of ammunition, nine Parrott 10-pound rifles with 900 rounds, nine James brass rifles with 900 rounds, three brass howitzers with 300 rounds, two brass boat howitzers with 200 rounds, and three brass 6-pound guns with 600 rounds. Of five Federal batteries that crossed Bull Run Creek, not one gun escaped.

At Harpers Ferry in September 1862, Confederate forces captured all the guns of the garrison—forty-nine fieldpieces and twenty-four mountain howitzers, a total of seventy-three guns with accoutrements and ammunition. And in June the next year at Winchester, the captured field artillery enabled the whole Second Corps of the Army of Northern Virginia to complete its equipment. Almost every gun in its batteries had been captured from the Federals.

The workhorse of the early war was the model 1841 bronze 6-pound field gun. These guns used a variety of ammunition of standard types—shot, shell, spherical case, and canister. In an effort to upgrade their performance, workers rifled many of them just before and during the war with a system of rifling developed by Gen. Charles Tillinghast James. These guns are sometimes called James rifles, which is a misnomer. Actually, the guns were rifled 6-pounders that used the conical James projectile, either bolt, shell, or canister.

Of all the captured field artillery pieces, two guns were especially favored. These were the model 1857 field gun, a bronze 12-pound smoothbore nicknamed the "Napoleon," and the model 1861 Ordnance rifle, an iron gun with 3-inch rifled bore sometimes called the Griffen or Rodman gun, the last also a misnomer. (It should be noted that many sources use the terms *brass* and *bronze* interchangeably when referring to field guns. This has become an accepted practice over the years, but the guns are actually bronze.)

The smoothbore Napoleon, probably the best-known gun of the Civil War, had a range of some 1,600 yards and fired shot, shell, spherical case, and canister. The tube weighed about 1,200 pounds, but mounted on a wooden carriage drawn by a six-horse team, it was very mobile. The ammunition chest contained thirty-two rounds—twelve shot, twelve case, four shell, and four canister—and weighed about 485 pounds. The gun was sturdy and easy to maintain. Loaded with canister, the Napoleon was deadly against massed troops at a quarter of a mile or closer. It was also a very safe gun for the crew. There are no known instances of this type of gun bursting in action.

The Ordnance rifle had a range of some 3,900 yards and weighed about 820 pounds. These rifled guns fired conical

> **. . . captured field artillery enabled the whole Second Corps of the Army of Northern Virginia to complete its equipment.**

projectiles—bolts (solid), shell, case, and canister—which were carried in a similar ammunition chest drawn by the same type of team as the Napoleon. The Parrott rifle, developed by Robert Parker Parrott, was another iron gun that saw extensive use in a variety of sizes. The most common in Confederate service were 10-, 20-, and 30-pounders, although larger guns were made. The 10-pounder had the same bore diameter, 3 inches, as the ordnance rifle and could accommodate the same type of ammunition, a great convenience in the field.

Another gun seen in some numbers was the model 1841 24-pound bronze field howitzer, which had a bore of 5.82

inches. Again, it used the same ammunition as the 6- and 12-pound guns. Canister of this size was highly effective against infantry or cavalry assaults on a fixed fortification. Other rather common fieldpieces included the model 1841 mountain howitzer and the 12-pound Dahlgren boat howitzer. Both guns had the same bore of 4.62 inches and used the same projectiles as the Napoleon.

In the category of heavy guns, the most common was the iron 32-pounder found in models 1821, 1829, 1841, 1845, and 1846. Weights of these guns varied from model to model, some short versions weighing about 3,500 pounds and long ones as much as 6,500 pounds. These were the guns so important to Confederate coastal and inland fortification defense. During the war many of these pieces were upgraded by rifling the smoothbore barrel and banding (reinforcing) the breech with a wrought-iron band. So modified, these guns became 6.4-inch rifles, for which a great many Confederate-made projectiles were developed.

A large number of mortars and of other guns of various calibers, large and small, saw service. The Confederates used everything that was available.

There was also a considerable diversity of ammunition for all these guns. Federal ammunition, unquestionably the most reliable, was much preferred because of its fuzing. Confederate-manufactured fuzes were notoriously unreliable. They would detonate prematurely, which endangered the gun crew, or not detonate at all, which was very demoralizing and hampered the effectiveness of Confederate artillery all during the war. This technological problem was never overcome. But necessity forced Confederate Ordnance to try to develop its own ammunition and fuzing because the captured superior ammunition was not always available. A dud rate of over 20 percent was not unusual.

Ammunition for smoothbore guns was relatively uniform by caliber, but that available for rifled guns was not. Patent projectiles and patent fuzes for the 3-inch Ordnance rifle and 10-pound Parrott were produced by Absterdam, Hotchkiss, Parrott, and Schenkl in at least bolt and shell configurations. All were very different, with the Hotchkiss round utilizing a lead driving band and the Schenkl round using a papier-mâché sabot. To further complicate matters, Confederate batteries more often than not comprised mixed-caliber guns, even batteries with only four guns. The study of such projectiles is a field all its own.

There is no question that Confederate artillery was a patchwork amalgamation of widely differing guns. But innovative adaptation and effective, sometimes brilliant, leadership played major roles in overcoming the obstacles. It has often been noted that at the end of the war the roads from Petersburg to Appomattox were blocked by guns with no teams to pull them. It cannot be said that the army surrendered for lack of ordnance.

BIBLIOGRAPHY

Alexander, E. P. "Confederate Artillery Service." *Southern Historical Society Papers* 11 (1883): 98–113. Reprint, Wilmington, N.C., 1990.

Davis, Graham. "Artillery at Southern Arsenals." *Southern Historical Society Papers* 12 (1884): 360. Reprint, Wilmington, N.C., 1990.

Kerksis, Sydney C., and Thomas S. Dickey. *Field Artillery Projectiles of the Civil War, 1861–1865.* Atlanta, Ga., 1968.

Kerksis, Sydney C., and Thomas S. Dickey. *Heavy Artillery Projectiles of the Civil War, 1861–1865.* Kennesaw, Ga., 1972.

Ripley, Warren. *Artillery and Ammunition in the Civil War.* New York, 1985.

Steuart, Richard D. "The Long Arm of the Confederacy." *Confederate Veteran* 35 (1927): 250–253. Reprint, Wilmington, N.C., 1985.

Thomas, Dean. *Cannons: An Introduction to Civil War Artillery.* Gettysburg, Pa., 1985.

Wise, Jennings Cropper. *The Long Arm of Lee; or The History of the Artillery of the Army of Northern Virginia.* 2 vols. Lynchburg, Va., 1915.

RUSS A. PRITCHARD

Imported English Artillery

As armed hostilities erupted, the Confederacy was faced with acute shortages of military supplies, particularly small arms and artillery. This critical problem was compounded by the South's inability to manufacture adequate stores.

To augment limited quantities of field and heavy artillery captured at former U.S. arsenals and fortifications, the Confederacy turned to the European market. Throughout the war, Great Britain was a prime supplier of artillery and munitions, although some French and Austrian field pieces were also imported through the blockade.

In England, Confederate purchasing agents were able to secure the most modern types of artillery available at the time. Although the quantity may have been inadequate, the quality was superb. Southern artillerists especially prized the guns manufactured by Armstrong, Blakely, and Whitworth.

Perhaps the most famous of the English manufactured artillery were the Whitworth guns. The concept created by Joseph Whitworth initially involved a rifled musket with a hexagonal bore that fired a hexagonal bore-shaped projectile. Although his rifled musket was not accepted by the British government, in the late 1850s he continued to refine and apply the proven concept to artillery. The best known of his hexagonal-bore cannons was the 12-pounder with 2.75-inch bore, which could be fired as a muzzleloader or breechloader.

Other hexagonal-bore Whitworths ranged in caliber from the tiny 3-pounder (1.65-inch) and 6-pounder (2.15-inch) to siege and heavy cannons such as the 32-pounder (3.75-inch), 80-pounder (5.0-inch), and 120-pounder (6.4-inch). Reports concerning the deployment of Whitworth guns around Charleston, Fort Fisher, and Gettysburg, for example, are found in the *Official Records of the War of the Rebellion* (1880–1901).

The Whitworth cannon may have been the most famous, but more commonly imported and employed in larger numbers were the guns manufactured by Capt. Alexander Theophilis Blakely, especially 12-pounder muzzle-loading rifles (3.5- and 3.6-inch). Various dome-shaped projectiles with soft lead sabot cups to expand into the rifling grooves have been excavated at sites in the western theater, the Deep South, and areas associated with the Army of Northern Virginia. Larger Blakely guns used during the war included the siege and heavy calibers of 4-inch, 6.4-inch, 7-inch, 7.25-inch, 8-inch, and a huge 12.75-inch gun that protected Charleston's inner harbor. Projectiles excavated in Virginia reflect Confederate usage of a 2.5-inch Blakely rifle, and shells recovered at Helena, Arkansas, were fired from a 3-inch Blakely rifle, although which side used this rifle is uncertain.

A few Armstrong 3-inch rifled guns were known to have been imported. Like some Whitworth cannons, Armstrongs were manufactured in both breech-loading and muzzle-loading versions. The breech-loading model appears to have used a conical projectile with a wide lead compression sabot covering much of the shell body. A cache of these was excavated in Virginia in the early 1960s. A second type of 3-inch projectile, also used in most larger-caliber guns, had a series of protruding pegs or shunts on the projectile body that matched and engaged the grooves of the rifled bore. Armstrong also produced 70-pounder (6.4-inch) and 150-pounder (8.5-inch) rifled cannons that saw service during the war.

The British-produced cannons were comparable to any made in the United States and probably were more technologically advanced. While their superior accuracy was a distinct asset to the Confederacy, ammunitions shortages due to the blockade of Southern ports and substandard Confederate-produced projectiles and fuzes often handicapped the potential of the imported Whitworth, Blakely, and Armstrong guns.

BIBLIOGRAPHY

Bartleson, John D. *Civil War Explosive Ordnance, 1861–1865.* Washington, D.C., 1972.

Dickey, Thomas S., and Peter C. George. *Field Artillery Projectiles of the American Civil War.* Atlanta, 1980.

Kerksis, Sydney C., and Thomas S. Dickey. *Field Artillery Projectiles of the Civil War, 1861–1865.* Atlanta, 1968.

Kerksis, Sydney C., and Thomas S. Dickey. *Heavy Artillery Projectiles of the Civil War, 1861–1865,* Atlanta, 1972.

Ripley, Warren. *Artillery and Ammunition of the Civil War.* New York, 1970.

C. A. HUEY

TURNER ASHBY.   LIBRARY OF CONGRESS

ASHBY, TURNER

ASHBY, TURNER (1828–1862), brigadier general. Born October 23, 1828, at Rose Bank, near Markham in upper Faquier County, Virginia, Ashby demonstrated his horsemanship talents at an early age by winning top prizes at jousting tournaments. While in his midtwenties, Ashby organized his friends into a cavalry company known as the Mountain Rangers to protect his neighborhood from ruffians accompanying the construction crews of the Manassas Gap Railroad. Following John Brown's raid at Harpers Ferry in mid-October 1859, Ashby's company mustered into the Virginia militia to perform guard and picket duty at Charles Town during the Brown trial and execution.

When civil war erupted sixteen months after Brown's execution, Ashby figured prominently in the plot to capture the Harpers Ferry arms factory and weapons' warehouses. Certain of Virginia's secession vote, Ashby and his brother Richard, along with former governor Henry A. Wise and other conspirators, persuaded Governor John Letcher to order Virginia militia to Harpers Ferry. When the Old Dominion seceded on April 17, Ashby immediately led forces in that direction. Unfortunately for the Virginians, as they awaited reinforcements on Bolivar Heights two miles west of Harpers Ferry, vigilant U.S. regulars torched the arsenal at 10:00 P.M. on April 18, destroying fifteen thousand small arms. Ashby led his cavalry into town too late to save the arsenal, but his men did help extinguish fires in the armory buildings.

While serving at Harpers Ferry during the spring of 1861, Ashby came under the command of Col. Thomas J. ("Stonewall") Jackson. Jackson assigned Ashby to guard Potomac River fords and bridges from Harpers Ferry fifteen miles downstream to Point of Rocks, Maryland. While in this capacity, Ashby's command assisted Maryland men across the river to join the Confederacy and interrupted Baltimore and Ohio Railroad traffic and the passage of boats on the Chesapeake and Ohio Canal. In addition, Ashby convinced Jackson and Jackson's successor at Harpers Ferry, Brig. Gen. Joseph E. Johnston, that he should be lieutenant colonel of the newly organized Seventh Virginia Cavalry. On July 23, 1861, Ashby received his official appointment as second in command of the Seventh Cavalry, but he soon exercised control over half the regiment, conducting independent operations away from the regiment's ailing commander, Col. Angus W. McDonald. When McDonald retired in February 1862, Ashby became the Seventh Cavalry's colonel on March 12.

During the summer and early fall of 1861, Ashby's mission was to protect the border counties of the lower Shenandoah Valley and to systematically destroy the Baltimore and Ohio Railroad between Harpers Ferry and Martinsburg. Meanwhile, the Confederate War Department had authorized Ashby to raise additional cavalry companies and to organize the first Confederate horse artillery (Chew's Battery). By March 1862, Ashby's Seventh Cavalry had ballooned into twenty-seven companies—nearly three times the size of a typical regiment. Such a large force proved impossible to organize and administer, and Ashby's ignorance of drill and discipline further reduced his cavalry's efficiency.

To correct this unpalatable situation, Jackson, in late April, stripped Ashby of his cavalry and ordered it to report to two infantry brigadiers. An indignant Ashby submitted his resignation and threatened to organize an independent command. Jackson quickly backed down, explaining in a letter to Gen. Robert E. Lee, "if I persisted in my attempt to increase the efficiency of the cavalry it would produce the contrary effect as Colonel Ashby's influence, [which] is very popular with his men, would be thrown against me." Jackson continued to object, however, to Ashby's promotion to brigadier general, once stating, "he has such bad discipline and attaches so little importance to drill, that I would regard it as a calamity to see him promoted." Despite Jackson's reservations, Ashby became a brigadier on May 23, 1862.

Although Ashby failed Jackson's discipline tests, the cavalry commander's incessant scouting and screening missions accounted for much of Stonewall's stealth and success during the cross-country movements of the Shenandoah Valley campaign. Yet on two occasions Ashby blundered. The first occurred at Kernstown, when Ashby misinformed Jackson, reporting that a retreating Union column consisted of only four companies of infantry. Jackson subsequently attacked on March 23, and when he encountered James Shields's entire division of nine thousand men, Stonewall was forced to retreat in his only defeat of the war. Ashby's second failure occurred following the defeat of Nathaniel P. Banks at Winchester on May 25. As the routed Federals fled north toward the Potomac, Ashby failed to cut off the Union retreat, primarily because his companies were scattered and many of his troopers were plundering captured wagons. As a disappointed Jackson noted in his official report, "had the cavalry played its part in this pursuit . . . but a small portion of Banks's army would have made its escape to the Potomac."

General Ashby's final role in the Valley campaign occurred as Jackson's army retreated south and east from Harrisonburg toward Port Republic. As the Confederates'

> . . . [Ashby's] reckless daring earned him the soubriquet "White Knight of the Valley," as well as much praise and respect.

rear guard, Ashby had frustrated and delayed Maj. Gen. John C. Frémont's advance in the main valley. On June 6, 1862, however, two miles south of Harrisonburg, the First New Jersey Cavalry, led by Sir Percy Wyndham, rashly attacked Ashby's position on Chestnut Ridge. Ashby annihilated Wyndham's cavalry, but the affair soon produced an infantry engagement. While Ashby was leading the Confederate infantry into action, a bullet from a Pennsylvania Bucktail pierced his heart, killing him instantly.

Though Ashby had lacked skills in military organization and ignored drill and discipline, his scouting abilities, equestrian skills, and reckless daring earned him the soubriquet "White Knight of the Valley," as well as much praise and respect. Stonewall Jackson's report of the Harrisonburg engagement provided an appropriate eulogy for him: "As a partisan officer I never knew his superior; his daring was proverbial; his powers of endurance almost incredible; his tone of character heroic, and his sagacity almost intuitive in divining the purposes and movements of the enemy."

Ashby, originally buried at the University of Virginia cemetery, was reinterred at the Stonewall Cemetery in Winchester in October 1866.

BIBLIOGRAPHY

Ashby, Thomas A. *Life of Turner Ashby.* New York, 1914. Reprint, New York, 1988.

Avirett, James B. *The Memoirs of Turner Ashby and His Compeers.* Baltimore, 1867.

Bushong, Millard K. *General Turner Ashby and Stonewall's Valley Campaign.* Verona, Va., 1980.

Dabney, R. L. *Life and Campaigns of Lt. Gen. Thomas J. Jackson.* New York, 1866. Reprint, Harrisonburg, Pa., 1988.

Neese, George M. *Three Years in the Confederate Horse Artillery.* New York, 1911. Reprint, Dayton, Ohio, 1988.

DENNIS E. FRYE

ATLANTA, GEORGIA

[*This entry is composed of two articles,* City of Atlanta, *which profiles the city during the Confederacy, and* Atlanta Campaign, *which discusses the military action there in 1864.* For further discussion of battles mentioned in these articles, see Andrews Raid; Kennesaw Mountain, Georgia; Tupelo, Mississippi; Wheeler's Raids.]

City of Atlanta

In 1860, Atlanta, Georgia, was the fastest growing city in the state; only Savannah and Augusta were larger. Four railroads converged in the city, making it the largest rail center south of Richmond-Petersburg. Peachtree, Marietta, Whitehall, and Decatur streets formed the commercial center. Its population included 7,800 whites, 1,900 slaves, and 23 free blacks. Slaves accounted for more than a third of the tax base.

Support industries for the railroads made the city a significant manufacturing center of the Southeast. Four large machine shops produced various kinds of steam engines, railway cars, and castings. The largest factory was the Scofield and Markham Rolling Mill, which specialized in the technologically demanding operations of rerolling iron rails and plates.

Two major newspapers served the city. The *Daily Intelligencer* and the *Gate City Guardian,* soon to be renamed the *Southern Confederacy,* staunchly supported John C. Breckinridge. Numerous other short-lived publications appeared throughout the war. Atlanta's religious life was overwhelmingly Protestant; of the city's thirteen congregations, only one was Roman Catholic. Most Atlantans were either Baptists or Methodists.

Primary and secondary educational opportunities were limited to family-hired tutors or private schools. The apprentice system served the majority of youths. The tiny Atlanta Medical College was the only institution of higher learning in the city.

In the presidential election of 1860, the city's moderate temperament was not stampeded. Compromise-minded John Bell carried the city with a plurality totaling 48 percent of the 2,230 votes cast, John C. Breckinridge came in second with 37 percent, and Stephen A. Douglas received only 15 percent.

Immediately following the news that Abraham Lincoln was the president-elect, Atlanta witnessed fevered recruiting activity by various militia groups, but on November 12, the mayor spoke to a large crowd at the courthouse, urging caution. Less than two weeks later the state legislature called for ten thousand troops to be raised and for a special state constitutional election to be held on January 2. Secessionists claimed that conditions had reached a point that precluded any compromise or debate. One of the most outspoken moderates, James M. Calhoun, a cousin of John C. Calhoun, was soon elected the city's wartime mayor, however.

The position of the moderates was destroyed when news of South Carolina's secession reached Atlanta in late December. A fifteen-gun salute at sunrise signaled the beginning of a day-long celebration. Similar activity marked Georgia's secession in mid-January.

The city council now actively promoted Atlanta as the perfect site for either the Confederate constitutional convention or the permanent capital of the Southern Confederacy. The "healthful" climate and Stone Mountain's granite failed to lure the Confederate Congress. Amid these unsuccessful attempts, the city welcomed newly elected President Jefferson Davis en route to Montgomery for his inauguration.

In mid-March, Alexander H. Stephens, the vice president of the Confederacy, visited the city, and Atlantans gave him a similar reception. At least fourteen volunteer units now drilled in the city. By August, Fulton County was the "banner county" of the state, having the largest number of volunteers in local units.

News of the firing on Fort Sumter sent Atlanta into another round of frenzied celebration. Citizens of a more realistic mind formed aid and relief associations to support the troops. One of the most prominent relief groups was the Saint Philip's Hospital and Aid Society, sponsored by the local Episcopal church. The city's twenty physicians agreed to treat families of volunteers free of charge. Several professional fund-raisers similarly supported the war effort. They usually contributed half of their gate receipts to the aid and relief associations. One of the most popular performers was the pianist slave "Blind Tom," who always played to packed houses.

Confederate contracts soon had the economy booming. Freight cars and railroad supplies were produced in record numbers. Bakeries turned out hardtack, the staple food of soldiers. Saddles, harnesses, and other cavalry necessities poured from many shops. Spirits of nitre, vinegar, alcohol, artillery fuses, uniforms, knapsacks, rifles, and revolvers were made by scores of firms.

The regional office of the Commissary Department relocated here early in the war, and the city served as headquarters of the state Commissary Department with a former mayor of Atlanta as its commander. The Confederate Quartermaster Department also had its headquarters in the city. Under military supervision, shoe and garment factories became the main source of supply for Braxton Bragg's army. The assistant medical director of the Western Department chose Atlanta for his office. By 1862, numerous hospitals operated in all sections of the city. Despite the heroic efforts of their staffs, however, these institutions were soon unable to care for the ever-increasing number of patients.

As the war continued, lawbreaking grew in direct proportion to the number of able-bodied men called to the front. Petty crime increased dramatically, though major felonies did

> ## Desperate women caused a food riot, and barter replaced the money economy.

not escalate nearly as rapidly. Both the municipal and state superior courts regularly had full dockets. Counterfeiting of paper currency constantly plagued the city. By 1862 the council felt the need to create a vigilance committee of twenty-five men to help the police force, constantly understaffed and ineffective, maintain law and order.

In 1862 Union strategy began to focus on Atlanta's railroads. With these lines destroyed, the city would be isolated and of no strategic use to the Confederates. Led by Capt. James J. Andrews, a small band of Federal soldiers disguised as civilians attempted to destroy the Western and Atlantic Railroad. When Andrews's raiders pirated the locomotive General at Big Shanty, Confederates pursued them on the engine Texas. "The Great Locomotive Chase" ended near Chattanooga where most of the Federals were captured and taken to Atlanta for trial as spies. Bragg's response was to declare martial law, but the order was ignored and the city continued about its business.

To provide additional protection for Atlanta, L. P. Grant commenced construction of fortifications around the city. The project was not fully implemented until the following summer when repeated defeat turned Confederate attention toward defensive operations.

Immediately, prices for even the most necessary and crudely made products soared. Flour rose to over twenty-two dollars a sack; shoes that normally sold for four dollars a pair cost over twelve dollars. By the summer of 1864, even these grossly inflated prices would be unimaginable bargains. Desperate women caused a food riot, and barter replaced the money economy. Grand juries repeatedly labeled inflation the city's most pressing economic problem.

Along with economic adversity, the city suffered through a series of epidemics. Smallpox, which made its first appearance at the end of 1862, reappeared throughout the war. A scarlet fever outbreak crippled the already weakened health of the populace, and all attempts at curtailing the disease

met with failure. In December, fire destroyed the largest military hospital in Atlanta.

Confederate losses in eastern Tennessee and northwestern Georgia drained the morale of the city, whose population had swelled to more than twenty-two thousand. The approach of William Tecumseh Sherman's forces along the Western and Atlantic tracks in the spring of 1864 added to the anxiety. All able-bodied men and boys were ordered to fight under the Army of Tennessee, commanded by Joseph E. Johnston, and defend Atlanta behind Grant's elaborate earthworks. Outnumbered two to one (100,000 Federals; 50,000 Confederates), Johnston prepared for the assault.

The Confederate government ordered most of the machinery and stores of the arsenal removed to more secure locations. The Quartermaster Department and many of the military hospitals were similarly evacuated. President Davis, under great public pressure for a victory, became increasingly impatient with Johnston and replaced him with aggressive John Bell Hood.

On July 20 Hood attacked Sherman at Peachtree Creek but was repulsed easily by the Northerners; Confederate casualties were high. Two days later, he again ordered his troops out of the trenches at the Battle of Atlanta, meeting with his second defeat in three days. Within a week he attacked at the Battle of Ezra Church. So great were Confederate casualties that Hood withdrew into the city and waited for Sherman's next move.

Sherman now laid siege to a city in collapse. Refugees, who earlier had sought haven in Atlanta, fought for space on every Macon-bound train. By the end of August fewer than three thousand Atlantans remained. Nearly every building in the city was damaged by bombardment. Looters roamed at will as exploding shells ripped open stores and homes. Mayor Calhoun met with the city council for the last time on July 18 and municipal government formally ceased to function.

At the end of August, Sherman moved his troops to Atlanta's southside, hoping to cut the last rail line from the city and lure Hood out. For the first time in forty days, Union siege guns did not fire, and Hood ordered an attack at Jonesboro. This was easily repulsed on the last day of August. Having lost four straight battles and 25 percent of his army in attacks, Hood evacuated Atlanta on September 1.

All Confederate ammunition and military stores that could not be evacuated were destroyed. Shortly after midnight, the city was rocked by a series of explosions as seven locomotives and eighty-one rail cars loaded with military supplies were blown up. At dawn Mayor Calhoun and a group of citizens surrendered the city, and by noon Federal troops occupied Atlanta. Within a few days, Sherman ordered civilians to evacuate, and about 1,700 left under a flag of truce.

Hoping to get Georgia completely out of the war, Sherman proposed negotiating with Governor Joseph E. Brown and Vice President Stephens. Both refused his overture and

Atlanta remained an occupied city until mid-November, when Sherman ordered the city's destruction. On November 15 most of the business district, but not the entire city, was burned. A heroic effort by Father Thomas O'Reilly saved some churches, residences, and City Hall from the torch. Sherman began his march across Georgia as the city smoldered.

Despite the widespread destruction, former residents quickly returned. One businessman wrote that the city was only a "dirty, dusty ruin." The city treasury held $1.64 in worthless Confederate currency. In less than a year, however, over 150 stores were open and Atlanta's trade was estimated to be 30 percent greater than before the war. The city's remarkable recovery as part of the New South would earn it national respect.

BIBLIOGRAPHY

Bowlby, Elizabeth C. "The Role of Atlanta during the War between the States." *Atlanta Historical Bulletin* 5 (July 1940): 177–195.

Bryan, T. Conn. *Confederate Georgia.* Athens, Ga., 1953.

Garrett, Franklin M. *Atlanta and Environs: A Chronicle of Its People and Events.* 3 vols. New York, 1954.

Harwell, Richard Barksdale. "Civilian Life in Atlanta in 1862." *Atlanta Historical Bulletin* 7 (October 1944): 212–219.

Key, William. *The Battle of Atlanta and the Georgia Campaign.* Atlanta, 1981.

Knight, Lucian Lamar. *History of Fulton County, Georgia.* Atlanta, 1930.

Kurtz, Wilbur G. *Historic Atlanta: A Brief History of Its Landmarks.* Atlanta, 1929.

Russell, James Michael. *Atlanta, 1847–1890: City Building in the Old South and the New.* Baton Rouge, La., 1988.

RALPH B. SINGER, JR.

Atlanta Campaign

The industrial and railroad heart of the cotton belt South, Atlanta was the focus of the crucial western campaign from May through September 1864 between Federal Maj. Gen. William Tecumseh Sherman and Confederate Gen. Joseph E. Johnston (until July 17) and Gen. John Bell Hood.

The campaign, which opened in the first week of May 1864, was the result of plans laid in February and March. When Ulysses S. Grant was elevated to the rank of lieutenant general and placed in command of all Union armies in February, he pieced together an uncomplicated grand strategy that called for the Army of the Potomac to concentrate on Robert E. Lee's Army of Northern Virginia, while Sherman, with three western armies, concentrated on the Army of Tennessee, then headquartered at Dalton, Georgia, under the command of General Johnston. The simultaneous application of pressure in both theaters would prevent the out-

numbered Confederates from shuttling reinforcements between East and West. Grant left the details of the western campaign to his lieutenant, telling him only that he should "move against Johnston's army, . . . break it up and get into the interior of the enemy's country as far as you can."

The largest of Sherman's three armies was the 60,000-man Army of the Cumberland commanded by Maj. Gen. George H. Thomas, the hero of both Chickamauga and Missionary Ridge. Next was the 25,000-man Army of the Tennessee (not to be confused with the Confederate Army of Tennessee) commanded by Maj. Gen. James B. McPherson. The smallest of the three was the 14,000-man Army of the Ohio under John A. Schofield. Altogether, Sherman's forces numbered nearly 100,000 men.

Opposing him at Dalton, Georgia, behind Rocky Face Ridge, was Johnston's Army of Tennessee consisting of 45,000 men organized into two corps—those of William J. Hardee and John Bell Hood. Leonidas Polk commanded a force of 14,000 men in Alabama and Mississippi, which could be called upon in a crisis.

In addition to his numerical inferiority, Johnston suffered from a lack of support in Richmond. Never popular with President Jefferson Davis, Johnston had made himself even more unpopular by declining to attempt an offensive into Tennessee over the winter of 1863–1864, claiming shortages in transport animals, bayonets, food, forage, and other necessities. Though many of Johnston's complaints were justified, his record was such that Davis and his military adviser, Braxton Bragg, were skeptical.

The campaign opened on May 5 when Federal skirmishers drove in Confederate pickets near Tunnel Hill and advanced against Rocky Face Ridge. The Confederate defenders at Mill Creek Gap west of Dalton had no trouble holding their positions, but six miles to the south at Dug Gap, the Twentieth Corps of Joseph ("Fighting Joe") Hooker threatened to push past two small Arkansas regiments. Johnston sent the crack division of Patrick Cleburne to the threatened point, and the Federals withdrew.

During the fighting near Dalton, McPherson's Army of the Tennessee embarked on a roundabout march to cut the Confederate army off from its line of transportation—the crucial Western and Atlantic Railroad. Johnston knew that there were Federal forces on the move behind the front, but he did not know in what numbers. This was mainly due to his inferiority in cavalry: his cavalry commander, Joseph Wheeler, was reluctant to expend his troopers in reconnaisance missions.

McPherson's troops passed through Snake Creek Gap eighteen miles south of Dalton on May 9 and advanced on the town of Resaca, defended by two Confederate brigades (about 1,400 men) under James Cantey. Though vastly superior in numbers, McPherson decided not to launch a direct assault and instead pulled back to await reinforcements.

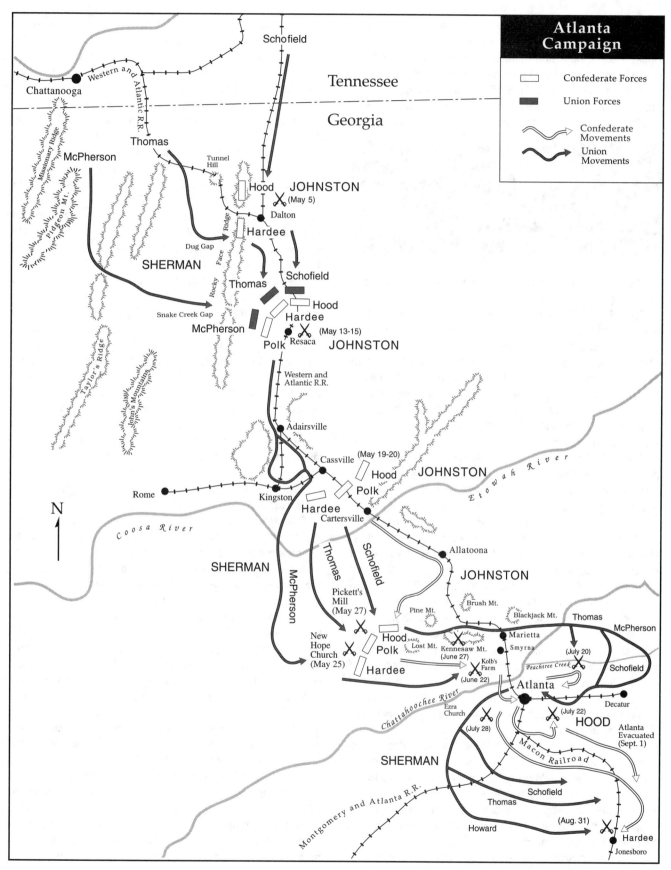

Atlanta Campaign

☐ Confederate Forces

■ Union Forces

Confederate Movements

Union Movements

Chattanooga

Western and Atlantic R.R.

Schofield

Tennessee

Georgia

Missionary Ridge

Pidgeon Mt.

McPherson

Thomas

Tunnel Hill

Hood

JOHNSTON (May 5)

Dalton

Dug Gap

Rocky Face Ridge

Hardee

SHERMAN

Snake Creek Gap

Thomas

Schofield

Hood

Hardee

McPherson

Polk

Resaca

(May 13-15)

JOHNSTON

Taylor's Ridge

John's Mountains

Western and Atlantic R.R.

Adairsville

Cassville

(May 19-20)

Hood

Polk

JOHNSTON

Rome

Kingston

Hardee

Cartersville

Etowah River

N

Coosa River

SHERMAN

McPherson

Thomas

Schofield

Allatoona

JOHNSTON

Pickett's Mill (May 27)

Pine Mt.

Brush Mt.

Blackjack Mt.

Thomas

McPherson

New Hope Church (May 25)

Hood

Polk

Lost Mt.

Kennesaw Mt. (June 27)

Marietta

Smyrna

(July 20)

Schofield

Hardee

Kolb's Farm (June 22)

Peachtree Creek

Atlanta

Decatur

(July 22)

HOOD

Ezra Church (July 28)

Atlanta Evacuated (Sept. 1)

SHERMAN

Chattahoochee River

Macon Railroad

Schofield

Montgomery and Atlanta R.R.

Thomas

Howard

(Aug. 31)

Hardee

Jonesboro

91

Johnston now faced threats from two directions. The main body of Federals continued to pound away at his lines on Rocky Face Ridge, and McPherson's army threatened his line of communications at Resaca. Uncertain which of these constituted the main Federal effort, Johnston waited until May 12 before taking the rest of the army south to join Cantey at Resaca. That day, he learned that Sherman was at

> **. . . Sherman was so frustrated by his inability to come to grips with Johnston, he decided to launch an all-out attack against the Confederate line.**

Snake Creek Gap, and he decided that Resaca was the site of the principal Federal effort.

The Battle of Resaca (May 13–15) was a meeting engagement: as the Confederates moved into position behind Camp Creek, the Federal army was forming in front of them. The battle commenced in midafternoon on May 13 and lasted until nightfall with neither side gaining an advantage. The fight continued the next day, and that evening the divisions of Alexander P. Stewart and Carter Stevenson attacked the Federal left. Their attack drove the enemy several miles and was halted only by nightfall.

The arrival of Leonidas Polk's Army of Mississippi gave Johnston a third corps and raised his effective strength to 60,000. He planned to renew the attack the next day (May 15), but reports that the Federals had gained a toehold on the southern bank of the Oostanaula River convinced him that he would have to evacuate Resaca in order to protect his line of communication. That night his army conducted the first of several evacuations. Confederate losses at Resaca were 500 killed, 3,200 wounded, and 1,400 missing. Federal casualties were more than 900 killed and 5,600 wounded.

Sherman's move around Johnston's left flank at Dalton and Resaca set a pattern for the campaign. With his superiority of numbers, Sherman kept Johnston's army pinned within its defensive line by a frontal assault and then sent a column around the flank attempting to cut the Western and Atlantic Railroad. Each time Johnston fended off the attack and blocked the probe, but each time he had to surrender territory to do so.

From Resaca, Johnston retreated first to Calhoun and then to Adairsville, ten miles to the south. There, he hoped, the narrow valley would allow his army to use the hills to the east and west to secure his flanks while he confronted the Federals. But investigation revealed that the valley was too broad and the hills too low to make such a plan feasible. Instead Johnston determined to ambush part of the Federal army. South of Adairsville, the road forked with one branch

heading due south to Kingston and another southeast to Cassville. By dividing his forces, Johnston anticipated that Sherman would do the same in pursuit. Johnston planned to unify his forces near Cassville and ambush whatever forces Sherman assigned to the Cassville road.

On May 19 all the Confederate forces were in position before first light, and Johnston issued a stirring call to battle to his troops. But at midmorning Hood, whose corps was assigned the principal role in the attack, reported that there were Federal forces on his flank and he was withdrawing. Johnston had no choice but to pull the army back to a ridge south of Cassville and invite the Federals to attack him. Even that strategy failed, for Hood and Polk argued that the position was vulnerable to Federal crossfire and urged Johnston to withdraw once again. On May 20 the Army of Tennessee conducted yet another evacuation, and the troops' morale fell.

The army halted at Allatoona three miles south of the Etowah River where it rested for three days. The peculiar geography of Allatoona made it a strong defensive site, and Sherman again looked to find a way around Johnston's position. Alerted by Wheeler's cavalry that Sherman had crossed the Etowah to the west, the Army of Tennessee moved westward in the predawn hours of May 24. The next day the armies clashed in the Battle of New Hope Church. The Federals launched five attacks, but each was beaten back. One Confederate soldier confided to his diary, "Such desperate fighting has never been witnessed in this army." The following day, May 27, the Federals tried to move around Johnston's right. At 4:30 in the afternoon Federal forces attacked Cleburne's division in the Battle of Pickett's Mill with similar results.

Calculating that since the Federals were moving to their left, their right might be vulnerable, Johnston asked Hardee to probe the Federal position, thus bringing on the Battle of Dallas (May 28). Hardee sent William Bate's division on a reconnaissance in force, but it was driven back as once again the attackers got the worst of it.

By June 4 it became evident that Sherman was returning to the line of the Western and Atlantic Railroad, and Johnston ordered the corresponding move eastward. The Army of Tennessee took up a position halfway between the Etowah River and Atlanta, anchored on a series of low hills. On one of those hills, Pine Mountain, Polk was killed by an artillery shell on June 14. His corps was given first to W. W. Loring and then to Alexander P. Stewart. When the Confederate left was turned once again, Johnston withdrew the army about two miles to Kennesaw Mountain.

The Army of Tennessee now occupied a very strong position. Big Kennesaw rises some seven hundred feet above the surrounding countryside and so dominated the area that a Federal infantryman speculated that Providence must have placed it there as a barrier to invasion. Little Kennesaw to the south was less imposing, and farther south the ground gave way so that the Confederate left was again the weak spot. Accordingly, Johnston sent Hood's corps to guard the left and extend the Confederate line. Hood, however, overstepped his orders and ordered an attack against the Federal right in the Battle of Kolb's Farm (June 22). Though Hood reported a victory, he suffered 1,000 casualties while inflicting only 350.

Despite the strength of the Confederate position, Sherman was so frustrated by his inability to come to grips with Johnston, he decided to launch an all-out attack against the Confederate line. He planned a feint against the lines on Kennesaw Mountain and then a massive assault against Confederate forces on the left where the divisions of B. Franklin Cheatham and Cleburne were posted. The Battle of Kennesaw Mountain (June 27) resulted in 3,000 Federal casualties and Confederate losses of only 552.

Despite this victory, Johnston began to argue that the Confederates' only chance was to destroy Federal supply lines. Both armies entrenched daily, making frontal assaults unthinkable—as Kennesaw Mountain proved. Johnston therefore asked President Davis to order Nathan Bedford Forrest's cavalry to operate against Sherman's supply lines. But Davis and Bragg had become even more disenchanted with Johnston. His continuous retrograde movements proved to them that he did not need reinforcements as much as he needed a fighting spirit.

Sherman turned Johnston's left once again a week after the Battle of Kennesaw Mountain, and Johnston retreated to Smyrna (July 3) and then to the Chattahoochee River (July 6). On July 9 Johnston retreated south of the Chattahoochee. He had, in effect, given up the last ditch, and Davis's patience was exhausted. On July 17 he relieved Johnston and appointed Hood, temporarily promoted to the rank of general, to command.

Throughout the spring, Hood had advocated offensive action in a series of letters to Davis, Bragg, and Secretary of War James A. Seddon. Now given his opportunity, he wasted little time. Johnston had told Hood that he planned to attack the Federal army as it crossed Peachtree Creek north of Atlanta. Adopting the idea, Hood sent the corps of Hardee and Stewart to execute it. The Battle of Peachtree Creek (July 20) was disappointing to the Confederates' hopes. Though they attacked aggressively, the battle was not well coordinated, and the Federals fought stubbornly. The Federals lost 1,800 to the Confederates' 5,000.

Two days later Hood sent Hardee's corps to attack McPherson's army east of the city in the Battle of Atlanta (July 22). This time the Confederates inflicted 4,000 casualties on the Federals, including McPherson himself, but they suffered nearly 7,500 casualties of their own, and the battle did not drive the enemy from the gates of the city.

Sherman spent a week trying to cut the city off from its rail connections to the south by means of cavalry raids conducted by Maj. Gen. George Stoneman and Brig. Gen. Judson Kilpatrick. Not satisfied with their indifferent success, he sent McPherson's former army, now commanded by Oliver O. Howard, to threaten the Montgomery and Atlanta Railroad southwest of Atlanta. Hood dispatched Stewart's corps to intercept, and the result was the Battle of Ezra Church (July 28) where once again the Confederates were beaten back with losses more serious than they could afford—nearly 5,000 men as compared to Federal losses of only about 560.

Having lost 17,500 men in three battles, Hood had little choice but to fall back into the city defenses. For a month, Sherman worked his way around the city attempting to cut off its rail communications with the rest of the South. The last battle for Atlanta was fought on August 31 at Jonesboro, fifteen miles to the south, where Hood assailed the Federal right hoping to prevent encirclement of the city. With the failure of that attack, Hood determined to abandon Atlanta, which he evacuated on September 1.

BIBLIOGRAPHY

Castel, Albert. *Decision in the West: The Atlanta Campaign of 1864.* Lawrence, Kans., 1992.

Connelly, Thomas L. *Autumn of Glory: The Army of Tennessee, 1862–1865.* Baton Rouge, La., 1967.

Hoehling, Adolph A. *Last Train from Atlanta.* New York, 1958.

Hood, John B. *Advance and Retreat: Personal Experiences in the United States and Confederate States Armies.* New Orleans, 1880. Reprint, Bloomington, Ind., 1959.

Johnston, Joseph E. *Narrative of Military Operations.* New York, 1874. Reprint, Bloomington, Ind., 1959.

McDonough, James Lee, and James Pickett Jones. *War So Terrible: Sherman and Atlanta.* New York, 1987.

McMurry, Richard M. "Confederate Morale in the Atlanta Campaign of 1864." *Georgia Historical Quarterly* 54 (1970): 226–243.

McMurry, Richard M. *John Bell Hood and the War for Southern Independence.* Lexington, Ky., 1982.

Sherman, William T. *Memoirs of William T. Sherman.* New York, 1875. Reprint, New York, 1984.

Symonds, Craig L. *Joseph E. Johnston: A Civil War Biography.* New York, 1992.

CRAIG L. SYMON

BAKER, ALPHEUS

BAKER, ALPHEUS (1825–1891), brigadier general. Baker was born May 23, 1825, in the Abbeville District, South Carolina. Educated in the law by his father, he was teaching school by the age of sixteen, in Abbeville, Lumpkin, Georgia, and Glenville, Alabama, where he settled. He also taught music and was admitted to the bar in Eufaula, Alabama, in 1849. In 1856, Baker, a Democrat, traveled to Kansas and returned home to arouse people to the importance of Kansas becoming a slave state.

In 1861, Baker was elected to the Alabama constitutional convention, representing Barbour County. He resigned his seat in the convention to enlist as a private in the Eufaula Rifles, subsequently a company in the First Alabama Infantry. Elected captain of the company, Baker led his men to Pensacola. In November 1861, he went to Tennessee and was elected colonel of the Fifty-fourth Alabama Regiment, which he led during the siege and Battle of New Madrid. He was captured at Island Number 10 on April 19, 1862, and imprisoned at Camp Chase and Johnson's Island.

> He resigned his seat in the convention to enlist as a private in the Eufaula Rifles. . . .

After exchange he became commander of the reorganized Fifty-fourth Alabama and led the regiment during the Vicksburg campaign. Seriously wounded in the Battle of Champion's Hill, Mississippi, May 16, 1863, Baker recovered and was promoted to brigadier general to date from March 5, 1864. Taking command of the Alabama brigade, Baker participated in the Atlanta campaign where he was again wounded at the Battle of Ezra Church on July 28, 1864. After brief service in the Department of the Gulf, his brigade was rushed to North Carolina to participate in the Carolinas campaign and the Battle of Bentonville March 19, 1865. He surrendered with his troops in North Carolina.

Baker, after the war, practiced law in Eufaula, Alabama. In 1878 he moved to Louisville, Kentucky, where he died October 2, 1891, and was buried.

BIBLIOGRAPHY

Faust, Patricia L., ed. *Historical Times Encyclopedia of the Civil War.* New York, 1986.

Owen, Thomas McAdory. *History of Alabama and Dictionary of Alabama Biography.* Vol. 2. Chicago, 1921.

Wakelyn, Jon L. *Biographical Dictionary of the Confederacy.* Edited by Frank E. Vandiver. Westport, Conn., 1977.

Warner, Ezra J. *Generals in Gray: Lives of the Confederate Commanders.* Baton Rouge, La., 1959.

JOHN R. WOODARD

BALDWIN, JOHN B.

BALDWIN, JOHN B. (1820–1873), congressman from Virginia. John Brown Baldwin's involvement with the Confederacy, although not unimportant, was overshadowed by his experiences during the secession crisis and, subsequently, during Reconstruction.

A prominent lawyer, Baldwin lived his entire life in Staunton, Virginia, the seat of Augusta County, one of the Whig citadels in a generally Democratic state. He served briefly in the legislature during the 1840s. He lost his seat, however, because he disagreed with the dominant public sentiment in the district, which favored legislative reapportionment on the basis of white population alone rather than on the traditional "mixed" basis that also gave weight to property, thereby favoring eastern Virginia. He campaigned in the 1860 presidential election for the Constitutional Union party, which won a narrow plurality in the state. Soon afterward he was elected to represent his home county in the Virginia convention of 1861.

There Baldwin and George W. Summers of Charleston led the nascent Union party, a coalition of conditional and unconditional Unionists, most of whom were former Whigs. He frequently participated in floor debate and also delivered a prodigious three-day Union oration. The most controversial and significant event in Baldwin's life occurred on April 4, 1861, when he met secretly with President Abraham Lincoln at the White House. Baldwin attempted without success to persuade Lincoln to preserve the peace and enable the upper South to remain in the Union. Never, he recalled, did he "make a speech on behalf of a client in jeopardy of his life, with such earnest solemnity and endeavor." That fateful interview impressed Baldwin as "a subject of more interest to me than anything that ever happened to me."

Baldwin's pro-Union stance was based on a belief that no irrepressible conflict divided North and South, and that few Northerners had any wish to interfere with slavery where it existed. He gave lip service to the idea that slavery as practiced in Virginia was "a right and a good thing," but he denied that the upper South and lower South had identical interests. Secession would, he warned, cut Virginia farmers off from their many Northern customers. Baldwin held out hope that the seceding states could be drawn back into the Union once it became apparent that the upper South would not join their bid for independence. For him, the Constitution contained more than adequate safeguards to protect the rights of slaveholders.

At no point during the critical six-week period between Lincoln's inauguration in early March and his proclamation for 75,000 troops in mid-April did a Southern Unionist in a position of authority have a comparably good opportunity to talk frankly with the new president. The Baldwin interview came about when Secretary of State William H. Seward urgently requested that Unionists in the Virginia convention send a spokesman to meet with Lincoln. Seward concealed

> **Baldwin's pro-Union stance was based on a belief that no irrepressible conflict divided North and South. . . .**

from Baldwin the full circumstances that prompted the summons—that Lincoln had decided to risk a resupply mission to Fort Sumter, in the harbor of Charleston, South Carolina, and that peace hung by a thread.

The most plausible version of the discussion between Lincoln and Baldwin suggests that the president greeted the Virginian with the question: "Why do you not adjourn that Convention?"

Baldwin replied that Unionists controlled the convention and could not reasonably adjourn it until some resolution of the national crisis took place. The Virginian followed with a plea that Lincoln remove Federal troops both from Fort Sumter and from Fort Pickens, offshore from Pensacola, Florida, the one other point in the seceded states that remained in Federal hands. Were he then to call a national convention and "settle this thing . . . by consultation and votes rather than by an appeal to arms," Lincoln might hold the upper South in the Union and give antisecessionists there "a stand-point from which we can bring back the seceded states."

Lincoln instead expressed reservations and hinted obliquely that he intended to try to feed the troops at Sumter.

"I told him that would not do," Baldwin recalled. Were fighting to occur, Virginia would be out of the Union "in forty-eight hours."

"Oh, sir," Lincoln responded, "that is impossible."

Baldwin retorted, "Mr. President, I did not come here to argue with you; I am here as a witness. I know the sentiments of the people of Virginia and you do not."

Lincoln thereupon told Baldwin, "I wish you had come sooner."

One of the inner circle of Virginia Unionists who debriefed Baldwin soon afterward vividly recalled his horror upon hearing that Lincoln wished Baldwin had come sooner. "I inferred from this remark of Mr. Lincoln, that he had taken a step, inconsistent with the view that you were urging upon him, that would result in war and bloodshed." Baldwin himself, who had gone to Washington "full of hope and confidence" about finding some basis for reaching "an understanding with Mr. Lincoln," returned to Richmond "much depressed and disappointed."

According to Baldwin, Lincoln never offered to evacuate Sumter in exchange for adjournment of the Virginia convention, nor did he make any "overture" or comment from which Baldwin "could infer it." Nevertheless, several days later Lincoln certainly did tell several visiting Virginians, among them the unconditional Unionist John Minor Botts, that Baldwin had summarily rejected an explicit offer to that effect. Botts concluded that Baldwin and his friends conspired to prevent Lincoln's offer from becoming known to the convention. The evidence suggests, however, either that Lincoln gave Botts a misleading version of his interview with Baldwin, or that Lincoln did not say to Baldwin what Baldwin thought he had said.

Virginia's secession and the start of the Civil War further depressed Baldwin. Deploring the "rabid" fever that seized many former Unionists, he voted against secession and predicted that "we are in danger of emerging from this revolution anything but a free people."

Baldwin nevertheless accepted appointment as inspector general of the state volunteers. Soon he was appointed colonel of the Fifty-second Virginia Infantry, raised at Staunton, which he commanded in the Allegheny campaigns in the fall of 1861. While still on duty in November 1861, Baldwin was elected over two opponents to the First Confederate Congress. He was reelected in May 1863, defeating the incumbent Virginia governor, John Letcher, an outcome that indicated popular discontent with the all-consuming war effort.

Baldwin's district encompassed parts of the fertile Shenandoah Valley. Not long after Congress convened in February 1862, the valley became the scene of intense fighting, as Thomas J. ("Stonewall") Jackson attempted to relieve growing Federal pressure on Richmond. For the duration of the war, or at least until Philip H. Sheridan's devastating campaign in the late summer and fall of 1864, Union and Confederate forces swept back and forth through the Shenandoah.

Baldwin, who served from the start of the First Congress in February 1862 until the final adjournment of the Second in March 1865, played an active role in the Confederate House. He held seats on the Committee of Ways and Means in both the First and Second Congresses, and in the latter he was selected to chair a Special Committee on Impressments. He attempted, as a congressman, to provide military and economic protection for his beleaguered constituents. More often than not, he voted to give President Jefferson Davis broad military authority to prosecute the war. At the same time, however, Baldwin sought to mitigate the impact of warfare on the civilian population and to maintain Southern food output, voting to exempt various classes of agricultural producers from military service.

Baldwin took pointed exception to impressment. Commanders in the field routinely impressed farm products to feed their armies. In so doing, they would strip bare an immediate locality rather than spread the burden over a wider area. Even if affected farmers were properly compensated—and often they complained that they were not—impressment caused local shortages and dislocations. In 1864 Baldwin sought to increase the tax-in-kind, which applied broadly to all producers, in order to lessen the inequalities that inevitably accompanied impressment. The shrinking perimeter of Confederate authority and the disintegration of transport doomed efforts to reform the impressment system, however.

Baldwin compiled an anti-administration record on some issues. Like other Union Whigs, he balked at proposals to suspend the writ of habeas corpus, and he opposed authorizing the enlistment of black soldiers. By the last months of the war in early 1865, he was more ready than most to acknowledge the hopelessness of the war effort and to seek a negotiated surrender.

Baldwin's most conspicuous public role occurred in the years immediately following the war. Elected to the General Assembly of the restored state government in October 1865, he was selected two months later as Speaker of the House. The so-called Baldwin legislature, dominated by "Conservative" ex-Confederates, occupied a powerful position in 1866.

That February the Joint Committee on Reconstruction took testimony from a number of Virginians, among them Baldwin. There the erstwhile Unionist denied that he had concealed from the Virginia convention of 1861 a peace overture from Abraham Lincoln. Baldwin also insisted that defeated Virginians accepted the results of the war and were working to establish equal civil rights for blacks and whites. He strongly objected, however, to any extension of political rights to blacks.

With near unanimity, the Baldwin legislature spurned the proposed Fourteenth Amendment, which would have reduced the representation of former Confederate states that did not allow black voting and would also have disqualified from office many prominent ex-Confederates. Voters in the North, however, elected a decisive majority of Republicans to Congress in late 1866. Overcoming bitter-end obstruction from President Andrew Johnson, Congress soon moved to abolish the existing governments in the South and to require approval of the Fourteenth Amendment. By the winter of 1867–1868, a Republican-dominated constitutional convention met to lay the foundations for a new Virginia government.

The adroit Baldwin and his brother-in-law, Alexander H. H. Stuart, were among the principals on the socalled Committee of Nine, organized in December 1868, which enabled white Virginia to escape further Reconstruction. They agreed to accept universal suffrage so long as voters had the opportunity to strike the proscriptive test oath and disfranchisement clauses of the new Constitution. The Committee of Nine also masterminded the nomination for governor of conservative Republican Gilbert C. Walker. The adoption of the modified Constitution and the election of Walker in July 1869 made Virginia the first ex-Confederate state to fall into conservative hands.

John B. Baldwin vaulted to prominence during the great crisis of 1860–1861. Virginia still had a larger number of slaves than any other state, and it occupied a central position as the secession drama unfolded. Had he and the Union Whigs at the Virginia convention been able to arrange a modus vivendi with the Lincoln administration, Baldwin could well have become a power in national politics. It was not, of course, to be. The man who believed secession "an absurdity and humbug" performed creditably for Confederate Virginia and continued to demonstrate his political acumen in the turbulent postwar years.

BIBLIOGRAPHY

Alexander, Thomas B., and Richard E. Beringer. *The Anatomy of the Confederate Congress: A Study of the Influences of Member Characteristics on Legislative Voting Behavior, 1861–1865.* Nashville, Tenn., 1972.

Crofts, Daniel W. *Reluctant Confederates: Upper South Unionists in the Secession Crisis.* Chapel Hill, N.C., 1989.

Interview between President Lincoln and Col. John B. Baldwin, April 4th, 1861: Statements & Evidence. Staunton, Va., 1866.

Journal of the Congress of the Confederate States of America, 1861–1865. 7 vols. Washington, D.C., 1904–1905.

Lowe, Richard. *Republicans and Reconstruction in Virginia, 1856–70.* Charlottesville, Va., 1991.

Maddex, Jack P., Jr. *The Virginia Conservatives, 1867–1879: A Study in Reconstruction Politics.* Chapel Hill, N.C., 1970.

Reese, George H., ed. *Proceedings of the Virginia State Convention of 1861.* 4 vols. Richmond, Va., 1965.

Yearns, Wilfred B. *The Confederate Congress.* Athens, Ga., 1960.

DANIEL W. CROFTS

THE BALLOON *INTREPID.* One of several Federal balloons in use during the Civil War, *Intrepid* was employed to reconnoiter the Battles of Fair Oaks and Seven Pines, May 3 to June 1, 1862. LIBRARY OF CONGRESS

BALLOON

Confederate experiments with balloons are not well known, unlike those of the Union's Thaddeus S. C. Lowe. An 1862 document on Union aeronautical activity during the Peninsular campaign contains the earliest mention of Confederate ballooning. Confusion exists about the balloon. Although two sites for balloon work are mentioned, the only documented use took place on the James River in 1862. Accounts of Confederate hot-air-filled cotton balloons and later coal-gas-filled silk balloons are unsupported. Another, undocumented, ballooning episode is suggested to have taken place at Charleston, South Carolina. [*See illustration with this article.*]

It is likely there was only a single Confederate balloon. This multicolored airship was constructed by Langdon Cheves and Charles Cevor in Savannah. They purchased silk, which was assembled and treated with gutta percha dissolved in naphtha to make it gas-proof.

The balloon was filled at the Richmond Gas Works and transported by rail. From about June 27, 1862, the balloon, tethered to either a boxcar or CSS *Teaser,* was used to observe Union troop movements. The Confederates, however, did not attempt to obtain an immediate tactical advantage by using a telegraph to direct artillery fire or troop movements according to the balloon's observations. Both balloon and tug were captured on July 4, 1862, when the tug ran aground.

It is unlikely Cevor and Cheves built a second balloon that was subsequently lost at Charleston; no evidence supports this speculation. Both men worked on the Charleston defenses, and accounts of their Virginia experiment may have been transposed to that city. The best source on Confederate ballooning uses Langdon Cheves's correspondence to show that one balloon was built in Savannah with multicolored silk bought for the purpose. The best descriptions of Civil War-era balloons can be found in the Union army's ballooning papers in the *Official Records.*

BIBLIOGRAPHY

Easterby, J. H. "Captain Langdon Cheves, Jr., and the Confederate Silk Dress Balloon." *South Carolina Historical Magazine* 44 (1943): 1–11, 99–110.

U.S. War Department. *War of the Rebellion: A Compilation of the Official Records of the Union and Confederate Armies.* Washington, D.C., 1880–1901. Ser. 3, vol. 3, pp. 252–319.

L. E. BABITS

BALL'S BLUFF, VIRGINIA

Fought October 21, 1861, some thirty-five miles upriver from Washington, this small battle on the Potomac River near Leesburg, Virginia, had great repercussions. Also called the Battle of Leesburg, it cost the Union force of 1,720 men 49 killed, 158 wounded, 553 taken prisoner, and 171 missing or drowned. Out of 1,709 Confederate men, 36 were killed, 117 wounded, and 2 taken prisoner.

The battle came about because George B. McClellan, commander of the Army of the Potomac, was heavily pressured by Radical Republican congressmen to advance against the Confederates in northern Virginia. McClellan, deciding to attack the isolated Confederate brigade at Leesburg, under Col. Nathan ("Shanks") Evans, telegraphed Gen. Charles Stone, commander of the Union division at Poolesville, Maryland, opposite Leesburg: "Perhaps a slight demonstration on your part would have the effect to move them." Stone was also informed by McClellan that George McCall's division of 12,000 would move upriver on the Virginia shoreline toward Leesburg via Dranesville.

Stone decided to cross the Potomac in a pincers movement. Willis Gorman's brigade would be the left pincer crossing at Edwards Ferry both to hold Evans in check and to link up with the advancing McCall. Meanwhile, a brigade commanded by the Radical Republican senator and colonel Edward D. Baker was to cross upriver at Smartt's Mill Ford to envelop Evans's extreme left flank. A small reconnaissance patrol was to scout between these two columns at Ball's Bluff. The patrol sent back an inaccurate report, which in turn led to its being ambushed by alert Confederate pickets of the Seventeenth Mississippi Infantry Regiment. This initial skirmish led to Union reinforcements moving across the Potomac to cross at Ball's Bluff instead of Smartt's Mill Ford, thus changing the entire axis of Stone's plan of assault.

At the same time, unknown to Stone—but not to Evans, who had captured a Union courier—McCall had turned around at Dranesville and marched back to his camps at Langley. These factors enabled Evans to first send Walter Jennifer's cavalry, William Duff's Mississippians, and the Eighth Virginia Infantry Regiment under Col. Eppa Hunton to

do battle around the Jackson house at 12:00 noon. Successful there, they then pushed the Union forces back to the edge of a cleared field of some eight to ten acres atop Ball's Bluff. Reinforcements on both sides now poured into the maelstrom, including Colonel Baker and three Union artillery pieces. Baker was killed just after 5:00 P.M. and his command was routed back across the Potomac into Maryland.

For his victory at Ball's Bluff, Colonel Evans was promoted to brigadier general to date from the day of the battle. On the Union side, this disaster three months to the day after First Manassas, combined with Baker's death, enabled the Radical Republicans in Congress to form the Joint Committee on the Conduct of the War. The committee met three times between December 1861 and March 1863 to investigate what had happened at Ball's Bluff. In February 1862 they illegally and falsely accused General Stone of treason and had him arrested without a writ of habeus corpus and thrown into the dungeon of Fort Lafayette and Fort Hamilton in New York Harbor for 189 days.

BIBLIOGRAPHY

Holien, Kim B. *Battle at Ball's Bluff.* Orange, Va., 1985.
Patch, Joseph D. *The Battle of Ball's Bluff.* Leesburg, Va., 1958.

KIM BERNARD HOLIEN

BALTIMORE RIOT

Baltimore in the spring of 1861 was a tinderbox. The secession crisis of the winter, complicated by depressed economic conditions, intensified sectional passions in Maryland. The bombardment of Fort Sumter and Abraham Lincoln's call for troops compounded the state's indecisiveness. Torn in their loyalties, Marylanders nevertheless opposed the coercion of the Southern states. Yet troops going by rail to the defense of Washington would have to pass through Baltimore.

On April 18 some Northern troops traveled through the city without incident. Police authorities, either unworried or merely neglectful, failed to make preparations for continued safe passages. On the following day, the public mood was more volatile. The legacy of the Know-Nothing riots in the 1850s, inflamed by the fiery rhetoric of Southern radicals and compounded by economic suffering, created a highly inflammatory atmosphere in Baltimore. News of the Sixth Massachusetts Regiment's arrival now provoked gathering mobs to obstruct its route. As the railway cars were drawn by horses through the city, crowds began to jeer and pelt the soldiers with stones and missiles. Disembarking from the coaches, the troops continued by marching to Camden

Street Station. Despite police efforts to maintain order and Mayor George Brown's symbolic act of walking at the head of the troops, rioting ensued. In the exchange of fire and missiles, four soldiers and a number of citizens lay wounded and dead.

Hysteria gripped Baltimore. A mass meeting that evening evoked extreme state rights statements from Governor Thomas Hicks. Municipal authorities, fearing the possibility of additional arrivals, cut Northern rail links to the city. A delegation was sent to Washington for consultations with alarmed Federal authorities. Meanwhile, Baltimoreans prepared for a siege. Finally, by April 28 the crisis had passed, and Unionist sentiment reasserted itself in the city. Gen. Benjamin F. Butler sealed Federal control over the city with his occupation of Federal Hill on the night of May 13. Yet the rioting left its scar, as evident in the state song:

> Avenge the patriotic gore
> That flecked the street of Baltimore,
> And be the battle queen of yore,
> Maryland, my Maryland!

BIBLIOGRAPHY

Brown, George William. *Baltimore and the 19th of April, 1861.* Baltimore, 1887.

Brugger, Robert J. *Maryland: A Middle Temperament, 1634–1980.* Baltimore, 1988.

Clark, Charles B. "Baltimore and the Attack on the Sixth Massachusetts Regiment, April 19, 1861." *Maryland Historical Magazine* 56 (March 1961): 39–71.

Radcliffe, George L. P. *Governor Thomas H. Hicks of Maryland and the Civil War.* Baltimore, 1901.

RICHARD R. DUNCAN

BANKING

Prior to the secession crisis, several Southern states had banking systems as solid and sophisticated as those in the North. Northern attempts to coordinate the transmission of financial information and banks' responses to crises had yielded a range of structures and mechanisms from clearinghouses (where bankers met daily to clear their balances with each other) and safety funds (early forms of deposit insurance) to free banking laws that permitted anyone to start a bank.

Several Southern states, however, had developed a much more effective solution to those problems—namely, branch banking, in which a bank could open offices in other locations without separate acts of the state legislature. Branching, which the North ignored, allowed rapid transfer of resources among branches, treating the resources of each individual as part of the whole. Most important, branching allowed for more efficient transmission of information about financial conditions from one branch location to another. At the onset of the Civil War, the South's banking system had emerged virtually unscathed from the panic of 1857 and had seen the culmination of a decade of impressive growth.

Secession, however, changed things immediately. In states that seceded first, banks felt instant effects. South Carolina banks suspended (i.e., ceased paying gold and silver coin, or specie, for their notes) in late 1860; a number of New Orleans factorage houses with liabilities exceeding $30 million suspended during the first two weeks of December. But Mobile and New Orleans banks continued to redeem notes for specie until fall 1861. In order to do so, they dramatically cut their lending and circulation. Even in the states that did not secede, banks had to reduce circulation and increase reserves. Deposits in Louisiana and North Carolina remained high, and little evidence exists to show that throughout the South bankers gave much thought to the practical problems of a war that would separate them from their Northern correspondents (banks in other locations in which banks regularly kept balances). Some minor expansion of lending occurred to Southern borrowers—attempts to carry friends of business acquaintances—but no coherent policy appears to have emerged. Nevertheless, all major categories of bank statistics showed declines from 1860 to 1861; circulation fell by $12 million, deposits by $5 million, specie by $4.5 million, and loans by $22 million. The number of banks also shrank from 119 to 104.

In addition to the deleterious effects of the secession crisis itself, the Confederacy and the states themselves exacted a toll on Southern banks. Alabama banks had to provide a $2 million loan to the state of Alabama and had to accept Confederate Treasury notes at par. Each bank had to contribute an amount proportional to its capital. At the level of the Confederate government, banks had a twofold obligation. First, they had to support the Confederacy by a direct loan (April 1861) to the government. They accomplished that by redeeming in coin their own notes that the banks paid for the government bonds, which constituted the collateral for the loan. Even though the banks had suspended specie payments, their notes traded at only a slight discount and, at the beginning of the war, were "as good as gold." As a result, the Confederacy did not (and probably could not) insist on receiving specie directly for the bonds. In May 1861, Secretary of the Treasury Christopher G. Memminger contacted a number of banks to ask for further loans from each of them, paying for them with $1,000 and $500 Treasury notes. Banks were expected to pay out in specie at par on the Confederate notes, although some discounted the notes early. At that point, Memminger well knew, as he told Louisiana bankers in September 1861, the value of

Confederate notes depended on the public's willingness to accept them as a circulating medium, not on the bankers' attitude.

A second obligation involved gaining the banks' participation in establishing the Confederate Treasury note currency. Achieving that meant convincing the New Orleans banks to participate in the program. But Louisiana's Constitution prohibited specie suspensions, and the New Orleans banks had remained absent from any of the banking conventions.

> **Three separate pressures combined to destroy the Southern banking system.**

Mobile's banks followed suit, continuing to pay specie. Thus the notion of a unified "national" currency never took hold.

Circulation of bank, local, private, and state issues rose 150 percent above the prewar average. The number of depreciated moneys rose dramatically, with the most discounted notes called shinplasters. Regardless of a bank's prewar position, that inflation would have undermined its notes' credibility even without the other problems brought on by the war. But three separate pressures combined to destroy the Southern banking system.

First, by offering their specie and notes for purchase of Confederate bonds, the banks assumed those bonds as collateral for their assets. When the Confederacy collapsed, the value of those bonds and hence those assets also collapsed.

Some assets would have remained, however, under other circumstances. Most Southern banks held large amounts of collateral in the form of Southern land (plantations) and property (chattel). The Union victories, combined with the perceived effects of the Emancipation Proclamation, eroded the value of those assets as well. That constituted the second process that destroyed the Southern banking system: even if a peace had been negotiated, if it came at the expense of slavery (as in some of the more desperate Southern ideas after 1864), the banks would have had virtually no assets left anyway.

Finally, Confederate and state policies during the war—independent of overall monetary policy and the one-third decline in money values—led to a staggering drain on a Southern bank's resources. One study has shown that a typical bank would have retained barely 36 percent of its assets by 1864, owing to taxation on stock, earnings, and various fees. What would the remainder of that bank's assets be worth if they consisted of slaves and Confederate bonds?

As if these pressures were not enough, banks in the Confederacy also had to deal with personnel problems and with the approach of enemy troops. Employees frequently moved in and out of civilian bank jobs, depending on the demands of the army or their families. Some bankers away at the front received instructions to return to their institutions. More disturbing were the problems associated with the impending arrival of Federal troops. Banks hid specie from the Union armies (as well as the Confederate government), and in one case a Tennessee banker escaped with his bank's specie to England and returned with it after the war to reopen his bank. Under other circumstances, banks saw Union troops issue counterfeit look-alike notes, which only further eroded the public's flagging confidence in paper money.

The collapse of the Southern banking system, although little appreciated by historians, constituted a dual tragedy. First, the dearth of financial institutions in the postbellum South led to major disruptions in commercial and agricultural lending. That, in turn, helped seal the fate of freedmen and whites alike by denying them access to credit under competitive circumstances. With virtually no banks in existence—and certainly no banks at all in direct, close competition—farmers and entrepreneurs either had to seek credit from furnishing merchants or other informal sources or, in the case of farmers, had to sharecrop. The record of black-owned insurance companies and savings and loans in the North suggests that at least *some* black-owned institutions would have appeared in a free market.

When combined with the undesirable and constrictive effects of the National Bank and Currency Acts, the ability of Southerners to start and grow banks almost vanished for decades. The second unappreciated aspects of Southern banking as it related to the Confederacy was that the Confederate experiment killed the extremely viable and healthy branch banking systems, almost unique to the South. Only in a few states—most notably California—did branching develop, and overall it remained absent from the political debates about banking that reformed the American system from the late 1800s to 1913. Thus, in addition to its other less than illustrious accomplishments, the Confederacy, through its failure, saddled much of the United States with an inferior unit banking system for years.

[*See also* Bonds; Currency; Shinplasters.]

BIBLIOGRAPHY

Ball, Douglas B. *Financial Failure and Confederate Defeat*. Urbana, Ill., 1991.

Calomiris, Charles W., and Larry Schweikart. "The Panic of 1857: Causes, Transmission, and Containment." *Journal of Economic History* 51 (December 1991): 807–834.

Morgan, James F. *Graybacks and Gold: Confederate Monetary Policy*. Pensacola, Fla., 1985.

Schweikart, Larry. *Banking in the American South from the Age of Jackson*. Baton Rouge, La., 1987.

Schweikart, Larry. "Southern Banks and Secession." *Civil War History* 31 (June 1985): 111–125.

LARRY SCHWEIKART

BAPTIST CHURCH

Practicing a pronounced belief in the autonomy of its individual congregations, the Baptist church was a perfect organizational analogue of the state rights orientation of many white Southerners. In 1860, nearly 650,000 white and black Southerners called themselves Baptist and had formed some 7,760 assemblies, scattered throughout the slaveholding states. Over 400,000 white Baptists were actively involved not only in evangelical enterprises but also in the major sectional questions of their day.

These folk contributed to Southern sectionalism in three ways. First, most Baptists believed and could justify through their reading of Scripture that slavery was a moral institution, as long as masters treated their slaves humanely. Second, Southern Baptists had divorced themselves from cooperative missionary enterprises with Northern Baptists during the 1840s and had established the Southern Baptist Convention, a fact that intensified their regional identification. Finally, during the critical decade of the 1850s, Baptist parsons and presses continually indicted Northern society as a source of sin, hypocrisy, and infidelity while upholding and, to some degree, attempting to transform Southern values and culture. In keeping with these ecclesiastical efforts, Baptist associations in all eleven seceding states passed resolutions that supported disunion, pledged support to the Confederacy, and offered intercession for the nascent nation. Basil Manly, a prominent Alabama Baptist clergyman, delivered the invocation at the inauguration ceremony for Jefferson Davis in February 1861.

During the secession winter, many Baptist writers and parsons proffered detailed advice concerning a proper course for Baptists and their political leaders to follow. In November 1860, James R. Graves, editor of the *Tennessee Baptist,* called for a convention of Southerners to demand ironclad protection of slavery in the territories through a federal slave code and in Southern states by means of a constitutional amendment and the rigid enforcement of the Fugitive Slave Law. If Northerners rejected these demands, then the South ought to secede as a unit. At the same time, the Alabama Baptist Convention argued that "the union of the states has failed" and pledged themselves to support the civil authorities who would protect the state's interest. Similarly, Mississippi Baptists urged immediate disunion as the best means to avert a civil war.

In contrast to Deep South Baptists, who came to support secession quickly, moderation characterized upper South Baptist responses to Abraham Lincoln's election and the secession crisis. For example, the *Biblical Recorder,* the Baptist paper in North Carolina, did not advocate secession until after Lincoln's call for troops following the shelling of Fort Sumter. But in both the upper and the lower South, Baptist leaders couched their cries for political action in evangelical terms. Secession would permit Southern Baptists to perform their religious duties unfettered by infidel notions of abolitionism and modernism.

Baptists supported the war effort in myriad ways. Approximately one hundred Baptist clergymen served as chaplains, and during 1862, the Southern Baptist Convention maintained an additional twenty-six missionaries in the field to work among the soldiers. Baptists supported interdenominational Bible societies and colportage efforts. Many Baptists, including clergymen, served as soldiers.

The vicissitudes of war brought subterranean stresses to the surface among Baptists, disrupting denominational schools and damaging church properties. Local associations lamented the loss of leadership, as parsons ministered at the front instead of in their prewar parishes. Some reform minded parsons, like Georgia's Nathaniel Macon Crawford, hoped to use secession as an opportunity to reform slavery. Recognizing slave marriages and making it legal to teach slaves to read typified these attempts. Evangelical enterprises among the slaves ultimately suffered, however, removing an important moral support for Southern separatism in the first place. Secession and slavery were good only if African Americans heard and responded to the true gospel. As a result, not a few Baptists interpreted Confederate defeat as a sign of divine displeasure. Baptists had not been faithful stewards of their holy message.

At the same time, Baptists could and did interpret their defeat not as Jehovah's rejection of their society but as a purifying process by which the "Lord chastens whom He loveth." Indeed, after the war, Baptists participated with other denominations in interfaith revivals that glorified the ideals that had prompted Southern secession. J. William Jones, a Virginia Baptist, became the best-known and one of the most influential of clerical exponents of Lost Cause religion. Gallant Confederates augmented biblical examples of righteous heroes in liturgical paeans to godly virtue. Jones led the attempt to rehabilitate the maligned image of Jefferson Davis and served as a longtime secretary-treasurer of the Southern Historical Society. He even utilized the failure of the Confederacy as a tool of religious conversion—mixing sacred and secular imagery into a hellfire and brimstone sermon. God could not have allowed the Confederacy to succeed with so many unconverted Southerners in its ranks. Along with many of his peers, Jones fought against what he perceived as immoral, modern tendencies in secular society, like skepticism, a threat he considered similar in nature to abolitionism. Prior, during, and after the war, Baptists looked to their scripture to defend their preindustrial world, including its racial mores, from what they considered infidelity.

[*See also* Lost Cause, *overview article.*]

BIBLIOGRAPHY

Daniel, W. Harrison. *Southern Protestantism in the Confederacy.* Richmond, Va., 1989.

Goen, Clarence C. *Broken Churches, Broken Nation: Denominational Schisms and the Coming of the Civil War.* Macon, Ga., 1985.

Mathews, Donald G. *Religion in the Old South.* Chicago, 1977.

McBeth, Harry Leon. *The Baptist Heritage: Four Centuries of Baptist Witness.* Nashville, Tenn., 1987.

Wilson, Charles Reagan. *Baptized in Blood: The Religion of the Lost Cause, 1865–1920.* Athens, Ga., 1980.

EDWARD RILEY CROWTHER

BARKSDALE, ETHELBERT

BARKSDALE, ETHELBERT (1824–1893), congressman from Mississippi. Barksdale was born in Tennessee and moved to Mississippi as a teenager. At the age of twenty-one, he became a journalist, as had his brother, William Barksdale—later a Confederate general killed at Gettysburg. Barksdale edited the *Democrat,* a newspaper in Yazoo City, Mississippi, from 1845 to 1850. Afterward, he moved to Jackson to edit the *Mississippian,* the official journal of the state.

In his first experience as a politician, he became a delegate to the Democratic National Convention that met in Charleston in 1860. At this convention, a split developed between the Northern supporters of Stephen A. Douglas for president and Southerners who wanted a plank endorsing Federal protection of slave property in the territories. Barksdale delivered a strong speech advocating the Southern point of view. Nevertheless, the convention was controlled by a small Douglas majority, and when the Southerners' position was defeated, Barksdale, along with the other members of the Mississippi delegation and the delegations from other Southern states, walked out and agreed to meet later in Richmond.

At that meeting of Southern Democrats, Barksdale served on the platform committee, which advocated that the Federal government "protect, when necessary, the rights of persons and property in the Territories." The Southerners then nominated John C. Breckinridge for president. Barksdale vigorously supported Breckinridge despite the likelihood of Abraham Lincoln's election; he wrote that if Lincoln were elected, "99 out of every 100 men" who supported Breckinridge would be for secession. Although Barksdale had not always been a secessionist, the events in 1860 drove him to support separation.

In the fall of 1861, Barksdale was elected to the First Congress and was easily reelected in 1863. In this political role, Barksdale became an active Confederate, enjoying argument and defending controversial positions. He once said that, if necessary, he would be willing to "throw aside the Constitution." He introduced measures in the First Congress allowing President Jefferson Davis to suspend habeas corpus and to impose martial law. He favored the draft, draft exemptions, and an agricultural tax—positions also favored by Davis. Later, when the Confederacy was seriously threatened, he advocated increasing the number of soldiers and introduced a bill allowing the arming of slaves. He argued for his position by reading a statement from Robert E. Lee that also supported arming slaves.

After the war, he resumed newspaper editing; this time he edited the influential *Clarion.* During Reconstruction, Barksdale deplored the bitterness and resentment of many white Mississippians; he counseled acceptance of the results of the war and advised giving rights to the freed blacks. Otherwise, he said, white Mississippians would lose to Radical Republicans all power to control affairs. Barksdale's newspaper called for whites to register, vote, and aid in the process of Reconstruction.

His popular and influential columns advocating the interests of small farmers led to his election to the U.S. Congress in 1882 and 1884. He was defeated, however, in campaigns for Congress in 1886, 1890, and 1892. Until his death, he lived and farmed at Oak Valley, a plantation in Yazoo County.

BIBLIOGRAPHY

Peterson, Owen. "Ethelbert Barksdale in the Democratic Convention of 1860." *Journal of Mississippi History* 14 (October 1952): 274–276.

Warner, Ezra J., and W. Buck Yearns. *Biographical Register of the Confederate Congress.* Baton Rouge, La., 1975.

RAY SKATES

BARKSDALE, WILLIAM

BARKSDALE, WILLIAM (1821–1863) U.S. congressman and Confederate brigadier general. Barksdale, born August 21, 1821, was a native of Tennessee who grew up an orphan in Mississippi. He served as a captain of commissary in the Mexican War, but saw no battle action. Barksdale won election to the U.S. House of Representatives in 1853 and was reelected every two years until the Civil War in campaigns marked by violent episodes that included a knife fight and a duel. In Washington the fiery Mississippian regularly engaged in vitriolic debate that led to baring of knives, a near duel, and a famous fistfight on the floor of the House in 1858. Despite the decade of noisy oratory, Barksdale was able to declare in 1860, "Never have I desired a dissolution of this union"—but the "sectional and hostile platform" of the

Republicans in that year prompted him to insist that the South must not accept Abraham Lincoln's goverance.

Barksdale served briefly in early 1861 as quartermaster general of the short-lived Army of Mississippi before becoming colonel of the Thirteenth Mississippi Infantry. He took the regiment to Virginia barely in time to take part in First Manassas, arriving on the Confederate far left near Chinn Ridge at the moment of decision. That fall Colonel Barksdale got into serious trouble for drunkenness. His superior, Gen. Nathan G. ("Shanks") Evans (himself notoriously intemperate), brought the colonel before a court-martial. Barksdale escaped the sentence of the court in part by giving "a solemn pledge" of temperance for the duration of the war and in part because he had meanwhile fought with distinction on the Edward's Ferry front during the Battle of Ball's Bluff.

Richard Griffith, a new brigade commander, recommended Barksdale for promotion in April 1862. The promotion came a few months later when Griffith fell mortally wounded during the Seven Days' Battles. As acting brigade commander, Colonel Barksdale won plaudits from both his division commander and Robert E. Lee. Promoted to brigadier general August 12, 1862, he led his command north with the army into Maryland after missing Second Manassas as part of the rear guard. He commanded it in a difficult and successful attack on Maryland Heights above Harpers Ferry and then participated in the brightest tactical moment for the Confederates at Sharpsburg, battering Sedgwick and Sumner in the West Woods.

General Barksdale's greatest day came on December 11, 1862, when he defended the riverfront in Fredericksburg against Federals attempting to cross. The next spring, on nearly the same ground, however, the general and his brigade came to grief when a vastly stronger Northern column forced them away from their rearguard post on Marye's Heights during the Chancellorsville campaign. At Gettysburg on July 2, 1863, William Barksdale led his seasoned veterans across the Emmitsburg Road in a successful assault on the Peach Orchard. As he rode at their head beyond the orchard toward Plum Run, the general fell from his horse struck by several projectiles. He died early the next day in enemy hands. In molding his Mississippi regiments into a potent force and leading them to distinction on several fields, Barksdale carved one of the best military records achieved by any of the antebellum political fire-eaters.

BIBLIOGRAPHY

Humphreys, Benjamin G. "Recollections of Fredericksburg." *Land We Love* 3 (1867): 443–460.
McKee, James W. "William Barksdale: The Intrepid Mississippian." Ph.D. diss., Mississippi State University, 1966.
Rand, Clayton. *Men of Spine in Mississippi.* Gulfport, Miss., 1940.

ROBERT K. KRICK

BARKSDALE'S MISSISSIPPI BRIGADE

This brigade of four Mississippi infantry regiments won one of the highest reputations as a fighting unit earned by any organization in the Army of Northern Virginia. The Thirteenth Mississippi was made up of companies from the state's east-central counties. Its first and best-known commander was William Barksdale. The Seventeenth came from Mississippi's far northern tier of counties, the Eighteenth was raised in west-central Mississippi, and the Twenty-first included companies from several widely separated regions.

The regiments had separate baptisms of fire at First Manassas and Ball's Bluff before they were united as a brigade under Gen. Richard Griffith in December 1861. After Griffith was mortally wounded at Savage Station, Barksdale became brigadier.

The Mississippi Brigade impressed an admiring Virginia major as "the finest body of men I ever saw . . . almost giants in size and power . . . and . . . almost without exception fine shots." When they screeched the rebel yell, the major wrote, "the volume of sound was tremendous." The men of the brigade performed ably throughout the war as some of Lee's most reliable shock troops. They won special distinction under Barksdale defending the riverfront at Fredericksburg in December 1862 and attacking to and beyond the Peach Orchard at Gettysburg. The brigade's most difficult day came on May 3, 1863, when it was driven from Marye's Heights near Fredericksburg, but because of the circumstances no discredit was attached to the brigade. Gen. B. G. Humphreys, who had been colonel of the Twenty-first, commanded the brigade after Barksdale's death at Gettysburg.

BIBLIOGRAPHY

Rietti, John C. *Military Annals of Mississippi.* [Jackson, Miss.?], 1895.
Rowland, Dunbar. *The Official and Statistical Register of the State of Mississippi.* Nashville, Tenn., 1908.
Stiles, Robert A. *Four Years under Marse Robert.* New York, 1903. Reprint, Dayton, Ohio, 1977.

ROBERT K. KRICK

BARRINGER, RUFUS

BARRINGER, RUFUS (1821–1895), brigadier general. The first—and possibly the only—Confederate general to meet Abraham Lincoln during the war was a lawyer prior to the attack on Fort Sumter. Barringer was born in Cabarrus

County, North Carolina, on December 2, 1821. He graduated from the University of North Carolina in 1842, and after studying law, he opened his legal practice in Concord. As a Whig, Barringer served in the State Assembly in 1848 and 1850 and was a Bell and Everett elector in 1860.

He was a strong Unionist and was so outspoken in his convictions that he once was publicly ridiculed on the streets of Charlotte. When he discerned that secession was imminent and that war was inevitable, however, he urged the legislature to arm the state and prepare for the coming conflict.

In April 1861, Barringer raised a company that became Company F, First North Carolina Cavalry. He was commissioned a captain on May 16. Barringer fought well with the

> **Though severely wounded in the face at Brandy Station, he "bore himself with marked coolness and good conduct"....**

Army of Northern Virginia in the Peninsular campaign, at Second Manassas, Sharpsburg, Fredericksburg, and Chancellorsville. He was still a captain in June 1863 when, though severely wounded in the face at Brandy Station, he "bore himself with marked coolness and good conduct," according to Wade Hampton, his commanding officer.

Barringer's rise in rank was rapid thereafter. He was promoted to major in August 1863, lieutenant colonel three months later, and brigadier general in June 1864, commanding four North Carolina cavalry regiments. His troopers were assigned to the division of William Henry Fitzhugh ("Rooney") Lee and served in that capacity until near the end of the war. A subordinate officer described the general as "prudent, methodical and cautious" on the battlefield.

Barringer's last of seventy-six engagements was fought at Namozine Church on April 3, 1865. Attempting to extricate a regiment from a perilous situation, he was captured by Jesse scouts, Union soldiers in Confederate disguise. He was taken to City Point, arriving at Federal headquarters at a time when Lincoln was visiting Ulysses S. Grant.

Barringer was in a tent preparing to shave when he heard a voice inquire, "Mr. President, have you ever seen a live Rebel general in uniform?" Lincoln replied, "No," at which point the flap of the tent was withdrawn and the first voice answered, "Here is one now." Lincoln greeted Barringer warmly. In the cordial conversation that ensued, the president recalled that in his years as a congressman, he had shared a desk with a Carolinian named Barringer. "That was my brother [D. Moreau Barringer]," the general said. Before parting, Lincoln wrote a note that he handed to Barringer. It was addressed to Edwin M. Stanton, asking that the secretary of war show special consideration to the prisoner. As a result of

the president's thoughtfulness, Barringer was sent to Fort Delaware rather than disreputable Old Capitol Prison in Washington.

By his marriage to Eugenia Morrison, Barringer was a brother-in-law of Thomas J. ("Stonewall") Jackson and D. H. Hill. In 1862 Jackson had offered Barringer the position of quartermaster on his staff. The kinsman declined the honor, saying he preferred to remain with his men.

Following his release from prison in August 1865, Barringer transferred his law practice to Charlotte where he was "a conspicuous figure in his military cape with his green bag in his hand." In a county that was strongly Democratic, Barringer joined the Republican party. He was a member of the constitutional convention in 1875 and an unsuccessful candidate for lieutenant governor in 1880. He retired in 1884 and devoted the remainder of his life to writing treatises on the war and advocating better education in the public schools. He died in Charlotte on February 3, 1895, and was buried there.

BIBLIOGRAPHY

Barringer, Paul B. *The Natural Bent.* Chapel Hill, N.C., 1949.
"Gen. Rufus Barringer." *Confederate Veteran* 9 (1901): 69–70. Reprint, Wilmington, N.C., 1985.
Hill, D. H., Jr. *North Carolina.* Vol. 4 of *Confederate Military History.* Edited by Clement A. Evans. Atlanta, 1899. Vol. 5 of extended ed. Wilmington, N.C., 1987.
Warner, Ezra J. *Generals in Gray: Lives of the Confederate Commanders.* Baton Rouge, La., 1959.

LOWELL REIDENBAUGH

BARTON, SETH MAXWELL

BARTON, SETH MAXWELL (1829–1900), brigadier general. One of four brothers to serve in the Confederate army, Barton was born at Fredericksburg, Virginia, on September 8, 1829. He was two months shy of his sixteenth birthday when, on July 1, 1845, he was admitted to the U.S. Military Academy. Barton graduated in 1849, ranking twenty-eighth in a class of forty-three that was distinguished chiefly by the fact that one of its members was author Stephen Vincent Benét, who ranked third. As a cadet, Barton was said to be "fond of reading and gave more attention to the pursuit of general knowledge than to the specific requirements of the course."

Barton's first assignment as a second lieutenant of infantry was at Fort Columbus in New York Harbor. A year later he was transferred to New Mexico. During his years on the frontier Barton was promoted twice, to first lieutenant in 1853 and to captain in 1857. He served as adjutant of the First Infantry from 1853 to 1857 and saw action against the Comanches the latter year.

Resigning his commission in June 1861 while at Fort Leavenworth, Barton offered his services to the South. He was commissioned a captain of infantry initially and then lieutenant colonel of the Third Arkansas on July 8. In early August, Barton wrote to Samuel Cooper, apprising the adjutant general of conditions in his command. "The clothing is mostly furnished from private sources," he revealed. Barton added that the muster rolls, though correct, "are not as intelligible as they should be for want of proper clerks." Last, the colonel lamented, "The want of stationary here may be well understood, from the fact that I have to tie up the muster rolls . . . with the ravelling of a tent cord."

Barton took part in the operations at Cheat Mountain and Greenbrier River and was acting chief engineer for Thomas J. ("Stonewall") Jackson's Romney campaign in January 1862. Jackson thought so highly of Barton that he recommended him for a brigadier's commission. The nomination was submitted to the Senate, withdrawn by Jefferson Davis a few days later, and ultimately confirmed on March 11, 1862. Barton's brigade was with E. Kirby Smith in East Tennessee and joined the defenses of Vicksburg in December 1862. He was captured on July 4, 1863, when that river bastion surrendered to Ulysses S. Grant, but he was exchanged almost immediately.

On September 21, Barton joined George E. Pickett's division, taking over the brigade that had been led by Lewis A. Armistead prior to his fall at Gettysburg. In the operations around New Bern, Barton was charged with "want of cooperation." He was censured again in May 1864 for his handling of troops south of the James River. He was relieved of command and, despite the petitioning for reinstatement by his regimental colonels, remained idle until late in the year when he took charge of a brigade in the defenses of Richmond. He was in George Washington Custis Lee's division in the retreat from the capital and was captured at Sayler's Creek on April 6, 1865. Barton was imprisoned at Fort Warren until July 1865.

After the war Barton resided in Fredericksburg where, it was said, he was "one of the finest chemists in the country." He died on April 11, 1900, while visiting his son in Washington, D.C., and was buried in City Cemetery, Fredericksburg.

BIBLIOGRAPHY

Compiled Military Service Records. Seth Maxwell Barton. Microcopy M331, Roll 17. Record Group 109. National Archives, Washington, D.C.

Hotchkiss, Jed. *Virginia.* Vol. 3 of *Confederate Military History.* Edited by Clement A. Evans. Atlanta, 1899. Vol. 4 of extended ed. Wilmington, N.C., 1987.

Obituary. *Daily Star* (Fredericksburg, Virginia), April 11, 1900.

LOWELL REIDENBAUGH

BARTOW, FRANCIS S.

BARTOW, FRANCIS S. (1816–1861), congressman from Georgia and colonel. Bartow was born into an affluent Savannah family on September 6, 1816. The son of an eminent physician, he was well educated at home before attending Franklin College (the University of Georgia), where he graduated with honors in 1835, and Yale Law School. He returned to Savannah in 1837 before completing his degree. He continued his study of law under Judge John McPherson Berrien and later married his daughter. Once admitted to the bar in 1839, he opened his own law practice and soon became active in state and local politics. He was elected as a Whig to two terms in the state house of representatives and one in the state senate in the 1840s, though he failed in his 1857 bid to represent Georgia's First District in Congress, when he ran on the Know-Nothing, or American party, ticket. Bartow was also active in local military endeavors, and from 1856 on, he served as captain of the Oglethorpe Light Infantry, an elite militia company made up of young men from Savannah's leading families. He had by then become a wealthy planter, and in 1860 he owned eighty-nine slaves.

Though once Unionist in sentiment, Bartow had by 1860 become both a Democrat and an ardent secessionist. Convinced that the Republican party and Abraham Lincoln were fanatics bent on the subjugation of the South, he campaigned actively for secession through the fall of 1860 in Georgia and other Southern states and supported the Southern Democratic candidate John C. Breckinridge in that fateful presidential race. His powerful speeches, once referred to as "logic on fire," proved persuasive. On December 28, 1860, he was speaking in Atlanta when word arrived of the burning of Fort Moultrie in Charleston, and he used the news to whip the crowd into frenzied support of South Carolina's course of action. Fulton County's delegates to the state secession convention in Milledgeville credited their pro-secession votes cast two weeks later to that speech. Bartow himself played a prominent role at that convention and was on the seventeen-member committee that drew up Georgia's ordinance of secession.

He was soon thereafter elected to the new Confederacy's Provisional Congress, which met in Montgomery in February. As chairman of its Committee on Military Affairs, Bartow succeeded in his push for gray uniforms for Confederate troops but failed in his attempt to limit volunteer military service to sixty-day terms. Others more sure of the inevitability of war, including Jefferson Davis, persuaded him to accept instead a twelve-month term of enlistment. Bartow had remained active in his leadership of the Oglethorpe Light Infantry and participated with it in seizing Fort Pulaski and Fort McAllister on the Savannah River from Federal hands. While in the Provisional Congress, he offered the service of his Savannah company to President Davis, thus making it, according to tradition, the first such company tendered for the Confederate cause.

Under the provisions of the Confederacy's permanent Constitution, which took effect in April, officials of the central government could not hold military positions as well, which forced a number of congressmen, including Bartow, to choose their means of service to the Confederacy. He resigned from the Provisional Congress and on May 21, took his Oglethorpe Light Infantry to Virginia. This move led to strenuous objections from Governor Joseph E. Brown, who had planned to use such units to build a state army. Bitter words were exchanged through correspondence, as Bartow remained defiant in denying the governor the right to choose how he would serve his new country.

On June 21, Bartow was elected colonel of the Eighth Georgia Infantry and served under Gen. Joseph E. Johnston in the lower Shenandoah Valley. From there they proceeded to Manassas, where on July 21 he led his own and four other regiments into the first battle of the war. After being wounded in the leg and having his horse shot from under him, he rallied his men for an assault on a Union battery on the Henry House Hill. There he was shot in the chest and died almost instantly. His final words, often cited later, were "They have killed me, boys, but the day is ours. Never give up the field."

Bartow's death made him one of the first and most honored Confederate martyrs. Fellow Georgia congressman Robert Toombs was among several to eulogize him on the floor of the Confederate Congress, which then adjourned for the day in his honor. His body was brought to Richmond and lay in state in the capitol. Gen. Lucius Jeremiah Gartrell of Georgia made much of the fact that he had caught the dying Bartow as he fell from his horse and was responsible for publicizing his final words. By December 1861, Cass County in northwest Georgia had been renamed Bartow County, and its congressman, Warren Akin, wrote his wife that "if we ever have another boy, I now feel like I will call him Bartow."

BIBLIOGRAPHY

Coleman, Kenneth, and Charles Stephen Gurr, eds. *Dictionary of Georgia Biography.* Vol. 1. Athens, Ga., 1983.

Henderson, Lindsey B. *The Oglethorpe Light Infantry.* Athens, Ga., 1961.

Knight, Lucian Lamar. *Reminiscences of Famous Georgians.* Vol. 2. Atlanta, 1908.

Northen, William W., ed. *Men of Mark in Georgia.* Vol. 3. Atlanta, 1908. Reprint, Spartanburg, S.C., 1974.

Wiley, Bell Irvin, ed. *Letters of Warren Akin, Confederate Congressman.* Athens, Ga., 1959.

JOHN C. INSCOE

Bate, William Brimage

BATE, WILLIAM BRIMAGE (1826–1905), major general, postwar governor of Tennessee, and U.S. senator. Bate was born on October 7, 1826, in what is now Castalian Springs, Tennessee. He received little formal education and left school soon after his father's death in 1842. For several years thereafter he worked as a clerk on a steamboat plying the rivers between Nashville and New Orleans.

Bate served in the Mexican War, becoming a lieutenant in the Third Tennessee Infantry Regiment. Upon returning to Tennessee, he edited a newspaper in Gallatin and served one term in the state legislature. After studying law at what is now Cumberland University, he established a practice in Nashville.

In 1854 Bate was elected attorney general of a district around Nashville. He was an ardent Democrat and in the late 1850s became a strong proponent of Southern rights. In 1860 he served as a Tennessee presidential elector for John C. Breckinridge, the Southern Democrats' presidential candidate.

In the spring of 1861 Bate—a staunch secessionist—played the key role in organizing the Walker Legion, a unit that evolved into the Second Tennessee Infantry Regiment. Bate joined the unit as a private, but he was soon elected captain of Company I and then colonel of the regiment. Mustered into Confederate service at Lynchburg, Virginia, the regiment spent an uneventful year there. Upon its reorganization in early 1862, it was transferred to the West to join what eventually became the Army of Tennessee.

At Shiloh on April 6, 1862, soon after he entered the battle, Bate was badly wounded in his left leg. The bullet broke two bones, and surgeons wanted to amputate the limb. Bate, however, held off the doctors with a pistol and had himself conveyed to a relative's home in Huntsville, Alabama, where he waited for the wound to heal.

Bate's wound kept him away from the army for ten months. His conduct at Shiloh, however, had won wide praise, and he was promoted to brigadier general on October 3, 1862. During his convalescence, he held minor administrative commands in northern Alabama and southeastern Tennessee. In February 1863 he returned to the Army of Tennessee where he was assigned to command a Tennessee-Alabama-Georgia brigade in the division of Maj. Gen. Alexander P. Stewart.

At Chickamauga, Bate, who still had to use crutches, had three horses shot from under him as he directed the Confederate attack. When the army was reorganized after Chickamauga, Bate's brigade was transferred to the division of Maj. Gen. John C. Breckinridge. Breckinridge soon took command of a corps, and Bate as the senior officer assumed command of the division.

Bate was one of the few Southern generals to give a creditable performance at Missionary Ridge in late November 1863. He and his men did not retreat from the battleground until advancing Federals chased off the units on both sides of his position and threatened to envelop the division.

Bate's army record in 1863 won widespread acclaim from both military figures and the Tennessee congressional delegation. On March 5, 1864, while the army was in its winter quarters at Dalton, Georgia, Bate was promoted to major general, to date from February 23. He was assigned to command a division in Lt. Gen. William J. Hardee's corps.

Bate turned in a mixed performance in the Atlanta campaign of 1864. On May 28, near New Hope Church, he did not keep tight control over his division. As a result, some of his officers, mistaking the sound of skirmishing for the signal to attack, threw their troops into an unsuccessful assault on a very strong enemy position. The Confederates lost some seven hundred men in the attack. At both Peachtree Creek (July 20) and Atlanta (July 22) Bate was hampered by difficult terrain and changing, sometimes unclear orders. As a result, he accomplished little in either battle. In early August, on the other hand, he caught the Northerners in a clever ambush southwest of Atlanta and inflicted several hundred casualties. In this affair, however, he was again wounded and spent six weeks recovering.

In the fall Bate returned to command his division in the Franklin and Nashville campaign. His men were engaged at Franklin on November 30 and at Murfreesboro on December 7. At Nashville on December 16 Bate's overextended division was posted to hold a poorly selected and incompetently fortified area on the Confederate left, which is now called Shy's Hill. The effort was hopeless, and a massive Federal assault overran the Southern position. The survivors from Bate's command joined the rest of the army in a mad flight southward.

> **In early August . . . he caught the Northerners in a clever ambush southwest of Atlanta and inflicted several hundred casualties.**

The Confederates finally got south of the Tennessee River where they were safe from pursuit and made their way to Tupelo, Mississippi. From there, part of the army was sent to join the Confederates in North Carolina, where Bate commanded a small corps in some of the closing operations of the war. At the time of the army's surrender, he was back in command of his division. After the surrender, he was paroled at Greensboro, North Carolina, on April 28, 1865.

Returning to Tennessee, Bate resumed the practice of law, worked to end Reconstruction in the state, and reentered Democratic politics. He served as a presidential elector in 1876 and was elected governor in 1882 and 1884. In 1886 he was named to the U.S. Senate where he served until his death on March 9, 1905. While in the Senate, he sponsored an 1893 bill that, in effect, repealed Reconstruction by ending Federal supervision of elections in the Southern states. Bate is buried in Nashville's Mount Olivet Cemetery.

BIBLIOGRAPHY

Hewitt, Laurence J. "William Brimage Bate." In *The Confederate General*. Edited by William C. Davis. Vol. 1. Harrisburg, Pa., 1991.
Kelly, Dennis. "Back in the Saddle: The War Record of William Bate." *Civil War Times Illustrated* 27, no. 8 (1988): 26–33.
Marshall, Park. *William B. Bate*. Nashville, Tenn., 1908.

RICHARD M. MCMURRY

BATON ROUGE, LOUISIANA

Located on the Mississippi River, Baton Rouge was the capital of Louisiana from 1850 to April 25, 1862, when Confederate authorities abandoned it a week before Union forces occupied New Orleans, eighty miles away. An unsuccessful Confederate attempt to recapture the town resulted in a battle against Union occupying forces on August 5, 1862. Briefly evacuated by the Federal army, Baton Rouge was reoccupied on December 17, 1862, and remained under Union control for the duration of the war.

In 1860 Baton Rouge had a population of 5,429, of whom 1,247 were slaves. In the presidential election that year, the town's voters cast 379 ballots for the Constitutional Union candidate, John Bell; 274 for the slavery expansionist, John C. Breckinridge; and 98 for the national Democrat, Stephen A. Douglas. Baton Rouge's livelihood was based on retail outlets serving the surrounding farms and plantations. Because these stores were supplied by riverboats, the economy could thrive only if peace prevailed and river traffic was undisturbed. With these economic facts in mind, a majority of Baton Rouge voters understandably supported the more moderate Bell and Douglas rather than the extremist Breckinridge.

As elsewhere in the Deep South, however, secessionists seized the initiative in Louisiana after Abraham Lincoln's election. On January 10, 1861 (sixteen days before Louisiana seceded from the Union), state military forces obtained the surrender of the Federal arsenal in Baton Rouge without firing a shot. In the euphoria that followed formation of the Confederacy, several units of troops were raised in the Baton Rouge area, of which the Fencibles, Delta

Rifles and Chasseurs à Pied were among the earliest and more prominent. After Louisiana joined the Confederacy, most residents of the community supported the Southern cause—at least during the single year in which they were free to do so.

On May 9, 1862, Union naval forces arrived in Baton Rouge from New Orleans and received the town's surrender without resistance. On May 28, Confederate guerrillas fired on Union sailors attempting to come ashore at Baton Rouge. Adm. David Farragut in retaliation ordered that the town be shelled, which caused considerable destruction and civilian distress. On the next day, 2,600 Union infantry arrived in Baton Rouge under the command of Brig. Gen. Thomas Williams. General Williams soon left for the vicinity of Vicksburg, Mississippi, to assist in the futile assault on that Confederate stronghold. When he returned to Baton Rouge in late July, his men were sick and physically exhausted from digging a useless canal aimed at diverting the Mississippi River around Vicksburg, which did not surrender until a year later.

In the meantime, Maj. Gen. Earl Van Dorn, the Confederate district commander, had decided to retake Baton Rouge. With the town restored to Confederate control, Van Dorn believed he could break the Union blockade of the mouth of the Red River and perhaps recapture New Orleans. Van Dorn ordered John C. Breckinridge, now a major general, to proceed by rail from Vicksburg with 5,000 men to Camp Moore, seventy miles northeast of Baton Rouge. There he would secure another thousand troops for the attack on Baton Rouge. But sickness and exhaustion from the intense summer heat had reduced the number of Breckinridge's men to about 3,400 by the time he left Camp Moore.

Breckinridge arrived at the Comite River, ten miles east of Baton Rouge, on August 4. Disease, hunger, and exhaustion had further reduced his units to only 2,600 men. Breckinridge divided his weakened force into two divisions, which commenced their attack at sunrise on August 5. On the right was Brig. Gen. Charles Clark's First Division, consisting of eight regiments, plus supporting artillery. On the left, the Second Division of Brig. Gen. Daniel Ruggles comprised six regiments, a battalion, and supporting artillery. On the Union side, General Williams commanded seven regiments.

Success of the Confederate attack would depend on the timely arrival of the ram *Arkansas* from Vicksburg. The mission of this heavily armed Confederate vessel was to sink or damage Union gunboats anchored in the river so that they could not fire over the heads of the Union garrison into Breckinridge's advancing columns. But *Arkansas* developed engine trouble just north of Baton Rouge and was abandoned and destroyed by its crew. Consequently, Union gunboat fire raked the Confederate units with devastating effect. Breckinridge called off his attack and withdrew to Port Hudson. Confederate losses were 467 killed, wounded or missing; Union casualties were 383 killed (including General Williams), wounded, or missing.

Federal forces left Baton Rouge on August 21 for New Orleans. But on December 17, Brig. Gen. Cuvier Grover returned with 8,000 Union troops, and Baton Rouge remained in Federal hands for the remainder of the war. It served as a staging base for Union operations against Port Hudson and Confederate-held northern Louisiana.

Baton Rouge accepted the reality of Federal occupation, and most citizens adjusted calmly to the presence of many blue uniforms. (The town had been predominantly Unionist in sentiment on the eve of secession.) Quite probably, saloon keepers, hotel owners, and restauranteurs pocketed many Yankee dollars providing the creature comforts of the Federal garrison. On the other hand, Baton Rouge became the destination of a large black migration from plantations in the vicinity, creating immense problems in housing, employment and sanitation. The Gothic statehouse burned during the occupation, and the war damage remained evident for years. The town did not become the state capital again until 1882.

BIBLIOGRAPHY

Carleton, Mark T. *River Capital: An Illustrated History of Baton Rouge.* Woodland Hills, Calif., 1981.
Moneyhon, Carl, and Bobby Roberts. *Portraits of Conflict: A Photographic History of Louisiana in the Civil War.* Fayetteville, Ark., 1990.
Winters, John. *Louisiana in the Civil War.* Baton Rouge, La., 1963.

MARK T. CARLETON

BATTLE, CULLEN ANDREWS

BATTLE, CULLEN ANDREWS (1829–1905), brigadier general. Battle, born June 1, 1829, was a native of Georgia, but moved with his family to Alabama in 1836. He graduated from the University of Alabama in 1850 and earned a name for himself as a lawyer and a political orator of stridently secessionist bent. Battle's only prewar military experience was as captain of a volunteer company raised during the John Brown affair. Two years later Captain Battle led the company into Confederate service as part of the Third Alabama Infantry. At the organization of the regiment, Battle won election as its major, and in July 1861 he was promoted to lieutenant colonel.

In the regiment's first battle, Seven Pines, its colonel was killed and Battle assumed command. He acted as colonel through the rest of 1862 and was wounded at the head of the regiment at both South Mountain and Sharpsburg, but his formal commission as colonel was not confirmed until March 26, 1863. Well before that date, Alabama politicians were pushing for Battle's promotion to brigadier general. As part of Rodes's Brigade, Battle led the Third at Chancellorsville, where he suffered two painful falls from horseback, and at Gettysburg. Battle was only Rodes's fourth choice as his replacement when promoted, but the Alabamian received his general's wreath August 20, 1863.

Despite two extended absences on sick leave, Battle commanded his brigade competently until a serious wound at Cedar Creek ended his war experience in October 1864. After the war Battle edited a newspaper in North Carolina. He died in Greensboro on April 8, 1905.

BIBLIOGRAPHY

Brewer, Willis. *Alabama.* Montgomery, Ala., 1872. Reprint, Tuscaloosa, Ala., 1964.
Freeman, Douglas S. *Lee's Lieutenants: A Study in Command.* 3 vols. New York, 1942–1944. Reprint, New York, 1986.
Hawthorne, J. B. *Cullen Andrews Battle.* N.p., 1905?

ROBERT K. KRICK

BATTLES, NAMING OF

Confederates and Federals sometimes differed in their designations of a particular engagement. D. H. Hill, lieutenant general, C.S.A., afterward wrote:

So many battle-fields of the Civil War bear double names, that we cannot believe the duplication has been accidental. It is the unusual which impresses. The troops of the North came mainly from cities, towns, and villages, and were, therefore, impressed by some natural object near the scene of the conflict and named the battle from it. The soldiers from the South were chiefly from the country and were, therefore, impressed by some artificial object near the field of action. In one section the naming has been after the handiwork of God; in the other section it has been after the handiwork of man.

Whether or not Hill's explanation is correct, his observation itself is borne out by a number of examples. Confederates named battles after such man-made objects as towns or settlements (Manassas, Leesburg, Boonsboro, Sharpsburg, Perryville, Murfreesboro) and buildings (Elkhorn Tavern, Gaines' Mill, Shiloh Church). Federals used the names of watercourses (Bull Run, the Chickahominy, Antietam Creek, Stones River) and other natural features (Ball's Bluff, Pea Ridge, Pittsburg Landing, South Mountain, Chaplin Hills).

But this distinction did not always hold, nor was the same pattern consistently followed. Although some Federals used the term "Pittsburg Landing," others, including Ulysses S. Grant, called the battle "Shiloh," as Confederates did. Originally Union officers reported one engagement as "Chaplin Hills," but eventually the designation "Perryville" came to be standard North as well as South. Both Confederates and Federals referred to artificial rather than natural objects in the case of "Mansfield" and "Sabine Cross Roads." And the pattern was reversed when the Confederates were impressed by a natural feature, "Ox Hill," and the Federals by a man-made structure, a residence known as "Chantilly."

In quite a few instances multiple names were used indiscriminately by both sides. An extreme example is the June 30, 1862, clash in Virginia that bore the names of a great variety of objects, all of them manmade (Glendale, White Oak Swamp Bridge, Frazier's or Frayser's Farm, Nelson's Farm, Charles City Cross Roads, New Market Road, Willis Church). Still other battles always and everywhere were known by but a single name (Gettysburg, for example).

Battles with Dual Names

Date of Battle	confederate Name	Federal NAME
July 21, 1861	First Manassas	Bull Run
Aug. 10, 1861	Oak Hills	Wilson's Creek
Oct. 21, 1861	Leesburg	Ball's Bluff
Jan. 19, 1862	Mill Springs	Logan's Cross Roads
Mar. 7-8, 1862	Elkhorn Tavern	Pea Ridge
Apr. 6-7, 1862	Shiloh	Pittsburg Landing
June 27, 1862	Gaines' Mill	Chickahominy
Aug. 29-30, 1862	Second Manassas	Second Bull Run
Sept. 1, 1862	Ox Hill	Chantilly
Sept. 14, 1862	Boonsboro	South Mountain
Sept. 17, 1862	Sharpsburg	Antietam
Oct. 8, 1862	Perryville	Chaplin Hills
Dec. 31, 1862– Jan. 2, 1863	Murfreesboro	Stones River
Apr. 1864	Mansfield	Sabine Cross Roads
Sept. 19, 1864	Winchester	Opequon Creek

BIBLIOGRAPHY

Boatner, Mark M., III. *The Civil War Dictionary.* New York, 1959.
Davis, Burke. *Our Incredible Civil War.* New York, 1960.

RICHARD N. CURRENT

BAYLOR, JOHN R.

BAYLOR, JOHN R. (1822–1894), colonel, territorial governor of Arizona, and congressman from Texas. John Robert

Baylor was born at Paris, Kentucky, July 27, 1822. As a child, Baylor moved with his father to Fort Gibson in the Indian Territory. Sent to Cincinnati for an education, he left school to live with an uncle near Rocky Creek, Texas.

A man of vigor and magnetism, he was elected to the Texas legislature and in 1855 was appointed agent to the Comanches on the Clear Fork of the Brazos. Baylor, however, came to possess a burning hatred of the Comanches and was dismissed. While helping to edit an anti-Indian newspaper, *The White Man,* in Weatherford, Baylor led 350 frontiersmen who forced the expulsion of the Indians from Texas in 1859.

With the coming of the Civil War, Baylor was selected as a lieutenant colonel in the Second Texas Mounted Rifles and given the responsibility of garrisoning the forts along the Lower Military Road from San Antonio to Franklin (El Paso). In July 1861, with less than four hundred men, Baylor invaded the Mesilla Valley from his base at Fort Bliss, Texas. After occupying the town of Mesilla, he forced the evacuation of Fort Fillmore and the surrender of six companies of the Seventh Infantry and two of Mounted Rifles at San Agustin Pass in the Organ Mountains. After creating the Confederate Territory of Arizona and appointing himself governor, Baylor issued a controversial order for the extermination of a band of Apaches near Pinos Altos. Referring to the order as an "infamous crime," President Jefferson Davis revoked Baylor's commission in the Confederate army. After the New Mexico campaign and a feud with Brig. Gen. Henry Hopkins Sibley, Baylor fought as a private at the Battle of Galveston and was elected to the Second Confederate Congress. In Richmond, he served on the Patents and Indian Affairs committees and supported a number of war measures but was opposed to martial law.

Baylor, who was active in politics after the war, died at Montell, Texas, on February 6, 1894.

BIBLIOGRAPHY

Baylor, George W. *John Robert Baylor.* Tucson, Ariz., 1966.
Finch, L. Boyd. "Arizona's Governors without Portfolio: A Wonderfully Diverse Lot." *Arizona Historical Quarterly* 26 (Spring 1985): 81–87.
Hall, Martin H. "Planter vs. Frontiersman." In *Essays on the American Civil War.* Edited by William F. Holmes and Harold M. Hollingsworth. Austin, Tex., 1968.
Thompson, Jerry. *John Robert Baylor: Texas Indian Fighter and Confederate Soldier.* Hillsboro, Tex., 1971.

JERRY THOMPSON

BEALE, RICHARD LEE TURBERVILLE

BEALE, RICHARD LEE TURBERVILLE (1819–1893), U.S. congressman and brigadier general. Beale, the descendant of seventeenth-century Virginia settlers, was born at Hickory Hill, Westmoreland County, May 22, 1819. He was educated at Dickinson College and the University of Virginia. He was admitted to the bar in 1839 and practiced law near his birthplace. Beale was a member of Congress from 1847 to 1849, a delegate to the state constitutional convention in 1851, and a state senator from 1858 to 1860.

In May 1861 Beale was mustered into Confederate service as a first lieutenant of "Lee's Legion" or "Lee's Light Horse." The legion was ordered to the aid of P. G. T. Beauregard on July 21, but arrived a day after the Battle of First Manassas. Beale was promoted to captain in July 1861 and to major in October. When the legion was merged with the Ninth Cavalry in the spring of 1862, he was appointed lieutenant colonel under William Henry Fitzhugh Lee. On the

> Dissatisfaction over details made concerning his regiment without his permission led Beale to submit his resignation three times. . . .

promotion of Lee to brigadier, Beale was appointed colonel of the regiment.

In December 1862, Beale led a bold expedition into Rappahannock County, capturing a Federal garrison without a single loss. Later Beale was cited by J. E. B. Stuart for repelling a threatened raid by Stoneman's cavalry.

Dissatisfaction over details made concerning his regiment without his permission led Beale to submit his resignation three times, on November 22, 1862, February 8, 1863, and August 25, 1863. In his third effort, Beale asserted he was "devoted as ever to Southern Independence" and asked to be allowed to raise a company of rangers or enlist as a private. His resignation was not accepted.

Beale played a prominent role in crushing Dahlgren's raid in January 1864 and assumed command of the brigade in August following the death of John Randolph Chambliss, Jr. Beale was recommended for brigadier by W. H. F. Lee in October. Wade Hampton and Robert E. Lee endorsed the recommendation, which was misplaced in the office of the adjutant general because an inordinate number of clerks had just been drafted for service in the field. The appointment was made on February 6, 1865.

Following the surrender Beale was paroled at Ashland, April 27, 1865. He resumed his legal practice and served a term in Congress from 1879 to 1881. He died on April 21, 1893, and was buried at Hickory Hill.

BIBLIOGRAPHY

Compiled Military Service Records. Richard L. T. Beale. Microcopy M331, Roll 19. Record Group 109. National Archives, Washington, D.C.

Hotchkiss, Jed. *Virginia*. Vol. 3 of *Confederate Military History*. Edited by Clement A. Evans. Atlanta, 1899. Vol. 4 of extended ed. Wilmington, N.C., 1987.

Warner, Ezra J. *Generals in Gray: Lives of the Confederate Commanders*. Baton Rouge, La., 1959.

LOWELL REIDENBAUGH

BEALL, JOHN Y.

BEALL, JOHN Y. (1835–1865), privateer and special agent. Beall was born January 1, 1835. His family, which pronounced the name "Bell," lived in Jefferson County, Virginia (present-day West Virginia). Beall attended the University of Virginia (1852–1853). Widely regarded as a young man of great promise, he had many friends and relatives prominent in the Confederate government.

His first military service was with a company formed in Jefferson at the time of the John Brown raid, called the Botts Grays. This unit became part of the Second Virginia Regiment, Stonewall Brigade. Beall, with Turner Ashby's cavalry at Harpers Ferry on October 16, 1861, was severely wounded, which forced an end to his regular service.

In February 1863 Beall was appointed acting master in the Confederate volunteer navy and was known forever afterward as "Captain Beall." From April to November 1863, Beall, assisted by a number of his neighbors, conducted active partisan warfare—privateering—on the Chesapeake Bay. On November 14, 1863, Beall was captured and subsequently imprisoned at Fort McHenry. He was exchanged in March 1864.

In September 1864 Beall was involved in operations aimed at freeing the Confederate officers imprisoned on Johnson's Island in Lake Erie. He led a party of twenty in the capture of the steamers *Philo Parsons* and *Island Queen*. But needing still more hardware to attack the formidable guard-ship USS *Michigan,* the Confederates arranged to purchase a lake ship, *Georgian,* and ordered cannon made for it at Guelph, Ontario. Believing incorrectly that Beall was managing this enterprise, U.S. officials pressed the Canadians to arrest him. The Canadians apprehended the wrong man and Beall escaped.

Late in 1864 Beall was part of a group that tried to intercept and release seven imprisoned Confederate general officers being moved from Johnson's Island to Fort Lafayette in New York. On December 16, near Suspension Bridge, New York, Beall and one young companion were captured. Beall tried to conceal who he was, but the companion testified against him, and Beall was tried and convicted as a guerrilla and spy.

Beall was hanged at Governor's Island, New York, on February 24, 1865. After Abraham Lincoln's assassination, there was some allegation that John Wilkes Booth, a friend of Beall's, had been motivated to kill the president in retaliation for not preventing Beall's hanging. Lost Cause devotees later lionized Beall as a heroic martyr.

BIBLIOGRAPHY

Markens, Isaac. "Defense of John Yates Beall."*Confederate Veteran* 35 (1928): 59–62. Reprint, Wilmington, N.C., 1985.

McNeilly, Rev. James H. "John Yates Beall: Account of his Thrilling Career for the South." *Confederate Veteran* 7 (1900): 66–69. Reprint, Wilmington, N.C., 1985.

Tidwell, William A., with James O. Hall and David Winfred Gaddy.*Come Retribution: The Confederate Secret Service and the Assassination of Lincoln.* Jackson, Miss., 1988.

U.S. War Department. *War of the Rebellion: Official Records of the Union and Confederate Navies.* Washington, D.C., 1894–1927. Ser. 1, vol. 3, p. 716; ser. 1, vol. 9, pp. 305–307, 318.

"Why Booth Killed President Lincoln." *Confederate Veteran* 9 (1902): 3–4. Reprint, Wilmington, N.C., 1985.

HERMAN HATTAWAY

BEAUREGARD, P.G.T.

BEAUREGARD, P. G. T. (1818–1893), general. Destined for a military career marked by controversy and conflict with superiors and colleagues, Pierre Gustave Toutant Beauregard was born at Contreras Plantation in St. Bernard Parish, Louisiana, just south of New Orleans, on May 28, 1818. Much has been made of his French creole origins, leading some to ascribe his later difficulties to aristocratic haughtiness derived from a fiery Gallic inheritance, but such theorizing stems largely from romantic notions of creole society. One of only eight full generals in the Confederate forces, he would see action in almost every theater of the Civil War, from the firing on Fort Sumter to a final surrender in the Carolinas during the last days of the conflict.

Beauregard entered West Point at the age of sixteen after several years at the French School in New York City, already a committed disciple of Napoléon Bonaparte and the military theorist Henri de Jomini. Immersion in this new Anglo-Saxon milieu led to his abandonment of the hyphen from the

P.G.T. BEAUREGARD.

Toutant-Beauregard family name, prelude to his eventual discarding of "Pierre" for his favored "G. T. Beauregard." Graduating second in the academy's class of 1838, he received a lieutenant's commission in the Corps of Engineers and quickly distinguished himself in building and repairing coastal fortifications at Pensacola, Florida, and near the mouth of the Mississippi in his native state.

Assigned to Winfield Scott's command at the outbreak of the Mexican War, he won that crusty soldier's praise for skillful reconnaissance missions in the campaign from Tampico to Mexico City, particularly impressing the general with the precision and acuity of his recommendations as to the best line of march against the enemy capital. Despite a brevet as major for bravery in the attack on Chapultepec, Beauregard came away from the war embittered against Scott, resentful that his contributions to victory had not won official commendation greater than that accorded fellow officers like Robert E. Lee and George B. McClellan. A comparable conceit as to his talents and accomplishments would continue to plague his relationships in the years ahead, and his scathing criticism of what he saw as the weaknesses in Scott's generalship revealed what would be an abiding tendency to accept conventional abstract theory rather than imaginative pragmatic execution as the measure of military performance.

From 1848 to 1860 Beauregard served as engineering officer in charge of "the Mississippi and Lake defences in Louisiana," and after 1853 as superintendent responsible for building the Federal Custom House at New Orleans, establishing in both assignments a reputation for superior engineering skills. After an unsuccessful try for the mayoralty of New Orleans in 1858, he enlisted the aid of Senator John Slidell, husband of his wife's sister, to win appointment in 1860 as superintendent of West Point. But his clear secessionist sympathies led to dismissal from the post on January 28, 1861, a mere five days after his installation.

Beauregard resigned his Federal commission effective February 20, 1861, and returned to Louisiana in expectation that he would be made commander of the state's now independent military forces, an appointment that went instead to Braxton Bragg. In resentful pride, he refused any other commission in the state army, enlisting perversely as a private in the Orleans Guards. That unit saw little of him, for Slidell and other influential political leaders had already pressed his claim with Jefferson Davis for appointment in the Confederate army. Convinced that the Louisianan's vaunted gunnery expertise made him particularly suited to the task, Davis commissioned him as brigadier general on February 27, 1861, with command of the Confederate and South Carolina forces aligned against the Federal garrison at Fort Sumter in Charleston Harbor.

Assuming his post on March 6, Beauregard quickly rearranged gun implacements on the Charleston Battery and the islands to its left and right to mount a circle of fire around

Fort Sumter in the center, confident that this concentration would keep at bay any Federal vessels attempting to reinforce the fortification and also allow for its destruction should that become necessary. His efforts proved highly effective. When negotiations with U.S. Maj. Robert Anderson, commander of the Federal garrison, failed to secure Union withdrawal from the island stronghold, Beauregard opened fire on Sumter during the early morning hours of April 12, and the fateful years of civil war had begun.

The events at Charleston made Beauregard an immediate Confederate hero, hailed as "Old Bory" and praised as one of the world's great soldiers. President Davis, the Confederate Congress, newspapers across the South, and smitten female admirers showered him with gratitude, while an equally responsive Northern editor placed a price on his head. If all this tended to reinforce an already prickly self-esteem, for the moment at least he gave no time to reveling in applause, but set about buttressing the defenses of Charleston by shifting the target of his batteries from Sumter to the harbor entrance.

Early in May 1861, he testily rejected a suggestion by Davis that he go to Pensacola to take Fort Pickens, thus crossing swords with his superiors for the first but not the last time. However much he might have offended the president, it did not keep Davis from appointing him in mid-May to command of the defenses of the Mississippi from Vicksburg to the Kentucky-Tennessee border. But by May 28 things looked dramatically different. Now the Confederate capital had been shifted to Virginia and new orders sped him on to Richmond.

Federal troops had crossed the Potomac to occupy Alexandria, pointing clearly to an impending attack upon the Confederate railroad junction at Manassas just north of the capital, and it was here that Davis and Robert E. Lee, his personal military adviser, wished Beauregard to take command. He did so on June 3, launching a dizzying round of activity centering on earthworks around Manassas, troop reorganization, and grandiose plans for a full-scale campaign into enemy territory across the Potomac, tactfully but resolutely rejected by his Richmond superiors. With a Federal attack obviously imminent, Davis and Lee ordered Gen. Joseph E. Johnston to move his army from the Shenandoah Valley to reinforce Beauregard. As the senior officer, Johnston had right of command of the joined forces, but recognizing Beauregard's longer presence on the scene and better knowledge of the terrain, he allowed his colleague to retain that prerogative, a courtesy Beauregard eventually repaid by asking Johnston to leave the field when actual fighting began.

Luckily for the Southern cause, Gen. Irvin McDowell's attack upon the Confederate positions just north of Manassas at Bull Run on July 21 preempted Beauregard's battle plan. As presented to a dismayed Johnston, that blueprint reflected many of the weaknesses of Beauregard's generalship. It abounded in a bewildering confusion of orders and lines of authority and gave little attention to possible responses of the adversary. Its implementation might well have spelled disaster for the Southern forces. But despite indescribable disarray and inefficiency in his headquarters, once the fighting began Beauregard revealed his essential strength as a commander, what historian Frank Vandiver has called a "soldier's greatest asset—battle sense." Skillfully countering McDowell's moves, he sent the Federal force reeling back toward Washington.

A grateful President Davis raised him to full generalship on the morning after the battle, confirmed when Congress dated his commission fifth in seniority behind only Adj. Gen.

> . . . he seemed indeed to be what one Richmond editor dubbed him, "Beauregard Felix," favorite of the gods.

Samuel Cooper, Albert Sidney Johnston, Robert E. Lee and Joe Johnston. Once again he heard his praises sung in all quarters of the South, and for a brief moment he seemed indeed to be what one Richmond editor dubbed him, "Beauregard Felix," favorite of the gods. Mindful of the troubles experienced in distinguishing friend from foe during the fighting at Manassas because of the similarity between the Confederate and Union standards, he added to his honors by designing the famous Southern battle flag, replacing the Stars and Bars.

His universal acclaim proved short-lived. To an old feud with Commissary Gen. Lucius B. Northrop over supposed lack of supplies to his troops, he now added a blustery dispute with Secretary of War Judah P. Benjamin for what he perceived as meddling interference with his command prerogatives. Davis attempted to calm these imbroglios but began to grow more impatient with Beauregard when it became clear that his complaints to opposition members of Congress fed increasing attacks upon administration policy. Disaffection increased with reports that the general had wide backing to contest for the permanent presidency in the coming elections ending the provisional status of the government.

But it was Beauregard's report to Congress on the Battle of Manassas that caused the greatest uproar. Although denying opposition claims that Davis had prevented pursuit of retreating Federal troops, the general implied that the taking of Washington had been nonetheless sacrificed by Davis's rejection of his original invasion plan and by the president's slowness in ordering Johnston's army to join forces with his own. Furious, Davis shot back that no such strategy had ever been presented to him and charged Beauregard with

attempting to exalt himself at his superior's expense. Unrepentant, Beauregard countered with a letter to the *Richmond Whig* in which he obliquely chastised Davis anew. His persistence struck many as sheer contumacy, and the heading of his communication—"Centreville, Va., Within hearing of the Enemy's Guns"—made him seem vainglorious and ridiculously pompous.

Whether on the initiative of his congressional friends or at the instigation of the president, late in January 1862, Beauregard was ordered west as second in command to Albert Sidney Johnston. As Johnston's position crumbled along the Tennessee-Kentucky border, he rejected Beauregard's pleas to mount a concentration of all available troops in defense of Fort Donelson against Ulysses S. Grant's certain attack, sending him instead to supervise the withdrawal of Gen. Leonidas Polk's army from Columbus, Kentucky.

Falling back all along their lines, Johnston and Beauregard gathered a force of some 35,000 men at Corinth, Mississippi. From there they moved on April 3 to attack Grant's army in camp at Pittsburg Landing on the west bank of the Tennessee River near a small church called Shiloh. Delay in the deployment of troops and careless noise in the undisciplined ranks convinced Beauregard that the element of surprise critical to his battle plan was now lost, and he urged postponement of the attack. Johnston demurred, and on April 6 the Confederates struck. From his position in the rear of the Confederate troops, Beauregard exercised more general command of the field than did Johnston, who threw himself into the thick of the fray like a corps leader until he fell fatally wounded. With Johnston's death Beauregard assumed full command and at day's end had almost forced Grant's army into the river. But the desperate weariness of his men led him to call a halt, and by next morning Don Carlos Buell's army had arrived to give Grant reinforcement sufficient to push back the exhausted Confederate foe.

Failure to clinch victory when it seemed in his grasp exposed Beauregard to renewed criticism by his enemies and even by one of his subordinates, Braxton Bragg. His own attempts to portray Shiloh as a misrepresented success only further diminished his reputation, an erosion heightened when Gen. Henry Halleck drove him from Corinth south to Tupelo. There, suffering from a chronic throat ailment from which he hoped to seek relief in Mobile, he turned temporary leadership of the Army of the West over to Bragg without authorization from Richmond, giving Davis the pleasure of ordering his immediate dismissal from command.

Determined to keep Beauregard out of the field, Davis next assigned him to head the Department of South Carolina and Georgia, headquartered at Charleston, where he arrived on September 15, 1862. Still convinced that the best way to protect the city lay in concentrating such firepower on the entrance to the harbor that Federal naval vessels would be unable to break through, he successfully hectored Richmond for increased matériel to strengthen his batteries and fortifications. In April 1863, he turned back a Union flotilla of nine ironclads and later that year withstood a siege by combined army and navy forces that inflicted heavy damage on Fort Sumter and surrounding island installations but failed to dislodge his hold on the city. In all, he had effectively managed what has been called "the war's longest and most skillful defense of a land point against attack from the sea."

During that extended standoff some additional opportunities had come his way. Lee wanted him to serve in northern Virginia while he led the campaign into Maryland and Pennsylvania, and Samuel Cooper invited him to aid Joe Johnston by guarding against Union incursions into Mississippi. But with his heart still set on an independent field command, Beauregard stubbornly rejected all such offers, until in April 1864, at Lee's instigation, he was given charge

> . . . he alone among the Confederate leaders anticipated Grant's move. . . .

of the Department of North Carolina and Southern Virginia, responsible for holding the southern approaches to Richmond.

The advance of the Army of the Potomac against Confederate forces in northern Virginia made Beauregard's mission vitally important, for loss of the Southern supply lines would spell almost certain collapse of Lee's attempts to hold the capital. When Union Gen. Benjamin Butler in early May moved troops up the James River to Drewry's Bluff, midway between Petersburg and Richmond, Beauregard managed to drive him back into a position bottled up between the James and Appomattox rivers, despite frequent interference from Davis and Bragg, now chief of staff. Again his critics charged that he had allowed an enemy force to escape destruction. His continuing reluctance to send reinforcements to Lee as Grant maneuvered to get his army between the Virginian and Richmond produced even more friction with his superiors.

Whatever his failings, he alone among the Confederate leaders anticipated Grant's move south of the James after the battle at Cold Harbor. While Lee for almost forty-eight hours remained ignorant of his opponent's whereabouts, Beauregard successfully blocked Grant's advance upon Petersburg until increasingly desperate communiqués convinced his skeptical colleague that it was indeed the full force of the Army of the Potomac pushing against his lines. Lee then moved quickly south and Petersburg was saved. It remains Beauregard's finest hour.

In the ensuing siege of Petersburg, he continued under Lee's direction, restive again in a subordinate position and frequently at odds with the high command. Bragg and Davis persisted in their long established animosity by charging him with various acts of malfeasance. He consequently welcomed assignment in October 1864 to head a new department called the Military Division of the West, with oversight of the armies of Gen. John Bell Hood in Georgia and Richard Taylor in Alabama.

Suggestive that the appointment represented primarily an attempt at political fence-mending by the administration, Davis severely limited Beauregard's authority in this new assignment, restricting him to basically advisory powers. Exploiting this opportunity, Hood won Beauregard's reluctant approval for a push into Tennessee but then proceeded to ignore the department commander in the campaign that led him to disaster at Nashville in December. Beauregard meanwhile proved incapable of divining William Tecumseh Sherman's objectives in his march east from Atlanta, failing to concentrate Confederate forces as the Federal juggernaut moved inexorably toward the sea. With his command widened to the Atlantic coast, he attempted to hold a line from Augusta to Charleston, where he expected the main Federal attack. But again Sherman confounded him, striking instead at Columbia in February 1865 and driving Beauregard's forces back into North Carolina before he could unite with those of Gen. William J. Hardee as they evacuated a now indefensible Charleston.

On the advice of Lee, a dismayed Davis dispatched Joe Johnston to take over Beauregard's command, leaving the Louisianan to direct rear-area troop movements and protect lines of communication. Apparently resigned to the war's inevitable conclusion, he declined appointment to small field commands in western Virginia and eastern Tennessee, preferring to remain under Johnston. When a gloomy April 13 conference with President Davis and Secretary of War John C. Breckinridge in Greensboro confirmed Lee's capitulation to Grant, Johnston surrendered his army to Sherman near Hillsboro, North Carolina, on April 26, 1865, and on May 1 Beauregard headed home to Louisiana.

Unlike most of his fellow Confederate generals, he found the postwar years generally prosperous and rewarding. Occasional moments of dejection in the Reconstruction period led to flirtation with various possibilities of foreign military service in Brazil, Romania, Egypt, Spain, and Argentina, none of which materialized, turning him to his old engineering skills. Appointed superintendent of the New Orleans, Jackson, and Great Northern Railroad late in 1865, he also served as president of the New Orleans and Carrollton street railway from 1866 until he was ousted as part owner of the company a decade later. Recovery from that setback came the next year, when he and Jubal Early began a long stint as supervisors of the drawings of the infamous Louisiana Lottery for reportedly handsome salaries. Some restoration of military status came with his appointment in 1879 as adjutant general and commander of the Louisiana militia, a position he held until 1888, when he was elected commissioner of public works for New Orleans.

Inevitably, passage of the years caught him up in a series of literary clashes with Joe Johnston over events at Manassas, with various promoters of Albert Sidney Johnston as the true hero of Shiloh, and with his old nemesis Jefferson Davis over just about everything, in a flurry of conflicting reminiscences. His chief contributions to the fray appeared in *The Military Operations of General Beauregard,* attributed to a friend, Alfred Roman, but essentially his own creation, and a *Century* magazine article, "The Battle of Bull Run," later expanded into *A Commentary on the Campaign and Battle of Manassas.*

After a brief illness he died in New Orleans on February 21, 1893. He was interred in that city's tomb of the Army of Tennessee in Metairie Cemetery, dominated, ironically, by the equestrian statue of Albert Sidney Johnston.

BIBLIOGRAPHY

Basso, Hamilton. *Beauregard, The Great Creole.* New York, 1933.
Beauregard, P. G. T. "The First Battle of Bull Run." *Century Illustrated Monthly Magazine* 19 (1884): 80–106.
Freeman, Douglas S. *Lee's Lieutenants: A Study in Command.* 3 vols. New York, 1942–1944. Reprint, New York, 1986.
Horn, Stanley F. *The Army of Tennessee.* Indianapolis, 1941.
Roman, Alfred. *The Military Operations of General Beauregard.* 2 vols. New York, 1884.
Vandiver, Frank E. *Their Tattered Flags: The Epic of the Confederacy.* New York, 1970. Reprint, Texas A & M University Military History Series, no. 5. College Station, Tex., 1987.
Williams, T. Harry. *P. G. T. Beauregard: Napoleon in Gray.* Baton Rouge, La., 1954.

JOSEPH G. TREGLE, JR.

BEAUVOIR

Developed in the late 1840s and early 1850s by Mississippi planter James Brown, this waterfront estate near Biloxi, Mississippi, was home to Jefferson Davis during the final twelve years of his life. The Beauvoir estate was dominated by a raised, single-story Greek Revival cottage and flanking pavilions. Having escaped the ravages of war, the property was purchased in 1873 by Davis family acquaintance and author Sarah Anne Ellis Dorsey, who gave her new home its French name because of the "beautiful view" of the Gulf of Mexico.

Responding to an offer from Mrs. Dorsey, Jefferson Davis decided to write at Beauvoir rather than develop and occupy his own property in the area. By February 1877, Davis was at work on *The Rise and Fall of the Confederate Government* in the east, or library, pavilion. He was assisted by personal

secretary William T. Walthall and Mrs. Dorsey. Upon her arrival in 1878, Varina Howell Davis replaced Mrs. Dorsey, whom she disliked. Despite Sarah Dorsey's intention to bequeath Beauvoir to Davis, he purchased the estate in 1879 for $5,500. The Davises, later joined by daughter Varina Anne ("Winnie"), entertained a variety of notables while residing at Beauvoir.

Following the deaths of Jefferson in 1889 and Winnie in 1898, Varina Davis sold the property for $10,000 to the Mississippi Division, United Sons of Confederate Veterans. The organization, in accordance with her wishes, leased the property to the state of Mississippi for a Confederate soldiers' home. The Jefferson Davis Memorial Home, from 1903 to 1957, provided shelter and care for about two thousand residents, including veterans and their wives, widows, and servants. Museum operations at the site were initiated in 1941 with the opening of the main house for tours. Today, the entire eighty-four-acre estate operates as a historic landmark.

BIBLIOGRAPHY

Davis, Varina. *Jefferson Davis, Ex-President of the Confederate States of America: A Memoir by His Wife, Varina Davis.* New York, 1890. Reprint ed. Introduction by Craig L. Symonds. Baltimore, 1990.
Strode, Hudson. *Jefferson Davis: Tragic Hero.* Vol. 3 of *Jefferson Davis.* New York, 1964.
Thompson, James W. *Beauvoir: A Walk through History.* Edited by Keith A. Hardison. Biloxi, Miss., 1988.

KEITH ANDERSON HARDISON

BEE, BARNARD E.

BEE, BARNARD E. (1824–1861), brigadier general. Though a South Carolinian by birth, Bee spent his formative years in Texas. He entered West Point in 1841, graduating four years later with a class standing of thirty-third. Bee served with distinction in the Mexican War and saw duty along the western frontier on the eve of the Civil War. He envisioned a terrible conflict if disunion became a reality. Not wishing to participate in such a struggle, he retired to his brother's ranch in Texas.

Bee's misgivings over secession disappeared when his native state pulled out of the Union. He resigned from the U.S. Army on March 3, 1861, before the firing on Fort Sumter. Bee began his Confederate service as a major, but on June 17, 1861, he received a brigadier-generalship and a brigade. At First Manassas on July 21, 1861, Bee tried to rally his troops as they retreated. He pointed to Thomas J. Jackson's stalwart brigade and exclaimed: "There stands Jackson like a

BARNARD E. BEE.

stone wall! Rally around the Virginians!" The sobriquet "Stonewall," which attached itself to Jackson and his Virginia brigade for the rest of the war, is still used. Bee fell with a mortal wound shortly after he uttered these famous words, and he died the next day. He was buried in Pendleton, South Carolina.

BIBLIOGRAPHY

Capers, Ellison. *South Carolina.* Vol. 5 of *Confederate Military History.* Edited by Clement A. Evans. Atlanta, 1899. Vol. 6 of extended ed. Wilmington, N.C., 1987.
Hennessy, John. "Stonewall Jackson's Nickname: Was It Fact or Was It Fiction?" *Civil War* 7 (March–April 1990): 10–17.

PETER S. CARMICHAEL

BEEFSTEAK RAID

During the dark early morning hours of September 14, 1864, Confederate cavalry Maj. Gen. Wade Hampton led 4,000 horsemen on a circuitous route toward Coggins Point, Virginia, just below the Union's general headquarters at City Point. The object was some 2,500 head of cattle to feed Robert E. Lee's war-weary and starving Army of Northern Virginia. The Beefsteak Raid, also known as the Hampton-Rosser Cattle Raid, was an overwhelming success with Confederates capturing the herd with few losses in manpower and much material gain.

On September 5, 1864, a Confederate cavalry scout named George D. Shadbourne had brought information of the herd kept by the Union army at Coggins Point, Virginia. Hampton promptly requested permission from General Lee to lead an expedition into Union lines to capture the cattle. With the Federal army daily tightening its hold on Lee's supply lines at Petersburg, the Army of Northern Virginia was suffering a severe lack of food. Lee consented, and Hampton quickly made plans for his surprise raid to commence on September 14.

By the morning of September 16, 1864, Brig. Gen. Thomas L. Rosser's Laurel Brigade had reached the Federal outposts that protected the cattle grazing peacefully on lush grassy fields. Rosser's men swiftly charged into the quiet Union camp of the First D.C. Cavalry. The First D.C. was a specially trained crack unit of cavalrymen armed with Henry repeating rifles. But taken by surprise, the Federals offered feeble resistance to the raiding graycoats who managed to capture nearly all the First D.C.'s officers. Rosser's men next challenged members of the Thirteenth Pennsylvania Cavalry who guarded the prized animals. They refused Rosser's demand to surrender, and a hot fight ensued with Confederates driving the Union cavalrymen back. The hungry Southerners eagerly seized cases of champagne, sardines, cigars, peaches, and other luxuries from abandoned sutler wagons. They then forced several Union civilian herdsmen to help them drive 2,486 cattle into a seven-mile-long column and headed toward Confederate lines.

When reports of the raid reached the Union command, Federals were incredulous over the speed and skill with which the Confederates had captured the cattle a mere six miles from Union central headquarters. Union gunboats had arrived on the James River to shell an enemy long gone. A detachment of Union cavalrymen set out in an angry search for the stolen cattle and their captors.

At 4:00 P.M. Rosser's men turned to fight the pursuing Federals at Ebenezer's Church. For four hours they held off the enemy while the rest of Hampton's troopers led the steers toward Confederate lines. By 9:00 the next morning, the raid had ended. Although the Federal forces outnumbered the Confederates twenty to one, Southern losses numbered a mere sixty-one; the surprised Federals had incurred some four hundred casualties.

The Beefsteak Raid brought enough meat to feed Lee's army for forty days and no doubt helped the Confederates survive their fourth winter of war. It proved one of the South's last dramatic cavalry sweeps into enemy territory and marked one of the largest cattle-rustling expeditions in U.S. history.

BIBLIOGRAPHY

Boykin, Edward. *Beefsteak Raid.* New York, 1960.

Cardwell, D. "A Brilliant Coup. How Wade Hampton Captured Grant's Entire Beef Supply." *Southern Historical Society Papers* 22 (1894): 147–156. Reprint, Wilmington, N.C., 1990.

Lykes, Richard W. "The Great Civil War Beef Raid." *Civil War Times Illustrated* 5, no. 10 (February 1967): 4–12.

McDonald, W.N. "Hampton's Cattle Raid." *Confederate Veteran* 31 (1923): 94–96. Reprint, Wilmington, N.C., 1985.

LESLEY JILL GORDON-BURR

BEERS, FANNIE

BEERS, FANNIE (1840?–?), hospital matron. Born in the North, probably in Connecticut, and well educated, Fannie married Augustus P. Beers, a Yale-educated Southerner, sometime in the 1850s. They resided in New Orleans where Fannie became an ardent Southern sympathizer. At the outbreak of the war she was visiting her mother while expecting a baby, but the infant died at birth. Fannie's known Confederate sympathies created much hostility in the community, so she and her small son, Georgie, fled to Virginia. Meanwhile, her husband had joined Dreaux's Battalion and was stationed in Virginia.

Fannie was obsessed with a desire to aid the Confederate cause, but at first her attempts to nurse the sick and wounded were discouraged because she was considered too young and delicate. At last she gained experience in a private hospital in Richmond called the Soldier's Rest, following which she became the matron of a hospital for Alabama soldiers where she worked for a few months until felled by illness.

Following a period of recuperation among her husband's relatives in Alabama, Fannie answered an advertisement during the summer of 1862 for a matron to help Dr. William T. McAllister organize the Buckner Hospital for Army of Tennessee troops at Gainesville, Alabama. During the course of the war, she moved with this hospital to Ringgold, Newnan, and finally, Fort Valley, all in Georgia. In her capacity as matron Beers supervised all aspects of hospital life that did not involve diagnosis, prescription, and surgery. She saw to it that the hospital was clean and the beds were properly supplied with linens. In addition she supervised the preparation and serving of food, personally cooking for and feeding the very ill. She helped care for and settle new patients and often sat with the dying during their last moments. While in Newnan her hospital contained a thousand beds.

Dissatisfied because so few patients were sent to Fort Valley, and driven by a need to serve, Beers asked to be assigned to a hospital nearer the front. After a few weeks in Macon, Georgia, she spent the winter of 1864–1865 in a very primitive tent hospital at Lauderdale Springs, Mississippi, where she nursed a number of soldiers through a smallpox epidemic. Broken in health, in February 1865 Beers returned for the duration of the war to her husband's relatives in Alabama where she experienced the destruction caused by Wilson's raid.

Where the Beers family lived immediately after the war is not known. Eventually they returned to New Orleans where she promoted remembrance of the Lost Cause by participating in veterans' gatherings and writing articles for the *Southern Bivouac,* of which she was at one time assistant editor. In 1888 she published *Memories: A Record of Personal Experience and Adventure during Four Years of War,* in which she recounted some of her hospital experiences as well as other wartime stories she heard from friends. Because she lost her Civil War diary and memorabilia during a raid, her book includes few specifics about time and people. She also included little information about her personal life. Her date of death is unknown.

BIBLIOGRAPHY

Beers, Fannie A. *Memories: A Record of Personal Experience and Adventure during Four Years of War.* Philadelphia, 1888. Reprint, Alexandria, Va., 1985.

Sifakis, Stewart. *Who Was Who in the Confederacy.* New York, 1988.

GLENNA R. SCHROEDER-LEIN

BELLE ISLE PRISON

In the summer of 1862, the Confederate authorities at Richmond relieved the overcrowding in their warehouse prisons for Union enlisted men by opening a camp on Belle Isle (or Island), an eighty-acre tract in the James River on which was already located an ironworks and workers' housing. The lower fifteen acres, where the prison was located, were flat and sandy. The proximity of the river's rapids and the connection to the south bank by a single railroad bridge simplified security. By mid-July, the island camp held 5,000 men. Though conditions during the first summer were relatively pleasant, they soon would make the island's name seem ironic indeed.

The opening of the prisoner exchange under the cartel of July 22, 1862, resulted in a rapid reduction of the prison population, and by September 23, the camp had closed. In January 1863, Belle Isle reopened at first as a temporary camp and then, with the breakdown of exchange, as a more permanent facility. In the camp's final form, the Confederates partially surrounded four to five acres with a deadline three feet wide by eight feet deep and with earthworks outside where the guards stood. A fenced walkway led to the river bridge. During the daytime the prisoners used the walkway to reach the river to drink, bathe, and use the sinks (latrines). Outside the prison were guards' quarters and a small hospital. Within the prison camp was a central thoroughfare from which radiated some sixty streets.

During the greater part of its history, the prison's commandant was Lt. Virginius Bossieux, a Virginian of French origin. Under him the prisoners were organized into squads of a hundred, headed by sergeants who called the roll and distributed rations.

By early fall 1863, the prison intended to hold 3,000 had some 6,300 captives. In early 1864, there were 8,000 or more within the camp. The overcrowded prisoners suffered greatly. To reduce escape attempts, they were not allowed access to the sinks after dark, so the ground became filthy. Although the Confederates supplied some tents, there were never enough, and prisoners either improvised shelter with pup tents made of blankets or simply burrowed in the soil. A few fires provided the only heat. The rations consisted of cornbread, rice, and occasional meat. Some prisoners tried to improve their lot by trading with one another and with the guards, using a variety of goods including prison-made jewelry and other souvenirs. Other prisoners stole scarce clothing, blankets, or food from one another.

In the winter of 1863–1864, the United States sent some clothing and food to the prisoners. The captive Union officers who distributed the goods—which many hungry prisoners quickly traded to guards for extra food—reported to their fellows and their government on the sad situation of the enlisted men. Though most sick prisoners were removed to hospitals on the island or in the city, deaths in the prison itself were numerous—ten or more men died each day. Because the prison was in full view of the Confederate capitol building, Union critics charged that Confederate leaders had to be aware of its deplorable conditions. This, together with the physical appearance of occasionally exchanged prisoners, was played up in Union propaganda.

> **By early fall 1863, the prison intended to hold 3,000 had some 6,300 captives.**

By the end of March 1864, the Confederates had removed all the Belle Isle prisoners to Andersonville, Georgia. During that summer, the temporary cessation of shipments to that equally congested pen caused a renewed accumulation of some 6,000 prisoners on Belle Isle. The worried Confederates supplemented their inadequate guards with two howitzers. In October, the Confederates transferred their new captives to Danville or (mostly) to Salisbury. Once again the Belle Islanders had gone from the frying pan to the fire. On February 10, 1865, the Confederates returned the island to its owners.

In the postwar period parts of the island served industrial functions. By the 1990s the city of Richmond had received title to the island and was contemplating recreational and historical uses for the prison site.

BIBLIOGRAPHY

Darby, George W. *Incidents and Adventures in Rebeldom: Libby, Belle-Isle, Salisbury.* Pittsburgh, 1899.

Hesseltine, William B. *Civil War Prisons: A Study in War Psychology.* Columbus, Ohio, 1930. Reprint, New York, 1964.

Parker, Sandra V. *Richmond's Civil War Prisons.* Lynchburg, Va., 1990.

FRANK L. BYRNE

BENJAMIN, JUDAH P.

BENJAMIN, JUDAH P. (1811–1884), U.S. senator, Confederate attorney general, secretary of war, and secretary of state. Born a British subject in the British West Indies on August 6, 1811, Benjamin was taken to the United States in his early youth. The child of Sephardic Jewish settlers, he was descended from families that could be traced back to fifteenth-century Spain.

Judah Benjamin's boyhood was much more steeped in Jewish culture and tradition than either Southern or Jewish historians have acknowledged. He was reared in Charleston, South Carolina, and grew to manhood in New Orleans, two of the largest Jewish communities in the United States in the early nineteenth century. His father was one of the twelve dissenters in Charleston who formed the first Reform Congregation of America. Although the records of Beth Elohim congregation were burned and we cannot know for certain, he probably was one of the first boys confirmed at the new reform temple, which was founded when he was thirteen years old. The character of a Jewish boy reared by a deeply involved Jewish family would be shaped by that experience the rest of his life.

He went to Yale Law School at fourteen, left under mysterious circumstances, and was admitted to the Louisiana bar in 1832. A strategic marriage to Natalie S. Martin, whose family belonged to the ruling creole aristocracy in New Orleans, propelled him into financial success and subsequently into a political career. He participated in the explosive growth of New Orleans between 1820 and 1840 as a commercial lawyer and political advocate for banking, finance, and railroad interests.

JUDAH P. BENJAMIN.

Benjamin prospered for a time as a sugar planter, helped organize the Illinois Central Railroad, and was elected to the Louisiana legislature in 1842. As a rising political star in the Whig Party, he was the first acknowledged Jew to be elected to the U.S. Senate (1852; reelected as a Democrat, 1858). In the Senate he was noted as an eloquent defender of Southern interests and has been ranked by some historians as one of the five great orators in Senate history, the equal of Daniel Webster and John C. Calhoun.

In Washington, he met Jefferson Davis (1853) and forged a friendship in an unusual confrontation. They were both intense and ambitious senators—Davis of Mississippi and Benjamin of Louisiana. Varina Howell Davis, the future First Lady of the Confederacy, wrote years later of them during this period, "Sometimes when they did not agree on, a measure, hot words in glacial, polite phrases passed between them." Because of a suspected insult on the floor of the Senate, Benjamin challenged Davis to a duel. Davis quickly and publicly apologized, and the incident of honor defended and satisfied drew them together in a relationship of mutual respect.

His wife had taken his only daughter, Ninnette, and moved to Paris in 1842. She joined him briefly after his election to the Senate, but returned again to Paris because of scandalous rumors about her in Washington. Thereafter Benjamin saw her once a year on trips to Paris. Only a fragment of a letter remains between them: "Speak not to me of economy," she wrote. "It is so fatiguing."

In the Senate, Benjamin was embroiled in the political turmoil leading to the Civil War, and he was frequently attacked on the basis of his religious background. Once in a debate on slavery when Senator Ben Wade of Ohio accused Benjamin of being an "Israelite with Egyptian principles," Benjamin is reported to have replied, "It is true that I am a Jew, and when my ancestors were receiving their Ten Commandments from the immediate Deity, amidst the thunderings and lightnings of Mount Sinai, the ancestors of my opponent were herding swine in the forest of Great Britain." It was a rare reply. Usually, when newspapers, political enemies, and military leaders insulted him with stinging phrases of religious prejudice, he almost never answered, but simply retained what observers called "a perpetual smile."

After secession, President Jefferson Davis appointed Benjamin as his attorney general on February 21, 1861. The president chose him because, in Davis's own words, Benjamin "had a very high reputation as a lawyer, and my acquaintance with him in the Senate had impressed me with the lucidity of his intellect, his systematic habits, and capacity for labor." Since the office of attorney general was a civilian post, the leadership in the capital considered it of little consequence, but this did not deter Benjamin. He plunged into the cabinet policy debates on all aspects of the Confederacy and developed a reputation as one who loved details, complexity, and problem solving. He became the administrator to the president, called by observers "the Poo Bah" of the Confederate government. At his first cabinet meeting, Secretary of War Leroy P. Walker said, "there was only one man there who had any sense, and that man was Benjamin." During his tenure at the Justice Department, Benjamin became a strong advocate of cotton diplomacy (the policy of shipping cotton to Europe as barter for arms and supplies, and of denying cotton to countries that did not support the South).

Davis then appointed Benjamin acting secretary of war in September, making the appointment permanent on November 21. By appointing a brilliant administrator without military experience, Davis could thereby be his own secretary of war, a position he had held in the Franklin Pierce administration. But Benjamin was a failure because when the war went badly on the battlefield, the military turned on him as a scapegoat. Frustrated generals who could not attack the president publicly had a convenient target in his secretary of war. As the Union forces struck back, criticism of Benjamin mounted. He was not a military man, and his orders, though flowing from constant meetings with the president, were treated as originating from him and were resented in the field as interference and amateurism.

Benjamin had highly publicized quarrels with Gen. P. G. T. Beauregard and Gen. Thomas J. ("Stonewall") Jackson. Beauregard called Benjamin in a letter to Davis "that functionary at his desk, who deems it a fit time to write lectures on law while the enemy is mustering at our front." Jackson threatened to resign, writing Davis that "with such interference in my command, I cannot be expected to be of much service in the field." Davis defended his "right hand," as Varina described Benjamin, who was working twelve and fourteen hours a day with Davis and was being blamed by the military for carrying out the president's orders.

Benjamin was berated by Northern generals as well. When Benjamin Butler, who commanded the forces that conquered New Orleans, issued a statement about the city, he said "the most effective supporters of the Confederacy have been . . . mostly Jews . . . who all deserve at the hands of the government what is due the Jew Benjamin."

The anger against Benjamin came to a head after the fall of Roanoke Island in early February 1862. Benjamin had been under intense pressure from Gen. Henry A. Wise at Roanoke and Governor Henry T. Clark of North Carolina to send many more men and arms to the garrison there. He had resisted for reasons that would not be known until twenty-five years after the war, and he accepted the subsequent public condemnation in silence to protect his country. Roanoke was sacrificed because to have done otherwise would have revealed to the enemy just how desperate the South was.

At the dedication of the Robert E. Lee monument in Richmond in 1890, Col. Charles Marshall, an aide-de-camp on General Lee's staff, read part of a letter from Benjamin, which revealed that President Davis had agreed to allow Benjamin to be publicly censured:

> I consulted the President whether it was best for the country that I should submit to unmerited censure or reveal to a Congressional Committee our poverty and my utter inability to supply the requisitions of General Wise, and thus run the risk that the fact should become known to some of the spies of the enemy, of whose activity we were well assured. It was thought best for the public service that I should suffer the blame in silence and a report of censure on me was accordingly made by the Committee of Congress.

When Benjamin resigned, Davis, as a reward for loyalty, promptly named him secretary of state.

On the subject of slavery, both Davis and Benjamin were "enlightened" Southerners whose attitudes were evolving. Most Jewish historians have understandably reacted with revulsion to the fact that Benjamin owned 140 slaves on a sugar plantation, and they have been unable to consider the question of his views on slavery with anything but embarrassed dismay. To comprehend Benjamin on this score, one must put him into context as a political figure against a backdrop of planter dogmatism and abolitionist fervor.

Such an exploration leads directly to an extraordinary episode of the war in which Benjamin played a central role: the effort to persuade Davis to issue a Confederate emancipation proclamation, which would promise slaves freedom in exchange for military service. That move, which began to take shape early in the war in the minds of military and political leaders but did not surface until 1864, is usually dismissed as a desperate gamble made at the end of the war to lure Britain into the fight. But as secretary of state, Benjamin's obsession all along had been to draw England into the war. Slavery, however, was a stumbling block because England had abolished slavery in 1833. As the clouds of defeat gathered, Benjamin spoke before ten thousand people in Richmond, delivering a remarkable speech in favor of a Confederate offer to free slaves who would fight for the South. Although the idea of arming slaves as soldiers was supported by Lee, who needed more men in the field, the public and political reaction was fierce. Howell Cobb, the former governor of Georgia, wrote that "if slaves will make good soldiers, our whole theory of slavery is wrong." Nevertheless, the Confederate Congress passed a partial version of the measure on March 13, but by then it was too late. Richmond fell less than a month later.

Benjamin's apparent change of personality after the war has puzzled historians. The utter secrecy and privacy of his later life is anomalous, given his earlier hunger for fame. No one can ever know, but certainly one key to understanding his silence after the war is his creation of a Confederate spy ring in Canada and the subsequent proclamation, conceived by the Union's secretary of war, Edwin Stanton, and issued by Lincoln's successor, President Andrew Johnson, for the arrest of Davis and seven Canadian Confederate spies after the Lincoln assassination. History, by means of the trials of the conspirators and by exhaustive investigations, has absolved both Benjamin and Davis from any responsibility. But the psychological and emotional impact on Benjamin of the long period of hysteria that followed the assassination must have taken its toll, especially since Lincoln's death fell on Good Friday and 2,500 sermons were given on Easter Sunday comparing Lincoln to a fallen Christ figure, as the nation acted out a passion play. There is no record of what Benjamin thought of the various published accusations against him.

If Benjamin's role in history has been misjudged by historians and was minimized even by participants, much of the responsibility for that lies with Benjamin himself. He chose obscurity early in the war with the unwavering decision that he could best serve the South by serving Davis and remaining in the presidential shadow. For reasons that have puzzled historians, Benjamin burned his personal papers—some as he escaped from Richmond in 1865 and almost all of the rest just before he died—and he left only six scraps of paper at his death. One historian has called him a "virtual incendiary."

Benjamin fled to England after the war and built a second career as a successful international lawyer. He was called to the bar (June 1866) after only five months' residence and achieved enormous financial success in his new home country. In 1868, he wrote a classic treatise on commercial law in

> **For reasons that have puzzled historians, Benjamin burned his personal papers—some as he escaped from Richmond in 1865 and almost all of the rest just before he died. . . .**

England (*Treatise on the Law of Sale of Personal Property*) known even today to law students as "Benjamin on Sales." In 1872, he became a queen's counsel, practicing with wig and robes in the House of Lords and appearing in 136 major cases.

Although he had been known in the U.S. Senate as an outstanding orator, in England he gave no published speeches on the war. He left no articles, essays, or books about his role in the war or any other aspect of it. Indeed, he made only two public statements in nineteen years that concerned the war. The first was a three-paragraph letter to the *Times* of London in September 1865, just after he arrived in England, protesting the imprisonment of Jefferson Davis. The second was a short letter in 1883 contradicting the charge that millions of dollars in Confederate funds were left in European banks under his control. There were no letters defending strategy or admitting error; nor does history record any war-related conversations with students or scholars. He spent a few evenings at dinner with Davis when the ex-president visited London five times between 1868 and 1883. Otherwise, he avoided nostalgic encounters with friends from the South. It is one of the enduring mysteries that Benjamin chose to erase all ties to his previous life. In fact, he never even returned to the United States.

Late in life, he retired and moved to Paris to be with his family. Benjamin died on May 6, 1884, and was buried in Pére Lachaise cemetery in Paris under the name of "Philippe Benjamin" in the family plot of the Boursignac family, the in-laws of his daughter. Three grandchildren died in childhood and no direct descendants survived. In 1938, the Paris chapter of the Daughters of the Confederacy finally provided an inscription to identify the man in the almost anonymous grave:

JUDAH PHILIP BENJAMIN
BORN ST. THOMAS WEST INDIES AUGUST 6, 1811
DIED IN PARIS MAY 6, 1884
UNITED STATES SENATOR FROM LOUISIANA
ATTORNEY GENERAL, SECRETARY OF WAR AND
SECRETARY OF STATE OF THE CONFEDERATE STATES
OF AMERICA, QUEEN'S COUNSEL, LONDON

In life, as in death, he was elusive, vanishing behind his agreeableness, his cordiality, his perpetual smile. To blend into the culture—whether Southern or English—was bred into him, a matter of the Jewish Southerner's instinct for survival. The public man celebrated on two continents sought a kind of invisibility, not unlike the private man nobody knew. Shunning his past, choosing an almost secret grave, with calculated concealment, he nearly succeeded in remaining hidden from history.

Since his death, Benjamin's life has remained relatively unchallenged in the images that have come down through history. Although historians have routinely called him "the brains of the Confederacy," they know relatively little about him. Many historians of the Civil War have referred to him as President Davis's most loyal confidant, but Davis himself in his 1881 memoir of the Confederacy, referred to Benjamin in the most perfunctory fashion, mentioning his name only twice in the 1,500-page, two-volume work. That is especially odd if, as Varina Davis testified in a letter written in 1889, Benjamin spent almost every day in the office with her husband and was a central figure in events.

Benjamin's image comes down through history as "the dark prince of the Confederacy," a Mephistophelian Jewish figure. Stephen Vincent Benét in *John Brown's Body* reflected the contemporary view of him:

Judah P. Benjamin, the dapper Jew,
Seal-Sleek, black-eyed, lawyer and epicure,
Able, well-hated, face alive with life,
Looked round the council-chamber with the slight
Perpetual smile he held before himself
Continually like a silk-ribbed fan.
Behind the fan, his quick, shrewd, fluid mind
Weighed Gentiles in an old balance. . . .

The mind behind the silk-ribbed fan
Was a dark-prince, clothed in an Eastern stuff,
Whole brown hands cupped about a crystal egg
That filmed with colored cloud. The eyes stared,
searching.

"I am a Jew, What am I doing here?"

Pierce Butler in 1907 and Robert Douthat Meade in 1943 wrote the two standard biographies of Benjamin in the first half of the twentieth century, pulling together the thousands of Civil War orders and letters to friends and family in England, France, New Orleans, Charleston, and elsewhere that he was unable to destroy after the war. Butler interviewed Benjamin's contemporaries, including Varina Howell Davis. Meade spent twelve years traveling—researching diaries, memoirs, and papers and interviewing family members and friends. His book revealed Benjamin to have been a gifted tactician with a philosophical nature and an urbane manner, a gourmet, an inveterate gambler, and a man whom women adored. Still, it acknowledged a paucity of material.

Meade and Butler also drew from the research of the spare beginnings of an unfinished biography by Francis Lawley, the Richmond and Washington correspondent of the London *Times* during the war, who became, according to Meade, "devoted to Benjamin, who doubtless helped to color his vivid dispatches with a sympathetic attitude toward the Confederacy." Benjamin kept up a relationship with Lawley for the rest of his life, but only six pages survive of the biography Lawley planned, along with fewer than a dozen letters.

Meade and Butler were both Southern historians unfamiliar with American Jewish history. Judaism for them represented strange and unsteady territory that they, perhaps too deeply ingrained with the attitudes of their time, were not prepared to explore. Butler, in 1907, treated Jewishness as if it were an unpleasant component of his admiring portrait, one that he was reluctant but duty-bound to include briefly. He referred to Benjamin's father as "that *rara avis,* an unsuccessful Jew" and described Benjamin in England as "this wonderful little Jew from America." Meade, writing during that sensitive period of the rise of Nazi Germany just before World War II, was more circumspect, yet observed that "like so many of Jewish blood today, Benjamin tended to become cosmopolitan." In the late 1930s, no Southern historian could convey the harshness of the anti-Semitism surrounding Benjamin without seeming prejudiced himself. In a steady drumbeat of insults in Richmond, Confederate opponents would later refer to Benjamin as "Judas Iscariot Benjamin," and, according to Mary Boykin Chesnut's diary, "Mr. Davis's pet Jew." The Jewish aspect of Benjamin's life and career was not fully examined until it was taken up in an 1988 biography, almost fifty years after the publication of Meade's book.

Historians have pointed out ways in which Jews and Southerners were alike—stepchildren of an anguished history—and yet different. Whereas the Jewish search for a homeland contrasted with the Southerner's commitment to place, Southern defenders of the Confederacy often used Old Testament analogies in referring to themselves as "the chosen people" destined to survive and triumph against overwhelming odds. Benjamin is fascinating because of the extraordinary role he played in Southern history and the ways in which Jews and non-Jews reacted to him. He was the prototype of the contradictions in the Jewish Southerner and the stranger in the Confederate story, the Jew at the eye of the storm that was the Civil War.

Objectively, with so few Jews in the South at the time, it is astonishing that one should appear at the very center of Southern history. Benjamin himself avoided his Jewishness throughout his public career, though his enemies in the Southern press and in the halls of the Confederate Congress never let the South forget it. The virulence of the times required a symbolic figure as a catalyst for an ancient hostility and perhaps contributed to his intentional elusiveness. As Bertram Korn pointed out in *American Jewry and the Civil War,* the nation both North and South experienced "the greatest outpouring of Judeophobia in its history" during the Civil War, and Benjamin was a convenient target.

Benjamin achieved greater political power than any other Jew in the nineteenth century—perhaps even in all American history. Although he was a nonpracticing Jew, he never attempted to deny his faith and contemporary society treated him as Jewish. Benjamin thus must stand as a symbol of American democracy and its openness to religious minorities. In spite of the bigotry surrounding him, not only was he elected to the U.S. Senate and appointed to three high offices in the Confederacy, but he was also offered an appointment as the ambassador to Spain and a seat on the U.S. Supreme Court. The nineteenth-century emancipation of the Jews, which began in Europe after the French Revolution, was as great a shock to Jews as were the centuries of persecution that preceded it. Benjamin was the main beneficiary of that emancipation and its most visible symbol in America.

In the final years before the war, Benjamin was widely admired nationally in both Jewish and non-Jewish communi-

ties for his prestige as a Southern leader and his eloquence as an orator. His election to the U.S. Senate was a watershed for American Jews. Because of the war, he became the first Jewish political figure to be projected into the national consciousness. Jews in the South were especially proud of his achievement because he validated their legitimacy as Southerners. A pivotal figure in American Jewish history, Benjamin broke down the barriers of prejudice to achieve high office. After him, it was more acceptable for Jews to be elected to office and to aspire to service in the councils of national power.

BIBLIOGRAPHY

Benjamin, Judah P. *Treatise on the Law of Sale of Personal Property, with Reference to the American Decisions, to the French Code and Civil Code.* 1868.

Butler, Pierce. *Judah P. Benjamin.* Philadelphia, 1907. Reprint, New York and London, 1980.

Evans, Eli N. *Judah P. Benjamin: The Jewish Confederate.* New York, 1988.

Meade, Robert Douthat. *Judah P. Benjamin, Confederate Statesman.* New York, 1943. Reprint, New York, 1975.

ELI N. EVANS

BENNING, HENRY L.

BENNING, HENRY L. (1814–1875), brigadier general. Benning was born in Columbia County, Georgia, on April 2, 1814, and graduated with honors from the University of Georgia in 1834. He studied law at Talbottown, Georgia, in the office of George W. Towns, a lawyer who would rise to become a member of Congress and governor of Georgia. Benning was admitted to the bar in 1835 at Columbus, and there he began the practice of law. He became the chief prosecutor for his circuit in 1838. In 1839 Benning joined his father-in-law in a law partnership and in 1855 was elected a justice of the Supreme Court of Georgia.

As strong a Democrat as he was an advocate of state rights, Benning served as vice president of the Democratic convention in Baltimore that nominated Sen. Stephen A. Douglas for the presidency in 1860. With the election of Abraham Lincoln and the rise of the secession movement, Benning was named a delegate to the Charleston convention in 1860 and was elected a delegate to the convention that adopted the ordinance of secession for the state of Georgia. He also served as a commissioner to the Virginia secession convention.

With the outbreak of hostilities, Benning entered Confederate service as colonel of the Seventeenth Georgia Infantry. Part of Robert Toombs's brigade, Benning's

Seventeenth Georgia fought gallantly on the Virginia Peninsula in the spring and early summer of 1862.

After little more than a year in the field, Henry Benning was elevated to the rank of brigadier general and placed in command of Toombs's old brigade, composed of four Georgia infantry regiments. Benning led these regiments, part of Gen. James Longstreet's First Corps of the Army of Northern Virginia, through the Battles of Second Manassas, Sharpsburg, Fredericksburg, and Gettysburg. Ordered to the western theater of war in the late summer of 1863, Benning and his men fought through the Battle of Chickamauga and the siege of Knoxville. Returning to the east, Benning led his regiments through the Battle of the Wilderness where he was severely wounded in the right shoulder. After recovering, he resumed command of his brigade in the fighting before Petersburg. Benning was with his old brigade when it surrendered with Gen. Robert E. Lee's Army of Northern Virginia on April 9, 1865.

Benning stood nearly six feet in height and was massive in frame. His commanding presence and deep voice made him a natural leader. Although not a professional soldier, he was an able and reliable commander. For his coolness under fire, courage, and steadfastness, his men gave him the sobriquet "Old Rock."

After the war, Benning returned to Columbus, Georgia, where he resumed the practice of law. He died while on his way to court on July 10, 1875, and was buried in Columbus.

BIBLIOGRAPHY

Cobb, James C. "The Making of a Secessionist: Henry L. Benning and the Coming of the Civil War." *The Georgia Historical Quarterly* 60, no. 4 (Winter 1976): 313–323.

Derry, Joseph T. *Georgia.* Vol. 6 of *Confederate Military History.* Edited by Clement A. Evans. Atlanta, 1899. Vol. 7 of extended ed. Wilmington, N.C., 1987.

Warner, Ezra J. *Generals in Gray: Lives of the Confederate Commanders.* Baton Rouge, La., 1959.

KENT MASTERSON BROWN

BENTONVILLE, NORTH CAROLINA

On March 19 through 21, 1865, the town of Bentonville, twenty-five miles southwest of Goldsboro, was the site of the Confederate's last major challenge to Gen. William Tecumseh Sherman's sweep through the Carolinas. Joseph E. Johnston's attempt to rout Sherman cost the Confederates 2,347 soldiers wounded, captured, or missing and the Federals 1,455 men.

By the early spring, Union troops had reached North Carolina in their ruinous push toward Richmond. Sherman's army headed north in two columns under the leadership of Generals John McAllister Schofield and Jacob Dolson Cox. Their ultimate objective was to reunite in Goldsboro, where they planned to resupply the troops with boots and clothing and establish a supply line to the coast.

From Petersburg and Raleigh, Robert E. Lee and Johnston speculated about Sherman's intentions and planned their strategy. Lee was intent on maintaining an unobstructed line of communication and supplies from Raleigh to Petersburg. Johnston did not have the manpower to attack Sherman's entire force: the Army of Tennessee had

> **Lee was intent on maintaining an unobstructed line of communication and supplies from Raleigh to Petersburg.**

suffered greatly during the Tennessee campaign; most of the officers had fallen during the disasters at Franklin and Nashville. Hence, Johnston preferred to strike before Sherman could reunite his army. Although Lee agreed that Johnston should attack, he urged caution; by the spring of 1865 the Confederacy could not afford unnecessary losses.

At Bentonville Johnston saw his chance. On March 16 Union Gen. Henry Slocum's troops ran into Confederate troops at Averasboro, and on March 18 Slocum and his men skirmished with Wade Hampton's cavalry until dark. Both sides withdrew that night, but, at dawn, the Confederate troops renewed their attack.

Sherman had expected Johnston to hinder his movement; he assumed that the danger to his troops had passed after Slocum and Hampton's clash at Averasboro. Therefore he moved to the right and joined Schofield en route to Goldsboro.

During the afternoon of the nineteenth, however, Joseph E. Johnston attacked Slocum yet again. At first Slocum thought that he confronted only cavalry, but it became increasingly apparent that he faced a sizable infantry force. Hence he sent a dispatch asking for support. The Confederates continued to launch attacks on the Union line until sundown. As night fell, the Confederates had not gained any ground, but they had not lost any either.

On March 20, massive numbers of Union reinforcements began to arrive, and the Confederates assumed a defensive position. Johnston remained optimistic, but by 4:00 P.M. the Union army had reunited in front of him. The Southerners hoped to wear down the Federal troops and subsequently launch a crippling attack. Union forces, however, moved to flank the Confederate left and advance on its rear. The

Southerners held off the Federal troops until the following evening (March 21), when Johnston ordered his troops to withdraw.

As the Confederate army headed northwest in the direction of Smithfield, the Union army offered virtually no pursuit. Sherman felt confident that he had sufficiently eliminated the threat from Johnston's army, and he and his troops headed, uncontested, for Goldsboro.

Johnston had succeeded in delaying Sherman at Bentonville, but only temporarily. Sherman charged on, and a month later, Johnston followed General Lee's example at Appomattox and surrendered his forces.

BIBLIOGRAPHY

Barrett, John Gilchrist. *North Carolina as a Civil War Battleground, 1861–1865.* Raleigh, N.C., 1980.
Luvaas, Jay. *The Battle of Bentonville: March 19–20–21, 1865.* Smithfield, N.C., 1965.

JENNIFER LUND

BIBLIOGRAPHY AND HISTORIOGRAPHY

During the years since 1865 writings about the Confederate South have become an industry all their own. Collectors and dealers continue to multiply, and their collections rival research libraries in the number and quality of titles. For some appreciation of the enterprise involved in Confederate collections, see Douglas Southall Freeman, *The South to Posterity: An Introduction to the Writing of Confederate History* (New York, 1951); Richard Harwell, *The Confederate Hundred: A Bibliophilic Selection of Confederate Books* (Urbana, Ill., 1964); and Richard Barksdale Harwell, *In Tall Cotton: The 200 Most Important Confederate Books for the Reader, Researcher and Collector* (Austin, Tex., 1978).

Major Themes of Historical Writing

Books about the Confederacy cover myriad subjects and themes. Although dividing them into broad categories risks oversimplification, three themes seem dominant in historical writings on the Confederate experience.

Apology. People who lose wars usually want urgently to explain or excuse their actions, attempting to vindicate themselves in print. Obvious examples are Jefferson Davis, *The Rise and Fall of the Confederate Government,* 2 vols. (New York, 1881), and Alexander H. Stephens, *A Constitutional View of the Late War between the States,* 2 vols. (Chicago, 1868–1870). Certainly Southerners of the Confederacy and

after have poured forth prose and poetry in an effort to justify the Lost Cause. Edward A. Pollard, for example, in *The Lost Cause: A New Southern History of the War of the Confederates* (New York, 1867), concluded:

> It would be immeasurably the worst consequence of defeat in this war that the South should lose its moral and intellectual distinctiveness as a people, and cease to assert its well-known superiority in civilization, in political scholarship, and in all the standards of individual character over the people of the North. . . . That superiority the war has not conquered or lowered; and the South will do right to claim and cherish it.

Pollard, of course, wrote his history in the ashes of defeat, reflecting a persistent Southern nationalism that is, at the least, understandable. Confederate history as apology, however, did not die with the generation that lived the history. Even at this writing, subtle and not-at-all-subtle manifestations of neo-Confederate sentiment abound in popular culture and supposedly serious scholarship. Indeed, the uses and perversions of Confederate history are a fertile topic for analysis in and of itself.

Continuity or Discontinuity. To what extent did the Confederacy provoke or provide fundamental change in the American South? Among those historians who emphasize the Confederate experience as collective trauma for Southerners, some contend that the war for national survival produced social crisis among Southern whites. The demands of an extended war and the sacrifices imposed by the Richmond government, the argument goes, opened class divisions within the so-called Solid South. Plain folk resented the "rich man's war and poor man's fight" imposed upon them by a government dominated by planters or planter interests. So the Confederacy failed because of social issues latent in the antebellum South. This point of view is present in works as otherwise diverse as Frank L. Owsley, *State Rights in the Confederacy* (Chicago, 1925), and Paul D. Escott, *After Secession: Jefferson Davis and the Failure of Confederate Nationalism* (Baton Rouge, La., 1978).

Other historians have agreed that the Confederate era was crucial in Southern life, but they emphasize more positive aspects of the experience. Examples of some works that share this emphasis, if little else, include Nathaniel W. Stephenson, *The Day of the Confederacy* (New Haven, 1919); Frank E. Vandiver, *Their Tattered Flags: The Epic of the Confederacy* (New York, 1970); Raimondo Luraghi, *The Rise and Fall of the Plantation South* (New York, 1978); and Emory M. Thomas, *The Confederate Nation, 1861–1865* (New York, 1979).

However much the scholars cited above may differ about the substantive impact of the Confederate experience, they do agree that the Confederacy and the war were major watersheds in Southern life. Other scholars demur. Perhaps the most thoroughgoing among this group was W. J. Cash, whose *Mind of the South* (New York, 1941) contended that the Confederacy was an expression of continuity and consensus. More recently, the collaboration of Richard E. Beringer, Herman Hattaway, Archer Jones, and William N. Still, Jr., *Why the South Lost the Civil War* (Athens, Ga., 1986), suggests among other things that Confederate Southerners were less than committed secessionists. This point echoes the idea of Kenneth M. Stampp in "The Southern Road to Appomattox," an essay in Stampp's *The Imperial Union: Essays on the Background of the Civil War* (New York, 1980), that significant numbers of Confederates never really embraced the cause with much zeal from the outset.

In league with historians who question the importance of the Confederate period in Southern life are scholars who argue that nothing really consequential in the South changed from the inception of the slave plantation system until the triple trauma of Great Depression, New Deal, and World War II. An articulate example of this contention is Numan V. Bartley's *The Creation of Modern Georgia* (Athens, Ga., 1983).

Southern Distinctiveness. From Jamestown to Fort Sumter, a period of almost 154 years, Southerners had been Americans, and after Appomattox Southerners again became Americans with arguably greater zeal than most. However ironic, it is often true that descendants of those people who fought long and hard to leave the United States have been the strongest patriots, 110 percent Americans, ever since the Civil War. Such observations and others have led many historians to emphasize the *American* identity of Southern Americans and so consider the Confederate interlude an anomaly. This emphasis is perhaps best expressed in a collection of essays by Charles G. Sellers, Jr., *The Southerner as American* (Chapel Hill, N.C., 1960), and best analyzed and understood in David Potter's *The South and the Sectional Conflict* (Baton Rouge, La., 1968) and C. Vann Woodward's *American Counterpoint: Slavery and Racism in the North-South Dialogue* (Boston, 1971).

On the surface, at least, the issue seems simple enough. But like most matters that touch on human experience, this one is pregnant with subtle complexities. Consider, for example, the eloquent passage from Douglas S. Freeman's *R. E. Lee: A Biography,* 4 vols. (New York, 1934–1935) about the aftermath of the Battle of Malvern Hill. Freeman writes:

Shattered bodies were everywhere and dead men in every contortion of their last agony. Weapons and the keepsakes of soldiers, caps and knapsacks, play-cards and pocket testaments, bloody heads with bulging eyes, booted legs, severed arms with hands gripped tight, torsos with the limbs blown away, gray coats dyed black with boys' blood—it was a nightmare of hell, set on a firm, green field of reality, under a workaday, leaden, summer sky, a scene to sicken the simple, home-loving soldiers who had to fight the war while the politicians responsible for bringing a nation to madness stood in the streets of safe cities and mouthed wrathful platitudes about constitutional rights.

The passage reflects Freeman's abhorrence of war, to be sure. But because he separates the "bloody heads with bulging eyes" from the "wrathful platitudes," Freeman encourages the notion that no connection existed between "the politicians" and "the simple, home-loving soldiers." Somehow, nice American boys found themselves killing each other for no good reason. They were all good Americans caught up in madness, Freeman implies, and the Southern soldiers were indistinct from their Northern adversaries. War is indeed madness. But to suggest that this war involved only "wrathful platitudes" trivializes the experience in which more than 600,000 men died.

Southerners had been and became again Americans. The Confederate experience, however, offers an opportunity to understand the Southern distinctiveness that seems to have sparked and sustained a terrible war.

A Selected Bibliography

Here follows a list of selected works arranged by topics touching on Confederate history. Because entries covering individual people and battles in this encyclopedia include pertinent bibliographies, this general bibliography omits biographies, battles, armies, ships, campaign studies, and personal narratives in all but a few cases. Also important is the fact that the list is of necessity only a sampling of a larger literature. In fact, the first category is a list of bibliographies.

Bibliographic Guides

These journals offer reviews and lists of published articles as well as articles that sometimes treat aspects of Confederate history. *Civil War History* (Kent, Ohio).

Journal of American History (Bloomington, Ind.).

Journal of Southern History (Baton Rouge, La.).

Cole, Garold L. *Civil War Eyewitnesses: An Annotated Bibliography of Books and Articles, 1955–1986.* Columbia, S.C., 1988.

Coulter, E. Merton. *Travels in the Confederate States: A Bibliography.* Norman, Okla., 1948.

Dornbasch, C. E., comp. *Regimental Publications and Personal Narratives of the Civil War: A Checklist.* 2 vols. New York, 1961–1971.

Link, Arthur S., and Rembert W. Patrick, eds. *Writing Southern History: Essays in Historiography in Honor of Fletcher M. Green.* Baton Rouge, La., 1965.

Nevins, Allan, James I. Robertson, Jr., and Bell I. Wiley, eds. *Civil War Books: A Critical Bibliography.* 2 vols. Baton Rouge, La., 1965–1967.

Thomas, Emory M. *The Confederate Nation, 1861–1865.* New York, 1979 (pp. 323–372, bibliography).

Manuscript and Archival Materials

Beers, Henry Putney. *Guide to the Archives of the Government of the Confederate States of America.* Washington, D.C., 1968.

National Historical Publications Commission. *Guide to Archives and Manuscripts in the United States.* Edited by Philip M. Hamer. New Haven, Conn., 1961.

U.S. Library of Congress. *National Union Catalog of Manuscript Collections.* Washington, D.C., 1961–.

Printed Primary Sources

Confederate Veteran. Edited by S. A. Cunningham. 40 vols. Nashville, Tenn., 1893–1932. Reprint, Wilmington, N.C., 1985.

Confederate Veteran Index. Edited by Louis Manarin. 3 vols. Wilmington, N.C., 1987.

Evans, Clement A., ed. *Confederate Military History.* 12 vols. Atlanta, 1899. Extended ed. in 19 vols. Wilmington, N.C., 1987–1989.

Johnson, Robert U., and C. C. Buel, eds. *Battles and Leaders of the Civil War.* 4 vols. New York, 1887–1888. Reprint, Secaucus, N.J., 1982.

Journal of the Congress of the Confederate States of America, 1861–1865. 7 vols. Washington, D.C., 1904–1905.

Matthews, James M., ed. *Statutes at Large of the Confederate States of America.* Richmond, Va., 1862–1864.

Moore, Frank, ed. *The Rebellion Record.* 11 vols. and supp. New York, 1861–1871.

Parrish, T. Michael, and Robert M. Willingham, Jr. *Confederate Imprints: A Bibliography of Southern Publications from Secession to Surrender.* Austin, Tex., 1987.

"Proceedings of the Confederate Congress." *Southern Historical Society Papers* 45, n.s. 7 (1925). Reprint, Wilmington, N.C., 1992.

Ramsdell, Charles W., ed. *Laws and Joint Resolutions of the Last Session of the Confederate Congress. Together with the Secret Acts of the Previous Congress.* Durham, N.C., 1941.

Southern Historical Society Papers. 52 vols. Richmond, Va., 1876–1959. Reprinted with 2 vol. index. Wilmington, N.C., 1990–1992.

U.S. Naval War Records Office. *Official Records of the Union and Confederate Navies in the War of the Rebellion.* 30 vols. and index. Washington, D.C., 1894–1927.

U.S. War Department. *War of the Rebellion: A Compilation of the Official Records of the Union and Confederate Armies.* 70 vols. in 128 parts. Washington, D.C., 1880–1901.

Periodicals

Most of the following are available in microform at good research libraries.

The Countrymen.
De Bow's Review.
Magnolia: A Southern Home Journal.
Record of News, History, and Literature.
Richmond Age: A Southern Monthly Eclectic Magazine.
Southern Cultivator.
Southern Field and Fireside.
Southern Illustrated News.
Southern Literary Messenger.
Southern Punch.

Physical and Graphic Materials

Art and Photographs

The Civil War: A Centennial Exhibition of Eyewitness Drawings. Washington, D.C., 1961.

Davis, William C., ed. *The Image of War, 1861–1865.* 6 vols. Garden City, N.Y., 1981–1984.

Frassantino, William A. *Antietam: The Photographic Legacy of America's Bloodiest Day.* New York, 1978.

Frassantino, William A. *Gettysburg: A Journey in Time.* New York, 1975.

Frassantino, William A. *Grant and Lee: The Virginia Campaigns, 1864–1865.* New York, 1983.

Guernsey, Alfred H., and Henry M. Alden, eds. *Harper's Pictorial History of the Great Rebellion.* 2 vols. New York, 1866–1868.

Miller, Francis T., ed. *The Photographic History of the Civil War.* 10 vols. New York, 1912.

Neely, Mark E., Jr., Harold Holzer, and Gabor S. Boritt. *The Confederate Image: Prints of the Lost Cause.* Chapel Hill, N.C., 1987.

Simpson, Marc. *Winslow Homer: Paintings of the Civil War.* San Francisco, 1988.

Maps

Cowels, Calvin D., comp. *Atlas to Accompany the Official Records of the Union and Confederate Armies.* 2 vols. Washington, D.C., 1891–1895.

Esposito, Vincent J., ed. *The West Point Atlas of American Wars.* 2 vols. New York, 1959.

A Guide to Civil War Maps in the National Archives. Washington, D.C., 1986.

Symonds, Craig L. *Gettysburg: A Battlefield Atlas.* Baltimore, 1992.

Geographical Guides

Cromie, Alice Hamilton. *A Tour Guide to the Civil War.* Chicago, 1965.

Kennedy, Frances H. *The Civil War Battlefield Guide.* Boston, 1990.

Stevens, Joseph E. *America's National Battlefield Parks: A Guide.* Norman, Okla., 1990.

Thomas, Emory M. *Travels to Hallowed Ground: A Historian's Journey to the American Civil War.* Columbia, S.C., 1987.

General Histories of the Confederate Period

Barney, William L. *Battleground for the Union: The Era of the Civil War and Reconstruction, 1848–1877.* Englewood Cliffs, N.J., 1990.

Brock, W. R. *Conflict and Transformation: The United States, 1844–1877.* New York, 1973.

Foote, Shelby. *The Civil War: A Narrative.* 3 vols. New York, 1958–1975.

Luraghi, Raimondo. *Storia della guerra civile americana.* Turin, Italy, 1966.

McPherson, James M. *Battle Cry of Freedom.* New York, 1987.

McPherson, James M. *Ordeal by Fire.* New York, 1982.

Parish, Peter J. *The American Civil War.* New York, 1975.

Randall, James G., and David Donald. *The Civil War and Reconstruction.* Boston, 1969.

Roland, Charles P. *An American Iliad: The Story of the Civil War.* Lexington, Ky., 1991.

Vandiver, Frank E. *Blood Brothers: A Short History of the Civil War.* College Station, Tex., 1992.

General Histories of the Confederacy

Coulter, E. Merton. *The Confederate States of America.* A History of the South, vol. 7. Baton Rouge, La., 1950.

Eaton, Clement. *A History of the Southern Confederacy.* New York, 1954.

Roland, Charles P. *The Confederacy.* Chicago, 1960.

Thomas, Emory M. *The Confederate Nation, 1861–1865.* New York, 1979.

Vandiver, Frank E. *Their Tattered Flags: The Epic of the Confederacy.* New York, 1970. Reprint, College Station, Tex., 1987.

Collected Essays

Belohlavek, John M., and Lewis N. Wynne, eds. *Divided We Fall: Essays on Confederate Nation-Building.* Saint Leo, Fla., 1991.

Bleser, Carol, ed. *In Joy and in Sorrow: Women, Family, and Marriage in the Victorian South, 1830–1890.* New York, 1991.

Clinton, Catherine, and Nina Silber. *Divided Houses: Gender and the Civil War.* New York, 1992.

Crow, Jeffrey J., Paul D. Escott, and Charles L. Flynn, Jr. *Race, Class and Politics in Southern History: Essays in Honor of Robert F. Durden.* Baton Rouge, La., 1990.

Donald, David, ed. *Why the North Won the Civil War.* Baton Rouge, La., 1960.

Gallagher, Gary W., ed. *Antietam: Essays on the 1862 Maryland Campaign.* Kent, Ohio, 1989.

Gallagher, Gary W., ed. *The First Day at Gettysburg: Essays on Confederate and Union Leadership.* Kent, Ohio, 1992.

Gallagher, Gary W., ed. *Struggle for the Shenandoah: Essays on the 1864 Valley Campaign.* Kent, Ohio, 1991.

Owens, Harry P., and James J. Cooke, eds. *The Old South in the Crucible of Civil War.* Jackson, Miss., 1983.

Potter, David. *The South and the Sectional Conflict.* Baton Rouge, La., 1968.

Robertson, James I., Jr., and Richard M. McMurry, eds. *Rank and File: Civil War Essays in Honor of Bell Irwin Wiley.* San Rafael, Calif., 1976.

Stampp, Kenneth M. *The Imperiled Union: Essays on the Background of the Civil War.* New York, 1980.

Woodward, C. Vann. *American Counterpoint: Slavery and Racism in the North-South Dialogue.* Boston, 1971.

Woodward, C. Vann. *The Burden of Southern History.* Rev. ed. Baton Rouge, La., 1968.

Wyatt-Brown, Bertram. *Yankee Saints and Southern Sinners.* Baton Rouge, La., 1985.

Extended Essays and Interpretive Works

Beringer, Richard E., Herman Hattaway, Archer Jones, and William N. Still, Jr. *Why the South Lost the Civil War.* Athens, Ga., 1986.

Degler, Carl N. *The Other South: Southern Dissenters in the Nineteenth Century.* New York, 1974.

Escott, Paul D. *After Secession: Jefferson Davis and the Failure of Confederate Nationalism.* Baton Rouge, La., 1978.

Faust, Drew Gilpin. *The Creation of Southern Nationalism.* Baton Rouge, La., 1988.

Hill, Louise B. *State Socialism in the Confederate States of America.* Charlottesville, Va., 1936.

Luraghi, Raimondo. *The Rise and Fall of the Plantation South.* New York, 1978.

McMurry, Richard M. *Two Great Rebel Armies: An Essay in Confederate Military History.* Chapel Hill, N.C., 1989.

McWhiney, Grady, and Perry D. Jamieson. *Attack and Die: Civil War Military Tactics and the Southern Heritage.* University, Ala., 1982.

Owsley, Frank L. *State Rights in the Confederacy.* Chicago, 1925.

Ramsdell, Charles W. *Behind the Lines in the Southern Confederacy.* Baton Rouge, La., 1944.

Stephenson, Nathaniel W. *The Day of the Confederacy.* New Haven, 1919.

Thomas, Emory M. *The Confederacy as a Revolutionary Experience.* Englewood Cliffs, N.J., 1971. Reprint, Columbia, S.C., 1991.

Wiley, Bell I. *Road to Appomattox.* New York, 1968.

Wyatt-Brown, Bertram. *Southern Honor: Ethics and Behavior in the Old South.* New York, 1982.

Secession

Barney, William L. *The Road to Secession.* New York, 1972.

Barney, William L. *The Secessionist Impulse: Alabama and Mississippi in 1860.* Princeton, 1974.

Crofts, Daniel W. *Reluctant Confederates: Upper South Unionists in the Secession Crisis.* Chapel Hill, N.C., 1989.

Ford, Lacy K., Jr. *Origins of Southern Radicalism: The South Carolina Upcountry, 1800–1860.* New York, 1988.

Inscoe, John. *Mountain Masters: Slavery and Sectional Crisis in Western North Carolina.* Knoxville, Tenn., 1989.

Johnson, Michael P. *Toward a Patriarchal Republic: The Secession of Georgia.* Baton Rouge, La., 1977.

McCardell, John. *The Idea of a Southern Nation: Southern Nationalists and Southern Nationalism, 1800–1860.* New York, 1972.

Potter, David M. *The Impending Crisis, 1848–1861.* New York, 1976.

Politics and Government

Alexander, Thomas B., and Richard E. Beringer. *The Anatomy of the Confederate Congress: A Study of the Influence of Member Characteristics on Legislative Voting Behavior, 1861–1865.* Nashville, Tenn., 1972.

Ball, Douglas B. *Financial Failure and Confederate Defeat.* Urbana, Ill., 1991.

Lee, Charles R., Jr. *The Confederate Constitutions.* Chapel Hill, N.C., 1963.

Moore, Albert B. *Conscription and Conflict in the Confederacy.* New York, 1924.

Patrick, Rembert W. *Jefferson Davis and His Cabinet.* Baton Rouge, La., 1944.

Ringold, May Spencer. *The Role of State Legislatures in the Confederacy.* Athens, Ga., 1966.

Robbins, John Brawner. "Confederate Nationalism: Politics and Government in the Confederate South, 1861–65." Ph.D. diss., Rice University, 1964.

Tatum, Georgia L. *Disloyalty in the Confederacy.* Chapel Hill, N.C., 1934.

Todd, Richard C. *Confederate Finance.* Athens, Ga., 1954.

Yearns, Wilfred B. *The Confederate Congress.* Athens, Ga., 1960.

State and Local Studies

Ash, Stephen V. *Middle Tennessee Society Transformed, 1860–1870: War and Peace in the Upper South.* Baton Rouge, La., 1988.

Barrett, John G. *The Civil War in North Carolina.* Chapel Hill, N.C., 1963.

Bergeron, Arthur W., Jr. *Confederate Mobile.* Jackson, Miss., 1991.

Bryan, T. Conn. *Confederate Georgia.* Athens, Ga., 1953.

Burton, Orville Vernon. *In My Father's House Are Many Mansions: Family and Community in Edgefield, South Carolina.* Chapel Hill, N.C., 1985.

Durrill, Wayne K. *War of Another Kind: A Southern Community in the Great Rebellion.* New York, 1990.

Escott, Paul D. *Many Excellent People: Power and Privilege in North Carolina, 1850–1900.* Chapel Hill, N.C., 1985.

Hermann, Janet Sharp. *The Pursuit of a Dream.* New York, 1981.

Kenzer, Robert C. *Kinship and Neighborhood in a Southern Community: Orange County, North Carolina, 1849–1881.* Knoxville, Tenn., 1988.

Kruman, Marc W. *Parties and Politics in North Carolina, 1836–1865.* Baton Rouge, La., 1983.

Paludan, Phillip Shaw. *Victims: A True Story of the Civil War.* Knoxville, Tenn., 1981.

Robertson, James I., Jr. *Civil War Virginia: Battleground for a Nation.* Charlottesville, Va., 1991.

Thomas, Emory M. *The Confederate State of Richmond: A Biography of the Capital.* Austin, Tex., 1971.

Thornton, J. Mills, III. *Politics and Power in a Slave Society.* Baton Rouge, La., 1978.

Wallenstein, Peter. *From Slave South to New South: Public Policy in Nineteenth Century Georgia.* Chapel Hill, N.C., 1987.

Wiener, Jonathan M. *Social Origins of the New South: Alabama, 1860–1885.* Baton Rouge, La., 1978.

Yearns, Wilfred Buck, ed. *The Confederate Governors.* Athens, Ga., 1985.

African Americans in the South

Brewer, James H. *The Confederate Negro: Virginia's Craftsmen and Military Laborers, 1861–1865.* Durham, N.C., 1969.

Cornish, Dudley T. *The Sable Arm: Negro Troops in the Union Army, 1861–1865.* New York, 1956.

Duncan, Russell. *Blue-Eyed Child of Fortune: The Civil War Letters of Colonel Robert Gould Shaw.* Athens, Ga., 1992.

Durden, Robert F. *The Gray and the Black: The Confederate Debate on Emancipation.* Baton Rouge, La., 1972.

Fields, Barbara Jeanne. *Slavery and Freedom on the Middle Ground: Maryland during the Nineteenth Century.* New Haven, 1985.

Genovese, Eugene D. *Roll, Jordan, Roll: The World the Slaves Made.* New York, 1974.

Glatthaar, Joseph T. *Forged in Battle: The Civil War Alliance of Black Soldiers and White Officers.* New York, 1990.

Johnson, Michael P., and James L. Roark. *Black Masters: A Free Family of Color in the Old South.* New York, 1984.

Mohr, Clarence L. *On the Threshold of Freedom: Masters and Slaves in Civil War Georgia.* Athens, Ga., 1986.

Wiley, Bell I. *Southern Negroes, 1861–1865.* New Haven, 1938.

Confederate Women

Clinton, Catherine. *The Plantation Mistress: Woman's World in the Old South.* New York, 1982.

Fox-Genovese, Elizabeth. *Within the Plantation Household: Black and White Women of the Old South.* Chapel Hill, N.C., 1988.

Friedman, Jean E. *The Enclosed Garden: Women and Community in the Evangelical South, 1830–1900.* Chapel Hill, N.C., 1985.

Massey, Mary Elizabeth. *Bonnet Brigades: American Women and the Civil War.* New York, 1966.

Rable, George. *Civil Wars: Women and the Crisis of Southern Nationalism.* Urbana, Ill., 1989.

Scott, Anne Firor. *The Southern Lady: From Pedestal to Politics, 1830–1930.* Chicago, 1970.

Wiley, Bell I., *Confederate Women.* Westport, Conn., 1975.

Society and Culture

Aaron, Daniel. *The Unwritten War: American Writers and the Civil War.* New York, 1973.

Andrews, J. Cutler. *The South Reports the War.* Princeton, 1970.

Bailey, Fred Arthur. *Class and Tennessee's Confederate Generation.* Chapel Hill, N.C., 1987.

Cunningham, Horace H. *Doctors in Gray: The Confederate Medical Service.* Baton Rouge, La., 1960.

Dumond, Dwight L., ed. *Southern Editorials on Secession.* New York, 1931.

Eaton, Clement. *The Waning of the Old South Civilization.* Athens, Ga., 1968.

Harwell, Richard B. *The Brief Candle: The Confederate Theatre.* Worcester, Mass., 1971.

Harwell, Richard B. *Confederate Music.* Chapel Hill, N.C., 1950.

Hill, Samuel S., Jr. *Religion in the Southern States: A Historical Study.* Macon, Ga., 1983.

Hill, Samuel S., Jr. *The South and the North in American Religion.* Athens, Ga., 1980.

Jimmerson, Randall C. *The Private Civil War: Popular Thought during the Sectional Conflict.* Baton Rouge, La., 1988.

Massey, Mary Elizabeth. *Ersatz in the Confederacy.* Columbia, S.C., 1952.

Massey, Mary Elizabeth. *Refugee Life in the Confederacy.* Baton Rouge, La., 1964.

Powell, Lawrence N. *New Masters: Northern Planters during the Civil War and Reconstruction.* New Haven, 1980.

Silver, James W. *Confederate Morale and Church Propaganda.* Tuscaloosa, Ala., 1957.

Wiley, Bell I. *Plain People of the Confederacy.* Baton Rouge, La., 1943.

Wilson, Edmund. *Patriotic Gore: Studies in the Literature of the American Civil War.* New York, 1962.

Economic Studies

Black, Robert C., III. *The Railroads of the Confederacy.* Chapel Hill, N.C., 1952.

DeCredico, Mary A. *Patriotism for Profit: Georgia's Urban Entrepreneurs and the Confederate War Effort.* Chapel Hill, N.C., 1990.

Dew, Charles B. *Ironmaker to the Confederacy: Joseph P. Anderson and the Tredegar Iron Works.* New Haven, 1966.

Goff, Richard D. *Confederate Supply.* Durham, N.C., 1969.

Lonn, Ella. *Salt as a Factor in the Confederacy.* New York, 1933.

Roland, Charles P. *Louisiana Sugar Plantations during the American Civil War.* Leiden, Netherlands, 1957.

Still, William N., Jr. *Confederate Shipbuilding.* Athens, Ga., 1969.

Vandiver, Frank E. *Ploughshares into Swords: Josiah Gorgas and Confederate Ordnance.* Austin, Tex., 1952.

Wise, Stephen R. *Lifeline of the Confederacy: Blockade Running during the Civil War.* Columbia, S.C., 1988.

Foreign Relations

Bernath, Stuart L. *Squall across the Atlantic: American Civil War Prize Cases and Diplomacy.* Berkeley, Calif., 1970.

Case, Lynn M., and Warren F. Spencer. *The United States and France: Civil War Diplomacy.* Philadelphia, 1970.

Crook, D. P. *The North, the South, and the Powers, 1861–1865.* New York, 1974.

Cullop, Charles P. *Confederate Propaganda in Europe, 1861–1865.* Coral Gables, Fla., 1969.

Ellison, Mary. *Support for Secession: Lancashire and the American Civil War.* Chicago, 1972.

Ferris, Norman B. *The Trent Affair.* Knoxville, Tenn., 1975.

Jones, Howard. *Union in Peril: The Crisis over British Intervention in the Civil War.* Chapel Hill, N.C., 1992.

Lester, Richard I. *Confederate Finance and Purchasing in Great Britain.* Charlottesville, Va., 1975.

Merli, Frank J. *Great Britain and the Confederate Navy, 1861–1865.* Bloomington, Ind., 1970.

Owsley, Frank L. *King Cotton Diplomacy: Foreign Relations of the Confederate States of America.* Rev. ed. Chicago, 1959.

Spencer, Warren F. *The Confederate Navy in Europe.* University, Ala., 1983.

General Military Studies

Barton, Michael. *Goodmen: The Character of Civil War Soldiers.* University Park, Pa., 1981.

Connelly, Thomas L., and Archer Jones. *The Politics of Command: Factions and Ideas in Confederate Strategy.* Baton Rouge, La., 1973.

Glatthaar, Joseph T. *March to the Sea and Beyond: Sherman's Troops in the Savannah and Carolinas Campaign.* New York, 1985.

Griffith, Paddy. *Battle Tactics of the Civil War.* New Haven, 1989.

Jones, Archer. *Civil War Command and Strategy: The Process of Victory and Defeat.* New York, 1992.

Jones, Archer. *Confederate Strategy from Shiloh to Vicksburg.* Baton Rouge, La., 1961.

Jones, Virgil C. *The Civil War at Sea.* 3 vols. New York, 1960–1962.

Linderman, Gerald F. *Embattled Courage: The Experience of Combat in the American Civil War.* New York, 1987.

Luvaas, Jay. *The Military Legacy of the Civil War: The European Inheritance.* Chicago, 1959.

Merrill, James M. *Battle Flags South: The Story of the Civil War Navies on Western Waters.* Rutherford, N.J., 1970.

Mitchell, Reid. *Civil War Soldiers.* New York, 1988.

Perry, Milton F. *Infernal Machines: The Story of Confederate Submarine and Mine Warfare.* Baton Rouge, La., 1965.

Robertson, James I., Jr. *Soldiers Blue and Gray.* Columbia, S.C., 1988.

Robinson, William N. *Confederate Privateers.* New Haven, 1928.

Royster, Charles. *The Destructive War: William Tecumseh Sherman, Stonewall Jackson, and the Americans.* New York, 1991.

Scharf, J. Thomas. *History of the Confederate States Navy.* New York, 1887. Reprint, New York, 1977.

Still, William N., Jr. *Iron Afloat: The Story of the Confederate Armorclads.* Nashville, Tenn., 1971.

Vandiver, Frank E. *Rebel Brass: The Confederate Command System.* Baton Rouge, La., 1956.

Weigley, Russell F. *The American Way of War: A History of United States Military Strategy and Policy.* New York, 1973.

Wiley, Bell I. *The Life of Johnny Reb: The Common Soldier of the Confederacy.* Indianapolis, 1943.

Woodworth, Steven E. *Jefferson Davis and His Generals: The Failure of Confederate Command in the West.* Lawrence, Kans., 1990.

The Lost Cause

Connelly, Thomas L., and Barbara L. Bellows. *God and General Longstreet: The Lost Cause and the Southern Mind.* Baton Rouge, La., 1982.

Foster, Gaines M. *Ghosts of the Confederacy: Defeat, the Lost Cause, and the Emergence of the New South.* New York, 1987.

Sutherland, Daniel E. *The Confederate Carpetbaggers.* Baton Rouge, La., 1988.

Wilson, Charles Reagan. *Baptized in Blood: The Religion of the Lost Cause, 1865–1920.* Athens, Ga., 1983.

[*For further discussion of historiographic shifts in the interpretation of the causes and outcome of the Civil War, see* Civil War, *articles on* Causes of the War *and* Causes of Defeat. *See also* Discography; Museums and Archives; *the extensive bibliography for the entry* Diaries, Letters, and Memoirs; *and the bibliographies of particular entries on battles and campaigns, biographical figures, governmental branches and departments, military units, ships, and states.*]

EMORY M. THOMAS

BIG BETHEL, VIRGINIA

The Civil War was less than two months old when this first significant military action in Virginia occurred. Even after the Old Dominion became the pivotal state in the Southern Confederacy, Federal troops continued to occupy Fort Monroe at the tip of the Virginia Peninsula. In command of that force was Maj. Gen. Benjamin F. Butler, a shrewd politician who owed his general's commission solely to his political power in Massachusetts. His second-in-command was Brig. Gen. Ebenezer W. Pierce, head of the Massachusetts Militia.

Early in June 1861, Butler learned that Confederates had constructed a battery emplacement at a bend in a branch of Black River at Big Bethel Church. The position was only eight miles northwest of Butler's outposts at Fort Monroe. The inexperienced Butler concluded that the 1,400 Southerners (mostly Col. D. H. Hill's First North Carolina and Maj. George Wythe Randolph's battery of howitzers) ought to be driven away. Butler thereupon organized an expedition of 4,400 men under General Pierce to do the job. Yet the grand strategy devised by Butler proved to be too sophisticated for the raw recruits under his command.

Butler's plan called for a march on the night of June 9–10, with a convergence of four separate regiments at the point of attack the next morning. Everything went wrong during the Federal movement. Nervous soldiers forgot the watchword; white badges issued for identification could not be seen in the darkness; some units were unable to find the roads they were supposed to take. The climax to the march came when two Federal regiments collided in the night and began shooting at each other. This brisk action alerted Confederates to the enemy's presence.

Late on Monday morning, June 10, with the temperature approaching ninety degrees, Federals lurched forward in an assault that quickly lost all semblance of order. Confederates squatting in the underbrush raked the Federals with musketry and cannon fire. Colonel Hill reported that his Southern troops "were in high glee, and seemed to enjoy it as much as boys do rabbit-shooting."

The one-sided contest lasted barely half an hour, after which Pierce's men fled back to their encampments in utter rout. Pierce had seemed bewildered throughout the contest. Instead of acknowledging defeat because of poor intelligence service and organizational breakdowns, Pierce blamed the outcome on the reluctance of New York colonels to obey a Massachusetts brigadier.

Union casualties were 18 killed, 53 wounded, and 5 missing. Among the dead was Maj. Theodore Winthrop, a globe-trotting journalist who was acting as Butler's military secretary. Southern losses were 1 killed and 7 wounded.

Later in the war, an action of such limited scope would have been termed a mere skirmish. Yet at this opening stage of hostilities, the steadfastness in battle of green Confederates sent encouragement through the South and gave credence to earlier boasts that "one Reb could lick ten Yankees any day." Richmond merchants proudly displayed battlefield relics in the windows of their shops. Conversely, Big Bethel sent a shock wave of embarrassment through the North.

BIBLIOGRAPHY

Dinkins, James. *1861 to 1865, by an Old Johnnie.* Dayton, Ohio, 1975.
Freeman, Douglas Southall. *Lee's Lieutenants: A Study in Command.* Vol. 1. New York, 1942. Reprint, New York, 1986.
West, Richard S., Jr. *Lincoln's Scapegoat General.* Boston, 1965.

JAMES I. ROBERTSON, JR.

BLEEDING KANSAS

The term *Bleeding Kansas* arose from a series of events that followed the passage of the Kansas-Nebraska Act in 1854. The act invalidated the restrictions on the expansion of slavery in the Missouri Compromise of 1820, initiating the struggle to make Kansas a free or slave state under the doctrine of popular sovereignty advocated by Senator Stephen A. Douglas of Illinois.

The conflicts in territorial Kansas from 1854 to 1861 involved much more than the slavery question; also at work were the insatiable hunger for both public and Indian lands, the desire by political parties for patronage appointments, competition for town sites, selection of railroad routes, and at times outright banditry and personal plunder. Yet the struggle between free-state and proslavery elements was evident even in some of these contests, and it was this controversial question that attracted national attention, with newspaper editors and politicians often exaggerating its significance.

Competition between the North and South resulted in organized efforts to encourage migration to Kansas. The New England Emigrant Aid Company was formed in Massachusetts, and more limited efforts were made in the South with the encouragement of such leaders as Col. Jefferson Buford of Alabama. In the subsequent patterns of settlement, proslavery groups were concentrated in the towns of Atchison, Leavenworth, and Lecompton and free-state settlers in Lawrence, Topeka, Manhattan, and Osawatomie.

When the time came to organize a legislature, armed proslavery Missourians crossed the border on election day 1855 to cast some of the 4,968 illegal votes against 1,210 lawful ones. Consequently the legislature and the laws it passed were denounced as bogus. The free-state groups

> **Raiders destroyed two free-state presses and burned a hotel occupied by the New England Emigrant Aid Company. . . .**

organized separately and held a constitutional convention in Topeka in October 1855, which proposed a constitution that would admit Kansas as a free state without benefit of an enabling act of Congress (usually required) but would provide for exclusion of free blacks and mulattoes from the state. Congress refused admission under this constitution.

A series of acts and threats of violence gave unhappy substance to the term *Bleeding Kansas.* Lawrence as the main seat of free-state activity became the locus of conflict in the so-called Wakarusa War in 1855, triggered when a proslavery settler killed his free-state neighbor over a boundary dispute. A military confrontation was prevented only by the intervention of the territorial governor, Wilson Shannon. A year later the city suffered an attack called the "sack of Lawrence" on May 21, led by the Douglas County proslavery sheriff Samuel J. Jones. Raiders destroyed two free-state presses and burned a hotel occupied by the New England Emigrant Aid Company and the home of the free-state leader Dr. Charles Robinson (later state governor). Upon receipt of this news John Brown, Sr., in the Osawatomie area set out to help protect Lawrence but turned back with his party of six men on May 24 to murder in especially brutal fashion five of his proslavery neighbors along Pottawatomie Creek. Two days before the sack of Lawrence, Senator Charles Sumner of Massachusetts had indicted the South in a speech, "The Crime against Kansas," which so provoked Congressman Preston Brooks of South Carolina that he beat Sumner with a cane on the floor of the Senate. The emerging Republican party thereupon coined the term "Bleeding Sumner."

The turmoil in Kansas had an impact upon the changing scene of political parties and the increased tension between the North and South. The declining Whig party sought to revive its fortunes by protesting the Kansas-Nebraska Act and its impact on the slavery issue. Its efforts between 1854 and 1856, however, were hampered by the increasing nativist opposition to Catholics and immigrants articulated by the Know-Nothing party. Attempts to fuse the interests of the two groups eventually failed. The new Republican party, which had tried to bring together one group of Whigs and Free-Soilers as early as the Jackson, Michigan, convention in 1854 , had succeeded by 1856 in becoming the major anti-Democratic party in the North. The Know-Nothings, then, can be viewed as a bridge or an intermediate phase between Whiggism and the expansion of Republicanism. The Republican party exploited in the North the proslavery sack of Lawrence and the attack on Sumner by distributing nearly a million copies of the "Crime against Kansas" speech.

National attention, both North and South, continued to focus on Kansas with the Lecompton convention meeting in the territorial capital in 1857. Delegates, elected primarily by proslavery voters (free-state electors abstained), crafted a proslavery constitution. Because it was not voted on by all the people in the territory, Senator Douglas was convinced that the principle of popular sovereignty had been violated. He broke with President James Buchanan in his opposition to the document, thereby losing much of the support once given him by fire-eaters in the South and contributing to the split in the Democratic party in the presidential election of 1860. Congress then passed the English bill, which provided for a popular vote on the Lecompton constitution. But even with the bill's provisions for generous public land grants for Kansas if the constitution were ratified, the document was rejected in the territory by a vote of 1,788 for and 11,300 against. Admission of the state into the Union was then delayed until 1861.

The violence that had flared intermittently in Kansas had caused an estimated fifty to over one hundred deaths. As late as 1858 five free-state men were killed in the Marais des Cygnes massacre by proslavery partisans.

Yet by the time Southern states were seriously debating secession, the Kansas question had become significantly muted. During the controversy over the Lecompton constitution, Governor H. R. Runnels of Texas had asserted that the rejection of Kansas as a slave state would further threaten the South, and he urged military preparations to protect the rights and honor of his state. Governor Joseph E. Brown of Georgia was equally concerned and threatened to call a convention to determine the status of Georgia if Kansas were rejected. But a Georgia citizen writing to Alexander H. Stephens expressed a more widespread view that there was little if any chance of Kansas becoming a slave state and that nothing more should be made of the issue. Many had come to realize that geographical and economic factors discouraged the expansion of slavery into Kansas and had contributed to the fact that there were only two slaves in the territory in 1860. Among the many newspaper editorials concerning secession, the *Charleston Mercury* in February 1860 was one of the very few, if not the only one, still arguing that the soil and climate of Kansas could sustain slavery. Other

newspaper editors and political leaders turned their attention in 1860 and 1861 to different issues.

[*See also* Republican Party; Sumner, Caning of.]

BIBLIOGRAPHY

Craven, Avery O. *The Growth of Southern Nationalism, 1848–1861.* A History of the South, vol. 6. Baton Rouge, La., 1953.

Dumond, Dwight L., ed. *Southern Editorials on Secession.* New York and London, 1931.

Gienapp, William E. *The Origins of the Republican Party, 1852–1856.* New York and Oxford, 1987.

Malin, James C. *John Brown and the Legend of Fifty-Six.* Philadelphia, 1942.

Potter, David M. *The Impending Crisis, 1848–1861.* New York, Hagerstown, San Francisco, and London, 1976.

Rawley, James A. *Race and Politics: "Bleeding Kansas" and the Coming of the Civil War.* Philadelphia and New York, 1969.

Robinson, W. Stitt. "The Role of the Military in Territorial Kansas." In *Territorial Kansas: Studies Commemorating the Centennial.* Lawrence, Kans., 1954.

Stampp, Kenneth M. *America in 1857: A Nation on the Brink.* New York and Oxford, 1990.

W. STITT ROBINSON

BLOCKADE

[*This entry is composed of three articles describing the Union strategy to prevent shipping through Southern ports and the Confederate efforts to combat that strategy:* An Overview; Blockade Running; *and* Blockade Runners. *For further discussion of the blockade and responses to it, see* Anglo-Confederate Purchasing; Charleston, South Carolina; Commerce Raiders; Erlanger Loan; Fort Fisher, North Carolina; Fort Wagner, South Carolina; Mobile, Alabama; New Orleans, Louisiana; New Plan; *Trent* Affair; Virginia; Wilmington, North Carolina.]

An Overview

The Union moved quickly to begin a blockade of the Confederacy. On April 19, 1861, Abraham Lincoln declared a blockade of the ports of South Carolina, Georgia, Alabama, Florida, Louisiana, and Texas, and eight days later extended it to Virginia and North Carolina. This was not intended to be a paper blockade. The object was to station enough ships to block entrance to or departure from Southern ports in order to prevent the South's obtaining essential war materials, to deny it the ability to export its cotton, and to deter Southern privateers and raiders from harassing Union shipping. But it also presented both diplomatic and physical problems for the North. Since the early years of the American Revolution, freedom of the seas and the defense of neutral rights had been an essential ingredient in American foreign policy. In pursuing its blockade of the Southern states, the North wished at the same time to avoid precedents that would hamper its own trade during future European wars. The attitude of Great Britain was helpful in achieving this objective, for the British did not want to insist on a freedom to trade that might be used against them in the future.

To close some 3,500 miles of coastline, the North had fewer than fifty ships in commission at the beginning of the war. Although the temporary Confederate policy of withholding cotton exports in an attempt to influence the British worked to the advantage of the blockaders, the Union navy had too few vessels to mount an effective blockade. So the North bought or chartered civilian vessels to fill immediate needs until more ships could be built. By the latter part of the war, nearly five hundred vessels were taking part in the operation.

During the first months, blockade runners found it comparatively simple to slip into Southern ports, but the blockade quickly became more effective. As direct entry into Southern ports from Europe became more difficult, goods intended for the Confederacy were sent on neutral vessels to Nassau in the Bahamas, Bermuda, or Havana. There they were transferred to Southern blockade runners who brought in both essential war materials and luxuries.

Dramatizing the possibilities for evading the blockade was the South's announcement in the fall of 1861 that James M. Mason and John Slidell, who were to represent the Confederacy in England and France, would proceed to Europe on a Confederate raider after running the blockade at Charleston. The Union strengthened its blockade off the port, but the two envoys were able to reach Havana on a chartered vessel. From there they attempted to travel to St. Thomas on the English ship *Trent*. *Trent* was stopped by a Union ship, and Mason and Slidell were taken to the North. For a few weeks there was fear of open conflict with England, but the crisis was defused. Neither side wanted war. American Secretary of State William H. Seward indicated that the action had not been authorized by the American government, the stern British protest stopped short of an ultimatum, and the North released the Southern emissaries.

The difficulty of blockading the numerous ports and inlets of the Confederacy and the necessity for better positioned Union bases persuaded the Union Navy Strategy Board that the blockade would have to be tightened by the use of amphibious operations to seize key inlets and provide new bases for Union vessels. The first of these operations was intended to make the blockade of Virginia more efficient. Union ships in the Chesapeake were being evaded by shallow draft vessels that connected Richmond and Norfolk by canal with the sounds of Virginia and North Carolina. Blockade runners made extensive use of this route in the early months of the war. But in late August 1861, a Union force attacked forts guarding Hatteras Inlet and captured Forts Clark and Hatteras. The latter was converted into a Union base.

An advantage for Confederate blockade runners was the distance of the Union bases at Hampton Roads and Key West from many of the ports and inlets that had to be blockaded. The Atlantic Blockading Squadron, based in Hampton Roads, found it difficult to police the whole area, and in the early fall of 1861 it was divided into northern and southern sections. Lincoln and his cabinet also accepted a proposal, presented by Secretary of the Navy Gideon Welles, for an attack on Port Royal. Situated between Charleston and Savannah, Port Royal possessed a fine natural harbor, capable of serving all the needs of the blockaders. In early November, a large Union force of some twelve thousand troops and numerous ships occupied Port Royal after the Confederates abandoned its defending forts. This led to the Union control of a whole string of sea islands and made possible further amphibious operations along the south Atlantic coast.

In the winter of 1861–1862, the Union tried again to make blockade evasion more difficult in the North Carolina–Virginia region. The North Carolina sounds continued to present great opportunities for blockade runners, and early in the new year the Union sent some 11,500 men to attack Roanoke Island. They hoped to capture the island and to move against the towns on Albemarle Sound to disrupt Confederate canal and rail communication. Not all the objects were attained, but Roanoke Island was taken and the noose around the South was drawn a little tighter.

In an effort to break the tightening cord, the Confederacy in March 1862 sent its ironclad CSS *Virginia* (previously the USS *Merrimack*) to try to break the Union blockade at Hampton Roads. *Merrimack* had been partially burned and scuttled by Union forces when Norfolk was taken by the Confederates early in the war. The Confederates had rebuilt it as an ironclad. The Union knew of this potential threat and had built its own ironclad—*Monitor*—to counter it. In trying to break the blockade, *Virginia* at first had some success, but *Monitor* fought it to a standoff, which left the blockade intact. The Confederacy experimented with ironclads and submarines throughout the war, but the North had the resources to counter all such efforts to break the blockade. The submarine CSS *H. L. Hunley* did succeed in sinking a blockading vessel off Charleston in February 1864 but did not return from the engagement.

In the first year of the war the Union had difficulty in mounting an effective blockade of the ports along the Confederate coastline in the Gulf of Mexico. Ultimately, the Union blockade in that region came to depend heavily on amphibious operations. Both New Orleans and Mobile provided great opportunities for Southern blockade runners. Of the two, New Orleans presented somewhat fewer problems for direct assault, and the Union determined to capture this vital Southern port. Preliminary footholds were gained in the fall of 1861, but the main attack was launched early the next year. In April, Flag Officer David G. Farragut combined forces with Commdr. David D. Porter and Gen. Benjamin Butler to capture the city, thereby delivering a powerful blow to Confederate trade. Mobile was too heavily defended to be taken, but Union forces put it under an increasingly stringent blockade. The North also launched a series of attacks against Texas ports.

In the early months of the war, Confederate privateers had caused considerable havoc to Union commerce, but as the blockade tightened in 1862 and 1863, and as neutrals refused to accept Confederate prizes in their ports, the main assault on Union merchant ships was launched by Confederate government raiders. From time to time these succeeded in slipping into Confederate ports. Also, blockade runners continued to bring in much needed supplies, usually sailing from neutral ports in the Caribbean.

A major problem experienced by the Confederacy was that of private owners of blockade runners seeking greater profits by importing scarce luxury goods rather than the necessities needed by Southern armies. The government first urged private blockade runners to carry military supplies, then made use of government-owned ships, and finally, in 1864 decreed that only necessary articles could be imported. Private owners were also ordered to provide half of the cargo space in their blockade runners for use by the Confederate government. Blockade runners continued to operate until the end of the war, but they never met all the needs of Southern armies.

In its efforts to prevent the activities of the blockade runners, the Union was prepared to interpret its maritime rights in ways that it had challenged in earlier years. The Union defended the doctrine of "continuous voyage," which had been used against the United States by Great Britain during the Napoleonic Wars. This doctrine allowed the seizure of ships trading between neutral ports if the cargo was ultimately destined for a blockaded port or, in the case of a ship carrying contraband, if it was destined for any port in enemy territory. American courts upheld the seizure of British ships destined for neutral ports when the cargo was ultimately intended for the Confederacy. In the *Peterhoff* case this doctrine was extended even to goods that were destined to come into the Confederacy overland from the Mexican port of Matamoros. (The Mexican-Texas border was used for widespread evasion of the blockade.).

The situation of both neutrals and Confederate blockade runners became more precarious after September 1862 when the Union Navy Department created a West India Squadron, with the intention of both protecting Union ships from Confederate cruisers and reducing the activities of blockade runners.

In the last two years of the war, evasion of the Union blockade became much more difficult, although runners were still able to enter some of the major Southern ports. Charleston was a heavily used point of entry until September 1863 when Union forces captured Fort Wagner. The city, however, was able to resist attack from the sea and remained in Confederate hands until 1865.

Mobile was another port that presented major problems for Union blockaders; it possessed formidable defenses against amphibious operations. Not until August 1864 did Farragut have the strength necessary to take the Mobile Bay forts, when he pressed ahead relentlessly with his famous cry, "Damn the torpedoes." Mobile itself was not occupied until the very end of the war, but the capture of the forts effectively closed the port to Confederate vessels.

By 1864 Wilmington, North Carolina, offered the most opportunities for blockade runners. It was the vital supply port for Confederate armies in Virginia and was also a port through which the South continued to export cotton. Access to the port by way of the Cape Fear River was defended primarily by Forts Fisher and Caswell. Until these were taken the port could not be closed. A strong Union attack on Wilmington's defenses failed in December 1864, but in January 1865 a large fleet and some eight thousand troops took Fort Fisher and closed the last major gap in the Union blockade.

The Union, however, never completely sealed the coastline of the Confederacy. Even in the last year of the war, half of the blockade runners were getting through. The Union blockade nevertheless was a success. Southern imports and exports dropped dramatically during the war. This was at a time when the Confederacy desperately needed increased imports to supply its armies and maximum sales of cotton to finance its huge war effort. Largely because of the Union blockade, Southern armies were undersupplied and Southern finances became increasingly chaotic as the war progressed. The South's lack of naval power allowed the North to pursue a relentless war of attrition.

BIBLIOGRAPHY

Anderson, Bern. *By Sea and by River: The Naval History of the Civil War.* New York, 1962.

Bernath, Stuart L. *Squall across the Atlantic: American Civil War Prize Cases and Diplomacy.* Berkeley, Calif., 1970.

Jones, Virgil C. *The Civil War at Sea.* 3 vols. New York, 1960–1962.

Nash, Howard P., Jr. *A Naval History of the Civil War.* South Brunswick, 1972.

Owsley, Frank. *King Cotton Diplomacy: Foreign Relations of the Confederate States of America.* 2d ed. Chicago, 1959.

West, Richard S., Jr. *Mr. Lincoln's Navy.* London, 1957.

Wise, Stephen R. *Lifeline of the Confederacy: Blockade Running during the Civil War.* Columbia, S.C., 1988.

REGINALD HORSMAN

Blockade Running

Throughout the Civil War, munitions, uniform material, leather, food, and other essential military and civilian goods poured into the Confederacy on board vessels known as blockade runners. These vessels were a vital element in the Confederate supply system. Before the war ended, blockade running would be sustaining the Southern armies, but at the beginning of the conflict few realized the tremendous volume of trade that would eventually exist between the Confederacy and the outside world.

In early 1861, the head of the Confederate Ordnance Bureau, Col. Josiah Gorgas, had three sources of supplies for the Confederate armed forces: goods on hand, home production, and imports. By using the arms seized in Federal arsenals, Gorgas had enough weapons and supplies to outfit the 100,000 men called out by President Jefferson Davis. Unlike others in the South, Gorgas did not believe that the war would be a quick one, and he knew that his on-hand stocks of munitions would soon disappear. In time, he planned to establish munition plants that would make the new nation self-sustaining, but Gorgas realized that until the

> Before the war ended, blockade running would be sustaining the Southern armies. . . .

factories could be completed, certain "articles of prime necessity" would have to be imported from Europe. Imports were supposed to be only a stopgap measure, something to fill the void between the depletion of existing stocks and the beginning of home production. But the Confederates were never able to meet their needs with domestic industry, and the flow of imports grew until it eventually became the most important element in the Confederate supply system.

In April 1861, in order to gain foreign supplies, Gorgas dispatched Capt. Caleb Huse to Great Britain to serve as a purchasing agent. Huse was later joined by Maj. Edward C. Anderson, and together they began work with Comdr. James Dunwoody Bulloch, the purchasing agent for the Navy Department. To provide funds for their agents the Confederacy contracted with the Charleston firm of John Fraser and Company, who sent bills of exchange to its Liverpool office of Fraser, Trenholm, and Company, from which cash was provided to the War Department's European officials. But even with the funds, the agents still faced two problems: the Confederacy's determination to follow a foreign policy known as "King Cotton," and the Federal blockade.

King Cotton. The blockade of the Southern coast had been established shortly after the firing on Fort Sumter.

Though in the beginning it was enforced by only a handful of vessels and its legality was questioned, it was recognized by the major European powers. At the same time, the British monarch, Queen Victoria, called upon her subjects to avoid giving assistance to either side.

Though disappointed by the European response, the Southerners were not worried because they believed that King Cotton would protect their new nation. King Cotton was an economic and political theory based on the coercive power of Southern cotton. The British textile industry imported 80 percent of the South's cotton. Without the cotton, the theory held, the industry would fail, and the entire economic fabric of Great Britain would collapse. In order to avoid that disaster, the British would have to intervene in the war on the South's side.

It was for this reason that during the summer of 1861, local politicians, merchants, newspapermen, and planters banded together to enforce an embargo keeping the South's cotton at home. Though never sanctioned by the government, the embargo was unofficially approved by Davis and his advisers, who felt it would bring Great Britain into the war. At the same time, in order to aid the financially disrupted planters, the Confederate government purchased over 400,000 bales of cotton. Initially viewed as a white elephant, this cotton eventually played an important role in the blockade-running system.

Though designed to bring the British into the war, the embargo also had the side effect of depriving Anderson, Huse, and Bulloch of a means to transport supplies. No vessels were coming from the South, and for the moment, British shippers were reluctant to go against the wishes of their queen or the guns of the Union navy. For the moment the purchasing agents were stymied, and for assistance they turned to the firm of Fraser, Trenholm, and Company, the Confederacy's European financial agents, for help in shipping their goods.

Fraser, Trenholm, and Company was a branch of the Charleston-based John Fraser and Company. Both were directed by George Alfred Trenholm. From his Charleston office Trenholm backed the cotton embargo, but at the same time allowed his partner in Liverpool, Charles K. Prioleau, to outfit a steamer to run the blockade. The vessel readied by Prioleau was the screw steamer *Bermuda,* organized as a private commercial venture. Prioleau agreed to sell cargo space to Anderson and Huse.

Though the agents felt the cost to be high, they also realized that this was their best opportunity to deliver their goods. They met Prioleau's price and on September 18, 1861, after an uneventful voyage, *Bermuda* successfully arrived at Savannah, Georgia, becoming the first steam blockade runner to reach the South. After landing its cargo, *Bermuda* returned to Liverpool with over two thousand bales of cotton. Profits were tremendous, and this example soon caused other firms to organize blockade-running ventures. Any hesitation brought on by the blockade or Queen Victoria's proclamation soon disappeared in the quest for money.

Although *Bermuda*'s success inspired additional blockade-running companies, it did little to relieve the problems confronting the Confederate purchasing agents. They still had no government-owned vessels to carry their munitions, and private firms were escalating their rates on government cargoes. Anderson, the senior agent, decided that it was in the best interest of the Confederacy to cut out the middleman and purchase a steamer. With financial help from the Navy Department agents, the steamer *Fingal* was obtained and sent through the blockade, arriving at Savannah in mid-November 1861. Equipment from the vessel was enough to outfit ten regiments. As Bulloch stated, the ship carried "the greatest military cargo ever imported into the Confederacy."

Besides the armaments, *Fingal* also carried Anderson and Bulloch. Anderson went on to Richmond where he pushed the concept of government-owned-and-operated blockade runners, but he found no backers. Neither the War Department nor the Navy Department would consider any involvement with blockade running. Officials preferred to leave it in the hands of private shippers while waiting for British intervention. Disillusioned with the results of his visit, Anderson returned to Savannah, where he served out the war as an artillery officer.

While Anderson began working on Savannah's defenses, Huse continued to purchase supplies in Europe, and since there were still no Southern vessels arriving in Great Britain, he contracted with local firms to carry the goods into the Confederacy. Huse's supplies arrived by two methods. He contracted for direct delivery to the South by British shippers, or he sent cargoes to Havana, Cuba, or Nassau, Bahamas, where they were transferred to steamers for the final run through the blockade. The latter system of transshipping proved more popular, and, by early 1862, vessels owned by British blockade-running companies and Trenholm's firms were operating between Havana and Nassau and the Confederacy. For their services, the private shippers charged the government extremely high rates, which Huse and other Southern agents had to meet.

Assisting Huse were Confederate consuls Charles J. Helm in Havana and Louis Heyliger in Nassau. Besides serving as government representatives, the two consuls had the crucial responsibility of making sure that cargoes received from Huse were properly transshipped. Both performed admirably, but because of the early capture of New Orleans, Heyliger soon found himself overseeing the bulk of the supplies coming from Great Britain.

During the spring and summer of 1862, Heyliger worked with private shippers to deliver vital munitions. The task posed problems. Even though Heyliger paid extraordinary fees for cargo space, he found that many companies refused to work with him, preferring instead to carry more profitable civilian goods rather than the bulky and often dangerous munitions. The best deals were made with Trenholm's firms, who gave the government preferred rates, though their patriotism never cut too deeply into their profit margin.

Although Trenholm's firms were on occasion willing to offer special deals to the Confederacy, British manufacturers cautiously regulated their involvement with Huse, being careful not to overextend their credit. By the end of 1862, the Confederate purchasing agent was £900,000 in debt and his means of payment seemed at an end. The ever-increasing premiums on bills of exchange soon ended their use and Huse had nearly expended his supply of specie. Without some form of exchange, Huse's operations would collapse. Then the Confederacy discovered a new use for King Cotton.

Cotton Bonds. When the South's cotton embargo failed to bring Great Britain into the war, many thought that the hundreds of thousands of cotton bales purchased by the government at the start of the war would become the predicted white elephant, but this was not the case. Cotton, so long an instrument of foreign policy, was now converted to a medium of exchange.

Following the lead of the Navy Department, the government began to use cotton to finance its overseas ventures. Employing the cotton purchased early in the war, the Confederacy issued a variety of cotton bonds. There were two ways to make a profit off the bonds: one could receive interest and redeem the bond at face value after a set length of time, or the holder could bring the bond to the Confederacy and receive cotton.

It was the latter method that made the bonds so popular. Cotton could be obtained in the South at about ten cents a pound and then sold in Great Britain for forty-eight cents a

> **Following the lead of the Navy Department, the government began to use cotton to finance its overseas ventures.**

pound, thus making a cotton bale purchased for $50 in Charleston worth nearly $250 on the Liverpool market. There was a wide variety of bonds, or as they were sometimes called, certificates. Even some of the Southern states, such as Georgia and North Carolina, issued them and used them to sponsor their own blockade-running ventures.

The use of the bonds allowed the Confederacy to pay off Huse's debt and provide him with new funds and credit for additional supplies. They were the basis for contracts between the South and its suppliers and were also used to finance the purchase and construction of blockade runners and warships. Private blockade-running ventures used them to guarantee outgoing cargoes for their steamers, because with the bonds and the right type of vessels, blockade running could be an extremely profitable business.

Using the bonds, many War Department bureaus, such as the Subsistence, Quartermaster, and Medical bureaus, withdrew their business from Huse and entered into one-sided partnerships with blockade-running companies—and there was never any shortage of such companies. The largest and most successful were the two companies operated by George Trenholm. Together his firms operated over thirty blockade runners and cargo vessels and grossed millions of dollars, which were reinvested in ships, cargoes, real estate, and Confederate bonds.

Other important firms included the Importing and Exporting Company of South Carolina, the Chicora Importing and Exporting Company, and the Charleston Importing and Exporting Company. These Charleston-based companies paid handsome dividends to their investors. Among the prominent British companies were the highly successful Anglo-Confederate Trading Company and the less lucrative Collie and Company. All these firms delivered civilian and military goods to the Confederacy. The civilian goods were immensely profitable since they were sold at outrageous wartime prices that contributed to inflation throughout the South.

The delivery of military goods also gave a good return, as the firms made extremely favorable contracts with the various War Department bureaus. One bargain, struck between the Confederacy and Crenshaw and Collie and Company, had the government paying 75 percent of all expenses plus the commission fees for the purchasing of ships and supplies, while allowing its civilian partners to use one-quarter of the cargo space for privately owned goods. Though a lopsided venture, the contract was similar to many issued during the war. Because of the need for supplies, most government agencies felt that a bad contract was better than no contract.

The Ordnance Bureau. The one notable exception to this arrangement was Gorgas's Ordnance Bureau. Like Anderson, Gorgas realized the advantage in using government-owned-and-operated vessels. Instead of making contracts with blockade-running firms, Gorgas had his agents purchase steamers in Great Britain. A depot headed by Maj. Norman S. Walker was established in St. George, Bermuda; from there the goods purchased and shipped by Huse were transferred to Ordnance Bureau steamers and sent to Wilmington, North Carolina, where they were met by Capt. James Sexias.

The Ordnance Bureau's blockade-running operation was under the control of Gorgas's brother-in-law, Maj. Thomas L. Bayne. Bayne supervised not only the landing and distribution of incoming cargo but also the purchasing and loading of government cotton. Initially Bayne's section worked out of Wilmington, but before the war ended, his command was upgraded to bureau status with agents at Charleston, Mobile, and St. Marks, Florida.

The line established by Gorgas and operated by Bayne employed five vessels. The most successful were *Cornubia, Robert E. Lee,* and *Eugenie,* captained by the furloughed Confederate naval officers Richard N. Gayle, John Wilkinson, and Joseph Fry, respectively. A typical cargo consisted of cases of Enfield rifles, cartridges, leather, knapsacks, stationery, sewing thread, lead, saltpeter, and uniform cloth. Though in service only from November 1862 to November 1863, Gorgas's vessels made forty-seven runs through the blockade. They delivered, among other things, nearly 100,000 Enfield rifles, tens of thousands of cartridges, and thousands of pounds of lead and saltpeter, all basic military necessities needed to keep the Confederate army alive.

The vessels operated by Gorgas were products of an ongoing maritime revolution brought about by blockade running. Steam warships had ended the days of sailing ships, and to counter their pursuers, the blockade runners also turned to steam engines. By the time the war ended, blockade running had helped launch a new generation of steam vessels, including the first successful commercial use of twin-screw-propeller vessels. The class of steamer that started the revolution was that found in the United Kingdom's coastal and cross-channel passenger trade, known as Clyde steamers. These were later replaced by iron- and steel-hulled vessels built exclusively for blockade running. Designed to carry an immense amount of cargo, these ships could make a profit of $100,000 on a single voyage from the Confederacy.

Blockade-Running Routes. The new vessels were needed. By December 1864, all of Gorgas's ships had been lost. At first the Confederate government did not replace them, but instead increased their reliance on private vessels. Operating out of Havana, Nassau, and Bermuda, the steamers delivered their cargoes to Charleston and Wilmington on the east coast and Mobile and Galveston in the Gulf of Mexico.

In the Gulf, Mobile grew in importance as an importation site for government supplies. From there supplies were sent to Selma and other western depots for distribution or use in munition plants. Down the coast, Confederate cargoes delivered to Galveston rarely crossed the Mississippi River. Logistics coupled with political instability in Mexico kept Texas from ever becoming a major landing site. What did come in remained in the Trans-Mississippi Department for use by the local military.

The Confederacy directed the majority of its shipments to Charleston and Wilmington where the goods could be easily transported to depots, factories, and armies. The most popular routes were from Nassau to Charleston and Bermuda to Wilmington. After the attack on Charleston during the summer of 1863, the bulk of the Nassau trade shifted to

Wilmington, making it the South's main port of entry and one of the most strategic points in the Confederacy.

The ships carrying supplies to the east coast had a very high success rate. During the war, runners were successful on over 75 percent of their runs, and most of the time the ships passed in and out unseen by the blockaders. The runners had the advantages of speed and surprise over their adversaries. Rarely would a cannon shell find its mark and even then the Union warships did not try to sink the blockade runners; when captured, most blockade vessels were taken north, condemned at prize courts, and sold with their cargoes at auction. The money was divided among the captors, thus making it far more advantageous for Northern crews to capture than to sink the runners.

Confederate Regulation of Blockade Running. Because of the high success rate and resulting profits, private companies dominated the trade until August 1863, when the Confederate government was finally forced to take an active hand in blockade running. Defeats at Gettysburg and Vicksburg had resulted in an increased demand for supplies and had dealt a severe blow to the Southern bond market, shattering the Confederacy's overseas finances. In order to revive the South's credit and gain new supplies, Secretary of War James A. Seddon turned to an expanded use of cotton. He ordered his commanders at Wilmington, Charleston, and Mobile to requisition cargo space for the shipment of government cotton. The operators of the blockade runners were paid a fair rate for the space, and any refusal would result in their vessels being seized.

This was only the beginning of Seddon's plans. In March 1864 his initial instructions were tightened and, with presidential approval, passed into law. The stricter regulations allowed the Confederacy to take up to 50 percent of a vessel's outgoing and incoming cargo space. This guaranteed that the South would be able to export its cotton to pay for European goods and would have stowage space for incoming supplies. At the same time Gorgas's bureau was expanded to supervise all government overseas shipping. In Europe, operations were consolidated under Colin J. McRae, who, in effect, became the Confederacy's European secretary of the treasury.

The unheralded McRae did a remarkable job in establishing a centralized system in Europe. He also revived Anderson's and Gorgas's plan for a line of Confederate-owned blockade runners. He ordered fourteen vessels in Great Britain and planned eventually to remove all private operators from the business of carrying government supplies.

McRae was soon joined by another official who also realized the importance of government-sponsored blockade running. During the summer of 1864, the Confederacy called upon the director of the largest blockade-running operation, George Alfred Trenholm, to become secretary of the treasury. Trenholm accepted the position, resigned from his companies, and set to work running the government's overseas operations. He promulgated additional, stricter regulations and made plans for the government's fourteen blockade runners being built in Great Britain. Only two of these specialized vessels, however, saw Confederate service before the war ended.

Even without these super–blockade runners, the flow of supplies continued. Under Trenholm's and McRae's guidance the Confederacy received more munitions during their tenure than at any time earlier, but the men were fighting a losing battle. The South, battered by Northern armies and suffering massive desertions from its own ranks, was running out of men. Nor could it keep its vital ports open. In August 1864 Mobile was captured; Wilmington was closed in early January 1865; and a month later Charleston was evacuated. The fall of these harbors cut the Confederacy's lifeline.

Because of the determined work of a few relatively unknown individuals, the economic power of cotton, and specialized steamers, the Confederate military was never without the means to fight. By Confederate records the South imported during the war 60 percent of its arms, 30 percent of its lead for bullets, 75 percent of the army's saltpeter, and nearly all its paper for cartridges. The majority of cloth for uniforms and leather for shoes and accoutrements came through the blockade, as well as huge amounts of metals, chemicals, and medicine. During the last months of the war, the Army of Northern Virginia received the bulk of its food via blockade runners. Though the lifeline was fragile and tenuous, it worked until the ports were captured. Defeat did not come from lack of materials. In fact, by the end of the war, the South had more munitions and goods than men; manpower was the one thing the blockade runners could not supply.

BIBLIOGRAPHY

Bradlee, Francis B. C. *Blockade Running during the Civil War and the Effect of Land and Water Transportation on the Confederacy.* Salem, Mass., 1925.

Gorgas, Josiah. "Notes on the Ordnance Department of the Confederate Government." *Southern Historical Society Papers* 12 (1884): 68–75. Reprint, Wilmington, N.C., 1990.

Hobart-Hampden, Augustus C. *Never Caught.* London, 1867.

Soley, James R. *The Blockade and the Cruisers.* New York, 1883.

Taylor, Thomas E. *Running the Blockade.* London, 1897.

Vandiver, Frank, ed. *Confederate Blockade Running through Bermuda, 1861–1865: Letter and Cargo Manifests.* Austin, Tex., 1947.

Wise, Stephen R. *Lifeline of the Confederacy: Blockade Running during the Civil War.* Columbia, S.C., 1988.

STEPHEN R. WISE

Blockade Runners

A blockade runner was any vessel that challenged the U.S. Navy's blockade of the Confederate coastline. Though a few Confederate warships such as *Nashville, Sumter,* and *Florida* and some privateers ran the blockade, the vast majority were cargo vessels that carried civilian and military supplies into the South and transported cotton to neutral ports. The motivating factor behind these ships was the profit derived from the sale of their cargoes.

Men served as captains of blockade runners for a variety of reasons. Such Southerners as Thomas Lockwood, Robert Lockwood, James Carlin, Louis Coxetter, and Robert Smith were motivated by both patriotism and the desire for profits. Others such as naval officers John Wilkinson, John Newland Maffitt, Joseph Fry, and Richard N. Gayle operated blockade runners under orders from the Confederate government. British citizens Joannes Wyllie, Johnathon Steele, Augustus Charles Hobart-Hampden, and the Irishman William Ryan ran blockade runners for adventure and profit. Whatever their motive, their skills were an important factor in a vessel's success or failure.

At the start of the war, many shipowners attempted to use sailing vessels, but quickly realized that they would not do. Sailing ships large enough to carry a profitable amount of cargo were easy marks for steam warships, and the small brigs, schooners, and sloops that could slip in and out of harbors and sounds had insufficient cargo capacity. After June of 1862, sailing ship blockade runners virtually disappeared along the east coast. They were used somewhat more often in the Gulf of Mexico, where many operated along the Texas coast; but supplies from east of the Mississippi River rarely crossed the river and imports coming into Texas had no impact on the war's major theaters.

To counter their steam-powered pursuers, the blockade runners turned to steam engines. Early in the war, before the blockade tightened, any steamer had a good chance of reaching a Southern port, and the first vessels to run the blockade were large, deeply laden ships such as the propeller-driven *Bermuda* and *Fingal.* Both were conventional merchantmen with large cargo capacities, but they had short careers because their deep drafts restricted them to main ship channels where eventual capture was inevitable. By the spring of 1862, the large steamers that had escaped capture were relegated to ferrying goods between Great Britain and Nassau, Bermuda, and Havana. From these ports a more elusive style of blockade runner was employed in order to avoid the Federal warships.

The steamship type that first began transshipping cargoes to and from the Confederacy were American-built coastal packets. These paddlewheel vessels were built with a low freeboard which, coupled with a wide beam, gave the steamers a shallow draft. They were sturdy and well adapted to negotiating the shallow southern coastline. Once their staterooms were removed, the vessels could carry between two hundred and five hundred bales of cotton.

Along the east coast such ships as *Gordon, Cecile,* and *Kate* became prominent blockade runners. *Kate,* a 477-ton packet measuring 165 feet by 29 feet, 10 inches by 10 feet, 4 inches, was successfully guided through the blockade twenty times by Capt. Thomas Lockwood. In the Gulf the New Orleans–based vessels *Matagorda* and *William G. Hewes* also became renowned blockade runners under the names *Alice* and *Ella and Annie.* Before its capture in 1864 off Mobile, *Alice,* commanded by Robert Smith, made eighteen trips through the blockade.

Though many packets were successful blockade runners, investors continued to seek out ships that could turn an even greater profit, and by early 1862, operators began using a style of paddlewheel steamer that had been developed for the United Kingdom's coastal and cross-channel passenger trade. Since many were built in and around Glasgow on the Clyde River, the ships were called Clyde steamers. Usually built with an iron hull, they were rugged, fast, and maneuverable and had a shallow draft and large cargo capacity that allowed them to carry from five hundred to one thousand bales of cotton. In a short time they became the mainstay of blockade running.

The first Clyde steamer to begin blockade running was *Herald,* a 450-ton iron-hulled sidewheeler that made 24 trips through the blockade before being destroyed off Wilmington. In all, over 80 Clyde steamers were converted to blockade runners. Among their ranks were the war's top runners, including the most successful, *Syren,* which made 33 trips in and out of Wilmington and Charleston. It was followed by *Denbigh* with 26 runs from Havana to Mobile and Galveston. Other ships of this class included *Alice,* with 25 trips; *Fannie,* with 20 trips; and the Confederate Ordnance Bureau's *Cornubia,* with 18 trips. Another well-known ship was *Margaret and Jessie,* which also made 18 trips and was considered the war's fastest blockade runner.

Although these ships were very successful, business interests demanded still better, and soon British dockyards were turning out ships built specifically for running the blockade. The first was *Banshee,* a steel-hulled 533-ton sidewheeler that measured 214 feet by 20 feet by 8 feet. In May 1863, it became the first steel-hulled vessel to cross the Atlantic Ocean. Then, under the command of Johnathon Steele, it became a successful blockade runner operating primarily between Nassau and Wilmington.

At first these ships were designed simply to meet the trade's basic requirements, but soon, seeking to increase profits, builders began to experiment with design and construction techniques, resulting in a revolution in shipbuilding. Engines were placed so that they were surrounded by coal bunkers to protect them from enemy shot. Many of the new runners were built of steel and designed with rounded deck structures, underwater blow-off pipes, hinged masts, and telescoping smokestacks. Builders experimented with paint schemes to camouflage the runners from enemy warships and increased engine size as well as the size and number of boilers. For additional speed, vessels were made longer with extremely narrow beams. Because of their design, the runners contained more cargo space than contemporary merchant ships.

The first generation of these super–blockade runners often suffered from many engineering and mechanical problems. *Banshee,* with steel plates of only ⅛ inch and ³⁄₁₆ inch, leaked badly, and others like the *Flamingo* spent more time being repaired than running the blockade. But builders soon overcame these problems and by the end of the war were producing such vessels as *Chicora, Lucy,* and *Fox,* which between them made fifty-two trips through the blockade without being captured. The epitome of the final generation of runners was *Colonel Lamb,* which was partially designed by Capt. Thomas Lockwood, the war's most successful blockade-running captain and the acknowledged "father of the trade." The 1,788-ton *Colonel Lamb* was the finest vessel built for blockade running. It measured 281 feet by 36 feet by 15.5 feet and could carry 2,000 bales of cotton, which translated into a profit of $100,000 on a single voyage from the Confederacy.

Though most blockade runners were sidewheelers, the war also saw the first successful commercial use of twin-screw-propeller steamers. Some fourteen of these novel vessels attempted to run the blockade, the most successful being *Annie,* which made thirteen trips. The twin screws proved to be sturdy, reliable vessels that combined light draft, speed, and great carrying capacity.

The specialized vessels used for blockade running were, for the most part, owned by private companies. But the Confederate Ordnance Bureau operated a line of blockade runners, and the Treasury Department also owned a few. In 1864, the government ordered fourteen super–blockade runners, but most were unfinished at the war's end.

The Confederate navy made use of some of its outdated Southern-built warships as runners and used the British-built twin-screw *Coquette* to transport cotton and supplies. The navy also employed the British-built *Juno* as a picket vessel at Charleston and in 1864 purchased at Wilmington the twin-screws *Atalanta* and *Edith* for use as commerce raiders. In Great Britain, Comdr. James Dunwoody Bulloch ordered a number of twin-screw vessels that were designed to serve as both blockade runners and commerce raiders, but none was finished in time to see active duty.

In all just under 300 steamers tested the blockade. Out of approximately 1,300 attempts, over 1,000 were successful. The average lifetime of a blockade runner was just over four runs, or two round trips. Some 136 were captured and another 85 destroyed.

By war's end, the blockade runners had evolved into very specialized vessels that carried out their missions with a high success ratio. They were so successful that the Federal navy converted captured blockade runners into gunboats and used them as blockaders, but even this could not stop the blockade runners from delivering their cargoes. Throughout the war, the Confederate military was well served by the runners.

Besides their impact on the war, blockade runners greatly influenced subsequent ship design. They expanded maritime technology by advancing the development and use of steel, twin-screw propulsion, enclosed ship bridges, fast hull forms, and camouflage paint schemes, all innovations that are still used in ship construction today.

BIBLIOGRAPHY

Foster, Kevin. "Phantoms, Banshees, Will of the Wisps and the Dare; or, the Search for Speed under Steam: The Design of Blockade Running Steamships." M.A. thesis, East Carolina University, 1991.

Price, Marcus. "Masters and Pilots Who Tested the Blockade of the Confederate Ports, 1861–1865." *American Neptune* 8 (April 1961): 81–106.

Wise, Stephen R. *Lifeline of the Confederacy: Blockade Running during the Civil War.* Columbia, S.C., 1988.

STEPHEN R. WISE

BLUFFTON MOVEMENT

The Bluffton movement, led by Robert Barnwell Rhett, Sr., of South Carolina, aimed to sever connections with the Democratic party, to challenge the leadership of John C. Calhoun, and to advance the cause of disunion. Launched on July 31, 1844, at a dinner in Rhett's honor in the low-country town of Bluffton, South Carolina, the movement quickly spread to the neighboring Beaufort, Colleton, Orangeburg, and Barnwell districts, enlisting men in the cause of separate state action against a hostile national government.

The causes of the movement were the abolition by Congress of the gag rule—the ban on antislavery petitions presented to Congress—and the tabling of the McKay bill, which would have lowered tariff duties, in the spring of 1844. Suspicious of ties with a national party composed of Northern as well as Southern members, Rhett wanted to repudiate the Democratic party and its presidential nominee, James K. Polk. Unlike Calhoun, who believed that the Democrats would protect Southern interests, Rhett feared that the Northern majority threatened to destroy slavery. Moreover, he was concerned about Northern Democratic equivocation on the annexation of Texas. Though Polk favored annexation and the Democratic platform advocated

CONFEDERATE $10,000 BOND.

GORDON BLEULER

territorial expansion, Rhett and the "Bluffton Boys" suspected that Northern Democrats could not be trusted to redeem those pledges after the election.

The movement revealed the beginning of a generational split in South Carolina politics. The Blufftonites were largely younger, inexperienced men drawn to the leadership of Rhett, who was twenty years younger than Calhoun. Hoping to secure the presidential nomination in 1848, Calhoun and his allies supported Polk, and their influence first weakened and then ended the Bluffton movement six weeks after it began. Rhett returned to the Calhoun fold. But a rising generation of leaders, too young to have experienced the nullification movement, had received their first schooling in Carolina radicalism. In time, they would be further emboldened to calculate the value of the Union.

BIBLIOGRAPHY

Boucher, Chauncey S. "The Annexation of Texas and the Bluffton Movement in South Carolina." *Mississippi Valley Historical Review* 6 (1919): 3–33.

Walther, Eric H. *The Fire-Eaters.* Baton Rouge, La., 1992.

White, Laura A. *Robert Barnwell Rhett: Father of Secession.* New York, 1931.

JOHN MCCARDELL

BONDS

Prior to 1861, Americans had financed their wars by three basic means: their government collected taxes, confiscated the property of alien enemies, and borrowed money from its citizens. Given the American distaste for heavy taxation and the inability of the Confederacy to seize and sell Unionist property by sequestration, the Confederate Congress had to depend heavily on loans to finance its war effort.

Loans came in several forms. The government issued Treasury notes, with or without interest, that could be used as money. Interest-bearing notes were intended to be closely held by investors. Circulating Treasury notes, if overused, would cause serious inflation. In addition, the Treasury needed to avoid selling securities that would fall due before the war was over; otherwise it would have to pay such debts at a time when it was hard-pressed to meet its current obligations. Therefore, government borrowing efforts had to be directed toward the sale of coupon and registered bonds, payable five or more years after their date of issue.

Confederate loans fell into several categories. The government could receive money on deposit and issue to the lender a certificate payable on demand, together with the accumulated interest. This kind of loan was styled a "call certificate."

Loans were secured by selling bonds, which were paid directly for goods and services or exchanged for money. To sustain the value of the bonds, tax revenues were needed. The Treasury also required a supply of gold and silver coins ("specie"), which would ensure that the interest on the public debt was paid with something of known and stable value. Without taking this step, the value of the bonds could not be maintained.

> **Unfortunately, the accumulation of a coin reserve was almost totally neglected. . . .**

Since the amount of money needed to finance the war was far greater than the banks, savings associations, and insurance companies could provide, massive bond sales made directly to the general public were needed. This meant that the bankers had to act as government loan agents; the Treasury also promptly set up government agencies (depositories) in areas where there were no banks.

Unfortunately, the accumulation of a coin reserve was almost totally neglected, and not until 1863 was an adequate system of loan offices set up. These errors were compounded by the illiquid character of the South's commercial agricultural economy. Cut off from its Northern and European cotton markets by the blockade, the Confederacy's capacity to borrow was greatly restricted.

Nevertheless, the Confederate States did sell $577 million of bonds and $291 million of call certificates. The funds procured from these sources provided the means for slightly less than one-third of the Confederacy's cash expenditures.

The first loan act, that of February 28, 1861, was authorized to cover $15 million of congressional defense appropriations. The purchasers were offered an 8 percent bond, whose payable coupons were made receivable for customs dues and the cotton export duty. But instead of insisting that the subscribers pay for these bonds with coin, as required by law, Secretary of the Treasury Christopher G. Memminger agreed to receive bank notes. As a result, the Confederacy received very little coin and had to suspend specie interest payments after July 1, 1862.

A second loan, dated May 16, 1861, authorized up to $20 million of ten-year 8 percent securities that were a combination of a bond and a call certificate. Because the loan could either be held to maturity or be converted upon demand into Treasury notes, it remained an attractive investment until July 1863, when Congress unilaterally changed the terms, damaging the government's credit.

The third loan, that of August 19, 1861, was the first attempt by Congress to pass a comprehensive law sustaining the value of $100 million of Treasury notes by making

them fundable into 8 percent bonds with serial maturities. The basic idea behind this loan was that the currency's value could be maintained by permitting the noteholder to purchase at face value in currency a bond whose interest was payable in coin. When specie payments were suspended, Confederate bonds became an unattractive investment because the interest was paid in rapidly depreciating Treasury notes that offered a very poor return to the investor. Bond sales languished, while nervous investors bought the $71 million of the 6 percent call certificates authorized by the act of December 24, 1861.

Efforts to sell general loans, such as that authorized on April 12, 1862, met with a poor response. Everyone preferred the 7.3 percent Treasury notes that were issued in lieu of the 8 percent bonds, simply because for only a modest reduction in interest, the holder could get a note usable as currency instead of a cumbersome bond. The act of October 17, 1862, authorizing a reduction in the interest paid on notes funded into bonds, resulted in the sale of almost $164 million of 8 percent and 7 percent bonds issued under the act of February 20, 1863.

Because of the large amount of bonds purchased under that act, the public bought only $21 million of the funding loan of March 23, 1863. Once again, the government was saved by the purchase of almost $74 million of call certificates. An attempt to sell bonds whose interest was payable in cotton (Act of April 30, 1863), resulted in only $12 million of sales, chiefly because the public correctly suspected that the government would refuse to pay the cotton or coin interest called for.

On February 17, 1864, Congress passed another act with a view to forcibly funding the entire outstanding currency into 4 percent bonds. About $361 million of these were sold and another $147 million of 6 percent nontaxable bonds and certificates of indebtedness were disposed of. Again, however, such revenues were nearly matched by the sales of 4 percent call certificates, which amounted to $135 million. By the end of 1864, even this inadequate source of funds dried up. The public, recognizing the inevitability of defeat, refused to advance any more money to a failing cause. As a result, a large number of prepared but unsold bonds were captured by the Federal forces at the end of the war.

[*See also* Erlanger Loan; Produce Loan.]

BIBLIOGRAPHY

Ball, Douglas B. *Financial Failure and Confederate Defeat*. Urbana, Ill., 1991.

Criswell, Grover C., Jr. *Confederate and Southern State Bonds*. Citrus, Fla., 1972.

Thian, Raphael P. *Register of the Confederate Debt*. Edited by Douglas B. Ball. Boston, 1972.

Todd, Richard C. *Confederate Finance*. Athens, Ga., 1954.

DOUGLAS B. BALL

BONHAM, MILLEDGE L.

BONHAM, MILLEDGE L. (1813–1890), brigadier general and South Carolina congressman and governor. Born in Edgefield District, December 25, 1813, Milledge Luke Bonham graduated from South Carolina College and practiced law in Edgefield. He served in the South Carolina General Assembly from 1840 to 1844 and in the U.S. House of Representatives from 1857 to 1860, filling the seat left vacant by the death of his cousin Preston S. Brooks. He had considerable military experience before the Civil War, commanding the South Carolina Brigade in the Seminole War and serving as lieutenant colonel with the Palmetto Regiment in the Mexican War.

Bonham anticipated the secession crisis as early as 1858, once remarking that Republican success "ought to be and will be the death signal of this Confederacy, come when it may." When the crisis broke in December 1860, he promptly resigned his seat in the House and went home. South Carolina sent him to Mississippi to help persuade that state to follow its action. At the outbreak of the war Bonham commanded the South Carolina militia with the rank of major general. He relinquished this position to accept a Confederate brigadier's commission under P. G. T. Beauregard. He commanded the South Carolina troops moving to the defense of Richmond and led his brigade throughout the First Manassas campaign. Mary Boykin Chesnut reported that an observer told her that " 'no general ever had more to learn than Bonham,' when he first saw him in command, and truly he believed no one ever learned more in a given time."

Although he served admirably, Bonham, when he was passed over for promotion, joined several other officers that autumn in protesting Jefferson Davis's policy of ranking officers from the "old army" over militia officers. He resigned his commission on January 29, 1862, having secured election to the First (regular) Confederate Congress. There he questioned Davis's initial plan for conscription, preferring to rely on volunteers until their numbers proved inadequate. Later, however, Bonham supported the administration's bill authorizing the president to suspend the writ of habeas corpus whenever he believed it necessary to do so.

When Governor Francis W. Pickens's term expired in December 1862, Bonham was chosen by the state legislature to replace him. The new governor inherited two major problems from his predecessor: coastal defense and military conscription. In the minds of many South Carolinians the two were closely intertwined. The state had contributed liberally to the Confederate army. Yet most of the South Carolinians were serving on the Virginia front or in the West at a time when the state's coastal region lay threatened. The taking of Port Royal by the Union navy in November 1861 had been a particularly hard blow. Many in the state questioned whether their defense was being neglected. As enlistments fell off, South Carolina adopted conscription even before it passed the Confederate Congress.

For all his previous differences with the Davis administration, Bonham was determined that South Carolina "in every legitimate way should sustain the Confederate authorities." In spite of the continuing drain of Carolina troops to other fronts and the unrelenting shelling and raiding of the Sea Islands in the Charleston area including Fort Sumter, he made good his inaugural promise to cooperate with the Confederacy in contrast to his neighboring governors in Georgia and North Carolina. While they made wide use of their discretionary powers in granting exemptions from conscription for state officers, Bonham refused to follow that course.

In yet another matter of exemptions, which arose shortly after he took office, Bonham worked diligently for compromise. On May 1, 1863, the Confederate Congress repealed the section of the Conscription Act that exempted overseers on large plantations. This threatened to place an economic hardship on South Carolina and ran contrary to state law, which provided for such exemptions. Bonham felt obligated to uphold the state statute. Until he could secure its repeal, which he did in December 1863, he recommended that South Carolinians exempt under state law claim a similar exemption with Confederate enrolling officers. He induced the latter to agree to this arrangement until he could bring the state statute in line with the new Confederate regulations. South Carolina continued on the course of cooperation until the end of 1864, when it reversed its policy of claiming no exemptions because of increasing dissatisfaction with the Davis government's failure to provide adequately for the state's defense and the immediate threat of invasion from William Tecumseh Sherman's army.

> **Mary Boykin Chesnut reported that an observer told her that " 'no general ever had more to learn than Bonham'. . . and truly he believed no one ever learned more in a given time."**

Meanwhile Bonham worked closely with his former commander General Beauregard, who had been placed in charge of South Carolina's defenses. When the general ordered the evacuation of Charleston by all noncombatants in February 1863, Bonham reluctantly agreed. When he then called up all white males beyond draft age for the defense of the city, the question arose of alien residents' liability for service. His predecessor had excused them, but Bonham refused to do so. The legislature backed his position in September 1863, with a law requiring alien residents to serve when needed. President Davis agreed to accept these state troops for three months' service (half the regular time) on the condition that South Carolina arm and equip them. The governor agreed to arm them but reported that resources for their supply were thin because of prior commitments to the Confederacy. For all these difficulties, Union efforts to take Fort Sumter failed twice in 1863, although Charleston continued under intermittent bombardment.

By the fall of 1863 Bonham began receiving reports from enrolling officers in the northwestern corner of the state that they were meeting with widespread resistance to conscription as well as desertion by those who had already served. This could be attributed not only to the Confederate military reverses of that summer but to local conditions as well. This region, which backed up against the mountains of North Carolina where many deserters found refuge, was mostly populated by nonslaveholders who had never been enthusiastic about secession. Bonham dispatched state troops to the area, obtained the cooperation of Governor Zebulon Vance of North Carolina in suppressing the disturbances, and called the legislature into special session. It responded with strong legislation making sheriffs and others liable to fines and imprisonment for failure to cooperate in curtailing draft evasion and desertion. It even agreed to a Confederate proposal to raise a special force from those not liable to conscription for special service against deserters. There was some improvement; but as the military and economic situation deteriorated further by the summer of 1864, conditions in that corner of the state once again worsened. All of Bonham's further efforts to curtail disaffection met with little success.

Yet another manpower problem confronting Bonham in 1863 was the need for slave labor to build and maintain coastal fortifications. This was not a new concern. The impressment of slaves for this purpose had begun early in the war, affecting primarily slave owners in the coastal areas. It met with little opposition initially; but as more slaves were taken for varying lengths of time by both state and Confederate authorities, the mood of the planters changed. Part of the problem lay in the inadequacy of supporting legislation relative to the length of impressment and compensatory pay to the owners. The legislature sought to remedy this by passing a law in December 1862, just as Bonham took office, limiting requisitions for slaves to thirty days' service and providing owners eleven dollars a month compensation. The law was flawed in many respects, however, including one provision that allowed owners to pay a dollar a day instead of furnishing a slave, an option many of them took. Enforcement was difficult, and only a few hundred slaves were recruited by this means in spite of Bonham's efforts to make the process work. Finally, in August 1863, Beauregard announced that his agents would assume responsibility for impressment. Some 3,500 slaves were now secured through impressment and voluntary action by their

owners, but this number soon dwindled as planters complained that their blacks were ill treated and not returned promptly and that their labor was needed at home. Enforcement became increasingly difficult, and Bonham was never able to solve the problem adequately.

Bonham was also confronted with popular dissatisfaction over the impressment of provisions and supplies for the Confederate army. This practice had been carried on informally since early in the war, arousing protest in South Carolina and elsewhere. When Congress formalized the procedure in the Confiscation Act of March 26, 1863, it became the new governor's specific problem. As complaints mounted, the governor brought the issue to the legislature's attention in its special session in September 1863. He indicated his displeasure at the frequently high-handed methods being used by Confederate commissioners and secured a legislative resolution supporting his position. While not specifically disavowing confiscation, both governor and legislature expressed concern that the law be administered evenly and fairly and only when absolute necessity dictated. Bonham conveyed these sentiments to Secretary of War James A. Seddon, who replied in a conciliatory fashion that he would investigate any complaints. As these continued to come in, Bonham brought the matter back to the legislature in November. It responded with resolutions asking the state's congressional delegation to work for change in Richmond. The governor was also requested to inform the state's citizens of their rights under the impressment law. Bonham continued to forward complaints to Seddon, but this problem, too, remained unresolved until war's end.

As Bonham's term came to an end in December 1864, it was evident that South Carolina faced imminent invasion. Over the governor's strong protest, the state had been ordered to give up most of its remaining cavalry for duty in Virginia the previous March. Now Bonham asked the legislature for authority to call up all males between sixteen and sixty for militia duty within the state with those between sixteen and fifty being allowed to go to Georgia in view of the menace in that direction. He also sought to have all militia forces and others deemed necessary for the state's defense declared exempt from Confederate service. The legislature promptly approved his request. This was a decided reversal of South Carolina's previous cooperation with the Confederacy, but the state's situation called for drastic action.

Following the completion of his term, Bonham again became a brigadier general of Confederate troops, commanding a cavalry brigade under Joseph E. Johnston until war's end. He then returned to his law practice in Edgefield. He served in the General Assembly during Presidential Reconstruction only to be sidelined during the Republican years. Active in the restoration of white rule, he was appointed state railroad commissioner in 1878 and continued in that position until his death on August 27, 1890.

BIBLIOGRAPHY

Bonham, Milledge Lipscomb. "Unpublished Biography of Milledge L. Bonham." Manuscript in South Caroliniana Library, University of South Carolina, Columbia.

Cauthen, Charles E. *South Carolina Goes to War, 1860–1865.* Chapel Hill, N.C., 1950.

Chesnut, Mary Boykin. *Mary Chesnut's Civil War.* Edited by C. Vann Woodward. New Haven, 1981.

Edmunds, John B., Jr. "South Carolina." In *The Confederate Governors.* Edited by W. Buck Yearns. Athens, Ga., 1985.

Freeman, Douglas S. *Lee's Lieutenants: A Study in Command.* Vol. 1. New York, 1942. Reprint, 1986.

WILLIAM E. PARRISH

BOOTH, JOHN WILKES

BOOTH, JOHN WILKES (1838–1865), assassin of Abraham Lincoln. Born in Maryland, the son of a slave-owning actor of English birth, Booth followed in his father's footsteps with a successful stage career, but his youth in Maryland made him a slavocrat in lifestyle—riding horses, shooting guns, holding violent opinions in politics, and disdaining blacks. He seems to have thought of himself as a Northerner but wrote in 1864, "My love (as things stand today) is for the South alone."

Although he left few letters for historians, Booth did compose two long political statements, one in the winter of 1860–1861 and the other in November 1864. The first justified secession as constitutional and blamed abolitionists for the nation's crisis. "This country was formed for the *white,* not the black man," he wrote in the later statement, and slavery was "one of the greatest blessings (both for themselves and us)" bestowed by "God . . . upon a favored nation." Intense identification with the Confederate cause and fear that Lincoln's reelection in 1864 would make him a dictator led Booth to begin planning that summer to kidnap Lincoln, take him to Richmond, and exchange him for Confederate prisoners of war.

Booth recruited Southern-sympathizing idlers, ex-Confederate soldiers, and a spy in Maryland for his kidnapping scheme and visited Montreal late in 1864, where he may have contacted Confederate agents. He decided very late to murder Lincoln. Acting as a self-styled "Confederate . . . doing duty *upon his own responsibility,*" he shot the president at Ford's Theatre in Washington, afterward shouting the Virginia state motto, "Sic semper tyrannis" [thus always to tyrants]. Confederate sympathizers helped hide him from pursuing soldiers, but he died on Virginia soil twelve days later, shot by a Union cavalryman.

[*See also* Lincoln, Abraham, *article on* Assassination of Lincoln; Espionage, *article on* Confederate Military Spies.]

BIBLIOGRAPHY

Hanchett, William. *The Lincoln Murder Conspiracies.* Urbana, Ill., 1983.

Tidwell, William A., with James O. Hall and David Winfred Gaddy. *Come Retribution: The Confederate Secret Service and the Assassination of Lincoln.* Jackson, Miss., 1988.

MARK E. NEELY, JR.

BORDER STATES

Composed of Delaware, Kentucky, Maryland, and Missouri, the border states were divided in their allegiance between the Union and the Confederacy. Geographically situated along a thousand-mile frontier dividing North from South, the border states in many ways resembled both sections.

In 1861 these four states possessed a total population of 2,137,000, of whom 430,000 were slaves. Although slavery was constitutionally legal in all, only in Kentucky did slaves represent a sizable portion of the population, reaching nearly 20 percent. Figures for Maryland, Missouri, and Delaware were substantially smaller, equaling only 13, 10, and 2 percent, respectively. At the same time, these states were similar to those in the North in that large numbers of immigrants, especially Germans and Irish, had settled in major port cities such as Baltimore, Louisville, and St. Louis. The major agricultural products of the region—corn, hemp, tobacco, horses, and mules—also reflected an interesting mixture of Northern and Southern farming.

Differences among the Border States. Although they occupied a position physically and demographically between the North and the South, the border states did not constitute a unit. Indeed, considerable geographic, social, political, and economic differences separated them along an east-west division. The Allegheny Mountains served as a barrier to trade and settlement and effectively partitioned Maryland and Delaware from Kentucky and Missouri. As a consequence, Kentucky and Missouri, settled largely by Virginians and Tennesseans, were economically oriented toward the Midwest and New Orleans, whereas Maryland and Delaware were linked more to the cities and markets of the Mid-Atlantic and New England states.

The border states also demonstrated little unity in the election of 1860, Maryland and Delaware voting for Southern Democrat John C. Breckinridge, Kentucky for Constitutional Unionist John Bell, and Missouri for Northern Democrat Stephen A. Douglas. Furthermore, Maryland and Delaware possessed large free black populations (the number of free blacks in Maryland nearly equaled the number of slaves), whereas in Kentucky and Missouri the number of free blacks in proportion to the overall population was negligible.

Attitudes toward Secession. As the secession crisis erupted, it was unclear which way the border states would go. Although their slave populations were considerably smaller than those of the eleven states that seceded, all but Delaware contained large, determined, and well-led secessionist minorities. In Maryland, where Southern rights Democrats controlled the legislature, secession activity centered in the southern tobacco-growing and eastern coastal counties and in the city of Baltimore. Only the refusal of Governor Thomas Hicks, a moderate Unionist, to convene the legislature prevented that body from forcing the state's secession. In Missouri, where the governor, lieutenant governor, Speaker of the house, and a majority of the Democratically controlled legislature supported disunion, secession found favor primarily among the farmers and planters of the rich Missouri River bottomlands. In Kentucky, a state noted for its long tradition of sectional compromise, secessionism tended to be concentrated in the planter-dominated Bluegrass region. Nevertheless, the vast majority of border state citizens overall sought to steer a middle course between Union and disunion. Efforts by secessionists to have conventions called to deliberate the question of separation were defeated in Maryland and Kentucky. And although a convention was held in Missouri, antisecession delegates quickly gained the upper hand and quashed any attempt to take their state out of the Union.

Indicative of their reluctance to choose sides, several politicians from the border states endeavored to mediate peace between the warring sections. In the U.S. Senate, John J. Crittenden offered a forlorn compromise that sought to restore the Union and preserve the institution of slavery. His fellow Kentuckian, Governor Beriah Magoffin, called on the governors of three midwestern states, as well as those of Missouri and Tennessee, to work together to avert civil war. All such attempts collapsed, however, in the wake of the firing on Fort Sumter and President Abraham Lincoln's call for volunteers. The governors of Missouri and Kentucky defiantly refused Lincoln's request, and those of Maryland and Delaware simply ignored the president.

Unwilling to face the difficult choice between Union and secession, two border states adopted a position of neutrality during the spring of 1861. When the Maryland legislature finally succeeded in pressuring Governor Hicks to call it into session, that body condemned the Federal government's war on the Confederacy but refused to consider an ordinance of secession. Instead, the legislators accepted the governor's recommendation that the state assume a position of neutrality. A desire to restore economic ties with the North and the continued Federal military buildup to protect Washington, D.C. (which was situated on the state's border with Virginia), however, made neutrality an impossibility. Similarly, in Kentucky, Governor Magoffin declared a policy of neutrality, all the while permitting Confederate recruiting agents to enter

the state and supplies to travel southward. Eventually, Kentucky was forced to abandon its fence-sitting when Confederate forces occupied the Mississippi River town of Columbus, triggering a Federal countermove into the state.

Only in Missouri did the state government make an overt attempt to join the Confederacy. There, Governor Claiborne F. Jackson mobilized the state militia and tried to seize the U.S. Arsenal in St. Louis. He was foiled by Union Capt. Nathaniel Lyon, who captured Jackson's entire force and drove secessionists from the state capital in Jefferson City. By the end of 1861, most of Missouri and Kentucky were

> Indicative of their reluctance to choose sides, several politicians from the border states endeavored to mediate peace between the warring sections.

firmly under Federal control. This, however, did not prevent their pro-secession governments from operating in exile. Indeed, Missouri and Kentucky enacted ordinances of secession, were admitted to the Confederacy as its twelfth and thirteenth states, and sent senators and representatives to the Congress in Richmond.

Effects on the Confederacy. In losing the border states, the Confederacy lost manpower and matériel that would have significantly increased its chances for success. The accession of Kentucky, Maryland, and Missouri would have added 45 percent to the white population of the seceded states, 80 percent to its manufacturing base, and almost 40 percent to its supply of mules and horses. The Confederacy also would have gained the highly defensible Ohio River, which traverses Kentucky's northern border for nearly five hundred miles, offering a shield to the South's vulnerable heartland.

Still, thousands of Missourians, Kentuckians, and Marylanders served in the Confederate army. Approximately one-fourth of the white men in Missouri, one-third of those in Maryland, and two-fifths of those in Kentucky who fought in the Civil War served in Southern units. Among them were some of the South's outstanding military leaders: Bradley Tyler Johnson and Isaac Trimble of Maryland; Sterling Price of Missouri; and Simon Bolivar Buckner, Albert Sidney Johnston, John Hunt Morgan, and John C. Breckinridge of Kentucky. In addition, border state politicians and military leaders known as the "western concentration bloc" influenced policy in Richmond by urging President Jefferson Davis to launch a campaign to reclaim Kentucky and plant the Southern banner on the banks of the Ohio.

The border states were the longest Federally occupied part of the South. Union troops entered Maryland in April, Missouri in June, and Kentucky in September of 1861. Only

Robert E. Lee's campaign in Maryland in September 1862 and that of Braxton Bragg in Kentucky during the same period seriously threatened the Union stronghold in those states. Even then, Confederate authorities were bitterly disappointed by the failure of Marylanders and Kentuckians to rally to the Southern cause. Incursions during 1864 by Jubal Early into Maryland and Sterling Price into Missouri also failed to elicit public support.

Despite the fact that the Lincoln administration cracked down on Southern sympathizers in the border states, jailing many without charges and confiscating the property of others, little could be done to shake the Unionism of their populations. Even Lincoln's Emancipation Proclamation, which aroused the fears of many border state slaveholders, failed to produce widespread disaffection or pro-Confederate sympathy.

[*See also* Early's Washington Raid; Kentucky; Missouri; Population; Sharpsburg Campaign.]

BIBLIOGRAPHY

Coulter, E. Merton. *The Civil War and Readjustment in Kentucky.* Chapel Hill, N.C., 1926.
Fields, Barbara Jeanne. *Slavery and Freedom on the Middle Ground: Maryland during the Nineteenth Century.* New Haven, 1985.
Hancock, Harold Bell. *Delaware during the Civil War: A Political History.* Wilmington, Del., 1961.
Harrison, Lowell. *The Civil War in Kentucky.* Lexington, Ky., 1975.
Parrish, William E. *Turbulent Partnership: Missouri and the Union, 1861–1865.* Columbia, Mo., 1963.
Smith, Edward Conrad. *The Borderland in the Civil War.* New York, 1927.

W. TODD GROCE

BOYCE, W. W.

BOYCE, W. W. (1818–1890), congressman from South Carolina. Boyce, unlike many of his fellow South Carolina politicians in the 1850s, was a reluctant secessionist. First elected to the U.S. Congress in 1852 as a state rights Democrat, he held relatively moderate views on secession, which linked him to the cooperationist camp. Fears of the Republican party led him to change his mind. In August 1860 he wrote that "negro equality, the only logical *finale* of which is emancipation," was the foundation upon which the party was built. Therefore, he cast his lot with those calling for secession if Abraham Lincoln was elected. When South Carolina adopted its ordinance of secession in December 1860, Boyce resigned his seat.

Although not a member of the secession convention, he was elected as one of the eight members of South Carolina's

delegation to the Montgomery convention. There he supported a constitution that was virtually identical to that of the United States with one exception. He and James Chesnut proposed that the constitution guarantee the right of secession. Only the South Carolina delegation favored the idea and it died. Along with fellow ex-congressman Lawrence Keitt, he supported Howell Cobb for the presidency.

In the Provisional Congress, Boyce was a member of the Postal Affairs and Inauguration committees. He also served on the committee that established the executive department. By the time the Confederate government had moved to Richmond, Boyce and Keitt were rumored to be leaders of a "coalition against Jeff Davis." That fall the "coalition" was being called a "party" and Richmond gossips were naming Boyce its primary leader. Some historians have even referred to anti-Davis politicians as the "Boyce Party."

Although word of his opposition to Davis circulated in South Carolina, it did not damage Boyce's relations with his constituents. In elections for the First and Second Congresses, he ran unopposed in South Carolina's Sixth Congressional District. He made no secret of his dislike for the president. In a March 1862 letter to James H. Hammond, Boyce wrote that "Davis is puffed up with his own conceit, and looks upon an independent opinion as an attack on him." "Common sense," he added, "he considers treason." Hammond shared the congressman's contempt and thought that the only hope for the South lay in impeaching Davis and calling for a convention of the states.

Among Boyce's main complaints were the president's thin skin, "West Point red tape," interference in military matters, and lack of boldness. The Confederacy was a revolution that initially had had a chance to succeed, but Davis's caution, Boyce thought, had foreordained the South's failure. He was fearful that the Confederacy would be "Davis-ized into nothing." Several weeks later, in another letter, he lamented, "Jeff Davis has brought us to the brink of ruin."

In Congress, Boyce was a member of several key committees including Ways and Means, Naval Affairs, and Currency. He vehemently opposed conscription but had no compunction about supporting legislation to destroy private property in the face of the enemy's advance. He advocated a scorched-earth policy so that Federal forces would find only desolation. In 1864, he proposed redeeming Confederate currency at its real, not face, value (about five cents on the dollar). This move would eliminate the need for other measures to stabilize the Confederate money supply. This proposal got nowhere. Although it was presented in opposition to legislation supported by the administration, there was not much reaction to it. The same could not be said for his espousing peace with the Union.

As early as February 1863, word leaked from secret House sessions that Boyce had suggested the South seek an accommodation with the states of the Old Northwest.

Nothing happened, but obviously it was an idea that Boyce thought had merit. He simply bided his time. Following Confederate victories at Spotsylvania and the Wilderness, he met with a group that included Senators William A. Graham of North Carolina, Herschel V. Johnson of Georgia, James L. Orr of South Carolina, and John W. C. Watson of Mississippi. The men thought that the time was propitious to work for a negotiated peace based upon Southern independence. On June 2, 1864, resolutions were introduced into both houses of Congress calling for the Confederate government to dispatch peace commissioners. That did not occur, but there were two abortive meetings between representatives of both governments—one at Niagara Falls and the other in Richmond. The meetings failed because each side presented nonnegotiable stipulations. The Confederacy insisted upon independence and slavery and the Union on reunion and the abolition of slavery.

In private, Boyce continued to stew over the president's policies: "It looks to me like we are going under the Jeff Davis lead very fast over the precipice. His intermeddling with the armies is usually disastrous, and he has no diplomacy." The Confederacy was "a country dying from the incompetency of its presumptuous chief." In October 1864, he let some of these same frustrations boil over into public print.

In August 1864, the Democratic convention had adopted a platform that called for cessation of hostilities and a convention of the states to restore peace. Distressed at the devastation the Confederacy was suffering, Boyce independently decided it was time to make the issue public. On September 29, he wrote an open letter to Davis that was released to the press several weeks later. It created a sensation.

In reviewing forms of government, Boyce concluded that a republic, "especially [in] the form of a Confederacy of free States," was designed to be a government for peace. Such a form of government was ill suited to prosecuting a war. A military dictatorship was the most effective form for waging war. "A Republic forced to the wall by a powerful enemy must end in despotism." In case anyone missed his drift, he spelled it out. Hadn't the South become a dictatorship? Boyce then listed what he considered examples of the Confederacy's slide into despotism: conscription "carried to its last limits" of taking men ages seventeen to fifty; direct taxes in clear violation of the Constitution; the issuance and then repudiation of vast sums of paper currency; the seizure and construction of railroads; the establishment of a state monopoly to control the exportation of staples; the ban on importation of luxuries; the taking of food from farmers "at our prices"; the suspension of the writ of habeas corpus; the use of passports, which "we used to think belonged to the iron despotism of Europe." Rhetorically, he asked Davis what greater powers could he have as a military dictator than the ones he enjoyed in 1864?

Boyce urged Davis to declare that the Confederacy was willing to accept an armistice and to agree to the call for a council of the states. By so doing, he would strengthen the chances for a Democratic victory in November 1864. The only hope for the Confederacy lay in doing what it could to advance the cause of the Democratic party in the North. The Democrats wanted peace and reconciliation, and they were "rational on the subject of slavery." The president had to act, and act soon, because Congress would not return to Richmond before the election. If Davis acted, there would be a real chance for real peace—one that would restore harmony. "The question," wrote Boyce, "rests with you. The responsibility is with you; the consequences will be with your country."

The letter appeared in Southern newspapers the second week of October. On the thirteenth, it was printed on the front page of the *Charleston Daily Carolinian* with a favorable notice from the *Columbus* (Georgia) *Sun*. For the next several weeks there was heated debate in the pages of the Southern press. Among the newspapers that thought the congressman's letter had merit were the *Raleigh Standard, Montgomery Mail, Mobile Tribune,* and *Lynchburg Virginian*. The *Charlotte News* called it treason.

In Columbia, the capital of South Carolina, a large gathering of citizens elected a committee that denounced Boyce's argument and called upon him to resign. The congressman was in town and defended himself ably, but he failed to alter the mood of the assembled throng. He refused to resign and his fellow citizens of Winnsboro rallied to his side.

The vehemence of Boyce's letter had the opposite effect from what he had intended. Instead of weakening and exposing the president, it elicited an outpouring of support for the beleaguered chief executive. Davis, emboldened by expressions of support from across the South, attacked Boyce's proposals. He did nothing to give war-weary voters in the North any indication that there might be a prospect of peace. And, by so doing, he did exactly what the congressman had predicted he would do: "traverse the same bloody circles you have been moving in for the past four years."

The South Carolina congressman was not deterred. He returned to Richmond where Mary Boykin Chesnut reported that despite his letter he had not "lost caste." She also reported that there was open talk of a "Boyce party" in Congress. There was never any formally organized faction, but likeminded politicians continued to meet. Following the failure of the Hampton Roads peace conference on February 3, 1865, Boyce realized that the only hope for the Confederacy was continued armed resistance. He urged that Robert E. Lee continue the fight by falling back to defensive positions in the Tennessee mountains.

Traditional interpretations of the Boyce letter have been that he was finished in South Carolina because of it. Certainly, Davis in his *Rise and Fall of the Confederate Government* ignores Boyce and the congressional peace movement. That omission—in fact, the entire publication—simply confirms Boyce's description of Davis's exalted opinion of himself.

In 1866, Boyce moved to the nation's capital and opened a law practice. Because he left the state, some have assumed that he was persona non grata in the Palmetto State. That really wasn't the case. At the turn of the century, the congressman was defended by a Fairfield County historian who noted that William Waters Boyce was a man who "had convictions and courage enough to express and maintain them. Had he lived in a wiser age, he would have been more appreciated."

BIBLIOGRAPHY

Beringer, Richard E. "Political Factionalism in the Confederate Congress." Ph.D. diss., Northwestern University, 1966.

Cauthen, Charles Edward. *South Carolina Goes to War, 1860–1865.* Chapel Hill, N.C., 1950.

Channing, Steven A. *Crisis of Fear: Secession in South Carolina.* New York, 1970.

Daily Carolinian (Charleston, S.C.), October 13–31, 1864.

Edrington, William. *History of Fairfield County, South Carolina.* Edited by B. H. Rosson, Jr. Tuscaloosa, Ala., n.d.

Taylor, Rosser H. "Boyce-Hammond Correspondence." *Journal of Southern History* 3 (August 1937): 348–354.

Woodward, C. Vann. *Mary Chesnut's Civil War.* New Haven, 1981.

Yearns, Wilfred B. *The Confederate Congress.* Athens, Ga., 1960.

WALTER B. EDGAR

BELLE BOYD. LIBRARY OF CONGRESS

BOYD, BELLE

BOYD, BELLE (1844–1900), spy. The most famous of the Confederacy's female operatives, Boyd was born in or near Martinsburg, Virginia (present-day West Virginia). Although most scholars agree that Boyd made important contributions to the Shenandoah Valley campaigns, some of the dramatic details of her memoir, *Belle Boyd, in Camp and Prison,* are still controversial. When Martinsburg came under Union occupation in 1861, Boyd's exploits included shooting at a Federal trooper who broke into her family's home (July 4, 1861) and charming attentive Union officers into divulging military information that she transmitted through secret messengers to Confederate leaders. During the fall of 1861 Boyd served as a courier for Gens. Thomas J. ("Stonewall") Jackson and P. G. T. Beauregard. Early in 1862 she was arrested by Union forces and detained for a week in Baltimore. In mid-May 1862, Boyd claims, she spied on a secret Union strategy session in Front Royal while crouched in a closet above the meeting room and then made a midnight ride of fifteen miles, through Federal sentries, to inform Col. Turner Ashby of her findings.

Boyd's most significant feat came on May 23, 1862, as General Jackson's forces approached Front Royal. Having obtained information on the status of Federal forces in the area, she dashed from Front Royal—on foot—to meet the advance guard of Jackson's troops. Caught in the crossfire of the opposing armies and waving her white bonnet to cheer on the Confederate troops, she reached Maj. Henry Kyd Douglas and reported that Jackson would have to hurry his attack in order to seize the town before retreating Federal forces burned its supply depots and bridges. Her message confirmed Jackson's own intelligence, and the Confederates were victorious.

Her deed sealed her status as a Confederate celebrity and resulted in her arrest on July 30, 1862, and imprisonment in Washington's Old Capitol Prison. She was released as part of a prisoner exchange a month later and sent to Richmond, Virginia, where she spent a few months among her admiring countrymen. Sometime in the winter of 1862–1863, she was appointed an honorary aide-de-camp, with the rank of captain, by General Jackson's headquarters.

In the summer of 1863 she returned to Martinsburg, only to be arrested again by Union forces. Her second incarceration at Old Capitol Prison lasted until December 1863, when she was released and banished South for the remainder of the war. In May 1864, she set sail for England, carrying Confederate dispatches. Her ship was captured by a Union vessel. She was sent to Canada and made her way to England, where, on August 25, 1864, she married Samuel Hardinge, Jr., the Union officer who had been put in charge of the captured blockade runner.

That winter, Hardinge was briefly incarcerated in America under suspicion of treason, and in order to support herself, Boyd wrote and published her memoirs in London. In 1866, after Hardinge's death, she took up acting. Later that year she returned to the United States, where she continued her acting career until 1869, when she married English businessman John Swainston Hammond. The couple was divorced in 1884, and in 1885 she married a young actor, Nathaniel Rue High, Jr., of Ohio. She toured the country giving recitals on her wartime experiences, earning the praise of Union and Confederate veterans alike. Boyd died of a heart attack in 1900 in Kilbourne City (Wisconsin Dells), Wisconsin, and was buried there.

BIBLIOGRAPHY

Boyd, Belle. *Belle Boyd, in Camp and Prison.* London, 1865. Reprint, New York, 1968.
Davis, Curtis Carroll. " 'The Pet of the Confederacy' Still? Fresh Findings about Belle Boyd." *Maryland Historical Magazine* 78 (1983): 35–53.
Scarborough, Ruth. *Belle Boyd: Siren of the South.* Macon, Ga., 1983.
Sigaud, Louis A. *Belle Boyd: Confederate Spy.* Richmond, Va., 1944.

ELIZABETH R. VARON

BRAGG, BRAXTON

BRAGG, BRAXTON (1817–1876), general and military adviser to Jefferson Davis. Bragg was born in Warrenton, North Carolina, on March 21, 1817. He attended West Point, graduating fifth in the 1837 class of fifty. He served in the Seminole Wars, where his health began its lifelong decline, and won two brevet promotions for gallantry during the Mexican War. In 1856, after marrying Eliza (Elise) Brooks Ellis, Bragg resigned from the army to become a successful sugar planter in Louisiana. When the state seceded in January 1861, the governor made Bragg a major general in command of the state's forces.

On March 7 President Jefferson Davis appointed Bragg brigadier general in the Confederate army. Ordered to Pensacola, Florida, Bragg quickly changed the volunteers he found there into drilled, disciplined soldiers. On September

12 Davis, pleased with Bragg's performance, promoted him to major general and on October 7 assigned him command of western Florida and all of Alabama.

In February 1862 Davis directed Bragg to proceed with his troops to Gen. Albert Sidney Johnston's army in northern Mississippi. Here Bragg shouldered two responsibilities—command of the Second Corps and chief of staff of the army—positions he held at the Battle of Shiloh. The Confederates attacked on April 6, slowly advancing throughout the day, despite the dispersal and tangling of corps, divisions, and brigades. Bragg commanded the forces near the center of the battlefield for several hours before moving to the Confederate right where the advance had stalled at the Hornet's Nest. Here he spent five hours directing piecemeal assaults before the Nest fell about 5:00 P.M. As the troops pushed forward, P. G. T. Beauregard, in command of the army since Johnston's death earlier in the day, called off the advance, an action that Bragg believed cost them the victory. By 2:00 P.M. the next day the Confederate line had collapsed before the weight of the reinforced Union army.

Bragg became a full general on April 12, 1862, the fifth ranking officer in the Confederacy. This promotion allowed Davis to assign Bragg to permanent command of the Western Department when Beauregard took an unauthorized sick leave. For a number of reasons, Bragg decided in July that an invasion of Kentucky could reap many benefits for the South. In anticipation of this move, he began an unprecedented transfer of an army by rail on the twenty-third. The move from Tupelo to Chattanooga—776 miles via six railraods—went without a hitch and proved to be the most successful part of the entire enterprise.

Advancing from Chattanooga on August 28 with 27,000 soldiers, Bragg encountered the enemy at Munfordville, where the heavily outnumbered Federal garrison of 4,000 surrendered on September 17. In an attempt to unite forces, Bragg traveled to Lexington to confer with Gen. E. Kirby Smith, leaving the army under his second in command, Gen. Leonidas Polk. As Federal Gen. Don Carlos Buell advanced, Polk disobeyed orders from Bragg, orders that might have enabled the Confederates to concentrate and defeat the Federals. Instead, Polk moved to Perryville where his deployment of the army for battle proved faulty. Bragg rejoined the army on October 8 and, despite Polk's mistakes, managed to push Buell's army back nearly two miles before the advance stalled. By midnight, however, Bragg began a retreat that ended in Tennessee. Despite the early promise of the Kentucky campaign, Bragg had achieved nothing of lasting value for the Confederacy.

Bragg next met the Federal army on December 31, 1862, about three miles northwest of Murfreesboro, in open farm country with small stands of thick cedar trees. Bragg ordered the Army of Tennessee, 35,000 strong, to pivot on its right, swinging northeast in an effort to force Gen. William S.

the cowardice or disobedience of Bragg's subordinate commanders allowed the Federals to escape.

Rosecrans, scenting the danger, hurriedly pulled his scattered corps together at Chickamauga Creek. On September 19 and 20 a mighty battle raged as Bragg attempted another grand pivot, hoping to force the Federals into McLemore's Cove and destroy them. The Army of Tennessee held its own through the nineteenth, and advanced at some points. That night the long-awaited Gen. James Longstreet arrived from Virginia, and Bragg reorganized the army into two wings, again hoping that a grand pivot would yield handsome results. Polk, however, attacked hours later than Bragg ordered and then allowed piecemeal assaults to exhaust his resources.

On the left, Longstreet formed his wing and waited for Polk's attack to produce results. Bragg, active on the field all day (contrary to Longstreet's postwar assertions), ordered Longstreet's troops forward at the precise moment a gap inadvertently opened in the Union line, thus initiating the famous breakthrough long credited solely to Longstreet. The timing of the assault and Longstreet's judicious troop deployment proved highly successful. The Union line broke and fled. The last Federal stand took place at Snodgrass Hill where Gen. George Thomas held fast until nightfall, covering the wild retreat of Rosecrans and the Federal army.

Moving the army to the heights overlooking Chattanooga, where Rosecrans had ensconced the Union army, Bragg spent the next several weeks quarreling with his subordinates and frittering away the advantages he had gained over the Federals at the Battle of Chickamauga. While his attention was thus occupied, the Federals replaced Rosecrans with Gen. Ulysses S. Grant. On November 24 Grant's forces easily swept the few Confederate soldiers deployed on Bragg's left off of Lookout Mountain and the following day chased the entire Army of Tennessee down the far side of the seemingly impregnable Missionary Ridge. On November 29 Bragg asked to be relieved from command. To Bragg's chagrin, Davis accepted the resignation with unseemly haste.

In February 1864, however, Davis, ever loyal to his friends, summoned the general to Richmond to serve as his military adviser, an office that allowed Bragg to wield considerable power among his army cohorts. Bragg served Davis and the Confederacy well during the eight months he spent in the capital city. The efficiency of several military institutions improved under his supervision, primarily through changes in department heads. In an extreme case Bragg initiated the dismantling of the Bureau of Conscription after finding it riddled with corruption. Davis relied heavily upon Bragg's understanding of military affairs, often seeking Bragg's expertise or opinion on a variety of matters. Bragg, however, never became a sycophant to Davis; indeed, the two often disagreed. Approaching his responsibilities with a characteristic intensity and devotion to duty, Bragg willingly shouldered

BRAXTON BRAGG. NATIONAL ARCHIVES

Rosecrans back beyond the Nashville Pike and to cut the Federal line of retreat. The grand pivot proved unsuitable on the rough and broken terrain, and, although Bragg managed to surprise Rosecrans, within an hour the Federals rallied, took strong positions, and fought fiercely for ten hours. On January 2, following a day of desultory firing, Bragg ordered an assault on a Union division threatening Polk's position. Eighty minutes of bloody combat convinced Bragg that the Federals could not be dislodged, and at 11:00 P.M. his army retreated from Murfreesboro.

For the next six months Bragg dallied in the Tullahoma area, reorganizing his army, quarreling with his subordinates, and caring for his ailing wife. In late June, Rosecrans again advanced, forcing Bragg to retreat to Chattanooga where he remained for several weeks. By late August Rosecrans began a flanking movement around the city, compelling Bragg to scurry southward in order to cover his line of communications. The Union's three corps were widely separated as they maneuvered through the mountainous country, and twice Rosecrans presented Bragg with excellent opportunities to strike the Federal forces in detail. Each time, however, censures and criticisms that otherwise would have fallen on Davis or, in at least one instance, Gen. Robert E. Lee. Unfortunately, Bragg's appointment as military adviser came too late in the war for him to make a great impact. Had he been assigned the post earlier, the Confederacy could have profited more from his considerable administrative talents.

In October 1864, while still performing the duties of military adviser, Bragg returned to field command when Davis ordered him to Wilmington, North Carolina, the last Confederate port remaining open to blockade runners. Bragg's performance here was shameful. He failed to prepare properly for anticipated attacks, and when the Federals made a concerted assault against Fort Fisher in January 1865, the commanding general stood by several miles away, wringing his hands and refusing to give credence to desperate appeals for aid from inside the fort. Bragg's explanations for his conduct were pusillanimous and illogical.

Bragg spent the last weeks of the Confederacy's life as a subordinate to Gen. Joseph E. Johnston, who, with the remnants of the Army of Tennessee, unsuccessfully attempted to block Gen. William Tecumseh Sherman's advance through North Carolina. As the Confederate government fled Richmond, Bragg joined Davis just in time to use his influence in convincing the president that the Confederacy had indeed been defeated. On May 10, 1865, as Bragg and his wife wended their way home, Union cavalry caught up with them near Concord, Georgia. Bragg was granted a parole on the spot and received no further trouble from the Federals; he died in Galveston, Texas, on September 27, 1876. He is buried in Magnolia Cemetery, Mobile, Alabama.

Bragg held a greater range of responsibilities than any other Confederate during the Civil War. He began in command of the Gulf coast fortifications at the start of the war; served as corps commander and chief of staff under Albert Sidney Johnston; was promoted to command of the Army of Tennessee, a position he held longer than anyone else, leading the western army to its northern high tide and to its one great victory; was one of only two people (the other was Lee) to serve as military adviser to the president; and ended his Civil War career as a subordinate field commander once again.

As an army field commander Bragg left much to be desired. Many factors contributed to his poor generalship. He suffered from myriad illnesses—migraine headaches, boils, dyspepsia, and rheumatism, to name a few—which frequently were brought on by stress. The diseases alone were enough to debilitate anyone, but the remedies he used to relieve his pain and discomfort may have been as damaging. He failed to inspire loyalty, confidence, or obedience in his subordinates, and he lacked the steadiness, the resolution, and the good luck of a successful field commander. A West Point–trained career officer, Bragg had little patience with his volunteer soldiers, and his harsh efforts to discipline them

seemed sometimes to go beyond the bounds of reason and necessity. Bragg also failed to learn from his mistakes, and to the end of the war he remained seemingly ignorant of the technological changes that required corresponding changes in tactics.

His personality may have been Bragg's greatest shortcoming. Although severely criticized and denigrated over the years, during his lifetime he had many staunch supporters, as evidenced by declarations of support and admiration even when he wielded little or no influence. Bragg, however, saw people in either black or white. Those he considered friends received his unwavering support and praise; all others he went out of his way to criticize and annoy. This flaw in his character frequently led to and exacerbated embarrassing quarrels with his subordinates, some of whom on two extraordinary occasions conspired together in petitioning Davis to remove Bragg from command of the Army of Tennessee. While serving as military adviser, Bragg took every opportunity to denigrate or thwart those he disliked, and he carried much of the responsibility for the removal of Joseph E. Johnston, a friend and supporter, from command of the Army of Tennessee in July 1864.

Bragg remains a study in contrasts and illuminates the Confederacy's serious misuse of talent. An able administrator, he spent most of the Civil War as a mediocre (at best) army field commander; although he maintained many loyal friendships, he went out of his way to create lasting enmities; sincerely devoted to the Confederate cause, he contributed greatly to its demise.

BIBLIOGRAPHY

Connelly, Thomas L. *Army of the Heartland: The Army of Tennessee, 1861–1862.* Baton Rouge, La., 1967.
Connelly, Thomas L. *Autumn of Glory: The Army of Tennessee, 1862–1865.* Baton Rouge, La., 1971.
Hallock, Judith Lee. *Braxton Bragg and Confederate Defeat.* Vol. 2. Tuscaloosa, Ala., 1991.
McWhiney, Grady. *Braxton Bragg and Confederate Defeat.* Vol. 1. New York, 1969. Reprint, Tuscaloosa, Ala., 1991.
Woodworth, Steven E. *Jefferson Davis and His Generals: The Failure of Confederate Command in the West.* Lawrence, Kans., 1990.

JUDITH LEE HALLOCK

BRAGG, THOMAS

BRAGG, THOMAS (1810–1872), governor of North Carolina, U.S. senator, and Confederate attorney general. A successful attorney, former two-term governor of North Carolina, and former U.S. senator, Bragg served as attorney general in Jefferson Davis's cabinet from November 21,

1861, to March 18, 1862. He was a capable man whose sentiments represented well the feelings of many North Carolinians. Bragg had been unenthusiastic about secession and privately doubted the Confederacy's prospects, yet he served faithfully in his four months in office and afterward continued to support the Confederate government.

Bragg was born on November 9, 1810, in Warrenton, North Carolina, and was one of six sons. Braxton Bragg, the Confederate general, was one of his brothers, and an older sibling, John, was a successful lawyer. Thomas Bragg studied first at Warrenton Academy and then in Middletown, Connecticut, at Norwich Military Academy. Returning to North Carolina to read law, Thomas followed John's example by studying under the supervision of Judge John Hall of Warrenton, a member of the North Carolina Supreme Court. In 1832 he was admitted to the bar.

Bragg opened a law practice in the town of Jackson in neighboring Northampton County and became a diligent, respected lawyer. Success in politics proved more difficult, however, because he was a Democrat in a strongly Whig county. Winning elections for county attorney and a single term in the state legislature in 1842, Bragg then had to be content with an advisory role in the party's state conventions until he received the Democratic nomination for governor in 1854. Bragg prevailed in a tight race and won reelection in 1856. As governor he stressed one of his party's popular issues, a wider franchise, and worked for internal improvements, expansion of railroads, and a better banking system.

Thomas Bragg was a reserved, sober, and conservative man who expressed himself confidently when asked but did not push for attention. He carried these traits into the higher positions that he occupied, beginning with his election to the U.S. Senate in 1859. As the sectional crisis deepened, Bragg remained loyal to the South but was distinctly unenthusiastic about secession. Saying little publicly, he indicated privately that he felt secession was impractical and unwise, no matter how justified. He doubted that the South was united or determined enough to endure a severe contest, despite the fervor that surrounded national politics. Honor, he wrote in his diary, had led Southerners in Congress to resign quickly after Abraham Lincoln's election. He himself did not withdraw from the Senate until March 6, 1861.

Back in North Carolina, Bragg helped prepare the state's military forces for the approaching conflict until he received an invitation from Richmond. Judah P. Benjamin, the Confederacy's attorney general, had taken over the responsibilities of the War Department ad interim after Alabama's Leroy P. Walker resigned, and Benjamin performed the duties of that arduous post so satisfactorily that President Davis decided to keep him there. Thus Benjamin's old post needed to be filled. Bragg enjoyed a fine reputation as a lawyer, but more important was the fact that he came from North Carolina. Already that state was furnishing disproportionate-

ly large quantities of men and matériel for the Confederate war effort, but Tarheel newspaper editors and politicians complained that their state was neglected and unappreciated. North Carolina had no one in the cabinet, and Davis remedied that deficiency with Bragg's acceptance of the office of attorney general.

In the brief four months that he discharged his responsibilities, Thomas Bragg addressed few matters of importance. Although he worked smoothly with President Davis, Bragg felt that he was rarely asked for advice on matters of significance. Legally, he worked to organize his department and rendered careful, conservative opinions on the few questions referred to him. Bragg advised the War Department, for example, that the government remained responsible for prop-

> **Although he worked smoothly with President Davis, Bragg felt that he was rarely asked for advice on matters of significance.**

erty taken by impressment. He also held that the Treasury Department should honor requisitions approved by the War Department without investigating their legality, and he wrote opinions on smaller questions such as pardons, the distribution of prize money for capture of a ship, or a clerk's salary. Many citizens contacted Bragg's office seeking his opinion on various acts of the Congress or administration. Wisely Bragg refused to comment, explaining that his duty under the law was to advise the president or other department heads. In his one report to Congress, he urged the establishment of a supreme court.

More striking than his official actions were Bragg's private comments in his diary. These revealed a lack of confidence in the cause that, though rarely voiced, was fairly widespread in the South and quite strong in North Carolina. On February 17, 1862, as the Provisional Congress expired, Bragg asked, "Will the Gov't endure? Can we repel the enemy? . . . I am by no means confident as to the issue." He found it difficult to take seriously the phrase "permanent government" and on February 20 wrote: "I must confess that taking a survey of our whole field of operations it seems to me that our cause is hopeless—God grant that I may be mistaken."

A month later Bragg left the cabinet for reasons that remain difficult to ascertain precisely. A Petersburg, Virginia, newspaper commented on his ill health, but since Bragg was enamored with neither his role in the cabinet nor the prospects of the cause, it is possible that he chose to end his service with the conclusion of the provisional government. The desire of Union Whigs to have a representative in the cabinet may also have played a role in Bragg's replacement by Thomas H. Watts of Alabama.

However pessimistic Bragg may have been privately, he continued to give public support to the Confederacy in North Carolina. He advised the government on sentiment in his state and accepted an appointment in 1864 to examine arrests under suspension of the writ of habeas corpus. When William W. Holden's *Raleigh Standard* began to agitate for peace, Bragg reportedly headed an effort to buy a paper and present an opposing, pro-Confederate viewpoint. After the war Bragg resumed the practice of law and was active in the Democratic party.

BIBLIOGRAPHY

Bragg, Thomas. Diary. Manuscripts Department, University of North Carolina at Chapel Hill.
Patrick, Rembert W. *Jefferson Davis and His Cabinet.* Baton Rouge, La., 1944.
Powell, William S., ed. *Dictionary of North Carolina Biography.* Vol. 1. Chapel Hill, N.C., 1979.

PAUL D. ESCOTT

BRANCH, LAWRENCE O'BRYAN

BRANCH, LAWRENCE O'BRYAN (1820–1862), U.S. congressman and Confederate brigadier general. Branch, born November 28, 1820, was the scion of a wealthy North Carolina family. He graduated from Princeton in 1838, practiced law in three Southern states, and served as president of a North Carolina railroad. Branch's sole antebellum military experience came as an aide for a few weeks in 1841 during the Second Seminole War. He represented his North Carolina district in the U.S. House of Representatives for three terms.

In 1861, Branch served for four months as quartermaster general of his home state. On September 20 he was commissioned colonel of the Thirty-third North Carolina Infantry and less than two months later was promoted to brigadier general—still without any real experience of war. In March 1862, Federals drove Branch out of New Berne. In Virginia two months later, Branch and his command were on the fringes of the Shenandoah Valley campaign, during which the new general exhibited considerable disdain for trained and professional military officers. On May 27, Branch commanded independently in another disaster, near Hanover Court House. The brigade then joined A. P. Hill's newly formed division and fought with it through the Seven Days' campaign.

Branch's Brigade performed solidly at Cedar Mountain, though not as well as he boasted in both public and private writings, and helped defend the army's left at Second Manassas. Hill's division arrived barely in time to save the day at Sharpsburg, and Branch led his troops into the confused fighting. Shortly after his climactic arrival, a Federal bullet killed him. Branch is buried in Raleigh, North Carolina.

BIBLIOGRAPHY

Branch, Lawrence O'Bryan. Papers, including autobiography. University of Virginia, Charlottesville.
Davis, Archie K. *Boy Colonel of the Confederacy: The Life and Times of Henry King Burgwyn, Jr.* Chapel Hill, N.C., 1985.
Freeman, Douglas S. *Lee's Lieutenants: A Study in Command.* 3 vols. New York, 1942–1944. Reprint, New York, 1986.
Hughes, John. *Lawrence O'Brian* [sic] *Branch.* N.p., 1884.

ROBERT K. KRICK

BRANDY STATION, VIRGINIA

This village, some seven miles northeast of Culpeper, Virginia, on the Orange and Alexandria Railroad, bordered the site of a June 9, 1863, battle that witnessed the largest clash of mounted units during the Civil War. By the narrowest of margins, Maj. Gen. J. E. B. Stuart wrestled a tactical victory from the Union cavalry under Brig. Gen. Alfred Pleasonton. Although they were defeated, Federal troopers demonstrated for the first time that they could hold their own against Stuart's soldiers. Imbued with a new sense of confidence, Union cavalry in Virginia became a formidable opponent for the rest of the war. Never again would Gen. Robert E. Lee's horsemen enjoy the degree of success that had marked their earlier campaigns. Southern casualties at Brandy Station amounted to 51 killed, 250 wounded, and 132 missing; the Federals lost 1,651.

The Rappahannock River divided the two antagonists after the smashing Confederate victory at Chancellorsville (May 1–4, 1863). Planning to launch a second raid of the North on June 9, Lee instructed Lt. Gen. Richard S. Ewell's Second Corps and Lt. Gen. James Longstreet's First Corps to abandon their camps in Culpeper County for the Shenandoah Valley. Stuart's troopers were to cross the Rappahannock the same day and screen the infantry's movements. Six batteries of horse artillery and five brigades of cavalry, totaling just more than 9,500 troopers and gunners, made up the Army of Northern Virginia's cavalry division. Supremely confident, as always, Stuart commanded the largest force of his career.

The night before the scheduled advance, Stuart's brigades were widely scattered along the Rappahannock. He hoped they could cross the river with little delay at dawn. Brig. Gen. Fitzhugh Lee's regiments were seven miles northwest of Stuart's headquarters at Fleetwood Hill, and Brig. Gen. William Henry Fitzhugh ("Rooney") Lee's soldiers bivouacked two miles west of the Rappahannock River and along the banks of the Hazel River. Brig. Gen. William E. ("Grumble") Jones's troopers spent the night along the Beverly's Ford Road, two miles south of the Rappahannock and not far from Saint James Church. Brig. Gen. Beverly H. Robertson's men rested southwest of Brandy Station on John M. Bott's farm. Brig. Gen. Wade Hampton's command also spent the night southwest of Brandy Station at Stevensburg. Because Stuart had failed to send pickets to the northern banks of the Rappahannock, he had little idea of the enemy's intentions.

Before the Confederates had stirred from their camps on June 9, Maj. Gen. Joseph Hooker had determined that Lee intended to move his army northward. The Northern commander ordered Pleasonton to take 11,000 cavalrymen and 3,000 infantry across the Rappahannock and "disperse and destroy the rebel force assembled in the vicinity of Culpeper." Pleasonton divided his command into two columns: the right wing under Brig. Gen. John Buford would cross at Beverly's Ford while the left wing under Brig. Gen. David M. Gregg would cross at Kelly's Ford. Both commands would reunite at Brandy Station and then push toward Culpeper where Pleasonton mistakenly believed Stuart's cavalrymen were encamped. He hoped to catch his adversary off guard, as Stuart edged his men to the banks of the river during the night of June 8. The Union officer, however, did not confirm reports that placed Confederate cavalry within a few hundred yards of the Rappahannock. A surprise was in store for both Pleasonton and Stuart in the morning.

Under a thick fog, Buford's men stormed past the Confederate pickets at Beverly's Ford around five in the morning. As the Northerners pounded down the Beverly's Ford Road, "Grumble" Jones roused his sleepy troopers, sending the exposed batteries of Maj. Robert F. Beckham a mile behind the lines to Saint James Church. Jones slowed Buford's rushing horsemen, slashing at the sides of the Union column with his nearest units, while Beckham sent canister flying down the road with the one cannon he had left at the front.

Jones reluctantly pulled his advanced regiments back to the high ground around Saint James Church. The entire brigade positioned itself west of the building; the artillerists were east of the church, extending the line just across Beverly's Ford Road. When the Federals raced across the exposed plain that rested below the Confederates, a barrage of shells, followed by a series of mounted counterattacks, sent the Northern cavalrymen scurrying to the woods. Although Jones had stabilized the Southern line, Stuart could not have been pleased by the enemy's fording of the

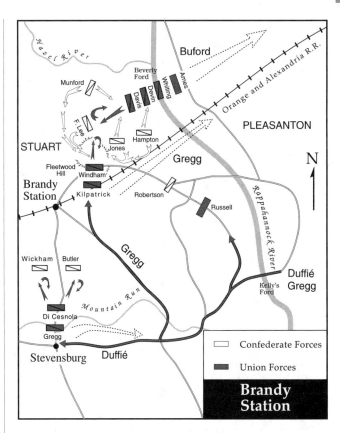

Rappahannock. With his brigades widely dispersed, he frantically called on his subordinates for assistance.

From his camp at Stevensburg, Hampton hurried to the front at 6:00, leaving one regiment at Fleetwood Hill and placing his other three units to the right of Beckham. On the western end of the line, Rooney Lee's brigade connected with the left flank of Jones's brigade. Lee posted his soldiers along Yew Ridge, a hulking eminence near the western tip of Fleetwood Hill. Hampton and Lee extended the line into the shape of a "huge crescent" that overlapped the flanks of Buford's troopers. To relieve the pressure from Hampton's probing skirmishers, Buford sent the Sixth Pennsylvania Cavalry against the Confederate center at Saint James Church. The Union soldiers made a gallant charge, as they fought hand to hand among Beckham's guns, but without sufficient support they were forced to retire. The failed attack brought a period of relative calm over this portion of the field.

The fighting now shifted toward Rooney Lee's position atop Yew Ridge, as Buford realized that the route to Brandy Station, via the Beverly's Ford Road, had been sealed off by the Confederates. Since 8:30 that morning, Buford had tested the enemy's left flank. Lee's troopers stood firm behind a stone wall until noon, when Federal infantry slipped around the end of the Southern line at Dr. Daniel Green's farm. Obliged to withdraw to the northwest end of Fleetwood Hill, Lee's soldiers now faced to the north and west. They waited for Buford to renew his assaults, as gunfire echoed two miles to their southeast. It warned of Stuart's newest threat.

About the time Hampton's men reinforced Jones at Saint James Church, Stuart learned of Gregg's crossing at Kelly's Ford. He sent the First South Carolina to the scene with the promise that Robertson's brigade would relieve them shortly. Gregg discovered that Robertson's troopers were galloping down the same road that he had planned to use to arrive at Brandy Station. Turning his column down a different road just west of Paoli's Mill, Gregg picked a less direct route to the battlefield, but it offered little Confederate resistance along the way. It was close to 9:00 when Gregg's hard-riding troopers passed Mount Dumpling. Fleetwood Hill was only two miles away, and Gregg ordered his men to attack the prominent eminence immediately. Only one Confederate cannon stood in the way of the Northern onslaught—an attack aimed at the rear of the Confederate line around Saint James Church. Stuart had been surprised for the second time that day.

The Southern cavalry chieftain mistakenly believed that Robertson's regiments could handle whatever enemy force had crossed Kelly's Ford. When Jones reported Federal activity around Brandy Station, Stuart quickly dismissed his subordinate's claim, remarking, "Tell General Jones to attend to the Yankees in his front, and I'll watch the flanks." Oblivious to the danger that lurked behind him, Stuart even disregarded the messages of Maj. Henry B. McClellan, a member of his staff, who watched the leading elements of Gregg's division steadily push toward Fleetwood Hill from the direction of Brandy Station. The lone Confederate cannon initiated a duel with three Union field pieces. The banging guns finally convinced Stuart that a potential disaster brewed behind his lines.

Stuart immediately ordered two regiments from Jones's brigade to Fleetwood Hill. Unit formations disintegrated as the troopers made a hard ride from Saint James Church. When Jones's cavalrymen reached the crest of the hill, they launched a ferocious attack that blunted the Union advance. Both sides continued to send reinforcements to the southern end of Fleetwood. Charge and countercharge characterized the next phase of the battle. The clash of sabers, not the ringing shots of pistols, pierced the air. It was a dramatic moment, but one that has created the false impression that the Battle of Brandy Station was limited to the ground surrounding Stuart's headquarters.

Four of Hampton's regiments followed Jones into the cauldron. Just as his troopers surged across the top of the hill, a fresh Union brigade under Col. Judson Kilpatrick struck opposite the terminus of Fleetwood. A confusing melee ensued and most of Kilpatrick's regiments were repulsed. Desperate to salvage the day, he called on the First Maine to make a final charge. The Union cavalrymen swept forward, gaining a temporary hold on Fleetwood Hill, but the momen-

tum of the assault carried the members of the First Maine a mile across the hill where they found themselves "cut off from all support." After their attack, Beckham placed all his available guns along the ridge, as the Confederates established permanent control of Fleetwood Hill.

Two hours of severe fighting had exhausted Gregg's division, and reinforcements were not at hand. His supporting division, under Col. Alfred N. Duffie, stumbled into Col. M. C. Butler's Second South Carolina at Stevensburg. Though Duffie could see Fleetwood, he made little attempt to break through the enemy's thin line. If Duffie had aggressively led his command, he could have aided Gregg at Brandy Station or marched to Culpeper to discover the disposition of Lee's infantry. With only two hundred men at hand, Butler's energetic defense saved Stuart from a potential fiasco.

After Gregg's battered command galloped off the field, heading toward the Rappahannock Railroad Bridge, Stuart consolidated his position along a two-mile front with Hampton on the right, stretched east across the Orange and Alexandria Railroad. Jones occupied the center of the line while Rooney Lee anchored the left flank, which bent around the northern rim of Fleetwood. Stuart wanted to pursue Gregg, but enemy activity on his left made this venture impossible, as Buford and Lee had been hotly engaged for most the afternoon.

Unlike Duffie, Buford tried to assist Gregg by concentrating his forces, mostly dismounted cavalry and infantry, against Lee's refused left flank. Just when Buford's men seized the northern crest of Fleetwood around 3:30, they received the order to retire to Beverly's Ford. Pleasonton had already

> **Stuart refused to admit that he had not been prepared for Pleasonton's assault but conceded that his troops nearly lost the field to the enemy.**

decided on a general withdrawal. Reports of Confederate infantry, the failure of Gregg's attack, and Buford's slow progress against Rooney Lee convinced Pleasonton that little more could be achieved south of the river.

Although Stuart could claim a tactical victory at Brandy Station, he had been badly surprised by Pleasonton, an incident that tarnished his reputation. After the battle, one Southern cavalryman wrote, "Stuart was certainly surprised and but for the supreme gallantry of his subordinate officers and men in his command it would have been a day of disaster and disgrace." In his official report, Stuart refused to admit that he had not been prepared for Pleasonton's assault but conceded that his troops nearly lost the field to the enemy. Stuart criticized Robertson for failing to block Gregg's advance and chastised Col. Thomas T. Munford, the temporary commander of Fitzhugh Lee's brigade, for his tardy arrival on the battlefield.

Stuart's insatiable need for approbation was not satisfied by his commanding officer, who offered few words of praise after Brandy Station. Lee must have been pleased by Stuart's aggressive leadership on the battlefield, which prevented the Federals from unmasking the location of the Confederate infantry. Nevertheless, criticism came from all circles and wounded Stuart's sensitive pride. A North Carolina woman wrote that "the more we hear of the battle at Brandy Station, the more disgraceful is the surprise." Mindful of public reaction to Brandy Station, Stuart tried to redeem himself in the coming campaign by launching a raid in Pennsylvania that possessed little military value and virtually paralyzed the entire army.

BIBLIOGRAPHY

Blackford, William W. *War Years with Jeb Stuart*. New York, 1945.

Coddington, Edwin B. *The Gettysburg Campaign: A Study in Command*. New York, 1968.

Gallagher, Gary W. "Brandy Station: The Civil War's Bloodiest Arena of Mounted Combat." *Blue & Gray Magazine* 8 (October 1990): 8–22, 44–53.

McClellan, Henry B. *The Life and Campaigns of Major-General J. E. B. Stuart, Commander of the Cavalry of the Army of Northern Virginia*. Boston, 1885.

Thomas, Emory M. *Bold Dragoon: The Life of J. E. B. Stuart*. New York, 1986.

U.S. War Department. *The War of the Rebellion: A Compilation of the Official Records of the Union and Confederate Armies*. Ser. 1, vol. 27, pts. 1–2. Washington, D.C., 1893.

PETER S. CARMICHAEL

BREAD RIOTS

There is no incident on the Confederate home front more misunderstood than the Richmond bread riot of April 2, 1863, and no civilian subject less studied than that of other food riots, mostly in the springs of 1863 and 1864, although New Orleans experienced a disturbance as early as July 1861. These events have been attributed to wartime inflation and a lack of adequate food supplies at fair prices.

A series of incidents that preceded the April 1863 disturbance in the Confederate capital helped cause it and explain why it occurred when it did. Specific local factors increased demand for shrinking supplies, exacerbating inflation that led to hoarding and speculation. Further irritants to a disgruntled population were the explosion of the Confederate ordnance laboratory on March 13, which killed more than sixty poor women, and a heavy snowfall the next week. The snow quick-

ly melted, making roads nearly impassable and causing flooding of the James River, which shut down the waterworks and public hydrants.

Crime and vice were common in Richmond, especially at night. The bread riot was organized violence on a large scale conducted openly. It was also political protest, planned and led by women, a purposeful rather than a spontaneous event.

Its timing was related to a series of outbreaks elsewhere. Atlanta, Georgia, had a food riot on March 16, 1863, as did Macon, Columbus, and Augusta about the same time. On a main rail link between Virginia and the lower South, Salisbury, North Carolina, witnessed a flour riot on March 18, when soldiers' wives raided merchants. Raleigh, High Point, and Boon Hill in the same state all experienced food riots that month. Mobile, Alabama, had one on March 25 (and a more serious incident in mid-April, as well as disturbances in August and on September 4). In Petersburg, Virginia, there was a bread riot on April 1. Most of these events were reported in Richmond papers, often with favorable editorial comments about the alleged hoarders, speculators, or profiteers who were targeted.

There had been talk about a protest in Richmond for several weeks, but final plans were made at a meeting held in Belvidere Baptist Church the night of April 1. Women from all over the city, particularly poorer neighborhoods, attended, as did some from outlying counties. Their participation indicates prior knowledge that something was about to happen.

The riot began before nine in the morning when Mary Jackson, a painter's wife, left her butcher's stall in the Second Market. Followed by a growing crowd of women and boys she marched to the Governor's Mansion. It is unclear whether Governor John Letcher actually addressed the group. The crowd became a mob when it surged out of Capitol Square, down Ninth Street, and invaded the business district on Main and Cary streets, sacking about twenty stores.

Mayor Joseph Mayo tried to quell the women by reading the Riot Act, but he was ignored. Governor Letcher called out the Public Guard, a state security force for the Capitol and other buildings, under its acting commander, Lt. Edward Scott Gay. There is no reliable evidence for the story that President Jefferson Davis took command of the Guard, ordering the men to prepare to fire while confronting the looters and giving them a deadline to disperse.

Estimates of the mob's size have ranged from a few hundred to twenty thousand, but careful scholars argue for about one thousand actual participants, as distinguished from spectators. Richmond's tiny police force was no match for the rioters. There are a few references in some accounts to bloodshed, shots fired, and injuries suffered, but none has been substantiated. The riot was over by eleven.

Forty-four women and twenty-nine men are known to have been arrested, but not all of them were charged or tried.

Court records later burned, so the disposition of many cases is unknown. Only twelve women were convicted, one of a felony. A majority were probably poor women, but others were or had once been members of the middle class, including at least eight of those arrested; a few owned land and even slaves. Male rioters got stiffer penitentiary sentences, four for felonies and two for misdemeanors.

The Confederate government failed in its attempt to censor news of the riot. Telegrams reached Danville and Lynchburg within hours. Reports were carried throughout the South by railroad passengers leaving Richmond and to the North by Union prisoners exchanged soon after the event. Most of the city's editors initially honored a request not to print articles about the incident, but John Moncure Daniel, a bitter critic of the Davis administration, blasted the authorities in his *Examiner* for their lenient treatment of the rioters, calling for a dictator to suppress lawlessness. He also attacked the women with ethnic, sexist, and religious slurs. Ironically, his colorful but distorted accounts are the basis for most historians' descriptions.

Sullen crowds gathered again on April 3, but were promptly dispersed by the City Battalion. Troops under Maj. Gen. Arnold Elzey, commander of the Department of Richmond, who had already withheld reinforcements from Lt. Gen. James Longstreet because of the crisis, strengthened Provost Marshal John Winder's men. Cannon were placed at the edge of the business district amid rumors of another riot planned for the night of April 10. The city moved quickly to enlarge its parsimonious welfare program.

Another rash of incidents the next spring suggests that the pinch of hunger became painful enough to move women to desperate action as their winter food supplies were exhausted. Savannah had a riot on April 17, 1864, and one occurred in Bladenboro, North Carolina, the same month. There are sketchy details about incidents in the last year of the war at Abingdon, Virginia; Lafayette, Alabama; Forsyth, Thomasville, and Marietta, Georgia; and Sherman, Texas.

Of their importance there can be no doubt. Historian Emory M. Thomas has called the Richmond riot "the best case study of the results of Southern food supply problems." Three levels of government in the capital were shaken, and all took steps to prevent another incident. Morale plummeted throughout the Confederacy. The food riots were a sign of urban unrest, similar to the yeoman discontent expressed in rural areas by women's raids on government storage depots, like that at Jonesville, North Carolina, in 1865. They were also disturbing evidence that the war had become a poor woman's fight, as well as a poor man's. Women who demonstrated in city streets and country crossroads and openly defied civil and military authorities hardly conformed to traditional Southern definitions of patriotism and female roles.

[*See also* Poor Relief; Poverty; Speculation.]

BIBLIOGRAPHY

Amos, Harriet E. "'All Absorbing Topics': Food and Clothing in Confederate Mobile." *Atlanta Historical Journal* 22 (1978): 17–28.

Chesson, Michael B. "Harlots or Heroines? A New Look at the Richmond Bread Riot." *Virginia Magazine of History and Biography* 92 (1984): 131–175.

Coulter, E. Merton. *The Confederate States of America, 1861–1865.* A History of the South, vol. 7. Baton Rouge, La., 1950.

Simkins, Francis Butler, and James Welch Patton. *The Women of the Confederacy.* Richmond, 1936.

Tice, Douglas O. "'Bread or Blood!': The Richmond Bread Riot." *Civil War Times Illustrated* 12 (1974): 12–19.

MICHAEL B. CHESSON

BRECKENRIDGE, JOHN C.

BRECKINRIDGE, JOHN C. (1821–1875), U.S. congressman, vice president, and presidential candidate, major general, and secretary of war. Breckinridge, who was born into one of Kentucky's most illustrious families, studied at Centre College, the College of New Jersey (Princeton), and Transylvania University. He practiced law briefly in Iowa and then in his home state. Major of the Third Regiment of Kentucky Volunteers, he arrived in Mexico too late for significant participation in the Mexican War. Breckinridge was elected to the Kentucky House of Representatives in 1849 as a Democrat and to the U.S. House in 1851 and 1853. In 1856 at age thirty-five he was elected vice president of the United States on the Democratic ticket with James Buchanan. In 1859, over a year before his term expired, the Kentucky legislature chose him for the Senate term beginning March 4, 1861. As the slavery controversy developed in the 1850s, Breckinridge had called for "perfect non-intervention" on the part of Congress on the issue of slavery in the territories.

When the Democrats split in 1860, Breckinridge became the candidate of the Southern party. Though he believed that a state had the right to secede, he denied that he was the secession candidate. Breckinridge lost his home state to Constitutional Unionist John Bell, but he carried eleven of the fifteen slave states and won 72 electoral votes to 39 for Bell and 12 for Stephen A. Douglas, the Northern Democratic candidate. But Republican Abraham Lincoln received 180 votes for a clear majority. As vice president, Breckinridge announced the election of Lincoln on February 13, 1861, when the electoral votes were officially counted.

Breckinridge hoped that some compromise would save the Union, but in the Senate he defended the actions of the Southern states. After the war started, he served on a six-man committee that formulated Kentucky's unique neutrality policy. When that troubled status ended in September 1861,

Breckinridge fled to Virginia to avoid arrest. The Senate expelled him on December 2.

Considered an important asset for the Confederacy, Breckinridge was commissioned brigadier general on November 2 and given the Kentucky Brigade in Gen. Simon Bolivar Buckner's Second Division in southern Kentucky. He helped organize the Confederate government of Kentucky, which was admitted into the Confederacy on December 10, 1861. One of the best of the "political generals," Breckinridge won the respect and admiration of most of his peers, with the conspicuous exception of irascible Braxton Bragg.

Breckinridge's first major engagement was at Shiloh where, in command of the Confederates' Reserve Corps, he performed well enough to merit promotion to major general as of April 14. After serving with Earl Van Dorn at Vicksburg, Breckinridge led an unsuccessful attempt to take Baton Rouge. Rejoining the Army of Tennessee, he incurred heavy casualties in his division at Murfreesboro in a charge ordered by Bragg. Several Kentuckians urged Breckinridge to seek a duel with his caustic commander.

Breckinridge then returned to the Vicksburg area and participated in Joseph E. Johnston's vain efforts to relieve that city. After it fell, he was ordered to rejoin Bragg's army in eastern Tennessee. At Chickamauga on September 19–20, 1863, Breckinridge's division was in D. H. Hill's corps. His assaults on the Federal left flank helped break the Union line but failed to destroy the army. Breckinridge commanded a corps on Lookout Mountain and Missionary Ridge above Chattanooga on November 25, 1863, when the Confederates were overrun. Bragg charged Breckinridge with drunkenness and removed him from command. But Confederate leaders had learned to discount Bragg's frequent accusations, and in February 1864 the Kentuckian was given command of the Department of Southwest Virginia. He built his command from scratch, and on May 15, with the aid of cadets from the Virginia Military Institute, he defeated Gen. Franz Siegel's larger force at New Market. It was perhaps Breckinridge's finest performance of the war.

Soon transferred to the Army of Northern Virginia, Breckinridge helped check Ulysses S. Grant at Cold Harbor. Then, as commander of a small corps, he accompanied Jubal Early on his raid to the outskirts of Washington. When they returned to the Shenandoah Valley, the Confederates were under intense pressure from Gen. Philip Sheridan's much larger force. Gen. John B. Gordon penned a vivid picture of Breckinridge at this stage of the war:

Tall, erect, and commanding in physique . . . he exhibited in marked degree the characteristics of a great commander. He was fertile in resource, and enlisted and held the confidence and affection of his men, while he inspired them with enthusiasm and ardor. Under fire and in extreme peril he was strikingly courageous, alert, and self-poised.

Later, Gen. Basil W. Duke also praised his fellow Kentuckian but added, "His chief defect as a soldier—and, perhaps, as a civilian—was a strange indolence or apathy which at times assailed him. . . . When thoroughly aroused he acted with tremendous vigour, . . . but he needed to be spurred to action. . . . He was at his best when the occasion seemed desperate."

After John Hunt Morgan's death on September 4, 1864, Breckinridge was returned to command of the Department of Southwest Virginia. Despite inadequate resources, he was able to fend off Union attacks against the vital saltworks in that area.

Meanwhile, the Department of War had become one of the most troubled spots in the Confederate government, and in February 1865 President Jefferson Davis appointed Breckinridge secretary of war. In 1861 Breckinridge had doubted that the Confederacy could win the war, and as he viewed the situation from his new position, he soon concluded that the cause was hopeless. He worked to bring the struggle to an honorable conclusion, which, in his view, rejected guerrilla warfare. "This has been a magnificent epic," he declared. "In God's name let it not terminate in a farce." When Richmond fell he was instrumental in preserving many of the military records.

Briefly with Lee, then with Joseph E. Johnston, and finally accompanying President Davis on his flight, Breckinridge made a daring and dangerous escape through Florida to Cuba. He went on to Europe and Canada where he remained in exile until President Andrew Johnson extended a general amnesty on Christmas Day, 1868. Breckinridge returned to his Lexington home in March 1869 after an absence of over eight years. Comparing himself to "an extinct volcano," he practiced law, worked for economic development in the state, and urged national conciliation until his death on May 17, 1875. He was only fifty-four.

BIBLIOGRAPHY

Davis, William C. *Breckinridge: Statesman, Soldier, Symbol.* Baton Rouge, La., 1974.

Davis, William C. "John C. Breckinridge." *Register of the Kentucky Historical Society* 85 (Summer 1987): 197–212.

Harrison, Lowell H. "John C. Breckinridge: Nationalist, Confederate, Kentuckian." *The Filson Club History Quarterly* 47 (April 1973): 125–144.

Heck, Frank H. *Proud Kentuckian: John C. Breckinridge, 1821–1875.* Lexington, Ky., 1976.

Klotter, James C. *The Breckinridges of Kentucky, 1760–1981.* Lexington, Ky., 1986.

LOWELL H. HARRISON

BRECKENRIDGE, ROBERT J.

BRECKINRIDGE, ROBERT J. (1800–1871), minister, politician, educator, and Unionist. Breckinridge was born into one of Kentucky's most illustrious families at Cabell's Dale, outside Lexington, on March 8, 1800. His father, John Breckinridge, became a U.S. senator and then attorney general in President Thomas Jefferson's cabinet; his mother, Mary Hopkins (Polly) Cabell Breckinridge, was related to several prominent Virginia families. He graduated from Union College, Schenectady, New York, in July 1819. Robert's health was poor, and he spent two years traveling and reading before studying law and receiving a license in 1824. But he was more interested in developing his farm, Braedalbane, in Fayette County than in building up his practice. Elected to the state house of representatives in 1824, he supported the conservative Old Court in a savage controversy over relief legislation. Reelected annually, he represented Fayette County until 1829.

Breckinridge's continued illness and the deaths of two of his children changed his attitude toward religion. He made a profession of faith in 1829 and decided to become a Presbyterian minister. He received his license to preach in April 1832 and then went to the Princeton Theological Seminary for further study. A few months later he accepted a call to Baltimore's Second Presbyterian Church. Robert's eloquence, persistence, and conviction that he was right soon made him a conspicuous but controversial figure in the denomination. He was largely responsible for the 1834 "Act and Testimony" that by 1837 had split the Presbyterians into New School–Old School factions. Breckinridge sided with the latter. During his stormy thirteen years in Baltimore he attracted national attention with his prolonged debates with Catholic spokesman (later Bishop) John Hughes and with Universalists.

Breckinridge and his wife spent a year abroad in 1836–1837 when he served as a church delegate. His fame as a controversialist was enhanced by an extended debate in Glasgow, Scotland, with George Thompson on the slavery question. By 1830 Breckinridge owned seventeen slaves, and the number continued to grow, although during his Maryland years he sent eleven freed blacks to Liberia. Breckinridge believed that slavery was wrong, but he insisted that it could be eliminated only through gradual, compensated emancipation, followed by colonization that would remove free blacks from the white community. His 1840 debates in Kentucky with Robert Wickliffe, the "Old Duke," resulted in other vitriolic exchanges. Breckinridge enraged both proslavery advocates and abolitionists, whom he denounced as extremists who endangered the nation.

When Kentucky's third constitutional convention met in 1849, emancipationists hoped to include in the new document a provision that would allow the legislature to consider emancipation whenever it wished. Breckinridge advanced a plan that would free at age twenty-five those slaves born after the adoption of Kentucky's new constitution but allow public authorities to hold them in service until they had earned enough to pay their way to Liberia. Although they polled over ten thousand votes collectively, all emancipationist candidates were defeated. Breckinridge attributed this defeat to the apathy of nonslaveholders.

In 1845 Breckinridge became president of Jefferson College in Pennsylvania. But his tenure there was unhappy, and in January 1847 he accepted an offer to become minister of the First Presbyterian Church in Lexington, Kentucky.

Breckinridge entered upon a new phase of his career in September when Governor William Owsley appointed him superintendent of public instruction. The office had been created in 1838, but six predecessors had done little to improve Kentucky's deplorable public schools. By the time of his resignation in 1853, Kentucky rivaled North Carolina for the best public school system among the slave states. Enrollments had soared and expenditures for education had increased dramatically. But his reforms also attracted opposition. He alarmed those who believed in the separation of church and state when he insisted that the Bible be adopted as the reading text in the elementary grades, and his advocacy of emancipation aroused protests. His presbytery finally ordered his pastoral relations dissolved and suggested strongly that he take a position at the new Danville Theological Seminary.

When the seminary opened on October 13, 1853, Breckinridge was named Professor of Exegetic, Polemic, and Didactic Theology. He remained at the seminary until 1869. Two of his best known books were published during his tenure there: *The Knowledge of God, Objectively Considered* (1858) and *The Knowledge of God, Subjectively Considered* (1859). He edited the *Danville Review* (1861–1865), which gave him an outlet for his political writings. His clashes with colleague Stuart Robinson, who referred to Breckinridge's "despotic and intolerant spirit," contributed to the schism between Northern and Southern factions of the Presbyterian church.

Despite poor health, Breckinridge was an imposing figure when he went to the seminary. Tall and slender, he had a full white beard and dark gray sideburns. Friends often referred to his kindness, his sense of humor, his capacity for affection and sympathy, his courage; opponents saw him as impulsive, combative, irritable, prejudiced, and vindictive. He was given to dogmatic opinions, which he seldom changed.

As the sectional crisis intensified, Breckinridge was a determined foe of secession. In an address in Lexington on January 4, 1861, he declared that if Kentucky did secede, it should form a confederation with Tennessee, Virginia, North

Carolina, Maryland, and Missouri. If that approach failed, he preferred that Kentucky remain separate rather than be swallowed up in a confederacy of all the slave states in which Kentucky would be a mere tool of the cotton states. When Governor Beriah Magoffin proposed calling a convention to determine the state's future, Breckinridge, fearing that it might result in secession, advised his associates to delay and defeat it by every possible means. If a convention was held, he asserted that its decision should be submitted to the people for approval. He conceded that the will of the people must then be accepted.

In June 1861, during the state's period of troubled neutrality, Breckinridge warned that secession and rebellion would ultimately destroy slavery. That institution would be

> Breckinridge warned that secession and rebellion would ultimately destroy slavery.

safe only in a sound Union. In order to save the old Union, he was willing to divide the territories between slave and free. Although he hoped to see slavery extinguished at some future date, he saw no practical way to deal with the large number of blacks in the cotton states except to continue slavery for the present.

Kentucky remained in the Union when its unique policy of neutrality ended in September 1861, and Breckinridge gave strong support to the war effort. Hailed as the "staunchest friend of the Union in the state," he was believed to have more influence with President Abraham Lincoln than any other Kentuckian. In his own family Breckinridge experienced the agonies of the divided country: two sons joined the Confederacy; two enlisted in Union forces. He supported the harsh measures of Gen. Stephen G. Burbridge and other Union officers who tried to suppress pro-Confederate sympathies and actions in the state. Because of his alleged influence with Lincoln, Breckinridge received numerous appeals for assistance, but he responded favorably to few of them. Instead, he declared that too few suspects were being arrested and that many of those who were arrested were being released too soon. "Treat them all alike," he demanded, "and if there are any among them who are not rebels at heart, God will take care of them and save them at least." Breckinridge insisted that violators of the law were not as entitled to its protection as those who obeyed. He did bend his principles occasionally, however, to help members of his family.

Yet Breckinridge disagreed upon occasion with Lincoln. He called the Emancipation Proclamation unnecessary, and he doubted its constitutionality. In 1849 he had declared that "emancipation is not the main thing—not even *a* main thing except as it may act on an object more important than itself,

Unity of race, and that the white race for Kentucky." Nevertheless, when Governor Thomas E. Bramlette's opposition to the enrollment of blacks for possible military service threatened to result in open warfare, Breckinridge was among those who persuaded the angered governor to accept the Federal policy.

In 1864 when most Kentuckians were opposed to the Lincoln administration, Breckinridge was a leader in organizing an Unconditional Union party in the state. When it failed to get the cooperation of the Union Democrats, the party held a convention and endorsed the crushing of the rebellion and restoration of the Union. Breckinridge went to Baltimore as a delegate to the national Union party and was elected temporary chairman. In his address he called for the end of slavery, rigorous prosecution of the war, restoration of the Union, and punishment of traitors. He campaigned hard for Lincoln's reelection. In one of his most controversial suggestions, he proposed that loyal Kentuckians not be paid for confiscated slaves until after the election and "let their votes be the test of their loyalty." Although military authorities blatantly interfered with the election in the state, George B. McClellan carried Kentucky by a wide margin over Lincoln.

Breckinridge was delighted by the collapse of the Confederacy, but he was disturbed by the postwar strength of the "Confederate Democrats" in Kentucky. He even feared for a time that war would begin again. Southern sentiment appeared dominant in his denomination, and in October 1865 he introduced a resolution that declared a majority of the Louisville presbytery was "in open rebellion against the Church, and in open contempt and defiance of her scriptural authority"; such members were "unqualified, unfit and incompetent" to participate in church affairs. His motion lost, 25 to 102, but the next year the Kentucky synod split into Northern and Southern branches. Critics of Breckinridge charged that he "would rule or ruin."

Breckinridge died in Danville on December 27, 1871, and was buried in Lexington. He had once remarked, "I am a wonder to myself." He was also a wonder to many of his contemporaries.

BIBLIOGRAPHY

Coulter, E. Merton. *The Civil War and Readjustment in Kentucky.* Chapel Hill, N.C., 1926. Reprint, Gloucester, Mass., 1966.

Gilliam, Will D., Jr. "Robert J. Breckinridge: Kentucky Unionist." *Register of the Kentucky Historical Society* 69 (October 1971): 362–385.

Gilliam, Will D., Jr. "Robert Jefferson Breckinridge, 1800–1871." *Register of the Kentucky Historical Society* 72 (July 1974): 207–223; (October 1974): 319–336.

Harrison, Lowell H. *The Antislavery Movement in Kentucky.* Lexington, Ky., 1978.

Howard, Victor B. "Robert J. Breckinridge and the Slavery Controversy in Kentucky in 1849." *Filson Club History Quarterly* 53 (October 1978): 328–343.

Klotter, James C. *The Breckinridges of Kentucky.* Lexington, Ky., 1986.

Tapp, Hambleton. "Robert Jefferson Breckinridge during the Civil War." *Filson Club History Quarterly* 11 (April 1937): 120–144.

Vaughan, William Hutchinson. *Robert Jefferson Breckinridge as an Educational Administrator.* Nashville, Tenn., 1937.

LOWELL H. HARRISON

BRICE'S CROSS ROADS, MISSISSIPPI

Also known as Tishomingo Creek and Guntown, the June 10, 1864, Battle of Brice's Cross Roads, west of Baldwyn, Mississippi, was the scene of Confederate Maj. Gen. Nathan Bedford Forrest's most spectacular victory. Forrest's numerically inferior force routed Brig. Gen. Samuel D. Sturgis's Union command. Sturgis's advance was designed, in large part, to keep Confederate cavalry raiders, particularly Forrest, from threatening Union Maj. Gen. William Tecumseh Sherman's vulnerable supply lines as he drove toward Atlanta. Forrest had actually begun such a raid when the Union advance into northern Mississippi compelled him to return.

Sturgis's expedition started in Memphis, Tennessee, and consisted of a combined infantry and cavalry force of 8,300, with 22 pieces of artillery and 250 wagons. Heavy rains slowed the Union column and this pace concerned Sturgis. On the evening of June 8, he held a conference at which he contemplated turning back to Memphis. Meanwhile, Forrest dispersed his 4,800 men so as to react to any line of advance the Federals might take.

On June 9 Sturgis massed his army on the Stubbs plantation, ten miles from Brice's Cross Roads. Confederate department commander Stephen D. Lee planned for Forrest to engage the Federals near Okolona. Forrest, however, held a council of war and informed his commanders that he intended to attack the Federals as soon as possible. He anticipated that Sturgis would send his cavalry to seize Brice's Cross Roads and then hurry his infantry along the muddy roads to reinforce them once the battle had begun. In this fashion Forrest predicted he could "whip" the cavalry first and then defeat the exhausted infantry as they reached the battlefield.

Although Forrest had hoped to reach Brice's Cross Roads first, Sturgis's 3,300 cavalry, under Brig. Gen. Benjamin H. Grierson, had been up since 5:30 A.M. and got there ahead of him. Lead elements of Grierson's cavalry easily dispersed a small Confederate patrol; but, as the Union cavalrymen fanned out along the Baldwyn Road, they encountered more Southerners.

At the same time, Sturgis allowed the infantry to prepare for the day at a more leisurely pace. Finally, about 7:00 A.M., the infantry formed to follow their comrades. This delay gave Forrest the opportunity to defeat the Union cavalry as he had planned.

Meanwhile, the combat was becoming more intense as both commands dismounted to fight amid the thick stands of blackjack and dense undergrowth. Forrest arrived at the scene and assumed command. Although heavily outnumbered, he used a series of sharp attacks to mask his numerical weakness, keep his opponents off balance, and hold the initiative. He added regiments into the line as they reached the field, constantly maintaining pressure on the Union cavalry.

By 1:00 P.M. the rest of Forrest's men and his artillery had arrived. Brig. Gen. Abraham Buford paused on his way only long enough to dispatch Col. Clark S. Barteau and 250 men to move along the farm lanes in an attempt to get into the Federals' rear. Shortly thereafter, the first of Sturgis's infantry staggered onto the battlefield, exhausted from struggling through the mire, and feeling the effects of the heat and humidity. As the infantrymen arrived, they slowly began to replace the cavalry on the front lines.

Following a brief lull, Forrest unleashed his entire command against the Federals, including a small force on the Union right flank and Barteau's men on the Union left. The fighting continued relentlessly for more than two hours as the Federals slowly gave ground. Finally, with his own lines shortened and his firepower concentrated, Forrest ordered the assault he felt sure would win the day.

The Confederates surged forward along the entire line, and first the Union right and then the left gave way. The Southerners continued to press home their assaults with vigor. In the confusion of the battle, and under constant pressure from their opponents, any Union hopes for an organized retreat disappeared. Finally, between 4:00 and 5:00 P.M., the Federal line collapsed. To make matters worse, some of the supply wagons had crossed the bridge over Tishomingo Creek and parked on the east side. Thus, when the Union line folded, the panicked teamsters entangled the wagons and blocked the bridge, creating a bottleneck that added to the confusion.

The Confederates spent the next two days hounding the retreating Federals. Forrest personally led the pursuit, until, faint with fatigue, he eventually had to be helped from his saddle. Other Southerners maintained the pressure on their battered opponents until they were themselves thoroughly exhausted. Indeed, the Federals were so badly routed that at one point an exasperated Sturgis remarked to a subordinate, "For God's sake, if Mr. Forrest will let me alone, I will let him alone." By June 13, Sturgis had his wish, as his shattered army finally reached the safety of Memphis.

On the day following the battle, Gen. S. D. Lee called Brice's Cross Roads "one of the most signal victories of the war for the forces engaged." Forrest's loss of 96 killed and 396 wounded was proportionately heavier than Sturgis's, but he inflicted far worse overall losses on the Federals—223 killed, 394 wounded, and 1,623 captured or missing. He also captured 16 artillery pieces, 176 wagons, 1,500 stand of small arms, and vast quantities of ammunition.

In the aftermath of the disastrous defeat, Sherman angrily observed to Secretary of War Edwin M. Stanton: "Forrest is the very devil, and I think he has some of our troops under cower." He vowed to send out two new commanders with orders to "follow Forrest to the death, if it cost 10,000 lives and breaks the Treasury." Nevertheless, Sherman's supply lines remained intact. Forrest had won his greatest victory, but it had proven to be of far greater tactical than strategic importance.

BIBLIOGRAPHY

Bearss, Edwin C. *Forrest at Brice's Cross Roads.* Dayton, Ohio, 1979.
Henry, Robert Selph. *"First with the Most" Forrest.* Indianapolis, 1944.
Wills, Brian Steel. *A Battle from the Start: The Life of Nathan Bedford Forrest.* New York, 1992.
Wyeth, John Allan. *Life of General Nathan Bedford Forrest.* New York, 1899. Reprint, Baton Rouge, La., 1989.

BRIAN S. WILLS

BRISTOE STATION, VIRGINIA

This village, eight miles south of Manassas on the Orange and Alexandria Railroad, was the site of an October 14, 1863, battle that was Confederate Gen. A. P. Hill's most stunning defeat of the Civil War.

By early autumn of that year, the opposing armies of Generals Robert E. Lee and George G. Meade faced each other again along the Rappahannock-Rapidan river line. Lee received word that Meade had transferred two Federal corps from his army to duty in Tennessee. The Confederate commander decided to go on the offensive to exploit this weakness. Lee's plan was to draw Meade away from the vital road junction of Culpeper and sever the Federal lines of communication with Washington. As the Southern army began a circuitous march on Meade's flank, the Federals rapidly fell back to the north.

On October 14, Hill's corps from Lee's army arrived on high ground overlooking Bristoe Station. Below was a Federal corps, seemingly caught in a horrendous traffic jam as men, horses, and wagons were trying to get across a ford on rain-swollen Broad Run. Hill immediately ordered an attack on what appeared to be an isolated and disorganized Federal force.

The first mistake made by the still-new Southern corps leader was in not reconnoitering the area with proper care. Hill's second error, which reflected his inexperience at corps level, was in sending only two brigades into action against a Federal host several times larger in size.

The two Confederate units—North Carolina brigades under Generals John Rogers Cooke and William Whedbee Kirkland—rushed across eight hundred yards of open fields. Too late Hill discovered that another Federal corps was also at Bristoe Station. It was posted along the railroad and squarely on the right flank of the attacking Southerners. Thus, massed Federals in a huge L-shaped line waited for two undersized brigades to charge into the angled line. It was one of the deadliest traps of the entire war.

The major fighting that afternoon lasted only forty minutes. Union musketry and artillery cut the attacking columns to pieces. A Tarheel soldier exclaimed that the Southern ranks "were mowed down like grain before a reaper." The Twenty-seventh North Carolina lost over half its men, including 33 of its 36 officers. Bristoe Station cost Hill almost 1,400 men killed, wounded, and missing, as well as five cannon seized in a brief Federal counterattack. Union casualties were fewer than 600 men.

Meade's army continued its withdrawal under cover of darkness. Rain was falling the next day when a shocked Lee rode with Hill over the battlefield. Southern bodies still lay scattered over the torn ground. Hill was trying to explain what happened when Lee uncharacteristically interrupted him: "Well, well, General, bury those poor men, and let us say no more about it."

Lack of supplies forced Lee to abandon his advance a few days later. The Confederates returned to the Rappahannock country and its rail connections with Richmond.

BIBLIOGRAPHY

Freeman, Douglas S. *Lee's Lieutenants: A Study in Command.* Vol. 3. New York, 1944. Reprint, New York, 1986.
Henderson, William D. *The Road to Bristoe Station.* Lynchburg, Va., 1987.
Humphries, Andrew A. *From Gettysburg to the Rapidan.* New York, 1883. Reprint, Baltimore, 1987.
Meade, G. G. *The Life and Letters of General George Gordon Meade.* Vol. 2. New York, 1913.
Robertson, James I., Jr. *General A. P. Hill.* New York, 1987.

JAMES I. ROBERTSON, JR.

BROCKENBROUGH, JOHN MERCER

BROCKENBROUGH, JOHN MERCER (1830–1892), brigade commander (1862–1863). Brockenbrough graduated from the Virginia Military Institute in 1850 and spent the prewar years as a prominent planter on Virginia's Northern Neck. The outbreak of war in 1861 prompted him to raise and equip a regiment from his neighborhood. Brockenbrough led this unit—which became the Fortieth Virginia Infantry—from 1861 until July 1863, at which time he resigned. Although he never rose above the rank of colonel, Brockenbrough commanded an entire brigade of Virginians through the desperate battles of 1862 and 1863 that forged the reputation of the Army of Northern Virginia as a peerless fighting force.

The pinnacle of Colonel Brockenbrough's career came with the performance of his troops at Chancellorsville in May 1863. But the resulting euphoria soon gave way to the despair of failure at Gettysburg in early July. Brockenbrough's Brigade was shredded on July 1, and the feeble remnants of that once-proud body of men were the first to collapse on July 3 in the famous Confederate assault. That misfortune was exceeded by the further disaster at Falling Waters, Maryland, on July 14, 1863. As the Confederate army withdrew across the Potomac River, Brockenbrough's handful of survivors found themselves encircled and eventually captured. The colonel was not present at the destruction of his brigade. A few weeks later Henry H. Walker, one of Brockenbrough's subordinates, was promoted to brigadier general over the colonel's head. The implied rebuke prompted Brockenbrough's resignation, and he finished the war as an officer of reserves.

Brockenbrough divided his time after the war between the Northern Neck and Richmond, where he died in 1892.

BIBLIOGRAPHY

Compiled Military Service Records. John Mercer Brockenbrough. Microcopy M324, Roll 853. Record Group 109. National Archives, Washington, D.C.
Krick, Robert E. L. *40th Virginia Infantry.* Lynchburg, Va., 1985.

ROBERT E. L. KRICK

BROOKE, JOHN MERCER

BROOKE, JOHN MERCER (1826–1906), naval officer. Born at Fort Brooke (present-day Tampa), Florida, Brooke joined the U.S. Navy as a midshipman in 1841, graduated from the Naval Academy in 1847, and was promoted to lieutenant in 1855. As a young naval officer, he invented deep-sea sounding leads that eventually made possible the laying of an Atlantic cable.

In April 1861, Brooke resigned his commission when Virginia seceded. He joined the Confederate navy as a lieutenant, and a June meeting with Secretary of the Navy Stephen R. Mallory led to his appointment to supervise work on armor and guns for CSS *Virginia.* His achievements are surprising, given his youth and lack of experience in these areas. Brooke was responsible for *Virginia's* slanted armor casemate, copied in other Confederate ironclads, as well as the idea of extensions of bow and stern under water. Friction between Brooke and constructor John D. Porter, who claimed credit for the ironclad's design, contributed to his subsequent lack of interest in the ironclad program.

In September 1862, Brooke was promoted to commander. In March 1863, he was named chief of the Confederate Bureau of Ordnance and Hydrography, a post he held until the end of the war. He designed a variety of ordnance for the Confederacy, including 32-pounder and 10- and 11-inch smoothbore guns. He is, however, best known for his double- and triple-banded rifled guns, produced in 6.4-inch, 7-inch, and 8-inch sizes. They were probably the finest rifled navy guns on either side in the war.

After the war, Brooke served as professor of astronomy, meteorology, and geography at the Virginia Military Institute from 1865 until 1899.

BIBLIOGRAPHY

Brooke, George M., Jr. *John M. Brooke: Naval Scientist and Educator.* Charlottesville, Va., 1980.
Brooke, John Mercer. "The *Virginia* or *Merrimac:* Her Real Projector." *Southern Historical Society Papers* 19 (1891): 3–34. Reprint, Wilmington, N.C., 1990.

SPENCER C. TUCKER

BROTHERS OF WAR

From a white population of 5.5 million people, the South sent about 1 million males—the very cream of its manhood—into Confederate service. Rare indeed was the family without some member in the armed forces. Owing to the always-urgent need for manpower at the front, many Southern families contributed a startling number of soldiers to the Confederate cause. As examples: ten sons and five sons-in-law of the Bledsoe family in Mississippi wore the gray; Mrs. Enoch Hooper Cook of Alabama saw her husband, ten sons, and two grandsons all enter military service.

Locally raised units were often termed a "cousinwealth" because of the presence in their ranks of so many kinsmen, and war's heavy hand struck hard at many households as a result.

Eighteen members of the same Bell family served in one infantry company. In the course of the war, six were killed and five died of disease. All six sons of David Barton of Winchester, Virginia, were soldiers in the Stonewall Brigade. Two were wounded and two were killed, one almost within sight of his home. Four Timberlake brothers were compatriots of the Bartons. All four were crippled by battle injuries. Four Carpenter brothers from Allegheny County, Virginia, were members of an artillery unit named for the oldest of the boys. He was killed in 1862 and succeeded in command by the next brother, who lost an arm in battle. The third sibling soon struggled home with a bullet wound in his lungs. The last of the brothers lost a leg in the closing weeks of the war.

Like all civil wars, the American struggle of the 1860s tore asunder many family loyalties. This was especially true in such border states as Virginia, Kentucky, and Tennessee, which, sandwiched between North and South with respect to geography, society, economics, and politics, caused family ties to snap traumatically. Three brothers-in-law of U.S. President Abraham Lincoln were Confederate officers. Two sons of Federal Adm. David D. Porter served in a Confederate artillery battery. John J. Crittenden, U.S. senator from Kentucky, also had two sons, one of whom, George, became a major general in the Confederate army, and the other, Thomas, a major general in the Federal forces. Both men survived the war.

Other brother-generals were not so fortunate. William Rufus Terrill and James Barbour Terrill were sons of a prominent Virginia legislator. The former graduated from West Point; the latter obtained his degree from the Virginia Military Institute. William Terrill served in the Union army, became a brigadier general in September 1862, and was killed a month later at Perryville, Kentucky. James Terrill joined the Confederate army and became a brigadier general on June 3, 1864, the day he was slain at Cold Harbor, Virginia. A brokenhearted father collected their bodies, took them home, and buried them in a single grave. The headstone read: "Here lie my two sons. Only God knows which was right."

BIBLIOGRAPHY

Eaton, Clement. *A History of the Southern Confederacy.* New York, 1954.
Robertson, James I., Jr. *The Stonewall Brigade.* Baton Rouge, La., 1963.
Wiley, Bell Irvin. *Confederate Women.* Westport, Conn., 1975.

JAMES I. ROBERTSON, JR.

BROWN, ALBERT GALLATIN

BROWN, ALBERT GALLATIN (1813–1880), Mississippi governor, captain, and congressman. Unlike many more privileged politicians of the period who were educated at prestigious schools, Brown was educated in the frontier schools of Mississippi. His father, a poor farmer, had brought his family from South Carolina to Mississippi in 1823 when Brown was ten years old. His early life on the farm created sympathies that earned him the reputation in Mississippi as the "poor man's friend." After studying at Mississippi College and Jefferson College, he read law and was elected a brigadier general of militia when he was just twenty years old. Soon he was elected to the state legislature and gained prominence by opposing the Bank of the United States.

A combination of his opposition to the Bank and his personal attractiveness helped him win election to the U.S. Congress in 1839. After refusing renomination, he became a circuit judge. Two years later he ran for governor on a platform calling for the repudiation of Union Bank bonds on the ground that they were not a debt of the state. He was elected by a large majority and served two terms during which he strenuously promoted education and help for the disadvantaged; he called for "a general system of common schools, which should be open to all and at which the poor should be educated gratis."

Brown returned to Congress as a senator in 1848. There he actively participated in the sectional debates. He usually allied himself with Jefferson Davis but was a stronger advocate of resistance to national authority than Davis was. He denied that the Federal government had the power to prohibit slavery in the territories. Agitated by the war with Mexico and the policy on slavery in acquired territory, Brown as governor had summarized in a message his position on state rights:

> The power to legislate in regard to slavery has not been delegated, and therefore does not belong to the federal government, but remains with the States respectively. The question in the Territories, it seems to me, must be left, as in the States, to be settled by the people who inhabit them.

He declared in 1858, "It is futile . . . to try to compromise the slavery question. The difference between the North and South is radical and irreconcilable." He also advocated the United States' taking Central America and converting it to slavery. Before the 1860 Democratic National Convention, Brown wrote to Stephen A. Douglas insisting that the platform at the convention must recognize both slavery in the territories and that slave property was equivalent to any other property.

The views of Mississippi's two senators, Brown and Jefferson Davis, now diverged. Brown spoke of the "radical and irreconcilable" split between the North and the South, whereas Davis, who traveled to New England for his health in 1858, delivered speeches supporting a strong Union. The newspapers at the time expressed some surprise at the contrasting positions. One wrote, "Jefferson used to be a ranting fire-eater, now he is a Union shrieking conservative. Albert Gallatin used to be a mild conservative, now he is a ranting fire-eater."

Brown's position on slavery was indeed radical. He enthusiastically justified the institution, declaring that a society with two classes—white and black—was superior to one divided along the lines of wealth, inheritance, occupation, or fate. During Brown's tenure in the Senate, Davis introduced a resolution calling for "protection of Constitutional rights in a Territory." Brown sought stronger wording, and he proposed an amendment to Davis's resolution, calling on Congress to pass laws that would "afford to slave property in the territories that protection which is given to other kinds of property." Davis's resolution passed overwhelmingly; Brown's amendment received only three votes.

Brown favored immediate secession when Abraham Lincoln was elected in 1860. He declared unequivocally, "The Union is dead and in process of mortification, and nothing remains to be done but to bury the rotten carcass." But despite his fire-eater sentiments, on November 22, 1860, at a conference called by Governor J. J. Pettus on the subject of secession, Brown initially sided with Davis and L. Q. C. Lamar in opposing a resolution to call a state secession convention. The resolution passed nevertheless, and the three dissenters then sided with the majority.

After Mississippi passed its ordinance of secession on January 9, 1861, Davis delivered a farewell address to the U.S. Senate, and two days later, Brown also resigned, saying but a few words, which were uncharacteristically temperate. After his resignation, Brown was elected to the Confederate Senate, but before he took his seat, he entered the Confederate army as a captain of the Brown Rebels, a company he had recruited. Assigned to the Eighteenth Mississippi Regiment, the company was commanded by Col. E. B. Burt and was sent to Virginia early in the war. It participated in the Battles of Manassas and Leesburg, where Colonel Burt was killed.

In the Senate, Brown headed the Committee on Naval Affairs. To ensure the survival of the Confederacy, he argued that the South's priority ought to be to "save the country first, and settle constitutional constructions afterwards." He introduced bills to restrict the production of cotton, draft all white men fit to serve, and free and draft 200,000 slaves. His committee proposed a volunteer navy for privateering. Stressing the honor and necessity of military service, Brown strongly opposed draft-exemption laws, which, he said, "stunk in the nostrils of the people." He denounced those who sought the security of government jobs rather than serving on the battlefield:

> While the young men of the country were day after day enduring uncomplainingly the hardships of the camp, parching under the noonday sun or wet with the dews of night, eating the commonest of food, wearing the coarsest apparel, aye, traveling barefoot over the flinty hills in the pursuit of the enemy, and content with eleven dollars a month, these clerks were quartered in snug apartments and employing their time in drawing up petitions for an increase of pay, and a consequent increase of comforts and luxuries.

Immediately after the war Brown dropped completely out of politics. In a letter published in 1867 in the *Jackson Clarion,* he seemed dramatically changed from the fire-eater of his Senate days. His appropriate role, he felt, was to keep quiet and not interfere in government. He accepted defeat, viewing the Confederacy as a conquered nation that must submit to its conqueror "as gracefully as possible." He urged the people of the state to "meet Congress on its own platform and shake hands" and claimed to be willing to "make the best of it."

In 1868, a controversy developed over a Reconstruction constitution for Mississippi, and a proposed constitution framed by a Republican convention was rejected by the voters. The document would have proscribed from public office every man who had had any connection with the Confederacy and who refused to take an oath swearing belief in the political and civil equality of all men. Brown and other influential Mississippians journeyed to Washington to consult with President Ulysses S. Grant. The president suggested removing the proscriptive clauses and submitting the constitution to another vote. Brown agreed that Grant's plan was the quickest solution and the best way to avoid "discord and disorder."

After the revised constitution was ratified, Brown again retired from politics to ride out the Republican administrations of Governors James L. Alcorn and Adelbert Ames. When Brown did speak out, he took a moderate and conciliatory position, advocating public education for both races, opposing separate black and white political parties, and encouraging black political involvement. He continued to scorn politics and refused all efforts to persuade him to run for office.

BIBLIOGRAPHY

Alexander, Thomas B., and Richard E. Beringer. *The Anatomy of the Confederate Congress: A Study of the Influences of Member Characteristics on Legislative Voting Behavior, 1861–1865.* Nashville, Tenn., 1972.

Cluskey, Michael W., ed. *Speeches, Messages, and Other Writings of the Hon. Albert G. Brown, a Senator in Congress from the State of Mississippi.* Philadelphia, 1859.

Ranck, James B. *Albert Gallatin Brown, Radical Southern Nationalist.* New York, 1937.

RAY SKATES

BROWN, JOSEPH E.

BROWN, JOSEPH E. (1821–1894), Georgia governor and U.S. senator. Born in South Carolina to a middle-class farm family that soon moved into the hill country of North Georgia, Joseph Emerson Brown completed his education at Yale Law School and then prospered in law and land speculation. In 1849 he won election to the state senate. He quickly emerged as a leader of the Democrats and in 1857 was elected governor. A skillful politician who understood the white masses of Georgia, he won reelection in 1859, 1861, and 1863. Generally a domestic liberal, in national affairs he became an ardent secessionist.

Governor Brown directed a strengthening of the militia and other military preparations, and after the election of Abraham Lincoln he warned against abolition, racial equality, and intermarriage as he championed immediate secession. When a convention of delegates was called to consider the issue, he refused to reveal the close vote between secessionists and cooperationists—those who opposed immediate secession and favored cooperation with other Southern states to win redress of their grievances. He ordered the seizure of Federal installations even before the convention formally voted to secede.

Following that vote on January 19 the governor worked forcefully to organize Georgia's considerable resources. He mobilized troops and equipment, but he did not fully cooperate with the new Confederate government, which was trying to mobilize the resources of a whole new nation. First, last, and always Brown was a Georgian, and he consistently defended traditional state rights, individual freedoms, and strict legalism against the encroachments of the Confederacy, no matter how great the emergency.

On April 12 the war began, and six days later, Brown called for volunteers. Thousands of new troops rallied but equipment was scarce, and Brown tried to keep departing Georgia troops from carrying weapons out of the state. He also attempted to maintain control of military units that were being integrated into the Confederate armed forces. This was only the beginning of his clashes with Confederate authorities.

But within the state Brown was a brilliant politician who understood his constituents in all their differences and variations from poor whites on up through wealthy planters. Most

JOSEPH E. BROWN.
LIBRARY OF CONGRESS

of all he understood the yeoman masses who would have to do most of the fighting and sacrificing, and in that respect he had clearer vision than President Jefferson Davis and his principal aides.

Early in the war Governor Brown worked hard to obtain adequate clothing and equipment for Georgia troops, and later he dispatched state purchasing agents all over the South and even abroad in chartered steamships, which often carried out state-owned cotton and brought back blankets, clothing, and medicine. He acted with equal vigor to look after the masses at home. He directed the state penitentiary to produce cotton cards so that thread could be prepared for spinning, and he also organized an efficient system for obtaining and fairly distributing scarce salt so that meat could be preserved. The governor also organized relief for the needy families of soldiers; during the last two years of the war his administration's heaviest expenditures   went into an extensive and effective welfare system that assisted the yeoman masses bearing the main burdens of the war. Brown greatly increased taxes during the war, but he made the system more progressive by exempting many of the poor and increasing the burden on the rich. Neither he nor anyone else in the Confederacy, however, could control the raging inflation that was undermining the whole Southern economy. Brown restricted cotton acreage, and the teetotaler Baptist governor further boosted food production by restricting distilling, which was a booming business in his own hill country of North Georgia. Within Georgia, Brown ran an efficient operation; indeed at that level he was very likely the most effective Southern governor, the state leader who got the most out of his beleaguered people.

But Governor Brown could not or would not see the larger picture, and all too often he ignored or rejected the need for Confederate unity, the obligation of the individual Southern states to close ranks behind the central government in Richmond if the rebellion was to have any real chance of success. From the beginning he had chafed at Confederate control, and in April 1862 he challenged the Confederates directly.

At that time the Confederate government, desperately short of troops, enacted the first national draft in American history. Immediately Brown challenged this dramatic but necessary expansion of Confederate power, denouncing it as "at war with all the principles for the support of which Georgia entered into this revolution." He tried to maintain control of all state military forces, but the legislature gave him only limited support, and the state supreme court backed the Confederates. Grudgingly Brown yielded, though he continued to protest as he rebuilt his state military forces with men too young or too old for conscription. Each time the embattled Confederates later expanded the age limits of the draft, the governor waged the same noisy struggle first to hold on to his army and then to rebuild it with older and younger recruits. Also he granted draft exemptions to thousands of state employees, including militia officers, setting a precedent that made it more and more difficult to enforce Confederate conscription throughout the crumbling Southland.

Brown also led his Georgians in opposition to impressment, especially the requisition of slave laborers by the Confederate army. He stopped the imposition of martial law in Atlanta in 1862 and frustrated Confederate efforts to seize the state-owned Western and Atlantic Railroad in 1863 and 1864. He frequently criticized Confederate tax and blockade-running policies. His opposition to the Davis administration reached a peak with his denunciations of arbitrary arrests and the suspension of the writ of habeas corpus, and early in 1864 the war-weary legislature backed him on this issue.

The governor did not always resist the Confederates, but his opposition grew steadily and led to an increasingly bitter correspondence with President Davis. Brown had the support of some powerful Georgians like Vice President Alexander H. Stephens and his brother Linton Stephens in the legislature and former secretary of state Robert Toombs and a growing number of planters and other influential people, but his main backing came from the yeoman masses. These were his people; he had sprung from this sturdy stock, and he, not the old planter elite, knew them best. And yet finally, whatever his intentions, he led them down the road to ruin with his state rights extremism.

Even the invasion of Gen. William Tecumseh Sherman's mighty army in 1864 did not dilute Brown's resistance to the fading Confederate government. Just at the time Atlanta fell to the invaders in September, Governor Brown furloughed the ten-thousand-man Georgia militia to keep it from coming under Confederate control. This left his state even more vulnerable to Sherman's devastating march to the sea, and though he rejected Sherman's peace feelers, Brown was soon calling for peace as morale plummeted all over the state.

The Confederates made one last desperate move late in the war by calling for the use of black troops—Southern slaves—in the Confederate army with the promise of freedom for honorable service, and Brown ran true to form. He denounced the plan as another dramatic departure from tradition. Once again, in the last days of the Confederacy, he showed himself unable or unwilling to make the adjustments necessary for victory in total war.

Inevitably defeat came in the spring of 1865 when Robert E. Lee surrendered in Virginia in April and the last scattered Confederates laid down their arms in May. Union troops arrested Governor Brown who was briefly imprisoned in Washington, D.C. Soon paroled, he returned to Georgia and supported the Reconstruction program of President Andrew Johnson who pardoned him in September. Opportunistically Brown supported Radical Reconstruction and served as chief justice of the state supreme court for two years, but when that regime collapsed in Georgia, he swung back to the Democrats. He prospered as a lawyer and businessman and served in the U.S. Senate from 1880 to 1890 when he resigned. Four years later one of Georgia's most successful and enduring politicians died at his home in Atlanta.

BIBLIOGRAPHY

Boney, F. N. "War and Defeat." In *A History of Georgia*. Edited by Kenneth Coleman. Athens, Ga., 1991.

Bragg, William Harris. *Joe Brown's Army: The Georgia State Line, 1862–1865*. Macon, Ga., 1987.

Bryan, T. Conn. *Confederate Georgia*. Athens, Ga., 1953.

Escott, Paul D. "Georgia." In *The Confederate Governors*. Edited by W. Buck Yearns. Athens, Ga., 1985.

Hill, Louise B. *Joseph E. Brown and the Confederacy*. Chapel Hill, N.C., 1939.

Parks, Joseph H. *Joseph E. Brown of Georgia*. Baton Rouge, La., 1977.

Thomas, Emory M. *The Confederate Nation: 1861–1865*. New York, 1979.

F. N. BONEY

BROWNLOW, WILLIAM G.

BROWNLOW, WILLIAM G. (1805–1877), Unionist editor, Reconstruction governor of Tennessee, and U.S. senator. William G. "Parson" Brownlow relished the role of scourge of the Confederacy. The career of this native Virginian and adopted Tennessean was characterized by a series of vehement, and sometimes violent, controversies. During his years as a Methodist circuit rider in the Appalachians his main talent was vilifying spokesmen of other religious denominations. Obliged by marriage to find more remunerative employment, Brownlow turned to journalism, which provided a fresh and larger outlet for his contentiousness. By 1861 Brownlow's slashing brand of journalism had earned his *Knoxville Whig* a circulation that surpassed that of all his competitors combined. By then he had also penned an anti-Presbyterian book, three anti-Baptist volumes, an anti-Catholic and anti-immigrant book, and one implacably hostile to the Democratic party.

> But when the crisis came he said, "I am for the Union though every other institution in the country perish."

Brownlow described himself as a "Federal Whig of the Washington and Alexander Hamilton school," and he opposed the doctrines of nullification and secession after 1832. He believed that slavery was countenanced by scripture, and he took the proslavery stance in a series of 1858 debates with abolitionist Abraham Pryne. But when the crisis came he said, "I am for the Union though every other institution in the country perish."

Anticipating an unfavorable verdict in the June 8, 1861, Tennessee referendum on disunion, he helped convene East Tennessee delegates who unsuccessfully petitioned for separate statehood for their Unionist region. His newspaper supported the Union even after Tennessee joined the Confederacy, and though he never overtly called for rebellion, his was the only newspaper in the Confederacy that opposed the existence of a Confederate government.

Under threat of indictment for treason, Brownlow left Knoxville for nearby Maryville. Soon afterward Unionists burned five important bridges. Brownlow denied complicity but was suspected. After a time, on receiving assurances from authorities in Richmond, he returned to Knoxville, only to be lodged in jail. Confederate Attorney General Judah P. Benjamin felt obliged to honor earlier assurances, so Brownlow was allowed to cross into Union lines near Nashville on March 15, 1862.

Within two weeks Brownlow had begun a speaking tour of Northern cities during which he recounted to his audiences the Confederate atrocities visited upon East Tennessee Unionists. That summer he penned *Sketches of the Rise, Progress, and Decline of Secession,* better known simply as *Parson Brownlow's Book.* Within a few months 100,000 copies were sold.

Brownlow returned to Knoxville with Ambrose Burnside's army in September 1863, and the first issue of the *Knoxville Whig and Rebel Ventilator* appeared on November 11. In January 1865, at a closely supervised wartime election, Brownlow was elected governor of Tennessee by 23,352 votes to 35 for his opponents. As Reconstruction governor he imposed a "damnesty oath" that excluded former Confederates from voting. By ratifying the Thirteenth, Fourteenth, and Fifteenth Amendments, Tennessee became the first Confederate state to be readmitted to the Union.

Brownlow's election to the U.S. Senate in 1869 roughly coincided with the enfranchisement of former Confederates and the end of Brownlowism in Tennessee. Two years after the expiration of his term in 1875, the "Fighting Parson" died in Knoxville.

BIBLIOGRAPHY

Coulter, E. Merton. *William G. Brownlow, Fighting Parson of the Southern Highlands.* Chapel Hill, N.C., 1937. Reprint, Knoxville, Tenn., 1971.

Humphrey, Stephen. *"That D—d Brownlow" Being a Saucy and Malicious Description of Fighting Parson William Gannaway Brownlow, Knoxville Editor and Stalwart Unionist . . . .* Boone, N.C., 1978.

Kelly, James C. "William Gannaway Brownlow, Part I." *Tennessee Historical Quarterly* 43 (Spring 1984): 25–43.

Kelly, James C. "William Gannaway Brownlow, Part II." *Tennessee Historical Quarterly* 43 (Summer 1984): 155–172.

JAMES C. KELLY

BROWNSVILLE, TEXAS

[*This entry includes two articles,* City of Brownsville, *which profiles the city during the Confederacy, and* Battles of Brownsville, *which discusses the military actions there.*]

City of Brownsville

The seat of Cameron County, Brownsville is located on the north bank of the Rio Grande, approximately twenty-five miles from the Gulf of Mexico. The city developed as a trading center in the late 1840s immediately upriver from a fort that had been constructed in 1846 by American troops across the Rio Grande from Matamoros, Mexico. The fort, and after it the city, were named for Maj. Jacob Brown, who was mortally wounded defending the post from bombardment across the river at the beginning of the Mexican War.

Brownsville's population in 1860 was 2,734, of whom approximately 75 percent were of Mexican origin or descent and 10 percent of European birth. Most of the rest of the population had come from elsewhere in the United States. Because labor was inexpensive, slavery never took root in the Rio Grande valley. According to the 1860 census, there were only seven slaves in Cameron County, all of whom lived in Brownsville.

The city's antebellum economy was based upon the cross-border trade and on the military garrison maintained by the U.S. Army. But before the Civil War, Brownsville was never more than an insignificant border town, its development retarded by its isolation from the rest of Texas and by the limited navigability of the Rio Grande. Bars at the mouth of the river restricted commerce to shallow-draft vessels. Major cargo had to be hauled from Brownsville overland to Point Isabel on the Gulf of Mexico.

When Texas seceded from the Union, U.S. forces peaceably abandoned all federal positions in the state, including their installation at Fort Brown, which was evacuated on March 20, 1861. Troops of the Texas Volunteers under Col. John S. ("Rip") Ford occupied Brownsville and other locations on the Rio Grande. Gen. Hamilton Prioleau Bee replaced Ford in command of Confederate troops at Brownsville in January 1863. The city was headquarters for the West Texas Sub-Military District, which stretched inland along the Rio Grande from the Gulf of Mexico to Eagle Pass and comprised about 1,200 troops.

Brownsville's significance in the Civil War resulted from the combined effects of the blockade imposed by the Union navy and the city's unique location on the border of a neutral nation with access to the ocean-borne commerce of the world. Like other Confederate port cities, Brownsville was blockaded—after a fashion. Beginning in early 1862, the Federals positioned themselves off Point Isabel. (The navy was prevented from effectively blockading the Rio Grande by its shallow depth and by a stipulation in the Treaty of Guadalupe Hidalgo, the instrument that made the Rio Grande the boundary between the United States and Mexico.) Rather than strangling Brownsville, the Union presence merely rerouted commerce across the border to Mexico, where, of course, the blockade did not apply. A flourishing pattern of trade developed that sustained the Confederate war effort in the Trans-Mississippi region and created several private fortunes. Cotton, the only significant Texas export, was drawn by wagon from all over the southwestern corner of the Confederacy to Brownsville, ferried across the Rio Grande to Matamoros, carted to the wharves that sprang up at the fishing village of Bagdad on the Mexican coast, transferred by lighter to vessels anchored in the Gulf of Mexico, and then shipped to the textile mills of Europe and the northeastern United States. Specie, weapons and ammunition, medicine, and other supplies moved in the opposite direction and entered the Confederacy.

This traffic was facilitated by an agreement that Colonel Ford negotiated with Mexican authorities in Matamoros and was orchestrated by three masters of the carrying trade, who placed their riverboats under Mexican registry after the war began—Charles Stillman, Mifflin Kenedy, and Richard King, the founder of the King Ranch. (The fluid political situation of Mexico, torn by factional conflict and distracted by the encroachment of the empire-building French under the leadership of Maximilian, added flavor to wartime life in Brownsville, particularly when losers in the latest turn of fortune took refuge there, but it did not materially hinder the flow of goods.) Thousands of ambitious people were attracted to the opportunities provided by the lucrative cotton trade. At times during the war, the number of inhabitants in the city swelled to ten times the 1860 population. As in any number of frontier boomtowns, law and order were frequent casualties of the explosive but temporary growth. Arthur J. L. Fremantle, a British officer who visited the area at the peak of its fortunes, concluded that "Brownsville was about the rowdiest town in Texas, which was the most lawless state in the Confederacy."

Brownsville's commercial contribution to the Confederate effort was limited by the greed and ingenuity of thieves and other opportunists and by the remoteness of the city from the heart of the South and the major theaters of war. This distance could be negotiated only by wagon trails; no railroad reached the city until after the war. Even so, it is clear that the Brownsville trade significantly aided the Confederate cause in the Trans-Mississippi theater. In one notable instance, Confederate troops in Little Rock, Arkansas, received a shipment of four thousand Enfield rifles that had been transported from England by way of Brownsville.

The notoriety of what became known as the "backdoor to the Confederacy" and a desire to forestall possible French designs on Texas eventually prompted Federal action. After Gen. Nathaniel P. Banks's defeat at Sabine Pass in 1863 dashed his plans to invade Texas from the east, he sent some seven thousand troops to the mouth of the Rio Grande. They landed on the Gulf coast on November 2, 1863, under the command of Napoleon J. T. Dana, and moved promptly inland toward Brownsville. Rather than defend the city, an outnumbered General Bee decided to abandon it. Before departing for Richard King's ranch, Confederate troops pushed their artillery into the Rio Grande and burned other military equipment as well as cotton awaiting export. The spreading fire, which set off an explosion in the magazine at Fort Brown, destroyed a significant portion of Brownsville. Federal troops moved into the city on November 6 and undertook repairs. They were soon followed by Abraham

Lincoln's appointee as provisional governor of Texas, Andrew J. Hamilton, who was prepared to govern the state from any toehold he could establish on its edge.

His regime was premature. In 1864, Ford organized a company he named the Cavalry of the West, comprising about 1,500 conscription-exempt volunteers, to drive what he called "a mongrel force of Abolitionists, negroes, plundering Mexicans, and perfidious renegades" out of the Rio Grande valley. To defend the Union position, Gen. Francis J. Herron, who had succeeded Dana at Brownsville, requested cavalry support from his superiors in New Orleans. He was instead ordered to evacuate the city. Failure to halt the contraband trade (the occupation merely forced the border crossing point upriver), the difficulty in maintaining a secure supply line to the Gulf, and the need to use their troops elsewhere induced the Federals in July 1864 to abandon Brownsville for the second time. Under pressure from Ford, Herron's troops withdrew from South Texas, except for a detachment left behind on the Gulf coast. Confederate troops reentered Brownsville on July 30, 1864, and remained in control of the city until the end of the war.

An attempt by Union forces to retake Brownsville in the spring of 1865 led to the last land battle of the Civil War. A month after Appomattox, but before the surrender of Confederate forces in the Trans-Mississippi Department, Federal troops under the command of Theodore H. Barrett advanced toward the city. On May 13, they encountered Ford's Cavalry of the West at Palmito Ranch, on the Rio Grande midway between Brownsville and the Gulf. The Texans routed Barrett's troops and drove them back to their position on the coast. When U.S. troops again attempted to occupy Brownsville two weeks later, they faced no opposition. The city had been abandoned on May 29 by Ford's unit, many of whom crossed the river to seek sanctuary in Mexico.

BIBLIOGRAPHY

Ford, John Salmon. *Rip Ford's Texas*. Edited by Stephen B. Oates. Austin, Tex., 1963.
Irby, James A. *Backdoor at Bagdad: The Civil War on the Rio Grande*. El Paso, Tex., 1977.
Kearney, Milo, ed. *More Studies in Brownsville History*. Brownsville, Tex., 1989.
Lea, Tom. *The King Ranch*. 2 vols. Boston, 1957.
Pierce, Frank C. *A Brief History of the Lower Rio Grande Valley*. Menasha, Wis., 1917.

GEORGE B. FORGIE

Battles of Brownsville

The keys to Federal border defenses in the lower Rio Grande valley of Texas were Fort Brown and its coastal outlet at Brazos Santiago. In April 1861, after the bombardment of Fort Sumter in South Carolina, Texas state forces under Col. John S. ("Rip") Ford captured the small Union garrison at Brazos Santiago along with several pieces of heavy artillery, several hundred stand of small arms, and thousands of dollars worth of government property. The Confederates then transformed the border community into a thriving port for shipping Confederate cotton across the Rio Grande. Agents transported cotton to Matamoros, where English and European ships waited with munitions and medicine, thereby circumventing the Federal blockade.

Brownsville became the focus of Federal military attention in 1863. Gen. Nathaniel Banks, with six thousand men under Maj. Gen. Napoleon Dana, landed at Brazos Santiago on the Gulf of Mexico on November 2. Twenty-four miles away in Brownsville, the few hundred Texan cavalrymen under Brig. Gen. Hamilton P. Bee withdrew, setting vast stores of cotton, gunpowder, and supplies ablaze before retreating. Four days later, Union troops occupied the city, closing that route for Confederate blockade running and beginning several months of occupation. Federal troops then advanced up the Rio Grande, eventually occupying all border towns up to Laredo.

In March 1864, a Confederate army of four hundred irregular cavalrymen under Texas Ranger Colonel Ford drove the Union troops back down the valley. In July, Ford and his troopers reoccupied Brownsville, driving the Union garrison to the coast. The Confederates then reopened the cotton trade with Matamoros. In September the Federals made an advance toward the city, but turned back after light skirmishing.

Entrenched Union troops maintained a tenuous hold at Brazos Santiago throughout the rest of the year, sending occasional raiding parties and scouts inland to skirmish with Confederate cavalry. On May 13, 1865, a five-hundred-man Union brigade composed of the Thirty-fourth Indiana Infantry, the Sixty-second U.S. Colored Infantry, and the Second Texas Cavalry (U.S.) under Col. Theodore Barrett marched inland to retake Brownsville.

On May 12, the Federals occupied a Confederate camp at Palmito Ranch east of the city. The following day, Colonel Ford and four hundred horsemen who called themselves the "Cavalry of the West," aided by a battery of Confederate artillery partially manned by French gunners from Mexico, attacked the Federal column. The Union troops, expecting a fairly easy advance since the principal Confederate armies had surrendered over a month earlier, fled back to Brazos Santiago. This Confederate victory marked the last land battle of the war. Two dozen Federals were killed or wounded while eighty-five were captured. Ten Texans were also wounded.

The Battle of Palmito Ranch had no impact on the war and served mainly as an ironic parting shot for the Southern cause. On May 26, 1865, Lt. Gen. E. Kirby Smith, commander of the Trans-Mississippi, began negotiations to surrender his command, which officially occurred on June 2.

BIBLIOGRAPHY

Evans, Clement A., ed. *Confederate Military History.* 12 vols. Atlanta, 1899. Extended ed. in 19 vols. Wilmington, N.C., 1987–1989.

Ford, John S. *Rip Ford's Texas.* Edited by Stephen B. Oates. Austin, Tex., 1963.

DONALD S. FRAZIER

BUCHANAN, FRANKLIN

BUCHANAN, FRANKLIN (1800–1874), naval officer. Buchanan was born in Baltimore, Maryland, on September 17, 1800. As the child of a prominent Maryland physician, he enjoyed a comfortable life while growing up. He received a commission in the U.S. Navy in January 1815 and served initially under Oliver Hazard Perry. Buchanan was promoted to the rank of lieutenant in 1825 and commander in 1841. Four years later, Secretary of the Navy George Bancroft chose him as the first superintendent of the newly created U.S. Naval Academy at Annapolis, Maryland. Buchanan served in the Mexican War as a sloop commander and later commanded Matthew C. Perry's flagship in the latter's expedition to Japan in 1852. Promoted to captain in 1855, Buchanan then commanded the Washington Navy Yard.

He resigned his commission in April 1861 and offered his services to the Confederacy the following August. Confederate Secretary of the Navy Stephen R. Mallory issued Buchanan a commission as captain on September 5. His first major assignment was as chief of the Office of Orders and Details in the Navy Department, where he made all assignments of personnel, helped to formulate naval policy, and acted as adviser to Secretary Mallory. On February 24, 1862, Buchanan became flag officer in command of the naval defenses on the James River. Moving to Gosport Navy Yard, Buchanan made the new ironclad ram CSS *Virginia* (formerly USS *Merrimack*) his flagship.

Buchanan took *Virginia* into Hampton Roads on March 8, 1862, to attack the Federal squadron there. His first target was the frigate *Cumberland.* After exchanging broadsides with this adversary, *Virginia* rammed it. *Cumberland* began sinking and threatened to take *Virginia* down with it because the ironclad's ram was stuck in its hull. Fortunately for the Confederates, the ram broke off, and the ship was freed to continue the attack. Buchanan turned *Virginia* toward the frigate *Congress,* whose captain ran the ship aground to avoid being rammed. An hour's pounding by *Virginia*'s cannons set *Congress* afire and killed and wounded dozens of

FRANKLIN BUCHANAN. Photograph by Mathew Brady, taken sometime between 1855 and 1861. NAVAL HISTORICAL CENTER, WASHINGTON, D.C.

its crew. The Federal captain then struck his colors and surrendered. Because fire from Federal shore batteries and sharpshooters prevented Buchanan from receiving the surrender, he ordered his gunners to destroy *Congress.* While supervising this destruction, Buchanan was wounded in the thigh by a rifle bullet. Subsequently, he yielded command of the operation to Lt. Catesby Jones.

Buchanan's wound prevented him from participating in the famous confrontation on the following day between *Virginia* and the Federal ironclad *Monitor.* He convalesced first at Norfolk and later moved to Greensboro, North Carolina. The Confederate Congress confirmed Buchanan's appointment as admiral on August 21, 1862, making him the ranking officer in the Confederate navy. In September, Mallory assigned Buchanan to command the naval forces in Mobile Bay, Alabama, hoping he would be more active and aggressive than his predecessor, Capt. Victor M. Randolph, had been. At Mobile, Buchanan won the respect not only of his command but of the army officers as well. This resulted in a spirit of cooperation between the two branches not found in other areas of the Confederacy.

Under Buchanan's command, the Mobile squadron had as its primary goal the defense of Mobile Bay rather than the breaking of the Union blockade. Buchanan had under him at first *Baltic,* a weak ironclad, and three wooden gunboats, *Morgan, Gaines,* and *Selma.* Work on two ironclad floating batteries, *Huntsville* and *Tuscaloosa,* and an ironclad ram, *Tennessee,* had begun at Selma, Alabama, that fall. Construction of a second ironclad ram, the sidewheeler *Nashville,* had commenced at Montgomery, Alabama, at about the same time. Buchanan had *Tennessee, Huntsville,* and *Tuscaloosa,* all of which were launched in February 1863, brought to the Mobile Navy Yard to receive their machinery, armament, crews, and iron plating. In June, *Nashville* reached the city to go through the same process of completion. The admiral kept his gunboats in the lower bay near Fort Morgan, Fort Gaines, and Fort Powell to help guard the bay entrances while he pushed for completion of the ironclads.

Buchanan had to endure delays in getting the work done and problems in obtaining cannon, armor plating, and seamen. These difficulties meant that the two ironclads would not reach completion that summer as Buchanan had hoped. When *Tennessee* was finally commissioned February 16, 1864, Buchanan ordered it taken into Mobile Bay, but the ironclad's deep draft prevented it from passing over the Dog River bar. Workmen constructed camels (wooden caissons), which they used to raise the ship and float it over the bar on May 18. Four days later, Buchanan shifted his flag from *Baltic* to *Tennessee.* Later that month, he planned an attack on the Union blockading fleet. *Tennessee* ran aground near Fort Morgan, delaying the strike, and Buchanan soon canceled the offensive because he considered the Federals too strong for his little squadron.

On August 5, 1864, Union Adm. David Farragut led his fleet against the Confederate forts and warships in the Battle of Mobile Bay. The superior Federal vessels quickly dispersed or destroyed the Confederate wooden gunboats, leaving *Tennessee* to face Farragut's squadron alone. Almost all the Union ships joined in the fray. Three gunboats rammed *Tennessee* but caused little damage. Buchanan, however, suffered a broken leg when an enemy shell knocked loose a port cover and it struck him. The Federal fire cut *Tennessee's* steering chains, making it impossible for the crew to change its position. When the ram's smokestack was shot away, the ship filled with smoke, and the crew could not answer the increasing hail of enemy shells. Commander James D. Johnston received Buchanan's permission to surrender the ironclad after an hour-long engagement.

Buchanan was taken to Fort Lafayette, New York, where he was held prisoner until February 1865. After his exchange, he was reassigned to Mobile but did not reach the city before its surrender in mid-April. Buchanan participated in the surrender of the Department of Alabama, Mississippi, and East Louisiana on May 8, 1865.

After the war, Buchanan returned to his home in Maryland. He served as president of Maryland Agricultural College, which later became the University of Maryland, for one year. He then retired to his home at Easton, where he lived until his death on May 11, 1874.

BIBLIOGRAPHY

Bergeron, Arthur W., Jr. "Franklin Buchanan." In *Dictionary of American Military Biography.* Edited by Roger E. Spiller. Vol. 1. Westport, Conn., 1984.

Lewis, Charles L. *Admiral Franklin Buchanan: Fearless Man of Action.* Baltimore, 1929.

Still, William N., Jr. *Iron Afloat: The Story of the Confederate Armorclads.* Nashville, Tenn., 1971.

Todorich, Charles M. "Franklin Buchanan: Symbol for Two Navies." In *Captains of the Old Steam Navy: Makers of the American Naval Tradition, 1840–1880.* Edited by James C. Bradford. Annapolis, Md., 1986.

Wells, Tom H. *The Confederate Navy: A Study in Organization.* University, Ala., 1971.

ARTHUR W. BERGERON, JR.

BUCKLAND MILLS, VIRGINIA

Eight miles east of Warrenton, Buckland Mills was the scene of a cavalry battle on October 19, 1863, between the divisions of J. E. B. Stuart and Hugh Judson Kilpatrick. Kilpatrick's Third Division was thoroughly routed by Wade Hampton's and Fitzhugh Lee's divisions, with the Union force suffering two hundred casualties to Stuart's thirty.

On October 17 Stuart, with Hampton's division, had moved as far east as the Little River Turnpike in Fairfax County. The next day, the Confederates began riding west along the Warrenton Pike when Stuart learned that Kilpatrick's division and six artillery pieces, with infantry, were on the move. Kilpatrick had been ordered to ascertain the Confederate positions, so he rode to Gainesville along the same pike. At Groveton the two forces met, and the Confederates slowly withdrew to Gainesville. At this point, Stuart and Fitz Lee, at Auburn (to the south), decided on a plan of attack for the nineteenth. Fitz Lee suggested that Stuart slowly retire before the Federals back to Warrenton, drawing Kilpatrick's division down the road. Fitz Lee would attack the Federal's left flank and rear once they had crossed Broad Run. Hampton was instructed to attack the Federal's front on the sound of Fitz Lee's guns. On October 19 Kilpatrick moved out at 8:00 A.M. toward Warrenton, driving Stuart's cavalry from Gainesville. At Buckland Mills, on Broad Run, the Confederates made a stand around 10:00 A.M. By noon Stuart had withdrawn farther up the Warrenton Pike to Chestnut Hill, about three miles west of Warrenton, and formed a line of battle, awaiting the Federal advance. Kilpatrick sent scouts forward at 1:00 P.M. to ascertain Stuart's position.

Kilpatrick then sent his Second Brigade, under George Armstrong Custer, to the front. Custer, in turn, put the Seventh Michigan Cavalry in the lead. This unit came within several hundred yards of Hampton's troopers, when Fitz Lee's Second Virginia, supported by the Confederate artillery, attacked Kilpatrick's left flank and rear. When Stuart heard the cannon, he ordered Hampton's First North Carolina to charge the Union horsemen. "I pressed them suddenly and vigorously in front," Stuart wrote. Initially the Federals resisted stubbornly, "but once broken the rout was complete," as the Seventh Michigan was driven back into the rest of Custer's Second Brigade. This caused Henry E. Davies's First Brigade, coming up the pike, to be driven in as well. The Confederates pursued Kilpatrick's troopers, "at full speed the whole distance" from Warrenton to Buckland. One Union trooper wrote, "The scene was one of great confusion and distress." In the rout, Custer's division recrossed Broad Run at Buckland Mills while Davies's remained on the western side of the stream. At this point Fitz Lee's division occupied the bridge at Broad Run, cutting Davies's men off and forcing them to leave the road in order to escape. "This they [the Federals] did pell-mell, in great disorder and confusion,

> **Kilpatrick then sent his Second Brigade, under George Armstrong Custer, to the front. Custer, in turn, put the Seventh Michigan Cavalry in the lead.**

to save themselves the best way they could; but a great many were captured, killed, and drowned, and a number of their wagons and ambulances were also captured in their flight," reported Col. Thomas Owen of Fitz Lee's brigade.

As Custer was pursued up the pike to Gainesville, Davies was chased cross-country to the Hay Market Road. Near Hay Market and Gainesville the Confederates encountered Federal infantry, which had come up to cover Kilpatrick's retreat. After initially engaging the infantry, Stuart's cavalry withdrew at nightfall and encamped near Buckland Mills. As Fitz Lee wrote in his report, Kilpatrick "was easily misled, . . . [and] his command was routed and pursued until after dark." Kilpatrick lost 150 men and eight wagons, and some 50 Federal infantrymen were captured. Stuart's force suffered 30 casualties in the "Buckland Races," as it came to be called by the Confederates.

BIBLIOGRAPHY

Blackford, William Willis. *War Years with J. E. B. Stuart*. New York, 1945.

McClellan, H. B. *The Life and Campaigns of Maj.-Gen. J. E. B. Stuart*. Richmond, 1885.

Thomas, Emory M. *Bold Dragon: The Life of J. E. B. Stuart*. New York, 1986.

Wells, Edward L. *Hampton and His Cavalry in '64*. Richmond, 1899.

KENNETH L. STILES

BUCKNER, SIMON BOLIVAR

BUCKNER, SIMON BOLIVAR (1823–1914), brigadier general and postwar governor of Kentucky. Born in Hart County, Kentucky, on April 1, 1823, Buckner entered West Point at the age of seventeen. He won the saber championship there and graduated eleventh in his class of twenty-five in 1844. He was teaching at West Point when he transferred to Winfield Scott's army to fight in the Mexican War. He was slightly wounded and breveted first lieutenant and captain. He returned to teach at West Point but transferred in 1849 in protest of compulsory chapel attendance. In 1855 he resigned from the army and went to Chicago to manage the estate inherited by his wife, Mary Jane Kingsbury. In 1858 he moved to Louisville, where he organized the Citizens' Guard company of militia and in 1860 took command of the state guard, the pro-Southern state militia.

At the outbreak of the Civil War, Buckner supported neutrality, and when the state legislature went Unionist, he resigned from the state guard. Turning down offers of a general's commission from Winfield Scott and Abraham Lincoln, he joined the Confederate army in September 1861. On the fourteenth, Albert Sidney Johnston appointed him brigadier general, and with 4,500 men he occupied Bowling Green, Kentucky.

When the Confederates withdrew from Kentucky, Buckner marched to Fort Donelson and commanded the right wing against Ulysses S. Grant's advancing army. Surrounded and outnumbered, Buckner agreed with Gideon Pillow and fort commander John B. Floyd that they should break through on Grant's left and escape. On the morning of February 15, 1862, the divisions commanded by Pillow and Buckner charged and drove back the enemy, opening the way to evacuate the fort or assault the Federal flank and rear. Pillow telegraphed Johnston that the battle was won. Then, apparently assuming that the Confederates could rest and finish the battle the next day, Pillow ordered the men back into their morning trenches. Buckner appealed the order to Floyd, but

Floyd upheld Pillow. When Buckner's men returned to their former positions, they were overwhelmed by advancing Federal troops and had to retreat still farther. After dark, Buckner, demoralized by the retrograde movement, inspected his lines and realized that his men were too exhausted to dig new trenches. "It was not your fault, my brave boys, it was not your fault," he declared. That night Buckner insisted on surrendering. Pillow wanted to fight, but he and Floyd fled and Nathan Bedford Forrest broke out, leaving Buckner to surrender. At daylight on February 16, he proposed a truce and his prewar friend Grant demanded "unconditional and immediate surrender."

Imprisoned at Fort Warren until August 1862, Buckner was exchanged and promoted to major general. During the Kentucky invasion he commanded a division in William J. Hardee's corps. At Munfordville, he had the unusual experience of advising Union Col. John T. Wilder on whether Wilder should surrender his 4,000-man garrison to Braxton Bragg's surrounding army of 27,000 men. Satisfied with Buckner's professional counsel, Wilder surrendered. On October 8, in the Battle of Perryville, Buckner skillfully deployed his artillery in an attack on Union Gen. James S. Jackson's division on the Union left, an assault that killed Jackson and forced his men from their position.

From December 1862 to April 1863, Buckner commanded the Department of the Gulf. Then, on May 12, 1863, he assumed command of the Department of East Tennessee. In late August, Bragg ordered him to evacuate Knoxville before the advancing army of Ambrose Burnside, which outnumbered Buckner's force. In the Battle of Chickamauga, on September 20, 1863, he commanded a corps in James Longstreet's left wing. In the late afternoon Buckner led his men in a frontal assault on the log breastworks on Snodgrass Hill, a position that seemed almost impregnable. They drove the enemy from their trenches and into the ravines beyond, where large numbers were captured. Subsequently, when Bragg failed to capitalize on the advantage and lost golden opportunities in the Chattanooga campaign, Buckner signed the petition demanding Bragg's removal.

After convalescing from an illness, Buckner served in several temporary assignments and on March 8, 1864, once again took over the Department of East Tennessee. On April 28, he was ordered to the Trans-Mississippi Department, where E. Kirby Smith recommended him for promotion to lieutenant general, effective September 20. Smith appointed him commander of the District of West Louisiana.

When the war ended, the War Department restricted him to Louisiana. He engaged in business in New Orleans before finally going home in 1868. Wealthy and influential, he was elected Democratic governor of Kentucky in 1887 and served four years with honesty and efficiency. In 1896 he ran for vice president for the Gold Democrat party. He died January 8, 1914, near Munfordville and is buried in Frankfort, Kentucky.

BIBLIOGRAPHY

Harrison, Lowell. "Simon Bolivar Buckner: A Profile." *Civil War Times Illustrated.* 16 (February 1978): 36–45.
Stickles, Arndt M. *Simon Bolivar Buckner: Borderland Knight.* Chapel Hill, N.C., 1940.

JAMES A. RAMAGE

BUMMERS

This term, probably from the German *bummler,* or "loafer," was applied, by Federals and Confederates alike, to the foragers of William Tecumseh Sherman's army on its March to the Sea from Atlanta and then northward through the Carolinas in the winter of 1864–1865. One veteran painted a verbal portrait of a bummer: "Fancy a ragged man . . . stealing his way through the pine forests far out on the flanks of a column. Keen on the scent of rebels, or bacon, or silver spoons, or corn, or anything valuable and you have him in your mind."

Initially, these foragers were selected from each regiment to do double duty as scouts and scavengers. Before dawn each day, they mounted horses (often taken from Southern plantations) and rode out on both flanks in advance of the army to secure supplies and to serve as a screen of mount-

> On the march through the Carolinas, the bummers made little pretense of attempting to protect private property. . . .

ed infantry that could provide advance notice of the approach of any Confederate force.

The foragers were ordered to avoid the destruction of private dwellings, the theft of personal property, and even the use of abusive language. But because they operated miles from their units, beyond effective command and control of their senior officers, they frequently ignored such orders. The term *bummer* was sometimes used to distinguish those who most frequently abused their authority, though within Sherman's army, anyone who served as a forager was a *bummer.* On the march through the Carolinas, the bummers made little pretense of attempting to protect private property, and they often burned whatever they could not steal. Plantation owners who tried to conceal their valuables discovered that the bummers were expert at discovering their hiding places.

So closely associated was Sherman's campaign with the activities of these foragers that they were given a place at the

BURIAL OF LATANÈ. An 1868 engraving by A.G. Campbell, after the painting by W.D. Washington. Photograph by Katherine Wetzel.
ELEANOR S. BROCKENBROUGH LIBRARY, THE MUSEUM OF THE CONFEDERACY, RICHMOND, VIRGINIA

end of each brigade during the Grand March of the armies through Washington at the end of the war. They rode through the capital in their ragged field uniforms with chickens and hams thrown across their saddles and plundered booty covering the pack mules they led.

BIBLIOGRAPHY

Glatthaar, Joseph T. *The March to the Sea and Beyond: Sherman's Troops in the Savannah and Carolinas Campaigns.* New York, 1985.
Harwell, Richard, and Philip N. Racine, eds. *The Fiery Trail: A Union Officer's Account of Sherman's Last Campaigns.* Knoxville, Tenn., 1986.

CRAIG L. SYMONDS

BURIAL OF LATANÉ

An enduring icon of the Lost Cause, the history and genre painting *The Burial of Latané,* touched the hearts of generations of Southerners despite what may seem to modern eyes only stilted composition and crude rendering.

Its inspiration came on June 13, 1862, when Capt. William Latané became the sole Confederate casualty of J. E. B. Stuart's reconnaissance on the Virginia peninsula. Latané's body was taken to a nearby plantation for burial. When enemy forces barred a local clergyman from the scene, the resident women conducted a funeral service themselves.

The incident inspired a popular poem and then the canvas executed by Richmond portraitist William D. Washington (1834–1870). It showed a pious matron preaching the burial service in an Eden-like bower that suggested the sacred beauty of the Southern landscape. Women gathering about the coffin symbolized the enduring strength of Confederate womanhood. Blacks assisting with the burial gave visual prominence to the Lost Cause myth of slave loyalty. And a well-clothed child decorating Latané's bier contradicted reports of home front poverty. Most important, *The Burial of Latané* offered reassurance to anxious wives and parents that their loved ones in arms would be buried with dignity and respect wherever they fell.

Washington's "touching and impressive scene," in the words of one early critic, caused a sensation when first exhibited in Richmond. And an 1868 engraved adaptation, offered for $1.50 a copy by publisher William Smith of New York, became a huge best-seller in the postwar South, where it was advertised as a "beautiful and appropriate ornament for any parlor."

BIBLIOGRAPHY

Faust, Drew Gilpin. "Race, Gender, and Confederate Nationalism: William D. Washington's Burial of Latané." *Southern Review* 25 (April 1989): 197–307.
Neely, Mark E., Harold Holzer, and Gabor S. Boritt. *The Confederate Image: Prints of the Lost Cause.* Chapel Hill, N.C., 1987.
Salmon, Emily J. "The Burial of Latané: Symbol of the Lost Cause." *Virginia Cavalcade* 29 (Winter 1979): 118–129.

HAROLD HOLZER

BURNETT, HENRY C.

BURNETT, HENRY C. (1825–1866), colonel and congressman from Kentucky. Henry Cornelius Burnett ranked as one of the most vocal members of the Confederacy's "Kentucky bloc"—generals and politicians determined to recapture Kentucky as part of an overall concentration in the West.

Born in Virginia, Burnett came to Kentucky as a child and attended the local academy at Hopkinsville. He later studied law and was admitted to the bar in Cadiz, Kentucky, in 1847. After practicing law and serving as clerk of the Trigg County Circuit Court, in 1855 Burnett was elected as a Democrat to the U.S. House of Representatives.

In October and November 1861, respectively, Burnett presided over both the southern conference and the sovereignty convention in Russellville, Kentucky. The November meeting established the Provisional Government of Kentucky which joined the Confederacy. Because of his active role in Kentucky's secession movement, Burnett was expelled from Congress on December 3, 1861. He was the only Kentucky representative ousted from office for his support of the South. The Provisional Government of Kentucky appointed Burnett a commissioner "with power to negotiate

. . . the earliest practicable admission of Kentucky into . . . the Confederate States of America." He also served as a colonel in the Eighth Kentucky Infantry and fought at Fort Donelson.

In 1861 Burnett was elected to the Provisional Senate and served in the First and Second Congresses as well. A strong supporter of President Jefferson Davis, Burnett criticized Gen. Braxton Bragg's disastrous 1862 invasion of Kentucky and attempted to mobilize partisan raiders to liberate the commonwealth from Union control. One of the most active Confederate senators, Burnett served on the Commerce, Judiciary, Claims, Military Affairs, and other influential committees. Though he favored Confederate conscription policies, Burnett expressed concern over violations of state rights. In February 1865, Burnett endorsed the arming of the slaves as a military necessity.

Following the war, Burnett practiced law and worked to advance the Democratic cause in Kentucky.

BIBLIOGRAPHY

Quisenberry, A. C. "The Alleged Secession of Kentucky." *Register of the Kentucky State Historical Society* 15 (1917): 15–32.
Wakelyn, Jon L. *Biographical Dictionary of the Confederacy.* Edited by Frank E. Vandiver. Westport, Conn., 1977.
Warner, Ezra J., and W. Buck Yearns. *Biographical Register of the Confederate Congress.* Baton Rouge, La., 1975.

JOHN DAVID SMITH

BURNSIDE'S EXPEDITION TO NORTH CAROLINA

This expedition began when Union Brig. Gen. Ambrose E. Burnside left Fort Monroe, Virginia, on January 11, 1862, with fifteen thousand men and eighty vessels of various descriptions. Subsequently, seventeen warships from the North Atlantic Blockading Squadron, commanded by Flag Officer Louis M. Goldsborough, joined Burnside's flotilla off the coast of North Carolina. The target of Burnside's expedition was Roanoke Island. Located behind the barrier islands of North Carolina's outer banks, the island provided access to the surrounding sounds and waterways of the state. Control of the island was vital to the success of any future operations against the ports and cities of eastern North Carolina.

Despite the size of the operation, Burnside and other Union military and political officials managed to keep the expedition's destination a secret. At one point, President Abraham Lincoln was supposed to have responded to a persistent questioner: "Now I will tell you in great confidence where they are going, if you will promise not to speak of it to any one . . . the expedition is going to sea!"

The Federals overcame repeated obstacles and endured numerous delays before they succeeded in clearing the sandbars at Hatteras Inlet and entering Pamlico Sound. During the considerable effort to coax the fleet into the sound, three of the ships and two of Burnside's officers were lost. Finally, on February 4, the entire Union armada was anchored safely in Pamlico Sound and prepared for action.

On the morning of February 5, the fleet proceeded toward Roanoke Island, with the warships escorting and protecting the packed troop transports. As the Federals neared the island, they were careful to conceal shipboard lights that might warn the defenders of their presence.

In actuality, the Southerners were already aware of the Union fleet's close proximity and had taken steps to upgrade

> ## The victory netted Burnside approximately 2,500 prisoners and cost the Southerners 23 dead. . . .

the island's defenses. Three forts were located on the northwestern shore, but none of these was adequately placed to prevent or effectively resist any landing in force on the center or southern end of the island. To man these positions, the Confederates scratched together a force of some 1,500 troops under Col. Henry M. Shaw, augmented by a small fleet of seven vessels under Capt. William F. Lynch. Confederate Secretary of War Judah P. Benjamin dispatched Henry A. Wise, the fiery brigadier general and former governor of Virginia, to assume command at Roanoke Island.

The new commander spent much of the ensuing time in Virginia, attempting to procure additional men, arms, and equipment. But by the time Burnside's expedition came steaming into Croatan Sound on February 7, 1862, the Confederates still had barely 3,000 men, poorly armed and ill-trained to resist the Federals. To compound matters, Wise suffered from an attack of pleurisy, which confined him to his headquarters on nearby Nags Head.

Admiral Goldsborough's fleet opened the engagement at 11:30 A.M. on February 7 and endured a very ineffectual fire from the Confederates. The Union navy quickly sank one ship and disabled another, and Lynch retreated with his remaining gunboats. Obstructions placed by the Southerners at the northern end of Croatan Sound proved of little nuisance to the attacking Federals.

This activity cleared the way for Burnside to land his forces, sometime around 3:30 or 4:00 P.M., on the beach at Ashby's Harbor at the center of the island. These troops came ashore on large surf boats, towed close to the shore by light-draft vessels. The naval warships provided covering fire with artillery, although the Federals did not actually need it. The Confederate commander had assigned a small force of men to delay the Federal landing, but these men failed to offer any resistance, and by midnight, 10,000 Union troops were ashore at Ashby's Harbor.

At 8:00 the next morning the Federals moved out to challenge the main Confederate defense line on Roanoke Island. Waiting for them at the northern end of the low-lying, sandy island were 1,500 Confederates and a three-gun battery. Surprisingly, none of the Southerners on hand knew how to fire the artillery pieces, and an officer had to rush over from headquarters on Nags Head to teach them. The Federals appeared before the lesson could be completed.

Burnside divided his men into three sections for the final assault. Leaving a holding force at the center of his line, he dispatched two brigades to strike the Confederates on either flank. These flanking forces struggled through thick undergrowth and marshes before arriving in position to attack the Southern lines. The combined assault proved too much for the defenders, who broke and fled. Seriously outnumbered and without the benefit of their entrenchments or the means to escape, the Confederates had no choice but to surrender.

The victory netted Burnside approximately 2,500 prisoners and cost the Southerners 23 dead, among them O. Jennings Wise, the son of General Wise. The Federals lost 37 killed, 214 wounded, and 13 missing in the operation. The loss of Roanoke Island struck a blow at Southern morale and, at the same time, gave a boost to Union spirits, sagging since First Manassas. Capturing the island also opened the way for further Union advances along the eastern seaboard of North Carolina. A Confederate congressional committee investigated the debacle but provided little more than a platform for Wise's recriminations against the department commander, Benjamin Huger, Secretary of War Benjamin, and others whom he blamed for the disaster.

BIBLIOGRAPHY

Johnson, Robert U., and C. C. Buel, eds. *Battles and Leaders of the Civil War.* 4 vols. New York, 1887–1888. Reprint, Secaucus, N.J., 1982.

Marvel, William. *Burnside.* Chapel Hill, N.C., 1991.

Thomas, Emory M. *Travels to Hallowed Ground.* Columbia, S.C., 1987.

U.S. Naval War Records Office. *Official Records of the Union and Confederate Navies in the War of the Rebellion.* Washington, D.C., 1894–1927. Ser. 1, vol. 6, pp. 549–600, 581.

U.S. War Department. *War of the Rebellion: A Compilation of the Official Records of the Union and Confederate Armies.* Washington, D.C., 1880–1901. Ser. 1, vol. 9, pp. 73–191.

BRIAN S. WILLS

BUTLER, MATTHEW CALBRAITH

BUTLER, MATTHEW CALBRAITH (1836–1909), major general and U.S. senator. Born in Greenville, South Carolina, Butler attended South Carolina College, but withdrew in 1856 after participating in a student riot. He studied law and was admitted to the South Carolina bar the following year. His marriage in 1858 to the daughter of Governor Francis W. Pickens led to a career in politics, and he was elected in 1860 to the South Carolina House of Representatives as a state rights advocate and Democratic secessionist.

Butler joined the call for a secession convention, and at the outbreak of hostilities, he resigned from the legislature to lead the Edgefield Hussars into Confederate service. An accomplished horseman, he joined Hampton's Legion in May 1861 and commanded a mounted unit at First Manassas. His actions there gained him recognition for his physical courage and tactical skill and earned him a promotion to the rank of major. During the Peninsular campaign, Butler displayed his mastery of cavalry tactics by successfully screening Confederate withdrawals and rapidly shifting to the offensive during the Battle of Williamsburg. He was promoted to colonel in August 1862, fought at Sharpsburg and Fredericksburg, and made a decisive contribution at Brandy Station in June 1863 by repulsing a Union flanking movement. He was wounded during this engagement by enemy artillery, resulting in the amputation of his right leg, but he was appointed brigadier general during his convalescence and returned to command in 1864 with no loss of enterprise or skill. Butler participated with distinction in numerous cavalry engagements including Hawes Shop and Trevillian Station and achieved the rank of major general in September 1864.

Butler returned to his law practice after the war and was again elected to the South Carolina legislature in 1866. Concluding that Republican rule was beyond reform, he joined forces with Martin Witherspoon Gary to return the Democratic party to power and restore the conservative regime. He assisted Gary in organizing the Red Shirt movement, Democratic gun clubs whose purpose was to intimidate and suppress the basic element of Republican power, the black voter. After the Democratic victory of 1876, Governor Wade Hampton appointed Butler to the U.S. Senate, where he served until 1894. Butler died in April 1909 in Washington, D.C.

BIBLIOGRAPHY

Brooks, U. R. *Butler and His Cavalry in the War of Secession, 1861–1865.* Columbia, S.C., 1909.

Williams, Alfred B. *Hampton and His Red Shirts: South Carolina's Deliverance in 1876.* New York, 1935.

ROBERT T. BARRETT

BUTLER'S WOMAN ORDER

Issued on May 15, 1862, from the headquarters of the Department of the Gulf in Union-occupied New Orleans, General Order No. 28 declared in part that "when any female shall, by word, gesture, or movement, insult or show contempt for any officer or soldier of the United States, she shall be regarded and held liable to be treated as a woman of the town plying her avocation." No other action during Gen. Benjamin F. Butler's controversial seven-month command of southern Louisiana raised more outcry than his eighty-two-word "woman order."

The directive was typical of the sternness with which Butler suppressed the disorder greeting his troops' arrival in New Orleans. While white men rioted, women sporting secessionist insignia turned up their noses and drew aside their skirts when passing Federal soldiers on the street. Others left streetcars and church pews whenever blue-clad conquerors entered. One woman emptied her slop jar on Adm. David Farragut's head as he walked beneath her balcony. Butler's patience snapped when another woman spat in the face of two Federal officers. The woman order followed hard upon this incident. Its implied authorization to treat demonstrative women as though they were streetwalkers struck a raw nerve in a community where harlotry had historically been widespread.

At home and abroad, the outcry against the woman order was loud and abusive. New Orleans's own creole general P. G. T. Beauregard was characteristic of Confederate commanders in using Butler's order to arouse his troops: "Men of the South! shall our mothers, our wives, our daughters and our sisters be thus outraged by the ruffianly soldiers of the North?" The Confederate state governor called on Southern soldiers to avenge this "foul conduct." Later in the year President Jefferson Davis branded Butler a common felon and ordered his immediate execution should he ever fall into Confederate hands. Meanwhile, on the floor of the British House of Commons, the prime minister, Lord Palmerston, called Butler's proclamation "infamous."

Butler imprisoned Mayor John Monroe for assailing the directive as uncivilized and un-Christian, but neither the Massachusetts general nor his troops ever executed the woman order. Local women thereafter behaved more circumspectly toward occupying troops, except for the prostitutes who reportedly pasted Butler's likeness in "the bottom of their tinklepots."

BIBLIOGRAPHY

Bragg, Jefferson Davis. *Louisiana in the Confederacy.* Baton Rouge, La., 1941.

Capers, Gerald. *Occupied City: New Orleans under the Federals, 1862–1865.* Lexington, Ky., 1965.

Foote, Shelby. *The Civil War: A Narrative, Fort Sumter to Perryville.* New York, 1958.

Holzman, Robert S. *Stormy Ben Butler.* New York, 1954.

Parton, James. *General Butler in New Orleans.* New York, 1864.

LAWRENCE N. POWELL

CABINET

The Confederate cabinet consisted of President Jefferson Davis, Vice President Alexander H. Stephens, and the secretaries of the six departments that composed the executive branch of the Confederate government: State, War, Justice, the Treasury, the Navy, and the Post Office. With several important exceptions, each of these departments replicated its counterpart in the prewar Union.

In organizational terms, most of the exceptions involved the offices of the attorney general, which, for the first time in American history, were given departmental status in the new Department of Justice. At the same time, the Confederacy failed to create a Department of the Interior. Its functions, such as the Bureau of Printing, the Patent Office, and territorial affairs, were transferred to Justice, which, as a consequence, was a much larger and more important department than the small suite of offices that served the Union attorney general. Another factor that greatly enhanced the attorney general's office was the decision not to establish a Confederate supreme court. In the absence of a supreme tribunal, the attorney general served as final interpreter of the constitutionality of legislation, a task made easier by the fact that state and Confederate district courts generally upheld war measures. Even so, had the Confederacy survived, these written interpretations of statutory and constitutional law might have provided an enduring basis for administrative centralization.

Although the formal organizational missions of the other departments closely corresponded to those in the prewar Union, most departments found their administrative challenges dramatically altered by the Civil War. For example, the Department of the Navy, under Stephen R. Mallory, began the war without a major vessel and soon lost easy access to international sea-lanes from Southern ports. Improvisation and, at times, brilliant ingenuity introduced the ironclad to modern warfare, but the construction of a large, or even small, oceangoing fleet was well beyond the material capacity of the South.

The Treasury Department was similarly hamstrung by an underdeveloped banking system, a shortage of gold bullion, and the limited utility of a plantation economy based on the export of cotton as a source of revenue for wartime govern-

ment operations. In all these respects, the challenge facing Confederate Treasury secretaries was very different from that faced by their prewar Union predecessors. Similar shortages of natural resources and productive capacity led the War Department to direct a wide program of confiscation, government-owned industry, and allocation of Southern manpower in order to mobilize men and matériel for the front. As was true of the other departments, these activities broke new ground in their innovative use of government authority and attempts at centrally directed economic coordination.

The two departments least changed by the war may also have been those least important to the Southern war effort. The Department of State had little to do beyond entertaining foreign representatives and giving advice to largely autonomous commissioners pursuing diplomatic recognition of the Confederacy in European courts. More active but also more mundane was the Post Office, which attempted the most thorough reproduction of prewar Federal organization. Absorbing with little change the antebellum system for delivering the mails, the Confederate Post Office moved letters in that part of the South that remained outside Federal control throughout the war.

> **The cabinet met frequently and. . . . Though these meetings were often indecisive, Davis appears to have heeded what advice was given.**

As his first cabinet, President Davis appointed Judah P. Benjamin of Louisiana, attorney general; Stephen R. Mallory of Florida, secretary of the navy; Christopher G. Memminger of South Carolina, secretary of the treasury; John H. Reagan of Texas, postmaster general; Robert Toombs of Georgia, secretary of state; and Leroy P. Walker of Alabama, secretary of war. In making these selections, Davis chose men who had been major rivals for the Confederate presidency or those his rivals recommended. He also gave geographical balance to his administration by allocating each of the states that seceded before the attack upon Fort Sumter at least one representative in the first cabinet. (Davis himself represented Mississippi.) As was also true in the Union, administrative

183

The Confederate Cabinet

POSITION	NAME	DATES OF SERVICE[1]
Attorney General	Judah P. Benjamin	Mar. 5–Nov. 21, 1861[2]
	Thomas Bragg	Nov. 21, 1861–Mar. 18, 1862
	Thomas H. Watts	Mar. 18 1862–Oct. 1, 1863
	Wade Keyes	ad interim, Oct. 1, 1863–Jan. 2, 1864
	George Davis	Jan. 2, 1864–Apr. 24, 1865[3]
Postmaster General[4]	John H. Reagan	Mar. 6, 1861–May 10, 1865[5]
President	Jefferson Davis	Feb. 18, 1861–May 10, 1865[6]
Secretary of the Navy	Stephen R. Mallory	Mar. 4, 1861–May 3, 1865[7]
Secretary of State	Robert Toombs	Feb. 21–July 24, 1861
	Robert M. T. Hunter	July 24, 1861–Feb. 22, 1862
	Williams M. Browne	ad interim, Mar. 7–Mar. 18, 1862[8]
	Judah P. Benjamin	Mar. 18, 1862–May 2, 1865[9]
Secretary of the Treasury	Christopher G. Memminger	Feb. 21, 1861–July 17, 1864
	George Trenholm	July 18, 1864–Apr. 27, 1865[10]
Secretary of War	Leroy Pope Walker	Feb. 21–Sept. 16, 1861
	Judah P. Benjamin	Nov. 21, 1861–Mar. 17, 1862[11]
	George Wythe Randolph	Mar. 18–Nov. 15, 1862
	Gustavus Woodson Smith	ad interim, Nov. 17–20, 1862
	James A. Seddon	Nov. 21, 1862–Feb. 5, 1865
	John C. Breckenridge	Feb. 6–May 3, 1865[12]
Vice President	Alexander H. Stephens	Feb.11, 1861–May 11, 1865[13]

[1]Unless otherwise indicated, starting date is date of confirmation by the Senate; ending date is date on which resignation became effective.

[2]Benjamin was appointed acting secretary of war on September 17, but the position was not made permanent and confirmed by the Senate until November 21. During the interim, Assistant Attorney General Wade Keyes ran the Justice Department.

[3]Ending date is that of the last cabinet meeting Davis attended, in Charlotte, North Carolina, after which he resigned.

[4]On February 25, 1861, Jefferson Davis nominated and the Senate confirmed Henry T. Ellet as postmaster general, but Ellet declined the appointment.

[5]Ending date is that of Reagan's capture by Union troops near Irwinville, Georgia.

[6]Starting date is that of Davis's inauguration; ending date is that of his capture by Union troops near Irwinville, Georgia.

[7]Mallory composed and dated his letter of resignation on May 2, following the cabinet meeting at Abbeville, South Carolina, but he did not present it to the president until the following day at Washington, Georgia. Mallory left the cabinet immediately, but Jefferson Davis's letter officially accepting his resignation is dated May 4.

[8]Browne had been running the state department since, at latest, February 22, 1861, but Jefferson Davis did not officially designate him secretary of state ad interim until March 7.

[9]Ending date is that of the cabinet meeting at Abbeville, South Carolina, after which Benjamin left the cabinet and fled the country, reaching Bimini on July 10.

[10]Ending date is that on which Trenholm submitted his letter of resignation. Trenholm left the cabinet immediately, although Davis's letter officially accepting the resignation is dated April 28. Davis then appointed John H. Reagan as secretary of the treasury ad interim, a position Reagan held until his capture by Union troops near Irwinville, Georgia, on May 10.

[11]Benjamin was appointed acting secretary of war on September 17, 1861, and he continued to run the department unofficially until March 24, 1862.

[12]Ending date is that of the remaining cabinet members' arrival at Washington, Georgia. Afterward, Breckinridge and John H. Reagan separated from the president with the intent of rejoining him later, but Breckinridge was unable to do so. He eventually fled to Cuba.

[13]Starting date is that on which Stephens took the oath of office; ending date is that on which he was arrested by Union cavalry at his home in Crawfordville, Georgia.

SOURCE: All dates are taken from Rembert W. Patrick, *Jefferson Davis and His Cabinet*, Baton Rouge, La., 1944.

ability and personal friendship played but minor roles in these early appointments. As a group, this cabinet lasted only from early March, when Reagan was appointed, until July 1861, when Toombs resigned in order to accept an appointment as brigadier general in the Confederate army.

Jefferson made in all sixteen appointments, aside from acting secretaries, to head the six Confederate departments. One man, Judah Benjamin, accounted for three of these as he was appointed, in succession, to Justice, War, and State. (He owed his survival to his close relationship with Davis; no other adviser so often or so influentially had the president's ear.) Benjamin, along with Mallory at Navy, Reagan at the Post Office, Davis as president, and Stephens as vice president, served in the cabinet throughout the life of the Confederacy. There was substantial turnover among the others. The War Department alone had five permanent secretaries, Justice had four, State had three, and the Treasury had two. The cabinet that sat between November 21, 1862, and September 8, 1863, had the longest tenure in terms of continuous membership. Along with Davis, Stephens, Mallory, and Reagan, that cabinet had James A. Seddon at War, Thomas H. Watts at Justice, Benjamin at State, and Memminger at Treasury. Even though these men served together for only ten months, they had the deepest influence upon the performance and development of their respective departments.

Under President Davis, the cabinet met frequently and, when it met, deliberated for hours. Though these meetings were often indecisive, Davis appears to have heeded what advice was given. For the most part, however, the cabinet served the president in other ways. One of these was as a structure for an immense delegation of authority over executive administration of the Southern war effort. With few exceptions, the secretaries, their assistant secretaries, and subordinate bureau chiefs were solely responsible for departmental operations within wide-ranging grants of statutory authority from the Confederate Congress. For the most part, Davis involved himself only in the detailed decision making of the War Department and, within its sphere, imposed his views only in military operations.

Another way that the cabinet served Davis was as a political lightning rod. Even though most departments were more or less autonomous of both legislative and executive direction, the deteriorating military position of the South and the ever-escalating demands that the war effort imposed upon civilians produced in the Congress repeated and bitter denunciations of executive performance. Although the president resisted many calls for the resignation of department secretaries, most of the turnover in his cabinet in fact reflected timely sacrifices to this congressional clamor.

[*See also* Judiciary; Post Office Department; Presidency; State Department; Treasury Department; War Department; *and biographies of numerous figures mentioned herein.*]

BIBLIOGRAPHY

Coulter, E. Merton. *The Confederate States of America, 1861–1865.* A History of the South, vol. 7. Baton Rouge, La., 1950.

Eaton, Clement. *A History of the Southern Confederacy.* New York, 1954.

Patrick, Rembert W. *Jefferson Davis and His Cabinet.* Baton Rouge, La., 1944.

Thomas, Emory M. *The Confederate Nation: 1861–1865.* New York, 1979.

Vandiver, Frank E. *Their Tattered Flags: The Epic of the Confederacy.* New York, 1970. Reprint, Texas A & M University Military History Series, no. 5. College Station, Tex., 1987.

RICHARD FRANKLIN BENSEL

CALHOUN, JOHN C.

CALHOUN, JOHN C. (1782–1850), author of the constitutional justification for secession. The son of a well-to-do slave owner who opposed ratification of the U.S. Constitution, John Caldwell Calhoun was born and raised in the up-country of South Carolina. He graduated from Yale College and then attended the Litchfield, Connecticut, law school of Tapping Reeve at a time when both institutions were under the control of extreme state-rights Federalists. Acquiring an up-country plantation and slaves, he looked upon himself as a kindly master, though he once ordered "30 lashes well laid on" as punishment for a runaway. Between 1810 and 1850 he served as a congressman, secretary of war (one of the best), vice president, senator, and secretary of state, while continually aspiring to be president.

At first, Calhoun assumed that the Federal government possessed broad powers, and he advocated an "enlarged policy" of protective tariffs, internal improvements, and a national bank. By 1828, however, he had reversed himself on the

> . . . Sovereignty, or the ultimate source of power within a body politic, resides in the people of each of the separate states.

tariff, which South Carolina cotton planters blamed for their economic troubles. Some talked of secession as a way out. Seeking a less radical alternative, Calhoun came up with the idea of nullification, which he presented anonymously in "The South Carolina Exposition" (1828) and later elaborated in various writings, especially in his posthumous *Discourse on the Constitution and Government of the United States* (1851).

His theory may be summarized as follows: Sovereignty, or the ultimate source of power within a body politic, resides in the people of each of the separate states. By ratifying the U.S. Constitution, these people delegated certain powers to the Federal government but gave up none of their sovereignty. The people of each state must therefore decide for themselves whether the Federal government, their agent, is at any time violating their instructions as given in the "constitutional compact." They can nullify any law they consider unconstitutional. The law then remains null and void within the state until three-fourths of all the states have ratified an amendment giving the Federal government the power in question. If this happens, the aggrieved state has a recourse: it can secede. To do so, it needs only to repeal its ratification of the U.S. Constitution.

According to Calhoun, the whole process was perfectly constitutional, but when South Carolina attempted to put his theory into practice by nullifying the tariff laws in 1832, President Andrew Jackson threatened to use force against the state, and Federal laws were never suspended within it. Realizing that one state alone could not effectively resist the Federal government, Calhoun thereafter devoted himself to uniting the South behind him and his principles. He did so by taking an extreme stand against antislavery activities of whatever kind. Slavery, he maintained, had a special place in the Constitution, for it was the only kind of property mentioned there (though not by name). Therefore, the Federal government, in the exercise of its legitimate powers, must always promote the interests of slave owners, and the free states must do nothing to interfere with its efforts.

Calhoun objected to the Compromise of 1850 primarily on the ground that it would increase the power of the North by admitting California as a free state. He now warned Northerners that the Southern states might leave the Union unless slavery was made absolutely secure. "If you are unwilling we should depart in peace, tell us so, and we shall know what to do, when you reduce the question to submission or resistance." Here was a hint that, unless secession was permitted, there would be war.

As Calhoun lay on his deathbed, his enemy Francis P. Blair wrote of him: " 'tis given out that having completed the ground work he does not look to live to enjoy it—poor old man, he resolved to die in giving birth to the Southern Confederacy." The formation of the Confederacy was delayed for eleven years, but Calhoun had indeed laid the groundwork for it. When South Carolina seceded, it followed exactly the procedure he had prescribed: an elected convention repealed the ratification of the U.S. Constitution. Other seceding states did the same. The Confederate Constitution embodied his principles in guaranteeing slavery and in acknowledging the sovereignty of the states, though it did not recognize the right of nullification or secession.

In 1860 Jefferson Davis had tried to incorporate a set of Calhoun's proslavery and state-rights resolutions in the Democratic party platform. As president of the Confederacy,

however, he needed to exert the powers of his government in enforcing conscription and other war measures. Vice President Alexander H. Stephens accused him of abandoning the state-rights principles of Calhoun and adopting the consolidationist heresy of Andrew Jackson. After the war, Davis as well as Stephens nevertheless claimed to be a faithful disciple of Calhoun. When Stephens gave his apologia the title *A Constitutional View of the Late War between the States* (1868–1870), he originated the designation "War between the States," which continues to serve as a reminder that a particular "constitutional view" underlay the attempt of Southerners to gain their independence.

BIBLIOGRAPHY

Calhoun, John C. *A Disquisition on Government and a Discourse on the Constitution and Government of the United States.* Vol. 1 of *The Works of John C. Calhoun.* Edited by Richard K. Cralle. Charleston, S.C., 1851.
Current, Richard N. *John C. Calhoun.* The Great American Thinkers Series. New York, 1963.
Dodd, William E. *Statesmen of the Old South; or, From Radicalism to Conservative Revolt.* New York, 1911.
Niven, John. *John C. Calhoun and the Price of Union.* Baton Rouge, La., 1988.
Wiltse, Charles M. *John C. Calhoun.* 3 vols. Indianapolis and New York, 1944–1951.

RICHARD N. CURRENT

CAMPBELL, JOHN A.

CAMPBELL, JOHN A. (1811–1889), associate justice of the U.S. Supreme Court and Confederate assistant secretary of war. Born in Washington, Georgia, the son of a distinguished lawyer, Campbell was educated at Franklin College (now the University of Georgia) and at West Point. The sudden death of his parent curtailed his military career and he returned home. A precocious youth, after studying law privately, he was admitted to the bar at nineteen. The following year he moved to Montgomery (later to Mobile), Alabama, where he practiced law, married, and served as a Democrat in the legislature several times. His rise to prominence as a brilliant member of the Alabama bar, gifted with an unusual memory and wide knowledge of history, made him an attractive public figure as well.

In 1850 he was named delegate to the Nashville Convention, where he avoided the sectional stridency of Robert Barnwell Rhett, William Lowndes Yancey, and other firebrands to help draft the conciliatory resolutions adopted by that body. At forty, Campbell had achieved a national reputation as a lawyer, and in March 1853, he was appointed an associate justice of the U.S. Supreme Court by Franklin

Pierce. His selection had been made at the request of jurists on the Court and was widely praised. He soon rose to equal the best on the bench and in the following years delivered many important opinions. In the controversial *Dred Scott* decision of 1854, he concurred with the majority ruling in holding that a slave was not a citizen and that the Missouri Compromise did not bestow citizenship upon him. At this time Campbell held no slaves, having earlier freed all he owned and thereafter employing as servants only free persons of color. A strict constructionist and state rights champion, he was also a strong Union man who repeatedly rose

> **"Resigned—and for a cause that he is hardly more than half in sympathy with. His is one of the hardest cases."**

above his section on many sensitive national issues. In 1860, in briefs before the Federal court at New Orleans, he opposed William Walker's filibustering ventures in Latin America as violations of America's neutrality laws.

Campbell's fearful concern for peace drew him into the Fort Sumter crisis in early 1861. Although strongly opposed to secession (Alabama had left the Union on January 11), he remained in Washington and on the bench, as he worked ceaselessly to promote compromise between the two sections. These efforts made him unpopular in Alabama and were not entirely met with sincerity by Secretary of State William H. Seward, spokesman for the new Lincoln administration, with whom he was negotiating. After weeks of efforts to reach an accord and thus avoid war (which he believed would be long and disastrous for the South), he was finally compelled to admit defeat. Abraham Lincoln refused to receive the Confederate commissioners sent by Jefferson Davis and, despite Seward's assurances that force would not be used to hold the fort, Lincoln sent the *Star of the West* with arms and men to Charleston. Many Southerners charged the judge with betrayal, Seward with duplicity, and Lincoln with open hostility to the South. Feeling that he had been misused, Campbell resigned and returned to Alabama.

"A resigned judge of the Supreme Court of the United States!" Mary Boykin Chesnut exclaimed in her famous diary. "Resigned—and for a cause that he is hardly more than half in sympathy with. His is one of the hardest cases." Hard it was, and though his motives were suspicious to many, in time it would be seen that his conduct, in the supreme crisis of his life, was above reproach.

Not until the fall of 1862 did Campbell agree to serve the Confederate cause. He had earlier moved his family to Richmond, where he was offered several positions of importance. Though he differed from Jefferson Davis, the latter

respected his gifts and his loyalty, and on October 22, acting upon the urgings of Secretary of War George Wythe Randolph, appointed Campbell assistant secretary. His assignment called for legal knowledge and administrative ability to help carry out the first military draft in America—which Randolph and the Confederate Congress had brought into being in April and September 1862.

In late November, Secretary Randolph suddenly quit his post (for personal reasons and differences with Davis), and Campbell found himself second in command in the War Office to another Virginian, James A. Seddon. A strong Southern nationalist, lawyer, and politician, Seddon threw the full force of his personality, class, and political connections into his stewardship. He was a man of independent thought and an able administrator. Campbell would work with him until the last weeks of the war, and between them developed a close and successful relationship. In time Seddon expanded the judge's purview and powers; the assistant secretary was charged with overseeing most of the routine of the department and its various bureaus, as well as drafting correspondence, especially with Southern governors over conscription and other matters.

Relations with other departments (Navy, Treasury) could at times be touchy, coordination with Adjutant and Inspector General Samuel Cooper not always harmonious, and orders to military leaders in the field difficult and unpleasant. But Campbell's customary detachment from personalities, evenhandedness, and steadfastness to duty strengthened the direction and effectiveness of the War Office—the busiest and most vital powerhouse of the Confederate government. To most, this tall, bald old gentleman, with deep penetrating eyes and sharp features, who dispatched orders with both alacrity and common sense, yet often with kindness, was the indispensable man in the Richmond bureaucracy. He ultimately emerged as the real power behind the scenes of the civilian war effort and, in the end, became what Gen. Josiah Gorgas observed: "the mainstay of the War Dept."

In the course of the war, Campbell differed with the Davis administration on major issues, and on several occasions he took issue with the president directly. He expressed his criticism respectfully to his superior or to his bureau chiefs. More a realist than most, he urged draconian measures when need warranted, as in matters of exemptions, martial law, taxes-in-kind, and impressment. He advocated control of the railroads, trading cotton with the enemy for food, and regulation of blockade runners. Eventually the War Department acquired a handful of runners to bring in munitions, medicine, and other essentials for the fighting forces. On larger issues, he was one with Seddon in urging a vigorous western theater strategic policy, early in 1863 stating bluntly that Davis was without any plan and seemed "to be drifting on the current of events." The next year, after the dual disasters of Gettysburg and Vicksburg, massive manpower shortages, and desertions, he urged that slaves be recruited as soldiers—knowing full well that freeing blacks for military service "would be the knell of slavery as it exists." By 1865 he realized that the war had been lost: "No money in the Treasury—no food to feed Gen. Lee's army—no troops to oppose Gen. Sherman—what does it all mean. Is [not] the cause really hopeless?"

It was, and yet Davis and the diehards held on. Campbell pleaded with the new secretary, John C. Breckinridge, to prepare for the inevitable collapse of the Confederacy. But first, and for the second time in his public life, he offered his talents as conciliator-mediator between the two governments in the special accords achieved by his old friend Francis P. Blair with the Lincoln administration—the Hampton Roads Conference.

For the better part of six hours, on February 3, 1865, Campbell, Robert M. T. Hunter, and Alexander H. Stephens conversed and talked history distant and present, all to the end of bringing about a cessation of hostilities. But as the Confederate peace commissioners had been instructed by Davis to negotiate only on a basis of Southern independence and Lincoln was holding firm to a restoration of the Union, the prospects for an armistice were doomed. Campbell later submitted his report of the transactions to the Confederate president and awaited events.

The end came on April 2, when Richmond was evacuated by the government, and Davis and most of the cabinet fled south. At considerable risk to himself, Campbell remained in the capital. Later he was successful in meeting with Lincoln and discussed at length proposals for peace and reconstruction (of at least the state of Virginia). With Robert E. Lee's surrender a few days later and Lincoln's assassination, these efforts came to nothing. Much to his surprise, on May 23 he was arrested by Federal authorities and confined to Libby Prison. Soon after, he was dispatched with Seddon and Hunter on a ship to imprisonment at Fort Pulaski, Georgia. Here he remained with many old associates for six months. Much of the time was passed in talk and thought of recent events and in correspondence with his family.

When finally released, he returned to his family and relocated to New Orleans. His property in Mobile had been destroyed by the invaders, and his house in Washington had been seized and sold for taxes. At fifty-four he set about rebuilding his law practice. Cases before Federal courts with periodic appearances before the Supreme Court, several on important national issues (such as monopolies, the Slaughterhouse cases, and Reconstruction tax issues), filled these last decades. Toward the end he was drawn back to Washington, but soon found his old haunt uncongenial and moved on to Baltimore, where he died. Campbell wrote and published chapters of an autobiography, which he regrettably never completed—a poignant loss to history, for the judge was an interesting man, honest, highly intelligent, often original in his thought, and a witness to much that posterity would love to know.

BIBLIOGRAPHY

Campbell, John A. *Reminiscences and Documents Relating to the Civil War.* Baltimore, 1887.

Connor, Henry Graves. *John Archibald Campbell, Associate Justice, 1853–1861.* Boston, 1920.

Jones, J. B. *A Rebel War Clerk's Diary at the Confederate States Capital.* 2 vols. Philadelphia, 1866.

Patrick, Rembert W. *Jefferson Davis and His Cabinet.* Baton Rouge, La., 1944.

Vandiver, Frank E., ed. *The Civil War Diary of General Josiah Gorgas.* University, Ala., 1947.

Younger, Edward, ed. *Inside the Confederate Government: The Diary of Robert Garlick Hill Kean.* New York, 1957.

JOHN O'BRIEN

CANADA

With the outbreak of the Civil War, Canada emerged as a potential battleground between North and South. The *Trent* affair (in which Confederate envoys en route to Europe were seized by U.S. officials) and the subsequent strain in U.S.-British relations in November and December 1861 raised the danger of war in Canada and unleashed animosities toward the inhabitants of the border states. Disaffected pro-Confederate elements in Canada merely increased the tensions. Much of Canadian opinion was outspokenly anti-Northern, some even pro-Southern. Conservative opinion, like that in Britain, claimed a dislike for American democratic institutions and "mob rule." Yet the North had its staunch supporters in the Canadian press; Canadian leaders hesitated to endorse the Confederate cause. Richmond reacted slowly to the possibilities of using Canada as a base for harassing the border states and encouraging anti-Union sentiment in the North. Southern leaders looked to Britain and France, not Canada, for effective intervention in the American conflict.

With the apparent Confederate failure to enlist support in Europe, the Richmond government in late 1863 prepared to use Canada as a second front in its war against the North. President Jefferson Davis absolved the Confederacy of any obligation to honor U.S. treaties. Pro-Southern forces in Canada could now ignore past barriers to offensive action, including the restraints imposed by Britain's official neutrality. Lord Charles Stanley Monck, governor general of Canada, informed Washington of Confederate plots, including one of November 1863 to release Southern prisoners being held at Johnson's Island in Lake Erie. Union officials alerted the area and forced the abandonment of the plot. In December Confederate conspirators succeeded in capturing the American-owned coastal steamer *Chesapeake* to convert it into a privateer. A U.S. naval vessel recaptured *Chesapeake* in Nova Scotian waters, and a boarding party apprehended a

Nova Scotian raider, John Wade, who managed to escape. When a Confederate legal expert failed to establish Confederate citizenship for the plotters, a New Brunswick magistrate declared the attack on *Chesapeake* an act of piracy, not the capture of a prize. A Halifax vice admiralty court ordered the ship returned to its owners. Washington dropped the case, unwilling to press for extradition to try British subjects for piracy.

Following the *Chesapeake* affair, the Confederate government moved at last to exploit Canada's anti-Northern sentiment. In April 1864 President Jefferson Davis appointed a commission consisting of Jacob Thompson of Mississippi, Clement C. Clay of Louisiana, and University of Virginia professor J. P. Holcombe, already in Canada, "to crystallize anti-Northern feeling in Canada and mould it into some form of hostile expression." At the outset the commission was aided by the overwhelming Union victories at Gettysburg and Vicksburg. Never had Canada appeared so vulnerable to U.S. power. Operating out of Queen's Hotel in Toronto, the commissioners planned a variety of border assaults from Maine to Ohio. They fostered a peace movement in the North to diminish support for the Union war effort, stepping up their activity as the 1864 election approached. One Confederate agent boasted that the Southerners in Canada would "do such deeds . . . as shall make European civilization shudder." Still the Southern efforts to defeat President Abraham Lincoln and undermine morale in the United States were few and inept. The Confederate agents in Canada suffered from a pro-Southern bias that rendered them ineffective; they recognized no legitimate or practical limits to their antiUnion plots.

> . . . **"to crystallize anti-Northern feeling in Canada and mould it into some form of hostile expression."**

In September 1864 the Virginian John Y. Beall planned an attack on Johnson's Island by gaining possession of USS *Michigan*. The plot failed when crew members apprehended Beall's accomplice, who had been sent abroad to drug them. In October some twenty Kentuckians, led by Lt. Bennett H. Young, attacked the Vermont town of St. Albans, robbing three banks and setting off a melee that resulted in one death. Gen. John A. Dix, commander of the Military District of the East, ordered his troops to pursue the raiders into Canada and either destroy them or bring them back for trial. Vermonters captured Young and others and turned them over to Canadian authorities. Later a Montreal court freed them.

Secretary of State William H. Seward warned London that the United States, if the raids continued, would terminate the

Rush-Bagot agreement of 1817 that demilitarized the U.S.-Canadian boundary and proceed to strengthen its border defenses. President Lincoln instituted a burdensome passport system to check movement across the border. Canadian opinion now became more contrite, troubled by the South's abuse of Canada's official neutrality. As peace returned to the border, Washington, in March 1865, terminated the passport system and reaffirmed the Rush-Bagot convention.

[*See also* Espionage, *articles on* Confederate Secret Service *and* Confederate Military Spies; Propaganda.]

BIBLIOGRAPHY

Crooks, David Paul. *The North, the South, and the Powers, 1861–1865.* New York, 1974.

Owsley, Frank Lawrence. *King Cotton Diplomacy: Foreign Relations of the Confederate States of America.* Revised by Harriet Chappell Owsley. Chicago, 1959.

Winks, Robin W. *Canada and the United States: The Civil War Years.* Baltimore, 1960.

NORMAN A. GRAEBNER

CAROLINAS CAMPAIGN OF SHERMAN

On December 22, 1864, Maj. Gen. William Tecumseh Sherman sent the following telegram to President Abraham Lincoln: "I beg to present you as a Christmas gift the city of Savannah." With this communication Sherman brought to a conclusion his dramatic March to the Sea. By all standard rules of strategy, his next move should have been the immediate transfer of his army by water to Virginia where Lt. Gen. Ulysses S. Grant had the Army of Northern Virginia bottled up behind fortifications at Petersburg. The Federal navy had the ships for this move, and both Lincoln and Grant supported the plan. Sherman, however, did not. He wanted instead to apply total war, as he had done in Georgia, to the Carolinas, especially the Palmetto State for its role in bringing on the conflict. He believed that by bringing the war to the Carolina home front his operations would have a direct bearing on the struggle in Virginia.

Sherman, a very persuasive individual, was granted permission for the Carolinas march, his position having been strengthened considerably by the news of Maj. Gen. George Thomas's near-annihilation of the Confederate Army of Tennessee at Nashville in mid-December 1864.

Sherman's plan of campaign called for feints on Charleston, South Carolina, and Augusta, Georgia, followed by a move on Columbia, South Carolina's capital city. From there he planned to march in a northeasterly direction first to

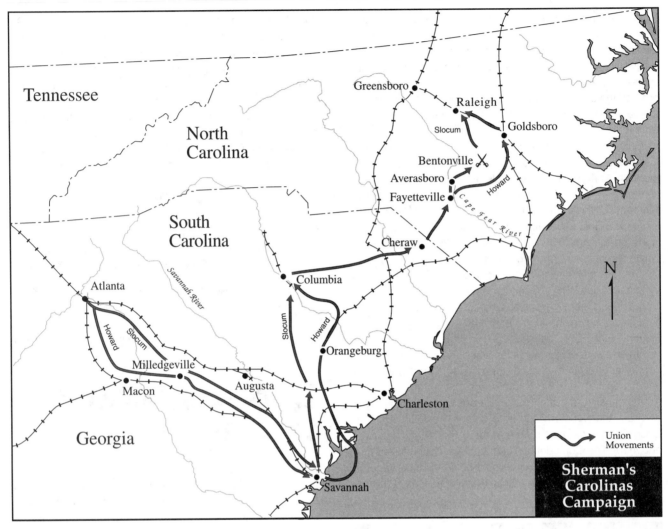

Fayetteville on the Cape Fear River in North Carolina and then to Goldsboro, which was connected to the North Carolina coast by two railroads. By this circuit he could cripple the chief lines of communication in the Carolinas as well as destroy all public and industrial property in his line of march. Furthermore, by bringing war to the home front, he felt certain that a defeatist psychology would be instilled in civilians and soldiers alike.

Since Sherman planned to sever all connections with his base at Savannah, the men would have to forage liberally in the countryside to survive. Army wagons could transport only a limited quantity of provisions, and no government supplies could be expected until the army reached the Cape Fear River. In an attempt to regulate the foraging parties, Sherman issued very strict orders, but as had been the case on the March to the Sea, there was a wide discrepancy between the orders and the actions of some of the men. Most of the outrages committed in the Carolinas were the work of "bum-

mers," self-constituted foragers who operated on their own and not under supervision.

By late January 1865, Sherman's sixty thousand veterans had begun crossing the Savannah River into South Carolina. The army was divided into two wings, the left commanded by Maj. Gen. Henry W. Slocum, the right by Maj. Gen. O. O. Howard. Each wing in turn comprised two corps, and each corps followed a different line of advance, forming a front over forty miles wide. Brig. Gen. Judson Kilpatrick was in charge of the cavalry.

When Sherman commenced his Carolinas campaign, the meager Confederate forces that might oppose him were scattered from Mississippi to Virginia, so by the second week in February the Federal army had penetrated well into South Carolina. On the twelfth, Orangeburg was occupied and five days later Columbia was in Sherman's hands. Much of South Carolina's capital city went up in flames on February 17. Burning cotton, high winds, and drunken Federal soldiers were to blame for this conflagration. "Though I never ordered it," Sherman said, "and never wished it, I have never shed any tears over the event, because I believe that it hastened what we all fought for, the end of the war." Lt. Charles A. Brown of the Twenty-first Michigan commented: "South Carolina may have been the cause of the whole thing, but she has had an awful punishment."

At Cheraw, the army's last stop in South Carolina, Sherman learned that Gen. Joseph E. Johnston had replaced P. G. T. Beauregard as commander of Confederate forces in the Carolinas and Georgia. He now concluded that his antagonist of the Atlanta campaign would somehow manage to unite his forces and give battle at a place of his own choosing. This Sherman had hoped to avoid.

On March 8 North Carolina for the first time felt the full weight of the Federal army. Sherman, assuming a friendly reception from North Carolina's pro-Union element, issued orders for the gentler treatment of the local citizens, but he did nothing to stop the burning of the state's great pine forests. North Carolina's turpentine woods blazed in "splendor as bummers touched matches to congealed sap in notches on tree trunks."

The most formidable obstacle in Sherman's path lay in the swirling waters of the Lumber River and the adjacent swamps. The region prompted him to remark, "It was the damnedest marching I ever saw." Fortunately for him, his engineers by now had become skilled at bridging streams and corduroying roads.

Federal cavalry crossed the Lumber on March 8. Upon learning that Confederate horsemen under Lt. Gen. Wade Hampton were nearby, Kilpatrick set a trap for him, only to have his own camp surprised by the enemy on the morning of the tenth. Kilpatrick escaped capture by hastily departing the bed of a female traveling companion. Eventually the Federals retook their camp. As a result there is some disagreement over who won the cavalry engagement at Monroe's Crossroads, contemptuously tagged by some as "Kilpatrick's Shirt-tail Skedaddle."

By engaging the Federals in battle, the horsemen in gray opened the road to Fayetteville. That night near the city, the Confederate cavalry under Hampton and Maj. Gen. Joseph Wheeler joined forces with Lt. Gen. William J. Hardee's small command, which had been moving north just ahead of Sherman. On the eleventh as the Federals entered the city from the south, the Confederates withdrew across the Cape Fear, burning the bridge behind them.

At Fayetteville Sherman ordered the arsenal destroyed along with other properties. He also took the opportunity to clear his columns of the vast numbers of white refugees and blacks following his army. He referred to them as "twenty to thirty thousand useless mouths."

From Savannah to Fayetteville, Sherman had managed his army in an almost flawless manner. From the Cape Fear to Goldsboro, however, it was a different story. He not only mistakenly placed little emphasis on Hardee's delaying action at Averasboro on March 16 but also allowed his own columns to become so strung out that Johnston came close to crushing one of the Federal corps near Bentonville. At this village, twenty miles west of Goldsboro, Johnston had skillfully managed on the nineteenth to concentrate his scattered forces, although a sparse group it was, totaling no more than 21,000 effectives. Seldom in history have so few been led in battle by so many officers of high rank. Present on the battlefield that day were two full generals of the Confederacy,

> "Though I never ordered it . . . and never wished it, I have never shed any tears over the event, because I believe that it hastened what we all fought for, the end of the war."

three lieutenant generals, and numerous brigadier and major generals.

Completely ignorant of Johnston's bold move, Sherman allowed his Fourteenth Corps to be caught off guard. For a while it seemed the Confederates would carry the day, but Federal reinforcements in the afternoon blunted Johnston's offensive. More Federal troops reached Bentonville on the twentieth, and by the next day Sherman had his entire army on the field. That night Johnston withdrew to Smithfield, ten miles to the west.

Though Bentonville was the largest battle fought on North Carolina soil (Confederate casualties, 2,606; Federal, 1,527), it was not one of the war's decisive engagements. Nevertheless, it must rank as an important battle. It marked the successful conclusion of Sherman's Carolinas campaign, and it was large in scope; 81,000 men were locked in combat over a three-day period.

At Goldsboro, Sherman's victorious troops linked up with Maj. Gen. John M. Schofield's command, and on March 25 the first train from the coast arrived. This completed the task Sherman had set for himself upon leaving Savannah.

After the war, Sherman commented that he would be remembered for the March to the Sea but that that operation was child's play compared to the Carolinas campaign. He characterized it as "one of the longest and most important marches ever made by an organized army in a civilized country. The distance from Savannah to Goldsboro is four hundred and twenty-five miles and the route embraced five large navigable rivers. . . . The country generally was in a state of nature with innumerable swamps . . . mud roads, nearly every mile of which had to be corduroyed. . . . We had captured . . . important cities and depots of supplies. . . . We had in mid-winter accomplished the whole journey . . . in fifty days . . . and had reached Goldsboro with the army in superb order."

The Federal march was a remarkable logistical feat that brought home to the people of the Carolinas the realities of war. Still, this operation had little direct bearing on Gen. Robert E. Lee's decision to surrender. It was the decisive Confederate defeat at Nashville coupled with the collapse of the transportation system in Virginia that paved the way for Appomattox.

[*See also* Bummers; Fort Fisher, North Carolina.]

BIBLIOGRAPHY

Barrett, John G. *Sherman's March through the Carolinas.* Chapel Hill, N.C., 1956.

Glatthaar, Joseph T. *The March to the Sea and Beyond: Sherman's Troops in the Savannah and Carolinas Campaigns.* New York, 1985.

Lewis, Lloyd. *Sherman, Fighting Prophet.* New York, 1932.

Luvaas, J. "Johnston's Last Stand—Bentonville." *North Carolina Historical Review* 33 (1956): 332–358.

JOHN G. BARRETT

CARY, HETTY

CARY, HETTY (1836–1892), Confederate belle. Hetty Cary, a well-known belle of Baltimore and Richmond society, endeared herself to the Confederacy forever when she and her sister Jennie and cousin Constance sang "Maryland, My Maryland" to Southern troops, just after the First Battle of Manassas. On that same occasion, Gen. P. G. T. Beauregard reportedly feted the Cary women in a mock ceremony wherein Hetty was dubbed a lieutenant colonel, Jennie a first lieutenant, and Constance a captain general. The Confederacy displayed a buoyant optimism during this early stage of war, and the Cary women symbolized a confident, even playful, sense of invincibility.

Although all three Cary women were well-known patriots, and Jennie Cary set the lyrics of "My Maryland" to the tune of "Lauriger Horatius," it was Hetty Cary who most captured the imagination of Lost Cause chroniclers—perhaps because of her striking looks and flair for the dramatic. The Civil War memoirs of Mrs. D. Giraud Wright described Hetty Cary as a "titian-haired" beauty with a "lilies and roses" complexion. Mrs. Wright reported that Hetty was once imprisoned at Fort McHenry for publicly wearing Confederate colors, and that on another occasion she had waved a Confederate flag from her Baltimore window as Federal troops passed by. Supposedly, the Union colonel below pronounced Hetty too beautiful to arrest.

Hetty Cary's 1865 wedding in Richmond, Virginia, to Confederate Col. John Pegram three weeks before his death on the Petersburg battlefield provided a final tragic flourish to her identification with the Confederacy. In 1879 Cary married Professor H. Newell Martin. She spent her remaining years teaching and touring Europe.

BIBLIOGRAPHY

Brock, Sallie A. *Richmond during the War: Four Years of Personal Observations by a Richmond Lady.* New York, 1867. Reprint, Alexandria, Va., 1983.

Harwell, Richard B., ed. *The Confederate Reader.* New York, 1957.

Simkins, Francis Butler, and James Welch Patton. *The Women of the Confederacy.* Richmond and New York, 1936.

Wright, Mrs. D. Giraud. *A Southern Girl in '61: The War-Time Memories of a Confederate Senator's Daughter.* New York, 1905.

VICTORIA E. BYNUM

CASTLE THUNDER PRISON

In August 1862, the Confederates opened this facility for the provost marshal of their capital's Eastern District. Their largest prison of its type, it consisted of three impressed commercial buildings on Cary Street near Libby Prison. The largest of the brick structures, Gleanor's Tobacco Warehouse and Factory, three and a half stories high, was divided into several large rooms and a number of cells. Gas and water were piped in, but because many of the windows were boarded up, the air was foul. The prison confined Confederate deserters, civilians, and political enemies. On either side were Whitlock's Warehouse, used for blacks and women, and Palmer's Factory, which held Federal deserters and others. These winglike prisons were connected by a wall, thus creating an enclosed yard for exercise by some of the prisoners. Newspapers gave the complex its ominous name, pairing it with another warehouse prison they called "Castle Lightning."

The first inmates were several hundred men transferred from Castle Godwin, a "Negro Jail" that had been used earlier as a provost prison. The Confederates intended Castle Thunder to hold 1,400 people, but, as in other prisons, its capacity was often exceeded. In mid-1863, the buildings held more than 3,000 prisoners. Among those confined in Castle Thunder in the course of the war were about 100 women, including accused spies, women who had disguised themselves as men to enter the Confederate army, and captured Unionists. Among the latter, the most famous was the first female U.S. Army surgeon, Dr. Mary Walker. Another woman achieved notoriety by naming her child born in the prison "Castellina Thunder Lee."

The prison's best-known head was Capt. George W. Alexander. A Georgia native, he was a prewar veteran of the Navy who had joined the Confederates, been captured in Maryland, and escaped from prison. In Richmond, he became part of the circle of Marylanders around Gen. John H. Winder, who made him an assistant provost marshal in charge of Castle Thunder. Alexander was a flamboyant man who sang in a Richmond theatrical, dressed all in black, rode a black horse, and used an enormous black dog named Nero to intimidate his prisoners.

Like many supervisors of provost prisons, Alexander believed that it required stern discipline to deal with social outcasts who frequently robbed one another and tried to escape. He punished one group by forcing them to stand outdoors in a winter rain for several days. Others he had flogged, hung by the thumbs, bucked and gagged, dressed in a "barrel shirt," and shut up in a tiny "sweat room." Rumors about such abuses led to an investigation by a committee of the Confederate House of Representatives in April 1863.

In his defense Alexander cited orders from General Winder to use corporal punishment. He also pointed to his creation of a thirty-bed hospital run by his wife and to his provision of a physician's supervision for the occasional branding of prisoners. The majority of the committee praised Captain Alexander, but a minority denounced his treatment of prisoners as unjust. In December 1863, Alexander was arrested for trading in Federal money and taking bribes from prisoners. Though acquitted by a court-martial, he was subsequently transferred to the Salisbury Prison. His successor, Capt. Lucien W. Richardson, a Virginian, succeeded better in maintaining order and improving conditions enough to win the praise of Confederate inspectors.

On the night of the fall of Richmond, guards removed the remaining prisoners. Castle Thunder's front door key was taken to New York where it was auctioned for the benefit of orphans of Union soldiers. Like several other prison officials, Captain Alexander found it expedient to leave the country, returning to Baltimore when the political climate cooled. The prison buildings were returned to their previous owners. In 1879, the Castle burned, and the site today is a corporation parking lot.

[*See also* Provost Marshal.]

BIBLIOGRAPHY

Blakey, Arch Frederic. *General John H. Winder, C.S.A.* Gainesville, Fla., 1990.

Byrne, Frank L. "Prison Pens of Suffering." In *Fighting for Time*. Vol. 4 of *The Image of War, 1861–1865*. Edited by William C. Davis. Garden City, N.Y., 1983.

Parker, Sandra V. *Richmond's Civil War Prisons*. Lynchburg, Va., 1990.

Radley, Kenneth. *Rebel Watchdog: The Confederate States Army Provost Guard*. Baton Rouge, La., 1989.

FRANK L. BYRNE

CAVALRY

The Confederate cavalry reigned supreme for the first two years of the Civil War. Even Philip Sheridan, the cavalry commander for Ulysses S. Grant's Army of the Potomac, wrote in his memoirs, "From the very beginning of the war the enemy had shown more wisdom respecting his cavalry than we. Instead of wasting its strength by a policy of disintegration he, at an early day, had organized his mounted force into compact masses, and plainly made it a favorite."

Part of the Southern superiority was probably due to the caliber of such leaders as J. E. B. Stuart, Wade Hampton, Fitzhugh Lee, and Nathan Bedford Forrest. But there were other reasons. The Confederate cavalry, early in the war, was organized into one independent, autonomous unit and acted as such. The regiments never suffered from the piecemeal detachment to individual infantry units that plagued the Federal mounted arm until 1863 when it too was organized into one unit. Stuart was given command of the cavalry of the Confederate Army of the Potomac (the precursor to Robert E. Lee's Army of Northern Virginia) in October 1861. In the West, the Confederate Army of Tennessee brigaded its cavalry in November 1862. It consisted of four brigades under Joseph Wheeler, John Austin Wharton, Nathan Bedford Forrest, and John Hunt Morgan.

Given this structure, the Confederates were able to introduce new tactics into cavalry doctrine—making large-scale mounted raids and putting cavalry into the battle to fight dismounted. Stuart conceived of the raid as a viable operation and other Confederate commanders followed suit, as did the Federals later in the war. The Confederates also introduced the tactic of having the cavalry ride to the strategic point on the battlefield to fight dismounted on a regular basis. Both these innovations rested upon the first—the new, and superior, organization of the Confederate cavalry.

Organization

In the Virginia theater, Stuart, and later Hampton and Fitz Lee, commanded the Army of Northern Virginia's cavalry, and Wheeler commanded the horsemen in the Army of Tennessee. The Army of Northern Virginia's cavalry began with about 1,700 troopers in six regiments in late 1861. By mid-1862 Stuart's division had grown to six brigades under Fitz Lee, William Henry Fitzhugh Lee, Beverly Holcombe Robertson, William Edmondson ("Grumble") Jones, Wade Hampton, and Albert Gallatin Jenkins, and numbered some 4,000 present for duty out of an aggregate of some 7,000. By mid-1863 the cavalry had grown to 10,000 men in seven brigades—much too large a force for its organizational makeup. Because of this, Stuart's division was broken into two divisions under Fitz Lee and Hampton, each with three brigades of two to four regiments.

Stuart's cavalry corps soon numbered 20,000 present and absent. Though the rolls contained nearly 20,000 names, only about a third might be present at any one time because of the way the cavalry had been established. Each trooper provided his own mount and was paid sixty cents a day for its use. When a trooper lost his horse, because of disease or battle wounds, he had to secure another, which usually meant traveling home to get another horse from the farm. As the war dragged on, it became harder and harder to find serviceable mounts, and this added to the number of cavalrymen absent because of sickness, wounds, or desertion.

In May 1864 the Army of Northern Virginia's cavalry was further enlarged organizationally into three divisions, with William Henry Fitzhugh Lee becoming the new major general. After Stuart was killed at Yellow Tavern in May 1864, Hampton was given command of the cavalry corps and Matthew Calbraith Butler was promoted to take Hampton's place in command of one of the divisions. By mid-1864 the number of cavalry had begun to decline. Of an aggregate of 14,418 in November, only 6,051 were present for duty, and 1,224 were dismounted. By the time of the surrender at Appomattox in April 1865, the cavalry numbered 134 officers and 1,425 enlisted men. It must be remembered, though, that a large portion of the Army of Northern Virginia's cavalry escaped from Appomattox to Lynchburg, some disbanding and riding home, others traveling south to continue the war in the Carolinas with Joseph E. Johnston's Army of Tennessee.

In 1862, the Army of Tennessee's four brigades comprised sixteen regiments in all. By January the next year, Wheeler's division numbered 8,300 men present for duty. In March a true cavalry corps was created for the Army of Tennessee when Wheeler's force was divided into three divisions under Morgan, Wharton, and William Thompson Martin. Each division had at least two brigades (Morgan's had three), with each brigade composed of two to five regiments. The corps' total strength was 6,872 men present for duty from an aggregate of 13,820. Forrest's division had two brigades of four and five regiments. By late 1863 Wheeler's troopers numbered 11,700 present of 28,000 on the rolls. In March 1865 this tally had dropped to 5,105 cavalrymen present of 7,042 on the rolls. On April 26, 1865, 175 officers and 2,331 enlisted men were paroled at Greensborough, North Carolina, when the Army of Tennessee surrendered.

Tactics

In addition to its initial superior organization, the Confederate cavalry's early ascendency over its Federal opponent stemmed from the less dogmatic approach its commanders took to the employment of mounted forces. Prior to the war, many of the future commanders of both North and South had been trained at West Point and Jefferson, and later Carlisle, Barracks. Their cavalry training revolved around Napoleon's maxims of war and the theories expounded by Henri de Jomini. These two Europeans believed that cavalry served a specific purpose on the battlefield as a supporting arm to the infantry and that its role within the army was limited. Basically, they thought that the cavalry was best suited for scouting, covering the army's flanks and rear, and charging infantry formations (but only after the main infantry attack) to ensure victory and cause confusion during the enemy's retreat. It was believed that cavalry could not act alone, either offensively or defensively, and that when in action cavalry should rely on the saber. These theories were mirrored in the doctrine and tactics taught within the U.S. Army prior to the Civil War.

The tactics that evolved from these theories were used throughout the war by the Confederate cavalry. At Manassas, independent companies like the famed "Black Horse Troop" of Warrenton and regiments of cavalry were used to seal the Southern victory by pursuing the retreating Federals across Stone Bridge, down the Warrenton Pike, to Centreville, and beyond. Throughout the war the Army of Northern Virginia and the Army of Tennessee used cavalry to scout the enemy's position and determine the intentions of the Union armies, both prior to Southern offensives and during the campaigns. Stuart's cavalry did an excellent job in covering Lee's flanks when the Army of Northern Virginia was marching south to the Rappahannock line in October 1862 after the Sharpsburg campaign. Stuart screened Lee's movements again when the Confederate army marched north on its way to Gettysburg in June 1863.

The cavalry was also used to control the area between the armies and to keep the Southern generals informed about Federal movements, intentions, and positions. In early 1861, prior to First Manassas, Stuart's horsemen did an excellent job of keeping Robert Paterson's Union force in the Shenandoah Valley from knowing the exact whereabouts of Joseph E. Johnston's army until after it had reached Manassas. After Manassas Stuart set up a line of outposts along the Potomac River to keep Johnston informed of enemy movements before him.

In April and May 1862, the Southern cavalry on the peninsula did another good job of keeping tabs on the Federals around Yorktown and covering John B. Magruder's withdrawal to Williamsburg. Throughout the war, whether along the Potomac, Rappahannock, Rapidan, or elsewhere, the Southern cavalry was used to cover the army's front by keeping tabs on the enemy before it, countering any Federal scouting raids, and warning of any major buildups that might signal an attack.

Throughout the war both Stuart's cavalry in Virginia and Wheeler's cavalry in the West were used to obtain supplies for their respective armies. This included everything from wagons, horses, and mules to uniforms, tents, money, and arms—horses and arms probably being the most important.

The charging of infantry formations by cavalry, in the traditional mounted attack was exemplified by Jubal Early's use of his cavalry at Fisher's Hill on October 18, 1864. As dawn broke, the Confederate cavalry, positioned prior to sunrise on the Federal right flank, stormed into Sheridan's encampment, driving the men out of their camp and back beyond Middletown. After Sheridan's successful counterattack, Early's cavalry covered the army's retreat by holding the pur-

> **Prior to 1862 it would have been thought foolish, and potentially disastrous, to send an army's cavalry force into enemy territory alone.**

suing Federals at bay while the infantry moved up the road and past key road and river crossings. From mid-March 1865 until Lee surrendered at Appomattox, covering the Army of Northern Virginia's rear was a full-time job for the cavalry as Grant relentlessly pushed Lee westward. This last campaign saw the Confederate cavalry mix mounted fighting with dismounted rearguard action to protect Lee's wagon trains and infantry formations from being surrounded and cut off.

Cavalry Raids. The most notable change in the use of cavalry, inaugurated by Stuart, was the large-scale mounted raid. Prior to 1862 it would have been thought foolish, and potentially disastrous, to send an army's cavalry force into enemy territory alone. But Stuart's "Ride around McClellan" in June 1862 changed that perception. Taking 1,200 men, Stuart covered 150 miles behind George B. McClellan's army to reconnoiter the Federal right flank and rear. By destroying considerable amounts of stores and capturing prisoners (with very little Confederate loss), Stuart changed the role of cavalry in this American war and established Confederate pre-eminence, at least until the Federals learned from their mistakes. During 1862 Stuart undertook three more raids, Forrest went on two, and Morgan conducted three.

Other famous raids by Stuart included assaults on Catlett's Station (August 22–23, 1862), Chambersburg (October 9–12, 1862), and Dumfries (December 26–31, 1862). During the raid on Catlett's Station, Stuart took 1,500 men to capture John Pope's headquarters. Besides destroying Federal stores, Stuart seized a large amount of money as well as Pope's papers, which gave Lee the information he needed to undertake the Second Manassas campaign. For Chambersburg, Stuart led 1,800 men into Pennsylvania to destroy machine shops and stores in the city and to round up about a thousand horses badly needed by the Army of Northern Virginia. The Dumfries raid was the fourth of a series of excursions against Ambrose Burnside's rear during

November and December 1862. Stuart and 1,800 troopers destroyed a large amount of property, capturing prisoners, horses, wagons, and arms. But in July 1863 Stuart undertook his disastrous Gettysburg raid. This time he went too far afield with his force, and instead of gaining intelligence for Lee or securing supplies in a quick strike, he got bogged down with his booty and effectively took himself out of the Gettysburg campaign.

Forrest led 1,000 men in July 1862 on his first raid and captured 1,000 Federals at Murfreesboro along with a million dollars worth of stores, destroying important railroad bridges along the way. This action delayed a planned Federal offensive and forced two Union divisions to be diverted from the front to guard the rail lines of the rear. Forrest's second raid, in December 1862, was aimed at the rail line connecting Grant's headquarters at Columbus, Kentucky, and Federal troops in northern Mississippi. Forrest's 2,500 men tore up the Mobile and Ohio Railroad during this foray.

In Morgan's first raid, in July 1862, 800 troopers captured 1,200 prisoners and a number of Federal depots while covering one thousand miles. This raid lowered Northern morale and delayed another planned Federal offensive. Morgan's October 1862 raid against Lexington, Kentucky, involved 1,800 men and resulted in the capture of a number of posts and the destruction of several key railroad bridges. In December 1862 he conducted a raid at the head of 4,000 men; they netted 1,800 prisoners and destroyed $2 million worth of Federal stores. But as had Stuart's raid at Gettysburg, Morgan's July 1863 Ohio raid ended in disaster. His force of 2,400 endured terrible fighting and covered a very long distance before surrendering at New Lisbon (Beaver Creek) on July 26. This failure, too, was the result of a mounted force being gone too long and too far from its main army, thus encountering stronger opposition and critical delays.

The tactic had been proven time and again: an independent body of cavalry could cover long distances in the enemy's rear, capturing stores and prisoners, gathering intelligence, and destroying vital supplies and lines of communication—if it were done quickly and with a force large enough to counter any opposition it might meet. These operations also forced the enemy to dedicate front-line troops to guard the rear from other mounted raiders or guerrilla forces, thus making the cavalry a force multiplier. The success of these raids, then, rested on several factors: the raiders had to be heavily armed (to defeat any opposition encountered); they had to be familiar with the terrain to be traversed; the operation had to be kept secret; and the force had to keep moving at all times.

Raiding continued as a main operation of the Confederate cavalry into the middle years of the war. But after Gettysburg, its usefulness began to ebb. This was due, in part, to the fact that the Federal cavalry had begun to operate as the

Confederates had all along—in large, independent bodies moving offensively and not just in reaction to Southern thrusts.

At the Battle of Brandy Station, the largest mounted clash of the war (involving some 10,000 cavalry), the Federal horsemen discovered they could ride and fight against Stuart as equals. On the morning of June 9, 1863, Alfred Pleasonton rode out of Fredericksburg and attacked Stuart's force as it guarded the Rappahannock River line. Under cover of a morning haze John Buford surprised William Edmondson ("Grumble") Jones's force and drove them to Brandy Station. At the same time David Gregg pushed Beverly Holcombe Robertson's men from Kelly's Ford. Just as Fleetwood Hill, the site of Stuart's headquarters, was about to be overrun by the Federals, Wade Hampton arrived and counterattacked, driving the Union force from the battlefield. Though Pleasonton retreated from the field, he had accomplished much. He had learned that Lee was moving north, he had surprised and humiliated the seemingly invincible Stuart, and he had shown his men that the Southern cavalry could be bested. As historian H. B. McClellan wrote, "It made the Federal cavalry. Up to that time confessedly inferior to the Southern horsemen, they gained . . . that confidence in themselves and in their commanders which enabled them to contest" the Southern cavalry from then on. By the time of the Gettysburg campaign, the Federal cavalry was gaining experience, its leaders were becoming bolder, its mounts were improving, and its equipment, superior to the Confederate arms, was at last plentiful. In addition, the numbers of Federal cavalry were growing.

Dismounted Fighting. The third important innovation that developed during the war was the large-scale use of dismounted cavalry in battle. By 1864, the Confederates were outnumbered and outgunned by the Federals. Confederate mounts were degenerating in both quality and quantity, and the cavalry could no longer attack en masse Federal cavalry formations—their numbers were too large. Nor could the Confederates ride with impunity around the Federal flanks and through the rear area, for the Southern horses were not up to such arduous tasks. As the Confederate army began to fight an almost exclusively defensive war, the chances to use the mounted arm in offensive charges or to follow up a victory with a mounted pursuit diminished—thus the turn to fighting as mounted *infantry.* Like brigading the cavalry and raiding, this innovation was eventually copied by the Federals.

One of the best examples of dismounted cavalry tactics was the role played by Stuart's cavalry in the Battle of the Wilderness in May 1864. The Federal army, under Grant, threw 127,000 troops, 21,000 of which were cavalry commanded by Sheridan, into this campaign. Lee's Army of Northern Virginia was composed of only 54,000 infantry and 9,000 cavalry, and the disadvantage in numbers had to be compensated for somehow. On May 5 Stuart's cavalry rode to Todd's Tavern, where they encountered Federal cavalry coming up a road. Here the Confederates dismounted and held the enemy in check until dark, fighting like infantry. The next day saw similar action near the intersection of the Catharpin and Brock roads. One Confederate diary entry reads, "Our regiment was moved to the front and dismounted to fight." Sheridan then moved his cavalry to Spotsylvania Court House, where Fitz Lee's men had ridden, dismounted, and erected barricades behind which to fight. This action allowed Lee to rush Anderson's corps to the crossroads and secure the Army of Northern Virginia's flank. The ability of Stuart's cavalry to move quickly to a strategic point, dismount, and hold the ground until rein-

> **"To charge into woods with the saber against . . . dismounted cavalry requires high courage, and is against immense odds."**

forcements arrived gave Lee the time he needed to move up a heavier force. The fighting continued on May 8 with the cavalrymen felling trees and building barricades to block the road. As one trooper wrote, "We boys of the cavalry were not much on using spades and shovels, but could use axes very well. We . . . cut down a long line of trees . . . and these made a pretty good obstruction to fight behind." By midmorning Lee's infantry had arrived and replaced the cavalry in the rifle pits.

This was the first battle in which the Confederate cavalry fought almost exclusively as infantry, but it was not to be the last. During Early's 1864 Shenandoah Valley campaign, dismounted cavalry was used extensively to slow the pursuit of Sheridan's Federal horsemen. Early's cavalry would fall back to important gaps or crossroads, dismount, and build barricades from which they were able to delay the Union forces. Prominent use was made of dismounted cavalry at Front Royal on September 20, Milford on September 22, and Luray on September 24.

Though true cavalry clashes did occur throughout 1864, dismounted fighting began to occupy more and more of the cavalry's time in battle, and it was the Confederates who adopted the practice first. In late 1863, the colonel of the First Vermont Cavalry ordered his men to charge a dismounted Confederate force in a tree line. His report stated, "To charge into woods with the saber against . . . dismounted cavalry requires high courage, and is against immense odds." The Federals' adherence in the beginning to the traditional European manner of cavalry fighting—mounted with saber in hand—derived, in part, from the philosophical outlook of

Union officers, particularly George B. McClellan who had studied and reported on European mounted training and tactics prior to the war. The Federals emphasized that the strength of the cavalry lay in its spurs and sabers and neglected to train its men in the tactics and weapons of dismounted combat. Their fondness for the saber caused them to be slow to adopt new tactics for fighting. Only after the Confederates used them to their advantage did the Federals follow suit. By war's end, though, after Union cavalrymen had learned to ride into battle, dismount, and fight on foot, the Federals again bested their Confederate adversary. They could put more men with greater firepower (because of their breech-loading repeating carbines) into the battle at a given time. Once again, the Federals had learned from the Confederates and gained the advantage.

Throughout the war, however, the Confederate cavalry was held in awe for its ability to strike quickly and deeply into enemy territory. After the fighting in the Wilderness, the infantry in the Army of Northern Virginia no longer joked about "never having seen a dead cavalryman." As one Southern artilleryman wrote, the Confederate cavalry "had shown itself signally possessed of the quality, that the infantry and artillery naturally admired most . . . obstinacy in fight." The Confederate cavalry became a major player in the army's campaigns. Its place in the history books was assured for the depth it added to the mounted arm.

[*See also* Beefsteak Raid; Brandy's Station, Virginia; Chambersburg, Pennsylvania; Early's Washington Raid; Forrest's Raids; Front Royal, Virginia; Gettysburg Campaign; Horses and Mules; Morgan's Raids; Price's Missouri Raid; Shenandoah Valley, *article on* Shenandoah Valley Campaign of Sheridan; Stoneman's Raids; Stuart's Raids; Wheeler's Raids; Wilderness Campaign; *and biographies of numerous figures mentioned herein.*]

BIBLIOGRAPHY

Averell, William Woods. *Ten Years in the Saddle: The Memoirs of William Woods Averell.* San Rafael, Calif., 1978.

Longacre, Edward G. *The Cavalry at Gettysburg.* Rutherford, N.J., 1986.

Starr, Stephen Z. *The Union Cavalry in the Civil War.* 3 vols. Baton Rouge, 1979.

Stiles, Kenneth Lamarr. "The Evolving Tactics of the 4th Virginia Cavalry: A Study of the Adaptability of Stuart's Cavalry, 1861–1865." M.A. thesis, Old Dominion University, 1988.

Sheridan, P. H. *Personal Memoirs of P. H. Sheridan.* 2 vols. New York, 1888.

Thomas, Emory M. *Bold Dragoon: The Life of J. E. B. Stuart.* New York, 1988.

Wyeth, John Allan. *That Devil Forrest: Life of General Nathan Bedford Forrest.* New York, 1899. Reprint, New York, 1959.

Young, Bennett H. *Confederate Wizards of the Saddle.* Boston, 1914.

KENNETH L. STILES

CEDAR CREEK, VIRGINIA

Ten miles south of Winchester, Virginia, Cedar Creek was the site of an October 19, 1864, battle that witnessed the destruction of Maj. Gen. Jubal Early's Army of the Valley. Never again would the Confederacy draw provisions from the Shenandoah Valley. Southern casualties amounted to around 2,900 men killed, wounded, or missing; the Federals lost 5,665.

Confederate debacles at Third Winchester (September 19) and Fisher's Hill (September 22) swept Early's troops from the lower Valley and allowed Maj. Gen. Philip Sheridan to lay waste to the region. When the Union army retreated, Early followed, arriving at Strasburg on October 13. A few miles to the north on the hills above Cedar Creek stood Sheridan's Army of the Shenandoah.

Early desired offensive action but realized that without reinforcements and supplies he had little hope of achieving a decisive victory. Gen. Robert E. Lee was not of the same mind. Discounting reports that had placed Sheridan's army at 35,000 to 40,000 men, Lee grossly underestimated the enemy's strength. He demanded that Early take his 10,000 rifles and "move against" Sheridan.

On October 17, Early sent Maj. Gen. John B. Gordon and Jedediah Hotchkiss, topographical engineer, to Massanutten Mountain. They discovered that the left flank of Sheridan's army was not prepared to resist a sudden assault. The Union Eighth Corps had encamped east of the Valley Turnpike while the Sixth and Ninth Corps had bivouacked west of the road and around the mansion Belle Grove.

Conferring with his subordinates the next day, Early approved one of the most audacious flanking maneuvers of the entire war. It called for Gordon to take three divisions— those of Brig. Gen. John Pegram, Maj. Gen. Dodson Ramseur, and Brig. Gen. Clement A. Evans—across the north fork of the Shenandoah at Fisher's Hill, skirt the end of Massanutten, cross the river again, and then form for an assault against the eastern flank of the camp of the Eighth Corps. Maj. Gen. Joseph B. Kershaw's division was ordered to move through Strasburg, cross Cedar Creek at Bowman's Mill, and coordinate his attack with Gordon. The remaining infantry division, commanded by Brig. Gen. Gabriel Colvin Wharton, would advance down the Valley Pike in a supporting role while Brig. Gen. Thomas Lafayette Rosser's horsemen were to protect Early's left flank.

Gordon's column moved out at 8:00 P.M. on October 18, stumbling across a mountain trail that resembled "a pig's path." Because victory depended on surprise, the soldiers removed equipment that might create noise and alert the enemy's pickets. After fording the Shenandoah for a second time, they went into position a half-mile east of the enemy's camp, just before 5:00 in the morning. Forty-five minutes later, concealed by a heavy fog, Gordon's troops and Kershaw's division stormed the Union camps. For the next three hours the Confederates drove the Eighth and Nineteenth Corps toward Middletown. Confident that he had attained a remarkable victory, Early told Gordon, "This is glory enough for one day." His soldiers had bagged eighteen pieces of artillery and 1,300 prisoners.

The Federals had formed a final defensive line three miles north of their camps. By 10:00 Early had edged his way toward the enemy, but the momentum of the Confederate assault had disappeared. Early believed that "it would not do to press my troops further." His men were exhausted and the famished soldiers abandoned the ranks to plunder Northern camps.

Away from his men when the fighting erupted, Sheridan had rushed to the scene where he massed his cavalry against Early's left flank. At 3:30 his troopers pounced on the exposed position. Up and down the line echoed the cry, "We are flanked," as the Confederates fell back in disorder. While trying to restore calm in his command, Ramseur, the youngest West Pointer to achieve the rank of major general in the Confederacy, received a mortal wound.

Early's army retreated to Fisher's Hill where the general bitterly remarked, "The Yankees got whipped and we got scared." Although his subordinates had flawlessly executed his plan, Early did not have sufficient numbers to compensate for surrendering the initiative to Sheridan. Defeat at Cedar Creek eliminated the Army of the Valley as an effective fighting force for the rest of the war. While Early headed south with his battered army, the morale of the Northern people soared. Together with the capture of Atlanta and Mobile Bay, Sheridan's triumphs in the Valley ensured Abraham Lincoln's victory in the presidential elections that November.

BIBLIOGRAPHY

Gallagher, Gary W., ed. *Struggle for the Shenandoah: Essays on the 1864 Valley Campaign.* Kent, Ohio, 1991.
Wert, Jeffry D. *From Winchester to Cedar Creek: The Shenandoah Campaign of 1864.* Carlisle, Pa., 1987.

PETER S. CARMICHAEL

CEDAR MOUNTAIN, VIRGINIA

This landmark in southern Culpeper County dominated the battlefield where Thomas J. ("Stonewall") Jackson fought a battle on August 9, 1862, that climaxed his last independent campaign. The fragmented Federal command in Virginia during August 1862 dictated Confederate strategy that led to the Battle of Cedar Mountain on the ninth and to Second Manassas at the end of the month. Robert E. Lee, recently victorious in the Seven Days' Battles, sent Jackson north to the vicinity of Gordonsville at the end of July to face the threat posed by a new Federal general, John Pope. Pope's strident anticivilian orders irritated Lee, who wrote to Jackson, "I want Pope to be suppressed." Lee referred to the Federal general with unaccustomed venom as "the miscreant Pope." While Gen. George B. McClellan's defeated army remained in the vicinity of Richmond, Jackson would head

> The first arrivals helped stitch together the . . . broken line; then more brigades wrested the initiative from the Federals.

north alone against Pope. When McClellan's army abandoned the Richmond line and headed back to the environs of Washington, Lee would go to join Jackson. The Southern strategy worked: Jackson trounced Pope at Cedar Mountain, and then Lee and Jackson together defeated Pope's army at Second Manassas as it was drawing major reinforcements from McClellan's returning troops.

Jackson started his army north from Orange County on August 7, but it made negligible progress because of intense heat and dust, and as a result of the commanding general's stubborn unwillingness to discuss details with subordinates. Confusion over terse marching orders on this day led to a bitter controversy between Jackson and A. P. Hill that persisted while both lived. Jackson's highest-ranking subordinate insisted, "I do not know whether we will march north, south, east, or west, or whether we will march at all." The army moved somewhat more smoothly on August 8, pushing through a corner of Madison County into Culpeper County, but even so the next morning a disconsolate Jackson telegraphed to Lee, "I am not making much progress."

On August 9, near noon, the head of Jackson's column came upon a Federal advance guard in the valley of Cedar Run, beneath the imposing bulk of a steep-sided ridge known as Cedar Mountain or—ominously—as Slaughter Mountain. There, on the farms of the Crittenden and Slaughter families, Jackson fought a meeting engagement with Federals under Gen. Nathaniel P. Banks, who commanded the advance elements of Pope's army. The contending forces reached the field piecemeal, many arriving after darkness ended serious fighting, but by the time of the late-afternoon climax Jackson had about twenty thousand men at his disposal and the Federals had fewer than fifteen thousand. The battle unfolded in searing heat of about 100°, making August 9 the hottest day on which major combat occurred in the Virginia theater during the war.

Confederate infantry opened the battle by driving Northern cavalry away from a position near the Crittenden house. Southern artillery reached the shoulder of Cedar Mountain after tremendous exertion. From there they dominated a large part of the field and afforded Jackson an impregnable right anchor for his position. While their troops filed into a haphazard and misshapen line without adequate high-level supervision, Jackson and Gen. Charles S. Winder supervised the Confederate half of an artillery duel that raged for more than an hour. Winder fell mortally wounded by a shell. Soon thereafter a small Federal attack force surged across a wide wheat field near the Confederate left under orders to drive away the Southern cannon in that quarter. Although Banks had no idea of the strength or positions of his opponents and sent far too few troops for the circumstances, the attackers fell upon a seam in the Confederate line and tore it apart. The three and a half Northern regiments rolled southward through Jackson's position, wreaking havoc as they flanked one unit after another.

The Federal advance nearly captured Stonewall Jackson himself. The Confederate general desperately sought to rally the shattered ranks of his nearest units, shouting to them to support him and waving a battle flag in one hand and his sword and scabbard in the other. Jackson's wife later wrote that her husband considered Cedar Mountain "the most successful of his exploits." He must have based that feeling on his personal involvement, with adrenaline surging through his veins as bullets flew past from three directions, because August 9 did not develop tactically as a masterpiece.

Jackson's personal efforts rallied many of his soldiers, but the tide turned in his favor primarily on the basis of substantial reinforcements who arrived quickly from Hill's division. The first arrivals helped stitch together the tattered and broken line; then more brigades wrested the initiative from the Federals and charged back through the wheat field to win the day. A battalion of the First Pennsylvania Cavalry galloped into the teeth of the Southern position in a forlorn attempt to stem the onslaught, but as darkness descended, Jackson's troops were advancing on every corner of the field.

During the night Federals arrived in great strength opposite Jackson. When a Confederate battery that pushed well to the front took a dreadful beating from several enemy artillery units, Jackson halted and consolidated his gains on what had been the initial Union position before the battle. He had lost about 1,400 casualties and inflicted about 2,600 on his foe.

On August 10 and 11 the two armies faced each other without renewing the serious fighting. The Confederates fell back into Orange County on the night of the eleventh. Jackson had achieved his purpose by blunting Pope's initia-

tive in north-central Virginia, defeating an exposed portion of the Federal army, and buying time for Lee to break away from Richmond in order to head for a junction with him. When Lee arrived the following week, he and Jackson collaborated on one of their most dazzling tactical ventures in the Second Manassas campaign.

BIBLIOGRAPHY

Allan, William. *The Army of Northern Virginia in 1862.* Boston, 1892. Reprint, Dayton, Ohio, 1984.
Grimsley, Daniel A. *Battles in Culpeper County.* Culpeper, Va., 1900.
Krick, Robert K. *Stonewall Jackson at Cedar Mountain.* Chapel Hill, N.C., 1990.

ROBERT K. KRICK

CENSORSHIP

The Union needed no spies because Confederate newspapers told everything there was "to be told," according to Mary Boykin Chesnut. Her observation describes the surprising degree of freedom of the press under a fledgling government that permitted almost absolute freedom of editorial expression and made diligent but often ineffective attempts to suppress vital military news. Most Southern editors exercised extreme discretion in what they published and engaged in an informal and voluntary censorship. Others, however, insisted on their right to publish anything. This included scathing attacks on elected officials and military commanders, criticisms of military strategy and government policies, and even sensitive military information. Nevertheless, the Richmond government, unlike its Union counterpart, never shut down a newspaper.

In his inaugural address, President Jefferson Davis stressed his administration's support for the constitutional guarantee of freedom of the press. Secretary of War George Wythe Randolph echoed this sentiment in 1862 when he expressed his hope that the war could be won without the suppression of a single newspaper. Taking advantage of the virtual immunity from interference, some Confederate papers, led by the *Charleston Mercury* and *Richmond Examiner,* subjected Davis, his cabinet, congressmen, and various military leaders to an unrestrained chorus of criticism, invective, and abuse. In response to the *Examiner*'s bitter denunciations, Judah P. Benjamin endeavored to have the newspaper closed down but failed to secure the support of the administration. Likewise, Speaker of the House Thomas S. Bocock, another victim of the *Examiner*'s intemperate remarks, urged the paper's destruction, but to no avail. Nathaniel Morse's *Augusta Chronicle* and the Unionist William W. Holden's *Raleigh Standard* consistently took what many regarded as treasonous editorial lines, yet the government never intervened. When some irate Georgia soldiers passing through Raleigh attacked the offices of the *Standard,* North Carolina Governor Zebulon Vance acted quickly to prevent the complete destruction of the paper's equipment. A rare instance of actual newspaper suppression occurred when Tennessee authorities arrested William G. ("Parson") Brownlow for treason and suspended publication of his *Knoxville Whig.* The Davis administration, however, pressured state officials to release the outspoken editor on condition that he agree to leave the South.

In 1863 the Judiciary Committee introduced into the Senate a sedition bill that would have curtailed freedom of expression and of the press, but it failed to pass. It was not until January 29, 1864, that the House, provoked by the increased frequency of press attacks on the government, approved a bill creating a Department of Inspection and Censorship. In the same year, however, Davis failed to obtain legislation that would have provided greatly strengthened government control over the press.

While strongly advocating freedom of expression, the government attempted to restrict access to sensitive military information. Congress excluded reporters from its sessions dealing with military matters and in the spring of 1861 passed laws giving the administration authority to control information sent over the telegraph and through the mail. Although censorship of mail dispatches occurred infrequently, government agents in telegraph offices, War Department officials, and army commanders were more zealous in suppressing military news.

The War Department, which initially relied on the cooperation and discretion of correspondents and their editors, gradually tightened its restrictions. Early on, Secretary of War Leroy P. Walker permitted reporters in the army camps on condition that they not report on troop dispositions, movements, and strengths. But in January 1862, the Army of the Potomac banished all correspondents, and the Confederate Congress made the publication of any news about disposition, movements, or numbers of army and naval forces a crime. Subsequently, reporters had to submit telegraphic dispatches to military authorities who frequently suppressed material they considered damaging. Army leaders, exercising virtually complete control over correspondents in their commands, not only reserved the right to dictate what was reported by telegraph but went so far as to exclude correspondents from their camps.

Gen. Braxton Bragg became notorious for his antagonism toward the press. In April 1861, during operations against Fort Pickens, Bragg had L. H. Mathews of the *Pensacola Observer* arrested for publishing information that supposedly jeopardized military security. Bragg frequently ordered censorship of telegraph reports; and when a Henry Watterson editorial critical of Bragg appeared in the *Chattanooga Rebel,* the general banned the newspaper

from his lines. In September 1863, John Linebaugh of the *Memphis Appeal* was arrested for treason. The grounds for the charge, never clear and subsequently dropped, may have been that he had filed a report concerning troop movements, but the charge may have been provoked by Linebaugh's criticisms of Bragg.

Other Confederate generals hostile to correspondents were Earl Van Dorn, Joseph E. Johnston, P. G. T. Beauregard, John Bell Hood, the always secretive Thomas J. ("Stonewall") Jackson, and Robert E. Lee. In July 1862, Van Dorn ordered fines or imprisonment for correspondents who wrote anything about troop movements or that undermined public confidence in commanding officers. Public and congressional protests, however, prevented Van Dorn from strictly enforcing the order. A report filed by the *Richmond Dispatch*'s William Shepardson in December 1861 so incensed Johnston that he banned correspondents from his

> **Military authorities . . . frequently suppressed material they considered damaging.**

command. And in 1864 as Johnston retreated across Georgia, military authorities censored all press dispatches from his army.

Official battle reports required presidential approval before publication, and Beauregard became the center of a mild controversy when a synopsis of his report of First Manassas appeared in the *Richmond Dispatch* without President Davis's authorization. While near Corinth, Mississippi, in May 1862, Beauregard ordered that all correspondents be shipped out on the first available train. Hood had a correspondent with him in Alabama during the fall of 1864 but refused to allow him to send telegraphic reports. The plainspoken Jackson openly expressed his contempt for newsmen. Military censors tried to limit news reports during the Seven Days' Battles, and not until Fredericksburg were Richmond newspaper correspondents allowed to accompany the Army of Northern Virginia to a major battle—and then their presence resulted from a bureaucratic error. P. W. Alexander, the South's most reliable reporter, however, found himself excluded from Lee's army on the eve of the battle.

Nevertheless, carelessness, lax enforcement, different interpretations of censorship rules, and indiscretions on the part of some journalists resulted in frequent leaks. Many generals believed that the failure to control the press significantly undermined the Confederate war effort. Bragg's defenders charged that the 1863 battles around Chattanooga had been lost because of newspaper reports. Shortly after the Seven Days' Battles, Lee criticized the *Richmond Dispatch* for revealing the disposition of his forces at the very time the Union army was on his front. In October 1863, Lee wrote Secretary of War James A. Seddon to protest Richmond newspaper accounts about his troop movements, which he claimed added to his difficulties. Lee was convinced that the enemy, having learned of Bragg's movement to Georgia from Savannah newspapers, had launched an attack on Wilmington. And after the war he bristled upon recalling that when James Longstreet went south in the summer of 1863, the newspapers told everything despite his best efforts to keep the matter secret.

What seems clear is that the legal and institutional apparatus to censor military information worked better in theory than in practice. It functioned best when journalists, acutely aware of their patriotic duty and dedicated to the cause, voluntarily exercised restraint in reporting on vital military matters.

[*See also* Habeas Corpus; Newspapers.]

BIBLIOGRAPHY

Andrews, J. Cutler. *The South Reports the Civil War*. Princeton, N.J., 1970.
Mathis, Robert Neil. "Freedom of the Press in the Confederacy: A Reality." *Historian* 37 (1975): 633–648.
Randall, James G. "The Newspaper Problem in Its Bearing upon Military Secrecy during the Civil War." *American Historical Review* 33 (January 1918): 303–323.
Towery, Patricia. "Censorship of South Carolina Newspapers, 1861–1865." In *South Carolina Journals and Journalists*. Edited by James B. Meriwether. Spartanburg, S.C., 1975.
Wilson, Quintus Charles. "A Study and Evaluation of Military Censorship in the Civil War." Masters thesis, University of Minnesota, 1945.

CHARLES MCARVER

Chambersburg, Pennsylvania

Chambersburg was the target of two raids by the cavalry of the Army of Northern Virginia, the first in October 1862 and the second in July 1864. J. E. B. Stuart passed through Chambersburg on October 10 and 11 during his second "Ride around McClellan." The Confederates captured and paroled some 300 Federal soldiers and confiscated a large number of horses, muskets, pistols, sabers, and other arms before destroying the rail lines, depot, and shops of the city. This raid also provided Lee with vital information about the Army of the Potomac's disposition and intentions.

The second raid was conducted by a much less disciplined force bent on retribution. In late July 1864, Maj. Gen.

Jubal Early ordered Brig. Gens. John McCausland and Bradley Tyler Johnson to cross the Potomac and ride to Chambersburg. Early wanted the Confederate raiders to take the town and demand a payment of $100,000 in gold or $500,000 in currency as retribution for Federal depredations committed in the Shenandoah Valley by Maj. Gen. John Hunter during the previous month. If the town did not pay the ransom, McCausland was to burn it to the ground.

Leaving their encampment at Martinsburg, McCausland's brigade of five regiments and Johnson's of two regiments and four battalions (a total of 4,000 men), accompanied by six pieces of artillery, crossed the Potomac River at McCoy's Ferry around daylight on July 29. The First and Second Maryland Cavalry units led the column and drove a small force of between 300 and 400 Federals from their front back to Hagerstown. After encountering light opposition throughout the day, the Confederates reached Mercersburg around 5:00 P.M. Here the Thirty-sixth Virginia Battalion drove the Federals out of the town, securing it so the Confederate column could close up and eat. After four hours of rest, McCausland led the men on to Chambersburg, skirmishing most of the way.

At 3:00 A.M. on July 30, the column was checked by Federal forces outside of Chambersburg. After two hours of fighting, the Federals withdrew and the Confederates occupied the fairgrounds outside the city. At 5:30 in the morning, the Twenty-first Virginia was sent into the town with the dismounted Thirty-sixth in support. McCausland entered Chambersburg, arrested the principal citizens and officials, and demanded that $100,000 in gold or $500,000 in currency be handed over under threat of torching the city. When the general was told that no more than $50,000 was available, the horsemen fired the city in fifty places. Some Confederates pillaged the shops and stores before burning the buildings, but others helped citizens evacuate prior to putting the torch to their structures. A number of the cavalrymen did not carry out the order to burn the town, including Col. W. E. Peters of the Twenty-first Virginia who was arrested when he refused to obey (he was later released). Some six thousand citizens lost their homes and the property damage totaled about $1.5 million. The Confederates left the town around noon. About two hours later, a Federal column under W. W. Averell, which had been chasing McCausland, rode into Chambersburg.

The Confederate raiders reached McConnelsburg around 5:00 P.M. and encamped. At sunrise on July 31, McCausland led his raiders to Hancock, which they reached a little after noon. Here the general demanded $30,000 and five thousand cooked rations for his troopers. During that night the men went on to Bevansville where they rested and fed their horses before starting out for Cumberland at sunrise. About 3:30 in the afternoon, the Southerners encountered a Federal force two and a half miles outside of Cumberland.

McCausland, not knowing the size of the Union force or the surrounding countryside, withdrew. By August 2, the raiders had reached Old Town on the Potomac where they captured a Union force after a brief artillery duel. Crossing the Potomac, the Southern raiders rode to Springfield and encamped. From there McCausland took his troopers to Oldfields, near Moorefield, where they rested.

> Somewhere in 1863 the war had changed. It was no longer a duel between gentlemen, but rather it had become more like a street fight. The horrors of total war had become commonplace by 1864.

Meanwhile Averell had crossed the Potomac, and he caught up with the Confederate raiders on August 6. The next day, the Union cavalry attacked McCausland's encampment at dawn, routing the entire force and capturing 27 officers (one of them being Johnson, who later escaped), 393 enlisted men, four artillery pieces, and four hundred horses. Disgusted with the undisciplined actions of the troopers throughout the raid—from stealing and looting to drunkenness and extorting money from the citizens of Chambersburg to spare their homes—Johnson reported, "Thus the grand spectacle of a national retaliation was reduced to a miserable hunkstering for greenbacks." He was also upset because McCausland had not informed him about the distribution of the troops in the encampment at Moorefield—which led to the routing of the brigades—and had not slept with his men, but stayed in town.

The action at Chambersburg was in marked contrast to the mounted raids undertaken earlier in the war. Where the raids of J. E. B. Stuart, Nathan Bedford Forrest, and John Hunt Morgan had tactical or strategic goals such as reconnaissance, disruption of the enemy's rear areas, or the capture of supplies, McCausland's raid was simply an act of revenge. Somewhere in 1863 the war had changed. It was no longer a duel between gentlemen, but rather it had become more like a street fight. The horrors of total war had become commonplace by 1864.

BIBLIOGRAPHY

Cooling, B. F. *Jubal Early's Raid on Washington, 1864.* Baltimore, 1989.

Corson, William Clark. *My Dear Jennie.* Edited by Blake W. Corson, Jr. Richmond, Va., 1982.

McClellan, H. B. *I Rode with Jeb Stuart: The Life and Campaigns of Major-General J. E. B. Stuart, Commander of the Cavalry of the*

Army of Northern Virginia. Richmond, Va., 1885. Reprint, New York, 1968.

KENNETH L. STILES

CHANCELLORSVILLE CAMPAIGN

This country intersection in Spotsylvania County, Virginia, became the focal point of a vast battlefield spread across some fifty square miles, on which Robert E. Lee and Thomas J. ("Stonewall") Jackson collaborated on April 29–May 6, 1863, for their greatest joint victory. Chancellorsville also was Jackson's last battle. His mortal wounding by the mistaken fire of his own men was one of the most important military events of the war.

After its resounding and easy victory in the Battle of Fredericksburg on December 13, 1862, Lee's Army of Northern Virginia spent the winter centered in that vicinity, but with flanks spread more than a dozen miles upstream and twice that far downstream. The Rappahannock River served as the military frontier between the contending countries; the Federal Army of the Potomac remained opposite Lee on the river's left bank. In the aftermath of the aptly named "Mud March" in January, President Abraham Lincoln replaced Ambrose E. Burnside with brash and boastful—but politically well-connected—Joseph Hooker. Hooker revamped his army's support functions, inaugurated an efficient intelligence service, and greatly improved morale. As he planned for spring campaigning, Hooker also produced an outstanding scheme designed to force Lee from the heights behind Fredericksburg that had proved so daunting a few months earlier.

Hooker intended to send his revitalized cavalry arm on a raid deep into the Confederate rear and at the same time to move his army far upriver and surprise Lee by crossing well west of Fredericksburg. The cavalry excursion faltered in attempts to get underway during mid-April as a result of bad weather and the lack of energy of its chief. The raiders finally departed on April 29 and spent a week ricocheting through central Virginia, harassed and controlled by a small Southern mounted detachment while Lee's main cavalry force remained with the army to perform vital screening and reconnaissance duties. A few weeks later during the Gettysburg campaign the same situation prevailed, only in reverse; it was as though the Federals had learned from their experience while the Confederates ignored the lesson they had taught so skillfully at Chancellorsville.

Meanwhile General Hooker put into motion his plan to move upriver to get behind Lee. The march covered consid-

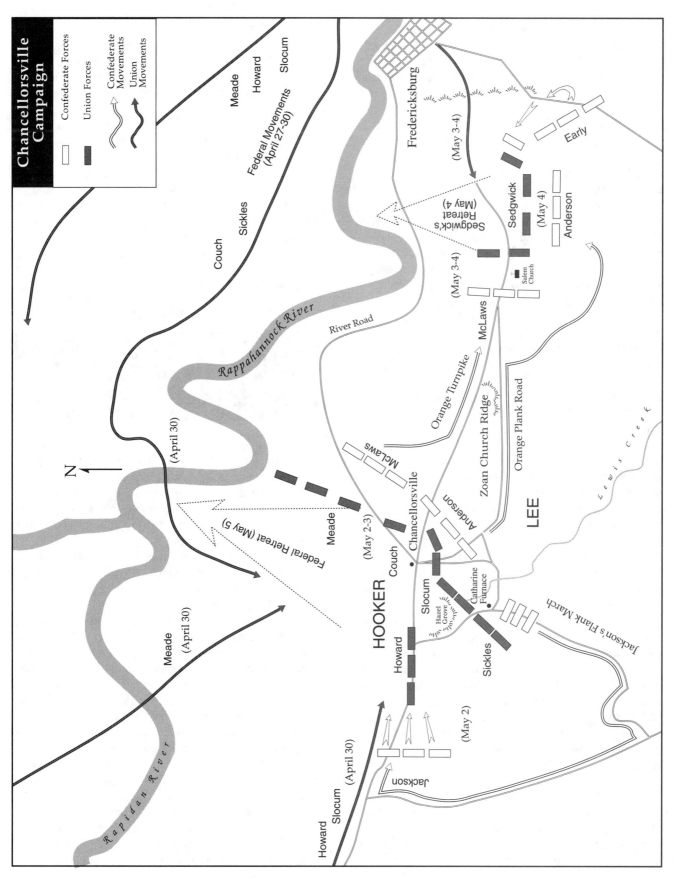

Chancellorsville Campaign

Confederate Forces
Union Forces
Confederate Movements
Union Movements

Federal Movements (April 27-30)

Meade
Howard
Slocum
Couch
Sickles

Rappahannock River

River Road

Rapidan River

N

Meade (April 30)

Meade (April 30)

(April 30)

Federal Retreat (May 5)

Meade

(May 2-3)

Chancellorsville

Couch

Slocum

Howard

Hazel Grove

Catharine Furnace

HOOKER

Sickles

(May 2)

Jackson

Howard
Slocum
(April 30)

Jackson's Flank March

McLaws

Orange Turnpike

Zoan Church Ridge

Orange Plank Road

Anderson

LEE

Lewis Creek

McLaws

(May 3-4)

Salem Church

Sedgwick's Retreat (May 4)

Sedgwick

(May 4)

Anderson

(May 3-4)

Fredericksburg

Early

erable distance and required heavy logistical support, but it succeeded remarkably well. By the end of April 30 Hooker had moved much of his army nearly thirty miles, crossed two rivers by various fords, and concentrated in the densely wooded Wilderness of Spotsylvania around Chancellorsville crossroads. "Chancellorsville" was not a town or even a hamlet, but rather a single building—a half-century-old inn at the intersection of the Orange Turnpike and Orange Plank Road. Hooker was unpopular with most of his high-ranking subordinates for various reasons, but his daring maneuver prompted Gen. George G. Meade to chortle, "Hurrah for old Joe! We're on Lee's flank and he doesn't know it." Hooker clearly was hoping that his coup would force the Confederate army to abandon its position and retire well to the south. He outnumbered Lee by more than two to one, having 130,000 men against 60,000, and could hardly imagine his opponent facing both those odds and the successful opening march by the Army of the Potomac.

By April 30 Lee did know where Hooker was and had boldly determined to gather his own army west of Fredericksburg to fight. The Federals had left a strong detachment feinting toward Fredericksburg, so Lee put Jubal Early in charge of a rear guard to face that threat. He hurried the rest of the Army of Northern Virginia in the direction of Chancellorsville. The few Confederates who had been retiring in the face of Hooker's host held a tenuous grip on the Zoan Church ridge east of Chancellorsville on the morning of May 1 when Lee and Jackson approached with the vanguard of the army. The Zoan ridge was not only strong high ground but also in the open, outside the seventy-square-mile morass known as the Wilderness. In the tangled Wilderness, Hooker would lose much of the advantage of his huge preponderance in numbers, so taking Zoan Church offered him a tremendous opportunity. The campaign turned in that moment when Stonewall Jackson arrived on the scene and ordered the corporal's guard of Confederates on hand to attack. The bravado that had sustained Hooker to this time evaporated in the face of a determined foe. During the rest of the campaign the Federal command story was one of steady spiritual deterioration. There was much talk at the time that Hooker was drunk, but the conventional wisdom soon emerged that he had given up his customary high alcoholic intake on assuming command and that the change had thrown his nervous system out of balance. Some reasonably strong contemporary evidence now available suggests that Hooker may indeed have been in liquor during the campaign.

From the Zoan Church ridge the Confederates pushed Hooker's troops steadily back toward Chancellorsville on May 1. Jackson orchestrated a tangled tactical combination of brigades, assigned in the order they arrived; ignoring divisional lines, they advanced westward on the roughly parallel Plank Road and Turnpike. The Confederates exploited an unfinished railroad grade as a third corridor through the Wilderness. Using that route, the Georgia brigade of Gen. Ambrose Ransom ("Rans") Wright slipped past the Federal right flank and forced it to swing northward nearly ninety degrees. The new configuration would be a central feature of the next day's operations.

At night on May 1 the Confederate high command gathered at a crossroads one mile from Chancellorsville to consider its options. Despite the enormous disparity in manpower that he faced, Lee was determined to assume the offensive. He had reconnoitered personally on his right during the day and found the ground there both heavily defended and nearly impassable. A small party of staff officers scouted through the brightly moonlit night directly toward Chancellorsville and came back to report that no opening offered in that direction. Through the night reports came in from a number of sources—a topographical engineer, a local

> **Darkness and the confusion inherent in the wide-ranging advance stopped Jackson's momentum a mile short of Chancellorsville.**

furnace operator, a Presbyterian clergyman who knew the region, and cavalry officers—suggesting that a way might be found to turn the Federal right. For Lee to move a column across his enemy's front, leaving a very small force as a decoy, violated the basic principles of war. To take such a risk when outnumbered more than two to one went beyond that to the verge of folly. Lee decided to go ahead.

When Jackson headed into the Wilderness early on May 2, he took some thirty thousand men with him, leaving Lee only about fifteen thousand with whom to face Hooker. For ten hours Lee feigned attacks and threw forward entire regiments as skirmishers responsible for scouting and screening the line. Tactical doctrine suggested that one or at most two of the ten companies in a regiment should provide a skirmish force in front of the main line of defense. At times Lee had no main line, just skirmishers. While Lee played his desperate game, Stonewall Jackson marched on a long looping route across Hooker's front and toward his right flank. Less than a mile into the march Jackson's men had to cross a high open spot that exposed them to Federal view. They double-timed through the ensuing artillery barrage and continued on their way. Aggressive Federal Gen. Daniel E. Sickles pushed infantry southward to interdict the Confederate movement. The Northern probe clashed with a rear guard near Catharine Furnace but did not deflect Jackson from his purpose.

Jackson rode near the head of his long column as it neared the point at which he and Lee had planned that the attackers should turn toward the enemy. He soon found that the Federal line stretched farther west than had been assumed; carrying through the original intention would not prove very effective. To meet this changed situation, Jackson marched farther north before turning east. Early in the afternoon his advance brigades arrived on a high wooded ridge that overlooked the unprotected right flank of the Union army. Hard marching and careful planning and daring had presented Jackson with one of the great opportunities of the war. As his brigades arrived, Jackson arranged them into a mighty attacking force two miles long, straddling the Orange Turnpike and overlapping the Federal line by a mile on each side. When two divisions had arrived, Jackson nodded to division commander Robert Rodes and said quietly, "You can go forward then."

The Confederates pouring out of the woods and screaming the rebel yell routed Federal Gen. O. O. Howard's Eleventh Corps and smashed two miles through the enemy positions. The bravest Northern defender could not stand long against a force that overlapped him on both sides as far as he could see. Flagrant disobedience of attack orders by Confederate Gen. Alfred H. Colquitt neutralized fully 40 percent of Jackson's line, but the rest surged irresistibly forward. The Federal position next beyond Howard's belonged to Sickles's troops, but most of them had marched south to investigate around Catharine Furnace, so Howard's retreat roared unchecked through the vacuum. For the rest of his life Hooker blamed Howard for the disaster (soon after the war he called Howard a "hypocrite . . . totally incompetent . . . a perfect old woman . . . a bad man"). In fact, no force of any sort could have faced successfully so massive a surprise attack in flank and rear.

Darkness and the confusion inherent in the wide-ranging advance stopped Jackson's momentum a mile short of Chancellorsville. As the general returned from a mounted reconnaissance beyond his amorphous front line at about 9:00 P.M., Confederates of the Eighteenth North Carolina Infantry fired in confusion on his party and wounded Jackson in three places. Early the next morning surgeons amputated his shattered left arm in a field hospital tent.

Cavalry Gen. J. E. B. Stuart assumed temporary command of Jackson's corps during the night of May 2–3 and prepared to drive the Federals from Chancellorsville. Southern artillerists identified an open knoll called Hazel Grove as the key to the battlefield, and Stuart prepared to seize it at dawn. Before Stuart could take Hazel Grove, Joe Hooker abandoned it. Confederate guns hurried to the hilltop and opened a steady fire that did much to win the day. Bitter and terribly confused woods fighting on May 3 between Hazel Grove and Chancellorsville exacted more casualties than had the dramatic actions of May 2, but in impenetrable obscurity. A knowledgeable Confederate officer who later wrote of the battle concluded resignedly, "It would be useless to follow in detail the desperate fighting which now ensued and was kept up for some hours." Its net result was gradual establishment of Confederate control around Chancellorsville. When Lee rode into the clearing around the house with his reunited army, the troops hailed him with a celebration so long and heartfelt that a staff officer wrote, "I thought that it must have been from such a scene that men in ancient days rose to the dignity of gods."

Lee's moment of triumph was interrupted when word arrived from near Fredericksburg that Early's rear guard had been penetrated by a Federal force under Gen. John Sedgwick. Lee suspended operations around Chancellorsville and sent reinforcements eastward under Gen. Lafayette McLaws. Near Salem Church, four miles west of Fredericksburg, part of the rear guard brought the Federals to a halt. McLaws handled his role poorly, and Lee went to the area in person on May 4 to arrange the attack that pushed Sedgwick back across the river during the night. The next night Hooker abandoned his position north of Chancellorsville and returned to the left bank of the Rappahannock, ending the campaign. Lee had suffered about thirteen thousand casualties; Hooker, eighteen thousand. The astonishing Confederate triumph under adverse circumstances is often, and aptly, called Lee's greatest victory, but its final act constituted a Southern disaster unequaled during the entire war. On May 10 Stonewall Jackson died at Guiney Station, south of Fredericksburg, removing what might have been the South's best hope for independence by military means.

The spectacular opening of the 1863 campaign at Chancellorsville presented Lee with an opportunity to raid north of the Potomac. He and his army, full of almost unlimited confidence in one another, carried their Chancellorsville momentum into Pennsylvania, but found a strikingly different set of circumstances at Gettysburg. There the ultimate consequence of Chancellorsville became apparent at a time "when every moment . . . could not be balanced with gold," in the words of a Confederate staff officer, who could only mutter sadly, "Jackson is not here."

BIBLIOGRAPHY

Alexander, Edward Porter. *Military Memoirs of a Confederate*. New York, 1907. Reprint, Dayton, Ohio, 1977.

Bigelow, John. *The Campaign of Chancellorsville*. New Haven, 1910. Reprint, Dayton, Ohio, 1983.

Ferguson, Ernest B. *The Souls of the Brave*. New York, 1993.

Hamlin, Augustus C. *The Battle of Chancellorsville*. Bangor, Me., 1896.

Hotchkiss, Jedediah, and William Allan. *The Battle-Fields of Virginia: Chancellorsville*. New York, 1867. Reprint, Baltimore, Md., 1985.

Krick, Robert K. "Lee's Greatest Victory." *American Heritage* 41 (March 1990): 66–79.

ROBERT K. KRICK

CHARLESTON, SOUTH CAROLINA

[*This entry is composed of two articles,* City of Charleston *and* Bombardment of Charleston. *See also* Davids; Fort Sumter, South Carolina; *H. L. Hunley.*]

City of Charleston

Founded in 1670 as Charles Town, the settlement was moved from its original site to a nearby peninsula at the confluence of the Ashley and Cooper rivers, which flowed into the Atlantic. The economy flourished with the export of low-country rice and the import of African slaves. Approximately 40 percent of all Africans involuntarily shipped to America entered across Charles Town's wharves. It became the principal city of the South and the capital of South Carolina. After the Revolutionary War, the city's name was changed to Charleston, and Columbia became the capital of the new state.

Postwar booms in the export of rice and the new staple of cotton sputtered during the 1820s, and Charleston's economy stagnated. The city's poor rail connections westward, its shallow harbor, and the lack of a variety of exports and of a pool of free, educated workers especially hurt small retailers and skilled laborers. The wealthy planter-merchant elite, however, prospered since the price of rice and luxury Sea Island cotton declined only slightly less than the cost of living.

The city was the economic, social, and cultural capital for the great planters of the low country. Here they built summer homes to escape the isolation and the sickly season on the plantations. They preempted the choice residential sites on the lower peninsula or its flanks where they could enjoy salubrious sea breezes and proximity to social institutions. They also brought their families to Charleston from January through March to enjoy the annual social season, which featured horse races, balls, concerts, and the theater. The planters' emphasis on family connections, sociability, and conspicuous leisure activities strongly influenced the city's character.

William Gilmore Simms was antebellum Charleston's most famous literary figure, but he was discontented with the city's intellectual life. The few citizens who were interested in ideas met periodically at Russell's Book Store and during the 1850s founded *Russell's Magazine,* the last of the Old South's literary publications. In the same decade the South Carolina Historical Society and the Carolina Art Association were founded. Physicians and naturalists made the greatest contributions to the city's intellectual life. Recognized nationally, Dr. Lewis R. Gibbes of the College of Charleston helped make the city the center of scientific activity in the Southeast.

During the late antebellum period local businessmen used their influence on City Council to invest municipal money in improving the city's rail connections. They revived its merchant marine and obtained funds to dredge the harbor, helping stimulate an economic boom. By the early 1850s Charleston had become the manufacturing center of the state, but its economy was soon in trouble again. Competing railroads siphoned off traffic, and the city's hinterland dependencies remained too few and too small to promote Charleston's growth. The city remained a colonial outlier of the northeastern regional system.

The faltering economy coupled with a steady stream of immigrants, sailors, and vagrants straggling into the port city seeking work caused growing unemployment. Prostitution flourished. With a population of 40,522 in 1859—it had declined about 2,500 since the beginning of the decade—the city of Charleston ranked twenty-second in the nation. It was the most populous of the South Atlantic ports and the major distribution center for the state. The out-migration of slaves and the immigration of Irish and Germans transformed Charleston from a city that was 53 percent black to 58 percent white, from a city dominated by a skilled black labor force to one in which two-fifths of the working class were white and 60 percent were foreign-born.

The inequality in the distribution of wealth was enormous in comparison to Northern cities: just over 3 percent of the 4,644 free white heads of households owned approximately half of the wealth in Charleston. Most Charlestonians owned neither land nor slaves, and class divisions were as obvious as racial divisions. Economically most whites living in the city had more in common with African Americans than with the white elite.

An increase in thefts and homicides, and rising Northern antislavery rhetoric, which Charlestonians feared would encourage slave insurrections, alarmed the propertied classes. Faced with these problems of social instability, they embarked on a program of reforms. They inaugurated a public school system, built a larger poorhouse, established a professional police force, and remodeled the jail. Charleston's problems were compounded by its large slave population for which there existed several separate agencies of social control.

In April 1860 the Democratic National Convention met in Charleston only to split quickly into Northern and Southern wings and arrange to reconvene elsewhere. When the national Republican party nominated Abraham Lincoln for president, Charleston became the South's leading publisher of secession pamphlets.

As the crisis worsened, the city's authorities harassed Charleston's 3,237 free blacks, including 122 of the city's mulatto aristocracy, themselves slaveholders. The police began a systematic door-to-door search and interrogation of the African American community. Poor free blacks unable to produce absolute proof of their emancipated status were reenslaved. The mulatto aristocracy was terrified. They faced the same fate. Previously, they had escaped police harassment because of their relationships with the white elite, but as the calls for secession grew louder, their white guardians fell silent. Many of Charleston's mulatto elite considered emigrating from the city but felt that they could not leave successful careers, take enormous losses through sale of their real estate, or even get safe passage out of South Carolina. But hundreds of less prosperous free blacks sold what they could, packed what they could carry, and fled. Some sold their property at huge losses and felt cheated by whites who took advantage of their predicament.

Following Lincoln's election, delegates from across South Carolina convened in Charleston where on December 20 they adopted the ordinance of secession from the Union. Bells rang throughout the city, cannons were fired, and volunteers jammed the streets.

On December 26 Maj. Robert Anderson commanding the U.S. garrison on Sullivan's Island moved his troops to Fort Sumter in Charleston Harbor. A few days later, in the first military encounter of the war, South Carolina troops seized three local sites occupied by Federal troops. In January the vessel *Star of the West* attempted to reinforce Fort Sumter, but it was fired on by batteries on Morris Island and turned back.

Following the formation of the Confederate States of America, Gen. P. G. T. Beauregard took command at Charleston. He redeployed the troops and rearranged the ring of batteries around Fort Sumter. When Major Anderson refused to surrender the fort, Beauregard ordered its bombardment on April 12, 1861. After Anderson surrendered the following day, his troops embarked for the North and Confederate soldiers occupied the fort. President Lincoln called for 75,000 volunteers and a blockade of Southern ports.

Gen. Robert E. Lee arrived in Charleston on November 6 to take command of the Military Department of South Carolina, Georgia, and Florida. The following day Hilton Head Island, Port Royal, and Beaufort fell to Union forces. Charlestonians panicked. In December a devastating fire swept across the city, and some suspected slave arsonists.

Union strategists were determined to seize Charleston, "the cradle of secession," to stop the daily manufacture of cartridges there and the building of ironclad vessels. The steam-powered workshops of the former U.S. arsenal located on the western edge of the city produced artillery shells and thousands of cartridges daily for the Confederacy. Construction was nearing completion on the 150-foot *Palmetto State,* commissioned by the Confederate government for harbor defense, and *Chicora,* a vessel protected by 500 tons of iron armor and mounting six guns, the cost of which was funded by the state of South Carolina. The third

ironclad built in the city during the war was named *Charleston.* The Federal high command also wanted to stem the flow of vast amounts of military supplies and luxury goods brought in by blockade runners. The first attack came in June 1862 when six thousand Federal troops landed southeast of the city and a fierce firefight erupted on James Island. Casualties were heavy on both sides and the Union forces retreated. In April 1863 nine Federal ironclads attacked Fort Sumter, but were forced to withdraw owing to Confederate fire and the threat of mines or submarine torpedoes, a weapon developed by the Confederate Torpedo Bureau that inaugurated a new era in naval warfare. The third attack, jointly planned by the army and navy, began in July when a large Union force occupied most of Morris Island. When the last Confederate redoubt could not be taken after heroic but costly attacks by black troops, Union forces began a bombardment of the city to force its surrender. The siege lasted for 587 days. Although the harbor defenses remained

> **Following Lincoln's election, delegates from across South Carolina convened in Charleston where on December 20 they adopted the ordinance of secession from the Union.**

too formidable for the Union navy, its increased surveillance and the occupation of Morris Island severely curtailed blockade running at Charleston.

Occasionally, daring military exploits boosted briefly the spirits of Charlestonians. In October the Confederate ship *David,* the first combat submarine, disabled a Union blockader off Charleston; in early 1864, *H. L. Hunley* became the first submarine to sink an enemy vessel.

By this time the city was deserted below Market Street where the Union shells could reach; above this point, the life and business of the city went on. In December Gen. William J. Hardee redeployed the demoralized troops around Charleston to meet an anticipated attack by Gen. William Tecumseh Sherman. But Sherman's destination was the state capital. In mid-February 1865 General Hardee decided that Charleston was no longer defensible, and it was evacuated. Union troops immediately seized the city. The following September a Northern reporter in Charleston described it as "a city of ruins, of desolation, of vacant homes, of widowed women . . . of deserted warehouses, of weed-wild gardens, of miles of grass-grown streets."

For nearly two centuries Charleston had been the most important city in the vast territory of the Carolinas and Georgia. From about 1837 to 1862 Southern policies had been largely determined by South Carolina, and South

Carolina had been largely controlled by Charlestonians. But in three years the city lost forever both its wealth and its influence.

BIBLIOGRAPHY

Burton, E. Milby. *The Siege of Charleston, 1861–1865.* Columbia, S.C., 1970.

Cauthen, Charles Edward. *South Carolina Goes to War, 1860–1865.* Chapel Hill, N.C., 1950.

Fraser, Walter J., Jr. *Charleston! Charleston!: The History of a Southern City.* Columbia, S.C., 1989.

Greb, Gregory Allen. "Charleston, South Carolina, Merchants, 1815–1860: Urban Leadership in the Antebellum South." Ph.D. diss., University of California, Riverside, 1978.

Johnson, Michael P., and James L. Roark, eds. *No Chariot Down: Charleston's Free People of Color on the Eve of the Civil War.* Chapel Hill, N.C., 1984.

Longton, William Henry. "Some Aspects of Intellectual Activity in Ante-Bellum South Carolina, 1830–1860: An Introductory Study." Ph. D. diss., University of North Carolina, Chapel Hill, 1969.

Marszalek, John F., ed. *The Diary of Miss Emma Holmes, 1861–1866.* Baton Rouge, La., 1979.

WALTER J. FRASER, JR.

Bombardment of Charleston

Early in the war Union military strategists determined to seize Charleston, the hated symbol of rebellion, to stop the daily manufacture of thousands of cartridges, the building of ironclads, and the flow of military supplies brought in by blockade runners. Following two unsuccessful attempts to take the city in June 1862 and April 1863, the Federals planned a joint army-navy operation. Following the capture of Morris Island and the reduction of nearby Fort Sumter by the army, Union vessels were to steam into the harbor and demand the surrender of the city.

In July a force of 6,000 Federal troops under Gen. Quincy A. Gillmore quickly occupied most of Morris Island. A heroic and costly attack by African American troops failed to overrun Fort Wagner, the Confederate strong point. This prevented the navy from executing its role in the operation since the harbor defenses remained formidable. General Gillmore dug in on Morris Island, constructed batteries, and trained his rifled long-range guns on Fort Sumter. One 200-pounder Parrott rifled gun was aimed at Charleston some four miles away.

On August 21, 1863, Gillmore sent a message to the commanding officer of Charleston, Gen. P. G. T. Beauregard, demanding the evacuation of Fort Sumter and Morris Island within four hours or bombardment of the city would commence. Beauregard dashed off a reply charging that by not giving "timely notice," Gillmore was committing "an act of . . . barbarity." But in the early morning hours of August 22,

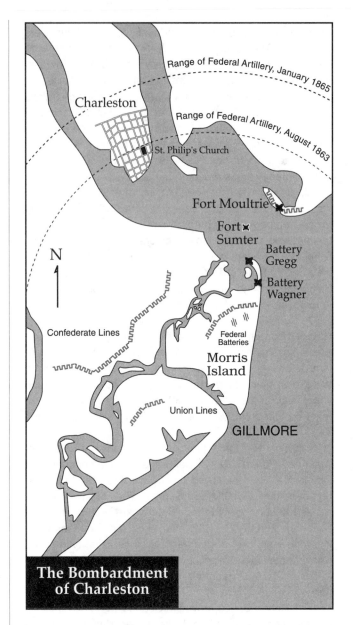

The Bombardment of Charleston

Gillmore ordered the bombardment to begin. It would continue for 587 days.

Charlestonians were angry and frightened. Those who could afford to took trains or carriages out of the city to safer communities. The poorer people remained. Authorities moved the post office, banks, and hospitals north of Calhoun Street, beyond the range of the Union artillery, and evacuated the city's orphans to Orangeburg.

The Union occupation of Morris Island and the increased surveillance by the Union navy severely curtailed blockade running while Federal land forces inched closer to the city. Confederate money depreciated and the costs of goods and services soared in Charleston. A few speculators in foodstuffs made huge profits, but destitution was widespread.

The bombardment of the city was sporadic until late 1863 when the shelling began with regularity. During nine days in January 1864, some 1,500 shells were fired into Charleston; occasionally they started fires. St. Philip's Church was hit repeatedly and its interior wrecked, and City Hall and the guard house were punctured with shell fragments. But because the city below Market Street was deserted, few people were killed during the bombardment.

With many of the city's firemen and police doing soldier duty, city services began to break down. Robberies increased dramatically. The bombardment, coupled with declines in student enrollments, severely impaired classroom instruction in the public schools.

General Beauregard was ordered to North Carolina in mid-April 1864 and Maj. Gen. Samuel Jones assumed command of the defenses of Charleston. By this time thousands of Union troops had occupied all of Morris Island, and their artillery was pounding Fort Sumter into rubble. During the summer fierce skirmishes broke out on islands around the city, and the Union artillery increased its shelling. Two of the worst days of the bombardment were September 30 and October 10 when 110 and 165 shells, respectively, fell into the city. During the fall several civilians were killed.

In October Lt. Gen. William J. Hardee arrived in Charleston to replace General Jones and take command of the remnants of the Department of South Carolina, Georgia, and Florida. About 12,500 soldiers—poorly trained, armed, clad, and fed—were concentrated around the city and Savannah. During mid-November Hardee turned over the defense of Charleston to Maj. Gen. Robert Ransom, Jr., and took hundreds of troops with him to defend Savannah against William Tecumseh Sherman, who was marching toward the city with 60,000 battle-hardened troops.

General Hardee evacuated Savannah in December and retreated toward Charleston where he redeployed 16,000 soldiers around the city. By January 1865 amphibious assaults on the city's defenses were increasing and Union shells were falling onto the Neck north of Calhoun Street. In mid-February Hardee concluded that it was no longer feasible to defend Charleston. During the night of February 17–18, the soldiers and most of the few remaining well-to-do evacuated the city and its defenses. Some 10,000 Confederate troops retreated northward up the peninsula.

On February 18 the Federals took possession of the city. The Union flag was raised over all public buildings and fortifications, and martial law was declared. One Union officer remarked that Charleston had fallen "after a siege which will rank among the most famous in history."

BIBLIOGRAPHY

Burton, E. Milby. *The Siege of Charleston, 1861–1865.* Columbia, S.C., 1970.

Fraser, Walter J., Jr. *Charleston! Charleston!: The History of a Southern City.* Columbia, S.C., 1989.

Sutor, Jack. "Charleston, South Carolina, during the Civil War Era, 1858–1865." M.A. thesis, Duke University, 1942.

WALTER J. FRASER, JR.

CHARLESTON SQUADRON

South Carolina's state navy was absorbed into Confederate service in April 1861 under Commdr. H. J. Hartstene. In November Capt. Duncan N. Ingraham assumed command, and in 1862 the Charleston Squadron acquired strength with the addition of the ironclads *Chicora* and *Palmetto State.*

On January 31, 1863, the squadron struck the Union blockade, seeking to open the city to outside commerce. The Charleston command declared the blockade broken, but little damage had been done and the city remained sealed. Soon after, Captain Ingraham was replaced as commander afloat by Capt. John Randolph Tucker of *Chicora.*

While the naval command concentrated on ironclads, Charleston was becoming a center for experimentation with mines and torpedoes. A cadre of young officers in the squadron pushed their superiors for action, and expeditions to attack Union monitors were organized. On October 5, 1863, Lt. William T. Glassell attacked USS *New Ironsides* with the torpedo boat *David.* The damage inflicted kept *New Ironsides* out of action for more than a year.

In late 1863 the ironclad *Charleston* was added to the squadron and became Tucker's flagship. Torpedo expeditions against the blockade continued (the submarine *H. L. Hunley*'s successful attack was under army command), but the ships and gunboats engaged in purely defensive operations for the rest of the war, bombarding the Union troops and batteries besieging the city. When Charleston was evacuated, the squadron was destroyed.

BIBLIOGRAPHY

Melton, Maurice. *The Confederate Ironclads.* South Brunswick, N.J., 1968.

Parker, William H. *Recollections of a Naval Life.* New York, 1883. Reprint, Annapolis, Md., 1985.

Rochelle, James H. *Life of Rear Admiral John Randolph Tucker.* Washington, D.C., 1903.

Scharf, J. Thomas. *History of the Confederate States Navy.* New York, 1887. Reprint, New York, 1977.

Still, William N. *Iron Afloat.* Nashville, Tenn., 1971.

MAURICE K. MELTON

CHARLOTTE NAVY YARD

The impending evacuation of the Gosport Navy Yard at Norfolk, Virginia, in May 1862 caused Navy Secretary Stephen R. Mallory to order the relocation of the facility's heavy machinery and ordnance stores. Officials chose the southern North Carolina city of Charlotte for the new yard because of its inland location and excellent rail connections with coastal ports. The government acquired a site bordered by two rail lines, and workers erected new structures. By year's end the Charlotte Navy Yard was producing gun carriages, projectiles, and other ordnance equipment. The addition of a large steam hammer permitted the forging of heavy propeller shafts, large anchors, and wrought-iron armor-piercing bolts unobtainable elsewhere in the Confederacy. The navy yard also produced torpedoes and wooden blocks and repaired locomotives. Many of the establishment's employees came with the machinery from Gosport. They were joined by local workmen and, in 1864, by skilled mechanics recruited in England.

Capt. Samuel Barron apparently was the installation's first commander but was replaced in October 1862 by Commdr. Richard L. Page. Page was followed in rapid succession by Capt. George N. Hollins and Commdr. Catesby Jones before again assuming command in May 1863. Chief Engineer Henry Ashton Ramsay superintended the works from the spring of 1864 until the end of the war.

With the rapid disintegration of the Confederacy in April 1865, the Charlotte Navy Yard was abandoned. Symbolic of that end was the destruction at the yard of the records of the Navy Department after their removal from Richmond.

BIBLIOGRAPHY

Alexander, Violet G. "The Confederate States Navy Yard at Charlotte, N.C., 1862–1865." *Southern Historical Society Papers* 40 (1915): 184–192. Reprint, Wilmington, N.C., 1991.
Donnelly, Ralph W. "The Charlotte, North Carolina, Navy Yard, C.S.N." *Civil War History* 5 (March 1959): 72–79.
Still, William N. *Confederate Shipbuilding.* 2d ed. Columbia, S.C., 1987.

A. ROBERT HOLCOMBE, JR.

CHATTAHOOCHEE

A wooden, twin-screw-propeller sail- and steam-powered gunboat measuring 130 feet in length, 30 feet in width, and 10 feet in depth of hold, *Chattahoochee* was built on the river for which it was named by David S. Johnston of Saffold, Early County, Georgia, pursuant to an October 19, 1861, contract with the Navy Department. Its armament consisted of a rifled and banded 32-pounder forward, a 9-inch Dahlgren smoothbore aft, and four 32-pounder smoothbores in broadside.

Under the command of Lt. Catesby Jones, *Chattahoochee* was commissioned January 1, 1863, and immediately began the monotonous task of defending the Apalachicola-Chattahoochee-Flint river system against anticipated Federal naval excursions from the Gulf of Mexico. The following May 27, while commanded by Lt. John J. Guthrie, *Chattahoochee* suffered a boiler explosion near Blountstown, Florida, which killed nineteen of its crew and resulted in its sinking. The vessel was raised several months later and taken to Columbus, Georgia, for repairs. Although lacking replacement boilers, *Chattahoochee* was placed into service for a brief time in the spring of 1864 when its crew, led by Lt. George W. Gift, participated in an abortive small-boat attack against Union blockaders off Apalachicola, Florida.

Still without operative steam machinery, *Chattahoochee* was scuttled to prevent capture twelve miles below Columbus soon after the April 16, 1865, fall of that city. In 1964 thirty feet of *Chattahoochee*'s stern was recovered and placed at the Confederate Naval Museum in Columbus.

BIBLIOGRAPHY

Castlen, Harriet Gift. *Hope Bids Me Onward.* Savannah, Ga., 1945.
Turner, Maxine. *Navy Gray: A Story of the Confederate Navy on the Chattahoochee and Apalachicola Rivers.* Tuscaloosa, Ala., 1988.

A. ROBERT HOLCOMBE, JR.

CHATTANOOGA, TENNESSEE

[*This entry includes two articles,* City of Chattanooga, *which profiles the city during the Confederacy, and* Chattanooga Campaign, *which discusses the military action there in 1863. See also* Wheeler's Raids.]

City of Chattanooga

At the beginning of the Civil War, Chattanooga was a little-known commercial and manufacturing town of 2,500 people, about a fourth of whom were African American slaves. Another 10 percent were free blacks. Despite its small size and relative obscurity, it was a community of great strategic importance because of its role as a transportation hub. The only rail route that provided an unbroken connection between Virginia and the West and another important line connecting the Deep South with the upper South converged in the little town that had been established only twenty-three years earlier as a river port. Before the war more than 45,000 bales of cotton were shipped by rail through Chattanooga annually to points north and to the Southern ports of Savannah and Charleston. The railroad was only one aspect of Chattanooga's importance as a transportation center. The town's key location on the Tennessee River linked it with the other important water transportation routes of the Southeast, and until the advent of the railroad in the 1850s, Chattanooga was almost totally dependent on the river for its livelihood.

During the secession crisis, Chattanoogans were a deeply divided people. Reflecting the town's location on the edge of Unionist eastern Tennessee, up to a third of its population openly opposed secession and voted to keep Tennessee in the Union. After the firing on Fort Sumter, however, Tennessee joined the Confederacy, and for the next two years Southern sympathies and authority prevailed in the town. Divided sympathies aside, Chattanooga was important for the contending armies because of its location. Its geographic importance became evident early in the war when Confederate troops garrisoned the area and converted the town into a major supply depot. Indeed, by early 1862, Chattanooga was a military community in almost every respect. Warehouses, barracks, hospitals, fortifications, and men in uniform everywhere became as much a part of the town as all of its civilian vestiges. With large armies present, the town's prewar population mushroomed as much as five-fold.

In the late summer of 1863, when Gen. William S. Rosecrans forced Braxton Bragg's Confederate army out of Tennessee, Union troops occupied Chattanooga. After a decisive victory at Chickamauga, Confederate forces moved north to try to recapture Chattanooga. For the next two months, Bragg's army besieged the town, cutting Federal supply lines and reducing Union troops and civilians to starvation rations. A large army under Ulysses S. Grant, however, broke the siege and dealt the Confederates a crushing defeat at Missionary Ridge on November 25. Chattanooga remained firmly under Union control until the end of the war and served as a key supply center for William Tecumseh Sherman's army as it moved into Georgia in the spring of 1864.

For the people of Chattanooga, the war years meant great social unrest and disruption, problems only exacerbated by the town's divided loyalties. During the first two years, the strong core of Unionists suffered persecution at the hands of their fellow citizens with Confederate leanings. Many Unionists were jailed, and scores of others fled to Federal-occupied areas. Confederate sympathizers, however, experienced the reverse when Chattanooga fell under Union control. Federal authorities confiscated the property of Southern sympathizers, jailed or expatriated others, and enforced strict martial law. In addition to maintaining control of the town's normal civilian population, Federal military authorities faced another major challenge. A large influx of former slaves added to the turmoil of the town in the summer of 1864.

Freed from the fetters of slavery, thousands of men, women, and children from Georgia, Alabama, and Tennessee flocked into Chattanooga seeking refuge and sustenance. With them came massive problems of hunger, disease, and civil unrest. For Union military authorities, dealing with social chaos in Chattanooga became almost as challenging as fighting the Confederate army. Even stricter martial law was established, and little by little, segregated tent cities for black refugees were set up, ringing the town. By the end of 1864, nearly four thousand black refugees lived in the makeshift tents and huts. At war's end, the Freedmen's Bureau assumed the administration of the refugee camps, instituting active educational and job placement programs for the former slaves.

With the return of peace in 1865, military authorities turned over to civilian authorities a town with serious problems. The strains of war had imposed a heavy financial burden on the municipal government, and most of the town's public buildings had been destroyed or rendered useless. A scourge of smallpox in the wake of the war lasted until the great flood of 1867 that washed away homes, industries, and a military bridge, keeping the town isolated for days.

Nevertheless, Chattanooga experienced a speedy recovery in the postwar years. The abundance of raw materials, its advantage as a transportation center, and cheap labor were successfully touted by local authorities to attract manufacturing enterprises. The development of business and industry by Northern investors immediately after the war spurred the local economy and helped city revenues rise to above prewar levels by 1870. The iron industry, in particular, boomed in the early 1870s, and the city's importance as a rail hub increased accordingly. Only twenty years after the war, the town was entered by nine trunk lines. Despite the many travails it had brought, the war served as a stimulus for the town's development. With its natural assets, its key geographic location, and large infusions of Northern capital in the immediate postwar years, Chattanooga changed from a simple crossroads town into a major industrial and commercial center.

BIBLIOGRAPHY

Bryan, Charles F., Jr. "The Civil War in East Tennessee: A Social, Political, and Economic Study." Ph.D. diss., University of Tennessee, 1978.

Govan, Gilbert E., and James W. Livingood. *The Chattanooga Country, 1540–1951: From Tomahawk to TVA.* New York, 1952.

Wilson, John. *Chattanooga's Story.* Chattanooga, Tenn., 1980.

CHARLES F. BRYAN, JR.

Chattanooga Campaign

A series of battles fought around Chattanooga, Tennessee, during October and November 1863, the campaign had ruinous consequences for the South. It cost the Confederacy some 6,700 killed, wounded, missing, or captured; the North suffered 5,800 casualties.

Following the defeat of the Federal Army of the Cumberland at Chickamauga on September 20, 1863, the routed Union troops had raced north through Rossville Gap to the safe haven of Chattanooga, Tennessee. On September 24, Gen. William Rosecrans, commander of the Northern soldiers in Chattanooga, withdrew from Lookout Mountain one

> **Rosecrans had no choice but to abandon Chattanooga or face the destruction of his 35,000-man army.**

of his brigades, which had originally been posted there to guard supply routes coming into the city from the west. Upon learning of this withdrawal, Gen. Braxton Bragg, commander of the Confederate Army of Tennessee, occupied this strategic mountain. He also fortified Missionary Ridge, which ran northeast to southeast on the east side of the city, and Lookout valley and Raccoon Mountain to the west.

In such a commanding position, Bragg, with about 46,000 effective troops, felt that Rosecrans had no choice but to abandon Chattanooga or face the destruction of his 35,000-man army. But Rosecrans, fearing to leave the comparative safety of the city with the Tennessee River guarding his rear, instead heavily fortified his front and awaited reinforcements. These troops consisted of two corps of about 16,000 men from the Army of the Potomac under Gen. Joseph Hooker, which began to arrive at Bridgeport, Alabama, twenty-seven miles west of Chattanooga, in the first part of October. There, the corps were assigned to guard the railroad that led back to Federal supply depots in Nashville.

At about the time that Hooker was beginning to arrive in Bridgeport, Bragg was despairing of Rosecrans abandoning Chattanooga voluntarily. He decided to starve the army out and ordered all river and rail traffic to the city stopped. In addition, Gen. Joseph Wheeler, who commanded the cavalry of the Army of Tennessee, took his troopers on a successful raid during the first week of October, destroying Federal wagon trains hauling supplies from the railhead in Bridgeport. (The Confederates had previously burned the railroad bridge that crossed the Tennessee River at Bridgeport, and consequently wagon trains had to negotiate a tortuous system of barely passable roads to reach Chattanooga, the trips sometimes taking up to twenty days

as compared to about an hour by rail.) As a result of Wheeler's raiding parties, Rosecrans had no choice but to put his soldiers on reduced rations.

When Gen. Ulysses S. Grant was appointed commander of the newly created Federal Military Division of Mississippi in mid-October, he relieved Rosecrans and assigned Gen. George H. Thomas as the new commander of the Army of the Cumberland. On October 23, Grant arrived in Chattanooga to talk over the situation with Thomas and Gen. William F. Smith, chief engineer of the Department of the Cumberland. Smith proposed an innovative plan that was to become known to history as the "Cracker Line." West of the city was a bend in the river called Moccasin Point. Smith's idea was to send 3,500 infantrymen under Gen. John B. Turchin, supported by three batteries of artillery, over an existing pontoon bridge to this neck of land and from there move them overland to a point on the east bank of the river opposite Brown's Ferry. At the same time, 1,500 more infantry under Gen. William B. Hazen were to drift downstream in fifty pontoon boats and drive in Confederate pickets guarding Brown's Ferry on the west bank. With that accomplished, the Federals on both sides would span the river with another pontoon bridge, allowing those soldiers on Moccasin Point to cross the Tennessee in force. The whole operation was to be supported by three divisions from Hooker's command, which would cross the Tennessee at Bridgeport and move to an area just west of Lookout Mountain. From Brown's Ferry, a road—entirely out of range of Southern artillery—led to another ferry on the river known as Kelley's. With Kelley's Ferry in Federal hands, it would be but a short steamboat run from Bridgeport to that point and a relatively safe eight-mile overland trip to Chattanooga.

The operation commenced well before dawn on October 27. Upon landing at Brown's Ferry and driving in the pickets, Hazen's men ran into about 400 of Gen. James Longstreet's troops, commanded by Col. William C. Oates, who temporarily held off the Federals, but could not do so for long. The pontoon bridge from Moccasin Point was in place that afternoon, and the Union plan went almost without a hitch. Only thirty-eight Federals and an undetermined but small number of Confederates were lost.

Advance elements from Hooker's command reached the vicinity of the village of Wauhatchie and Lookout valley not far from Brown's Ferry on the evening of the twenty-eighth. There, they were attacked in a night fight by Longstreet's troops. After a sharp battle, however, the Confederates ceased firing about 3:30 the next morning, and the Cracker Line was secure. The besieged Union garrison in Chattanooga was soon receiving food and ammunition: the first steamboat arrived at Kelley's Ferry on the first of November.

As a result of Longstreet's withdrawal from Lookout Mountain, Grant was able to garrison the south side of the

Tennessee River with about 20,000 troops, and Bragg then was forced to end his siege of Chattanooga.

On November 5, Longstreet and his 12,000 troops were ordered to leave the Chattanooga area and move to Knoxville to confront the Union army's Ninth Corps under Gen. Ambrose E. Burnside. Under the circumstances, Bragg could ill afford to lose that many men while Grant was gaining strength every day. Longstreet was incredulous at the order, but felt that he might be able to beat Burnside quickly and return to the Confederate lines at Chattanooga in time for the impending battle. Grant, for his part, when he learned of Longstreet's departure, immediately began formulating plans to smash Bragg's lines on Missionary Ridge. The stage was set for Confederate disaster.

On November 13, 17,000 Federal troops of the Army of the Tennessee arrived at Bridgeport; these soldiers were mostly veterans of the Vicksburg campaign under the command of Gen. William Tecumseh Sherman. Gen. Henry W. Halleck, general-in-chief of the Union armies, had ordered Sherman to relieve Chattanooga, but to repair rail lines as the soldiers came forward. Impatient for Sherman to come to his aid, however, Grant had canceled Halleck's order on October 27. Sherman arrived in Chattanooga on November 14, and Grant ordered him to reconnoiter the northern end of Missionary Ridge. Following a discussion with Grant of a plan of battle to defeat the Confederates on the ridge, Sherman returned to Bridgeport and brought his troops up through Lookout valley to Brown's Ferry to reinforce the Federal army and prepare for the coming action.

Before a full attack could take place on Missionary Ridge, a strategic foothill to the east of Chattanooga, called Orchard Knob, had to be secured. On the morning of November 23, two divisions under Gen. Philip Sheridan and Gen. Thomas Wood were sent out of Chattanooga in the direction of Orchard Knob as if on a grand parade, though the movement was, in fact, a reconnaissance in force of the foothill. The Confederates, observing from Missionary Ridge, were taken in, and before they could respond appropriately, the Union divisions rushed the Southern defenses on Orchard Knob and won a quick, decisive victory. The Federal army then moved out of Chattanooga and forward to new positions facing the Confederate lines on Missionary Ridge.

To assault Bragg's army, Sherman was to attack the Confederate right on the northern end of the Ridge, while Hooker, after moving his men into position across Chattanooga valley, attacked Bragg's left. In the meantime, Thomas's Army of the Cumberland would hold the center of the Federal line in reserve, merely threatening the Confederate center or, if necessary, coming to the aid of either flank attack. The Union assault was set for November 25.

While Sherman was moving his troops across the Tennessee River at Brown's Ferry and into position on the left of the Army of the Cumberland during the foggy, rainy day of November 24, Hooker's Federals, too, were on the move. At about 8 o'clock that morning, Hooker ordered one of his divisions, Gen. John W. Geary's, to cross Lookout Creek and assault the southern position on the side of Lookout Mountain. Later in the day the divisions of Gen. Charles Cruft and Gen. Peter J. Osterhaus, about 10,000 men, were to follow. These Federals faced about 2,700 Confederates under the command of Gen. John Jackman, who had dug in a strong line around the Craven home on the slopes of the mountain. In addition, scattered over the mountain were another 4,000 Southerners.

Taking Lookout Mountain, however, was not Hooker's main objective. Rather, by crossing Chattanooga valley between Lookout Mountain and Missionary Ridge, he planned to clear that area of Confederate troops, take the town of Rossville, and bring himself up into position on the right of the Federal lines to attack Bragg's left flank and possibly move to his rear. Nevertheless, if he saw an opportunity to clear the Southerners from the heights of Lookout Mountain, he planned to exercise that option. He did see an opportunity that day and took advantage of it.

After crossing Lookout Creek, the advancing Federals climbed up the steep western slope of the mountain in fog so thick the men could barely see in front of them. Working their way around to the northern side, they continued their arduous climb up the nearly vertical walls of the mountain. After battling the Federals all day, the Southerners withdrew to Missionary Ridge that night, and the Stars and Stripes were planted atop Lookout Mountain for all to see on the bright

> **With orders from no one, the soldiers . . . rose in a brilliant, unstoppable assault.**

morning of November 25. The Battle of Lookout Mountain—known to history as "The Battle above the Clouds"—was, in truth, not much of a battle by Civil War standards. Because of the dense fog and rain, neither side could see the other very clearly, and Union artillery, firing on the mountain from Moccasin Point, was ineffective. With Hooker's capture of Lookout Mountain, however, Grant had in effect a relatively straight line of battle on Missionary Ridge, with little danger now on his flanks.

The Battle of Missionary Ridge began on the morning of the twenty-fifth. By the previous evening, Sherman had gained an advanced position on Bragg's right in the foothills below the ridge, and Hooker was moving steadily in the direction of Bragg's left. At 11:00 A.M., Sherman assaulted the Confederate right, but made little progress. Under the nominal command of Gen. William J. Hardee, Bragg's right had just been reinforced by Gen. Patrick Cleburne's division.

Cleburne, considered one of the finest fighting generals of the Confederacy, had been sent on November 23 to help Longstreet in his efforts against Burnside. But as Bragg finally came to realize Grant's intentions, Cleburne had been hurriedly recalled from Chickamauga Station and had arrived in time to fortify the northern end of Missionary Ridge, blunting Sherman's assault.

Off toward the southern end of the ridge, Hooker had stalled at Chattanooga Creek waiting for a pontoon bridge to be built so he could cross his command.

Meanwhile, in the center, after being stripped of a corps and then a division to aid Sherman, the Army of the Cumberland, with three divisions remaining, sensed disaster on the Union left and right. At 3:00 P.M., Thomas, who had been given a halfhearted order by Grant to advance his troops, decided to take matters into his own hands. Forming Sheridan's and Wood's divisions of Granger's Corps, along with Gen. Richard Johnson's and Gen. Absolam Baird's divisions as support, he attacked through Orchard Knob. At first the Union soldiers were bogged down in the Confederate trenches they had captured at the foot of the ridge, but the unrelenting Southern artillery fire aimed at them elicited an amazing response. With orders from no one, the soldiers of the Army of the Cumberland rose and, in a brilliant, unstoppable assault, charged up the six hundred feet to the Confederate center on the crest of Missionary Ridge. The attack broke and routed the Confederate center, and soon all the Southern units from left and right followed the retreat down the opposite side of Missionary Ridge, across Chickamauga Creek, and, by early morning on November 26, through Ringgold Gap. This retreat in effect ended the Chattanooga campaign.

The battles around Chattanooga had significant results for the North. The city and its railroads were now under permanent Federal control, and in the spring of 1864, Sherman would use Chattanooga as a staging area for his Atlanta campaign. The railroads would, in turn, supply his successful assault on the Deep South. Grant would become commander-in-chief of all the Federal armies and lead the Union to victory in April 1865.

BIBLIOGRAPHY

Connelly, Thomas L. *Autumn of Glory: The Army of Tennessee, 1862–1865.* Baton Rouge, La., 1971.

Downey, Fairfax D. *Storming of the Gateway: Chattanooga, 1863.* New York, 1960.

Horn, Stanley F. *Tennessee's War, 1861–1865.* Nashville, Tenn., 1965.

Taylor, Benjamin F. *Missionary Ridge and Lookout Mountain.* Chicago, 1872.

Tucker, Glenn. "Chattanooga!" *Civil War Times Illustrated,* August 1971.

WARREN WILKINSON

CHESNUT, JAMES

CHESNUT, JAMES (1815–1885), brigadier general and congressman from South Carolina. Although Chesnut was a member of President Jefferson Davis's inner circle, his military and political accomplishments have been eclipsed by the writings of his wife, Mary Boykin Chesnut, whose perceptive diary of Southern society during the war has become a major source of knowledge about life in the Confederacy.

Chesnut was a South Carolinian of distinguished lineage who broke with the family's planter tradition and sought a career in public service. His Princeton training was followed in 1835 by the study of law under the famous Charlestonian James Louis Petigru, who was considered the undisputed leader of the South Carolina bar. It doubtless was Petigru's competence in the practice of law and not his politics that was attractive to the young Chesnut. Petigru frequently represented slaves and spoke out against disunion at every opportunity. Chesnut, considered a political moderate by his contemporaries, did not dispute Petigru's antisecession philosophy, but he was firmly convinced that "commerce, culture, and Christianity derived their 'chief earthly impulse' from slavery." This principle guided Chesnut as he entered public office in 1840, the same year he wed Mary Boykin Miller.

Between 1840 and 1858 Chesnut served several terms in both the state legislature and senate. In 1858 he was unanimously elected to the U.S. Senate, where his oratorical skills immediately made him conspicuous among fellow Southerners. During the tumultuous months following John Brown's raid, Chesnut assailed the abolitionists, and after Abraham Lincoln's election he had the distinction of being the first senator from the South to resign his seat in protest.

As a member of South Carolina's secession convention, Chesnut helped draft the document that dissolved the Union, and in February 1861, he traveled to Montgomery, Alabama, to represent the Palmetto State in the Provisional Confederate Congress. Here Chesnut nurtured a friendly relationship with Jefferson Davis, which paid tremendous dividends during his Confederate career.

Chesnut was in Charleston as the crisis over the Federal occupation of Fort Sumter worsened. Without prior military experience, Chesnut's role in this affair was relegated to that of a volunteer aide to the commander of the Confederate forces, Brig. Gen. P. G. T. Beauregard, but his contribution was arguably his greatest of the war.

On April 11, 1861, Beauregard sent Chesnut and two fellow aides, Capt. Stephen D. Lee and Col. Alexander Chisolm, to Fort Sumter to demand the evacuation of the fort. Federal commander Maj. Robert Anderson handed Chesnut a written refusal and remarked in passing that the garrison had food enough to last only a few more days. This news Chesnut relayed to Beauregard and a telegram was sent to the

Confederate capital requesting further instructions. In reply, Beauregard was directed to avoid needless bloodshed and not injure the fort unnecessarily, if Anderson would state the time he would evacuate the fort. Chesnut returned to Fort Sumter to negotiate the evacuation details, provided he found Anderson's departure schedule acceptable. Otherwise Chesnut had full authority to order the bombardment to commence. Anderson's response contained numerous provisos that Chesnut found unsatisfactory, so he drafted a reply stat-

> **Chesnut had full authority to order the bombardment to commence.**

ing that in one hour the Southern guns would open fire. At 4:30 A.M., April 12, 1861, the Civil War began.

For the next thirty-four hours Chesnut witnessed the bombardment from his assigned post on Morris Island. About 1:00 in the afternoon of April 13, with fires blazing out of control inside Fort Sumter, the Union garrison surrendered. Chesnut carried this news to the Confederate commander in Charleston, but he had little opportunity to savor the hero's welcome he received. Beauregard sent him for the third time in as many days to Fort Sumter, accompanied this time with a fire engine and a surgeon.

Early June found Chesnut leaving his beloved South Carolina. While retaining his seat in the Confederate Congress, Chesnut followed Beauregard to northern Virginia, where the Southern army took up a defensive position around Manassas Junction. Many hours were spent on horseback as the general and his aide studied the topography of the Bull Run valley. When not escorting the general, Chesnut served as judge advocate and carried correspondence to Davis detailing Beauregard's never-to-be-attempted plan for a grand but impractical offensive that later was the subject of considerable controversy. At the First Battle of Manassas, Chesnut relayed orders to the regimental commanders, led the legion of South Carolinians in their final charge after their leader Wade Hampton was wounded, and joined in the pursuit of the fleeing Federals in the company of Capt. John Lay's Virginia cavalry squadron.

For his early military contributions and as a special favorite of Davis, Chesnut could have requested and received a commission, as he did for others. But his aristocratic code was "too high South Carolina" to have anyone intercede on his behalf. He remained in Congress through the fall of 1861 despite some speculation that he might not win reelection in December. When the votes were tallied, Chesnut indeed lost his seat, which his wife attributed to political maneuvering and his aversion to "electioneering for such a place as Senator." The loss was diminished somewhat

when Chesnut agreed to serve on the South Carolina Executive Council, which was designed to circumvent the powers of an ineffective governor. The council, described by Mary Chesnut as "trouble-bringing—and no glory-giving," was charged with controlling all aspects of the military affairs of the state. Council business periodically took Chesnut to Richmond, where he found pleasurable company with the president and Robert E. Lee.

In the fall of 1862 an official aideship on the staff of President Davis was offered to Chesnut, a position he eagerly accepted. As the president's representative, Chesnut examined the lengthy lines of fortifications constructed around Richmond and traveled throughout the Confederacy on inspection trips. On April 30, 1864, Chesnut was commissioned brigadier general of reserves and returned to South Carolina to finish out the war. As commander of the state reserve forces, Chesnut organized local opposition to William Tecumseh Sherman's advance through Georgia and South Carolina.

James Chesnut returned to his plantation, Mulberry, after the war, dabbled in politics, and died at age seventy from the effects of a stroke. He was buried in the family cemetery near Camden, South Carolina.

BIBLIOGRAPHY

Chesnut, Mary Boykin. *Mary Chesnut's Civil War.* Edited by C. Vann Woodward. New Haven, 1981.

Doubleday, Abner. *Reminiscences of Forts Sumter and Moultrie in 1860–61.* New York, 1876. Reprint, Spartanburg, S.C., 1976.

Nevins, Allen. *The War for the Union.* New York, 1959.

U.S. War Department. *The War of the Rebellion: A Compilation of the Official Records of the Union and Confederate Armies.* Washington, D.C., 1880–1901. Ser. 1, vol. 1, pp. 59–62.

DAVID R. RUTH

CHESNUT, MARY BOYKIN

CHESNUT, MARY BOYKIN (1823–1886), diarist. The author of the finest firsthand account of the social world of the Confederacy, published as *Mary Chesnut's Civil War,* Chesnut was born on March 31, 1823, in Statesburg, South Carolina, first child of Mary Boykin and Stephen Decatur Miller, state senator and former U.S. congressman. Miller, a proponent of nullification, was elected governor when Mary was five and in 1830 won a U.S. Senate seat.

Mary's formal education in Camden and Charleston ended in 1838 with her father's death. At seventeen, she married James Chesnut, Jr., only surviving son of one of the largest land and slaveholders in the state, and went to live at Mulberry Plantation south of Camden. The Chesnuts were childless, and during the next two decades Mary found few emotional or intellectual outlets other than the voracious reading that would later inform her famous record of the war years. James was elected in 1858 to the U.S. Senate and took Mary to Washington where she formed friendships with many prominent Southern legislators and their wives.

After Abraham Lincoln's election, Chesnut resigned his Senate seat and went to Montgomery as delegate to the Confederate Provisional Congress. In Montgomery, Mary's hotel quarters served as the first of her remarkable wartime salons, to which the men and women who were creating a new nation came to socialize, exchange information, and—eventually—to grieve. Mary began a private diary in February 1861, candidly recording what she saw and heard, conscious of the magnitude of the events into which she had been drawn and attuned to the ironies and jealousies around her. (Seven volumes of her wartime journals survive, covering most of 1861 and three months in 1865.) A close friend of Varina Davis and an ardent supporter of the president, she observed and recorded as early as February 1861, "these men have brought old hatreds & grudges & spites from the old Union. Already we see they will willingly injure our cause to hurt Jeff Davis."

Mary Chesnut found herself in an excellent position to view the upheavals of her world. In March 1861, James, as aide to P. G. T. Beauregard, participated in the negotiations over Fort Sumter, and Mary recorded the attack from her vantage point on a rooftop. In Richmond, she waited with Varina Davis for news of Manassas, visited the first wounded of the war, heard over and over the dreaded "dead march," and at times expressed anguish in her journal over what she regarded as the foolishness of most men. "Jeff Davis ill & shut up," she wrote in August, "& none but *noodles* have the world in charge."

Frustrated at her woman's role as mere observer, she was troubled by her husband's lack of ambition for the spotlight. By the close of 1862, she had convinced James to accept a colonelcy and return to Richmond where he served for the next fifteen months as personal aide to Davis. Mary found lodgings near the White House of the Confederacy, and the Chesnut home was constantly filled with people seeking patronage, support, respite, or recuperation from the chaos of war. In her journal, Mary recorded everything: wartime romances, quarrels, parties, funerals, constant rumors, and firsthand reports of battles—both military and political.

In April 1864, General and Mrs. Chesnut returned to Columbia, where Mary worked at Louisa McCord's hospital and again kept open house, entertaining Davis himself in October. In early 1865 she fled to Lincolnton, North Carolina, and following Robert E. Lee's surrender, to Chester, South Carolina. There, as always, governors, generals, and friends flowed through her tiny rented rooms—among the last of them, Varina Davis and her children.

Chesnut ceased keeping her journal in June 1865, uncertain of the future. Mulberry had been ravaged; the Chesnut fortune was gone and the lands tangled in debt. Mary took over running the household, made a home for less fortunate family members, operated a small dairy business that brought in the family's only cash, and experimented with literary projects. In the next twenty years, she tried her hand at

> **"These men have brought old hatreds & grudges & spites from the old Union. Already we see they will willingly injure our cause to hurt Jeff Davis."**

fiction, but her most compelling task was the preparation of her journals for publication.

After a first attempt in the mid-1870s, she began a full-scale expansion and revision in 1881, retaining the diary format and allowing no anachronisms or hindsight to intrude. The book was still unfinished when she put the more than 2,500-page manuscript aside in late 1884 to struggle with the last illness and death of both James and her mother. Embroiled in legal entanglements and herself suffering from a recurring heart condition, Chesnut could not return to her book before her own death on November 22, 1886.

Prior to her death, Chesnut had asked a much younger friend to take responsibility for her journals: Isabella Martin (the "irrepressible Isabella" of the revised journal), who, following the war, had become a schoolteacher in Columbia. Martin made little effort to find a publisher until, in 1904, she met a New York writer and journalist, Myrta Lockett Avary, who read the journals and insisted they be published. The firm of D. Appleton agreed and arranged for several long excerpts to appear in the *Saturday Evening Post* under the title "A Diary From Dixie." The Appleton edition appeared in 1905 as *A Diary from Dixie, as Written by Mary Boykin Chesnut, Wife of James Chesnut, Jr., United States Senator from South Carolina, 1859–1861, and afterward an Aide to Jefferson Davis and a Brigadier-General in the Confederate Army*. Edited by Martin and Avary with a heavy hand, it contained only about half the manuscript (most of the material dealing with Camden and Columbia, for example, was cut). In 1947, a second edition entitled *A Diary from Dixie* was published, edited by novelist Ben Ames Williams, who again cut out much material and "smoothed up" Chesnut's writing. Neither edition made clear that the manuscript was in fact a much expanded, changed, and thoroughly restructured version of the original journal. Not until the 1981 publication of *Mary Chesnut's Civil War*, edited by C. Vann Woodward, was the full revised journal as Chesnut wrote it made available to the public. Woodward's edition, which clarified the precise nature of Chesnut's work, was awarded the Pulitzer Prize.

Chesnut's panorama of her times ranges from the plantation to the corridors of the capitol. A veritable "Who's Who" of the Confederacy, it provides particularly vivid portraits of the Davises, the Lees, the Louis T. Wigfalls, C. Clement Clays, John Smith Preston and his family, Stephen R. Mallory, John Bell Hood, Wade Hampton, Robert M. T. Hunter, and Joseph E. Johnston, as well as her own family members and hundreds of ordinary people from spies and shopkeepers to slaves. The book reveals a surprising range of interests and viewpoints among the members of Chesnut's circle. Strongly partisan, she was conscious of historical context from the first, and within her kaleidoscopic picture of the effects of war on everyday lives, she discerned pattern and meaning.

Chesnut offers a richly textured view of the concerns of women; indeed she was herself a complex and paradoxical woman. Private, intellectual, and often lonely, she was magnetic, charming, sought after. She loathed slavery from girlhood and asserted in March 1861, "[Senator Charles] Sumner said not one word of this hated institution which is not true," but she viewed blacks through the racist lens of her time and place. Admiring the Southern woman as noble, she nevertheless linked the plight of women to that of slaves. Gifted with wit, an ironic eye, a passionate intellect and heart, and objectivity about her own shortcomings and those of her world, Chesnut provides us a stunning eyewitness account of the society that was the Confederacy.

BIBLIOGRAPHY

Chesnut, Mary Boykin. *Mary Chesnut's Civil War*. Edited by C. Vann Woodward. New Haven, 1981.

Chesnut, Mary Boykin. *The Private Mary Chesnut: The Unpublished Civil War Diaries*. Edited by C. Vann Woodward and Elisabeth Muhlenfeld. New York, 1984.

Fox-Genovese, Elizabeth. *Within the Plantation Household: Black and White Women of the Old South*. Chapel Hill, N.C., 1988.

Muhlenfeld, Elisabeth. *Mary Boykin Chesnut: A Biography*. Baton Rouge, La., 1981.

Wiley, Bell Irvin. *Confederate Women*. Westport, Conn., 1975.

Wilson, Edmund. *Patriotic Gore: Studies in the Literature of the American Civil War*. New York, 1962.

ELISABETH MUHLENFELD

CHICKAMAUGA

The iron-hulled, schooner-rigged, twin-screw-propeller steamship *Edith* was built by John & William Dudgeon of Millwall, London, in 1864. It measured 370 gross tons, 174.1 feet long, 25.1 feet in beam, and 14.2 feet in depth of hold. *Edith* was jointly owned by the Confederate government

(three-quarters) and by Crenshaw & Collie, a private company. It made nine successful runs through the blockade, carrying mixed government and private freight.

The Confederate navy bought *Edith* at Wilmington, North Carolina, for use as a commerce raiding cruiser in September 1864. Commissioned CSS *Chickamauga* by 1st Lt. John Wilkinson, it was armed with a 12-pounder rifle forward, a 32-pounder rifle aft, and a 64-pounder rifle amidships. *Chickamauga,* with a complement of approximately 120 men, left Wilmington October 29, 1864, cruised off New York approaches, called at Bermuda (November 7–15), and returned to Wilmington on November 18. It captured seven vessels: two barks, two schooners, and the clipper ship *Shooting Star* were destroyed; two barks were bonded and set free.

An anticipated second cruise was canceled to help defend Wilmington. A detachment from *Chickamauga*'s crew manned a two-gun naval battery in defense of Fort Fisher during the first attack (December 20–27, 1864). Of thirty-two men working the guns, nineteen were killed or wounded. During the second attack (January 12–15, 1865), the gunboat carried reinforcements and shelled attacking troops. It escaped capture at the fort and harried the Union advance up the Cape Fear River until scuttled on January 25 near Indian Wells, North Carolina, to block the river. The wreck was subsequently raised, removed, and converted to a fast fruit carrier.

BIBLIOGRAPHY

Scharf, J. Thomas. *History of the Confederate States Navy*. New York, 1887. Reprint, New York, 1977.

Wilkinson, John. *The Narrative of a Blockade Runner*. New York, 1877. Reprint, Alexandria, Va., 1984.

Wise, Stephen R. *Lifeline of the Confederacy: Blockade Running during the Civil War*. Columbia, S.C., 1988.

KEVIN J. FOSTER

CHICKAMAUGA CAMPAIGN

The Battle of Chickamauga on September 19 and 20, 1863, was a decisive Confederate victory after three defeats—at Gettysburg, Vicksburg, and Knoxville. Although the Confederates did not retake Chattanooga, their objective, the victory brought new life to their cause. Chickamauga was one of the few Civil War battles fought with Southern troops (66,000) outnumbering Union troops (58,000). The victory came at a high price, however, with the Confederacy reporting nearly 18,000 casualties, and the Union, nearly 16,000.

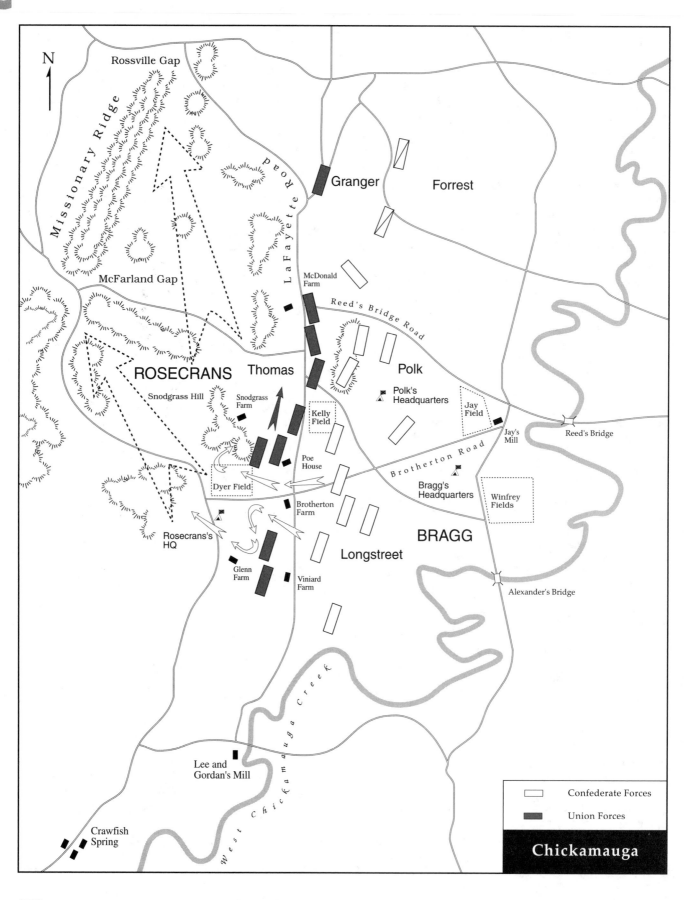

N

Rossville Gap

Missionary Ridge

LaFayette Road

Granger

Forrest

McFarland Gap

McDonald Farm

Reed's Bridge Road

ROSECRANS

Thomas

Polk

Polk's Headquarters

Jay Field

Snodgrass Hill

Snodgrass Farm

Kelly Field

Jay's Mill

Reed's Bridge

Poe House

Brotherton Road

Dyer Field

Bragg's Headquarters

Winfrey Fields

Rosecrans's HQ

Brotherton Farm

BRAGG

Glenn Farm

Longstreet

Viniard Farm

Alexander's Bridge

West Chickamauga Creek

Lee and Gordan's Mill

Crawfish Spring

	Confederate Forces
	Union Forces

Chickamauga

Known for its ferocity, the battle was often described by the men who fought it as a soldiers' fight. In many areas, the underbrush would not allow the use of artillery, leaving small units of infantry to do the fighting on their own, and the thick woods and smoke from battle made it difficult for officers to control their commands. But because both armies were composed of veterans by this time, officer control was not as important as it might have been.

The Chickamauga campaign began in early summer when the Union Army of the Cumberland moved from Murfreesboro toward Confederate defensive positions around Tullahoma, Tennessee. The Army of Tennessee, commanded by Gen. Braxton Bragg, fell back into the shelter of Chattanooga after the Union army, under Maj. Gen. William S. Rosecrans, carried out a series of skillful maneuvers that threatened the Confederate supply lines.

The Union military objective then became the important railroad hub of Chattanooga. Bragg fully expected to be overwhelmed by a Union force of over 100,000 men as he prepared to defend this vital Confederate position. In addition, the Confederate high command felt Chattanooga, because of the geography, was the last position strong enough to stop the invading Northern army. (The ridges surrounding the city only opened up to possible Union attack at one point, Lookout Valley, west of the town.)

Confederate commanders were slow in establishing a strategy, allowing the Union plan to take shape. From the end of July until September 9, the Union Army of the Cumberland set off on a maneuver that took Bragg by surprise. Rosecrans divided his army, sending two corps south to cross the Tennessee River in Alabama and one corps north. Bragg believed that the corps moving north of Chattanooga was the primary force. The Union plan worked. On September 9, the Confederates abandoned Chattanooga and moved south to block the Union advance into North Georgia by way of LaFayette.

Bragg had trouble determining where the various Union corps were located. Between September 11 and 17, he tried several probing movements in an effort to isolate and destroy the corps one by one in the mountain coves of North Georgia. He was unsuccessful, so on September 17, he decided on a plan that would place the now-reinforced Army of Tennessee between Chattanooga and the widely separated corps of the Union army. Bragg selected two crossings over the West Chickamauga Creek—Reed's Bridge and Alexander's Bridge—which he assumed would put him well north of the Union left flank at Lee and Gordon's Mill, about ten miles south of Chattanooga. Once the Confederates were across the Chickamauga, they could use the creek as an anchor on the left, push the Union corps back into the narrow mountain coves west of LaFayette, and destroy them.

With his army still widely scattered, Rosecrans now realized he had to concentrate his forces before the Confederates severed his supply lines with Chattanooga. He ordered his two southernmost corps—those of Maj. Gen. George H. Thomas and Maj. Gen. Alexander McCook—to move north as quickly as possible and concentrate at the little town of Crawfish Spring. This maneuver was carried out by the eighteenth. That evening, the Union left was extended three miles north of Lee and Gordon's Mill along the LaFayette Road and north of Bragg's crossing points on the Chickamauga Creek. Union cavalry had attempted to keep the Confederates east of the creek on the eighteenth, but the cavalry was outnumbered and the Southerners were able to cross at both locations late in the afternoon.

Early on the morning of Saturday, September 19, George Thomas sent Brig. Gen. John Brannan's division east of the LaFayette Road toward Reed's Bridge in order to capture an isolated Confederate brigade reported to be on the west side of the Chickamauga Creek. Brannan met Brig. Gen. Nathan Bedford Forrest's cavalry corps at the edge of the Jay field, just west of Jay's Mill. As Forrest was drawn into battle, he realized he was facing infantry, and he quickly searched out Confederate infantry for help. Soon there was fighting along a mile-long front extending from the Reed's Bridge Road south into the Winfrey fields. As both sides committed additional units to the battle, the woods and fields south of Reed's Bridge Road erupted with fierce fighting that spread south for almost four miles.

Meanwhile Rosecrans moved his headquarters from Crawfish Spring to a local farmstead, which brought him closer to the center of the fighting.

As the battle on the north end of the field began to subside, assaults intensified on the Union center and right. In the early afternoon, an attack against the Union center by Confederate Maj. Gen. Alexander P. Stewart's division broke through the Union line at the Poe house. Stewart's division pushed that of Brig. Gen. H. P. Van Cleve across the LaFayette Road, west through the Poe fields, and into the North Dyer fields and the Tan yard. Stewart, being unsupported, was forced to retire after heavy losses when he was hit on both flanks.

Around 2:00 P.M., a fierce contest occurred around the Viniard farm less than a mile east of Rosecran's headquarters and still farther south from where the fighting had begun. Rosecrans ordered Brig. Gen. Jefferson C. Davis forward to seek the Confederate line, and he was soon hotly engaged with Brig. Gen. Bushrod Rust Johnson's division and Col. Robert Trigg's brigade. Davis was forced back across the LaFayette Road into the fields west of the Viniard house, but he was soon reinforced by two brigades. Facing withering fire from Col. John Wilder's artillery, Johnson and Trigg were forced to retire to the woods east of the LaFayette Road.

As darkness covered the battlefield, fighting broke out in the center of the Confederate line. Maj. Gen. Patrick Cleburne's division, moving west from Jay's Mill along

Brotherton Road, struck at the Union line confronting two Southern divisions. Two brigades from B. Franklin Cheatham's division supported Cleburne's men. After an hour of confused fighting, both sides retired with heavy losses. Confederate Brig. Gen. Preston Smith and Union Col. Philemon Baldwin were both killed.

That evening, Braxton Bragg reorganized his army, dividing it into two wings, the right commanded by Lt. Gen. Leonidas Polk and the left by Lt. Gen. James Longstreet. Longstreet, who arrived about midnight, had no time to scout the field and was not familiar with the terrain.

Rosecrans, at his headquarters, held a council of war with his corps commanders and staff. He was advised to withdraw and take defensive positions along Missionary Ridge to pro-

> ## Chickamauga was one of the few Civil War battles fought with Southern troops outnumbering Union troops.

tect Chattanooga. But thinking he had won the day, he decided to stay and force Bragg from the field.

Bragg had ordered Polk to strike the Union left at daylight on the twentieth, but the battle did not get underway until midmorning. This so infuriated Bragg, he later ordered Polk's arrest. The delay, however, did give Longstreet an opportunity to look over his wing formations.

When the battle began, the Confederates met with success on their right near the McDonald farm. Two brigades of Maj. Gen. John C. Breckinridge's division enveloped the Union left and gained the rear of the northernmost Union position. Being unsupported in the attack, however, Breckinridge had to retire when faced with a flank attack from the last of the Union reserves. The Confederates, along the center of their line, had three divisions poised in the thick woods east of the Brotherton farm.

Just before noon as the battle moved south all along the line, about 11,000 Confederates crossed the LaFayette Road on a mile-long front. They caught the Union troops in Wood's division in an administrative marching formation, as they moved from their position in the Brotherton fields north to close up with another division. This unsupported movement of troops (in response to an unverified order by Rosecrans to Wood) and the timing of the Confederate's attack, led to the defeat of the Union army at Chickamauga. Longstreet's troops poured through the gap in the Union lines, causing a general rout of the Union center and right.

Brief but effective countercharges by isolated Union regiments and brigades gave George H. Thomas time to gather retreating units to form a new line facing south around the Snodgrass farm. Thomas's part of the original line east of the

LaFayette Road continued to hold through the afternoon of the twentieth. The new line on Snodgrass Hill was in serious trouble when reinforcements under Maj. Gen. Gordon Granger arrived. Because Rosecrans and two of his corps commanders left the field when the Confederate breakthrough occurred, Thomas, a Southerner by birth, was now the ranking Union officer. All afternoon, the Confederates assaulted the Federals on Snodgrass Hill. There were minor successes, but it was not until dark that the Union regiments, under Thomas's orders, began to fall back north through Rossville and McFarland gaps in Missionary Ridge toward Chattanooga.

The Confederates had won an important tactical victory, but they failed to follow up their success with quick pursuit. Instead, Bragg, feeling he had failed to destroy the Union army according to his plan, decided to lay siege to the defeated Union army in Chattanooga. Over the next two months, the Confederates tried to starve the Union army into submission. But the Federals received supplies and reinforcements until they were strong enough to break the siege in late November 1863 in the Battles of Orchard Knob, Lookout Mountain, and Missionary Ridge.

Twenty-seven years after the Battle of Chickamauga, Union and Confederate veterans returned to create the Chickamauga and Chattanooga National Military Park, the first such park. It was to be used as a place for military and historical study. It was also a place of healing for old bitter feelings between the two sides.

BIBLIOGRAPHY

Boynton, Henry V. *The Chickamauga National Military Park.* Cincinnati, Ohio, 1895.
Connelly, Thomas L. *Autumn of Glory: The Army of Tennessee, 1862–1865.* Baton Rouge, La., 1971.
Davis, William C. *The Orphan Brigade.* Baton Rouge, La., 1983.
Tower, R. Lockwood, ed. *A Carolinian Goes to War: The Civil War Narrative of Arthur Middleton Manigault.* Columbia, S.C., 1983.
Tucker, Glenn. *Chickamauga—Bloody Battle in the West.* Dayton, Ohio, 1961.

JOHN F. CISSELL

CITADEL, THE

The Citadel originated out of the fears of the white population of antebellum South Carolina. In 1822, the discovery of free black Denmark Vesey's slave insurrection conspiracy in Charleston prompted the state's legislature to authorize the construction of a fortified armory, or citadel, to defend the city from similar disturbances in the future. Funding lagged, however, until the nullification crisis of the early 1830s when state leaders, facing possible conflict with Federal troops, hastily appropriated over $200,000 to complete The Citadel in Charleston and The Arsenal in the capital city of Columbia.

In 1842, the legislature combined the two facilities into an institution of higher education, the South Carolina Military Academy. Students spent one year at The Arsenal and their final three years at The Citadel. The cadets guarded the weapons at the two sites while receiving "a broad and practical education" in military and academic disciplines. Graduates were not required, and most did not elect, to pursue a career in the armed forces, but their four years of military training gave them the skills to function as a sort of informal reserve officer corps in case of a large mobilization.

South Carolina began such a mobilization after it seceded from the Union in December 1860. Cadets from The Citadel played an important role in setting up defensive implacements around Charleston Harbor. On the morning of January 9, 1861, cadets stationed at an artillery battery on nearby Morris Island spotted and fired three shots at *Star of the West,* a merchant vessel that had been dispatched by President James Buchanan to resupply the federal garrison at Fort Sumter. The ship survived what was the first hostile fire of the secession crisis but was forced to abandon its mission. Three months later, Citadel cadets were also present at, and may have participated in, the more famous bombardment of Fort Sumter.

Over the next four years, a large percentage of The Citadel community participated in the conflict. Discounting 14 alumni who died before the spring of 1861, 226 men graduated from The Citadel between 1846 and 1864. Of them, 209 entered the armies of the Confederacy. Twenty-nine served as noncommissioned soldiers, 2 as chaplains, 11 as surgeons, and 167 as officers. The highest rank was achieved by Johnson Hagood (class of 1847), Micah Jenkins (1854), Evander McIvor Law (1856), and Ellison Capers (1857), all of whom rose to brigadier general. Forty-nine of the graduates died in the Confederate armies, 94 suffered nonfatal wounds, and 16 became prisoners of war. Citadel alumni took part in the great majority of the major engagements of the war.

In a separate category were 36 cadets who left the academy in 1862 to form their own cavalry company, the Cadet Rangers. Incorporated into the Sixth South Carolina Cavalry, they performed routine duties until March 1864 when their unit was sent to reinforce a division of the Army of Northern Virginia under Maj. Gen. Wade Hampton. The Cadet Rangers skirmished against Federals in Virginia and engaged elements of William Tecumseh Sherman's advancing Union army on the routes leading into Columbia.

The Citadel continued to operate for all but the last four months of the war. The legislature exempted students from the draft and placed them in a special branch of the state militia subject to mobilization only by order of the governor.

Perhaps as a result, enrollment at the academy increased from 125 cadets in late 1861 to 325 in late 1864.

Throughout the war, the governor ordered the cadets out of class periodically to provide support services for the Confederacy. Cadets drilled recruits, mounted defensive fortifications, manufactured ammunition, protected arms depots, guarded Union prisoners, and performed picket duty along Charleston's southern defensive perimeter. On one occasion, in December 1864, the battalion of state cadets suffered eight casualties in a skirmish with Union forces at Tulifinny Creek. Afterward, the cadets marched to Spartanburg in the western part of the state where the governor had moved the seat of his collapsing administration. Four months later, in the wake of Robert E. Lee's surrender, the governor placed the cadets on what turned out to be an indefinite furlough.

The Civil War took a significant toll on the South Carolina Military Academy. The Arsenal was burned when Sherman's army passed through Columbia in February 1865. That same month, Union forces spearheaded by black troops entered Charleston, occupied The Citadel, and closed it as an academic institution.

The Citadel reopened as a state-owned military college for men in 1882. Soon thereafter, it resumed paying homage to the Confederacy. Indeed, very late into the twentieth century, "Dixie" was regularly played by the school's band at Friday afternoon parades, the Confederate battle flag was a common sight at athletic contests, and the most prestigious academic scholarship awarded by the college was named "The Star of the West."

BIBLIOGRAPHY

Baker, Gary R. *Cadets in Gray: The Story of the Cadets of the South Carolina Military Academy and the Cadet Rangers in the Civil War.* Columbia, S.C., 1989.

Bond, Oliver J. *The Story of The Citadel.* Richmond, 1936. Reprint, Greenville, S.C., 1989.

Thomas, John Peyre. *History of the South Carolina Military Academy.* Charleston, S.C., 1893.

WINFRED B. MOORE, JR.

CITIZENSHIP

The American Constitution recognized dual American citizenship—that of the nation and that of the state. Early Supreme Court decisions gave the state the claim to precedence. It was not until the adoption of the Fourteenth Amendment in 1868 that U.S. citizenship became primary and that of the state derivative. The permanent Constitution of the Confederacy made one significant change in the matter of citizenship. As a concession to state rights, federal jurisdiction was removed from controversies between citizens of different states, leaving such matters entirely to state courts. The Confederacy inherited the remaining U.S. laws and rulings on citizenship when Congress ordered the continuation of all U.S. laws not inconsistent with the Confederate Constitution.

The only subsequent change was a law of August 22, 1861, conferring all the rights of citizenship upon noncitizens in the army and promising them full citizenship after the war in any state of their choice if they would renounce all other allegiance and swear to uphold the Confederate Constitution and its laws.

The naturalization laws inherited from the United States required five years of continued residence in a Confederate state, a declaration of intent at least two years before admission to citizenship, a renunciation of past allegiance, and an oath to support the Confederate Constitution and that of the state in which the person resided. Thus Congress implied that allegiance to the state was as important as that to the Confederacy.

Several efforts were made to give the states a stronger role in the process. In January 1862 Congress passed a bill repealing all existing laws of naturalization and putting the process entirely in the states' hands. President Jefferson Davis vetoed it on the grounds that it did not protect the right of foreigners living in the Confederacy and that it violated a constitutional provision that Congress set the rules for naturalization. Several efforts to pass a similar bill were made, but all failed.

Alien enemies residing in the Confederacy suffered the tribulations of wartime. A law of August 8, 1861, required all alien enemies to leave the Confederacy within forty days. Under the sequestration laws, the courts issued thousands of writs of garnishment against their property. Both Confederate and state courts refused to hear cases when

> ## [The Confederate] Congress implied that allegiance to the state was as important as that to the Confederacy.

the plaintiff was an alien enemy. Those Union sympathizers who kept their sympathies secret and did not resort to treasonable activities, however, seem to have escaped with both life and property intact.

The possibility that Confederates who fell into enemy hands might be treated as rebels never materialized. Though the United States never recognized the Confederacy, it regarded the Southern nation as a belligerency, and captured Confederate soldiers and alien enemies were treated

as legitimate prisoners of war. Confederates abroad suffered no discrimination, though Confederate agents could never confer officially with foreign governments.

[*See also* Confiscation; *article on* Confederate Sequestration; Foreigners; Northerners.]

BIBLIOGRAPHY

Kettner, James H. *The Development of American Citizenship, 1608–1870.* Chapel Hill, N.C., 1978.

Moore, Albert B. *Conscription and Conflict in the Confederacy.* New York, 1924.

Robinson, William M., Jr. *Justice in Grey: A History of the Judicial System of the Confederate States of America.* Cambridge, Mass., 1941.

Yearns, Wilfred B. *The Confederate Congress.* Athens, Ga., 1960.

W. BUCK YEARNS

CIVIL LIBERTIES

On February 22, 1862, the president of the Confederate States of America proclaimed in his inaugural address that his administration would continue to cherish and preserve the personal liberties of citizens. Protecting individual rights was a paramount reason for secession, and the Confederate Constitution (Article I, Section 9) incorporated all of the guarantees of civil liberties found in the amended U.S. Constitution. Jefferson Davis boasted that, in contrast to the United States of America, which continued to exercise "tyrannical" authority as it had in suppressing civil liberties in Maryland, "there has been no act on our part to impair personal liberty or the freedom of speech, of thought, or of the press."

Events in the next few months demonstrated the great difficulty of maintaining such a position while fighting an unlimited modern war for the Confederacy's survival. This war forced the mobilization of most human and material resources and the centralization of authority, processes that inevitably challenged individual liberties as well as state rights. If the Confederate government assiduously protected civil liberties, its war effort could be undermined by spoken and written criticism, unfettered movement of people and information, and severe shortages of troops. If, however, it restricted the spoken and written word and the activities of its citizens or suspended civil government and the writ of habeas corpus, it risked alienating the public whose support was essential for military success.

Faced with this dilemma and hard-pressed on the battlefield, Confederate leaders at both the national and the state levels heatedly debated civil libertarian issues. Military necessity ultimately dictated the three areas in which they reluctantly, but legally, restricted civil liberties: declaring martial law, conscripting men into military service, and suspending the privilege of the writ of habeas corpus. In each case, unlike President Abraham Lincoln, President Davis adhered to strict constructionist principles and persuaded Congress to pass appropriate enabling legislation before he approved restrictions on civil liberties.

On February 27, 1862, Congress authorized the president to suspend the privilege of the writ of habeas corpus and to declare martial law in areas threatened by the enemy. Davis immediately placed Norfolk and Portsmouth under martial law so that the military could arrest and detain disloyal individuals. Then on March 1, in a controversial and perhaps excessive attempt to curtail spying and criminal activity in the vulnerable capital, Davis appointed Gen. John H. Winder the military governor of Richmond. Within a year, Congress permitted generals to declare martial law so they could enforce conscription and maintain public order near the front. This was especially detested in Unionist strongholds, such as eastern Tennessee, and in locales with burgeoning peace societies, such as Alabama, northeastern Mississippi, and southwestern Virginia. Within his own administration Davis faced a harsh and outspoken critic, Vice President Alexander H. Stephens, who repeatedly denounced martial law, conscription, and the suspension of habeas corpus as unnecessary violations of civil rights that undermined the integrity of the Southern republic. These issues further polarized Confederate politics into pro- and anti-Davis factions.

In the spring of 1862, with casualties mounting and one-year volunteers heading home, the Confederacy resorted to conscription. This infringement upon personal liberty incensed many Southerners, including several outspoken generals. Critics recalled the denunciation of forced service in the Declaration of Independence and, ironically, noted its similarity to slavery. Governor Joseph E. Brown of Georgia called Davis an "emperor" and began a lengthy debate on the unconstitutionality of conscription. Citing state rights, Governor Zebulon B. Vance exempted North Carolina officials from the despised draft. Some judges even issued writs of habeas corpus to free draftees.

The widespread opposition to conscription convinced Congress to permit President Davis to suspend the privilege of the writ of habeas corpus three separate times for a total of sixteen months. They justified these suspensions and the repeated use of martial law as necessary for apprehending thousands of draft evaders and keeping them in the ranks. Yet such measures inevitably produced further dissent among Southerners. Georgia's legislature unanimously condemned the third suspension, and state legislators in Mississippi and Louisiana passed hostile resolutions.

Southern newspapers took Davis to task, violently attacking him, his administration, and his generals for interfering with habeas corpus, imposing conscription, and abusively enforcing the Impressment Act. The fiercely independent press undermined morale on the home front and ignored the censorship restrictions intended to protect the military. Congress passed a law in January 1862 making it a crime to publish news about Confederate land and naval forces. Yet neither national nor state authorities ever suppressed such outspoken journals as the *Richmond Examiner,* the *Charleston Mercury,* or the *Raleigh Standard.* Eventually, several prominent generals closed their camps to reporters, and irate troops and vigilantes destroyed a few presses.

Early in 1863 the Confederate Senate considered a sedition bill that would have curtailed freedom of the press and of speech. The measure died because most Southern legislators were avid proponents of free speech. Among the most vociferous was Henry S. Foote of Tennessee, who compiled a "shocking catalogue" of his government's questionable arrests following the suspension of habeas corpus. For example, General Winder jailed John Minor Botts, a former U.S. congressman, for declaring his neutrality, and the Reverend Alden Bosserman for openly praying for the defeat of "this unholy rebellion." Most preachers and teachers accepted the restrictions on free speech in the South's closed society. But some who merely questioned the course of events lost jobs, and staunch Unionists fled northward. Others secretly supported peace societies, and angry mobs and zealous soldiers forcibly expelled a few. In lieu of specific legislation, the public pressures that had long stifled discussion about slavery now tried to impose loyalty to the Confederacy through intimidation and book burning.

As death and deprivation intensified public disaffection, tighter restrictions upon Southerners proved counterproductive. Disloyal words and deeds became too widespread to curtail. By early 1865, despite presidential pleas, Congress refused to sanction further suspensions of the writ of habeas corpus. De jure and de facto proscriptions of civil liberties repeatedly generated profound controversies, but ultimately they had only marginal impact on the demise of the war-torn Confederacy.

[*See also* Conscription; Habeas Corpus; Military Justice.]

BIBLIOGRAPHY

Beals, Carleton. *War within a War: The Confederacy against Itself.* Philadelphia, 1965.

Eaton, Clement. *A History of the Southern Confederacy.* New York, 1954.

Ramsdell, Charles. *Behind the Lines in the Southern Confederacy.* Baton Rouge, La., 1944.

Robbins, John B. "The Confederacy and the Writ of Habeas Corpus." *Georgia Historical Quarterly* 55 (1971): 83–101.

Tatum, Georgia Lee. *Disloyalty in the Confederacy.* Chapel Hill, N.C., 1934.

BLAKE TOUCHSTONE

CIVIL SERVICE

The Confederate government had more than 70,000 civilian employees at its peak, compared to 100,000 for the Union. The administration was organized into six departments: a staff of 29 in the State Department; 125 in the Department of Justice; 1,016 in the Navy Department; 2,780 at the Treasury; 9,183 in the Post Office; and 57,124 civilians in the War Department.

Some efforts were made at formalizing procedures. The Ordnance Bureau used competitive science examinations for its skilled positions. The postal service organized a formal training school for clerks and officers. The Treasury Department established written work regulations. The standard workday in the State Department and the Treasury was 9:00 A.M. to 3:00 P.M., in contrast to the eleven-hour average in industry in that era. But senior officials were expected to put in whatever hours were necessary.

Cabinet secretaries received $6,000 per year; clerks' salaries generally ranged from $700 to $1,500 and did not keep pace with inflation. Bureau chief Robert Kean complained in 1863 that his $3,000 salary went only as far as $300 "in ordinary times." In at least three instances, government workers went on strike for higher pay: postal clerks at Richmond and women at the Brown's Island arsenal (twice).

Civil servants were exempted from military service. But 2,000 clerks from all departments were organized into a military home guard, which was called out periodically to defend the Richmond capital.

The postal service was the first department organized. This was accomplished largely because Postmaster General John H. Reagan had persuaded five high-ranking Southern officials of the U.S. Post Office to join the Confederacy, bringing with them organizational documents, and because he absorbed nearly intact the U.S. postal service of the Southern states, as personnel shifted their allegiance. The Union maintained U.S. mail service throughout the South (and collected receipts from Confederate postmasters) until June 1, 1861.

At peak strength, the postal service employed 9,183: 72 at the central office; 7,009 postmasters and 93 clerks; 1,950 mail contractors; and 59 telegraph workers. Clerks in the Richmond Post Office earned $700 to $800 per year. They went on strike from August 21 through 23, 1863, until the postmaster general agreed to press Congress for a pay increase. The service showed a financial surplus every year, and Reagan boasted that he had needed proportionately only half the personnel that the U.S. Post Office had used.

The Department of State, usually the most prestigious in a government, was the smallest of the Confederacy's departments and was described as a "backwater office." It had only 29 staff members: the secretary ($6,000), four clerks ($1,000 to $1,500), a messenger ($500), and a porter ($360) in the central office, and 22 commissioners and agents in the diplomatic service. Secretary Robert Toombs remarked that there was so little to do that he "carried the State department in his hat."

The Department of Justice had a roster of 126: 14 in its central office; 16 district judges throughout the Confederacy, each with a district attorney and marshal, plus a total of 54 clerks; and 10 in other offices. The Constitution provided for a supreme court, but it was never established. The attorney general appointed judges (whose salaries ranged from $5,000 in Louisiana to $2,500 in Florida), issued patents (75 in 1862), and provided legal opinions for the other departments (217 in all).

Military officers headed the five bureaus of the Navy Department, but a civilian staff of 16 was employed at its Richmond headquarters and approximately 1,000 civilian laborers at its more than a dozen shipyards, laboratories, cannon foundry, and powder mill. Clerks earned salaries of

> **The Confederate government generally attracted effective civil servants. Governmental operations were reasonably efficient despite the lack of resources.**

$1,000 to $2,100, messengers $500, and laborers an estimated $800 per year. The department was noteworthy for its developments in ironclad ships, the submarine, and torpedo mines, all of which transformed naval warfare.

Next to the military, finance was the gravest issue for the Confederacy. The Treasury Department had some 2,780 civilian employees: 562 clerks and messengers and 14 officials in its central office; 400 customs collectors (a declining number as the Union blockade intensified); and 1,789 appraisers, tax collectors, and other staff.

Secretary Christopher G. Memminger promulgated a written set of work regulations providing for a six-month probationary period for new employees before "permanent commission," a six-hour workday, and standards of conduct. The rules drew some criticism, and one man was fired for "communication to a Richmond newspaper." Chief clerk Henry Capers attributed the dissent to the disposition of Southerners: "To command was so much the nature of our people that it was, of all things, most repugnant to their natures to be commanded."

The department employed a large number of women as "note clippers" and "note signers." The currency was lithographed, but, unlike modern procedure, the signatures of officials were added by hand. The so-called Treasury girls faced a quota of 3,200 notes to sign per day and had their pay docked ten cents for each note spoiled. Women clerks were paid $65 per month in 1863. Although this rate matched that of male postal clerks, it was barely half the standard $125 per month for men in comparable Treasury positions.

The War Department was by far the largest office, with an estimated 57,124 civilian employees. There were 277 clerks and other staff at Richmond headquarters. Wartime constraints forced even small economies: envelopes from correspondents were turned inside out and reused.

The Ordnance Bureau operated 17 arsenals, foundries, and powder mills employing by 1865 some 3,691 white men and 2,245 black men, plus a number of women. In addition, 13,228 government miners dug for gunpowder ores and 11,500 constructed railroads and fortifications: 1,500 whites and 10,000 slaves and freedmen. The Conscription Bureau had 2,443 agents, the Tax Collection Bureau 2,965, and the Supply Service 12,533. The Medical Corps operated dozens of hospitals with a civilian staff of 8,250.

Women were employed in great numbers in the War Department: 3,300 as nurses, matrons, and laundresses in the hospitals, and at least 5,000 making clothing in the quartermaster factories. An 1863 explosion in a Brown's Island "condemned cartridge" refitting shop killed 45 women and 2 men. Later that year, a wage strike there raised government pay from $2.50 to $3.00 per day. By 1864, married women were earning $7.00 per day and single women $5.00. Another strike by 100 women, seeking to eliminate the differential, was unsuccessful. In their wartime work, women proved themselves as capable as men.

The Confederate government generally attracted effective civil servants. Governmental operations were reasonably efficient despite the lack of resources. But the Confederacy did not match the levels of centralization and administrative coordination among departments that marked the U.S. government under Abraham Lincoln.

[See also African American Forgeworkers; Conscription; Judiciary; Medical Department; Navy Department; Ordnance Bureau; Patent Office; Post Office Department; State Department; Niter and Mining Bureau; Taxation; Treasury Department; War Department.]

BIBLIOGRAPHY

Capers, Henry D. *Recollections of the Civil Service of the Confederate Government.* Atlanta, 1887.

Jones, John B. *A Rebel War Clerk's Diary.* Edited by Earl S. Miers. New York, 1961.

Kaufman, Janet E. "Treasury Girls." *Civil War Times Illustrated* 25 (May 1986): 32–38.

Kean, Robert G. H. *Inside the Confederate Government.* Edited by Edward Younger. New York, 1957.

Van Riper, Paul P., and Harry N. Scheiber. "The Confederate Civil Service." *Journal of Southern History* 25 (1959): 448–470.

JAMES J. HORGAN

CIVIL WAR

[*For discussion of the course of the war itself, see entries on particular battles and states.*]

Names of the War

With the echo of the first shot in April 1861, Americans began arguing over a name for the conflict. The debate has waned with the passing decades, but it still has not ended. By far the most popular of the titles is "The Civil War." Both sides used the term throughout the four-year struggle. In the South, generals such as Lee, Longstreet, and Gordon, as well as wartime Richmond newspapers, referred to the war by that name. The term's opponents, concentrated in the South, argue that "The Civil War" suggests a rebellion against lawful authority. It also implies that two different sections of the nation were fighting for control of a single government, when in fact the Confederacy was seeking to exist independently. Justifications for the name are that the struggle came within the definition of civil war expounded by many philosophers of that day, that the conflict was indeed a civil war in areas like Missouri, Tennessee, and Kentucky, and that the term is short, convenient, and less controversial than any of the other names.

"War between the States" has been a favorite Southern appellation since the conflict ended. Not used during the war itself, the term came into use with the publication in 1868 of Alexander H. Stephen's *A Constitutional View of the Late War between the States.* It enjoyed its highest boost in popularity during the Spanish-American War, when Americans of North and South joined together in a common cause. Southern congressmen once sought to make the term the official title, but a resolution to that effect was tabled. An objection to this name is that it is long and cumbersome. Further, the Southern nation was a confederation of eleven sovereignties, with much more involved than merely state rights. This title is thus misleading.

The Union counterpart in titles is "War of the Rebellion." Northerners at the time considered the South to be in rebellion, and many Confederates seemed to take pride in being called "Rebels." This name is too long, however, and it is also erroneous because it was a full-scale war, with two organized governments respecting the rules of war. Yet "War of the Rebellion" continues to live as the title of the 128 huge volumes containing the official records of the Union and Confederate armies.

Two names, "Second American Revolution" and "War for Southern Independence," were outgrowths of Confederate beliefs that their struggle paralleled the colonists' fight in the 1770s to break away from British control. Foreign writers often referred to the North-South contest as "The

Confederate War," and a Maryland writer proposed "War of Secession." Both terms, however, suggest that secession was the primary cause of the war, which then puts the blame for hostilities solely on the South.

In many parts of the old Confederacy today, "The War" is a phrase that needs no explanation. Other titles with short-lived appearances have included "War of Sections," "The War for Nationality," "Conflict of the Sixties," "The War against Slavery," "The Uncivil War," "The Brothers' War," "War against the States," and "The Lost Cause."

Among the somewhat facetious names given by Southerners are "The Yankee War," "The Southern Defense against Northern Aggression," and "Mr. Lincoln's War." By far the most diplomatic of all the titles for the American struggle is "The Late Unpleasantness."

[*See also* Battles, Naming of.]

BIBLIOGRAPHY

Fish, Carl Russell. *The American Civil War.* New York, 1937.
Roller, David C., and Robert W. Twyman, eds. *The Encyclopedia of Southern History.* Baton Rouge, La., 1979.

JAMES I. ROBERTSON, JR.

Causes of the War

During the Civil War, few people on either side would have dissented from Abraham Lincoln's statement in his second inaugural address that slavery "was, somehow, the cause of the war." After all, had not Jefferson Davis, a large slaveholder, justified secession in 1861 as an act of self-defense against the Lincoln administration, whose policy of excluding slavery from the territories would make "property in slaves so insecure as to be comparatively worthless . . . thereby annihilating in effect property worth thousands of millions of dollars"? And had not the new vice president of the Confederate

> ## The United States, said Stephens, had been founded on the false idea that all men are created equal.

States of America, Alexander H. Stephens, said in a speech at Savannah on March 21, 1861, that slavery was "the immediate cause of the late rupture and the present revolution" of Southern independence? The old confederation known as the United States, said Stephens, had been founded on the false idea that all men are created equal. The Confederacy, by contrast, "is founded upon exactly the opposite idea; its

foundations are laid, its cornerstone rests, upon the great truth that the negro is not equal to the white man; that slavery, subordination to the superior race, is his natural and moral condition. This, our new Government, is the first, in the history of the world, based on this great physical, philosophical, and moral truth."

Historical Views of the Causes of the War

For at least a half century after the war, this remained the predominant interpretation of its causes. In 1913 the foremost Civil War historian of his day, James Ford Rhodes, declared definitively that "of the American Civil War it may safely be asserted that there was a single cause, slavery." Although no historian today would put it quite so baldly, most of them would agree with the basic point. But during the century and a quarter since the guns ceased firing, dissenters from this viewpoint have provoked many rhetorical battles over the causes of the war.

Early Dissension. Two of the earliest dissenters were none other than Jefferson Davis and Alexander Stephens. After 1865 slavery was a dead and discredited institution. It no longer seemed appropriate, as it had in 1861, to emphasize it proudly as the reason for secession. To salvage honor and assert a sound constitutional basis for their lost cause, Stephens and Davis now insisted that Southern states had seceded and gone to war not to protect slavery but to vindicate state sovereignty. In *A Constitutional View of the War between the States,* which invented the favorite Southern name for the conflict three years after it was over, Stephens maintained that "the War had its origin in opposing principles" concerning not slavery and freedom but rather "the organic Structure of the Government of the States. . . . It was a strife between the principles of Federation, on the one side, and Centralism, or Consolidation, on the other." And Davis, writing his book *The Rise and Fall of the Confederate Government* in the 1870s, insisted that the Confederates, like their forefathers of 1776, had fought solely "for the defense of an inherent, unalienable right . . . to withdraw from a Union into which they had, as sovereign communities, voluntarily entered. . . . The existence of African servitude was in no wise the cause of the conflict, but only an incident."

The Progressive Theory. This virgin-birth theory of secession became widely accepted among Southern whites: the Confederacy had been conceived by no worldly cause but by constitutional principle. Thus the Civil War was a war of Northern aggression against Southern rights, not a war to preserve the American nation and, ultimately, to abolish slavery. By the 1920s, though, the notion that a people would go to war over principles had become suspect among historians. Human behavior, most of them thought, is rooted in materialism. The "Progressive school" dominated American historiography from the 1920s to the 1940s. This school posited a clash between interest groups and classes as the central theme of American history: industry versus agriculture, capital versus labor, railroads versus farmers, manufacturers versus consumers, and so on. The real issues of American politics, in this interpretation, revolved around the economic interests of these contesting groups: tariffs, taxes, land policies, industrial and labor policies, subsidies to business or agriculture, and the like.

The Progressive school explained the causes of the Civil War within this interpretive framework. The war transferred to the battlefield a long-running contest between plantation agriculture and industrializing capitalism, and the industrialists emerged triumphant. It was not primarily a conflict between North and South: "Merely by the accidents of climate, soil, and geography," wrote the foremost Progressive historian Charles A. Beard, "was it a sectional struggle"—the accidental fact that plantation agriculture was located in the South and industry mainly in the North. Nor was it a contest between slavery and freedom. Slavery just happened to be the labor system of plantation agriculture, as wage labor was the system of Northern industry. For some Progressive historians, neither system was significantly worse or better than the other—"wage slavery" was as exploitative as chattel bondage. In any case, they said, slavery was not a moral issue for anybody except a tiny handful of abolitionists; its abolition was a mere incident of the destruction of the plantation order by the war. The *real* issues between the North and the South in antebellum politics were the tariff, government subsidies to transportation and manufacturing, public land sales, and related questions on which manufacturing and planting interests had clashing viewpoints.

This interpretive synthesis proved a godsend for a generation of mostly Southern-born historians who seized upon it as proof that slavery had little to do with the origins of the Confederacy. The Nashville Fugitives, an influential group of historians, novelists, and poets who gathered at Vanderbilt University and published in 1930 a famous manifesto, *I'll Take My Stand,* set the tone for the new Southern interpretation of the Civil War's causes. It was a blend of the old Confederate apologia voiced by Jefferson Davis and the new Progressive synthesis created by Charles Beard. The Confederacy fought not only for the constitutional principle of state rights and self-government but also for the preservation of a stable, pastoral, agrarian civilization in the face of the overweening, acquisitive, imperialistic ambitions of an urban-industrial Leviathan. The real issue that brought on the war was not slavery—this institution, wrote one of the Nashville Fugitives, "was part of the agrarian system, but only one element and not an essential one"—but rather such matters as the tariff, banks, subsidies to railroads, and similar questions in which the grasping businessmen of the North sought to advance their interests at the expense of Southern farmers and planters. Lincoln was not elected in 1860 in the name of freedom over slavery; rather, his election represented the ascendancy of tariffs and railroads and factories over agriculture and the graces of a rural society. The result was the triumph of acquisitive, power-hungry robber barons over the highest type of civilization America had ever known—the Old South. It was no coincidence that this interpretation emerged during the same period that the novel and movie *Gone with the Wind* became one of the most popular literary and cinematic successes of all time; history and popular culture on this occasion marched hand in hand.

Revisionism. An offshoot of this interpretation of the Civil War's causes dominated the work of academic historians during the 1940s. This offshoot came to be called revisionism. The revisionists denied that sectional conflicts between

> The war was brought on not by genuine issues but by extremists on both sides. . . .

North and South—whether over slavery, state rights, or industry versus agriculture—were genuinely divisive. The differences between North and South, wrote one of the leading revisionists, Avery Craven, were "no greater than those existing at different times between East and West." The other giant of revisionism, James G. Randall, suggested that they were no greater than the differences between Chicago and downstate Illinois.

Such disparities did not have to lead to war; they could and should have been accommodated peacefully within the political system. The Civil War was therefore not an irrepressible conflict, as earlier generations had called it, but *The Repressible Conflict,* as Craven titled one of his books. The war was brought on not by genuine issues but by extremists on both sides—rabble-rousing abolitionists and Southern fire-eaters—who whipped up emotions and hatreds in North and South for their own partisan purposes. The passions they aroused got out of hand in 1861 and erupted into a tragic, unnecessary war that accomplished nothing that could not have been achieved by negotiation and compromise.

Of course, any such compromise in 1861 would have left slavery in place. But the revisionists, like the Progressives and the Vanderbilt agrarians, considered slavery unimportant; as Craven put it, the institution of bondage "played a rather minor part in the life of the South and the Negro." Slavery would have died peacefully of natural causes in another generation or two had not fanatics forced the issue to armed conflict. This hints at another feature of revisionism: while blaming extremists on both sides, revisionists focused most of their criticism on antislavery radicals, even antislavery moderates like Lincoln, who harped on the evils of slavery and expressed a determination to rein in what they called "the Slave Power." This had goaded the South into a defensive response that finally caused Southern states to secede to free themselves from the incessant pressure of these self-righteous Yankee zealots. Revisionism thus tended to portray Southern whites, even the fire-eaters, as victims reacting to Northern attacks; it truly was a war of Northern aggression.

Slavery

Since the 1950s, however, historiography has come full circle to Lincoln's assertion that "slavery was, somehow, the cause of the war." The state rights, Progressive, agrarian, and revisionist schools seem moribund if not actually dead. To be sure, echoes of some of these interpretations can still be heard. Economic conflicts of interest, for example, did occur between the agricultural South and the industrializing North. These conflicts emerged in debates over tariffs, banks, land grants, and similar issues. But these matters divided parties and interest groups more than North and South. The South in the 1840s and 1850s had its advocates of industrialization and protective tariffs and a national bank, just as the North had its millions of farmers and its low-tariff, anti-bank Democratic majority in many states. The Civil War was not fought over issues of the tariff or banks or agrarianism versus industrialism. These and similar kinds of questions have been bread-and-butter issues of American politics throughout the nation's history, often generating a great deal more friction and heat than they did in the 1850s. But they have not caused any great shooting wars. Nor was the Civil War a consequence of false issues trumped up by demagogues or fanatics. It was fought over real, profound, intractable problems that Americans on both sides believed went to the heart of their society and its future.

In 1858 two prominent political leaders, one of whom expected to be elected president in 1860 and the other of whom *was* elected president, voiced the stark nature of the problem. The social systems of slave labor and free labor "are more than incongruous—they are incompatible," said Senator William H. Seward of New York. The friction between them "is an irrepressible conflict between opposing and enduring forces, and it means that the United States must and will, sooner or later, become either entirely a slaveholding nation, or entirely a free-labor nation." In Illinois, senatorial candidate Abraham Lincoln launched his campaign with a theme taken from the Bible: "A house divided against itself cannot stand." The United States, he said, "cannot endure, permanently, half *slave* and half free. . . . It will become *all* one thing, or *all* the other." The policy of Lincoln's party—and Seward's—was to "arrest the further spread of [slavery], and place it where the public mind shall rest in the belief that it is in the course of ultimate extinction."

Sectionalism. When Seward and Lincoln uttered these words, the free and slave states had coexisted peacefully under the same Constitution for seventy years. They shared the same language, legal system, political culture, social mores, religious values, and a common heritage of struggle to form the nation. Yet by the late 1850s, Southern spokesmen agreed with Lincoln and Seward that an irreconcilable conflict within a house divided into free and slave states had split the country into two antagonistic cultures. "In this country have arisen two races," said a Savannah lawyer—and he meant not black and white but Northern and Southern —"two races which, although claiming a common parentage, have been so entirely separated by climate, by morals, by religion, and by estimates so totally opposite to all that constitutes honor, truth, and manliness, that they cannot longer exist under the same government."

What lay at the root of this antagonism? Slavery. It was the sole institution not shared by North and South. Both had cities, farms, railroads, ports, factories, colleges, literary societies, poets, poverty, wealth, slums, mansions, capitalists,

> **"On the subject of slavery the North and South . . . are not only two Peoples, but they are rival, hostile Peoples."**

workers, riverboats, gamblers, thieves, racial segregation, immigrants, Protestants, Catholics, Jews, ethnic and class conflict, and almost anything else one might name—but only one had slavery. That "peculiar institution" defined the South. The *Charleston Mercury* stated in an editorial in 1858 that "on the subject of slavery the North and South . . . are not only two Peoples, but they are rival, hostile Peoples." When the members of a South Carolina planter family who contributed four brothers to the Confederate army learned of Lincoln's election as president, they agreed that "now a stand must be made for African slavery or it is forever lost." In going out of a Union ruled by Yankee fanatics, "we . . . are contending for all that we hold dear—our Property—our Institutions—our Honor. . . . I hope it will end in establishing a Southern Confederacy who will have among themselves slavery a bond a union stronger than any which holds the north together."

Slaves were the principal form of wealth in the South. The market value of the 4 million slaves in 1860 was $3 billion—more than the value of land, or cotton, or anything else in the slave states. It was slave labor that made it possible for the American South to grow three-quarters of the world's cotton, which in turn constituted half of all American exports. But slavery was much more than an economic system. It was a means of maintaining racial control and white supremacy. Northern whites were also committed to white supremacy. But with 95 percent of the nation's black population in the South, the region's scale of concern with this matter was so much greater as to constitute a different order of magnitude and create a radically different set of social priorities.

The economic, social, and racial centrality of slavery to "the Southern way of life" focused the region's politics overwhelmingly on defense of the institution. Many Southern leaders in the age of Thomas Jefferson had considered slavery a "necessary evil" that would eventually disappear from this land of liberty. But with the rise of the cotton kingdom, slavery had become in the eyes of Southern whites by the 1830s a "positive good" for black and white alike. Proslavery pamphlets and books became a cottage industry. Their main themes were summed up in the title of a pamphlet by a clergyman published in 1850: *A Defense of the South against the Reproaches and Encroachments of the North: In which Slavery Is Shown to Be an Institution of God Intended to Form the Basis of the Best Social State and the Only Safeguard and Permanence of a Republican Government.* The foremost defender of slavery until his death in 1850 was John C. Calhoun, who noted proudly that "many in the South once believed that slavery was a moral and political evil. That folly and delusion are gone. We see it now in its true light, and regard it as the most safe and stable basis for free institutions in the world" and "essential to the peace, safety, and prosperity" of the South.

The defensive tone of much of the proslavery argument was provoked by the rise of militant abolitionism in the North after 1830. William Lloyd Garrison, Theodore Weld, Wendell Phillips, Frederick Douglass, and a host of other eloquent crusaders branded slavery as a sin, a defiance of God's law and of Christian ethics, immoral, inhumane, a violation of the republican principle of liberty on which the nation had been founded. Although the radical abolitionists did not get far in the North with their message of racial equality, the belief that slavery was an unjust, obsolete, and unrepublican institution—a "relic of barbarism" as the new Republican party described slavery in its 1856 platform—entered mainstream northern politics in the 1850s. "The monstrous injustice of slavery," said Abraham Lincoln in 1854, "deprives our republican example of its just influence in the world—enables the enemies of free institutions, with plausibility, to taunt us as hypocrites."

Expansion of Slavery. But it was not the *existence* of slavery that polarized the nation to the point of breaking apart. It was the issue of the *expansion* of slave territory. Most of the crises that threatened the bonds of union arose over this matter. The first one, in 1820, was settled by the Missouri Compromise, which balanced the admission of Missouri as a slave state with the simultaneous admission of Maine as a free state and banned slavery in the rest of the Louisiana Purchase territory north of 36°30′ while permitting it south of that line. Paired admission of slave and free states during the next quarter century kept their numbers equal. But the annexation of Texas as a huge new slave state—with the

potential of carving out several more within its boundaries—provoked new tensions. It also provoked war with Mexico in 1846, which resulted in American acquisition of three-quarters of a million square miles of new territory in the Southwest. This opened a Pandora's box of troubles that could not be closed.

Convinced that the "slave power" in Washington had engineered the annexation of Texas and the Mexican War, the "antislavery power" in Congress determined to flex its muscles. In 1846 David Wilmot of Pennsylvania introduced in the House of Representatives a resolution banning slavery in all territory that might be conquered from Mexico. By an almost unanimous vote of all Northern congressmen against the virtually unanimous vote of all Southern representatives, the resolution passed—because the larger Northern population gave the free states a majority in the House. Equal representation in the Senate enabled Southerners to block the Wilmot Proviso there. But this issue framed national politics for the next fifteen years.

The most ominous feature of the Wilmot Proviso was its wrenching of the normal pattern of party divisions into a sectional pattern. On most issues before 1846, Northern and Southern Whigs had voted together and Northern and Southern Democrats had done likewise. But on the Wilmot Proviso, Northern Whigs and Democrats had voted together against a solid alliance of Southern Whigs and Democrats. This became the norm for all votes on any issue concerning slavery—and most of the important national political issues in the 1850s did concern slavery. This sectional alignment reflected a similar pattern in social and cultural matters. In the 1840s the two largest religious denominations, the Methodists and Baptists, had split into separate Northern and Southern churches over whether a slave owner could be appointed as a bishop or missionary of the denomination.

In addition to a growing conviction in the North that slavery was contrary to the teachings of Christ, a secular free-labor ideology had become the dominant Northern worldview. It held up the ideals of equal opportunity, equal rights, the dignity of labor, and social mobility. Slavery represented the opposite. It denied equal opportunity and rights, degraded the concept of labor, and blocked social mobility. Most important, it afflicted poor but aspiring white men as well as slaves. "Slavery withers and blights all it touches," wrote a free-labor advocate. "It is a curse upon the poor, free, laboring white men. . . . They are depressed, poor, impoverished, degraded in caste, because labor is disgraceful." Wherever slavery goes, said a New York congressman in 1849, "there is in substance no middle class. Great wealth or hopeless poverty is the settled condition."

The national political controversy focused on slavery in the territories because though the Constitution protected the institution in the states where it existed, Congress could presumably legislate the status of territories. And equally important, the territories represented the future. In 1850 they constituted more than half of the landmass of the United States. From 1790 to 1850 the territories that became states accounted for more than half of the nation's increase in population. As that process continued, the new territories would shape the future. To ensure a free-labor destiny, Northerners wanted to keep slavery out of these territories. In 1848 a new political party, the Free-Soil party, was founded on this platform. "We are opposed to the extension of slavery," declared a Free-Soil newspaper, because if slavery goes into a new territory "the free labor of the states will not. . . . If the free labor of the states goes there, the slave labor of the southern states will not, and in a few years the country will teem with an active and energetic population." And eventually, the expansion of free territory and the containment of slavery would make freedom the wave of the future, placing slavery "in the course of ultimate extinction," as Lincoln phrased it.

That was just what Southerners feared. The North already had a majority in the House; new free states would give them a majority in the Senate as well as an unchallengeable domination of the electoral college. "Long before the North gets this vast accession of strength," warned a South Carolinian, "she will ride over us rough shod, proclaim freedom or something equivalent to it to our Slaves and reduce us to the condition of Haiti. . . . If we do not act now, we deliberately consign our children, not our posterity, but *our children* to the flames."

This argument swayed white nonslaveholders in the South as much as it did slaveholders. Whites of both classes considered the bondage of blacks to be the basis of liberty for whites. Slavery, they declared, elevated all whites to an equality of status and dignity by confining menial labor and caste subordination to blacks. "If slaves are freed," maintained proslavery spokesmen, whites "will become menials. We will lose every right and liberty which belongs to the name of freemen." The Northern threat to slavery thus menaced all whites. Nonslaveholders also agreed with slaveholders that the institution must be allowed to go into the territories. Such expansion might increase their own chances of becoming slave owners. The attempt by Northern Free-Soilers to exclude slavery from the territories united Southern whites in a conviction that Northerners were trying to place a stigma on the South of "degrading inequality . . . which says to the Southern man, Avaunt! you are not my equal, and hence are to be excluded as carrying a moral taint." The South could not tolerate such an insult. "Death is preferable to acknowledged inferiority."

The controversy over slavery in the region conquered from Mexico led to a crisis that almost provoked secession in 1850. In the end, the complex Compromise of 1850 narrowly averted this outcome. The essential features of the Compromise admitted California as a free state and divided the remainder of the Mexican Cession into two large territo-

ries, New Mexico and Utah, whose residents were given the right to decide for themselves whether or not they wanted slavery. (Both territories subsequently legalized slavery, but few slaves were taken there.)

State Rights and Slavery. The Compromise of 1850 also included a concession to the South in the form of the Fugitive Slave Law that gave unprecedented powers to the Federal government. This raises an important point about the state rights theory. State rights, or sovereignty, was a means rather than an end, an instrument more than a principle. Its purpose was to protect slavery from the potential hostility of a national majority. Southern political leaders from the 1820s to the 1840s jealously opposed the exercise of national power for a variety of purposes. "If Congress can make banks, roads, and canals under the Constitution," said Nathanial Macon of North Carolina, "they can free any slave in the United States." Calhoun, the South's leading political philosopher, formulated an elaborate constitutional structure of state rights theory to halt any use of Federal power that might conceivably be construed at some future time as a precedent with negative consequences for slavery.

At the same time, though, Southerners were not averse to using national power in defense of slavery. Indeed, this was a more reliable instrument than state rights. And the South had the power to wield. During forty-nine of the seventy-two years from 1789 to 1861 a Southerner—and slaveholder—was president of the United States. Twenty-four of the thirty-six Speakers of the House and presidents pro tem of the Senate were from the South. At all times during those years a majority of Supreme Court justices were Southerners. This happened because, though the South had only a minority of the national population, it usually controlled the Jeffersonian Republican party and, after 1828, the Democratic party, which in turn usually controlled the government. Southern domination of the Democratic party increased during the 1850s, so that even though both Democratic presidents in that decade—Franklin Pierce and James Buchanan—were Northerners, they were beholden to Southerners and did their bidding.

The usefulness of this national power had been demonstrated in the 1830s when Congress imposed a gag rule to stifle antislavery petitions and the post office banned antislavery literature from the mail in Southern states. But the Fugitive Slave Law of 1850 provided an even more striking example. It was the strongest manifestation of national power thus far in American history. It overrode the laws and officials of Northern states and extended the long arm of Federal law, enforced by the army and navy, into Northern states to recover escaped slaves and return them to their owners. Senator Jefferson Davis, who later insisted that the Confederacy fought for the principle of state sovereignty, voted with enthusiasm for the Fugitive Slave Law. When Northern state legislatures and courts invoked state rights and individual liberties against this Federal law, the U.S. Supreme Court with its majority of Southern justices reaffirmed the supremacy of national law to protect slavery.

Calhoun died in 1850, and during the following decade the South moved further away from his principles of state sovereignty and used its leverage in the Democratic party to wield greater national power than ever. Jefferson Davis was one of the principal architects of this process. As secretary of war in President Franklin Pierce's cabinet, he helped persuade a reluctant Pierce to cave in to Southern demands for repeal of the Missouri Compromise restriction on slavery in the territories north of 36°30′. Pierce endorsed repeal as a party measure; so did Senator Stephen A. Douglas of Illinois, who

> Southerners were not averse to using national power in defense of slavery. Indeed, this was a more reliable instrument than state rights.

knew that he would need Southern votes if he expected to win the presidency. Patronage and pressure induced just enough Northern Democrats to vote for the Kansas-Nebraska Act in 1854 to obtain its passage.

But this turned out to be the first of several Pyrrhic victories for the South. It drove tens of thousands of angry Northern Democratic voters out of the party and gave birth to the Republican party, which by 1856 had become the second major party in the North. Running on the Wilmot Proviso platform of excluding slavery from the territories, the Republicans carried most Northern states in the presidential election of 1856. James Buchanan won the election only because of Southern support. Open warfare between proslavery and antislavery settlers in Kansas spilled over into the halls of Congress, where fistfights broke out between Northern and Southern representatives, members came armed to the floor of Congress, and South Carolinian Preston Brooks caned Senator Charles Sumner of Massachusetts into unconsciousness at his seat in the Senate. Presidents Pierce's and Buchanan's actions—and nonactions—favored the proslavery side in Kansas. Under heavy Southern pressure, Buchanan in 1858 even went so far as to endorse the fraudulently ratified Lecompton constitution to bring Kansas into the Union as a slave state. Kansas "is at this moment," the president told Congress, "as much a slave state as Georgia or South Carolina." This was too much for most remaining Northern Democrats, who followed Douglas's leadership and broke with the president to defeat the Lecompton constitution.

Each incident in the Kansas controversy propelled more Northern voters into the Republican party. So did the

Supreme Court's *Dred Scott* decision in 1857 in which five Southern and one Northern Democratic justice overturned precedents to rule that Congress had no power to prohibit slavery in the territories. This made slavery legal not only in Kansas but in every other territory as well. But this would remain a barren right unless the territorial legislatures enacted and enforced a slave code. In Kansas, where antislavery settlers were in a clear majority by 1858, there was faint chance of that. So Southern politicians, led by Jefferson Davis, made their boldest bid yet to use national power in the interest of slavery. They introduced in Congress a Federal slave code for the territories and demanded its endorsement by the Democratic National Convention in 1860.

Meanwhile the abolitionist John Brown, who had gained experience as an antislavery guerrilla fighter in Kansas, led a quixotic but violent raid to seize the Federal armory at Harpers Ferry in Virginia. He planned to arm the slaves and foment a chain reaction of slave uprisings throughout the South. The raid was a total failure: Brown and most of his followers were captured or killed; Brown was hanged. This affair sent shock waves of fear and outrage through the South. It also confirmed Southern convictions that loss of control of the national government would be fatal. U.S. Marines commanded by Robert E. Lee had captured Brown. But what if the Federal government had been in Republican hands? Southerners equated John Brown with all abolitionists, and abolitionists with the "Black Republicans."

The Brown raid formed the backdrop of a bitter contest for Speaker of the House in the 1859–1860 session of Congress. The Republican candidate gained a plurality but not the necessary majority of votes. For eight weeks the donnybrook went on. Congressmen hurled bitter insults at one another, and one observer reported with perhaps some exaggeration that on the floor of the House "the only persons who do not have a revolver and a knife are those who have two revolvers." A Southerner wrote that a good many slave-state congressmen wanted a shoot-out in the House; they "are willing to fight the question out, and settle it right there. . . . I can't help wishing the Union dissolved and we had a Southern confederacy." At one point during the contest, the governor of South Carolina wrote to one of his state's representatives: "If you upon consultation decide to make the issue of force in Washington, write or telegraph me, and I will have a regiment in Washington in the shortest possible time."

The Speakership fight was finally settled by election of a nonentity. A few weeks later, Southern delegates walked out of the 1860 Democratic National Convention when Northerners refused to accept a platform endorsing a Federal slave code for the territories. All efforts to reunite the severed party failed, and the bolters nominated a "Southern rights" candidate. This ensured the election of Abraham Lincoln, who carried every Northern state and therefore the election. For the South, this was the handwriting on the wall.

They had lost control of the government, probably permanently. It was not state rights they had contended for in this contest. It was national power, power that they had held and had used to secure the Fugitive Slave Law, the Kansas-Nebraska Act, the *Dred Scott* decision, and other measures to protect slavery. But every such victory had driven more Northern voters into the anti–slave power camp, which finally elected a president who believed slavery a "monstrous injustice" that should be "placed in the course of ultimate extinction." So seven slave states left the Union and formed the Confederate States of America.

> **"If the minority have the right to break up the Government at pleasure, because they have not had their way, there is an end of all government."**

Secession. But that did not necessarily mean war. The government could have acquiesced in the division of the United States into two nations. Some Northerners did propose to "let the erring sisters depart in peace." But most were not willing to accept the dismemberment of the United States. They feared that toleration of disunion in 1861 would create a fatal precedent to be invoked by disaffected minorities in the future, perhaps by the losing side in another presidential election, until the United States dissolved into a dozen petty, squabbling, hostile autocracies. The great experiment in republican self-government launched in 1776 would collapse, proving the contention of European monarchists and conservatives that this upstart republic across the Atlantic could not last. "The doctrine of secession is anarchy," declared a Cincinnati newspaper in an editorial similar to hundreds in other newspapers. "If the minority have the right to break up the Government at pleasure, because they have not had their way, there is an end of all government." Even the lame-duck President Buchanan, in his last message to Congress in December 1860, said that the Union was not "a mere voluntary association of States, to be dissolved at pleasure." The founders of the nation "never intended to implant in its bosom the seeds of its own destruction, nor were they guilty of the absurdity of providing for its own dissolution." If secession was legitimate, said Buchanan, the Union became "a rope of sand" and "our thirty-three States may resolve themselves into as many petty, jarring, and hostile republics. . . . The hopes of the friends of freedom throughout the world would be destroyed. . . . Our example for more than eighty years would not only be lost, but it would be quoted as conclusive proof that man is unfit for self-government."

No one held these convictions more strongly than Abraham Lincoln. "Perpetuity . . . is the fundamental law of all national governments," he declared in his inaugural address on March 4, 1861. "No State, upon its own mere motion, can lawfully get out of the Union." Later in the year, Lincoln told his private secretary that

> the central idea pervading this struggle is the necessity that is upon us, of proving that popular government is not an absurdity. We must settle this question now, whether in a free government the minority have the right to break up the government whenever they choose. If we fail it will go far to prove the incapability of the people to govern themselves.

But even this refusal to countenance the legitimacy of secession did not make war inevitable. Moderates on both sides sought a compromise formula. Nothing availed to stay the course of secession in the seven lower South states. Delegates from these states formed the Confederate States of America in February 1861, elected Jefferson Davis president, and proceeded to establish a new nation with the appearance of permanence. But the other eight slave states were still part of the United States when Lincoln took the oath of office. He hoped to keep them there by assurances that he had no intention or right to interfere with slavery in the states and by refraining from hostile action against the Confederate states, even though they had seized all Federal property and arms within their borders—except Fort Sumter and three other less important forts. By a policy of watchful waiting, of maintaining the status quo, Lincoln hoped to allow passions to cool and enable Unionists to regain influence in the lower South. But this hope was doomed. Genuine Unionists had all but disappeared in the lower South, and Fort Sumter became a flash point of contention.

A large brick fortress on an artificial granite island in the middle of Charleston Bay, Fort Sumter could not be seized by the Confederates as easily as other Federal property had been, even though it was defended by only some eighty-odd soldiers. Lincoln came under great pressure from conservatives and upper South Unionists to yield the fort as a gesture of peace and goodwill that might strengthen Southern Unionism. After leaning in this direction for a time, Lincoln concluded that to give up Sumter would do the opposite; it would demoralize Unionists and strengthen the Confederacy. Fort Sumter had become a master symbol of sovereignty. To yield it would constitute de facto recognition of Confederate sovereignty. It would surely encourage European nations to grant diplomatic recognition to the Confederate nation. It would make a mockery of the national government's profession of constitutional authority over its own property.

So Lincoln devised an ingenious plan to put the burden of decision for war or peace on Jefferson Davis's shoulders. The garrison at Fort Sumter was about to run out of provisions in April 1861. Giving advance notice of his intentions, Lincoln sent a fleet toward Charleston with supplies and reinforcements. If the Confederates allowed unarmed boats to bring in "food for hungry men," the warships would stand off and the reinforcements would return north. But if they fired on the fleet, the ships and the fort would fire back. In effect, Lincoln flipped a coin and told Davis: "Heads I win; tails you lose." If the Confederate guns fired first, the South would stand convicted of starting a war. If they let the supplies go in, the American flag would continue to fly over Fort Sumter. The Confederacy would lose face; Unionists would take courage.

Davis did not hesitate. He considered it vital to assert the Confederacy's sovereignty. He also hoped that the outbreak of a shooting war would force the states of the upper South to join their fellow slave states. Davis ordered Gen. P. G. T. Beauregard, commander of Confederate troops at Charleston, to open fire on Fort Sumter before the supply ships got there. At 4:30 A.M. on April 12, Confederate artillery started the Civil War by firing on Fort Sumter. After a thirty-three-hour bombardment in which the Confederates fired four thousand rounds and the skeleton crew in the fort replied with a thousand—killing no one on either side in the first clash of this bloodiest of wars—the burning fort lowered the American flag in surrender. As Lincoln put it four years later in his second inaugural address: "Both [sides] deprecated war; but one of them would *make* war rather than let the nation survive; and the other would *accept* war rather than let it perish. And the war came."

[See also Compromise of 1850; Cornerstone Speech; Declaration of Immediate Causes; Dred Scott Decision; Election of 1860; Expansionism; Fort Sumter, South Carolina; Fugitive Slave Law; Harpers Ferry, West Virginia, *article on John Brown's Raid;* Kansas-Nebraska Act; Missouri Compromise; Nullification Controversy; Secession; State Rights; Sumner, Caning of; Wilmot Proviso; *and biographies of numerous figures mentioned herein.*]

BIBLIOGRAPHY

Barney, William L. *The Road to Secession: A New Perspective on the Old South.* New York, 1972.
Cooper, William J., Jr. *The South and the Politics of Slavery, 1828–1856.* Baton Rouge, La., 1978.
Craven, Avery. *The Coming of the Civil War.* 2d ed., rev. Chicago, 1957.
Current, Richard. *Lincoln and the First Shot.* Philadelphia, 1963.
Fehrenbacher, Don E. *The Dred Scott Case: Its Significance in American Law and Politics.* New York, 1978.
Foner, Eric. *Free Soil, Free Labor, Free Men: The Ideology of the Republican Party before the Civil War.* New York, 1970.
Freehling, William W. *The Road to Disunion: Secessionists at Bay, 1776–1854.* New York, 1990.
McCardell, John *The Idea of a Southern Nation: Southern Nationalists and Southern Nationalism, 1830–1860.* New York, 1979.
Nevins, Allan. *The Emergence of Lincoln.* 2 vols. New York, 1950.
Nevins, Allan. *Ordeal of the Union.* 2 vols. New York, 1947.
Potter, David M. *The Impending Crisis, 1848–1861.* New York, 1976.
Potter, David M. *Lincoln and His Party in the Secession Crisis.* 2d ed. with new preface. New Haven, 1962.
Pressly, Thomas J. *Americans Interpret Their Civil War.* 2d ed., with new introduction. Princeton, 1962.
Stampp, Kenneth M. *America in 1857: A Nation on the Brink.* New York, 1990.
Stampp, Kenneth M. *And the War Came: The North and the Secession Crisis, 1860–61.* Baton Rouge, La., 1950.

JAMES M. MCPHERSON

Strategy and Tactics

The strategy and tactics of the Civil War reflected the influence of the Napoleonic Era, with its appealing popular belief that wars could be won in climactic battles. They also reflected the engineering curriculum at West Point, which helped American officers adapt the products of the Industrial Revolution to local conditions. The curriculum at West Point, which supplied most of the leading officers on both sides, spent little time on European warfare, although Dennis Hart Mahan had organized the Napoleon Club at the academy in order to encourage extracurricular study of the subject. Nevertheless, only a few officers had read any of the work of Antoine Henri de Jomini, the principal interpreter of Napoleon's campaigns. Jomini's allegedly rigid prescriptions for warfare conducted along geometric lines and his emphasis on limited war were not generally accepted doctrine. Technology, training, and the practical engineering education received by the leading Civil War generals, not Jominian influence, determined the limits of thought that would decide wartime strategy (planning the allocation of resources to achieve the military goals of a war or campaign) and tactics (the utilization of those resources when an engagement was pending or actually under way).

Tactics

The tactics employed by the Union and Confederate armies were much the same. During the early months of the war formations were generally quite irregular, as green officers and their equally green troops were just learning tactics, and outmoded tactics at that. Later, the armies frequently relied mainly on one or two lines of two ranks each, in close order, perhaps a thousand men long, and sometimes followed skirmishers (soldiers who precede the main body to discover or delay the enemy). These lines might attack similar lines in close formation, much as in the days of the inaccurate smoothbore musket. Or they might shoot at or charge lines in entrenchments or behind breastworks.

In either event, the rifle-musket, developed in the 1850s, made such tactics quite obsolete. The invention of the minié ball—a bullet with a hollow base that would expand upon firing so as to catch the rifling grooves in the gun barrel—so improved the accuracy and range of the musket that battles were more deadly than in the past. Properly used, the Civil War rifle-musket made it extremely difficult to destroy an opponent who was comparably equipped and manned. Armies could be defeated and badly crippled, but they would survive to fight another day.

The combination of new weapons technology, frontal assaults, and commonsense use of the ax and spade made the Civil War the bloodiest of American wars. Under such conditions it did not take men in the ranks long to learn to dig in with amazing speed when their safety required it (Union troops approaching Atlanta could entrench for the night in less than an hour). Thus, judicious use of trenches or breastworks gave the defense a significant advantage, sometimes estimated at three to one, over an offense of equal size. The resulting carnage, especially to the attacker, appalled many officers. Union Gen. William Tecumseh Sherman, for example, attempted with some success to employ skirmishers instead of the customary two-rank line as a way to avoid the extraordinary casualties usually suffered by troops attacking a well-protected adversary equipped with rifle-muskets.

Although Civil War officers welcomed new technology, they did not always grasp its significance when applied to the fate of their soldiers. Close-order frontal assaults had become foolish, so tactical turning movements, in which part of one's force was stealthily moved to the flank or rear of the enemy, were often attempted in order to avoid bloody frontal encounters. The commander on the tactical defensive, however, knowing the dangers of frontal assault to the tactical offensive, preferred to receive his enemy from the front. Therefore, the defender either changed front, retreated, or kept his flanks so well guarded by troops or features of the terrain that effective tactical turning movements were frequently impossible. Frontal assaults sometimes became inevitable if there were to be any battle at all. Under the circumstances, by the middle of the war, generals on the defensive put much thought into field fortifications and entrenchments and sometimes discovered that the men had thought out the problem for themselves and prepared trenches on their own initiative.

Professional officers on both sides were also receptive to other new technology, notably the steam engine and the telegraph. Steamboats played a vital role, making river supply and combat practical, and one cannot underestimate the role of the rickety Southern rail network in supporting Confederate strategy. Rail movement between main armies in Virginia, Tennessee, and Mississippi facilitated redeployment of small detachments from all over the Confederacy in order to hit the Union army at its perceived weak spots.

Clearly, speedy steam transportation gave new meaning to the Jominian concept of interior lines, which supposed an advantage to a force that was closer to separated enemy contingents than they were to each other, and therefore permitted that force to concentrate first against one enemy contingent and then the other before they would be able to concentrate in response. Steam could provide an advantage equivalent to interior lines to the side that had the most conveniently located railroads. In theory, possession of interior lines could be countered by simultaneous advances of two or more forces of the adversary. The most notable examples of simultaneous advances are the campaigns of Ulysses S. Grant and Sherman during the last year of the war, although Abraham Lincoln and H. W. Halleck had ordered such advances in late 1862. But such movements required swift relay of information and orders. Thus, the telegraph was an essential partner with the steamboat and railroad in permitting coordinated advances or rapid concentrations.

Strategy

The technology of transportation, information, and rifle muskets, plus extensive use of entrenchments, created the stalemate that marked the Civil War. The major goal of strategy on both sides was to break that stalemate. American generals had learned about the defensive power of entrenchments at West Point and saw the offensive potential of the turning movement in the Mexican War. Indeed, the turning movement was the motif of most Civil War campaigns, because it was a potentially effective means of breaking the impasse by avoiding bloody frontal offensives against entrenchments. Yet armies moved over great distances and still fought bloody battles without decisive result.

Opening Strategies. Initially the Union considered a logistic strategy, as typified by the proposals of Winfield Scott, the general in chief of the Union army, who had demonstrated the utility of the turning movement in the Mexican War. Scott sought to avoid bloody battles caused by attacking large armies. Instead, he sought to deprive the Confederacy of military resources. A naval blockade would be established along the Confederacy's coastline, and an army of eighty thousand men and another naval force would operate on the Mississippi River to turn Southern positions and bisect the Confederacy. Labeled the "Anaconda Plan" because it was aimed at squeezing the Confederacy to death, Scott's plan was not adopted because of the impatience of Union politicians who expected quick victory.

Nevertheless, progress along the Mississippi was satisfactory, and the Union had substantial control of the river after July 1863. On the other hand, the Union blockade of the Atlantic and Gulf coasts was not particularly effective. Many blockade runners got through the blockade successfully. At the port of Wilmington alone, for example, over 80 percent of Confederate attempts to run the blockade were successful. This result was replicated elsewhere, as the Confederacy purchased vessels with high speeds and low profiles that made it relatively easy to evade the blockade. Moreover, ships of the blockading squadrons were limited by the amount of coal they could carry. Rapid consumption of fuel and frequent breakdowns meant much time spent off-station either recoaling or repairing.

President Jefferson Davis initially attempted a comprehensive defense of the entire Confederacy, as illustrated in 1861 when Albert Sidney Johnston did not concentrate his troops pending possible enemy threats in Kentucky, but rather established what historian Archer Jones has characterized as a "system of strong points with troops attached to them," called a cordon defense. Davis admitted this decision to be wrong after setbacks at Fort Henry, Fort Donelson, and Roanoke Island, because it dispersed Confederate forces rather than concentrated them. The early emphasis on territorial defense, however, not only met the political need to sustain morale but also served the military need to protect Confederate resources. For example, with the only important ironworks in the Confederacy in 1861 located in Richmond—the Tredegar company—that city's defense became vital.

The New Confederate Strategy. Davis soon rejected passive defense and pursued instead an "offensive-defensive" strategy that frequently employed raids. Davis's strategy was also politically motivated: by going on the offensive, he might influence Northern elections and increase the chance of foreign recognition. In this effort time was on the Confederates' side; the longer they could keep armies in the field, the greater the political impact of their offensive victories.

Offensive-Defensive. Davis's strategy called for a defensive posture that would emphasize the strategic turning movement for both offensive and defensive purposes. In the strategic (as opposed to tactical) turning movement, one placed one's own army at a favorable point on the adversary's line of communication, forcing him to recover his communications by attacking on ground of one's choice. In this way, one could seize the advantage of the tactical defensive when on the strategic offensive. Although relying on defense, stressed historian Frank E. Vandiver, Confederates would exploit opportunities for counterattacks. The offensive-defensive enabled the South to take maximum advantage of its vast geography and the supremacy of the defense. Confederates were forced to trade space for time. A retreating force moved faster than its pursuer, for it could hinder pursuit by destroying bridges, blocking roads, or taking up rails, and while it moved toward its base it gathered more troops as it relieved itself of the obligation to guard bridges, junctions, and population centers. Some historians have been critical of the offensive-defensive; E. Merton Coulter, for example, thought that the defensive was a disaster for the Confederacy, and T. Harry Williams believed that a defensive war meant a long war, a disadvantage to the side with inferior resources. Yet it seems difficult to imagine a better strategy, taking all Southern circumstances into account.

The shift to the offensive-defensive was illustrated by the way in which Confederates met the 1862 threat to Richmond posed by the approach of the Army of the Potomac under George B. McClellan. In order to avoid frontal conflict, McClellan himself planned a strategic turning movement. He went around Joseph E. Johnston by moving his troops south on Chesapeake Bay to Union-held Fortress Monroe, at the tip of the peninsula formed by the York and James rivers. By moving up the peninsula and threatening Richmond, McClellan hoped to force Johnston onto the tactical offensive, thereby giving McClellan the defensive advantage. Typically, turning movements failed to trap defending armies,

> Southerners also used the railroad, steamboat, and telegraph for counteroffensive concentrations that embraced almost the entire Confederacy. . . .

except at Vicksburg and Appomattox, but they frequently forced retreats. They also provoked counteroffensives to regain lost territory or prevent losing more. Thus the threat to Richmond posed by McClellan's turning movement caused Confederates to attack at Fair Oaks and the Seven Days' Battles, where the South lost a larger percentage of forces engaged than the Federals. The affair was a tactical victory for the Union, but Confederates won a significant strategic and political battle when they forced McClellan back, a move that led to his evacuation of the peninsula. The results were not decisive, however, and McClellan's withdrawal only set the stage for future bloody battles.

Southerners also used the railroad, steamboat, and telegraph for counteroffensive concentrations that embraced almost the entire Confederacy, as in the Shiloh and Chickamauga campaigns. Prior to the Shiloh campaign, Halleck, Grant, and Flag Officer Andrew Foote had conducted a grand turning movement in the West, capturing Forts Henry and Donelson in February 1862, turning the Confederates out of Columbus and Nashville, and forcing them to abandon their cordon defense. Under the influence of P. G. T. Beauregard, however, Confederates used the railroad, steamboat, and telegraph to prepare a counteroffensive to win back western Tennessee in spring 1862 by concentrating in northern Mississippi troops from all over the middle and western South. This plan was in accord with Davis's offensive-defensive strategy; the goal was to drive back Grant, who was on the Tennessee River, before the army of Gen. Don Carlos Buell could join him. Surprise at Shiloh was complete, and Grant was driven back to the protection of his gunboats. Maneuverable armies with rifle-muskets proved virtually indestructible, however, and when Buell reached Grant the tables were turned. Confederates lost their gains on the second day and withdrew to Corinth, Mississippi, evacuating it a month later when menaced by Halleck's leisurely advance. Since the South lost a greater percent of forces engaged than the North, the campaign proved to be a military defeat, and the loss of territory produced serious political attrition in the Confederacy.

The Confederate counteroffensive concentration at Chickamauga came in response to Gen. Braxton Bragg's retreat from Tennessee to northern Georgia in the summer of 1863. After threatening to turn Buell and forcing the Union general to retreat to the Ohio River, Bragg was himself forced back by Buell's successor, William S. Rosecrans, who conducted a series of turning movements against him. Bragg's retreat, however, provided the Confederates the occasion to

> **Throughout the war, the Confederate leadership had relied on raids to supplement major offensive and defensive movements.**

implement a long-contemplated offensive plan—to make another concentration by rail. Part of a corps from the Army of Northern Virginia under the command of James Longstreet, plus other troops from eastern Tennessee, Mississippi, and northern Georgia, were sent to Bragg. Longstreet arrived in time to take an important part in the September 1863 Battle of Chickamauga, driving the Union forces into Chattanooga, where they remained under siege for over a month. Although the two most important Confederate concentrations in space, Shiloh and Chickamauga, did not lead to ultimate Confederate victory, they nonetheless bought time and caused Union planners to prepare their future course of action more carefully than they had before.

Politics and Raids. As the war progressed, Davis added a political element to his strategy. Tentatively in 1862, but definitely in 1864, he sought to influence Union politics, with some limited success, as the peace Democrats illustrated in their 1864 platform. Understanding the political overtones of Davis's thinking helps to understand some otherwise inexplicable Confederate actions, notably the 1862 movements north by Robert E. Lee and Bragg, and the 1864 replacement with the aggressive John Bell Hood of Joseph E. Johnston. Both actions were attempts to undermine Northern morale by inflicting defeats upon the Union Army and thus affect Federal elections.

Davis's plans to influence the Union elections of 1864 depended upon clear Confederate victories, and Johnston's retreats, however skillful, did not contribute to a political

strategy because they were perceived as defeats by Confederate civilians. Johnston was therefore replaced by Hood, who attacked Sherman, failed to drive him back, and retreated into the defenses around Atlanta. Once more Sherman employed a turning movement, forcing Hood's withdrawal from Atlanta on September 2, 1864. Because of Atlanta's symbolic significance, Confederate morale was significantly weakened.

Throughout the war, the Confederate leadership had relied on raids to supplement major offensive and defensive movements. Raids maintained the offensive initiative and involved a minimum of bloody contact with the enemy. They were part of a logistic strategy aimed at crippling the Federals by undermining their supply. For example, in late 1862 Grant, using Memphis as his base, had advanced south along the railroad in an attempt to turn Vicksburg from favorable ground to the east. The Confederates stopped him at Oxford, Mississippi, when Earl Van Dorn raided Grant's supplies at Holly Springs and Nathan Bedford Forrest simultaneously raided Grant's railroad in Tennessee. These raids, involving a minimum of contact with the Federals, temporarily stopped the advance of a 40,000-man Union army. The Confederate raids forced Grant to cope with attacks on his railroads and supply depots by basing his army on the river, keeping limited communications, using interior lines, and living off the land. Grant persisted, until in April 1863 he crossed his troops over to the west bank of the Mississippi, marched south of Vicksburg, and ferried back to the east bank. Grant turned Vicksburg and forced the surrender of the city and 29,000 men on July 4, 1863.

Raids also had political effect. The cavalry raids that defeated Grant's December 1862 march on Vicksburg, frustrated the summer 1863 advance of Buell on Chattanooga, and delayed for months offensive action by Rosecrans against Bragg all raised Southern morale. Although such small raids were very helpful to the Confederate cause, major moves north, such as Lee's raid into Maryland in 1862, Bragg's invasion of Kentucky in 1862, and Lee's raid into Pennsylvania in 1863, proved to be less valuable owing to heavy casualties and the political attrition created by civilians' perceptions of defeat when the Confederate armies withdrew, as raiders inevitably had to do. Although it seemed so to those on the home front, Sharpsburg was not part of an invasion, for Lee aimed not to occupy territory, but only to supply his troops on Northern soil, gather recruits, encourage foreign recognition, influence the Union's fall elections, and encourage Northern peace movements. Lee's hopes were largely in vain, for although he won a tactical victory at Sharpsburg, Confederates suffered twice the percentage of casualties than the Union and then retreated. Confederate civilians, untutored in the subtleties of military strategy, looked upon the battle as a defeat, perceiving that Confederates had gained territory and then lost it.

Events proceeded no better for Lee in 1863. He planned a second raid across the Potomac into Pennsylvania to secure supplies from Union territory, leaving the resources of the Shenandoah Valley available for the following fall. As in 1862, however, the Confederacy ran a risk. If Lee returned to Virginia too soon after major battle, the public on both sides would assume that he had been defeated. Nevertheless, Lee attacked in a three-day battle at Gettysburg, was twice repulsed, and withdrew. Even if Lee had won a tactical victory, withdrawal, and the consequent drop in civilian morale, would have been inevitable: his foragers were unable to fan out widely in the face of the enemy. Some scholars have seen in Lee's operations an effort to win the war by destroying the enemy army in battle. But his use of raids for supply makes this thesis doubtful. Like so many other Confederates, Lee hoped for victory by political means, expecting the Republican party to be displaced by Democratic peace advocates in the 1864 elections.

The New Federal Strategy. Even with the fall of Atlanta in 1864, the war was still in a strategic stalemate. After three years, Tennessee was the only Confederate state to be substantially restored to the Union. The problem of continued stalemate has caused historians such as Archer Jones and Russell F. Weigley to reinterpret Grant's later strategy. Grant understood the importance of river transport, and if he appeared to rely on a strategy of attrition, it was not by choice. Once Grant became general in chief, writes Weigley, he sought "the utter destruction of the Confederacy's capacity to wage war," although he preferred enemy destruction that was due to "capture, not . . . attrition and ultimate annihilation." In the spring of 1864 now General in Chief Grant recognized the difficulties of weakening the Confederates by conquering enough of the South to deprive them of supplies and recruits. Progress was too slow and garrisons in occupied territory absorbed too many men.

Instead Grant planned to use simultaneous advances to counter Confederate interior lines. The telegraph naturally played a vital role in Grant's plans, which called for raids to isolate Confederate soldiers from their supplies by destruction of the railroads and other facilities that provided them. But none of the raids took place until November 1864, when Sherman began his march from Atlanta through Georgia to Savannah. Facing token opposition, Sherman took only a month to devastate an area of Georgia about 50 miles wide and 250 miles long. By February 1865 he had turned north to raid the Carolinas. Sherman saw clearly the tremendous political and military impact such raids would have on Confederate morale and desire to continue the war.

While Sherman was making his way to Atlanta, Grant kept Lee so busy in Virginia that he could not again send Longstreet west, but Grant's efforts to gain decisive victories only forced Lee into the trenches around Petersburg and Richmond and began a siege. This dubious achievement cost Grant so many casualties that Northern morale was seriously compromised. Confederate civilians took heart from Grant's difficulties, but by April 1865 he had finally stretched Confederate defenses so thin that Lee was forced to evacuate Richmond and Petersburg and flee west, hoping to turn south into North Carolina and join Joseph E. Johnston. Lee got as far as Appomattox Courthouse, where he was turned by Union troops and surrendered to Grant on April 9, 1865. The Confederate attempt to unite Lee and Johnston failed.

The military, social, and political will of the Confederacy was drained. The South was not defeated by a strategy of annihilation, for 326,000 men were still available at the end of 1864, but desertion had almost doubled in the previous nine months, and the Southern army was well on its way to exhaustion. Steady attrition destroyed Southern morale, will, and psychological capacity to resist. Events had forced the Union to adopt a raiding logistic strategy, and in the end, as Archer Jones remarks, "political attrition had won the war before the military attrition of Grant's logistic strategy could bring military victory." But Davis's offensive-defensive strategy, supplementing a defensive posture with raids, turning movements, and offensive concentrations, had enabled the Confederacy to fight much longer than anyone could have predicted from a simple comparison of Union and Confederate resources.

[*For further discussion of specific technological advances in weaponry, see* Arms, Weapons, and Ammunition. *See also entries on the numerous biographical figures and campaigns and battles mentioned herein.*]

BIBLIOGRAPHY

Beringer, Richard E., Herman Hattaway, Archer Jones, and William N. Still, Jr. *Why the South Lost the Civil War.* Athens, Ga., 1986.

Hattaway, Herman, and Archer Jones. *How the North Won: A Military History of the Civil War.* Urbana, Ill., 1983.

Jones, Archer. *Civil War Command and Strategy: The Process of Victory and Defeat.* New York, 1992.

Mahon, John K. "Civil War Infantry Assault Tactics." *Military Affairs* 25 (Summer 1961): 57–68.

Nelson, Larry E. *Bullets, Ballots, and Rhetoric: Confederate Policy for the United States Presidential Contest of 1864.* University, Ala., 1980.

Vandiver, Frank E. "Jefferson Davis and Confederate Strategy." In *The American Tragedy: The Civil War in Retrospect.* Edited by Bernard Mayo. Hampden-Sydney, 1959.

Vandiver, Frank E. *Rebel Brass: The Confederate Command System.* Baton Rouge, La., 1956.

Vandiver, Frank E. *Their Tattered Flags: The Epic of the Confederacy.* New York, 1970.

Weigley, Russell F. "American Strategy from Its Beginnings through the First World War." In *Makers of Modern Strategy: From Machiavelli to the Nuclear Age.* Edited by Peter Paret, with Gordon A. Craig and Felix Gilbert. Princeton, 1986.

RICHARD E. BERINGER

Causes of Defeat

Efforts to explain the causes of Confederate defeat in the Civil War have generated a great deal of controversy over the past century and a quarter. The debate began with the publication in 1866 of *The Lost Cause* by Richmond journalist Edward Pollard, who blamed Jefferson Davis, and it continues today. Yet despite all the efforts to determine "Why the North Won" or "Why the South Lost"—the difference in phraseology is sometimes significant—there is no consensus among students of the war. The best way to approach the problem is to review the principal explanations for Confederate defeat with an eye to the defects and virtues of each.

Major Explanations

Most interpretations fall into one of two categories: internal or external. Internal explanations focus mainly or entirely on the Confederacy and usually phrase the question as "Why did the South lose?" External interpretations look at both the Union and the Confederacy and often phrase it as "Why did the North win?" No matter which approach they take, most analyses assume, at least implicitly, that Union victory was inevitable. But this is a fallacy. The Confederacy had several opportunities to win the war and came close to doing so more than once.

Overwhelming Numbers and Resources. The earliest and perhaps most durable explanation of Confederate defeat is an external one. It was advanced by Robert E. Lee himself in his farewell address to his soldiers at Appomattox: "The Army of Northern Virginia has been compelled to yield to

> **"The Army of Northern Virginia has been compelled to yield to overwhelming numbers and resources."**

overwhelming numbers and resources." This explanation enabled Southerners to preserve their pride in the courage and skill of Confederate soldiers, to reconcile defeat with their sense of honor, even to maintain faith in the righteousness of their cause while admitting that it had been lost. The Confederacy, in other words, lost the war not because it fought badly, or because its soldiers lacked courage, or because its cause was wrong, but simply because the enemy had more men and guns.

This thesis remains alive and well today. In a symposium at Gettysburg College in 1958 on "Why the North Won the Civil War," historian Richard N. Current reviewed the statistics of Northern demographic and economic preponderance—two and one-half times the South's population, three times its

railroad capacity, nine times its industrial production, and so on—and concluded that "surely in view of the disparity of resources, it would have taken a miracle . . . to enable the South to win. As usual, God was on the side of the heaviest battalions." And in 1990, Civil War historian Shelby Foote declared that "the North fought that war with one hand behind its back." If necessary, "the North simply would have brought that other arm from behind its back. I don't think the South ever had a chance to win that war."

Many Southerners, however, began to question this overwhelming-numbers-and-resources thesis soon after the war, and by the twentieth century many of them had rejected it. This explanation did credit to Confederate skill and courage in holding out for so long against such great odds, but it seemed to do little credit to their intelligence. After all, Southerners in 1861 were well aware of their disadvantages in numbers and resources. Yet they went to war confident of victory. Were they naive? Irrational? Inexcusably arrogant?

As they pondered this matter, numerous Southerners—and non-Southerners—concluded that overwhelming numbers and resources were not the cause of Northern victory after all. History offered many examples of a society winning a war against greater odds than the Confederacy faced. The outstanding example in the minds of everyone in 1861 was the United States in its War of Independence against the most powerful nation in the world. In our own post-Vietnam generation we too are familiar with the truth that victory does not always ride with the heaviest battalions.

To win the Civil War, Union armies had to invade, conquer, and occupy the South and to destroy the capacity of Confederate armies to wage war and of the Southern economy to sustain it. But victory for the Confederacy did not require anything like such a huge effort. Confederate armies did not have to invade and conquer the North in order to win the war; they needed only to hold out long enough to force the North to the conclusion that the price of conquering the South and crushing its capacity to wage war was too high, as Britain had concluded in 1781 and as the United States concluded with respect to Vietnam in 1972. Most Southerners thought in 1861 that their resources were more than sufficient to win on these terms. And even after losing the war, many of them continued to insist they could have won. Former Confederate Gen. Joseph E. Johnston wrote in the 1870s that the Southern people had not been "guilty of the high crime of undertaking a war without the means of waging it successfully." And former Gen. P. G. T. Beauregard wrote in 1884: "No people ever warred for independence with more relative advantages than the Confederacy."

Although Johnston's and Beauregard's memoirs had a self-serving quality—they too blamed Jefferson Davis, partly in order to deflect blame from themselves—their assertions find plenty of echoes in modern studies. Most historians in the twentieth century have rejected the overwhelming-num-

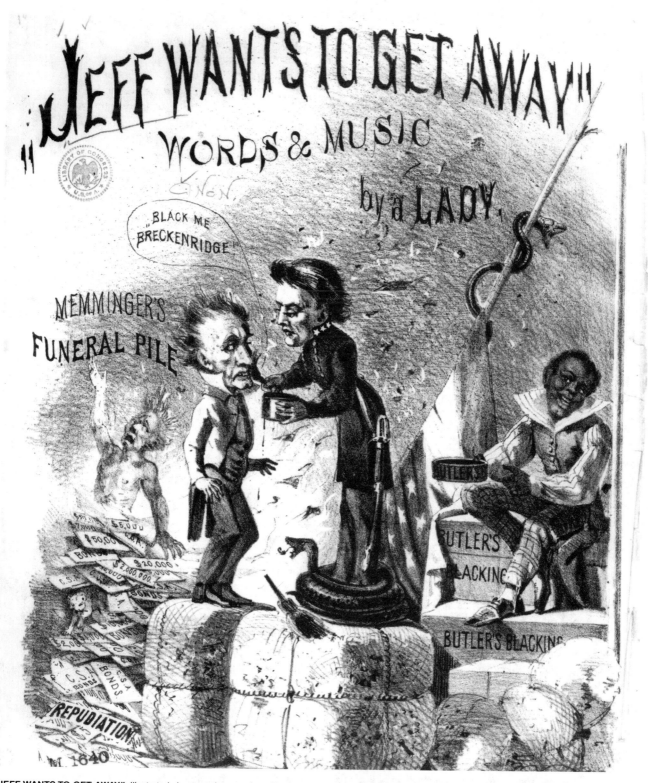

"JEFF WANTS TO GET AWAY." Illustrated sheet music cover for a Northern song lampooning the imminent collaspe of the Confederacy. Jefferson Davis, standing on a bale of cotton, demands that John C. Breckenridge "black me" (presumably to facilitate his escape.) At left, Secretary of State Christopher G. Memminger drowns in worthless Confederate bonds. "Butler's Blacking" at right probably refers to the Union general Benjamin F. Butler, who had forced the Confederacy to recognize the status of African American troops. A copperhead, symbol used by Republicans to vilify Peace Democrats, curls around Breckinridge's feet. Another coils around the broken staff of a Union flag. Lithography by Alexander McLean on wove paper. Published in St. Louis, Missouri, 1864. LIBRARY OF CONGRESS bers-and-resources thesis as a sufficient explanation for Confederate defeat. Instead, they have advanced a variety of *internal* explanations.

Internal Conflicts. One such approach focused on what might be termed the internal-conflict thesis. Several variations on this theme have emerged. One of the earliest and most persistent was spelled out by Frank Owsley in his book *State Rights in the Confederacy,* published in 1925. Owsley maintained that the centrifugal force of state rights fatally crippled the central government's efforts to prosecute the war. Owsley singled out Governors Joseph E. Brown of Georgia and Zebulon Vance of North Carolina as guilty of obstructive policies, of withholding men and arms from the Confederate army to build up their state militias, and of petty political warfare against the Davis administration. On the tombstone of the Confederacy, wrote Owsley, should be carved the epitaph: "Died of State Rights."

A variant on the state rights thesis focuses on the resistance by many Southerners, including Vice President Alexander H. Stephens, to such war measures as conscription, certain kinds of taxes, suspension of the writ of habeas corpus, and martial law. Opponents based their denunciations of these "despotic" measures on grounds of civil liberty, or state rights, or democratic individualism, or all three combined. This opposition crippled the army's ability to fill its ranks, obtain food and supplies, and stem desertions. It hindered the government's ability to curb antiwar activists who divided the Southern people and sapped their will to win. The persistence during the war of the democratic practices of individualism, dissent, and carping criticism of the government caused historian David Donald in 1958 to amend that inscription on the Confederacy's tombstone to: "Died of Democracy."

Three flaws mar the power of the internal-conflict thesis to explain Confederate defeat. First, recent scholarship has demonstrated that the negative effects of state rights sentiment have been much exaggerated. State leaders like Brown and Vance did indeed feud with the Davis administration. But at the same time these governors as well as others took the initiative in many areas of mobilization: raising and equipping regiments, providing help for the families of soldiers, organizing war production and supply, building coastal defenses, and so on. Rather than hindering the efforts of the government in Richmond, the activities of states augmented them. "On balance," concludes a recent study, "state contributions to the war effort far outweighed any unnecessary diversions of resources to local defense."

As for the died-of-democracy thesis, it appears that, on the contrary, the Confederate government enforced the draft, suppressed dissent, and suspended civil liberties at least as thoroughly as did the Union government. The Confederacy enacted conscription a year before the Union and raised a larger proportion of its troops by drafting than did the North.

And though Abraham Lincoln used his power to suspend the writ of habeas corpus and to arrest antiwar activists more vigorously than did Jefferson Davis, the Confederate army suppressed Unionists with as much ruthlessness, especially in eastern Tennessee and western North Carolina, as Union forces wielded against Copperheads in the North or Confederate sympathizers in the border states.

This points to a second flaw in the internal-conflict thesis: we might term it "the fallacy of reversibility." If the North had lost the war—which came close to happening on more than one occasion—the same thesis of internal conflict could be advanced to explain *Northern* defeat. Bitter divisions existed in the North over conscription, taxes, suspension of habeas corpus, martial law—and significantly, in the case of the North, over emancipation as a war aim. If anything, the opposition was more powerful in the North than in the South. Lincoln endured greater vilification than Davis during much of the war. And Lincoln had to face a campaign for reelection in the midst of the most crucial military operations of the war—an election that for a time it appeared he would lose, an outcome that might well have led to peace negotiations with an independent Confederacy. This did not happen, but its narrow avoidance illustrates the intense conflict within the Northern polity that neutralized the similar but perhaps less divisive conflicts within the South as an explanation for Confederate defeat.

Third, one might ask whether the internal conflicts between state and central governments or among different factions and leaders were greater in the Confederacy than they had been in the United States during the Revolution. Americans in the war of 1776 were more divided than Southerners in the war of 1861, yet the United States won its independence and the Confederacy did not. This suggests that we must look elsewhere for an explanation of Confederate defeat.

Internal Alienation. Similar problems taint another interpretation that overlaps the internal-conflict thesis. This one might be termed the internal-alienation argument. Much scholarship recently has focused on two large groups in the South that were or became alienated from the Confederate war effort: nonslaveholding whites, and slaves.

The nonslaveholders were two-thirds of the Confederacy's white population. Many of them, especially in mountainous and up-country regions of small farms and few slaves, opposed secession in 1861. They formed significant enclaves of Unionism in western Virginia where they created a new Union state, in eastern Tennessee where they carried out guerrilla operations against the Confederacy and contributed many soldiers to the Union army, and elsewhere in the upland South. Other nonslaveholders who supported the Confederacy and fought for it became alienated over time because of ruinous inflation, shortages of food and salt, high taxes, and a growing suspicion that they were risking their lives and property to defend slavery. Clauses in the conscription law that allowed a drafted man to buy a substitute and exempted from the draft one white man on every plantation with twenty or more slaves gave rise to a bitter cry that it was a rich man's war but a poor man's fight. Many families of soldiers suffered malnutrition as food shortages and inflation worsened. Bread riots occurred in parts of the South during

> **About one-third of the border-state whites actively supported the Confederacy, and many of the remainder were at best lukewarm.**

1863—most notably in Richmond itself. Numerous soldiers deserted from the army to return home and support their families. Several historians have argued that this seriously weakened the Confederate war effort and brought eventual defeat.

The alienation of many Southern whites was matched by the alienation of a large portion of that two-fifths of the Southern population that was black and slave. Slaves were essential to the Confederate war effort. As the South's principal labor force, they enabled the Confederacy to mobilize three-quarters of its white men of military age into the army—compared with about half in the North. Slavery was therefore a source of strength to the Confederacy, but it was also a source of weakness. Most slaves who reflected on their stake in the war believed that a Northern victory would bring freedom. Tens of thousands voted with their feet for the Union by escaping to Federal lines, where the North converted their labor power and eventually their military manpower into a Union asset. This leakage of labor from the Confederacy and the unrest of slaves who remained behind retarded Southern economic efficiency and output.

The alienation of these two large blocs of the Southern people seems a plausible explanation of Confederate defeat. But some caveats are necessary. The alienated elements of the American population in the Revolution were larger than those in the South during the Civil War. Many slaves ran away to the British, and the Loyalists undoubtedly weakened the American cause more than disaffected nonslaveholders weakened the Confederate cause. It is easy to exaggerate the amount of nonslaveholder alienation in the South; some historians have done precisely that. And though large numbers of slaves ran off to Union lines, this happened only where Union military and naval forces invaded and controlled Confederate territory—an external factor—and the great majority of slaves remained at home.

But perhaps the most important weakness of the internal-alienation thesis is that same fallacy of reversibility men-

tioned earlier. Large numbers of the Northern people were bitterly alienated from the Lincoln administration's war policies. Their opposition weakened and at times threatened to cripple the Union war effort. About one-third of the border-state whites actively supported the Confederacy, and many of the remainder were at best lukewarm Unionists. Guerrilla warfare behind Union lines occurred in these regions on a larger scale than in Unionist areas behind Confederate lines. The Democratic party in the free states denounced conscription, emancipation, certain war taxes, the suspension of habeas corpus, and other measures. Democrats exploited these issues in an aggressive attempt to paralyze the Lincoln administration. The peace wing of the party—Copperheads—opposed the war itself.

If the South had its class conflict over the theme of a rich man's war and poor man's fight, so did the North. If the Confederacy had its bread riots, the Union had its more dangerous and threatening draft riots. If many soldiers deserted from Confederate armies, a similarly large percentage deserted from Union armies until late in the war. If the South had its slaves who wanted Yankee victory and freedom, the North had its Democrats and border-state whites who strongly opposed emancipation and withheld support from the war because of it. Internal alienation, therefore, provides no more of a sufficient explanation for Confederate defeat than internal conflict, because the similar—perhaps greater—alienation within the North neutralized this factor, too.

Lack of Will. Another explanation for Confederate defeat overlaps the internal-conflict and internal-alienation theses. This one can be termed the lack-of-will thesis. It holds that the Confederacy could have won if the Southern people had possessed the will to make the sacrifices necessary for victory. In his book *The Confederate States of America,* the North Carolina–born E. Merton Coulter declared flatly that the Confederacy lost because its "people did not will hard enough and long enough to win." And in 1986 the four authors of *Why the South Lost the Civil War* echoed this conclusion: "We contend that lack of will constituted the decisive deficiency in the Confederate arsenal."

The lack-of-will thesis has three main facets. First is an argument that the Confederacy did not have a strong sense of nationalism. The Confederate States of America, it is said, did not exist long enough to give their people that mystical faith called nationalism or patriotism. Southerners did not have as firm a conviction of fighting for a country, a flag, a deep-rooted political and cultural tradition, as Northerners did. Southerners had been Americans before they became Confederates, and many of them—especially former Whigs—had opposed secession. So when the going got tough, their residual Americanism reemerged and triumphed over their newly minted, glossy Confederate nationalism.

This is a dubious argument. If the rhetoric of Confederate nationalism did not contain as many references to abstract symbols or concepts like flag, country, Constitution, and democracy as did Union rhetoric, Southerners felt a much stronger and more visceral commitment to defending land, home, and family from invasion by "Yankee vandals." In this sense, Confederate nationalism was if anything stronger than its Union counterpart. In their letters and diaries, Southerners expressed a greater determination to "die in the last ditch" than Northerners did. As the Confederate War Department clerk John Beauchamp Jones expressed it in his diary in 1863, the Southern people had far more at stake in the war than did Northerners: "Our men *must* prevail in combat, or lose their property, country, freedom, everything. . . . On the other hand, the enemy, in yielding the contest, may retire into their own country, and possess everything they enjoyed before the war began."

A Union officer who was captured in the Battle of Atlanta on July 22, 1864, and spent the rest of the war in Southern prisons, wrote in his diary on October 4 that from what he had seen in the South "the End of the War . . . is some time hence as the Idea of the Rebs giving up until they are completely subdued is all Moonshine they submit to privations that would not be believed unless seen." The Southern people persisted through far greater hardships and suffering than Northern people experienced. Northerners almost threw in the towel in the summer of 1864 because of casualty rates

> ## Some Southerners began to wonder if God was on their side after all.

that Southerners had endured for more than two years. Thus it seems difficult to accept the thesis of lack of will stemming from weak nationalism as a cause of Confederate defeat.

A second facet of the lack-of-will interpretation is what might be termed the guilt theme—the suggestion that many Southern whites felt moral qualms about slavery, which undermined their will to fight a war to preserve it. The South, wrote historian Kenneth M. Stampp, suffered from a "weakness of morale" caused by "widespread doubts and apprehensions about the validity of the Confederate cause." Defeat rewarded these guilt-ridden Southerners with "a way to rid themselves of the moral burden of slavery," so a good many of them, "perhaps subconsciously, welcomed . . . defeat." Other historians with a bent for social science concepts agree that the Confederates' morale was undermined by the "cognitive dissonance" of fighting a war to establish their own liberty but at the same time to keep 4 million black people in slavery.

This also seems doubtful. To be sure, one can turn up quotations from Southern whites expressing reservations about slavery, and one can find statements by Southerners

after the war expressing relief that it was gone. But the latter are suspect in their sincerity. And in any event one can find far more quotations on the other side—assertions that slavery was a positive good, the best labor system and the best system of social relations between what were deemed a superior and an inferior race. As one study of former slave owners after emancipation expressed it, "nothing in the postwar behavior and attitudes of these people suggested that the ownership of slaves had necessarily compromised their values or tortured their consciences."

In any case, most Confederates thought of themselves as fighting not for slavery but for independence. If slavery weakened Southern morale to the point of causing defeat, it should have weakened American morale in the Revolution of 1776 even more, for Americans of that generation felt more guilt about slavery than did Southerners of 1861. That sentiment helped produce the abolition of slavery in Northern states and the large number of manumissions in the upper South in the generation after 1776. And it is hard to see that Robert E. Lee, for example, who did have reservations about slavery—and about secession for that matter—made a lesser contribution to Confederate success than, say, Braxton Bragg, who believed firmly in both slavery and secession.

A third facet of the lack-of-will interpretation focuses on religion. At the outset, Southern clergymen preached that God was on the side of the Confederacy. But as the war went on and the South suffered so much death, disaster, and destruction, some Southerners began to wonder if God was on their side after all. Perhaps, on the contrary, he was punishing them for their sins. "Can we believe in the justice of Providence," asked one prominent Confederate, "or must we conclude that we are after all wrong?" Several historians have pointed to these religious doubts as a source of defeatism and loss of will that corroded Confederate morale and contributed to Southern defeat.

But note the phrase *loss of will* in the preceding sentence: not *lack,* but *loss.* There is a difference—a significant difference. A people whose armies are destroyed or captured, railroads wrecked, factories and cities burned, ports seized, countryside occupied, and crops laid waste quite naturally lose their will to continue the fight because they have lost the means to do so. That is what happened to the Confederacy. If one analyzes carefully the lack-of-will thesis as it is spelled out in several studies, it becomes clear that the real topic is *loss* of the will to carry on, not an initial *lack* of will. The book *Why the South Lost the Civil War,* which builds its interpretation around the *lack*-of-will thesis, abounds with *loss*-of-will phraseology: Union military victories "contributed to the *dissolution* of Confederate power and will . . . *created* war weariness and *destroyed* morale. . . . The loss of Atlanta and Sherman's march, combined with Lincoln's reelection, severely *crippled* Confederate will to win. . . . By 1865 the Confederacy had *lost* its will for sacrifice" (italics added).

This is the right way to put it. The cause-effect relationship is in the correct order: military defeat caused loss of will, not vice versa. It introduces external agency as a crucial explanatory factor—the agency of Northern military success, especially in the eight months after August 1864. The main defect of the lack-of-will thesis and of the internal-conflict and internal-alienation theses discussed earlier is that they attribute Confederate defeat to factors intrinsic to the South and tend to ignore that outside force battering away at the Confederacy. Thus the authors of *Why the South Lost the Civil War* conclude flatly, in the face of much of their own evidence, that "the Confederacy succumbed to internal rather than external causes." The overwhelming-numbers-and-resources interpretation at least had the merit of recognizing the external aspects of Confederate defeat, although the weaknesses of that interpretation remain.

Inferior Leadership. Another category of interpretation with an external dimension might seem to resolve the dilemma of explanation. This one focuses on leadership. Numerous historians of both Northern and Southern nativity have argued that the North developed superior leadership that became the main factor in ultimate Union victory. This literature deals mainly with three levels of leadership.

First, generalship: The Confederacy benefited from better generalship in the first half of the war, particularly in the eastern theater and at the tactical level. But by 1864 a group of generals, including Ulysses S. Grant, William Tecumseh Sherman, and Philip Sheridan, had emerged to top commands in the North with a grasp of the need for coordinated offensives in all theaters, a concept of the total-war strategy necessary to win this conflict, the skill to carry out the strategy, and the relentless determination to keep pressing it despite a high cost in casualties. In this interpretation the Confederacy had brilliant tactical leaders like Lee, Stonewall Jackson, Nathan Bedford Forrest, and others who also showed strategic talent in limited theaters. But the South had no generals who rose to the level of overall strategic ability demonstrated by Grant and Sherman. Lee's strategic vision was limited to the Virginia theater, where his influence concentrated Confederate resources at the expense of the western theaters in which the Confederacy suffered from poor generalship and where it really lost the war.

The second level where numerous historians have identified superior Northern leadership is in management of military supply and logistics. In Secretary of War Edwin M. Stanton, Quartermaster General Montgomery Meigs, Assistant Secretary of the Navy Gustavus Fox, Chief of U.S. Military Railroads Herman Haupt, and many other officials the North developed by 1862 a group of top- and middle-level managers who organized the Northern economy and the flow of supplies to Union armies with unprecedented efficiency and abundance. The Confederacy could not match Northern skill in organization and administration. In this interpretation, it was not the North's greater resources but its better management of those resources that won the war.

Third, presidential leadership: Lincoln proved to be a better commander in chief than Davis. A surprising number of Southern-born historians join Northerners in this conclusion. Two quotations to illustrate the point: Northerner James Ford

> **"If the Union and Confederacy had exchanged presidents with one another, the Confederacy might have won its independence."**

Rhodes wrote at the beginning of the twentieth century that "the preponderating asset of the North proved to be Lincoln." And in 1960 the Southern-born historian David Potter put it even more strongly: "If the Union and Confederacy had exchanged presidents with one another, the Confederacy might have won its independence."

This may overstate the case. In any event, a broad consensus exists that Lincoln was more eloquent than Davis in expressing war aims, more successful in communicating with the people, more skillful as a political leader in keeping factions working together for a common goal, better able to endure criticism and work with his critics. Lincoln was flexible and pragmatic, and possessed a sense of humor that helped him survive the stress of his job; Davis was austere, rigid, humorless, with the type of personality that readily made enemies. Lincoln had a strong physical constitution; Davis was frequently prostrated by illness. Lincoln picked good administrative subordinates (with some exceptions) and knew how to delegate authority; Davis went through six secretaries of war in four years and spent a great amount of time on petty administrative details that he should have left to subordinates. A disputatious man, Davis sometimes seemed to prefer winning an argument to winning the war; Lincoln was happy to lose an argument if it would help win the war. Davis's well-known feuds with two of the Confederacy's top generals, Beauregard and Joseph E. Johnston, undoubtedly hurt the South's war effort.

The thesis of superior Northern leadership seems more convincing than other explanations for Union victory. But once again, caveats are in order. With respect to generalship, even if the North did enjoy an advantage in this respect during the last year or two of the war, the Union army had its faint-hearts and blunderers, its McClellan and Pope and Burnside and Hooker who nearly lost the war to superior Confederate leadership in the East despite what was happening in the West. On more than one occasion the outcome seemed to hang in the balance because of *incompetent* Northern military leadership.

As for Union superiority in the management of production and logistics, this was probably true in most respects. The Northern war effort could draw on a wider field of entrepreneurial skills to mobilize men, resources, technology, industry, and transportation than could the South. Yet the Confederacy could boast some brilliant successes in this area of leadership. Ordnance Chief Josiah Gorgas almost literally turned plowshares into swords, building from scratch an arms and ammunition industry that kept Confederate armies better supplied than had seemed possible at the out-

> **If the presidential election had been held in August 1864 . . . Lincoln would have lost.**

set. The Rains brothers, George and Gabriel, accomplished miracles in the establishment of nitrate works, the manufacture of gunpowder, and the development of the explosive mines (then called torpedoes) that were the Confederacy's most potent naval weapon. Secretary of the Navy Stephen R. Mallory's boldness and resourcefulness turned out to be a pleasant surprise. What seems most significant about Confederate logistics is not the obvious deficiencies in railroads and the commissariat—to cite two notorious examples—but rather the ability of some Southern officials to do so much with so little. Instead of losing the war, their efforts went far toward keeping the Confederacy fighting for so long.

Finally, what about Lincoln's superiority to Davis as commander in chief? This might seem self-evident. Yet Lincoln did make mistakes. He went through a half-dozen failures as commanders in the eastern theater before he found the right general. Some of his other military appointments and strategic decisions could justly be criticized. And as late as the summer of 1864, when the war seemed to be going badly, when Grant's forces had suffered enormous casualties to achieve a stalemate at Petersburg and Sherman seemed equally stymied before Atlanta, Lincoln came under great pressure to negotiate peace with the Confederacy. To have done so would have been to admit Northern defeat. Lincoln resisted the pressure, but at what appeared to be the cost of his reelection. If the presidential election had been held in August 1864 instead of November, Lincoln would have lost. He would thus have gone down in history as an also-ran, a loser unequal to the challenge of the greatest crisis in the American experience. And Jefferson Davis might have gone down in history as the great leader of a war of independence, the George Washington of the Southern Confederacy.

That this did not happen was owing to events on the battlefield—principally Sherman's capture of Atlanta and Sheridan's striking victories over Jubal Early in the Shenandoah Valley. These turned Northern opinion from deepest despair in the summer to confident determination by November. This transformation of the Northern will illustrates the point made earlier that the will of either the Northern or the Southern people was primarily the result of military victory rather than a cause of it. Events on the battlefield might have gone the other way on these and other occasions during the war. If they had, the course of the war might have been quite different.

The Factor of Contingency

It is this element of contingency that is missing from generalizations about the cause of Confederate defeat, whether such generalizations focus on external or internal factors. There was nothing inevitable about Northern victory in the war. Nor was Sherman's capture of Atlanta any more inevitable than, say, McClellan's capture of Richmond in June 1862 had been. There were several major turning points, points of contingency when events moved in one direction but could well have moved in another. Two have just been mentioned: McClellan's failure to capture Richmond and Sherman's success in capturing Atlanta. The latter, coupled with Sheridan's victories in the Shenandoah Valley, proved to be the final and decisive turning point toward Union triumph. Two earlier moments of contingency that turned in favor of the North were of equal importance, however.

The first occurred in the fall of 1862. Confederate offensives during the summer had taken Southern armies from their backs to the wall in Mississippi and Virginia almost to the Ohio River and across the Potomac River by September. This was the most ambitious Confederate effort to win European recognition and a victorious peace on Union soil. But in September and October Union armies stopped the invaders at Sharpsburg and at Perryville, Kentucky. This forestalled European intervention, dissuaded Northern voters from repudiating the Lincoln administration by electing a Democratic House of Representatives in the fall of 1862, and gave Lincoln the occasion to issue the Emancipation Proclamation, which enlarged the scope and purpose of the war.

The other major turning point came in the summer of 1863. Before then, during the months between Union defeats at Fredericksburg and Chancellorsville, a time that also witnessed Union failures in the western theater, Northern morale and especially army morale dropped to its lowest point in the war. The usually indomitable Capt. Oliver Wendell Holmes, Jr., recovering from the second of three wounds he received in the war, wrote during the winter of 1862–1863 that "the army is tired with its hard and terrible experience . . . . I've pretty much made up my mind that the South have achieved their independence."

But then came the Battle of Gettysburg and the capture of Vicksburg. This crucial turning point produced Southern cries of despair. At the end of July 1863 Ordnance Chief Gorgas wrote:

> One brief month ago we were apparently at the point of success. Lee was in Pennsylvania. . . . Vicksburgh seemed to laugh all Grant's efforts to scorn. . . . Now the picture is just as sombre as it was bright then. . . . It seems incredible that human power could effect such a change in so brief a space. Yesterday we rode on the pinnacle of success—today absolute ruin seems to be our portion. The Confederacy totters to its destruction.

Predictions in July 1863 of the Confederacy's imminent collapse turned out to be premature. More twists and turns marked the road to the end of the war. This only accentuates the importance of contingency. All the factors discussed in this essay—numbers and resources, leadership, will, internal conflicts and alienation—formed the context of the specific events of the war. Separately or collectively, in complex and indirect ways, they influenced the direction that events took at crucial points of contingency. To understand why the Confederacy lost, in the end, we must turn from large generalizations that imply inevitability and study instead the contingency that hung over each military campaign, each battle, each election, each decision during the war. The chain of cause and effect from each of these events to the next will enable us, as with the piece-by-piece completion of a jigsaw puzzle, to get the big picture into some kind of focus.

[See also African Americans in the Union Army; Civil Liberties; Class Conflicts; Conscription; Desertion; Morale; Nationalism; Slavery, article on Slavery during the Civil War; State Rights; Taxation.]

BIBLIOGRAPHY

Beringer, Richard E., Herman Hattaway, Archer Jones, and William N. Still, Jr. Why the South Lost the Civil War. Athens, Ga., 1986.

Boritt, Gabor S., ed. Why the Confederacy Lost. New York, 1992.

Coulter, E. Merton. The Confederate States of America, 1861–1865. A History of the South, vol. 7. Baton Rouge, La., 1950.

Donald, David, ed. Why the North Won the Civil War. Baton Rouge, La., 1960.

Escott, Paul D. After Secession: Jefferson Davis and the Failure of Confederate Nationalism. Baton Rouge, La., 1978.

Faust, Drew Gilpin. "Altars of Sacrifice: Confederate Women and the Narratives of War." Journal of American History 76 (1990): 1200–1228.

Faust, Drew Gilpin. The Creation of Confederate Nationalism: Ideology and Identity in the Civil War South. Baton Rouge, La., 1988.

Hattaway, Herman, and Archer Jones. How the North Won: A Military History of the Civil War. Urbana, Ill., 1983.

Owsley, Frank L. State Rights in the Confederacy. Chicago, 1925.

Scarboro, David D. "North Carolina and the Confederacy: The Weakness of States' Rights during the Civil War." North Carolina Historical Review 56 (1979): 133–149.

Tatum, Georgia Lee. Disloyalty in the Confederacy. Chapel Hill, N.C., 1934.

Thomas, Emory. The Confederate Nation, 1861–1865. New York, 1979.

Wesley, Charles H. The Collapse of the Confederacy. Washington, D.C., 1922.

Wiley, Bell Irvin. The Road to Appomattox. Memphis, Tenn., 1956.

Woodworth, Steven E. Jefferson Davis and His Generals: The Failure of Confederate Command in the West. Lawrence, Kans., 1990.

JAMES M. MCPHERSON

Losses and Numbers

The Civil War was the bloodiest war in the history of the United States. An estimated 1,166,850 American soldiers became casualties in this conflict, 665,850 of whom died. Disease killed almost twice as many men as bullets and shot. Inadequate medical facilities and a lack of understanding of the germ theory caused many wounded to perish from infection long after the fighting had ended. Table 1 illustrates the distribution of casualties in both Union and Confederate armies.

> **The Confederate propensity to attack also led to enormous losses.**

Battlefield casualties resulted from a variety of innovations in technology compounded by a profound lack of updated tactics. This gap between technology and tactics—sometimes referred to as the "Tec-Tac Disjoint"—killed many men needlessly. Both armies continued to employ linear tactics even in the face of the withering fire of newly perfected rifled weapons, dooming many of their troops. The Confederate propensity to attack also led to enormous losses that the South could ill afford. Later in the war, however, both Union and Confederate armies increasingly relied on entrenchments. Table 2 lists the war's ten bloodiest battles, which accounted for 38 percent of all battlefield casualties.

The staggering losses were more damaging to the South, since the North had a sizable advantage in population. In part, the war was decided by attrition. Napoleonic tactics, still in use by most Civil War leaders, advocated moving masses of troops into one cataclysmic battle that would decide the war. In the Civil War, however, huge armies constantly bludgeoned each other, but very few decisive battles occurred. In the end, the North's ability to replace losses in the field was a decisive factor in victory.

Table1. Civil War Casualties

CASUALTIES	UNION	CONFEDERATE	TOTAL
Died of Disease	224,000	140,000[a]	364,000
Died in Prison	30,200	26,000[a]	56,200[a]
Missing, Presumed Dead	6,750	not available	
Other Nonbattlefield Deaths	34,800	not available	
Total Nonbattlefield Deaths	**295,750**	**166,000[a]**	**461,750[a]**
Killed in Action	67,100	54,000	121,100
Died of Wounds	43000	40,000	83,000
Total Battlefield Deaths	**110,100**	**94,000**	**204,100**
Total War-Related Deaths[b]	**405,850**	**260,000[a]**	**665,850[a]**
Nonmortally Wounded	275,000	226,000	501,000
Total Battlefield Casualties[c]	385,100	320,000	705,100
Total Casualties[d]	**680,850**	**486,000[a]**	**1,166,850[a]**

[a]Approximate figure.

[b]Total nonbattlefield deaths plus total battlefield deaths.

[c]Total battlefield deaths plus nonmortally wounded.

[d]Total war-related deaths plus nonmortally wounded.

SOURCE: Data taken from Thomas L. Livermore, *Numbers and Losses in the Civil War in America, 1861–1865*, Boston, 1901, and from E. B. Long and Barbara Long, *The Civil War Day by Day: An Almanac, 1861–1865*, Garden City, N.Y., 1971.

Table 2. Ten Battles with the Highest Casualties

BATTLE	DATE	CASUALTIES		
		UNION	CONFEDERATE	TOTAL
Gettysburg	July 1–3, 1863	17,684	22,638	40,322
Seven Days	June 25–July 1, 1862	9,796	19,739	29,535
Chickamauga	Sept. 19–20, 1863	11,413	16,986	28,399
Spotsylvania	May 8–19, 1864	17,500	10,000[a]	27,500
Wilderness	May 5–6, 1864	17,666	7,500[a]	25,166
Shiloh	Apr. 6–7, 1862	13,047	10,694	23,741
Sharpsburg	Sept. 17, 1862	11,657	11,724	23,381
Chancellorsville	May 1–4, 1863	11,116	10,746	21,862
Second Manassas	Aug. 29–30, 1862	10,096	9,108	19,204
Murfreesboro	Dec. 31,1862–Jan. 2, 1863	9,220	9,239	18,459

[a]Approximate figure.

SOURCE: Data taken from Thomas L. Livermore, *Numbers and Losses in the Civil War in America, 1861–1865*, Boston, 1901, and from E. B. Long and Barbara Long, *The Civil War Day by Day: An Almanac, 1861–1865*, Garden City, N.Y., 1971.

Not to be discounted was the role of immigrants, African Americans, and whites from the border states. An estimated 178,892 free blacks and former slaves—93,346 from the seceded states—served in the Union army, a manpower resource the South did not have. Nearly 500,000 foreign-born troops also served in the armies of the North. Furthermore, the majority of white men from the slaveholding border states of Delaware, Kentucky, Maryland, and Missouri fought for the North; only approximately 185,000 served in the Confederate army. But even discounting these blacks, immigrants, and border state whites, the North still enjoyed a tremendous advantage in its reserve of military-age men. In all, two and a quarter million men served in the Union army and approximately 900,000 served the Confederacy. Tables 3

Table 3. Population and Military Manpower in 1860

	NORTH[a]	SOUTH[b]	BORDER STATES[c]
Total Population[d]	19,086,250	9,101,450	3,211,897
Total Males Age 10 to 49[e]	6,128,138	2,837,819	1,019,340
White Males Age 10 to 49	6,057,644	1,712,064	850,552
Black Males Age 10 to 49	70,494	1,125,755[f]	168,788[g]

[a]Includes California, Connecticut, Illinois, Indiana, Iowa, Maine, Massachusetts, Michigan, Minnesota, New Hampshire, New Jersey, New York, Ohio, Pennsylvania, Oregon, Rhode Island, Vermont, and Wisconsin. Population of U.S. territories not included.

[b]Includes the eleven states that had seceded by May 20, 1861: Alabama, Arkansas, Florida, Georgia, Louisiana, Mississippi, North Carolina, South Carolina, Tennessee, Texas, and Virginia.

[c]Includes Delaware, Kentucky, Maryland, Missouri and the District of Columbia.

[d]Includes males and females of all races and ages.

[e]Includes males of all races. Although the age group fifteen to thirty-nine is commonly regarded as the appropriate pool of military manpower, this table lists ten years of age as the lower limit to reflect the fact that, as the war went on, youths age ten to fifteen became eligible for duty. The Union did not draw heavily on the youngest cadre of would-be soldiers, but the Confederates did enlist substantial numbers of fourteen- and fifteen-year-old boys toward the end of the war. Similarly, this table lists forty-nine as the upper age limit because, as the war continued, increasingly older men were called upon to serve, particularly in the Confederacy. At the outbreak of the conflict, the most common age of those enlisting was eighteen years.

[f]Includes 1,088,464 slaves and 37,291 free blacks.

[g]Includes 131,708 slaves and 37,080 free blacks.

SOURCE: Roger L. Ransom, *Conflict and Compromise: The Political Economy of Slavery, Emancipation, and the American Civil War*, Cambridge, Mass., 1989, pp. 90–91. Computed from figures in U.S. Census Office, Eighth Census [1860], Population, Washington, D.C., 1864. Total population of the South is listed as 360 persons higher than reported in the census, reflecting an upward adjustment of 360 slaves for the original purposes of the table.

Table 4. Military Strength[a]

	UNION			CONFEDERATE		
	PRESENT	ABSENT	TOTAL	PRESENT[b]	ABSENT	TOTAL
Army Strength, July 1861	183,588	3,163	186,751	—	—	112,040[c]
Army Strength, Jan.1862	527,204	48,713	575,917	258,680	68,088	326,768
Army Strength, Jan. 1863	698,802	219,389	918,191	304,015	145,424	449,439
Army Strength, Jan. 1864	611,250	249,487	860,737	277,970	186,676	464,646
Army Strength, Jan. 1865	620,924	338,536	959,460	196,016	204,771	400,787
Total Manpower, 1861–1865		2,213,000[d]			900,000[e]	

[a]Unless otherwise noted, all figures from E. B. Long and Barbara Long, *The Civil War Day by Day: An Almanac, 1861–1865*, Garden City, N.Y., 1971. Because of the inaccurate procedures used during the war to record troop strength and the difficulty after the war of collecting those records and assessing their validity, these figures are at best approximations. Union figures for January 1862 and following were calculated for January 1 of each year listed. Corresponding Confederate figures were actually calculated for December 31 of the previous year.

[b]For Confederates this table lists as present only those figures Long and Long in *Civil War Day by Day* classify as "aggregate present," not those classified as "present for duty," which tend to be 40,000 to 50,000 men lower at each point.

[c]Separate present and absent figures not available. Total figure taken from Thomas L. Livermore, *Numbers and Losses in the Civil War in America, 1861–1865*, Boston, 1901.

[d]Includes both army and navy. Army alone totals 2,129,000 men. Figures taken from U.S. Census Bureau, *Historical Statistics of the United States, Colonial Times to 1970*, Washington, D.C., 1975, pt. 2, ser. Y856–Y857, p. 1140.

[e]Includes both army and navy. This figure, taken from Roger L. Ransom, *Conflict and Compromise: The Political Economy of Slavery, Emancipation, and the American Civil War*, Cambridge, Mass., 1989, is an approximation of the greatest number of men likely to have fought for the South. Livermore in *Numbers and Losses* has calculated that 1,003,600 men served, but this number is probably inflated. On the low end of the spectrum is the figure of 750,000 men, calculated by Long and Long in *Civil War Day by Day*. James M. McPherson in *Battle Cry of Freedom: The Civil War Era*, New York, 1988, calculates a more likely figure of 882,000 men by extrapolating from records of surviving Confederate veterans in 1890. According to Ransom, McPherson's method of calculation may slightly overestimate the number of deaths between 1865 and 1890.

and 4 show the distribution of Union and Confederate populations and military strength during the conflict.

All of these statistics translate into a Civil War soldier's grim reality. The chances of death or dismemberment were very high, with nearly 30 percent of all Union troops and 48 percent of Confederate troops becoming casualties. As an illustration, consider a typical company of one hundred men.

In Federal armies, six would be killed on the battlefield or from wounds, eight would die of disease, and fifteen others would be wounded. In a Confederate company, ten would die as a result of combat, sixteen would fall to disease, and twenty-two would be wounded.

[*See also* Health and Medicine, *articles on* Sickness and Disease *and* Battle Injuries.]

BIBLIOGRAPHY

Livermore, Thomas L. *Numbers and Losses in the Civil War in America, 1861–65*. Boston, 1900. Reprint, Dayton, Ohio, 1986.

Long, E. B. *The Civil War Day by Day: An Almanac, 1861–1865*. Garden City, N.Y., 1971.

McWhiney, Grady, and Perry Jamieson. *Attack and Die: Civil War Military Tactics and the Southern Heritage*. Tuscaloosa, Ala., 1982.

Ransom, Roger L. *Conflict and Compromise: The Political Economy of Slavery, Emancipation, and the American Civil War*. Cambridge, Mass., 1989.

DONALD S. FRAZIER

CLARK, HENRY T.

CLARK, HENRY T. (1808–1874), governor of North Carolina. Born into a prominent planter family, Henry Toole Clark was raised on a plantation near Tarboro, North Carolina. He graduated from the University of North Carolina in 1826. Although he read law and was admitted to the bar, Clark spent most of his adult life supervising his family's extensive holdings. He served as a state senator from Edgecombe County from 1850 to 1861, and in 1858, as a secession Democrat, was elected Speaker of the Senate, then the second most powerful post in North Carolina government. When Governor John W. Ellis died in July 1861, Clark was appointed by the legislature to serve as governor until his term as senator ended in August 1862.

Although intelligent and a hard worker, Clark was politically unambitious and uninspiring as a leader. His greatest contribution as governor was his successful mobilization of North Carolina troops for the war effort and his outfitting of some fifty regiments for the cause. When he asked the War Department to furnish North Carolina troops with supplies, his request was denied on the ground that the blockade made it impossible for the central government to help. The legislature then passed a law requiring the state to equip its own troops. In a deal made with the Confederate Quartermaster Department, North Carolina agreed to furnish its troops with clothes, shoes, and blankets in return for commutation money. No other Confederate state made such an agreement.

Under Clark's leadership, North Carolina also proved resourceful in providing arms and ammunition to its troops. In September 1861, the state established a powder mill for munitions production in Raleigh. In October, the governor sent an agent to Europe to purchase arms and ammunition for state troops (North Carolina was the only state to buy arms directly from Europe). He had his adjutant general let out contracts with firms across the state to produce weapons. And in April 1862, he sent agents into every coun-ty to buy, borrow, or impress firearms in the hands of citizens. In all, he obtained about 51,000 stand of arms for state troops during his administration.

Federal forces in August 1861 captured Forts Hatteras and Clark and in February 1862 took Roanoke Island. By May, Federal forces had control of all of coastal North Carolina except for Wilmington and the lower Cape Fear region. Clark received blame from across the state for the loss of the sound region. The governor in turn accused Richmond of neglecting the defense of coastal North Carolina.

Clark was keen to repress any sign of disloyalty in the state. In an effort to raise a state force quickly to help defend the coastal region, in March 1862 he had ordered a draft of one-third of the state militia. In reaction, militant Unionists in the central counties of Randolph and Davidson held meetings in which leaders demanded peace and reunion. Clark sent in 300 troops to quell the insurrection. Earlier in July 1861, he had sent 160 troops into the same region to put down a "rebellious disturbance" by an underground band of reunionists who drilled under the U.S. flag and pledged themselves to fight for the Union.

Governor Clark played a key role in establishing the Salisbury Prison, the first prisoner-of-war camp in the Confederacy. He suggested the Salisbury site because the town was an important railroad terminus and grain-producing center. It also contained an abandoned three-story cotton mill near the railroad that could house up to 2,000 prisoners. Clark offered to furnish state troops to serve as prison guards. By March 1862, there were about 1,500 prisoners at Salisbury.

Clark chose not to run for election in 1862, and fellow party members did not urge him to do so. Clark was not a viable candidate: besides blaming him for the Federal occupation of the coastal region, citizens resented his enforcement of the conscription laws. Zebulon Vance, candidate of the new Conservative party (mostly prewar Unionists and old-line Whigs) won the contest.

Clark was a man of unblemished character, but the times called for a forceful leader, and that he was not. After the inauguration of Vance, Clark returned to his plantation at Tarboro, where he remained until his death in 1874.

BIBLIOGRAPHY

Barrett, John G. *The Civil War in North Carolina*. Chapel Hill, N.C., 1963.

Crabtree, Beth G. *North Carolina Governors, 1585–1975*. Rev. ed. Raleigh, N.C., 1974.

Iobst, Richard W. "Henry Toole Clark." In *Dictionary of North Carolina Biography*. Vol. 1. Edited by William S. Powell. Chapel Hill, N.C., 1979.

Mercer, Gary Garnall. "The Administration of Governor Henry Toole Clark, 1861–1862." Master's thesis, East Carolina College, 1965.

WILLIAM THOMAS AUMAN

CLASS CONFLICTS

In recent decades, the social history of the Confederacy has received substantial scrutiny, especially the role that class divisions among whites played in the South's eventual defeat. Much of this research has involved nonslaveholding men and women, significant numbers of whom became restive under Confederate rule. The areas of the Confederacy least dominated by plantation slavery were most disaffected, although debate continues as to the degree to which this class-based resistance undermined the Confederacy.

Personal ownership of slaves represented one measure of wealth and social standing, a critical benchmark in view of the importance of slavery in the sectional crisis. In 1860, three-quarters of Southern families owned no slaves; these families were concentrated in areas not suited to plantation agriculture, most notably the Appalachian and Ozark mountains. The social geography of the South thus dictated that regional differences would take on class overtones. These social cleavages had political ramifications as well. Before the war, farmers in the mountains and upper Piedmont generally backed the Democratic party, particularly in the lower South. Distrustful of centralized authority and Whiggish planters' social pretensions, they preferred the limited government espoused by the Democrats. The demands of the Confederate state would challenge their preference for small, locally based government.

After the election of Abraham Lincoln, nonslaveholder-dominated areas hesitated over the calls for secession. Opposition to immediate secession correlated with nonslaveholding, with the poorest mountain areas rejecting disunion decisively. In the upper South, nonslaveholding majorities prevented secession prior to the firing on Fort Sumter. After Lincoln's call for troops in April 1861, many rallied to the Confederacy in the face of invasion, especially in the lower South. Others lapsed into a passive acquiescence, but in eastern Tennessee and western Virginia, majorities opposed secession even after hostilities began.

Most white Southerners strongly supported the new republic for the first year of the war, but the demands of mobilization placed increasing pressures on the home front. Even wealthy slaveholders felt the impact, for the institution of slavery was vulnerable. Secession unsettled the plantations, since the slaves understood their status hinged on the outcome of the conflict. Furthermore, the Confederate practice of requisitioning slaves for fortification labor had a disruptive effect. The laborers were frequently ill-treated, and they always returned home with increased knowledge of the location of the nearest Federal army. The overriding issue was security; the departure of thousands of young white males for the front left the discipline of the slaves to untried hands. Young boys, old men, and women tried to overawe the

slaves, and many expressed worry about the outcome. One man feared in May 1861 that "our entire white population will volunteer" and the "slaves will become our masters, if they can."

The planters' concerns carried substantial weight, for slaveholders were overrepresented in Confederate government. Several Southern governors retained rifles in state armories, while the central government had hundreds of thousands of volunteers it could not arm. Similarly, local officials demanded that troops and militia remain near home, where they could assist in the case of raid or insurrection.

> **Strong planter opposition long prevented the Davis administration from considering the use of black troops, and even after Davis endorsed the policy.**

When Confederate authorities resorted to conscription in 1862, they took measures to maintain security and production on the plantation. The law allowed draftees to hire substitutes, which encouraged wealthier potential conscripts to buy their way out. One South Carolina woman complained to President Jefferson Davis about these "big men about towns," adding that they were "no serviz to us at home." Several Confederate generals wrote in 1864 that "more than 150,000" men employed substitutes, adding that the soldiers thus furnished were of poor quality and frequently deserted. The conscription laws also exempted various classes from service, including one overseer or supervisor on plantations with more than twenty slaves. The stated goal was "to secure the proper police of the country," and some three to four thousand individuals reportedly utilized the provision.

One of the more striking instances of planter influence occurred late in the war. Strong planter opposition long prevented the Davis administration from considering the use of black troops, and even after Davis endorsed the policy, the Confederate Congress blocked their use until only days before Appomattox.

The solicitude accorded planters heightened the disaffection among others. With reason, nonslaveholder-dominated regions felt they bore a disproportionate burden. Military service removed a major portion of their labor force. The women and children left behind found it difficult to raise enough food, and it was hard for authorities to find and transport enough to aid them. The blockade cut off consumer goods, while catastrophic depreciation overcame the Confederate currency, amounting to some 9,000 percent inflation overall by the last days of the war. This severely hurt those poorer families primarily dependent on soldiers' pay, which remained eleven dollars per month for privates. And even this sum was often late; for example, in the Trans-Mississippi Department soldiers were months behind in receiving their pay, which was depreciating all the while.

The fiscal policies of the Confederate government augmented such hardships. The Confederate Congress avoided most levies against plantations or slaves, and Treasury Secretary Christopher G. Memminger opposed direct taxation on constitutional grounds. Thus the government adopted other means of raising funds, with dire social effects. The tax-

> **The conscription issue became the focal point for class resentment, especially the twenty-slave exemption.**

in-kind seized 10 percent of the agricultural surplus of all farms. Requisition agents roamed across the South, seizing food at government prices, which were well below the market price. For example, by July 1864 the agents were paying only 20 percent of the prevailing price of corn to farmers. The secretary of war himself described this as a "harsh, unequal, and odious mode of supply."

The conscription issue became the focal point for class resentment, especially the twenty-slave exemption. That provision achieved "universal odium," one Confederate congressman observed, but despite modifications it was not repealed until the closing days of the war. The various exemptions inspired complaints of a "rich man's war and a poor man's fight." As several North Carolinians observed, "the common people is drove of[f] in the ware to fight for the big mans negro," while the slaveholder himself was making money at home. Rich speculators provided a scapegoat for rampant inflation and shortages. The *Richmond Examiner* commented that the "disposition to speculate upon the yeomanry of the country . . . is the most mortifying feature of the war."

The tax-in-kind seized 10 percent of the agricultural surplus of all farms. With implementation of the draft, lukewarm Confederates now faced a choice of military service or overt opposition. Resistance was less onerous for those with few possessions to sacrifice. Draft evaders gravitated toward the mountains and frontier areas, where it was easier to escape detection. This process concentrated disaffection in the very areas that had opposed secession, as did the departure of Confederate supporters for the army. When Confederate authorities tried to apprehend fugitives, the latter banded together to resist. Deserters and draft evaders dominated large areas.

Bitter conflict in northern Alabama illustrates these larger trends. Many small farmers initially tried to sit out the war. As one mountaineer wrote, the Confederates wanted "to git you

pumpt up to go to fight for their infurnal negroes," and afterward "you may kiss there hine parts for o they care." With conscription, those trying to avoid the draft found it increasingly difficult to cultivate their farms without being captured. By 1862, thousands of guerrillas were roaming through the region, subsisting on food seized from Confederate sympathizers. As Confederate reprisals increased, the Federal occupation of the Tennessee valley provided escape, and nearly three thousand Alabama whites joined the First Alabama Cavalry and other Union regiments. The North's army recruited disproportionately from the poorest and most isolated hill counties. A study of one loyalist stronghold, Winston County, has revealed that Union enlistees substantially outnumbered Confederates and that the Union soldiers owned less land and were drastically poorer than their Confederate neighbors. This pattern was evident in nonplantation areas throughout the South, and Union recruitment attained substantial proportions as Northern troops penetrated the region. Some 100,000 whites from the Confederate states joined the Union army, including 30,000 from Tennessee and a roughly equal number from what would become West Virginia. This number is dwarfed by the 850,000 to 900,000 who served the Confederacy; nevertheless it represented a substantial drain on Southern manpower.

Although most overt resistance to the Confederacy occurred in the mountains or other inhospitable terrain, support eroded elsewhere, too. In eastern North Carolina, the arrival of Union troops in 1862 prompted something approaching class war in Washington County. Bands of Unionist irregulars appropriated the property of Southern sympathizers, culminating in a major Confederate massacre of Union collaborators and blacks. In the cities, swollen with refugees, rampant inflation and food shortages prompted repeated unrest. Food riots occurred in Mobile, Atlanta, and Macon. Even in Richmond, crowds of women chanting "bread or blood" broke into stores in April 1863. While cities remained securely under Confederate control, overt Unionist displays were suicidal, but as Federal troops entered one city after another, they were frequently welcomed by the urban poor and foreign-born. In occupied New Orleans, for example, large numbers of workingmen collaborated with the Union administration in efforts to reconstruct the state.

The Richmond government faced increasing political difficulties, and by 1863 several states had elected anti-administration governors and congressmen. The anti-Davis faction defies easy categorization, being composed in part of state rights proponents from the plantation areas who continued to support the Confederacy. Anti-administration men from the up-country were more willing to consider a negotiated peace, but both groups collaborated to protect their states from the demands of the Confederate government.

To some extent, the state rights controversies that bedeviled the Confederate government can be seen as a response by local officeholders to the growing disaffection. Governor Joseph E. Brown of Georgia, for example, was considered the spokesman of the small farmers of northern Georgia. Governor Brown had denounced conscription as unconstitutional, and he exempted thousands of local officials and militia officers from the draft. In North Carolina, William W. Holden actually ran for governor in 1864 on a peace platform, and though he lost, he ran strongly in the mountainous western portion of the state. Covert "reconstructionist" sentiment became increasingly common among state and local officials. In Alabama, for example, a clandestine "peace society" was reportedly widespread in the Confederate army, and some army officials were surreptitiously exploring surrender terms before Richmond fell.

> The growing incidence of desertion provided an obvious index of spreading disaffection.

The growing incidence of desertion provided an obvious index of spreading disaffection. The first wave of desertion coincided with the draft legislation of 1862, which involuntarily extended the enlistments of many volunteers. As one Mississippi private observed, many of his comrades had left and added that "a heap says if their familys get to suffering they will go." As defeat followed defeat these numbers grew. After the Battle of Nashville in December 1864, the Southern army largely evaporated in the course of retreat. Robert E. Lee himself wrote during the siege of Petersburg that "hundreds of men are deserting nightly and I cannot keep the army together unless examples are made of such cases." In the spring of 1865 some 40 percent of Confederate troops east of the Mississippi were absent without leave, totaling some 100,000 Southern soldiers by war's end. Although desertions occurred among all social classes, it seems clear that the privations of the nonslaveholding families were a major cause. Without official censorship, soldiers were well aware of the hunger and violence their families faced at home. As one desperate wife wrote, "before God, Edward, unless you come home we must die." Many such men decided that their families came before an increasingly hopeless cause.

With the Confederate surrender at Appomattox, class tensions contributed to postwar disorder, especially as reflected in continuing conflict between Unionists and their late Confederate adversaries. Returning soldiers from both armies set out to avenge personal or family feuds, and violence remained pervasive. These conflicts took on political overtones, as individuals tried to use the judicial process to punish wartime misdeeds. Wartime Unionists saw themselves as victims of persecution, as Presidential Reconstruction returned Confederate sympathizers to local office. The continuing polarization was the major source of scalawag sentiment during Military Reconstruction. White Republican votes were concentrated in the poorer mountain and hill areas that had been most opposed to secession, and in which wartime Unionist sentiments had been most pronounced. In later years, these areas would be supportive of independent and populist insurgencies, too.

It is possible to exaggerate the significance of class differences within the Confederacy. Nonslaveholders did comprise the bulk of the Southern army, and most soldiers remained committed to independence until the war's final days. Still, substantial disaffection existed behind Confederate lines. Class resentment was not the only relevant variable, but it was a major one, given the widespread perception that nonslaveholders bore an excessive share of the war's privations. In order to prevail, Southerners probably needed more unity than their stronger adversary. They failed to achieve it, and class conflict represented one salient cause.

[*See also* Bread Riots; Conscription; Desertion; Impressment; Inflation; Morale; Peace Movements; Planters; Poverty; Society; Speculation; Tax-in-Kind; Unionism.]

BIBLIOGRAPHY

Crofts, Daniel. *Reluctant Confederates: Upper South Unionists in the Secession Crisis.* Chapel Hill, N.C., 1989.

Current, Richard Nelson. *Lincoln's Loyalists: Union Soldiers from the Confederacy.* Boston, 1992.

Durrill, Wayne K. *War of Another Kind: A Southern Community in the Great Rebellion.* New York, 1990.

Escott, Paul D. *After Secession: Jefferson Davis and the Failure of Confederate Nationalism.* Baton Rouge, La., 1978.

Hahn, Steven. *The Roots of Southern Populism: Yeoman Farmers and the Transformation of the Southern Upcountry, 1850–1890.* New York, 1983.

Rable, George C. *Civil Wars: Women and the Crisis of Southern Nationalism.* Urbana, Ill., 1989.

Thomas, Emory. *The Confederate Nation, 1861–1865.* New York, 1979.

MICHAEL W. FITZGERALD

CLAY, CLEMENT C.

CLAY, CLEMENT C. (1816–1882), congressman from Alabama and Confederate representative in Canada. Clement Claiborn Clay was born December 13, 1816, at Huntsville, Alabama. He was the son of Clement Comer Clay, an Alabama politician who served as governor in 1836 and 1837 and was named to the U.S. Senate shortly before the expiration of his term. As a result of his outspoken support of the secession movement, Clement Comer Clay was arrested by Federal troops after they occupied northern Alabama and was kept under military arrest for some time. Because of the similarity of the two men's names, Clement Claiborn Clay added Junior to his name and is often referred to as Clement C. Clay, Jr.

Young Clay graduated from the University of Alabama, receiving a bachelor's degree in 1834 and a master's degree in 1837. During his father's term as governor, he served as his private secretary and then studied law at the University of Virginia. He was admitted to the bar in 1840 and joined his father's law practice in Huntsville. Clay also operated a plantation called Wildwood in Jackson County and was the editor of the *Huntsville Democrat* from 1840 until 1842.

A member of the Democratic party, Clay was elected to the Alabama General Assembly in 1842 and was reelected in 1844 and 1845. While completing his last term, Clay was elected by the legislators as judge of the Madison County Court in 1846, serving until 1848 when he resigned. In 1853 Clay ran for the U.S. House of Representatives but was defeated. That winter, the Alabama legislature elected him to the U.S. Senate, and he was unanimously reelected in 1859.

While in the Senate, Clay championed the cause of state rights and supported John C. Calhoun's interpretation of the U.S. Constitution, arguing that Congress had no power over slavery in the states, that the territories were joint property of the states, that Congress had no right to make any law discriminating between the states or depriving them of their full and equal rights in any territory, and that any law interfering with slavery was a violation of the Constitution.

Clay was especially outspoken in his opposition to Justin S. Morrill's land grant act to aid colleges. Morrill's proposal that the Federal government donate public land to support higher education in each state in proportion to its population passed the House of Representatives in April 1858, but was opposed by Clay in the Senate. Basing his arguments on state rights, he declared that the legislation "treats the States as agents instead of principals, as the creatures, instead of the creators of the Federal government." Because of his opposition and that of other Southern senators, it was not until February 1859 that the Morrill Act passed the Senate, and then it was vetoed by President James Buchanan.

Clay also supported the admission of Kansas into the Union under the provisions of the Lecompton constitution enacted by the proslavery Kansas legislature. The Lecompton constitution called for a vote on slavery by the citizens of Kansas. One article guaranteed the right of property in slaves and specified that should it be rejected by the voters, a constitution without slavery would be enforced but the right of property in slaves who were already in Kansas would not be abolished. The Lecompton constitution first was approved by the voters of Kansas when antislavery forces boycotted the election. Ultimately, however, Kansas was not admitted under the Lecompton constitution, which was later repudiated by a majority of the settlers.

Clay remained in the Senate until Alabama adopted its ordinance of secession on January 11, 1861. He was one of five Southern senators who made dramatic speeches on the floor before walking out of the chamber.

With the formation of the Confederate States of America, Clay was offered the position of secretary of war by President Jefferson Davis, but he declined the post in favor of Leroy P. Walker. Shortly afterward, in November 1861, the Alabama General Assembly elected Clay to the first regular session of the Confederate Senate on the tenth ballot by a vote of sixty-six for Clay, fifty-three for Thomas H. Watts, and five for

> **Clay remained in the Senate until Alabama adopted its ordinance of secession.**

George P. Beirne. Clay drew a two-year term and took his seat in February 1862. He was appointed to the Commerce, Conference, and Military Affairs committees. During his career in the Senate, Clay was a strong supporter of Secretary of Navy Stephen R. Mallory and was named chairman of a special joint committee to investigate the administration of the Navy Department. Clay apparently used his influence to exonerate Mallory.

Clay also supported the passage of legislation that would restrict a Confederate supreme court from having appellate jurisdiction over state courts in what was one of the strongest debates on state rights in the Confederate Congress. (A supreme court was never established.) He also authored legislation to conscript foreign nationals into the Confederate army. Clay's state rights stance also was evident when he joined with Alabama's other senator, William Lowndes Yancy, to protest to President Jefferson Davis that they were "mortified" because Alabama troops were being placed under the command of officers from other states.

Much of Clay's work in the Senate was devoted to mobilizing the Confederacy for total war. He became disheartened by what he perceived to be a lack of total support for the war effort on the part of many Southern officials, once writing that he was "sick of the selfishness, demagogism and bigotry that characterize a large portion of those in office." When Clay learned "how many are growing rich in the Commissary and Qr. Masters Departs. by defrauding the Government and the people and yet are unchecked," he said he could hardly stand to continue in public service.

Throughout his term of office, Clay was a staunch supporter of President Davis and often a confidante of Varina Howell Davis, the president's wife. She once wrote to Clay to express her concern over the toll the task of governing the Confederacy was taking on her husband's health, telling him that the "President hardly takes time to eat his meals and works late at night." Clay became one of Davis's closest advisers on foreign policy. In fact, he, along with Benjamin H. Hill, Howell Cobb, and Robert M. T. Hunter, became the chief administration leaders in the Senate.

Clay, however, privately blamed much of Davis's problems with Congress on the Confederate president's personality, which Clay described as being that of a complex and inscrutable man who would not ask for or receive counsel. Davis, said Clay, seemed bound to go exactly the way his friends advised him not to go. Clay lamented that he had difficulty being friends with Davis and regretted that Davis "will be in a minority." Although Clay nevertheless was one of Davis's strongest supporters, he was honest and open in his dealings with other Southern leaders, even the anti-Davis faction, and as such maintained their respect throughout his term of office.

His loyalty to Davis, however, cost him the support of many of his constituents, for Davis's policies were not well received by many Alabamians. When Clay stood for reelection in 1863, he was defeated by Richard W. Walker. Clay then joined his wife in Petersburg, Virginia, where he attempted to negotiate a deal to purchase 100,000 bales of cotton to be sold overseas by the Confederate government. The scheme was never completed.

In late April 1864, Clay and Jacob Thompson were appointed Confederate representatives to Canada, to join James P. Holcombe who was already there. It was to be a secret assignment that Clay commented he could not enjoy; he accepted it only "with extreme reluctance, thro' a sense of duty to my country, & will do my best to serve her faithfully & efficiently." He left Petersburg on April 30 and traveled to Wilmington, North Carolina, where on May 6, he, Thompson, and their secretary, William W. Cleary, boarded a blockade runner for the trip to Canada via Bermuda. They reached Halifax, Nova Scotia, on May 19 and were joined by Holcombe.

Clay was entrusted with about $100,000 to finance his Canadian operations. One of his primary duties was to disrupt the North's war-making potential by sending secret agents south into the United States to contact copperheads, pro-Southern sympathizers, and members of the Knights of the Golden Circle and the Sons of Liberty. Two of Clay's most successful agents were Thomas H. Hines and John B. Castleman, who tried to persuade Illinois, Indiana, and Ohio to withdraw from the Union, form a northwestern confederacy, and enter into an alliance with the South. In addition they hoped to purchase several Northern newspapers and to disrupt the North's financial base through the spread of disinformation on the gold market.

Clay and his agents also had been given $25,000 with which to help Confederate prisoners held on Johnson's Island in Lake Erie escape to Canada. From there, they were to be shipped South through the blockade to rejoin their units, or they could remain in Canada to aid the Southern movement. Clay and the others recruited almost a hundred of the escapees who were willing to continue their service to the South.

Neither Clay nor Thompson, however, had the temperament to encourage a revolution. Eventually, they clashed over their objectives, and Thompson moved his base of operations to Toronto, Holcombe settled at Niagara Falls, and Clay moved to St. Catherines, Ontario.

Of more importance were Clay's secret contacts with Northern copperheads to seek a negotiated end to the fighting. Clay's counterpart in the North was Horace Greeley, who, although an abolitionist, hoped to end the slaughter on the battlefield through negotiations. When Greeley learned that Clay and Charles Francis Adams, whom he referred to as "two ambassadors of Davis & Co.," were in Canada with what he believed to be "full and complete powers for a peace," he pressured President Abraham Lincoln to meet with them. In arguing with Lincoln, Greeley pointed out that "our bleeding, bankrupt, almost dying country also longs for peace; shudders at the prospect of fresh conscriptions, or further wholesale devastations and of new rivers of human blood." Greeley's arguments reflected the growing pacifism and defeatism that by the summer of 1864 had added to the increased demand for a negotiated settlement of the war in the North. Faced with a Democratic call for an immediate cessation of hostilities, Lincoln's prospects for the 1864 election were dimming. Although he had little faith in the success of Greeley's proposal, in reply to his request Lincoln agreed to talk "with any person anywhere professing to have any proposition of Jefferson Davis in writing, for peace, embracing the restoration of the Union and the abandonment of slavery."

> **Clay was entrusted with about $100,000 to finance his Canadian operations.**

Greeley was named the intermediary between Clay and Lincoln and was empowered to inform the Confederate commissioner of the North's intention to enter into talks with responsible negotiators. On July 15, 1864, Lincoln informed Greeley that "I not only intend a sincere effort for peace, but I intend that you shall be a personal witness that it is made," and he extended to Clay, Thompson, Holcombe, and G. N. Sanders, whom he called Confederate "commissioners," a formal letter of safe conduct to the national capital. Armed with Lincoln's letter, Greeley traveled to Niagara Falls on July 17 to talk with Clay and the others, but he was disappointed when he learned that they were not duly accredited representatives of the Confederate government. The men explained that their presence was unofficial and could not be acknowledged by Southern authorities. They promised, however, that if they were guaranteed safe conduct to Washington, D.C., and from there to Richmond, they could secure the necessary approval. Afterward Lincoln was convinced that Clay and the others were present not to negotiate a peace between the Union and the Confederacy but to incite peace activists in the North to obstruct the war effort. As a result, he declared that he would negotiate only with certified representatives of the South who were willing to restore the peace, preserve the Union, and abolish slavery.

Clay and his colleagues also wanted to influence the Democratic National Convention held in Chicago in August 1864, in the hopes of electing a Democratic president and negotiating an end to the war. The Democrats were badly divided between copperheads and those supporting the North's war effort, and many Northerners feared that Clay would be able to influence and perhaps even control the

> **Many Northerners feared that Clay would be able to influence and perhaps even control the Democratic nomination.**

Democratic nomination. This rumor was so widespread that some newspapers reported that Clay had prepared a platform to be adopted by the Democratic delegates. It was said to call for the war to be continued only to restore the Union as it was before the fighting started, with "no further detriment to slave property" and permanent slave status for all blacks "not having enjoyed actual freedom during the war."

Seventy Confederate supporters led by Hines and Castleman did infiltrate Chicago during the Democratic convention, but they had to flee the city when the delegates adjourned. Splitting up, a third headed South and a third returned to Canada; the twenty-two remaining Confederates joined Hines and Castleman and traveled to south-central Illinois where they planned to destroy military supplies and disrupt railroad traffic in the St. Louis, Missouri, area. The plan failed, and in late October and early November, Hines's and Castleman's men returned to Chicago where they hoped to lead an armed uprising in conjunction with the presidential election; they were discovered, however, and most were arrested. This ended the Northwest Conspiracy.

Another major effort to encourage pro-Southern sentiment in the North took place on November 25, 1864, when eight Confederates led by Col. Robert M. Martin succeeded in setting fire to ten hotels, three theaters, and some vessels in the harbor of New York City. Although this caused much excitement, little actual damage was done and no uprising occurred because ten thousand Federal reinforce-

ments had been sent to the city to discourage copperhead activities.

In October 1864, Clay gave $2,462 to Lt. Bennett H. Young to underwrite a Confederate raid on St. Albans, Vermont. Planned by Clay and Young, this was one of the most spectacular Confederate raids of the war. Young and twenty men quietly infiltrated St. Albans on October 18 and spent the day reconnoitering its defenses. The following day at 3:00 P.M. the Confederates robbed St. Albans's banks of $200,000 and herded its citizens onto the village green. The Southerners then tried to set fire to several hotels and other buildings, seized horses from the streets and livery stables, and shot up the town, wounding three civilians, one of whom later died. After occupying the village for about forty-five minutes (during which time Young claimed they were Confederate soldiers despite the fact that they were not uniformed or carrying a flag), the Southerners mounted the horses they had seized and rode for the Canadian border fourteen miles away.

Word quickly spread of the attack, and troops were rushed to the region. When the Confederates crossed the border into Canada, they abandoned their weapons and horses and separated. Pursuing Northerners crossed into Canada and captured seven of the troopers as well as Young. Canadian authorities then arrived and took charge of the prisoners. Eventually fourteen of the raiders were captured, and on November 7, 1864, they were brought to trial in Montreal Police Court. Clay paid $6,000 to hire three well-known attorneys to defend Young and the others. The Confederates asked for a delay to secure copies of their commissions from Richmond, and eventually the case was dismissed because the court had no jurisdiction; the arrests had not been made with warrants signed by the governor-general. Five of the raiders were rearrested, released again, and arrested a third time before they were finally released on bail and fled to Europe.

In seven months, Clay and the other Confederate representatives in Canada had spent more than $500,000, but had failed to instigate a northwestern revolution, negotiate a peace, nominate a peace candidate on the Democratic ticket, or seriously disrupt the North's war effort. They did cause much hysteria with their raids and terrorist activities. Realizing he could accomplish nothing more, Clay sailed from Halifax for Bermuda on January 13, 1865. In Bermuda he boarded a blockade runner and sailed to Charleston, arriving on February 2. On the tenth, he rejoined his wife in Macon, Georgia.

After the Confederate surrender, Clay decided to abandon his homeland and started on horseback for Texas. During the journey he learned that President Lincoln had been assassinated and that he had been implicated as one of the conspirators. When he discovered that a reward had been offered for his capture, Clay abandoned his plan to go to Texas and rode 150 miles to surrender to Federal authorities back in Macon. He was arrested and taken to Augusta, Georgia, where he was shipped, along with Davis, to Fortress Monroe, Virginia, and imprisoned.

Although never brought to trial, Clay was not released until May 1866 after his wife pleaded with President Andrew Johnson for his freedom. He returned to Wildwood and resumed his law practice. His health had deteriorated during the war, and he declined to reenter politics. Clay died on January 3, 1882, in Madison County. His papers, which are preserved at Duke University Library in Durham, North Carolina, offer some of the best insights into the inner workings of the Confederate government during the war and shed light on the various personalities involved.

BIBLIOGRAPHY

Brewer, W. *Alabama: Her History, Resources, War Record, and Public Men from 1540 to 1872.* Montgomery, Ala., 1872.
Fleming, Walter L. *Civil War and Reconstruction in Alabama.* New York, 1905.
Nuermberger, Ruth K. *The Clays of Alabama: A Planter-Lawyer-Politician Family.* Lexington, Ky., 1958.
Owen, Thomas M. *History of Alabama and Dictionary of Alabama Biography.* Chicago, 1921.
Pickett, Albert J. *History of Alabama and Incidentally of Georgia and Mississippi from the Earliest Period.* Birmingham, Ala., 1900.
Saunders, James E. *Early Settlers of Alabama.* New Orleans, La., 1899.
Wood, Gray. *The Hidden Civil War: The Story of the Copperheads.* New York, 1942.

KENNY A. FRANKS

CLAY-CLOPTON, VIRGINIA

CLAY-CLOPTON, VIRGINIA (1825–1915), society leader and suffragist. Virginia Tunstall was born in Nash County, North Carolina, the daughter of Dr. Peyton Randolph Tunstall and Ann (Arrington) Tunstall. Her mother died when she was a young child, and she was raised by relatives in Tuscaloosa, Alabama, who were politically prominent members of the planter and merchant class. She graduated in 1840 from the Nashville (Tennessee) Female Academy. On February 1, 1843, she married Clement Claiborne Clay of Huntsville, Alabama, who in 1853 was elected to the U.S. Senate. Childless and without household responsibilities, Virginia Clay was able to direct her considerable social talents to cultivating the political elite of the nation's capital.

In January of 1861, the Clays left Washington with the general withdrawal of the Southern senators. During the war, Clement Clay served in the Confederate Congress and as an adviser to Jefferson Davis. Despite the occupation of her family home in Huntsville in 1862 by Northern troops, Virginia Clay was buffered from much of the hardships of the war by her wealth and social position. In 1865, her husband was accused of complicity in the assassination of Abraham Lincoln and was imprisoned in Fort Monroe with Jefferson Davis. Virginia Clay played a leading role in securing his release eleven months later by writing letters to influential political figures and personally appealing to President Andrew Johnson.

Reduced financially by the war, the Clays took up farming in Huntsville. Clement Clay never recovered from the defeat of the Confederacy and died in 1882. Virginia Clay was remarried on November 29, 1887, to David Clopton, a justice on the Alabama Supreme Court. Upon his death in 1892, she took the name Clay-Clopton. She became an early and key figure in the Southern women's suffrage movement, serving as president of the Alabama Equal Rights Association from 1896 to 1900. In 1905 she published a volume of memoirs, *A Belle of the Fifties,* which focused upon her years as a Washington social figure and on her experiences during the Civil War.

BIBLIOGRAPHY

Bleser, Carol, and Frederick Heath. "The Clays of Alabama: The Impact of the Civil War on a Southern Marriage." In *In Joy and in Sorrow: Women, Family and Marriage in the Victorian South.* Edited by Carol Bleser. New York, 1991.
Nuermberger, Ruth. *The Clays of Alabama: A Planter-Lawyer-Politician Family.* Lexington, Ky., 1958.
Sterling, Ada. *A Belle of the Fifties: Memoirs of Mrs. Clay of Alabama, Covering Social and Political Life in Washington and the South, 1853–1866. Put into Narrative Form by Ada Sterling.* New York, 1905.
Wiley, Bell I. *Confederate Women.* Westport, Conn., 1975.

LEEANN WHITES

CLEBURNE, PATRICK

CLEBURNE, PATRICK (1828–1864), major general. Born in County Cork, Ireland, March 16, 1828, Patrick Ronayne Cleburne was the son of a fairly well-to-do doctor. In 1846 he failed a medical school entrance examination and, believing he had disgraced his family, enlisted in the British army. In September 1849 he purchased his discharge from the army and three months later arrived in New Orleans.

After clerking for a few months in Cincinnati, Cleburne was hired to manage a drugstore in Helena, Arkansas. The Irishman fit well into the small frontier community, joining the Masons, the Episcopal church, the Sons of Temperance, and (until 1856 when he became a Democrat) the Whig party. He also studied law. In 1855 he became a naturalized citizen, and in the next year he was admitted to the bar.

In 1860 citizens in the Helena area organized a military company called the "Yell Rifles." Cleburne enlisted as a private. He was soon elected captain to command the company. After Arkansas's secession, the company entered state service as part of the First Arkansas Infantry Regiment. On May 14, 1861, Cleburne was elected colonel of the regiment. He was an excellent officer and put his British army experience to good use.

That summer the regiment joined Brig. Gen. William J. Hardee's force at Pittmans Ferry, near Pocahontas, in northeastern Arkansas. There, on July 23, Cleburne and his command transferred from Arkansas to Confederate service.

Assignment to Hardee's command was, in many ways, the key event in Cleburne's Civil War career. A strong friendship developed between the two officers, and Cleburne's Confederate service—for better and worse—became tied inextricably to Hardee's.

That fall Hardee's command joined Gen. Albert Sidney Johnston's army at Bowling Green, Kentucky. Hardee was named major general to command a division, and Cleburne became commander of one of his brigades consisting of the First and Fifth Arkansas regiments, the Sixth Mississippi, and the Fifth Tennessee. The same skills and knowledge that made Cleburne a fine regimental commander enabled him to turn his brigade into one of the Confederate army's finest units.

Johnston was forced to evacuate Bowling Green in February 1862. He retreated to Corinth, Mississippi, where he organized troops collected from all over the Old Southwest into what eventually became the Army of Tennessee. Cleburne was promoted to brigadier general (to date from March 4, 1862) to command his brigade in Hardee's Third Corps of that army. At Shiloh Cleburne's brigade lost 1,013 of its 2,700 men—the heaviest loss of any Southern brigade in the battle. Cleburne himself received high praise for his conduct.

After Shiloh the Confederates were forced back into Mississippi, and the army's new commander, Gen. Braxton Bragg, determined to transfer the army to Tennessee. Along with the troops of Maj. Gen. E. Kirby Smith, he then marched into Kentucky. Bragg created a two-brigade provisional division under Cleburne and sent it to reinforce Smith's column advancing from eastern Tennessee. At the Battle of Richmond, Kentucky, on August 30, Cleburne was wounded in the jaw and was absent from his command about three weeks.

Cleburne was back with his brigade at the Battle of Perryville on October 8 and was twice wounded. In December, after the army had withdrawn to middle Tennessee, he was promoted to major general with date of rank set at November 23. He thus became the highest-

PATRICK CLEBURNE.   Library of Congress

ranking military officer of foreign birth in the Confederate army. He was assigned to command a division in Hardee's corps.

With his new command, Cleburne fought at Murfreesboro and was with the army on the retreat to North Georgia in the late summer of 1863. He participated in the great Confederate victory at Chickamauga in September and especially distinguished himself at Missionary Ridge and at Ringgold Gap in November where he covered the Confederate retreat to Dalton, Georgia.

Meanwhile, a civil war had erupted among the generals of the Army of Tennessee, and Cleburne had followed Hardee into the group that opposed Bragg. Most historians of the army believe that membership in the anti-Bragg faction hurt Cleburne's chances for further promotion. In January 1864 Cleburne proposed that the Confederacy free slaves and incorporate them into its armies. This proposal was rejected, and it too damaged Cleburne's chances for higher command.

Cleburne led his division through the Atlanta campaign of 1864 with his accustomed skill. He especially distinguished himself at Pickett's Mill and Atlanta. At Jonesboro, Hardee commanded a two-corps force, and Cleburne commanded Hardee's corps.

After the fall of Atlanta Hardee was sent away from the army. Maj. Gen. B. Franklin Cheatham took command of the corps, and Cleburne returned to his division. At Franklin,

Tennessee, on November 30, Cleburne went with his division into the desperate assault on the Federal works. His troops overran an advanced Northern position and swept on toward the main line. Two horses were killed under Cleburne as he moved forward with his men. Then Cleburne, on foot and with his hat in one hand and his sword in the other, disappeared into the holocaust. A few seconds later a bullet struck just below his heart; he died instantly. Buried first in Rose Hill Cemetery, Columbia, Tennessee, his body was soon taken to St. John's Churchyard at nearby Ashwood. In 1870 the body was moved to what is now Magnolia Cemetery in Helena, Arkansas.

Cleburne's career illustrates very well the problems the Confederates faced in the West. The internal politics of the Army of Tennessee that helped block his well-earned promotion also did much to bring about the Southern defeat in the all-important western theater.

BIBLIOGRAPHY

Buck, Irving A. *Cleburne and His Command.* Jackson, Tenn., 1959.
Durden, Robert F. *The Gray and the Black: The Confederate Debate on Emancipation.* Baton Rouge, La., 1972.
Nash, Charles Edward. *Biographical Sketches of Gen. Pat Cleburne and Gen. T. C. Hindman.* Little Rock, Ark., 1898. Reprint, Dayton, Ohio, 1977.
Perdue, Howell, and Elizabeth Perdue. *Pat Cleburne: Confederate General.* Hillsboro, Tex., 1973.
Woodworth, Steven E. *Jefferson Davis and His Generals: The Failure of Confederate Command in the West.* Lawrence, Kans., 1990.

RICHARD M. MCMURRY

CLOPTON, DAVID

CLOPTON, DAVID (1820–1892), congressman from Alabama. Born on September 29, 1820, in Putnam County, Georgia, Clopton graduated from Randolph-Macon College in Virginia in 1840. He was admitted to the bar in 1841 and practiced law first in Griffin, Georgia, and then in Tuskegee, Alabama. In 1859 Clopton was elected as a Democrat to the U.S. House of Representatives.

When Alabama passed the secession ordinance in January 1861, Clopton, an ardent secessionist, returned to the state. In 1861 he enlisted as a private in the Twelfth Alabama Infantry and was promoted to assistant quartermaster with the rank of captain. Clopton was elected as a representative to the First and Second Confederate Congresses and served on the Claims, Naval Affairs, Illegal Seizures, and Medical Department committees. Although not an obstructionist, he was reluctant to grant expansive powers to the Confederate central government. He supported the arming of slaves, drafting of speculators, and Confederate control of commerce. He introduced proposals to moderate such existing programs as conscription and taxation.

In March 1866 Clopton opened a successful law practice in Montgomery and returned to politics in 1874 when the Democratic party was restored to power in Alabama. In 1878 he was elected to the Alabama legislature and in 1884 was appointed an associate justice on the Alabama Supreme Court, where he remained until his death in Montgomery on February 5, 1892.

BIBLIOGRAPHY

McMillan, Malcolm C. *The Alabama Confederate Reader.* University, Ala., 1963.
Owen, Thomas McAdory. *History of Alabama and Dictionary of Alabama Biography.* 4 vols. Chicago, 1921.
Thornton, J. Mills, III. *Politics and Power in a Slave Society: Alabama, 1800–1860.* Baton Rouge, La., 1978.
Wakelyn, Jon L. *Biographical Directory of the Confederacy.* Edited by Frank E. Vandiver. Westport, Conn., 1977.
Warner, Ezra J., and W. Buck Yearns. *Biographical Register of the Confederate Congress.* Baton Rouge, La., 1975.

SARAH WOOLFOLK WIGGINS

COBB, HOWELL

COBB, HOWELL (1815–1868), congressman from Georgia and major general. Howell Cobb was born at Cherry Hill, Jefferson County, Georgia, on September 7, 1815. He was the oldest of seven children and brother of Thomas R. R. Cobb, who would be the chief designer of the Confederate Constitution. In 1819 the Cobb family moved to Athens, home of Franklin College (the University of Georgia), where Howell acquired a Jacksonian Democratic bias against nullification before graduating in 1834. About a year later he married Mary Ann Lamar, daughter of a wealthy middle Georgia merchant-planter. They settled in Athens.

Admitted to the bar in 1836, Howell's political career began the following year with his appointment as solicitor general of the state's western district. He was elected to Congress in 1842 from the Sixth Georgia District and repeatedly reelected as a Democrat for the rest of the decade. Chosen Speaker of the 31st Congress, he helped steer through that body the Compromise of 1850. The next year his Georgia friends organized the Union party and elected him governor. Meanwhile his leadership in the state Democratic party had gone to others, while his support of Democratic presidential candidate Franklin Pierce in 1852 infuriated the Unionists. A politician without a party, he resumed his law practice after leaving the governorship in 1853. Two years later, running as a Democrat, he easily recaptured his old congressional seat. Back in Washington, Cobb was soon hobnobbing with Democratic leaders. It paid off with his appointment in 1857 as secretary of the treasury by President James Buchanan. His conflict with the Georgia Democrats had taught Howell that to resonate with folks back home he had to move resolutely toward separatism.

On December 7, 1860, U.S. Secretary of the Treasury Cobb resigned from President James Buchanan's cabinet. A few days later he set out for his home in Athens, Georgia. He had scarcely settled when he headed for northern Georgia to turn the sentiment among old Unionist friends into passion for secession. But despite the best efforts of this born-again state rights advocate, many Unionist delegates were chosen on January 2, 1861, to attend the mid-January convention in Milledgeville, the state capital.

On the eve of the convention Cobb took his message to a gathering of friends and delegates at the Macon home of his brother-in-law, John B. Lamar. He implored his listeners to mute Unionism, a tactic he believed would permit the convention to take Georgia out of the Union with a minimum of bickering. Although not a delegate, Cobb accompanied Lamar and his guests to nearby Milledgeville and was honored with a chair on the convention floor. On January 19 he wired his son that the ordinance of secession had been adopted. The convention completed its work by naming ten delegates to a convention of seceded states to meet in Montgomery, Alabama, on February 4. Cobb and Robert Toombs were chosen delegates-at-large along with eight district delegates. One of the latter was Cobb's younger brother Thomas. The Cobbs had fared well, thanks to Howell's prominence and zeal.

Georgia's delegates to the Montgomery convention assembled with those from South Carolina, Florida, Alabama, Mississippi, and Louisiana. The convention unanimously chose Cobb as its presiding officer. In a short acceptance speech, the incipient Confederacy's first leader announced that separation from the United States was "perfect, complete, and perpetual." He continued by urging a cordial welcome be extended to those Southern states not yet in the fold, adding emphatically that peace must be maintained not only with the late sister states of the North but with the world at large as well. He concluded by predicting for the Confederacy an "era of peace, security, and prosperity."

That Cobb was accorded the distinction of being chosen the Confederacy's first leader was an acknowledgment of his skill as a negotiator. Whether he was being rewarded or punished is not altogether clear. Impassioned secessionists may have been playing a clever game. His plea for peace recalled his dexterity during the drafting of the Compromise of 1850 when, according to his critics, he had given away too much. By electing him president of the Montgomery convention they were withholding the bigger prize, president of the

HOWELL COBB. LIBRARY OF CONGRESS

Confederacy. Although Cobb denied he had been the victim of such intrigue, some of his friends believed otherwise.

With the drafting of the Constitution of the Confederate States of America, the Montgomery convention became the Provisional Congress. Cobb was convinced that its crowning achievement was the unanimous adoption on March 11 of the Constitution. None had labored more diligently than his brother in framing the document that Howell proclaimed was the "ablest ever prepared . . . for a free people." Perhaps next in importance to the adoption of the Constitution was Cobb's administration of the oath of office to President Jefferson Davis on February 18. Although pleased with the selection of Davis by the Congress, Cobb was distressed by the choice of Alexander H. Stephens as vice president. Surmounting almost two decades of political rivalry between the two was Cobb's conviction that his fellow Georgian's Unionism had survived the birth of the Confederacy.

Having met twice in Montgomery, Congress moved the capital of the Confederacy to Richmond in late May. It would hold three meetings there. Until it adjourned sine die on February 17, 1862, Cobb was its presiding officer. Meanwhile he began a second career. Assisted by relatives and friends, during the summer of 1861 he recruited the Sixteenth

Georgia Infantry Regiment. Congress rewarded him on August 28 by approving his nomination for a colonelcy.

Recruitment received a mighty boost on July 21 from the defeat of Union forces at First Manassas. Cobb agreed with his brother, also a colonel, that it "has secured our independence." Howell predicted the blockade would soon be lifted and peace would follow quickly. His boundless optimism was contagious, and nine hundred Georgians joined the Sixteenth Regiment to celebrate the imminent independence of the Confederacy.

By mid-August Howell's troops were quartered at Camp Cobb, located about a mile from the state house, which was the new headquarters of the Provisional Congress. Cobb's life of political leadership and soldiery continued for eight months. Soldiery promptly presented a litany of woes. Early in September the regiment was ravaged with mumps and measles, about thirty cases proving fatal in five weeks. Meanwhile a special agent dispatched to Savannah to pick up a shipment of Enfield rifles discovered that Governor Joseph E. Brown had confiscated them. When Cobb learned what had happened, he lost his self-control, excoriated Confederate authorities, and demanded such interference cease. His demand produced a thousand rusty rifles. Cleaned and polished, they moved an official of the State Department to congratulate the Georgian on having the best guns in the Confederate army. In mid-October his son boasted that the colonel had progressed enough to shout drill orders from horseback.

On October 18 and 19 Cobb moved his troops to the Yorktown area, where they joined Gen. John B. Magruder's Army of the Peninsula. Cobb quickly developed a liking for "Prince John." Both Cobb and his brother, whose Georgia Legion was encamped nearby, believed the general was competent, though somewhat excitable, and that he was unfairly charged with a weakness for strong drink. The clammy atmosphere of the lower peninsula defied Cobb's morale-boosting improvisations. He felt unappreciated as he prepared to depart for the final session of the Provisional Congress. His brother, likewise beset with gloom, joined him in addressing a letter to the War Department requesting transfer of their commands to Georgia. The request unheeded, Cobb set out for Richmond on October 18. He arrived amid excitement over the seizure by USS *San Jacinto* of two Confederate envoys aboard the British merchantman *Trent*. Cobb believed this act was a violation of international rights.

Once invited by presidents to confer on important matters of state, Cobb was to be granted no such courtesy by President Davis. Rather, Davis dismissed the *Trent* affair with a single reference before the opening of the final session of the Provisional Congress. As the prospect of England's entering the war faded, Secretary of the Treasury Christopher G. Memminger, lamenting to Cobb that the *Trent*

affair had ended as it did, trusted that further complications "between them and England" would yet end the blockade. Cobb was to cling to the hope that England would go after the "cowardly Yankee" government.

The final session of the Provisional Congress lasted about three months. This was a difficult time for Cobb. When he was in Richmond, Magruder urged him to return to Yorktown; when he was with his troops, politicians wanted him in Richmond. Magruder's continual alarms over a likely attack may have been aimed at keeping Cobb on the lower peninsula. They became a routine of camp life, Cobb conceding that without "this amusement" soldiers would forget the war and become unfit. That many of them wished to return home with their arms at the end of their twelve months' enlistment was far more upsetting to Cobb than the general's monotonous alerts. The Georgian expressed his concern to Memminger, urging that Davis instruct all generals to see that discipline was tempered with kindness. Memminger responded that Davis had promised to do all he could to soften the "old habits" of the professionals, concluding on the

> That many of them wished to return home. . . at the end of their twelve months' enlistment was far more upsetting to Cobb.

considerate note that Cobb would soon be "up here" to help legislate on his concern.

When Cobb returned to Richmond in mid-January 1862, the Provisional Congress was entering its final weeks. Its leader was approaching the end of a political career that had spanned over a quarter century. For the first time he was dejected over the Confederacy's prospects. This was partly due to his presumption that Gen. George B. McClellan was about to deliver a crushing blow. Helping to push him closer to defeatism was a rumor that Savannah was about to be attacked. In desperation Cobb joined three fellow Georgians in urging a scorched-earth reception. Although his fears proved groundless and his call for destruction went unheeded, Confederate reverses in February convinced him of the necessity of putting the torch to homes and fields.

As he arose before the Provisional Congress on February 17 to deliver his valedictory, Cobb lacked his earlier optimism. After excoriating the enemy and extolling the Confederacy as true to the "conservative principles" of the Founding Fathers, he pronounced Congress adjourned. Five days later, on Washington's birthday, he called into session the House of Representatives of the newly elected bicameral Congress of the Confederate States of America, administered the oath of office to Speaker Thomas S. Bocock, and summarily became a warrior statesman without portfolio.

On March 8, 1862, Cobb took charge of the newly formed Second Brigade. Recently promoted to brigadier general, he now commanded over five thousand troops consisting of four regiments, including the Sixteenth Georgia and that of his brother. While conducting a chase after Federals in North Carolina, he was ordered to join Magruder on the peninsula in accordance with a plan prescribed by Gen. Robert E. Lee to concentrate forces near Richmond. His brigade took a position across the Warwick River from the Northerners. There was little action until April 16. Then a short but hot fight took place around Lee's Mill. In this, his first test under fire, Cobb was satisfied he had handled his men well. By late June Confederate forces had withdrawn to within a few miles of Richmond. On the twenty-fifth the Seven Days' Battles began, with Magruder putting on a show of force in front of the capital. Two days later McClellan began his retreat to Harrison's Landing with Southern forces in vigorous pursuit. After losing an artillery duel and failing to overrun a rear guard at Malvern Hill on July 1, the Confederates spent the next day burying their dead. Of Cobb's men engaged in this action, one-third had been killed or wounded.

Cobb needed a rest, but having attended two fruitless parleys with Union officers on the subject of prisoner exchanges, he was asked by General Lee to try again. He refused and went home instead. Within a month he was back with the Second Brigade, now assigned to Gen. Lafayette McLaws's division of the Army of Northern Virginia. Maryland was about to be invaded and Cobb's destination was Crampton's Gap in South Mountain. On September 14 McLaws ordered Cobb to hold the Gap "if it costs the life of every man." A disaster ensued. The Second Brigade was badly mauled and its commander blistered by the staccato expletives of McLaws. Because other passes could not be sealed either, the Battle of Sharpsburg (September 17) was indecisive. Although the invasion failed, the Army of Northern Virginia survived. The hapless Cobb was sent to the Gulf coast.

Acting on instructions from Lee, the War Department ordered Cobb to report to Gen. P. G. T. Beauregard in Charleston. Early in November the Georgian conferred with the general about his assignment to the newly created Military District of Middle Florida, one of seven in Beauregard's department. With headquarters in Quincy, middle Florida was a rich agricultural area fronting on the Gulf of Mexico between the Suwannee and Choctawhatchee rivers. It was formed to defend vital rivers, particularly the Apalachicola and its tributaries, against Federal gunboats, to protect plantations and saltworks from raids, and to discourage collusion between Federal blockaders and Unionist Southerners.

Cobb planned to secure the coast with troops and seal the important river by filling its channel with obstacles. These operations required more than the thousand troops on duty when Cobb arrived. Warning the War Department in early

March against the "delusion of an early peace," he requested five thousand men. Although denied his request, he was permitted to woo volunteers by suspending conscription. When Cobb left for another duty station in September, he had raised about half the number of troops he had requested.

In August 1863, Cobb was in Atlanta conferring with Gen. Braxton Bragg, commander of the Army of Tennessee, planning the defense of Georgia. As he was preparing to return to Quincy, he received orders to tidy up the assorted recruits Governor Brown had assembled in Atlanta. Thus was born the short-lived Georgia State Guard. Until its demise in February 1864, the State Guard supplied a few troops for Bragg and for defense units in North Georgia and Savannah as well. Cobb used it to track down deserters, stragglers, and

> **Because immediate action was not taken on his proposal, he conveyed . . . his conviction that Congress was lack-brained.**

profiteers. His new assignment made him a participant in the disaster that was unfolding in Georgia, and it enabled him to renew contacts with Richmond. He met with Davis twice in Atlanta, and when he learned that the controversial Bragg was to be replaced, he headed for Richmond to plead for his choice as successor. He was pleased with the appointment of Gen. Joseph E. Johnston.

Having been promoted on December 3, Cobb arrived in Richmond as a major general. He promptly expressed concern over the absence of a comprehensive military plan, conferred with the president, and submitted to the leaders of Congress a plan that would authorize him to recruit from the State Guard a new command. Because immediate action was not taken on his proposal, he conveyed to Vice President Stephens his conviction that Congress was lack-brained.

Cobb was relieved to be back in Georgia. He promptly visited the Army of Tennessee and predicted "Old Joe" Johnston would drive the Federals out of the state. In an unofficial letter to the president, he explained that this could be done by means of a strong drive into Tennessee. Meanwhile enlistments in the State Guard were expiring and with them Cobb's command.

For over a month Cobb was without a unit. Finally Congress acted and on April 5 the War Department braced itself for the Confederacy's last effort in the Southeast by ordering Cobb to Macon to establish headquarters for the Georgia Reserve Force. With the heaviest concentration in Macon, fewer than five thousand troops, many of them part-time soldiers, were strung between Savannah and Columbus to repel hostile forays against railroads south of Atlanta. On

July 30 Cobb repulsed Gen. George Stoneman's raiders in a sharp clash east of Macon, thereby setting the stage for the capture of some six hundred raiders and their commander.

With the fall of Atlanta on September 2, 1864, matters had become critical enough to oblige Davis to visit Georgia. Arriving in Macon on the twenty-fourth, he joined Cobb in paying a visit to the Army of Tennessee encamped about twenty-five miles south of Atlanta. When the two returned to Macon, Cobb was greeted with an additional assignment. Richmond had finally put together an overall military plan, a part of which was a new command known as the District of Georgia. It embraced Macon, Columbus, and Augusta and was responsible to the Army of Tennessee. On the twenty-eighth Cobb received orders to serve as its commander. He now had two commands, but few troops. (Yet, despite this lack of manpower, he opposed recruiting slaves. He would write the secretary of war in January 1865 that "if slaves will make good soldiers our whole theory of slavery is wrong.")

From Macon, Cobb and Davis went to Augusta where on October 2 they conferred with Beauregard, newly appointed commander of the Military District of the West. Cobb returned to Macon hoping to contribute his troops to a general confrontation with the enemy. This hope was destroyed on November 15, when Gen. William Tecumseh Sherman left Atlanta in flames and began his slash-and-burn March to the Sea. Although one of Cobb's plantations became a victim of Sherman's raiders, Cobb believed that they were less devastating than the reverses suffered by the Army of Tennessee. Early in January he confessed to Davis that his despair over Sherman's outrages paled beside his unease over southwestern Georgia, where his family had gone to escape the raiders. He believed that this food basket of the Confederacy was sitting on a potential slave insurrection that could easily be ignited by the inflammable Sumter Prison at Andersonville.

With over twelve thousand "splendidly equipped" troops under Maj. Gen. James H. Wilson rampaging eastward across Alabama, southwestern Georgia suddenly acquired importance. Cobb was ordered to turn Wilson back. He had half as many men, poorly equipped. Before undertaking his final military assignment, he made a fruitless appeal to Davis for more troops.

On April 11 the sinking Confederacy's birthplace caught a glimpse of its first leader, whose devotion and faith were vanishing. In conference with the governor of Alabama it was decided that Cobb would not try to defend Montgomery; rather, he would make a stand at Columbus. Six days later Columbus fell. Cobb escaped with six hundred men under cover of darkness. Upon reaching Macon he was handed a dispatch from Beauregard dated April 20 announcing an armistice. Two days later Cobb surrendered to Wilson, was arrested, and while on the way to prison was parolled by President Andrew Johnson.

After the war Cobb practiced law in Macon, was pardoned on July 4, 1868, and on October 9 dropped dead in the lobby of New York's Fifth Avenue Hotel. He was buried in Athens.

BIBLIOGRAPHY

Coulter, E. Merton. *The Confederate States of America, 1861–1865.* A History of the South, vol. 7. Baton Rouge, La., 1950.

Foote, Shelby. *The Civil War: A Narrative.* 3 vols. New York, 1958–1974.

Franklin, John Hope. *The Emancipation Proclamation.* Garden City, N.Y., 1963.

McFeely, William S. *Frederick Douglass.* New York, 1991.

McPherson, James M. *Ordeal by Fire: The Civil War and Reconstruction.* New York, 1982.

Montgomery, Horace. *Howell Cobb's Confederate Career.* Tuscaloosa, Ala., 1959.

Simpson, John Eddins. *Howell Cobb: The Politics of Ambition.* Chicago, 1973.

Thomas, Emory M. *The Confederate Nation, 1861–1865.* New York, 1979.

HORACE MONTGOMERY

COBB, THOMAS R. R.

COBB, THOMAS R. R. (1823–1862), constitutional authority, secessionist, congressman from Georgia, and brigadier general. Thomas Reade Rootes Cobb was born in Jefferson County, Georgia, on April 10, 1823, reportedly weighing an incredible twenty-one and a half pounds. He was named for his mother's father, Thomas Reade Rootes of Fredericksburg, Virginia, at whose home, Federal Hill, his parents had been married.

The brilliant Georgian finished atop his graduating class at Franklin College (later the University of Georgia) and passed the state bar while only eighteen years of age. His prodigious intellect and an immense capacity for hard work yielded legal and literary accomplishments of significance during his twenties and then placed him at the forefront of Georgia secessionists. Cobb published *The Supreme Court Manual* (Athens, 1849) when he was twenty-six. Two years later his *Digest of the Statute Laws of the State of Georgia* (Athens, 1851) won for him an enviable reputation because of its importance, thoroughness, and skillful presentation.

As controversy over slavery intensified, Cobb undertook a scholarly study of legal and historical precedents on the subject. The resulting book remains an important exposition of Southern arguments, including justification of the status quo on the basis of biblical tenets. *An Inquiry into the Law of Negro Slavery in the United States of America to which is Prefixed an Historical Sketch of Slavery* (Philadelphia, 1858) offered elaborate scientific, sociological, economic, and philosophical grounds as support for the South's peculiar institution. Predictably, *An Inquiry* attracted wide support in the South and generated bitter invective in the North. Cobb himself owned twenty-three slaves in 1860.

In addition to his legal and scholarly endeavors, Cobb expended considerable energy on education and religious activities. His steady involvement in Georgia politics grew to overwhelm all other considerations as the secession crisis intensified. After Abraham Lincoln's election Cobb delivered a fiery address to the state legislature that, in the words of Alexander H. Stephens (whom Cobb loathed), "did more . . . in carrying the State out, than all the arguments and elo-

> ## Cobb campaigned feverishly, attending rallies, writing articles and letters, and orating across the state.

quence of all others combined." When the legislature called for a convention to consider secession, Cobb campaigned feverishly, attending rallies, writing articles and letters, and orating across the state. Cobb carried on his crusade with such ardor that he reminded his sister-in-law of "the Methodist Circuit Riders I used to know in my childhood—so thoroughly infused with the Spirit and the righteousness of the cause—that no physical discomfort dampens his zeal."

Cobb's efforts reached fruition when the convention, in which he sat after winning election by a tiny margin, adopted the ordinance of secession. Cobb served as chairman of the working committee to revise the state constitution and was one of ten Georgia delegates to the convention of seceding states that met on February 4, 1861, in Montgomery. That body, with Tom's elder brother Howell presiding, approved a provisional constitution and became the Provisional Congress of the Confederate States. The younger Cobb worked on various projects with his accustomed zeal, stalking out of meetings and engaging in bitter verbal jousts when events went against his precepts. Among the legislation he introduced were bills banning importation of slaves, protecting international copyrights, controlling Sunday mail carriage, and protecting Southern cotton. Cobb wore homespun clothes to the sessions in ostentatious token of his resistance to Northern imports. He thought many of his colleagues guilty of "selfishness, intrigue, low cunning and meanness," writing in April that the "atmosphere of this place is positively tainted with selfish ambitious schemes for personal aggrandizement." Almost every Confederate leader fell short in Cobb's eyes.

The proud and sensitive Georgian inevitably clashed with an equally prickly Jefferson Davis. The new president "is

chatty and tries to be agreeable," Cobb told his wife, but "is not great in any sense of the term." In February, while differing with Davis over some relatively unimportant legislation, Cobb wrote, "I shall strive hard to pass it over his head, it will do my soul good to *rebuke* him at the outset of his vetoing." He and Davis remained on uneasy terms for the rest of Cobb's life, with the result that Cobb's military service in the field was haunted by real or imagined episodes of negative influence from the executive mansion.

By the late spring of 1861 Cobb had determined to raise a unit for military service. His sole military experience to date had been unwarranted interference with the Confederacy's civil authorities on behalf of hometown troops. Cobb's temperance enthusiasm, religious ardor, and political quarrels had colored such military dealings as had come his way. He considered a Confederate setback early in the war to be "attributable entirely to a drunken, Godless general" willing to fight on a Sunday morning. The defeat might even be blamed on the president who, "obstinate as a mule," insisted on appointing such infidels. In the throes of enthusiasm for a local company headed for war, townspeople called on Cobb one Sunday for a patriotic speech, but he substituted "a lecture of five minutes length on Sabbath-breaking." In that stern spirit Tom Cobb undertook the task of raising a unit of civilians and turning them into soldiers, in an arena of which he knew precisely nothing.

Cobb fell upon the notion of organizing a legion—a military establishment that encompassed artillery, cavalry, and infantry in a single unit. The idea had popular appeal but no utility whatsoever in mid-nineteenth-century warfare. The novice soldier, however, had political power at his disposal adequate to smother the opposition of professional military men, and on August 28, 1861, Congressman Cobb became Colonel Cobb of Cobb's Georgia Legion. Companies of the legion had been reaching Richmond during the summer and going into a camp of instruction nearby.

The new colonel split his time between legislative duties in the Congress and attempts to put his troops into shape. Richard B. Garnett, a veteran soldier destined for Confederate prominence, contributed substantially to the latter effort from his post as second in command of the legion. The cavalry major, Pierce Manning Butler Young, was a brilliant military leader, but Cobb disliked his personality. In fact, the mercurial Cobb waxed wrathful against almost every one of his officers at one time or another. No doubt numbers of them suffered terribly under the circumstances. They had company in their misery in the form of Cobb's superiors in the War Department, whose efforts to integrate the colonel's misbegotten legion into the country's armed forces ran afoul of Congressman Cobb's political clout. His immediate superior for an extended period was his brother Howell, a spectacularly maladroit political general but, of course, an easy man for Tom to please.

Although most of the men in the ranks had less occasion to experience Cobb's mood swings, some of them thought poorly of him. Elijah H. Sutton of one of the Georgia regiments in Cobb's Brigade wrote that both Cobb brothers were failures in the eyes of their men. Howell was a "whipped cur" in battle and full of "incompetency." After Howell's resignation and Tom's death, a new brigadier "soon gained the love of the men, something the Cobbs failed to do." Sutton hinted that Tom Cobb bled to death at Fredericksburg when stretcher-bearers refused to brave a dangerous stretch of road to hurry their general to the rear. Another enlisted man later bluntly claimed that a Confederate comrade mistreated by the general inflicted the wound that killed him. Both stories were almost certainly inaccurate, but their very existence suggests some broad dissension among the soldiery.

Other observers, however, thought that Cobb met his military obligations well. Benjamin L. Mobley of the legion thought Cobb "the best Colonel in the Confederate States" because "he dont let his men stand garde when it is raining or when it is cold." Mobley also liked his colonel's fighting spirit when Cobb said in a speech excoriating Northerners "that he wanted to hate them so bad that he would feel just as well with a stold sheep on his back as [with a] piece of yankee goods." Henry D. McDaniel, a bright young man who later became governor of Georgia, wrote soon after Cobb's death, "I admired him more, perhaps, than any other son of my state."

Cobb's Legion, the happy and the grumbling alike, received orders on September 11, 1861, to move to Virginia's peninsula. There the men spent nearly eight months of only occasionally lively duty, much of the time under the command of the excitable Gen. John B. Magruder. Colonel Cobb quickly discovered to his dismay that the legion would not be—could not be—used en masse. The military verities that had made the legion concept obsolete dictated that Cobb's cavalry and artillery and infantry must serve where needed at various points of the compass. With a paranoia that oozed from many of his letters, Cobb insisted that such pragmatic use of the South's military resources constituted "malignant persecution" by "Davis and his minions." He threatened to resign unless his superiors ceased using his cavalry as they thought best. Cobb identified, perhaps unconsciously, the basic issue when he wrote that spreading out his troops "is most mortifying to my pride."

By the time Robert E. Lee assumed command of the army near Richmond, Cobb had been in the field for nine months, but had not yet seen any intense combat. Lee irritated Cobb as much as other professional officers had. The general was "haughty and boorish and supercilious in his bearing and is particularly so to me," Cobb wrote. In fact he loathed all West Point graduates as a group, since "self-sufficiency and self-aggrandizement are their great controlling characteristics." But by the fall of 1862, Lee's calm poise had accomplished the remarkable feat of muting Cobb's antipathy, even as the Georgian remained steadily hostile toward some of the army's command and intermittently unhappy with most of the rest.

Colonel Cobb saw limited action with his legion's cavalry during the Seven Days' Battles, and his units arrived too late to take part in the Second Battle of Manassas. The components of the legion met their baptism of fire in sustained battle action during the Maryland campaign, during which Howell Cobb failed badly at Crampton's Gap; but Tom Cobb missed this action, having gone home on leave. When he returned to the army that fall, Cobb worked energetically in political circles to effect the transfer of his legion to another theater in hopes that a change of environment might bring him the satisfaction that so persistently eluded him. Although he had sought promotion to general officer's rank for months, Cobb now loudly announced he would refuse to accept such a commission. Nevertheless, when the promotion came, on November 1, 1862, Cobb received it gladly and assumed command of the brigade that had belonged to his brother.

General Cobb's brigade held the most famous Confederate position on the battlefield at Fredericksburg, the Sunken Road and Stone Wall at the foot of Marye's Heights. In that stronghold Cobb moved among his men on December 13, 1862, as the initial Federal attacks built up on the broad killing plain stretching below the heights. A member of his brigade wrote four days later, "Our brave and beloved Genl Cobb . . . pulled off his hat & waving it over his head exclaimed 'Get ready Boys here they come' & they did come *sure.*" Cobb's Georgians readily repulsed the attacks against them all through the afternoon, but they did so without their general's leadership after the first phase of the action. A piece of Federal iron "just grazed . . . the right thigh" of the general "and struck the left where it lodged, breaking the bone & lacerating the femoral artery." The stricken general died just after 2:00 P.M. at a nearby field hospital. Ironically, he had taken his mortal wound within clear view of Federal Hill, his mother's family home at the edge of Fredericksburg, only a few hundred yards from the Sunken Road. According to a contemporary, Lee said on December 14 in an informal eulogy, "If we gain our independence we will need such a man as General Cobb was to give our country tone and character abroad."

BIBLIOGRAPHY

Cobb, Thomas R. R. "Extracts from Letters to His Wife, February 3, 1861–December 10, 1862." *Southern Historical Society Papers* 28 (1900): 280–301.

Cobb, Thomas R. R. *An Inquiry into the Law of Negro Slavery in the United States of America to which is prefixed an Historical Sketch of Slavery.* Philadelphia, 1858.

Cobb, Thomas R. R. Papers. University of Georgia, Athens; Duke University, Durham, N.C.; Georgia State Archives, Atlanta.

McCash, William B. *Thomas R. R. Cobb.* Macon, Ga., 1983.
Porter, Rufus K. "Sketch of General T. R. R. Cobb." *Land We Love* 3 (1867): 183–197.

ROBERT K. KRICK

COLD HARBOR, VIRGINIA

This crossroad tavern, some ten miles northeast of Richmond, was the site of a battle during the 1864 campaign waged by Federal forces under Lt. Gen. Ulysses S. Grant against Richmond and the Army of Northern Virginia commanded by Gen. Robert E. Lee.

After the Battles of the Wilderness and Spotsylvania and the maneuvering along the North Anna River in May 1864, Grant moved his Army of the Potomac southeast across the Pamunkey River to Cold Harbor. (In effect, Grant was moving along the circumference of a circle from north of Richmond to a point east of the city.) On May 31 Grant's cavalry drove back a small force of Confederates and seized the road junction at Cold Harbor.

On June 1 Lee made an effort to regain the road junction, but the attempt failed. Both sides continued to feed troops into the area and to entrench, so that soon there were two six-mile-long parallel lines of earthen fortifications running roughly from northwest to southeast.

The Federal line from right to left consisted of the Ninth Corps, the Fifth Corps, the Eighteenth Corps, the Sixth Corps, and the Second Corps. The Confederate line from left to right was made up of the Second Corps under Maj. Gen. Jubal Early, the First Corps under Lt. Gen. Richard Heron Anderson, and the Third Corps of Lt. Gen. A. P. Hill. The southeastern ends of both lines were very close to the Chickahominy River. The weather was hot and humid. Skirmishing flared along the lines on June 1 and 2, although there was no significant change in the armies' positions.

Grant had planned to make a general attack on Lee's position on the morning of the second. He postponed it, however, first until 5:00 P.M. that day and then until 4:30 A.M. on the third. Grant's main effort was to be made by the Second, Sixth, and Eighteenth Corps (the left and center of his line) against Hill and Anderson (the right and center of Lee's position). The other Northern corps were to demonstrate against the Confederates in their fronts to draw attention from the real points of attack.

The Federal commander seems to have believed that the heavy fighting of the previous month had demoralized and weakened Lee's men. If the Northerners could break through the Cold Harbor line, they could destroy Lee's army, capture Richmond, and for all practical purposes end the war.

The Union soldiers knew better. Unlike Grant who had spent the war's first three years in the West, they had fought the Army of Northern Virginia for three years and Lee for two. Tradition has it that many Federal soldiers, realizing the strength of the Southern fortifications, wrote their names on slips of paper and pinned them to their uniforms so that their bodies could be identified after the battle.

The engagement itself was a short, fairly simple affair. Each of Grant's three attacking corps moved against the Confederate works in its front. The terrain and the opposing lines were such that the attacking Union columns diverged as they advanced. Each assaulting force was therefore exposed to fire from the defenders in its front as well as to that from Southerners on its flanks.

Bravery and numbers could not overcome such handicaps. The Northerners overran a few advanced Confederate outposts, but Lee's main line was far too strong to be carried. Several Federals got to within fifty yards of the main Southern works; a few to within thirty. Col. James P. McMahan carried the flag of the 164th New York regiment to the top of the Confederates' main fortification before he was shot down. Within fifteen minutes the battle, for all practical purposes, was over, and the Federal generals soon canceled plans for follow-up attacks.

Grant's army had numbered about 108,000 men in early June; Lee's about 59,000. The Federal attack at Cold Harbor cost Grant about 7,000 men. Lee lost perhaps 1,500. Grant's much heavier losses were made worse by his stubbornness. After the battle he refused to ask for a truce to bury his dead and retrieve his wounded because to do so would be to admit defeat. Not until June 7 did Grant request permission to send out parties to aid any surviving wounded soldiers and to bury those who had been killed or died from their wounds.

Soon after Cold Harbor, Grant decided on his next move. He would make no more direct attacks on the Army of Northern Virginia. He would break away from Lee's front, cross the James River, and strike for Petersburg, some twenty-three miles south of Richmond. Early on June 13 Lee's scouts brought him word that Grant's army had disappeared.

BIBLIOGRAPHY

Dowdey, Clifford. *Lee's Last Campaign: The Story of Lee and His Men Against Grant, 1864.* Boston, 1960.
Humphreys, A. A. *The Virginia Campaign of 1864 and 1865.* New York, 1883.
Trudeau, Noah André. *Bloody Roads South: The Wilderness to Cold Harbor, May–June 1864.* Boston, 1989.
Wheeler, Richard. *On Fields of Fury: From the Wilderness to the Crater: An Eyewitness History.* New York, 1991.

RICHARD M. MCMURRY

COLUMBIA, SOUTH CAROLINA

The capital of South Carolina, Columbia is located in the geographical center of the state on a bluff overlooking the Congaree River. It played a significant role in the Confederacy from the meeting of the South Carolina secession convention on December 17, 1860, to the burning of the town during the occupation by William Tecumseh Sherman's army on February 17 and 18, 1865. Established as the state capital in 1786, Columbia had grown by 1860 to a population of 8,052. More than 3,500 of the residents were African Americans, only 250 of whom were free. The visual center of the town was the new State House, whose cornerstone had been laid in 1851 but which was still under construction. South Carolina College, founded in 1801, was located south of the State House, and the business district was clustered closely around Richardson (later Main) Street to the north. Businesses were interspersed with private dwellings. There was a market–town hall, four hotels, ten churches, and fourteen schools. Columbia was a large cotton marketing center, with warehouses and brokers located in Cotton Town on Upper Boundary (later Elmwood) Street on the town's northern border.

> **Intense excitement gripped Columbia when the state legislature met on November 5, 1860. . . .**

Intense excitement gripped Columbia when the state legislature met on November 5, 1860, and chose presidential electors, calling on the twelfth for a state convention to assemble on December 17. The streets filled with crowds as prominent leaders spoke from hotel balconies. At the annual meeting of the state agriculture society, the president denounced the Republican party as "vulgar, coarse, and insolent." It was, he said, "restricted by no Constitution, and only impelled by hatred to the slaveholder and his slave." South Carolina College professor Joseph LeConte said that secession was in the air "like a spiritual contagion."

The state convention met in the Baptist church and declared the state's intention to secede, but it adjourned to Charleston when local cases of smallpox were reported. When news of secession reached Columbia from Charleston, it was greeted with bonfires, cannons, bell-ringing, and parades. P. F. Frazee, an abolitionist carriage maker, was whipped, tarred and feathered, and exiled to the North because of his views.

Local militia companies volunteered for Confederate service, and a training camp was established first at the fair-grounds and later at Lightwood Knot Springs. A prisoner of war camp for Union officers, called Camp Sorghum by inmates because of the poor rations, was located on the west bank of the Congaree River. State offices for Confederate bureaus in Columbia included the Conscription, Medical, Commissary, Quartermaster, and Paymaster departments.

In 1862 Confederate printing operations were moved to Columbia from Richmond. "Government girls" were employed to print currency and bonds. A military hospital opened at the fairgrounds, and in 1862 it moved to the South Carolina College campus. Professor Joseph LeConte supervised the largest Confederate medical manufacturing facility at the fairgrounds, and a niter works for the making of gunpowder opened at the state hospital.

Local businesses also aided the war effort. The Saluda Factory on the west bank of the Congaree produced woolen cloth, and others made socks, buttons, shoes, uniforms, and hats for the army. On the Columbia Canal a mill produced gunpowder, and local foundries manufactured bayonets, swords, and cannonballs.

Persons engaged in these activities and refugees from the low country swelled the population to some 25,000 by 1865. Many people could not afford food at inflated prices, and a Corn Association was formed in April 1863 to distribute food. By September, 2,000 people were receiving relief. In 1864 the Board of Relief listed 1,100 names. Citizens used locally made soap, sea salt, and sorghum in place of manufactured products. No coffee was available, so they brewed beverages from parched sweet potatoes, okra seed, peanuts, and other substitutes.

As prices increased, there was public criticism of speculators and "extortioners." Increased supplies of paper money further depreciated its value. The cost of cloth produced by a local factory was attacked so fiercely that the owners sold out at half price. Flannel cloth soon cost forty dollars a yard. By January 1865, local merchants refused to accept Confederate currency for provisions.

The women of Columbia opened a soldiers' rest home in the Charlotte Railroad depot in late 1861. After it was moved to the South Carolina Railroad depot, it was enlarged and renamed the Wayside Hospital. Some 75,000 wounded soldiers are said to have been given aid. In 1862 the Ladies' Hospital opened near the Charlotte depot.

To raise funds for relief and hospital work the women of the town held concerts, dances, fairs, and suppers. The most elaborate event was the Great Bazaar held in the State House in January 1865. Booths represented every Southern state, and almost all items produced in the Confederacy were on sale. The remarkable amount of $350,000 was raised.

As the war continued, Columbia was used as a place of safe storage by low-country residents for silver plate, bank funds, and valuable possessions. The bells of St. Michael's Church in Charleston were sent to Columbia, as was the library of the College of Charleston. But by 1865 town law enforcement was breaking down. The gaslights went unlighted, and burglary was common.

In January 1865 General Sherman left Savannah and marched into South Carolina. At the request of the citizens of Columbia, Gen. Robert E. Lee ordered 2,000 cavalry under the command of Wade Hampton to defend Hampton's home. On February 16 Sherman's army arrived before Columbia and from a hill west of the Congaree River began to shell the South Carolina Railroad depot, troop concentrations, and other strategic points.

Sherman issued Special Field Order Number 26, instructing Gen. O. O. Howard to cross the river, occupy the town, and destroy public buildings, transportation, and manufacturing. They were to spare libraries, asylums, and private homes, however. Meanwhile, Confederate officials began an evacuation of the town. Sizable amounts of Confederate and

> ## Another lasting dispute was who was to blame for the destruction.

state property were lost. Hampton ordered the cotton warehouses emptied and the cotton burned outside of town. For lack of transport facilities, the cotton was rolled into the streets. Before he left Columbia, however, Hampton canceled the order to burn the cotton.

During the night of February 16-17, Confederate troops withdrew, and stragglers and town residents plundered the warehouses and depots. Cotton was ignited and powder exploded at the South Carolina Railroad depot. The Charlotte depot was set on fire by the departing troops. On the morning of February 17, Mayor Thomas J. Goodwyn surrendered Columbia to the advancing Union army. As the troops entered the town, local citizens plied them with the ample stores of wine and whiskey.

After nightfall on February 17 more fires broke out. Local fire companies were overwhelmed, and Union troops were ordered to extinguish the fires. A powerful wind came out of the northwest, fanning the flames. Accounts tell of sparks filling the air and blazing shingles blowing from one building to another. Roving bands of civilians and soldiers—both black and white—destroyed property, threatened citizens, and spread fires. Finally, between 1:00 and 2:00 in the morning troops were called in to restore order. The wind subsided about 3:00, and by 5:00 the streets were clear. Two soldiers had been killed, thirty persons wounded, and 370 arrested. Among them were officers, soldiers, and civilians.

On the morning of February 18 General Howard began locating shelters for the homeless. He established tight security in the city and turned over all food and supplies not need-

ed by the army for distribution to citizens. He gave rifles and ammunition to the mayor to use for protection once the army left. Meanwhile Sherman ordered the destruction of railroads, bridges, and war matériel stored in the area. On February 20 the Union army marched northward out of Columbia.

For three months seven thousand to eight thousand persons were issued daily rations. Towns as far away as Augusta and Charlotte sent supplies by wagon. After the surrender of the Confederate armies in the East in April, local and state government passed into the hands of the military. On May 25 troops of the Twenty-fifth Ohio Regiment arrived in Columbia, and the era of Reconstruction began.

Two major questions remained about the burning of Columbia—the extent of the fire and who was responsible. A few days after the fire Southern author William Gilmore Simms made a survey of Columbia and listed 1,386 buildings destroyed. A recent study by historian Marion B. Lucas, however, indicates the loss of 458 structures, including 193 public buildings. The major destruction was limited to the central business district—about one-third of the city.

Another lasting dispute was who was to blame for the destruction. Ten days after the fire Wade Hampton accused Sherman: "You laid the whole city in ashes, leaving in its ruins thousands of old men and helpless women and children." In his official report Sherman claimed to have saved what remained of the city and blamed Hampton for "filling it with lint, cotton, and tinder." In a series of newspaper articles in March and April 1865, Simms concluded that Sherman was responsible, and a local committee of citizens laid the blame on the Union soldiers. In 1873 the Mixed Commission on British and American Claims concluded that blame "was not to be ascribed to either the intention or default of either the Federal or confederate officers." A collection of data made by Senator Coleman L. Blease in 1929 and 1930 contained no new evidence. Marion Lucas concluded in his 1976 study that "the fire was an accident of war." Confederate confusion over whether the cotton was to be burned was reckless. Citizens giving whiskey to Union soldiers was inexcusable. Failure of Union officers to end the rioting in the city was careless. Only when the wind subsided was the fire controlled.

BIBLIOGRAPHY

Cauthen, Charles E. "Confederacy and Reconstruction." In *Columbia, Capital City of South Carolina, 1786–1936*. Edited by Helen K. Hennig. Columbia, S.C., 1936.

Edgar, Walter B., and Deborah K. Woolley. *Columbia, Portrait of a City*. Norfolk, Va., 1986.

Lucas, Marion B. *Sherman and the Burning of Columbia*. College Station, Tex., 1976.

A. V. HUFF, JR.

COMMERCE RAIDERS

Raiders were naval warships that preyed upon the merchant ships of enemy nations. Commerce raiding, or *guerre de course*, was a strategy employed by weaker naval powers against nations with a large merchant marine. Raiders drove up insurance rates on the enemy's merchant shipping and caused many ships to flee to the protection of other countries' flags. They could be a powerful tool in economic warfare. Successful commerce raiders often forced the enemy to pursue them rather than participate in military actions against home shores. They generally sought to avoid contact with enemy warships because of their light armament.

The Confederacy employed both public (naval) and private (privateer) forms of commerce raiding. Commissioned naval vessels were sent to distant sea lanes to hunt, capture, or destroy traders. Privately owned, government-licensed warships, called privateers, generally sought to capture merchant vessels for profit in waters closer to home. Privateers had nearly become obsolete with the advent of steam propulsion. The Treaty of Paris of 1856 outlawed privateering and regulated government commerce raiding. The United States and Spain, alone among the major maritime nations, refused to sign. Thus neither the United States nor the Confederate States had renounced privateering when the Civil War began.

One of President Jefferson Davis's first actions in office was his April 17, 1861, call for privateers to be licensed. Letters of marque, the government commission papers of privateers, were issued quickly; within two months over a dozen prizes had been brought into Southern ports. Privateering vessels required speed, minimal armament, and a relatively small crew. Most were small, fast schooners and brigs,

> **Privateering vessels required speed, minimal armament, and a relatively small crew.**

although some were steamships. Most privateers operated in the waters around weakly blockaded ports, dashing beyond the safety of friendly coastal defenses to snatch a prize sailing near shore. A few privateers made cruises off the New England coast and in the Caribbean. Several ships were quite successful, but economic considerations led to the demise of privateering. By mid-1863 larger numbers of blockaders patrolling the coast decreased the chance to earn a profit in privateering while the potential profit from blockade running increased.

The naval vessels best suited for commerce raiding could make long cruises, had speed sufficient to run from more powerful ships, and an armament to match any adversary that could catch them. Generally, these vessels had full sailing rigs to minimize coal consumption, and steam engines driving a propeller to add speed for chasing and running. Government cruisers generally operated in areas far removed from Southern shores; indeed only five of the twelve most successful commerce raiders were ever in a Confederate port.

Commerce raiders, both naval and private, caused many problems for neutral nations. Foreign governments trod a narrow path to avoid favoring one side or the other in the struggle. Early in the war, as a result of President Abraham Lincoln's proclamation of blockade, Great Britain and France recognized the Confederacy as a belligerent. The recognition of belligerency allowed the infant nation to purchase stores and weapons. Both Great Britain and France, however, forbade the belligerents to recruit or fit out expeditions in their territory. Thus, vessels and their armament could be purchased in Europe, but ordnance could not be fitted, nor the crew engaged, at the time of sailing. This prevented several Confederate raiders from sailing after being purchased in Great Britain and France. Warships of both the Confederacy and the Union were allowed to replenish coal occasionally in neutral ports but could not recruit or engage the enemy while in neutral waters. Violations of the duties of neutrals and of their sovereignty caused a number of diplomatic incidents and led, after the war, to the international arbitration of the *Alabama* Claims.

Neutrality restrictions also prevented Confederate privateers and government warships from bringing prizes into foreign waters. This prohibition led to the slow death of privateering for economic reasons: prizes had to be brought into port and sold for profit. It also led to the destruction, rather than the appropriation, of prizes taken by government cruisers. After seven prizes captured by the raider *Sumter* were allowed to go free from Cienfuegos, Cuba, in 1861, Confederate cruisers destroyed prizes rather than attempting to send them to the South by way of neutral ports.

The first Confederate government commerce raider to prey on Northern shipping was the small steam-auxiliary *Sumter*, which sailed on June 30, 1861. The steamer was converted in New Orleans from a passenger-cargo vessel into an ocean cruiser. Under its talented captain, Raphael Semmes, *Sumter* captured eighteen Union vessels in a seven-month cruise through the Gulf of Mexico and the North Atlantic. Suffering from worn-out engines and boilers, *Sumter* was laid up and later sold at Gibraltar.

The next Confederate raider to sail was the former passenger steamer *Nashville*. It was seized at Charleston, armed with two small 12-pounder cannons, and commissioned CSS *Nashville*. Under Lt. Robert Pegram it made a voyage in 1861 from Charleston to Southampton, England. *Nashville* destroyed the U.S. clipper ship *Harvey Birch* in the

English Channel on the outward voyage; on the return trip it burned another Union vessel. The Confederate navy sold it as unsuitable for its use, and the next owner converted *Nashville* into a blockade runner.

Several exceptional groups of Confederate commerce raiders used whaleboats and small schooners to hunt prizes. Acting as maritime guerrillas, these men employed impudence, stealth, local knowledge, and careful planning to strike at unarmed Union merchant vessels, and occasionally warships, in waters throughout the Confederacy. Three maritime guerrillas were particularly successful: John Taylor Wood, John Y. Beall, and John Clibbon Braine.

Commander John Taylor Wood, CSN, captured seven Union vessels between October 1862 and February 1864. He conducted raids in whaleboats that had been carried to various river landings atop wagons. Wood became President Davis's naval aide and eventually commanded *Tallahassee*, a more capable vessel. At the war's end, Wood and several other prominent Confederates escaped to Cuba through Florida waters in a stolen small boat.

Master John Y. Beall, CSN, of Matthews County, Virginia, became the "Mosby of the Chesapeake," capturing small Union vessels on the bay. Beall and a party of watermen destroyed four Federal schooners on September 19, 1863. Beall was captured and imprisoned in November 1863, but was paroled in March 1864. He then organized a breakout attempt from Point Lookout Prison, Virginia, that failed. Leading another raiding party, he seized the steamers *Philo Parsons* and *Island Queen* on September 19, 1864. On December 16 of that year, while trying to free seven Confederate prisoners being moved to Fort LaFayette in New York, Beall was captured by Union forces. They hanged him as a spy at Governor's Island, New York Harbor, on February 24, 1865, although he was a warrant officer operating under orders.

Another Confederate commerce raider, John Clibbon Braine, sailed with clandestine parties of Confederates on board passenger steamers. Braine and his companions captured the steamer *Chesapeake* in December 1863, the steamer *Roanoke* in September 1864, and the schooners *St. Mary's* and *Spafford* in March 1865.

The largest Confederate commerce raiding program was based on the work of James Dunwoody Bulloch and other naval officers in Europe. They ordered vessels built for government service in foreign shipyards and arranged delivery of the armament and crew at some remote point. The first of Bulloch's ships completed was the cruiser *Florida*. Built on the plans of a British Royal Navy cruiser at Birkenhead, England, it sailed on March 22, 1862. *Florida* met the steamer *Bahama* in the Bahama Islands and received guns and crew. The raider was partially armed and commissioned August 10, 1862, but the men discovered that crucial parts of its guns had been left behind. *Florida* had to run the blockade

in and out of Mobile, Alabama, for additional crewmen and ordnance parts. Operating under three captains, *Florida* captured thirty-seven Union merchant vessels. The Confederates converted one of its prizes, the bark *Clarence,* into a lightly armed cruiser. *Clarence* and a succession of armed prizes, the barks *Tacony* and *Archer,* captured twenty-three further vessels. *Florida* was captured and towed from the harbor of Bahia, Brazil, by USS *Wachusetts* in violation of Brazilian neutrality. The United States promised to return *Florida* to Brazil, but the ship "accidentally sank" before the promise could be kept.

The most successful Confederate raider was CSS *Alabama.* It sailed on July 29, 1862, from Liverpool and met two ships carrying its officers, crew, and armament at Terceira in the Azores. On August 24, Raphael Semmes commissioned the ship CSS *Alabama.* It cruised the North Atlantic and sailed into the Gulf of Mexico where it sank the blockader USS *Hatteras* off Galveston, Texas. *Alabama* captured sixty-nine vessels, sinking fifty-eight of them. In the South Atlantic, Semmes commissioned the captured bark *Conrad* as the subsidiary cruiser CSS *Tuscaloosa.* It in turn captured two vessels. After a cruise through the Indian and Atlantic oceans, *Alabama* met and was sunk by the Union cruiser USS *Kearsarge* in battle off the coast of Cherbourg, France, in the English Channel.

Another purchasing agent, Capt. Matthew Fontaine Maury, CSN, bought the new iron, sail-auxiliary screw steamship *Japan* at Dumbarton, Scotland, for conversion into a cruiser. The ship left Scotland on April 1, 1863, and met the steamer *Alar* off Ushant, France, to receive arms and supplies. Its commander, William L. Maury, commissioned the vessel CSS *Georgia* on April 9, 1863. Maury burned five of the nine ships that he captured during a seven-month cruise in the Atlantic. When the iron hull proved unsuitable for a cruiser, *Georgia* was decommissioned at Liverpool and sold.

Another of Matthew Maury's purchases was not as successful. On November 24, 1863, the former Royal Navy cruiser *Victor* left Sheerness, England, under suspicion of violating British neutrality laws. Outside of British territorial waters it was commissioned CSS *Rappahannock.* The ship was to meet *Georgia* off the French coast to receive armament, but severe machinery problems forced it to put in at Calais, France, for repairs. The ship was found unsuitable for service as a cruiser and sat out the remainder of the war as a station ship at Calais.

American protests to the British government following the successes of *Florida, Alabama,* and *Georgia* led to the seizure of several vessels on suspicion of their violating British neutrality. The first was a small cruiser, *Alexandra,* being built as a gift for the Confederate government. A second, more substantial cruiser, similar to *Alabama,* was seized in Glasgow for similar reasons. This steam-auxiliary sailing ship, named *Canton* or *Pampero,* might have been a formidable commerce raider had it been commissioned.

When highly suitable vessels could not be found for commerce raiding, the Confederacy pressed other ships into service. In the summer and fall of 1864, two blockade runners were converted into commerce raiders while in Confederate ports. The runner *Atalanta* became the raider CSS *Tallahassee* and later CSS *Olustee;* the runner *Edith* became CSS *Chickamauga.* Navy Secretary Stephen R. Mallory chose John Taylor Wood, who had done well in guerrilla raids on Chesapeake Bay, as *Tallahassee*'s first commander. *Tallahassee-Olustee* captured and destroyed thirty-five vessels during two cruises. *Chickamauga* sank four during a single short cruise.

The last Confederate commerce raider to operate was the full-rigged clipper steam-auxiliary ship *Shenandoah.* Formerly the merchant vessel *Sea King, Shenandoah* cruised against the New England whaling fleets in the Pacific and Arctic. It captured thirty-seven vessels and burned thirty-two. Its commander, James Waddell, did not learn that the war had ended until August 2, 1865. *Shenandoah* sailed for the United Kingdom, arriving November 6, 1865, the last Confederate military unit to fly the national ensign.

A number of vessels intended for commerce raiding were nearing completion when the war ended. Four enlarged and improved *Alabama*-type corvettes built in France and six fast twin-screw steamers built in Great Britain were never delivered to the Confederacy. The French government prevented the corvettes from sailing, and the Confederacy sold the ships to raise money for other projects. The six guerrilla raiders built on the *Tallahassee* model were fast twin-screw steamers with a small sailing rig. They were designed to pay for themselves first by running the blockade and then by making dashes against coastal commerce, fishing fleets, and Northern seacoast cities. These ten ships were ultimately dispersed to the Prussian, Brazilian, and Peruvian navies.

Following the end of the war, the United States brought suit against Great Britain, holding that that country was liable for not exercising "due diligence" to prevent the depredations of the commerce raiders purchased there. An international tribunal of arbitration was established in Geneva, Switzerland, to decide the case. Great Britain, found liable for the acts of *Florida, Alabama, Shenandoah,* and their tenders, settled the case in 1873 by paying the United States $15.5 million in gold.

Confederate raiding of Northern merchant fleets was among the most successful programs of the government. The commerce raiders did great damage to the Northern economy. Over three hundred vessels were destroyed and many hundreds more were sold to foreigners to prevent financial ruin if captured by a raider. It took the U.S. merchant fleet over forty years to recover from the depredations of the Confederate commerce raiders.

[*See also* Alabama Claims; Anglo-Confederate Purchasing; Enchantress Affair; *and entries on the ships* Alabama, Florida, Georgia, *and* Shenandoah.]

BIBLIOGRAPHY

Bulloch, James D. *The Secret Service of the Confederate States in Europe; or, How the Confederate Cruisers Were Equipped.* 2 Vols. New York, 1884. Reprint, New York, 1959.

Dalzell, George W. *The Flight from the Flag: The Continuing Effect of the Civil War upon the American Carrying Trade.* Chapel Hill, N.C., 1940.

Forrest, Douglas French. *Odyssey in Gray: A Diary of Confederate Service, 1863–1865.* Edited by William N. Still. Richmond, Va., 1979.

Lester, Richard I. *Confederate Finance and Purchasing in Great Britain.* Charlottesville, Va., 1975.

Merli, Frank J. *Great Britain and the Confederate Navy, 1861–1865.* Bloomington, Ind., 1970.

Robinson, William Morrison, Jr. *The Confederate Privateers.* New Haven, 1928.

Semmes, Raphael. *Memoirs of Service Afloat during the War between the States.* Baltimore, 1869. Reprint, Secaucus, N.J., 1987.

KEVIN J. FOSTER

COMMISSARY BUREAU

On February 26, 1861, President Jefferson Davis signed a bill creating the Commissary Bureau (or Subsistence Department) whose function was to provide rations for the Confederate States army. The bureau was headed first by Col. Lucius B. Northrop of South Carolina (March 27, 1861–February 16, 1865) and then by Brig. Gen. Isaac M. St. John of Georgia (February 16, 1865, to the end of the war).

> Custom dictated that each commander of a division, brigade, or regiment assign quartermaster duties to one of his officers.

The bureau was originally designed to operate with one colonel who was to serve as commissary general, four captains called commissaries, and as many lieutenants (subalterns) of the line, called assistant commissaries, as were necessary to accomplish the bureau's mission. On March 14 and May 16, 1861, acts of Congress slightly altered the rank structure and added two more officers. Civilians were hired as clerks, and by 1863 the bureau employed thirty-six in Richmond.

Following the precedent established in the prewar U.S. Army, the commissary general was supposed to run a simple senior office with a minimum of personnel. His subordinates in the office would handle functional areas, such as the procurement of bacon or beans, and ensure that the right number of rations reached the right group of soldiers. Each of the major armies had a staff officer assigned as commissary. This relieved the commanding general of the onerous details of ordering the correct amount of bread or beans for subordinate units and ensuring that food got to where it was supposed to go. Often the officer was an experienced commissary with direct ties to the bureau and strong loyalty to the commissary general. This practice occasionally led to divided allegiance between the unit commander and the commissary general.

Custom dictated that each commander of a division, brigade, or regiment assign quartermaster duties to one of his officers. These men were usually not professional commissaries or experienced in supply matters. They rarely wanted this unglamorous job and often treated it as a curse or a sign of the commander's displeasure. Thus, commissary problems, because of divided loyalties and lack of attention by commanders, multiplied. These problems proved to be a major impediment to the combat efficiency of the Confederate army from its inception and were accentuated as the size of the army grew.

The problem of feeding the Confederate armies was exacerbated by Davis's choice of Lucius B. Northrop as the commissary general. Northrop, a West Point graduate in the class of 1833, had been dropped from army rolls in 1848 because of a string of sick furloughs. Davis, then U.S. secretary of war, had reinstated him eight months later, but Northrop's ill health kept him in South Carolina where he became a doctor. Northrop resigned his U.S. Army commission January 8, 1861, and on March 13, Davis offered him a captain's billet in the Commissary Bureau. Apparently because he was unable to find anyone else who would take the job as commissary general, Davis named Northrop to the post. Thus, the Confederacy had to make do with an inexperienced individual of dubious health in a vital position.

Northrop rapidly had subsistence matters in a shambles. Legislation passed on March 6, 1861, had provided that enlisted men, both regular and provisional, were to receive one ration a day. That ration, like so much else in the Confederacy, was based on prewar U.S. Army standards: ¾ pound of pork or bacon or 1¼ pounds of fresh or salt beef, and 18 ounces of bread or flour, or 12 ounces of hard bread, or 1¼ pounds of corn meal. In addition, units were to receive ample supplies of peas, beans, or rice; coffee; sugar; vinegar; tallow; soap; and salt. But in the agriculturally rich Confederacy, Northrop and his department failed miserably to provide even this simple staple diet to the South's common soldiers.

Not content with the process of procuring foodstuffs and distributing them to the army, Northrop soon attempted to control all food production in the Confederacy, and his bureaucratic nature added to the distribution problems. He maintained that the bureau could mass-purchase vital raw materials where they were cheapest, transport them to be processed, and then stockpile or distribute the product to the hungry armies. But he soon ran afoul of currency shortages, wartime inflation, transportation difficulties, and spoilage of perishables.

The plight of the Confederate army at Manassas, Virginia, in the spring and summer of 1862 illustrates the damage that Northrop did and foreshadowed the failure of the bureau throughout the war. As soon as the army started gathering at Manassas, Northrop ordered commissaries not to purchase local wheat because it cost more than wheat in south-central Virginia. Wheat would be shipped by railroad to Richmond to be milled into flour and subsequently shipped to the army farther north. Each stage added to the flour's cost and tied up limited rail assets. Thus officers at Manassas watched flour, raised and milled locally, being loaded onto trains going to Richmond, while government flour was being off-loaded from the same train. Northrop's policy of mass purchase was good in theory, but when applied it overburdened the limited Confederate railroad system. It also often left, as in the case of Manassas, vital assets of the Confederacy within easy reach of the enemy.

In addition to Northrop's inexperience and unrealistic economic ideas, other factors combined to ensure the Commissary Bureau's failure. Spiraling inflation caused prices for goods to escalate rapidly out of the purchase range of the commissaries. They were forced to resort to impressment to provide foodstuffs to satisfy the ever-increasing appetite of the army. Impressment, an emergency power granted under the Constitution, allowed government agents to commandeer private property as long as the owner was justly compensated. But the issue of just compensation was regulated by the commissary general and did not reflect local market prices. Commissaries often impressed goods at prices far below their true market value.

Impressment combined with the South's degrading transportation system, both rail and horse, detrimentally effected those Southerners living nearest the railroads. Unable to transport goods great distances, commissaries overburdened areas that were convenient to lines of communication. Thus, a farm owner near a railroad could be "impressed to death" by having his crops and horses taken while his peers in hard-to-reach rural areas would be unaffected. This practice led to numerous complaints and charges of corruption by the Confederate Congress.

As early as March 1862, commissaries in Tennessee were under investigation, and after the summer of 1862, the bureau was the target of a continual string of congressional investigations and special committees. In its attempt to control the bureau, Congress on December 31, 1864, debated an Act to Protect the Confederate States against Frauds. Senator George N. Lester of Georgia voiced the feelings of most of the Confederacy. He gave his support to the act and stated:

> From one end to the other of the Confederacy loud voices of complaint come up [that] . . . the quartermasters and commissaries . . . are growing vastly rich by fraud, corruption, mismanagement, and illegitimate use of public property and money entrusted to their custody and disbursement.

By 1865 charges of corruption were so strong that Congress attempted to legislate the Commissary Bureau almost out of existence and send the majority of the over two thousand civilians and soldiers controlled by the department to duty with the army. President Davis vetoed the bill because it would have been detrimental to the army.

Complaints by Robert E. Lee and other Confederate commanders led to the far more competent Brig. Gen. Isaac M. St. John replacing Northrop on February 16, 1865. St. John was a Yale graduate and had been an engineer and in the railroad business before the war. His skillful handling of the Niter and Mining Bureau led to his position as commissary general. But even St. John's skill could not overcome the problems created by Northrop and inflation, limited assets, and degraded railroads in the short life left to the Confederacy.

Civil War scholar James I. Robertson, Jr., has said that the Army of Northern Virginia did not lose any battles because of a lack of ammunition. The same cannot be said for a lack of rations. The Confederate soldier faced two enemies, the Federals and hunger. In the end both of these enemies won.

[*See also* Impressment.]

BIBLIOGRAPHY

Coulter, Merton E. *The Confederate States of America, 1861–1865.* A History of the South, vol. 7. Baton Rouge, La., 1950.

Davis, Jefferson. *Jefferson Davis, Constitutionalist: His Letters, Papers and Speeches.* Jackson, Miss., 1923.

Eaton, Clement. *A History of the Southern Confederacy.* New York, 1954.

Goff, Richard D. *Confederate Supply.* Durham, N.C., 1969.

U.S. War Department. *War of the Rebellion: A Compilation of the Official Records of the Union and Confederate Armies.* Washington, 1880–1901. Ser. 4, vol. 1, pp. 869–879.

Vandiver, Frank E. *Rebel Brass: The Confederate Command System.* Baton Rouge, La., 1956.

Weinert, Richard P. *The Confederate Regular Army.* Shippensburg, Pa., 1991.

P. NEAL MEIER

COMMUNITY LIFE

The degree to which community life in the South was altered during the years of the Confederacy is one of the central topics of Southern history. A primary difficulty is defining exactly what composed a Southern community before the war. For the vast majority of Southerners, both free and slave, antebellum community life encompassed a rural existence. Although substantial urban centers such as Richmond, Charleston, and New Orleans existed and exhibited distinctive characteristics, for most Southerners community life centered on their rural county of residence. These counties did contain some market towns and county seats, but population centers rarely numbered more than a thousand inhabitants.

Although their county was the fundamental administrative unit that governed their public lives, on a day-to-day basis the private lives of most Southerners centered on their rural

> **In 1863 crop production in the South stood far below prewar levels.**

neighborhood, an area of about fifty to a hundred square miles in which they and their relatives and friends were born, married, and died. These self-contained rural neighborhoods, which usually were named after the predominant river or creek in the area, were focused on a general store, post office, and church. In some areas of the South the rural neighborhood even defined the political party identification of most of its residents.

The events at the outset of the Civil War reflected the degree to which these rural neighborhoods had been the center of antebellum Southern community life. For years before 1861 they had formed the basis of the local militia. Hence, when the Southern states seceded and joined the Confederacy, the antebellum militia units could be rapidly transformed into state military companies that formed the basis of the Confederate army. For example, the militia unit in the northeastern rural neighborhood of Flat River in Orange County, North Carolina, produced the Flat River Guards under the command of the officers who had directed the antebellum volunteer company of the same name.

The fact that the military units consisted of men who resided in the same rural neighborhood and county was very important in the early years of the war. This link between community life and military structure probably eased the difficult transition many Southern soldiers must have experienced when for the first time in their lives they traveled far outside their community of birth. To share this experience with neighbors not only made the transition easier but also gave a community-based meaning to the cause for which these men were fighting. Since most Southern white men did not own slaves, they clearly could not have been motivated to risk their lives solely to protect other men's property. But once the public accolades and excitement that accompanied enlisting ended and these men found themselves on the battlefield, the fact that their companies were composed of relatives and neighbors provided them with a sense that they were fighting the war to defend their communities. But, in turn, as the war progressed and the first companies suffered casualties, soldiers who were not residents of the same rural neighborhood or even the same county had to be recruited to fill the ranks. The traditional sense of camaraderie must have severely declined, resulting in diminished morale.

The rural neighborhood basis of community life was also important for civilians during the Confederacy. During the initial mobilization in 1861 most Southern states, which were unprepared for war, relied on the counties and especially the rural neighborhoods to supply the troops with basic necessities. Much of this activity was led by the women's aid societies that were formed in nearly every town and neighborhood in Southern counties. The first task of the societies was to clothe the soldiers in the local companies. To do this, they raised money by holding concerts and other public events. The money was then used to buy material from which the societies sewed the company uniforms and blankets. The pace of the activity of the aid societies usually began to slacken within a year of mobilization, as the states acquired the resources to supply their troops and the civilian population began to experience shortages.

On the home front the war had a distinct impact on community life. Although the impact was most obvious in communities that became battlefields or were invaded by the enemy, life in other communities, too, was altered. For example, all Southern communities witnessed the departure of men between the ages of eighteen and forty-five. It was not unusual for at least 70 percent of the men of that age group to be absent from their community for some period during the war.

The departure of these men had a profound social and economic impact on community life. As they went off to war, the marriage and birth rates in most communities declined sharply. The impact of this development was not confined to the years of the Confederacy. With as many as one-fourth to one-third of all Confederate soldiers having died, many Southern women were never able to marry. Further, the departure of so many men also caused a severe decline in the labor force since the vast majority of families did not own slaves. As a result, by 1862 and increasingly in 1863 crop production in the South stood far below prewar levels and every community experienced the resulting inflation.

The loss of so many men also forced Southern county governments to assume far greater responsibilities for the welfare of their residents than before. County courts began to appropriate what had before the war been unheard of sums to provide relief for the wives and children of soldiers who could not care for themselves. Often the money was raised by taxing masters for their slaves at rates that would never have been possible before the conflict.

Although initially the county courts provided direct grants of money to the needy, it became apparent that this method was insufficient, as inflation caused Southern farmers to increase the prices they charged for their products. Hence, the counties found it necessary to send agents to other communities and even other states to purchase corn and other foodstuffs for distribution directly to the needy. In some communities the local government used the tax-in-kind law passed by the Confederate Congress in April 1863 to collect one-tenth of all farm products. Finally, many local governments began to attempt to fix prices to restrain the ravages inflicted by inflation. Hence, where before 1861 Southern rural neighborhoods had been largely self-sufficient, during the last two years of the war they were forced to provide for the basic needs of a substantial share of their population and to intervene in the economy in ways never before considered legitimate for local government.

Besides the growing need to provide for the welfare of many of their residents, the economy of Southern communities was influenced by the tremendous civilian relocation that accompanied Union invasions of outlying regions of the Confederacy. For example, when the Union army invaded the Albemarle Sound of North Carolina in 1862, large numbers of planters and their slaves in the region rapidly relocated upcountry. These refugees not only bid up the cost of supplies in the communities where they resettled, thereby worsening the problem of inflation; their decision to relocate their slaves caused other disruptions. Many of these low-country slaves were leased out to Piedmont masters who had little concern about their well-being. Further, the influx of slaves who had heard of and sometimes witnessed a Union invasion, combined with the shortage of white men, held the potential for significant conflict. In an extreme example, within a two-week period in 1863 two masters in Orange County, North Carolina, were murdered by their slaves.

The threat to traditional community norms not only came from changes in the slave community. Although scholars disagree over the extent of social unity among Southern whites before the war, there is general agreement that during the years of the Confederacy the degree of social tension increased. The change in social relations among whites can be observed in three communities in different regions of North Carolina. In Washington County, a low-country community that experienced invasion very early in the war, social unity declined rapidly when the property interests of yeoman farmers and planters clashed, as yeomen disagreed with the way planters led recruitment efforts and supported the draft. In turn, the yeoman challenge caused planters to tighten their control over local courts and the militia. By June 1862 yeomen with Unionist sympathies, combined with tenant farmers and white laborers, had begun to confiscate the property of planters who had moved up-country to avoid the Union invasion of the region. When planters tried to reassert their antebellum level of control, guerrilla warfare ensued.

Guerrilla warfare also characterized the decline in unity at the other end of North Carolina in the mountain community of Shelton Laurel in Madison County. Here the nature of class tension was far more complex than in Washington County, for Confederate supporters in this community tended to be both the wealthiest and the poorest residents, whereas the sympathies of Unionists were shaped by their physical distance from the slave population. When by the fall of 1862 the deprivations of war as well as the threat of conscription had led local Unionists to raid a village in their community, locally based Confederate forces responded in January 1863 by attacking civilians whom they believed to be Unionists. After capturing a number of men, most of whom had not participated in the raid, the Confederates murdered thirteen of them ranging in age from thirteen to sixty.

Although most Confederate communities did not experience the violence that shattered the traditional order of Washington County and Shelton Laurel, few could avoid the growth of dissension against the war effort. Even in Orange County, a Piedmont North Carolina county that did not face Union invasion until after Robert E. Lee's surrender to Ulysses S. Grant, after two years of war a marked decline in

> **There is general agreement that during the years of the Confederacy the degree of social tension increased.**

morale created political dissension. As early as August 1863 at meetings in the community there were calls for convening a peace convention. By the fall of 1864 some community leaders advocated peace even at the price of emancipation.

Although the Civil War clearly altered Southern community life during the years of the Confederacy, the long-term impact is less evident. Despite leaving their own communities for the first time as a result of the war and experiencing life in other communities where they served, once the war ended and they returned home the common goal of most Confederate soldiers was to reestablish as closely as possible their prewar lives. With the major exception of the effects of emancipation, white Southerners largely succeeded in re-

creating a community life similar to that which had existed before the Confederacy.

[*See also* Class Conflicts; Conscription; Crime and Punishment; Marriage and Divorce; Morale; Religion; Slavery, *article on* Slave Life; Society; State Socialism.]

BIBLIOGRAPHY

Burton, Orville Vernon. *In My Father's House Are Many Mansions: Family and Community in Edgefield, South Carolina.* Chapel Hill, N.C., 1985.

Campbell, Randolph B. *A Southern Community in Crisis: Harrison County, Texas, 1850–1880.* Austin, Tex., 1983.

Durrill, Wayne K. *War of Another Kind: A Southern Community in the Great Rebellion.* New York, 1990.

Escott, Paul D. *After Secession: Jefferson Davis and the Failure of Confederate Nationalism.* Baton Rouge, La., 1978.

Harris, J. William. *Plain Folk and Gentry in a Slave Society: White Liberty and Black Slavery in Augusta's Hinterlands.* Middletown, Conn., 1985.

Kenzer, Robert C. *Kinship and Neighborhood in a Southern Community: Orange County, North Carolina, 1849–1881.* Knoxville, Tenn., 1987.

Paludan, Phillip Shaw. *Victims: A True Story of the Civil War.* Knoxville, Tenn., 1981.

ROBERT C. KENZER

COMPROMISE OF 1850

In the 1840s Americans' enthusiasm for expansion collided with growing antislavery sentiments, and the resulting controversy spurred a search for some formula to resolve the issue of slavery in the territories. The Compromise of 1850 was the most comprehensive effort by Congress to solve territorial and slavery-related problems. For a few years it was applauded and sometimes revered, but by 1854 its flaws and new territorial disputes had revealed the failure of this legislation to remove the causes of conflict.

President James K. Polk entered the White House in 1845 determined to add territory to the United States, and the war with Mexico expanded the nation's borders to the Pacific Ocean. The Wilmot Proviso, however, offered in 1846 by David Wilmot, a representative from Pennsylvania who belonged to Polk's own Democratic party, exposed the internal dangers of such continental visions. Wilmot proposed that slavery be prohibited from any lands gained from Mexico. Though his idea never became law, it polarized Congress and aroused state legislatures, North and South.

In the 1848 presidential campaign, Democrat Lewis Cass advanced an idea that became known as "popular sovereignty." Although Congress at some point would have to approve statehood for a new territory, Cass suggested that it should "in the meantime" stay out of territorial questions, allowing the people living there "to regulate their own concerns in their own way." This was an attractive formula to many, but it raised doubts among Southern leaders, who insisted that slaveholders had a right to carry slaves into any territory during the territorial stage. Many Northerners, on the other hand, wanted and expected settlers to prohibit slavery before statehood. For political benefit Democrats interpreted Cass's idea differently to Northerners and Southerners, but distrust of Cass in the South helped elect his Whig opponent, slave-owning Zachary Taylor.

The gold rush of 1849 forced these divisive issues onto Congress's agenda as more than eighty thousand people streamed into California. President Taylor urged them to apply for admission into the Union, and they did so, proposing a state constitution that barred slavery. California's application threatened to end for the foreseeable future the balance between free and slave states in the Senate. Immediately some Southerners objected that California should be a slave state or that the Missouri Compromise line should at least be extended westward to the Pacific. Nine Southern states sent representatives to the Nashville Convention, which asserted slaveholders' rights and endorsed extension of the Missouri Compromise line. President Taylor remained adamant for California's admission, but his sudden death in July 1850 left the decision to Congress.

> **The legislation anticipated disagreement and provided for appeal of a territorial legislature's action directly to the U.S. Supreme Court.**

In these circumstances the venerable and respected Henry Clay, who had played a prominent part in the compromises of 1820 and 1833, assumed a central role. In January 1850 the Whig leader proposed an overall settlement packaged as one piece of legislation, the "omnibus bill." Stephen A. Douglas of Illinois, a rising star in the Democratic party, assisted Clay. The senators' proposals encompassed five major areas. First, California would enter the Union as a free state. Second, new territories called New Mexico and Utah would be organized in the Southwest with governments empowered to legislate on "all rightful subjects . . . consistent with the Constitution." This ambiguous phrase, interpreted differently by Southerners and Northerners, continued the confusion inherent in Cass's original proposal. In fact, the legislation anticipated disagreement and provided for appeal of a territorial legislature's action directly to the U.S. Supreme Court. Third, Texas would give up its claims to a more extensive western bound-

ary, and in exchange the United States would assume the state's public debt. Fourth, the slave trade in the District of Columbia would be ended. And fifth, a stronger fugitive slave law for the nation would be enacted.

For six months Clay and Douglas worked to arrange support for the omnibus bill, but when it finally came to a vote, it was defeated. The prospect of an overall adjustment had not been attractive enough to overcome sectional objections. With Clay sick and absent from Washington, Douglas devised another strategy. He proposed the five elements of the compromise as five separate bills, hoping to piece together different majorities for each part of the compromise. The strategy worked, and by September 17 the Compromise of 1850 had become law. Each bill had gained a majority, although the bulk of Northern and Southern congressmen voted against each other in every instance but one.

Crowds in the capital celebrated the passage of the compromise, and initially political leaders hailed it as a settlement of the issues that threatened to divide the nation. In 1852 Franklin Pierce, who pledged to support the compromise, won a smashing victory in the presidential election. The views of his Whig opponent, Winfield Scott, were unknown, and Free Soil candidate John P. Hale openly repudiated the compromise. Thus, this legislation seemed to have won broad acceptance and growing prestige. By 1854, however, the peacemaking properties of the legislation had vanished.

What caused this great reversal? First, the Compromise of 1850 had skirted, rather than settled, the controversy over what rights proslavery and antislavery settlers had in the territories. The ambiguous language of the bill provided no formula to guide the future. Northerners continued to believe that slavery could and should be prohibited from the territories, whereas Southerners insisted that they had the right to carry slaves into any territory before it became a state. In 1850 one witty observer had remarked that Congress was passing a lawsuit rather than a law, and truly the compromise did nothing to settle the status of slavery in the territories. Thus, in 1854, when territorial organization for Kansas and Nebraska was considered, bitter disputes broke out anew. Second, the Fugitive Slave Law contained questionable features that soon fueled controversy. African Americans who were alleged to be escaped slaves had no opportunity in legal proceedings under the law to challenge that claim, and Federal commissioners received ten dollars for each fugitive they returned to slavery but only five dollars for alleged fugitives they set free. These provisions violated the beliefs many held about fair play and the right to a trial by jury. Moreover, under the Fugitive Slave Law, gripping human dramas began to occur in Northern towns and cities as freedom-loving men and women, some of whom had lived in the North for decades, were arrested and remanded to slavery. The Compromise of 1850 had proved, in the words of historian

David Potter, to be only an "armistice," not "a true compromise."

[*See also* Georgia Platform; Bleeding Kansas; Dred Scott Decision; Fugitive Slave Law; Missouri Compromise; Wilmot Proviso.]

BIBLIOGRAPHY

Campbell, Stanley W. *The Slave Catchers: Enforcement of the Fugitive Slave Law, 1850–1860.* Chapel Hill, N.C., 1961.
Hamilton, Holman. *Prologue to Conflict: The Crisis and Compromise of 1850.* Lexington, Ky., 1964.
Potter, David M. *The Impending Crisis, 1848–1861.* New York, 1976.

PAUL D. ESCOTT

CONFEDERATE STATES OF AMERICA

[*This entry serves as a general introduction to the history of the Confederacy. For further discussion of the origin of the Confederacy, see* Civil War, *article on* Causes of the War; Nationalism; Secession; State Rights. *For further discussion of Confederate government and politics, see* Cabinet; Congress; Constitution; Diplomacy; Judiciary; Politics; Presidency; Public Finance; *and articles on particular states. For further discussion of Confederate society, economy, and culture, see* Community Life; Economy; Nationalism; Slavery; Society. *For further discussion of the Civil War and its effects on the Confederacy, see* Army; Civil War; Morale; Navy; Prisoners of War. *See also biographies of numerous figures mentioned herein.*]

Some Southerners came to believe that the South possessed a character quite distinct from that of the North, distinct enough to qualify the region for separate nationhood. They looked upon themselves as constituting a suppressed nationality comparable to the Irish or the Polish, though they could hardly claim a distinctive language, religion, or tribal history.

There were, of course, real differences between the North and the South. The most important consisted of the relatively rapid industrialization of the one section and the persistence of a slavery-based agricultural economy in the other. Cotton and slavery might have provided an adequate basis for Southern nationality and independence—if American nationalism and the spirit of Union had been less strong than they proved to be. Southern nationalists did not want war, but war came, and as a result their experiment with independence was brief, lasting only from 1861 to 1865.

Sectionalism and Secession. Ever since the founding of the American republic, sectionalism had erupted in a Union-threatening crisis from time to time. At the constitutional convention of 1787, the project for a "more perfect Union" was endangered when Northern and Southern delegates disagreed on such questions as the prohibition of slave imports. The Union seemed at risk in 1819 when a controversy arose over the admission of Missouri as a slave state, and again in 1832 when South Carolina nullified Federal tariff laws. An even more serious crisis occurred in 1850; it resulted from a number of sectional disputes, the most serious of which concerned the status of slavery in the territories. Compromises enabled the Union to survive each of these crises.

So long as political parties remained national in membership, partisanship offset sectionalism and made compromise possible. Then, in the 1850s, partisanship gave way to sectionalism as the Whig party disappeared, the Democratic party split, and the new Republican party gained strength. President George Washington had warned in his Farewell Address (1796) that the Union would be imperiled if a time should ever come when parties were organized on a geographical basis, with a party of the North and another of the South. By 1860, that time had arrived. The party of the North, the Republicans, now elected their presidential candidate, Abraham Lincoln, though they failed to win a majority in either house of Congress.

South Carolinians made Lincoln's election the occasion for adopting an ordinance of secession and declaring South Carolina an independent state on December 20, 1860. In doing so, they followed a theory and a procedure that John C. Calhoun had formulated years earlier. According to Calhoun's doctrine of state sovereignty and state rights, secession was a perfectly legal and constitutional process. By February 1, 1861, the other six states of the lower South—Mississippi, Florida, Alabama, Georgia, Louisiana, and Texas—had followed South Carolina's example, though some secessionists justified their action on the basis of a revolutionary rather than a constitutional right, citing the precedent of July 4, 1776.

In the slave states of the upper South and the border, leaders hoped for a compromise that would preserve the Union, and with that object in view Virginia invited the rest of the states, North and South, to a peace convention, which met in Washington, D.C., but accomplished nothing. Meanwhile another convention sat in Montgomery, Alabama, and organized a provisional government for the Confederate States of America.

The seceded states had taken over most of the Federal property within their borders. A few forts remained under Federal control, most conspicuously Fort Sumter in Charleston Harbor. Confederate policy, as set in a resolution of the Provisional Congress, looked to the acquisition of these forts by negotiation if possible and by force if necessary. Lincoln, however, announced his intention to "hold, occupy, and possess" all the forts and other Federal property, and he refused to deal with commissioners from the Confederacy. When a Federal relief expedition approached Charleston Harbor, the Confederates opened fire on Fort Sumter, April 12, 1861, and compelled its surrender on April 14. The next day Lincoln called upon the states remaining in the Union for troops to enforce Federal laws in the states that had withdrawn from it.

The governors of Virginia, Tennessee, Arkansas, North Carolina, Missouri, Kentucky, and Delaware rejected Lincoln's call. Virginia and Tennessee began at once to give military support to the Confederacy, without waiting for the referenda that eventually showed majorities in both states in favor of secession. Conventions in Arkansas and North Carolina soon voted to secede. Extralegal bodies later proclaimed the secession of Missouri and Kentucky, and the Confederacy claimed both of these states also. Both were represented in the Confederate Congress, but their legitimate governments and a majority of their people remained loyal to the Union.

Constitution and Government. Montgomery remained the Confederate capital until July 1862, when the government moved to Richmond, Virginia. Meanwhile the Montgomery convention performed three functions: it chose a provisional president and vice president, served as a Provisional Congress, and drew up a constitution for the Confederacy.

For president, the convention selected Jefferson Davis, recently a U.S. senator from Mississippi and formerly a secretary of war and a professional soldier. For vice president, the choice was Alexander H. Stephens, long a congressman from Georgia. Both men had been moderates rather than fire-eaters, or extreme secessionists. Both were later elected, without opposition, to regular terms in office.

The Provisional Congress reenacted all U.S. laws not inconsistent with the Confederate Constitution, and this document was an exact copy of the U.S. Constitution except for certain significant changes. For instance, the president was given an item veto, and he and the vice president were limited to a single six-year term. Protective tariffs were prohibited. So were slave importations, but the institution of slavery itself was guaranteed. As Stephens declared, the "cornerstone" of the Confederacy was the same as that of slavery—the principle of the inequality of the white and black races.

After the unicameral Provisional Congress (1861–1862), there were two regular Congresses (1862–1864, 1864–1865). Each of these, like the U.S. model, consisted of a House and a Senate. Of the 267 men who, during the life of the Confederacy, served as senators or representatives, almost a third had been members of the U.S. Congress at one time or another, and one had been a U.S. president—John Tyler.

The Confederate Congress established six departments: State, Treasury, War, Navy, Justice, and Post Office. These duplicated the U.S. departments except for Justice, which the United States had not yet created, and Interior, which the Confederacy omitted. The new postal service succeeded the old without a break, the Southern employees of the U.S. government becoming employees of the Confederate government overnight.

Heads of departments changed frequently, so that Davis's cabinet had much less stability than Lincoln's. The most influential of Davis's cabinet advisers was Judah P. Benjamin, successively attorney general, secretary of war, and secretary of state.

The Confederate Constitution provided for a judiciary with a supreme court, but Congress included no such high tribunal when setting up a court system.

Diplomacy. At first, the Confederates looked confidently to Europe for assistance that would enable them to establish their independence. They were encouraged by the example of the Revolutionary War, in which France had intervened to help the rebellious English colonies succeed. They were further encouraged by the doctrine of King Cotton: they thought Great Britain and France were so dependent on Southern cotton that the two powers, to maintain their supply, would step in and end the war, with the Confederacy intact.

The Confederates promptly sent missions to Britain, France, Russia, and other countries to seek recognition and aid. It looked for a time as if Britain would go to war with the United States after a U.S. warship seized two of the Confederate emissaries, James M. Mason and John Slidell, from the British steamer *Trent* while they were on their way abroad (November 1861). But neither the British nor any other government ever officially received a diplomat from the Confederacy or recognized it as a member of the family of nations.

Britain did recognize the belligerency, though not the independence, of the Confederacy when Queen Victoria issued her proclamation of neutrality (May 13, 1861). Other countries did the same. This meant that they would extend to the Confederacy the rights of a nation at war under international law.

The British government violated its neutrality to the extent of allowing British shipbuilders to sell *Alabama* and other warships to the Confederacy. These, constituting the main force of the Confederate navy, engaged in commerce raiding on the high seas. They had access to foreign ports but not to their own, which were shut off by the Union blockade. Arguing that the blockade was ineffective and hence illegal, the Confederates tried unsuccessfully to persuade the British to break it.

When Emperor Napoleon III of France set up a puppet government in Mexico, the Confederates were willing to give it recognition (thus disregarding the Monroe Doctrine) in return for French recognition of their own government, but nothing came of this idea.

In the end, Confederate diplomacy failed partly because the European interest in Southern cotton was offset by other economic interests. More important, the European powers were divided, and Russia was conspicuously friendly to the United States. Neither Britain nor France dared risk intervention so long as the Confederacy had not clearly demonstrated its ability to survive with very little outside help.

The Army. The president of the Confederate States, like the president of the United States, was commander in chief of the army and navy. Except for what coordination President Davis could provide, the Confederacy had no unified command until near the end of the war, when Robert E. Lee became general in chief. Originally, both a Regular Army and a Provisional Army were contemplated, but the Regular Army never developed, and the Provisional Army fought the war.

Troops were recruited for this army directly as individuals and indirectly as members of state militias, which the governors furnished. From the outset men were impressed, or drafted, into state militias, but the Confederacy in its direct recruiting relied on volunteers until April 16, 1862, when its

> **The Confederacy had no unified command until near the end of the war, when Robert E. Lee became general in chief.**

Congress passed the first national conscription act in American history. This act applied at first to able-bodied men from eighteen to thirty-five and eventually to those from seventeen to fifty. It exempted state officeholders, workers in a variety of presumably indispensable occupations, and one owner or overseer for every twenty slaves. It also exempted men who could provide substitutes. All these provisions were unpopular, and most were modified before the end of the war.

Volunteers continued to enlist and did so in about the same numbers as were conscripted. How many men, all together, served in the Confederate army can only be guessed at. The most reliable estimate is 850,000 to 900,000, or somewhat less than half as many as served in the Union army, but a much higher proportion of the white population. At any given time the effective strength of the armed forces was considerably less than the numbers on the rolls. Many were absent without leave—as many as two-thirds in late 1864 according to Davis himself. Some deserters joined the enemy, and so did some draft evaders. More than 100,000 such "tories" fought on the Union side.

The Confederacy also lost considerable numbers as prisoners of war. In 1862 the Federal and Confederate authorities agreed to a cartel providing for a regular and large-scale exchange of prisoners. The arrangement soon broke down

because Davis refused to exchange black prisoners or their white officers and declared Benjamin F. Butler and his subordinates "outlaws" to be executed if captured. As Union prisoners accumulated, the Confederates were unable to provide suitable facilities for all of them, and terrible suffering resulted at Andersonville and other Southern prisons. Still, Union General in Chief Ulysses S. Grant was unwilling to renew the cartel, since the return of prisoners would benefit the Confederacy more than the Union, the Confederacy being more desperately in need of additional troops.

So desperate were Confederate leaders by 1865 that they finally decided to recruit slaves, but the war ended before any blacks actually served as Confederate soldiers.

Strategy. To maintain their independence, the Confederates needed not to win the war but only to keep the Federals from winning it. The Confederacy did not possess sufficient human and material resources to overwhelm the North in any case. Hence Davis adopted an essentially defensive though by no means entirely passive strategy. It was offensive-defensive. Throughout the war, while undertaking to repel Federal advances, the Confederates also made extensive counterthrusts from time to time.

Thus in 1862 Thomas J. ("Stonewall") Jackson sped northward down the Shenandoah Valley to threaten Washington and draw Federals away from beleaguered Richmond. Robert E. Lee and Braxton Bragg made simultaneous movements into Maryland and Kentucky, movements that culminated in the Confederate recapture of Harpers Ferry and in Confederate retreats from Sharpsburg, Perryville, and Murfreesboro.

In 1863 Lee invaded Pennsylvania with the twofold objective of intensifying the war-weariness of the North and relieving the pressure on Vicksburg, which was under siege. He retreated from Gettysburg and the Confederates surrendered Vicksburg on the same day, July 4, 1863.

Again in 1864, when Federals were hemming in Richmond and Petersburg, Jubal Early attempted to divert them by raiding the outskirts of Washington. And finally, after the fall of Atlanta, John Bell Hood attacked the Federals at Nashville, only to be routed.

Meanwhile John Hunt Morgan, Nathan Bedford Forrest, and Joseph Wheeler made cavalry raids into Unionheld areas of the South and even into Kentucky, Indiana, and Ohio.

The Confederate strategy did not prevent the steady loss of territory to the Federals. After only a little more than a year of war, the Confederacy had lost control of northeastern Virginia, stretches of the coast from North Carolina to Florida, and a large part of both Tennessee and Louisiana, including the state capitals, Nashville and New Orleans. By the end of 1863 more than half of the original Confederacy had been isolated from the Richmond government because of Federal penetration, and by the end of 1864 no more than three states—most of Virginia and North and South Carolina—remained under the government's control.

This does not necessarily mean that the Davis policy was ill-advised. "If it did not win the war," as historian Frank Vandiver has written, "the offensive-defensive did enable the Confederates to outlast their resources—ample proof of the soundness of the strategy and the strategist."

The Economy. Far inferior to the Union in both human and material resources, the Confederacy at the start could claim only about two-fifths as many people (a third of them slaves), one-fourth as much bank capital, and one-tenth as great a manufacturing capacity. The Confederacy did produce more corn and livestock per capita, and it had a large potential asset in its cotton crop.

The Confederates failed to make timely and adequate use of the cotton as a basis for foreign credit. Hence financing the war proved difficult. Bullion and coin were relatively scarce, and the Confederates had to rely much more on the issue of paper money and much less on taxation and borrowing than the Union did.

The consequence was extreme inflation. This was made worse by a scarcity of many commodities, a scarcity that was due to the blockade and to extensive hoarding, which in turn was exacerbated by the government's policy of impressment, that is, the seizure of goods at arbitrary prices. Inflation was also intensified by the shrinkage of Confederate-held territory and the resulting increase in the ratio of currency to commerce as people in the occupied areas sent their Confederate money to what was left of the Confederacy, where the paper retained at least a little of its nominal value.

Transportation suffered from the inadequacy of the railroads, which had serious gaps to begin with. True, the Confederates were the first to reinforce an army by rail in the midst of battle, and their railroads gave the presumed advantage of "interior lines" some reality. Still, the government failed to take effective control of the railroad system until late in the war. By then, the tracks and rolling stock had deteriorated badly, and the gaps had grown worse with the loss of key junctions such as Chattanooga and Atlanta. River and coastal shipping similarly was obstructed by enemy occupation.

Horses and mules, together with horse-drawn and mule-drawn vehicles, played a larger role in Confederate life, both military and civilian, than did railroad trains or riverboats. In the beginning the Confederacy was well supplied with horses and mules, but these were rapidly used up, and replacements were hard to get. By 1863 there was a serious shortage.

The Confederates acquired some munitions and other war matériel by seizures of U.S. arsenals, purchases abroad, and captures on the battlefield. But they had to depend mainly on expanding their few existing facilities, such as the Tredegar Iron Works in Richmond, and on developing new ones. The government tried to stimulate war-related manufactures by various means, among them the granting of draft exemptions to needed laborers. There were remarkable achievements in the production of salt, nitrates, and other necessities, but not enough to meet all the military and civilian requirements. Even when a surplus of commodities, such as foodstuffs, existed in one place, there were often shortages in other places because of the transportation difficulties.

Economic exhaustion eventually set in. As Charles W. Ramsdell has said, "The Confederacy had begun to break down *within,* long before the military situation appeared to be desperate."

Society. The war brought significant, if not all of them permanent, changes in Southern society, especially in the role of women, the relationship of classes, and the position of blacks.

Women took up responsibilities that formerly had belonged to men. They assisted the war effort directly by encouraging men to enlist, by sewing for soldiers and nursing them, and by serving as spies, among whom the most famous were Belle Boyd and Rose O'Neal Greenhow. They ran farms and plantations and worked at factory and government jobs. As diarists and memoirists, most notably Mary Boykin Chesnut and Catherine Ann Edmondston, they left the best literature embodying the wartime experience.

At least for the duration, women were liberated from the romantic antebellum stereotype of the lady on the pedestal, though certainly not from family obligations and the necessity of work. The hardships of the farm eventually caused many wives to call their soldier husbands home, thus depriving the army of men instead of inducing them, as earlier, to enlist.

Planters could no longer base their prestige solely on the land and slaves they owned. A heroic war record also counted, and men of no previous high standing, such as Stonewall Jackson, rose to positions of leadership and fame. At the same time, class consciousness grew among small farmers and day laborers, who expressed their feelings in the common saying that it was "a rich man's war and a poor man's fight." Mobs of women occasionally engaged in bread riots, demanding price reductions and looting stores of groceries and other merchandise.

Black men and women, as slaves, kept the plantations going and thus enabled an unusually high proportion of white men to be absent in the army. Blacks also gave direct assistance to the military as construction gangs, teamsters, cooks, and the like. Afterward, members of planter families liked to tell of retainers who had remained loyal to them throughout the war.

Yet the slaves constituted at least as much of a liability as an asset to the Confederacy. They did not revolt, as whites had feared they would, but—especially after Lincoln's

Emancipation Proclamation (January 1, 1863)—they flocked to the camps of oncoming Federals and assisted them as spies, guides, and laborers. About 100,000 blacks from the South (and others from the border states and the North) joined the Union army. In short, the slaves themselves contributed mightily to the final defeat of the Confederacy and the destruction of slavery—the institution upon which the Confederacy was based.

> **Politics pitted President Davis . . . and his faithful followers against a growing number of opponents. . . .**

Politics. Political parties did not emerge in the Confederacy, though there remained in many cases a distinction between old Democrats and former Whigs. Politics, often virulent, nevertheless persisted in the form of rivalries for power and disagreements over governmental methods and even aims. These dissensions seriously weakened the Confederacy.

Politics pitted President Davis, always a Democrat, and his faithful followers against a growing number of opponents, the foremost of whom was Vice President Stephens, once a Whig. Davis, burdened with responsibility as he was, took a fairly broad view of the powers of the central government. Stephens became increasingly extreme in his devotion to state rights. He and other critics of Davis blamed him for practically everything that went wrong in the Confederacy.

Some of the severest critics were state governors. Davis had to contend with especially troublesome resistance from Joseph E. Brown of Georgia and Zebulon Vance of North Carolina. These governors wanted to keep control of their own state militias, and they objected both to Confederate conscription and to its enforcement by suspension of the writ of habeas corpus. Brown kept many Georgia soldiers inside the state, and Vance accumulated stocks of war matériel for the exclusive use of North Carolina troops.

Confederate nationalism had to compete not only with state rights but also with persisting Unionism. This was most pervasive in the Appalachian Mountains and in the adjoining hill country, where slaves were few. Fifty-two counties of northwestern Virginia rejoined the Union as the state of West Virginia in 1863. A third of the counties of Tennessee, those in the eastern part of the state, would probably have rejoined the Union as East Tennessee if Federal armies had established control there as early as they did in northwestern Virginia. From the outset Confederate leaders had worried about popular tendencies toward "reconstruction," and these tendencies increased with military reverses, multiplying

casualties, economic hardships, and a consequent lowering of public morale.

Peace movements gained ground, particularly in North Carolina and Georgia. In North Carolina a secret society known as the Red Strings (or Heroes of America) cultivated defeatism, and William W. Holden ran for governor as a peace candidate in 1864. (He was easily defeated by Vance, who called for keeping up the war effort.) In Georgia, Stephens and Brown advocated negotiating with the enemy. Stephens was willing to settle for guarantees of state rights in a reunited nation, but Davis refused to consider anything short of peace with independence. Davis insisted on this as his minimum terms when he authorized Stephens and other envoys to meet with Lincoln and his secretary of state, William H. Seward, in the Hampton Roads conference of February 1865. Lincoln took the position that the war would end only when the Confederates laid down their arms, and before long they had no real choice except to do so.

BIBLIOGRAPHY

Beringer, Richard E., Herman Hattaway, Archer Jones, and William N. Still, Jr. *Why the South Lost the Civil War.* Athens, Ga., 1986.

Coulter, E. Merton. *The Confederate States of America, 1861–1865.* A History of the South, vol. 7. Baton Rouge, La., 1950.

Eaton, Clement. *A History of the Southern Confederacy.* New York, 1954.

Roland, Charles P. *The Confederacy.* Chicago, 1960.

Thomas, Emory M. *The Confederate Nation, 1861–1865.* New York, 1979.

RICHARD N. CURRENT

CONFEDERATE VETERAN

Published in Nashville, Tennessee, from 1893 until 1932, the *Confederate Veteran* became the most popular Southern magazine of its time because it marketed the myth of the Lost Cause, a romantic and emotional defense of the fallen Confederacy. Sumner Archibald Cunningham, the founder, typified his readers, a coterie of unreconstructed Southerners. Initially printed as a leaflet to report donations for the Jefferson Davis Memorial at Richmond, Virginia, the maiden issue of *Veteran* contained reminiscences, personal recollections of battles, accounts of United Confederate Veteran activities, and the defeatist poetry of Chaplain Abram Ryan interspersed with the listing of funds.

Reader response encouraged Cunningham to launch his leaflet as a regular monthly. Averaging thirty pages in length with distinctively Confederate covers, *Veteran* included personal anecdotes, nostalgia masquerading as Civil War history, Ku Klux Klan testimonials, and flowery obituaries submitted by a growing readership. With this blend of vindication, censorship, racism, and death, Cunningham created a golden past for white Southerners to remember: the Lost Cause. Accordingly, *Veteran* became the official organ of the United Confederate Veterans, the United Daughters of the Confederacy, the Sons of Confederate Veterans, and the Confederate Southern Memorial Society.

Veteran's popularity peaked in 1906 with 21,000 subscribers, but gradually the relentless march of time decimated readership and created serious funding problems for Cunningham. After his death at age seventy in 1913, the magazine struggled on until 1932 when time and economic depression ended publication.

BIBLIOGRAPHY

Connelly, Thomas L. *The Marble Man, Robert E. Lee.* New York, 1977.

Cresap, Bernarr. "The Confederate Veteran." *Alabama Review* 12, no. 4 (1959): 243–257.

Evans, Josephine King. "Nostalgia for a Nickel: The Confederate Veteran." *Tennessee Historical Quarterly* 48, no. 4 (1989): 238–244.

Foster, Gaines M. *Ghosts of the Confederacy: Defeat, the Lost Cause, and the Emergence of the New South.* New York, 1987.

Goff, Reda C. "The Confederate Veteran Magazine." *Tennessee Historical Quarterly* 331, no. 1 (1972): 45–60.

White, William. *The Confederate Veteran.* Tuscaloosa, Ala., 1962.

JOSEPHINE S. KING

CONFISCATION

[*This entry is composed of two articles,* Confederate Sequestration *and* Federal Confiscation, *which discuss the seizure of enemy property by the Confederate and U.S. governments.*]

Confederate Sequestration

Since the earliest conflicts between nations, belligerents have exercised the right to confiscate enemy property. The Civil War was no exception to this rule. Indeed, both the Confederate Congress and the U.S. Congress passed laws relating to the capture and disposition of enemy property.

After Abraham Lincoln's March 4, 1861, inauguration, Confederate Secretary of the Treasury Christopher G. Memminger sent a circular to all U.S. civil authorities still residing in the South. In this letter, Memminger ordered that they pay all outstanding debts due the United States to the Confederate Treasury. Just two months later, in May, the Confederate Congress passed a law that required all debts due to individuals or businesses in the North be paid to the Confederate Treasury. Congress followed up on these initiatives in an attempt to ensure the moneys owed to the Federal government would be deposited in the very limited Confederate Treasury.

The Confederates did not rely only upon the collection of these debts. In response to—and retaliation against—the U.S. Confiscation Act of August 6, 1861, the Confederate Congress passed the Sequestration Act on August 30, 1861. Although the Sequestration Act was modeled after the Union statute, it was in actuality much harsher. Whereas the Union's August 1861 act called for the seizure of all property, including slaves, used to "aid the rebellion," the Confederacy's Sequestration Act authorized agents to seize *all* property belonging to alien enemies still residing in the Confederate States as of May 21, 1861—three months before the passage of the act. Congress also directed that agents be appointed to enforce the provisions of the law: they were to hunt out alien enemy property, confiscate it, and sell it. The law was amended on February 15, 1862, to allow those Southerners whose property had been seized by the Federals to be compensated for their losses.

The district courts and the Board of Sequestration Commissioners provided the machinery used to enforce the Sequestration Act. As the judges appointed to hear the cases well knew, the act had to be administered with discretion to ensure that innocent citizens were not unduly punished—and impoverished.

Some Southern jurists questioned the constitutionality of the act. South Carolina's Confederate District Court judge, former U.S. Circuit Court judge A. G. Magrath, declared the act legal and constitutional on the grounds that the right to wage war included the right to seize property. Many in the Palmetto State, and the Confederacy as a whole, disputed this definition of war powers, maintaining that the Confederate Congress had no specific power that enabled them to seize enemy property. Citing precedents from 1794, these judges and attorneys argued that the United States had dispensed with the policy of confiscating enemy property and had signed a treaty with England guaranteeing that the practice would be abolished. They also argued that the Confederate Sequestration Act did not correspond to the Federal Confiscation Act because that statute limited the Union to confiscating only those articles defined as contraband of war, be they confiscated Confederate exports or other goods seized and deemed necessary for the war effort.

Defenders of the law, including the Confederate attorney general, maintained that independent, sovereign nations were definitely granted the power to confiscate enemy property. Since the Confederate States was as much an independent country as any European nation, these attorneys argued, the Confederacy was fully justified in adopting the policy of sequestration. In building this defense, the Confederacy's attorneys were forced to adopt a broad view of constitutional powers: they implied that they accepted the notion of a strong central government, equipped with the authority to enact sweeping war powers. In adopting this view, they belied the very foundation of the Confederate nation: state rights.

The Confederate Congress amended the Sequestration Act several times. On October 15, 1861, an assemblage of planters and merchants in Macon, Georgia, urged that the confiscation of alien property date from the date of the bill's passage, not three months retroactively. Toward the end of the war, Congress broadened the act still further: that body directed that anyone who fled the Confederacy without the permission of President Jefferson Davis or the commanding officer in charge of the Trans-Mississippi would be treated as an enemy alien and hence would have his property seized.

The individual Confederate states also enacted state-level versions of the Sequestration Act. In these instances, Confederate agents seized everything from tobacco and cotton to pianos, city property, and ship cargo. Some accounts note that Confederates confiscated three thousand acres of land in Florida; agents netted $500,000 from aliens residing in the capital city of Richmond; and even Thomas Jefferson's Monticello went on the auction block because its owner was a New Yorker serving in the Union navy.

Despite all the litigation and the operation of the sequestration commissioners, the Confederacy realized very little tangible gain from the enforcement of the act. Unfortunately, information on the amount of money and property seized remains scant; many figures are deemed unreliable. Still, historians have documented that between January 1 and September 30, 1863, and January 1 and September 30, 1864, $6,102,070.39 was deposited in the Confederate Treasury. In gold, this figure amounted to $380,000.

> **Thomas Jefferson's Monticello went on the auction block because its owner was a New Yorker . . . in the Union navy.**

In spite of the active enforcement program, the Sequestration Acts proved to be unsuccessful. Secretary Memminger and others within the Confederate government expected to garner large sums from the confiscation of Northern property. The reality—less than a million dollars in gold—belied that expectation. Indeed, any hope that the seizure of enemy property would help make the Confederacy rich must have been dashed after only two years when it became evident that the money was just not there. Still, the Confederates saw fit to broaden their view of war powers and saw nothing constitutionally wrong with seizing the property of an enemy power. This shows that Southerners were fully

cognizant of the changes that could occur to ideological conceptions when confronted by the realities of a modern war.

[*See also* Northerners.]

BIBLIOGRAPHY

Coulter, E. Merton. *The Confederate States of America, 1861–1865.* A History of the South, vol. 7. Baton Rouge, La., 1950.

Klingberg, Frank W. *The Southern Claims Commission.* Berkeley, Calif., 1955.

Randolph, Nowlin. "Judge William Pinckney Hill Aids the Confederate War Effort." *Southwestern Historical Quarterly* 68 (1964): 14–28.

Schwab, John Christopher. *The Confederate States of America, 1861–1865: A Financial and Industrial History of the South during the Civil War.* New York, 1901. Reprint, New York, 1968.

Turner, Martha L. "The Cause of the Union in East Tennessee." *Tennessee Historical Quarterly* 4 (1981): 366–380.

MARY A. DECREDICO

Federal Confiscation

The Union government's Confiscation Acts of 1861 and 1862 had their origins in the North's desire to facilitate the war effort, to punish the Southerners, to do something about slavery, and to lay the groundwork for a meaningful Reconstruction. As early as July 4, 1861, Secretary of the Treasury Salmon P. Chase suggested that the confiscated property of "insurgents" could help pay for a Union victory. Shortly thereafter, Republican Lyman Trumbull introduced a confiscation bill in the Senate that, with some modification, became law on August 6, 1861.

Some Democrats, especially those from slaveholding border states, expressed concern over the bill's potential disruptive impact on slavery and on the prospects of an early reconciliation with the seceded states. The law, however, was technically limited in its scope, especially since it had real force only where Federal authority existed. It gave the president the authority to confiscate property used "in aiding, abetting, or promoting" the Confederate cause, but it specifically limited the Federal government's grasp over slave property to those slaves actively employed in the Confederate war effort. The Federal government was to pursue confiscation through the courts and could do so without having the owner of the property present at the proceedings.

This Confiscation Act remained in effect throughout the war, but a second more comprehensive law addressed some of its inadequacies. In December 1861 Lyman Trumbull introduced in the Senate the new confiscation bill that finally became law on July 17, 1862. The bill became Congress's primary legislative attack on slavery. Unlike the first Confiscation Act, which had passed quickly in the rush of early wartime legislation, this one served as a catalyst for prolonged debate on more expansive issues, including the role of Congress in the conduct of the war, the nature of secession, and the role of confiscation and land redistribution in reconstructing the South. After it passed along partisan lines, Senator Orville Browning, who had broken with his fellow Republicans on this measure, petitioned Abraham Lincoln to veto the bill. He argued that because the bill would permanently confiscate an individual's property it violated the Constitution's attainder clause. Lincoln was ready to oblige him because of his own constitutional reservations but signed the bill after Congress passed a joint resolution explaining that the law would not be retroactive, nor would confiscation extend beyond the lifetime of the individual who fell under its provisions. (The Supreme Court eventually upheld the constitutionality of both Confiscation Acts in 1870 in *Miller v. U.S.*)

In its final form the Confiscation Act of 1862 gave the courts the option to punish treason with death or fine and imprisonment. As with the earlier act, proceedings could be conducted without the presence of the accused. Individuals found to be aiding the rebellion could be fined and imprisoned. Both classes were disqualified from holding political office. Furthermore, the president was empowered to confiscate immediately the property of Confederate government officials and military officers, former officials of the United States, and individuals who owned property in loyal territory. Individuals involved in the rebellion outside these classes had sixty days from a presidential proclamation to abandon the rebellion or suffer confiscation of all their property.

Although confiscation remained a judicial proceeding, the new law gave the military a significant role in the way in which it dealt with the slavery issue. Slaves "shall be deemed captives of war, and shall be forever free of their servitude and not again held as slaves" if they escaped from disloyal masters to Union lines, were captured by Union forces, or were deserted by their owners and came under Union control. The law also gave the president the authority to employ slaves "for the suppression of this rebellion, and for this purpose he may organize and use them in such manner as he may judge best for the public welfare." It also rendered inoperative the Fugitive Slave Law except for loyal slave owners and gave the president the authority to initiate colonization of slaves freed by the law.

Ultimately, enforcement of both Confiscation Acts depended on the president and, particularly, his attorney general, Edward Bates, a Missouri Republican. Both lacked enthusiasm for confiscation, and Lincoln would use it only when it would help him achieve his primary goal: the restoration of the Union. In New Orleans in late 1863 and early 1864, for example, presidential pardons removed most of the individuals who would have been subjected to the provisions of the law. And President Andrew Johnson's liberal pardon policy after the war's end had a similar effect throughout the South. Ultimately, a relatively inconsequential amount of

Confederate property in the North and the South was confiscated. The Captured Property Act of March 3, 1863, actually produced much more revenue for the government; captured property, almost 95 percent of which was cotton, netted about $25 million by May 1868. The government reaped about $300,000 from the Confiscation Acts.

The message contained in the laws, however, suggested an importance that went beyond anything measured in dollars and cents. The Confiscation Act of 1861 signaled the beginning of the North's move toward total war, and it indicated a willingness on the part of Congress to violate the sanctity of private property to make war on the South's aristocracy. Furthermore, the Confiscation Acts identified slaveholding with disloyalty. With the passage of the Confiscation Act of 1862, the safety of slave property in the loyal border states was threatened, and it could no longer be assumed that a black man or woman was a slave. The Confiscation Acts along with the Emancipation Proclamation and other wartime measures had a disruptive effect on the institution of slavery. Slaves learned of the measures through masters' reactions and the grapevine, picked up ideas about property redistribution, deserted their masters, and gave every indication that they knew the provisions of the second law well enough to defend their freedom by claiming to have belonged to disloyal masters. Ultimately, confiscation gave the army de facto power to free slaves. In the fall of 1862, for example, Gen. William Tecumseh Sherman ordered his men to treat the slaves who came within their lines as free until courts could give a final ruling.

Southerners reacted to these laws with anger and fear. In 1861 the Confederate Congress passed the Alien Enemies Act on August 8 and the Sequestration Act on August 30 probably in retaliation for the first Confiscation Act. The former gave aliens the options of becoming Confederate citizens, leaving the South, or being treated as enemies; the latter authorized the confiscation of their property. The Federal threat of confiscation gave Confederate propagandists ammunition to stir up hatred of the enemy by reminding Southerners that the loss of wealth was the price of defeat. Fear of confiscation prompted Confederate commanders and slaveholders near Union lines to remove able-bodied slaves. The Confiscation Acts combined with Reconstruction measures caused a lingering fear of confiscation into the 1870s, despite the fact that the issue was last brought up in Congress in March 1867.

[*See also* Contraband.]

BIBLIOGRAPHY

Berlin, Ira, et al., eds. *The Destruction of Slavery.* Ser. 1, vol. 1 of *Freedom: A Documentary History of Emancipation, 1861–1867.* Cambridge, Mass., 1985.

Lucie, Patricia M. L. "Confiscation: Constitutional Crossroads." *Civil War History* 23 (December 1977): 307–321.

Randall, James G. *Constitutional Problems under Lincoln*. 2d ed., rev. Urbana, Ill., 1951.

Shapiro, Henry D. *Confiscation of Confederate Property in the North*. Ithaca, N.Y., 1962.

Syrett, John. "The Confiscation Acts: Efforts at Reconstruction during the Civil War." Ph.D. diss., University of Wisconsin, 1971.

PAUL A. CIMBALA

CONGRESS

Upon voting to secede from the United States, the conventions of the seven original Confederate states sent delegations equal to their 1860 congressional representation to Montgomery, Alabama, to form a new nation. Fearful of delay, they adopted with only one day's discussion a one-year Provisional Constitution, which converted the Montgomery convention into the new government's legislative body. Congressmen from states that later seceded were elected by their convention or legislature. Thus, there were no popularly elected Provisional congressmen. In all, the Confederate Congresses had representatives from eleven seceded states and the extralegal Confederate governments of Kentucky and Missouri, plus nonvoting representatives from Arizona Territory and the Cherokee, Chickasaw, Choctaw, Creek, and Seminole Indian nations.

The average Confederate congressman was well off financially, with a median estate worth $47,000. Sixty-four percent had served in state legislatures and 32 percent in the U.S. Congress. Only 10 percent had had no previous political experience. Professionally they ranged from horse breeder to financier. At least 92 had been Whigs and most of these had

> **Congress acquired a body of laws by adopting all U.S. laws consistent with the Confederate Constitution.**

been conservative on secession. At least 138 had been Democrats and most of them had been early secessionists. Political experience and wealth were greatest in the Provisional Congress, somewhat less in the First, and even less in the Second, though this decline was relatively slight.

The Provisional Congress. The Provisional Congress met until February 17, 1862. The Provisional Constitution permitted plural officeholding, so a number of members served both in Congress and in the army, a privilege denied by the Permanent Constitution. Voting was by state, as it had been in the Philadelphia Convention, and a tied vote in a delegation left that state's vote uncounted.

The business of nation building occupied the first months. Congress acquired a body of laws by adopting all U.S. laws consistent with the Confederate Constitution. It elected Jefferson Davis president and Alexander H. Stephens vice president, and then established executive departments much like those of the United States. Other aspects of government, such as a postal system, the judiciary, and citizenship and naturalization systems, were also carried over with little change. Congress contracted for the regular publication of its laws and had the major laws published in a newspaper in each state. The Senate and House rules were adopted almost bodily from the U.S. Congress, but recording of debates was left to newspaper reporters, with frequent secret sessions making adequate reporting impossible.

The delegates to Montgomery had hoped for a government without political parties, and to a large extent they succeeded. Old habits, however, could not be so easily abandoned. In private correspondence the erstwhile secessionists, Unionists, Democrats, and Whigs expressed distrust of their former political opponents. These feelings were of some importance in determining how people voted in elections, but there is no evidence of any significant voting alignment within Congress based on past politics until the Second Congress. Without specific party lines to guide them, therefore, each congressman had to decide for himself how he would vote.

This political vacuum worked in President Davis's favor. He was never without his congressional critics, but during the first year the war was going well and people were confident of victory. Demands upon them were relatively light. Criticism of the president was therefore mainly personal or doctrinal and did little to affect the course of legislation. Whigs and Unionists argued that Davis denied them patronage. Some secessionists felt that he was secretly a reconstructionist. Scattered armchair experts disliked his military policies. Extreme state rights advocates disliked his frequent vetoes. Meanwhile administration measures went through Congress almost intact, and the newspapers jeered at the legislature as being a "register of Executive decrees." Underneath all this, another factor operated in Davis's favor: during wartime people generally assume that their political and military leaders know best what to do, and that overt opposition borders on treason. Nothing but the firmest conviction would allow the Provisional Congress to tamper with administration requests.

Confederate leaders originally hoped to finance the government on a low tariff income, but as an interim device Congress authorized an issue of $1 million in Treasury notes guaranteed by a tax of $\frac{1}{8}$¢ per pound on cotton exported. It also provided for a Provisional Army of 100,000 militia volunteers, ordered the president to arm and equip them as he wished, and established a general staff.

The Fort Sumter affair necessitated a called session of Congress, but there seemed to be no alarm. On May 16

Congress authorized the issue of $20 million in fiat Treasury notes and $50 million in 8 percent bonds for general investment and for money pledged from the sale of agricultural produce—the first produce loan. This quick and easy financing set Congress on the road to a monetary policy based on Treasury notes and bond issues to absorb surplus currency. Congress now removed all restrictions on the number of volunteers who might be accepted in the army and bypassed the states by letting the president receive independent companies. The president was also given the right to control all telegraphic operations. On May 21 Congress finally established a tariff system that was to last for the duration. The leading rate was 15 percent on most commonplace items, with raw materials paying somewhat less and luxuries somewhat more.

> **Congress now removed itself from diplomatic strategy and accepted the administration's policy of cotton diplomacy.**

Congress now removed itself from diplomatic strategy and accepted the administration's policy of cotton diplomacy. It prohibited the export of cotton and other staples except through Confederate ports or into Mexico, trying to cut off all supplies going to the United States and to force Europe to break the blockade and come get what it wanted. Some congressmen wished to buttress the policy with a promise of a lower tariff to any nation recognizing the Confederacy, but this movement floundered and was dropped.

The victory at First Manassas did little to influence the next sessions of Congress. It authorized a call for 400,000 volunteers and let the president accept units of specialists and local defense. During the winter it enacted several feeble acts to induce volunteering and reenlistments, none of them very successful. Finally the Provisional Congress ordered a war tax of fifty cents on each one hundred dollars of goods named by the Treasury Department.

The Provisional Congress had spent much of its first month in writing a constitution for the permanent government of the Confederacy. The new Constitution provided for a Congress identical to that of the United States, and elections for representatives were held on the first Wednesday in November 1861. Each state had its former Federal representation and used old election procedures. Most states allowed absentee voting by soldiers and refugees at army camps and other designated places. Traditional politicking would have seemed divisive; candidates usually announced themselves briefly in newspapers and did little personal campaigning. A few districts engaged in vigorous battles over local issues, but national policy was seldom a subject of debate. Voters tended to support men whom they had favored before the war. Democrats and secessionists were popular at this time, and the election returns gave them about a three-to-two majority in the First Congress. Five state legislatures chose one former Whig and one former Democrat, and eight legislatures chose two former Democrats. The overall pattern of those elected seemed basically like that of the Provisional Congress.

The First Congress. When the First Congress convened on February 18, 1862, it was evident that the one-year volunteers were weary of military service. There was the possibility that more than half of them would not reenlist, and President Davis was compelled to ask for the conscription of all able-bodied men between the ages of eighteen and thirty-five. On April 16 Congress, over the objections of the Atlantic seaboard states above Florida, enacted such a law. It then conferred blanket exemptions on a long list of occupations whose personnel was deemed more important to the home front than to the army. That fall Congress extended the conscription age to forty-five but refused to reduce the number of class exemptions. By the end of 1863 the need for troops was becoming desperate, and on February 17, 1864, Congress set the conscription age from seventeen to fifty and pared the exemption list drastically.

Demands for changes in these laws occupied much of Congress's time. The first law had let eligible men offer substitutes. This obviously favored the wealthy, and Congress finally drafted both the substitutes and those who had hired them. Planters had been allowed one exempt overseer for every twenty slaves they owned, but this elitist practice had severe critics. In the end, Congress exempted only those overseers so employed before February 16, 1862. After a bitter debate, state rights advocates secured the exemption of all state officers certified by their governor as necessary for proper government.

Wedded to conservative financing, Secretary Christopher G. Memminger continued asking for more Treasury notes, backed by faith in the government and payable in specie after the war. He also requested great amounts of bonds into which currency could be invested and which would be exchangeable directly for agricultural products. Congress gave him most of what he requested, but people preferred to spend their rapidly inflating currency quickly rather than buy bonds. Near the end of the First Congress Memminger reported that funding was going badly, and at his suggestion Congress enacted a forced funding law, which set up a schedule by which currency would gradually decline to worthlessness unless funded into bonds. In January 1863, it levied its first significant tax on property, income, licenses, and businesses, plus a 10 percent tithe on slaughtered hogs and agricultural products.

The First Congress dealt with other matters of only slightly less importance. In their need for supplies, army agents often ruthlessly seized them from producers and wholesalers. The Impressment Act of March 26, 1863, permitted the seizure of agricultural products and military supplies at a "fair" price and established a system of arbitration whereby a former owner might negotiate a better price. Congress also permitted the destruction of property if it were in danger of being captured. On February 6, 1864, the legislature ordered that no major staple crop or military stores could be exported except under regulations established by the president, and it outlawed the importation of luxuries. Despite almost violent debate on the subject, Congress on three occasions gave the president authority to suspend the right of habeas corpus when deemed necessary.

Congress was noticeably reluctant to take any initiative in two areas. It left to the president all decisions about what manufactories were needed for the war effort, but when asked by the War Department it quickly encouraged private individuals to manufacture guns, ammunition, clothing, and other army accoutrements. It also flirted with the idea of price control to stem inflation, but never managed more than a vestige of such regulation.

By 1864 an important new alignment had appeared in the legislature. The Confederacy was now divided into what historians Alexander and Beringer term "exterior" and "interior" districts. Exterior districts were those occupied by the enemy and therefore little affected by the legislation of Congress. Their voters naturally preferred congressmen who would support any measure that might help redeem their homes. Interior districts were those still within Confederate jurisdiction and in which its laws could be enforced. They supported congressmen who would heed local grievances as well as tend to issues of national survival.

The Second Congress. Politics reverted to type during elections for the Second Congress during mid-1863. Louisiana, Missouri, Tennessee, and Kentucky—now almost entirely exterior areas—held elections by general ticket, with each voter casting his ballot for one congressman from each district; other states continued to vote as before. The major issue now was the Davis administration and critics were in full cry. Usually they attacked the one or two programs that most closely affected their districts, but in the southeastern seaboard states they arraigned the government on almost everything. Past politics became openly important, and the general aura of discontent and war weariness helped candidates who had urged caution in 1860. In the Second Congress two-thirds of the new men were former Unionists and three-fifths were Whig. These men, however, were no less loyal Confederates than the two-term congressmen and remained so to the end of the war. They simply did not want a war that demanded further sacrifices.

In the Second Congress, which met on May 2, 1864, a congressman's former party, his secession stand, and the exterior or interior status of his district became ever more important in determining his vote. The First Congress had carried legislation about as far as it could go, and now the administration could ask only for refinements in the laws. The voting alignments, however, too often took precedence over national survival and made constructive legislation almost impossible. Meanwhile a peace movement was gaining momentum. But the president insisted that the North already knew the conditions on which the Confederacy would make peace and that further negotiations would signal irresolution. The result was that no significant law was enacted during the first session.

The last session of Congress, which began on November 9, 1864, was marked by a legislative stalemate. A majority of congressmen were now from exterior districts, but enough of them were willing to ally with interior-district men on certain issues to block new administrative programs. Until the last week, the administration won only two victories. There was talk in and out of Congress of depriving Davis of his constitutional prerogative as commander in chief and persuading Gen. Robert E. Lee to take full military command. Davis scotched this plan on February 6, 1865, by naming Lee general in chief, knowing that Lee would not exercise a broader command. Davis also virtually ended the peace agitation in Congress at about the same time by sending a commission to meet with Northern representatives, but he instructed them to accept peace only with independence. After the inevitable failure, Congress officially vowed to continue the war until victorious.

Meanwhile other matters were at a standstill. Congress refused all requests for financial reform and on December 28, 1864, merely extended the funding deadline to July 1, 1865. A few days before Congress ended, so many men had left Richmond that there was barely a quorum in the House and some compromise was absolutely essential. On March

> After the inevitable failure, Congress officially vowed to continue the war until victorious.

13 Congress let the president call upon the states for as many slaves as he wished to serve as soldiers, but left it to the individual state to decide whether such men should be freed. There were 125,000 men still exempt or detailed. Davis wanted all exemptions ended and the men subject to detail to the army or the home front as the president wished; on March 16, 1865, Congress kept a few exemptions and let the president detail the rest. On March 18 Congress ordered that goods impressed must be paid for at market prices. On the same day the legislature gave the president his only outright defeat; it refused to pass a new habeas corpus suspension.

All these desperation laws of Congress's last week were of course too late to be of any value.

Confederates generally had a low opinion of their Congress. Those approving President Davis's leadership chided Congress for tampering with administration requests; those critical of the administration considered Congress too submissive. Pragmatically, Congress had little alternative to such submissiveness. Survival of the Confederacy was uppermost in the minds of everyone, even congressmen, and legislative chaos would have been ruinous. As Alexander and Beringer so well demonstrate, past politics, position on secession, economic factors, and local conditions often influenced voting, but until late 1864 there is little evidence of bloc voting. In the Second Congress a definite Whig-Unionist versus Democrat-secessionist alignment began to emerge, as well as the important interior versus exterior district alignment. It was now obvious that the new congressmen were not decisively committed to Southern independence at the expense of their districts. By then, however, the limits of legislation had been reached and no obstructionist alignment had any measurable effect on the conduct of the war.

[See also Conscription; Economy; Habeas Corpus; Impressment; Montgomery Convention; New Plan; Poor Relief; Public Finance; State Rights; State Socialism; entries on particular states; and biographies of numerous figures mentioned herein.]

BIBLIOGRAPHY

Alexander, Thomas B., and Richard E. Beringer. The Anatomy of the Confederate Congress: A Study of the Influences of Member Characteristics on Legislative Voting Behavior, 1861–1865. Nashville, Tenn., 1972.

Beringer, Richard E. "A Profile of the Members of the Confederate Congress." Journal of Southern History 33 (1967): 518–544.

Curry, J. L. M. Civil History of the Government of the Confederate States with Some Personal Reminiscences. Richmond, Va., 1901.

Davis, Jefferson. The Rise and Fall of the Confederate Government. 2 vols. New York, 1881. Reprint, New York, 1958.

Journal of the Congress of the Confederate States of America, 1861–1865. 7 vols. Washington, D.C., 1904–1905.

Yearns, Wilfred B. The Confederate Congress. Athens, Ga., 1960.

W. BUCK YEARNS

CONSCRIPTION

The survival of the Confederacy depended on its ability to outlive the Civil War, and endurance required a proficient military force. When the Southern states went to war in April 1861, eager volunteers swelled the ranks of the army to defend their homeland and earn glory and fame. But by the end of the year, Southern soldiers were eager to return home. They had learned the reality of war: long hours of boredom, exhausting marches, and the ever-present threat of death. Self-preservation demanded that the Confederate government assume the liability of equipping the army with soldiers.

The Confederate government ultimately passed three conscription acts. These three measures were the most controversial pieces of legislation passed by the Confederate Congress. Conscription initiated heated debates between the states and the central government, sparked class conflict among Southerners, and created hostility between volunteers and conscripts in the army. Southerners had founded the Confederate States of America on the premise of the sovereignty of each state, and a national conscription law threatened the supremacy of state governments. Yet the need to fight a successful war dictated that the central government appropriate a great deal more power than Southerners had anticipated.

By December 1861, the war promised to be long and costly. Amassing a stable and effective army became a priority for Confederate leaders. The twelve-month volunteers, who had joined the army during the first flush of excitement, were now older and wiser and looking forward to returning to their homes before the end of winter. Confederate President Jefferson Davis and Secretary of War George Wythe Randolph began discussing the problem of keeping the veterans in the army and adding to their ranks as well. They turned to the idea of a national draft as a means of recruiting manpower and coordinating the war effort among the states.

First Conscription Act

The first Conscription Act became law April 16, 1862. It drafted for military service all white males between the ages of eighteen and thirty-five for a period of three years unless the war ended sooner. The law required that soldiers who had already enlisted serve three years from their original date of enlistment. To honor their patriotism, the government offered the twelve-month men sixty-day furloughs and allowed them the privilege of reorganizing and electing their officers. For newcomers, the act included a grace period that granted them the option of volunteering before conscription forced them into the army. Volunteers could elect their officers, or they could volunteer for an existing unit, permitting them to fight alongside friends or relatives.

The government also recognized the need to ensure that an adequate labor force remained at home to foster the nation's industrial and agricultural resources. Five days after passing the Conscription Act, Congress amended the bill by exempting from the draft individuals employed in occupations germane to the war effort and the maintenance of the country. Those exempted included Confederate and state officials; laborers employed for the war effort, such as factory hands, miners, and foundry workers; mail carriers and telegraph operators; railroad employees; teachers who had at least twenty pupils; ministers; druggists; hospital attendants; and the physically and mentally disabled. The secretary of war reserved the power to exempt specific superintendents and laborers in the cotton and wool industries. Six months later, the government added journalists, postmasters, physicians, and conscientious objectors to the list. Conscientious objectors reserved the option to provide a substitute or pay five hundred dollars into the Confederate Treasury.

To Southerners, the most antagonistic element of the act was the overseer clause, or the Twenty-Slave Law. This clause exempted one white male for every plantation with twenty slaves. In part, planters wanted assurance that they could maintain control over their slaves in the wake of

> Substitution not only heightened class conflict among Southerners but also placed unqualified men in the army and lowered morale. . . .

Lincoln's Emancipation Proclamation. But most Southerners viewed the overseer clause as a means for the slaveholding class to avoid the draft.

The clause evoked such criticism that seven months later the legislature revised the law. Following May 1, 1863, the clause pertained only to plantations belonging to minors, women, or disabled planters. To prevent men from suddenly becoming overseers merely to evade the draft, the exempted person had to have been employed as an overseer prior to April 16, 1862. In addition, the law required the owner of the plantation to pay five hundred dollars to the Confederate Treasury. When even this failed to curtail abuse of the clause, the War Department began enrolling overseers and then detailing them to the plantations during harvesting season.

The overseer clause, even in its mitigated form, still aroused a great deal of class conflict among Southerners, as did the equally egregious substitution clause. This provision allowed an individual, referred to as a principal, to hire a substitute to fulfill his obligations as a conscript. The government expected that wealthy industrialists would use this clause to continue their work to the benefit of the Confederacy. In reality, it became a way for the wealthy to avoid a war that the less fortunate could not escape.

Southerners subject to the draft regarded substitution as blatant class favoritism, and they deplored exemption on the ground that so many men used it as a means of evading conscription. Employers sold positions that granted exemption to those who could afford it. Similarly, money could persuade certain physicians to sign a disability voucher. Despite its deleterious effect on national morale, the exemption clause

remained law for the duration of the war, and Congress did not abolish substitution until December 1863.

Substitution not only heightened class conflict among Southerners but also placed unqualified men in the army and lowered morale among the soldiers. Many resourceful individuals made a career of posing as substitutes during the war. They would accept payment from a principal, enlist in the army, desert, and then repeat the cycle, thus making a living from the bounties. Those substitutes who did not desert at the first chance were often men who did not meet the physical qualifications for soldiering. The substitute market employed a large number of underage boys and overage men who did not have the physical stamina to fight at the front.

The Conscription Act engendered a great deal of opposition from state officials. Many felt the act was unconstitutional and that it conflicted with state rights ideology. Yet eventually, most state governors, whether they believed in the constitutionality of a national draft or not, recognized the need for conscription and agreed to work with the central government. They did, however, share a resentment toward the Confederate conscription officers who usurped the positions of state officials.

Governor Joseph E. Brown of Georgia was the most infamous exception to this attitude among the governors. Brown believed in state rights at all costs and fought to retain the sovereignty of state governments. He argued against the necessity of the draft, asserting that Georgia had always produced more than its quota of men for the army. He hindered the recruiting process by issuing large numbers of exemptions to Georgians called by conscription and resisted the enrollment of the state militia, declaring that he needed the men in Georgia for local protection. Though other governors would balk at the increasing power of the central government, Brown remained the most vehemently opposed to any challenge to state authority.

Second Conscription Act

Five months after the inauguration of the first act, the army continued to want for soldiers. Southerners had displayed enormous ingenuity in eluding the enrollment officers by finding work that qualified them for exemption, by spending a fortune in substitutes, and by outright deception. On the heels of the horror at Sharpsburg, where both armies suffered thousands of casualties, the Confederate Congress issued a second Conscription Act on September 27, 1862. With it, they hoped to create a more stringent law that would eliminate the instances of misuse and put more men on the battlefields.

The second Conscription Act enabled the president to enlist white males between the ages of eighteen and forty-five. At the time, Davis recruited only men eighteen to forty, but the Confederate losses at Vicksburg and Gettysburg forced him to call on forty-to-forty-five-year-old males as well.

Despite the discord it had engendered, the substitution clause remained intact in September 1862. In addition, the government extended the list of exemptions once again. Davis and his administration hoped that, by conscripting men between thirty-five and forty-five years old, they could eliminate the number of men available to serve as substitutes and hence reduce exploitation of the system. By extending the number of exemptions, they attempted to ensure that enough men remained in industrial and agricultural occupations to keep the nation functioning. The abuses continued, however, and the second Conscription Act did little to appeal to latent patriotism.

Southerners received the second act in much the same way they had reacted to the first—with anger and resentment. By conscripting men as old as forty-five, Congress depleted the number of men remaining at home to plant crops and serve in local defense. Poorer families, whose survival depended on an ample number of bodies to plant and harvest and who could not afford to buy a substitute, suffered the greatest hardships under the extended draft.

Southern outrage regarding the conscription acts manifested itself most intensely in the mountain regions. In these areas, a large percentage of the population did not share the viewpoints of their state politicians, who frequently favored the wealthier constituencies living in the lowlands. In fact, many nonslaveholding mountain inhabitants espoused Union sentiment and felt no obligation to fight for the Confederacy. Most important, the majority of these people barely subsisted on the food they grew each year; they could not spare an able-bodied man.

As the war ground on, organized resistance to the draft intensified, particularly in the mountain regions of eastern Tennessee, North Carolina, Alabama, and Mississippi. Armed men joined together to aid one another in eluding the enrollment officers and to fight them off when necessary. By the end of the war, a number of enrollment officers had lost their lives to men who were desperate to avoid conscription.

Desertion became more common as the war progressed. As the South's resources diminished, so did the soldiers' rations. Deteriorating conditions in the camps and disintegrating morale, caused by the Confederate defeats during the summer of 1863 and despondent letters from their families, compelled men by the thousands to turn homeward.

In a vain attempt to recover his troops, Jefferson Davis issued a Proclamation of Amnesty to all deserters in August 1863. He revoked the usual punishments of incarceration or death for anyone who would return to the army during the stated grace period. When that failed, he suspended the writ of habeas corpus in the areas where draft evasion was most successful.

Difficulties with enforcement and coordination of conscription plagued authorities; the enterprise needed organi-zation. When conscription first became law, its administration and execution had fallen to the Adjutant and General Inspector's Office. Under the guidance of this office, individual states recruited and organized units. In December 1862, the Confederacy established a Bureau of Conscription, which took responsibility for enrolling all troops east of the Mississippi River. This act further empowered the central government to allocate manpower to the indigent areas.

From its inception, the Bureau of Conscription clashed with military officers who desired a more efficient and less bureaucratic method of raising soldiers. Braxton Bragg took direct action and authorized Brig. Gen. Gideon Pillow to establish a recruiting bureau of his own, which operated in direct competition with the Bureau of Conscription in Richmond. Pillow and his men engaged in field recruiting in Alabama, Mississippi, and Tennessee. Pillow experienced a great deal of success with military conscription, but the legality of his methods came into question, and the government subsequently abolished his independent bureau. Within a short time, however, he was recruiting once again in Joseph E. Johnston's department. While employed under Johnston, however, Pillow was not able to wield the power he had enjoyed under Bragg; from Richmond, the Bureau on Conscription closely audited his work. When John S. Preston became superintendent of the Bureau of Conscription in August 1863, he set out to reorganize its structure and increase its efficiency. Under his direction, the bureau eventually abolished military conscription altogether.

During 1863, the Confederacy suffered severe setbacks, including, in the last months of the year, Bragg's defeat at Chattanooga. The Bureau of Conscription could not recruit soldiers fast enough to replace the casualties, and once again, the government modified the conscription laws.

Third Conscription Act

The Conscription Act of February 17, 1864, revealed the desperation that would soon pervade the Confederate government. Extending the draft to include males seventeen to fifty, the bureau planned to detail older conscripts, or to assign them to local reserve units, thus freeing younger men to fight on the front. Authorities received instructions to reserve Confederate and state civil service positions for those unable to fight. In addition, to keep the men in the ranks, the government offered one-hundred-dollar government bonds, at 6 percent interest, to any noncommissioned officers or privates who did not desert.

Congress also used this Conscription Act to amend once again the overseer clause. Reflecting the decline in the worth of Confederate money, plantation owners would no longer pay five hundred dollars to the public treasury for each overseer; instead they had to produce a bond guaranteeing one hundred pounds of bacon or of beef and pork for every physically sound slave on their plantations. In addition, any surplus goods grown on the plantations had to be sold to the government at a fixed price.

The third act also eliminated almost half of the authorized exemptions. In an attempt to curtail the abuses generated by the exemption system, the Conscription Bureau now filled positions formerly held by laborers immune to the draft by detailing enlisted men. This provision gave the central government virtual dominion over the Confederate labor force.

The most astonishing provision of the new Conscription Act was that which authorized the government to employ up

> **The secretary of war despaired of adding any more white Southerners to the ranks.**

to twenty thousand free blacks and slaves. Although they did not propose to arm the slaves in early 1864, Southerners prepared to use them and free blacks for special detail, such as building fortifications and working in munitions factories.

The Conscription Act of 1864 and the heavy losses on the field further exacerbated conflict between the Confederate government and the state governments. The war was going badly. It had seriously depleted state resources, and even civilians faced severe deprivations. Individual states turned on the central government and blamed the president and Congress for their woes.

By the end of 1864, military commanders, desperate for soldiers, had turned against the Bureau of Conscription. The third act had not placed an adequate number of men at the front, and commanders cited the inefficiency of the Conscription Bureau as the reason. They had a point; during the early months of 1864, the bureau had issued more exemptions than it had received conscripts. Bragg, in particular, began pushing to reinstate military conscription.

President Davis and the secretary of war despaired of adding any more white Southerners to the ranks. They had already called out all men between seventeen and fifty; those who had not presented themselves for duty to this point were not likely to do so now. So, in desperation, Davis made the shocking proposal to arm slaves.

In March 1865, Congress made provisions to "recruit" slaves for field service. It carefully stipulated that the master must assent to the use of his slave for military service, that recruitment would not drain any state of more than 25 percent of its slave population and, especially important, that the slave would retain his slave status.

In March Congress also conceded to the abolishment of the Bureau of Conscription. Generals of state reserve forces, who reported directly to the War Department, received

orders to take charge of enforcing the Conscription Acts. But by 1865, Southerners were no more eager to join the army than they had been in 1862.

A national conscription law was an extreme act for a confederation founded on the principle of the sovereignty of its individual states. It was bound to create conflict and unrest. Yet winning the war necessitated a degree of coordination, and with the Conscription Acts, Congress did attempt to lend organization to the war effort. It also strove to place unwilling soldiers at the front.

The number of soldiers the Conscription Acts added to the military ranks remains uncertain—perhaps ninety thousand conscripts reached the front. The Conscription Acts did encourage volunteerism and, in 1862, prevented the twelve-month veterans from leaving the army.

Ironically, although the Conscription Acts were intended to save the Confederacy, they no doubt promoted disunity within the nation. The substitution clause and the Twenty-Slave Law aggravated class tensions between Southerners, and the states rebelled against the power the Bureau of Conscription imparted to the national government. Yet the enactment of a national conscription law demonstrated how far some Southerners were willing to go to realize their dream of an independent South.

[*See also* Army, *articles on* African Americans in the Confederate Army *and* Manpower; Class Conflict; Desertion; Habeas Corpus; Morale; State Rights.]

BIBLIOGRAPHY

Brooks, Robert Preston. *Conscription in the Confederate States of America, 1862–1865.* Cambridge, Mass., 1917.

Escott, Paul D. *After Secession: Jefferson Davis and the Failure of Confederate Nationalism.* Baton Rouge, La., 1978.

Mitchell, Memory F. *Legal Aspects of Conscription and Exemption in North Carolina, 1861–1865.* Chapel Hill, N.C., 1965.

Moore, Albert Burton. *Conscription and Conflict in the Confederacy.* New York, 1924.

Thomas, Emory M. *The Confederate Nation, 1861–1865.* New York, 1979.

JENNIFER LUND

CONSTITUTION

The states that left the American Union in 1860 and 1861 brought with them a rich tradition of constitutionalism. Many Southern leaders explained their support for secession in terms of the failure of the federal compact. Most blamed Northerners for failing to live up to their obligations, although some thought it was structural flaws in the U.S. Constitution that made secession necessary.

The Provisional Constitution of the Confederate States of America signed on February 8, 1861, created a compact among six Deep South states. The Permanent Confederate Constitution, signed on March 11, 1861, created a political structure for what became the eleven-state Confederate nation. Both documents were similar to the U.S. Constitution. The differences between the two reflected the political struggles that had led to secession.

The Montgomery Convention and the Provisional Constitution. On February 4, 1861, forty-three delegates from South Carolina, Alabama, Mississippi, Georgia, Florida, and Louisiana assembled in Montgomery, Alabama, to write a provisional constitution for the Confederate States of America. The convention finished its work four days later. Such speed was possible because of the "mania for unanimity" among the delegates and because the Provisional Constitution was something of a cross between the Articles

> There was no serious debate over the name of the new nation—the "Confederate States of America". . . .

of Confederation and the U.S. Constitution and borrowed heavily, in language and concepts, from both documents. Like the Articles of Confederation, the Provisional Constitution created a unicameral Congress in which each state had a single vote. Borrowing from the British system, the Provisional Constitution allowed cabinet members to serve in Congress and stipulated that Congress choose the president. Like the Constitution of 1787, it provided for a president with a veto power and enumerated powers for the Confederate Congress similar to those given to the U.S. Congress. There were also a number of substantive differences between the Provisional Confederate Constitution and the Constitution of 1787.

Under this document Jefferson Davis became president of the fledgling nation and formed a government. By its own terms the Constitution was to last no more than a year, but it was in operation for only thirty-one days before the delegates wrote and signed a permanent constitution. The preamble of the Provisional Constitution reflected the state rights philosophy and Protestant culture of its framers: "We, the Deputies of the Sovereign and Independent States of South Carolina, Georgia, Florida, Alabama, Mississippi, and Louisiana, invoking the favor of Almighty God . . . ."

The Permanent Constitution. Under the terms of the Provisional Constitution, the Montgomery convention reconstituted itself as the Provisional Congress of the Confederate States of America until such time as a permanent constitution could be adopted and a permanent congress elected.

There was no serious debate over the name of the new nation—the "Confederate States of America" reflected what the founders thought they were creating.

The delegates who gathered in Montgomery reflected, in their occupations, their interest in politics, and their stake in slavery, the elite of the society they represented. In early March when the Texas delegation arrived, their numbers rose to fifty. Of these, forty-two were lawyers and thirty-three described themselves as planters (including twenty-seven of the lawyers). Forty-eight were native Southerners, forty-nine were slaveowners. Twenty-one owned at least 20 slaves and one owned 473. Thirty-eight were college graduates. Almost all had extensive political experience: twenty-three had served in the U.S. Congress; sixteen were former or sitting judges, including two state chief justices; two had been in national cabinets, and a third had been in the cabinet of the Republic of Texas. Oddly, one of the most influential members of the convention had no political experience per se. Thomas R. R. Cobb, the "James Madison" of the Confederate Constitution, had never held an elective office, although he had been the first reporter of the Georgia Supreme Court. He was also one of the South's foremost legal scholars and the author of the influential *An Inquiry into the Law of Negro Slavery* (1858).

On February 9, the day after the signing of the Provisional Constitution, members of the Provisional Confederate Congress appointed a twelve-man committee, chaired by South Carolina's secessionist leader Robert Barnwell Rhett, Sr., to draft a permanent constitution. Other important members of the committee included Thomas R. R. Cobb and Robert Toombs of Georgia; James Chesnut, Jr., of South Carolina; and Wiley Harris, a skilled Mississippi lawyer. On February 28 Rhett presented the Congress with a draft of a permanent Constitution. For the next ten days the Montgomery delegates functioned as a Congress during the morning and as a constitutional convention during the afternoon and evening. On March 11, 1861, the Montgomery convention adopted this document and sent it on to the seceded states for ratification.

Structurally the U.S. and Confederate Constitutions are nearly identical. Both have a preamble and seven articles, and both create a national president, a bicameral legislature, and a court system. The only major structural difference is that the first twelve amendments to the U.S. Constitution were incorporated, almost word for word, into the main body of the Confederate Constitution.

The Confederate Constitution is often seen as a document for a nation based on state rights and limited government. To a great extent this is true, but the document also vested the national government with some centralizing powers. Like the U.S. Constitution, the Confederate document had a necessary and proper clause, a supremacy clause, and a clause requiring all state officials to swear allegiance to the national government. Article I, Section 9 of the Confederate Constitution had a habeas corpus suspension provision that was identical to that of the U.S. Constitution. These certainly gave the national government power to act.

In addition, innovations in the Confederate Constitution gave the new government more power in some respects than the U.S. government had. The president was limited to one term, but that term was for six years. Thus he may have had more opportunity to implement his policies than his counterpart in Washington. The Confederate president had a line-item veto and the right to dismiss at will all cabinet members. Incorporating aspects of a parliamentary system, the document stipulated that Congress could grant cabinet officers "a seat upon the floor of either House, with the privilege of discussing any measures appertaining to his department." This gave the administration an advantage in getting its programs through Congress that the U.S. president lacked. Robert Toombs thought these provisions strengthening the executive branch were the most important differences between the two constitutions.

The most significant differences between the two, however, lay in the Confederate provisions limiting the power of the national government, protecting state rights and, most important, protecting slavery.

A limited government. A persistent complaint of antebellum Southerners had concerned the national government's assumption of increased power after 1789. Reflecting the divergent views of state rights advocates and nationalists were the fights over the establishment of a national bank, the 1828 "Tariff of Abominations," the doctrine of nullification, and the constitutionality of the federal government's funding internal improvements. Thus, the Confederate preamble differed significantly from that of the U.S. Constitution in order to cure what were seen as defects allowing centralization. Unlike its federal counterpart, the preamble did not state that the central government was to "provide for the common defense" or "promote the general welfare." It also contained an explicit reference to state sovereignty (discussed below) and a direct appeal for the "favor and guidance of Almighty God."

Article I granted the Confederate Congress the legislative powers "delegated" in the Constitution. This was a major limitation on the power of the Confederate government. The enumerated powers clauses (Art. I, Sec. 8) limited taxes to those providing "revenue necessary to pay the debts, provide for the common defence, and carry on the Government of the Confederate States." This clause specifically forbade any "bounties" or taxes "to promote or foster any branch of industry." Section 8 absolutely prohibited the Congress from appropriating money for "internal improvements intended to facilitate commerce" except for those directly connected to navigation, harbors, and rivers. Under this Constitution there would be no support for national roads, railroads, or other such improvements.

It also provided that the executive branch could propose appropriations and needed only a simple majority in Congress to have them adopted, whereas appropriations originating with Congress needed a two-thirds majority to pass. This particular provision strengthened the president vis-à-vis Congress but generally it made the national government less flexible than that of the United States. The Constitution also required that all appropriations be for exact amounts and declared that there could not be "extra compensation to any public contractor, officer, agent or servant." The absolute prohibition on "impa[i]ring the right of property in negro slaves" limited the use of slaves for war activities. These provisions, combined with the lack of a common defense clause in the preamble, were significant departures from the U.S. Constitution and at least potentially hampered the operations of a government that was about to fight a major war with a far richer and more powerful adversary.

Finally, in a move to eliminate patronage (which could have undermined the president's power to run the government), the Constitution prohibited the president from removing civil servants except for "dishonesty, incapacity, inefficiency, misconduct, or neglect of duty." The president, however, retained the explicit power to fire cabinet members and diplomats without cause.

During the war itself the Davis government was able to overcome some, but not all, of the constitutional obstacles to a strong government. President Davis amassed considerable power, but at great cost to his political capital. During the war the Davis administration often suppressed civil liberties to a greater extent than its counterpart in Washington. Only five days after Davis took office the Confederate Congress adopted legislation allowing the suspension of habeas corpus. Davis sporadically imposed martial law on Richmond and other major cities. In some areas of the Confederacy, like eastern Tennessee, martial law led to the summary executions of a few civilians and the mass incarceration of others. By the end of the war, Vice President Alexander Stephens and other leading politicians no longer supported the administration, in part because of Davis's "betrayal" of Southern Constitutional principles. "Our liberties, once lost," he declared, "may be lost forever."

State rights. Directly tied to the limitations on the national government was a respect for state rights. Some scholars have argued that the Confederate Constitution was so extreme on this issue that the Confederacy was doomed to lose the war. Others dispute this point. In any event, even a cursory glance at the document shows that in respecting state rights—and simultaneously limiting the power of the central government—the Confederate Constitution created a government that was quite different from that in place in the Union.

The state rights tone was set in the preamble, which added to "We, the people of the Confederate States," the significant phrase, "each State acting in its sovereign and independent character." Article I allowed the states to impeach "any judicial or other Federal officer, resident and acting solely within the limits of any state." Such an officer would then be tried by the Confederate Senate. This provision was never implemented during the life of the Confederacy. Nevertheless, the threat of impeachment may have undermined the ability of Confederate officials to enforce unpopular laws and policies in their state. Article I, Section 10, also allowed states to impose their own import and export duties, something prohibited to the states remaining in the Union.

> "We, the people of the Confederate States, each State acting in its sovereign and independent character."

Southern distrust for the national judiciary was apparent in the drafting of Article III of the Confederate document. A key provision of the U.S. Constitution is the clause creating diversity jurisdiction by giving the federal courts the power to hear cases "between Citizens of different States." The Confederate Constitution lacked such a provision, which in practice meant that civil suits between citizens of different states would have to be litigated in state courts. This undermined the nationalization of law and jurisprudence, and had the Confederacy survived, it probably would have led to unnecessary complications in litigation and complaints about the failure of litigants to get a fair trial in a neutral forum. Moreover, in a nation that was predicated on state rights and local interests, the abolition of diversity jurisdiction could have led to a judicial and business climate that would have hampered economic development. The Confederate Constitution also failed to include the phrase "law and equity" in granting jurisdiction to the national courts. This is generally seen as a concession to the civil law system in Louisiana and its vestiges in Texas. A final bow to state rights, and one that could have led to enormous instability, was a provision allowing a constitutional convention to be called on the demand of just three states.

During the war, state judges issued writs of habeas corpus directed against military officers trying to impose Confederate conscription. Without a functioning court system, which the Constitution would have allowed but did not mandate, the Davis administration and the Confederate military could only respond to these manifestations of state rights with suspensions of martial law.

Slavery. Far from a "peculiar institution," slavery was, as Confederate Vice President Alexander Stephens declared, "the cornerstone" of the Confederacy. As such, it was pro-

tected even more in the Confederate Constitution than it had been in the proslavery U.S. Constitution of 1787.

The most obvious difference between the two documents lay in their use of the term *slavery.* In deference in 1787 to some of the Northern delegates who thought their constituents might oppose the Constitution if the word appeared, the framers of the U.S. Constitution substituted such phrases as *other persons, such persons,* and *persons owing service* for the word *slaves.* No such problems arose in the framing of the Confederate document. The blatantly proslavery Confederate Constitution contains the words *slave* or *slavery* ten times in seven separate clauses.

As their predecessors had in the Philadelphia Convention of 1787, the South Carolina delegates in Montgomery wanted to count slaves fully for representation. South Carolina had a larger percentage of slaves than any other state and would have gained by their full representation. The delegates in Montgomery, however, must have understood that a full counting of slaves would have discouraged the other Southern states, with smaller percentages of slaves, from joining the Confederacy. Thus, the convention chose to continue the Federal compromise by maintaining the three-fifths clause for determining congressional apportionment.

The frequent refusal of Northern states to cooperate in the rendition of fugitive slaves had been a major irritant in the antebellum period. The Montgomery delegates did not, however, substantially alter the fugitive slave clause in their Constitution. There were probably two reasons for this. First, they were writing a constitution for a slaveholders' republic, and it was unlikely that any Confederate state would ever adopt legislation similar to the Northern personal liberty laws. Second, a substantial change in the wording of the clause would have undermined the Southern argument that the meaning of the clause in the U.S. Constitution was clear and that secession was justified by the North's refusal to fulfill its constitutional obligations.

The Confederate Constitution also mirrored, but surpassed, the federal Constitution on the issue of the slave trade by absolutely forbidding the operation of the African slave trade. This was done over protestations of South Carolinians, who wanted the matter left to Congress. Prohibiting the trade was not an indication of antislavery sentiment but the result of the distaste for the African trade by some slave owners, fear of Africans themselves, and the fear that Europe would not recognize the Confederacy if it did not unequivocally prohibit the trade. Permitting the trade also might have discouraged Virginia and Maryland from entering the Confederacy because of the excess of slaves in those states. Those states might not have wanted foreign competition with their interstate slave trade.

On all other issues the Constitution created a thoroughly proslavery republic. The Constitution authorized Congress to *limit* the importation of slaves from other nations and states but did not prohibit it altogether as current federal law did. The Constitution absolutely prohibited any law "impa[i]ring the right of property in negro slaves." Reflecting Southern states' rejection of Northern states' decisions that had freed the slaves of visitors, Article IV guaranteed that the citizens of each Confederate state "shall have the right of transit and sojourn in any State of this Confederacy, with their slaves and other property; and the right of property in said slaves shall not be thereby impaired." The Constitution's fugitive slave clause reiterated this right. Finally, the Constitution affirmed the proslavery holding of Chief Justice Roger B. Taney in the U.S. Supreme Court *Dred Scott* decision, by declaring that slavery could never be prohibited from any Confederate territory. At the same time, however, the Confederate authors jettisoned Taney's implausible argument that the national government could not regulate the territories. Thus, their territory clause accomplished two proslavery goals. It guaranteed both slavery in the territories and the ability of Congress to counter any antislavery movement that might arise in the Confederate hinterlands.

Ratification. On March 11 the Montgomery convention unanimously adopted the new Constitution. The next day Howell Cobb, president of the convention, sent the Constitution to the states for their approval. The ratification of five states would complete the process. On March 12 the Alabama secession convention debated and ratified the document by a vote of 87 to 5; on March 16 the Georgia convention read and ratified the Constitution by a unanimous vote of 260 to 0; on March 21, after some political maneuvering, Louisiana ratified 94 to 10; on March 23 the Texas Secession Convention approved the Constitution 126 to 2 after almost no debate; and on March 26 Mississippi ratified it by a vote of 78 to 7. The Confederate Constitution was now in force.

Radicals delayed ratification in South Carolina. Robert Barnwell Rhett, Sr., wanted to amend the document to prohibit any free state from entering the Confederacy. But finally, on April 3, South Carolina ratified by a vote of 138 to 21. The negative votes represented not latent Unionist sentiment but the proslavery extremism in the Palmetto State. After ratification the South Carolina convention proposed amendments to eliminate the three-fifths provision and count all slaves for representation; to prohibit free states from joining the Confederacy; to repeal the constitutional prohibition on the slave trade; and to prohibit the government from going into debt, except in the event of war.

Finally, on April 22, Florida ratified the Constitution with a vote of 50 to 0. By this time fighting between the Union and the Confederacy had begun. By the end of June, North Carolina, Arkansas, and Virginia had joined the Confederacy. Tennessee adopted an ordinance of secession in May and placed the Confederate Constitution before the voters, who endorsed it in August by a vote of 85,753 to 30,863. Rump governments in Kentucky and Missouri also eventually endorsed the Confederate Constitution, but those states remained firmly in the Union throughout the war.

[*See also* Congress; Conscription; Dred Scott Decision; Fugitive Slave Law; Habeas Corpus; Judiciary; Montgomery Convention; Presidency; *and* State Rights.]

BIBLIOGRAPHY

Beringer, Richard E., Herman Hataway, Archer Jones, and William N. Still, Jr. *Why the South Lost the Civil War.* Athens, Ga. 1986.

Carpenter, Jesse T. *The South as a Conscious Minority: A Study in Political Thought.* New York, 1930.

Fehrebacher, Don. E. *Constitutions and Constitutionalism in the Slaveholding South.* Athens, Ga., 1989.

Finkelman, Paul. "Slavery and the Constitutional Convention of 1787: Making a Covenant with Death." In *Beyond Confederation.* Edited by Richard Beeman, Stephen Botein, and Edward C. Carter II. Chapel Hill, N.C., 1987.

Lee, Charles Robert, Jr. *The Confederate Constitutions.* Chapel Hill, N.C., 1963.

McCash, William B. *Thomas R. R. Cobb: The Making of a Southern Nationalist.* Macon, Ga., 1983.

Nieman, Donald. "Republicanism, the Confederate Constitution, and the American Constitutional Tradition." In *An Uncertain Tradition: Constitutionalism and the History of the South.* Edited by Kermit L. Hall and James W. Ely, Jr. Athens, Ga., 1989.

Owsley, Frank. *States Rights and the Confederacy.* Chicago, 1925. Reprint, Gloucester, Ma., 1961.

Thomas, Emory. *The Confederate Nation, 1861–1865.* New York, 1979.

PAUL FINKELMAN

CONSTITUTIONAL UNION PARTY

Comprising members of the old Whig and American parties, the Constitutional Union party organized for the presidential election of 1860. The party proposed to remove the slavery question from the political arena and adopted an ambiguous platform that supported the Constitution, the Union, and the enforcement of the laws of the United States.

In February 1860, thirty prominent leaders from among the old Whigs and Americans—including John J. Crittenden, William C. Rives, and Washington Hunt—issued an appeal to the American people, denouncing both the Democratic and the Republican parties and calling for the organization of a new party. Believing that the public was tired of slavery agitation, organizers of the Constitutional Union party felt they could relieve sectional strife by remaining silent on the slavery issue.

The first Constitutional Union National Convention was held at Baltimore in May 1860. Here party members nominated John Bell of Tennessee for president and Edward Everett of Massachusetts for vice president. Bell's conservatism on the slavery issue and his large slaveholdings made him an appealing candidate both to Northern moderates and to upper South Unionists. Also at the Baltimore convention, Constitutional Unionists declared all party issues secondary to preservation of the Union, and they denounced Breckinridge Democrats as disunionist conspirators.

As the November election approached, party members hoped that moderate Republicans, sensing defeat for their candidate, would vote for the Constitutional Union ticket to prevent a Democratic victory. Constitutional Unionists also thought that the division within the Democratic party between Stephen A. Douglas and John C. Breckinridge might convince Democrats that neither nominee would win and thus they would support John Bell in order to defeat Abraham Lincoln. Bell, however, received only 12.6 percent of the popular vote, carrying the three upper South states of Virginia, Kentucky, and Tennessee.

Throughout the secession winter of 1860–1861, Bell and other Constitutional Union party leaders urged Lincoln to adopt conciliatory measures toward the South. The outbreak of the Civil War ended all hopes of a peaceful reconciliation and signaled the demise of the Constitutional Union party.

[*See also* Whig Party.]

BIBLIOGRAPHY

Crofts, Daniel W. *Reluctant Confederates: Upper South Unionists in the Secession Crisis.* Chapel Hill, N.C., 1989.
Dumond, Dwight Lowell. *The Secession Movement, 1860–1861.* New York, 1931.
Parks, Joseph Howard. *John Bell of Tennessee.* Baton Rouge, La., 1950.

BRUCE W. EELMAN

CONTRABAND

From early modern times, the Western nations have elaborated increasingly detailed conventions of warfare governing persons and property. During the eighteenth century, the term *contraband of war* came into vogue to designate forbidden articles of commerce—chiefly arms and ammunition—that neutral nations might not furnish to belligerents in time of war. By the nineteenth century the term also applied to such articles captured from one belligerent by another. The Civil War stretched the meaning of the term in new and unforeseen directions.

The process began with the war scarcely a month old, when four escaped slaves forced the issue. The men had been impressed into service to build Confederate fortifica-

tions on Virginia's lower peninsula. They sought refuge at Fortress Monroe, the Union-held position at the tip of the peninsula, commanded by Gen. Benjamin F. Butler, a shrewd Massachusetts politician.

Prevailing Federal policy steadfastly supported the property rights of slaveholders, but Butler viewed that principle through the prism of his circumstances. Facing an array of slave-built earthworks, he had no doubt of the military usefulness of impressed slaves. If their masters considered them property, why could not the United States do the same, to deny the Confederacy the benefit of their labor and to turn it to the Union's advantage? On such a basis, he offered pro-

> **The North's designation of escaped and captured slaves as contraband of war caught the South on the horns of a dilemma.**

tection to the fugitives. Although at first he did not invoke the words *contraband of war,* the designation "contrabands" rapidly gained currency both in his command and throughout the North. In August 1861, Congress ratified the notion into law with the Confiscation Act, which authorized the seizure of all property (slaves included) used for belligerent purposes and freed the affected slaves.

Union soldiers lost no time putting the contrabands to work performing mundane camp chores. But during the spring and summer of 1862, as Union forces advanced into the Confederacy, the army required military laborers more than servants. Congress obliged first by prohibiting members of the armed forces from returning runaway slaves to their masters and second by passing a strengthened Confiscation Act and a new Militia Act, which freed the slaves of all disloyal persons and authorized the wholesale employment of former slaves in the Union war effort.

After President Abraham Lincoln issued the Emancipation Proclamation, the size of the contraband population soared. Concentrated mostly in the plantation regions of the Union-occupied South, it numbered several hundred thousand by the end of the war. Able-bodied men served as soldiers and military laborers; women were put to work as farm laborers under the direction of plantation lessees or army-appointed "superintendents of contrabands." Those incapable of labor took refuge at "contraband camps," where the army and Northern benevolent societies provided food, shelter, clothing, and other amenities. Such assistance provoked a wide-ranging debate over its economic and social implications, strains of which echoed into the twentieth century.

The North's designation of escaped and captured slaves as contraband of war caught the South on the horns of a dilemma. Neither politicians nor ideologues could find a means to undercut the contraband logic, except by continuing to sing the antebellum refrain that slaves loved their masters and had no desire to seek refuge with the Northerners. Although Confederate planners understood the importance of slave labor to their cause, they struggled in vain to halt the transformation of slaves into contrabands.

The popularity of the designation "contraband" arose largely from its wry play upon the contradictory nature of slaves as persons and property. Ironically, it also helped perpetuate an association of other-than-human attributes to the former slaves that lingered in the North as well as the South long after the dust of war had settled.

[*See also* African Americans in the Union Army; Confiscation, *article on* Federal Confiscation Acts.]

BIBLIOGRAPHY

Berlin, Ira, et al., eds. *Freedom: A Documentary History of Emancipation, 1861–1867.* 4 vols. to date. Cambridge, England, 1982–.
Butler, Benjamin F. *Private and Official Correspondence of Gen. Benjamin F. Butler during the Period of the Civil War.* Vol. 1. Norwood, Mass., 1917.
Gerteis, Louis S. *From Contraband to Freedman: Federal Policy toward Southern Blacks, 1861–1865.* Westport, Conn., 1973.
Quarles, Benjamin. *Lincoln and the Negro.* New York, 1962.

JOSEPH P. REIDY

COOK, PHILIP

COOK, PHILIP (1817–1894), politician and brigadier general. Cook was born in Twigg County, Georgia, on July 30, 1817. He attended Oglethorpe University near Milledgeville and graduated from the University of Virginia Law School in 1841. A state senator when war broke out, he enlisted as a private in the Macon County Volunteers, which became the Fourth Georgia Infantry. Initially the unit was assigned to Portsmouth, Virginia, where Cook was made adjutant. After the Seven Days' Battles near Richmond, during which he was wounded at Malvern Hill, he was commissioned a lieutenant colonel, and on November 1, 1862, following the Battle of Sharpsburg, he was commissioned colonel of the regiment. At Chancellorsville he was again wounded and took three months to recover. During this period he was elected to the Georgia state senate and served for forty days before rejoining the army for a short time. He returned to Georgia to serve out his senate term during the 1864 session.

Upon the death of Gen. George Pierce Doles at Bethesda Church, Colonel Cook was promoted to brigadier general, his commission bearing the date August 5, 1864. He participat-

ed in Gen. Jubal Early's Valley campaign and then joined Gen. Robert E. Lee's army at Petersburg. During the Battle of Fort Stedman on March 25, 1865, he was again wounded and taken to a hospital in Petersburg. Cook was captured when the city fell, and he was not paroled until July 30, 1865.

He returned to Americus, Georgia, where he practiced law until 1880. He served as a member of the constitutional convention of 1865, in Congress from 1873 to 1883, and as secretary of state of Georgia in 1890. He died in Atlanta on May 21, 1894, and is buried in Macon, Georgia.

BIBLIOGRAPHY

Derry, Joseph T. *Georgia.* Vol. 6 of *Confederate Military History.* Edited by Clement A. Evans. Atlanta, Ga., 1899. Vol. 7 of extended ed. Wilmington, N.C., 1987.
Johnson, Allen, ed. *Dictionary of American Biography.* Vol. 2. New York, 1964.
Warner, Ezra J. *Generals in Gray: Lives of the Confederate Commanders.* Baton Rouge, La., 1970.

CHRIS CALKINS

COOPERATIONISTS

Those politicians in the Deep South who opposed separate state action during the secession crisis of 1860 to 1861 were called cooperationists. Among their leaders were James H. Hammond of South Carolina, James L. Alcorn of Mississippi, Jeremiah Clemens and Benjamin Fitzpatrick of Alabama, and Herschel V. Johnson and Alexander H. Stephens of Georgia.

Despite their predominantly Democratic leadership, cooperationists were strongest in counties that had voted for the Constitutional Union party in 1860 and areas with few slaves, such as the mountains of northern Alabama and Georgia and the pine barrens of south central Georgia. Lacking a centralized organization, a coherent philosophy, or a coordinated strategy, cooperationists included genuine secessionists who believed that independence could best be achieved through cooperative action, conditional Unionists who opposed secession until a last effort at compromise had been made, and others who supported the cooperationist position primarily as a means of fending off radical action.

Demoralized by the secession of South Carolina in December 1860, the cooperationists nonetheless made strong showings in convention elections elsewhere in the Deep South, particularly in Alabama, Georgia, and Louisiana. Within the conventions they attempted to delay secession by sponsoring resolutions calling for a Southern convention and for a popular referendum on any secession ordinance. Ultimately, the cooperationists were unable to mount an effective challenge to the immediate secessionists. Indeed, as one state after another seceded from the Union, the secessionists turned the cooperative argument on its head by asserting that the only practical means of attaining a unified South was for the remaining slave states to join them in forming an independent Confederacy.

BIBLIOGRAPHY

Barney, William L. *The Secessionist Impulse: Alabama and Mississippi in 1860.* Princeton, 1974.

Johnson, Michael P. *Toward a Patriarchal Republic: The Secession of Georgia.* Baton Rouge, La., 1977.

Potter, David. *The Impending Crisis, 1848–1861.* New York, 1976.

Thornton, J. Mills, III. *Politics and Power in a Slave Society: Alabama, 1800–1860.* Baton Rouge, La., 1978.

Wooster, Ralph A. *The Secession Conventions of the South.* Princeton, 1962.

THOMAS E. JEFFREY

COPPERHEADS

The label was a smear term applied to Democratic critics of the Lincoln administration. Although many dictionaries still define "Copperhead" as "a Northern sympathizer with the South during the Civil War," some recent historians have characterized Democratic dissenters in the North more realistically, discrediting Radical Republican rhetoric and presenting the Copperheads simply as conservative and partisan critics.

Radical Republicans, led by Whitelaw Reid, the editor of the *Cincinnati Gazette,* sought to discredit Democratic dissenters in the upper Midwest by equating them with a poisonous snake that had a brown-blotched body and copper-colored head. After Democratic victories in the fall 1862 election, the Republicans intensified their smear campaign, invariably referring to the Democratic party as the Copperhead party and to its candidates as Copperheads. Some even referred to the conservative members of President Abraham Lincoln's cabinet as Copperheads.

Democratic dissent reached high tide during the first six months of 1863: in Indiana and Illinois the so-called Copperhead state legislatures feuded with their Republican governors; union military failures fostered a sense of defeat; many opposed Lincoln's emancipation measures; and widespread violations of civil rights (including the arbitrary arrest of Clement L. Vallandigham for alleged disloyalty on May 5, 1863) aroused resentment. Moreover, Federal conscription was highly unpopular in many quarters.

But Copperheadism, linked to the peace movement throughout the war, faded during the second half of the year as Union military victories at Gettysburg and Vicksburg lessened criticism of the Lincoln administration. Propeace Democratic gubernatorial candidates lost several election contests: Vallandigham in Ohio, George W. Woodward in Pennsylvania, and Thomas Seymour in Connecticut. The smear campaign was also instrumental in these defeats inasmuch as it discredited the Copperheads as pro-Southern and traitorous in their outlook.

Besides Vallandigham, Woodward, and Seymour, other well-known Copperheads included Samuel Medary (editor of the *Crisis* in Ohio), Wilbur F. Storey (editor of the *Chicago Times*), Dennis A. Mahony (editor of the *Dubuque Herald*), Daniel W. Voorhees (congressman from Indiana), Horatio Seymour (governor of New York), and Benjamin Wood (congressman and editor of the *New York Daily News*).

Radical Republicans, claiming that the Copperheads belonged to subversive secret societies, transformed three organizations into bogeymen in order to discredit the Democrats, influence elections, and serve as an excuse to organize Union Leagues (Republican-controlled secret patriotic societies). The three were Knights of the Golden Circle, Order of American Knights, and Sons of Liberty.

George W. L. Bickley, while residing in Cincinnati in 1859, had founded the Golden Circle as an agency to convert a part of northern Mexico into a personal fief and perhaps annex it to the United States. Early in the war he lived in Knoxville, Tennessee, where he tried to re-create the Golden Circle and work for the secession of Kentucky. Despite Republican contentions, not a single castle of the Knights of the Golden Circle existed north of the Ohio River during the war years.

The Order of American Knights, founded by Phineas C. Wright (a former resident of New Orleans) in St. Louis in early 1863, received considerable publicity in the Northern press during the last two years of the war. An "Occasional Address of the Supreme Commander" expressed an abhorrence of President Lincoln's "unconstitutional acts," including emancipation, and glorified state rights. Wright's incompetence and shabby reputation spelled failure for the largely paper-based organization. Col. John P. Sanderson, stationed in St. Louis, wrote "a grand exposè" of the O.A.K. in 1864. Sanderson imagined that the "traitorous organization" had half a million members in the upper Midwest, with Vallandigham as head of the Northern branch and Confederate General Sterling Price commanding the Southern branch. Sanderson's suppositions found their way into Judge Advocate General Joseph Holt's report on subversive societies, printed as political propaganda preceding the 1864 presidential election.

The Sons of Liberty, based in Indianapolis, was founded by Harrison H. Dodd in early 1864. "Its objective and purposes, " a Dodd-printed booklet stated, "are the maintenance of constitutional freedom and State's rights, as recognized and established by the founders of our republic." No known chapters existed outside of Indianapolis, yet Dodd convinced Vallandigham, at the time an exile in Canada, to accept the nominal headship of the Sons of Liberty. Dodd's actions regarding a New York–to–Indianapolis arms shipment and suggestion of "a revolution" gave Republican leaders the chance to devise a devastating exposé and make arrests that led to two Indianapolis-based treason trials and much adverse publicity for the Sons of Liberty. Some detectives manufactured suppositions that also linked the S.L. to the Camp Douglas conspiracy.

Some Confederate agents in Canada and officials in Richmond accepted the Republican political propaganda at face value and supposed that a northwestern Confederacy was a possibility. Gen. P. G. T. Beauregard, for example, wanted Southern governors to issue a joint statement urging the upper Midwest to set up its own confederacy, promising friendship and free use of the Mississippi River.

[*See also* Northwestern Conspiracy; Peace Movements.]

BIBLIOGRAPHY

Gray, Wood. *The Hidden Civil War: The Story of the Copperheads.* New York, 1942.
Klement, Frank L. *The Copperheads in the Middle West.* Chicago, 1960.
Klement, Frank L. *Dark Lanterns: Secret Political Societies, Conspiracies, and Treason Trials in the Civil War.* Baton Rouge, La., 1984.
Klement, Frank L. "Economic Aspects of Middle Western Copperheadism." *Historian* 14 (1951): 27–44.

FRANK L. KLEMENT

CORINTH, MISSISSIPPI

The battle fought on October 3 and 4, 1862, in Corinth was one of three engagements (Perryville and Sharpsburg were the others) that had as their result the blunting of the Confederates' great fall 1862 offensive. In the summer of 1862 Gen. Braxton Bragg, commanding the Army of Tennessee, shifted his army from northeastern Mississippi—the scene of its recent operations—to eastern Tennessee and Kentucky. When Bragg departed for his new field of activity, he left behind in Mississippi two independent Southern forces. One, commanded by Maj. Gen. Earl Van Dorn, consisted of some cavalry and a division of infantry under Maj. Gen. Mansfield Lovell. Its strength was about 7,000 men. The other force (some 17,000 men) was commanded by Maj. Gen. Sterling Price. It was made up of two divisions—one under Brig. Gen. Dabney H. Maury and the other under Brig. Gen. Louis Hèbert.

Van Dorn was the senior general, but he had no authority over Price unless their forces were united. Price, who loathed Van Dorn for personal reasons, had orders from Bragg to try to keep the Federals from sending troops from Mississippi to oppose Bragg in Tennessee. Van Dorn wanted to operate against the Northerners in western Tennessee.

At first ignoring Van Dorn, Price seized Iuka, Mississippi, on September 13. Several days of operations there forced him to withdraw to Ripley, where on the twenty-eighth he united with Van Dorn. Losses had reduced Southern strength to about 22,000, but Van Dorn decided to strike for Corinth—

> Speed . . . was the key to Confederate success. The Southerners had to overrun Corinth before even more Federals could be brought in.

an important rail center that the Confederates had to capture if they were to advance farther northward.

Corinth was defended by 23,000 Federals commanded by Maj. Gen. William S. Rosecrans. The force consisted of four divisions under Maj. Gen. Charles Hamilton and Brig. Gens. David Stanley, Thomas Davies, and Thomas McKean. Other Federal forces were not far off and could quickly be rushed to Rosecrans's aid. Speed, therefore, was the key to Confederate success. The Southerners had to overrun Corinth before even more Federals could be brought in to reinforce the defenders. As he advanced, Van Dorn feinted at several towns, hoping to prevent the Federals from learning his objective and to keep them divided as long as possible.

Believing that Rosecrans's defenses on the northwest side of Corinth were the weak point in the Union position, Van Dorn struck there on the morning of October 3. Had he been on the face of a clock, his army would have been deployed on a line curving around from 10 to 1. Lovell's division was on his right, Maury's in his center, and Hèbert's on his left. Rosecrans had three of his divisions formed on a corresponding line—McKean facing Lovell, Davies in front of Maury, and Hamilton opposing Hèbert. Stanley was in reserve.

Lovell led off the Confederate attack at 9:00 A.M. Van Dorn hoped that his onslaught would compel Rosecrans to shift troops from the right and center of the Union line. Then Maury and Hèbert would strike. Soon all of the Southern divisions were pushing forward. Throughout that "terrible hot day" the Confederates slowly drove Rosecrans's men two miles back toward the center of the line. Four separate times the Federals tried unsuccessfully to stay the Confederate advance. By 5:00 P.M. Rosecrans was pushed back to in the heavily fortified inner line of defenses.

Van Dorn was convinced that one more effort would bring complete victory. He soon found, however, that the Northerners were still full of fight, and his officers came to him with reports of heavy casualties, low supplies of ammunition, and exhausted, hungry, and thirsty men who could fight no more that day. Van Dorn suspended the attack. He would finish Rosecrans on the fourth.

During the night medical personnel sought to help those wounded in the day's battle. Supply officers distributed what ammunition they had. The men sought water, food, and what rest they could get. Meanwhile, the generals pondered what they should do to prepare for the renewed battle.

> **Corinth . . . featured inept generals leading a courageous rank and file.**

Rosecrans brought Stanley's division into his line between Davies and McKean. The new Federal position, curving around the center of the clock, was anchored on five small forts (called "batteries"), the most important of which was Battery Robinett, near the center of the Union line.

Van Dorn planned to attack early on October 4. At 7:00 A.M., several hours after the assault was to get underway, Hébert, who was to lead off the effort, reported that he was too sick to exercise command. Brig. Gen. Martin E. Green was quickly assigned to his place, but it took him until 10:00 A.M. to get the division launched into its advance. Lovell, meanwhile, did almost nothing. The bulk of fighting fell on Maury and Green.

Once the attack got underway it did not last long. Some of Green's men broke through the Federal line, but they ran short of ammunition and were driven back. Parts of Maury's division fought their way into the streets of Corinth itself and battled the Federals house to house. Meanwhile, the rest of Maury's charge shattered on the fortifications of Battery Robinett where, in fierce fighting, the Federals held. The Confederates who had gotten into the town fled or were killed or captured. Van Dorn, realizing that Union reinforcements were approaching and that continued efforts to take the town would result in the complete destruction of his army, decided to withdraw.

For several days the Northerners attempted a pursuit, but they too were nearing exhaustion. By October 11 the Confederates had reached the relative safety of Holly Springs. Within a few weeks both sides in Mississippi had shifted their attention to Vicksburg and the struggle for control of the Mississippi River.

Van Dorn reported his losses at Corinth and on the retreat at 594 men killed, 2,162 wounded, and 2,102 missing (many captured, some deserted). Rosecrans listed 315 killed, 1,812 wounded, and 232 captured or missing.

For the Confederates, Corinth, like so many of the war's western battles, featured inept generals leading a courageous rank and file. The combination of brave soldiers and weak command could not overcome the great courage of the Federal troops who were backed by superior resources and commanded by better generals.

BIBLIOGRAPHY

Castel, Albert. *General Sterling Price and the Civil War in the West.* Baton Rouge, La., 1968.

Cockrell, Monroe F., ed. *The Lost Account of the Battle of Corinth and the Court Martial of Gen. Van Dorn.* Jackson, Tenn., 1955.

Hartje, Robert G. *Van Dorn: The Life and Times of a Confederate General.* Nashville, Tenn., 1967.

Lamers, William M. *The Edge of Glory: A Biography of General William S. Rosecrans.* New York, 1961.

RICHARD M. MCMURRY

CORNERSTONE SPEECH

Delivered by Confederate vice president Alexander H. Stephens on the night of March 21, 1861, at the Athenaeum in Savannah, Georgia, this speech became notorious for its declaration that the Confederate government's "cornerstone" rested on the inequality of the races and the institution of black slavery.

Delivered extemporaneously, the speech began with praise for the "improvements" the Confederate Constitution had made on the older one, such as the banning of a protective tariff and federal financing of internal improvements. The Constitution also set the slavery question to rest forever, Stephens said, and during the long justification of the institution that followed he uttered the phrase that gave the speech its name. He went on to commend the breadth and wealth of the Confederacy and its wise and conservative Congress and expressed the belief that the new nation would soon be enlarged by the border states. The prospect of war had diminished, but the South, though desirous of peace with all, had to be ready to fight. He warned against factionalism in the South and praised its policy of free trade. If true to itself and its destiny, he concluded, the South would not fail.

The speech was widely reported. Thoughtful Southerners, including Jefferson Davis, deplored Stephens's emphasis on slavery rather than the politically advantageous theme of state versus national sovereignty. Northern reaction was uniformly hostile. The abolitionist press used the speech to demand harsh measures from Abraham Lincoln. The speech's value to the Union cause, one Northern paper later judged, was "incalculable."

BIBLIOGRAPHY

Avary, Myrta Lockett, ed. *Recollections of Alexander H. Stephens: His Diary Kept When a Prisoner at Fort Warren, Boston Harbor, 1865; Giving Incidents and Reflections of His Prison Life and Some Letters and Reminiscences.* New York, 1910.

Cleveland, Henry. *Alexander H. Stephens in Public and Private: With Letters and Speeches, Before, During, and Since the War.* Philadelphia, 1886.

Schott, Thomas E. *Alexander H. Stephens of Georgia: A Biography.* Baton Rouge, La., 1988.

THOMAS E. SCHOTT

COTTON

In 1858 Senator James Henry Hammond of South Carolina replied to Senator William H. Seward of New York:

> Without the firing of a gun, without drawing a sword, should they [Northerners] make war upon us [Southerners], we could bring the whole world to our feet. What would happen if no cotton was furnished for three years? . . . England would topple headlong and carry the whole civilized world with her. No, you dare not make war on cotton! No power on earth dares make war upon it. Cotton is King.

Hammond, like most white Southerners, believed that cotton ruled not just in the South but in the United States and the world. Many economists agreed. In 1855, David Christy entitled his influential book *Cotton Is King.* Cotton indeed drove the economy of the South, affected its social structure, and, during the Civil War, dominated international relations of the Confederacy through "cotton diplomacy."

Cotton in the Antebellum Period

In the early eighteenth century, long-staple cotton was grown in Georgia and on the Sea Islands of South Carolina, but it depleted the soil and proved unprofitable to market. The intensive and laborious hand method of picking out cotton seeds severely restricted the amount of cotton that could be prepared for making into cloth. Cotton could not compete with rice and indigo for commercialization, and Southern colonialists experimented with the crop primarily for domestic use. Despite some increased cotton production during a tobacco depression between 1702 and 1706, few attempted to produce cotton commercially before the Revolutionary War.

Extensive production of cotton awaited the advent of Eli Whitney's cotton gin in the spring of 1793. To separate the seed from the cotton, gins first used spikes placed on rollers and then saws. The influence of the gin was instantaneous; soon Southern mechanics set up gins as far west as Mississippi. By 1804 the cotton crop was eight times greater than it had been the previous decade. The cotton gin made practical the use of the heavily seeded short-staple cotton, which could be grown in upland areas more readily than long-staple cotton. An increase in market demand growing out of England's textile industry ensured favorable prices and spurred the ascension of the short-staple cotton industry.

Cultivation of cotton, on both small and large farms, utilized relatively simple methods. Hoe ridge cultivation was developed after 1800 with ridges set apart about three to six feet, depending on the fertility of the land. After 1830 farmers used V-shaped harrows, which were converted into cultivators, side harrows, and double shovels. (Harrows raked soil with metal teeth to remove debris and smoothed out and leveled the soil once broken; cultivators turned the soil under; shovels were used as more traditional plows and also turned the soil over while digging deep furrows.) Cultivation procedures changed little throughout the nineteenth century. A bed for the cotton had to be prepared by clearing out the old stalks from the previous crop. Sometimes these stalks were beaten down with clubs, but if they were large (four to five feet), they had to be pulled by hand. Manure or commercial fertilizer was placed as deeply as possible in the furrow. Usually the cotton bed was built up in February and March. The actual planting of the cotton seed in most areas was in April: early planters risked frost; late planters risked dry spells. Planting was done by hand. In about a month, the plants were thinned. The crop was cultivated with a sweep plowed between the rows four or five times and hoed by hand three or four times. In the middle of June, when they were anywhere from six inches to a foot high, the cotton plants bloomed. Around the last of July or first of August, forty-two to forty-five days after they had blossomed, the cotton bolls opened. Picking usually began about August 20. Most of the crop was ginned immediately after picking.

Cotton prices fluctuated wildly over the years. Prices were high until 1819, then down, up, and down again. In 1837 they hit a crisis low and remained rather low until 1848. Prices rose sharply in 1849 and 1850 but dropped in 1851, though not as low as previously. Throughout the remainder of the 1850s prices rose.

The average amount of seed cotton used to make a 400-pound bale of lint ranged from about 1,200 to 1,400 pounds. The bales had to be transported from the gins to a local market and then on to larger markets. Cotton was shipped to market continually from September through January. Wagons loaded with bales of cotton often lined roads. The moving of cotton demanded better roadbeds, sometimes even plank roads, near market towns. River transportation to seaports was common from market towns located on rivers or canals. Major cities grew up at railroad stations as rail lines began to link the hinterland to ports and then to the Northeast and Midwest.

Improvements in the production and transportation of cotton and the new demand for the fiber led to a scramble for greater profits. To reap the most profits and to provide the labor needed for cotton picking, a large number of slaves were imported into South Carolina and Georgia, and slave labor became a valuable market throughout the South. The way into the Southern aristocracy was through the ownership of land and slaves, and the way to get land and slaves was to grow cotton: the crop provided the cash and credit to buy both. At this time, too, the cotton kingdom pushed ever westward with planters searching for new and richer soils to grow more white cotton with the labor of more black slaves. Ironically, just as abolitionist sentiment was increasing in the United States, the invention of the cotton gin instigated a deeper entrenchment of slavery into the Southern economy and society.

The Southern aristocracy, which slavery created, dominated Southern society and inhibited the development of efficient methods for soil use. In the face of soil exhaustion, Southern planters needed to extend control into the fresh lands of the western territories. Hence, territorial expansion became a sectional issue as both North and South realized that western lands were essential for the survival of Southern slave culture.

Most discussions of cotton dwell on the short period when cotton did rule as king. This "mature" period of cotton and slavery was not necessarily typical of or relevant to the earlier periods of plantation agriculture that accompanied the emergence of cotton monoculture. Discussions also tend to treat the South as one unit rather than the large and varied region it was. The cotton kingdom extended west through Texas and north about six hundred miles up the Mississippi River valley.

Antebellum history often seems dominated by scenes of plantations worked by slaves. Although thousands of large plantations employed slave labor and produced most of the South's cotton, numerically there were more small farmers, mostly whites, who cultivated the upland areas. Many of these yeomen were subsistence farmers and produced only a surplus of cotton for market. Southern farmers who did not grow cotton sold some of their foodstuff to the planters. Cotton could bring prosperity or depression, according to changes in the market, and these fluctuations meant very differing experiences for whites, slaves, and antebellum free blacks of each different region of the South.

When at its peak, the demanding cultivation and transportation of cotton required the labor of the majority of men, women, and children in the rural South. Most Southern life was regulated by the agricultural economy, and more and more over time, this came to mean the cotton economy. Although free workers and slaves pursued a diversity of agricultural and industrial occupations in the antebellum South, by 1850 the routine of taking care of the white-blossomed, white-bolled short-staple cotton plants increasingly typified rural Southern existence.

By 1860, cotton ruled the South, which annually exported two-thirds of the world supply of the "white gold." Cotton ruled the West and Midwest because each year these sections sold $30 million worth of food supplies to Southern cotton producers. Cotton ruled the Northeast because the domestic textile industry there produced $100 million worth of cloth each year. In addition, the North sold to the cotton-growing South more than $150 million worth of manufactured goods every year, and Northern ships transported cotton and cotton products worldwide.

Cotton in the Confederacy

As the U.S. cotton industry developed, other countries became more dependent on cotton produced in the American South. The power of cotton allowed the Confederacy to employ cotton diplomacy as its foundation for foreign relations during the Civil War; Southerners attempted to use cotton to pressure countries such as England and France into the war on behalf of the Confederacy. Southern leaders were convinced that the key to their success lay in gaining international recognition and help from European powers in breaking the blockade that the Union had thrown up around coastal areas and ports and that was increasingly effective as the war went on. (Although the Union blockade never thoroughly sealed the Confederate coastline, it was successful in causing Southern imports and exports to drop drastically at a time when the Confederacy needed to fund its huge war efforts.)

Southerners saw cotton as the great leverage in this effort, and at the time this made sense. More than three-fourths of the cotton used in the textile industries of England and France came from the American South. Between a fifth and a fourth of the English population depended in some way on the textile industry, and half of the export trade of England was in cotton textiles. About a tenth of the nation's wealth was also invested in the cotton business. The English Board of Trade said in 1859 that India was completely inadequate as a source of raw cotton; England apparently was dependent on the American South for cotton. This concept of King Cotton led many Southerners to believe that England and France would have to intervene in the Civil War in order to save their own economies. The Confederacy began applying pressure on the neutral powers through a voluntary embargo of cotton. Although Congress never formally established the embargo, local "committees of public safety" prevented the shipping of cotton from Southern ports.

To exploit their leverage, the Confederate States sent William Lowndes Yancey, Pierre A. Rost, and A. Dudley Mann to England in the spring of 1861 to confer with Lord Russell, the British foreign secretary. As a result, the British and French granted the Confederacy belligerency status. It was a small victory, probably not very effective in helping the Confederacy. The cotton diplomats failed to arrange with England a denunciation of the blockade or the negotiation of a commercial agreement, let alone diplomatic recognition of the Confederacy.

Regardless of wishful beliefs and England's real economic dependence on cotton, at the time of the outbreak of the Civil War an overabundance of cotton existed in Europe.

> **In the face of soil exhaustion, Southern planters needed to extend control into the fresh lands of the western territories.**

Furthermore, British hostility to slavery decreased the likelihood of intervention. Moreover, it was not in the vested interests of the neutral powers, particularly Great Britain, to denounce the blockade. The Confederate government attempted to convince the Europeans that the Federal blockade was ineffective and thus illegal under the terms of the 1856 Treaty of Paris. The Confederacy failed to acknowledge that Great Britain, as the world's foremost naval power, would desire to let stand any blockade, regardless of its legality or actual effectiveness. And to make matters even worse, the South's voluntary embargo undercut its own argument that the Federal blockade was porous.

Although the South never succeeded in convincing foreign powers to intervene against the North, cotton diplomacy was successful in obtaining financial help from abroad. This came in the form of loans and bonds, which Confederate Treasurer Christopher G. Memminger guaranteed with cotton. The Confederate Treasury Department issued $1.5 million in cotton certificates during the war for acquisitions abroad. One such loan backed by cotton was the Erlanger loan, signed on October 28, 1862, and modified on January 3, 1863. This loan, amounting to $15 million, was secured by cotton. At the time cotton was worth twenty-four pence a pound, and the Erlanger loan made cotton available to holders at six pence per pound.

This reliance on cotton for the security of loans, bonds, and certificates placed a great deal of responsibility on the Produce Loan Office, whose agents had to ensure that planters would fulfill government subscriptions of cotton at a time when many planters were unwilling to sell to the government. Ultimately, however, cotton enabled the Confederacy to realize $7,678,591.25 in foreign exchange.

The Confederacy also hoped to raise tax revenue on the sale of cotton abroad. On February 28, 1861, Congress passed an act levying an export duty of $\frac{1}{8}$ of a cent per pound on all cotton shipped after August 1 of that year. The government hoped to raise $20 million through the export tax in order to pay a $15 million loan funded by an issue of 8 percent bonds. But because of the tightening blockade and the South's own voluntary cotton embargo, the measure raised only $30,000. When the secretary of the treasury lobbied to have this minuscule tax raised, opposition from the planter class kept Congress from increasing it, even when the Confederacy's finances were desperate.

To a degree, planter opposition also undercut Southern efforts to shift from cotton production to the planting of foodstuffs. The Confederacy was convinced it could become self-sufficient. It would produce all the food and cotton it needed, and revenue from cotton could buy weapons, blankets, and other manufactured goods until the Confederacy started manufacturing its own. Planters believed that the yeomen and poor would fight in the army and that slaves would continue to produce food and the South's greatest weapon, cotton.

By the spring of 1862, however, there was already an abundance of cotton and a shortage of foodstuffs. In April 1862 yeomen soldiers could not go home to plant spring crops, and their families would again have no food. To encourage the growth of foodstuffs, every Southern cotton-producing state attempted to limit the amount of cotton that could be grown. State governors issued proclamations urging planters to reduce their cotton acreage by as much as four-fifths and encouraging them to plant enough wheat, corn, and beans to feed themselves, their slaves, the armies in the field. The planters responded, cutting their usual acreage of cotton to about half and devoting the rest to food crops. Many planters even had enough surplus foodstuffs to sell to the families of the yeoman poor whose husbands and sons were away in the war. Still, the planters did not reduce their cotton production as much as the state and Confederate governments wanted. Some scholars argue that this is an example of how the Confederacy contributed to its own defeat by refusing to disturb the interests of the planter class.

But even with resistance by the planters, the shift to the production of foodstuffs combined with the drain in manpower and the eventual Union occupation created a drastic drop in cotton production as the war dragged on: 4.5 million bales were grown in 1861; 1.5 million in 1862; 500,000 in 1863; and only 300,000 in 1864. As production dropped, the price of cotton skyrocketed on the world market, and blockade runners decided the risks were worth taking; cotton-exporting corporations formed throughout the cotton kingdom. In addition, Mexico traded cotton directly across the Texas border.

In an attempt to control the flow of cotton to Europe and rectify the declining economy, Southern politicians in late 1863 introduced an approach called the "New Plan." Through this series of administrative actions and congressional laws, the Confederate government became directly involved in blockade running. Rather than making contracts for supplies payable in cotton, the government itself began selling the cotton abroad and buying supplies with the proceeds, thereby cutting out the middlemen. The plan's supervisor, Colin J. McRae, gained direct control over cargo space on blockade runners. Those who refused to accept a fair rate to transport cotton for sale by the government would have their vessels confiscated. The War Department increasingly turned to the sale of cotton to purchase needed supplies, and by the end of 1863 it had reserved fully one-third of all cargo space on blockade runners.

As a result of these measures and other financial consolidations under the plan, Confederate foreign financing was greatly improved and 27,229 bales of cotton were exported for $5.3 million in sales. But because of the Confederacy's early confidence in the diplomatic leverage of King Cotton, it did not institute measures such as the New Plan soon enough to make a considerable impact on the war effort. The South could not keep its vital ports open or continue to endure Northern attacks on the battlefield.

If the Confederate government was able, albeit partially and belatedly, to gain control over the cotton trade with Europe, it had much less success in curtailing the cotton trade with the Union. On May 21, 1861, the Confederate Congress prohibited the sale of cotton to the North. Yet an illicit trade across military lines flourished between Southern cotton farmers and Northern traders. President Abraham Lincoln gave licenses to traders, who followed the Union army into the South. On March 17, 1862, the Confederacy gave state governments the right to destroy any cotton that might fall into the hands of the Union army. Some devoted Confederates burned their own cotton to keep it out of enemy hands. Other Southerners, however, discovered that Union agents were willing to pay the highest prices in over half a century for cotton or offered badly needed supplies as barter. Ironically, valuable currency for cotton from the North saved some small Southern farmers from starvation. But this selling of cotton to the North undermined Confederate nationalism, as did the official Confederate trading of cotton with the North conducted in the last years of the war.

As the price of foodstuffs reached astronomical heights and Confederate currency became worthless with inflation, the smuggling of cotton out of the South to the North increased. Women whose husbands had been killed or were away at the battlefield or in prison were heavily involved in forming these caravans. Rich planters and factors also made large deals with Federal officials. The situation became totally absurd when cotton was sold to Federal troops to get supplies for the Confederate army. Even President Lincoln approved an arrangement to send food for Robert E. Lee's troops at Petersburg in exchange for cotton for New York. Ulysses S. Grant stopped this exchange because he was attempting to cut off Lee's supplies, but other such exchanges occurred throughout the Civil War.

Some scholars have written with hindsight that the Confederacy might have been more successful, had it pursued a different strategy with its cotton. If Confederate leaders had confiscated all the cotton in the South and stored it, they could have used it as a basis to obtain credit from European nations. With credit, some scholars believe, the Confederacy could have bought a navy strong enough to break the Union blockade. Others argue that the Confederate government would have been better served if it had made cotton, not gold, the basis of its currency.

Although the Civil War ended the slave plantation system, it did not end the South's legacy of cotton. Cultivation of the crop had worn out much of the land. Many planted up and down on slopes, which then eroded. The concentration on cotton production meant complete reliance on a one-crop system; crop rotation was uncommon and farmers did not plow under clover or peas to restore humus to the soil. Diminishing fertility of cotton lands was a major problem farmers continued to face after the Civil War.

[See also Blockade, overview article; Diplomacy; Erlanger Loan; Expansionism in the Antebellum South; Farming; New Plan; Plantation; Produce Loan; Slavery; Urbanization.]

BIBLIOGRAPHY

Ball, Douglas. *Financial Failure and Confederate Defeat*. Urbana, Ill., 1991.

Burton, Orville Vernon. *In My Father's House Are Many Mansions: Family and Community in Edgefield, South Carolina*. Chapel Hill, N.C., 1985.

Gates, Paul. *The Farmer's Age: Agriculture, 1815–1860*. New York, 1960.

Gray, Lewis Cecil. *History of Agriculture in the United States to 1860*. 2 vols. Washington, D.C., 1932.

Hilliard, Sam Bowers. *Atlas of Antebellum Southern Agriculture*. Baton Rouge, La., 1984.

Owsley, Frank L. *King Cotton Diplomacy*. 2d ed. Chicago, 1959.

Powell, Lawrence, and Michael Wayne. "Self-Interest and the Decline of Confederate Nationalism." In *The Old South in the Crucible of War*. Edited by Harry P. Owens and James J. Cook. University, Miss., 1983.

Ramsdell, Charles W. *Behind the Lines in the Southern Confederacy*. Baton Rouge, La., 1944.

Todd, Richard Cecil. *Confederate Finance*. Athens, Ga., 1954.

Woodman, Harold D. *King Cotton and His Retainers*. Lexington, Ky., 1968.

ORVILLE VERNON BURTON and
PATRICIA DORA BONNIN

CRIME AND PUNISHMENT

The patterns of crime and punishment that emerged during the years of the Confederacy were unique partly because of the South's distinctive past and partly because of the inevitable disruptions of a wartime society. Before the Civil War, whites were most frequently prosecuted for crimes of violence, a pattern grounded in the belief that white crime was motivated not by evil but by passion. Assault, dueling, and carrying a concealed weapon were all common offenses during the antebellum years. So too were horse theft and counterfeiting, two offenses that clearly threatened the economic order and that most likely resulted from greed rather than need.

During wartime many of the customary rules of order ceased to apply, a fact that had a major impact on the nature and extent of unlawful behavior. As the relatively orderly society of the antebellum era began to disintegrate, so did traditional legal processes. Lacking any systematic record of crime statistics, historians must piece together information from contemporary accounts and from legislation enacted by Confederate states to deal with criminal activity. Taken together, this evidence leaves the impression that criminal behavior was on the rise as Confederate fortunes declined. Beginning in 1862, as the Confederacy experienced greater casualties and military defeats, particularly in the West, more sacrifice was demanded at home. At first the rural areas paid the heavy price of war, but by 1863 urban areas were facing serious food shortages. These developments, coupled with high inflation, heavier taxation, conscription laws, and poor transportation, created a fertile atmosphere for increased crime.

There is no better evidence for intensified unlawful behavior than Confederate legislation and various local ordinances that imposed martial law and authorized the government to suspend fundamental civil rights. Such efforts, however, proved ineffective as the war advanced. When local courts charged with enforcing the criminal law were disrupted, law enforcement became impossible. In areas where invasion seemed imminent, state legislatures authorized the courts to move to safer locations. But these moves did not solve the problem of court personnel—clerks, attorneys, witnesses, defendants—being absent because of wartime responsibilities. Some states tried to keep the courts in business by allowing men over the age of sixty to serve as jurors and clerks to serve as attorneys. States such as Alabama and Mississippi authorized the continuance of cases when key participants were away at war. Such efforts, however, were apparently insufficient.

During the last years of the Confederacy, governments resorted to the military to maintain law and order, but the military itself could do little. In fact, contemporary observers in states such as Virginia, North Carolina, and Louisiana complained about defense units in local communities themselves engaging in crime.

Early in the war the Confederacy turned its attention to slave resistance. To be sure, the presence of slavery posed special problems for white wartime society. Although black labor aided the war effort, at the same time the Confederacy witnessed an increase in theft, malingering, resistance, and running away among slaves. The fragile mechanisms of law enforcement during the war led to a much greater incidence, in particular, of theft. In Savannah near the end of the war, for example, more than half the arrests made by police were of slaves, whereas the prewar figure had been less than 20 percent. Since police power by this time was so diminished, the actual incidence of slave crime was probably much greater. In wartime Tennessee, theft by slaves grew as the institution itself began to fall apart. African Americans especially sought horses and mules for easy sale.

Confederate states responded by strengthening slave codes. In 1861, Florida put the militia on patrol duty, requiring weekly rounds. In other states, special slave patrols were created by county courts or justices of the peace, authorized to act more often and to impose stiffer penalties for neglect of duty. As slave crime became an increasing concern of the Confederacy, punishments were made more severe. Regulations were tightened on the sale of whiskey to slaves, and some states made arson, larceny, and burglary subject to much harsher penalties.

Although the data is scarce, unlawful behavior among whites was probably greater than among slaves. One Arkansas observer noted in 1861 that there are "more dangers from bad white men among us than from the poor slaves." Offenses committed by whites included property crimes (such as theft, arson, animal stealing, and counterfeiting), crimes of violence (assault, riot, rape, murder, poi-

> Although black labor aided the war effort, at the same time the Confederacy witnessed an increase in theft . . . and running away among slaves.

soning), and crimes against morality (gambling, drinking, breaking the Sabbath).

One of the most vexing offenses of the Confederate years was theft, clearly on the rise because of wartime shortages. Planter complaints in the records blamed the "lower classes," but the poor were severely deprived and believed that the wealthy were not suffering at all. In one western Georgia county, more than one hundred people were prosecuted for theft from 1861 to 1865, whereas very few suspected thieves had been brought to court before the war. Suspects were also prosecuted in groups, a fact that reflects the unlawful activity of gangs of deserters or draft evaders. Banditry was very rare in the antebellum years, but common in the Confederacy. These dangerous groups of men, sometimes teenagers, had only one objective—plunder—which they might commit murder to achieve. There was little lawful response to their actions, especially in areas where conscription had depleted the male population, except for defensive efforts by communities themselves.

Other crimes on the rise during the Confederacy were counterfeiting, made a capital crime; prostitution, particularly at winter encampments; murder, often associated with matters of loyalty; and carrying concealed weapons. Confronted by alarming food shortages and by increased efforts to distill grain into more profitable alcohol, state legislatures enacted

> ... the poor were severely deprived and believed that the wealthy were not suffering at all.

stiff penalties for distillers, but such laws could not be effectively enforced.

Records from individual states all point to increases in crime and the inability to control it. Georgia, for example, experienced a substantial rise in property and misdemeanor offenses during the war years. In North Carolina, slave owner Jonathan Worth noted with dismay that "theft, robbery, and almost every other crime are common in almost all the rural districts." By 1865, anarchy seemed to prevail in two Piedmont counties as judges refused to hold court. Rural areas of Tennessee were populated by gangs that apparently operated without restraint. Newspapers from the state leave the impression that property crime was widespread. Evidence from Virginia reveals many cases of gambling, theft, and robbery-related murders. In 1862, the Richmond city council must have been responding to increased crime when it made a request for more jails, although studies show that lawbreakers faced few penalties. The Confederacy generally prescribed harsh punishments to deter rising crime. In South Carolina, for example, arson was made a capital offense. A horse thief in Alabama faced the gallows. In Arkansas, the death penalty was meted out to those convicted of such offenses as slave stealing, forgery, perjury, incest, and kidnapping.

Clearly, the disruption and deprivation of war, particularly as 1865 approached, led to increased criminal activity across the South. As the records show, however, with their attention and resources focused on the war, there was little that Confederate governments could do to enforce laws or to capture and punish offenders.

[*See also* Bread Riots; Civil Liberties; Counterfeiting; Desertion; Dueling; Habeas Corpus; Military Justice; Prostitution.]

<hr>

BIBLIOGRAPHY

Ash, Stephen V. *Middle Tennessee Society Transformed, 1860–1870*. Baton Rouge, La., 1988.

Ayers, Edward L. *Vengeance and Justice: Crime and Punishment in the 19th-Century American South*. New York, 1984.

Escott, Paul D. *Many Excellent People: Power and Privilege in North Carolina, 1850–1900*. Chapel Hill, N.C., 1985.

Ramsdell W., Charles. *Behind the Lines in the Confederacy*. Baton Rouge, La., 1944.

Ringold, May Spencer. *The Role of the State Legislatures in the Confederacy*. Athens, Ga., 1966.

DONNA J. SPINDEL

CRITTENDEN COMPROMISE

In December 1860, Kentucky senator John J. Crittenden proposed a comprehensive set of resolutions designed to avert secession and war. These resolutions became known as the Crittenden Compromise following their December 18 referral to the Senate Committee of Thirteen, a special committee set up to review methods for diffusing the sectional crisis.

Crittenden, nationally known for his past compromising efforts, offered the South protection by giving slavery in the slave states a permanent constitutional status while simultaneously allaying Northern fears of unchecked slave expansion. The Crittenden Compromise comprised six unamendable constitutional amendments: the first and most important restored and extended the old Missouri Compromise line by protecting slavery south of 36°30′ but prohibiting the institution north of the line, and citizens in territories were to decide for themselves whether new states would enter the Union free or slave; the second amendment prohibited Congress from abolishing slavery on government property in slave states; the third forbade the abolition of slavery in the District of Columbia unless it was abolished in both Maryland and Virginia, and not then without consent of the inhabitants or compensation to the owners; the fourth protected interstate transportation of slaves; the fifth compensated claimants of fugitive slaves rescued by mobs; and the sixth prohibited future constitutional amendments that would overturn these guarantees.

Initially, it appeared as if these resolutions had a real chance for passage. Upper South Unionists embraced the Crittenden Compromise as the only hope of avoiding secessionist victory in their states. Many in the Republican ranks were also sympathetic to conciliatory measures. President-elect Abraham Lincoln, however, made it clear that he would not waver on his commitment to contain slavery where it already existed. Although Lincoln was agreeable to some of the resolutions, his opposition to the restoration of the 36°30´ line made passage of the compromise impossible.

Following its failure in the Committee of Thirteen, Crittenden brought his compromise directly before the Senate on January 3, 1861, and called for a national plebiscite on the resolutions, arguing that the American people supported the compromise. On January 16, however, the Senate voted down Crittenden's appeal 25–23. The failure of the Crittenden Compromise ended any hope of halting the secession movement by congressional action. Lincoln's opposition to the compromise was a major setback to Southern Unionism.

BIBLIOGRAPHY

Crofts, Daniel W. *Reluctant Confederates: Upper South Unionists in the Secession Crisis.* Chapel Hill, N.C., 1989.
Kirwan, Albert D. *John J. Crittenden: The Struggle for the Union.* Lexington, Ky., 1962.
Potter, David M. *Lincoln and His Party in the Secession Crisis.* New Haven, Conn., 1942.

BRUCE W. EELMAN

CROSS KEYS AND PORT REPUBLIC, VIRGINIA

These tiny villages in the central Shenandoah Valley were the scene of consecutive victories by Thomas J. ("Stonewall") Jackson's army on June 8 and 9, 1862, which climaxed his Valley campaign. During the first week of June, Jackson retreated steadily southward up the valley on the west side of fifty-mile-long Massanutten Mountain. Federals under Gen. John C. Frèmont followed on his heels, while another enemy force under Gen. James Shields hurried southward on a parallel route east of the Massanutten. By June 4 Jackson had focused his intentions on the vicinity of Port Republic, south of the southern tip of the mountain and at the confluence of two rivers that formed the south fork of the Shenandoah River. There the ground would offer him the chance to face first one and then the other of his pursuers.

When Jackson turned southeast off the Valley Pike toward Port Republic, Northern cavalry assailed his rear guard near Harrisonburg on June 6. The Confederates repulsed the thrust, but the army's cavalry chieftain, Turner Ashby, was killed in the skirmish. At dawn on Sunday, June 8, Jackson had part of his army encamped on high ground across the river from Port Republic. Gen. Richard S. Ewell commanded a Confederate force that remained about four miles north of Port Republic on the Harrisonburg Road, around the Cross Keys settlement. Early on the eighth a small Union cavalry

detachment burst into Port Republic and nearly cornered Jackson in his headquarters on the southern edge of town. Three of his staff members fell into enemy hands. A handful of Confederates stalled the cavalry raiders long enough for friendly infantry to hurry to the rescue.

Meanwhile Frèmont approached Ewell's position and began a series of attacks that accomplished nothing. Ewell had spread four brigades across the crest of a long curving ridge rising from the south bank of Mill Creek. Strong artillery clusters guarded his line, especially on its left and center. Hours of artillery exchanges punctuated by an occasional brief Union infantry assault produced no results of consequence except casualties. The hottest fighting at Cross Keys developed on the Confederate right, where Ewell's feisty subordinate, Brig. Gen. Isaac Trimble, took the initiative. When the Eighth New York approached to point-blank range, Trimble unleashed the deadly fire of about a thousand muskets. The Eighth New York suffered in a few minutes about one-third of the total loss among the more than two dozen regiments in Frèmont's army. Trimble then surged forward onto Frèmont's left flank and curled it up. Acting under Jackson's general orders, Ewell rejected repeated pleas by Trimble for a further advance. When darkness closed the fighting, the Federals had lost nearly 700 men from a strength of 12,000, and Ewell had lost about 300 from his 5,000.

During the night of June 8–9, Jackson hurriedly cobbled together an awkward bridge over one of the rivers at Port Republic. He moved his army across it and northeast of the village early on the ninth in the overly ambitious hope that he could defeat Shields's advance guard there and then turn and go after Frèmont again. The Federals waiting on the river plain below Port Republic numbered no more than 4,000, but they enjoyed the cover of a farm lane perpendicular to Jackson's line of advance. More important, they had the use of a clearing atop a finger of the Blue Ridge that reached down toward the main road. Artillery atop that ridge at the Lewis family's "coaling," or charcoal manufactory, dominated the plain and decimated Jackson's troops. For a time Jackson pushed forward just two regiments of his old brigade, together with some badly outmatched guns. His first attempts to get above the dominant Federal artillery pieces and drive them away failed miserably. As some of Ewell's troops began to arrive from Cross Keys in time to stabilize the bad situation near the river, Gen. Richard Taylor's Louisiana brigade scrambled through the densely thicketed mountainside toward the guns. The crisis of the battle came when the Louisiana men stormed into the coaling for a hand-to-hand fight over the artillery. After seemingly endless minutes of intensely violent personal encounters, the Federals regained the ground. Taylor finally secured the coaling and assured Jackson of victory. The much smaller Federal force broke and ran northward, having stood up stoutly to three times their numbers. Jackson lost more than eight hundred men. During the rout that followed Taylor's success atop the coaling, the Confederates gathered up hundreds of prisoners, who brought the otherwise moderate Federal loss to slightly more than one thousand casualties.

Stonewall Jackson's double victory at Cross Keys and Port Republic put the crowning touch on his spectacular three-month Shenandoah Valley campaign. The two battles forced the pursuing Federals to retire out of range, giving Jackson the opportunity to succor his weary army unhindered in the bountiful valley for a week. Then, free from the threat posed earlier by Frèmont and Shields, Jackson and his army headed across the mountains toward Richmond. There they joined with Gen. Robert E. Lee and the Army of Northern Virginia to drive away the Federal army besieging the Confederate capital.

BIBLIOGRAPHY

Allan, William. *History of the Campaign of Gen. T. J. (Stonewall) Jackson in the Shenandoah Valley of Virginia.* Philadelphia, 1880.
Kelly, Henry Brooke. *Port Republic.* Philadelphia, 1886.
Tanner, Robert G. *Stonewall in the Valley.* Garden City, N.Y., 1976.
Taylor, Richard. *Destruction and Reconstruction.* New York, 1879.

ROBERT K. KRICK

CUBA

The jewel of Spain's remaining colonial empire, Cuba was of great interest to the Confederacy as a market for its cotton in exchange for durable goods. With a population of 1,396,530 (1,015,977 free, the majority of whom were white, of Spanish origin; 370,553 slave), Cuba was also of concern to the Union, which saw it as a source of support for the Southerners.

Spain maintained an official policy of neutrality during the Civil War but did not honor the Union blockade of the South until 1863 when it proved effective. In the first eighteen months of the war the South traded cotton in Havana for clothing, food, shoes, medicine, and other durable goods. Cuba was also the point of departure for Southern diplomats bound for Europe.

The Union seized dozens of blockade runners in Cuban waters, which created diplomatic tensions between Spain and the United States. The Cuban colonial government tolerated some economic relations with the South until it became obvious that the Confederacy would lose the war. In the early months of the war it was not uncommon to see dozens of Confederate ships in Havana Harbor. By the fall of 1863 that no longer was the case.

The Civil War led to an increase in abolitionism on the island following the end of hostilities on the North American continent. The threat of annexation to the United States, a long-standing source of tension between the United States and Cuba, declined during the early 1860s. Cuba, however, had little effect on the Civil War.

BIBLIOGRAPHY

Cortada, James W. *Spain and the American Civil War: Relations at Mid-Century, 1855–1868.* Philadelphia, 1980.
Thomas, Hugh. *Cuba: The Pursuit of Freedom.* New York, 1971.

JAMES W. CORTADA

CURRENCY

[*This entry is composed of three articles that discuss Confederate monetary policy, legislation to enact this policy, and the notes and coins that were issued in the Confederacy:* An Overview; Congressional Money Bills; *and* Numismatics. *For further discussion of the Confederate monetary system, see* Bonds; Inflation; Shinplasters; Treasury Department.]

An Overview

On November 1, 1860, just before the election of Abraham Lincoln, the currency of the eleven states that formed the Confederacy consisted of approximately $63 million of gold, silver, and copper coins together with about $85 million of notes put out by 144 state-chartered banks (some with branches) that existed in eight states. Three states—Arkansas, Mississippi, and Texas—had no banks.

The election of Lincoln caused a run on the banks, which, with the exception of those in Louisiana and a few in Alabama, promptly suspended the payment of coin on their notes and deposits. Gold and silver coins were immediately hoarded, and although the Confederacy took possession of three U.S. mints, for all practical purposes it never issued any coins of its own.

Since the banks were, for the most part, prohibited by state law from issuing notes under the denomination of $5, there was no means of effecting small transactions. Various state governments required that the banks issue low-denomination notes, including notes under a dollar. State bank note issues increased to approximately $125 million by 1865.

The state governments were prohibited by the Provisional Constitution from issuing their own notes, although the Permanent Constitution discarded this provision. As a result, most state legislatures avoided the issue of any but high-denomination, interest-bearing notes until February 18, 1862, when the new Constitution went into effect. Thereafter, there was a flood of notes ranging in denomination from 5 cents up to $500. Total outstanding state issues in 1865 came to about $65 million.

Cities and counties also issued a large amount of currency. In Virginia, Louisiana, and Texas such emissions were especially numerous and were motivated by the need to furnish the public with change, to raise funds for war mobilization, and to cover general expenses. Creditworthy private individuals and corporations (such as railroads and manufacturers) printed and circulated their own notes as a means of raising funds and making change. Such notes were usually repayable in goods and services or were made redeemable in Confederate Treasury notes in multiples of $5, $10, or $20. Local government and private issues are thought to have exceeded $25 million.

The major element in the Southern currency from 1861 through 1865 was undoubtedly the Treasury notes put out by the Richmond government. Starting in 1861 with a mere authorization of $1 million, this currency reached $800 million in early 1864. Despite the reform act of February 17, 1864, it was once again at that level by early 1865.

As the territory under Confederate rule shrank, Federal legal tender notes and fractional currency steadily infiltrated into the South. By the end of the war, distrust of the local money had reached the point where even the Confederate troops insisted upon being paid in Union currency. This desire for something of real value proved well founded after the war when the entire Southern money stock became practically worthless. Nearly all the banks failed, paying only a few cents on the dollar. Payment on the government issues was prohibited by the fifth section of the Fourteenth Amendment.

BIBLIOGRAPHY

Ball, Douglas B. *Financial Failure and Confederate Defeat*. Urbana, Ill., 1991.
Criswell, Grover C., Jr. *Confederate and Southern State Currency*. Citrus, Fla., 1976.
Lerner, Eugene. *Money, Prices and Wages in the Confederacy, 1861–1865*. Chicago, 1954.
Schwab, John C. *The Confederate States of America, 1861–1865: A Financial and Industrial History of the South during the Civil War*. New York, 1901.

DOUGLAS B. BALL

Congressional Money Bills

Operating at first with a $500,000 loan from Alabama, Congress quickly established its monetary policy. On March 9, 1861, it authorized the issue of $1 million in interest-bearing Treasury notes. This proved hopelessly inadequate, and on May 16 Congress authorized $20 million notes and $50 million in 8 percent bonds. Secretary Christopher G.

Memminger denied any danger of inflation, and on August 19 Congress authorized $100 million more notes, followed on December 24 by another $50 million new bond issues accompanying all note issues. Memminger had asked for more interest-bearing notes that could be held as investments, but the last three issues were non-interest-bearing notes more likely to be circulated than held for investment or retired into bonds.

The same pattern continued in 1862, with Congress authorizing three more issues of fiat Treasury notes and more bonds into which they might be funded. Funding, however, went slowly, and by 1863 $410 million in notes were circulating.

In 1863 Congress tried to stem inflation by forced funding. On March 23 it ordered a gradual reduction of the interest rate of bonds into which notes could be funded; after a certain date they would be acceptable only for government dues. In the same act, however, Congress authorized Memminger to issue $50 million of notes a month. Meanwhile the rapid inflation made bonds an increasingly poor investment.

On February 17, 1864, Congress boldly ordered that notes should be funded at a gradual reduction of their face value; on January 1, 1865, they would be abolished by a 100 percent tax. But most notes continued circulating at declining value, and on December 29 Congress extended the funding deadline to July 1, 1865.

There is little doubt that this flood of fiat money and the resulting inflation and speculation were major factors in demoralizing the Confederate home front.

BIBLIOGRAPHY

Ball, Douglas B. *Financial Failure and Confederate Defeat*. Urbana, Ill., 1991.
Lerner, Eugene M. "Monetary and Fiscal Programs of the Confederate Government, 1861–1865." *Journal of Political Economy* 62 (1955): 20–24.
Matthews, James M., comp. *Statutes at Large of the Confederate States of America*. Richmond, Va., 1861–1864.
Todd, Richard C. *Confederate Finance*. Athens, Ga., 1954.
Yearns, Wilfred B. *The Confederate Congress*. Athens, Ga., 1960.

W. BUCK YEARNS

Numismatics

In February 1861, when the Confederacy was established, the Treasury took over the mints in New Orleans, Dahlonega, and Charlotte. Acting on the public demand for a new coinage, the Treasury ordered the New Orleans mint to provide new designs and dies. A fifty-cent piece was prepared, but after only four pieces were struck, the collar for the edge reeding broke. The four coins were distributed to various officials. Three are now in museums and the fourth, the piece captured with President Jefferson Davis's baggage in 1865, is now worth approximately $500,000.

Without a coinage, the Confederate currency was practically confined to paper money. Yet the South had so shunned the mechanical arts that there were only eight security engravers in the whole country. Only three of these engravers had any experience with steel plate work; the rest were stationers or lithographers. Thus the first currency order was placed in New York on March 13, 1861, with the National Bank Note Company. The four type notes that were made (known as "Montgomeries" because they were issued from that city) are the most beautiful produced for the Confederacy. But when war broke out, the Treasury had to fall back on the Southern firms.

An agreement was signed May 13, 1861, with the New Orleans branch of the American Bank Note Company. Although the six designs printed were excellent, that firm's three workmen could not produce enough currency to pay for a war. Accordingly, other contracts, calling for lithographic work, were signed with Hoyer and Ludwig in Richmond. This firm took until November 1861 to finish only $17 million of notes. Moreover, the designs were merely crude copies of Northern security work. As such, they were vulnerable to counterfeiting.

To overcome this problem, Thomas Bell was sent by Treasury Secretary Christopher G. Memminger in August 1861 to New York, where he hired, with the assistance of the American Bank Note Company, two of its steel plate engravers, William Leggett and Edward Keating. Together they established a Confederate security printing establishment. At the same time, agents in Europe hired Scottish lithographers, while the banks lent their note plates, three of which were converted into plates for Treasury notes. Thanks to these measures and the seizure of the American Bank Note Company branch in New Orleans, note production increased. But the continued use of poor lithographs and the failure to standardize denomination designs paved the way for a wave of counterfeiting in September 1862.

To meet this crisis, the Treasury Department organized a contest. Every printing firm submitted new designs for the Confederate currency utilizing original work. The new designs, it was hoped, would check counterfeiting and speed production. All the winning entries were provided by Edward Keating and George Dunn, a Scottish lithographer. Starting with the issue dated "December 2, 1862," the high-denomination notes were printed from copper plates and had green backs. The $20 and lower notes were all lithographed; the $20, $10 and $5 note backs were blue—hence the "blue back" nickname given Confederate currency. The $2 and $1 notes had no backs because they were not worth copying.

The accepted designs included portraits of Mrs. Lucy H. Pickens, the wife of South Carolina's governor, and George

Wythe Randolph, secretary of war, on the $100 note; President Davis on the $50 note; Vice President Alexander H. Stephens on the $20 note, and Robert M. T. Hunter, former secretary of state, on the $10 note. In addition, the $5 bill honored Treasury Secretary Christopher G. Memminger and the Richmond capitol building, the $2 note had a portrait of Secretary of State Judah P. Benjamin, and the $1 note bore a picture of Alabama Senator Clement C. Clay.

Under an act of March 23, 1863, the engraved dates were altered from "December 2, 1862," to "April 6, 1863." A fifty-cent note was added with an image of President Davis copied from a Confederate stamp.

Finally, by an act of February 17, 1864, the Treasury ordered design changes to differentiate the new issues from the old. Accordingly, new backs were ordered in Europe and a red tint was added to the faces of every note. In addition, a battle scene was substituted for the Columbia capitol building on the $10 bill, and a $500 note honoring Gen. Thomas J. ("Stonewall") Jackson was added. The European-made backs were intercepted by the Union fleet, and Keatinge hurriedly prepared crude new blue backs for the $5 to $100 notes.

In 1865, the Confederate bills became war souvenirs or play money. Ten years later, there were a sufficient number of collectors to result in the publication of the first comprehensive catalogs. Prices were low, ranging from five cents or less for common 1862 to 1864 notes up to $5 to $10 for better items. Even in 1945, common Confederate notes could be bought for ten cents and the $1,000 and $500 "Montgomery" notes were priced at only $60.

With the Civil War Centennial of 1961 through 1964, prices rose rapidly. By the end of 1991, an uncirculated $1,000 "Montgomery" was worth over $18,000, and even the commonest Confederate notes in new condition commanded $15. Fascination with the Civil War in Europe drove up demand and prices. Despite the large quantities issued, the price of Confederate money seems destined to continue its rise in the future.

BIBLIOGRAPHY

Ball, Douglas B. "Confederate Currency Derived from Banknote Plates." *Numismatist* 85, no. 3 (March 1972): 339–352.

Ball, Douglas B. "The Confederate Currency Reform of 1862." In *America's Currency 1789–1866.* New York, 1985.

Ball, Douglas B. *Financial Failure and Confederate Defeat.* Urbana, Ill., and Chicago, 1991.

Slabaugh, Arlie R. *Confederate States Paper Money.* Iola, Wis., 1991.

DOUGLAS B. BALL

DAHLGREN PAPERS

Following the aborted Kilpatrick-Dahlgren cavalry raid on Richmond (February 28–March 3, 1864), Col. Ulric Dahlgren was killed while attempting to return to Union lines. Soon after Dahlgren's death young William Littlepage, a local schoolboy, searched Dahlgren's pockets and discovered papers that produced a storm of controversy. They contained various inflammatory statements, including references to burning Richmond and killing President Jefferson Davis and his cabinet.

The publication of the Dahlgren papers in the Richmond newspapers fanned the flames of hatred and prompted cries for retribution. Eventually Gen. Robert E. Lee wrote to Gen. George G. Meade, asking him if his government had approved or sanctioned the violent actions proposed in the captured letters. Meade disavowed the statements but wrote his wife of "collateral evidence in my possession," suggesting he believed the papers genuine.

Dahlgren's supporters quickly sprang to his defense and insisted the papers were either forged or planted on the fall-

> ### [They proposed] burning Richmond and killing President Jefferson Davis and his cabinet.

en warrior. All those intimately involved in the raid, including its leader Gen. Judson Kilpatrick, denied the published statements concerning the burning of Richmond and the killing of Davis and the Confederate cabinet. Others claimed the transposition of the *h* and *l* in Dahlgren's signature on one of the documents proved they were forgeries.

Any impartial investigation into the controversy became frustratingly difficult because none of the original Dahlgren papers survived. During the 1950s, however, historian V. C. Jones thoroughly reviewed the issue and refuted theories that claimed the papers were false because of Dahlgren's name being misspelled. He noted that of the three separate papers concerning the raid, the two with the most damning statements had no signature. To establish the papers' authenticity he documented a chain of possession and offered testimony from virtually every prominent Confederate authority who claimed to have seen the documents. His findings are still valid today.

[*See also* Kilpatrick-Dahlgren Raid.]

BIBLIOGRAPHY

Dahlgren, Admiral John A. *Memoir of Ulric Dahlgren.* Philadelphia, 1872.
Jones, Virgil Carrington. *Eight Hours before Richmond.* New York, 1957.

MICHAEL J. ANDRUS

DANVILLE, VIRGINIA

Located in south-central Virginia, less than five miles from the North Carolina border, the city of Danville was a primary supply center for the Confederacy during the Civil War. From a population of 3,689 (1,674 white; 1,466 slave; 202 free black; 347 other) in 1860, the city expanded to almost 6,000 by the end of the war. In the decade before the war the major economic activity of the region was tobacco, and by 1860 Danville had become the third largest processing center of the crop in the state. Moreover, because it was the only urban center in the county, the city contained a variety of other businesses—shoes, clothing, blacksmith, flour and meal—to sustain the needs of the townspeople and the neighboring countryside.

Its citizens, like the vast majority of Southerners, were conservative in their outlook on life. To get ahead they advocated hard work and frowned on consumption of liquor, so much so that they banned its sale within city limits. The city council also instituted a slave patrol to control the black population and limit their access to the city.

In 1861 the majority of the city's residents opposed secession, believing that the South could best defend its rights by remaining in the Union. When Virginia called for a convention to decide the issue, the people elected William T. Sutherlin, a moderate Unionist, to represent them. To many in Danville the argument for or against secession revolved around its economic consequences. In the end, they opposed Virginia leaving the Union because they believed that secession would bring disruption and chaos to the local economy. Lincoln's call for troops changed the disposition of the townspeople, however, and thereafter they willingly supported the Confederate cause.

The fear that the local economy would decline proved to be unfounded. In fact, the city became a major economic beneficiary of the conflict. The war caused existing manufacturers, especially of shoes and clothing, to expand their production dramatically, and it led to the development of new industries—munitions, coal, and fertilizer—as well. A primary factor in this increased productivity was the city's strategic location. Situated far behind the front lines, businesses could operate without fear of enemy interference. This security led several manufacturing companies in Richmond and Petersburg to transfer their operations to Danville. The city had direct rail connections with Richmond, and in May 1864 the War Department completed construction on a railway that connected the city with Greensboro, North Carolina, which facilitated the transportation of supplies from the Deep South.

In the last two years of the war the morale of the townspeople declined considerably, with numerous individuals failing to meet their responsibilities. In January 1864 the citizens petitioned the War Department to have Union prisoners removed from the city. Danville served as the last capital of the Confederacy from April 3 to April 10, 1865, when President Jefferson Davis transferred the government there after the fall of Richmond.

BIBLIOGRAPHY

Ballard, Michael. *The Long Shadow.* Jackson, Miss., 1988.
Davis, William C. *Jefferson Davis: The Man and His Hour.* New York, 1991.
Hattaway, Herman, and Archer Jones. *How The North Won: A Military History of the Civil War.* Urbana, Ill., 1983.
Siegel, Frederick F. *The Roots of Southern Distinctiveness: Tobacco and Society in Danville, Virginia, 1780–1865.* Chapel Hill, N.C., 1987.

MICHAEL G. MAHON

DAVIDS

The torpedo boat *David* gave its name to other torpedo boats of the same or similar specifications. The name derived from its size relative to Goliath-sized Union ships. Its mission was to glide in under the guns of a blockader and detonate a spar torpedo beneath the waterline. Using such a ship was exclusively a Confederate tactic—though Union Lt. William B. Cushing destroyed *Albemarle* from a launch carrying a spar torpedo. The psychological effect of the Davids upon Union blockaders and the resulting restriction on their movements greatly outweighed actual losses.

The prototype *David* was built in Charleston in 1863 by the Southern Torpedo Company, a group of private investors who later gave control of the ship to the Confederate navy. Its mission determined the design. A 50-foot keel, 6-foot beam, and 5-foot draft satisfied requirements for a small craft. The essential design feature was a 10-foot metal spar extending from the prow; to this was fixed a spar torpedo armed with 60 or more pounds of powder capable of damaging or sinking the largest ship.

A steam engine propelled the cigar-shaped hull at five to seven knots as the ship darted through the Union fleet, seeking its target. Iron plating furnished protection both from attacking ships and from its own exploding torpedo. *David* offered a very low profile because tanks in the hold could be filled to submerge the hull up to the pilot's cabin and smokestack; thus the ship could be almost entirely concealed beneath the water's surface.

On October 5, 1863, *David* attacked the 3,486-ton ironclad *New Ironsides,* a ship of immense symbolic significance to the entire Union as well as the Charleston blockading fleet. Lt. William Glassel commanded, Engineer James H. Tomb manned the engines, Seaman James Sullivan managed the spar, and Walker Cannon piloted *David* to the target. *New Ironsides* was not sunk, but the exploding torpedo badly damaged both the ship and the fleet's morale. The design and its initial success drew praise from U.S. Adm. John A. Dahlgren.

David's success fueled interest in manufacturing more such ships. In a construction system where standardized design and parts were virtually unknown, some attempt was made to issue uniform specifications for a David: 30-, 46-, or 50-foot length and 5- to 6-foot draft. The one exception was a 160-foot David "Number Six" at Charleston. Of about fifteen vessels built, most were at least partially ironclad. The spar on later versions was usually longer by several feet than *David's* 10-foot spar.

Of four wooden Davids built at Richmond for service on the James—*Hornet, Scorpion, Wasp,* and *Squib*—the latter was made famous when Lt. Hunter Davidson commanded an attack on USS *Minnesota* at Newport News. He failed to sink the ship but was promoted to commander for his daring.

At Charleston in March and April 1864, Engineer Tomb commanded a David against USS *Memphis* and USS *Wabash.* Though neither attack inflicted damage on the ships, the psychological effect was devastating. As ships in Charleston anchored close alongside within protective nets, blockade runners moved more freely. *Torch, Midge,* and eight unnamed Davids were also laid down at Charleston.

In January 1865, *St. Patrick,* built at Selma, Alabama, seriously alarmed the crew of USS *Octorara* and other block-

DAVID. The torpedo boat off the U.S. Naval Academy at Annapolis, Maryland, duing the late 1860's.   NAVAL HISTORICAL CENTER, WASHINGTON, D.C.

aders at Mobile. At the Columbus (Georgia) Naval Iron Works, *Viper* transported men fleeing the last battle of the war in April 1865. Victorious Union men captured numerous Davids, regarding them as a curiosity. *Midge* was transported to the Brooklyn Navy Yard and another to Annapolis as trophies of war.

BIBLIOGRAPHY

Perry, Milton F. *Infernal Machines: The Story of Confederate Submarine and Mine Warfare.* Baton Rouge, La., 1965.
Scharf, J. Thomas. *History of the Confederate States Navy from Its Organization to Surrender of Its Last Vessel.* New York, 1887. Reprint, New York, 1977.
Silverstein, Paul H. *Warships of the Civil War Navies.* Annapolis, Md., 1989.
Turner, Maxine. *Navy Gray: A Story of the Confederate Navy on the Chattahoochee and Apalachocola Rivers.* University, Ala., 1988.

MAXINE TURNER

DAVIS, GEORGE

DAVIS, GEORGE (1820–1896), congressman from North Carolina and attorney general. Davis was born March 1, 1820, at Porter's Neck, New Hanover County, North Carolina, on his father's plantation. His forebears included two governors of South Carolina. He graduated at the head of his class from the University of North Carolina in 1838 and was admit-

ted to the bar two years later. He established his practice in Wilmington and acquired a reputation for eloquence at the bar and for brilliance as a historical scholar and lecturer.

Politically, he was identified with the Whig party until that party's demise. He joined the Constitutional Union party in 1860, prompted by his dedication to the Union and the party's policy of reconciliation. A member of the Washington peace conference of February 1861, he deplored the conference's failure to arrive at mutually acceptable terms, but felt constrained to join the secession movement.

Davis was chosen in June 1861 by moderate secessionists as a delegate-at-large from North Carolina to the Provisional Congress. But three months later he was elected for a two-year term in the Confederate Senate, where he distinguished himself as one of his state's strongest nationalists. After he was defeated for a second term in September 1863, he was named by Jefferson Davis on the last day of the year as attorney general. He served in that office with distinction until the Confederacy's collapse.

Perhaps his most important contribution as a cabinet member was the friendly advice he gave to Jefferson Davis in an effort to improve the thin-skinned president's relations with his critics and Congress.

After the war he was imprisoned for several months at Fort Hamilton, New York, and then paroled on January 2, 1866. In greatly reduced circumstances, Davis devoted himself to restoring his law practice and his career as a railroad lawyer. Although declining to seek public office, he threw his weight against the radicals' proposed constitution of 1868. When it was approved nevertheless, Davis and others of like mind labored successfully to have it reformed in 1875. He died February 23, 1896, and was buried in the Wilmington, North Carolina, Oakdale Cemetery.

BIBLIOGRAPHY

Ashe, Samuel A. *Biographical History of North Carolina.* Vol. 2. Greensboro, N.C., 1907.
Powell, William S., ed. *Dictionary of North Carolina Biography.* Vol. 2. Chapel Hill, N.C., 1986.

RICHARD BARDOLPH

DAVIS, JEFFERSON

DAVIS, JEFFERSON (1807 or 1808–1889), U.S. senator, U.S. secretary of war, and president of the Confederate States of America. Davis was born on June 3, probably in 1807 (he sometimes put it in 1808), in Christian County (present-day Todd), Kentucky, the son of Samuel and Jane (Cook) Davis. In about 1811 the family settled near Woodville, Mississippi. After two years at St. Thomas College, near Springfield, Kentucky, Davis entered Jefferson College in Mississippi and later transferred to Wilkinson County Academy. He joined the junior class at Transylvania University, Lexington, Kentucky, in the fall of 1823. Influenced by his elder brother, Joseph E. Davis, Jefferson entered the U.S. Military Academy in September 1824. Cadet Davis compiled a good academic record as well as a fairly large number of demerits. He ranked twenty-third out of thirty-three in the graduating class and was commissioned brevet second lieutenant of infantry on July 1, 1828.

Routine assignments took him to various frontier posts and to some Indian fighting. In September 1832 he received the surrender of the famed Sauk chief Black Hawk and escorted his prisoner from Prairie du Chien, Wisconsin Territory, to Jefferson Barracks, Missouri. Promoted to first lieutenant of dragoons, May 10, 1834, Davis led several expeditions into hostile Kiowa and Wichita villages. A year later on May 12, 1835, he submitted his resignation from the army.

Davis married Sarah Knox Taylor (daughter of Zachary Taylor) on June 17 at her aunt's house near Louisville, Kentucky. The couple went immediately to Mississippi, where brother Joseph had provided Jefferson eight hundred acres to clear, build on, and on which to start a planter's life. Both Jefferson and "Knoxie" contracted a severe fever in late August or early September, and on September 15, 1835, she died. Desolate and gravely ill, Davis traveled to Havana, Cuba, in the winter to recover. He returned to Mississippi via New York and Washington. He lived in seclusion—working on his plantation (Brierfield), reading, and learning his brother's views on slave management, which were considered comparatively liberal. Gradually he became a knowledgeable and successful planter whose slaves are reported to have held him in high regard.

Nearly ten years passed before Davis emerged from his seclusion. When he did, he entered Mississippi politics and married again. Varina Howell, a Natchez girl not twenty when she married Davis on February 25, 1845, became the mainstay of his life. Independent, sometimes willful, Varina irritated Davis at first, but after a period of adjustment, she shared his trials and triumphs, fought battles for him, bore him four sons and two daughters, and loved him always.

Davis was elected to Congress that year and when the Mexican War began he was elected colonel of a volunteer regiment from Vicksburg. With it he joined his former father-in-law's army at Carmargo, Mexico. General Taylor advanced against Monterrey, and Davis's Mississippi regiment played an important role in the campaign. Davis and his Mississippians remained with Taylor while much of his army joined Gen. Winfield Scott's campaign from Vera Cruz to Mexico City. Mexico's leader, Gen. Antonio Lopez de Santa Anna, attacked Taylor in the expectation of annihilating a weakened American force. At the victorious Battle of Buena Vista, Davis and his Mississippi riflemen did heroic duty. Wounded, Davis returned to the United States to find himself a hero.

The Mississippi legislature presented him a sword of honor and appointed him in 1847 to fill out an unexpired Federal senatorial term. Reelected in 1850, Democrat Davis went on to prominence in the Senate and in Federal affairs. He became chairman of the Military Committee of the Senate and proved to be a bureaucrat with remarkably progressive ideas—new weapons always caught his attention and he remembered the success of the new percussion rifles he had provided for his Mississippians. During his term Davis's cultural interests led him to take a leading role in developing the Smithsonian Institution.

Senator Davis could be heard expressing the Southern position on national issues often and eloquently. He disliked the Compromise of 1850 and favored extension of the Missouri Compromise line to the Pacific as a solution to the slavery problem.

In the 1850s Davis came to inherit the mantle of John C. Calhoun as the leading Southern spokesman. But party and doctrinal loyalty led him to resign his Senate seat in 1850 to enter, belatedly, the governor's race in Mississippi against Henry S. Foote. Foote took a moderate stance toward the Great Compromise and seemed to be riding a rising feeling of Unionism. Davis had once before been in a raucous campaign for a forlorn hope, but had usually held appointive office and had not really been a cracker-barrel politician; now he disciplined himself to doff his natural hauteur and stump as much

JEFFERSON DAVIS. Pre-Civil War portrait by Mathew Brady, c. 1860.

of the state as time and his precarious health permitted. He talked of the need for a united South, one committed to protecting its rights within the Union; he reached for votes from the poor whites, a class long ignored under a Mississippi oligarchy. He lost, by barely a thousand votes, and returned, in his words, to "quiet farm-labors, until the nomination of Franklin Pierce, when I went out to advocate his election." Davis became President Pierce's secretary of war.

His penchant for innovation, already seen during his Senate stint, grew with his new position. Convinced by experience that western military operations required new methods, Secretary Davis brought in camels for use in the desert. He introduced new infantry tactics, pushed the substitution of iron for wooden gun carriages, increased the number of rifles and rifled muskets capable of using the new minié cartridge, and modernized the ordnance at some of the coastal forts.

He had long advocated a transcontinental military railroad and, as secretary of war, surveyed various routes for that line. During his secretaryship he had charge of expanding the U.S. Capitol and sometimes served as acting navy secretary.

Mississippi returned Davis in March 1857 to a Senate facing serious national problems. Davis viewed the future with increasing gloom. The Kansas-Nebraska Act of 1854 had repealed the Missouri Compromise and opened lands west of Missouri to local option on slavery. A protracted war between pro- and antislavery settlers in Kansas Territory dragged on through the 1850s until the whole country lamented "Bleeding Kansas." This crisis finally disrupted the party system as the Whig party expired and the anti-South and antislavery Republican party took its place.

Increasingly the cotton South turned to Davis as adviser and defender. He made no apologies for slavery since he considered it the best adjustment of capital to labor, far better than the industrial system of the North where laborers were subjected to "humiliation and suffering." Davis saw slavery in the South as "moral, a social and political blessing." Protecting slavery meant, also, protecting sovereign state rights in the Union. Davis's defense of the South threw him into combat with the "Black Republican" party. Seeking to preserve the Democratic party as the last national forum of compromise between the sections, he opposed Stephen A. Douglas's popular sovereignty doctrine enshrined in the Kansas-Nebraska Act. Initially a proponent of the act, Davis came to see it as a snare and a delusion, since "squatter sovereignty," as he called it, would allow territories to pass laws annulling Southerners' constitutional property rights.

From a constitutional issue, slavery rose to become a moral issue, and political rhetoric inflamed the national conscience. Davis spoke often on the slave issue. And he hewed hard to his love for the Union. As late as the spring of 1860 he thought the Union safe but felt, rightly enough, that danger came not from differences but from politics and politicians.

He knew, after 1858, that preserving the Union would be difficult in 1860, an election year that might see the Republicans winning and ensconcing an "abolition president" in the White House. He considered that tantamount to ending the nation—the South could not live under an abolitionist administration because constitutional protection would disappear.

Jefferson Davis came to his views on Southern rights through reading, discussion, and iron logic. Devoted to the nation by lineage, history, and patriotism, Davis nonetheless believed in the compact theory of the Union, which held that the states were sovereign, that they had yielded sovereignty by joining the Union, and that they could reclaim it by seceding. As pressure built against slavery and against the cotton system through the 1850s, Davis became louder in his calls for Southern rights within the Union, but he urged moderation and restraint to save the Republic.

Appointed in December 1860 to the Senate Committee of Thirteen charged with finding a solution to the crisis, Davis saw little hope and reluctantly advised secession and the formation of a Southern confederacy.

Anguished, ill, and weary, Davis made a farewell speech to the Senate on January 21, 1861, which stated clearly the South's position and reasons for leaving the Union. He and his family left Washington for Brierfield Plantation on January 22. Back in Mississippi he accepted a commission as major general of state troops, but at Brierfield he received word of his election as president of the Provisional Government of the Confederate States of America.

He did not want the job. He felt better qualified for military command, but dutifully accepted the political post. Why his reluctance about the presidency? He knew the problems ahead for the new Confederacy—the probability of war and the South's unreadiness—and he disliked the kind of politicking the presidency required. Was he the right man? Yes. On balance, the South called its best to lead its quest for independence. Davis had national, even international, renown, the respect of friends and foes, a judiciousness valuable in raucous times, a balancing realism, a need to be needed, and proper presidential probity.

In his inaugural address at Montgomery, Alabama, on February 18, 1861, Davis spoke of his hope for peace, described the South's course to secession, stressed the Confederacy as a product of evolution, not revolution, announced Southern dedication to agriculture and to free trade, and made a firm declaration: "We have entered upon the career of independence, and it must be inflexibly pursued." He urged creation of a national army and navy and spoke prophetically of his own future:

Experience in public stations . . . has taught me that care and toil and disappointment are the price of official elevation. You will see many errors to forgive, many deficiencies to tolerate, but you shall not find in me either a want of zeal or fidelity to the cause that is to me highest in hope and of most enduring affection.

An expected state rights advocate, Davis became almost immediately an unexpected Confederate nationalist. A constitutionalist, he used that document to strengthen the central government. A national army that superseded the state militias became the main bastion of his administration. When the government took control of military operations within Confederate borders, the states lost more power than they guessed.

Davis picked his cabinet with an eye toward state representation, toward old political lines, and toward ability. His first picks were not uniformly good, notably the secretary of war, Alabamian Leroy P. Walker; the secretary of state, Georgia's Robert Toombs; and the secretary of the treasury,

South Carolinian Christopher G. Memminger. His two best appointees were Louisianan Judah P. Benjamin who as attorney general headed the new Department of Justice, and Floridian Stephen R. Mallory as secretary of the navy. Benjamin would become a close presidential confidant and Mallory an innovative, resourceful navy builder.

Through early negotiations with Abraham Lincoln's government about Federal property in the South, Davis learned quickly that diplomacy, far from being a gentlemanly enterprise, was a practice in deceit. Failure of negotiations led to the Fort Sumter crisis in April 1861. That fort athwart Charleston Harbor boasted old ordnance and a small garrison, but its Union banner flouted Confederate sovereignty. Davis made a decision, over some cabinet objections, and Confederate guns began firing at Fort Sumter on April 12, 1861. War began.

Davis organized his armies with skill, although critics suggested that he meddled with generals too much and stuck by such controversial cronies as Gen. Braxton Bragg and Commissary Gen. Lucius B. Northrop beyond reason. To some extent Davis served as his own war secretary—that six men filled that title indicates problems—and, like most chief executives, he relied on people he knew to get things done. If he did hold a tight rein on some generals, many of them needed it; to generals he trusted, such as Robert E. Lee, he gave help and scant advice.

He understood morale building and, in order to weld Virginia to the Confederacy, moved the capital to Richmond in late May 1861.

From the start he offered a hard war program to a laissez-faire Congress. His urging produced a Conscription Act in 1862 that saved the Confederate armies as first enlistments expired; he supported an impressment program that generated much public resentment as the armies commandeered supplies for the men and animals; despite his own predilections he urged tough taxes on land, cotton, and slaves, and endorsed a unique tax-in-kind to be paid with food, forage, cloth, or animals; he accepted also the produce loan, which was designed to extract more staples in return for Confederate paper. But neither he nor Congress could condone the truly draconian taxes needed in a new and warring nation.

Necessity brought Davis to varied innovations. As war eroded his country and its people, he forced himself to become a much more public figure, spoke often, made several "swings around the Confederacy" to rekindle flagging faith, and maintained a prodigious correspondence with critics, friends, and restive governors. Toward the last he even proposed limited slave emancipation in return for national service.

Some things he ought to have done he could not bring himself to do. Although Congress provided authority virtually to nationalize the railroads, Davis did not press its enforcement—it smacked too much of federalism. Nor did he deal harshly with an increasingly critical press. Where Lincoln suppressed seditious publications, Davis did not; he stuck by freedom of expression. He suspended the writ of habeas corpus only under congressional authority, never under assumed war powers.

As the war ran against his country, Davis worked harder for longer hours, pushed his wretched health beyond limits, and became estranged from Congress and from most of the public. He found the state rights policies of many governors almost inconceivable in a period of crisis and frowned on cajoling reluctant patriots. Congress often balked at the president's war program, but grudgingly followed his lead. His own dedication was sometimes seen as haughty aloofness, but a close reading of his state papers and his letters shows his fiery devotion unflagging to the end.

As president he had the task of devising a national strategy for victory, and he adopted the offensive-defensive as the best way to use interior lines and inferior Southern resources against Northern strength. Under this plan, Southern armies would conserve men and matériel, retreat in the face of superior forces (if state rights governors permitted), and wait for a moment of Southern superiority. He applied this strategy in Maryland and Kentucky in 1862 and in the West. When he found that old-fashioned command structures failed under the vastness of the war, he tried a new theater-command idea that might well have worked had Joseph E. Johnston, the general picked for the command, been bold.

At the end, his dream of independence fading, Davis remained first and last the foremost Confederate. When General Lee evacuated Richmond on April 2, 1865, Davis led a refugee government to Danville, Virginia, and then moved southward in hopes of getting across the Mississippi and continuing the struggle. He was captured at Irwinville, Georgia, on May 10, 1865.

He had done as well as anyone could to create a Southern nation. Although he lacked Lincoln's facility with language, at times he approached eloquence in talking of the cause he nearly won. He created a revolutionary state, and when the dream was lost and his country gone, he could take some consolation in a legacy of honor.

Davis served a harsh two-year prison stint at Fort Monroe while awaiting a treason trial and achieved at last a mite of martyrdom. Varina's ceaseless efforts to free him, combined with those of many others in the North and South, finally succeeded. Released from prison on bail in May 1867 (he was never brought to trial), Davis continued his life in the Confederacy. Never wavering in his belief in the cause, never admitting error, he continued to argue the constitutional right of secession and the legitimacy of the Confederacy. Financially strapped, he worked at tasks that friends provided, tried various business schemes that failed, and at last found refuge at Beauvoir, a charming house belonging to a

lifelong friend near Biloxi, Mississippi. There he spent his last years writing his history of the war and his country. In June 1881, Davis's two-volume *Rise and Fall of the Confederate Government* appeared. A heavy, badly organized book, product of Davis and several collaborators, it was Davis's view of the whole Confederate experience and decidedly his book as he flayed his enemies and praised his friends: Joseph E. Johnston and P. G. T. Beauregard ranked as villains, while Bragg and Northrop came off well. Davis's second book, *Short History of the Confederate States,* published in 1889, lacked anger, presented a more balanced view of the war, and showed real literary quality.

Personal tragedy dogged much of Davis's life. Not only did he lose his first wife early, but also his four sons died before him. One of them, Joseph Evan, was killed in a fall from a White House balcony on April 30, 1864.

In his last years, Davis became a hero, seen as a long-neglected symbol. On his rare public appearances he came increasingly to advocate reunion and reconciliation. He died on December 5, 1889, aged eighty-two, survived by Varina and two daughters, Margaret and Varina Anne ("Winnie").

[*See also* Beauvoir; Davis Bend; Presidency.]

BIBLIOGRAPHY

Davis, Jefferson. *The Rise and Fall of the Confederate Government.* 2 vols. New York, 1881.

Davis, Varina H. *Jefferson Davis, Ex-President of the Confederate States of America: A Memoir by His Wife.* 2 vols. New York, 1890.

Davis, William C. *Jefferson Davis: The Man and His Hour, A Biography.* New York, 1991.

Dodd, William E. *Jefferson Davis.* Philadelphia, 1907.

Eaton, Clement. *Jefferson Davis.* New York, 1977.

Monroe, Haskell M., James T. McIntosh, Lynda L. Crist, Mary S. Dix, and Richard Beringer, eds. *The Papers of Jefferson Davis.* 7 vols. to date. Baton Rouge, La., 1971–.

Patrick, Rembert W. *Jefferson Davis and His Cabinet.* Baton Rouge, La., 1944.

Rowland, Dunbar, ed. *Jefferson Davis, Constitutionalist: His Letters, Papers, and Speeches.* 10 vols. Jackson, Miss., 1923.

Strode, Hudson. *Jefferson Davis.* 3 vols. New York, 1955–1964.

Woodworth, Steven E. *Jefferson Davis and His Generals: The Failure of Confederate Command in the West.* Lawrence, Kans., 1990.

FRANK E. VANDIVER

DAVIS, JOSEPH E.

DAVIS, JOSEPH E. (1784–1870), Mississippi planter and elder brother and adviser to Jefferson Davis. Born in Georgia the eldest of ten children of whom Jefferson was the youngest, Joseph Emory Davis grew to manhood in Kentucky and read law in Mississippi. As a prosperous

Natchez lawyer Davis accumulated land and in midlife moved to Hurricane, a large cotton plantation on the Mississippi River below Vicksburg where he became one of the wealthiest planters in the state. He was known for his innovative slave management, establishing a slave jury to decide disputes and allowing workers to keep what they earned beyond their worth as field hands.

Davis served as a father figure for his brother. He gave him land adjacent to Hurricane on which to develop a cotton plantation and, as an active Democrat, fostered Jefferson's political career. Shortly after the outbreak of the Civil War, Joseph, at Jefferson's request, went to Richmond to assist the Confederate president and his family. But after a few weeks he returned to Mississippi to attend to his and his brother's plantations. He continued to send Jefferson his opinions of Confederate generals and the conduct of the war.

In April 1862 Joseph Davis and his family fled from Hurricane when Federal raiders looted and burned the plantation. Officers of the Union navy, then the army, and finally the Freedmen's Bureau attempted to set up a model community for freed slaves at Davis Bend, the 11,000-acre loop of land that had contained the plantations of the Davis brothers and John A. Quitman, ex-governor of Mississippi. They enjoyed only modest success. For the next three years the elderly Davis was a refugee struggling to provide for his many dependents, as the armies swept back and forth across Mississippi. After the war Davis spent the last five years of his life seeking to rebuild his fortunes.

[*See also* Davis Bend.]

BIBLIOGRAPHY

Davis, Jefferson. *The Papers of Jefferson Davis.* Vol. 1. Edited by Haskell M. Monroe, Jr., and James T. McIntosh. Vols. 2–3. Edited by James T. McIntosh. Vols. 4–6. Edited by Lynda Laswell Crist. Baton Rouge, La., 1971–1989.
Hermann, Janet Sharp. *Joseph E. Davis, Pioneer Patriarch.* Jackson, Miss., 1990.
Hermann, Janet Sharp. *The Pursuit of a Dream.* New York, 1981.

JANET SHARP HERMANN

DAVIS, VARINA HOWELL

DAVIS, VARINA HOWELL (1826–1906), first lady of the Confederacy. It is one of the Civil War's rich ironies that Varina Howell Davis became First Lady of the Confederacy, for she was unsuited by personal background and political inclination for the role. Born into the planter class in Mississippi in 1826, she received an excellent education at a girls' academy in Philadelphia and at home with a private tutor. Her father, William B. Howell, was an active member of the Whig party, and she grew up in a household where people took politics seriously and discussed them with gusto. She was a straightforward, candid, and outspoken girl, and her personality was always at odds with the role of the Southern "lady."

When she met Jefferson Davis at a Christmas party in 1843, she was a tall seventeen-year-old with large expressive eyes, and she was already known for her dry wit. Davis was a rich widower in his mid-thirties who had only recently recovered from the death of his first wife, Knox Taylor Davis. Her impressions of Davis were mixed: she thought he was arrogant and aloof, but also handsome, well-spoken, and cultivated. Her initial doubts gradually faded, however, and she fell in love with him. He also fell in love, attracted to her fine mind and good looks. The couple married on February 26, 1845.

The marriage was charged with struggle from the beginning, starting with an inheritance dispute. Joseph E. Davis, Jefferson's older brother and manager of the family's large estate, devised a will that excluded Varina from inheriting any of the Davis property. She protested immediately, but to no avail—Jefferson told her to accept his brother's decision. She felt further alienated from her husband when he enlisted in the army to fight in the Mexican War without consulting her. It was becoming clear that Jefferson simply accepted the sex roles of his era and expected her to do what he told her to do. By the time he returned from war in 1847, the couple had become estranged. When he was appointed to the U.S. Senate, he left her at home in Mississippi for almost a year to punish her.

Somehow the Davises reconciled and she went to Washington, but other conflicts plagued the marriage, often because Jefferson Davis continued to make arbitrary decisions without consulting his wife. He controlled the family's finances and even decided whether Varina could visit her relatives. In what became a typical pattern in the relationship, she would protest his decisions and then eventually acquiesce. She had no other choice. If she wanted a divorce—which she never mentioned in writing—it would have been almost impossible to obtain under Mississippi law. Moreover, she had no income of her own, and it would have been difficult to return to her parents because by the late 1840s her father was going bankrupt. In the 1850s the Davises had four children, but they were never able to resolve their power struggles.

Varina Davis retained her Whiggish sympathies through the 1850s, even though her husband was a Democrat, and like many Southern Whigs she was alarmed by the secession crisis of 1860 and 1861. She told several close friends and relatives that it was foolish for Southern states to leave the Union and that the Confederacy would never survive. After her husband became president, she reluctantly joined him in Richmond to spend what she later called four of the worst years of her life.

Few people seem to have known of her opposition to secession, but she nonetheless became a controversial figure. Members of Richmond's society called her direct manner crude and unrefined; the First Lady was not deemed to be a proper lady. Some politicians, surprised by her astute understanding of contemporary issues, accused her of meddling in the president's decisions. In fact she seems to have exercised little political influence over her husband, but her extraordinary behavior was enough in and of itself to draw criticism.

The First Lady got off to a bad start in the summer of 1861 by appearing at public receptions when she was visibly pregnant, something that very few politicians' wives did in the nineteenth century. She could also be blunt-spoken, according to a man who met her in Richmond in 1862. He described her as "very smart, . . . quite independent, says what she pleases and cuts at people generally." Furthermore, Varina Davis had an acute sense of the ridiculous, which got her into trouble. At a dinner party she attended, a general's wife remarked that the underdrawers for an entire Confederate regiment had mistakenly been made with two right legs. She burst out laughing, much to the horror of the other guests.

As the war ground on, Varina Davis continued to depart from the traditional female role. As early as 1862, she envi-

sioned a hard life after the war and told her husband she would take a paying job outside the home if necessary. She also began selling off her personal possessions—clothing, china, and books—to build up cash reserves. Her personal life was further marred by the tragic death of her young son Joseph, who died in a freak accident in 1864 when he broke his neck in a fall. As she told one of her friends, she was relieved when the Confederacy collapsed and the war ended in 1865.

Yet the postwar era was also filled with challenges for Varina Davis. Her husband served two years in federal prison, and after he was released in 1867 he was never able to support his family. Continually at the edge of destitution, the Davises never again owned a home. Varina Davis gradually took over the management of their household affairs as her husband's health declined. After he died in 1889, she moved to Manhattan, where she lived for the rest of her life. Still fending off poverty, she nonetheless created an interesting life, writing for newspapers and magazines. Many of her publications focused on the war, and they often reflected her conviction that secession had been a terrible mistake. It certainly cast a long shadow over her life, even though she had never wanted to be the Confederate First Lady.

BIBLIOGRAPHY

Cashin, Joan E. "Varina Howell Davis." In *Portraits of American Women*. Edited by G. B. Barker-Benfield and Catherine Clinton. New York, 1991.

Davis, Jefferson. *The Papers of Jefferson Davis*. 6 vols. Edited by James T. McIntosh, Lynda L. Crist, Mary Seaton Dix, et al. Baton Rouge, La., 1971–1986.

Evans, Eli N. *Judah P. Benjamin: The Jewish Confederate*. New York, 1988.

Rable, George C. *Civil Wars: Women and the Crisis of Southern Nationalism*. Urbana, Ill., 1989.

Woodward, C. Vann, ed. *Mary Chesnut's Civil War*. New Haven, 1981.

JOAN E. CASHIN

VARINA HOWELL DAVIS. Miniature by John Wood Dodge, 1849. Watercolor on ivory, 6.5 by 5.3 centimeters.
NATIONAL PORTRAIT GALLERY, SMITHSONIAN INSTITUTION, WASHINGTON, D.C.

DAVIS BEND

Site of the adjoining plantations of Jefferson Davis, his older brother Joseph E. Davis, and Mississippi Governor John A. Quitman, Davis Bend was an 11,000-acre loop of land on the Mississippi River about twenty-five miles down the river from Vicksburg in Warren County.

In 1818 Joseph Davis began acquiring land on Davis Bend and settled there in 1827. His Hurricane Plantation (named after an 1825 storm) was situated on the western end of the loop. The land (some 5,000 acres), crops, and his personal property made him one of the wealthiest men in

Mississippi by 1860. Hurricane House, built in the 1830s, was a three-story mansion famed for its size, elegance, and conveniences. Numerous outbuildings and spectacular grounds and gardens completed the estate, including a replica Greek temple for the owner's office and library.

Brierfield, located on the southwestern curve of Davis Bend, comprised about 1,800 acres and was named for the dense tangle of greenery that had to be cleared when Jefferson Davis moved there in 1835. His house, completed about 1850, was smaller and plainer than Hurricane, a rambling wooden one-story structure designed by the owner with a classic central hall, capacious rooms and fireplaces, and traditional galleries front and rear.

In April 1862 both plantations were abandoned and Hurricane was burned by Union forces in June. The Freedmen's Department (a precursor of the Freedmen's Bureau) used the Davis plantations beginning in 1863. Four years later they were sold by Joseph Davis (Jefferson Davis was then a Federal prisoner) to Benjamin Montgomery, his former slave. Isolated after the river changed Davis Bend to Davis Island in 1867 and plagued by flooding, the property was difficult to farm and manage, leading the Montgomery family to default. After years of litigation following Joseph Davis's death, Jefferson Davis regained control of Brierfield in 1878; Brierfield House survived until destroyed by fire in 1931. Hurricane remained in the Davis family until 1897 and Brierfield until 1953.

BIBLIOGRAPHY

Davis, Jefferson. *The Papers of Jefferson Davis*. 7 vols. to date. Baton Rouge, La., 1971–.

Everett, Frank E., Jr. *Brierfield: Plantation Home of Jefferson Davis*. Hattiesburg, Miss., 1971.

Hermann, Janet Sharp. *Joseph E. Davis, Pioneer Patriarch*. Jackson, Miss., 1990.

Hermann, Janet Sharp. *The Pursuit of a Dream*. New York, 1981.

LYNDA LASSWELL CRIST

DEARING, JAMES

DEARING, JAMES (1840–1865), brigadier general. Dearing, born April 25, 1840, was a native Virginian who attended the U.S. Military Academy. He was performing well academically in his third year at West Point, despite a generous ration of demerits, when his native state seceded and he resigned. Dearing was commissioned as lieutenant in a Louisiana artillery unit just days before First Manassas and served in that capacity for seven months. A Virginia battery selected Dearing as its captain early in 1862. He led that company with notable valor at Williamsburg and Seven Pines, where

Gen. James Longstreet commended his "conspicuous courage and energy." Dearing also played a brief role near the climax of Second Manassas.

In January 1863, Dearing won promotion to major and command of an artillery battalion in George E. Pickett's division. His guns supported the division's famous charge on July 3 at Gettysburg. Early in 1864, Dearing left artillery service to command a cavalry detachment under Pickett with rank of colonel. His successful role in the 1864 operations near the coast of North Carolina earned Dearing the wreath of a brigadier general on April 29, 1864, four days after his twenty-fourth birthday. The new general fought with distinction at Drewry's Bluff and Petersburg in May and June. For much of 1864 his mixed brigade of Georgia and North Carolina units served at widely separated points, sometimes independently and sometimes as part of a division. Near the end of the war Dearing assumed command of the noted Laurel Brigade of Virginia cavalry. He was mortally wounded at its head on April 6, 1865, and died seventeen days later. Dearing was one of the youngest Confederate generals and the last to die from battle wounds. He is buried in Lynchburg, Virginia.

BIBLIOGRAPHY

Dearing, James. Papers. Virginia Historical Society, Richmond; Historical Society of Pennsylvania, Philadelphia; University of Virginia, Charlottesville.

Halsey, Don P. *Historic and Heroic Lynchburg*. Lynchburg, Va., 1935.

Parker, William L. *General James Dearing*. Lynchburg, Va., 1990.

ROBERT K. KRICK

DEATH AND MOURNING

One of the most famous images to come out of the South's wartime experience was of the funeral of a young Confederate officer. William D. Washington's 1864 painting *The Burial of Latané* immortalized the mourning ritual for twenty-nine-year-old Capt. William Latané, a Virginian killed in a skirmish near Richmond in June 1862. His brother John, who was with him when he died, took the body to a nearby plantation for burial. With the men away at war, the women, slaves, and children of the area fulfilled their promise to John Latané to give his brother a proper burial. A former editor for the *Southern Literary Messenger*, John R. Thompson, wrote a poem about the incident, and a verse from it appears on the marker over Latané's grave: "A brother bore his body from the field . . . but woman's voice read over his hallowed / dust the ritual of the dead." Washington's painting, frequently reproduced in the postbellum South, came to symbolize the Lost Cause and Southerners' response to the loss of so many of its young men.

Death and mourning were pressing matters to people experiencing a bloodbath. The casualty rate made Southerners acutely aware of mortality. Out of a potential military population of about a million, 750,000 soldiers served in the Confederate armies, and approximately 250,000 died during the war—about one in four Southern white men of military age in contrast to the Northern rate of one in ten. Individual battles, such as those at Sharpsburg, Shiloh, and Gettysburg, resulted in death on a scale that Americans had never seen before. In addition to battle deaths, disease killed both soldiers and civilians in unprecedented numbers; the ratio of those dying from disease to those killed in battle was close to two to one. Infectious diseases of childhood, such as mumps and measles, were killers of young country boys newly exposed to them. Camp diseases, including malaria, dysentery, and diarrhea, proved fatal to many soldiers as well.

Southerners of the mid-nineteenth century were accustomed to death. Growing up mostly in rural places, they were used to the slaughtering of livestock and the hunting of animals. Infant mortality rates were high and the death of family members not uncommon. But despite this familiarity, the scale of wartime carnage, the bullets and cannonballs tearing comrades apart, the sights and sounds and smells of mortality, hit soldiers hard. Death often came suddenly and left its memory in blood on survivors. Soldiers saw gruesome scenes of mutilated bodies and swollen corpses.

The men dealt with the psychological trauma in a number of ways. Some adopted a public attitude of indifference. Others went into despair, often developing hardened attitudes to inure them to the brutalities around them. Many engaged in grim humor, displaying a plain folk realism. During the siege of Petersburg, one wizened veteran cooking bacon was almost hit by a minié ball that disturbed his fire, and he complained: "Plague take them fellows. I 'spect they'll spile my grease yet before they stop their foolishness." A story told in the Confederate ranks was that one Yankee body would kill an acre of land but a Southerner's bones would fertilize it forever.

Most typically, Confederate soldiers accepted fatalistically the hard realities of death in war. Coming mainly from evangelical Protestant homes, they looked upon death as part of God's plan, and godliness became a protective armor. Imbued with the confidence of holy warriors at the beginning of the conflict, they trusted God to protect individual soldiers. But the length of the war and its bloodiness undermined this attitude. The good died all too often. It was hard enough to accept the death of an individual at home, but battle deaths eluded their understanding. How could such grotesque deaths be part of a divine plan, they wondered.

Fear of death was connected to the widespread revivalism in Confederate armies. As the casualty rates mounted and the war stretched on year after year, these soldiers in an evangelical age tried "to get right with God," to gain the assurance of salvation. As many as 150,000 soldiers may have professed religion during the war. Denominations encouraged revivalism by distributing death-focused tracts with such titles as *Prepare for Battle* and *A Word of Warning for the Sick Soldier. Sufferings of the Lost* predicted an eternity of fire and brimstone for the unrepentant, but *Mother's Parting Words to Her Soldier Boy,* issued to nearly 250,000 soldiers, promised hope after death; in heaven, home and family would be reunited.

Soldiers drew strength from this reassurance of an afterlife but feared an impersonal death. They saw comrades die anonymously and rest in unmarked graves, and they were

> **Soldiers seeking an honorable, decent death tried to invest it with meaning by facing death with bravery. . . .**

worried that their deaths would go unreported to their loved ones at home, that their remains would be treated with disrespect. Some soldiers pinned their names on their uniforms before battles; others carried letters from wives who could be notified of their death. But some men avoided attempts at identification, fearing that to prepare for death was to invite it.

Soldiers seeking an honorable, decent death tried to invest it with meaning by facing death with bravery and sacrificial gallantry. In recounting the tales of battle, much attention was given to the context in which the death occurred and whether the deceased had died illustrating the manly ideal. Burial carried an especially heavy burden of meaning. A Confederate soldier who suffered through the Battle of Gettysburg recalled that "the worst of all was we did not get to bury our dead."

Letters of condolence were a vital part of the mourning process. Soldiers clung to memories of home; writing of a friend's death, they often explicitly evoked scenes of childhood happiness in their letters. Soldiers typically avoided dwelling on death in their correspondence, both to save their home folks worry and to boost their own morale. But when they had to write in sympathy to a family about a comrade's death, the letter became a battlefront obituary. The writer would give the mourning family details of the casualty, including where and when the soldier fell, whether the death was instantaneous or prolonged, and what had happened to the remains. He would end with praise for the soldier's character and courage.

The rising tide of the dead as the war continued weakened morale, perhaps even more on the home front than on the battlefield. Confederate rhetoric taught that women as well as men had to sacrifice for the cause. Once the protectors of family, women now had to give up husbands and fathers, brothers and sons, for the Confederacy. Alone at home, they themselves faced the fear of death from illness, childbirth, and attacks on civilian populations. Bread riots hit Southern cities near the end of the war, led by women facing death by starvation for themselves and their children.

Women not only made sacrifices but also celebrated their martyred men. They transformed mourning from a private ceremony to a ritual with public meaning; by sanctifying the men who fought and died for the Confederacy, they sanctified the cause itself. But as the war dragged on and demands on soldiers and their families increased, women who faced the deaths of their loved ones in battle and at home became alienated. "My husband is my country," wrote one woman. "What is country to me if he be killed?" In the last year of the war, its emotional toll mounted, and, ironically, mourning seemed to lose its intensity. "People do not mourn their dead as they used to," wrote diarist Kate Stone in the spring of 1864. Soldiers had become hardened to the fighting and the death around them, and military hospitals were seen as places treating the injured and the dead with little respect.

Historians who argue for a collapse of the Confederate will to fight as a factor in its defeat can point to the accumulated effects of Southerners living with death as part of that collapse.

[*See also* Burial of Latané; Funerals.]

BIBLIOGRAPHY

Faust, Drew Gilpin. "Altars of Sacrifice: Confederate Women and the Narratives of War." *Journal of American History* 76 (1990): 1200–1228.

Mitchell, Reid. *Civil War Soldiers: Their Expectations and Their Experiences.* New York, 1988.

Wiley, Bell I. *The Life of Johnny Reb.* Indianapolis, 1943.

CHARLES REAGAN WILSON

DEBT

Debts within the Confederacy fell into four categories: those of the Confederate government, those of the states, those of local governments, and the obligations of private individuals to Northerners. The governmental debts were all repudiated after the war; private debts frequently proved impossible to collect as many Southern firms and citizens went bankrupt in 1865.

Confederate Debt. The Confederacy started out with no debt, but the outbreak of war in April 1861 forced the government to borrow heavily by issuing Treasury notes, bonds, and certificates of indebtedness payable on demand. These debts rapidly mounted.

At the end of the Provisional government on February 17, 1862, the total debt was $163.3 million of which $95.8 million was represented by Treasury notes, $41 million by loans, and $26.4 million in overdue army pay and other obligations. By January 1, 1863, the debt equaled $605.8 million, of which $410 million was in Treasury notes, $145 million in bonds, and $50 million in unpaid bills.

The debt expanded geometrically during 1863. Total indebtedness by January 1864 came to $1,340 million of which $791 million was in Treasury notes, $537 million in foreign and domestic bonds, and $150 million in past due army payments. Despite belatedly passed tax laws, the

> **The governmental debts were all repudiated after the war; private debts frequently proved impossible to collect. . . .**

Confederate debt by October 31, 1864, had risen to $1,863 million. Treasury notes fell to $709 million, and the funded debt was $804 million, with over $350 million of unpaid obligations. Economists generally agree that the primary cause of this rapid increase in the public debt lay in the absence of a productive internal revenue system.

State Debts. At the start of secession, the acknowledged debts of the eleven Confederate states were approximately $98 million. Since the states, particularly at the beginning of the war, were actively levying troops, their expenses were heavy. The states also furnished small-denomination notes as a substitute for hoarded silver coins and provided relief to soldiers' families and to the cotton planters, who were unable to export their produce.

Moreover, the state governments, pandering to the public opposition to the war tax, paid this levy on behalf of their citizens. They did so by selling state bonds for Confederate Treasury notes, which were paid over to the Confederacy.

So far as the prewar bonds were concerned, the states generally allowed the interest to accumulate on them until after the war, when the state finances had to be completely reorganized. This unpaid interest accounts in most cases for the reported increase in state debts in 1865.

Figures for the additional funded debt emitted during the war are not readily available. State governments did sell some bonds. The total funded indebtedness of the Southern states incurred on behalf of the Confederate cause was probably over $50 million.

War expenses, coupled with a limited borrowing ability and a reluctance to raise enough taxes to cover anything like the current expenses, inevitably resulted in the issue of large quantities of state Treasury notes. Total issues outstanding in 1865 exceeded $65 million, although because of funding operations and redemptions, the total amount issued may well have exceeded $100 million.

City and County Debts. Very few records of local government expenditures have survived from the Confederate era. Cities other than New Orleans, the South's largest metropolis, had limited credit. Consequently, to judge by the few surviving specimens in the numismatic market today, city and county bond issues were neither numerous nor in large amounts. Bond issues in even the richest Louisiana parishes frequently came to less than $15,000 and were used largely for arming and organizing local military units.

The note issues of towns and counties are better known, largely because many of them were approved by the state governments. There are also many surviving notes, which are sold to collectors today.

The largest issues of such currency occurred in Virginia, Louisiana, and Texas where practically all the counties and parishes issued notes and many of the cities and towns did so. The total in Virginia alone was $2.5 million. In South Carolina, which forbade local government scrip, such issues were practically confined to Charleston, while in other states only a handful of towns and about 15 percent of the counties emitted notes. The total of such issues came to about $12.5 million as compared to about $3 million of local government bonds.

Private Debts. As was typical of a quasi-colonial economy, the South depended for its commercial liquidity upon funds borrowed from outside the region. These were usually used by the local businessmen who lent the planters money in anticipation of the harvest to move the crops in the fall and import goods in the spring. In early 1861, the crop advances had been paid off and the usual $60 million of credits on merchandise had been curtailed to only $40 million by uneasy Northern lenders.

In addition, Northerners had made permanent investments in the South by purchasing government bonds and bank and railroad securities and by mortgage lending. Thus when the Federal government decreed the confiscation of Southern assets held in the North, the Confederate Congress retaliated in kind. The congressmen thought that as Northerners owned 30 percent of all Southern corporate capital and debt (which they valued at $300 million, although the number was nearer to $100 million), the sale of these investments and the collection of debts due Northerners would result in at least $100 million of cash for the Confederate Treasury. But these calculations proved to be wildly optimistic.

Leaving aside the unrealistic estimate, there were a variety of reasons the Confederacy managed to collect only $12 million from this program. Many Southerners wanted to maintain their Northern business relationships. Consequently, the New Orleans banks paid off $4 million of Northern debts after the war began, and many persons refused to report their obligations or Northern holdings in their corporations. Some also foresaw that if they paid such funds over to the Confederacy, they might have to pay twice in the event of a Union victory.

If anyone in the South had supported secession with a view to evading payment of their debts, the final outcome was a great disappointment. The war not only destroyed the value of all Confederate-related assets but left the Southerners obligated to pay their Northern creditors both the principal of what they owed and a four-year accumulation of interest as well.

The rapid and irresponsible accumulation of Confederate and state debts adversely affected government credit and the economy at large. A bloated currency led to hyperinflation, shortages of goods, and a general collapse of morale, military and civilian. By 1862, the public began to fear that the burgeoning debt would be completely or partially repudiated. Thus farmers refused to sell their crops to the Confederate agents. The army then resorted to seizing goods under impressment laws. Since owners were paid little or nothing for their crops, such actions alienated the victims while discouraging the production and distribution of food. Thus the growing public debt was among the factors contributing to Confederate defeat.

[*See also* Bonds; Confiscation; Currency; Impressment; Taxation.]

BIBLIOGRAPHY

Ball, Douglas B. *Financial Failure and Confederate Defeat.* Urbana, Ill., 1991.

Hawk, Emory Q. *Economic History of the South.* New York, 1934.

Schwab, John Christopher. *The Confederate States of America, 1861–1865.* New York, 1901.

Todd, Richard Cecil. *Confederate Finance.* Athens, Ga., 1954.

DOUGLAS B. BALL

DECLARATION OF IMMEDIATE CAUSES

The Declaration of the Immediate Causes of Secession was adopted by the South Carolina secession convention to explain the reasons for the state's withdrawal from the Union. The declaration was drafted by a special committee of the convention, chaired by Christopher G. Memminger, a long-time South Carolina congressman and future Confederate secretary of treasury.

The declaration represented the views of the more moderate members of the convention. Another document, the Address to the People of South Carolina, drafted by a committee chaired by Robert Barnwell Rhett, Sr., reflected the philosophy of the radical faction in the convention.

The declaration stated that South Carolina and other states had asserted their rights of freedom and sovereignty in the Declaration of Independence, the peace treaty signed with Great Britain in September 1783, and the Federal Constitution ratified in 1788. The declaration noted that in recent years the Northern states had refused to fulfill their constitutional obligations to the Southern states, especially in regard to fugitive slaves. The election of a president whose opinions and purposes were hostile to the Southern institution of slavery left South Carolina no recourse but to dissolve the union existing between the states and to resume its position as a separate and independent state.

The declaration was debated by the convention on December 24, 1860. An effort by Maxcy Gregg, a member of the radical faction, to table was defeated by a 124 to 31 vote, and the convention, after some minor amendments, passed the declaration.

BIBLIOGRAPHY

Channing, Steven A. *A Crisis of Fear: Secession in South Carolina.* New York; 1970.

Journal of the Convention of the People of South Carolina Held in 1860, 1861, and 1862, Together with the Ordinances, Reports, Resolutions. Columbia, S.C., 1862.

May, John Amasa, and Joan Reynolds Faunt. *South Carolina Secedes.* Columbia, S.C., 1960.

Wooster, Ralph A. *The Secession Conventions of the South.* Princeton, N.J., 1962.

RALPH A. WOOSTER

DEMOCRATIC PARTY

The American party system that emerged in the 1830s took deep root in the South as it did elsewhere in the country. The system was a highly mobilized, deeply divided one, in which Democrats and Whigs regularly confronted each other in intense election and legislative battles. In the Southern states, both parties competed effectively on a regionwide basis (with the exception of South Carolina, where the two-party system never developed). In the 1830s and 1840s the Democrats enjoyed their greatest Southern support in Mississippi, Alabama, Texas, Arkansas, and Florida, but they were closely competitive in the rest of the region as well.

In addition to their electoral strength, Southerners, such as James K. Polk, John C. Breckinridge, Howell Cobb, John Slidell, Jefferson Davis, and the editor Thomas Ritchie, also played significant roles in the national party, shaping its outlook, articulating its perspective, managing its activities, and

advancing its policies. Between 1836 and 1860, Southerners appeared on every Democratic presidential ticket.

The party's commitment to limited government included nonintervention with slavery where it existed and resistance to demands, when they arose, that slavery be abolished or its extension limited. Although Southerners were a minority within the party as a whole, their interests, when different from those of other Democrats, were safeguarded by such procedural devices as the need of a candidate to garner two-thirds of a national convention's votes before a nomination for president could be made.

When the crisis over the expansion of slavery into new territories began in the mid-1840s, the Democrats repeatedly demonstrated their commitment to leaving the South to pursue its own practices in peace and to sustaining its claim to equal treatment in the new territories. Democrats defended Southern rights and values within the Union even at the ultimate cost of Northern votes. And as the party became identified with appeasing Southerners in the matter of slavery extension, some Northerners reacted violently enough to contribute to a fundamental electoral realignment that severely weakened the party as a national force.

Many Northern Democrats resisted Senator Stephen A. Douglas's successful attempt in 1854, at Southern insistence, to repeal the Missouri Compromise prohibition of slavery in the federal territories above the line of 36° 30´ north latitude. Three years later the Democratic administration of President James Buchanan, again at Southern insistence, demanded that Congress accept Kansas's proslavery Lecompton Constitution. Douglas believed the Lecompton Constitution to be fraudulently ratified and a corruption of the notion of popular sovereignty, and he refused to accept any further moves by the party to guarantee slavery in the territories. A bitter and devastating internal party fight followed, and a significant number of Northern Democrats left their party in disagreement and disgust.

As a result, while keeping its national status and role, in the 1850s the center of gravity of the Democracy shifted South. This meant that, in addition to traditional Democratic policy preferences on economic development and issues of the role and power of government, the Democratic attitude toward slavery expansion became more favorable to Southern interests and more aggressive in its support for them. The Republican party built itself as a major political force by stressing how far the Democrats had become a tool of Southern interests.

There continued to be ideological congruence on a range of traditional Democratic policies among the factions. But they could not resolve their differences over how far to guarantee the right of slaveholders to take their property into new territories under Federal protection. In 1860, the fatal split led to two different Democratic candidates contesting for the surviving Democratic vote: Douglas, the national candidate, and

Breckinridge, the candidate of the Southern wing. This catastrophic national breach was the prelude to the secession crisis in which Southern Democrats divided between strong Southern rights men who led the secession movement, on the one hand, and on the other, various factions of administration supporters and more pro-Union types, including some who still followed Douglas despite his hostility toward the notion of a territorial slave code.

After secession and the establishment of the Confederacy, Democrats played important political roles in the new nation. The Confederacy's top leadership—Jefferson Davis and such cabinet members as Robert M. T. Hunter and Judah P. Benjamin, among many others—were all prominent prewar Democrats who continued to dominate the policies and politics of their homeland. The Democratic commitment to limited government remained a hallmark of their policies as well. Although wartime exigencies inevitably led to the centralization of power in the Confederacy, its very strong state rights tradition more than echoed prewar Democratic advocacy in a way that Whiggery did not.

Political divisions within the Confederacy were persistent and bitter in constitutional conventions and state legislatures, in Congress, and ultimately in the electoral arena. Although formal partisanship and party organization was discouraged and never officially existed, partisan memories and differences, under other names and in fragmented fashion, often affected policies, attitudes, and behavior in the Confederate States. And there was a Whig-dominated revulsion against the Democratic leaders of the Southern nation expressed in state and congressional elections in the upper South in 1862 and 1863. But all of this remained localized and unsustained in the absence of formal national institutions of electoral and policy mobilization and management: caucuses, partisan newspapers, national committees, and regular conventions.

In the North during the Civil War, the Democratic party remained strong and vigorous, although it was now the minority party there, owing to the loss of its Southern wing. Generally, most Northern Democrats supported the war against secession, but though hostile to the Confederacy, they provided continuous and sturdy opposition to the Lincoln administration, challenging what they believed to be Republican lust for revolutionary changes in American society, including the end of slavery. At the same time, an important peace wing in the party fought strenuously to end the war and allow the South to do as it wished. They were strong enough to include a peace plank in their national platform in 1864. Confederate leaders hoped for Democratic victory in the nation, but their hopes were in vain. Although the racism and tenacious, crabbed conservatism of many Democrats attracted hundreds of thousands of votes in the North, their search for peace without victory and their willingness to appease the South allowed the Republicans to brand all

Democrats as Southern sympathizers, even traitors to the Union in time of peril. One Republican newspaper, the *New York Evening Post,* blasted them, not untypically, as the party of "Dixie, Davis and the devil."

This war-induced Southern coloration of the Democratic party remained a potent issue in national politics for more than a generation after Appomattox. "Waving the Bloody Shirt" of Unionism against Democrats was standard Republican practice into the 1890s. Although a "solid South" favorable to the Democrats also ultimately was a product of the Civil War and its aftermath, the pro-Southern tone of the party over the course of America's most dramatic and defining episode as a nation severely handicapped Democratic efforts to regain control of national politics until well into the twentieth century.

[*See also* Bleeding Kansas; Copperheads; Election of 1860; Fugitive Slave Law; *and biographies of numerous figures mentioned herein.*]

BIBLIOGRAPHY

Alexander, Thomas P., and Richard E. Beringer. *The Anatomy of the Confederate Congress: A Study of the Influences of Member Characteristics on Legislative Voting Behavior, 1861–1865.* Nashville, Tenn., 1972.

Escott, Paul. *After Secession: Jefferson Davis and the Failure of Confederate Nationalism.* Baton Rouge, La., 1987.

Freehling, William W. *The Road to Disunion: Secessionists at Bay, 1776–1854.* New York, 1990.

Johannsen, Robert. *Stephen A. Douglas.* New York, 1973.

Kruman, Marc. *Parties and Politics in North Carolina, 1836–1865.* Baton Rouge, La., 1983.

Nichols, Roy F. *The Disruption of the American Democracy.* New York, 1948.

Silbey, Joel H. *A Respectable Minority: The Democratic Party in the Civil War Era, 1860–1868.* New York, 1978.

JOEL H. SILBEY

DESERTION

Although desertion was as prevalent in the Union army as in the Confederate forces, the North's overwhelming superiority in numbers made such defections a comparatively minor annoyance for the Union, whereas for the South they were disastrous. In the spring of 1862 Confederate desertion had progressed alarmingly, and by the latter half of the war hundreds of regiments could not muster so much as half of their paper strength. In the wake of the Battle of Sharpsburg (September 17, 1862), Gen. Robert E. Lee told President Jefferson Davis that deserters and stragglers had deprived him of a third to a half of his effective force and "were the main cause of . . . retiring from Maryland."

The War Department's official estimate disclosed that there were by June 30, 1863, 136,000 absent from the three Confederate armies of Lee, Braxton Bragg, and John C. Pemberton; and in September 1864, Davis told a Macon, Georgia, audience that two-thirds of the army was absent without leave. If half of them would return, he said, victory would be within the Confederacy's grasp. The gravity of the statistics becomes clear when it is recalled that the entire effective strength of the Confederate army never exceeded 500,000 at any one time, and that at Gettysburg (July 1–3, 1863) the Confederacy's troops numbered only 75,000.

Thirty years after Appomattox, North Carolina's future chief justice Walter Clark became editor of the five-volume *Histories of the North Carolina Regiments*. The individual authors of its regimental histories made almost no reference

> ## If half of them would return, he said, victory would be within the Confederacy's grasp.

to desertion as a factor in the war, but Clark himself candidly wrote that "the evil became so great that it overcame all bounds and together with the breakdown in the finances of the Confederacy it was the cause of its overthrow."

As the war progressed, attitudes of both soldiers and civilians toward deserters softened from vociferous outrage to grudging tolerance and not infrequently to unconcealed sympathy. In midsummer of 1863 a conscription official in South Carolina reported to the Richmond government that "it is no longer a reproach to be known as a deserter," and early in 1865, Gen. John S. Preston, superintendent of the Confederate Bureau of Conscription, declared that "so common is the crime, it has in popular estimation lost the stigma which justly pertains to it, and [deserters] are everywhere shielded by their families and by the sympathies of many communities."

It is, of course, impossible to establish with precision the motives that prompted any particular soldier to abandon the Confederate colors, but much can be learned from letters written by troops in the ranks now reposing in private collections, public and private libraries, archives, and museums; from wartime newspapers; and from the *Official Records of the War of the Rebellion*. The latter contains hundreds of dispatches by Federal commanders in which data drawn from interviews with Southern defectors were transmitted to Union headquarters, as well as quantities of letters in which Confederate officers and civilians discuss the causes of the flight from duty.

Some soldiers were by temperament, experience, or for reasons of health less able than their comrades to cope with hunger, cold, rain, sleeplessness, disease, wounds, and exposure. Many were pitifully ignorant of the war's issues; many were depressed by dispiriting letters from home; and some, as they contemplated the plight of their families on hardscrabble farms in the rural hinterlands felt that they were choosing between deserting the army or deserting their families in a cause they only dimly understood. The more pious troopers found it hard to bear the sights and sounds of wickedness that offended their eyes and ears at every turn, and others were more grievously distressed than their tent-mates by news from home about the depredations of marauding bands of deserters, vandals, and Confederate cavalrymen who "borrowed" their poultry and livestock for food.

Perhaps the most frequent complaints were the scarcity of rations, the sporadic payment of their paltry wages, the unavailability of furloughs, and the news of peace meetings on the home front. The rigors of campaigning and of combat were, of course, a severe trial, to say nothing of the tedium of inactivity during the long winter months, which was hard on rustics pining for a furlough that never came, ignorant of their military obligations. Mystified by the rules of discipline and the Articles of War, they had little understanding of the gravity of their offense. There were, in fact, men in all social ranks who were—at least from time to time—far from convinced that the cause was worth the compulsory military service they were called upon to perform in what many considered a "rich man's war and a poor man's fight."

Official response to the problem included measures to prevent desertions; to return escapees to the ranks; to round up draft dodgers; and to punish wrongdoers both to deter other runaways and to penalize defections. The authorities confronted a dilemma in the desperately outnumbered Confederacy. If deserters were severely punished, they could not be immediately, if at all, returned to duty; and if the draft laws were aggressively enforced in seriously disaffected areas, loyalty to the cause would falter. But if a policy of leniency were pursued, regiments in the field would be seriously thinned.

Efforts to raise the enlisted man's morale and ease his hardships included the provision of food and other necessities to his hard-pressed family, supplemented by appeals to those at home not to write gloomy letters to men in the army. Generals also ordered regimental commanders to read to the troops at assembly the sections of the Articles of War that bore upon straggling, desertion, and insubordination.

In times of heightened discouragement, following hard fighting, exhausting marches, exposure to hunger and weather, and disheartening news of defeats, the Confederacy made such efforts as its meager means permitted to scour the country for additional rations and supplies (notably shoes and blankets), to distribute occasional rations of whiskey, and to improve opportunities for recreation and for worship.

But when, despite these efforts, desertion continued unabated, the authorities would experiment briefly with the tightening of discipline. A few particularly incorrigible offenders might be publicly executed, furloughs virtually suspended, and even minor offenses punished with unaccustomed vigor. But such strategems did little to reduce disaffection and were periodically abandoned until another surge of exasperation prompted another attempt.

To prevent troops from dropping out of line, commanders published stringent orders regulating such conduct, and frequent roll calls, sometimes three or four in an hour, kept a check upon soldiers' whereabouts. The most severe command issued by General Lee to curb desertion and straggling was his general order (perhaps never seriously enforced) instituting a system of "file closers," assigning to every tenth man on the march the duty of keeping a fixed bayonet and loaded pistol at the ready to cut down men who showed evidence of breaking from the ranks. The object, Lee sadly explained, was to "make the avoidance of duty more dangerous than its performance."

Sometimes the granting of furloughs was suspended altogether, either because the men simply could not be spared or because furloughed men all too frequently failed to return. The number of furloughs was often tied to the number of men present for duty, a policy calculated to give every aspirant for a leave a stake in the whole regiment's attendance record. To tighten controls further, an order might stipulate that a regimental commander must accompany a certificate of furlough with his affirmation "that none are absent without leave since the publication of this order."

Until the critical summer of 1863, newspapers throughout the Confederacy were crowded with paid notices calling for the return of specifically named deserters, carefully identified as to regiment and company, and offering thirty dollars for each runaway apprehended. The tactic was eventually abandoned as a failure, for it yielded almost no harvest. In some tragic instances soldiers published as deserters were in fact not runaways at all but were discovered to have been killed in action or to have died of wounds or disease.

Several times a conciliatory policy was undertaken whereby the government offered amnesty to soldiers who would return by a specified date and pledged that they would not be punished. When the offer brought little response, the date was extended, but even this indulgence proved unavailing in the end. Contemporary records do show, however, that thousands of absentees went home fully intending to return to duty after looking to the spring plowing and planting and did in fact drift back to their units.

When efforts to prevent desertion and to persuade recusants to return disappointed official hopes, the Confederate authorities turned increasingly to more aggressive measures by stricter enforcement of military regulations, the Articles of War, and state laws forbidding civilians to harbor or assist runaways. The twentieth Article of War prescribed that troops who were "convicted of having deserted . . . shall suffer death, or such other punishments as, by sentence of a court martial, shall be inflicted." In addition the Confederacy assigned to various civil and military agencies the duty of hunting down and capturing fugitives to be returned to their units for trial and sentencing.

Because the Articles of War did not clearly distinguish between "desertion" and "absence without leave," those charged with enforcement were disposed to shrink from relentlessly pursuing absentees and dealing out the full penalties. Desertion, literally construed, was the abandonment of military service with *intent not to return*—a point all but impossible to establish. In short, hunting deserters was always a sprawling, widespread, but unsuccessful enterprise.

Not infrequently deserters chose not to return to their own homes where they might encounter official pursuers, but congregated in mountainous or wooded regions where enthusiasm for the Confederacy was at best grudging. When militia units were dispatched to duty in such "deserter country," it was by no means unusual to discover that their quarry were more numerous and better organized and armed than they themselves were. Not a few Confederate deserters chose to cross over to Union lines where, in relative comfort and safety, they were separately interviewed for military information to be forwarded to Union headquarters.

Runaways who were apprehended and convicted by courts-martial were subjected to various punishments, among them detention in military prisons, subjection to ball-and-chain confinement, bread and water diets, stoppage of pay, branding with the letter D, hanging by the thumbs, and "bucking and gagging." More severe were the infliction of a stipulated number of lashes (usually thirty-nine or fifty, "well laid on") and long prison terms at hard labor. Most fearful of all was the death penalty, in nearly all cases by firing squad but occasionally by hanging. The records of courts-martial in the National Archives confirm the conclusion that only a relatively small number of deserters sentenced to death actually suffered the extreme penalty. The court-martial's proceedings were sent upward through the chain of command to the secretary of war for review and then to President Davis for final determination. In hundreds of cases, death sentences stopped there and were mercifully revoked by the president and replaced by lesser penalties.

By modern standards, however, the death penalty was by no means rare. A special study of its application to the men of North Carolina's regiments has disclosed that approximately two hundred of the state's convicted deserters were executed while their assembled comrades were compelled to look on as a warning not to bring the same fate upon themselves. Because North Carolina supplied approximately a fifth of enlistments, it may perhaps be assumed that the total Confederate executions approached a thousand.

Only a small fraction of the Confederacy's deserters were in fact apprehended and sentenced, and it seems safe to say that a similarly small proportion of those convicted were actually put to death. There can be little doubt that capital punishment was resorted to not primarily to punish the transgressor but to afford examples for those contemplating defection. There is, moreover, no evidence to suggest that the imposition of the death penalty was in any significant degree more effective than lesser penalties in curbing the propensity of a surprising number of Civil War soldiers, North and South, to yield to the impulse to abandon their more steadfast comrades.

[*See also* Class Conflict; File Closers; Military Justice; Morale.]

BIBLIOGRAPHY

Bardolph, Richard. "Confederate Dilemma: North Carolina Troops and the Desertion Problem." *North Carolina Historical Review* 66 (January and April 1989): 61–86; 179–210.

Dodge, David. "The Cave-Dwellers of the Confederacy." *Atlantic Monthly* 68 (1891): 514–521.

Lonn, Ella. *Desertion during the Civil War*. New York, 1928. Reprint, Gloucester, Mass., 1966.

Martin, Bessie. *Desertion of Alabama Troops from the Confederate Army*. New York, 1932.

Moore, Albert B. *Conscription and Conflict in the Confederacy*. New York, 1924. Reprint, New York, 1963.

Robertson, James I., Jr. *Soldiers Blue and Grey*. Columbia, S.C., 1988.

Wiley, Bell I. *The Life of Johnny Reb*. Baton Rouge, La., 1971.

RICHARD BARDOLPH

DIARIES, LETTERS, AND MEMOIRS

No event in American history has provoked more extensive and heated commentary on the part of participants than the Civil War. Recognized, even before it began, by people on both sides as a historic—for some a missionary—confrontation to determine the future course and identity of the United States, the war seemed to demand that those who had lived through it record their experience and reflect upon its larger significance. But for those who had lived within or fought for the Confederate States of America, the significance was greater yet. The defeat of the Confederacy and emancipation of the slaves, followed by the abolition of slavery, bequeathed a special and uniquely conflicted legacy to the white and black residents of the erstwhile seceding states.

Personal or firsthand accounts of life within the Confederacy and of the war to defend it abound and take a variety of forms. Diaries and journals kept during the war interweave the experiences of specific individuals with the vicissitudes of the struggle. In varying degree, depending upon the sophistication of the author, these are crafted literary documents, some of which were revised for publication by the author, others of which have been rescued from oblivion by editors and historians who have recognized their special value. Letters, written during the war and subsequently published, normally embody greater spontaneity, since their authors usually had no thought of publication. Memoirs, which most often were written after the cessation of hostilities and explicitly intended for publication, tend to subordinate representations of the author to an evaluation of the events the author observed or participated in. Memoirs, too, frequently served to justify the author's evaluation of battles, strategies, policies, or events, and, if relevant, the author's role in them.

Chronicling Momentous Events. Before the news of Abraham Lincoln's election to the presidency raced through the Southern states, white Southerners of both sexes and all ages put pen to paper to record their private experience of what they sensed would prove momentous events. At the beginning of June 1860, Catherine Ann Devereux Edmonston, in Halifax County, North Carolina, began the diary that she would keep throughout the war, noting that although she had previously commenced diaries, she had always left off, "perhaps from weariness, perhaps from an absolute dearth of events."

Beginning in 1860, she and other Southerners had a plethora of events to reflect upon and record. At an accelerating rate, the war forced itself into the most isolated and previously uneventful lives. In the most common pattern, men were drawn into politics and battles while women remained at home to cope with the management of rural households, hostile troops and marauders, the ever more burdensome dearth of supplies, and, eventually, the upheaval of emancipation. But the lines between men's and women's experience of the war were never entirely neat. Some women participated directly in the political and military circles of Richmond and other cities. Others, who founded and staffed hospitals for the wounded and dying, lived intimately with the human cost of the conflict. As the Union's war effort broadened into William Tecumseh Sherman's policy of systematic devastation, women found themselves the direct objects of military attack. And all women were vulnerable to the disruptions and deprivations that followed in the wake of mobilization, military conflict, and, ultimately, defeat. Nor were men, notwithstanding their special concern with military events, impervious to or isolated from the disruption of civilian life.

The four years of the Civil War and the Confederacy decisively shaped Southern life and consciousness for the ensuing century and beyond. White Southerners initially turned to diaries and journals because they knew themselves to be living during a momentous historical epoch, to be living through revolutionary events. Fighting for Southern independence and the preservation of slavery as a social system, they knew that the outcome of the struggle would result in the recognition of a new nation or in their subjugation. So they wrote of their experience in the knowledge that even its most mundane details would one day be of interest to others.

If white Southerners kept their diaries and journals while uncertain of the outcome, they published them when the outcome had been decided. The shadow of defeat thus hangs over the Southern accounts of the war and the Confederacy that we read today. Consider the case of Mary Boykin Chesnut, the most celebrated Confederate diarist of all. Born into one political family of the slaveholding elite and having

> ... women's diaries provide the most extensive information about life on the home front. . . .

married into an even more influential and wealthy one, she spent much of the war in the company of the innermost circles of the Confederacy. Her published diary appropriately begins on February 18, 1861, the day of Jefferson Davis's inauguration as provisional president of the Confederacy. The concluding entry, July 26, 1865, begins, "I do not write often now—not for want of something to say, but from a loathing of all I see and hear. Why dwell upon it?"

Between 1865 and her death on November 22, 1886, Mary Chesnut turned periodically to revising her diary for publication. In her case, thanks to the scholarship of Elisabeth Muhlenfeld and C. Vann Woodward, we can follow the progress of successive revisions and, accordingly, recognize at least some of the considerations that led her subtly but tellingly to rewrite her account under the influence of unfolding events. Revisions similar to, if not as extensive and self-conscious as Mary Chesnut's, almost certainly shaped the published diaries and journals of others as well.

Mary Chesnut's diary especially reveals the tension that permeates most, if not all, Confederate diaries and journals between the writer's concern to provide a chronicle of events and his or her concern to provide an autobiographical portrait. Thus she interweaves accounts of conversations among influential or not-so-influential participants and descriptions of life in various parts of the Confederacy with reflections upon herself—her role in events, other people's reactions to her, her character, and her feelings. In this respect, the diaries and journals of the Confederacy normally embody interpretations of the struggle on the part of those who are desperately assessing the consequences of defeat, attempting to justify their own actions and roles, worrying about their own and their region's future place in the newly consolidated

Union, or trying to construct from the bitterness of defeat a history or memory in which future generations of Southerners might take comfort and pride. But if all the diaries and journals, in greater or lesser degree, reflect their writer's concern with self-portraiture and the worthiness of their section's cause, many also provide invaluable information on the waging of the struggle at the front, in political circles, and at home.

Women's Diaries. For obvious reasons, women's diaries provide the most extensive information about life on the home front, although letters from absent husbands frequently include information—and, not infrequently, directives—on how things should be done. Women from different parts of the South and with different levels of income detailed discrete versions of a general story of hardship and, as the years passed, deprivation and devastation. As a young woman, Lucy Rebecca Buck in Front Royal, Virginia, lived through several periods of occupation by both Union and Confederate troops. She especially registered the destruction of the fences upon her family's farm and the demands to feed the occupiers. Like Lucy Buck, Kate Stone, from a well-to-do Louisiana slaveholding family, experienced the war as a young woman. As the fighting around Vicksburg intensified and the forts and cities around it fell, Federal gunboats and soldiers came to dominate their lives. In resistance, Kate's mother burned twenty thousand dollars worth of cotton rather than allow the invaders to capture it. Supplies of food and clothing dwindled, relations with slaves deteriorated, and in 1863 the family, like many others of the region, migrated with 130 slaves and what possessions they could salvage to Tyler, Texas, where they spent the remainder of the war.

Parthenia Hague spent the war as a schoolteacher on a large plantation in southern Alabama. As the blockade of the coast between Mobile and New Orleans tightened, especially after the capture of Ship's Island in September 1861, she and the family with whom she was living began to feel the pinch of dwindling imports. In her diary, published in 1888, she proudly recounted her own and the other white women's ingenuity in devising substitutes for the luxuries they had previously enjoyed. She described in especially loving detail their growing skill in the production of cloth and clothing, from spinning and weaving to dyeing and sewing. Since, before the war, elite white women were unlikely to have used walnuts for brown dye or even to have known that they could, we may assume that she and her friends received invaluable instruction from slave women, who had been dyeing cloth for "Sunday clothing" for their own families throughout the antebellum period.

Because of shortages caused by the blockade, the escalating inflation of the Confederate dollar, the failure and devastation of crops, and the depredations of enemy troops, unaccustomed economic hardships permeated white Southern women's experience and recollections of the war.

As a result, many others like Parthenia Hague also wrote of the ways in which they were forced to make do and the goods they had to do without.

But while women's lives on farms and plantations ranged from uncomfortable to dangerous, some women's lives in the cities assumed a cast of frenetic gaiety, characterized by the feeling that one should dance tonight for tomorrow one may die. Years later, Thomas Cooper De Leon published his recollections of those days and that mood. In a diary that was never published, Meta Morris Grimball worried about the effect that the new laxness in social mores would have upon her daughters. And after the war, Emma Holmes still wrote disapprovingly of the festive mood that had prevailed in Charleston as late as 1865.

Other women, however, lived intimately, as nurses, with the more somber face of the war. Throughout the South many, such as Virginia Davis Gray in Arkansas, sewed clothes for soldiers and nursed the wounded in their own homes or in hospitals. Phoebe Yates Pember, who served as a hospital matron in Richmond, provided a careful account of hospital organization and nursing activities.

Most diarists focused upon what they considered the most dramatic aspects of their experience, notably the arrival of enemy troops, the burning of plantations and farms, and the departure of slaves. Mary Sharp Jones and her pregnant daughter, Mary Sharp Jones Mallard, kept a journal of their harrowing experience of the ruthlessness of Sherman's soldiers who pillaged and occupied their plantation, Montevideo, during the March to the Sea. Eliza Frances Andrews, who edited the diary of her youth for publication in 1908, described her growing fear of the Northerners as she traveled in late 1864 and early 1865 across the route of Sherman's march through Georgia. What she saw redoubled her fears of the enemy: "Yankee, Yankee, is the one detestable word always ringing in Southern ears. . . . They thwart all my plans, murder my friends, and make my life miserable." As a seventeen-year-old, Emma LeConte personally experienced the terror of Sherman's approach. After surviving the destruction and pillaging of Columbia, South Carolina, she wrote of feeling unconquered and of hating the Federals more than ever, viewing the very name *Yankee* as "a synonym for *all* that is *mean, despicable* and *abhorrent*."

Other women, like Elizabeth Hardin who described the confusion that overtook Nashville after the fall of Fort Donelson, penned their own accounts of civilians' direct encounters with military activities. Burning cities, scorched countryside, and looted plantations indeed brought the war into Southern homes—although none so much as the news of a dead or wounded friend, cousin, father, brother, husband, or son.

For many slaveholding women the response of their own former slaves to the news of the Emancipation Proclamation seemed the irreducible moment of truth—the final destruc-

tion of the world they had known and the devastating knowledge that they might never have understood the slaves they had thought they knew well. One diarist after another has her own example of disillusionment—of the slave, frequently a trusted house servant whom she had considered virtually a member of the family, who took off without so much as a good-bye. Mary Chesnut was taken aback when, in 1865, her friends the Martins left Columbia "and their mammy, the negro woman who had nursed them, refused to go with them. That daunted me."

Many slaveholding women found it hard to accept the simple fact that their former slaves wanted to be free, and even those who acknowledged the desire for freedom had great difficulty in understanding what freedom meant. Diaries teem with women's accounts of their problems with the former slaves who did remain, but now had to be treated like the free laborers they were. Ella Gertrude Clanton Thomas had an especially difficult time in coming to terms with those of her

> . . . letters permit us to glimpse the experiences and perceptions of less affluent and less well educated Southerners who found the time and the words. . . .

former slaves who stayed. On the other hand, Catherine Edmonston was frankly relieved to be free of the responsibility for hers. Since men's absence had forced many women to assume unaccustomed responsibilities of farm and plantation management, their difficulties with former slaves concerned labor in the fields as well as service in the house. The departure of slaves confronted many former slaveholding women with the desperate situation women on small farms had contended with throughout the war. And what slaveholding women registered as unimaginable burdens, former slave women embraced as new, if uncertain, opportunities.

Letters. Like diaries and journals, letters between friends or family members provide an immediate impression of the confusion and challenges of everyday life and the mounting problems during the final years of the conflict. Robert Manson Myers's edition of the letters of the men and women of the family of Charles Colcock Jones, a Presbyterian minister and the owner of large slaveholdings in Liberty County, Georgia, conveys the immediate response of the members of a highly educated elite family to the disasters that were falling upon them.

Throughout the war, Southerners wrote to friends and kin in the North about their views and experiences. In March 1861, Sue Sparks Keitt of South Carolina explained the decision to secede to a Northern friend, denouncing the intentions of the "Black Republicans." And Sarah Lamb, whose husband was the commanding officer of Fort Fisher, North Carolina, wrote regularly to her parents in Providence, Rhode Island, about life in the blockade-running city.

Letters became a lifeline that bound those who were separated by the fighting. Typically, soldiers wrote to the parents, siblings, wives, or sweethearts they had left at home of the travails of life at the front, and those at home wrote of their growing difficulties. Winston Stevens of the Second Florida Cavalry and his wife, young Octavia, who remained to cope with their plantation in Florida, corresponded about the hardships they both confronted and, toward the end, worried about the departure of the slaves and the threat of insurrection. In a similar vein, Isaac Hall, a private from Bienville Parish, Louisiana, and his wife, Mary, exchanged accounts of their respective problems. Many yeoman men, like William Stoker of Texas, worried about their wives and their farms. Stoker knew that enemy soldiers might mistreat women whose husbands were away; he also knew that women could be unfaithful. And like so many small farmers, he was especially aware of how hard it would be for women to plant and harvest crops or find help for doing so.

More than diaries and journals, which were primarily written by those who had education and leisure, letters permit us to glimpse the experiences and perceptions of less affluent and less well educated Southerners who found the time and the words to communicate with the family members and friends from whom they were separated. Leander Huckaby, who served in the Eleventh Mississippi Infantry in the Peninsular campaign and who spelled pneumonia "new monia," wrote to his wife of his experiences and his concern for the maintenance of their farm. Letters such as these, by ordinary people whose words usually would not have been preserved, bring alive the suffering, discomfort, and physical danger that were a daily reality for innumerable Southerners.

Freedmen's Bureau Papers. African American Southerners—whether slaves, escaped slaves, free blacks, or emancipated slaves—were even less likely than the less affluent whites to keep journals and diaries, to write letters, or to have their letters preserved. But from the start— although at an accelerating rate following the news of the Emancipation Proclamation—more and more black Southerners came in contact with the agents of the Freedmen's Bureau, who received letters from and about them, took affidavits from them, and generally monitored their situation.

Although the papers of the Freedmen's Bureau obviously differ from those of private individuals, they nonetheless offer direct testimony to at least some of the experiences and aspirations of those who were attempting to extricate themselves from slavery—those who were claiming their freedom. In this respect, the edition of the papers of the Freedmen's Bureau for the war years contributes an essential dimension to an understanding of the Confederacy. What some

Southerners experienced as a traumatic defeat, other Southerners experienced as the dawn of a new era.

A Political Diary. From the beginning, life in the Confederacy unfolded under the shadow of mobilization for and conduct of a war. The business of war dominated the operations of the Confederate government, which was born of the determination to defend Southern independence and died with Southern defeat on the battlefield. J. B. Jones, who, four days before the firing on Fort Sumter, fled South from Philadelphia, where he had been editing a proslavery newspaper, the *Southern Monitor,* spent the years of the war in Richmond as clerk to the five successive Confederate secretaries of war. During those years, Jones, an accomplished professional writer, kept an extensive diary of the events and personalities he witnessed at first hand.

Jones's diary captures the quality of life in Richmond, the intrigues and tensions that frequently pervaded the civilian and military leadership of the Confederacy, and the ways in which the war pervaded the consciousness of Confederate purpose. Sitting in the War Office, he was always among the first to learn of military successes, defeats, and shortages. He was also privy to the jockeyings for position and what he sometimes took to be the failure to appreciate talent. In March 1862, for example, he noted, "Price, Beauregard, Walker, Bonham, Toombs, Wise, Floyd, and others of the brightest lights of the South have been somehow successively obscured. And Joseph E. Johnston is a doomed fly, sooner or later, for he said, not long since, that there could be no hope of success as long as Mr. [Judah P.] Benjamin was Secretary of War." Since the words had been spoken at a dinner table, he observed, they would reach the ears of the secretary. And three days later he penned the deadpan entry, "Mr. Benjamin has been promoted. He is now Secretary of State."

Even as the pace of events accelerated and Southern prospects looked ever less hopeful, Jones retained his cool, understated tone. In the fall of 1864, he dispassionately recorded, "Sherman left a burning Atlanta at his back and started his 'March to the Sea.' " Two days later, noting that the Confederate Senate had passed a resolution requesting that Jefferson Davis limit the number of exemptions from military service that governors might grant, he wryly added, "This will, perhaps, startle Governor Smith of Virginia, who has already kept out of the army at least a thousand." Perhaps, Jones reflected, "it will hit Governor Brown of Georgia, also; but Sherman will hit him hardest."

A passionate and occasionally acerbic Confederate, Jones was a proslavery man and a Southern nationalist. His diary, published in 1866 shortly after the Confederate defeat and before the more self-consciously crafted diaries that appeared during the final decades of the nineteenth century, ranks among the most illuminating and comprehensive accounts of the day-by-day progress of the Confederacy.

Military Memoirs and Diaries. Although a civilian, Jones's experience in the War Department afforded him a special position from which to appreciate the constant encroachment of the war effort on every aspect of Southern life. Gen. Edward Porter Alexander spent those same years upon the field of battle with the Army of Northern Virginia, participating in both Manassas campaigns, as well as the Sharpsburg campaign, the Battles of Fredericksburg and Chancellorsville, and the Gettysburg campaign. During the final year of the war, he was present at Wilderness, Spottsylvania, the siege of Petersburg, and Appomattox. Not until 1897 did Alexander, at his children's prompting, begin to write the story of his experience. After completing a massive manuscript, he began to polish sections, which he published to great acclaim in 1907 as *Military Memoirs of a Confederate.* The more personal sections, which he kept back, were not identified, collected, and published until 1989, when they appeared as *Fighting for the Confederacy.*

Alexander's *Military Memoirs,* which were admired by President Theodore Roosevelt and countless historians, stand as a model of an objective, almost scholarly account of the Army of Northern Virginia as seen by a participant, in keeping with Alexander's own ambition to tell the story professionally. For that very reason, the *Military Memoirs* excluded many of his personal responses and, especially, his candid assessment of other participants. *Fighting for the Confederacy* breaks that silence, permitting readers to glimpse, for example, a complex portrait of Gen. Robert E. Lee as not merely a brilliant commander but a man of humor, frustration, anger, and his share of pettiness. More important, it offers an immediate and wonderfully detailed picture of army life that is all the more gripping for being told by a man who had firsthand knowledge of the business of war—of the importance of terrain, of supplies, of chains of command, of railroads, and all the rest. And even at his most candid, Alexander retains the responsible commander's respect for those with whom he was working and fighting. The point of his book is the immediate evocation of experience, not an after-the-fact ascription of blame.

Alexander's *Fighting for the Confederacy,* while an exemplary narrative of life on the Confederate battlefront, does not stand alone. The writings of innumerable ordinary soldiers who attempted, in memoirs, diaries, or letters, to capture their personal experience in specific battles or locations may now be seen as so many small pieces in an immense mosaic of collective memory. Leonidas Torrence, a corporal in the Twenty-third (formerly Thirteenth) North Carolina Infantry, penned his own account of the Peninsular, Sharpsburg, Chancellorsville, and Gettysburg campaigns, including the bout of measles that kept him, like so many others, out of action for a period. John Tucker, a sergeant in the Fifth Alabama Infantry, wrote of many of the same campaigns, including accounts of how he provisioned his troops with help

from civilians by plundering Union camps and by foraging. John Johnston, who served in the Seventh and Fourteenth Tennessee cavalries and participated in the Confederate withdrawals from Tennessee, Mississippi, and Georgia, later recalled the experience of being under fire, when the tension mounted so high that the hours went by like minutes. The feeling dissipated as one became "indifferent to time and danger." But after the fighting had ceased, he and his comrades experienced an indescribable feeling of delight and relief.

Even as the war was raging, soldiers and civilians alike expressed criticism of its general conduct and frequently of Jefferson Davis or specific commanders. Edwin Hedge Fay, who served first as a sergeant in Webb's (Louisiana) Cavalry Company and then as captain of the Office of the Chief of the Topographical Bureau, District of West Louisiana and Arkansas, had scant patience with the war or the army, which he constantly schemed to leave so as to go home to his family. Valerius Cincinnatus Giles, a captain in the Fourth Texas Infantry, wondered in his diary about Gen. Braxton Bragg's failure to follow up the victory at Chickamauga with a pursuit of Gen. William S. Rosecrans's army. Sam Watkin's well known memoir, *"Co. Aytch" Maury Grays,* is similarly very critical of Bragg's generalship throughout the war. Thomas Jewett Goree, captain in the First Corps of the Army of Northern Virginia and aide-de-camp to Gen. James Longstreet, never spared other officers in his letters and even ranked them according to their drinking habits. He deplored President Davis's failure to take Washington after the First Battle of Manassas and reproached him for his misunderstanding of his generals, especially Joseph E. Johnston.

Memoirs as Apologia. The generals had their own quarrels with one another that were born in the bitterness of mounting reverses and festered long after the war. Gen. John Bell Hood's memoir of the Army of Tennessee, which he commanded, began as a report to the Confederate Congress on his failure in the Franklin and Nashville campaign but, by 1880, had grown into a full-fledged book, which Gen. P. G. T. Beauregard arranged to have published as part of his own continuing struggle with Jefferson Davis and Gen. Joseph E. Johnston. Johnston had already aired his position, to which Hood was responding, in his *Narrative of Military Operations* (1874). In 1891, Beauregard followed up Hood's counterattack with his own commentary, justifying the wisdom of his actions and his role in the army. Gen. James Longstreet, bitter over the criticism of his alleged failure at Gettysburg, used his memoirs published in 1896 to defend his record.

For all the bitterness among the former generals of the Confederacy, Robert E. Lee escaped virtually unscathed and avoided the elaborate self-justifications so many of the others indulged in. His posthumously collected *Wartime Papers* offer an extensive picture of his relations with the military and civilian leaders of the Confederacy as well as with his own family. Jefferson Davis did not get off so lightly. On his shoulders fell the principal responsibility for the entire government of the Confederacy, including much of the burden for the conduct of the war. In keeping with the magnitude of that responsibility, Davis cast his apologia as a defense of the Confederacy itself, acknowledging by his choice of subject that his life and reputation would remain inextricably tied to the office he had held. His two-volume work, *The Rise and Fall of the Confederate Government* (1881), provided an extensive exploration of constitutional issues and govern-

> ## Long before Davis began . . . his account, others had taken up the work of justification.

mental policies, but it remained, above all, a monumental effort of self-justification.

Long before Davis began, much less finished, his account, others had taken up the work of justification. Well before Appomattox, Albert Taylor Bledsoe had begun his classic justification for secession, *Is Davis a Traitor, or Was Secession a Constitutional Right Previous to 1861?* (1866). Bledsoe was not alone in his concern to justify something larger than personal reputation. General Lee himself is said to have admonished Bledsoe in the wake of Appomattox, "Doctor, you must take care of yourself; you have a great work to do; we all look to you for our vindication." The overwhelming magnitude of the Civil War as a political and military crisis led many other Southerners to reflect upon it as a judgment upon their society and values.

Religion and the Lost Cause. During the war, in letters and diaries, Southerners explored their consciences and sought to understand the ways in which the crisis through which they were living might reflect a divine judgment. Few doubted the legitimacy of their cause, or even the legitimacy of slavery, but they did worry that they must strive to live their chosen lives as better Christians than they had in the past. Col. David Lang, who served in the Eighth Florida Infantry at Gettysburg, Cold Harbor, and Petersburg, wrote approvingly in his letters of the revivalism that he saw sweeping the Army of Northern Virginia in September 1863. His and others' concerns echoed those of the Southern divines who, throughout the war, had preached Fast Day sermons calling their people to account and urging them to justify their actions by their faith.

Even after defeat, Southerners generally perpetuated this religious commitment in their recollections of the faith that had animated the troops. In January 1892, Basil Gildersleeve, the eminent classical scholar who had served in the Confederate army until he was wounded in 1864, warmly recalled the deep religious feeling of the army and its

leaders in the *Atlantic Monthly*. His recollections seconded the firsthand accounts that Rev. J. William Jones had collected and published in *Christ in the Camp* (1888).

Others, however, experienced defeat as a direct challenge to the faith that had informed their conviction of the righteousness of their cause. On October 8, 1865, Ella Gertrude Clanton Thomas wrote in her diary that the abolition of slavery had forced her to acknowledge "how intimately my faith in revelations and my faith in the institution of slavery had been woven together." Following emancipation and the defeat of the Confederacy, her "faith in God's Holy Book was terribly shaken." Even prayer could not assuage her doubts, for when she opened the Bible "the numerous allusions to slavery mocked me. Our cause was lost. Good men had had faith in that cause. Earnest prayers had ascended from honest hearts—Was so much faith to be lost? I was bewildered—I felt all this and *could not* see God's hand."

Gertrude Thomas did not publish the diary in which she recorded the doubts that wracked her in the wake of defeat. Shaken at the collapse of her world, she set herself to putting her life back together as best she could. Others throughout the South did the same. And most of them made their peace with defeat as an expression of God's will without repudiating their previous certainty that they had fought for his cause against the Antichrist. But soul-searching and moments of doubt there were, even as the struggle to reconstruct private lives merged with a larger struggle to reconstruct sectional pride. Men like Bledsoe and Lee recognized the importance of reclaiming the righteousness and legitimacy of the Confederacy, if only to justify the sacrifices that the war had extracted from so many. Davis and his generals believed that they must defend their reputations before the bar of history. Many private citizens with no public honor to defend had a harder time of it. At least in the short run, the devastation of their lives seemed to swamp their concerns about the meaning of the struggle.

But as the South began to recover and lives resumed some semblance of a normal pattern, Southern men and women began to collect and sort their memories. And as they did, they began to reclaim their own experience of the past. Since the 1880s, the publication of diaries, journals, memoirs, and letters that capture the events and meaning of the war to those who, on the front or at home, participated in it has continued virtually unabated. Taken together, the disparate personal records of those who lived in and through the Confederacy—from the memoirs of generals to the letters of ordinary soldiers, from the diaries of elite ladies to the plaintive letters of farm wives, from the letters and affidavits of slaves and former slaves to the reflections of ministers and intellectuals—constitute the living witness, if not necessarily the "vindication" that Lee feared the South might lack, a testimonial to the spirit and conviction of those who survived and those who did not.

[For further discussion of letters from the war front, see Soldiers. *See also biographies of numerous figures mentioned herein.]*

BIBLIOGRAPHY

Diaries and Journals

Andrews, Eliza Frances. *The War-Time Journal of a Georgia Girl.* Edited by Spencer Bidwell King, Jr. Macon, Ga., 1960.

Breckinridge, Lucy Gilmer. *Lucy Breckinridge of Grove Hill: The Journal of a Virginia Girl, 1862–1864.* Edited by Mary D. Robertson. Kent, Ohio, 1979.

Buck, Lucy Rebecca. *Sad Earth, Sweet Heavens: The Diary of Lucy Rebecca Buck during the War between the States, Front Royal, Virginia, December 25, 1861–April 15, 1865.* Edited by William P. Buck. Birmingham, Ala., 1973.

Burge, Dolly Sumner Lunt. *Diary.* Edited by James I. Robertson, Jr. Athens, Ga., 1962.

Chesnut, Mary Boykin. *Mary Chesnut's Civil War.* Edited by C. Vann Woodward. New Haven, 1981.

Coleman, Ann Raney. *Victorian Lady on the Texas Frontier: The Journal of Ann Raney Coleman.* Edited by C. Richard King. Norman, Okla., 1971.

Crossley, Martha Jane. "A Patriotic Confederate Woman's War Diary, 1862–1863." Edited by H. E. Sterkx. *Alabama Historical Quarterly* 20 (1958): 611–617.

Dawson, Sarah Morgan. *A Confederate Girl's Diary.* Edited by James I. Robertson, Jr. Bloomington, Ind., 1960.

Edmonston, Catherine Ann Devereux. *Journal of a Secesh Lady: The Diary of Catherine Ann Devereux Edmonston, 1860–1866.* Edited by Beth Gilbert Crabtree and James W. Patton. Raleigh, N.C., 1979.

Gray, Virginia Davis. "Life in Confederate Arkansas: The Diary of Virginia Davis Gray, 1863–1865." Edited by Carl H. Moneyhon. *Arkansas Historical Quarterly* 42 (Spring 1983): 47–85; 42 (Summer 1983): 134–169.

Grimball, Meta Morris. Journal. Grimball Family Papers. Southern Historical Collection. University of North Carolina Library.

Hague, Parthenia Antoinette. *A Blockaded Family: Life in Southern Alabama during the Civil War.* Edited by Elizabeth Fox-Genovese. Lincoln, Neb., 1991.

Hardin, Elizabeth Pendleton. *The Private War of Lizzie Hardin: A Kentucky Confederate Girl's Diary of the Civil War in Kentucky, Virginia, Tennessee, Alabama, and Georgia.* Edited by G. Glenn Clift. Frankfort, Ky., 1963.

Holmes, Emma. *The Diary of Miss Emma Holmes, 1861–1866.* Edited by John F. Marszalek. Baton Rouge, La., 1979.

Ingraham, Mrs. Alfred. "The Vicksburg Diary of Mrs. Alfred Ingraham (May 2–June 13, 1863)." Edited by W. Maury Darst. *Journal of Mississippi History* 44 (May 1982): 148–179.

Jones, J. B. *A Rebel War Clerk's Diary.* Edited by Earl Schenck Miers. New York, 1961.

Jones, Mary Sharp, and Mary Sharp Jones Mallard. *"Yankees a' comming": One Month's Experience during the Invasion of Liberty County, Georgia, 1864–1865.* Edited by Haskel Monroe. Tuscaloosa, Ala., 1959.

Kean, Robert G. H. *Inside the Confederate Government.* New York, 1957.

LeConte, Emma. *When the World Ended: The Diary of Emma LeConte.* Edited by Earl Schenck Miers. New York, 1957.

Morgan, Sarah. *The Civil War Diary of Sarah Morgan.* Edited by Charles East. Athens, Ga., 1991.

Pember, Phoebe Yates. *A Southern Woman's Story: Life in Confederate Richmond, Including Unpublished Letters Written from the Chimborazo Hospital.* Edited by Bell Irwin Wiley. Jackson, Tenn., 1959.

Smedes, Susan Dabney. *Memorials of a Southern Planter.* Edited by Fletcher M. Green. New York, 1965.

Stone, Kate. *Brokenburn: The Journal of Kate Stone, 1861–1868.* Edited by John Q. Anderson. Baton Rouge, La., 1955.

Thomas, Ella Gertrude Clanton. *The Secret Eye: The Journal of Ella Gertrude Clanton Thomas, 1848–1889.* Edited by Virginia Ingraham Burr. Chapel Hill, N.C., 1990.

Torrence, Leonidas. "The Road to Gettysburg: The Diary and Letters of Leonidas Torrence of the Gaston Guards." Edited by Haskell Monroe. *North Carolina Historical Review* 36 (October 1959): 476–517.

Tucker, John S. "The Diary of John S. Tucker: Confederate Soldier from Alabama." Edited by Gary Wilson. *Alabama Historical Quarterly* 43 (1981): 5–33.

Letters

Barr, James Michael, ed. *Confederate War Correspondence of James Michael Barr and Wife Rebecca Ann Dowling Barr.* Taylors, S.C., 1963.

Glover, Robert W., ed. "The War Letters of a Texas Conscript in Arkansas." *Arkansas Historical Quarterly* 20 (1961): 355–387.

Goree, Langston James, ed. *The Thomas Jewett Goree Letters.* Vol. 1. Bryan, Tex., 1981.

Groene, Bertram H., ed. "Civil War Letters of Colonel David Lang." *Florida Historical Quarterly* 54 (1976): 340–366.

Herd, Elmer Don, Jr., ed. "Sue Sparks Keitt to a Northern Friend, March 4, 1861." *South Carolina Historical Magazine* 62 (April 1961): 82–87.

Hodges, Ellen E., and Stephen Kerber, eds. "Children of Honor: Letters of Winston and Octavia Stephens, 1861–1862." *Florida Historical Quarterly* 56 (1977): 45–74.

Hodges, Ellen E., and Stephen Kerber, eds. " 'Rogues and Black Hearted Scamps': Civil War Letters of Winston and Octavia Stephens, 1862–1863." *Florida Historical Quarterly* 57 (1978): 54–82.

McInty, Garnie W., ed. "The Human Side of War: Letters between a Bienville Parish Civil War Soldier and His Wife." *North Louisiana Historical Association Journal* 13, nos. 2–3 (1982): 59–81.

Reynolds, Donald E., ed. "A Mississippian in Lee's Army: The Letters of Leander Huckaby." *Journal of Mississippi History* 36 (February 1974): 53–67; 36 (May 1974): 165–178; 36 (August 1974): 273–288.

Thomas, Cornelius M. Dickinson, ed. *Letters from the Colonel's Lady: Correspondence of Mrs. (Col.) William Lamb Written from Fort Fisher, N.C., C.S.A., to Her Parents in Providence, R.I., U.S.A., December 1861 to January 1865.* Winnabow, N.C., 1965.

Wiley, Bell Irwin, ed., with Lucy E. Fay. *This Infernal War: The Confederate Letters of Edwin H. Fay.* Austin, Tex., 1958.

Memoirs

Alexander, Edward Porter. *Fighting for the Confederacy: The Personal Recollections of General Edward Porter Alexander.* Chapel Hill, N.C., 1989.

Alexander, Edward Porter. *Military Memoirs of a Confederate: A Critical Narrative.* New York, 1907.

Beauregard, P. G. T. *A Commentary on the Campaign and Battle of Manassas.* New York, 1891.

Davis, Jefferson. *The Rise and Fall of the Confederate Government.* 2 vols. New York, 1881.

De Leon, Thomas Cooper. *Belles, Beaux, and Brains of the '60s.* New York, 1909.

De Leon, Thomas Cooper. *Four Years in Rebel Capitals: An Inside View of Life in the Southern Confederacy, from Birth to Death.* Edited by E. B. Long. New York, 1962.

Gildersleeve, Basil. "The Creed of the Old South." *Atlantic Monthly* 69 (January 1892): 75–87.

Giles, Val C. *Rags and Hope: The Recollections of Val C. Giles, Four Years with Hood's Brigade, Fourth Texas Infantry, 1861–1865.* Edited by Mary Lasswell. New York, 1961.

Hood, John Bell. *Advance and Retreat: Personal Experiences in the United States and Confederate Armies.* Edited by Richard N. Current. Bloomington, Ind., 1959.

Johnston, John. "The Civil War Reminiscences of John Johnston, 1861–1865." Edited by William T. Alderson. *Tennessee Historical Quarterly* 13 (1954): 65–82, 156–178, 244–276, 329–354; 14 (1955): 43–81, 142–175.

Johnston, Joseph E. *Narrative of Military Operations.* New York, 1874.

Jones, Rev. J. William. *Christ in the Camp; or, Religion in Lee's Army.* Richmond, Va., 1888.

Lee, Robert E. *The Wartime Papers of Robert E. Lee.* Edited by Clifford Dowdey and Louis H. Manarin. Boston, 1961.

Longstreet, James. *From Manassas to Appomattox: Memoirs of the Civil War in America.* Philadelphia, 1896. Reprint, edited by James I. Robertson, Jr. Bloomington, Ind., 1960.

Watkins, Sam R. *"Co. Aytch" Maury Grays: First Tennessee Regiment; or, A Side Show of the Big Show.* Nashville, Tenn., 1882. Reprint, edited by Bell I. Wiley. Jackson, Tenn., 1952.

Collections and Secondary Sources

Berlin, Ira, Barbara J. Fields, Thavolia Glymph, Joseph P. Reidy, and Leslie Rowland, eds. *The Destruction of Slavery.* Ser. 1, vol. 1 of *Freedom: A Documentary History of Emancipation, 1861–1867.* [Freedmen's Bureau papers.] New York, 1985.

Elliott, Colleen Morse, and Louise Armstrong Moxley Easley, eds. *The Tennessee Civil War Veterans Questionnaires.* Compiled by Gustavus W. Dyer and John Trotwood Moore. Columbia, S.C., 1985.

Harwell, Richard Barksdale, ed. *The Confederate Reader.* New York, 1957.

Horn, Stanley F., ed. *Tennessee's War, 1861–1865: Described by Participants.* Nashville, Tenn., 1965.

Jones, Katharine M. *Ladies of Richmond, Confederate Capital.* Indianapolis, Ind., 1955.

Jones, Katharine M., ed. *Heroines of Dixie: Confederate Women Tell Their Story of the War.* Indianapolis, Ind., 1955.

Rawick, George P., ed. *The American Slave: A Composite Autobiography.* 19 vols. Westport, Conn., 1972.

Rawick, George P., ed. *The American Slave: A Composite Autobiography.* Supplement. 12 vols. Westport, Conn., 1977.

ELIZABETH FOX-GENOVESE

DIPLOMACY

From the outset of the Civil War Confederate leaders sought to exercise the prerogatives of nationhood by securing European recognition and, through direct negotiations, to tap whatever foreign interests might exist in the perpetuation of an independent Southern republic. As early as March 1861 President Jefferson Davis, with the approval of the Confederate Congress, appointed William Lowndes Yancey, Pierre A. Rost, and A. Dudley Mann as commissioners to Great Britain, France, Russia, and Belgium, empowering them with the authority to establish diplomatic relations with those countries. Their instructions, prepared by Secretary of State Robert Toombs, emphasized the need to confirm the South's legitimacy as an independent nation—its long and careful deliberations that had led to separation, its constitutional government, its strength and determination to defend its political integrity. The Confederacy's free trade and liberal navigation policies, Toombs added, would ensure accessible and profitable markets for the manufactures of Europe. Toombs instructed the commissioners to propose treaties of friendship, commerce, and navigation with the nations of Europe when they received official recognition.

Early Optimism for Recognition. Confederate leaders had reason to anticipate the triumph of their diplomacy. Britain's powerful conservative classes, long cynical toward the democratic experiment in America, saw clearly that the Civil War placed democratic institutions on trial. The United States itself had passed beyond the control of the Old World, but if the American people were determined to demonstrate the failure of their political institutions, reactionary Europe could encourage them in their effort so that the work of destruction might triumph. In July 1861 *Blackwood's Magazine* declared: "It is precisely because we do *not* share the admiration of America for her institutions and political tendencies that we do not now see in the impending change an event altogether to be deplored." Even much of Britain's liberal sentiment turned instinctively against the North. Sympathetic to the idea of self-determination, it questioned Washington's right to employ force in repressing the will of a minority that preferred independence. Many British liberals, moreover, were attracted to the South's free trade principles. Edouard de Stoeckl, the Russian chargé d'affaires in Washington, observed that British leaders anticipated the elimination of an Atlantic rival. "The Cabinet in London," he reported, "is watching attentively the internal dissensions of the Union and awaits the result with an impatience which it has difficulty in disguising."

During April 1861 the Confederate objective of securing Europe's recognition seemed propitious. If many in Britain favored the breakup of the American Republic for moral, political, and economic reasons, French emperor Napoleon III understood that his dream of a colonial empire in Mexico would face far less challenge from an independent Confederacy than from a reconstructed Union. Shortly after the Fort Sumter crisis in April, Henri Mercier, the French minister in Washington, proposed to British minister Lord Lyons that they seek authority to recognize the Confederacy at the appropriate moment. The United States had recognized other countries without regard to their revolutionary origins. Lyons agreed in principle but believed that their governments should carry the responsibility for determining the time and mode of the decision, especially since recognition would damage British relations with the government in Washington. For Stoeckl the rupture between North and South was irrevocable; strict impartiality between the warring sections would serve no European interest. "The recognition of the Southern Confederacy by France and England," he wrote on April 14, "will offer us a very natural excuse to follow their example in recognizing a *fait accompli*."

Conscious of Confederate weakness on the high seas as well as the North's immense shipping trade, President Davis, on April 17, issued a proclamation offering letters of marque and reprisal for privateers to prey on Northern commerce. Two days later President Abraham Lincoln, determined to deprive the Confederacy of all foreign imports, announced a blockade of the entire Southern coast. Lincoln, with the overwhelming support of the North, recognized but one objective: the reforging of the Union. Secession was unacceptable. Unless the North retreated from its demand for Southern capitulation, Confederate vice president Alexander H. Stephens responded, "no power on earth can arrest or prevent a most bloody conflict." Pursuing uncompromisable goals, the North and South after the firing on Fort Sumter faced total war. Lincoln's secretary of state, William H. Seward, reaffirmed the North's determination when, on April 23, he informed the governor of Maryland that the United States, under no circumstances, would permit the issues

> **. . . the United States, under no circumstances, would permit the issues between North and South to be settled by foreign arbitrament.**

between North and South to be settled by foreign arbitrament. Any Anglo-French effort at mediation, he warned Mercier and Lyons, would constitute unwarranted intervention calling for total resistance.

Seward had warned Lyons earlier that, if war came, Britain would need to forgo the importation of Southern cotton for a time. The British minister observed that his country required Southern cotton and would obtain it one way or another. With news of the war, however, Queen Victoria, on May 13, issued a proclamation of neutrality, recognizing the South as a belligerent. France, Spain, the Netherlands, Brazil, and other maritime states followed the British lead. The Lincoln administration, joined by congressional leaders, resented deeply the European recognition of Southern bel-

ligerency. Seward responded by informing the British and French governments that the conflict between North and South was not war but a local insurrection of no legitimate concern to foreign powers. Seward instructed U.S. diplomats abroad to prevent any European recognition of the Confederate States of America. Lincoln added that Confederate privateering was piracy and all engaged in it would be treated as pirates.

Mann reached London on April 15; Yancey and Rost two weeks later. On May 3 they gained an informal interview with British foreign minister Lord John Russell. The commissioners argued the legitimacy of the Confederacy's existence, its determination to survive under its Constitution, and its intention to cultivate peaceful and mutually profitable relations with other countries. Such evidences of nationhood, they said, merited recognition. Russell declared that the matter rested with the cabinet; meanwhile he would not comment. Rost moved on to Paris where Count de Morny, a confidant of Emperor Louis Napoleon, informed him that France and England had agreed to pursue identical policies toward the Confederate States, but that recognition was merely a matter of time. Britain and France, he said, understood their interests in Southern independence. In mid-July the commissioners reported that British opinion was undergoing an encouraging change, more and more convinced that the North could not subdue the South.

Washington discovered during April that the Confederate government had dispatched commissioners to the European capitals. Seward warned the French government that the United States would regard any communication between it and the Southern agents as injurious to American dignity and honor. When he learned that Lord Russell in London had received the commissioners informally, he prepared a letter, his famed Number 10 of May 21, so menacing that Lincoln modified some passages and eliminated others. Even in revised form the dispatch was little less than an ultimatum, suggesting that the United States would break diplomatic relations if Russell persisted in seeing the Southern envoys. Charles Francis Adams, the new U.S. minister, arrived in Britain on May 13, the day of the queen's proclamation. A few days later, in an interview with Russell, he condemned the British decision. Then on June 10 Adams received Seward's dispatch of May 21. He now informed Russell that any further relations between the British government and the Confederate commissioners, whether official or not, would constitute a manifestation of hostility toward the United States. Russell assured Adams that conversation was not recognition, and that he had no intention of seeing the Confederates again. Throughout the summer of 1861 Seward condemned the British and French governments for behaving as if the United States were at war. The country, he argued, faced a domestic disturbance that it would dispose of in its own way.

The Failure of King Cotton. What gave the South its presumption of success in its quest for European recognition was the alleged power of cotton. Toombs reminded the commissioners in March that the annual yield of British manufacturing based on Southern cotton totaled $600 million. "The British Ministry," he observed, "will comprehend fully the condition to which the British realm would be reduced if the supply of our staple should suddenly fail or even be considerably diminished." *De Bow's Review* predicted that the blockade would be "swept away by the English fleet of observation hovering on the Southern coasts to protect . . . the free flow of cotton to English and French factories." If cotton was king, the South had only to embargo that commodity to force Britain to destroy the blockade. The Confederate Congress refused to establish a formal embargo, but Committees of Public Safety in the Southern seaports effectively halted the export of cotton to Europe. Having burned much of the 1861 cotton crop, the South had little to sell. The Confederacy gambled that the shortage of cotton would destroy British adherence to the blockade. The added realization that the blockade, maintained largely by lightly armed merchant vessels, was ineffective reinforced this conviction. The Treaty of Paris (1856) had declared not only that a neutral flag covers enemy goods, except contraband, but also that a blockade, to be legally binding, must also be effective. Still the British government, ignoring the blockade's weakness as well as its doubtful legality, treated it with great circumspection. The dearth of cotton for shipment not only failed to eliminate the blockade but also created resentment and the unwanted impression that the blockade was effective. The huge surplus of raw cotton in British and French warehouses merely compounded the evidence of King Cotton's weakness.

In September President Davis, with congressional support, assigned separate commissioners to the principal governments of Europe. He appointed Mann to Brussels, James M. Mason to London, and John Slidell to Paris. The new secretary of state, Robert M. T. Hunter of Virginia, instructed Mason to explain to the British government the true position of the Confederate States as an independent, permanent, and constitutional nation. The North, Hunter added, had rejected peaceful separation and then subjected the South to a barbarous, uncivilized war. In taking up arms the Confederate States appealed to the world, not for aid and alliances, "but for the moral might which they would derive from holding a recognized place as a free and independent people." Six months of fighting, including the Confederate victory at Manassas in July, had demonstrated the South's capacity and determination to maintain its independence. If recognition must finally come, it appeared the duty of nations to place their moral weight immediately on the side of peace.

The *Trent* Affair and the U.S. Blockade. Mason and Slidell, with secretaries George Eustis and James Macfarland, left Charleston on October 12, ran the Union blockade, and made their way to Havana. There, on November 7, they embarked on *Trent,* a British mail steamer bound for England. On the following day Capt. Charles Wilkes of USS *San Jacinto* removed them and their secretaries from the British vessel, permitting *Trent* to continue on its voyage. Wilkes took the Confederates to Fortress Monroe and then to Boston. Confederate officials and writers took hope from the realization that Wilkes had defied international law and insulted the British flag. Hunter assumed that the British, in protecting the right of asylum, would avenge the insolence. Britain, declared the Confederate press, would suffer an unmitigated insult or go to war. "If the insult goes unresented," the *Southern Literary Messenger* advised, "another too flagrant to be borne will inevitably follow."

From London the Confederate commissioners reported a wave of anger and resentment. They reminded Russell on November 27 that the Federal action was a violation of international law, not justified under any treaty between Britain and the United States. If Confederate citizens merited the protection of the British flag, the cabinet had no choice but to demand the restoration of Mason and Slidell to their former positions. In his response of December 7 Russell declined to enter into any discussion of the *Trent* case, but the British government had already demanded the instant restitution of the captured Confederate leaders; unless the North yielded, Rost observed, war was certain. Seward recognized the justice of the British case, as well as the warlike mood of the British people, and brought the controversy to a deliberate end. With the release of Mason and Slidell, Yancey predicted, the British government would maintain a "frigid neutrality" toward the Confederacy. As the year ended, the Confederate commissioners could only lament the apparent control that Seward and Adams exerted over European policy.

Mason, Slidell, and their secretaries reached London on January 29, 1862. Slidell and Eustis departed for Paris the following morning. Mason found himself surrounded by Confederate sympathizers, but the ministry, he reported, remained reticent on the questions of blockade and recognition. In late January the British Foreign Office submitted to Europe's governments the Union practice of clogging harbors by sinking ships loaded with stones; all agreed that the damage to Charleston Harbor was an outrage. The British government complained to Washington but in no way challenged the legitimacy of the Federal blockade. On February 7 Mason requested and received an interview with Lord Russell; it resolved nothing. Mason concluded that the British cabinet would act on the blockade if pressed by the House of Commons, but the debates of early March convinced him that Parliament would never force any change in British policy. Indeed, on February 11 Russell informed Lyons that as long as the Federal government maintained ships in sufficient numbers, not to prevent access to any harbor, but merely to render entering or leaving dangerous, Britain would regard the blockade as effectual under international law.

Slidell, on February 5, asked French minister Antoine Édouard Thouvenel for an interview. Thouvenel informed Rost that the French government would welcome a discussion of the blockade but was not prepared to entertain the question of recognition. If the Federal blockade was so ineffective, Thouvenel asked Slidell, why did so little cotton reach neutral ports? French merchants had asked Slidell that same troubling question. Slidell explained that the blockade runners were generally small vessels; for them turpentine provided greater profit than an equal volume of cotton. Slidell acknowledged that the blockade, despite its ineffectiveness, still managed to eliminate large neutral vessels whose owners preferred to avoid risks. In reporting his interview Slidell advised Hunter that "two or three steamers arriving at Havre with cotton on French account, after having run the blockade, would go further to convince people here of its inefficiency than all the certified lists from our customhouses." Slidell added that France was sympathetic to the Confederate cause and would challenge the blockade if Britain, with its greater interests, would take the initiative. Unfortunately, Slidell observed in March, British policy was not promising. Russell's definition of a blockade, he complained to French officials, merely resuscitated the discarded notion of paper blockades.

Confederate Public Relations Efforts and Pro-Southern Sympathies. Confederate leverage in seeking European recognition required not only the power to compel attention but also popular sympathy for the Southern cause. In large measure the Confederate commissioners carried the burden of informing Europe's political and business leaders of the validity, strength, and promise of the Southern independence movement. But in November 1861 Hunter dispatched Henry Hotze, a young and able journalist, to direct the Confederacy's educational program in Europe. In London Hotze detected not only the North's near monopoly of the news but also the strange capacity of its agents to antagonize through exaggerated claims to power. Hotze quickly gained access to the *London Post* and by April 1862 was writing editorials for the *Standard* and the *London Herald,* a leading opposition paper. In May he established his own journal, the *Index.* Determined to influence British leaders, Hotze avoided giving offense. His fair and accurate reporting of battles and commercial opportunities won respect and a wide British following.

Meanwhile President Davis sent Edwin de Leon to France as a Confederate agent. De Leon failed from the outset. Slidell denied him the support required to gain access to French leaders of importance. With de Leon's dismissal in late 1863, Hotze took up the Confederacy's educational program in France. His fairness again gave him access to important news agencies. He won widespread support among French officials, merchants, shipbuilders, and others who favored the Confederacy, but he could not undermine French liberal attachment to the United States. However pervasive Europe's pro-Confederate sympathies, they had no bearing on the decisions of the European governments.

For many Europeans Northern industrial and financial advantages had at first created doubts that the South could sustain even a defensive war. But the rout of the Union forces at Manassas in July 1861 dispelled the illusion of a certain and easy Northern victory. The Southern commissioners reported that the Confederate triumph produced a powerful sensation in Europe. Benjamin Moran, assistant secretary in the U.S. legation in London, lamented: "This defeat will have a bad effect for the North in Europe, & will raise the hopes of the rebels." On August 14 the commissioners reminded Lord Russell that Britain had recognized countries that had demonstrated far less capacity to maintain their independence than had the Confederacy at Manassas. Russell offered no response.

Yet so lacking in energy and purpose was the Northern war effort that foreign observers now questioned the capacity of the Union to reconquer the South. Not even the Federal capture of Fort Henry, Fort Donelson, and New Orleans between February and April 1862 convinced the British of Northern superiority. "All the successes of the North," Lord Russell observed in April, "do not persuade me they can conquer the South." The Federal capture of New Orleans challenged the illusion of Confederate power, but Gen. George B. McClellan's retreat from Richmond in early July confirmed the widespread conviction among European observers that the Union was doomed. "It is plain," declared the *Times* (London), "that the time is approaching when Europe will have to think seriously of its relations to the two belligerents in the American war." In Parliament William S. Lindsay advocated British mediation to end the apparently interminable and pointless struggle. Lindsay withdrew the motion when Prime Minister Lord Palmerston warned Parliament that mediation meant war.

Mason noted in June that the gradual exhaustion of the cotton supply was driving British sentiment toward the Confederacy. He described the impact on Lancashire:

> The cotton *famine* (as it is now every where termed), prevailing and increasing in the manufacturing districts, is attracting the most serious attention. Parochial relief . . . is found utterly inadequate to prevent *actual starvation* of men, women, and children, who, from such causes, are found dead in their houses. Private contributions . . . do not and cannot remove the sufferers from the starvation point; and very soon they must be left to die, unless aid is afforded from the treasury.

Clearly British policies that deprived the mills of Southern cotton were becoming matters of public concern, especially as the Lancashire mills in 1862 began to deplete the stores of raw cotton in British warehouses. By July Britain's stock of 1.2 million bales had declined to 200,000; by September only 100,000 remained, with the mills consuming 30,000 bales a week. This proved to be the climax of the cotton famine, although unemployment and destitution among the mill workers continued. During 1863 both the cotton supply and employment began to recover, partially from successful blockade running in the South and partially from increased imports of raw cotton from India, China, Brazil, and Egypt. In France the cotton famine and recovery corresponded to that of Great Britain.

By July 1862 the high cost of British neutrality and the Confederate successes in the field had convinced Mason and Slidell that the time had come to demand formal recognition as a matter of right. But under strong advice from

> **. . . Britain's refusal to grant recognition merely prolonged a ruinous and hopeless war.**

friends in Parliament, they agreed to await a more opportune occasion. Responding to the news of Confederate successes in Virginia, Slidell, on July 20, gained an interview at Vichy with the French emperor, who stressed his troubles in Mexico and fear of a collision with the United States. Slidell then argued the Confederate case for immediate recognition in a long letter to Thouvenel. The Confederate States, he wrote, now stood before the world as an established nation meriting immediate recognition. During their conversation on July 23, Thouvenel advised Slidell to withhold his demand. "In a few weeks," said the French minister, "when we shall have further news from the seat of war, we can better judge the expediency of so grave a step, and the English Government may perhaps then be prepared to cooperate with us, which they certainly are not now." When Slidell urged mediation and assured Thouvenel that the South would welcome it, Thouvenel responded that both Mercier and Lyons insisted that an offer of mediation would create exasperation in the North and achieve nothing. In London, on July 24, Russell explained British reluctance to offer mediation by observing that neither the North nor the South would compromise its objectives. Mason responded that all Europe understood the finality of the separation; Britain's refusal to grant recognition merely prolonged a ruinous and hopeless war. Russell observed that the ultimate outcome of the American war remained uncertain. When the South had finally resisted all efforts to conquer it, other countries might justly recognize its independence. That time had not arrived.

In September Mason and Slidell assured Judah P. Benjamin, Confederate secretary of state since March, that

the British and French governments were reconsidering their previous decisions to avoid any involvement in American affairs. In mid-September the earl of Shaftesbury, returning from a vacation in the south of France, visited Slidell in Paris to inform him that Britain was fast approaching a decision to intervene. The British ministry, encouraged by the South's victory in the Second Battle of Manassas in late August, had taken up the question of mediation. Palmerston, responding to Second Manassas, penned a note to Russell on September 14: "The Federals . . . got a very complete smashing. . . . Even Washington and Baltimore may fall into the hands of the Confederates. If this should happen, would it not be time for us to consider whether in such a state of things England and France might not address the contending parties and recommend an arrangement upon the basis of separation?"

The Confederacy's Opportunity Passes. On September 14 and 15 Gen. Robert E. Lee moved his forces into Maryland. When the news of Lee's costly battle at Sharpsburg and the Confederate retreat across the Potomac reached Europe in late September, Slidell predicted that the Northern success in checking the Southern advance would serve as another pretext for British procrastination. Indeed, on October 2 Palmerston reminded Russell that mediation based on separation would benefit the South; the North, therefore, would resist such interference until additional Southern victories compelled it to capitulate. Ignoring Palmerston's caution, William E. Gladstone, chancellor of the exchequer, declared at Newcastle on October 7: "Jefferson Davis and other leaders have made an army, and are making, it appears, a navy, and they have made what is more than either, they have made a nation." Supported by Gladstone, Russell in mid-October prepared a memorandum arguing for mediation; the cabinet, including Palmerston, rejected it.

In Paris Slidell, on October 26, informed the new French minister, Edouard Drouyn de Lhuys, that the British cabinet, except for Gladstone, stood firm against mediation. If the French government favored the Confederacy, as the emperor insisted it did, the time had come for France to act alone. Two days later the emperor called Slidell to St. Cloud and again expressed his sympathy for the South. To act without Britain, however, would render France vulnerable to British policy and expose it to Washington's wrath. He informed Slidell, however, that on October 15 the king of Belgium had advocated a joint French-British-Russian proposal for a six-month armistice with a lifting of the Federal blockade. Slidell doubted that Britain and Russia would accept mediation; nor was he convinced that the emperor would act. Yet on November 8 Mason reported that Britain and Russia had received such a proposal. On that day the Russian government informed the British Foreign Office that it had rejected the emperor's strategy. On November 12 the British cabinet, convinced that the North would reject mediation, reached the same decision. With good reason Richmond's dismay over the failure of mediation was profound; never again would the European powers consider such a direct involvement in the American war.

In January 1863 Mason, responding to Benjamin's repeated instructions, pressed Lord Russell on the issue of the blockade. Mason protested the British refusal to explain why, in its modification of the doctrine of blockade, it denied the Confederacy the historic rights of belligerency. Russell repeated what he had written to Lord Lyons in February 1862, that the Declaration of Paris did not demand that a port be blockaded so that no vessel could gain access, whatever its size or the prevailing conditions. Storms and winds, he argued, could not render a blockade nonbinding on neutrals. Mason responded in February that nowhere did the

> ## Lee's surrender terminated the Confederacy's diplomatic effort in Europe.

Declaration of Paris refer to winds or storms or the nature and size of vessels engaged in blockade running. One vessel, wrote Mason, had evaded the blockade at Charleston thirty times. Russell terminated the exchange on February 27 by asserting that he had explained the British position and did not care to discuss it further. In Paris Slidell took hope from assurances that French sentiment continued to favor the South. The emperor, he wrote in January, would pursue mediation again, either alone or with the concurrence of Britain and Russia. As the weeks passed, Mann in mid-March expressed his growing disillusionment:

> So far as I can judge . . . the chances for an early European recognition of our independence, have not increased in the slightest degree. . . . The Emperor of the French seems to be just as far as ever from taking the initiative in this regard.

No longer did Confederate successes in the field—the victory at Fredericksburg in December or even that at Chancellorsville in May—seem to matter.

Naval Purchases Abroad. Even as the British government rejected Southern appeals for recognition or any direct intervention in the American war, it enabled the Confederacy to achieve remarkable successes on the high seas. As early as May 1861 Confederate Secretary of the Navy Stephen R. Mallory instructed James D. Bulloch of Georgia to buy or order six vessels in England to prey on Northern commerce. At the same time the Confederate Congress appropriated funds for the purchase of two ironclads and dispatched James H. North to procure them in France under the

assumption that the French government favored the destruction of the blockade. Bulloch, finding no cruisers available, contracted for the construction of two vessels. North discovered that France was not prepared to sell ironclads. Eventually, in May 1862, he arranged for the construction of a giant ironclad by the Thompson works of Glasgow. In July Bulloch contracted with the Laird Brothers of Birkenhead for two rams.

As early as February 1862 the U.S. consul in Liverpool, Thomas H. Dudley, reported to Adams that Liverpool shipbuilders were constructing a Confederate cruiser, *Oreto.* Lord Russell insisted that an Italian company had ordered the ship. *Oreto* cleared for Palermo but sailed to the Bahamas where, armed and equipped, it became the Confederate commerce raider *Florida.* During April Adams learned that another Confederate cruiser, *No. 290,* was under construction in Liverpool. Too late Russell ordered the vessel stopped. It departed suddenly in July, acquired armament in the Azores, and became the famed Confederate raider *Alabama.*

Despite Adams's continued warnings that one day the United States would demand compensation for the damage wrought by British-made Confederate commerce raiders, the British permitted additional vessels to escape during the early months of 1863. But in September Adams threatened the British government with war if it permitted the Laird rams, then in the water, to escape. In seizing them the British government terminated the Confederate acquisition of British-made vessels. Cruisers already in the Atlantic continued their devastating assaults on Northern commerce. Later Russell, in conversation with Adams, condemned the South for making Britain the base of its maritime operations.

Final Diplomatic Efforts. As late as June 1863 Slidell continued to press the French government for recognition, arguing that the capacity of the Confederate States to maintain their independence was beyond question. He informed the emperor that the British cabinet denied recognition not because it doubted the South's eventual success but because it desired the breakup of the Union and was confident of a Confederate victory. France could stop the prolonged conflict by recognizing the Confederacy. The emperor responded that any proposal for recognition submitted to the London government to stop the war would reach Washington and expose an isolated France to U.S. retribution. At risk was not only French commerce but also the entire French effort in Mexico. France could not afford to move without Britain. Again, during the parliamentary debates of July, Palmerston, supported in his judgment by the Union victories at Vicksburg and Gettysburg, refused to budge. Concluding that Britain would never recognize Mason, Benjamin on August 4 instructed him to conclude his mission and, with his secretary, withdraw from London.

Mason received Benjamin's letter on September 21 and informed Russell of his impending departure. Russell, in a brief note, observed that he had explained the British refusal to recognize him on previous occasions. "These reasons," he concluded, "are still in force, and it is not necessary to repeat them." Having lost faith in Britain, Benjamin turned to France for support in breaking the blockade; the French government, still refusing to act unilaterally, rejected responsibility for Europe's acceptance of the blockade as well as any intention of courting trouble by challenging it.

Throughout 1864 Confederate leaders hoped that their assertions of ultimate victory would still bring the needed European support. By summer the Confederacy's fate in the courts of Europe hinged on the success or failure of Gen. Ulysses S. Grant's assault on Richmond. Mason, now in London under a broad commission to serve the Confederacy wherever he might be effective, reported optimistically in June that a Southern victory in Virginia would still compel the British ministry to act. In Paris Slidell complained that the French emperor was too concerned with his problems elsewhere, but still agreed with Mason that a decisive Confederate victory at Richmond would lead to Anglo-French intervention.

To reassure Europe of the South's determination to win, the Confederate Congress, on June 14, issued a manifesto to the governments of Europe, which declared that the South, in its quest for immunity against external interference, committed its cause to "the enlightened judgment of the world." In his final appeal to Europe on December 27, 1864, Benjamin wondered why Britain and France, despite the South's continued resistance, had refused to recognize its independence. Concluding at last that the explanation lay in slavery, he dispatched Duncan F. Kenner, a member of Congress from Louisiana, on a secret mission to convey to Mason and Slidell his offer of emancipation in exchange for recognition. In Paris the emperor informed Slidell that such an offer would not have influenced his decision. Mason returned to London where, on March 14, 1865, Palmerston presented an identical response. Britain's earl of Donoughmore observed that two years earlier the offer might have mattered; in March 1865 Grant's campaign had eliminated the issue.

Lee's surrender terminated the Confederacy's diplomatic effort in Europe. Richmond's perennial pursuit of European recognition and trade was a major element in the entire Confederate war effort. Europe's recognition of Southern independence would have created diplomatic havoc in Washington. European defiance of the Federal blockade would have opened the South to the massive imports the Confederate war effort required. That Washington escaped such potentially costly external challenges was a measure of Seward's success in convincing the European governments that, whatever their interests in Southern independence, they could not intervene diplomatically without risking war. Europe's disinclination to fight the United States bound any

European support of the Confederacy to the conviction that the South could triumph on its own. That conviction was never realized.

[*See also* Blockade, *overview article;* Canada; France; Great Britain; Laird Rams; Mexico; Propaganda; State Department; Trent Affair; *and biographies of numerous figures mentioned herein.*]

BIBLIOGRAPHY

Adams, Ephraim Douglas. *Great Britain and the American Civil War.* 2 vols. New York, 1925.

Callahan, James Morton. *Diplomatic History of the Southern Confederacy.* New York, 1901.

Case, Lynn M., and Warren F. Spencer. *The United States and France: Civil War Diplomacy.* Philadelphia, 1970.

Crook, David Paul. *The North, the South, and the Powers, 1861–1865.* New York, 1974.

Ellison, Mary L. *Support for Secession: Lancashire and the American Civil War.* Chicago, 1973.

Ferris, Norman B. *The Trent Affair: A Diplomatic Crisis.* Knoxville, Tenn., 1977.

Jordan, Donaldson, and Edwin J. Pratt. *Europe and the American Civil War.* Boston, 1931.

Meade, Robert Douthat. *Judah P. Benjamin: Confederate Statesman.* New York, 1943.

Merli, Frank J. *Great Britain and the Confederate Navy, 1861–1865.* Bloomington, Ind., 1970.

Owsley, Frank Lawrence. *King Cotton Diplomacy: Foreign Relations of the Confederate States of America.* Revised by Harriet Chappell Owsley. Chicago, 1959.

NORMAN A. GRAEBNER

DIRECT TAX ACT

At the time the Confederacy was established in February 1861, there had been no direct taxation of real estate or personal property in the United States since the War of 1812. Instead, the chief fiscal tool of the Federal government had been import duties. With a view to getting rid of the protective tariffs, some Southerners had proposed the abolition of the customs houses and the imposition of direct taxation. But fearful of any system in which the taxpayers knew how much they were paying, Congress retained the customs dues.

The Provisional Constitution of the Confederacy provided either that direct taxes could be apportioned among the states, each state to pay a fixed amount based on the last census (the old Federal system), or that the Confederacy, in the absence of a census, could levy a tax based on a fixed percentage of the assessed value of all property. Because the Confederacy never took a census of its own and refused to use the Federal census of 1860, and because the Permanent Constitution had no alternative provision for levying and collecting such a tax, the power of levying direct taxes expired to all practical purposes with the end of the provisional government on February 18, 1862.

In the congressional session on May 8, 1861, Secretary of the Treasury Christopher G. Memminger sought authorization to impose a direct tax on the Southern people. But lacking a letter of support from President Jefferson Davis for this radical measure, Congress tabled Memminger's request and asked him to furnish a report on direct taxes at its next session in July 1861.

In preparing this report, the secretary discovered that each state used a system unique to itself, so that Congress would have to devise its own program. He therefore proposed that $25 million be raised through a tax of fifty-four cents on each hundred dollars of assessed property. To be taxed were real estate, slaves, and personal property such as stocks, bonds, cattle, and merchandise.

Resistance to the war tax authorized by the act of August 19, 1861, was noisy and prolonged. Unable to attack this proposal on legal grounds, opponents claimed that a tax equal to only 2.5 percent of the South's Gross National Product would provoke armed resistance and the collapse of the Confederacy. The plain fact was that both within and outside Congress most owners of large slaveholdings expected to have their $3.5 billion stake in slavery protected without their having to make any sort of contribution for that purpose. They also assumed that the war would be short and Southern independence secured at little or no cost to themselves. Secretary Memminger inadvertently assisted such delusions by failing to make clear the direct connection between inadequate taxation and defeat. Gazeway B. Lamar, a Georgia banker, presciently observed that the Southern people must be prepared to pay heavy taxes. Otherwise, they might as well surrender immediately and hand over their slaves for emancipation by the Federal authorities.

Yet the law as finally enacted was riddled with exemptions that reduced tax yields by a third. Moreover, lacking prior experience in such measures, Congress made numerous drafting errors. Collection and assessment times were put off to too distant a day. No provisions were made for paying the assessors and collectors, for reimbursing them for their expenses, or for securing the cooperation of sheriffs, who held the state tax records. Moreover, in the interest of economy, too few personnel were provided for, so that the effectiveness of the tax depended upon the integrity of the taxpayer.

As finally passed, the act called for the appointment of a chief collector in each state and a collector in each county assisted by at least two assessors. Each citizen was to furnish a list of taxable property by a specified date. The necessity of collecting the tax directly from the public might be avoided if a state assumed the tax. In that case, the state would receive a 10-percent rebate on the amount it paid.

Payment had to be in specie or Confederate Treasury notes only.

As a fiscal measure, this tax was not a success. There were long delays getting suitable persons to fill the various posts. The state governments issued their own currency in exchange for Confederate notes, thereby frustrating the whole purpose of the tax, which was to reduce inflation by retiring some of the excess Treasury notes. Assessments and checking the veracity of property declarations were hindered by states' giving encouragement to their sheriffs not to cooperate with the Confederate assessors. Moreover, because there was no centralized guidance from Richmond, appraisals varied widely from state to state. This was particularly true of slaves, whose average declared prices were much too low.

Texas and Mississippi, in the hope of evading payment entirely, refused to assume the tax, and the Treasury had to collect directly from the citizens. Only South Carolina took the Confederate records and collected the tax from its own citizens. Without doubt, however, the greatest deficiencies of the act were its failure to impose the tax each year for the duration of the war and its failure to demand a larger revenue of at least $40 million to $80 million a year.

BIBLIOGRAPHY

Ball, Douglas B. *Financial Failure and Confederate Defeat*. Urbana, Ill., and Chicago, 1991.

Schwab, John Christopher. *The Confederate States of America, 1861–1865: A Financial and Industrial History of the South during the Civil War*. New York, 1901.

Todd, Richard C. *Confederate Finance*. Athens, Ga., 1954.

DOUGLAS B. BALL

DISCOGRAPHY

Commercially recorded record albums featuring music of the Civil War date back to the 1940s, but it was only in the 1960s that recordings were issued that had some element of authenticity and were accompanied with adequate annotations. With the coming of compact discs in the late 1980s, many of these albums were reissued in digital sound. This discography deals with recordings that are widely available to a general audience. The issue number refers to the compact disc (CD) release unless otherwise indicated; most commercial companies have discontinued vinyl long playing (LP) versions of their albums.

Some albums attempt to include a cross section of the war's different types of music, and others feature a specific type or genre. One of the most faithful attempts to re-create the parlor music and sentimental songs of the age is New

World Records' *Songs of the Civil War* (CD 202–2). Since parlor music especially was equally popular in the South and the North, the album relates to the Confederacy as much as the Union and contains rare recordings of popular songs like Will S. Hays's "Drummer Boy of Shiloh," as well as splendid notes and song texts. A related collection, though more focused on Northern songs, is *Who Shall Rule This Nation (Songs of Henry Clay Work,* Nonesuch LP 71317).

Far fewer of the original Confederate band books survived the conflict than did their Northern counterparts, but the 1st Brigade Band has recorded several albums of Southern band music. The 1st Brigade Band, perhaps the best-known of the modern groups re-creating the sound of the brass band, uses authentic period instruments and arrangements from the old books. Their various tapes and LPs are issued through the Heritage Military Music Foundation in Milwaukee. One of their most interesting is *Gen. Rob't E. Lee's Favorite 26th N.C. Band* (vol. 8, cassette only), a collection of quicksteps, marches, and dance tunes taken from the books of the Twenty-sixth North Carolina Band. *Band Music of the Confederacy* (vol. 4, LP only) celebrates and re-creates the music of the legendary Eleventh Mississippi Infantry Regimental Band, thought by some to be the best in the Confederacy. A third collection, *Dixie's Land* (vol. 7, cassette only), contains more concert and marching fare from various sources, as well as occasional vocals.

There is no authentic comprehensive collection of traditional or folk music from the South, but Confederate camps were filled with the sound of ballad singing and fiddle playing. During the 1930s and 1940s, the Library of Congress recorded in the field dozens of folk songs and tunes, but many of these are available only at the Archive of Folk Culture in Washington. A sample of them may be found on an LP issued by the Library of Congress, *Songs and Ballads of American History and the Assassination of Presidents* (AFS L29); this contains "Booth Killed Lincoln," "The Southern Soldier," and "The Battle of Antietam Creek," all taken from vintage field recordings. Less authentic but well interpreted is a larger collection of folk music, Folkways' *Songs of the Civil War* (SFW 5717, 2 cassettes), designed to accompany Irwin Silber's book of the same name; artists include Pete Seeger, the New Lost City Ramblers, and others. The fiddle tunes of the era are presented in two tapes on the Pearl Mae label by instrumentalist Jim Taylor and fiddler Bruce Green; these are *Falls of Richmond* and *Little Rose Is Gone.* Both tapes have good annotations and are full of tunes that either were known in the war or have associations with the Confederacy.

Several popular recordings feature modern interpretations of songs from the conflict. These often fail to use authentic settings or styles, but they are more accessible to modern listeners. One of the best is *Tennessee Ernie Ford Sings Songs of the Civil War* (Capitol, 2 CDs, C2 95705), a compilation of two LPs (*Songs of the North* and *Songs of the South*) origi-

nally issued in 1961. Framed by spare, modern arrangements, Ford's booming baritone lends itself well to "Stonewall Jackson's Way" and "Bonnie Blue Flag," among others. A more recent set of interpretations is *Songs of the Civil War* (Col. CK-CD 48607, CD or cassette), drawn from a PBS television show by the same name. The Southern half of the set features modern country and bluegrass singers like John Hartford, Waylon Jennings, Hoyt Axton, and Kathy Mattea, often in sparse, appealing settings featuring acoustic instruments. Sweet Honey in the Rock, based in Washington, adds several good renditions of spirituals. A series of cassettes beginning with *Songs of the CSA* has been produced by Birmingham singer and songwriter Bobby Horton, and it has the distinction of being one of the few series devoted exclusively to songs of the Confederacy.

Several recent collections offer a cross section of all sorts of music, from folk to popular to military. The first of these was the CBS/Legacy set *The Confederacy* (CB 47123), an opu-

> **Far fewer of the original Confederate band books survived the conflict than did their Northern counterparts. . . .**

lent set issued in the 1960s and containing elaborate photographs and song notes. Produced by classical expert Goddard Leiberson, the set features formal singers and heavily orchestrated backgrounds that had little resemblance to the actual music of the 1860s. Mercury's set *Music of the Civil War* (LP, SR12–7701) contained a wider selection of music but was marred by sound effects and narration. Perhaps the most popular recent Civil War set is the sound track to the Ken Burns PBS television series, *The Civil War* (Elektra Nonesuch 9 79256–2, CD or cassette). Though the famous theme song for the series, "Ashokan Farewell," is a modern composition dating from 1984, many other pieces on the album are evocative, well performed, and authentic. Many vocal tunes, however, are heard only as piano solos.

The most elaborate attempt to recapture the actual sound of the music of the age is Time-Life Music's *The Civil War Music Collector's Edition* (R–103–12, CD or cassette). Drawing on performers both known and unknown, the producers have assembled fifty performances on three CDs. They include not only parlor songs, band music, and folk music but also spirituals, fife and drum music from camp duty, and minstrel show music. A large booklet accompanies the set and chronicles just how rich and complex the music of the age was.

With the increasing popularity of spoken word recordings ("audio books") in the late 1980s, a number of Civil War books have become available in this format. Recorded

Books, Inc., of Prince Frederick, Maryland, has issued a number of such tapes, including Adrian Cronauer's reading of *Andersonville Diary* (5 cassettes, RBI 88090). Dick Estell's reading of James I. Robertson, Jr.'s, biography *General A.P. Hill: The Story of a Confederate Warrior* is one of the most polished of these performances, available from Books on Tape (10 cassettes, BOT 2455). Bierce's famous "Occurrence at Owl Creek Bridge" is available on a number of tape editions, including that of Mark Hammer (RBI, 2 cassettes, 82041). Noteworthy too is Alan Bergreen's reading of Bruce Catton's *The Civil War: A Short History* (RBI, 5 cassettes, 85440).

CHARLES K. WOLFE

DIXIE

The most popular song associated with the Confederate cause, "Dixie," had its origins in a term that had been used to denote the South since the 1850s. The ultimate source of *Dixie,* the term, is obscure, but two favorite explanations for it are the popularity of the term *Mason-Dixon Line* and the use by the Citizens' Bank and Trust Company of Louisiana of its own currency notes in which the ten-dollar notes bore the French word for "ten," *dix.* Whatever its origin, by the end of the 1850s, *Dixie* was being used to denote the South.

The song itself originally bore the title "I Wish I Was in Dixie's Land" and was composed, ironically, in the heart of New York City. One rainy day in April 1859, in an old, chilly boardinghouse, a forty-four-year old minstrel singer named Dan Emmett was struggling to produce a new song for the troupe he was with, Bryant's Minstrels. A native of Mount Vernon, Ohio, Emmett had earlier been an army fife player and a circus band musician, but by the 1840s he was writing songs for the new type of entertainment springing up, the minstrel show. His "Old Dan Tucker" had become a favorite in these new shows, and since then he had written dozens of others. Now he had to come up with a finale for Bryant's show.

Emmett later recalled that as he started to work out a new song, the phrase "I wish I was in Dixie" kept running through his mind; his wife had used the phrase to complain about northern winters. He picked up a tin whistle and began to work out a melody and in less than an hour had the first verse and chorus. The song had its formal debut at Mechanics Hall in New York on April 4, 1859. "It made a tremendous hit," Emmett recalled, "and before the end of the week everybody in New York was whistling it." Sheet music publication soon followed—in 1860 by Firth, Pond and Company, and later by dozens of unauthorized companies. By the fall of 1860, the song had made its way into the South

and was even used as the basis for an anti-Lincoln campaign song. Though it continued to be popular in the North, by 1861 the South had made it its own. It was played at Jefferson Davis's inauguration in Montgomery in 1861, and Gen. George E. Pickett ordered it played at the famous charge at Gettysburg. Since the original text of the song had little in it about the war or war issues, Albert Pike added some new words with a refrain that concluded, "To arms! To arms! And conquer peace for Dixie!"

In later years, controversy arose as to whether Emmett had really composed the song. A Louisville publisher insisted that two of his writers had made the song by fitting new words to an older folk tune known by Southern blacks, and others argued that the song first came from black stevedores on the Mississippi River. No effective proof of this ever surfaced, though, and Emmett's claim is generally accepted today.

By the end of the nineteenth century, "Dixie" had become a favorite anthem at various Confederate reunions and a staple in fiddling contests throughout the South. Often accompanied by rebel yells and the waving of the Confederate banner, by the mid-twentieth century the song had become popular with high school bands who used it as a rally song at local football games. The song's connotations and association with the Lost Cause were still so powerful that by the 1980s the playing of the song at high school games became mired in controversy, and many school administrators banned it from school events.

[*See also* Mason-Dixon Line.]

BIBLIOGRAPHY

Harwell, Richard B. *Confederate Music.* Chapel Hill, N.C., 1950.
Heaps, Willard A., and Porter W. Heaps. *The Singing Sixties: The Spirit of Civil War Days Drawn from the Music of the Times.* Norman, Okla., 1960.

CHARLES K. WOLFE

DRED SCOTT DECISION

As the slave of army surgeon John Emerson, Dred Scott had lived on a military base in Illinois and at Fort Snelling, in Wisconsin Territory, which was made free by the Missouri Compromise. In 1850 a St. Louis court, following Missouri precedents dating from 1824, found Scott had become free while living outside Missouri, a slave state, and once free, he remained free despite his return to Missouri. In 1852 the Missouri Supreme Court, articulating the proslavery ideology and hostility to the North that would eventually lead to secession, rejected its own long-standing precedents:

Times are not as they were when the former decisions on this subject were made. Since then not only individuals but States have been possessed of a dark and fell spirit in relation to slavery, whose gratification is sought in the pursuit of measures, whose inevitable consequence must be the overthrow and destruction of our government. Under such circumstances it does not behoove the State of Missouri to show the least countenance to any measure which might gratify this spirit.

In 1854 Scott began a new suit in the U.S. District Court against John F. A. Sanford, a New Yorker who had recently become the executor of Emerson's estate after Emerson's widow, and initial executor, had remarried. Scott argued he was a citizen of Missouri and sued Sanford in federal court because there was a diversity of citizenship between the two parties. Sanford answered that blacks, whether free or in bondage, could *never* sue as U.S. citizens in a federal court. Judge Robert W. Wells ruled that *if* Scott was free, then he was a citizen of Missouri for purposes of federal diversity jurisdiction. After a trial, however, Judge Wells ruled that Scott was still a slave. Scott then appealed to the U.S. Supreme Court. At issue was more than the status of Scott and his family: the Missouri Supreme Court's decision challenged Congress's authority to prohibit slavery in any federal territory. The central political issue of the 1850s was now before the Supreme Court.

The end of the Mexican-American War had left the nation in possession of vast amounts of land (known as the Mexican Cession) including the present-day states of New Mexico, Arizona, California, Utah, and Nevada. Much of this land was below the Missouri Compromise line, and thus theoretically open to slavery. With the acquisition of this territory and the rise of proslavery thought and Southern nationalism, Southerners were no longer content to be shut out of the western territories. The Kansas-Nebraska Act (1854), which partially repealed the Missouri Compromise by allowing slavery in the territory immediately to the west of Missouri under a concept of popular sovereignty, led to a mini-civil war in Kansas and the formation of the Republican party in the North. In the 1856 presidential election this two-year-old party, pledged to stop the spread of slavery into the territories, carried all but five Northern states.

The avidly proslavery Chief Justice Roger B. Taney of Maryland used *Dred Scott v. Sandford* [sic] (1857) to decide these pressing political issues in favor of the South. Taney's two most controversial points were (1) that the Missouri Compromise was unconstitutional because Congress could not legislate for any federal territories acquired after 1787 and because freeing slaves in the territories constituted a taking of property without due process, in violation of the Fifth Amendment; and (2) that blacks, even those in the North with full state citizenship, could never be U.S. citizens.

Taney asked: "Can a negro, whose ancestors were imported into this country, and sold as slaves, become a member of the political community formed and brought into existence by the Constitution of the United States, and as such become entitled to all the rights, privileges, and immunities guaranteed by that instrument to the citizens?" Rigorously applying a jurisprudence of original intent, Taney answered with a resounding no. In an analysis that was historically incorrect and shocking to the North, Taney asserted that when the Constitution was adopted blacks were universally considered "beings of an inferior order, and altogether unfit to associate with the white race, either in social or political relations; and so far inferior, that they had no rights which the white man was bound to respect; and that the negro might justly and lawfully be reduced to slavery for his benefit."

In dissent Justice Benjamin Robbins Curtis, of Massachusetts, noted that in 1787 free blacks were citizens of five states and thus they were also citizens of the United

> **Robert W. Wells ruled that *if* Scott was free, then he was a citizen of Missouri. . . . After a trial, however, Judge Wells ruled that Scott was still a slave.**

States when the Constitution was adopted. Curtis also argued that under a "reasonable interpretation of the language of the Constitution" Congress had the power to regulate slavery in the federal territories. This dissent heartened Northerners like Horace Greeley who wrote that Taney's decision was an "atrocious," "wicked," "abominable," "false," "detestable hypocrisy" built on "shallow sophistries." The *Chicago Tribune* expressed the reaction of many Northerners: "We scarcely know how to express our detestation of its inhuman dicta, or to fathom the wicked consequences which may flow from it."

But, not all Northerners opposed the decision. Northern Democrats hoped the decision would destroy the Republican party by essentially declaring its "Free-Soil" platform to be unconstitutional and once and for all end the national debate over slavery in the territories. In the words of the New York *Journal of Commerce,* the decision was an "authoritative and final settlement of grievous sectional issues."

The decision also undermined Northern Democrats, however, whose strength had been grounded in the party's appeal to popular sovereignty. Under popular sovereignty settlers would decide for themselves if they wanted slavery in a territory. This system appealed to American concepts of democratic rule and Northern negrophobia. Northern Democrats hoped popular sovereignty would keep both slaves and blacks out of the territories. At the same time, however, popular sovereignty allowed Northern Democrats to appease their Southern colleagues who opposed restrictions on slavery in the territories.

Just as Taney's decision undermined Republican Free-Soil politics, so it undermined Democratic popular sovereignty. Under *Dred Scott* the settlers of a territory, like the Congress, were precluded from restricting slavery. This made popular sovereignty meaningless and took away from Northern Democrats their most potent weapon. Stephen A. Douglas, the most prominent proponent of popular sovereignty, told his Illinois constituents that settlers could still keep slavery out of most of the territories by not passing laws that would protect slave property. This led Southern Democrats to demand a federal slave code for the territories and helped set the stage for the split within the Democratic party in 1860.

Taney doubtless thought his powerful fifty-four-page decision would finally open all the territories to slavery while undermining the Republican party. "Taney's opinion," historian Don Fehrenbacher has written, "proves to be a work of unmitigated partisanship, polemical in spirit though judicial in its language, and more like an ultimatum than a formula for sectional accommodation. Peace on Taney's terms resembled . . . a demand for unconditional surrender." The decision was, as historian Harry Jaffa has written, "nothing less than a summons to the Republicans to disband."

But instead of disbanding, Republicans successfully made Taney and the decision the focus of their 1858 and 1860 campaigns. In his "house divided" speech (1858) Abraham Lincoln argued that Taney's opinion was part of a proslavery conspiracy to nationalize slavery and a prelude to future proslavery jurisprudence. He warned of "another Supreme Court decision, declaring that the Constitution of the United States does not permit a *state* to exclude slavery from its limits." He told the voters in Illinois, and by extension the entire North, that "we shall *lie down* pleasantly dreaming that the people of Missouri are on the verge of making their state *free;* and we shall *awake* to the *reality,* instead, that the Supreme Court has made *Illinois* a *slave* state."

Such arguments, combined with such other issues of the day, led a majority of Northerners to vote Republican in 1860; that in turn led to secession and the creation of the Confederacy.

[*See also* Bleeding Kansas; Compromise of 1850; Democratic Party; Fugitive Slave Law; Kansas-Nebraska Act; Missouri Compromise; Republican Party; Sumner, Caning of; Wilmot Proviso.]

BIBLIOGRAPHY

Erlich, Walter. *They Have No Rights: Dred Scott's Struggle for Freedom.* Westport, Conn., 1979.
Fehrenbacher, Don E. *The Dred Scott Case: Its Significance in American Law and Politics.* New York, 1978.
Finkelman, Paul. *An Imperfect Union: Slavery, Federalism, and Comity.* Chapel Hill, N.C., 1981.
Jaffa, Harry V. *The Crisis of the House Divided: An Interpretation of the Issues in the Lincoln-Douglas Debates.* New York, 1959.
Potter, David M. *The Impending Crisis: 1848–61.* New York, 1976.

PAUL FINKELMAN

DREWRY'S BLUFF, VIRGINIA

Also called Fort Darling, the fortified position atop Drewry's Bluff overlooking the James River played a vital role in defending the water approaches to Richmond, about seven miles away.

As the Union Army of the Potomac under Maj. Gen. George B. McClellan prepared to blast the Confederates out of their defenses at Yorktown in May 1862, Gen. Joseph E. Johnston determined to evacuate the Yorktown line and retreat farther up the Virginia Peninsula toward Richmond. In doing so, however, he compelled the evacuation of Norfolk. To prevent the capture of the Confederate ironclad *Virginia,* its crew destroyed the ship, leaving the James River open to ascent by the Union navy.

The Federals naturally determined to take advantage of *Virginia*'s absence, and in mid-May the Union ironclads *Monitor* and *Galena* escorted three wooden warships upriver. The best place to challenge this small fleet of Union vessels was at Drewry's Bluff. The high ground would afford Confederate artillery with a clear field of fire and be difficult to hit from the river below. The narrowness of the river at that point and the installation of sunken vessels as obstructions would further hinder the Federals. Gen. Robert E. Lee sent a brigade of infantry to support the position, while the crew from *Virginia* arrived to serve the heavy guns in the works.

Although the Confederates carried out their improvements in haste, the natural advantages of the position soon became apparent. When the Federal fleet arrived on May 15, 1862, neither of the ironclads could elevate its guns sufficiently to return the Confederate fire. Furthermore, the obstructions prevented them from attempting to run past the fort. As the Southern crews watched from above, all the while pouring fire into the vessels below, *Monitor* and *Galena* maneuvered futilely. As the fighting continued, *Galena* began to suffer damage from the Confederates' heavy shells. After four hours of battle, the Union ships moved off. *Galena* sustained more damage and casualties than any of the other vessels, but limped to safety. Still, the Confederates at Drewry's Bluff had thwarted the Federal attack.

On May 16, 1864, Drewry's Bluff again became the scene of fighting. A Union landing at Bermuda Hundred earlier in the month threatened to leave the Confederate capital and the city of Petersburg below it vulnerable to attack. Union Maj. Gen. Benjamin F. Butler, commanding the 39,000-man Army of the James, failed to press his advantage, however. He lost precious time as he cautiously moved along the peninsula of land between the James and Appomattox rivers. The Confederates had time enough to concentrate their forces and stop Butler's advance, whereupon the Union commander retreated to Bermuda Hundred.

Butler's position was too strong to be attacked directly, but Gen. P. G. T. Beauregard was willing to pit his 20,000 men against them in the open. Hoping to bring Butler out of his defenses, Beauregard sent Maj. Gen. Robert Frederick Hoke to Drewry's Bluff. This was enough to convince the Federals to leave their lines.

On May 12, Butler advanced almost half of his force toward Drewry's Bluff, leaving behind enough infantry to hold his defenses. On the next day, the Federals attacked the Confederate works with some success, but once again, rather than following up his initial success, Butler vacillated. He formed a defensive line with Maj. Gens. Quincy A. Gillmore and William F. Smith on the left and right, respectively.

> The assault soon spread along the broad front of the opposing forces, but the poor visibility continued to disrupt the attacking columns.

In the meantime, Beauregard reached Drewry's Bluff and received welcome reinforcements. He hoped to launch an attack of his own, now that he had succeeded in luring Butler away from his defenses. Early on the morning of May 16, Confederates under Maj. Gen. Robert Ransom, Jr., slammed into the Union right flank. The Southerners enjoyed great initial success, but as the fighting progressed in the early morning fog, the attack became disjointed.

The assault soon spread along the broad front of the opposing forces, but the poor visibility continued to disrupt the attacking columns. The Federals managed to launch a counterattack that stymied any further Confederate inroads. By midmorning, the fighting had begun to slacken, and despite a half-hearted attempt by the Southerners to strike at Butler as he retreated to his defenses, the battle was over. The fighting had cost the Federals almost twice as many men as the Confederates—4,160 to 2,506—and had ended Butler's threat to Richmond and Petersburg. By the end of the next day, May 17, Beauregard had put the "cork" in the "bottle" and sealed Butler into his lines at Bermuda Hundred, where he could do no further harm.

BIBLIOGRAPHY

Johnson, Robert U., and C. C. Buel, eds. *Battles and Leaders of the Civil War.* 4 vols. New York, 1887–1888. Reprint, Secaucus, N.J., 1982.

Robertson, William Glenn. *Back Door to Richmond: The Bermuda Hundred Campaign, April–June 1864.* Baton Rouge, La., 1987.

U.S. Naval War Records Office. *Official Records of the Union and Confederate Navies in the War of the Rebellion.* Washington, D.C., 1894–1927. Ser. 1, vol. 7, pp. 269–270, 352–370.

U.S. War Department. *War of the Rebellion: A Compilation of the Official Records of the Union and Confederate Armies.* Ser. 1, vol. 11, pt. 1, p. 636; ser. 1, vol. 36, pt. 2, pp. 6–269.

BRIAN S. WILLS

DUELING

The duel was an important element of life in the Confederacy, with roots going back to the antebellum period. Although widely outlawed in the region before the Civil War—in Virginia as early as 1776 and even in South Carolina by 1812—dueling had been invested with great significance by those antebellum Southerners who continued the practice, closely tying it to concepts of honor and social position. After dueling largely disappeared from the North during the early national period, it also became a symbol of a distinctively Southern way of life. Thus, as white Southerners confronted the questions of honor and nationalism brought on by the war, dueling took on a notable role in the Confederate states.

Although it is impossible to say how many duels were fought during the war, many contemporary observers believed that the crisis increased the incidence of dueling. It infiltrated army life, as officers resorted to duels to settle private scores. The most noted such duel resulted in the 1863 killing of Ransom Calhoun, a nephew of John Calhoun, by Alfred Rhett, the son of fire-eater Robert Barnwell Rhett. And it entered Confederate politics and government, as vitriolic debate brought challenges, threats, and sometimes combat between political figures or between those in government and, especially, their journalistic critics.

After the war, dueling declined rapidly. Although a few duels were fought and challenges issued into the 1890s, these were isolated affairs that met with increasing public disapproval. The culture of honor having been eclipsed, its most visible manifestation could no longer be sustained.

BIBLIOGRAPHY

Chesnut, Mary Boykin. *Mary Chesnut's Civil War.* Edited by C. Vann Woodward. New Haven, 1981.

Coulter, E. Merton. *The Confederate States of America, 1861–1865. A History of the South*, vol. 7. Baton Rouge, La., 1950.

Wyatt-Brown, Bertram. *Southern Honor: Ethics and Behavior in the Old South.* New York, 1982.

DICKSON D. BRUCE, JR.

DUKE, BASIL C.

DUKE, BASIL C. (1815–?), physician and brigadier general. Born near Orangeburg, Mason County, Kentucky, on March 31, 1815, Basil C. Duke was educated in private schools and studied under Dr. N. R. Smith before graduating from the University of Maryland's Medical School in 1834. Afterward he opened a private practice in Mayslick, Kentucky. A Whig, Duke actively supported the Constitutional Union party in the presidential election of 1860. He later became a staunch Democrat.

Although not an ardent secessionist, Duke at the outbreak of the Civil War enlisted as a private in the Fifth Kentucky Volunteer Infantry commanded by Col. John S. Williams. Commissioned as the regiment's surgeon, Duke was promoted to brigadier general. Throughout the remainder of the war, he served on the medical staff of Confederate organizations along the border states. He was named chief of the medical staff of the Army of Eastern Kentucky in 1861, and the following year he was made the medical director of Southwestern Virginia, East Tennessee, and Eastern Kentucky, which was commanded by Humphrey Marshall. Duke saw action with Kentucky troops at Middle Creek, Kentucky; Princeton, Virginia; during the Kanawah valley, West Virginia, campaign; and throughout Virginia and Tennessee between 1861 and 1865.

When the war ended, Duke returned to Mayslick, resumed his medical practice, and became a leading Kentucky physician.

BIBLIOGRAPHY

Mosgrove, George D. *Kentucky Cavaliers in Dixie: The Reminiscences of a Confederate Cavalryman.* Jackson, Tenn., 1957.
Warner, Ezra J. *Generals in Gray: Lives of the Confederate Commanders.* Baton Rouge, La., 1959.

KENNY A. FRANKS

DUKE, BASIL WILSON

DUKE, BASIL WILSON (1838–1916), brigadier general and historian. Duke was born May 28, 1838, in Scott County, Kentucky. After he earned a law degree at Transylvania University, he opened a law practice in St. Louis, Missouri. In June 1861, he married Henrietta Hunt Morgan, sister of John Hunt Morgan.

Active in the Missouri secessionist movement, Duke was sentenced to death in absentia by a secessionist vigilance committee. He was elected a first lieutenant in Morgan's Lexington Rifles, a part of the Second Kentucky Cavalry; after promotion to colonel, Duke commanded the regiment. He was wounded at Shiloh, but recovered to participate in Morgan's great Ohio raid in 1863, where he was captured along with the rest of Morgan's command. A prisoner of war for a year before being exchanged, he returned to Confederate service, was promoted to brigadier general in September 1864, and commanded a cavalry brigade that served in Kentucky and Virginia until Appomattox. With Robert E. Lee's surrender, Duke was ordered to provide Jefferson Davis's escort as he fled Richmond. He was captured during a decoy mission to lead Federal troops away from Davis.

After the war, Duke resumed his law practice in Louisville and was elected to the Kentucky House of Representatives in 1869. He wrote, among other works, *A History of Morgan's Cavalry* (1867) and *The Reminiscences of General Basil W. Duke, C.S.A.* (1911), and edited *Mid-Continent* and *Southern* magazines. Duke died on September 16, 1916.

BIBLIOGRAPHY

Brown, Dee Alexander. *The Bold Cavaliers.* Philadelphia, 1959.
Mosgrove, George D. *Kentucky Cavaliers in Dixie: The Reminiscences of a Confederate Cavalryman.* Jackson, Tenn., 1957.
Warner, Ezra J. *Generals in Gray: Lives of the Confederate Commanders.* Baton Rouge, La., 1959.

PAUL F. LAMBERT

EARLY, JUBAL

EARLY, JUBAL (1816–1894), lieutenant general. Early was one of the Confederacy's most able corps commanders and an architect of the cult of the Lost Cause. "Old Jube" fought in most of the major campaigns of the Army of Northern Virginia and held an independent command in the Shenandoah Valley late in the war. Although he should be considered just behind Thomas J. ("Stonewall") Jackson and James Longstreet in ability, Early's reputation suffered because of losses to Union Maj. Gen. Philip Sheridan in 1864 and because of a cantankerous personality that won from Robert E. Lee the fond epithet of "my bad old man" but also created friction with fellow officers.

Jubal Anderson Early was born November 3, 1816, in Rocky Mount, Franklin County, Virginia, the third of ten children. His father was a prominent farmer, his mother from a family with large slaveholdings. Young Jubal entered the U.S. Military Academy at West Point in 1833, performing better in academics than in discipline and graduating eighteenth of fifty in the class of 1837, which included Joseph Hooker, John C. Pemberton, and John Sedgwick. Commissioned second lieutenant July 1, 1837, Early as part of Company E, Third Artillery, participated in the Seminole War in Florida (1837–1838) and then went to Tennessee to assist with Indian removal. Before learning of his promotion to first lieutenant, to date from July 7, 1838, Early had begun the process of resigning from the army, effective July 31, 1838.

Returning to Rocky Mount, Early studied law and set up practice in 1840. He became active in the Whig party, representing Franklin County for a term in the Virginia General Assembly. In 1843, Early was appointed commonwealth's attorney for Franklin, a post he held until 1852. In between came service in the Mexican War. As major of the First Virginia Regiment, he performed garrison duty in northern Mexico under Zachary Taylor, seeing no combat but contracting the rheumatism that afflicted him throughout his life. He was honorably discharged August 3, 1848.

When the secession crisis came, Early won a seat as delegate to the Virginia secession convention, which convened in Richmond on February 13, 1861. Franklin County voters selected Early, a staunch Unionist, presumably because of the county's tobacco ties with markets in the North. Early's

cautious approach earned him the nickname "the Terrapin from Franklin." Even after the climactic events at Fort Sumter and the Federal call for troops to put down the rebellion, Early voted on April 17 with the fifty-five delegates hoping to remain in the Union. When the ordinance passed, he barely hesitated before offering to help with the military defenses of Virginia, claiming that the U.S. Constitution still prevailed but that "that does not prevent our State authorities from repelling invasion." After the war, Early wrote that any doubts about secession "were soon dispelled by the unconstitutional measures of the authorities at Washington and the frenzied clamor of the people of the North for war upon their former brethren of the South."

For the next four years, the man called "Old Jube" or "Old Jubilee" by his troops would assert his forceful character on the battlefield. Named colonel on May 16, 1861, he led the brigade at First Manassas that turned the tide of battle late in the day on the Confederate left. For these efforts he was promoted to brigadier general, to date from July 21. At the Battle of Williamsburg on May 5, 1862, he was severely wounded in the shoulder but recuperated in time to rejoin the army at Malvern Hill on July 1. Commanding a brigade under Richard Ewell in Jackson's wing of the army, Early fought at Cedar Mountain, Second Manassas, and Harpers Ferry. Old Jube's performance at Sharpsburg garnered the praise of Lee and Jackson for repelling withering Federal assaults on the Confederate left near the Dunkard Church. At the Battle of Fredericksburg on December 13, Early's men again sealed a breach during a crucial moment in the Union attack on the Confederate right.

By the end of 1862, Early had also proved himself to be one of the true characters in the army. He had a knack for challenging superiors without repercussion. While marching to Fredericksburg in late November, Jackson questioned why he saw so many stragglers in the rear of Early's column. Early cracked that Jackson witnessed the straggling "probably because he rode in the rear of my Division." The severe Jackson reportedly only smiled at the blunt reply. Early also was one of the few people who could swear in front of Lee, who overlooked such indiscretions because of Early's talents for command. Others, however, did not so readily forgive his acerbic nature. Brig. Gen. G. Moxley Sorrel wrote that Early's "irritable disposition and biting tongue made him anything but popular," and Confederate soldier Henry Kyd Douglas found him "arbitrary, cynical," and "personally disagreeable." Both, however, offered high praise for his abilities. Early himself knew the impression he had on others, but did not care.

In appearance, Early was considered striking with dark piercing eyes and a gray patriarchal beard broken at times by a smile like that of a possum. He rode into battle wearing a slouch hat topped by a black ostrich plume. Rheumatism bent his six-foot frame, making him appear shorter and older than he was. He punctuated a piping, nasal voice (which one person likened to an old woman's) with streams of tobacco juice and stinging oaths that impressed many with their originality. Arriving at Lynchburg, Virginia, in 1864, he raised himself in the saddle to yell to Federal cavalry: "No buttermilk rangers after you now, you God-damned Blue-Butts!"

Promotion to major general did not come until January 17, 1863. At that time he was also confirmed as permanent commander of Ewell's former division. As Lee and Jackson outmaneuvered Union Maj. Gen. Joseph Hooker at Chancellorsville (May 1–3), Early guarded Marye's Heights above Fredericksburg against Maj. Gen. John Sedgwick. The

> **Early overstated Longstreet's culpability in an attempt to absolve Lee from criticism.**

Union forces proved too much for Old Jube's smaller command, but the Confederates on May 4 regrouped with Lee's army to push Sedgwick back over the Rappahannock.

In June 1863, Lee steered his army northward to conduct a raid that culminated at Gettysburg. With the death of Jackson at Chancellorsville, Ewell had ascended to command of the Second Corps, which included Early's division. To them fell the task of clearing the Union Eighth Corps under Maj. Gen. Robert H. Milroy from Winchester, Virginia. On June 14, Early's men successfully stormed a Federal fort northwest of town in what became the Second Battle of Winchester. Early's men continued through the Cumberland Valley into Pennsylvania, brushing aside the minimal resistance from emergency militia and traveling to the Susquehanna River at Wrightsville until receiving the call from Lee to concentrate toward Gettysburg. The march fortuitously placed Early's men on the enemy's right flank in the late afternoon of July 1, just in time to help shatter the Eleventh Corps under Maj. Gen. O. O. Howard and chase it through town toward Cemetery Hill.

What happened next became one of the great "what ifs" of the Civil War. Lee ordered Ewell to take Culp's Hill, if practicable. Early and Ewell both believed their men too disorganized to seize the moment. After the war, Early and Longstreet waged a bitter war of words over this and other

actions at Gettysburg in some of the most celebrated articles written about the conflict. Each blamed the other for contributing to Confederate defeat. Some historians believe Ewell (and secondarily Early) acted appropriately based on information of the time. Nonetheless, Early overstated Longstreet's culpability in an attempt to absolve Lee from criticism.

Early continued to show promise for higher command, although his progress was not unblemished. He took part in a disaster at the Rappahannock Bridge on November 7, 1863, but performed better in the Mine Run campaign at the end of November, leading the Second Corps when Ewell fell ill. In December, he was sent to western Virginia to disrupt rail lines of the Baltimore and Ohio and canvass the countryside for supplies. At the Wilderness on May 5 and 6, 1864, Early refused to launch a flank attack on the Federal right because he believed an enemy force would prevent the maneuver (despite testimony to the contrary from John B. Gordon). Although Lee needed to prod Early to make the successful attack, he valued his lieutenant enough to give him the Third Corps at Spotsylvania when A. P. Hill fell ill. Early returned briefly to divisional command before taking over the Second Corps when Lee removed Ewell.

The new lieutenant general, with promotion to date from May 31, 1864, shortly received exciting orders. Union forces under Maj. Gen. David A. Hunter were advancing up the Shenandoah Valley with the ultimate destination of Lynchburg. If the railroad link in that town were severed, and the Valley controlled by the Federals, then a vital granary and invasion route would be lost. On June 12, Lee ordered a twofold mission: clear Hunter and his army out of the Valley and then head north to threaten Baltimore and Washington in the hope that Ulysses S. Grant would divert troops from the Richmond-Petersburg theater. With his small Army of the Valley, numbering from 8,000 to never more than 14,500, Early from June to November marched more than 1,600 miles while fighting seventy-five battles and skirmishes. His men chased Hunter from the valley in mid-June, raided Maryland, collected levies of $220,000 from Hagerstown and Frederick, defeated a scratch force under Lew Wallace at Monocacy Junction on July 9, and threatened to enter Washington, D.C., on July 11. Many criticized Early for failing to take the city, but the fight at the Monocacy River had delayed the advance, allowing two divisions of the Union's Sixth Corps to file into the defenses and limit the chances of success. Early's campaign nevertheless had caught Grant by surprise and forced the diversion of the Sixth and Nineteenth Corps that would have faced the Army of Northern Virginia.

Grant now ordered Philip Sheridan to assemble an Army of the Shenandoah to deny Lee the Valley's resources. In three battles—Third Winchester on September 19, Fisher's Hill on September 22, and Cedar Creek on October 19— Sheridan defeated the Confederates. At Cedar Creek, however, Early had conducted a surprise flank attack that routed two corps and forced another to withdraw until Sheridan delivered a decisive counterattack later that day.

Many Southerners blamed Early for the loss of the Valley, although it is doubtful anyone else could have prevented it. He made errors in the placement of his troops but overall conducted an excellent campaign that rivaled Jackson's performance of 1862. The fall defeats, however, removed the area from the Confederates and contributed to a turn in Northern morale that ensured President Abraham Lincoln's reelection in November.

After a defeat of his thousand-man force on March 2, 1865, at Waynesboro, Early finally was removed by Lee, who still had faith in his lieutenant but recognized his "bad old man" had lost the confidence of soldiers and authorities. Artillerist E. Porter Alexander after the war wrote that Early had "proved himself a remarkable corps commander," adding that his "greatest quality perhaps was the fearlessness with which he fought against all odds & discouragements."

After Lee's surrender, Early fled first to Texas and then to Mexico, finally arriving in Canada in July 1866 where he wrote his memoirs. He returned to the United States in 1869, after President Andrew Johnson pardoned former Confederates, and settled in Lynchburg to practice law. In 1877 he became a commissioner of the Louisiana State Lottery, which allowed him to pursue his lecture tours and writing for various Confederate military studies. The former Unionist became an unreconstructed rebel who wore only gray and never apologized for his actions, including the burning of Chambersburg, Pennsylvania, on July 30, 1864, which he ordered as retribution for Union destruction in the Shenandoah Valley.

As an officer in both the Association of the Army of Northern Virginia and the Southern Historical Society, Early had an enormous influence on the writing of Civil War history. He helped fashion the cult of the Lost Cause, elevating Lee to saintlike status and arguing that the agrarian South never lost a battle but only succumbed to overwhelming numbers churned out by a greedy, industrial North. As long as Old Jube lived, wrote historian Robert Stiles, "no man ever took up his pen to write a line about the great conflict without the fear of Jubal Early before his eyes."

Early maintained his cantankerous ways until 1894. On February 16, he took a fall from which he never recovered and finally died on March 2. He was buried in Spring Hill Cemetery in Lynchburg.

BIBLIOGRAPHY

Bushong, Millard K. *Old Jube: A Biography of General Jubal A. Early.* Boyce, Va., 1955. Reprint, Shippensburg, Pa., 1988.
Early, Jubal Anderson. *Autobiographical Sketch and Narrative of the War between the States.* Philadelphia, 1912. Reprint, Wilmington, N.C., 1989.
Early, Jubal A. *A Memoir of the Last Year of the War for Independence, in the Confederate States of America, Containing an Account of His Commands in the Years 1864–1865.* Toronto, 1867.
Freeman, Douglas S. *Lee's Lieutenants: A Study in Command.* 3 vols. New York, 1942–1944. Reprint, New York, 1986.
Osborne, Charles C. *Jubal: The Life and Times of Jubal A. Early, CSA, Defender of the Lost Cause.* Chapel Hill, N.C., 1992.
Stiles, Robert. *Four Years Under Marse Robert.* New York, 1903. Reprint, Dayton, Ohio, 1977.

WILLIAM ALAN BLAIR

EARLY'S WASHINGTON RAID

With about 14,000 men, Lt. Gen. Jubal Early in July 1864 raided Maryland, defeated a small force at Monocacy Junction, threatened to enter Washington, D.C., and forced the Union to divert the better portion of two corps that would have been pitted against the Army of Northern Virginia. Early lost about 700 and the Federals 1,300 of their roughly 7,000 men during the major action of the campaign at the Monocacy River on July 9.

Early conducted the raid as the second half of a two-part plan by Gen. Robert E. Lee first to clear the Shenandoah Valley of Union soldiers and then to threaten Washington and Baltimore to compel Ulysses S. Grant to siphon troops from Petersburg. Recently promoted to command the Second Corps of the Army of Northern Virginia, "Old Jube" started for

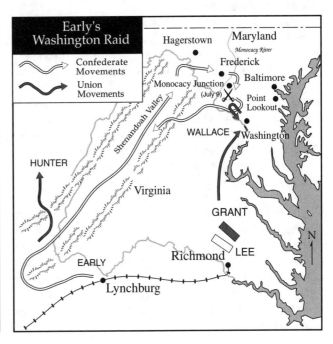

Lynchburg on June 13 to prevent Union Maj. Gen. David A. Hunter from seizing the town and severing a vital east-west rail link. Although Hunter commanded 18,000 men against Early's 12,000, the Union general apparently lost his nerve, retreated to the west on June 19, and handed the valley to the Confederates.

Early seized the chance Hunter's departure presented; by July 5, the vanguard of the newly christened Army of the Valley had begun crossing the Potomac at Shepherdstown. Complicating Early's advance was a vaguely defined scheme to free Confederate prisoners of war at Point Lookout, below Baltimore. Lee wanted Early to incorporate the men into the Army of the Valley but could supply his lieutenant with few details on how the escape would be managed. Early sent cavalry toward Baltimore to cut rail lines and be in position to aid the escaped Confederates—something that never occurred because Federals learned of the escape plan. With the remainder of the army, Early traveled through many of the sites of the 1862 Maryland campaign. At Hagerstown and Frederick he forced levies totaling $220,000.

Union Maj. Gen. Lew Wallace, meanwhile, had used his own initiative to establish a force at Monocacy Junction, several miles south of Frederick, where he could protect roads leading to Baltimore and Washington as well as a rail line of the Baltimore and Ohio. To bolster his force of reserves, Wallace received last-minute reinforcement from seasoned veterans of James B. Rickett's division of the Sixth Corps. Wallace stationed most of his men where they could guard two bridges—a wooden structure for the Georgetown Road and an iron one for the Baltimore and Ohio rail line a half mile to the north. He also sent a portion of his troops two miles farther to the north to protect the Baltimore Pike from Robert Rodes's Confederate division.

After testing the Union positions with artillery and a demonstration that Wallace repulsed, Early concluded that he would have to ford the Monocacy to flank the Union position. John McCausland's cavalry fortuitously provided the way when the men crossed the river roughly a mile below the bridge and ran into the Union left. Early decided that Dodson Ramseur's division would hold the center while John B. Gordon's division followed the cavalry's path to attack the Federal left. Gordon advanced with three brigades, attacking en echelon from the right under brigadiers Clement A. Evans, Zebulon York, and William Terry. After emerging from woods seven hundred yards from the Union soldiers, Gordon's men needed to mount three charges across a field choked with shocks of wheat and broken by a stream to force the Federals from three positions along wooden fences, a stone fence, and finally the cuts along the Georgetown Road. General Evans went down with a serious wound early in the attacks. By 4:30 P.M. the work was done; Wallace's men retreated toward Baltimore and the road to Washington lay open to Early's men.

Shortly after noon on July 11, Early scanned the outer defenses of Washington while the remainder of his army finished an arduous march in extreme heat along dust-choked roads. Early correctly judged his men to be too fatigued to attack works manned by 100-day men, invalids, and heavy artillery. The delay, however, proved fateful. During the night, the remainder of the Sixth Corps under Maj. Gen. Horatio G. Wright filed into the defenses. They would soon be bolstered by the Nineteenth Corps under William H. Emory. Wallace's defense at the Monocacy had delayed Early's men just enough to allow reinforcements to arrive.

Early spent July 12 skirmishing with Union soldiers, but decided to withdraw rather than risk an attack that would have proved far too costly, even if successful. The Confederates recrossed the Potomac at White's Ford, July 13 and 14, having raided the North successfully and having forced Grant to part with troops that could have helped in the campaign against Lee.

BIBLIOGRAPHY

Cooling, B. Franklin. *Jubal Early's Raid on Washington: 1864.* Baltimore, 1989.

Gallagher, Gary W., ed. *Struggle for the Shenandoah: Essays on the 1864 Valley Campaign.* Kent, Ohio, 1991.

Vandiver, Frank E. *Jubal's Raid: General Early's Famous Attack on Washington in 1865.* New York, 1960.

Worthington, Glenn. *Fighting for Time; or, The Battle that Saved Washington and Mayhap the Union.* Baltimore, 1932.

WILLIAM ALAN BLAIR

ECHOLS, JOHN

ECHOLS, JOHN (1823–1896), brigadier general. A prominent Virginian but somewhat obscure Confederate officer, Echols was born March 20, 1823, in Lynchburg. At his 1840 graduation from Washington College in Lexington, he and twenty of his classmates established the alumni association of that institution. Echols studied law at Harvard and started a legal practice in Staunton. He successively became commonwealth attorney, member of the state's general assembly, and delegate to the Virginia secession convention.

Appointed lieutenant colonel of the Twenty-seventh Virginia, Echols led the regiment at First Manassas. Promotion to colonel occurred shortly after. At Kernstown, Echols suffered a severe arm wound, but his gallantry brought an April 16, 1862, advance to brigadier general. A huge man (six feet, four inches tall, 260 pounds), he served most of the remainder of the war in western Virginia. He was in the action at Droop Mountain and commanded the Confederate right at New Market. In both Jubal Early's raid on Washington and the second Shenandoah Valley campaign, Echols's troops played a support role. He was in command of southwestern Virginia at Robert E. Lee's surrender. Echols guarded President Jefferson Davis on his flight from Danville to Augusta.

Echols had an impressive postwar career. He became a prominent Staunton businessman, served on the Committee of Nine in the restoration to the Union of his native state, and was instrumental in the expansion of the old Virginia Central Railroad into the Chesapeake and Ohio rail system. Echols served on the board of visitors of both Washington and Lee University and Virginia Military Institute. He died May 24, 1896, of Bright's disease in Staunton, where he is buried.

BIBLIOGRAPHY

"Gen. John Echols." *Confederate Veteran* 4 (1896): 316–317. Reprint, Wilmington, N.C., 1985.
Hotchkiss, Jedediah. *Virginia.* Vol. 3 of *Confederate Military History.* Edited by Clement A. Evans. Atlanta, 1899. Vol. 4 of extended ed. Wilmington, N.C., 1987.

JAMES I. ROBERTSON, JR.

ECONOMY

The Confederate States of America faced many problems during its four-year existence, and many if not most of them were related to mobilizing and paying for the war effort. During the war, the Southern economy underwent many permutations. Most scholars agree that Confederate fiscal and monetary policies weakened the Southern economy and thus hastened, if not caused, eventual Southern defeat. Nevertheless, despite the many flaws in economic policymaking, the Confederate economy did manage to support the war effort for four years. In the process, the Southern economy was transformed from its antebellum roots.

In 1861, the eleven states that formed the Confederacy contained 9 million people, of which close to 4 million were bondsmen. These inhabitants lived in an overwhelmingly agricultural economy: cotton was indeed king and represented almost 70 percent of all U.S. exports. The vast majority of Southerners farmed, and those who realized profits usually plowed them back into land and slaves.

Still, many Southerners had, during the decade immediately preceding the firing on Fort Sumter, awakened to the perils of a staple crop economy. Commercial conventions and the press began trumpeting the need to diversify as early as the 1840s. In the beginning, the voices of J. D. B. De Bow, William Gregg, and Daniel Pratt appeared to be voices in the South's agrarian wilderness, but by the 1850s, these stalwart boosters of economic diversification began to attract an audi-

ence. During the 1850s, their boosterism bore fruit, as Southerners began to invest in nonagricultural pursuits. Southerners increased railroad mileage almost 300 percent; they poured millions into industrial establishments such as cotton and rolling mills; and they improved the value of the products they produced by close to 300 percent. By 1860, the South contained over 20,000 manufacturing establishments, which employed over 110,000 workers and represented a capital investment of $95,974,585—an increase of more than 100 percent over 1850 totals.

> ## The South's share of national manufacturing actually dropped between 1850 and 1860.

But despite such impressive totals, the Southern states still lagged well behind the more industrialized North. Indeed, the South's share of national manufacturing actually dropped between 1850 and 1860. Moreover, the growth was uneven: some states in the Deep South contained few industrial establishments and even fewer rail lines, while states such as Virginia and Georgia housed most of the factories and about one-third of the railroads. (These figures are based upon the *Statistical View of the United States . . . Compendium of the Seventh Census,* 1850, and the *Eighth Census of the United States: Manufactures,* 1860. The census takers used different categorizations for manufacturing and other pursuits; consequently, there may be slight variations. These figures are drawn for the Southern states, defined as the eleven states of the future Confederacy.) In short, the South expanded dramatically, but the rest of the nation grew even more rapidly. Consequently, when the Confederate States formed, they produced one-twentieth the amount of pig iron and had one-twenty-fourth the number of locomotives and one-seventeenth the amount of cotton and woolen goods that the North had.

This nation of farmers was undaunted by the task it faced. Though many in Montgomery (and later Richmond) realized that the Confederacy faced formidable handicaps, most were confident that indigenous resources and foreign purchases could provide all the nascent country needed to defeat the Union.

Foreign Trade

Initially, both Union and Confederate officials concentrated upon European sources for supply. This was not unusual: though the North had an established manufacturing base, it, like the South, was woefully deficient in war matériel. Consequently, the first skirmishes between the two sides took place in the financial and manufacturing centers of England and the Continent.

Until about 1862, Confederate procurement policies abroad were marked by their haphazard nature. To be sure, Confederate purchasing agents were dispatched to Europe to buy, usually on credit, badly needed war goods. For the first year and a half, foreign purchases were paid for with specie, foreign bills of exchange, and credit. Eventually, the Treasury Department relied upon Confederate bonds and cotton certificates to pay for foreign goods.

Finding adequate sources of funds and credit were problems for the Confederacy's foreign agents, but they were by no means the only ones. Most of the agents represented different bureaus within the Confederate government. As a result, competition ensued between the Ordnance and Navy departments, and others. This competition hindered Confederate purchasing efforts and gradually led to an overhaul of the system. Colin McRae became the Confederacy's sole government agent in 1863. After that year, McRae apportioned funds for foreign goods among the various departments and oversaw the general financing of war matériel with cotton. Had this reorganization taken place sooner, Confederate financial and purchasing operations abroad would have been enhanced significantly.

Davis and others within the Congress realized that the new nation needed foreign goods, but they also believed that Europe needed Southern cotton more. Consequently, they were confident that a self-imposed blockade on cotton shipments abroad would force Britain and France to intervene to secure an uninterrupted flow of cotton. This policy was endorsed by the press, planters, factors, and other businessmen involved in the production and shipment of cotton. Although Congress never passed a law prohibiting cotton exports, the states and localities passed restrictive measures that had the desired effect. These measures were enforced by local committees of public safety.

The states and localities that enacted restrictive legislation lifted those restrictions beginning in 1862. By the time the Confederacy did this, the Union's naval blockade was in place. Davis and others assumed that the existence of a "paper blockade" in defiance of international law would force Britain and France to intervene to break the Union blockade, but such was not the case. Nor did the Confederate government make an effort initially to circumvent the Union cordon and thus send 400,000 stockpiled bales of cotton overseas. Instead, Davis encouraged private firms to do so. Nonetheless, Confederate purchasing agent Caleb Huse bought four steamers for the government to use in running the blockade. These vessels ran the gauntlet forty-four times without a loss.

The continued competition between Confederate agents overseas and the success of these Confederate blockade runners convinced the South's European emissaries and chief agent McRae that the government should become actively involved in blockade running. Congress finally acceded to the request and passed a law in 1863 requiring all blockade-running vessels to carry at least one-third to one-half of their cargo on government account. Congress grudgingly followed up on this law a year later when it passed an initiative that prohibited the importation of luxuries and gave Davis the authority to regulate all cotton shipments sent out of the Confederacy. The results of this experiment in state socialism were impressive: Davis reported that all the problems with the old system of individual runners had been eliminated. Cotton was being shipped to Europe where it played a key role in financing purchases of badly needed war matériel and in boosting Confederate credit overseas. Had this government oversight been undertaken sooner, there is no doubt that the South would have been able to obtain more supplies and would have been able to finance its foreign operations more efficaciously.

Mobilizing for War

President Jefferson Davis initially may have misjudged the extent of the Union blockade, but he did not underestimate the North's war-making capacity. Indeed, Davis placed top priority on obtaining arms, ammunition, and other accoutrements of war for his armies. The War Department's Ordnance Bureau rose to the challenge of equipping the Southern armies.

The chief of the Ordnance Bureau was Josiah Gorgas. This Pennsylvania-born officer was a godsend to the Confederacy; he worked miracles. He knew that the whole Confederacy contained only two mills capable of rolling and rerolling iron. He immediately contracted with the Tredegar Iron Works and the Atlanta Rolling Mill (later renamed the Confederate Rolling Mill) for badly needed iron bar and plate. With government aid in the form of lucrative advances to firms that would convert to government production, and with the establishment of Confederate arsenals, depots, an ammunition laboratory, and powderworks, Gorgas succeeded in creating what one scholar has termed a military-industrial complex. Gorgas himself noted in his diary that "where

> **Cotton was being shipped to Europe where it played a key role in financing purchases. . . .**

three years ago we were not making a gun, pistol, nor a sabre, no shot or shell [except at the Tredegar Iron Works]—a pound of powder—we now make all these in quantities to meet the demands of our large armies." Statistics bear out Gorgas's statement. The Atlanta Rolling Mill produced almost 400,000 pounds of sheet iron for the Confederate Navy Department in 1862 alone. The Augusta Powder Works churned out, among other things, 110 twelve-pound guns,

4.6 million lead balls, over 10 million small arms cartridges, and 174 gun carriages. The Tredegar Iron Works produced over 200 pieces of heavy siege, field, and seacoast ordnance a year and, in 1862 alone, manufactured 351 such guns.

Gorgas also drew upon the expertise of smaller manufacturers. The Ordnance Bureau directed local and regional arsenals to let contracts with interested parties to produce assorted accoutrements for the War Department. The response was immediate. Hardware shops, gunsmiths, and others converted existing facilities into small factories to produce war matériel.

The Quartermaster Department oversaw the mobilization of the economy for the supply of the armies. The first quartermaster general, Col. Abraham C. Myers, was not as capable as Gorgas, nor did he have enough supplies on hand—uniforms, blankets, tents, and the like—to clothe and equip all the soldiers who took up Confederate arms. Consequently, Myers offered cash bonuses to those who initially supplied their own. He then placed advertisements in newspapers throughout the South soliciting contracts for uniforms, clothing, blankets, and tents. The response to these entreaties was immediate. Established textile firms and budding entrepreneurs took advantage of lucrative contracts to produce for the Quartermaster Department.

The euphoria among the manufacturers soon waned, however, and the department found itself with less goods than anticipated. The problem lay in the system: competitive bidding led manufacturers to sell more goods on the open market where greater profits could be made. Those manufacturers then reneged altogether on government contracts. These problems were soon exacerbated by the loss of two key quartermaster depots in Nashville and New Orleans. To compensate, Myers directed local agents to impress needed raw materials for government factories, and he saw to it that factories kept their workers via draft exemptions.

Myers was soon faced with the necessity of reorganizing the bureau. He did not survive the reorganization: he was replaced by Brig. Gen. Alexander R. Lawton in 1863. Lawton went even further than Myers. He renegotiated all contracts and lowered the profit ceiling from 75 percent to 33⅓ percent. He kept manufacturers with government contracts faithful by making them dependent upon the department for raw materials and labor exemptions. Though accounts are fragmentary, it appears that all factories with quartermaster contracts were required to earmark two-thirds of their output for the department.

The early successes of the Ordnance and Quartermaster bureaus were gradually forgotten after 1863. From that year until the end of the Confederacy, all Confederate bureaus were increasingly faced with problems that did not go away and that reflected graver problems in the Confederate economy. As time passed, machinery and spare parts wore out and could not be replaced because raw materials were lacking. Replacement parts and supplemental goods could not be obtained because the Union blockade's increased effectiveness cut down on the amount of cargo that could be garnered from outside sources. Indigenous sources of raw materials were slowly but steadily lost as the Union military continued its conquest of the Southern heartland. When raw materials were obtained it was often to little effect. In 1864, Davis and the War Department issued General Order No. 77, which rescinded exemptions for virtually all detailed laborers. Consequently, all private firms lost their skilled workers to the Confederate army. (It should be noted, however, that the Ordnance and Niter and Mining bureaus successfully appealed this ruling and were able to maintain, with only a slight reduction, their work force.) Some factories went bankrupt because the government could not pay for contracted goods. Quartermaster General Lawton estimated that his bureau owed factories with government accounts over $5 million by 1865.

Other problems in production were related to other weaknesses within the Confederate economy. The breakdown of the Southern transportation system proved decisive in the final demise of the Confederate war effort. The South's failure to maintain its limited rail network doomed most supply efforts: both raw materials destined for factories producing war goods and foodstuffs bound for the armies or urban centers were often left at the depot for want of transportation. So too, the South's failure to create an adequate credit system to buy supplies from domestic and foreign sources seriously handicapped the Confederacy's ability to support its war effort completely.

Despite these problems, the Confederacy's military mobilization should still get high marks. The South did manage to expand its antebellum manufacturing base enough to sustain its field armies, for the most part, for four years. But this was achieved at a high cost: the government's mobilization policies profoundly affected the domestic economy and resulted in much hardship for the Southern people.

Fiscal Policy

Jefferson Davis vested the task of overseeing the Confederate economy with Christopher G. Memminger, a lawyer from South Carolina who had only limited experience in business and financial affairs. The secretary of the treasury enumerated several measures to finance the war effort during the early months of the Confederacy, including war taxes, tariffs, the floating of bonds, and the acquisition of overseas credit. Few of these initiatives proved adequate to sustain the economy's war-making capabilities.

From the beginning, Memminger and the Treasury Department relied upon loans to finance the war effort. As early as February 28, 1861, Congress passed the Act to Raise Money for the Government and to Provide for the Defence of the Confederate States of America. This loan, the so-called $15 million loan, instructed Memminger to issue $15 million in bonds or stock certificates bearing 8 percent interest, paid semiannually in specie. The loan was to be paid for with an export duty on cotton. Unfortunately, the loan proved difficult to administer: all banks within the Confederacy had suspended specie payments almost immediately after secession. This merely compounded the more serious problem of a general dearth of hard currency in the Confederacy to pay the interest on the bonds subscribed. In order to solve this problem, Memminger altered the loan subscription policies slightly to allow payment in bank notes of exchange. This loan was fully subscribed and did aid the Confederacy in its early days. Still, as most knew, it was not enough. Consequently, the Treasury Department turned to other types of loans.

Produce Loans. The most successful and longest lived loans were produce loans, which Congress authorized on May 16, 1861, at Memminger's request. Fifty million dollars worth of twenty-year bonds were, according to the law, to be sold for "specie, military stores, or for the proceeds of sales of raw produce or manufactured articles, to be paid in the form of specie or with foreign bills of exchange." The act also directed the Treasury to issue $20 million in Treasury notes that were to be used by the people to pay all taxes. Antebellum newspaper editor and tireless Southern booster J. D. B. De Bow was placed in charge of the loan's administration.

The Southern people reacted favorably to the loan. In fact, so many people subscribed that it was extended by $100 million more in August 1861. This extension was funded by a war tax on property and was designed to continue to bolster Confederate credit overseas and help curb the inflationary nature of the currency by taking excess Treasury notes out of circulation. Over time, however, the enthusiasm for the produce loans began to wane. Many agricultural producers disliked the government's call to pay for the bonds on a set day—it implied the government could choose a day when agricultural prices were very low, thus forcing farmers to sell at a loss. These complaints led many farmers to urge Congress to pass legislation guaranteeing them relief. Some went so far as to urge the government to buy all crops. These plans for state subsidies and government control of produce died quietly.

Congress followed the produce loans with the issue of more Treasury notes: an April 18, 1862, law called for $250 million in Treasury stocks, notes, and bonds to be issued. At Memminger's request, the law allowed individuals to exchange goods in kind for the notes. These regulations were further refined less than a month later, when the Treasury Department instructed bond officials to buy only cotton with the bonds.

Subscribers to the produce loan were also urged to pay their subscriptions, especially since cotton was selling well on the open market. Here, however, many farmers and planters balked, for they believed that the price of cotton differed in various parts of the Confederacy. Farmers also demanded that payment for their cotton be made in Treasury notes, a negotiable form of de facto legal tender, instead of non-negotiable Confederate bonds with a lengthy term of maturity.

The Treasury's renewed emphasis on cotton was understandable. Cotton was garnering good prices, and many believed it could be used to finance more foreign purchases. Consequently, Memminger began to issue cotton certificates. These were to be offered in Europe as collateral for any war purchases made by Southern agents.

The Erlanger Loan. Many disagreed with the stockpiling of cotton to finance foreign purchases; with the Union blockade reducing exports, it appeared more and more unlikely that the South would be able to get all its warehoused cotton to Europe. Still, that cotton was to serve as the collateral on the Confederacy's $15 million Erlanger loan.

The Erlanger loan was negotiated October 28, 1862, between Confederate agent John Slidell and the French banking house of Emile Erlanger and Company. The final agreement (completed in January 1863) called for the Erlanger House to float a $15 million loan. The Confederate Congress was to borrow 75 million francs, using 7 percent bonds based on cotton as collateral. The Erlanger loan was an initial success, but the military fortunes of Confederate armies soon dampened enthusiasm for the loan. Indeed, news of Confederate defeats depressed the market in 1863, but renewed successes in 1864 buoyed it back up. By February 1865, almost all the loan had been sold for $7.7 million—just over half its face value. Still, the Erlanger loan played a pivotal role in Confederate financial operations, for it restored Southern credit abroad and allowed Southern agents to contract for more war matériel.

As might be expected, the resort to loans and the printing press created unprecedented levels of inflation. As the stock of money increased, so too did price levels. The urban populations were especially hard hit by prices that seemed to spiral out of control. Indeed, by the end of 1863, the general price index in the eastern Confederacy was over two thousand times what it had been in January 1861; by the beginning of 1865, that index was over five thousand times the 1861 levels. State and local governments did attempt to address this problem by fixing prices and by establishing city stores for the poor. But often these initiatives merely added to the inflationary spiral by encouraging hoarding.

Taxation. High prices and charges of speculation and hoarding were heard throughout the Confederate South. Again, government programs did little to arrest these problems; in fact, they may have exacerbated them. In an ongoing effort to feed the Southern troops and ensure that farmers and planters did their share for the Confederate cause,

Congress passed the Impressment Act on March 26, 1863, and the Tax-in-Kind Acts on April 24, 1863. Secretary of the Treasury Memminger urged the passage of a tax-in-kind for several reasons: it would help provide subsistence for the army; it would keep the Confederate government from having to impress needed agricultural goods from the civilian population; it would remove the government from the marketplace for food, thus increasing the amount available for civilian consumption; it would relieve the flood of currency in circulation; and it would be a tax easy to collect and less easy to evade. The tax-in-kind called for all Southern farmers and planters to contribute one-tenth of their agricultural products and one-tenth of their slaughtered hogs to the Treasury and War departments, the chief administrators of the tax. Government agents, known derisively as T.I.K. men, would assess the value of farm products and tell the producers what their tax would be. The goods would then be collected and funneled to district-level administrators who would see that the food was forwarded to the armies.

The tax-in-kind proved to be one of the most unpopular measures ever passed. All farmers resisted the assessment process and argued that the agricultural tithe was merely a euphemism for impressment. Farmers were also plagued by phony agents who stole goods at random. Finally, many of the goods destined for the troops never reached them because the overburdened Confederate railroads could not transport them; tons of produce rotted at government depots as a result. The chorus of protest against the law resulted in its eventual amendment. In February 1864, Congress allowed farmers to pay the tax on sweet potatoes in cash, and those who had a relative in the ranks were exempted altogether. By 1865, all individuals had the option to pay the tithe in cash.

The Confederate Congress passed the Impressment Act also in 1863. It was born out of the Commissary and Quartermaster departments' need to acquire food, transportation, and slave labor to build fortifications, drive wagons, and assist in the general war effort. One historian has noted that the act merely legalized what the armies and the bureaus were already practicing: the seizure of goods to support the armies at the front lines. Again, the Southern people resisted—and resented—the law because it allowed the army to impress food and other supplies at government-fixed prices that were often 50 percent below the prevailing market rates. Farmers and merchants, when they were reimbursed by impressment agents, were paid in badly depreciated Confederate scrip. As with the tax-in-kind, the impressment process encouraged individuals to hoard goods—despite stiff penalties for those found evading the law. It also contributed to the downward trend of civilian morale. Fear of seizures, the lack of confidence in Confederate money, and the perception that the government was becoming a centralized tyranny created popular bitterness and resentment,

which only added to the malaise that dominated the home front by the beginning of 1864.

The Confederacy's resort to such measures as the tax-in-kind and impressment reflected the government's failure to develop an adequate tax system. In 1861, most Confederate officials believed that the war would be short and thus could be financed through import and export duties. In February 1861 the Provisional Congress passed a temporary tariff based upon the 1857 U.S. tariff. The next month, Congress levied additional duties on imports of iron, coal, cheese, lumber, and paper and placed a tax on all ships passing into Southern ports. Unfortunately for Secretary Memminger, these duties amounted only to approximately $3.5 million because of the increased effectiveness of the Union's naval blockade.

Memminger saw the failure of this policy and began to advocate the levying of a direct tax on real property. The tax would be used to pay the interest on foreign loans and would reduce the redundancy of the currency because it would be paid in Treasury notes. Memminger pleaded his case in May 1861, but Congress and the president balked: both feared the people would resent the intrusion of government and the cost of a direct tax. Memminger was also stymied by the Confederate Constitution, which mandated that all taxes be apportioned according to population, a stipulation that required a census. Given the instability occasioned by the war, the taking of a census was manifestly impossible. Congress did incorporate tax provisions in its 1861 loan acts, including one that levied a tax of one-half of 1 percent on all Southern taxable wealth. Memminger estimated that $26 million could be realized from this levy. To sweeten the law—and to obviate the need to establish a national tax-gathering mechanism—the law allowed the states to decrease the tax

> ## As with the tax-in-kind, the impressment process encouraged individuals to hoard. . . .

by 10 percent if the state assumed the tax for its residents. As might be expected, the states followed the law as they interpreted it. Most floated state bonds to pay for the tax instead of adding the half of 1 percent tax to state taxes. Ultimately, about $18 million was collected under these provisions.

The failure to tax in adequate measure continued to force the Confederate government to rely on notes, loans, and bonds. But by 1863, this policy had created a debt so huge that the government could not even pay the interest on it. As bonds and notes continued to be printed, inflation spiraled. Consequently, many people began to lobby for the enactment of a general tax law. Congress responded and on April

24, 1863, passed the nation's first comprehensive tax: it placed an 8 percent ad valorem tax on all farm products and established a list of license, occupational, income, and profit taxes. The law did not tax income from earnings or profits from land, because these items were covered under the Tax-in-Kind Act.

Opposition to the tax law surfaced immediately. Many found its provisions complicated and inequitable. Most could evade it altogether if they chose to do so. In the end, the law raised only approximately $82 million, which could not begin to cover all the Confederacy's debts.

Given the shortcomings of the 1863 tax law, President Davis and Congress decided to levy a direct tax—in violation of the constitutional mandate of a census. On February 17, 1864, Congress provided for a 5 percent tax to be levied on all real and personal property. The act also called for levies on profits, jewelry, and other luxury items. Taxes on land and slaves were to be based on 1860 values. Once again, the people protested, and the collection of the tax was largely stymied.

Impact of Failed Economic Policy

The failure to develop an adequate tax law, continued inflation, a spiraling debt, redundant currency, and other financial problems forced Memminger to resign in June of 1864. In his place, Davis appointed a man who was no stranger to financial circles: businessman George Trenholm of the well-known Charleston firm of Fraser and Trenholm. Trenholm immediately set out to reduce the amount of money in circulation and thus stop inflation. Trenholm also advocated that duties be paid on exports and imports. The Congress endorsed his funding measures but refused to implement his recommendation on trade duties.

The desperate situation of Confederate finances did not go away as the new year of 1865 dawned. Trenholm was forced to tell Congress that he had to have at least $500 million in order to keep the government and the war effort going for the first six months of 1865. Davis, too, urged the Congress to pass some supplemental tax law so the Confederacy could continue to exist, but Congress merely increased the rates of the 1863 law. This expedient could not save the Confederacy; Gen. Robert E. Lee surrendered before any more money was collected for the nation's coffers.

There is no doubt that the Southern economy during the Civil War was a decisive factor in the Confederacy's defeat. Misguided policies during the early months of the conflict and later resistance to needed initiatives doomed the Confederacy. The South's rejection of taxes and the government's inability to communicate the need for sacrifice and certain specific financial measures created a vicious cycle. The failure to enact a comprehensive and long-term economic policy that would distribute the economic burden

equally created hardships behind the lines and popular fears of government tyranny. Bureaucratic and congressional mistakes and the resulting domestic hardship did much to destroy civilian support for the war effort.

On the other hand, mobilization policies did not fail the South. The Confederate bureaus were able to take a small manufacturing base and convert it to war production. The success of the War Department's efforts in particular proved that good management and far-seeing entrepreneurs could make a difference.

Although Confederate economic policies get mixed marks and economic weaknesses proved crucial in the South's defeat, there is little doubt that the war years unleashed a revolution in the economic life of the nation. Government encouraged and took over needed war industries; people converted small shops and larger factories to war-related production; they lobbied for tax and poor relief from the government; and all were subjected to forcible seizures of products deemed essential for the war effort. The Southern economy, overwhelmingly agrarian in 1860 was, in five short years, transformed into an industrial one. For the first time, many individuals embraced and encouraged a more balanced, diversified economy; many others saw the need for far-reaching policies and programs; still others embraced the notion of activist government. The Confederacy may have self-destructed economically in 1865, but the road to that self-destruction left a legacy that would be called upon in the postwar era.

[*See also* Banking; Blockade; Bonds; Bread Riots; Civil Service; Cotton; Currency; Debt; Extortion; Farming; Impressment; Inflation; Labor; Lead; Mining; New Plan; Ordnance Bureau; Plantation; Poverty; Public Finance; Quartermaster Department; Rice; Salt; Saltpeter; Slavery; Speculation; State Socialism; Substitutes; Sugar; Taxation; Textile Industry; Tobacco; Transportation; Treasury Department; *and biographies of numerous figures mentioned herein.*]

BIBLIOGRAPHY

Ball, Douglas B. *Financial Failure and Confederate Defeat.* Urbana, Ill., 1991.

Coulter, E. Merton. *The Confederate States of America, 1861–1865.* A History of the South, vol. 7. Baton Rouge, La., 1950.

DeCredico, Mary A. *Patriotism for Profit: Georgia's Urban Entrepreneurs and the Confederate War Effort.* Chapel Hill, N.C., 1990.

Dew, Charles B. *Ironmaker of the Confederacy: Joseph R. Anderson and the Tredegar Iron Works.* New Haven, 1966.

Goff, Richard. *Confederate Supply.* Durham, N.C., 1969.

Lerner, Eugene M. "Inflation in the Confederacy." In *Studies in the Quantity Theory of Money.* Edited by Milton Friedman. Chicago, 1956.

McPherson, James M. *Battle Cry of Freedom.* New York, 1988.

Owsley, Frank L. *King Cotton Diplomacy: Foreign Relations of the Confederate States of America.* 2d ed. Chicago, 1959.

Thomas, Emory M. *The Confederate Nation, 1861–1865.* New York, 1979.

Todd, Richard Cecil. *Confederate Finance.* Athens, Ga., 1954.

MARY A. DECREDICO

EDGED WEAPONS

Edged Weapons in the Army

Edged weapons were already obsolete by the mid-nineteenth century, made so by the rifle-musket, breech-loading carbine, and revolver. Swords, however, were still considered a badge of rank by officers and a necessary inconvenience for cavalry and mounted artillery. Foot artillery needed short swords as camp tools and for clearing fields of fire. Bayonets were useful to infantry as digging implements, candle holders, and spits for cooking meats. Such weapons were infrequently used in combat.

Confederate edged weapons came from various sources. Without doubt the largest numbers were captured from Federal installations in the South or gleaned from the battlefield during the early months of the conflict. The most popular model, and the most functional, was the U.S. model 1860 cavalry saber. Surprising numbers of this model with strong Confederate provenance exist today in the collections of the Museum of the Confederacy at Richmond, Virginia. Many Confederates who had previously been career officers in the U.S. Army carried their prewar service swords, model 1850 foot officer's and model 1850 staff and field officer's types. Gens. Robert E. Lee and Thomas J. ("Stonewall") Jackson are notable individuals who did so. It was a popular practice to carry war trophies, engraved or presentation Federal swords taken in action from an adversary.

Importation of edged weapons from England and the Continent greatly supplemented the South's supply of swords, sabers, cutlasses, bayonets, and knives. England supplied a considerable number of iron-mounted pattern 1853 sabers, and some brass-mounted variations made by Robert Mole are sometimes encountered. Model 1822 officer's swords were also imported in some quantity. In some cases blades were etched with Confederate motifs and hilt decoration altered in similar fashion. Soligen, Germany, also supplied many thousands of blades to the American market, both North and South. French models were imported in lesser quantities. Gen. J. E. B. Stuart is known to have carried a French saber made by Devisme of Paris, as did Lee at the close of the war.

The smallest number, but certainly the most interesting, are those rare weapons made within the Confederacy. These were handmade in limited numbers. Surviving specimens exhibit the whole spectrum of quality and craftsmanship. With the beginning of hostilities, dozens of companies Edged Weapons in the Armybegan manufacture of edged weapons in Alabama, Georgia, Louisiana, North and South Carolina, Tennessee, and Virginia. No makers have been positively identified in Arkansas, Florida, Mississippi, or Texas, but there are many unmarked specimens whose maker and place of fabrication are unknown. The majority of these swords were copies of existing Federal patterns, but there were some notable exceptions.

The firm of Thomas, Griswold, and Company, New Orleans, designed and manufactured some of the finest swords made in the South. The masterpiece produced by this shop is the sword made for Gen. Sterling Price now in Richmond's Museum of the Confederacy. The heavily gilt guard bears the coat of arms of the state of Missouri; the grip is ivory in the form of an ear of corn. Aguider Dufilho, also of New Orleans, made blades of exceptional quality. One of his designs features a pelican feeding its young between the raised letters *CS* cast in the brass guard. The pelican was part of the state seal of Louisiana. Both Dufilho and Thomas, Griswold ceased production with the Federal occupation of New Orleans in 1862.

Nashville, Tennessee, boasted two extensive sword manufacturers who shared expertise. In their short period of operation, the Nashville Plow Works, also known as Sharp and Hamilton, and the College Hill Arsenal produced a variety of distinctive edged weapons. Similarities of manufacture and the commonality of component parts turned out by the two firms indicate their degree of cooperation. Leech and Rigdon, also known as the Memphis Novelty Works, operated in Memphis until the capture of the city. This firm produced at least four different models of edged weapons for officers and enlisted men. The company also made sword belts, sword belt plates, and spurs. The loss of Louisiana and Tennessee deprived the Confederacy of some of its finest and most distinctive sword makers.

> **Bayonets were useful to infantry as digging implements, candle holders, and spits for cooking meats.**

The most prolific sword manufacturer in the Confederacy was the firm of Boyle, Gamble, and MacFee of Richmond and its affiliated companies of Boyle and Gamble and Company, and Mitchell and Tyler. These firms produced a wide variety of officer's swords and sabers, some exceptional quality pieces with etched blades, enlisted men's sabers, saber bayonets, and artillery short swords. Surviving specimens indicate a large and diverse operation. The company also repaired swords, etched blades, and furnished replacement scabbards for those damaged in the field.

The Confederate States Armory, a private enterprise run by Louis Froelich in Kenansville, North Carolina, produced a most distinctive sword of his own pattern with the letters *CSA* cut out within the cast brass guard. Froelich made several other types of swords, an unusual cavalry saber, and a considerable number of cutlasses, side knives, and short swords of his own design. Also in North Carolina was the Raleigh Bayonet Factory, a major source of Confederate-made socket and saber bayonets. Although none is marked or has been positively identified, surviving correspondence indicates that the operation was not a small one.

Kraft, Goldschmidt, and Kraft in Columbia, South Carolina, produced a variety of high-quality edged weapons and fitted some early double-edged European blades to cavalry hilts, resulting in an unusual saber.

The companies of E. J. Johnston and William J. McElroy in Macon, Georgia, were closely allied with the ordnance complex at that location. Both firms are known for their officer's swords, although their quality seems to vary from sword to sword. Louis Haiman and Brother and A. H. DeWitt were located in Columbus, Georgia, and were also allied with the ordnance complex there. The Haiman products are quite varied, almost as if the swords were made to order. The basic patterns are unique to the firm and usually follow no known Federal pattern. Few products of DeWitt have survived, although documentation suggests that the firm made several edged weapons.

The company of James Conning, in Mobile, Alabama, produced a significant number of edged weapons, most of them utilitarian, although some were fine copies of antebellum U.S. swords. Before the war Conning had been a jeweler, and the quality of many of his officer's swords is evidence of his trade.

Also surviving today are numerous unmarked swords and sabers, obviously made in very limited numbers, some by competent swordsmiths but more by untrained small cutlers and blacksmiths. It must be realized that there was no single existing sword foundry in the South when the war commenced. Tremendous effort and enthusiasm were required to produce the wide range of edged weapons that remain. Total production of many firms may have numbered only a few thousand swords or even a few hundred or less. Any Confederate edged weapon is relatively rare today.

[*See also* Joe Brown's Pikes.]

BIBLIOGRAPHY

Albaugh, William A., III. *Confederate Edged Weapons.* New York, 1960.
Albaugh, William A., III. *Photographic Supplement of Confederate Swords.* Washington, D.C., 1963.
Albaugh, William A., III. *Photographic Supplement of Confederate Swords with Addendum.* Orange, Va., 1979.
Albaugh, William A., III, and Richard D. Steuart. *Handbook of Confederate Swords.* Harriman, Tenn., 1951.
Edmunds, Frederick R. "Collecting Confederate Swords: The Mystique." *Bulletin of the American Society of Arms Collectors,* no. 52 (1985): 9–23.
Edmunds, Frederick R. "The Edged Weapons of Kenansville, North Carolina." *Bulletin of the American Society of Arms Collectors,* no. 54 (1986): 11–24.

RUSS A. PRITCHARD

Edged Weapons in the Navy

Edged weapons prescribed by naval ordnance instructions for shipboard use included boarding pikes, cutlasses, battle axes, and bayonets for use with shoulder arms. In addition, officers carried swords purchased at their own expense. Sheath knives were forbidden, but jackknives, useful tools aboard ship, were allowed.

Sizable numbers of edged weapons fell into Confederate hands at the beginning of the war. At Gosport Navy Yard in Norfolk, Virginia, retreating Federals left behind 2,111 pikes and 411 battle axes. These were later supplemented by locally made weapons and by imports from Europe, particularly Britain.

Intended for use in repelling boarders, the boarding pike consisted of a seven-inch-long iron tip attached to the end of an eight-foot-long hardwood staff. The pattern in Federal use in 1861 was the model 1816, and the few surviving Confederate-made naval pikes follow this design, although some substitute brass for iron.

Probably the most distinctive of naval weapons, the cutlass was a short sword used primarily in boarding operations. Most Southern-made cutlasses were either imitations of the straight-bladed U.S. model 1841 or variations that closely resembled the artillery short sword. Cook & Brother and Thomas, Griswold & Company of New Orleans produced some of the South's finest cutlasses, and Robert Mole of Birmingham, England, manufactured many of those imported through the blockade. When supplies were short and the need immediate, the navy typically improvised: at New Orleans, one hundred machetes were purchased, apparently for use as cutlasses.

The navy issued battle axes to designated members of crews for use in cutting through boarding nets and rigging or for fire fighting. Though no contracts are known to have been issued for the manufacture of battle axes, the navy did purchase similar civilian tools such as shingling hatchets as substitutes. Naval crews used a wide variety of bayonets, the kind depending on the shoulder arm the man carried. One type, the British Enfield navy cutlass bayonet used with the short Enfield sea-service rifle, served two purposes, as its name implies.

The Confederate government commissioned a naval officer's sword to be manufactured by Robert Mole in England. The sword bears a distinctive pommel cap in the shape of a dolphin head, a brass guard containing the seal or arms of the Confederate navy, and etchings of tobacco and cotton leaves on the blade. It is often found with the markings of Firmin & Sons and Courtney & Tennant, British military outfitters and Confederate importers, respectively. Another popular model was the L. Haiman & Brothers sword made in Columbus, Georgia. In addition, many officers who had previously served in the U.S. Navy continued to carry their U.S. model 1852 naval officer's sword throughout their Confederate service.

BIBLIOGRAPHY

Albaugh, William, III. *Confederate Edged Weapons.* New York, 1960.
Albaugh, William, III. *A Photographic Supplement of Confederate Swords.* Washington, D.C., 1963.
Brown, Rodney H. *American Pole Arms, 1526–1865.* New Milford, Conn., 1967.
Lord, Francis. *Civil War Collector's Encyclopedia.* Vol. 1. New York, 1965.
Todd, Frederick P. *American Military Equipage, 1851–1872.* New York, 1980.

A. ROBERT HOLCOMBE, JR. and CHARLES V. PEERY

EDUCATION

[*See also* Childhood; Slavery, *article on* Slave Life; *and entries on numerous biographical figures mentioned herein.*]

Primary and Secondary Education

Although antebellum Southerners generally accepted the value of an education and responsibility for the schooling of orphans and children of the indigent, few were willing to endorse, much less fund, widespread public schooling. Communities instead relied upon denominational schools, private academies, or, for the well-to-do, family tutors. To their supporters, such insular schools possessed several advantages: they were devoid of bureaucratic interference, closely reflected local mores, and were easily formed, or disbanded, as circumstances warranted.

And yet by 1860 several prominent Southerners had spoken out in favor of wider educational opportunities. Christopher G. Memminger of South Carolina, Thomas R. R. Cobb and Joseph E. Brown of Georgia, and especially the Reverend Calvin H. Wiley of North Carolina were outspoken proponents of state-supported schools. Thus despite legislative inertia and a general suspicion that such a system would be both abolitionist and socialist, several state assemblies by 1861 had initiated literary funds through which communities received financial aid. Louisiana, for example, funded free schools as early as 1847 despite strong protest by the state's Catholic community, and Virginia by 1860 enjoyed a fund sufficient to defray tuition and books for some fifty thousand indigent children scattered throughout 3,197 primary schools. Several of the larger cities, too—Charleston, Mobile, New Orleans, and Norfolk, for instance—adopted their own local tax-supported institutions. Private classrooms nevertheless continued to dominate, effectively denying a large segment of the population a basic education. Whereas several literary funds might allow children one or two dollars toward tuition expenses at nonpublic institutions, schools such as Virginia's Danville Female Academy charged twenty-five dollars per session for courses of instruction.

Whatever the type of school, resentment of Northern methods was nearly universal. Much of the dislike reflected the South's dependence on outside sources for educational materials. Even basic school equipment had to be purchased elsewhere. As for the many Northern teachers throughout the South, "Let us in no instance," one observer commented, "employ raw Yankee teachers. Let them all be watched, and let them know they are objects of suspicion." Books, however, attracted the loudest protests. There were few textbooks published in the South, and thus educators were constantly reacting to what they perceived to be biased passages and interpretations. *De Bow's Review,* for example, protested that whereas a basic geography text devoted two pages to Connecticut onions and broom corn, the Louisiana sugar industry rated only ten lines. Several Northern publishers worsened the situation by adding surcharges to titles shipped South, disguising offensive books by merely replacing the title page, or marketing editions with only a few pages or passages removed or obliterated.

The war provided an opportunity to start anew. But Confederate textbooks were often too difficult for the age group for which they were intended; others were only slight revisions of standard Northern texts; and all of them suffered from a lack of skilled printers and adequate supplies of paper. The South did produce a variety of titles, but as economic conditions deteriorated, the region increasingly turned back to those Northern books that survived.

It was not long before teachers and students were in short supply as well. In the first rush of patriotism, academies lost many of their students to the army. In a Blount County, Alabama, school, for instance, twenty-two of the twenty-three boys over sixteen volunteered. Girls, too, were eager to help the cause. Sallie Eola Reneau attempted to form a company of "Mississippi Nightingales," complete with military uniforms and sidearms; in Columbia, South Carolina, schoolgirls organized benefits to raise money for Hampton's Legion; and the *Nashville American* reported on the little girl who remarked to a passing soldier that she would study hard "if you will whip the Yankees good for us."

Like their pupils, many teachers left for the army. In an effort to retain instructors, the Confederate government in 1862 exempted from the draft all male teachers with at least twenty students and two years' experience. Unfortunately, the public-service gesture attracted more derision than praise. That combined with the declining state of the schools led instructors to lament, "Away with the thought that teaching is an easy life," for "in no occupation is labor—exhausting, nervous labor—more demanded." Such conditions, continued enlistments, and the public's declining perception of educators in time led to a severe shortage of qualified teachers. North Carolina, for example, in 1860 included 2,164 licensed male teachers, but in 1863 only 525. Women refugees filled some slots, and disabled veterans took others, but it was not enough. Alabama authorities were hardly alone in resorting to teacher competency examinations, nor were they unique in having to admit that leniency was necessary in many cases "where peculiar hardships would exist if the above provisions were rigidly enforced."

Schools had to adapt as best they could. For example, female boarding academies in Morehead City, North Carolina, and Huntsville, Alabama, cleverly offered situations "secure from danger, either of epidemics or war's alarms." Others fought for professional standards, banding together in statewide organizations or within the Confederate States Educational Association, formed in 1861 and still active in the last months of the war. Teachers did their part as well. In the face of rocketing inflation, a Vicksburg teacher, Madge Brown, readily accepted "wood and potatoes, butter and pumpkins" for pay.

By 1863, however, teachers and administrators increasingly had to defend their school's very existence in the face of greater national need. Jefferson Davis expressed his support of continued school terms, but many publicly funded institutions disappeared as local and state governments reallocated scarce funds. Louisiana managed as late as 1865 to retain its literary fund, whereas Florida, Texas, and Virginia withheld varying amounts to sustain the war effort. To retain public support, some schools took on expanded roles. In Raleigh, the North Carolina Institution for the Deaf and Dumb and the Blind instructed its students in the manufacture of rifled-musket cartridges. But as the war progressed, and defeat appeared more certain, the schools' primary function took on new meaning. In 1863 Eliza Burleson Sivley instructed her son "to content yourself to remain at school for an education is about all we can give you and can't be taken from you and will do you more good than wealth."

Supporters also pointed out that eliminating schools only accomplished at home what the enemy was attempting on the battlefield, the destruction of Southern society; schools, after all, were "where the young mind and heart of the State are trained for virtuous and useful enterprise, imbued with patriotic sentiments and fitted for the grave responsibilities which devolve upon the citizens of a free country." In the end, though, declining enrollments, teacher shortages, low morale, inadequate funds, scarce supplies, and adverse public opinion combined to defeat the best efforts of Southern educators. As diarist Mary Boykin Chesnut commented, "wait until you have saved your country before you make preachers and scholars."

BIBLIOGRAPHY

Kennerly, Sarah Law. "Confederate Juvenile Imprints: Children's Books and Periodicals Published in the Confederate States of America, 1861–1865." Ph.D. diss., University of Michigan, 1956.

Parrish, T. Michael, and Robert M. Willingham, Jr., comps. *Confederate Imprints: A Bibliography of Southern Publications from Secession to Surrender.* Austin, Tex., and Katonah, N.Y., 1987.

Stillman, Rachel Bryan. "Education in the Confederate States of America, 1861–1865." Ph.D. diss., University of Illinois at Urbana-Champaign, 1972.

Weeks, Stephen B. *Confederate Text-Books: A Preliminary Bibliography.* Washington, D.C., 1900.

EDWARD D. C. CAMPBELL, JR

Higher Education

Prior to the Civil War, higher education found a significant measure of support among the white population of a number of the states eventually forming the Confederacy. The impetus for the development of Southern higher education grew out of the region's increasing isolationist tendencies fueled by powerful economic, cultural, intellectual, political, and religious forces. As the abolitionist cries intensified and the sectional crisis deepened throughout the 1840s and 1850s, a strong sentiment emerged among the region's wealthiest and most influential families that Southern students needed to be educated in their own region away from what they perceived to be the unsympathetic, radical, and seditious intellectual influences of the North. As the South became increasingly suspicious of nonindigenous intellectual currents, there was a corresponding increase in efforts to establish new academies and colleges. Colleges were seen as vital elements for the preservation of a Southern culture and way of life.

Impeding the development of higher education, however, was the inability of the region to develop a system of preparatory (elementary and secondary) schools. This absence of preparatory schools forced the region's institutions to devote considerable resources to elementary and secondary-level instruction. Thus many of the colleges founded in the antebellum South were by late-nineteenth-century standards actually primary or secondary schools. Even the best Southern colleges were forced to offer extensive preparatory programs. Although the quality of many Southern institutions that called themselves colleges was necessarily suspect, their numbers are impressive. There were only nine colleges in America at the time of the Revolution; by 1850 there were approximately 240 with almost half of them in the South. In the middle of the nineteenth century, the South led the nation in the number of colleges, faculty members, and college students in proportion to its population. Specific enrollment contrasts are enlightening: in 1860 the South had one college student for every 247 white inhabitants; the North counted one student for every 703 residents.

On the eve of the Civil War, South Carolina College (antecedent of the University of South Carolina) reported an enrollment of 184, and East Tennessee University (later renamed the University of Tennessee) enrolled approximately 110 students each year, although about 66 percent of these students were in a preparatory or precollege-level department. The University of Mississippi at Oxford registered approximately 100 students each year, and the University of North Carolina counted 461 students from nearly half the states of the nation. A similar situation existed in Athens, Georgia, where enrollment in the late 1850s reached 159. A law school was established there, and the faculty grew in size and stature, boasting of such distinguished scholars as Joseph and John LeConte and William Louis Jones, all recognized leaders in the nation's scientific and academic communities. These figures compare favorably with Northern institutions. In the 1860–1861 school year, Rutgers enrolled 124, Princeton 314, and Michigan, one of the largest American institutions, 614 students. At the University of Wisconsin the enrollment surpassed 300 only twice during the entire decade of the 1850s.

In the years immediately preceding the war, Wake Forest College in North Carolina was a comfortable if not prosperous institution. Unencumbered by debt, it possessed an endowment and physical plant valued at $100,000. In Spartanburg, South Carolina, Wofford College experienced a steady expansion. In the six years following its founding in 1854, enrollment increased from 24 to 79 and plans were under way to increase its endowment of $69,000 to $200,000. Its library contained 1,000 volumes, and a museum was on the drawing boards.

Thus the antebellum period was, for Southern higher education, a period of both material prosperity and intellectual advancement. Individual institutions experienced modest expansion of financial support and enrollment. Faculties, in general, were academically respectable and included a number of nationally recognized scholars.

The Civil War drastically altered the situation, as students and faculty were scattered and physical plants damaged or destroyed. In September 1861, the University of Tennessee attempted to open but could do so only for a few weeks before suspending operations; most of its students had joined the military and its buildings had been commandeered by the Confederate army. By January of 1862 the army had turned the buildings into a lodging for the wounded. From September 1863 to June 1865 Union forces expropriated the

> ... students and faculty were scattered and physical plants damaged or destroyed.

university, and during this occupation one of its seven buildings, as well as the library and scientific equipment, was destroyed. The grounds of the university were also substantially damaged by Union troops, with trees and shrubs removed to make way for ramparts and other fortifications. The university reopened on March 1, 1866, but could find only students in need of preparatory work. It was not until 1868 that the university enrolled a freshman class of 11 students.

The wartime suspension of operations and the experiences of the University of Tennessee were not unique among the colleges of the Confederacy. By the summer of 1861, 75 of the 123 students enrolled at the University of Georgia were in the military, and the university struggled to remain open. As the military fortunes of the Confederacy declined, additional students and faculty entered military service, and during the fall of 1863 the university suspended operations. Its buildings were converted to war use and were subsequently utilized as a hospital for Confederate soldiers, as a refugee camp for families displaced by the fighting, and ultimately as headquarters for Union troops, who remained until the fall of 1865. For the most part, however, the buildings escaped the most severe damages of war, and on January 6, 1866, the university reopened with 78 students.

The University of Mississippi in Oxford, although forced to suspend operations in the fall of 1861, suffered virtually no damage during the war, and just three months after the surrender at Appomattox it reopened with 193 students. Conditions were less favorable at the University of Alabama, which had to suspend operations for most of the war. Virtually all its buildings had been burned and most of the library lost. An attempt to reopen in 1865 was aborted when only one student arrived for classes. The situation was also bleak at Wofford College; its endowment—which had been loyally invested in the Confederate government—evaporated. Similarly Wake Forest College suspended operations in 1862 and saw its $100,000 in assets reduced to about $11,000. When it finally reopened in 1866, its buildings were badly in need of repair, and it could count only 22 of 67 students as at the college level; the remainder were in preparatory classes.

Emory in Atlanta suspended operations in the fall of 1861 and remained closed for the duration of the war, as did South Carolina College, which closed during the early months of 1862. The College of Charleston also closed for the war. It reopened in 1866, but it was not until 1878 that enrollment reached 50, a figure comparable to the antebellum period. The conflict virtually destroyed the University of the South in Sewanee, Tennessee. With prewar assets in excess of $500,000, the university had aspired to be an educational center for the entire South. It emerged from the war with its buildings burned, its founder, Bishop Polk, dead, and its assets greatly devalued.

> ## The war profoundly effected the colleges and universities of the Confederacy.

At the conclusion of the war, 4,000 Union soldiers occupied the village and campus of the University of North Carolina at Chapel Hill. The university possessed $200,000 in worthless securities and debts of over $100,000. Closed for the war, the university attempted to reopen in 1868, but lacking adequate financial support it closed again in 1871. It resumed instruction in 1875 with a faculty of 7 and about 70 students, considerably reduced from its 1857–1858 enrollment of over 400 students in nine departments.

The war profoundly effected the colleges and universities of the Confederacy. Colleges that prospered in the antebellum era were forced to suspend operations during a conflict that saw endowments lost, the tax base weakened, students and faculty in disarray, and facilities often in ruins. It was not until decades later that a revitalized South witnessed (with the exception of efforts long under way at the University of Virginia) real attempts to build true universities in Nashville, Chapel Hill, and Durham that would eventually rank with the best in the nation.

BIBLIOGRAPHY

Cartter, Allan M. "The Role of Higher Education in the Changing South." In *The South in Continuity and Change*. Edited by John C. McKinney and Edgar T. Thompson. Durham, N.C., 1965.

Coulter, E. Merton. *College Life in the Old South*. 2d ed. Athens, Ga., 1983.

Dyer, Thomas G. *The University of Georgia: A Bicentennial History, 1785–1985*. Athens, Ga., 1985.

Hollis, D. W. *University of South Carolina*. 2 vols. Columbia, S.C., 1951, 1956.

Montgomery, James Riley, Stanley J. Folmsbee, and Lee Seifert Greene. *To Foster Knowledge: A History of the University of Tennessee, 1794–1970*. Knoxville, Tenn., 1984.

Sansing, David G. *Making Haste Slowly: The Troubled History of Higher Education in Mississippi*. Jackson, Tenn., 1990.

JOSEPH M. STETAR

Military Education

Military academies were established in the south starting in 1839 with the Virginia Military Institute (VMI) at Lexington and the South Carolina Military Academy at the Citadel in Charleston in 1842. By 1861, these two famous colleges had been joined by similar institutions in all the Confederate states. Either through state sponsorship of public colleges or through state donations to private colleges, military education was flourishing in the South at the time of secession. The antebellum South led the nation in military academies per capita, prompted in part by the martial traditions of plantation slave society. The Federal government had also encouraged this kind of education by sending army officers as advisers to various college campuses, both military and civilian.

During the 1840s and 1850s, military colleges continued to spring up across the South. Col. Robert T. P. Allen founded the Kentucky Military Institute in 1845. Maj. George Alexander started the Arkansas Military Institute at Tulip, Arkansas, in 1850. That same year, Jefferson College in Natchez, Mississippi, resumed its military training, the state providing muskets and accoutrements. In 1851, Col. Arnoldus Brumby, West Point class of 1835, started the Georgia Military Institute in Marietta, which was later donated to the state of Georgia. In Tennessee, the Western Military Institute at Tyree merged with the economically troubled University of Nashville to become the Nashville Military Institute. South Carolina added another campus, the Arsenal, at Columbia. Maj. D. H. Hill, later a Confederate lieutenant general, opened the North Carolina Military Institute at Charlotte in 1859. Louisiana State Seminary of Learning and Military Academy opened at the same time, under Superintendent William Tecumseh Sherman. Colonel Allen left Kentucky and opened the Texas Military Institute at Bastrop in 1860.

Alabama led the South in the number of military colleges with two private academies at Glenville and La Grange. Both received generous state support. In 1860, Alabama made martial training compulsory at the University of Alabama, making it a military academy of sorts.

The military institutes trained the students in tactics and drill. The manual of arms and the school of the soldier were emphasized, as were parade ground formations. Formal dress parades were frequent. Everyday life at the schools was harsh, regimented, and run on the West Point model. Cadets wore their uniforms at all times; civilian clothes were forbidden. The men lived four to a room, which was typically furnished by each cadet with an iron bedstead, a pine table, a mirror, a wash basin and foot tub, a bucket and dipper, a washstand, and a candlestick. Games of chance, including checkers, chess, and backgammon, were barred. Reading was restricted to course materials. In the classroom, cadets learned engineering, mathematics, tactics, architecture, French, English, natural and experimental philosophy, history, chemistry, rhetoric, and the law of nations. In many states, including Alabama and Georgia, at least one scholarship was awarded to a student from each county. This practice spread military education and militarism throughout the state.

These colleges produced hundreds of officers and non-commissioned officers for the Confederacy, with the Virginia Military Institute leading the way. In 1861, VMI claimed 433 living graduates and 654 nongraduates. That year, Virginia raised 64 regiments of infantry, heavy artillery, and cavalry, and VMI graduates commanded 22. An additional 790 commissioned officers of other ranks came from VMI. Of the 1,902 students who attended VMI from its opening to 1865, 1,781 served in the Confederate army. Though neither of the national service academies was in the South, 294 West Point graduates served the Confederacy, 144 as generals. The Citadel also contributed: of its 224 living graduates prior to 1860, 193 served the Confederacy. These included 4 generals, 17 colonels, 10 lieutenant colonels, 22 majors, 58 captains, 62 lieutenants, and 20 noncommissioned officers. Of these men, thirty-nine died in combat.

At the beginning of the war, many cadets of the various military academies served as drill instructors. High-ranking officers who were unschooled in formal tactics submitted to the training of teenaged students as the Confederacy built its army. Sometimes as individuals, other times as a company, cadets could be found at many of the principal training camps in the South during the opening months of the war. Protected from conscription in most states, cadets continued their studies until the proximity of battle intervened.

When the time came, the cadets also fought. Many simply left school on their own and joined the army. On other occasions, however, cadet battalions were deployed as units. A unit of cadets from the Citadel claimed to have fired the first shot on Fort Sumter in Charleston Harbor on April 12, 1861. In May 1864, the 177 cadets of the Georgia Military Institute (GMI) turned out to repel Sherman's invasion. Still dressed in their flashy school uniforms, these boys came under fire for the first time at Resaca on May 14. Later attached to the Georgia Militia Division under Maj. Gen. Gustavus Smith, the GMI students fought around Atlanta and opposed Sherman's march to Savannah. In all, over a dozen GMI cadets were killed or wounded.

The most famous instance of cadets fighting was at the Battle of New Market, Virginia, on May 15, 1864. Some 247 students from VMI joined Confederate Maj. Gen. John C. Breckinridge's ad hoc force to repel a Union invasion of the Shenandoah Valley. Ten cadets died and 47 were wounded in the fighting.

The Southern military academies also produced famous faculty members. Besides the aforementioned Hill and Sherman, Lt. Gen. Thomas J. ("Stonewall") Jackson taught at VMI. Bushrod Rust Johnson, military superintendent of the University of Nashville, became a Confederate major general. Colonel Allen led Texas troops in Virginia, Arkansas, and Louisiana.

The Civil War destroyed most of these schools. Union troops razed the buildings of VMI and GMI. The loss of students and faculty also hampered school operations. By the end of Reconstruction, all Southern military schools had disappeared save for the Citadel and Virginia Military Institute. The Southern military education tradition was upheld in postbellum years by state agricultural and mechanical colleges established under the Morrill Land Grant Act.

[*See also* Virginia Military Institute.]

BIBLIOGRAPHY

Baker, Gary R. *Cadets in Gray: The Story of the Cadets of the South Carolina Military Academy and the Cadet Rangers in the Civil War.* Columbia, S.C., 1989.
Conrad, James Lee. "Training in Treason." *Civil War Times Illustrated* 30 (September–October 1991): 22–29, 62–64.
Franklin, John Hope. *The Militant South.* Cambridge, Mass., 1956.
Napier, John Hawkins, III. "Military Schools." In *The Encyclopedia of Southern Culture.* Edited by Charles Reagan Wilson and William Ferris. Chapel Hill, N.C., 1989.
Wise, Henry A. *Drawing Out the Man: The VMI Story.* Charlottesville, Va., 1978.

DONALD S. FRAZIER

Women's Education

The fortunes of the Confederacy had a decisive impact on women's education only in the long run. The vicissitudes of war frequently affected specific schools, academies, and colleges, but the wartime education of Southern women did not differ significantly from the education they had received before.

Throughout the antebellum period, many elite Southern women had received a remarkably sophisticated education in literature, history, languages, art, and music, although typically they spent only a few years at school. As a result of the slow development of public schools in the South, girls of wealthy families mainly received their early education at home from their mothers, a governess, or a tutor. Less affluent white women, especially those who lived in the countryside without access to a town, might receive some basic education from their mothers or in an old field or Sabbath school. Slave women, who received no formal education, were not supposed to learn to read, although some did, usually taught by a slaveholding woman.

During the 1850s, the number of female academies and colleges in the South expanded dramatically, testifying to a broad interest among the elite in women's education. Indeed, during the decade the South outpaced the North in the chartering of women's colleges. Many, although not all, of these institutions were closely associated with one of the Protestant denominations, most commonly the Methodists, and were directed by ministers. Many academies encouraged religion among their students. Instruction at Judson College in Alabama included the Bible and other religious texts, and once a semester the college held a series of revival services. Ella Gertrude Clanton Thomas regarded her conversion as one of the high points of her stay at Wesleyan College.

Whether religious or secular, schools invariably embodied a strong commitment to the education of women in Christian morals and were designed to prepare students for their distinct roles as women. Even those that prided themselves on offering an extensive and rigorous education that might include geography, mathematics, Latin, and rudimentary science firmly opposed what they perceived as a Northern tendency to encourage an interest in women's rights. Politics was discussed, sometimes hotly, in women's seminaries and colleges, but nowhere do we find evidence that the young women strayed far, if at all, from the views considered appropriate to a slave society. The South resisted the Northern and midwestern trend toward coeducation and discouraged women of "good" families from becoming teachers.

As early as June 1861, alarm over the mobilization for war led parents to withdraw their daughters from the highly respected Salem College in North Carolina, so that during that summer the school had empty places for the first time in recent memory. But as the war progressed, parents came to believe that their daughters would be safer in Salem than at home, especially if home was in a war-torn region. By 1862, girls were streaming into Salem, which became more crowded than ever and remained so throughout the rest of the war. Wesleyan College in Macon also stayed open throughout the war, except for a few weeks, although during the final year the school dropped its requirement that students master French as a second language, presumably because of a decline in the number of teachers.

Many academies and colleges suffered the loss of teachers, some of whom returned to the North or chose to serve the Confederacy as soldiers or nurses. Others closed because their buildings were requisitioned for the war effort. The Auburn Masonic Female College in Auburn, Alabama, which occupied a fine new brick house, became a hospital for Confederate soldiers; during the latter part of the war the Montevallo Female Institute in Montevallo, Alabama, quartered the soldiers camped in the town. After the war, both

institutions eventually returned to their educational missions, although the Auburn Masonic Female College served for a brief period as a furniture factory before becoming a school for girls and boys. The Tuscumbia Female Academy in Tuscumbia, Georgia, which had been founded in 1826, did not survive the war. Having been closed during the hostilities, the building was eventually used for the Public School of Tuscumbia.

The abiding consequences of the defeat of the Confederacy pushed Southern women's education in new directions. Most dramatic was a growing acceptance of

> ... the defeat of the Confederacy pushed Southern women's education in new directions.

women as teachers. The collapse of their fortunes forced many families to rely, at least in part, on income that women could earn, and teaching offered the most acceptable occupation. The gradual emergence of a comprehensive public school system also generated a need for teachers and new opportunities for women. Thus, during the final quarter of the nineteenth century, the South began to follow the path of the feminization of teaching that had characterized the North before the war.

Formal education for former slave women emerged during the war. The establishment of schools for freed women and men on the Sea Islands during those years was a response as much to the desires of the former slaves themselves as to the missionary zeal of the Northerners who taught them and testified to their eagerness for education. Following the war, Southern African Americans struggled to create schools, educating their women as fully as possible and increasingly training them to become teachers for the next generation.

Although the Confederacy promoted no distinct new developments in women's education, it proved remarkably successful in perpetuating the tradition of educating elite women that had prevailed before the war. The defeat of the Confederacy, however, ensured the emergence of new educational opportunities for poor white and former slave women and new possibilities for all Southern women to take up careers as teachers.

BIBLIOGRAPHY

Blandin, I. M. E. *History of Higher Education of Women in the South prior to 1860*. Washington, D.C., 1975.

Griffin, Frances. *Less Time for Meddling: A History of Salem Academy and College*. Winston-Salem, N.C., 1979.

Swint, Henry Lee. *The Northern Teacher in the South, 1862–1870*. New York, 1967.

Young, Elizabeth Barber. *A Study of the Curricula of Seven Selected Women's Colleges of the Southern States.* New York, 1932.

ELIZABETH FOX-GENOVESE

ELECTION OF 1860

The election of 1860 led to the secession of some of the states that formed the Confederate States of America, but to this day historians are not sure why. The platform of the victorious Republican party dropped its 1856 denunciation of slavery as a "relic of barbarism" comparable to polygamy, and instead pledged the "maintenance inviolate of . . . the right of each state to order and control its own domestic institutions." Though the platform opposed slavery's expansion into the territories and the reopening of the African slave trade, many knowledgeable Southerners doubted the West would sustain slave agriculture and many opposed the slave trade agitation. The Republican candidate, Abraham Lincoln, carried a consistent antislavery record, but he was so little known outside Illinois and so widely regarded as a nonentity sure to be controlled by others that he, personally, could hardly have weighed as a factor. Honoring regnant political custom, he did not campaign or offer any remarks for publication from his nomination on May 18 to his election on November 6.

The Constitutional Union party, embracing conservative Whig remnants, on May 9 had nominated John Bell of Tennessee with no platform. The Democratic party had convened their national nominating convention in Charleston, South Carolina, in April, but no candidate was nominated until June. Southern delegates wanted a platform pledging Congress and the executive to protect slave property in the territories. The minority platform, drafted by Democrats who supported the nomination of Stephen A. Douglas of Illinois, left it to the Supreme Court to decide what power Congress or territorial legislatures held over slave property in the territories. After the minority platform was adopted by the full convention, the Alabama delegation led those of Mississippi, Louisiana, South Carolina, Florida, Texas, Georgia, and some delegates from Delaware and Arkansas out of the convention.

The Democrats reconvened in Baltimore on June 18. When they refused to let bolting Southern delegates back in, the Virginia, North Carolina, and Tennessee delegations withdrew along with parts of the Maryland, Kentucky, Missouri, Arkansas, California, and Oregon delegations. Douglas gained the nomination. On the next day the (mostly) Southern Democrats nominated John C. Breckinridge of Kentucky on a platform that demanded federal protection of slave property in the territories until statehood. It also urged the acquisition of Cuba and the building of a Pacific railroad while condemning the acts of state legislatures that frustrated execution of the Fugitive Slave Act.

The party contest for popular votes that ensued, though lively, did little to inform or educate voters. The political campaign of that summer was bewildering. Despite the critical issues looming in the sectional party split, the Republicans, drawing on their old Whig heritage, somehow set the tone by running a copy of the old Harrison log-cabin-and-hard-cider campaign of the 1840s. The Republicans ran what has been called a "hurrah" campaign, characterized more by spectacle and vociferous cheering for their candidate than by emphasis on or explanation of the planks in their platform. They slighted issues and scoffed at threats of disunion. The other parties scurried to match the Republicans' marching clubs and torchlight parades.

Essentially the contest boiled down to a Breckinridge-Bell struggle in the South and a Lincoln-Douglas struggle in the North. Voters learned little about the candidates from the other section of the country except what the candidates from their own section wanted them to hear. Perceptions of Lincoln and Douglas in the South were terrifyingly distorted. Breckinridge's image in the North was equally skewed. Breckinridge made one speech in the campaign, breaking with tradition, but Douglas shattered tradition altogether, campaigning throughout the North in the summer and venturing into the upper South late in the summer. After news from the states that held their gubernatorial elections in October showed that Lincoln would win Pennsylvania and Indiana and with them the presidential election, Douglas plunged into the Deep South in the autumn. Most historians

> The party contest for popular votes that ensued . . . did little to inform or educate voters.

have written admiringly of his attempts to save the Union in this campaign by warning the South against secession in the event of Lincoln's election.

Like all elections up to that time in American history, the election of 1860 was a collection of state elections, and party strategies varied from state to state. Some Southern radicals hoped for Republican victory in order to bring about secession all the faster. Naturally, in the upper South, an area likely to become the bloody doormat over which armies marched in the event of disunion and civil war, the Breckinridge forces stressed their Unionism (and downplayed its conditional quality). In the Deep South they especially urged Southern unity—perhaps to extract concessions from the Republicans, perhaps to start the process of secession and independence. Motives varied greatly and are difficult for historians to

Presidential Election of 1860

	REPUBLICAN	DEMOCRAT	SOUTHERN DEMOCRAT	CONSTITUTIONAL UNION
Alabama	0	13,651	48,831	27,875
Arkansas	0	5,227	28,732	20,094
Delaware	3,815	1,023	7,337	3,864
Florida	0	367	8,543	5,437
Georgia	0	11,590	51,889	42,886
Kentucky	1,364	25,651	53,143	66,058
Louisiana	0	7,625	22,681	20,204
Maryland	2,294	5,996	42,282	41,760
Mississippi	0	3,283	40,797	25,040
Missouri	17,028	58,801	31,317	58,372
North Carolina	0	2,701	48,539	44,990
South Carolina	Did not hold a popular vote for presidential electors.			
Tennessee	0	11,350	54,709	69,274
Texas	0	Fused with Bell	47,548	15,438
Virginia	1,929	16,290	74,323	74,681

assess. Most Breckinridge leaders seem to have doubted they could win. Few put much faith in achieving victory ultimately by throwing the election into the House of Representatives. And both Bell and Breckinridge forces depicted themselves as the best guarantors of slavery's survival; the former maintained that the best chances lay *within* the Union.

Despite the fatalism of many Southern politicians about the outcome on November 6, voting totals rose in every Southern state—in some by great margins. Estimates of voter turnout are not available for the South, but it appears to have been good there and may have been as high as 82 percent in the North.

Breckinridge carried all the future states of the Confederacy except Virginia (which included the Unionist area that would secede to form West Virginia in three years) and Tennessee, both of which went to Bell. Most historians have been quick to point out, however, that Breckinridge's opposition, if united, carried 55 percent of the Southern vote.

Secessionist Democrats emerged from the election with unity sufficient to take the Deep South out of the Union. Republican victory thus prompted secession in several states, but only the threat of military coercion after the firing on Fort Sumter provoked the secession of some of the states that formed the Confederacy.

[*See also* Constitutional Union Party; Democratic Party; Lincoln, Abraham, *article on* Image of Lincoln in the Confederacy; Republican Party; *and entries on particular states.*]

BIBLIOGRAPHY

Crenshaw, Ollinger. *The Slave States in the Presidential Election of 1860.* Baltimore, 1945.

Historical Statistics of the United States: Colonial Times to 1970. 2 vols. Washington, D.C., 1975.

Johannsen, Robert W. *Lincoln, the South, and Slavery: The Political Dimension.* Baton Rouge, La., 1991.

Potter, David M. *The Impending Crisis, 1848–1861.* New York, 1976.

MARK E. NEELY, JR.

ELECTION OF 1863

This election, coming on the heels of serious military reverses in the summer of 1863, changed the nature of Confederate politics. On July 4 Gen. Robert E. Lee withdrew from Gettysburg after defeat there. On the same day Gen. John C. Pemberton surrendered his army and the city of Vicksburg to Gen. Ulysses S. Grant. In June, Gen. Braxton Bragg had been maneuvered out of his base at Tullahoma, Tennessee, and withdrew his army to Chattanooga, which he soon abandoned.

Although the Confederate armies bounced back to win some victories, notably at Chickamauga in September 1863, the morale of the home front deteriorated under the impact of the military setbacks, combined with inflation, conscription, impressment, and long casualty lists. Pathetic letters from home to soldiers at the front painted graphic pictures of starvation, fears of slave unrest, and marauding bands of deserters from both armies. Many soldiers, responding to these letters, returned home and were among the voters in 1863. In some locations, discontent was channeled into action by various peace societies, some of which even ran candidates.

Almost 40 percent of the 137 members of the Second Congress were new to that body, for many incumbents who had been secessionists in 1860 and 1861 were turned out of office. Among the new congressmen, over two-thirds had opposed secession in 1861. The results had party implications: in 1861 Democrats had tended to be secessionists, and former Whigs, Unionists; three-fifths of the new congressmen in 1863 had once been Whigs. These men had gone with the Confederacy once the decision for secession was made; but their initial hesitation seemed to recommend them to the voters in the crisis of 1863. Moreover, some of the new members composed a "peace party," bringing a fresh ideological stance into Congress. Some desired a restoration of the Union; others believed that peace with independence could still be won at the conference table if President Jefferson Davis were not too stubborn to negotiate.

This political change was not confined to Congress. Former Whigs (mostly former Unionists) increased their strength in almost every Confederate state legislature, and some were elected governors. In Alabama the voters picked a former Whig in the gubernatorial election for the first time in the state's history—even though the Whig party itself was long dead.

The Second Congress, meeting in its initial session May 2, 1864, presented a striking contrast to the First Congress. Almost two-thirds of the members of the first House had been Democratic or secessionist; in the second House the balance was about even. Not counting areas where normal elections could not be held because of the presence of Federal troops, the voters elected former Unionists to replace secessionists in fifteen districts and returned incumbent former Unionists in another sixteen. Most of these thirty-one seats in the second House represented districts in the Appalachians and the adjacent Piedmont.

Much of the change was due to peace sentiment. Jehu A. Orr of Mississippi told the electorate during his campaign that he would do his best to achieve an honorable peace and that he believed secession had been a great mistake. The contraction of Confederate-controlled territory also resulted in legislative turnover. Many of the reelected secessionists came from "phantom constituencies," districts that were controlled by the Union army. For such areas, notably Kentucky, Missouri, and much of Tennessee, ballots could be cast only by soldiers and refugee civilians. Had normal elections been held throughout the Confederacy, the result would probably have been a resounding defeat for those who had originally favored secession.

The North Carolina contingent in the Second Congress included eight newcomers, some of them apparently elected through the influence of peace societies. The Tarheel delegation was now composed of ten former Union Whigs and only two former secession Democrats (one a holdover senator and the other an incumbent who reclaimed his seat by a mere ten-vote margin). Some Confederates were so alarmed by Tarheel behavior that they feared a second revolution, and in fact much of the change in voting behavior in the Second Congress was due to bloc voting by the North Carolina delegation. James Madison Leach of North Carolina, for example, declared that he had opposed secession for twenty years; James T. Leach, North Carolina, avowed that he was an early advocate of reconstruction; and another North Carolinian frankly admitted that he ran for the Second

> **Similarly, the new congressmen were less willing to use slaves as soldiers. . . .**

Congress because he opposed Davis's war measures and wanted to stay out of the military.

For the most part, the Unionists in the Second Congress were opposed to the rigorous policies of the Davis administration, which they thought were encroaching upon their constitutional rights. The new congressmen and their incumbent allies were less willing than other congressmen to curtail draft exemptions and more willing to restrict the zeal of quartermasters who impressed supplies for the army and paid less than market prices for what they took. The impact of the 1863 elections was especially notable on the issue of the suspension of the writ of habeas corpus. By 1864 suspension was being used to prevent the emasculation of the draft law by judges who would issue writs to get soldiers out of the army. Some legislators who opposed conscription attacked it indirectly by appealing to the individual's right to be free of arbitrary detention by government authority. Similarly, the new congressmen were less willing to use slaves as soldiers than were their more experienced colleagues. In contrast, those voting for draconian measures in support of the war effort usually represented occupied districts, notably Missouri, Kentucky, and parts of Tennessee and Virginia. These delegates could vote in full confidence that their constituents would not feel the effects of harsh impressment, sweeping conscription, or suspension of the writ of habeas corpus.

The turnover in membership also meant that the Second Congress would be less unified than its predecessor. Although political parties never developed in the Confederacy, the change in the composition of the membership in the Second Congress, the legislative issues of the last

Congress, and the stress of a losing war effort exacerbated political divisions and led to the development of factions that might have become the basis of a two-party system if the Confederacy had survived. Analysis of legislative voting in the Second Congress reveals deep cleavage between former Union Whigs and former secession Democrats. More important, however, legislative behavior in the Second Congress was closely correlated with the location of a congressman's home in relation to the Union army.

In short, by the fall of 1863, Confederate-controlled territory had diminished and the cost of secession had become apparent to Confederate voters, who turned away from original secessionists. Even so, the new members—though differing in attitude from the old—were generally familiar to the voters. There was no electoral revolution; most of the new members were simply familiar names whose previous behavior was more symbolic of caution than that of the men they displaced.

[*See also* Conscription; Habeas Corpus; Impressment; *and entries on particular states.*]

BIBLIOGRAPHY

Alexander, Thomas B., and Richard E. Beringer. *The Anatomy of the Confederate Congress: A Study of the Influences of Member Characteristics on Legislative Voting Behavior, 1861–1865.* Nashville, Tenn., 1972.

Beringer, Richard E. "A Profile of the Members of the Confederate Congress." *Journal of Southern History* 33 (November 1967): 518–541.

Beringer, Richard E. "The Unconscious 'Spirit of Party' in the Confederate Congress." *Civil War History* 18 (December 1972): 312–333.

"Proceedings of the Confederate Congress." *Southern Historical Society Papers* 44–52 (1923–1959). Reprint, Wilmington, N.C., 1991–1992.

Yearns, Wilfred B. *The Confederate Congress.* Athens, Ga., 1960.

RICHARD E. BERINGER

ELKHORN TAVERN, ARKANSAS

Also known as the Battle of Pea Ridge, the fighting in Benton County, Arkansas, on March 7 and 8, 1862, secured Union control of Missouri. The Confederates suffered around 1,500 men killed, wounded, and missing, and the Federals lost slightly less than 1,400.

Pro-Confederate Missourians under Maj. Gen. Sterling Price had been trying to gain the upper hand in their home state since the summer of 1861. After Union Brig. Gen. Nathaniel Lyon was killed in August in the Wilson's Creek campaign to drive them out of the state, Price had moved into the interior where the pro-Southern Missouri State Guard had captured Lexington. Price, however, was unable to capitalize on his victory and had been forced to retreat into Missouri's southwest corner where he established his base at Springfield.

Price hoped that he could gain enough support from Richmond to move back into Missouri and had been trying to persuade Brig. Gen. Ben McCulloch, who commanded Confederate troops in northwest Arkansas, to help him. But the two men disagreed over how this could be accomplished; as a result of this dispute, the government created the Trans-Mississippi District of Department No. 2 and placed Maj. Gen. Earl Van Dorn in command. Van Dorn arrived at Little Rock, Arkansas, late in January and began plans for an invasion of Missouri that he expected to culminate in the capture of St. Louis.

To oppose the Confederates, the Union government had appointed Brig. Gen. Samuel R. Curtis over the newly created Southwestern District of Missouri. Curtis's objective was to protect the state from the Confederates and if necessary drive them farther south. He took command of the Army of the Southwest, which consisted of the First Division under Brig. Gen. Franz Sigel, the Second under Brig. Gen. Alexander S. Asboth, the Third under Brig. Gen. Jefferson C. Davis, and the Fourth under Col. Eugene A. Carr. Sigel, however, was second in command of the entire army; therefore, his division was actually under Col. Peter J. Osterhaus. After arriving at Rolla, Curtis began to move his 10,250 men, and on February 13, 1862, his army marched into Springfield, taking the town without a battle.

The Confederates retreated before him; Price had joined McCulloch in the Boston Mountains near Fayetteville in northwestern Arkansas. Van Dorn arrived on March 2 and divided his new Army of the Southwest, numbering around 16,500, into two divisions. Price still headed the Missourians, while McCulloch oversaw two brigades of Texas, Arkansas, and Louisiana troops, with the infantry under Col. Louis Hébert and cavalry under Brig. Gen. James McQueen McIntosh. In addition, Brig. Gen. Albert Pike, who commanded Indians from the Five Southern Tribes, was summoned from the Indian Territory. On March 4 Van Dorn had his army on the move and reached Little Sugar Creek two days later.

Curtis, learning of the Confederate advance, pulled back to a defensive position where Telegraph Road, which ran north and south, crossed the creek. His line, just below the Missouri border, was near an inn known as Elkhorn Tavern and three miles south of a 150-foot-high plateau called Pea Ridge. Believing that the attack would come from the direction of Fayetteville, Curtis closed Telegraph Road with felled trees and dug earthen fortifications in the Little Sugar Creek valley, making any attack from the south or southwest perilous.

Van Dorn recognized the futility of an assault on such a strong position. Therefore, he decided to envelop the Federal army and hit it in the rear, destroying Curtis's link with Missouri Unionists and breaking his supply line. During the night the Confederates moved around Curtis's right flank down a local road that paralleled Telegraph Road, the Bentonville Detour. But the Confederates had been on the march for three days, and by the morning of March 7 the men were tired and cold. Price's Missourians reached the crossing of the Bentonville Detour and Telegraph Road first; the roads met in Cross Timber Hollow just over three miles north of the tavern. But since McCulloch's Confederates lagged behind, Van Dorn decided to split the attack. Price's Missourians would move straight down Telegraph Road, while McCulloch would hit Curtis several miles west of Elkhorn Tavern near the tiny village of Leetown. This decision meant that the engagement became two battles.

Curtis was not deceived; he knew the Confederates had moved around his flank and had turned much of his army to the rear facing north. Without waiting for Van Dorn to attack him, he pushed his army forward. Osterhaus's and Davis's divisions encountered McCulloch's men just north of Leetown while Carr met Price's advance down Telegraph Road. Van Dorn's decision to split his army proved to be a bad one, as McCulloch and McIntosh were killed near Leetown and Hébert was captured. This left one wing of the battle without a leader, and by midafternoon the remnants of McCulloch's division retreated to the Bentonville Detour. In the meantime Van Dorn accompanied Price's division through Cross Timbers Hollow toward Pea Ridge. After Southern artillery weakened the Federal position on the plateau, Confederates climbed the embankment west of Elkhorn Tavern and drove the Federals back. The fighting ended as night fell with the Confederates holding the tavern and key positions on Telegraph and Huntsville roads. Survivors from the Leetown fight joined Van Dorn at this location and waited to renew the battle the next day.

On the morning of March 8 the two armies had consolidated their troops. Curtis deployed his four divisions facing north while Van Dorn formed a defensive line near the tavern. But Van Dorn was short of ammunition, and when the battle opened, the Confederates fell back under heavy artillery fire and soon began to scatter. By 11:00 A.M. the battle was over, and Curtis could claim a well-deserved and decisive victory.

The Battle of Elkhorn Tavern was one of the few major engagements in the Trans-Mississippi. The Confederate defeat ensured that the Union would retain control over Missouri, and Van Dorn, who significantly outnumbered the Federals, must be faulted for his failure to adapt to the situation as it developed. Moreover, the defeat may have influenced Richmond's decision to relegate the Trans-Mississippi to a secondary role in the war; Van Dorn's army was transferred to the east side of the Mississippi River at the end of the month. This decision had far-reaching consequences, as it appeared that the Confederate government was abandoning the Trans-Mississippi. Although there would be future Confederate raids into Missouri, this engagement proved the pivotal battle for control of the state.

BIBLIOGRAPHY

Bearss, Edwin C. "The First Day at Pea Ridge, March 7, 1862." *Arkansas Historical Quarterly* 17 (Summer 1958): 132–154.

Brown, Walter L. "Pea Ridge: Gettysburg of the West." *Arkansas Historical Quarterly* 15 (Spring 1956): 3–16.

Castel, Albert. "A New View of the Battle of Pea Ridge." *Missouri Historical Review* 62 (January 1968): 136–151.

Hartje, Robert George. *Van Dorn: The Life and Times of a Confederate General.* Nashville, Tenn., 1967.

Hughes, Michael A. "A Forgotten Battle in a Region Ignored. Pea Ridge, or Elkhorn Tavern, Arkansas—March 7–8, 1862." *Blue & Gray Magazine* 5 (January 1988): 8–36.

Pea Ridge National Park. "The Battle of Pea Ridge, 1862." Pamphlet. Rogers, Ark., n.d.

Shea, William L., and Earl J. Hess. "Pea Ridge." In *The Civil War Battlefield Guide.* Boston, 1990.

Shea, William L., and Earl J. Hess. *Pea Ridge: Civil War Campaign in the West.* Chapel Hill, N.C., 1992.

ANNE J. BAILEY

EMANCIPATION PROCLAMATION

In the Preliminary Emancipation Proclamation of September 22, 1862, President Abraham Lincoln declared that, as of January 1, 1863, "all persons held as slaves within any State, or designated part of a State, the people whereof shall then be in rebellion," would be "forever free." In the final Emancipation Proclamation of January 1, 1863, he designated all of the Confederacy as still in rebellion except for certain Louisiana parishes and Virginia counties and the entire state of Tennessee. Most of the excepted areas were those under the presumed control of Federal forces. Eastern Tennessee was not yet under such control but could hardly be considered "in rebellion," since its people were overwhelmingly pro-Union. Lincoln justified the proclamation as "a fit and necessary war measure," and so he could not logically have applied it to the border slave states or to the Federally occupied portions of the South—areas in which his government was not waging war.

Newspapers in the Confederacy ridiculed Lincoln's action. They accused him of leaving the slaves in bondage where he had the power to free them and pretending to emancipate them where he had no power to do so. Yet the papers also denounced the proclamation as a call upon the slaves to revolt. Especially worrisome were its clauses advising freed slaves to "abstain from all violence, unless in necessary self-defense," and stating that "such persons" would be "received into the armed service of the United States."

The Confederate government took steps to retaliate. In a January 12, 1863, message to his Congress, Jefferson Davis characterized the proclamation as "a measure by which millions of human beings of an inferior race" were being "encouraged to a general assassination of their masters." He recommended dire punishment for captured white officers of black troops. Congress responded with a joint resolution containing the following provisions: such officers were to be tried by military courts, which could impose the death penalty;

> **Eventually the Confederates indicated a willingness to issue their own emancipation decree if, by doing so, they could be assured of foreign recognition.**

black soldiers, if formerly slaves, were to be handed over to state governments for return to their previous owners.

The Davis government was temporarily strengthened by the popular reaction to Lincoln's policy, which at first had a unifying effect on Confederate citizens. Even the most persistently anti-Davis newspaper, the *Richmond Examiner,* endorsed Davis's stand, charging Lincoln with "the most startling political crime in American history." The preliminary announcement disheartened Unionists in eastern Tennessee and caused Thomas A. R. Nelson and other leaders to switch their loyalty from Lincoln to Davis. Andrew Johnson, the Unionist governor of Tennessee, feared that still others would go over to the Confederate side, and he was much relieved when Lincoln excluded the entire state from the final proclamation.

The Confederacy was seriously weakened, however, by the long-term effects of Lincoln's emancipation policy. Early on, Davis feared that it would handicap Confederate efforts to gain recognition and intervention from abroad. His diplomatic and propaganda agents overseas, aware of "the universal hostility of Europe to slavery," also worried that Lincoln's action would draw European sympathy and support away from the Confederacy. To counteract this threat of the proclamation, Confederate propagandists included in the June 11, 1863, issue of their periodical, the *Index,* an "Address to Christians throughout the World," in which a number of prominent Southern preachers testified that the abolition of slavery would be "an interference with the plans of Divine Providence." Eventually the Confederates indicated a willingness to issue their own emancipation decree if, by doing so, they could be assured of foreign recognition. Their

failure to obtain such recognition was due, at least in part, to Lincoln's proclamation.

For the Confederacy, the proclamation had even more disastrous consequences through its influence on the slaves. Though nearly all of them were illiterate, they soon learned about the promise of freedom to come on January 1, 1863. Some Mississippi militiamen in Confederate service requested permission to go home before then—"as the negroes are making their brags that by the first of January they will be free as we are and a general outbreak is expected about that time." Here and there throughout the South the rumor ran that slaves were preparing to rise on the appointed day. To strengthen control over them, Congress amended the Conscription Act on October 11, 1862, so as to exempt one man as owner or overseer for every twenty slaves on a plantation (the Twenty-Slave Law). Actually, slaves responded to the proclamation not by attempting to revolt but by heading for the nearest Union army camp. They were already fleeing in that direction; now, with freedom as the lure, the numbers increased. Approximately 100,000 from the Confederate states (along with other blacks from the Northern and border states) sooner or later joined the Union army.

By stimulating the movement of laborers and soldiers to the Union side, the proclamation threatened to worsen the already serious manpower shortage of the Confederacy. As early as January 10, 1863, Gen. Robert E. Lee warned the secretary of war about the consequences of the "savage and brutal policy" that Lincoln recently had proclaimed. There is an "absolute necessity," Lee wrote, "to increase our armies, if we desire to oppose effectual resistance to the vast numbers that the enemy is now precipitating upon us." It proved impossible to increase the armies sufficiently, however, and a year later Gen. Patrick Cleburne concluded that the South was losing the war because it lacked the manpower of the North. As a result of the proclamation, Cleburne said, "slavery, from being one of our chief sources of strength," had become "one of our chief sources of weakness." He therefore suggested that the Confederacy take the drastic step of recruiting its own army of slaves. When Congress finally authorized such a step, on March 13, 1865, the earlier joint resolution concerning the proclamation was revised. Instead of warning the North against recruiting "negroes," the resolution now warned only against recruiting "our negro slaves."

At the Hampton Roads peace conference, on February 3, 1865, the proclamation emerged as an issue in the discussion between Lincoln and representatives of the Confederacy. Vice President Alexander H. Stephens (according to his own account) asked Lincoln what permanent effect, if any, the proclamation would have on the slaves. "Would it be held to emancipate the whole, or only those who had, at the time the war ended, become actually free under it?" Lincoln (again, according to Stephens's account) replied that this was a question for the courts. "His own opinion was, that as the proclamation was a *war measure,* and would have effect only from its being an exercise of the war power, as soon as the war ceased, it would be inoperative for the future." Doubting, as he did, the postwar validity of the proclamation, Lincoln helped to bring about the adoption of the Thirteenth Amendment, which made the question moot.

Whether or not the proclamation would have conferred legal and lasting freedom on any slave, it certainly brought at least a degree of practical freedom to the multitudes that it encouraged to escape from bondage. By thus depleting the human resources of the Confederacy, while also helping to deter foreign intervention, the proclamation contributed mightily to the Confederacy's ultimate defeat.

[*See also* African Americans in the Confederacy; African American Troops in the Union Army; Contraband; Juneteenth; Slavery; Thirteenth Amendment.]

BIBLIOGRAPHY

Coulter, E. Merton. *The Confederate States of America, 1861–1865.* A History of the South, vol. 7. Baton Rouge, La., 1950.
Franklin, John Hope. *The Emancipation Proclamation.* Garden City, N.Y., 1963.
Wiley, Bell I. *Southern Negroes, 1861–1865.* Baton Rouge, La., ∂1938. Revised ed., Baton Rouge, La., 1974.

RICHARD N. CURRENT

ENCHANTRESS AFFAIR

The brig *Enchantress* was taken by the Confederate privateer *Jeff Davis* on July 6, 1861, off the coast of Delaware. A prize master and five seamen from the Confederate vessel attempted to take the prize into a Southern port. But sixteen days after her capture, *Enchantress* was retaken by the Union warship *Albatross.* The six Confederates were imprisoned in Philadelphia, tried for piracy (October 22–28, 1861), and convicted.

When an international conference meeting in 1856 had agreed to declare privateering illegal, the United States had declined to sign the agreement. Nevertheless, in 1861 the U.S. government decided to accept the argument that privateering was piracy, and the *Enchantress* affair gave it the opportunity to do so. The five members of the brig's crew were sentenced to death as pirates.

The sentence, however, was never carried out. Confederate president Jefferson Davis threatened retaliation for what he described as "a practice unknown to the warfare of civilized man, and so barbarous as to disgrace the nation which shall be guilty of inaugurating it." If any Confederate privateersmen were executed, he said, captured Union officers would be treated in accordance with the disposition of the

imprisoned crew. Ultimately, the captured privateersmen and the prize muster were declared prisoners of war, and many were eventually exchanged.

The *Enchantress* case was one of several involving captured Confederate privateers that persuaded Lincoln's government to drop its decision to treat their crews as pirates.

BIBLIOGRAPHY

Coulter, E. Merton. *The Confederate States of America.* A History of the South, vol. 7. Baton Rouge, La., 1959.
Robinson, William. *The Confederate Privateers.* Columbia, S.C., 1990.

WILLIAM N. STILL, JR.

ENGINEER BUREAU

The Confederate Engineer Bureau was born with the recognition that precautionary measures needed to be taken by the new Confederacy to protect itself in the event of attack. Although the Confederate Congress formally authorized the formation of the Engineer Bureau on March 7, 1861, by designating an engineer force of a number of commissioned officers together with one hundred "sappers and miners and pontoniers," the bureau, as a central authority, played little or no role in Confederate engineering in the early stages of the war. What engineering was done to secure the defenses at Charleston Harbor, Savannah, Mobile Bay, Pensacola, the Mississippi River, the North Carolina coast, the river approaches in Tennessee and Kentucky, and the Virginia coast and peninsulas was accomplished by departmental commanders and their own staff engineers, not by any coordinated effort from the Engineer Bureau.

From the inception of the bureau until the late summer of 1861 Maj. Josiah Gorgas, chief of the Ordnance Department, served as its unofficial head. On August 3, 1861, Maj. Danville Leadbetter of Alabama was ordered to Richmond to assume command of the bureau. Although Leadbetter remained in titular command of the bureau until the fall of 1862, he was unable to render efficient service as bureau chief. Sent to Chattanooga in November 1861, Leadbetter never returned to Richmond.

On September 24, 1862, Lt. Col. Jeremy Francis Gilmer was named chief of engineers. The date of Gilmer's appointment marked the true emergence of the bureau as a central agency. Gilmer set about trying to coordinate engineering efforts in the far-flung Confederacy by making frequent inspections of important defensive installations. In spite of Gilmer's tremendous efforts, the bureau was hampered by chronic shortages of manpower and matériel as well as finances. Like the Ordnance and Commissary departments,

PONTOON BRIDGE.

the Engineer Bureau required a large budget to finance the construction of forts, earthworks, bridges, railroads, and mobile engineering and construction equipment. As the war progressed, finances dwindled, crippling the bureau's efforts to provide necessary defenseworks and to supply armies in the field with necessary equipment.

Although the South had relied upon slave labor for its economic survival up to and through the war, the Engineer Bureau was never able to use slave labor to augment manpower shortages in any systematic manner. The very limited natural resources of the South further reduced the bureau's attempts to build railroads, bridges, and fortifications. Even its efforts to unify major railroad lines inside the Confederacy failed, owing to lack of manpower, iron rails, and government support for the control of the otherwise privately owned railroad lines.

Among the responsibilities assigned to the Engineer Bureau was the preparation of maps. In the field, most mapmaking was performed by staff topographers in the respective armies. But in countless engagements in all theaters of war, the lack of adequate maps hampered the armies. The central mapmaking efforts of the Engineer Bureau, however, were not very successful. The bureau assigned numerous survey teams to the peninsula, Richmond, northern Virginia, Fredericksburg, Chattanooga, Vicksburg, the Trans-Mississippi, and other locations, but to little avail. The lack of adequate manpower and the unavailability of necessary supplies, including paper, hampered the effort from the beginning.

It was not until the end of 1862 that the Confederacy recognized the need for organizing engineer regiments with pioneer and bridge equipment. Of all the efforts of the bureau, the initiative to organize these regiments met with the greatest success. Gilmer had suggested forming such units in the Army of Northern Virginia as early as the fall of 1862. Although not enthusiastic about the idea, Gen. Robert E. Lee finally agreed to the formation of an engineer regiment in his army. Such an organized engineer command accompanied the Army of Northern Virginia on its invasion of Pennsylvania in the summer of 1863, laying pontoon bridges across the Potomac at Falling Waters. A similar engineer regiment was formed in the Army of Tennessee in early 1863, and other engineer commands were formed in western Virginia, the Department of the Carolinas, Georgia, and Florida, and the Department of the Trans-Mississippi.

It was the organized First Regiment of Engineers of the Army of Northern Virginia that helped Lee rapidly establish his defense works at Spotsylvania Court House in May 1864 and Cold Harbor in June 1864. The efforts of the First Engineers at laying pontoon bridges over the James River at Chaffin's Bluff near Richmond, building and strengthening the defense works at Petersburg, and maintaining the rail lines in and out of Richmond and Petersburg helped Lee defend the capital city longer than it otherwise could have been done. The First Regiment of Engineers surrendered at Appomattox Courthouse with the rest of Lee's army.

The Third Regiment of Engineers accompanied the Army of Tennessee throughout the campaign from Dalton, Georgia, to the fall of Atlanta, laying bridges and overseeing the construction of fortifications and the maintenance of railroads. The regiment was divided after the fall of Atlanta, a portion following Gen. John Bell Hood's advance into Tennessee and a portion remaining with Gen. William J. Hardee and, ultimately, Gen. Joseph E. Johnston.

Although the Engineer Bureau represented an attempt to centrally coordinate the defense of the Confederacy, coordination never occurred. Partly because the war had progressed too far before the bureau itself became coordinated and partly because of the lack of manpower, matériel, and finances, the bureau was unable to perform effectively the task it was assigned. As well, in a Confederacy where central authority was politically abhorrent, the bureau's task was thwarted by uncooperative private interests and departmental commanders who jealously guarded their own territories of command.

Aside from the success of the bureau in forming engineer regiments that served in the major theaters of war and in providing critical bridging and railroad maintenance work, the most notable engineering efforts in the Confederacy were performed by departmental and local commanders and their staff engineers without the direction of the Engineer Bureau.

[*See also* Forts and Fortifications; Transportation.]

BIBLIOGRAPHY

Nichols, James L. *Confederate Engineers.* Tuscaloosa, Ala., 1957.
Thomas, Emory M. *The Confederate Nation, 1861–1865.* New York, 1979.

KENT MASTERSON BROWN

ERLANGER LOAN

Negotiated between the Confederate States of America and Emile Erlanger and Company of Paris, the Erlanger Loan was issued on March 19, 1863, in five European cities and raised £1,759,894 ($8,535,486 gold value) for Confederate use in Europe. It was secured by government-owned cotton in the Confederacy and provided that cotton would be delivered in the Confederacy to the bondholders on demand.

The Erlanger family had become prominent in banking in Germany in the early nineteenth century under the leadership of Raphael Erlanger. By midcentury, the family, originally Jewish, had converted to Christianity, and Raphael Erlanger had become a baron. He sent his son, Frederick Emile, to establish a branch of the family business in Paris. The firm issued railroad and government bonds, and Emile became friendly with the emperor, Louis Napoleon.

John Slidell, Confederate commissioner to France, cultivated the friendship of many businessmen, bankers, and others with connections to the emperor. Slidell was aware that by mid-1862, the Confederacy was severely restricted in its ability to place funds in Europe to pay for its shipbuilding and munitions-purchasing programs. The Confederacy had, during the first year of the war, sent to Europe nearly all of the bills of exchange that had accumulated in the South before the Federal blockade stopped all normal shipping in early June 1861. Although numerous small vessels ran the blockade, only small amounts of cotton were carried to Europe during the first year to earn new exchange. The Confederate government was slow to develop a blockade-running program of its own and hesitated to risk shipping the limited amounts of gold and silver that it held. Confederate paper money had, of course, no value in Europe. When Emile Erlanger and Company proposed a bond issue for the Confederacy, Slidell highly recommended it, not only as a means of meeting the financial crisis, but also for political purposes, since Erlanger was influential with the emperor. It may have been relevant also that Slidell's daughter and Emile Erlanger were soon to become engaged to be married.

Erlanger's original offer to issue £5 million at 8 percent interest, with the Confederacy receiving 70 percent of the face value and paying a commission of 5 percent to the firm, was rejected by the Richmond authorities as much too expensive. They agreed to allow the firm to issue £3 million, at 7 percent interest with the South receiving 77 percent and paying a 5 percent commission, only because they hoped that it would increase Slidell's ability to elicit favorable decisions from Louis Napoleon. A provision that bondholders could convert their bonds into cotton in the Confederacy with the right to export it was an important incentive for investors, since the price of cotton in Europe was quite high.

The firm issued the bonds at 90 percent of face value in London, Liverpool, Paris, Amsterdam, and Frankfurt, and the issue was an immediate success. Within two weeks, however, the price sagged to 87 and Erlanger feared that subscribers might not make the remainder of their installment payments. The firm secretly bought in the market to sustain the price and induced the Confederates to provide funds to continue the effort. The price was sustained and all payments were made, but the Confederates had bought back nearly half of the loan. During the next year, Erlanger was able to resell many of these bonds, and the Confederates were able to use many others in payment of debts. In the end, the Confederate government had sold bonds with a face value of £2,391,000 and had raised £1,759,894 in Europe at an effective annual interest rate of a little over 12 percent. The price of the bonds became an indicator of European estimates of the likelihood of Confederate independence.

It is impossible to determine whether the bond issue increased Slidell's influence at the court of Louis Napoleon. The Erlanger loan was successful, however, in providing funds in Europe to continue Confederate military and naval purchases in 1863.

BIBLIOGRAPHY

Ball, Douglas B. *Financial Failure and Confederate Defeat.* Chicago, 1991.

Gentry, Judith Fenner. "A Confederate Success in Europe: The Erlanger Loan." *Journal of Southern History* 36 (May 1970): 157–188.

Lester, Richard I. *Confederate Finance and Purchasing in Great Britain.* Charlottesville, Va., 1975.

Owsley, Frank Lawrence. *King Cotton Diplomacy: Foreign Relations of the Confederate States of America.* 2d ed., rev. Chicago, 1959.

Thompson, Samuel Bernard. *Confederate Purchasing Operations Abroad.* Chapel Hill, N.C., 1935.

JUDITH FENNER GENTRY

ESPIONAGE

[*This entry is composed of three articles*: Confederate Secret Service, *which overviews the organization and operations of Southern espionage efforts;* Federal Secret Service, *which discusses Northern espionage during the Civil War; and* Confederate Military Spies, *which profiles notable Southern espionage agents. For further discussion of Confederate attempts to influence the war and Northern opinion through espionage, see* Copperheads; Lincoln, Abraham, *article on* Assassination of Lincoln; Northwestern Conspiracy; *and* Propaganda. *For further examination of Confederate innovations in the field of espionage, see* Signal Corps *and* Torpedoes and Mines. *See also biographies of numerous figures mentioned herein.*]

Confederate Secret Service

According to records discovered as recently as 1990, the Confederacy spent approximately $2 million in gold on Secret Service activities—a princely sum for those days and many times the amount spent by the Union for similar purposes. The Confederate Secret Service covered a wide range of operations from classic espionage penetration of the Federal government in Washington to the development of secret weapons for use behind enemy lines. Secret Service operations also included assistance to Gen. Robert E. Lee and other field commanders in the collection of tactical intelligence and an ambitious attempt to capture President Abraham Lincoln as a hostage. Most important of all, the Secret Service engaged in a serious clandestine political effort to create a peace movement in the North.

The Confederate Secret Service, like the modern American intelligence community, comprised a group of organizations created at different times for distinct purposes and originally with no unifying concept of operations. Experience, however, was an active teacher, and before the war's end legislation was introduced into the Confederate Congress to bring the diverse activities together into a Special and Secret Service Bureau—the Confederate version of a central intelligence agency.

In early 1861, while the Confederate government was still in Montgomery, Alabama, Jefferson Davis began to employ secret agents for political missions abroad. The most successful early espionage operation, however, appears to have been organized by Virginia before that state had formally joined the Confederacy. The most notorious agent of this effort was a Washington hostess, Rose O'Neal Greenhow, who used her social connections and her sexual attractions to elicit a flow of useful information about Federal military preparations in the Washington area. Her greatest success was to alert the Confederates in northern Virginia to Gen. Irvin McDowell's movement from Washington toward the railroad junction at Manassas, which resulted in the Union defeat at the 1861 battle there.

The Confederate espionage network in Washington that included Greenhow continued throughout the war to supply intelligence in support of the government in Richmond, and the network also provided direct support to General Lee's Army of Northern Virginia. Its information enabled Lee to anticipate General Grant's Wilderness campaign and even informed him of Grant's basic strategy of making a flanking maneuver after each frontal encounter. Lee thus was able to prepare roads in order to get ahead of and stop Grant's moves.

The War Department also assigned skilled Secret Service agents to various Confederate generals for specific campaigns. For example, Lt. Henry Thomas Harrison was assigned to Gen. D. H. Hill in North Carolina in early 1863 and later to Gen. James Longstreet for the Gettysburg campaign. Harrison was credited with alerting Longstreet to George Meade's movements into Pennsylvania that resulted in the battle.

Conventional wisdom says that the North was industrial and the South agricultural, but the war brought a spate of technical innovations from Southern inventors. Some of these inventions were weapons like underwater mines that could be used more effectively if they and their technology could be kept secret. As a result, a number of activities, like mine laying and the development of timed detonators for sabotage, were considered by the Confederates as Secret Service activities and protected by special security arrangements.

> ## Their chief success was the destruction of the Union army's main supply base. . . .

Similarly, the Confederate Signal Corps, another innovation, depended on the security of its signaling and the cipher systems used for important messages. As a result, it did not seem illogical to the Confederates to charge their Signal Corps with the mission of managing a secret courier line between Washington and Richmond for the delivery of important messages from Confederate agents in the North. Once the Signal Corps was involved in clandestine operations via the secret line, it was a small step to have both the Signal Corps and the War Department espionage apparatus managed by the same people.

The idea of using signal flags to send messages over the battlefield was first advanced before the war by surgeon Albert James Myer of the U.S. Army. The Confederates used the system in time to help win the First Battle of Manassas, but the Union army failed to implement the idea until the Confederates had demonstrated its success. The Confederate Signal Corps also ran its secret line between Richmond and Washington continuously throughout the war. It was still in operation when General Lee surrendered on April 9, 1865.

The practical use of underwater explosives was first demonstrated in the James River near Richmond in the summer of 1861 by Comdr. Matthew Fontaine Maury, who had established an enviable reputation as a scientist through his work on oceanography. The use of mines was further developed by the Confederate War Department's Torpedo Bureau, under Gen. Gabriel J. Rains, and by the Navy Department's Submarine Battery Service under first Maury and then Lt. Hunter Davidson.

The Confederates also organized groups of saboteurs, called Strategic Corps, to plant explosives at depots, factories, bridges, river shipping facilities, and other targets behind Union lines. Their chief success was the destruction of the Union army's main supply base at City Point, Virginia, on August 9, 1864. A Strategic Corps team planted a bomb on a ship at the dock, which caused several other ships loaded with ammunition to explode, showering Ulysses S.

Grant's neighboring headquarters with debris and inflicting widespread damage. Other teams burned ships on the Mississippi and Ohio rivers and attacked logistics targets in the rear of Union armies.

The most important Secret Service operation of the entire Confederate effort was the attempt to turn widespread disaffection with the war and the Lincoln administration into an effective peace movement. Preparations for this operation began in 1863, and it was launched in April 1864 when Jefferson Davis approved the allocation of $1 million in gold to Jacob Thompson, a former U.S. secretary of the interior who had been selected to head the operation. Thompson's overt mission was to serve as a Confederate commissioner in Canada to search for peace with the U.S. government. (Since Canada was a British possession and Britain did not recognize the Confederacy, Thompson could not be appointed as a minister or ambassador; therefore, the title "commissioner" meant only that the Confederates had commissioned him to act on their behalf.)

There was a covert side to Thompson's mission, however. If no progress was made toward peace, Thompson was to attack the Union war effort by clandestine operations from Canada. To provide him with the technical means necessary for such operations, Clement C. Clay, a former U.S. senator, was also appointed a commissioner. Clay apparently represented the interests of the War Department.

The Confederates promoted an existing secret political group, the Knights of the Golden Circle, as a means of organizing the opposition to the war. Many local chapters of the Knights operated on a quasi-military basis, and some were armed and willing to consider a revolt to express their disaffection. The Confederates tried to induce the Copperheads, as they were called, to take coordinated action against the war. The primary focus was to be Chicago where the Copperheads and a cadre of Confederates infiltrated from Canada were to free the thousands of Confederate prisoners of war held there. The target date was August 1864, and the attack was to be accompanied by revolts or demonstrations in other cities in Illinois, Indiana, and Ohio. The copperheads, however, could never be brought to act, and the operation was eventually penetrated by Federal agents who arrested several of the key plotters in November 1864.

In the meantime, other operations were attempted by the Confederates in Canada. One of the leading Secret Service operatives, John Y. Beall, tried to free the Confederate prisoners on Johnson Island in the harbor of Sandusky, Ohio, but was frustrated when his supporting team got cold feet. Another team, led by Lt. Bennett H. Young, tried to burn St. Albans, Vermont, and made off with over $200,000 in U.S. currency and negotiable paper.

The Confederates in Canada also apparently recruited John Wilkes Booth in July 1864 to organize an attempt to abduct President Lincoln. Booth had help from Richmond but appears to have been directed primarily from Canada. He tried once to capture Lincoln in March 1865, but failed. At that point, Richmond apparently decided it was too late to try again and planned instead to blow up the White House to disrupt coordination between Grant and William Tecumseh Sherman. An explosives expert was sent to assist Booth, but he was captured on his way into Washington. In the absence of his technical adviser and unable to contact knowledgeable superiors, Booth apparently decided to approximate the damage that would be caused by an explosion by attacking simultaneously several officials who would likely have been involved in such an explosion. The result of Booth's decision was the assassination of Lincoln and the wounding of Secretary of State William H. Seward on April 14, 1865. None of the other targets was attacked. Booth was assisted in his escape by several elements of the Secret Service, but he was caught and killed by Union cavalry on April 26, 1865.

The end of the war found the Confederate espionage net in Washington and the Signal Corps' secret line still in operation. More important, the Confederate apparatus in Canada, now under the direction of Gen. Edwin Grey Lee, who had replaced Thompson, was still intact and had Secret Service money to operate with. For several months Lee and his colleagues acted almost like a Confederate government in exile, turning out propaganda denying Confederate complicity in the Lincoln assassination and defending individuals accused of crimes by the Federal government.

Like all clandestine operations, the Confederate Secret Service had failures as well as successes, but on the whole, the efforts were imaginative and made contributions to the Confederate war effort that have never been recognized.

BIBLIOGRAPHY

Bakeless, John. *Spies of the Confederacy*. Philadelphia and New York, 1970.

Baker, Gen. L[afayette] C. *History of the United States Secret Service*. Philadelphia, 1867.

Nelson, Larry. *Bullets, Bayonets, and Rhetoric: Confederate Policy for the United States Presidential Contest of 1864*. University, Ala., 1980.

Perry, Milton F. *Infernal Machines*. Baton Rouge, La., 1965.

Stern, Philip Van Doren. *Secret Missions of the Civil War*. New York, 1959.

Tidwell, William A., with James O. Hall and David Winfred Gaddy. *Come Retribution: The Confederate Secret Service and the Assassination of Lincoln*. Jackson, Miss., and London, 1988.

WILLIAM A. TIDWELL

Federal Secret Service

As in the new Confederacy, intelligence and espionage in the Union emerged more out of necessity, accident, and experimentation than from any organized plan. Indeed, many in the Northern high command still held to the eighteenth-century notion that spying was a contemptible practice beneath the dignity of soldiers. No systematic attempt was made during and immediately after secession to gather reliable military information. Instead, the Union leaders simply relied upon what came to them via rumor and exaggerated newspaper claims. When Gen. Irvin McDowell led his army into Northern Virginia in the campaign culminating in humiliating defeat at Manassas on July 21, 1861, he did not even have a good map of the countryside.

In fact, the first—admittedly ineffective—attempts to arm Abraham Lincoln's armies with information came from the agents of a civilian detective, Allan Pinkerton. Lincoln had known him prior to the war, and it was Pinkerton who discovered a plot to assassinate Lincoln during his trip to Washington to be inaugurated. Foiling the plot endeared Pinkerton to Lincoln, and also called his name to the attention of another former acquaintance, Gen. George B. McClellan. First in western Virginia, and then in Washington, when McClellan replaced the hapless McDowell, Pinkerton was called on to use his stable of "detectives" to provide information on contract. At McClellan's behest, Pinkerton, though always a civilian, organized what he chose to call the U.S. Secret Service, though in fact it never held any official military or governmental status or sanction.

Pinkerton's was a twofold mission: in Washington he was to keep an eye on Confederate sympathizers and ferret out spies; when McClellan's Army of the Potomac was on campaign, Pinkerton would serve on his staff without official rank and manage the efforts of spies and scouts in collecting information about enemy troops. At the former task Pinkerton proved to be rather effective. He caught noted Southern agent Rose O'Neal Greenhow and saw her imprisoned, and had a number of other suspected traitors either arrested or driven out of the city.

In the field, however, Pinkerton proved to be one of the war's notable failures. He knew nothing of military intelligence—few did—nor of how to interpret what information he acquired. From his Chicago detective agency and elsewhere he assembled a small corps of agents, all civilians, whom he sent behind enemy lines charged with learning whatever they could of Confederate numbers, positions, morale, equipment, and anticipated movements. The value of Pinkerton's reports was in the first place predicated on the quality of what was sent to him. His agents were sometimes effective, like Timothy Webster, who operated in the Confederacy for months under cover before being caught and hanged. But they were not trained military men and women who knew the value or import of what they saw. Moreover, they all were prone to accept rumor as fact. And when their reports came back to Pinkerton, he compounded the problem by apparently devising a formula of his own for converting *reported* numbers of troops into *actual* numbers—which always came out much higher. Thus, in April 1862 when only 17,000 Southerners faced McClellan at Yorktown, Pinkerton told the general that there were 120,000! Even when Pinkerton succeeded in enumerating every unit in the army facing McClellan that summer, he still tripled their actual numbers in his reports. In part this may have been because Pinkerton read his man McClellan very well, and the general always preferred to believe himself too heavily outnumbered to risk a fight. When McClellan was finally eclipsed in the fall of 1862, Pinkerton disappeared from the war with him.

Despite the lack of an organized beginning to Federal espionage and intelligence gathering, many generals besides McClellan employed their own agents, though usually for limited times and specific purposes. Moreover, once Union armies began to occupy Confederate territory, information started coming into the camps on its own, chiefly from Union sympathizers seeking protection and from runaway slaves, or "contrabands," who flocked to the Federal banners in the thousands. Each commander dealt with such information as he chose, although most turned responsibility for it over to the army provost marshal general, who was already charged with managing the fugitives themselves.

The first attempt at a systematic military gathering of information emerged in the western theater, under the guidance of Ulysses S. Grant. In October 1862, as he was planning his overland drive toward Vicksburg, Grant selected Brig. Gen. Grenville M. Dodge for command of a division in his army, with authority for organizing and operating a spy network to provide Grant with intelligence on enemy numbers and movements. Dodge was a perfect choice, having already built and commanded the First Tennessee Cavalry, a regiment of mounted scouts operating in Missouri and Arkansas. He also operated another regiment of loyal western Tennesseeans who provided information on the enemy in their region.

Upon receiving the assignment from Grant, Dodge went to work and quickly produced something far more effective and efficient than Pinkerton's dime novel–style operation. Secrecy was a byword. Only Dodge knew the identity of all of his agents, most of them civilians; they were frequently noted in dispatches only by numbers. He equipped them with Confederate money for their work behind enemy lines and paid them for their services with profits from the sale of confiscated cotton. Although the total number of his agents may never be known, at least 117 would serve him at one time or another, and his network would, by the end of the war, include operatives in almost every Confederate state east of the Mississippi except Florida.

Any kind of information was of interest to Dodge. Given the deplorable quality of road and terrain maps of the Southern states, Dodge—himself an engineer—constantly used information from his people to update the charts he provided to Grant. During the Vicksburg campaign itself, Dodge

kept Grant constantly informed of Confederate numbers and positions, allowing the Federals to apply numerical superiority where it counted, while ignoring lesser enemy forces that Pinkerton and McClellan would have exaggerated into legions. Dodge even gave his operatives bogus information about Federal movements as gifts for Confederate commanders in order to win their confidence, thus inaugurating counterintelligence and double agents. Not only did Dodge's network gather information. It also collected Southern spies, constantly thwarting Confederate operatives, including the capture and eventual execution of Sam Davis, the boy spy later virtually canonized in the Lost Cause pantheon for dying rather than revealing the names of his fellow spies.

Dodge managed his small intelligence empire, while still leading his combat division, until he was wounded in the Atlanta campaign. Thereafter it functioned largely on its own under the hand of William Tecumseh Sherman, having already set a model for effectiveness as the most widely flung and far-reaching intelligence network of the war.

Meanwhile, spy work in the eastern theater had progressed at a more leisurely and less professional pace. Following the disappearance of Pinkerton in November 1862, espionage floundered without firm management until the spring of 1863 when Gen. Joseph Hooker engaged Col. George H. Sharpe to head the newly formed Bureau of Military Information in March. A Rutgers and Yale graduate, Sharpe was colonel of the 120th New York Infantry, but more likely it was his proclivity for drinking and high living that grabbed the equally fun-loving Hooker's attention. Yet if he was a bit of a dissipate, Sharpe was also a born spy master. In his first major task, providing Hooker with data on Robert

> [Baker's methods included] . . . midnight arrests, incarceration without habeas corpus, and involuntary confessions.

E. Lee's army prior to the Chancellorsville campaign, Sharpe assessed Confederate numbers down to less than one-fourth of 1 percent—a margin of error of only 150 men out of some 60,000. He performed nearly as well during the Gettysburg campaign, but then commenced his most dramatic service when Grant came east in 1864.

Through contacts as yet unknown, Sharpe managed to get through to Samuel Ruth, Union-sympathizing superintendent of the Richmond, Fredericksburg, and Potomac Railroad, and Elizabeth Van Lew, both operating in the Confederate capital itself. Ruth furnished information on troop movements, supplies, and the condition of the South's rail network, and helped escaped Federal prisoners find their way to safety. He even sent information for Federal raiding parties who destroyed portions of his own rail line when it carried valuable matériel for the Southern war effort. Van Lew, a woman regarded as odd and therefore not suspected by her high society Richmond friends and neighbors, was Ruth's associate in some of this work. "Crazy Bet" visited Northern prisoners in Richmond's prisons and then conveyed military information gleaned from them through the lines to Sharpe. From these and other sources, many of them Confederate officers whom she flattered into indiscreet revelations, Van Lew derived a mass of information that she wrote in code on onionskin paper and hid inside empty eggshells, sending them in the keeping of her servants to Union lines. Upon the fall of Richmond in April 1865, one of Grant's first calls was at the Van Lew mansion to extend his thanks.

While Sharpe assumed the field intelligence role once performed by Pinkerton, the duty of keeping an eye on traitors and spies within Washington itself, and much of the North, fell to the National Detective Police, created in 1863 under the management of Lafayette C. Baker. His counterintelligence efforts, for the most part effective, were sometimes crude and brutal, including midnight arrests, incarceration without habeas corpus, and involuntary confessions.

Even as late as 1865 there was no uniform coordination of all Union intelligence activities. Baker reported to the secretary of war; Sharpe to George G. Meade or Grant; Dodge's network to Sherman's staff; and a host of other operatives to their individual employers. As a result methods and effectiveness varied widely, but in the main, by mid- or late 1863 Union armies across the map were getting good information and using it well. At the same time they were successfully subverting most Confederate efforts at gathering good intelligence and performing acts of espionage behind Federal lines.

BIBLIOGRAPHY

Baker, Lafayette C. *History of the United States Secret Service.* Philadelphia, 1867.
Fishel, Edwin. "The Mythology of Civil War Intelligence." *Civil War History* 10 (1964).
Hirshson, Stanley P. *Grenville M. Dodge.* Bloomington, Ind., 1967.
Pinkerton, Allan. *The Spy of the Rebellion.* New York, 1888.
Time-Life Books. *Spies, Scouts and Raiders.* Alexandria, Va., 1985.

WILLIAM C. DAVIS

Confederate Military Spies

The Confederate spies who were successful at their missions and never bragged about their successes remain largely unknown. We know the most about those spies who either were caught in the act or talked at some point about their wartime experiences.

The men and women who served as spies supporting the Confederate military effort were a diverse group representing many aspects of Southern society. The two attributes that come closest to describing them as a group were their commitment to the Southern cause and their lack of qualification for combat service. Even this second attribute is not completely descriptive, however, for though many of the spies were women, physically disabled men, or wounded veterans no longer able to serve in the field, the young soldiers who served as cavalry scouts proved to be so capable at collect-

> **Confederate spies belonged to a number of different organizations that together formed the Confederate Secret Service.**

ing information under pressure that a number of them were drawn into the clandestine world of espionage.

When the Confederates began to create the institutions that were needed for combat, they had the help of a number of men who knew clandestine operations to the extent that it was known by the U.S. government before the war. In addition, a number of immigrants in both the North and the South had had personal experience in the clandestine activities associated with various republican revolutions in Europe in the decades before the Civil War. The Confederates may also have had some help from British or French intelligence agents who saw the weakening of the United States as one possible outcome of a Confederate victory. The net effect was that the Confederates had available nearly all the know-how then in existence to help them organize the collection of information they needed to defend themselves against the Northern armies.

Confederate spies belonged to a number of different organizations that together formed the Confederate Secret Service. Scholars are still trying to piece together the history of these organizations, but some parts of the story are well known.

Rose O'Neal Greenhow. The first Confederate spy to gain widespread recognition was Rose O'Neal Greenhow, widow of a respected agent of the U.S. State Department. She was noted for her intelligence and had a great deal of political experience—much more than was usual for a woman in those days. She had lived in Mexico and California and had known most of the American presidents and cabinet officers from the time of Andrew Jackson down to Abraham Lincoln's predecessor, James Buchanan. The great spokesman for the Southern point of view, John C. Calhoun, had been her friend and tutor. As an active member of Washington society and a successful hostess, Greenhow knew or was acquainted with nearly everybody of any consequence in the American government before the arrival of Lincoln.

When the leading Southerners left Washington in early 1861 to begin the organization of the Confederate government, it would have been only natural for them to think of Rose Greenhow as somebody who might be able to help them gather information about the activities of the Northerners who remained behind. She was recruited into an espionage organization by Thomas Jordan of the provisional army of Virginia. Jordan taught her a simple cipher system for her communications and arranged a courier network to deliver her reports to the Virginia forces across the Potomac River. When the Virginia forces were incorporated into the Confederate army in June 1861, Jordan became a member of the staff of Gen. P. G. T. Beauregard, the Confederate commander, and continued to manage Greenhow and the other members of the espionage organization to which she belonged.

Greenhow exploited her contacts among government officials, particularly her friendship with Senator Henry Wilson of Massachusetts, who had succeeded Confederate President Jefferson Davis as chairman of the Senate Military Affairs Committee. In July she was able to send a message to Jordan alerting him to the plans of Union Gen. Irvin McDowell for an advance into Virginia. McDowell's venture ended with Union defeat at the First Battle of Manassas, and Greenhow was widely credited in Confederate circles with having provided the information that made victory possible.

Greenhow's chief drawbacks were her flamboyant personality and her ardent belief in the Southern cause. Combined, these attributes kept her from maintaining the low profile that would have been more suitable for a successful spy. She was arrested by Union detectives on August 23, 1861, and kept under house arrest or in prison until mid-1862 when she and two other Confederate women spies were freed and sent to the Confederacy.

Greenhow, while in prison, continued to contact some of her informants and to forward their information, but after her release the Confederates sent her to England to promote sympathy for the Southern cause. On her return to the Confederacy in October 1864, she was drowned while trying to reach shore from her stranded blockade runner.

Augusta Morris and Catherine Baxley. The other women sent south with Rose Greenhow were Augusta Hewitt Morris and Catherine Virginia Baxley. These two women did not achieve the notoriety that surrounded Greenhow, but they had longer careers in espionage.

Morris apparently returned to the North using the alias "Mrs. Mason" and continued to work for the Confederacy. One of the leading Confederates in Washington was Thomas Green, who lived in a mansion only three blocks from the White House. In 1863 Green was reported by Union detec-

tives to be working with a Mrs. Mason and traveling to Baltimore two or three times a week in order to mail information to Richmond. (The Confederates used the U.S. mails heavily in their courier system. A report in a double envelope would be mailed to a collaborator who would remove the outer envelope and hand the inner one to a courier who would carry it across the Potomac and deliver it in Richmond.)

On May 3, 1864, Morris was given $10,500 from the Incidental and Contingent Expenditures fund of the Confederate War Department. This was a large sum for those days and probably represented a payroll for an espionage organization such as the one reporting to Green.

Baxley also returned to the North and was provided with a cipher system for communication with the Confederate State Department and the South's clandestine organization in Canada. Her mission probably involved carrying information and messages between Canada and Richmond through Union territory. She was arrested again by the Union in early 1865 and remained in prison until the war was over.

Belle Boyd. Another woman who achieved some notoriety as a Confederate spy was a young Virginian named Belle Boyd. During 1861 around Martinsburg, Virginia (present-day West Virginia), and in 1862 near Front Royal, Virginia, Boyd served as a courier and spy for the Confederate forces in the area. She appears to have had little or no training in the craft of espionage and exposed herself unnecessarily to arrest by the Federal forces, but she talked her way out of a number of close calls and managed to provide Col. Turner Ashby and Gen. Thomas J. ("Stonewall") Jackson with some extremely useful information on Federal troop movements and strengths. She was arrested in June 1862 and confined in the Old Capitol Prison in Washington. In August of the same year she was sent south in an exchange of civilian prisoners. She returned to Martinsburg, was arrested again, and sent south once more.

On May 8, 1864, Boyd sailed from Wilmington, North Carolina, on a blockade runner, carrying dispatches for Confederate agents in Europe. Her ship, *Greyhound,* was captured, and Boyd (who had destroyed the dispatches in her care) was sent to the North for interrogation. She was finally released by her captors and sent to Canada.

On June 12, 1864, Miss Belle Boyd and maid checked into the St. Lawrence Hall Hotel in Montreal and were assigned rooms 136 and 137. On June 15, the Reverend Stuart Robinson, a Presbyterian minister from Louisville, Kentucky, who was assisting the Confederate clandestine organization in Canada, checked into the same hotel and was assigned room 138. It would appear that the Confederates were anxious to keep track of Boyd and to verify her continued loyalty to the Confederacy.

In due course Boyd went on to England where she was married on August 25, 1864, to Ensign Samuel Hardinge, recently of the U.S. Navy. He had commanded the prize crew that had taken *Greyhound* into port and had fallen in love with Boyd. Unfortunately, he did not live long thereafter, and Boyd became a widow at twenty-one. After the war, she spent the remainder of her life as an actress and lecturer trading on her notoriety as a former Confederate spy.

Other Female Agents. There were several other female spies who provided outstanding service to the Confederacy. Early in the war, Antonia Ford of Fairfax County, Virginia, added to the information provided by Rose Greenhow, and later after the Confederate partisan Col. John S. Mosby began his operations in northern Virginia, Ford provided him with valuable tactical information. Sarah Slater and Josephine Brown worked between Richmond and Canada, mostly during 1864 and 1865. The sisters Ginnie and Lottie

> [Conrad headed a team sent to] . . . determine if it would be feasible to capture Lincoln as a hostage.

Moon were raised in Ohio by a Virginia father. When war came, they went south and found useful employment in gathering information and carrying messages for the Confederates in Kentucky and Tennessee and in the Trans-Mississippi area. After the war, they continued their unconventional activities, working for women's suffrage and other causes.

Still other women worked for the Confederate clandestine effort in a variety of circumstances, but there were also a number of men who provided invaluable information to the Confederacy.

Daniel Lucas. A good example of male espionage agents who were not qualified for combat was Daniel Bedinger Lucas of Jefferson County, Virginia (present-day West Virginia). Lucas was a graduate of the University of Virginia and a lawyer. In 1861 he served on the staff of Gen. Henry A. Wise, a former governor of Virginia, in his campaign in western Virginia, but Lucas suffered from a congenital deformity that prevented him from engaging in the physical activity demanded by field duty. He returned to Richmond where he was active in the management of espionage and other secret operations. In late 1864 he went to Canada to assist Gen. Edwin Grey Lee who had been sent there to change the direction of the clandestine activities being organized against the North.

After the war, Lucas practiced law in West Virginia, was appointed to a short term as a U.S. senator from that state, and became a justice of the West Virginia Supreme Court of Appeals. He was discreet in conversation and writings about his wartime clandestine experiences, and as a result, the

details of his years with the Confederate Secret Service are not known.

John Palmer. One of the most successful of the Confederate spies was John Williamson Palmer, a correspondent for the *New York Tribune.* Palmer had impeccable credentials and freedom of access behind Union lines. His dispatches, printed under the byline "Altamont," were widely read and exceptionally perceptive concerning Confederate strategy. What was not so obvious was that he was in an excellent position to report on Union strategy and to make sure that his interpretation of Confederate strategy represented the view the Confederates wanted the Union to have. Palmer played this difficult and dangerous game for about two years, but finally he gave it up—possibly because of the nervous strain involved—and spent the final years of the war in Richmond writing letters carrying Confederate propaganda. These letters were put into the Union mail system for delivery, thus appearing to have originated in the North.

Thomas Conrad. Another successful Confederate spy was Thomas Nelson Conrad, who operated a boys' school in connection with the Dumbarton Avenue Methodist Church in Georgetown in the District of Columbia. At the beginning of the war, Conrad helped the Confederate clandestine organization in Washington—probably the same one to which Rose Greenhow belonged. In 1862, however, Conrad was arrested and sent south in an exchange of civilian prisoners. Conrad went to work for the Secret Service of the Confederate War Department and made numerous trips into Union territory. In 1863 he was in Montgomery County, Maryland, just north and west of the District of Columbia, and from that point he observed the movements of the Union army north toward Gettysburg.

The youthful Captain Conrad took great delight in devising disguises that would fool enemy detectives, and he chose to try them out on the Confederates protecting Richmond to prove their effectiveness. The Confederate provost marshals, however, did not like being fooled. One of their ledgers, now in the U.S. National Archives, was used to record persons clearing the provost checkpoint on entering or leaving Richmond. It contains a list of aliases known to have been used by Captain Conrad—they were on the lookout for him.

Later Conrad, as a lay Methodist preacher, became a chaplain in the Third Virginia Cavalry and served at the same time as one of Gen. J. E. B. Stuart's cavalry scouts. In the spring of 1864 he was sent by Jefferson Davis to report on the movements and destination of the corps being assembled near Annapolis, Maryland, by Northern Gen. Ambrose Burnside.

The following September he was sent to Washington as head of a small team to observe the movements of President Lincoln and determine if it would be feasible to capture Lincoln as a hostage. While in Washington, Conrad stayed at the home of Thomas Green, who had worked with Augusta Morris. Conrad reported that Lincoln's capture was possible. In November 1864 he was sent back to the Potomac River to organize an espionage line, paralleling the existing secret line of the Confederate Signal Corps, in order to report information pertinent to the operation to abduct Lincoln. He was captured by the Union navy on the night of April 16, 1865, and kept in prison for some weeks.

After the war, Conrad held various teaching positions and served as the first president of the institution that later became the Virginia Polytechnic Institute and State University.

Henry Harrison. Another highly successful Confederate spy was Henry Thomas Harrison of Mississippi who worked as a scout and spy against Ulysses S. Grant's forces in Tennessee and Mississippi. For a time he operated under the direction of Thomas Jordan, who had directed Rose Greenhow before being transferred to the Confederate Army of Tennessee.

Later Harrison moved to the eastern area to work against the Union forces in North Carolina and Virginia. He was particularly successful in providing information to Gen. James Longstreet during the Gettysburg campaign. Later Harrison was assigned to duty behind Union lines in New York City, but the nature of his mission there is not known.

Sam Davis. A less successful Confederate scout in the Army of Tennessee was young Sam Davis of the First Tennessee Infantry. He was recruited by Capt. Henry Shaw, who operated under the alias of Coleman, to join a group of scouts collecting information for Gen. Braxton Bragg, then in command. The group successfully collected a great deal of important information behind Union lines and then scattered to make their way individually back to Confederate territory. Davis was picked to carry the essential papers; the other members of the group would not have anything incriminating on them if caught.

As it transpired, Davis, Shaw, and other members of the group were captured, but only Davis could be proved to be working for the Confederate Secret Service. His Union captors pressed him to identify "Coleman," but he refused. He was tried as a spy, although he had been captured in uniform. He was sentenced to be hanged and at the last moment was offered a pardon if he would tell where Coleman could be found. Although Coleman was a fellow prisoner, Davis refused to point him out and gave his life for the cause.

John Wilkes Booth. Another ardent supporter of the Southern cause was John Wilkes Booth, whose sister, Asia Booth Clark, wrote that her brother had told her that he was a spy for the Confederacy. A good deal is known about Booth's activities in 1864 and 1865 while he was trying to organize the capture of President Lincoln as a hostage, but very little is known about his activities before he was drawn into that plot.

Booth appears to have been recruited to head the team for the capture operation in late July 1864. He abandoned his other activities for the Confederate Secret Service and in August and September wound up an oil venture and other personal affairs. He recruited several people to help in the operation and in October 1864 went to Canada, where he met leading members of the Confederate Secret Service in Montreal. A trip to Washington in November overlapped with Captain Conrad's stay for a few days. In late November and December Booth made trips to southern Maryland to organize the route his team would take when they had captured Lincoln. Finally, in March 1865, the team set out to seize the president but were frustrated when Lincoln changed his itinerary.

The Confederates then sent Lt. Thomas F. (Frank) Harney, an explosives expert, to Washington in a scheme to blow up the White House during a meeting of key officials in order to disrupt coordination between Grant's and Sherman's armies. Harney, however, was caught on his way into Washington, and Booth took it upon himself to approximate the damage that would have been caused by an explosion. He tried to organize simultaneous attacks against Lincoln, Vice President Andrew Johnson, Secretary of State William Seward, and Secretary of War Edwin Stanton. As it turned out, only Lincoln was murdered and Seward injured by his attacker.

Booth escaped through southern Maryland, but Union troops caught and killed him on April 26, 1865. Four of his associates were hanged in June of that year, and several others served prison sentences of varying lengths.

P. C. Martin. A Confederate spy of a radically different type was P. C. Martin, an importer and liquor dealer from Baltimore. Martin left Maryland early in the war to escape arrest for his pro-Southern activities. He settled in Montreal where he became the leader of the Confederate clandestine activity in that city.

He helped organize an ambitious plan to free the Confederate prisoners of war held on Johnson Island in the harbor of Sandusky, Ohio, but the plan was frustrated when word of it got out. After Booth's departure in October 1864, Martin took the actor's theater wardrobe on a ship down the St. Lawrence to run the blockade into the Confederacy. The ship was wrecked and Martin was drowned. Booth's wardrobe was recovered in 1865.

Walter Bowie. One of the most intriguing Confederate spies was Walter Bowie of Prince George's County, Maryland. Bowie was a prominent young lawyer in Upper Marlboro, Maryland, when the war broke out. He went south to volunteer his services to the Confederacy and served for some months in a staff position in Richmond. In 1862, he returned to Maryland to take charge of the courier and reporting system supporting the Confederate espionage organization in Washington that Rose Greenhow had belonged to. He was apprehended and imprisoned in the Old Capitol Prison in Washington, but he managed to escape with the help of the Confederate underground organization in that city.

Bowie acquired a reputation as a guerrilla operating in southern Maryland and eventually joined the partisan unit in northern Virginia commanded by John S. Mosby, but his reputation appears to have been based on a confusion of identities. There were three Walter Bowies in the Confederate army in Virginia, and their records were sometimes mixed up (they still are today). During the Civil War when news was often circulated by word of mouth, there was ample opportunity for one Walter Bowie to be credited with the actions of

> [They hatched a] . . . scheme to blow up the White House during a meeting of key officials. . . .

another. One of the other Walter Bowies, for instance, was a graduate of the Virginia Military Institute who spent several months operating in southern Maryland as the head of a raiding team belonging to the Confederate volunteer navy. It is likely that his activities were credited to the Walter Bowie from Prince George's County.

One of Bowie's duties in managing the espionage network was to prepare summaries of information collected by the entire organization. A summary that has survived among the papers of Col. Charles Venable of Robert E. Lee's staff shows that in April 1864 Bowie reported to Lee General Grant's preparations for the campaign of 1864. Bowie's report was quite accurate and even outlined the tactic of repeatedly moving to the flank of Lee's army that Grant employed when the campaign opened in May 1864.

Mosby's force had become well established in northern Virginia, and Bowie was sent to join his unit where he found that Walter Bowie of the volunteer navy had preceded him. Mosby took over the task of maintaining contact with the Confederate clandestine organization in Washington while the Maryland Bowie, as a lieutenant of one of Mosby's companies, was sent with a small team to southern Maryland with the ostensible mission of seizing the governor of Maryland. This mission coincided in time with Conrad's mission to investigate the possibility of capturing Lincoln and was probably related to it.

Bowie moved through southern Maryland, passed around Washington to the north, and tried to return to Virginia through Montgomery County north and west of the District of Columbia. In the course of that passage Bowie's party was ambushed by local citizens, and Bowie was killed.

Robert Coxe. A different type of agent was Robert Edwin Coxe of Georgia. Coxe was a wealthy planter who had lived in Europe for several years before the war. In 1863 he moved his family to Canada and established himself in St. Catharines, Ontario, near Niagara Falls. The proximity to Niagara provided excellent cover for the meeting of clandestine agents. A museum (which still exists) on the Canadian side of the falls kept a book in which visitors recorded their signatures. An agent could visit the museum and sign the book without attracting attention. Somebody at the museum or another visitor would inspect the book periodically and, when an expected signature appeared, send word to St. Catharines. In due course a representative of the Confederate Secret Service would turn up to meet the visiting agent at a prearranged location. Under cover of tourist traffic, this arrangement lasted through the remainder of the war without being discovered.

In June 1864, the former U.S. senator Clement C. Clay, one of the Confederate commissioners in Canada, moved into Coxe's house in St. Catharines along with the former U.S. consul Beverly Tucker. Clay and Tucker conducted a number of clandestine operations from this location while Coxe went to Maine, then to Poughkeepsie, New York, and finally to Washington, D.C. After the assassination of Lincoln, Coxe was arrested, but he was later released for lack of evidence.

In addition to the people mentioned above, there were a number of others known to have been involved in Confederate clandestine operations, but we have little information about them. These include Benjamin Franklin Stringfellow, who served as a cavalry scout and was in Washington to deliver a diplomatic message when the war ended; Channing Smith, another cavalry scout who was commissioned in late 1864 and sent for some special assignment with Mosby; Emile Longmare, who worked with the copperheads in the North to promote an antiwar movement; Vincent Camalier, who worked as a smuggler of contraband and crossed the lines with word of impending Union movements; Augustus Howell of Prince George's County, Maryland, who was almost caught up in Booth's assassination operation; and Thomas Harbin, an agent of the Confederate War Department who worked with Booth and his team.

The dedication of these and other Confederate spies is obvious. Many of them received no money for their pains, and most who were paid received little more than their expenses. They were individuals doing what they could for the cause in which they believed.

BIBLIOGRAPHY

Bakeless, John. *Spies of the Confederacy.* Philadelphia and New York, 1970.

Foster, G. Allen. *The Eyes and Ears of the Civil War.* New York, 1963.

Grimes, Absalom. *Absalom Grimes: Confederate Mail Runner.* Edited by M. M. Quaife. New Haven, 1926.

Kane, Harnett T. *Spies for the Blue and Gray.* New York, 1954.

Ross, Ishbel. *Rebel Rose.* New York, 1954.
Stern, Philip Van Doren. *Secret Missions of the Civil War.* New York, 1959.
Tidwell, William A., with James O. Hall and David Winfred Gaddy. *Come Retribution: The Confederate Secret Service and the Assassination of Lincoln.* Jackson, Miss., 1988.

WILLIAM A. TIDWELL

EVANS, NATHAN ("SHANKS")

EVANS, NATHAN ("SHANKS") (1824–1868), brigadier general. Born in Marion, South Carolina, Evans was a controversial officer whose early success at First Manassas was obscured by disputes with subordinates and superiors alike throughout the war. After graduating from West Point in 1848, Evans was appointed to a cavalry regiment and sent west where he gained renown as an Indian fighter. When South Carolina seceded, he was appointed colonel of state troops and eventually went to Virginia to join the Confederate army.

At First Manassas, Evans, with the assistance of Barnard E. Bee and Wade Hampton, took the initiative without prior orders to hold off a Federal force of about 17,000 trying to outflank the Southerners near the Stone Bridge. Evans's determined defense with a force of barely 5,000 saved the Confederate left, allowing the Southern forces to win the battle. Commended for his courage and skill by superiors, Evans appeared to have a bright future. After his brigade routed Federal troops at Ball's Bluff, he was promoted to brigadier general and placed in command of the Third Military District.

> **Evans had his accusers arrested and court-martialed with inconclusive results.**

He subsequently served at Second Manassas, South Mountain, and Sharpsburg, and in the Vicksburg campaign.

Despite his initial successes, Evans by late 1862 had become involved in disputes over his conduct. At the Battle of South Mountain, subordinates accused him of drunkenness and cowardice under fire. Evans had his accusers arrested and court-martialed with inconclusive results. He himself was court-martialed for disobeying orders but was acquitted. In spring 1863 his superiors reported unfavorably on the conditions of his brigade in North Carolina. P. G. T. Beauregard finally removed him from command, calling him incompetent. Although he later returned to duty, he remained in obscurity for the rest of the war.

After the war, Evans became principal of a high school in Midway, Alabama, where he died. He is buried in Cokesbury, South Carolina.

BIBLIOGRAPHY

Freeman, Douglas S. *Lee's Lieutenants: A Study in Command.* 3 vols. New York, 1942–1944. Reprint, New York, 1986.
Warner, Ezra J. *Generals in Gray: Lives of the Confederate Commanders.* Baton Rouge, La., 1959.

FRITZ P. HAMER

EWELL, RICHARD S.

EWELL, RICHARD S. (1817–1872), lieutenant general. One of seventeen men to attain the rank of lieutenant general in the Confederate military, Richard Stoddard Ewell was a key figure in the eastern campaigns. He served as a division commander under Gen. Thomas J. ("Stonewall") Jackson early in the war and then replaced Jackson after his death as head of the Second Corps in Gen. Robert E. Lee's Army of Northern Virginia.

A native of Virginia, Ewell graduated thirteenth in the West Point class of 1840, and served mostly in the Far West with the cavalry during the twenty years prior to the Civil War. He saw limited action in the Mexican War.

Ewell entered Confederate service in April 1861. He commanded a brigade at the Battle of First Manassas but was not directly involved in the combat.

In March 1862 Ewell (now leading a division) went to the Shenandoah Valley to join Jackson in his campaign against Union Gen. Nathaniel Banks. Though Jackson was the overall commander, Ewell's men did most of the fighting. His troops engaged and routed the Federals in the opening battle at Front Royal on May 23, 1862. Two days later, moving against Banks at Winchester, Ewell made the initial attack, and one of his brigades under Gen. Richard Taylor led a final charge that routed the enemy. After Jackson retreated to avoid a pincer by Federal Gens. John C. Frémont and James Shields that threatened his rear, Ewell personally planned, directed, and won a battle with Frémont at Cross Keys on June 8, 1862. When Jackson attacked Shields early the next morning, Ewell led the men who captured a Federal artillery battery on the coaling ground above Port Republic, resulting in a Southern victory.

In June 1862, Ewell moved with Jackson to Richmond to join Lee in defending the Confederate capital under siege by Union Gen. George B. McClellan. He fought in only one of the five battles (Gaines' Mill, June 27, 1862); after taking terrible losses in an unsuccessful attack against an entrenched enemy, he held his tenuous line until Southern reinforcements came up to make the final, victorious charge.

Ewell moved north with Jackson after the Seven Days' Battles to confront Federal Gen. John Pope leading the newly formed Army of Virginia. After defeating the leading Union element under Banks at Cedar Run on August 9, 1862, Jackson and Ewell raced north on a flanking march to Pope's rear. They opened the Battle of Second Manassas at Groveton on August 28, 1862, where Ewell was shot in his right knee. The wound resulted in the amputation of his leg.

While Jackson continued the campaign, moving with Lee into Maryland, Ewell returned to Richmond to recuperate. He was nursed by the sweetheart he had lost to another during his youth, Lizinka Campbell Brown, who was now a wealthy widow.

In May 1863, just as Ewell was well enough to return to duty, Jackson was wounded at Chancellorsville. Jackson died on May 10, 1863, and Ewell was named as his replacement to head Lee's Second Corps. Prior to his rejoining the army, Ewell married Lizinka on May 24 and they enjoyed a brief honeymoon. He then led his corps north toward Pennsylvania.

Marching down the Shenandoah Valley, Ewell stopped to engage Union Gen. Robert Milroy at Winchester. He gained a spectacular victory on June 14, 1863, and then moved northward, intent on capturing Harrisburg, the capital of Pennsylvania. Just prior to his attack, Lee recalled Ewell to Gettysburg, where the enemy under Gen. George Meade was concentrating.

Ewell attacked the Northern flank on July 1, 1863, and drove the Federals from the field. Although Ewell has been criticized by some for not continuing to assault the enemy, who had retired to Cemetery Hill, this assertion ignores the facts. The Federals' position was strongly manned. Had he charged the heights, Ewell would have been easily repelled and would have suffered devastating losses to his command. The next day Lee attacked the Union left with Gen. James Longstreet's corps. Late in the day, when Meade drew men from his right (fronting Ewell) to hold off this threat, the chance arose for Ewell to drive a wedge into the Northern line. But he was not ready, and his delayed charge, mounted piecemeal, failed.

Following their defeat at Gettysburg, Lee and his army retreated back to Virginia. Ewell spent the winter of 1863–1864 along the Rappahannock River. Not completely recovered from the amputation of his leg, he considered relinquishing command, but Lizinka (who had joined him that winter) would not hear of it. She took the unprecedented step of assuming charge of his affairs while he rested to regain his strength.

In May 1864, Gen. Ulysses S. Grant led the Federals south against Lee. Ewell made initial contact with the enemy in the Wilderness on May 5, 1864, showing consummate skill

as he fought off the repeated Federal charges. Grant, facing a stalemate, took his army around Lee's right, and the two met again at Spotsylvania. At first the battle was inconclusive. Thinking that Grant would once again maneuver, Lee started to withdraw Ewell's artillery just as the Northerners renewed their assault at sunrise on May 12, 1864. Without his guns, Ewell was quickly overrun, losing half his corps before he finally restored his line. He was so distraught over the casualties to his command, however, that he became sick and was forced to go on leave. When he reported for duty on May 31, Ewell found that Lee had replaced him with Jubal Early.

Assigned to Richmond, Ewell managed the city's defenses above the James River. After repeated unsuccessful attempts to regain a field command, Ewell became so disillusioned that when Lizinka proposed in late December that she take the oath of allegiance to the Union in order to regain her properties in the North, Ewell agreed to assist her in committing treason. She left Richmond for St. Louis on March 24, 1865. Less than two weeks later, Ewell led his ragtag assortment of troops after Lee toward Appomattox. He was captured on April 6 during the Battle of Sayler's Creek and imprisoned at Fort Warren in Boston Harbor.

Released in July 1865, Ewell retired to Spring Hill, Tennessee, where Lizinka owned a large plantation. He became a gentleman farmer. During the winter of 1872, Ewell fell ill with pneumonia. When his spouse attempted to nurse him back to health, she contracted the disease and died on January 22. Forty-eight hours later, Ewell joined his wife in death.

BIBLIOGRAPHY

Hamlin, Percy. *The Making of a Soldier.* Richmond, Va., 1935.
Hamlin, Percy. *Old Bald Head.* Strasburg, Va., 1940.
Martin, Samuel J. *The Road to Glory: Confederate General Richard S. Ewell.* Indianapolis, Ind., 1991.

SAMUEL J. MARTIN

EXPANSIONISM IN THE ANTEBELLUM SOUTH

The myth of a monolithic, unchanging slave South distorts the history of the slavocracy. Thus the Civil War supposedly matched the entire South against the North. But, in fact, the four border states never left the Union, West Virginia seceded from Virginia, and over 100,000 Confederate residents joined Abraham Lincoln's army. So too, before the Civil War, the South supposedly massed unanimously behind the so-called positive good of perpetual slavery. But, in fact, most upper South residents considered slavery a temporary evil. They hoped to remove blacks and slaves from their half of the South. Meanwhile, important lower South clergymen considered slavery short on Christian blessings. They urged state legislatures to protect slaves' families and access to Christianity. Most owners derided such suggestions as meddling interference, not proslavery Christianity.

These divergent viewpoints within the South, involving the pivotal matters of whether slaveholders' absolute power should be perpetuated, limited, or removed to other locales, put into perspective another fundamental Southern intramural contest, that concerning whether slavery should be expanded into new territories. According to the standard account, Southerners combated only Northerners in pre-Civil War controversies over territorial expansion, with "expand or perish" the Southerners' persistent motto. So when Abraham Lincoln won the presidency in 1860 pledging no expansion of slavery, Southerners supposedly concluded that the Union, not slavery, must perish.

The expand-or-perish interpretation, while concentrating the causes of secession into three vivid words, actually reduces a complex phenomenon to a caricature. The oversimplification is useful only to warn all who study Southern slaveholding that variations over time and space must be noticed. Southern beliefs about the *economic* necessity for expansion especially fluctuated. Convictions about slaveholders' *political* need for expansion flourished more consistently—with some important exceptions. The exceptions predominated in the climactic 1850s, when expand-or-perish thinking was particularly erratic. As the Civil War approached, South Carolina's planters, who feared they might perish without disunion, worried that Southern territorial expansion, especially into the Caribbean, might remove slavery from their state. In contrast, New Orleans merchants, who thought they might perish without Caribbean expansion, believed that disunionism could cripple expansionism. The border South's prosperous residents, who often supported territorial expansion as a way to remove slavery from their area, still hoped that expansionism would perish if disunion resulted.

Just as Southern attitudes about territorial expansion changed from one place to another, so the expansion issue changed from one era to another. Southern drives for more territory accelerated from 1793 to the mid-1830s, met opposition in the 1840s, and turned around again in the 1850s, as the Southern economy veered from half recession to unrelieved depression to almost universal prosperity. A paradox illuminates the point: the fallacious myth of universal Southern enthusiasm for expansion during the era of sectional controversy, from 1844 to 1860, fits the facts—*before* 1844. As for the period before 1793, then Southern zeal for expansion could scarcely be found.

From 1793 to 1843, Southern expansionists were making up for earlier Southern generations' characteristic lack of desire for new territorial acquisitions, but they had not yet developed the fears of later generations that exotic territorial adventures could destroy old cultural stabilities. During the eighteenth century, the slave South had been predominantly a seaboard civilization, usually (though not always) uninterested in spreading west of the coastal colonies. Native Americans—Creeks, Choctaws, Seminoles, and Cherokees—had cultivated some of what became upland South Carolina and Georgia, northern Mississippi and Alabama, and western Tennessee. Non-English peoples had controlled the rim of the Anglo lower South, including the French-owned areas of what became Louisiana and Arkansas, and the Spanish-owned areas of what became Texas, Florida, and southern Alabama and Mississippi.

Eighteenth-century entrepreneurs did not yet covet what became the southernmost tier of the United States, because they could not conceive of a lucrative crop suitable for North

> **Just as Southern attitudes about territorial expansion changed from one place to another, so the expansion issue changed from one era to another.**

America's westward, noncoastal tropics. They considered lower South latitudes too tropical for the upper South's staple crop, tobacco, and not tropical enough for South America's staple crops, sugar and coffee. Only the South Carolina and Georgia coastal malarial swamps could support the colonial lower South's most coveted crop, rice; and only the Sea Islands near the coast could support the secondary staple, silky Sea Island cotton. West of the coast, some colonial South Carolinians grew indigo for a limited market, lost after the American Revolution. Other Carolinians produced the cheaper grades of cotton, also commercially limited without a then-uninvented gin to separate seeds from fibers. So while black slaves outnumbered white citizens more than eight to one in Georgia and especially South Carolina coastal areas, almost four out of five North American slaves toiled north of the future cotton kingdom. Slaves especially peopled the upper South tobacco belts, although whites still outnumbered blacks.

Southern Consensus for Expansionism

Eli Whitney's invention of the cotton gin in 1793 at last sent lower South entrepreneurs swarming to southwestern frontiers soon densely populated by slaves. Two simultaneous economic and political developments accelerated the population surge from the oldest South to the new cotton frontier. Almost at the moment when the cotton kingdom required more slaves, Congress abolished the African slave trade (1807). And almost at the moment when the newer South's economy ascended, the older South's economy declined. In upper South tobacco belts, debilitated soil and poor prices produced chronic stagnation. In South Carolina's coastal rice swamps, land was more worn and profits less fabulous than in colonial times; and in that state's up-country area, the first cotton spree had yielded the first cotton-exhausted soil. Throughout these eastern locales, struggling planters needed to shrink their operation or lose their property. Out in the southwestern cotton kingdom, buoyant developers, now legally barred from buying slaves from Africa, competed for contracting slaveholders' unneeded bondsmen. As a result, some 750,000 blacks were relocated from 1790 to 1860. The lower South's share of slaves in the United States leapt from 21 to 59 percent over these years.

In the wake of slavery's spread over previously uncultivated tropical regions, slave sellers in older areas had the cash to finance a modest postboom survival economy. Slave buyers in new cotton areas had the laborers to produce a post–eighteenth century bonanza. The process of paying leaner Peter to fatten hungry Paul, however, served more than economic desires. Among planters who wanted to preserve slavery, slave buying was the key to consolidating slavery's lower South empire. Among Southerners who wanted to remove slavery and blacks from their area, slave selling was the key to producing an all-white upper South. That anti-slavery rationale for an expansion of slavery even came to appeal to some Southern opponents of slavery who had earlier opposed slaveholder expansionism. In the eighteenth century, before the cotton expansion, Thomas Jefferson of Virginia had considered slavery's expansion wrong. But by 1820, after the cotton kingdom was well established, Jefferson called expansionism right. If slavery were to be bottled up in old areas, he thought, fearful whites would never free the densely concentrated blacks. If slavery were to be "diffused" into new areas, on the other hand, whites would more readily emancipate the scattered slaves. "Diffusion" was the key word. It united Southerners who hoped to remove all slaves from their declining area with Southerners who wanted more slaves to proceed toward their advancing area.

That unanimity imperiled both Native American landowners inside the lower South's domain and foreign landowners just outside. Newly expansive slave owners, while wishing the lower South swept of alien whites and Native Americans, especially sought to remove neighbors who encouraged slave resistance. The most menacing resistance came not from the few groups of slave insurrectionists, who always were quickly quashed, but from the more numerous individual runaways, who ultimately helped defeat Confederate armies. During the Civil War, runaways increased when

slaveholders' enemies massed close by; and in the early nineteenth century, foreigners and Native Americans were uncomfortably close to the new cotton kingdom.

In Spanish Florida, for example, some Spaniards, Seminoles, and an occasional Englishman encouraged Georgia and South Carolina slaves to flee. In the face of this unrest, slaveholders argued that either the government must protect property or property holders must protect themselves. Farther north, on the Tennessee frontier, Andrew Jackson had become a vivid symbol of that maxim. In 1818,

> **... before the cotton expansion, Thomas Jefferson of Virginia had considered slavery's expansion wrong.**

President James Monroe ordered General Jackson to chastise some Seminoles who were troubling whites on the United States side of the Spanish Florida border. Jackson did more. He chased Seminoles over the Spanish border, seized their fort, killed several of their chieftains, hanged two Englishmen said to be their accomplices, and expelled a Spanish garrison from Pensacola.

Southern statesmen, in a pattern that would become crucial in the 1850s, divided along geographic lines on the wisdom of such adventuring as Jackson's. Southwestern frontiersmen cheered Jackson's raid. But South Carolina's John C. Calhoun (privately) and Kentucky's Henry Clay (publicly) deplored private raids that arguably exceeded governmental authorization. Nevertheless, southwesterners, South Carolinians, and border Southerners alike urged public government to oust aliens and make private assaults unnecessary. After the Missouri controversy of 1819 through 1821, slaveholders' motivations were increasingly political as well as economic. More lower South land would mean more Southern states and thus more defenders of slavery in Congress.

Safer Southern frontiers would also mean safer American frontiers. That nationalistic reason for expansion southward especially prevailed before the Missouri controversy but lingered long after. Such patriotism enabled Southern leaders to rally a national consensus to evict foreigners and Native Americans from the entire lower South during the first four decades of the nineteenth century. In 1803, President Thomas Jefferson, as part of the Louisiana Purchase, bought the future slave states of Louisiana, Arkansas, and Missouri from the French. In 1819, another Virginian president, James Monroe, taking advantage of the Spanish weakness that Jackson's raid had revealed, purchased the future state of Florida and southern areas of Mississippi and Alabama from Spain. In the 1830s, yet another Southern president, Jackson himself, deported Native Americans to reservations across the Mississippi River. And in 1844, the last antebellum president from Virginia, John Tyler, brought four decades of unanimous Southern zeal for expansion to a climax—and to an end—with his insistence that the Union annex Texas. That republic had secured its independence from Mexico in 1836, which had secured its independence from Spain in 1819.

President Tyler sought a national consensus to make the United States the latest nation with sovereignty over the vast Texas acreage. He thus did not emphasize one aim of fellow Southern expansionists: increasing the South's power in Congress. He did, however, reemphasize slaveholders' problems with neighbors perceived as hostile. If neighboring enemies incited slaves, Jackson had said and Tyler now repeated, slaveholders must be able to control the contiguous land. Jackson had worried about allegedly slave-inciting Spaniards, Englishmen, and Seminoles in Spanish Florida, which abutted Georgia. Tyler thought that English antislavery influence might eventually prevail in the Texas Republic, which abutted Louisiana and Arkansas. Better to annex another area contiguous to the lower South, Tyler declared with the aging Jackson's support, than to expose the slavocracy to antislavery neighbors.

Tyler reiterated not only Jackson's determination to take over contiguous areas but also Jefferson's desire to acquire outlets for relocation of slaves. A new economic slump throughout the South, moreover, lent urgency to Jefferson's old argument for diffusing slaves away. In the 1840s the adolescent southwestern cotton kingdom, no less than the aging colonial South, endured economic crisis. Cotton prices, which had averaged 16.4 cents a pound in 1835 and 1836, plunged in the 1840s, after the devastating panic of 1837, to an average of 7.9 cents a pound. Only an exorbitant yield could compensate for these 50 percent lower prices, and only virgin lands could spawn 50 percent higher yields. Not even the relatively undeveloped Southwest now seemed sufficiently unscarred. An unspoiled Texas would provide an economic safety valve, said Tyler, to drain redundant slaves away from decaying slaveholding areas.

This newest safety valve argument continued to promise racial as well as economic relief. If no Texas outlet was secured, annexationists warned, the black population would swell in states suffering economic decline. If economic depression then persisted, whites would flee from excess blacks. Were Texas to be annexed, on the other hand, slaveholders would be able to sell unneeded slaves through the outlet. Here, in pristine form, was the agrarians' expand-or-perish argument. Unless slavery could spread into new areas, the slaveholders' depressed economy would collapse and the South's racial order would crumble. Add to this formula for disaster the possibility that English abolitionists in Texas, right across the Louisiana-Arkansas border, would incite blacks to flee or pillage or worse. This logic yielded a clear choice: increase the number of Southern congressional seats and double the lower South's land by adding Texas to the Union or expect a racial inferno. That exclusively Southern reason for national expansion, however, made Northerners increasingly resistant to American Manifest Destiny, slaveholder-style.

Collapse of the Southern Consensus

If the Southern expand-or-perish argument had remained unchallenged in the mid-1840s and had pervaded the 1850s, no historian would be able to deny that a monolithic South had been united behind slave diffusion. But in Texas annexation times, the expansionists' diffusion argument inspired, in dialectical fashion, the first Southern breach over the question of slavery's expansion. In 1844, Southern Democrats, with rare border South exceptions, massed behind the expand-or-die thesis. When Southern Democrats thus insisted, reluctant Northern Democrats almost had to appease their party brethren, for the Democratic party was always stronger in the South than in the North. In contrast, when Northern Whigs insisted, Southern Whigs could hardly defy their party allies, for Whiggery was always stronger in the North than in the South. In 1844, after Southern Democrats relentlessly demanded Texas and after Northern Democrats reluctantly acquiesced and Northern Whigs contemptuously disapproved, Southern Whigs were driven to ask whether slavery would in fact perish unless the institution could diffuse into Texas.

That query undercut lower South unanimity on the expand-or-perish dogma. How, after all, could the single new slave state of Texas save slavery, in or out of Congress, if the institution drained out of eight border and upper South states and out of South Carolina too? Furthermore, how could cotton production in virgin Texas rescue the cotton South from a depression caused by cotton overproduction? Annexation, warned Whig South Carolina Congressman Waddy Thompson, would "very soon" remove slavery from "Maryland, Virginia, North Carolina, Tennessee, and Kentucky." Even in aging South Carolina, he feared, slavery would become "an incumbrance which we shall be glad to get rid of; and . . . it will afford me very little consolation in riding over my fields, grown up in broom-sedge and washed into gullies, to be told that . . . slavery still exists and is prosperous" in Texas.

Kentucky's Henry Clay, Whig nominee for president in 1844, reversed Waddy Thompson's lower South logic. Although a large border South slaveholder himself, Clay looked for the day when the South could rid itself both of slaves and of free blacks. He declared Texas annexation desirable in the abstract, because more slaves would then be diffused from the upper South. But he saw diffusion as not worth either a foreign war or a sectional controversy. A statesman's "paramount duty," he declared, was "preserving the Union," not saving slavery, a "temporary institution."

Slavery a "temporary institution"! Preserving the Union the "paramount duty"! With those four words, Henry Clay underscored, as if in Civil War blood, the difference between the border and lower Souths in their priorities about slavery, expansionism, and Unionism. But if the lower South's Waddy Thompson, hoping to keep slaves in South Carolina, and the border South's Henry Clay, hoping to keep all Americans in the Union, rejected annexation for contrary Whig reasons, the Whigs' alliance against Texas almost killed expansionism. Three months after the Democrats' ultra-expansionist James K. Polk defeated Clay in the November 1844 presidential election, the U.S. Senate nearly rejected the admission of Texas into the Union. The margin for Texas was thin, 27–25, because only three of fifteen Southern Whigs joined with the unanimously pro-Texas Democratic senators. Despite continued Whig opposition, the Democrat–led administration and Congress annexed Mexican territories from Texas to the Pacific, including California, in the Mexican Cession of 1848.

In the half century since the invention of the cotton gin, U.S. expansionism in lower South latitudes had swept across the continent. That omnivorous territorial expansion, achieved in the 1840s despite increasing Southern opposition and greater Northern opposition, bid fair to override all obstacles once again in the 1850s. During that presecession decade, Southern attempts to control Kansas, California, New Mexico, Arizona, Cuba, Nicaragua, and Mexico periodically convulsed the nation, helped provoke the election of Abraham Lincoln in 1860, and helped lead to the formation of the Confederacy. Yet all latter-day Southern expansion efforts failed, in part because Northerners massed powerfully against them, and in part because Southerners failed to mass unanimously for them.

The lack of unanimous Southern zeal for expansion in the 1850s stemmed, first of all, from expansionism's very success. During the presecession decade, there was no way slaveholders could cultivate all the Texas, Arkansas, and California acres previously acquired. There was also no way most Southerners could still think that the slave South would perish economically. As the 1840s ended, so did the post-1837 depression. The prosperity of Southerners in the 1850s, with the exception of South Carolina rice farmers, exceeded pre-1837 levels. Cotton prices, which had averaged under 8 cents a pound in the 1840s, averaged 11 cents a pound in the 1850s. The lower South now needed more slaves to exploit unused land, not more outlets for unneeded slaves. Meanwhile, the upper South, also enjoying better times, no longer needed to sell slaves to survive. So lower South demand for slaves exceeded the supply, and the price of slaves soared 70 percent between 1850 and 1860.

One remarkable proposed solution demonstrated how completely times had changed. In the 1840s, many declining Southerners, growing too much cotton on too many tired acres, had sought fresh lands as a way to export excess blacks. In the 1850s, some booming Southerners, growing too little cotton with too few laborers, sought to import Africans as a way to develop excess land. A lower South movement to reopen the African slave trade grew with stunning rapidity in the mid-1850s. By buying slaves from Africa, ran one rationale for the proposed panacea, the lower South could expand its cotton kingdom continually without contracting the upper South's number of slaves counterproductively. With the upper South keeping its slaves while the lower South consolidated a hemisphere-wide empire, went the dream, Southern states, ever more numerous in Congress, would transcend the debilitating divisiveness of Texas annexation.

But the proposal caused a worse divisiveness. In the upper South, angry slave sellers noted that by seeking to reopen the African slave trade, slave buyers in the lower South were seeking to slice prices, even to cut U.S. sellers out of the market altogether. Reopening the trade would also defy Federal laws, enrage the North, and lead to disunion. After this upper South outcry, the lower South proposal sank almost as fast as it had arisen. But by urging that the South had overly abundant territory and insufficient slaves, the lower South finished off the Texas-outlet logic.

In yet another indication that the economic side of the planters' expand-or-perish rationale had become past history, the only remaining group of economically perishing planters tended now to oppose territorial expansion. South Carolina coastal rice aristocrats suffered through a crippling economic slide in the 1850s, with the value of the rice crop sinking 25 percent below 1840s levels. South Carolina upcountry cotton producers fared better, but their economic recovery was less spectacular than Southwesterners'. Some 7,000 whites and 70,000 South Carolina blacks departed for the cotton frontier in the 1850s, preserving that stagnating state's distinction as the only slave-exporting lower South state. The state also retained its distinction as the only declining eighteenth-century locale of slavery that exported slaves and still crusaded to keep slavery forever.

That singular determination to retain departing slaves turned most South Carolinians against tropical meccas. Waddy Thompson had put it well in Texas times: who would stay in depleted Carolina if they could go to virgin El Dorados? John C. Calhoun came around to a similar attitude in 1846, opposing a southwestern drive to acquire all of Mexico. Leading South Carolinians continued to harbor such views of proposed Caribbean expansion in the 1850s. Mexico seemed full of non-American peons, Cuba full of free blacks, and the Southwest full of coarse frontiersmen. "It is not by bread alone that man liveth," intoned South Carolina's revered Francis Sumter in 1859. "We want some stability in our institutions."

Many South Carolinians opposed a supposedly destabilizing Caribbean empire because they favored a supposedly stabilizing disunion revolution. These disunionists hoped that outside the Union and beyond unsettling Northern attacks, a settled South could flourish. They feared that if the Union did acquire vast tropical lands, restless southwesterners would never decide to secede. Still, a taste for staying home and distaste for expansionism swept up the powerful South Carolina Unionist, U.S. Senator James Henry Hammond, just as it did the secessionists. "I do not wish," said Hammond, "to remove from my native state and carry a family into the semi-barbarous West."

While South Carolinians, the most avid disunionists, usually considered slaveholder expansion into raw land the semibarbarous road toward extinction, New Orleans businessmen, the most important proponents of Caribbean expansion, also cared little about acquiring new agricultural land. These avid imperialists instead longed for new urban markets. New York City and other northeastern urban centers were routing New Orleans in the competition for midwestern trade. In response, New Orleans merchants dreamed of commanding South American trade from U.S. ports in the Caribbean. It was not planters but the South's most expansive merchants who feared they might perish unless the North American republic spread over South America.

New Orleans merchants, as capitalist as any Northerner, and South Carolina planters, more anticapitalist than any other Americans, clashed not only over whether capitalistic hustle was salutary but also over the most effective means of Southern survival. Most South Carolinians favored disunion as a way to escape the materialistic North. Most New Orleans capitalists favored the Union as a means to acquire a materialistic empire. If we exert enough pressure on Northern Democrats, New Orleans newspapers editorialized, the party will use the Union's power to acquire first Cuba's harbors and then other lucrative Caribbean ports. If we fail to leave the Democratic party and the Union, responded many South Carolinians, we will be left hopelessly behind in a riotously expansive nation.

That climactic Southern intramural war undercuts an important latter-day explanation for slaveholder expansionism. The Southern slave labor system, runs some historians' argument, generated less efficient laborers and less entrepreneurial owners than the Northern free labor system; and hence, without constant expansion to fresh lands, Southerners supposedly feared that their allegedly anachronistic system would perish. Evidence for that interpretation derives from the Texas annexation struggle in the 1840s, when the cotton South was staggering economically. But during the climactic struggle over Caribbean expansion in the 1850s, when cotton growers were booming, up-to-date New Orleans capitalists became the avid Southern territorial expansionists, South Carolina's not-very-capitalist planters generally

became anti-expansionists, and southwestern slaveholders, whatever they thought of Cuba, were seeking more slaves so they could pile up higher profits than Northern employers of free laborers could muster.

With the economic aspect of agrarians' expand-or-perish conception now vanished, and with economic expand-or-perish imperatives now impelling only the nonagrarian merchants, the political taproot of Southern agriculturalists' expansion became preeminent. Throughout the eras when Southerners sought more land, then more safety valves, and then more markets and more slaves, defensive defiance was these slaveholders' political style. Slaveholders' aggressive

> An "Africanized" island commanding the Gulf, ninety miles from Florida, could not be tolerated.

defensiveness usually took the form of drives for more congressional seats and especially for more secure borderlands, lest Northerners overwhelm slaveholders from without and corrode hinterlands from within. The old concern about slaveholders' vulnerable outposts, however, shifted in the 1850s from lower South to border South latitudes. True, near the Mexican border, lower South expansionists continued to complain about Mexican seduction of fugitive slaves. That argument helped impel abortive efforts to acquire Mexico in the 1850s. Near the Gulf of Mexico, other lower South expansionists focused on Cuba. They claimed that English abolitionists wished to emancipate (or, as the word went, "Africanize") Cuba, just as Englishmen had wished to emancipate Texas. An "Africanized" island commanding the Gulf, ninety miles from Florida, could not be tolerated. But Southerners farther from the Gulf considered English-inspired "Africanization" less creditable than in Texas times.

With a lower South reaching from the Atlantic to the Pacific now acquired, the greater border menace seemed to be northward, where more Northerners seemed to be helping slaves escape from the border South. This shift in the direction of greatest Southern concern created a revealing phenomenon: Southern congressmen cared less about California and Cuba, on the one hand, than about the Fugitive Slave Law and Kansas, on the other. During the crisis of 1850, Southerners demanded the opportunity to make California a slave state; and especially in southern California, cotton plantations would have enjoyed fabulous yields. But Southerners in Congress surrendered California to the North in exchange for a new Fugitive Slave Law. That edict was especially designed to protect the border South, where less plantation slavery was possible. Four years later, Southern drives to acquire Cuba and to open up Kansas to slavery came to a climax at practically the same moment. Cuba, already a slave island and more tropical than the most tropical lower South, possessed even more fertile land for slaveholders than did California. In contrast, Kansas, difficult to win for slavery and located northward in the border South temperate zone, could never sustain cotton and offered less potential for other plantation crops as well. Yet in 1854, Southern congressmen fought harder for the Kansas-Nebraska Act than for Cuba. Subsequently, Southern congressmen more insistently demanded that the Union admit Kansas than that the nation acquire Cuba.

These Southern priorities exasperated William Marcy, a New York Democrat and Franklin Pierce's secretary of state. The South's demand for Kansas, wrote Marcy, "has sadly shattered our party in all the free states," depriving "it of that strength which . . . could have been more profitably used for the acquisition of Cuba." Marcy's irony could as easily have been applied to 1850, when the South's insistence on a dubiously enforceable Fugitive Slave Law ruptured Southern sympathy in the North and deflected Southern energies from southern California, which was so highly adaptable to slaveholding.

Such priorities were less bizarre than Marcy thought. A now land-rich South understandably put lower priority on the acquisition of California and Cuba, both lush but neither located on a slaveholder's porous border. The higher priority involved consolidation of the vulnerable border South. Inside that embattled middle ground between the free labor North and the heavily slaveholding South, many inhabitants often hoped that their relatively few slaves would drain southward. Meanwhile, some Northern neighbors hoped to entice border

> ## Cuba . . . possessed even more fertile land for slaveholders than did California.

fugitive slaves northward. The border slave state of Missouri, already surrounded on two sides by free labor Illinois and Iowa, could not save slavery, so Missouri slaveholders said, if a free labor Kansas menaced it from a third border. With this critical argument for the Kansas-Nebraska Act, Missourians reemphasized one constant in the changing story of Southern expansionism. Whether in Louisiana in 1803 or Florida in 1819 or Texas in 1844 or Kansas in 1854, Southerners feared slaves would flee from borderlands unless land could be seized from enemies over the border.

But if the entire South put its highest priority on controlling the Kansas borderlands, southwestern congressmen continued to support the lesser priority of Cuba. As U.S. Senator Albert Gallatin Brown of Mississippi put it, "I want Cuba, and I know that sooner or later we must have it, . . . for the plant-

ing or spreading of slavery" and to expand slaveholders' congressional power. Presidents Franklin Pierce (1853–1857) and James Buchanan (1857–1861), both Northern Democrats, tried to meet this demand by buying Cuba from Spain. When Spain would not sell, Pierce's ministers to Spain, England, and France issued the famous Ostend Manifesto (1854), warning that if Spanish possession of Cuba endangered America, "by every law, human and divine, we shall be justified in wresting it."

Spain would not be bullied, whereupon Caribbean expansionists embraced so-called filibustering. Antebellum Americans used that term (linguistically derived from *freebooter*) to connote private armies that hoped to sail from a U.S. port, land in a Caribbean nation, lead an allegedly popular revolution, and annex the supposedly liberated nation to the United States. Such private invasions, which arguably culminated in John F. Kennedy's Bay of Pigs fiasco in Cuba in the 1960s, bore a resemblance to Andrew Jackson's incursion into Florida in 1818. A disproportionate percentage of 1850s filibusterers came from Jackson's Tennessee frontier. The most successful filibusterer, Tennessee's William Walker, briefly captured Nicaragua in the mid-1850s. The Jackson-Walker raiding spirit found its perfect financial complement in the New Orleans mercantile community's worried imperialism.

The combination of New Orleans cash and Tennessee adventurism might have been lethal to Caribbean nations—if the U.S. government had failed to enforce the Neutrality Law of 1818, which forbade U.S. citizens from invading foreign nations. But Northerners would have condemned any president who allowed lawless Southerners to capture a slaveholder's empire (and hence gain more congressional votes). Northern Democrats always preferred to appease the South a good deal while standing firm against Southern demands a little, thus keeping the party electable in the North and overwhelming in the South. In pursuit of that politic goal, Northern presidents sought legal purchase of Cuba while imprisoning illegal filibusterers. Only a relentlessly unified South might have budged Presidents Pierce and Buchanan from that seemingly balanced statecraft.

Southerners could not muster unanimous support for illicit private raids on Caribbean nations any more than they could for reopening the African slave trade or for Jackson's 1818 strike on Florida. Just as John C. Calhoun had considered Jackson an enemy of hierarchy and order, so most South Carolinians usually considered the filibusterers to be disorderly pirates who were seeking to seize disorderly nations. Just as Henry Clay had feared that Jackson's raid (and, later, Texas annexation) would disrupt the Union, so many upper South Democrats declared piracy in Cuba not worth disunion in America. With Southerners fighting Southerners, Northern Democratic presidents could follow Northern constituents' desires. Thus, Federal judges and naval officers blocked critical filibuster expeditions before invasions reached the targeted nations, aborting especially the plot of former Mississippi governor John Quitman to capture Cuba in 1855 and the assault by William Walker on Nicaragua in 1857.

Although Southerners were as badly divided on filibustering as on reopening the African slave trade, they were more united on the issue of Kansas. Yet irresolution plagued even this main Southern expansionist effort of the 1850s. By securing the Kansas-Nebraska Act in 1854, Southerners acquired the right to race Northern settlers to Kansas. Instead of speeding to Kansas, however, most migrants to the Southwest headed for more tropical virgin lands in Texas and Arkansas. With more Northerners peopling Kansas, not even determined Southern congressmen could pressure enough Northern Democrats to admit Kansas as a slave state in defiance of most Kansans' wishes.

Not enough Northerners appeased the South because too many Southerners deserted. In 1858, the House of Representatives rejected Kansas as a slave state by a vote of 120–112. If the six upper South ex-Whigs who voted "no" had voted "yes," the South would have had its sixteenth slave state. Southern opposition, having almost defeated Texas, had blocked the acquisition of Kansas for the South. The only southward expansion to triumph in the 1850s was the Gadsden Purchase (1853) of a strip of lower California—an acquisition aimed at building railroads, not planting cotton.

The frenetic Southern expansion efforts of the 1850s, which upset most Northerners yet acquired not one slave state, contrasted dismally with the sustained expansion efforts of 1793 to 1843, which had distressed few Northerners and had secured a lower South empire. But back in the heady pre-Texas days, all Southerners had cherished expansionist objectives, even if some had winced at Jackson's methods. With Southern unanimity over expansionist goals dissolving and Northern protests rising, Southerners were fortunate that Texas squeaked through; and no luck could thereafter win further expansion of the slavocracy. Even in Kansas, despite the Kansas-Nebraska Act, late antebellum slave society's demands eventually outran its power. Disunited Southerners could not forever successfully defy the more numerous and, in the end, equally resolute Northerners.

Northern Republicans of the 1850s would have dismissed the notion that Southern division hindered Southern expansion. They believed in that decade that everywhere they looked, whether toward Cuba or Nicaragua or Kansas or Mexico, Southerners were seeking to take over the Union and the hemisphere. Moreover, whenever Republicans called slavery too immoral to be allowed to spread, Southerners responded that Republicans must silence their hateful slander.

Republicans were right that *some* Southerners wanted every inch of New World space in the 1850s and that *no*

Southerner could abide Northern insult. By calling slavery too barbarous to spread, Republicans took the expansion issue beyond pragmatic considerations, such as whether Caribbean acquisitions would depopulate South Carolina, to patriotic considerations, especially whether Southerners were respectable people. Republican moral condemnation generated a charged Southern vocabulary: would Southerners "submit" or "resist"? In this white man's egalitarian nation, white males could not "submit" to charges of

> By calling slavery too barbarous to spread, Republicans took the expansion issue beyond pragmatic considerations. . . .

moral inferiority without surrendering their self-respect and honor. Indeed, a failure to "resist" moral condemnation itself had practical consequences in a Southern world still divided on the morality of permanent slavery. If border Southerners submitted to Republican insult, these disbelievers in slavery's permanence would be lost to the slavocracy. Waverers must instead be rallied to resent the Republicans. If clergymen who criticized slaveholders' Christian imperfections saluted Republicans' antislavery morality, no Southerner would listen to them. Internal reformers must instead castigate outside agitators. All factions of Southern opinion thus had a pragmatic stake in condemning Northern critics.

This verbal aggressiveness once again illuminated the most constant aspect of Southern expansionism, whatever the changing economic motives: besieged Southerners' defiance of detractors, whether by rebutting insult or by seeking additional congressional seats or by fortifying vulnerable hinterlands. And curse the Republicans they constantly did. Along with their scorn came expansionist proposals, each more extreme than the last, and all of them, taken together, giving off the illusion of a consolidated civilization, even of a conspiratorially united slavocracy. But if resentment of Republican condescension was almost universal, support of filibusterers or endorsement of reopening of the African slave trade or a move to Kansas was not. So, too, in the secession crisis, while the necessity of resisting Lincoln's antislavery criticism was acknowledged almost universally, the necessity of resisting only outside the Union was not. After antiexpansionist South Carolinians precipitated disunion, proexpansionist Louisianans felt compelled to follow their lower South brethren. But border Southerners felt a countervailing compulsion: to save the Union. Here again, the Southern politics of the 1850s, so often aimed at making border areas more Southern than Northern, had failed.

The resulting Southern disunity would prove to be even more fatal to Confederate armies than it had been to

Caribbean filibusterers, the reopening of the African slave trade, and the securing of Kansas. In war even more than in peace, the infuriated Southerner was an awesome force. But not even the South's fabled courage could ultimately defeat the more numerous Northerners, plus the border South third of Southern white folk, plus the runaway sixth of Southern black folk. And fugitive slaves, by fleeing toward Northerners during the Civil War, proved that prewar Southern expansionists' fears of nearby "aliens" had been all too prescient.

[See also Bleeding Kansas; Compromise of 1850; Democratic Party; Fugitive Slave Law; Imperialism; Kansas-Nebraska Act; Missouri Compromise; Wilmot Proviso.]

BIBLIOGRAPHY

Brown, Charles H. *Agents of Manifest Destiny: The Lives and Times of the Filibusters.* Chapel Hill, N.C., 1980.

Freehling, William W. *Secessionists at Bay, 1776–1854.* Vol. 1 of *The Road to Disunion.* New York, 1990.

Horsman, Reginald. *Race and Manifest Destiny: The Origins of American Racial Anglo-Saxism.* Cambridge, Mass., 1981.

Lander, Ernest M., Jr. *Reluctant Imperialists: Calhoun, the South Carolinians, and the Mexican War.* Baton Rouge, La., 1980.

May, Robert E. *The Southern Dream of a Caribbean Empire, 1854–1861.* Baton Rouge, La., 1973.

Merk, Frederick. *Manifest Destiny and Mission in American History: A Reinterpretation.* New York, 1963.

Potter, David. *The Impending Crisis, 1848–1861.* New York, 1976.

Rauch, Basil. *American Interest in Cuba: 1848–1855.* New York, 1948.

Remini, Robert V. *Andrew Jackson and the Course of American Empire, 1767–1821.* New York, 1977.

Smith, Justin H. *The Annexation of Texas.* New York, 1911.

Takaki, Ronald T. *A Pro-Slavery Crusade: The Agitation to Reopen the African Slave Trade.* New York, 1971.

Urban, C. Stanley. "The Idea of Progress and Southern Imperialism: New Orleans and the Caribbean, 1845–1861." Ph.D. diss., Northwestern University, 1943.

Walker, William. *The War in Nicaragua.* Mobile, Ala., 1860.

WILLIAM W. FREEHLING

EXTORTION

As part of their effort to unite the South around a coherent set of ideals, Confederate cultural and political leaders struggled to identify the particular virtues of the South and to purge themselves of any accompanying vices. Wanting to consider themselves morally superior to the greed they claimed had overwhelmed the economic system of the North, leading Confederates hoped to root out their own greediest practices.

Foremost among those was what Southerners called extortion. As historian Drew Gilpin Faust has pointed out, since the eve of secession, "southerners had been citing the growing materialism of American, and especially northern, society as a fundamental justification for independence." Religious and political speakers drew on the South's heritage of republican ideology to claim that special economic privilege threatened to undermine the region's particular virtues of self-sufficiency, personal independence, and mutual respect among the classes. Southerners defined extortion as using a position of power to make unfair profits. Under this heading fell such practices as creating monopolies on goods, speculating on cotton and food crops, hoarding goods to

> The impressment agents then became the enemies, appearing to work in tandem with corrupt marketers to deprive farmers of a just return on their goods. . . .

raise prices, and setting prices on necessities beyond reasonable limits. To Southerners who believed that their society adhered to values of personal integrity and respect rather than those of a faceless marketplace, these were offenses against public morality and suggested that the South was becoming too much like the North. The practices mocked Southerners' claim to have a country based on religious principles and to understand the basic truths of political economy.

People who manipulated the economy for selfish purposes had long faced criticism in the South, but the opportunities the war presented for both production and marketing intensified economic developments that were well underway. In the 1850s far more Southerners than ever were turning to commercial agriculture, and those with money were investing in a wide range of commercial ventures, especially manufacturing and the railroads. Accusing fellow Southerners of extortion was a way to raise general concerns about the growing importance of a commercial economy, and then to blame the problem on the region's most obvious offenders. Accusations of extortion could thus serve a cathartic function for much of society.

The issue became most heated over food shortages and increases in food prices. Households unable to support themselves were newly dependent on local stores. A main problem with food supplies was impressment by the military. After the Confederate Congress passed the impressment law, farmers lived in fear of getting less than market prices for crops seized by the government. The impressment agents then became the enemies, appearing to work in tandem with corrupt marketers to deprive farmers of a just return on their goods and consumers of a just price. General store owners who hoarded food and raised prices seemed especially offensive in a time of sacrifice. In towns and cities from

Richmond to Mobile, women mounted protests and then riots against the unfairness of high food prices and the unavailability of basic items. As historian Paul Escott has noted, the general popularity of the goals of these riots shows how fully most Southerners had accepted the idea that government and financial interests were working together unfairly.

As the war dragged on and Confederate troops met failure after failure, Southerners looked in many directions for scapegoats. With unseen forces apparently sapping the region's economic fortunes, many Southerners blamed Jewish bankers and immigrant merchants. This tendency continued the long-standing fear held by native-born Protestant Southerners that outsiders came to the South only to cheat them out of their money. Jews offered obvious targets for numerous reasons. Along with their historical stereotype as Shylocks, many did not work in the fields, many owned stores, and they were not part of the Protestant churches that were so important as agents of community life. Congressman Henry S. Foote wildly estimated that Jews made up nine-tenths of the region's merchants and speculated that they would own most of the wealth in the South by the end of the war.

Southerners generally agreed that too many were taking advantage of the war. As a Montgomery, Alabama, newspaper noted, "the whole country is ringing with denunciations of the extortioners." Some claimed that the profiteering followed economic logic and saw no reason to try to stop it, but they were the minority. The difficulty lay in what to do about extortion. The Confederate Senate debated a bill to restrict overpricing and excessive speculation, and seven states passed laws against those practices. A law in South Carolina set a 75 percent limit on the amount of profit resalers could make, and other states passed similar laws. The vagueness of the issue and the fear of stifling production limited such laws to symbolic importance, but that should not minimize their significance. By condemning the various forms of extortion so frequently, Southerners could believe that they were fighting for ideals far higher than money.

[*See also* Bread Riots; Speculation.]

BIBLIOGRAPHY

Escott, Paul D. *Many Excellent People: Power and Privilege in North Carolina, 1850–1900.* Chapel Hill, N.C., 1985.

Faust, Drew G. *The Creation of Confederate Nationalism: Ideology and Identity in the Civil War South.* Baton Rouge, La., 1988.

Silver, James W. *Confederate Morale and Church Propaganda.* New York, 1967.

Thomas, Emory M. *The Confederate Nation: 1861–1865.* New York, 1979.

TED OWNBY

FAMILY LIFE

In Southern culture, kin relationships were central to an individual's self-image and standing in the community. More than any other region, the South placed the family at the center of social life; it was the chief forum for socialization, education, and community.

White Families

Southern white families during the Confederacy lived in an agrarian society with few cities. Many farmed land they did not own, and most had few or no slaves; only a small proportion cultivated large plantations with many slaves. The economic responsibilities on these family farms varied with the wealth of the family, but their structures were similar. Nuclear, extended, or augmented families had male heads and reinforced the patriarchal culture.

Patriarchy defined both the Northern and the Southern family, but the patriarchal nature of Southern society, unlike that in the North, was primarily agrarian. In a farming community, everyone in the household worked at producing food and daily necessities, and the father was in charge. Of course, differences in family structure and functions of family members varied according to economic status. But scholars no longer accept the old mythology of a bifurcated distinction between a white aristocratic family with a strong paternalistic father and a poor white family whose father was more interested in alcohol and fishing than his home. Actually, Southern families, rich and poor, held many values in common. Notions of honor and virtue, of parental priority in the family, of the importance of religion, were shaped and shared by varied groups of white Southerners.

Southern culture held children in high regard; they were a major source of pride and satisfaction for their parents. In wealthy families, childhood was a time to play and to study under a tutor or private schoolteacher. Poorer rural families could not afford the luxuries and concentrated attention that planters gave their children. Nevertheless, they worked together daily, and, with the seasonal rhythms of farm life, rainy days, Sundays, and holidays, the family had some recreational time together. Close bonds developed, and family members demonstrated strong feelings of affection for one another.

Southern society consisted of farms dispersed throughout neighborhoods, which were usually networks of interlocking families. Many white Southerners were born, married, had children, and were buried, all within a family context in an area of ten to twenty miles. Intermarriage within families heightened the significance of kinship bonds. In many instances among rich and poor whites, brothers in one family married sisters in another. This pattern of sibling exchange is often confused with cousin marriage. Wealthy clans formed interlocking relationships through marriage. Family linkages, important factors in political alliances and allegiances, often led to an individual's acquiring a leadership role in the community, the state, or ultimately the Confederacy.

It was men from these kinship networks who rushed off to defend their families and communities when the Confederacy called for troops. The family and kinship nature of neighborhoods initially gave an advantage to the Southern soldiers.

> **Family linkages . . . often led to an individual's acquiring a leadership role. . . .**

Local men formed companies identified by county and neighborhood. Brothers, cousins, and in-laws stood shoulder to shoulder. Some entire companies were made up of relatives, often with a single surname. For example, Company I of the Twentieth South Carolina Volunteers, raised in 1862, had thirty-four men whose surnames were "Gunter," and most of the others were nephews, uncles, and cousins. Fighting with one's family strengthened a man's courage and helped ease the massive dislocation he felt upon leaving home for the first time. Moreover, he felt constrained not to let down his family by deserting or running in the face of danger.

The Civil War, of course, caused great disruption in the Southern family. So many men of military age, sometimes as much as 70 percent of those eighteen to forty-five years of age, were absent from Southern communities. Even some boys as young as thirteen and men as old as sixty left for the battlefront. The family lost moral authority over the boys in the army; moreover, in Southern society, where masculinity was associated with power, children at home sometimes used the opportunity of their father's absence to test their mother's control. Initially many of the men going off to war rushed through whirlwind courtships and quick marriages. With so many casualties and some survivors' deferring marriage, the birthrate declined significantly during the war years.

The Civil War brought separation, economic distress, and death, and family life reflected these changes. Physical closeness and family togetherness no longer maintained a sense of community, so news reports, letters, fleeting visits, and a vague notion of a common purpose had to take their place. The absence of fathers created great stress, which is reflected in correspondence among Southern family members. Wives mediated between fathers and children, writing to their husbands about home life and their offspring. Letters of some elite families indicate strained marriages.

Although divorce was illegal in some Southern states, one study suggests that before the war some wealthier women sought divorce and accused their husbands of abuse, particularly blaming "Demon Rum." During the war armies attracted camp followers, and prostitution flourished at winter camps. And too, nonslaveholding men, many of them serving as soldiers, accused their wives of adultery and sought divorce. Prior to the war, Southern churches traditionally were very involved in the personal lives of members. Church committees monitored the conduct of their members and helped with domestic problems, and some churches formally accused men of physical abuse of their families. These discipline committees became less active as the war continued.

Just as concern for family led to large initial enlistments, concern for the family may have ultimately led to Confederate defeat. As family and kin in a given unit were replaced by men from other areas as the war went on, the neighborhood meaning of the war was diluted. Also, when the wealthy used their family influence to get safer positions such as in home guards, class tensions caused morale problems. More important, Southern fighting men ultimately were compelled to weigh duty to country against love of family. Hunger on the home front forced many to place the welfare of their families above loyalty to the cause. Because the Confederate government failed to provide sufficient relief for the families of soldiers, many men deserted to keep their families from starving. When the government could no longer provide families with subsistence levels of food, Confederate women desperately petitioned officials for food and furloughs for their husbands. Some of these women, moreover, encouraged their menfolk to desert.

Men also felt the need to protect their families from the growing crime on the home front. Crime of all sorts increased as bandits, guerrillas, and soldiers roamed the countryside. Women left alone were particularly vulnerable. Scholars have argued that the heavy desertion rate, particularly in the last year, was one reason the South lost the war. But scholars have not fully explored the war's impact. Children bore a heavy burden of responsibility on family farms, working long

hours beside their mothers and other relatives; poorer white children worked in war industries. Approximately every third white family lost a father, son, or brother, and many children were orphaned. In the face of death, families provided support and love, and nearly every Southern family sheltered disabled veterans.

One of the most important roles of Southern women was their willingness to sacrifice their loved ones to the Confederate cause. But they also found that the exigencies of war enabled them to make a more substantial contribution to family and community life than they had previously had the opportunity to make. Women ran farms, businesses, and their communities with increasing confidence as the war progressed. These changes in their lives, however, were probably short-lived, as after the war they returned to their more limited antebellum roles.

Demographers have cited a "male gap" in the South during and after the war. In 1870 in Georgia, for instance, white women outnumbered men by thirty-six thousand. Thus, some women never married. The mother-child ratios indicate that significantly fewer children were born during the 1860s. The demographic stability of the North after the war is explained by the continuing inflow of immigrants; however, preliminary analysis of the white South reveals that demographic stability quickly returned to that region as well, even without immigration. The Civil War brought to the white families of the South their most traumatic moment, but despite its effects, most of the structures and values of Southern white families survived.

Black Families

If the Civil War was traumatic for Southern white families, who, for the most part, enthusiastically supported the Confederacy, it was even more traumatic for African Americans already vulnerable under slavery. War necessarily entailed anxiety and apprehension. Then, with the defeat of the Confederacy, came freedom, citizenship, and the legal recognition of marriage and family.

Despite debate among historians on the nature of the slave family, strong evidence suggests that monogamous marriage was the norm. Planters' records often list slaves in family units. The demographic vitality of the slave population of the southern United States required a social base—stable families that provided physical, emotional, and cultural support for childbirth and child rearing. And, despite the most difficult circumstances, the slave family in the South was typically a male-dominated nuclear family (father, mother, and children), the prevailing form the world over.

Families provided economic benefits through family gardens and also, to some extent, shielded their members emotionally from the hardships of slavery. Having a spouse to love, to accompany, and to grow old with was important in the difficult circumstances of slavery. Slave children worked alongside parents daily, and on Sundays families traveled to and from church together. Slave children played games and listened to the folktales of parents and extended family members.

Slave owners saw slave families as a means to increase the labor force and also to enhance their control and plantation stability. For example, family ties and responsibilities deterred slaves from running away. Some planters offered incentives for slaves to marry and ritualized slave marriages; others merely allowed them. Nevertheless, slave marriages were acknowledged by the community if not by the law. Divorce also was acknowledged, and children born out of wedlock carried no stigma.

Slave families were inescapably vulnerable to separation at someone else's whim. Although most masters sanctioned slave marriages, some owners separated families, even while proclaiming they did not want to. A master's vacation or extended visit included his personal slaves, who might have preferred to remain at home with their own families. Slaves were rented, willed, given, sold, and purchased according to the needs of owners, and the slaves' desire for family autonomy counted for nothing. While the ideology of paternalism moved some masters to decline profitable sales in order to avoid breaking up slave families, this same ideology led to the sale of some slaves in order to maintain social control through the threat of additional sales in the future.

The Civil War immediately separated families, both black and white, although demographic patterns were not as dramatic for African Americans as for Southern whites. White refugees often took their slaves when they moved, thereby disrupting slave families. Slaves feared the evacuation of plantations as they had estate dispersals. Husbands and wives owned by different masters were particularly apprehensive about relocation during the Civil War.

Just as white soldiers left their homes to join regiments, some slaves had to go with their masters to the front lines to act as valets and cooks. Slaves could not or were not allowed to write, but often sent messages to loved ones with travelers or in the slave owners' letters. Even more slaves were separated from their families when impressed to work on fortifications. The standard of living for most of these African Americans, generally men, was at best minimally adequate. In an occasional military or industrial job, however, slaves could do extra work to earn income for their families at home or to purchase transportation for visits. Sometimes slaves hired out to the government were given leaves of absence to visit families, and employers sometimes linked family visitation to overtime work.

Free blacks had a different role during the Civil War. While early in the war some Southern states permitted free blacks to muster into local or state militia units, none allowed African Americans to serve as regular soldiers. Yet some light-skinned free blacks became "honorary white men" and actu-

ally enlisted and fought for the Confederacy. Families of Confederate free blacks, whether volunteers or impressments, were not eligible for even the meager aid furnished to whites by state and local governments.

Although the war was hard on the African American families whose husbands and sons were forced into Confederate service, the war decidedly benefited the black family by increasing its autonomy. Freedom for slaves did not await the Emancipation Proclamation. Especially in more remote rural areas, as institutional control and close personal supervision of slaves lessened, slave families attained greater personal freedom. While masters were away at war, slaves took advantage of the situation. They expanded their own garden spots and traditional space around their cabins, and black women spent more time with their own families and in their own homes. Parental authority, especially of the father, increased when the white boss was away at the front. In many cases slaves refused to submit to punishment, demanded wages from owners, slipped away to become Union "contraband," or enlisted in the Federal army.

> **White refugees often took their slaves when they moved, thereby disrupting slave families.**

During the last two years of war, church reformers in the South argued that slave marriages must be legalized and not violated by whites. As slaves were liberated by Union forces or escaped to federal lines, many were eager to "legitimize" their marriages and have their children formally baptised and recognized.

The Civil War also altered escape patterns; before the war it was solitary young men who had run away. During the Civil War the number of families who escaped together noticeably increased. As the war and Union troops presented a real opportunity for slaves, more families and kin groups, sometimes even entire plantation communities, attempted to gain their liberty. Family commitment among slaves, however, also worked to deter escape; some slaves opted to remain at home rather than risk losing contact with their family.

The Confederacy may arguably have lost the Civil War because of the commitment of African Americans to family. Union black troops made a significant difference in the manpower of the Union army. Runaway slaves and free African Americans understood that the Union Army offered them an opportunity to rescue family and kin still slaves in the South. The white commander of the black First South Carolina Volunteers explained that his men "had more to fight for than whites. Besides the flag and the Union, they had home and wife and child." According to one Union recruiter, when he asked a group of African Americans at St. Helena Island to enlist "to fight for themselves [and] . . . protect their wives and children from being sold away from them, and told of the little homes which they might secure to themselves and their families in after years, they all rose to their feet, the men came forward and said 'I'll go,' the women shouted, and the old men said 'Amen.' "

African American families suffered a higher percentage of lost loved ones. Black Union soldiers were treated as traitors and not as prisoners of war by Confederates. Confederate soldiers often took no quarter when facing black troops. The gruesome massacre after the surrender at Fort Pillow vividly illustrates the racism and dangers that black soldiers faced. Two-thirds of all black soldiers were killed, some literally crucified and burned.

Defeat for the Confederacy certainly did not mean defeat for all Southerners. States with a majority black population actually won the Civil War. With freedom wrought by the Civil War, former slaves immediately began the search for family members sold and separated during slavery. Slave families demanded valid and legal marriages. Even as many Southern whites began restricting freedom for former slaves, they saw the need to allow black families. One newspaper quoted a typical comment: "Freedom from being sold on the block and separated from his wife and children is all the freedom he ought to have."

African Americans celebrated their newfound freedom by keeping and strengthening their family life. The black family and demographic stability of the African-American community held firm.

[*See also* Marriage and Divorce; Morale; Slavery, *article on* Slave Life.]

BIBLIOGRAPHY

Bleser, Carol, ed. *In Joy and in Sorrow: Women, Family, and Marriage in the Victorian South.* New York, 1991.

Burton, Orville Vernon. *In My Father's House Are Many Mansions: Family and Community in Edgefield, South Carolina.* Chapel Hill, N.C., 1985.

Bynum, Victoria E. *Unruly Women: The Politics of Social and Sexual Control in the Old South.* Chapel Hill, N.C., 1992.

Censer, Jane Turner. *North Carolina Planters and Their Children, 1800–1860.* Baton Rouge, La., 1984.

Escott, Paul D. " 'The Cry of the Sufferers': The Problem of Welfare in the Confederacy." *Civil War History* 23, no. 3 (1977): 228–240.

Gutman, Herbert G. *The Black Family in Slavery and Freedom, 1750–1925.* New York, 1976.

Kenzer, Robert C. *Kinship and Neighborhood in a Southern Community: Orange County, North Carolina, 1849–1881.* Knoxville, Tenn., 1987.

Mohr, Clarence L. *One the Threshold of Freedom: Masters and Slaves in Civil War Georgia.* Athens, Ga., 1986.

Rable, George C. *Civil Wars: Women and the Crisis of Southern Nationalism.* Urbana, Ill., 1989.

ORVILLE VERNON BURTON

FARMING

On the eve of the Civil War, farming in the South had assumed a patchwork quality. There were, of course, thousands of large plantations employing mainly slave labor in the river bottoms of the Old Southwest and on the South Atlantic coast. But tens of thousands more small farmers, mostly white, cultivated the uplands, some of whom farmed for a subsistence and a surplus of cotton, corn, tobacco, or hogs, while still others were content to avoid markets altogether. Within these crop cultures, there labored many others, not properly called farmers, but without whom crops could not be planted or harvested. Most conspicuously, women labored in the home to raise children, make cloth, prepare food, and produce commodities for local trade in their truck gardens, milking barns, and chicken pens.

These various kinds of farming arose not from personal preference but from a conflict over the shape of Southern agriculture that had begun in the 1830s and would end only with the Populist revolt in the 1890s. As plank roads, river improvements, and later railroads connected the Southern interior to northeastern and midwestern markets, large farmers seized the opportunity to make ever greater profits. In some but not all parts of the South, they used the power of state and local government to require others to fence their animals in place of enclosing crops and to hunt game and range hogs only in designated places, thus limiting access to what had been common lands. Developers also required by means of cash taxes that small farmers help build and pay for an infrastructure of roads, cotton weighing platforms, and other public buildings that made commercial farming profitable. In the early 1840s, these development measures had begun to place commercial growers and subsistence farmers in conflicting positions.

By 1860, then, three kinds of farmers labored on the land in the Old South—large planters who produced a staple crop, mostly cotton, with slave labor for sale in distant markets; large commercial farmers who employed tenants and day laborers to produce livestock, corn, and wheat, also for distant markets; and smaller farmers and the women and children in their households who produced a subsistence for themselves and sometimes a surplus, usually for sale or for barter in the neighborhood. This tripartite social formation also produced two distinct classes of dependents, slaves on the one hand and poor white tenants and laborers on the other. When the war began, secessionists supposed that the South's farmers would rise as one to defend the new nation, but that was not the case. The war, in fact, exacerbated differences among farmers as well as disrupting the production of agricultural products.

Farmers in the Confederacy first felt the impact of the war during the financial crisis of late 1860 and early 1861. As secession became nearly a certainty, creditors began to call in their debts due from Southern commercial farmers, both large and small, and after secession credit disappeared entirely. At the same time, trade in farm commodities ground to a halt as banks began to hoard specie after the Union blockade of the Southern coast took hold. Cotton and wheat lay on docks and in barns, and a new Confederate war tax on property forced farmers to either borrow scarce money or sell crops at ruinously low prices. Those farmers who had most thoroughly committed themselves to supplying markets outside the South took the first blow in the conflict.

Smaller semisubsistence farmers did not begin to feel the pinch until the fall of 1861. By that time, the first wave of volunteers had served in summer campaigns after having taken care to plant their crops the previous spring. In the fall, however, as the fighting continued, soldiers could not return home to help harvest those crops. The task fell to women and children who found themselves both shorthanded and without animals to haul crops from the fields to barns or to markets; the Confederate army had purchased or impressed thousands of horses, mules, and oxen in the summer of 1861. Moreover, it became nearly impossible to preserve pork in December because the price of salt had skyrocketed—by a factor of twelve in Savannah between May and October 1861. Before the war, salt had been imported mainly as ballast in ships that would carry away cotton, ships that in 1861 remained blockaded in Southern ports. The result was a subsistence crisis on many Southern farms during the first winter of the war. Between November 1861 and March 1862, six Confederate states approved legislation for the relief of indigent families left behind by men serving in either state militias or the Confederate army.

In April 1862, the Confederate government's Conscription Act began a massive and forced removal of labor from the countryside at the worst possible moment. But the act did not effect everyone equally. On small farms, young men between the ages of eighteen and thirty-five, both heads of households and agricultural laborers, were unable to plant spring wheat and corn, thereby leaving their families at the mercy of local markets in foodstuffs. At the same time, large planters, being exempt themselves from the draft, instructed their slaves to plant corn and wheat and beans instead of cotton, thus ensuring not only a subsistence for slaves but also a large marketable crop in foodstuffs that would command premium prices among the poor during the next fall and winter. Moreover, a severe drought that summer parched the crops and reduced yields for all farmers, and the Confederate army itself consumed a large portion of the South's foodstuffs and cloth. It also commandeered much of the best pasture land in the Shenandoah Valley and the Tennessee River basin to graze horses used by the cavalry and the quartermaster corps. Finally, the war itself disrupted planting in many parts of the Confederacy, especially on the South Atlantic coast where Union raiders regularly penetrated one hundred miles or more inland, and in parts of middle Tennessee, the Mississippi delta, and southern Louisiana occupied by Union armies.

By the fall of 1862, the price of corn, produced now mainly on large plantations, had risen to $2.50 per bushel, well beyond the purchasing ability of ordinary farm families. Confederate soldiers received only about eleven dollars per month, and part of that paid the soldiers' own expenses: a uniform, shoes, and tobacco. Not surprisingly, many of those soldiers deserted and returned home to harvest what little had been planted the previous spring. As one farmer in Mississippi wrote in December 1862, "We are poor men and are willing to defend our country but our families first and then our country." The crops had failed, however, and many were forced to purchase corn at inflated prices. In a Mississippi county, for example, one local notable wrote that six hundred families there had a father or son in the army and could not afford to eat. "The Bread is here," he argued, "but owing to the High price is beyond the reach of these poor people."

Many blamed speculators for the scarcity and high price of foodstuffs, but small farmers themselves had contributed to the inflated prices, especially of corn. Confederate taxes, unlike most local taxes, had to be paid in cash, and therefore many converted their corn, rye, wheat, and barley into liquor, which, being easily transportable and in great demand as

> As one farmer in Mississippi wrote . . . "We are poor men and are willing to defend our country but our families first and then our country."

usual, could be sold in distant cities and to Confederate soldiers for specie. Yet the Confederate government remained the real culprit in these difficulties. Its conscription laws had confiscated the labor supply on small farms and its new taxes had the effect of converting foodstuffs into a marketable luxury.

As a result, many small farmers began to organize actively against not only military service but also the Confederacy itself; both had undercut the independent economy that they had gone to war to preserve in the first place. Farmers in the mountains barricaded themselves in hollows; others in Piedmont North Carolina closed the borders of several counties against Confederate recruiting agents; and many in Tennessee, Arkansas, and northern Alabama organized themselves into guerrilla bands. Moreover, many Southern communities included disaffected yeoman families who hid male relatives by day and fed and comforted them by night.

But that strategy only preserved the men; it did not make their labor available to their families.

In 1863, inflation destroyed any hope the Confederate government might have had of mobilizing smaller farmers in its favor. The continued absence of labor on small Southern farms meant that little had been planted in the spring of 1863, and less harvested the following fall. Farmers in Virginia harvested only about one-third of their normal crop. In addition, the spring wheat in Georgia and Alabama suffered from rust and the corn from a severe drought. The price of corn rose that summer from three dollars to ten dollars per bushel. Moreover, the supply of cloth dwindled in the countryside. Southern textile mills diverted all their efforts to the production of uniforms, blankets, and tents for the army, leaving little or nothing for a population that was still wearing clothing manufactured three years earlier. Farmers' wives found it impossible to make their own cloth, mainly as a result of a shortage of cards with which to straighten cotton and wool fibers. For small farmers and their families food and clothing had become not just pricey, but impossible to obtain or even to produce at home.

In the spring of 1863, poor women in the South took the matter directly to the authorities. In a dozen or more places in the Confederacy, women rioted for fair prices that would enable poor men and women to acquire the common necessities of everyday living. In Salisbury, North Carolina, women working in government textile mills invaded stores and offered what they called "government prices" for flour, bacon, and molasses; these were prices that had been set by a local board under the terms of the Impressment Act and had lagged behind inflation. When their demands were refused, the women simply seized the items they needed. In Richmond, more than a thousand women met at the capitol building and then looted downtown stores of food and clothing. Poor men and women in the countryside did much the same when they threatened "to organize and commence operations" if food and clothing did not soon become available. As one farmer in Bladen County, North Carolina, put it: "Some of us has been traveling for the last month with the money in our pockets to buy corn & tryd men that had plenty & has bin unable to buy a bushel." Planters were "holding on for a better price . . . so as to take all the soldiers wages for a fiew bushels," and that was not fair. "The time has come," he concluded, "that we the comon people has to hav bread or blood & we are bound boath men & women to hav it or die in the attempt."

But the worst was yet to come. In 1864, inflation placed all commodities of any kind out of the reach of ordinary farmers. In February of that year, flour sold in Richmond for $250 per barrel, corn for $30 per bushel, and bacon for $6.50 per pound. Moreover, the Confederate government began to impress at a government price much below market prices all goods of any use to the army. Farmers located near railroads typically lost all their grain and livestock, and large portions of eastern North Carolina were commandeered as pasture for the Army of Northern Virginia's cavalry because pastures in the Shenandoah Valley were now both worn out and vulnerable to Union attack. The final blow came with Union advances into southern Virginia, the Mississippi delta, Tennessee, and northern Alabama, and with William Tecumseh Sherman's march through Georgia and the Carolinas. The devastation of farms in the Confederacy was complete.

In the end, the war to preserve the Southern countryside had transformed it. It had bankrupted commercial farmers and destroyed their capital for a generation. It had turned many poor white farmers against both the Confederate government and neighboring planters. And it had freed the slaves who, after the war, would compete with white farmers for scarce land and credit and later flood the Southern market for agricultural labor, thereby driving down wages. But the war had also created new possibilities. Southern farm men and women who had protested the imposition of unjust prices during the war would do so again in the Southern Alliance and the Populist party. And Southern commercial farmers who had struggled against the deadweight of slavery before 1860 would seize the opportunity to produce a New South rooted in highly commercialized investment agriculture.

[*See also* Bread Riots; Class Conflict; Conscription; Cotton; Desertion; Food; Impressment; Inflation; Plain Folk; Rice; Slavery; Substitutes; Sugar; Taxation; Tobacco.]

BIBLIOGRAPHY

Ash, Stephen A. *Middle Tennessee Society Transformed, 1860–1870: War and Peace in the Upper South.* Baton Rouge, La., 1988.

Auman, William Thomas. "Neighbor against Neighbor: The Inner Civil War in the Central Counties of Confederate North Carolina." Ph.D. diss., University of North Carolina, 1988.

Hahn, Steven. *The Roots of Southern Populism: Yeoman Farmers and the Transformation of the Georgia Upcountry, 1850–1890.* New York, 1983.

Ramsdell, Charles W. *Behind the Lines in the Southern Confederacy.* Baton Rouge, La., 1944.

Simkins, Francis Butler, and James Welch Patton. *The Women of the Confederacy.* Richmond, Va., 1936.

WAYNE K. DURRILL

FAST DAYS

Jefferson Davis proclaimed nine days of fasting between June 1861 and March 1865. Along with national fasting days, the governors and legislatures of several states proclaimed occasional days of either thanksgiving or humiliation. Most stores closed, and, when possible, military companies suspended drills. With roots deep in American religious history, fast days have long sounded a call for sacrifice and unity in the name of a high religious goal. Denying themselves food to show religious and political unity may well have held a special meaning for people being asked to sacrifice food for the war effort. Fast days were also times for collecting money for the cause: the call for self-denial served as a call for contributions.

Official days of fasting were part of the effort by Confederate leaders to create the national unity necessary to fight a long and difficult war. Fast-day preachers and secular speakers proclaimed that Southerners were fighting a holy war that pitted a people of high moral standards against a people driven by greed and consumed by immorality. Linking the religious mission of the Confederacy to the stories of the Old Testament, they claimed to represent a new chosen people. One church periodical asserted that military success at Manassas, Chancellorsville, and Chickamauga had followed specific days of fasting.

Preachers used the occasion to castigate Southerners for a host of sins that seemed to stand in the way of the military effort and of the purity of their cause. Drunkenness and adultery seemed especially tempting to men away from their homes, dishonest financial dealings seemed too available with the economic disruption of the war years, the possibility of corruption among political officials seemed more likely with the new powers the government was assuming, and the abuse of slaves seemed more of a problem with opportunities for escape increasing.

On days of fasting, Southerners were urged to examine whether they were living up to the highest of their ideals and to consider the consequences of failure. As Georgian Charles Colcock Jones, Jr., wrote from an army camp, "the nation must be brought to feel their sins and their dependence upon God, not only for their blessings but for their actual salvation from the many and huge dangers which surround us."

It is not easy to determine how fully white Southerners answered the calls for fasting and humiliation. Discussions of the fasts appear often in the letters and diaries of the wealthy, but they are much harder to find in the documents left by the ordinary folk. For example, the diaries of South Carolina farmer David Golightly Harris mentioned the first of the Confederacy's nine fast days, but not the other eight. The call for public fasting ran up against two important Southern traditions. One was a religious tradition that stressed individual conversion rather than group rituals. The second was a political tradition that stressed personal independence rather than obedience to central authority. Despite their less than complete acceptance, however, the fast days were important examples of calls for self-examination and sacrifice.

BIBLIOGRAPHY

Chesebrough, David B., ed. *"God Ordained This War": Sermons on the Sectional Crisis.* Columbia, S.C., 1991.
Daniel, W. Harrison. "Protestantism and Patriotism in the Confederacy." *Mississippi Quarterly* 24 (1971): 117–134.
Faust, Drew G. *The Creation of Confederate Nationalism: Ideology and Identity in the Civil War South.* Baton Rouge, La., 1988.
Myers, Robert Manson, ed. *The Children of Pride: A True Story of Georgia and the Civil War.* New Haven, 1972.
Racine, Philip N., ed. *Piedmont Farmer: The Journals of David Golightly Harris, 1855–1870.* Knoxville, Tenn., 1990.
Silver, James W. *Confederate Morale and Church Propaganda.* New York, 1967.

TED OWNBY

FILE CLOSERS

The main assault formation used by Civil War soldiers, North and South, was well over two hundred years old when the war began. Based on a system invented by Gustavus Adolphus in the mid-1600s, Civil War assault formations were generally linear to take advantage of the firepower of the musket. Soldiers, facing their enemy, lined up shoulder to shoulder in lines that were two deep, one directly behind the other. These lines, separated by thirteen inches, were called ranks. A file was the formation that resulted from positioning one soldier behind the other. Officers and noncommissioned officers—for instance, the commanding officer and first sergeant or sergeant major—took their places as prescribed by regulations.

The tactical manuals of the day stated: "The remaining officers and sergeants will be posted as file closers, and two paces behind the rear rank." The file closers were to ensure that the formation stayed in strict alignment as it advanced. When casualties occurred, as they inevitably did in Civil War assaults, and men dropped out of formation, the file closers ordered men in their vicinity to move to the right or left to fill the hole the casualty created.

As the Civil War came to its bloody close and discipline broke down in the Confederate armies, file closers were given another, far more deadly, assignment. On February 22, 1865, Gen. Robert E. Lee issued General Order Number 4, directing that file closers on the march were to prevent straggling and that in action they were always to have "loaded guns and fixed bayonets." They were to maintain discipline and

use such degree of force as may be necessary. If any refuse to advance, disobey orders, or leave the ranks to plunder or to retreat, the file-closer will promptly cut down or fire upon the delinquents.

Lee's harsh order giving peremptory execution authority to file closers was generally ignored. In an army where comradeship was more important than military discipline, for one Confederate soldier to shoot or bayonet another was more than even General Lee could ask for from his men.

BIBLIOGRAPHY

Hardee, William J. *Rifle and Light Infantry Tactics.* Philadelphia, 1855.

Mahon, John K. "Civil War Infantry Assault Tactics." In *Military Analysis of the Civil War.* Millwood, N.Y., 1977.

Scott, H. L. *Military Dictionary.* New York, 1864.

U.S. War Department. *War of Rebellion: Official Records of the Union and Confederate Armies.* Washington, D.C., 1880–1901. Ser. 1, vol. 46, pt. 2, pp. 1249–1250.

P. NEAL MEIER

FILM AND VIDEO

Documentary Film and Video

At most only several minutes long, the first motion pictures depended heavily on instantly recognizable and popular subjects such as the Civil War to attract audiences. Newsreels of current events—the earliest form of documentary—were especially suitable. The activities of the Grand Army of the Republic and other Northern veterans' groups dominated most of the first productions, but the South, too, provided material for scores of brief silent documentary films. Universal Film's Animated Weekly, International News, Mutual Weekly, Reel Life, Screen Telegram, and the Selig-Tribune recorded Confederate veterans' reunions at Macon (1912), Arlington National Cemetery (1913), Gettysburg (1913), Atlanta (1914), Richmond (1915), Birmingham (1916), Washington, D.C. (1917), Corinth (1926), Tampa (1927), Little Rock (1928), and Charlotte (1929). A 1925 Pathe Weekly news short of a Dallas reunion even featured eighty-two-year-old veteran A. B. Willy introducing his new bride to his former compatriots.

Besides showing the usual parades and encampments, these early films occasionally included interviews with former Confederate soldiers, with the spoken words printed on cards. The productions also included insights into the sometimes unreconstructed Southern mind-set. A 1914 Animated Weekly news film depicted a delegation of United Confederate Veterans preparing to urge Congress to add the Cross of Saint Andrew to the U.S. flag. More remarkable, the Gaumont Weekly series filmed reunions of former slaves and their former masters in Birmingham (1913) and Washington, D.C. (1916).

There were far more instances, however, of sectional reconciliation. A 1909 Columbia Photograph Company newsreel featured President William Howard Taft meeting with assembled Confederate and Union veterans in Petersburg, Virginia. Several films (1914, 1917, 1923) recorded Woodrow Wilson reviewing veterans' parades or greeting members of the United Daughters of the Confederacy. Perhaps most moving to audiences both North and South were the documented returns of captured battle flags to Confederate or Union groups or representatives.

Many of the silent shorts, especially those marking the war's fiftieth anniversary, emphasized how quickly the past was fading. A 1911 Powers Studio film featured veterans' distant reminiscences; in 1912 the Edison company depicted disabled veterans at Hampton, Virginia; the Lubin company in 1913 presented elderly former Confederate and Union soldiers reunited at Gettysburg. Still later, in 1923, several newsreel companies recorded the U.S. Marines' reenactment of Pickett's Charge, watched by veterans too infirm to do more than feebly stand aside and cheer. An Urban-Kineto production, *Romantic Richmond* (1924), presented a city filled with both wartime memories and old soldiers.

The various film companies also captured the increasingly strong Southern urge to memorialize the Lost Cause. A 1918 Universal Animated Weekly newsreel recorded Virginia governor Henry Carter Stuart gratefully accepting the sword of the late Camille J. Polignac, a French nobleman and esteemed Confederate major general. Monument dedications in cities large and small were frequent subjects, but none more so than the Confederate Memorial at Stone Mountain, Georgia. International News featured sculptor Gutzon Borglum three times in 1924, his angry destruction of the models the next year, the appointment of a successor, Augustus Lukeman, in 1926, and scenes of the dedication (with a separate version distributed only in Atlanta) in 1928.

But while those productions recorded current news events, several film companies, government agencies, and corporations also began experimenting with retrospective views. The Mutual Film Corporation, for example, in 1916 included tours of Chattanooga, Chickamauga, Gettysburg, Montgomery, Vicksburg, and the Richmond defenses in its *See America First* series. A ten-minute 1921 Ford Motor Company documentary was among the first to explore Civil War personalities and causes. And in another innovation, the U.S. Army Signal Corps produced several training films utilizing Confederate and Union troop movements, including *Concentrations for the Battle of Gettysburg* (1924).

With the advent of sound recording in the late 1920s, film's dramatic possibilities increased. The Signal Corps, for instance, recorded Marshall Foch's 1936 visit to Richmond where he reviewed Civil War veterans. A year later, the Virginia Conservation Commission financed *Richmond under Three Flags,* which featured the Confederate Memorial

Institute's Battle Abbey shrine. The Smithsonian Institution in 1934 filmed archaeological excavations at the Shiloh National Monument in Tennessee, and the National Park Service funded *Heart of the Confederacy* (1937) and *They Met at Gettysburg* (1938), the latter featuring Confederate veteran William H. Jackson's tour of the battlefield. Southern military history furnished especially useful lessons during World War II. The U.S. Army's 1941 animated eight-minute training film, *The Battle of Chancellorsville,* presented basic strategic and tactical concepts to inductees.

Controlling production, distribution, and theaters, too, the major Hollywood studios during the 1930s produced the most documentaries—mostly as brief fillers to accompany their major releases. More travelogue than documentary, Warner Brothers' *The Blue and the Gray* and *Dixieland* (both 1935) presented tours of Southern monuments. The studio's Vitaphone subsidiary in 1937 presented *Under Southern Stars,* an account of Lee and Jackson at Chancellorsville. Sometimes feature films were severely recut as documentaries. MGM's *Tennessee Johnson,* released in 1942, provided enough footage five years later for two educational films: *Jefferson Davis Declares Secession* and *Johnson and Reconstruction.* Newsreels also remained popular, in the 1930s and 1940s featuring centenarian Confederate veterans, reunions in Biloxi (1930) and Chattanooga (1942), the famed 1938 Gettysburg reenactment, and a remarkable 1942 Movietone News short of aged veterans beside army trainees at Fort Oglethorpe, Georgia.

By the 1950s changes in audience demographics and the Federal government's antitrust actions dismantling the studios' long-time monopoly of all phases of film production and presentation caused a decline in commercial documentary filmmaking. Besides, there were few veterans left alive to film. The government, however, continued production: the U.S. Navy in 1958 and 1959 produced studies of the maritime war; the army in 1957 completed a brief film on Civil War photography; and the Defense Department in 1956 sponsored four thirty-minute films on the struggle to end slavery. Corporations such as E. I. du Pont Nemours, McGraw-Hill, and Nationwide Insurance also funded several films.

The rapid growth of television, especially network news divisions, fostered scores of dramatized documentaries. The CBS News *You Are There* series narrated by Walter Cronkite included programs on the Emancipation Proclamation (1955), death of Stonewall Jackson (1955), capture of John Wilkes Booth (1956), the Appomattox surrender (1956), and the attack on Fort Sumter (1957). The NBC network countered with *Gentleman's Decision* (1961), a dramatization of Lee's surrender. A St. Louis television station in 1955 produced *The War between the States* and *The War's Aftermath* for its *Young USA* program.

Animated maps and period photography dominated documentary and educational films in the post-1945 years.

Productions such as MGM's *The Battle of Gettysburg* (1959) emphasized military maneuver, a tendency particularly evident in the site-specific films produced during and after the Civil War Centennial for battlefield parks, historic sites, and museums. Coronet Instructional Films, the Encyclopaedia Britannica, and Film Associates of California were among the few educational film producers that attempted any analysis of Confederate economic, geographic, social, and political conditions. In the 1970s television, too, retreated from Civil War topics; producer David Wolper's re-creation of the trial of Henry Wirz, commander of Andersonville prison, was among the rare exceptions.

Two recent productions—*The Divided Union* (1987) and *The Civil War* (1990)—in effect have carried documentary explorations of the Confederacy to the extreme in both length and variety of period images. Produced and written by Ken Burns, Ric Burns, and Geoffrey C. Ward for PBS affiliate WETA, of Washington, D.C., the nine-part *Civil War* won more than a dozen awards, including two Emmys and a George Foster Peabody citation. Although less familiar, the five-hour *Divided Union,* created by English producer-director Peter Batty, also balances period photography and artwork, newsreel footage, and excerpts from Civil War letters, diaries, and personal reminiscences in a presentation of both Confederate and Union military history. *The Divided Union* differs, though, in that it also includes considerable footage of reenactments by living-history interpreters, a recently popular and rapidly expanding mode of quasi-documentary film that includes, for example, introductions to Civil War era weaponry, battlefield and site tours, and histories of various engagements. Companies such as Time-Life, which distributes *The Video History of the Civil War,* produce the films primarily for home distribution.

BIBLIOGRAPHY

Fielding, Raymond. *The American Newsreel, 1911–1967.* Norman, Okla., 1972.
Jacobs, Lewis, comp. *The Documentary Tradition.* New York, 1979.
Spehr, Paul C., comp. *The Civil War in Motion Pictures: A Bibliography of Films Produced in the United States since 1897.* Washington, D.C., 1961.

EDWARD D. C. CAMPBELL, JR.

Fictional Presentations

David O. Selznick hesitated to purchase the film rights to Margaret Mitchell's *Gone with the Wind.* Knowing the odds against any Civil War movie earning a profit, particularly after the recent disaster, *So Red the Rose,* Selznick had to be repeatedly prodded into action. The Civil War required a heavy investment in props, costumes, and complex settings, and such movies required deftly handled, inoffensive stories that could play in theaters both North and South.

The same factors had influenced the production of silent films, but the early motion pictures' briefer format helped alleviate several cost factors. More important, because the war remained such a vivid event for most audiences, fictional films in many instances served as exciting retrospectives. Hundreds of these early films featured Southern stories. Produced by studios such as Biograph, Broncho, Champion, Edison, New York Motion Picture, Triangle, and Universal, the films often revolved around themes of sectional reconciliation. In *A Reconstructed Rebel,* for example, a former Confederate fights as a U.S. Marine in Honduras. Thomas H. Ince produced perhaps the most outlandish of the type, *A*

> **Because the war remained such a vivid event for most audiences, fictional films . . . served as exciting retrospectives.**

Southern Cinderella (1913), with the beautiful Southern Cinderella left under the care of her wicked Yankee stepmother. Vitagraph's *The Carpenter; or the Stranger in Gray* (1914) was the most extreme example of the genre: a mysterious Christ-like carpenter brings peace to a family divided by the war.

The Kalem studio's *Southern Boy of '61* (1911) was one of numerous stories in which a Confederate spares a blue-uniformed family member encountered in battle. Many more Civil War plots were, however, more overtly Southern in tone. In D. W. Griffith's *In Old Kentucky* (1909), the protagonist abandons his family rather than listen to Unionist sentiment; in *The Flag of His Country* (1910), a Southern wife deserts her husband after his enlistment in the Federal army. A few were more ambivalent. In Griffith's *The Honor of His Family* (1910), a Confederate officer kills his son for desertion under fire and then to spare the family reputation places the body among his fallen Southern comrades. Other productions harped on the sometimes violent hatreds spawned by the war. In the Selig studio's *Brother against Brother* (1909), rival siblings try to murder one another; in *The Boomerang* (1913), a Union soldier kills his father, a Confederate officer who had deserted him years before; and in *A Rose of the South* (1916), two lifelong friends kill each other in battle, determined to die true to their respective causes. Wartime events and legends furnished several early movie plots; *Barbara Frietchie,* for example, became a staple for several studios, with productions released in 1908, 1911, 1915, and 1924.

Usually presented as loyal slaves and acted by whites in blackface, African American characters were a prominent part of numerous Confederate stories. In both *The Confederate Spy* (1910) and *The Informer* (1912), "happy, contented, and well cared for" blacks defend their masters' homes against Union troops. Uncle Wash, in *Hearts and Flags* (1911), protects his mistress from foragers. The famous minstrel performer Lew Dockstader, playing the title role in *Dan* (1914), rescues his master from Union captors. D. W. Griffith's *His Trust* and *His Trust Fulfilled* (both 1911) tell of the slave Old George, charged with protecting the plantation during the war. After his master's death in battle, it is George who cares for his owner's child—and his sword.

Several directors attempted large-scale productions years before D. W. Griffith's *Birth of a Nation* (1915). Thomas H. Ince, for example, completed an expensive five-reel epic, *The Battle of Gettysburg* (1913), approximately an hour long and complete with special bookings and advance tickets. Released the same year, the Kalem studio's *Shenandoah* included hundreds of extras in Virginia battle scenes. Almost as many reels in length, it was cut at the last moment, as the studio feared no one would sit through so long a picture. Griffith had no such fears. Adapted from clergyman Thomas Dixon's novel and successful play *The Clansman,* Griffith's monumental epic was, in fact, a second attempt at filming the story. The Kinemacolor studio had initiated a color version of Dixon's story shot at authentic Southern locations, but the company eventually ran afoul of financial and technical problems.

Griffith also ran short of money but remained determined that his production be realistic in every detail. Although his interpretation of the war and black-white relations aroused strident protests, his depictions of military life were universally praised. Griffith studied minute details of uniform types, weapons, and fortifications, often arriving on locations with a stack of books under one arm and his pockets overflowing with scribbled notes. In his earlier films such as *The Battle* (1911), Griffith had already experimented with filming swirling scenes of combat; thus for *Birth of a Nation* he was able to stage elaborate scenes of combat so exciting that even Northern audiences found themselves sometimes cheering for the besieged Confederates.

Still studied and debated for its interpretation of the antebellum and postwar South, *Birth of a Nation* also deserves attention for its view of the war itself. Griffith and his technicians attempted to evoke the conflict's massive sweep, variety, and losses on a scale that has never been repeated. Facing financial constraints himself, David Selznick did not even seriously consider adding such large-scale combat scenes to *Gone with the Wind.* Released only a week after *Birth of a Nation,* Cecil B. DeMille's *The Warrens of Virginia* was produced on a smaller scale but was equally biased in its scenes of African American unrest, Confederate dead, and the destroyed Southern landscape. (The film was remade in 1924 with less success.)

Buster Keaton's *The General* (1926), based on James J. Andrews and his Union raiders' attempt to destroy a Confederate rail route, used the war as a comic foil. The Kalem studio had used the same plot for *The Railroad Raiders of '62* (1911); Walt Disney would again in 1956. Filmed in Oregon, Keaton's masterpiece, despite its farcical spirit, included several well-directed battle scenes and a period narrow-gauge railway. Moreover, Bert Haines and Devereaux Jennings provided a cinematography that captured much of the feeling of Mathew Brady's Civil War images. In 1939, an elderly Keaton appeared in yet another Civil War film, *Mooching through Georgia.*

By the advent of sound films in the late 1920s, studios had found the Civil War an increasingly awkward subject. Although movies about the prewar South provided escapist entertainment, productions on the Confederacy itself tended to alienate the predominantly non-Southern moviegoer. One way around the impasse was to rely on spy stories, stories that audiences perceived more as mysteries than as sectional dramas. *Secret Service* (1931), for example, first produced as a silent film in 1915 and again in 1919, depicted a Union infiltrator at work in Richmond; *Operator 13* (1934) starred Marion Davies as a disguised mulatto spy. Also safe were musicals such as *The Littlest Rebel* (1935) starring Shirley Temple and Bill ("Bojangles") Robinson.

Hollywood nevertheless occasionally ventured into more serious plots. The 1928 version of *The Little Shepherd of Kingdom Come* (first adapted from the John Fox, Jr., novel in 1920) starred Richard Barthelmess as a Kentucky-raised lad torn between secession and the Union. Hardly as ambivalent was Paramount's *So Red the Rose* (1935), loosely adapted from a Stark Young novel. Simultaneously premiered in each of the former Confederate capitals and with advertisements to "see the Old South ride again," it was a box-office disaster. The movie's setting was so romanticized and its characters so stereotyped, even within the context of films made in the 1930s, that black actor Daniel Haynes at first refused to work in Hollywood again, and director King Vidor, a Southerner, avoided even mentioning the film in his later autobiography. Small wonder David Selznick was nervous in adapting Margaret Mitchell's *Gone with the Wind.*

GWTW, as it became popularly known, consumed at least seven script writers, including F. Scott Fitzgerald, as well as six directors but opened in Atlanta at last in December 1939. It proved so popular that the South's smaller and fewer movie theaters often had to delay showings so that Selznick and the film's distributor, Metro-Goldwyn-Mayer, could meet the demand of larger audiences elsewhere. Like *Birth of a Nation, GWTW*'s scenes were carefully researched. Griffith served as his own expert; Selznick hired his, including Atlanta historian Wilbur G. Kurtz. And although, like Griffith's film, the Civil War scenes comprised the shortest portion of *GWTW,* the crowded hospitals, the battlefield covered with dead, the panic at the fall of Atlanta, seemed even starker in contrast.

Despite *Gone with the Wind*'s enormous success, few similar films followed, in part because Confederate themes hardly complied with the government's World War II restrictions that films comport with Allied war aims to free suppressed peoples. *Dark Command* and *Virginia City* (both 1940), Civil War westerns, were permissible, in large part because of their more neutral setting. Studios eventually produced scores of such western films, including *Escape from Fort Bravo* (1953), Sam Peckinpah's *Major Dundee* (1965), the Italian-made *The Hills Run Red* (1967), *The Outlaw Josie Wales* (1976), and *The Long Riders* (1980). Similarly, *The Raid* (1954), directed by Argentinian Hugo Fregonese, depicted an attack by Confederate marauders on a small Vermont town. Although set in the South, *Tap Roots* (1948) and *Shenandoah* (1965) were acceptable, as both depicted families opposed to the war; *Band of Angels* (1957) seemed more a vehicle for its star (Clark Gable) than its setting; and *The Horse Soldiers* (1959), directed by John Ford, focused on its Union protagonists.

Television has provided a middle ground, with miniseries that move characters and incidents between the opposing sides. The CBS network touted the eight-hour *The Blue and the Gray* (1982) as an educational production, and ABC advertised its twelve-hour *North and South* Civil War segments (1986) as a "novel for television." Like many of their precursors, both films were elaborate costume romances with ample chances for fictional characters to encounter historical personalities, reconfirming that the genre presents not so much significant historical events interpreted with incidental stories as the reverse—fiction embellished with period detail.

BIBLIOGRAPHY

Campbell, Edward D. C., Jr. *The Celluloid South: Hollywood and the Southern Myth.* Knoxville, Tenn., 1981.

Cassidy, John M. *Civil War Cinema: A Pictorial History of Hollywood and the War between the States.* Missoula, Mont., 1986.

Spears, Jack. *The Civil War on the Screen and Other Essays.* New York, 1977.

Spehr, Paul C., comp. *The Civil War in Motion Pictures: A Bibliography of Films Produced in the United States since 1897.* Washington, D.C., 1961.

EDWARD D. C. CAMPBELL, JR.

FIRE-EATERS

Southern proslavery and state rights extremists were termed the fire-eaters in the two decades before the Civil War. The image evoked by the term was that of swaggering hotheads intent on breaking up the Union in their defense of slavery and Southern rights. The most famous of the fire-eaters were Edmund Ruffin of Virginia, an agricultural reformer; Robert Barnwell Rhett, Sr., of South Carolina, an editor and low-country planter; and William Lowndes Yancey of Alabama, a lawyer and gifted orator.

The fire-eaters were the ideologues of secession. They identified the ownership of slaves as the most fundamental of all Southern rights and insisted that Southern honor and equality could accept no outside interference with the institution of slavery. They pushed traditional state rights doctrines to the logically extreme position that states could peacefully withdraw from the Union.

Too impatient and scornful of compromise to be entrusted with positions of political power, the fire-eaters turned to agitation to spread their message that Southern honor and security demanded separate nationhood. Through speeches, pamphlets, editorials, and committees of correspondence they popularized secession as a constitutional right among the Southern white masses.

Although blocked in their secessionist efforts during the sectional crisis over the Compromise of 1850, the fire-eaters played a key role in the secession movement of 1860 and 1861. They were instrumental in the breakup of the national Democratic party over the issue of Federal protection of slavery in the territories and fully exploited Southern fears over Abraham Lincoln's election. Nevertheless, they were soon shunted aside as more moderate politicians assumed control of the new Confederate government.

BIBLIOGRAPHY

Barney, William L. *The Road to Secession.* New York, 1972.
Craven, Avery. *Edmund Ruffin, Southerner.* New York, 1932.
DuBose, John. *The Life and Times of William Lowndes Yancey.* Birmingham, Ala., 1892.
McCardell, John. *The Idea of a Southern Nation: Southern Nationalists and Southern Nationalism.* New York, 1979.
White, Laura A. *Robert Barnwell Rhett: Father of Secession.* New York, 1931.

WILLIAM L. BARNEY

FLAGS

The Confederate Flag

During its four years of existence, the Confederacy adopted three official flags. The first was adopted on March 14, 1861, by the Provisional Congress then meeting in Mobile, Alabama. Its design, credited to Nichola Marschall of Marion, Alabama, combined a field consisting of three equal horizontal bars (red, white, and red) with a blue canton or union (the top quarter of the flag nearest the staff or halyards) in the upper hoist corner extending through the upper red and center white bars. (The hoist is the part of the flag along the flagstaff and also refers to its height or width; the fly is the distance from the flag staff to the end of the flag and also refers to its length.) The canton bore a circle of white stars equal to the number of states in the Confederacy. When first adopted, seven states were represented. By year's close, as additional states seceded, the number grew to thirteen. This flag came to be nicknamed the "Stars and Bars."

No official proportions were established for this flag, although the first ordered for Congress was proportioned 9 to 14, hoist (width) to fly (length). Lacking specifications, flag makers set their own proportions. The most common among surviving flags are 2 to 3, 3 to 5, 5 to 9, 3 to 4, and 1 to 2 (all hoist to fly). Similar discretion was permitted in the arrangement of stars. Although a circle of stars was the most common arrangement, many flags were made with a central star as well, often larger than those in the ring of the circle. Star patterns other than circular were also tolerated.

Because of its deliberate similarity to the Stars and Stripes, the Stars and Bars was judged inadequate. After an initial, unsuccessful attempt to modify the flag by eliminating the white bar and all but four of the stars, on April 19, 1862, the Flag Committee of the new Congress proposed an alternate design, consisting of a red field traversed by a white St. Andrew's cross having at its center a blue shield bearing a golden sunburst. This proposal, however, died in the House, and nearly a year later (April 22, 1863), the committee proposed another design. This design combined a field of three horizontal bars (white, blue, and white) with a square canton extending two-thirds of the hoist, having as its design the Southern Cross battle flag of the eastern Confederate armies. On May 1, this design was amended by eliminating the central blue bar and was adopted by both houses. This new national flag was soon nicknamed the "Stainless Banner" for its dominating white field.

Although the congressional proposal called for proportions of 1 to 2 (hoist to fly), both the navy and the Quartermaster Department of the army quickly modified the flags made for those services to the more practical proportions of 2 to 3. Variations were also produced by nongovernmental makers. These included variants made in Mobile devoid of the canton's central star and several made in Mississippi without the white border to the St. Andrew's cross of the canton.

In calm weather, however, a limply hanging Stainless Banner was often mistaken for a flag of truce. Accordingly, on March 4, 1865, Congress revised the design by adding a red vertical bar to the fly end of the field equal in width to the white portion next to the canton, and at the same time they proportioned the flag 2 to 3. Although the new flag was also to have its canton reproportioned 3 to 5, nearly all surviving examples are simply modified second national flags and accordingly have square cantons. The last national flag was short-lived, as the surrender of Confederate ground forces in April and May ended the Confederacy.

BIBLIOGRAPHY

Cannon, Devereaux D. *The Flags of the Confederacy: An Illustrated History.* Memphis, Tenn., 1986.
Madaus, Howard Michael. "Rebel Flags Afloat: A Survey of the Surviving Flags of the Confederate States Navy, Revenue Service, and Merchant Marine." *Flag Bulletin* 25, nos. 1–2 (1986): 1–78.
Preble, George Henry. *Origin and History of the American Flag.* Philadelphia, 1917.
Thian, Raphael. *Documentary History of the Flag and Seal of the Confederate States of America, 1861–'65.* Washington, D.C., 1880.

HOWARD MICHAEL MADAUS

Military Flags

The national and state flags of the Confederacy identified political entities, and early in the war many of both types were presented to military units. The inadequacy of these flags for distinguishing battlefield combatants resulted in the development of another class of flags for the use of army units. The evolution of these military battle flags took different directions in each of the main theaters of operation.

East of the Appalachians, the most famous of the battle flags, that of the Army of Northern Virginia, was devised in September 1861. As a result of confusion over flags at First Manassas, the senior officers of the major field armies, Gens. P. G. T. Beauregard and Joseph E. Johnston, modified a design that had been submitted as a national flag by William Porcher Miles of South Carolina. Miles's design consisted of a rectangular red field traversed by a blue St. Andrew's cross edged in white and bearing white stars equal to the number of Confederate states. Beauregard added a border, and Johnston altered the proportions to square.

The initial 120 flags of this design were made from silk, but shades of pinks were used, owing to a shortage of red silk in Richmond. The borders were yellow, and, reflecting Kentucky's neutrality, only twelve stars graced the cross. Subsequent issues of this flag were manufactured from bunting seized at Norfolk or later imported through the blockade. Although interior dimensions and materials could vary, the basic design was uniform in the east throughout the war. The bunting flags were square, with a red field traversed by a dark blue St. Andrew's cross edged with a narrow strip of white. After 1861, thirteen white five-pointed stars decorated

the arms of the cross. Except for two issues made in early 1862 with orange borders, all were bordered in white. Although intended to be made in three sizes (2½, 3, and 4 feet square respectively for cavalry, artillery, and infantry), in practice, the smallest size was quickly discontinued, the cavalry using infantry flags instead. Significantly, the design of this flag was never officially promulgated by the War Department; rather the design was carried to the western theater by Beauregard and Johnston when they were transferred.

When Beauregard arrived in the western theater in early 1862, he found three other battle flag designs had been adopted by units in the Army of the Mississippi Valley (later the Army of Tennessee). Two forces had adopted rectangular blue battle flags while in Kentucky: William J. Hardee's corps a flag bordered in white and bearing a white central disk, and Leonidas Polk's corps a flag traversed by a red St. George's cross, edged in white and bearing eleven to thirteen white stars. Earl Van Dorn's corps (the Army of the West) brought from the Trans-Mississippi theater a flag featuring a rectangular red field bordered in yellow and bearing thirteen scattered white stars and a white crescent in the upper hoist corner. Only Braxton Bragg's corps from the Florida coast had arrived without a distinctive flag. Beauregard furnished this corps with a battle flag that differed from its eastern counterpart only by having twelve six-pointed stars and pink or yellow borders.

The absence of uniformity of battle flags in the western army was partly corrected in 1864. After Johnston took command, he reinstated the design of the eastern battle flag, now rectangular in configuration and without exterior borders. A new army corps added to the Army of Tennessee in May 1864 from the Department of Mississippi and East Louisiana brought battle flags of similar shape and pattern but bearing only twelve stars. Johnston's desire for uniformity, however, was frustrated when Patrick Cleburne's division was permitted to retain its battle flags featuring a blue field bordered in white and bearing a white central disk.

After Van Dorn's departure from the Trans-Mississippi Department, little effort was made to institute battle flags there until 1864. A few conforming to the eastern theater's design were presented to units, but they were usually rectangular, bore neither exterior borders nor edging on the blue cross, and frequently had a central star larger than those on the arms of the cross. A variant of this design, blue with a red cross, served as the battle flag for John G. Walker's Texas Division in 1864. Sterling Price's Missouri Division also received battle flags in 1864 featuring a blue field bordered on three sides in red and bearing a white Latin cross. This design copied a similar pattern that had been made in early 1863 for the Missouri Brigade in Mississippi and which, shortly before Vicksburg's surrender, was modified by Gen. John C. Pemberton by changing the field color to red and the borders to white.

BIBLIOGRAPHY

Crute, Joseph H., Jr. *Emblems of Southern Valor: The Battle Flags of the Confederacy.* Louisville, Ky., 1990.

Madaus, Howard Michael, and Robert D. Needham. *The Battle Flags of the Confederate Army of Tennessee.* Milwaukee, Wis., 1976.

Madaus, Howard Michael, and Robert D. Needham. "Unit Colors of the Trans-Mississippi Confederacy." *Military Collector & Historian* 41, nos. 3–4 (1989): 123–141, 172–182; 42, no. 1 (1990): 16–21.

Todd, Frederick P. "Confederate Colors and Flags." In *American Military Equipage, 1851–1872.* Providence, R.I., 1972.

HOWARD MICHAEL MADAUS

State Flags

The Southern states, in seceding, were claiming to resume their status as independent republics, and accordingly many adopted distinctive national flags. These fell into three broad categories.

Prior to the war, only the state militias had consistently required flags. Most conformed to the flag known between 1796 and 1841 as the "national standard," which consisted of a blue field emblazoned with the coat of arms of the United States. As early as 1839 South Carolina had substituted the palmetto tree for the U.S. symbols on the flags for its militia. After toying with other variations, on January 28, 1861, its legislature adopted a similar blue flag, having a white palmetto in its center and a white crescent in the upper hoist corner.

Shortly after seceding, Virginia followed South Carolina's example, and on April 30, 1861, the Virginia convention adopted a flag consisting of a blue field fringed in white on its fly and bearing the state's coat of arms in its center in full color. Scrolls over and below the figures bore the state's name and its motto *sic semper tyrannis* ("thus always to tyrants").

Although South Carolina and Virginia were the only Southern states to adopt state flags adapted from the old national standard, unofficial flags having blue fields with the state's coat of arms were made and presented to Confederate volunteers from Maryland, North Carolina, Georgia, and Louisiana in 1861. The Confederate-allied Missouri State Guard also adopted a blue field with the Missouri coat of arms in gold in its center the same year.

In those states with minimal militia traditions, the flags tended to follow a different model: the flag of the United States. Although Florida on September 13, 1861, adopted a state flag modeled after the first Confederate national flag, an earlier state flag, selected on January 13, 1861, had combined a field of thirteen red and white horizontal stripes with a blue canton bearing a white five-pointed star. Louisiana followed Florida's earlier example and adopted a state flag on

February 11, 1861, that joined thirteen horizontal stripes alternating blue, white, and red with a red canton bearing a yellow five-pointed star. The single stars on these little-used flags bore a common kinship with another group of Southern state flags: those that emphasized the single five-pointed star as a symbol of independence.

In 1861, a flag consisting of a blue field bearing a white five-pointed star was popularized in the Southern states through the song "The Bonnie Blue Flag." Although historical precedents for this flag existed in the 1810 flag of the Republic of East Florida and the Texan independence flags of 1836 and 1839, there is little evidence of a direct lineage from these earlier flags. Rather, the idea of the design seems to have emanated from the Flag Act of 1818, which stipulated that a star be added to the U.S. flag on the Fourth of July after the admission of a new state to the Union. Conversely the flags with a single star would symbolize the withdrawal of a state from the Union.

Several Confederate states adapted this concept in 1861. Alabama's unofficial flag featured its name in white above a white star set in a blue field. Mississippi, on January 26, 1861, adopted a flag with a field of white bordered and fringed in red and bearing a full-color magnolia tree in its center. The design was completed by the addition of a blue canton containing a white star. Texas, upon seceding in February, unofficially revived its 1839 independence flag, which joined a vertical blue bar bearing a white star to two horizontal bars (white over red). North Carolina's flag, adopted on June 22, 1861, copied many elements of the Texas flag. The Carolina flag also consisted of two horizontal bars (blue over white) joined to a red vertical bar on the hoist. The red bar bore a white five-pointed star surrounded by the dates of the state's Mecklenburg Resolution and of its secession, both in white.

Despite their emphasis on state rights, the Southern states made little effort to promote their flags. Only Virginia and North Carolina provided state flags to their volunteer forces during the conflict. Indeed, three Confederate states, Arkansas, Kentucky, and Tennessee, never adopted flags, though the last made an abortive effort in 1861 to adopt one that simply substituted the state's coat of arms for the stars of the Confederacy's first national flag.

BIBLIOGRAPHY

Cannon, Devereaux D. *The Flags of the Confederacy: An Illustrated History.* Memphis, Tenn., 1986.

Hubbs, G. Ward. "Lone Star Flags and Nameless Rags." *Alabama Review* 39, no. 4 (1986): 271–301.

Smith, Whitney. *The Flag Book of the United States.* New York, 1970.

HOWARD MICHAEL MADAUS

FLORIDA

With votes split in the 1860 election among Southern Democrat John C. Breckinridge (8,543), Constitutional Unionist John Bell (5,437), and Democrat Stephen A. Douglas (367), the state of Florida seceded from the Union on January 10, 1861. Out of a population of 140,424 (77,746 white, 61,745 slaves, and 932 free African Americans), the state contributed roughly 15,000 soldiers to the Confederate cause. Approximately 1,200 white Floridians and nearly as many African Americans served in the Union armies. At least a third of the Florida soldiers in the Confederate armies lost their lives in battle or from disease.

Contributions to the Confederacy. Although the number of soldiers furnished by Florida was relatively modest, the state made significant contributions to the Confederate cause in military leadership and in valuable foodstuffs. Among the major leaders from Florida was Stephen R. Mallory, the Confederate secretary of navy. Despite a shortage of conventional ships and weapons, Mallory was ahead of Union Secretary of Navy Gideon Welles in recognizing the changes that were taking place in naval warfare. Mallory utilized shell guns, screw propellers, torpedoes, armored ships, and even submarines in naval combat. A crude submarine, *H. L. Hunley,* claimed the sinking of the blockader *Housatonic* outside Charleston Harbor in February 1864, the first such sinking in history.

Another military leader from Florida was Gen. W. W. Loring, who, when he surrendered with Gen. Joseph E. Johnston in April 1865, was the senior major general on field duty with the Confederate armies. The colorful E. Kirby Smith, another Floridian, commanded Confederate forces west of the Mississippi River and was the last Confederate general in the field when he surrendered to Gen. E. R. S. Canby on May 26, 1865.

The production of salt was a major Florida contribution to the Confederacy. The industry was concentrated around St. Andrews Bay (near present-day Panama City) and in Taylor County along the Gulf of Mexico (Apalachee Bay). Great kettles of seawater were evaporated over large furnaces to obtain salt used to preserve meat for Robert E. Lee's armies. The product was so important that Floridians were exempted from conscription to manufacture it.

After the surrender of Confederate forces at Vicksburg in 1863, another of Florida's strengths came into play. Cattle driven from the open ranges in the state compensated in large part for the Confederate loss of Texas cattle and helped the South carry on the war for two more years. Florida supplied Confederate armies with more than 25,000 cattle and 10,000 hogs in 1864.

The state also provided sugar, syrup, and hides to the Confederate cause, and its inland rivers and inlets served as harbors for blockade runners throughout the war. New Smyrna in East Florida and Apalachicola in West Florida became bases from which smuggled goods were distributed.

Secession and the War in Florida. In January 1861, rural Florida faced a new national existence with no cities or factory system, and with only about four hundred miles of railroads and a thousand free skilled laborers within its borders. On February 4, delegates from Florida and other seceding states met at Montgomery, Alabama, and agreed upon a provisional government for the Confederate States of America, with a constitution to be returned to the states for ratification. The Florida secession convention reassembled on February 26 and unanimously adopted the Constitution.

Governor Madison S. Perry quickly ordered the seizure of all Federal arsenals by state militia troops. The men occupied arsenals at Chattahoochee, Fort Marion at St. Augustine, and Fort Clinch at Fernandina, but failed to dislodge Federals at Fort Pickens on Santa Rosa Island in Pensacola Bay and the fifty troops in Fort Taylor at Key West. The Union commander at Fort Barrancas at Pensacola was Lt. Adam

> ... its inland rivers and inlets served as harbors for blockade runners throughout the war.

Slemmer of the First Artillery. When a large Confederate force prepared to attack the fort, Slemmer, with no orders or authorization from the Union command in Washington, ordered his force of eighty-one men to move to Fort Pickens at the western extremity of Santa Rosa Island. This contingent held the fortress until President Abraham Lincoln was inaugurated and subsequently sent reinforcements. Strategic Pensacola Harbor became a Union command post for capture of Confederate blockade runners. Fort Taylor, located on the west shore of the Key West island, remained in Union hands throughout the war. Since the townspeople of Key West were mostly Confederate sympathizers, Union intelligence officers stationed at Fort Taylor collected information here about Confederate military operations to send to Washington.

John Milton, inaugurated in October 1861 as Florida's wartime governor, was pleased with Confederate plans for defense of the approaches to Apalachicola, the harbor and railroad terminus at Fernandina, the port of Jacksonville, and other coastal towns. But in February 1862, Governor Milton was dismayed when these plans were abandoned. Pressures from Federal forces in Tennessee and Kentucky brought a sweeping order to the Florida department to send all men and supplies northward to defend the northwestern border of the Confederacy. A month later only two thousand Confederate troops remained in the state. Coastal defenses were dismantled and military ordnance was moved into the interior. Governor Milton reflected the temper of Floridians when he wrote to President Jefferson Davis that "the Confederacy has abandoned most of Florida to the mercy and abuse of the Lincoln government." Nevertheless, Milton, according to Davis biographer Rembert Patrick, was among the most loyal and cooperative state rights governors in his dealings with Davis.

The movement of Confederate troops inland enabled the Federal navy to gain effective control of and occupy at will the east coast of the United States extending from Port Royal, South Carolina, to Key West, Florida. This in turn enabled blockade squadrons to keep watch on the Florida-based blockade runners. On March 3, 1862, the Federals took control of Fernandina and Fort Clinch on Amelia Island, and a Federal garrison occupied Fort Clinch for the duration of the war. In that same month Union forces moved southward to occupy Jacksonville and St. Augustine. Incapable of effective resistance, Confederate sympathizers moved into the interior, where the Federals followed them. The Northerners conducted raids, freed slaves to obtain army recruits, destroyed military stores, and then withdrew. They returned to Jacksonville in October 1862 and March 1863 for the same purposes. Raiders coming in from the gulf destroyed the saltworks at Cedar Key and Apalachicola on several occasions, but the Confederate workers soon returned and resumed their saltmaking.

Florida's interior—the area between the St. Johns and Apalachicola rivers and including the capital city of Tallahassee—remained in Confederate hands throughout the war. Capt. John Jackson Dickison, a legendary Civil War hero in Florida, deployed a little band of old men and young boys in guerrilla warfare in defense of the state's interior. Dickison, a middle-aged, well-to-do plantation owner at Orange Springs, Florida, when the war began, organized a

> **Incapable of effective resistance, Confederate sympathizers moved into the interior, where the Federals followed them.**

cavalry unit known as the Leo Dragoons. His militia unit was assigned as home guards defending the west bank of the St. Johns River, gateway to the interior. He deployed his little band of cavalry to strategic positions for ambushing Northerners who ventured west of the St. Johns River.

Throughout the summer and fall of 1863 and January of 1864, Florida enjoyed almost a year of respite from significant Federal attacks. This virtual armistice was broken in February 1864 when five thousand Federal troops from lower South Carolina and upper Georgia embarked aboard trans-

ports for an invasion of northeast Florida. Union objectives were to stop the flow of cattle and other foodstuffs from moving northward to General Lee's armies, to free the slaves, and to enlist them in the Union armies. The Federal forces reached Jacksonville on February 7 and moved westward in the direction of Lake City. Despite critical need for troops elsewhere, General Lee ordered reinforcements to assist Gen. Joseph Finegan, commander of the East Florida Military District, in repelling the invaders.

General Finegan withdrew his small force ahead of the Union advance until he received the reinforcements and found a strong defensive position near the village of Olustee located thirteen miles east of Lake City. His men took up position on a line about a mile and a half long running between Ocean Pond on the north and a large cyprus swamp on the south and waited for the advancing Union army. Gen. Truman A. Seymour, the Union commander, had added about five hundred ex-slaves to his original force. Around the middle of the day on February 20, the two forces engaged in the Battle of Olustee. Repeated assaults by the Union forces were repelled at very close range by the Confederates artillery and small arms. By a little after six in the evening the Confederates had forced the Union men to retreat, which was made easier by the fact that General Seymour had failed to bring all of his forces to the battle.

Olustee, though a minor battle with respect to the number of men involved, had the highest percentage of casualties, both Union and Confederate, of any battle in the war. The Union lost 40 percent of its force in dead, wounded and missing men while the Confederate forces reported casualties of 20 percent. Though the Confederates were unable to follow up their victory, it was decisive. Seymour's army departed from Florida; the interior and the supply lines for shipment of foodstuffs to the Confederate armies remained secure. Historian Rembert Patrick contends that the Olustee victory may well have enabled the South to carry on the war for an added year.

The Home Front. Floridians were asked to endure hardships and make sacrifices to solve wartime problems. The state budget averaged $500,000 per year during the war. Previously it had never exceeded $50,000 per year. Because tax collections were sometimes suspended and tax payments were irregular, especially in the enemy-held areas of Florida, the only way for the state to pay for war expenditures was to borrow money. The legislature authorized treasury notes and twenty-year bonds, but the bonds did not sell well and were used to pay creditors who would take them. The total amount of treasury notes issued during the war was $2,236,640.38, of which only $397,370.36 was redeemed. The Civil War cost Floridians $2,225,000 in addition to the capital that had been invested in some 65,000 slaves.

The Confederate government, in order to meet financial obligations, assessed Florida and other states a tax according to the population. More painful and of more direct affect on Floridians was the Confederate Impressment Act of 1863, which permitted Confederate or state officials to enter homes, seize surplus foods and items needed for war, and leave IOUs for payment to the occupants.

Outfitting the troops with arms, ammunition, clothing, and equipment soon became a major problem. Florida's legislature first appropriated $100,000 for this purpose, but this was just a drop in a very large bucket. The Confederate government provided no help. Consequently, some troops were not provided with even basic equipment, which lowered morale. Wealthy planters organized military units and provided some of the equipment, and often they were elected as the units' officers. The Ladies Military Aid Societies were given $10,000 worth of material, appropriated by the Florida legislature, to make uniforms, but there was never enough clothing, shoes, and blankets. Hospitals, doctors, and nurses were also in short supply. To ease the situation, Florida opened the Howard Grove Hospital in Richmond to care for its sick and wounded fighting on the Virginia front. It was supported by contributions of food and money from Floridians and an appropriation of $30,000 from the legislature.

With four-fifths of Florida men absent from their homes, women who lived on plantations and depended on slave labor found their lives greatly changed. In the early years of the war, slaves often stayed on the plantations, but eventually they left, leaving their mistresses to do the tasks they had performed. The plantation women had to learn how to fell trees, roll logs, clear fields, and plant crops. They also continued their traditional tasks of weaving, knitting, and canning foods.

Military supplies for the Confederacy were brought to Florida by blockade runners—small boats that slipped out of Florida bays and inlets often at night to evade capture by Federal gunboats. In the first year of the war the business of running the blockade was usually conducted through legal channels with clearance papers approved by the Confederate customs or military officials. Sponsors of these enterprises promised to import supplies for government use in return for permission to export cotton, tobacco, and naval stores. But as the war progressed and Federal forces strengthened the blockade, dwindling supplies and increased demand encouraged the runners to import consumer goods without authorization. Catherine Cooper Hopley, an English tutor on Governor Milton's plantation, wrote of profiteers who sold scarce imported goods at exorbitant prices both to consumers and to the Confederate government. Quinine, used for many medical purposes, sold for $20 an ounce. Flour that would have brought $10 a sack upon arrival was sold to the Confederate government in the quartermaster's depot for $30 to $50. Rum, purchased in Cuba for 17 cents a gallon, was sold in Florida for $25 a gallon. Governor Milton, in his letters to President Davis, complained that goods manufac-

tured in the North were shipped to the Bahamas, covered with English stamps, and then sold at a profit in Florida. Milton argued that this profiteering did damage to Confederate morale that outweighed any good for consumers, and in 1864 he asked that the Confederacy halt the approval of papers for the runners. The Confederate government, however, did not agree. The Confederacy, in fact, encouraged the trade with Northern markets and toward the end of the conflict tried to reserve as much cargo space as possible with the blockade runners.

Regardless of the Confederate success in defending the interior of Florida, the day of the Confederacy was soon over. Lee surrendered on April 9, 1865, and Johnston on April 26. On May 10, Gen. E. M. McCook reached Tallahassee and accepted the surrender of the capital and the eight thousand Confederate troops remaining in Florida. Governor Milton, in a message to the Florida legislature, declared that "death would be preferable to reunion," and asserted that this was "the sentiment of all true Southern men." These were not idle words: the governor took his own life on April 1, 1865. The majority of war-weary Floridians did not share Milton's view. A few went into exile in Latin America, but most shared the feeling of a returning veteran who said, "Thank God, it is over, one way or another."

[*For further discussion of battles and cities in Florida, see* Fort Pickens, Florida; Olustee, Florida; Tallahassee, Florida.]

BIBLIOGRAPHY

Davis, William Watson. *The Civil War and Reconstruction in Florida.* New York, 1913.
Hopley, Catherine C. *Life in the South from the Commencement of the War.* London, 1863.
Johns, John E. *Florida during the Civil War.* Gainesville, Fla., 1963.
Tebeau, Charlton. *A History of Florida.* Coral Gables, Fla., 1980.

MERLIN G. COX

FLORIDA

The wooden cruiser *Florida* was 192 feet long and displaced 700 tons. Its all-rifle armament consisted of two 7-inch Blakely rifles and six 6-inch Blakely rifles. The ship had a screw propeller that could be lifted out of the water when under sail. Although *Florida*'s speed averaged 9½ knots, its maximum speed was 12 knots. crew's size varied but averaged 100 men and 20 officers. A sister ship to *Alabama,* it was the first cruiser constructed in England. It was built from the modified plans of a Royal Navy gunboat by William C. Miller and Sons of Liverpool, and the engines were the work of Fawcett and Preston, also of Liverpool. In order to conceal the ship's real identity, it was built under the name of *Oreto,* supposedly for the Italian government. Construction on *Florida* began in June 1861, and it sailed for Nassau on March 22, 1862, posing as an ordinary merchant ship.

After some difficulty the ship left Nassau under command of Lt. John N. Maffitt, who could not begin his cruise immediately because *Florida* lacked an adequate crew and critical parts of armament. In addition, some men aboard had yellow fever. Maffitt, trying unsuccessfully to complete his equipment and roster of men in Cuba, took *Florida* on a daring daylight run through the Union blockade into Mobile on September 4, 1862. The need for tedious repairs prevented the ship's departure until January 17, 1863.

During the first cruise *Florida* captured twenty-five ships, nineteen of which were destroyed and six were bonded. The practice of bonding referred to a form of ransom where the owner agreed to pay a specified amount after the war to the Confederacy for not burning his ship. Three prizes were outfitted as cruisers, and these vessels, *Tacony, Clarence,* and *Lapwing,* captured twenty-two more ships. Of these captures, fifteen were destroyed, six were bonded, and one, *Archer,* was recaptured by Union forces. Directly or indirectly *Florida* captured forty-seven prizes during the first cruise. Lt. C. W. Read commanded one prize used as a cruiser. Read ended his cruise by capturing the armed revenue cutter *Caleb Cushing* at Portland, Maine, and blowing it up.

After months at sea, *Florida* was refitted at Brest, France, remaining there from August 23, 1863, until February 10, 1864. By this time, Maffitt, ill and exhausted, asked to be relieved of his duty. While the ship was at Brest, Comm. J. N. Barney took over its command and supervised the repairs. Ill health, however, prevented his continuing, and he was replaced by Lt. Charles M. Morris. *Florida*'s second cruise, considerably less successful than the first, accounted for the capture of thirteen prizes, eleven of which were destroyed and the other two bonded. The crew found far fewer enemy ships this time out, in part because many U.S. ships were either tied up in port or had been transferred to foreign flags.

Florida was captured in the neutral port of Bahia, Brazil, on October 7, 1864, by the U.S. warship *Wachusetts,* a sister ship of *Kearsarge,* which had already sunk *Alabama.* *Wachusetts* commander Napoleon Collins sailed *Florida* to Hampton, Virginia, where it sank.

BIBLIOGRAPHY

Boykin, Edward. *Sea Devil of the Confederacy: The Story of the Florida and Her Captain John Newland Maffitt.* New York, 1959.
Bulloch, James D. *The Secret Service of the Confederate States in Europe or How the Confederate Cruisers Were Equipped.* 2 vols. New York, 1883.
Owsley, Frank L. *The C.S.S. Florida: Her Building and Operations.* Tuscaloosa, Ala., 1987.

FRANK LAWRENCE OWSLEY

FLOYD, JOHN B.

FLOYD, JOHN B. (1806–1863), politician and brigadier general. Born June 1, 1806, in Montgomery County, Virginia, John Buchanan Floyd served as governor from 1848 to 1852. His political service to the Democratic party secured his appointment as President James Buchanan's secretary of war (1857–1860). After bitter criticism by Northern politicians and the press for alleged transfer of arms and equipment from Northern to Southern arsenals and contractor indiscretions within the War Department, he was commissioned a Confederate brigadier in 1861. He served in the West Virginia campaign under Robert E. Lee, being involved in small battles at Cross Lanes, Carnifix Ferry, and Gauley Bridge. Sent west in December 1861 with his brigade of Virginia troops, he joined Albert Sidney Johnston's forces in western Kentucky.

As senior brigadier, Floyd assumed command on the Cumberland River at Fort Donelson, Tennessee, in February 1862 just as Ulysses S. Grant's joint army-navy expedition invested the work (having captured nearby Fort Henry on the Tennessee River a week before). Although hampered by divided leadership (there were three brigadiers besides himself), unclear and conflicting orders from Johnston, a jealous but largely untested army of over fifteen thousand men, and an untenable static defense position, Floyd stymied Union forces for three days while Johnston conducted a retreat of the main army from Bowling Green to Nashville.

JOHN B. FLOYD. LIBRARY OF CONGRESS

Nonetheless, in a comedy of errors, fouled communications, amateurish tactical bungling, and loss of nerve, Floyd and his fellow officers (Gideon Pillow, Simon Bolivar Buckner, Bushrod Rust Johnson) relinquished the initiative, failed to extricate their army, and were forced to surrender to Grant. In a famous opéra bouffe scene of passing command, Floyd and Pillow fled with the Virginia brigade (and miscellaneous portions of the garrison), thereby earning the enmity and scorn of friend and foe alike for the remainder of the war.

Floyd subsequently escaped to Nashville and aided in restoration of order and transfer of army supplies from the city. But because he had deserted his command, he was subsequently removed from other positions of command in the Confederate service. Active as a Virginia militia major general in southwestern Virginia, Floyd organized partisan bands to combat Union incursions, but his health broke, resulting in his early death in August 1863 near Abingdon, Virginia. Known to posterity for the Fort Donelson disaster, Floyd represented the typical nineteenth-century political general whose ambitions exceeded his military talents to the detriment of the Confederacy.

BIBLIOGRAPHY

Barnwell, Robert W. "General John B. Floyd." *Confederate Veteran* 39 (April 1931): 141–142.
Connelly, Thomas Lawrence, and Archer Jones. *The Politics of Command: Factions and Ideas in Confederate Strategy.* Baton Rouge, La., 1973.
Warner, Ezra. *Generals in Gray: Lives of the Confederate Commanders.* Baton Rouge, La., 1959.

B. FRANKLIN COOLING

FOLK NARRATIVES

Folklorists study three types of folk narratives: myths, legends, and folktales. *Myths* are those narratives set in a prehistoric past that deal with the actions of gods and supernatural beings. *Legends* are stories set in the historic past and told to convey what the teller feels is truth; or, at least, they allow for an element of belief or disbelief. *Folktales* are fictional stories told primarily for entertainment, although they may contain a moral or illustrate some generally accepted truth. There are four broad categories of folktales that have been distinguished by folklorists. These include animal tales (such as "The Tar Baby"), wonder tales (such as "The Smith Outwits the Devil"), jokes and anecdotes, and formula tales (such as "The Old Woman and Her Pig" or "The House That Jack Built"), which are cumulative, catch, or endless tales. Viewed from this stance, there are no myths about the Confederacy. It is true, as scholar Richard M. Dorson has

suggested, that the war left no coherent body of folk sagas in its wake; nevertheless, legends and folktales were abundant on both sides of the conflict.

Although Confederate soldiers told both legends and folktales, their activity in this regard is, for a variety of reasons, less well known than the narrative traditions concerning the Confederacy that have lingered on to the present. One of the chief reasons is that, because of the ongoing conflict, folklorists at the time of the war were not collecting folk narratives from soldiers on either side. Even if conditions had permitted, there likely would have been little interest in such collections, because most nineteenth-century folklorists were concerned with the traditions of American Indians, African Americans, or other groups considered to be outside of mainstream society. Thus, only through perusal of diaries, journals, and newspaper articles or from orally preserved accounts can one discover what traditional stories Confederate soldiers told. The interests of American folklorists have expanded considerably since the Civil War. Consequently, a great deal more is known about the folk narrative traditions that lingered on after 1865 pertaining to the war than about the narrative traditions that existed during the war.

Available information suggests that the folk narratives told by soldiers consisted mainly of legends and jokes. Many of the legends dealt with famous personalities such as Abraham Lincoln. One characteristic Southerners persistently attached to the president was that he was a drunk, and many stories circulated around campfires that purported to give the truth about his legendary binges. But just as often the tales told by fighting men dealt with less well-known personalities. Stories about hairbreadth escapes by rank-and-file soldiers became the stuff of legends, as did yarns about the hardships of war. Other favorite legend topics included the activities of guerrillas, haunted burial grounds, and battlefields.

Jokes were numerous and extremely varied and often conveyed the toll of the war on an individual level. Typical is a humorous tale recorded in the *Memorial Reminiscences* of the Confederate Women of Arkansas. According to this yarn, a tired and war-weary Confederate was cooling his feet in a stream and trying to mend his ragged coat when he was visited by a mounted Union soldier who said, "Hi, there, Johnny Reb. I've got you this time." To this the Confederate soldier replied: "Yes, and a hell of a git you got." Often the jokes that were told had nothing to do with the war or its personalities. Ribald jokes were especially popular with the troops but are even less well documented than other forms of folk narrative. Some famous persons, such as Governor Zebulon Vance of North Carolina, achieved renown among the troops and the general populace for their skill at telling jokes, and many widely traveled yarns became attached to them. One widely known tale attributed to Vance concerned a rabbit that sprang from the bushes during the Battle of Malvern Hill. The rabbit darted in front of the troops who called out, "Run, run, run!" An officer then asked Vance if he should shoot the animal. Vance replied no and called out, "Run, little cottontail! I'd run too if I wasn't governor of North Carolina." Other personalities, in particular Lincoln, were the subject of jokes, both ribald and "clean."

Those people left at home related the same types of narratives that were told by those in the ranks, but the civilians' stories encompassed a broader range. Animal tales and wonder tales, for example, were commonplace on the home front but rarely told in military camps. Many of the narratives related by civilians, though, dealt with the war; the activities of guerrillas, known in many communities as jayhawkers, were one of the most frequent subjects of legends. Indeed, a whole series of episodic cycles has grown up around Beanie Short, a guerrilla who operated in the Cumberland region of northern Tennessee and southern Kentucky. These narratives focus on his raiding activities, his treacherous death, and his buried treasure. If legend is to be believed, most guerrillas amassed sizable treasures, which they buried and have never been found.

Some traditional stories told during the Confederacy were related from the viewpoint of African Americans. The most widely told dealt with the freedom of blacks, their abilities as soldiers, and humorous comments on race relations. In Virginia a black woman was asked if she had run away from her master, to which she replied no, saying her master had run away from her. In Vicksburg, a black boy stood still while a shell landed almost at the feet of his party, which consisted of himself, a Catholic nun, and a convalescent Confederate soldier. After the soldier leaped to safety, the boy threw the smoldering shell away just before it exploded. When asked by the nun why he did not act earlier, he answered that he had too much respect for white people to do something like that while a white gentleman was standing there. Of course, such tales were also told by some whites.

Most Confederate folk narratives were short, consisting of a single episode, and were relatively uncomplicated. Exceptions would be the wonder tales and some of the animal stories, but these had no connection with the war and were commonplace before the 1860s. Legends were told by most people, but folktales were likely related by only a few star narrators. Both types of narratives differed in one other important way—namely, the manner of their telling. Both legends and folktales were told anywhere two people congregated but legends were related in a matter-of-fact, relatively undramatic style whereby the narrator let the text speak for itself and did not attempt to improve the story with dramatic flourishes. Folktale narrators, on the other hand, were usually more animated and dramatic when delivering their yarns. The difference in presentation styles was, of course, mainly due to the manner in which the narrators and their audiences

regarded legends and folktales. Those telling the former generally thought of themselves as merely relaying factual information, whereas those telling the latter viewed their task as one of providing entertainment.

BIBLIOGRAPHY

Aarne, Antti, and Stith Thompson. *The Types of the Folk-Tale.* Helsinki, Finland, 1928. Reprint, Bloomington, Ind., 1964.
Botkin, B. A. *A Civil War Treasury of Tales, Legends and Folklore.* New York, 1960.
Dorson, Richard M. *America in Legend: Folklore from the Colonial Period to the Present.* New York, 1973.
Roberts, Leonard W. *Up Cutshin and Down Greasy: Folkways of a Kentucky Mountain Family.* Lexington, Ky., 1959.
Roberts, Nancy. *Civil War Ghost Stories and Legends.* Columbia, S.C., 1992.
Wiley, Bell Irvin. *The Common Soldier in the Civil War: The Life of Johnny Reb.* Indianapolis, Ind., 1943. Reprint, Baton Rouge, La., 1986.
Wilgus, D. K., and Lynwood Montell. "Beanie Short: A Civil War Chronicle in Legend and Song." In *American Folk Legend: A Symposium.* Edited by Wayland D. Hand. Berkeley, Calif., 1971.

W. K. MCNEIL

FOOD

In the Confederacy, food varied from plentiful to inadequate, depending on what could be produced, acquired, and transported. People who could afford staples and luxury items or lived where the war had little physical impact ate relatively well. But shortages of food were common and many soldiers, refugees, urban dwellers, people living near battlefields, and poor farmers suffered hunger or malnutrition by the latter half of the war.

In 1860, the South produced an adequate amount of food to feed its citizens, especially rice, wheat, corn, pork, sugar, sweet potatoes, peas, and beans. But once the war started, spoilage, inadequate and disrupted transportation systems, impressment, poor weather, destruction of crops, a shortage of producers, and the occupation of food-producing regions by Federal troops caused many Southerners to experience hunger.

Food shortages hit the Confederacy almost as soon as the war began. Coffee, tea, salt, and sugar disappeared, and by 1863, meat, butter, and lard were also in limited supply. Military rations proved inadequate after the early months of war. Food was a daily concern for Confederate soldiers and a major topic in letters they wrote home. Some feared hunger more than the enemy. In their writings, they bemoaned Spartan helpings, spoiled meat, and persistent shortages of pork, butter, coffee, fruits, vegetables, and flour. Insufficient food fostered desperation, depression, lethargy, and often an inability to fight and survive disease and battle wounds. Nutritional deficiencies led to night blindness, and rancid food, unripened fruit, and polluted water caused dysentery, worms, and typhoid.

The Confederate Subsistence Department contracted with Southern farmers for grains and meat to feed the army, but the department was the most poorly organized of all governmental agencies. Adding to its problems were speculators who overcharged the government and farmers who hoarded food. Orders often were ignored. Rations might sit at food depots for days because there was no way to transport them.

> **The men became resourceful in locating outside sources of food and less picky about what they ate and how it was prepared.**

Typical military fare included hardtack (crackers), corn meal, fresh beef, and sometimes rice, field peas, or potatoes. Soldiers drank coffee substitutes, alcohol, and water, though the latter often had to be purified, disguised, or drunk with one's eyes closed. Initially, the army specified generous rations for infantry and officers based on U.S. Army rations. Rarely were specifications met, however, and rations declined significantly as the war dragged on—so much so that by 1864 soldiers often ate a day's food supply at one meal.

The men became resourceful in locating outside sources of food and less picky about what they ate and how it was prepared. Soldiers foraged for additional supplies in the countryside, purchased affordable extras when near a town or farm, and sometimes stole from a farmer's field. They hunted deer, possums, muskrats, squirrels, and wild fowl to add variety and protein to their diet. Men cooked a dough mixture of flour, grease, and water. Pieces of meat were skewered on sticks and held over the fire, since cooking implements were scarce. When wood was unavailable, they ate their food raw. During active campaigning, they either cooked prior to marching or ate nothing more than crackers and water. A few regiments had black slaves as cooks, but most men managed on their own. Occasionally, a bakery or central kitchen provided breads and foods for several regiments, but usually rations were distributed as needed.

More fortunate soldiers had other sources of food. Some received food boxes or trunks from relatives or soldiers' or ladies' aid societies. From family larders and fields came hams, turkeys, pickles, vinegar, cakes, catsup, and breads. But as the war progressed, limited or disrupted transportation made it increasingly difficult to deliver such food to the

designated recipient without a personal agent. Occasionally soldiers purchased home-cooked foods and fresh vegetables at wayside stands, but these were rare.

While all soldiers suffered hunger or consumed inedible fare at one time or another during their military service, some men had an especially miserable time of it. Braxton Bragg's Army of Tennessee faced desperate hunger during 1863. His soldiers moved southward from Murfreesboro through land that had been picked clean by Federal and Confederate troops and commissary agents. Though Florida beef and corn meal rations were available, Robert E. Lee's Army of Northern Virginia had priority before the Army of Tennessee. Troops at Fort Donelson in 1862, D. H. Hill's division during the 1862 spring campaign, and the soldiers defending Vicksburg in the spring and early summer of 1863 faced near starvation. The Army of Northern Virginia was well fed marching north into Pennsylvania but famished on its retreat from Gettysburg. During the Virginia campaign of 1864, Lee's army was described as "half clothed, half fed." No longer could that state provide enough food for the military, and supplies had to be secured from the Deep South. By June 1864, four crackers and a quarter-pound of meat a day comprised rations in Lee's army. Marching toward Appomattox, his men became even more desperate. Some did not eat for days, and others consumed corn kernels intended for the horses.

Officers ate better than the average soldier, although Lee reportedly was abstemious in his eating habits. Most generals exhibited some sensitivity to their hungry troops, and leaders like Bragg repeatedly demanded more and better provisions. Yet piles of rations spoiled at depots when orders were misunderstood, railroad cars and wagons were unavailable to transport the food, or armies changed their marching plans and missed intended supplies.

Hospital food ranged from nourishing to inedible, depending on supplies from local farmers and the presence of female nurses who were sensitive to patients' needs. Chimborazo Hospital in Richmond had its own bakeries, slaughterhouse, and kitchens to feed thousands of patients. Ladies' aid societies often prepared hams, turkeys, biscuits, and pies for the wounded. Nevertheless, soldiers complained about hospital meals, and those who could travel preferred home care where food was tastier, cleaner, and more plentiful.

The diet of civilians varied significantly but generally was better than that of the common soldier. Residents of middle Georgia, Alabama, South Carolina, and Texas were not significantly affected until Federal troops moved in and destroyed food supplies, crops, farm tools, and animals. The wealthy of Richmond, Augusta, Mobile, and the low-country plantations rarely experienced hunger until the end of the war. They could afford the staples and delicacies that made it through the blockade; their main complaints were high prices and unscrupulous speculators. Wealthy families continued to enjoy oysters, bacon, fresh shrimp and crab, tea, vegetables, fruits, a bit of sugar, and even fine flour for cakes. Varina and Jefferson Davis were criticized for eating extremely well while thousands in Richmond went hungry.

Yet more typical behavior was scrimping, preserving, and developing greater self-sufficiency. A new sense of asceticism developed even among some of the privileged. The lower and middle classes tightened their belts. Some Southerners ate only two meals a day, and mothers often sacrificed their own food to feed thin and hungry children. Torrential rains and droughts in several Southern states spoiled or burned out corn and vegetable crops in 1862 and 1863. Many urban and rural poor fell victim to inflation, as it put what little was available out of reach. Many urban women begged or scavenged.

In addition, food shortages prevailed for civilians because military needs came first. As farmers entered the army and became consumers rather than producers and women took charge of planting, less food was available. The shortages, high prices, and hunger fostered great discontent on the home front, and women wrote letters complaining to the Confederate government and begging husbands and sons to come home. So desperate were some women in towns in North and South Carolina, Alabama, and Georgia that they took to the streets to protest or riot. To counter the growing unease, public support for hungry soldiers' families was essential. States such as North Carolina, Georgia, and Louisiana enacted laws to distribute rations or cash payments to malnourished families.

Other issues concerning food fostered further discontent on the home front. Confederate agents ordered and purchased food to feed the soldiers, but farmers became increasingly reluctant to sell when promissory notes failed to be paid and severe inflation ate into any funds they received. Impressment laws, enacted in 1863, were unpopular. Fearing the seizure of their produce, farmers often refused to market their crops in some cities despite the growing need for food. When families failed to cooperate with the government, agents often took food with or without paying.

Farmers faced other problems, too. Given limited transportation, they found it increasingly difficult to reach markets to sell or purchase food. State laws encouraged farmers to grow corn rather than cotton, but some ignored such demands. Fearing that cotton or corn crops might fall into Federal hands, Southerners burned fields as enemy troops approached. Confederate soldiers from Lee's army journeyed to the North Carolina mountains in search of new food sources and stole what they needed from local farms.

Refugees crowding into Southern cities put more pressure on limited urban resources, especially food supplies. Few refugees could carry food when they fled their homes, and those who moved in with friends or into crowded boarding houses found food supplies scarce and expensive.

Owing to the increasing shortage of grains, some states enacted prohibition laws during the war. Yet such laws usually were ignored or, at least, were difficult to enforce. Alcohol was a pleasurable indulgence for many, especially war-weary soldiers, and its medicinal uses made it essential.

The greatest food shortage in the Confederacy was salt, which, before the outbreak of war, had been imported primarily from Europe and the Northern states. The blockade exacerbated the limited supply, and Federal troops gradually occupied the areas containing the Confederacy's sources of salt; only Saltville, Virginia, remained an important mine throughout the four years. Because salt was essential for preserving meat and for seasoning, its shortage caused both the Confederate and the state governments to search for other sources, including seawater, new salt mines, and artesian wells. So desperate was the need for salt that states exempted from military service those who labored in the mines. Families often begged soldiers serving near the coast to send them salt. Others resorted to a primitive means of extracting and reusing the salt from dirt floors of smokehouses. High prices and scarcity forced many to abandon salt as a preservative; instead they dried their meat, experimented with other spices, or restricted themselves to fresh meat when it was available.

Coffee was sorely missed, and no substitute adequately replaced it. Southerners concocted alternative brews from parched corn, wheat, acorns, okra seed, chicory, dandelions, persimmon seeds, and even potato peelings. Tea also became scarce. Women substituted sassafras or strawberry leaves, boiled grasses, or drank plain hot water with milk. Little sugar was available once Federal troops occupied Louisiana, and Southerners substituted molasses, maple syrup, sorghum, honey, or fruit syrups as sweeteners—or did without.

Because of the shortage of pork and beef, civilians ate more fish and fowl. Thus, ironically, those Southerners who *were* adequately fed probably, in some respects, consumed a better diet during the war than before it, with less fat, sugar, and red meat, and more vegetables and legumes in their daily fare. Meals improved in summer and early fall with the appearance of fresh vegetables and fruits and the harvesting of corn and wheat. Fortunate families expanded the size of their gardens and orchards if they could obtain seeds. Lucky Southerners who owned a cow enjoyed milk and butter. Wheat flour, especially finely ground, disappeared, and cooks used other grains such as corn and rice. Some whites observed that their food resembled what slaves had always consumed.

Women became resourceful cooks and meal planners. They scavenged for fresh berries and roots, baked mock apple pie made with crackers instead of apples, and learned how to revive rancid butter. The urban poor rummaged through discarded garbage for tidbits. Newspapers carried stories providing advice on how to cook with available foods. *The Confederate Receipt Book,* compiled in 1863, testifies to the creative use of scarce foods. Privileged Southerners sometimes did without, holding "starvation parties" where no food was served.

Slaves' diets changed little during the war since they had always depended on corn, pork, field peas, biscuits, and molasses. They too faced shortages and consumed less meat and fresh foods, but most ate better than the average Confederate soldier. Many continued to fish, hunt, and garden to supplement their meal offerings. Probably many worked fewer hours in the absence of male masters and therefore perhaps had lighter caloric needs. And because some masters could no longer afford to feed their slaves, more were rented out.

Food, then, was a matter of daily concern for soldiers and civilians during the four long years. Thousands went hungry on the battleground and the home front. Some historians feel that the will of the South would have been stronger had sufficient food been available for everyone. Some even argue that food ultimately affected the war's outcome.

[*See also* Bread Riots; Extortion; Farming; Impressment; Inflation; Salt; Speculation; Substitutes; Tax-in-Kind.]

BIBLIOGRAPHY

Confederate Receipt Book: A Compilation of over One Hundred Receipts, Adapted to the Times. Richmond, Va., 1863. Reprint, with introduction by E. Merton Coulter. Athens, Ga., 1960.
Gates, Paul W. *Agriculture and the Civil War.* New York, 1965.
Goff, Richard D. *Confederate Supply.* Durham, N.C., 1969.
Lonn, Ella. *Salt as a Factor in the Confederacy.* New York, 1933.
Massey, Mary Elizabeth. *Ersatz in the Confederacy.* Columbia, S.C., 1952.
Stevens, John K. "Hostages to Hunger: Nutritional Night Blindness in the Confederate Armies." *Tennessee Historical Quarterly* 48 (1989): 131–143.
Taylor, Robert A. "Rebel Beef: Florida Cattle and the Confederate Army, 1862–1864." *Florida Historical Quarterly* 67 (1988): 15–31.
Wiley, Bell I. *The Life of Johnny Reb.* Baton Rouge, La., 1971.

SALLY G. MCMILLEN

FOOTE, HENRY S.

FOOTE, HENRY S. (1804–1880), Tennessee governor and congressman. Historians who have mentioned Henry Stuart Foote at all have not been kind to his memory. Charles S. Sydnor viewed him as the Clement L. Vallandigham of the South, and E. Merton Coulter said he was "choleric," "excitable," "incorrigible," "eccentric," "irascible," "voluble," and "restless." Clement Eaton described him as "a little man, always barking and snapping, . . . a consummate dema-

gogue." But worse still, most historians have done what Foote would have abhorred: they have ignored him. Thomas Hart Benton swore not even to mention his name in his *Thirty Years' View.* When others have referred to him, the comments have been negative. His only biographer, John Edmond Gonzales, suggests that he was a "political chameleon"—aligning himself with first one political party and then another.

Contemporaries had little better to say of him. Jefferson Davis, a fellow Mississippian, found him a thorn in his side in both the U.S. Senate and the Confederate presidency; Davis, who fought him physically and verbally, denounced him as "a

> . . . he was a "political chameleon"—aligning himself with first one political party and then another.

constitutional liar." A colleague in the Confederate Congress described him as a "nuisance" whose conduct on the floor of Congress often was "disgraceful," and a Richmond newspaper editor said he was a "loose and inaccurate thinker."

On the other hand, his Nashville postwar law partner, Arthur S. Colyar, saw him as "one of the brightest intellects on the American continent," but also observed that he was "the most changeable of men." A Mississippian, writing some fifteen years after Foote's death, regarded him as a "foeman worthy of the steel of the ablest opponent of whatever cause espoused." No one questioned his skill at debate and repartee. He had a good basic knowledge of law; indeed, the Nashville Bar Association declared at the time of his death that he had had no equal as a trial lawyer. As a journalist, lawyer, writer, and lawmaker, he was successful. As a politician, he won—perhaps—his share of the contests. Always on the move, he was respected if not loved whether in Alabama, Mississippi, California, Texas, Tennessee, Richmond, or Washington.

Foote was born in Fauquier County, Virginia, February 28, 1804. After graduation from Washington College at the age of fifteen, he studied law and was admitted to the bar at Richmond when nineteen. During his lifetime he established residence and practiced law in half a dozen states and the District of Columbia, in addition to residing for some months in exile in England and Canada.

Foote first settled in Tuscumbia, Alabama, in 1823, where he married, practiced law, and edited a newspaper. His vitriolic journalistic style soon led to a duel with John A. Winston, later governor of Alabama. Neither man was hurt, but Foote was barred from the practice of law in Alabama for three years. Undaunted, he gathered up his family and moved to Mississippi, living and practicing law successively in

Jackson, Natchez, and Vicksburg. His support of Andrew Jackson made him known throughout much of Mississippi, and he was elected to the legislature in 1837. At about the same time, he developed a strong interest in the independence movement in Texas and, after paying an extended visit to that new republic, published in 1841 a two-volume work, *Texas and the Texans*.

But his primary interest was politics, not law and journalism, and he aligned himself with the Democratic party in Mississippi, becoming one of the party's most respected leaders. He served, with Jefferson Davis, as a presidential

> ## Foote's propensity for fighting anyone and everyone got him into serious trouble. . . .

elector in 1844 and vigorously supported James K. Polk because of Polk's willingness to annex Texas. In 1847 he was elected to the U.S. Senate.

In Washington, Foote became one of the architects of the Compromise of 1850, although his colleague Davis, and indeed all of the Mississippi House delegation, bitterly opposed the measure. But he saw the compromise as a means of preserving the Union; as a strong Union supporter in a state where secession already was being discussed, he risked his political future to work for the measure's passage. In 1851, boldly heading the Union Democrats, he announced for governor and was elected by a small majority over Davis, a state rights Democrat—a feat attributable to his oratorical abilities and his powers of persuasion.

He was unhappy as governor because his interests lay primarily in national politics. He had supported Franklin Pierce for president and hoped for a cabinet post but received "a cruel blow" when the president ignored him and appointed Jefferson Davis secretary of war. He offered his candidacy for U.S. Senate in 1854, but the legislature, controlled in large measure by state rights Democrats, elected Albert Gallatin Brown. Soon, in typical Foote fashion, he resigned the governorship a few days before he had finished one term and moved to San Francisco, where he joined his two sons-in-law in the practice of law. By the end of the decade, however, he had returned to Mississippi and again entered politics with vigor. In 1859, he announced for Congress, but because of his Unionist proclivities, he received little encouragement. He withdrew and by midsummer had established a residence and law practice in Nashville.

Foote had been in Nashville less than six weeks when he became aligned with the Democratic party with a view to exerting influence in the presidential election of 1860. Months before Democrats assembled in Charleston to nominate a

presidential candidate, Foote had announced his support for Stephen A. Douglas. Alarmed at the Republicans' gains in 1856 and viewing that party as a prime instigator of disunion, he predicted that the Southern states would secede should a Republican be elected. The Illinois Democrat, he said, was the only person who could satisfy all sections and maintain peace.

Douglas's defeat was upsetting to Foote, and he confidently predicted that Abraham Lincoln would bring secession and war. Remembering the Southern convention of 1850, he urged Governor Isham G. Harris and other Tennessee Democrats to call a conference of representatives from the Southern states to meet in Nashville. The fifteen slaveholding states should attempt to secure certain guarantees from the Republicans, he said; that failing, they should declare the Union at an end and withdraw in concert. The last thing they should do, he asserted, was to secede in piecemeal fashion. But these efforts failed, and Foote turned his attention to Tennessee. He worked with Governor Harris and the secessionist Democrats to accomplish separation in the Volunteer State, becoming one of the many former sincere Unionists who gave up hope for a peaceful settlement after Lincoln was inaugurated.

In the early fall of 1861, Foote became a candidate for the Confederate Congress from the Fifth District. He won handily over two opponents, and in early February 1862, he departed for Richmond. He wasted no time in leading the opposition to the administration and soon was at war with Davis and most of the cabinet. He accepted with difficulty the fall of Forts Henry and Donelson and the occupation of Nashville, calling for the dismissal and censure of Secretary of War Judah P. Benjamin and Naval Secretary Stephen R. Mallory. Benjamin, he said, was unfit to hold a cabinet post and Mallory was "utterly incompetent." But he saved most of his invective for his old nemesis, President Davis; he was a person, Foote said, who would establish a dictatorship to serve his own ends, who had only "power for mischief," who was basically corrupt, and who might best serve his country if placed in a mental institution. (He had characterized Thomas Hart Benton in roughly these same terms a decade earlier when both served in the U.S. Senate.)

Foote's propensity for fighting anyone and everyone got him into serious trouble in Richmond, and he occasionally despaired of his life. He had remembered Washington as a place where he had been threatened with fists and guns, but men of the Deep South also fought with knives and clubs. He had only to refer to Alabama Congressman E. S. Dargan as a "damned rascal" when the Alabamian lunged at him with a bowie knife. When Foote ridiculed a congressman from Arkansas, the two came to blows before being separated. When a Richmond editor called upon Congress to censure and expel him for his general conduct, he reacted in such a manner that the editor threatened to kill him. The editor persuaded Congressman William G. Swan to carry a written challenge to Foote, but the irascible Nashvillian responded so violently that Swan stabbed him with the only weapon at hand—an umbrella. The two were arrested and placed under a peace bond by a Richmond magistrate.

Foote referred to himself as the champion of the people against the aggressions of a selfish administration. As such, he boasted that he carefully read all bills introduced, and he presented a large number himself. He bitterly opposed the suspension of the writ of habeas corpus by Earl Van Dorn around the Vicksburg area and attacked Braxton Bragg for imposing martial law in Atlanta. He insisted upon a careful investigation after each battle the Confederacy lost, and he frequently criticized the Davis administration for withholding information on the conduct of the war. He investigated the commissary and cited the waste and profiteering he uncovered. Generally anti-Semitic, he wanted to expel all Jewish traders from the South and constantly urged Davis to dismiss Benjamin from his cabinet. He urged people to accept Confederate paper money, wanted Congress to make it legal tender, and publicly declared that anyone who refused to accept Confederate notes was "deserving of the Penitentiary."

Foote was disturbed that the new government was not accepted in Europe, and on this matter he and President Davis agreed. Davis was critical of both France and England because they appeared to be "unfriendly," and Foote introduced a resolution urging Davis to recall the Southern envoys from every country that had not granted recognition by May 1, 1863.

Foote and Davis also agreed on the wisdom of trying to persuade the states of the Old Northwest to withdraw from the war. Southern Illinois, Indiana, and Ohio, in large measure, had been settled by migrants from Confederate states, and their sentimental attachment to the land of their birth remained strong. The Northwest was tied to the South by the vast Mississippi River system, and common economic bonds. Also, the peace element in the Democratic party in those states had won important victories in the fall 1862 elections. Both Foote and Davis urged leaders in those states to force Lincoln to make peace and recognize the independence of the South. The matter became one of the many subjects upon which Foote repeatedly addressed Congress.

If there was one characteristic that Foote consistently displayed, it was his inconsistency. Invariably, in matters affecting his political life he fled when the going got rough. So it was with his relationship with the Confederacy. Early in his congressional career he had predicted a short war and an early victory for the South. Always impatient, he urged that the war be taken to the enemy; he would expend a million men and $2 billion, if need be, to take the war into the North and rake those states with fire and sword. It was the Northern people who must be made to feel the harshness of war, he

said; their "cupidity" and "semi-barbarous and insatiable lust for . . . domination had started the war," and they must be made to suffer.

He rejoiced in his first few months in Richmond that the Southern people daily became "more enthusiastic and resolute and far more confident as to the ultimate outcome of the struggle." So encouraged was he with victories in the

> **He . . . believed that a negotiated peace might at least preserve slavery.**

East in the late fall of 1862 that he suggested that commissioners be sent to Washington to propose terms of a just and lasting peace guaranteeing Southern independence. He believed the South had so much support among the common folk of the North that a refusal by the administration would result in a revolt of such magnitude that Lincoln would be deposed. But as Northern armies took Tennessee, the West, and much of the Southwest and ultimately closed in on Atlanta and on Lee in Virginia, he turned to Washington to beg for peace at almost any price.

When Congress convened in November 1864 after a brief recess, Foote expressed a belief that the Confederacy could not hold on beyond spring of the next year. He had given up on Southern independence but believed that a negotiated peace might at least preserve slavery. Congress, however, published a manifesto declaring that the Confederacy would never give up short of independence and then enacted a measure making negotiation with the enemy punishable by fine and imprisonment.

Foote nevertheless was determined to sound out the Federal authorities. He and his wife secretly fled toward Union lines but were overtaken on January 10, 1865, by Confederate troops some thirty-seven miles beyond the picket lines and within five miles of Union troops. Mrs. Foote was permitted to proceed, but Foote was briefly confined in Fredericksburg and then permitted at his request to return to Congress in Richmond. As his colleagues debated censure and expulsion, he fled again—this time successfully—and on January 28 was received across enemy lines and imprisoned. Although he wrote letters to Lincoln, the press, and some of the cabinet members, he was in large measure ignored.

When Andrew Johnson became president, he ordered Foote to either leave the country within forty-eight hours or stand trial for treason and rebellion. Foote fled to Montreal, from where he wrote numerous letters pleading not for the Confederacy but for his own liberty and the right to live in the United States. He wrote Johnson of his hope for peace and prosperity for America and to affirm that he was ready to take the oath of allegiance. To fellow Tennesseans, he wrote advising them to ratify the Thirteenth Amendment and swear allegiance to the United States. Finally, in late August 1865, Johnson permitted him to return to the country. By that time he had taken the oath of allegiance, publicly endorsed black suffrage, and assured all that he would not become involved again in politics.

After Foote paid an extended visit to his daughter and her husband, William M. Stewart, a U.S. senator from Nevada, he lived in St. Louis for a year, writing and speaking. By the summer of 1867, he was back in Nashville and had become affiliated with the conservative Democrats. He campaigned for the Democratic presidential candidate in 1868, and, though the Radical Republicans won the presidency, the conservatives in Tennessee were returned to power. Foote apparently had little confidence in Ulysses S. Grant, but he urged Tennesseans to support the president—another instance of his ambivalence and opportunism.

Writing had been not only a profitable venture for Foote but therapeutic. Early in 1866, Harper and Brothers published his *War of the Rebellion,* a lengthy work covering the colonial period through 1864 but emphasizing the past fifteen years. He saw nothing "irrepressible" about the conflict, but attributed it to a "blundering generation" of the fifties and sixties—the "sectional factionists." In 1873 he moved to Washington where he practiced law and wrote a series of articles for a Washington newspaper. These were collected and published as *Casket of Reminiscences* in 1874. Then, in 1876, he published his last book, *The Bench and Bar of the South and Southwest;* critics complimented the "new" Foote for the absence from this work of the usual vitriolic comments about people he did not like.

By the time his last book circulated, he was back in Tennessee and affiliated with the Republican party, the same party he had vilified since its formation in 1854. Republicans composed the minority party in the Volunteer State, and leaders welcomed him gladly. They named him an elector for the state at large, and he used his position to describe Democrats repeatedly as "unscrupulous men," dishonest and corrupt. Rutherford B. Hayes's victory in 1876 was pleasing to Foote, who for the next four years divided his time between Nashville and Washington. In 1878 he was elected permanent president of the Republican State Convention, and a few men even talked of him for governor. He was seventy-four by that time, however, and a Nashville newspaper described him as "a decrepit old gentleman with a fiery red head, almost entirely bald, . . . leaning heavily on a stout gold-headed cane."

Late in 1878, Hayes appointed him superintendent of the U.S. Mint at New Orleans, where he was well received. By the end of the following year he had become seriously ill and departed in April 1880 for Nashville, where he died on May 19. Former governor Joseph E. Brown of Georgia attended his funeral, and Gen. William Brimage Bate and former Confederate congressmen Robert Looney Caruthers and Arthur Colyar were pallbearers. He was buried in Mt. Olivet Cemetery.

BIBLIOGRAPHY

Chambers, William Nisbet. *Old Bullion Benton: Senator from the New West.* Boston, 1956.
Coulter, E. Merton. *The Confederate States of America, 1861–1865.* A History of the South, vol. 7. Baton Rouge, La., 1950.
DeBerry, John H. "Confederate Tennessee." Ph.D. diss., University of Kentucky, 1969.
Eaton, Clement. *Jefferson Davis.* New York, 1977.
Gonzales, John Edmond. "The Public Career of Henry Stuart Foote, 1804–1880." Ph.D. diss., University of North Carolina, 1957.
Warner, Ezra J., and W. Buck Yearns. *Biographical Register of the Confederate Congress.* Baton Rouge, La., 1975.

ROBERT E. CORLEW

FORD, ANTONIA

FORD, ANTONIA (1838–1871), spy. The daughter of a prominent merchant in Fairfax Court House, Virginia, Ford began her career as a spy in 1861 by passing information she gathered from Union forces in her hometown to Confederate leaders Col. J. E. B. Stuart and Gen. P. G. T. Beauregard. Although the exact nature of Ford's espionage activities is unclear, they seem to have been appreciated by Stuart, who rewarded Ford, on October 7, 1861, with a commission as an honorary aidede-camp.

Gen. Lafayette C. Baker, chief of Union counterintelligence, was aware of Ford's reputation: in March 1863, in the wake of Col. John S. Mosby's famous capture of Gen. Edwin H. Stoughton in Fairfax Court House, Baker placed a female counterspy in Fairfax to entrap Ford. Ford allegedly revealed to the counterspy that she had aided Mosby, and as a result, she was arrested on March 13, 1863, and committed to Old Capitol Prison in Washington, D.C. A few months later, Ford was released and sent on to Richmond as part of a prisoner exchange. Mosby in later years adamantly maintained that Ford had nothing to do with the Stoughton incident.

A year after Ford's arrest, on March 10, 1864, she married the Union officer who had arrested her, Maj. Joseph C. Willard. The couple settled in Washington, D.C., where Antonia Ford died in 1871.

BIBLIOGRAPHY

Bakeless, John. *Spies of the Confederacy.* Philadelphia, 1970.
Kane, Harnett T. *Spies for the Blue and Gray.* New York, 1954.

ELIZABETH R. VARON

FOREIGNERS

Contrary to popular myth, the Confederate States of America was not an entirely homogeneous society. The eleven states of the Confederacy had a white population of almost 5.5 million, of whom nearly a quarter of a million, or about 4 to 5 percent, were alien. The foreign-born percentages in two states were surprisingly high—Texas, over 7 percent, and Louisiana, over 11 percent—and Florida and Virginia each had more than 2 percent. In all Confederate states except Texas, the Irish were more numerous than any other ethnic group, followed by the Germans and the English.

The Home Front. The Germans created a German belt of sorts in south-central Texas where by their very numbers and geographic isolation they were able to reconstruct much of their Old World culture. In Texas and Virginia, the immigrants cultivated distinctive Texas-German and Shenandoah-German dialects, agricultural practices, housing styles, arts and crafts, food preparations, and folkways. The rural Germans, like other groups of immigrants living in the backcountry of Alabama, Tennessee, and North Carolina, did not significantly affect the balance of Confederate political power. In fact, most rural immigrants in the Confederacy largely eschewed politics, turning instead to their own institutions, and thus provided no challenge to the Confederacy's insistence on slavery and a conservative social order.

On the other hand, immigration did have a major effect upon the Confederacy's urban life. In many ways, the presence of immigrants in Southern cities made those urban areas less Southern and more Northern in appearance. Ethnic churches, presses, musical societies, theaters, beer gardens, and fraternal organizations took their places within the heart of the Confederacy. Through such port cities as New Orleans; Galveston, Texas; Mobile, Alabama; Savannah, Georgia; and Charleston, South Carolina, many hopeful immigrants arrived. But because of poverty, disease, or circumstance they often remained in the poorest neighborhoods near the wharves and warehouses. As their numbers grew in these cities and in such river cities as Memphis and Louisville, an immigrant-related political backlash emerged.

On the eve of the Civil War the immigrant population in the urban South decidedly changed the size, character, and composition of the working classes in Southern cities. The foreign-born became the major source of free labor in all key Confederate river and port cities. As the immigrants assumed positions in drayage, smithing, fitting shops, and taxi and hotel services, they drove blacks into manual labor and the resulting economic competition created additional strains in race relations.

The poverty of the immigrants and their tenuous relationship with Southern blacks made them suspect in the eyes of native-born white Southerners. Southern politicians viewed the immigrants as a danger to the urban social order and thus supported the enlarging of police forces—often ironically by hiring the foreign-born themselves—to control immigrant and black behavior. Nativism emerged, directed especially at the Irish Catholics who were accused of rowdyism, drunkenness, and consorting with blacks (even though they competed with them for jobs). Confusing causes with consequences, when disease and epidemic broke out in the poorest sections of Southern cities, white Southerners immediately concluded that immigrants threatened their region. Election riots involving Irish immigrants only fanned the fires of nativism. Defenders of the Confederacy proclaimed that the presence of immigrants in the South only brought to Southern cities all the social, economic, political, and cultural ills of the North.

Nevertheless, nativism did not consume Southern cities as it did those in the North because most immigrants remained either apolitical or staunchly supportive of slavery and the Confederate cause. Urban politicians eventually even acknowledged the immigrant presence by adding German and Irish names to the ballot, but Southern immigrants remained as yet too unorganized to create an effective political base.

The Military. Foreigners in the Confederacy occupied virtually every socioeconomic category. Some rose to prominence as politicians, lawyers, editors, or doctors, and many found their calling in military service. As might be expected, significant foreign companies were raised from areas with diverse, cosmopolitan populations such as Mobile, Alabama, and New Orleans, Louisiana. Various units comprised men of Irish, German, Scottish, French, Spanish, Mexican, Italian, and Chinese backgrounds.

Many of these men enlisted in the colorful regiments known as Zouaves. Organized in 1831 in Algeria, the Zouaves eventually admitted Europeans into their ranks. Like their namesakes, the Confederate Zouaves were noted for their gaudy dress of baggy trousers, short open jackets with extravagant embroidery, white gaiters, and turban headdresses. Perhaps most famous among the Confederate Zouaves were the Louisiana Zouaves, a name given to at least three regiments commonly known as the Tigers. Composed mainly of French, Italians, and creoles, the Louisiana Tigers were recruited from the most undisciplined and irreverent elements of New Orleans. Although they had a reputation as chronic troublemakers, their performance on the battlefields was impressive.

Another group of foreigners in the Confederate army was the European Brigade. Formed in February 1862 as the Union army advanced into Louisiana, the brigade was composed mostly of Europeans living in New Orleans. Among its numbers were 2,500 Frenchmen, 800 Spaniards, 500 Italians, 400 Germans, Dutchmen, and Scandinavians, and

500 Swiss, Belgians, Englishmen, Slavonians, and Austrians. The European Brigade performed yeoman duty during the Federal capture of New Orleans. With few Confederate troops left in the city, Mayor J. T. Monroe called upon the brigade, under Col. Paul Juge, to maintain law and order in the Crescent City. When Confederates threatened to burn the city rather than submit to Union control, the European Brigade suppressed the movement. Mayor Monroe prevailed upon Juge, who had planned to retire, to keep his men under arms until order was restored and the transition to Federal control was completed. The European Brigade disbanded in May 1862. It was given much credit by the mayor and the citizens of the city for maintaining the public order and preventing wanton destruction of life and property during very frightening times. Much like native-born Confederates the foreign-born served in the home guards to provide local defense, to preserve order, to guard property and commissary stores, to stand guard at prison camps, and to do provost duty in general.

Only two foreign-born Confederates attained the rank of major general. Irish-born Patrick Cleburne distinguished himself at the Battles of Shiloh; Richmond, Kentucky; and Franklin. His British military background, discipline, and charm earned him the respect of his men and admiration of his superiors despite opposition from some Southerners because of his foreign birth. The Frenchman Camille J. Polignac fought at the Battles of Shiloh and Corinth and in the Red River campaign. When he died in 1913 he was the longest surviving Confederate major general. The dashing Prussian-born cavalryman Heros von Borcke was perhaps the most widely known foreigner in the Confederate army. Chief of staff and close friend to Gen. J. E. B. Stuart, von Borcke participated in all of Stuart's campaigns and flamboyantly carried into battle what was reputedly the largest sword in the Confederacy.

[See also Cleburne, Patrick; Germans; Irish; Louisiana Tigers; Polignac, Camille J.; Population.]

BIBLIOGRAPHY

Jones, Terry L. *Lee's Tigers: The Louisiana Infantry in the Army of Northern Virginia.* Baton Rouge, La., 1987.

Lonn, Ella. *Foreigners in the Confederacy.* Chapel Hill, N.C., 1940. Reprint, Gloucester, Mass., 1965.

Silverman, Jason H. *Beyond the Melting Pot in Dixie: Immigration and Ethnicity in Southern History.* Lexington, Ky., forthcoming.

Silverman, Jason H. "Stars, Bars, and Foreigners: The Immigrant and the Making of the Confederacy." *Journal of Confederate History* 1 (1988): 265–285.

JASON H. SILVERMAN

FORREST, NATHAN BEDFORD

FORREST, NATHAN BEDFORD (1821–1877), lieutenant general. Forrest was born in Chapel Hill, Tennessee, on July 13, 1821. Although he had barely six months' formal education, Forrest assumed responsibility for his family at the age of sixteen following his father's death. Life in the Southern backcountry, the demands of Southern honor, and a constant struggle for control conditioned his life.

Forrest supported his family until 1842, when he moved to Hernando, Mississippi, to go into business with an uncle. In 1851, he relocated to Memphis, Tennessee, where he engaged extensively in the slave trade, establishing one of the largest such operations in the region. With the money he obtained, he rose from semisubsistence to planter status, acquiring substantial plantation property in Coahoma County, Mississippi. Throughout his prewar years, Forrest held various public offices and positions of authority: constable in Hernando; coroner in DeSoto County, Mississippi; lieutenant in the DeSoto Dragoons (Fifty-first Regiment, Mississippi Militia); and alderman in Memphis from 1858 to 1859 and in 1860.

Following Tennessee's secession from the Union, Forrest enlisted as a private in Capt. Josiah White's Tennessee Mounted Rifles (Seventh Tennessee Cavalry) with his youngest brother and fifteen-year-old son. Shortly afterward, the governor of Tennessee summoned him to Memphis and authorized him to raise a battalion of mounted troops, which later became known as the Third Tennessee Cavalry Regiment. As a lieutenant colonel, Forrest recruited and equipped his command, mostly at his own expense. In his first substantial combat experience at Sacramento, Kentucky, on December 28, 1861, he demonstrated the traits that characterized him as a soldier throughout the war by employing envelopment tactics and engaging the enemy personally.

In February 1862, Forrest established a reputation for boldness when he led his men out of Fort Donelson before its surrender, after having participated actively in its defense. Following his election as colonel, the cavalry commander fought at Shiloh, suffering a severe wound during the final phase of that battle. Subsequently, he assumed a new command, later known simply as Forrest's cavalry brigade, and promptly won promotion to brigadier general following a daring raid against the Union garrison at Murfreesboro, Tennessee, on July 13, 1862.

In mid-December 1862, Forrest crossed the Tennessee River into the western part of the state on a raid designed to sever Maj. Gen. Ulysses S. Grant's supply lines. For two and a half weeks, Forrest's cavalrymen used bluff and bluster to capture railroad depots, burn supplies, and disable miles of

NATHAN BEDFORD FORREST.

track and trestlework. Forrest succeeded in eluding his pursuers until December 31, when he fought a pitched battle at Parker's Crossroads. He was on the verge of winning the battle when a second Union force appeared, at which point he was fortunate just to extricate the bulk of his command. Nevertheless, Forrest succeeded in crippling Grant's supply lines and thwarting that general's initial assault against Vicksburg, Mississippi.

On February 3, 1863, Forrest's command suffered a defeat at Dover, Tennessee, while under the overall command of Maj. Gen. Joseph Wheeler. Then, following redeeming victories at Thompson and Brentwood, Tennessee, Forrest successfully halted a raid in April and May 1863 by Union Col. Abel Streight against the Western and Atlantic Railroad. In the climax to his pursuit, the Confederate cavalryman again used psychology and deception to compel a numerically superior force to surrender to him. Forrest was a master of this kind of warfare. In the case of his confrontation with Abel Streight, he employed false couriers from phantom units and moved the minimal number of troops at hand so as to artificially inflate his command.

Forrest's cavalry participated in Braxton Bragg's retreat from central Tennessee, his evacuation of Chattanooga, and the subsequent battle along Chickamauga Creek, Georgia. Following the victory over William S. Rosecrans's Federals at Chickamauga, Forrest urged but failed to convince Bragg to pursue the defeated enemy. Angry at his superior's ineptitude and resenting Bragg's previous treatment of him, Forrest bitterly denounced Bragg and won a transfer to an independent command in Mississippi.

For the third time in his military career, Forrest raised a command, known simply as Forrest's cavalry corps, with new recruits and conscripts joining a small nucleus of veterans.

Promoted to major general on December 4, 1863, he led raids against Federal communications and supply lines in Tennessee and Alabama and blunted various Union raids into Mississippi throughout 1864. In April, he conducted a raid into western Tennessee that culminated in the capture of Fort Pillow. In the latter stages of that battle, Forrest lost control of his men, who killed members of the black Tennessee Unionist garrison who should have been spared.

In June, Forrest ably defeated and routed a superior force of Union infantry and cavalry at Brice's Cross Roads. In July, he helped turn back another Federal invasion force at Tupelo, although he suffered a temporarily disabling wound while directing the pursuit of the retreating Union troops. After recovering from his wound, Forrest engaged in a generally successful effort to destroy the railroads of northern Alabama and central Tennessee and decimated the river supply depot at Johnsonville, Tennessee. He cut short the Johnsonville expedition to march with John Bell Hood in that general's disastrous Tennessee campaign in November and December 1864. Forrest's outstanding conduct of the rear guard in Hood's retreat from Nashville, Tennessee, saved the Army of Tennessee from further destruction.

Forrest returned to Mississippi to reorganize his cavalry command. During this period he received a promotion to lieutenant general to date from February 28, 1865. In the closing months of the war, Forrest attempted to restore the condition of his command to resist further Union advances. Despite his preparations, he was unable to prevent a vastly superior force under Brig. Gen. James Harrison Wilson from dispersing his command and capturing Selma, Alabama, in March and April 1865. Forrest regrouped his men a final time before surrendering them at Gainesville, Alabama, in May.

Following the war, Forrest struggled to regain control over his life during Reconstruction and in the face of a series of business failures. For some years, he served as president of and worked diligently to promote the Selma, Marion, and Memphis Railroad. Contrary to his avowal at the end of the war to remain quietly at home, he embraced the budding Ku Klux Klan and assumed the role of first grand wizard of the secret organization. Never completely adjusting to the new realities of the postwar years, Forrest helped restore white Conservative Democrats to power and sought to reassert white supremacy in the South. He died in Memphis on October 29, 1877, having failed to recoup his prewar fortune.

Nathan Bedford Forrest stands as one of the foremost cavalry raiders of the war. His ferocity as a warrior was almost legendary. His claim to have slain one more enemy soldier in personal combat than the twenty-nine horses killed beneath him only added to the legend. Forrest fought by the simple maxim "Forward men, and mix with 'em." He understood, perhaps better than most, the basic premise of war: "War means fighting and fighting means killing."

BIBLIOGRAPHY

Henry, Robert Selph. *"First with the Most" Forrest*. Indianapolis, 1944.

Jordan, Thomas, and J. P. Pryor. *The Campaigns of Lieut. Gen. N. B. Forrest, and of Forrest's Cavalry*. New Orleans, 1868.

Lytle, Andrew. *Bedford Forrest and His Critter Company*. New York, 1931.

Mathes, J. Harvey. *General Forrest*. New York, 1902.

Wills, Brian Steel. *A Battle from the Start: The Life of Nathan Bedford Forrest*. New York, 1992.

Wyeth, John Allan. *Life of General Nathan Bedford Forrest*. New York, 1899. Reprint, Baton Rouge, La., 1989.

BRIAN S. WILLS

FORREST'S RAIDS

Gen. Nathan Bedford Forrest conducted three principal cavalry raids against Federal garrisons and supply lines in his native state of Tennessee during the Civil War. He undertook forays behind Union lines throughout his career, but those in July 1862 against the Union garrison at Murfreesboro, in December 1862 and January 1863 against Union lines in western Tennessee, and in November 1864 against the Union depot and storage facility at Johnsonville, established his reputation as one of the South's foremost cavalry raiders.

The first of these raids occurred in July 1862, when Colonel Forrest, already recommended for promotion to brigadier general for his conduct at Fort Donelson and Shiloh, took his cavalry command across the Tennessee River. At McMinnville he received reinforcements and prepared for a push on the Union garrison at Murfreesboro. Arriving at the town early on July 13, Forrest divided his men into three groups. The first was to attack the nearest Union camp of the Ninth Michigan Infantry and the Seventh Pennsylvania Cavalry, the second was to storm the town, and the third was to hit the camp of the Third Minnesota on the farthest side of Murfreesboro.

Forrest expected the operation to proceed smoothly, but complications developed. The Federals in the town surrendered, but the others quickly rallied after the surprise attack and put up a stubborn defense. Forrest led his men against the Minnesotans, capturing their camp and some prisoners. As his troopers pinned down these Federals, he rode off to supervise the fighting in the other camp. When one of his officers recommended that they break off the raid before Union reinforcements arrived, Forrest answered characteristically, "I did not come here to make half a job of it. I mean to have them all."

Through the astute use of bluff, Forrest soon convinced both of the remaining Union commanders to surrender. His victory netted the Confederates 1,200 prisoners and sub-stantial stores of weapons and equipment. He had inflicted casualties of 29 killed and 120 wounded while sustaining losses of 25 killed and 40 to 60 wounded.

Forrest's second major raid into Tennessee took place between December 11, 1862, and January 2, 1863. In compliance with orders to destroy the Union supply lines in western Tennessee, Brigadier General Forrest set out from Columbia, Tennessee, on December 11 to wreck the track and trestlework of the Mississippi Central and the Mobile and Ohio Railroads.

The Southerners reached the Tennessee River crossing at Clifton on December 15, pushing across the river on flatboats by late the next night. As the Confederates moved toward Jackson, Tennessee, they encountered Union troops under Col. Robert G. Ingersoll. The two forces clashed, with the Southerners routing and capturing much of Ingersoll's command, including the colonel, 147 men, and two 3-inch Rodman cannons.

Forrest then used several ploys to deceive Brig. Gen. Jeremiah C. Sullivan into believing that the Confederates were in front of Lexington in superior numbers. Sullivan obliged Forrest by concentrating his forces and conceding the countryside to the Southerners. Forrest seized the opportunity to dispatch forces to attack depots and destroy track and bridges north and south of the town. He left a thin screen of horsemen to maintain the deception and rode on to capture Humboldt and Trenton.

On December 23, Forrest took Union City and continued to destroy rail lines in the region. In his December 24 report, he noted with satisfaction: "We have made a clean sweep of the Federals and [rail]roads north of Jackson." On Christmas Day, Forrest moved his command to the southeast, with an eye to returning to Confederate lines. Finding that Federal gunboats and burned bridges on the Obion River blocked his path, he located an old, unstable bridge the Federals had ignored, had his men shore up the structure, and pushed his command across the river.

Forrest faced a final obstacle before he could reach the safety of Confederate lines. Union Col. Cyrus Dunham had placed his brigade onto the Confederates' path at Parker's Cross Roads. On December 31, Forrest decided to strike these Federals, capture them if possible, and proceed. Using his artillery and flanking attacks to great advantage, Forrest had almost succeeded when other Federals appeared in his rear, and he was fortunate just to extricate his command from the trap. His men escaped the pincers and reached the crossing at Clifton. Brushing aside a final effort to stop him, Forrest had his men across the river by January 2, 1863.

Despite the rough handling at Parker's Cross Roads, Forrest's western Tennessee raid was a success. Coupled with Brig. Gen. Earl Van Dorn's capture of Maj. Gen. Ulysses S. Grant's forward supply base at Holly Springs, Mississippi, Forrest's actions crippled Grant's initial assault on Vicksburg.

The third of his Tennessee raids began on October 24, 1864, when Major General Forrest's cavalry command left their base at Jackson, Tennessee. On October 28, the Confederates reached the Tennessee River near Fort Heiman and placed batteries along the bank, concealing them from view. For the next two days, their artillery sparred with Union gunboats and steamers. The Southerners succeeded in capturing and temporarily converting the Union gunboat *Undine* and the steamer *Venus* to Confederate service. Although Forrest lost both ships in subsequent fighting, his crews managed to escape capture and his plans for an attack on the massive depot and storage facility at Johnsonville remained intact.

In the meantime, Forrest began to deploy his troops and artillery across the river from the depot. His cannoneers wrestled their guns into place and concealed them. By 2:00 P.M. on November 4, all was ready. The Confederate gunners, their weapons targeted from as close a range as the terrain would permit, blasted the Union supply base with devastating effectiveness. By nightfall, the entire bank was ablaze.

In the Johnsonville raid, Forrest's men had destroyed four Union gunboats, fourteen transports, twenty barges, and an estimated $6.7 million worth of Federal property. Sherman noted stoically, "That devil Forrest was down about Johnsonville, making havoc among the gunboats and transports." Forrest was also, as in his previous Tennessee raids, enhancing his reputation as a raider.

BIBLIOGRAPHY

Henry, Robert Selph. *"First with the Most" Forrest.* Indianapolis, 1944.
Jordan, Thomas, and J. P. Pryor. *The Campaigns of Lieut.-Gen. N. B. Forrest, and of Forrest's Cavalry.* New Orleans, 1868.
Morton, John Watson. *The Artillery of Nathan Bedford Forrest's Cavalry.* Nashville, Tenn., 1909.
Wills, Brian Steel. *A Battle from the Start: The Life of Nathan Bedford Forrest.* New York, 1992.
Wyeth, John Allan. *Life of General Nathan Bedford Forrest.* New York, 1899. Reprint, Baton Rouge, La., 1989.

BRIAN S. WILLS

FORT DELAWARE PRISON

Fort Delaware was a fortification built of cut stone on Peapatch Island to control the navigation of the Delaware River. The fort was near the New Jersey side of the river opposite Delaware City, Delaware. Just after the war's start, the United States used it to hold political and naval prisoners. In the spring of 1862, to handle the growing number of Confederate army prisoners, the Federals built shed barracks inside the fort intended for two thousand men. During the period of exchange under the cartel of July 22, 1862, the fort often served as a way station for officers and enlisted men en route to City Point, Virginia. With the breakdown of exchange in 1863, the Federal authorities declared Fort Delaware to be a regular prison depot and built outside the walls of the original fort additional barracks intended to hold five thousand prisoners.

From 1863 to 1865, the commanding officer of Fort Delaware was Brig. Gen. Albin Francisco Schoepf. A refugee of Austrian-Polish birth, he had received military training in Europe and was a protégé of Joseph Holt, the powerful judge advocate general of the army. Prisoners' complaints against him sometimes reflected antiforeign prejudices, but since Schoepf tried to be verbally conciliatory, especially to captive officers, they often deflected their grievances to his adjutant, Capt. George W. Ahl, whom they blamed for much of what they disliked about the prison. Ahl headed a unit formed from Confederate deserters who supplemented the militia that made up the principal guard force. These ex-Confederates were inevitably a prominent target of the hatred of the prisoners, who charged them with deliberate cruelty.

Officer prisoners, who were carefully segregated from enlisted men, complained, but they recognized that their housing and usual ability to buy additional food from the civilian provisioner meant that their condition was better than that of the common soldiers. As in other prisons, officers could entertain themselves by reading, holding informal classes and minstrel shows, gambling, and even preparing a manuscript newspaper. But all prisoners complained that the rations of bread and meat served in mess halls were inadequate in both quality and quantity. Even the water was deficient; that used for cleaning came from ditches and the river and was polluted by the fort's own sewage. Drinking water brought in by boat from nearby Brandywine Creek was marginally less noxious. Complaints of dampness in a prison barely above river level were endemic, and indeed in July 1863, the new barracks sank into the mud and several threatened to tip over.

Ill health, including typhoid fever, was to be expected, and in September 1863, 327 men died out of 8,822. A month later, smallpox broke out, yet the U.S. commissary general of prisoners rejected the complaint even of the surgeon general that the fort was not a suitably healthy prison site. And in fact the monthly death toll did decline in 1864, even though the prison reached a maximum population of 9,174. Because literate, vocal officers were among the prisoners, conditions at Fort Delaware elicited frequent denunciations by the Confederate government and newspapers, and the fort became one of the more dreaded prisons in Southern eyes.

Fort Delaware's location convenient to the warring lines guaranteed that it would continue to be used when exchange resumed in 1865, and it was not finally abandoned as a military prison until August 1865. The fort itself was used in the Spanish-American and other wars and then became a Delaware state park. The prison's most significant monument is on the New Jersey shore: the 2,436 Confederate graves in the Finns Point National Cemetery.

BIBLIOGRAPHY

Byrne, Frank L. "Prison Pens of Suffering." In *Fighting for Time*. Edited by William C. Davis. Vol. 4 of *The Image of War, 1861–1865*. Garden City, N.Y., 1983.

Hesseltine, William B. *Civil War Prisons: A Study in War Psychology*. Columbus, Ohio, 1930. Reprint, New York, 1964.

Rich, Edward Robins. *Comrades!* Easton, Md., 1898.

Wilson, W. Emerson. *Fort Delaware*. Newark, Del., 1987.

FRANK L. BYRNE

FORT FISHER, NORTH CAROLINA

Situated at the mouth of the Cape Fear River, Fort Fisher guarded the approaches to the port of Wilmington, North Carolina. A mammoth earthwork, the fort assumed strategic importance late in the war because Wilmington, a favorite base for blockade runners, remained the last major port open for the Confederacy. In December 1864 and January 1865 the Federal command launched two attacks on Fort Fisher that featured a huge number of ships and massive artillery bombardments. On January 15, the fort fell to combined sea and land assaults.

Work began on Fort Fisher in April 1861. In July 1862 Col. William Lamb assumed command and continued the construction of the largest earthwork in the Confederacy and one of the largest in the world. Shaped like a letter L, with the

> **Forty-eight guns looked out from behind sandbagged and revetted walls that stood twenty feet high. . . .**

angle pointing in a northeasterly direction out to sea, the fort placed its long side toward the seacoast and threw its short side across a narrow peninsula. Forty-eight guns looked out from behind sandbagged and revetted walls that stood twenty feet high and twenty-five feet thick. Heavy traverses lay between the gun chambers and thus protected gunners from explosions nearby. A shallow ditch, a log palisade, and a mine field further protected the land approach to the fort.

Several other forts lined the Cape Fear River, but Fort Fisher was the key installation. Its size and big guns had kept the Union fleet several miles out at sea. So much hard labor, by slaves and conscripts, had gone into the making of the fort that during Reconstruction, Republicans angled for votes among poorer whites and blacks by warning that the Democrats planned to rebuild it.

On September 2, 1864, U.S. Secretary of the Navy Gideon Welles won approval for his proposal to attack Fort Fisher. After Rear Adm. David Farragut declined command of the naval expedition because of illness, the assignment was given to Rear Adm. David D. Porter. Gen. Benjamin F. Butler headed the troops of the Federal army that would attack following a bombardment. On the Confederate side, Gen. Braxton Bragg was in overall command at Wilmington, with Gen. W. H. C. Whiting immediately responsible for the defense of the city and its approaches. Colonel Lamb commanded the Confederates at the fort. Fifty-six vessels, the largest U.S. armada assembled to that time, sailed to the fort and anchored in a semicircle one-half mile away. Twenty-five hundred Federal troops landed to assault fewer than eight hundred Confederates in the fort.

The first attack began on the night of December 23 as Federal sailors towed an old ship laden with powder and explosives to within three hundred yards of Fort Fisher. General Butler had conceived this idea, believing that a huge explosion could do great damage, but the blast was without consequence. So also was a tremendous bombardment on the twenty-fourth. "Never since the invention of gunpowder," wrote Colonel Lamb, "was there so much of it harmlessly expended as in the first day's attack on Fort Fisher." Another huge bombardment on Christmas Day prepared the way for Butler's ground attack, but when his men had come to within fifty yards of the fort, he ordered a retreat, and the first attack was over.

Admiral Porter asked Gen. Ulysses S. Grant for the same troops and a different commander, and on January 13, 1865, the second battle began with Maj. Gen. Alfred H. Terry landing 8,000 Federal troops against 1,500 Confederates in the fort. Two days of bombardment that General Whiting characterized as "beyond description" did considerable damage to the fort, wounded many of its defenders, and led the Confederate commanders to call for reinforcements from Bragg. Only 350 men arrived. On January 15 a Federal force of 6,000 stormed the fort, now manned by about 1,200 Confederates. Vicious hand-to-hand fighting wavered both ways, but precise support from the navy's guns helped ensure a Federal victory. About 10:00 P.M. on January 15 the Confederates surrendered, having received no effective relief from General Bragg, who had at hand 6,000 troops under Gen. Robert Frederick Hoke and three artillery batteries.

The fall of Fort Fisher deprived the Confederacy of its last connection with the rest of the world. In the second attack

Federal forces had lost 670 soldiers and about 400 sailors. The Confederates suffered approximately 500 casualties, including General Whiting (who later died in prison) and Colonel Lamb. Fifteen hundred Confederates were taken as prisoners. Admiral Porter, who wrote that "no one could form the slightest conception of these works . . . who had not seen them," estimated that his fleet expended fifty thousand shells in its attack. In February Federal forces followed up their victory by moving against General Hoke's forces and on February 22 captured Wilmington.

[*See also* Wilmington, North Carolina.]

BIBLIOGRAPHY

Barrett, John G. *The Civil War in North Carolina.* Chapel Hill, N.C., 1963.
Gragg, Rod. *Confederate Goliath: The Battle of Fort Fisher.* New York, 1991.

PAUL D. ESCOTT

FORT HILL

The South Carolina plantation home of American statesman John C. Calhoun was originally named Clergy Hall when it was built in 1803 and served as a Presbyterian manse during the early settlement of the old Cherokee Indian boundary. Calhoun acquired the property in 1825 through his mother-in-law, although while serving as vice president, he continued to live in the Georgetown section of the District of Columbia. Financial and domestic considerations hastened a decision to return to the South, and he moved his family to Clergy Hall the following year.

Calhoun renamed the house Fort Hill and transformed the original structure of vernacular up-country design into a Greek Revival plantation home of commanding presence, with broad views of the surrounding 1,100-acre estate. Fort Hill allowed Calhoun to indulge his avocation of agriculture. It did not, however, distract him from the political events of the day. In the summer of 1831 the nullification controversy was developing into a national crisis. From his office, located behind the main house, Calhoun wrote the "Fort Hill Address," which gave intellectual focus to the gathering forces of Southern nationalism.

Fort Hill remained a Calhoun family property for nearly forty years after Calhoun's death in 1850. Plantation lands were under cultivation throughout the Civil War, and after the conflict, crops were tended by former Calhoun family slaves working as paid laborers.

Fort Hill came through the Civil War unscathed. After the war, there were Federal troops in the nearby town of Pendleton, but their few acts of vandalism were confined to the town itself. Since 1889, Fort Hill has been the site of Clemson University, a legacy of Calhoun's son-in-law, Thomas Green Clemson.

BIBLIOGRAPHY

Cook, Harriet Hefner. *Fort Hill: John C. Calhoun Shrine.* Revised by Carol C. Brannon. Clemson, S.C., 1970.
Freehling, William W., ed. *The Nullification Era: A Documentary Record.* New York, 1967.
Wilson, Clyde N., and W. Edwin Hemphill, eds. *The Papers of John C. Calhoun.* 20 vols. to date. Columbia, S.C., 1977.

ROBERT T. BARRETT

FORT PICKENS, FLORIDA

One of three forts that guarded the entrance to Pensacola Bay, Florida, Fort Pickens almost became the site of the first shots of the Civil War. Early in January 1861 a combination of quick thinking by the Federal commander and Southerners' hesitation saved the fort from Confederate capture. By April 16, 1861, the Union had a thousand men and four warships at Fort Pickens, and its possession was never seriously challenged. With the Union forces firmly entrenched in the bay, Confederates could not fully utilize the Pensacola Navy Yard, and by the spring of 1862 all of Pensacola was in Union control.

Secession winter, 1860–1861, found the small Union force at Pensacola threatened with isolation. Fort Pickens along with Forts McRee and Barrancas were key positions for defense of the harbor and the valuable Pensacola Navy Yard. During December and early January, Alabama militia joined Florida secessionists at Pensacola to aid in wresting the forts from U.S. control. But on January 10, the same day that Florida seceded from the Union, Federal forces at Fort Barrancas abandoned their position for the more formidable location at Fort Pickens on the western tip of Santa Rosa Island. This stone garrison contained numerous cannons, thousands of projectiles, loose shot, and several pounds of powder. The Federal lieutenant had only eighty-one men, and the fort, unused since the Mexican War, had fallen into disrepair. Southerners attempted to obtain a peaceful surrender over the next few days, but the small contingent of Federals stood firm. A confrontation seemed only a matter of time.

Confederates soon received word that the warship *Brooklyn* was en route to reinforce Pickens with two hundred men. Two former U.S. senators quickly moved to forestall the outbreak of hostilities. Stephen R. Mallory and John Slidell joined other leaders of the soon-to-be-formed

Confederacy in determining that "the possession of the Fort was not worth one drop of blood to us." They approached President James Buchanan with a simple compromise. If he called off the Federal expedition, the state troops that had massed at Pensacola would not attack. Buchanan agreed. On January 29, 1861, *Brooklyn* dropped anchor in the harbor and waited.

After Abraham Lincoln's inauguration in March, the situation began to change. Denying the validity of the quasi armistice, Lincoln sent orders on March 12 to land the company and reinforce the fort, but the ship's commander delayed the landing for a month. Finally, on April 12, the same day Confederates fired on Fort Sumter, two hundred Union men with supplies and ammunition disembarked at Fort Pickens. They were soon joined by an additional eight hundred men.

Between April 12, 1861, and May 9, 1862, five engagements occurred, including incidents of burning, attempted infantry invasions, and artillery duels. In early October Brig. Gen. Braxton Bragg sent a thousand men to make a clandestine attack on the fort. The resulting Battle of Santa Rosa Island ended with Confederates in full retreat and Federals shaken by the surprise. Both sides claimed victory, but the battle left the same stalemate in place that had existed since early spring. On May 9, 1862, the Confederates burned and abandoned their position at Pensacola.

BIBLIOGRAPHY

Bearss, Edwin, "Civil War Operations in and around Pensacola." *Florida Historical Quarterly* 36 (1957): 125–165; 39 (1961): 231–255.

Dickison, J. J. *Florida.* Vol. 11 of *Confederate Military History.* Edited by Clement A. Evans. Atlanta, 1899. Vol. 16 of extended ed. Wilmington, N.C., 1989.

Tilley, John Shipley. *Lincoln Takes Command.* Chapel Hill, N.C., 1941.

LESLEY JILL GORDON-BURR

FORT PILLOW MASSACRE

The Confederates originally constructed the earthwork fortification on the Mississippi River, north of Memphis, to protect the water approaches to that city. Fort Pillow was situated on a high bluff on the eastern bank, overlooking the river. After the Confederates evacuated the fort in 1862, it became part of the chain of Federal garrisons employed to protect communications and supply lines in the region. In 1864, Maj. Lionel F. Booth commanded a garrison there, variously estimated at between 557 and 580 black and white troops of the Thirteenth Tennessee Cavalry, the Eleventh U.S. Colored Troops, and Battery F of the Fourth U.S. Colored Light Artillery.

In March and April 1864, Maj. Gen. Nathan Bedford Forrest determined to attack the isolated Union garrison as part of a raid into western Tennessee and Kentucky. The first Confederates arrived before Fort Pillow in the early morning hours of April 12, under the command of Brig. Gen. James R. Chalmers. Chalmers succeeded in driving the Federals into their innermost entrenchments and deployed his men. Forrest arrived at 10:00 A.M. to find Fort Pillow virtually surrounded, with Confederate sharpshooters situated on high ground, enabling them to fire directly into the fort. Forrest reconnoitered and placed additional sharpshooters.

These sharpshooters had already profoundly affected the fighting at Fort Pillow. At 9:00 A.M., Confederate fire had struck Booth in the chest as he stood near one of the earthwork's portholes. Maj. William F. Bradford assumed command, although he continued to use Booth's name in negotiations with the Confederates.

Under this covering fire, Forrest's men seized a row of Union barracks and outlying rifle pits. This success convinced the Confederate general that he was now in a position to storm the fort. But, typically, Forrest preferred to take the fort through negotiation, if possible. To that end, at 3:30 P.M., he sent in a demand for the unconditional surrender of the garrison, warning, "Should my demand be refused, I cannot be responsible for the fate of your command."

Bradford insisted upon having an hour to consult with his officers. Forrest, worried that he might use the time to obtain reinforcements, granted him twenty minutes. The Confederate commander also dispatched troops to the riverbank to prevent an approaching Union transport vessel from landing and impatiently rode to the scene of the truce negotiations. Finally, Bradford declared that he would not surrender. Forrest rode back to his lines and issued orders for an assault.

The Confederates rushed across the relatively short distance to the fort and scaled the parapet. As they swarmed into Fort Pillow, firing point-blank into the defenders, the Federal garrison retreated. In such an eventuality, the Union commanders had planned to rely upon the gunboat *New Era* to drive off the pursuing Southerners and thereby enable the garrison to escape. As the garrison broke for the riverbank below, however, the fighting became chaotic and Bradford was unable to execute the plan. Many of the Federals tried to surrender. Others ran for their lives. Still others fired as they withdrew, apparently hoping to prolong the defense until help could arrive.

Remaining outside Fort Pillow, Forrest lost control of events inside the fort and on the riverbank below. Pent-up anger and racial animosity led some of the Confederates to give their opponents no mercy. Casualty figures demonstrate that members of the fort's garrison, especially black troops, suffered an inordinately high number of deaths. Although the Confederates were the attacking party, they lost just 14 killed and 86 wounded, while the Federal defenders lost 231 killed, 100 wounded, and 226 captured. The victorious Southerners took prisoner only 58 of the 262 black troops engaged.

The Northern press immediately labeled the events at Fort Pillow a "massacre." A U.S. congressional committee investigated the affair, calling witnesses and accumulating often gruesome testimony. The committee determined that a massacre had occurred at the fort. Forrest denied the charges, but the exertions that he and other Confederate officers had to take to prevent unnecessary killings are the most telling testimony that such slaughter took place and that, for however long, he was powerless to prevent it. In any event, as commander of the troops on the scene, Forrest was responsible.

BIBLIOGRAPHY

Castel, Albert. "The Fort Pillow Massacre: A Fresh Examination of the Evidence." *Civil War History* 4 (1958): 37–50.
Cimprich, John, and Robert C. Mainfort, Jr. "The Fort Pillow Massacre: A Statistical Note." *Journal of American History* 76 (December 1989): 830–837.
Cimprich, John, and Robert C. Mainfort, Jr. "Fort Pillow Revisited: New Evidence about an Old Controversy." *Civil War History* 28 (December 1982): 293–306.
Maness, Lonnie E. "The Fort Pillow Massacre: Fact or Fiction."*Tennessee Historical Quarterly* 45 (Spring 1986): 287–315.
Wills, Brian Steel. *A Battle from the Start: The Life of Nathan Bedford Forrest*. New York, 1992.

BRIAN S. WILLS

FORT PULASKI, GEORGIA

The Confederate surrender of Fort Pulaski, following an intense two-day Union artillery bombardment (April 10–11, 1862), eliminated Savannah, Georgia, as a blockade-running seaport. Located on Cockspur Island and named for Count Casimir Pulaski, the Polish hero of the American Revolution, this pentagonal masonry fort made of 25 million bricks was completed in 1847. On January 6, 1861, it was seized by the Georgia militia.

Union plans for a naval blockade of the Confederacy included the capture of Fort Pulaski. By November Northern troops had landed on nearby Tybee Island, with Capt. Quincy A. Gillmore designated commander of the projected bombardment. Gillmore's men began erecting eleven batteries containing 36 heavy guns and mortars at ranges varying between 1,650 and 3,400 yards. Fort Pulaski mounted 48 cannons with a garrison of 385 officers and men command-

ed by Col. Charles H. Olmstead. Brig. Gen. Robert E. Lee, who years earlier had sited and begun building the fort and who now commanded Confederates in Georgia, South Carolina, and eastern Florida, believed Fort Pulaski to be invulnerable.

After sunrise on April 10, 1862, Olmstead confidently rejected Gillmore's surrender summons, saying, "I am here to defend this Fort, not to surrender it." Union artillery opened fire at 8:15 A.M. Fort Pulaski replied shortly after. By evening the beginnings of a breach were plainly visible in the southeast wall. Incoming harassment fire throughout the night hampered repairs. Exchange of fire resumed the second morning. Northern gunners exploited the expanding breach by aiming shells through it and across the parade ground to strike the fort magazine. With sixteen cannon dismounted and his defenders endangered by the probable explosion of 40,000 pounds of gunpowder, Olmstead at 2:00 P.M. hoisted a bedsheet and Gillmore rowed over to receive a formal surrender.

During the two-day bombardment 5,275 shot and shell had been hurled against Fort Pulaski. Mortars proved ineffectual. The decisive breach had been cut almost entirely by three large rifled cannon, which led Northern artillerists to predict correctly that rifled ordnance would "revolutionize such warfare."

BIBLIOGRAPHY

Bryan, T. Conn. *Confederate Georgia*. Athens, Ga., 1953.
Gillmore, Quincy A. "Siege and Capture of Fort Pulaski." In *Battles and Leaders of the Civil War*. Edited by Robert U. Johnson and C. C. Buel. Vol. 2. New York, 1888. Reprint, Secaucus, N.J., 1982.
Lawrence, Alexander A. *A Present for Mr. Lincoln: The Story of Savannah from Secession to Sherman*. Macon, Ga., 1961.

DENNIS KELLY

FORTS AND FORTIFICATIONS

[*This entry is composed of two articles that discuss the use of coastal fortifications, tower defenses, frontier forts, and field fortifications in the Confederacy:* An Overview *and* Field Fortifications. *For further discussion of the construction, armament, and management of these forts and fortifications, see* Artillery *and* Engineer Bureau. *For further discussion of their role in the Civil War, see* Fort Fisher, North Carolina; Fort Pickens, Florida; Fort Pulaski, Georgia; Fort Stedman, Virginia; Fort Sumter, South Carolina; Fort Wagner, South Carolina; *and entries on the numerous battles and campaigns mentioned herein.*]

An Overview

At the onset of the Civil War, the Confederacy found itself in possession of a wide range of formerly Federal coast defense and frontier forts. These installations and others built during the war would play a major role in the defense of the Confederate States.

Fortification building was not an arcane science; the U.S. Army had a long history of developing fortified installations, dating back to before the American Revolution. The standard guide of the time was *A Complete Treatise on Field Fortification,* written in 1836 by Dennis H. Mahan, professor of military and civil engineering at the U.S. Military Academy. Mahan's engineering doctrine was the dominant influence in the development of fortifications, addressing all aspects including permanent and field (temporary) defenses, establishing clear lines of fire, planning for defense, trenches, revetments (support facings for ramparts), and the like. Mahan's work effectively served as the bible on the subject and was widely used by both sides during the war. Indeed, in the preface Mahan stated that his work was "a book not for study alone, but one which the officer can take with him into the camp, and consult at any moment." Though the clouds of sectional violence had already been long gathering by the time Mahan's work was published, few could imagine that its tenets would be followed by Americans fighting Americans.

> **At the start of the war there was some hesitation . . . over the employment of fortifications.**

The development of fortifications normally required the efforts of trained engineers. During the prewar period the Corps of Engineers was the elite branch of the army, receiving the top graduates of West Point. Among their ranks were several officers who would later find fame while serving in the Confederate army. Superintending engineer from 1848 to 1849 for the construction of Fort Gaines, on Dauphin Island at the entrance to Mobile Bay, was Capt. P. G. T. Beauregard. Fort Alafia, an 1849 temporary defense erected in Polk County, Florida, was built under the supervision of 1st Lt. John C. Pemberton, Fourth U.S. Artillery. Army Engineer Lt. Col. Robert E. Lee designed the plans for Fort De Soto, a major coastal defense on Mullet Key in Tampa Bay, Florida; when the fort was finally built in 1898, Lee's original plans were utilized. The lessons learned by these and other future Confederate staff and field officers were well applied during the Civil War.

At the start of the war there was some hesitation on both sides over the employment of fortifications. One major reason was that no one believed the war would last long enough to require serious fortification programs; both South and North fully expected to sweep the battlefield of the foe at the first opportunity, quickly bringing the conflict to an end. It was also felt that these structures were not appropriate as devices of modern civilized warfare. The violence of the combat and effectiveness of modern weaponry quickly disabused the participants of this notion.

As the war intensified, it became apparent that often the combatants felt secure only if they were dug in somewhere. Southern field commanders quickly recalled that the use of fortifications, whether of earth, logs, rails, or other material, gave the advantage to the defense. A standard axiom of the time was that good troops would be able to hold the line against three times their number. As a result, throughout the war much time and energy was spent by both sides digging trenches and erecting fortifications.

The fortifications utilized by the Confederate States during the war generally fell into the categories of coastal fortifications, field forts, tower defenses, and frontier forts.

Coastal Fortifications

The earliest seacoast defenses of the United States were built of varying designs, utilizing earth, stone, brick, and other natural materials. There had been two recognized periods of construction before 1816, when a board established by President James Madison planned and oversaw the construction of the third phase of seacoast defenses. The board was headed by a French military engineer, Simon Bernard, who followed the work of Marquis de Vauban, a fortification engineer who revolutionized fort design and construction in France. Bernard designed several forts that would later be used by the Confederacy, including Fort Morgan at the entrance of Mobile Bay. Another member of the board, Bvt. Lt. Col. (later Brig. Gen. and Chief of Engineers) Joseph G. Totten, was responsible for several other installations that rank as some of the most impressive harbor defenses ever produced. These included Forts Sumter, Pickens, and Pulaski.

The board recommended that nearly two hundred new forts and batteries be built, but only a few were actually constructed, with some effort spent on upgrading existing installations. The resulting works were known as the "Third System." Several examples of these permanent forts were acquired by the Confederacy in 1861. The Third System forts were of uniform brick and stone construction, designed to withstand the current threat of wooden sailing ships armed with smoothbore cannons possessing a range of about one mile. The forts were massive, vertical-walled structures, normally polygonal in plan with from four to seven faces. They combined a strong, durable structure with a high concentration of armament and substantial firepower. The method used to multiply the available firepower was the extensive use of casemated gun emplacements, which provided additional protection to the guns and crews, enabled more aiming flexibility, and permitted multiple tiers of guns to be installed. Depending upon the size and location of the defense, the planned armament could run from fewer than fifty guns up to nearly four hundred.

Following secession, the majority of the existing coastal defense forts along the southern Atlantic seaboard and Gulf coast were quickly captured or turned over to state forces. For his part, the outgoing president James Buchanan made no real effort to reinforce the Union forts remaining in the seceding states. In several cases state militias simply marched in and took possession, as occurred during the first week of January 1861 when Governor Thomas O. Moore ordered Louisiana troops to seize the Federal forts in that state. Alabama state troops seized Forts Morgan and Gaines on Mobile Bay that same week.

The first Federal shots of the war came in Pensacola, Florida, on the night of January 8 when a guard at Fort Barrancas, immediately west of the Pensacola Navy Yard, fired at a group of men who approached the fort and failed to respond to challenges. Shortly afterward the Federal troops ferried across Escambia Bay under the command of 1st Lt. Adam Slemmer and occupied Fort Pickens on Santa Rosa Island. The Southerners successfully occupied the Navy Yard, Fort Barrancas, and nearby Fort McRee, but Pickens remained in Union hands, effectively denying the use of Pensacola to the Confederacy.

Where the Confederates were able to seize well-maintained forts, they found strong, lasting defenses. One example was Fort Jackson, built by the United States on the Mississippi River below New Orleans between 1822 and 1832 on the former site of Spanish Fort Bourbon. A star-shaped pentagon, the fort's walls were twenty-five feet above the water line of a moat that completely surrounded it. The walls were constructed of red brick to a thickness of twenty feet, with reinforced gun foundations of red and gray granite. In the center of the fort was a defensive barracks intended as a bombproof shelter capable of accommodating five hundred men. The entire structure rested on foundations made of three layers of cypress logs, topped by cypress two-by-fours used as a leveling device and all made airtight by being submerged in water.

Many of the coastal forts, however, had been unoccupied for several years or at best had seen only small maintenance garrisons. A number of the forts acquired by the Confederacy were in deplorable condition after several years of neglect. Foundations had shifted, walls were collapsing, the wind and rain had washed away parapet platforms, and fittings had rotted away. Lacking guns and facilities for personnel to return these acquisitions to service, the Confederate engineers faced a stiff test in readying the defenses.

When possible the coastal fortifications were reinforced with supporting installations. At major seaports these addi-tional placements became rather extensive, a prime example being the Savannah River approaches in Georgia. The two existing masonry forts acquired by the Confederate defenders were Forts Jackson and Pulaski; additional defenses included Forts Beaulieu, Boggs, Brown, Lee, McAllister, Mercer, and Rose Dew, and Battery Jones. This pattern of enhancing the defenses was regularly repeated elsewhere.

The Confederacy's strongest forts had been designed to handle extended shelling by smoothbore artillery and naval guns. Indeed, the Union fleet's bombardment and running of Forts Jackson and St. Phillip below New Orleans in late April 1862 did only superficial damage. But the Union's introduction of rifled guns at Fort Pulaski, Georgia, that same month made these forts effectively obsolete. Following the Federal bombardment of Fort Sumter in April 1863, General Beauregard, commander of the Charleston defenses, noted in an official report that the use of rifled guns and ironclads on masonry forts had irrevocably changed the defensive equation.

Surprisingly, it turned out that the fortification material best suited for defense against the Northern rifled cannon was any sort of yielding substance that could be shoveled back into place easily, such as sand. Union Brig. Gen. Quincy Gillmore, the engineer who devised the assaults on Fort Pulaski and later on the Charleston defenses, reported that though his cannons had holed Fort Pulaski, causing its surrender, an even larger bombardment had negligible effect on Fort Wagner outside Charleston. Wagner, built of sand, survived multiple attempts at breaching, as the sand would fall back into the area that had been displaced.

Forts that were of primarily earthen construction lent themselves to even longer survival. Fort McAllister of the Savannah defenses was bombarded by the Federal navy on January 27, February 1, and March 3, 1863. Each time, the defenders dug their cannons out of the dirt that had been piled up by the shelling and resumed firing. In the case of Fort Sumter, which was assaulted regularly from April 1863 to February 1865, the breaches in the walls were packed with gabions (wickerwork filled with stones and dirt), sand, cotton bales, and rubble. The fort held, but like the few other remaining permanent forts in Confederate hands, it was doomed by the overwhelming manpower of the North and the collapse of the Confederacy itself.

Field and Semipermanent Forts

The prewar emphasis had been on large masonry installations, but the Civil War witnessed a widespread use of entrenchments and earthen fortifications built by soldiers as the need arose. Early in the hostilities, the idea of digging trenches and doing earthwork was frowned upon, the prevailing feeling being that the manual labor required was beneath the dignity of soldiers. Those who did engage in fortification work were often given the epithet of "dirt-diggers."

Throughout the war the South relied primarily on slave labor when available to build its forts and trenches.

Although the Confederates made little use of earthworks during the earlier campaigns, they increasingly utilized earthen fortifications, often enabling them to hold the field, even when they were outnumbered. By war's end, the field fortifications were the most common type to be found, owing to their relative ease of construction and applicability to changing defensive needs. By Appomattox the Confederates had built thousands of earthen fortifications throughout the South, ranging from quickly erected battlefield defenses to major networks protecting whole cities, transport routes, and waterways.

The basis for field fortifications was the trench, which, if necessary, could be built rapidly while under fire or, if time permitted, could be rather extensive. As men worked to excavate the trench, the dirt was piled up in front, providing a parapet, or defensive platform. As time permitted, parapets would be raised, strong-point redoubts (rectangular earthworks) and redans (triangular earthworks) erected, and defensive ditches built in front of the earthworks. Bombproofs against artillery fire were often constructed at forts by leaning timbers against the inner walls and covering them with earth. If there was no timber, the parapets might be made as much as fifteen feet thick to stop artillery fire. A head log, under which the men could fire, was frequently utilized with some sort of skid or device placed to ensure that the log wouldn't roll back on the defenders if struck by a projectile.

Individual gun batteries were usually earthen and were erected for the purpose of supporting major installations or defending a specific approach. These battery positions required extensive work, including laying floor planking and providing protective space for the gun crews. They were normally equipped with only one or two cannons, and sandbags and gabions were often used to build up the shoulders of the gun embrasures to provide the gun crews with more cover. In the field, battery positions were usually not very substantial, owing to their temporary nature, and often they were built hurriedly wherever possible with whatever materials were at hand. One example was Battery or Fort Powell, one of the Confederate defenses of Mobile Bay, which was erected on a sandbar off Cedar Point at the western entrance of the bay.

In advance of the defense, trees would be felled with their tops facing the direction of the enemy and the tips of the branches sharpened into spikes, resulting in devices called abatis. Closer to defense (if time allowed), sharpened sticks were placed in the ground, again facing the enemy, giving the appearance of a picket fence laid almost on its side. Known as palisades, or chevaux-de-frise, these served the same purpose as abatis but gave the defending riflemen a clearer view of the approaching enemy.

In the field, the Confederates quickly learned the value of fortifications. Immediately following their victory at First Manassas, a network of trenches and redoubts was constructed to allow them to preserve their position. This included the substantial use of "Quaker guns," logs that were shaped and blackened to appear like emplaced artillery. With George B. McClellan's move for Richmond via the peninsula, the Confederates evacuated their Manassas battlefield fortifications and starting working on a string of defenses in advance of the Union army, which included the utilization of Lord Cornwallis's old defenses in the vicinity of Yorktown. These field forts served the purpose admirably, causing no end of delays for McClellan and forcing him to bring heavy siege guns up the peninsula with great difficulty. The Southerners continued a pattern of building defenses and then falling back, first through Williamsburg and then to the outskirts of Richmond. When the Confederate army broke out during Lee's Seven Days' campaign, it was the Federals who were forced to rely on rapidly erected defenses, building them and then withdrawing, for protection.

Later in the war, during William Tecumseh Sherman's Atlanta campaign, practically every foot from Ringgold to Atlanta was entrenched, fortified, and laced with obstructions by the Southern defenders. One singular earthen fortification type developed for this series of defenses was the "Shoupade" redoubt, named for its designer, Brig. Gen. Francis Shoup, chief of artillery for Gen. Joseph E. Johnston. Shoup designed the redoubts to follow the lay of the land along the north bank of the Chattahoochee River and provide supporting fire to one another. The fortifications were of triangular design, built of logs and earth ten to twelve feet high in front, with each to be defended by a company of about eighty men. The structures were placed roughly eighty feet apart, linked by heavy palisades with two artillery pieces between each strong point. The resulting line was effectively impregnable and, most important, gave Johnston much flexibility in moving the body of his army behind the line to repel any crossing.

The Federals nevertheless managed to cross the river in several locations on the night of July 8, 1864, and Johnston once again traded terrain for position. Over General Shoup's opposition, the Army of Tennessee was pulled back from the Chattahoochee River line, and these unique structures were not combat-tested. Johnston's army withdrew into Atlanta, where boundary defenses had already been erected.

As with Atlanta, lengthy strings of more permanent earthen defenses were erected at numerous important locations across the South, including Vicksburg, Mobile, Charleston, Petersburg, and Richmond. At locations like Charleston, the new defenses were erected to work in concert with the established masonry forts. At the inland cities, the defensive lines were built from scratch.

Richmond was the initial primary target of the Union army, and under the auspices of General Lee, the Confederates started fortifying the city in July 1861. The first hastily constructed defenses were completed in 1862 at Drewry's Bluff overlooking the James River (these being subsequently reinforced). The James was further fortified below the mouth of the Appomattox River, with additional defenses placed at Jamestown Island, Hardin's Bluff, Mulberry Island, and Day's Point. When possible, civilian and both slave and free black labor was utilized, but the work proceeded very slowly and the Richmond defenses were not effectively completed until the summer of 1864.

As originally planned, the fortification line was to include eighteen closed or semiclosed forts with seven supporting outerworks equipped with 218 heavy guns. As completed, the defenses included an outer line located about ten miles from the capital, stretching for over sixty-five miles around the city. Key earthen forts included Fort Harrison, Fort Darling (on Drewry's Bluff), Fort Hoke, Fort Johnson, and Fort Stephens. Toward the end of the war, these substantial

> **Less permanent installations were still erected when needed to fulfill short-term defensive requirements or to counter an expected move by the enemy.**

defenses were bolstered by the emplacement of mines and ship hulks sunk in the channel of the James. The Confederate fortifications in defense of Petersburg to the south were similarly substantial, including Forts Baldwin, Gregg, Whitworth, Mahone, and Walker, and Battery 45 and Battery Pegram. Taken together, the Richmond and Petersburg defenses made the region one of the more heavily defended portions of the Confederacy, but the loss of Petersburg in the spring of 1865 made Richmond's defenses superfluous.

In the western theater, Maj. Samuel H. Lockett, chief engineer under Lt. Gen. John C. Pemberton, erected a similar network on a smaller scale for the defense of Vicksburg, Mississippi. Lockett took advantage of the natural lay of the bluffs rising above the Mississippi River, erecting an effectively impregnable series of fortifications and earthworks on the last continuous ridge around the town, linked by trenches and rifle pits. These defenses included Square Fort (Fort Garrott), Fort Hill, the Second Texas Lunette, Third Louisiana Redan, Salient Works, Railroad Redoubt, South Fort, and others.

Less permanent installations were still erected when needed to fulfill short-term defensive requirements or to counter an expected move by the enemy. During a two-week span in March 1863, a Confederate detachment out of Vicksburg under the command of Brig. Gen. W. W. Loring erected seven earthen forts in the vicinity of Greenwood,

Mississippi, in order to prevent the Union from running gunboats and transports down to the Yazoo River. The primary defense was Fort Pemberton, erected at a point where the Tallahatchie and Yazoo rivers closed to within two hundred yards of each other. Equipped with one 32-pounder and three 12-pounder rifles, one 3-inch Whitworth, one 10-pounder Parrott rifle, one 20-pounder Parrott rifle, and one 8-inch naval gun, Pemberton was supported by six other defenses ranging along the Tallahatchie and Yalobusha rivers: Forts Ann, LeFlore, Moore, and Texas, and Middle Fort and Lower Fort. Assisting in the defense was the steamer *Star of the West* (of Fort Sumter fame), which was sunk in the Tallahatchie River.

One of the key strategies for the North during the prosecution of the war was the policy of coordination between the Union army and the fleet. In response, the Confederacy found it imperative to continue the development of semipermanent fieldworks at obvious choke points and on commanding ground, throughout both the western and the eastern theaters. Examples include the fortifications erected at Island Number 10, Fort Henry, and Fort Donelson in the west. Fort Donelson, on the Cumberland River in Tennessee, covered some ninety-seven acres with earthworks, rifle trenches and water batteries.

The Fort Blakely–Spanish Fort complex on Mobile Bay was equally impressive. Blakely consisted of a four-mile-long barricade of pine logs covered with mud and sand and fronted with dense abatis. The fort boasted nine lunettes (crescent-shaped earthworks) and was armed with thirty-five artillery pieces in addition to siege mortars; its flanks were covered by the marshes of the Appalachee River. Spanish Fort, historically a defensive position for Mobile, was equally impressive. Located seven miles from the Confederate city, it consisted of three redoubts (Spanish Fort, Fort Alexis, and Red Fort), linked by rifle pits that stretched some 2,500 yards from the Appalachee River to Bayou Minette. At the base of the works was a deep ditch six feet in width, with the inner side next to the forts protected by telegraph wire fencing, an elaborate chevaux-de-frise, and a line of thick abatis, all backed up by heavy artillery.

Charleston, South Carolina, was considered the single most heavily armed and best defended port on the Atlantic seaboard. The main defenses included Third System masonry Fort Sumter and Fort Moultrie (Sullivan's Island) as well as the earthworks of Battery Gregg and Battery Wagner, both of which were located on Cumming's Point. To back up the mid-harbor defenses, the Confederates built several batteries in Charleston proper, including White Point (or "South") Battery, between the Cooper and Ashby rivers. The inner harbor defenses never saw action, as the Union fleet never penetrated the harbor.

At Mobile Bay and other locations, earthen coastalinlet fortifications served an additional purpose: providing protection for blockade runners. These riverine defenses often employed combinations of rafts, mines, booms, pilings, and fire vessels to further obstruct the rivers and outlets. Fort Forrest, a Confederate seven-gun redoubt opposite Roanoke Island, North Carolina, was placed to take advantage of a double line of sixteen sunken vessels and a system of pilings in the Croatan Sound.

The single strongest earthworks complex of the Confederacy was Fort Fisher, the key to the Cape Fear defenses in North Carolina. Expansion of the existing Battery Boles commenced in July 1863 on timbers stacked fifteen to twenty-five feet thick, with sand covering and marsh grass planted over the resulting structure. An L-shaped fort evolved, with its angle pointing northeast out to sea. The eastern face, running 1,900 yards down the beach, was the vertical arm. At its southern tip was the massive Mound Battery, equipped with two long-range guns. About a mile from the mound and near the tip of Confederate Point on the river side was Battery Buchanan. A line of rifle pits protected the rear of the fort in case of an attack from the river. Located below Wilmington, Fort Fisher staunchly protected the approaches to that port, making Wilmington the last major Confederate port available to blockade runners.

Tower Defenses

One final form of fixed fortification that saw limited use in the Confederate States was the tower defense. Earlier tower defenses had been built under the Federal Third System, primarily in the South. Either rectangular or circular in plan, these multistory structures mounted a few weapons arranged in such a way as to provide fire in all directions. These fixed-point defenses were commonly referred to as Martello towers, after a similar structure on the Bay of Martello in Corsica.

Notable examples included Tower Dupre (otherwise known as Battery Dupre) and a similar structure near Proctorsville, both constituting part of the New Orleans defenses. Dupre was located about four miles below the mouth of Bayou Bienvenue on Lake Borgne; hexagonal in shape, it had loopholes in the first floor for riflemen, and embrasures, or slotlike openings, on the second floor adequate for six cannons. Other five 24-pounder cannons were placed in a lunette water battery at the base of the tower.

The tower defense at Proctorsville was lower down on Lake Borgne and protected the terminus of the Mexican Gulf Railroad. A square, three-floored structure about forty-eight feet high, the top floor of the defense had embrasures for four cannons, the second floor had loopholes and embrasures for rifles, and the ground floor contained quarters and the magazine. Though this structure was considered important enough to be manned during 1861 by Company B, Twenty-first Louisiana Infantry, neither it nor Dupre played a role in Confederate operations in the New Orleans vicinity.

Frontier Forts

Although the last form of defensive works employed by the Confederates were called forts, they were not truly developed fortifications. The numerous frontier installations covering the western approaches to the United States were normally open posts, consisting of several buildings, stables, barracks, guardhouse, and the like, built out of whatever materials were available (stone, adobe, sticks). Built during the 1840s and 1850s to guard the frontier as American settlers pushed westerly (or as conflicts with Indians arose), these dragoon and cavalry outposts and camps were themselves continually abandoned with new posts being built farther west.

As with the major permanent installations in the East, the western forts had been poorly manned and maintained because of insufficient regular army personnel. For those that remained in active service in Texas and New Mexico Territory, the secession of the Southern states created a serious problem. Brig. Gen. David E. Twiggs, the Federal commander in Texas (and later a Confederate general), surrendered all the Federal property under his command to the Confederates in April and May 1861, leaving most of the forts unmanned. State militia forces immediately occupied a few. Ironically, one of the posts that was garrisoned by the Confederates was Fort Davis in southwestern Texas, which had been named in 1854 for Secretary of War Jefferson Davis. But a serious lack of manpower and materials, combined with a need to defend the Trans-Mississippi Confederacy, left the majority of the frontier forts unoccupied by the South.

Some did see Confederate use during the war, although they were employed primarily as frontier supply bases and protection against Indians. Fort Bliss, Texas, for example, served as headquarters for Confederate activities in the far Southwest until August 1862. A few of the remaining Spanish presidios were also occasionally utilized by the Confederates, one being the Presidio of Nuestra Señora del Pilar y Gloriosa San José, also known as the Presidio of San Elizario, about twenty-five miles below El Paso.

The Confederates also built several new installations along the Gulf coast, notably in the vicinity of the major ports of Corpus Christi and Galveston, as well as at the entrances of major tributaries. An example of the latter was Fort Sabine, erected to defend the approaches of the Sabine River. It was successfully defended by a force under the command of Lt. Dick Dowling on September 8, 1863 (in the process, the thrown-together Confederate force managed to sink two Union gunboats). As the North closed down river accesses to Texas, these forts, too, were abandoned.

Armament

The early armament used by the Confederates in their fortifications was primarily 24- and 32-pounders. When possible, the Southerners used whatever was left behind at the former Federal posts; field fortifications relied upon regular field artillery. In general, though, providing defensive weaponry for the Confederacy remained a catch-as-catch-can proposition throughout the war and often led to an eclectic mix of firepower. An example was Battery Beauregard, built on Sullivan's Island as part of the Charleston defenses. By the end of the war, it was equipped with one 10-inch Columbiad smoothbore, one 8-inch Columbiad which had been rifled and banded, three 8-inch seacoast howitzers, three 32-pounders rifled and banded, two 24-pounders rifled and banded, one 6-pounder smoothbore, and one 6-pounder rifled.

Even when field commanders received cannons, there was no guarantee that the weapons would contribute to the success or strength of the fort. Early in the war the commander of the Louisiana defenses submitted a request for guns to the Confederate War Department. The secretary of war replied that 125 32-pounders had been ordered from the Norfolk Navy Yard for shipment to New Orleans. By the end of the year, only 95 of these guns had been delivered, and they had arrived without sufficient amounts of powder.

Even if powder had been provided, these guns were still of limited use; the War Department had neglected to send carriages, chassis, or implements. The pattern was repeated elsewhere: Fort Pulaski, built for 146 pieces, had only 20 installed. Fort Sumter had about 60 of its 135 in place. Fort Cobb, a battery located below Elizabeth City in Pasquotank County, North Carolina, utilized 4 guns taken from a sunken ship. Moreover, there was practically no reserve of heavy cannons available to replace those that might be damaged in service or to arm the temporary works being erected.

At no time during the war was the Confederate arms industry able to adequately supply the medium and heavy guns and accoutrements required for the defenses. Both sides suffered from this problem initially, but the North's industrial strength provided increasing supplies of adequate artillery for its fixed and field fortifications as the war progressed, whereas the Confederacy's inadequacies only worsened.

As the fighting went on, the South's temporary fortifications were steadily abandoned in the face of an overpowering Union army. Many of the permanent forts went earlier, as the North attained control of the Atlantic seaboard, Gulf coast, and inland waterways. The defenders of Vicksburg held out for forty-seven days, withstanding two assaults by Ulysses S. Grant's army, before General Pemberton surrendered the "Gibraltar of the Confederacy." Fort Fisher lasted until January 1865, finally succumbing to a combined Union land and naval assault that saw more than 2 million pounds of ordnance thrown at the structure. The two attacks on the fort constituted the single heaviest land-sea battle of the war.

The last to fall was Fort Tyler, Georgia, overlooking the town of West Point on the Chattahoochee River. Described as a "strong bastioned earthwork" thirty-five yards square, surrounded by a ditch twelve feet wide and ten feet deep, the fort was protected by an abatis and mounted two 32-pounders and two fieldpieces. On Easter Sunday, April 16, 1865, Fort Tyler (under the command of Brig. Gen. Robert Charles Tyler) was attacked by a Federal brigade. The fort surrendered following Tyler's death. Thus ended Confederate use of permanent and fortifications.

BIBLIOGRAPHY

Bergeron, Arthur W. "Confederate Coastal Defenses in Louisiana." *Periodical: Journal of the Council on America's Military Past* 13, no. 4 (1985): 29–39.

Biggs, Greg. "The 'Shoupade' Redoubts: Joseph E. Johnston's Chattahoochee River Line." *Civil War Regiments: A Journal of the American Civil War* 1, no. 3 (1991): 82–93.

Coleman, James C., and Irene S. Coleman. *Guardians of the Gulf: Pensacola Fortifications, 1698–1980.* Pensacola, Fla., 1982.

Holden, W. C. "Frontier Defense in Texas during the Civil War." *West Texas Historical Association Yearbook* 4 (1928): 16–31.

Hunt, O. E., ed. *Forts and Artillery.* Vol. 5 of *A Photographic History of the Civil War in Ten Volumes.* New York, 1911. Reprint, New York, 1957.

Lewis, Emanuel Raymond. *Seacoast Fortifications of the United States: An Introductory History.* Annapolis, Md., 1970.

Mahan, D. H. *A Complete Treatise on Field Fortification.* New York, 1836. Reprint, New York, 1968.

Peterson, Harold L. *Forts in America.* New York, 1964.

Prucha, Francis Paul. *A Guide to Military Posts of the United States, 1789–1895.* Madison, Wis., 1964.

Roberts, Robert B. *Encyclopedia of Historic Forts: The Military, Pioneer, and Trading Posts of the United States.* New York, 1988.

Young, Rogers W. "The Construction of Fort Pulaski." *Georgia Historical Quarterly* 20 (1936): 41–51.

MARK MORGAN

Field Fortifications

Rifle pits, trenches, and breastworks—field fortifications—were unknown to eager volunteers rushing to the colors in the first eight months of 1861. Until the 1850s, the foot soldier's standard firearm was a percussion musket with an effective range of 70 yards, a figure no greater than the Brown Bess and Charleville flintlock muskets carried by his grandfather in the Revolutionary War. The infantry advanced, halted, fired, and charged in the linear formations perfected by Napoleon Bonaparte, the century's foremost soldier.

The rifle-musket adapted by the U.S. Army in the mid-1850s and destined to be the Civil War's standard infantry weapon had an effective range of 600 yards. Although a muzzle loader, a trained soldier utilizing it could fire two aimed rounds a minute. This giant leap forward in weapons technology doomed the linear tactics of Napoleon, in which artillery was the queen of battle and a mass charge of caval-

FASCINES IN THE CONFEDERATE TRENCHES AT PETERSBURG, VIRGINIA.

ry, boot to spur, usually determined the victor. This revolution in weaponry gave a decided tactical advantage to the defenders, and as the war progressed field fortifications became increasingly sophisticated and significant.

In 1861 and through the Battle of Shiloh (April 6–7, 1862), soldiers North and South frowned on the use of field fortifications. It was believed that the labor required to throw them up was undignified, unworthy of a volunteer, and would sap morale. Many officers argued that masked batteries and trenches were uncivilized, and advocates of entrenching were labeled "dirt-diggers." Gen. Robert E. Lee, an early champion of construction and use of earthworks for defense of ports and harbors against amphibious attack, was derisively called the "King of Spades."

In the months before Shiloh, the Confederacy, determined to fight a defensive war, devoted much effort by both soldiers and impressed slaves to the construction of earthen fortifications to cover the approaches to their Centreville and Manassas Junction encampments. These included batteries (emplacements for one or more cannons); redoubts (enclosed works with four angles and four fronts); redans (works with two fronts and three angles); lunettes (works with three or more angles, their rear open to interior lines); and trenches (ditches with the soil thrown up front), fronted by an abatis, usually of felled timber or sharpened stakes. When Maj. Gen. George B. McClellan arrived on the peninsula in the first week of April 1862 and began his march on Richmond, he found his way barred by the Yorktown-Warwick

line. The Confederate left was anchored on the 1781 British Yorktown works, their parapets greatly thickened and the ditches widened and deepened, with their center posted behind the Warwick River, dammed at four points to create water barriers, and their right on Skiff Creek. The dams and other points where the river could not be flooded were covered by earthen batteries and entrenchments. These defensive works caused McClellan to pause from April 5 to May 4 to construct breaching batteries, seriously compromising his campaign.

At Williamsburg, on May 5, the Confederates used previously constructed redoubts and batteries to batter McClellan's vanguard and were enabled then to undertake a successful retrograde into the Richmond defenses. As they closed on the eastern approaches to Richmond, Union engineers marked out and soldiers constructed earthworks, from which McClellan, a former Corps of Engineers officer, proposed to invest the city. These works served the Union well when they were assailed by the Confederates at Seven Pines (May 31–June 1) and in the Seven Days' Battles (June 26–July 1). At Seven Pines, Ellerson's Mill (June 26), and Gaines' Mill (June 27), these works shielded the defenders as they inflicted disproportionate losses in killed and wounded on the attacking Southerners. At Gaines' Mill the Federals, because of time constraints, sheltered themselves behind fence rails, knapsacks, and blanket roll barricades.

In the East, except for the Harpers Ferry siege (September 12–15, 1862) when the defenders employed previously prepared earthworks, neither the Army of the Potomac nor the Army of Northern Virginia again made more than limited use of field fortifications until mid-December at Fredericksburg. At the latter fight, the Confederates, sheltered in rifle pits and trenches and behind stone walls, supported by artillery emplaced behind earthen parapets, inflicted frightful casualties on the attackers.

At Forts Henry, Donelson, and Pillow, and Island Number 10 in the West, defensive earthwork perimeters were thrown up by the Confederates on lines laid out by their engineers to cover the approaches to heavy batteries commanding the rivers at these key strongholds. These entrenched camps, along with the large defending forces at Donelson and Island Number 10, were captured by the Union.

After Shiloh, Maj. Gen. Henry W. Halleck hastened to the front and directed the advance on Corinth (April 28–May 30, 1862). He pushed ahead continually, but his troops entrenched after every forward movement and invaluable time was lost throwing up trenches, when vigorous scouting and patrolling would have revealed that they would be of little use.

At Murfreesboro (December 31, 1862–January 2, 1863), both beligerents entrenched and underscored the vital role that "dirt-diggers" played when the armies assumed defensive stances. The breastworks erected by Maj. Gen. George H. Thomas's wing shielding the Lafayette Road (September 19–20) facilitated his stand "like a rock" at Chickamauga. Confederate engineers delineated three lines of earthworks at Missionary Ridge, but the topography was against them and they were stormed by Thomas's troops on November 25. Both at Vicksburg and at Port Hudson in the late spring of 1863, Confederates posted in the trenches defending the perimeters of these bastions hurled back their attackers with prohibitive losses. In early July, Vicksburg and Port Hudson, cut off from reinforcements, surrendered to investing Union armies.

In the East in 1863, Maj. Gen. Joseph Hooker, after gaining General Lee's flank at Chancellorsville, lost confidence and pulled back into the Wilderness and entrenched, which proved his undoing. At Gettysburg neither army made a concerted effort to entrench. Union soldiers for the most part utilized man-made and natural features. Later the same year, at Mine Run (November 26–December 2), both armies made extensive use of field fortifications as they marched, maneuvered, and skirmished.

The war roared toward a bloody and terrible climax in 1864. With Ulysses S. Grant in charge and the implementation of his sustained offensive strategy, soldiers in the two major Union army groups, and the Confederate Army of Tennessee in the West and the Army of Northern Virginia in the East now maneuvered with "a rifle-musket in one hand and a shovel in the other." All levels of command from general to private now knew that breastworks gave a decisive edge

to the defenders. It was recognized that veteran troops shielded by field fortifications could fight off at least three times their number of attackers. Units, on coming into the presence of the enemy, habitually deployed from column into line, and their commanders sent out skirmishers. Experienced officers examined the terrain to locate the best ground for entrenching, and the soldiers turned to. They stacked arms, secured tools from the wagons, or, if under fire, made use of bayonets, mess plates, or cups to entrench their section of the line.

In woods, trees were felled, positioned, and covered with earth. If no timber was available, the superior slopes of the parapet, if artillery was a hazard and there was sufficient time, were given a thickness of fifteen to twenty-two feet. Against small arms fire, two feet sufficed. Head logs positioned on skids were commonplace.

These field works—trenches and rifle pits—were thrown up by the rank and file with little oversight from field officers. During the war's final year, the soldiers, whenever they halted in the presence of the enemy, entrenched before kindling fires or preparing food. These improvised works were abandoned with the same unconcern with which they were erected. European officers visiting the armies were surprised at seeing average infantrymen accomplishing what in their armies was the province of engineer and sapper battalions.

In Virginia from the Rapidan to Richmond and on to Petersburg, General Lee's veterans fighting from behind

> **All levels of command from general to private now knew that breastworks gave a decisive edge to the defenders.**

earthworks savaged their assailants. From the time Maj. Gen. George G. Meade's Army of the Potomac crossed the Rapidan on May 4 until it crossed the James on June 14 through 16, Grant's losses nearly equaled the strength of Lee's army encountered in the Wilderness (May 5–6). At Petersburg and on the eastern approaches to Richmond during the next nine months, Union losses in killed, wounded, and prisoners were only slightly less than the total defending force on March 29, 1865.

William Tecumseh Sherman's experience with field fortifications in the Atlanta campaign that carried his army from Ringgold Gap across the Chattahoochee (May 7– July 8) was similar, but his losses were far less than those suffered by Grant's eastern army. Unlike Grant, Sherman skillfully used the terrain and superior numbers to first probe and then maneuver Gen. Joseph E. Johnston's Confederates out of ten successive lines of earthworks. Only at Kennesaw

Mountain on June 27 did Sherman launch a frontal assault on Johnston's field fortifications, but he soon called off the attack and went back to outflanking the foe.

The realities of the technological revolution in weaponry and the response of the Civil War soldier to it through the use of field Forts and Fortificationsfortifications are as much a part of survival in warfare today as 130 years ago. The much-boasted initiative of the American soldier impressed itself in no aspect of military art more than in the development and construction of earthworks during the Civil War.

BIBLIOGRAPHY

Fieberger, G. J. *A Textbook on Field Fortifications.* New York, 1900.
Hogane, James T. "Reminiscences of the Siege of Vicksburg." *Southern Historical Society Papers* 2 (November 1883): 223–227, 291–297, 484–489. Reprint, Wilmington, N.C., 1990.
Hunt, O. E. *Entrenchments and Fortifications.* Vol. 5 of *The Photographic History of the Civil War.* Edited by Francis Trevelyn Miller. 10 vols. New York, 1911.
Nichols, James L. *Confederate Engineers.* Confederate Centennial Studies. Edited by W. S. Stanley Hoole. Tuscaloosa, Ala., 1957.

EDWIN C. BEARSS

FORT STEDMAN, VIRGINIA

This fort, located near Petersburg, was the site of a battle fought March 25, 1865, that was Gen. Robert E. Lee's last tactical offensive movement in the nine-and-a-half-month Petersburg campaign. Lee's plan was to find a weak point in the Federal line, punch through that portion of the enemy entrenchments, and force their abandonment. He could then shorten his line defending Petersburg and detach a force to go to Gen. Joseph E. Johnston's aid in North Carolina and stop his adversary, Maj. Gen. William Tecumseh Sherman. The troops could then return with Johnston and deal with the forces under Gen. Ulysses S. Grant.

General Lee entrusted the selection of the point of attack to Lt. Gen. John B. Gordon. Gordon chose the area between a section of the Confederate defenses known as Colquitt's Salient and the Union's Fort Stedman, where the lines were about 150 yards apart. The Ninth Corps under Maj. Gen. John G. Parke held this section of the Federal siege lines. The fort was named for Col. Griffin A. Stedman, Eleventh Connecticut Infantry, who had been killed near the site in 1864. The earthen structure was surrounded by a moat four feet deep and half full of water; it was thirteen feet from the bottom of the moat to the top of the parapet. To the north of the fort were the Ninth and Tenth Batteries; to the south the Eleventh and Twelfth Batteries, as well as Fort Haskell six hundred yards away.

General Lee committed Gordon's entire corps to the assault supported by reserves from Longstreet's and Hill's Corps. If they were successful, a body of cavalry was to be sent through the broken line and wreak havoc in the rear of the Federal army.

At 4:00 A.M. the attack began with ten thousand to twelve thousand infantry arranged in three compact columns, the cavalry being held in reserve. Hitting the Federal lines and breaking through, the Confederates captured Fort Stedman, the adjacent Tenth Battery, and nine cannon, eleven mortars, and nearly a thousand prisoners (many escaped in the later stages of the battle), including Brig. Gen. Napoleon B. McLaughlin.

As the Confederates poured through the gap, one column moved north toward the Ninth Battery, and the other headed straight for the rear of the Federal army. The third was to move down the lines against Fort Haskell and capture the Eleventh and Twelfth Batteries. But heavy resistance at the fort caused the Confederate movement to falter and finally give way. At the other points of attack, the Southerners also lost their momentum.

Newly arriving Federal reinforcements in the field under Brig. Gen. John F. Hartranft stalled the Confederates around 8:00 A.M., and Gordon ordered a withdrawal. The Union loss amounted to 75 killed, 419 wounded, 523 missing; the Confederates, 1,600 killed and wounded, 1,900 captured. Four days later Grant began his final offensive movement, which culminated in the fall of Petersburg on April 3.

BIBLIOGRAPHY

Gordon, John B. *Reminiscences of the Civil War.* New York, 1911.
Hartranft, John F. "The Recapture of Fort Stedman." In *Battles and Leaders of the Civil War.* Edited by Robert V. Johnson and C. C. Buel. Vol 4. New York, 1888. Reprint, Secaucus, N.J., 1982.
Hodgkins, William H. *The Battle of Fort Stedman, March 25, 1865.* Boston, 1889.
Kilmer, George L. "Gordon's Attack at Fort Stedman." In *Battles and Leaders of the Civil War.* Edited by Robert V. Johnson and C. C. Buel. Vol. 4. New York, 1888. Reprint, Secaucus, N.J., 1982.
Trudeau, Noah Andre. *The Last Citadel: Petersburg, Virginia, June 1864–April 1865.* Boston, 1991.

CHRIS CALKINS

FORT SUMTER, SOUTH CAROLINA

The scene of the opening battle of the Civil War, Fort Sumter was located on an artificial island inside the entrance to

FORT SUMTER, SOUTH CAROLINA. Interior view of the fort, April 14, 1861, after its evacuation by Maj. Robert Anderson. The north end of the two-tiered west barracks and the barbette of the adjacent north channel face are visible.
NATIONAL ARCHIVES

Charleston Harbor. A pentagon, with brick walls about three hundred feet long, forty feet high, and eight to twelve feet thick, the fort was still under construction in 1860. To it, on the night of December 26, Maj. Robert Anderson moved his garrison of U.S. troops from Fort Moultrie at the edge of the harbor entrance, where he and his men had been exposed to the threat of attack by South Carolinians.

Having declared their state an independent republic, the South Carolinians resented the presence of what was to them a foreign flag, and they looked upon Anderson's move to Fort Sumter as an act of aggression. They considered it another hostile act when, in January 1861, the Buchanan administration sent the unarmed merchant ship *Star of the West* with reinforcements for the fort. As the ship approached Charleston Harbor, South Carolina shore batteries opened fire and compelled it to turn back.

The Confederate government early established its policy with regard to the two principal forts remaining under Federal control in the seceded states. On February 15, 1861, the Provisional Congress in Montgomery secretly resolved that "immediate steps should be taken to obtain possession of Forts Sumter and Pickens . . . either by negotiation or force." President Jefferson Davis thereupon sent to Washington three commissioners—Martin J. Crawford, John Forsyth, and A. B. Roman—to try negotiation. He ordered P. G. T. Beauregard to Charleston to take command of the harbor and make preparations for the use of force.

In Washington the Confederate commissioners failed to get an audience with any member of the Lincoln administration, but Secretary of State William H. Seward communicated with them through a go-between. The commissioners thought it a great diplomatic victory for the Confederacy when Seward pledged that his government would not, without notice, undertake to change the situation at Sumter. As Commissioner Crawford reported, the Confederate States "were not bound in any way whatever to observe the same course" (but were left free to continue their preparations for attack). "We think, then, that the policy of 'masterly inactivity,' on our part, was wise in every particular."

Such inactivity displeased Governor Francis W. Pickens and his fellow South Carolinians, who demanded immediate action. "The President shares the feeling expressed by you that Fort Sumter should be in our possession at the earliest possible moment," Secretary of War Leroy P. Walker assured Governor Pickens on March 1, but cautioned: "Thorough preparations must be made before an attack is attempted, for the first blow must be successful."

General Beauregard proceeded to extend and enlarge the batteries surrounding and targeting the fort. His preparations practically complete, he advised the Davis government on March 27 that the expulsion of Anderson from Sumter "ought now to be decided on in a few days." Davis gave Beauregard the following instructions on April 2: he should be ready to strike whenever the commissioners withdrew from

Washington, and meanwhile he should cease to allow Anderson the privilege of buying groceries in Charleston.

On April 8 the Davis government heard from the commissioners that they had met a final "refusal" and considered their mission at an end. This news alone would have been sufficient to trigger an assault on Sumter, but even more ominous news arrived in Montgomery on the same day. A telegram from Beauregard said Governor Pickens had just received a message from President Abraham Lincoln to the effect that "provisions would be sent to Sumter peaceably, otherwise by force." Secretary Walker immediately replied to Beauregard: "Under no circumstances are you to allow provisions to be sent to Fort Sumter."

Davis and his cabinet decided not to wait for the arrival of Lincoln's expedition but, instead, to risk the onus of firing the first shot. On April 10 Walker on behalf of Davis ordered Beauregard to demand immediate evacuation of the fort and, if refused, to "reduce" it. Anderson the next day rejected the demand but said he and his men would be "starved out in a few days." Walker then authorized Beauregard to "avoid the effusion of blood" if Anderson would state a time for his withdrawal and would agree meanwhile not to fire unless fired upon. Beauregard sent James Chesnut, Roger A. Pryor, and two aides by boat to present this offer to Anderson after midnight. Anderson promised to hold his fire and to evacuate in three days—unless he should receive "controlling instructions" or "additional supplies." Chesnut and Pryor told him his reply was unsatisfactory and a bombardment would begin in an hour.

The bombardment began at 4:30 on the morning of April 12, 1861. Anderson was unable to make much of a response, completely outgunned as he was. He received no assistance from Lincoln's expedition, which proved a fiasco. The leading warship *Powhatan* had been misdirected to Fort Pickens, other vessels had been delayed by a storm, and the rest stood helplessly offshore. Cannon balls battered the brick walls of the fort while hot shot set fire to the wooden buildings inside. Anderson surrendered at noon on April 14. All his eighty-four soldiers and forty-three laborers had survived, but two men died as a result of a gun explosion during the surrender ceremonies.

Among Confederate leaders it had been an axiom that a clash at Sumter would induce Virginia and other states of the upper South and the border to secede. None of these states did so immediately, but Virginia, Tennessee, Arkansas, and North Carolina seceded in consequence of Lincoln's call for troops on April 15. Southerners generally rallied to the support of the Davis government. Northerners did the same with respect to the Lincoln administration. Most of them believed the Confederates had convicted themselves of war guilt, but the Confederates accused Lincoln of having deliberately provoked the attack. Davis, in *The Rise and Fall of the Confederate Government* (1881), still felt called upon to explain: "He who makes the assault is not necessarily he who strikes the first blow or fires the first gun."

In 1863, U.S. forces made two unsuccessful attempts to retake Sumter and capture Charleston. The U.S. flag was not again raised over the fort until April 14, 1865, exactly four years after the surrender.

[*See also* Star of the West.]

BIBLIOGRAPHY

Current, Richard N. "The Confederates and the First Shot." *Civil War History* 7 (1961): 357–369.
Swanberg, W. A. *First Blood: The Story of Fort Sumter.* New York, 1957.

RICHARD N. CURRENT

FORT WAGNER, SOUTH CAROLINA

Fort Wagner and Battery Gregg were the principal land defenses of Morris Island, which commanded the only approach for large vessels entering Charleston Harbor. The fort was an enclosed earthwork that extended entirely across a narrow point of the island and prevented the enemy from threatening Battery Gregg by land. Between July 10 and 18, the fort was assaulted by Federal forces. The successful defense by the Confederates manning the fort set back by months the Union's plan to capture Charleston.

In July 1863 a Federal army-navy force commanded by Brig. Gen. Quincy A. Gillmore and Rear Adm. John Dahlgren planned to seize Morris Island as a preliminary step in the effort to reduce the defenses of Charleston and ultimately capture the city. On July 10, Brig. Gen. George C. Strong successfully landed his brigade of 3,700 men upon Morris Island, despite resistance from the island's garrison. Strong lost 15 killed and 91 wounded. Confederate losses were 294.

On July 11, Strong ordered a daylight assault on Fort Wagner by three regiments. The fort had been reinforced the evening before, bringing its numbers up to approximately 1,200 defenders. Strong's attack was repulsed with the loss of 49 killed, 123 wounded, and 167 missing. The Confederate garrison lost 6 killed and 6 wounded.

Following this unsuccessful assault, heavy artillery was placed on the island. To cover the placement of the siege artillery, the Federal naval vessels subjected the fort to heavy bombardment on July 15–17. A second assault to capture the fort was planned for the evening of the eighteenth. To prepare the way for the infantry attack the fort was subjected to an extraordinarily heavy all-day bombardment by both

Dahlgren's naval vessels and the land batteries. The garrison of the fort at this time consisted of 1,300 men, 13 heavy guns, and 1 light field battery. Despite the weight of the Federal bombardment, Confederate losses did not exceed 8 killed and 20 wounded.

At dusk the Federal infantry, consisting of Strong's and Col. H. S. Putnam's brigades, supported by Brig. Gen. Thomas G. Stevenson's brigade—altogether 6,000 men—advanced upon the fort. Spearheading the assault was the Fifty-fourth Massachusetts, a black regiment under the command of Col. Robert G. Shaw. Although the Federals managed to gain a foothold in the fort, they were eventually driven out. General Strong was mortally wounded, Colonel Putnam was killed, and five out of Strong's six regimental commanders were killed or wounded. Union losses totaled 246 killed, 880 wounded, and 389 missing. The Confederate garrison, under the command of Brig. Gen. William Booth Taliaferro, suffered losses of 36 killed, 133 wounded, and 5 missing.

General Gillmore now abandoned the effort to capture Fort Wagner by direct assault and undertook siege operations to reduce the fort. By September 6, his forces had reached the ditch surrounding the fort and an assault on the fort was ordered for the seventh. The Confederates, however, abandoned the fort during the night. Losses during the siege operations for the Federals were 71 killed, 278 wounded, and 9 missing. Confederate losses through August 21 were 38 killed and 150 wounded.

BIBLIOGRAPHY

Bryan, E. K. "Defence of Fort Wagner." In *Histories of the Several Regiments and Battalions from North Carolina in the Great War, 1861–1865.* Edited by Walter Clark. Vol. 5. Goldsboro, N.C., 1901.
Twiggs, H. D. D. "The Defence of Battery Wagner." *Southern Historical Society Papers* 20 (1892): 166–183. Reprint, Wilmington, N.C., 1990.
U.S. War Department. *War of the Rebellion: A Compilation of the Official Records of the Union and Confederate Armies.* Washington, D.C., 1880–1901, Ser. 1, vol. 28, pts. 1–2.

D. SCOTT HARTWIG

FRANCE

France responded to the outbreak of war in America with interests so varied and conflicting that they prevented the nation from pursuing a consistent policy toward the Confederacy. From the outset Emperor Louis Napoleon expressed sympathy for the Southern cause. Yet his deep involvement in European affairs had created potential enemies on the Continent, and any unilateral decisions that antagonized Washington would expose French commerce as well as the emperor's burgeoning Mexican venture to Northern retaliation. Napoleon had undertaken commitments in Mexico that he could not sustain. The process of intervention began in July 1861 when the Mexican government repudiated its international obligations. In the London Convention of October 30, Britain, France, and Spain, all harboring grievances against Mexico, agreed to occupy the country but not to interfere in its right to form its own government. Privately Napoleon, supported by Mexican monarchists, favored a European-controlled monarchy. A stabilized Mexico,

> **. . . Emperor Louis Napoleon expressed sympathy for the Southern cause.**

Napoleon wrote on October 9, would attract European capital, increase European trade, supply European Textile mills with cotton, and terminate both Mexican outrages and encroachments from the United States.

When in the spring of 1862 the French minister in Mexico, Dubois de Saligny, announced France's opposition to the Mexican government of Benito Juarez and its support for the Mexican monarchists, the British and Spanish forces withdrew. Thereafter the reinforced but isolated French army faced a hostile Mexican populace as well as effective Mexican guerrillas. Still Napoleon persisted in his misadventure. Confederate leaders concluded that Napoleon's massive defiance of the Monroe Doctrine would ultimately fail without the support of an independent South ready to accept a French vassal state in Mexico. For Napoleon, however, salvation lay not in adopting the Confederate cause but in avoiding a unilateral confrontation with the United States. To escape that danger the French emperor required British support. This reality, operating in an atmosphere of sometimes immense cordiality between the French government and the Confederacy, sustained a recurring Confederate anticipation of French recognition even as it assured profound disillusionment at the end.

Confederate presumptions for success also rested on French perceptions of Southern military superiority and the alleged power of cotton. Such presumptions were not without merit. The French minister in Washington, Henri Mercier, believed from the outset that the South would emerge victorious and therefore deserved recognition. Then in September French foreign minister Antoine Édouard Thouvenel informed Mercier of the growing cotton famine in France. The cotton Textile districts, he wrote, were facing disaster. Mercier responded by urging British and French recognition of the Confederacy and breaking of the blockade as soon as the public was prepared to assume the risks. When Mercier approached U.S. Secretary of State William H. Seward in late October with Thouvenel's demand for cotton, Seward retorted that France required Northern wheat more than Southern cotton. Any European intervention in the American contest, he warned, would produce both a wheat famine and war. As the year ended, proSouthern sympathies in the French government as well as France's desire for cotton had failed to produce recognition or any defiance of the Federal blockade.

In late January 1862 James M. Mason and John Slidell, commissioners assigned to Britain and France respectively, reached London after having been taken from the British packet *Trent* and briefly held in the United States. Slidell continued to Paris to take up the questions of recognition and the blockade. For months the Confederacy had gathered evidence that the blockade was ineffective and therefore illegal by the standards embodied in the Treaty of Paris (1856). Thouvenel refused to defend the blockade but wondered why so little cotton reached European ports if the blockade was ineffective. Slidell acknowledged that owners of large cotton-carrying vessels preferred to avoid the risks of blockade running. Slidell concluded that French officials would challenge the blockade if Britain, with its greater maritime interests, would take the initiative. But British foreign minister Lord John Russell had already declared that any blockade was binding as long as some danger of capture existed. Russell's definition, Slidell complained, committed France to a paper blockade as long as the emperor refused to act independently.

Privately, French officials challenged the legality, even the morality, of the blockade. On April 11 William S. Lindsay, pro-Confederate member of the English Parliament, reminded Louis Napoleon in Paris that in three months the cotton famine in Britain and France would become intolerable. It was, moreover, Europe's acceptance of the blockade that unfairly compelled the South to fight without access to European manufacturers. The emperor offered sympathy and declared his willingness to send a fleet to the Southern coasts, but only if England would send an equal force. At the same time Mercier, with Seward's permission, traveled to Richmond and there, on April 16, sought to obtain from Secretary of State Judah P. Benjamin a firsthand estimate of the South's capacity and determination to win. Seward assumed that Mercier would find the South in disarray. Instead, Benjamin informed Mercier that Southerners would never dishonor themselves "by reuniting with a people for whom [they felt] unmitigated contempt as well as abhorrence." Benjamin reminded Mercier that the Federal blockade was ineffective, that he could name twenty ports where the United States had never stationed a warship. Mercier could only acknowledge to Thouvenel his embarrassment over French policy.

Slidell believed that the Confederate victories of June and July 1862, especially in Virginia, presented the opportune time to demand French recognition as a right won on the bat-

tlefield. Thouvenel, on July 23, advised Slidell to withhold his demand until additional Confederate victories would compel Britain to act. Confederate successes had raised the issue of European mediation to terminate the war. Slidell suggested to Thouvenel that the South would welcome mediation, but Mercier had warned Paris that any offer of mediation would merely antagonize the North and achieve nothing. Slidell reported to Benjamin on August 24: "We are still hard and fast aground here. Nothing will float us off but a strong and continued current of important successes in the field." Such victories remained elusive. Yet on October 28 the emperor welcomed Slidell to St. Cloud and declared his intention to propose a joint British-French-Russian mediation to end the war. The emperor declared his preference for a six-month armistice, with Southern ports open for commerce. In early November Louis Napoleon submitted his tripartite proposal to Britain and Russia only to have it rejected by both countries.

During subsequent months it became apparent, despite continued French promises of intervention, that France would not move without Britain. When the parliamentary debates of July 1863 revealed that the British ministry remained firm in its adherence to Northern demands, Benjamin and Slidell exerted renewed pressure on France to act alone; again they failed. Édouard Drouyn de Lhuys, the new French foreign minister, denied France's responsibility for Europe's acceptance of the blockade and repeated the plea that France was too vulnerable to defy the U.S. government without British support.

Benjamin expressed his final disillusionment with French policy in September 1864, complaining that the emperor had persistently exhibited a friendship for the South and yet, with equal persistence, had maintained open and cordial relations with the North. France had shown a minimum of hospitality to Confederate ships in French ports and had failed to deliver war vessels promised to the Confederacy. The emperor's subservience to the anti-Confederate policies of London and Washington, Benjamin concluded, had been total. French neutrality had favored the Union; the Confederacy could only submit in silence.

[*See also* Mexico; Monroe Doctrine; Trent Affair.]

BIBLIOGRAPHY

Blumenthal, Henry. *A Reappraisal of Franco-American Relations, 1830–1871.* Chapel Hill, N.C., 1959.
Carroll, Daniel B. *Henri Mercier and the American Civil War.* Princeton, 1971.
Case, Lynn M., and Warren F. Spencer. *The United States and France: Civil War Diplomacy.* Philadelphia, 1970.
Owsley, Frank Lawrence. *King Cotton Diplomacy: Foreign Relations of the Confederate States of America.* Revised by Harriet Chappell Owsley. Chicago, 1959.
Sears, Louis M. *John Slidell.* Durham, N.C., 1925.

NORMAN A. GRAEBNER

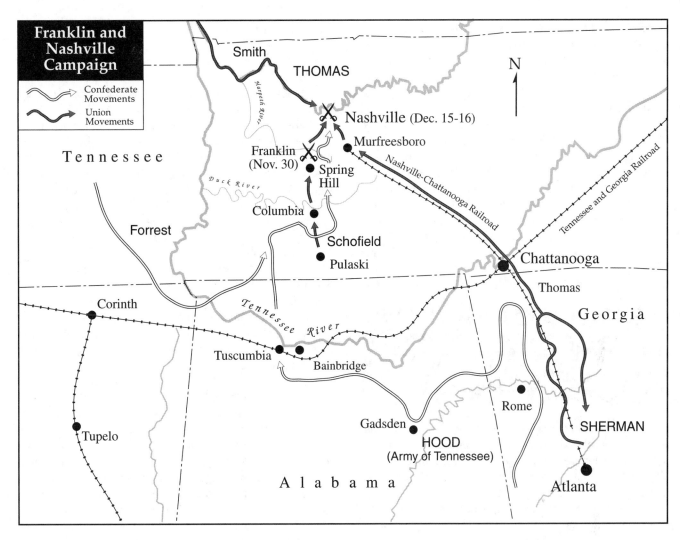

FRANKLIN AND NASHVILLE CAMPAIGN

In early September 1864, after the close of the Atlanta campaign, the Confederate Army of Tennessee camped at Palmetto, Georgia, a few miles southwest of Atlanta. The army was exhausted and, like its opponents, needed to regroup before beginning the next round. While the soldiers rested, Southern leaders developed plans to pry the Federals out of Atlanta and to get them out of Georgia.

The Confederate strategy was hammered out between September 25 and 27 during a visit to the army by President Jefferson Davis. The chief executive and Gen. John Bell Hood, the army's commander, reasoned that operations against the railroad connecting the Federals occupying Atlanta with their base at Chattanooga, Tennessee, would compel them to withdraw northward to protect their line of supply. If all went well, the Southerners would eventually lure their enemy into an area where the Confederates could fight at an advantage. A Southern victory in North Georgia would go far to offset the past summer's defeats; if it came in time, it might also affect the 1864 election in the North.

In early October Hood moved into northwestern Georgia, striking eastward against the railroad as he went. His army—about 40,000 men—was divided into three infantry corps (commanded by Lt. Gen. Alexander P. Stewart and Stephen D. Lee and Maj. Gen. B. Franklin Cheatham), a cavalry corps (under Maj. Gen. Joseph Wheeler), and an independent cavalry division (under Brig. Gen. William Hicks Jackson). After doing extensive damage to the railroad, Hood moved west. He reached Gadsden, Alabama, on October 20.

The Federal army followed Hood, but one Northern corps was left to hold Atlanta. When Hood moved into Alabama, the Union commander, Maj. Gen. William Tecumseh Sherman, posted his army just west of Rome, Georgia. Sherman refused to be drawn farther westward. Instead, he soon detached part of his force to protect Tennessee and with the rest returned to Atlanta. On November 15 he marched off across Georgia for Savannah on the Atlantic coast.

Realizing that Sherman was not going to chase him across Alabama, and that it was unlikely he could move fast enough to head off the Federals in Georgia, Hood hatched the idea of marching into Tennessee. A threat to Nashville should force the Unionists to abandon Georgia. If it did not, the mere presence of a Southern army in middle Tennessee might confuse the Union plans. A Confederate victory in Tennessee would restore Southern morale and prestige. It might even be possible, Hood fantasized, for the Confederates to win in Tennessee and then move to Virginia and join the army there for one great battle that would bring Confederate independence. Hood decided upon this scheme without consulting either the government or Gen. P. G. T. Beauregard, his immediate military superior. When

> **The generals, without clear orders, did not know how their units were deployed, where they were, or what they were doing.**

informed of Hood's intentions, Beauregard insisted that Wheeler's cavalry be detached to oppose Sherman. To replace Wheeler, Beauregard promised Hood the cavalry of Maj. Gen. Nathan Bedford Forrest, then with Southern forces in Mississippi.

Execution of Hood's plan depended on speed. Every hour's delay gave the Unionists more time to prepare for his coming. Over the next several weeks a combination of poor planning and administration, logistical problems, and the need to link up with Forrest forced Hood to drift westward to Tuscumbia. Not until November 20 did Hood get all of his army across the Tennessee River, and on the twenty-first the Southerners started for middle Tennessee.

Maj. Gen. George H. Thomas commanded the Federals defending Tennessee. His force consisted of the Fourth Corps (Maj. Gen. David Stanley), the Twenty-third Corps (Maj. Gen. John M. Schofield), and assorted cavalry and garrison units. In all, there were about 65,000 Federal troops in the area, but many of them were posted along the railroad between Nashville and Chattanooga. Reinforcements from the Mississippi Valley and other points were on the way to Nashville. Thomas stationed Schofield with 30,000 men at Pulaski to observe Hood and delay his march while he assembled the rest of his force at Nashville.

When Hood moved forward, Schofield pulled back to the Duck River at Columbia. There the Southerners found him when they arrived on November 26. On the next day, the Federals crossed the river and destroyed the bridges, but

they remained in position to block Hood's direct route to Nashville.

Hood decided to swing east of Columbia, cross the river at a ford, and then march northwest to Spring Hill where he would regain the road to Nashville. Historians have usually depicted Hood as maneuvering to cut Schofield off from Nashville and destroy his force. It seems more likely, however, that Hood was thinking only in terms of getting to Nashville ahead of Schofield, not in terms of destroying him.

Whatever his intent, Hood moved to execute it during the night of November 28–29. Forrest's cavalry, Cheatham, Stewart, and one division of Lee's corps marched off to swing around to Spring Hill. The rest of Lee's corps, almost all of the artillery, and the wagons remained in front of the Federals at Columbia.

By noon on November 29, Forrest's horsemen were near Spring Hill where they encountered small bodies of Northerners east of the town. Throughout the afternoon Confederate infantry arrived and deployed in the fields east of the road. Meanwhile, the Federals—aware of Hood's maneuver—were gradually pulling out of their river line and marching northward.

Confusion reigned among the Confederates. Units moved back and forth. The generals, without clear orders, did not know how their units were deployed, where they were, or what they were doing. Hood's staff—there was no chief of staff—simply broke down, and his control of the army dissolved. Messages from Hood were sometimes not delivered to corps commanders. Many reports from the field did not reach army headquarters. Hood made a few ineffective attempts to get some of his units onto the Columbia-Franklin road, but an almost total misunderstanding of how his army was aligned frustrated his efforts. (Hood believed that his men were deployed facing westward; they, in fact, faced to the north.) Finally, an exhausted Hood fell asleep in a nearby house. Confederate soldiers settled down for the night east of the road, and the Federals marched north to safety.

The Confederate breakdown at Spring Hill has never been satisfactorily explained. Some historians have thought that one or more of the Southern generals were drunk, under the influence of drugs, or off visiting some local ladies. More likely, Hood's own weaknesses as a commander (he typically did not ensure that his orders were obeyed), his poor administration of the army, his apparent lack of any definite plan, the absence of a functioning staff, and the fact that he had been up for more than twenty hours and was simply too tired to go on all combined to produce the chaos.

On November 30 Schofield had his men in position at Franklin while his engineers worked to prepare crossings over the Harpeth River. Hood's Confederates followed the Federals north. Late that afternoon Hood threw his army into a massive frontal assault on Schofield's position at Franklin.

The Southerners overran an advanced Federal work and then continued on to smash into the very strong Union line. In places Hood's men broke through, but Northern reserves poured into the fight and eventually pushed the Southerners back. Many of the Confederates then rallied and attacked again and again. Some Federal officers reported a dozen separate attacks on their positions. Not until nine or ten at night did the fighting fade away. Schofield then crossed the river and continued his march to Nashville.

The Federals reported 2,326 men (of some 28,000 engaged) lost at Franklin. Hood lost about 5,000 (of 28,000), including twelve general officers and fifty-five regimental commanders. The leadership of the army had been shot away. Two Southern brigades were commanded after the battle by captains. One regiment numbered only thirty men.

Despite his heavy losses at Franklin, Hood decided on December 1 to follow Schofield northward. In truth, he had little choice. He obviously could not overtake Sherman who was far across Georgia, and to withdraw southward would be to abandon middle Tennessee, demoralize the army, and admit defeat. To remain at Franklin would not accomplish anything. Perhaps Hood could get reinforcements from the Trans-Mississippi; perhaps the Federals at Nashville would be content to wait out the winter; perhaps they would attack and give him and his men a chance to reverse the situation that had existed at Franklin. Nashville itself was too strongly fortified for the weakened Confederates to assault, but they could build their own works and perhaps hold them against an attack.

In early December Hood's crippled army deployed outside Nashville on a long east-west line to cover most of the major roads running south from the city. While the Southerners worked to fortify their position, Thomas continued to build up his army in the city. The Federals were joined by the Sixteenth Corps (Maj. Gen. A. J. Smith) as well as by some 5,200 men brought up from garrison posts in Tennessee and new troops shipped from the North. Thomas, a systematic officer, wanted to prepare a force that would do a thorough job of wrecking Hood's army. Meanwhile, Hood made the Confederate situation even more desperate by sending off most of his cavalry and some infantry to Murfreesboro to operate against the Nashville-Chattanooga railroad.

The task of organizing the cavalry, and then bad weather, delayed the Federal attack until December 15. When Thomas struck, his plan was brilliant. He distracted Hood with an early probe against the right of the Confederate line and then launched an overwhelming assault against its left. Enveloped on their left, the Southerners fell back to a new, shorter line along the Brentwood Hills a few miles to the south.

On the afternoon of December 16, Thomas assaulted Hood's new line. While Union infantry attacked at several points, a massive artillery barrage pulverized the Southerners. Late in the day Northern cavalrymen were again able to envelope the Southerners' left, and the Confederates there found themselves under attack from three directions. At about 4:00 P.M., Hood's line collapsed, and his men fled southward.

For the next several days the Confederate army moved toward the Tennessee River with Union cavalry nipping at its heels. Lee's corps, the least beaten Southern unit (it had been on the Confederate right on December 16 and had not been involved in the debacle on the left of Hood's line), covered the retreat. Things were a bit easier for the Confederates after December 18 when they got across the Duck River at Columbia. On Christmas day the leading units reached the Tennessee near Bainbridge, Alabama, and by December 28 the last of Hood's men had crossed. The Confederates moved west to Corinth, Mississippi, and then south to Tupelo.

Thomas lost 2,562 men in the Battle of Nashville out of about 50,000 engaged. Hood had an estimated 23,000 troops in the battle. His losses are not known. The best estimates put his killed and wounded at about 1,500. The Northerners reported that they took 4,500 prisoners during the battle and while the Southerners were retreating to the Tennessee River. Doubtless, many other Confederates deserted and went to their homes. On December 31 Hood's army reported 18,708 officers and men "present for duty."

Hood's Franklin and Nashville campaign, in the words of one Confederate officer, was "a complete and disastrous failure." It was the worst-managed major military operation of the war. For all practical purposes, it destroyed the Army of Tennessee. Hood himself was relieved from command on January 23, 1865, and the army never again fought as a unit. Parts of it were sent off to help defend Mobile; other units set out for North Carolina to reinforce the Confederates there. Some arrived in time for the final skirmishes in the East; others were strung out all across Mississippi, Alabama, Georgia, and the Carolinas when the war ended.

BIBLIOGRAPHY

Connelly, Thomas Lawrence. *Autumn of Glory: The Army of Tennessee, 1862–1865.* Baton Rouge, La., 1971.

Cox, Jacob D. *The March to the Sea: Franklin and Nashville.* New York, 1889.

Daniel, Larry J. *Soldiering in the Army of Tennessee: A Portrait of Life in the Confederate Army.* Chapel Hill, N.C., 1991.

Hay, Thomas Robson. *Hood's Tennessee Campaign.* New York, 1929.

Horn, Stanley F. *The Decisive Battle of Nashville.* Baton Rouge, La., 1956. Reprint, Knoxville, Tenn., 1968.

McDonough, James Lee, and Thomas L. Connelly. *Five Tragic Hours: The Battle of Franklin.* Knoxville, Tenn., 1983.

Sword, Wiley. *Embrace an Angry Wind: The Confederacy's Last Hurrah: Spring Hill, Franklin, and Nashville.* New York, 1992.

RICHARD M. MCMURRY

FREDERICKSBURG CAMPAIGN

The town of Fredericksburg, Virginia, at the falls of the Rappahannock River, which numbered 5,022 inhabitants in 1860, was the site of a victory for the Army of Northern Virginia on December 13, 1862, that must be reckoned its easiest major triumph of the war. Ambrose E. Burnside assumed command of the Federal Army of the Potomac on November 7 and at once determined to move it southeast toward Fredericksburg, hoping to interpose between Robert E. Lee and Richmond and thereby to gain either tactical or strategic advantages. Lee's army at the time was scattered in the lower Shenandoah Valley and in Piedmont Virginia, taking advantage of the harvest season while recuperating from the difficult Maryland campaign. Burnside promptly sought information about Southern strength around Fredericksburg by means of a cavalry reconnaissance. On November 8 Capt. Ulric Dahlgren, later notorious for a controversial raiding scheme around Richmond, led several dozen Union horsemen into the town. They surprised a handful of Confederate cavalrymen in Fredericksburg but found no other defenders.

The Federals advanced down the left bank of the Rappahannock toward Fredericksburg while Lee with forward elements of his army attempted to keep pace across the river. Burnside had divided his army into three "grand divisions," an innovation that did not survive his tenure in command. Gen. E. V. Sumner, leading the grand division at the head of the army, reached the heights opposite Fredericksburg on November 17. With most of Lee's regular

> **The civilians evacuated the town in bitter cold weather amid haunting scenes of suffering. . . .**

infantry still two days away, Sumner looked across the river at a tiny Confederate detachment consisting of a few artillery pieces and a few hundred untested infantry. The shining opportunity for the Federals came to naught, however, as they equivocated about crossing, even though a broad and rocky stretch of river at the north edge of town was readily negotiable.

Burnside arrived on the scene on November 19. So did Confederate Gen. James Longstreet. On the twentieth Lee reached Fredericksburg, and the Northern chance to take uncontested control of the strong ground west of town had vanished. With that position in Federal hands, Lee would have been obliged to head southward another twenty miles

to the next strong point. Burnside had called for a pontoon train with which to effect his river crossing, but it did not come for weeks. The orders that reached the train's operators had not conveyed any sense of urgency. Meanwhile the Federals had threatened to bombard the city of Fredericksburg on the premise that its cover was useful to Lee's army. The civilians evacuated the town in bitter cold weather amid haunting scenes of suffering that moved the Army of Northern Virginia to sympathy and eventually to an outpouring of donated funds to help support the refugees.

The bombardment of Fredericksburg finally came soon after the pontoons arrived. Early on December 11 Burnside sent engineer troops down to the river, which was more than four hundred feet wide, to build pontoon bridges at three points. The bridge builders had little difficulty at the crossing a mile below town; they eventually put down three spans there. The two crossing points in town proved to be far more dangerous for the engineers. Veteran riflemen of William Barksdale's Mississippi brigade held the waterfront in town, enjoying ample protection in basements and behind walls. The virtually unopposed crossing below town doomed any Confederate hope that the Federals could be held beyond the river permanently—indeed, why should they not be allowed into the city to try their luck on the killing plain beneath the heights where Lee's army waited in supreme confidence? Lee had left two divisions far downstream, however, and until D. H. Hill and Jubal Early could bring those troops up to lend a hand, the Confederates needed to buy some time. Barksdale's men provided a day's delay for that purpose.

Burnside's engineers pushed their first boats into the icy river (the thermometer read 24° at 7:00 A.M. in a nearby city), anchored them, and began to lay boards for the bridge flooring. Before they had reached midpoint in the stream, the growing light allowed the Mississippians to find them in their rifle sights and drive them away. After repeated costly and frustrating efforts, Burnside ordered that some 150 cannon on the heights above the river be fired on the town to clear away the opposition. Within an hour the artillery hurled several thousand rounds into Fredericksburg's buildings. "I believe," one of the Mississippians wrote, "there was not a square yard in the city which was not struck by a missile of some kind." After the guns ceased, the bridging teams attempted to resume work, but the Confederates met them with fire not at all diminished by the heavy shelling. The turning point at the river crossing came when three Northern regiments jumped into the pontoon boats and turned them into assault craft, crossing the river in the face of steady losses in order to drive away the Confederates and establish what apparently was the first literal bridgehead in American military history.

Barksdale's troops fell back reluctantly through the streets of Fredericksburg, contesting each block and ensuring the completion of their task. They had earned a full day for Lee to use in consolidating his position. The rest of the army, which had been watching Barksdale's men from the amphitheaterlike high ground around the city, cheered them as they came back from their hard day's work.

Burnside did not attack on December 12. He occupied the day in moving his troops across the river and laying plans. Those Federals in the city on the twelfth indulged in a carnival of looting and destruction of civilian property entirely unprecedented in the Virginia theater of the war. By 1864 such behavior would become a tacit Federal war policy, but in December 1862 it was new, and it embarrassed some Northern officers while outraging the Confederates who looked on helplessly. Their chance for revenge was not long in coming.

Lee's line at the foot of the high ground behind Fredericksburg ran for seven miles along irregular contours carved out by geological forces. Immediately west of the city a commanding ridge rose sharply from an open plain. Farther to the Confederate right the ground sloped up from the river much more gradually. On Lee's right center the ridge lay a good deal farther west than it did on his left or on his far right. As a result, a deep re-entrant angle in the line (a deep bulge swerved away from the attackers) created a zone in which Burnside could not consider attacking. Lee's position was really not vulnerable to frontal assault at all, but if one had to be made (and politicians and newspapers were pressuring Burnside to move), it would have to come against the shoulders of the re-entrant. Burnside determined to attack directly out of town against the ridge there and at the same time to move against Lee's far right near Hamilton's Crossing.

December 13 dawned foggy, but the mist cleared by midmorning and an Indian summer day (56° at 2:00 P.M.) burst upon nearly 200,000 soldiers approaching mortal combat. Lee had almost 80,000 men arrayed on his strong line and Burnside brought about 115,000 troops to battle. Gen. William B. Franklin, commanding on the Federal left, followed the army commander's vague orders about moving against the enemy by organizing an attack westward from the Bowling Green Road. His first alignment fell prey to one of the most famous individual feats of the war. Maj. John Pelham of Alabama and a small detachment moved rapidly from spot to spot firing a single cannon and managed by means of a daunting enfilade fire to confuse the Federal effort for nearly an hour.

When the Northern assault finally rolled forward, it came under intense artillery fire from Confederate guns emplaced on Prospect Hill, near the right of Stonewall Jackson's line. After extensive counterbattery fire, the Union attack went forward again. This time it found an unguarded point on the line, and a division of Pennsylvanians poured through. For the second consecutive battle Jackson had allowed a curious lethargy about defensive matters to land him in trouble. The

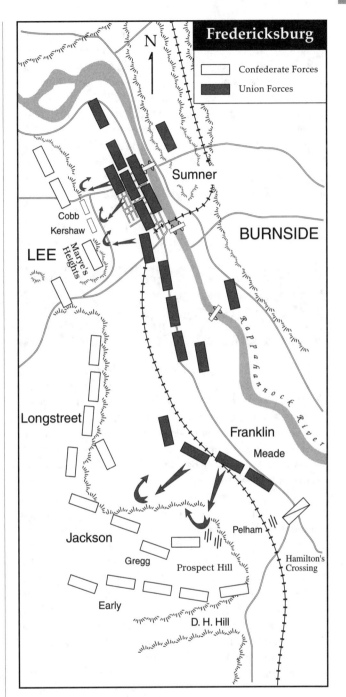

Pennsylvanians, who were commanded by Gen. George G. Meade, penetrated deep into the Confederate position and mortally wounded Gen. Maxcy Gregg of South Carolina. The success of the breakthrough, however, was temporary and largely illusory. Jackson was holding the Confederate right with roughly one-half of Lee's strength, yet his line covered only about one-fifth of the army's front. That alignment resulted not from Confederate prescience but from simple good fortune. When Early and D. H. Hill brought their divisions back to the army's position from far downstream, using the time bought by Barksdale's defense of the riverfront, they piled them up behind their comrades in Jackson's corps. There was no time to juggle the entire front. Meade's men ran into more Southern reserves than they could hope to deal with, and soon the Northerners were obliged to retrace their steps under pressure from pursuing Confederates.

Franklin's brief success with Meade's division constituted the only marginally bright spot of the battle for the Union army. While Meade and his men advanced and retreated, their comrades several miles to the north had opened a series of attacks that turned into one of the most one-sided and hopeless butcheries of the war. The ridge just behind Fredericksburg included a stretch six hundred yards long

> **[It] . . . turned into one of the most one-sided and hopeless butcheries of the war.**

through which the deep Sunken Road traversed its base. The road had a retaining wall of stone on the town side that became famous enough to be treated as a proper noun. Confederate infantry behind the Stone Wall enjoyed protection as thorough as any devised later in the war by military engineers. For a half-mile toward town from this ready-made fortress, the ground lay bare, broken only by a few fences and a half-dozen houses. A pronounced swale around a canal ditch offered the attacking Union soldiers a bit of cover, but the ditch was bridged poorly and in few places. Northerners moving across that bare plain would face terrible punishment from Confederate artillery on Marye's Heights (as the ridge above the road was known, after the family that owned part of it). The attackers might form under a little protection in the swale, but they would have to move toward the Stone Wall without cover of any sort. The only possible result would be a bloody disaster, with casualties in the thousands, the fatal multiplier being how many doomed brigades Burnside fed into the carnage.

That brief early winter afternoon, on one of the shortest days of the year, must have seemed an eternity to the thousands of Northern boys who took their turns lining up and then plunging bravely over the crest toward the Sunken Road, without a hope of success. Confederates in the road and on the hills behind it shot about eight thousand of the attackers without losing more than a thousand men. Gen. Thomas R. R. Cobb of Georgia commanded the brigade that opened the battle defending the Sunken Road. He fell mortally wounded early in the action. Joseph B. Kershaw's South Carolinians joined the Georgians in the road, and other Southern units participated—almost unnecessarily—from nearby vantage points. When darkness put an end to the

slaughter, no man of the attacking force had come close to the wall.

The Confederate command, apparently unaware of the degree of havoc wreaked upon their foe, expected a renewal of the attacks the next day. Burnside was of the same mind and even proposed leading a desperate assault in person, but wiser counsels prevailed. Southerners entrenched portions of their infantry line on December 14, the first such extensive field fortifications on a Virginia battlefield, but they found no occasion to use them until fighting resumed the following spring in the same location. Burnside recrossed his hard-won pontoon bridges under cover of a noisy storm on the night of December 15–16 and ended a campaign that had been an unmitigated disaster for the Union cause. Burnside had lost nearly thirteen thousand men while inflicting fewer than five thousand casualties on his enemy. The Battle of Fredericksburg closed the 1862 campaign in Virginia on an extremely high note for Lee's army and the South. For nearly five months the winter season would suspend active campaigning. When the war resumed in the spring of 1863, Lee's army would show tremendous confidence, based on its success at Fredericksburg, as it faced a new Federal commander.

BIBLIOGRAPHY

Allan, William. *The Army of Northern Virginia in 1862.* Boston, 1892. Reprint, Dayton, Ohio, 1984.

Freeman, Douglas S. *Lee's Lieutenants: A Study in Command.* Vol. 2. New York, 1943. Reprint, New York, 1986.

Henderson, George Francis Robert. *The Campaign of Fredericksburg.* London, 1886.

Scales, Alfred M. *The Battle of Fredericksburg.* Washington, D.C., 1884.

Whan, Vorin E., Jr. *Fiasco at Fredericksburg.* State College, Pa., 1961.

ROBERT K. KRICK

FREE MARKETS

The disruption of farming in the wartime South; inadequate transportation facilities; droughts, disease, and destruction; the voracious appetite of armies; and the Union blockade—all these caused the price of food to rise sharply in the South's urban centers. The poor of the cities suffered the greatest privations. To help feed them, some city governments supported the establishment of charity markets supplied by private individuals; other urban governments cooperated with benevolent organizations to provide food for the indigent; and still other cities appropriated public funds for poor relief.

One of the earliest and most extensive free markets subsidized by private contributions began in New Orleans. For instance, during the ten days it was open during December 1861, an average of 1,850 families received provisions daily. During March 1862 alone, $16,249 in donations paid for foodstuffs to distribute to the poor. After the city fell to Union forces, the Federals continued direct food relief for the indigent. Mobile, Alabama, also had a free market provided by private citizens. By March 1863 they had contributed $30,645 in cash to purchase food, including 6,000 bushels of corn, for distribution to the needy. Natchez, Mississippi, had two free markets supplied by private individuals; they were open two mornings a week so that the poor could draw rations of food.

In the capital of the Confederacy a rising tide of refugees swelled the ranks of the destitute. During December 1862, the Richmond City Council appropriated $20,000 to get the needy through the winter and the following year appropriated another $150,000. In late 1864, the council established a Board of Supplies to scour the countryside for food, transport it to Richmond, and provide for its storage and distribution. By the end of the war, the city government was cooperating with the Union Benevolent Society of Richmond to purchase and distribute food on a regular basis to 4,500 persons, but there was never enough to feed adequately all the people of the city.

In Charleston, South Carolina, beef that had sold for 15 cents per pound in 1861 cost $3 per pound by 1863, and corn sold for $225 a bushel. The city government was spending $10,000 monthly to feed about 3,000 poor people. But farmers balked at bringing food into the city when the bombardment began, and as refugees increased, rations had to be pared in half. To meet the needs of feeding the poor, the Charleston government created a Subsistence Committee, which sent agents into the countryside with public funds to buy produce. With the cooperation of the military authorities, the city council also contracted with the railroads to bring into Charleston thousands of pounds of rice, meal, peas, and potatoes, some of which was distributed to the poor.

The creation of free markets supported by both private donations and public expenditures in the South's major cities undoubtedly saved thousands from suffering and even starvation. It may also have prevented more food riots than occurred.

BIBLIOGRAPHY

Capers, Gerald M. *Occupied City: New Orleans under the Federals, 1862–1865.* Lexington, Ky., 1965.

Fraser, Walter J., Jr. *Charleston! Charleston!: The History of a Southern City.* Columbia, S.C., 1989.

Gates, Paul W. *Agriculture and the Civil War.* New York, 1965.

Thomas, Emory M. *The Confederate State of Richmond: A Biography of the Capital.* Austin, Tex., 1971.

WALTER J. FRASER, JR.

FREE PEOPLE OF COLOR

[*This entry is composed of two articles that discuss the lives and contributions of free people of color in the Confederacy:* Free Blacks *and* Free Creoles of Color. *For further discussion of the role of free people of color in the Confederate armed forces, see* Army, *article on* African Americans in the Confederate Army, *and* Navy, *article on* African American in the Confederate Navy.]

Free Blacks

For all practical purposes, the Confederacy was the most biracial society in North America from 1861 to 1865. Among the three tiers of this beleaguered community of whites, slaves, and free blacks, perhaps the last experienced the most complex and difficult lives in the shadow of bondage. A typical free black was either an African American ex-slave legally manumitted (either by a white person or through self-purchase) or someone born free, whose freedom was inherited through parents or some other antecedent, usually a white grandparent. Though most were "full-blooded blacks" (persons without white ancestry), a large number were mulattoes, persons of mixed black and white ancestry, sons and daughters of upper- or middle-class white men and free black or slave women.

According to the 1860 census, there were nearly 250,000 free blacks in the antebellum South, tenacious survivors in a sea of slavery whose numbers had increased by 12 percent (mulattoes by 2 percent) from the previous decade despite a combination of lower fertility, higher mortality rates, and prejudice. Their number in the seceded states was some 132,760. Forty-four percent of the Confederacy's free blacks resided in Virginia. The number in that state was exceeded only in the border state of Maryland, where 83,942 lived. Free blacks composed 1.4 percent; slaves, 35 percent; and whites, 60 percent of the Southern population. They were the most urbanized of African Americans; approximately 40 percent resided in towns and cities, and 15 percent of these dwelled in some of the Confederacy's largest municipalities: New Orleans, 10,689; Charleston, 5,478; Richmond, 2,576; Norfolk, 1,046; Mobile, 817; Savannah, 705; and New Bern, North Carolina, 689.

They functioned on the fringes of urban Southern society, living, working, and practicing traditional Judeo-Christian-American standards of morality and responsibility, yet maintaining their own identity. They recognized the limitations of their lives and the considerable power whites possessed over them. Free blacks quietly established and maintained networks of social, religious, educational, and benevolent organizations for mutual support, creating an outlying black-based economy and thus maintaining their quasi-independence. They worked chiefly as day laborers, farmhands, waiters, barbers, cooks, seamstresses, and nurses but also as mechanics, tailors, carpenters, hairdressers, bricklayers, clerks, blacksmiths, and wheelwrights. Treated as a third-rate, possibly subversive caste, free blacks were expected to know and obey state criminal codes concerning them, no matter how onerous or unfair. Georgia, Texas, and Virginia established legislative controls under which these blacks could voluntarily enslave themselves, an outgrowth of antebellum laws proposed or enacted for the enslavement of the Southern free black class. Similar wartime measures to force exile or enslavement upon them were contemplated but either failed to be passed or enforced; these were vigorously resisted by free blacks and their white allies.

> **Mindful of their precarious status, most free blacks maintained a low public profile.**

Any black person was presumed to be a slave in the Confederate States of America unless he or she proved otherwise. As one of several obligatory survival skills, free blacks quickly learned to highlight their unique status by appending "f. c. p." (free colored person), "f. m. c." or "f. m. o. c." (free man of color), "f. n." (free Negro), "f. n. w." (free Negro woman), "f. w. c." (free woman of color), or "f. p. o. c." (free person of color) to their correspondence and legal documents. They were denied access to most public facilities or forced to accept separate, unequal accommodations. They were prohibited from selling or purchasing liquor, medicine, and firearms; from owning dogs, boats, and books or papers other than deeds or registers of their manumission; from purchasing train tickets, returning from visits to the North, or having sexual relations with whites. Their children, denied access to public education, were taught in underground schools, churches, and private homes by sympathetic whites and courageous blacks or were sent North.

As living reminders that not all African Americans were born to be slaves and as victims of the peculiar institution's oppressive customs, free blacks could not hold certain occupations or under most circumstances testify in court against whites who had assaulted or cheated them. Vigilante groups and citizen and home guard patrols monitored their movements. They were forbidden to hold meetings without the presence of whites or to have unsanctioned contacts with slaves. They were required to carry badges or passes at all times and were intimidated into remaining in their homes at night. They had few, if any, civil rights, and usually the greater their percentage in proportion to the white population in a given area, the more likely the communities were inclined to enact repressive measures, particularly in Virginia, Georgia,

and North and South Carolina. Free blacks were expected to obey these laws and pay taxes, though they could not vote or hold public office.

Despite these limitations on employment, mobility, and residency, several became substantial owners of real estate, personal property, and slaves. One respected black Richmond resident, ex-slave Gilbert Hunt, owned slaves, a house, and associated property valued at more than two thousand dollars at his death in 1863. In the same city, several free blacks purchased four city lots worth four thousand dollars on behalf of their Union Burial Ground Society in 1864. Henderson Goings of Albemarle County, Virginia, was a prosperous farmer who owned seventy-five acres of land on which he grew corn, oats, potatoes, and wheat. There was a limited bilingual free black aristocracy in New Orleans, which distanced itself from non-French-speaking, non-slave-owning blacks and established schools for its children. Black slave owners were common in Louisiana and were known for being just as harsh toward slaves as white planters. Some of these men, Jordan Noble among them, raised companies of slave laborers on behalf of the South.

Mindful of their precarious status, most free blacks maintained a low public profile. Nevertheless, some deliberately identified with the Confederate cause (in some locales, up to 25 percent), though in practice they were more likely to be loyal to a particular town, county, or state rather than the Confederacy. This was a stratagem for survival, an effort to preserve their free status in the face of the pressures and suspicions of their white neighbors. Free black farmers, for example, sold crops and hired out their slaves to the government. One such family, the Ellisons of Charleston, earned nearly $24,000 between 1862 and 1864 from their agriculture.

Between January and July 1861 nearly three thousand free blacks in Tennessee, Virginia, South Carolina, and Georgia volunteered to serve the Confederacy, and South Carolina's blacks signed memorials attesting to their willingness to fight. Giles Price of Thomasville, Georgia, and John Rapier of Alabama publicly spoke and wrote on behalf of the South. Approximately eighty Savannah blacks offered to serve in any capacity for the duration of the war, and Joe Clark, a Columbus, Georgia, barber, sought official permission to raise a company of free blacks. Charlottesville, Virginia, free blacks offered their property and services to the town council and promised to faithfully serve anywhere in the state.

But not all free blacks were eager to embrace the cause of Southern nationhood. Some collaborated with and spied for Union forces. Plots of black insurrections were suspected, and minor outbreaks were suppressed throughout the region until the end of the war. Black pro-Union organizations across Virginia met during 1864 and 1865 to map out ways to undermine the Confederacy.

Compelled to use every resource, the Confederacy considered free blacks an integral component of its war effort, even though the drafting of slaves was extremely unpopular, its legality challenged by slaveholders as an infringement of their property rights. Free black volunteers, however, were sought and accepted for noncombatant military duty, and their numbers, though small in comparison to impressed slaves, released white males for the army. Louisiana, Georgia, Mississippi, South Carolina, and Virginia were among states that passed legislation for their employment and authorized their transfer to duty under the Confederate government. In February 1864, the Confederate Congress ordered free black men between the ages of eighteen and fifty to be impressed as laborers. Volunteers or conscripts, skilled or unskilled, these blacks received the same pay and rations as white soldiers and in many instances were organized at camps of instruction, formed into companies, and sent to fortifications, hospitals, factories, and similar facilities. Some were seized by press gangs or forced to pay 10 percent of their wages to extortionists to avoid conscription, fines, or imprisonment. A few even conspired with Confederate officers to substitute their slaves and shared the wages with the whites.

The most ironic development of military employment was the Confederacy's belated recognition of its need for black soldiers. Black military companies had been organized in Tennessee as early as April 1861; Louisiana and Alabama blacks served as militia members and marched in review with white regiments in February 1862; at the same time Virginia legislators tentatively discussed plans to enroll free black soldiers.

The Negro Soldier Law of March 13, 1865, called for the enlistment of 300,000 black troops, primarily slaves, to be formed into regiments, battalions, and brigades. Shortly before and after that time until the fall of Richmond, newspaper editorials and advertisements urged free blacks to enlist for the good of the nation. These solicitations hinted at postwar racial reforms and improved, albeit limited, black civil rights. Conceivably, there was a time when such appeals might have received an enthusiastic response from black Southerners, but by 1865 racial memories could not be so easily disregarded. An Atlanta free black was quoted in a January 1865 newspaper as refusing to enlist because he did not have a country nor had he ever had one. But crumbling logistics and near-exhaustion of resources on the eve of final Confederate defeat prevented implementation of this unprecedented entreaty.

Free black adroitness in maintaining a circumscribed freedom in the midst of slavery demonstrated a focused sense of purpose. White Confederates could have learned much about cultural endurance from them.

After Appomattox several free black families expected to wield political, religious, economic, and social leadership in the African American community. But they were out of touch with the black masses. As free blacks they had distanced themselves from slaves, curried favor with the white power structure, boasted of their antebellum freedom (as opposed to slaves "shot free" by the war, the Emancipation Proclamation, or the Thirteenth Amendment), or taken snobbish advantage of their privileged status in the antebellum South. When they sought to lead and speak on behalf of blacks, the freed people preferred the leadership of fellow ex-slaves, and having been a slave became a prerequisite for black-to-black political support. It would be a generation before Southern blacks could redefine themselves as a community embodying a collective history, trust, and self-preservation.

BIBLIOGRAPHY

Berlin, Ira, Barbara J. Fields, Thavolia Glymph, Joseph R. Reidy, and Leslie S. Rowland, eds. *The Destruction of Slavery.* Ser. 1, vol. 1 of *Freedom: A Documentary History of Emancipation, 1861–1867. Selected from the Holdings of the National Archives of the United States.* New York, 1985.

Blackerby, H. C. *Blacks in Blue and Gray: Afro-American Service in the Civil War.* Tuscaloosa, Ala., 1979.

Burnham, Philip. "Selling Poor Stephen." *American Heritage* 44, no. 1 (February–March 1993): 90–97.

Durden, Robert F. *The Gray and the Black: The Confederate Debate on Emancipation.* Baton Rouge, La., 1972.

Johnson, Michael P., and James L. Roark. *Black Masters: A Free Family of Color in the Old South.* New York, 1984.

Nelson, Bernard H. "Legislative Control of the Southern Free Negro, 1861–1865." *Catholic Historical Review* 32 (April 1946): 28–46.

Wesley, Charles Harris. *The Collapse of the Confederacy.* Washington, D.C., 1937.

Wiley, Bell Irvin. *Southern Negroes, 1861–1865.* New Haven, 1938.

Williams, George Washington. *History of the Negro Race in America from 1619 to 1880.* New York, 1882.

ERVIN L. JORDAN, JR.

Free Creoles of Color

In Louisiana and in the port cities of Alabama and Florida, native-born Catholic creoles of color of Latin European and African descent distinguished the lower South's free black population at the time of the Civil War. By 1860 New Orleans, with a free black population of 10,939 in an urban population of 170,024 (144,601 white; 14,484 slave), and Mobile, with 817 free blacks in a total population of 29,258 (20,854 white; 7,587 slave), possessed large, tightly knit communities of French- and Spanish-speaking creoles of color. In Florida, with 932 free blacks in a state population of 140,423 (77,746 white; 61,745 slave), most of the free black residents of the port cities of Pensacola, St. Augustine, Key West, and Jacksonville were either the creole descendants of the region's early Spanish and African inhabitants or West Indian émigrés.

These creoles, brought within United States borders by the Louisiana Purchase (1803) and the acquisition of West Florida (1810) and Florida (1819), prospered during the early decades of American rule. Acquiring a degree of recognition from the treaties with France and Spain and benefiting from the persistence of a relatively flexible tripartite racial order, free creoles exercised a comparatively high level of economic and social mobility. Creole artisans in New Orleans, Mobile, and Pensacola excelled in such varied occupations as cabinetmaker, tailor, shoemaker, mason, cigar maker, butcher, barber, and blacksmith. In New Orleans, highly educated free creoles of color pursued careers as architects, engineers, brokers, doctors, literary artists, and musicians, and in rural Louisiana, a few *gens de couleur* accumulated great wealth as slaveholding planters.

The presence of an intermediate class of free people of color proved inimical to the region's planter elite, however. Beginning in the 1840s, state legislators in Alabama and Florida enacted laws requiring free persons of color to choose a white guardian. By 1855 such guardians supervised the activities of over half of Mobile's free blacks. Finally, between 1858 and 1860 state legislatures throughout the lower South admonished free persons of color to choose their own masters and become slaves for life. Some creoles fled the rising tide of white oppression. In Pensacola the number of creole residents dropped precipitously from 350 in 1850 to 130 in 1860. In New Orleans the size of the free black population declined from 15,072 in 1840 to 10,689 in 1860.

Threatened with violence, expulsion, and confiscation of property after Louisiana seceded on January 26, 1861, the city's community of creoles of color mobilized to safeguard their community. In a defensive action, free black volunteers proffered their services to Confederate officials. In Mobile and in small creole enclaves in the outlying Louisiana parishes of Natchitoches, Pointe Coupée, and Plaquemines, free black leaders undertook similar measures. Though the Confederacy refused to enlist the men in the Regular Army, local officials in New Orleans and Mobile accepted the creole companies into their local militias. By November 1861 Louisiana Confederate Governor Thomas O. Moore had enrolled 1,500 free black soldiers in New Orleans in the First Native Guards, Louisiana Militia, and white officials inducted over 3,000 free black soldiers into the state militia units. However, officials assigned them neither arms nor supplies and confined their activities to company drills.

Within a year of their enlistment, the city's Native Guards militiamen confirmed Confederate fears of questionable black allegiance. In January 1862 authorities noted the free black regiment's high rate of absenteeism, and when Commodore David G. Farragut's naval bombardment forced

the Confederates to evacuate the city in April 1862, the Native Guards refused to leave. Shortly after Gen. Benjamin F. Butler, the commanding officer of the Union army, occupied the city, the creole militiamen volunteered their services to the Union general. In August, Butler authorized the induction of the First Native Guards. By December, 3,122 free creoles of color and blacks filled three regiments of Louisiana Native Guards officered by both blacks and whites. At the Battle of Port Hudson in 1863, the desperate courage of creole officer André Cailloux and his fellow soldiers of the First and Third Native Guards helped to dispel doubts in the Union army and the United States regarding blacks' ability to fight.

Long before Cailloux and his colleagues enlisted in the Union army, however, the city's free creole intelligentsia had possessed a well-developed ideology of social and political radicalism. During the repression of the antebellum decades, slaveholding as well as nonslaveholding creoles of color developed an intense antagonism toward the governing planter elite. Disaffected activists tapped the ongoing current of political radicalism in nineteenth-century Europe and the Americas. In the city's romantic literary movement, some creole intellectuals, like thinkers in France and Haiti, channeled their discontent into their literary works. Others joined the

> **The presence of an intermediate class of free people of color proved inimical to the region's planter elite, however.**

spiritualist movement, a radical new religious sect whose origins lay in the French socialism of Charles Fourier. With the Federal occupation of the city, they launched an aggressive campaign for equal rights.

Simultaneous with the Native Guards' official induction into the Union army in September 1862, a cadre of influential creoles of color launched a French-language biweekly newspaper, *L'Union*. The editors of the paper condemned slavery, reviled the Confederacy, and urged their readers to support the Union cause. They immediately seized upon the issue of military service to demand equal citizenship. The predominantly creole First Native Guards, the paper insisted, already possessed a legitimate claim to citizenship in view of the role of the regiment's Haitian and Louisiana forebears in the American Revolution and the War of 1812. The paper's bold editorialists even criticized President Abraham Lincoln. Attacking his plan to colonize free blacks and freedmen in Central America, they urged the nation to adopt racial policies modeled after the emancipation and enfranchisement decrees of France's Second Republic.

In 1864, after Federal officials in New Orleans dismissed their demands for suffrage, creole leaders centered at

L'Union redirected their efforts to Washington. In March their representatives met with the president. Though Lincoln evaded their request for the franchise, the men succeeded in laying their case before the nation. Their actions signaled the onset of a national campaign for black civil rights.

BIBLIOGRAPHY

Berlin, Ira. *Slaves without Masters: The Free Negro in the Antebellum South.* New York, 1974.

Blassingame, John W. *Black New Orleans, 1860–1880.* Chicago, 1973.

Hirsch, Arnold R., and Joseph Logsdon. *Creole New Orleans: Race and Americanization.* Baton Rouge, La., 1992.

Kolchin, Peter. *First Freedom: The Responses of Alabama's Blacks to Emancipation and Reconstruction.* Westport, Conn., 1972.

McPherson, James M. *The Negro's Civil War: How American Negroes Felt and Acted during the War for the Union.* New York, 1965. Reprint, Urbana, Ill., 1982.

CARYN COSSÉ BELL

FRIETCHIE, BARBARA

FRIETCHIE, BARBARA (1766–1862), Unionist and subject of a poem by John Greenleaf Whittier. When Robert E. Lee's army entered Frederick, Maryland, in the fall of 1862, Barbara Frietchie was an ailing, ninety-six-year-old resident of that community. Frietchie died in December but was immortalized when Whittier's poem about her appeared in the October 1863 issue of the *Atlantic Monthly.*

In the Whittier tribute, Frietchie's flag flying outside her window incited the wrath of Thomas J. ("Stonewall") Jackson, who ordered his men to shoot the Union banner down. When Frietchie appeared at the window and demanded that the troops "shoot at this old gray head," instead, Jackson was shamed. "Who touches a hair of yon gray head," he said to his men, "dies like a dog! March on!"

Jackson did march through Frederick, a border town, on September 10, 1862, on his way to Harpers Ferry. Nonetheless, most contemporary and historical accounts suggest that the Confederate commander had no encounter with Frietchie, although there were flag-waving episodes involving some of the many Unionist residents of Frederick. Two days later, many of the townspeople turned out to cheer and wave flags when the Union troops entered Frederick, and it is believed that Barbara Frietchie was active during this patriotic demonstration.

Soon after the appearance of Whittier's poem, Southern commentators were quick to deny the story's authenticity. Confederates seem to have taken particular offense at the poem's cut at Jackson, recently killed at Chancellorsville and often lionized as a symbol of Southern chivalry. The implication that Jackson had ordered his men to fire on an old woman's house and was then shamed by the woman's fury apparently was especially galling to Confederate sensibilities.

BIBLIOGRAPHY

Cole, Adelaide. "Of Dame Barbara and Her Legend." *Indiana Social Studies Quarterly* 37 (1984): 54–57.

Quynn, Dorothy M., and William R. Quynn. "Barbara Frietschie." *Maryland Historical Magazine* 37 (September 1942): 227–254.

Seilheimer, George O. "The Historical Basis of Whittier's 'Barbara Frietchie.'" In *Battles and Leaders of the Civil War.* Vol. 2. Edited by Robert U. Johnson and Clarence C. Buel. New York, 1888. Reprint, Secaucus, N.J., 1982.

NINA SILBER

FRONT ROYAL, VIRGINIA

This village in the northern Shenandoah Valley, at the confluence of the north and south forks of the Shenandoah River, was the site of a battle on May 23, 1862, that ruptured the strategic status quo and opened the way for Thomas J. ("Stonewall") Jackson's victorious Valley campaign. In a surprise attack at a point the Federals considered secure, Jackson inflicted nearly one thousand casualties on his foe while suffering only a few dozen himself.

Two months before the Battle of Front Royal, Jackson had suffered a tactical reverse at Kernstown that forced him to retreat south up the valley and take shelter in the mountain fastness of Swift Run Gap. He emerged at the end of April and made a circuitous march that led to the victory at McDowell on May 8. For the next two weeks Jackson gathered forces from various quarters and moved east and then north toward Strasburg, where Union Gen. Nathaniel P. Banks had entrenched his army. On May 21 Jackson swerved eastward from New Market and crossed Massanutten Mountain through the only gap along its fifty-mile length. The next day and into May 23 the Confederate column pressed steadily down the narrow subvalley running northward from Luray, heading toward an isolated Federal detachment guarding the railroad at Front Royal. As he neared his target, Jackson pointed his advance guard up the winding Snake Grade near Asbury Chapel, heading toward the Gooney Manor Road that curled along the western shoulder of the Blue Ridge. At the same time Southern cavalry swarmed across the south fork of the Shenandoah River at McKoy's Ford and rode northwest with the mission of breaking the rail line between Strasburg and Front Royal. The cavalry succeeded in its mission after a fight at Buckton Station that killed two promising young Southern officers.

Jackson's careful and devious approach along the mountainside enabled him to make a surprise appearance on the outskirts of Front Royal. When Confederates of the First Maryland Infantry, who had been chafing to leave the army at the expiration of their initial enlistments, learned that their counterparts of the Union First Maryland held Front Royal, they charged into the town. Gen. Richard Taylor's Louisiana brigade dashed into the streets with the Marylanders and soon put the vastly outnumbered Northern force to rout. The ecstatic townspeople who flocked into the streets posed as much impediment to the attackers as did the fleeing foe.

Federals set fire to the crucial bridges near town as they retreated, but pursuing Confederates, with Jackson in their midst leading by example, threw burning timbers into the river and forced their way across. The absence of his artillery, which was mismanaged by the army's chief of that arm, hampered Jackson's pursuit, but he pushed ahead with elements of the Sixth Virginia Cavalry. The mounted men brought the enemy to bay around a house and orchard less than three miles north of the bridge, near Cedarville. Jackson hurled his handful of cavalrymen against the new Federal concentration, exploiting the momentum his surprise had generated. The Southern horsemen galloped up the road four abreast and shattered the last resistance, but at the cost of heavier losses than their friends in the infantry had suffered all day; one color-bearer went down with more than twenty bullets in his body.

As his men rounded up the Federal survivors, Jackson began planning for operations designed to take advantage of the golden opportunity that his hard marching and carefully prepared surprise had won for him. The result was his major victory at the Battle of Winchester two days later.

BIBLIOGRAPHY

Allan, William. *History of the Campaign of Gen. T. J. (Stonewall) Jackson in the Shenandoah Valley of Virginia.* Philadelphia, 1880.
Hale, Laura Virginia. *Four Valiant Years in the Lower Shenandoah Valley.* Strasburg, Va., 1973.
Taylor, Richard. *Destruction and Reconstruction.* New York, 1879.

ROBERT K. KRICK

FUGITIVE SLAVE LAW

A revealingly unanswerable question illuminates blacks' influence on whites' history. Did fugitive slaves more disrupt the Union before 1860 or the Confederacy thereafter? During the Civil War, approximately one in six slaves fled to Union armies or territories. Approximately one in six of these runaways joined the Union's ultimately liberating army. The fugitives undermined the Confederacy's racial order, damaged its economic production, and swelled the ranks of its armed assaulters. Black runaways also created the Union's contraband problem, for although Lincoln's armies fought to secure obedience to Federal laws, which included the Fugitive Slave Law of 1850, could soldiers fight the slaveholders and also return slave property? Finally, the fugitives complicated the issue of the purpose of the war. A war effort at first aimed only at preserving the white people's Union came to need those 100,000 black soldiers. But would ex-slaves fight for exclusively white liberty? The 600,000 self-liberated fugitives, by raising these issues, helped cause a war initially fought on other grounds to spawn black emancipation.

Before the Civil War, too, black fugitives had disrupted white people's controversies. Without runaway slaves, the explosive fugitive slave issue would not have existed, and the equally explosive territorial expansion issue would have been more manageable. Southern expansionist drives were aimed, to a large degree, at deterring fugitive slaves. Southerners feared that if antislavery proponents controlled the other side of the slavocracy's borders, whether in Texas or Kansas or Florida, more slaves would flee toward freedom. If one can imagine a South without a fugitive slave problem, a much-longer-enduring antebellum Union becomes conceivable.

But this slaveholders' republic without fugitive slaves is ultimately unimaginable. American dreams of freedom inspired blacks, too, and flight was the slaves' most promising avenue to liberty. One black betrayer, by alerting whites to an insurrection plot, could destroy a group revolt, but a single fugitive could run as far as skill and luck allowed. A slave escaping from the border states, especially, shortened the long odds against successful flight and heightened the impact of the escape. Border blacks who freed themselves dampened the border South's not-so-great enthusiasm for slavery and challenged the North's not-so-serene compliance with the slaveholders. Successful fugitives could also become inspiring orators and writers, celebrating blacks' journey toward freedom, as did Frederick Douglass in his magnificent speeches and autobiography.

With the Fugitive Slave Law of 1850, the white establishment sought to abort the black slaves' major method of including themselves in white aspirations and history. An earlier Federal fugitive slave law, passed in 1793, had fallen victim to *Prigg v. Pennsylvania* (1842), wherein the U.S. Supreme Court had declared that state authorities need not help enforce a Federal law. That Fugitive Slave Law depended on state enforcement, for few Federal judges and policemen yet existed.

The new Fugitive Slave Law, the South's major gain from the Compromise of 1850, established one-man bureaucracies. A commissioner, appointed by Federal judges, received total authority over runaway slaves; a commissioner could demand that any Northerner help capture alleged fugitives;

and subsequently, a commissioner was judge and jury of last resort. Accused fugitives had no right to testify in their own behalf or to secure writs of habeas corpus. The commissioner was paid five dollars if he freed the alleged fugitive, ten dollars if he extradited the black to the South. Extra paperwork for extradition supposedly justified the extra payment, but many Northerners considered it a bribe—the symbol of an unspeakably despotic law.

In exchange for Northern acquiesence in allegedly despotic Federal machinery to return fugitives, Southerners agreed to the admission of free-labor California into the Union. After that Compromise of 1850 tradeoff, slaveholders demanded that their theoretical gain, the return of fugitive

> **Accused fugitives had no right to testify in their own behalf or to secure writs of habeas corpus.**

slaves, be realized. Contrary to popular myth, then and now, they largely received their due. Ninety percent of the 322 fugitives tried under the Fugitive Slave Law were remanded to their owners. But the other 10 percent made the headlines, and well-publicized stories of successful defiance weakened the law's deterrent effect on potential fugitives. The notoriety of the few who escaped the commissioners also poisoned Southern opinion of the North, just as the dispatching of blacks southward, without judge or jury, lowered the North's opinion of the South. Seldom has a law 90 percent successful so dismally failed.

Some famous exceptions to the usual, but ultimately less important, smooth return of fugitives included the rescue by Boston blacks in 1851 of Shadrack, a Virginia slave, from a courthouse; he was then sent to freedom in Canada. That same year a Syracuse mob rescued Jerry, a Missouri slave, from a police station, with the same eventual result: freedom in Canada. Also in 1851, a Maryland slaveholder, Edward Gorsuch, went with his son to Christiana, Pennsylvania, in pursuit of his fugitive slaves. A local black leader, William Parker, barricaded the fugitives in his house, with largely free blacks standing guard. When Gorsuch persisted, gunfire cracked, and the master was slain and his son badly wounded. The slaves got away to Canada, as did William Parker. Gorsuch's murderers remained at large.

A still more publicized fugitive slave incident involved a black returned to enslavement. In 1854, a Virginia fugitive, Anthony Burns, was arrested in Boston and ordered remanded to the South. Important intellectuals plotted to spring the literate slave from jail, but their plan failed and a policeman was killed. Fifty thousand angry Bostonians flooded the streets, demanding that Burns be freed. But at a cost of $100,000, a phalanx of policemen plus a U.S. infantry com-

pany and a detachment of artillery sliced a path through the protesters, and Anthony Burns set sail for Virginia. He soon voyaged back north, after Bostonians purchased his freedom.

Those huge numbers—$100,000, 50,000 Bostonians—did overwhelm in Southern memories the 290 slaves peaceably returned. Northern states' personal liberty laws also helped pave the Southern path toward secession. These laws affirmed that Northern state officials could not cooperate with Federal Fugitive Slave Law enforcers. Some personal liberty laws also reaffirmed free blacks' legal rights, including the right to secure a writ of habeas corpus. But states had no authority over Federal legal processes, and personal liberty laws never liberated a fugitive from a commissioner. The personal liberty laws chiefly served to express Northerners' sense of the Fugitive Slave Law: that it was outrageously un-American, and tyrannical, particularly in requiring all free citizens to hunt down a brave escapee from despotism. Southerners ultimately tried to secede in part from that insulting opinion. But secession and the Civil War only gave Northerners more power to aid more fugitives—a slaveholders' problem that no Union or Confederacy could solve.

[*See also* Compromise of 1850; Contraband; Dred Scott Decision.]

BIBLIOGRAPHY

Campbell, Stanley. *The Slave Catchers: Enforcement of the Fugitive Slave Law, 1850–1860.* Chapel Hill, N.C., 1968.
Galpin, W. Freeman. "The Jerry Rescue." *New York History* 43 (1945): 19–34.
Gara, Larry. *The Liberty Line: The Legend of the Underground Railroad.* Lexington, Ky., 1961.
Pease, Jane H., and William H. Pease. *The Fugitive Slave Law and Anthony Burns.* Philadelphia, 1975.
Slaughter, Thomas P. *Bloody Dawn: The Christiana Riot and Racial Violence in the Antebellum North.* New York, 1991.

WILLIAM W. FREEHLING

FUNERALS

The Civil War wrought a major change even in American funeral customs. Prior to the struggle, undertakers were cabinetmakers or hardware store owners who supplied casket, hearse, and team for the funeral service. Families of any means buried their deceased in wooden coffins; the less affluent wrapped the body in a blanket or sheet. Any viewing of the remains in the interval between death and burial was of short duration. Cooling boards and ice chests, in which ice was placed beneath the corpse as a temporary preservative, were sometimes used for prominent figures. The inadequacy of this practice, however, especially in the heat of summer, gave rise to a popular jingle: "Soon ripe, soon rotten; soon gone, but not forgotten."

Then came civil war, and with unprecedented numbers of men fighting, unprecedented numbers died. Grief-stricken families wanted the remains of their heroes, but how to transport the dead from battlefields to destinations hundreds of miles away was a major problem. The condition of the decomposing corpse when it finally reached home was of equal concern.

Two developments resulted. One was the rise of professional undertakers who handled remains in an orderly and knowledgeable fashion. Allied to this was the perfection of embalming through the arterial injection of fluid. The first embalming fluids had an arsenic base. They petrified rather than preserved (and hence were eventually outlawed by federal statute.) Nevertheless, with embalming and large-scale production of metallic, airtight coffins, it became possible in the Civil War to ship home untold numbers of fallen soldiers. Funeral services were held months after death, in either public or family cemeteries. Psalm-readings, prayers, sometimes a eulogy, and often one or more hymns comprised the usual burial service.

BIBLIOGRAPHY

Habenstein, Robert W. *The History of American Funeral Directing.* Milwaukee, 1955.

Robertson, James I., Jr. "The Development of the Funeral Business in Georgia." *Georgia Review,* Spring 1959.

JAMES I. ROBERTSON, JR.

GAINES' MILL, VIRGINIA

[*This entry discusses the battle of June 27, 1862. For discussion of the battle of May 31 through June 12, 1864, see* Cold Harbor.] Site of the third of the Seven Days' Battles fought on the outskirts of Richmond, Virginia, Gaines' Mill witnessed fighting between Robert E. Lee's Army of Northern Virginia and Union Maj. Gen. George B. McClellan's Army of the Potomac. The battle raged throughout most of the day of June 27, 1862, leaving the Confederates exhausted victors. Estimated casualties among the 57,018 Southerners numbered 8,751 dead, wounded, and missing; Federal losses totaled 6,837 killed, wounded, and missing out of 34,214 men.

On June 26, 1862, Lee had tried and failed to destroy Union Maj. Gen. Fitz John Porter's isolated Fifth Corps positioned north of the Chickahominy River, northeast of Richmond. The Battle of Mechanicsville, or Beaver Dam Creek, ended badly for the Confederates. Lt. Gen. Thomas J. ("Stonewall") Jackson's failure to arrive from the Shenandoah Valley in time to move behind and assail the enemy's flank left the attacking Confederates to falter before a well-entrenched enemy. Southerners took a great loss in casualties. That night, Porter withdrew to the southeast, closer to the remainder of McClellan's army. Lee followed in hot pursuit.

Near Gaines' Mill, south and east of New and Old Cold Harbor, Porter halted and turned to face the Confederates. His men soon formed a strong semicircular defense on a plateau behind Boatswain's Swamp just above the Chickahominy River. Federals dug themselves into the Virginia mud, south and east of a stream, and awaited the pursuing Confederates.

Soldiers of Gen. A. P. Hill's Light Division were the first to approach the Federal position, and they immediately formed into charging columns. Over the next several hours the brigades of Maxcy Gregg, William Dorsey Pender, Lawrence O'Bryan Branch, Joseph R. Anderson, James Jay Archer, and Charles W. Field stormed across the boggy swamp to assault the enemy lines. Each fell back before the deadly blaze of artillery and infantry gunfire.

At one point, Lee tried to divert the enemy's attention from its center by sending James Longstreet's division to the right of Hill's men. They too met with strong resistance and retreated to Confederate lines.

The bulk of Lee's army was on the field; only Jackson's fourteen brigades were absent. Jackson again was late, apparently directed down the wrong road, which almost brought his troops through Gaines' Mill. He countermarched four miles and finally arrived on the field around 3:00 P.M. But Jackson, hesitant to jump into the fray without knowledge of battle positions and plans, still waited and watched. Meanwhile the fight raged on with Confederate losses mounting and Union reinforcements on the way.

It was not until 7:00 that evening that all of Lee's men were in place and poised to move forward in one last coordinated assault. Four thousand fresh troops under Brig. Gen. John B. Hood and Col. Evander M. Law spearheaded a dramatic charge on the Union center. The remainder of Lee's army attacked on either flank. The fight grew hot and severe, and as darkness enveloped the field, Porter's men retreated. A last effort by the Federal cavalry to stem the tide of storming Confederates proved futile. Mounted men from the Fifth and Second U.S. Cavalry were easy targets for infantry rifle fire, and they soon turned to join the retreat. That night Porter again slipped farther south, this time to reunite with the rest of McClellan's withdrawing army.

The costly Southern victory had revealed disturbing problems in Lee's command structure. All-day delays, misinformation, inaccurate maps, garbled orders, and an overall lack of communication had greatly hindered Lee's ability to fight with his full strength against Porter's single corps.

Gaines' Mill again revealed the aggressive fighting spirit Lee had displayed at Mechanicsville. Over the next few days Lee would persist in his quest to destroy McClellan's army, but engagements at Savage's Station, Frayser's Farm, and Malvern Hill only resulted in more losses to Lee's army; he won no decisive victories. Nevertheless, Lee did succeed in forcing McClellan eventually to withdraw his massive army entirely from the peninsula. Not for another two years would a Union force come as close to threatening the Confederate capital.

BIBLIOGRAPHY

Catton, Bruce. *Mr. Lincoln's Army.* Garden City, N.Y., 1951.
Cullen, Joseph P. "Gaines's Mill." *Civil War Times Illustrated* 3, no. 1 (April 1964): 11–17.
Dowdey, Clifford. *The Seven Days: The Emergence of Lee.* Boston, 1964.

Freeman, Douglas S. *Lee's Lieutenant's: A Study in Command.* 3 vols. New York, 1942–1944. Reprint, New York, 1986.

LESLEY JILL GORDON-BURR

GALVANIZED YANKEES

Although the origin of the term *Galvanized Yankees* is obscure, it has two exactly opposite meanings—both are correct. The primary meaning refers to the 6,000 Southern soldiers who deserted the Confederate cause, joined the Union army as the First through Sixth Regiments, U.S. Volunteers, and spent the rest of the war fighting Indians on the western frontier. The second meaning refers to Northern soldiers who deserted the Federal army and joined the Confederate army, although these soldiers were sometimes referred to as "Galvanized Rebels."

Both groups of Galvanized Yankees were usually recruited from prisoner of war camps. There they chose to fight against their former flag rather than undergo the deprivation and possible death the camps offered. Many, however, changed uniforms only as a ruse to return to their former colors. Consequently, the Galvanized Yankee units experienced high desertion rates (one in seven) when they were in the vicinity of their former comrades. Desertion rates notwithstanding, the turncoat soldiers often fought well for their new country, as in the case of Northerners fighting for the South at Egypt Station, Mississippi, and of the U.S. Volunteer Regiments in the West.

BIBLIOGRAPHY

Brown, D. Alexander. *The Galvanized Yankees.* Urbana, Ill., 1963.

Haw, Joseph R. "The Last of the C.S. Ordnance Department." *Confederate Veteran* 34 (1926): 451. Reprint, Wilmington, N.C., 1985.

Laurie, Clayton. "Two-Sided Adventure." *Civil War Times Illustrated* 24 (June 1985): 40.

McLender, L. "About Some 'Galvanized Yanks.'" *Confederate Veteran* 13 (1905): 249. Reprint, Wilmington, N.C., 1985.

P. NEAL MEIER

GALVESTON, TEXAS

[*This entry includes two articles,* City of Galveston, *which profiles the city during the Confederacy, and* Battle of Galveston, *which discusses the military action there in 1863. See also* Harriet Lane.]

City of Galveston

In 1860 the second largest town in Texas contained a population of 7,307, including 2,688 European immigrants—a majority from Germany—as well as 1,178 slaves and 2 free blacks. On the eve of the Civil War, Galveston ranked as the major U.S. port on the Gulf of Mexico west of the Mississippi River and fifth among Southern seaports in trade. Despite some concern about the impact on commerce, a majority of voters in Galveston favored Southern Democrat John C. Breckinridge in 1860 and secession in 1861.

Once war began, Galvestonians volunteered for several military companies, including ones in Hood's brigade, Waul's legion, and Cook's artillery regiment. Confederates constructed fortifications and brought in cannon to defend the important island port. The first Union blockading ship appeared in July 1861. A Federal squadron of several vessels occupied the harbor on October 4, 1862, and Confederate troops retreated to the mainland. A counterattack by land and water on January 1, 1863, by Gen. John B.

> **Several merchants moved their operations to Houston and focused on trade through Mexico.**

Magruder captured one warship, drove the others from the harbor, and reoccupied the town. The Union blockade resumed quickly and continued to the end of conflict in 1865. Despite the threat of a Federal force on the coast below Galveston in the fall of 1863, the port did not face another attack. Almost three hundred immigrants avoided conscription because they were foreign citizens and about fifty Unionists left with the Union navy.

Most Confederate blockade runners from Galveston escaped the Federal ships, but the use of smaller vessels and visits by fewer ships per year reduced the export of cotton by at least two-thirds. Several merchants moved their operations to Houston and focused on trade through Mexico. A few small rope and iron manufacturers continued in operation. Many middle- and upper-class families became refugees in Houston to escape possible shelling and occupation. Working men faced unemployment and shortages but received some aid from charitable groups organized primarily by women.

Citizens and Confederate officers held some dances and celebrations. Yet the war disrupted social patterns in church services and schools on several occasions. Shortages, inflation, and the partial breakdown of local government led to thefts, the use of fences for firewood, and occasional violence. Confederate troops mutinied briefly in August 1863, and soldiers' wives protested the following summer over pay and food problems. Yellow fever caused more than 250 deaths in September 1864. Slavery also faced wartime changes as refugees took one-third of the bondsmen off the island. The Confederate army used slave labor to build fortifications. A few slaves escaped to the Union naval vessels, while the remainder welcomed the Union army on June 19, 1865, which became the popular date for celebrating emancipation in Texas.

Postwar Galveston recovered rapidly with trade nearing the prewar level by 1866. Its population had grown to 13,818 in 1870, which ranked the town first in Texas.

BIBLIOGRAPHY

Barr, Alwyn, "Texas Coastal Defense, 1861–1865." *Southwestern Historical Quarterly* 65 (1961–1962): 1–30.
McComb, David G. *Galveston: A History.* Austin, Tex., 1986.

ALWYN BARR

Battle of Galveston

In the early morning darkness of January 1, 1863, Confederates recaptured Galveston, the principal seaport on the Texas coast and key to the blockade of the western Gulf of Mexico. Its recapture provided a Confederate morale boost while denying the Union navy a base in the region. It also prevented a Union invasion of Texas from that city. Galveston continued to be an important blockade-running port for the rest of the war.

In October 1862, Union sailors and marines had seized the town after its Confederate garrison withdrew. Adm. David Farragut then requested that an army garrison be sent. On Christmas Day, a 260-man Union detachment composed of three companies of the Forty-second Massachusetts Infantry under Col. Isaac Burrell arrived to secure the town. Anchored off shore along the roadstead and in Galveston Bay were the gunboats of Commdr. William B. Renshaw's squadron, including USS *Clifton,* USS *Westfield,* USS *Sachem,* USS *Owasco,* USS *Corypheus,* and the revenue cutter USS *Harriet Lane,* as well as half a dozen coal tenders and troop transports.

Gen. John B. Magruder, the commander of the Department of Texas, used a surprise land-sea attack to retake the city. Magruder's battle fleet consisted of *Bayou City,* a river steamer, and *Neptune,* a coastal mail packet. Confederate shipworkers in Houston outfitted both vessels with bow cannons and piled cotton bales along the decks as makeshift armor. Accompanying the two cottonclads were two steamboats, *Lucy Gwinn* and *John F. Carr,* serving as wood tenders.

Magruder loaded his fleet with 300 volunteer sharpshooters to act as boarding parties. An additional 1,500 men, along with a dozen pieces of artillery, crossed over to Galveston Island on the night of December 31, 1862. At 4:00 A.M. on New Year's Day, Magruder ordered his troops to open fire. The Union fleet returned the fire with murderous ferocity, scattering the Texan gun crews. A Confederate infantry assault against the Forty-second Massachusetts also disintegrated. At dawn, Magruder aborted the attack.

Taking advantage of the distraction on shore, the Confederate naval forces attacked. Texan sharpshooters cleared the deck of *Harriet Lane* as a boarding party captured the ship. The Confederates then boldly sent a flag of truce to Commander Renshaw, ordering him to surrender his entire fleet. Mistaking the Confederate vessels for ironclad rams, Renshaw ordered his fleet out of Galveston Bay, abandoning the infantry on shore. His flagship, *Westfield,* was hard aground, and Renshaw ordered it destroyed; a premature explosion killed him and twelve crewmen.

Thirty Texans were killed, and another 130 were wounded in the Confederate victory. *Neptune* sank in shallow water and *Bayou City* was severely damaged. Union losses were 21 killed, 36 wounded, and 250 captured. In addition to taking *Harriet Lane* and causing *Westfield* to be scuttled, the Confederates captured three coaling vessels.

BIBLIOGRAPHY

Evans, Clement A., ed. *Confederate Military History.* 12 vols. Atlanta, 1899. Extended ed. in 19 vols. Wilmington, N.C., 1987–1989.
Hayes, Charles Waldo. *Galveston: A History of the Island and the City.* 2 vols. Austin, Tex., 1974.
Noel, Theophilus. *A Campaign from Santa Fe to the Mississippi: Being a History of the Old Sibley Brigade from Its First Organization to the Present Time; Its Campaigns in New Mexico, Arizona, Texas, Louisiana and Arkansas in the Years 1861–2–3–4.* Shreveport, La., 1865. Reprint, edited by Martin Hardwick Hall and Edwin Adams Davis. Houston, Tex., 1961.

DONALD S. FRAZIER

GARLAND, AUGUSTUS HILL

GARLAND, AUGUSTUS HILL (1832–1899), congressman from Arkansas and postwar governor, U.S. senator, and U.S. attorney general. Born June 11, 1832, in Tipton County, Tennessee, Garland was educated at St. Mary's College in Lebanon, Kentucky, and St. Joseph's College in Bardstown, Kentucky. While in school he was strongly influenced by his admiration for Henry Clay.

Returning to Washington, Arkansas, in 1852, Garland began reading law and formed a law firm with his stepfather,

AUGUSTUS HILL GARLAND.

Thomas Hubbard, and worked for Simon T. Sanders, the county and circuit court clerk for Hempstead County. In 1856 he moved to Little Rock where his law practice became one of the most prestigious in the state.

The defeat of the American party candidates in the 1856 election left the Democratic party, led by the Johnson "Family," in control of Arkansas politics. When the 1860 election began, Garland participated in an opposition convention, assembling the group generally recognized as the successor to the Whig-American party coalition. In the national election that fall Garland was an elector for the Constitutional Union party.

At the January 1860 term of the Arkansas Supreme Court, Garland lost a series of appeals dealing with the taxation of swamp and overflowed lands, and he spent the summer preparing to carry his appeal to the U.S. Supreme Court. On the day after Christmas, he was enrolled as an attorney before the Court.

By the time Garland returned to Little Rock late in January 1861, the state was full of excitement over the coming election that would decide whether to call a secession convention. Garland immediately announced his candidacy for one of Pulaski County's two seats in the convention. With no time to publish his thoughts on secession, he declared that he agreed with the views of Joseph Stillwell, another candidate in Pulaski County.

Garland was a conservative Unionist. He opposed separate state secession and urged cooperation with the border states. He suggested calling a convention of all slaveholding states to adopt the Crittenden Resolutions. As the only cotton-growing state left in the Union, Arkansas would benefit from a monopoly on trade, he argued, and he urged the people to make the state one of the strongest in the Union instead of one of the weakest in the Confederacy.

In February the people of Arkansas voted to call a convention to consider the question of secession, but the convention had a strong Unionist contingent. Garland and Stillwell were elected by 550 votes over their secessionist opponents. The secession convention began on March 4, 1861, the same day that Abraham Lincoln was inaugurated. The Unionist leaders—Garland, his brother Rufus Garland, Hugh F. Thomasson, and W. W. Watkins—adopted a two-part strategy. They worked to defeat efforts to draw up a secession ordinance and suggested waiting to see what Lincoln would do. After agreeing to submit the question of secession or cooperation to the voters, the convention adjourned on March 21.

The convention reconvened on May 6, however, in reaction to Lincoln's call for troops and immediately adopted a secession ordinance. Garland voted for the ordinance reluctantly in the hope of continuing to influence the course of events. Next the convention considered whom to send to the Confederate Congress. The first nomination went to former senator Robert Ward Johnson; the second to Garland. He was elected on the first ballot. While the convention turned to rewriting the state constitution, Garland headed for Montgomery to join the Provisional Congress. When he took his seat he was the youngest member of that body; he would become one of only twenty-eight men to serve in all three Congresses.

After Congress reconvened in Richmond, Garland was appointed to the Public Lands and the Finance committees. It was in committees that Garland built a reputation for hard work and scholarship. His first major motion was a resolution calling on the Finance Committee to investigate the expediency of declaring Treasury notes and bonds legal tender. This resolution was the beginning of a long controversy over legal tender that was never resolved. By the time discussion of the matter was dropped in 1864, notes were accepted as legal tender though they had never been designated as such.

Congress adjourned in August and Garland returned to Arkansas to seek election to the First Congress as a representative of the Third District. His main opponent was Jilson P. Johnson of Desha County, an early secessionist and part of the Johnson Family. Garland waged a vigorous campaign, and, certain he had won when the unofficial totals were announced, he left for Virginia for the final session of the Provisional Congress.

By the time he reached Richmond, Congress was already in session. Garland was appointed to the Judiciary

Committee in addition to his other assignments, which was in keeping with his interest in constitutional law. During this session the committee was dealing with issues relating to the seizure of property. Resolutions introduced by Garland led this inquiry in two directions. He proposed allowing citizens whose goods or property had been confiscated by Federal authorities to recover their losses by seizing land owned by U.S. citizens, and amending the Sequestration Act to exempt the property of free blacks who had been forced to leave the slave states. Garland accepted the absolute right of a government to seize alien enemy property, but he sought to protect property owners from loss.

Meanwhile a problem had developed over the November election. Arkansas Governor Henry Rector had announced the results of the election on the basis of official returns sent to the secretary of state by the county clerks. According to these returns Garland had received 2,157 votes, Jilson Johnson, 2,125 votes, and four other candidates, fewer numbers of votes, giving Garland a plurality. But Johnson announced that he was contesting the election because of problems in the returns from Arkansas County. Garland at first ignored Johnson's challenge, but the House of Representatives accepted it and sent the matter to the Committee on Elections. The committee, deeply divided along party lines, was determined to work slowly and carefully. During the course of the controversy it issued a number of reports and asked the principals to provide evidence several times.

Although the status of his congressional seat was uncertain, Garland decided to run for the Senate. When Confederate senators were chosen in 1861, R. W. Johnson had used his influence as head of the Family to ensure his own selection, but he had drawn a short term and had to seek reappointment in 1862. Garland had gotten more votes than Johnson in the balloting for seats in the Provisional Congress, so he apparently felt the time was ripe to remove the Family from power.

Garland, Johnson, and a third candidate were invited to address the General Assembly. Garland, in his speech, put special emphasis on the financial difficulties facing the Confederacy, referring to the need to make notes and bonds legal tender and discussing a bill for new taxes. He then turned to the topic of ending the war. Garland argued that the cost of the war to both sides in men and money was such that it should end soon. He urged that the Confederacy stay ready for war but make an offer for peace. The final vote came two days later: Johnson received forty-six votes on the twelfth ballot, and Garland forty-two.

Garland had better luck with his congressional seat. When the third session of the First Congress convened in January 1863, more evidence concerning the contested election was sent to the Committee on Elections. Jilson Johnson, however, decided to withdraw his suit, the committee was dismissed, and Garland retained his seat.

He was now able to immerse himself in committee work. In addition to the Judiciary Committee, he was a member of committees on Enrolled Bills and on the Medical Department. He also served on various committees dealing with matters ranging from homesteads for disabled veterans to plans for retaliation against the United States for attempts to enforce the Emancipation Proclamation.

At the close of the First Congress, Garland sent a report to his constituents outlining major legislation and focusing on financial matters. The last part of the report was directed at boosting morale. Calling on civilians to support the government and the army, Garland mentioned in passing that he felt the conventions being held to organize a Unionist government for Arkansas were of no importance.

When the Second Congress convened in May 1864, Garland was made chairman of the Committee on Territories and Public Lands and was again appointed to the Judiciary Committee. He also served on the Special Committee to Inquire into the Charges against W. R. W. Cobb.

The climax of Garland's summer came with his election to the Confederate Senate. Taking his seat in November 1864, Garland was appointed to the Committee on Post Offices and Post Roads. In the next month he introduced twelve bills, resolutions, and memorials on subjects ranging from the salaries of civil officers to limiting the number of slaves employed by the army.

Garland was increasingly concerned about the Confederacy's ability to maintain itself. His ideas on the economy reached final form in January 1865, when he offered a resolution calling for the Judiciary Committee to study the need for a Home Department. Such a department, he urged, should have broad powers for the development, management, and control of the South's internal resources. But the growing military crisis did not make an expansion of government powers attractive, and this resolution died in committee.

Garland brought to Congress his belief in constitutionalism and his faith in a strong central government. He supported the Davis administration on most issues. In letters to his constituents he always emphasized money and military matters and explained them in detail, for he felt these were the things of greatest interest to the people. But his own primary interests lay in two other areas—the suspension of the writ of habeas corpus and the establishment of a supreme court.

In 1862 Congress gave President Jefferson Davis the power to suspend the writ of habeas corpus and declare martial law in areas threatened by invasion. Although the law was applied sparingly nationwide, in Arkansas Gen. Thomas C. Hindman, and later Lt. Gen. Theophilus H. Holmes, exceeded this authority by issuing a series of directives curtailing the power of the civil authorities, establishing price controls, suspending the writ of habeas corpus, and declaring martial law. Garland was horrified.

With this firsthand knowledge of how martial law and suspension of habeas corpus could be misused, Garland was absolutely opposed to the extension of the law when it expired in February 1863. A new, more limited law for the suspension of habeas corpus was passed in February 1864. When the Second Congress convened in May, several members felt they had a mandate to repeal the law even though it was about to expire, and the matter was sent to the Judiciary Committee. The majority of the committee supported renewing the law, but in a minority report issued May 28, 1864, Garland and Burgess Sidney Gaither of North Carolina favored letting the law expire. Garland gave three major reasons the law should be allowed to lapse: first, the law allowed too much discretion about whom to arrest; second, it violated judicial independence by allowing the president to appoint investigating committees for matters normally handled by the courts; and finally, it tended to lower civilian morale. Neither the majority nor the minority report recommended any action, and the law was allowed to expire.

The effort to establish a supreme court for the Confederacy also preoccupied Garland. The Judiciary Act of March 16, 1861, defined the powers of a supreme court, but its organization was suspended in July 1861, delaying its operation without destroying its proposed authority. Bills introduced in 1862 to organize the court never came to a vote.

In April 1863, in a report written by Garland, the House Judiciary Committee recommended the passage of the Senate supreme court bill, with an amendment to give the court appellate jurisdiction over state courts. Garland felt this jurisdiction was essential for the stability of the South in that it would ensure the equal enforcement of Confederate laws. Although his viewpoint was well received, the House postponed action on the bill and it died when Congress adjourned in January 1864.

By late 1864 Garland knew that the war had been lost. Disgusted with the Senate for spending its time and energies fighting with President Davis, Garland left Richmond in late February 1865 to return to Arkansas.

In May, Confederate Governor Harris Flanagin authorized him to confer with Federal authorities to arrange terms for the restoration of peace and order. Garland accepted the commission and went to Little Rock, where he met with Gen. J. J. Reynolds and Unionist Governor Isaac Murphy. When Garland presented Flanagin's plan for unifying the state, Reynolds and Murphy went as far as they could in being conciliatory. They agreed to give the army a chance to disband and promised not to arrest the Confederate civil officers unless ordered to do so. But they refused to recognize the county officers in southern Arkansas.

With the war over, Garland turned his attention to personal matters. He prepared an application for a pardon to be sent to President Andrew Johnson. He stressed that he had been elected to the Confederate Congress as a conservative, that he never called for harsh measures against the Unionists, and that he was always opposed by the secessionists. He included letters of recommendation written by an impressive array of prominent officials, all of whom backed his pardon as a way of securing conservative support for the government and as a step toward restoration of peace and order. The pardon was granted July 15, 1865.

Next Garland sought to reestablish his law practice. Among the matters needing attention was the case of *McGee v. Mathis,* and related cases, which he had filed with the U.S. Supreme Court during the December 1860 term. When Garland checked the records in July 1865 he discovered that the cases were still on the docket. This posed a dilemma. He wanted to attend to the cases, but he could not take the Iron-clad Oath, which required all federal officeholders, including lawyers practicing in federal courts, to swear that they had neither supported nor served in any government that was opposed to the U.S. government.

In October 1865 Garland filed a petition asking that he be allowed to return to practice before the Court without taking the oath. The case, titled *Ex parte Garland,* challenged the oath's constitutionality. It was the first attempt by a Southerner to use the judicial system to ameliorate punishment of the ex-Confederates. In his petition Garland reminded the Court that he had been sworn as an attorney of the Supreme Court in December 1860 and that he had filed briefs and arguments in a number of cases that were pending when Arkansas seceded. He wanted to resume the duties he had taken on before the war, but he could not take the oath without committing perjury. He argued that all laws requiring an oath are repugnant to the Constitution and are therefore null and void; he further argued that if the oath was valid, his presidential pardon relieved him of having to take it. On January 14, 1867, the Court ruled that the law requiring the oath was unconstitutional. The decision restored to Garland, but only Garland, his right to practice before the Supreme Court without taking the oath. As a practical matter, other Southern lawyers could have petitioned the Court for readmission, basing their argument on Garland's victory; but the oath was quietly dropped to avoid the continuing litigation.

Garland now turned to the political arena. In 1868 he led Arkansas conservatives in an unsuccessful fight to prevent the ratification of a new constitution. He was also chairman of the Arkansas delegation to the Democratic National Convention. But as the final measures of Congressional Reconstruction were put into place, Garland withdrew from public affairs.

An adviser to Arkansas Democrats throughout Reconstruction, Garland returned to public life in 1874 when Joseph Brooks and his supporters tried to oust Elisha Baxter from the governor's office. During the Brooks-Baxter War which followed, Garland was a leader of the Baxter forces, devising a strategy that led to the reaffirmation of Baxter as the rightful governor and to the calling of a constitutional convention. When the new constitution was ratified, Garland was elected governor. Hampered by economic and political pressures, he reestablished conservative government and was the symbol of the end of Reconstruction in Arkansas.

In 1877 Garland was chosen for a seat in the U.S. Senate. While there he worked for legislation of both regional and national impact, including federal aid to education, relief for disaster victims, construction of a levee system, and establishment of a national health agency.

The high point of Garland's public life came with his appointment as U.S. attorney general in 1885. Long noted for his legal scholarship, he issued meticulously written opinions dealing with matters ranging from land patents to federal appointments. Garland returned to private life in 1889, establishing a law practice in Washington, D.C. On January 26, 1899, he died while arguing a case before the Supreme Court.

BIBLIOGRAPHY

Alexander, Thomas B., and Richard E. Beringer. *The Anatomy of the Confederate Congress: A Study of the Influences of Member Characteristics on Legislative Voting Behavior, 1861–1865.* Nashville, Tenn., 1972.

Dougan, Michael B. *Confederate Arkansas: The People and Politics of a Frontier State in Wartime.* University, Ala., 1976.

Kerby, Robert L. *Kirby Smith's Confederacy: The Trans-Mississippi South, 1863–1865.* New York, 1972.

Newberry, Farrar. *A Life of Mr. Garland of Arkansas.* N.p., 1908.

Thomas, David Y. *Arkansas in War and Reconstruction, 1861–1874.* Little Rock, Ark., 1926.

Woods, James M. "Devotees and Dissenters: Arkansas in the Confederate Congress, 1861–1865." *Arkansas Historical Quarterly* 38 (Autumn 1979): 227–237.

BEVERLY WATKINS

GARNETT, RICHARD BROOKE

GARNETT, RICHARD BROOKE, (1817–1863), brigadier general. A member of Tidewater aristocracy, Garnett was born November 21, 1817, at the family mansion in Essex County, Virginia. In 1841 he and his cousin, Robert Selden Garnett, graduated in the same West Point class. Dick Garnett fought against the Indians in Florida and the West.

In May 1861, the handsome officer with blue eyes, wavy hair, and closely cropped beard accepted appointment as a Confederate major. Promotion to brigadier general in the Provisional Army came in November. When Gen. Thomas J. ("Stonewall") Jackson moved up to command of the Shenandoah Valley defenses, Garnett succeeded him at the head of the Stonewall Brigade.

His first battle, at Kernstown in March 1862, was Garnett's undoing. With his troops low on ammunition and Federals threatening both flanks, Garnett on his own sought to save his brigade by ordering it to fall back from the front. This withdrawal forced Jackson's whole force to abandon its position. Jackson promptly removed Garnett from command and initiated court-martial proceedings. They were never held because of the press of war. A staff officer who knew Garnett well remarked that he "was ever thereafter anxious to expose himself, even unnecessarily, and to wipe out effectually by some distinction in action, what he felt to be an unmerited slur upon his military reputation."

Garnett campaigned zealously to get a new command and soon was given a brigade in Gen. George E. Pickett's division. He led it well in the 1862 Sharpsburg campaign. On July 3, 1863, Garnett's brigade was in the front rank of the Pickett-Pettigrew charge at Gettysburg. Extremely ill, the general was wearing a heavy overcoat in spite of the heat. Garnett got to within twenty yards of the Federal lines when he disappeared in the gunsmoke and confusion. His riderless horse soon galloped toward the rear. Presumably, Federal soldiers stripped his dead body of its sword and other insignia before burying Garnett in one of the mass graves on the battlefield.

BIBLIOGRAPHY

Harrison, Walter H. *Pickett's Men: A Fragment of War History.* Gaithersburg, Md., 1987.

Pierce, John E. "The Civil War Career of Richard Brooke Garnett: A Quest for Vindication." M.A. thesis, Virginia Polytechnic Institute and State University, 1969.

Robertson, James I., Jr. *The Stonewall Brigade.* Baton Rouge, La., 1963.

JAMES I. ROBERTSON, JR.

GEORGIA

A record turnout in the 1860 election in Georgia gave Southern Democrat John C. Breckinridge a plurality of 51,893 votes, but Constitutional Unionist John Bell tallied 42,886 and Northern Democrat Stephen A. Douglas, 11,580. On January 19, 1861, a popularly elected convention voted to secede from the Union, and the initial narrow margin of 166 to 130 revealed again the ambivalence that had surfaced in the earlier presidential election. With a population of 1,057,286 (including 465,698 blacks of whom all but 3,500 were slaves) Georgia contributed approximately 120,000 troops to the Confederacy. That plus a booming agriculture centered around King Cotton, a rapidly expanding industrial base including many textile mills, and an extensive railroad network radiating out from the hub of Atlanta to the other growing cities of Savannah, Augusta, Macon, and Columbus made the Empire State of the South second only to Virginia within the Confederacy.

The state's political leaders adjusted quickly to the rush of events as a new order emerged. In Montgomery, Alabama, Georgians played a major role at the convention that established the new Confederate government. Howell Cobb presided over the assembly, which became the Provisional Congress, his younger brother Thomas R. R. Cobb played the major role in drafting the Confederate Constitution, Alexander H. Stephens became vice president of the new nation, and Robert Toombs accepted the post of secretary of state. Back home the state convention functioned as a legislature for a while and also formulated a new state constitution, again largely the work of Thomas Cobb. Governor Joseph E. Brown, an ardent secessionist, seized scattered Federal installations and mobilized troops and equipment, but he was less enthusiastic about cooperating with the new Confederate government, an ominous sign. Then on April 12 war erupted, and most of the upper South joined the Confederacy.

Governor Brown's Policies. Brown's call for volunteers on April 18 brought forth thousands of new troops, but equipment was scarce, and he tried to keep weapons from being carried out of the state by departing Georgia forces. This and his efforts to control military units and appoint their officers led to increasing clashes with Confederate officials.

Brown was loyal to the Confederacy, but he was more devoted to old Southern traditions like state rights, individual freedoms, and strict legalism, and he refused to subordinate them in the interest of the centralized war effort that was necessary for victory. Nevertheless Brown was an able administrator and a brilliant politician who understood his white constituents and rallied them to support Georgia's war effort, if not always the Confederacy's. Thus when he ran for an unprecedented third term in November he won easily, as he did again in 1863.

In April 1862 the Confederate government enacted the first national draft in American history, and Brown, convinced that it was unconstitutional, led the opposition. He tried to maintain control of all militia and other state troops, but the legislature gave him only limited support and the state supreme court sided with the Confederates. Grudgingly he yielded and rebuilt state forces with men too young or too old for the draft. Then each time the embattled Confederates later expanded the age limits of the draft, he waged the same struggle first to hold on to his own state army and then to rebuild it with older and younger recruits. He also granted

draft exemptions to thousands of state employees, including militia officers, setting a precedent other states followed in their erratic enforcement of the unpopular conscription law.

Governor Brown also led his people's opposition to impressment, especially the requisition of slave laborers by the Confederate army. He blocked the imposition of martial law in Atlanta in 1862, as well as Confederate efforts to control the state-owned Western and Atlantic Railroad the following years. He often criticized Confederate tax and block-

> **Brown sometimes cooperated with the Confederate government, but more often he was intransigent. . . .**

ade-running policies. His resistance to the Davis administration in Richmond peaked with attacks on arbitrary arrests and the suspension of the writ of habeas corpus, and early in 1864 he gained legislative backing on this issue. Brown sometimes cooperated with the Confederate government, but more often he was intransigent; increasingly the governor and the president engaged in bitter, hostile correspondence.

Brown had influential allies in his struggle against the Confederate government. Vice President Stephens, too, soon began to quarrel with the president, and by mid-1863 he was spending most of his time in Georgia denouncing the Davis "despotism." His brother Linton Stephens pursued the same policy in the state legislature. Robert Toombs served only briefly as secretary of state and then as an army officer; by 1863 he too had returned to Georgia and joined the anti-Davis faction. These powerful politicians spearheaded the state rights crusade in Georgia, which increasingly undermined the Confederate war effort on the home front.

But Brown's main allies were the white masses whom he consistently championed. Early in the war he acted to supply Georgia troops with adequate clothing and equipment, and later he sent state agents far afield and even abroad with chartered steamships to acquire what was needed. He showed equal concern for the ordinary folks on the homefront. The governor ordered the state penitentiary to manufacture cotton cards so thread could be prepared for spinning, and he obtained and efficiently distributed scarce salt for preserving meat. He organized relief for the needy families of soldiers, and by the last two years of the war he had set up an extensive and expensive welfare system to assist the yeoman masses who bore the heaviest burdens of the war. Governor Brown pushed through the legislature a program of tax reforms, and he boosted food production by reducing cotton acreage and restricting distilling. Within Georgia, Brown ran an efficient operation with a special concern for the white masses, but he remained an ardent advocate of state rights and failed to channel the state's resources fully into the Confederate war effort.

Georgia's Economy. The state's resources were formidable. Its impressive prewar industries expanded rapidly if unevenly. Heavy industry boomed mostly in the fast-growing cities. The Confederates built a huge gunpowder mill in Augusta, and the railroad center of Atlanta had one of the few large rolling mills in the South. All five major cities had at least one arsenal, and growing towns like Athens, Dalton, and Rome also expanded operations, as all manner of military equipment was manufactured by Confederate and state plants and private factories fulfilling government contracts.

The state's large textile industry operated at full blast, but could not expand owing to a shortage of machinery. Shoe factories operated at full capacity, too, mostly fulfilling army contracts, but demand remained greater than supply. Iron production increased only a little.

Overall, Georgia's businesspeople, manufacturers, and managers worked effectively, though some profiteers helped fuel rampant inflation. Skilled and ordinary laborers, augmented by women and blacks, also performed well, but shortages of labor, capital, and machinery hindered all efforts to match the Northern industrial machine that was simply too powerful.

The state's prewar railroad system was quite extensive, and it ran well for several years. But no new lines were built, and overburdened equipment began to break down. Finally invading Union armies literally tore up the deteriorating system.

Overall Georgia's economy was sound in 1861, but the demands of the war were too great, and soon a ruinous inflation began to sweep through the land. Like the central government, Georgians relied too much on loans and not enough on taxes to finance the war, and soon the Confederacy, the states, banks, and even private businesses were pumping out floods of paper money, which became increasingly worthless. Hard money faded away, goods became scarce, and prices soared. By 1864 corn was selling in Atlanta for ten dollars a bushel and Irish potatoes for twenty dollars a bushel while soldiers at the front earned only eleven dollars a month!

Disaffection Increases. The snowballing inflation helped erode morale on the home front. Even in the early days of wartime enthusiasm, Unionism had persisted, especially in the hills of North Georgia where not even Governor Brown's political skills could restrain growing hostility to the war effort. As the war dragged on and casualties mounted and battles were lost, disaffection increased everywhere. Unpopular Confederate policies like conscription and impressment were magnified by the criticisms of the state's leaders. And always inflation worked its destructive way, convincing many Georgians that their world was out of control, that they might even lose the war. Moreover, the Emancipation Proclamation

and the Union's increasing recruitment of black troops, mostly former slaves, prodded the South's most sensitive nerve.

More and more soldiers deserted the army to come home and look after their families, and a peace movement surfaced in western Georgia. Early in 1864, with William Tecumseh Sherman's huge army poised to invade North Georgia, a special session of the legislature denounced Confederate policies and toyed with the idea of peace negotiations. By the time Sherman captured Savannah at the end of 1864, many white Georgians had simply given up, as they watched their old way of life vanish.

The War's Impact on Blacks. Black Georgians, nearly half of the population, experienced the war very differently than whites. At the start they had no enthusiasm for secession and the new Confederacy. Indeed, during this formative period they endured a wave of terror, including lynchings, and the harsh slave code was made even more repressive.

Some slaves lived much as they always had, but as more and more white men marched off to war, many blacks found new opportunities. Some went with Confederate troops to the front as cooks, teamsters, and servants, and others were impressed to work on fortifications. Some were moved away from the threat of Union invasion, and others entered booming war industries. All this disrupted the slave system (and many black families) as change swept through the South.

Some blacks remained obedient, but others saw a new day dawning and became increasingly restless. Occasionally rumors of insurrection surfaced only to die out quickly. The few individual slaves who did strike out received summary treatment at the hands of courts or mobs. Many others ran away, a traditional method of resistance that greatly increased during the war. At first runaways headed in a steady trickle for the Union-held Sea Islands on the coast. Later they fled by the thousands to Sherman's invading army; he did not want them, but many stayed anyway. By then they knew that the North was winning and that its victory would mean the end of slavery. Many blacks became more assertive, discomfiting whites.

Although wartime privations hit blacks even harder than whites, many labored on under strict supervision. As in peacetime, they had no real choice; the slave system employed relentless and often brutal force. In agriculture, in new fields like hospital work and railroad and other transportation facilities, and especially in industry, slave laborers made a massive, indeed essential contribution to the South's war effort. At the same time traditional forms of resistance like loafing, stealing, and sabotage increased, as many blacks prayed for Union victory and helped the invading armies when they could. Like whites, black Georgians watched the old regime disintegrate as they struggled to survive in the rising chaos.

The desperate Confederate government moved to exploit black manpower fully in late March 1865 when it offered freedom for honorable service in the decimated ranks of its armies. The Union had been recruiting black Southerners for its armed forces since the spring of 1862 when field hands from the liberated Sea Islands along the South Carolina and Georgia coast were enlisted. Most of the Union's almost 200,000 black troops came from the North or from those areas of Dixie that were occupied before mainland Georgia. The Confederate decision to emulate the Northerners came far too late in the war—Robert E. Lee's army would surrender in less than three weeks—and, of course, Governor Brown and the legislature denounced the whole idea. White Georgia could not bring itself to make such a radical change even in the midst of total war.

Changing Roles of Women. Women on the home front also carried a heavy burden. With more and more men joining the army, they had to fill the gaps, and many for the first time actually managed farms and plantations. This was "man's work" and challenging enough in normal times, but wartime shortages and disruptions and the growing restiveness of the slaves multiplied the difficulties. Finally, women faced the ultimate horror—invasion and occupation by an enemy army.

But they persevered, ran things as normally as possible, and did what had to be done. The number of female teachers increased rapidly, and for the first time some white women like Madame M. C. Cazier of Savannah went to work as nurses in hospitals as far away as Richmond. Others got out old looms and spinning wheels to make clothing for their families and for soldiers, and some swelled the ranks of female wage earners in the booming factories. Women sponsored aid societies and wayside homes for the troops; they staged "starvation parties," plays, dances, bazaars, and other social events for the cause. Young women cut short their courtships amid a flood of wartime marriages that often ended suddenly on distant battlefields. A few belles partied through the war, or tried to, but most women faced up to the hard conditions. After the war many lived on as embittered spinsters and widows, passing their hatred on to later generations of Georgians who learned to say "Yankee" with a snarl.

As inflation steadily priced luxuries and then essentials out of reach, women had to improvise. They created substitute foods like coffee made from acorns, and occasionally they became so desperate for scarce items, especially food, that they banded together and looted government or private supplies in Atlanta, Augusta, Columbus, Macon, Milledgeville, and smaller towns. The increasing number of prostitutes reflected the general breakdown of law and order as the war dragged on.

Most women lived in isolated rural areas and faced intense loneliness. They worked hard, closed ranks with friends and kinfolk, became more active in their churches, and wrote letters to loved ones in the army. These sometimes lengthy and often unsophisticated letters concentrated on local affairs, often mixing humor and gossip with serious business matters, and they powerfully affected morale in the army. Some radiated optimism and patriotism, but gloomy or desperate letters encouraged desertion, which became a major problem as the war continued. Increasingly deserters, bushwhackers, and looters roamed through the countryside, and toward the end Sherman's soldiers sent thousands of citizens and slaves refugeeing into southwestern Georgia and other supposedly secure areas.

The Toll on Institutions. Georgians tried to maintain normalcy in the midst of the growing confusion. Many younger and older white men remained at home; many of draft age found it easy to avoid conscription by hiring a substitute or wangling a medical deferment or occupational exemption. They and black slavepower and white womanpower succeeded in carrying on much as usual—but only for a while.

Twelve daily urban newspapers and sixty smaller journals continued to publish with no real interference from authorities, and some carried Maj. Charles H. Smith's humorous Bill Arp stories, a running "cracker" commentary on the war that became a popular book in 1868. Early in 1863 publishers in Augusta organized the Press Association of the Confederate States to try to share resources and reduce costs, but as the war continued newspapers shrank in size and quality, and many finally faded away as Confederate Georgia crumbled. Book and magazine publishing experienced a similar decline, though Richard Malcolm Johnston during these years published his *Georgia Sketches* describing humorous events in the lives of ordinary folks. The thirteen-year-old Joel Chandler Harris, working as a printer's assistant on a plantation near Eatonton, first heard the African American folktales that later became the basis for his Uncle Remus stories.

Georgia's shaky education system faltered badly. Colleges closed as their students marched off to war, and the state's new white public education system collapsed as funds were shifted to wartime activities. Counties took up the slack as best they could, but many youngsters had no school to attend, and some ended the war little better educated than the children of slaves.

The state's churches were less devastated. Many ministers had opposed secession, but the great majority rallied around the war effort. Though they were draft exempt, some volunteered for combat, and others became hospital commissioners or chaplains in the army, which experienced periodic religious revivals. Ministers at home carried on their good works among increasingly distressed congregations, trying to boost morale. Some championed a liberalization of the slave code as the tide of battle turned against the South.

Military Events in Georgia. Ultimately, of course, the war was decided on the battlefield. Hundreds and then thousands of Georgia soldiers fell, but at first the carnage was far away in Virginia or the West. Then the Union navy began to blockade the coast, brushing aside a feeble Confederate "mosquito fleet" of a few riverboats. By March 1862 Union forces had occupied all the Sea Islands, and the following month their powerful new artillery overwhelmed Fort Pulaski at the mouth of the Savannah River, effectively sealing off the city of Savannah. In the summer of 1863 an amphibious attack destroyed the town of Darien, but five naval bombardments failed to demolish Fort McAllister, a new earth and stone fortification at the mouth of the Ogeechee River.

Probes along the coast continued as the Union blockade tightened, but the real threat to Georgia came from the interior. At first only a few raids threatened the vital Western and Atlantic Railroad running from Chattanooga to Atlanta, and in September 1863 a Southern victory at Chickamauga relieved the pressure. But then Ulysses S. Grant and Sherman took command of the Union forces.

Late in November at Lookout Mountain and Missionary Ridge, Union attacks sent the Confederate army reeling back into northwestern Georgia. Grant moved on to face Lee in Virginia, and in the spring of 1864, Sherman's army of nearly 100,000 men moved south along the Western and Atlantic Railroad toward Atlanta. Joseph E. Johnston's army of 55,000 men fought a series of delaying actions and even threw back the attacking Federals at Kennesaw Mountain near Atlanta with heavy losses. But always Sherman's troops flowed around the Southern flanks, and by summer Atlanta was besieged.

President Jefferson Davis replaced cautious Johnston with reckless John Bell Hood who squandered troops in poorly coordinated attacks and then marched north to escape encirclement. On September 2 Sherman's troops occupied Atlanta; only the fall of Richmond could have stunned the South more. In the North Abraham Lincoln's reelection in November was virtually assured, which in turn meant that the Union war effort would not falter.

Sherman sent sufficient troops after Hood's army to finish it off later in Tennessee. Then he forced all remaining civilians to leave Atlanta and began planning his famous "march to the sea." During this crucial period Governor Brown furloughed ten thousand state troops to keep them out of Confederate control. He and Stephens at first rejected Sherman's peace feelers, but soon the governor was openly calling for peace as morale plummeted throughout the state.

On November 10, after burning most of what remained of battered Atlanta, Sherman cut all supply and communication lines and led 63,000 battle-hardened veterans into the heart of the state against only token resistance. Some expected him to follow the route of an earlier unsuccessful cavalry raid and head for Macon and Andersonville where 13,000 Union prisoners of war had already died in appalling squalor. But instead he followed the main rail line toward Savannah, tearing up track as he went. He relaxed discipline, spread his men over a forty-to-sixty-mile front, and ordered the destruction of bridges, mills, factories, salt supplies, and other

resources. His men responded all too eagerly and despoiled homes and private property as well, though they generally refrained from murder and rape. On November 22 they entered the capital at Milledgeville, destroyed production facilities, and looted a little, but they did not damage government buildings, including the statehouse where they held a mock session of the legislature and rescinded the ordinance of secession (by a unanimous vote).

Concentrating their numbers more, they moved on in a southeastern direction along the Central of Georgia Railroad. A month later they approached Savannah as the ten-thousand-man Confederate garrison retreated northward. On December 22 Sherman and his troops marched triumphantly into the state's largest city, offering it to President Lincoln as a Christmas present. Old Savannah gave up without a fight; Confederate Georgia had had enough.

Georgians knew they were beaten, but the war dragged on for a few more months. After resting and refitting, Sherman's army headed north into South Carolina on February 1. The final blow in Georgia came from an entirely new direction. Only a few days after Lee surrendered at

Georgians knew they were beaten, but the war dragged on for a few more months.

Appomattox, Union Gen. James H. Wilson and thirteen thousand crack cavalrymen slashed into western Georgia from Alabama, scattered Gen. Howell Cobb's few thousand militiamen, captured Columbus on April 16, and burned its many factories. Wilson's troopers rode on to capture Macon on April 20, and Governor Brown surrendered the last state troops early in May. Brown, Stephens, Cobb, and a few other Georgians were briefly imprisoned, but Toombs escaped to Europe.

One final Confederate drama remained to be played out in Georgia. President Davis had fled south from Richmond early in April, and the remnants of his government held its last official meeting at the well-to-do Georgia town of Washington not far from the Carolina border. Davis rode on farther south, hoping to carry on somehow, and Union troops captured him near Irwinville, Georgia, on May 10, only a few days before the last Confederate soldiers surrendered in Texas.

The war was finally over. White Georgians faced the bleak reality of total defeat. Black Georgians gained freedom, but the promise of equality soon turned to ashes. For generations all Georgians would be haunted by the awesome struggle of the war.

[*For further discussion of battles and campaigns fought in Georgia, see* Andrews Raid; Atlanta, Georgia, *article on*

Atlanta Campaign; Chickamauga Campaign; Fort Pulaski, Georgia; March to the Sea, Sherman's. *For further discussion of Georgia cities, see* Atlanta, Georgia, *article on* City of Atlanta; Macon, Georgia; Savannah, Georgia, *article on* City of Savannah. *See also* African Americans in the Union Army; *and biographies of numerous figures mentioned herein.*]

BIBLIOGRAPHY

Boney, F. N. "War and Defeat." In *A History of Georgia.* Edited by Kenneth Coleman. Athens, Ga., 1991.

Bryan, T. Conn. *Confederate Georgia.* Athens, Ga., 1953.

DeCredico, Mary A. *Patriotism for Profit: Georgia's Urban Entrepreneurs and the Confederate War Effort.* Chapel Hill, N.C., 1990.

Escott, Paul D. "Georgia." In *The Confederate Governors.* Edited by W. Buck Yearns. Athens, Ga., 1985.

Hill, Louise B. *Joseph E. Brown and the Confederacy.* Chapel Hill, N.C., 1939.

Johnson, Michael P. *Toward a Patriarchal Republic: The Secession of Georgia.* Baton Rouge, La., 1977.

Lane, Mills, ed. *War is Hell: William T. Sherman's Personal Narrative of His March through Georgia.* Savannah, Ga., 1974.

Mohr, Clarence L. *On the Threshold of Freedom: Masters and Slaves in Civil War Georgia.* Athens, Ga., 1986.

Parks, Joseph H. *Joseph E. Brown of Georgia.* Baton Rouge, La., 1977.

Schott, Thomas E. *Alexander H. Stephens of Georgia: A Biography.* Baton Rouge, La., 1988.

Thomas, Emory M. *The Confederate Nation: 1861–1865.* New York, 1979.

F. N. BONEY

GEORGIA

The iron-hulled, brig-rigged cruiser *Georgia* measured 210 feet long, 27 feet in beam, 15 feet in depth of hold, 1,150 tons displacement, and 648 tons gross. Two boilers provided steam to steeple-type, geared condensing engines, yielding a trial speed of 13.66 knots. The ship was built in 1863 by Alexander Denny & Company of Dumbarton, Scotland. Confederate foreign purchasing agent Commdr. Matthew Fontaine Maury bought the vessel for the Confederate navy using English shipowner Thomas Bold as cover. The aliases of *Japan* and *Virginian* enhanced secrecy during building. *Georgia* was armed from the tug *Alar* off Ushant, France, and commissioned CSS *Georgia,* April 9, 1863, by Commdr. William L. Maury. Armament consisted of two 10-pounder Whitworth guns, two 24-pounder guns, and a 32-pounder Blakely rifle.

Georgia cruised the north and south Atlantic Ocean against the Northern merchant fleet. On the coast of Morocco, *Georgia* fired on a large group of raiders attacking a shore party, an incident called the "Confederacy's only foreign war." During its cruise *Georgia* captured nine Union merchantmen. It burned the ships *Dictator, Constitution, Bold Hunter,* and clipper bark *Good Hope;* bonded the ships *Prince of Wales, George Griswold, City of Bath,* and *John Watt;* and allowed the bark *J. W. Seaver* to go free. *Georgia's* cruise was cut short owing to the rapid fouling of its iron hull, which caused a dangerous loss of speed.

On May 10, 1864, *Georgia* was decommissioned, disarmed, and sold to a private Liverpool merchant for Mediterranean trade. USS *Niagara* captured it in international waters, and it was then condemned by a prize court and sold into U.S. service. Later sold to Canadian owners, *Georgia* continued in New England and Canadian maritime trade until lost on the coast of Maine in 1878.

BIBLIOGRAPHY

Lyon, David John. *The Denny List.* London, 1975.

Merli, Frank J. *Great Britain and the Confederate Navy, 1861–1865.* Bloomington, Ind., 1970.

Morgan, James Morris. *Recollections of a Rebel Reefer.* London, 1918.

Scharf, J. Thomas. *History of the Confederate States Navy.* New York, 1887. Reprint, New York, 1977.

Spencer, Warren F. *The Confederate Navy in Europe.* University, Ala., 1983.

KEVIN J. FOSTER

GEORGIA PLATFORM

The Georgia Platform was adopted in December 1850 by a special convention called to consider the state's response to the Compromise of 1850. The Platform announced that, although Georgia did not approve of the Compromise, the state would "abide by it as a permanent adjustment of this sectional controversy." It further specified that Georgia "will and ought to resist, even (as a last resort) to a disruption of every tie which binds her to the Union," any congressional act that repealed or altered the Fugitive Slave Law, that restricted or suppressed the slave trade, or that abolished slavery in the District of Columbia.

Since these were all matters settled by the Compromise, the effect of the Platform was to admit Georgia's acquiescence in the Compromise's principal provision, namely, the admission of California to the Union as a nonslaveholding state. It was this provision that had so excited the Southern states, since it upset the balance of slave and free states in the Senate. Many Southern political leaders feared that the Compromise represented an attempt to enact the Wilmot Proviso, which sought to ban slavery from territories acquired as a result of the Mexican War, and which had passed the House of Representatives but failed in the Senate.

By introducing the slavery question at the national level, the Compromise disrupted party lines in the South and began the formation of new alliances. In Georgia, Whigs, led by Robert Toombs, and Democrats, led by Howell Cobb, joined ranks to form the Constitutional Union party. Highly respected and safe on the slavery question, these men gave repeated assurances that the Compromise did not threaten slavery. They stood in opposition to fire-eaters led by Governor George W. Towns, who sought to precipitate secession of the Southern states. Though less vocal or numerous than in other states, especially South Carolina and Mississippi, the secessionists in Georgia posed a serious threat to the supporters of the Union in that state. And since Georgia was the first state to hold a convention to determine a position on the Compromise, all eyes were focused on Milledgeville when the convention assembled.

The position of "conditional Unionism" as articulated in the Georgia Platform quickly found support in the states of the upper South as well as in Alabama and Louisiana. Thus isolated, secessionists in South Carolina and Mississippi had little success in advancing their cause. The Georgia Platform thus lessened sectional tensions. It also stated clearly the consequences of further congressional interference with slavery, giving warning that any renewal of the slavery question would put the Union at risk.

[*See also* Compromise of 1850; Fugitive Slave Law.]

BIBLIOGRAPHY

Montgomery, Horace. *Cracker Parties*. Baton Rouge, La., 1950.
Shryock, R. H. *Georgia and Union in 1850*. Durham, N.C., 1926.

JOHN MCCARDELL

GETTYSBURG CAMPAIGN

Following the Union defeat at Chancellorsville in May 1863, Robert E. Lee sought approval from the Confederate government to mount an invasion of Maryland and Pennsylvania with his Army of Northern Virginia. The North was becoming increasingly despondent over the progress of the war with the repeated failures of the Northern armies and their attendant high casualties. Lee believed he could build momentum for the growing Northern peace movement by shifting his army to Northern soil and inflicting a defeat upon the Federal Army of the Potomac. Operations in Pennsylvania would also allow Lee to provision his army from the rich agricultural areas of Pennsylvania's Cumberland Valley, while relieving Virginia from the destructive presence of contending armies.

Finally, Harrisburg, the Pennsylvania capital, could be threatened or perhaps temporarily captured, adding further embarrassment to the Lincoln administration and fuel for the peace movement.

Lee's proposal initially met with opposition in Richmond. There was concern over the security of the Confederate capital while Lee moved north. Some thought was also given to detaching elements of Lee's army to help break the siege of Vicksburg, Mississippi, by the Federal army of Ulysses S. Grant. It was also discussed whether Lee himself, with major elements of his army, should be shifted to Tennessee to mount an offensive against the Federal army under William Rosecrans. Lee's opinion ultimately prevailed, and it was agreed the invasion should take place. It was hoped that by taking the offensive in the east, the Federal forces threatening Vicksburg and Chattanooga would be forced to detach troops to drive Lee out of Pennsylvania.

In preparation for the invasion, Lee reorganized his army into three corps of approximately 20,000 men apiece. The First Corps remained under Gen. James Longstreet's command. The Second Corps (Stonewall Jackson's old corps) was placed under Gen. Richard S. Ewell. The Third Corps, under Gen. A. P. Hill, was formed with elements of Jackson's old corps and with new troops from outside the army. The cavalry division, under Gen. J. E. B. Stuart, was reinforced to six brigades. Lee's total strength was approximately 75,000 men and 280 guns.

The leading elements of Lee's army left their camps near Fredericksburg, Virginia, on June 3. Ewell and Longstreet's corps led the way, screened by Stuart's cavalry, while Hill remained behind temporarily to observe and deceive the Federals.

The Union Army of the Potomac, under Gen. Joseph Hooker, was aware that Lee was on the move, but was uncertain of the Confederate's intentions. On June 9, he ordered his cavalry commander, Gen. Alfred Pleasonton, to conduct a reconnaissance in force, with 11,000 men, across the Rappahannock in the direction of Brandy Station. Pleasonton surprised the Confederate cavalry, and the largest cavalry battle of the entire war ensued. Although Stuart recovered from his initial surprise and forced Pleasonton back, the battle caused him great embarrassment. Stuart's losses were 523 out of approximately 10,000, while Pleasonton lost 837.

Brandy Station failed to check the movement of the Army of Northern Virginia, and the leading elements of the army entered the Shenandoah Valley on June 12. Hooker received definite intelligence concerning this on the thirteenth and promptly issued orders for his army to withdraw from the line of the Rappahannock and march north to a new point of concentration around the Centreville, Virginia, area.

While Hooker's army repositioned itself and Hill and Longstreet marched toward the Valley, Ewell's Second Corps arrived before Winchester, Virginia. Garrisoning Winchester

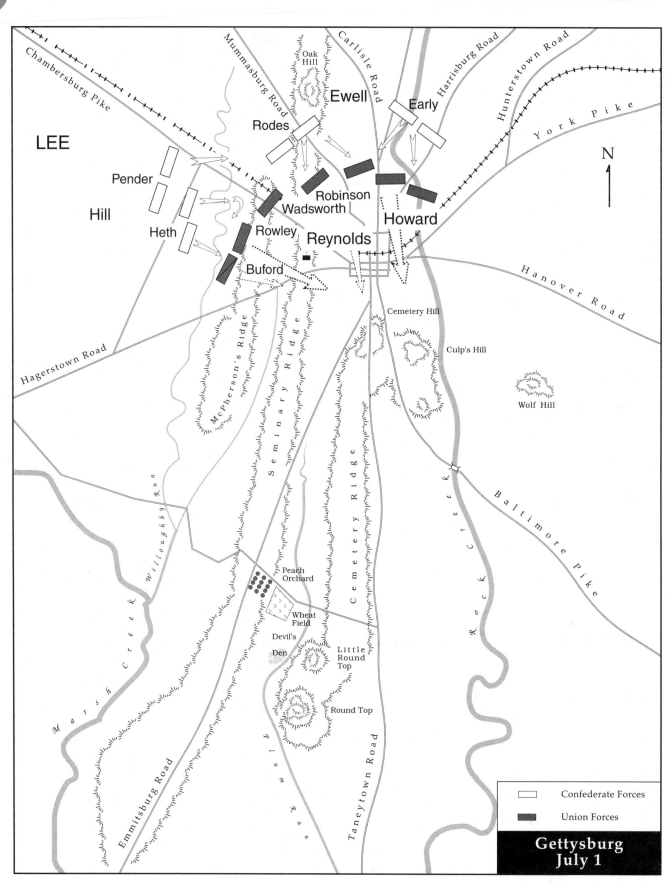

Chambersburg Pike

Mummasburg Road

Oak Hill

Carlisle Road

Harrisburg Road

Hunterstown Road

York Pike

Ewell

LEE

Rodes

Early

N

Pender

Hill

Robinson

Wadsworth

Howard

Heth

Rowley

Reynolds

Buford

Hanover Road

Cemetery Hill

Culp's Hill

Hagerstown Road

McPherson's Ridge

Seminary Ridge

Cemetery Ridge

Wolf Hill

Baltimore Pike

Rock Creek

Willoughby Run

Marsh Creek

Peach Orchard

Wheat Field

Devil's Den

Little Round Top

Round Top

Emmitsburg Road

Plum Run

Taneytown Road

☐ Confederate Forces

■ Union Forces

**Gettysburg
July 1**

was Gen. Robert Milroy's Second Division of the Eighth Corps, numbering approximately 9,000 men. Ewell launched a skillfully conducted attack late on the fourteenth and penetrated Milroy's defenses. That night, at 2:00 A.M., Milroy attempted to retreat but ran into a trap laid by Ewell. The Federals were routed and Milroy lost 4,443 men, most of whom were captured. Ewell's losses were 269.

Into Pennsylvania. On June 15, the leading elements of Lee's army entered Pennsylvania. By the twenty-fourth, Ewell's entire corps was bivouacked near Chambersburg, Pennsylvania. Hill's corps crossed the Potomac into Maryland on the same day with Longstreet's corps a day's march behind. In what proved to be one of the crucial decisions of the campaign, Lee gave discretionary orders to Stuart to take three of his brigades and march north, crossing the Potomac either east or west of the Blue Ridge Mountains, and eventually to take position on Ewell's right in Pennsylvania. Given the choice, Stuart chose to cut across the rear of the Federal army, crossing well east of the Blue Ridge.

Stuart's raid encountered numerous obstacles in its effort to circuit the Union rear. Powerful infantry columns forced him to make time-consuming detours in his march and an improved and aggressive Federal cavalry engaged him in several skirmishes that caused further delays and detours. Stuart captured a supply train of 125 wagons and 400 prisoners, but it was small compensation for Lee who was deprived of his best cavalry during the critical days of the campaign. Stuart would not rejoin the army until July 2.

By June 28, both Longstreet's and Hill's corps were camped in the vicinity of Chambersburg. Ewell's corps pushed farther east to threaten Harrisburg. Robert Rodes's and Edward Johnson's divisions occupied Carlisle, while Jubal Early's division marched to York, Pennsylvania. On the morning of the twenty-eighth, troopers of Albert Gallatin Jenkins's cavalry brigade advanced to within four miles of Harrisburg. This was to be the deepest Confederate forces penetrated into Pennsylvania, for Lee was forced to cancel the operations against Harrisburg and order Ewell to withdraw from his advanced positions owing to alarming news about the Federal army.

Without Stuart to provide him with timely and accurate information about the enemy, Lee was uncertain of the exact position of the Federal army. He believed it was still south of the Potomac. But on June 28 he was startled to learn through a spy, James Harrison, that the Federal army was massed in the vicinity of Frederick, Maryland, thirty miles south of Gettysburg. If the Federals moved west across South Mountain they would be on Lee's line of communications to Virginia. To prevent this, Lee issued instructions to bring about a concentration of his army east of the mountains in the vicinity of Cashtown, Pennsylvania, about ten miles west of Gettysburg. By positioning his army east of the mountains,

Lee posed a threat to both Harrisburg and Baltimore, and he believed this would keep the Federals off his line of communications.

By the twenty-eighth, the Federal army was under new leadership. Hooker had resigned over differences with the War Department regarding the Harpers Ferry garrison. In his place Lincoln appointed Gen. George G. Meade to command. Meade pushed his 93,000 men north from Frederick on a broad front. The left brushed the Catoctin Mountains, while the right stretched nearly thirty miles east. Meade's plan was to cover Baltimore and relieve Harrisburg. When this was accomplished, he would seek battle on the most favorable terms. During the final days of June, Meade's numerous cavalry, which was skillfully screening the front of his advancing army, provided him with strong evidence that Ewell had withdrawn from Harrisburg and that Lee's army was concentrating west of Gettysburg. In response to this Meade shifted the weight of his army to the left and began a gradual concentration of his army toward the Pennsylvania crossroads town. On June 30, John Buford's division of Federal cavalry marched to Gettysburg to secure the town and scout the region. They encountered a Confederate infantry brigade, which withdrew westward without an engagement.

The Confederate brigade belonged to Henry Heth's division of Hill's corps. Its commander reported the presence of Buford in Gettysburg, but Hill was skeptical. The Federal army was still believed to be in Maryland. Nevertheless, Hill planned to investigate. Heth and William Dorsey Pender's divisions, approximately 13,000 men, were ordered to march on Gettysburg on July 1. Their orders were to drive the Federal cavalry away but to halt if infantry was encountered. Lee did not want a general engagement to be precipitated with his concentration east of the mountains uncompleted.

The Federals also planned to move powerful forces to Gettysburg on July 1. Both the First and Eleventh Corps were under orders to march to Gettysburg to Buford's support, and four other corps were to move within supporting distance. The stage was set for the meeting of the opposing armies.

Day One. Contact was made at 5:30 A.M. on July 1 when the advance of Heth struck a picket post of Buford's division. Heth pushed on and encountered a dismounted line of Federal cavalry about two miles west of Gettysburg. Believing it was infantry, Heth deployed two brigades of infantry and pressed rashly ahead. About this time, Maj. Gen. John F. Reynolds, commander of the Union First Corps, arrived upon the battlefield. Exercising the discretion Meade had provided him, Reynolds decided to commit his First Corps and the Eleventh, as they arrived, to the engagement.

Between 10:30 and 11:00 A.M. a meeting engagement between Heth and James Wadsworth's division of the First Corps took place. Heth was soundly beaten, losing several hundred prisoners and the opportunity to seize Gettysburg

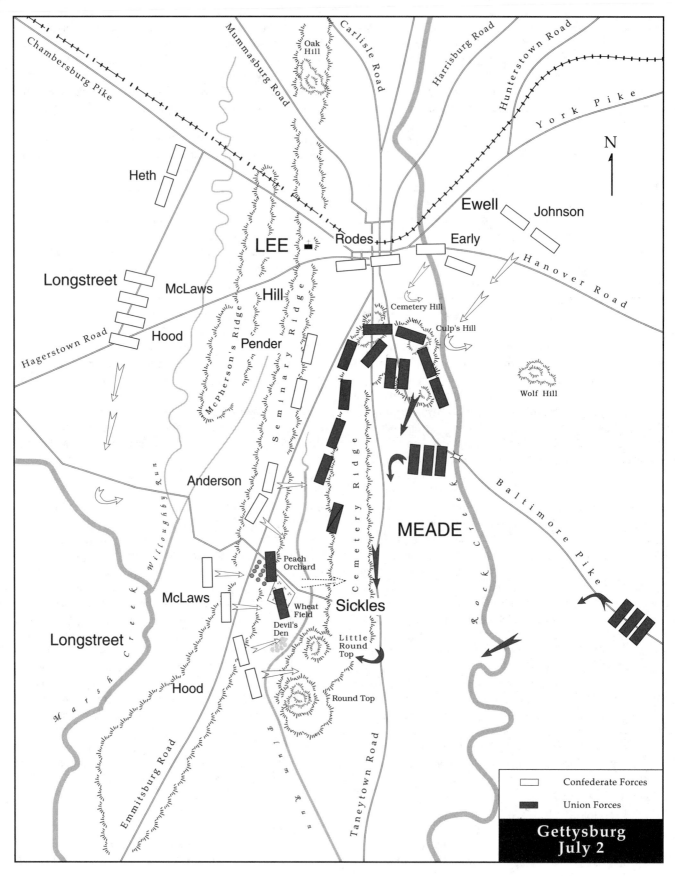

Chambersburg Pike

Mummasburg Road

Oak Hill

Carlisle Road

Harrisburg Road

Hunterstown Road

York Pike

Heth

Ewell Johnson

N

LEE Rodes Early

Hanover Road

Longstreet McLaws

Hill

Cemetery Hill

Pender

Culp's Hill

Seminary Ridge

Hood

McPherson's Ridge

Wolf Hill

Willoughby Run

Anderson

Cemetery Ridge

MEADE

Rock Creek

Baltimore Pike

Peach Orchard

Marsh Creek

McLaws

Wheat Field

Sickles

Longstreet

Devil's Den

Little Round Top

Hood

Round Top

Plum Run

Emmitsburg Road

Taneytown Road

Confederate Forces

Union Forces

Gettysburg July 2

cheaply. The Federals, although victorious, lost Reynolds, who was killed early in the fighting. They had, however, gained room and time to arrange a defense from which they could delay the Confederates and screen the strong defensive terrain that rose up south of Gettysburg.

Learning of Heth's contact with the enemy, Ewell diverted the march of Early and Rodes to approach Gettysburg from the north. At 1:30 P.M. the action was renewed with Rodes launching an uncoordinated attack upon the First Corps. Lee had arrived upon the battlefield and attempted to prevent the battle from escalating out of control. It was soon evident, however, that this was impossible, and at 2:30 P.M. he permitted Heth's division to advance to Rodes's support. Early arrived from the north and attacked around 3:00 P.M., inflicting a crushing defeat upon the Eleventh Corps. Heth and Rodes had a more difficult time with the First Corps and lost heavily in their attacks. Late in the afternoon, Hill sent Pender in to relieve Heth and he and Rodes cleared the First Corps from their positions west of town. The Federals fell back in considerable disorder through Gettysburg to Cemetery Hill, immediately south of town, where they were rallied and reorganized by Generals O. O. Howard and Winfield Scott Hancock.

Hill's corps was too exhausted to attempt to complete the Southern victory by attacking Cemetery Hill. Lee therefore sent Ewell directions to carry the hill if it was "practicable" to do so. But Ewell had his own problems and was unable to mount an attack before night brought an end to the fighting. Out of approximately 42,000 men engaged, over 9,000 Federals and approximately 6,800 Confederates were casualties.

Although a Confederate tactical victory, the first day of fighting had been a strategic Union victory. The Federals had gained the advantage of position on ground they had selected. Lee, still without Stuart, was thrust into the role of the attacker, over ground he did not know. But battle had been joined, and Lee was determined to exploit his victory of July 1 by renewing the battle the next day.

Day Two. The early morning of July 2 was spent in reconnoitering the Federal position. Lee was uncertain how heavily the Federals had been reinforced during the night. They were found to be holding a horseshoe-shaped position, running from Culp's Hill to Cemetery Hill and down Cemetery Ridge, where Lee was told the Federal left flank rested. Upon this information he developed his battle plan. Longstreet was directed to take John Bell Hood's and Lafayette McLaws's divisions and conduct a covered march to gain a position that would place them upon the Union left flank. Their attack would be supported by Richard Heron Anderson's division of Hill's corps. It was believed at Lee's headquarters that these three divisions, numbering approximately 20,000 men, would crush the exposed Federal flank. Ewell's orders were to demonstrate against Culp's Hill and Cemetery Hill to pin the Federal defenders in place. If opportunity offered, however,

he was given the discretion to deliver a full-scale attack. Longstreet was opposed to the operation and offered his opinion that the Confederates should attempt to outmaneuver the Federals to gain a position from which Lee could fight on the defensive. Lee was unmoved and the offensive was set in motion over Longstreet's objections.

Unknown to Lee, nearly the entire Army of the Potomac was in his front. By forced marches Meade had concentrated his army during the night. Only the Sixth Corps, thirty-five miles distant at Manchester, Maryland, was absent, and it was en route and expected by mid- to late afternoon. Meade had skillfully deployed his army to take advantage of the natural strength of the terrain. His left, contrary to the report of Lee's reconnaissance officers, rested not on Cemetery Ridge but on Little Round Top, nearly three-quarters of a mile south of where Lee believed the Federal flank to be. This sector of the Federal front was to be held by the Third Corps. But its commander, Gen. Daniel E. Sickles, was dissatisfied with his position and shortly after 2:00 P.M. he advanced his entire corps nearly one-half mile in advance of the army's general line. The line Sickles occupied extended for nearly one mile and formed a vulnerable salient angle at the Peach Orchard.

Longstreet's flank march occupied the entire morning and was further delayed when Longstreet discovered Sickles's corps in a completely unexpected position. Not until nearly 3:00 P.M. was Longstreet prepared to open his pre-assault bombardment. A sharp artillery duel ensued for nearly one-half hour. At 3:30, Longstreet's infantry stepped off. Devil's Den and Little Round Top were struck first. The efforts of Meade's chief engineer, Gen. Gouvenour K. Warren, managed to avert disaster on Little Round Top by seeing that infantry from the Fifth Corps were sent to its defense. They arrived not a moment too soon. The battle ebbed and flowed, but ultimately the Federals prevailed.

From Devil's Den the battle spread north to the Wheatfield and then the Peach Orchard. Meade hurried the Fifth Corps to Sickles's aid and stripped troops from elsewhere on his line. The heavy blows of Longstreet's and Anderson's brigades proved too much, however, and around 6:00 P.M. Sickles's line collapsed and streamed east in retreat. Uncommitted elements of the Fifth Corps, a division of the Twelfth Corps from Culp's Hill, and the Sixth Corps, which was beginning to reach the field, managed to stabilize the situation and check the victorious Confederates.

On Lee's left, Ewell had opened an artillery bombardment the moment he had heard the sound of Longstreet's guns. Federal guns responded and an hour-long duel ensued, the result of which was that Ewell's guns were completely silenced. Nearly two hours later Ewell sent his infantry forward. Johnson's division assailed Culp's Hill while two brigades of Early's division attempted to storm Cemetery Hill. Johnson's troops gained abandoned Federal entrenchments near the southern base of Culp's Hill, but the summit was

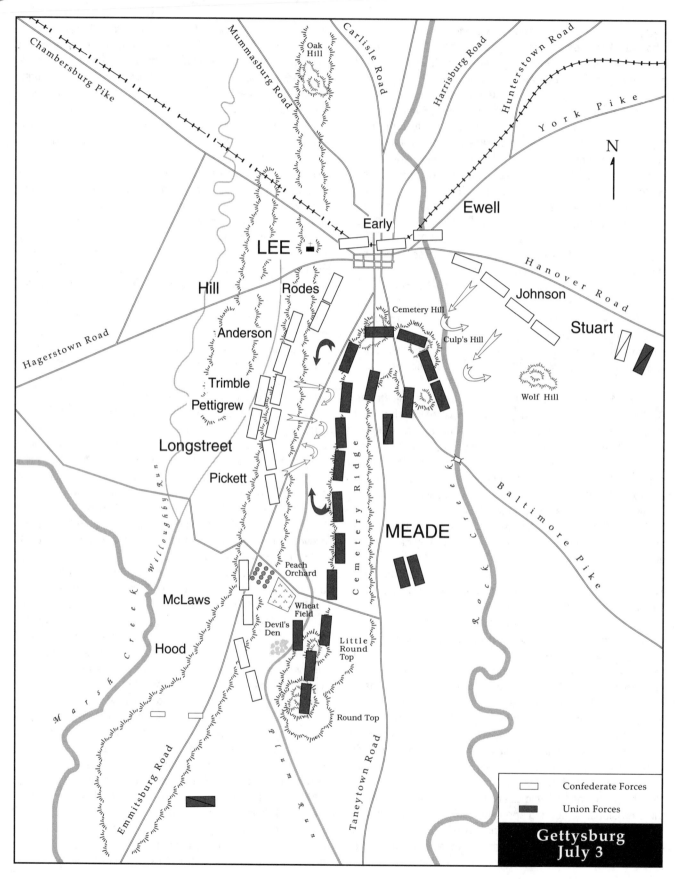

Gettysburg
July 3

Confederate Forces

Union Forces

defended by a brigade of New York troops who could not be dislodged. On Cemetery Hill, Early's brigades stormed up the hill, routing several regiments of the Eleventh Corps and getting in among some of the Federal artillery. But they were counterattacked by a brigade of the Second Corps and other Eleventh Corps regiments and driven off the hill. This action marked the end of the second day's fighting. At least 16,500 men or more were casualties.

After the war controversy developed over the cause of the Confederate failure to realize victory on July 2. Former Confederate Gens. William Dorsey Pendleton and Jubal Early selected James Longstreet as the scapegoat. Pendleton published an account affirming that Lee had actually instructed Longstreet to attack the Federals at daylight. Longstreet was also accused of deliberately dragging his feet out of opposition to Lee's plan during his corps flank march into position.

Although Longstreet did not support Lee's plan of attack and was guilty of a sulky and obstinate demeanor on July 2, Pendleton's and Early's charges were inaccurate and without substance. There was no early morning attack order, and although Longstreet's flank march was in some respects poorly managed, there is no evidence that Longstreet attempted to sabotage Lee's plan by delaying his corps march into position.

Day Three. Lee's confidence was unshaken by the failures of the second and he determined to continue the struggle on July 3. "The general plan was unchanged," wrote Lee. Longstreet, reinforced by George E. Pickett's division, which had been guarding wagon trains in Chambersburg, was to renew the attack, apparently at daylight. Johnson's division, heavily reinforced during the night, was to storm Culp's Hill at the same time. Stuart's cavalry, which had at last found the army, was instructed to march beyond the army's left flank and position itself to threaten the Federal rear.

Unfortunately for Lee, his plans were never realized. Meade seized the initiative and counterattacked on Culp's Hill at 4:30 A.M. Longstreet, who may have misunderstood what Lee wished, had prepared orders around sunrise for his corps to attempt to maneuver around the round tops and gain the Federal flank. Under the circumstances, concerted action was now impossible, and Lee was forced to modify his plan of attack. He now determined to launch a massive frontal assault designed to break the Federal center on Cemetery Ridge. A preattack bombardment by nearly 140 guns would cripple the Federal defenders, and then the divisions of Pickett and Pettigrew and one-half of Trimble's (slightly over 12,000 men) would advance over one mile of open ground and smash through the Union defenses. It was a bold, daring plan, and Longstreet, who was given the task of directing the attack, was adamantly opposed. Lee, however, was determined to make the effort, and Longstreet was compelled against his better judgment to carry out the plan.

At 1:00 P.M. the artillery cannonade opened. Between 80 and 100 Federal guns responded, and one of the largest artillery duels of the war ensued. Thick clouds of smoke covered much of the field and hindered the view of the artillerymen on both sides, causing gunners of both armies to overshoot their targets. After nearly one and one-half hours of intense firing, the Federal artillery ceased fire under orders to conserve their ammunition. By the time the bombardment stopped at 3:00, the Confederate artillery had exhausted its supply of long-range ammunition and was unable to support the infantry.

The Southern infantry emerged into view shortly after 3:00. Their perfectly preserved lines of battle extended for nearly one mile. The Federal artillery reopened at this time and inflicted terrible losses on the attackers but failed to check them. As the Southern infantry loomed nearer, the Federal infantry added its small-arms fire to the canister of the artillery and the Confederates fell by the hundreds. Federal infantry swung out on both Confederate flanks, which were exposed and unsupported, inflicting more losses and chaos. A small group of men, principally from Pickett's division and led by Gen. Lewis A. Armistead, managed to penetrate the Federal position briefly, but they were quickly overwhelmed. By 4:00 the attack had been repulsed with tragic loss. Between 5,500 and 6,000 Confederate soldiers were casualties, with perhaps as many as 1,000 being killed.

Elsewhere on the field, Johnson's division, after sustaining heavy losses, had retired from Culp's Hill by late morning. Stuart fared no better. His march east was detected, and powerful Federal cavalry units moved to engage him. Several miles east of town a cavalry action ensued that was indecisive, but it was successful in checking Stuart's forward progress.

The Army of Northern Virginia was spent and exhausted. Imperfect casualty figures give its losses at 4,427 killed, 12,179 wounded, and 5,592 missing. Its losses were undoubtedly higher, probably as many as 28,000. The Army of the Potomac had likewise suffered dreadfully: 3,155 killed, 14,529 wounded, and 5,365 missing.

Lee maintained his position on July 4 in hopes that Meade would attack him. He did not, and that night the army commenced its retreat under a heavy rain that helped slow the Federal pursuit. Lee's advance guard arrived at Williamsport, Maryland, on the sixth and discovered the Potomac swollen by rains and impassable. Lee entrenched his army on strong terrain and went to work building a pontoon bridge. Meade had brought his army up by the thirteenth and contemplated an assault, but called it off when the majority of his senior officers advised against it. That night, the pontoon bridge had been completed and the Potomac had fallen so that it was fordable, and Lee withdrew to Virginia. A rearguard action took place on the fourteenth between Buford's cavalry and elements of Heth's and Pender's divisions. The Confederates lost 719 prisoners and General Pettigrew, who was mortally wounded.

The Gettysburg campaign was over. On July 4, Vicksburg surrendered to Grant. The South, with its limited resources and manpower, was faced with a continuing struggle. The North's sagging morale was encouraged by the Union victories, and the peace movement lost its momentum. Although Lee's army had survived to fight another day, it had suffered crippling losses from which it never fully recovered. One Confederate lieutenant may have summarized best what Gettysburg meant for the South when he wrote, "we gained nothing but glory and lost our bravest men."

[See also Brandy Station, Virginia; Winchester, Virginia.]

BIBLIOGRAPHY

Coddington, Edwin B. *The Gettysburg Campaign: A Study in Command.* New York, 1968.

Frassinito, William. *Gettysburg: A Journey in Time.* New York, 1975.

Freeman, Douglas S. *Lee's Lieutenants: A Study in Command.* 3 vols. New York, 1942–1944. Reprint, New York, 1986.

Hassler, Warren W., Jr. *Crisis at the Crossroads.* University, Ala., 1970.

Johnson, Robert U., and C. C. Buel, eds. *Battles and Leaders of the Civil War.* 4 vols. New York, 1887–1888. Reprint, Secaucus, N.J., 1982.

Pfanz, Harry W. *Gettysburg: The Second Day.* Chapel Hill, N.C., 1987.

Stewart, George R. *Pickett's Charge.* Boston, 1959.

Tucker, Glenn. *High Tide at Gettysburg.* Indianapolis, 1958. Reprint, Dayton, Ohio, 1988.

D. SCOTT HARTWIG

GIBSON, RANDALL LEE

GIBSON, RANDALL LEE, (1832–1892), brigadier general, U.S. congressman and senator. Gibson was born September 10, 1832, in Woodford County, Kentucky. His family home was the plantation Live Oaks in Terrebonne Parish, Louisiana. After earning a law degree from the University of Louisiana, he served as military attaché with the American embassy in Spain and then opened a law practice and established a sugar plantation in Terrebonne Parish.

When the Civil War began, Gibson became aide-de-camp for Louisiana Governor Thomas O. Moore before being commissioned a captain in the First Louisiana Artillery in March 1861. In August 1861 he was promoted to colonel of the Thirteenth Louisiana Infantry, which he commanded at the Battle of Shiloh. There he assumed command of the Louisiana Brigade after its commander, Brig. Gen. Daniel Weisigner Adams, was wounded and lost his right eye. Gibson also fought at Perryville, Murfreesboro, and

Chickamauga. Promoted to brigadier general on January 11, 1864, Gibson served in the Atlanta campaign and in Lieut. Gen. John Bell Hood's invasion of Tennessee. His military career ended with his command of the Louisiana Brigade in the defense of Spanish Fort, near Mobile, Alabama, in March 1865. During the fighting, Gibson's force of less than 2,000 lost 93 killed, 350 wounded, and 250 captured.

After the war, Gibson opened a law firm in New Orleans. He was elected to Congress in 1872 but was denied his seat by Radical Republicans. He was elected again to Congress in 1874 and served four terms. Gibson was instrumental in persuading President Rutherford B. Hayes to withdraw troops from Louisiana and end Reconstruction. In 1882 he was elected to the U.S. Senate and was reelected in 1888. He played a major role in founding Tulane University. Gibson died in Hot Springs, Arkansas, on December 15, 1892, and is buried at Lexington, Kentucky.

BIBLIOGRAPHY

Evans, Clement A., ed. *Confederate Military History.* 12 vols. Atlanta, 1899. Extended ed. in 19 vols. Wilmington, N.C., 1987–1989.

Johnson, Robert U., and C. C. Buel, eds. *Battles and Leaders of the Civil War.* 4 vols. New York, 1887–1888. Reprint, Secaucus, N.J., 1982.

KENNY A. FRANKS

GILMER, JOHN A.

GILMER, JOHN A. (1805–1868), congressman from North Carolina. John Adams Gilmer's most significant contribution to the Confederacy was his effort to thwart its inception. By comparison, his role was a congressman during the last year of the war was quite secondary.

No Southern Unionist during the secession crisis faced so excruciating a dilemma as Gilmer, a member of the U.S. House of Representatives who lived in Greensboro, North Carolina. At the behest of New York Senator William H. Seward and his alter ego Thurlow Weed, President-elect Abraham Lincoln secretly invited Gilmer to serve in his cabinet. The offer was designed to show that Southerners had no reason to fear the new Republican president. Until a larger segment of Southern opinion became so persuaded, however, any individual Southerner who accepted a cabinet position would squander his political influence and destroy his political base. In the end, Gilmer refused the offer.

Gilmer lived in a distinctive part of the South. Although he himself owned more than fifty slaves, Guilford County and the adjacent North Carolina Piedmont were characterized by modest landownings and yeoman farming rather than plantation slavery. A substantial number of Quakers also lived there and opposed slavery on principle. These circumstances together with an eagerness for transportation improvements and a long-standing resentment of the eastern-dominated state government combined to give the Greensboro region a decided Whiggish orientation and a political outlook that had no room for Southern rights posturing.

A successful lawyer, Gilmer served in the state senate for several terms starting in 1846. There he promoted internal improvements, especially the North Carolina Railroad, and worked to expand the scope of public education. He took a strongly Unionist stance during the 1850 crisis. Defeated in an 1856 race for governor on the American party (Know-Nothing) ticket, he was elected to Congress in 1857.

Gilmer was among the handful of Southerners to vote with Republicans and Douglas Democrats in 1858 against the admission of Kansas as a slave state under the Lecompton constitution. Despite ferocious criticism of his Kansas vote by North Carolina Democrats, he won reelection in 1859. Gilmer gained a degree of national visibility in December 1859 when

> . . . Gilmer blamed the immediate crisis on a conspiracy among Southern Democrats.

the Southern Opposition (or "South Americans" as the two dozen former Whigs in the House sometimes designated themselves) put his name forward as a candidate for Speaker of the House. He supported the 1860 presidential candidacy of John Bell, who was nominated by the Constitutional Union party. Lincoln, however, swept the North, provoking the states of the Deep South to secede.

Although not enthusiastic about offering a cabinet appointment to someone "who opposed us in the election," Lincoln judged that Gilmer was the most suitable of several Southern Unionists promoted by Seward and Weed. Gilmer, however, found the cabinet offer perplexing. It did indicate that Lincoln wanted to aid Southern Unionists. But Gilmer believed that the appointment by itself would not calm the uproar in the South and he dreaded the abuse he would face. Uncertain how to respond, Gilmer consulted confidentially with other antisecessionists. His predecessor in Congress, Edwin G. Reade, "strongly urged Mr. Gilmer to accept." Maryland Congressman Henry Winter Davis, the most audacious member of the Southern Opposition, emphatically agreed: it was "a matter of life or death."

Gilmer thereupon tried to persuade Lincoln and the Republican party to offer more substantive reassurances. The North Carolinian pointed out that "apprehensions of real danger and harm to them and their peculiar institution" had "seized" the people of the South. Gilmer considered a "gen-

erous and patriotic" concession on the vexing territorial issue the best way for Republicans to arrest the secession contagion. He believed that the compromise package proposed by Kentucky Senator John J. Crittenden would stop secession dead in its tracks.

Gilmer, who privately bewailed the unreasonable behavior of "my maddened brethren of the South," urged Republicans to treat Southern symptoms with an appropriate palliative. "Yield to them this useless and foolish abstraction of Congressional protection to slavery in the Territories," he implored Weed. In Gilmer's opinion, the North could safely grant to deluded Southerners "this silly boon for which they so furiously struggle," because the most stringent protection for slavery in the territories "would come as near making slave states, as the drying up of the Mississippi, could be secured by a law of Congress."

For Gilmer, the territorial issue was a "mere abstraction," created by extremists North and South. The North, he thought, had no need to prohibit slavery from an arid region to which it would never spread in any case. The South, however, was equally wrongheaded to fear that slavery in the states could not survive without Federal protection for slavery in the territories.

The impasse, even if rooted in misperceptions and political one-upmanship, had explosive potential. "We are in real trouble," Gilmer wrote to a friend in January 1861. "There is real danger at hand—I can't say that I have lost all hope, but . . . the prospects are gloomy in the extreme. I often shed tears in silence."

As much as any Republican, Gilmer blamed the immediate crisis on a conspiracy among Southern Democrats. Within the previous year, he charged, they had split their national party, falsely represented themselves as having no plans to disrupt the Union in the case of Lincoln's election, and then treacherously reversed themselves after the election to argue that disunion was the only way to preserve the peace and safety of the South. Their demand that Congress protect slavery in the territories seemed to Gilmer a transparent pretext, made in the expectation that the North would never allow it.

Unfortunately for Southern Unionists, Republicans gagged at the Crittenden Compromise's promise to protect slavery in all territory south of 36° 30', now held or "hereafter acquired." They considered such language an open invitation to conquer new slave territory in the Caribbean and Latin America. Gilmer and the more flexible Southern Unionists thereupon indicated that they would accept the so-called border state plan, which prohibited either Congress or a territorial legislature from interfering with slavery in existing territory south of 36° 30'. This least dogmatic territorial compromise avoided both "protection" and "hereafter acquired."

Gilmer's speech to the House on January 26, 1861, stirred an emotional response. He implored his listeners to avert the "dreadful calamity" of civil war. More accurately than most of his countrymen, Gilmer foresaw that any clash of arms would so arouse the South as to make reunion impossible, except at the price of massive bloodshed. One reporter claimed never to have seen such an effect as was produced by this "honest appeal of a great heart." When Gilmer finished speaking, "dozens of Republicans and Southern Union men rushed forward to congratulate him." Conciliatory Republicans told reporters that "some compromise must be made to keep John A. Gilmer from being carried down by the secession tide."

Southern Unionists, attempting to reverse the drift of public opinion in their home states, mailed an unprecedented avalanche of pro-Union speeches and documents to citizens in the upper South. The effort was coordinated by Joseph C. G. Kennedy, head of the U.S. Census Bureau, and paid for by Gilmer, probably the wealthiest of the congressmen involved. A squad of twenty clerks addressed the mailings, which

> **Secessionists soon protested that "Gilmer and company . . ." were flooding the South with "submission and coercion speeches."**

Union congressmen then franked for free delivery. Night after night, from the close of office hours until midnight, the mailing operation continued. Secessionists soon protested that "Gilmer and company," working with "the Census Bureau and the Black Republicans," were flooding the South with "submission and coercion speeches."

Elections held in the upper South in February 1861 demonstrated that Unionist efforts had an effect. Fewer than one-third of the delegates elected on February 4 to the Virginia convention favored secession. Virginia voters also specified by more than two-to-one that any action of the convention must be approved by popular referendum. The results in Tennessee on February 9 and North Carolina on February 28 added to secessionist woes. Voters in both states narrowly refused even to countenance the calling of a convention. Had either convention met, it would have been dominated by Union delegates.

Unfortunately for the Unionists, Lincoln and the majority of the Republican party continued to oppose any direct compromise on the territorial issue. That circumstance, together with indications that Lincoln planned to deliver a hard-line inaugural address, finally prompted Gilmer to refuse the cabinet post.

Seward, who was soon to become secretary of state in the new cabinet, scrambled to repair the growing breach between Lincoln and the upper South. The adroit New Yorker quietly persuaded a minority of Republicans in Congress to vote for a constitutional amendment guaranteeing the safety of slavery in the states. He then got Lincoln to endorse the amendment and to adopt a more peaceful and conciliatory tone in his inaugural address. Republicans in Congress also organized three new western territories without any language to prohibit slavery. Four days after Lincoln took office, Gilmer took a hopeful view. "What more," he asked rhetorically, "does any reasonable Southern man expect or desire?"

The North Carolinian dispatched a sheaf of letters to Seward, describing the desperation of secessionists in the upper South. Their "only hope," he noted, was that fighting might break out between the seceded states and the Federal government. In order to "avoid a collision," Gilmer advised, Lincoln should surrender the two remaining Federal outposts in the Deep South—Fort Sumter in the harbor of Charleston, South Carolina, and Fort Pickens, offshore from Pensacola, Florida. Allow the Deep South to remain "out in the cold for awhile." After it became plain that the upper South would not follow, the secession movement would self-destruct.

For several weeks from mid-March to early April, Southern Unionists such as Gilmer dared to believe that Lincoln had adopted a "let-alone" policy and that the great crisis had been surmounted. In fact, of course, Lincoln decided to try to hold Fort Sumter, notwithstanding the likelihood that Confederate forces would strike to wrest it from him. Doubtful that the Union could be restored peacefully, the new president judged that his options had narrowed to peaceable separation or war.

The accumulating evidence that the administration had decided to risk a confrontation threw Gilmer into a profound depression. "I am so deeply disturbed that my heart seems to melt within me," he wrote to Seward on April 11. "If what I hear is true that we are to have fighting at Sumter or Pickens, it is what the disunionists have most courted, and I seriously apprehend it will drive the whole South into secession."

Ten days later, his worst apprehensions fulfilled, Gilmer wrote a final letter to Seward. Its tone, unlike many other last letters sent North the week after the firing on Sumter, was not bellicose, but rather reflective and despairing. With his Union-saving hopes in ruins and his only son already serving in a Confederate volunteer company, Gilmer took a bleak view of the future. "All hope is now extinguished," he mourned. "As matters now stand, there is a United North against a United South, and both marching to the field of blood."

Gilmer was elected to the May 1861 convention that removed North Carolina from the Union. He voted with other Union Whigs to identify that action as an act of revolution rather than secession. Otherwise Gilmer played no conspicuous role in Confederate North Carolina until the midpoint of the war.

By the summer of 1863, however, following the catastrophic Confederate defeats at Vicksburg and Gettysburg, a groundswell of discontent swept the state. Antiwar sentiment flourished among the yeomen of the Piedmont, few of whom had favored secession in the first place. Conscription not only forced them to fight for a cause that many did not support; it also left nonslaveholding families without able-bodied males to perform farm work. Increasingly severe food shortages resulted.

Under the circumstances, original secessionists in North Carolina lost all political influence. Elections for the Second Congress, held in August 1863, produced the most militantly anti-administration delegation ever to represent any Confederate state. Nine of the ten, among them Gilmer, were former Union Whigs. Several, notably James T. Leach and George W. Logan, opposed all war measures and plainly would have welcomed restoration of the Union.

Although Gilmer necessarily stood in the anti-administration camp, his position in the context of the North Carolina delegation was more that of a pro-war moderate. He had close ties to Governor Zebulon Vance, a former colleague from the last fateful U.S. Congress before the war started. Vance walked a delicate tightrope. He sharply criticized Jefferson Davis for infringing on civil liberties and exceeding his authority as president. By so doing, however, Vance and like-minded conservatives worked to appease growing peace sentiment and thereby reconcile restless North Carolina to continued struggle for the Confederate cause.

During his tenure in Congress, which extended from May 1864 until shortly before the end of the war in March 1865, Gilmer attempted to develop more equitable tax laws and supply systems. The downward spiral of Confederate military fortunes inevitably thwarted his initiatives. Like other North Carolinians, Gilmer objected whenever the Davis administration moved to suspend the writ of habeas corpus. He also opposed arming slaves.

Gilmer did not support the resolution put forward by James T. Leach in November 1864, which indicated a readiness to abandon the quest for independence. He did, however, work to persuade Davis to send a delegation to the Hampton Roads conference of February 3, 1865. There Confederate spokesmen discovered that Lincoln and Seward insisted upon reunion as the basis for any settlement of the war. Shortly afterward, Gilmer proposed a dual government, or "diet," in which Union and Confederate congresses and executives would remain separate but function in a coordinated manner. His proposed halfway house between independence and reunion won scant support.

Gilmer estranged himself from the North Carolina peace faction, and even from his close friend and ally, Senator William A. Graham, when he went out of his way to give eleventh-hour public support to the continued military struggle. By sharing a platform on February 9, 1865, with Secretary of State Judah P. Benjamin, Gilmer identified himself with bitter-enders at a time when most North Carolinians were working behind the scenes for a negotiated surrender. Gilmer's position was made all the more awkward when Benjamin demanded enlistment of black soldiers.

The end of the war left Gilmer in "great distress," musing about uprooting to the free states in order to "begin life again." That did not happen. He remained in Greensboro, where he continued to provide his former slaves with food, clothing, farm implements, and medical care. Gilmer's "extraordinary humanity and regard for his slaves" was "proverbial in his neighborhood." They were reported to be "substantially free" long before emancipation.

Gilmer's situation was complicated by politics. William W. Holden, who was appointed governor by President Andrew Johnson soon after the end of the war and who had earlier spearheaded the North Carolina peace movement, hoped to remain in power. Holden feared, however, that prominent Union Whigs such as Vance, Graham, and Gilmer might gain greater popular support because of their stronger Confederate credentials. Holden therefore persuaded Johnson to withhold pardons for his would-be rivals. Gilmer "was once ultra right," Holden noted, "but he went far astray" during the war. Not until near the end of 1865 did Gilmer receive his pardon.

Conservatives did topple Holden, at least temporarily. He lost the election in November 1865 to former Whig Jonathan Worth, state treasurer during the Confederate period. Presently, however, Congress suspended the state governments organized under Johnson's auspices. Holden returned for another stormy tenure as governor in 1868 after enactment of the Reconstruction Constitution, which enfranchised blacks.

Gilmer traveled to Philadelphia in August 1866 to attend the National Union Convention, at which Conservatives from both North and South attempted unsuccessfully to devise a strategy to counter Republican Reconstruction policy. His health deteriorated by early 1867, however, and he died in May 1868.

Gerald W. Johnson, a native of Greensboro who became a well-known journalist and political commentator, wrote a perceptive biographical sketch of Gilmer in the 1920s. Although "now unknown to all save a few specialists," Johnson observed, Gilmer was a tragic and appealing figure who had appeared briefly in "the spotlight of history." Illuminated in the midst of a terrible storm, he was then "lost in the night."

BIBLIOGRAPHY

Alexander, Thomas B., and Richard E. Beringer. *The Anatomy of the Confederate Congress: A Study of the Influences of Member Characteristics on Legislative Voting Behavior, 1861–1865.* Nashville, Tenn., 1972.

Crofts, Daniel W. *Reluctant Confederates: Upper South Unionists in the Secession Crisis.* Chapel Hill, N.C., 1989.

Hamilton, J. G. deRoulhac, and Max R. Williams, eds. *The Papers of William Alexander Graham.* 7 vols. to date. Raleigh, N.C., 1957–.

Jeffrey, Thomas E. *State Parties and National Parties: North Carolina, 1815–1861.* Athens, Ga., 1989.

Journal of the Congress of the Confederate States of America, 1861–1865. 7 vols. Washington, D.C., 1904–1905.

Kruman, Marc W. *Parties and Politics in North Carolina, 1836–1865.* Baton Rouge, La., 1983.

Sitterson, Joseph Carlyle. *The Secession Movement in North Carolina.* Chapel Hill, N.C., 1939.

Yearns, Wilfred B. *The Confederate Congress.* Athens, Ga., 1960.

DANIEL W. CROFTS

GIST, STATES RIGHTS

GIST, STATES RIGHTS, (1831–1864), brigadier general. Gist was born in Union District, South Carolina, September 3, 1831. His father, an ardent disciple of John C. Calhoun, chose his son's unusual name to demonstrate his own political sentiments. After studying at South Carolina College and Harvard Law School, the young Gist practiced as an attorney. He also served in the South Carolina military forces and in 1861 was adjutant and inspector general of the state army.

Going to Virginia in 1861, Gist served as a volunteer aide-de-camp on the staff of Brig. Gen. Barnard E. Bee. At First Manassas (July 21), when all the officers of the Fourth Alabama Regiment became casualties, Gist took command of the regiment and directed it throughout the remainder of the battle.

Gist was back in South Carolina during the winter of 1861–1862, laboring to raise troops for the state. On May 20, 1862, he was appointed a Confederate brigadier general. For a year he served in the Carolina coast defenses.

Sent to Mississippi in May 1863, Gist commanded a brigade there and at the Battle of Chickamauga (September 20, 1863). In 1864 Gist commanded his brigade in the Atlanta campaign. Wounded there on July 22, Gist was absent from duty for about a month. At Franklin (November 30), he was mortally wounded as he advanced with his men in the great Confederate charge on the Federal works. He died in a field hospital that night.

Gist was first buried in a nearby cemetery, but his body was later moved to Trinity Episcopal Church Cemetery in Columbia, South Carolina.

BIBLIOGRAPHY

Cisco, Walter Brian. *States Rights Gist: A South Carolina General of the Civil War.* Shippensburg, Pa., 1991.

Warner, Ezra J. *Generals in Gray: Lives of the Confederate Commanders.* Baton Rouge, La., 1959.

RICHARD M. MCMURRY

GLORIETA PASS, NEW MEXICO

The battle fought March 28, 1862, at Glorieta Pass marked the end of Confederate expansion in the Southwest and was the turning point in Brig. Gen. Henry Hopkins Sibley's attempt to seize New Mexico.

After defeating the main Union forces at Val Verde on February 21 and bypassing Fort Craig, Sibley planned to concentrate his 2,000 Texans near the last Federal outpost, Fort Union, in the northeast corner of the territory. A 200-man Confederate detachment remained at Albuquerque to watch movements by the Fort Craig garrison. A second force of about 350 men under Maj. Charles Pyron, occupied the capital. A third column, composed chiefly of some 800 foot soldiers under Lt. Col. William Read Scurry, took a circuitous route through the mountains, planning to rendezvous with Pyron near Glorieta Pass in the Sangre de Cristo Mountains east of Santa Fe.

On March 26, Pyron, proceeding with the plan, blundered into the vanguard of a 1,300-man army of mostly Colorado volunteers under Col. John Slough at the west end of Glorieta Pass known as Apache Canyon. Pyron, taken by surprise, saw a third of his troops captured, while the Federals lost less than a dozen before withdrawing. Scurry, alerted to Pyron's danger, led his men in a freezing night march and reached Apache Canyon the next morning.

On March 28, after a quiet day of waiting, the 1,300-man Federal force divided, with about 450 making a flank march over a rugged mesa to strike the Confederate rear while the balance marched down the pass. Scurry, unaware of the enemy plans, left a hundred-man detachment at the mouth of Apache Canyon to guard the wagons and led the remaining 950 Texans toward Slough's command in Glorieta Pass.

The two forces met at 11:00 A.M. near Pigeon's Ranch. The Federals were thrown back in confusion before taking position around the adobe ranch buildings. The battle was fought as a number of disjointed gun duels throughout the afternoon until Scurry ordered a three-pronged attack against the Union line around 4:00 P.M. The Confederates turned the Federal right, forcing the Colorado volunteers back to another line farther down the pass. The Confederates did not pursue; darkness ended the battle. Thirty-six Texans had been killed, 70 wounded, and some 25 captured; the Federals counted 38 killed, 64 wounded, and about 20 captured.

During the day, however, disaster had struck the Confederate rear. The Union flank detachment under Maj. John Chivington routed the Texan wagon guard at midafternoon, burning some ninety wagons and killing over eight hundred draft animals. The destroyed supplies constituted the bulk of the Confederate commissary and crippled Sibley's campaign.

On March 29, Scurry withdrew his force to Santa Fe, where Sibley and the rest of the army met him. After a week's delay, the Texans retreated, evacuating New Mexico Territory and Confederate Arizona forever by June.

BIBLIOGRAPHY

Alberts, Don E., ed. *Rebels on the Rio Grande: The Civil War Journal of A. B. Peticolas.* Albuquerque, N.M., 1984.
Colton, Ray C. *The Civil War in the Western Territories.* Norman, Okla., 1959.
Hall, Martin H. *Sibley's New Mexico Campaign.* Austin, Tex., 1960.
Josephy, Alvin M., Jr. *The Civil War in the American West.* New York, 1991.

DONALD S. FRAZIER

GORDON, JOHN B.

GORDON, JOHN B., (1832–1904), major general, U.S. senator, and governor of Georgia. The descendant of Scottish immigrants and of a Revolutionary War soldier, Gordon was born in Upson County, Georgia, February 6, 1832, and for more than forty years was one of the most celebrated citizens of the state.

Gordon attended the University of Georgia but did not graduate. In 1854 he studied law in Atlanta and by the end of the year had passed his bar examination and was a partner in an established law firm. When the legal profession failed to provide the income he expected, Gordon moved to the state capital of Milledgeville in November 1855. There he obtained employment as a newspaperman covering the general assembly. By the end of the decade, however, he was in northwestern Georgia working with his father in developing coal mines.

Shortly after the bombardment of Fort Sumter, Gordon helped organize a company of volunteers from Georgia, Alabama, and Tennessee that styled itself the "Raccoon Roughs." On May 15 the company was mustered into Confederate service as part of the Sixth Alabama Infantry Regiment, with Gordon as major and his brother Augustus as captain. After training in Corinth, Mississippi, the regiment departed for Virginia. There it occupied the extreme right of P. G. T. Beauregard's line on July 21. While other regiments routed the Federals at First Manassas, however, the Sixth Alabama only waited, marched, and countermarched.

Gordon's rise in the command structure was spectacularly rapid. He was promoted to colonel on April 28, 1862; to brigadier, November 1, 1862; and to major general, May 14, 1864.

JOHN B. GORDON. NATIONAL ARCHIVES

Gordon fought valiantly whenever his command was engaged. At Seven Pines, where he lost 60 percent of his troops, he was placed in temporary command of Robert Rodes's brigade when that officer was incapacitated by wounds. Gordon's brigade led Robert E. Lee's vanguard into Maryland in September 1862 and engaged the enemy at South Mountain. In the words of Rodes, Gordon fought in a "manner I have never heard or seen equalled during the war." D. H. Hill, the division commander, added: "Gordon excelled his former deeds at Seven Pines and in the battles around Richmond. Our language is not capable of expressing a higher compliment."

Gordon's brigade was in the thickest of the fighting at Sharpsburg, a battle in which the general was wounded five times, once in the head. Only a bullet hole in his hat prevented him from drowning in his own blood as he lay unconscious on the ground. He was nursed back to health by his wife, who had left their two sons with her mother-in-law in Georgia to accompany the general to the war. "I owe my life to her incessant watchfulness night and day," said Gordon, "and to her tender nursing through weary weeks and anxious months."

By the spring of 1863 the general, of "striking appearance and commanding presence . . . six feet tall, thin and straight as a rail but muscular and powerful of build," was back in action, commanding a brigade under Jubal Early at Chancellorsville. In the Gettysburg campaign, he led Early's column to York and Wrightsville. Rejoining the main Confederate force at Gettysburg, Gordon took an active part in the first day's engagement north and west of the town. An officer who glimpsed Gordon riding a black stallion that day called the sight "the most glorious and inspiring thing . . . standing in his stirrups bareheaded, hat in hand, arms extended, and, in a voice like a trumpet, exhorting his men. It was superb, absolutely thrilling." Gordon did not consider his actions the next two days "of sufficient importance to mention."

At Spotsylvania, Gordon's men shouted their famous "Lee to the rear!" order to the commanding general while Gordon rode to the front of his troops and reestablished the Confederate line, thereby turning imminent disaster into victory.

In June 1864, Gordon's brigade was detached from the forces around Richmond and participated in Early's Shenandoah Valley campaign. Gordon's men helped drive David O. Hunter from the Valley and delivered a crushing blow to Lew Wallace at Monocacy on the aborted raid on Washington. Gordon then took part in the Battles of Third Winchester, Fisher's Hill, and Cedar Creek before rejoining Lee in the defenses of Petersburg.

His last major action occurred on March 25, 1865, when he directed a predawn attack on Fort Stedman, hoping to breach the Union lines and permit some of Lee's troops to escape to North Carolina and join Joseph E. Johnston. Initially, the attack carried the works, but lack of support and confusion in the darkness eventually doomed the venture. The thirty-three-year-old lawyer who possessed "the personality and genius for war" commanded the Second Corps on the retreat from Petersburg and surrendered at Appomattox.

Returning to Georgia, Gordon resumed the practice of law, this time in Atlanta, and entered Democratic politics. He lost a gubernatorial bid in 1868 but was elected to the U.S. Senate in 1873. Shortly after his reelection in 1879, Gordon resigned to enter the employ of a major railroad company. He served as governor from 1886 to 1890, after which the legislature again elected him to the Senate.

The popular soldier-statesman served as commander-in-chief of the United Confederate Veterans from the inception of the organization in 1890 until his death on January 9, 1904. He was buried in Oakland Cemetery, Atlanta.

BIBLIOGRAPHY

Early, Jubal A. "Leading Confederates on the Battle of Gettysburg." *Southern Historical Society Papers* 4 (1877): 243–244, 254–258. Reprint, Wilmington, N.C., 1990.

Eckert, Ralph Lowell. *John Brown Gordon: Soldier, Southerner, American.* Baton Rouge, La., 1989.

Gordon, John Brown. *Reminiscences of the Civil War.* New York, 1903.

Ockenden, I. M. Porter. "Gordon, Commander in Chief, U. C. V." *Confederate Veteran* 12 (1904): 56–59. Reprint, Wilmington, N.C., 1985.

Tankersley, Allen P. *John B. Gordon: A Study in Gallantry.* Atlanta, 1955.

LOWELL REIDENBAUGH

GORGAS, JOSIAH

GORGAS, JOSIAH, (1818–1883), chief of ordnance of the Confederate army. Born July 1, 1818, at Running Pumps, Pennsylvania, Gorgas was the son of Joseph Gorgas and Sophia Atkinson. Appointed to the U.S. Military Academy in 1837, he graduated sixth in his class in 1841 and selected the Ordnance Corps for his service. His first assignment was to Watervliet Arsenal near Troy, New York. He traveled for a year in Europe (1845–1846) and then joined Gen. Winfield Scott's expeditionary force to Mexico. His good work in placing guns for the Vera Cruz siege and in servicing ammunition needs made Gorgas commander of the ordnance depot there. But a bout with yellow fever plus the tedious routine of the depot eroded much of the glamour of the Mexican War for him. A carper, he complained much about people and conditions, but his sound war service taught him, and several important superiors, something of his native competence in ordnance matters. Mexican service also introduced him to many younger officers who would work with and against him during the Civil War.

Gorgas's natural independence sometimes translated into a resentment of superiors, and this involved him in a petty but lasting dispute with Secretary of State James Buchanan and Secretary of War William L. Marcy—a controversy that cost Gorgas a brevet promotion for Mexican services and hampered his entire U.S. Army career.

Routine ordnance duties throughout the 1840s and 1850s took Gorgas to installations in the Deep South and to scattered arsenals in the North. At Mount Vernon Arsenal in Alabama, he met Amelia Gayle, daughter of a former governor of Alabama. He and Amelia were married on December 26, 1853. She soothed the roughness of Josiah's personality, but could not heal the wound left by the dispute with Buchanan. She bore Josiah two sons (one, William Crawford, would be a conqueror of yellow fever) and four daughters.

Promotions were slow for this dark-haired soldier with steady eyes, a large nose, and a straight mouth hidden by a full beard. When the Civil War came, he was a captain in command of Frankford Arsenal in Philadelphia. At first Gorgas hesitated to join the new Confederate army, but continuing troubles with superiors pushed him at last to accept a commission (effective April 8, 1861) as major in the artillery of the Confederate States with assignment to the important duty of chief of ordnance. Gen. P. G. T. Beauregard, who knew him slightly, had urged his appointment on President Jefferson Davis. He proved one of the most effective of Davis's appointees.

The challenges facing Gorgas were staggering. The South had few manufacturing facilities, only one large foundry capable of casting heavy cannon (in Richmond, Virginia), and although each state had an armory, arsenals capable of repairing or making arms were few. Across the Confederacy Gorgas counted only 159,010 small arms of all kinds, about 3.2 million cartridges of various calibers, powder enough for another million and a half bullets, and an indeterminate amount of cannon powder. Close to 3 million percussion caps were counted, along with saltpeter and sulphur enough to make an additional 200 tons of powder. Supplies were scattered across different states; governors tended to guard their hoards with parochial jealousy.

> His efforts led to the purchase of blockade runners for his and other supply departments. . . .

Gorgas's first efforts were directed toward scavenging every battlefield, next toward creating or expanding existing industrial capacities, and finally toward the importation of all kinds of ordnance stores from the North and from Europe. He developed mineral resources through a Niter and Mining Corps. Various arsenals were overhauled and modernized; small ordnance shops were established in Tennessee, Mississippi, Virginia, and Texas. Gorgas hoped to create a centralized procurement and distribution plan that would rely on a few large works from which arms and munitions would be distributed to the railheads near field armies. But he soon realized that the rail system of the South inhibited such a centralized procurement plan, and without that luxury, he had to rely on decentralized distribution.

By 1862, Gorgas had turned his attention increasingly to blockade running as an essential source of cannons, powder, lead, copper, arms, and other ordnance needs. He successfully urged creation of a Bureau of Foreign Supplies to organize overseas purchasing. His efforts led to the purchase of blockade runners for his and other supply departments, and an efficient system of transshipment in Bermuda, Nassau, and Cuba. From 1861 to 1865 about 600,000 small arms reached the South. From December 1863 to December 1864, 1,933,000 pounds of saltpeter and 1,507,000 pounds of lead arrived.

Gorgas's programs succeeded. On April 8, 1864, he confided in his diary that

it is three years ago today since I took charge of the Ordnance Department. . . . I have succeeded beyond my utmost expectations. From being the worst supplied of the Bureaus of the War Department it is now the best. . . . Where . . . we were not making a gun, a pistol nor a sabre, no shot nor shell . . . —a pound of powder—we now make all these in quantities to meet the demands of our large armies.

On November 19, 1864, he was promoted to brigadier general.

Gorgas performed logistical miracles to the end of the war. Perhaps his greatest strength was his judgment of subordinates. He picked able men to run his installations and to serve with the field armies, and he backed his men strongly. He and his department did more than any other supply agency to sustain the Confederacy.

After the war, failure in an iron-making venture at Brierfield, Alabama, led Gorgas to become, on July 1, 1869, head of the junior department of the nascent University of the South at Sewanee, Tennessee, and finally head of that institution (July 10, 1872). A stormy tenure there ended with his appointment in July 1878 as president of the University of Alabama. He enjoyed the town of Tuscaloosa and was a quick success with the faculty and student body. The Alabama move restored his self-confidence, but his happiness was brief. Illness forced Gorgas to resign the presidency in September 1879. Appointed librarian, he lived with his family on the university campus until his death on May 15, 1883.

BIBLIOGRAPHY

Vandiver, Frank E., ed. *The Civil War Diary of General Josiah Gorgas.* University, Ala., 1947.
Vandiver, Frank E. *Ploughshares into Swords: Josiah Gorgas and Confederate Ordnance.* Austin, Tex., 1952.

FRANK E. VANDIVER

GOSPORT NAVY YARD

Located across the Elizabeth River from Norfolk, Virginia, Gosport was the largest and best equipped naval yard in the United States in 1861. Norfolk was an important port and shipbuilding center from the colonial period, and Gosport was chosen as the site for a naval yard in the years after the War of 1812. In 1830 the navy opened its first stone dry dock at the yard. By 1861 the yard occupied a rectangular area about three-quarters of a mile long and a quarter of a mile wide. Yard facilities included a granite dry dock, two large ship houses, a third ship house under construction, riggers and sail lofts, sawmills, timber sheds, spar and mast storage sheds, foundries, machine shops, boiler shops, an ordnance magazine, and an ordnance laboratory. The Gosport Navy Yard also served as the storage site for over three thousand naval cannons, most important of which were some three hundred new Dahlgren shell guns.

Commandant of the yard in 1861 was Commo. Charles S. McCauley, a fifty-two-year-old navy veteran. Either under repair or anchored off the yard that spring were the sailing sloops *Plymouth* and *Germantown,* the brig *Dolphin,* ships-of-the-line *Delaware* and *Columbus,* and two frigates, *Columbia* and *Raritan.* Former ship-of-the-line *Pennsylvania* served as an unarmed receiving ship, and the ship-of-the-line *New York* was still on the stocks. The most important vessel at Gosport was the five-year-old steam frigate *Merrimack,* in dry dock for repairs. In March, the steam sloop-of-war *Cumberland* anchored off the yard.

In early April 1861, Federal Secretary of the Navy Gideon Welles, concerned over the fate of *Merrimack,* requested that McCauley make it ready for departure as quickly as possible. When McCauley replied that this would take a month, Welles ordered the U.S. Navy's engineer-in-chief, Benjamin F. Isherwood, to make the repairs. Isherwood went to Gosport with Commdr. James D. Alden, who was to command *Merrimack* when the repairs were finished; they arrived on April 14. He had *Merrimack* ready by the seventeenth, but McCauley refused to let him raise steam. Isherwood later charged that McCauley was drunk; other sources suggest that he was simply confused and indecisive.

Isherwood had *Merrimack'*s boiler fires alight the next morning, but he could not persuade Commander Alden to sail the ship out in defiance of McCauley. Both officers returned to Washington. Secretary Welles promptly sent Commo. Hiram Paulding to relieve McCauley.

Although the gates into the yard were locked, a loud mob had gathered just outside them, convincing McCauley that thousands of Virginia troops were about to attack. On April 20 he ordered all the ships in the yard burned and scuttled. Upon his arrival, Paulding confirmed these orders and extended them to include the entire yard.

The destruction was not fully effective. Civilians and Virginia soldiers raced into the yard as soon as the defenders abandoned it and extinguished most of the fires. Although all the vessels at the yard, with the exception of *Cumberland* and *Pawnee,* were set afire, *Plymouth, Delaware,* and *Columbus* sank with little damage. Neither powder charges at the dry dock nor those at the powder magazine exploded. The sail loft, rigging loft, gun carriage depot, and two of the ship houses were totally burned, but all the other buildings were saved intact. Confederate naval authorities seized over a thousand guns, thousands of tons of supplies, and even uniforms from various storehouses within the yard, and recovered some four thousand shells from the harbor waters.

Most important, in the undamaged dry dock, *Merrimack* sank with fire damage confined to its rigging and upper deck. Not only was the hull of the ship salvageable; within a watertight magazine below decks were over two thousand 10-pound cartridges.

Union forces recaptured the navy yard in May 1862. Despite extensive destruction of the yard's facilities by the retreating Confederates, the yard formed an important part of Union naval control of the Hampton Roads area for the remainder of the war.

BIBLIOGRAPHY

Beach, Edward L. *The United States Navy: 200 Years.* New York, 1986.
Wertenbaker, Thomas J. *Norfolk: Historic Southern Port.* Durham, N.C., 1931.
Still, William N., Jr. *Iron Afloat: The Story of the Confederate Armorclads.* Nashville, Tenn., 1971.

ROBERT S. BROWNING III

GOVERNORS

By 1860 all Southern states had governors elected by those citizens eligible to vote for members of the lower house of the general assembly except South Carolina, whose governor was elected by the assembly. All American governors under the first state constitutions had little authority, but the practical matter of efficient government compelled gradual change. By 1860 Southern governors had gained considerable independence from the legislatures, but they were not yet as powerful constitutionally. The power they had gained lay not so much in a strengthened executive branch as in their ability to curb legislative authority. The typical governor could delay legislation passed by the assembly but had little appointive power. It is true that every state that entered the Confederacy named the governor as its commander in chief, but this power was almost untested.

When the Confederacy began its war for independence, the old practice of decision making by legislatures proved inadequate. The citizenry had to be persuaded to make great sacrifices and consider defeat unthinkable; producers and merchants had to be induced to give the war their first priority; soldiers had to be supplied. A central government could provide the basic war measures and some methods of implementing them, but the South was not yet ready for this degree of central authority. And even if it had been, geography and the state of the economy would have prevented the imposition of much more centralism than actually occurred. To wage a successful war, the Confederate government had to have the full cooperation of the states. The extent of each state's cooperation can largely be measured by the actions of its governor.

Charisma and Leadership. In any struggle for independence against great odds, strong leadership is pivotal. All the first Confederate governors except John Letcher of Virginia had been secession leaders who obviously had the respect of their people. As their responsibilities increased during war, so did their visibility. How dedicated each of them was to victory offered guidance to their people, who usually responded to the war as their governor seemed to respond. With certain exceptions, then, the governors represented the collective sentiment of their constituents.

Twenty-eight men served as Confederate governors. Most were in their forties, and only Charles Clark of Mississippi and Harris Flanagin of Arkansas were Northern-born. All who were governor during secession were Democrats, and all but three of these had advocated secession upon Abraham Lincoln's election. In the last years of the Confederacy, when discontent was rampant, voters turned mainly to ex-Whigs and former Unionists. Most governors had been lawyers and half of them had college or university degrees. Most were politically experienced and six had had military experience. As a whole, they were quite representative of mid-nineteenth-century American political leadership.

Alabama, Florida, Louisiana, Kentucky, Mississippi, Tennessee, Texas, and Virginia began their Confederate years with governors clearly intent upon success. They made sound preparations for war, and when it came they acted decisively. They publicly sought to preserve state and individual rights, but also accepted the need for sacrifice. Possibly J. J. Pettus of Mississippi was overzealous in his support of wartime legislation, but he was reelected overwhelmingly; and Andrew B. Moore of Alabama had malcontents from the first whom he could not beguile. These eight governors were no better or worse managers than the other five original Confederate governors, but they had a symbolic quality that established their states' rapport with the Confederate war program.

The other secession governors failed to become charismatic pro-Confederate leaders. Joseph E. Brown of Georgia did so deliberately; Claiborne F. Jackson of Missouri was politically inept; John W. Ellis of North Carolina was too retiring; Francis W. Pickens of South Carolina was too inert; and Henry M. Rector of Arkansas was apparently too scatterbrained.

Only seven of the postsecession governors served long enough for their image to be of much consequence. John G. Shorter of Alabama and John Milton of Florida became governors early in the Confederacy and established themselves as protagonists of both state and nation. Henry W. Allen of Louisiana, Milledge L. Bonham of South Carolina, Francis R. Lubbock of Texas, and William ("Extra Billy") Smith of Virginia took office midway through the war. They were fair-minded,

dedicated officials, and it would be difficult to imagine executives operating under such difficulties to have been more successful. None of them had a compelling personality, but all projected a grim determination that would be the last hope of the Confederacy. Zebulon Vance of North Carolina quickly became the paradigm of a state and individual rights fanatic, and both he and his state actually appeared to be anti-Confederate despite their enormous contributions to the war.

The quality of leadership of the eight remaining governors varied much but mattered little. The tenure of Henry T. Clark of North Carolina was very brief. Thomas H. Watts of

> **The quality of leadership of the eight remaining governors varied much but mattered little.**

Alabama served the last seventeen months of the war and made serious efforts at leadership, but by 1864 disaffection was so great that he seemed too pro-Confederate for Alabamans and too pro-Alabama for Richmond. Richard Hawes of Kentucky, Clark of Mississippi, and Thomas C. Reynolds of Missouri made valiant efforts to do something constructive, but their states were largely in Federal hands. Flanagin of Arkansas, Andrew G. Magrath of South Carolina, and Pendleton Murrah of Texas took office near the end of the war and were both inactive in and sometimes obstructive to the war effort.

Cooperation with Richmond. Though the image that a governor projected was important to the morale of his state, what he did was even more important. There was a vast uncertainty regarding the proper course of action. Bred under state rights doctrine, he now had to accept the exigencies of war. Upon the enactment of Confederate laws on conscription, impressment, and suspension of habeas corpus, most governors protested automatically. Some—Brown of Georgia and Vance of North Carolina—complained so stridently that they were condemned more for their words than for their deeds. But after making their protests, and occasionally forcing slight compromises, the governors were generally cooperative.

An examination of the careers of the Confederate governors indicates that fifteen of them cooperated effectively with the war policies of the central government. Some were more nationalistic than their legislatures and suffered politically for their zeal. These men were Smith and Letcher of Virginia, Pickens and Bonham of South Carolina, Perry and Milton of Florida, Moore and Shorter of Alabama, Moore of Louisiana, Pettus of Mississippi, Clark and Lubbock of Texas, Jackson of Missouri, George W. Johnson of Kentucky, and Isham G. Harris of Tennessee. Certain inevitable obstacles often hampered good execution of Confederate policies in a state, but within recognized limits these governors deserve good marks for nationalism.

Several others would like to have been more effective Confederates but were unable to do so. Ellis and Clark of North Carolina were too passive; Allen of Louisiana and Rector of Arkansas were cut off from Richmond by enemy occupation; Hawes and Reynolds were refugee governors. Five governors came to office when the war was already lost. Watts of Alabama, Magrath of South Carolina, Murrah of Texas, and Charles Clark of Mississippi hoped to salvage something either by separate state action or by continuing the war in the Southwest, but none of their desperate efforts succeeded. Flanagin of Arkansas simply gave up and did nothing.

Only Brown of Georgia and Vance of North Carolina significantly hampered the war effort. Both were fanatical state righters and their constant carping undoubtedly fed the discontent developing in their states; both men willingly shouldered this resentment. Brown was the more destructive. Vance won the right to exempt state employees from military service and other, smaller victories, but on most matters he cooperated, albeit grudgingly. Brown differed with Richmond

> **Only Brown of Georgia and Vance of North Carolina significantly hampered the war effort.**

more, quarreled more violently, and won more victories over the central government.

Management. Equally important as charisma and the degree of cooperation with Richmond was a governor's executive ability. What power the Southern governors had acquired by 1860 was largely in negative control over legislation. But legislatures at this time were basically conservative, disliking taxation and preferring to interfere as little as possible in the state economy or the personal affairs of the citizens. This system could not operate effectively under the strain of constant demands from Richmond and ever-increasing problems at home. State governors now had to initiate virtually all the necessary legislation and to expand their power as commander in chief to unprecedented levels.

To exercise these new powers, governors often found themselves vying more with their own legislatures than with Richmond. The Florida and South Carolina legislatures even created a plural executive to diffuse executive power, though this worked badly in Florida and it soon returned to a single executive. But the need for emergency action usually prevailed. There would be a need for a law, the governor would specify what was needed, and generally the legislature would comply. Thus the national pattern also became the state pattern.

The first major duty of the governors was to raise volunteers for the Confederate provisional army. They had started doing so even before secession and soon had far more volunteers than the War Department could accept. The governors protested bitterly when so many volunteers were encamped at home at state expense; nevertheless, these men were available to Richmond at a moment's notice. Legislatures all wanted local defense forces and these the governors provided, though they never proved to be effective defenders.

One of the greatest contributions the states made, even under Brown and Vance, was in matériel for the army. The work in this area was ad hoc and improvisational. Governors found themselves suddenly saddled with a variety of duties without precedent: collecting weapons, manufacturing ammunition, negotiating contracts for the manufacture of all sorts of army needs, sending out purchasing agents and blockade runners to buy everything from meat to muslin, and begging clothing from churches and ladies' organizations. Moreover, they had to compete with Confederate purchasing agents. Selfish localism naturally dictated that one's own volunteers had first call upon such goods, leaving the War Department to outfit less fortunate soldiers.

All governors took seriously their position as commander in chief of state forces. They seized Federal installations on their own initiative, and those outside the main battle zones unwillingly took charge of their own defenses. They impressed slaves and free blacks for labor; they obtained from their legislatures or simply arrogated to themselves the right to restrict cotton planting, to arrest peace activists, to ban distilling, to restrict hoarding and speculation, and even to declare martial law. The governors of Georgia, South Carolina, and Texas even ventured into foreign diplomacy.

Some of the new policies were startlingly modern. All tried to allocate money or food to soldiers' families. Arkansas failed in this, but Georgia succeeded magnificently: its welfare expenditures dominated the state's budget for the last two years of the war. Salt was a vital preservative and every governor had carte blanche authority to acquire it. Cotton and wool cards were vital and scarce, and governors either imported them or ordered their manufacture. As unimportant as these efforts may seem, the home front could not have survived as long as it did without them.

To finance this work, conservative antebellum practices had to be abandoned. The financial history of each state shows regular demands by governors for appropriations and almost immediate responses by the legislatures in the form of fiat money and bond issues or new taxes. The Georgia state budget exceeded the state's appropriations for the entire decade of the 1850s. Refugee governors virtually carried their state treasury in their saddlebags and spent it at their own discretion. Thus with rare exceptions the governor asked and the legislature complied—an illustration of executive dominance during wartime. Obviously many of these expenditures were for military purposes, but events were creating such distress among civilians that for the first time in American history individual welfare was considered a government responsibility. The Civil War was indeed putting the Southern states and their governors through a revolutionary experience.

[*See also* State Rights; *biographies of particular governors; and entries on particular states.*]

BIBLIOGRAPHY

Escott, Paul D. *After Secession: Jefferson Davis and the Failure of Confederate Nationalism.* Baton Rouge, La., and London, 1978.

McMillan, Malcolm C. *The Disintegration of a Confederate State.* Macon, Ga., 1986.

Moore, Albert B. *Conscription and Conflict in the Confederacy.* New York, 1924.

Owsley, Frank L. *State Rights in the Confederacy.* Chicago, 1925. Reprint, Gloucester, Mass., 1961.

Ringold, Spencer. *The Role of State Legislatures in the Confederacy.* Athens, Ga., 1966.

Yearns, Wilfred B. *The Confederate Congress.* Athens, Ga., 1960.

W. BUCK YEARNS

GRAHAM, WILLIAM A.

GRAHAM, WILLIAM A., (1804–1875), governor of North Carolina, U.S. secretary of the navy, and congressman from North Carolina. William A. Graham enjoyed the broadest national reputation of any North Carolinian during the late antebellum era. Successively U.S. senator (1840–1843), governor (1845–1849), secretary of the navy in the cabinet of Millard Fillmore (1850–1852), and nominee for vice president on the Whig party ticket with Winfield Scott in 1852, Graham deplored North-South antagonism. Strongly antisecessionist in 1861, he struggled throughout the war and afterward to prevent the upheaval from becoming a full-scale assault on property and privilege.

Graham was a prominent lawyer. He was also a very large slaveholder, especially by the standards of North Carolina, where whites outnumbered blacks two to one. He held over fifty slaves at his home plantation in Orange County and several dozen others on absentee properties in the southwestern part of the state (where he had lived when young) and in adjacent South Carolina. Considered a paternalistic owner, Graham occasionally encountered sharp complaints from his overseers: "I have taken More from Your Negroes than I ever taken before and More Than I ever will A gain," one wrote. Graham's indulgence would "Spoil any Negro in the world."

As the Kansas controversy subsided in late 1858 and 1859, Graham hoped that "the flame of slavery agitation" would die down for want of new fuel. Political parties, he predicted, would have to "appeal to public sentiment on topics more expansive and general than opposition to, or zeal for the establishment of slavery in a territory." Graham looked equally askance at Northern alarms that slavery might soon be fastened upon the free states and at Southern claims that Free-Soilers hoped to ignite slave insurrections in the South. Neither could take place, he judged, "without a Revolution of the bloodiest character," an outcome "not desired by one man in a hundred of either section."

In 1860 Graham and like-minded Southern moderates created the Constitutional Union party, hoping thereby to reinvigorate the traditional Whig electorate and to exploit the rupture of the Democratic party. Never expecting to carry sufficient states to win an outright majority in the electoral college, Constitutional Unionists hoped instead that their candidate, former U.S. senator John Bell of Tennessee, would carry a number of Southern states and that the victory of fusion tickets in several Northern states would throw the election into the House of Representatives. There they anticipated that Union-saving dynamics, similar to those engineered by Henry Clay in 1820, 1833, and 1850, might dampen sectional animosity and set the stage for Bell's selection as president.

As that prospect faded and the Republican candidate, Abraham Lincoln, appeared likely to win, Graham warned the South against rashly disrupting the Union because it had lost the presidential election. Lincoln's election, even if "a calamity deeply to be deplored," posed no unmistakable danger. Only hostile actions would justify a drastic response. Lincoln's capacity to do harm would be limited, furthermore, because he would control neither Congress nor the Supreme Court.

The abrupt secession of seven Deep South states during the winter of 1860–1861, before Lincoln's inauguration, created an extraordinary crisis. Would the slave states of the upper South, among them North Carolina, follow the lead of the lower South? Or would they be able to arrange some sort of Union-saving compromise? For Graham and most other North Carolina Whigs, the only safe course lay in compromise.

In his view, secession meant war: "the idea that there will be no war because the Northern people will not fight is absurd." Graham also feared that war would have exactly the opposite effects than that which secessionists expected. Were the South to fight and lose, slavery would "certainly be abolished." Even were the South to fight and win, the exodus of runaway slaves from Virginia would become a torrent and the slave system of North Carolina would soon stand in jeopardy.

The possibility that Graham might play a key role in resolving the crisis became a topic of speculation during the secession winter. By appointing a prominent Southerner to his cabinet, Lincoln might indicate his commitment to peaceful compromise. As one of the best-known Unionists in the nonseceding slave states, Graham found his name mentioned repeatedly in newspapers. The prospect was not one he welcomed, nor was it one that would be offered. Lincoln and his managers did think the idea had promise, but they preferred to find a Southerner who currently held elective office. Lincoln's choice was John A. Gilmer, a congressman from Greensboro, North Carolina, and a close friend of Graham's. Gilmer, who regularly sought advice from Graham, agonized for two months before declining.

Graham did, however, participate vigorously in efforts to keep North Carolina in the Union. Nominated by antisecessionists in his home county to a state convention, Graham and his running mate, a Union Democrat, won overwhelming victories. Union strength proved so formidable that a narrow majority of voters statewide refused even to allow the convention to meet, fearing any process that might result in secession. Graham continued to advocate peaceful restoration of the Union. He had little hope that any successor government could secure "so much freedom, prosperity, and safety."

The clash at Fort Sumter and Lincoln's subsequent proclamation calling for 75,000 volunteer troops appalled Southern Unionists such as Graham. The proclamation came at a time "when the public mind in all the eight slave holding states that had not seceded, was settling down in the conviction that the forts were to be evacuated and repose was to be allowed." Rather than support a "war of conquest . . . against our brethren of the seceding States," Graham renounced the Union. "However widely we have differed from, and freely criticized the course taken by these States," they were "closely united with us, by the ties of kindred, affection, and a peculiar interest." At the same time, Graham confessed to "a painful sadness." Disunion was a catastrophe "that ought to have been prevented."

Graham could not avoid extensive involvement with the Confederate war effort. Five of his sons served in the army; all, miraculously, survived. Graham, elected in May 1861 to the convention that withdrew North Carolina from the Union, attempted unsuccessfully to present the state's action as revolution rather than secession (many former Unionists remained unconvinced that a state could secede from the Union). In December 1861, anticipating themes that reverberated in North Carolina for the duration of the war, Graham complained that a proposed loyalty oath and sedition law violated civil liberties. He made pointed reference to the plight of ten thousand Quakers, who had religious scruples against both sworn oaths and the bearing of arms.

The impact of the war increased in 1862. Federal troops occupied parts of eastern North Carolina. Heavy fighting in Virginia exacted a high price in blood and treasure, fueling increased demands for manpower and supplies. Confederate conscription and the suspension of the writ of habeas corpus raised fears about military despotism. Food shortages added to civilian miseries, as did soaring prices. Under the circum-

stances, former Unionists gained control over the state government, riding a wave of popular discontent against original secessionists.

Graham, who refused numerous suggestions that he himself run for governor, was one of an inner sanctum of prominent former Whigs who masterminded the landslide victory of former congressman Zebulon Vance, then an officer in the Confederate army. Proclaiming themselves "Conservatives," the erstwhile Unionists insisted that independence could be secured without sacrificing civil liberties or subordinating civilian government to military authority. Elected to the state senate in August 1862 at the same time Vance was chosen governor, Graham soon afterward was selected by the new legislature to fill one of the state's seats in the Confederate Senate. His term would not begin, however, until 1864.

Conservatives found it a burdensome task to maintain North Carolina's loyalty to the Confederacy. Following catastrophic defeats at Gettysburg and Vicksburg in the summer of 1863, dozens of peace meetings took place in the state to urge the opening of negotiations that might end the war. Support for a state convention, seen by some as a way to withdraw North Carolina from the Confederacy, grew during the subsequent winter and spring. The tendency of haughty Virginians and South Carolinians "to undervalue North Carolina" also stirred popular resentment.

Graham resisted admonitions to speak out against the growing peace movement. He also counseled Vance and others to maintain critical distance from the immensely unpopular Confederate government in Richmond. "The masses of the people are so wearied by the war," Graham privately observed, "that, if they can find candidates to represent their opinions, they may give us a delegation in Congress for unconditional peace." Graham himself saw no alternative to continued military struggle. He feared, however, that the war would, whatever its outcome, "destroy the institution of slavery" within two years.

So matters stood in May 1864 when Graham's term in the Confederate Senate began. There he and the delegation of Union Whigs from North Carolina compiled the most anti-administration voting record in the Second Confederate Congress. Graham's arrival in Richmond coincided with the bloodiest month of fighting in the entire war, as Robert E. Lee's Army of Northern Virginia tried desperately to blunt Ulysses S. Grant's offensives. North Carolina's relations with President Jefferson Davis reached a new low. Conscription of seventeen- and eighteen-year-olds and of men between forty-five and fifty eroded the already diminished supply of agricultural labor, raising the prospect of even more acute food shortages. Graham denounced renewed suspension of the writ of habeas corpus, regarded by many as a direct response to North Carolina peace sentiments and resistance to conscription. Such Confederate high-handedness "touched a nerve of exquisite sensibility" among people who had sacrificed prodigally for the Confederate cause. Conciliation, he advised, would secure more genuine loyalty than "force or terror."

Graham and like-minded North Carolina Conservatives aided Governor Vance, who overcame a challenge from William W. Holden to win reelection in August 1864. While continuing to give lip service to the cause of independence, Holden had shown greater readiness than other Conservatives to appease popular discontent with the war. Vance insisted that a state convention, favored by Holden, would throw North Carolina "into the arms of Lincoln" and force the state's soldiers "to fight alongside his negro troops in exterminating the white men, women and children of the South." The governor combined forthright support for continuation of the armed struggle with blunt criticism of the Davis government and of original secessionists. Vance's strong defense of habeas corpus did much to maintain his popularity.

Nothing, however, could reverse the crumbling military fortunes of the Confederacy. Just as Graham returned to Richmond in November 1864 for the reconvening of Congress, Lincoln won reelection, thereby frustrating lingering Southern hopes for negotiated independence. William Tecumseh Sherman then began his devastating march through Georgia. Soon John Bell Hood would lead the Army of Tennessee to destruction. Facing a desperate military emergency, Robert E. Lee and others proposed the enlistment of black troops, with promises of freedom to the recruits and their families. Graham would have none of it. Such "wild schemes" were "a confession of despair," illustrating that "military men are but poor Judges of the policy of a nation." Enrolling black soldiers would be "equivalent to a dissolution of the Confederacy."

Graham worked unsuccessfully behind the scenes during February and March 1865 to effect a negotiated surrender, recognizing the hopelessness of continued military resistance. He and John A. Campbell, former U.S. Supreme Court justice and assistant Confederate secretary of war, favored accepting Lincoln's apparent offer, made at the Hampton Roads conference of February 3, 1865, to provide amnesty and to restore property other than freed slaves. Campbell, one of three Confederate officials who had conferred with Lincoln, also understood him to say that the South could, by returning to the Union, block or delay general emancipation, as contemplated in the pending Thirteenth Amendment to the Constitution, which had already passed Congress. On March 2, 1865, Graham and two other members of the Senate met with President Davis to urge capitulation.

His counsels unheeded, Graham returned to North Carolina in mid-March 1865. He warned Governor Vance that Lee's army would be destroyed within thirty days and suggested that North Carolina should act unilaterally. As the governor vacillated, the Confederacy, by then reduced to a shrinking remnant of North Carolina and Virginia, fought to

the bitter end. Two of Graham's sons were wounded in last-ditch hostilities around Petersburg.

Graham's postwar career was eclipsed by his profound disagreement with the Republican party's approach to Reconstruction. Selected by the state legislature for a U.S. Senate seat in November 1865, Graham and other members-elect from the ex-Confederate states were not allowed to take their seats. Although ready to protect black property rights and to allow for limited black testimony in court,

> **... Graham believed voting should be "jealously reserved to the white race."**

Graham believed voting should be "jealously reserved to the white race." He thought that disabilities placed on former Confederate officeholders by Section III of the Fourteenth Amendment interfered with the right of voters to choose their own officials. Contemptuous of the Military Reconstruction Acts of 1867, he advised North Carolinians to remain under military rule rather than call a convention to write a new state constitution. Graham attended the National Union Convention in Philadelphia in August 1866 and was appointed to the board of the Peabody Educational Fund in 1867.

In a letter to Governor Vance written late in the war, Graham pronounced an epitaph on the efforts of "the conservative men, who opposed the revolution while there was a chance to avert it, but when it became inevitable, have nobly done their duty, in endeavouring to give it success." No North Carolinian stood higher in the estimation of his peers, but the profound challenges posed by secession, war, and Reconstruction swept him rudely aside.

BIBLIOGRAPHY

Alexander, Thomas B., and Richard E. Beringer. *The Anatomy of the Confederate Congress: A Study of the Influences of Member Characteristics on Legislative Voting Behavior, 1861–1865.* Nashville, Tenn., 1972.

Crofts, Daniel W. *Reluctant Confederates: Upper South Unionists in the Secession Crisis.* Chapel Hill, N.C., 1989.

Hamilton, J. G. deRoulhac, and Max R. Williams, eds. *The Papers of William Alexander Graham.* 7 vols. to date. Raleigh, N.C., 1957–.

Jeffrey, Thomas E. *State Parties and National Parties: North Carolina, 1815–1861.* Athens, Ga., 1989.

Journal of the Congress of the Confederate States of America, 1861–1865. 7 vols. Washington, D.C., 1904–1905.

Kruman, Marc W. *Parties and Politics in North Carolina, 1836–1865.* Baton Rouge, La., 1983.

Sitterson, Joseph Carlyle. *The Secession Movement in North Carolina.* Chapel Hill, N.C., 1939.

Yearns, Wilfred B. *The Confederate Congress.* Athens, Ga., 1960.

DANIEL W. CROFTS

GRANBURY, HIRAM BRONSON

GRANBURY, HIRAM BRONSON, (1831–1864), brigadier general. Granbury was born in Copiah County, Mississippi, and studied at Oakland College in Rodney, Mississippi. He moved in the early 1850s to Waco, Texas, where he practiced law and held the post of chief justice of the county court (an executive, not a judicial office).

He helped organize and was named captain of the Waco Guards, which became part of the Seventh Texas Infantry Regiment. In November 1861 he was elected major. Captured at Fort Donelson (February 1862), Granbury was soon exchanged, and on August 29, 1862, he became colonel of the regiment. For the rest of 1862 and most of 1863 he and his regiment were assigned to the Department of Mississippi and East Louisiana.

In the fall of 1863 Granbury's regiment went to Georgia to reinforce the Army of Tennessee. At Missionary Ridge (November 23–25) Granbury took command of the brigade when Brig. Gen. James Argyle Smith was wounded. Granbury's handling of the brigade at Ringgold Gap (November 27) on the retreat from Chattanooga won wide praise. On March 5, 1864, he was appointed brigadier general (with date of rank set at February 29).

Granbury commanded his brigade through the Atlanta campaign and in the Franklin and Nashville campaign. At the Battle of Franklin (November 30) he was killed leading his men in the great assault on the Federal works.

Granbury was buried at Franklin, but in 1893 his body was moved to the Granbury Cemetery in Granbury, Texas—a town named for him.

BIBLIOGRAPHY

Hewitt, Lawrence L. "Hiram Bronson Granbury." In *The Confederate General.* Edited by William C. Davis. Vol. 3. Harrisburg, Pa., 1991.

Warner, Ezra J. *Generals in Gray: Lives of the Confederate Commanders.* Baton Rouge, La., 1959.

RICHARD M. MCMURRY

GREAT BRITAIN

Prior to the Civil War, nineteenth-century relations between the United States and Great Britain were influenced by mutual resentments that had festered since the American Revolution and had been amplified during the War of 1812. Those historic antagonisms were reinforced by a series of crises that developed with disturbing regularity. Britain and the United States confronted disagreements over the Canadian rebellion, fishing and trade agreements, and disputed boundaries with Maine and Oregon. American efforts to annex California and Texas and control Central American nations brought the prerogatives of both countries into conflict and left the British with the impression that Americans were "most disagreeable fellows" at best. British officials and elements of the ruling gentry maintained a jaundiced view of Americans and harbored suspicions that the country was capable of all manner of international mischief.

The sectional crisis that led to the Civil War in 1860 fueled British fears that the country might resolve its internal problems through some form of international adventure. Britons and Canadians were both apprehensive about the fact that Americans openly expressed designs for the annexation of Canada to compensate for the loss of the Southern states. Those reservations appeared to be reinforced by President-elect Abraham Lincoln's choice of the aggressive William H. Seward as secretary of state. Seward was often outwardly antagonistic toward the British and had been a supporter of annexing Canada, which he considered "ripened fruit which must fall." Lord Lyons, British minister to the United States, reported that he thought that Seward would be "dangerous," as he frequently employed the Anglo-American relationship as "good material" for his brand of politics. Lyons considered Seward typical of American politicians of "second rate station and ability."

British perception of the Southern United States appears to have been somewhat different from the view held of the North. Though English evangelists soundly condemned the slaveholding South, many Britons felt a close, if only economic, relationship with the American Southeast. Southern cotton had become an essential element of the British textile economy, and manufacturing concerns found ready markets for industrial products in the agricultural South. The cotton-related industry in Great Britain had grown to approximately 80 million pounds sterling in the decade prior to the Civil War, and the mills of Lancashire and West Derbyshire consumed more than 2.5 million bales annually. By 1860 a large percentage of the British population was dependent upon the textile industry, and most recognized the implications of any disruption of the cotton trade. Unlike the general attitude toward the North, where problems with Canada were focused, British attitudes toward the South and Southern attitudes toward Britain were based on mutually beneficial economics and were characterized by a spirit of friendliness and even admiration.

Unfortunately for the Confederacy, that relationship began to deteriorate almost immediately after secession. In April 1861 President Lincoln proclaimed a blockade of Southern seaports. The blockade, designed to isolate the Confederacy politically and economically, threatened the cotton trade. A month later Queen Victoria issued a proclamation of neutrality. In spite of a highly antagonistic reaction in the North, the British proclamation assisted the United States: it forbade British subjects to engage in sympathetic activities on behalf of the Confederacy, forced recognition of the Union blockade, and prevented the fitting out of warships in British ports. The United States was quick to point out, however, that the declaration benefited the Confederacy by recognizing the South's status as a belligerent. That recognition undermined the United States' position that the South's secession from the Union was an internal affair. It also provided a degree of protection for Confederate military personnel by making it difficult for the United States to treat them as criminals or pirates.

Although Victoria's proclamation proved to be important to Confederate survival, Southerners were convinced that Great Britain's need for cotton would ultimately lead to its supporting the Confederate cause. In response to the Union blockade the Confederacy declared a cotton embargo. Southerners shared a firm belief in King Cotton diplomacy. By starving the mills of Lancashire and West Derbyshire, the South could create sufficient economic and political pressure to force Great Britain to recognize the Confederacy and perhaps even provide military assistance. The *Charleston Mercury* summed up the argument in June 1861, reminding the South that "the cards are in our hands and we intend to play them out to the bankruptcy of every cotton factory in Great Britain and France or the acknowledgement of our independence."

The Confederate cotton embargo had a predictable impact on the British textile industry. In Lancashire the dwindling supply of cotton resulted in the closing of mills and the

> ## The Confederate cotton embargo had a predictable impact on the British textile industry.

loss of thousands of jobs. That economic disaster resulted in considerable pressure to recognize the Confederacy and no small amount of interest in active British military intervention in America. But in spite of the pressure, British politicians stoically refused to be drawn into the conflict and even adopted measures designed to ensure that war materials were not shipped from Great Britain to either belligerent. Britain wanted no part of a war with the United States. The impact of the "cotton famine" would be nominal compared to the effect of an embargo on wheat from the United States. It would be cheaper to subsidize the cotton industry than to go to war and perhaps risk internal strife or revolution. In fact, while the cotton industry suffered, the woolen industry advanced. Shipbuilding, too, benefited from Confederate and specula-

tive demands for British vessels. British resistance to involvement in American affairs was also based on the belief that the Confederacy could win its independence without assistance—a belief held until it was too late to provide assistance. For the Confederacy, King Cotton diplomacy proved to be a bitter disappointment, and British failure to recognize or assist the South elicited open expressions of resentment in the Confederacy.

Although the cotton embargo failed to have the desired political impact on Britain's policy toward the Confederacy, the Union navy provided an incident that almost achieved the Confederate political objective of provoking war between the United States and Great Britain. On November 8, 1861, Capt. Charles Wilkes forcibly removed newly appointed Confederate commissioners James Mason and John Slidell from the royal mail steamer *Trent* and took them as prisoners to Fort Warren in Boston Harbor. News of Mason's and Slidell's capture was received with public enthusiasm in the United States, but Britons were outraged by Wilkes's contempt for the sovereignty of a British vessel. The British press demanded release of the prisoners and an apology. The gravity of the *Trent* affair resulted in the creation of a War Committee in the cabinet. The committee mulled the options and after determining that Wilkes had acted illegally, considered preparing for war with the United States. Confederates were also indignant, but at the same time they were elated over the possible international consequences of Wilkes's actions. Southern newspapers reflected the general sentiment that the United States would not back down and that Britain would not stand for the violation of its neutrality. In spite of the high level of tensions between the United States and Great Britain, war was averted when Secretary of State Seward issued an apology and confirmed that Mason and Slidell would be released. The passions subsided, but the affair reinforced the British perception of Northern animosity.

The equitable resolution of the *Trent* affair was another disappointment for the Confederacy—a disappointment compounded by the reception that Mason and Slidell received, once they arrived in Europe. Slidell was able to gain a sympathetic audience with Napoleon III, but Lord John Russell refused to officially recognize Mason and treated his overtures with an indifference that surprised the Confederate State Department and angered Southerners. Throughout 1862 Mason attempted to achieve recognition for the Confederacy without success. Regardless of the impact of the Union blockade, the *Trent* affair, and the Confederate cotton embargo, Great Britain was not willing to be drawn into America's internal conflict. Although many Britons were openly sympathetic to the Confederate cause, the government refused to intervene. By the summer of 1862 the British refusal to recognize the Confederacy or its envoys had produced open resentment in the South. Southern newspapers called for the expulsion of British consuls residing in the

Confederacy and the recall of Confederate commissioners in Great Britain. The *Richmond Enquirer* in April 1863 labeled Great Britain "our worst and deadliest enemy" aside from the United States. After being continually rebuffed by Lord Russell, Mason left London for Paris in August 1863, and the Confederacy broke off efforts to establish official relations with Great Britain.

Although Great Britain denied the Confederacy recognition, the South received valuable, if clandestine, assistance from the British. In spite of the declaration of neutrality, Confederate agents in Great Britain worked effectively to secure military supplies and equipment. To a great degree the industrial capacity of the Confederacy was enhanced by weapons and war matériel obtained from Great Britain in exchange for cotton and other marketable agricultural products. British shipbuilders supplied vessels for a variety of Confederate purposes. The majority were employed in running cargoes through the Union blockade. In spite of the efforts of the U.S. Navy, fast steamships maintained limited Confederate foreign commerce throughout the war. Other vessels were acquired to be fitted out as commerce raiders. Ships like *Alabama, Florida,* and *Shenandoah* put to sea from English shipyards and destroyed hundreds of U.S. merchant vessels.

During the postwar arbitration of claims against Great Britain for the destruction inflicted by Confederate commerce raiders, it was estimated that British war matériel and unofficial support for the Confederacy extended the rebellion for as much as two years. Had it not been for the efforts of Charles F. Adams, U.S. minister to Great Britain, the amount of support would have undoubtedly been greater. Adams employed every device at his disposal to ensure the strict maintenance of British neutrality. Although he was not always successful, his efforts contributed significantly to frustrating Confederate diplomacy and procurement. His relentless pursuit of U.S. objectives at the Court of St. James was in no small way responsible for the lack of success registered by Confederate foreign policy and the ultimately unsatisfactory nature of relations with Great Britain.

[*See also* Alabama Claims; Anglo-Confederate Purchasing; Blockade, *overview article;* Propaganda; Trent Affair.]

BIBLIOGRAPHY

Adams, Ephram Douglass. *Great Britain and the Civil War.* 2 vols. New York, 1958.

Callahan, James Morton. *Diplomatic History of the Southern Confederacy.* Springfield, Mass., 1957.

Cullop, Charles P. *Confederate Propaganda in Europe, 1861–1865.* Coral Gables, Fla., 1969.

Ellison, Mary. *Support for Secession: Lancashire and the American Civil War.* Chicago, 1972.

Ferris, Norman B. *Desperate Diplomacy: William H. Seward's Foreign Policy, 1861.* Knoxville, Tenn., 1976.

Jenkins, Brian. *Britain and the War for the Union.* 2 vols. Montreal, Canada, 1974, 1980.

Owsley, Frank Lawrence. *King Cotton Diplomacy: Foreign Relations of the Confederate States of America.* 2d ed. Chicago, 1959.

Vanauken, Sheldon. *The Glittering Illusion: English Sympathy for the Southern Confederacy.* Washington, D.C., 1989.

GORDON WATTS

GREENHOW, ROSE O'NEAL

GREENHOW, ROSE O'NEAL, (1815–1864), spy. A popular Washington, D.C., hostess, the Maryland-born Greenhow joined the spy ring of Col. Thomas Jordan, Gen. P. G. T. Beauregard's adjutant general, as soon as the war broke out. Greenhow, whose late husband had worked for the State Department, assiduously mined her contacts in the U.S. government for military secrets that might be helpful to the Confederacy. Her greatest accomplishment came in the days before the Battle of First Manassas (July 21, 1861), when she sent cipher messages via secret couriers to General Beauregard, informing him of Gen. Irvin McDowell's marching orders and troop strength. Her information influ-

ROSE O'NEAL GREENHOW. A portrait with one of her four daughters.
NAVAL HISTORICAL CENTER, WASHINGTON, D.C.

enced Jefferson Davis to send Gen. Joseph E. Johnston to reinforce Beauregard; Johnston's men turned the tide of the battle.

On August 23, 1861, Greenhow was arrested by Allan Pinkerton, head of the Union army's secret service. Though incarcerated in her home, Greenhow managed, through visitors, to transmit information on Union forces to Jordan. She was transferred to Old Capitol Prison in January 1862 and paroled that June on the condition that she not return to the North during the war. In August 1863 Greenhow went abroad as an unofficial diplomat for the Confederacy in England and France; her prison chronicle, *My Imprisonment and the First Year of Abolition Rule at Washington,* was published in London that year. Greenhow drowned on October 1, 1864, when the British steamship carrying her back to the Confederacy ran aground off North Carolina. She was buried in Wilmington, North Carolina, on October 2, 1864, with full military honors.

BIBLIOGRAPHY

Greenhow, Rose O'Neal. *My Imprisonment and the First Year of Abolition Rule at Washington.* London, 1863.
Ross, Ishbel. *Rebel Rose: Life of Rose O'Neal Greenhow, Confederate Spy.* New York, 1954.
Sigaud, Louis A. "Mrs. Greenhow and the Rebel Spy Ring." *Maryland Historical Magazine* 41 (1946): 173–198.

ELIZABETH R. VARON

GUERILLA WARFARE

Historically, guerrilla wars are brutal, savage affairs waged by small groups of men among the mountains, forests, and swamps. The irregular conflict which occurred in the Confederate States of America during the years 1861 through 1865 was no exception. For pro-Confederate Southeners guerrilla warfare was a way of disrupting Northern invasion and occupation. Pro-Union Southerners, on the other hand, engaged in the "little war" to resist Confederate domination. Although it never achieved decisive military results, partisan activity enabled thousands of civilians behind the lines to strike at the enemy while retaining a semblance of their former peaceful lives.

Early Guerrilla Activity in the Border States. The first large-scale guerrilla actions took place on the western border even before the Civil War started. From May 24, 1856, when a group of abolitionists led by John Brown murdered five Southern settlers in Kansas, guerrilla warfare had raged on the frontier. Bands of Free-Soil and proslavery marauders burned, robbed, and killed in an effort to drive the other from "Bleeding Kansas." When war officially came in 1861, many on the Kansas-Missouri border were already veterans of irregular warfare.

Although Missouri, a slave state, remained technically in the Union, an active minority led by Governor Claiborne F. Jackson worked hard for secession. Consequently, hundreds of Kansas Unionists, fearful of being cut off from the North and nervous over a potential Confederate invasion, joined in bands and marched over the state line. Clad in blue and flying the U.S. flag, the Kansas jayhawkers showed virtually no restraint in their zeal to crush rebellion in Missouri. "Jayhawking" soon became synonymous with brigandage. In the autumn of 1861, Senator James Lane led a small army of fellow Kansans into Missouri and left a trail of death and desolation in his wake. The climax came on September 23, when the jayhawkers looted and burned the city of Osceola. Smaller bands of Kansans led by James Montgomery, Marshall Cleveland, and others also roamed western Missouri, stealing slaves and livestock, burning homes, barns, and crops, and murdering any man who protested.

The most notorious gang of jayhawkers was that led by Charles Jennison. Composed largely of antislavery militants, horse-thieves, and common criminals, Jennison's regiment lent savagery to an already bloody border war. In addition to theft, arson, and murder, torture and probably rape joined the list. As a warning to others, Jennison personally sliced off the ears of his victims.

It was largely the vicious, indiscriminate forays of Jennison that finally compelled Federal authorities to force the jayhawkers from the border. By the winter of 1861–1862, however, much of western Missouri was a wasteland, and hundreds, perhaps thousands, of Missourians who might otherwise have remained loyal to the Federal government suddenly became bitter, and often active, enemies.

Although Missouri rebels made several thrusts into Kansas in response to jayhawker raids, it was not until the following year, 1862, that full-scale guerrilla warfare reached the state. Led by William Clarke Quantrill, a twenty-four-year-old Ohio schoolteacher, Missouri partisans, called bushwhackers, launched a series of strikes into Kansas that all but paralyzed the state. On March 7, Aubrey was raided, in September, Olathe was looted, and a month later Shawnee was destroyed. Other bands as well as Quantrill's terrorized Unionists in Missouri, skirmished with cavalry patrols, and harassed Federal garrisons in the western part of the state. Although numerically superior, the Unionists were no match for the better-mounted, better-armed guerrillas. Hence, while blue-clad troops held the towns, colorfully dressed bushwhackers ruled the countryside.

Throughout the rest of Missouri a similar situation existed. In the northeast, Joseph Porter recruited hundreds of men and then laid ambuscades for his Federal pursuers. Farther south, the dashing "Swamp Fox of the Confederacy," M. Jeff Thompson, operated in the bootheel of Missouri, surprising

Northern patrols and sniping at Union gunboats on the Mississippi.

Across the river, the pattern was repeated. Although Kentucky was a slave state, most of its citizens remained neutral or loyal to the Union. As the regular conflict moved south, however, many of those left behind engaged in a bitter contest to gain control of the state. Unionist home guards, ill-disciplined and vengeful, scoured their communities testing the loyalty of neighbors and settling old scores. As a result, numerous bushwhacking bands sprang up.

In an attempt to tap the growing discontent behind enemy lines, both in Kentucky and elsewhere, the Confederate government legitimized guerrilla organizations by passing on April 21, 1862, the Partisan Ranger Act. Many guerrilla leaders, including Quantrill, officially enrolled their men. Federal

> ## Unionist home guards . . . scoured their communities testing the loyalty of neighbors and settling old scores.

commanders, however, refused to extend such recognition, and although there were exceptions, Southern partisans were to be hanged or shot when captured. "Pursue, strike, and destroy the reptiles" ran a typical Union decree.

In May 1862, Maj. Gen. John C. Breckinridge sent a number of men, including Adam Johnson, back into Kentucky to recruit troops for the Confederacy. After skirmishing with Federals in the streets of his hometown, Henderson, and surprising a Union detachment near Madisonville, Johnson led his recruits on a raid across the Ohio River. There, on July 18, he seized the arsenal at Newburgh, Indiana. Johnson's act spread panic across southern Indiana and neighboring Ohio. Throughout the summer Johnson remained in Kentucky, employing his men as guerrillas to burn bridges, attack garrisons, and eventually pin down enough Federal troops to facilitate the invasion later that year of a Confederate army led by Gen. Braxton Bragg.

Early Guerrilla Activity in the Deep South. Although most guerrilla activity was centered in the disputed border states and was waged largely by Confederate partisans, increasingly the Deep South became a scene of irregular Unionist operations. Stretching from the Ohio River to northern Georgia, the Appalachian Mountains rose like an island of discord in the heart of the new nation. Isolated and long ignored, many of the impoverished mountaineers of the region saw little to gain from secession and much to lose in a "rich man's war and a poor man's fight." After passage of the Confederate Conscription Act on April 16, 1862, with its numerous exemptions that favored the wealthy, their fears seemed justified.

The rugged Shelton Laurel region of North Carolina became a stronghold of anti-Confederate activity where deserters, draft dodgers, and Unionist guerrillas found refuge. After partisans made an unusually bold raid on nearby Marshall, January 8, 1863, Brig. Gen. Henry Heth, commander of the Department of East Tennessee, sent in a regiment. Subjected to sniper fire the moment they entered Shelton Laurel, the angered soldiers flogged and tortured several women to gain information. Then, on January 18, the troops rounded up over a dozen men and boys and shot them the following day. Though intended as a warning, the killings did little to curb mountain bushwhacking.

Elsewhere throughout the South, pockets of revolt and lawlessness materialized as the war dragged on. In the panhandle of Florida, gangs of deserters, criminals, and other "lay-outs" roamed the hardscrabble hills, raiding farms for food, loot, and liquor. On the west coast of the state, William Strickland led a band of freebooters who, emerging from their sanctuary in the swamps, spent the nights prowling nearby plantations and carrying off slaves, food, and plunder. In 1863, Strickland organized his gang into the Union Rangers, and in exchange for arms and equipment, he supplied Federal gunboats with food and information. Farther south, near Tampa, small bands of partisans sparred with Southern troops and drove off cattle intended to feed hungry Confederates to the north.

Although most Southerners had welcomed secession, many slaveless farmers in the uplands of Alabama and Mississippi, in the rural parishes of Louisiana, and in the German settlements of northern Texas had quietly opposed it. After passage of the Conscription Act, however, simple indifference to the Confederate cause in these regions often erupted into antigovernment violence. Secret societies sprang up, loyalist neighbors were threatened, and when enrollment officers tried to enforce the draft, they were chased, beaten, and sometimes killed. In Winston County, Alabama, Unionists worked to form their own Free State, and other Tories in the northwest corner of the state considered merging with the mountain regions of Tennessee and Georgia to create the nonslave commonwealth of Nickajack. When Col. A. D. Streight led a Federal cavalry raid through Alabama and Georgia in April 1863, companies of local Unionists eagerly served as guides.

Farther west, not only did pockets of pro-Union sentiment exist in the poorer parishes of Louisiana, but after the Federal capture of New Orleans early in 1862, pro-Confederate guerrillas also became active. When a Northern landing party was fired upon by a band of bushwhackers at Baton Rouge on May 28 of that year, Adm. David Farragut ordered his gunboats on the Mississippi to shell the town. Several months later Farragut's cannon also opened on Donaldsville for a similar occurrence. Organized gangs of criminals, runaway slaves, and deserters from both armies also preyed upon the state, robbing, raping, and murdering indiscriminately. One group operated from the Atchafalaya Swamp where the Teche region to the west and the Lafourche country to the east were equally accessible to their forays.

Like its neighbor to the south, Arkansas was also beset by guerrillas of both flags. In the east, Confederate bushwhackers led by James McGhee and Joseph Barton harassed traffic on the Mississippi and burned half a dozen Federal steamers. To the northwest, bands of Unionists clashed with Confederate partisans in the Ozark Mountains.

Similarly, guerrillas under John McNeill and John D. Imboden in rugged western Virginia fought savagely against both Unionist partisans and Federal troops.

William Clarke Quantrill. By the spring of 1863 Quantrill was on the minds of all Kansans. Because of his success the year before, the people of the state saw no reason to be optimistic about the coming summer. Already several ominous incidents had occurred, including a daring raid to Diamond Springs in May by Richard Yager's bushwhackers. Consequently, Federal Brig. Gen. Thomas Ewing, Jr., recently appointed to the border command, instituted a series of tough policies.

In an effort to prevent raids into Kansas, Ewing first established a system of stations along the state line. At each camp the general placed over one hundred well-armed and equipped cavalrymen. Next, Ewing recruited a number of spies who successfully infiltrated the partisan ranks. Finally, to deny support to the guerrillas, the general rounded up "several hundred of the worst" sympathizers in western Missouri and prepared to send them south. This last act would have tragic consequences. Hunted like animals themselves, the bushwhackers were outraged at the mistreatment and exile of their families and plotted retaliation. When a brick guardhouse collapsed in Kansas City on August 13, 1863, killing five of the women and children, their thirst for revenge mounted.

No place in America was more hated by Quantrill's followers than Lawrence, Kansas. Not only had the city served as a Free-Soil citadel during the 1850s, but the New England colony was also home to Senator James Lane, the jayhawker who had burned Osceola two years before. In addition, Lawrence was a sanctuary for runaway slaves and headquarters of the Red Legs, a gang of Unionist guerrillas.

One week after the prison disaster, on the morning of August 21, Quantrill and over four hundred bushwhackers, including Frank James and Coleman Younger, halted at the edge of Lawrence. Not only had Federal spies been unable to warn Ewing of the guerrillas' plans, but a captain commanding the border station at Aubrey, Kansas, offered no serious opposition when they crossed the state line. The officer also failed to send any word west. Hence, at 5:00 A.M. the three thousand people of Lawrence were asleep when

Quantrill charged into the town. For the next several hours the guerrillas roamed Lawrence unhindered, robbing stores, burning homes, and murdering unarmed citizens. Although Senator Lane escaped and the Red Legs were absent that day, the second largest city of Kansas was in ashes and over 150 men and boys lay dead when the Missourians finally left. Thousands of Federal troopers and Kansas militiamen pursued the bushwhackers, but by skillful management Quantrill led his command to the woodlands of Missouri and safety the following day.

Four days after the massacre, on August 25, 1863, Thomas Ewing issued General Order No. 11. In part, the edict decreed that all Missourians residing in three of the counties bordering Kansas were to be expelled from the land and their crops and forage destroyed. Two weeks later the order had been carried out, as one officer put it, "to the letter." The suffering and hardship imposed on innocent and guilty alike were extreme, and Order No. 11 proved to be the harshest military act of the war aimed at a civilian population. Because most troops enforcing the edict were Kansans, it was also certain that the ensuing death and destruction in Missouri would equal, if not greatly surpass, that of Lawrence.

In mid-September, Ewing sent thousands of Federal cavalrymen on a massive sweep through the woodlands of western Missouri in a bid to crush the guerrillas. Several skirmishes occurred and a number of partisans were slain, but once again Quantrill eluded his pursuers.

On October 6, 1863, as he was passing through the southeastern corner of Kansas, Quantrill halted to attack the Union fort at Baxter Springs. Although several defenders were killed, the assault was soon repulsed. A short time later, however, the guerrilla leader encountered a Federal wagon train just north of the fort. Unaware of partisans in the area, Maj. Gen. James Blunt and his escort paused to watch the blue-clad bushwhackers, assuming they were troopers from the fort. Before Blunt realized his mistake, the guerrillas charged and quickly overwhelmed his command. Although the general and several of his men escaped, eighty-five others were killed, including the band musicians and James O'Neal, an artist for *Frank Leslie's Illustrated Newspaper*.

A wave of horror swept the North upon learning of the events in Kansas. For the first and only time the guerrilla war in the West overshadowed the battlefields of the East.

John S. Mosby. In January 1863, Confederate Gen. J. E. B. Stuart detached a private from his command, John S. Mosby, and directed him to take nine volunteers into Union-occupied northern Virginia and engage in irregular operations. Opposed to secession initially and an "indifferent soldier" at first, the twenty-nine-year-old Mosby, after joining Stuart's cavalry, had proven himself to be a daring trooper, courier, and scout. As a guerrilla leader, the former lawyer displayed a talent for war that soon became legendary. By the time his career ended he had achieved the rank of colonel and his field of operations, the region between the Blue Ridge and Bull Run mountains, had become known to friend and foe alike as "Mosby's Confederacy."

Immediately after crossing enemy lines, Mosby's tiny band went on the attack, harassing Union outposts, stealing horses, destroying equipment, and capturing surprised Federal soldiers by the score. On March 9, 1863, at Fairfax, Mosby gained national attention when he roused from bed and captured Brig. Gen. Edwin Stoughton. The embarrassment to the Union army was compounded when Mosby brazenly retreated with his prisoner in full view of the Federal fortifications at Centreville. The feat won Mosby a captaincy and enabled him to officially organize his growing company into the Forty-third Battalion of Partisan Rangers.

Later that month, near Chantilly, Mosby's Rangers were pursued by a force more than twice as large. Again, on April 1, while they were camped along the Potomac River, a similar Federal column surprised them. In each instance, however, the captain turned on his attackers, inflicting heavy casualties and taking more than a hundred prisoners.

In addition to hit-and-run raids and almost continuous skirmishing, the Virginia partisans burned bridges on the Orange and Alexandria Railroad and tore down miles of telegraph wire. On May 30, 1863, with the aid of a small fieldpiece, Mosby ambushed a locomotive near Manassas and set the cars on fire. As a result, Federal troops needed on front lines were detailed to guard railroads, patrol highways, and serve as escorts.

Unlike guerrillas in the West, Mosby's Rangers normally wore Confederate uniforms, paroled or sent their captives south, and generally conducted themselves according to the rules of warfare. But, as in the West, a large and sympathetic population in northern Virginia provided the guerrillas with food, shelter, information, and recruits. A wide variety of men were attracted to Mosby's company. Discharged veterans, soldiers on furlough, even convalescents, were drawn by the informal come-and-go nature of the command. Local farm boys from Virginia and Maryland were swept up by the romance associated with independent cavalry. A considerable number of deserters and freebooters also joined, lured by the prospect of easy plunder. Under Mosby's leadership, however, the conglomerates were honed into a highly effective fighting force.

Because of atrocities committed by bushwhackers in the West, as well as the penchant for plunder all guerrilla bands displayed, including Mosby's, powerful Southern voices were raised calling for a repeal of the Partisan Ranger Act, arguing that irregular warfare was barbaric, uncontrollable, and injurious to the cause. Even Robert E. Lee, whose own father had fought the British as a partisan, harbored doubts. Finally, in February 1864, the Confederate Congress revoked the act and a short time later Secretary of War James A. Seddon

ended government sanction of all guerrilla groups—with two exceptions. Only John McNeill's partisans in western Virginia and Mosby's in the north were to remain officially recognized by Richmond.

In mid-May 1864, as Ulysses S. Grant pushed south on his great spring offensive against Lee, Mosby's men struck railroad bridges and supply trains in the Federal rear. Then when Confederate Gen. Jubal Early began a diversionary thrust toward Washington, Mosby joined him and soon succeeded in severing rail and wire communications between the U.S. capital and Harpers Ferry for two days.

Returning south, Mosby attacked a pursuing Union column at Mount Zion Church and all but annihilated it, taking over fifty prisoners and leaving another fifty dead and wounded. On the morning of August 13, as Union Gen. Philip Sheridan and his army were invading the Shenandoah Valley, Mosby and three hundred Rangers surprised a section of his supply train near Berryville. Seventy-five wagons were seized or destroyed, almost a thousand head of livestock stolen, and over two hundred Federals taken prisoner.

Later, in an effort to construct another supply line for Sheridan's army, labor gangs set to work rebuilding the Manassas Gap Railroad. Mosby's men attacked furiously, tearing up rails, driving off work crews, even derailing two construction trains. Thousands of Federal troops soon arrived, however, making further raids suicidal. Nevertheless, in a brilliant counterstroke, Mosby raced north and struck Sheridan's "secure" supply line, the Baltimore and Ohio Railroad. On October 14, 1864, the guerrillas derailed a train near Harpers Ferry and stole $170,000 in U.S. payroll funds. Admitting defeat, the Federals suspended all work on the Manassas Gap Railroad.

Various stratagems were devised to crush Mosby. One plan called for the organization of an elite body of sharpshooters, armed with Spencer repeating rifles, to hound Mosby's trail until he was destroyed. On November 18, 1864, Mosby's lieutenant, Adolphus Richards, ambushed and wiped out the one-hundred-man unit. Another antiguerrilla tactic was to arrest the populace in Mosby's Confederacy and destroy their mills, barns, and crops. This caused terrible suffering, but Mosby continued to operate freely. An even more severe measure was the execution of captured Rangers. Although it proved the most difficult decision of his life, Mosby, in an effort "to prevent the war from degenerating into a massacre," ordered captured Federals hanged in retaliation. Summary executions on both sides then ceased.

On January 30, 1865, while visiting Richmond, Mosby was honored by the Confederate House of Representatives. A few days later the Senate paid a similar tribute, making the "Gray Ghost" the only partisan of the war accorded such recognition.

John Jackson Dickison. After the Federal occupation of eastern Florida early in the war, Capt. John Jackson Dickison of the Second Florida Cavalry withdrew his command across the St. Johns River. Although isolated and far from lines of support, Dickison chose to fight rather than retreat. Utilizing the swampy environment deftly, Dickison's company staged a series of amphibious assaults, sweeping up Federal pickets, scattering Union raiding parties, and returning runaway slaves. Although he seldom led more than a hundred men, the captain's ceaseless guerrilla attacks ultimately prevented the Northerners from extending their control over central Florida.

On the night of May 19, 1864, Dickison's men crossed the St. Johns and captured nearly sixty Federals at Welaka and Fort Gates. Several nights later, near Palatka, the guerrillas ambushed the Union gunboat *Columbine* as it was passing

> **Probably no guerrilla anywhere waged war more ruthlessly than William Anderson, known to later generations as Bloody Bill.**

downriver, capturing or killing one hundred Federals and destroying the boat. Later that summer Dickison audaciously attacked a large Union force at Gainesville, killed, wounded, or captured over two hundred men, and then pursued the rest for miles. Once again, on the night of October 24, 1864, the Confederates surprised a Federal raiding party near Magnolia, inflicted heavy casualties, and chased the survivors into the swamps.

William Anderson. Probably no guerrilla anywhere waged war more ruthlessly than William Anderson, known to later generations as Bloody Bill. A native of Missouri, he was living in Kansas when the war began. In 1862, after Unionists murdered his father, Anderson returned to Missouri and joined the bushwhackers. When one of his sisters was killed in the Kansas City prison disaster the following year, the twenty-four-year-old guerrilla dedicated the remainder of his short life to the slaughter of Unionists. Several days after his sister's death, Anderson rode to Lawrence with Quantrill where he reportedly shot fourteen men in cold blood. Six weeks later he killed perhaps as many in the massacre at Baxter Springs.

On June 12, 1864, Anderson and his company, clad in blue uniforms, rode up to a fourteen-man Federal patrol near Kingsville, Missouri, and killed or captured all but two. The prisoners were shot, the bodies were stripped, and one man was scalped. Two days later the bushwhackers attacked a wagon supply train and killed eight more Federals. The following month Anderson's gang crossed the Missouri and in succession shot or hanged eight men and slashed the throat of a ninth. On July 15, Anderson raided Huntsville, Missouri, killed one man, and stole between $30,000 and $100,000. A

week later the bushwhackers burned the railroad depot at Renick and pulled down miles of telegraph wire. The following day Anderson ambushed a Federal patrol, killed two, and then mutilated them.

Throughout the summer Anderson's gang roamed Missouri, burning bridges, bushwhacking patrols, and committing uncounted atrocities. Many, including Anderson himself, adorned their bridles with scalps. Some wore necklaces of human ears.

On September 27, 1864, Anderson and eighty bushwhackers, including Frank and Jesse James, raided Centralia, Missouri. Shortly before noon a train pulled into the station. Among those on board were over twenty Union soldiers, many returning home on furlough. The troops were stripped, lined up, and shot. With the depot and train in flames Anderson and his men rode south a few miles to a stand of timber where several hundred bushwhackers were camped. Shortly after Anderson left, over one hundred Union militiamen entered Centralia. Viewing the carnage and destruction, the militia immediately set off in pursuit. Aware of the Federals' presence, a squad of guerrillas lured them into ambush where they were surrounded and hopelessly outnumbered. The fight became a massacre in minutes. Those who surrendered were subjected to terrible torture. Some were clubbed to death, and others were pinned to the ground with bayonets. Wounded men had their throats cut and many were scalped. Some were beheaded. Throughout the ordeal, those waiting their turn were forced to watch. In all, over 150 Federals died at Centralia. "The war has furnished no greater barbarism," wrote a horrified Union general.

Other Guerrilla Activities Late in the War. Elsewhere throughout the South, because their loved ones had suffered death, injury, or outrage at the hands of Unionists, a number of guerrillas now waged remorseless vendettas. Sam Hildebrand stalked the forests of southern Missouri, dealing out death to dozens. Similarly, Champ Ferguson of Tennessee haunted the Cumberlands, shooting, stabbing, and mutilating Unionists wherever he found them. Before he was finally hanged, Ferguson claimed over one hundred victims.

The response to guerrilla warfare had also become more brutal. Unlike most commanders, who were content to simply shoot or hang captured bushwhackers out of hand, William Tecumseh Sherman believed the punishment should fit the crime. When torpedoes (land mines) laid along the track threatened to sever his rail communications as he fought south toward Atlanta in the summer of 1864, the general authorized his commanders to place prisoners in a car and pull it forward with a rope to test the track for additional mines. In the event no prisoners were available, suspected Southern civilians would do. "Make somebody suffer" summed up Sherman's response to partisans and their abettors.

By 1864, the situation in Kentucky verged on anarchy. Because of the Emancipation Proclamation and the Federal enlistment of black troops, slave owners loyal to the Union felt betrayed. Many who had formerly favored the Federal government now went to war against it. Guerrilla bands led by Ike Berry, Marcellus Clarke, and a score of others sprang up overnight. In an attempt to suppress the revolt, Maj. Gen. Stephen Burbridge issued a series of draconian laws, including confiscation of property and the execution of five guerrillas for every loyalist killed. Except for adding to the death and destruction, however, the acts accomplished little.

Of all the states that suffered from guerrilla warfare, however, none suffered more than Missouri. By 1864 few counties had been spared. Gangs of vengeful Unionist militia scoured the state, beating, torturing, and murdering Confederate sympathizers. Equally vicious bands of bushwhackers led by John Thrailkill, George Todd, and others roamed almost at will, ambushing Federal patrols, terrorizing the populace, and bringing life in Missouri to a standstill. Trains were attacked, stage lines stopped, and steamboats that braved the rivers subjected to almost constant sniper fire. To run the gauntlet on the Missouri, pilots in St. Louis asked and received a thousand dollars for a single trip to Kansas. Terrified Unionists fled their farms and huddled in garrisoned towns that, for all practical purposes, became little more than islands surrounded by vast killing fields. "The very air seems charged with blood and death," wrote a Kansas City editor.

The last significant guerrilla actions of the war occurred in Virginia. While Mosby was recovering from a serious wound, Adolphus Richards remained active throughout the winter. In addition to sparring with Federal patrols, Richards's men in late January 1865 destroyed a fifteen-car train on the Baltimore and Ohio near Ashby's Gap. An even more spectacular success came on February 21 when partisans under Jesse McNeill slipped into Cumberland, Maryland, and captured Union Gens. Benjamin Kelley and George Crook.

With the war reaching its climax in the spring of 1865 and the South facing imminent defeat, many, including Jefferson Davis, suggested that the Confederate army should disperse and wage guerrilla war. But General Lee forbade it. Drained by four years of desperate fighting, his nation in ruins, Lee ordered his men to lay down their arms and return home. With the partisans scattered in remote regions, it took weeks before some ceased operations. Many drifted home and tried with varying degrees of success to live normal lives. Others, fearing retaliation, moved elsewhere. A few, like Frank and Jesse James, either could not or would not surrender.

On April 21, 1865, twelve days after Lee's surrender, John Mosby disbanded his Rangers. Three weeks later, in one of the last skirmishes of the war, William Quantrill was shot near Bloomfield, Kentucky. Ironically, the career of perhaps the best-known partisan on either side was ended by Federal guerrillas.

The hatred engendered by the irregular war lingered long after hostilities ceased. Thousands who had never heard a cannon had been touched by the guerrilla conflict. The bitterness could be partly measured in the postwar years by the severity of Federal Reconstruction, and it could be seen in newspaper headlines describing bank robberies, train holdups, and murders committed by former bushwhackers. In the Appalachians, the Ozarks, and other regions, generations would be required to heal the wounds inflicted by the guerrilla war.

[*See also* Bleeding Kansas; Centralia Massacre; Chambersburg, Pennsylvania; Mosby's Rangers; *and biographies of numerous figures mentioned herein.*]

BIBLIOGRAPHY

Brownlee, Richard S. *Gray Ghosts of the Confederacy: Guerrilla Warfare in the West, 1861–1865.* Baton Rouge, La., 1958.

Castel, Albert. "The Guerrilla War." *Civil War Times Illustrated* 13 (October 1974): 4–50.

Castel, Albert. *William Clarke Quantrill: His Life and Times.* New York, 1962.

Fellman, Michael. *Inside War: The Guerrilla Conflict in Missouri during the American Civil War.* New York, 1989.

Goodrich, Thomas. *Bloody Dawn: The Story of the Lawrence Massacre.* Kent, Ohio, 1991.

Hall, James O. "The Shelton Laurel Massacre: Murder in the North Carolina Mountains." *Blue & Gray* 8, no. 3 (February 1991): 20–26.

Jones, Virgil Carrington. *Ranger Mosby.* Chapel Hill, N.C., 1944.

Paludan, Phillip S. *Victims: A True Story of the Civil War.* Knoxville, Tenn., 1981.

Siepel, Kevin H. *Rebel: The Life and Times of John Singleton Mosby.* New York, 1983.

Starr, Stephen Z. *Jennison's Jayhawkers: A Civil War Cavalry Regiment and Its Commander.* Baton Rouge, La., 1973.

Wert, Jeffry D. *Mosby's Rangers.* New York, 1990.

THOMAS GOODRICH

HABEAS CORPUS

The so-called great writ of liberty, an order that can be given by any judge requiring authorities to produce prisoners in court and to explain the law by which they are held, was specifically protected by the Confederate Constitution. That document copied the language of the U.S. Constitution and stated in Article I, "The privilege of the writ of habeas corpus shall not be suspended, unless when in cases of rebellion or invasion the public safety may require it."

Despite military invasions by Federal forces in 1861 and considerable endangerment of public safety in certain areas of the Confederacy, President Jefferson Davis, who shared the customary American view that only Congress could suspend the writ of habeas corpus, did not act until the Confederate Congress on February 27, 1862, empowered him to suspend the writ in "such cities, towns and military districts as shall, in his judgment, be in such danger of attack by the enemy as to require the declaration of martial law for their effective defence."

Martial law had been imposed in the case of invasion only once in American history that anyone could remember—by Gen. Andrew Jackson at New Orleans in 1815. Though many Americans, North and South, held strong opinions on the subject, perhaps none possessed firm knowledge of the consequences of such action in a great civil war. Besides, suspending the writ of habeas corpus and imposing martial law were not the same thing (or, at least, are not so regarded by modern legal authorities who do not look upon suspension as an invitation to try civilians in military courts). The act of the Confederate Congress, which equated the two, was but a sign of general confusion on the subject. Moreover, military authorities had already arrested many civilians before the writ was suspended, and the second floor of the notorious Castle Thunder military prison in Richmond was reserved for civilians throughout the war.

As soon as he had the power, Davis used it, putting Norfolk and Portsmouth, Virginia, under martial law on the very day the bill became law. He then placed Richmond under martial law on March 1, 1862. Gen. John H. Winder, commander of the Department of Henrico, which included Richmond, quickly grew infamous for his attempts to rule the city. He outlawed liquor sales and recruited government detectives among Maryland refugees (he was from Maryland himself), who proved extremely unpopular with the Virginians.

The inevitable reaction by libertarians, state righters, factional opponents, and defeatists caused Congress to pass a bill on April 19, 1862, stipulating that the authorization would expire thirty days after the opening of the next legislative session. Indeed, the authority lapsed on September 17, 1862, but was renewed on October 13, to last until February 13, 1863. The reauthorization dropped mention of martial law but did not outlaw, limit, or clarify its use. The legislators allowed Davis's authorization to lapse in 1863, a congressional election year, and despite the efforts of ardent advocates of presidential authority like Mississippi Congressman Ethelbert Barksdale, habeas corpus remained a Confederate privilege for almost a year.

Habeas corpus served as a mini-judicial review in some instances, and nowhere more clearly than in controversies involving conscription. Any judge who thought conscription unconstitutional, and many did, could release civilians from enrollment or conscripts from military control with a habeas corpus writ. In the North, which retained active political parties throughout the war, these judges tended to come from the opposition Democratic party. In the Confederacy, such judges seem to have been concentrated within the boundaries of disaffected states, especially North Carolina. Another uncooperative state was Georgia, and Vice President Alexander H. Stephens proved to be more Georgian than Confederate on this and many other issues and bitterly opposed suspension.

Defeatism and opposition to central authority flourished, and by late 1863 the need for reauthorization seemed acute to the president, who was especially worried about alleged disloyalty in North Carolina. His message to Congress of February 3, 1864, consisted of one long plea for a new bill authorizing suspension of the writ of habeas corpus. Davis mentioned a wide variety of cases where he deemed the power necessary: to suppress secret conspiracies and disloyal meetings, to keep judges from preventing generals from marching, to control desertion, to enforce conscription, to protect Richmond from spies, and to combat communication with the enemy. On February 17, 1864, Davis received what proved to be his last congressional authorization to suspend the writ. This authority had expired by August 1864, and numerous efforts to draft and pass another bill failed.

"The turning of the tide against the Confederacy," historian Frank L. Owsley concluded in 1925, coincided with the refusal of its Congress "to empower the President to suspend the writ of habeas corpus and to establish martial law." Owsley added "that after August 1, 1864, when the last act suspending the writ had expired, the fortunes of the South never rose again." More recent and specialized studies have chosen instead to praise Jefferson Davis and other Confederate authorities for their benign record on civil liber-

> **Virtually all authorities would agree that Davis was constitutionally more circumspect than Abraham Lincoln. . . .**

ties. Virtually all authorities would agree that Davis was constitutionally more circumspect than Abraham Lincoln, who quickly assumed the authority and suspended the writ of habeas corpus in some areas less than two weeks after the firing on Fort Sumter and throughout the nation in certain kinds of cases for more than two years. By contrast, Davis always asked his Congress before suspending habeas corpus and enjoyed the authority to suspend for only some sixteen months of the war. Moreover, the Confederacy, though it allowed minor infractions to be punished by military courts in urban areas under martial law, never employed trials by military commission—essentially courts-martial for civilians—after disallowing a brief experiment with such justice in Texas. It was the use of these by the Lincoln administration that the U.S. Supreme Court roundly condemned in *Ex parte Milligan* in 1866.

Perhaps the most important writ of habeas corpus issued in Confederate history came from Judge James W. F. Allen of a Virginia circuit court. The writ was served on Gen. John D. Imboden's provost marshal, who was holding W. E. Coffman, a civilian from Rockbridge County sentenced to death by a court-martial in December 1863 for communicating with the enemy. Imboden would have ignored the writ, but the provost marshal had telegraphed the War Department immediately and Richmond authorities instructed obedience. This saved the Davis administration a potential martyr like Clement L. Vallandigham in the North and thus made favorable appraisals of the Confederacy's record on civil liberties much easier in later years.

How the internal security system actually operated in those periods when the writ of habeas corpus was suspended in the Confederacy simply is not known. While the Confederate Congress was considering the expiration of the suspension in February 1863, it demanded an account of civilian prisoners held by War Department authority, and the Davis administration submitted lists from prisons in Richmond and Salisbury, North Carolina. The government held 302 such prisoners at that time, and the total, adjusted for population differential, is proportionate with analogous numbers for the Lincoln administration in the same period. This suggests, despite the obvious dissimilarities in formal approach to this constitutional question, that actual practice in the Confederacy may have been roughly similar to that in the North. Moreover, those Confederate civilians most likely to be unsympathetic with the cause never enjoyed the privilege of the writ of habeas corpus: the slaves. The Union's president did not enjoy any such degree of control over millions of potentially disaffected persons in the North as the president of the Confederacy did over the slaves.

BIBLIOGRAPHY

Alexander, Thomas B., and Richard E. Beringer. *The Anatomy of the Confederate Congress: A Study of the Influences of Member Characteristics on Legislative Voting Behavior, 1861–1865.* Nashville, Tenn., 1972.
Robbins, John B. "The Confederacy and the Writ of Habeas Corpus." *Georgia Historical Quarterly* 55 (Spring 1971): 83–101.
Robinson, William M., Jr. *Justice in Gray: A History of the Judicial System of the Confederate States of America.* Cambridge, Mass., 1941.

MARK E. NEELEY, JR.

HAMPTON, WADE

HAMPTON, WADE (1818–1902), lieutenant general, governor of South Carolina, and U.S. senator. Born in Charleston to a family of great wealth and distinction, Hampton spent his early years at Millwood Plantation and graduated from South Carolina College in 1836. He studied law, but returned to Millwood as a planter and also acquired vast land holdings in Mississippi.

Hampton considered public service more as an obligation than an opportunity and served in the South Carolina house of representatives from 1852 to 1857 without distinction. His election to the state senate in 1858, however, coincided with events that stirred him, and his was a voice for moderation and restraint amid a rising chorus calling for secession and Southern independence. Although the Hamptons were among the largest slaveholders in the South, he opposed reestablishing the African slave trade and believed that the South could resolve its differences within the Union. Nevertheless, when appealing for Southern unity and respect for constitutional law, he declared from the floor of the state senate in December 1859, "Unless every patriot in our land strikes once more for the Constitution, I see not how the Union can be or should be preserved."

WADE HAMPTON. HARPER'S PICTORAL HISTORY OF THE GREAT REBELLION

Hampton had little influence on the events that followed, and at the outbreak of war he resigned from the state senate and volunteered for Confederate service as a private soldier. Recognizing the power and influence of the Hampton name, Governor Francis W. Pickens instructed Hampton to raise a military command and secured for him the rank of colonel in the Confederate army. Hampton's call to arms was enthusiastically answered by the sons of the master class, and within days Hampton's Legion was formed.

Tall and powerfully built, Hampton epitomized the Southern ideal of a gallant warrior, and in his first engagement, in July 1861 at First Manassas, was praised for his contribution to the Confederate victory. Promoted to brigadier general the following year, he was successful in reducing the enemy threat in actions preliminary to Seven Pines. Hampton was heavily engaged in this battle and sustained a wound that forced him from command.

During his convalescence in South Carolina, he came to realize that the Federal advantages in both men and matèriel were a fatal combination and became convinced that the South could not sustain a prolonged war. With this in mind, he returned to his command in June 1862 determined to press for an early victory and participated in the decisive stage of the campaign to sweep enemy troops from the approaches to Richmond. Maneuvering in the vicinity of White Oak Swamp, Hampton found himself behind the enemy's right flank and prepared to exploit this unexpected position. Gen. Thomas J. ("Stonewall") Jackson hesitated, however, and Hampton waited with growing anger and frustration as the advantage passed from Confederate hands and the main battle developed at Malvern Hill. Out of loyalty to Jackson, Hampton kept his counsel, but felt that a decisive defeat of the Army of the Potomac had been within their grasp and that they had lost a strategic opportunity.

While harassing the ensuing Union retreat from Virginia, Hampton was transferred to the cavalry, where he served as senior brigadier to Maj. Gen. J. E. B. Stuart. Stuart and Hampton were contrasts in temperament and leadership. Their military success masked their differences, which nevertheless broke through the surface when Hampton on one occasion wrote, "I suppose Stuart will as usual give all the credit to the Va. brigades. He praises them on all occasions, but does not often give us credit." Hampton fought at Sharpsburg in September 1862 and the following month returned with Stuart to Maryland, where they humiliated the Army of the Potomac with a series of bold maneuvers. After the Battle of Fredericksburg, Hampton led a series of daring raids behind enemy lines, which secured his fame as a leader of cavalry.

Hampton participated in some of the bloodiest fighting of the war during the spring and summer of 1863. In June he charged with his cavalry at Brandy Station, where his brother Frank was killed by enemy infantry. Less than a month later, Hampton sustained heavy losses to his command and was himself severely wounded in hand-to-hand fighting at Gettysburg. He expressed a tempered optimism when he wrote from the hospital at Charlottesville, "I am doing well. . . . Our army is in good condition after its horrible and *useless* battle." He returned to the field in November with a promotion in rank to major general and assumed divisional command of the cavalry under Stuart.

With the initiative shifting to the enemy, Hampton spent the early months of 1864 defending Confederate lines and recruiting fresh troops in his native state. In early May he was

> **Hampton sustained heavy losses to his command and was himself severely wounded in hand-to-hand fighting. . . .**

engaged in the Wilderness campaign when Stuart, protecting Richmond's outer defenses, was killed by enemy cavalry. With Stuart dead, Hampton reported directly to Robert E. Lee, and in August he was given overall command of the cavalry. Hampton reorganized his troops and led them in defense of Petersburg. It was during a heavy engagement in late October that his son, Preston, temporarily assigned to his staff, was fatally wounded while charging the enemy. This personal loss transformed the war for Hampton: he no longer hoped for an honorable peace but now sought to avenge his son's death.

In January 1865 Hampton was ordered to South Carolina to rally defenses against the threatened enemy invasion. Soon after his arrival, he was promoted to lieutenant general, one of only three general officers without formal military training to achieve this rank. Hampton, unable to deter the enemy advance, evacuated his troops to North Carolina, where he was among the last of the Confederate high command to surrender.

After the war, Hampton returned to South Carolina, where he led the efforts to defeat the Reconstruction government and restore the conservative regime to power. Rejecting the extremes of racial politics, he campaigned as a moderate Democrat and was elected governor in 1876 and again in 1878. After resigning the governorship, he was elected to the U.S. Senate, where he served from 1879 to 1891. Hampton died in April 1902.

BIBLIOGRAPHY

Cauthen, Charles E., ed. *Family Letters of the Three Wade Hamptons, 1782–1901.* Columbia, S.C., 1953.
Freeman, Douglas S. *Lee's Lieutenants: A Study in Command.* 3 vols. New York, 1942–1944. Reprint, New York, 1986.
Hampton, Wade. "What Negro Supremacy Means." *Forum* (June 1888): 383–395.
Sheppard, William Arthur. *Red Shirts Remembered: Southern Brigadiers of the Reconstruction Period.* Atlanta, 1940.
Wellman, Manly Wade. *Giant in Gray: A Biography of Wade Hampton of South Carolina.* New York, 1949.

MARK E. NEELY, JR.

HAMPTON ROADS CONFERENCE

Held on the U.S. steamer *River Queen* off Fort Monroe at Hampton Roads, Virginia, on February 3, 1865, this four-hour conference between ranking officials of the Federal and Confederate governments failed to achieve any tangible results despite hopes on both sides. President Abraham Lincoln and Secretary of State William H. Seward represented the United States; the Confederate delegation included Vice President Alexander H. Stephens, Senator Robert M. T. Hunter, and John A. Campbell, a former Supreme Court justice now serving as assistant secretary of war.

The meeting originated in a peace initiative proposed in late 1864 by Francis P. Blair to Lincoln, that both sides cease fighting and join forces against Napoleon III's troops in Mexico. Lincoln had no interest in this idea, but he was willing to talk to the Confederates and allowed Blair to explore the possibility. In several trips to Richmond, Blair secured Jefferson Davis's agreement for the conference. Though he held little hope for its success, Davis had political reasons of his own for sanctioning the meeting. He hoped what he regarded as the conference's inevitable failure would blunt the burgeoning peace movement in the Confederate Congress and in several states. The conference was almost aborted by a protracted disagreement on the diplomatic language of the Confederate commissioner's instructions. But Gen. Ulysses S. Grant's unabashed enthusiasm for the conference and his personal plea to Lincoln succeeded in removing this difficulty.

The mutually incompatible aims of both sides, not to mention the near-hopeless military situation of the Confederacy, guaranteed failure even before the talks began. Reunion and an end to the rebellion were for Lincoln sine qua non. Davis's instructions to his delegation spelled out its mission as "an informal conference" for "securing peace between the two countries." Stephens, who knew the only chance for the Confederacy was an armistice, tried several times to bring up Blair's Mexican plan. Lincoln rebuffed the suggestion each time, as well as Hunter's bid for an armistice. Nothing without reunion, he said. Blair's had been an unofficial mission.

Turning to the subject of slavery and the treatment of Confederate leaders, Lincoln promised leniency. He also held out the possibility of compensation—up to $400 million—to slave owners for their confiscated slaves. There would be no backing down on the Emancipation Proclamation: the courts would have to sort out tangled questions of its applicability that the Confederates raised. In any event, Seward said, the Thirteenth Amendment had just passed the U.S. Congress, thereby rendering such questions moot upon its ratification. Since both slavery and the rebellion were doomed, Lincoln urged the Confederates to lay down their arms and return to their former allegiance to save further bloodshed. On this note the conference ended.

The failure of the conference to achieve peace served the Davis administration in two ways. Southerners took Lincoln's insistence on reunion as a humiliating demand for unconditional surrender, and this rekindled momentarily a fierce war spirit across the ravaged Confederacy. The conference's failure also muffled the administration's many congressional foes.

BIBLIOGRAPHY

Kirkland, Edward Chase. *The Peacemakers of 1864.* New York, 1927.
McPherson, James M. *Battle Cry of Freedom: The Civil War Era.* New York, 1988.

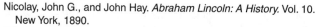
Nicolay, John G., and John Hay. *Abraham Lincoln: A History.* Vol. 10. New York, 1890.

Stephens, Alexander H. *A Constitutional View of the Late War between the States: Its Causes, Character, Conduct and Results, Presented in a Series of Colloquies at Liberty Hall.* Vol. 2. Philadelphia, 1870.

THOMAS E. SCHOTT

HAMPTON'S LEGION

"Legions" were permitted and organized only in the early stages of the Civil War. A legion was a miniature army in that it contained all three military components: infantry, artillery, and cavalry. Ten such units existed in the Confederate armies. The most famous in the group was the South Carolina legion of Wade Hampton.

One of the wealthiest planters in the antebellum South, Hampton had known a life of splendid luxury. He was a state legislator and ardent Southern nationalist when the war began. Hampton promptly diminished his fortune by recruiting a legion that, if necessary, could fight independently. In less than a week after his initial call, thirty South Carolina companies volunteered for Hampton's unit. This was more than twice the number that could be accommodated. Hampton's Legion came to consist of six infantry companies, four cavalry companies, and a battery of artillery sporting six new and revolutionary Blakely guns.

The highest-born of the Palmetto State served as privates in such companies as the Columbia Zouaves and Edgefield Hussars. Officers came exclusively from the socially elite class. The legion also boasted a veritable platoon of black servants who prepared meals and attended to other tasks.

Hampton trained and splendidly equipped his unit at Camp Hampton, a few miles outside Columbia. The legion received a royal welcome upon its early summer arrival at Richmond, Virginia. One of its field officers boasted that the unit was "by all odds the finest looking and best drilled body of men that has left" South Carolina.

When battle became imminent at Manassas, Hampton speedily boarded his unit on a train and rushed northward. The companies marched three miles from the railroad depot straight into the war's first major battle. Hampton's second-in-command, Lt. Col. Benjamin J. Johnson, was killed almost immediately. This left the legion with no experienced field officer. Federals enfiladed the Carolinians' position and soon had Hampton's force surrounded on three sides. Legion officers did not possess enough military knowledge to know when to retreat. Hence, the legion stubbornly maintained its position and fought gallantly until superior officers persuaded Hampton to retire to a less exposed sector. The unit suffered casualties of 121 of the 600 engaged. Among the wounded

was Colonel Hampton, who barely escaped death when a bullet grazed his skull.

In November 1861, Hampton received promotion to brigadier general. His legion then became part of Gen. James Longstreet's division. It fought in the 1862 Peninsular campaign. The legion ceased to exist shortly thereafter when the infantry companies were merged with the brigade of Gen. John Bell Hood, the cavalry units became part of Col. Thomas Lafayette Rosser's command, and the artillery was redesignated as Hart's South Carolina Battery. Four officers in Hampton's Legion eventually became Confederate generals.

[*See also* Hampton, Wade.]

BIBLIOGRAPHY

Brooks, U. R., ed. *Stories of the Confederacy.* Columbia, S.C., 1912.

Heller, J. Roderick, III, and Carolyn A. Ayres, eds. *The Confederacy Is on Her Way up the Spout: Letters to South Carolina, 1861–1864.* Athens, Ga., 1992.

Wellman, Manly Wade. *Giant in Gray: A Biography of Wade Hampton of South Carolina.* New York, 1949.

JAMES I. ROBERTSON, JR.

HARDEE, WILLIAM J.

HARDEE, WILLIAM J. (1815–1872), lieutenant general. Hardee was born October 12, 1815, on the troubled Georgia-Florida border, site of almost continuous warfare for more than a generation. Coming from a military family, he was expected to enter West Point, which he did in 1834. Upon graduation in 1838 he joined the Second Dragoons, serving briefly in Florida before going to France in 1840 to attend the Royal Cavalry School at Saumur. He returned to his regiment in 1842 and went with it to the Mexican border where, to his humiliation, he was captured in the first engagement of the war. He put this embarrassment behind him during Winfield Scott's march from Vera Cruz to the city of Mexico, being breveted twice for conspicuous service. Having been previously detailed as a special training officer for the Second Dragoons, Hardee continued this work, in which he excelled, at Carlisle Barracks after the war. Frontier duty in Texas followed, with Hardee engaging in several campaigns against Indian marauding parties.

In 1853 Secretary of War Jefferson Davis directed Hardee to prepare a system of light infantry tactics for the U.S. Army and Militia. Basing his work on a French manual born of the experience in the Algerian wars, Hardee completed his work early in 1855. His *Rifle and Light Infantry Tactics* became the standard by which Federal and Confederate soldiers trained and maneuvered. Service as senior major and chief training officer in Davis's hand-picked Second Cavalry followed. In 1856, he returned to West Point as commandant, an office he changed significantly.

Hardee resigned from the army in January 1861 and became colonel of the First Regiment of Georgia Volunteers. Davis called him to Montgomery in February where he worked with the president, Leroy P. Walker, and P. G. T. Beauregard to prepare an elaborate bill for the organization of the Confederate army. In March, Hardee, who had resigned from his Georgia post, became colonel of the First Regiment of Infantry. He commanded Fort Morgan, Alabama, until June, when he became a brigadier assigned to defend the Arkansas border and to organize troops there for service in the Confederate army.

Hardee remained in Arkansas until September 1861. He and Gideon Pillow participated in a poorly conceived invasion of Missouri, which failed for lack of transportation and cooperation. Hardee, however, managed to train and equip a splendid brigade of Arkansas troops. These men would become the heart of Hardee's division, his corps, and the Army of Tennessee. No finer troops existed in the Confederacy. Hardee also began the development of a group of subordinate officers who would excel in the war. His alter ego, Patrick Cleburne, headed the list.

Hardee's brigade crossed the Mississippi in September 1861, marching rather than being transported by water, and took position at Bowling Green, Kentucky, in October. That fall he vigorously trained his men, conducting marches and operations to the north and east. Hardee headed a division by this time, and in December 1861, he became commander of the Army of Central Kentucky.

Disasters at Mill Springs and Donelson that winter rendered Bowling Green untenable, and Hardee took the army south through Tennessee. At Shiloh he led a corps, the front line of Joseph E. Johnston's army, and fought well. In the Kentucky campaign that fall, Hardee, now a lieutenant general, led a wing. At Perryville he again performed well, spotting a gap in the center of the Union line and throwing Cleburne's division into it, a movement that broke the enemy right. At Murfreesboro, in December 1862, Hardee was at his best, leading a magnificent envelopment that crushed William S. Rosecrans's right wing.

Because of ongoing quarrels with Braxton Bragg, Hardee, in August 1863, was transferred from the army to reorganize the exchanged men of the Vicksburg garrison. Thus he missed Chickamauga, where he was sorely needed. At Chattanooga, in November, Hardee's troops held off William Tecumseh Sherman's attacks and formed the defense behind which Bragg was able to extricate his army.

Offered command of the Army of Tennessee in December 1863, Hardee declined, believing Johnston better suited for that command. In the Atlanta campaign under Johnston, Hardee led his corps skillfully in successive actions. When

John Bell Hood took command in July 1864, however, Hardee's corps turned to the offensive and wrecked itself in severe fighting at Peachtree Creek and Atlanta. Hardee performed poorly in the former battle, capably in the latter. At Jonesboro he led a beaten army against breastworks and failed. Relieved from the Army of Tennessee at his own request, over the pleas of Davis, Hardee took command of the Department of South Carolina, Georgia, and Florida and attempted to defend eastern Georgia against Sherman's army. He continued to organize resistance against Sherman as the latter pushed north into the Carolinas in early 1865. At Averasborough and Bentonville he fought well albeit with desperation. To the day the Army of Tennessee surrendered, Hardee demonstrated why the men he commanded and the Army of Tennessee regarded him as "Old Reliable."

Following the war Hardee tried plantation life and then moved to Selma, Alabama, where he became for several years president of the Selma and Meridian Railroad. He died in Wytheville, Virginia, November 6, 1873, on an annual family trip to White Sulphur Springs.

BIBLIOGRAPHY

Hughes, Nathaniel C., Jr. *General William J. Hardee, C.S.A.* Baton Rouge, La., 1965.
Pickett, William D. *Sketch of the Military Career of William J. Hardee, Lieutenant-General, C.S.A.* Lexington, Ky., 1910.

NATHANIEL CHEAIRS HUGHES, JR.

HARPERS FERRY, WEST VIRGINIA

[*This entry is composed of three articles:* Arsenal and Armory, *which discusses the establishment and contents of the U.S. installation;* John Brown's Raid, *which discusses the 1859 raid by abolitionist John Brown; and* Battle of 1862, *which discusses the battle won at the site by Thomas J. ("Stonewall") Jackson. For further discussion of the arms captured by Confederates at Harpers Ferry, see* Small Arms, *articles on* Captured U.S. Small Arms *and* Altered U.S. Small Arms.]

Arsenal and Armory

President George Washington recommended that Congress establish federal armories and arsenals to ensure adequate arms production for self-defense for the fledgling United States. Congress approved the legislation in 1794, and Washington selected Springfield, Massachusetts, as the site of the first national armory and Harpers Ferry, Virginia, as the site of the second. Washington favored Harpers Ferry because of the water power generated at the confluence of the Potomac and Shenandoah rivers; the abundance of raw materials, such as iron ore for gun barrels and timber for stocks; its location in Virginia, which would provide a Southern armory in Washington's home state and an economic boost to the Potomac valley; and its proximity to the new federal capital, located only sixty-two miles down the Potomac.

Production of small arms at Harpers Ferry did not begin until 1800, however, because of difficulties with land purchases and inadequate skilled labor to construct the factory and water power works. From 1800 to 1861, the armory pro-

> ## Interchangeable parts manufacturing also was pioneered at Harpers Ferry.

duced over 620,000 rifles and muskets, with annual employment ranging between 250 and 425 workers. With the exception of the period from 1841 to 1854, when ordnance officers ran the Harpers Ferry establishment, a civilian superintendent managed the armory's overall operations, and a civilian master armorer supervised weapon designs and day-to-day production of the small arms. Both the armory (the factory complex where weapons were manufactured) and the arsenal (the warehouse for weapons' storage) fell under the auspices of the Ordnance Bureau, a branch of the government within the War Department under control of the secretary of war.

Harpers Ferry weapons accounted for numerous innovations in federal arms manufacturing. The 1803 model was the first military rifle produced at a federal armory, its handsome half-stock, octagonal barrel, and brass fittings reflecting the influence of Pennsylvania rifle artisans. Percussion technology replaced the antiquated flintlock with adoption of the 1842 model percussion smoothbore musket. The first percussion rifle produced by the government was the 1841 model "Mississippi" rifle. Improvement upon the individual percussion cap system occurred with development of the 1855 model rifle and 1855 model rifle-musket. These weapons utilized a Maynard primer system, which advanced a percussion tape onto the breech cone each time the weapon was cocked. Although the Maynard primer saved loading time by eliminating the fumbling percussion cap, the tape jammed easily and often was ruined by moisture; hence this system saw no use during the Civil War.

Interchangeable parts manufacturing also was pioneered at Harpers Ferry. John H. Hall, a Maine inventor who contracted with the government in 1819 to produce one thou-

sand breech-loading rifles, developed a system of tools, machinery, and gauges in his rifle works along the Shenandoah River that "succeeded in establishing methods for fabricating arms exactly alike, and with economy, by the hands of common workmen." By developing precision machinery that produced uniform parts, Hall doomed craft-oriented production. His American System of manufacturing, he believed, "formed the taproot of modern industrialism."

Another Harpers Ferry invention that changed the character of warfare was the Burton bullet, better known as the miniè ball. James H. Burton served as master armorer at Harpers Ferry from 1849 to 1854, and during his tenure, he perfected a hollow-based, conical-shaped lead bullet that expanded and gripped the rifling of a gun barrel upon discharge of the powder. Since the bullet was slightly smaller than the barrel's interior caliber, for the first time an infantryman could load a rifle as quickly as a musket (three times per minute). As a result, the Burton bullet antiquated the inaccurate musket and enabled the U.S. Army to adopt the much deadlier rifle as its primary small arm.

Despite these innovations at the Harpers Ferry armory, production consistently lagged behind its sister armory at Springfield. Reasons include persistent droughts, which reduced water power and shut down machinery; an infirm work force that was constantly battling disease; inept managers who practiced political patronage and promoted the regional economy above the national interest; and craft-oriented workers who resisted the introduction of machine technology. In an attempt to correct these problems, the Ordnance Bureau between 1841 and 1854 replaced the civilian superintendents with professional ordnance officers who rebuilt and retooled the armory, transforming it, according to historian Merritt Roe Smith, into one of the five "most progressive manufacturing establishments of its type" in the country.

Abolitionist John Brown eyed the Harpers Ferry armory for its products rather than for its progressive manufacturing. Approximately 100,000 weapons were stored at the arsenal in 1859—weapons Brown intended to seize and distribute throughout the South in an attempt to end slavery. On Sunday night, October 16, 1859, Brown and his eighteen followers captured the undefended armory and arsenal, but Brown failed to escape. Local militia soon surrounded the government buildings, and at dawn on October 18, U.S. Marines, under command of Lt. Col. Robert E. Lee, charged the armory fire engine house and captured Brown, ending the raid. Although Brown's men had removed a few guns, these were soon recovered, and the bullet-damaged armory buildings were quickly repaired.

Sixteen months following Brown's raid, Virginia seceded from the Union. Seizure of the Harpers Ferry armory and arsenal became a primary target of a group of secessionists led by former Virginia governor Henry A. Wise and including

Turner and Richard Ashby, John D. Imboden, and former armory superintendent Alfred M. Barbour. On April 17, 1861, the date of Virginia's official secession vote, these secessionists received permission from Governor John Letcher to advance the state militia to seize the armory and arsenal. The following day, Barbour arrived in Harpers Ferry and announced Virginia's intention. His public pronouncement also warned Lt. Roger Jones and his small garrison of forty-five U.S. regulars guarding the federal property. Subsequently, Jones ordered gunpowder placed throughout the armory and arsenal buildings as he prepared for their destruction. At 10:00 P.M. on April 18, with three hundred Virginia militia only one mile from Harpers Ferry, Jones torched the federal property and withdrew his force into

> Jones ordered gunpowder placed throughout the armory and arsenal buildings. . . .

Maryland. The flames totally consumed the two arsenal buildings, destroying fifteen thousand small arms. Most of the armory was saved, however, as local residents extinguished the fires before much damage occurred.

With Harpers Ferry now located on the border between North and South, Virginia officials decided to dismantle the armory and ship its machinery south to Richmond, Virginia, and Fayetteville, North Carolina. Col. Thomas J. ("Stonewall") Jackson, who commanded at Harpers Ferry, superintended the transfer of most of the machinery. When the Confederates abandoned Harpers Ferry on June 15, 1861, the armory buildings were burned, leaving only brick skeletons as a reminder of the once-thriving small arms factory.

Federal armies occupied Harpers Ferry in 1862 and reroofed some of the armory buildings for quartermaster and commissary storage. The armory also housed Confederate prisoners and served as Gen. Philip Sheridan's primary supply depot during the 1864 Shenandoah Valley campaign. Following the war, the United States decided not to reestablish its armory at Harpers Ferry, and the property was sold at public auction in 1869.

BIBLIOGRAPHY

Imboden, John D. "Jackson at Harpers Ferry in 1861." In *Battles and Leaders of the Civil War.* Edited by Robert U. Johnson and C. C. Buel. Vol. 1. New York, 1887. Reprint, Secaucus, N.J., 1982.

Smith, Merritt Roe. *Harpers Ferry Armory and the New Technology.* Utica, N.Y., 1977.

Villard, Oswald G. *John Brown, 1800–1859: A Biography Fifty Years After.* New York, 1909.

DENNIS E. FRYE

John Brown's Raid

John Brown's attack on the Harpers Ferry armory and arsenal (October 16–18, 1859) sent shock waves throughout the North and South. In a violent attempt to rid the country of slavery, Brown chose Harpers Ferry as his initial target because of the 100,000 weapons stored in the U.S. Arsenal. He planned to seize these rifles and muskets for his army of slaves—an army Brown would recruit, train, and use to conduct guerrilla warfare throughout the Southeast. Slaves emancipated by his forces would find safe refuge in the strongholds of the Appalachian Mountains, where Brown intended to establish his own nation, backed by a constitution that would guarantee freedom for all.

Brown launched his bold scheme on a dreary Sunday evening, October 16, 1859. At 10:00 P.M., he and eighteen followers began marching from the Kennedy farm, their isolated headquarters in Maryland five miles north of Harpers Ferry. By midnight, the raiders had possession of the armory and arsenal and the bridges leading into Harpers Ferry. With these initial targets secured, Brown sent raiding parties to seize hostages and slaves from prominent estates in the vicinity. One of these hostages was Lewis Washington, the great-grandnephew of George Washington, whom Brown wanted as a symbol of his revolution. In the opening hours, no shots had been fired and no opposition encountered. The attack had surprised the community and the U.S. government.

About 1:00 A.M., however, Heyward Shepherd, a free black baggage porter for the Baltimore and Ohio Railroad, panicked when confronted by Brown's men and was shot as he tried to escape. The gunfire awakened Dr. John W. Starry, who resided near the railroad; upon investigation, he discovered Shepherd's mortal wound and learned of the raiders' intention to free the slaves. Brown's men then made a critical error. Instead of retaining Starry, they allowed him to slip away into the Monday morning darkness. Starry quickly galloped to nearby Charles Town, where he sounded the alarm and alerted local militia. Within hours, hundreds of militiamen from Virginia and Maryland were descending upon Harpers Ferry, blocking all avenues of escape for Brown and his men.

Brown compounded his problems by allowing an eastbound passenger train to proceed through Harpers Ferry. The conductor telegraphed notice of the raid, and word quickly arrived in Washington of the trouble. President James Buchanan then ordered a contingent of ninety Marines from the Washington Naval Yard to Harpers Ferry. Lt. Col. Robert E. Lee, at home on leave at Arlington, received instructions to proceed to the town and take command of the situation. Lt. J. E. B. Stuart, who delivered the War Department orders to Lee, accompanied the colonel. By the early morning of October 18, Marines had surrounded John Brown, now trapped within the small brick fire-engine house of the armory.

Just before dawn on the eighteenth, Lee sent Stuart to the barricaded doors of the engine house to demand Brown's surrender. Brown refused and then stated his terms of safe passage into Maryland and Pennsylvania for himself, his few remaining men, and his eleven hostages. Instructed not to parlay, Stuart backed away from the door and waved his hat, signaling the Marines to attack. The first attempts to beat down the doors with a sledgehammer failed. A dozen Marines then used a ladder as a battering ram, and a door was penetrated. Marine Lt. Israel Greene quickly dashed into the building and, confronting Brown, badly wounded him across the head and neck with his saber. Two raiders were bayoneted and killed; two others were captured. No hostages were injured during the attack.

The episode exacted a heavy toll. Ten of Brown's raiders had been killed or mortally wounded, including two of his sons. Four townspeople had died, including the Harpers Ferry mayor. One Marine had been mortally wounded during the attack on the engine house.

Brown was transported to Charles Town, the seat of Jefferson County, Virginia, where he was tried for murder, treason, and inciting slave insurrection. His trial commenced on October 27 and lasted over three days. A jury found him guilty of all charges, and on November 2, Judge Richard Parker sentenced him to be hanged. One month later, on December John Brown's Raid2, 1859, with his gallows surrounded by thousands of Virginia militiamen, Brown was executed. Then the silence of the moment was broken by the voice of J. T. L. Preston of the Virginia Military Institute: "So perish all such enemies of Virginia! All such enemies of the Union! All such foes of the human race." Yet, just before his death, Brown had handed his jailer a note, with a prophecy: "I, John Brown," it opened, "am now quite certain that the crimes of this guilty land will never be purged away but with blood."

Reactions to Brown's raid, the trial, and his execution propelled the country into a fervent emotional debate over the issue of slavery. Leading Southerners, alarmed by Brown's "direct stab at the peculiar institution" and dismayed by Northern support for Brown's overt violence, warned of the impending breakup of the Union. Jefferson Davis, speaking to the U.S. Senate, declared, "Have we no right to allege that to secure our rights and protect our honor we will dissever the ties that bind us together, even if it rushes us into a sea of blood?" The *Charleston Mercury* announced, "The day of compromise is passed. . . . The South must control her own destinies or perish." And the *Richmond Enquirer* dolefully noted, "The Harpers Ferry invasion advanced the cause of Disunion more than any other event . . . since the formation of the Government."

Influential Northerners, in contrast, praised John Brown as a martyr. Ralph Waldo Emerson described him as "the Saint" whose death made "the gallows glorious like the cross." Henry David Thoreau elevated him to "an angel of light," and Louisa May Alcott called him "Saint John the Just." Church bells throughout the North tolled in Brown's honor on his execution day, and public prayer meetings and gun salutes proclaimed a pro-Brown sentiment. Incensed by the Northern reaction, South Carolina invited the Southern states to a secession meeting, but the convention failed to materialize, in part because the governor of Texas declared the South Carolina response premature and certain to lead to the destruction of the Union.

John Brown and his failed thirty-six-hour raid upon Harpers Ferry drove the nation to the brink of civil war. His martyrdom in the North and the intense hatred for him in the South led a Kansas paper, the *Lawrence Republican,* to observe, "It is safe to say that the death of no man in America has ever produced so profound a sensation."

BIBLIOGRAPHY

Boyer, Richard O. *The Legend of John Brown: A Biography and a History.* New York, 1973.
Oates, Stephen B. *To Purge This Land with Blood: A Biography of John Brown.* New York, 1970.
Sanborn, Franklin B. *Life and Letters of John Brown.* Boston, 1885.
Villard, Oswald Garrison. *John Brown, 1800–1859: A Biography Fifty Years After.* Boston and New York, 1911.

DENNIS E. FRYE

Battle of 1862

Harpers Ferry was the site of a battle on September 13 through 15, 1862, in which Thomas J. ("Stonewall") Jackson captured 12,500 prisoners, the largest surrender of U.S. troops during the Civil War. Jackson's success at Harpers Ferry enabled Robert E. Lee to cease his withdrawal from Maryland and fight the Battle of Sharpsburg on September 17.

Robert E. Lee and the Army of Northern Virginia commenced the first invasion of the North on September 3, 1862, when thirty-five thousand bedraggled Confederates began splashing across the Potomac River at White's Ford northeast of Leesburg, Virginia. When the army arrived unchallenged at Frederick, Maryland, twenty miles north of the Potomac, Lee halted the advance to rest his troops and to monitor Northern reaction to his incursion into Union territory.

While at Frederick, Lee became particularly concerned about the fourteen thousand Federals who remained south of his army at Harpers Ferry and Martinsburg, blocking access to vital communication and supply lines into the Shenandoah Valley. To remove this threat from his rear, Lee on September 9 issued Special Order 191, a bold and complicated strategic

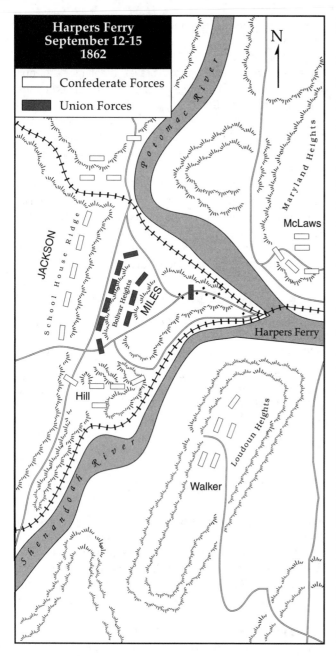

**Harpers Ferry
September 12-15
1862**

☐ Confederate Forces
■ Union Forces

N

Potomac River

Maryland Heights

McLaws

JACKSON

School House Ridge

Bolivar Heights

MILES

Harpers Ferry

Hill

Shenandoah River

Loudoun Heights

Walker

move designed to eradicate the Union garrisons in the lower valley.

Special Order 191 divided the army into four parts. Three columns, comprising six divisions and totaling twenty-three thousand men, would march upon Harpers Ferry from three directions, seize the three mountains surrounding the town, and hence trap the Federals between the hills. Lee and the remainder of the army, meanwhile, would await reunion of the scattered Confederates at Boonsboro, Maryland, twenty miles north of the Ferry. Lee selected Maj. Gen. Thomas J. ("Stonewall") Jackson to direct the Harpers Ferry mission, and he allowed only three days for its completion.

Although the division of his army in enemy territory posed a hazard, Lee considered the risk minimal. His primary opponent, Maj. Gen. George B. McClellan and the Army of the Potomac, had moved cautiously and slowly toward Rockville, Maryland; but Lee considered this a defensive posturing for the protection of Washington and Baltimore, not an aggressive march toward the Confederates operating around Harpers Ferry. If and when McClellan appeared on the horizon, Lee intended to have his army reunited on a battleground of his choosing.

On Wednesday morning, September 10, implementation of Special Order 191 commenced. Maj. Gen. John G. Walker and his division of two thousand men waved farewell to Maryland and recrossed the Potomac into Loudoun County, Virginia, where eyes turned northwest toward their target— Loudoun Heights—a steep bluff overlooking Harpers Ferry from the south bank of the Shenandoah River. Maj. Gen. Lafayette McLaws and the seven thousand soldiers comprising his division, along with Richard H. Anderson's division, marched southwest from Frederick toward Maryland Heights, the high ridge dominating Harpers Ferry from north of the Potomac. Stonewall Jackson, with fourteen thousand men from his own division and the divisions of Richard S. Ewell and A. P. Hill, pushed west from Frederick. Jackson marched through Middletown and Boonsboro to Williamsport, where he crossed the Potomac and promptly frightened the Union garrison at Martinsburg into a hasty retreat south toward Harpers Ferry. From all directions of the compass, Confederates were tramping across the countryside in a three-pronged pincer movement directed at Harpers Ferry.

The Federals knew they were coming. Col. Dixon S. Miles, commander of the Harpers Ferry garrison, had received scout reports and telegraph messages informing him of the danger. Consequently, at the outset of the invasion, Miles had deployed his forces in anticipation of a Confederate attack. But Miles had badly miscalculated. The fifty-eight-year-old West Point graduate believed an infantry attack against Bolivar Heights—a low-lying ridge one mile west of Harpers Ferry—would be the main Confederate target. Miles thus placed the bulk of his garrison, or nearly eight thousand men, upon Bolivar Heights. This number increased to ten thousand when the Martinsburg garrison arrived on September 12. Another poor judgment by the Harpers Ferry commander involved enemy artillery. Miles did not believe the Confederates could drag long-range cannon over a thousand vertical feet to the crests of Maryland and Loudoun Heights. Hence, the Union commander defended Maryland Heights with only two thousand men and placed no Federal soldiers on Loudoun Heights. Even if Maryland and Loudoun Heights fell to the Southern infantry, Miles considered these positions relatively harmless since Confederate small-arms fire from the ridge tops would be too far removed and isolated to cause damage to his garrison.

Miles's miscalculations proved fortunate for the Confederates, who were experiencing their own problems. River crossings and mountain gaps had slowed the Confederate march toward Harpers Ferry and had further debilitated infantrymen already suffering from lack of shoes and a paucity of food. In addition, Jackson's circuitous and fatiguing march through western Maryland and the lower valley encompassed fifty-one miles in seventy-two hours. Further complicating the situation were time constraints. Special Order 191 stipulated that the Harpers Ferry mission be completed by September 12, but the twelfth arrived and passed without any Confederates reaching their targets. Because the Southerners had fallen behind schedule, McClellan's accidental discovery of Special Order 191 on September 13 further aggravated Lee's problems as the Federal commander boasted he had "all the plans of the Rebels" and would "catch them in their own trap."

Finally, on September 13, Confederates began taking their Harpers Ferry objectives. Walker occupied Loudoun Heights without firing a shot. Jackson's fourteen thousand men blocked escape from the west by settling upon School House Ridge, a linear rise paralleling the main Federal position on Bolivar Heights. The brigades of Joseph B. Kershaw and William Barksdale, both of McLaws's command, waged a six-hour battle on the crest of Maryland Heights before the Federals finally withdrew. By dusk on the thirteenth, Confederates completely encircled Harpers Ferry, and their artillerymen began clearing roads and hauling artillery to the crests of Maryland and Loudoun Heights.

Union commander Miles, recognizing his predicament, desperately sent couriers searching for McClellan and assistance. McClellan responded on September 14 by attacking three gaps in South Mountain to "cut the enemy in two and beat him in detail." Confederate resistance stalled the Union advance, however, and provided Jackson with one additional day to conquer the Harpers Ferry position.

Confederate cannoneers began bombarding Miles's garrison at 2:00 P.M. on Sunday the fourteenth. Although the hail of shell demoralized the Federals, most found refuge in deep ravines, and few were injured by the ironstorm. To ensure a quick end to the siege, Jackson, during the night of the fourteenth, transferred fifteen guns to a plateau on Loudoun Heights to enfilade the ravines sheltering the Federals. Stonewall also ordered Hill's three thousand men to flank the Union left on Bolivar Heights by attaining a position on the Chambers Farm. With his garrison now outflanked and outgunned, Colonel Miles surrendered shortly after 8:00 A.M. on September 15.

The fruits of victory for Jackson included seventy-three pieces of artillery, thirteen thousand small arms, two hundred wagons, and 12,500 prisoners—the largest capitulation of U.S. troops during the Civil War. Jackson's loss included 39 killed and 247 wounded. The Confederate victory at Harpers

Ferry temporarily halted General Lee's retreat from Maryland and allowed him to stand at Sharpsburg, where Jackson's forces reunited with the army on September 16 and 17.

BIBLIOGRAPHY

Frye, Dennis E. "Drama between the Rivers: Harpers Ferry in the 1862 Maryland Campaign." *Antietam: Essays on the 1862 Maryland Campaign.* Edited by Gary W. Gallagher. Kent, Ohio, 1989.

Frye, Dennis E. "Stonewall Attacks: The Siege and Capture of Harpers Ferry." *Blue and Gray Magazine* 5, no. 1 (1987): 7–27, 47–63.

U.S. War Department. *War of the Rebellion: A Compilation of the Official Records of the Union and Confederate Armies.* Washington, D.C., 1880–1901. Ser. 1, vol. 19, pts. 1–2.

Walker, John G. "Jackson's Capture of Harpers Ferry." In *Battles and Leaders of the Civil War.* Edited by Robert U. Johnson, and C. C. Buel. Vol. 2. New York, 1888. Reprint, Secaucus, N.J., 1982.

White, Julius. "The Capitulation of Harpers Ferry." In *Battles and Leaders of the Civil War.* Edited by Robert U. Johnson, and C. C. Buel. Vol. 2. New York, 1888. Reprint, Secaucus, N.J., 1982.

DENNIS E. FRYE

HARRIS, ISHAM G.

HARRIS, ISHAM G. (1818–1897), governor of Tennessee and U.S. senator. Harris ranks as one of the most significant figures in nineteenth-century Tennessee politics. He held public office for over five decades and played an influential role in shaping his state's history. Born on a farm in Franklin County, Tennessee, in 1818, Harris received a limited formal education. After teaching himself the law, he moved to Paris, Tennessee, opened a legal practice, and joined his brothers in a lucrative mercantile business. His marriage into a prominent planter family enhanced his standing in the community.

With the help of his father-in-law, Harris plunged into the political arena, working actively on behalf of Democratic candidates on all levels. A skilled orator and effective proponent of party issues, he easily won election to the state senate in 1847, using the issue of slavery to arouse voter support. Throughout his antebellum political career, Harris addressed other important issues such as banking, tariffs, and internal improvements, but defending slavery always was an integral part of his message.

Once in the Tennessee General Assembly, the senator lost no time in transferring the politics of slavery from the campaign trail to the legislative halls. A year later, Harris skillfully used the preservation of the peculiar institution and condemnation of northern abolitionists to win an overwhelming election to the U.S. Congress. The congressman's two-term record was not particularly distinguished, but without fail

Harris sided with the South in every debate and roll call. Gerrymandered out of office by a Whig-controlled legislature in 1851, Harris stayed away from politics for four years. He moved his growing family to Memphis and established himself as a leading attorney in the local bar. In 1855, Governor Andrew Johnson appointed him associate justice of the Tennessee Supreme Court.

After a brief stint on the bench, Harris reentered politics and easily won election for governor over a weak Whig opponent. Assuming office at a time of economic distress, he proposed legislation to reform state banking and restructure state currency. These measures, however, met with little success. Despite limited achievements in his first term, Harris was renominated and elected in a landslide victory for another term in 1859.

With the United States on the verge of disunion, Harris's second term proved far more eventful than his first. Early in the secession crisis, the Tennessee governor asserted his jealous regard for Southern state rights. During the 1860

> **With the United States on the verge of disunion, Harris's second term proved far more eventful than his first.**

presidential election, Harris campaigned tirelessly for Southern Democrat candidate John C. Breckinridge, insisting that voting for anyone else was a vote against Tennessee and the South. With the election of Abraham Lincoln and the subsequent secession of the lower Southern states, Harris began to openly question his state's future in the Union.

In January 1861, Harris called a special session of the General Assembly and recommended that the legislature submit a referendum to the people to vote for or against a secession convention. Although the convention was voted down overwhelmingly in February, the governor continued to advocate secession. After the firing on Fort Sumter, Harris issued an electrifying rejection of Lincoln's call for volunteers, proclaiming that "Tennessee will not furnish a Single Man for the purpose of Coercion but 50,000 if necessary for the defense of our rights and those of our southern brothers."

The governor then convened a special session of the General Assembly and rammed through ordinances declaring Tennessee independent and joining the state with the Confederacy. Harris had the ordinances submitted to the people in another statewide referendum on June 8. This time, with the exception of large numbers of dissenters in eastern Tennessee, the citizenry voted overwhelmingly to support secession.

Well in advance of the official vote, Harris committed his state to the Confederate cause. On May 1 (more than a month before the referendum) he appointed commissioners who signed an agreement with the Confederate government establishing a military league between Tennessee and the Confederate States and providing that Tennessee would immediately be under the "direction of the president of the Confederate States." He began raising and arming troops and constructing defenses to overcome the state's vulnerable geographic situation. Within a matter of weeks, the governor mobilized over 100,000 men and gradually turned them over to the Confederacy. The state army that Harris built eventually became the nucleus of the western Army of Tennessee. Internal divisions within the state continued to occupy the governor's time. At first he dealt leniently with the eastern Tennessee Unionists, but when his efforts met with little success, he clamped down sternly by arresting leaders and stationing more troops in the region.

By all measures, Harris performed brilliantly in overseeing the organization, equipping, and training of a large army under adverse conditions. Nevertheless, he made a fatal mistake in organizing the state's defensive lines. One of his earliest strategic moves was to commit state forces to the defense of the Mississippi River, while virtually ignoring the Tennessee and Cumberland rivers. Certain that Kentucky would remain totally neutral throughout the conflict, Harris argued that the only threat of invasion existed in the far west. Early in 1862, his short-sighted strategy had disastrous results. With the fall of Forts Henry and Donelson to a Union army under Ulysses S. Grant, Nashville was left wide open to capture. Harris ordered the evacuation of state government to Memphis.

For all practical purposes, Harris's governorship ended with the fall of Nashville. A handful of legislators who had followed him to Memphis drafted meaningless bills, but their efforts were futile. When Memphis surrendered to enemy forces in June, the governor once again fled and volunteered his services as an aide to the Confederate military. He became a member of the staffs of Albert Sidney Johnston, Braxton Bragg, Joseph E. Johnston, and John Bell Hood, serving in virtually every campaign of the Army of Tennessee until the end of the war. In late 1864, he was seriously considered for command of a cavalry brigade, but his refusal to relinquish his title as governor barred him by law from accepting the opportunity.

At war's end, Harris became a fugitive from justice. Pushed by Governor William G. Brownlow, the eastern-Tennessee-controlled General Assembly declared Harris guilty of treason and issued an award for his arrest. Two years later, however, the former governor was able to return to Memphis from exile in Mexico and England. He resumed the practice of law for several years, but the call of politics returned him to public office when he was elected to the U.S. Senate in 1877. Harris remained well entrenched in the Senate for twenty years, holding membership in several key committees. He consistently expressed the views of the Tennessee Bourbon Democrats, championing agrarian demands for paper money, free silver, bank reform, and tariff reduction. Along with the majority of Southern Democrats, he regularly supported measures restricting the rights and suffrage of African Americans. He died in Washington in June 1897 and was buried with full Confederate military honors in Memphis.

BIBLIOGRAPHY

Connelly, Thomas L. *Army of the Heartland: The Army of Tennessee, 1861–1862.* Baton Rouge, La., 1967.
Horn, Stanley F. "Isham G. Harris in the Pre-War Years." *Tennessee Historical Quarterly* 19 (1960): 195–207.
Watters, George W. "Isham G. Harris, Civil War Governor and Senator from Tennessee, 1818–1897." Ph.D. diss., Florida State University, 1977.

CHARLES F. BRYAN, JR.

HARRIS, WILEY POPE

HARRIS, WILEY POPE (1818–1891), congressman from Mississippi. Harris, unlike most of his influential contemporaries, was a native Mississippian who could trace his lineage to Gen. Wade Hampton and George Washington. His father, once a wealthy Georgian, lost his property and died when Harris was only three years old. The boy was adopted by his uncle, for whom he was named. He attended the University of Virginia for two years and continued his study of law at Lexington, Kentucky. He practiced law in Mississippi from 1840 until 1847, when he was appointed circuit judge; subsequently he was elected to that same position and served until 1850.

In 1851 Harris was a delegate to a state convention called during the secession crisis of 1849–1851. The secession controversy had split Mississippi politicians into two camps— those favoring compromise and those like Jefferson Davis who wanted to protect slavery at any cost. Harris found himself caught in the controversy. At the convention, the majority advocated compromise, seeking to avoid any disruption of relations with the U.S. government. But Harris was a member of the minority who, though preferring to avoid secession, nevertheless declared it to be a "rightful remedy" if Southern demands were ignored and Northern policy was "pressed to a point deemed dangerous to the independence, and safety of the institutions of the States." Harris continued to believe that the Compromise of 1850 had produced only a "temporary repose" and, worse, had contributed to Northerners believing they could successfully "urge their policy to its extreme possibilities in the territories."

Harris served in the U.S. Congress from 1853 to 1855. During his tenure, he frequently warned of the growing power of the Federal government and of the diminishing strength of the states. He pointed out that the central government with an army, a navy, and vast revenues at its command was in a dominant position. Federal officials felt "more exalted" than state officials, and the shift in the balance of power was becoming dangerous.

In January 1861 Harris was a delegate to the constitutional convention that adopted the ordinance of secession. Reuben Davis, in his description of the convention, described Harris as "one of the most extraordinary men this State has ever produced." Davis wrote that Harris's name suggested to all Mississippians "the image of a tall, slender figure, crowned by a most intellectual head. Nature seems to have endowed him with all the qualities requisite in a great lawyer and a magnificent orator."

Looking back in later life to the troubled period of 1861, Harris in his unpublished autobiography described the thinking of Mississippi's leaders about the wisdom and justice of secession. Mississippians were divided between cooperation and secession. Harris clearly fit in the latter category, but his position was more thoughtful than that of the fire-eaters. In favoring secession, he felt that cooperationists were being indecisive, merely dragging out the inevitable with meetings and debate. He was certain that if Mississippi seceded, other states would follow, and he predicted two scenarios: one, that the border states would secede, thus preventing war "because the conquest of the slave States would be impossible," or two, the border states would not secede and instead would be "instruments of a settlement." Therefore, Harris expected no war. He also underestimated the North's determination and overestimated its dependence on cotton and commerce with the South. He believed the Northern people would "soon tire of a war which would entail such costly sacrifices." Harris admitted overlooking many considerations because of his "absorbing anxiety" over the consequences of secession.

Harris was chosen by unanimous vote on the first ballot to attend the Provisional Congress in Montgomery in 1861. While there, he scorned delay and proposed that the members dismiss preliminaries and move to a general election. He served on several committees, including Judiciary, Military Affairs, and Public Lands. One of his proposals was to impose a tax on slaves, which reflected his lack of sympathy with slaveholders; he himself had none. In his autobiography he commented that slave owners were unpopular as a class and "deserved to be unpopular." He wrote, "The ostentation at home and abroad drew upon them actual antipathy everywhere," adding that they "were generally ignorant, bigoted and intolerant of contradiction."

After his hard work at the Provisional Congress, it is surprising that he did not run for a seat in the regular Congress.

Instead, he returned to the practice of law where he could exercise his legal expertise.

As he saw the North gain the advantage in the war, Harris began to hope for a peaceful settlement, but he realized "there could be no peace without the humiliation of the South." He wrote letters promoting the idea of some kind of "adjustment," but no one was interested. In the end he realized the South "had made a sad mistake."

During Reconstruction Harris was dismayed by the alienation and depression suffered by the state, which had neither a national nor a state government it could respect. "It is a dreary life we lead here," he wrote, "with a national government ever suspicious and frowning, imperious and hostile, and a home government feeble, furtive, false, and fraudulent." And he sought amelioration: "We are in a new world. . . . It is better that we hang a millstone about our necks than cling to these old issues."

BIBLIOGRAPHY

Alexander, Thomas B., and Richard E. Beringer. *The Anatomy of the Confederate Congress: A Study of the Influences of Member Characteristics on Legislative Voting Behavior, 1861–1865.* Nashville, Tenn., 1972.
Warner, Ezra J., and W. Buck Yearns. *Biographical Register of the Confederate Congress.* Baton Rouge, La., 1975.

RAY SKATES

HARRISON, HENRY THOMAS

HARRISON, HENRY THOMAS (1832–?), scout and spy. A native of Tennessee, Harrison entered Confederate service in early 1861 as a civilian scout in northern Virginia and became a scout in Mississippi in 1862. He signed reports there as "H. T. Harrison, Secret Agent." One picture shows him in the uniform of a second lieutenant, holding a revolver and pointing to a simple numerical cipher printed on cardboard.

Called to Richmond in January 1863, he reported to Secretary of War James A. Seddon and was assigned to Gen. James Longstreet. While on temporary duty with Gen. D. H. Hill in North Carolina, Harrison was captured near New Bern by a Union patrol on March 21, 1863. He was released on April 13 when his complex cover story held up. No longer able to spy in North Carolina, he was sent back to Longstreet.

On June 2, 1863, Col. Moxley Sorrel of Longstreet's staff furnished Harrison with two hundred dollars in U.S. currency and ordered him to Washington to track Union troops as they set out to counter Robert E. Lee's invasion of Maryland and Pennsylvania. Harrison reached Longstreet near Chambersburg, Pennsylvania, on the night of June 28. As Longstreet wrote later, Harrison brought "information more accurate than a force of cavalry could have secured." This is generally credited with changing the disposition of Lee's army before the Battle of Gettysburg. During the last year of the war, Harrison was in New York City engaged in undisclosed clandestine activities.

In a letter from Baltimore, dated April 7, 1866, Harrison told his wife, Laura: "I write on the eve of a journey, and will not see you for some time, perhaps never." Later she learned that he was in the gold fields of Montana Territory. The last word of him there came in the spring of 1867. Thinking her husband dead, Laura remarried. After an absence of over thirty-four years, Harrison unexpectedly turned up on November 20, 1900, seeking to see his two daughters. Turned away, he went to Cincinnati. From there he wrote to Laura's brother in March 1901 that he was going to San Francisco. Then Harrison disappeared for good.

BIBLIOGRAPHY

Hall, James O. "The Spy Harrison." *Civil War Times Illustrated* 24, no. 10 (February 1986): 19–25.
Longstreet, James. *From Manassas to Appomattox.* Philadelphia, 1896. Reprint, Millwood, N.Y., 1985.
Longstreet, James. "Lee's Invasion of Pennsylvania." In *Battles and Leaders of the Civil War.* Vol. 3. Edited by Robert U. Johnson and C. C. Buell. New York, 1888. Reprint, Secaucus, N.J., 1982.
Sorrel, G. Moxley. *Recollections of a Confederate Staff Officer.* Edited by Bell Irvin Wiley. Jackson, Tenn., 1958.

JAMES O. HALL

HART, NANCY

HART, NANCY (fl. 1862), Confederate guide and spy. Whether Nancy Hart actually lived is unknown; the story of her exploits may well be a legend. In any event, she is said to have lived in obscurity in the mountain district of West Virginia. She was a staunch supporter of the Confederacy and with the outbreak of the war volunteered her services to Thomas J. ("Stonewall") Jackson as a guide to lead his men along hidden mountain trails to surprise Federal garrisons. She proved so adept a guide that the Federals offered a reward for her capture.

In July 1862 Hart was captured at Summerville, West Virginia, by Companies A and F of the Ninth Virginia Volunteer Infantry commanded by Lt. Col. William C. Starr. At the time an itinerant photographer was at Summerville and persuaded Starr to allow him to photograph Hart. As the dark-haired young woman was positioned before the camera, her guards placed a military hat on her head. Somehow Hart managed to grab a guard's musket and kill him. Then she rushed outside, mounted Starr's horse, and galloped away to safety.

At 4:00 A.M. on July 25, Hart returned to Summerville along with two hundred Confederate cavalry under Maj. R. A. Bailey. The Southerners surprised Starr's men, seized the town, and captured Starr and several other members of his command. After burning two houses and a commissary storehouse and destroying two wagons, Hart and the Confederates withdrew taking with them several horses and mules as well as captured arms and ammunition.

BIBLIOGRAPHY

Miller, Francis T., ed. *The Photographic History of the Civil War*. 10 vols. New York, 1911.
U.S. War Department. *The War of the Rebellion: A Compilation of the Official Records of the Union and Confederate Armies*. Washington, D.C., 1880–1901. Ser. 1, vol. 12, pt. 2.

KENNY A. FRANKS

HAWES, RICHARD

HAWES, RICHARD (1797–1877), major and Confederate governor of Kentucky. Born in Caroline County, Virginia, Hawes moved to Kentucky with his parents in 1810. A graduate of Transylvania University, he practiced law and engaged in hemp manufacturing. He served as a Whig in both the legislature and Congress. Hawes became a Democrat in the 1850s and supported John C. Breckinridge for president in 1860. He took a leading role during the secession crisis, serving as a member of the bipartisan legislative committee that recommended neutrality for the state. When that failed Hawes went with the Confederacy. Commissioned a major, he served briefly with Humphrey Marshall's command in eastern Kentucky.

When Provisional Governor George W. Johnson died on April 9, 1862, from wounds received at Shiloh, Hawes succeeded him. He had to lead a government-in-exile, however, for the Union controlled Kentucky. The situation changed when Confederate Gen. Braxton Bragg invaded the state in late August. After a quick trip to Richmond to secure assurances of support there, Hawes followed Bragg. In a ceremony held in the House chamber at Frankfort on October 4, he was formally installed as governor, but that afternoon Union artillery began shelling the town, and Hawes and Bragg abandoned the capital in haste. Hawes attempted to maintain a shadow government thereafter, sometimes in Richmond, more often with Kentucky troops in the Army of Tennessee,

but he admitted in 1863 that he was "almost powerless." At war's end, he returned to Paris, Kentucky, and resumed his law practice. Elected to local judgeships, he continued on the bench until his death.

BIBLIOGRAPHY

Clift, G. Glenn. *Governors of Kentucky*. Cynthiana, Ky., 1942.
Connelly, Thomas L. *Autumn of Glory: The Army of Tennessee, 1862–1865*. Baton Rouge, La., 1971.
Harrison, Lowell H. "Kentucky." In *The Confederate Governors*. Edited by W. Buck Yearns. Athens, Ga., 1985.

WILLIAM E. PARRISH

HAYS, HARRY THOMPSON

HAYS, HARRY THOMPSON (1820–1876), brigadier general. Born on April 14, 1820, in Wilson County, Tennessee, Hays attended St. Mary's College in Baltimore. He then practiced law in New Orleans and became active in the Whig party. He fought with the Fifth Louisiana in the Mexican War.

When the Civil War began, Hays became a colonel of the Seventh Louisiana Infantry and fought at First Manassas and in Stonewall Jackson's 1862 Shenandoah Valley campaign with Richard Taylor's brigade. Hays was severely wounded at Port Republic but returned to duty at Sharpsburg. He had been commissioned a brigadier general on July 25, 1862, and succeeded Taylor as commander of the Louisiana brigade. Hays fought at Fredericksburg, Chancellorsville, and Gettysburg, but was seriously wounded again at Spotsylvania. After he recovered, Hays was transferred to the Trans-Mississippi Department in July 1864 where he searched for absentees from the Army of Northern Virginia until Robert E. Lee's surrender. No longer needed for this duty, he replaced William Robertson Boggs in command of the District of Louisiana. On May 10, 1865, E. Kirby Smith promoted Hays to major general, although this was not approved by Richmond.

After the war, Hays returned to New Orleans where he served as sheriff of Orleans Parish until Philip Sheridan removed him from the office in 1866. He later practiced law with Gen. Daniel Weisiger Adams. Hays died on August 21, 1876, and is buried in Washington Avenue Cemetery, New Orleans.

BIBLIOGRAPHY

Jones, Terry L. *Lee's Tigers: The Louisiana Infantry in the Army of Northern Virginia*. Baton Rouge, La., 1987.

Seymour, W. J. *The Civil War Memoirs of Captain William J. Seymour.* Baton Rouge, La., 1991.

ANNE J. BAILEY

HEALTH AND MEDICINE

[*For further discussion of medicine in the Confederacy, see* Hospitals; Nursing. *For discussion of the organization of medical services in the Confederate army, see* Medical Department.]

Sickness and Disease

The spectrum of sickness and disease among military personnel was similar to that in the general population, both North and South. Disease prevention was hampered by the era's lack of understanding of the basis of disease (germ theory was unknown) and consequent ignorance of the importance of hygiene and antisepsis. Many symptoms, such as fever, diarrhea, and dysentery, were regarded as diseases and treated as such.

The civilian population in the South was subject to a variety of medical problems, some of which were unique to the region. Puerperal fever was often a complication following childbirth; it is now known to be caused by bacteria, but ignorance led to the death of new mothers. Malaria and yellow fever, both transmitted by mosquitoes, were common in much of the coastal south. Tuberculosis was found in cities where crowding existed but was more of a problem in the urban North. Lack of previous exposure would be fatal to soldiers crowded in camps. Common childhood diseases were not widespread in the largely rural population, and the absence of immunity led to serious problems for new recruits.

The military population, beset by constant fatigue, exposure, poor nutrition, inadequate clothing, lack of shelter, and deficient camp hygiene, was especially vulnerable to illness. A healthy fighting force required, above all, the exclusion of those who were unfit for the rigors of military life. But for a volunteer army motivated by patriotic fervor, there was great pressure to accept many who were unsuitable, and the difficulty of fielding sufficient numbers as the war continued increased such pressure.

In the primarily rural South, many men had not been exposed to the usual childhood diseases. Thus waves of measles with its complications of respiratory infections swept through the susceptible troops in their crowded camps of instruction. These measles epidemics were greatest early in the war. Many rural recruits also had not been immunized against smallpox. Although army medical authorities were

familiar with vaccination and practiced it at various times and locations, this disease took a large toll.

Complicating the medical picture was the fact that many new recruits did not know the basic rules of hygiene. Further, ignorance of proper food preparation—evidenced by burned bread and greasy fried food—resulted in soldiers' suffering chronic indigestion, diarrhea, and abdominal pains.

A lack of proper clothing and shoes, especially in inclement weather, plagued the Confederacy throughout the war, as did its inability to transport sufficient nutritious food. Frequently, preserved meat was unfit to eat, vegetables were absent, and fresh beef a rarity. Outbreaks of scurvy occurred. Troops often had to drink impure water, teeming with pathogens, with disastrous results.

The most debilitating medical problems of Confederate soldiers were the intestinal disorders diarrhea (abnormally liquid and frequent bowel movements) and dysentery (loose, bloody bowel movements). These were caused by a variety of then unknown bacteria and viruses as well as inadequate and poorly cooked food. Improper placement of latrines with subsequent contamination of drinking water, coupled with a reluctance to use latrines, exacerbated the problem. Further, the general debility caused by these illnesses weakened many men and made them more susceptible to other illnesses. Given their myriad causes, diarrhea and dysentery were also extremely difficult to cure. Their incidence progressively increased during the war. They were responsible for more deaths than gunshot wounds, and more soldiers were discharged from the army because of them than because of battlefield injuries. An estimated 94,000 Confederates died from wounds; some 164,000 are believed to have died of disease.

Diarrhea and dysentery were treated with a variety of remedies, which shared the common effect of astringency in the hope of halting the watery intestinal discharge. Such treatment was almost entirely ineffective. A few physicians recognized that a well-prepared, balanced diet was helpful in some cases, but this was tried only in a few rear-echelon general hospitals.

Typhoid fever (a specific, bacterially caused disease), typhus fever (a group of diseases caused by the tick-borne *Rickettsia*), and "common continued fevers" (as they were called) were other major medical problems. Typhoid fever, which included gastrointestinal manifestations, killed at least a quarter of its victims. It was primarily a disease of new soldiers and was rarely seen in veteran armies because protective immunity developed. Typhus had among its effects aches and fevers. "Common continued fevers" were an ill-defined group of illnesses with some of the manifestations of typhoid.

Another transmissible disease, malaria, was endemic in the mid-nineteenth-century South. Now known to be caused by a mosquito-borne protozoan, the disease was then believed to be caused by "miasmas" arising from stagnant water. In the Southern coastal states during the warm months, there was an average of two reported cases of malaria for each soldier enrolled, indicating numerous recurrences of this debilitating illness. Quinine had been isolated from cinchona bark in 1822 and was known to be effective in the treatment of malaria. But adequate supplies of quinine were halted by the Federal blockade in late 1862. Various local remedies—such as turpentine and extracts of dogwood and willow bark—were reportedly partly effective.

Pneumonia, now known to be caused by a variety of bacterial and viral organisms, was considered a single disease and was treated variously by diet, whiskey, opium, and quinine when available. Respiratory diseases unexplainably were more prevalent among Confederate than Union soldiers; all other diseases were present in proportionate numbers in both armies. Pulmonary tuberculosis, rheumatism, and venereal diseases were among the other debilitating illnesses of which there was little understanding; thus, treatment for them was ineffective.

Confederate medical authorities labored heroically to deal with the medical problems of those under their care. But like their counterparts in the North, they were hindered by their lack of understanding of the cause of the diseases they were called upon to treat. Unlike their Union counterparts, they were also hampered by limited supplies of the medications they needed and the ever-tightening Federal blockade against imports.

BIBLIOGRAPHY

Adams, George W. *Doctors in Blue: The Medical History of the Union Army in the Civil War.* New York, 1952.

Cunningham, Horace H. *Doctors in Gray: The Confederate Medical Service.* Baton Rouge, La., 1958.

Medical and Surgical History of the War of Rebellion. 6 vols. Washington, D.C., 1875–1888. Reprinted as *The Medical and Surgical History of the Civil War.* Edited by James I. Robertson, Jr. 14 vols. Wilmington, N.C., 1990–1991.

Shryock, Richard H. "A Medical Perspective on the Civil War." In *Medicine in America: Historical Essays.* Baltimore, 1966.

Steiner, Paul E. *Disease in the Civil War.* Springfield, Ill., 1968.

Wiley, Bell I. *The Life of Johnny Reb.* Baton Rouge, La., 1970.

HERBERT M. SCHILLER

Battle Injuries

Traumatic battle injuries and their treatment fall into the realm of surgical disease. Because few physicians in the Confederate army had any military surgery experience, they found Dr. J. Julian Chisolm's *A Manual of Military Surgery for the Use of Surgeons in the Confederate States Army* invaluable. Confederate Surgeon General Samuel Preston Moore continually ordered his surgeons to submit records of the outcome of their treatments and procedures, for it was only through review of such reports that advances in treatment could be maintained. But like their Union counterparts, Confederate surgeons disliked record keeping and understandably postponed the onerous task until they had treated the wounded. During active campaigning, intensive medical care might be required for days, and maintenance of accurate records was not possible. This, along with the fact that almost all the Confederate Medical Department's records were burned in Richmond in April 1865, has limited the study of Confederate battle injuries and treatment.

> ## Most wounds were caused by the slow-moving lead conical minié ball. . . .

Wartime surgery was chiefly concerned with the repair of mangled bodies and the care of the infections that invariably followed wounds. Ether and chloroform anesthesia had been known since the 1840s; chloroform was much preferred and seems to have been readily available in the South during the war. Surgeons reported few deaths from its administration.

Most wounds were caused by the slow-moving lead conical minié ball, which, when entering the body, dragged fragments of skin and clothing with it and introduced contaminated, potentially infectious material. The soft ball would shatter any bone it struck and be itself distorted in shape. Should the ball continue farther it would produce massive tissue destruction. If it left the body, the gaping exit wound would be markedly disproportionate to the original size of the projectile.

Bullet wounds constituted approximately 93 percent of battlefield injuries; those from artillery projectiles, 6 percent; and those from sabers or bayonets, less than 1 percent. The anatomic distribution of bullet wounds was 71 percent in the extremities, 18 percent in the torso, and 11 percent in the head and neck.

The farther an injury from the trunk, the better the outcome: wounds to the extremities were rarely fatal; seven out of eight soldiers survived such injuries, albeit many with a missing or useless limb. Wounds in other parts of the body were more often fatal. Abdominal wounds had an overall fatality rate of 87 percent, and perforating injuries to the small intestine were invariably fatal. Wounds involving the colon showed up to 40 percent fatality, and those entering the peritoneal cavity but not damaging any abdominal organs were 25 percent fatal. Only 20 percent survived fracture of the pelvis. Penetrating thoracic wounds showed an overall fatality rate of 60 percent. Examination of bodies of men killed in action on battlefields has revealed that 82 percent of the mortal wounds were in the head, neck, or chest. Twelve percent of the fatalities resulted from abdominal injuries, and these were primarily a result of liver or aortic laceration with subsequent hemorrhage. Only 5 percent of the fatalities resulted from wounds of the extremities, and these too were the result of hemorrhage.

Hemorrhage among those who survived their initial wound and were brought to a field hospital was not a major problem. Those with major hemorrhage had already died on the field. Patients with hemorrhage were treated with tourniquets or compresses, although the former were frowned upon. Actually, of bleeding problems following traumatic wounds, only 10 percent occurred in the first twenty-four

> **Controversy between preserving limbs or amputating them because of wound damage continued throughout the war.**

hours. During the "intermediary" period, from the first twenty-four hours until the onset of the inevitable wound infection, the incidence of bleeding complications would begin to increase. Hemorrhage would peak at the time of the "separation of the slough," when an area of infection and dead tissue would begin to separate from the underlying living tissue. During this dangerous time arteries might reopen and bleeding resume when the dead tissue came away.

Surgical cases in which arteries had been tied also were subject to hemorrhage and suppuration. The cause of the hemorrhage was the removal of the suture around the vessel. In major surgery and amputations, the major arteries were tied off. Unsterile silk, linen, or cotton thread was used, and the ligature was left hanging out of the wound. Soaked with serum and blood, it was an excellent wick by which bacteria found their way into the swollen wound. During his daily rounds the surgeon would pull on the ligature to see if the artery had become shriveled and if the dead blood vessel would pull free; this usually meant that a firm blood clot had formed and the vessel had become sealed. Unfortunately, if such a clot had not formed, the end of the artery would pull free and hemorrhage would begin.

Controversy between preserving limbs or amputating them because of wound damage continued throughout the war. If the limb was badly damaged or had a compound fracture (one in which the bone protrudes through the skin) with splintering, immediate amputation was indicated. The risk of conservative treatment in such cases, with the intervening probing for the bullet and fragments of bone, was development of one of the "surgical fevers" and at best a subsequently useless limb. Local excision of bone and soft tissue damage was more dangerous than amputation.

Debate over the proper amputation technique—whether or not to leave a flap of skin to cover the raw stump—continued throughout the war. The former involved tying the ends of

arteries with the attendant risks. The latter was quicker but required removal of more of the limb. In cases of mass casualties after a battle, speed was critical, for the removal of damaged tissue, before it had time to become infected and gangrenous, was imperative. Dealing with any associated wound infections several days later seemed less of a problem.

In the 1860s bacteria were not known to cause infection; sterile technique was unknown. Postoperative infections associated with pus formation were seen so often in the healing of wounds, whether from injury or surgical treatment, that they were regarded as part of the healing process. These complications were known as "surgical fevers" and covered a spectrum of postoperative bacterial infections including erysipelas, pyemia, tetanus, osteomyelitis, and hospital gangrene. Hospital gangrene was almost invariably fatal. Its cause is unclear, but it seems to have resulted from a mixed infection by *Clostridium,* the bacteria that causes gas gangrene, and other bacteria associated with abscess formation. Pyemia ("blood poisoning") was invariably fatal and caused by widespread blood-borne infection. Soldiers in otherwise poor health—fatigued, malnourished, crowded, and depressed—were more susceptible to these complications.

Despite the state of medical information in 1860, Confederate surgeons seem to have been generally competent and achieved results equal to their Union counterparts.

BIBLIOGRAPHY

Adams, George W. *Doctors in Blue: The Medical History of the Union Army in the Civil War.* New York, 1952.

Chisolm, J. Julian. *A Manual of Military Surgery for the Use of Surgeons in the Confederate States Army.* 3d ed. Columbia, S.C., 1864. Reprint, Dayton, Ohio, 1983.

Cunningham, Horace H. *Doctors in Gray: The Confederate Medical Service.* Baton Rouge, La., 1958.

Wiley, Bell I. *The Life of Johnny Reb.* Baton Rouge, La., 1970.

HERBERT M. SCHILLER

Medical Treatments

Twentieth-century accounts of medical treatment during the Civil War make it sound like little more than a hodgepodge of folk remedies. Medical therapeutics in mid-nineteenth-century America was largely based on the medical properties of plants and was administered in elixirs, decoctions, ointments, poultices, and compounded powders and pills. There was, however, a scientific basis to much of the therapy, consistent with the state of medical knowledge in that era. Review of texts on therapeutics from the 1840s and 1850s reveals that more than two-thirds of the substances then considered effective were of vegetable origin.

These medicines, and other supplies, were plentiful in Southern cities at the beginning of the war, but they could not be expected to last long. Although supplies captured from the enemy provided an occasional bonanza, this was not a reliable source. Shortly after fighting began, the War Department sent Caleb Huse to Britain to serve as purchasing agent abroad. Although his primary charge was the obtaining of ordnance, part of his budget was for medical supplies. An office of the Medical Department was established at Nassau to coordinate the exchange of cotton and the collection of medical supplies to be brought in by blockade runners. Another source of needed medical supplies was the cotton-starved North. This government-sanctioned trade occurred along the Mississippi River, especially south of Memphis, but was erratic and produced only a little medicine. Individuals sympathetic with the Confederacy occasionally smuggled medicine across the changing borders, but such goods were few in number.

Early in the war the Medical Department established some eight depots under the supervision of physician medical purveyors who bought, stored, and distributed supplies. By war's end, such sites had increased fourfold. Many were located near ports of entry and near the manufacturing centers that arose throughout the Confederacy.

With external supplies unsure at best, it fell to the Confederate Medical Department to develop its own pharmaceutical laboratories. The nine major facilities were located in North and South Carolina, Georgia, Alabama, and Texas. Pharmacists and chemists staffed the facilities. Alcohol was distilled from grain, and white poppies were cultivated for gum opium, necessary for the production of morphine. Locally manufactured chloroform was plentiful. Many of the pharmaceutical facilities had their own botanical farms to supply needed medical plants.

Under the direction of Surgeon General Samuel Preston Moore, Francis P. Porcher, a teacher of materia medica and therapeutics (equivalent to today's pharmacology) in the then-closed medical school in Charleston, began his *Resources of the Southern Fields and Forests, Medical, Economical, and Agricultural,* which discussed the medical properties of over four hundred native plants. The book was referenced to dozens of other books of materia medica, some of them of recent publication. Copies of Porcher's book were sent to medical officers, and extracts were published in local newspapers to encourage the collection of needed plants. Circuit riders from the medical depots collected plants and encouraged citizens to help. By the middle of the war, eight tons of herbal medicines had been prepared and thirty-two tons of roots and leaves awaited processing.

Among the illnesses thought to respond to herbal remedies were acute diarrhea and dysentery, which, depending on their severity, were sometimes treated with cathartics to speed the removal of the offending agent. Chronic disorders of the bowels were treated with products with astringent properties—for example, decoction of root of blackberry, dried bark of dogwood, sweet-scented water lily, ground root of cranesbill, root of marsh rosemary, pomegranate rind, tea of water pepper, syrup of unripe persimmons, tea of black alder bark and berries, decoction of white oak bark, and black oak galls. The problem in treating diarrhea and dysentery this way was that they were only symptoms of a variety of infectious and noninfectious diseases, not diseases themselves. Interestingly, most of the items mentioned by Porcher are included in George B. Wood's authoritative and contemporary *Treatise on Therapeutics and Pharmacology, or Materia Medica.* In short, these remedies were state of the art for their time.

Malaria was a disease whose true cause was unknown but that could be effectively treated with quinine, isolated from the bark of the cinchona tree. In the absence of quinine, the Medical Department recommended a mixture of dogwood, poplar, and willow bark mixed with whiskey. The use of these tree barks, separately or together, was recognized by Wood in his text. Scurvy was yet another disease whose cause, although not completely known, was felt to be related to a diet deficient in fresh fruit and meat. Confederate medical authorities recognized that sorrel eaten as a salad or in soup was a cure or preventive of scurvy. Other diseases or groups of diseases of uncertain cause were frequently grouped according to presenting signs and patient symptoms. Pneumonias, urethral discharges resulting from venereal diseases, pelvic pain, and the urinary burning of bladder infections were treated as if they were diseases themselves. Civilians also suffered from problems in addition to those experienced by the men in uniformed service. Because adult males were absent from small farms, food production decreased, and the ability of families to earn money to purchase necessities, such as clothing and staples, became increasingly limited. Scarcity of food and increasing costs caused malnutrition in the women, old men, and children left behind. Public assistance by local government was largely unknown, although churches and some communities provided a small amount of relief for a few. The availability of medical care became increasingly limited by the absence of doctors and medicines needed by the military.

A large variety of remedies that experience had shown effective or that relieved certain symptoms of disease were available, and those used by the Confederate physicians differed little from those employed by their Union counterparts. Although these remedies seem curious today, they represented what was felt to be sound medical treatment, based on reports by reputable physicians in Europe and America during the previous fifty years. Some possessed merit; others did not. They did reflect, however, the trial-and-error observations recorded in medical journals and texts of the day. It would not be until the physiological changes that accompany particular diseases were understood that a more rational approach to medical treatment could be instituted.

BIBLIOGRAPHY

Blake, John B. "Women and Medicine in Ante-Bellum America. "*Bulletin of the History of Medicine* 39 (March–April 1965): 99–123.

Cunningham, Horace H. *Doctors in Gray: The Confederate Medical Service.* Baton Rouge, La., 1958.

Medical and Surgical History of the War of Rebellion. 6 vols. Washington, D.C., 1875–1888. Reprinted as *The Medical and Surgical History of the Civil War.* Edited by James I. Robertson, Jr. 14 vols. Wilmington, N.C., 1990–1991.

Porcher, Francis P. *Resources of the Southern Fields and Forests, Medical, Economical, and Agricultural.* Charleston, S.C., 1863. Reprint, New York, 1970.

Wood, George B. *Treatise on Therapeutics and Pharmacology, or Materia Medica.* Philadelphia, 1856.

HERBERT M. SCHILLER

Medical Training

Medical training in the middle third of the nineteenth century varied greatly among the schools. In addition to the few university-affiliated schools, some of which maintained standards of educational excellence, proprietary schools abounded. These latter, run for profit and owned and operated by physicians, offered shortened instruction. The usual course of classroom lectures consisted of theory and practice (medicine), materia medica (pharmacology), chemistry, anatomy, surgery, and obstetrics. The course of instruction at good schools might last one year, while that at proprietary schools was much shorter, in some cases six weeks or less. Rarely was a school affiliated with a hospital; none offered much in the way of practical experience with patients. If clinical experience was obtained it was through apprenticeship to an established physician. State licensing boards did not exist. Most trained physicians were products of the proprietary schools and it was these men who staffed the medical corps. Prior to the war there was little emphasis in the South on surgery and Health and Medicinenone on military medicine or surgery. Most Southerners seeking formal medical education attended schools in the North or abroad in preference to the Southern medical schools located in Charleston, Charlottesville, Augusta, Richmond, Mobile, and Nashville. The curriculum of these six schools was similar to that of the most prominent institutions in the Northeast; the course of instruction lasted about six months. As in the North, many proprietary schools also existed, producing marginal practitioners at best.

During the first months of the war, all the reputable Southern medical schools closed except the Medical College

of Virginia. Located in Richmond, this school quickly adapted to wartime conditions. In addition to attending lectures, the students studied wounds and diseases firsthand in the numerous city hospitals as well as the field hospitals of the Army of Northern Virginia. During the course of the war, the Medical College of Virginia graduated four hundred students. But these new doctors and the existing physicians were hardly sufficient to care for the 600,000 Confederate soldiers mobilized during those years.

To provide some continuing education for military physicians, the Surgeon General's Office oversaw the publication of a medical journal as well as several texts on military surgery. And with the ever-tightening blockade preventing the importation of medicines, the surgeon general encouraged Francis P. Porcher to publish a medical botany in 1863 to provide guidance on the use of native herbs in the treatment of disease.

BIBLIOGRAPHY

Chisolm, J. Julian. *A Manual of Military Surgery for the Use of Surgeons in the Confederate States Army.* 3d ed. Columbia, S.C., 1864. Reprint, Dayton, Ohio, 1983.

The Confederate States Medical and Surgical Journal. 2 vols. Richmond, Va., 1862–1864. Reprint, Metuchen, N.J., 1976.

Cunningham, Horace H. *Doctors in Gray: The Confederate Medical Service.* Baton Rouge, La., 1958.

Porcher, Francis P. *Resources of the Southern Fields and Forests, Medical, Economical, and Agricultural.* Charleston, S.C., 1863. Reprint, New York, 1970.

HERBERT M. SCHILLER

HEISKELL, J. B.

HEISKELL, J. B. (1823–1913), a congressman from Tennessee. The eldest of nine children of the editor and publisher of the *Knoxville Register,* one of the most respected and influential newspapers in the region, Joseph Brown Heiskell graduated from East Tennessee College (1840), read law under Finley Gillespie of Madisonville, and commenced his practice in Monroe County before relocating in Rogersville and marrying a daughter of John A. McKinney, a prominent member of the Rogersville bar. Like his father and uncle before him, Heiskell occupied a seat in the Tennessee legislature (1857–1859), where he chaired the committee that prepared the first legal code for the state.

A staunch Whig, Heiskell opposed secession but joined the rebellion after Abraham Lincoln's call for volunteers and ran on a pro-Confederate ticket for the Provisional Congress. Although he lost the August 1861 election for the First District of Tennessee by an overwhelming margin to Unionist T. A. R. Nelson, he was elected to the First Confederate Congress three months later, after the legislature had redistricted the state and many Unionists stayed away from the polls.

Taking his seat in Richmond on February 18, 1862, the opening day of the first session, Heiskell served continually and rarely missed a vote through the end of the second session in mid-October later that year. A member of the Judiciary and War Tax committees, he introduced as many as twenty-one bills and resolutions. Most had to do with fiscal matters, though one measure sought to facilitate the production of small arms, another called for an investigation of ordnance factories in Richmond, and another would have allowed draft exemptions to persons engaged in the manufacture of iron, lead, and copper, of whom there was a considerable number in upper eastern Tennessee.

During his first two sessions in office, Heiskell proved to be decidedly pro-administration, arguing and voting in favor of two conscription bills and the suspension of the habeas corpus writ. At the same time he firmly believed that it was the

> [Heiskell] advocated the taking of hostages in retaliation for the capture and imprisonment of Southern citizens and other noncombatants. . . .

duty of the Confederate government to remunerate its citizens for losses sustained during the war, and he supported regulating by law the seizure and impressment of private property for the use of the military. Undoubtedly the most intriguing (and controversial) proposal introduced by Heiskell was his resolution of September 10, 1862, in which he advocated the taking of hostages in retaliation for the capture and imprisonment of Southern citizens and other noncombatants—that is, to arrest for the purpose of later exchanging not mere farmers and mechanics but "men prominent in their respective neighborhoods for their adhesion to the anti-slavery, black republican, anti-Christian government in Washington."

In the third and fourth sessions, from January 1863 to February 1864, Heiskell sponsored another twenty bills, distinguishing himself as one of the more active members of the Tennessee delegation, despite obtaining a leave of absence so that he could return home, where he served conspicuously as a voluntary aide-de-camp for Confederate forces in the area. Back in Richmond, Heiskell remained concerned about military affairs in eastern Tennessee, as witnessed by his calls for investigations of the Confederate disaster at Fishing Creek, Kentucky (in which his brother, Carrick W. Heiskell, then a captain of the Nineteenth Tennessee Infantry, had participated), and the operations of Gen. John S. Williams at Blue Springs, Tennessee. Perhaps the most curious measure he brought forward during this period was a January 1864 reso-

lution that instructed the congressional doorkeeper to regulate the heating in the House "so as to preserve a temperature not higher than sixty-two degrees Fahrenheit." On major issues he generally stood by the president, voting in favor of a direct tax, the third Conscription Law, and the abolition of the practice of hiring substitutes for military service. He also assumed a hard-line position on a proposed prisoner of war exchange, approving (though in the minority) Jefferson Davis's refusal to recognize Gen. Benjamin F. Butler as a legitimate Federal exchange agent. Congress's vote on this issue prompted Heiskell's resignation in February 1864, some ten days before Congress adjourned.

Reelected unanimously to the Second Confederate Congress, Heiskell assumed increased responsibilities by serving on as many as five committees. Contrary to what has been written, he continued to play an active role in government, contributing ten additional pieces of legislation during the first session. For example, in May 1864, in the midst of the Wilderness campaign, he was the chief sponsor in the House of a bill authorizing President Davis to suspend the writ of habeas corpus and declare martial law in Richmond. Yet he also differed with Davis by criticizing the inequality of prices paid under impressment laws, complaining bitterly about the performance and abilities of the postmaster general, and, in his last recorded action in Congress, voting with the majority on June 14, 1864, against turning over control of the railroads to the Confederate military.

By the time Congress reconvened in November 1864 for what turned out to be its final session, Heiskell was in the enemy's hands, having been captured some three months earlier while at home. The details of his surrender are sketchy, but according to published reports it appears that he walked to meet the Federals before they entered Rogersville, prompting President Abraham Lincoln to question whether Heiskell "was scared and wanted to save his skin." The object of intense, high-level negotiations for a special prisoner exchange that never materialized, Heiskell remained confined in Camp Chase, Ohio, until the end of hostilities. In the meantime arrangements were made for his salary and mileage per diem to be drawn by his wife, Sarah, to help care for their five children.

Following the war, Heiskell moved to Memphis, where he reestablished his legal practice and was joined by his brother, Carrick, and fellow congressional colleagues Landon Carter Haynes and William G. Swan, among other eastern Tennessee èmigrès. Although he was excepted from Andrew Johnson's amnesty proclamation of May 1865, there is no record that he requested a pardon or ever received one. Nevertheless, this unreconstructed Confederate who early in the war had vowed never to "affiliate with a people who are guilty of an invasion of [Southern] soil" eventually held public office again, serving as a delegate to the state constitutional convention in 1870 and as attorney general and court reporter of Tennessee (1870–1878), before rejoining his Memphis law firm. Interestingly, one of Heiskell's sons, Frederick, an 1872 graduate of Washington and Lee University, married a daughter of Senator Lucius Q. C. Lamar of Mississippi, a New South spokesman.

BIBLIOGRAPHY

Green, John W. *Law and Lawyers.* Jackson, Tenn., 1950.
Journal of the Congress of the Confederate States of America, 1861–1865. 7 vols. Washington, D.C., 1904–1905.
Thomas A. R. Nelson Papers. McClung Collection. Knox County Public Library, Knoxville, Tenn.
U.S. War Department. *War of the Rebellion: A Compilation of the Official Records of the Union and Confederate Armies.* Washington, D.C., 1880–1901. Ser. 1, vol. 39, pt. 2, pp. 299–300, 303.
Warner, Ezra J., and W. Buck Yearns. *Biographical Register of the Confederate Congress.* Baton Rouge, La., 1975.

R.B. ROSENBURG

HELM, BENJAMIN HARDIN

HELM, BENJAMIN HARDIN (1831–1863), brigadier general. Born into a prominent Bardstown, Kentucky, family on June 2, 1831, Helm was a brother-in-law of Mrs. Abraham Lincoln (through his 1856 marriage to Emily Todd). He graduated from the U.S. Military Academy in 1851, ninth of forty-two in his class. On October 9, 1852, he resigned from the U.S. Army, in which he was a second lieutenant in the Second Dragoon Regiment. A "Southern rights Democrat," he practiced law, sat in the state legislature (1855–1856), and served as state's attorney (1856–1858).

At the beginning of the Civil War Helm declined an offered appointment as major (paymaster) in the Federal army. While Kentucky tried to remain neutral, he served as an assistant inspector general of the state guard. He was, however, a Confederate supporter, and as early as May 1861 he applied for a commission in the Southern army. He helped recruit the First Kentucky Cavalry Regiment for Confederate service and on October 19, 1861, was commissioned as the regiment's colonel.

Promoted to brigadier general March 14, 1862, Helm served in Mississippi and Louisiana until February 15, 1863, when he was assigned to command what had been Brig. Gen. Roger W. Hanson's brigade in the Army of Tennessee. Helm was wounded on September 20, 1863, at the Battle of Chickamauga and died the next day. His body was first buried in Atlanta, Georgia, but in the 1880s it was moved to the Helm Cemetery in Elizabethtown, Kentucky.

BIBLIOGRAPHY

McMurtry, Robert G. "Confederate General Ben Hardin Helm." *Filson Club Historical Quarterly* 32 (1958): 311–328.
Warner, Ezra J. *Generals in Gray: Lives of the Confederate Commanders.* Baton Rouge, La., 1959.

RICHARD M. MCMURRY

HELPER, HINTON ROWAN

HELPER, HINTON ROWAN (1829–1909), abolitionist. Helper was born in the North Carolina up-country, the son of a small farmer. In the mid-1850s, after writing a book about his failed attempt to strike it rich in California's gold fields, he wrote *The Impending Crisis of the South: How to Meet It,* a 413-page tome that attacked slaveholders for forcing onto nonslaveholders a political economy that enriched the few while preventing economic development in the South as a whole. In the book, Helper called for uncompensated emancipation of all slaves and for their subsequent colonization outside the United States.

When the *Impending Crisis* was first published in New York in 1857, it provoked little stir in either the North or the South, much to Helper's disappointment. He therefore moved to New York and sought to market the work through a variety of schemes. All were unsuccessful, although he did manage to persuade Horace Greeley to give the book a favorable review in the *New York Tribune.* During the presidential campaign of 1859, Greeley also raised $19,000 to pay for about 100,000 copies of a shorter edition of the book, *The Compendium of the Impending Crisis,* which was then distributed widely by the Republican party as a campaign document. The book, however, first came to national attention during the contest for Speaker of the House of Representatives in January 1860 when John B. Clark, a Democratic congressman from Missouri, presented a resolution calling *The Impending Crisis* "insurrectionary and hostile to the domestic peace and tranquility of the country." Clark argued that no one who endorsed its principles, as had Republican nominee John Sherman of Ohio, was "fit to be Speaker of this House." The ensuing controversy gave the Democrats, the minority party in the House, a means by which to brand the Republicans a party of disunion and thereby defeat Sherman's bid for the Speaker's chair. Thereafter, Southern Democrats pointed to *The Impending Crisis* as proof that the Republicans planned to abolish slavery immediately and destroy the South.

Helper realized little profit from *The Impending Crisis* or the controversy that it produced, however, and spent the remainder of his life working in poorly paying civil service jobs, serving as a collection agent for private debts, and writing four other unprofitable books, three of them violently racist in tone. He died by his own hand, bitter and virtually penniless, in Washington, D.C.

BIBLIOGRAPHY

Bailey, Hugh C. *Hinton Rowan Helper: Abolitionist-Racist.* University, Ala., 1965.
Helper, Hinton Rowan. *The Impending Crisis of the South: How to Meet It.* Edited by George M. Frederickson. Cambridge, Mass., 1968.

WAYNE K. DURRILL

HENRY AND DONELSON CAMPAIGN

The Tennessee and Cumberland rivers in western Kentucky and middle Tennessee from February 3 through February 16, 1862, witnessed the creation of a vital link in the ultimate Union victory. Joint operations between land and naval forces on these rivers proved capable of surmounting Confederate position defense and indecisive leadership to capture Forts Henry and Donelson. In this campaign Ulysses S. Grant, together with his naval colleague Andrew Hull Foote, effected the first major penetration of the Confederacy in the West. Drawing upon antebellum perception of western rivers as valuable travel arteries of communication and commerce, Union authorities settled on the Mississippi valley with its tributary rivers like the Tennessee and Cumberland as the proper avenues of advance. The Confederate theater commander, Gen. Albert Sidney Johnston, was virtually powerless to blunt such an advance, although command mistakes on his part accelerated the opportunity.

Political, economic, and military strategic goals of the Lincoln administration in the West ultimately rested upon reopening western rivers. Johnston, whose responsibilities stretched from the Appalachian Mountains to beyond the Mississippi River, had neither men nor matèriel to conduct a proper defense of such a vast area. He concentrated his poorly trained, mostly sick, and inadequately supplied force of forty thousand men at strong points like Columbus, Kentucky, on the Mississippi, and Bowling Green, Kentucky, astride the Louisville and Nashville Railroad. He relied upon two earthen fortifications, constructed by the Tennessee state government about twelve miles apart in frontierlike Stewart County, Tennessee, to hold where the twin rivers bisected his defense line. Inadequately sited, constructed haltingly by slave gangs and soldiers, neglected by the high

command, Forts Henry and Donelson were overlooked by Johnston and senior Confederate officials until the moment of crisis. Yet these forts guarded the vital upper heartland where rich mineral and agricultural resources and important cities like Clarksville and Nashville, the Tennessee state capital and munitions center, lay directly behind Johnston's forward defenses. The rivers held the key to unlocking this treasure for the Union.

Northern ownership of most of the steamboat fleet on western rivers denied this resource to the Confederacy. But during the autumn of 1861 the Union government saw the merit in forging a gunboat flotilla. When teamed with steamboats as troop transports, the means of mounting a strike force to crack Johnston's line became apparent. Henry W. Halleck, Federal commander of the Department of Missouri, balked at first, fearing Johnston's perceived strength and the inadequacies of his own subordinates, and having misgivings about Grant. But Grant and Foote finally secured Halleck's grudging support for a rapid attack via the rivers.

The Union expeditionary force of fifteen thousand men, supported by seven gunboats, some armored, departed river staging areas like Cairo, Illinois, and Paducah, Kentucky, on February 3. Riding floodwaters of the swollen Tennessee, they moved virtually undetected to within striking distance of Fort Henry by February 6. Here, Kentuckian Lloyd Tilghman tried desperately to finish an uncompleted Fort Heiman on high ground across from a flooded Fort Henry and prepare his defenses. He was unprepared when Grant and Foote struck and only barely ordered his infantry to escape overland to Fort Donelson. Tilghman remained behind with a "forlorn hope" of about a hundred artillerymen to conduct an "honorable" defense against the gunboats. Meanwhile, Grant's soldiers became mired in the mud as his divisions under Generals John Alexander McClernand and Charles Ferguson Smith attempted to move on the forts by country roads.

Foote refused to be slowed by the army. Under orders from Grant to effect a coordinated attack, the gunboats pushed forward and engaged Tilghman's heavy seacoast fortress guns by early afternoon on February 6. The ensuing battle proved no contest. The Confederate gunners damaged several of the gunboats before virtually all their cannon were rendered inoperable and carnage was widespread among the gunners. Foote demanded unconditional surrender (the first rendering of that phrase) and Tilghman had no choice. Federal naval personnel simply rowed through the fort's sally port onto a flooded parade ground to take the Confederate's sword. Fort Henry cost the Union forces eleven killed, thirty-one wounded, and five missing. Tilghman suffered five killed and eleven wounded, with the rest of his force remaining at the fort captured.

The effect of the Union victory was electric. As Grant consolidated his position on the high ground around Fort Henry

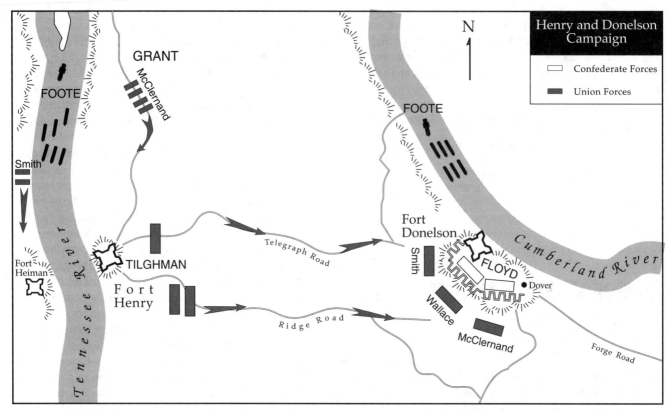

in preparation to moving on to Fort Donelson, the navy again took the initiative. A flotilla under Comm. S. L. Phelps raided 150 miles up the Tennessee River, cutting the railroad bridge above Fort Henry, spreading havoc along the way, and destroying quantities of war matériel. Before being stopped near Muscle Shoals, Alabama, this demonstration of Union naval power sent shock waves among Confederate military and the public alike. Lincoln's gunboats had become a "superweapon." Meanwhile, on February 7, Johnston realized his Bowling Green position was no longer tenable and ordered a retreat to Nashville. He sent subordinates with their commands to cover his flank at Fort Donelson.

Johnston eventually dispatched John B. Floyd, Gideon Pillow, Simon Bolivar Buckner, and Bushrod Rust Johnson, together with upwards of eighteen thousand Confederates to defend Fort Donelson. His instructions were vague, but, in his mind at least, the army was to conduct a holding action long enough for the main Army of Central Kentucky to retire behind the Cumberland at Nashville. With Floyd (the most inexperienced of the generals) as senior commander, and none of the four a leader of first rank at this point in the war, the stage was set for disaster. Unit commanders and their men, while equally untried, were more combative, but with the exception of cavalry led by an unknown Tennessee colonel, Nathan Bedford Forrest, no Confederates contested Grant's march from Fort Henry on February 12. Union forces moved into position virtually without opposition, while Foote's

flotilla steamed back down the Tennessee, up the Ohio, and thence up the Cumberland to help.

Action at Fort Donelson began on February 13. While awaiting Foote's arrival, Grant issued instructions to McClernand and Smith to move into position but avoid any general engagement with the Confederates. Contrary to orders, both McClernand and Smith nudged forward in probing attacks that were repulsed. At one point, with the weather warm and balmy, dry leaves in front of a battery position caught fire, threatening Union wounded with horrible death. Their adversaries leaped from their rifle pits to help save them in a touch typical of later scenes in this war between brothers. By nightfall, Grant realized that Fort Donelson would be no easy repetition of the earlier victory. He ordered reserves forward from Fort Henry to form a third division under Lew Wallace and awaited Foote to make a naval attack the next day.

The youthful Union soldiers had jettisoned blankets and overcoats during the warm overland march from Fort Henry, but now the spring weather turned bitterly cold and blizzard-like overnight. Fires were forbidden on both sides, and everyone suffered. February 14 found two shivering armies capable of little more than sharpshooting and skirmishing. That afternoon, however, the Union navy approached Fort Donelson's two water batteries. This time the battle proved no contest for the gunboats. Confederate artillerists occupied commanding heights and had had weeks of training. Foote chose to run his ironclads close in toward the enemy guns, and the Southern gunners exacted a terrible toll. Virtually all the Union gunboats suffered damage, Foote was wounded, his flagship a shambles, and the myth of Lincoln's gunboats was shattered forever. Amid shouts of victory by the Confederates, their generals decided to escape the Fort Donelson trap.

At dawn the next day, Pillow's and Buckner's divisions went forward with a rush through the frozen countryside in an effort to beat back McClernand's division blocking the roads to Nashville and freedom. They succeeded handsomely. By noon not only was McClernand routed, but the roads lay wide open. Grant remained unaware of the impending disaster, having left headquarters that morning to consult with the wounded Foote aboard his flagship. McClernand's calls for help finally caused Lew Wallace to wheel his command into a blocking position to stymie the Confederate drive. Grant received word of the defeat and returned to rally his army. He told McClernand and Wallace, "Gentlemen, the position on our right must be retaken" and left it to them to accomplish the mission. Summoning his old West Point mentor, C. F. Smith, he explained that the Confederates had undoubtedly evacuated some of their lines to conduct the assault and ordered Smith to drive forward and capture the fort. More anxiously, he sent a dispatch to Foote saying that the army was in danger and asking for naval intervention.

Meanwhile, the Confederate generals dithered, argued, misread one another's concept of mission, and lost the initiative and hence the battle. Floyd and Buckner understood that once victory had been attained, the army would march off, leaving artillery and rear-area troops to the mercy of the enemy. Pillow demurred, wanting to hold Tennessee soil as long as possible and to evacuate the whole garrison. In the end, with the hour late and Union counterattacks beginning to press the tired Confederates, the four men decided to retire for the night, gather up supplies, wounded, artillery, and the like, and evacuate at dawn on February 16. But C. F. Smith's division had knifed forward and captured Buckner's outer defense line, thus breaching Confederate fortifications and causing the Kentuckian to have grave reservations about further defense.

Confederate scouts searched for avenues of escape that night. Army doctors counseled that the men could not survive crossing frozen creeks and the long trek to Nashville. Buckner became gripped by battle fatigue and fears of Smith's division; Pillow urged continued resistance; Floyd vacillated. Time was wasted, and in a midnight council that has since defied understanding, a decision was made to surrender to Grant on the morrow. Forrest stalked angrily into the night, vowing to escape. Floyd and Pillow, fearing punishment at the hands of Union authorities, similarly deserted, passing command to Buckner in the famous opèra bouffe episode derided by subsequent generations. Floyd's three-

thousand-man Virginia brigade, Pillow's personal staff, and uncounted hundreds of others evaded the Union dragnet over the days after the surrender. But when Buckner sent a flag of truce to his opponent that night, the Confederate fighting men became enraged and nearly mutinied at this betrayal by their leaders.

Eventually, Buckner met with his old army friend Grant in the hamlet of Dover, within Confederate lines. Grant demanded unconditional surrender, and Buckner, though aghast at such treatment from an old colleague, was powerless to refuse. Grant telegraphed Halleck later that day: "We have taken Fort Donelson and from 12,000 to 15,000 prisoners including Generals Buckner and Bushrod Johnson; also about 20,000 stand of arms, 48 pieces of artillery, 17 heavy guns, from 2,000 to 4,000 horses, and large quantities of commissary stores."

When this news reached Johnston at Nashville, he was shocked, since all previous news from the fort indicated victory. Nashvillians rioted and fled the city in droves, with Buell's army eventually occupying the capital on February 24. Johnston could provide no defense. Aided by Floyd, Pillow, and Forrest, his forces evacuated as much Confederate property as possible, but his retreat did not stop short of northern Alabama and Mississippi. Union forces stood poised to end the rebellion all over the upper South. But, as fatigued and battered in victory as the Confederates were in defeat, Grant's men could not move quickly. Moreover, their generals fell to bickering, and momentum slipped from their grasp. Johnston was able to regroup to fight another day.

Still, a Confederate field force was swept into Northern prison camps. Western and much of middle Tennessee as well as all of Kentucky were reclaimed for the Union. Hopes of early European recognition of the Confederacy were dashed, and Johnston's reputation as the South's greatest warrior was destroyed. The fall of Forts Henry and Donelson changed the war in the West overnight. Flagging spirits in the North were revived, and a deep wedge was driven into the South. The Southern home front began its wavering trend toward eventual collapse in a war of attrition.

BIBLIOGRAPHY

Connelly, Thomas L. *Army of the Heartland: The Army of Tennessee, 1861–1862.* Baton Rouge, La., 1967.

Cooling, Benjamin Franklin. *Forts Henry and Donelson: The Key to the Confederate Heartland.* Knoxville, Tenn., 1987.

Grant, Ulysses S. *Personal Memoirs.* Vol. 1. New York, 1885. Reprint, Cutchogue, N.Y., 1990.

Hamilton, James. *The Battle of Fort Donelson.* South Brunswick, N.J., 1968.

Simon, John Y., ed. *The Papers of Ulysses S. Grant.* Vol. 4. Carbondale, N.Y., 1972.

B. FRANKLIN COOLING

HEROES OF AMERICA

A secret, underground, pro-Union organization (often called Red Strings because a piece of red string in a lapel or on a window or door served as a secret sign of membership) composed of militant Unionists, deserters, and draft dodgers—and to some extent, slaves and free blacks—the Heroes of America existed in North Carolina, Virginia, West Virginia, Tennessee, the District of Columbia, and possibly other states during the Civil War. Its main mission was to protect its members from Confederate authorities. The HOA also provided needy members with food and other necessities, maintained an underground railroad on which members could be spirited to the Union lines, encouraged disloyalty on the home front and desertion in the ranks of the Confederate army, fostered the formation of armed, anti-Confederate guerrilla units, provided military intelligence to Federal troops, and promoted class conflict in the Confederacy by inducing the poor to join by promising a postwar distribution of the property of wealthy planters.

During the war it was rumored that the HOA originated within Union lines and was introduced into the Confederacy by special Federal agents. But the balance of the evidence now available suggests that the secret society was founded in central North Carolina, probably in Davidson County (the environs of present-day Lexington), where so many of its known leaders lived. It likely had its roots in a secret underground association of approximately five hundred armed Unionists who mustered under the U.S. flag in Davidson and the adjoining counties of Forsyth, Guilford, and Randolph. Witnesses reported that this band of militant Unionists, headed by John Hilton of Davidson County, favored the "coercion policy of Lincoln" and were prepared to "strike for the old Union." In July 1861, Confederate troops aborted this threatened insurrection of disloyalists.

One of the main leaders and organizers of the HOA was Dr. John Lewis Johnson, a druggist and physician, who lived in the Abbotts Creek community in southern Forsyth County. Perhaps because he was pressured by Confederate authorities to volunteer for the army or face charges of disloyalty, he joined the ranks as a substitute in 1862. By 1863, Johnson was serving in a Confederate hospital in Raleigh. The Tarheel capital, where the Grand Council of the Heroes of America was first organized, thereafter became a center of HOA activity.

In the summer of 1863, William W. Holden, editor of the influential Raleigh *North Carolina Standard,* embarked on his campaign for peace. Holden and his Peace party followers—influenced by the movement of some Northern Democrats for peace and reunion with a constitutional guarantee of slavery for the returning Southern states—demanded that Confederate authorities, or the states acting in convention together, make a permanent peace with the North.

The HOA supported the peace movement. Johnson is on record as having taken part in a Peace party rally near Raleigh in July 1863. Many other disloyalists took part in peace meetings, especially in the central and western Piedmont. The U.S. flag was hoisted at peace meetings in Wilkes and Rowan counties.

The 1863 phase of the peace movement culminated in an insurrection of deserters and draft dodgers across the central counties in September. A brigade of Confederate troops was sent in to suppress the uprising. The Heroes of America, through a clever network of secret dugout caves, managed to conceal hundreds of the men from the hunters. When the troops left a neighborhood, the men in hiding emerged from their dens and returned to aid their families and to offer protection and support to those whose husbands or sons had been captured.

A raid by Confederate soldiers in September left Holden's press in ruins, but the redoubtable editor renewed his activities in January 1864. President Jefferson Davis reacted by suspending the writ of habeas corpus. Undaunted, Holden challenged the incumbent, Zebulon Vance, in the 1864 gubernatorial contest on a peace platform.

In July, as a tactic to cow Holden supporters, newspapers backing Vance exposed the Heroes of America to the public for the first time during the war. Prompted by a promise from Vance to be lenient with those who voluntarily came forward, dozens of men publicly confessed their membership in the society and asked pardon from the governor for allowing themselves to be "misled" into joining it. The press revealed the secret signs, passwords, and rituals of the HOA. Holden was accused of being a leader of the society. With most of his supporters fearing reprisals, including arrest for disloyalty, few showed up at the polls to vote for him, and Vance won by a landslide. After Holden's loss to Vance, the HOA ceased to play a role in the politics of Confederate North Carolina.

In October 1864, Johnson, who had been ordered to duty at the front (probably as punishment for his Peace party activities), decamped with a company of Confederate troops to the Federal lines. He then went to Washington, D.C., where he initiated into the HOA Daniel Reeves Goodloe (a Republican and abolitionist from North Carolina), Benjamin Sherwood Hedrick (a Patent Office examiner and native Tarheel who had been fired in 1856 from his professorship at the University of North Carolina for expressing pro-Republican and antislavery sentiments), and John G. Barrett (the commissioner of patents). A National Grand Council of the Heroes of America with Hedrick at its head was established in Washington. In 1870, Goodloe testified before a Senate committee that during the war Johnson had also initiated Abraham Lincoln and Ulysses S. Grant into the Heroes of America. If this is true, it is likely that Lincoln and Grant kept their membership quiet because the Republican party,

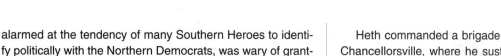

alarmed at the tendency of many Southern Heroes to identify politically with the Northern Democrats, was wary of granting publicity to the Heroes of America or to the peace movement that many of them supported.

In the fall of 1864, an investigation by Confederate detectives revealed that the HOA was widespread and powerful in southwestern Virginia. An informant reported that the secret order had been introduced into the area in the fall of 1863 by one Horace Dean of North Carolina. Montgomery County alone was said to harbor eight hundred members, including the sheriff, several justices of the peace, and other local government officials. By the winter of 1864, bands of deserters and disloyal county officials, many of whom belonged to the HOA, controlled southwestern Virginia.

During the Civil War the Heroes of America played an important role in the demise of the Confederacy. At first composed solely of die-hard Unionists, the ranks of the order by midwar had become swollen by the addition of thousands of disaffected citizens, especially deserters and draft dodgers. Together, they spread dissension, disorder, and disloyalty in the army and on the home front.

[*See also* Peace Movements; Unionism.]

BIBLIOGRAPHY

Auman, William T., and David D. Scarboro. "The Heroes of America in Civil War North Carolina." *North Carolina Historical Review* 58 (1981): 327–363.

Hamilton, J. G. de Roulhac. "The Heroes of America." *Publications of the Southern History Association* 40 (1907): 10–19.

Shanks, Henry T. "Disloyalty to the Confederacy in Southwestern Virginia, 1861–1865." *North Carolina Historical Review* 21 (1944): 118–135.

Tatum, Georgia Lee. *Disloyalty in the Confederacy.* Chapel Hill, N.C., 1934.

WILLIAM THOMAS AUMAN

HETH, HENRY

HETH, HENRY (1825–1899), major general. Heth, born December 16, 1825, was a Virginian of distinguished lineage who graduated from the U.S. Military Academy in 1847 and served the U.S. Army well for the next fourteen years. After he joined his home state's forces upon secession, Heth spent the early part of the war primarily in western Virginia. As a brigadier general, he failed miserably at the Battle of Lewisburg in May 1862. Nonetheless, his friendship with Robert E. Lee earned him a field position with the Army of Northern Virginia in January 1863. Heth purportedly was the only officer in the army whom Lee addressed by his given name.

Heth commanded a brigade and temporarily a division at Chancellorsville, where he sustained a minor wound. A few weeks later, the Virginian advanced to the rank of major general and received permanent division command. On July 1, 1863, Heth achieved the dubious distinction of precipitating the epic fight at Gettysburg. His division stumbled into Federal troops that day and became so heavily engaged as to make disengagement impossible. During the battle he sustained his second wound in as many months.

Although Heth spent the last two years of the war as a solidly reliable division commander in the Army of Northern Virginia, he never advanced beyond mediocrity. His division fought well on virtually every field, but Heth rarely displayed strategic initiative. The highlight of his late-war career came at Reams's Station on August 25, 1864, when the general personally bore a battle flag at the head of his men as they carried a Union position. Heth surrendered his division at Appomattox.

After the war he held a variety of jobs. He died September 27, 1899, from the effects of Bright's disease. He is buried in Hollywood Cemetery, Richmond.

BIBLIOGRAPHY

Connolly, Thomas. *An Irishman in Dixie.* Columbia, S.C., 1988.

Morrison, James L., Jr., ed. *The Memoirs of Henry Heth.* Westport, Conn., 1974.

ROBERT E.L. KRICK

HILL, A. P.

HILL, A. P. (1825–1865), lieutenant general. Considered the finest division commander in Confederate service, and Lee's principal lieutenant in the last year of the war, A. P. "Little Powell" Hill has become the personification of the life and death of the Army of Northern Virginia. Both Robert E. Lee and Stonewall Jackson called for him on their deathbeds.

Ambrose Powell Hill was a product of Piedmont Virginia landed gentry. Born November 9, 1825, near Culpeper, he received a private education before his 1842 appointment to West Point. While on summer furlough from the academy in 1844, the tragedy of Hill's life occurred. He contracted gonorrhea. The disease's bacteria, unknown to anyone, lodged in his urinary tract and created strictures that eventually would bring debilitating illness.

An eight-month sick leave forced Hill to drop back a year at West Point. At his 1847 graduation, he stood fifteenth in his class. The new artillery lieutenant arrived too late in Mexico to see action. Seven years of duty assignments followed in Mexico, Texas, and Florida. In 1855 Hill transferred to the

A.P. HILL   NATIONAL ARCHIVES

U.S. Coastal Survey Service in Washington. His 1859 marriage to Kitty Morgan McClung would produce four daughters.

With the outbreak of civil war, Hill became colonel of the Thirteenth Virginia. He saw no major action for a year. Nevertheless, his proven talents in organization, drill, and discipline led to his promotion on February 26, 1862, to brigadier general. His baptism in battle came on May 5 at Williamsburg. Hill's successful attack at a critical moment swept Union forces from his front, and he won praise as the most conspicuous brigadier on the field. On May 26, he received promotion to major general and command of the largest division (six brigades) in all of the Confederate armies.

It was in the Seven Days' counteroffensive by Lee that the Powell Hill of history emerged. Directed to attack the Federal right flank in concert with Stonewall Jackson's forces, Hill grew impatient at Jackson's tardiness and assaulted on his own. His division took heavy casualties at Mechanicsville and equally severe losses the next day at Gaines' Mill. On June 30, the divisions of Hill and James Longstreet fought a bloody but inconclusive engagement with Federals at Frayser's Farm. Hill blamed all three defeats on Jackson's failure to provide necessary and expected support.

A post–Seven Days' argument with Longstreet resulted in the latter placing Hill under arrest. Lee intervened and transferred Hill to Jackson's command. An even stronger clash of wills developed. On August 8, Jackson criticized Hill for poor marching procedures on the move to intercept Gen. John

Pope's advance. But Hill's timely arrival the following day in the Battle of Cedar Mountain was instrumental in the Southern victory. Similarly, Hill's steadfastness in beating back repeated Union attacks at Second Manassas elicited high praise.

By then, "Little Powell" was a familiar figure in the ranks. Five feet, nine inches tall, he weighed but 145 pounds. His curly hair was chestnut-colored and worn long. Hazel eyes flashed during battle or anger. Disdaining uniform and insignia, Hill customarily wore calico shirts—his favorite being bright red in color.

Lee's army was marching into Maryland on September 4, when Jackson's patience with Hill's casual marching style snapped. He placed Hill under arrest for insubordination. Hill obtained temporary release a week later and participated dutifully in the capture of Harpers Ferry. On September 17, in one of the most dramatic moments of the war, Hill's Light Division dashed into battle at Sharpsburg after a seventeen-mile forced march and saved Lee's army from almost certain destruction.

For seven months thereafter, Hill and Jackson waged an increasingly bitter exchange of charges and countercharges that did credit to neither man. An inexplicable gap in Hill's lines at the Battle of Fredericksburg added fuel to the controversy. The quarrel ended with Jackson's death following Chancellorsville. On May 26, 1863—a year to the day of his last promotion—Hill was assigned as a lieutenant general in command of the newly formed Third Corps in Lee's army. It was Hill's troops who opened the Battle of Gettysburg. Sickness limited the general's activities, and his debut as a corps commander was less than spectacular.

Hill partially redeemed himself on the retreat to Virginia with a smashing repulse of Federals at Falling Waters, Maryland. Yet on October 14, he suffered his worst defeat when he precipitately launched an attack against powerfully entrenched Federals at Bristoe Station. Hill was a central figure in Lee's attacks the following May against Ulysses S. Grant's army in the Wilderness. Illness then forced him to relinquish command for two weeks. Lingering effects from gonorrhea had produced a slow blocking of the kidneys.

The general prematurely struggled back to duty and performed badly in May 23 fighting at the North Anna River. With his health somewhat improved by the end of the month, Hill made a speedy arrival at Petersburg on June 18 and helped prevent that gateway city to Richmond from falling into Union hands. Throughout the long besiegement that followed, Hill commanded the southern half of Lee's defenses. He did so brilliantly. One high-ranking officer observed that from June 1864 through March 1865, "every Federal effort to break Lee's right was met and defeated by General Hill with promptness and without heavy loss on his part."

Victories, always against heavy odds, came after engagements at Jerusalem Plank Road, Weldon Railroad, the

Crater, Reams's Station, Peeble's Farm, Jones's Farm, and Burgess's Mill. Lee relied heavily on the little general throughout the months of entrapment. Not once did Hill disappoint him.

These accomplishments came in spite of worsening health. Malfunctioning kidneys slowly produced uremia. For most of February and March 1865, Hill was unable to perform his duties. The general tried to regain his strength with rest at the James River estate of a kinsman. He painfully returned to the front only two days before Grant's all-out assault on April 2 against Lee's position. It was barely dawn that morning when Hill was fatally shot through the heart while trying to reestablish his lines. He is buried in Richmond beneath a statue to his memory.

A Richmond newspaper stated in 1864 that Hill was "the abiding strength and dependence of Lee's army." Gen. William Mahone later said of him: "A more brilliant, useful soldier and chivalrous gentleman never adorned the Confederate army."

BIBLIOGRAPHY

Hassler, William W. *A. P. Hill: Lee's Forgotten General.* Chapel Hill, N.C., 1979.
Pender, William Dorsey. *The General to His Lady.* Chapel Hill, N.C., 1965.
Robertson, James I., Jr. *General A. P. Hill.* New York, 1987.
Schenck, Martin. *Up Came Hill.* Harrisburg, Pa., 1958.

JAMES I. ROBERTSON, JR.

HILL, BENJAMIN H.

HILL, BENJAMIN H. (1823–1882), congressman from Georgia. Benjamin Harvey Hill was born into a modest farm family in Hillsboro, in Jasper County, Georgia, on September 14, 1823, the seventh of nine children. When he was ten, he moved with his family to Troup County in western Georgia's newly opened Creek Indian lands. He was the second of his family to attend college, entering the University of Georgia in 1841, where he proved to be far more of a scholar than his older brother who was also on campus at the time. Ben Hill graduated in three years at the head of his class. A year later he married Caroline E. Holt, of a politically and socially prominent Athens family. After admission to the bar, he moved to LaGrange, Georgia, and opened a law practice. His successful practice soon earned him a large estate and by 1860 fifty-seven slaves.

Hill took an active interest in politics and proved to be an accomplished orator, though his political career was characterized by repeated fluctuations in party affiliation and factional alignments, leading contemporaries and historians alike to judge him an opportunist. He first ran for office as a Whig and was elected to a single term in the Georgia legislature in 1851. As a Know-Nothing, he ran unsuccessfully for Congress in 1855 and for governor in 1857, losing the latter race soundly to a relatively unknown Democrat, Joseph E. Brown. But it was in the presidential campaign of 1856 that Hill first gained a statewide reputation. In his support of Millard Fillmore's attempt at presidential reelection, he clashed with two of the state's most prominent Democrats, Robert Toombs and Alexander H. Stephens, and challenged them to debates. His stinging attack on Stephens in a Lexington debate and on Toombs in their encounter the next

> His insults led Stephens to challenge him to a duel, though Hill declined to fight. . . .

day in Washington, Georgia, earned Hill widespread attention as a brash young "giant-killer." His insults led Stephens to challenge him to a duel, though Hill declined to fight the "frail invalid."

In 1859 Hill was elected to the state senate and from that platform became an increasingly outspoken Unionist. Though he threw his support to John Bell and his Constitutional Union party in the 1860 presidential election, he also pushed without much success a fusion scheme by which Georgia supporters of John Breckinridge, Stephen A. Douglas, and Bell would agree to throw their votes to the one who, on the eve of the election, looked most likely to defeat Abraham Lincoln.

In December he was elected by his Troup County constituents to represent their antisecessionist views at the state secession convention in Milledgeville. "May they who would destroy the Union in a frolic," he wrote on accepting his role as convention delegate, "have the wisdom to furnish our children a better." Still convinced that the South's grievances could be more effectively addressed within rather than outside the Union, Hill, along with Herschel V. Johnson, Alexander Stephens, and others, continued to argue against secession. Yet when a test vote he put forward for further negotiation indicated that the majority of the convention favored immediate secession, he capitulated, voting with the majority and signing the state's ordinance of secession. Yet he displayed his unhappiness over this turn of events openly, saying that he assisted with the dissolution of the Union as he "would bury a benefactor." This statement embittered some local secessionists who, in the midst of their celebration in Milledgeville, burned him in effigy.

Hill soon pledged his support for the new Confederacy, however, and was rewarded with election as one of Georgia's ten delegates to the Provisional Congress that met in

Montgomery in February 1861. In November the Georgia legislature selected him as one of the state's two Confederate senators (along with Robert Toombs, who refused to serve), a position Hill continued to hold throughout the war. At age thirty-nine, he was that body's youngest member.

When Congress convened in Richmond in February 1862, Hill was named chairman of the Senate Judiciary Committee. From that position, he soon stirred dissension with his determined effort to establish a Confederate supreme court. Though the Constitution drawn up in Montgomery the year before authorized the creation of such a court, many state rights advocates in and out of Congress, including Governor Brown and other Georgia congressmen, opposed it as yet another effort toward centralizing on the part of the Davis government. Hill was vocal in the lively debate over the issue in March 1862, which led to a violent collision on the Senate floor with Alabama senator William Lowndes Yancey. In response to insults from Yancey, Hill hurled a glass inkstand at him, grazing his cheekbone. Further infuriated when Yancey calmly ignored this blow from behind, Hill rushed at him with a chair but was restrained by other senators. Though Hill's persistence eventually led to the bill's passage in the Senate in 1863, it was buried in the House and a Confederate supreme court never materialized.

On this and on other matters, Hill was a particularly vocal adherent to Jefferson Davis and his administration and cultivated the perception that he was the president's spokesman in the Senate. Davis referred to him as "Hill the faithful" and once said of him, he "stood by me when all others forsook our cause. . . . His pen and voice were on my side when I most needed them. They were equal to ten thousand bayonets—and I will not forget his services." Two other much-debated issues on which Hill demonstrated his loyalty to presidential policy were conscription and suspension of the writ of habeas corpus. In both cases, his support took the form of direct attacks on Governor Brown.

The matter of conscription was the first to seriously distance President Davis from Brown. Davis felt the need for mandatory military service of white male citizens as early as the spring of 1862 and pushed the first Conscription Act through Congress in April. Brown at first refused to cooperate and wrote of his strenuous objections to Davis throughout the summer. When a second act extending the age limit of conscripts to forty-five was passed in September, Brown became defiant and turned to his legislature in an effort to secure a state law opposing it. In messages to the General Assembly of Georgia he condemned the president's actions as unconstitutional and a direct denial of the states' right to protect their own territory and citizens. Hill spent much of the fall in Georgia as an unofficial emissary of Davis, attempting to counteract the effects of the governor's charges. When Brown continued to defy the act after his own state supreme

court upheld its validity, Hill went before the state legislature on December 11 and delivered an incendiary speech in which he defended both the need and the legitimacy of conscription and attacked Brown for the irrationality of his arguments against it and for undermining the war effort.

Three acts by Congress between February 1862 and August 1864 gave President Davis the prerogative to suspend the writ of habeas corpus. Although these measures were widely condemned by Georgians, including Brown, Ben Hill again proved fully supportive of this presidential privilege, insisting that it was a necessary war measure and as such did not violate a citizen's constitutional rights.

These clashes created such enmity between Senator Hill and Governor Brown that when Brown ended his third term in 1863, several of his political enemies, including Alexander Stephens, felt Hill was the natural challenger for the gubernatorial race that year. But Hill, recognizing Brown's continued popularity among Georgians and not wanting to risk his own influential position in Richmond, declined the opportunity to oppose him. Hill did exert his influence to keep Robert Toombs, as outspoken a critic of Davis as Brown was, from winning the state's second Senate seat. Herschel V. Johnson,

> **In response to insults from Yancey, Hill hurled a glass inkstand at him, grazing his cheekbone.**

far less hostile to the Confederate administration, easily defeated Toombs, much to Hill's satisfaction. Hill's biographer called Johnson's victory "the last great victory of Hill for the administration."

Hill's staunch loyalty to the administration wavered briefly in the face of the peace movement that was gaining momentum in the spring of 1864. He opposed a resolution by the vice president's brother, Linton Stephens, that Georgia as a single state could initiate peace negotiations with the Union government. But he was more conciliatory on this issue than he had been on others and reasoned with Stephens that such a plan would be effective only if undertaken by the Southern states acting together through a convention. Nothing came of such proposals, as Georgians became preoccupied with their defense against William Tecumseh Sherman's invasion.

Hill returned home from Richmond and took an active and highly visible role in rallying morale, as in a speech in Macon in which he urged continued resistance to Sherman, who he warned planned to exterminate Georgians and repopulate the state with "Yankees." On behalf of the Confederate War Department, he traveled to the southwestern part of the state to urge planters there to give up much-needed cotton and other supplies they were hoarding for army use. At Davis's request, Hill constantly urged Georgia draft evaders and deserters to come forward in the Confederacy's great hour of need; his persistence was such that he aroused animosity among some yeomen in the state and criticism from state newspapers.

When Sherman himself made overtures of peace to Georgia officials in October 1864, Hill convinced Jefferson Davis that nothing short of a presidential appearance in the state could counteract peace sentiment in Georgia. Davis made the trip accompanied by Hill, and despite controversial statements by the president blaming Confederate troops for their failure to defend Atlanta adequately, nothing came of Sherman's attempts to negotiate with state officials.

Hill was also influential behind the scenes at the Hampton Roads conference on February 3, 1865. Lincoln and William H. Seward met aboard a steamer off the Virginia coast to discuss peace terms with a Confederate commission headed by Vice President Alexander H. Stephens. When Governor Brown urged the Georgia legislature to back a Southern convention to negotiate a peace settlement, Hill, alarmed that Stephens might tell Lincoln of this proposal, intervened and persuaded his fellow Georgian not to pass along Brown's idea at the conference. Though nothing came of the conference (the Union leaders would consider nothing short of unconditional surrender), Hill maintained that it had served a valuable purpose in that it silenced the Southern peace movement and strengthened resolve for a fight to the finish. He undertook a speaking tour of the state in which he attempted to rally Georgians to renewed support for the war effort. Defeatism was rampant enough at that point to make his campaign a failure and himself a target of ridicule and hostility, but it also earned Hill a postwar reputation as having been "the last to accept secession, and the last to accept defeat." On March 11, 1865, in his hometown of LaGrange, he delivered one of his most moving appeals, which is thought to have been the final speech made by a Southerner on behalf of the Confederacy.

After Robert E. Lee's surrender at Appomattox a month later, Hill returned home, where he took great satisfaction in the fact that most of his former slaves chose to stay with him. In May, Federal authorities came to his home, arrested him and Confederate naval secretary Stephen R. Mallory who was visiting him at the time, and took both to New York, where they were imprisoned at Fort Lafayette. Hill remained a prisoner for over two months until his parole by President Andrew Johnson in July.

Hill retired from public life until 1867, when he moved to Athens, Georgia, and emerged to deliver a series of well-publicized and widely circulated speeches denouncing the recently passed Reconstruction Act and the entire Southern policy of the Radical Republicans. He urged Georgians to defy the policy and harshly condemned those Southerners who cooperated with Reconstruction measures. He maintained that such actions by Congress were unconstitutional and urged President Johnson to block enforcement. In December 1867, he was unanimously elected president of a conservative convention held in Macon, where he lashed out at black suffrage policies and vowed that Georgians would "not be brought under the dominion of the Negro." His rhetoric over the next three years became particularly critical of the "cowardly" cooperationism of former governor Joseph Brown and of current governor Rufus Bullock, whom he labeled a "stupid express agent." His newspaper column "Notes on the Situation" in the *Augusta Chronicle and Sentinel,* published regularly during this period, gained him national attention.

Then suddenly in December 1870, Hill switched sides and announced his acquiescence to Reconstruction policy and urged his fellow Georgians to do likewise. Continued opposition, he maintained, was futile and a misuse of political energies that could be diverted to other, more pressing issues. This unexpected flip-flop on Hill's part was probably related to his recent membership in the Western and Atlantic's leasing company, which forced him to make peace with the Northern radicals who controlled the company. The man so recently hailed for his courage in speaking out against what many Georgians viewed as despotic rule was now denounced as a turncoat and a traitor and once again seen as a mere opportunist. His involvement with the company, as much as his political sellout, so offended Georgia conservatives that he was ostracized from state politics for the next five years.

In the meantime, he also embraced the New South cause and became one of its earliest spokesmen, long before Henry Grady began touting the same message. Hill gave what many consider his most effective speech before University of Georgia alumni in 1871, when he extolled the merits of modernized agriculture, more efficient use of natural resources, and a more broadly based educational system.

After moving to Atlanta in 1872, Hill reentered the political fray and was elected to Congress from the Ninth District in 1875. He quickly reasserted himself as a defender of Southern rights when in January 1876 he confronted James G. Blaine, the congressman from Maine seeking the Republican presidential nomination that year, on the floor of the House of Representatives. After Blaine "waved the bloody shirt" with insulting remarks about Jefferson Davis and his responsibility for the atrocities at the Andersonville prison, Hill rose and made a stirring and well-received defense of Davis, demanding that "this reckless misrepresentation of the South stop right here." Hill was elected to the U.S. Senate in January 1877 and served in the office he had so long coveted until a painful malignancy on his tongue rendered him speechless (for one of the era's most accomplished orators, an irony not lost on his contemporaries). It led to throat cancer in 1881 and death at home in Atlanta on August 16, 1882.

BIBLIOGRAPHY

Bryan, T. Conn. *Confederate Georgia.* Athens, Ga., 1953.

Coleman, Kenneth, and Charles Stephen Gurr. *Dictionary of Georgia Biography.* Vol. 1. Athens, Ga., 1983.

Conway, Alan. *The Reconstruction of Georgia.* Minneapolis, Minn., 1966.

Hill, Benjamin Harvey, Jr. *Senator Benjamin H. Hill of Georgia: His Life, Writings, and Speeches.* Atlanta, 1891.

Knight, Lucian Lamar. *Reminiscences of Famous Georgians.* 2 vols. Atlanta, 1907.

Pearce, Haywood J., Jr. *Benjamin H. Hill: Secession and Reconstruction.* Chicago, 1928.

Yearns, Wilfred B. *The Confederate Congress.* Athens, Ga., 1960.

JOHN C. INSCOE

HILL, D. H.

HILL, D. H. (1821–1889), lieutenant general. Born July 12, 1821, in the York District, South Carolina, Daniel Harvey Hill was the youngest of eleven children. Boyhood illnesses left him with a pain-racked spine for most of his life but did not prevent him from pursuing a military career.

Hill entered the U.S. Military Academy at West Point in 1838, graduating twenty-eighth of fifty-six in the class of 1842. As a brevet second lieutenant, he was assigned to the First Artillery in August 1842, was transferred to the Third Artillery on October 20, 1843, and was promoted to full second lieutenant on October 13, 1845. During the war with Mexico, he served first under Zachary Taylor at Monterrey and then with Winfield Scott in the Mexico City campaign. Conspicuous bravery earned Hill promotion to first lieutenant on March 3, 1847, with brevets as captain for Contreras and major for Chapultepec.

Hill resigned from the army February 28, 1849, and settled into life as an educator. He served as professor of mathematics at Washington College, Virginia (1848–1854), and Davidson College, North Carolina (1854–1859). The opening of the Civil War found Hill as superintendent and professor of mathematics and artillery at the North Carolina Military Institute.

Elected colonel of the First North Carolina on May 11, 1861, Hill repulsed inept Federal charges at the Battle of Big Bethel Church, south of Yorktown, Virginia, on June 10. This effort won him promotion to brigadier general, to date from July 10, 1861, and assignment to improve defenses in North Carolina. Hill returned to Virginia on November 16 to serve under Gen. Joseph E. Johnston. As a major general, to date from March 26, 1862, Hill led a division under Johnston at Williamsburg (May 5, 1862) and Seven Pines (May 31–June 1), and under Gen. Robert E. Lee at Mechanicsville, Gaines' Mill, and Malvern Hill (June 26–July 1, 1862). From July through August, he left Lee's army to command the Department of North Carolina but did not enjoy the experience. Before rejoining the Army of Northern Virginia on September 2, Hill helped build up the defenses in the Richmond-Petersburg area that would become important in the latter stages of the war.

With a combative personality that served better on the battlefield than off, Hill increasingly alienated those who controlled his advancement. None doubted his courage or leadership: he often exposed himself to fire just to settle his men. His fighting spirit and willingness to place himself in danger made him popular with the soldiers in his command, but his carping rankled fellow officers and superiors who called Hill a "croaker" because of his despondent talk and tactless complaining. In battle reports, the North Carolinian criticized superiors—including Lee—for mismanaging the spring 1862 battles around Richmond.

Although the repercussions of such challenges would not become fully apparent until late 1863, Hill's personality may have made him an inviting target for those who wanted either to slight his abilities or to find a convenient scapegoat. In the Maryland campaign of 1862, he was incorrectly accused of having lost the Confederate battle plan (Special Orders No. 191) that fell into Union hands. Hill also received less than his due for employing his minimal force to delay the advance of the Army of the Potomac over South Mountain near Boonsborough on September 14, 1862. At Sharpsburg, his division stood up well in the horror of what became called the "Bloody Lane."

Yet when Lee reorganized the army in October, he did not see Hill as having potential for corps command. Lee believed him "an excellent executive officer" with not "much administrative ability. Left to himself he seems embarrassed and backward to act." Poor health, coupled with the sting of not receiving promotion to lieutenant general, caused Hill to submit his resignation from the army on January 1, 1863. Thomas J. ("Stonewall") Jackson, Hill's brother-in-law, was among those who persuaded the North Carolinian to remain in the service.

Hill subsequently accepted an appointment as a corps commander under Braxton Bragg in the Army of Tennessee, where he contributed to the Confederate victory at Chickamauga (September 19–20, 1863), but he shortly became embroiled in a bitter dispute with his commander. Bragg had alienated many of his chief officers, who signed a petition calling for the general's dismissal. Bragg incorrectly blamed Hill as the petition's author. President Jefferson Davis supported Bragg against Hill, who became the only officer relieved from command. The experience cost him promotion to lieutenant general, which Davis declined to put through for confirmation, and caused some unfairly to equate Hill with the missed opportunities of the Chickamauga campaign.

Hill spent the remainder of the war trying to clear his record and win meaningful command, but he managed only a series of relatively minor positions. Beginning on May 5, 1864, Hill became a volunteer aide to General P. G. T. Beauregard, serving in whatever capacity was most needed. This included commanding a division for several days, going to Lynchburg to help organize the defense against Union Maj. Gen. David Hunter, and returning to the Richmond-Petersburg area to perform duties as inspector general of trenches. Occasionally, other officers requested Hill's services, but he lacked the support of Davis and Bragg, who had since become military adviser to the president. Hill ended his military career first as commander of the District of Georgia in mid-January 1865 and then under Johnston in North Carolina. He fought at Bentonville (March 19–20) and surrendered with Johnston's forces at Durham Station on April 26.

After the war, Hill remained in North Carolina and published a monthly magazine, *The Land We Love,* from 1866 to 1869 and a weekly newspaper, *The Southern Home.* The gap between him and Lee widened as Hill refused to accept blame for the lost order or to back down from criticism of his former commander. After 1877, Hill returned to a college campus, this time serving as the president of Arkansas Industrial University (the future University of Arkansas) until 1887 and then the Middle Georgia Military and Agricultural College in Milledgeville from 1885 to 1889. He died of cancer while in Charlotte, North Carolina, on September 24, 1889, and was buried in Davidson College Cemetery.

BIBLIOGRAPHY

Bridges, Hal. *Lee's Maverick General: Daniel Harvey Hill.* New York, 1961. Reprint, Lincoln, Nebr., 1991.

Freeman, Douglas S. *Lee's Lieutenants: A Study in Command.* 3 vols. New York, 1942–1944. Reprint, New York, 1986.

Johnson, Robert U., and C. C. Buel, eds. *Battles and Leaders of the Civil War.* 4 vols. New York, 1887–1888. Reprint, Secaucus, N.J., 1982.

WILLIAM ALAN BLAIR

H.L. HUNLEY

The Confederate submarine *H. L. Hunley* was the first undersea warship to sink an enemy vessel in combat. Despite the importance of the act and the fame that resulted, many details of the submarine's history are uncertain. The submarine was the last in a series of privateer submersibles built by a consortium of investors and engineers in New Orleans,

Louisiana, and Mobile, Alabama. To reward private initiative, the Confederacy offered prize money equaling 20 percent of the value of any Union warship sunk. The submarine partners planned to earn prize money sinking Federal warships.

The partners originally included James R. McClintock and Baxter Watson, machinists and engineers; Robert Ruffin Barrow, financier; and Horace L. Hunley and Henry J. Leovy as surety on the privateer bond. The men first built a submarine called *Pioneer* in New Orleans in 1862. The submarine received a privateering commission but apparently never saw action before being destroyed when the city fell.

Hunley, McClintock, and Watson moved to Mobile, Alabama, and built another submarine there. The machine was constructed in the shop of Thomas B. Lyons and Thomas W. Parks and may have been named *American Diver.* Hunley financed the construction of the hull and research to develop an "electro-magnetic engine" to propel it. An effort to produce an electric engine for it failed, and instead a hand-operated crank turned by four men was installed. *American Diver* was lost, without loss of life, in rough seas off Fort Morgan in an attempted attack on the Federal fleet.

Hunley lost little time in building another submarine. He retained one-third interest and sold the remainder to E. C. Singer, R. W. Dunn, B. A. Whitney, and J. D. Breaman. Constructed as a larger version of *American Diver,* the new submarine was propelled by nine men, with one man steering and controlling depth and the other eight turning a crank propeller. The new vessel apparently was first called *Fish Boat,* but was later renamed *H. L. Hunley.* The boat was described as about thirty feet long, four feet wide, and five feet deep. The submarine would sink an enemy ship by passing beneath it and allowing a towed explosive "torpedo" to detonate *H. L. Hunley* against the ship's side. Control of the towed torpedo proved too uncertain, and it was later mounted on a spar projecting beyond the bow.

H. L. Hunley was tested at Mobile and then sent by railroad flatcar to Charleston, South Carolina. Large Union naval targets, and chances for helping the Confederacy and earning prize money, were more plentiful off that port. McClintock, operating as skipper, took the submarine on several trips against the blockaders off Charleston Harbor but failed to meet the enemy. In late August 1863, the Confederate government seized the submarine and replaced the crew with naval volunteers from the ironclads *Chicora* and *Palmetto State,* under Lt. John A. Payne. On August 29, 1863, while learning to operate the submarine, Payne accidentally sank it, killing five men.

The sub was raised and repaired and placed under Horace Hunley and Lt. George E. Dixon of the Twenty-first Alabama Volunteers. The two men trained another naval crew in September, but a second accidental sinking on October 15 killed Hunley and seven crewmen. Dixon per-

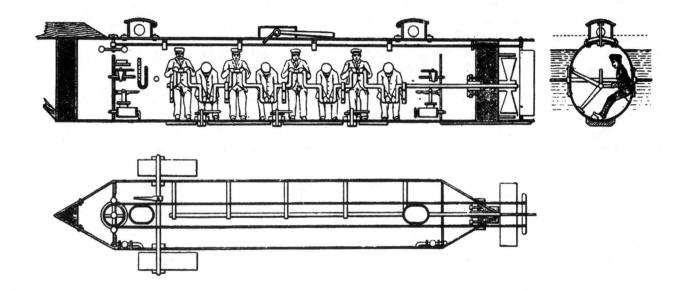

H. L. HUNLEY*. Cutaway plan by William A. Alexander, 1863.

suaded Gen. P. G. T. Beauregard to allow another attempt against the steam sloop USS *Housatonic.* The sub was raised a second time, refitted, and a new crew trained. On February 17, 1864, Dixon and a mixed navy and army crew attacked *Housatonic.* The torpedo sank the blockader but may have also sunk *Hunley.* The submarine did not return from its raid and has never been found.

Two modern reconstructions of *Hunley* have been built by local groups working with city museums and technical schools, one in Charleston in 1966 and 1967, and one in Mobile in 1990. Each is located at the city museum. They were based primarily on a painting by Conrad Wise Chapman, now in the Museum of the Confederacy at Richmond, and on somewhat hazy recollections of the builder and various witnesses. No contemporary plans are known to exist. Both modern ships were of welded construction with simulated rivet detailing. Neither should be termed an exact replica, but a conjectural reconstruction, as accurate as research and modern techniques allowed at the time of its construction.

BIBLIOGRAPHY

Duncan, Ruth H. *The Captain and Submarine CSS H. L. Hunley.* Memphis, Tenn., 1965.

Kloeppel, James E. *Danger beneath the Waves: A History of the Confederate Submarine H. L. Hunley.* College Park, Ga., 1987.

Perry, Milton F. *Infernal Machines: The Story of Confederate Submarine and Mine Warfare.* Baton Rouge, La., 1965.

Robinson, William Morrison. *The Confederate Privateers.* New Haven, Conn., 1928.

U.S. Naval War Records Office. *Official Records of the Union and Confederate Navies in the War of the Rebellion.* Washington, D.C., 1894–1927. Ser. 1, vol. 15, pp. 229, 231, 238, 327–337, 366–367, 528, 592; ser. 1, vol. 16, p. 427; ser. 2, vol. 1, pp. 104, 256.

KEVIN G. FOSTER

HODGE, GEORGE BAIRD

HODGE, GEORGE BAIRD (1828–1892), acting brigadier general and congressman from Kentucky. Hodge was born in Fleming County, Kentucky, in April 1828. The son of a prominent planter, he attended briefly the Mayville Seminary in Kentucky. In 1845 he was commissioned a midshipman and served on USS *Cumberland,* USS *Alleghany,* and USS *Raritan.* He remained in the navy until 1850, when he resigned as a lieutenant. Hodge then studied law and opened a practice in Newport, Kentucky, where he also became active in politics. In 1852 he ran unsuccessfully for the U.S. Congress as a Whig. He then joined the Democratic party, winning a seat in the Kentucky state legislature in 1859, which he held until 1861. He was also an elector on the John C. Breckinridge ticket in 1860.

At the beginning of the Civil War, Hodge, a staunch state rights advocate, was sympathetic to the Southern cause, but only reluctantly supported secession. He served as a member of the Executive Council of the provisional government of Kentucky in 1861. He also enlisted in the Confederate army as a private under Gen. Simon Bolivar Buckner. Kentucky's secession governor, George W. Johnson, appointed Hodge to represent Kentucky in the Provisional Confederate Congress. Then in January 1862 Hodge was elected to represent northern Kentucky's Eighth Congressional District in the First Congress.

Hodge alternated his time between the army and the Congress, but he preferred life in the military and the contributions he could make there. He was soon promoted to captain because of his family and political connections and was made adjutant general on Breckinridge's staff. Hodge was able to improve his standing after showing gallantry at the Battle of Shiloh, resulting in his promotion to major on May 6, 1862. He continued as Breckinridge's adjutant general, and exactly one year later he attained the rank of colonel.

With this promotion, Hodge first served for a short time as inspector general at Cumberland Gap. He then commanded William Preston's cavalry under Maj. Gen. Joseph Wheeler and Brig. Gen. Nathan Bedford Forrest. Moving through eastern Tennessee, this brigade took part in the Chattanooga operations and, after fighting at Chickamauga, rode in Wheeler's raid of northern Georgia in October 1863. Hodge's actions in these campaigns brought special commendation from Wheeler and labeled him a cavalry hero. For his efforts, Hodge was appointed brigadier general on November 20, 1863, but the Senate failed to confirm the rank.

Throughout this period, Hodge had continued to hold his congressional seat, although he was seldom present. When he was there, he frequently offered and supported firm military legislation. His voting record on conscription was strong, and in February 1863 Congress passed a resolution he had proposed calling for all captured black Union soldiers to be held until they could be returned to their masters. Captured freedmen were to be "sold into perpetual bondage, for the purpose of raising a fund to reimburse citizens of the Confederacy who have lost their slave property." As a representative from a Union-occupied district, Hodge also supported other stern economic measures as necessary for the Confederacy to survive. His continual absence from the House, however, did not allow him to work as effectively as he could have to obtain relief for his home state. Remaining in his cavalry command, he decided not to run for election to the Second Congress in the fall of 1863.

In August 1864 Hodge's name was resubmitted for promotion to brigadier general, but once again it went unconfirmed by the Senate. Nevertheless, he was assigned to head the District of Southwest Mississippi and East Louisiana. Under him the command began to deteriorate, bringing complaints of poor leadership from his critics. In January 1865 Hodge was brought up on formal charges of

incompetency and cowardice. Although he successfully defended his record against these accusations, Forrest requested that he relinquish his command of the district and relieved him in March, ordering him to Richmond for special assignment. The disillusioned Hodge refused to go and remained in Meridian, Mississippi, where on May 10, 1865, he surrendered and was paroled as a brigadier general.

After the war, Hodge reopened his law practice in Newport, Kentucky, and once again became involved in politics. In 1872 he was an elector on Horace Greeley's presidential ticket. He was elected to the state senate a year later as a Democrat and served there until 1877, when he moved to Longwood, Orange County, Florida, to become a farmer. He died there on August 1, 1892.

BIBLIOGRAPHY

Alexander, Thomas B., and Richard E. Beringer. *The Anatomy of the Confederate Congress: A Study of the Influences of Member Characteristics on Legislative Voting Behavior, 1861–1865.* Nashville, Tenn., 1972.

Davis, William C. *Breckinridge: Statesman, Soldier, Symbol.* Baton Rouge, La., 1974.

Henry, Robert S. *"First with the Most" Forrest.* Indianapolis, Ind., 1944.

Yearns, Wilfred B. *The Confederate Congress.* Athens, Ga., 1960.

ROBERT F. PACE

HOLCOMBE, JAMES P.

HOLCOMBE, JAMES P. (1820–1873), congressman from Virginia, diplomat, and secret service agent. A native of Powhatan County, Virginia, Holcombe came from a background unlikely for an ardent secessionist. The eldest son of an antislavery doctor who freed his bondsmen and moved to Indiana, Holcombe attended Yale and studied law at the University of Virginia. Like his father, he moved to the Midwest, where he wrote legal treatises, but he later returned to Virginia and eventually taught law at the university in Charlottesville. A Presbyterian, Holcombe and his wife, Ann Selden Watts, had six children.

Holcombe resigned his professorship in 1861 and harnessed his oratorical skills and state rights advocacy to win election to Virginia's secession convention. Elected to the House of Representatives (1862–1864), he bent his state rights principles to the harsh demands of war, even supporting heavy taxation and government intrusion into the economy. After standing down from his congressional seat, Holcombe went in early 1864 to Nova Scotia to sort out claims involving the capture of the Federal ship *Chesapeake* by unauthorized Southern privateers and to organize the return of Confederate soldiers in Canada.

He pursued the latter objective indifferently until new, more aggressive Confederate commissioners arrived. With one of these, Clement C. Clay, Holcombe was drawn into the shadowy machinations of the Confederate intelligence service. He helped Clay begin a correspondence with Horace Greeley, ostensibly about peace negotiations but in fact designed to encourage Northern opposition to Lincoln. When he returned to Richmond, he urged Secretary of State Judah P. Benjamin to expand efforts to disrupt Northern morale. Among other schemes, he advocated promoting anarchy in the North to persuade the northwestern states to secede from the Union.

After the war he ran a private school, first on his Bedford County farm and later at Capon Springs, West Virginia, where he died.

BIBLIOGRAPHY

Gaines, William H., Jr. *Biographical Register of Members, Virginia State Convention of 1861, First Session.* Richmond, Va., 1969.

Tidwell, William A., with James O. Hall and David Winfred Gaddy. *Come Retribution: The Confederate Secret Service and the Assassination of Lincoln.* Jackson, Miss., 1988.

Warner, Ezra J., and W. Buck Yearns. *Biographical Register of the Confederate Congress.* Baton Rouge, La., 1975.

NELSON D. LANKFORD

HOLLY SPRINGS, MISSISSIPPI

Located thirty-five miles southeast of Memphis, Tennessee, on the Mississippi Central Railroad, this northern Mississippi town was the site of a raid by Confederate Gen. Earl Van Dorn on December 20, 1862. As a result of this raid, Gen. Ulysses S. Grant was forced to abandon his drive down the Mississippi Central Railroad aimed at capturing Vicksburg, Mississippi. The Union lost 1,500 men captured and over $1,500,000 in destroyed supplies.

In the fall of 1862, Gen. Ulysses S. Grant drove south from Tennessee into Mississippi. He established a supply base at Holly Springs, planning to use the facilities of the Mississippi Central to support his drive. As part of his advance, Grant ordered his cavalry under the command of Col. Theophilus L. Dickey to raid the Mobile and Ohio Railroad. Dickey, with eight hundred men, moved out of Spring Dale, Mississippi, on December 14.

Lt. Col. John Griffith commanded the Texas Cavalry Brigade in Gen. John C. Pemberton's army at Grenada,

Mississippi. He recommended that Pemberton concentrate the cavalry under the command of Gen. Earl Van Dorn in order to raid Grant's supply base at Holly Springs. Pemberton agreed and on December 12, he placed Van Dorn in charge of a cavalry force made up of brigades commanded by Colonels Griffith, William H. Jackson, and Robert McCulloch. Griffith commanded the Sixth, Ninth, and Twenty-seventh Texas Cavalry; Jackson's force was made up of Mississippi and Tennessee cavalry; and McCulloch commanded the First Mississippi Cavalry and the Second Missouri Cavalry. The total force was approximately 3,500 men.

Van Dorn informed the three brigade commanders of the raid, emphasizing that their only chance of success was absolute secrecy—they were to tell their men nothing. The brigade commanders, knowing they faced a long ride, weeded out any troopers and horses that would not be able to keep pace.

On the evening of December 17, Van Dorn and his men moved out of Grenada along the Ponotoc road. Many of the men thought they were after Dickey's column, known to be along the Mobile and Ohio Railroad. Van Dorn, however, wanted to avoid Dickey's column, if possible. But in spite of his efforts, the Union force brushed the rear of the Southerners.

When he left Ponotoc, Van Dorn avoided any road leading directly toward Holly Springs, hoping this deception would lead the Northerners into believing he planned to strike into Tennessee. The men went into camp on the evening of the eighteenth, still ignorant of their objective. That afternoon Van Dorn had sent one of his men ahead to scout the town, and he reported back late that evening that the garrison had no knowledge of the approaching column.

While Van Dorn conferred with his brigade commanders, the men ate and fed their horses. The column then countermarched along the Ripley road until it came to the Holly Springs turnoff. As the Confederates approached the town, they posted guards at every farmhouse to ensure that no one warned the Federals they were coming. Van Dorn also increased the pace of the column. He wanted to reach Holly Springs ahead of any Northern scouts.

About 10:00 P.M. on the nineteenth Van Dorn halted for a final briefing. He also separated Griffith's Brigade from the main force and sent it along a side road that would bring it into Holly Springs from a different direction. When it became apparent that the columns would reach the town before daylight, Van Dorn ordered the commanders to stop five miles away and await sunrise. An hour before dawn, the men moved out in columns of four with guns loaded, but uncapped. McCulloch's brigade led on the main road. The First Mississippi and First Missouri of this brigade were to attack the Union cavalry. The Second Missouri had orders to dismount and attack any infantry they encountered. The Texans were to charge from the east and mop up any Federals around the depot. In addition, Griffith had orders to set up a roadblock south of town. Jackson was to approach from the north to cut off any Northerners escaping in that direction.

When Dickey had brushed against the Southerners close to Ponotoc, he had sent scouts to report their presence to Grant, but owing to a misunderstanding, the scouts did not depart immediately. Dickey did not discover this until later. When he did, he sent other scouts to Grant, but they were too late. Luckily, Grant had received word from other sources that raiders were on the loose. He warned his depot commanders to keep a sharp lookout. When Col. Robert C. Murphy, commander at Holly Springs, received this message, he ordered his cavalry commander to be ready to join a pursuit column. Murphy had under his command the 101st Illinois Infantry, detachments of the Twentieth and Sixty-second Illinois, and six companies of the Second Illinois Cavalry.

On the morning of the twentieth an African American informed Murphy that 5,000 Confederates were advancing on Holly Springs along the Ripley road. Murphy tried to order the crews manning two trains at the depot to alert the garrisons north and south of the town, and he set the infantry to work building barricades out of cotton. It was too late.

Van Dorn's men captured the Union pickets without firing a shot. With the pickets captured, Griffith's Confederates were able to surprise the Northerners at the depot and capture them after firing only a few shots. Among their prisoners was Colonel Murphy. McCulloch's First Mississippi then charged to the fairgrounds where the Union cavalry camped. The First Missouri followed, mopping up elements of the 101st Illinois. At the fairgrounds they surrounded the Union cavalry and, after a hard fight, forced them to surrender. With this action, Holly Springs was in Confederate hands. In addition to the supplies captured, they paroled 1,500 Northern soldiers. Van Dorn set up pickets, knowing that Grant would learn of his location the minute he cut the telegraph wires. After allowing his men to reequip with the best supplies, Van Dorn ordered the rest destroyed. Grant's wife and several other Union women who were in the town were not harmed.

At 4:00 P.M. the Confederates rode out of Holly Springs, their work completed. The destruction of the Holly Springs supply base, along with Nathan Bedford Forrest's raids in western Tennessee, forced Grant to abandon his advance down the Mississippi Central Railroad. This delayed the capture of Vicksburg for six months.

BIBLIOGRAPHY

Bearss, Edwin C. *Decision in Mississippi*. Little Rock, Ark., 1962.
Dupree, J. G. "The Capture of Holly Springs, Mississippi." *Mississippi Historical Society* 4 (1901): 49–61.
Hartje, Robert G. *Van Dorn: The Life and Times of a Confederate General*. Nashville, Tenn., 1967.

GEORGE A. REAVES III

HOLMES, THEOPHILUS H.

HOLMES, THEOPHILUS H. (1804–1880), major general. Born November 13, 1804, in Sampson County, North Carolina, Theophilus Hunter Holmes graduated from West Point in 1829, forty-fourth out of forty-six. He earned a brevet for gallantry in the Seminole War and a second one in the Mexican War. He resigned from the Federal army in April 1861.

Commissioned a brigadier general in the Confederate army that June, he commanded the troops at Fredericksburg and was promoted to major general in October. He led a division during the Seven Days' Battles but was criticized for his actions at Malvern Hill. On July 16, 1862, he was given command of the Trans-Mississippi Department, replacing the efficient but unpopular Thomas C. Hindman. Holmes was a poor choice for the position and frequently used his personal friendship with Jefferson Davis as an excuse for disregarding orders. Known as the "Old Granny General," Holmes was frequently ill, and some suspected that he had "softening of the brain." He proved unequal to his task and in February 1863 was replaced by E. Kirby Smith. In March 1863 Holmes was assigned to command the District of Arkansas, including the Indian Territory and Missouri. In an attempt to relieve Vicksburg, Holmes unsuccessfully assaulted Helena, Arkansas, on July 4, 1863. Early the next year he learned that several Arkansas politicians were working for his removal. Rather than face dismissal Holmes resigned on March 16, 1864, and the next month he was placed in command of North Carolina reserves.

He died near Fayetteville, North Carolina, on June 21, 1880, and is buried there.

BIBLIOGRAPHY

Bailey, Anne J. *Between the Enemy and Texas*. Fort Worth, Tex., 1989.
Castel, Albert. "Theophilus Holmes: Pallbearer of the Confederacy." *Civil War Times Illustrated* 16 (1977): 10–17.
Kerby, Robert L. *Kirby Smith's Confederacy: The Trans-Mississippi South, 1863–1865*. New York, 1972.
Park, Joseph H. *General Kirby Smith, C.S.A.* Baton Rouge, La., 1954.

ANNE J. BAILEY

HONOR

Winston Churchill once claimed that the Civil War was the last to be fought among gentlemen. The concept of honor played a salient part in the war as well as in its causes and aftermath. Although a Northern concept of honor can be identified, the Southern version has caught the historical imagination. Indeed, some scholars consider the Southern code of honor, as it is often called, a foundation stone of regional distinctiveness and cultural continuity to the present day—even though the ethic has shrunk under the influences of national homogenization over the past fifty years.

For most of American history, the Southern people, white and black, were largely agrarian folk. They were scattered in small communities across an enormous and still underdeveloped countryside. As a result, white Southerners of the Civil

> ## White Southerners of the Civil War era were more likely to adhere to the precepts of honor than contemporary Northerners. . . .

War era were more likely to adhere to the precepts of honor than contemporary Northerners, whose economy and social life had become rather urbanized. According to an older generation of scholars, the Southern white male was alleged to have demonstrated a sensitivity to personal insult, a romantic notion of cavalier virtues and valor, a devotion to proper manners and the dictates of hospitality, a colorful deference toward women, and a sense of rugged individualism. The 1932 edition of the *Encyclopedia of the Social Sciences* encapsulated this commonly held view. The writer explained, "Honor represents a strong personal sense of socially accepted dignity or socially expected conduct." Margaret Mitchell's *Gone with the Wind* (1935) was the most popular literary work to bathe that sentiment in pleasing nostalgia.

Historians have lately applied a more anthropological and psychological definition of honor to the Southern ethic. They claim that the Southern code involved much deeper social, racial, and political issues than simply ballroom manners or horseback tournaments in imitation of scenes from Walter Scott's novels. The sociology of honor embraces internal and external features. Thus, the ethic may serve as a mediator between individual and group aspirations and the judgment of the watching world. Anthropologist Julian Pitt-Rivers observes that "honor felt becomes honor claimed, and honor claimed becomes honor paid." In other words, a white Southerner's sense of identity was directly linked to public recognition.

In the Southern patriarchal and agrarian order, hierarchies of diverse forms shaped social relations—male over female, personal prosperity over poverty, respected lineage over family obscurity, education over illiteracy, age over youth, and, above all, white over black. These moral polarities were strictly observed. A gentleman of refined family ori-

gins, learning, and wealth expected to have his status confirmed by the community. In the lower ranks of society, men assumed their distinctive places in the social and racial order. Yet they insisted upon a rough egalitarianism to create what might be called a "people's timocracy," that is, the notion that virtually *all* white men and their womenfolk had a claim for respect. The well-born and wealthy could not be too lordly without risking retaliation for encroaching on the dignity of inferiors, and even the lowliest white woodchopper deemed himself superior to any black, slave or free.

If a white male Southerner did not attain public notice of his claim to status, the resulting stain of contempt could scarcely be tolerated. Rejection meant, in a phrase, "social death," a stripping of independence, the stigma of shame, which was the very opposite of honor. Violence might well ensue as the only means of reasserting one's self-regard.

In contrast to the Southern view was the Northern concept of honor. The commercial and industrial revolution that so energized the economy prepared the North for a more institutional approach to the question of honor. Under the inspiration of a revised, New Testament theology, an inner voice of caution and self-discipline—the conscience—was supposed to animate the Northerner. Unlike shame, guilt did not involve public exposure and therefore was less ruinous to self-regard. Pursuing the dictates of conscience, Northerners were likely to believe, was the essence of liberty. Their definition of liberty, unlike the Southern variety, did not include a right to enslave others. In contrast to the face-to-face style of Southern exchange, the Northern code of behavior stressed obedience to law and reliance upon the written word. Nor could Northerners understand why Southerners demanded community consensus, enforced at times by mob action in the suppression of dissent. The South's decision to leave the Union appeared as a childish, impulsive act soon to be repented, not the act of an aggrieved and honorable people.

For the Northerner, honor was perceived as duty to God and Union. The concept also incorporated the idea of personal dignity. A Northern gentleman, it was assumed, would not demean himself to notice insult, certainly not to the extremity of engaging in a duel. As Northerners saw the matter, ritual violence was a vestige of barbarism. Abrasive or brusque conduct should not entail receipt of a blow or a note to demand a lethal exchange of gunfire. Ex-Confederate General Nathan Bedford Forrest, for instance, after the war issued a challenge to a Northerner who disputed his status as a gentleman. Forrest's adversary simply ignored the summons.

On a collective scale, too, honor had sectional meanings. White Southerners became increasingly disaffected within the Union for precisely the same reasons that they might react to an indignity on an individual level. Only so long as white Southerners thought their adversaries recognized their moral and political parity were many willing to remain in the Union. Throughout the first half of the century each sectional dispute had weakened that allegiance. First the abolitionists provoked fury in the South. Then antislavery politicians echoed the radicals' charges that slaveholders fell below the standards of civilized, Christian society. When Northern congressmen strenuously objected to a draconian fugitive slave bill in 1850 and posed unwelcome conditions for its passage, for instance, a secessionist fire-eater declared, "We cannot stay in the Union any longer with such dishonor attached to the terms of our remaining." The admission of Kansas as a slave state concerned "a point of honor," declared Representative Preston Brooks of South Carolina in 1856. Soon afterward, during the Kansas debate, he illustrated his convictions. On the Senate floor, he inflicted nearly murderous blows on the head of antislavery Senator Charles Sumner of Massachusetts. Not only had Sumner attacked the Southern way of life, he had also questioned the loyalty of South Carolina troops in the Revolutionary War and personally insulted Brooks and his cousin Andrew Butler. Brooks's allies excused his conduct, claiming that Senator Sumner did not merit the option of a duel but had to be thrashed. Dueling required a social and moral equality of the parties; a horsewhipping or caning appropriately addressed the provocations of an underling.

For many in the lower South, the election of "Black Republican" Abraham Lincoln in the fall of 1860 was a calculated outrage against the South. Its leaders had long threatened disunion under such circumstances, but much to Southern chagrin, Northern politicians disregarded the warning. When Lincoln gave his mobilization order after the fall of Fort Sumter in April 1861, upper South whites were convinced that he sought to deprive them of their freedom and their honor. Both threats, the reasoning went, obliged them to unite with their kindred in the lower slave states. Throughout the secession crisis of 1860 and 1861, fire-eaters accused Southern Unionists of abject cowardice. Submission to Northern rule was an invitation to perpetual enslavement and loss of manhood, they claimed.

Honor also played a role in the conduct of the war itself. Historian Grady McWhiney argues that a singular stress upon martial valor, theatrical bravado, and even recklessness distinguished a number of Confederate leaders. J. E. B. Stuart, John B. Magruder, Thomas J. ("Stonewall") Jackson, Nathan Bedford Forrest, even Robert E. Lee, were among them. Statistics on casualties under circumstances of both offense and defense, however, do not bear out the charge of Southern rashness in battle. On the other hand, at the beginning of the war, Northern military caution was pronounced. It was partly attributable to anxieties that Southern bellicosity was greater than the martial zeal of city-dwelling and self-confessedly "effete Yankees." That myth later dissolved. Yet, from start to finish, Southern women expected and indeed

insisted that their defenders pledge themselves to "the law of Knightly honour and chivalry," as Catherine Edmonston of North Carolina put it.

In the organization of the Southern army, the strictures of honor found a place as well. No doubt its mandate inspired enlistments and generally aided morale. To refuse to fight or to return home early, some believed, would leave a stain upon the family escutcheon. But it could have a negative impact, also. When, as sometimes happened, a Southern officer was voted out of command by his troopers, he usually resigned his commission. He considered the removal a defacement of his honor. William Faulkner's great-grandfather's election defeat as a colonel inspired the novelist to fictionalize the incident in *The Unvanquished.* In another area of military life, punishments included ways to strip a soldier of his dignity by subjecting him to the ridicule and execration of fellow troopers. Shaving heads, standing on whiskey barrels, riding rails, wearing a sign labeled "thief," or whippings of varying severity were among the devices to shame an offender. Northern officers also sometimes subjected their miscreants to humiliating penalties of this sort.

Honor, which has always been considered an essential inspiration in military life, was especially apparent in the upper ranks of command. Throughout the war, some egocentric Southern generals disputed their location on seniority lists. They disobeyed commands given by alleged inferiors and repudiated other signals of implied inferiority, occasionally with disastrous repercussions. When, for instance, Jefferson Davis placed Joseph E. Johnston fourth on the list of five full generals, the irate Virginia West Pointer protested. The ranking "seeks to tarnish my fair fame as a soldier and a

> Some egocentric Southern generals . . . disobeyed commands given by alleged inferiors and repudiated other signals of implied inferiority, occasionally with disastrous repercussions.

man," he wrote. The alleged affront denied him the symbolic meaning of his "father's Revolutionary sword," bequeathed "without a stain of dishonor." Johnston's *amour propre,* as well as that of his high-strung commander in chief, severely damaged the relations of the two leaders when cooperation was vital to Confederate success.

Honor also helped assuage the humiliation of defeat. To lose the struggle by no means chastened white Southerners into heartfelt submissiveness. Repudiation of Confederate debts, even emancipation could be rationalized as war casualties. But not so Republican attempts to invest the freed people with equal protection of the law. Likewise, Federal occupation and then Congressional Reconstruction seemed a conspiracy to debase the conquered whites by rendering white men virtually powerless in comparison with the former slaves. Reaction to such interferences even received sexual expression. Robert Dabney of Davidson College, for instance, warned that under the new regime, former Confederates were "subjugated to every influence from without, which can be malignantly devised to sap the foundation of their manhood, and degrade them into fit material for slaves." He therefore called upon the women to help rouse Southern men to resist the baleful consequences. God had not favored the South, Dabney and others reasoned, as punishment for the Old Testament sins of debauchery, haughtiness, and greed. Slaveholding and disunionism—both honorable and justifiable—were no more condemned by God, Dabney was persuaded, than by the whites themselves.

Thus, the Southern ethic of honor, with its emphasis upon familial, rank-conscious values, assisted in the coming of the war and provided a rationale for continuing white oppression of blacks. That habit of mind, which justified bloody violation of federal and state criminal law, eventually helped in the overthrow of Reconstruction governments and the return of ex-Confederates to positions of power.

To be sure, the ascriptions of honor, particularly regarding race, colored attitudes above the Mason-Dixon Line as well as below it. Copperhead Democrats in the North defended Southern mores. Nor did all Southerners subscribe wholeheartedly to the venerable and primitive code as briefly sketched here. Instead, some adopted, to a degree, the Christian code of conscience and guilt and rejected reliance upon honor and shame. Nonetheless, honor played a major, but elusive role in the tragic history of mid-nineteenth-century America.

[*See also* Class Conflict; Dueling; Sumner, Caning of.]

BIBLIOGRAPHY

Adams, Michael C. C. *Our Masters the Rebels: A Speculation on Union Military Failure in the East, 1861–1865.* Cambridge, Mass., 1978.

Greenberg, Kenneth S. *Masters and Statesmen: The Political Culture of American Slavery.* Baltimore, 1985.

Hattaway, Herman, and Archer Jones. *How the North Won: A Military History of the Civil War.* Urbana, Ill., 1983.

McWhiney, Grady, and Perry D. Jamieson. *Attack or Die: Civil War Military Tactics and the Southern Heritage.* University, Ala., 1982.

Pitt-Rivers, Julian. "Honor." In *International Encyclopedia of the Social Sciences.* Vol. 6. Edited by David L. Stills. New York, 1986.

Smith, T. V. "Honor." In *Encyclopedia of the Social Sciences.* Vol. 7. Edited by R. A. Seligman. New York, 1932.

Wyatt-Brown, Bertram. *Southern Honor: Ethics and Behavior in the Old South.* New York, 1982.

Wyatt-Brown, Bertram. *Yankee Saints and Southern Sinners.* Baton Rouge, La., 1985.

BERTRAM WYATT-BROWN

HOOD, JOHN BELL

HOOD, JOHN BELL (1831–1879), lieutenant general. Born in Owingsville, Bath County, Kentucky, on June 1, 1831, Hood spent his boyhood years in neighboring Montgomery County. His parents were descendants of pioneer stock and solid members of Kentucky society. His father attended medical school, and though he did not take a degree, he opened a practice in Bath County. After the members of his family moved to Montgomery County in 1835, their fortunes were reversed when Hood's maternal grandfather died and left them 225,000 acres of land and a sum of cash. As a result young Hood thereafter led a comfortable life.

Hood won appointment to West Point on February 27, 1849, and graduated in 1853, finishing forty-fourth in a class of fifty-two. He was appointed brevet second lieutenant in the Fourth U.S. Infantry and was stationed in the West. Later, he was transferred to a detachment of dragoons and appointed second lieutenant in the Second U.S. Cavalry. The dragoons were stationed in Texas, and it was at this time that Hood formed his lifelong attachment to the Lone Star State, especially appreciating its rough pioneer spirit. Although he spent relatively few years there, he came to identify strongly with Texas. For the most part his duties on the frontier were uneventful, though he was once wounded while campaigning against the Indians.

With the secession of Texas, Hood resigned his commission in the U.S. Army on April 17, 1861, and headed east to Richmond, where he volunteered his services to the Confederate government. Assigned to the rank of captain and then major, Hood rose rapidly in command until he was given charge of the newly organized Fourth Texas Infantry, which he whipped into shape with stiff discipline and organization. As a young officer, Hood was a splendid physical specimen. He stood six feet, two inches, was broad at the shoulders, narrow at the hips, and had a full head of blondish auburn hair with a provocative off-color cowlick. He had a long, lean face and great sad eyes of a hypnotic blue.

His service record with the Confederate army in the East, especially after First Manassas and the Peninsular campaign, reads like a history of the Army of Northern Virginia. He quickly established a reputation as a fighting general and demonstrated that quality on many fields. Hood served with distinction at Williamsburg, the Seven Days' Battles (especially at Gaines' Mill), Second Manassas, Sharpsburg (Antietam), and Fredericksburg. He missed the Confederate victory at Chancellorsville in May 1863, but fought at Gettysburg where he was severely wounded in the left arm. Although he recovered sufficiently to resume command, he never regained the full use of his arm. Hood was promoted to brigadier general to rank from March 3, 1862, and to major general to rank from October 10, 1862.

JOHN BELL HOOD.

At times brilliant as a brigade and divisional commander, Hood was always a fierce fighter. Robert E. Lee regarded Hood's men as shock troops to be used in the most desperate situations, and at that assignment they never failed. Hood fought with an intensity he passed on to his men. His unit, though he commanded it for less than six months, was known throughout the war as Hood's Texas Brigade and was composed mostly of Texans who came east at the beginning of the war.

In the fall of 1863, Lee transferred an entire corps of his army, including Hood, to Tennessee, where it joined the Army of Tennessee under the command of Braxton Bragg in an attempt to defeat the Federal army under William S. Rosecrans. This move ended Hood's association with Lee and the army in the East. Hood's command arrived from Virginia in time to participate in the greatest battle fought in the West, Chickamauga, where Hood lost his right leg. Not expected to recover from his wound at first, he survived, but was never the same physically and perhaps emotionally. Recovery was slow, but by early winter of 1864 he was fit to return to duty.

Promoted to lieutenant general on February 1, 1864, with date of rank set at September 20, 1863, Hood was ordered to return to the Army of Tennessee as a corps commander under Bragg, a man whom he neither liked nor trusted.

Hood's association with the army in Tennessee became a tapestry woven of intrigue, defeat, humiliation, and near-annihilation. Shortly after Hood's return to the army, Joseph E. Johnston replaced Bragg as commander, largely as a result of a series of squabbles within the high command. Hood was directly involved and was accused of having undermined his old commander in an attempt to ingratiate himself with his superiors. Johnston, consequently, never quite trusted Hood, and Hood returned the favor by continuing the criticism he had leveled at Bragg. When Johnston was relieved from command of the Army of Tennessee, Hood succeeded him on July 17, 1864. He was promoted to full general with temporary rank on July 18, 1864.

Having begun the war commanding about a thousand men, Hood now found himself in charge of an entire army numbering many thousands. Though he had succeeded at the previous level, he was not equal to his new task. Against the advice of many, Hood attacked William Tecumseh Sherman's army in a series of battles around Atlanta, and he continued these assaults until he had seriously crippled his army. Successive losses at Peachtree Creek, Ezra Church, and Jonesboro cost Hood the fighting edge of his army as well as the city of Atlanta, which was evacuated on September 1. Instead of attempting to block Sherman's March to the Sea, Hood turned north into Tennessee to threaten Sherman's rear and cut his line of supply and communication. Sherman, however, refused to take the bait and turn northward, leaving Hood instead to contend with Federal troops under John M. Scofield and George H. Thomas (both classmates of Hood's at West Point).

In a series of rash and ill-prepared battles, Hood succeeded in nearly destroying what was left of his army. After much maneuvering through middle Tennessee, he attacked the well-entrenched Federals under Scofield at Franklin on November 30, 1864. Despite staggering losses and the demoralization of much of his army, Hood pushed his troops on to Nashville where he deployed and awaited attack from both Scofield and Thomas. When it came, the Federal assault was delivered with such weight of numbers and ferocity that it was over in a matter of hours. Confederate military history records no rout more thorough than that sustained by Hood at Nashville. A despondent Hood was now relieved from command at his own request. In May 1865 he surrendered at Natchez, Mississippi, having never been returned to command.

As a soldier, Hood was without peer in the Confederate army as a leader at the brigade and divisional levels. He was able to inspire his men and make them follow him despite the odds. His troops, man for man, were judged perhaps the best combat troops in the Army of Northern Virginia. Above the divisional level, however, Hood was a failure. As an administrator, he lacked the most basic of skills, and as a strategist he was rash, impulsive, and inappropriately aggressive. To be sure, he suffered from physical handicaps after the loss of his arm and leg, although to his credit, he never used this as an excuse for failure. Hood demonstrated both distressing traits—shifting responsibility to subordinates and intriguing against superiors, to name but two—and attractive qualities— courage, dash, devotion to an ideal, gallantry, and charm. In the end, however, it was his inability to recognize his own weaknesses and to make realistic adjustments to the changing circumstances of war that brought about his downfall.

After the war, he made his home at New Orleans where he engaged in the cotton business and married Anna Marie Hennen. Shortly before Gettysburg, Hood met and fell deeply in love with Sally ("Buck") Preston, daughter of John S. Preston of South Carolina. After at least two refusals of marriage, Sally finally agreed to an engagement, despite strenuous objections from her family. This was after Chickamauga. By the time the Franklin and Nashville disaster had come and gone, so had their relationship. The union between Hood and Sally Preston was never consummated and the two parted company at war's end never to see each other again. His business thrived and his family lived well. Yet for all his apparent happiness, Hood spent the remaining years of his life writing his war memoir, *Advance and Retreat,* which was full of apologies, bitterness, and hostility. Before Hood found a publisher for the book, a final calamity befell him. In 1878 and 1879 a yellow fever epidemic in New Orleans forced the closing of the cotton exchange and brought ruin to a number of local businessmen, Hood among them. He lost his wife and a daughter to the fever in August 1879, and on August 30, he too died of the disease. He left behind heavy debts and ten orphaned children for whom no financial provision had been made. Friends had his memoirs published and sold for the benefit of the children. Hood was laid to rest in Matairie Cemetery, New Orleans.

BIBLIOGRAPHY

Dyer, John. *The Gallant Hood.* Indianapolis, 1950.
Freeman, Douglas S. *Lee's Lieutenants: A Study in Command.* 3 vols. New York, 1942–1944. Reprint, New York, 1986.
McMurry, Richard M. *John Bell Hood and the War for Southern Independence.* Lexington, Ky., 1982.
O'Connor, Richard. *Hood: Cavalier General.* New York, 1949.
Warner, Ezra J. *Generals in Gray: Lives of the Confederate Commanders.* Baton Rouge, La., 1959.

TERRENCE V. MURPHY

HOOD'S TEXAS BRIGADE

This brigade was organized on November 1, 1861, at Dumfries, Virginia, from thirty-two volunteer infantry companies recruited in Texas. The original brigade included the First, Fourth, and Fifth Texas Infantry and the Eighteenth Georgia Infantry. These three Texas regiments were the only units from that state to serve in Robert E. Lee's Army of Northern Virginia.

In all, Hood's Texas Brigade fought in thirty-eight engagements. After the Battle of Seven Pines on May 31, 1862, the eight infantry companies of Hampton's South Carolina Legion were added to the brigade. The Texans became famous at the Battle of Gaines' Mill on June 27. In this battle, the brigade was credited with breaking the Union line and putting the enemy to flight. The unit continued its heavy fighting at Second Manassas and Sharpsburg. In October 1862, the Third Arkansas Infantry replaced the Eighteenth Georgia and Hampton's Legion, giving the brigade its final organization. As part of Lt. Gen. James Longstreet's corps, the unit fought at Gettysburg, Chickamauga, and Knoxville. At the Battle of the Wilderness, the brigade stemmed the Federal assault at the Widow Tapp farm, earning the unit lasting glory but at the cost of half its men. The Texas Brigade participated in the battles around Petersburg before surrendering with Lee's army at Appomattox.

The brigade holds a number of records for its staggering loss rate. In six major battles—Gaines' Mill, Second Manassas, Sharpsburg, Gettysburg, Chickamauga, and the Wilderness—the unit lost 3,470 killed, wounded, or missing. The most terrible period for casualties, however, came early in the brigade's career when it suffered 1,780 casualties in the eighty-three days between Gaines' Mill, June 27, 1862, and Sharpsburg, September 17, 1862. Through recruitment and replacements, an estimated 4,500 men served in its ranks. At Appomattox, only 476 were left to surrender.

Regiments within the brigade also suffered record losses. The First Texas Infantry is credited with having the highest percentage loss for a Confederate unit on a single day: 82.3 percent. Over 150 men of this regiment fell in twenty minutes of heavy fighting in Miller's Cornfield at Sharpsburg. Overall, the brigade lost 64.1 percent casualties for the day, ranking it third of any brigade in the war for a single day's loss.

During the war, Hood's Texas Brigade was commanded by several officers. The original commander was Louis T. Wigfall, who resigned to join the Confederate Senate early in 1862. He was replaced by Brig. Gen. John Bell Hood, a West Point graduate and veteran of the Texas frontier. Hood received promotion to division command in midsummer, leaving Col. William Tatum Wofford in command of the brigade. Brig. Gen. Jerome Robertson led the brigade through the fall of the year and throughout 1863. Then Brig. Gen. John Gregg commanded the brigade until his death at Darbytown Road on October 7, 1864. Command then fell to a succession of regimental officers including Col. C. M. Winkler, Col. Fredrick S. Bass, and Col. Robert H. Powell.

BIBLIOGRAPHY

Fletcher, William A. *Rebel Private, Front and Rear.* Beaumont, Tex., 1908. Reprint, Washington, D.C., 1954.

Polley, J. B. *Hood's Texas Brigade.* New York, 1910.

Simpson, Harold B. *Gaines' Mill to Appomattox.* Hillsboro, Tex., 1963.

DONALD S. FRAZIER

HORSES AND MULES

Together with the vehicles they pulled, horses and mules played a much larger role in the Civil War (but have received much less attention) than railroad trains or riverboats. Mounts were indispensable for cavalry, and draft animals for gun carriages, supply wagons, and ambulances. Besides their military uses, horses and mules were necessary for civil transportation and farm production, for which purposes oxen also served.

Possessing an inferior railroad system, the Confederate States depended on horses and mules to an even greater extent than did the United States. To Confederates, this seemed a matter of little concern at first, for suitable animals then appeared to be plentiful. In 1860 the South, consisting of the fifteen slave states, had less than 40 percent of the people but 45 percent of the horses, 90 percent of the mules, and 52 percent of the oxen in the country as a whole. Southern saddle horses were reputed to be superior to Northern horses in quality as well as quantity. Southerners prided themselves on their knowledge of horseflesh, their skill at breeding and training, and their general horsemanship.

Not all this livestock remained available to the Confederacy, however. Among the Southern states, Missouri was first and Kentucky second in the raising of horses, and Kentucky led in the production of mules. Though the Confederacy claimed both Missouri and Kentucky, it no longer had easy access to either of the two states after the first year of the war. Much of the output of other important breeding states—notably Virginia, Tennessee, Louisiana, and Texas—was lost as the Union armies advanced and the area under Confederate control shrank.

Even at the outset the Confederacy was deficient in the production of certain items necessary for the employment of horses and mules—feed, vehicles, and other manufactures. Concentrating on such profitable crops as cotton and tobacco, Southerners depended largely on Northern farms for hay. They looked to Northern factories for most of their wagons and carriages; the rest, those of local manufacture, often used wheels and other mass-produced parts that came from the North.

During the first two years of the war, the existing supply of horses was steadily depleted. Many were killed in battle, worn out by hard usage, or felled by disease, especially during an epidemic that caused severe losses to the Army of Northern Virginia (as well as the Army of the Potomac) in September 1862. Many of the surviving animals were in poor condition. They suffered from shortages of hay and fodder, veterinary surgeons and hospitals, and facilities for winter care. Emaciation was particularly to be seen in the areas of frequent campaigning, where the contending armies used up all the forage.

By the summer of 1863 the Confederacy faced a crisis, the "sources for the supply of horses and mules being well-nigh exhausted in the Confederate States," as the quartermaster general was informed. Jefferson Davis referred to him a proposal to "introduce horses and mules from Mexico, California, and Europe." The quartermaster general replied that several hundred mules had been purchased in Texas and were "awaiting a safe opportunity" to cross the Mississippi River. It was questionable whether they would be of much use, however, for they were "generally small." Horses from Mexico, California, Texas, and New Mexico might be useful for the cavalry "if very judiciously selected," but wild mustangs would be "entirely useless." As for obtaining horses from Europe, that was "certainly impracticable." It became impracticable also to bring many from west of the Mississippi, once the Federals had captured Vicksburg and Port Hudson and taken control of the river.

"For the future I see nothing left us but to procure animals from the enemy's country," an officer advised the quartermaster general in July 1863. The quartermaster general sent funds with Robert E. Lee's army for the purchase of horses during the Pennsylvania campaign, hoping to get as many as

> During the first two years of the war, the existing supply of horses was steadily depleted.

two thousand in Maryland. Instead, Lee left behind quite a few of his own horses when he returned from Gettysburg. John Hunt Morgan obtained some remounts during his 1863 raid into Indiana and Ohio, and he gathered a large herd from Federal stables during an 1864 raid into Kentucky. Other forays into enemy territory brought in as many as a thousand at a time. Still, the total captured fell far short of the requirements, and the numbers were offset by losses to Federal raiders. According to William Tecumseh Sherman, his foragers collected fifteen thousand mules and a great many horses just during the march from Atlanta to Savannah.

Originally the Confederate government bought animals, feed, vehicles, and equipment in the open market. As inflation worsened, however, the government began to seize these along with other goods from the owners, paying them less than market prices. An "average figure" of $350 was set in 1863 for first-class artillery and wagon horses and $300 for first-class mules. For wagons with iron axles, a higher price was allowed than for the more primitive kind with wooden axles. Rates were also set for the hire of teams, wagons, and drivers and for the labor of baling hay and fodder and shelling and bagging corn.

To tighten its control over the supply of animals and vehicles, the Confederate government centralized its system of procurement and distribution in 1863. The inspector general of field transportation was henceforth to take charge of "all inspections, purchases, impressments, and issues of field transportation (including artillery horses)." The Confederacy was to be divided into districts in each of which an officer was to "control the subject." Thus competition from state purchasing and impressment agents would be reduced if not eliminated. The Mississippi governor, who had impressed 619 horses for his state's service, now agreed to turn them over to the Confederate government, which was to pay the state for their use and reimburse it for any losses.

While the government procured draft animals for the army, cavalrymen had to provide their own mounts. The owner was paid forty cents a day for the use of his horse and was reimbursed if the animal was killed in action—but not if it was captured, disabled, diseased, or worn out. The man would have to find his own remount or be transferred to the infantry or the artillery. Many more cavalry horses were disabled or worn out than were killed, and the owners were hard put to pay for replacements. A man might have difficulty buying another horse even if his first one died in action, for with scarcity and inflation the purchase price became much higher than the reimbursement, which was based on the original evaluation. Davis himself pointed out: "it may thus not unfrequently happen that the most efficient troops, without fault of their own—indeed, it may be because of their zeal and activity—are lost to the cavalry service."

The government was responsible for equipping the cavalry horses but was not always able to equip them adequately. The saddles, inferior to the McClellan saddles of the U.S. cavalry, often proved "ruinous to the backs of horses." There came to be a "want of horseshoes and horseshoe nails, forges, and transportation therefor," as well as a shortage of blacksmiths. During Lee's Pennsylvania campaign "many valuable horses were lost owing mainly to the want of shoes."

The scarcity of horses, mules, feed, equipment, and vehicles had grave consequences for the Confederacy. Its cavalry, far better than the Union's in the beginning, deteriorated from 1863 on. To save horses for the field artillery, the Confederates more and more substituted mules for other hauling, but still had to eliminate some artillery as well as a number of transports and ambulances. Civil transportation and the economy suffered as impressment officers took the best horses, mules, and vehicles for the military and left farmers and planters with rickety carts and wagons and decrepit, if any, teams. Oxen meanwhile became less available as draft animals, since owners often had to slaughter them for food. In 1865 the head of the Bureau of War, Robert G. H. Kean, listed seven "causes of the failure of Southern independence," the fifth of which was the following: "Want of horses for transport and artillery; country stripped by impressment of horses, which straightway perished for want of forage; this want due to defective transportation by railroad and wagon, and limited supply in any given area of country."

BIBLIOGRAPHY

Ramsdell, Charles W. "General Robert E. Lee's Horse Supply, 1862–1865." *American Historical Review* 35 (1930): 758–777.

Vandiver, Frank E. *Rebel Brass: The Confederate Command System*. Baton Rouge, La., 1956.

U.S. War Department. *War of the Rebellion: A Compilation of the Official Records of the Union and Confederate Armies*. Ser. 4, vol. 2. Washington, D.C., 1900.

RICHARD N. CURRENT

HOSPITALS

The Confederacy at the outbreak of the Civil War had no well-established system of hospitals to care for its sick and wounded soldiers. Few hospitals existed in the prewar South because most nineteenth-century Americans cared for sick family members at home. Hospitals, or almshouses as they were frequently called, were regarded as asylums for the indigent. For the working poor, the newly arrived immigrant, and the merchant seaman, the few antebellum hospitals offered a level of health care previously unavailable to those who did not have home care. The United States maintained no general military hospitals before 1861, and the few marine hospitals located in the South's port cities and towns could not begin to meet the medical needs of the Confederacy.

The Confederate government established a Medical Department in February 1861 but failed to foresee the need for an organized hospital system until after First Manassas. When newly appointed Surgeon General Samuel Preston Moore arrived in Richmond in July 1861, he faced the overwhelming task of providing care for the large numbers of sick and wounded soldiers who had streamed into the Confederate capital. Soldiers were placed in temporary hospitals set up in tobacco warehouses, churches, barns, hotels, schools, and other large buildings, and many were cared for in private homes. Fearful that widespread epidemics might result from housing patients in crowded and poorly ventilated facilities, Moore embarked on an aggressive building scheme in the summer of 1861. The Provisional Congress appropriated fifty thousand dollars for this purpose in August. Moore advocated the construction of pavilion-style general hospitals. These facilities consisted of three to five divisions of individual ward buildings designed to accommodate about six hundred patients each. The wards were constructed from undressed pine planks and included many windows and doors for maximum ventilation.

Private Facilities. While the Confederate Medical Department developed its system of general hospitals, private citizens and charitable organizations provided much of the care for soldiers away from the front. Some forty-four private hospitals were organized in Richmond in the weeks after First Manassas. The citizens of Memphis formed the Southern

> A congressional investigating committee found inadequate medical supplies, surgical instruments, food, nurses, transportation facilities, and record-keeping. . . .

Mothers' Society and established a hospital that served the western army until June 1862. In Alabama, a group of Montgomery women opened the Ladies Hospital or Soldiers' Home in the early months of the war. The Nashville Hospital Association, organized by a committee of local women, administered the Gordon Hospital in the Tennessee capital.

In July 1861, Sally L. Tompkins opened and equipped at her own expense a private hospital in the home of Judge John Robertson of Richmond. When the Confederate Congress passed legislation requiring military control of all hospitals housing soldiers, Tompkins appealed to President Jefferson Davis to continue her role as administrator of the Robertson Hospital. Davis, impressed by the hospital's exceptional record of returning men to the field, ensured its continuance by commissioning Tompkins a captain in the cavalry. Other private hospitals, however, though equally successful at nursing men back to health, were not extended the same privilege, and most were closed or absorbed into the Confederate Medical Department by 1863.

Staff Organization. General hospitals were administered by a surgeon-in-charge who served as the chief medical officer and oversaw the prudent management of the hospital fund. This fund, created from moneys generated by the commutation of rations, was used to purchase food and other supplies for soldiers. The surgeon-in-charge, assisted by surgeons serving as division heads, also dealt with desertion, drunkenness, gambling, and other disciplinary problems among the patients. Congress authorized one assistant surgeon or contract surgeon for every seventy patients, but hospitals seldom had a full complement of physicians. Surgeons

were also assisted by hospital stewards, clerks, and ward masters who handled routine duties such as cleaning wards, managing supplies, and maintaining records.

Hospital surgeons provided emergency medical treatment and operated on the wounded, primarily amputating limbs following military engagements. But the vast majority of their time was spent treating the sick with the primitive and sometimes lethal therapeutics of the era. On the other hand, they were well aware of the importance of good diet to the healing process and did their best to see that patients were properly nourished. Unfortunately, however, Confederate hospitals often lacked the foodstuffs necessary, and patients faced the same daily rations no matter what their prescribed diet.

Combating Poor Conditions. In spite of the tremendous strides made by the Confederate Medical Department in organizing a hospital system during the first year of hostilities, it failed to meet the needs of the army. A shortage of beds was not the only problem facing the system. A congressional investigating committee found inadequate medical supplies, surgical instruments, food, nurses, transportation facilities, and record-keeping practices in the military hospitals.

Congress passed key legislation in 1862 and 1863 to alleviate the problems. The most significant was the Act to Better Provide for the Sick and Wounded of the Army in Hospitals. This statute, enacted after an extensive debate on the merit of female nurses, allowed the appointment of hospital matrons. As early as August 1861 the Provisional Congress had authorized hospital attendants, but these hired nurses and cooks, mostly freed or enslaved African Americans, along with volunteer nurses, convalescing soldiers, and members of various Catholic orders, had failed to provide adequate nursing care. The new legislation authorized for each hospital two matrons, two assistant matrons, and two ward matrons per ward. The chief matron had authority "over the entire domestic economy of the hospital," and the assistants supervised laundry and patients' clothing. Ward matrons prepared beds, monitored food preparation, and administered medicines. A number of prominent women accepted appointments as matrons, including Phoebe Yates Pember, chief matron of the Georgia Division of Chimborazo Hospital; Emily Mason, matron of Winder Hospital; Mary Pettigrew, matron of the Virginia Division of Chimborazo and of hospitals in Raleigh; Juliet Opie Hopkins, matron of the Alabama Division of Chimborazo; Louisa Cheves McCord, matron of hospitals in South Carolina; and Ella King Newsom, Kate Cummings, Mrs. William P. Gilmer, and Fannie Beers, matrons of hospitals serving the Army of Tennessee. Nevertheless, Confederate society never regarded hospital employment as respectable work for women.

In the spring of 1863, Congress ordered the establishment of "way hospitals" at railroad junctions and in major towns to supplement the small hospitals established by private citizens. Enterprising men and women in South Carolina organized the first wayside hospitals in the Charleston and Columbia depots of the South Carolina Rail Road Company during the summer of 1861. These facilities provided care for soldiers on medical furlough.

The legislation that authorized matrons also required the Medical Department to assign soldiers to hospitals according to their home states. In theory, this would group soldiers with the same manners and customs together and enable officers to locate the hospitalized sick and wounded more readily. It was also meant to facilitate the distribution of provisions sent by the various state governments and relief associations for particular groups of soldiers. In reality, this practice was difficult to follow and was often ignored by the surgeons.

Medical conditions in the hospitals were as satisfactory as could be expected given the Confederacy's shortage of medical supplies and physicians. Congress monitored conditions throughout the war, and the early reports were quite favorable, although Congress considered closing Richmond hospitals for a thorough cleaning in 1863. The lack of cleanliness and prevalence of contagious disease proved to be formidable foes for hospital personnel. Soldiers followed the same poor sanitary practices in the hospitals that had turned their camps into cesspools. Conditions were particularly bad following battles, when the hospitals were filled to capacity and the stench of rotting flesh permeated the air.

> **. . . Congress considered closing Richmond hospitals for a thorough cleaning in 1863.**

These conditions, combined with the era's limited understanding of the nature of illness, made the hospitals virtual breeding grounds for disease. To combat the situation, surgeons attempted to separate the sick from the wounded, particularly the erysipelas and gangrene patients, and the surgeon general issued numerous directives concerning hospital conditions.

Eastern Hospitals. Chimborazo Hospital, one of the largest and most famous of Confederate general hospitals, was constructed on a high plateau overlooking the James River just east of Richmond. This pavilion-style facility served as the prototype for other general hospitals. Dr. James Brown McCaw of Richmond accepted the post of commandant in October 1861 a few weeks before the hospital admitted its first patients. Chimborazo, a complex of 120 buildings including soup houses, icehouses, kitchens, mess halls, morgues, bathhouses, a bakery, and a brewery, operated as a self-sufficient post. Its five divisions accommodated about 600 patients each. McCaw, an innovative and efficient administrator, purchased food and supplies unavailable through military channels and acquired two canal boats to transport the

purchases to the hospital via the James River and Kanawha Canal. Almost 78,000 patients were hospitalized at Chimborazo during the course of the war, including 17,000 treated for battle wounds.

Other major hospitals in Richmond included Jackson, Howard's Grove, Stuart General, Louisiana General, and Winder. The Winder Hospital opened in April 1862 under the command of Surgeon Alexander G. Lane. The hospital, spanning 125 acres on the western outskirts of Richmond, was organized into six divisions; its capacity of 4,800 patients made it the largest facility in the Confederacy. Winder had a dairy, icehouse, extensive gardens, and a highly productive bakery. Like Chimborazo, it maintained two canal boats. Winder admitted some 76,000 patients, treating 64,683 with the loss of 3,259 soldiers between its opening and March 1, 1865. A fire in January 1864 and the general decline in the Richmond hospital census resulted in its temporary closing in 1864.

Petersburg and Lynchburg also served as hospital centers for the army in Virginia, along with facilities in Charlottesville, Danville, and Liberty where an eight-hundred-bed hospital was situated adjacent to the Virginia and Tennessee Railroad. North Carolina, South Carolina, and Florida maintained hospitals modeled after Virginia facilities.

Western Hospitals. In the latter part of the war, Chattanooga and Atlanta served as medical centers for the western army. Samuel Hollingsworth Stout, one of eight medical directors of hospitals in the Confederacy, was largely responsible for the development and success of the hospital program in the West. A medical pioneer, Stout designed wards with just two rows of bunks to reduce the amount of "impure gases generated by patients," which were thought to affect others. He ordered his subordinates to barter and forage on a regular basis, to plant gardens, and to build bakeries. Stout acquired a printing press to print forms for his hospitals and saved funds for the purchase of food and supplies.

Chattanooga's hospitals served as the models for others in the western theater. Academy, Foard, Gilmer, and Newsom hospitals were relocated prior to the Battle of Chickamauga, with their original organization intact. By 1863, the western hospitals were constantly being moved south in the face of the advancing Union forces. To Stout's credit, he selected the best sites for the hospitals, areas of high elevation adjacent to railroads in localities where the citizens could provide supplies. Like their counterparts in the East, however, Stout's western hospitals were hampered by the vagaries of the Confederate transportation system and the inability of the commissary and quartermaster to keep up with the mobile hospitals.

The hospital system in the Trans-Mississippi was small in comparison to the operations maintained by Stout for the Army of Tennessee and the large network in the eastern theater. The Medical Department maintained general hospitals in Shreveport, Louisiana; Little Rock, Arkansas; and Houston and Galveston, Texas. These facilities proved inadequate in the latter years of the war. Military and civil authorities established field hospitals, converted hotels, and enlarged existing state institutions to accommodate the increasing number of sick and wounded following the escalation of hostilities in the far West.

Specialized Facilities. The Medical Department organized a number of specialized hospitals in Georgia, including the Empire Hospital in Macon for gangrene patients, the

> **The Confederates also established special hospital facilities in their prisons for Union soldiers.**

Ophthalmic Hospital in Athens for patients with eye disorders, the Polk Hospital in Macon for hernia patients, and a hospital in Kingston for severe venereal disease cases. Tuberculosis patients were treated in Richmond's General Hospital Number 24, and separate wards were established at Howard's Grove for smallpox patients. The Louisiana Hospital in Richmond provided facilities for mental patients toward the end of the war. In February 1865, Congress established orthopedic hospitals "for the exclusive treatment of cases of old injuries and deformities from gun shot wounds."

The Confederates also established special hospital facilities in their prisons for Union soldiers. Located in tobacco warehouses or factory buildings, these small facilities were staffed and administered much like the general hospitals. Members of the Provisional Congress inspected prison hospitals early in the war and declared that Union soldiers were receiving adequate care and sustenance. Prison hospitals continued to offer satisfactory medical care until the cessation of prisoner exchanges. But, as the Confederacy's fortunes waned, so did conditions in prison hospitals.

The Final Record. After the initial medical crises in both the East and the West, the Confederate Medical Department had built a large and generally efficient hospital system. By 1864, the department was operating 154 facilities in eight states. Among the innovations were the design of the pavilion-style hospital, forerunner of the modern general hospital; the organization of the mobile hospital, prototype for future military medical units; and the development of specialty hospitals. The Confederate hospital experience demonstrated the importance of good nursing care and allowed women to enter the workplace. Most important, it helped change Southerners' perceptions about hospital care. Men who had never before been in a hospital learned they could be nursed back to health in one. It would not be until after

Reconstruction that modern hospitals emerged on a large scale across the United States, but the Civil War had hastened the movement.

[*See also* Health and Medicine; Medical Department; Nursing.]

BIBLIOGRAPHY

Chisolm, J. Julian. *A Manual of Military Surgery for the Use of Surgeons in the Confederate States Army.* 3d ed. Columbia, S.C., 1864. Reprint, Dayton, Ohio, 1983.

Cullen, Joseph P. "Chimborazo Hospital." *Civil War Times Illustrated* 19 (January 1981): 36–42.

Cumming, Kate. *Kate: The Journal of a Confederate Nurse.* Edited by Richard B. Harwell. Baton Rouge, La., 1959.

Cunningham, Horace H. *Doctors in Gray: The Confederate Medical Service.* Baton Rouge, La., 1958.

Medical and Surgical History of the War of Rebellion. 6 vols. Washington, D.C., 1875–1888. Reprinted as *The Medical and Surgical History of the Civil War.* Edited by James I. Robertson, Jr. 14 vols. Wilmington, N.C., 1990–1991.

Pember, Phoebe Yates. *A Southern Woman's Story: Life in Confederate Richmond.* Edited by Bell I. Wiley. Jackson, Tenn., 1959.

Peters, Joseph P. "Confederate Hospitals during Civil War Days." *Southern Hospitals* 34 (January 1966): 21–25.

Straubing, Harold E., ed. *Bullets, Bandages, and Beans: Personal Narratives by Hospital Workers in the U.S. Civil War.* Canton, Ohio, 1991.

JODI KOSTE

HOTCHKISS, JEDEDIAH

HOTCHKISS, JEDEDIAH (1828–1899), major and topographer. A native of Windsor, New York, Hotchkiss, who became known as "mapmaker of the Confederacy," spent his youth in the North and was educated at the Windsor Academy. In 1847, after a year of teaching, he set out on a walking tour through the Cumberland Valley into western Virginia and the Shenandoah Valley. Attracted by the beauty of the region, Hotchkiss accepted a position as tutor for the Daniel Forrer family in Staunton. Eventually this family school evolved into the Mossy Creek Academy, a widely known school for boys. In 1858 Hotchkiss organized the Loch Willow School at Churchville, which he operated until the Civil War began.

When the war came, Hotchkiss closed his school and volunteered his services to his adopted homeland. Because of his self-taught mapmaking skills, he made a nearly unique contribution to the Confederate military effort. At the outset of the war, generals on both sides demanded maps, and few were available. The historian T. Harry Williams has noted that, as in many areas, the North had the advantage in mapmaking skills and resources but that the South produced some very capable mapmakers; he called Hotchkiss "possibly the foremost mapmaker of the war."

Hotchkiss drew maps for Gen. Robert S. Garnett before the Battle of Rich Mountain in western Virginia in July 1861 and witnessed the Confederate defeat there. Afterward Hotchkiss became ill and retired for several months to recuperate at home. By March 1862 he felt fit again and sought a position on the staff of Lt. Gen. Thomas J. ("Stonewall") Jackson of the Second Corps, Army of Northern Virginia. Jackson made Hotchkiss his topographical engineer and set him the task of making a map of the Shenandoah Valley from Harpers Ferry to Lexington. Henceforth, Hotchkiss carried out reconnaissance and drew maps for the general until Jackson's death in May 1863. Thereafter he performed the same services for Gens. Richard S. Ewell and Jubal Early until the end of the war.

Hotchkiss sketched most of the maps while on horseback, using different colored pencils to note the chief characteristics and peculiarities of the terrain as well as troop positions, roads, and residences. The sketches were often critical in the planning of military operations by Jackson, Ewell, and Early. Hotchkiss knew the ground and usually guided the generals unerringly as they planned their moves. In a sense, his eyes were the eyes of the Second Corps. Hotchkiss also kept a journal, which is one of the most useful of Civil War military diaries because of his staff role with the leading figures directing the Confederate military efforts in Virginia.

After the war Federal authorities in Virginia ordered Hotchkiss to surrender his maps. Hotchkiss carried his protest against confiscation of the maps to Washington where he obtained a private conference with Ulysses S. Grant. Grant agreed that Hotchkiss should retain the maps and offered to pay him for copies of selected maps that might have future military use.

Hotchkiss knew the maps had great historical value, and he hoped to use them himself to illustrate accounts of the war. Indeed, his maps appeared in many books. In 1867 a New York firm published *The Battlefields of Virginia*. Written with William Allan, who had been chief of ordnance for the Second Corps, the account drew upon Hotchkiss's maps and journals and official records of both sides to summarize the major battles in Virginia from Fredericksburg to Chancellorsville. The book also included a firsthand account of Stonewall Jackson's death penned by his doctor, Hunter McGuire. Hotchkiss corresponded with many writers who drew upon both his maps and his memories. Among these were early Jackson biographers John Esten Cooke and the Englishman G. F. R. Henderson. In the early nineties, he supplied more than 120 maps to the editors of the *Atlas to Accompany the Official Records of the Union and Confederate Armies*. Hotchkiss worked for many years on a military history of the war in Virginia, which was published in

1899 as part of Clement A. Evans's series *Confederate Military History*.

With his intimate knowledge of the Army of Northern Virginia, Hotchkiss became a popular lecturer on the Civil War. Using chalk to illustrate his talks, he fascinated audiences in the North and South, often lecturing on "Reminiscences of Stonewall Jackson's Campaign in the Valley of Virginia." He also turned his geographical knowledge and mapmaking skills to other advantage. Known by 1890 as the "Father of Booms," Hotchkiss as author, lecturer, geological authority, editor of an industrial journal, and friend of Northern and English investors was one of Virginia's most persistent advocates of industrialism in the late nineteenth century.

Hotchkiss's maps and journals on the Civil War remained in private hands for nearly fifty years after his death in 1899, but in 1948, the Library of Congress acquired the materials.

BIBLIOGRAPHY

LeGear, Clara Egli, comp. *The Hotchkiss Map Collection*. Washington, D.C., 1951.

McDonald, Archie P., ed. *Make Me a Map of the Valley: The Civil War Journal of Stonewall Jackson's Topographer*. Dallas, Tex., 1973.

Roper, Peter. *Jedediah Hotchkiss: Rebel Mapmaker and Virginia Businessman*. Shippensburg, Pa., 1992.

Thomas, Jerry B. "Jedediah Hotchkiss, Gilded Age Propagandist of Industrialism." *Virginia Magazine of History and Biography* 84 (1976): 189–202.

JERRY BRUCE THOMAS

HUMPHREYS, BENJAMIN GRUBB

HUMPHREYS, BENJAMIN GRUBB (1808–1882), brigadier general and Reconstruction governor of Mississippi. Because of his mother's death when he was nine, Humphreys left Mississippi to spend his early school years in Kentucky and New Jersey. In 1824 he returned home and worked briefly as a store clerk. A year later, he was appointed to West Point, where he joined the class of Joseph E. Johnston, Robert E. Lee, and other Civil War figures. Despite a good record, Humphreys, after a Christmas riot, was expelled from the academy along with thirty-eight others. He then became overseer of his father's plantation in Claiborne County and at the same time studied law. He was elected in 1838 to the state house of representatives and in 1839 to the state senate. In 1846 he bought land on the banks of the Yazoo River in Sunflower County, and after clearing it for cultivation, he moved there with his family.

When war erupted, Humphreys joined the Sunflower Guards and was elected captain. After being commissioned colonel on September 11, 1861, he was assigned to the Twenty-first Mississippi Regiment, First Mississippi Brigade, Army of Northern Virginia. The brigade was commanded by Brig. Gen. William Barksdale. In June 1863 Humphrey's regiment moved north into Pennsylvania with Robert E. Lee's army. At the Battle of Gettysburg, Humphreys's Twenty-first Regiment was heavily engaged. On the second day the brigade, fighting as a part of Longstreet's Corps, attacked the Union left; General Barksdale was killed in the attack. As the only Mississippi field officer not killed or wounded, Humphreys assumed command of the brigade. In September 1864 Humphreys, now a brigadier general, led the Mississippi Brigade to Georgia and participated with Longstreet in the defeat of the right wing of Rosecrans's army at Chickamauga. Humphreys commanded his brigade in the siege of the Union army at Chattanooga and fought through November and December in difficult conditions with few rations and supplies in the campaign against the Federal works at Knoxville. In May 1864 Humphreys's brigade, now back with Lee's army in Virginia, participated in the Wilderness campaign. He also fought with Jubal Early in the Shenandoah Valley. In September at Berryville, Virginia, Humphreys received a gunshot wound that disabled him for the remainder of the war.

After the war, Humphreys was elected governor of Mississippi in October 1865 despite the fact that he had not been pardoned by President Andrew Johnson. Humphreys, calling himself "an unpardoned rebel," sought to renew his allegiance to the United States and to show the victors that the days of the fire-eating secessionists were over. Because of his high rank in the Confederate army, President Johnson only reluctantly sent a pardon, but Humphreys was inaugurated.

In office, he supported a moderate position in the legislative debate on the freedmen question and criticized attempts to reconstitute slavery through restricting the rights of the ex-slaves. The bill that passed was more moderate than the one promoted by extremists, but it did severely restrict the rights of ex-slaves and eventually became the basis for the Mississippi Black Code.

Because of his opposition to Military Reconstruction, Humphreys was removed from office in 1867. Gen. Irwin McDowell, who commanded the Mississippi district, then appointed Union Gen. Adelbert Ames provisional governor, but Humphreys refused to vacate his office. Faced with his intransigence, a detail of soldiers forcibly evicted him and took over the statehouse. Even after his ejection from the capitol, the governor and his family continued to occupy part of the executive mansion until they were finally marched out between a file of military guards.

In 1868, under the new Republican constitution, Humphreys again ran for the governorship. The voters elect-ed him but rejected the new constitution, which proscribed the rights of many Confederates. As a result, the state continued to be governed by a military governor.

BIBLIOGRAPHY

Rainwater, Percy Lee, ed. "The Autobiography of Benjamin Grubb Humphreys." *Mississippi Valley Historical Review* 20 (1934): 231–255.

Roland, Dunbar. *History of Mississippi: The Heart of the South.* Vol. 2. Chicago, 1925. Reprint, Spartanburg, S.C., 1978.

RAY SKATES

HUNTER, ROBERT M. T.

HUNTER, ROBERT M. T. (1809–1887), secretary of state, congressman from Virginia, and commissioner to the Hampton Roads peace conference. The second Confederate secretary of state was born April 21, 1809, at Mount Pleasant in Essex County, Virginia. After graduating from the University of Virginia in 1828, he studied law and was admitted to the Virginia bar in 1830.

From 1834 to 1837 Hunter served in Virginia's House of Delegates. Though elected as an independent, he allied himself with the anti-Jackson state rights Whigs. As an opponent of Old Hickory, he voted against legislative efforts to instruct Virginia's senators to support Thomas Hart Benton's expunging resolution and opposed Virginia's endorsement of the specie circular. On the other hand, to the dismay of the Whigs, he refused to endorse state internal improvements or the enlargement of banking establishments.

In 1837 Hunter, running as a "Sub-Treasury, Anti-Clay, state rights Whig," was elected to the U.S. House of Representatives. To the distress of the national Whigs, he consistently supported Martin Van Buren's subtreasury plan. Hunter's peculiar political independence proved advantageous after the Twenty-sixth Congress convened in December 1839. When the House deadlocked over the election of a Speaker, each party saw enough of its own principles in the Virginian to elect him as a compromise candidate, and at the age of thirty, Hunter became the youngest man ever to fill the position. But by attempting to act as a nonpartisan Speaker, he pleased neither party and let pass an opportunity to build a base of political support.

During the presidential campaign of 1840, Hunter issued a public letter stating that he would support neither President Martin Van Buren nor the Whig, William Henry Harrison, in the autumn election. Virginia Whigs were offended at what they considered yet another act of rebellion from a renegade who was nominally in their party. In 1841, when Hunter sought reelection with the endorsements of both parties, the

ROBERT M. T. HUNTER. Portrait made during Hunter's tenure as secretary of state. NAVAL HISTORICAL CENTER, WASHINGTON, D.C.

Whigs repudiated him. Local Democrats nominated Hunter and he retained his seat in Congress, but he had effectively ended his association with the Whig party. The Whigs retaliated by voting him out of office in 1843.

In the race for the presidency in 1844, Hunter, acting with a group of Virginia colleagues, tried to engineer a victory for John C. Calhoun by attempting to change the rules of the national nominating convention to favor minority candidates. Although they failed to win the nomination for Calhoun, they managed to deny Van Buren the party's nod. Instead, dark horse James K. Polk was nominated for and won the White House.

In March 1845, Hunter returned to the House of Representatives, where he led the fight for the retrocession of Alexandria County (later Arlington County) from the District of Columbia to Virginia. In 1847 the Virginia legislature sent Hunter to the U.S. Senate. As chairman of the Senate Finance Committee, he steered through Congress the tariff of 1857.

During the crisis over the settlement of the Mexican Cession, Hunter stood in opposition to the Clay compromise proposals. He ultimately voted for the Fugitive Slave Law and the organization of New Mexico and Utah; he opposed the admission of California, the abolition of the slave trade in the District of Columbia, and the settlement of the boundary dispute between Texas and New Mexico. After the death of Calhoun during the compromise debate in March 1850, Hunter, along with Jefferson Davis of Mississippi and Robert Toombs of Georgia, took over the direction of the Southern Democrats. The three came to be known as the "Southern Triumvirate."

Hunter was widely mentioned as a possible Democratic nominee for president in 1860, and his native state supported him when the party convened in Charleston. After a deadlock developed, however, and the delegates reconvened in Baltimore, Hunter threw his support to John C. Breckinridge, the eventual nominee of the Southern branch of the party.

As conditions deteriorated after the election of Abraham Lincoln, Hunter was one of three senators from the border states chosen to sit on the Committee of Thirteen that ultimately proposed the Crittenden Compromise. In an attempt to defuse the situation at Fort Sumter, on January 2, 1861, he introduced a resolution that would have required the president to retrocede any fort, dockyard, arsenal, or other such Federal installation upon proper application by a state legislature or convention. In response to Republican obstinacy, Hunter joined his senatorial colleague James M. Mason and eight Virginia congressmen in calling for a convention to avert sectional crisis by redrawing the Constitution.

Hunter presented his own proposals for restructuring the Federal government in a speech before the Senate on January 11, 1861. In a plan derived directly from principles enunciated by John C. Calhoun during the debate over the Compromise of 1850, Hunter called for constitutional amendments declaring that Congress had no power to abolish slavery in the states, the District of Columbia, or Federal dockyards, forts, and arsenals and that Congress could not abolish, tax, or obstruct interstate slave trade. He demanded a constitutional guarantee that fugitive slaves would be restored to their rightful owners or that the state providing refuge would compensate the slave owner for his lost property. To prevent a president from fomenting insurrection and circumventing the Constitution through patronage, Hunter called for a dual executive. One president would be elected from each section. While one president served in the White House for four years, the other would sit as president of the Senate; at the close of four years, they would switch offices. No bill could be passed without the consent of both.

He also proposed restructuring the Supreme Court. The chief executive from each section would appoint five justices. These justices would have the power to call before them any state that did not fulfill its constitutional obligations, including the return of fugitive slaves. If a state were found guilty, the rights of its citizens would be abrogated, and any other state in the Union could tax their property or commerce.

Hunter's plan had no support, and he resigned his Senate seat in March. After the Old Dominion seceded from the

Union, the Virginia secession convention named Hunter one of its five delegates to the Provisional Confederate Congress, then meeting in Montgomery. Once he had taken his seat, he lobbied intensely for the removal of the Confederate capital to Richmond or another Virginia city.

After the resignation of Robert Toombs, Hunter accepted appointment as secretary of state, a post he held from July 24, 1861, until February 22, 1862. One of his first acts was to adopt the principles of the Paris Conference of 1856 governing privateering, neutral flags, and blockades. Refusing to recognize a paper blockade, he insisted that blockades must be effective to be in force.

Displeased with the progress that the three Confederate commissioners to Great Britain—A. Dudley Mann, Pierre A. Rost, and William Lowndes Yancey—were making in winning recognition for the Confederacy, Hunter recalled Yancey and reassigned Mann and Rost. He dispatched his old colleague James M. Mason to England with instructions to stress that the Confederacy would offer low tariffs to the industrial giant. Mason was directed to recall to the British that they had in the past extended diplomatic recognition to other break-away nations, including the South American colonies that declared independence from Spain, and Greece when it declared itself free of the rule of the Ottoman Empire. Hunter sent John Slidell to France with similar instructions. Both representatives were seized from the British mail packet *Trent* shortly after the ship departed Havana on November 8. Although Hunter and other members of the administration hoped that the *Trent* incident would offer Britain an excuse to declare war on the United States, the English did not seize the opportunity. Hunter initiated a mission to Spain that proved similarly unsuccessful.

A slow and ponderous man, Hunter might have made an admirable secretary of state in ordinary times, but he was not suited for policy-making in a revolutionary emergency. In February 1862 he yielded his post as head of the State Department and then took a seat in the Confederate Senate, where he was elected president pro tem. He continued to dabble in diplomatic affairs by serving on the Foreign Relations Committee; he also sat on the Conference and Finance committees.

In the Senate, Hunter took a keen interest in the Confederacy's financial woes, especially attempts to limit inflation. Recognizing the need to restrict the amount of unsecured paper money, he preferred selling Treasury bonds below par over issuing depreciated currency. At one point he proposed that each taxpayer, in exchange for a bond, should contribute one-fifth of his total income to the Confederate government to finance the war; this measure failed to pass the House. During the next session, Hunter proposed a tax-in-kind, which was enacted. He also introduced a bill on January 23, 1863, gradually reducing interest rates on Treasury bonds from 8 percent to 6 percent and limiting the

amount of bonds the secretary of the Treasury could issue monthly to $50 million. The miserable condition of the Confederacy's finances by March 3, 1865, forced Hunter to defend his economic vision in the Senate, where he blamed the failure to halt rampant inflation on "impaired publick confidence."

As 1864 closed, Hunter objected to a bill exempting cargoes of vessels owned by individual states from restrictions on imports and exports; he feared that all trade would pass from the national government to the states. Instead, he proposed lifting all restrictions on importation. He also offered an amendment to a bill to provide supplies to the army that would have allowed commanding generals to impress whatever supplies they required for the use of their armies.

In general Hunter supported the Davis administration until the matter of freeing and arming the slaves came up in February 1865. Hunter opposed the move as unconstitutional and a blatant violation of state rights, but he was forced to vote in support of the measure because of strict directions to do so from the Virginia General Assembly.

> [Hunter] proposed that each taxpayer . . . should contribute one-fifth of his total income to the Confederate government to finance the war.

Early in 1865, Francis Preston Blair, a political colleague of Hunter's since the Jacksonian period, appeared in Richmond to urge a meeting between the warring sides to conclude a peace. Blair warned that if the conflict continued much longer, the United States would be forced to overwhelm the South by offering its forfeited lands to the people of Europe. Under Blair's initiative, a peace conference was arranged for February 3 on board the steamboat *River Queen* in Hampton Roads. Davis commissioned Hunter, Vice President Alexander H. Stephens, and Assistant Secretary of War John A. Campbell to meet with Lincoln and Union Secretary of State William H. Seward. The Confederate commissioners were instructed by Davis to begin discussing "the issues involved in the existing war, and . . . securing peace to the two countries."

Stephens expected to improve the Southern bargaining position by suggesting that the two sections reunite to revive the Monroe Doctrine and force Napoleon III out of Mexico, although Hunter thought this a feeble suggestion. Lincoln refused to negotiate on any basis other than reunion and abolition, although he held out a small hope that the abolition might be a compensated one. He also categorically refused to discuss anything further while the South was in arms. Hunter reminded Lincoln that Charles I had treated with the

Parliamentarians during the English Civil War. According to the Virginian, the president "laughed, and said that `Seward could talk with me about Charles I, he only knew that Charles I had lost his head.'" Hunter could not accept such "an absolute submission both as to rights and property, . . . a submission as absolute as if we were passing through the Candine forks," and the conference broke up.

Although he believed the South's defeat was inevitable, Hunter returned to Richmond and in a public address urged greater prosecution of the war. In March, however, after a consultation with Robert E. Lee on the military situation, he seized an opportunity to seek a cease-fire during which questions about slaveholders' property rights and the status of the rebellious states could be answered. On this occasion, he worked with William A. Graham, John A. Campbell, James L. Orr, and William C. Rives to introduce a resolution in the Confederate Senate calling on Davis to propose through Lee an armistice to reestablish peace and union and to settle whether the seceded states would retain their former rights and privileges if they returned to the Union. Sympathetic members of the Senate, however, determined that Davis's mind was set against suing for peace and that the resolution would do no good. They had not acted on the peace resolution when Congress adjourned for the last time.

At the conclusion of the war, Ulysses S. Grant called for Hunter's arrest, and he was imprisoned in Fort Pulaski, Georgia, until January 1866. During Hunter's incarceration, Benjamin F. Butler took great delight in devastating the Virginian's lands in Essex County. Upon being paroled, Hunter returned to Fonthill, his 3,100-acre plantation near Lloyds, Virginia, and again took up farming and the practice of law.

In 1867 and 1868 Hunter served as a delegate to Virginia's Underwood convention. He supported the resulting new state constitution minus its two clauses that disfranchised all former state and local Confederate officials and that required a loyalty oath as a qualification for public office. (As a result of a compromise engineered by the Committee of Nine, these two clauses were separately voted on by the electorate and defeated.) Under the new order, he served as state treasurer beginning in 1874 and grappled with the problem of the payment of Virginia's enormous prewar debt. He was defeated for reelection in January 1880 by one of William Mahone's Readjuster candidates.

As vice president of the Southern Historical Society, Hunter engaged in heated public correspondence with Jefferson Davis over the reasons for the calling of the Hampton Roads peace conference and the policy of conscripting and emancipating blacks. The dispute was made all the more bitter because the point of contention was so small. Davis maintained he had agreed to the meeting only because Blair had asked for it and produced a corroborative letter from Judah P. Benjamin to back his argument. Hunter stressed the public pressure to bring the war to an end because of the rapidly diminishing resources of the South and backed his recollection of the peace conference with letters from the other two commissioners. Hunter also produced an account of the "Origin of the Late War," published in 1876 in the *Southern Historical Society Papers,* which defended the South's decision to secede as the only possible response to repeated Northern aggression. At the urging of Calhoun's children, he gave serious consideration to writing a full-scale biography of the South Carolinian to enshrine his principles and protect his memory but decided that such a work from his hand would hurt rather than help his former mentor and colleague.

In his declining years, Hunter was named collector of the port of Tappahannock by Grover Cleveland. Two years later, on July 18, 1887, he died at Fonthill and was interred in the family cemetery at Elmwood.

BIBLIOGRAPHY

Ambler, Charles Henry, ed. *Correspondence of Robert M. T. Hunter, 1826–1876.* In *Annual Report of the American Historical Association for the Year 1916.* Washington, D.C., 1918.

Crow, Jeffrey J. "R. M. T. Hunter and the Secession Crisis, 1860–1861: A Southern Plan for Reconstruction." *West Virginia History* 34 (1972–1973): 273–290.

Davis, Jefferson. "The Peace Commission: Letter from Ex-President Davis." *Southern Historical Society Papers* 3 (1876–1877): 208–214. Reprint, Wilmington, N.C., 1990.

Fisher, John E. "The Dilemma of a States' Rights Whig: The Congressional Career of R. M. T. Hunter, 1837–1841." *Virginia Magazine of History and Biography* 81 (1973): 387–404.

Hitchcock, William S. "Southern Moderates and Secession: Senator Robert M. T. Hunter's Call for Union." *Journal of American History* 59 (1972–1973): 871–884.

Hunter, Martha T. *A Memoir of Robert M. T. Hunter.* Washington, D.C., 1903.

Hunter, Robert M. T. "Origin of the Late War." *Southern Historical Society Papers* 1 (1876): 1–13. Reprint, Wilmington, N.C., 1990.

Hunter, Robert M. T. "The Peace Commission of 1865." *Southern Historical Society Papers* 3 (1876–1877): 168–176. Reprint, Wilmington, N.C., 1990.

Hunter, Robert M. T. "The Peace Commission: Hon. R. M. T. Hunter's Reply to President Davis' Letter." *Southern Historical Society Papers* 4 (1877–1878): 303–318. Reprint, Wilmington, N.C., 1990.

Simms, Henry H. *Life of Robert M. T. Hunter: A Study in Sectionalism and Secession.* Richmond, Va., 1935.

SARA B. BEARSS

IMBODEN, JOHN D.

IMBODEN, JOHN D. (1823–1895), brigadier general. Born near Staunton, Virginia, on February 16, 1823, John Daniel Imboden practiced law in Staunton and represented that district for two terms in the Virginia legislature prior to the war. As a conspirator in the plot to capture the Harpers Ferry armory and arsenal, Imboden's first military operation occurred on April 19, 1861, less than 30 hours after Virginia's secession, when the captain marched his Staunton Artillery into Harpers Ferry.

Following his promotion to brigadier general on January 28, 1863, Imboden conducted his most famous campaign. From April 20 to May 27, 1863, Imboden, in cooperation with Brig. Gen. William Edmondson ("Grumble") Jones, marched his command of 3,400 men through northwestern Virginia to destroy railroad bridges and collect horses, mules, and cattle for the Confederacy. Imboden's route carried him 400 miles in 37 days. Torrential spring rains and mud slowed their progress, but his force destroyed eight railroad bridges, captured over $100,000 worth of Federal animals and supplies, and rounded up 3,100 cattle.

Imboden returned to the valley, and his next notable exploit was the surprise and capture of an entire Federal regiment, or nearly five hundred men of the Ninth Maryland Infantry, at Charles Town, on October 18, 1863. Imboden's final campaign occurred during the summer and fall of 1864, when he led his cavalry brigade in operations with Lt. Gen. Jubal Early. Typhoid fever forced the general from active duty to a prison command in Aiken, South Carolina, when he finished out the war.

During the postwar period, Imboden helped develop the coal mining industry in southwestern Virginia. Following his death on August 15, 1895, he was buried in Richmond.

BIBLIOGRAPHY

Imboden, John D. "Stonewall at Harpers Ferry in 1861." In *Battles and Leaders of the Civil War*. Edited by Robert U. Johnson and C. C. Buel. Vol. 1. New York, 1887. Reprint, Secaucus, N.J., 1982.

Imboden, John D. "Reports of Brig. Gen. John D. Imboden, April 29–June 1, 1863." In *War of the Rebellion: A Compilation of the Official Records of the Union and Confederate Armies.* Ser. 1, vol. 25, pt. 1. Washington, D.C., 1889.

Warner, Ezra J. *Generals in Gray: Lives of the Confederate Commanders.* Baton Rouge, La., 1959.

DENNIS E. FRYE

IMPERIALISM

Imperialism played a role in the origins of the Confederate States of America. When dis-Unionists argued the case for secession, they sometimes voiced predictions that an independent Southern nation would grow into a vast empire for slavery—that the new country would extend its domain and institutions southward into Mexico, Central America, the islands of the Caribbean Sea, and even the farthest reaches of South America. Such pronouncements, in many instances, were merely rhetoric designed to persuade Southerners that the potential benefits of secession outweighed its risks. However, Article IV, Section 3, of the Confederate Constitution, with its provision that the Confederacy could acquire new territory and that slavery was to be legal in such acquisitions, suggested that the new nation might follow an imperialistic course.

Confederate imperialism derived from the Southern expansion movement of the 1850s, when many Southerners reached the conclusion that American extension into Latin regions would benefit their section. They looked southward for new slave states that would enhance their political power in Washington. They also anticipated other advantages from southward expansion, including plantation opportunities, the elimination of northern Mexico as a haven for fugitive slaves, wealth from control of isthmian transit routes, improved Southern trade with the Pacific coast and Asia, and an outlet for the surplus black population of the upper South. Virginian Matthew Fontaine Maury, who as superintendent of the U.S. Naval Observatory helped plan an expedition by two U.S. naval officers to explore the Amazon River, hoped that Virginia planters would one day take their slaves to Brazil, thus relieving his state of the danger of race war. Some Southern expansionists anticipated that U.S. acquisition of the Spanish colony of Cuba, which already had slavery, would enhance the competitive position of the South's sugar planters in world markets: since U.S. acquisition of the island would terminate the African slave trade to Cuba, labor costs there, and thus the price of Cuban sugar, would rise.

Southern pressure for America's territorial and commercial expansion southward influenced American diplomacy. President Franklin Pierce completed the Gadsden Purchase from Mexico and tried to pressure Spain into selling Cuba. President James Buchanan sought land cessions from Mexico, asked the U.S. Congress to authorize an American protectorate over Mexican Chihuahua and Sonora, supported the efforts of the Louisiana Tehuantepec Company to procure transit concessions across Mexico's isthmus, and tried to purchase Cuba. Southern politicians, diplomats, and entrepreneurs played key roles in these projects. From 1849

> **Native Tennessean William Walker conquered and ruled Nicaragua in the mid-1850s.**

to 1860, the slave states provided much of the leadership, manpower, and support for the era's illegal filibustering (that is, private, military) expeditions. The most important of these expeditions attacked Cuba, Mexico, and several of the states of Central America. Native Tennessean William Walker conquered and ruled Nicaragua in the mid-1850s. Even though Walker had no intention of seeking Nicaragua's annexation to the United States, many Southerners rallied to his cause, especially after he legalized slavery there in September 1856.

Prominent Southern radicals became involved with the filibusters. Edmund Ruffin met with Walker during the Southern Commercial Convention at Montgomery, Alabama (1858). William Lowndes Yancey, C. A. L. Lamar, Roger A. Pryor, Albert Gallatin Brown, and John A. Winston aided filibusters in a support capacity. Mississippi secessionist John A. Quitman agreed to lead a filibuster army against Spanish forces in Cuba. Such contacts between notorious radicals and the filibusters attracted attention from the nation's press. This publicity, combined with the secrecy that necessarily cloaked planning for illegal military expeditions, gave rise to charges by antislavery Republicans, Southern anti-imperialists, and foreign observers that the whole tropical expansion movement was part of a secessionist conspiracy. The Knights of the Golden Circle, a filibuster organization that aspired to create a new slave empire with Cuba at its center and embracing the Deep South, most of the border slave states, Central America, the West Indies, and parts of Kansas and South America, conformed to this conspiracy interpretation. Southern imperialism, however, was less an agenda for separate nationhood than a program to avert the necessity of a separate nation. It enjoyed broad public support throughout the South, especially in the Gulf states.

Important Southern politicians who did not favor immediate secession, including Jefferson Davis, Alexander H. Stephens, John Slidell, and Judah P. Benjamin, advocated slavery's southward extension and worked toward that end, sometimes in collaboration with the filibusters.

The frustration of Southern imperialism intensified the alienation of the slave states from the Union and thus became a contributing cause to Southern secession. Northern Presidents Pierce and Buchanan, though willing to acquire territory through diplomatic channels, enforced U.S. neutrality statutes against filibustering expeditions. Their efforts prevented Quitman's planned strike against Cuba in 1854 and 1855, and contributed to Walker's downfall in Nicaragua in 1857 and his inability to reconquer that country in the years that followed. Antislavery Republicans in Congress opposed legislation to facilitate the purchase of Cuba. Many Southerners interpreted Northern obstruction of tropical expansion projects as evidence that the South's population was being reduced to second-class status within the Union; Northern hostility to slavery's southward extension appeared an indictment of their way of life. One of the last prewar efforts to resolve sectional strife, the so-called Crittenden Compromise, addressed these perceptions. This proposal (December 1860) would have reinstated the Missouri Compromise line and extended it to the Pacific Ocean, protecting slavery in any territory "hereafter acquired" south of the 36°30´ parallel latitude—a seeming invitation to slavery's future thrust into the tropics. President-elect Abraham Lincoln and the Republican party rejected the plan.

Had the Confederacy established its independence, it likely would have attempted expansion into the tropics. Warfare with the North, however, precluded such initiatives. Confederate armies did invade vulnerable areas of the Union with hopes of incorporating those areas into the new nation. But Confederate penetration of the New Mexico Territory and the states of Kentucky, Missouri, and Maryland was hardly an example of imperialism—which implies rule over subject peoples. The Confederacy made part of New Mexico into the Confederate territory of Arizona, under the expectation of eventual statehood, and recognized Missouri as its twelfth state. Southern imperialism, with its dream of a vast slave empire, died at the beginning of the Civil War.

[For further discussion of Southern efforts to acquire additional territory, see Expansionism. See also Crittenden Compromise; Cuba; Mexico.

BIBLIOGRAPHY

Barney, William L. *The Road to Secession: A New Perspective on the Old South.* New York, 1972.

Brown, Charles H. *Agents of Manifest Destiny: The Lives and Times of the Filibusters.* Chapel Hill, N.C., 1980.

Genovese, Eugene D. *The Political Economy of Slavery: Studies in the Economy and Society of the Slave South.* New York, 1967.

May, Robert E. *The Southern Dream of a Caribbean Empire, 1854–1861.* Baton Rouge, La., 1973.

McCardell, John. *The Idea of a Southern Nation: Southern Nationalists and Southern Nationalism, 1830–1860.* New York, 1979.

Rauch, Basil. *American Interest in Cuba: 1848–1855.* New York, 1948.

Walker, William. *The War in Nicaragua.* Mobile, Ala., 1860. Reprint, Tucson, Ariz., 1985.

ROBERT E. MAY

IMPRESSMENT

The Confederacy's need for supplies prompted the Congress to enact an impressment law on March 26, 1863. As with other initiatives passed in an effort to obtain goods for the war effort, the Impressment Act created severe dissension on the home front.

The act established state boards of commissioners throughout the South. President Jefferson Davis and the state governors were each entitled to appoint one person to the board. This board served two functions: it mediated disputes between impressment agents and the individual whose property was to be impressed, and it fixed prices for goods set to be impressed by government agents. The board published the list of prices frequently so as to keep in step with fluctuations on the markets. Still, the lists rarely reflected the prevailing market price.

Local impressment agents administered the law. They traveled throughout the South and surveyed the stocks of farmers, merchants, and others with products deemed necessary for the government. The agent and the farmer or merchant would assess the value of the property chosen for impressment. The individual whose property was impressed was either paid in full in Confederate scrip at the time or was issued a certificate entitling him to payment upon redemption later.

Apparently, the civilian population voiced little opposition to the impressment measure until the summer of 1863. Then the floodgates of protest opened. With the nation reeling from the military debacles at Gettysburg and Vicksburg, and with Confederate currency rapidly depreciating in value, Southerners were less than pleased to see impressment price lists that set prices well below market values. These rates—which were often 50 percent below the market price for the good—infuriated farmers and small businessmen alike who were squeezed by inflation and government demands. It came to be assumed that if the government impressed your goods for the army's use, you would take a loss. Southerners were also bothered by the haphazard way impressment agents enforced the law. Moreover, the burden of impressment was not distributed equally: those living near the Confederate field armies or near transportation depots were hit hardest. Similarly, Southerners were preyed upon by fake impressment agents who used counterfeit certificates as licenses to steal from neighbors. These were real problems, but for many, what irked them most about the law was its wastefulness: too often impressed foodstuffs, supposedly destined for the field armies, rotted at depots because agents failed to obtain transportation prior to the impressment or because transportation could not be found.

From the beginning of the war, military authorities also impressed slaves to work on fortifications or to serve as teamsters, nurses, or cooks. As with the impressment of foodstuffs and other supplies, this impressment was administered by local military authorities—Congress did not regulate impressment procedures until the 1863 law. After 1863, Congress insisted that the impressment of slaves and military goods conform to the laws of the state where the slave was impressed.

The owners of impressed slaves were paid thirty dollars a month or whatever wage may have been agreed upon in advance. In the event the impressed slave was killed while working for the government, the owner was entitled to be reimbursed in full. Masters nonetheless were often resistant to allowing impressment agents to spirit off their slaves. Planters found that impressed slaves were not treated well and were kept past the time specified in the government contract. In addition, the government was slow to pay, and when it did, it always paid in worthless Confederate currency. In short, many owners found impressment to be an economic liability. Nonetheless, military authorities found slave labor to be imperative for the war effort, especially as the tide turned against the Confederacy. By February of 1864 the govern-

> It came to be assumed that if the government impressed your goods for the army's use, you would take a loss.

ment wanted to hire a minimum of twenty thousand slaves; if the slave owners did not volunteer their chattels, the government reserved the right to impress them.

Scholars have been unable to calculate the amount of goods impressed. Authorities on the Confederate financial system, however, have speculated on the amount. Since Treasury notes were issued largely to pay for impressed goods, the amount of notes issued during the course of the Impressment Act's existence provides a rough estimate of what impressment brought to the Confederate government. Over $500 million worth of vouchers and notes were still unpaid as late as March 1865.

The unpopularity of the impressment system and the inequities it represented almost preordained its demise. By the end of the war, the Impressment Act was a dead letter, and the government found itself forced to pay for goods at market prices.

BIBLIOGRAPHY

Ball, Douglas B. *Financial Failure and Confederate Defeat.* Urbana, Ill., 1991.
Coulter, E. Merton. *The Confederate States of America, 1861–1865.* A History of the South, vol. 7. Baton Rouge, La., 1950.
Todd, Richard Cecil. *Confederate Finance.* Athens, Ga., 1954.

MARY A. DECREDICO

INDIANS

Native Americans who lived in the Confederate States of America and in Indian Territory possessed common cultural traditions. These ranged from a mixed economy of agriculture and hunting, to a villagelike settlement pattern, to a profound respect for the supernatural. Extensive interaction with Europeans, including intermarriage, had dramatically altered these traditional ways of life of the Southern Indians. Well before 1861, many of the tribespeople had adopted Euro-American clothing and housing styles, engaged in plantation-style agriculture that included slave labor, welcomed formal education, and adopted Christianity.

The most notable of the Southern Indians were the so-called Five Civilized Tribes—the Choctaws, Chickasaws, Creeks, Seminoles, and Cherokees. These people's ancestral domains extended from the Great Smokey Mountains westward to the Mississippi River, and from the Tennessee River southward to the Gulf of Mexico. The cultural transformation within their communities was particularly dramatic after 1800. The syllabary of the great Sequoyah (which enabled the Cherokees to achieve literacy in their own language), the adoption of a written constitution and code of laws by the Cherokees and the Choctaws, and a general acceptance of slavery illustrated the nature and extent of the change.

Little of this impressed Southern whites, however. The tribes possessed lands that were both fertile and mineral-rich, lands they wanted for their own use. They brought pressure upon the government of the United States to remove the Southern Indians from their ancestral homes, preferably beyond the Mississippi River. Although considered as early as 1801, removal did not become a clear national policy until 1830 when President Andrew Jackson secured congressional approval of the General Removal Act. In the decade that followed, the Five Civilized Tribes were forced to leave their homelands and take up new ones in Indian Territory. But not all of the Indians made the move; some avoided it by taking refuge in isolated hills or swamps, where they remained in virtual obscurity until removal pressures subsided. Thereafter and during the era of the Confederacy, these remnant bands lived lives of economic deprivation, political disfranchisement, and social alienation.

With their population of 50,000, the Five Civilized Tribes held title to virtually all of Indian Territory. The Quapaws, Senecas, and Seneca-Shawnees occupied small reservations in the northeast corner. Originally natives of Arkansas, 450 Quapaws were removed to Indian Territory after 1834. A Northern people, the Senecas of Sandusky ceded their Ohio lands in 1832, after which some 275 of them moved to Indian Territory. The same year a mixed band of 252 Senecas and Shawnees, also from Ohio and known as Eastern Shawnees, followed them, arriving only a few months later.

In the southwestern quadrant of Indian Territory, some 2,000 Native Americans lived in 1861 on lands leased from the Choctaws and Chickasaws. Plains Indian in cultural characteristics, these included the Wichitas and affiliated tribes, Caddos, Comanches, and Absentee Shawnees, among others. The Wichitas were the original occupants of the area, indeed of all of Oklahoma, and the Caddos were recent arrivals (1859) from Louisiana via Texas. The Penateka Comanche band came with the Caddos out of Texas, as did the Absentee Shawnees, although other Absentee bands had lived along the Canadian River since the 1830s.

With a reserve in Kansas, the Osage Indians were not technically an Indian Territory tribe. But for centuries they had seen themselves as sovereigns over the region, hunting

> **The treaties with the Five Civilized Tribes gave each the right to send one nonvoting delegate to sit in the Confederate House of Representatives. . . .**

where they wished and terrorizing anyone who objected. Peace and stability in the territory required the cooperation of the Osages.

Although there were Chickahominy Indians in Virginia, Lumbees in North Carolina, Catawbas in South Carolina, and Tunicas and Houmas in Louisiana, when the Confederate States government thought of Indian peoples they thought primarily of the tribes of Indian Territory. Recognizing the strategic necessity of drawing them into the Confederacy's orbit, the Provisional Congress in March 1861 resolved to send a commissioner to the territory to negotiate treaties of alliance. Accordingly, President Jefferson Davis appointed Albert Pike, a native of New England and now a prominent Arkansas lawyer, as commissioner to all the Indian tribes west of Arkansas. Legislation passed in May "for the protection of certain Indian tribes" became the substance of Pike's instructions. The Richmond government expected to secure the support of the Indians because of their Southern background, the military withdrawal of the United States from the territory, and Washington's failure to pay the tribes for their land.

Pike's first stop was Park Hill, the governmental center of the influential Cherokee Nation, where he arrived in early June 1861. There he found the tribe divided in its support of the Confederacy and Chief John Ross intent upon preserving a neutral course. Pike respected Ross's position and moved on to North Fork Town in the Creek Nation where, on July 10, he signed a treaty with the Creeks despite considerable opposition among the fullbloods. Unanimous in their support of the South, the Choctaws and Chickasaws signed two days later; a divided Seminole Nation signed on August 1. In these treaties the Confederates assumed all the financial obligations of the old treaties with the United States, made explicit pledges that the Indians' land would not be organized into official territories, guaranteed slavery, granted procedural rights in Confederate courts, and gave the tribes the privilege of sending delegates to Congress. For their part, the Indians agreed to become allies of the South in the current conflict.

From North Fork Town, Pike moved farther west to negotiate with the tribes of the Wichita Agency. On August 12 he signed one treaty with the Wichitas, Caddos, and affiliated tribes, and another one with the nonreservation Plains Comanches. The treaties encouraged the tribes "to prepare to support themselves, and live in peace and quietness," all under the laws and protection of the Confederate States.

While Pike was treating with the Plains tribes, he received word that the Cherokees were finally willing to negotiate with the Confederacy. The defeat of Union forces at Wilson's Creek in Missouri (August 10), the increasing belligerency of mixed-ancestry Cherokee slaveholders, the desire to retain the unity of the tribe, and the attractive offers made by Pike had caused Chief Ross to abandon his neutral posture. The treaty signed on October 7 was similar to those signed in June by the other four of the Five Civilized Tribes.

Pike used the occasion of the Cherokee treaty to negotiate with the neighboring Quapaws, Senecas, Eastern Shawnees, and Osages. Signed on October 2 and 4, these treaties recognized the four tribes as wards of the Confederate government and parties to the existing war, guaranteed slavery (which none of them practiced), and committed the Richmond government to generous annuities. These treaties, along with those signed by the Five Civilized Tribes and the Plains tribes, brought Pike's mission to a successful close. With only minor modifications, all of the treaties were ratified by the Confederate Congress.

It was one thing for the Richmond government to secure treaties of alliances with the tribes of Indian Territory, but it was something else again to carry out the provisions of the treaties. To facilitate that task the Confederate Congress authorized the establishment of a Bureau of Indian Affairs within the War Department (March 1861), the creation of a regional superintendency (April 8, 1862), and the appointment of six tribal agents. Jefferson Davis appointed David Hubbard of Alabama as the first commissioner of Indian affairs. Hubbard was followed by S. S. Scott (1862–1863) and R. W. Lee (1864).

Political squabbling prevented the appointment of a superintendent, but agents were selected. Serving rather consistently in their posts during the course of the war were John Crawford as Cherokee agent, Douglas Hancock Cooper as Choctaw and Chickasaw agent, Israel G. Vore as Creek agent, J. J. Murrow as Seminole agent, J. L. Harmon as agent for the Plains tribes, and A. J. Dorn as agent for the Osages, Quapaws, Senecas, and Seneca-Shawnees. Preoccupation with war and the scarcity of resources, however, left the Bureau of Indian Affairs largely a paper organization.

The treaties with the Five Civilized Tribes gave each the right to send one nonvoting delegate to sit in the Confederate House of Representatives at Richmond. Elias C. Boudinot took his seat as the Cherokee representative on October 2, 1862; Robert McDonald Jones acted as the Choctaw-Chickasaw delegate after January 17, 1863; and Samuel Benton Callahan, a trusted white man, represented the Creeks and Seminoles beginning May 30, 1864. The three introduced legislation affecting Indian Territory and participated in debate, but like the Bureau of Indian Affairs, their impact upon Confederate-Indian relations was negligible.

The treaties with the Five Tribes also called for the creation of a postal system. The postmaster general of the Confederacy, John H. Reagan of Texas, sought to meet those commitments by maintaining the thirteen routes and twenty-nine offices formerly established by the United States. Most of his plans were stillborn, however, because Indian Territory was early dominated by military events. Apparently only the routes and offices paralleling Red River remained in operation after 1863. Even then most mail was generated by military personnel and dispatched by courier to post offices in Texas or Arkansas.

Although never officially recognized by the Richmond government, tribal people other than those in Indian Territory contributed to the Confederacy. Most notable was a 400-man eastern Cherokee battalion attached to North Carolina's Thomas Legion, which engaged in several sharp skirmishes guarding the western approaches to the state. The 180-man First Mississippi Choctaw Infantry Battalion helped defend Vicksburg in 1863, but during the course of the battle it was captured by Union troops and met an uncertain fate. The

Alabama and Koasati peoples in Louisiana also raised a Confederate unit.

Historians have often debated why remnant Indian groups in the Southern states and larger tribes in Indian Territory should have fought on behalf of the very people who had dispossessed them of their ancestral lands only thirty years before. There is no clear answer. Economic, cultural, and family ties provide a partial explanation. Important too in Indian Territory were the activities of Southern sympathizing tribal agents and border state pressure groups. Less tangible but just as significant was the remarkable ability of the Southern Indian tribes to use history to their advantage—in this case agreeing to forget the trauma of removal in order to win firmer recognition of tribal sovereignty. In retrospect the move was not particularly prudent, but it was an independent one. Alliance with the Confederacy was above all, then, an expression of independence.

[See also Elkhorn Tavern, Arkansas; Indian Territory; Wilson's Creek Campaign; and numerous figures mentioned herein.]

BIBLIOGRAPHY

Brown, Walter L. "Albert Pike, 1809–1891." Ph.D. diss., University of Texas, 1955.

Foreman, Grant. The Five Civilized Tribes. Norman, Okla., 1934. Reprint, Norman, Okla., 1982.

Hudson, Charles. The Southeastern Indians. Knoxville, Tenn., 1976.

McNeil, Kenneth. "Confederate Treaties with the Tribes of Indian Territory." Chronicles of Oklahoma 42 (1964–1965): 408–420.

Wilson, T. Paul. "Delegates of the Five Civilized Tribes to the Confederate Congress." Chronicles of Oklahoma 53 (1975): 353–366.

W. DAVID BAIRD

INDIAN TERRITORY

With boundaries roughly identical to those of present-day Oklahoma, Indian Territory in 1861 was an unofficial designation for that area assigned by treaty to Native American tribes who had been removed to it from their eastern ancestral domains in the 1820s and 1830s. Those with the largest tracts were the Choctaws, Chickasaws, Creeks, Seminoles, and Cherokees—the so-called Five Civilized Tribes. In the northeastern corner the Quapaws, Senecas, and Shawnees occupied much smaller tracts, and in the southwest the Wichitas, Caddos, Absentee Shawnees, and Comanches inhabited lands leased from the Choctaws and Chickasaws. Some 3,000 to 4,000 Indians from the territory enlisted in the Confederate army during the Civil War. It was also the site of numerous skirmishes and battles.

Indian Territory in 1860 was only sparsely populated. Best estimates place the total number of Indians at just under 53,000, or less than one person per square mile, with the Cherokee, Choctaw, and Creek nations having the largest populations. The western two-thirds of the territory was virtually uninhabited, with the Plains tribes numbering no more than 2,000 people. Living among the Indians were some 3,000 mostly Southern-born whites and 8,376 black slaves, nearly 60 percent of whom were held by the Cherokees and Choctaws.

The sectional debate that raged in the United States during the 1850s was only dimly reflected in Indian Territory. Slavery was the focus of much discussion and the cause of tribal division, but the phrase "state rights" was meaningless. Yet tribal leaders were seriously disturbed by Republican rhetoric during the presidential campaign of 1860 that proposed expropriation of tribal lands for white settlement. When Abraham Lincoln was elected, the Indians expected the worst. Trusted advisers and friends confirmed and played upon their fears.

Many tribal leaders, therefore, welcomed the formation of the Confederate States of America. Cherokees of mixed ancestry led by Stand Watie organized the Knights of the Golden Circle to advance the Southern cause and to counteract the Keetoowahs, an antislavery society of full bloods influenced by missionaries. Choctaw Robert M. Jones, a large slaveholder, argued that opponents of Southern secession should be hanged. That the destiny of Indian Territory lay with the Confederacy seemed clear when, in early May 1861, U.S. troops abandoned Forts Washita, Arbuckle, and Cobb along the western frontier and withdrew to Kansas.

In the summer and fall of 1861, the Five Tribes and the Quapaws, Senecas, Shawnees, Osages, Comanches, Wichitas, and affiliated tribes all signed treaties of alliance and entered new bureaucratic relationships with the Confederacy. Simultaneously, the Richmond government organized a separate military department for Indian Territory commanded by Brig. Gen. Albert Pike (subsequently by William Steele, Samuel Bell Maxey, and Douglas Hancock Cooper) and composed of both Indian and non-Indian, largely Texas, regiments. Indian units and their officers were recruited from members of the Five Civilized Tribes. By 1864 they formed one division of three brigades (a Cherokee, a Choctaw-Chickasaw, and a Creek-Seminole, commanded respectively by Stand Watie, Tandy Walker, and D. N. McIntosh). The Indian division had a reported strength of 3,260, but the effective fighting force was surely less than 1,000.

Not everyone in Indian Territory supported a Confederate alliance. Among its opponents was the Creek fullblood and slaveholder Opothleyahola and some 7,000 of his followers, all of whom proclaimed loyalty to the old treaties with the United States. In late 1861, 1,400 Confederate Indian and

Texas troops commanded by Cooper engaged in three sharp battles with the dissidents (Round Mountain on November 19, Chusto-Talasah on December 8, and Chustenahlah on December 25) in an effort to force them into submission. Although one of Cooper's fullblood Cherokee regiments deserted en masse at Chusto-Talasah, the Confederate onslaught forced the Creek leader to retreat from Indian Territory and seek refuge in Kansas.

By early 1862, therefore, Confederate Indian troops controlled all of Indian Territory. That position of strength soon deteriorated, especially after the defeat of Southern forces at Elkhorn Tavern, Arkansas (March 6–8, 1862). Although

> ## The resulting chaos reduced Confederate military activity in Indian Territory to isolated raids and private justice.

based entirely upon circumstantial evidence, subsequent charges by Federal officers that Cherokee soldiers scalped the dead demoralized Indian Territory units. Following the battle, General Pike retreated with much of his command deep into the Choctaw Nation (twenty miles north of Texas) where he built defensive positions. He directed the Cherokee and Creek-Seminole regiments to patrol the Kansas border and along the Arkansas River.

The victory at Elkhorn Tavern encouraged the Union command to invade Indian Territory from Kansas in June 1862. Organized by Col. William Weer, the so-called Indian Expedition included eight white units and two Indian military units as well as several thousand returning refugees. Weer's troops pushed virtually unopposed a hundred miles south to Fort Gibson. At nearby Park Hill, Cherokee Chief John Ross welcomed the Union troops as liberators; and deserters from John Drew's Cherokee Confederate regiment, who had not been paid in months, volunteered for service, enough to organize the Third Indian Home Guard Regiment. Despite this reception and bright prospect, a failure of leadership and rumors of a counterattack caused the Union troops to withdraw back to Kansas, taking Chief Ross and as many as two thousand Cherokee refugees with them.

Southern forces were unable to capitalize upon the collapse of the Indian Expedition. Among the Cherokees two tribal governments vied for legitimacy, one recognizing John Ross as chief and the other acknowledging Stand Watie. There was not much more stability in the Confederate command. General Pike, unable to get requested supplies and believing his authority undermined, resigned in protest, only to be arrested by his subordinate and successor, General Cooper. The resulting chaos reduced Confederate military activity in Indian Territory to isolated raids and private justice.

Southern forces were in no position to challenge seriously a second Union invasion that began in April 1863. An Indian brigade composed of three loyalist regiments and commanded by Col. William A. Phillips occupied Fort Gibson with only minimal opposition. Three months later, Maj. Gen. James G. Blunt led a three-thousand-man force down the Texas Road and across the Arkansas River to attack five thousand Confederates commanded by General Cooper camped at Honey Springs. After a sharp battle on July 17, the poorly supplied Southern troops retreated from the field. They ultimately found safety in camps along Red River, where they were shortly joined by some fifteen thousand family members who abandoned their homes rather than suffer the wrath of Union forces that now controlled the northern two-thirds of Indian Territory.

Honey Springs was the decisive battle of the Civil War in Indian Territory. Thereafter Confederate operations were guerrilla-like activities designed to interrupt Union supply lines to Fort Blunt (old Fort Gibson). On such "scouts" Gen. Stand Watie and his First Indian Brigade were most effective, especially in capturing the steamer *J. R. Williams* (June 15, 1864) and, in conjunction with Texas troops commanded by Brig. Gen. Richard Montgomery Gano, a supply train of three hundred wagons at Cabin Creek (September 19, 1864). Less effective but more terrorizing were forays by Col. William Quantrill into the northeast corner of Indian Territory. Col. Tandy Walker's Second Indian Brigade gave more respectable support in the Confederate victory at Poison Springs, Arkansas (April 18, 1864).

The fall of Richmond and the capitulation of Gen. Robert E. Lee in April 1865 made further resistance of Confederate Indian troops in Indian Territory futile. On May 26, Lt. Gen. E. Kirby Smith surrendered the white Confederate command in Indian Territory, and the three tribes most tenacious in their commitment to the South surrendered through their chiefs: the Choctaws on June 19, the Cherokees on June 23, and the Chickasaws on July 14. Stand Watie, who acted on behalf of the Cherokees, was the last Confederate general to surrender.

The military contribution of Indian Territory to the Confederate war effort was marginal. Despite the place of the territory in its grand strategy, the Confederate high command never allocated sufficient resources to Indian and non-Indian troops operating there. In December 1863, at least one thousand of the Five Tribes enlistees were without guns of any kind, and those that were armed were generally not present in camp, often composing as little as 25 percent of the aggregate force. Without arms, discipline, or training, Indian troops fought bravely but with only minimal effect.

The tribes of Indian Territory paid dearly for their participation in the Civil War. The conflict left some of them so divided that factional disputes plagued their communities a century later. For them the war was an internecine struggle, with pro-Southern tribespeople devastating the property of their pro-Northern kinsmen, and vice versa. By 1865, there were few structures in Indian Territory that had not been torched at least once. And there were virtually no cattle, some 300,000 of them having been driven off by white entrepreneurs from Kansas or Arkansas.

Estimates that the tribes suffered losses of as much as one-third of their populations seem much too high. Yet we do know that 1,018 of the 3,530 Indians who enlisted in Union regiments died during their service. Assuming a higher loss among Confederate troops and an even greater number of deaths among noncombatants, Indian Territory may have lost as much as 20 percent of its Indian population, or 10,000 individuals.

An even greater cost was the loss of nationhood. Declaring that acceptance of Confederate alliances had abrogated all existing treaties, U.S. officials demanded that Indian Territory tribes negotiate new ones. Signed in 1866 and 1867, these required substantial land forfeitures, consent to the construction of railroads across tribal domains, and participation in an intertribal government, among other things. Put differently, the treaties were designed to open up Indian Territory to alien economic and political interests. The subsequent invasion culminated fifty years later in the loss of the Native Americans' land base and national identity and in the creation of the state of Oklahoma.

[*See also* Copperheads; Elkhorn Tavern, Arkansas; Indians; *and articles on particular Indian tribes and numerous figures mentioned herein.*]

BIBLIOGRAPHY

Doran, Michael F. "Population Statistics of Nineteenth Century Indian Territory." *Chronicles of Oklahoma* 53 (1975–1976): 492–515.

Franks, Kenny A. *Stand Watie and the Agony of the Cherokee Nation.* Memphis, Tenn., 1979.

Gaines, W. Craig. *The Confederate Cherokees: John Drew's Regiment of Mounted Rifles.* Baton Rouge, La., 1989.

Grayson, G. W. *A Creek Warrior for the Confederacy: The Autobiography of Chief G. W. Grayson.* Edited by W. David Baird. Norman, Okla., 1988.

Rampp, Lary C., and Donald L. Rampp. *The Civil War in Indian Territory.* Austin, Tex., 1975.

W. DAVID BAIRD

INFANTRY

During Gen. Philip Sheridan's victorious 1864 Shenandoah Valley campaign, a veteran Federal officer noted that, though outnumbered and repeatedly defeated, the Confederate infantry often inflicted more casualties than they took. They were better shots, he decided, than his own men and more skilled in taking cover, fighting like Indians or hunters. Also, in emergencies their regiments could move rapidly in an apparently disorderly swarm without losing their cohesion, offering less of a target than the orderly ranks the Federals tried to maintain. (It must be noted that this difference was most pronounced in the eastern theater, in actions between the Army of Northern Virginia and the Army of the Potomac; in the

> They were better shots, he decided, than his own men and more skilled in taking cover, fighting like Indians or hunters.

west, where Federal soldiers often had much the same civilian backgrounds as their opponents and Federal leadership was more aggressive, it was less evident.)

Several major factors contributed to this combat efficiency of the Confederate infantry. The government wisely attempted to keep its existing regiments filled with volunteers and conscripts rather than allowing them to dwindle away from battle casualties and sickness while raising more new regiments (as was done in the North for political reasons). Mixed in with veterans under experienced officers, these replacements quickly learned both the formal and the practical aspects of soldiering. The combat efficiency of Confederate infantry regiments therefore remained generally constant, as compared to the U.S. forces, which were a mixture of badly under-strength veteran units and fat newly raised regiments, green as gourds from colonel to drummer boy.

Organization

The basic Confederate infantry organization was the regiment. Its organization was practically identical with that of a U.S. regiment: ten companies (each consisting of three officers and approximately ninety-five enlisted men); a small regimental headquarters (colonel, lieutenant colonel, major, adjutant, quartermaster, surgeon, assistant surgeon, sergeant major, quartermaster sergeant, commissary sergeant, hospital steward, and two "principal musicians"); and sometimes a band. The major noticeable difference between the two sides was that each Federal regiment had its own chaplain.

During the first year of the war, the Confederate infantry included a number of odd units—separate companies and battalions (formations with three to eight companies), and so-called legions. These last were inspired by famous Revolutionary War formations, such as "Light-Horse Harry" Lee's legion of light infantry and light dragoons, which had proven highly effective in the irregular warfare waged in the Southern states. Probably the outstanding Civil War example was Hampton's Legion—organized, uniformed, armed, and equipped by Wade Hampton of South Carolina—an eight-company battalion of infantry, four companies of cavalry, and two of artillery. It soon proved impossible, however, to employ such legions as units in large-scale warfare. Hampton therefore recruited his infantry up to regimental strength and transferred the cavalry and artillery to regiments of their respective arms. Some separate battalions remained in existence throughout the war, but many of them were added to existing regiments or combined to form new ones.

A varying number of regiments—usually four or five—formed a brigade, a basic tactical formation at this time. Brigades were made up of regiments from the same state (a notable exception in the Army of Northern Virginia was its lone Arkansas regiment, which was lumped into its Texas Brigade); whenever possible they were commanded by an officer from that state. Brigades were frequently identified by name—usually that of the commander under which it originally won distinction—rather than by its number. Thus the Virginia Brigade, which Gen. Thomas J. Jackson led at First Manassas, was known as the Stonewall Brigade for the rest of its much-battered existence. The Texas Brigade referred to itself as Hood's Texans even after John Bell Hood had left the Army of Northern Virginia. Sometimes the practice became confusing: at Gettysburg, for example, McGowan's Brigade was first commanded by J. Johnston Pettigrew and then by J. K. Marshall; Archer's Brigade was led by Birkett Davenport Fry. A different type of nickname was that adopted by some Kentucky troops after the Federal occupation of their home state—the Orphan Brigade.

Until the winter of 1862–1863 the Army of Northern Virginia's infantry brigades might include a company of artillery, a practice that continued for approximately a year more in the western Confederate armies.

Several—usually four or five—brigades of infantry, with several companies of artillery, constituted an infantry division. (In contrast, until February 1863 most Federal divisions also included a regiment or more of cavalry.) An average of four infantry divisions and additional artillery made up a corps; several corps (with cavalry, reserve artillery, engineers, and service troops) formed an army. Thanks to the Confederate practice of keeping existing infantry regiments as near full strength as possible, their infantry formations usually were stronger than their Federal equivalents; a Confederate infantry brigade of 1862 through 1864 could put approximately as many rifles into line as a whole Federal division. Only when the Confederate conscription could no longer furnish sufficient replacements did their infantry units dwindle away like the veteran Federal regiments.

Though most of the Confederate states raised separate battalions of sharpshooters, there is little evidence that many of these were trained, armed, or employed as such. Instead, like other separate battalions, they frequently were later consolidated to form standard infantry regiments. However, during the 1864 campaign many infantry brigades of the Army of Northern Virginia organized 180-man corps of picked soldiers for outpost service, sniping, and patrolling. These corps were divided into four-man groups, each of which lived and fought as a team. These organizations proved highly useful, especially for fighting in thick woods such as the Wilderness.

Mounted infantry were infantrymen given horses or mules for greater mobility; they moved mounted, but dismounted to fight. In the East they appeared largely in the more irregular Confederate forces in the Shenandoah Valley, but in the West they were relatively common. Though useful in raids and in advance or rearguard actions, especially in broken country, Confederate mounted infantry had two major weaknesses. Being armed with unhandy, long muzzle-loading muskets, it was relatively helpless if caught while mounted by Federal cavalry: dismounted, with every fifth man detailed to hold horses, it seldom could stand off attacks by superior numbers of enemy infantry for any great length of time—a mission that Federal mounted infantry units armed with Spencer repeating rifles could accomplish handily.

Clothing and Equipment

Though the first year of the war saw gentlemen's companies with smart uniforms, elaborate camp equipment, and black body servants for each private, the average Confederate infantryman of 1861–1862 could be only sketchily equipped. This became something of a virtue for he soon preferred to travel light. Knapsacks (packs) were discarded as too cumbersome; most soldiers substituted the traditional American "horseshoe roll," rolling their blankets up lengthwise (inside an oilcloth or rubber blanket if they had one), slinging it over the left shoulder, and fastening its ends together behind the right hip. Extra articles of clothing could be rolled up inside the blanket. Alternatively, the soldier might make a short roll of his blanket and sling it across the middle of his back on a narrow strap or thong. A shortage of suitable material made blankets a difficult item to procure. Northern observers reported Confederates using varicolored quilts or strips of carpet, the latter sometimes with a central slit cut in them so they could be worn as ponchos. Captured U.S. blankets and civilian ones in all colors were also common.

The haversack (a plain canvas bag, roughly a foot square, with a flap cover and often a removable inside bag for small articles) slung at the soldier's left hip held his rations and few personal possessions. Over it would hang his canteen. His leather cartridge box with its forty rounds of ammunition usually was worn on the waist belt, handy to his right hand; between it and the belt buckle was a small leather pouch for percussion caps. The bayonet was carried in a leather scabbard suspended from a frog on the left side of the waist belt, under the haversack and canteen.

Confederate equipment as a whole showed great variety—prewar militia issue, obsolete U.S. material found in seized arsenals, different European models smuggled in through the blockade, captured material, and various domestic manufactures. Soldiers frequently added two practical items, a large tin cup and a "side" (bowie) knife, which was more of a tool than a weapon. Some veterans claimed that Confederate infantrymen tended to discard their bayonets (which were seldom actually bloodied in combat) and even their cartridge boxes and cap pouches, preferring to stuff cartridges and caps into their pockets. Considering the limited pocket space the Confederate jacket and trousers provided, this last story should be regarded with suspicion.

Recent research, confirmed by contemporary photographs, indicates that the Confederate infantryman was, contrary to received tradition, generally well supplied with clothing. Quartermaster Department records show a steady issue of clothing, if not smart uniforms, to the troops. Perhaps the Army of Northern Virginia's most ragged period was during the Second Manassas and Sharpsburg campaigns of August through September 1862, when its first locally procured uniforms (especially shoes) were wearing out and the Quartermaster Department was just beginning to develop an efficient supply system. By 1865 raggedness reemerged in troops from states such as Florida, which could not provide adequate support. Other states, such as North Carolina, however, had a surplus of uniforms on hand in 1865. Clothing supply for the Confederate western armies was less reliable but appears to have been generally adequate. America was rough campaigning country: after a few weeks in the field new uniforms would be showing heavy wear and tear.

The standard infantry uniform was a gray forage cap, a short, single-breasted gray jacket, sky-blue trousers, and heavy shoes. Naturally there were many variations, especially in the shades of gray cloth available. A frequent substitute for gray was "butternut," yellowish-brown shades obtained by dyes made from walnut hulls and copperas. Trousers were often gray or butternut, instead of blue, and many soldiers replaced their issue caps with soft slouch hats of many patterns. The showy zouave uniforms of 1861 soon disappeared, though one or two Louisiana regiments may have retained theirs for some time. The Second Alabama and Fourth Arkansas infantry in 1863 wore reddish homespun and broad-brimmed wool hats. The Forty-seventh Georgia had uniforms of blue-striped brown ticking. Requiring uniforms in a hurry before the Battle of Shiloh, the Second Texas received undyed clothing which reminded them of shrouds. Some prisoners taken in 1863 had English-manufactured jackets and overcoats of excellent dark-blue cloth. In the Wilderness in 1864, a North Carolina brigade in new uniforms of unusually dark gray were mistaken for Yankees and shot up—along with Lt. Gen. James Longstreet—by another Confederate unit.

Shoes were a major problem. Imports from England were gradually throttled, and domestic production was seriously hampered by a shortage of leather. By 1863 shoes were being made with canvas uppers, which came apart in wet weather. By 1864 some unfortunate infantrymen were receiving shoes with iron-bound wooden soles. In consequence, dead or captured Northerners were frequently stripped of their footgear.

Parts of Federal uniforms, which might also be taken from captured supply depots, were commonly worn. Although sky-

> ## . . . after a few weeks in the field new uniforms would be showing heavy wear and tear.

blue trousers were regulation for Confederates, the use of blue coats and overcoats was considered a violation of the laws of warfare, and Confederate commanders usually ordered such articles redyed or discarded. It could result in unfortunate incidents. A. P. Hill's attack on the Federal left flank at Sharpsburg probably owed part of its success to the fact that his men had replaced their tattered outfits with blue uniforms they had just captured at Harpers Ferry, and the Federals could not readily distinguish friend from foe.

The general appearance of Confederate infantry was marred by a thriftless element that neglected its clothing and equipment, preferring to go ragged rather than care for it or carry a change of shirts and underwear. A good many of them (like some Federal soldiers) seem to have had a personal aversion to soap and water; in 1864 a Federal cavalryman described prisoners from the Eighth South Carolina Infantry Regiment as having the aroma of aged billy goats. Ironically, such men became the "ragged rebels" of Confederate tradition—supposedly the epitome of the Confederate infantryman and one of the South's most beloved myths.

Weapons

The Confederate infantryman's standard weapon was the rifle-musket, a long-barreled, muzzle-loading, percussion-ignition, rifled weapon that fired the so-called minié ball. Besides the rifle-musket, there was the rifle, a weapon with a shorter, heavier barrel, usually equipped with a sword bayonet. The Confederates also had a few special sharpshooters' rifles, the most prized of which seems to have been the short, English-manufactured, caliber .45 Whitworth. When fitted with a telescope sight, it was reportedly accurate up to eight hundred yards.

The first Confederate infantry organized in 1861 were haphazardly armed with weapons taken from seized U.S. arsenals in their territory, those already in the possession of their state militias, and whatever could be purchased in Europe or the Northern states before hostilities began. (It is estimated that approximately 600,000 small arms were brought into the South by blockade runners.) Such sources were later supplemented by the hastily developed Confederate arms industry and by captured weapons.

Though some Confederate infantry, especially in the West, were initially armed with flintlock muskets, smoothbores, shotguns, and hunting rifles, by late 1862 and early 1863 the average Confederate infantryman had received a modern rifle-musket or rifle. The English-made caliber .557 Enfield rifle-musket and short rifle were reportedly the most popular, but various U.S. models—either captured or Southern-manufactured—were also common. Some one hundred thousand good Austrian Lorenz caliber .54 rifle-muskets added variety. It should be noted that Federal infantry were not much better armed than the Confederates during the war's first two years; even in 1863, at Vicksburg and Gettysburg, some Federal soldiers turned in their obsolete smoothbore muskets and replaced them with captured rifle-muskets.

In general, these weapons were accurate at up to six hundred yards and could kill at one thousand. Their percussion firing mechanism functioned even in bad weather, which had left the flintlock musket useless except as a long handle for its bayonet. Their major weakness was a comparatively slow rate of fire. A fresh, well-trained soldier with a clean rifle-musket could fire three rounds a minute, but as continued firing fouled its barrel the rate of fire would drop to two rounds a minute, or less.

Tactics

The rifle-musket's increased range and accuracy forced considerable changes in tactics. American officers—Confederate and Federal—whose last combat service had been in 1846 and 1847 against Mexican troops armed with smoothbore flintlock muskets with an effective range of barely two hundred yards, now found themselves in a new, far more deadly sort of war. Artillery could no longer attempt to unlimber within three hundred yards of enemy infantry and demolish it with canister without quickly taking prohibitive losses. Cavalry charges against unbroken infantry became next to impossible, and infantry attacks were risky, costly affairs. In short, the infantryman with his rifle-musket dominated the battlefield; the effectiveness of his fire led to the increasing use of field fortifications.

Both opponents began the war with the same drill manuals and the same tactics, modifying the latter to fit the improvements in infantry weapons. If the changes seem slow and insufficient to modern readers, it must be remembered that it probably was late 1862 before the majority of infantry on either side had modern rifle-muskets and the need for change became apparent. Also, the rifle-musket's relatively slow rate of fire made it necessary to use masses of men in both the attack and the defense. At Fredericksburg, Robert E. Lee's defensive line in the Sunken Road at the foot of Marye's Heights was four men deep, each line firing in turn and then passing to the rear to reload. An attacking army normally expected heavy losses and so commonly adopted deep formations, to be certain of getting enough men into its objective to hold it against counterattacks. At Shiloh in 1862, Confederate Gen. Albert Sidney Johnston's initial attack on the Federal left flank was delivered by two corps, one behind the other, with two more corps held in column as reserves. At Gettysburg, the right flank of Pickett's charge was three brigades deep; at Atlanta in 1864, John Bell Hood formed his brigades with their regiments in column (one behind the other), thus giving them a depth of eight to twelve men.

The common formation used by an infantry regiment in action throughout the war was the "line of battle"—its companies abreast in a two-deep line, with the regimental colors in the center. One company usually would be deployed as skirmishers from one hundred to three hundred yards in front of their regiment, depending on the terrain. In wooded or broken country, this skirmish line would be strengthened, sometimes with half the regiment being so engaged. During prolonged fighting in such areas, whole regiments might be deployed in heavy lines of skirmishers, individual soldiers taking cover and firing at will.

A typical infantry division attack formation was in three lines, each composed of one or more brigades. (The composition of each line would be based on the number of brigades present, their relative strength, and the tactical situation.) The leading brigade would be in line of battle, its regiments advancing abreast, preceded by one or two lines of skirmishers who probed forward to locate and develop the enemy position. The second line, also deployed in line of battle, followed approximately 250 yards behind. The third line

> **Cavalry charges against unbroken infantry became next to impossible, and infantry attacks were risky, costly affairs.**

might be similarly deployed or held in "column of fours" for rapid movement to a point of danger or opportunity.

Once hostile contact was made, the first line pushed up to absorb the skirmishers and attacked. This seldom was a dashing bayonet charge; instead it often broke down into an "advance by rushes," elements of the first line working forward, sometimes gradually, from one bit of cover to the next, with pauses to build up the fire superiority to cover the next rush. If the first line stalled, the second line would be fed in to restore the momentum of the attack, followed if necessary by the third line. The assaulting force, at the moment of collision with the enemy, would thus consist of two or three lines merged into one heavy, disorderly wave, the individual regiments badly intermixed. Only forceful personal leadership by officers and noncommissioned officers of all grades could keep it under the necessary minimum of control to ram the attack home. Even then, it might fail, especially if the enemy had had time to entrench and so was sheltered from infantry and artillery fire.

Perhaps the most marked tactical feature of the Civil War was the employment of hasty entrenchments, made of whatever materials were available. These were little used before late 1863, but after experiencing the protection afforded by sunken roads at Fredericksburg and Sharpsburg and stone farm fences at Gettysburg, the average soldier on both sides concluded that it was wise to dig in. Through 1864 and 1865, unless utterly exhausted, troops in the vicinity of the enemy, even if they were under orders to attack, would habitually entrench as soon as they halted, using their tin cups, halves of discarded canteens, and knives.

In action, infantry officers of all grades had to be quick to detect gaps in the enemy's front and to maintain tight contact with the friendly units to their front and flanks. A gap of any size between units might allow the enemy to wedge into their front and roll up their line in both directions, while an open flank not covered by alert patrols was an invitation to disaster, troops in line formation being very vulnerable to attacks from the flank and rear.

Though his war ended in defeat, the Confederate infantryman had won an outstanding reputation for hard fighting, swift marching, endurance amid hardships, and sheer pugnacity. He nevertheless had remained a thorough individualist, much given to straggling, unauthorized foraging, absence without leave, and general indiscipline.

Officers whom the Confederate infantryman trusted could lead him against any danger. But such trust was hard-

> **. . . Confederate infantry could accomplish wonders—but at a cost the South could not afford.**

earned, the Southern infantryman being persnickety and demanding of his officers. He disliked strict West Pointers (particularly for officers below the grade of general), regarded men from other states as unreliable foreigners, and scorned any tendency toward pomp and circumstance. Above all, he expected nothing less from every officer, whether new lieutenant or general, than unhesitating, outstanding courage and personal leadership. Both victory and defeat killed or disabled large numbers of such officers; eventually it became impossible to replace them with men of equal courage and competence. A British observer conclud-

ed that Confederate infantry could accomplish wonders—but at a cost the South could not afford.

[*See also* Civil War, *article on* Small Arms; Uniforms.]

BIBLIOGRAPHY

Coggins, Jack. *Arms and Equipment of the Civil War.* Garden City, N.Y., 1962.

Comminger, Henry S. *The Blue and the Gray.* Vol. 1. New York, 1950.

Department of Military Art and Engineering, U.S. Military Academy. *Supplemental Material: Weapons of the Civil War and Organization and Tactics.* West Point, N.Y., 1959–1960.

Elting, John R. *American Army Life.* New York, 1982.

Freeman, Douglas S. *Lee's Lieutenants: A Study in Command.* 3 vols. New York, 1942–1944. Reprint, New York, 1986.

Todd, Frederick P., ed. *American Military Equipage.* Vol. 2. Providence, R.I., 1977.

Watkins, Sam R. *Co. Aytch.* New York, 1962.

Wiley, Bell I. *The Life of Johnny Reb.* New York, 1943. Reprint, Baton Rouge, La., 1986.

JOHN R. ELTING

INFLATION

During the four short years of its existence, the Confederacy was plagued by a classic case of hyperinflation. This inflation destroyed the value of the government's currency and its credit and thus its capacity to supply its armies. Ultimately it contributed heavily to the destruction of the civilian population's morale and to the Confederacy's defeat.

The causes of this inflation included a bloated currency and public concern regarding the ultimate worth of the Richmond government's Treasury notes. This feeling was accentuated by the Union ban against the circulation of Confederate money in territory under Federal control. Inflation was also strongly influenced by the malfunctioning of the internal transportation system, military impressments, and the Federal blockade.

At the time the Confederate government was established in February 1861, the circulating medium of the eleven states of the Confederacy amounted to approximately $85 million in bank notes and $46 million in gold, silver, and copper coins. Three years later, before the Forced Funding Act of February 17, 1864, ordered the holders of Treasury notes to buy bonds or else have their money declared worthless, the currency of the country was approximately $1.115 billion, consisting of $900 million in Treasury notes, $125 million in bank notes, and $90 million in state, local government, and private scrip. Thus the currency was 8.5 times its prewar size. This growth was caused not only by massive government expenditures (greatly increased by the inflation) but also by the failure to regulate the circulation of $215 million worth of competing currencies.

Inflation was further promoted by the absence of effective and timely internal taxes to sop up the excess currency.

The value of the currency and the inflation were affected by a number of factors over which the government had only varying degrees of control. For example, Union military victories followed by Federal rules prohibiting the circulation of Confederate notes in occupied territory caused such notes to be sent to the regions still under Richmond's control. Thus by 1864, with at least a third of its land area and people under occupation, the real increase in the currency in the area remaining under Confederate control was more nearly 11, not 8.5, times the prewar circulation.

The inflation was reflected in the price of gold expressed in paper money and the prices of domestic and imported goods. So far as the gold value of paper money was concerned, Treasury notes were at par with gold during much of 1861. Confederate money enjoyed a considerable advantage over other currencies because it circulated without discount or exchange charges throughout the whole country. By the beginning of 1862, however, five gold dollars commanded six in Treasury notes. In January 1863, a gold dollar was worth three paper dollars, and by early 1864, the ratio had risen to about 1–20, with rates as high as 1–40 being posted west of the Mississippi River, where the residents had long held a strong aversion to paper money.

The gold premium advanced most quickly during times of Union victories and more slowly during periods when the tide of battle favored the Confederates. The premium declined only twice, first in mid-1864, when a forced funding act and the recall of old notes of exchange for new ones temporarily reduced the size of the currency. The second occasion was in March 1865, when the Treasury sold its gold coin for Treasury notes in order to pay the Army of Northern Virginia. Just before the capture of Richmond, in March 1865, the ratio was around sixty Treasury dollars to one in gold.

The prices for such imported goods as coffee, which could not be easily restocked because of the blockade, increased very rapidly. Southern merchants, denied Northern credits, had not been able to stock up with imported or Northern goods and supplies of these were soon exhausted. By January of 1864, the premium on such goods was 41 times prewar prices, nearly twice the gold premium. The differential would have been even higher except that many people could no longer afford such luxuries and had to do without or use local substitutes. After the "New Plan" regulating imports and exports went into effect on February 17, 1864, there was a modest decline in prices. But prices resumed their rise, reaching 88–1 after Wilmington was captured in early 1865.

The prices of domestically made goods up until the second half of 1863 grew more rapidly than the gold premium. By April 1863, domestic goods were priced 6.25 times higher than in 1861, whereas the gold premium in paper was only 4.5. Thereafter, the prices of domestically made goods,

chiefly food, declined when compared with gold, so that by January 1865, the gold-to-paper ratio was 1–53, whereas the domestic price index was only 38.5 times the prewar level.

This apparent anomaly can be attributed to a number of factors. Domestic food production rose, so more food was available. On the other hand, the breakdown in the railroad system made it difficult to move surpluses from where they were produced to where they were needed. In addition, the military impressment officers seized produce at artificially low prices before it could reach the cities, so that food prices were artificially raised in urban areas.

Wages and salaries, particularly of those working directly or indirectly for the government, were seldom raised and never on a scale sufficient to keep pace with inflation. This inflicted severe economic hardship on many people, thus further undermining public morale, particularly among soldiers, many of whom deserted.

Confederate government efforts to retard or reverse the inflation proved inadequate and sometimes harmful. The plan to limit the currency by making Treasury notes fundable into bonds failed because the Treasury did not take the needed measures to make the interest payable in coin.

Because taxes were low, were levied late, and favored the planters, the government's fiscal revenues were inadequate to reduce the currency. Treasury efforts to reduce expenses and inflation by levying taxes-in-kind and by impressing provisions at artificially low prices only fueled inflation by encouraging nonproduction, hoarding, and speculation. The supply of food produced or marketed near cities or the armies declined, thereby further increasing the shortages and high prices.

Similarly, the three-year delay in enacting regulations governing foreign trade encouraged high-priced luxury imports, provided no incentive to import necessities, and drew off badly needed foreign exchange. This negligence further promoted economic disintegration. Inflation, like so many other difficulties, was a problem for which the Confederates did not have timely or adequate remedies.

[*See also* Bonds; Bread Riots; Currency; New Plan; Speculation; Taxation.]

BIBLIOGRAPHY

Lerner, Eugene. *Money, Prices and Wages in the Confederacy, 1861–1865.* Chicago, 1954.
Schwab, John C. *The Confederate States of America, 1861–1865: A Financial and Industrial History of the South during the Civil War.* New York, 1901.

DOUGLAS BALL

JACKSON, CLAIBORNE F.

JACKSON, CLAIBORNE F. (1806–1862), governor of Missouri. Born in Fleming County, Kentucky, Claiborne Fox Jackson moved to Missouri when he was twenty, settling in Arrow Rock. He became involved in the mercantile business and banking while also actively pursuing a career in politics. He served in the Missouri House of Representatives from 1836 to 1848 and in the state Senate from 1848 to 1852. Here he allied himself with Senator Thomas Hart Benton, the longtime leader of Missouri Democratic politics, and became a leader in the Central Clique, a group of politicians who dominated affairs at Jefferson City.

In the aftermath of the Mexican War, Jackson became an ardent champion of the extension of slavery into the new territories, drafting resolutions to that effect in the legislature. This led to his break with Benton, who refused to support that issue. The resultant split kept Missouri Democratic politics in turmoil throughout the 1850s, although the Democrats managed to retain the governorship. Jackson tried to play a conciliatory role during this period and was rewarded by being

> . . . he did pursue against
> overwhelming odds a course
> he believed was best for his
> state and the South.

named the state's first banking commissioner in 1857 while also serving as state Democratic chairman. Thomas L. Snead, who was his aide during the Civil War, described Jackson as "tall, erect and dignified; a vigorous thinker, and a fluent and forcible speaker, always interesting, and often eloquent . . . with positive opinions on all public questions, and the courage to express and uphold them."

In 1860 Jackson became the consensus candidate of the party for governor, something he had long sought. Almost immediately he was confronted with the split in the national Democratic party. Although sympathetic to the Breckinridge wing of the party, he realized that his best chance for election came from remaining loyal to the regular Douglas Democrats, a move that proved successful.

At his inauguration on January 3, 1861, however, Jackson revealed his true sentiments by warning that Missouri would have to join the slaveholding states in secession if the North tried coercion in any form against those who were leaving the Union. He asked the General Assembly to call a convention to determine Missouri's future course while also seeking a strengthening of the state militia.

In the days that followed, Jackson worked actively to prepare the militia for the future possibility of secession. He sent his lieutenant governor, Thomas C. Reynolds, to Washington to confer secretly with Southern leaders there as to the best course of action. The legislature approved his recommendation for a convention, but when it met on February 28 it adopted a course of strict neutrality, taking a wait-and-see attitude with regard to any future action. Following the firing on Fort Sumter, President Abraham Lincoln requested four thousand three-month volunteers from Missouri. Jackson rejected this call for Missouri troops as "illegal, unconstitutional and revolutionary; in its objects inhuman and diabolical." At the same time he met secretly with Southern sympathizers in St. Louis to determine the best course of action to secure the U.S. arsenal in that city with its sixty-thousand-stand of arms.

Calling the legislature into special session, Jackson sought unprecedented powers over the state militia while also ordering that organization into week-long statewide encampments the first week of May. This latter move served as a coverup for an attempt to seize the U.S. arsenal at St. Louis as the militia established Camp Jackson on the outskirts of that city. That plot was thwarted by decisive action on the part of Capt. Nathaniel Lyon, in command of the facility, who ringed the arsenal's approaches with a series of defensive positions. Meanwhile Jackson sent secret emissaries to President Jefferson Davis at Montgomery and to the recently seceded state of Virginia seeking aid. Davis responded by forwarding two 12-pound howitzers and two 32-pound guns from the arsenal at Baton Rouge, which arrived at Camp Jackson disguised as "Tamaroa marble." On the final day of the encampment, Lyon surrounded Camp Jackson with ten thousand men and forced the surrender of the militia. While Lyon marched his prisoners to the arsenal, rioting broke out, and twenty-eight persons were killed.

The legislature now promptly passed Jackson's militia bill, giving the governor expanded powers. Jackson appointed Sterling Price to head a reorganized "Missouri State Guard."

Missouri quickly became an armed camp as the new organization moved forward. Price arranged a truce with the Union forces in St. Louis, now commanded by Gen. William S. Harney. But this broke down after ten days as rumors circulated that Jackson was continuing to strengthen his forces in the interior of the state. A *New York Herald* reporter, visiting Jefferson City, found Confederate flags much in evidence.

When Lyon replaced Harney, he made it clear in a personal confrontation with Jackson and Price at St. Louis on June 11 that he intended to assert Union authority over the entire state. Jackson now called for fifty thousand volunteers to defend the state and abandoned Jefferson City, retreating to a more defensible position at Boonville as Lyon moved up the Missouri River to occupy the capital. Following a brief skirmish at Boonville in which Lyon quickly dispersed state guardsmen led by Jackson, the governor and Price retreated to southwest Missouri to reorganize their forces.

Jackson, accompanied by former senator David Rice Atchison, hastened to Richmond in mid-July where he secured an agreement from Jefferson Davis to pay Missouri troops in the field as soon as the state seceded. Returning to New Madrid, which the Confederates had recently occupied, Jackson learned that he had been deposed by a reconvened state convention and replaced with a pro-Union provisional government. Undaunted, he issued a proclamation on August 5 declaring Missouri a free and independent state under authority presumably given him by the legislature. Returning to Memphis, Jackson discovered that the Confederate Congress had appropriated $1 million for Missouri troops cooperating with its armies.

Hastening through Arkansas, Jackson learned that Price had defeated a Union force under Lyon at Oak Hills, Missouri, and moved on to Lexington. There Jackson rejoined him and called the legislature to meet at Neosho to formally withdraw Missouri from the Union. Unable to hold their position at Lexington, the State Guard retreated once more into southwest Missouri. A rump session of the state legislature met at Neosho on October 28 and passed an ordinance of secession. Jackson's emissaries in Richmond promptly signed an alliance with the Confederacy whereupon the legislature made provision for Missouri's representatives in the Confederate Congress and authorized the governor to issue $10 million in defense bonds to underwrite the cost of Missouri's war effort. Jackson now traveled to New Orleans to secure arms for the State Guard. He also managed to float the recently authorized defense bond issue.

Union forces under Gen. Samuel R. Curtis had meanwhile pushed Price out of Missouri. Jackson rejoined Price in time for the Battle of Elkhorn Tavern in early March. Thereafter he established a temporary capital at Camden, Arkansas. Sometime during the winter he managed to bring his wife and family south, together with twenty handpicked slaves. They were settled on a farm in Red River County, Texas. In July 1862, Jackson conferred with his fellow governors in the Trans-Mississippi at Marshall, Texas, and cooperated with them in dealing with problems in that theater. That fall he established reception camps along the Missouri-Arkansas border for those Missouri recruits wishing to join Confederate forces.

In mid-November 1862 Jackson contracted pneumonia and died at Little Rock after a confinement of several weeks. Though one might question the practical wisdom of Jackson's actions in 1861, he did pursue against overwhelming odds a course he believed was best for his state and the South. Certainly he was deeply attached to both.

BIBLIOGRAPHY

Kirkpatrick, Arthur R. "Missouri's Secessionist Government, 1861–1865." *Missouri Historical Review* 45 (January 1951): 124–137.

Knox, Thomas W. *Camp-Fire and Cotton-Field: Southern Adventure in Time of War.* Cincinnati, Ohio, 1865.

Parrish, William E. *A History of Missouri.* Vol. 3. Columbia, Mo., 1973.

Parrish, William E. "Missouri." In *The Confederate Governors.* Edited by W. Buck Yearns. Athens, Ga., 1985.

Snead, Thomas L. *The Fight for Missouri from the Election of Lincoln to the Death of Lyon.* New York, 1888.

WILLIAM E. PARRISH

JACKSON, THOMAS J. ("STONEWALL")

JACKSON, THOMAS J. ("STONEWALL") (1824–1863), lieutenant general. Stonewall Jackson ranks among the most brilliant commanders in American history. Even though his field service in the Civil War lasted but two years, his movements continue to be studied at every major military academy in the world. He was an artillerist who excelled in infantry tactics, a devout Christian merciless in battle, a man of eccentricities but one motivated by an inflexible sense of duty. Jackson's death at the midway point of the war was the greatest personal loss that the Confederacy suffered. Many writers then and now insist that had he lived, the outcome of the South's attempt at independence might have ended differently.

No general ever rose from humbler beginnings. Jackson was born January 21, 1824, at Clarksburg deep in the mountains of what is now West Virginia. Although Jacksons were longtime residents of the area, his father was a struggling attorney with mounting debts. Jackson was only two years old when the father and an infant sister died of typhoid fever. For four years the widow and three children were virtual

THOMAS J. ("STONEWALL") JACKSON. This portrait by George W. Minnes, from the Matthew Brady collection, was taken two weeks before Jackson's death on May 10, 1863.

NATIONAL ARCHIVES

wards of the town. Mrs. Jackson remarried, but her new husband was unable financially to care for the children. They were sent individually to live with relatives. Jackson's mother died a year after the breakup of the family.

The lad grew up under the care of an uncle who ran lumber and grist mills in Lewis County, south of Clarksburg. Jackson developed into a sturdy youth accustomed to hard work and outdoor activities. The absence of parents also made him withdrawn and introspective in personality. Local tutors, plus a love of reading, provided him with a limited education.

Jackson went to the U.S. Military Academy in 1842 only after the first appointee from his congressional district decided not to pursue a military education. Few cadets ever entered West Point with less scholastic preparation than Jackson. Moreover, the mountain lad was introverted, awkward, and lacking in social graces. He made few friends during the four years at the academy. Using impassivity as a protection, Jackson concentrated all of his energies on learning. Determination, patience, and hours of studying by day and night accomplished his goal. Rising from near the bottom of his class at the start, Jackson ranked seventeenth of fifty-nine cadets at his 1846 graduation.

War had already been declared with Mexico when Jackson entered the army as a lieutenant in the Third U.S. Artillery. He proceeded at once to Mexico. His battery saw no action for six months, and Jackson openly despaired of getting into battle. In March 1847, however, he participated in the assault on Vera Cruz; other engagements followed, with Jackson cited for gallantry at Contreras and Chapultepec. By the end of the war, Jackson held the rank of brevet major. None of his West Point classmates had done as well in Mexico.

Jackson returned to the States and reported for duty at Fort Hamilton on Long Island, New York. By then he had developed an increasing interest in religion. (In Mexico, he had had several discussions about Catholicism with the bishop of Mexico City, but found the services too formal.) In September 1848, Jackson received baptism and attended a number of communions at an Episcopal church adjacent to Fort Hamilton. His duties as assistant quartermaster and occasional member of courts-martial left Jackson free to pursue his fondness for reading. History was his favorite subject. Jackson also maintained a steady correspondence with his beloved sister, Laura, who was married and lived in Beverly, Virginia. He continued through the years to make periodic visits to this only surviving member of his immediate family.

Apprehensions over health were an ongoing concern to Jackson. Chronic discomfort, especially with his stomach, liver, and kidneys, soon convinced him that his troubles were punishment from God for his sins. Jackson sought relief from several New York physicians. When hydrotherapy seemed to ease his pain, Jackson became an ardent devotee of water

treatments and thereafter regularly visited spas whenever possible. He likewise made physical exercise a part of his daily routine. Although many of his problems may have been the result of hypochondria, his weak eyesight and poor hearing were real and plagued him after his Mexican service.

In December 1850, Jackson's company transferred to Fort Meade in the remote interior of Florida. The artillerist uncharacteristically became embroiled in arguments with his commanding officer, Maj. William H. French. Jackson was soon under arrest for accusing French of having an affair with his maid. Meanwhile, Jackson had received an offer to become professor of artillery tactics and optics at the Virginia Military Institute in Lexington, Virginia. The academy was small, having been in existence barely a dozen years; nevertheless, it offered Jackson both a challenge and a change of scenery. He resigned his army commission and reported to the institute on the eve of the 1851–1852 school year.

"The Major" spent a fourth of his life at VMI. Only three months after his arrival in Lexington, Jackson joined the Presbyterian church and rapidly became one of the most devout Calvinists of his age. He found solace in constant prayer and strength through an inflexible faith. He attended every service at the Lexington Presbyterian Church. To the amusement of the congregation, Jackson slept through at least part of every service. He always sat bolt upright, his back never touching the pew. In that way, Jackson said, the pain of discomfort was punishment for his disrespectful naps.

Jackson's name and that of VMI are permanently intertwined—but not because of the professor's classroom performance. He was too skilled in artillery principles to be able to present it effectively. Having no background in the other subjects he taught—acoustics, analytical mechanics, astronomy, and physics—Jackson was forced to study as he taught. Memorizing lectures the night before he gave them, he was unable to expand upon or deviate from presentations. A question from a cadet, and Jackson could only repeat verbatim what he had previously said on the subject.

At the same time, the professor was a disciplinarian who tolerated nothing less than absolute attention and response from cadets in class. Jackson was personally responsible for the expulsion of a half-dozen cadets from VMI. At least two of them challenged him to duels; one threatened to kill him on sight. Cadets called him "Major Jackson" to his face. Behind his back, he was "Tom Fool," "Old Blue Light," "crazy as damnation," "the worst teach that God ever made," and similar derogations.

Giving credence to many of those disparagements were a number of eccentricities that Jackson regularly exhibited. He would often thrust his arm into the air without warning and then make several pumping motions with it (in order to make his blood circulate better, he explained). Jackson on occasion would forget to eat; he seemed always wrapped in inner concentration; his reticence sometimes led him to stare in darkness at a blank wall; he ate only foods he disliked; he walked with exaggerated strides; on the few occasions when he laughed, Jackson threw back his head, opened his mouth widely, and emitted no sound whatsoever. He was unquestionably a "town character," Lexingtonians said with a shake of their heads.

On the other hand, Jackson displayed a number of qualities that impressed those who knew him well. Devotion, duty, and determination were his bywords. He was honest to a fault, extremely conscientious, and pleasant in the confines of small, private gatherings; his dependability won friends just as his piety won respect. In the latter years of the 1850s, Jackson organized and taught a black Sunday School class

> ... Jackson turned to an aide and exclaimed joyfully: "He who does not see the hand of God in this is blind, sir, blind!"

for slaves and freedmen, in open defiance of a Virginia law that forbade blacks from congregating in public.

Jackson married twice, both times to daughters of Presbyterian ministers. His first marriage, to Elinor Junkin of Lexington in 1853, ended when she died in childbirth fourteen months later. In 1857 he married Mary Anna Morrison of Davidson, North Carolina. That union, extraordinarily bound by Christian love, produced one surviving daughter.

Thoughts of a possible civil war began with Jackson in December 1859, when he and part of the VMI cadet corps were among the witnesses at the execution of abolitionist John Brown. Jackson remained a strong Unionist until he thought his beloved Virginia threatened by Federal coercion. At the secession of his state, he dutifully offered his services to the Confederacy. He left Lexington on April 20, 1861, never again to see his adopted town.

When Jackson and a contingent of cadets arrived in Richmond to serve as drill instructors for thousands of recruits gathering for military service, the ex-professor hardly resembled an impressive soldier. It had been fourteen years since Jackson had last seen combat. He was then thirty-seven, five feet, ten inches tall, with extended forehead, sharp nose, thick beard, and high-pitched voice. Unusually large hands and feet were the extremities of a 170-pound frame. Jackson rode a horse awkwardly, body bent forward as if he were leaning into a stiff wind. His uniform for the first year of the war consisted of battered kepi cap pulled down almost to his nose, the well-worn blue coat of a VMI faculty member, and boots that reached above his knees.

Appearance was deceiving. Jackson swept into war with cool professionalism and complete confidence in himself. Something else was there that molded Jackson into an out-

standing general. He reduced his burning faith to military logic. The great national catastrophe that had descended was a trial ordained by God to test the faith of man. Therefore, as Jackson viewed it, the Civil War was a religious crusade to regain the Almighty's favor. Christian faith and the Confederate cause were, for Jackson, one and the same. He proved to be demanding, steel-cold, even pitiless, in the field because he was fighting on the order of Joshua, Gideon, and other commanders of Old Testament fame.

His field dispatches, official reports, and home correspondence all contained references to "the blessings of God" and "an all-wise Providence." At the height of one of his greatest victories, Jackson turned to an aide and exclaimed joyfully: "He who does not see the hand of God in this is blind, sir, blind!"

Appointed a colonel of infantry on April 27, 1861, Jackson's first orders were to return to the Shenandoah Valley and take command of gaudily dressed militia and inexperienced volunteers rendezvousing at Harpers Ferry. The new commander assumed his duties with a stern and heavy hand. Units theretofore accustomed to parades underwent hours of daily drill; incompetent officers were sent home; all liquor in the town was poured into the streets; artillery emplacements and picket posts quickly ringed the area. Jackson taught the ignorant, corrected the errant, and punished the insubordinate. An officer who returned to Harpers Ferry after Jackson took command stated in wonder: "What a revolution three or four days had wrought! I could scarcely realize the change."

In less than a month, fresh troops swelled the Confederate garrison to such a size that Gen. Joseph E. Johnston assumed command. Jackson's accomplishments, however, bore personal dividends. On June 17, 1861, he was promoted to brigadier general and given a brigade of five infantry regiments from the Shenandoah Valley. His first duty as a general was to help destroy railroad property at nearby Martinsburg. ("If the cost of the property could only have been expended in disseminating the gospel of the Prince of Peace," Jackson observed.) On July 2, Jackson and one of his regiments easily repulsed a Federal probe near Falling Waters, Virginia.

The most famous nickname in American history came to Jackson and his brigade on July 21 at Manassas. When a Union army moved into Virginia to seize the railroads at Manassas Junction, the forces of Johnston and P. G. T. Beauregard combined to resist the advance. The all-day battle was actually a collision between two armed mobs seeking to become armies. Jackson's brigade was posted back of the crest of Henry House Hill, an eminence that commanded the Confederate left. In early afternoon Federals broke through the first lines of the defenders and swept up the hill in anticipation of victory. Jackson ordered his men to the hilltop. Gen. Barnard E. Bee, seeing the force in position, shouted to his faltering South Carolina troops: "Look, men! There stands Jackson like a stone wall! Rally behind the Virginians!"

Stonewall Jackson's line held fast in hours of vicious combat. A late-afternoon counterattack by fresh Confederate regiments sent exhausted Federals in retreat toward Washington. The South had gained a victory and found a hero.

In the next three months, Jackson and his Stonewall Brigade lay quietly encamped near Centreville. Promotion to major general (retroactive to August 7) came with orders in November for Jackson to take command of the defenses of the Shenandoah Valley. He established his headquarters at Winchester, organized his small force, and obtained the use of Gen. W. W. Loring's small Army of the Northwest. On New Year's Day, 1862, Jackson embarked on an expedition to clear Federals from nearby railroad stations and Potomac River crossings. Owing primarily to sleet storms and wretchedly cold weather, the ensuing Romney campaign achieved little but underscored Jackson's always-present determination to strike the enemy.

Jackson returned with his men to Winchester after ordering Loring's troops to remain in the field at Romney. Loring complained to the War Department. Secretary of War Judah P. Benjamin ordered Jackson to recall Loring. Jackson did so and then submitted his resignation from the army because of what he regarded as unwarranted interference with his authority. Governor John Letcher and other friends succeeded in persuading Jackson to remain in command. Secretary Benjamin yielded, and Loring was transferred elsewhere.

This affair demonstrated that like all mortals of unswerving purpose, Jackson was convinced of his own infallible judgment. "Old Jack," as his troops affectionately called him, was nevertheless exceedingly contentious with many of his immediate subordinates. These prickly relationships—with such officers as Gens. Turner Ashby, Richard Brooke Garnett, Charles S. Winder, and A. P. Hill—often marked, and marred, Jackson's career. He was never apologetic about wounding the pride of others. "Through life," Jackson insisted, "let your principal object be the discharge of duty."

His greatest achievement was the 1862 Shenandoah Valley campaign. That spring, Jackson's responsibilities were twofold: to block any Union advance into the valley, and to prevent Federals there and at Fredericksburg from reinforcing George B. McClellan's army moving on Richmond. When Jackson began his offensive, a Federal officer later commented, the Confederate general "began that succession of movements which ended in the complete derangement of the Union plans in Virginia."

Rebuffed at Kernstown on March 23, Jackson retired up the valley. He appeared suddenly at McDowell on May 8 and sent a Federal force in retreat. Then his "foot cavalry" marched rapidly northward down the valley. On May 23, Jackson overpowered the Federal garrison at Front Royal,

drove the main Federal army from Winchester two days later, and then fell back when three Federal armies totaling 64,000 soldiers began converging on Jackson's 17,000 Confederates. On June 8 and 9, Jackson inflicted defeats on his pursuers at Cross Keys and Port Republic. He had thwarted every Union effort made against him. He did so through a combination of hard marches, knowledge of terrain, unexpected tactics, singleness of purpose, heavy attacks concentrated at one point, and self-confidence arising from the belief that God was on his side.

Jackson shifted his army to Richmond to assist Robert E. Lee in the counterattack against McClellan. "Old Jack's" role in the Seven Days' Battle was critical and became controversial. He failed to make his expected June 26 arrival at Mechanicsville and the battle that exploded there; he was also late the next day in reaching the field at Gaines' Mill. On June 30, whether from fatigue or lack of directives from Lee, Jackson remained inactive at White Oak Swamp while conflict raged a few miles away at Frayser's Farm. It was a less-than-sterling performance by the general who had brilliantly whipped Union armies in the Shenandoah Valley.

Thereafter, Jackson won new laurels with every engagement he fought. On August 9, at Cedar Mountain, he defeated the vanguard of Gen. John Pope's army. Later that month, Jackson executed the flank movement for which he became both feared and famed. He swung his men almost sixty miles around Pope's right, captured the main Federal supply depot in the rear of Pope's army, launched an attack of his own at Groveton, and then held off Pope's army at Second Manassas until Lee's forces arrived and sent the Union forces reeling in defeat. In Lee's Maryland campaign the following month, Jackson's troops overwhelmed the large Federal garrison at Harpers Ferry before rejoining Lee's army for the Battle of Sharpsburg. Jackson successfully withstood heavy Federal assaults throughout that morning and gave affirmation to the nickname "Stonewall."

Reorganization of the Army of Northern Virginia came in the autumn. On October 10, 1862, Jackson was appointed lieutenant general and placed in command of half of Lee's forces. Jackson spent weeks polishing his corps: reshuffling officers, replenishing men and supplies, and personally seeing that religious services, Bibles, and tracts werepresent in the ranks. A widening disagreement with one of his division commanders, A. P. Hill, overshadowed much of that period.

Jackson's forces repulsed with comparative ease a major Federal assault at the December Battle of Fredericksburg. Four months of inactivity followed, in which Jackson oversaw the preparation of his 1862 battle reports, worked hard at enkindling a deeper religious spirit in his soldiers, and knew genuine happiness when Anna Jackson visited her husband with the five-month-old daughter he had not seen.

Spring 1863 brought a new advance from the Federal army. In the tangled confusion of the Virginia Wilderness,

Jackson performed his most spectacular flanking movement. A twelve-mile circuitous march brought Jackson and 28,000 men opposite Gen. Joseph Hooker's unprotected right. Late in the afternoon of May 2, Jackson unleashed his divisions in an attack that drove routed Federals some two miles before darkness brought the battle to a standstill. Jackson was anxious to continue pressing forward. For the only time in the Civil War, he rode out to make a personal reconnaissance of the enemy's position. He was returning through thick woods to his own lines when Confederates mistook the general and his staff for Union cavalry and opened fire.

Three bullets struck Jackson. One shattered the bone in his left arm below the shoulder. Following amputation of the limb, Jackson was taken to the railhead at Guiney's Station for possible transfer to a Richmond hospital. Pneumonia rapidly developed. Jackson had always expressed a desire to die on the Sabbath. Around 3:15 on Sunday afternoon, May 10, 1863, he passed away quietly after saying: "Let us cross over the river and rest under the shade of the trees."

The general is buried beneath his statue, the centerpiece in Stonewall Jackson Cemetery, Lexington, Virginia.

[*See also* Loring-Jackson Incident.]

BIBLIOGRAPHY

Chambers, Lenoir. *Stonewall Jackson.* 2 vols. New York, 1959.

Henderson, G. F. R. *Stonewall Jackson and the American Civil War.* 2 vols. London, 1898.

Jackson, Mary Anna. *Memoirs of "Stonewall" Jackson, by His Widow.* New York, 1892. Reprint, Dayton, Ohio, 1976.

Robertson, James I., Jr. *The Stonewall Brigade.* Baton Rouge, La., 1963.

Vandiver, Frank E. *Mighty Stonewal.* New York, 1957. Reprint, Texas A & M University Military History Series, no. 9. College Station, Tex., 1988.

JAMES I. ROBERTSON, JR.

JACKSON, MISSISSIPPI

City of Jackson

Located on the Pearl River in the center of the state, 44 miles from Vicksburg and the Mississippi River to the west and 93 miles from Meridian to the east, Jackson, Mississippi, was the state capital and a railroad, commercial, and manufacturing center at the beginning of the Civil War. In 1860 its population stood at 3,798 people (2,178 whites, 1,601 slaves, and 19 free blacks). Among the whites were Germans, Irish, Italian, and French.

As the state capital, Jackson was the site of the Mississippi secession convention of January 1861.

Mississippi was the second state to secede from the Union, its ordinance citing the protection of slavery as the reason for its action. As the delegates voted in the chambers of the House of Representatives in what today is called the Old Capitol, citizens crowded the lawn outside. The announcement of the 84–15 vote for separation caused wild cheering and the presentation of a blue silk flag with a single white star to the president of the convention. The scene so inspired an

> ## There was a rush of men to arms, and . . . church bells were melted down for cannon.

Irish actor named Harry McCarthy, the story goes, that later that same day he wrote the song "The Bonnie Blue Flag." The lyrics were printed in a local newspaper, and he sang it to an enthusiastic audience that night at the concert hall.

Governor J. J. Pettus immediately began making war preparations for the city, acquiring, for example, some heavy artillery. There was a rush of men to arms, and in the enthusiasm, church bells were melted down for cannon. By the summer, however, many Jacksonians had come to believe that the war would be short and criticized Pettus's activities. In these early months, in fact, life in Jackson continued little changed from its prewar rhythm. The circus and the famous Christie's Minstrels made their annual visits in 1861. Commercial activity on State Street continued. The hotels remained full, shops and stores were busy, and functions at the concert hall attracted large audiences. The Baptist, Catholic, Christian, Episcopal, Methodist, and Presbyterian churches were filled on Sundays, and the five elementary schools remained open. The train ride on the Southern Railroad between Jackson and Vicksburg took two hours and forty-five minutes, excellent time by contemporary standards. The buying and selling of slaves continued, though whites worried about a war-inspired increase in runaways. The city's major newspaper, the weekly *Jackson Mississippian*, advertised the availability of "negro dogs" for five dollars an hour or twenty dollars per capture. As the war progressed, the newspaper also printed notices of deserters from the Confederate army.

Early war rumors had Jacksonians edgy. In the summer and fall of 1862 the city became a Confederate and state command center for logistics, coordination of railroads, mobilization of slaves for construction of defenses, and deployment of state troops. John C. Pemberton arrived in the fall of 1862 to coordinate the Confederate war effort against Ulysses S. Grant's activities to the north and Nathaniel P. Banks's threat from the south. Rifle pits and forts were built to the north, west, and south of the city, the Pearl River protecting the east. Grierson's Raid through the eastern part of the state in the spring of 1863 cut the railroads between the city and Meridian to the east and Louisiana to the south. The raid also encouraged the mobilization of all able-bodied men and the institution of daily drill. Military authorities took over business property surrounding the capitol.

The war first came home to Jackson during Grant's Vicksburg campaign of 1863. After marching down the west bank of the Mississippi River, Grant crossed over to the east side near Bruinsburg and quickly placed his troops between Pemberton's forces, now in Vicksburg, and Joseph E. Johnston's, recently arrived in Jackson. Grant first turned his army against Jackson and from May 14 through 16, 1863, drove the Confederate forces from the city. He then ordered William Tecumseh Sherman to destroy Jackson's war-related facilities and the railroads tying the city to Vicksburg and the rest of the state. After Vicksburg's capture on July 4, Grant ordered Sherman back to Jackson to evict Johnston again, and he did further damage between July 17 and 23, 1863. On his way to Meridian in early 1864, Sherman passed through Jackson once more from February 5 through 7.

Union occupations of the city caused Governors J. J. Pettus and Charles Clark to move the state government to safer locations. Thus, while Jackson remained Mississippi's capital throughout the war, it housed the state government for only a brief time from May 1863 until the Confederate surrender in the spring of 1865. During Sherman's second visit to Jackson in July 1863, however, a group of prominent citizens held a meeting with delegates from nearby towns in the hopes of creating a new government and returning to the Union. Sherman was cooperative, but the movement never gained widespread popular support.

With the coming of the enemy, life in Jackson underwent substantial change. Destruction was so widespread that the city gained the title "Chimneyville." In reality, the damage was inflicted primarily on factories, warehouses, and railroads. Many structures remained standing, including the capitol building. Fighting in the environs resulted in the presence of Confederate wounded and deserters. Many Jacksonians left the city for safer residence, and during Union sieges, some people lived in tents along the Pearl River. Economic activity was severely curtailed, and goods of all sorts were in short supply. Food was scarce, age-old coffee substitutes were revived, and homespun clothing appeared. As inflation made unbacked Confederate paper money increasingly worthless, money became a major problem for the state government and its citizens.

When the fighting ended in the spring of 1865, Jackson was restored as capital of a state impoverished by the ravages of war. Its population in 1866 stood at 3,406 people, 425 fewer whites and 113 more blacks than in 1860. Mississippi underwent a mild Reconstruction and provided leadership in the South's postwar restoration of white conservative rule.

BIBLIOGRAPHY

Bettersworth, John K. *Confederate Mississippi: The People and Policies of a Cotton State in War Time.* Baton Rouge, La., 1943. Reprint, Philadelphia, 1978.

Bettersworth, John K. "The Home Front, 1861–1865." In *A History of Mississippi.* Edited by Richard Aubrey McLemore, 2 vols. Jackson, Miss., 1973.

Jackson. Vertical File. Mississippi Department of Archives and History, Jackson.

Ranlett, S. A. "The Capture of Jackson, Mississippi." In *Civil War Papers Read before the Massachusetts Commandery of the Military Order of the Loyal Legion of the United States.* Boston, 1900.

Russell, William Howard. *My Diary North and South.* New York, 1954. Reprint, Philadelphia, 1988.

JOHN F. MARSZALEK

Battle of Jackson

During the Vicksburg campaign, Gen. Ulysses S. Grant considered the capture of Jackson, Mississippi, a strategic objective not because it was the state's capital but because of its location. If the Union army controlled Jackson, it would hold the high ground between the Yazoo and Big Black rivers, from which it could attack Vicksburg from the east. Defended by Gen. John C. Pemberton's forces, Vicksburg was a crucial site on the Mississippi, and Jackson could be a stepping-stone to its capture. Jackson was also a major railroad junction.

At the end of April 1863, Grant occupied Grand Gulf, twenty-eight miles south of Vicksburg at the mouth of the Big Black River. With him was a force of 24,000 men. On May 8, Gen. William Tecumseh Sherman joined him, swelling the

> On July 16, during the night, the Confederates quietly abandoned Jackson undetected by Sherman or his men.

number of men to 40,000. Grant was now able to move with three corps—Gen. James B. McPherson's, Gen. John A. McClernand's, and Sherman's. On May 11, Sherman's corps, accompanied by Grant, was briefly detained by a burning bridge and a skirmish with William Wirt Adams's brigade. At the same time, McPherson's corps met Gen. John Gregg's brigade at Raymond, a few miles from Jackson. Expecting a small enemy force, Gregg, with only 2,500 men, instead had to fight a force three times the size of his own. Nevertheless, Gregg held his ground for more than four hours. When he heard that Union reinforcements were on the way, Gregg ordered withdrawal to Jackson. The Confederates suffered about 500 killed or wounded; the Union forces, about 400. When Gen. Joseph E. Johnston, Pemberton's immediate superior, arrived in Jackson from Tennessee to witness the Confederate retreat and to find the enemy with no significant obstacle between it and Vicksburg, he lamented, "I am too late."

On the next day, May 14, the Federal troops under Sherman and McPherson moved on Jackson. Sherman's corps came up the Mississippi Springs Road from Raymond, while McPherson's advanced on the Clinton Road. During a heavy rainstorm, a battalion of sharpshooters and artillery fire delayed their progress long enough for the Confederates to remove supplies, for Johnston had already decided to abandon the city without a fight. The Union forces had a fairly easy entry; one of Sherman's units located an unmanned line of entrenchments, and his men came unopposed up the railroad from the south. The Confederates had even failed to burn a critical bridge that provided easy access into town. Johnston's Confederates evacuated northward up the Canton Road. Estimates put the Union casualties at 300; the Confederate at less than 400.

After spending the night of May 14 in Jackson, Grant and McPherson's corps moved quickly toward Vicksburg. Sherman's corps was ordered to remain in Jackson for twenty-four hours to destroy railroads and Confederate supplies. Jackson suffered heavy damage; Union troops destroyed railroad tracks and much public and private property. As Sherman wrote, "Jackson, as a railroad center or government depot of stores and military factories, can be of little use to the enemy for six months." Disorder reigned and wanton destruction, even of the Catholic church, followed. Sherman blamed the unjustified acts on "bad rum" drunk by his troops. On May 16, while Johnston's forces were moving to join Pemberton to defend Vicksburg, Sherman's corps set out quickly for that city.

Immediately after the fall of Vicksburg on July 4, the victorious Grant, instead of celebrating, ordered Sherman back to Jackson, which he felt was crucial to protect the Mississippi River from Confederate interference. After Vicksburg, "I did want rest," Sherman wrote, "but I ask nothing until the Mississippi River is ours, and Sunday and 4th of July are nothing to Americans till the river of our greatness is free as God made it."

On July 5, Sherman, with eleven infantry divisions, moved against Johnston, positioned near the Big Black River. Johnston, who believed Sherman's force to be double his, fell back to Jackson behind heavy entrenchments, which, anchored on the Pearl River both north and south, ringed the town. Skirmishes failed to turn Sherman away. And on July 12, the Confederates bombarded his troops with heavy-caliber, long-range artillery. The Federal troops were repulsed. They lost about 500 men and three battle flags. Despite this success, Johnston feared that Sherman would surround the city with his superior numbers. To Jefferson Davis, he wrote, "The enemy is evidently making a siege which we cannot resist." On July 16, during the night, the Confederates quietly abandoned Jackson undetected by Sherman or his men. Johnston crossed the Pearl River, burning bridges behind him. His losses had been lighter than Sherman's—Confederate casualties (killed, wounded, and missing) were 600; Union casualties were 1,132. Low casualties notwithstanding, discipline and desertions were problematic, and Johnston had felt defeat was inevitable. Retreat was to him the wisest course. Sherman did not pursue Johnston because of "the intense heat, dust, and fatigue" of his troops. He wrote that the 30,000 men retreating with Johnston would probably "perish by heat, thirst, and disappointment."

Sherman's troops moved into Jackson on July 17. Sherman assigned Gen. Frank P. Blair's division to guard private property and prevent looting—a mission that Blair apparently failed to perform with much energy. Jackson was again sacked, plundered, and burned. Sherman condemned the lack of discipline "that reflects discredit on us all," but he hastened to add that the conduct was "confined to a few men." On July 24, the Federal troops once again moved out of Jackson.

Jackson was occupied two more times during the war. On the evening of February 5, 1864, Federal troops on their way to Meridian entered the town after clashing with the cavalrymen under Gen. William Wirt Adams and Col. Peter Starke, who could do little against Sherman's 20,000 men. The troops left the next day. In early July 1864, Sherman, still trying to eliminate danger from the feared Gen. Nathan Bedford Forrest, sent Union forces under the command of Gen. Henry Slocum from Vicksburg to keep reinforcements from getting to Forrest. Slocum's forces occupied Jackson, although only briefly, for a fourth time on this mission.

BIBLIOGRAPHY

Grant, U. S. *Personal Memoirs of U. S. Grant*. Edited by William S. McFeely. New York, 1982.
Sherman, William T. *Memoirs of William T. Sherman*. Edited by William S. McFeely. New York, 1984.
U.S. War Department. *War of the Rebellion: A Compilation of the Official Records of the Union and Confederate Armies*. Washington, D.C., 1880–1901. Ser. 1, vol. 24, pts. 1–3.

RAY SKATES

JAMES RIVER SQUADRON

Created in the spring of 1862, the James River Squadron served as a crucial part of the Confederate defenses on the

James River below Richmond until its vessels were destroyed by their own crews in the spring of 1865.

Aware of the possibility of a Federal attack up the James River, the Confederates built a number of shore batteries along the river and supplemented them with several small civilian steamers converted into gunboats. The first of these was the gunboat *Patrick Henry,* a former river steamer commanded by Capt. John R. Tucker. Added later was the former screw-tug *Teaser,* armed with a single 32-pound gun. In early 1862, with the ironclad CSS *Virginia* nearing completion, Secretary of the Navy Stephen R. Mallory combined the vessels on the James River to form the James River Squadron commanded by Flag Officer Franklin Buchanan aboard *Virginia.* Buchanan's squadron was supplemented by the addition of the wooden gunboats *Jamestown, Raleigh,* and *Beaufort,* which escaped to the James River after the Federal capture of Roanoke Island in the Carolina sounds. The unarmored vessels supported *Virginia* during its epic struggle with USS *Monitor.* In May, after the Confederates were forced to abandon Norfolk and scuttle *Virginia,* the remaining vessels took refuge above the batteries and river obstructions at Drewry's Bluff. Several were stripped of their armament for additional shore batteries. The remaining gunboats joined the shore batteries in repelling a Union foray up the river on May 15, 1862.

Aside from minor raiding sorties, the squadron participated in no major operations during the rest of 1862 or 1863. Capt. French Forrest, former Confederate commander of the Gosport Navy Yard, succeeded Buchanan as squadron commander and played a role in having *Patrick Henry* turned into the home of the Confederate Naval Academy in October 1863. Although the Federals captured *Teaser* in late 1862, the strength of the squadron was increased by the addition in 1862 of the ironclad *Richmond* and in 1863 the ironclads *Fredericksburg* and *Virginia II.* Like *Richmond,* these newer ironclads were shallow-draft, casemated vessels. They mounted four guns in varying calibers and configurations, but typically two of these were large-shell guns and two were large-caliber rifled pieces. Along with the ironclads, the wooden gunboats *Nansemond, Hampton,* and *Drewry* and the small steam launches *Torpedo, Scorpion, Wasp,* and *Hornet* had joined the squadron by the start of 1864. The gunboats were armed with a variety of cannons, but the launches had only a single spar torpedo apiece for armament.

With a nucleus of three strong ironclads, the James River Squadron was the most powerful group of vessels ever assembled by the Confederacy. Disappointed by Forrest's apparent lack of initiative, Mallory replaced him with Commdr. John K. Mitchell in January 1864. By this time, however, the Federals had effectively blocked the river just above City Point with a combination of submersible mines and sunken hulks. Led by the ironclads, Mitchell's squadron fought a series of engagements in the summer of 1864, driving off Union working parties and assisting in the defense of shore installations. When flooding carried away some of the river obstructions in January 1865, Mitchell seized the chance to attack the Federal supply city at City Point. In the darkness, though, both *Virginia II* and *Richmond* ran aground and came under fire from Union shore batteries. Supported by the wooden gunboats and *Fredericksburg,* the stranded vessels eventually got free. *Virginia II,* however, was damaged and the small gunboat *Drewry* was blown up after being abandoned by its crew. Mitchell's foray thus failed, as did a bold attempt in early February to put the small launches on wheels and move them overland to attack the Union ships at City Point.

On February 18, 1865, Rear Adm. Raphael Semmes, former captain of *Alabama,* took command of the squadron. Morale was low. Many officers and men served as gunners ashore. Semmes and the squadron were powerless to prevent the fall of Richmond, and on April 3 he ordered the ships scuttled to prevent capture. With the remaining crewmen, Semmes fled inland to Danville, Virginia. There the remnant of the James River Squadron dissolved on May 1 after receiving word of the surrender of Gen. Joseph E. Johnston. Among the last to surrender were the naval cadets of *Patrick Henry.* After serving as guards of the final gold supply of the Confederacy, the young officers were given forty dollars a piece and sent home.

[*See also entries on the ship* Virginia.]

BIBLIOGRAPHY

Gibbons, Tony. *Warships and Naval Battles of the Civil War.* New York, 1989.
Johnson, Robert U., and C. C. Buel, eds. *Battles and Leaders of the Civil War.* 4 vols. New York, 1887–1888. Reprint, Secaucus, N.J., 1982.
Scharf, J. Thomas. *History of the Confederate States Navy.* New York, 1887. Reprint, New York, 1977.
Still, William N., Jr. *Iron Afloat: The Story of the Confederate Armorclads.* Nashville, Tenn., 1971.

ROBERT S. BROWNING III

JENKINS, ALBERT GALLATIN

JENKINS, ALBERT GALLATIN (1830–1864), congressman from Virginia and brigadier general. Jenkins was born November 10, 1830, at Greenbottom, Cabell County, Virginia (now West Virginia). Educated at Marshall Academy, Jefferson College, and Harvard Law School, he practiced law in western Virginia and served in the U.S. Congress from 1857 to 1861.

After leaving Congress that year, Jenkins enlisted recruits for the Border Rangers (a Virginia militia group) and was elected captain of the unit on May 20. Three other cavalry units recruited from western Virginia were also placed under his command. Their first recorded expedition took place in June, when they rode to Point Pleasant on the Ohio River and seized a number of Union sympathizers.

On July 16 at the Battle of Scary Creek, Kanawha County, West Virginia, Jenkins commanded the Border Rangers, which carried the flag for the battle. After early fighting and a

> ... he and his men crossed the Ohio River and became the first force to raise the Confederate flag on Ohio soil.

retreat, Jenkins rallied with Capt. James M. Corns and the Sandy Rangers to capture the field. They took Col. Charles A. DeVilliers of the Eleventh Ohio Volunteers and Col. William E. Woodruff of the Second Kentucky and his staff prisoner. Jenkins incurred a slight wound.

Jenkins was appointed aide to Gen. John B. Floyd with the rank of colonel on August 24 and formed the Eighth Virginia Cavalry from the Border Rangers, Sandy Rangers, and other cavalry units. His commission as lieutenant colonel of the Eighth Cavalry was dated September 24, 1861. In November Jenkins with his cavalry unit and Col. John Clarkson with the Wise Legion Cavalry staged a surprise raid on Camp Paxton, a Union recruitment camp at Guyandotte. There they captured about a hundred recruits and marched them to the railhead at Newbern, Virginia.

In early 1862 Jenkins was elected to the First Confederate Congress and resigned his field commission on February 20. He served as a member of the standing committees of Printing and of Territories and Public Lands.

Jenkins, after receiving an appointment as brigadier general of cavalry, resigned from Congress on August 5 and assumed command of forces in Monroe County. He and 550 cavalrymen then embarked on a five-hundred-mile raid through West Virginia. On September 4 he and his men crossed the Ohio River and became the first force to raise the Confederate flag on Ohio soil.

Jenkins, during the winter of 1862–1863, helped organize the Sixteenth and Seventeenth Virginia Cavalry regiments encamped near Salem. By spring, he commanded the Cavalry Brigade of the Army of Western Virginia, headquartered at Dublin under Maj. Gen. Samuel Jones. The Jenkins Brigade consisted of five Virginia cavalry regiments and three battalions. Jenkins made another raid into western Virginia in

March. Leading companies of the Eighth and Sixteenth Cavalries, he rode to Hurricane Bridge in Putnam County where he attacked a small fort defended by three companies of U.S. infantry. After several hours and few casualties, Jenkins broke off and moved on to Point Pleasant. There his cavalry attacked a Union force barricaded in the courthouse before withdrawing deeper into Virginia.

Jenkins and his brigade, part of the vanguard of forces moving into Pennsylvania that June, gathered cattle and horses around Chambersburg to supply the Confederate army. On June 28 he and his men were on the hills surrounding Harrisburg, the state capital. Before they could take the town, however, Jenkins received orders to move to Gettysburg. They arrived there on the afternoon of July 1 and were assigned to guard prisoners. While scouting enemy positions the next day, Jenkins was wounded in the head. He was cared for at a house in Gettysburg until the Confederates retreated into Virginia, where he spent a number of weeks recuperating.

Some sought that fall to have Jenkins promoted to major general. A petition to this end was sent to the Confederate secretary of war and was marked to "file for consideration when there is a division to which an appointment can be made."

Jenkins resumed command of his brigade by January 1864 and set about recruiting and organizing cavalry troops in western Virginia and West Virginia. He was appointed cavalry commander of the Department of Western Virginia with headquarters in Dublin that spring.

When Federal forces under Gen. George Crook threatened the Virginia and Tennessee Railroad and Confederate stores at Dublin in May, Col. John McCausland moved his brigade to defensive positions on Cloyds Mountain. Jenkins arrived there on the night of May 8 and assumed command. The next morning, he changed the Confederate positions over the objections of McCausland and others.

During the ensuing Federal attack, Jenkins ordered a charge by the Forty-fifth Virginia regiment and Beckley's Battalion, which penetrated Federal lines but was repulsed. As the Confederates were retreating, Jenkins rode forward to rally them, but a musket ball struck him in the left arm and he fell from his horse. He was captured after the Confederates retreated further to New River Bridge. On May 13, Federal surgeons, after consulting with Confederate surgeons, amputated his arm. But eight days later, he suffered a secondary hemorrhage, supposedly when an orderly knocked loose a ligature used to clamp off an artery. Jenkins died early in the morning of May 21, 1864.

In February 1866 Jenkins's body was moved to the family cemetery at Greenbottom, West Virginia. In 1891, he was again reinterred by the United Confederate Veterans in the Confederate plot in Spring Hill Cemetery, Huntington, West Virginia, where he rests today.

One of the Richmond newspapers in 1863 described Jenkins as being "about five feet ten inches high, well formed and of good physique; dark hair, blue eyes, and heavy brown beard; pleasing countenance, kind, affable manners, fluent and winning in conversation, quick, subtle and argumentative in debate." He was an experienced debater and dynamic public speaker.

BIBLIOGRAPHY

Dickinson, Jack L. *Eighth Virginia Cavalry.* Lynchburg, Va., 1986.
Dickinson, Jack L. *Jenkins of Greenbottom: A Civil War Saga.* Charleston, W. Va., 1988.
Geiger, Joe. *Civil War in Cabell County, West Virginia.* Charleston, W. Va., 1991.
Lowry, Terry. *The Battle of Scary Creek.* Charleston, W. Va., 1982.
Rosanna Blake Confederate Collection. Morrow Library, Marshall University, Huntingon, W. Va.

JACK L. DICKINSON

JOE BROWN'S PIKES

At the outbreak of the Civil War, the Confederacy suffered acute shortages of weapons, and state and national officials concocted various schemes to remedy the problem. The governor of Georgia, Joseph E. Brown, proposed the use of pikes to arm Southern troops. The advent of firearms had rendered the pike obsolete, but some armies continued to use the weapon for ceremonial purposes. Pikes were easy to produce and conjured the image of Greek or Swiss phalanxes cutting their way to victory.

In the spring of 1862, with the Confederate States facing a critical shortage of small arms, Maj. Gen. Thomas J. ("Stonewall") Jackson suggested to the governor of Virginia that recruits be supplied with pikes as their principal weapon. Gen. Robert E. Lee approved the idea and requested that a thousand be forwarded to Jackson as early as possible. Subsequently, Lee wrote that pikes were in production and said he would approve their requisition.

Although the shortage of arms subsequently eased, with stocks on hand supplemented by weapons captured from the Federals, some leaders, most notably Governor Brown, continued to advocate the production and use of pikes. He ordered the manufacture of thousands of them for his Georgia state troops.

Production of the weapons included several modern versions of the style of pike used by the Swiss to cut the bridle reins of charging cavalrymen, who would then be easy targets for more conventional weapons. Other variations appeared, such as a pike with a collapsible blade, which was apparently a safety feature for times when the pike was not in use. Most of these weapons were locally manufactured and designed for Georgians. Thus this style came to be labeled "Joe Brown's Pikes."

BIBLIOGRAPHY

Lord, Francis A. *Civil War Collector's Encyclopedia: Arms, Uniforms, and Equipment of the Union and Confederacy.* New York, 1963.
Wiley, Bell Irvin. *The Life of Johnny Reb: The Common Soldier of the Confederacy.* Indianapolis, 1943.

BRIAN S. WILLS

JOHNSON, ANDREW

JOHNSON, ANDREW (1808–1875), military governor of Tennessee, and vice president and president of the United States. Johnson, the only member of the U.S. Senate from a seceding state to remain loyal to the Union, was born the son of a Raleigh, North Carolina, innkeeper whose death left the family in poverty. Bound out as an apprentice tailor, Johnson learned his trade and the rudiments of reading and writing at the shop. He broke his apprenticeship articles after three years, ultimately settling in Greeneville, Tennessee, where he practiced his trade and became active in local politics. Between 1829 and 1842 Johnson served as alderman and then mayor of Greeneville and as a state legislator. From 1843 to 1853 he served in Congress.

Johnson cultivated a reputation as a radical Democratic representative of the workingmen, artisans, and small farmers who predominated in the hilly country of eastern Tennessee. As he sought statewide office, however, Johnson became a strong advocate of the rights of slaveholders in the Union. A united Democratic party elected him governor for two terms (1853–1857) and then to the U.S. Senate in 1857, where he took a firm proslavery stand. In the presidential election of 1860 he supported the Breckinridge-Lane ticket of the proslavery wing of the Democratic party. Nonetheless, Johnson was not comfortable in the extreme proslavery camp. He did not agree that a state had a constitutional right to secede, and it would become clear that he bore a powerful emotional attachment to the Union.

When the states of the Deep South began to secede after the election of Abraham Lincoln to the presidency, Johnson took a much firmer pro-Union stand than most upper South and border-state congressmen. As Southern senators resigned their seats, he assailed them and was bitterly denounced in return. His course was controversial in Tennessee, where he emerged as the leading Unionist, but it made him a hero in the North and gave him a national reputation.

Johnson defeated his state's secessionists at first, but he could not dam the wave of secessionism that swept Tennessee after the firing on Fort Sumter and Lincoln's call for troops. Johnson was driven from Tennessee and took an active role in devising war measures in the Senate.

By 1862 Union forces had occupied Nashville and surrounding areas of central Tennessee. Hoping to make the state an example that would undermine support for the Confederacy among reluctant secessionists, Lincoln made Johnson a brigadier general of volunteers and appointed him military governor of the state, with instructions to establish a loyal civil government to take its place in the Union.

Johnson immediately set to work creating a political organization to serve as a vehicle for restoration, but a variety of factors frustrated his efforts. Unlike eastern Tennessee, central Tennessee was firmly secessionist. The few Unionists were conservative Whigs, deeply committed to slavery and suspicious of the radically Democratic Johnson. Only after sullen resistance did central Tennesseans obey orders requiring all who had aided the rebellion to take oaths of loyalty or to promise to desist from disloyal action. Despite eastern Tennessee's strategic importance, Johnson was unable to persuade the Union military commanders in Tennessee to secure a political base for loyalism by liberating his home region. Nor could he get Lincoln or the War Department to intercede. The commanders proved unwilling even to commit the resources necessary to make Nashville itself secure militarily. Few people were willing openly to espouse Unionism when Confederate troops might return at any time. Moreover,

> **Johnson was determined to complete restoration of the state government before ascending to the vice presidency in March 1865.**

the commanders refused to recognize Johnson's final authority over matters of civil government, insisting that they retain ultimate control of law enforcement and other matters of military concern. Bickering took up a good deal of Johnson's energy.

The uncertain future of slavery also inhibited the establishment of a Unionist political organization. Johnson himself had defended slavery, and he doubted he could secure much support for antislavery Unionism in Tennessee. When runaway slaves gathered around the Union military encampments in Tennessee, Johnson favored using them as military laborers but opposed organizing them as fighting units. But proslavery Unionists turned out to be lukewarm in their condemnation of disloyalty and reluctant to act to restore loyal government. Johnson gravitated toward more radical

Unionists, who began to attack slavery and to demand that only ardent Unionists participate in the restoration process. After Lincoln issued the preliminary Emancipation Proclamation in the fall of 1862, Johnson endorsed emancipation in Tennessee and the recruitment of African Americans as soldiers. With this, conservative Unionists repudiated both Johnson and Lincoln. The divisions among Unionists, who probably remained a minority in central Tennessee, rendered establishment of a Unionist government impossible.

In December 1863 Lincoln took reconstruction matters into his own hands, promulgating proclamations offering amnesty to Southerners who took an oath of loyalty and outlining a procedure whereby they could restore civil governments whenever their number equaled 10 percent of the 1860 presidential electorate in their states. Lincoln's proclamations galvanized Johnson into action, but he insisted upon a more rigorous oath and a more limited electorate. As a result his efforts sputtered once more.

As he attempted to restore Tennessee's state government on a radical basis, Johnson also undertook extensive speaking tours in the North to help Union election campaigns. He proved a popular political attraction and reconfirmed his position as the leading Unionist of the South. As such, and because he was more radical than Lincoln and a Democrat, Johnson seemed an ideal running mate for Lincoln in 1864. The party convention nominated him in June and he was elected in November.

Johnson was determined to complete restoration of the state government before ascending to the vice presidency in March 1865. An irregularly chosen constitutional convention met in January and proposed amendments to the state constitution that abolished slavery and made key state offices appointive by the governor. These were to be submitted to the people for ratification, with election of a governor and state legislature to follow. On February 22, 1865, 25,000 voters—compared to 145,000 who had voted in the 1860 presidential election—ratified the amendments almost unanimously. Johnson resigned his military commission and governorship on March 3, 1865, and was inaugurated vice president of the United States the following day.

Johnson succeeded to the presidency upon the death of Lincoln on April 15, 1865. As president, he undertook a more lenient program of Reconstruction than he had followed as military governor. Where Lincoln had not already appointed provisional governors, Johnson issued proclamations doing so. The governors were to appoint temporary state officials and to recommend persons for appointment to Federal offices. They were to call constitutional conventions, insisting only on the abolition of slavery, nullification of ordinances of secession, and repudiation of Southern war debts. By an amnesty proclamation Johnson pardoned nearly all Confederates who would take a loyalty oath. Pardoned

Confederates were permitted to participate in the Reconstruction process and often took leading roles in the reestablished governments.

As president, Johnson opposed extending voting privileges to black Americans, vetoed Federal legislation to protect their civil rights, and worked to defeat the Fourteenth and Fifteenth Amendments to the Constitution. The bitter conflict Johnson's course engendered with the Republican-controlled Congress led to his impeachment in 1868. He was acquitted by one vote and served out his term, retiring in 1869. In 1875 he was again elected senator from Tennessee, but he died the same year.

BIBLIOGRAPHY

Hall, Clifton R. *Andrew Johnson: Military Governor of Tennessee.* Princeton, 1916.
Maslowski, Peter. *Treason Must Be Made Odious: Military Occupation and Wartime Reconstruction in Nashville, Tennessee, 1862–1865.* Millwood, N.Y., 1978.
Trefousse, Hans L. *Andrew Johnson: A Biography.* New York, 1989.

MICHAEL LES BENEDICT

JOHNSON, BRADLEY TYLER

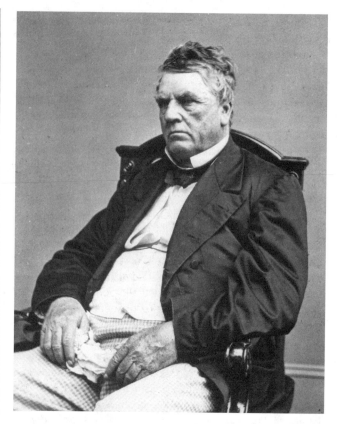

BRADLEY TYLER JOHNSON. NATIONAL ARCHIVES

JOHNSON, BRADLEY TYLER (1829–1903), brigadier general. Johnson graduated from Princeton University in 1849 and was admitted to the Maryland bar in 1851. A leader in the state Democratic party, Johnson fervently worked for self-determination in Maryland. His sense of honor and devotion to his state led him to form a militia company in his hometown of Frederick, Maryland, which became part of the First Maryland Infantry. Johnson was elected major and later was promoted to lieutenant colonel (July 1861) and to colonel (March 1862). The First Maryland fought at First Manassas, served under Gen. Thomas J. ("Stonewall") Jackson during the 1862 Shenandoah Valley campaign, and participated in the Seven Days' Battles. In August 1862, the unit was mustered out of service, and Johnson joined the staff of Stonewall Jackson.

Johnson was assigned temporary command of Gen. John Robert Jones's brigade during Second Manassas and acted as provost marshal of Frederick in the Sharpsburg campaign. He next served on a military court in Richmond. In November 1863, Johnson assumed command of the Maryland Line and in June of the next year was promoted to brigadier general to replace Gen. William E. ("Grumble") Jones, who was killed in the Battle of Piedmont. In Gen. Jubal Early's raid on Washington in July 1864, Johnson led an aborted attempt to

liberate Confederate prisoners at Point Lookout, Maryland. Johnson and Gen. John McCausland led the raid on Chambersburg, carrying out Early's orders to burn the town. After Johnson's brigade was routed at Moorefield, West Virginia, in August, he and McCausland disputed responsibility for the disaster. Johnson requested a court of inquiry, but none was ever convened. Johnson's brigade participated in the 1864 Shenandoah Valley campaign, and in November, he was relegated to command a prison at Salisbury, North Carolina, where he served until the close of the war.

After the war, Johnson practiced law in Richmond and served in the Virginia state senate. He wrote and spoke frequently on the war, demonstrating his eloquence, humor and passion for the South. Johnson died at Amelia, Virginia, and is buried in Loudon Park Cemetery, Baltimore.

BIBLIOGRAPHY

Goldsborough, William W. *The Maryland Line in the Confederate Army.* Baltimore, Md., 1900. Reprint, Gaithersburg, Md., 1987.
Hartzler, Daniel D. *Marylanders in the Confederacy.* Westminster, Md., 1986.
Johnson, Bradley T. *Maryland.* Vol. 2 of *Confederate Military History.* Edited by Clement A. Evans. Atlanta, 1899. Vol. 2 of extended ed. Wilmington, N.C., 1987.

Newman, Harry Wright. *Maryland and the Confederacy.* Annapolis, Md., 1976.

Warner, Ezra J. *Generals in Gray: Lives of the Confederate Commanders.* Baton Rouge, La., 1959.

JOHN E. OLSON

JOHNSON, BUSHROD RUST

JOHNSON, BUSHROD RUST (1817–1880), major general. A native of Belmont County, Ohio, Johnson was born October 7, 1817, and graduated in 1840 from the U.S. Military Academy. For the next seven years Johnson served with the Third U.S. Infantry. He took part in the Seminole and Mexican wars and, for six months following the fall of Mexico City, served as depot commissary at Vera Cruz. He resigned from the army in October 1847 and took a teaching position at the Western Military Institute in Georgetown, Kentucky. For four years (1851–1855) he doubled as a teacher and superintendent. During the same period he held commissions in the militia of Kentucky (1849–1854) and Tennessee (1854–1861).

Commissioned a colonel at the start of the war, Johnson was promoted to brigadier, January 24, 1862, and was in command of the garrison at Fort Henry when it fell in February 1862. He was captured in that action but escaped a few days later when the Federals took over Fort Donelson. Johnson was severely wounded at Shiloh, but he recovered in time to take part in Braxton Bragg's invasion of Kentucky. At Chickamauga, Johnson was the first to spot a gap in the Union line and exploit it fully "with the coolness and judgment for which he was always distinguished," according to D. H. Hill.

While Johnson was with James Longstreet in eastern Tennessee, influential friends stumped for his advancement. Alexander P. Stewart reported that he had "utmost confidence in his fitness" to command a division. Longstreet affirmed that Johnson "has courage, skill and ability to an eminent degree. . . . I have found him always ready, with able suggestions, and the desire to execute them." Simon Bolivar Buckner extolled Johnson's "gallantry and ability." Patrick Cleburne and B. Franklin Cheatham added their voices to the clamor for a major general's commission, which came on May 21, 1864.

The Ohioan transferred to Virginia for the spring campaign of 1864. He opposed Benjamin Butler's assault on the Richmond and Petersburg Railroad and took part in the engagement at Drewry's Bluff, where he captured the enemy's guns but lost more than one-fourth of his division.

After commanding South Carolina troops at the Battle of the Crater, Johnson saw his division shattered at Sayler's Creek and was without a command when he surrendered at Appomattox.

Johnson returned to Tennessee and became chancellor at the University of Nashville. He also arranged to conduct a collegiate department at the Montgomery Bell Academy as a preparatory school. When a depression forced that institution to close its doors in 1874, Johnson moved to Brighton, Illinois, where he died on September 12, 1880. He was buried in nearby Miles Station. A century later, however, his remains were exhumed and reburied next to those of his wife in Nashville, Tennessee.

BIBLIOGRAPHY

Compiled Military Service Records. Bushrod Rust Johnson. Microcopy M331, Roll 141. Record Group 109. National Archives, Washington, D.C.

Cummings, Charles M. *Yankee Quaker, Confederate General.* Rutherford, N.J., 1971.

Porter, James D. *Tennessee.* Vol. 8 of *Confederate Military History.* Edited by Clement A. Evans. Atlanta, 1899. Vol. 10 of extended ed. Wilmington, N.C., 1987.

LOWELL REIDENBAUGH

JOHNSON, HERSCHEL V.

JOHNSON, HERSCHEL V. (1812–1880), Georgia governor, Democratic vice presidential candidate, congressman, and president of Georgia's constitutional convention. Herschel Vespasian Johnson was among Georgia's most influential antebellum politicians. As Stephen A. Douglas's vice presidential running mate in 1860, he played a central role in the secession crisis as one of the Deep South's strongest Unionist voices, while consistently advocating state rights policy before and during the Civil War.

Johnson was born on September 18, 1812, in Burke County, Georgia, the son of a modest planter. He was educated at private schools, including the Monaghan Academy in Warrenton, Georgia, and in 1831 entered the University of Georgia, graduating in 1834 in a class that included Alexander H. Stephens, who became a lifelong friend and close political ally. Johnson married Ann F. Polk, the daughter of a Maryland Supreme Court justice, a niece of President James K. Polk, and a cousin of Bishop (and later Confederate general) Leonidas Polk.

Johnson studied law for a year in Augusta, where he opened a successful practice after passing the bar in 1835. Four years later, he used his earnings to purchase a large Jefferson County plantation called Sandy Grove, which he managed while practicing law in a new partnership in nearby Louisville, Georgia. It was in Louisville that Johnson first became involved in politics, and in 1840, at the age of twenty-eight, he was approached by local Democrats to run for Congress. He declined but made a strong impression as an effective stump speaker when campaigning for the Democratic nominee that year, for his own unsuccessful bid for Congress in 1843, and for his wife's uncle, James K. Polk, in the presidential election of 1844. Johnson's hard-hitting oratory had by then attracted statewide attention. Though he lost a gubernatorial bid in 1847, the man who defeated him, Governor George W. Towns, appointed him to fill the remaining year of Walter T. Colquitt's vacated U.S. Senate seat. During his brief term in Washington, Johnson made several speeches on the Senate floor in which he took strong pro-Southern stands on the Mexican War, on Texas's admission to the Union, and on slavery's protection from any interference from Congress, either in states where slavery existed or in present or future territories.

Johnson returned from Washington in March 1849 and in July was elected to a four-year term as superior court judge of the Ocmulgee District. As an outside observer of the sectional crisis that erupted the following year over California's bid for statehood, he continued to maintain a hard-line defense of state sovereignty and argued that any new territory should be divided equally into slave and nonslave states. He initially opposed the terms of the Compromise of 1850 and challenged fellow Georgian Howell Cobb's conciliatory stance in Congress. Only when disruption of the Union seemed the likely alternative did he reluctantly accept the compromise.

In 1853, with his judicial term drawing to a close and encouraged by Georgia Democrats' support the year before for nationalist presidential nominee Franklin Pierce for whom he had actively campaigned, Johnson ran for governor. He was elected by a narrow margin over Whig candidate Charles J. Jenkins, author of the Georgia platform of 1850. During his two terms as governor (1853–1857), Johnson retreated from his earlier fire-eating stance and moved to a more moderate position on sectional issues. He supported Stephen Douglas's Kansas-Nebraska Act in 1854, having much earlier advocated its principle of popular sovereignty as the determinant of a territory's status in regard to slavery. Its failure disappointed him greatly, and he was quite vocal in denouncing the ensuing violence on the part of extremists on both sides. Though he remained staunch in his commitment to state rights principles, he became more outspoken in his opposition to secession or any other threat to national unity.

Johnson retired to Sandy Grove at the end of his second term as governor in November 1857, to preside over what by 1860 amounted to over 3,600 acres of land and 117 slaves. He vowed that his political career was behind him, but his decision proved short-lived when the presidential election

three years later brought the sectional crisis to a critical juncture. Johnson was convinced that Stephen Douglas offered the only hope for a Democratic candidate with viable appeal on both sides of the Mason-Dixon Line. He attended the party's convention in Charleston and worked hard to maintain party unity and gain the nomination for the Illinois senator. Though his efforts proved futile at the abortive convention, Johnson impressed enough delegates there to win their nomination as Douglas's vice-presidential running mate when the Democrats met again in Baltimore. Johnson accepted the nomination reluctantly as his "patriotic duty." The party had by then split, with the Southern wing nominating John C. Breckinridge as its presidential candidate in yet another convention. Most Georgia Democrats aligned themselves with this movement and were critical of Johnson's refusal to do likewise. Johnson was in fact the only Georgian still present at the "national" convention when Douglas won the nomination.

In an unpublished autobiography, Johnson described the reception that awaited him when he returned to Georgia after the convention. In the towns and villages he passed through on the train, "crowds would gather at the windows to get a glance at the man . . . who deserved the gallows, for alleged treason to the rights of the South, who, as they supposed, had abandoned his friends and his hearthstone, for the poor price of the Vice-Presidency." Throughout a speaking tour of the state, he was greeted with hostility and resentment and was told by friends and former political associates that his present linkage with Douglas "was fatal to all my future prospects and would not only consign me to obscurity, but to political infamy." He also made an extensive campaign tour through the northern and midwestern states, traveling over four thousand miles between New York and Iowa. There he faced a more favorable, if guarded, reception than that at home.

Though never as optimistic as Douglas that Northern commitment to the Union could carry their ticket to victory over Abraham Lincoln, Johnson was sorely troubled by the election's outcome and its aftermath. Despite his loss of support within Georgia, he traveled around the state in late November and December urging Georgians not to follow the rash course of South Carolinians in seceding. Though he was consistent in his insistence that the Southern states had a constitutional right to secede, he was equally adamant that Lincoln's election alone was not enough justification to do so. He preached the logic of a wait-and-watch policy of taking no action until the new president assumed office late in March and had a chance to negotiate a settlement of the crisis.

As a delegate to Georgia's secession convention in Milledgeville in January 1861, Johnson urged delay and proposed a stopgap measure of having delegates from all Southern states, both in and out of the Union, meet in Atlanta in February and draw up their own terms to present to

Lincoln and to Congress as an alternative to secession. Up until this point, Johnson had been closely aligned with fellow cooperationists Benjamin H. Hill and Alexander H. Stephens. Though Hill encouraged him to continue pushing for the measure whenever the opportunity for a vote on it came up, Stephens felt the lengthy list of demands and conditions it included was completely unworkable and refused to support it, which led to a temporary rift between Johnson and the soon-to-be Confederate vice president. Nevertheless, when the measure was put to a vote as "Johnson's Substitute" to Eugenius Aristides Nisbet's ordinance of secession, minority

> ## Yet he remained pessimistic regarding its chances for survival. . . .

support for it proved surprisingly strong. In one of a series of votes on January 19, Johnson's proposal received 133 votes as opposed to 164 for Nisbet's move for immediate secession.

Once Georgians had voted themselves out of the Union, Johnson, like most other Unionists, pledged his support for the new Confederacy. Yet he remained pessimistic regarding its chances for survival, writing soon afterward that "I felt that the State of Georgia would soon be launched upon a dark, uncertain and dangerous sea. I was never so sad before." He once again retired to his plantation, too old for military service and too unpopular for elective office. "I think my public career is ended," he confided to Alexander Stephens, then at the Confederacy's Provisional Congress in Montgomery. "My adhesion to Douglas and the North was fatal."

But Johnson's retirement plans proved as premature then as they had in 1857. In November 1862, the state legislature elected him to replace John W. Lewis in the Confederate Senate. A year later he was reelected for a full term, so that he served in Richmond from January 16, 1863, until the war's end.

Throughout his wartime congressional career, Johnson remained consistent in adhering to his state rights principles. He opposed conscription, the suspension of the writ of habeas corpus, and the establishment of a Confederate supreme court. He even took the radical step of proposing an amendment to the Confederate Constitution that would have authorized the right of peaceful secession of an individual state from the Confederacy. He was strongly criticized for this move in Georgia newspapers, particularly the *Savannah Republican.* He later explained to this newspaper that the purpose of the proposal was not to encourage secession, which he felt should never be more than a last resort. But in the event that such extreme action was felt necessary, he said, the "object of the amendment is to sheath forever the

sword of civil war. . . . The aggrieved State may withdraw without the shedding of fraternal blood and take her position among the family of nations to work out her destiny as best she can." After stirring much controversy, Johnson was forced to withdraw the bill on a procedural technicality, and the issue was never raised again.

Despite his considerable political stature before the war, Johnson was not a dominant force in the Confederate Congress. As he later explained in his autobiography, "I did not pretend to make myself prominent in the Senate, because I found that my views were so averse to the policy of the administration, and the effort to enforce them so hopeless, that I contented myself with giving my views mildly and in few words and in voting according to the convictions of my judgment."

Perhaps more surprising than his relatively passive role in the Senate was the staunch loyalty to Jefferson Davis that Johnson maintained behind the scenes, revealed primarily through his correspondence with Davis's far less supportive vice president. Johnson journeyed from Richmond to Milledgeville in November 1863 for the primary purpose of thwarting a meeting of Georgia legislators openly hostile to the president. He subsequently wrote to Stephens, "Differing as I do from the President in several particulars, yet I am satisfied that a warfare on his administration will be disastrous. It will discourage the army; divide the people at home and weaken the energies of the country. One revolution at a time is enough."

Johnson chided Stephens on his involvement in the efforts among Georgians to undermine and discredit President Davis. In a series of letters in March 1864, he denounced the vice president's lengthy absences from Richmond and his failure to use his position to constructively shape or influence administration efforts. Johnson accused his friend of advocating impeachment proceedings against Davis and denounced his measures as foolhardy and misguided. "You are the Vice President & a part of the Executive branch of the Government," he wrote. "How deeply to be lamented that holding that relation you should feel it to be your duty to avow your hostility to & advise the Legislature to array the States against the Government! Nothing has yet occurred which fills me with so much gloom and sadness. . . . From Gen'l [Robert] Toombs and Gov. Brown I expected rashness—I did not expect it of you."

Johnson played an ambivalent role in the peace movement that emerged in 1864. He was one of the few senators active in efforts that were much more conspicuous among members of the lower house. In June 1864, he was part of a coalition of congressional peace advocates that, in the wake of Confederate victories at Spotsylvania and in the Wilderness, sought to lobby both houses of Congress to initiate negotiations with the Lincoln administration to end the war with Southern independence intact. But resolutions introduced by the coalition's spokesmen to send peace commissioners to Washington were soundly rejected by both houses.

After Atlanta's fall two months later, however, as the prospect of Georgians negotiating a separate peace with William Tecumseh Sherman was discussed, Johnson showed little enthusiasm for such an initiative. Despite rumors that Sherman had approached both him and Governor Joseph E. Brown to discuss terms for Georgia's reentry into the Union, Johnson denied any serious consideration of the option. In an open letter to "Several Gentlemen of Middle Georgia" on September 25, 1864, he maintained

> . . . though deeply resentful of Radical Republican rule in the state, he refrained from speaking out against it. . . .

that "there can be no peace upon any honorable terms so long as its present rulers are in power." Far from inspiring the Federal government with a sense of justice or magnanimity, he said, any Southern peace sentiments in the wake of Atlanta's fall and Richmond's imminent capture by Ulysses S. Grant would be construed "as intimidation on our part and would stimulate and intensify the war spirit of the North." He advised his fellow Georgians that such a "confession of overthrow" could lead to no better than terms of unconditional surrender, which he knew they were not yet ready to concede.

In December 1864, Sherman's troops overran Johnson's Sandy Grove plantation, ransacking but not destroying it. By the war's end, Johnson could take little satisfaction in his prescience four years earlier regarding its outcome and the disastrous effects on the South, for he was among those facing financial ruin as he returned home in April 1865 to resume his law practice and rebuild his plantation.

But again, his attempt to return to private life was interrupted by political responsibilities. When the state constitutional convention met in Milledgeville in October 1865, Johnson was chosen as its president. Under the terms of its short-lived Constitution, the legislature met in January 1866 and elected Johnson and Stephens, recently released from prison, to the U.S. Senate. The lack of proper repentance implied by the quick conversion of these high-ranking Confederate officials into Federal officeholders compelled the Radical Republican Congress to bar their entry and deny them their seats. Johnson reacted with a combination of relief and resentment at this indignity. He wrote Stephens that he had had no desire to go to Washington and found the one "prospect of relief" in the fact that "for the present, I can play Senator and also stay at home & attend to my profession." In

response to Stephens's musings over whether to relinquish the office to a Georgian less offensive to Northern sensibilities, Johnson urged him to stand firm. "They have elected you with full knowledge of your objections & your ineligibility (according to Radical tests). Therefore, keep me company in the agreeable task of staying at home, until we can be allowed to take our seats."

That time never came, and Johnson's political career, in effect, was over. He practiced law and managed his plantation, and though deeply resentful of Radical Republican rule in the state, he refrained from speaking out against it, despite frequent invitations to do so. In 1873 Governor James M. Smith appointed Johnson to the superior court judgeship of Georgia's middle circuit, a position he accepted despite increasingly poor health in order to alleviate his continued financial hardship. He served in that position until his death at Sandy Grove on August 16, 1880.

BIBLIOGRAPHY

Bryan, T. Conn. *Confederate Georgia.* Athens, Ga., 1953.

Conway, Alan. *The Reconstruction of Georgia.* Minneapolis, Minn., 1966.

Flippin, Percy Scott. *Herschel V. Johnson of Georgia: State Rights Unionist.* Richmond, Va., 1931.

Flippin, Percy Scott, ed. "From the Autobiography of Herschel V. Johnson." *American Historical Review* 30 (January 1925): 311–336.

Johnson, Michael P. *Toward a Patriarchal Republic: The Secession of Georgia.* Baton Rouge, La., 1977.

Knight, Lucian Lamar. *Reminiscences of Famous Georgians.* Vol. 2. Atlanta, 1908.

Mellichamp, Josephine. *Senators from Georgia.* Huntsville, Ala., 1876.

Phillips, Ulrich Bonnell. *Georgia and State Rights.* Washington, D.C., 1902. Reprint, Yellow Springs, Ohio, 1968.

JOHN C. INSCOE

JOHNSON'S ISLAND PRISON

In October 1861, Lt. Col. William Hoffman, the U.S. commissary general of prisoners, examined the Lake Erie islands for a prison site and selected as the most practicable a three-hundred-acre island in Sandusky Bay, some two-and-three-quarters miles from Sandusky, to which prisoners could be brought by rail and from which they could be moved by boat. On the island, half of which Hoffman leased from its owner and namesake, Leonard B. Johnson, there was a forty-acre clearing on which Hoffman had buildings for guards and prisoners erected. For the latter there were ultimately thirteen two-story barracks in a fifteenacre enclosure surrounded by a high plank fence with platforms for guards and two block-houses with small cannons. At this early stage of the Civil War, the U.S. authorities thought that Johnson's Island would hold all their prisoners.

The prison almost immediately began to be used mainly for officer prisoners up to the rank of general, with the first arriving on April 10, 1862. The highest number held before the commencement of regular exchange was 1,462 at the end of August 1862. After a temporary reduction, exchanges broke down and the total rose to 2,763 by the end of 1863 and to a peak of 9,423 by January 1865.

Throughout most of its existence, Ohioans administered Johnson Island. When creating the prison, Hoffman arranged for the appointment of William S. Pierson as commander. Though lacking military experience, Pierson was a former mayor of Sandusky and able to administer what began as a small institution. He became major of the locally recruited Hoffman Battalion, ultimately enlarged to the 128th Ohio Volunteer Infantry Regiment, which made up the core of the guard force. In January 1864, Brig. Gen. Henry D. Terry took command, bringing with him five additional regiments for guards. Complaints of indiscipline and bad physical conditions continued under Terry as they had under Pierson. On May 8, 1864, the adjutant general of Ohio, Charles W. Hill, took command for the remainder of the war. He instituted a thorough cleaning of the buildings and grounds.

Part of the explanation for the filth on the island was that the rock that underlaid the scant topsoil impeded drainage and made it difficult to dig adequate sinks (latrines). Pure wells were also hard to provide and pumping water from the lake was not always feasible, especially in winter. Winter exacerbated the problems because, though the island was very like a resort in summer, it was brutal in the cold season, especially for prisoners accustomed to a Southern climate and furnished with insufficient blankets and clothing. In 1864 when the Union authorities in retaliation for alleged Confederate mistreatment of Union prisoners reduced rations and cut off most purchases from the sutler and the delivery of gift boxes, prisoners began to complain of severe hunger. Indicative of the reality of their suffering was the organization of a "rat club" for hunting, eating and selling rats to other prisoners. Far more common diversions were theatricals, handcrafts, reading, classes, and religious services.

Inevitably, escape was a preoccupation of the prisoners. Attempts at tunneling were almost never successful, but it was sometimes possible to deceive the guard at the gate or to scale the wall at night and then cross to the mainland on winter ice. Even then, rewards posted for escapees often induced recapture; still, a few prisoners reached Canada and were able to run the blockade into the Confederacy.

Some other escaped prisoners became involved in attempts by Confederate agents in 1864 and 1865 to launch irregular attacks on the United States, to encourage insurrection, and especially to free Confederate prisoners from Northern camps. A rescue of the Johnson's Island prisoners and a conspiracy among the inmates to aid the effort had been rumored in 1863, and the Federals had begun to mount cannons in earthworks and to station near the island the ship *Michigan,* the only armed vessel on the Great Lakes. Confederate agents in Canada plotted to capture the vessel and free the prisoners. They sent an escaped prisoner to prepare the way and, in September 1864, sent a party headed by John Yeats Beall, an acting master in the Confederate navy, which captured two lake steamers. But Beall's crew lost heart before trying to seize *Michigan,* and he was later captured out of uniform on U.S. soil and hanged for violation of the laws of war. Thus failed the most formidable raid on Johnson's Island.

In 1865, first the resumption of exchange and then the end of the war rapidly emptied the prison. In September, the handful of remaining prisoners was transferred. By the following June, the buildings had been sold and the post abandoned. Parts of the site were used for orchards, quarrying, and summer resorts. In the mid-twentieth century a causeway was built to connect the island and the shore. Though remnants of the fortifications remain, the only publicly owned memorial is the cemetery whose 206 graves attest to the fact that this prison for officers was less fatal than many. A statue of a Confederate soldier gazes toward the South.

BIBLIOGRAPHY

Barrett, John G., ed. *Yankee Rebel: The Civil War Journal of Edmund DeWitt Patterson.* Chapel Hill, N.C., 1966.
Frohman, Charles E. *Rebels on Lake Erie.* Columbus, Ohio, 1965.
Hesseltine, William B. *Civil War Prisons: A Study in War Psychology.* Columbus, Ohio, 1930. Reprint, New York, 1964.
Shriver, Philip R., and Donald J. Breen. *Ohio's Military Prisons in the Civil War.* Columbus, Ohio, 1964.

FRANK L. BYRNE

JOHNSTON, ALBERT SIDNEY

JOHNSTON, ALBERT SIDNEY (1803–1862), general. Johnston, a distinguished soldier of three republics, was born February 2, 1803, in Washington, Kentucky, and was educated in private schools and at Transylvania University. He graduated from the United States Military Academy in 1826, standing eighth in his class.

Johnston had an unusually versatile military career. He served in the Black Hawk War as adjutant to the commanding general, as senior general, and, later, as secretary of war of the Republic of Texas, as a staff officer in the Battle of Monterrey in the Mexican War, as paymaster of U.S. troops stationed in the frontier forts of Texas, as colonel of the elite Second Cavalry Regiment, and as the commander of the U.S. force sent to quell the incipient Mormon rebellion in Utah Territory.

Upon the secession of his adopted state, Texas, Johnston resigned his U.S. commission and joined the Confederacy. His former fellow cadet and now close friend, Jefferson Davis, immediately appointed him a full general in the army of the Confederacy and placed him in command of the western theater of operations. Heavily outnumbered and indecisive in his early moves, Johnston lost Forts Henry and Donelson in February 1862 to a Federal offensive led by Brig. Gen. Ulysses S. Grant, thereby opening the region to Union penetration along the Tennessee and Cumberland rivers. But Johnston redeemed himself two months later by concentrating his forces at Corinth, an important rail center in northern Mississippi, and surprising Grant in the Battle of Shiloh, April 6 and 7. Johnston was killed the first day of the engagement while his lines were still advancing. He was buried in the Texas State Cemetery in Austin.

BIBLIOGRAPHY

Johnston, William Preston. *The Life of General Albert Sidney Johnston.* New York, 1878.

Roland, Charles P. *Albert Sidney Johnston: Soldier of Three Republics.* Austin, Tex., 1964.

Schaller, Frank. "A Review of the Life and Character of the Late General Albert Sidney Johnston, C.S.A." In *The Spirit of Military Institutions.* Edited by Auguste F. Marmont. Columbia, S.C., 1864.

CHARLES P. ROLAND

JOHNSTON, JOSEPH E.

JOHNSTON, JOSEPH E. (1807–1891), general. Johnston was the son of Peter Johnston, a distinguished soldier in the command of "Light-Horse Harry" Lee in the War for Independence. From this association came a long friendship between the two veterans' sons—Joseph E. Johnston and Robert E. Lee.

Joseph Eggleston Johnston was born February 3, 1807. When he was four the family moved from Prince Edward County, Virginia, to the southwestern part of the state, near Abingdon, where Peter Johnston was a circuit judge. Both the new location and the family's kinships gave young Joseph ties to what was to become a powerful, informal network of prominent Confederates called the "Abingdon bloc."

Johnston graduated from the U.S. Military Academy in 1829, thirteenth in a forty-six-man class. His friend Robert E.

JOSEPH E. JOHNSTON. NATIONAL ARCHIVES

Lee stood second. For most of the rest of his life Johnston would place behind Lee, and there are hints that, despite their friendship, Johnston experienced twinges of jealousy toward his more distinguished classmate.

Except for a few months when he was employed as a civil engineer, Johnston remained in the service until he resigned in 1861 to join the Confederacy. Johnston's story for those thirty-two years was the usual one of a career military officer whose assignments took him from New York to Florida to Mexico. Meanwhile, he steadily made his way up through the grades of the army's hierarchy while acquiring a reputation as a brave, competent officer. Commissioned into the Fourth Artillery as second lieutenant in 1829, Johnston served in the Mexican War and was named lieutenant colonel of the First Cavalry in 1855. Wounded in the wars against the Seminole Indians in Florida and in the Mexican War, he won frequent praise for heroism.

In 1860 Johnston's career took an upward turn when the position of quartermaster general of the army became vacant. Johnston was selected for the coveted post, which carried with it promotion to the staff grade of brigadier general. He was now both a brigadier general (staff grade) and a lieutenant colonel (permanent grade). For once, he had surpassed Lee, who remained a lieutenant colonel. On April 22, 1861, Johnston resigned to go with Virginia into the Confederacy.

When Johnston reached Richmond, he found Robert E. Lee a major general in command of the state army. The governor named Johnston to the same grade. Soon, however, the state decided that it needed but one major general, and Johnston was reduced to brigadier general.

Displeased with his demotion in the state army, Johnston transferred to Confederate service as a brigadier general (then the highest grade in that army). Johnston was sent to command the Southern forces gathering at Harpers Ferry, Virginia. He was to organize and train the troops and defend the town. Almost immediately, however, Johnston concluded that Harpers Ferry could not be held. After a brief squabble with the government, he evacuated the town and fell back to Winchester.

In July Johnston took his army to reinforce the Confederates at Manassas. There, in the first great battle of the war, the South won a victory. As the senior officer present, Johnston commanded the victors, and after the battle, he remained in command of all Confederate troops in the area.

In September Johnston fell into a row with the Southern government about his rank. He and four other officers had been named to the new grade of full general. Confederate law stipulated that former army officers joining the Confederacy would be ranked within each grade by the relative rank they had held in the U.S. Army. Johnston believed he would be ranked by his staff grade of brigadier general and would therefore be the highest-ranking Confederate officer. To his dismay, he found himself ranked fourth, after Samuel Cooper, Albert Sidney Johnston, and Lee.

President Jefferson Davis later justified the placement on the grounds that Johnston was ranked by his permanent grade of lieutenant colonel, not by his staff grade of brigadier general. The reasons for Davis's decision are unknown. Some historians have speculated that Davis and Johnston had long been personal enemies or that their wives had engaged in a dispute of some sort. Others have argued that Davis had supported another candidate for the quartermaster general vacancy in 1860 and used the matter of Confederate rank to strike back at Johnston. It is also possible that Davis simply distrusted Johnston's abilities and wanted to make sure that he would never exercise command over Albert Sidney Johnston or Lee.

Whatever the reason for this action, Davis's decision was unfair to Johnston and probably illegal. Cooper was ranked by his staff grade. (Cooper, however, was in a staff position in both armies; the others were in command of troops in the Southern army.) Fair and legal or not, Davis's decision stood. It was wise because it meant that Johnston would never be

in position to hamper Lee. The real problem, of course, was that Confederate law made no provision for the different types of grade that existed in the U.S. Army.

Throughout the winter of 1861–1862 Johnston carried on an increasingly bitter correspondence with Davis and other officials about his rank, the organization and supply of his army, and the general war policy that the Confederacy should follow. As the differences between the general and the president grew more heated, many of Davis's political and military enemies realized that Johnston made a good point man for their attacks on the administration. Increasingly Johnston became identified with the opponents of the president. At the same time Davis began to lose whatever confidence he had in Johnston's ability to handle an army.

On May 31, 1862, at the Battle of Seven Pines, Johnston was seriously wounded. Because he would be incapacitated for some months, Davis on June 1 named Lee to take his place. Lee soon won such a string of victories that there would never be a question of any other officer commanding the main army in Virginia.

Johnston was able to return to duty in November. By then the South had suffered several disasters in the area between the Appalachian Mountains and the Mississippi River then known as "the West." Davis decided to send Johnston to the West as an overall commander for Confederate forces in Tennessee and Mississippi. The president hoped that Johnston would be able to coordinate those two armies and, by transferring troops from one to the other, combine their resources to defeat a Union threat to either.

Unfortunately for the Southerners, the Federals were strong enough to mount simultaneous operations against more than one point, and the Confederates were usually unable to ascertain what their enemy was doing. Johnston lacked faith in Davis's scheme to shift troops around to defeat the enemy, and he was unwilling to assume responsibility for ordering such movements. Instead, Johnston offered the impracticable proposal of shifting troops from west of the Mississippi to help defend Vicksburg.

The result was a disaster for the South. By mid-May one Confederate army was cooped up in Vicksburg, Mississippi, and was slowly being starved into surrender. Davis ordered Johnston to Mississippi to assume personal command of the effort to raise the siege. Johnston was either unable or unwilling to take any meaningful action, and on July 4 the city and its army surrendered.

From the Confederate point of view the Vicksburg campaign was a debacle from start to finish. As soon as it was over, Davis and Johnston fell into an unseemly squabble over who was responsible for the loss of the city, its army, and enormous quantities of invaluable railroad equipment. Johnston, his wife, his staff officers, and his political and military friends exchanged letters among themselves in which they expressed the belief that Davis's hatred for Johnston had become so great that the president would do anything to disgrace him. It is hard to escape the belief that the Johnston coterie was becoming at least mildly paranoid about the government's attitude toward the general. Johnston also made available to Davis's critics, such as Senator Louis T. Wigfall, information about the campaign that they were able to use in their attacks on the president.

For several months after the loss of Vicksburg, Johnston was in what amounted to exile in Mississippi. There Davis doubtless would have been glad for him to remain. In December 1863, however, Davis had to find a new commander for the Army of Tennessee, the Confederates' major military force in the West. After considering several alternatives, he had to name Johnston to the post because there was no better choice. At the end of the year Johnston reached Dalton, Georgia, and assumed his new command.

By May 1864 Johnston had done a creditable job of rebuilding the strength and morale of the Army of Tennessee. The old mistrust of the government remained, however, and he and the Richmond authorities were never able to agree on a plan for the summer's campaign. Davis wanted Johnston to advance and reestablish Confederate control over Tennessee. Johnston thought he was not strong enough for such an offensive move. Johnston also believed that Davis was withholding supplies and reinforcements. He would not tell the government what he intended to do, and he constantly complained about whatever suggestions were made to him.

When the Federals advanced against Johnston at Dalton, he was unable to hold his position and fell back into the heart of Georgia. By mid-July, Johnston had backed his army south to Atlanta. He had lost more than twenty thousand men, given up valuable territory in North Georgia, abandoned the right bank of the Chattahoochee River (thereby exposing the great Confederate industrial complex in central Alabama), demoralized many of his soldiers, and thrown some Southern political figures into a near panic. The government was still in ignorance of whatever plans he may have had to defend Atlanta.

In mid-July, Davis, his patience finally exhausted, removed Johnston from command of the army and replaced him with Gen. John Bell Hood. Johnston, with a small group of loyal officers, retired to Macon, Georgia. For seven months he and his wife traveled about the fast-shrinking Confederacy while his political allies continued their assaults on the Davis administration for its handling of the war in general and its treatment of Johnston in particular.

In February 1865 Davis recalled Johnston to active service—mostly at the request of Lee who had been named general-in-chief of the Confederate armies. Johnston was ordered to assume command of troops in the Carolinas and halt the advance of a Union force that had marched across Georgia and was heading north toward Virginia. The effort

was hopeless, and on April 26 in North Carolina, Johnston surrendered his army.

In the years after the war Johnston lived in Virginia, Alabama, and Washington, D.C. He worked in the transportation ("express") business, as a railroad president, and later as a commissioner of railroads. From 1879 to 1881 he served in the U.S. House of Representatives from Virginia. He devoted much of his time and energy to writing. His chief work, *Narrative of Military Operations Directed during the Late War between the States,* was published in 1874. Like almost all Civil War generals' memoirs, it is self-serving and presents a one-sided view of events. Johnston died March 21, 1891. He was buried in Baltimore.

Johnston's reputation has probably changed more drastically than that of any other Confederate general. For decades historians who based their work on postwar memoirs praised his military abilities. Recent writers, using more reliable sources, have revised that opinion, and as a result his reputation has precipitously declined.

BIBLIOGRAPHY

Connelly, Thomas L. *Autumn of Glory: The Army of Tennessee, 1862–1865.* Baton Rouge, La., 1971.
Connelly, Thomas L., and Archer Jones. *The Politics of Command: Factions and Ideas in Confederate Strategy.* Baton Rouge, La., 1973.
Jones, Archer. *Confederate Strategy from Shiloh to Vicksburg.* Baton Rouge, La., 1965.
Lash, Jeffrey N. *Destroyer of the Iron Horse: General Joseph E. Johnston and Confederate Rail Transport, 1861–1865.* Kent, Ohio, 1991.
McMurry, Richard M. "'The Enemy at Richmond': Joseph E. Johnston and the Confederate Government." *Civil War History* 27 (1981): 5–31.
Symonds, Craig L. *Joseph E. Johnston: A Civil War Biography.* New York, 1992.
Woodworth, Steven E. *Jefferson Davis and His Generals: The Failure of Confederate Command in the West.* Lawrence, Kans., 1990.

RICHARD M. MCMURRY

JONES, CATESBY

JONES, CATESBY (1821–1877), naval officer. Born April 15, 1821, in Fairfield, Virginia, Catesby ap Roger Jones entered the U.S. Navy as a midshipman in 1836. He was promoted to lieutenant in 1849 and remained in that rank until he left the service in 1861. His career in the U.S. Navy was characterized by the normal ship-to-shore rotation. In the 1850s he worked with Lt. John A. Dahlgren in experiments with naval ordnance. This experience would result in his appointment to similar work in the Confederate navy.

Upon the secession of Virginia, Jones resigned his commission and was appointed a captain in the Virginia State Navy. On June 10, 1861, he was commissioned a lieutenant in the Confederate navy and assigned to command naval batteries on Jamestown Island. Jones's experiments with the effect of naval gunfire on sloping iron armor led to his appointment as executive officer of the ironclad CSS *Virginia.* As second in command he participated in the March 8, 1862, engagement in which USS *Cumberland* and *Congress* were destroyed by *Virginia.* When Capt. Franklin Buchanan was wounded, Jones assumed the command and was in charge

> **Jones's experiments with the effect of naval gunfire on sloping iron armor led to his appointment as executive officer of the ironclad CSS *Virginia.***

the following day when the Confederate armorclad fought USS *Monitor.* He resumed the position of executive officer when Buchanan's replacement took command.

After the destruction of *Virginia* in early May 1862, Jones commanded, successively, river batteries at Drewry's Bluff on the James River near Richmond, the wooden gunboat *Chattahoochee* on the Chattahoochee River near Columbus, Georgia, and the naval ordnance works at Charlotte, North Carolina. On May 9, 1863, he was ordered to take charge of the Confederate Naval Iron Works at Selma, Alabama. Under his direction this facility cast more than a hundred large naval guns. Jones commanded the ironworks until they were captured by Union forces on April 2, 1865.

After the war Jones established residence in Selma and formed a partnership with John M. Brooke and Robert D. Minor, fellow Confederate naval officers, to purchase war supplies in the United States for foreign governments. The company was never successful despite extensive travel by Jones in the United States and a trip to Peru. On June 20, 1877, Jones died after being shot by a neighbor over a quarrel between their children.

Jones was highly respected by his peers both in the Confederate and the U.S. navies. Adm. David Dixon Porter remarked after the war that he had regretted the loss of only two officers from Union service, Jones and Brooke.

BIBLIOGRAPHY

Mabry, W. S. *Brief Sketch of the Career of Captain Catesby Ap R. Jones.* Selma, Ala., 1912.

Still, William N., Jr. *Iron Afloat: The Story of the Confederate Armorclads.* Columbia, S.C., 1986.

WILLIAM N. STILL, JR.

JONES, J. B.

JONES, J. B. (1810–1866), writer. Born in Baltimore on March 6, 1810, John Beauchamp Jones grew up in Kentucky and Missouri. He became a successful novelist—his *Wild Western Scenes* (1841) sold 100,000 copies—but he achieved greater recognition as a journalist. In the 1840s Jones settled near Philadelphia where he wrote many novels portraying frontier society and in 1857 established the *Southern Monitor,* a weekly journal that defended Southern rights within the Union.

In *Secession, Coercion and Civil War* (1859) Jones sought to temper the passions of secession, but the Fort Sumter crisis caused him to move to the new Confederate capital at Montgomery. Here he was hired by the War Department as a clerk and began to compose his important diary. "At fifty-one I can hardly follow the pursuit of arms; but I will write and preserve a diary of the revolution. . . . To make my diary full and complete as possible is now my business," he wrote on April 29. He made almost daily entries until April 19, 1865. Early the next year *A Rebel War Clerk's Diary* was published in two volumes—his supreme achievement, the most consulted and quoted primary source for events in wartime Montgomery and Richmond.

Jones's *Diary* presents portraits of Jefferson Davis and other leaders that are among the best contemporary likenesses in Civil War literature. His daily record of activities in the War Office, under five secretaries and numerous bureau chiefs, colonels, and generals, provides much of the inner history of the Confederacy. Also important to social and economic historians are his observations on inflation and the daily prices of necessities; military historians value his faithful reports of weather conditions.

From Jones's pages one can discern the pain and privations of the common people, the self-interest and narrowness of politicians and military men, and the anguish accompanying a failing cause. Using terse, direct language, often colored by anger, stereotypes, and prejudice, Jones is a personal and lively chronicler. He lacks the literary qualities of Mary Boykin Chesnut, however, and the objectivity and deeper perception of Robert Garlick Kean, whose diary, *Inside the Confederate Government,* was published in New York in 1957. Jones's style—tough and combative—masks the fears of a father of a large family eking out survival on a small salary in Richmond's wildly inflationary economy.

With the fall of Richmond, Jones moved back to Philadelphia, where he oversaw the publication of his book. In October 1865 he gave testimony in the Henry Wirz trial in Washington, defending the commandant of Andersonville from charges of willful neglect and starvation of Union prisoners of war (and defending the Confederate administration as well). Soon after, he succumbed to declining health and died in Burlington, New Jersey, on February 4, 1866, while the *Diary* was in press. It enjoyed a large publication and has been reprinted, in whole or part, at least three times. A modern scholarly edition is a major need of Confederate historiography.

BIBLIOGRAPHY

Freeman, Douglas S. *The South to Posterity.* New York, 1939. Reprint of revised edition, Wilmington, N.C., 1983.
Jones, J. B. *A Rebel War Clerk's Diary at the Confederate States Capital.* 2 vols. Philadelphia, 1866. Revised ed. by Earl Schenck Miers. New York, 1958.

JOHN O'BRIEN

JONES, WILLIAM EDMONDSON "GRUMBLE"

JONES, WILLIAM EDMONDSON "GRUMBLE" (1824–1864), brigadier general. Sour-visaged, belligerent, fully deserving of his nickname "Grumble," Jones lived a short and stormy life. He was born May 3, 1824, in southwestern Virginia's Washington County. An 1848 graduate of West Point, he had nine years of duty at frontier posts stretching from Texas to Washington Territory. The death of his bride in an 1852 shipwreck left Jones permanently embittered. In 1857 he resigned from the army and became a semirecluse on his Glade Spring farm.

Virginia's secession led Jones to organize a mounted company that became part of the First Virginia Cavalry. He soon succeeded J. E. B. Stuart as colonel of the regiment and later commanded the equally renowned Seventh Virginia Cavalry. On September 19, 1862, Jones received promotion to brigadier general and command of the Laurel Brigade. Gallant conduct at Brandy Station in June 1863 brought Jones additional fame. His piercing eyes, long beard, high-pitched voice, penchant for profanity, and farmer's attire in battle made him an easily recognizable general.

Long-standing enmity between Jones and Stuart soon reached the explosive stage. In October, Jones was court-martialed from the Army of Northern Virginia and sent to command the isolated Department of Southwest Virginia and East Tennessee. He performed well in the Knoxville campaign and later at the Battle of Cloyds Mountain, Virginia. On June 5, 1864, in a sharp fight at Piedmont with Gen. David Hunter's Federals, Jones was struck in the forehead by a bullet and killed instantly. He is buried in the Glade Spring Presbyterian Church cemetery.

"Grumble" Jones was a hard-fighting and thoroughly dedicated soldier. He won a reputation as "the best outpost officer" in Robert E. Lee's army. Yet a running feud with his superior officer proved to be his downfall.

BIBLIOGRAPHY

Blackford, William W. *War Years with Jeb Stuart.* New York, 1945.
"'Grumble' Jones." *Civil War Times Illustrated* 7 (June 1968):35–41.
Thomas, Emory M. *Bold Dragoon: The Life of J. E. B. Stuart.* New York, 1986.

JAMES I. ROBERTSON, JR.

JONES COUNTY, MISSISSIPPI

According to legend, in 1864 the pro-Union populace of Jones County, Mississippi, formed a revolutionary government, adopted a declaration of independence, and formally seceded from Mississippi and the Confederate States of America. This new nation called itself the Republic (or Confederacy, or Kingdom) of Jones. When Mississippi and the Confederacy subsequently attempted to enforce their sovereignties in the county, the Republic of Jones organized its own army and navy and declared war on its parent states. The Republic of Jones, so the story goes, maintained its existence until the defeat of the Confederacy the following year. For the past century and a quarter, this tale has been retold regularly in the national press and entertainment media.

The facts behind this legend indicate that the epithet "Republic of Jones" did, indeed, originate in events that occurred in 1864 in Jones County, Mississippi, but the history of the matter differs quite sharply from the legendary accounts. By 1864, Jones County, Mississippi, had been known whimsically for more than a generation as "The Free State of Jones" because of its geographical remoteness, its lack of formal government and social amenities, and the independent, uninhibited lifestyle of its pastoral citizens. Like other frontier counties, Jones had little share in the cotton and slave economics and politics of the state, and most of its scattered population opposed secession. Nevertheless, when war came, the three thousand white people of Jones County provided two full companies and parts of six others to Southern armies.

Because of its isolation and sparse population, Jones County during the war became a haven for Confederate army deserters, some of whom banded together to plunder the local citizens and resist capture by Southern troops. In early 1864 Sherman's march to Meridian drove the Confederate army briefly from the state. Thinking that Federal troops had come to southeastern Mississippi to stay, some of the deserters sought to justify their robberies, assaults, evictions, and even killings of local citizens by representing such crimes as political acts. There is little to suggest, however, that the mass of these stragglers were any more ideologically committed to the Union than they were to the Confederacy.

In mid-1864 Confederate efforts to quell deserter freebooting in Jones County inspired the newspaper *Courier,* of Natchez, a town long since under Union occupation, to lampoon the idea of secession by claiming that the rustic pineywoodsmen of the Free State of Jones had seceded from Mississippi just as that state had seceded from the Union. A month later, this burlesque was taken up by the *New Orleans Daily Picayune.* The spoof was then taken literally by elements of the Northern press, which portrayed the military policing in Jones County as Confederate attempts to suppress a civilian political revolt. In time, these different versions of the story merged with Jones County oral tradition to produce the modern legend of the Republic of Jones.

BIBLIOGRAPHY

Leverett, Rudy. *Legend of the Free State of Jones.* Jackson, Miss., 1984.

Montgomery, Goode. "Alleged Secession of Jones County." *Publications of the Mississippi Historical Society* 8 (1904): 13–22.

Natchez Courier, July 12, 1864.

New Orleans Daily Picayune, July 17, 1864.

New York Tribune, August 1, 1864.

RUDY LEVERETT

JUDICIARY

The Confederacy's judicial system was a subject of controversy from the start, and Congress never established in full the system called for by the new nation's constitutions. In a departure from the Federal system, circuit courts were never created. Subsequently, bitter divisions over principle and personalities prevented organization of both a supreme court and a court of claims, which had been planned. The court of claims would have heard lawsuits against the Confederate government in the same way that the U.S. Court of Claims—established in 1855—handled suits against the U.S. government. Nevertheless, a judicial system resting on state courts and Confederate district courts functioned without paralyzing confusion or variances in rulings. State courts, following precedents established in the U.S. system, customarily upheld the powers of the central government.

The judicial clauses of the Provisional Constitution sought to continue cases interrupted by secession by extending judicial powers to all cases in law and equity arising under the laws of the United States. (Most Southern states had both law courts and courts of equity; the latter, following English practice, supplemented law courts by applying general principles of justice in circumstances not covered by the law.) But other features, beyond this practical provision, soon occasioned controversy. The Provisional Constitution called for a single judicial district in each state, which meant that the number of district courts that had existed under the United States was reduced by more than half. This undesirable situ-

> **The Confederacy's judicial system was a subject of controversy from the start. . . .**

ation produced the only amendment made to either Confederate constitution, when in May 1861 Congress received the authority to define districts as it deemed appropriate.

The Provisional Constitution also called for a supreme court, and the Judiciary Act of March 16, 1861, envisioned that this high court would exercise appellate jurisdiction over state courts—a disturbing idea to many. The supreme court was to consist of all the district court judges assembled together. Experience in the states had shown that this was not a satisfactory procedure, and observers pointed out that western judges would have difficulty traveling to Richmond in a timely manner. Consequently, on July 31, 1861, Congress suspended the supreme court until it could be organized under the Permanent Constitution.

Battles over the role of the judiciary grew more heated as the Provisional Congress debated a permanent Constitution. To radical state rights thinkers in the Congress, the court system had been one of the chief engines of centralization and usurpation under the United States. One senator declared that if John Marshall's abilities had not made the U.S. Supreme Court so powerful, the Union would still be in existence. Questions of state versus Confederate authority presented themselves in almost every clause of the section on the judiciary, and changes adopted for the Permanent Constitution foreshadowed subsequent controversy.

First, state rights radicals, in March 1861, succeeded in eliminating the jurisdiction of Confederate courts over disputes between citizens of different states. Failing in several other limitations of central authority, they attacked the most important point: appellate jurisdiction for the Supreme Court over decisions rendered in state courts. On this point the radicals nearly prevailed, but a divided delegation from Florida denied them a majority, and thus the Permanent Constitution called for a supreme court that was not explicitly restricted and crippled as the state rights men wished. Battles over the nature of the court, however, would continue in the First Congress.

Another change made to Article III of the Provisional Constitution eliminated language giving the Confederate judiciary power over all cases of law and equity. This deletion respected state rights, since Louisiana and Texas operated under the Roman legal tradition, which lacked separate courts of equity. The distinction between law and equity, however, remained for most of the states, and Congress could have given its district courts power over cases of law and equity there. Instead it eventually prevented them from entering cases of equity wherever "plain, adequate remedy may be had at laws."

The Permanent Constitution called for a court of claims, but Congress never established one. In the absence of that court the executive departments, the Board of Sequestration Commissioners, and the district courts handled the relevant work. Provision was made for a court of admiralty to sit in Key West, but since the Confederacy never controlled that city, the admiralty court never became a reality.

In accordance with the Permanent Constitution, President Jefferson Davis asked the First Congress on February 25, 1862, to establish a supreme court. Although Congress considered the matter in 1862 and 1863, it failed to act. Soon after Davis's request, bills were introduced calling for a supreme court consisting of one chief justice and three associate justices. Senator Benjamin H. Hill of Georgia argued that a government without a supreme court would be "a lame and limping affair," but both houses let the matter drop without a vote in 1862. The next year Hill proposed a similar bill, and the conflicts that had stalled consideration came out into the open.

Supporters of a supreme court argued that the nation needed clarity and consistency in its laws and sought to allay concerns that there would be a usurpation of state power within the Confederacy. On that point, however, many legislators—led by men such as Clement C. Clay, William Lowndes Yancey, Louis T. Wigfall, and Robert W. Barnwell—were extremely sensitive. The key question was whether a supreme court would be free to enforce Confederate law as the supreme law of the land. Without appellate jurisdiction over state courts, a supreme court was superfluous, yet appellate jurisdiction seemed likely to Clay to "favor the consolidation of the government." Yancey warned that it would "chain" the states to central authority. According to historian W. Buck Yearns, all but four senators wanted a supreme court, but only six of them were willing to grant the appellate jurisdiction that would make it meaningful.

Politics and personalities also played a role in the battle over a supreme court. With elections approaching in 1863, some congressmen were reluctant to go on record as giving the central government any additional power. Other congressmen thought they knew who would be appointed to the court if it were established, and their opposition to certain individuals became opposition to the court. Tennessee's representative, Henry S. Foote, asserted that he would "never consent to the establishment of a supreme court of the Confederate States so long as Judah P. Benjamin shall continue to pollute the ears of majesty Davis with his insidious counsels." Others feared that Assistant Secretary of War John A. Campbell, a former justice of the U.S. Supreme Court and a very able lawyer, would become chief justice and promote central power in the Confederacy just as John Marshall had done in the United States. In the end, the Senate passed a bill for a watered-down supreme court, but the House let the matter drop, and the Confederacy had to proceed without the highest court called for by its Constitution.

Confederate district courts were organized and judges appointed. Under the Judiciary Act they were instructed to follow state laws and state court practices as well as enforce Confederate laws. But they were often busy with traditional civil and criminal matters and especially with habeas corpus cases involving soldiers seeking to avoid military service. Because the Confederate judicial system was so weak and truncated, it was the state courts that proved to be most influential.

In a striking irony, the Davis administration turned to and relied upon state courts to uphold the powers of the central government. No issue presented the question of central versus state power more sharply or elicited more angry threats from governors than conscription. On this question President Davis and several state governors thoroughly debated the powers of the Confederacy and brought strongly opposed viewpoints into the open. In the absence of a supreme court, Davis took the contested questions into state courts, where Confederate authority was affirmed.

> **Politics and personalities also played a role in the battle over a supreme court.**

In September 1862, Governor Joseph E. Brown of Georgia thundered against the second conscription act, charging that it struck down Georgia's "sovereignty at a single blow." Brown even declared that "no act of the government of the United States prior to the secession of Georgia" had been so injurious to constitutional liberty, and he obtained resolutions from his legislature to support him. In similar fashion South Carolina's governor and executive council insisted that any man exempted by state law from the militia was also exempt from conscription and threatened to issue a "countervailing order" against any Confederate conscription officer who tried to enroll such individuals.

In response Jefferson Davis was unbending on principle and conciliatory on procedure. He defended the constitutionality of the conscription law at length to Governor Brown, and he bluntly wrote South Carolina's leaders that "if a State may free her citizens at her own discretion from the burden of military duty, she may do the same in regard to the burden of taxation, or any other lawful duty, payment or service." That would deny the Confederacy the right "to enforce the exercise of any delegated power and would render a Confederacy an impracticable form of Government." Yet Davis also promised the Palmetto State's leaders that he would release any soldier whose exemption was upheld by South Carolina courts, and he assured Senator Benjamin Hill that he relied "on the decision of the Supreme Court of Georgia to remove the difficulties."

In these two states, as well as in Virginia, Alabama, Texas, Florida, and Mississippi, President Davis won his tests of the constitutionality of conscription. In Georgia the decision of the state supreme court was unanimous and was greeted by spectators with an outburst of applause that forced the chief justice to call for order. The decision of the Texas Supreme Court declared that the "power to raise and support armies is an express constitutional grant to the Congress of the Confederate States, and there is no limitation as to the mode or manner of exercising it. When Congress calls for the military service of the citizen . . . the right of the State government must cease or yield to the paramount demand of Congress." Thus state courts upheld the supremacy of Confederate law on a vital question and continued to do so. Although individual judges, such as Richmond Pearson of North Carolina, sometimes caused much concern, the South's judicial system proved to be "fragmented in structure but centralized in substance," in the words of historian Emory Thomas.

There were undoubtedly several reasons for this surprising outcome. The facts that the administration's measures were necessary and that opponents offered no alternatives may have had some influence. Perhaps more salient was the fact that the permanent Constitution authorized Congress to "make all laws which shall be necessary and proper for carrying into execution" the powers granted to the national legislature. The power to make war and the power to raise and support armies were among those grants of authority. Even in a confederation whose members were historically jealous of state prerogatives and state sovereignty, the logic of having a central government to wage war against external enemies remained clear.

In addition, the judges who staffed the courts of the Southern states had learned their law in the judicial system of the United States. They, as well as the attorneys general of the Confederate States, referred to past decisions in U.S. history for guidance and often cited decisions of U.S. courts as precedents. Although Southern jurists may have believed that the Federal government had usurped state authority, they were not unfamiliar with the idea of a central government supreme in its defined sphere. The crisis of war surely called out for such a government in the South. It was fortunate for the Confederacy that the absence of a supreme court did not greatly multiply the problems under which it already labored.

[*See also* Conscription; Crime and Punishment; Habeas Corpus; State Rights.]

BIBLIOGRAPHY

Coulter, E. Merton. *The Confederate States of America, 1861–1865.* A History of the South, vol. 7. Baton Rouge, La., 1950.
Escott, Paul D. *After Secession: Jefferson Davis and the Failure of Confederate Nationalism.* Baton Rouge, La., 1978.
Moore, Albert Burton. *Conscription and Conflict in the Confederacy.* New York, 1924.
Robinson, William M., Jr. *Justice in Grey.* Cambridge, Mass., 1941.
Thomas, Emory M. *The Confederate Nation, 1861–1865.* New York, 1979.
Yearns, Wilfred B. *The Confederate Congress.* Athens, Ga., 1960.

PAUL D. ESCOTT

JUNETEENTH

June 19 (or "Juneteenth") is observed by African Americans in Texas to commemorate the official emancipation of slaves in the Lone Star State following the end of the Civil War.

Although Gen. Robert E. Lee capitulated to Gen. Ulysses S. Grant at Appomattox Courthouse on April 9, 1865, the Trans-Mississippi Department did not surrender until June 2, and a shortage of transport vessels delayed for over two weeks the arrival of Union forces in Texas. On June 19, 1865, Gen. Gordon Granger landed in Galveston and proclaimed the freedom of the state's slaves. Subsequently, African Americans in Texas have celebrated June 19 annually as their true emancipation day.

During the late nineteenth century, the typical Juneteenth celebration was a day-long event commencing with a parade complete with brass bands and representatives of the leading African American churches, fraternal orders, and social clubs. A barbecue, speeches, sporting events, and dancing (sometimes concluding with an evening ball) would follow.

Although the popularity of the celebration diminished after World War II, it never completely died out. Employers complained that many of their African American employees used Juneteenth as an excuse to take the day off, and some civil rights activists preferred that their constituents pay more attention to contemporary efforts to gain full equality. The growing interest in African American history during the late

1960s and early 1970s fueled public recognition for Juneteenth commemorations. In 1972, the Texas legislature passed a resolution proclaiming June 19 to be a "holiday of significance to all Texans and, particularly, to the blacks of Texas." As such, this event fosters community spirit among blacks and also serves as a source for racial interaction in communities throughout the state.

BIBLIOGRAPHY

Barr, Alwyn. *Black Texans: A History of the Negroes in Texas, 1528–1971.* Austin, Tex., 1973.

Rice, Lawrence D. *The Negro in Texas, 1874–1900.* Baton Rouge, La., 1971.

Watriss, Wendy. "Celebrate Freedom: Juneteenth." *Southern Exposure* 5 (1977): 80–87.

JAMES M. SORELLE

KANSAS-NEBRASKA ACT

In 1854, Congress passed the Kansas-Nebraska Act, repealing part of the 1820 Missouri Compromise. That previously sacrosanct agreement had divided Federal territories acquired in the Louisiana Purchase (1803) at the 36°30′ geographic line, with slavery permitted southward (including south of the slave state of Missouri) but prohibited northward (including west and north of Missouri) whenever Congress authorized settlement of these areas. In 1824, Illinois, to Missouri's east and outside the Louisiana Purchase area, banned slavery after a historic struggle. In 1846, Iowa, carved out of Louisiana Purchase territory to Missouri's north, extended the 36°30′ ban from the territorial to the statehood stage by entering the Union as a free-labor state. If Congress had authorized settlers to enter the Louisiana Purchase territory to Missouri's west without repealing the 36°30′ proscription of slavery, Missouri, with only 10 percent of its population enslaved, would have been guaranteed a third nonslaveholding neighbor.

In 1854, Missouri's very powerful Senator David R. Atchison warned several equally powerful Southern Democrats, living with him in a Washington, D.C., boardinghouse, that slavery in Missouri could not then endure. Its neighbors would both inspire Missouri slaves to flee and stimulate Missouri's 88 percent majority of nonslaveholders to rout the slaveholders. Congress, declared Atchison, must instead repeal the 36°30′ ban when opening the area for settlement. Then, he promised, Missouri slaveholders would seize their western hinterlands and consolidate their regime.

The final form of the Kansas-Nebraska Act, drawn to Atchison's specifications, repealed the Missouri Compromise ban on slavery in Kansas Territory, located west of Missouri, and in Nebraska Territory, located north of Kansas Territory. The majority of settlers in each, decreed Congress, would decide slavery's fate. An area previously reserved for one section was here turned into a prize for the winner of an endurance race, involving which section would send more settlers to the two territories.

Most Northerners loathed having to compete for an area previously declared theirs. Congress nevertheless passed the minority section's law, for first Atchison's boardinghouse mates, then almost all Southern Democrats, and then most Southern Whigs supported the Missourian—and because Northern Democrats could not then defy Southern Democrats. Particularly, Illinois Senator Stephen A. Douglas, the Northern Democrats' congressional leader, wished to open Kansas and Nebraska Territories to settlers, for he wanted whites and railroads to develop the West. He also hoped to win the presidential nomination of a revitalized Democratic party. These objectives required Southern Democrats' support, and the price of their support was legislation that allowed settlers rather than congressmen to determine a locality's institutions—precisely Douglas's popular sovereignty principle. So after Southern Democrats insisted, Douglas made repeal of the Missouri Compromise his cause, as did President Franklin Pierce, another Northern Democrat.

> An area previously reserved for one section was here turned into a prize for the winner of an endurance race, involving which section would send more settlers to the two territories.

The ensuing law helped inspire the rise of Douglas's Illinois rival, Abraham Lincoln, and more broadly, the rise of the Democratic party's new rival, the Republican party. The Kansas-Nebraska Act also provoked armed combat in what became known as Bleeding Kansas. Although proslavery Missourians reached that pre–Civil War battleground first, more antislavery Northerners ultimately arrived. Yet in 1857 and 1858 Southerners demanded that Douglas support the admission of Kansas into the Union under the Kansas proslavery minority's proposed Lecompton constitution, which protected slavery. When Douglas balked at this defiance of what the majority of Kansans wanted, Southerners blamed him for the congressional decision that rejected the Lecompton constitution. After Douglas won the Democratic party's presidential nomination in 1860, most Southern Democrats seceded from the party. With the Democrats split, the Republican Lincoln won the presidency, and a Southern Confederacy beckoned.

[*See also* Bleeding Kansas.]

BIBLIOGRAPHY

Freehling, William W. *Secessionists at Bay, 1776–1854.* Vol. 1 of *The Road to Disunion.* New York, 1990.

Johannsen, Robert W. *Stephen A. Douglas.* New York, 1973.

Nichols, Roy F. "The Kansas-Nebraska Act: A Century of Historiography." *Mississippi Valley Historical Review* 43 (1956): 187–212.

Rawley, James A. *Race and Politics: "Bleeding Kansas" and the Coming of the Civil War.* Philadelphia and New York, 1969.

Roy, P. Orman. *The Repeal of the Missouri Compromise.* Cleveland, 1909.

WILLIAM W. FREEHLING

Keitt, Lawrence

KEITT, LAWRENCE (1824–1864), congressman from South Carolina and colonel. Keitt, one of South Carolina's most outspoken advocates of secession, was elected to the U.S. House of Representatives in 1852. While in Congress, he twice resigned his seat. In 1856, he accompanied fellow South Carolinian Preston Brooks to the U.S. Senate chamber where Brooks beat Senator Charles Sumner senseless. During the fray, Keitt used his own cane to keep away others who tried to come to Sumner's defense. A special House committee recommended expelling Brooks and censuring Keitt. When Northern congressmen couldn't muster the votes to expel Brooks, they turned their wrath on Keitt. He was censured and promptly resigned his seat. In a special election, the voters of his district turned out in record numbers and voted overwhelmingly to return him to Congress.

By the summer of 1860, with Abraham Lincoln's election a certainty, Keitt was in the forefront of those calling for South Carolina's secession. Like Robert Barnwell Rhett, Sr., he was strongly radical on the question and had little patience for cooperationists and none for Unionists. Some have interpreted his behavior as a reaction to the murder of his ill brother by slaves in Florida. His speeches and correspondence do contain numerous references to slave insubordination, plots, and conspiracies.

Keitt was in Columbia when news of Lincoln's election came. He was a popular figure in the state capital and was serenaded by the excited crowds. On at least one occasion, in response to the clamor, he addressed a throng gathered outside his hotel. Elected a delegate to South Carolina's secession convention, he resigned his seat in Congress the day the convention met in Columbia.

In the convention, he remarked that he had "been engaged in this movement" since the day he first embarked on a political career. And when the ordinance of secession was adopted, he said that he was pleased that the convention had "carried the body of this Union to its last resting place, and now we drop the flag over its grave." When the convention was preparing its "Declaration of the Immediate Causes which Induce and Justify the Secession of South Carolina," Keitt was among those who refused to shy away from the question of slavery as a primary cause. "It is," he said, "the great central point from which we are now proceeding." He was defeated in a bid to be one of the commissioners to confer with the government in Washington over the status of Federal property in South Carolina, but he was elected to be one of the state's eight delegates to the Montgomery convention.

Keitt, like Rhett, found in Montgomery that his reputation had preceded him. For most of his political career he had played a negative role. After years of criticizing the existing central government, he found it difficult to participate in creating a new one for the Confederacy and seldom spoke. According to Alexander H. Stephens, Keitt said his wife had advised him "to keep his mouth shut and his hair brushed." Whether because of his reputation as an obstructionist or his wife's admonition, he played only a modest role in the convention.

Keitt was named to a five-person committee to draft the rules governing the convention. Other than that, his contributions centered on efforts to amend the proposed constitution. He led the South Carolina delegation's attempts to eliminate the three-fifths clause for taxes and representation. South Carolina was willing to pay more taxes (it could well afford to) in return for a larger congressional delegation. Initially, the amendment passed, but later the convention reversed itself and the three-fifths clause remained. He also supported an amendment giving Congress the authority to reopen the slave trade, a measure that was defeated.

In the maneuvering for the presidential election, Keitt and James Chesnut torpedoed Rhett's candidacy. Keitt and W. W. Boyce strongly favored Howell Cobb of Georgia and worked for his election. With persuasion, the South Carolina delegation went for Jefferson Davis, but Boyce and Keitt were openly reluctant. On the evening of the election, a crowd gathered at the Exchange Hotel to serenade Vice President Stephens. He spoke to the jubilant crowd, and then Keitt was called upon to make some remarks. As a radical secessionist he assured the assemblage that the new government was in good hands with Davis and Stephens. Above all else, he noted, the Union was dead!

Back in South Carolina's convention, Keitt argued against ratification of the Confederate Constitution. He was part of a very small minority, however, and when the vote was taken, both he and Rhett were recorded as voting yes.

Upon his return to Montgomery for the second session of the Provisional Congress, Keitt resumed his role as government critic. Later, en route to Richmond with the Chesnuts, he pronounced "Jeff Davis a failure—and his cabinet a farce." Needless to say, it did not take long for these Davis loyalists to spread the word. By July, Richmond gossips were already talking about the "coalition against Davis." Keitt and Boyce were rumored to be among the leaders "of the party forming against Mr. Davis."

Lawrence Keitt was an unhappy man. As one of the earliest and most ardent secessionists, he had expected to become a power broker in the new government. His reputation as something of a Hotspur and his impolitic criticism of Davis doomed him to a minor role at best. Realizing the futility of his situation and dreaming of military glory, the congressman refused to stand for election to the First Congress.

> He added that if he could not withdraw his forces, he intended to assault the enemy at first light the next day.

Back home, he raised a regiment of eight hundred men, the Twentieth South Carolina Volunteers. He was elected colonel, and from mid-January to March 1862, he organized and trained the unit. Keitt was excited about being in uniform and wrote glowing letters to his wife, Sue. In June 1862, when John C. Pemberton reorganized the Department of South Carolina, Georgia, and Florida, Keitt was given command of the defenses of Sullivan's Island in Charleston.

Four months later, Davis replaced Pemberton with P. G. T. Beauregard. The new commander enhanced Keitt's command to include the area between the Cooper and South Santee rivers. It was a difficult area to defend. The coast was riven with innumerable inlets, creeks, and tidal marshes. Most of the white population had abandoned the area. Keitt wanted to divide his command to defend several potential invasion sites, but Beauregard ordered him to keep his forces concentrated in the Charleston area. In May and June 1863, the Twentieth South Carolina was chasing Union raiding parties south of the port city.

On July 18, Union troops attacked Fort Wagner on Morris Island. Following the failure of the Fifty-fourth Massachusetts to take the Confederate position, a six-week siege commenced. On August 1, Fort Wagner was added to Keitt's command. He visited the island on several occasions to view the ever more successful Union attempts to breach the works. On September 5, he sent a message to Beauregard from Fort Wagner that the fortifications were no longer tenable. Beauregard told him to hold. The situation was desperate. Union sappers (specialists in field fortifications) were literally at what was left of the walls. Constant shelling kept the defenders in their bombproofs. When they ventured out to try to repair the parapets or get some fresh air, they usually became casualties. On September 6, Keitt wrote, "The retention of the post after to-night involves the sacrifice of the gar-

rison." He added that if he could not withdraw his forces, he intended to assault the enemy at first light the next day. Late in the afternoon, Beauregard agreed to the abandoning of Wagner.

As soon as darkness fell, Keitt began evacuating his men. He remained with the rear guard and was among the last Confederates to leave Morris Island early on the morning of September 7. The withdrawal was done so stealthily that as close as the Union forces were, they did not realize it had taken place. There were only a few glitches. The powder magazines failed to blow up because of faulty fuses, and two barges of men were captured. Nevertheless, it was a successful operation and more than one thousand men were saved for further Confederate service. Beauregard commended him for his actions. With Sullivan's Island now within reach of Federal guns, the Twentieth South Carolina was moved to Mount Pleasant on the mainland opposite the city.

In the fall of 1863, Keitt, who had long dreamed of becoming a general officer, decided to take matters into his own hands. He obtained leave and journeyed to Richmond to press his case in person. He was on a quixotic quest. He had never tempered his early criticism of Davis and continually expressed such sentiments as "to be a patriot, you must hate Davis," or, "His [Davis's] imbecility has been as mischievous as treachery." Such comments circulated in government circles and further damaged what was already a lost cause. Nor did Keitt's champions—Major General Pemberton and Congressmen Boyce and Louis T. Wigfall—help matters. All were known Davis critics. In addition, the superintendent of conscription reported that the number one violator of the Conscription Act of 1862 was Col. Lawrence M. Keitt. Keitt accepted volunteers in excess of his unit's authorized strength. This was a clear violation of the law that was designed to raise as many men as possible for front-line units. The South Carolinian tap-danced on this issue and maintained that he had done nothing illegal.

In his meeting with Davis and War Department officials, Keitt agreed to raise a second regiment (this one to be cavalry) in the hopes that this would bring him a star. Back home he found recruiting far more difficult in late 1863 than it had been eighteen months earlier. The promotion was not forthcoming. The president, through channels, always found a reason to say no. Keitt seemed to accept that but was offended that Davis had neither the good manners nor the manly courage to answer him personally.

In May 1864, the Twentieth South Carolina was ordered to Virginia. Twice, Keitt loaded his men on trains only to have his order rescinded and his unit sent to James Island to repel possible Union advances. After a week of this uncertainty, the tired and exhausted unit boarded railroad cars for the northern front. On May 30, Keitt met with Davis and asked that the Twentieth South Carolina be assigned to Kershaw's Brigade. The president granted his request, and much to his surprise and delight, Keitt found himself the senior colonel in the brigade. As such, he became its acting commander. Keitt was pleased, but the brigade's veterans "felt and saw at a glance" Keitt's "inexperience and want of self-control."

The Army of Northern Virginia was maneuvering near Cold Harbor. On June 1, Keitt was directed to do a reconnaissance of the area along the brigade's front. Instead he formed his entire brigade along an old road. He ordered the line to advance. Astride his iron-gray charger with saber held high, the brigade's acting commander led the charge. The left side of the line broke under Federal shelling. In trying to rally his troops, Keitt was an inviting target for enemy marksmen. Felled by a musket ball in the liver, he lingered a day and died on June 2.

At Cold Harbor, Colonel Keitt's inexperience and impetuousness resulted not only in his own death but also in that of many brave men of Kershaw's Brigade. Historian Douglas S. Freeman singled out Keitt in the introduction to his third volume of *Lee's Lieutenants:* "The competent Generals who escaped bullets and disease were hampered in almost every action by some man who, like Keitt at Cold Harbor, . . . was unable to meet the exactions of the field." It's a scathing indictment of the secessionist who sought glory on the battlefield and found only death.

Keitt's body was returned to South Carolina, and he was buried in Orangeburg during a downpour of rain. There were the usual tributes in the press, but one contemporary source was noticeably silent. Although in South Carolina at the time of Keitt's death, Mary Boykin Chesnut makes no mention of it in her famous diary. Earlier she had written that Keitt was "quick as a flash. No one gets the better of him." And when he was in Richmond in 1863 lobbying for promotion: "Our old tempestuous Keitt breakfasted with us yesterday. I wish I could remember half of the brilliant things he said." "Quick," "tempestuous," "brilliant," are words that capture the spirit of the man who was in the vanguard of the movement to break up the Union. They are a fitting epitaph.

BIBLIOGRAPHY

Burton, E. Milby. *The Siege of Charleston, 1861–1865.* Columbia, S.C., 1970.

Cauthen, Charles Edward. *South Carolina Goes to War, 1860–1865.* Chapel Hill, N.C., 1950.

The Correspondence between the Commissioners of the State of South Carolina to the Government at Washington and the President of the United States; together with the Statement of Messrs. Miles and Keitt. Charleston, S.C., 1861.

Dickert, D. Augustus. *History of Kershaw's Brigade, with Complete Rolls of Companies, Biographical Sketches, Incidents, Anecdotes, Etc.* Newberry, S.C., 1899.

Herd, Don Elmer, Jr. "Chapters from the Life of a Southern Chevalier: Lawrence Massillon Keitt's Congressional Years, 1853–1860." M.A. thesis, University of South Carolina, 1958.

Merchant, J. Holt, Jr. "Lawrence M. Keitt, South Carolina Fire-Eater." Ph.D. diss., University of Virginia, 1976.

Woodward, C. Vann, ed. *Mary Chesnut's Civil War.* New Haven, 1981.

WALTER B. EDGAR

KELLY'S FORD, VIRGINIA

During this battle, fought on November 7, 1863, the Army of Northern Virginia lost 2,023 soldiers and Federal troops sustained 264 casualties while forcing the Confederates to retreat farther southward into Virginia.

As the Confederate army prepared to bivouac for the winter, President Abraham Lincoln pressured Gen. George G. Meade to strike the retreating Southerners before the onset of winter complicated maneuvers. From his headquarters near Warrenton, Meade formulated a plan to attack Robert E. Lee's troops on the banks of the Rappahannock River.

The summer campaign of 1863, culminating in the horror of Gettysburg, had weakened the Army of Northern Virginia. More recently, the upset at Bristoe Station in October 1863 had further troubled General Lee. He began moving his cold and weary army back toward the Rappahannock, settling along the southern bank of the river near Kelly's Ford in early November.

The topography of the area around Kelly's Ford strongly favored an enemy approaching from the North. The high northern bank made defense from the southern position perilous at best. To hinder any Union attempts to cross the river, Robert Rodes placed the Second North Carolina Regiment close to the shore. Its fire would allow the rest of the army to get into a defensible position farther from the northern bank. Jubal Early and Rodes had positioned their divisions on the southern side of the river in a line that reached for miles on either side of Kelly's Ford. Guarding against a surprise attack, Harry Thompson Hays's brigade manned a number of rifle pits on the northern bank of the Rappahannock. Hays's troops maintained ties to the rest of the army by way of a pontoon bridge located several hundred yards above the remains of the Orange and Alexandria Railroad crossing.

The morning of November 7, Federal troops advanced on Kelly's Ford. As they clashed with the Second North Carolina, Rodes sent in the Thirtieth North Carolina for support. But this unit panicked and sought cover in some abandoned buildings. In the confusion, Union troops captured both regiments, and by midafternoon the Northerners had forced their way across the river. There they exchanged fire with Richard E. Anderson's division until dark, ultimately pushing the Southerners back into their trenches.

On the opposite bank, reports that the Federals were heading north toward the bridgehead prompted Early to reinforce Hays and his men. He sent a large segment of Robert

F. Hoke's brigade, under the command of Archibald C. Godwin in Hoke's absence, to help Hays's men defend the rifle pits.

As darkness descended on the battle, the firing diminished. Because a nocturnal attack was unprecedented, Lee did not believe that the Union would move on his army that night. With Hays and Godwin holding the redoubts on the northern bank, Lee made plans to attack the Union army at Kelly's Ford the next morning.

In the evening, however, during a cold rain, the Fifth and Sixth Federal army corps, under the direction of Gen. John Sedgwick, initiated an attack at the bridgehead. On the southern side of the river, Early watched in dismay as only a few Confederates managed to escape. Early had lost 1,674 men and four guns.

Dislodged from their position on the northern bank and with a substantial force of Union troops already across the river, the Confederates could no longer hold Kelly's Ford. They retreated that night to a position between Culpeper Courthouse and Brandy Station. The next morning Lee moved the army to more favorable ground south of the Rapidan. Despite his victory at Kelly's Ford, Meade succeeded in gaining only an insubstantial amount of ground. As 1863 came to a close, the Northern commander failed to achieve the blow to the Southern army that Lincoln so desperately wanted.

BIBLIOGRAPHY

Freeman, Douglas S. *Lee's Lieutenants: A Study in Command.* 3 vols. New York, 1942–1944. Reprint, New York, 1986.

Graham, Martin F., and George F. Skoch. *Mine Run: A Campaign of Lost Opportunities, October 21, 1863–May 1, 1864.* Lynchburg, Va., 1987.

U.S. War Department. *War of the Rebellion: A Compilation of the Official Records of the Union and Confederate Armies.* Washington, D.C., 1894–1927. Ser. 1, vol. 29, pp. 553–635.

JENNIFER LUND SMITH

KEMPER, JAMES LAWSON

KEMPER, JAMES LAWSON (1823–1895), major general. A native of the Virginia Piedmont, Kemper was born June 11, 1823, in Madison County. He graduated in 1842 from Washington College in Lexington, saw limited service in the Mexican War as a captain of Virginia volunteers, and then established a law practice in his home area. Elected five times to the Virginia General Assembly, Kemper also chaired

JAMES LAWSON KEMPER. NATIONAL ARCHIVES

the state committee on military affairs and was president of the board of visitors of the Virginia Military Institute. In 1861 he resigned as Speaker of the House of Delegates to enter the Confederate army.

Appointed colonel of the Seventh Virginia, he led the regiment from First Manassas through Seven Pines. On June 3, 1862, Kemper received a brigadier's commission and took command of a Virginia brigade formerly led successively by James Longstreet, Richard S. Ewell, and A. P. Hill. That unit became part of George E. Pickett's division. Kemper won praise for gallantry at Second Manassas and Sharpsburg. A man of "solid qualities and sound judgment," he became known for high-flown oratory before and after battles.

On July 3, 1863, Kemper and his troops were on the extreme right in the first line of the Pickett-Pettigrew attack at Gettysburg. Kemper was captured after being shot in the groin. Subsequently exchanged, he was unable to resume field service. Kemper was promoted to major general on September 19, 1864, and commanded Virginia's reserve forces for the remainder of the war.

He resumed his law practice in Madison County, became a postwar orator of renown, and in 1874 was elected governor of Virginia. After his April 7, 1895, death in Orange

County (where he is buried), a eulogist said of Kemper: "A Virginian, he loved his State with all the force of an ardent and earnest nature."

BIBLIOGRAPHY

Hotchkiss, Jed. *Virginia.* Vol. 3 of *Confederate Military History.* Edited by Clement A. Evans. Atlanta, 1899. Vol. 4 of extended ed. Wilmington, N.C., 1987.
Riggs, David F. *Seventh Virginia Infantry.* Lynchburg, Va., 1982.
"The Southern Cause." *Southern Historical Society Papers* 30 (1902): 366–368. Reprint, Wilmington, N.C., 1991.

JAMES I. ROBERTSON, JR.

KENNER, DUNCAN F.

KENNER, DUNCAN F. (1813–1887), congressman from Louisiana and diplomat. By birth and circumstance Duncan Farrar Kenner was a child of the Old South. Temperament and history made him a father of the New South. Born to a wealthy and influential Southern family, Kenner possessed all the advantages of the ruling class. He attended private academies in New Orleans, graduated from Miami College in Ohio (the alma mater of several Confederate generals and politicians), studied law with John Slidell, traveled widely throughout the northern United States and Europe, grew rich planting sugar cane and breeding horses, and maintained these advantages by serving in the Louisiana legislature.

Though among the largest and wealthiest slaveholders in Louisiana, Kenner, like scores of other Southerners, had mixed feelings about slavery. Uncertain of its permanent and tangible benefits to the South, he considered slavery a generally wasteful, unproductive institution that impeded the economic development of the South and exaggerated its dependence on an unsympathetic, increasingly hostile North. Kenner's experiences sustained these impressions. He saw firsthand the expansive and productive character of the Northern free labor economy, and he recognized that both Northern and European sentiment had turned against slavery.

Despite his reservations, Kenner chose to defend slavery and to work toward the creation of an independent Southern republic dedicated to its preservation. Though he did not participate in the Louisiana secession convention, he endorsed its actions and represented Louisiana at the Montgomery convention. For Kenner, unlike his friend Judah P. Benjamin, secession was no mere contrivance that held promise of reconstructing the Union along lines favorable to the slaveholding South. It was, rather, a genuine expression of Southern independence and an opportunity to create a Southern republic. At the Montgomery convention, Kenner called for expedient, resolute action in establishing the new nation. He proposed that the convention act as a provisional congress, authorized to create a confederation of states and to adopt a constitution defining its character and governing its affairs.

Without much debate and with little hesitation, the delegates adopted Kenner's proposal. The Provisional Congress focused its efforts on establishing a permanent government, creating executive departments, defining their powers, and regulating their operations. On several issues Kenner was a visible and assertive nationalist. He advocated the creation of an active national government, patterned on the United States and endowed with sufficient powers to guarantee Southern independence and forge a national identity. He favored the selection of a nationalist president (the entire Louisiana delegation endorsed Jefferson Davis from the beginning), opposed the right of secession for the states of the new confederation, called for the adoption of a protective tariff, promoted government subsidies for railroad improvement, advocated strict confiscation and sequestration laws, and urged the development of a more diversified economy.

In the constitutional convention and permanent Congress, Kenner was less conspicuous and, to some degree, less assertive. For reasons most Southerners understood and applauded, the convention rejected his proposals establishing a protective tariff and other high tax measures aimed at

> **At the Montgomery convention, Kenner called for expedient, resolute action in establishing the new nation.**

the agricultural South. On the issue of slavery, Kenner, like all delegates, was an ardent supporter of the rights of masters. The Montgomery convention gave slavery a prominent place in the Confederate Constitution, referring to it by name, guaranteeing its protection in the territories, and permitting its unrestricted transportation throughout the Confederate states. Kenner agreed with these provisions, though apparently he believed they provided inadequate protection against the encroachment of government. He offered an amendment to the Constitution restricting Congress's authority over slavery and augmenting the rights of property in slaves. And though the convention defeated Kenner's particular proposal, the Confederate Constitution limited severely the government's authority and opportunity to "impair" the rights of Southern masters.

During the first weeks of the war, Kenner, like many congressmen, seemed absorbed with the routine of government, apparently content to let Jefferson Davis determine national policy and conduct national affairs. As chairman of the Ways and Means Committee, Kenner devoted himself to committee assignments, concentrating on matters of public debt and financing. But he had no illusion about the tenacity of the Lincoln government and its commitment to the preservation of the "old" Union. And he was convinced that victory in the war would be neither swift nor complete. From the beginning, Kenner pressed for both military preparation, including a limited conscription, and European recognition. After Federal armies occupied southeastern Louisiana in 1862, including Kenner's congressional district, he called for an even more vigorous prosecution of the war and a more audacious foreign policy. In Congress he opposed the many exemptions granted from military service, including the infamous Twenty-Slave Law, urged the impressment of slaves for military purposes, and endorsed the suspension of the writ of habeas corpus. In private discussions with his friend Secretary of State Benjamin and with President Davis, he recommended the use of all economic and diplomatic resources, including the emancipation of slaves, to end the political stalemate and gain independence.

The Federal occupation of Louisiana, the collapse of chattel slavery in the sugar parishes, and the reemergence of Unionism among whites convinced Kenner that the Confederacy could not win its independence or establish a national identity on the battlefield. The South would never gain its independence unless it obtained European recognition and massive financial and military assistance. Its unbending commitment to slavery barred any legitimate hope of securing foreign recognition and forcing the Lincoln government to submit to Southern independence. Kenner maintained that emancipation should be seen strictly as a wartime measure, designed to secure recognition and independence. He insisted as well that Confederate emancipation was not an invitation for foreign mediation or an overture for reunification with the Union. And, as the Federal contract labor system and free-state movement in Louisiana indicated, emancipation did not imply abandoning white supremacy.

At the insistence of Benjamin and Davis, Kenner kept these sentiments to himself. President Davis considered them unwarranted, though Secretary of State Benjamin thought them merely premature. Kenner's proposals took on greater relevance in the last weeks of the war. Late in 1864, following Lincoln's disheartening reelection and in the wake of massive Confederate desertions and casualties, Secretary Benjamin persuaded President Davis to send Kenner to Europe. Davis gave Kenner near plenary power to negotiate recognition in exchange for limited, gradual emancipation.

After weeks of exhausting travel, Kenner arrived in Europe, eager to complete his mission and confident of its success. The Confederate emissaries, especially John Slidell and James M. Mason, did not share Kenner's enthusiasm or confidence. In the context of events, their pessimism was jus-

tified. The principal European powers, particularly France and Great Britain, were never convinced that an independent Southern republic was in their best interests. Despite its pretensions and expectations, the Confederacy had few relevant economic and cultural ties with Europe—certainly none that justified diplomatic recognition and a permanent division of the American Union. And though slavery was an important diplomatic issue, by 1865 the issue had lost its relevance. The British government recognized Lincoln's commitment to a disciplined, workable emancipation that would not disrupt production, risk investment, or unnecessarily divide Northern public opinion. The British cabinet concluded that recognition would only prolong the war, jeopardizing investment and threatening the destruction of the Union.

Kenner's mission also ignored domestic political circumstances. The Lincoln government was committed to a thorough restoration of the Union. It rejected mediation and discounted recognition, pursuing instead military victory and permanent emancipation. The Confederacy too dismissed mediation, demanding recognition, financial assistance, and permanent slavery. The mission did not fail because the South had lost the war. Military victory belied both recognition and emancipation. The Kenner mission failed because it denied the fundamental reality of the war: the Southern states had abandoned the Union and formed the Confederacy to preserve slavery. Southern independence and national identity were impossible without slavery.

With the final defeat of Confederate forces, Kenner reasserted his allegiance to the Union and returned home to Louisiana. He also returned to public life, serving as a state senator and advocate of the New South. He wanted the North to leave the South alone to deal with its immense economic and social problems. "Our people desire no further agitation, discord, or revolutions," he wrote to Governor James Madison Wells. "We desire nothing but peace and the opportunity to repair our shattered fortunes."

BIBLIOGRAPHY

Alexander, Thomas B., and Richard E. Beringer. *The Anatomy of the Confederate Congress: A Study of the Influences of Member Characteristics on Legislative Voting Behavior, 1861–1865.* Nashville, Tenn., 1972.

Bauer, Craig A. "The Last Effort: The Secret Mission of the Confederate Diplomat, Duncan F. Kenner." *Louisiana History* 22 (1981): 67–95.

Blumenthal, Henry. "Confederate Diplomacy: Popular Notions and International Realities." *Journal of Southern History* 32 (1966): 151–171.

Brauer, Kinley J. "British Mediation and the American Civil War: A Reconsideration." *Journal of Southern History* 38 (1972): 49–64.

Brauer, Kinley J. "The Slavery Problem in the Diplomacy of the American Civil War." *Pacific Historical Review* 46 (1977): 439–469.

Price, Grady Daniel. "The Secret Mission of Duncan F. Kenner, Confederate Minister Plenipotentiary to Europe in 1865." M.A. thesis, Tulane University, 1929.

Warner, Ezra J., and W. Buck Yearns. *Biographical Register of the Confederate Congress.* Baton Rouge, La., 1975.

Yearns, Wilfred B. *The Confederate Congress.* Athens, Ga., 1960.

TERRENCE W. FITZMORRIS

KENNESAW MOUNTAIN, GEORGIA

The Confederate victory at Kennesaw Mountain on June 27, 1864, was a setback in Union Maj. Gen. William Tecumseh Sherman's Atlanta campaign. But though a tactical success for the Southerners, it proved a strategic reverse for Confederate Gen. Joseph E. Johnston.

Johnston, after delaying Sherman's 100,000-man army across sixty miles of northern Georgia, took a blocking position with 65,000 men across Lost, Pine, and Brushy mountains. He opened communications with Richmond officials to bring cavalry forces from Mississippi to cut the Union railroad supply line, a plan later disapproved by President Jefferson Davis.

Sherman resumed his advance on June 8, deploying his superior numbers farther toward his right than Johnston could defend with a lesser force. On June 14 Lt. Gen. Leonidas Polk was killed on Pine Mountain. Threatened with envelopment at Lost Mountain, Johnston withdrew his left wing behind Mud Creek, but Union pressure at a salient in the center held by Lt. Gen. William J. Hardee led Johnston to withdraw his army on the night of June 18–19 to a previously selected position astride Kennesaw Mountain. In an arc-shaped line west of Marietta, the Confederates protected the Western and Atlantic Railroad, their supply link with Atlanta.

Advancing, Sherman made contact along the Confederate front while extending to his right to threaten the railroad. Two Union corps reached the vicinity of Kolb's farm on June 21. Johnston reacted by transferring Lt. Gen. John Bell Hood's corps of eleven thousand from right to left. Hood exceeded Johnston's orders and attacked on June 22, suffering severe losses. Although defeated at Kolb's farm, Hood extended the flank beyond Sherman's reach.

Believing his foe to be stretched thin, Sherman abandoned flanking maneuvers for a direct attack. His plan for destroying Johnston's army called for deceptions on either flank while two strikes pierced the center. Johnston remained confident.

At 8:00 A.M., June 27, Sherman's plan went into effect following an artillery bombardment. A feint attack at the north end of Kennesaw Mountain produced negligible results. In the meantime, three Union brigades numbering 5,500 men moved to attack the mountain's southerly spur, called Pigeon Hill. The Federals easily overran the skirmish line but soon became pinned down at close range on the hill's slope. Heavy Confederate fire coming from strong earthworks held by Maj. Gen. Samuel G. French's division paralyzed this assault.

Two miles farther south, the main Union attack of eight thousand infantry got started an hour behind schedule. The Federals charged in five dense brigade columns. Fighting from behind earthworks the Confederate divisions led by Maj. Gens. Patrick R. Cleburne and Benjamin F. Cheatham inflicted frightful losses on the attackers. Savage handto-hand fighting took place at a projecting salient called the "Dead Angle." Although two Union brigades simultaneously assaulted the angle's apex and south flank, Cheatham's soldiers bravely held fast, repulsing them. The battle was over by noon. Sherman was personally chagrined by the result. He lost three thousand men compared to Johnston's one thousand.

When Sherman later learned that a subordinate's movement around the Confederate's south flank had gained a favorable position, he reverted to his flanking maneuvers. On July 2 Johnston withdrew from Kennesaw Mountain to Smyrna, satisfied with having delayed Sherman for nearly a month and inflicted disproportionate losses.

BIBLIOGRAPHY

Cox, Jacob D. *Atlanta.* New York, 1881. Reprint, Dayton, Ohio, 1987.

Kelly, Dennis P. *Kennesaw Mountain and the Atlanta Campaign.* Atlanta, 1991.

Symonds, Craig L. *Joseph Johnston: A Civil War Biography.* New York, 1992.

Womack, Robert J. *Call Forth the Mighty Men.* Bessemer, Ala., 1987.

DENNIS KELLY

KENTUCKY

Although John C. Breckinridge, the Southern Democratic candidate for president in 1860, was a favorite son, Kentucky voters favored John Bell, the Constitutional Union candidate. Republican Abraham Lincoln received only 1,364 votes in the state of his birth. With an 1860 population of 1,155,684 (919,484 whites, 225,483 slaves, 10,684 free blacks, 33 Indians), Kentucky provided some 100,000 soldiers to the Union, including the Home Guard, and between 25,000 and 40,000 to the Confederacy. Over 20,000 of the Union soldiers were blacks.

Sentiment was badly divided in the commonwealth when the war began. Slavery was an obvious tie with the South, the Kentucky Resolutions of 1798 and 1799 had enunciated the doctrine of state rights, and the Mississippi River trade had forged strong economic bonds. Many Kentuckians had Southern backgrounds, and the state's culture bore a Southern flavor. Yet Kentucky had a strong nationalistic tradition, and Henry Clay and John J. Crittenden had become famous as compromisers who sought mutually acceptable solutions to the sectional crises. Railroads were changing transportation patterns, and Kentucky was becoming more closely associated with the North.

Political Developments. On May 20, 1861, the pro-Southern governor Beriah Magoffin declared Kentucky's neutrality after rejecting both Union and Confederate requests for troops following the attack on Fort Sumter. A select group of six political leaders tried to formulate a policy for state defense, but it failed when Unionists would not accept Magoffin on a special board to manage state preparedness.

Two elections during the summer of 1861 demonstrated that the Unionists had a clear majority. In the congressional campaign Unionists such as A. M. Starling effectively charged that the Confederacy would destroy the lucrative slave trade by reopening the African slave trade and that the South wanted "Kentucky to stand between her & danger, to be her battleground." Unionist candidates won nine of ten seats, losing only in the extreme western end of the state. After the state legislative election on August 5, Unionists had 76–24 and 27–11 margins in the house and senate, more than enough to override gubernatorial vetoes.

Lincoln moved cautiously, for, as he wrote, "I think to lose Kentucky is nearly the same as to lose the whole game." Recruiting camps outside the state, such as Camp Joe Holt in Indiana and Camp Boone in Tennessee, welcomed Kentuckians who were eager to fight, and clandestine agents operated within the state. After the August election Unionists established Camp Dick Robinson in Garrard County, and Lincoln refused to remove it.

War came to Kentucky in early September 1861 when Confederate Gen. Gideon Pillow seized Columbus on the Mississippi River. Gen. Ulysses S. Grant quickly occupied Paducah, and rival forces moved into the northern and southern portions of the state. The General Assembly ordered only the Confederates to withdraw, but that directive was ignored.

Gen. Albert Sidney Johnston, given command of Confederate forces west of the Appalachian Mountains, established a line across southern Kentucky with key positions at Cumberland Gap, Bowling Green, Forts Henry and Donelson on the Tennessee and Cumberland rivers, and Columbus. Gen. Robert Anderson, the hero of Fort Sumter, became the Federal commander in the state, but he soon gave way to Gen. William Tecumseh Sherman, who was in turn replaced by Gen. Don Carlos Buell. Numerous skirmishes occurred, but neither army was prepared to fight, and each commander was convinced that he was greatly outnumbered.

Confederates held meetings in Russellville in late October and mid-November and established a provisional state government that was admitted into the Confederate States of America on December 10, 1861. Its capital was Bowling Green, but its jurisdiction extended no farther than Confederate troops advanced. This government withdrew with the Confederate army in mid-February 1862. When Governor George W. Johnson, a wealthy Scott County farmer, was killed at Shiloh, the ten-man council selected lawyer Richard Hawes as his successor. The Confederate government returned briefly with Braxton Bragg and E. Kirby Smith in the late summer, 1862, and Hawes was installed at Frankfort. But he soon left the state with the Confederate army, and for the rest of the war the Confederate government of Kentucky was in exile.

Although Governor Magoffin carefully executed orders from the legislature, Unionists did not trust him, and many of

> **Slaves who served became free, and after March 3, 1865, their wives and children were also freed.**

his powers were removed. In August 1862 he resigned, and James F. Robinson completed his term. In 1863 Union Democrats nominated Thomas E. Bramlette who easily defeated Charles A. Wickliffe, the regular Democratic candidate, for governor. Both parties distanced themselves from the Lincoln administration, which had become more unpopular because of the Emancipation Proclamation, even though it did not apply to Kentucky. In the 1864 presidential election, Lincoln, running on a Union party ticket, was decisively defeated in the state by Gen. George B. McClellan.

During the last two years of the war Bramlette claimed with some justification that Kentucky was being treated as if it were a Confederate state. He was especially incensed by the Union decision to use black troops. John J. Crittenden had spoken for many Kentuckians when he declared, "I would rather see our young men brought home as corpses than see them saved by such unsoldierly means," but the war's insatiable demands for manpower forced adoption of the policy. Col. Frank L. Wolford, commander of the famed First Kentucky Cavalry (U.S.), was dismissed from service for his outspoken opposition, and in the spring of 1864 Bramlette nearly broke with the national administration. The Reverend Robert J. Breckinridge, believed to be the Kentuckian with the most influence with Lincoln, helped prevent an open rupture. Kentucky began black enlistments, for slaves as well as freemen, in April 1864. Slaves who served became free, and after March 3, 1865, their wives and children were also freed. Loyal masters were supposed to receive $300 from the Federal government for each slave lost. Slaves had been assessed at $107,494,527 in 1860; the figure in 1864 was only $34,179,246. Kentucky had stubbornly rejected Lincoln's efforts to introduce compensated emancipation, and the discredited institution lingered in the state until adoption of the Thirteenth Amendment to the Federal Constitution in December 1865.

Military Action in Kentucky. The first battle of significance in Kentucky came at Mill Springs (Logan's Crossroads) toward the eastern end of Johnston's line. On January 19, 1862, Gen. George H. Thomas defeated a Confederate force that attacked him under the command of Generals George B. Crittenden and Felix K. Zollicoffer. Zollicoffer was killed when he rode into the Union lines, and the Confederate casualties of 519 were double the Union losses. Most of the Confederates escaped across the flooded Cumberland River.

More critical were the early 1862 losses of Forts Henry and Donelson. Anticipating that the battle for Kentucky would be fought in the Bowling Green area, Johnston did not visit the forts, and he allowed a confused command situation to develop there. Fort Henry on the Tennessee River fell to Andrew H. Foote's Union navy gunboats on February 6. Ten days later Grant acquired the nickname "Unconditional Surrender" when Simon Bolivar Buckner, his West Point classmate and friend, surrendered some seventeen thousand men at Donelson. With the two great rivers open to Federal gunboats, Johnston abandoned Kentucky and withdrew south of the Tennessee River to protect his supply lines. The Battle of Shiloh, fought on April 6–7, 1862, in which both Johnston and George Johnson were killed, should have been fought in Kentucky.

The Confederates made another major invasion of the state in the late summer of 1862. Gen. E. Kirby Smith almost annihilated a Union force of 6,500 near Richmond on August 30 and soon occupied Lexington and Frankfort. Then he scattered his forces across the bluegrass and made little effort to cooperate with Braxton Bragg, who headed a larger invading force. Bragg did not reach Glasgow until September 14, and when he delayed at Munfordville to force the surrender of some 4,000 Unionists, General Buell reached Louisville before Bragg could threaten it. Smith and Bragg did not coordinate their efforts, and when Kentucky's largest battle of the Civil War was fought at Perryville on October 8 the Confederates used only some 15,000 troops, one-third of the number in the state. The Confederates made gains in savage fighting, but they had secured few enlistments in Kentucky, and Bragg and a council of war decided to withdraw. After some unkind remarks about cowardly Kentuckians, Bragg became the Confederate officer most hated by Kentuckians, especially those fighting under his command.

During the rest of the war Kentucky was held by Union forces except for occasional Confederate raids, most notably those led by John Hunt Morgan. His spectacular incursions embarrassed Union commanders who failed to intercept him and resulted in considerable damage to Union facilities. The destruction of the massive railroad trestles on the Louisville and Nashville Railroad line near Elizabethtown was especially damaging. Other Confederates entered the state from time to time. Occasionally, a unit would remain in the commonwealth for a few weeks, recruiting men and horses and allowing some of the troops to visit briefly with their families. Such raids pinned down a substantial number of Federal troops who tried to defend key points against sudden attacks.

Of course, many Kentuckians on both sides fought outside the state, practically all of them in the armies west of the mountains. The most famous Confederate unit was the "Orphan Brigade," the First Kentucky Brigade. Of the many Federal units, Wolford's "Wild Riders" of the First Kentucky Cavalry was one of the best.

During the last two years of the war guerrillas spread destruction across the state and brought about savage repressive measures from harried Union commanders. "Sue Mundy" (Jerome Clarke) and William Clarke Quantrill were among the most infamous. Public reaction to the repressive measures reinforced the opposition to emancipation and the use of black troops, so that a War Department official reported in 1864 that "a large majority of Kentuckians are today undoubtedly disloyal." A more tactful general, John M. Palmer, replaced Gen. Stephen G. Burbridge on February 10, 1865, but there were few changes in Union policy. There was some truth to the later assertion that Kentucky joined the Confederacy after the war was over.

The Home Front. Despite guerrilla depredations, Kentucky did not suffer the economic destruction visited upon several Southern states. But losses were heavy whenever large military units passed through an area. Fences became firewood, horses and mules volunteered for military service, chickens and hogs disappeared, vegetables and fruit were devoured. The Shaker communities at Pleasant Hill and South Union were hurt severely by visits from both armies. On the other hand, the war provided markets for almost anything that could be raised or manufactured, and many Kentuckians benefited from the boom. The farm price index (1860 =100) rose as high as 210 in 1864, and since the general price index increased only to 182, farmers on the average profited from the war economy. The decline in manpower led to a reduction of 4 million acres in croplands. Nonagricultural wages rose more slowly than prices, and the average worker lost close to a third of real purchasing power by 1865. Louisville was by far the state's largest city and manufacturing center, and its position on the Ohio River and as a terminus for the Louisville and Nashville Railroad contributed to its prosperity.

The Civil War affected nearly every aspect of life in the state. The educational system that had made real progress during the 1847–1853 administration of School Superintendent Robert J. Breckinridge lost ground and was ill prepared to deal with postwar problems, including education for the blacks. Slavery's extinction created complex social and economic problems with which the state was not prepared to cope. The differences among Kentuckians brought strains and often divisions to many institutions and may have contributed to some of the famous postwar feuds. Harriet Means of Ashland wrote that "I would not *dare* to give a large party now for fear the ladies would all get into a free fight." It is impossible to measure the loss of the thousands of men who were killed or maimed in the conflict, or who died from disease, or who were never able to adjust to the postwar era.

For most Kentuckians, the Civil War was one of the most traumatic experiences in their lives; later, some of them gave it a romantic gloss that became part of the Kentucky heritage. As for the state, slavery was ended, realistic limits were set to state rights, and an alliance was forged with the Southern Democratic party. Although other factors were also involved, postwar Kentucky was never as important nationally as it had been before 1861.

[*For further discussion of battles and campaigns fought in Kentucky, see* Henry and Donelson Campaign; Morgan's Raids; Paducah, Kentucky; Shiloh Campaign.]

BIBLIOGRAPHY

Connelly, Thomas L. *Army of the Heartland.* Baton Rouge, La., 1967.
Connelly, Thomas L. *Autumn of Glory.* Baton Rouge, La., 1971.
Coulter, E. Merton. *The Civil War and Readjustment in Kentucky.* Chapel Hill, N.C., 1926.
Harrison, Lowell H. *The Civil War in Kentucky.* Revised edition. Lexington, Ky., 1988.
Harrison, Lowell H. "The Civil War in Kentucky: Some Persistent Questions." *Register of the Kentucky Historical Society* 76 (January 1978): 1–21.
Johnston, J. Stoddard. *Kentucky.* Vol. 9 of *Confederate Military History.* Edited by Clement A. Evans. Atlanta, 1889. Vol. 11 of extended ed. Wilmington, N.C., 1988.
McDowell, Robert Emmett. *City of Conflict: Louisville in the Civil War.* Louisville, 1962.
Speed, Thomas. *The Union Cause in Kentucky.* New York, 1907.

LOWELL H. HARRISON

KERSHAW, JOSEPH B.

KERSHAW, JOSEPH B. (1822–1894), major general. Descended from forebears prominent in military and political arenas, Kershaw was born at Camden, South Carolina, January 5, 1822. His grandfather, also named Joseph, had emigrated from England and played an active role as a colonel in the Revolutionary War. His father, John, served

several terms as mayor of Camden, was a county judge, a member of the state legislature, and a one-term member of Congress.

Orphaned at seven, Joseph Kershaw attended local schools and the Cokesbury Conference School in the Abbeville District. Leaving after a brief period there, Kershaw went to Charleston where he clerked in a dry goods store. The job paled quickly, and he returned to Camden, read law, and was admitted to the bar in 1843. At the start of the Mexican War Kershaw wore the uniform of a first lieutenant with the DeKalb Rifle Guards of his hometown. His stay in

> While defending the Sunken Road at Fredericksburg, he displayed "great coolness and skill," in the words of E. Porter Alexander.

Mexico was cut short by a fever that forced his early return to Camden where he resumed his law practice and was elected to the state legislature in 1852.

Kershaw was a member of his state's secession convention and in February 1861 was elected colonel of the Second South Carolina Infantry, which he had recruited. The regiment occupied Morris Island during the bombardment of Fort Sumter. Kershaw led the regiment at First Manassas as part of Milledge L. Bonham's brigade. Promoted to brigadier general, February 13, 1862, and given command of the brigade following Bonham's resignation, Kershaw fought in the Peninsular campaign and Seven Days' Battles and helped capture Maryland Heights during the reduction of Harpers Ferry. While defending the Sunken Road at Fredericksburg, he displayed "great coolness and skill," in the words of E. Porter Alexander. The South Carolinian also fought with distinction at Chancellorsville. On the second day at Gettysburg, as Lafayette McLaws's division embarked on its assault against Little Round Top, Kershaw appeared "cool, composed and grand, his steel-gray eyes flashing the fire he felt in his soul," wrote D. Augustus Dickens, brigade historian.

Transferred west with James Longstreet in September 1863, Kershaw arrived at Chickamauga in time to help crush the Federal right flank. He also participated in the Knoxville campaign before the corps was recalled to Virginia.

On May 6, 1864, Kershaw was riding with Longstreet and Micah Jenkins through the Wilderness when a mistaken volley from William Mahone's troops across the Plank Road ripped through the group. As his men prepared to return the fire, Kershaw dashed to the head of the column, shouting "They are friends!" His prompt action averted further bloodshed, although Longstreet was severely wounded and Jenkins was killed.

On May 18, shortly after he took part in the Battle of Spotsylvania, Kershaw was promoted to major general. He joined Jubal Early in the Shenandoah Valley campaign of 1864 but was ordered back to Richmond in September. While en route to the capital, he received news of Early's defeat at Winchester. He hastened back to the valley where he opened the attack at Cedar Creek. Kershaw eventually moved into the defenses of Petersburg and marched westward in April 1865. He was captured at Sayler's Creek and imprisoned at Fort Warren until August 12.

Returning to his law practice in Camden after the war, Kershaw was elected to the legislature in 1865 and became president of the senate. In later years he was elected judge of the Fifth District, a position he held until failing health intervened. He was appointed postmaster of Camden in 1893 and died April 13, 1894. He was buried in Quaker Cemetery, Camden.

BIBLIOGRAPHY

Alexander, E. Porter. "The Battle of Fredericksburg." *Southern Historical Society Papers* 10 (1882): 455. Reprint, Wilmington, N.C., 1990.

Capers, Ellison. *South Carolina.* Vol. 5 of *Confederate Military History.* Edited by Clement A. Evans. Atlanta, 1899. Vol. 6 of extended ed. Wilmington, N.C., 1987.

Dickert, D. Augustus. *History of Kershaw's Brigade.* Dayton, Ohio, 1976.

McLaws, Lafayette. "Gettysburg." *Southern Historical Society Papers* 7 (1879): 88–90. Reprint, Wilmington, N.C., 1990.

Warner, Ezra J. *Generals in Gray: Lives of the Confederate Commanders.* Baton Rouge, La., 1959.

LOWELL REIDENBAUGH

KILPATRICK-DAHLGREN RAID

This raid, named for Union Gen. Judson Kilpatrick and Col. Ulric Dahlgren, began on February 28, 1864, with the avowed purpose of freeing Union soldiers held in Richmond's Libby Prison and Belle Island. Over the next four days, 4,000 handpicked Federal cavalrymen clashed with a scattered force of 500 Southern soldiers and home guard units to the west and north of Richmond. In the end, the Federals lost 340 men, 583 horses, and much equipment and never reached close proximity to either of the two prisons.

In mid-February 1864 Union intelligence reported that the Confederate capital's meager defenses left it especially vulnerable to a cavalry raid. The boisterous and ambitious H. Judson Kilpatrick sought the approval of President Abraham Lincoln for a surprise raid that would free prisoners and

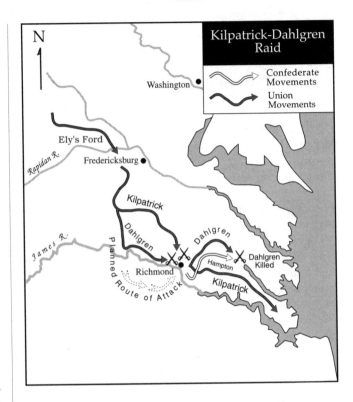

wreak havoc on the Confederate capital. Lincoln gave his enthusiastic support, hoping that Kilpatrick would bring some positive results to the Union war effort.

On the night of February 28, Kilpatrick set out with his men toward Ely's Ford on the Rapidan River. Included in his force was young Ulric Dahlgren. The earnest son of navy officer John Dahlgren was to lead a detachment of cavalry across the James River and attack from the south, while Kilpatrick's main force entered the city from the north. Gen. Robert E. Lee had predicted such a raid four months earlier and was well prepared for this one. As sleet and rain fell in torrents, Confederate spies spread the word of the Union plans and alerted city defenses of the enemy approach. By the time Kilpatrick's men arrived, the Confederates were ready.

Federals first sensed trouble soon after Dahlgren split away from Kilpatrick's main force on February 29. Kilpatrick unexpectedly met strong resistance five miles north of Richmond. After fighting several hours, he withdrew to the east and then, after hesitating, turned to resume battle. Maj. Gen. Wade Hampton and his small force of three hundred cavalrymen came from behind. In the ensuing darkness Kilpatrick's exhausted men doggedly fought the Confederates, but the Union general's fighting spirit was gone and he again turned to retreat eastward toward Federal lines.

Meanwhile, Dahlgren with his detachment of five hundred men found the James River swelled from the recent rains.

When Dahlgren tried instead to enter Richmond from the west, he met stiff resistance from G. W. Custis Lee's local defense brigade. This force of armory workers and government clerks blocked Dahlgren's planned approach. In the confused retreat, Dahlgren and one hundred of his men became separated. Trying to reach the safety of Union lines, Dahlgren stumbled upon an ambush in King and Queen County. He was killed instantly, and most of the remaining Federals surrendered.

Papers found on Dahlgren's body by a teenaged boy revealed that the raiding cavalrymen planned more than simply freeing prisoners. The papers detailed Federal intentions to burn the city and kill Jefferson Davis and his cabinet. Richmond newspapers soon published the papers, and Southerners were outraged. They demanded an investigation and explanation from Federal authorities. Union officials first claimed that the papers were forgeries and later admitted only to Dahlgren's guilt.

The extent of Union involvement in the plans to burn Richmond and kill Confederate civilian leaders remains unclear. But in March 1864, the mere allegation of such dark intentions was enough to strengthen Southern resolve to persevere in the war.

[See also Dahlgren Papers.]

BIBLIOGRAPHY

Dahlgren, John. *Memoir of Ulric Dahlgren.* Philadelphia, 1872.
Jones, V. C. *Eight Hours before Richmond.* New York, 1957.
Riggs, David F. "The Dahlgren Papers Reconsidered." *Lincoln Herald* 83 (1981): 658–667.
Thomas, Emory M. "The Kilpatrick-Dahlgren Raid—Part I and II." *Civil War Times Illustrated* 16–17 (February—April 1978): 4–9, 26–33.

LESLEY JILL GORDON-BURR

KNOXVILLE AND GREENEVILLE CONVENTIONS

The Knoxville Convention of May 30 and 31, 1861, and the Greeneville Convention of June 17 through 20, 1861, represented eastern Tennessee Unionists' challenge to the state's secession crisis. Although they failed to prevent Tennessee's alliance with the Confederacy or to establish a separate pro-Union state, they gave powerful voice to anti-Confederate sentiment, provided leadership for those opposed to the Southern cause, and required the Confederate government to allocate precious resources to Tennessee's mountain dis-

tricts. Because of its dependence upon the strategically vital East Tennessee and Virginia Railroad to carry troops from the Deep South to the eastern theater of war, the Confederacy had to retain the region regardless of its inhabitants' expressed wishes.

A people with scant commitment to slavery or commercial agriculture, eastern Tennesseans had long felt alienated from planter-dominated middle and western Tennessee. On February 9, when the entire state had voted against

> On June 8, middle and western Tennesseans overwhelmingly endorsed secession, but eastern Tennesseans rejected it by a 68 percent vote.

Governor Isham G. Harris's call for a secession convention, eastern Tennesseans with a negative vote of 81 percent were far more emphatic than western Tennesseans at 65 percent and middle Tennesseans with only 51 percent. But the bombardment of Fort Sumter and Abraham Lincoln's subsequent call for volunteers galvanized the Tennessee legislature to declare separation from the Union on May 6 and to schedule a plebiscite for June 8.

Reacting to this in mid-May, fifteen prominent Knox County Unionists, including William G. Brownlow and Oliver Perry Temple, met in Temple's law office and called for a Union convention. Whigs in politics, they found common cause with their longtime Democratic party foe Senator Andrew Johnson. Emboldened by editorials in Brownlow's *Knoxville Whig* and Johnson's passionate rhetoric, over 400 delegates assembled at Knoxville's Temperance Hall on May 30 and 31 and chose Congressman Thomas A. R. Nelson as their presiding officer. Though a nondelegate, Johnson addressed the convention, which thereafter passed resolutions condemning the June plebiscite, urging Tennesseans to reject secession, and empowering Nelson to convene a second convention should events warrant.

On June 8, middle and western Tennesseans overwhelmingly endorsed secession, but eastern Tennesseans rejected it by a 68 percent vote. Arguing that the referendum had been won by force and fraud, Nelson called a second convention at Greeneville on June 17, but only 285 delegates gathered. Some earlier supporters had reluctantly accepted the plebiscite's verdict, and others—most notably Andrew Johnson—had fled the state. Transient Confederate troops constantly threatened the delegates, and a passing Louisiana regiment ate the conventioneers' breakfast. Nonetheless, the convention entertained truculent proposals advocating armed resistance and eastern Tennessee statehood, but eventually it passed calmer resolutions expressing an "earnest desire" that eastern Tennessee remain neutral territory and requesting the Nashville government to allow the region separate statehood. Not surprisingly, the convention's three-man commission to the Tennessee legislature found an unsympathetic audience.

Whatever the conventions' lack of success, they served notice of eastern Tennessee's resistance to joining the Confederacy. Over thirty thousand of its inhabitants would enroll in Union regiments, others fought as guerrillas, and when Ambrose Burnside's Union army marched into the region in 1863, his soldiers were greeted as liberators.

BIBLIOGRAPHY

Bryan, Charles F., Jr. "A Gathering of Tories: The East Tennessee Convention of 1861." *Tennessee Historical Quarterly* 34 (Spring 1980): 27–48.

Campbell, Mary E. R. *The Attitude of Tennesseans toward the Union, 1847–1861.* New York, 1961.

Henry, J. Milton. "The Revolution in Tennessee, February, 1861 to June, 1861." *Tennessee Historical Quarterly* 18 (Summer 1959): 99–118.

Queener, Verton M. "East Tennessee Sentiment and the Secession Movement, November, 1860–June, 1861." *East Tennessee Historical Society's Publications,* no. 20 (1948): 59–83.

Temple, Oliver Perry. *East Tennessee and the Civil War.* Cincinnati, Ohio, 1899.

FRED ARTHUR BAILEY

KNOXVILLE CAMPAIGN

Located on the Holston (now Tennessee) River in eastern Tennessee, Knoxville was the object of an unsuccessful Confederate siege against Federal forces in the fall of 1863. While Gen. Braxton Bragg was investing Chattanooga during that period, he requested that President Jefferson Davis order Gen. James Longstreet, with whom Bragg could not get along, to assault the Union Army of the Ohio in Knoxville. The Federals, numbering about 12,000 infantry and 8,500 cavalry under Gen. Ambrose Burnside, had been quartered there since taking the city on September 2. Bragg's intention was not only to get rid of Longstreet but also to divert Northern concentration from Chattanooga.

Although furious with Bragg for splitting the Confederate command, Longstreet had no choice but to follow orders, and on November 5, he started his 17,000-man force north. The journey was difficult, and eight days later, they had traveled only sixty miles, reaching the town of Sweetwater. There the general had expected rations and supplies, but they were not forthcoming. Berated by Bragg for taking too much time, and with his troops exhausted, hungry, and ragged, Longstreet pushed on nevertheless.

Realizing that Longstreet was approaching, Burnside sent a force of 5,000 troops to confront him. Burnside knew he could not defeat the superior number of Confederates, but he wanted to keep Longstreet busy so that he could not return to Chattanooga and assist Bragg's army when the Federals there attacked those troops. Longstreet, on November 13, ordered three brigades of Gen. Joseph Wheeler's cavalry to take and hold the heights across from Knoxville on the south-

> **One Union officer even lit the fuses of cannon balls and rolled them down into the tightly bunched gray ranks. . . .**

ern bank of the Holston River. Wheeler, after being slowed by two regiments of Federal horsemen, arrived at the river on November 15, but found the heavily armed heights impregnable. With no chance of victory, he and his troopers rode back to rejoin Longstreet.

In the meantime, the Southern infantrymen were thirty miles southwest of Knoxville fording the Little Tennessee River at Loudon, when Longstreet received word that the Union troops were a few miles east of him across the river and seemingly retreating to Knoxville. Longstreet headed for Lenoir's Station, about eight miles northeast of Loudon, hoping to cut them off. But the Federals moved quicker, and by the time Longstreet arrived in Lenoir on November 16, they were gone.

Longstreet nevertheless pressed on hard, hoping to destroy Burnside's troops at the crossroads of Campbell's Station, fifteen miles southwest of Knoxville. Learning of a shortcut, Longstreet sent Gen. Lafayette McLaws's division forward on that route, while the division of Gen. Micah Jenkins pressed the Federals from the rear. But Burnside discovered the Confederate plan and rushed forward a division to outrun McLaws to Campbell's Station. The Federals arrived first, taking up defensive positions along the Kingston and Concord roads. The Confederate attacks that day were poorly coordinated and gained nothing, and as a result, Burnside's soldiers, protected by some seven hundred Federal cavalry acting as a rear guard, were able to withdraw after dark. Making a forced march along the Kingston Road, the Union infantrymen retired to Knoxville.

Right behind the Federals followed Longstreet's men. Approaching the city, the Confederates routed a Federal cavalry force commanded by Gen. William Sanders. Sanders was killed, the only Southern-born Union general to meet that fate in the Civil War. Taking up positions around Knoxville, Longstreet laid siege to the town.

Capt. Orlando Poe, Burnside's chief engineer, had built stout defensive forts and earthworks around Knoxville's eastern, northern, and western perimeter; the Holston River covered the southern side. In the northwestern corner of these defenses was located a strong work known as Fort Sanders. Longstreet determined to attack there, but after a couple of aborted assaults, he briefly shelved Sanders as an objective. After being reinforced with two brigades numbering about 2,600 men under Gens. Bushrod Rust Johnson and Archibald Gracie, Jr., however, on November 29 Longstreet decided to strike the fort at dawn.

Prior to the attack, the ground in front of the fort had been reconnoitered by the Confederates, but they failed to realize that a ditch surrounding Sanders was between six and eight feet deep. Added to that, the fort's walls at ground level were thirteen feet high and sloped forty-five degrees, making an average total of twenty difficult feet that had to be climbed before the attackers could gain access to the interior of the work. And if those conditions were not enough to ensure failure, cold, wet weather had covered the earth of the fort with ice.

Unaware of what lay in store for them, the Confederate attack proceeded as scheduled—and met with disaster. With Longstreet's soldiers caught in the ditch, Federals on the fort's parapets slaughtered them mercilessly. One Union officer even lit the fuses of cannon balls and rolled them down into the tightly bunched gray ranks, creating havoc. Recognizing unqualified defeat after twenty minutes of fighting, Longstreet called off the assault. Confederate losses in that short battle amounted to 129 killed, 458 wounded, and 226 missing, while the Federals lost 5 killed and 8 wounded.

During the fight, Longstreet received a telegram from Jefferson Davis informing him that Bragg's forces had been routed at Chattanooga and ordering him to abandon Knoxville and reinforce Bragg. Longstreet, though, with the intention of keeping Federal reinforcements from harassing Bragg's army, stayed in the Knoxville area until the night of December 4, when he withdrew to the northwest. A Federal pursuit engaged in—and lost—one last battle with the Confederates at Bean's Station, Tennessee, on December 14. This action effectively ended the siege of Knoxville.

Total losses for the siege were 1,142, exclusive of cavalry, for the Confederates out of approximately 20,000 engaged, and 693 for the Union out of about 12,000 infantry effectives. The Confederacy suffered an even greater check to its cause as a result of splitting the forces at Chattanooga, thereby ensuring major defeats there and at Knoxville.

U.S. War Department. *War of the Rebellion: A Compilation of the Official Records of the Union and Confederate Armies.* Washington, D.C., 1880–1901. Ser. 1, vol. 31, pts. 1 and 3.

WARREN WILKINSON

BIBLIOGRAPHY

Johnson, Robert U., and C. C. Buel, eds. *Battles and Leaders of the Civil War.* Vol. 3. New York, 1888. Reprint, Secaucus, N.J., 1982.

Longstreet, James. *From Manassas to Appomattox.* Philadelphia, 1896. Reprint, Bloomington, Ind., 1960.

Seymour, Digby Gordon. *Divided Loyalties: Fort Sanders and the Civil War in East Tennessee.* 2d ed. Knoxville, Tenn., 1990.

L

LABOR

[*This entry includes two articles that discuss the workers on the Confederate home front and battlefront, the conditions under which they labored, and their contributions to the Confederacy:* An Overview *and* Skilled Labor. *See also* African American Forgeworkers; Bread Riots; Civil Service; Farming; Inflation; Mining; Plain Folk; Plantation; Powder Works; Sailors; Shelby Iron Company; Shipyards; Slavery; Soldiers; Textile Industry; Tredegar Iron Works.]

An Overview

Making war entails hard work on the part of civilians and soldiers alike. The Confederacy's war effort differed fundamentally from the Union's in that it mobilized slaves as well as free persons. As Confederate leaders often boasted, slavery provided both the rationale for the rebellion and the practical means for achieving victory. With slave laborers producing the goods that sustained soldiers as well as civilians, white men could focus upon the fight. At home and afield, in service and out, residents of the Confederate states shouldered the heavy burden of war.

The Battlefront. The dangerous work of combat fell almost without exception upon men and disproportionately upon the small farmers and laborers who constituted the bulk of the white population. The job paid little, and the amenities were few. Soldiers ran a comparatively high risk of occupational injury or death, from microbes as well as miniè balls. Even apart from the hazards of combat, soldiers performed arduous duty virtually on a daily basis.

The work began with basic training, where fresh recruits endlessly practiced using firearms and moving in tactical formations of several dozen to several thousand men. Soldiers in cavalry and artillery units had to perfect similar skills, coordinating the movements of animals with those of men. Artillerists also worked on positioning, sighting, and firing cannon. In all, despite times of comparatively light duty—even downright boredom—soldiers in both armies viewed training as hard work.

Whether or not soldiers saw marching in the same light, they understood that when the walking stopped, work would begin: clearing brush and trees, pitching camp, constructing shelter. Some of these tasks, like cooking, tidying the living area, and washing and mending clothes, were traditionally women's work. Others, like digging fortifications, currying horses, and loading and unloading wagons, were traditionally slaves' work. Soldiers who possessed artisan skills ranging from blacksmithing to shoemaking often continued to ply their trades while in service. And, through need if not predilection, most soldiers became expert tinkerers, fashioning natural materials and broken or abandoned equipment into useful articles.

Slaves, too, worked in direct support of field armies, for the most part as personal servants, cooks, and laborers. During the first year of the war, slaves attended owners in the enlisted ranks as well as in commissioned offices. Over time, however, only officers retained their servants; the slaves of private soldiers either returned home or found employment with the army. They cooked for their owners' bunkmates or for entire companies of soldiers; they worked as teamsters or laborers for the quartermaster or subsistence departments; they tended the sick and wounded or buried the dead for the medical corps.

Most slaves in Confederate employ, however, did the heavy, disagreeable, and often dangerous work of moving earth and trees to construct fortifications, roads, and bridges. Commanders who anticipated Federal attack routinely impressed slaves from surrounding plantations to serve in labor battalions. Impressment orders usually obligated masters to furnish 10 percent of their able-bodied adult slaves, with tools and rations, for thirty days' service.

Impressed slaves often worked under hard-driving overseers. If the intensity and regimentation of such labor offered slaves little opportunity for rest, at times the confusion provided cover for escape, as the "contrabands" who in May 1861 approached Union Gen. Benjamin F. Butler's lines at Fortress Monroe, Virginia, testified. Over time, masters as well as slaves devised strategies to avoid impressment. Nonetheless, impressed slaves labored prodigiously; extant earthworks on battlefields across the South bear mute testimony to their diligence.

The Home Front. The war reshaped labor on the home front no less than on the war front. From the start of the war, Confederate military strategists had comfortably assumed that plantation slaves working in their accustomed ways would raise food enough for soldiers and civilians alike. But industrial self-sufficiency was another matter, given the paucity of the antebellum infrastructure. Entrepreneurs, artisans, and laborers would need to contribute their respective skills and energies to produce the arms and ammunition; the flour and pork; the clothing and other textiles; the saddles, harnesses, and other leather products; the wagons, gun carriages, and other wood products—in short, the innumerable necessities of modern warfare. In the best of times, reallocation of material and human resources would have been difficult; the Union blockade and the success of Federal armies beginning in the spring of 1862 compounded the difficulty.

In the circumstances, shopkeepers and artisans in the luxury trades had to adjust. Carriage makers could fashion caissons as well as phaetons, and clocksmiths could make and repair small arms as well as timepieces. Other artisans likewise contributed their skills to the war effort, working either in private establishments with government contracts or in the numerous facilities established and operated by the Confederate government throughout the South.

For various reasons, ordnance establishments assumed pride of place among these works. The Ordnance Department employed thousands of metalworkers, molders, and men skilled in the use of machinery to cast cannon and shot, make and repair small arms, and fabricate ammunition. Thousands of carpenters and brickmasons made additions and repairs to existing structures. These skilled workers represented such a valuable component of the civilian labor force that conscription legislation pointedly exempted them from military service. Many an artisan—native-born Southerners as well as German and Irish immigrants—availed himself of the exemption, in some cases for reasons of Unionist politics, in others for family considerations. Still others believed they best served the cause by remaining at their workbenches.

Both private and government employers paid skilled workers well, but as the war progressed, rising inflation undercut the artisans' wages. Beginning in 1863, skilled workers protested against their losing battle with the high cost of living. In various cities of the Confederacy, typographers and telegraphers struck for higher wages; by 1864 workers in every branch of government service from the post office to the Ordnance Department were doing the same, as were both skilled and unskilled workers employed by government contractors.

Although skilled workers did not monopolize popular opposition to inflation—as the well-known women's bread riots of 1863 demonstrate—the workers' protests were significant for several reasons. First, the work stoppages and slowdowns threatened production of vital war matèriel. Second, the attack on inflation had potentially broad appeal among the Confederate citizenry. Third, even if the protest did not ultimately address larger political questions, officials feared

that it might. Accordingly, they squelched strikes by drafting the strikers into military service.

Women in the Work Force. Although not subject to conscription, southern women were drawn into the vortex of war in countless ways. Even before the first shot had been fired, the wives and daughters of black belt planters and women from the urban commercial and professional classes formed societies to knit socks and sew uniforms and flags for their men. After the fighting began, they also practiced a strict domestic economy aimed at achieving self-sufficiency in necessities and at conserving scarce resources. With similar fervor, some women of the upper classes went to work as clerks and bookkeepers in private shops and government offices, though traditional opposition to work outside the home limited such employment. Accordingly, upper-class women tended to focus their energy on volunteer services as nurses, schoolteachers, and members of committees to relieve the suffering of soldiers' families.

Slave women had to accommodate to their owners' new concerns, without, however, sacrificing their perspective on unfolding events or their ultimate objectives. In the short run, this accommodation meant additional hours of spinning and weaving after housework was completed. In the long run, it entailed even greater contributions to the orderly functioning of households. But, ironically, as mistresses became increasingly dependent upon their slaves, the slaves became less dependent upon them.

On yeoman farms and in urban tenements, women could ill afford the luxury of voluntary labor for the public good. With few if any slaves at their command, farm women assumed new agricultural chores to supplement their customary dairying, cooking, housekeeping, and child-rearing. Whereas farm women in the North faced similar challenges, they contended with no comparable dearth of work animals and, indeed, benefited from a proliferation of mechanical inventions to compensate for the shortage of workers.

Southern women of the urban working classes also struggled for subsistence, but within the context of earning sufficient wages for necessities and rent. By removing the men, conscription severely reduced the earning power of working class households. Although the resulting shortage of men created job openings for women and children, soaring inflation reduced the purchasing power of their earnings. The well-known bread riots of 1863 hint at urban women's mounting frustration with these circumstances, but, despite the protests, conditions got worse instead of better.

Agricultural Work. Confederate agriculture could scarcely have escaped the reallocation of men and resources. Both yeoman farms and slave plantations experienced the effect, but in different ways and with different—though equally profound—results. On the farms the combination of conscription and the Confederate tax-in-kind created a subsistence crisis, which the most determined exertions of the soldiers' wives and children could not alleviate. During 1864 and 1865, growing numbers of soldiers deserted to assist their families. Arriving home, they often found little if any food, fields grown over in weeds, and wagons and stock confiscated. In many cases, they labored in vain to reverse the deterioration that had occurred in their absence. Many had little alternative but to mortgage their land for the means of subsistence, thereby committing their future to commercial agriculture in order to liquidate their debts. The long-term consequences of these new patterns played themselves out through the rest of the nineteenth century.

> **Although not subject to conscription, southern women were drawn into the vortex of war in countless ways.**

Slave Labor. As the war dragged on, both private employers and Confederate authorities of necessity turned to slaves to meet their production goals. In time, the Niter and Mining Bureau as well as the Ordnance, Quartermaster, Subsistence, and Medical departments employed large numbers of slaves. Most of these men and women, hired from their masters by the year, worked as laborers, although men with skills in the building or mechanical trades worked in their specialties. Some evidence also suggests that employers promoted unskilled slaves into jobs of skill or responsibility as the need arose. By the end of the war, such slaves had managed to bargain for various perquisites not enumerated in the initial agreements of hire; these included extensive travel privileges and cash payments for overtime work.

On the plantations, the shift from staples to foodstuffs altered field routines and, as a result, larger patterns of employing slave laborers. The absence of military-age men decreased supervision, despite provisions for one exemption per each twenty slaves (later modified to one exemption per each ten slaves). On many plantations, slaves worked essentially on their own, with little or no oversight by owners or overseers. They raised grains and vegetables, in most circumstances more fearful of Confederate tax-in-kind officials than of Northern soldiers.

On the plantations where masters or overseers remained in control, slave-grown foodstuffs provided subsistence for families, black and white, and a surplus for tax purposes and exchange in local markets. Even in the midst of war, plantation slaves were capable of producing bountiful harvests, as Federal armies repeatedly learned, perhaps none more appreciatively than that of William Tecumseh Sherman. If soldiers in the trenches at Petersburg endured maddening hunger, the fault lay with the transportation system rather than the plantation system.

By itself, the shift from staples to cereals guaranteed an aggregate decrease in the amount of labor performed by plantation slaves, a pattern that continued into the postwar years. But slaves in large portions of the South ceased laboring altogether on behalf of the Confederacy by fleeing from their owners. Some 500,000 escaped to Union-occupied areas of Tennessee, the Mississippi valley, the Carolina low country, and the Chesapeake Tidewater. Other slaves fled to Union armed forces wherever they operated, upsetting the balance of power between masters and slaves throughout the Confederacy. The system of plantation labor was far different in December 1864 from what it had been in December 1860. Though still the foundation of agricultural production, it was chipping badly around the edges.

These changes in turn dramatically affected Confederate labor policy during the closing months of the war, in no respect more so than in the matter of enlisting slave men into military service. Despite the continuing need for slaves to work in fields and factories, and despite the obvious irony of relying upon slaves to resuscitate the struggle on behalf of perpetuating slavery, Confederate leaders felt that the exhaustion of white manpower left no other choice. Critics of the policy contended that the short-term objective of prolonging the fight subverted the original purpose of the war: if slaves were fit for combat, then they were not fit for slavery. Appomattox settled the debate.

In sum, the Civil War significantly altered traditional labor relations in the South even before emancipation thoroughly revolutionized them. Not just masters and slaves experienced the consequences. With white women plowing, white men cooking, black women supervising big houses, and black men bearing arms, it was clear how profoundly war could change the course of human events.

BIBLIOGRAPHY

Berlin, Ira, et al., eds. *Freedom: A Documentary History of Emancipation, 1861–1867.* 4 vols. to date. Cambridge, England, 1982–.

Brewer, James H. *The Confederate Negro: Virginia's Craftsmen and Military Laborers, 1861–1865.* Durham, N.C., 1969.

Coulter, E. Merton. *The Confederate States of America, 1861–1865.* A History of the South, vol. 7. Baton Rouge, La., 1950.

Eaton, Clement. *A History of the Southern Confederacy.* New York, 1954.

Escott, Paul D. *After Secession: Jefferson Davis and the Failure of Confederate Nationalism.* Baton Rouge, La., 1978.

Thomas, Emory. *The Confederacy as a Revolutionary Experience.* Englewood Cliffs, N.J., 1971.

Wiley, Bell Irvin. *The Life of Johnny Reb: The Common Soldier of the Confederacy.* Baton Rouge, La., 1943.

Wiley, Bell Irvin. *Southern Negroes, 1861–1865.* New Haven, 1938.

JOSEPH P. REIDY

Skilled Labor

Despite the popular enthusiasm generated by secession, the success of the Confederacy depended upon creating an industrial infrastructure capable of prosecuting war against an economic powerhouse. In comparison with the rest of the nineteenth-century world, the Confederacy had little cause for shame. Railroads spanned the region, iron foundries dotted the Appalachians and its foothills, and workshops of considerable variety and output flourished in the interior as well as along the coast. But for the Confederacy to win the war it would have to sustain itself in manufactures; therefore, the existing infrastructure would have to be expanded and integrated. Confederate government officials, working largely through the War Department's assorted bureaus, laid the plans for this effort. Skilled workers transformed the designs into reality.

Every Confederate state boasted both free and slave artisans. The former practiced trades whose origins lay in colonial times if not earlier: they fashioned wood, metal, leather, and other raw materials into items for use in homes, farms, and businesses. Blacksmiths and related ironworkers were an especially distinctive group, with growing importance in the nascent industrial economy. As railroads spread from the 1830s until the start of the war, these blacksmiths and ironworkers labored in mills and workshops building, repairing, and operating machinery of increasing complexity and sophistication. A small but noteworthy number of these metalworkers were free men of color. In Charleston and New Orleans, in particular, their ironwork set a standard for artistry as well as craftsmanship.

Other skilled workers were slaves. These included plantation blacksmiths, carpenters, coopers, and jacks-of-all-trades, as well as a host of urban craftsmen. Although most urban slave artisans were building tradesmen—carpenters and masons, in particular—others worked in the specialties that catered to the needs of urban populations. Some worked with iron and other metals of potential use to the military.

As war clouds gathered, civilians and government officials contemplated how to achieve industrial self-sufficiency. Foundries throughout the region would produce the lighter work, and such establishments as the Atlanta Rolling Mill and the renowned Tredegar Iron Works in Richmond would handle the heavy work, which in addition to rails and ordnance soon also included armor plate for warships.

Confederate planners calculated the need for additional industrial productivity beyond that represented by extant facilities. Rather than rely entirely upon private enterprise, they envisioned a direct government role. The chief architect of this plan was Josiah Gorgas, head of the Ordnance Department. Under his direction, the government began manufacturing cannons, small arms, and ammunition at sites across the South.

From start to finish, managers of workshops both private and government-sponsored faced a shortage of skilled workers. Recognizing this, lawmakers designing the conscription law that took effect in spring 1862 exempted pilots, telegraph operators, printers, and employees of railroads, riverboat companies, mines, furnaces, and foundries. By the fall of 1862, as the impact of conscription upon industrial production became clearer, lawmakers expanded the protected list.

In addition to the well-known provisions covering overseers for every twenty slaves, the revised guidelines exempted millers, tanners, saltmakers, shoemakers, blacksmiths, wagon makers, charcoal makers, and employees of wool and cotton factories, paper mills, and government arms-making facilities. In practice, the conscripts were selected from among all men of eligible age, and then those deemed eligible for exemption were detailed on special service to remain in their civilian occupations. Conscription officers reviewed

> Confederate planners calculated the need for additional industrial productivity. . . .

each case periodically, returning to his unit each man whose skills were no longer required on the home front.

Artisans generally favored the exemptions out of a variety of motives ranging from personal to political. The needs of their families often loomed large. Certain craftsmen plied trades essential to the well-being of their communities. Among individual artisans throughout the Confederacy and among organizations of certain tradesmen in the cities of the upper South, lingering Unionism explains the popularity of exemption. Whether their Unionism was rooted in opposition to slavery, or family ties to the Union, such men were less than enthusiastic arms-bearers in the Confederate cause. In fact, when pressed into service against their will, such men often crossed over the lines to the Northerners.

Artisans detailed from the army faced certain particular burdens. Legislation of spring 1863 had limited the pay of men on detached service to the regular soldier's pay plus a ration. Such soldier-artisans often found themselves working alongside paroled Federal prisoners or foreign-born men earning several times that amount. Only in mid-1864 did new legislation allow for higher wages, to the satisfaction of the men but the consternation of their employers.

For artisans no less than other Confederate civilians, inflation undercut the purchasing power of their wages, however high. Skyrocketing prices also sapped morale. As early as 1863, certain skilled workers—telegraphers and typographers, in particular—began striking for increased wages to keep pace with the rising cost of living. In 1864, such stoppages became routine in government-operated as well as privately owned facilities. So rampant were these actions and so potentially disruptive to production that Confederate authorities adopted a policy of breaking strikes by drafting the strikers. Workers often resorted to individual acts of defiance—expressed most frequently by desertion-to protest the government's failure to control the cost of necessities.

In the circumstances, shop superintendents turned increasingly to boys, women, and slaves to meet production targets. They promoted semiskilled operatives into skilled positions, hoping that experience would prove an adequate teacher. They employed women to fill vacancies left by men. And they relied especially upon slave laborers to perform both skilled and semiskilled work. Statistics from Tredegar indicate the magnitude of these changes. On the eve of the war, the company's main facility employed approximately 1,000 white men and fewer than 100 slaves, but by late 1864, there were roughly 200 slaves and 400 white men at work there. At the latter date, slaves made up roughly half of the 2,000 persons employed in all the company's facilities.

In the end, state-sponsored industrialization both drew out skills latent within the Southern population and focused that talent with remarkable efficiency and effect. Skilled laborers helped lay the foundation for postwar industrial development, which for various reasons, both economic and political, fell short of the potential that had been drawn out by the exigencies of war.

BIBLIOGRAPHY

Brewer, James H. *The Confederate Negro: Virginian's Craftsmen and Military Laborers, 1861–1865.* Durham, N.C., 1969.

Dew, Charles B. *Ironmaker to the Confederacy: Joseph R. Anderson and the Tredegar Iron Works.* New Haven, 1966.

Escott, Paul D. *After Secession: Jefferson Davis and the Failure of Confederate Nationalism.* Baton Rouge, La., 1978.

Moore, Albert Burton. *Conscription and Conflict in the Confederacy.* New York, 1924.

Vandiver, Frank E. *Plowshares into Swords: Josiah Gorgas and Confederate Ordnance.* Austin, Tex., 1952.

JOSEPH P. REIDY

LAIRD RAMS

Two iron-hulled, steam-powered ironclad warships were built by the firm of John Laird and Sons of Birkenhead, United Kingdom, for James D. Bulloch, chief Confederate naval purchasing agent in Europe. The ships, considered among the most formidable naval weapons of their time, incorporated some of the ideas of Capt. Cowper Coles of the Royal Navy, a leading designer of ironclads. Built between April 1862 and August 1863, they displaced 1,423 tons (light); they measured 224.5 feet long, 42.5 feet in beam, and 15.5 feet in depth of hold. A two-cylinder, horizontal direct-acting engine of 1,450 indicated horsepower drove a single screw propeller. Auxiliary power was provided by their bark sailing rig. Their two polygonal turrets were designed to carry two nine-inch, 220-pounder Armstrong guns. These turrets were protected by 5-inch iron armor over 22-inch teak and iron backing. The raised, armored forecastle and poop were designed to carry two 32-pounders, and the hull was covered with iron plate armor, which tapered from 4.5 inches at midship to 3 inches at the bow and 2 inches at the stern.

Their intended names in the Confederate navy were CSS *North Carolina* and CSS *Mississippi,* and great things were expected of them. Bulloch believed that they might have a "conclusive" answer to "the question of the blockade"—they could take the war to the coastal cities of the North.

The distinguishing feature of these vessels was a heavy iron beak, a ram, that projected forward about seven feet from the bow. The introduction of steam propulsion to warships had revived an ancient tactic of sea war by transforming such ships into formidable battering rams, allowing them to sink an enemy vessel by smashing its hull. Naval officers considered the rams to be among the most powerful weapons of sea war, but for the most part these vessels did not perform as well as expected.

Such ships, however, posed a special challenge to existing definitions of neutrality. Bulloch suspected that, in the aftermath of the *Alexandra* trial (which held that British firms could build ships for the Confederacy so long as those ships were not equipped with armaments while in Britain), the crown might reconsider its neutral obligations and take steps to prevent the departure of the rams. He therefore arranged their sham sale to the French firm of Bravay and Company of Paris, ostensibly for a future sale to the Egyptian navy. To enhance the subterfuge, the ships were given the cover names of *El Tousson* and *El Monassir.* This clandestine operation did not fool the British ministers, however. As the rams neared completion in late 1863, the government seized them while it conducted an extensive investigation in Paris and Cairo and came to the conclusion that the departure of these ships would not be in the national interest. And so, in May 1864, the Admiralty—"with a law suit in one hand and the valuation in the other"—made an offer to Bravay that the firm could not refuse. The rams thus became the property of the Royal Navy and were commissioned HMS *Scorpion* and HMS *Wivern.* They served the Queen's navy with no particular distinction until the early years of the twentieth century.

In addition to their intrinsic interest as secret weapons and technological innovators, the Laird Rams had another aspect of importance. They set off a crisis in Anglo-American affairs. The United States wanted Great Britain to stop the ships from leaving Liverpool, but British internal law did not clearly require the government to do so. The situation forced Lord John

Russell and his cabinet colleagues into a reappraisal of their neutral obligations. As the British debated their correct course in the matter, the American minister, Charles Francis Adams, wrote his famous—and much misunderstood—"this is war" note to the Foreign Office. In it he threatened a rupture of diplomatic relations between the two countries if Britain did not cease its "warlike" activity—that is, its supposed complicity in constructing a Confederate navy and allowing the rams, vessels equipped for war, to join that navy. The crisis brought on by the rams drove the British to confiscate those ships and to impose greater restrictions on Bulloch's procurement efforts. Russell's decision effectively thwarted Confederate efforts to build a navy in British yards. September at Birkenhead, no less than July at Gettysburg, doomed the South.

[See also Laird Shipyards.]

BIBLIOGRAPHY

Bulloch, James Dunwoody. *The Secret Service of the Confederate States in Europe: or, How the Confederate Cruisers Were Equipped.* 2 vols. New York, 1884. Reprint, New York, 1959.

Jones, Wilbur D. *The Confederate Rams at Birkenhead.* Tuscaloosa, Ala., 1961.

Merli, Frank J. "The Confederate Navy." In *In Peace and War: Interpretations of American Naval History, 1775–1984.* Edited by Kenneth J. Hagan. 2d ed. Westport, Conn., 1984.

Merli, Frank J. *Great Britain and the Confederate Navy, 1861–1865.* Bloomington, Ind., 1970.

Parkes, Oscar. *British Battleships, 1860–1950: A History of Design, Construction, and Armament.* Hamden, Conn., 1971.

Spencer, Warren. *The Confederate Navy in Europe.* University, Ala., 1983.

KEVIN J. FOSTER and FRANK J. MERLI

LAIRD SHIPYARDS

The William Laird and Sons Company was founded by John Laird, Jr., and William Laird, who had a history of successful construction of merchant and military ships. Located on the English River Mersey, across from the harbor of the city of Liverpool, the company was one of the earliest shipyards to build iron ships and by 1842 had built forty-four. In 1839 it constructed the iron paddle packet *Dover* for the British navy and in 1842 the iron paddle frigate *Guadalupe* for the Mexican government. At 788 tons *Guadalupe* was the largest iron vessel that had ever been constructed.

During the American Civil War the Lairds contracted with Confederate navy agent James Dunwoody Bulloch for the construction of *Alabama* and two ironclad rams. The *Alabama* contract was signed on August 1, 1861, and the ship was completed on June 15, 1862. The shipbuilders, following Bulloch's design, constructed a unique vessel for its

day: it was powered by both steam and sail, and it had a device to lift the propeller out of water when under sail only, large storage areas for provisions to enable the ship to stay at sea for long periods of time, passages for the passing of ammunition to the deck guns, and a condenser to convert seawater into drinking water.

During its cruise of twenty-three months under Capt. Raphael Semmes, the ship destroyed more enemy vessels than any other ship in naval history. Its destructive cruise raised the question of British culpability, which in turn led to the Geneva Arbitration Tribunal that in 1873 ordered Great Britain to pay $15.5 million to the United States for failure to prevent delivery of the ship to the Confederate navy.

The two ironclad rams Bulloch contracted for were formidable ships designed to operate in the shallow American coastal and river waters in order to raise the Union blockade and even to lay siege to certain Northern cities. The ships were 230 feet long, 42 feet at the extreme width, with a draft fully loaded of 15 feet. Made of wood with iron siding, they were powered by both sail and steam. Their most distinctive feature was a seven-foot iron ram protruding from the bow below the water level.

Largely because of the destructive *Alabama* cruise, the British government had become sensitive to Washington complaints and to reports submitted to it by the U.S. consul in Liverpool. Before the rams were completed, the British government seized them in 1864, thus preventing delivery to the Confederate navy. The Laird rams served well and long in the British navy as *Scorpion* and *Wivern*. Because the British domestic law to impose its neutrality on British subjects was outdated, the Lairds were not punished, despite the later decision of the Geneva tribunal.

The William Laird and Sons Company still operates on the Mersey River and maintains a Confederate museum that concentrates on *Alabama* and the Laird rams.

[See also Alabama Claims; Laird Rams; *and entry on the ship* Alabama.]

BIBLIOGRAPHY

Baxter, James Phinney. *The Introduction of the Ironclad Warship.* Cambridge, Mass., 1933. Reprint, Hamden, Conn., 1968.

Bulloch, James D. *The Secret Service of the Confederate States in Europe; or, How the Confederate Cruisers Were Equipped.* 2 vols. Liverpool, 1883. Reprint, New York, 1959.

Spencer, Warren F. *The Confederate Navy in Europe.* University, Ala., 1983.

Spencer, Warren F. "Ships for the South: James D. Bulloch, Confederate Agent in Europe." In *Divided We Fall: Essays on Confederate Nation Building.* Edited by John M. Belohlavek and Lewis N. Wynne. Saint Leo, Fla., 1991.

Summersell, Charles Grayson. *CSS Alabama, Builder, Captain, and Plans.* University, Ala., 1985.

WARREN F. SPENCER

LAMAR, L. Q. C.

LAMAR, L. Q. C. (1825–1893), framer of Mississippi's ordinance of secession, lieutenant colonel, diplomat, U.S. congressman, and Supreme Court judge. Lucius Quintus Cincinnatus Lamar, a native of Georgia, graduated from Emory College at Oxford, Georgia, in 1845. He married the daughter of Augustus Baldwin Longstreet, president of Emory College. When Longstreet resigned to become the president of the University of Mississippi, Lamar followed, taking a job as a mathematics professor despite his legal education and his preference for the law.

By 1851, Lamar had become an advocate of state rights, speaking out publicly in opposition to California's admission as a free state and earning a reputation as an eloquent and forceful speaker. Lamar was elected from Mississippi to the U.S. House of Representatives in 1857 and reelected in 1859. By this time, he was a vigorous spokesman for Southern interests, though he denied being a secessionist. As a delegate to the Charleston Democratic National Convention in 1860, Lamar sided with moderate Southern Democrats, opposing Southern withdrawal over the issue of territorial rights. Yet when the representatives of the Southern states withdrew, Lamar joined them. The election of Abraham Lincoln convinced him that secession was inevitable, and he began planning for a Southern nation. He resigned his seat in Congress and as a member of Mississippi's secession convention drafted the ordinance of secession.

At the beginning of the war, Lamar helped raise a regiment and became a lieutenant colonel. He insisted that the time for speeches and statesmanship was over. He was, nonetheless, depressed over the prospects of a long and bloody war, and while encamped at Richmond, he began to suffer attacks that left him temporarily unconscious and paralyzed on one side. After recuperating in Mississippi, he returned to Richmond and fought in the battle at

> **The remainder of his life proved to be the most important and productive of his career.**

Williamsburg, taking command of his regiment upon the death of Col. C. H. Mott. One-fifth of the regiment's men were casualties. Afterward, Lamar suffered another attack and was again forced to return home.

In late 1862 Lamar was appointed a special commissioner to seek Russian recognition of the Confederacy. He traveled as far as London and France, where he was received and entertained as a diplomat. The Confederate Senate realized, however, that Russia was unlikely to recognize a nation

that advocated slavery. It did not confirm Lamar's commission, and he returned to Richmond.

Near the end of 1863, Lamar was sent by the Davis administration to Georgia to quell growing opposition to Confederate policies. Again, he suffered the poor health that would recur the rest of his life. In December 1864 he was commissioned judge advocate of the military court of the Third Army Corps, Army of Northern Virginia.

After the war, although disfranchised, Lamar worked in Mississippi to promote conciliation, and in 1866 he returned to the university as a professor of ethics, metaphysics, and law. In 1870, during Republican rule, Lamar was forced to resign his professorship and to return to the practice of law.

The remainder of his life proved to be the most important and productive of his career. Pardoned from the disabilities imposed on Confederate officials, he served in the U.S. House of Representatives from 1872 to 1877 and in the U.S. Senate from 1877 to 1885. In 1885 he became President Grover Cleveland's secretary of the interior, and in 1888 Cleveland appointed him to the Supreme Court. He served until 1892 and died a year later.

BIBLIOGRAPHY

Cate, Wirt Armistead. *Lucius Q. C. Lamar: Secession and Reunion.* Chapel Hill, N.C., 1935.
Mayes, Edward. *Lucius Q. C. Lamar: His Life, Times, and Speeches.* Nashville, Tenn., 1896.

RAY SKATES

LANIER, SIDNEY

LANIER, SIDNEY (1842–1881), poet, critic, and musician. Sidney Clopton Lanier's importance for the Confederacy was at least as great after his death as before. Born in Macon, Georgia, and educated at Oglethorpe, Lanier volunteered for the local regiment, the Macon Volunteers, just before graduation in the spring of 1861. He was first posted to Norfolk, Virginia, with his regiment. He saw his first action at Drewry's Bluff in 1862 and survived the Seven Days' Battles later that summer and Chancellorsville in 1863. He served in the Signal Corps at Fort Boykin and aboard blockade runners based in Wilmington, North Carolina. He was captured in November 1864 and spent several months in Federal prison camps. He bribed his way out in February 1865.

Lanier's health, never robust, was ruined by the war and imprisonment. He died of the effects of consumption in 1881. Because of his relatively brief life, his frail health, and his popular poems and orations, he became, after his death, the "Keats of the Confederacy." His suffering, anecdotes of his flute playing under extreme hardship (in prison, in camp between actions), his extremely romantic philosophy (a blend of German and Oriental idealism and mysticism), and his proto-Agrarian political essays (e.g., "The New South," 1880) combined to make Lanier the focal point of cultural reconstruction in the South. Hamilton Wright Mabie wrote of Lanier after his death:

> Lanier was distinctively a national poet—one who felt the stir of the vast movement of coordination which did not begin with the close of the war, but which revealed itself then for the first time, and who expressed in the depth and largeness of his poetic conception neither the sentiment of New England nor of the South, new or old, but of that America which is to be also much larger, more significant, more influential, richer in appeal to the imagination than the provinces of which it is composed.

BIBLIOGRAPHY

Mabie, Hamilton Wright. "The Poetry of the South." *International Monthly* 5 (1902): 200–223.
Mims, Edwin. *Sidney Lanier.* Boston, 1905.
Rubin, Louis D., Jr. "The Passion of Sidney Lanier." In *William Elliott Shoots a Bear: Essays on the Southern Literary Imagination.* Baton Rouge, La., 1975.
Starke, Aubrey Harrison. *Sidney Lanier: A Biographical and Critical Study.* Chapel Hill, N.C., 1933.

MICHAEL KREYLING

LAW, EVANDER MCIVOR

LAW, EVANDER MCIVOR (1836–1920), brigadier general. There was an unfortunate tendency among many Confederate generals to engage in bitter disputes with their fellow officers. Some feuds, such as that between Joseph E. Johnston and P. G. T. Beauregard, are well known. Another bitter and less familiar feud, between two talented and ambitious young brigadiers, involved Evander McIvor Law and Micah Jenkins.

Law was born at Darlington, South Carolina, on August 7, 1836, and graduated from the Citadel in the class of 1856. He taught, along with Jenkins, at Kings Mountain Military Academy in South Carolina and then moved to Alabama. In early 1861 Law entered Confederate service and soon became lieutenant colonel of the Fourth Alabama Infantry. He was severely wounded at First Manassas and after his recovery was promoted to colonel.

He commanded a brigade from the Seven Days' Battles through the Sharpsburg campaign, was frequently praised by superiors, and was appointed brigadier general on October 13, 1862. Law commanded John Bell Hood's division admirably at Gettysburg after Hood was wounded; he led it again when Hood was wounded at Chickamauga. When temporary command of the division went to Jenkins, who ranked Law by three months, their rivalry was so intense that corps commander James Longstreet appointed a third officer to replace Hood. Longstreet preferred charges against Law, but they were dropped. Law commanded his brigade until he was severely wounded at Cold Harbor in 1864. He never returned to the Army of Northern Virginia but commanded a cavalry brigade in the Carolinas campaign of 1865.

After the war, Law was active in education and in the United Confederate Veterans. He was one of the last surviving Confederate generals when he died at Bartow, Florida, on October 31, 1920.

BIBLIOGRAPHY

Law, Evander McIvor. "From the Wilderness to Cold Harbor." In *Battles and Leaders of the Civil War.* Edited by Robert U. Johnson and C. C. Buel. Vol. 4. New York, 1888. Reprint, Secaucus, N.J., 1982.
Law, Evander McIvor. "On the Confederate Right at Gaines's Mill." In *Battles and Leaders of the Civil War.* Edited by Robert U. Johnson and C. C. Buel. Vol. 2. New York, 1888. Reprint, Secaucus, N.J., 1982.
Law, Evander McIvor. "The Struggle for 'Round Top.'" In *Battles and Leaders of the Civil War.* Edited by Robert U. Johnson and C. C. Buel. Vol. 3. New York, 1888. Reprint, Secaucus, N.J., 1982.
Wheeler, Joseph. *Alabama.* Vol. 7 of *Confederate Military History.* Edited by Clement A. Evans. Atlanta, 1899. Vol. 8 of extended ed. Wilmington, N.C., 1987.

J. TRACY POWER

LAWTON, ALEXANDER R.

LAWTON, ALEXANDER R. (1818–1896), brigadier general, quartermaster general, and U.S. ambassador to Austria. A graduate of West Point (1839) and Harvard University Law School (1843), Lawton before the war was a lawyer in Savannah, Georgia, president of a railroad, state legislator, militia colonel, and ardent secessionist. Acting on the orders of Governor Joseph E. Brown, he commanded the First Georgia Militia Regiment when it seized Federal Fort Pulaski at Savannah before Georgia had seceded.

When war broke out, Lawton was promoted to brigadier general (April 13, 1861) and directed the defense of the Georgia coast. In June 1862, commanding a Georgia brigade, he joined Thomas J. ("Stonewall") Jackson in the Shenandoah Valley. Lawton fought in the Seven Days' Battles and replaced Richard S. Ewell when he was wounded at

Second Manassas. Although badly wounded at Sharpsburg while in command of Ewell's division, he returned to service in May 1863.

President Jefferson Davis appointed Lawton, over his strong objections, quartermaster general in August 1863. (Lawton replaced Col. Abraham C. Myers, whose wife supposedly had called Mrs. Varina Davis a "squaw" because of her dark complexion.) In his new post he was to provide Confederate soldiers with uniforms, shoes, nonordnance equipment, and transportation, a virtually impossible task in the inflation-wracked and politically divided Confederacy. His efficiency diminished by state governors who controlled vital war matèriel, Lawton nevertheless increased by thousands the number of uniforms and blankets sent to the Army of Northern Virginia. In a January 1865 letter to the Confederate Congress he reported, "The Army has been fully provided."

After the war, Lawton entered Georgia state politics. In 1887, President Grover Cleveland appointed him ambassador to Austria. He died in New York and is buried in Savannah.

BIBLIOGRAPHY

Coulter, Merton E. *The Confederate States of America, 1861–1865. A History of the South*, vol. 7. Baton Rouge, La., 1950.

Eaton, Clement. *A History of the Southern Confederacy*. New York, 1954.

Vandiver, Frank E. *Rebel Brass: The Confederate Command System*. Baton Rouge, La., 1956.

Weinert, Richard P. *The Confederate Regular Army*. Shippensburg, Pa., 1991.

P. NEAL MEIER

LEACH, JAMES MADISON

LEACH, JAMES MADISON (1815–1891), lieutenant colonel and congressman from North Carolina. James Madison Leach fought for the Confederacy in 1861 and represented North Carolina in the Second Confederate Congress. As a determined foe of the policies of President Jefferson Davis, Leach gave voice to much of the discontent and restiveness with war measures that characterized his state. Although he supported demands for peace, on occasion he differed with his outspoken cousin, Congressman James T. Leach, over the latter's peace proposals.

Born on January 17, 1815, at his family's plantation in Randolph County, North Carolina, James Madison Leach attended Caldwell Institute in Greensboro and the U.S. Military Academy. He then studied law under an older brother and, after obtaining his license in 1842, opened a practice in Lexington, where he resided the rest of his life. A remarkably effective advocate, Leach was renowned as a defense lawyer and is said to have prevailed in seventy of seventy-one murder cases, losing only the first case he handled.

Throughout his life he was a strong proponent of education and internal improvements. Elected to the North Carolina House of Commons in 1848 as a Whig, Leach promoted education and supported the Railroad Act of 1849, which committed the state to building the North Carolina Railroad.

> **. . . Leach developed a record as a foe of all administration programs.**

Leach served in the state legislature for ten years and then ran for the U.S. House of Representatives against a Democratic incumbent, winning election by a large majority.

As the secession crisis grew, Leach took a consistent stand against secession. As soon as Abraham Lincoln called for volunteers to put down the rebellion, however, he changed his stance. He canceled a tour on which he was speaking against secession and rushed home to raise a company of volunteers. Chosen as captain of his company, Leach became lieutenant colonel upon organization of the Twenty-first Regiment, North Carolina Troops. He fought at First Manassas and saw other action in Virginia before he resigned on December 23, 1861.

By 1863 discontent with the war had become pronounced in North Carolina, and the state elected new congressmen in eight out of ten districts. Five of the newcomers were avowed peace candidates. When one of these, Congressman-elect Samuel H. Christian, died in March 1864, Leach ran for the seat and won easily on a pledge that he would seek peace with independence.

In the Second Congress Leach developed a record as a foe of all administration programs. He gave his approval to resolutions declaring that Secretaries Judah P. Benjamin, Christopher G. Memminger, and John H. Reagan were incompetent, and he voted to override every presidential veto. Opposition to the suspension of the writ of habeas corpus was one of his special causes. On December 5, 1864, Leach introduced a resolution declaring "that the privilege of the writ of *habeas corpus* is one of the great bulwarks of freedom, and that it ought not to be suspended except in extreme cases . . . that the people of this Confederacy are united in a great struggle for liberty, and that no exigency exists justifying its suspension." Later that year and in January 1865 he tried unsuccessfully to win the House's approval of this statement. Leach's efforts prompted a North Carolina captain to declare that the congressman "has thrown more obstacles in the way of my arresting deserters . . . than any ten men in this County." Leach also fought Jefferson Davis's proposal to arm and emancipate Southern slaves, offering an amendment to prohibit the government from arming the slaves, mustering them into Confederate service, or "at any time" using them as soldiers.

James M. Leach urged the government to initiate peace negotiations, and by April 1865 he believed that North Carolina should pursue separate state negotiations on its own. But he drew a distinction between his support for peace and that of his colleague and cousin James T. Leach. On November 25, 1864, James M. Leach refused to support his cousin's peace resolutions (which won only three votes) and, to the delight of the *Richmond Examiner,* told the House "that there was no member from North Carolina who desired peace upon any terms [other] than eternal separation from the North."

Many of Leach's other efforts in Congress seemed designed to relieve his constituents from the heavy demands of the Confederate war effort. He worked to exempt from the tax-in-kind tenant farmers and nonslaveholders who "produce no surplus, but only a support." Similarly he called for the exemption of "such number of mechanics and artisans as shall be indispensably necessary to carry on the mechanical and industrial pursuits of the country." In January 1865 Leach tried unsuccessfully to exempt in each county one blacksmith and one miller for every two thousand people and one tanner and one shoemaker for every four thousand residents. He presented memorials from slaveholders concerned about the health of their impressed bondsmen, but he also sought repeal of the exemption for those who owned or managed fifteen or more slaves.

After the Civil War Leach rebuilt his fortune through successful legal work and remained active in politics. During Presidential Reconstruction he served in the North Carolina Senate from 1865 to 1868 and became a leader among the conservatives who opposed Congressional Reconstruction. Leach chaired the committee that denounced the proposed Fourteenth Amendment and urged its rejection. As a Conservative (later Democrat) Leach won election to Congress in 1870 and 1872 but declined to run a third time. He worked for the Democratic party in the 1876 and 1880 elections and returned to his state's General Assembly as a senator in 1879. Leach died on June 1, 1891, and was buried in Hopewell Church Cemetery.

BIBLIOGRAPHY

Alexander, Thomas B., and Richard E. Beringer. *The Anatomy of the Confederate Congress: A Study of the Influences of Member Characteristics on Legislative Voting Behavior, 1861–1865.* Nashville, Tenn., 1972.
Hamilton, J. G. de Roulhac. *Reconstruction in North Carolina.* New York, 1914.
Journal of the Congress of the Confederate States of America, 1861–1865. 7 vols. Washington, D.C., 1904–1905.
Powell, William S., ed. *Dictionary of North Carolina Biography.* Vol. 3. Chapel Hill, N.C., 1988.
"Proceedings of the Confederate Congress." In *Southern Historical Society Papers.* 51–52 (1958–1959). Reprint, Wilmington, N.C., 1992.

PAUL D. ESCOTT

LEACH, JAMES T.

LEACH, JAMES T. (1805–1883), congressman from North Carolina. James T. Leach of North Carolina served in the House of Representatives of the Second Congress of the Confederate States. Elected in 1863 as an avowed peace candidate, Leach quickly became one of the most energetic and determined foes of Jefferson Davis's administration. His career illustrates the Confederacy's difficulty in establishing firm loyalty to a new government and reflects the extremes of discontent that developed in response to the South's plight. Leach's actions in Congress also reveal the kinds of issues that aroused opponents of the government.

Born in 1805 into a prominent family in Johnston County, North Carolina, James Thomas Leach studied first law and then medicine, earning a diploma from Jefferson Medical College in Philadelphia. He returned home and practiced medicine, and occasionally some law, for the rest of his life. Marrying Elizabeth Willis Boddie Sanders in 1833, Leach built his home on his family's Leachburg Plantation and gradually purchased the parcels of land inherited by his brothers and sisters. By 1860 he owned and managed a large plantation with forty-seven slaves. It is said that his policy in acquiring slaves was to purchase only those who wished to earn their freedom. He encouraged self-improvement among his white neighbors, also, by opening a free school in his home and later building schoolhouses nearby. He took orphaned boys and destitute women into his house and urged improved farming methods upon his neighbors.

In prewar politics Leach was an old-line Whig. He served one term in the North Carolina Senate (1858–1860), during which he became an ally of State Treasurer Jonathan Worth, a conservative who possessed a keen empathy for common farmers and cared little about the territorial issues that were dividing the nation. During the secession crisis Leach took a staunchly pro-Union position. He argued vigorously against secession, opposing that step even after Abraham Lincoln called for volunteers in April 1861. These pro-Union convictions cost Leach reelection to the state legislature.

In 1863 Leach ran for the Confederate House of Representatives as one of several disaffected North Carolina peace candidates. Campaigning in his district against three strong supporters of the Confederate government, Leach denied the right of secession and openly pledged himself to seek "a just, honorable and lasting peace." He won election easily. His broadside to "Fellow-Citizens of the Third Congressional District," published in September 1863, immediately placed him among the leadership of the peace movement in the Second Congress.

In Richmond, Leach was appointed to the committees on Post Offices and Post Roads and on Territories and Public Lands, but he devoted most of his energy to larger questions of policy. He spoke out against "reckless legislation . . . endorsed by the President and the mighty strides now making toward a military despotism." To Leach there was "too much of brass button and bayonet rule in the country," and he declared that the central government should "leave the execution of some of its laws to the people at home." In May 1864 he condemned suspension of the writ of habeas corpus and introduced a resolution "declaring the supremacy of the civil over the military law." He also introduced resolutions denouncing secret sessions and "defining the rights of the States in furnishing soldiers."

Leach was solicitous of the needs of his constituents, seeking to increase the pay of soldiers and to "exempt soldiers' families from the payment of the tithes [tax-in-kind] when there is not more than is necessary for the comfortable support of the family." But his primary initiatives in the House were three joint resolutions, offered in May 1864, November 1864, and January 1865, in favor of peace negotiations. His resolutions of May 23, 1864, condemned the usurpations of the United States but called for the appointment of commissioners to seek a ninety-day armistice. The second set of resolutions, presented on November 25, 1864, frankly called the South's decision to secede because Lincoln had won the presidency a mistake, declaring that that decision had brought a train of "fearful consequences not contemplated by those who advocated" secession. Although these resolutions proposed that the South enter peace negotiations when the United States recognized the "reserved rights of the States" and guaranteed the "rights of property," they received only three votes (from Leach and two other North Carolina representatives). On January 23, 1865, Leach offered his last set of peace resolutions, which blamed the United States for violations of the federal Constitution, cruelty, and "acts of wantonness," but nevertheless sought an armistice. On March 1, 1865, he offered resolutions approving the appointment of Robert E. Lee as general-in-chief and recommending that "he be invested with powers to treat for peace." Two weeks later he alone opposed the House's concurrence in a Senate resolution that pledged Southerners to fight on to independence rather than accept dishonorable peace terms.

Leach fought the Davis administration to the end of his time in office, blasting the president's proposal to arm slaves and promise them the reward of freedom. Such a policy, Leach raged, "would be wrong in principle, disastrous in practice, an infringement upon the States' rights, an endorse-

ment of the principle contained in President Lincoln's emancipation proclamation, an insult to our brave soldiers and an outrage upon humanity." During his term Leach criticized cabinet officers, opposed the administration's economic proposals, sought to broaden exemptions, and voted to override every presidential veto.

After the Civil War Leach became an ally of William W. Holden and late in 1866, when conservatives were denouncing the proposed Fourteenth Amendment, joined in a call for a new Reconstruction government in North Carolina. He remained active in local affairs and became a dedicated prohibitionist, resigning from his position as county commissioner in 1875 rather than certify anyone as a "qualified" barroom operator. Leach died on March 28, 1883, and was buried in the family cemetery near Mount Zion Church in Johnston County, North Carolina.

BIBLIOGRAPHY

Alexander, Thomas B., and Richard E. Beringer. *The Anatomy of the Confederate Congress: A Study of the Influences of Member Characteristics on Legislative Voting Behavior, 1861–1865.* Nashville, Tenn., 1972.

Hamilton, J. G. de Roulhac. *Reconstruction in North Carolina.* New York, 1914.

Journal of the Congress of the Confederate States of America, 1861–1865. 7 vols. Washington, D.C., 1904–1905.

"Proceedings of the Confederate Congress." *Southern Historical Society Papers* 51–52 (1958–1959). Reprint, Wilmington, N.C., 1992.

Yearns, Wilfred B. *The Confederate Congress.* Athens, Ga., 1960.

PAUL D. ESCOTT

LEAD

A Confederate government of highly limited resources often had to utilize blockade runners and contracts with private firms in order to obtain badly needed war supplies. Lead was among the most vital of these commodities. Without it, weapons had no ammunition.

So scarce was lead in the wartime South that soldiers would collect bullets from battlefields and send them to arsenals in the rear to be melted down and recast. Southern officials issued appeals requesting citizens to strip their homes of all lead articles such as pipes, roofs, window weights, and common utensils. Blockade runners did a brisk business in lead importation: over 1.5 million pounds entered the Confederacy by this means in one thirteen-month period.

Small lead mines existed in eastern Tennessee and Arkansas. But as Col. William Broun of the Confederate Ordnance Department later stated: "Our lead was obtained chiefly, and in the last years of the war entirely, from the lead mines at Wytheville, Va. The mines were worked night and day, and the lead converted into bullets as fast as received. The old regulation shrapnel shells were filled with leaden balls and sulphur. The Confederacy had neither lead nor sulphur to spare, and used instead small iron balls and filled with asphalt."

Wytheville's state-owned mines had supplied George Washington's army with bullets in the American Revolution. After the new nation came into being, Virginia sold the mines to two Austin brothers. (Stephen F. Austin, the "Father of Texas," was a son of one of the owners.) The mines at Wytheville—the quarries themselves were at Austinville, seven miles away—were a thriving business when civil war came.

Of the three types of lead mined there, sulphuret (or "blue ore") was the most abundant. It was either crystalline or granular in structure and easily recognizable from the carbonate and oxide varieties of lead. The C.S. Niter Corps monitored production, with Gen. Josiah Gorgas of the Niter and Mining Bureau in overall charge of operations. When conscription drained manpower from the mines, Confederate officials impressed slaves to continue the work. Output at the Wytheville mines averaged about 80,000 pounds monthly. In all, these mines produced 3,283,316 pounds of lead for the Confederacy.

By 1864 Union officials regarded the Wytheville quarries as the most important target in southwestern Virginia. Federal raiding parties went into action as soon as the Virginia and Tennessee Railroad and nearby points were secured. Gen. William W. Averell made a stab at Wytheville on May 11 but was driven off by Confederate cavalry under Gen. John Hunt Morgan. On December 17, several mounted regiments of Gen. George Stoneman's force captured the

> **When conscription drained manpower from the mines, Confederate officials impressed slaves to continue the work.**

mines, poured oil on the equipment, and set fire to the works before returning to their base.

Persistent miners repaired the damage and, on March 22, 1865, resumed operations. Confederates managed to repulse an April 5 attempt by Federals to seize the mines. Two days later, however, a heavier assault by Union cavalry routed the defenders. The lead works were destroyed a second time, only two days before Robert E. Lee's surrender at Appomattox.

In all the Confederacy consumed 10 million pounds of lead in the manufacture of the 150 million cartridges used by its armies.

[*See also* Niter and Mining Bureau.]

BIBLIOGRAPHY

Marvel, William. *Salt, Lead and Rail.* Lynchburg, Va., 1992.
Vandiver, Frank E. *Ploughshares into Swords: Josiah Gorgas and Confederate Ordnance.* Austin, Tex., 1952.
Walker, Gary G. *The War in Southwest Virginia, 1861–65.* Roanoke, Va., 1975.

JAMES I. ROBERTSON, JR

LEE, EDWIN GRAY

LEE, EDWIN GRAY (1836–1870), colonel and acting brigadier general. Lee was born at Leeland, near Shepherdstown, Virginia, May 27, 1836. Nicknamed Ned, this distant kinsman of Robert E. Lee and future son-in-law of Gen. William N. Pendleton attended the Hallowell School in Alexandria and graduated from William and Mary, after which he practiced law.

At the beginning of the war Lee was commissioned a second lieutenant in the Second Virginia Infantry. He was an aide to Thomas J. ("Stonewall") Jackson at Harpers Ferry and saw action at First Manassas. When the army was reorganized in the spring of 1862, Lee was elected lieutenant colonel of the Thirty-third Virginia. He regarded the grade as unsatisfactory inasmuch as he was superior to John F. Neff, who was chosen colonel. He threatened to resign but, on the counsel of Alexander Pendleton, his brother-in-law, and others, he eventually agreed to serve in the subordinate role. At Cedar Mountain, Lee had the rare distinction of commanding his superior officer, Colonel Neff, who had been placed under arrest by Charles S. Winder over a minor policy matter and had gone into battle without his sword or authority.

Following the death of Neff at Second Manassas, Lee commanded the Thirty-third at Fredericksburg. Ill health, caused by the hardships of military life, forced Lee to resign in December 1862. He was recommissioned a colonel a few months later and given duty in Richmond.

In June 1864, Lee was assigned to Staunton, Virginia, with orders to organize local troops for defense of the Shenandoah Valley. He was appointed brigadier general on September 20, 1864. Two months later he was given a six-month leave of absence because of failing health. His nomination to the grade of brigadier was rejected by the Senate on February 24, 1865, although he apparently continued to appear on the rolls at that rank until the end of the war.

Shortly before the surrender, Lee and his wife, Susan, ran the blockade and went to Montreal on a secret mission for the government. Returning to the United States in 1866, he continued to struggle against the ravages of lung disease. He died at Yellow Sulphur Springs, Virginia, August 24, 1870, and was buried in Lexington.

BIBLIOGRAPHY

Hotchkiss, Jed. *Virginia.* Vol. 3 of *Confederate Military History.* Edited by Clement A. Evans. Atlanta, 1899. Vol. 4 of extended ed. Wilmington, N.C., 1987.

Lee, Susan P. *Memoirs of William Nelson Pendleton.* Philadelphia, 1893.

Levin, Alexandra Lee. *This Awful Drama: General Edwin Gray Lee, C.S.A., and His Family.* New York, 1987.

Warner, Ezra J. *Generals in Gray: Lives of the Confederate Commanders.* Baton Rouge, La., 1959.

LOWELL REIDENBAUGH

LEE, FITZHUGH

LEE, FITZHUGH (1835–1905), major general, postwar governor of Virginia, and U.S. diplomat. Born at Clermont, in Fairfax County, Virginia, Fitz Lee was the grandson of Henry ("Light Horse Harry") Lee and great-grandson of George Mason. Lee attended the U.S. Military Academy from 1852 to 1856, while his uncle, Robert E. Lee, was superintendent. Graduating forty-fifth out of forty-nine, he excelled in horsemanship. His equestrian skills earned him a position with the Second U.S. Cavalry in Texas. For two years, he served on the frontier fighting Comanches, where he received a critical wound to his lungs that nearly cost him his life. He returned to West Point as an instructor in 1860.

In May 1861, Lee resigned from the U.S. Army and returned to Virginia. In September, after serving as adjutant to Brig. Gen. Richard S. Ewell during the Battle of First Manassas, he received a commission as lieutenant colonel of the First Virginia Cavalry. Lee led scouting and raiding parties against the Federals picketed in northern Virginia and often left taunting notes for former comrades in the U.S. Army.

Serving under Maj. Gen. J. E. B. Stuart, he received high praise from his commander and was promoted to colonel in the spring of 1862. He joined Stuart for the Ride around McClellan during the Peninsular campaign and was cited for his "zeal and ability." In July, Lee was promoted to brigadier general in command of the Second Brigade. He continued to serve with the Army of Northern Virginia, seeing limited action at Second Manassas and Sharpsburg. During the winter of 1862–1863, he made successful hit-and-run attacks against the Federal army.

On March 17, 1863, one of Lee's taunting messages drew a response from Gen. William Averell, who launched a raid across the Rapidan River at Kelly's Ford. Fitz Lee's small command outside of Culpeper, Virginia, drove the larger invading force across the river for a marginal victory.

At Chancellorsville, Lee's reconnaissance provided key information that the Federal right flank was "in the air" and vulnerable to an attack. This prompted the renowned flank attack led by Gen. Thomas J. ("Stonewall") Jackson on May 2 that resulted in the Confederates' strategic victory. In September, Lee was promoted to major general commanding the Second Division of the cavalry corps.

In 1864, Lee distinguished himself at Spotsylvania, Yellow Tavern—where he assumed command after Stuart was mortally wounded—and Trevilian's Station. During the battle at Winchester on September 19, Lee received a serious wound to his thigh, which kept him out of service until January 1865. At Five Forks, Lee's military reputation was tainted when his attendance at the notorious shad bake (a fish fry given by a fellow officer some distance from his force's position) resulted in his absence from the battle front. He redeemed himself by delaying Gen. Philip Sheridan's pursuit of the retreating Army of Northern Virginia.

After the war, Lee tried farming at his home, Richlands, in Stafford County, Virginia, but he soon turned to politics and was elected governor of Virginia in 1886. He was the U.S. consulate general in Havana, Cuba, from 1896 to 1898. During the Spanish-American War, Lee served as a major general in the U.S. Army. He died on April 29, 1905, in Washington, D.C., and was buried in Hollywood Cemetery in Richmond, Virginia.

BIBLIOGRAPHY

Bond, Frank. "Fitz Lee in the Army of Northern Virginia." *Confederate Veteran* 6, no. 9 (1898): 420–423. Reprint, Wilmington, N.C., 1985.

Nichols, James A. *General Fitzhugh Lee: A Biography.* Lynchburg, Va., 1989.

Warner, Ezra J. *Generals in Gray: Lives of the Confederate Commanders.* Baton Rouge, La., 1959.

KAREN G. REHM

LEE, GEORGE WASHINGTON CUSTIS

LEE, GEORGE WASHINGTON CUSTIS (1832–1913), major general. Born September 16, 1832, at Fort Monroe, Virginia, the first child of Mary Custis Lee and Robert E. Lee, Custis Lee spent much of his life coping with the burden of his father's fame. At West Point he graduated first in the class of 1854, exceeding his father's record (second in the class of 1829). Commissioned in the Corps of Engineers (like his father), Custis Lee served on several construction projects before resigning May 2, 1861, in response to the secession of Virginia.

Lee secured a place on the military staff of President Jefferson Davis and spent most of the war in Richmond.

Rewarded with promotions for faithful service, Lee became a brigadier general on June 25, 1863, and a major general on October 20, 1864.

By turns eager for command in the field but unsure of his capacity to lead in combat, Lee was often ill during the war. He remained on Davis's staff because the president wanted him and because his father needed him. The elder Lee relied upon his son to express his views to the president and to keep him informed about policies and politics within the administration.

Lee finally did command a reserve regiment of industrial workers on the retreat from Richmond, but had to surrender himself and his men at Sayler's Creek on April 6, 1865. After the war Lee taught engineering at the Virginia Military Institute in Lexington. Following his father's death, Custis Lee became president of Washington and Lee University from 1871 to 1897. He died on February 18, 1913.

BIBLIOGRAPHY

Freeman, Douglas S. *R. E. Lee: A Biography.* 4 vols. New York, 1934–1935.
Nagel, Paul C. *The Lees of Virginia: Seven Generations of an American Family.* New York, 1990.

EMORY M. THOMAS

LEE, ROBERT E.

LEE, ROBERT E. (1807–1870), general. Born at Stratford, Westmoreland County, Virginia, on January 19, 1807, Lee was the fourth of five children (the third son) of Ann Hill Carter Lee and Henry ("Light-Horse Harry") Lee. Two children of Harry Lee's first marriage also lived with the family. Robert Lee did not remain very long at Stratford. His father had been a hero in the Revolution, governor of Virginia, and a member of Congress; but by the time of Robert's birth, Lee's fortunes were in serious decline. Harry Lee's debts

> **Throughout his young manhood and middle age people called him the best-looking man in the army.**

forced him into prison in 1809 and compelled the family to move to Alexandria, Virginia, in 1810. Then in 1812 Harry Lee sustained serious injuries in Baltimore helping an editor defend his newspaper against a mob outraged over editorials opposing the War of 1812. In May 1813, he sailed away to the Caribbean, ostensibly to recoup his fortune and recov-

er his health, leaving family and creditors behind. Light-Horse Harry Lee died on Cumberland Island, Georgia, in 1818 without having seen his family again.

Ann Lee raised her children in very modest circumstances and tried to teach them standards of conduct in the hope that they would avoid their father's mistakes. After attending schools in Alexandria, Robert Lee managed to secure an appointment to West Point. Rather suddenly he left the company of his mother and sisters, for whom he had cared during his adolescence, and in 1825 entered the exclusively male society at West Point.

His mother's precepts, his academic background, and his quick, precise mind all served Lee well at West Point. He finished second in the class of 1829 and garnered not one demerit during his four years at the academy. Lee's success earned him an appointment in the Engineer Corps at a time when the U.S. government was willing to support public projects. His first assignment was at Cockspur Island in the Savannah River preparing the foundation of what much later became Fort Pulaski.

Approximately a month following his graduation from West Point, Ann Lee died, and Robert Lee began his career in the military with a small inheritance (about ten slaves) and roots in his extended family. Although Lee made friends in Savannah, he spent his leaves in northern Virginia increasingly in the company of Mary Custis, the only child of Mary Fitzhugh Custis and George Washington Parke Custis, the adopted son of George Washington. Lee was extraordinarily handsome then, and throughout his young manhood and middle age people called him the best-looking man in the army. He was about five feet, ten or eleven inches tall, with a fit, medium build and nearly perfect posture. A guest at his son's wedding in 1859 claimed that Lee outshone the entire company, and those who saw him on horseback insisted that he appeared even more imposing riding than afoot.

Mary Custis and Robert Lee married in July 1831 at Arlington, the Custis estate just across the Potomac from Washington. The young couple began life together in officers' quarters at Fort Monroe, Virginia, Lee's second duty assignment. They had seven children between 1832 and 1846. The Lees and their children often lived at Arlington while Lee served in the Engineer Department in Washington, and Mary Lee remained with the children at Arlington when duty called Robert Lee to St. Louis and later to the Mexican War.

Lee served on the staff of Winfield Scott during the campaign from Vera Cruz to Mexico City in 1847. He became a member of Scott's "little cabinet," his inner circle of advisers, and Lee's talent, energy, and daring were especially conspicuous at Cerro Gordo and Chapultepec. He emerged from the war with Scott's unabashed admiration and the brevet (temporary) rank of colonel.

In 1852 Lee returned to West Point as superintendent, and in 1855 he transferred from staff assignments to com-

ROBERT E. LEE. This April 20, 1865, photograph by Mathew Brady was taken under the back porch of Lee's home near Richmond, Virginia, shortly before Lee became president of what is today known as Washington and Lee University. NATIONAL ARCHIVES

mand of cavalry troopers on the Texas frontier. When his father-in-law died in 1857, Lee began a protracted leave as executor of Custis's estate.

Custis had dabbled in many enterprises and had done none of them very well. Unfortunately for Lee, Custis had not done a very good job of making his will either. So Lee attempted to unsnarl affairs associated with Custis's estate, a task he never quite completed in his lifetime.

Lee was still working at Arlington in October 1859 when reports of a slave insurrection sent him hurriedly to Harpers Ferry in command of a detachment of marines. He confronted John Brown and a few of his followers barricaded in a fire engine building with thirteen hostages. The situation was tense, but Lee managed to capture Brown and put down his raid without harming Brown's hostages.

In 1860 Lee returned to Texas and duty, having had his fill of farming on his father-in-law's estates. In February 1861, he returned to Arlington in response to the secession crisis. He rejected an opportunity to command the principal field army charged with suppressing the rebellion, choosing instead to offer his services to Virginia and the Southern Confederacy. Lee resigned his commission in the U.S. Army on April 20, 1861, and on April 23 accepted command of the armed forces of Virginia. In this capacity Lee organized the mobilization of Virginia troops and on June 10 surrendered his men and equipment to the Confederate government for the national army and navy. Thereafter Lee served as informal adviser to President Jefferson Davis and remained for the most part in the new capital at Richmond.

On August 31, 1861, Lee became a full general in the Confederate army. By this time he was in western (present-day West) Virginia attempting to unscramble egos and thwart a Union campaign in the Kanawha Valley. Lee failed in both undertakings and returned to Richmond on October 31. Less than a week later Davis sent Lee to command the Department of South Carolina, Georgia, and Florida and to confront Federal incursions along the Southern coast.

Lee arrived in South Carolina on the very day a Federal combined arms force captured Port Royal. Subsequently he worked to contain the enemy invasion and to organize the defense of the coastal region. He concluded that the Confederacy lacked the ships, men, and guns to defend the barrier islands and so contracted the chain of defensive positions up rivers to sites where the guns available would have some chance of stopping Union gunboats. Lee's plans were sound, but his design forced coastal residents to flee inland with their slaves and thus made refugees of some rich and powerful Confederates.

In March 1862, Davis recalled Lee to Richmond and made him, in effect, his chief of staff. Lee was again an adviser while others commanded armies. He did perform a valuable service as buffer between the president and Joseph E. Johnston, who commanded the primary Confederate army in Virginia. In the process of countering Union Gen. George B. McClellan's Peninsular campaign, Davis and Johnston seemed overconcerned about personal prerogatives, and Lee was able to filter some of the vitriol out of communications between the two men. Otherwise, though, Lee worked hard at thankless tasks while McClellan's blue host came steadily closer to Richmond.

Then on May 31, 1862, Johnston committed his army to what became the Battle of Seven Pines, and as the inconclusive fighting wound down, Johnston was seriously injured. On June 1 Davis gave Lee command of Johnston's army and in so doing placed Lee in charge of the Confederacy's tottering fortunes.

Lee withdrew the army into the outskirts of Richmond and ordered the men to prepare elaborate field fortifications. So in the public mind, Lee became "the King of Spades" as well as "Granny Lee" for his supposed overcaution. Lee, however,

> He rejected an opportunity to command the principal field army . . . choosing instead to offer his services to Virginia. . . .

was already making plans that were anything but defensive and cautious. He reorganized Johnston's army and renamed it the Army of Northern Virginia—all while in the face of the enemy. He sent J. E. B. Stuart and the cavalry to scout McClellan's right flank, a reconnaissance that became known as Stuart's "Ride around McClellan" because he circled the entire Federal army. Lee shifted divisions of troops to attack the Federal right flank and summoned Thomas J. ("Stonewall") Jackson's Shenandoah Valley army to strike the Federal rear. The result of these actions was the Seven Days' Battles (King's School House, Mechanicsville, Gaines' Mill, Frayser's Farm, White Oaks Swamp, and Malvern Hill) from June 25 through July 1, 1862. After the nearly constant and always bloody fighting, the Federals lay inert under cover of their gunboats at Harrison's Landing on the James River, twenty-three miles from Richmond. Lee was suddenly a hero, and the Confederacy seemed saved. But Lee was frustrated: he had wanted not merely to drive the enemy away but to destroy McClellan's army altogether.

The Seven Days' Battles began a year of success for Confederate arms. Lee continued to seek his enemies' destruction and marched to the old battlefield at Manassas to strike the forces of John Pope. While Jackson fixed Pope's attention and fended off Federal attacks, Lee maneuvered James Longstreet and the other half of the Confederate army to strike Pope's flank. Second Manassas was a resounding Confederate victory, but still less than Lee's dream of annihilating a major Union army.

In the hope of fighting a decisive battle on Northern soil, Lee led his army into Maryland as part of a dual offensive in that state and in Kentucky. En route, however, a copy of Lee's invasion order fell into Union hands and under the eyes of McClellan, who was once more in command of the primary Union army in the East. Lee scrambled to reconcentrate his forces while McClellan moved cautiously to strike Lee's divided command. The armies met at Sharpsburg, Maryland, across Antietam Creek, and the battle became the bloodiest single day of the war. The Army of Northern Virginia barely survived a tactical draw, but Lee abandoned his invasion and retreated back into Virginia.

The campaigns of 1862 in Virginia concluded on the Rappahannock River at Fredericksburg on December 13. Ambrose E. Burnside, next to command the Federal Army of the Potomac, attacked Lee's army entrenched south of the city. The result was a massacre of Federal troops, who never breached Lee's lines.

The spring of 1863 brought a new Federal commander to challenge Lee. Joseph Hooker attempted to sweep across the Rappahannock and strike Lee's flank and rear. Lee set most of his army in motion to meet Hooker, and the armies collided in a sparsely settled region near a crossroads called Chancellorsville. Then Lee learned that Hooker's flank was unsecure, and he dispatched Jackson with his entire corps to envelop the Federals. Jackson's attack was devastating, but in the wake of the success, Jackson himself fell, accidentally wounded at the hands of some of his own troops. With J. E. B. Stuart in charge of Jackson's corps, Lee was able to unite the two wings of his army and press Hooker severely. But even at Chancellorsville in what many consider Lee's greatest battle, the Army of Northern Virginia was unable to destroy the Army of the Potomac.

Still hoping for a climactic victory, Lee once more marched north, this time into Pennsylvania. He met the Federals and the new commander George G. Meade at Gettysburg. On July 1, 1863, the Confederates captured the town and drove their enemies onto Cemetery Hill and Ridge. But Richard S. Ewell, in command of one of Lee's three corps, stopped, following to the letter Lee's orders against a general engagement before the entire army arrived. The next day, July 2, Longstreet's corps sought the Federal left flank, found it, and fought a desperate but drawn battle at Little and Big Round Tops and within Devil's Den. Late in the day Stuart arrived with news of his raiding, but with no reliable reconnaissance reports of the strength and disposition of Meade's army. Nevertheless, Lee determined to attack again—to make one last attempt at a battle of annihilation. He decided to try to break the center of the Federal lines on Cemetery Ridge.

Pickett's Charge was a debacle reminiscent of Malvern Hill. Lee took the risk because he believed he had to in order to achieve victory. He had come too far, worked too hard, to

shrink from what he perceived to be the moment of truth. He lost.

After the Army of Northern Virginia had limped back into northern Virginia in August, Lee submitted his resignation to the president. He pointed out that he had been ill the previous spring (likely with the heart disease that eventually killed him) and had never really recovered. He argued that because he had not been successful, the president should install another in his place. Davis declined to accept the resignation and told Lee that he knew no one better to command the army.

Lee, however, was still unwell. He was compelled to conduct his abortive Bristoe Station campaign (October 9–22) from a wagon instead of horseback. Yet Bristoe Station and Mine Run, which followed in November, demonstrated that Lee was still intent on victory and still capable of stratagems designed to lay waste his enemy.

Throughout the winter of 1863–1864 Lee labored to conserve his resources and himself. He ordered rigorous inspections throughout his army to ensure that men and equipment would be ready for the spring and to emphasize the need to husband their dwindling supplies. His new opponent was Ulysses S. Grant, now commander in chief of Union armies. Grant elected to exercise his far-flung command from a headquarters in Meade's army opposite Lee.

During the first week of May in 1864 Grant crossed the Rapidan River and plunged into an area known locally as the Wilderness. Lee let the Federals cross the river and waited to strike until the Wilderness compelled the Federals to disperse their superior numbers and even the odds. From a tactical perspective Lee won in the Wilderness; but Grant did not withdraw and lick his wounds as other Union commanders had done. Grant put his army in motion, east and south, to try to force his way between Lee and Richmond. Lee was just resourceful enough to block Grant's march at Spotsylvania Court House. There the armies again came to grips, and again Grant recoiled and resumed his drive to the east and south. Lee continued his canny counterpunching until the armies came near Cold Harbor, very close to the site of the fighting two years before at Gaines' Mill. Then Grant tried to break through the center of Lee's long line and failed disastrously.

In the wake of Cold Harbor, however, Lee lost his enemy: Stuart was dead, and his cavalry was unable to determine Federal intentions. When Grant's army reappeared, it was south of the James marching on Petersburg, a crucial railroad junction south of Richmond. Inspired fighting and blind luck held Petersburg long enough for Lee to reinforce the defenders. Then Lee again became the "King of Spades." He used trenches to compensate for his inferiority in numbers and held his lines around Petersburg and the line of forts north of the James, east of Richmond, for the next nine and a half months.

Both commanders attempted to break the trench stalemate. For his part Lee dispatched Jubal Early to Lynchburg, down the Shenandoah Valley, and to the outskirts of Washington in hopes of fighting Federals outside of prepared fortifications. And Lee attempted to break the Federal lines and trap his enemies in their holes on several occasions. Ultimately, though, he was himself trapped in a war of attrition that he had worked to avoid. Eventually, on April 1, 1865, Lee's lines became too thin and too short; he had to evacuate his works and Richmond on April 2.

> Even as he lived, Lee became a legend. . . . Lee became something of a Christ figure for the defeated Southern Confederates.

The Army of Northern Virginia survived in flight for only one week. On April 9, 1865, Lee surrendered to Grant at Appomattox Courthouse. The Confederacy lived little longer than Lee's army.

In peace Lee stood for sectional reconciliation. He accepted the presidency of Washington College in Lexington, Virginia, and attempted to educate a new generation of Southerners to cope with an altered reality in the South. He established a balance in the curriculum between the traditional classical education and the more practical disciplines in science and engineering. He introduced elective courses and supplanted the many rules governing student conduct with one: students should conduct themselves as gentlemen. In Lee's mind conducting oneself as a gentleman was essentially a matter of selfless concern for other people. "The great duty in life," he once wrote, "is the promotion of the happiness and welfare of others."

Even as he lived, Lee became a legend. Southerners needed Lee to prove that good people can and do lose and to demonstrate that success in battle or elsewhere does not necessarily denote superiority. Lee became something of a Christ figure for the defeated Southern Confederates.

Cardiovascular troubles, probably dating from the war period, increasingly plagued Lee in Lexington. During the spring of 1870 he took an extended trip into the Deep South, ostensibly for his health, more likely as a farewell tour. Because he knew or sensed that he was dying, he agreed to sit for a portrait and pose for a statue, acts he had loathed in the past, during the summer of 1870.

Then one evening in the fall Lee came home late from a vestry meeting and suffered a stroke as he attempted to bless his supper. He lingered a time in a passive state, and on October 13, 1870, he died.

[See also Arlington House; Army of Northern Virginia; Lee Memorial Association; Lee Monument Association.]

BIBLIOGRAPHY

Connelly, Thomas L. *The Marble Man: Robert E. Lee and His Image in American Society.* New York, 1977.

Dowdey, Clifford. *Lee.* Boston, 1965.

Dowdey, Clifford, and Louis H. Manarin, eds. *The Wartime Papers of R. E. Lee.* Boston, 1961.

Freeman, Douglas S. *R. E. Lee: A Biography.* 4 vols. New York, 1934–1935.

Lee, Robert E. [Jr.]. *Recollections and Letters of General Robert E. Lee.* Garden City, N.Y., 1924.

Sanborn, Margaret. *Robert E. Lee.* 2 vols. Philadelphia, 1966–1967.

EMORY M. THOMAS

LEE, STEPHEN D.

LEE, STEPHEN D. (1833–1908), lieutenant general. Lee was born September 22, 1833, at Charleston, South Carolina. His mother died when he was quite young, and he and a sister were raised by their financially unsuccessful physician father. Stephen was named for one of his uncles, who ran a military boarding school where Stephen received all of his early formal education. Appointed to West Point, he graduated in 1854, seventeenth out of forty-six.

Lee spent nearly seven years on active duty in the U.S. Army. He saw combat in Florida during the Third Seminole War and along the Kansas-Missouri border. Lee impressed his superiors with his organizational and administrative capabilities. The young Lee displayed no deep concern for politics, but his sentiments were unquestionably proslavery and thoroughly Southern.

At the outset of the Civil War, Lee was appointed a captain in South Carolina's regular artillery service. He served during the Fort Sumter episode as an aide-de-camp to Brig. Gen. P. G. T. Beauregard. The ensuing year constituted the high point of his practical military education. He emerged distinguished from the mass of other junior officers, reflecting and always infusing professionalism. Above all else, he had a certain air of competence. Some observers perceived him to be dashing and inspiring, and many were impressed with his ingenuity and his courage. Although he was bold in combat—some critics later would say he was audacious to a fault—he never attracted notice for any oddity.

Lee rose eventually to become a lieutenant general at thirty, the youngest man in the war to attain that rank. He did not attain independent command until 1863 and oversaw only small bodies of troops until August 1864. Lee commanded an artillery battery during late 1861 and an artillery battalion in the Peninsular campaign. He briefly headed the Fourth Virginia Cavalry early in mid-1862 and won notice as an artillery commander at Second Manassas and at Sharpsburg. Lee defeated William Tecumseh Sherman at

Chickasaw Bayou, helped with the defense of Vicksburg, and commanded all the cavalry in Mississippi in late 1863 and early 1864. He rose to military department command, the only one of Nathan Bedford Forrest's superiors to work well with that eccentric genius. He finally attained a corps command with the Army of Tennessee.

Late in the war Lee married a Mississippi woman and thereafter lived in his wife's home, which is now a museum and historical pilgrimage headquarters. After the war Lee worked as an insurance salesman, served in the Mississippi senate, and headed the A. & M. College of Mississippi. He was deeply committed to and involved with the establishment and early management of the Vicksburg National Military Park and helped found the United Confederate Veterans, which he served as commander in chief during the last four years of his life. He died May 28, 1908, and is buried in Friendship Cemetery, Columbus, Mississippi.

BIBLIOGRAPHY

Davis, William C., ed. *The Confederate General*. Vol. 4. Harrisburg, Pa., 1991.
Hattaway, Herman. *General Stephen D. Lee*. Jackson, Miss., 1976.

HERMAN HATTAWAY

LEE, WILLIAM HENRY FITZHUGH

LEE, WILLIAM HENRY FITZHUGH (1837– 1891), major general and U.S. congressman. Born May 31, 1837, to Mary Custis Lee and Robert E. Lee at Arlington, "Rooney" Lee attended Harvard, inspired a damning passage in classmate Henry Adams's *Autobiography* ("the Southerner has no mind"), and left without graduating to accept a direct commission in the U.S. Army in 1857. Lee resigned his commission in 1859 to marry and become a farmer at White House on the Pamunkey River in Virginia.

After Virginia seceded, Lee enlisted in the Confederate army, initially as a captain of cavalry. He served with W. W. Loring in western (present-day West) Virginia during the summer and fall of 1861. By early 1862 he was at Fredericksburg in command of the Ninth Virginia Cavalry. He led this regiment on J. E. B. Stuart's Ride around McClellan in June 1862 and served with Stuart in the Army of Northern Virginia thereafter. Promoted to brigadier general for bravery at South Mountain, Lee participated in raids and reconnaissance during the period in which Confederate cavalry dominated in the East. Then at Brandy Station on June 9, 1863, Lee suffered a wound in his leg and was cap-

tured soon after while he recuperated at his wife's home near Richmond.

Imprisoned at Fort Monroe and Fort Lafayette until exchanged in March 1864, Lee afterward resumed active service. On April 23, 1864, he became at the age of thirty-six the youngest major general in the Confederate army. By the time his father surrendered at Appomattox, Lee was second in command of cavalry in the Army of Northern Virginia.

After the war Lee rebuilt his farm and his life. His first wife had died while he was a prisoner of war, and in 1867 he remarried. Lee became president of the Virginia Agricultural Society, state senator (1875–1878), and U.S. congressman (1886–1891). Likely the most successful of the Lee children, Rooney Lee died October 15, 1891.

BIBLIOGRAPHY

Freeman, Douglas S. *R. E. Lee: A Biography*. 4 vols. New York, 1934–1935.
Thomas, Emory M. *Bold Dragoon: The Life of J. E. B. Stuart*. New York, 1986.

EMORY M. THOMAS

LEE MEMORIAL ASSOCIATION

The Robert E. Lee Memorial Association is a nonprofit organization that owns and operates Stratford Hall Plantation, Lee's birthplace in Westmoreland County, Virginia. It was formed in 1929 under the leadership of Mrs. Charles D. Lanier to purchase Stratford. The Great House and outbuildings at Stratford were restored under the direction of noted architect Fiske Kimball. The all-female governing board has a member from each state of the Union, the District of Columbia, and Great Britain. A leading benefactor and board member was Mrs. Alfred I. duPont, in whose honor a research library was named at its inception in 1980.

Stratford was built by Thomas Lee about 1738. Two signers of the Declaration of Independence, Richard Henry Lee and Francis Lightfoot Lee, grew up there. A later resident was General Lee's father, Henry ("Light Horse Harry") Lee, the brilliant Revolutionary War cavalry leader. His wife, Ann Hill Carter Lee, gave birth to their fourth son, Robert Edward, at Stratford on January 19, 1807. Lee lived at Stratford for only three and a half years, however. The plantation was sold by the Lee family in 1822 and remained in other private hands until purchased by the association.

The mission of the association today is to preserve and interpret Stratford and to educate the public on the historical significance of Robert E. Lee and other family members. In 1981 the association initiated an annual summer seminar for history teachers. It sponsors special events and annual open houses on General Lee's birthday and July 4. Special tours include one on Children's Days. Others concern architecture, the farm, gardens and decorative arts.

[*See also* Lee Monument Association.]

BIBLIOGRAPHY

Armes, Ethel. *Stratford Hall: The Great House of the Lees.* Richmond, Va., 1936.
Dill, Alonzo T., and Mary Tyler Cheek. *A Visit to Stratford and the Story of the Lees.* Stratford, Va., 1986.
Nagel, Paul C. *The Lees of Virginia: Seven Generations of an American Family.* New York, 1990.

C. VAUGHAN STANLEY

LEE MONUMENT ASSOCIATION

The Lee Monument Association, which played an important role in ensuring the prominent place of Robert E. Lee among the heroes of the Lost Cause, first organized in 1870 shortly after the general's death. At the behest of Jubal Early, veterans of the Army of Northern Virginia met in Richmond, resolved to erect a monument to Lee in the former Confederate capital, and began a regionwide fund-raising campaign. Initially the association competed with similar groups, including the Lee Memorial Association that dedicated a statue to Lee at Washington and Lee University in 1883.

In 1886, Virginia Governor Fitzhugh Lee, a veteran and nephew of the Confederate commander, reorganized the Lee Monument Association under a board composed of state officials and representatives from Richmond's Ladies' Lee Memorial Association, which had raised more money than any other group. With Fitzhugh Lee's leadership and contributions from Early and Lee Camp, a newly formed Confederate veterans' group in Richmond, the reorganized Lee Monument Association raised the remainder of the necessary funds. Its board selected a sculptor, Frenchman Jean Antoine Merciè, chose a site on the edge of one of Richmond's growing suburbs, and dedicated the statue's base in 1887. Three years later, on May 29, 1890, a crowd of over 100,000 gathered to watch the unveiling of Merciè's majestic mounted Lee and to celebrate not only the general but the Confederacy. Later, when statues to other Confederate leaders were erected near that of Lee, Richmond's Monument Avenue became a major shrine to the Lost Cause.

[*See also* Lee Memorial Association.]

BIBLIOGRAPHY

Connelly, Thomas L. *The Marble Man: Robert E. Lee and His Image in American Society.* New York, 1977.
Foster, Gaines M. *Ghosts of the Confederacy: Defeat, the Lost Cause, and the Emergence of the New South, 1865 to 1913.* New York, 1987.

GAINES M. FOSTER

LETCHER, JOHN

LETCHER, JOHN (1813–1882), governor of Virginia. Letcher grew up in the comfortable middle class in Lexington, Virginia, in the Shenandoah Valley. Optimistic and gregarious, he became a lawyer and for a while edited a local newspaper. Politics was his real calling, and Letcher gradually rose as a moderate Jacksonian Democrat. As a delegate to the state convention of 1850–1851, he helped write a more liberal constitution for Virginia, and in return the voters in his district elected him to Congress for four consecutive terms from 1851 to 1859. There he was a moderate conservative as the South came under increasing pressure from the rising Republican party. In 1859 he won the governorship in a close contest with the disintegrating Whig party.

On January 1, 1860, forty-six-year-old Letcher and his large family moved into the governor's mansion in Richmond to begin his four-year term as the nation stumbled toward civil war. Still a moderate, he championed "prudence and moderation . . . conciliation and compromise" and only grudgingly went along with increased military preparations. In the November presidential election he supported Stephen A. Douglas, the Northern Democratic candidate, and after Abraham Lincoln's victory, he unsuccessfully resisted the calling of a state convention. Only after war erupted, Lincoln called for troops, and the Virginia convention voted to secede did Letcher lead his state out of the Union and into the new Confederacy.

Now Governor Letcher was the wartime leader of the most powerful state in the Confederacy; he had a new role to play. Working frantically to mobilize Virginia for total war, Letcher performed efficiently, and even many secessionists conceded that he was finally doing well. He appointed Matthew Fontaine Maury and other able men to his Advisory Council, and aware of his own lack of military experience, he often followed their suggestions. Letcher appointed Robert E. Lee to command the Virginia forces, and among the many other officers he commissioned was Thomas J. Jackson, soon to be known as "Stonewall."

Virginia's rapid mobilization produced more volunteers than weapons, but even so the governor loaned some scarce equipment to other states. A practical man, he knew the Southern states had to cooperate to win. Even more important, he realized that they would have to close ranks behind the Confederate government, which was now moving to Richmond. Letcher's confidence in President Jefferson Davis encouraged his cooperation with the Confederates as did the presence of massive Federal forces on Virginia's borders. But mainly common sense told him that old concepts of state rights, individual freedoms, and strict legalism would have to yield to the immediate demands of the war effort. This pragmatic acceptance of Confederate leadership was the hallmark of his administration.

Soon the war became a grinding battle of attrition, and the Confederacy in April 1862 acted to hold its one-year volunteers in the ranks and to mobilize able-bodied civilians by enacting the first national draft in American history. A storm of protests arose, and some states never fully cooperated with this radical but necessary measure. In private correspondence with other Southern governors Letcher denounced the new draft as unnecessary and unconstitutional, naively assuming that each state would effectively mobilize its own manpower, but he also advised his fellow governors to support Confederate conscription for the duration of the war and only then to challenge it in the courts. Again Letcher followed a win-the-war-first policy, and publicly he ordered Virginia officials to enforce the new draft.

He also cooperated with Confederate call-ups of Virginia's rapidly dwindling militia forces, despite protests from affected counties. Uneasy about vulnerable areas of the state, he backed a small, independent state force, the Virginia State Line, which did not accept men eligible for the draft. Despite Confederate complaints the governor uncharacteristically continued to support this inept little "army" until the legislature disbanded it in February 1863.

Letcher wanted the Line to protect vital saltworks in the southwestern part of the state. The South needed this essential preservative, and Virginia had some of the main sources. In the fall of 1862 the legislature passed the problem of fair distribution at reasonable prices on to the governor and gave him sweeping new powers. Letcher became the salt czar of Virginia, but he failed to establish an efficient statewide system. He hesitated to seize uncooperative saltworks and to fix prices, and he often got tangled in red tape. Early in 1863 the legislature transferred his powers to another state agency, but the salt program continued to falter.

At every level Southerners had difficulty establishing sweeping new administrative policies, and they failed to control inflation. Governor Letcher often denounced "speculators" and "extortioners," but neither he nor the legislature nor any Confederate officials could long check soaring prices that were undermining the South's economy.

Letcher also failed to prevent the Northwest's secession from the state of Virginia, but this too was a problem beyond his or the Confederates' control; the Unionists in that region were too powerful. He also failed to rouse his people with stirring oratory; his speeches were usually loaded with tedious accumulations of facts and statistics.

Clearly he had weaknesses as a popular leader, but he seldom wavered in his selfless support of the Confederate war effort, even as attacks on the Davis administration escalated. Letcher tolerated Confederate impressment of civilian property, a practice he detested and had hesitated to employ in his salt program. Even the impressment of slaves, which infuriated many planters, gained the resigned support of the governor who wanted above all to win the war.

Letcher's continuing cooperation with the Confederates became increasingly unpopular with the conservative people of Virginia. The legislature moved from complaints to actual

> **Letcher's continuing cooperation with the Confederates became increasingly unpopular with the conservative people of Virginia.**

investigations of his salt program, his support for impressment, and especially his call-ups of militia units. Letcher defended himself ably—he was handling difficult programs that were vital to the war effort—and he was never officially censured. Nevertheless, the legislators' message was clear: do not be so quick to put Confederate needs before the traditional rights and privileges of Virginians.

An experienced politician, Letcher understood, and he did ease up a little, but basically he continued to support President Davis's administration. During 1863, the last year of his governorship, the Confederates and to a lesser extent the Virginia legislature took over many of Letcher's responsibilities as he planned to continue his career by running for the Confederate Congress in his old congressional district. His supporters conducted a brief campaign, but on May 28 he lost to the incumbent. The voters had spoken: Letcher had been too much a Confederate and not enough a Virginian. Shaken by this first major defeat at the polls and economically hurt by the raging inflation in Richmond, he completed his term of office, still hoping that President Davis and General Lee could achieve victory.

Early in January 1864 Letcher and his family returned to Lexington where he continued to support the Confederate war effort as a private citizen. In June a Union army briefly occupied Lexington, and the Northern troops destroyed a few mills and salt supplies, the Virginia Military Institute, and Letcher's home—another crude but clear recognition of his service to the Southern cause.

Early in the spring of 1865 the battered Confederacy finally collapsed, and on May 17 Letcher was arrested and taken to Washington where he remained in prison for almost seven weeks. Paroled on July 10, he returned to Lexington, championed sectional reconciliation, and resumed the practice of law. In the mid-1870s he served a term in the state legislature, but his health declined rapidly. On January 26, 1882, he died at home, once again an American, a Southerner, and a Virginian.

BIBLIOGRAPHY

Boney, F. N. "Governor Letcher's Candid Correspondence." *Civil War History* 10 (1964): 167–180.

Boney, F. N. *John Letcher of Virginia: The Story of Virginia's Civil War Governor.* University, Ala., 1966.

Boney, F. N. "John Letcher: Pragmatic Confederate Patriot." In *The Governors of Virginia: 1860–1978.* Edited by Edward Younger and James Tice Moore. Charlottesville, Va., 1982.

Boney, F. N. *Southerners All.* Macon, Ga., 1990.

Boney, F. N. "Virginia." In *The Confederate Governors.* Edited by W. Buck Yearns. Athens, Ga., 1985.

Dabney, Virginius. *Virginia: The New Dominion.* New York, 1971.

Thomas, Emory M. *The Confederate Nation: 1861–1865.* New York, 1979.

F. N. BONEY

LIBBY PRISON

In March 1862, the Confederates required the Richmond, Virginia, firm of Libby and Son, ship chandlers and grocers, to vacate its premises so that it could be used to hold prisoners. The Libbys left behind their business sign, which gave their name to one of the Confederacy's better known prisons. Located on Cary Street with the James and Kanawha Canal and the James River itself in the rear, it was a brick building about 300 feet long and 103 feet deep. Although it seemed to be one structure, interior brick walls divided it into thirds. It had three floors plus a basement. Barred windows, many of

> **City water drawn from the James provided for drinking and washing and also flushed primitive water closets. . . .**

them unglazed, provided ventilation. City water drawn from the James provided for drinking and washing and also flushed primitive water closets, a rare amenity in Civil War prisons.

Libby's commander during most of the war was Thomas P. Turner. A Virginian who had attended but not completed both West Point and Virginia Military Institute, he began as a lieu-

tenant and ended as a major. He also supervised other Richmond prisons. The jailer under him was an enlisted man, the unrelated Richard R. Turner. A prewar overseer, Dick Turner was a large, often angry and violent man whom most prisoners came to despise and in their recollections often confused with his superior. Prisoners also tended to dislike the officious clerk, Erasmus Ross. The staff came to include blacks captured from the Union who were made to do cleaning and other menial work. The guards were drawn from local military companies.

Because of its division into several parts, it was possible to segregate several types of prisoners within Libby. At first a few political prisoners were held there, but soon it was used exclusively for prisoners of war. Although some privates were occasionally held in certain rooms later in the war, the Confederates used Libby almost entirely as an officers' prison. Because the headquarters of the Richmond prisons was in the building, many men who were being taken elsewhere were brought in to be registered, and thus a large number of prisoners later recalled having been "in Libby." During the war perhaps 125,000 prisoners actually stayed in Libby, of whom about 40,000 to 50,000 were held for a prolonged time.

The prison was most crowded between May 1863, when regular exchange of officers ceased, and May 1864, when the Confederates transferred most of the officers, using Libby thereafter mainly for transients. During the congested period, over three thousand officers complained of lack of space, cold, vermin, and short rations. Most of the officers, however, had access to money with which they purchased additional comforts, and their hardships never approximated those of the enlisted men imprisoned at Richmond nor did more than a handful die. Nonetheless, because many were highly literate they were able to circulate their understandable complaints about their imprisonment and quickly made Libby infamous.

Unhappy prisoners sometimes escaped individually, and on February 9, 1864, 109 made the Civil War's best known escape through a tunnel, with 48 being recaptured. Correctly believing that some of the others had been helped by sympathizers in the city, the Confederates attempted to stop signaling through hand gestures and cloths by shooting at prisoners who appeared at windows. In March 1864, in an effort to intimidate the prisoners and prevent an uprising in support of the Kilpatrick-Dahlgren raid on Richmond, the Confederates buried several hundred pounds of gunpowder in the basement. They later claimed that since they had informed the prisoners, this was simply a bloodless warning, but the Federals effectively featured it in their propaganda during and after the war. At the war's end, the United States used Libby for a time to confine Confederates, including Dick Turner. After reverting to commercial uses, the building was dismantled in 1888 and 1889, reerected as a museum in

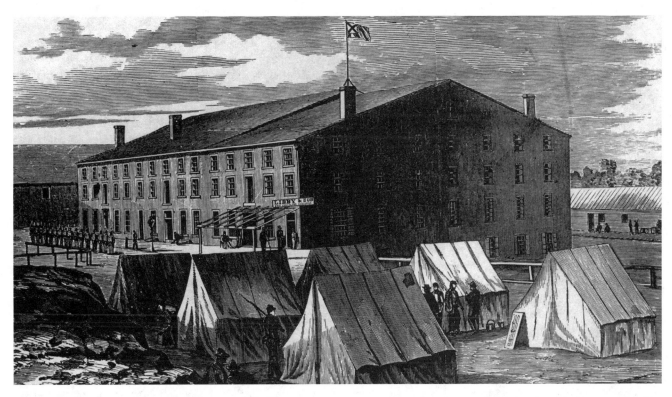

LIBBY PRISON, RICHMOND, VIRGINIA. Sketch from a photograph.

Chicago, and later demolished. There are remnants of it still in that vicinity.

BIBLIOGRAPHY

Byrne, Frank L. "Libby Prison: A Study in Emotions."*Journal of Southern History* 24 (1958): 430–444.
Byrne, Frank L. "Prison Pens of Suffering." In *Fighting for Time*. Vol. 4 of *The Image of War, 1861–1865*. Edited by William C. Davis. Garden City, N.Y., 1983.
Hesseltine, William B. *Civil War Prisons: A Study in War Psychology.* Columbus, Ohio, 1930. Reprint, New York, 1964.
Parker, Sandra V. *Richmond's Civil War Prisons.* Lynchburg, Va., 1990.

FRANK L. BYRNE

LINCOLN, ABRAHAM

[*This entry is composed of two articles*, Image of Lincoln in the Confederacy, *which discusses Confederates' views of the Republican ticket in the 1860 presidential election and of Abraham Lincoln himself, and* Assassination of Lincoln, *which discusses John Wilkes Booth's plot to assassinate Lincoln. For further discussion of Confederates' views of*

Lincoln, see Election of 1860 *and* Republican Party. *For further discussion of the plot to assassinate Lincoln, see* Booth, John Wilkes, *and* Espionage, *articles on* Confederate Secret Service *and* Confederate Military Spies.]

Image of Lincoln in the Confederacy

The presidential election of 1860 did little to educate voters of the South about Abraham Lincoln, the Republican candidate. The campaign was waged in the North as a contest between Northern Democrats and Republicans, and in the South, between Southern Democrats and Constitutional Unionists; little dialogue between the sections occurred. The distorted image of Lincoln as an abolitionist (which he had never been) carried over into the Confederacy. Once war broke out, Confederates added to this core image of radicalism the usual scurrilous allegations made by one belligerent about the other.

The Confederates' descriptions of Lincoln in the press and popular literature mostly constituted perverse opposites or antic caricatures of his genuine traits. A teetotaler, Lincoln was assumed by Confederates to be a habitual inebriate. Although he had little formal education, their depiction of him as an ignorant illiterate would repeatedly be refuted by public letters and speeches of memorable eloquence and clarity. Lincoln may have seemed a coward to swaggering and militant secessionists because of his unfortunate decision to heed advisers' fears of assassination and to travel in secret through Baltimore to Washington for his inauguration in 1861. Yet from youthful tests of physical strength on the frontier to reckless exposure to enemy fire when Confederates neared Washington in 1864, Lincoln proved generally oblivious to problems of personal safety. Likewise, to depict Lincoln as a corrupt profiteer, as Confederates occasionally did, was to run counter to his consistent personal honesty in money matters. All such images were quite off the mark.

A more durable accusation focused on alleged atrocities committed by Union soldiers in the South during the war. Jefferson Davis himself initiated this tactic even before First Manassas. On July 20, 1861, the Confederate president jeered at Lincoln's recent message to the U.S. Congress and denounced to the Congress in Richmond as "rapine" the destruction of "private residences in peaceful rural retreats," the "outrages [i.e., rapes] committed on defenseless females by soldiers," and the "deliberate malignity" of denying medicines to "the sick, including the women and children" by declaring them contraband of war—in short, "waging an indiscriminate war upon. . . all, with a savage ferocity unknown to modern civilization." William Tecumseh Sherman's image would come to bear the brunt of these accusations, levied from 1861 to this day in the South, while in the end Lincoln's would by and large escape them.

One Confederate accusation, also raised early by Jefferson Davis, would stick: that the North's president was a tyrant who crushed civil liberties and rode roughshod over the U.S. Constitution. This charge, consistent with Southern antebellum complaints about Northern policies, also served Davis well, as historian Paul Escott has shrewdly observed, in keeping the focus of the Confederate citizenry on preserving white liberty from Northern aggression rather than on defending black slavery, an institution whose profits were not enjoyed equally by all classes of Southern citizens. Finally, unlike the demonic pieces of character assassination and popular billingsgate, this charge had some substance. Denouncing Lincoln's arrogation to himself of the power to suspend the privilege of the writ of habeas corpus, Davis said in the summer of 1861, "We may well rejoice that we have forever severed our connection with a government that thus tramples on all the principles of constitutional liberty."

When Lincoln announced the preliminary Emancipation Proclamation on September 22, 1862, he fulfilled Southern fears of his abolitionism. On this issue popular vituperation could hardly be distinguished from the criticism by high-ranking Confederate officials. Virtually all regarded it as a monstrous and criminal invitation to slaves to murder their masters. Davis said in his January 12, 1863, message to Congress, that the document "encouraged [slaves] to a general assassination of their masters," but he added the sophisticated argument that emancipation would mean "extermina-

tion" of the black race in America, as they would surely die out in hopeless competition with the allegedly superior white race.

Eventually Davis himself embraced emancipation (as a reward for black military service), but the desperate idea came too late in Confederate history to be put into effect. Davis's increasing difficulties in quelling dissent, desertion, and draft resistance also led him to adopt a policy on civil liberties that Confederate critics in the press likened to Lincoln's. In other words, Davis and Lincoln came to fight the war in similar ways, as historian David Donald pointed out in 1978, using conscription and avoiding realistic taxation. Yet to this day most historians retain images of Davis and Lincoln as opposites.

The notion, born of Lincoln's reputation for personal charity and forgiveness, that Lincoln would not have reconstructed the Southern racial order had he lived contained genuine power to soften Lincoln's image in the South after the war was over. Eventually, Davis's reputation would fall, even among Southerners, and Lincoln's would rise.

In truth, the Confederate view of Lincoln contained little beyond what Northern Democrats said of Lincoln during the Civil War. For example, Roger B. Taney's decision in *Ex parte Merryman,* declaring Lincoln's suspension of the writ of habeas corpus illegal, became Confederate propaganda when it was reprinted in Jackson, Mississippi, and New Orleans during the war. And *Abraham Africanus I,* a political pamphlet published in New York in 1864, would have found a welcoming audience in the Confederacy. Only the intensity of feeling against Lincoln was greater among Confederates than among his determined Northern critics-and even the intensity was finally matched by John Wilkes Booth and his little band of Confederate sympathizers.

BIBLIOGRAPHY

Davis, Michael. *The Image of Lincoln in the South.* Knoxville, Tenn., 1971.

Donald, David Herbert. *Liberty and Union: The Crisis of Popular Government, 1830–1890.* Boston, 1978.

Escott, Paul D. *After Secession: Jefferson Davis and the Failure of Confederate Nationalism.* Baton Rouge, La., 1978.

MARK E. NEELY, JR.

Assassination of Lincoln

"Damn the rebels! This is their work," exclaimed U.S. Secretary of the Navy Gideon Welles when he first learned of Lincoln's assassination. Many other Northerners naturally leaped to the same conclusion, and President Andrew Johnson issued a proclamation on May 2, 1865, offering rewards for the arrest of Jefferson Davis along with Jacob

Thompson, Clement C. Clay, Beverly Tucker, and George N. Sanders, identified as "rebels and traitors . . . harbored in Canada," for conspiring to procure the murder of President Lincoln. These prominent Confederates escaped prosecution, but the military trial of Booth's co-conspirators and Maryland associates was guided by the theory that the assassination was a Confederate plot.

That now seems very unlikely, though many persons active at one time or another in the Confederate cause were involved with John Wilkes Booth, the actor who shot Lincoln and who identified himself as "a Confederate . . . doing duty *upon his own responsibility.*" Booth's original idea, hatched in the overheated election summer of 1864, was to kidnap Lincoln, take him to Richmond, and perhaps exchange him for Confederate prisoners of war. Late in the year Booth visited Montreal, where he stayed in a hotel notorious as a haunt of Confederate agents. In Maryland and Washington he recruited for his political crime two former Confederate soldiers, Samuel Arnold and Michael O'Laughlin; an escaped Confederate prisoner of war, Lewis Payne; a Confederate spy, John H. Surratt; and at least two other men.

By the time he gathered the conspirators, Booth had lost his opportunity (he planned to capture Lincoln as he rode to the Soldiers Home, where the president slept during Washington's hot summer months). When he decided instead to kidnap Lincoln from a theater—the president's appreciation of drama was well known—several men dropped out of Booth's plot. Very late he decided on assassination rather than kidnapping. He shot the president on April 14, 1865, and Payne gravely wounded Secretary of State William H. Seward. Apparently the conspirators hoped, by killing high government officials, to bring about a change that would yet save the Confederacy.

> . . . prominent Confederates escaped prosecution, but the military trial . . . was guided by the theory that the assassination was a Confederate plot.

Booth escaped for a time after the murder and was aided by the Confederate spy Thomas A. Jones of Maryland, who years later wrote a book about these experiences. A Union cavalryman finally shot the assassin dead against orders.

Attempts by the U.S. War Department to implicate Confederate officials stumbled conspicuously in 1866 when a congressional committee discovered that government witness Sanford Conover and others had given perjured testimony. The cooling of Civil War passions caused further decline in belief in the existence of a Confederate assassination plot. Gradually, the theory triumphed that the crime

was entirely Booth's inspiration, and even his pro-Confederate political motivation was soft-pedaled by (unconvincing) assertions that he was a deranged actor whose career was faltering.

Eventually some sentimentalists emphasized the expressions of dismay heard in the states of the Confederacy at the time of Lincoln's assassination. In truth, plenty of joy was also expressed in the South, and there exists no systematic, statistical evaluation of the evidence for Southern feelings about the murder of the Confederacy's nemesis, Abraham Lincoln.

BIBLIOGRAPHY

Davis, Michael. *The Image of Lincoln in the South.* Knoxville, Tenn., 1971.

Hanchett, William. *The Lincoln Murder Conspiracies.* Urbana, Ill., 1983.

Tidwell, William A., with James O. Hall and David Winfred Gaddy. *Come Retribution: The Confederate Secret Service and the Assassination of Lincoln.* Jackson, Miss., 1988.

MARK E. NEELY, JR.

LITERATURE

[*This entry is composed of two articles,* Literature in the Confederacy, *which discusses literature written in the South during the Confederacy, and* The Confederacy in Literature, *which discusses depictions of the Confederacy in literature written after the Civil War.*]

Literature in the Confederacy

Writing during the Civil War focused on the war itself and its ramifications, for the topic not only offered opportunities to established authors to develop and expand traditional themes, methods, and subject matter but also opened the way for fresh materials and approaches from new writers as well. William Gilmore Simms, Paul Hamilton Hayne, Henry Timrod, and other well-known authors continued to contribute poetry, essays, lectures, and fiction to Southern periodicals and newspapers, and such relatively new names as James Ryder Randall, Francis Orray Ticknor, and Abram Joseph Ryan began to appear in various publications. Over the four years of the war a respectable body of belles lettres made its way into print.

In the beginning, getting into print was not too difficult. One of the first calls, along with the demand for troops to fight the war, was for a literature to explain, defend, and celebrate the new nation. There had been summonses for a Southern literature since the 1840s, but the establishment of a Confederate government in 1861 led immediately to the realization that the new nation must have its own literature soon. And nowhere was this need better encapsulated than in Timrod's odes "Ethnogenesis" (February 23, 1861) and "The Cotton Boll" (September 3, 1861). These poems posit a laureatelike speaker who celebrates the new nation's past and present and prophesies a future for it in which its mission—not unlike that perceived by the United States after World War II—is to share its "mighty commerce" and many "blessings" with "mankind."

The country's purpose defined, Simms, Hayne, John Esten Cooke, John R. Thompson, and other writers of standing celebrated battles and leaders in verse on Fort Sumter, Manassas, Vicksburg, Gettysburg, Petersburg, and Richmond and on P. G. T. Beauregard, J. E. B. Stuart, Thomas J. Jackson, Robert E. Lee, and Jefferson Davis. Relative newcomers like Randall, Ticknor, Margaret Junkin Preston, and John Williamson Palmer joined the chorus. Palmer's poems, and many others, were often attributed to anonymous sources, and his best-known lyrics, "Stonewall Jackson's Way" (1862) and "In Martial Manner" (1863), made their own way without benefit of the poet's reputation.

Eloquent and patriotic poetry could readily be printed in magazines and newspapers in the early days of the conflict, but by 1864, after paper, personnel, and equipment shortages and the failure of publishers to pay contributors or of subscribers to pay for subscriptions, the number of periodicals was reduced drastically. Despite the popularity of verse in newspapers, few volumes of it were published during the period, although John H. Hewitt's *War: A Poem with Copious Notes, Founded on the Revolution of 1861–1862* (1862), Theophilus Hunter Hill's *Hesper, and Other Poems* (1861, 1863), Joseph H. Martin's *Smith and Pocahontas: A Poem* (1862), William M. Martin's *Lyrics and Sketches* (1861), and Preston's *Beechenbrook* (1865) were exceptions. Much of this poetry dealt with themes and material familiar to and widely accepted by both poets and readers.

Prose, on the other hand, could not always be so readily exchanged among newspapers as verse could. Accordingly, fiction, especially novels, more frequently appeared in book form. Serial fiction and short stories, their natural popularity notwithstanding, were usually in limited supply. Over the life span of the Confederacy, for example, fewer than thirty novels were printed or reprinted, including Augustus Baldwin Longstreet's *William Mitten* (1864), James Dabney McCabe, Jr.'s, *Aide-de-Campe* (1863), and Augusta Jane Evans's *Macaria* (1864), the most popular of all Confederate novels, and one that was written to support the Confederacy. It was characterized by the author as "the bodyguard for the liberty of the Republic." Several novels were republished-Nathaniel Beverly Tucker's *Partisan Leader* (1862), for instance. Some editions of English novels appeared, such as Charles Dickens's *Great Expectations* (1863), George Eliot's *Silas Marner* (1863), and William Makepeace Thackeray's

Adventures of Philip (1864), as well as translations of a few German and French novels. Victor Hugo's *Les Misèrables* (1863–1864) was a particular favorite of Confederate soldiers. Also available were books of humorous tales and sketches, including George W. Bagby's *The Letters of Mozis Addums to Billy Ivvins* (1862), Richard Malcolm Johnston's *Georgia Sketches* (1864), and H. O. Judd's *Look Within for Fact and Fiction* (1864), and some drama was published, such as J. J. Delchamps's *Love's Ambuscade* (1863), McCabe's *The Guerrillas* (1863), and William Russell Smith's *The Royal Ape* (1863).

Few of the more significant Southern writers published books during the period of the Confederacy, however. Hayne and Thompson, for example, collected their poems and attempted to send them to England for publication, but the manuscripts were lost in the blockade. Simms contributed one backwoods novel, "Paddy McGann," to the *Southern Illustrated News* in 1863, but it did not appear in book form until a century later. Cooke's *Life of Stonewall Jackson* was brought out by Ayres and Wade in Richmond in 1863, but his newspaper sketches of his experiences in the war were not published as a book until 1867 and his novels on the war did not begin to appear until it was over. Indeed, much good writing during the period—both poetry and prose—was neither collected nor put into book form until later, much later in the case of Randall's *Poems* (1908), Simms's *Paddy McGann* (1972), Mary Boykin Chesnut's *Diary* (1905), and William J. Grayson's *Autobiography* (1990).

Confederate publishers were scattered throughout the new nation in Raleigh, Nashville, Columbia, Charleston, Augusta, Macon, Atlanta, and New Orleans. Both West and Johnston, and Ayres and Wade, were based in Richmond, S. H. Goetzel and Company in Mobile, and Burke, Boykin, and Company in Macon. Evans and Cogswell in Charleston was one of the largest firms, but despite a prewar list that included several of Simms's novels and plays, it published little belles lettres during the war. By 1863 shortages led to books being bound in wallpaper and printed on crude wrapping paper. Many firms failed under such conditions.

Magazines and newspapers faced the same hardships. Few of the journals (almost a hundred at the beginning of the war) lasted until the cessation of hostilities. The best of them were short-lived and by 1864 could seldom pay their contributors. In May of that year, for example, Hayne sought with partial success to barter his verse for medicine with Ayres and Wade, publishers of *Southern Illustrated News* (1862–1865), who owed him $180 for contributions printed since January.

The plight of newspapers by this time was even more serious. Paper could seldom be found and printing equipment could not be kept repaired sufficiently to publish regularly. With the loss of territory resulting from the war, many papers folded or were forced to move their offices from place to place, as in the well-known flight of the *Memphis Appeal* from its original base to towns in Mississippi, Alabama, and Georgia, a situation that led it to be referred to frequently as the "Moving Appeal."

The literature of the Confederacy, as may be expected, achieved mixed results. Limited by time and the pressure of events, writers found it difficult to sustain works of any length. Simms's "Paddy McGann," Longstreet's *William Mitten,* and Evan's *Macaria* are not important novels in an aesthetic sense, and the short fiction by Bagby, Johnston, and others was hardly any more significant. The best prose on the war appeared later in novels and tales by Sherwood Bonner, George Washington Cable, Cooke, Joel Chandler Harris, Grace King, Mary Murfree, and Thomas Nelson Page, among others, and in history, biography, and diaries by Chesnut, Cooke, King, and Page. The greatest achievement in the period's literature, however, was the short poetry the war inspired. Randall's "Maryland, My Maryland," Palmer's "Stonewall Jackson's Way," and Ticknor's "Little Giffin" express patriotic fervor and have the right touch, and Timrod's lyrics are clearly the ultimate accomplishment of Confederate literature. His "Ethnogenesis," "The Cotton Boll," "A Cry to Arms," "Carolina," "Spring," "Christmas," "The Unknown Dead," and the memorial "Ode" (1866) represent a body of poetry on the war excelled only by the Northerners Walt Whitman in *Drum-Taps* (1865) and Herman Melville in *Battle-Pieces* (1866). Not a massive literary achievement, assuredly, but one not unworthy of the Lost Cause.

[*See also* Diaries, Letters, and Memoirs; Lanier, Sydney; Newspapers.]

BIBLIOGRAPHY

Hubbell, Jay B. *The South in American Literature, 1607–1900.* Durham, N.C., 1954.

London, Lawrence F. "Confederate Literature and Its Publishers." In *The James Sprunt Studies in History and Political Science.* Edited by J. C. Sitterson. Chapel Hill, N.C., 1959.

McKeithan, Daniel M., ed. *A Collection of Hayne Letters.* Austin, Tex., 1944.

Moore, Rayburn S., ed. *A Man of Letters in the Nineteenth-Century South: Selected Letters of Paul Hamilton Hayne.* Baton Rouge, La., 1982.

Muhlenfeld, Elisabeth. "The Civil War and Authorship." In *The History of Southern Literature.* Edited by Louis D. Rubin, Jr., et al. Baton Rouge, La., 1985.

Oliphant, Mary C. Simms, et al., eds. *The Letters of William Gilmore Simms.* 6 vols. Columbia, S.C., 1952–1982.

Parks, Edd Winfield, and Aileen Wells, eds. *The Collected Poems of Henry Timrod: A Variorum Edition.* Athens, Ga., 1965.

Parrish, T. Michael, and Robert M. Willingham, Jr., comps. *Confederate Imprints: A Bibliography of Southern Publications from Secession to Surrender.* Austin, Tex., 1987.

Sears, Stephen W., ed. *The Civil War: A Treasury of Art and Literature.* New York, 1992.

RAYBURN S. MOORE

The Confederacy in Literature

In his bitter requiem for the fallen Confederacy, "The Conquered Banner," Father Abram J. Ryan predicted that "its fame on brightest pages, / Penned by poets and by sages, / Shall go sounding down the ages." But even the unreconciled bard might have been amazed by the extent to which his prophecy was fulfilled, for the fact is that for well over a century the clash between the Confederacy and Union became the single most popular event in American history for fiction writers and poets.

The first to appear were those, on both sides of the struggle, who had lived through it. Among immediate postwar Southern poets, only Sydney Lanier saw much active com-

> . . . as Johnny Rebs, the Southern armies, for most readers, *were* the Confederacy. . . .

bat; his first book, a little-known novel called *Tiger-Lilies* (1867), recorded his life as soldier and prisoner of war. More successful was John Esten Cooke, who as an active participant and staff officer had gained an insider's view. Beginning in 1866 with *Surry of Eagle's-Nest,* Cooke devoted seven novels to the course of the war. But he avoided depicting the horrors of combat and instead focused on portraying heroes like Robert E. Lee, J. E. B. Stuart, and Thomas J. ("Stonewall") Jackson as avatars of the Cavaliers who, in regional myth, had fathered the Southern nation. Realism in fiction was not the mode of the day. When a Northern veteran, John W. De Forest, attempted to set down the bloodiness of battle in scenes in *Miss Ravenel's Conversion from Secession to Loyalty* (1867), he knew that readers would shrink from such gross depiction. But his novel, which also retroactively championed abolitionism, was the most faithful to actuality of any long fictional work before Stephen Crane's *The Red Badge of Courage* (1895).

Whether viewed as gallant defenders of their homeland or as Johnny Rebs, the Southern armies, for most readers, *were* the Confederacy; the domestic scene, by comparison, was thin material. But, as the scars of battle faded, writers of the defeated South embarked on a campaign of regional justification that swept the North as well. By 1888, Albion W. Tourgée, who had described his disillusioning experiences during Reconstruction in *A Fool's Errand* (1879), charged that American writing, particularly that class called "local color," had become "not only Southern in type but distinctly Confederate in sympathy." The prevailing mood was romantic nostalgia. Now that the South presented no military danger, its quixotic attempt to establish an aristocratic empire could take on the special glamour reserved for lost causes. The primary promulgator of this romanticized history was Thomas Nelson Page, whose *In Ole Virginia* (1887) and other works portrayed a vanished world of grace and honor.

Less lofty in social status were the dialect tales of Joel Chandler Harris, which replaced the image of the black as the pious and suffering Uncle Tom with the sly and engaging Uncle Remus; for the first time the rich oral tradition of black people found its way into popular writing. Harris's many other books also dealt with the middle Georgia region, most notably *Tales of the Home Folk in Peace and War* (1898). A countertrend soon became observable in the work of George Washington Cable. Though he had served as a Confederate cavalryman, Cable became increasingly liberal in his views

> By the 1890s, the historical romance had become the dominant genre throughout the nation.

about the plight of the freed blacks. He had gained wide popularity with his tales of Louisiana creoles; but when he turned to direct social criticism of the region in such books as *Dr. Sevier* (1884) and *John March, Southerner* (1894), he was treated as an apostate.

By the 1890s, the historical romance had become the dominant genre throughout the nation. The spate of newer romancers drew heavily upon types their predecessors had established—the Southern belle, the chivalrous young officer, the cantankerous old father, the faithful black retainer—and their settings were often the tall-pillared plantation home as well as the field of battle. But their plots grew more melodramatic, and the love interest became central to reader appeal. Typical of this school was Mary Johnston, whose *The Long Roll* (1911) features a Confederate captain who fights both for the cause and for the hand of his lady. Another staple plot is pivotal to Thomas Dixon's *The Southerner* (1913), whose heroine is loved by two brothers who espouse opposite sides. Dixon is also responsible for the most blatant example of the racism that could not be entirely eradicated from many Southerners' memories, *The Clansman* (1905), which furnished the plot for D. W. Griffith's *The Birth of a Nation* (1915). Even writers who were better known for other work turned to the Southern romance; examples are Winston Churchill's *The Crisis* (1901) and Upton Sinclair's *Manassas* (1906). One author, however, soon had enough of the moonlight-and-magnolia ambience; Ellen Glasgow, proclaiming that "what the South needs is blood and irony," soon proceeded to give it both, though her only novel that directly deals with the Confederacy is an early one, *The Battle-Ground* (1902).

The 1920s and 1930s saw the rise and flowering of what has been dubbed the "Southern Renaiscence"—a remark-

ably wide-ranging and acute reexamination of the legacy of the region's past. Chief among these poets, novelists, and critics were John Crowe Ransom, Donald Davidson, Robert Penn Warren, Cleanth Brooks, Merrill Moore, Andrew Lytle, and Allen Tate. These were the "inheritors"—those who by birth, ancestry, and early residence had roots deep in the Southern experience. They were hardly uncritical defenders, but they saw a decline of once-valued moral and ethical imperatives in a modern world of materialism and commercialism—views they set forth in their manifesto *I'll Take My Stand* (1930). These ideas also became themes in the literature they produced. Notable examples are the novels of Warren, particularly the Cass Mastern section in *All the King's Men* (1946), *Band of Angels* (1955), and *Wilderness* (1961). Characteristic, too, of this newer historical awareness are Andrew Lytle's *The Long Night* (1936) and Caroline Gordon's *None Shall Look Back* (1937). Allen Tate, a biographer of Stonewall Jackson and Jefferson Davis, also produced a novel, *The Fathers* (1938), an antisentimental inquiry into the moral ambiguities of the Civil War. This attitude is also central to his poem "Ode to the Confederate Dead" (1936), in which a modern man, pausing at a cemetery, ponders his relationship to the past which these buried soldiers had represented. The war is also recalled in Donald Davidson's "Lee in the Mountains" (1938); here the great general, now a college president in Virginia, reflects on his battles and his hopes for mercy and justice for his compatriots.

The greatest writer of the Renaiscence was, of course, William Faulkner, whose centrality to American writing about the South can only be suggested here. The great-grandson of a Confederate colonel, Faulkner was obsessed by all periods of Southern history, but the complex reasons for the South's defeat are central to the body of his work. A key text here is the novella "The Bear" (in *Go Down, Moses,* 1942), in which Ike McCaslin renounces his inheritance of the family plantation because of what he perceives as the human misuse of God-given land and the further curse put upon it by slavery. Among the works more directly dealing with the Confederacy are *Absalom, Absalom!* (1936), *The Unvanquished* (1938), and a number of short stories.

The 1930s and succeeding decades saw a continuation of the historical romance. Escapist reading about a vanished and glamorous past was undoubtedly the main reason for their popularity. A few, however, were characterized by a more careful portrayal of historical events and greater attention to the central fact of slavery and the legacy it had left. A representative selection would include Hervey Allen's *Action at Aquila* (1938), John Peale Bishop's *Many Thousands Gone* (1931), James Boyd's *Marching On* (1927), DuBose Heyward's *Peter Ashley* (1932), MacKinlay Kantor's *Andersonville* (1955), Joseph Stanley Pennell's *The History of Rome Hanks* (1944), a trilogy by T. S. Stribling (*The Forge,*

1931, *The Store*, 1932, *Unfinished Cathedral*, 1934), Ben Ames Williams's *House Divided* (1947), and Stark Young's *So Red the Rose* (1934). In a class by itself, because of its astonishing continued worldwide popularity both as book and film, is Margaret Mitchell's *Gone With the Wind* (1936). More recent examples are Shelby Foote's *Shiloh* (1952) and John Jakes's best-selling trilogy: *North and South* (1982), *Love and War* (1984), and *Heaven and Hell* (1987).

Whatever readers are looking for—from mere light entertainment to a desire to know more about the South and the nation it created—the Confederacy shows no present signs of dying as a subject for literature.

[*See also* Lanier, Sydney.]

BIBLIOGRAPHY

Aaron, Daniel. *The Unwritten War.* New York, 1973.
Bain, Robert, Joseph M. Flora, and Louis D. Rubin, Jr. *Southern Writers: A Biographical Dictionary.* Baton Rouge, La., 1979.
Bridges, Emily. *The South in Fiction.* Chapel Hill, N.C., 1948.
Hubbell, Jay B. *The South in Southern Literature, 1609–1900.* Durham, N.C., 1954.
Lively, Robert A. *Fiction Fights the Civil War.* Chapel Hill, N.C., 1957.
Wilson, Edmund. *Patriotic Gore.* New York, 1962.

J. V. RIDGELY

LOMAX, LUNDSFORD LINDSAY

LOMAX, LUNDSFORD LINDSAY (1835-1913), major general. Lomax was born November 4, 1835, in Newport, Rhode Island, where his father was stationed as an army major of ordinance. Young Lomax received his early education in Virginia, the family home state. He graduated in 1856 from West Point, joined the Second U.S. Cavalry, and saw frontier service against the Indians until his April 2, 1861, resignation from the army.

Lomax received a captain's commission and spent the first two years of the Confederacy in the West on the staffs of Gens. Ben McCulloch, Earl Van Dorn, and Joseph E. Johnston, respectively. In the spring of 1863, at the urging of his lifelong friend, Fitzhugh Lee, Lomax came east and accepted the colonelcy of the Eleventh Virginia Cavalry. Solid performances at Brandy Station and Gettysburg brought July 23, 1863, promotion to brigadier general. Most of Lomax's remaining service was in the Shenandoah Valley. After elevation to major general on August 10, 1864, he commanded Jubal Early's cavalry in the second Shenandoah Valley campaign. On March 29, 1865, Lomax succeeded Early in command of what was left of the Valley District.

LUNDSFORD LINDSAY LOMAX.   LIBRARY OF CONGRESS

He became a postwar farmer in Fauquier County and married a cousin of Gen. William H. Payne. In 1885 he began a four-year tenure as president of what is now Virginia Tech. He spent the next six years aiding in the compilation of the U.S. War Department's *Official Records of the Union and Confederate Armies.* In later years, as a commissioner of the Gettysburg battlefield park, Lomax played a leading role in the erection of the dominant Virginia monument across from Cemetery Ridge. He died May 28, 1913, and is buried in Warrenton, Virginia.

BIBLIOGRAPHY

Armstrong, Richard L. *Eleventh Virginia Cavalry.* Lynchburg, Va., 1989.
Hotchkiss, Jed. *Virginia.* Vol. 3 of *Confederate Military History.* Edited by Clement A. Evans. Atlanta, 1899. Vol. 4 of extended ed. Wilmington, N.C., 1987.
"Maj. Gen. L. L. Lomax." *Confederate Veteran* 21 (1913): 450. Reprint, Wilmington, N.C., 1985.

JAMES I. ROBERTSON, JR.

LONGSTREET, JAMES

LONGSTREET, JAMES (1821–1904), lieutenant general. Born January 8, 1821, on his grandparents' plantation in the Edgefield District, South Carolina, Longstreet spent most of his youth outside Gainesville, Georgia. After his father died in 1833, his mother sent him to live with his uncle, Augustus Baldwin Longstreet, humorist, minister, and an ardent secessionist in 1860, while she relocated in Alabama. James received an appointment to West Point from Alabama (Georgia's slots were filled) and entered the academy in 1838. His academic record was hardly impressive; he graduated fifty-fourth of sixty-two in the class of 1842.

With a brevet second lieutenant's commission in hand, Longstreet served with the Fourth U.S. Infantry at Jefferson Barracks in Missouri and in Louisiana. Transferring to the Eighth Infantry in 1845, he was stationed in Florida until the outbreak of the Mexican War. From 1847 to 1849, Longstreet served as regimental adjutant and fought under Gens. Zachary Taylor and Winfield Scott. Always brave and alert, Longstreet was wounded while charging the Mexican bastion at Chapultepec. His gallant behavior earned him brevets as captain on August 20 and major on September 8, 1847. After the war, Longstreet saw duty in Texas where he received a captain's commission on December 7, 1852. On July 19, 1858, he was promoted to major in the Paymaster Department in Albuquerque, New Mexico Territory. Longstreet tendered his resignation from the U.S. Army on June 1, 1861.

Longstreet (called "Old Pete" by his men) was made a brigadier general, dated June 17, and led a Virginia brigade

> ## Longstreet often lacked finesse when dealing with his fellow officers and civilian officials.

near Manassas Junction. He did not see action at First Manassas on July 21, but he had been engaged three days earlier at Blackburn's Ford where he repelled an advancing Federal brigade. The fight at Blackburn's Ford demonstrated the superiority of the defense and probably influenced Longstreet's tactical thinking for the rest of the war. He almost always preferred receiving the enemy's assault and then striking back with a well-directed counterattack.

Longstreet often lacked finesse when dealing with his fellow officers and civilian officials. Though he received a promotion to major general, dated October 7, 1861, he risked his career by supporting Gen. Joseph E. Johnston in his dispute with Jefferson Davis over strategy and by blaming the president for the army's failure to capture Washington after

Manassas. His arrogant manner and strong opinions rankled subordinates and superiors alike. Longstreet became moody and withdrawn after he lost three of his four children to scarlet fever in January 1862.

When Johnston shifted his forces to the peninsula in the spring of 1862, Longstreet directed many of the complex movements and handled responsibilities beyond his rank. During a rearguard action at Williamsburg on May 5, Longstreet tenaciously held his ground, allowing the bulk of Johnston's force to continue its retreat. He did not, however, enjoy success at Seven Pines on May 31. Johnston's confusing orders resulted in an argument between Longstreet and Maj. Gen. Benjamin Huger, which delayed the Confederate advance. Longstreet made matters worse by swinging his troops farther south than Johnston had intended, but he redeemed himself by aggressively fulfilling his orders during the Seven Days' campaign (June 25–July 1). Longstreet especially impressed his new commander, Gen. Robert E. Lee, who told Davis that "Longstreet is a Capital soldier."

When Lee reorganized the Army of Northern Virginia after the Seven Days' Battles, he gave Longstreet the right wing, which included five divisions, while giving Maj. Gen. Thomas J. ("Stonewall") Jackson only three. At Second Manassas Longstreet arrived on the field on August 29, just to the right of Jackson. Although urged by Lee to launch an attack immediately, Longstreet warned that a premature assault would not allow him to concentrate his forces. Lee acquiesced, permitting Longstreet to bring his entire command to bear on the enemy the next day, when he drove the Federals off in confusion.

Longstreet further enhanced his reputation at Sharpsburg, Maryland, on September 17. Conspicuously wearing a pair of carpet slippers because of a foot injury, Longstreet was omnipresent, encouraging his men and even holding his staff officers' horses so they could operate the cannon of a depleted battery. One of his subordinates remembered that Longstreet was "like a rock in steadiness when sometimes in battle the world seemed flying to pieces." Throughout the day he brilliantly shifted his troops to meet each Union threat. When Longstreet returned to headquarters that night, Lee embraced him and exclaimed, "Ah! here is Longstreet; here is my old *war-horse*" (which led to Longstreet's being called "Lee's War Horse" on occasion). Lee pushed for Longstreet's promotion to lieutenant general, which was approved, dated October 9. With the boost in rank, he also received command of the First Corps.

The Battle of Fredericksburg on December 13, 1862, must have confirmed Longstreet's faith in superiority of the defense. In repulsing over 25,000 Federals at Marye's Heights, he not only took advantage of the natural terrain but improved it with entrenchments. Longstreet, in fact, deserves credit as one of the first officers to demonstrate the decisive

JAMES LONGSTREET.
HARPER'S PICTORIAL HISTORY OF THE GREAT REBELLION

advantage in constructing fieldworks. During the winter, he ordered the use of traverses—earthen walls that cut across a trench and protected the flanks of the men inside.

Unable to feed his army adequately at the beginning of 1863, Lee dispatched Longstreet with two divisions of the First Corps to the area south of the James River. Although he furnished his troops with sufficient supplies, Longstreet cautiously besieged Suffolk and decided against a major assault. Controversy surrounded Longstreet's decision, since he himself had admitted that the place could be captured. Some detractors point to this failure as proof that he was not aggressive. A British observer, however, wrote that Longstreet "was never far from General Lee, who relies very much upon his judgement. By the soldiers he is invariably spoken of as 'the best fighter in the whole army.' " Because Longstreet was on detached service, he missed the Battle of Chancellorsville but marched with the army into Pennsylvania.

Longstreet and Lee collided over strategy during the Gettysburg campaign. Longstreet had favored a concentration of forces in the West, but Lee insisted on a raid into the North. Longstreet felt comfortable with his superior's plan as long as Lee would retire to a strong defensive position and force the Federals to assault the Army of Northern Virginia. When Lee decided to attack the Northern position south of

Gettysburg on July 2, Longstreet felt betrayed. Lee, in fact, rejected Longstreet's suggestion to flank the Union left that day, instructing his subordinate to press straight ahead. Unusually apathetic and sluggish in his movements, Longstreet nevertheless launched a fierce assault through the Peach Orchard and Wheat Field which nearly captured Little Round Top.

Lee continued his frontal assaults the next day against Cemetery Hill. Longstreet adamantly opposed such a move, desiring a flanking maneuver instead. Lee held firm, however, and ordered Maj. Gen. George E. Pickett's division and elements of the Third Corps to strike the Union center. Before the attack, Longstreet told artillerist Col. Edward Porter Alexander that "I do not want to make this charge. I do not see how it can succeed." Alexander thought Longstreet "obeyed *reluctantly* at Gettysburg, on the 2nd and 3rd. But it must be admitted that his judgment in both matters was sound and he owed it to Lee to be reluctant, for failure was *inevitable.*" After the battle, Longstreet privately expressed the hope that all of Lee's subordinates would share responsibility for the army's defeat and that Lee would still enjoy the South's full support.

Longstreet and two of his divisions were detached to the Army of Tennessee after Gettysburg, a plan consistent with Longstreet's strategic view that emphasized a concentration of Confederate forces in the western theater. At Chickamauga on September 20, 1863, Longstreet exploited a gap in the enemy's line, routing the entire Union army, an accomplishment that earned him a new nickname—"Bull of the Woods." He followed this triumph with a poor showing during the siege of Chattanooga when he allowed the Federals to gain a foothold at the base of Lookout Mountain at the end of October.

Longstreet also became embroiled in the feud surrounding Gen. Braxton Bragg that fall. Longstreet fueled divisiveness among the officers in the Army of Tennessee by openly criticizing Bragg. Rumors surfaced that Longstreet would replace Bragg as the army's new commander, but Jefferson Davis suggested that Longstreet receive an independent command and move toward Knoxville, which he did on November 5. A few weeks later the mission ended in failure, marking the nadir of Longstreet's career as he feuded with his subordinates, notably Maj. Gen. Lafayette McLaws, while his men suffered from a lack of rations and clothing.

Longstreet and his two divisions returned to Virginia in April 1864, a welcome addition to the Army of Northern Virginia. One of Lee's staff officers wrote to Longstreet: "I really am beside myself, General, with joy of having you back. It is like the reunion of a family."

Longstreet recaptured his former glory at the Battle of the Wilderness on May 6 by completing a forced march and then directing a counterattack that saved the Confederate right flank. In circumstances remarkably similar to the wounding of

Stonewall Jackson the previous year, Longstreet's own men fired at the general and his staff, hitting the First Corps commander in the throat and right arm—a serious injury that required an extended period of absence. Because his officer corps had been thinned, Lee desperately needed the services of his lieutenant for the rest of the Overland campaign and beginning of the siege of Petersburg. One Confederate staff officer felt "very anxious that Genl. Longstreet should get back to the army . . . Genl. Lee needs him not only to advise with, but Genl. Longstreet has a very suggestive mind and none of the other Lt. Genls. have this."

With a husky voice and a paralyzed arm, Longstreet returned to the First Corps in October. The general's condition presented Lee with a perfect opportunity to reassign his subordinate to a less critical post, but Lee immediately gave Longstreet command of the army's left flank, a line that stretched north of the James River. After the Federals broke through the Petersburg defenses on April 2, 1865, Longstreet guided his own troops as well as remnants of the Third Corps during the retreat to Appomattox. When a fellow officer suggested that Longstreet impress upon Lee the need to surrender, Longstreet sharply rebuked him, saying that only Lee could make that decision and that he would follow the general to the end.

Longstreet's reputation declined precipitously after the war, largely owing to the efforts of a cadre of Southern officers headed by Jubal Early. Through the *Southern Historical Society Papers,* these men blamed Longstreet for the loss at Gettysburg and characterized him as a sulky, insubordinate officer who consistently undermined Lee's operations. Longstreet's published criticism of Lee's actions at Gettysburg in the *Philadelphia Weekly Times* of November 3, 1877, and February 28, 1878, and his affiliation with the Republican party after the war made him a convenient scapegoat for the South's defeat. Edward Porter Alexander, who had been at Gettysburg, noted that "Longstreet's *great* mistake was not in the *war,* but in some of his awkward and apparently bitter criticisms of Gen Lee." The negative sentiments held against Longstreet are reflected in an 1876 letter written by Early: "He [Longstreet] is sincerely purporting to lay claim to the chief glory for the seven days around Richmond, but the rebut I gave him on that head has taken the wind out of his sails."

Nevertheless, although Longstreet did not always agree with Lee's decisions, they maintained a warm relationship and respected each other professionally. Lee frequently camped next to Longstreet, and a British observer noted in 1863 that the friendship between the two officers was "quite touching-they are almost always together." Longstreet exhibited shortcomings as an independent commander and lacked delicacy in dealing with subordinates. In combat, however, he had few equals. Unlike Stonewall Jackson who frequently attacked in a piecemeal fashion, Longstreet delivered well-coordinated assaults by concentrating his forces against a specific point.

Pardoned on June 19, 1867, Longstreet, through connections with the Republican party, obtained a number of governmental appointments, including surveyor of the port of New Orleans in 1869; postmaster at Gainesville, Georgia, in 1879; U.S. minister to Turkey in 1880; and Federal marshal for northern Georgia in 1881. President William McKinley appointed him U.S. commissioner of railroads in 1897. Longstreet spent the remaining years of his life near Gainesville where he died on January 2, 1904.

BIBLIOGRAPHY

Alexander, Edward Porter. *Fighting for the Confederacy: The Personal Recollections of General Edward Porter Alexander.* Edited by Gary W. Gallagher. Chapel Hill, N.C., 1989.
Eckenrode, H. J., and Bryan Conrad. *James Longstreet: Lee's War Horse.* Chapel Hill, N.C., 1933. Reprint, Chapel Hill, N.C., 1986.
Longstreet, James. *From Manassas to Appomattox.* Philadelphia, 1896.
Piston, William Garrett. *Lee's Tarnished Lieutenant: James Longstreet and His Place in Southern History.* Athens, Ga., 1987.
Sorrel, G. Moxley. *Recollections of a Confederate Staff Officer.* New York, 1905. Reprint, Dayton, Ohio, 1978.

PETER S. CARMICHAEL

LORING, W. W.

LORING, W. W. (1818–1886), Confederate major general and Egyptian Army officer (1869–1879). William Wing Loring was born December 4, 1818, in Wilmington, North Carolina. His long military career probably included more of interest before and after the Civil War than during his four Confederate years. He was fighting Seminoles at the age of fourteen and held a commission when he was eighteen. Loring won a seat in the Florida legislature while in his early twenties and was commissioned as captain in the U.S. Army during the Mexican War. He came out of that war a brevet colonel and missing an arm. Loring remained in the army until 1861, at which time he was by far its youngest colonel.

After a brief stint as a Confederate colonel, Loring received brigadier general's rank on May 20, 1861. He participated in the complex and disappointing campaigns in northwestern Virginia in 1861 before receiving orders to collaborate with Thomas J. ("Stonewall") Jackson early in 1862. The two generals soon found themselves in violent disagreement over the location of winter quarters assigned to Loring's men. Richmond sided with Loring, who was promoted in the midst of the controversy. After commanding near Charleston, Virginia, in 1862, Loring went west to join John C. Pemberton's army. He evaded the Vicksburg entrapment and commanded a division in the army led by Joseph E. Johnston and then by John Bell Hood, participating in the late-1864 disasters in Tennessee. Loring surrendered with Johnston in North Carolina.

General Loring went to Egypt in 1869 to accept a commission as brigadier from the khedive. During a decade in that service Loring earned decorations and promotion. For the last seven years of his life the veteran officer lived in New York and Florida. He died December 30, 1886, and was buried in St. Augustine, Florida.

[See also Loring-Jackson Incident.]

BIBLIOGRAPHY

Loring, William W. *A Confederate Soldier in Egypt.* New York, 1884.
Wessels, William L. *Born to Be a Soldier.* Fort Worth, Tex., 1971.

ROBERT K. KRICK

LORING-JACKSON INCIDENT

In the winter of 1861–1862 Maj. Gen. Thomas J. ("Stonewall") Jackson conducted a controversial winter campaign in the mountains and the Shenandoah Valley of northwestern Virginia. After receiving reluctant approval for his plans, Jackson was reinforced by troops under Brig. Gen. William W. Loring.

The small Army of the Valley left Winchester on New Years' Day, 1862, and occupied the town of Romney two weeks later, after difficult marching and countermarching in snow and sleet. Jackson's troops fought the bitter weather, widespread illness, and each other more than they did the Federals and were in no condition to continue the campaign. Loring and his men, to make matters worse, were near mutiny over Jackson's supposed incompetence and favoritism toward his own brigades. Jackson, however, ordered Loring to occupy Romney for the winter while the rest of the army returned to Winchester and operated from there.

When Loring complained to Secretary of War Judah P. Benjamin, Benjamin ordered Jackson to send Loring back to Winchester immediately. Though Jackson complied with Benjamin's order, he tendered his resignation on January 31, 1862, protesting, "with such interference in my command I cannot expect to be of much service in the field."

A host of allies, including Governor John Letcher of Virginia, pressured Jackson to stay and persuaded him to withdraw his resignation in mid-February. The Romney campaign was overshadowed by the bitter Loring-Jackson dis-

pute, with the result that Confederate civil authorities would not overlook Jackson's insistence on military authority again.

BIBLIOGRAPHY

Chambers, Lenoir. *"Stonewall" Jackson.* Vol. 2. New York, 1959.
Tanner, Robert G. *Stonewall in the Valley: Thomas J. "Stonewall" Jackson's Shenandoah Valley Campaign, Spring 1862.* Garden City, N.Y., 1976.
Vandiver, Frank E. *Mighty Stonewall.* New York, 1957. Reprint, Texas A & M University Military History Series, no. 9. College Station, Tex., 1988.

J. TRACY POWER

LOST CAUSE

[*This entry is composed of two articles,* An Overview,*which discusses changing Southern interpretations of the Civil War and Confederate defeat, and* Iconography, *which discusses graphic and sculptural depictions of Confederate heroes and military incidents. See also* Burial of Latanè; Civil War,*articles on* Causes of War *and* Causes of Defeat; Confederate Veteran; Film and Video; Juneteenth; Literature, *article on* The Confederacy in Literature; Memorial Day; Memorial Organizations; Monuments and Memorials; Southern Historical Society; Volck, Adalbert.]

An Overview

The Lost Cause, the title of Edward A. Pollard's 1866 history of the Confederacy, first referred to the South's defeat in the Civil War, but in time it came to designate the region's memory of the war as well.

Appomattox brought defeat, desolation, and despair to the white South. Almost at once, Southerners began to memorialize their failed cause, establishing Confederate Memorial Day and dedicating funeral monuments to the Confederate dead. These activities, usually held in cemeteries, evoked mourning and melancholy even as they honored the soldiers. They formed part of a larger process through which white Southerners assimilated defeat. Former Confederates reexamined their defense of slavery and decision to secede from the Union and judged both legal and moral. To explain their defeat, some Southerners pointed to the Confederates' personal sins, such as drinking or swearing. But most Southerners proclaimed the South blameless, sought solace in biblical promises that God tested those whom he loved best, and concluded that God had chosen the South for some great destiny. Having decided God had not abandoned them, white Southerners sought other explanations for their defeat. A few leaders blamed each other; others questioned the unity, discipline, or commitment of the Southern people. Almost no one criticized the fighting mettle of Confederate soldiers; rather, their heroism was praised.

In the 1870s the process of coming to terms with defeat entered a new phase. Jubal A. Early and a few other former Confederate leaders organized the Southern Historical Society (SHS), which, through its publications and the other Southern writings it endorsed, established certain "truths" about the Confederate cause: the South had not fought to preserve slavery; secession was a constitutional and justifiable response to Northern violations of the national compact; and Robert E. Lee and Thomas J. ("Stonewall") Jackson were perfect heroes whose very existence testified to Confederate nobility. When explaining Confederate defeat, Early and the SHS offered two not altogether consistent explanations: James Longstreet's tardiness at Gettysburg led to the loss of the war, and the Confederate armies succumbed only to overwhelming numbers and resources.

Beginning in the late 1880s, the mourning and self-examination of the early postwar years gave way by the turn of the century to a popular celebration of the war. Communities throughout the South dedicated Confederate monuments. A few of these statues memorialized generals or other leaders, but most honored the common soldiers and took the form of a lone soldier, often at rest, atop a tall shaft on the court-house square or a central street. In 1889 the United Confederate Veterans formed and chose as its leader John B. Gordon, a Confederate general committed to a New South and reconciliation with the North. Within a decade, the United Daughters of the Confederacy and the Sons of Confederate Veterans organized. All three groups participated in annual reunions of Confederate veterans, which became regional festivals that drew huge crowds. Some scholars argue that this turn-of-the-century Confederate celebration expressed a civil religion that preserved a distinctive regional identity and Lost Cause mentality. It did indirectly foster white supremacy, state rights, and Democratic party solidarity, as well as incorporate most of the positions held by the SHS. But its rituals primarily celebrated the sacrifice and heroism of the soldiers and vindicated the honor of the South. The celebration thereby rendered the Lost Cause a glorious memory with much of the war's pain, passions, and such issues as slavery or independence expunged. In fact, it did little to revive wartime ideology or forge a distinctively regional identity, but instead reinforced Southerners' deference to leaders and loyalty to country, now the reunited nation.

In 1898 the Spanish-American War allowed the South to demonstrate its loyalty and honor under fire. In the war's wake, and amid a national resurgence of racism that rendered reconciliation among whites easier, most Northerners joined in the celebration of the Confederate soldiers. Robert E. Lee became a national hero, and Blue-Gray reunions demonstrated the North's respect for its former foes. With

Northern acknowledgment of Southern honor and with regional confidence restored, the Confederate celebration lost much of its intensity. As the twentieth century progressed, fewer Confederate monuments were erected. As the veteran generation died off, Confederate reunions became less spectacular, and in 1932 the old soldiers held their last major review. Sons' and daughters' organizations persisted, but neither assumed the central role in Southern society the veterans had held. With this decline of the organizations and ceremonies of the Lost Cause, no one interpretation of the war dominated Southern culture as it once had.

Southern academics and other intellectuals developed independent, conflicting interpretations of the war. In their 1930 manifesto, *I'll Take My Stand,* the Nashville agrarians sought to counter both New South commercialism and the ills of modern industrial society by promoting an image of an agrarian South, although one that all but ignored the existence of slavery. Thereafter a few conservative Southern

> . . . the mourning and self-examination of the early postwar years gave way by the turn of the century to a popular celebration of the war.

intellectuals similarly evoked the memory of the Old South and the Confederacy in opposition to modern developments they disdained. A larger number of Southern intellectuals, however, rethought their society's celebration of the Confederacy. Novelist William Faulkner, journalist W. J. Cash, historian C. Vann Woodward, and others saw slavery as central to the sectional confrontation, stressed the Civil War's devastating effects on the South, and claimed that defeat helped create a distinctive regional mentality characterized by guilt and an appreciation for human limitations. By the 1960s, a few historians influenced by this tradition even attributed Confederate defeat to guilt over slavery which had led to a failure of Confederate nationalism. Not all historians embraced such explanations; over the course of the century scholars attributed the war to a conflict of civilizations, a blundering generation, the collapse of the political party system, and a host of other factors. They offered myriad explanations of Confederate defeat, although perhaps the overwhelming-numbers-and-resources argument remained preeminent. Most Southern historians and intellectuals, though, emphasized the importance of slavery to the conflict and viewed the war as more tragic than did the Confederate celebration or twentieth-century popular culture.

A few scholars find popular acceptance of failure, guilt, and human limits, which they label the Lost Cause mentality, in twentieth-century country music. Such sentiments appeared in many country songs, but that probably reflected the hard realities of Southern rural and lower-class life rather than any influence of the Lost Cause. The popular memory of the Civil War more often took heroic form. Novels and films-especially the silent classic *Birth of a Nation* and one of the most popular movies of all time—*Gone with the Wind*—portrayed the Old South as a conservative but romantic place that suffered a terrible defeat. Yet in most, as in *Gone with the Wind,* Confederates appeared as heroic figures who survived, if not triumphed, in the end, and slavery seemed a benign if not beneficial institution. Once again, an absence of concern about the plight of African Americans made it easier for both Northern and Southern whites to honor the heroes of the Southern cause. With twentieth-century popular culture's glorification of the Confederacy, following its celebration at the turn of the century, many white Southerners even joked that the South had not actually lost the war, which suggested that the heritage of defeat had ceased to be very important to or even very real for them. Rather than displaying some special caution or wisdom rooted in defeat, white Southerners became among the most patriotic of Americans; the Lost Cause had primarily fostered respect for the military and unquestioning patriotism.

The Civil War Centennial, more a Northern than a Southern celebration, did little to reverse the decline of interest in the Lost Cause or to reshape its definition. Rather, the centennial further demonstrated the increasing commercialization and trivialization of the memory of the war. During the civil rights revolt of the 1950s and 1960s, many white Southerners did revive the use of Confederate symbols, especially the Confederate flag and "Dixie," in behalf of segregation and white supremacy. They thereby did much to reverse what the turn-of-the-century Confederate celebration had done to render them symbols of honor and loyalty to country. In the 1980s continued display of the Confederate flag exacerbated tensions between white and black Southerners. By then blacks who objected to Confederate symbols as an assertion of white supremacy probably reacted more to the battles of the 1960s than to those of the 1860s. But with few exceptions, black Southerners had never participated in or embraced the Lost Cause. For them the Civil War brought not defeat but deliverance from slavery. They gloried not in Confederate legions but in their ancestors' participation in a Union army that brought emancipation, which many black communities after the war, and into the present, celebrated on January 1, June 19, or various other dates.

These conflicts over Confederate symbols exposed, more than anything else, the nation's failure to establish a biracial society after it emancipated the slaves, but they also revealed that the Civil War remained important for some Southerners. Even in the 1970s and 1980s, many people, not just Southerners, reenacted Civil War battles. The Daughters of the Confederacy and Sons of Confederate Veterans persisted; many of their members continued to interpret the war much as the SHS had. But only a small minority of Southerners participated in reenactments or descendants' organizations; for the majority, Confederate symbols and evocations of the Lost Cause had little fixed meaning and little clear relationship to the issues that motivated Confederates from 1861 through 1865. When a neoconservative Harvard student flew the Confederate flag out her window to challenge liberal calls for cultural diversity on campus; when a country-music singer bragged that if the South had won the war, murderers would be hanged and the day Elvis Presley died would be a national holiday; and when an advertisement for an Atlanta hotel featured William Tecumseh Sherman's picture and told patrons "Say Sherman sent you" to receive a discount, then defining any specific ideological or cultural content to the Lost Cause became difficult, if not futile. Moreover, in the 1980s most white Southerners displayed limited knowledge of or interest in the history of the Civil War. One survey found that just 39 percent of white Southerners claimed to have had an ancestor in the Confederate army; another 37 percent did not know if their ancestors had fought or not. Only 30 percent of the same respondents admitted they had a great deal of interest in Southern history, though another 51 percent claimed to have some interest.

By the 1990s the memory of the Civil War had not totally disappeared from Southern culture, but certainly the specificity and power of the Lost Cause had dramatically declined.

BIBLIOGRAPHY

Connelly, Thomas L., and Barbara L. Bellows. *God and General Longstreet: The Lost Cause and the Southern Mind.* Baton Rouge, La., 1982.

Foster, Gaines M. *Ghosts of the Confederacy: Defeat, the Lost Cause, and the Emergence of the New South, 1865–1913.* New York, 1987.

Kirby, Jack Temple. *Media-Made Dixie: The South in the American Imagination.* Athens, Ga., 1986.

Neely, Mark E., Jr., Harold Holzer, and Gabor S. Boritt. *The Confederate Image: Prints of the Lost Cause.* Chapel Hill, N.C., 1987.

Pressly, Thomas J. *Americans Interpret Their Civil War.* New York, 1962.

Weaver, Richard M. *The Southern Tradition at Bay: A History of Postbellum Thought.* Edited by George Core and M. E. Bradford. New Rochelle, N.Y., 1968.

Wilson, Charles Reagan. *Baptized in Blood: The Religion of the Lost Cause, 1865–1920.* Athens, Ga., 1980.

Wilson, Charles Reagan. " 'God's Project': The Southern Civil Religion, 1920–1980." In *Religion and the Life of the Nation: American Recoveries.* Edited by Rowland A. Sherrill. Urbana, Ill., 1990.

GAINES M. FOSTER

Iconography

One of the great ironies of Confederate iconography is that while the cause lived, it was rarely depicted in the popular arts, but after it was lost, it was widely celebrated in postwar graphics. In yet a further irony, much of this retrospective Lost Cause parlor art was created not by Southern publishers but by Northern ones eager to profit from the reopening of the Southern marketplace, where the native print industry had all but died during the war.

Lost Cause icons—engravings and lithographs of the Confederacy's great heroes and most famous military incidents—came pouring off the presses in New York, Philadelphia, Boston, and Chicago after 1866. So did sentimental genre scenes illuminating Southern defeat and suffering, typified by Currier & Ives's lithograph of a Confederate

> **Lost Cause prints proliferated as long as the fashion for home art itself endured.**

veteran returning to a war-ravaged home, a print aptly titled *The Lost Cause.* A landmark example of the Lost Cause icon was the print of William D. Washington's painting, *The Burial of Latanè,* published in 1868 and popular for generations. As late as 1863 the Virginian who owned the original canvas noted that throughout his life he had seen "many of the steel engravings hanging on the walls of this county and neighboring counties," adding, "I really believe that these engravings helped to hold the Southern People together as one after the war."

Another important Lost Cause icon celebrating two wartime generals, *The Last Meeting of Lee and Jackson,* first appeared in a print adaptation in New Yorker Frederick Halpin's 1872 engraving. It won far greater acclaim and acceptance than the original E. B. D. Julio painting on which it was based.

Robert E. Lee and Thomas J. ("Stonewall") Jackson, together with Jefferson Davis, constituted a Lost Cause "trinity" of icons portrayed more often in prints than any other Confederate heroes. Jackson, surprisingly, proved an object of fascination for Northerners, perhaps because this "Cromwell in Gray" seemed more comprehensible to the Puritan Union culture than cavaliers like Lee. Currier & Ives even celebrated Jackson's martyrdom in a reverential deathbed print granting him a wholly military setting for his final moments, when in fact Jackson had died in a house, not a tent.

Davis had a checkered career in Lost Cause art. At first he was mercilessly lampooned in caricatures that vivified the story that he had donned hoopskirts to evade capture by Union troops. But Davis recovered from this symbolic emasculation when he was shackled at Fortress Monroe. Overnight he became a living martyr of the Lost Cause, and his reemergence was celebrated in engraved and lithographed tributes from then until his death in 1889.

No Confederate hero inspired as many prints—or as consistently reverential ones—as did Robert E. Lee. Although the enfeebled Confederate print industry had been unable to produce a single Lee portrait while the war raged, Northern publishers filled the void once the war ended, first portraying him nobly in defeat in an array of Appomattox prints in 1865. Lee's death in 1870 ignited demand for his image, and when competing memorial associations organized fund-raising appeals to erect statues in Lexington and Richmond, both offered Lee prints as premiums. "A grateful people," one observer reported, "gave of their poverty gladly" to purchase the prints—one of which showed Lee in beatific close-up, the other astride his beloved horse, Traveller.

Lost Cause prints proliferated as long as the fashion for home art itself endured. A journalist visiting a Mobile home in 1871 noted what had become true of innumerable Southern dwellings after the war: "Upon the walls were portraits of Gen. R. E. Lee, and Stonewall Jackson, and Jefferson Davis." Added the eyewitness: "Indeed, the first two mentioned I see everywhere in the South, in private as well as in public houses."

Financed in part by the sale of popular prints, Edward Virginius Valentine's recumbent statue of Robert E. Lee was installed in 1883 atop the general's tomb in the chapel of Washington College in Lexington, Virginia. In 1890, the Lee Monument Association's heroic equestrian statue of Lee by sculptor Marius Jean Antonin Mercie was unveiled before a throng of 100,000 in Richmond. An orator for the occasion declared it a blessing that "future generations may see the counterfeit presentment of this . . . bright consummate flower of our civilization."

Completion of these two Lee monuments ushered in a golden age of Confederate statuary. The city of Richmond, in particular, was soon crowded with dazzling sculpture, including a series of large equestrian statues of Jackson, J. E. B. Stuart, and others, crowning the same broad avenue where the Mercie Lee had been installed.

Atlanta, too, became an important outdoor gallery of public icons. The installation of one such tribute, Solon Borglum's sculpture of Gen. John B. Gordon, may best be remembered because it ushered in the saga of the most ambitious of all Confederate sculpture memorials-and also the most disastrous.

Around 1915, a journalist named John Graves and the president of the national United Daughters of the Confederacy, Mrs. Helen Plane, conceived of the idea of a Confederate Memorial for one of the South's grandest vistas: the face of Stone Mountain, Georgia. Appropriately, they turned to Solon Borglum's brother, Gutzon Borglum, who would later sculpt Mount Rushmore.

Borglum's plans proved even more ambitious than Graves's and Mrs. Plane's. Dismissing their proposal for a mere Lee portrait as nothing more than a "stamp on a barn door," Borglum conceived of a far grander monumental frieze that would portray artillery and infantry, and colossal sculptures of Lee, Jackson, and Davis. He began work in 1915, but was interrupted by World War I. Work resumed in 1922, and on January 19, 1924—Lee's 117th birthday—the Stone Mountain Monumental Association unveiled the massive head of Lee.

This proved the apex of the movement to create Confederate memorial statuary. Soon after, Borglum began feuding with the Monumental Association over artistic details and money. When the Association fired him, he destroyed all his models, leaving Stone Mountain permanently unfinished—a monument not only to Lee but to the passionate, three-generation-long effort to create permanent sculpted tributes to Confederate heroes.

BIBLIOGRAPHY

Buttre, J. C. *Catalogue of Engravings for Sale by J. C. Buttre & Co.* New York, 1884.

Connelly, Thomas L. *The Marble Man: Robert E. Lee and His Image in American Society.* Baton Rouge, La., 1977.

Neely, Mark E., Jr., Harold Holzer, and Gabor S. Boritt. *The Confederate Image: Prints of the Lost Cause.* Chapel Hill, N.C., 1987.

Smith, Rex Alan. *The Carving of Mount Rushmore.* New York, 1985.

HAROLD HOLZER

LOUISIANA

As part of the Confederacy's Trans-Mississippi Department, Louisiana was on the military periphery during much of the Civil War. The capture of New Orleans by Federal forces on May 1, 1862, was a pivotal event, but the state's major battles seem like skirmishes compared to Virginia's titanic struggles. For the conflict's last three years, two governments vied for control of the Pelican State: a military-dominated Unionist regime centered in New Orleans and a Confederate administration that was repeatedly forced to shift its state capital farther north. Exercising tenuous authority over southern Louisiana (designated the Department of the Gulf by occupying authorities), the Unionist state government played an important role in molding federal race and Reconstruction policy.

If the state was confined to the military sidelines, white Louisianians were often in the thick of things. Masses of them mobilized for war. Approximately 56,000 whites enlisted in Confederate armies, while another 10,000 served in the state militia. Together they represented 64 percent of Louisiana's white military manhood as of 1860 (men between the ages of thirteen and forty-five). Louisianians in gray mostly saw action beyond state borders, in places like Shiloh, Manassas, and Malvern Hill. New Orleans's famed Washington Artillery served more or less continuously with Robert E. Lee's Army of Northern Virginia, although a battery fought in Tennessee. Roberdeau Wheat's Louisiana Tigers, comprising roustabouts from the New Orleans waterfront, participated in every major campaign in Virginia, Maryland, and Pennsylvania. Moreover, Louisiana made important contributions to the Confederacy's top brass. Creole Gen. P. G. T. Beauregard, who commanded Confederate forces in Charleston during the bombardment of Fort Sumter, led Southern armies to victory at First Manassas. Braxton Bragg, one of eight full generals commissioned by the Confederacy (Beauregard was another), went from being a colonel on Louisiana Governor Thomas O. Moore's staff to overall commander of the Army of Tennessee. Richard Taylor, Zachary's son, served with distinction under Thomas J. ("Stonewall") Jackson before assuming charge of the newly formed District of Western Louisiana (as Confederate-controlled northern Louisiana was called) in August 1862.

Several civilians left their mark on the Confederacy. Without question the smartest man in Jefferson Davis's cabinet was former U.S. Senator Judah P. Benjamin, whose portfolio variously included Justice, War, and State. John Slidell, Benjamin's Senate colleague, became Confederate Commissioner to France, and Judge Pierre A. Rost joined in the Confederacy's first diplomatic mission to Europe. Confederate Congressman Duncan F. Kenner, chairman of the Ways and Means Committee, spearheaded the eleventh-hour effort by the expiring Richmond government to barter emancipation for European intervention.

Secession

As a general rule, support for the cause of Southern rights was strongest in states with large slave populations. But Louisiana, one-half of whose 1860 population of 708,000 was black, is a case apart. John C. Breckinridge, for example, the Southern Democratic presidential candidate during the 1860 presidential election, polled less than 45 percent of the vote—his lowest proportion in the Gulf South and second lowest among the eleven states that eventually formed the Confederacy. The south Louisianian sugar industry's dependence on tariff protection accounts for some of this residual Unionism. Another explanation was yeoman dissent in places like Winn Parish, historically a seedbed of radical protest. But most of the state's surprisingly buoyant Unionism can be traced to the influence of New Orleans, the South's largest and oldest city, and home to a quarter of the state's population. Linked to national markets by the Mississippi River, the city's largely Northern-born commercial community was reluctant to cut its lifeline to the free states. Pro-Union feeling was even stronger at the bottom of the white social structure, where recent immigrants predominated. (Nearly 40 percent of New Orleans's 1860 population was foreign-born.) Angry that Stephen A. Douglas had outpolled Breckinridge in every New Orleans district, Senator Slidell complained that "here in the city seven-eighths of the vote for Douglas were cast by the Irish and Germans." Had it not been for strict registration laws that reduced the number of immigrant voters, Breckinridge's statewide percentage would likely have been even smaller. Later in the war thousands of New Orleans's foreign-born residents joined the Union army.

Because of the strength and breadth of pro-Union sentiment, Louisiana's secessionists pulled out all stops to sever the state's ties with Washington. Calling the legislature into special session shortly following Abraham Lincoln's election, Governor Moore declared: "I do not think it comports with the honor and self-respect of Louisiana as a slaveholding state, to live under the government of a Black Republican president." Moore was an immediate secessionist; he favored separate state action, as opposed to the strategy of having Louisiana leave the Union in concert with other slave states. Before the secession convention met, he ordered state militiamen to seize federal military installations in Baton Rouge, New Orleans, and along the river. The election for convention

> ... a resolute secessionist minority had brilliantly undermined the conditional Unionism of Louisiana's white majority.

delegates took place in a climate of intimidation. The immediate secessionists, organized into various home guards, vigilance committees, and Southern rights associations, placed those favoring compromise on the defensive. In New Orleans, South Carolina native Benjamin A. Palmer, the city's foremost Presbyterian minister, delivered a two-hour fire-breathing sermon that effectively silenced the wavering Unionists within his up-scale congregation.

Immediate secessionists scored a narrow 52-to-48-percent victory on January 7, 1861, because many demoralized Unionist voters stayed home on election day. Compared to the presidential election two months earlier, turnout among rural voters had dropped by nearly a quarter. Owing to the fact that seats in the secession convention were apportioned on the basis of total population, this slim electoral majority for disunion ballooned into an 80-to-44 margin in the delegate count. On January 26 the ordinance of secession passed by a vote of 113 to 17, despite the lonely prediction by the

Unionist judge James Taliaferro of war and anarchy. As was the case in most states that joined the Confederacy, Louisiana never submitted its secession ordinance to a popular vote. Abetted by the cross-pressures of regional loyalty and racial hysteria, a resolute secessionist minority had brilliantly undermined the conditional Unionism of Louisiana's white majority.

Military Action

Trainloads of embalmed corpses and wounded soldiers from Shiloh were still arriving in New Orleans in early April 1862 when a Federal flotilla under Adm. David Farragut steamed up the Mississippi toward the Confederacy's largest port. Seventy-five miles downriver, near Forts Jackson and St. Phillip, Confederate defenders had strung a makeshift defensive chain of vessels and a fire raft across the Mississippi, but Farragut's fleet successfully ran the gauntlet on April 24. Five days later the Union navy dropped anchor outside the New Orleans levee; two days after that, following Union Gen. Benjamin F. Butler's capture of Fort Jackson, Farragut raised the Stars and Stripes over the U.S. Custom House on Canal Street in downtown New Orleans. Meanwhile, Mayor John Monroe's obstructionism had given Confederate Gen. Mansfield Lovell enough time to evacuate the four thousand troops still in the city and torch the cotton stacked near the riverfront.

The fall of New Orleans opened up southern Louisiana for Union army forays, and they were not long in coming. Farragut's fleet forced the surrender of Baton Rouge on May 12 and then continued upstream to threaten Vicksburg. Three months later, on August 5, 1862, Confederate troops under Gen. John C. Breckinridge drove the Union garrison back to New Orleans, but had to abandon the state capital for the second and final time in December 1862. Even before retaking Baton Rouge, blue-clad soldiers began punching their way up and down the state's major north-south bayous, disrupting plantation routine and forcing wide-scale planter refugeeing to Texas. In October 1862, for example, the Bayou LaFourche expedition resulted in the loss of southeastern Louisiana to a Federal force under the command of Gen. Godfrey Weitzel.

The next spring another Union expedition, this one up Bayou Teche, farther to the west, tried to squeeze Confederate troops out of southern Louisiana altogether. By this time, Louisiana had been reassigned to Gen. E. Kirby Smith's Trans-Mississippi Department and placed under the command of Richard Taylor in the District of Western Louisiana. To clear an invasion path to Texas, in early April 1863 the Department of the Gulf's new commander, Nathaniel P. Banks, moved against Taylor's scattered Confederate forces west and north of Brashear City. Banks's army was three times larger than Taylor's, and his gunboats threatened to outflank every defensive position Confederates managed to erect on the narrow neck of land between the bayou and the swamps. There was some sharp fighting at Irish Bend on April 14, but most of the campaign consisted of rearguard skirmishing. Burning bridges as they went, Confederates retreated from New Iberia through Vermilionville and Opelousas. By May 7 Banks had reached Alexandria, the traditional dividing point between Franco southern and Anglo northern Louisiana, obliging Taylor to relocate his headquarters to Natchitoches. The Confederate state government meanwhile had fallen all the way back to Shreveport.

The expulsion of Southern forces from southwestern Louisiana was only temporary. Less than a week after arriving in Alexandria, Banks redeployed the bulk of his army against Maj. Gen. Franklin Gardner's Confederate garrison at Port Hudson, twenty-five miles north of Baton Rouge. Port Hudson was the southern hinge on the Confederacy's remaining door to the Trans-Mississippi West. Throughout the winter and spring of 1863 Ulysses S. Grant had been hammering away at the northern hinge at Vicksburg. After reaching Vicksburg's rear in May, Grant expected his Louisiana counterpart to join him for the final blow. But Banks, reluctant to become Grant's second fiddle, moved on Port Hudson instead.

Situated, like Vicksburg, on a hairpin curve of the Mississippi River, Port Hudson was fortified along a several-mile front approachable only through thick forests and deep ravines, some of them blocked by felled trees. Enjoying a huge manpower advantage (40,000 to 5,700), Banks twice tried to take the Confederate works by frontal assault, only to suffer stunning casualties. Thereafter he settled in for a protracted siege, which included tunneling mine shafts under Confederate lines. Union forces were ready to detonate explosive charges beneath Gardner's fortifications, when the Confederate commander surrendered Port Hudson on July 9, 1863. Gardner realized Vicksburg's fall five days earlier ruled out Confederate forces coming to the relief of his beleaguered garrison. The Confederacy was now cut in two, and Taylor's troops were forced to regroup in northern Louisiana. Conceived to unify Louisiana under Unionist rule, liberate Texas, and capture stores of cotton, Banks's Red River campaign in the spring of 1864 was the last major military action on Louisiana soil. Having cleared Confederate forces from Alexandria, Bank's 27,000-man army waited until the Red River rose high enough to permit Como. David Porter's gunboats to float past the double rapids above the city. Because Banks enjoyed the supporting fire of Union gunboats, Taylor was leery of giving battle near the river. But the Union commander threw away his naval advantage by leaving the river road for a shorter inland route to Shreveport. Taylor furiously attacked Banks's advancing columns at Mansfield on April 8, 1864, throwing them back in confusion. The next day he followed up with another assault on Federal forces dug in at Pleasant Hill. Banks thereupon fell back to the Mississippi River, where naval transports carried his army to the safety of New Orleans.

Banks's abortive Red River campaign effectively concluded full-scale military operations in the Confederate District of Western Louisiana. Guerrilla bands composed of deserters and camp followers from both sides desolated the no-man's-land between Union and Confederate lines, especially in north central Louisiana, where arson and rustling were rampant. They were active in the contraband trade in cotton, which boomed after Confederate and Federal officials concluded the illicit commerce was mutually beneficial. The guerrilla bands became more wanton as defeat swelled the ranks of Confederate desertion.

The Civil War inflicted wholesale destruction on Louisiana. During the Teche campaign, for example, footsore soldiers from both armies plundered mules and horses, carts and carriages, as they marched up the bayou. The following year Alexandria was badly burned, and each side blamed the other. The most devastating Southern loss may have been the destruction of the saltworks at Avery Island, which, since its founding in May 1862, had produced more than 22 million pounds of salt for the Confederacy.

Government and Politics

Avery Island is one of the better-known examples of Confederate involvement in the economy. But there were others, especially under Governor Henry W. Allen, a Confederate brigadier general who had been wounded in the Battle of Baton Rouge. Assuming office in January 1864, Allen built state laboratories to provide medicine, erected an iron foundry in Shreveport, opened trade with Mexico to secure arms and scarce civilian goods, and distributed free cotton cards to enable hard-pressed families to spin their own cloth. He was keenly concerned with the welfare of soldiers' families. Under his administration state stores were established to provide affordable necessities to the common folk and soak up surplus state treasury certificates. Allen was also one of the first prominent Confederates to advocate arming the slaves. Historian Douglas S. Freeman described him as "the single great administrator produced by the Confederacy."

In part because of Allen's governing style, relations between Richmond and Confederate state authorities never deteriorated to the degree they did in Georgia and North Carolina. To be sure, there was ongoing friction over Louisiana's defenses. Governor Moore wrangled with the Davis administration about keeping munitions and soldiers within the state. Sharp words were exchanged over Richmond's choice of military commanders for Louisiana. But comparatively speaking, these difference never festered into open sores. Allen and Moore both cooperated with Davis's efforts to strengthen the value of Confederate currency, which was worth more in Louisiana than almost anywhere else. The Confederate legislature also helped dampen class conflict by postponing debt and tax collections. As for partisanship, according to historian Jefferson Davis Bragg, "Politics of the ordinary sort took a vacation in Louisiana during the war."

Politics, ironically, did not take a holiday in the Federal Department of the Gulf. New Orleans was a hotbed of political controversy. From almost the moment the city fell into Union hands, President Lincoln looked on Louisiana as a laboratory for field-testing Federal race and Reconstruction policy, and his two political generals were eager assistants. Of the two, Butler was more controversial because of his brusque treatment of recalcitrant Confederate sympathizers. His relief and public works program offered employment to thousands of destitute whites, especially from immigrant households, and laid the groundwork for the Free State party, which eventually metamorphosed into the postwar Republican party. Banks, on the other hand, tilted to the wealthy sugar planters and New Orleans merchants who controlled the conservative Union movement.

Butler's and Banks's clashing Reconstruction priorities were shaped by their different approaches to black free labor. The Department of the Gulf had been exempted from the Emancipation Proclamation, but that technicality did not prevent thousands of slaves from fleeing to Union lines. To give only one illustration, almost eight thousand bondsmen flocked to the five-mile-long caravan that trailed Banks's Teche expedition back to New Orleans. As contraband camps swelled with black refugees, Butler induced the slaves to return to plantations by ordering planters to pay wages and prohibiting the use of the whip. In contrast, Banks, who was cultivating political support among old slave owners, cut wages and used Federal provost marshals to bolster planter authority. Both generals, however, sought to enlist African Americans in the Union military, once arming the slaves became official policy. Over twenty-four thousand black Louisianians served in blue, the most from any state. Two of their regiments—one composed of prewar free blacks, the other of slaves—fought with valor in the bloody May 27 assault on Port Hudson.

Just as Federal race policy was framed with reference to Louisiana developments, so was early Reconstruction policy. In December 1862, a year before Lincoln unveiled his own plan of Reconstruction, two south Louisiana Unionists were elected to Congress, though they served only temporarily and as delegates. Lincoln's mild program—which authorized a return to civilian rule whenever 10 percent of the 1860 white population swore allegiance to the United States—resulted in the 1864 election of a Unionist state government under Michael Hahn and a new constitution that abolished slavery but stopped short of enfranchising blacks. Andrew Johnson applied Lincoln's Louisiana model to the rest of the

former Confederacy when he succeeded the slain president, only to have Congress overthrow the wartime plan in favor of a Reconstruction program based on black suffrage.

That turn toward radicalism vindicated New Orleans's self-confident free black community. Since 1862 its leaders had been arguing that justice and the future safety of the country dictated giving blacks citizenship. Creole blacks had also been in the forefront of the effort to arm African Americans. Both policies were eventually adopted, but their most persistent advocates were seldom elevated to positions of leadership in the new political order. Whites from outside the state had captured control of the Republican party.

The Civil War ended in Louisiana when Kirby Smith surrendered the Trans-Mississippi Department on May 26, 1865. By this time most of his command had decamped for home fires. The final accounting of Louisiana's failed bid to switch national loyalties was a 73 percent decline in farm value, a 70 percent decline in livestock value, unenumerated machinery losses, broken levees, destroyed railroads, and a terrible loss of young life—a demographic calamity by any definition.

[*For further discussion of battles and cities in Louisiana, see* Baton Rouge, Louisiana; New Orleans, Louisiana; Port Hudson, Louisiana; Red River Campaigns. *See also* Butler's Woman Order; and Louisiana Tigers; *and biographies of numerous figures mentioned herein.*]

BIBLIOGRAPHY

Bragg, Jefferson Davis. *Louisiana in the Confederacy.* Baton Rouge, La., 1941.

Dew, Charles B. "The Long Lost Returns: The Candidates and Their Totals in Louisiana's Secession Election." *Louisiana History* 10 (Fall 1969): 353–369.

McCrary, Peyton. *Abraham Lincoln and Reconstruction: The Louisiana Experiment.* Princeton, 1978.

Moneyhon, Carl, and Bobby Roberts. *Portraits of Conflict: A Photographic History of Louisiana in the Civil War.* Fayetteville, Ark., 1990.

Ripley, C. Peter. *Slaves and Freedmen in Civil War Louisiana.* Baton Rouge, La., 1976.

Winters, John D. *The Civil War in Louisiana.* Baton Rouge, La., 1963.

LAWRENCE N. POWELL

LOUISIANA TIGERS

The name "Louisiana Tigers" derived in 1861 from the Tiger Rifles, a Zouave company in Roberdeau Wheat's Battalion. Wheat's men became so notorious for thievery, brawling, and drunkenness that the battalion soon became known as the Louisiana Tiger Battalion. When other Louisiana commands showed similar behavior, the name was applied to all the Louisiana troops in the Army of Northern Virginia. Almost without exception the units that became notorious for bad behavior were New Orleans commands. The fact that hundreds, if not thousands, of Tigers could not speak English made them even more conspicuous. In fact, many units drilled completely in French for the first year of the war.

There were the approximately thirteen thousand infantry from the Pelican State who served in the Army of Northern Virginia. Originally comprising nine regiments and five battalions, the Tigers were eventually consolidated into two brigades in the Second Corps. The First Louisiana Brigade was com-

> **The Tigers fought in every major battle of the eastern theater and at times played a crucial role in them.**

posed of the Fifth, Sixth, Seventh, Eighth, and Ninth Louisiana Volunteers; the Second contained the First, Second, Tenth, Fourteenth, and Fifteenth Louisiana Volunteers.

The Tigers fought in every major battle of the eastern theater and at times played a crucial role in them. At First Manassas, Wheat's Battalion first engaged the enemy and delayed them for a crucial time. Under Richard Taylor the First Louisiana Brigade marched through the Shenandoah Valley in 1862 with Thomas ("Stonewall") Jackson, who gave it much of the credit for winning the battles of Front Royal, Winchester, and Port Republic. At Second Manassas, William Edwin Starke's Second Louisiana Brigade earned fame by holding the famous railroad cut with rocks after running out of ammunition. Starke was later killed at Sharpsburg, where the First Louisiana Brigade, now under Harry Thompson Hays, lost 60 percent of its men in thirty minutes. Francis Nicholls led the Second Louisiana Brigade at Chancellorsville and lost his foot during Jackson's celebrated flank attack. Hays's brigade aided Jubal Early in holding the enemy at Fredericksburg and gained acclaim for winning some temporary success at Salem Church.

During the Gettysburg campaign, Hays's brigade made the critical charge that captured Winchester, and the Second Louisiana Brigade captured six hundred Federals at Stephenson's Depot, Virginia. At Gettysburg, Hays's men helped rout the Northerners on the first day and briefly broke the Union line and captured two batteries on Cemetery Hill on July 2. The year ended in disaster when over six hundred of Hays's men were captured during a surprise attack on their position at Rappahannock Station on November 7. Both brigades suffered heavily in the Wilderness, where Leroy A. Stafford, commanding the Second Louisiana Brigade, was mortally wounded.

Because of the heavy losses, the two brigades were consolidated under Hays but kept their separate organizations.

Hays was wounded at Spotsylvania on May 9. The Second Louisiana Brigade was mostly overrun and captured at the Mule Shoe, but Hays's brigade played a crucial role in containing the Union breakthrough on the Confederate left. The consolidated brigade, under Zebulon York, accompanied Early to the Monocacy and Washington and fought well throughout the Shenandoah Valley campaign of Sheridan. When York was wounded at Third Winchester, William Raine Peck took command until early 1865. In the last days of the war, the Louisiana Brigade, under Col. Eugene Waggaman, led the attempted breakout of Petersburg at Fort Stedman and was among the last troops to leave the city. At Appomattox only 376 Tigers remained. During the war about 3,300 Tigers had died and at least 10 percent deserted.

See also Foreigners *and biographies of numerous figures mentioned herein.*]

BIBLIOGRAPHY

Jones, Terry L. *The Civil War Memoirs of Capt. William J. Seymour: Reminiscences of a Louisiana Tiger.* Baton Rouge, La., 1991.
Jones, Terry L. *Lee's Tigers: The Louisiana Infantry in the Army of Northern Virginia.* Baton Rouge, La., 1987.

TERRY L. JONES

LOWRY, ROBERT

LOWRY, ROBERT (1830–1910), brigadier general and postwar governor of Mississippi. Born March 10, 1830, in Chesterfield District, South Carolina, Lowry moved with his family to Tennessee and then on to Tishomingo County, Mississippi. Raised by an uncle who was a judge in Raleigh, Mississippi, he became a lawyer and served in the Mississippi State Senate.

In 1861 he joined and was quickly elected major of the Sixth Mississippi Infantry Regiment. On May 23, 1862, he became the regiment's colonel. In 1863 he was with the Confederate forces that tried to prevent the capture of Vicksburg, and he won much praise for his performance in the Battle of Port Gibson on May 1. In the following year he was with the Army of Tennessee in the Atlanta and Franklin and Nashville campaigns. At the Battle of Franklin (November 30, 1864), he took command of the brigade when Brig. Gen. John Adams was killed. Seizing a flag, he bravely led the men on in the assault.

Maj. Gen. W. W. Loring called him "an officer of the first order," and in February 1865 he was promoted to brigadier general. He served in the Carolinas campaign of 1865 and surrendered with the Southern forces there. He was paroled at Greensboro, North Carolina (probably on May 1).

Lowry was active in state politics after the war. He served in the legislature, helped overthrow the Republican Reconstruction government, and was twice elected governor (1881, 1885). He died in Jackson on January 19, 1910 and is buried in the city cemetery in Brandon, Mississippi.

BIBLIOGRAPHY

Jones, Terry L. "Robert Lowry." In *The Confederate General.* Edited by William C. Davis. Vol. 4. Harrisburg, Pa., 1991.
Warner, Ezra J. *Generals in Gray: Lives of the Confederate Commanders.* Baton Rouge, La., 1959.

RICHARD M. MCMURRY

LUBBOCK, FRANCIS R.

LUBBOCK, FRANCIS R (1815–1905), governor of Texas and lieutenant colonel. A native South Carolinian born October 16, 1815, Francis Richard Lubbock was a prominent rancher and politician in Texas prior to the Civil War and a resident of Velasco, near Houston, Harris County. He was elected lieutenant governor of the state in 1857 but was not reelected two years later. In 1860 he was a delegate to the Democratic National Convention at Charleston and supported the Southern rights faction that walked out of the convention. Following the election of Abraham Lincoln, Lubbock became a strong advocate of secession.

In 1861 Lubbock was elected governor over Edward Clark, and upon taking office he began to organize the state for defense. At his suggestion a board was created to direct military preparations, a frontier cavalry regiment was organized, and funds were raised to support these measures. As a member of the military board, Lubbock actively encouraged the development of war industries in the state. Private firms received contracts for the construction of a foundry, a percussion-cap factory, and other munitions works. Machinery was acquired to make cloth and shoes at the state penitentiary.

In the summer of 1862, Lubbock joined with the governors of Arkansas and Louisiana to ask the Confederate government to establish a branch of the Treasury in the Trans-Mississippi, to send more supplies to the district, and to provide additional troops. Lubbock was concerned particularly with the problems on the frontier and feared that the removal of able-bodied men from the state increased the threat of Indian attacks in the West. President Jefferson Davis responded by increasing the autonomy of the Trans-Mississippi region and sending General Theophilus H. Holmes to take command of it.

Lubbock decided not to run for reelection in 1863. He served on the staff of Gen. John B. Magruder who com-

manded Confederate forces in Texas. He then joined the staff of Gen. John Austin Wharton, who was named commander of Gen. Richard Taylor's cavalry division following the death of Gen. Thomas Green on April 12, 1864. Lubbock was with Wharton in the cavalry action against the Federal rear guard as Gen. Nathaniel Banks retreated from his Red River campaign that spring. In 1864 Lubbock went to Richmond where he received a lieutenant colonel's commission and served on the staff of President Davis as an adviser on Trans-Mississippi affairs.

At the war's end Lubbock accompanied Davis in his effort to escape Union capture, but he was taken with him at Irwinville, Georgia. Lubbock was sent to Fort Delaware where he remained for several months. After being paroled, he returned to Texas, living in Houston, Galveston, and Austin and actively participating in Democratic party politics and holding public office. Lubbock died at Austin on June 22, 1905.

BIBLIOGRAPHY

Lubbock, Francis R. *Six Decades in Texas: The Memoirs of Francis R. Lubbock.* Austin, Tex., 1900.
Yearns, W. Buck, ed. *The Confederate Governors.* Athens, Ga., 1985.

CARL H. MONEYHON

LYNCHBURG, VIRGINIA

A tobacco manufacturing center before the Civil War, the city of Lynchburg in the course of the conflict became one of the principal supply depots for the Confederate forces operating in Virginia. The primary reason for this was the city's strategic location far behind the front lines. The Confederate War Department could stockpile vast quantities of supplies—munitions, foodstuffs, clothing—secure in the knowledge that they were safe from the enemy. In addition, the city had direct railroad connections with Richmond and Petersburg to the east, Charlottesville and Gordonsville to the north, and Knoxville, Tennessee, to the west, which enabled the Confederacy to transport men and materials quickly and efficiently. Over time Lynchburg increased in importance, becoming by 1864 an indispensable source of supply for the Army of Northern Virginia.

The Federals were aware of how valuable Lynchburg was to the Confederate war effort, and on June 6, 1864, Lt. Gen. Ulysses S. Grant directed Maj. Gen. David Hunter, commander of the Federal forces in the Shenandoah Valley, to occupy the city. To accomplish his mission Grant wanted Hunter to move east of the Blue Ridge Mountains at Staunton, join forces with Maj. Gen. Philip H. Sheridan's cavalry nearby, and advance on Lynchburg from the north, destroying the southern branch of the Orange and Alexandria Railroad as he went. But when Hunter reached Staunton he did not move east of the mountains and unite with Sheridan; instead, he elected to continue up the valley on his own and approach Lynchburg from the west. He occupied Lexington on June 11, and after destroying everything of value, he passed through the Blue Ridge Mountains via Buford's Gap and began his advance on Lynchburg, reaching the outskirts of the city on June 17.

When the Federals occupied Lexington, Gen. Robert E. Lee foresaw that Lynchburg would be their next objective, and he moved quickly to protect his supply base. On June 12

> ## Lynchburg . . . became one of the principal supply depots for the Confederate forces operating in Virginia.

he sent Lt. Gen. Jubal Early and the entire Second Corps of the Army of Northern Virginia, approximately eight thousand men, west to defend the city and defeat Hunter. A lack of rolling stock delayed the Confederates' arrival, but by midday of June 17 Early and half of his command had reached the city. Prior to Early's arrival, the city had been protected by nine thousand troops commanded by Maj. Gen. John C. Breckinridge, half of which were reserve forces made up of several disorganized infantry units, the cadets of the Virginia Military Institute, and invalids from the hospitals.

Confined to bed because of an injury, Breckinridge called upon Lt. Gen. D. H. Hill to take charge of the city's defense. Hill established a defensive line just outside the city limits, but after surveying the field Early created a second line of breastworks covering both sides of the Salem Turnpike about two miles from the city. That night half of the Second Corps, Breckinridge's division, and about fifteen pieces of artillery took up positions along the advance line of defense while the reserve forces occupied the interior line of works.

When Hunter descended on Lynchburg he commanded an army composed of two divisions of infantry, two divisions of cavalry, and several batteries of artillery, a total of about eighteen thousand men. If he had acted boldly and decisively, he could have captured the city with few difficulties; but because he was under the impression that he was greatly outnumbered, he failed to do so. On the afternoon of the seventeenth, his artillery opened fire on the Confederate positions, but no infantry assault was attempted. The next day Hunter ordered several small-scale attacks, but they were easily repulsed and he made no further attempts to seize the city. When he discovered that Early had arrived, Hunter immediately issued orders for the army to retreat. That night under the cover of darkness he led his command back toward the Shenandoah Valley.

Compared to other engagements, the Battle of Lynchburg, in terms of troops involved, was not very large, but it did have a significant impact on the course of the war in Virginia in 1864. When Hunter withdrew, Early pressed his rear guard hard and sent his cavalry over the Blue Ridge to prevent Hunter from retreating down the valley. Unable to use the valley as an avenue of escape, Hunter had no choice but to retreat into the mountains of West Virginia, taking his army out of the war for several weeks and leaving the valley unprotected. With no one to oppose him, Early marched down the valley, crossed over the Potomac River, and threatened Washington, D.C.

Early's raid and his continued presence in the lower valley, in turn, compelled Grant to alter his plans to defeat the Confederate forces in Virginia. To protect the Union's capital and drive the Confederates from the valley, he had to transfer two full corps from the Army of the Potomac to northern Virginia. The departure of nearly forty thousand men severely limited Grant's offensive capabilities; unable to penetrate or outflank his opponents' defenses, he had to place Richmond and Petersburg under siege. Hunter's failure also caused Grant to abandon his idea of attacking Richmond from the west, and Lynchburg remained a vital supply base for the Confederates until the end of the war.

BIBLIOGRAPHY

Blackford, Charles M. "The Campaign and Battle of Lynchburg."*Southern Historical Society Papers* 30 (1902): 279–331. Reprint, Wilmington, N.C., 1991.

Catton, Bruce. *Grant Takes Command.* New York, 1968.

Freeman, Douglas S. *Lee's Lieutenants: A Study in Command.* 3 vols. New York, 1942–1944. Reprint, New York, 1986.

Johnson, Robert U., and C. C. Buel, eds. *Battles and Leaders of the Civil War.* Vol. 4. New York, 1888. Reprint, Secaucus, N.J., 1982.

MICHAEL G. MAHON

MCCAUSLAND, JOHN

McCAUSLAND, JOHN (1836–1927), brigadier general. Born in St. Louis, Missouri, September 13, 1836, the son of Irish immigrants, McCausland graduated from the Virginia Military Institute in 1857. While a professor at VMI, he went with a number of cadets to witness the hanging of John Brown in Charlestown.

Upon Virginia's secession he formed the Rockbridge Artillery but declined its command. Later, however, he organized troops in the Kanawha Valley and assumed command of the Thirty-sixth Virginia Infantry with the rank of colonel. He was present at the surrender of Fort Donelson, Tennessee, in 1862 but escaped with his troops to safety. After serving with the infantry in southwestern Virginia until May of 1864, he was promoted to brigadier general and given command of a cavalry brigade.

JOHN MCCAUSLAND.   LIBRARY OF CONGRESS

McCausland saved Lynchburg, Virginia, by delaying David Hunter's advance until reinforcements could arrive. He then led a gallant charge at Monocacy, Maryland, and took his cavalry to the suburbs of Washington, D.C., at the head of Jubal Early's army.

In July of 1864 he was ordered by General Early to Chambersburg, Pennsylvania. He demanded $500,000 as retribution for damage caused by Hunter in the Shenandoah Valley. When the townspeople refused to pay, McCausland ordered the town burned. On the retreat from Chambersburg, his cavalry was surprised at Moorefield and many of his men were captured.

McCausland served throughout the Shenandoah Valley campaign and was present at Appomattox. Once again he refused to surrender; instead he cut his way through the Union lines and returned home.

Threats arising from the episode at Chambersburg caused him to flee to Europe and Mexico for two years. After his return, McCausland spent the rest of his life farming in Mason County, West Virginia. At his death on January 22, 1927, he was survived only by Felix Robertson as the last Confederate general.

BIBLIOGRAPHY

Brown, James Earl. "The Life of Brigadier General John McCausland." *West Virginia History* 5 (1942): 1094.
Lewis, Thomas A. *The Shenandoah in Flames.* Alexandria, Va., 1987.
Scott, J. L. *Thirty-Sixth Virginia Infantry.* Lynchburg, Va., 1987.

J. L. SCOTT

MCCOMB, WILLIAM

MCCOMB, WILLIAM (1828–1918), brigadier general. Born in Mercer County, Pennsylvania, November 21, 1828, McComb moved to Tennessee in 1854 to superintend the construction of a flour mill at Price's Landing on the Cumberland River.

At the outbreak of the war McComb enlisted as a private in Company L of the Fourteenth Tennessee Infantry. He was promoted to lieutenant shortly thereafter and was adjutant of the regiment during the Cheat Mountain campaign. McComb was with W. W. Loring's division during Thomas J. ("Stonewall") Jackson's Romney expedition and, upon the reorganization of the army in the spring of 1862, was elected major of the Fourteenth Tennessee. In that role he participated in the engagements around Richmond. Because of deaths among officers of higher rank, McComb rose rapidly and became colonel of the regiment, September 2, 1862, shortly after Second Manassas.

For several months in 1864 fellow officers sought promotion for McComb. A petition containing the signatures of many officers stated that he had earned promotion "by his gallantry on many a hard contested field—by his uniformly strict discipline—his close and earnest attention to his duties." Henry Heth also recommended promotion, calling McComb "a gallant and deserving officer." Robert E. Lee declared that McComb was the "best officer to command the brigade" formed by the consolidation of James Jay Archer's old brigade with that of Bushrod Rust Johnson even though he was not the senior colonel. McComb was commissioned a brigadier, February 27, 1865.

After his parole at Appomattox, McComb resided in Mississippi and Alabama for several years. He moved to Louisa County, Virginia, in 1869 and engaged in farming for nearly fifty years.

McComb was one of the last six surviving general officers of the Confederacy when he died at his plantation, July 21, 1918. He was buried in Louisa County.

BIBLIOGRAPHY

Compiled Military Service Records. William McComb. Microcopy M331, Roll 170. Record Group 109. National Archives, Washington, D.C.

"The Last Roll." *Confederate Veteran* 26 (1918): 404. Reprint, Wilmington, N.C., 1985.

Porter, James D. *Tennessee.* Vol. 8 of *Confederate Military History.* Edited by Clement A. Evans. Atlanta, 1899. Vol. 10 of extended ed. Wilmington, N.C., 1987.

Warner, Ezra J. *Generals in Gray: Lives of the Confederate Commanders.* Baton Rouge, La., 1959.

LOWELL REIDENBAUGH

MCCULLOCH, BEN

MCCULLOCH, BEN (1811–1862), brigadier general. Born November 11, 1811, in Rutherford County, Tennessee, the elder brother of Gen. Henry Eustace McCulloch, Ben moved to Texas in 1835 at the urging of his friend Davy Crockett and fought in the Texas Revolution. He served a term in the Republic of Texas legislature and was a well-known Indian

fighter. He led Texas Rangers in the Mexican War and in the late 1840s joined the California gold rush. He served as sheriff of Sacramento County from 1850 until 1852 and then returned to Texas to become a U.S. marshal.

When Texas seceded, McCulloch became a colonel of state troops and took the surrender of Federal forces under David Emanuel Twiggs at San Antonio. Commissioned a brigadier general on May 11, 1861, he was assigned to command in Arkansas. His troops fought with the Missourians under Sterling Price at Oak Hills. Because of a personality clash between McCulloch and Price, the Confederate government created the Trans-Mississippi District in January 1862 and sent Maj. Gen. Earl Van Dorn to take command. In Van Dorn's attack at Elkhorn Tavern, Arkansas, McCulloch directed the right wing and was fatally wounded by a Union sharpshooter on March 7, 1862. McCulloch refused to wear the Confederate uniform and was dressed in his customary black velvet when shot through the heart. He is buried in Austin in the Texas State Cemetery beside his father, a brigadier general in the War of 1812.

BIBLIOGRAPHY

Hughes, Michael A. "A Forgotten Battle in a Region Ignored . . . Pea Ridge, or Elkhorn Tavern, Arkansas—March 7–8, 1862: The Campaign, the Battle, and the Men Who Fought for the Fate of Missouri." *Blue & Gray Magazine* 5 (1988): 8–36.

Nunn, W. C., ed. *Ten More Texans in Gray.* Hillsboro, Tex., 1980.

Pea Ridge National Park. "The Battle of Pea Ridge, 1862." Pamphlet. Rogers, Ark., n.d.

Wright, Marcus, J., comp., and Harold B. Simpson, ed. *Texas in the War, 1861–1865.* Hillsboro, Tex., 1965.

ANNE J. BAILEY

MCCULLOCH, HENRY EUSTACE

MCCULLOCH, HENRY EUSTACE (1816–1895), brigadier general. McCulloch was born December 6, 1816, in Rutherford County, Tennessee, the younger brother of Ben McCulloch. After moving to Texas in 1837 Henry served as sheriff of Gonzales County, fought in several Indian campaigns, and commanded a company of Texas Rangers in the Mexican War. He was elected to the state legislature in 1853 and the Texas senate in 1855.

McCulloch, when the Civil War began, was a U.S. marshal. The secession convention appointed him a colonel and authorized him to demand the surrender of the U.S. forts on the northwestern frontier. McCulloch briefly headed the Department of Texas and was made commander of the

Submilitary District of the Rio Grande early in 1862. He was promoted to brigadier general in March 1862. McCulloch took command in the eastern district of Texas and forwarded over twenty-thousand Texans toward Little Rock. In September he joined them and took command of a division of Texas infantry. In December he was replaced by Maj. Gen. John G. Walker and was assigned a brigade. McCulloch fought at Milliken's Bend on June 7, 1863, but his performance was so poor that he was transferred to an administrative post. In September 1863 he took over the Northern Subdistrict of Texas and remained there until the war's end.

Although he apparently had little talent for leading troops, McCulloch was an excellent administrator. Following the war he engaged in shipping cattle to Cuba, and worked for the railroad, and was appointed superintendent of the Asylum for the Deaf and Dumb in Austin, a position he held until he retired in 1879. He died in Rockport, Texas, on March 12, 1895, and is buried in Seguin.

BIBLIOGRAPHY

Bailey, Anne J. *Between the Enemy and Texas.* Fort Worth, Tex., 1989.

Wright, Marcus J., comp., and Harold B. Simpson, ed. *Texas in the War, 1861–1865.* Hillsboro, Tex., 1965.

ANNE J. BAILEY

MCDOWELL, THOMAS D.

McDOWELL, THOMAS D. (1823–1898), congressman from North Carolina. Born on January 4, 1823, in Bladen County, North Carolina, McDowell graduated from the University of North Carolina in 1843 and commenced planting in his native county. He served three terms as a Democrat in the house of commons (1846–1851) and another three in the state senate (1852–1855, 1858–1859). Like most North Carolina Democrats, he espoused the constitutional right of secession; nonetheless, he opposed disunion until after Abraham Lincoln's call for troops. Although he owned fifty-seven slaves in 1860 and ran a plantation valued at $65,000, McDowell later claimed that he would have readily "consented to a just and equitable plan of gradual emancipation . . . at any time before the war."

Elected to the secession convention in May 1861, McDowell resigned that position to take a seat in the Provisional Congress. There he generally supported the measures of the Davis administration, his principal concern being the defense of the North Carolina coast. He was subsequently elected without opposition to the First Congress and served on the Commerce Committee. A staunch adherent to the state rights school of politics, he became increasingly disenchanted with the centralizing tendencies of the Davis administration, voted against the suspension of habeas corpus, and opposed most of the administration's economic and military measures. He was not a candidate for reelection in 1863.

McDowell quickly reconciled himself to the outcome of the war, claiming that the abolition of slavery had "relieved [me] of the greatest trouble of my life." Avoiding politics, he concentrated instead on the management of his agricultural interests. He died at his plantation on May 1, 1898.

BIBLIOGRAPHY

Alexander, Thomas B., and Richard E. Beringer. *The Anatomy of the Confederate Congress: A Study of the Influences of Member Characteristics on Legislative Voting Behavior, 1861–1865.* Nashville, Tenn., 1972.

Powell, William S. *Dictionary of North Carolina Biography.* 4 vols. to date. Chapel Hill, N.C., 1979–.

Wakelyn, Jon L. *Biographical Dictionary of the Confederacy.* Edited by Frank E. Vandiver. Westport, Conn., 1977.

Warner, Ezra J., and W. Buck Yearns. *Biographical Register of the Confederate Congress.* Baton Rouge, La., 1975.

THOMAS E. JEFFREY

MACKALL, WILLIAM W.

MACKALL, WILLIAM W. (1817–1891), brigadier general. Mackall was born in Cecil City, Maryland, January 18, 1817, and graduated in 1837 from West Point eighth in a class of fifty. A career soldier, he was wounded in the Seminole War and wounded and brevetted in the Mexican War. He resigned from the U.S. Army on July 3, 1861, to join the Confederate army.

In March 1862 Brigadier General Mackall took command of New Madrid and Island Number 10, where on April 7 he surrendered with 3,500 men to the Federals. Exchanged in August 1862, Mackall held minor posts until he became Gen. Braxton Bragg's chief of staff on April 17, 1863. Mackall served Bragg and the Army of Tennessee well, particularly during Bragg's frequent illnesses. Although he supported Bragg and attempted to ease the general's burdens, Mackall became dissatisfied with his position, believing Bragg did not clearly define his duties and too often interfered in what Mackall considered his own administrative domain. On October 16, 1863, Mackall left Bragg. He returned to his old position, however, in January 1864 when Gen. Joseph E. Johnston replaced Bragg as commander of the Army of Tennessee. When Gen. John Bell Hood, in turn, took the command in July 1864, Mackall again asked to be relieved of duty. He held no further military assignments.

Mackall always believed he failed to receive deserved promotions because as a Marylander he had no one in the South to promote his interests out of either familial or political motives. He retired to farm in Virginia until his death in Fairfax County on August 12, 1891.

BIBLIOGRAPHY

Gow, June I. "Chiefs of Staff in the Army of Tennessee under Braxton Bragg." *Tennessee Historical Quarterly* 27 (1968): 341–360.
Gow, June I. "Military Administration in the Confederate Army of Tennessee." *Journal of Southern History* 40 (1974): 183–198.
Hallock, Judith Lee. *Braxton Bragg and Confederate Defeat.* Vol. 2. Tuscaloosa, Ala., 1991.
Mackall, William W. *A Son's Recollections of His Father.* New York, 1930.

JUDITH LEE HALLOCK

MCLAWS, LAFAYETTE

McLAWS, LAFAYETTE (1821–1897), major general. McLaws, who was born January 15, 1821, in Augusta, Georgia, attended the U.S. Military Academy at West Point, where he graduated in the class of 1842, ranking forty-eighth among fifty-six graduates. For nearly two decades after graduation McLaws performed routine duty in seven states, the Indian Territory, and Mexico. When the Civil War broke out, he had been stuck at the rank of captain for almost ten years.

McLaws served briefly as a quartermaster in Georgia early in 1861 before receiving appointment as colonel of the Tenth Georgia Infantry on June 17. He took his new command to Virginia, where he made a strong enough impression on the Confederacy's military hierarchy to win promotion to brigadier general on September 7, 1861, and to major general on May 23, 1862. McLaws's commission as major general was dated earlier than that of most of the other division commanders in the Army of Northern Virginia. As a result, he outranked most of that army's more familiar division commanders.

For two years McLaws led a sturdy division in Robert E. Lee's army that included Joseph B. Kershaw's South Carolina brigade, William Barksdale's (later Benjamin Grubb Humphreys's) Mississippi brigade, and the two Georgia brigades commanded by Thomas R. R. Cobb (later William Tatum Wofford) and Paul J. Semmes (later Goode Bryan). McLaws managed to weld his brigades into a solid fighting force noted for its defensive prowess. In the words of a staff officer, McLaws "was an officer of much experience and most careful. Fond of detail, his command was in excellent condition, and his ground and position well examined and reconnoitered."

McLaws saw action on Virginia's peninsula early in 1862 under John B. Magruder, whose judgment he soon came to distrust. In Maryland during September 1862, McLaws commanded with marked success on Maryland Heights and then led his division to a great, if lucky, triumph in the West Woods near Sharpsburg. At Fredericksburg, McLaws executed an assignment that played to his strength when he guarded the riverfront. He was, wrote an observant artillerist, "about the best general in the army for that sort of job."

Perhaps because he irritated Lee by his lack of initiative around Salem Church in May 1863, McLaws did not receive either of the promotions to corps command issued later that month. At Gettysburg, McLaws was so disgusted with James Longstreet, who had been his mentor, that he called him "a humbug, a man of small capacity, very obstinate, not at all chivalrous, exceedingly conceited, and totally selfish." The deadly impact of the rift on McLaws's career became apparent in the aftermath of Longstreet's botched Knoxville campaign that fall when Longstreet brought six formal charges against him. Five of them were patently absurd, as attested by dozens of witnesses, and the sixth was misrepresented. Although the War Department overturned the one negative finding and censured Longstreet for his behavior, the corps commander remained far more important to Lee's army than did McLaws.

McLaws spent the rest of the war in defense of Savannah, vainly attempting to stem William Tecumseh Sherman's onslaught and then following the Southern retreat northward. After the war the general lived in straitened circumstances. In 1886 he declared, "I am without means, having lost all." He died July 22, 1897, at Savannah, Georgia.

BIBLIOGRAPHY

Freeman, Douglas S. *Lee's Lieutenants: A Study in Command.* 3 vols. New York, 1942–1944. Reprint, New York, 1986.
McLaws, Lafayette. Papers. Southern Historical Collection, University of North Carolina, Chapel Hill; Duke University, Durham, North Carolina.

ROBERT K. KRICK

MCLEAN, WILMER

MCLEAN, WILMER (1814–?), army volunteer. In 1861 McLean was a forty-seven-year-old Virginian who owned a farm near Manassas Junction. Too old to fight but an ardent Confederate, he did what he could to support the Southern cause. In June 1861 he assisted Gen. P. G. T. Beauregard in a reconnaissance of the local countryside and soon after permitted the Confederates to place a signal station on his property. Beauregard used his house as army headquarters during the affair at Blackburn's Ford on July 18—the first engagement between the two opposing armies in Virginia. After the First Battle of Manassas, he worked as a volunteer for the Confederate Quartermaster Department.

By the spring of 1862, however, his dedication to the cause had waned considerably. He saw nothing but waste and mismanagement in the Quartermaster Department, and he grew tired of donating his time for free while others were reaping tremendous profits through speculation. In March 1862, he sold his home and began speculating in the sugar market, traveling widely throughout the South.

Toward the end of 1863, he returned to Virginia and settled down in a house at Appomattox Court House—a small peaceful village some two hundred miles from Manassas—with the hope of never seeing another soldier. He lived there in quiet seclusion until April 9, 1865, when Gen. Robert E. Lee used his residence to surrender the Army of Northern Virginia.

BIBLIOGRAPHY

Foote, Shelby. *The Civil War: A Narrative.* Vol. 3. New York, 1974.
Gallagher, Gary W., ed. *Fighting for the Confederacy: The Personal Recollections of General Edward Porter Alexander.* Chapel Hill, N.C., 1989.
McPherson, James M., ed. *Battle Chronicles of the Civil War.* Vol. 5. New York, 1989.

MICHAEL G. MAHON

MACON, GEORGIA

Proclaimed "Queen Inland City of the South," Macon dominated the economy of central Georgia. Situated on the fall line of the Ocmulgee River and at the intersection of the Central of Georgia Railroad and the Macon and Western Railroad, the city served the heart of the state's cotton belt. This rail center linked Atlanta, Columbus, Americus, Milledgeville, Augusta, and Savannah.

Macon's population was 8,034 in 1860, making it the fifth largest Georgia city. Famed poet and resident Sidney Lanier boldly declared its future as the "cultural capital of the young South" and the "next American Athens." Residents numbered 5,337 whites, 2,664 slaves, and 33 free blacks. Ironically, the free black population was 55 less than in 1850. Bibb County, with Macon as its county seat, was the only one in the area to have a white population majority. One-fifth of the city's residents were foreign-born and 60 percent of the white households owned slaves. Planters headed 9 percent of resident families; 37 percent described themselves as "professionals, merchants, manufacturers, or proprietors." Master craftsmen and journeymen also headed 37 percent of families; semi-

skilled and day laborers composed 14 percent. Overseers headed 2 percent of households, and the remaining 1 percent included widows and the retired or unemployed.

Almost all slaves worked as domestics, building tradesmen, proprietors of small shops (typically the city's barbers were blacks), or laborers on the railroad. Many negotiated with their masters to permit them to operate their own small businesses, free from daily contact with their owners. Urban

> Its location . . . ensured its relative safety from either land or water assault until late in the war.

slaves experienced only limited opposition in engaging in such commercial ventures.

The minuscule free black population worked primarily in the construction trades, domestic service, or other service occupations. A notable exception was Solomon Humphries who purchased his family's freedom from his plantation master, became a successful merchant, made a fortune, and was widely respected.

Macon's economy rested primarily on King Cotton. One-seventh of Georgia's total production was baled in the city on the eve of the Civil War and transported via rail or river to Northern or European mills. The railroad and its supporting iron industry also were major elements of the economy. The Macon and Western Railroad boasted a cash surplus of $131,000 in 1860 and paid a 9 percent dividend. The Central of Georgia Railroad connected the city with Savannah, the state's busiest deepwater port, enabling Maconites to enjoy seafood as "common luxuries" in winter and cheap ice in summer. Several roundhouses attested to the importance of rail transportation to the city's economic vitality.

In the presidential election of 1860, Maconites voted for either John Bell of the Constitutional Union party or John C. Breckinridge, the proslavery nominee of the fragmented Democrats. Bell carried the city by a small margin, while Breckinridge won the state. The announcement of Abraham Lincoln's victory forced the city's moderates to join the secession camp or cease public political discussion.

Lincoln's election caused the city to begin preparing for armed conflict with the Federal government. On November 8 the Minutemen announced their unit's uniform style and color. The following week a Committee of Safety prepared to take "protective measures" within the city. The Macon volunteers unfurled their unit's colors with fifteen stars in anticipation of the formation of the Southern nation. Sidney Lanier soon joined this unit, which was one of Georgia's first to fight at the Virginia front. During the war, twenty-six companies of infantry, artillery, and cavalry went into battle. The city's

Camp Oglethorpe was a major staging location for soldiers ordered to the front. No county in the Confederacy sent more troops in proportion to its population than Bibb, and roughly one-tenth of the county's white males died in the war.

While the recently established *Macon Telegraph* urged the electorate to guard against hasty action on the part of their representatives in the legislature, Mayor M. S. Thomson, the first of Macon's three Civil War mayors, also urged careful thought and tried to maintain public order. In mid-December the city chose three delegates to the state secession convention. One of these, Eugenius A. Nisbet, drafted the Georgia Ordinance of Secession, which declared the state an independent republic on January 19, 1861. Troops from Macon had already been ordered by Governor Joseph E. Brown to seize Fort Pulaski near Savannah.

Numerous aid societies, most patterned after the Macon Ladies Soldiers' Relief Society, contributed to war preparations even before the fall of Fort Sumter. These groups sewed, solicited contributions, and tended the sick and wounded. They were instrumental in converting the Macon Hotel, the vacant Georgia Academy for the Blind, and other buildings into treatment facilities as casualties mounted. Arrival of wounded from Chickamauga transformed City Hall into a hospital.

The city enjoyed unique security from enemy assault during the first years of war. Its location in the heart of the Piedmont and upstream from the shoals at the confluence of the Ocmulgee and Altamaha rivers ensured its relative safety from either land or water assault until late in the war.

The Confederate government established three ordnance installations in the city in 1861. An armory for manufacturing and repairing small arms, an arsenal for molding cannons and other heavy arms, and a laboratory for producing ammunition became major employers. These factories ranked in size only behind the Tredegar Iron Works in Richmond and the Selma, Alabama, Ordnance Works. Other government offices quickly located in the city. A Quartermaster Depot, the Medical Purveyor's Office, and a steam bakery produced necessities. By war's end, the Confederate government controlled a great portion of the city's land and labor, both free and slave. Over a thousand slaves and several hundred white civilians worked in these factories. The Confederate Treasury Department used Macon as a depository for $1.5 million in gold.

Private businesses, though plagued by chronic labor and material shortages, similarly prospered. Articles for military and civilian use—from steam engines, cotton presses, and sawmills to spurs, swords, pistols, and uniforms—poured from the city. The twin problems of rampant inflation and shortages of food and cloth precipitated a riot by some Macon women in 1864.

Though the Georgia Academy for the Blind moved to Fort Valley, Wesleyan College managed to remain open through-out the war. Public entertainment provided welcome diversion from the hardships. Residents supported and regularly attended various stock companies whose productions ranged from *Macbeth* to *Pizzaro*.

By 1864, Macon was exhibiting the overcrowding, lawlessness, disease, and disorder of a refugee city. Dislocated civilians, wounded and ill soldiers, and prostitutes poured in following Confederate defeats in northern Georgia and Alabama.

In the spring of 1864, the Army of Georgia Reserves and Georgia Militia, commanded by Howell Cobb, headquartered in Macon. Union forces under the command of George Stoneman raided the city on July 30, but they were repulsed and failed in their attempt to free Union officers held as prisoners of war. Earthworks now guarded the city's perimeter.

Following the fall of Atlanta, Macon anticipated a direct Union attack. Because Cobb's militia numbered only 1,500, the armory was dismantled and removed to keep it from falling into enemy hands. The city did escape Sherman's March to the Sea as he swept across the state from the ashes of Atlanta to Savannah. With the Union capture of the state capital, Milledgeville, Macon's City Hall served as the capitol building until war's end.

Cobb surrendered the city to Union commander James H. Wilson on April 20, 1865, eleven days after Appomattox. Though some looting and pillaging occurred, Macon fared better than many occupied cities, for Wilson and Cobb cooperated in maintaining order. Nor had the city sustained substantial war-related damage.

James Johnson, the presidentially appointed provisional governor of Georgia, inspected Macon in mid-July and found the city rebuilding. Businesses reopened and banking revived, though barter was still widely used. Tracks and rolling stock of the Central of Georgia Railroad were repaired and the company refinanced. Most of the residents who had fled during the war's final months returned quickly; by decade's end the population had grown to over seven thousand and Macon continued its dominance of central Georgia.

BIBLIOGRAPHY

Anderson, Nancy B. *Macon: A Pictorial History.* Virginia Beach, Va., 1979.

Reidy, Joseph P. "Masters and Slaves, Planters and Freedmen: The Transition from Slavery to Freedom in Central Georgia, 1820–1880." Ph.D. diss., Northern Illinois University, 1982.

Simms, Kristina. *Macon: Georgia's Central City.* Chatsworth, Calif., 1989.

Young, Ida, Julius Gholsow, and Clara Nell Hargrove. *History of Macon, Georgia.* Macon, Ga., 1959.

RALPH B. SINGER, JR.

MCRAE, COLIN J.

MCRAE, COLIN J. (1812–1877), Mississippi governor and congressman, and chief financial agent for the Confederacy in Europe. McRae was born in Sneedsboro (present-day McFarlan), North Carolina, on October 22, 1812. In 1817 his family moved to Mississippi where his father became a well-established merchant and trader. Eventually the family settled in Pascagoula, Mississippi, on the Gulf coast; however, as his father's business expanded, the family maintained another home in Mobile, Alabama. McRae, although he was a Presbyterian, attended the Catholic College of Biloxi, Mississippi, for one year.

McRae's father died in 1835, and he took over the operation of the family's extensive mercantile business and assumed responsibility for his ten brothers and sisters. McRae quickly became a respected cotton commissioner and was one of the most successful businessmen along the Gulf coast, where he operated a fleet of coastal trading vessels. He also invested heavily in railroad development and real estate. He was one of the founders of Mississippi City, located about eighteen miles west of Biloxi. In addition he owned thousands of acres of land and many slaves.

Active in Mississippi politics, McRae was appointed a general of militia, and in 1838 he was elected to the Mississippi legislature. In 1840, he moved his base of operations to Mobile and entered into a partnership with Burwell Boykin as commission merchants. He also became involved in Democratic politics during this period. During the 1840s, McRae formed a business arrangement with his brother John J. McRae to promote the Mobile and Ohio Railroad and later the Mobile and New Orleans Railroad. The brothers also became slave dealers, real estate brokers, and land speculators. John McRae went on to become a U.S. senator from 1851 to 1852, governor of Mississippi from 1854 to 1858, a member of the U.S. House of Representatives from 1858 until secession, and a member of the Confederate House of Representatives from 1861 to 1863.

Colin McRae was a staunch secessionist, and in January 1861 he was elected to represent Mobile County in the Provisional Congress of the Confederacy. He was named to the Finance Committee as well as the Engrossment and Enrollment, Buildings, and Naval Affairs committees. He was also appointed to the Special Committee for the Inauguration of the President and Vice-President.

Because of his vast mercantile interests, McRae was concerned with keeping the port of Mobile open and argued strongly for its defense, pointing out its value as a major shipping point in correspondence with Confederate officials. He suggested that the Confederate navy construct four patrol boats to protect Mobile's harbor area. In addition he opposed transferring large numbers of Alabama troops to the regular army, insisting that they remain under state control and be used to protect Alabama. Because he understood the importance of commerce to the Federal government and realized that one way to weaken the North's war effort was to cripple its overseas trade, McRae also pushed for the issuance of letters of marque to Southern privateers who would scour the oceans in search of Northern shipping.

McRae did not stand for reelection. Instead he became involved in equipping the Southern military and entered the arms and munitions business. In 1861, he became an agent of the Confederate Ordnance Bureau, working in an unofficial capacity until July 16, 1862, when he was appointed an Ordnance Bureau agent for the Confederacy and the state of Alabama.

In 1861 he became interested in the construction of a major arms foundry at Selma, Alabama. Selma offered an ideal location: it was inland and therefore safe from a seaborne assault, it had excellent river and rail connections, and it was close to the coal and iron deposits of central Alabama. In addition, there existed in the city a small foundry and machine shop, the Selma Manufacturing Company, which the Confederacy could purchase for $35,000. In March 1865, President Jefferson Davis approved McRae's plan and authorized the purchase of the Selma company and the construction of an arms and munitions center. In addition to his official connection with the Selma ordnance works through his Confederate and Alabama commissions, McRae had a personal financial interest in the operation.

McRae spent much time putting the plan into effect, traveling to New Orleans to purchase equipment. The Selma operation developed into one of the largest iron manufacturing centers in the South, second only to the Tredegar Iron Works in Richmond, Virginia. Eventually the entire operation

> McRae . . . became involved in equipping the Southern military and entered the arms and munitions business.

was taken over by the Confederate War and Navy departments. At the peak of its production, the Naval Arms Foundry at Selma employed three thousand workers and specialized in casting heavy cannons as well as operating an arsenal, powdermill, ironworks, and navy yard. It was at Selma that the Confederacy built the machinery and hulls for its naval vessels.

During the fall of 1862, McRae purchased cotton throughout the South and arranged for its shipment through the blockade to European markets, where it would be sold or exchanged for arms and munitions. The operation was so successful that during the first two years of the conflict

European arms dealers were the principal source of Confederate weapons and military equipment.

In January of 1863 McRae served as the European manager of the Erlanger loan, negotiated with Emile Erlanger and Company of Paris, France. In return for Confederate bonds backed by cotton, Erlanger agreed to market a loan of 5 million pounds sterling in Europe for a fee equal to 5 percent of the bond issue. At the time cotton was considered an excellent financial investment for Europeans, and bond purchasers were offered two options for redeeming their investment: they could take possession of the cotton that backed the loan in New Orleans at the close of the war for a price of six pence a pound, or if they wanted their cotton before the war ended, they could demand that it be delivered to points within the Confederacy not more than ten miles from a railway or navigable stream for shipment at the bondholders' risk and expense.

The bonds were discounted 40 percent, and Erlanger was secretly allowed to take over the bonds at 77 percent and sell them in foreign financial markets at 90 percent of face value. Although the rates were exorbitant, they were not out of line with the interest charged on other loans of the period. The arrangement also allowed Erlanger and Company to repurchase the bonds, with Confederate capital, as a means of supporting the market and preventing their value from plunging. Because the bonds were backed by cotton, their successful distribution depended on the willingness of purchasers to speculate on the price of cotton.

The agreement allowed Erlanger and Company to make an enormous profit of about 13.5 million francs. The arrangement was criticized by many; however, the loan and subsequent bond issue provided the South with $15 million with which to continue the war effort, and it proved to be the mainstay of Confederate purchasing power in Europe. In spite of its drawbacks, the loan underwrote most of the arms purchases made by the Confederacy abroad until 1864, and at the time its terms were about the best that McRae could have negotiated. The value of the bonds fluctuated greatly during the war years, and the price of cotton rose and fell as the Federal blockade restricted trade and new cotton-producing areas were opened in Egypt. When the war ended the bonds became worthless, but their holders continued to scheme for their redemption for several years.

McRae returned home briefly in 1863 to complete the transfer of the Selma operation to the Confederate government. That same year he was named the chief Confederate overseas financial agent and devoted most of his time and energy to maintaining the South's credit, an increasingly difficult task as the North began to assert its supremacy on the battlefield and the Union's navy tightened its blockade of Southern ports.

At first the blockade was enforced by only one warship responsible for approximately three hundred miles of coastline. It had little effect on Southern trade with Europe and caused McRae little trouble. By 1864, however, the Federal navy had grown from 42 warships to 671 vessels, and their stranglehold on the South threatened to cut communications with other countries. Although McRae did everything possible to maintain trade, his efforts failed, and with the fall of Wilmington, North Carolina, which was evacuated by Southern forces on February 11, 1865, his task became impossible.

In October 1863, McRae suggested a plan to Confederate officials to reestablish Southern credit. First, he proposed the revoking of all contracts in which profits or commissions were allowed. Second, he demanded that a single contracting or purchasing officer be appointed for the War Department and another for the Navy Department. Third, he wanted to appoint a general agent in Europe with broad discretionary powers who would control all Southern credit, raise money, and take charge of all contracting and purchasing agents abroad. Fourth, McRae wanted the Confederate government to take control of all exports and imports, allowing nothing into or out of the South unless it was on a government account or an account of a bondholder demanding cotton. Finally, he urged that Confederate officials seize all cotton and tobacco in the South at a price fixed by Congress. This, he pointed out, would allow the government, rather than speculators, to make a profit. The plan was approved by President Davis and his cabinet and enacted into legislation in January 1864. McRae hoped that through these measures the Confederacy could restructure its credit by maintaining a monopoly on the shipping of cotton. It came too late in the war effort, however, to have much effect.

In the fall of 1864, at the urging of Secretary of State Judah P. Benjamin, McRae embarked on a secret mission to recruit Poles, who had unsuccessfully rebelled against Russia earlier that year, into Confederate service. In August 1864, four Polish officers had run the Federal blockade and offered their services to President Davis in return for the Confederacy setting aside an area in which the exiles could settle. Davis agreed and authorized the Poles to organize their own military units. On September 1, Benjamin ordered McRae to oversee the arrangements to ship the exiles to Mexico and from there into the Confederacy. He was not to induce any Poles to volunteer; they had to offer their services on their own. McRae was given 50,000 British pounds from the Secret Service fund to carry out the plan. The project failed to generate support among exiles, and in February 1865, McRae admitted to Benjamin that the recruitment effort had not succeeded.

With the downturn in Confederate military fortunes, several holders of Southern bonds in Europe sued McRae in an effort to force payment of their notes. In every instance the courts ruled in McRae's favor and acquitted him of any legal obligation. At the end of the war McRae returned to

Mississippi and reestablished many of his former businesses.

When Davis was indicted for treason in 1867, McRae was among those supplying funds for the defense. Although Davis was charged under a statute enacted in 1790, Federal prosecutors never brought the matter to trial, as the defense maintained that the Fourteenth Amendment precluded any further punishment of ex-Confederates. After numerous delays the charges were dropped, and Davis was released under the provisions of a presidential proclamation of general amnesty in December 1868.

In the fall of 1867, McRae joined a group of Confederate expatriates to form a colony of exiles in Central America. He purchased a plantation and mercantile establishment at Puerto Cortès in Honduras. Applying his business talents to the new endeavor, McRae quickly became involved in the cattle and mahogany trade and expanded his mercantile business. He was joined in Honduras by his brother John and one of their sisters. John died in British Honduras (present-day Belize) while visiting Colòn in May 1868 and was buried there. Colin McRae also died in British Honduras in February 1877 and was buried beside his brother.

BIBLIOGRAPHY

Brewer, W. *Alabama: Her History, Resources, War Record, and Public Men from 1540 to 1872.* Montgomery, Ala., 1872.
Davis, Charles S. *Colin J. McRae: Confederate Financial Agent.* Tuscaloosa, Ala., 1961.
Eaton, Clement. *A History of the Southern Confederacy.* New York, 1954.
Fleming, Walter L. *Civil War and Reconstruction in Alabama.* New York, 1905.
Huse, Caleb. *The Supplies for the Confederate Army: How They Were Obtained in Europe and How Paid For.* Boston, 1904.
McRae, John Colin. Letters. Alabama State Department of Archives and History. Montgomery, Ala.
Thompson, Samuel B. *Confederate Purchasing Operations Abroad.* Chapel Hill, N.C., 1935.

KENNY A. FRANKS

MAFFITT, JOHN N.

MAFFITT, JOHN N. (1819–1886), naval officer and commander of blockade runners. Maffitt enlisted in the U.S. Navy in 1832 and resigned his commission in 1861 after twenty-nine years of service, including fourteen in the coastal survey. This latter service was probably responsible for the success of his blockade running.

Maffitt was commissioned a lieutenant in the Confederate navy in May 1861. His first command was *Savannah,* flagship of Josiah Tattnall's squadron, which tried to prevent the capture of Port Royal. His next assignment was as captain of a blockade runner. At Nassau on May 6, 1862, Maffitt took command of *Oreto,* which soon became *Florida.* Unable to begin his cruise immediately because of an inadequate crew, incomplete armament, and yellow fever among his men, he began an odyssey in Cuba that eventually took the ship on a spectacular run through the Union blockade in full daylight at Mobile, a feat he accomplished by disguising *Florida* as an English warship. He finally began his first cruise on January 17, 1863. Although he constantly encountered difficulty in supplying his ship, Maffitt captured twenty-five merchant ships. His auxiliaries seized another twenty-two, making the captures attributed to *Florida's* first cruise a total of forty-seven.

After leaving *Florida* Maffitt returned to duty as a blockade runner and briefly commanded the ram *Albermarle* in 1864. His superiors, fearing that the aggressive Maffitt would lose *Albermarle,* had him removed. He climaxed his career by running the blockades at Wilmington, Charleston, and Galveston with *Owl.* Maffitt served for a time in the British merchant service before returning to his home in North Carolina, where he spent his remaining years on a small farm near Wilmington.

BIBLIOGRAPHY

Boykin, Edward. *Sea Devil of the Confederacy: The Story of the Florida and Her Captain John Newland Maffitt.* New York, 1959.
Dalzell, George W. *Flight from the Flag.* Chapel Hill, N.C., 1940.
Owsley, Frank L. *The C.S.S. Florida: Her Building and Operations.* Tuscaloosa, Ala., 1987.

FRANK LAWRENCE OWSLEY

MAGOFFIN, BERIAH

MAGOFFIN, BERIAH (1815–1885), governor of Kentucky. Magoffin was born in Harrodsburg, Kentucky, on April 18, 1815. He graduated from Centre College in 1835 and completed the law course at Transylvania University in 1838.

A Democratic stalwart, Magoffin was a delegate to several national conventions and a frequent candidate for presidential elector. Elected to the state senate in 1850, he was defeated for lieutenant governor in 1855. Magoffin won the governorship in 1859 over Joshua F. Bell, 76,187 to 67,283. His troubled administration was dominated by the sectional crisis and the Civil War.

Magoffin never concealed his Southern sympathies. He accepted slavery, and he charged that the Republicans ("obstinate in spirit, and sullen in temper") had violated Southern rights in regard to the territories and fugitive slaves. Although he believed in the right of secession, Magoffin hoped that collective demands from the slave states would force the North to make concessions. If compromise failed, he predicted that Kentucky would go with the other slave states.

When his efforts to secure a compromise failed, Magoffin advocated calling a convention to determine the state's policy, but Unionist legislators refused it for fear that it might be a plot to take Kentucky out of the Union. After the fall of Fort Sumter, Magoffin rejected the Union call for troops; Kentucky would supply "no troops for the wicked purpose of subduing her Sister Southern States." But he also refused to supply troops to the Confederacy, and he helped formulate Kentucky's neutrality policy, which he proclaimed on May 20, 1861.

After summer elections the Unionist majorities in the legislature easily overrode his vetoes. When opposing forces entered the state in early September, the legislature ordered him to demand the withdrawal of only the Confederates. When his veto failed, Magoffin obeyed the directive; he explained that his oath of office required him to obey the will of the majority, regardless of his own views. He puzzled his opponents by retaining his office and denouncing the Confederate government of Kentucky that was established in November. But his efforts to halt what he saw as Federal vio-

> . . . the legislature ordered him to demand the withdrawal of only the Confederates.

lations of constitutional rights convinced his opponents of his pro-Confederate stance, and the legislature stripped him of many of his powers. His position became increasingly untenable. But the lieutenant governor had died in 1859, and Magoffin would not accept Speaker of the Senate John F. Fisk as his successor. After secret negotiations, Fisk resigned as Speaker on August 16, 1862, and was replaced immediately by James F. Robinson. Two days later Magoffin resigned as governor, Robinson replaced him, and Fisk was reelected Speaker.

Magoffin retired to his Harrodsburg farm and law practice. Chicago real estate investments made him wealthy. When the war ended, he urged Kentuckians to ratify the Thirteenth Amendment and extend civil rights to blacks. Magoffin served a term (1867–1869) in the statehouse. He died on February 28, 1885, and was buried at Harrodsburg.

BIBLIOGRAPHY

Commonwealth of Kentucky. House of Representatives. *Journal.* 1859–1862.
Commonwealth of Kentucky. Senate. *Journal.* 1859–1862.
Coulter, E. Merton. *The Civil War and Readjustment in Kentucky.* Chapel Hill, N.C., 1926.
Dues, Michael T. "The Pro-Secessionist Governor of Kentucky: Beriah Magoffin's Credibility Gap." *Register of the Kentucky Historical Society* 67 (July 1969): 221–231.
Harrison, Lowell H. "Beriah Magoffin, 1859–1862." In *Kentucky's Governors, 1792–1885.* Edited by Lowell H. Harrison. Lexington, Ky., 1985.
Harrison, Lowell H. "Governor Magoffin and the Secession Crisis." *Register of the Kentucky Historical Society* 72 (April 1974): 91–110.

LOWELL H. HARRISON

MAGRATH, ANDREW G.

MAGRATH, ANDREW G. (1813–1893), district judge and governor of South Carolina. Born in Charleston February 8, 1813, Magrath attended Catholic Bishop John England's school and graduated from South Carolina College in 1831. After attending Harvard Law School and reading law, he was admitted to the bar in 1835. He served in the state legislature in 1840 and 1842. Magrath married Emma C. Mikell in 1843. He was a cooperationist in the secession crisis of 1852 and joined James L. Orr's National Democratic faction in 1856. He was elected to the Democratic National Convention but resigned to become federal district judge.

After Abraham Lincoln's election in 1860, Magrath resigned from the judiciary, declaring that "the Temple of Justice, raised under the Constitution of the United States, is now closed." He was elected to the secession convention and on December 30, 1860, became secretary of state. He served on the Executive Council until 1862. Then he was appointed Confederate district judge. Although he held the Conscription and Sequestering acts constitutional, his opinions increasingly reflected a state rights position. He declared the war tax on securities unconstitutional. His later decisions made him popular with the anti–Jefferson Davis faction.

On November 16, 1864, Magrath urged Senator James Chesnut, Jr., a leader of the pro-Davis faction, to run for governor. Mrs. Chesnut noted: "I take it for granted he wants to be governor himself, and to use Mr. Chesnut in the canvass as a sort of lightning rod." Chesnut refused, and four names emerged: John Smith Preston and Samuel McGowan, who were pro-Davis, and Magrath and A. C. Garlington, anti-Davis. On December 14 Magrath won on the sixth ballot. He declared his efforts would be directed toward defending the state equally from the Union and from the Confederate government.

The legislature gave Magrath power to exempt from Confederate service whomever he deemed necessary for the defense of the state and restricted the power of the Confederacy to impress slaves in South Carolina. With

William Tecumseh Sherman's invasion imminent, Magrath urged Davis to save Charleston.

In January 1865 Magrath received word that P. G. T. Beauregard had ordered the evacuation of the garrison there. The governor appealed to Davis and Robert E. Lee, and Davis sent a brigade of Charlestonians. Meanwhile, Magrath appealed unsuccessfully to the governors of Georgia and North Carolina. By February the state was

> On May 15, 1865, Union Gen. Quincy A. Gillmore charged Magrath with treason.

invaded, and the governor urged citizens to defend their homes and to destroy or remove what was of value to the enemy. With Sherman before Columbia on February 16, Magrath moved to Winnsboro, Union, and then Spartanburg. He called the legislature to meet in Greenville on April 25, but no quorum appeared. Magrath returned to Columbia and ordered other state officials to do the same. After Joseph E. Johnston's surrender on April 26, Magrath demanded that Confederate supplies be turned over to the state.

On May 15, 1865, Union Gen. Quincy A. Gillmore charged Magrath with treason. The governor suspended the functions of his office, and on May 25 he was arrested and imprisoned at Fort Pulaski. On November 23, 1865, President Andrew Johnson ordered Magrath released. Shortly afterward he married Mary McCord (his first wife having died) and moved to Charleston. He resumed the practice of law until his death on April 9, 1893.

BIBLIOGRAPHY

Cauthen, Charles E. *South Carolina Goes to War, 1860–1865.* Chapel Hill, N.C., 1950.
Edmunds, John B., Jr. "South Carolina." In *The Confederate Governors.* Edited by W. Buck Yearns. Athens, Ga., 1985.

A. V. HUFF, JR.

MAGRUDER, JOHN B.

MAGRUDER, JOHN B. (1807–1871), major general. Born in Port Royal, Virginia, Magruder graduated from West Point in 1830. Serving in the First United States Artillery, he earned distinction in the Mexican War. Magruder, who became known as "Prince John," was fond of finery, drink, and revelry, which made him a conspicuous figure but raised questions about his competency among his superiors. On April

20, 1861, shortly after Virginia seceded from the Union, Magruder resigned his brevet lieutenant colonel commission in the U.S. Army. He received a Confederate commission as colonel on May 21, 1861, to date from March 16, 1861. Promotion came rapidly: he became a brigadier general on June 17 and a major general on October 7, 1861.

Command of the Confederate troops on the peninsula in May 1861 offered Magruder a critical assignment. He defeated the Federals at Big Bethel, a minor skirmish on June 10, which won him acclaim throughout the South. A more serious threat materialized in the spring of 1862, when Gen. George B. McClellan's Union army plodded up the peninsula. To slow the Federal advance, Magruder brilliantly disguised the numerical weakness of his force. His subterfuges stalled McClellan at Yorktown for an entire month. This allowed Gen. Joseph E. Johnston to shift his forces to the peninsula and assume overall command there. Magruder's performance, however, did not impress Johnston. His criticisms reached Jefferson Davis whose estimation of Magruder fell considerably.

Magruder's part in the Seven Days' Battles remains the most controversial aspect of his career in Confederate service. While Gen. Robert E. Lee concentrated the bulk of his forces on the Confederate left, Magruder and Gen. Benjamin Huger were left with 25,000 men to stave off more than 65,000 Federals south of the Chickahominy River. Repeating his tactics on the peninsula, Magruder deluded McClellan into believing that he faced a superior force. As Lee chased the retreating Federal army, Magruder joined the pursuit on June 28. The dapper Virginian suddenly became lethargic, punctuated by occasional outbursts of anger. Physical exhaustion, an allergic reaction to some medicine, and the mental strain of holding Lee's thin right flank had taken a toll on Magruder. He did not handle his troops energetically at Savage's Station on June 29 or the next day at Frayser's Farm. At Malvern Hill on July 1, Magruder fell apart. One Confederate officer observed that there was a "wild expression" in Magruder's eyes and "his excited manner impressed me at once with the belief that he was under the influence of some powerful stimulant."

The press singled out Magruder for the failure to destroy McClellan's command while Lee and Jackson largely escaped criticism. Persistent rumors of his drunkenness largely explains why Magruder became a scapegoat of the Seven Days' Battles. Shortly thereafter, he was transferred to the Trans-Mississippi and assigned to Texas in October 1862. Magruder protected the state's coast and launched a successful raid against Galveston on the first day of 1863. In 1864, Magruder detached most of his troops to Gen. Richard Taylor in Louisiana. He stayed in Texas with his small force until the end of the war.

After the war, Magruder emigrated to Mexico, where he served in the army of Maximilian. Magruder returned to the

United States after Maximilian's regime fell. He died in Houston, Texas, on February 18, 1871.

BIBLIOGRAPHY

Capers, Ellison. *South Carolina.* Vol. 5 of *Confederate Military History.* Edited by Clement A. Evans. Atlanta, 1899. Vol. 6 of extended ed. Wilmington, N.C., 1987.
Gallagher, Gary W. "The Fall of 'Prince John' Magruder."*Civil War Times Illustrated* 19 (August 1989): 8–15.

PETER S. CARMICHAEL

MAHONE, WILLIAM

MAHONE, WILLIAM (1826–1895), major general and U.S. senator. Mahone was born December 1, 1826, in Southampton County, Virginia. He was the grandson of veterans of the War of 1812 and son of a tavernkeeper who commanded a militia regiment during the Nat Turner insurrection.

As a youth, Billy Mahone carried mail from Jerusalem (Courtland) to Hill's Ford (Emporia) and was described as a congenial chap and a whiz at the gaming table. With financial aid from friends, he attended the Virginia Military Institute, graduating in 1847. During his two years as a teacher at the Rappahannock Military Academy, Mahone continued his studies and was appointed engineer of the Orange and Alexandria Railroad and later of the Norfolk and Petersburg line.

Offering his services to the state upon its adoption of the ordinance of secession, Mahone was appointed quartermaster general of Virginia and then colonel of the Sixth Virginia Infantry. He took part in the capture of the Norfolk Navy Yard, commanded the Norfolk district until it was abandoned, and then joined the Army of Northern Virginia for the remainder of the war.

As commander of a brigade at Seven Pines, Mahone was criticized by D. H. Hill for creating a gap in the Confederate line. But at Malvern Hill he was lauded by John B. Magruder who said he "could not speak too highly" of Mahone and his men. James Longstreet also praised Mahone for his performance at Second Manassas where a severe wound incapacitated Mahone for the Maryland campaign.

Longstreet was in the forefront of those urging that Mahone, who was commissioned a brigadier on November 16, 1861, be promoted to major general. In February 1863, he called his subordinate "one of our best brigadiers and . . . worthy of promotion." Richard Anderson, Robert E. Lee, and members of Congress also endorsed him. But when the promotion came on June 1, 1864, Mahone immediately declined it, apparently because it was only a temporary advancement. He was promoted to the permanent rank of major general on August 3 to date from July 30, when Mahone and his division performed heroically at the Battle of the Crater. Commenting on Mahone's feat of first containing the Federals and then routing them, W. H. Stuart of the Sixty-first Virginia wrote: "The whole movement was under his immediate and personal direction, and to him, above all, save the brave men who bore the muskets, belongs the honor and credit of recapturing the Confederate lines."

Billy Mahone, "short, spare and long-bearded, always in gray slouch hat and peg-top trousers, eyes blue and restless, voice thin and piping," surrendered at Appomattox and returned to his railroad interests in Virginia. He took an active part in politics as an organizer of the Readjuster party. He lost a bid for the gubernatorial nomination in 1877, but won a seat in the U.S. Senate in 1880 when he became identified with the Republican party. He made his home in Washington during his later years and died there October 8, 1895. He was buried in Blandford Cemetery, Petersburg, his adopted city.

BIBLIOGRAPHY

Blake, Nelson Morehouse. *William Mahone of Virginia.* Richmond, Va., 1935.
Bridges, Hal. *Lee's Maverick General: Daniel Harvey Hill.* New York, 1961.
Compiled Military Service Records. William Mahone. Microcopy M331, Roll 162. Record Group 109. National Archives, Washington, D.C.
Hotchkiss, Jed. *Virginia.* Vol. 3 of *Confederate Military History.* Edited by Clement A. Evans. Atlanta, 1899. Vol. 4 of extended ed. Wilmington, N.C., 1987.

LOWELL REIDENBAUGH

MALLORY, STEPHEN R.

MALLORY, STEPHEN R. (1811–1873), U.S. senator and Confederate secretary of the navy. Mallory was born at Port of Spain on the island of Trinidad, British West Indies. His father was a construction engineer from Connecticut, and his mother was Irish. The Mallorys left Trinidad when Stephen was about a year old and lived at several places before settling in Key West in 1820. Stephen's formal education was rudimentary, consisting of six to twelve months in a country school near Blakely, Alabama, at age nine and about three years at a Moravian academy at Nazareth, Pennsylvania. He helped his mother run her boardinghouse at Key West after his father's death. In 1833 he became inspector of customs at Key West and read voraciously to improve himself. Having decided to become a lawyer, he studied law under Judge

William Marvin from 1830 to 1834 and was soon admitted to the Florida bar. He commanded a small vessel in campaigns against the Seminoles in the Everglades (1836–1838). In July 1838, he married Angela Moreno, a Spanish woman from Pensacola. From 1837 to 1845, he was county judge of Monroe County and was named collector of the port at Key West in 1845.

In 1850, the Florida legislature elected Mallory (a Democrat) as a U.S. senator, and he was reelected in 1856. Appointed chairman of the Naval Affairs Committee in 1853, he unsuccessfully supported appropriations for the development of an ironclad floating battery that was something of a forerunner of Confederate armorclads. His Naval Retiring Board removed Matthew Fontaine Maury from active duty in 1855, prompting much criticism. This board and other reforms designed to streamline the navy's personnel became the model for the Union Navy Department's reorganization during the Civil War. In 1858, President James Buchanan offered to appoint Mallory minister to Spain, but he declined the appointment.

Although he had been a strong supporter of the South while in the Senate, Mallory opposed secession. Nevertheless, he resigned on January 21, 1861, after Florida left the Union. Offered the post of chief justice of the state's Admiralty Court, he turned it down. Mallory's political enemies accused him of preventing the Florida authorities from seizing Fort Pickens in January 1861, but he had conferred with and received support from senators from other Southern states in advising against bloodshed at that time. Mallory did use his influence with Buchanan to keep warships from entering Pensacola Harbor and to prevent reinforcements from being landed at the fort.

Jefferson Davis named Mallory head of the Navy Department on February 25, 1861. He had not sought the office and was unaware of his nomination. One reason for his appointment was that he came from Florida, which was allotted a prominent cabinet position because of the date of its secession. Mallory had also had experience in naval affairs during his long career, and he had shown great interest in innovations and improvements in both ship design and naval ordnance. The Florida delegation to Congress opposed his nomination because of their misunderstanding of his actions involving Fort Pickens. Mallory's was the only appointment delayed in the Congress, though he was ultimately confirmed on March 4. He and Postmaster General John H. Reagan were the only two men who remained in their cabinet positions throughout the conflict.

Mallory's department at the beginning of the war consisted of approximately twelve small ships and some three hundred officers who had left the U.S. Navy. Although he allowed these officers to retain their Union ranks, he based promotions entirely on gallant or meritorious conduct. In May 1863, Mallory persuaded Congress to create the Provisional Navy.

STEPHEN R. MALLORY. NAVAL HISTORICAL CENTER, WASHINGTON, D.C.

Through it, he could promote young and energetic officers, which was a significant reform. One of Mallory's major accomplishments as secretary was recruiting and training sailors for the navy. Many of these men transferred to their vessels from the army, despite some opposition by several secretaries of war.

To create a navy, Mallory had to purchase ships built abroad or have them built there. The department also issued thirty-two contracts from June 1861 to December 1862 for construction of gunboats and other vessels within the Confederacy. He emphasized the building of several powerful ironclads. Mallory wrote in May, "I regard the possession of an iron-armored ship as a matter of the first necessity." He hoped to use ironclads to break the Union blockade of the Southern coast. After Mallory called for acquisition of an ironclad, Congress appropriated $2 million to purchase or construct such ships in Europe.

Capt. James D. Bulloch was sent to England to purchase ironclads that could sink the wooden blockaders, and fast commerce raiders that would clear the oceans of Northern merchant ships. Mallory hoped the activities of the commerce raiders would draw blockaders away from the Southern ports. Bulloch succeeded in having *Florida* and *Alabama* constructed by the Laird shipyards and turned over to Confederate commanders. Lt. James H. North also went to Europe to purchase one or more existing ironclads. Although he failed to buy such a vessel, he did have construction of an ironclad ram *(Stonewall)* started in Scotland. It was eventually sold to Denmark before its completion and was acquired by the Confederacy from that country, though too late to participate in the conflict. Bulloch's efforts to obtain two additional ironclad rams from the Laird shipyards in Liverpool failed when the British government gave in to Union diplomatic pressure and seized them in October 1863 before they were completed.

> **The warships that did go in search of the raiders were mostly older and heavier vessels that would have been of little use in patrolling the coastline.**

To help pay for these activities, Mallory sent other agents to Europe with the authority to promise cotton for ship construction. This use of cotton bonds set a precedent, and the government authorities in Richmond tried to make better use of their large cotton reserves. In 1863, after the Navy Department's funds began dwindling, Mallory became involved in blockade running and ordered Bulloch and Comdr. Matthew Fontaine Maury to buy a speedy runner to take cotton to Europe. Eventually Bulloch acquired three vessels, which brought him sufficient amounts of cotton to finance his work. Mallory kept these operations small so that they would not interfere with those of the War Department, which conducted most of the blockade running.

Mallory put some of his best officers, men like Raphael Semmes and John N. Maffitt, aboard the commerce raiders because of the importance he attached to their activities. The efforts of his raiders failed to secure one of the objectives for which he had obtained them. Though these vessels destroyed millions of dollars of Northern shipping, the Union government chose to accept the loss of its merchant ships rather than weaken or abandon the blockade. The warships that did go in search of the raiders were mostly older and heavier vessels that would have been of little use in patrolling the coastline.

To create a navy in the South, Mallory acquired gunboats through purchase, construction, and capture. He set up workshops for producing naval supplies and machinery and foundries for casting cannons and projectiles. As with his overseas program, the naval secretary stressed construction of ironclads. The design he preferred was that of a casemated, armor-plated wooden vessel similar to the floating battery he had supported in the 1850s. Mallory intended for the first of his ironclads to attack the Union blockading ships and open Southern ports. He also hoped that his gunboats would be seagoing vessels that would take the war to the North.

None of them, however, was seaworthy, nor did any possess adequate engines for such ambitious projects.

Confederate work crews at Norfolk raised the frigate *Merrimack* from where it had been scuttled. It was converted into an ironclad ram and renamed *Virginia*. Mallory contracted for construction of four armored vessels on the Mississippi River, two at New Orleans and two at Memphis. Various delays prevented completion of all of these gunboats. At New Orleans, *Louisiana* had to be used as a floating battery because its machinery could not propel it against the flow of the river. Memphis fell before the two vessels there were finished, but one, *Arkansas,* was taken up the Yazoo River in Mississippi and completed there. That ship, too, had problems with faulty engines, which led ultimately to its being blown up by its crew to avoid capture.

After the summer of 1862, however, Mallory changed both the mission and the size of his new ironclads. Their primary duty became the defense of the Confederacy's rivers and harbors by supporting the masonry and earthen fortifications that guarded those areas. Instead of the large, deep-draft vessels designed by Lt. John M. Brooke, Mallory switched over to smaller and lighter ironclads based upon the plans of John L. Porter, chief naval constructor. The loss of Norfolk and New Orleans forced Mallory to establish new shipyards at various places in the interior. In addition to facilities at Richmond and Charleston, ironclad construction was started or completed at Selma, Mobile, Oven Bluff, and Montgomery, Alabama; Columbus, Georgia; Shreveport, Louisiana; Yazoo City, Mississippi; and Whitehall and Edward's Ferry, North Carolina. Despite their weaknesses, the presence of vessels such as *Tennessee* at Mobile Bay caused Union naval authorities to delay or even cancel attacks on Southern ports.

At first, the Confederate navy could obtain new cannons only from the Tredegar Iron Works in Richmond. Mallory sent Lt. Catesby Jones to Selma, Alabama, in the spring of 1863 to assume control of a foundry there that had been converted to produce heavy ordnance, armor plate, and projectiles. From January 1864 to March 1865, the Selma works turned out fifteen rifled and banded cannons designed by John Brooke. With the rifled pieces produced in Richmond, the Selma guns meant that the navy never had a shortage of modern armament for its vessels. Naval ordnance works at Atlanta, Richmond, Charleston, and Charlotte manufactured gun carriages and other equipment. A powder mill established originally at Petersburg, Virginia, was moved to Columbia, South Carolina, and after 1864 it was producing all the navy's needs.

Mallory played an active and early role in the development and use of torpedoes, or mines. The use of these devices became one of the most successful aspects of the navy's activities during the war. Confederate minefields helped keep the Union navy from entering Charleston Harbor and delayed the attack on Mobile Bay. By the end of the war, torpedoes had sunk or damaged forty-three enemy vessels, including four monitors. These devices destroyed more Federal warships than did all the Confederate gunboats. Mallory also supported the development and employment of torpedo boats and submarines. One of the first submarines was *Pioneer,* which was built at New Orleans. It was scuttled upon the fall of the city, having never had an opportunity to attack the enemy. *H. L. Hunley* became the first submarine in history to attack and sink an enemy vessel, the steam sloop *Housatonic.* A number of semisubmersible torpedo boats called Davids were constructed at Charleston, and the Confederates were planning to build a model that could venture into the open sea. Because of this latter development, one historian has stated that the Davids might have become a more prominent offensive weapon if the war had lasted longer.

The construction of the Eads ironclads at St. Louis for the Union navy concerned Mallory greatly. Because of them, he decided that it was more important to defend New Orleans from the north than from the Gulf of Mexico. In early April 1862, Flag Officer George N. Hollins at Memphis received a message from Como. William C. Whittle at New Orleans that Flag Officer David G. Farragut's Union squadron had entered the Mississippi River. Whittle asked Hollins to come to his assistance. Hollins did so and telegraphed Mallory asking permission to order his vessels southward. He felt that his wooden gunboats would be more effective against Farragut's wooden ships than against the ironclads. Mallory declared that it was more important to oppose the latter, and he even proposed sending the ironclad *Louisiana* northward. He thought that the forts on the lower river would be able to stop Farragut.

When the Federal squadron steamed past the forts, forced the destruction of the ironclads *Mississippi* and *Louisiana,* and captured New Orleans, Mallory was virtually incapacitated by the distress he suffered as a result of these disasters. He came under severe criticism not only for the fall of the Crescent City but also for the loss of Norfolk, Memphis, and *Virginia,* which all occurred about the same time. In August 1862, the Confederate House of Representatives called for an investigation into the Navy Department's role in these events, and a joint committee conducted hearings for about a year and a half. In its report, however, the committee exonerated Mallory from any guilt and praised him for the achievements his department had accomplished so far.

Occasionally, Mallory directed his subordinates to attempt unusual or unrealistic schemes. His message to Capt. Franklin Buchanan in March 1862 suggesting that *Virginia* sail into the Atlantic Ocean and attack New York City was one such order. In February 1863, he proposed an expedition whereby sailors would use small boats to carry them at night to Union monitors stationed off the coast. Once aboard, the men would douse the ironclads with inflammable substances

and set them afire. A lieutenant went to Charleston to set up such a force, but the project was stopped by the naval commander there in favor of using spar torpedoes. This small unit was called the Special Service Detachment, and ten boats were acquired for it. By September, the force had been broken up and the project abandoned without any attacks on the blockaders.

Mallory and his wife were well liked by Richmond society, even though they were not well known there when the war started. One historian has written of the Floridian that "his wit, his powers as a raconteur, his genial manners and frank courtesy soon won general esteem." The Mallory home accommodated a number of distinguished visitors to the capital during the course of the war. Mallory was not only adept at spinning tales and flattering the ladies, but he cooked well and mixed excellent mint juleps. Despite the long hours he devoted to his job, he found time to relax with his family.

In mid-January 1865, Mallory urged his naval commander at Richmond, Flag Officer John K. Mitchell, to sortie down the James River with his squadron and attack the giant Federal base at City Point. He hoped that, if they were successful in destroying the base, the Confederates would force Ulysses S. Grant to break off his siege of Richmond and Petersburg. Mitchell delayed sending his vessels downstream, and when they finally moved, their attempt failed. This plan of Mallory's had a fair chance of succeeding. If it had, it might have delayed Grant's operations for some months. Disappointed with Mitchell's handling of this affair, Mallory soon replaced him with Adm. Raphael Semmes.

> **Occasionally, Mallory directed his subordinates to attempt unusual or unrealistic schemes.**

Mallory accompanied Jefferson Davis and the cabinet in the retreat from Richmond to Danville in early April. They then spent a week at Greensboro, North Carolina. At Charlotte, Davis asked his cabinet about accepting the agreement signed by Gen. Joseph E. Johnston and Maj. Gen. William Tecumseh Sherman. With four other cabinet members, Mallory advised Davis to accept the convention's terms, rejecting a proposal that the Confederacy turn to guerrilla warfare. He did not believe that it would succeed and recognized that the Southern people no longer supported the war effort. Mallory went with Davis as far as Washington, Georgia, where, on May 3, 1865, he resigned and left the party to join his family at LaGrange. Mallory did not intend to try to escape from the South.

Most historians have treated Mallory's performance as secretary of the navy better than did many of his contemporaries. The press, public, and politicians criticized him frequently for inefficiency, lack of aggressiveness, and, in some cases, doing too much himself. Given the gigantic difficulties under which he worked, Mallory accomplished a great deal and can be ranked as one of the best Confederate cabinet members. He was intelligent and not reluctant to heed the advice of his staff and his naval officers. Mallory worked well with Davis and most of his fellow cabinet members. His imagination, hard work, and enthusiasm for his job all contributed to his success. Joseph T. Durkin, Mallory's chief biographer, concluded, "He was by no means a great administrator, but he was a conscientious, methodical, and generally reliable one."

After leaving Davis's entourage, Mallory went briefly to Atlanta and then traveled on to LaGrange. On the night of May 20, he was arrested with Senator Benjamin H. Hill in the latter's home and was imprisoned at Fort LaFayette in New York Harbor. Mallory was released on parole on March 10, 1866, and joined his family at Bridgeport, Connecticut. His health had deteriorated because of the pressures of the war years and the months he had spent in prison. Mallory returned to Pensacola in July 1866 and resumed his law practice. He opposed black suffrage and Radical Reconstruction, expressing his views in numerous editorials in the *West Florida Commercial*. Mallory died at his home early on November 12, 1873, and was buried in St. Michael's Cemetery.

[*See also* Navy, article on Navy Department.]

BIBLIOGRAPHY

Clubbs, Occie. "Stephen Russell Mallory, the Elder." Master's thesis, University of Florida, 1936.

Durkin, Joseph T. *Stephen R. Mallory: Confederate Navy Chief.* Chapel Hill, N.C., 1954. Reprint, Columbia, S.C., 1987.

Hendrick, Burton J. *Statesmen of the Lost Cause: Jefferson Davis and His Cabinet.* New York, 1939.

Mallory, Stephen R. Papers. Southern Historical Collection, University of North Carolina, Chapel Hill.

Melvin, Philip. "Stephen Russell Mallory, Naval Statesman." *Journal of Southern History* 10 (1944): 137–160.

Patrick, Rembert W. *Jefferson Davis and His Cabinet.* Baton Rouge, La., 1944.

Still, William N., Jr. *Iron Afloat: The Story of the Confederate Armorclads.* Nashville, Tenn., 1971.

Wells, Tom H. *The Confederate Navy: A Study in Organization.* University, Ala., 1971.

ARTHUR W. BERGERON, JR.

MALVERN HILL, VIRGINIA

On July 1, 1862, the last major confrontation of the Seven Days' Battles between Maj. Gen. George B. McClellan's Army of the Potomac and Gen. Robert E. Lee's Army of Northern Virginia took place at Malvern Hill. The site was located on high ground five miles from the Union base at Harrison's Landing on the James River. McClellan had chosen this naturally strong position to make his last stand before reaching Harrison's Landing and the safety of the gunboats waiting there.

For the sixth time in seven days, the opposing armies massed to confront each other in battle. Lee had achieved his goal of relieving pressure on Richmond by driving McClellan away from the city, but had failed to accomplish his overriding aim of annihilating the Army of the Potomac. He had devised several masterful plans to destroy the Federals, but on every occasion the failure of one or more of his subordinates and the consequently uncoordinated attacks left the Southerners short of their objective and badly bloodied. At one point during the battle of Malvern Hill, Lee answered an officer's concern that McClellan might escape: "Yes, he will get away because I cannot have my orders carried out."

Calculating that McClellan's men were demoralized by the steady repetition of fighting and retreat and believing that one final push might accomplish his elusive goal of destroying the enemy army, Lee determined to attack. The decision would prove costly. The Union position was a formidable one. Maj. Gen. Fitz John Porter's men had been preparing it since the day before, and its creeks and ravines ensured that any attacking columns would be funneled into a frontal assault. With as many as 100 Union artillery pieces dotting the high ground and another 150 in reserve, the Confederates would be heavily pounded.

Despite warnings from Maj. Gen. D. H. Hill, Lee gave his approval for the advance. To prepare for the attack, Maj. Gen. James Longstreet suggested that the Confederates mass their artillery so as to create a powerful cross fire. But the Southerners failed to bring more than a fraction of their artillery into play, and when batteries came forward, the Federals quickly pounded them into silence or retreat.

Lee assigned the task of assaulting McClellan's right flank to Maj. Gen. Thomas J. ("Stonewall") Jackson's troops. He directed Maj. Gen. John B. Magruder to form his men on Jackson's right. Next to Magruder would come Maj. Gen. Benjamin Huger's division. The exhausted soldiers under Longstreet and Maj. Gen. A. P. Hill would remain in reserve.

True to form in this series of battles, Lee's plan for the attack miscarried. Because of faulty communication, the Confederates thought McClellan might be retreating, when in fact he was not.

About 3:30 P.M. Brig. Gen. Lewis A. Armistead of Huger's division advanced. This was to have been the signal for a general offensive along the line, made with artillery support. That support was missing, however, and the Federal guns hammered the exposed Confederates. Huger's men had little choice but to seek cover. But as D. H. Hill's men moved past them, the Union cannons had no shortage of targets, and Hill's men suffered badly from the fire. Magruder's men had marched away and then countermarched, and as they reached the battlefield, they too began to feel the brunt of the Federal artillery fire. The Union projectiles tore wide gaps in the Confederate lines. As daylight faded, the Southern brigades continued to feed themselves into a bloody maelstrom. Darkness finally brought the fighting to an end, and the Federals moved away to their base at Harrison's Landing.

On the slopes of Malvern Hill, Lee had lost a staggering 5,355 casualties; McClellan, 3,214. Mercifully for the combatants, the bitter fighting at Malvern Hill ended the Seven Days' Battles. In assessing what he had seen that day, D. H. Hill observed, "It was not war—it was murder."

BIBLIOGRAPHY

Cullen, Joseph P. *The Peninsula Campaign, 1862: McClellan and Lee Struggle for Richmond.* Harrisburg, Pa., 1973.

Freeman, Douglas S. *Lee's Lieutenants: A Study in Command.* 3 vols. New York, 1942–1944. Reprint, New York, 1986.

Johnson, Robert U., and C. C. Buel, eds. *Battles and Leaders of the Civil War.* 4 vols. New York, 1887–1888. Reprint, Secaucus, N.J., 1982.

Sears, Stephen W. *To the Gates of Richmond: The Peninsula Campaign.* New York, 1992.

U.S. War Department. *War of the Rebellion: A Compilation of the Official Records of the Union and Confederate Armies.* Washington, D.C. Ser. 1, vol. 11, pt. 1, pp. 67–70; ser. 1, pt. 2, pp. 495–497.

BRIAN S. WILLS

Manassas, First

Ten hours of combat near Manassas, Virginia, on July 21, 1861, changed the way a nation viewed war. Both Federals and Confederates came to these fields confident of swift, relatively bloodless victories. They left behind more than 800 dead and 2,700 wounded. They also left behind any illusions that the war could be won or lost on a single Sunday afternoon. Wrote Confederate Samuel Melton: "I have no idea that they intend to give up the fight. On the contrary, five men will rise up where one has been killed, and in my opinion, the war will have to be continued to the bloody end."

As the confluence of the Orange and Alexandria and the Manassas Gap railroads, Manassas Junction assumed preeminent importance for the Confederates in the summer of 1861. Defending at Manassas were 22,000 Confederates under the command of P. G. T. Beauregard. Beauregard knew his force to be insufficient to stop a Union overland advance on Richmond. Instead, Confederate success depended on the ability of a second Confederate army (10,000 men) in the Shenandoah Valley under Joseph E. Johnston to move swiftly to Beauregard's support when the Federals advanced. Johnston's army would move to Manassas Junction via the Manassas Gap Railroad.

On July 16, 1861, Union Gen. Irvin McDowell led 33,000 slightly trained soldiers out of Washington and Alexandria toward Manassas. Beauregard quickly sent word to Johnston and then assumed a defensive position along Bull Run. His line extended for nearly eight miles, from the Stone Bridge on the north to Union Mills on the south.

On July 18 the Federals tested the Confederate center at Blackburn's Ford. In a sharp skirmish that left 83 Union troops killed or wounded, Confederates under James Longstreet repulsed the Federals. Convinced that he could not force his way across Bull Run, McDowell, at Centreville, spent the next two days searching for an undefended ford. The Confederates made good use of the Union delay. Johnston's army slipped away from a Union force under Robert Patterson in the Shenandoah Valley and took the trains to join Beauregard at Manassas Junction. By July 21, Beauregard's and Johnston's combined forces totaled 32,000, only 1,000 less than the Federals.

McDowell's search along Bull Run uncovered an undefended crossing at Sudley Ford, about two miles north of the Confederate left at the Stone Bridge. On Sunday morning, July 21, McDowell's army moved forward in three columns. Two of them were diversionary—one toward Blackburn's and Mitchell's Ford in the Confederate center and the other toward the Stone Bridge. At 6:00 A.M. a Union 30-pounder Parrott rifle, drawn to its position near the Stone Bridge by a team of ten horses, fired the first shot of the first major land battle of the Civil War.

Meanwhile the main Union column (13,000 men with five batteries) marched northwestward toward Sudley Ford, bent on crossing the stream and sweeping southward behind the Confederates. The march proceeded slowly but without incident until about 8:30 A.M. At that time Confederate signal officer E. P. Alexander, on the Wilcoxen farm about eight miles south of the Stone Bridge, by chance spotted the Union column. Alexander immediately sent warning to Col. Nathan Evans, whose two regiments had charge of defending the Confederate left: "Look out for your left, you are turned." At the same time, Evans received warning of the Union flanking movement from his pickets near Sudley. Leaving 200 men to defend the Stone Bridge, Evans moved with his remaining 900 to block the Union flanking column. His job: delay the Federals long enough for Confederate reinforcements from the center and right to arrive.

Evans met the head of the Federal column on the slopes of Matthew's Hill. For perhaps thirty minutes his two regiments fought alone, while the Federals piled troops from Ambrose Burnside's and Andrew Porter's brigades into the fight. At about 11:00 A.M. Confederate reinforcements

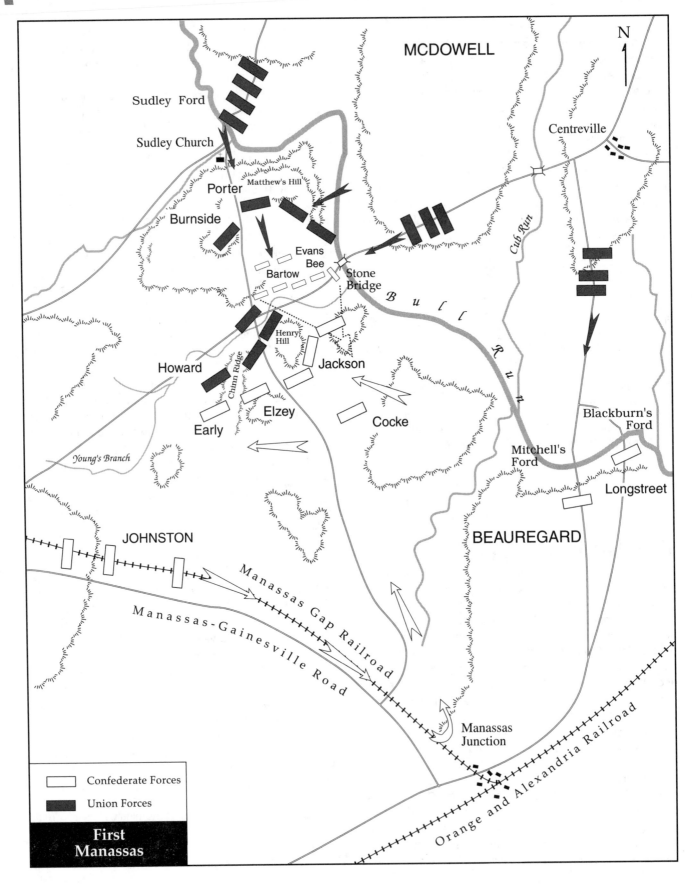

MCDOWELL

N

Sudley Ford

Centreville

Sudley Church

Matthew's Hill

Porter

Burnside

Evans
Bee
Bartow
Stone
Bridge

Bull Run

Cub Run

Howard
Henry Hill
Chinn Ridge
Jackson

Early
Elzey
Cocke

Blackburn's
Ford

Young's Branch

Mitchell's
Ford

Longstreet

JOHNSTON

BEAUREGARD

Manassas Gap Railroad

Manassas-Gainesville Road

Manassas
Junction

Orange and Alexandria Railroad

| | Confederate Forces |
| | Union Forces |

**First
Manassas**

arrived. Four regiments under Barnard E. Bee and Francis S. Bartow moved up on Evans's right. Along fence lines and in pine thickets the battle raged. But the Federals, outnumbering the Confederates by nearly 10,000 men, soon lapped around both Confederate flanks. The Southern lines gave way. Soon nearly 3,000 Confederates were streaming rearward to the heights of Henry Hill.

Had McDowell continued his assault at this moment, the battle might have ended as a crushing Confederate defeat. But the Federal advance stopped on Matthew's Hill. The delay gave Beauregard and Johnston the time they needed to rush reinforcements to Henry Hill to stabilize the shattered Confederate line. Thomas J. Jackson's Virginia brigade arrived first and formed behind a thirteen-gun line of artillery on the southeastern edge of Henry Hill. Behind these Virginians the fugitives from Matthew's Hill rallied. By 2:00 P.M. the Confederates on Henry Hill were presenting a strong front. It was a rejuvenation made possible only by Union delay.

At about 2:30 the Federals moved against Jackson's line on Henry Hill, first with Charles Griffin's and James B. Ricketts's batteries of artillery and then with infantry. Jackson's regiments met the Federals with a fire that routed the infantry and devastated Ricketts's battery. Later Griffin moved two of his Union cannons to within two hundred yards of the Confederate line. The Thirty-third Virginia lunged forward and captured them—the first tangible Confederate success of the day. Then the Second and Fourth Virginia of Jackson's brigade charged and captured Ricketts's battery, too. The tide of the battle turned.

For the next ninety minutes the fighting surged across Widow Henry's farm. The Confederates captured and recaptured the Union cannons three times. In this fighting General Bee and Colonel Bartow became the two highest-ranking Confederates to die in the battle. Beauregard and Johnston haphazardly threw regiments into the battle as they arrived; a frantic procession of crises allowed for little coordination. McDowell, too, fed regiments into the fight singly, or at best in pairs, until by 4:00 he had few regiments left to send forward (about half the Union army remained east of Bull Run and never joined the battle). A final advance by the Eighth and Eighteenth Virginia of Philip St. George Cocke's brigade drove the last Federals off Henry Hill into the valley of Young's Branch.

Foiled in his efforts to dislodge the Confederates from Henry Hill by direct attack, McDowell tried finally to flank the Confederates by sending a brigade under O. O. Howard over Chinn Ridge, around the Confederate left. But before Howard could manage the movement, Johnston had directed two fresh brigades under Jubal Early and Arnold Elzey to Chinn Ridge. When Howard's four regiments crested the ridge, they found themselves caught in a pocket of Confederate fire. Elzey attacked. Howard's regiments broke after a brief fight.

With that, from right to left, McDowell's lines began to crumble.

Harassed by Confederate artillery fire, disorganized Union regiments retreated the way they had come—some northward across Sudley Ford, a few eastward across Stone Bridge. The Confederates followed and opened fire on the Federals as they struggled across the bridge over Cub Run, about a mile east of Bull Run. A shell overturned a wagon on the bridge. The Federals panicked. "Before the third shell struck near us, every man as far as the eye could see seemed to be running for very life," recorded one Federal. For hours, frightened Union soldiers and a few hundred civilians who had come out from Washington to catch a glimpse of the battle jammed the roads leading to the Union capital. The Confederates, nearly as disorganized in victory as were the Federals in retreat, did not pursue beyond Cub Run and later returned to their bivouacs along Bull Run.

The battle produced several heroes for the Confederates. Johnston and Beauregard were foremost. Evans received

> **Beauregard and Johnston haphazardly threw regiments into the battle as they arrived; a frantic procession of crises allowed for little coordination.**

just praise for his delaying action in the morning, and Elzey garnered much notice for his decisive attack on Chinn Ridge in the afternoon. But the most famous would be Jackson. His brigade had provided a focal point for rallying the fugitives from the morning fight on Matthew's Hill. And in the afternoon, his regiments had engineered the initial capture of Ricketts's and Griffin's guns. On these fields Jackson won his sobriquet "Stonewall."

The 387 Confederate dead and 1,582 wounded initially did little to dim Southern euphoria over the victory. One Southern soldier told his wife, "Sunday last . . . was the happiest day of my life, our wedding-day not excepted. I think the fight is over forever." But Confederate glee soon yielded to the realization that the Federals had no intention of giving up. Strategically, the battle changed little in the Virginia theater; each side simply returned to its starting point to prepare for the next campaign. And people North and South soon realized that the next campaign would be infinitely larger and bloodier. It would be shown that First Manassas elevated the war to a higher, more awful and costly level. The next campaign would involve not 30,000 Federals but almost 130,000. And by 1864 the hundreds lost at Manassas would pale in comparison to the thousands lost at Gettysburg, the Wilderness, and a dozen other fields. But no battle of the war—perhaps no battle in American history—would have so dramatic an emotional impact as First Manassas.

BIBLIOGRAPHY

Beattie, Russell H., Jr. *Road to Manassas.* New York, 1961.

Davis, William C. *Battle at Bull Run.* Garden City, N.Y., 1977.

Freeman, Douglas S. *Lee's Lieutenants: A Study in Command.* 3 vols. New York, 1942–1944. Reprint, New York, 1986.

Gallagher, Gary W., ed. *Fighting for the Confederacy: The Personal Recollections of General Edward Porter Alexander.* Chapel Hill, N.C., 1989.

Hennessy, John. *The First Battle of Manassas: An End to Innocence.* Lynchburg, Va., 1989.

Johnston, Robert M. *Bull Run, Its Strategy and Tactics.* Boston, 1913.

U.S. Committee on the Conduct of the War. *Report of the Joint Committee on the Conduct of the War.* Washington, D.C., 1863.

JOHN J. HENNESSY

MANASSAS, SECOND

War came a second time to the plains of Manassas in August 1862—this time in a form bigger, bloodier, and strategically more significant than in 1861. More than 100,000 troops participated in the battle, leaving behind more than 23,000 casualties (9,000 Confederate). Robert E. Lee's decisive victory over Federal Maj. Gen. John Pope and the Army of Virginia here laid the groundwork for his first raid into the North. Conversely, it brought the Union war effort to a dangerously low ebb. The aftermath of Second Manassas represented perhaps the South's best opportunity to win the war.

After his successful repulse of Union Gen. George B. McClellan's Army of the Potomac in the Seven Days' Battles around Richmond, Lee turned his attention northward to a second Union threat: the newly formed Army of Virginia, commanded by Pope. Fearful that Pope would menace the Virginia Central Railroad—Richmond's communications with the Shenandoah Valley—or, worse, move on Richmond from the northwest, Lee on July 15 dispatched a force under Thomas J. ("Stonewall") Jackson to confront Pope. Jackson and Pope eyed each other across the Rapidan River until August 9, when Jackson attacked an exposed part of Pope's army near Cedar Mountain, just south of Culpeper. Though a Confederate victory, after the battle Jackson had to retire across the Rapidan in the face of increasing Union numbers.

On August 15, confident that McClellan intended no further trouble in front of Richmond, Lee and James Longstreet joined Jackson near Gordonsville. Anxious to force Pope out of central Virginia before McClellan's army, now retiring from the Virginia Peninsula, could join him, Lee hunted for a chance to strike Pope or at least drive him back. From August

17 until August 25 the armies sparred, first along the Rapidan and then, after a short retreat by Pope, along the Rappahannock.

On August 25, 1862, Lee found an opening. Holding Longstreet with 30,000 men in front of Pope, Lee sent 24,000 men under Jackson (about half the army) on a wide flanking march around Pope's right flank. They first marched northward to Salem and then turned to the southeast, through Thoroughfare Gap and Gainesville. On the evening of August 26 Jackson's troops cut the Orange and Alexandria Railroad—the Federal supply line—at Bristoe Station and Manassas Junction. In thirty-six hours Jackson's men had marched fifty-four miles to the rear of the Union army. Few strategic maneuvers of the war would surpass this one in nerve and effectiveness.

Surprised and outmaneuvered, Pope turned away from the Rappahannock and fanned out in search of Jackson's command. Jackson spent August 27 pillaging the stores at Manassas and beating back two mild Union advances. That night he set fire to the remaining plunder and marched northward to elude Pope. On August 28 he assumed a position in woods and behind ridges north of the Warrenton Turnpike near Groveton. There, Jackson knew, he could monitor the Federal march and perhaps lure Pope into battle. At the same time he would be in position to await the arrival of Lee and Longstreet, then marching to join him with almost 30,000 men.

Jackson and his troops passed a quiet day on August 28 until about 5:30 P.M. Then Jackson received word of a Union column (Rufus King's division) marching eastward on the Warrenton Turnpike, only a few hundred yards in front of his position. After watching the Union troops march unwarily by for several minutes, Jackson ordered an attack. Soon shells burst above the Federal column. Union brigade commander John Gibbon ordered his regiments to turn off the road and move against the Confederates. For the next ninety minutes the fighting raged on the Brawner and Dogan farms. Though Jackson outnumbered the Union division in front nearly three to one, he was unable to launch a coordinated assault sufficient to overwhelm the Federals. Instead the battle amounted to a brutal, largely static musketry fight waged from behind fence lines. Darkness brought an end to the indecisive fighting. Among the Confederate casualties was Richard S. Ewell, who would lose his leg and be absent from the army for nine months.

Though Jackson had failed to destroy King's division, he had revealed his position to Pope, who responded by ordering his entire army to converge on Jackson's position. The next morning, August 29, Jackson discovered that King had retreated but that additional Union troops had arrived on Henry Hill to the east. He deployed his troops along the cuts and fills of an old unfinished railroad and prepared for battle.

Meanwhile, the rest of the Confederate army, led by Lee and Longstreet, moved to join Jackson. Following Jackson's

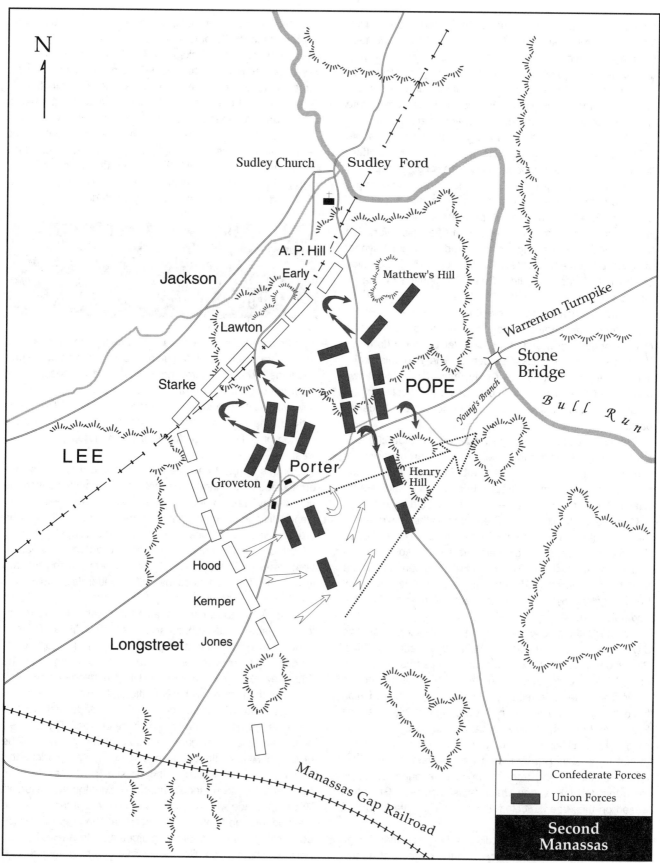

N

Sudley Church   Sudley Ford

A. P. Hill

Jackson   Early   Matthew's Hill

Lawton

Starke   POPE

LEE   Porter

Groveton   Henry Hill

Hood

Kemper

Longstreet   Jones

Warrenton Turnpike

Stone Bridge

Bull Run

Young's Branch

Manassas Gap Railroad

	Confederate Forces
▮	Union Forces

Second Manassas

earlier route, Longstreet on August 28 pushed aside a Union force at Thoroughfare Gap. Resuming the march the next morning, the head of Longstreet's column reached the battlefield at about 10:00 A.M. Longstreet formed on Jackson's right, extending his line southward across the Warrenton Turnpike for more than a mile. Once formed, the Confederate line resembled a huge pair of jaws, ready to snap shut.

John Pope knew nothing of Longstreet's presence south of the turnpike on August 29. Instead he focused all his attention on Jackson. During the morning Franz Sigel's corps and John F. Reynolds's division moved against Jackson along a two-mile front. In what amounted to a protracted heavy skirmish, the Federals managed no progress against Jackson's lines. During the afternoon Pope intensified his efforts. At 3:00 Cuvier Grover's brigade launched a violent bayonet attack that threatened to dislocate part of A. P. Hill's division on the left of Jackson's line. Only hard fighting by Maxcy Gregg's brigade of South Carolinians and Edward L. Thomas's Georgia brigade drove the Federals back.

An hour later another Union charge, this by Col. James Nagle's brigade, plunged into Alexander Lawton's (formerly Ewell's) division, in Jackson's center. The Federals maintained their position for minutes only, until an advance by two brigades of Starke's division to Lawton's right relieved the pressure against Jackson's center and forced the Federals back.

The largest Union attack of August 29 came at 5:00 P.M., and it came against the most beleaguered part of Jackson's line: A. P. Hill's division on the left. Parts of three Union brigades surged against Gregg's brigade on a knoll southeast of Sudley Church. In an episode that would become part of Confederate lore, General Gregg unsheathed his grandfather's Revolutionary War sword and paced his line: "Let us die here, my men, let us die here," he said. Despite Gregg's urgings, his men yielded. The left of Hill's line bent back more than three hundred yards. Only the timely arrival of Jubal Early's brigade restored the Confederate front and forced the Federals to retreat.

Lee had little to do with the fighting on Jackson's front this day. Instead, he focused on launching an attack against Pope's dangling left flank. But in this he was frustrated. First Longstreet prudently requested time to examine the ground to his front. Then Lee received word of a threatening Union force hovering opposite Longstreet's right flank (this was Fitz John Porter's corps along the Manassas-Gainesville road). Not until almost 5:00 would Lee decide this force meant no trouble. But by then it was too late to launch an attack. Instead, Longstreet mounted a reconnaissance in force that ran into strong Union resistance near Groveton. Based on this, Lee canceled all plans for an attack against Pope's left.

The repulses of August 29 did nothing to dissuade Pope from continuing the battle. Indeed, on the morning of August 30 he concluded that the Confederates were retreating. At noon he launched a pursuit—one of the shortest of the war. Lee, Longstreet, and Jackson had, of course, gone nowhere. Pope decided to renew his attacks against Jackson's line. He remained unaware of Longstreet's presence opposite his left.

At 3:00 P.M. Pope launched his largest attack of the battle: more than 5,000 men under the command of Fitz John Porter surged against Starke's division on Jackson's right. In the battle's most intense burst of fighting, Jackson's men clung tenaciously to their position on the unfinished railroad, though in places the Federals closed to within ten yards. After thirty minutes of fighting many Confederates ran out of

> **After thirty minutes of fighting many Confederates ran out of ammunition. Some met the Union attack with stones.**

ammunition. Some met the Union attack with stones. This was, wrote one Federal, "an unlooked for variation in the proceedings." The rock-throwing episode would become the most famous incident of the battle. It lasted only moments, however, until Confederate reinforcements from Hill's division arrived. The Federals retreated, pelted all the while by the cannon of S. D. Lee's battalion, a few hundred yards to the west.

Porter's retreat threw the Union line into a spasm of disorganization. Lee and Longstreet simultaneously sensed the opportunity. Lee ordered Longstreet to attack—to seize Henry Hill and cut off the Union retreat. At the same time, he ordered Jackson to "look out for and protect Longstreet's left." Less than thirty minutes after receiving orders to advance, Longstreet had more than 20,000 soldiers moving forward toward the Union left. Less than 3,000 Federals stood in their path.

John Bell Hood's division, along the Warrenton Turnpike, led Longstreet's assault. Near Groveton the Texas Brigade struck and demolished a brigade of New York troops commanded by Gouverneur K. Warren. One Union regiment, the Fifth New York, had more men killed here than any other infantry regiment in any other battle of the war.

Next, Hood's men routed a Union brigade just west of Chinn Ridge, capturing a battery in the process. Then, joined by Nathan Evans's brigade, Hood ascended the west slope of Chinn Ridge into the face of Col. Nathaniel McLean's brigade of Ohioans. Soon the division of James Lawson Kemper arrived on Hood's right. Col. Montgomery Corse's Virginia brigade wheeled left down the crest of the ridge and crashed into the flank of the Union line. The Federals resisted stoutly, buying time for reinforcements to arrive. For the next hour both sides piled troops into the most intense sustained fighting of the battle. The fighting here would be decisive; it would determine the magnitude of the Union defeat.

While the combat raged on Chinn Ridge, Jackson stood still on the north flank. This in turn allowed Pope to pull troops from the right of his line and put them into position on Henry Hill. By the time the Federals yielded on Chinn Ridge—which they did only after buying precious time and extracting heavy Confederate casualties—four brigades of Union troops were waiting on Henry Hill. David Rumph Jones's division led the Confederate advance against Henry Hill, joined soon by Richard Heron Anderson's division and Cadmus Wilcox's brigade. But an hour of assaults left the Federals unmoved. Darkness brought an end to the fighting. The beaten but intact Union army retreated from the field that night.

The next day Lee moved again to cut off Pope's retreat to Washington by again sending Jackson on a flank march. This time, however, Pope responded promptly. He blocked Jackson's march near Germantown and then attacked him with two divisions. The resultant Battle of Ox Hill on September 1 ended in stalemate after two hours of combat in a driving rainstorm. The battle, which claimed the lives of Union Gens. Isaac Stevens and Philip Kearny, marked the end of the campaign.

The Second Manassas campaign helped chisel the identity of the Army of Northern Virginia. The army's three dominant figures assumed the roles they would henceforth play. Lee showed himself to be the master strategist—patient, trusting of subordinates, and incredibly bold. It would be his most successful campaign. By swift marching and unmatched daring, Jackson showed himself to be the master creator of opportunities. His strategic brilliance during the last week of August 1862 was second only to his Shenandoah Valley campaign. And Longstreet showed himself to be cautious—prudently so, it would prove—but swift, strong, and decisive once moved. On no other battlefield would he contribute more to Confederate victory.

Bringing a Union army to the brink of destruction—and indeed the Union cause to the edge of collapse—cost Lee some 9,000 casualties. More than 16,000 Federals fell or were captured during the campaign. The victory at Second Manassas bared the strategic table for Lee. From here he moved unfettered into Maryland, where what was perhaps the Confederacy's greatest hope for victory perished on the banks of Antietam Creek.

BIBLIOGRAPHY

Allan, William. *The Army of Northern Virginia in 1862*. Boston, 1892. Reprint, Dayton, Ohio, 1984.

Freeman, Douglas S. *Lee's Lieutenants: A Study in Command*. Vol. 2. New York, 1943. Reprint, New York, 1986.

Gordon, George H. *History of the Campaign of the Army of Virginia, under John Pope: From Cedar Mountain to Antietam*. Boston, 1880.

Hennessy, John J. *Return to Bull Run: The Campaign and Battle of Second Manassas*. New York, 1992.

Hennessy, John J. *Second Manassas Battlefield Map Study*. Lynchburg, Va., 1991.

Johnson, Robert U., and C. C. Buel., eds. *Battles and Leaders of the Civil War*. Vol. 2. New York, 1888. Reprint, Secaucus, N.J., 1982.

Ropes, John C. *The Army under Pope*. New York, 1881. Reprint, Wilmington, N.C., 1989.

Stackpole, Edward J. *From Cedar Mountain to Antietam, August-September, 1862*. Harrisburg, Pa., 1959.

JOHN J. HENNESSY

MARCH TO THE SEA, SHERMAN'S

Union Gen. William Tecumseh Sherman completed the Atlanta campaign with the capture of that Georgia city on September 2, 1864. He allowed the Confederate Army of Tennessee under Gen. John Bell Hood to escape destruction, however, and on October 3 found himself chasing Hood back toward Chattanooga over the same ground he and Gen. Joseph E. Johnston had contested during the recently completed campaign. Frustrated, Sherman reached back to a lifetime of civilian and military experiences and decided to undertake something different. Instead of continuing to try to protect his railroad supply line by chasing Hood all over Georgia, he would send Gens. George H. Thomas and John M. Schofield with some 60,000 troops to Tennessee to handle Hood, while he cut loose from his supply line with approximately 62,000 of his best troops and marched across Georgia to the Atlantic Ocean.

In later years, Sherman called his action nothing more than a change of military base from Atlanta to Savannah, but actually he implemented psychological warfare, demonstrating to Confederate soldiers and the civilian population that the Confederacy could not defend its home front and therefore was doomed. He saw his raid as the only way to end the war quickly. It was much more effective and humane, he believed, than slaughtering troops in conventional warfare.

As he had done in his raid on Meridian, Mississippi, in early 1864, Sherman divided his invading force into two approximately equal wings (under O. O. Howard and Henry W. Slocum) with Hugh J. Kilpatrick's cavalry protecting the flanks. Since he had no supply line, the army was to consume the twenty-day rations it carried with it and the three thousand beef cattle driven along behind. For the rest, it would live off the countryside. The army left Atlanta on November 15, destroying the city's war-making capacity but leaving many of its structures standing. Opposing it was a varied collection of Confederate troops numbering perhaps

8,000: mainly Joseph Wheeler's cavalry corps and Gustavus W. Smith's Georgia militia. On November 17, William J. Hardee became overall Confederate commander in Georgia, but he could do little to stop Sherman and concentrated his small military force on fortifying Savannah. Hood and his Army of Tennessee were far away to the rear, still hoping to draw Sherman into Tennessee.

The March to the Sea covered about fifteen miles a day. The two columns traveled along separate paths, sometimes as far as fifty miles apart, throwing out foragers (bummers) in all directions to supply the troops. Sherman tried to make it appear that he was moving against Macon, Augusta, or Savannah and then brought his wings together to capture Milledgeville, the wartime state capital, on November 23. This indirect approach confused the outmanned Confederates and made their task even more impossible.

There were a number of skirmishes during the march, including those at Lovejoy on November 16; Griswoldville on November 22; Ball's Ferry, November 24 through 25; Millen Grove, December 1; Rocky Creek Church, December 2; Thomas's Station, December 3; Brier Creek, December 4; and Ebenezer Creek, December 7. The most memorable encounter of the march occurred on November 22 at Griswoldville, ten miles outside of Macon. Union troops brushed aside the attacking Georgia militia and to their horror found that the dead were young boys and old men. Wheeler and Smith could never offer any significant opposition to the advancing Union force. Sherman's casualties for the entire campaign were only around 2,200 men.

As the troops marched, they terrorized the countryside. Physical assault against civilians was rare, but destruction and confiscation of property was widespread. Food was regularly taken, though at times Southerners in need were helped. Clothes and household furnishings were often carried away or destroyed. It was not a scorched earth policy, however, because everything in the path of the invaders was not routinely burned. Only property connected with slavery and Union prisoners of war was systematically destroyed. For example, dogs were killed because of their use in chasing fugitive slaves and escaping Union prisoners.

There was a great deal of destruction in Georgia during the March to the Sea, but Sherman's troops were not the sole perpetrators. Ironically, Confederates helped him create the terror of war on civilians. The plundering by Confederate deserters and elements of Wheeler's cavalry, as well as runaway slaves and Union deserters, intensified the havoc. Sherman regularly wished there was some other way to end the conflict, but he was convinced there was none.

Slaves played an important role in the march. Many ran away from their masters and acted as spies for the army, and even those who simply stood by the roadside and cheered the advancing troops buoyed the soldiers with their exuberance. Sherman, whom the slaves viewed as a conquering

messiah, found them an encumbrance to his army, though he treated them with respect on the personal level.

Union officers and men as a rule agreed with their commander's position that the thousands of fugitives following the army were a nuisance. There were some soldiers who were kind to the slaves, but military attitudes were usually racist at worst and condescending at best. On December 9, Gen. Jeff C. Davis, commander of the Fourteenth Corps, demonstrated army attitudes with his actions at Ebenezer Creek. Davis's unit, with black fugitives to the rear and Joe Wheeler's Confederate cavalry not far behind, was crossing the creek on pontoon bridges. As soon as the troops had crossed, the bridges were removed, and the blacks were left stranded. Fearing for their lives at the hands of Wheeler's approaching cavalry, the fugitives made desperate attempts to cross the creek. Many tragically drowned in the effort. Davis and Sherman never admitted any blame.

By December 10, only Savannah and nearby Fort McAllister stood in the way of Sherman's reaching the sea. He chose his old division from Shiloh, now under William B. Hazen, to assault the fort, and this force easily overran the garrison on December 13. William J. Hardee still held Savannah, and on December 17 Sherman demanded its surrender. He clamped a siege on the city, but, as he had in Atlanta, he allowed the Confederate force to escape when he took Savannah on December 21. Meanwhile, John M. Schofield defeated John Bell Hood at Franklin, Tennessee, on November 30, and George H. Thomas finished the job at Nashville on December 15 and 16. It was a happy Sherman who telegraphed Abraham Lincoln on December 22 offering Savannah as a Christmas gift.

Upon entering the city, Sherman continued his psychological warfare, but now he put his troops on their best behavior to show the populace the benefits of returning to the Union. He wanted Confederates to know that he believed in a hard war but a soft peace. He wanted them to quit fighting so that more death and destruction would be unnecessary.

The March to the Sea confused, frustrated, frightened, and angered the people of the Confederacy. At its start, Georgians were encouraged to rise up in opposition and burn what they could not carry away from the invaders. In the midst of the campaign, rumors were rife about the size, location, and activities of the invaders. Their arrival in an area created panic and helplessness. Throughout, Confederate newspapers predicted imminent disaster for the Federals and criticized Sherman for raiding rather than fighting, but desertions increased in Robert E. Lee's army in Virginia and the optimism of the Confederate populace plummeted. From Savannah, Sherman marched through the Carolinas during the early months of 1865, moving toward a juncture with Ulysses S. Grant against Lee in Virginia. The March to the Sea was a harbinger of modern total war, and it created the fodder for later Lost Cause arguments that Sherman was a villian and the Confederate leaders were corresponding exemplars of virtue.

[*See also* Bummers; Savannah, Georgia, *article on* Savannah Campaign.]

BIBLIOGRAPHY

Cox, Jacob D. *The March to the Sea—Franklin and Nashville.* Introduction by Nat C. Hughes. New York, 1882. Reprint, Wilmington, N.C., 1989.

DeLaubenfels, David J., ed. "With Sherman through Georgia: A Journal [John Rzeha]." *Georgia Historical Quarterly* 41 (September 1957): 288–300.

Glatthaar, Joseph T. *The March to the Sea and Beyond: Sherman's Troops in the Savannah and Carolinas Campaign.* New York, 1985.

Hitchcock, Henry M. *Marching with Sherman.* Edited by M. A. deWolfe Howe. New Haven, 1927.

Jones, James P. "General Jeff C. Davis, U.S.A., and Sherman's Georgia Campaign." *Georgia Historical Quarterly* 47 (March 1962): 231–242.

Marszalek, John F. *Sherman: A Soldier's Passion for Order.* New York, 1992.

Marszalek, John F. "W. T. Sherman, Was He Really a Brute?" *Blue and Gray* 7 (December 1989): 46–51.

JOHN F. MARSZALEK

MARINE CORPS

Section 5 of "An Act to provide for the organization of the Navy," passed by the Provisional Congress of the Confederate States on March 16, 1861, established a Corps of Marines, commanded by a major and consisting of six companies. An amendatory act, passed May 20, 1861, expanded the corps to ten companies and elevated the grade of the commanding officer to that of colonel. All laws and regulations of the U.S. Marine Corps not inconsistent with these acts were applied to the government of its Confederate counterpart.

Lloyd J. Beall, former paymaster in the U.S. Army, was appointed colonel of the Confederate States Marines on May 23, 1861. Colonel Beall served throughout the war as the first and only commanding officer of the corps. Fifty-six officers were appointed to the corps during the war period. Nineteen were formerly officers of the U.S. Marine Corps, four had served in the U.S. Navy or Coast Survey, three were appointed directly from civilian pursuits, one, the commandant, with service in the U.S. Army, and the rest came from the ranks of the Provisional Army of the Confederate States.

The Confederate States Marines served in many of the coastal operations of the war: Pensacola, 1861–1862; Port Royal, November 5–7, 1861; Hampton Roads, March 8–9, 1862; New Orleans, April 24, 1862; Drewry's Bluff, May 15, 1862; Charleston Harbor, 1863–1865; Mobile Bay, August 5, 1864; and Fort Fisher, December 24–25, 1864, and January 13–15, 1865. Marines also served ashore at Second Drewry's Bluff, May 13–16, 1864; Fort Gaines, August 5–8, 1864; Savannah, December 11–20, 1864; Sayler's Creek, April 6, 1865; and Spanish Fort (Fort Blakely), April 9, 1865.

Marine Guards served aboard many of the warships of the Confederate States Navy including the commerce raiders CSS *Sumter, Georgia, Tallahassee (Olustee), Chickamauga, Stonewall,* and *Shenandoah.* One solitary Marine, Capt. Becket K. Howell, cruised aboard CSS *Alabama.*

The headquarters of the marines was located at Richmond, Virginia. Three companies garrisoned the post at Drewry's Bluff from May 1862 until the evacuation of Richmond in April 1865. Companies were regularly assigned to the naval stations at Mobile, Alabama, and Savannah, Georgia, with detachments on duty at various times at the navy yards at Richmond, Charleston, South Carolina, and Wilmington and Charlotte, North Carolina.

The marines were utilized on numerous occasions as a rapid deployment force, being called upon for missions to Charleston Harbor in February 1862 and the proposed attack upon the Federal prisoner of war compound at Point Lookout, Maryland, in July 1864. Marines also assisted in the capture of USS *Underwriter* at New Berne, North Carolina, February 2, 1864, and USS *Waterwitch* off Ossabaw Island, Georgia, June 3, 1864.

The irresistible tide of Federal ground and naval forces eliminated the Confederate naval bases at Savannah, Charleston, and Wilmington during late 1864 and early 1865. Contingents of Marines from those stations made their way to the post at Drewry's Bluff, where they were organized with sailors into a naval battalion under the command of Capt. John R. Tucker. The majority of marines were killed or captured at the Battle of Sayler's Creek on April 6, 1865. A few managed to escape, only to surrender at Appomattox on April 9, 1865. Others, components of a naval brigade made up of shipless crew from the James River Squadron, surrendered at Greensboro, North Carolina, on April 28, 1865. The last organized force of Confederate Marines, the remnant of the Mobile Company, surrendered north of that city on May 10, 1865.

BIBLIOGRAPHY

Donnelly, Ralph W. *The Confederate States Marine Corps: The Rebel Leathernecks.* Shippensburg, Pa., 1989.

Gardner, Donald R. "The Confederate Corps of Marines." Master's thesis, Memphis State University, 1973.

Sullivan, David M. "Leathernecks in Gray: A Perspective of the War through the Letters of Confederate States Marine Officers." *Journal of Confederate History* 1, no. 2 (1988): 351–386.

DAVID M. SULLIVAN

MARMADUKE, JOHN SAPPINGTON

MARMADUKE, JOHN SAPPINGTON (1833– 1887), major general and postwar governor of Missouri. Both Marmaduke's father and his uncle served as Missouri's governor, the first in 1844 and the latter in 1860. The younger Marmaduke attended Yale and Harvard before accepting a cadetship at West Point, graduating in 1857, and then serving in Utah during the Mormon War.

Though his father favored the Union, Marmaduke in 1861 resigned his commission in the Federal army and was made colonel of cavalry in the Missouri State Guard. He commanded the militia at Boonville against government forces under Nathaniel Lyon and was so embarrassed by their poor showing that he resigned his colonelcy and rode to Richmond, receiving a commission as first lieutenant in the Confederate army in 1861. Wounded at Shiloh, he displayed a brilliant leadership that earned him promotion to brigadier general. Marmaduke was transferred to the Trans-Mississippi Department in August 1862, assuming command of Confederate cavalry in Arkansas and Missouri and making frequent raids. In December, he led a division at Cane Hill and Prairie Grove, Arkansas, and the following January was repulsed at Springfield trying to strike the Federal line of communications from Rolla. That summer, he participated in battles at Helena and Little Rock, and in the spring of 1864 he led troops in defensive operations against Frederick Steele's Arkansas campaign, engaging at Jenkins's Ferry and Pine Bluff.

In September 1863, while at Little Rock, Marmaduke engaged in a duel with fellow cavalry division commander, Lucius M. Walker. (Marmaduke had voiced doubts about Walker's courage in battle, leading Walker to challenge him.) The duel resulted in Walker's death.

In May 1864, while participating in the Red River campaign, Marmaduke's horsemen surprised Steele's wagon train at Poison Springs, Louisiana. Attacking the Federal escort of 1,200 men, comprised mainly of the First Kansas Colored Infantry, Marmaduke's men killed or captured nearly a third of the bluecoats—including as many as one hundred black soldiers who, after being wounded or captured, were murdered by vengeful Confederates.

In the fall of 1864, Marmaduke commanded Sterling Price's cavalry during the famous raid into Missouri, participating in battles at Pilot Knob, Little Blue River, and Westport before being captured while conducting a rearguard action at the Marais des Cygnes River in Kansas. On March 18, 1865, while imprisoned at Fort Warren, Massachusetts, for the duration of the war, Marmaduke was made a major general, the last appointed in the armies of the Confederacy.

Elected governor of Missouri in 1884, Marmaduke died during his last year in office.

BIBLIOGRAPHY

Britton, Wiley. *The Civil War on the Border.* New York, 1890.
Castel, Albert. *General Sterling Price and the Civil War in the West.* Baton Rouge, La., 1968.
Monaghan, Jay. *Civil War on the Western Border, 1854–1865.* Lincoln, Nebr., 1955.
O'Flaherty, Daniel. *General Jo Shelby: Undefeated Rebel.* Chapel Hill, N.C., 1954.

CHRISTOPHER PHILLIPS

MARRIAGE AND DIVORCE

During the Civil War, separation, economic devastation, and death placed tremendous stress on Southern marriages. Societal expectations encouraged husbands and wives to cope with these stresses in gender and race-specific ways: white men by displaying active courage, white women through stoic suffering. Slave men and women were expected, first and foremost, to remain loyal to their white "families." But though societal expectations shaped the effects of the war on Southern marriages, they often did so in unintended ways. Many women displayed uncommon boldness in confronting marital crises foisted on them by war; many slaves and former slaves struggled against their white "masters" to solidify their own marital and family ties in the emerging New South.

The letters and diaries of upper-class Southern white women have proven especially useful to scholars of the Civil War. Studies of the marriages of Jefferson and Varina Howell

> **Many women displayed uncommon boldness in confronting marital crises. . . .**

Davis, Clement and Virginia Tunstall Clay, and J. Jefferson and Ella Gertrude Clanton Thomas indicate that the final defeat of the Confederacy strained the marriages of some elite families to the breaking point. They also suggest that some planter-class wives adjusted to defeat more easily than their husbands did. Ella Gertrude Thomas, Virginia Clay, and Varina Davis all built rich public lives after the war and became the stronger, even dominant, partners in their marriages. While defeat of the Confederacy understandably demoralized their powerful husbands, subjecting all three to recurring bouts of depression and despondency, the efforts by these women to achieve economic and psychic survival in the war-devastated South released them from traditionally ornamental, passive roles.

Court records provide yet another window on Confederate marriages. The Civil War brought changes in who was likely to seek a divorce, and why. A study of nineteenth-century divorce patterns in central North Carolina provides cases in point. During the antebellum era, women—most of them from the slaveholding classes—far outnumbered men in seeking divorce. Disaffected wives typically charged husbands with wasting property, desertion, adultery, or physical abuse, often committed during drunken "frolics." In contrast, during and immediately after the war, men sought divorces in larger numbers than women. The overwhelming charge lodged against wives was adultery, typically committed while husbands were away at war. Husbands seeking divorce were often of yeoman rather than planter backgrounds, suggesting that economic devastation also contributed substantially to the war's shattering of Southern marriages.

A high rate of marital failure in the wake of the Civil War may also have resulted from the haste with which many marriages were contracted during its early years. The abandonment by many young people of traditional forms of courtship and, especially, marriages between Confederate women and Union soldiers shocked older Southerners. When Eleanor Swain, the daughter of University of North Carolina president David Swain, married a Union general, many of the families' friends refused to attend the wedding and some never spoke to Eleanor again.

The Civil War wreaked special havoc on the marriages of slaves. The forced separation of slave families was not a new practice, but occurred more frequently during the war. Confederate state governments impressed many slaves into military and industrial employment, in the process separating husbands from wives and parents from children. Slaves' increasing difficulty in keeping marriages intact created complex and painful situations, such as that of one couple reunited in a refugee camp in 1864—after each had married someone else.

Postwar Reconstruction transformed African American marriages. Freedom from slavery and the gaining of citizenship through the Fourteenth Amendment to the Constitution enabled former slaves to search for lost partners and to legalize their marriages. These were monumental gains, but they did not assure African American couples happy or stable marriages. The efforts by many white Southerners and Northerners to reestablish white supremacy in the postwar South burdened blacks' marriages in a variety of ways. Labor contracts between white landowners and former slaves and forced apprenticeships of former slave children, for example, put some African American husbands and wives at odds with one another and with their former masters. These people were forced to choose what was more important in the uncertain New South: the exercise of one's freedom (relative at best for blacks by 1872) or immediate economic security. Like white couples, most black couples managed to endure these difficult times, but postwar divorce records reveal the wartime stresses that fractured some marriages.

[*See also* Family Life.]

BIBLIOGRAPHY

Bleser, Carol, ed. *In Joy and in Sorrow: Women, Family, and Marriage in the Victorian South.* New York, 1991.

Bynum, Victoria E. *Unruly Women: The Politics of Social and Sexual Control in the Old South.* Chapel Hill, N.C., 1992.

Clinton, Catherine, and Nina Silber, eds. *Divided Houses: Gender and the Civil War.* New York, 1992.

Rable, George C. *Civil Wars: Women and the Crisis of Southern Nationalism.* Urbana, Ill., 1989.

Scott, Anne Firor. *The Southern Lady: From Pedestal to Politics, 1830–1930.* Chicago, 1970.

VICTORIA E. BYNUM

MARSHALL, HENRY

MARSHALL, HENRY (1805–1864), congressman from Louisiana. Marshall was born in Darlington District, South Carolina, and attended Union College at Schenectady, New York, in the late 1820s. In the mid-1830s, he moved to De Soto Parish, Louisiana, the site of his future plantation, Land's End. In 1860, Marshall owned eight thousand acres and 201 slaves. His total net worth of $206,000 made him one of the largest plantation owners to serve as a Confederate congressman.

In January 1861, Marshall was selected from the district comprising the parishes of De Soto, Natchitoches, Sabine, and Caddo as the senatorial delegate to the Louisiana secession convention. This convention in turn elected him as a representative to the Montgomery convention, soon to become the Provisional Congress. As a member, Marshall sought to strengthen the Constitution's state rights orientation by removing any language from the document that endowed electors with a dual identity as citizens of the Confederacy and of the individual states. In the Provisional Congress he served as chairman of the Committee on Public Lands and maintained his state rights convictions by opposing the Davis administration on issues such as direct taxation, centralized control over military affairs, and increased presidential powers.

After his election from the Fifth Congressional District to the First Congress, Marshall continued his anti-administration stance while serving on the Claims, Quartermaster's and Commissary Departments, Military Transport, Conference, Inauguration, Patents, and Territories and Public Lands committees. In 1863, he chose not to run for reelection and retired to his plantation where he died on July 13, 1864.

BIBLIOGRAPHY

Alexander, Thomas B., and Richard E. Beringer. *The Anatomy of the Confederate Congress: A Study of the Influences of Member Characteristics on Legislative Voting Behavior, 1861–1865.* Nashville, Tenn., 1972.

Wakelyn, Jon L. *Biographical Dictionary of the Confederacy.* Edited by Frank E. Vandiver. Westport, Conn., 1977.

Warner, Ezra J., and W. Buck Yearns. *Biographical Register of the Confederate Congress.* Baton Rouge, La., 1975.

Yearns, Wilfred B. *The Confederate Congress.* Athens, Ga., 1960.

LESLIE A. LOVETT

MARSHALL, HUMPHREY

MARSHALL, HUMPHREY (1812–1872), U.S. diplomat, brigadier general, and congressman from Kentucky. Born in Frankfort, Kentucky, Marshall was the nephew of antislavery leader James G. Birney and a relative of Supreme Court Chief Justice John Marshall. At West Point, he graduated forty-second in a class of forty-five in 1832. He became a member of the Mounted Rangers, but resigned after a year to study law. In 1833 he opened a practice in Louisville, Kentucky, became a planter, and fought in the Black Hawk War. Upon his return, he entered politics, serving on the Louisville City Council. By the late 1830s Marshall had become active in the state militia and was promoted to the rank of lieutenant colonel in 1846. In the war with Mexico, he fought as a colonel in the First Kentucky Cavalry.

When Marshall returned from Mexico, he concentrated his efforts on politics. A member of the Whig party, he was elected to the U.S. House of Representatives in 1849. He remained in Congress until 1852, when President Millard Fillmore, in return for Marshall's support of the administration, appointed him minister to China. Returning to the United States in 1854, Marshall reentered the House the next year as a member of the Know-Nothing (American) party. By 1859 he had become a secessionist and left Congress, although he later tried to save the Union and favored an armed neutrality. Marshall supported Democrat John C. Breckinridge for president in 1860, but when the Confederacy was formed, he labored to keep Kentucky neutral.

Marshall's opinions changed drastically, however, when Confederate Maj. Gen. Leonidas Polk moved a small garrison into southern Kentucky and Lincoln responded by sending a large army of occupation. This action convinced Marshall that Kentucky remained in the Union only because of coercion by the Federal government, and he sought an appointment in the Confederate army. Commissioned a brigadier general on October 30, 1861, he was indicted for treason and had to flee his home state. Marshall was placed in command of an independent department, the Army of Southwest Virginia. His brigade fought along the Big Sandy River on the Kentucky–West Virginia border against Union forces under Gen. James A. Garfield. They attained minor success at Middle Creek in January 1862 and at Pound Gap in March. Marshall's greatest military success was a minor affair in which he forced Union Gen. J. D. Cox's troops back from Princeton, West Virginia, on May 16 and 17, 1862.

Generally resentful of his assignment to the western Virginia mountains, Marshall resigned his commission on June 16, 1862. With the planned invasion of Kentucky an important part of Confederate strategy, however, the Southerners needed Kentuckians in places of command to arouse Confederate loyalties in the state. Marshall's superiors put this argument to him, and he accepted reappointment as brigadier general on June 19.

He moved his troops westward into Kentucky in September to join Gen. Braxton Bragg in his campaign to rid the state of Federal troops. Marshall held little regard for Bragg and joined Gen. E. Kirby Smith in politicking against him. Marshall marched his brigade slowly through eastern Kentucky, with no apparent urgency to reach its objective. When Bragg reached the rendezvous at Lexington, he found that few of the troops he was supposed to meet were present—Marshall had bivouacked his men some thirty miles east of Lexington. Marshall did connect with Bragg, eventually, but he and his troops rarely took their positions in time to take part in a maneuver. Bragg was finally forced to retreat from Kentucky, and Marshall was granted permission to take his own route back to western Virginia. He received no significant military assignments after that.

Marshall, who was not an impressive military leader, weighed more than three hundred pounds and expressed a deep belief in spiritualism. In addition, his discipline was too lax for him to command volunteers effectively. His penchant for leniency was so well known that one of his officers made a standing offer to "eat the first man the general should shoot for any crime." Marshall tired of his command and resigned his commission again on June 17, 1863. This time, no one tried to dissuade him. He traveled to Richmond, Virginia, and opened a law office.

Marshall then put his political background to use and was elected to represent the Eighth District of northern Kentucky in the Second Congress. While there, he became the leader of the Kentucky contingent and was a prominent member of the Military Affairs Committee. Marshall opposed Jefferson Davis's administration at every turn, disagreeing especially with the president's choice of generals. He was particularly critical of Bragg, accusing him of incompetence in the Kentucky campaign. Bragg had similar feelings toward Marshall, asserting that in the Mexican War Marshall and his men did "some fine running & no fighting." Regarding Marshall's abilities as a congressman, Bragg called him a "humbug and a superficial, tho' fluent fool." In Congress, Marshall did not support Davis's call for the suspension of habeas corpus or for heavy taxation. He did, however, back conscription and impressment. As a representative from a federally occupied region, Marshall's main goal was to organize another invasion of Kentucky. He believed that an efficient raid could be effective against the Federals and would free his home state of Union domination. Although this invasion never happened, Marshall agitated for it throughout his term in office.

Marshall remained in Congress until its final adjournment on March 18, 1865. Upon the collapse of the Confederacy, he fled to Texas to escape any possible treason charges that might still be outstanding. Marshall returned to Louisville in 1866 and opened a law office. He had limited success with this practice but remained in Louisville until his death on March 28, 1872.

BIBLIOGRAPHY

Alexander, Thomas B., and Richard E. Beringer. *The Anatomy of the Confederate Congress: A Study of the Influences of Member Characteristics on Legislative Voting Behavior, 1861–1865.* Nashville, Tenn., 1972.

Johnston, J. Stoddard. *Kentucky.* Vol. 9 of *Confederate Military History.* Edited by Clement A. Evans. Atlanta, 1899. Vol. 11 of extended. ed. Wilmington, N.C., 1988.

McWhiney, Grady. *Braxton Bragg and Confederate Defeat.* Vol. 1. New York, 1969.

Thomas, Emory M. *The Confederate Nation: 1861–1865.* New York, 1979.

Vandiver, Frank E. *Their Tattered Flags: The Epic of the Confederacy.* New York, 1970. Reprint, Texas A & M University Military History Series, no. 5. College Station, Tex., 1987.

Yearns, Wilfred B. *The Confederate Congress.* Athens, Ga., 1960.

ROBERT F. PACE

MASON, JAMES M.

MASON, JAMES M. (1798–1871), congressman from Virginia and diplomat. Though by middle age James Murray Mason had attained the high office his prominent Virginia family had raised him to expect, he could not have anticipated that he would be remembered most because of the actions of others rather than his own. As the grandson of Revolutionary giant George Mason, he grew up with the arro-

gant confidence of a member of the Virginia gentry. He was born in the northern corner of the state that was then part of the District of Columbia, and he graduated from the University of Pennsylvania. After studying law at William and Mary, he settled in Winchester, Virginia, on a modest estate called Selma.

Mason served in the Virginia legislature in the 1820s and sat in the state's constitutional convention of 1829 and 1830, where he upheld backcountry interests against those of the Tidewater. After a single term in the U.S. House of Representatives (1838–1839), he won election in 1847 to the U.S. Senate and remained there until the secession crisis.

A state rights Democrat, Mason moved in the congenial company of his fellow Virginia senator Robert M. T. Hunter and South Carolinian John C. Calhoun. He served as chair-

> "Here we are," Mason wrote his wife, "on the deep blue sea; clear of all the Yankees."

man of the Senate Foreign Relations Committee and drafted the Fugitive Slave Law that was part of the Compromise of 1850. Like Calhoun, whose constitutional views he admired, Mason viewed sectional antagonism as something too deep to be assuaged by palliative measures. For him, Abraham Lincoln's election spelled the end of the Union. He left the Senate on March 28, 1861—nearly a month before Virginia seceded—and served briefly in the Provisional Congress in his old role as Foreign Relations chairman.

Mason's greatest challenge came when Jefferson Davis appointed him the fledgling Confederacy's diplomatic commissioner to Great Britain. Mason's letter of instruction came from his fellow Virginian Hunter, whose own Confederate reincarnation in 1861 was as secretary of state. Hunter told Mason to go to London immediately and present the South's request for diplomatic recognition not as "revolted provinces or rebellious subjects" but as a "new Confederacy and a new Government." In words hardly suited to such a proud nation, he suggested that Mason remind the English—erroneously thought to be in great need of cotton—that the supply of that staple to Britain from an independent South "would be as abundant, as cheap and as certain as if these States were themselves her colonies."

On his way to Charleston in search of a ship to run the blockade, Mason traveled in the company of another former U.S. senator, John Slidell, a Louisianan sent by the Confederacy as emissary to France. Slidell took his family with him and, like Mason, was also accompanied by a secretary of legation. At first they planned to take the steamship *Nashville,* but an unexpected increase in activity by the blockading Northern ships made them consider going to

JAMES M. MASON. NATIONAL ARCHIVES

Mexico before embarking. When they concluded that the overland route would unduly delay their mission, they found another ship, a privateer with a shallower draft than the *Nashville* and a better chance of eluding the blockading vessels. On the evening of October 11, 1861, *Gordon* slipped out of Charleston in a driving rain and through the blockade without incident. "Here we are," Mason wrote his wife, "on the deep blue sea; clear of all the Yankees."

The ship arrived in the Bahamas three days later. On learning that the only regularly scheduled British vessel leaving from Nassau stopped, inconveniently, at New York, the commissioners decided to continue on to Cuba where they expected to find passage to the West Indies and then to London. When they reached Havana they were feted by sympathetic Spanish citizens and introduced by the obliging British consul general to Cuban authorities as diplomats of the Confederacy. They made no attempt to keep their mission a secret. Capt. Charles D. Wilkes of the warship USS *San Jacinto* learned of their presence when he put in at a port down the coast. He quickly cast off for Havana in hopes of capturing them when their ship put out to sea. The common knowledge in the Cuban capital that the Southerners had booked passage on the British mail packet *Trent* eliminated guesswork for Wilkes. On November 8 *San Jacinto* intercepted *Trent* on the high seas, and Wilkes, ignoring the cautions of his executive officer not to spark an international incident, did just that.

After firing shots across the mail packet's bow, Wilkes sent across a boarding party to take prisoner the two Confederate diplomats whose names would ever after be linked in history. For Mason and Slidell, their diplomatic role was beginning much sooner than expected. After much glowering, brandishing of bayonets, and hurling of insults between members of the boarding party and the largely Southern company of passengers, *Trent* gave up its soon-to-be-famous passengers. Though the Northern sailors did not search the British ship for papers or take it as a prize, seizing the two commissioners and their assistants was enough. While Slidell was gathering his bags to leave the mail packet, his wife asked who commanded *San Jacinto*. When told it was someone she knew, she blurted out the bald truth before Mason could stop her: "Captain Wilkes is playing into our hands!"

The incident lasted less than three hours but reverberated across the ocean for weeks to come. As *San Jacinto* sailed up the coast, often within sight of Confederate territory, Mason while pacing the decks lectured his secretary on how this act of "piracy" would force the British to join hands with the South. On November 24 *San Jacinto* dropped anchor in Boston Harbor and turned over its captives to the prison at Fort Warren. Mason and Slidell were ushered into their spartan but clean and warm quarters—an eighteen-by-eighteen-foot room that the two men shared. It was not an uncomfortable arrangement. Far from eating prison gruel in a damp cell, the Southerners enjoyed professionally cooked meals replete, as one disgusted Bostonian reported, with "champagne, fruit, cigars, English papers and letters of sympathy." "Indeed," Mason admitted, "we have a better daily table than any hotel affords."

While Mason and Slidell languished in enforced idleness, the diplomatic furor raged outside the walls of Fort Warren. Learning that Confederate emissaries had been taken at gunpoint from a British ship, the cabinet in Westminster wrestled with a way to avoid war, but as a precaution postponed planned reductions in military spending. Outside the corridors of Whitehall the British press concluded that the government could do no less than demand release of the commissioners and a formal apology from the American government. Some London editors (including one Karl Marx) argued that any war between Britain and the North would suit only the slave owners' purposes and for that reason must be avoided. But reinforcements sent to the British garrison in Canada reminded everyone that the incident could indeed lead to the result Mason so fervently prayed for in his cell in Boston Harbor. While in prison, the Virginia diplomat wrote afterward, he bet a fellow Southern inmate fifty barrels of corn that the British would demand his freedom.

When the American press learned of the outrage the *Trent* affair was causing in England, newspapers spread the fear of imminent conflict with Great Britain throughout the North. A prominent British correspondent in Washington wrote that if war broke out between his country and the North, "Old Nick will be unchained for some time to come." In Fort Warren, Mason and his companions read with enjoyment these reports on the apparent slide toward war their arrest had triggered.

The British cabinet finally composed an ultimatum demanding release of the diplomats and an apology. But as one of his last public acts, Prince Albert, consort of Queen Victoria, altered the text to soften it and provide the Americans with a face-saving retreat by saying the British government hoped Wilkes had not acted on higher authority. Formal presentation of the ultimatum to Secretary of State William H. Seward did not take place until December 23. A hint of the American response had been contained in earlier denials by Abraham Lincoln that his government had ordered Wilkes's action. On December 27 the crisis passed when Seward told the British ambassador that Mason and Slidell would be released without condition.

The Confederate detainees were surreptitiously bundled out of Fort Warren and transferred to a British warship that took them away in an icy gale to Bermuda and then on to London. Mason arrived to a hero's welcome in the Mayfair town houses and country homes of influential British sympathizers. Ominously, though, the government officially ignored him. Though he cultivated all the right elements in industry, press, and Parliament, Mason could not effect the goal he

> **A last semiofficial act was to publish . . . a refutation of Secretary of War Edwin Stanton's charge that the Lincoln assassination was engineered by the Confederate government.**

came to achieve—recognition of the Confederacy. In July 1862 he complained that "the Government here is tardy and supine" but hoped the success of Confederate arms and a shortage of cotton would change their minds. He wrote frequently to Lord Russell, secretary of state for foreign affairs, but could not gain an audience. Russell turned aside Mason's entreaties by writing rather offensively that if the Confederacy ever achieved "stability and permanence" it would be recognized: "That time, however, has not, in the judgment of Her Majesty's Government, yet arrived." Late in the war Mason did meet with Lord Palmerston but went away disappointed each time.

Perhaps the Confederate emissary could have achieved the diplomatic recognition Richmond desired, but Mason seems to have accepted defeat too easily. Certainly he could have shown more energy and more tenacity in pursuit of an admittedly difficult goal. Had he done so, his explanations for

his failure would have sounded less like attempts to blame others for his own shortcomings.

By autumn 1862 Mason had abandoned his purely diplomatic approach and helped secure loans and facilitate commercial transactions for the South. The next August President Davis decided that because the British had refused his request for recognition, Mason should consider his mission "at an end" and leave London. Mason did as instructed but wrote a plaintive dispatch after he reached Paris saying he was "at some loss to know whether it was intended that I should remain for the present in Europe." He wrote his wife from his flat near the Arc de Triomphe, "I am plodding on in this Babel, but with little in it to interest me. . . . I have seen nothing in Paris. . . . In truth I have not the heart or spirit to gaze after new things." In the fall of 1863, however, he was appointed the Confederate commissioner on the Continent and traveled back and forth between London and Paris. He despaired of ever convincing the British of the rightness of his cause: "The so-called antislavery feeling seems to have become with them a sentiment akin to patriotism."

Up to the end of the war, even when the last Atlantic ports had fallen to Northern assaults, Mason continued to send his forlorn dispatches by blockade runner to Nassau and Bermuda in hopes that they would get through. In March 1865 he was still corresponding with Secretary of State Judah P. Benjamin about such irrelevancies as the missing Confederate seal he had dispatched the previous year. Even after learning of the evacuation of Richmond, he wrote that "the war will go on to final success." A last semiofficial act was to publish in the London *Index,* a news sheet subsidized by Confederate money, a refutation of Secretary of War Edwin Stanton's charge that the Lincoln assassination was engineered by the Confederate government.

Mason planned to sail for Canada in September 1865 after seeing Benjamin, who escaped from Richmond and made his way to London and eventual success as a barrister there. Mason did not leave as expected, however, and was not reunited with his family in Canada until the following April. Under the aegis of President Andrew Johnson's amnesty, the diplomat returned to Virginia in 1869, visibly older, his step slow and heavy. He could not return to Selma. Like the homes of many Southerners, it had been put to the torch during the war. After a long, gradual decline, Mason died on April 28, 1871, in Alexandria, Virginia.

[*See also* Trent Affair.]

BIBLIOGRAPHY

Biographical Directory of the United States Congress, 1774–1989. Washington, D.C., 1989.

Ferris, Norman B. *The Trent Affair: A Diplomatic Crisis.* Knoxville, Tenn., 1977.

Mason, Virginia. *The Public Life and Diplomatic Correspondence of James M. Mason.* New York and Washington, D.C., 1906.

Wakelyn, Jon L. *Biographical Dictionary of the Confederacy.* Westport, Conn., 1977.

NELSON D. LANKFORD

MASON-DIXON LINE

Because of disputed boundaries between English colonies in America, arising from conflicting statements in colonial charters issued by various kings of England in the seventeenth and eighteenth centuries, English surveyors and astronomers were sent to North America to locate and establish legal boundaries.

During the years 1763 through 1767, Charles Mason and Jeremiah Dixon surveyed the boundaries of three colonies, Delaware, Maryland, and Pennsylvania. The line of the latter two was surveyed westward 244 miles. Opposition by Indian tribes delayed its completion until 1784. The survey cost $75,000 and was paid by William Penn and Lord Baltimore. An eight-foot-wide vista was cut through the forests and small stone markers placed at each mile post, with larger stone markers bearing the coats of arms of Penn and Baltimore at five-mile intervals. In ensuing years many markers fell or were appropriated by settlers. In 1900 through 1902 the line was resurveyed and stabilized.

Between the Revolution and the Civil War, the line acquired additional significance as the border between Northern states that had eliminated African slavery and Southern states that retained the institution. In 1820 Missouri, west of the Mississippi River, was admitted as a slave state, with slavery prohibited in the remaining territory north of 36°30´.

Immediately prior to the Civil War, Southern slaveholding states were called "Dixie," presumably derived from the word Dixon, and popularized in a minstrel show song in 1859. The term Mason-Dixon Line has continued in use in the twentieth century to distinguish between Northern and Southern states of the American Union.

BIBLIOGRAPHY

Mason, A. Hewlett, ed. *The Journal of Charles Mason and Jeremiah Dixon, 1736–1768.* Vol. 76 of *Memoirs of the American Philosophical Society.* Philadelphia, 1969.

Matthews, Edward B., ed. *Report on the Resurvey of the Maryland-Pennsylvania Boundary Part of the Mason and Dixon Line.* Harrisburg, Pa., 1909.

Miers, Earl Schenck. *Border Romance: The Story of the Exploits of Charles Mason and Jeremiah Dixon.* Newark, Del., 1975.

Poitiaux, Robinson Morgan. *The Evolution of the Mason and Dixon Line.* Richmond, Va., 1902.

PERCIVAL PERRY

MAURY, D. H.

MAURY, D. H. (1822–1900), major general and U.S. diplomat. Educated at the University of Virginia and West Point, Dabney Herndon Maury had fifteen years' experience in the U.S. Army by the time the Civil War began in 1861. He had served with distinction during the Mexican War, published a tactics manual for mounted rifles, taught as an instructor at West Point, and fought Indians on the frontier. When his native state of Virginia seceded from the Union, Maury submitted his resignation papers to the U.S. Army. The army refused to accept his resignation and Maury found himself instead dismissed for his traitorous request. Nonetheless, he

> **Maury was one of the founding members of the Southern Historical Society. . . .**

quickly left his post in New Mexico and arrived in Richmond in July 1861 to offer his military services to the Confederacy.

Maury's first assignment was as a cavalry captain. After a brief stint stationed on the Rappahannock River under Gen. Theophilus H. Holmes, Maury went west to join Gen. Earl Van Dorn's Trans-Mississippi Department. Maury once wrote that his only "application for services ever made during the war was for service in the field of the Army of Northern Virginia." The Confederate army never granted that request, and Maury spent the entire war far west of his native state.

At the Confederate defeat at Elkhorn Tavern, Arkansas, in March of 1862, Colonel Maury's performance in the face of failure greatly impressed Van Dorn. Promotion to brigadier general came within a week.

As a brigadier general in the Army of the West, Maury competently led Confederates through the Battles of Iuka and Corinth. During the winter of 1862–1863 he won promotion to major general. In late December 1862 his division went to the aid of Stephen Dill Lee at Vicksburg, Mississippi. On April 15, Maury received new orders to go to Knoxville, Tennessee, as commander of the Department of East Tennessee. He hoped this would keep him closer to home, but in six weeks he changed posts again.

In May 1863, Maury became commander of the District of the Gulf with headquarters in Mobile, Alabama, and he and his family settled in Mobile for the duration of the war. Maury later described this assignment as an "interesting and agreeable command." It was not an idle one. For the next two years he devoted his energy to keeping Mobile and its important bay free from Federal control. He was also responsible for diverting enemy raids sent into Mississippi and Alabama. In April 1864, Federals managed to take control of Mobile Bay, but Maury stubbornly fought to defend the city until the following spring. In April 1865 he finally acquiesced to superior forces and surrendered his command. For Dabney Maury, as for other Confederate officers, his years as a soldier had come to a bitter end.

Maury's postwar years were varied, taking him from Virginia to Louisiana before he served as the U.S. minister to Colombia. Most pertinent to the history of the Confederacy, Maury was one of the founding members of the Southern Historical Society and served as its chairman for twenty years. As part of this organization Maury joined other Southerners in working to recover and make available for publication Confederate records of the war.

BIBLIOGRAPHY

Hotchkiss, Jed. *Virginia.* Vol. 3 of *Confederate Military History.* Edited by Clement A. Evans. Atlanta, 1899. Vol. 4 of extended ed. Wilmington, N.C., 1987.

Maury, Dabney H. *Recollections of a Virginian in the Mexican, Indian and Civil Wars.* New York, 1894.

Warner, Ezra J. *Generals in Gray: Lives of the Confederate Commanders.* Baton Rouge, La., 1959.

LESLEY JILL GORDON-BURR

MAURY, MATTHEW FONTAINE

MAURY, MATTHEW FONTAINE (1806–1873), naval officer. Appointed an acting midshipman at the age of nineteen, Maury served for over thirty-six years in the U.S. Navy, during which time he won international recognition for his pioneering work in the fields of navigation, hydrography, and meteorology. Following Virginia's secession from the Union, Maury resigned his commission to serve in defense of his native state. He was immediately appointed by Governor John Letcher to serve on an advisory council charged with mobilizing state defenses. On April 23, 1861, Maury was commissioned a commander in the Virginia State Navy. He retained this rank when the state navy was incorporated into the Confederate navy on June 10.

In late spring 1861, Maury began a series of experiments with torpedoes, or underwater mines. He believed that, for a nation lacking the resources to construct a large navy, torpedoes offered a cheap and effective alternative for defending Southern waterways from Union warships. Although initially skeptical, Confederate Secretary of the Navy Stephen R. Mallory came to endorse Maury's ideas, and in the fall of 1861 the Confederate Congress appropriated moneys for a torpedo development program. Maury's researches led to

MATTHEW FONTAINE MAURY. Pictured with Raphael Semmes (at right), commander of the commerce raider *Alabama*.
NAVAL HISTORICAL CENTER, WASHINGTON, D.C.

building a torpedo with an improved electric detonator, the first used successfully in warfare.

Maury also advocated the construction of steam-powered gunboats to protect Southern waters. The gunboats he envisioned were shallow-draft and highly maneuverable, and mounted large-caliber rifled guns. Such vessels, Maury argued, could be quickly and economically built and, in large numbers, would be capable of driving Federal ships from the South's rivers and bays. The Confederate Congress was impressed enough with his proposal to appropriate $2 million to build one hundred of these gunboats. Yet Maury had scarcely begun supervising work on these craft when the program was abruptly canceled. The success of CSS *Virginia* against the Union blockading fleet at Hampton Roads had convinced the Confederate government that it should apply its limited resources to the building of ironclad warships.

In late summer 1862, Maury was ordered to England as a special agent with instructions to purchase ships for the Confederate government. Over the next two and a half years, he used his worldwide fame as a scientist to promote publicly the cause of Southern independence among the British people. In addition, he continued his experiments on electric torpedoes, the results of which were forwarded to the Navy Department. He also arranged for the purchase of two ships to serve as commerce raiders. One of these vessels, the screw steamer *Georgia,* made nine captures.

On May 2, 1865, knowing that the collapse of the Confederate government was imminent, Maury set sail for Texas with $40,000 worth of torpedo equipment in a last-ditch effort to help the Southern cause. Arriving in Havana twenty days later, he learned that the war was over. Because he fell into three of the six categories of Confederates exempted from the Federal government's 1863 amnesty proclamations (he was a U.S. Navy officer who had resigned and aided the South, an agent of the Confederate government, and a Confederate naval officer above the rank of lieutenant), Maury was unable to return to Virginia until July 1868. He was then appointed a professor of physics at Virginia Military Institute, a position he held until his death.

BIBLIOGRAPHY

Corbin, Diana F. M. *A Life of Matthew Fontaine Maury, U.S.N. and C.S.N.* London, 1888.
Lewis, Charles L. *Matthew Fontaine Maury: The Pathfinder of the Seas.* Annapolis, Md., 1927.
Williams, Frances L. *Matthew Fontaine Maury: Scientist of the Sea.* New Brunswick, N.J., 1963.

CHARLES E. BRODINE, JR.

MECHANICSVILLE, VIRGINIA

Also known as Beaver Dam Creek and Ellerson's Mill, the first major confrontation of the Seven Days' Battles between Gen. Robert E. Lee's Army of Northern Virginia and Maj. Gen. George B. McClellan's Army of the Potomac took place on June 26, 1862, near the small village of Mechanicsville, east of Richmond. As McClellan brought his army within sight of Richmond, he planned to use heavy artillery to shell the Confederate capital into submission from behind well-established entrenchments. Lee refused to wait for McClellan to perfect his plans, however. Using intelligence gathered by Brig. Gen. J. E. B. Stuart, he decided to seize the initiative and attack Maj. Gen. Fitz John Porter's 30,000-man corps while the latter remained separated from the rest of the Union army by the Chickahominy River. Lee planned to supplement his forces with Maj. Gen. Thomas J. ("Stonewall") Jackson's Army of the Shenandoah Valley. If all went according to plan, Jackson would smash into the flank and rear of Porter's command while Confederates under Maj. Gens. A. P.

Hill, D. H. Hill, and James Longstreet struck the Federals from the front. About one-third of Lee's army under Maj. Gens. John B. Magruder and Benjamin Huger would remain in the entrenchments to defend Richmond. Once the Federals in their front began to withdraw, they were to join the attack as well.

On June 25, the day before the Confederate offensive, Federals under Brig. Gen. Joseph Hooker clashed with Southerners under Huger at Oak Grove. Although neither side gained much advantage from the fighting, McClellan recalled Hooker when he became aware of Jackson's approach. An overwhelming sense of foreboding filled him. He informed Secretary of War Edwin Stanton: "I will do all that a General can do with the splendid Army I have the honor to command & if it is destroyed by overwhelming numbers can at least die with it & share its fate."

The fighting at Oak Grove had no effect upon the timetable for the Confederate assault on Porter, but the delay of Jackson's march threatened to wreck the schedule completely. A. P. Hill had his men ready to strike early in the day, waiting only for the flanking force to appear. As the day wore on with no word from Jackson, Hill grew impatient and decided to proceed without him. At 3:00 P.M., the Confederates swept through Mechanicsville, driving the Federals from the village. This cleared the way for D. H. Hill's and Longstreet's men to cross the Chickahominy. Under the weight of the Confederate advance, Porter's troops withdrew to geographically strong positions along Beaver Dam Creek.

Despite the strength of the Union lines, A. P. Hill sent his men against the Federals in a frontal assault. Hill first attempted to strike the Union right flank with Brig. Gen. Joseph R. Anderson's command, supported by the brigades of Gens. James J. Archer and Charles W. Field. Artillery and small arms fire hammered the Confederates and repulsed the attack. As Brig. Gen. William D. Pender's men reached the field they joined the assault, attacking the Union left flank. The Federals quickly cut Pender's command to pieces and the attack degenerated into confused, disjointed, and ineffectual stabs at the Union line.

Late in the day, Lee decided to gamble on one final assault to turn Porter out of his formidable defenses. He ordered the first of D. H. Hill's brigades, under Brig. Gen. Roswell S. Ripley, into action on Pender's right. Coincidentally, President Jefferson Davis, watching the action on the field, issued an order similar to Lee's without the latter's knowledge. Ripley's men advanced against the same strong positions opposite Ellerson's Mill and suffered the same fate as Pender's men. Darkness finally ended any further bloody assaults.

Lee had counted upon precision from his subordinates to carry out his plan. Jackson's failure to arrive in a timely manner and A. P. Hill's impetuosity cost the Confederates 1,484 casualties. In contrast, the Federals whom Lee sought to annihilate lost 361. Nevertheless, the Confederate commander had seized the initiative from his Union counterpart. McClellan would spend the remainder of the Seven Days' Battles hoping to do little more than save his army from destruction.

BIBLIOGRAPHY

Cullen, Joseph P. *The Peninsula Campaign, 1862: McClellan and Lee Struggle for Richmond.* Harrisburg, Pa., 1973.

Freeman, Douglas S. *Lee's Lieutenants: A Study in Command.* 3 vols. New York, 1942–1944. Reprint, New York, 1986.

Johnson, Robert U., and C. C. Buel, eds. *Battles and Leaders of the Civil War.* 4 vols. New York, 1887–1888. Reprint, Secaucus, N.J., 1982.

Sears, Stephen W. *George B. McClellan: The Young Napoleon.* New York, 1988.

Sears, Stephen W. *To the Gates of Richmond: The Peninsula Campaign.* New York, 1992.

BRIAN S. WILLS

MEDALS AND DECORATIONS

Medals and decorations, as they are understood today, had no real tradition in the American military at the time of the Civil War. Although the Congress had periodically voted to award special presentation swords or gold medals to high-ranking officers and rewarded officers' bravery with brevet rank, there were no badges of recognition for enlisted men. The Medal of Honor, the first U.S. decoration, was not established until 1862. The Confederates, raised in this tradition, which in part stemmed from American disdain of what was considered to be aristocratic European foppery, therefore had no particular reason to establish medals or decorations. As a result, although the Confederate Congress authorized the president to bestow "medals with proper devices" and "badges of distinction," little was actually done to recognize individual bravery, and the few systems that did exist were largely locally created.

A "Roll of Honor" system was implemented within the various armies, with the intention of recognizing valor and serving as a substitute until medals were issued, but the medals were in fact never struck and the Roll of Honor tended to become a quota system in which companies voted on a prescribed number of recipients for the honor. Since, in many cases, far more men were deserving of the honor than received it, most companies refused to vote at all, and the system was largely a failure.

The only medals known to have been actually presented to Confederate soldiers were what was known as the "Davis Guard Medals." This was a small round silver medal, made out of Mexican silver dollars, with "Sabine Pass . . . Sept 8th . . . 1863" engraved on one side and "DG" and a Maltese cross on the other. President Davis presented forty-two of these medals to the members of the Davis Guard, a company of the First Texas Heavy Artillery, for their defense of the fortifications at Sabine Pass, Texas, in 1863.

Medallions were struck in France during the war for presentation to the members of the Stonewall Brigade, but they did not reach this country until after the war was over. They were offered for sale at veterans' reunions after 1895. All other Southern decorations, such as the United Daughters of the Confederacy's Southern Cross of Honor, were postwar decorations awarded to veterans or their families.

BIBLIOGRAPHY

Stiles, Robert. *Four Years under Marse Robert.* Washington, D.C., 1903.

Todd, Frederick P. *American Military Equipage, 1851–1872.* Vol. 2. Providence, R.I., 1977.

LES JENSEN

MEDICAL DEPARTMENT

[This entry discusses the organization of medical services in the Confederate army. For a more detailed discussion of Confederate army hospitals, see Hospitals. *For a broader discussion of medical care, see* Health and Medicine; Nursing.] Organization of the Confederate States Medical Department began in March 1861, with the appointment of a surgeon general, four surgeons, and six assistant surgeons. The woeful inadequacy of this staff became quickly apparent, and the department was soon enlarged to meet the needs of both the field armies and the general hospitals.

The first surgeon general, David Camden De Leon, served only from May 6 to July 12, 1861. On July 30, Dr. Samuel Preston Moore, a career military surgeon, replaced him. Moore presided over the Medical Department for the remainder of the war. The surgeon general was assigned the rank of colonel (later brigadier general); surgeons, the rank of major (later colonel); and assistant surgeons, the rank of captain. Medical officer uniforms consisted of a cadet gray tunic with black facings and a stand-up collar. Trousers were dark blue with a black velvet stripe, edged with gold cord, running the length of the leg. White gloves, a star on the collar, a green silk sash, and a cap with the letters "M.S." completed the uniform. Surgeons rarely wore this dress in the field, however.

The surgeon general was responsible for the administration of the Medical Department and the hospitals; he appointed medical officers and directed their work. During the rapid expansion of the Medical Department in the early months of the war, some incompetent physicians entered the service. Moore devised a system of examinations to remove many of these dangerous individuals. He also oversaw and encouraged the publication of professional texts for use by medical personnel.

Units of the Medical Department paralleled those of the military departments. Each army had a medical director who reported to his military commander and to the surgeon general. The chief surgeon of each army division, who was free of regimental medical duties, reported to the army medical director. Brigade surgeons, who retained regimental responsibilities, reported to the chief surgeon. Finally, each regiment had a surgeon and assistant surgeon; the first reported to the brigade surgeon.

Hospital administrative districts were not necessarily the same as those of the military departments. Each hospital was supervised by a surgeon, who reported to one of eight medical directors of hospitals, who in turn reported to the surgeon general. Confusion existed during the first two years of the war because the local military commander or army medical directors could also issue orders to the hospital surgeons. But the interlocking lines of authority were separated in March 1863, so that hospital surgeons reported solely to the medical directors of hospitals who reported solely to the surgeon general.

The general hospitals, located in cities behind the lines of active campaigning, were organized so that state residents could be kept together. Although hospitals usually occupied both fixed structures and movable pavilions, in times of heavy fighting, churches, hotels, and private homes were pressed into service. Under optimal conditions, the Medical Department tried to maintain a ratio of one surgeon for 80 patients, but this sometimes had to be stretched to one surgeon for up to 250 patients. The department also established a system of "wayside hospitals" along railroads for use by furloughed and discharged soldiers returning home.

During the course of the war approximately 1,200 surgeons and 2,000 assistant surgeons served in the Confederate army, and 26 surgeons and 93 assistant surgeons served in the Confederate navy aboard ships and at five naval hospitals.

BIBLIOGRAPHY

Cunningham, Horace H. *Doctors in Gray: The Confederate Medical Service.* Baton Rouge, La., 1958.

Miller, Francis T., ed. *The Photographic History of the Civil War.* 10 vols. New York, 1911. Reprint, New York, 1957. 7:237–296, 349–352.

HERBERT M. SCHILLER

MEMMINGER, CHRISTOPHER G.

MEMMINGER, CHRISTOPHER G. (1803– 1888), secretary of the treasury. Christopher Gustavus Memminger was born at Neyhinger in the Duchy of Württemberg on January 9, 1803; he was one of two foreign-born members of the Confederate cabinet. Brought to the United States in 1806, when he was orphaned, he was admitted in 1807 to the Charleston, South Carolina, Orphanage.

In 1814, he came to the attention of Thomas H. Bennett, a trustee of the orphanage and an antebellum governor of South Carolina. Bennett took Memminger into his home, assumed his guardianship, and later adopted him into his own large family. This arrangement was highly beneficial to Memminger, who gained thereby not only a happy home but the patronage of a powerful benefactor and the support of his able sons. Memminger could never have prospered to the same degree in his legal, political, and business careers or gained access to Charleston's closely knit, aristocratic society without this connection.

In 1819, Memminger graduated from South Carolina College in Charleston. Subsequently, he studied law with his uncle, Joseph Bennett, and was naturalized as an American citizen and admitted to the bar in early 1824. In his youth, Memminger displayed not only a considerable ability for hard work but also strong religious convictions. Even as a student he demonstrated a tendency toward the strict observance of rules and devotion to principles that both helped and hindered his effectiveness in public life.

Once launched on his legal career, Memminger, with his ability to present complicated legal matters in a lucid manner, soon became a leading member of the South Carolina bar. By 1860, he was a director of several companies and the owner of at least fifteen slaves, a large Charleston house, a plantation, and a summer home in Rock Hill, North Carolina. His estate, worth over $200,000, made him a Southern aristocrat.

His political career started with his serving one term as alderman in Charleston (1834–1836). During that period, he visited New England to study its educational system and on his return instituted a school board (on which he sat for many years) and free public schools for his own city. Subsequently, he served almost continuously as a member of the South Carolina Assembly (1836–1860). In that capacity he played an innovative role in promoting state support of public education, particularly the College of South Carolina.

During the nullification crisis of 1832 and 1833, Memminger had been a moderate Unionist. But he steadily became disillusioned with the Union, and by early 1860, after John Brown's raid on Harpers Ferry, he had become an

CHRISTOPHER G. MEMMINGER. A late-nineteenth-century photograph. NAVAL HISTORICAL CENTER, WASHINGTON, D.C.

advocate of secession on the basis of unified Southern action. In keeping with this plan, the South Carolina legislature sent him to Virginia to solicit the commonwealth's support for a simultaneous withdrawal of all the slave states from the Union. Because the Virginians were too badly divided to make a decision, the mission was a failure. It was significant that this reverse was attributed to Memminger's alleged lack of oratorical skills and his less than ingratiating manner.

In 1860, South Carolina seceded and Memminger was selected to go to Montgomery, Alabama, as part of the state's delegation. Before his departure, he had given some consideration to the legal needs of an independent Southern nation and had published his conclusions in "Plan of a Provisional Government for the Southern Confederacy." On the strength of this, Memminger at Montgomery was elected chairman of the committee to draft a provisional constitution. His work on that project was finished on February 8, 1861.

On February 18, Jefferson Davis arrived in Montgomery and took the oath of office as president. The next day he appointed Memminger as secretary of the treasury. The appointment was a surprise, particularly as Davis and Memminger were not acquainted. Mary Boykin Chesnut, in an addendum to her famous diary, claimed that Davis had planned to make Robert W. Barnwell, of South Carolina, secretary of state and Robert Toombs, of Georgia, secretary of the treasury. Barnwell declined the proffered honor and told Davis that the South Carolina delegation wanted Memminger at the Treasury. Davis shuffled his cabinet accordingly, moving Toombs to the State Department. Only after the appointment was announced was it discovered that the South Carolina delegation was allegedly "mortified." He was not, after all, a leading figure in South Carolina.

The new secretary's professional qualifications for his office were very limited. He was honest, hard-working, and genuinely devoted to the new country. He had been a director of the Farmers Exchange Bank of Charleston for many years and had served as a member or chairman of the South Carolina Assembly's Finance Committee from 1836 to that date. But South Carolina's finances offered an atypical experience for a man about to face record deficits, for the state budget was practically always balanced and the tax assessments on land had been frozen since 1840. Memminger thus had no experience with a modern internal revenue system of the sort that the Confederacy would need if it were to have an effective fiscal program.

Memminger was also a Jacksonian Democrat with a preference for a currency comprised solely of gold and silver coin. In two cases during the 1840s, Memminger had tried to strip some of the South Carolina banks of their charters for not paying gold or silver on their notes during a panic. His opposition to irredeemable bank notes included an emphatic distaste for a legal tender currency put out solely on the central government's credit. Yet Memminger swiftly found himself, contrary to his wishes, compelled to use Treasury notes to cover a considerable part of his expenditures.

Moreover, he had a fundamental fear of a strong central government and passionately believed in laissez-faire. He himself had voted for or moved amendments to the Constitution removing the general welfare clause and inserting a provision against government aid to any group. These restrictions were later to thwart plans for the government acquisition of or control over the cotton crop.

No less serious were his personality deficiencies. As a lawyer, he believed that all actions were either legal or illegal without any ambiguities. Still worse, he would declare a proposed solution to a problem illegal without exploring alternative approaches. When one of his proposals was rejected, he would passively accept defeat and fail to pursue the matter further. If the South were to succeed in its bid for independence, it needed to approach its problems in a pragmatic and innovative manner and with a will to persevere in the face of resistance.

Moreover, though witty and friendly within his family circle, Memminger in public life exhibited an austere personality that soon got him into trouble. He offended many members of Congress by insisting that they make appointments to see him and not just drop by. He told department employees to attend to their duties and not engage in idle conversations. His demands were reasonable enough, but he put them so tactlessly as to create much ill will.

More seriously, Memminger also quarreled with members of the cabinet. He refused to refund to Postmaster General

> **. . . the Treasury met with little approval and much condemnation both during and after the war.**

John H. Regan the gold the post office had deposited in the Treasury until President Davis ordered him to do so. Memminger also upbraided the secretaries of war and the navy for their failure to use bonds to make payments and for their habit of making sudden demands for funds on the Treasury.

Other government officers complained that Memminger was overly preoccupied with legal technicalities, was slow and uncooperative in meeting their needs, and ungraciously acted as if he had been imposed upon whenever they requested his assistance. He also shared the public delusion that the war would not last long and was convinced therefore that no extraordinary measures were needed. His administration of the Treasury met with little approval and much condemnation both during and after the war. In retrospect he was clearly miscast for the role he was called upon to play.

Many of these problems would have been mitigated had Memminger exploited an important asset—his cordial personal relationship with the president. But Memminger apparently hesitated to invoke his chief's aid—to secure orders from Davis to other members of the cabinet requiring that they cooperate with him or support his financial proposals on the floor of Congress.

The secretary had no sooner organized his department with the help of former Washington officials than hostilities commenced on April 12, 1861. When Congress reconvened in May, Memminger laid before it a war finance plan based on suggestions made by John C. Calhoun in 1816. This program called for financing the war through the issue of Treasury notes, whose value would be sustained by making them fundable into bonds paying interest in coin. As a means of checking any redundancy of the currency thus emitted, not only would the circulation be limited by funding, but direct internal taxes were to be levied sufficient to pay the interest and the maturing principal.

The success of this plan required certain administrative actions. Among the most important was procuring the necessary Treasury notes and bonds from the printers. Memminger knew that the number of local printers was inadequate for the country's needs. Nonetheless, he opposed the creation of a Southern equivalent of the Bureau of Engraving and Printing on the doctrinaire ground that such a body would encourage the use of Treasury notes after the war, a policy he adamantly opposed. He also felt that the rights of the printers as independent contractors took precedence over the Treasury's needs. Under these circumstances, the printers were practically encouraged to do slipshod work and to be late in making deliveries. This left the entire government, particularly the army, without funds for paying the soldiers or furnishing them with essential supplies. This in turn directly promoted desertion.

Besides needing an ample supply of currency to pay the government's bills, the secretary needed a stock of coin with which to pay the interest on the public debt. Memminger failed to accumulate a reserve and refused to borrow for public use the idle coin in the banks' vaults. As a result, not only did coin payments on the debt go into default after July 1862, but bond prices in terms of gold fell, making the funding of notes financially unattractive. Thus one of the key means of sustaining the value of the Treasury notes was improvidently lost. Bond sales also depended upon opening offices to make bond purchases easy for the public. Yet prior to 1863, wanting to avoid unnecessary expense, Memminger failed to use the legal authority given to him to establish more offices. As a result, note funding and bond sales were significantly diminished.

To ensure the circulation of the Treasury notes, Memminger called together a bankers' convention in Richmond on July 24, 1861. At his suggestion, the banks agreed to receive and pay out such notes, thus making them the currency of the country. Thanks to this wise measure, the secretary secured credit for his issues without having to resort to a legal tender law as was the case in the North. This gain was unfortunately offset by the secretary's refusal to follow the advice of some bankers and others to curtail by coercion or voluntary means the issuance of rival currencies. Here again, Memminger refused to pursue the matter because it would impinge on the banks' state-granted privilege of issuing their own notes.

Another important matter was procuring from Congress adequate internal revenues. Memminger knew that the blockade would diminish customs receipts and that the cotton export duty would provide little revenue. Taxes on real estate, personal property (including slaves), incomes, and sales were clearly required.

In May 1861, Memminger asked for a direct tax, but since the president sent no message backing him, Congress put off consideration of this unpopular step until July. Then, again without support from the president or the cabinet, Memminger tried to secure the passage of a modest $25 million tax bill. Congress, after bitter debate and opposition from the large slaveholders, reluctantly complied.

Despite ample warnings from the bankers that the war tax of August 19, 1861, needed to be doubled or quadrupled in order to provide even minimal revenues, Memminger did not request any new levies in 1861. Nor did he assert himself during all of 1862. Instead, he made only weak tax proposals in very general terms. Still worse, he wasted precious time on an abortive forced-loan plan (in essence a 20 percent income tax in return for which the taxpayer would be given 6 percent bonds) and a scheme calling for a state guarantee of the Confederate debt. He did not force the tax issue until January 1863, when he belatedly procured a supporting message from President Davis. Even then, his proposals were of questionable legality and were not accompanied by draft legislation.

In consequence, the tax law of April 24, 1863, enacted two years after the war began, was seriously deficient. It did not tax slaves, despite the secretary's observation that the war was being fought to protect their $3.5 billion investment in slavery. The law also taxed other items far too lightly and ordered few collections before January 1864. As a result the currency grew to nearly $900 million and the country was overwhelmed by a disastrous inflation.

Several other economic matters also required Memminger's attention. The blockade had rendered the export of the South's cotton crop difficult, and the public was

> . . . after three years in office, Memminger found himself a discredited man.

clamoring for a scheme that would harness Southern staples to the war effort.

For a while, Memminger temporized, opposing and then supporting proposals that would have the government buy the cotton crop. In October 1861, the secretary finally decided, at the behest of the bankers, to declare such a plan illegal. Had the question been reformulated as a loan by the planters to the government (the Treasury was purchasing with bonds the goods and services needed by the army), then something could have been done. As it was, a cotton purchasing operation was put off until April 1862. This resulted in planter resistance to taxation, added to the costs of acquisition, and seriously delayed shipments abroad on the government's account.

A closely related question was whether, under the King Cotton doctrine, cotton shipments should be withheld with a view to coercing Great Britain and France to recognize the Confederacy. Memminger opposed the vigilante committees that were trying to prevent cotton exports, but did so solely on legal grounds. He made no effort to check their activities and refused to make a public issue of the question. As a result, they seriously inhibited the export of cotton, which Memminger knew to be essential.

A third cotton-related question was whether the government should take an active role in organizing blockade-running operations. At George A. Trenholm's suggestion, the secretary proposed to the cabinet that the Confederacy buy two available shipping lines to promote direct trade with Europe. Thwarted by the opposition of the cabinet and his own inability to convince the president of the necessity of making this purchase, Memminger dropped any further effort to buy or lease ships on the Treasury's account. The abdication of responsibility in this area to the War Department greatly delayed cotton shipments.

Finally, given the shortage of foreign exchange from the sale of produce abroad, the secretary, who had to cover War and Navy department expenditures, realized early on that a foreign loan was urgently needed. He requested and received authority to sell bonds abroad by the act of May 16, 1861. But he failed to pursue the matter, and by 1863, when the so-called Erlanger loan was floated in Europe, the tide of battle had turned against the South. As a result, the Treasury had to borrow money on onerous terms and the funds realized were too little and too late to maintain the government's credit in London or to meet the Confederacy's pressing economic and military needs.

By February 1864, after three years in office, Memminger found himself a discredited man. Congress paid little or no attention to his recommendations. The currency had practically lost its value, the government's credit at home and abroad was badly damaged, and the tax structure was unfair and ineffective.

In May 1864, the House of Representatives passed a resolution of no confidence in the secretary, and Memminger, weary of his thankless task, promptly resigned in July after Congress adjourned. He was succeeded by his good friend and fellow South Carolinian George A. Trenholm.

With Charleston under siege and his home within the range of Union guns, Memminger retired to his summer home at Rock Hill, North Carolina, where he remained for the duration of the war. His home in Charleston was captured and pillaged in February 1865 and the property confiscated and later used as an orphanage for black children.

Unlike many of his fellow Confederate leaders, Memminger was neither arrested nor imprisoned. He procured a pardon in 1867 and resumed his business activities and law practice. He also participated in the bitter debates that followed the war, defending himself against unfair or inaccurate accusations regarding his role in the Confederacy's defeat.

In 1876, he was once again elected to the South Carolina Assembly. As part of the first legislature since the overthrow of the Radical Republicans in Columbia, he played a key role in reorganizing the state's finances. He was instrumental in preventing the government from abolishing the statewide public school system, which had been one of the major accomplishments of Reconstruction in the state. Overcoming bitter resistance, he also established with state support a college for blacks.

Retiring from public life in 1879, Memminger died in Charleston on March 7, 1888.

[*See also* Public Finance; Treasury Department.]

BIBLIOGRAPHY

Ball, Douglas B. *Financial Failure and Confederate Defeat.* Urbana, Ill., 1991.

Capers, Henry Dickson. *The Life and Times of C. G. Memminger.* Richmond, Va., 1893.

Dowdey, Clifford. *Experiment in Rebellion.* Garden City, N.Y., 1946.

Hendrick, Burton J. *Statesmen of the Lost Cause: Jefferson Davis and His Cabinet.* New York, 1939.

Lee, Charles Robert, Jr. *The Confederate Constitutions.* Chapel Hill, N.C., 1963.

Schwab, John Christopher. *The Confederate States of America, 1861–1865: A Financial and Industrial History of the South during the Civil War.* New York, 1901.

Todd, Richard Cecil. *Confederate Finance.* Athens, Ga., 1954.

DOUGLAS B. BALL

MEMORIAL DAY

The celebration of Confederate Memorial Day, an annual ceremony honoring the Confederate dead, began in the spring of 1866. That January women in Columbus, Georgia, issued a public call to decorate Confederate graves, and for this they are sometimes credited with establishing the holiday. Jackson and Vicksburg, Mississippi, along with several other Southern communities, have challenged Columbus, Georgia's, claim. Most likely, several communities acted independently. The idea apparently grew out of the private decoration of soldiers' graves, though Southerners also borrowed from similar customs in other cultures.

During the next fifty years, more and more Southern communities celebrated the holiday, usually under the charge of a ladies' memorial association or, later, the United Daughters of the Confederacy. The date of the observance varied from place to place. In the Deep South most communities celebrated April 26, the anniversary of Joseph E. Johnston's surrender; in South and North Carolina towns more commonly chose May 10, the date of Thomas J. ("Stonewall") Jackson's death and Jefferson Davis's capture; towns in Virginia and other areas celebrated on still different dates. After Davis's death in 1889, some communities and a few states began to observe the holiday on his birthday, June 3.

As with the date, the nature of the celebration took various forms in different communities and changed over time. In the early years, citizens in some towns simply went together to the cemetery and decorated the graves. In others they held more formal programs that included hymns, prayers, and speeches in defense of the soldiers' honor and the nobility of the Southern cause. In either case, the central ritual was the placing of greenery or flowers on the Confederate graves. These ceremonies both honored the fallen soldiers and allowed survivors to mourn, thereby distancing themselves from the cause but still expressing hope for its, and their, eventual vindication. As a sense of vindication developed in the 1880s and 1890s, the tone of the celebration changed. The central ritual remained the decoration of the graves, but

> ... Confederate soldiers had come to serve as symbols not of rebellion but of loyalty to leaders and country.

the occasion became somewhat less funereal and more festive. Bands now participated, often playing "Dixie," and speeches became more common. During the same years, a few cities invited Union veterans to participate with the former Confederates. The new practices reflected changes in the Lost Cause. The passions and issues of the war had begun to dissipate, and Confederate soldiers had come to serve as symbols not of rebellion but of loyalty to leaders and country.

As the veterans died and interest in the Lost Cause faded during the twentieth century, the holiday became less important in Southern culture. By the end of World War II, many communities no longer held celebrations; today only a few do. Eight Southern states still recognize Confederate Memorial Day, although not all of them close state offices on that day. Florida and Georgia observe April 26, South and North Carolina May 10, and Kentucky and Louisiana June 3. Alabama and Mississippi, making concessions to modern practices, celebrate the fourth Monday in May as Confederate Memorial Day.

BIBLIOGRAPHY

Confederated Southern Memorial Association. *History of the Confederated Memorial Associations of the South.* New Orleans, La., 1904.

Foster, Gaines M. *Ghosts of the Confederacy: Defeat, the Lost Cause, and the Emergence of the New South, 1865–1913.* New York, 1987.

Wilson, Charles Reagan. *Baptized in Blood: The Religion of the Lost Cause, 1865–1920.* Athens, Ga., 1980.

GAINES M. FOSTER

MEMORIAL ORGANIZATIONS

Efforts to honor the Confederate dead began shortly after the war ended. Although several groups claimed to be first, probably the earliest memorial organization was founded in Columbus, Georgia, in March 1866 by a group of women determined to decorate the graves of soldiers; in July of the same year, the women of the Soldiers' Aid Society of Wilmington, North Carolina, formed the Ladies' Memorial Association of Wilmington for the same purpose. Similar local groups developed in all parts of the South, with goals limited to decorating graves with flowers, often on a day set aside for the purpose. These efforts eventually became Confederate Memorial Day, an annual event whose date varies from state to state.

More widespread memorial organizations were founded in the later 1860s and the 1870s. Some of the organizations were military in nature, such as the Association of the Army of Northern Virginia and the Association of the Army of Tennessee. A variety of local and state organizations were formed, especially in Richmond and other cities. These groups held annual reunions, arranged for burial of soldiers, and provided benevolence for needy veterans and families. They celebrated Confederate Memorial Day throughout the South; memorials were also held on the death of Jefferson Davis and other Confederate leaders. They were joined by the Southern Historical Society (1869) and the Lee Memorial Association (1870), whose goals included preserving the Southern past and glorifying its heroes.

The Confederate Veterans, an umbrella organization of local groups, was founded in 1889 in New Orleans and quickly became a prominent Southern organization. Its first commander in chief was Gen. John B. Gordon, who retained his post until 1904. This group, which restricted membership to veterans, sought both to memorialize the war and to provide needed services to its increasingly elderly membership. Several other umbrella organizations were also formed, including the Sons of the Confederacy (1896), which allowed male descendants of veterans to join, and the United Daughters of the Confederacy (1895), which included any female relative of men who had served. The United Daughters of the Confederacy created the Children of the Confederacy (1896), a group committed to keeping the memory of the Confederacy alive among young people. The offi-

cial organ for these groups and others was the *Confederate Veteran,* a periodical started in Nashville in 1893 by Sumner A. Cunningham, who remained its editor for twenty-one years.

The United Confederate Veterans was a large-scale organization: its peak membership was 80,000, about one-third of the surviving veterans in 1903. Organized along military lines, it sponsored local meetings of individual camps and annual national reunions. The organization devoted its attention to organizing public ceremonies such as dedications of monuments and Memorial Day celebrations, relief efforts for veterans and their families, drives to persuade Southern state governments to provide pensions and establish soldiers' homes, and burial societies to bury the dead from battlefields, locate and mark graves, care for cemeteries, and pay for funerals. It also boasted a Historical Committee (1892) to oversee the writing of Confederate history, aid state historical associations, and help support Confederate museums. The United Confederate Veterans met jointly with the Grand Army of the Republic in 1913 at Gettysburg, where they reenacted Pickett's charge. The group's last reunion was held in Selma, Alabama, in 1950, with one veteran in attendance.

The United Daughters of the Confederacy (UDC) shared many of the concerns of the United Confederate Veterans and added new activities of their own. Because lineal descendants of Confederate women and nieces of soldiers were included, the organization continues to the present day. In addition to raising money for monuments, caring for graves, engaging in relief work, and sponsoring local, state, and national meetings, the UDC has worked to ensure that Confederate history is taught according to its convictions. To this end it has sponsored scholarships, raised funds for libraries at home and abroad, opened "relic rooms" throughout the South to preserve Confederate artifacts, and led in the development of the Confederate Museum in the old White House of the Confederacy in Richmond. The UDC also offered the Cross of Honor beginning in 1900; this was a medal bestowed for their endurance on men who had served in the Confederate army or navy. Later, they offered the Cross of Military Service to lineal descendants of Confederate veterans who served in other U.S. wars.

The UDC had a notable ability to raise funds for monuments. Many towns owed their courthouse statue of local Confederate leaders to the UDC, which also developed many national projects, alone or in conjunction with other groups. One monument was a memorial to "the faithful slave," a massive boulder placed at Harpers Ferry in 1931 to commemorate former slave Heyward Shepherd, who refused to join John Brown's raid. Another, sponsored jointly with the United Confederate Veterans, was a memorial to the women of the Confederacy. The two groups disagreed about whether women's martial or nurturing aspects should be celebrated in the design, but the conflict was ultimately decided in favor of the men's design for a nurturing figure. The monument was dedicated in 1906. Monuments were also erected in honor of Varina ("Winnie") Davis, the original daughter of the Confederacy; Thomas J. ("Stonewall") Jackson; Robert E. Lee; Jefferson Davis; Henry Wirz, the Andersonville commandant who was executed as a war criminal; other military leaders; and various battlefields.

[*See also Confederate Veteran*; Lee Memorial Association; Memorial Day; Monuments and Memorials; Soldiers' Homes; Southern Historical Association.]

BIBLIOGRAPHY

Foster, Gaines M. *Ghosts of the Confederacy: Defeat, the Lost Cause, and the Emergence of the New South, 1865 to 1913.* New York, 1987.

Poppenheim, Mary B., et al., eds. *The History of the United Daughters of the Confederacy.* 2 vols. N.p., n.d.

White, William W. *The Confederate Veteran.* Tuscaloosa, Ala., 1962.

Wilson, Charles Reagan. *Baptized in Blood: The Religion of the Lost Cause, 1865–1920.* Athens, Ga., 1980.

MARLI F. WEINER

MEMPHIS, TENNESSEE

An important Mississippi River port, Memphis was the fastest growing and second largest city in the state in 1861. It was the sixth largest city in the Confederacy with a population of 22,263 including 3,684 slaves, 198 free blacks, and 18,381 whites. About 60 percent of the free population was American-born; the immigrant population was largely German and Irish.

The economy of the city was based primarily on the wholesale distribution of merchandise within a radius of 150 miles and the cotton market; the city was the trade center for the region's cotton planters. The delivery of merchandise into Memphis and the shipment of cotton out to textile mills, mainly in the Midwest and Northeast, made the city one of the busiest river ports in the United States. Four railroads provided overland transportation.

In addition to retail and wholesale merchants, Memphis advertised twelve wagon builders, six carriage makers, nine slave dealers, five book and job printers, four iron railing manufacturers, three flour mills, two brass and iron foundries, a railcar builder, a sugar refinery, and a brewery. The cotton trade involved approximately 125 firms that provided the services of buyers, brokers, and factors, and the facilities of gins, warehouses, oil processors, and mills.

The people of Memphis hesitated at first to join the secession movement, but when the polls opened on June

8, 1861, for a second state ballot on the question, only five Memphians cast their votes to remain in the Union. At a mass meeting a few days before, three thousand people had voted to declare the city independent of the United States and specified that if Tennessee did not follow suit, Memphis should withdraw from the state and become part of Mississippi. The young men of the city demonstrated an especially strong commitment to the South, organizing seventy-two volunteer companies for the Confederate army.

Its Mississippi River location made Memphis a target of strategic importance. The Federal high command early determined to split the South and supply its own armies in the West by controlling the river from St. Louis to the Gulf of Mexico.

In the late winter of 1862, the Union army broadened its campaign in the West by seizing control of the Cumberland and Tennessee rivers and occupying Nashville, the state capital. Just before the fall of Nashville, Memphis had welcomed Governor Isham G. Harris and a number of state officials seeking a safe haven for the seat of government. Harris convened the legislature in the city on February 20, but, in the absence of a quorum on succeeding days, he adjourned the body March 20 and departed to join Tennessee troops in the field.

Moving down the Mississippi, Union forces captured Confederate river defenses in a brisk battle at New Madrid, Missouri, on March 13. Within a month they surged farther downstream to assault and take possession of Island Number 10.

After the Union victory at the Battle of Shiloh (April 6–7), the Confederate command in the West withdrew most of its forces into northern Mississippi, leaving Memphis protected by garrisons at Forts Randolph and Pillow. When these troops were ordered to Mississippi on June 1, the city's defense was left to eight Confederate gunboats. But the gunboat defense was unsuccessful. On June 6 a Federal fleet of six gunboats and four rams challenged the defenders, and in just over an hour it controlled the river at Memphis. Only one Confederate gunboat escaped downriver; the others were sunk, burned, or run aground.

The U.S. flag was raised in Memphis the same day, and Union troops instituted military rule that lasted past the end of the war. By nightfall approximately one thousand Memphis residents, alarmed by the capture of their city, had fled southward by rail. Using impressed slave labor, the Union army hastened to erect Fort Pickering, an impressive installation that could accommodate ten thousand soldiers. Never attacked, Pickering was important primarily as a symbol of Union control.

Command of the city was held in succession by at least ten Union army officers. Generals Ulysses S. Grant, William Tecumseh Sherman, Stephen A. Hurlbut, and Cadwallader

C. Washburn had the most active tenures. The administration of Military Governor Andrew Johnson at Nashville had little effect on Memphis until near the end of the war, when the governor called for statewide elections.

A flotilla of trading boats had followed the invading army into the port, bringing both new merchandise and new merchants to the city. From the first, the Federals encouraged the resumption and extension of commercial activities by businessmen old and new. With increasing success, they induced planters to bring their cotton to market in the face of Confederate insistence that it be withheld. By 1863 commerce was exceeding prewar levels.

The high levels of economic activity were due in important part to smuggling or underground trade with the Confederates, well represented in the nearby rural countryside by partisans and guerrillas. Union troops were never able to clear West Tennessee of the irregular Southern units who funneled smuggled supplies to regular army forces. The importance to the South of a Union-controlled Memphis was recognized by the various Federal commanders. They surely agreed with their colleague General Washburn when he declared in 1864, "Memphis has been of more value to the Southern Confederacy since it fell into Federal hands than Nassau." In response, Washburn clamped down on trade so stringently that commerce in Memphis came to a virtual standstill during the last few months of the war.

Although most white residents of the city were strongly sympathetic with the Confederacy, very few seemed to expect that they would be liberated by the Southern army. Hopes were raised for a few hours on August 21, 1864, when Gen. Nathan Bedford Forrest led a detachment of cavalrymen into the heart of the city to divert Federal attention from Confederate troop movements in northern Mississippi. Forrest took a number of prisoners and withdrew before the surprised enemy could offer significant resistance. The quick raid was the last combat action of the war at Memphis.

Using bluffs, threats, and intimidation, the military commanders of the city tried unendingly to return the loyalty of the populace to the Union. Recalcitrant Confederate sympathizers were sometimes jailed and often threatened with banishment. Loyalty oaths, required of merchants and other holders of privilege licenses, were promoted for the entire citizenry. Although by January 1863 it was estimated that at least 15,000 citizens had taken the oath, skeptical generals tried other measures of loyalty. General Hurlbut ordered all civilians not employed by government to register either as loyal to the United States, enemy of the United States, or subject of a foreign power. In less than thirty days, 11,652 had registered as loyal, 661 as subjects of foreign powers, and 10 as enemies. General Sherman demonstrated the consequences of disloyalty when he burned the nearby town of Randolph in retaliation for its harboring Southern guerrillas who fired at Union gunboats.

Despite flight to the south by some of its citizens and the absence of a large number in the Confederate military service, the population of Memphis grew and generally prospered from 1862 to 1865. By 1866, the city held approximately 35,000 people: 21,000 whites and 14,000 blacks.

The commanding generals interfered very little in the operation of local government. They insisted that the city government fulfill its responsibilities, especially in the areas of police and fire protection, street maintenance, schools, and the administration of recorders' or police courts. An exception to this general practice of restraint was an act by General Washburn in 1864. Doubting the loyalty of a popularly elected mayor, Washburn set aside the results of the city election,

> **"Memphis has been of more value to the Southern Confederacy since it fell into Federal hands than Nassau."**

declared martial law, and appointed to office all of those just elected with the exception of the mayor. A popular election a year later returned the ousted mayor to office.

Believing it to be in their best interests for life in the city to go on as normally as possible, Federal commanders usually gave free rein to educational, cultural, religious, fraternal, and social practices. One result was that public schools operated without interruption; another was that the school board incorporated schools for blacks into the city system in 1864. There were limits to freedom such as the prohibition of "treasonous" or pro-Confederate statements at all public functions, including worship, and the banning of all pro-Southern newspapers. The publisher of the *Daily Appeal* fled southward with his presses and continued to publish from points in Mississippi and Alabama. The *Appeal* was returned to Memphis after Appomattox.

The greatest change the war brought to Memphis was the unprecedented influx of blacks who first came as refugee slaves and remained to become free. Because they were runaways from neighboring plantations, the blacks had no jobs and no means of support. Some were impressed to work on military fortifications, but most eventually were placed in refugee camps just outside the city. From the camps they were employed to plant and harvest agricultural produce needed by the Union army. In November 1864, the army attempted to recruit five companies of black soldiers but at first raised only two. Other blacks volunteered soon afterward, probably attracted by a generous cash enlistment bonus put up by local whites.

Spared significant war damage, Memphis emerged from the conflict with its infrastructure largely intact and its commerce thriving. The greatest concern of the city in 1865 was the uncertainty of future relationships between the newly freed blacks and the white majority.

BIBLIOGRAPHY

Capers, Gerald M., Jr. *The Biography of a River Town; Memphis: Its Heroic Age*. Chapel Hill, N.C., 1939.

Harkins, John E. *Metropolis of the American Nile*. Edited by Charles W. Crawford. Cambridge, Md., 1982.

Hooper, Ernest Walter. "Memphis: Federal Occupation and Reconstruction, 1862–1870." Ph.D. diss., University of North Carolina, Chapel Hill, 1957.

Keating, John M. *History of the City of Memphis and Shelby County, Tennessee, with Illustrations and Biographical Sketches of Some of Its Prominent Citizens*. 2 vols. in 1. Syracuse, N.Y., 1888.

Parks, Joseph H. "A Confederate Trade Center under Federal Occupation: Memphis, 1862 to 1865." *Journal of Southern History* 7 (August 1941): 289–314.

Parks, Joseph H. "Memphis under Military Rule, 1862 to 1865." *East Tennessee Historical Society Publications*, no. 14 (1942): 31–58.

Young, John Preston, ed. *Standard History of Memphis, Tennessee, from a Study of the Original Sources*. Knoxville, Tenn., 1912.

WALTER T. DURHAM

MERIDIAN CAMPAIGN

In the winter of 1863–1864, Gen. William Tecumseh Sherman decided to remove all Confederate threats to the Mississippi River. The river at Vicksburg was now under Union control, but east of Vicksburg the countryside was not secured. Of special interest was Meridian, a town in east-central Mississippi. Because two railroads—the Mobile and Ohio and the Southern—crossed there, the town was critical to Confederate communications and supply. After a visit to his home in Ohio, Sherman traveled down the Mississippi, now full of ice, to Memphis. There he gathered troops for a march to Meridian to break up the two railroads and, he hoped, "to punish the rebel General Forrest." Nathan Bedford Forrest posed a threat to the crucial Union supply routes in Tennessee.

Sherman planned to gather about 10,000 men from Gen. Stephen A. Hurlbut's forces in Memphis, journey downriver on steamers, and collect an equal number of men from Gen. James B. McPherson in Vicksburg. He would also send a force from Vicksburg up the Yazoo River to confuse the Confederates about his main goal—Meridian. Several infantry companies, under the command of Col. James H. Coates, were to leave Vicksburg on five transports, protected by five gunboats, and move toward Yazoo City. They would destroy means of crossing the river, take as much cotton as possible, and encourage the planters to cooperate with the Union in return for free access to the port of Vicksburg. In addition, Gen. William Sooy Smith was to move overland

through northeast Mississippi from Memphis to Meridian with a cavalry force of 7,000. Sherman warned Smith about General Forrest and his "peculiar force."

Disembarking at Vicksburg, Sherman's forces moved on February 3 directly for Meridian. Responsible for protecting the area was Confederate Gen. Leonidas Polk, who was headquartered at Meridian. He had only 9,000 men plus Gen. Stephen D. Lee's cavalry corps of 7,500 men. Sherman had confused the Southerners by feinting an attack at Mobile, and they had located some of their resources there. General Forrest, coming from Tennessee with about 3,000 men, was in the northeastern part of the state.

As Sherman was leaving Vicksburg, Colonel Coates was receiving Confederate artillery fire on his Yazoo expedition. He disembarked to engage Gen. Lawrence Sullivan Ross's Texas Brigade. The Texans, some protected by a log fortification and some fighting on foot at twelve paces with pistols, forced the Union soldiers to fall back and move away down the river.

On February 4, Sherman's forces met General Lee's cavalry and skirmished with Gen. Wirt Adams's brigade near Jackson. The skirmishing continued almost nonstop—one skirmish on February 5 continued for eighteen miles—but the superior Union forces could not be checked.

Sherman's troops, on the morning of February 6, occupied Jackson, Mississippi's capital, about ninety miles from Meridian. Two Confederate divisions arrived too late to defend the city. As the Union troops left Jackson on the seventh, the Confederates attacked but, because of the closed ranks of the Union army, could neither inflict significant damage nor slow its progress.

Coates had occupied Yazoo City but left to go upriver to Greenwood, collecting cotton along the way. He returned downriver, and about six miles from Yazoo City went ashore. Here his forces again met General Ross's cavalry, which launched a heavy attack; one part of Coates's force was surrounded for four hours but refused three times to surrender. Eventually, after the Union soldiers were able to unite in a well-defended position, the Confederates left Yazoo City. The next day their opponents also evacuated.

Meanwhile, against lessening resistance, Sherman moved to Decatur, a hamlet about twenty miles west of Meridian, and bivouacked for the night. During the late hours, Wirt Adams's cavalry attacked, and Sherman, who had been left unguarded because of a mix-up, came close to being captured before the Southerners retreated.

By February 14, Sherman and his men had reached Meridian, having traveled 150 miles in eleven days. In Meridian they began a systematic campaign of destruction. For five days they laid waste to arms and supplies with "axes, crowbars, sledges, clawbars, and with fire." According to Sherman, "Meridian, with its depots, store-houses, arsenal, hospitals, offices, hotels, and cantonments no longer exists."

His troops set to work tearing up the railroads that ran both north-south and east-west for about twelve miles each way. They also ravaged the surrounding area, destroying roads, bridges, culverts, and sawmills. With this mission fulfilled, their other goal, to destroy Forrest, remained; but in Sherman's words, "In this we failed utterly."

Gen. William Sooy Smith had been ordered to start from Memphis on February 1 to seek out Forrest, but he delayed leaving for ten days. On his way, his 7,000 men encountered Forrest's troops near West Point. On February 21 the two sides skirmished for an hour and a half. As the Union forces withdrew, moving north, Forrest and his cavalry followed. After Forrest decided that Smith and his forces "had begun a rapid and systematic retreat," he gathered reinforcements and charged their rear. The retreating men stopped their northern flight twice to resist the pursuit, but without success. In all, Forrest pursued Smith for about eighty miles. Smith's casualties (killed, wounded, and captured) were 388; Forrest's, 144. Had Forrest waited a few days before attacking, he might have been even more successful. At the time, General Lee was moving to join him but did not get to the area until February 23. Lee was disappointed at the mix-up; even with combined forces the Confederates would still have been outnumbered by Smith's command.

> **"Meridian, with its depots, store-houses, arsenal, hospitals, offices, hotels, and cantonments no longer exists."**

By February 20, Sherman had grown weary of waiting for Smith and had received no word of his misfortunes, so he and his troops started slowly back to Vicksburg. In fact, Sherman did not learn what had happened to Smith for about a week, and he never forgave Smith for his failure.

Sherman arrived back in Vicksburg at the end of February. The Meridian expedition had given him experience in the kind of warfare he would practice so successfully on his march through Georgia. His troops had proved capable of traveling great distances—in one short month they had marched from 360 to 450 miles—and they had been able to live off the land. Sherman also practiced the destructiveness for which he became renowned. The Union casualties were fairly low: of the total of 912, only 5 officers and 108 enlisted men were killed, 385 were wounded, and 414 were captured or missing. Total Confederate casualties are unknown.

BIBLIOGRAPHY

Henry, Robert S. *"First with the Most" Forrest.* Indianapolis, 1944. Reprint, Jackson, Tenn., 1969.

Lee, Stephen D. "The War in Mississippi after the Fall of Vicksburg, July 4, 1863." *Publications of the Mississippi Historical Society* 10 (1909): 47–52.

U.S. War Department. *War of the Rebellion: A Compilation of the Official Records of the Union and Confederate Armies.* Washington, D.C., 1880–1901. Ser. 1, vol. 32, pt. 1, pp. 164–391.

RAY SKATES

METHODIST CHURCH

The Methodist Episcopal Church, South (MECS), which had been organized in 1844 after American Methodists split on the issue of slavery, was a bulwark of Confederate nationalism. During the war Methodists endorsed and participated in the fast days and the Confederate government's invocations of scripture to support the cause, helping to make religion the foundation of Confederate nationalism and evangelical language the metaphorical means of expressing hopes for victory and alleviating the horrors of war. In sermons and denominational publications, Methodists cast the Confederacy as the redeemer nation, the New Israel, and called on church members to sacrifice for the noble cause. Led by Methodist Bishop George Foster Pierce of Georgia, clergy emphasized moral discipline and civic duty and railed against the democratic "anarchy" of Northern society.

Methodists administered to soldiers directly by means of chaplains, semimonthly organs such as the *Soldier's Paper* (published in Richmond) for troops in Virginia and the Carolinas, and the *Army and Naval Herald* (Macon, Georgia) for those in the western theater, and numerous short, pocket-size religious tracts. The most important wartime religious events were the revivals in the ranks, beginning in 1863 and recurring in spasms thereafter. Perhaps as many as 150,000 soldiers were "born again" during the war, many of them Methodists won over by the hard preaching of Methodist chaplains or by the appeals found in Methodist devotionals and published sermons. Methodist churchmen also tried to reform soldiers' behavior. Officers otherwise indifferent to religious concerns supported moral reform efforts as a way to improve discipline. Methodists such as the Reverend R. N. Sledd, in an 1861 sermon in Petersburg, Virginia, linked personal moral victory with Southern independence. Methodists joined other Protestant denominations in stocking camp libraries with religious tracts and newspapers and running Bible classes that taught both scripture and the need to give up strong drink, cursing, and gambling.

The revivals and moral reforms among soldiers were not equaled at home, creating another gulf between soldier and citizen and, for a time, elevating the male convert-soldier to a higher spiritual and moral plane than men and women at home. The former had faced death, the latter only hardship.

Such differences affected the psychological and social adjustments Southerners had to make both in and out of the church after the war.

Methodist activity and authority declined as the war disrupted the normal ecclesiastical business of the MECS. The General Conference, scheduled to meet in New Orleans in 1862, was canceled after Union troops occupied the city. Several bishops convened in Atlanta, but no important denominational business was transacted. State conferences met irregularly. Still, the MECS managed to publish its denominational papers and tracts, which became the principal means of maintaining church identity and authority.

The war affected local churches in many ways, most profoundly in the loss of ordained church leadership and the interruption of organized religious life. Preachers rushed to the colors in 1861, some enlisting as privates. Most Methodist clergy who joined the Confederate army went in either as elected officers of military units or as chaplains of regiments. Two hundred Methodists served as chaplains, more than any other single denomination. Still others, however, were drafted. The absence of ministers was disruptive enough, but the loss of stewards, class leaders, and other church officials disrupted church management in numerous congregations. Sabbath schools were suspended, and in areas close to battles, church buildings were sometimes converted to hospitals. In towns it was still possible to find Sabbath services, but in the rural areas already dependent on itinerant ministers Methodist contact ebbed. Plantation missions especially suffered. Amid such confusion, people left the church. Others found an ecumenical fellowship among other Protestants equally isolated or disrupted in their normal church practices. Such wartime unions helped build the broad Southern evangelical Protestant canopy under which common white folks gathered after the war, irrespective of denominational rivalries among ministers.

Whatever the internal confusion, Southern Methodists were galvanized in their Southern identities during the war. The war divided further the Northern and Southern Methodist churches. Northern Methodists supported the war with a fervor unmatched by any other denomination, invoking the church militant to justify a crusade to crush secession, end slavery, and remake Methodism. From the Southern perspective, it was bad enough that Union troops occupied local Methodist churches as quarters, but worse was Secretary of War Edwin M. Stanton's November 1863 directive giving Northern Methodist bishops authority over all MECS houses of worship in which "a loyal minister . . . appointed by a loyal bishop of said church does not officiate." Especially in the Gulf states, Northern clergymen pursued an aggressive takeover policy to keep Confederates from using pulpits to promulgate "treason" and to curb any "lapse into semi-barbarism" by Southerners. Embittered Southern Methodists recalled such indignities whenever talk of Methodist reunion later cropped up; indeed, the memories of wartime sufferings at the hands of Union troops and ministers became a rallying cry for continued Southern Methodist independence after the war and served also to invigorate the Lost Cause movement. Like the Old Testament Jews who had lost the temple to invaders, Southern Methodists joined other Southern Protestants in viewing themselves as a chosen people who must reclaim their holy city from infidels.

Black Methodists responded differently to wartime stresses. The absence of white ministers led to greater assertions of religious leadership among blacks in biracial churches. The collapse of slavery in the face of Union advances disordered the social relations between white and black Methodists. At the same time, Northern missionaries and teachers challenged traditional local white authority. The Northern Methodists' special effort to recruit blacks angered white Southern Methodists. So, too, did the efforts of the African Methodist Episcopal church (AME church) to educate Southern black Methodists and recruit them as members.

Black membership in the MECS fell from 207,000 in 1860 to 78,000 in 1866. Blacks left the MECS in part because of Northern recruitment efforts (which largely occurred in towns and cities) but mainly because Southern blacks had taken religious matters into their own hands. Local religious leaders led the way out of the MECS. Although black and white Southern Methodists shared a common theology and polity, blacks had chafed at their social status in and out of the church. Most black Methodists joined the AME church, which set up conferences as early as 1865 in South Carolina and then colleges and a seminary to train ministers; others formed the Colored Methodist Episcopal church in 1870 following an amicable withdrawal from the MECS; and others gravitated toward the AME Zion church. The exodus of black Methodists left the MECS almost wholly a white denomination by the 1870s and made possible the segregation of Southern churches that preceded Jim Crow law in the South. At first, the MECS bemoaned the loss, but by the 1880s it had accepted, even welcomed, the segregation.

After the war many white Southern Methodist ministers endorsed the Lost Cause movement. Former army chaplains relived the war in their sermons, recalling the religious community forged in battle and wartime revivals. The celebration of the war restored masculine authority within the church and society, and the demand for moral uprightness and integrity that accompanied ministerial claims of being God's chosen people led to an emphasis on religious, social, and political orthodoxy and attempts to enforce strict moral codes of behavior.

Methodist bishop D. S. Doggett gave the invocation at the dedication of the Stonewall Jackson statue in Richmond in 1875, the event usually regarded as the symbolic beginning of the Lost Cause movement. Extremely influential evangelist Sam Jones, a Georgia Methodist, regularly preached at veterans' reunions; Methodist bishop Atticus Haygood became a prominent booster; and Methodist publications such as the *Christian Advocate* often ran poems and paeans to the Lost Cause. For ten years from its founding in 1867, the Reverend Albert T. Bledsoe's chauvinistic *Southern Review* was the most important organ in the Lost Cause movement, and after 1890 the Methodist-controlled *Confederate Veteran* assumed that mantle. From such thinking, Methodists like Oscar Fitzgerald warned against foreign immigration and Northern influence corrupting a "new South," whereas others such as John C. Calhoun Newton, in his book *The New South and the Methodist Episcopal Church, South* (1887), feared the New South creed portended "low mammon worship."

By ennobling the memory of the war and the Old South, including slavery, the Southern Methodists played a central role in forging a regional civil religion that fused together church interest and public identity. This became the MECS's principal legacy from the war and spoke volumes on the social and political transformation in Southern Methodism. It had metamorphosed from its inclusive, biracial, antislavery, antiestablishment colonial past into separate white and black Methodist churches and an MECS that, along with the Southern Baptist church, had come to embody the region's social and political establishment.

BIBLIOGRAPHY

Dvorak, Katharine L. *An African-American Exodus: The Segregation of the Southern Churches.* Brooklyn, N.Y., 1991.

Faust, Drew Gilpin. "Christian Soldiers: The Meaning of Revivalism in the Confederate Army." *Journal of Southern History* 53 (1987): 63–90.

Silver, James W. *Confederate Morale and Church Propaganda.* Tuscaloosa, Ala., 1957.

Sweet, William Warren. *The Methodist Episcopal Church and the Civil War.* Cincinnati, 1912.

Wiley, Bell Irvin. *The Life of Johnny Reb: The Common Soldier of the Confederacy.* Indianapolis, 1943.

Wilson, Charles Reagan. *Baptized in Blood: The Religion of the Lost Cause, 1865–1920.* Athens, Ga., 1980.

RANDALL M. MILLER

MEXICO

Confederate dealings with Mexico were influenced not by King Cotton directly but by the geographical relationship. Mexico was beyond the Union blockade. Thus, it could supply the South, particularly the Trans-Mississippi Department, with metals, saltpeter, powder, sulphur, blankets, textiles, and foodstuffs, and in turn, cotton and other Southern commodities could be exported safely. Some Confederate officials on the border noted the potential for commerce with Europe through Mexico, although with less optimism when the Mexican Liberals commanded the frontier than later when the forces of French-inspired Austrian Archduke Maximilian controlled the border. In sum, the question was whether Confederate officials in Richmond would recognize that diplomatic efforts in Mexico involved the benefits to be derived from trade with the world through Mexico and from the moral support of recognition by Mexico.

In May 1861, the Confederate government appointed John T. Pickett its minister to Mexico to stymie the expected U.S. diplomatic offensive. Many of Pickett's actions, including

> The Confederacy adopted a conservative diplomatic style, when a more revolutionary, dynamic approach was required. . . .

those that brought him criticism, were consistent with his instructions. On the one hand, he was told to proceed with convenient speed to the Republic of Mexico. On the other hand, he was allowed to converse freely with local authorities at Veracruz. This state rights view demonstrated the Confederate State Department's failure to understand the Mexican Liberals' desire to establish an effective central government. Although committed to state rights domestically, the Confederacy should have adjusted its policy for export.

Once in contact with the Mexican government, Pickett was to point out that Southerners had always been Mexico's best friends and that both peoples, involved in agriculture and mining, had similar interests in obtaining cheap foreign manufactured goods and relied upon similar labor systems, slavery and peonage. He was to stress that the Confederacy expected strict neutrality in the troubles north of the border; official recognition of the Confederacy was not necessary. His instructions were open to interpretation, and Pickett carried them out in a manner that made clear his contempt for Mexico and Mexicans. His mission was also handicapped by the history of Southern slave expansionism and the filibustering expeditions of the 1850s.

During his months in Mexico, Pickett was volatile, unthinking, imprudent, hasty, a heavy drinker—all qualities that should have disqualified him for office. It was not just his personal characteristics, however, but also his instructions that contributed to the failure of his mission. The message he bore stressed the positive values of slavery, an agricultural economic system, and a decentralized state government system. It served only to persuade the Liberal government that its future was more secure in association with the North if it wished to abolish peonage, centralize government authority, create a national economic structure, attract foreign trade and investment, and end filibustering.

When King Cotton proved a weak weapon to induce European action to ensure Southern independence, a new Confederate policy in 1862 attempted to use Mexico as a pawn to be sacrificed in order to convince Napoleon III to abandon neutrality. The Confederacy was willing to overlook the Monroe Doctrine, to forgo (or at least postpone) expansion into Mexico, and to guarantee Napoleon III's position in that country against the United States in return for French recognition, which Southern leaders believed would trigger a U.S.-French military clash.

In the period from 1862 to 1865, Confederate relations with Mexico were complicated by the unstable situation in that country. A joint French, British, and Spanish intervention in 1862 quickly became a unilateral French project, and the concurrent rumors of Maximilian's pending coronation as Mexican emperor encouraged the Confederate leaders. They assumed that Maximilian's Mexico would be a sympathetic and ideologically reliable neighbor. Recognition would be forthcoming; so might a military alliance, since the South was willing to bargain away the Monroe Doctrine for an alliance. Although President Benito Juàrez's government favored the North, it made no effort to block Confederate trade along the northern frontier and used every opportunity to increase its revenue from that trade.

The Confederacy sent William Preston to Mexico in 1864 on a mission to alleviate its failing fortunes. His instructions recognized the realities of the Confederate position. The touchy question of recognition was set to one side by declaring that the public reception of Preston would be equivalent to de facto recognition. But he was instructed to pursue a military alliance and commercial privileges, especially along the frontier. Maximilian, however, refused to receive Preston.

In attempting to solve their mutual border problems, Confederate and Mexican officials at the border twice came close to perfecting "treaties" (without instructions in both instances) that would have implied mutual recognition. The Hamilton P. Bee–Albino Lòpez (February 1863) and James E. Slaughter–Tomàs Mejàia (December 1864) accords—which regulated border relations and trade—simulated international agreements because they were enforced equally upon citizens of both nations. Still, the Confederacy's chief difficulties in obtaining desirable relations along the border lay not in the Mexican nation but within its own outlook.

The Confederacy adopted a conservative diplomatic style, when a more revolutionary, dynamic approach was required to accomplish the tasks that lay before it. It did not need the preservation of the international status quo. Its claim to existence had created a change. It needed the most favorable revision of international commerce and power that it could effect. If it were to achieve this goal, the Confederacy required trading partners and the moral and material support of recognition. Precisely these two items received low priori-

ty from the Confederate high command until near the end of the war. In Mexico, for example, Pickett and Josè Augustàin Quintero, the Southern agent in northern Mexico, were instructed to maintain friendly relations, to seek Mexico's neutrality, and above all, to make it clear that the Confederacy would not tolerate Mexico's granting special privileges to the United States. Only if other matters went smoothly were they to seek formal trade ties. Despite these priorities, Quintero immediately pushed for close trade ties, but his labor went unrewarded because his superiors lacked interest.

Often dismissing the Confederate diplomatic failure in Mexico in terms of Pickett's personality or the ill timing of the Preston mission, historians overlook the broader aspects. Abler diplomats might have quieted the fears of Mexicans, but the conservative worldview behind the Confederacy's instructions demonstrated the inability of the South to understand its own neighbor. To instruct an agent to the Liberal government to emphasize a mutually shared interest in slavery, agriculture, and state rights was shockingly ignorant in light of the decade-long Mexican civil war during which the Liberals had fought to abolish peonage, establish a centralist government, create the basis for an industrial-commercial economy, and displace an agrarian, aristocratic elite. Furthermore, for the Confederate leadership not to focus upon drawing maximum advantage from the Texas-Mexico border reflected a mentality that was woefully out of place in the industrializing nineteenth century. In sum, the South was badly out of tune with its times, clearly in relation to Mexico and very likely elsewhere as well.

BIBLIOGRAPHY

Daddysman, James W. *The Matamoros Trade: Confederate Commerce, Diplomacy, and Intrigue.* Newark, N.J., 1984.

Fuentes Mares, Josè. *Juàrez y la intervenciòn.* Mèxico, 1962.

McCormack, Richard B. "Los Estados Confederados y Mèxico." *Historia Mexicana* 4 (1966): 337–357.

Owsley, Frank. *King Cotton Diplomacy.* Rev. ed. Chicago, 1959.

Schoonover, Thomas. *Dollars over Dominion: The Triumph of Liberalism in Mexican–United States Relations, 1861–1867.* Baton Rouge, La., 1978.

Tyler, Ronnie C. *Santiago Vidaurre and the Southern Confederacy.* Austin, Tex., 1973.

THOMAS SCHOONOVER

MILITARY JUSTICE

The Confederate Constitution empowered Congress to establish rules for the government of Confederate soldiers. Soon there arose a system of military justice based almost entirely on the Articles of War and the army regulations of the

United States, which had been derived from the system of Great Britain.

Initially, the Confederate War Department's Adjutant and Inspector General's Office was charged with review and custody of documents pertaining to military justice, but in February 1864, a new bureau, the Judge Advocate's Office under Maj. Charles H. Lee (after April under Maj. William S. Barton), assumed responsibility.

The main topics of the Articles of War adopted on March 6, 1861, were military offenses and the courts of inquiry and courts-martial that were the disciplinary procedural bodies available to deal with them. These offenses included common crimes such as insubordination, drunkenness, fighting, absence without leave, and desertion, and less common ones such as mutiny, threats or violence against superiors, cowardice, and misbehavior in action.

Courts of inquiry were fact-finding bodies ordered by President Jefferson Davis, or convened at the request of an accused, to investigate the responsibility of officers for affairs or accusations or imputations against officers or men. These courts, composed of up to three officers, plus a judge advocate to act as recorder, could summon witnesses and administer oaths, but they could not initiate an opinion and could punish only for contempt. Court findings sometimes led to the convening of courts-martial.

> **Robert E. Lee and many other commanders had become convinced that the existing system was not ensuring prompt and certain punishment.**

General courts-martial, composed of five to thirteen officers, all senior in rank to the accused, tried officers and men, as well as sutlers, drivers, and all others paid by the army. Initially, only general officers commanding field armies and colonels commanding departments could convene these courts, but by 1865 generals commanding cavalry forces not directly part of an army command, officers commanding separate departments, and generals commanding reserve forces had this authority.

Special or regimental courts-martial consisted of three officers convened to try noncapital offenses committed by soldiers or persons paid by the army. Convening authorities were officers commanding regiments or corps, or garrisons, forts, barracks, or other places where the troops were from different arms of the service.

Judge advocates prosecuted, summoned witnesses, swore in the members of the court, and were then sworn in by the court president who kept order and conducted court business. Convictions were wrought by simple majority, except death sentences which required a two-thirds majority. Sentences were carried out upon approval of the convening authority who could mitigate or suspend sentence. Only President Davis could approve sentences passed on general officers.

Once the army was on the march an expedient was the drumhead court-martial, which executed its judgments immediately. In addition, for noncapital offenses, commanding officers meted out summary justice without reference to formal judicial process. Sentences were often unfair and capricious, usually involving some form of corporal punishment, extra duty, confinement, or reduction in rank.

By 1862 Robert E. Lee and many other commanders had become convinced that the existing system was not ensuring prompt and certain punishment of offenders. The legal necessity to convene each court-martial, not always an easy or timely task during active operations, meant delays, which often resulted in witnesses being unavailable. More delay resulted from the requirements to forward charges to general headquarters before the accused could be ordered to trial and to return the findings to the convening authority for review before sentences could be executed. These shortcomings led to a sharp increase in offenses as offenders mistook the system's slowness for immunity.

The response, embodied in an act of October 9, 1862, was a new type of tribunal: a permanently open military court for each army corps in the field. These courts had three members (colonels) and a judge advocate (captain) appointed by President Davis, plus a court-appointed provost marshal to execute orders and a clerk to record decisions. By 1864, twelve corps, cavalry divisions, all military departments, northern Alabama, and each state had courts. Judges and courts could be transferred as required, and corps and department commanders could detail field officers as members. Although it was not the intent that military courts eliminate courts-martial, their inherent advantages caused a lessening of courts-martial jurisdiction.

Military courts could try all offenses against the Articles of War and the customs of war, crimes against Confederate or state law, and all cases of murder, manslaughter, arson, rape, robbery, and larceny committed by military personnel and prisoners of war outside the Confederate States, where military courts exercised powers equal to Confederate States district courts. They could summon civilian witnesses, for example, and hold them until they agreed to testify. In the case of treason, ambiguity about the applicability of the Articles of War to civilians caused disputes about the jurisdictions of civil and military courts. Military courts (and courts-martial) were not subject to appellate jurisdiction of civil courts.

One shortcoming that could not be legislated for was the tendency to leniency shown by tribunals. The long-term effect was a tide of straggling and desertion that by 1864 threatened to engulf the army. Nor did leniency help instill the desired respect for and obedience to orders that would have made best use of the experience, tenacity, and courage of the Confederate soldier. As Lee observed, many opportunities were lost and many lives uselessly sacrificed because of indiscipline.

[*See also* Desertion; Provost Marshal.]

BIBLIOGRAPHY

Confederate States War Department. *Regulations for the Army of the Confederate States, 1863*. Richmond, Va., 1863. Reprint, Harrisburg, Pa., 1980.

Robinson, William M. *Justice in Grey: A History of the Judicial System of the Confederate States of America*. New York, 1941.

Wiley, Bell I. *The Life of Johnny Reb*. New York, 1943. Reprint, Baton Rouge, La., 1971.

KENNETH RADLEY

MILITARY TRAINING

The turning of raw recruits into soldiers for the Confederacy virtually mirrored the same activity in the Union, both being based upon the system of the prewar U.S. Army. Drill and weapons training were designed to instill subordination in the soldiers, produce instant and unquestioning obedience to commands, and facilitate the orderly movement of large numbers of men quickly and effectively on the battlefield. Most officers relied on either Winfield Scott's 1835 *Infantry Tactics* or the simpler and more popular *Rifle and Infantry Tactics* written by William J. Hardee (now a Confederate general) and known simply as *Hardee's Tactics*.

Although details varied in these and the other manuals used (in volunteer regiments it was often left up to individual officers to choose whichever manual they preferred), virtually all shared features in common. Men were expected to learn to obey commands as given by bugle or drum, since a voice would not carry far in battle. As many as fifty different such commands had to be learned, not all of them applicable to all soldiers and units.

The basic drill unit was the company, though practice in squad and battalion drill was also required. Regimental drill was as large as most evolutions went, but a few brigades actually practiced full brigade drill early in the war before discovering its impracticability. In his early months in uniform, a Johnny Reb might expect to spend several hours a day practicing his evolutions. This did not include just parade ground maneuvers. Practice in line of march—usually four abreast—was also required. Separate branches like the artillery and cavalry had their own distinctive drill and training regimens.

In the early days, weapons training also occupied much time and practice until handling them became second nature. Silas Casey's 1862 *Infantry Tactics* reduced the loading and firing of the rifled musket to a dozen commands and twenty discrete actions, and Confederate manuals did much the same. Of course, the men quickly learned how to load and fire, but the object of the drill was to have them do so in unison in order to deliver a shattering volley at the command to fire. Even more time was devoted to bayonet practice, with dozens of commands and positions being studied for using the bayonet as virtually a saber at the end of the rifle. Ironically, the bayonet saw almost no practical combat use and inflicted fewer than four wounds out of a thousand.

Attempted almost universally at the outset, all but the most basic and rudimentary training disappeared from most of the Confederate forces after 1863, especially when regiments were reduced by casualties from nearly a thousand to only two hundred or so and with whole companies numbering a mere thirty to forty. Still, though haphazard and ersatz like so much else in the Southern war effort, training in the Confederate forces definitely left its mark in producing one of the most effective groups of fighting men in history.

BIBLIOGRAPHY

Davis, William C. *Fighting Men of the Civil War*. London, 1989.

Robertson, James I., Jr. *Soldiers Blue and Gray*. Columbia, S.C., 1988.

Wiley, Bell I. *The Life of Johnny Reb*. Baton Rouge, La., 1971.

WILLIAM C. DAVIS

MILTON, JOHN

MILTON, JOHN (1807–1865), governor of Florida. Nominated for governor on the twenty-third ballot by a Democratic convention that also declared for secession, John Milton, a Jackson County planter and slave owner, defeated Constitutional Unionist Edward Hopkins in a close election in November 1860. Under Florida law he would not take office until October of the following year. Thus he had the frustrating experience of seeing his predecessor, the lame duck Madison S. Perry, with the support of the General Assembly, make critical decisions regarding the direction the state was to follow while appointing his friends and supporters to key positions, particularly in the military. Milton believed in a state militia to be controlled by the governor, whereas Perry felt the Confederate government should take full responsibility for military affairs.

Further complicating Milton's situation was the continued exercise of constituent power by the extralegal secession convention, which overrode on occasion both the executive and the legislature. The state attorney general refused to support Milton's challenge of the convention's constitutional authority, and for a while Milton had to share power with a four-man executive council. Moreover, the passage of the Confederate Conscription Act of 1862 signaled the end of Milton's state militia and left him with limited power over the meager state resources.

An ardent secessionist, a firm believer in slavery, and a particularly strong supporter of the concept of state rights, Milton nevertheless soon came to realize that it was essential during the wartime emergency that unity and harmony prevail among the central government and the states. Although he protested strongly to President Jefferson Davis over decisions and policies that he felt were invasions of state sovereignty, he nevertheless urged his fellow Floridians to acquiesce for the common good. Chief among these policies were conscription, exemptions, blockade running, and impressment. Believing conscription to be unconstitutional but a matter for a judicial body to decide, Milton supported it strongly and urged his constituents to volunteer rather than wait to be drafted. While other governors dispensed exemptions liberally, Milton felt that all men who could carry arms should be liable for military service and was much more select in allowing exemptions. He also differed with governors who attempted to evade central government regulation of blockade running by having private ships transfer their ownership to individual states. His strongest reservations were over impressment of private property for public use. He did not deny the right of Confederate government to take such property, but he continually disputed with the central government over the methods by which impressment was carried out and sought to regulate it rather than forbid it in Florida.

Governor Milton was one of the most cooperative and staunchest supporters of the Confederacy of any of the Southern governors, several of whom he criticized for placing local priorities over those of the central government. He maintained throughout his administration a continuing cordiality with Jefferson Davis, even naming one of his sons for the president.

The frustrations of his administration coupled with mounting distress over the declining fortunes of the Confederacy caused him to take his own life on April 1, 1865.

BIBLIOGRAPHY

Parker, Daisy. "Governor John Milton." *Tallahassee Historical Society Annual* 3 (1937): 14–21.
Parker, Daisy. "John Milton, Governor of Florida: A Loyal Confederate." *Florida Historical Quarterly* 20 (1942): 346–361.
Tebeau, Charlton W. *A History of Florida.* Coral Gables, Fla., 1971.

WILLIAM H. NULTY

MINE RUN CAMPAIGN

South of the Rapidan River and twenty-five miles east of Fredericksburg, at Mine Run, Virginia, the Army of Northern Virginia met advancing Federal troops in a stalemate that lasted from November 27 to December 2, 1863. During the course of the campaign, 1,653 Federal troops were killed, wounded, or captured, while the Confederates lost 601 soldiers.

As intense cold descended on Virginia near the close of 1863, Robert E. Lee's army prepared for a respite from the year's campaigning. Farther north, Gen. George G. Meade received information that Lee had left the lower fords on the Rapidan, the Orange Road, and the Orange Plank Turnpike exposed. Meade viewed this oversight as a means to deliver a surprise attack on his enemy. Quietly his troops prepared to cross the Rapidan and advance on the Southerners.

Meade lost the element of surprise early on in his mission. Heavy rains and swollen streams forced him to postpone his plans for two days. By the time he mobilized his troops on the twenty-sixth, Lee had already received news of his impending advance.

Unsure of whether Meade planned to head for Richmond or to attack the Confederate right flank, Lee prepared to meet either possibility. He would attack the Union flank as it marched southward or, in the case of a direct assault, he would aggressively defend his rear lines.

Weather conditions and rugged terrain affected both armies. Streams remained dangerously high and further slowed Meade's already tardy movements. Poor visibility in the dense woods caused Confederate commanders to use particular caution.

Anticipating Meade's arrival, Lee sent the Second Corps north to Locust Grove to meet the Army of the Potomac. Jubal Early's division moved first, followed by Robert Rodes's. Lee instructed Edward Johnson's division to take an alternate route to the rendezvous point.

When Early and Rodes arrived at Locust Grove, they found that Federal troops had preceded them. Because of the uncertain terrain, the Southerners decided to delay their attack until Johnson, who was traveling a more circuitous course, joined them.

Before Johnson arrived in Locust Grove, he met with Union bullets. George Hume Steuart's brigade, at the rear of the column, came under particularly brisk fire. At 4:00 P.M., Steuart ordered a counterattack against the Federals. By the end of the day, the Confederates had twice repelled Union advances. During the engagements, both armies had suffered substantial casualties.

During the next four days, the Southern army dug trenches that successfully repulsed Union advances. The armies engaged in occasional fire through the bitter cold and a somber veil of rain. Behind Union lines, Meade issued orders for a massive attack to begin at 8:00 A.M. on the thirtieth. Before dawn, however, G. K. Warren, who was responsible for the assault to the Confederate right, discovered that his enemy had resolutely reinforced and fortified during the night. The Confederate trenches appeared impregnable; sensing a catastrophic disaster, Warren canceled his attack. Upon receiving Warren's dispatch, Meade called off the entire maneuver.

After sitting in trenches for four days, Lee resolved to take the offensive. On December 1, he ordered Richard Heron Anderson's and Cadmus Marcellus Wilcox's division to attack the Union left. The next morning his troopers advanced on the Federal lines only to find that Meade had retreated during the night.

Meade's campaign across the Rapidan had come to nought. Neither side had won any strategic gains. Yet Confederate troops successfully repulsed the Union advance, and Lee had learned a valuable lesson concerning the efficacy of trenches. Following the rebuff at Mine Run, the Army of the Potomac retreated back across the Rapidan and settled in for the winter.

BIBLIOGRAPHY

Freeman, Douglas S. *Lee's Lieutenants: A Study in Command.* 3 vols. New York, 1942–1944. Reprint, New York, 1986.

Graham, Martin F., and George F. Skoch. *Mine Run: A Campaign of Lost Opportunities, October 21, 1863–May 1, 1864.* Lynchburg, Va., 1987.

Thomas, Emory M. *The American War and Peace, 1860–1877.* Englewood Cliffs, N.J., 1973.

U.S. War Department. *War of the Rebellion: A Compilation of the Official Records of the Union and Confederate Armies.* Washington, D.C., 1880–1901. Ser. 1, vol. 29, pp. 823–907.

JENNIFER LUND SMITH

MINING

In the Confederacy, mining was largely conducted in Virginia where large amounts of iron, coal, and limestone fed the many iron furnaces along the Allegheny frontier, the Shenandoah Valley, Wythe County, and Richmond. Coal and iron mined in Alabama supplied the ironworks at Selma, at Dade City in Georgia, and at Sewanee in Tennessee. Coal fueled railways, steamboats, and factories. Gold mined in the Appalachian field in South Carolina, Virginia, North Carolina, Georgia, and Alabama supplied mints at Charlotte, North Carolina, and Dahlonega, Georgia. Copper mined at Copper Hill, Tennessee, was used in electrical wire for telegraph lines.

Mines, operated like plantations with slave miners and white overseers, were usually pits dug around surface outcrops. But some mines were more deeply sloped tunnels, and in the Richmond coalfield at Dover, Midlothian, and Clover Hill, slaves dug vertical shafts as deep as six hundred feet. Material was broken by miners wielding picks and bars or exploding black powder in holes drilled into the mine face with hand augers. Breakings were shoveled into carts and hauled from the mine by mules.

Without these mines, supplies of coal, iron, gold, and copper would have been limited to imports through the blockade and amounts seized at the beginning of the war. Union campaigns through Tennessee, Georgia, and down the Shenandoah Valley left only Richmond as the source of iron and coal. The Tredegar Iron Works at Richmond cast over a thousand cannons, in addition to armor plate, shells, shot, and components for arms, machinery, and railways. The Richmond coalfield supplied over 100,000 tons of coal annually.

[*See also* Niter and Mining Bureau; Railroads; Telegraph; Tredegar Iron Works.]

BIBLIOGRAPHY

Bruce, Kathleen. *Virginia Iron Manufacture in the Slave Era.* New York, 1968.

Eavenson, Howard N. *The First Century and a Quarter of the American Coal Industry.* Pittsburgh, Pa., 1942.

Rickard, T. A. *A History of American Mining.* New York, 1932.

Wilkes, Gerald P. *Mining History of the Richmond Coalfield of Virginia.* Charlottesville, Va., 1988.

WALTER R. HIBBARD, JR.

MISCEGENATION

The etymological roots of *miscegenation* are *miscere* (Latin, "to mix") and *genus* ("race"). Practically speaking, however, miscegenation has occurred in all civilizations whenever two different peoples have encountered each other. Genetic blending is as much a part of history as is cultural exchange, as evidenced by the triracial (Caucasian, Semitic, and Negroid) origins of such African groups as the Mandingo.

In the recorded history of North America, racial mixing occurred first between Europeans and Native Americans and then between both groups and the transplanted Africans. Although sexual relations with both the indigenous population and the enslaved blacks were overtly discouraged by most European officials, such taboos were impossible to enforce. With time, white-Indian mixing was gradually to lose its stigma, leaving white-black relations as the primary target of the cursed term *miscegenation*.

The earliest European-Americans attempted to make ethnic terminology a fairly exact science, but precision proved impossible. The Spanish reportedly developed over a hundred words (reputed numbers vary) denoting different racial mixtures. The French colonials had far fewer such designations, and the English even less. Within the bounds that became the continental United States, the most common terms were *mulatto* (half-black and half-white), *quadroon* (one-quarter black and three-quarters white), *octoroon* (one-eighth black and seven-eighths white), *mestizo* (part-Indian, part-white in Latin-oriented communities), *half-breed* (in British-oriented societies), and *griffe* (part-black, part-Indian, perhaps part-white). The ethnic composition of racially mixed individuals could be cited with presumed certainty in the first two or three generations, but the identification system collapsed with the intermingling of subsequent offspring. Officials often guessed, as demonstrated by records that describe nonwhites as "mulatto in color," or *pardo* (light-skinned mixed race). The inevitable result was the general absorption of Indian mixtures into one of the three dominant cultures and the general categorization of all black-white people as mulatto, regardless of exact composition.

Miscegenation is popularly associated with the American South, that being the area in which slavery survived the longest and in which most blacks resided. The rate of miscegenation was highest in states to the north, however. The percentage of mulattoes amid the enumerated African American population of the free states in 1850 was 28.96 percent; in the South that year, mulattoes constituted only 10.14 percent. In 1860, the corresponding figures were 30.95 percent (North) and 12.30 percent (South).

To some extent, the Northern numbers were inflated by Southern white fathers who sent mixed-race children to the free states after Southern manumission laws were tightened. Economics and demographics, however, appear to have played a stronger role. Both domestic servants and craftsmen were more likely to be of mixed race, and most Northern blacks lived in towns and cities where their skills were the most marketable. By contrast, the South's free mixed residents were as likely to be rural as urban. Their tendency to intermarry within their caste—as a means of maintaining what was considered to be prestige in a prejudicial social system—created a highly visible brown class that has led casual observers to assume more Southern mixing than actually occurred.

The latest studies on miscegenation in the slave regime also belie some other traditional conclusions. The sexual use of female field hands by white planters and overseers was not the common pattern, nor were instances in which several black slaves on a single plantation bore mixed-race children. More at risk was the household servant, and the typical scenario was likely to be a long-term relationship that bore the characteristics of a common-law marriage. The most

detailed study yet available, focusing upon Anglo-Alabama (which excludes the French and Spanish influence of the Gulf coast), has documented a high incidence of bachelorhood or widowerhood among the white fathers of mixed-race children.

Other figures speak to greater family stability among the mixed-race population than has been previously assumed. The fact that 60 percent of antebellum Alabama's free mulattoes had mulatto parents is a seemingly obvious but nonetheless needed reminder that every mulatto was not the result of a new incident of miscegenation. Among the remaining 40 percent, the fact that exactly half had white fathers and exactly half had white mothers clearly exposes another carefully nurtured myth: that black-white mixing was the result of male white licentiousness and that all white females abhorred the thought of interracial alliance. In Alabama, where interracial marriages were not penalized until 1852, unions of white wives and mulatto husbands can be documented in all corners of the state.

> **"Why should I mind if my husband has that child every other year by a nice colored woman?"**

Less quantifiable is the extent to which white wives tolerated, even encouraged, miscegenous concubinages both during and after slavery. Current studies on child spacing and marital relations, as well as the observations of nineteenth-century census takers North and South, point to a spreading effort by white females to limit the size of their families—abstinence being the method of choice before modern manufacturing and medicine offered other options. Among those who could afford it, concubinage was a practical alternative. As expressed by one Southern farm wife of the early twentieth century: "Why should I mind if my husband has that child every other year by a nice colored woman?"

The offspring of such congenial or tacitly tolerated concubinages were likely to be accorded special treatment by both the family and the community. Under the slave regime, they were often freed, educated, or trained in a trade, or given favored positions on the plantation if manumission was not possible. The conspicuous concubinage of Richard Mentor Johnson, vice president under Andrew Jackson, and the more discreet affair attributed by some to Thomas Jefferson are frequently cited examples. Innumerable others exist, such as the lifestyle of the Revolutionary era Indian trade czar and war financier George Galphin, of whom a contemporary (General Thomas S. Woodward, himself part Indian) wrote: "Of the five varieties of the human family, he [Galphin] raised children from three, and no doubt would have gone the whole hog, but the Malay and Mongol were out of his reach." Like Johnson, Galphin provided well for his offspring. His legitimate white daughter wed Georgia's Governor John Milledge. One half-black daughter, Barbara Galphin Holmes, was handsomely endowed at the time of her marriage to Galphin's British-born partner. It is not surprising that contemporary census takers were color-blind—perhaps they saw "green" better than "black"; when they visited the Holmes household, they recorded the widowed Barbara as the white mistress of a number of black slaves. Her quadroon son became a prominent doctor, marrying and living as white in the antebellum South. As with most such families, however, not all lines of descent prospered. By the close of the antebellum era, the free, mixed-race Galphins had proliferated, but most who bore that well-known surname lived in exceedingly modest circumstances.

Less studied by the historical community—and less understood—are the triracial (white, black, and Indian) isolate groups that have peopled both the North and the South. Anthropological scholars have long analyzed their culture. Genealogical literature is now documenting their origins. From the Carmels of Ohio and the Moors of Delaware to the Cubans of Virginia, the Lumbees and Haliwas of North Carolina, the Melungeons and Ramps of Appalachia, the Brass Ankles and Turks of South Carolina, and the Redbones who scattered their clusters from South Carolina to Texas, these groups have certain characteristics in common. Specific families are usually traceable back to a miscegenous incident in the 1600s or 1700s, from which time they were accorded a nebulous but intermediate social status between black and white. Most members of these groups maintained that status by intermarrying with other black-white or Indian-white people.

With time, as black-white miscegenation became more common and the social order felt more threatened, African ancestors were likely to be forgotten by these families, Indian forebears would be only vaguely remembered, and swarthiness became commonly attributable to "Portuguese" descent. In some regions, the revised family trees were accepted by the larger social order; elsewhere they were not. Public recollection of a family's African ancestry was commonly influenced by a subjectively complex consideration of economic status, physical features, and social behavior. Even the lightest descendants of well-known triracial groups—though they voted, served in local militia companies, and married whites—were likely to find that their communities had long memories whenever someone wished to embarrass or discredit them.

Being of mixed racial ancestry was obviously no guarantee of success, although most successful free blacks were mulattoes. Perhaps their better education and training, their close relationship to whites, their distinguishing color, and the financial benefits provided to some by their parents combined to give them an advantage in life. Such cities as Philadelphia, Charleston, and New Orleans developed highly cultured and respected communities of free mulattoes. Rural areas such as Natchitoches Parish, Louisiana, and Horry County, South Carolina, spawned free people of color who earned wealth and status through the slave plantation system. As a generality, however, antebellum families who acknowledged their mixed origins and operated within the socially approved sphere were more apt to be successful than those who denied their past in an effort to live as white.

In post–Civil War America, the "mulatto elite" or "brown aristocracy" lost its niche as a separate caste, falling—politically and legally, if not always socially—to the top level of a subordinate class generically termed *black*. The efforts of these families to maintain themselves as a distinct stratum within the black subculture provided the educated leadership that African America needed to progress—even though many nonmixed blacks resented the perceived superiority of browns and tans. In retrospect, it is not surprising to find that a majority of "black" politicians during and after Reconstruction were of visibly mixed ethnicity. Ultimately, it is ironic that so many of the modern civil rights leaders have been descended from black-white relationships of earlier centuries. The dominant white race in America sowed, itself, the seeds of leadership that would overthrow its own concept of white supremacy.

BIBLIOGRAPHY

DeMarce, Virginia E. "'Verry Slitly Mixt': Tri-racial Isolate Families of the Upper South—A Genealogical Study." *National Genealogical Society Quarterly* 80 (1992): 5–35.

Fogel, Robert William, and Stanley L. Engerman. *Time on the Cross: The Economics of American Negro Slavery.* New York, 1974.

Johnson, Michael P., and James L. Roark. *Black Masters: A Free Family of Color in the Old South.* New York, 1984.

Mills, Gary B. *The Forgotten People: Cane River's Creoles of Color.* Baton Rouge, La., 1977.

Mills, Gary B. "Miscegenation and the Free Negro in Antebellum 'Anglo' Alabama: A Reexamination of Southern Race Relations." *Journal of American History* 68 (June 1981): 16–34.

Williamson, Joel. *New People: Miscegenation and Mulattoes in the United States.* New York, 1980.

Woodward, Thomas S. *Woodward's Reminiscences of the Creek, or Muscogee Indians.* Montgomery, Ala., 1859.

GARY B. MILLS

MISSISSIPPI

Some Mississippians who witnessed the state's secession in 1861 had also witnessed the admission of Mississippi to the Union in 1817. Yet most citizens in 1861 were immigrants, mostly from the older states of the South, for Mississippi was in many ways a frontier still growing and only beginning to develop settled institutions. In 1820 the state had had 75,448 inhabitants—42,176 whites and 33,272 nonwhites, 32,814 of them slaves. Forty years later on the eve of secession, the population had grown more than tenfold to 791,305—353,899 whites and 437,406 nonwhites, among whom 436,631 were slaves. Mississippi's whites were overwhelmingly of English and Scotch-Irish lineage. Only tiny pockets of Germans and Irish in towns like Vicksburg, Natchez, and Jackson and a few descendants of eighteenth-century French settlers living along the Gulf coast added ethnic flavor. Mississippi's slaves had largely been brought from the older states of the South to furnish labor for the booming cotton economy.

In 1860 Mississippi's society was overwhelmingly rural and the economy was almost wholly agrarian. Only 17,702 people lived in towns. Aside from some villages and hamlets, the state had only four towns of any consequence: Natchez (6,612), Vicksburg (4,591), Columbus (3,308), and Jackson (3,191). Cotton was the state's chief cash crop, and food crops, especially corn, were also produced in abundance. Most of Mississippi's planters along with their slaves lived in the western half of the state. Except for the Tombigbee Prairie, which also contained some plantations, eastern Mississippi was a land of small farmers; some owned a few slaves, and others none. This demographic division also marked a rough political division. Though never dominant, Whigs were most numerous in the plantation counties along the Mississippi River, while the small farmers and small planters were largely Democrats. Culturally in 1860, Mississippi was just emerging from its frontier past. The University of Mississippi began operation in 1848; public schools were founded in Natchez, Vicksburg, Columbus, and Jackson; a "lunatic asylum," a penitentiary, roads, and railroads had been built.

In the forty years before secession, Mississippi's slave population increased more than thirteenfold. In 1820 slaves constituted 43 percent of the population; in 1860, 55 percent. Washington and Issaquena counties on the Mississippi River counted 92 percent of their populations as slave; Jones in the southeast and Tishomingo in the northeast were respectively only 12 percent and 20 percent slave. Slave labor was considered essential for cotton production, and personal wealth of Mississippians in slave property exceeded $400 million.

Antebellum Sectional Crises. Slavery emerged as a bitterly divisive national issue in the aftermath of the Mexican War (1849–1851). Should the territories acquired from Mexico be open to slavery or not? Mississippi's governor during those years was John Anthony Quitman, a Democrat, a Southern nationalist, and a fire-eater. He counseled secession should the national government attempt to regulate slavery. Most Whigs and some Unionist Democrats, led by

Senator Henry S. Foote, called for moderation and compromise. The crisis was averted when voters elected a Unionist majority to a secession convention called by Quitman. Sealing the Unionist victory, Foote narrowly defeated Jefferson Davis for the governorship in 1851.

The emotional events of the 1850s—the Kansas controversy, the rising popularity of the Free-Soil position, and the increasingly strident demands of the abolitionists—undercut the Mississippi Unionists and strengthened the appeal of fire-eaters like Quitman, Governors John Jones McRae and J. J. Pettus, and Senator Albert Gallatin Brown. The breakup of the national Whig party in the mid-1850s left many Mississippi Unionists without a party base, and the Democratic leadership was dominated by secessionists.

The crisis peaked in the presidential election of 1860. Governor Pettus, both U.S. senators (Brown and Jefferson Davis, the most moderate of Mississippi's secessionist leaders), and the entire House delegation recommended that a secession convention be called if Abraham Lincoln, a former Free-Soil Whig but now a Republican, was elected. Mississippi's delegation to the Democratic National Convention refused to support Stephen A. Douglas and walked out when the convention rejected a plank guaranteeing the rights of slavery in new territories.

Three candidates appeared on the November ballot in Mississippi: Douglas of Illinois, nominee of the Democratic party; John C. Breckinridge of Kentucky, nominee of the Southern Democrats; and John Bell of Tennessee, nominee of the Constitutional Union party. Lincoln was not on the bal-

> **In 1860 Mississippi's society was overwhelmingly rural and the economy was . . . agrarian.**

lot. Breckinridge had the support of the secessionist Democrats in Mississippi, and Bell was backed by Unionists and many former Whigs. The Mississippi electorate gave Breckinridge 40,464 votes, Bell 25,335, and Douglas 3,636.

Lincoln's election precipitated the state's secession. Governor Pettus called the legislature into session and recommended that it issue a call for elections to a secession convention. In the elections held on December 20, 1860, immediate secessionists won a large majority of the seats—about seventy-five out of a hundred. The delegates met on January 7, 1861, at the statehouse in Jackson and elected William Barry, an immediate secessionist, as president. Efforts by cooperationists and Unionists first to postpone secession and then to submit the question to the people in a referendum failed, and on January 9, Mississippi's ordinance of secession, drafted by L. Q. C. Lamar, was passed. Mississippi thus became the second state to secede.

Within a month all seven of the lower Southern states had left the Union, and on February 4, 1861, delegates convened at Montgomery, Alabama, to form a Confederate government. The secession convention chose nine delegates to represent Mississippi. Over the next two months delegates to the Provisional Congress at Montgomery wrote a constitution and formed a government headed by Jefferson Davis of Warren County, Mississippi. In late March Mississippi's secession convention reconvened at the statehouse in Jackson and ratified the new Constitution. By then war fever was rising, and Governor Pettus had already begun to form military units, gather arms, and look to the defense of Mississippi.

The War in Mississippi. When the war began, Mississippi occupied a key place in Union strategy. The state lay in the heart of the Deep South, a strategic crossroads. The Mississippi River, a central objective for Union forces from the earliest days of the war, wound along the state's entire western border. Consequently, countless battles, raids, and skirmishes were fought within Mississippi. Nearly all the many engagements fell into three major campaigns—the campaign for Corinth in 1862, that for Vicksburg in 1862 to 1863, and that for eastern Mississippi in 1864 to 1865.

The war came to Mississippi in earnest during the early spring and summer of 1862. Having breached the South's first defensive line at Forts Henry and Donelson, Gen. Ulysses S. Grant descended the Tennessee River. Disembarking at Pittsburg Landing near a country church called Shiloh, Grant aimed his army at Corinth, twenty miles to the south. He hoped to destroy the Memphis and Charleston Railroad, a major east-west Confederate communications route. Gens. Albert Sidney Johnston and P. G. T. Beauregard had already gathered a Confederate army at Corinth. Johnston's army attacked Grant's forces around Pittsburg Landing. In two of the bloodiest days of the war, the Confederates dealt Grant a severe blow but failed to destroy him. Grant was briefly relieved, and over the next two months, the Union army, now under Gen. Henry W. Halleck, crept slowly south toward Corinth. As the Union force advanced, it grew in strength, and the Confederates, commanded by Beauregard since the death of Johnston at Shiloh, were forced to evacuate. Corinth was occupied on May 29, 1862.

Meanwhile, up from the Gulf of Mexico came a major threat to southwestern Mississippi. In early April 1862, Adm. David Farragut established a base on the Gulf coast and aimed his fleet at the lower Mississippi River. He took New Orleans on April 24, 1862, and proceeded upriver. He reached Natchez on May 12, demanded that town's surrender, and appeared off Vicksburg on May 18. In June, Farragut fought his way upriver past the Vicksburg batteries and was joined by a Union fleet from Memphis. For a month they bombarded and threatened the town. But Farragut lacked an army, and Vicksburg was well defended from the river side. Falling water in the river and the appearance of the Confederate ironclad *Arkansas* convinced Farragut he should abandon his attempt to take Vicksburg. On July 27 he weighed anchor and headed downriver.

Almost as Farragut was withdrawing, another attack on Vicksburg was being mounted, this time from upriver and with a powerful army. General Grant had barely escaped a career-ending disaster at Shiloh, while Gen. William S. Rosecrans successfully defeated a counteroffensive by Maj. Gen. Earl Van Dorn to reclaim northeast Mississippi and western Tennessee (Battle of Corinth, October 3–4, 1862). Grant then prepared to move against Vicksburg. He began his campaign in November 1862 by sending Maj. Gen. William Tecumseh Sherman downriver with forty thousand men on steamboats supported by Rear Adm. David D. Porter's fleet of gunboats. Sherman planned to tie Confederate Gen. John C. Pemberton's Confederate army to the Vicksburg defenses and make an assault on the town bluffs if possible. Meanwhile Grant would start south through central Mississippi to invest Vicksburg from the rear. Late in December, Grant's base at Holly Springs was destroyed by Van Dorn, and Sherman's assault on the Chickasaw Bluffs north of Vicksburg was repulsed by greatly inferior Confederate forces.

Sherman withdrew and established a base twenty miles north of Vicksburg while Grant retreated to Memphis. Ever tenacious, Grant then brought his forces downriver to join Sherman's force. His army reunited by the end of January, Grant determined to try again. For almost three months he tried to flank the Vicksburg defenses by sending amphibious expeditions through the tortuous, flooded waterways north of Vicksburg. Finally, on April 17 Admiral Porter ran his gunboats and steamboats by the Vicksburg batteries while Grant's army marched overland through Louisiana and

> In two of the bloodiest days of the war, the Confederates dealt Grant a severe blow but failed to destroy him.

recrossed the river at Bruinsburg. Grant then moved rapidly toward Jackson, hoping to keep Joseph E. Johnston's new and growing Confederate force from combining with Pemberton's army. Over the next nineteen days, Grant's army marched two hundred miles, living mostly off the country. He fought five victorious engagements at Port Gibson (May 1), Raymond (May 11), Jackson (May 14), Champion's Hill (May 16), and the Big Black River (May 17). By May 19 Pemberton was back inside the entrenchments surrounding Vicksburg. After two unsuccessful assaults on Pemberton's lines, Grant settled down for a forty-seven-day siege. Pemberton surrendered his army on July 4, 1863.

During 1864, campaigning in Mississippi shifted into the eastern and northeastern regions. Union forces had two objectives—to lay waste the economy of the unoccupied sections of Mississippi and to tie down the dangerous cavalry forces of Nathan Bedford Forrest. Sherman was beginning his campaign from Chattanooga to On three occasions from February to July 1864 Union armies marched out from Memphis only to be repulsed by Forrest. On February 3 Sherman set out from Vicksburg to cut a swath across Mississippi to Meridian, a major rail center and supply depot for Confederate forces. To keep Forrest occupied, he ordered Gen. William Sooy Smith to March from Memphis to Meridian. Sherman on February 14 reached Meridian, where he destroyed the railroads and Confederate stores. Smith never came. Ten days late leaving Memphis, he encountered an entrenched Forrest near Okolona. When Smith decided to withdraw, Forrest attacked and harassed Smith's forces for eighty miles. On June 10, Maj. Gen. Samuel D. Sturgis, under orders from Sherman to find and defeat Forrest, met a fate worse than Smith's. While advancing from Memphis, Sturgis was attacked near Brice's Crossroads by Forrest and was defeated utterly, losing a fourth of his men. A month later yet another Union army under Gen. A. J. Smith left Memphis to confront Forrest. The two armies clashed at Tupelo (Harrisburg) on July 14–15 in a bloody but drawn battle. Smith was forced to withdraw, but he had dealt the Confederates over thirteen hundred casualties.

Forrest then moved into Tennessee to threaten Sherman's lines of communication, and for the remainder of the war campaigning in Mississippi was limited to Union raids against railroads.

The Home Front. At first, Mississippians met the war with considerable enthusiasm. Military companies were formed faster than they could be equipped and mustered into Confederate forces; Governor Pettus suffered considerable criticism for being "too slow." Though support for the war was high in 1861 and 1862, problems on the home front were apparent very early.

Cotton, Mississippi's prewar economic staple, proved to be a burden during wartime. It produced little cash and was certainly inedible. The secession convention appointed a committee to encourage farmers to plant corn and wheat, and by mid-1862, the government was seeking to restrict the planting of cotton. Yet, despite such efforts, cotton planting continued, and frequently planters illegally sold their cotton to the enemy. When Mississippi needed food, it got cotton.

In 1860 Mississippi's wealth was primarily in land and slaves. Except for railroad and levee building and lumbering, Mississippi industries were related to agriculture. Although in 1860 Mississippi produced a fourth of the nation's cotton, the state had few textile mills, and by 1864 only one had survived

Federal destruction. For clothing, women had to resort to using old spinning wheels and looms.

During the war Mississippi was in conflict not only with the Union but also with the Confederate government. Governor Pettus felt that Confederate support for the state's defense was inadequate, and thus he wanted Mississippi secured with troops under its own control. In addition, Mississippians opposed the Confederacy's monopolizing the state's railroads, its interference with the state's sovereignty, and its punishment of state citizens for such crimes as contraband trade. Citizens especially opposed military seizure of property without fair payment. As the war continued, many Mississippians blamed Jefferson Davis and the Confederacy for their suffering.

Civil order in the state soon broke down. After the fall of Vicksburg, local government faltered, taxes went uncollected, courts ceased to function, and government services disappeared. County government, never overly active even before the war, was practically inoperative at war's end. After May 14, 1863, when the city of Jackson fell to Grant, the state government could no longer meet there and became an itinerant, meeting successively at Enterprise, Columbus, and Macon. Governor Charles Clark, inaugurated on the steps of the Columbus courthouse in 1863, had never occupied the statehouse or the governor's mansion in Jackson. By 1864 legislative sessions had become brief and infrequent.

Disorder intensified throughout the war. Vigilance committees gained power, and blacks who had been essential to cotton production abandoned the plantations and farms. Farm work fell disproportionately on women and old men. Taxes went unpaid, for many plantations had been simply abandoned. Many nonslaveowning yeomen who complained of "a rich man's war and a poor man's fight" defected from the Confederate cause, and parts of Mississippi became a refuge for deserters.

War-weariness and defeatism grew. In the biennial elections of 1863, many fire-eaters were defeated by more moderate opponents, and some old radicals like Albert Gallatin Brown and Ethelbert Barksdale began to talk of reconstruction. In 1865, after the surrender of the last Confederate forces in Mississippi, Governor Clark sought to return to the state capital from which Governor Pettus had fled in May 1863. Clark ordered the legislature to assemble at the statehouse on May 18, 1865.

Clark's assumption that Union authorities would allow Mississippi's wartime government to reestablish control was mistaken. On May 20 the legislators convened, but after meeting for only an hour they were disbanded by Union Brig. Gen. E. D. Osband. At the same time, Osband ordered Governor Clark to vacate his office in the statehouse and to turn over the state archives to Union military authorities. Clark protested the illegality of the order, but he complied on May 22. He was later arrested and imprisoned in Fort Pulaski at Savannah, Georgia, and remained in custody there until October 11.

Certainly Mississippi's greatest wartime loss, both immediate and long term, lay in casualties. The census of 1860 showed 70,295 white male Mississippians between the ages of eighteen and forty-five. State enlistments during the war totaled 78,000. Of those, about 20,000 (26 percent) died from wounds or disease. Some Mississippi units were all but wiped out. The Vicksburg Sharpshooters went to war with 124 men; 1 returned. The Quitman Guard of Pike County marched off to battle with 125 men; 25 returned. Other units were decimated in single battles. The Sixth Mississippi Regiment lost 300 of 425 men at Shiloh; the Sixteenth Mississippi at Sharpsburg lost 63 percent of those present; at Chickamauga, the Twenty-ninth Mississippi lost 53 percent. The wounded and maimed remained uncounted. In 1865 the legislature ordered a survey to determine the number of veterans who needed artificial legs and suggested establishing a factory to produce them. In 1866 the legislators appropriated $30,000 to pay for artificial limbs.

[*For discussion of battles fought in Mississippi, see* Brice's Crossroads, Mississippi; Corinth, Mississippi; Holly Springs, Mississippi; Meridian Campaign; Shiloh Campaign; Tupelo, Mississippi; Vicksburg Campaign. *For discussion of Mississippi cities, see* Jackson, Mississippi, *article on* City of Jackson. *See also* Barksdale's Mississippi Brigade; Jones County, Mississippi; *and biographies of numerous figures mentioned herein.*]

BIBLIOGRAPHY

Bearss, Edwin C. *Decision in Mississippi.* Little Rock, Ark., 1962.
Bettersworth, John K. *Confederate Mississippi: The People and Policies of a Cotton State in Wartime.* Baton Rouge, La., 1943.
McLemore, Richard A. *A History of Mississippi.* Vol. 1. Hattiesburg, Miss., 1973.
Rainwater, Percy L. *Mississippi: Storm Center of Secession, 1856–1861.* Baton Rouge, La., 1938. Reprint, New York, 1969.

RAY SKATES

MISSOURI

On October 28, 1861, a rump session of the Missouri legislature met at Neosho and passed an ordinance of secession removing the state from the Union. One month to the day later the Confederate Congress formally received Missouri as the twelfth state in the new nation. The state's representatives and senators, initially chosen by the legislators and later by its troops in the field, sat in the Confederate Congress for the remainder of the war. But the legislature enacting secession had been deposed three months earlier, together with the remainder of the state government, by a state convention originally called in February to decide the issue of secession. By the time of this action, the state had been overrun by Union troops except for its extreme southwestern and southeastern corners. This legislature never met again, yet the government-in-exile, headed by Governors Claiborne F. Jackson and Thomas Caute Reynolds, continued a shadow existence in Arkansas and Texas until the war's end, cooperating with Confederate authorities in the Trans-Mississippi theater.

Missouri in 1860 was a state in flux. Originally pioneered by Southerners from Virginia, Kentucky, and Tennessee in the early nineteenth century, its population had grown by 75 percent during the 1850s. Much of that growth had come from the North (180 percent increase) and abroad (110 percent increase), so that by 1860 the Northern- and foreign-born outnumbered the Southern-born in the state's population for the first time. The majority of the foreign-born were Irish and Germans concentrated near St. Louis, although they spread out along the Missouri River as far west as Cole County. Of the 1,182,012 persons living in Missouri, only 114,931 (1 in 9) were slaves, by contrast with a ratio of 1 to 4 1/2 thirty years earlier. Most of these latter lived in the counties bordering the Mississippi and Missouri rivers, working as either farm laborers or domestic servants. Only 59 of the state's 24,320 slaveholders owned more than 40 slaves. The free black population was relatively small and concentrated mainly in St. Louis. They pursued a variety of occupations from boat hands to barbers and caterers. Many were descended from creole blacks who had come with the French in the eighteenth century.

The election of 1860 found Missourians badly divided among the four contending groups at both the state and the national levels. Claiborne F. Jackson, longtime champion of slavery expansion, was elected governor by remaining loyal to the national (Douglas) Democrats, although Sample Orr, the candidate of the Constitutional Unionists, ran him a close second. These two parties also garnered 70 percent of the popular vote in the presidential contest, with Stephen A. Douglas gaining the state's electoral vote over John Bell by a mere 429 votes. Clearly most Missourians wanted to avoid the extreme positions of the Republicans and the Breckinridge Democrats. Yet at his inauguration, Governor Jackson made it clear that his sympathies lay with the South in the secession crisis. Lieutenant Governor Reynolds paid a secret visit to Washington to confer with Southern congressional leaders as to the best course for Missouri to pursue. Upon his return he organized a prosecessionist paramilitary group called the Minute Men to counteract the pro-Union home guard already established by Congressman Frank Blair.

The Missouri legislature provided for the calling of a state convention in late February 1861 to discuss secession. Overwhelmingly conditional Unionist, it voted to take a wait-

and-see attitude inasmuch as none of the surrounding states had taken any action and the state's conservative business interests realized they had increasing economic ties to the East via a developing rail network to counter their Mississippi River ties to the South.

Although temporarily thwarted in their desire to take Missouri into the Southern Confederacy, Jackson and Reynolds began laying plans for more overt action. Their key concern was the U.S. arsenal in south St. Louis with its sixty-thousand stand of arms. At a secret meeting with their St. Louis militia commander, Gen. Daniel Marsh Frost, the two men agreed to call a statewide militia muster as a cover-up to enable the St. Louis militia to seize the arsenal and its arms. They also called the state legislature into special session in the hope of persuading it to reorganize the militia with stronger gubernatorial control. Simultaneously Jackson curtly rejected furnishing Missouri's quota of four thousand volunteers when President Abraham Lincoln issued his call for troops in the aftermath of Fort Sumter. Congressman Blair promptly volunteered his home guards, many of whom came from St. Louis's German population, to fill the ranks. They were quickly mustered in, armed from the arsenal, and stationed in defensive positions guarding the approaches to that facility.

The St. Louis militia were thus thwarted but went into encampment at Camp Jackson on the western edge of the city on May 6. Their counterparts in western Missouri seized the small Federal arsenal at Liberty. Governor Jackson meanwhile wrote Jefferson Davis seeking assistance. The Confederate president forwarded several cannons disguised as Tamaroa marble, from the Baton Rouge arsenal up the Mississippi. Learning of this and dismayed during an undercover drive through the camp's streets by his sighting of pro-Confederate street signs, Gen. Nathaniel Lyon surrounded Camp Jackson with Federal troops on May 10, the day it was scheduled to disband, and demanded its surrender as a pro-Confederate operation. As he marched his prisoners to the arsenal, shots rang out, and in the ensuing melee twenty-eight persons were killed. The Missouri legislature promptly gave the governor powers to reorganize the militia into the Missouri State Guard. Jackson appointed former governor Sterling Price, who had seen service in the Mexican War, as the guard's new head, and recruitment began in earnest.

A temporary truce was obtained, but this broke down on June 11. Deeming Jefferson City indefensible, Jackson abandoned his capital, and it was promptly occupied by Lyon's forces moving up the Missouri River. Following brief battles at Boonville and Carthage, Jackson, Price, and the State Guard retreated into southwestern Missouri. Union troops poured into Missouri from Kansas, Iowa, and Illinois, and the state remained occupied for the duration of the war.

Governor Jackson, accompanied by former senator David R. Atchison, hastened to Richmond where he secured promises of Confederate cooperation as soon as Missouri withdrew from the Union. Price, meanwhile, with the cooperation of Gen. Ben McCulloch from Arkansas, defeated Lyon at Oak Hills near Springfield on August 10 and then advanced without McCulloch on Lexington where he captured a small Union garrison on September 20. Unable to hold that advanced position, he retreated to Neosho where the rump session of the legislature taking Missouri out of the Union was held.

At the end of 1861 Price was driven from the state by Union troops under Gen. Samuel R. Curtis. He joined forces with the Confederates under Gen. Earl Van Dorn, only to be defeated by Curtis at the Battle of Elkhorn Tavern (March 7–8, 1862). After this Price took the bulk of the State Guard into the Confederate army, where he was commissioned

> ### . . . shots rang out, and in the ensuing melee twenty-eight persons were killed.

major general. Included was a small group of guardsmen who had been serving under M. Jeff Thompson in southeastern Missouri. Transferred east of the Mississippi, the Missourians arrived too late to assist Albert Sidney Johnston at Shiloh. Other Missouri troops, who had regularly enlisted in the Confederate armed forces, were present at Shiloh as well as at Forts Henry and Donelson earlier.

Meanwhile the Confederates sent raiders under Col. Joseph Porter and other troops from Arkansas back into Missouri to recruit Southern sympathizers and harass Union outposts in the summer of 1862. They met with varying success as far as recruitment was concerned, but they did play havoc with Union forces and supplies throughout the state.

Price led his troops against the Union forces under Ulysses S. Grant at Iuka and Corinth in September and October 1862 before he returned west of the Mississippi in early 1863. Most of the Missourians reluctantly remained east of the Mississippi and fought through the Vicksburg campaign. After coming off parole, many of them were later involved in the Chattanooga, Atlanta, and Franklin and Nashville campaigns. Other Missouri forces fought with Price in the various Arkansas campaigns of 1863 and 1864. Four times they launched raids into their home state under John Sappington Marmaduke (January and April 1863), Joseph O. Shelby (October 1863), and Price (September 1864). The first three raids were merely meant to harass Union outposts and secure recruits and supplies. The last raid was a major attempt to regain sufficient control of the state to reinstall a government at Jefferson City.

In the interim, Confederate guerrillas, led by William Clarke Quantrill and others, infested Missouri and kept the state in constant turmoil throughout the war. A native of Ohio,

Quantrill had migrated to the Missouri border in 1857 at the age of twenty as the proslavery agitation in Kansas was reaching its climax. When Charles Jennison's pro-Union jayhawk raiders struck western Missouri in random reprisals and looting in 1861, Quantrill organized a guerrilla band to retaliate. Some joined up for sheer excitement. Others, like the Younger brothers and their cousins the James boys, had seen farms looted and relatives slain by the jayhawkers. Fierce fighting followed all along the border. Union commanders in turn proclaimed martial law and pursued a stringent policy of harassment against Confederate sympathizers through arbitrary arrests, assessments, and banishments.

The climax along the border came in the summer of 1863 when Union Gen. Tom Ewing placed a number of women related to the guerrillas in a makeshift prison which collapsed, killing several. In retaliation Quantrill led his gang

> ... most of Missouri's Confederate leaders went into exile in Mexico where they joined forces with Maximilian.

across the border on August 21 to raid Lawrence, Kansas, long an antislavery stronghold. He left the town in flames and at least 150 dead. Ewing now issued his Order No. 11 forcing all persons in a four county area living more than a mile from Union posts to abandon their homes on the grounds that they had aided and abetted the guerrillas over time. Thereafter Quantrill's band broke up into smaller units and spread to the interior of the state. While Quantrill's guerrillas gained the greatest notoriety, they had many counterparts, some legitimately pro-Confederate and some merely organized thieves, who roamed Missouri throughout the war spreading havoc in their wake.

Governor Jackson meanwhile maintained a shadow government-in-exile at Camden, Arkansas, until his death at Little Rock in December 1862. Then Lieutenant Governor Reynolds, who had exiled himself to his native South Carolina, went quickly to confer with Confederate authorities and Missouri's congressmen at Richmond before assuming control of the remnant of Missouri's Confederate government in the West. Following the Union capture of Little Rock in September 1863, Reynolds established his capital at Marshall, Texas. From there he cooperated with Gen. E. Kirby Smith in the Trans-Mississippi Department, coordinating the efforts of Missouri troops, encouraging continued guerrilla activity in his home state, and working with other western governors to establish an effective Confederate presence west of the Mississippi with diminishing success.

Two of Reynolds's notable accomplishments were his recommendations for a "Western Preferred Mail" system and a

Treasury branch that could handle claims against the Confederacy without prior referral to Richmond and could engrave and sign government notes and bonds. He accompanied Sterling Price on his September 1864 raid into Missouri, hoping to reestablish his government at Jefferson City. This raid proved a dismal failure, however, and he retired with Price's force back into Arkansas.

At war's end, most of Missouri's Confederate leaders went into exile in Mexico where they joined forces with Maximilian. After his attempt to secure an empire in Mexico failed, they slowly drifted back to Missouri where many of them ultimately found prominent places in postwar Democratic politics.

All told, Missouri furnished some 30,000 men to the Confederate armed forces as opposed to the over 100,000 Missourians who served the Union. Yet there were many more unnumbered Missourians who sympathized with the Confederacy and lent it assistance through guerrilla activities within the state. Many were reluctant or unable to leave their homes to serve elsewhere, but their bitter partisanship kept Missouri in a state of turmoil whose memory lasted well into Reconstruction.

[*For further discussion of battles and campaigns fought in Missouri, see* New Madrid and Island Number 10; Price's Missouri Raid; Wilson's Creek Campaign. *See also* Guerrilla Warfare; Missouri Compromise; *and biographies of numerous figures mentioned herein.*]

BIBLIOGRAPHY

Brownlee, Richard S. *Gray Ghosts of the Confederacy: Guerrilla Warfare in the West, 1861–1865.* Baton Rouge, La., 1958.

Castel, Albert. *General Sterling Price and the Civil War in the West.* Baton Rouge, La., 1968.

Fellman, Michael. *Inside War: The Guerrilla Conflict in Missouri during the American Civil War.* New York, 1989.

Kirkpatrick, Arthur R. "Missouri's Secessionist Government, 1861–1865." *Missouri Historical Review* 45 (January 1951).

Parrish, William E. *A History of Missouri. Volume III, 1860 to 1875.* Columbia, Mo., 1973.

Parrish, William E. "Missouri." In *The Confederate Governors.* Edited by W. Buck Yearns. Athens, Ga., 1985.

WILLIAM E. PARRISH

MISSOURI COMPROMISE

When Missouri applied for statehood in 1819, Representative James Tallmadge of New York moved to amend the new state's constitution to eliminate slavery. Excepting only Louisiana itself, Missouri would be the first state to be carved out of the vast expanse of the Louisiana Purchase. Its disposition would tip the existing balance of slave and free states. Of even graver potential consequence for the South, the amendment if passed threatened to "dam up Southerners in a sea of slaves" and abrogate the understanding that underpinned the Union, that the Federal government had no constitutional right to interfere with slavery in the states.

The proposed amendment gave rise to a firestorm of public controversy, evoked virtually all the pro- and antislavery arguments that would subsequently wrack the Union, illuminated the potential of the slavery issue to divide political parties along sectional lines, and brought threats of secession. "This momentous question, like a fire bell in the night, awakened and filled me with terror," Thomas Jefferson wrote; "I considered it at once as the knell of the union." Tempers cooled only after a compromise made possible by the adept legislative maneuvering of Henry Clay: Missouri and Maine entered the Union without restriction, one slave and one free; and slavery was prohibited in the great bulk of the Louisiana territory north of 36°30′.

The controversy gave rise to a resurgent "Old Republicanism" in the South in the 1820s that helped to bring Andrew Jackson to power in 1828 and to usher in the "second party system." Dependent on support from both North and South, the Jacksonian party worked to quiet discussion of the slavery question for a generation. When abolitionist pressure and the desire to build a transcontinental railroad through the unorganized area north of 36°30′ made this no longer possible, latter-day Jacksonians repealed the territorial prohibition with the Kansas-Nebraska Act (1854), and in 1857 the Supreme Court declared in the Dred Scott decision that the prohibition had never been constitutional, ruling that Congress had no power to prohibit slavery in the territories. With the effective repeal of the Missouri Compromise the national party system collapsed, all the slavery issues came once more to the fore, and secession quickly followed.

[See also Dred Scott Decision; Kansas-Nebraska Act.]

BIBLIOGRAPHY

Brown, Richard H. "The Missouri Crisis, Slavery, and the Politics of Jacksonianism." *South Atlantic Quarterly* 65 (1966): 55–72.
Moore, Glover. *The Missouri Controversy, 1819–1821.* Lexington, Ky., 1953.

RICHARD H. BROWN

MOBILE, ALABAMA

[*This entry includes three articles:* City of Mobile, *which profiles the city during the Confederacy;* Battle of Mobile Bay, *which discusses the naval battle of 1864; and* Mobile Campaign, *which discusses the 1865 Union campaign to capture the city.*]

City of Mobile

Mobile, Alabama, the state's only seaport and the Confederacy's second largest Gulf port, virtually lost its cotton trade during the war owing to the Federal blockade and Confederate embargo. Escaping direct attack until the end of the war, the city of 30,000 in 1860 grew to about 45,000 in 1865 as it served the Confederacy as a site for training camps, recreation, and medical care.

Before the war virtually all local commercial activities, from marketing cotton to obtaining goods for planters in the interior, served the cotton trade that undergirded Mobile's economy. The city's hinterland encompassed rich cotton-producing areas in Alabama and Mississippi. Planters in both states with access to the Alabama-Tombigbee River system that flowed into the Mobile River used Mobile as their cotton market. By 1860 Mobile had surpassed all Southern ports except New Orleans as a cotton exporter. Cotton usually made up 99 percent of the total value of exports from antebellum Mobile. Lumber and lumber products, the export ranking second in value, accounted for only 1 percent of the total value of exports.

With cotton as the basis for its economy, Mobile, as much as any other Southern port, remained essentially undiversified. Many people provided services directly related to marketing cotton or entertaining planters who visited the city, and few entered other economic pursuits. A substantial portion of profits from transactions in cotton left Mobile for northeastern American cities as well as for Liverpool and Le Havre, where international firms handled many of the transport, insurance, and market arrangements for Alabama cotton. In the 1850s, to encourage the commercial independence and diversification of the local economy, civic boosters promoted railroads, direct trade, and manufacturing. All their efforts achieved limited success. For its major lines of commerce the port still depended on its river system and Mobile Bay, which flowed into the Gulf of Mexico.

A culturally diverse work force supplied the labor for the city. Most skilled workers were white, while slaves supplied much of the semiskilled and unskilled labor. They worked as domestics, draymen, mechanics, and press hands. In 1860 half of Alabama's free blacks lived in Mobile where they constituted about 3 percent of the free labor force. Stiff competition had developed among laborers in Mobile and other Southern ports in the late antebellum years when increasing numbers of white immigrants sought jobs formerly held by slaves and free blacks. By 1860 the free male labor force of Mobile consisted of 50 percent foreign-born, 34 percent Southern-born, and 16 percent Northern-born. Irish and German workers predominated among the foreign-born. Free

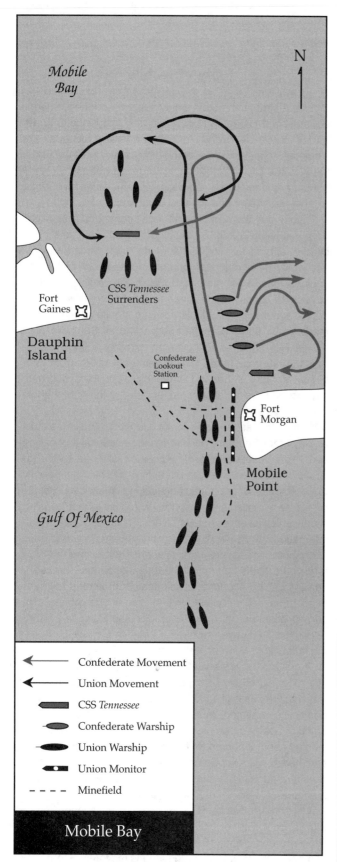

Mobile Bay

Mobile Bay

Fort Gaines

Dauphin Island

CSS *Tennessee* Surrenders

Confederate Lookout Station

Fort Morgan

Mobile Point

Gulf Of Mexico

N

← Confederate Movement

← Union Movement

— CSS *Tennessee*

— Confederate Warship

— Union Warship

— Union Monitor

---- Minefield

women, white and black, comprised about one-tenth of the total free work force in Mobile.

In the 1860 presidential election, because of their concerns for maintaining financial and commercial ties between the North and the South, Mobile's voters registered preferences for moderate candidates, with 71 percent choosing Constitutional Unionist John Bell or National Democrat Stephen A. Douglas. Of major Southern ports, only New Orleans exceeded Mobile's support for moderates. Shortly after the election, however, the citizens began shifting their sympathies from moderation to secession. In the campaign for delegates to the Alabama secession convention, both major newspapers, the *Mobile Register* and the *Mobile Advertiser,* adopted cooperationist positions, but local voters favored secessionist delegates by a two-to-one majority. Native Southerners, especially slaveholders, provided many of the votes for secessionists, while nonslaveholders born in the North gave important support to cooperationists. After the passage of Alabama's ordinance of secession on January 11, 1861, Southern loyalty for secessionists eventually overrode Unionist sentiment. Mobilians supported the Confederacy hoping that it would, among other things, end their colonial relationship to the North and spur urban growth in their city.

At the outset of the Civil War the location of Mobile made it a prime target, one of ten key Southern seaports, for Union blockaders. Initially the blockade proved ineffective, with the Federals closing off only the main entrances to Mobile; the side entrances, coast, and inlets remained unguarded. In early 1862 trade continued without much interruption between New Orleans, Mobile, and Havana by bayou and inland channels. But immediately after the capture of New Orleans in April 1862, blockade running decreased sharply, and Adm. David Farragut's capture of Mobile Bay in August 1864 essentially halted it.

Despite the blockade, Mobile's gay social life continued into the war. Residents and visitors observed local social customs such as gentlemen calling on the ladies of their acquaintance on New Year's Day. Naval officers visited fashionable homes, whose hosts and hostesses they entertained in turn with shipboard balls, dinners, and moonlight cruises. A local newspaper dubbed Mobile the "Paris of the Confederacy." Some of the most fashionable homes where Mobilians entertained visiting generals, politicians, and literary figures were those of Octavia Walton Le Vert, Mary Walker Fearn, Augusta Jane Evans, and Gen. Dabney Herndon Maury, commander of the Department of the Gulf from the summer of 1863 to the end of the war. Numerous balls and concerts benefited needy groups of soldiers and civilians. As touring companies curtailed their travels during the war, the Mobile Theatre relied heavily on local actors to maintain its offerings of plays. Visitors, particularly soldiers, composed the bulk of audiences.

A variety of local hospitals provided good medical care to soldiers and civilians. Five hospitals that were operating when the war began continued in service. From 1861 through 1864 Confederate authorities built or renovated older buildings to provide seven additional hospitals for soldiers and sailors. Local women formed charitable associations to give supplies and services to patients in the hospitals. Augusta Evans even personally established and equipped a convalescent hospital on the grounds of her home.

With the blockade cutting imports through the port and Federal occupation and Confederate impressment interfering with transport of goods from the hinterland of Mobile, food shortages and inflation troubled residents. Municipal authorities sponsored a Free Market that served hundreds of poor citizens. Private organizations labored to meet needs: the Volunteer Relief Committee solicited private funds to aid the destitute, the Mobile Military Aid Society employed soldiers' dependents to sew uniforms for Alabama companies in the Confederate army, and the Mobile Supply Association hired agents to procure foodstuffs from areas north of Mobile, ship them to the city, and sell them at cost. All of these efforts failed to avert a bread riot staged in 1863 by women who were irate at shortages and high prices. Their protest sparked municipal authorities to call for new charitable groups to canvass the city, identify needy families, and solicit donations for them; these efforts apparently succeeded in relieving many in distress.

Its isolation from the war allowed Mobile to provide notable educational and publishing activities for the Confederacy. Although local public and private schools reduced operations during the war and the Medical College of Alabama in the city closed its doors, Spring Hill College continued to hold its regular sessions, even with fluctuations in numbers of students and faculty. By 1865 enrollment had reached an all-time high as parents, including high-ranking Confederate officers, placed their sons in the college to protect them against the draft. Two presses in Mobile enjoyed expansion of business because of the war. W. G. Clark and Company published the *Mobile Advertiser and Register,* as well as repeated printings of readers for Southern children by Adelaide de Vendel Chaudron. S. H. Goetzel and Company published William J. Hardee's *Rifle and Light Infantry Tactics,* Augusta Jane Evans's *Macaria,* and a variety of other books.

The Confederate embargo and the Union blockade substantially reduced the trade in cotton through Mobile for the duration of the war. Disruption of foreign trade persisted after the war as Union occupying forces, which took the city in April 1865, closed the port to foreign trade until late in August. The city survived the war intact, only to lose four-fifths of its warehouse facilities on May 25, 1865, when the ordnance depot exploded, killing as many as three hundred people and destroying more than twenty blocks. Rebuilding began in the fall.

As much as Mobilians tried to revive their prewar commerce in cotton, it failed to equal earlier volume. While agriculture adjusted to the changes brought about by war and emancipation, production of cotton in Mobile's hinterland declined. Throughout Alabama cotton production did not reach 1860 levels until the 1890s. Receipts of cotton in Mobile and exports through the port lagged far behind the boom years of the 1850s, averaging during Reconstruction about 60 percent of the 1850s average. Changes in railroad networks accounted for much of the diversion of cotton away from Mobile. The export trade in lumber, however, grew markedly.

Postwar commercial developments required extensive harbor improvements, especially the deepening of the ship channel through the bay to the city docks, and harbor improvements required substantial Federal aid. Before the Civil War the U.S. government had financed dredging the channel through Choctaw Pass to ten feet, but this channel had shoaled to seven and one-half feet by 1865. From 1870 to the mid-1890s Federal funds paid for deepening and widening the channel, and these improved port facilities served an increasingly diversified export and import trade.

Mobile in 1860 had ranked seventh in population of major Southern cities and twenty-seventh among all American cities. Disruption of the cotton trade caused by the war precipitated a decline, and Mobile never again achieved as much regional or national prominence as it had in 1860 when cotton was king.

BIBLIOGRAPHY

Amos, Harriet E. "'All-Absorbing Topics': Food and Clothing in Confederate Mobile." *Atlanta Historical Journal* 22 (1978): 17–28.

Amos, Harriet E. *Cotton City: Urban Development in Antebellum Mobile.* University, Ala., 1985.

Amos, Harriet E. "From Old to New South Trade in Mobile, 1850–1900." *Gulf Coast Historical Review* 5 (1990): 114–127.

Bergeron, Arthur W., Jr. *Confederate Mobile.* Jackson, Miss., 1991.

McLaurin, Melton, and Michael Thomason. *Mobile: The Life and Times of a Great Southern City.* Woodland Hills, Calif., 1981.

HARRIET E. AMOS DOSS

Battle of Mobile Bay

This naval battle occurred on August 5, 1864, with Confederates fighting to retain control of Mobile Bay, Alabama. Union forces under Rear Adm. David G. Farragut led a fleet of four monitors and fourteen wooden warships into the harbor, past the formidable Fort Morgan, to engage the Confederacy's few wooden ships and single ironclad.

During the early morning hours of August 5, Union ships, fastened together in pairs, moved cautiously behind the monitors into the harbor, aware that the bay floor was lined with torpedoes. Confederates, well entrenched in Fort Morgan, quickly manned their guns and unleashed a terrific rain of fire upon the enemy. One Union ship fell victim to a mine. As four wooden Confederate ships joined the fray, Union vessels returned the deadly fire. Confederate Adm. Franklin Buchanan, famous for commanding *Virginia* at Hampton Roads, ordered *Tennessee* to head straight for the fleet as it moved out of range of Fort Morgan. Several Union ships quickly maneuvered to surround the Southern vessel, spraying its iron sides with solid shot. The effect was devastating. With the ship severely damaged and Buchanan himself seriously injured, *Tennessee* surrendered to the victorious Federals. By 10:00 A.M. the Battle of Mobile Bay was over.

The battle ended in a Federal victory with the Union losing 319 men out of a total of 3,000. Mobile itself held out for another eight months, but the battle closed the port to the outside world, led to the surrender of the ironclad *Tennessee,* and cost the South 312 men killed, wounded, or captured.

BIBLIOGRAPHY

Bergeron, Arthur W., Jr. *Confederate Mobile.* Jackson, Miss., 1991.
Bowles, R. C. "The Ship Tennessee." *Southern Historical Society Papers* 21 (1893): 291–294. Reprint, Wilmington, N.C., 1990.
Johnson, Robert U., and C. C. Buel, eds. *Battles and Leaders of the Civil War.* Vol. 4. New York, 1888. Reprint, Secaucus, N.J., 1982.
Thomas, Emory M. "'Damn the Torpedoes': The Battle of Mobile Bay." *Civil War Times Illustrated* 16, no. 1 (1977): 5–9.

LESLEY JILL GORDON-BURR

Mobile Campaign

The Mobile campaign took place from March 17 to April 12, 1865, during the final weeks of the Civil War. Mobile Bay had fallen to the Union navy in August 1864, but for eight additional months the enemy could not drive Confederates from the seaport. Thirty miles from the Gulf of Mexico, Mobile had served as a crucial port for the blockaded Confederates. It was here that Southerners built ironclads and rams to fight against the Union navy. As the Civil War entered its fourth year, a renewed Union offensive commenced in an effort to capture the city. A combined force of naval and land units laid siege to two forts surrounding Mobile. For nearly a week, Confederates offered spirited resistance but could not match the overwhelming numerical superiority of the enemy. On April 12 the Federals entered Mobile to find the city empty of Confederate soldiers. Determined and desperate, the remaining Southerners vainly sought to escape toward Montgomery. For the Confederacy the loss of Mobile was anticlimactic; three days earlier Gen. Robert E. Lee had surrendered to Gen. Ulysses S. Grant at Appomattox Courthouse in Virginia. The Confederacy would soon be no more.

After the fall of the Mississippi River to Federal control in July 1863, Union Adm. David G. Farragut had sought to wrest Mobile Bay from the Confederacy. He laid plans in January 1864 for the campaign, but it was not until early August 1864 that operations commenced against the well-fortified bay. Four hundred guns, three forts, numerous torpedoes, and

> **As the Civil War entered its fourth year, a renewed Union offensive commenced in an effort to capture the city.**

floating mines defended Mobile. If an enemy invasion was going to come, Confederates were not going to make it easy. The resulting Battle of Mobile Bay was a spirited one, combining ironclad monitors and wooden vessels. Mines exploded and monitors rammed; when the smoke cleared the Confederates had lost their single ironclad *Tennessee* and the Federals had Fort Gaines and Mobile Bay.

As winter warmed to spring 1865, the city of Mobile remained in Southern hands. While Union Maj. Gen. William Tecumseh Sherman triumphantly marched through Georgia, South Carolina, and into North Carolina, and Gen. Ulysses S. Grant tightened his grip on Richmond, the scant number of defenders at Mobile poised ready for attack.

On March 17 Union troops embarked on a new mission to capture Mobile once and for all. This combined naval and land offensive included 20 ships and 45,000 men. Maj. Gen. Dabney Herndon Maury, commander of the District of the Gulf, defended Mobile with a mere 10,000 Confederates, 300 guns, and 5 gunboats. Federals from two directions converged on the city: 13,000 from Pensacola, Florida; the remainder, supported by gunboats, from the mouth of the bay in the east. On March 27, Federals drew near Spanish Fort, part of the inner works that defended the city from the east. From March 27 to April 8 a siege of Spanish Fort ensued. Four thousand Confederates fought eight times their strength, 32,000 Union soldiers. Over 50 siege guns and nearly 40 fieldpieces pounded into Spanish Fort's meager defenses. A final infantry assault ended the siege at midnight, April 8. Union troops captured over 3,000 prisoners and 40 guns.

Meanwhile the other contingent of Federals from Pensacola moved toward Fort Blakely, five miles north of Spanish Fort. On April 1, five miles outside of the fort, a Union cavalry detachment clashed with defending Confederates and drove them back to within a mile of the fortification. Confederates lost seventy four men while the attacking cavalrymen suffered only two casualties. Thirteen thousand enemy cavalry and infantry then laid siege to the Confederate works. A single division under Missourian Maj. Gen. Francis Marion Cockrell and a brigade commanded by William T. Thomas mustered what strength they could to fight against overwhelming odds. When Spanish Fort fell on April 8, the Federals increased their numbers at Blakely to 45,000. On April 9 the final infantry engagement of the Civil War occurred when the enemy staged a frontal assault on the besieged works. Within twenty minutes all defense had crumbled and remaining Confederates waved the white flag of surrender.

Three days later Maury evacuated Mobile, leaving 500 prisoners and 50 guns to the victorious Federals. By afternoon the mayor of Mobile had formally surrendered to Union control. Maury, with 4,500 men and 27 guns remaining, retreated with his supply train north toward Montgomery. On May 4 they too yielded to the Union.

The Mobile campaign was costly and had little effect on the war's outcome. Federals lost a total of 1,417 men; Confederate soldiers killed, wounded, missing, and captured numbered over 4,000. So many lives lost left a bitter taste in the mouth of General in Chief Grant. He later wrote:

I had tried for more than two years to have an expedition sent against Mobile when its possession by us would have been of great advantage. It finally cost lives to take it when its possession was of no importance, and when, if left alone, it would have within a few days fallen into our hands without any bloodshed whatever.

BIBLIOGRAPHY

Johnson, Robert U., and C. C. Buel, eds. *Battles and Leaders of the Civil War.* 4 vols. New York, 1887–1888. Reprint, Secaucus, N.J., 1982.

McFeely, Mary D., and William S. McFeely, eds. *Memoirs and Selected Letters: Ulysses S. Grant.* New York, 1990.

Thomas, Emory M. "'Damn the Torpedoes. . . .': The Battle for Mobile Bay." *Civil War Times Illustrated* 16, no. 1 (April 1977): 5–9.

LESLEY JILL GORDON-BURR

MOBILE SQUADRON

This was the Confederate naval force that defended Mobile from 1862 to 1865. It was commanded by Como. Victor M. Randolph until August 15, 1862, when he was replaced by Adm. Franklin Buchanan who served until his capture on *Tennessee* August 5, 1864. Como. Ebenezer Farrand then commanded the squadron until it surrendered May 5, 1865.

The vessels in the Mobile Squadron were either converted merchant ships or among those built in Selma and Mobile.

In 1862 it included five vessels. *Baltic* was a partly armored sidewheel river towboat armed with four guns and scrapped in July 1864. *Morgan* and *Gaines,* wooden sidewheel gunboats carrying eight guns, were built in 1862. *Selma,* originally named *Florida,* was a coastal packet steamer built in Mobile in 1856. Cut down, reinforced, and partly armored, it joined the squadron in 1862. *Tennessee,* added to the squadron in July 1864, was probably the strongest ironclad built by the Confederacy. It carried six heavy guns and 6-inch armor set at a 30-degree angle.

These vessels, except for *Baltic,* formed the squadron that fought at Mobile Bay. Only *Morgan* escaped either capture or destruction. The ship's captain, Como. George W. Harrison, claimed that *Morgan* grounded in shallow water and could not rejoin the battle. As a result of this action, Adm. Franklin Buchanan accused Harrison of cowardice. He was, however, exonerated and was still in command of *Morgan* in March 1865. Other ships, most of them also built at Selma and Mobile, which joined the squadron after this were *Tuscaloosa,* a four-gun ironclad; *Huntsville,* an incomplete ironclad used as a floating battery; and *Nashville,* a heavily armored sidewheel ironclad built in Montgomery and Mobile. These vessels defended Mobile until the squadron's surrender on May 4, 1865.

[*See also* Mobile, Alabama.]

BIBLIOGRAPHY

Civil War Naval Chronology, 1861–1865. 6 vols. Washington, D.C., 1961–1966.

Jones, Virgil C. *The Civil War at Sea.* 3 vols. New York, 1961–1962.

Potter, E. B. *Illustrated History of the United States Navy.* New York, 1971.

Register of Officers of the Confederate States Navy, 1861–1865. Washington, D.C., 1931.

Scharf, John Thomas. *History of the Confederate States Navy from Its Organization to the Surrender of Its Last Vessel.* New York, 1887.

FRANK LAWRENCE OWSLEY

MONTGOMERY, ALABAMA

Montgomery became the focus of national attention in February 1861 when the city became the first capital of the Confederate States of America. Situated near the headwaters of the Alabama River, Montgomery had served as the state capital since 1849. Although Mobile was the largest city in Alabama in 1860, Montgomery claimed the next largest population, with about 9,000 citizens, of whom some 4,000 were black. Planters, lawyers, and the more successful entrepreneurs dominated the city. Often they owned slaves. That fact distinguished them from the majority of the citizens who owned no human chattel or other assets of the affluent. Most of Montgomery's population had been born in the United States, although some were of European origin. A few free blacks (seventy in 1860) lived in Alabama's capital city, but the vast majority of blacks were slaves.

Agriculture represented the most important source of wealth, and slaves produced much of that prosperity. The river city, located in Alabama's alluvial black belt, was a center of cotton commerce. Montgomery flourished in the decade preceding the Civil War. Evidence of growth—imposing Italian-style mansions, new churches, a growing popula-

> **The Provisional Constitution provided that until otherwise decided Montgomery would be the [Confederate] capital. . . .**

tion—testified to the prosperity. A theater opened to much acclaim in 1860. By then Montgomery had ceased to be a rough frontier town.

Yet Montgomerians worried about the future. The debate over the extension of slavery threatened to break up the Union. A series of crises, climaxing with Abraham Lincoln's election in 1860, convinced most that secession was necessary, and no city in Alabama was as blatantly secessionist in outlook as Montgomery. William Lowndes Yancey, a resident and fire-eater, had advocated separation as early as 1850. John C. Breckinridge carried the city easily in the election of 1860. Relatively few Montgomerians approved the cautious course recommended by Stephen A. Douglas. Despite having spoken in Montgomery just days before the election, he received only 112 votes.

The national Republican victory led to the establishment of the Confederate States of America. At Montgomery, on January 11, a secessionist convention voted to leave the Union. That decision, rendered in the capitol building, which looked down Market Street, was anticipated, and hundreds of citizens had gathered. Cannon blasts, the raising of flags, pealing church bells, and an extended celebration followed well into the night.

Six lower South states had cut their ties with the Union by the end of January. It remained for those states to form a government. Montgomery hosted the convention that consummated the Confederacy. The city's selection was due largely to its central location and convenient river and railroad facilities. Montgomery was transformed in early February by arriving politicians, soldiers, newspaper reporters, and certainly office seekers. As a *New York Herald* correspondent

observer, Montgomery had "become a focal point of interest to the whole nation" and "when the present times shall have become historic, Montgomery will be read of as the scene of one of the most wonderful revolutions." Visitors jammed the city's two hotels, the Exchange and the Madison House, crowded its dirt streets, and, pleased merchants noted, spent large sums of money.

Convening in the capitol, thirty-seven delegates began secret deliberations on February 4. Within days much of the vital work was completed: the Provisional Constitution was drafted and a vice president, Alexander H. Stephens, and a president, Jefferson Davis, were elected. The arrival of Davis several days later occasioned more festivities. That evening, at the Exchange, Yancey assured the gathered crowd, "the man and hour have met."

The Provisional Constitution provided that until otherwise decided Montgomery would be the capital, and the city took on the trappings of a government seat. A downtown building was converted into an executive complex where Davis and his cabinet members conducted government business. Varina Howell Davis arrived soon, and the first family moved into a two-story residence. The social scene reminded some of Washington. Mary Boykin Chesnut, the famous diarist, described a dinner party as "brilliant," and Howell Cobb, president of the convention, wrote after attending a ball that he had never seen "so ample a repast." In the meantime, Montgomery became the destination of some men who would soon be well known: P. G. T. Beauregard, Raphael Semmes, Joseph E. Johnston, and Braxton Bragg numbered among the visitors.

But in March, war loomed. President Lincoln stated in his inaugural address that the Union was perpetual. Compromising efforts, such as a peace convention, failed, and tension intensified at Fort Sumter when Federal forces refused to evacuate. From Montgomery, on April 12, orders were telegraphed to General Beauregard, and Confederate batteries opened fire on the fort in Charleston Harbor.

The beginning of the war forced a decision on the remaining Southern states in the Union. Within a month, five more states joined the Confederacy. Among them was Virginia and a move was soon underway to make Richmond the capital. Inadequate accommodations in Montgomery and its hot climate motivated some who favored removal. Some members of Congress argued that Virginia's safety, linked to the security of the entire Confederacy, was dependent upon locating the government there. Considerable support existed for maintaining Montgomery as the capital, but on May 20 a vote for removal barely carried.

Montgomery nevertheless remained important to the Confederacy. The city was on a major railroad thoroughfare, and thousands of troops passed through each month, with some entering one of the seven military hospitals. Montgomery also served as a major supply depot. Huge quantities of food, especially corn, were gathered there for the armies. Over the railroad lines leading in and out of the city, supplies were transported to the front. Small arms were also manufactured in Montgomery and a niter works operated.

In 1862, Federal troops occupied parts of northern Alabama and Montgomerians began to fear for their safety. If the enemy overran Mobile, and there was speculation of that, citizens worried about an approach from the south. But it was not until July 1864 that Federal forces threatened central Alabama. Even then Gen. Lovell Rousseau's troops only destroyed railroad track east of Montgomery, temporarily slowing the resupply of Confederate troops defending Atlanta.

A more serious threat materialized in early April 1865. Forces under Gen. James Wilson swept down from northern Alabama and defeated outnumbered Confederates at Selma. The enemy reached Montgomery on April 12. Although defensive works existed, Mayor Andrew Noble surrendered the city without a fight. The Union troops spared Montgomery but did burn some rolling mills and the small arms factory. Montgomery, where the Confederacy had been born, had fallen. On that same day, in Virginia, Robert E. Lee surrendered to Ulysses S. Grant.

[See also *Montgomery Convention*.]

BIBLIOGRAPHY

Flynt, J. Wayne. *Montgomery: An Illustrated History.* Woodland Hills, Calif., 1980.

Jones, James Pickett. *Yankee Blitzkrieg: Wilson's Raid through Alabama and Georgia.* Athens, Ga., 1976.

Napier, John H. "Montgomery during the Civil War." *Alabama Review* 4 (April 1988): 103–131.

Patrick, Rembert. *Jefferson Davis and His Cabinet.* Baton Rouge, La., 1944.

WILLIAM WARREN ROGERS, JR.

MONTGOMERY CONVENTION

Held in Alabama's capitol building from February 4 to May 21, 1861, this convention of delegates from the seven originally seceded states—South Carolina, Georgia, Florida, Alabama, Mississippi, Louisiana, and Texas (whose delegates arrived late)—launched the Confederate government. In addition to choosing a provisional president and vice president, the convention wrote provisional and permanent constitutions and, after organizing itself into a Provisional Congress, passed a spate of legislation to set the machinery of the new government in motion and gear it for war.

Each state in the convention was allowed the same number of delegates as its delegation in the Federal Congress at Washington: one for each representative and two at-large delegates. The convention operated unicamerally, however. Each state was allowed only one vote. Chosen by the secession conventions in their respective states, the vast majority of the fifty men who served in Montgomery were well-to-do planters and lawyers of considerable political experience. Sixty percent were Democrats; the other 40 percent, Whigs. All in all, they comprised a broad cross section of the South's traditional political leadership. The composition of the convention belied the revolutionary nature of the business it was about. Almost half of its delegates were Unionists or cooperationists who had been either outright opponents or at best lukewarm supporters of secession. Fire-eating radicals were distinctly underrepresented at Montgomery.

Because of the convention's decision to hold most of its sessions in secret, both contemporary observers and later historians found it difficult to learn details of the convention's actions and deliberations. Although not popular with the press, the decision for secrecy at Montgomery was never seriously questioned by the delegates. All of them recognized the need to attract foreign recognition of the Confederate States. Presenting a united and self-confident front to the world (including the United States) thus became an overriding imperative at Montgomery. The delegates naturally wanted to minimize any reports of dissension and disagreement among themselves. Equally important was avoiding any hint of precipitousness. At all costs, the Southern experiment had to appear reasoned, moderate, and justified.

It was if anything even more important that it appear this way to the border states. The slave states still remaining in the Union—who though not officially represented at the convention had all sent observers—played a crucial role in its deliberations. Devoted to the American Union, yet bound economically and temperamentally to the lower South, the border states constituted a potential infusion of vast resources for the new Southern nation if they could be induced to join it. Hence their sensitivities and desires had to be consulted at almost every turn.

The Confederate Constitution. After electing Georgian Howell Cobb as president of the convention, the thirty-seven delegates then on hand set about their work with little dissension or debate. On the convention's second day, it adopted rules drawn up by Alexander H. Stephens of Georgia and named a Committee of Twelve headed by Christopher G. Memminger of South Carolina to frame a provisional government. This committee, using a draft Memminger brought with him as a basis, produced the Provisional Constitution in only two days. The convention adopted it unanimously on February 8. On the following day, the convention, sitting now as the Provisional Congress of the Confederate States, named another committee of twelve members (chaired by

Robert Barnwell Rhett, Sr., of South Carolina) to draft a permanent constitution. This committee reported its draft of the permanent Constitution to the Provisional Congress (sitting as a constitutional convention) on the last day of February. Following extensive discussion and the adoption of several amendments, the convention unanimously approved the draft on March 11.

Confronted with the immediate need to reassure the border states of the essential conservatism of their movement, the delegates adopted a fundamental law closely resembling the Constitution of the United States. Indeed, except for a few important differences, it was copied verbatim from that revered document. The main differences were features that more closely guaranteed state rights and protected the institution of slavery. Other changes made minor, but significant improvements in governmental machinery. The preamble bluntly declared that each state acted "in its sovereign and independent character" to form not "a more perfect Union" but a "permanent federal government." State legislatures were allowed to impeach agents of the federal government

> But the overriding necessity for presenting a united front to the world dictated that . . . pre-election politicking be carried out behind closed doors.

acting solely within the boundaries of a state. Nonetheless, state officers were bound by oath to support the Confederate Constitution, which along with Confederate laws and treaties was the "supreme law of the land." Although there was some sentiment for explicitly allowing the right of secession in the document, neither it nor John C. Calhoun's theory of state nullification of Confederate statutes was included.

Avoiding circumlocutions, the Confederate Constitution called a slave a slave. It explicitly protected the institution of slavery in the states and any territories that might be acquired. But in several ways the convention refused to adopt more radical proslavery provisions. For example, the importation of slaves from abroad was prohibited. This provision not only preserved a hallowed prohibition of the old Constitution but also indirectly endorsed the upper South's economic stake in the interstate slave trade. The convention also voted to preserve the three-fifths clause as the basis for apportioning representation in the new Congress. The Confederacy was indeed to be a slaveholding republic, but most of its founding fathers balked at stirring up needless antagonism among nonslaveholders, especially with the destiny of the border states still much in doubt. Nor were extreme Southern nationalists successful in passing an amendment barring free states from future membership in

the Confederacy. Moderates led by Alexander Stephens blocked this move to limit the future expansion of the new republic.

Enshrining two long-held Southern beliefs, the Constitution allowed a tariff for revenue, but not one for protecting domestic enterprises, and it forbade central government appropriations for internal improvements. Other features of the Constitution aimed at greater economy and efficiency in the management of fiscal affairs. Congress was allowed to appropriate money only by a two-thirds vote in both houses, and the amount and purpose of each appropriation had to be explicitly spelled out. The president was allowed a single-item veto of appropriations bills. Although this provision strengthened the executive, as did another that allowed cabinet members nonvoting seats on the floor of Congress, the branch was weakened by limiting the president to a single six-year term. Interestingly, the Confederacy retained the electoral college system to elect its executive officers. Although it was widely disliked, no one could devise a suitable alternative.

Choosing a President and Vice President. The choice of president for the Confederacy engendered the most interest in Montgomery. But the overriding necessity for presenting a united front to the world dictated that the choice be unanimous and that pre-election politicking be carried out behind closed doors. The fact of secrecy not only clouded the process for contemporaries but has made it equally baffling to historians. There was no shortage of qualified candidates. As long-standing secessionists, both William Lowndes Yancey of Alabama and Rhett had good claims on the office. Georgia had three experienced, qualified politicians meriting consideration: Cobb, Stephens, and Robert Toombs. Even Robert M. T. Hunter of Virginia had some support.

For one reason or another none of these candidates was acceptable to the majority. Fire-eaters Yancey and Rhett were anathema to the border state conservatives, whom the delegates in Montgomery studiously avoided offending. The diminutive Stephens, on the other hand, had opposed secession until the very moment Georgia left the Union, and as an ex-Whig, he lacked the proper party pedigree among supporters of the movement for Southern independence. Fiery Robert Toombs suffered the same disability, although he had embraced secession earlier, and he may have further hurt his chances by gross overindulgence in alcohol at Montgomery. Cobb let it be known that he did not want the office. All three Georgians, moreover, suffered the identical stigma of lacking the unanimous endorsement of their own delegation, which was hardly surprising given the deep political and personal animosities among that state's delegates.

From the first there appears to have been a strong current in favor of Jefferson Davis of Mississippi for the presidency. A Democrat and moderate secessionist with experience in the national House and Senate as well as in the cabinet as secretary of war, Davis also had military experience, having graduated from West Point and served with distinction during the Mexican War. Besides being on almost everyone's short list of candidates, Davis had the important endorsements of Virginia's two pro-secession senators, James Mason and Hunter. When the state delegations caucused on the evening of February 8, Mississippi, Florida, and Alabama had lined up solidly behind Davis. By the following morning, only the Georgians remained divided, but to preserve harmony they promptly acquiesced. The convention elected Jefferson Davis provisional president unanimously on the afternoon of Saturday, February 9.

At the same time, it elected Alexander H. Stephens provisional vice president. The choice did not turn out to be a particularly happy one, but as in so many decisions taken at Montgomery, political imperatives overshadowed more practical alternatives. Obviously the most populous and powerful state of the Deep South could not be slighted. And as the foremost antisecessionist in the South, Stephens seemed the logical choice to attract and weld conditional Unionists and cooperationists to the new government. Stephens took the oath of office on February 11; Davis was inaugurated a week later, three days after his arrival in Montgomery.

The Provisional Congress. The Montgomery convention quickly became for the South the successor to the Federal government. After study by committee, it adopted the Stars and Bars as the national flag. It dispatched commissioners to foreign powers and to Washington to negotiate for Federal property within the Confederacy. It passed a law continuing all Federal legislation in force until November 1860, so long as these laws were consistent with the Confederate Constitution or not explicitly repealed by Congress, and it formed a committee to revise U.S. laws to fit the Confederacy. It also voted to retain the existing customs agents in the South.

The most urgent task confronting the convention was organizing and equipping an army. The Provisional Congress had initially created both a Regular Army and a Provisional Army, authorizing the recruitment of 100,000 troops who would serve either six-month or one-year enlistments. After the war started, this number was raised to 400,000 who would serve either for three years or for the duration of the conflict.

Raising money for the new government presented an almost equally pressing problem. Reluctant to strain loyalty by imposing taxes, Congress elected to rely on loans. On February 28, it passed the first major piece of financial legislation: the issue of $15 million worth of twenty-year 8 percent Treasury bonds. The onset of the war required the issue of another $50 million worth of these bonds in mid-May. Because of the dearth of hard money in the South, this law authorized payment for the bonds either in military supplies or with agricultural or manufactured products as well as

specie. This so-called produce loan became a key feature of future Confederate financing. Noteworthy, too, was a provision of the law allowing the Treasury to issue $20 million worth of non-interest-bearing notes, paper currency, which would be redeemable in gold two years after the close of hostilities. This was the first wave in what became a flood of increasingly worthless paper money.

On May 21, Congress elected to move the capital of the Confederacy to Richmond, Virginia, thus bringing the Montgomery convention to a close. On balance, the convention had performed its task admirably. During its three and a half months of existence, it had in relative harmony set up a viable government, elected executive officers for it, produced its fundamental law, and begun the formidable task of setting it on a war footing. It had, in fact, formalized the South's "conservative revolution."

[*See also* Congress; Constitution; Presidency; *and biographies of numerous figures mentioned herein.*]

BIBLIOGRAPHY

Coulter, E. Merton. *The Confederate States of America, 1861–1865.* A History of the South, vol. 7. Baton Rouge, La., 1950.

Lee, Charles Robert, Jr. *The Confederate Constitutions.* Chapel Hill, N.C., 1963.

Randall, J. G., and David H. Donald. *The Civil War and Reconstruction.* 2d ed. Lexington, Mass., 1969.

Thomas, Emory M. *The Confederate Nation: 1861–1865.* New York, 1979.

Yearns, Wilfred B. *The Confederate Congress.* Athens, Ga., 1960.

THOMAS E. SCHOTT

MONUMENTS AND MEMORIALS

[*This entry contains two articles discussing the statues, buildings, parks, and battlefields that honor and preserve the memory of the Confederacy and the Civil War:* An Overview *and* Battlefields. *For further discussion of Confederate monuments and memorials, see* Lee Monument Association; Lost Cause; *and* Memorial Organizations.]

An Overview

On a courthouse lawn stands a single stone soldier, at ease but facing north to challenge any Yankee advance. This stereotype of the Confederate monument has become one of the most common symbols of the South, especially for those from outside the region. Many Confederate monuments do look just like that, but the stereotype ignores the diversity of monument designs and oversimplifies the movement that produced them.

Southerners erected monuments not just to the common soldiers but to prominent Confederate leaders. There are several monuments to Robert E. Lee, the most honored individual, including a recumbent statue at Washington and Lee University, a towering standing figure in New Orleans, and a massive, mounted likeness on Monument Avenue in Richmond, Virginia. Monument Avenue also boasts statues to Matthew Fontaine Maury, J. E. B. Stuart, Thomas J. ("Stonewall") Jackson, and Jefferson Davis. Statues of Davis and Jackson were erected in other cities as well, and their likenesses, along with that of Lee, were carved into the face of Stone Mountain, Georgia, the most massive of Confederate monuments, which was first conceived in 1915 but not completed until 1970.

Long before, Southerners erected still other types of monuments, including a few to Confederate women and one, in Fort Mill, South Carolina, to Confederate Catawba Indians. But most Confederate monuments, as the popular stereotype suggests, honored the memory of the common soldiers. The overwhelming majority were erected in the first fifty years after the war, usually through a popular fund-raising effort led by a local women's memorial association or, later, a United Daughters of the Confederacy (UDC) chapter. The inscriptions these groups chose, of varying lengths and eloquence, praised the Confederate soldiers' honor, devotion to country, and sometimes their cause as well. The form selected for the monuments varied, too, from a towering rock pyramid in Richmond's Hollywood Cemetery to a reclining lion in Atlanta's Oakland Cemetery. Baltimore and at least two other cities chose designs that included an allegorical figure for fame. Despite some diversity, however, patterns in design and placement do emerge and help elucidate the development of the Lost Cause, which produced the monuments.

The first Confederate monument, a simple stone pillar, was erected in a cemetery in Cheraw, South Carolina, in 1867. During the following two decades most towns that dedicated Confederate monuments placed them in cemeteries and chose some sort of funereal design for them, usually an obelisk or other simple shaft, topped by an urn or a draped cloth. In placing funeral statues in cemeteries, and in celebrating the newly established Confederate Memorial Day, Southerners mourned the death not only of beloved friends and relatives but of their cause and would-be nation. Like mourning in other contexts, the process allowed them to assimilate the loss of the war and distance themselves from the failed cause.

In the late 1880s and 1890s, funereal designs became less common in Confederate monuments, and statues of soldiers, not uncommon before, became typical. Some of these statues had intricate bases. Some of the soldiers on them were cast of bronze; a few struck a heroic pose or carried a flag. But the lone marble soldier, standing at rest or even leaning on his rifle, atop a relatively simple shaft came to dominate designs. At about the same time, thoroughfares and, especially after 1900, courthouse lawns replaced cemeteries as the locations usually chosen for Confederate monuments. And the number of monuments erected increased dramatically; the overwhelming majority of Confederate monuments were dedicated between 1895 and 1915. A desire to honor aging veterans before they died no doubt contributed to the increasing pace of memorialization. But the rise in the number of monuments and, more important, the new sites and design selected for them also reflected the growing sense of vindication Southerners felt at the turn of the century. Statues honoring the Confederacy, placed not in an isolated cemetery but in the very center of the community, testified to Southerners' conviction that their cause had been noble and their soldiers heroic and manly. Through their choice of a lone soldier, in effect celebrating a representative faithful common man, Southerners may also have sought to reinforce the values of loyalty to country and deference to leaders at a time of political unrest and social change. Probably this is why there was relatively little renewed sectionalism accompanying the dedication of the monuments. The soldiers on most monuments were symbolically as well as figuratively at rest, and fewer than half of them faced North—most faced the direction the courthouse did.

Commercialism also contributed to the increase in the number of monuments and similarity in design after 1900.

> The soldiers on most monuments were symbolically as well as figuratively at rest, and fewer than half of them faced North. . . .

Two or three companies participated in this, but none more than the McNeal Monument Company. This Marietta, Georgia, firm dispatched traveling agents to drum up business, offering free marble breadboards to officers of UDC chapters who signed with them, promising easy credit terms, and advertising Confederate memorial drinking fountains that combined "Art, Sentiment, and Utility." A few towns actually erected a memorial fountain.

Such commercialization suggests that the popular need for memorialization had begun to decline; after 1915 comparatively few Confederate monuments were erected, although one was put up as late as 1980. As the twentieth century progressed, some existing monuments fell into disrepair or had to be relocated to make way for automobile traffic. More recently, a few Confederate monuments became objects of controversy when African Americans complained that they honored slavery and racism. Monuments, though, have been far less frequently embroiled in controversy than the Confederate flag, perhaps because, unlike the flag, Confederate monuments rarely became symbols of white opposition to civil rights in the 1950s and 1960s. In fact, though Confederate monuments remain prominent in the symbolic landscape of Southern literature, and are a historic part of the physical landscape of the region, and occasionally a Southern town will repair or refurbish its monument and set aside a day of celebration, they hardly seem vital symbols of the modern South.

BIBLIOGRAPHY

Davis, Stephen. "Empty Eyes, Marble Hand: The Confederate Monument and the South." *Journal of Popular Culture* 16 (Winter 1982): 2–21.

Emerson, Bettie A. C. *Historic Southern Monuments: Representative Memorials of the Heroic Dead of the Southern Confederacy.* New Orleans, 1911.

Foster, Gaines M. *Ghosts of the Confederacy: Defeat, the Lost Cause, and the Emergence of the New South, 1865 to 1913.* New York, 1987.

Widener, Ralph W., Jr. *Confederate Monuments: Enduring Symbols of the South and the War between the States.* Washington, D.C., 1982.

Wilson, Charles Reagan. *Baptized in Blood: The Religion of the Lost Cause, 1865–1920.* Athens, Ga., 1980.

Winberry, John J. "'Lest We Forget': The Confederate Monument and the Southern Townscape." *Southeastern Geographer* 23 (November 1983): 107–121.

GAINES M. FOSTER

Battlefields

Civil War monuments, memorials, and parks—much visited reminders of the war—still fire passions, as evidenced by conflicts between Civil War buffs, preservationists, and developers at Manassas and Brandy Station. The first successful effort to protect a Civil War battlefield occurred in 1864. On April 30, ten months after the battle and six months after Abraham Lincoln had spoken his immortal words at the dedication of Soldiers' National Cemetery, the state of Pennsylvania chartered the Gettysburg Battlefield Memorial Association (GBMA) to commemorate the "great deeds of valor . . . and the signal events which render these battle grounds illustrious." The association, composed of members from Northern states that had sent troops into the battle, was interested in acquiring only lands where the Army of the Potomac fought on July 1 through 3, 1863. By 1890, the association had acquired 470 acres.

By the late 1870s Union soldiers and unit associations were becoming interested in memorializing themselves and their comrades on the battlefields where they had fought. The first memorials had been erected by the participants while the guns still roared. In 1861, following their victory at First Manassas, Georgia soldiers positioned a column honoring Col. Francis Barlow, killed in that battle. Twenty months later, in the spring of 1863, soldiers of Col. William B. Hazen's brigade built a monument and wall enclosing the gravesites of their comrades who had fallen in defense of the Round Forest on December 31, 1862, at Murfreesboro. Union troops posted at Vicksburg on July 4, 1864, placed a memorial at the site where on July 3, 1863, Maj. Gen. Ulysses Grant and Lt. Gen. John C. Pemberton met to discuss terms for the Confederate surrender. Then in June 1865, U.S. regulars built two pyramidal stone monuments on the Manassas battlefields—one at the Henry House and the other at the unfinished railroad grade.

Even at the time that Lincoln spoke at Gettysburg, plans were afoot to erect in Soldiers' National Cemetery a national monument. The proposed monument, designed by J. G. Batterson, featured a column crowned by Liberty, with four seated figures at the base representing History, Industry, War, and Prosperity. It was finally dedicated on July 1, 1870. Previous to this, two memorials had been completed and positioned in the cemetery. These were the First Minnesota Urn in 1867 and a statue of Maj. Gen. John E. Reynolds, cast from bronze cannon tubes by the sculptor John Quincy Adams Ward, in August 1872.

No monuments were erected on the GBMA's lands for some fifteen years after the battle. Meanwhile, Union veterans of Gettysburg looked back on the war as the most significant event of their lives, and they took actions to memorialize themselves and their dead comrades. The first unit to do so at Gettysburg was the Second Massachusetts Infantry in 1879, when a lettered granite block was affixed to a boulder positioned near Spangler's Spring. Other regiments and batteries rushed to emulate the Second Massachusetts, and by 1890 more than three hundred memorials and monuments had been sited on lands administered by the GBMA. Nearly $1 million had been expended on this work.

Meanwhile, veterans of the Battle of Chickamauga, following a proposal made by Union veterans H. V. Boynton and Ferdinand Van Derveer, held a reunion at Crawfish Spring in 1889. They organized the Chickamauga Memorial Association to seek the creation of a memorial park that, unlike the one at Gettysburg, would honor both armies and be administered by the U.S. government. The veterans were politically powerful, and with a spirit of reconciliation abroad, Congress acted promptly. On August 19, President Benjamin Harrison, himself a veteran of the Army of the Cumberland in its Tennessee and Georgia campaigns, signed into law a bill establishing Chickamauga and Chattanooga National Military Park, the nation's first. Under the leadership of a three-man commission, lands were purchased, troops' positions determined and marked, roads built, and state memorials and unit monuments erected. On September 18 through

Civil War Battlefields and Monuments Administered by the National Park Service

NAME[1]	LOCATION	DATE ESTABLISHED
Andersonville National Historical Site	Ga.	Oct. 16, 1970
Antietam National Battlefield Site (redesignated a national battlefield, 1978)	Md.	Aug. 30, 1890
Appomattox Courthouse Monument (redesignated a national historical park, 1954)	Va.	June 18, 1930
Arkansas Post National Memorial	Ark.	July 6, 1960
Brice's Cross Roads National Battlefield Site	Miss.	Feb. 2, 1929
Chickamauga and Chattanooga National Military Park	Ga., Tenn.	Aug. 19, 1890
Colonial National Memorial (redesignated a national historical park, 1936)	Va.	July 3, 1930
Cumberland Gap National Historical Park	Ky., Tenn., Va	June 11, 1940
Fort Donelson National Military Park (redesignated a national battlefield, 1985)	Tenn.	Mar. 26, 1928
Fort Jefferson National Monument	Fla.	Jan. 4, 1935
Fort Sumter National Monument	S.C.	Apr. 28, 1948
Fredericksburg and Spotsylvania County Battlefields Memorial National Military Park	Va.	Feb. 14, 1927
Gettysburg National Military Park	Pa.	Feb. 11, 1895
Glorieta Pass Battlefield Unit (addition to Pecos National Historical Park)	N.Mex.	June 27, 1990
Gulf Islands National Seashore	Fla., Miss.	Jan. 8, 1971
Harpers Ferry National Monument (redesignated a national historical park, 1963)	W.Va., Md.	June 30, 1944
Kennesaw Mountain National Battlefield Site (redesignated a national battlefield park, 1935)	Ga.	Feb. 8, 1917
Manassas National Battlefield Park	Va.	May 10, 1940
Monocacy National Battlefield	Md.	Oct. 21, 1976
Pea Ridge National Military Park	Ark.	July 20, 1956
Petersburg National Military Park (redesignated a national battlefield, 1962)	Va.	July 3, 1926
Richmond National Battlefield Park	Va.	Mar. 2, 1936
Rock Creek Park (includes Fort Stevens)	D.C.	Sept. 27, 1890
Shiloh National Military Park	Tenn.	Dec. 27, 1894
Stones River National Military Park (redesignated a national battlefield, 1980)	Tenn.	Mar. 3, 1927
Tupelo National Battlefield Site (redesignated a national battlefield, 1961)	Miss.	Feb. 21, 1929
Vicksburg National Military Park	Miss.	Feb. 21, 1899
Wilson's Creek National Battlefield Park (redesignated a national battlefield, 1970)	Mo.	Apr. 22, 1960

[1] For a list of battles with dual names, see the article *Battles, Naming of.*

20, 1895, the park was dedicated in impressive ceremonies by Vice President Adlai Stevenson before a huge audience that included forty thousand veterans.

Five years before, on August 30, 1890, Congress had authorized an Antietam National Battlefield Site to include only token tracts, scattered about the "landscape turned red," where monuments and markers were to be placed. Then, in late December 1894, President Grover Cleveland signed into law legislation creating Shiloh National Military Park to commemorate the three armies of the Southwest—two Union and one Confederate—on the ground upon which they

fought. Less than two months later, on February 11, 1895, the president approved an act establishing Gettysburg National Park. The lands administered by GBMA were transferred to the United States, and the commission authorized by the legislation moved to acquire lands where both armies fought, mark and memorialize Confederates as well as Union soldiers, and restore the historic scene. On February 21, 1899, Vicksburg National Military Park was authorized.

The landscape of the five Federal Civil War parks created before 1900, unlike those established after 1916, features an unsurpassed collection of military and memorial art—statues, obelisks, temples, busts, reliefs—that date from the mid-1860s to the 1890s. These works of art, numbering in the thousands, were funded by the Federal and state governments, veterans, families and friends, and associations. Their creation provided commissions for sculptors and artists ranging from journeymen to giants such as Augustus St. Gaudens, Daniel Chester French, and Gutzon Borglun. From the 1890s through 1910, these works of art were important sources of income for bronze foundries and stonecutters.

Congress did not create another Civil War military park until 1917, when Kennesaw Mountain National Battlefield Site was established on Cheatham Hill where, three years before, veterans of "Fighting Dan" McCook's brigade had dedicated a monument funded by the state of Illinois. By that time, even the youngest of the veterans were in their mid-seventies and no longer had the clout to campaign and secure money for construction of battlefield monuments.

The two largest and, at the time of their construction most costly, battlefield memorials are the Illinois and the Pennsylvania memorials, the former at Vicksburg and the latter at Gettysburg. The Illinois memorial, resembling Rome's Pantheon, was dedicated in 1906 and features, on bronze and stone tablets, the names, by unit, of 36,290 soldiers from the state who participated in the Vicksburg campaign. The Pennsylvania temple, also listing its sons—approximately 33,000—who fought at Gettysburg, was dedicated in 1910.

At Shiloh in 1917, the United Daughters of the Confederacy's memorial by Frederick Hibbard was unveiled. It features two panels. In relief on the right are the heads of eleven young Southern soldiers as they march into battle, faces bright and heads held high. On the left, the relief depicts the heads of nine Confederates returning from Shiloh, their heads drooping and the fire of battle gone from their eyes. On a center pedestal are two bronze figures representing Death and Darkness snatching the laurels of victory from a third female figure, the Confederacy.

At Chickamauga, unlike the other four nineteenth-century parks, there were until the 1970s no monuments to generals, as this was deemed to be a soldiers' battle. The New York memorial, atop Chattanooga's Lookout Mountain, features a column with two soldiers, Billy Yank and Johnny Reb, with hands clasped in reconciliation. The theme of national reconciliation engendered by joint reunions, the establishment of Federal battlefields, and common sacrifices in the Spanish-American War came to fruition in the early twentieth century. Maryland at Antietam in 1900 and Missouri at Vicksburg in 1917 erected and dedicated imposing memorials honoring on the same structure their sons who fought in blue and in gray.

During the same years (1880–1917) that these major commemorative works were erected, thousands of memorials in stone and bronze appeared on courthouse squares in cities, towns, and villages, North and South, to remember local sons. A number of these—Indianapolis's Soldiers and Sailors Memorial, Boston's tribute to Robert Gould Shaw and the Fifty-fourth Massachusetts, and the memorials honoring Matthew F. Maury, Thomas J. Jackson, Jefferson Davis, Robert E. Lee, and J. E. B. Stuart on Richmond's Monument Avenue—became landmarks of late twentieth-century America, though others are too frequently looked upon merely as traffic problems. They remain, however, reminders of an era in our history when men fought to the death for principles too often out of vogue today.

BIBLIOGRAPHY

Craven, Wayne. *Sculptures at Gettysburg.* Philadelphia, 1982.
Lee, Ronald F. *The Origin and Evolution of the National Military Park Idea.* Washington, D.C., 1973.
Mackintosh, Barry. *The National Parks: Shaping the System.* Washington, D.C., 1991.
Walker, Steve, and David R. Riggs. *Vicksburg Battlefield Monuments.* Jackson, Miss., 1984.

EDWIN C. BEARSS

MOON SISTERS

Virginia B. Moon (1844–1925) and Charlotte Moon Clark (1829–1895) were ardent Confederates from Oxford, Ohio, who carried dispatches between military officers in the Confederacy and Democratic dissenters in Ohio who opposed Lincoln's policies and worked in secret to aid the Confederate cause. In 1862 Lottie, who had married Judge Jim Clark of Hamilton, Ohio, relayed Confederate papers through Union lines to Kentucky; later she carried dispatches from Toronto, Canada, to Virginia, and then to Cincinnati, Ohio. Meanwhile, her younger sister, Ginnie, a resident of Memphis, Tennessee, was serving as a courier in her own right.

Early in 1863 Ginnie was arrested in Cincinnati for carrying Confederate mail and contraband. In her memoirs she proudly reports that she swallowed a secret dispatch from Confederate sympathizers in Ohio intended for Confederate authorities in Mississippi to prevent it from falling into her captors' hands. When Lottie, herself in Cincinnati at the time, heard of Ginnie's predicament, she intervened by appealing to the head of the Union Department of the Ohio, Gen. Ambrose E. Burnside, who happened to be an old suitor of Lottie's. The sisters soon after were cleared of any charges of espionage and paroled in the spring of 1863 to go to their respective homes, where they were kept under surveillance.

The Clarks eventually relocated to New York, where Lottie took up a career as a novelist and journalist. Ginnie served as a Confederate spy in Memphis for a few months after her arrest in Ohio. When Union officers ordered her to leave Memphis, she made her way to Newport News, Virginia, where she was held in custody for a month at Fortress Monroe by Gen. Benjamin Butler. She returned to Memphis after the war. Late in life, she moved to Hollywood, California, and became a motion picture actress.

BIBLIOGRAPHY

Jarecka, Louise L. "Virginia Moon, Unreconstructed Rebel." *Delphian Quarterly* 30 (1947): 17–21.
Kane, Harnett T. *Spies for the Blue and Gray*. New York, 1954.
Smith, Ophia D. *Old Oxford Homes and the People Who Lived in Them*. Oxford, Ohio, 1941.

ELIZABETH R. VARON

MOORE, THOMAS O.

MOORE, THOMAS O. (1804–1876), governor of Louisiana. Moving to Louisiana in his mid-twenties, the North Carolina–born Moore had become the largest sugar planter in Rapides Parish by the eve of the Civil War. A lifelong Democrat, he served on the police jury and then represented this central Louisiana parish in both houses of the state legislature, before winning easy election to the governor's seat in 1859.

He used his office to abet the Louisiana secession movement. Declaring it dishonorable for Louisianans "to live under the government of a Black Republican president," Moore two weeks after Lincoln's election called the legislature into special session in order to prepare for a secession convention election, and he kept up the disunionist momentum by calling out the state militia and ordering it to seize Federal property before Louisiana had officially left the Union. The martial activity intimidated many Louisiana Unionists.

Until Maj. Gen. Richard Taylor (Zachary's son) was made head of the Department of Louisiana in July 1862, Moore functioned as both chief executive officer and military commander of Louisiana. After the April 1862 capture of New Orleans, however, Moore's effective authority seldom reached beyond northern Louisiana. Moore made indigent relief, especially for soldiers' families, an urgent priority of his administration. The militia and state finances also absorbed much of his attention. Like many Confederate governors, Moore wrangled with Richmond over troop deployments, military supplies, and local defenses. He once withheld arms from the Southern army. But Moore also tried to consolidate Confederate nationalism by banning illicit trade with Union-occupied territory and sponsoring "Confederate Associations" to boost morale and patriotism.

After leaving office, Moore refugeed in Texas in 1864, fled to Mexico and Cuba in 1865, returned to his devastated Rapides plantation in 1866, and died at his home in 1876.

Though ranking him below his successor, Henry Watkins Allen, historians generally believe Moore's stewardship of Confederate Louisiana deserves more credit than it has received.

BIBLIOGRAPHY

Bragg, Jefferson Davis. *Louisiana in the Confederacy*. Baton Rouge, La., 1941.
Cassidy, Vincent H. "Louisiana." In *The Confederate Governors*. Edited by W. Buck Yearns. Athens, Ga., 1985.
Davis, Edwin Adams. *Heroic Years: Louisiana in the War for Southern Independence*. Baton Rouge, La., 1964.
Odom, Van D. "The Political Career of Thomas Overton Moore, Secession Governor of Louisiana." *Louisiana Historical Quarterly* 26 (October 1943): 975–1054.
Owsley, Frank. *State Rights in the Confederacy*. Chicago, Ill., 1925. Reprint, Gloucester, Mass., 1961.

LAWRENCE N. POWELL

MORALE

Like an army that cannot fight on without rations, a new nation fighting for its very existence cannot maintain the struggle without strong, sustaining morale among its military and civilian populations. Thus morale was of vital importance to the Confederacy. The Southern nation obviously possessed spirit enough to engage in four years of a war that was the bloodiest and most destructive in U.S. history. Yet it can be said that Confederate morale proved deficient. During the Civil War the South's morale underwent a disastrous decline until ultimately, as historian Charles Wesley argued long ago, the collapse of the Confederacy came from within. Although no single factor by itself explains the South's defeat in a massive, complex, and multifaceted struggle, morale lay at the heart of the Confederacy's demise. Many scholars today view morale as the Achilles heel of the South in the grinding war it had to fight.

Before the first guns fired on Fort Sumter, Confederate morale was high, but a closer examination reveals that popular sentiments were neither uncomplicated nor untroubled. The South had traveled a long, rough, and somewhat unlikely road to secession. Throughout the 1850s only a small minority of radicals had desired the breakup of the Union, and their calls for a united stand by all the Southern states were ignored. After Abraham Lincoln won the presidential election in 1860, the strategy of separate state secession unfolded. Led by South Carolina, six Deep South states left the Union and formed a new confederacy. But even in the

Deep South public opinion had been closely divided in states such as Georgia and Louisiana, and strong Unionist feelings existed elsewhere, as in Alabama. Moreover, crucial upper South states had refused to join the new nation.

Scholars have drawn different conclusions about this situation, but its significance for Confederate nationalism and unity should not be missed. Charles Roland, after surveying the secession of the lower South states, declared that they were "swept out by a great emotional folk movement. Notwithstanding the presence of large Unionist minorities in some of the states, it is doubtful that any similar political rupture in modern history has been supported by as high a proportion of the population."

Roland is probably right, yet in July of 1861 the *Richmond Examiner* stated a different and equally valid view. "Loyal as the great mass of our people are," wrote the *Examiner*'s editors, "there is yet no doubt that the South is more rife with treason to her own independence and honour than any community that ever engaged before in a struggle with an adversary." The Confederate States were in the process of forming a new government and nurturing new loyalties. Those profoundly committed to a Southern nation were few, whereas those who loved the Union and left it reluctantly were many. The solidification of Southern nationalism still lay ahead.

Regional Loyalty versus Confederate Nationalism

With the outbreak of hostilities, a large portion of the slaveholding upper South quickly entered the Confederate fold. Yet the accession of Virginia, North Carolina, Tennessee, and Arkansas to the cause only made the task of building Confederate nationalism more challenging. These states, faced by the necessity of choosing sides, had acted upon a strong sense of regional loyalty. Identification with the South, however, was not the same thing as dedication to a Confederate nation. In the upper South and elsewhere, moderate and substantially Unionist sentiments had to be turned in a new direction and harnessed for a new cause. A Confederate identity had to evolve from Southernness, and devotion to a new nation had to replace loyalty to revered American traditions.

These facts dictated the selection of moderate leaders and conservative policies at Montgomery. Fire-eating radicals, such as William Lowndes Yancey of Alabama who had pioneered in Union-hating and calls for secession, were omitted from high positions. Their day was over, and the task of consolidating a much more diverse and moderate public opinion, marked by historic affection for the Union, was at hand. President Jefferson Davis took the essential first step toward building a sense of Confederate nationalism by portraying the new Southern nation as the true carrier of American traditions. In the face of a degenerate, aggressive North, Davis argued, the Confederacy had become the guardian of the Founding Fathers' legacy. The purpose of the new Southern nation was to "perpetuate the principles" of American constitutional liberty.

This appeal to traditional national values helped unite a region faced with imminent invasion. After Lincoln called for troops, Unionists and secessionists joined together in defense of their threatened home, the South. An outpouring of regional loyalty produced 500,000 volunteers for military service in the summer of 1861—more men than the Confederate government could arm or equip and more than it would subsequently field at any one time. Morale was strong and robust.

The Phases of Morale

Yet the spirit of Confederate nationalism needed further development, or its weakness might become apparent. Events on the battlefield, on the home front, and in the halls

> **The Confederate victory at First Manassas produced jubilation and some unrealistic expectations.**

of government would have a great effect on national unity and popular morale. To understand this process, one must consider both the phases of Southern morale and the forces that affected it positively or negatively.

Early Optimism. In the summer of 1861 the morale of the Southern people was running at high tide. Swept along by the strong wave of loyalty to their region, Southerners joined the army and prepared for their first battle. The Confederate victory at First Manassas produced jubilation and some unrealistic expectations. By fall the massive preparations of the enemy had tempered overoptimistic emotions, and some disputes had arisen within the Confederacy that pointed to future difficulties. But the government of the new nation was becoming an organized fact, the South had fielded impressive armies of its own, and no major disaster had befallen the cause. Unfortunately for Confederate patriots, however, this period of enthusiasm and high hopes lasted only until the spring of 1862.

The Reality of War Intrudes. Around April of 1862 a second phase of Confederate morale began, one that would last until July 1863. In this phase unpleasant realities began to crowd out initial high hopes, and totally unexpected aspects of life in the Confederacy made themselves felt. Conscription signaled the beginning of these new facts. For the first time in American history, the central government passed laws to compel its citizens to serve in the armies. Necessity required Confederate leaders to take this step because bounties, furloughs, and other inducements had failed to lure new enlistments. Ordinary citizens who had joined the army for a year now wanted to return home and plant their crops. "The spirit of volunteering had died out," admitted Secretary of War James A. Seddon.

In this second phase other internal and external problems of fundamental importance to morale appeared. Bitter disputes over questions of policy arose, as the potent issue of state rights reared its head. A growing, activist central government displeased both planters and leaders who had expected something very different in a Southern government. At the same time, Confederate policies generated deep divisions in the population along class lines. Financial and economic difficulties deepened, and the first food riots occurred in Southern cities.

On the battlefield Southern troops won some victories, but Union forces made significant territorial gains, especially with the fall of New Orleans and Forts Henry and Donelson. Any hope for a brief war was fading, and reasons to doubt the Confederacy's staying power were multiplying. When Confederate offensives into Maryland and Kentucky both

> **Lee's defeat in Pennsylvania shattered all hopes of winning . . . independence through successful offensive action.**

failed in the fall of 1862, Jefferson Davis had cause to remark that Southerners were entering "the darkest and most dangerous period we have yet had."

Thus from April 1862 to July 1863 the skies over the new nation were darkening. Yet in this period the Confederacy also marshaled its strength and resisted the forces weakening it. Government measures largely stemmed desertion from the armies, and the military situation was far from hopeless. On occasion, a notable success, such as the victory at Chancellorsville, stimulated hopes for a revival of Confederate fortunes. The decline in morale had not become uncontrollable.

Impact of Vicksburg and Gettysburg. A third and far more ominous phase in Confederate morale arrived with the shocking defeats at Vicksburg and Gettysburg in July 1863. It took some days for accurate news of these disasters to reach the population, but once they did, no one could deny their depressing significance. Robert E. Lee's defeat in Pennsylvania shattered all hopes of winning Confederate independence through successful offensive action. The strongest Southern army had been driven back and had no option thereafter but to assume a defensive posture. Any realistic hope of foreign recognition and aid, long sought but already unlikely, had to be given up. With the capture of Vicksburg, the Confederacy itself was cut in two. The resources of the Trans-Mississippi West fell out of reach, and

the Gulf states lay open to Federal invasion from armies in Mississippi or Tennessee. Jefferson Davis admitted that these defeats submerged him "in the depths of . . . gloom," and so dedicated a Confederate as Josiah Gorgas confided to his diary, "Today absolute ruin seems our portion. The Confederacy totters to its destruction."

After this turning point, internal forces of disintegration outpaced the government's efforts to hold the Confederacy together. On the home front, resistance to conscription and impressments grew rapidly. As poverty deepened, thousands of suffering yeoman families quietly withdrew their support from the cause, and more politically active Confederates, particularly in North Carolina and Georgia, began to agitate openly for peace. The army's strength, which had already begun to fall, now plunged sharply downward as the flow of deserters widened into a racing stream. The government began using detachments of seasoned troops to round up concentrations of deserters, but without permanent effect.

The words of Confederate officials documented this increasingly desperate, third phase of morale. Assistant Secretary of War John A. Campbell asked on July 25, 1863, whether "so general a habit" as desertion should be considered a crime when some 40,000 to 50,000 men were absent without leave and 100,000 evaded duty in some manner. On November 26, 1863, Secretary of War Seddon reported that "the effective force of the Army is generally a little more than a half, never two-thirds, of the numbers in the ranks." By the middle of 1864 the army's strength had fallen to 195,000 present out of 316,000 enrolled. Senator Herschel Johnson of Georgia advised Jefferson Davis in 1864 that "the disposition to avoid military service is . . . general," and Maj. S. B. French reported at the end of this period that "in all the States impressments are evaded by every means which ingenuity can suggest, and in some openly resisted."

Morale was very low, but the Confederate cause was not yet seen as hopeless, for the North also was war-weary and staggering beneath the conflict's heavy burdens. Abraham Lincoln sometimes despaired of his reelection, and pro-peace elements in the Democratic party were working hard to control their party's platform and presidential nomination. Jefferson Davis pursued a strategy of encouraging Northern peace advocates while doing everything that could be done to present the stiffest possible resistance on the battlefield. State leaders joined Davis in predicting extermination and degradation at the hands of a depraved enemy unless the South prevailed. The end of this policy, and of the third phase in Confederate morale, approached as William Tecumseh Sherman's troops neared Atlanta.

Morale at Low Tide. "Our all depends on that army," wrote Mary Boykin Chesnut. "If that fails us, the game is up." Unfortunately for Confederates, she was right. Atlanta fell, and the Richmond war clerk J. B. Jones lamented that "our fondly-cherished visions of peace have vanished like a mirage of the desert." Although Jefferson Davis exhorted his countrymen to fight on, he had to admit that "two-thirds of our men are absent . . . most of them absent without leave." Not long after Sherman's strategic breakthrough, Lincoln won reelection, and Southerners knew that Confederate defeat was only a matter of time.

In this final phase in the level of morale, most sources of support for the Confederacy were evaporating. Only the central government and those determined soldiers who stayed with the armies remained resolute. For a few more months the government tried desperate expedients and brave men in gray fought on, but most Southerners were resigned to defeat before Lee arrived at Appomattox.

Forces Affecting Morale

The spirit of Confederates was tested in many ways during the Civil War. Events naturally affected morale as Southern armies met defeats in battle and as Union pressure helped damage a mismanaged economy. But internal forces also had a serious impact on morale. Opposition to the government flourished among both planters and small farmers, and class resentments among the poor caused a steadily increasing number to withdraw their support from the war effort.

The Effect of the War. It is self-evident that defeats on the battlefield worked powerfully to depress Confederate morale. The Confederacy was a beleaguered new nation, and after the first year no Southerner could deny that the cause was losing ground. As time went on, the lengthening litany of defeats eroded confidence among even the stoutest patriots. The connection between military reverses and declining morale is manifest in the correlation between key defeats and trends in desertion. Moreover, it was inevitable that the human cost of the South's struggle for independence would produce a reaction. As the world marveled at the unprecedented carnage Americans were inflicting on one another, hundreds of thousands of Southern homes went into deep mourning. In America's bloodiest war, the South bore the brunt of destruction.

There was another, paradoxical side, however, to the effects of war. Armed conflict strengthened Southern morale by creating an intense and unifying hatred of the enemy. War always forces its combatants to depersonalize the foe in order to cope with the psychological trauma of killing, and civilians share in this process. Moreover, hostile images of the Yankee had long been current in Southern culture. The Civil War provided reason to magnify these negative images enormously. Cultural conceptions of honor contributed to the process, as Southerners judged their opponents by standards the latter did not share.

Confederate political leaders did all they could to intensify these attitudes. From the first days of the Confederacy, Jefferson Davis depicted the United States as a consolidat-

ed despotism where corruption reigned and freedom was extinguished. Soon after the fighting started, he began a steady practice of denouncing the Union as an uncivilized, inhuman, and brutal foe. Governors and state legislators added bitter criticisms of the "ruthless barbarity" of an enemy that intended to impose the vilest forms of subjugation upon the South. To the *Charleston Mercury,* Northerners were "civilized savages . . . plunderers, liars, fanatics." When other newspapers, such as the *Richmond Enquirer,* spoke of Northerners' "extreme malignity toward us," they were accelerating a potent social process. Southerners were unifying themselves by defining their foe as so hateful and despicable that no thought of reunion could be entertained. In this way, the war generated feelings that supported Confederate morale and endured long after the Confederate government disappeared.

Confederate Policy and Planters. Another factor affecting morale involved fundamental problems related to the class system and the economy. These caused so much frustration and resentment that many questioned whether the government deserved their support. An indicator of the severity of the Confederacy's social problems is the fact that dissatisfaction appeared from an early date at the two extremes of the social scale. For differing reasons, both wealthy planters and small yeoman farmers became alienated from the cause.

The large plantation owners discovered that life under the Southern government was shockingly different from their expectations. They had sought to insulate their holdings from change, to guard their world against the intrusions of "Black Republicans." In order to shield slavery and plantation agriculture, they had embarked on a quest for independence that involved them in a massive war. But soon it became evident that the necessities of fighting the war clashed radically with the ends they pursued.

Davis's administration sought firmly and resolutely to build the strong central government needed to fight the North.

> **. . . after the first year no Southerner could deny that the cause was losing ground.**

Control of the armies, conscription of men, impressment of supplies, and suspension of the writ of habeas corpus showed by early 1862 that the Confederate government was going to lead with a strong hand. Davis sincerely believed that all his measures were constitutional, especially given the government's powers to make war and raise armies. But such steps surprised many in the planter class. They had expected a weak and limited central government in a nation devoted to state rights. Instead they saw a behemoth in

Richmond whose bureaucracy became larger, in proportion to population, than the government of the North.

Moreover, this central government adopted policies that intruded directly into the affairs of each plantation. Not content with impressing goods, the Confederacy began to impress slaves. Despite the fears of slave owners concerning the treatment of their valuable property, the government commandeered slave labor to dig trenches, build fortifications, and otherwise assist the armies. Davis supported efforts to change what the planters grew by urging them to shift from cotton to food crops. Whenever Federal forces moved deeper into the Confederacy, army officers confiscated planters' stores of cotton and burned it to keep it from falling into the hands of the enemy. By 1863 the tax-in-kind was taking from planters and other farmers a portion of all their food crops. In 1864 new legislation required planters, as a means of keeping their overseers, to promise under bond to provide one hundred pounds of bacon and one hundred pounds of beef for each able-bodied slave. The government had become directly involved in plantation affairs.

These policies caused consternation and provoked harsh attacks on the government in the political arena. Early in the war representatives of the planter class began to express profound ideological dissatisfaction with the central government. Georgia's governor, Joseph E. Brown, who charged that conscription controverted "all the principles for which Georgia entered into this revolution," was the policy's most outspoken critic, but he was not the only one. Congressmen and newspaper editors joined in denouncing the South's new government as traitorous to the Confederacy's basic purposes. The *Charleston Mercury,* for example, quoted Linton Stephens with approval in 1862 when he condemned conscription as "the very embodiment of Lincolnism, which our gallant armies are today resisting."

Jefferson Davis defended his policies and put them into operation despite the opposition. Eventually, as the Confederacy's situation became more desperate, a few critics realized that Davis and the South had no alternative and dampened their criticism. But much damage had been done to Confederate morale. Leaders of public opinion had questioned the legitimacy of their new government and argued, in effect, that it was unworthy of the people's allegiance. Such criticism did more than express planters' dissatisfaction. It depressed morale generally and impeded the process of building support for the new nation.

The Deteriorating Economy. The serious financial and economic problems of the Confederacy also damaged morale for common citizens as well as planters. The government held little specie, raised very little revenue through taxes (partly because planters objected to them), and printed far too much money. As a result uncontrollable inflation ravaged the economy. Moreover, shortages of many commodities that the South was accustomed to buy from Europe

or the North quickly developed. Hoarding made shortages worse, and profiteering aggravated the inflation of prices. The economic situation deteriorated steadily and caused many in disgust to condemn the government.

If these economic setbacks were inconvenient for wealthy planters, they were devastating to poorer white citizens. Although small farmers were largely self-sufficient in normal times, most needed a few essential items they could not produce. Salt was a vital preservative for meat, and most families also purchased such items as coffee, sugar, some clothing, and tools. Inflation and shortages quickly drove prices of these commodities out of reach, and instances of hoarding enraged the citizenry. The governors of several states denounced speculation, and newspapers joined in the outcry over greed and the lack of patriotism. In 1861 the *Richmond Examiner* declared, "This disposition to speculate upon the yeomanry of the country . . . is the most mortifying feature of the war." One year later it judged "native Southern merchants" as worse than Yankees and lamented, "The whole South stinks with the lust of extortion." The Rome, Georgia, *Weekly Courier* quoted the Bible against extortioners, and the *Atlanta Daily Intelligencer* warned that because of extortion, "want and starvation are staring thousands in the face."

In fact, the causes of hunger went beyond hoarding and profiteering. Drought or crop failures occurred in years of war as well as peace and naturally depressed morale. But in addition the Confederacy itself sometimes seemed responsible for suffering, as families were victimized by impressment or abuses by the military. Florida's governor complained that soldiers had taken the last milk cows from starving families of soldiers, and in 1864 Secretary of War Seddon admitted that "the most scandalous outrages" had occurred in Mississippi. One woman wrote that the troops camped on her land had not hesitated to "catch up the fowls before my eyes." Commenting in 1862, the *Richmond Enquirer* reported, "We often hear persons say, 'The Yankees cannot do us any more harm than our own soldiers have done.'"

Even more serious was the shortage of labor on small farms caused by volunteering and conscription. An early warning sign of this problem was the flood of letters in 1861 from rural districts lamenting the absence of blacksmiths and other artisans. Soon thereafter many more nonslaveholding families began to appeal for exemptions or furloughs of the husbands or sons who were their chief source of labor. Increasingly on one-man farms, wives and children found that they could not keep up the work of cultivation unaided. As the Edgefield, South Carolina, *Advertiser* explained, "The duties of war have called away from home the sole supports of many, many families. . . . Help must be given, or the poor will suffer." A desperate woman named Elizabeth Leeson wrote to Secretary of War Seddon in 1863: "I ask [you] in the name of humanity to discharge my husband[;] he is not able to do your government much good and he might do his children some good. . . . The rich has aplenty to work for them." The suffering of soldiers' families was a critical danger to the Confederacy. Military and political officials agreed that letters from suffering loved ones led to many desertions. As an anonymous Virginian wrote to Secretary of War Seddon, "What man is there that would stay in the armey and [k]no[w] that his family is sufring at home?"

Hunger and speculation were destroying people's morale. One acquaintance of Jefferson Davis advised the president that speculation was "the cause of thousands of good men leaving their posts." In 1863 an enrolling officer reported from the hill country of South Carolina that previously loyal citizens were supporting deserters. Citing "the speculations and extortions so rampant throughout the land," he wrote that these civilians "swear by all they hold sacred that they will die at home before they will ever be dragged forth again to do battle for such a cause."

Class Resentment. The most corrosive factor in the decline of yeoman morale was class resentment, a sense of class injustice. Elizabeth Leeson had voiced the feeling that her family was sacrificing heavily while rich slaveholders had "aplenty to work for them." Perhaps this aspect of "a rich man's war and a poor man's fight" was unavoidable, given the fact that most Southern whites did not own slaves. But Confederate laws and policies magnified the advantage possessed by slaveholders and convinced many nonslaveholders that they were being asked to do much more than their fair share. Nothing damaged Confederate morale more than this conviction of class discrimination and social injustice. The outcry against unfair government policies was intense.

Objections to favoritism in the raising of troops arose in the summer of 1861. After volunteers began to exceed the Confederacy's supply of arms, the government announced that it would arm and accept only long-term volunteers. Companies that could arm and equip their own men, however, were still allowed to enroll for only twelve months' service. In practice, only wealthier men could bear the costs of raising twelve-month units. This policy, admitted Albert T. Bledsoe, chief of the Bureau of War, created "no little dissatisfaction in the country." William Brooks, the presiding officer at Alabama's secession convention, reported that leading men had struggled to encourage enlistments among nonslaveholders in Perry County. Just when leaders had "partially" changed the sentiments of men who "not unfrequently declared that they will 'fight for no rich man's slaves,'" the Confederacy declared its new policy. These "poor laboring men," Brooks pointed out, compared their lot to "slaveholders [who] can enter the army and quit it at the end of twelve months. . . . I leave you to imagine the consequences."

Angry feelings proliferated with the adoption of conscription. The law provided for exemptions for the disabled or unfit and for a variety of occupations, such as transportation workers, miners, and state and Confederate officials. Complaints of favoritism in the application of the law arose almost immediately. Officeholders tended to be from the upper classes, and some states declared that thousands of them were essential to the operation of the government. Careless administration of the law also produced inequities. An anonymous Georgian, for example, complained to the War Department that it was "a notorious fact if a man has influential friends—or a little money to spare he will never be enrolled." Judge Robert S. Hudson of Mississippi warned President Davis that incompetence or favoritism by enrolling

> **Many nonslaveholders already believed that the war's benefits would accrue primarily to slaveholders. . . .**

officers had created much "disloyalty, discontent, and desertions." In 1864 Congressman Robert Henry Whitfield of Virginia urged an investigation of exemption boards in the name of "common justice to the poor and uninfluential."

Far more serious was the resentment created by two other features of the conscription law: substitution and the exemption of overseers. The government permitted a conscript, if he had the means, to hire someone to go to war in his place. To the *Richmond Examiner* this ability to pay for a substitute was "the best proof of the citizen's social and industrial value," but, needless to say, many poorer citizens regarded it as an unjust privilege for the rich. Mary Boykin Chesnut wrote in her diary about planters' sons who had "spent a fortune in substitutes," and Confederate documents recorded that at least fifty thousand men escaped the dangers of battle by hiring a substitute. As early as 1862 Secretary of War George Wythe Randolph condemned the "great abuses" of substitution, which had become "a regular business," but not until the beginning of 1864 did Congress end this divisive and unpopular system.

The exemption of overseers, which had been demanded by planters and state officials, created an even greater storm of protest. Because Congress, in October 1862, exempted one white man for every twenty slaves under his supervision, this statute soon was denounced as the "twenty-nigger law." Many nonslaveholders already believed that the war's benefits would accrue primarily to slaveholders; now it seemed that slaveholders would also avoid the war's dangers. "Never did a law meet with more universal odium," observed one congressman, "than the exemption of slave-owners. . . . Its influence upon the poor is most calamitous, and has awakened a spirit and elicited a discussion of which we may safely predict the most unfortunate results." The legislature of North Carolina soon bowed to popular pressure and protested to Congress about the "unjust discrimination" of the law, but Congress enacted only mild restrictions on the exemption of overseers. Planters gladly paid a tax imposed on overseers, who thus continued to enjoy safety in a war that was killing unprecedented numbers of Southerners. The situation fed a popular impression, as Senator James Phelan of Mississippi observed, that "nine tenths of the youngsters of the land whose relatives are conspicuous in society, wealthy, or influential obtain some safe perch where they can doze with their heads under their wings."

Meanwhile, the families of nonslaveholding soldiers faced grinding poverty and suffering. The Confederate government, struggling against enormous problems, was not providing the essentials of economic or physical security. Moreover, as the conviction spread that government policies were discriminatory and unjust, the Confederacy's demands for sacrifice increased. These pressures on morale became insupportable. Coupled with growing evidence of defeat on the battlefield, class resentments and the sheer difficulty of surviving in the Confederacy caused hundreds of thousands of citizens to withdraw their active support from the war effort.

In March 1864, an impressment officer in South Carolina encountered an uncooperative and frustrated citizen. "The sooner this damned Government [falls] to pieces," he said, "the better it [will] be for us." He was ready to compromise and "get back into the old Union." Like most Southerners, this man had sacrificed much for the cause, and he probably had little love for Yankees. But he was one of many whose patience was exhausted. He was angered by the unexpected or unfair policies of his government and disgusted by its inability to provide basic economic or physical security. For him, as for most Southerners, loyalty to his region had not grown into a sustaining devotion to Confederate nationalism. The corrosive and depressing forces that sapped morale had proven too great.

[*See also* Bread Riots; Class Conflict; Conscription; Desertion; Extortion; Impressment; Inflation; Nationalism; Poverty; Speculation; Taxation.]

BIBLIOGRAPHY

Beringer, Richard, Herman Hattaway, Archer Jones, and William N. Still, Jr. *Why the South Lost the Civil War.* Athens, Ga., 1986.

Escott, Paul D. *After Secession: Jefferson Davis and the Failure of Confederate Nationalism.* Baton Rouge, La., 1978.

Lonn, Ella. *Desertion during the Civil War.* New York, 1928. Reprint, Gloucester, Mass., 1966.

Owsley, Frank L. *State Rights in the Confederacy.* Chicago, 1925. Reprint, Gloucester, Mass., 1961.

Ramsdell, Charles W. *Behind the Lines in the Southern Confederacy.* Edited by Wendell H. Stephenson. Baton Rouge, La., 1944.

Silver, James W. *Confederate Morale and Church Propaganda.* Tuscaloosa, Ala., 1957.

Tatum, Georgia Lee. *Disloyalty in the Confederacy.* Chapel Hill, N.C., 1934. Reprint, New York, 1970.

Thomas, Emory M. *The Confederate Nation, 1861–1865.* New York, 1979.

Wesley, Charles H. *The Collapse of the Confederacy.* Washington, D.C., 1937.

Wiley, Bell Irvin. *The Plain People of the Confederacy.* Baton Rouge, La., 1943. Reprint, Gloucester, Mass., 1971.

PAUL D. ESCOTT

MOREHEAD, JOHN MOTLEY

MOREHEAD, JOHN MOTLEY (1796–1866), North Carolina governor and congressman. Morehead was born in Pittsylvania County, Virginia, July 4, 1796. In his infancy he moved with his family to Rockingham County, North Carolina, and graduated in 1817 from the University of North Carolina, where he demonstrated a remarkable flair for scholarship. Two years later he was licensed to practice law and was elected from Rockingham County to serve in the Virginia House of Commons in 1821 and 1822. Upon moving to Guilford County to practice law, he represented Guilford in the House from 1826 to 1828.

In 1835 he sat as a delegate to his state's constitutional convention where he worked on behalf of efforts to reform the system of representation in order to promote greater equality between eastern and western sections of the state. His early identification with the stimulation of railroad building and other internal improvements—particularly for the western counties—drew him from the Jacksonian wing of the Democratic party into a position of leadership in the Whig party. In 1840 and 1842 he was elected to two terms as governor. Again, he gave his best efforts to foster railways and waterways against the strong (and sometimes successful) opposition of his Democratic foes.

After retiring from the governorship, Morehead again devoted himself to business and his law practice, serving for several years as president of the North Carolina Railroad and as an organizer of the Western North Carolina Railroad. From 1859 to 1861 he was returned to the general assembly.

A slave owner himself, he candidly expressed disapproval of the institution on moral grounds but shrank from association with abolitionists because, he was at pains to point out, the system was an existing fact, recognized by federal and state constitutions and statutes, and because, he warned, the hasty and forced liquidation of slavery would produce civil, social, and economic convulsions.

In the presidential election of 1860 Morehead supported John Bell, the nominee of the Constitutional Union party, and upon Abraham Lincoln's election denied that this turn of events in and of itself justified secession of the slave states. Indeed, as the crisis deepened he still declared himself a conservative, opposed to the dissolution of the Union. He gladly accepted appointment to serve as the head of North Carolina's five-man delegation to the Washington peace conference of February 1861. "I came here to act for the Union—the whole Union," he said upon his arrival. "I recognize no *sides,* no party."

While he was in Washington, his state voted on February 28 on the question of calling a convention to consider secession. His own county voted 2,771 to 113 against holding a convention, and the state at large, though by a much smaller majority, also voted in the negative. Tempers continued to rise, however, and a special session of the legislature on its own motion voted to convoke a convention to meet on May 20. There an ordinance of secession was adopted and the state ratified the Constitution of the Confederate States.

The failure of the Washington conference to achieve an accommodation was a heavy disappointment to Morehead. Though he continued to resist the secession movement, nevertheless when his state did secede he became a sturdy Confederate loyalist and remained so throughout the war.

Before the legislature adjourned on May 28, it elected eight delegates, including State Senator Morehead, to sit in the Provisional Congress. That body had, by this time, already completed two sessions in Montgomery, Alabama. It was not until the next session commencing on July 20 in Richmond that Morehead and his North Carolina associates took their seats. The Provisional Congress ceased to exist on February 17, 1862, and with that, Morehead's formal political career closed after forty years of public life. He died in 1866 and was buried in the Greensboro, North Carolina, First Presbyterian Church, which later became the Greensboro Historical Museum.

Some authorities argue that though Morehead's brief participation in the Confederate Congress was relatively

> **"I came here to act for the Union—the whole Union. . . . I recognize no *sides,* no party."**

obscure, he exerted real influence unofficially through his personal association with President Jefferson Davis, who looked upon him as a trusted friend and adviser. He also served as North Carolina's member of the Congress's Committee on the Financial and Commercial Independence of the Confederate States, and it was in that capacity that he played an important role in securing the extension of the Richmond and Danville Railroad from the Confederate capital to Greensboro, North Carolina.

Perhaps Morehead's principal service to the Confederacy was rendered long before the secession crisis, in the form of his sponsorship of internal improvements, especially rail-

roads, in North Carolina in the 1840s and 1850s. These provided crucial links in the future Confederacy's transportation lines, which proved in time to be of critical importance in shaping the Confederacy's economic and social development and in adding to its ability to wage war.

Morehead was, by contemporary accounts, a man of impressive persona, with a gift for persuasive oratory. He is usually ranked as one of the state's strongest nineteenth-century governors, and his principal biographer has characterized him as the "Father of Modern North Carolina."

BIBLIOGRAPHY

Konkle, Burton Alva. *John Motley Morehead and the Development of North Carolina.* Raleigh, N.C., 1922.
Powell, William S., ed. *Dictionary of North Carolina Biography.* Vol. 4. Chapel Hill, N.C., 1990.

RICHARD BARDOLPH

MORGAN, JOHN HUNT

MORGAN, JOHN HUNT (1825–1864), brigadier general and guerrilla raider. Born June 1, 1825, in Huntsville, Alabama, Morgan grew up in Lexington, Kentucky, where he attended Transylvania University. In the Mexican War he fought as a first lieutenant in the Kentucky cavalry, participating in the Battle of Buena Vista, February 23, 1847. A manufacturer of hemp in Lexington, Morgan organized and commanded an artillery company in the state militia from 1852 through 1854. In 1857 he formed the Lexington Rifles, a volunteer infantry company that joined the pro-Southern state guard militia in 1860. A Confederate from the beginning, he wired President Jefferson Davis on April 16, 1861, offering to serve as a recruiter. He raised a Confederate flag on his woolen factory, declaring that henceforth he would sell only uniforms of Confederate gray. When Kentucky decided to stay in the Union, he and the Lexington Rifles left for the war on September 20, 1861, rendezvousing with two hundred other men at Bloomfield, Kentucky. The group elected Morgan to lead them to Confederate lines in western Kentucky.

From October 1 to October 27, 1861, he conducted raids behind the lines on his own authority. Then, on October 27, he was sworn in and elected captain of a cavalry company. Continuing guerrilla warfare, he had, by March 1862, achieved many small victories that made him a famous folk hero, the "Francis Marion of the war." To many Southerners he represented the ideal of the romantic cavalier. His success inspired the popular movement for guerrilla war that culminated in the Partisan Ranger Act of April 21, 1862, which authorized the president to commission companies, battal-

JOHN HUNT MORGAN. LIBRARY OF CONGRESS

ions, and regiments to conduct guerrilla war behind enemy lines.

Promoted to colonel on April 4, 1862, he commanded a squadron at Shiloh. Gen. P. G. T. Beauregard increased his command to 325 men, and by the time of Morgan's promotion to brigadier general on December 11, 1862, it had grown to a division of 3,900. Discarding the saber, Morgan armed his raiders with infantry rifles and Colt revolvers. They lived off the land and traveled light; their only wheels were two mountain howitzers for each brigade. He used horses to provide mobility, to hit and run. In skirmishing, he deployed the artillery and dismounted the men to fight as infantry. For intelligence, he sent out scouts and intercepted telegraph messages. On the march, he used a system of rolling guards protecting the flanks and leapfrogging to the front when the column passed. He usually kept his opponents confused by sending out feints and fake telegrams.

In the first two years of the war, Morgan's raids made a mockery of Federal attempts to protect border state Kentuckians. After the first Kentucky raid, General in Chief Henry W. Halleck admitted, "The stampede among our troops was utterly disgraceful." Andrew Johnson, military governor of Tennessee, concluded that Morgan's raids undermined Federal authority and the efforts to strengthen loyalty to the Union. William Tecumseh Sherman proclaimed that Morgan and the other Confederate raiders were the most dangerous men of the war and would have to be killed or captured.

In reaction to a raid at Gallatin, Tennessee, Union Gen. Don Carlos Buell concentrated his entire cavalry force of 700 men under Gen. Richard W. Johnson and ordered them to seek out and destroy Morgan. Johnson boasted that he would return "with Morgan in a bandbox." On August 21, 1862, he located Morgan near Gallatin, but after two mounted assaults with sabers, the Union cavalry scattered in wild retreat, losing 21 dead, 47 wounded, and 176 missing, including General Johnson, who was captured by his prey.

Morgan's greatest contribution to the Confederate war effort was the diversion of Union troops and resources to defend against his raids. By mid-December 1862, the Union army had 20,357 men guarding communication lines and supply depots in the West. Morgan and other raiders forced the Union to channel men and resources into the construction of stockades to defend railroad trestles and the reconstruction of tunnels, bridges, track, and telegraph lines. But because of Morgan, the Union commanders strengthened their cavalry and organized mounted infantry, and by the summer of 1863, the stronger Union cavalry ended the advantage the Confederate raiders had enjoyed. Morgan's men now suffered a series of defeats.

Attempting to restore morale and efficiency, Morgan marched into Indiana and Ohio without authority and was captured and imprisoned. Many Southerners nevertheless praised him for carrying the war to the enemy. He escaped from the Ohio penitentiary on November 27, 1863, and served as commander of the Department of Western Virginia and East Tennessee from June to August 22, 1864. He was killed on September 4 in Greeneville, Tennessee, attempting to escape from Federal cavalry under Gen. Alvan C. Gillem. Given a state funeral in Richmond, Virginia, he was buried in Hollywood Cemetery and then reinterred with honor in 1868 in Lexington, Kentucky.

[*See also* Guerrilla Warfare; Morgan's Raids.]

BIBLIOGRAPHY

Ramage, James A. *Rebel Raider: The Life of General John Hunt Morgan.* Lexington, Ky., 1986.

Thomas, Edison H. *John Hunt Morgan and His Raiders.* Lexington, Ky., 1975.

JAMES A. RAMAGE

MORGAN'S RAIDS

Col. John Hunt Morgan, with a brigade of 867 cavalrymen, marched from Knoxville, Tennessee, to Cynthiana, Kentucky, on the first Kentucky raid, July 4 through 28, 1862, recruiting 300 men and eluding a Union force of 3,000 under Gen. G.

Clay Smith. President Abraham Lincoln wired: "They are having a stampede in Kentucky. Please look to it!" Morgan exaggerated Southern sympathy and encouraged the Confederate high command to assume that the people of Kentucky would rise in support of an invading Confederate army.

In early August 1862 civilian informers reported that the twin tunnels behind enemy lines on the Louisville and Nashville Railroad seven miles north of Gallatin, Tennessee, were weakly guarded by 375 infantrymen under Union Col. William P. Boone. Morgan prepared for a raid on Gallatin by sending teenage couriers to arrange for food and forage

> **Morgan's men surprised the Federals and captured them, including Boone, without firing a shot.**

along the seventy-five-mile passage from Sparta to Gallatin. Marching light and under cover of darkness, the raiders reached Gallatin before dawn on August 12, and learned from civilians that Boone's 124 guards were asleep on the courthouse lawn and Boone was sleeping in the hotel with his wife. Morgan's men surprised the Federals and captured them, including Boone, without firing a shot. The soldiers defending the tunnels surrendered with no resistance, and civilians participated in the destruction of the tunnels. The Louisville and Nashville Railroad was Gen. Don Carlos Buell's main artery of supply, and this, the most strategic guerrilla raid of Morgan's career, shut it down, suspending Buell's advance on Chattanooga for ninety-eight days and giving the initiative to Gen. Braxton Bragg for the invasion of Kentucky.

Morgan commanded 2,140 men in a raid on Union Col. Absalom B. Moore's brigade of 2,100 at Hartsville, Tennessee. In a frontal assault on December 7, 1862, Morgan lost 21 men and another 104 were wounded, but the raiders killed 58, wounded 204, and captured 1,834. The purpose of the Christmas raid, December 22, 1862, to January 1, 1863, was to destroy the two Louisville and Nashville Railroad trestles north of Elizabethtown, Kentucky. Morgan's division of 3,900 succeeded, closing the railroad for five weeks and diverting 7,300 troops from the Union army in the Battle of Murfreesboro.

On the "Great Raid," July 1–26, 1863, Morgan's 2,500 men raided through Indiana and Ohio. On July 19, at Buffington Island, Ohio, the pursuing Union cavalry organized by Gen. Ambrose Burnside and commanded by Generals Edward H. Hobson and Henry M. Judah, captured 700 of Morgan's men. Morgan retreated and was captured on July 26 near West Point, Ohio. The raid delayed Burnside's

advance into East Tennessee for one month and boosted Southern morale.

Morgan was incarcerated in the Ohio State Penitentiary. He escaped on November 27, 1863, and with two thousand men, raided from southwestern Virginia into Kentucky from May 30 to June 12, 1864, confiscating horses in Lexington and advancing to Cynthiana. There, on June 12, his command was defeated by the cavalry brigade of Stephen G. Burbridge.

Discipline broke down, and after the raid the Confederate War Department charged Morgan with allowing "excesses and irregularities" relating to the armed robbery of the Farmer's Bank of Kentucky in Mount Sterling and other banks. The men who robbed the banks distributed the money among themselves. Robbery of nongovernmental funds was illegal, as was withholding stolen funds from the Confederate government. Morgan was charged with allowing bank robbery in the Union state of Kentucky, and on August 30, 1864, he was suspended, pending a court of inquiry scheduled for September 10. Six days before the inquiry was to commence, Morgan was killed in Greenville, Tennessee, while attempting to escape from Union cavalry that had surrounded his headquarters and separated him from his men.

[*See also* Morgan, John Hunt.]

BIBLIOGRAPHY

Duke, Basil W. *History of Morgan's Cavalry.* Cincinnati, Ohio, 1867.
Ramage, James A. *Rebel Raider: The Life of General John Hunt Morgan.* Lexington, Ky., 1986.

JAMES A. RAMAGE

MOSBY, JOHN S.

MOSBY, JOHN S. (1833–1916), partisan officer. Enlisting as a private in the First Virginia Cavalry in May 1861, Mosby eventually became a scout for J. E. B. Stuart. In January 1863, with Stuart's approval, Mosby began guerrilla operations in northern Virginia. For the next two years the Forty-third Battalion of Virginia Cavalry, or Mosby's Rangers, waged partisan warfare against Union troops and supply lines.

A small, thin, restless man of absolute fearlessness, Mosby, called the "Gray Ghost," was a natural guerrilla leader. He recruited and organized his command, disciplined its youthful members, and plotted the raids. He possessed a keen intellect, an untiring energy, and an iron will. Few, if any, Confederate units reflected its leader more than Mosby's Rangers.

Mosby operated from the counties of Fauquier and Loudoun that became known as "Mosby's Confederacy."

From this base, the Rangers attacked Union wagon trains, railroad lines, and troop detachments. His mission, as he said, was "to weaken the armies invading Virginia by harassing their rear."

Wounded three times, Mosby forged the battalion into one of war's finest commands. Robert E. Lee regarded him highly and cited him more often in reports than any other officer. Mosby provided Lee with valuable information and seized hundreds of prisoners and large quantities of arms, equipment, horses, and supplies.

Mosby rose to the rank of colonel and, at war's end, commanded two battalions of eight companies. Refusing to surrender, he disbanded his command on April 21, 1865. His record was unmatched by any other Confederate partisan officer.

Unlike many Southerners, Mosby accepted the defeat of the Confederacy. He resumed his legal practice and eventually worked in the Federal government. He served under Republican administrations as a consul in Hong Kong, in the General Land Office, and as an attorney in the Department of Justice. Mosby died in the nation's capital and was buried in "Mosby's Confederacy," in Warrenton, Virginia.

[*See also* Mosby's Rangers.]

BIBLIOGRAPHY

Jones, Virgil Carrington. *Ranger Mosby.* Chapel Hill, N.C., 1944.
Siepel, Kevin H. *Rebel: The Life and Times of John Singleton Mosby.* New York, 1983.
Wert, Jeffry D. *Mosby's Rangers.* New York, 1990.

JEFFRY D. WERT

MOSBY'S RANGERS

Officially designated the Forty-third Battalion of Virginia Cavalry, Mosby's Rangers was a guerrilla unit under the command of John S. Mosby; it operated in northern Virginia from the winter of 1863 until the end of the war. During that twenty-eight-month span, the rangers became the most effective and feared partisan command in the Confederacy.

In January 1863, Mosby, a cavalry officer, and fifteen men undertook guerrilla operations in the Virginia counties south and west of Washington, D.C. Within five months, so many volunteers had joined the unit that Mosby received permis-

GROUP OF MOSBY'S RANGERS.

sion to organize the command into a unit of the Army of Northern Virginia. At Rector's Cross Roads on June 10, Mosby organized Company A, Forty-third Battalion of Virginia Cavalry. By war's end, the command consisted of two battalions of eight companies, and at least 1,900 men had served in the unit.

Mosby's Rangers operated from a base in the counties of Fauquier and Loudoun, which became known as "Mosby's Confederacy." There civilians concealed, sheltered, and fed the rangers while acting as an information and warning network. From this base, the guerrillas operated eastward toward the Union capital, westward across the Blue Ridge Mountains into the Shenandoah Valley, and northward across the Potomac River into Maryland.

From Mosby's Confederacy, the rangers stood across the supply and communication lines of invading Union armies. Union wagon trains, railroad cars, outposts, and troop

> Although Mosby had hundreds of men at hand, he seldom took more than several dozen with him on a raid.

detachments became the rangers' targets. Each raid was plotted carefully by Mosby, and when his men struck, they did so swiftly in daylight or darkness. By forcing Federal officers to guard the wagons and railroads, the rangers drained the strength of the invading enemy and became a constant factor in Union campaign strategy.

Although Mosby had hundreds of men at hand, he seldom took more than several dozen with him on a raid. The nature of the warfare demanded secrecy and celerity, and small bodies of mounted men were most effective. Raids lasted usually two or three days, with the rangers returning to their base before dividing the spoils and disbanding. The unit's successes came at a high cost, however: the rangers incurred casualties of between 35 and 40 percent, with nearly five hundred rangers spending some time in Federal prisons.

Their various exploits and raids brought the rangers wartime fame and an enduring legacy—the capture of a Union general at his headquarters; the seizure of a railroad train and $178,000 in Union greenbacks; and the relentless campaign against Philip H. Sheridan's Union army in the Shenandoah Valley.

On April 21, 1865, Mosby disbanded the command, refusing to surrender it. The rangers had provided Robert E. Lee with valuable intelligence and captured hundreds of enemy soldiers and hundreds of thousands of dollars worth of material, but they did not lengthen the war in Virginia or alter its basic nature.

BIBLIOGRAPHY

Jones, Virgil Carrington. *Ranger Mosby.* Chapel Hill, N.C., 1944.
Wert, Jeffry D. *Mosby's Rangers.* New York, 1990.

JEFFRY D. WERT

MURFREESBORO, TENNESSEE

In early December 1862 the Lincoln administration urged the new commander in middle Tennessee, Gen. William S. Rosecrans, to start a campaign against Braxton Bragg's 37,700-man Army of Tennessee at Murfreesboro. Though still exhausted by the long Perryville, Kentucky, campaign of October and weakened by the detachment of 7,500 men to Vicksburg under Gen. Carter Stevenson, Bragg's army was still a formidable fighting force. On December 26, Rosecrans marched the three wings of his 43,400-man army out of Nashville toward the Confederates at Murfreesboro. Because of bad weather and the delaying attacks of Confederate cavalry under Gen. Joseph Wheeler, Rosecrans's army took until December 30 to cover the thirty-mile route.

On the morning of December 31, Rosecrans hoped to hold with his right wing under Gen. Alexander McCook while his left under Gen. Thomas Crittenden advanced at 8:00 A.M. across the fords of Stones River to crush the Confederate right. McCook's wing had not prepared any defenses and were poorly positioned to repulse a Confederate attack. Bragg planned to launch an all-out assault with two of Gen. William J. Hardee's divisions (under Gen. Patrick Cleburne and Gen. John P. McCown) against the Union right. Gen. Leonidas Polk's corps would advance simultaneously, with the units joining in a giant wheeling movement to roll up the Union center. Prior to battle, Polk's command was reorganized. Two of Gen. B. Franklin Cheatham's brigades were exchanged for two of Gen. Jones Mitchell Withers's, which resulted in poorly coordinated attacks along that front. Gen. John C. Breckinridge's division of Hardee's corps was to hold east of Stones River to guard the Confederate right and act as a reserve to exploit any Confederate successes.

Before the Union advance began, Hardee's forces struck McCook's wing at 6:00 A.M. McCown's division quickly routed two Union brigades, capturing one general (August Willich) and mortally wounding another (Edward Kirk). Cleburne's division soon followed, moving into the Union rear and forcing back two of the Federals' brigades. Two brigades of Gen. Jefferson C. Davis's division joined with Gen. Philip Sheridan's division in successfully resisting the initial uncoordinated attacks of Polk's corps.

Hardee's command had broken into the Union rear and captured McCook's headquarters and the Gresham House, field hospital for the right wing. Confederate cavalry under Gen. John Austin Wharton also rode into the area, chasing off Union ammunition wagons and threatening the Nashville Pike. With ammunition running low and under mounting pressure from front and rear, Davis's and Sheridan's divisions retreated toward the pike.

By 9:00 A.M. it was obvious to Rosecrans that his right had been pushed back and his last supply route, the Nashville Pike, was threatened. He countered by calling off his attack and sending Gen. Lovell Rousseau's division into a cedar forest north of the Wilkinson Pike to link up with Sheridan and protect the rear of Gen. James Negley's division. Two of Gen. Horatio Van Cleve's brigades and one of Gen. Thomas Wood's were to hold the area farther west along the Nashville Pike.

The Confederates continued their advance into the Union rear. McCown's division of three brigades, which had advanced farther west than planned, now turned east in an uncoordinated attack and was repulsed by Union reserve infantry and artillery. This action resulted in the death of one brigade commander, Gen. James Edwards Rains, who was shot through the heart, and temporarily destroyed the effectiveness of these units.

Negley's division and parts of Sheridan's and Rousseau's division were soon caught in a pocket just north of the Wilkinson Pike with the Confederates on three sides. Sheridan's exhausted division pulled out, followed by Rousseau. Pressure from Gen. Patton Anderson's Mississippi brigade forced Negley's units, which were in danger of being cut off, back to the Nashville Pike. By noon, despite a spirited defense by Col. Oliver Shepherd's regular brigade, the Confederates of Polk's corps had driven through the forest of cedars to a large cotton field bordering the Nashville Pike. But there the drive stalled, owing to lack of artillery support to counter the Union batteries along the pike. The Confederates' artillery had been unable to follow through the dense cedar woods and limestone outcroppings. Col. Francis Walker of the Nineteenth Tennessee later claimed that if even one battery could have been brought up, the South would have won the day completely.

Cleburne's division, farther west, continued pushing the Union forces toward the Nashville Pike. At one point in the afternoon Gen. Bushrod Rust Johnson's brigade had captured the pike but was repulsed by a Union counterattack by re-formed units. Johnson complained, "At the moment in which I felt the utmost confidence in the success of our arms, I was almost run over by our retreating troops. Our men were in sight of the Nashville Pike. . . . Had we held this position the line of communication of the enemy would have been cut." By 3:00 P.M. the Confederate attacks in the area faltered, with the men exhausted and lacking support.

While Confederate attacks on the left enjoyed some success, Withers's advances along the Nashville Pike made little progress against the Union line at the Round Forest, a half acre of mature hardwoods along the Nashville and Chattanooga Railroad. Earlier, at approximately 10:00 A.M., Col. James Chalmer's brigade of Mississippians had advanced against the Round Forest position held by Col. William Hazen's brigade. But Chalmers's unit retreated when its line was broken by the ruins of the Cowan House and it tried to re-form under a deadly Union crossfire. Gen. Daniel Smith Donelson's Tennessee brigade immediately advanced against the same position, but their attack on the Round Forest also faltered.

> ## The Confederates' artillery had been unable to follow through the dense cedar woods. . . .

Bragg asked Breckinridge at 10:00 A.M. for two brigades to reinforce Hardee's drive farther west, but they were delayed as a result of what they thought was a Union threat from the north. When they finally arrived at 1:00 P.M., they were thrown instead against the Union line at the Round Forest, which had been reinforced. After these two brigades failed, Bragg called for Breckinridge to send two more against the same position. At about 3:30 P.M. Gen. William Ballard Preston's and Col. Joseph Palmer's brigades advanced. Union Colonel Hazen was impressed by the "dreadful splendor" of the Confederate line stretching into the distance. These units too were repulsed by the deadly Union fire in the last major Confederate attack of the day.

Overall, however, the first day of fighting at Murfreesboro had ended in a Confederate victory. The Federals' right and center had been crushed and only their Round Forest position on the left had held. Rosecrans could barely hold on to his last supply line, the Nashville Pike. Casualties on both sides had been high (approximately 17,000), making December 31, 1862, the bloodiest single day of the war in Tennessee.

For Bragg, nightfall ushered in a happy new year, and he sent an exultant victory telegram to Richmond: he had driven the Union forces from nearly every position, inflicted heavy casualties, and captured supply wagons, thousands of soldiers, and thirty-one pieces of artillery. The Confederates expected the Union army to retreat to Nashville and lick its wounds. The fighting, however, was not yet over, for that evening Rosecrans determined to make a stand. He pulled back from the Round Forest and ordered the battered Union army to dig in along the Nashville Pike.

January 1, 1863, saw only minor action as Bragg waited for the supposedly defeated Union force to retreat. Rosecrans sent three brigades of Van Cleve's division and one of Gen. John Palmer's division across the river at McFadden's Ford to a position that threatened Bragg's right.

Bragg ended the period of inactivity the next day at 4:00 P.M., ordering four brigades of Breckinridge's division to attack the Union units east of the river. Breckinridge argued with Bragg against making the charge, which he considered suicidal, and Gen. Roger Hanson of the Orphan Brigade reportedly volunteered to shoot Bragg instead of attacking. Despite the protests, the attack went forward. After initial success in routing two Union brigades, the Confederate line advanced toward McFadden's Ford. Although the Confederates pushed the second Union line across the river, they soon ran into the massed fire of fiftyseven Union artillery pieces on the west side. The artillery fire caused many casualties, including Hanson, who fell mortally wounded. Negley's division made a successful counterattack, which was joined by other Union units.

Breckinridge's attack had resulted in about 1,700 casualties, representing 38 percent of those who advanced. For this sacrifice Bragg had nothing to show, but had actually lost ground as well as three Confederate cannons. Breckinridge, upon seeing the gaps in the ranks of his old unit, cried out, "My poor Orphans! My poor Orphan Brigade! They have cut it to pieces!"

The day's outcome left the Army of Tennessee disheartened. Polk complained to Bragg in a letter, "I greatly fear the consequences of another engagement at this place." With the rain increasing and his army exhausted, Bragg decided to abandon Murfreesboro and retreat south to Shelbyville and Tullahoma on January 3. Two days later, Rosecrans's army occupied Murfreesboro.

Both armies suffered high casualties. Union losses were 12,700, or 29 percent of those engaged, while the Confederates lost 9,870, representing 27 percent of their force. Although the Union victory was not decisive, it gave a psychological boost to a war-weary North. Bragg's staff blamed him for turning a hard-fought victory into defeat by retreating. The bickering and morale problems that plagued Bragg and his command continued to fester as a result of this lost opportunity.

BIBLIOGRAPHY

Cozzens, Peter. *The Battle of Stones River: No Better Place to Die.* Chicago, 1990.

Davis, William C. *The Orphan Brigade.* Garden City, N.Y., 1980.

Johnson, Robert U., and Buel, C. C., eds. *Battles and Leaders of the Civil War.* Vol. 3. New York, 1888. Reprint, Secaucus, N.J., 1982.

McDonough, James Lee. *Stones River: Bloody Winter in Tennessee.* Knoxville, Tenn., 1980.

Spearman, Charles M. "The Battle of Stones River." *Blue and Gray Magazine* 6, no. 3 (1988): 8–30, 36–45.

Stevenson, Alexander. *The Battle of Stones River near Murfreesboro, Tennessee.* Boston, 1884. Reprint, Gettysburg, Pa., 1983.

U.S. War Department. *War of the Rebellion: A Compilation of the Official Records of the Union and Confederate Armies.* Washington, D.C., 1880–1901. Ser. 1, vol. 20, pt. 1, pp. 166–979.

CHARLES M. SPEARMAN

MUSEUMS AND ARCHIVES

Studying and interpreting Confederate history is a fascinating and time-consuming process. Important research collections are housed in numerous archives, libraries, and museums across the United States, many of which are located in the Southern states that once formed the Confederacy. Resources such as manuscripts, printed works, photographs, other artwork, and contemporary physical artifacts are equally important components in the research process. To contact the public or private facilities that specialize in Confederate history, consult the published directories that describe historical agencies in general, or consult any of the several published catalogues and guides to specific collections.

The largest and most important archival collections are housed in the National Archives and the Library of Congress, both of which are located in Washington, D.C. These facilities have vast quantities of materials related to Confederate civil and military affairs, as well as the papers of prominent politicians and military leaders. Both institutions have published guides to their collections, Henry Putney Beers's *The Confederacy: A Guide to the Archives of the Government of the Confederate States of America* (1968, 1986) and John R. Sellers's *Civil War Manuscripts: A Guide to Collections in the Manuscript Division of the Library of Congress* (1986). Another essential access tool is the *National Union Catalog of Manuscript Collections (NUCMC)* and its index, copies of which are at all major research libraries around the country.

Visual images of the Confederacy, including photographs, paintings, prints, drawings, and portraits, are available at the National Archives, the Library of Congress, and the National Portrait Gallery. Access to the latter two collections is available through Hirst D. Milhollen and Donald H. Mugridge's *Civil War Photographs, 1861–1865: A Catalog of Copy Negatives Made from Originals Selected from the Mathew B. Brady Collection in the Prints and Photographs Division of the Library of Congress* (1961) and the Smithsonian Institution's *National Portrait Gallery Permanent Collection Illustrated Checklist.* Other important photograph collections are housed at the United States Army Military History Institute, Carlisle Barracks, Pennsylvania, and the Valentine Museum in Richmond, Virginia. In addition, numerous examples of Confederate artwork are housed in other facilities in the United States. For an example, consult Virginius C. Hall, Jr.'s, *Portraits in the Collection of the Virginia Historical Society: A Catalogue* (1981).

Maps, atlases, and related cartographic items are especially important to the study of military history. Guides to the collections in Washington, D.C., are Richard W. Stephenson's *Civil War Maps: An Annotated List of Maps and Atlases in the Library of Congress*, 2d ed. (1989), and *A Guide to Civil War Maps in the National Archives* (1986). Other maps are more readily available in the *Atlas to Accompany the Official Records of the Union and Confederate Armies* (1891–1895) and in the numerous secondary sources that are at most research facilities.

State-run libraries and archives and historical societies in those states that once formed the Confederacy also have significant collections. An overview of this level of the study of Confederate history is found in James C. Neagles's *Confederate Research Sources: A Guide to Archive Collections* (1986). Many of the state-run collections have individually published guides; for an example, see the Florida Department of State, Division of Library and Information Services, Bureau of Archives and Records Management, *Guide to the Records of the Florida State Archives* (Tallahassee, Fla., 1988).

Other materials at state facilities concentrate on the Confederate period of individual state governments, the state military regiments that constituted the Confederate army, and the compiled service and pension records of individual soldiers and their widows. The state of North Carolina, for example, has an extensive regimental history and troop roster publication begun in 1966, *North Carolina Troops, 1861–1865,* covering the artillery, cavalry, and infantry. State facilities often contain the papers and diaries of prominent citizens and military men as well as those of ordinary citizens. Many house collections of wartime newspapers and Confederate imprints. Their collections of related photographs and artwork capture the wartime life and surroundings of the individual states.

Other important primary source collections are in the custody of major state and private university libraries, large city or county governments, independently operated historical societies and libraries, or in private collections.

The Southern Historical Collection, which covers the whole of Southern history, is housed at the Wilson Library at the University of North Carolina at Chapel Hill. It features *A Guide to Manuscripts* (1970) and a supplement (1976).

The Virginia Historical Society in Richmond, the center for the study of Virginia history, features Waverly K. Winfree's *Guide to Manuscript Collections of the Virginia Historical Society* (1985). The society's Confederate collections include the bulk of Robert E. Lee's papers and papers of military notables Thomas J. ("Stonewall") Jackson, J. E. B. Stuart, A.

P. Hill, and Jubal Early, and materials on various Virginia military regiments.

Items related to Jefferson Davis, Albert Sidney Johnston, and postwar veterans' organizations are on deposit in the Howard-Tilton Memorial Library at Tulane University and are accessed through the *Inventory of the Louisiana Historical Association Collection* (1983).

The Huntington Library in San Marino, California, houses a valuable Civil War collection including papers of Joseph E. Johnston and Stuart that are described in the *Guide to American Historical Manuscripts in the Huntington Library* (1979).

The Eleanor S. Brockenbrough Library at the Museum of the Confederacy in Richmond has an important postwar collection of Davis materials; papers of Lee, Jackson, and Stuart; regimental items pertaining to the theater of operations of the Army of Northern Virginia; and a fine collection of Confederate currency and bonds.

The William Stanley Hoole Special Collections Library at the University of Alabama has a collection of Davis papers, the diaries and papers of Josiah Gorgas, the records of the Shelby Iron Works, and materials related to the wartime history of the state as a whole.

The Hargrett Rare Book and Manuscript Library at the University of Georgia houses the Permanent Constitution of the Confederacy, the papers of Howell Cobb, and a large collection of Confederate imprints.

Confederate artifacts reflecting the material culture of the wartime South are housed in museums throughout the United States. In some instances institutions that are not formally designated as museums, such as state-run historical agencies, will have collections of three-dimensional objects that date from the Confederate years. In addition, there are fine collections in the possession of private citizens.

Some Confederate museums have direct ties to the wartime years, in that the particular facility may have served as a residence of a prominent citizen, a military headquarters, or a postwar veterans' meeting hall. In turn, this added significance often helped with the acquisition of artifacts. During the 1890s, certainly prompted by the twenty-fifth anniversary of the war years, Confederate museums were established in Richmond, New Orleans, Charleston, and other cities. Former Confederates, from individuals in the top ranks of government down to ordinary soldiers or their descendants, began donating wartime possessions to these and other custodial institutions for posterity. The practice continued well into the twentieth century, and the verbal anecdotes that often accompanied the donations add as well to the store of narrative histories concerning the Confederate experience. Today, the museums that study the Confederacy are more than relic halls, and they are actively engaged in the preservation, study, and interpretation of the wartime South for national audiences.

The Museum of the Confederacy in Richmond houses one of the nation's largest Confederate collections. Founded in 1890 and opening in 1896, the museum features collections of flags, uniforms, edged weapons, firearms, and a variety of other wartime military and domestic effects. Also housed there are personal effects of Davis, Lee, Jackson, and Stuart. The monumental oil painting *The Last Meeting of Lee and Jackson,* by E. B. D. Julio, is on display. Adjacent to the museum is the White House of the Confederacy, the wartime residence of Davis and his family. Fully restored to its mid-nineteenth-century appearance, the building features a fine collection of furniture and decorative arts, many of which were used by the Davis family. In addition, the muse-

> Today the museums that study the Confederacy are more than relic halls, and they are actively engaged in preservation, study, and interpretation. . . .

um also houses the Eleanor S. Brockenbrough Library, which is its research facility.

Other important and historic buildings associated with the Confederacy include the First White House of the Confederacy and the Alabama Capitol, both in Montgomery. Jefferson Davis's last home, Beauvoir, in Biloxi, Mississippi, is where he wrote his two-volume memoir, *The Rise and Fall of the Confederate Government.*

The Confederate Museum in New Orleans was founded in 1891 and is located in the former meeting hall of the city's United Confederate Veterans. The featured holdings include possessions of Davis, uniforms of P. G. T. Beauregard and Braxton Bragg, flags, weaponry, and oil paintings. The museum's archival and manuscript holdings are on deposit at the Howard-Tilton Memorial Library at Tulane University.

The Confederate Museum in Charleston was opened in 1894 by Confederate veterans, and today the facility is operated by their descendants. The museum's holdings include both military and civilian artifacts from the firing on Fort Sumter to William Tecumseh Sherman's March to the Sea.

The Virginia Historical Society in Richmond, founded in 1831, houses the Maryland-Steuart Collection, one of the nation's finest collections of Confederate firearms, edged weapons, and military accoutrements. The *Four Seasons of the Confederacy,* a series of military murals painted by Charles Hoffbauer, is another of the society's many treasures. The research arm of the society is nationally renowned for its holdings on the Civil War in Virginia.

The Confederate Naval Museum in Columbus, Georgia, houses the remains of CSS *Jackson (Muscogee)* and the remains of CSS *Chattahoochee.* Both vessels were in active service before being destroyed to avoid capture by Union forces. The museum holds other naval artifacts and ship models and features exhibitions on the Confederate navy and marine corps.

[*See also* Beauvoir; Memorial Organizations.]

BIBLIOGRAPHY

American Association for State and Local History. *Directory of Historical Organizations in the United States and Canada.* 14th ed. Edited by Mary Bray Wheeler. Nashville, Tenn., 1990.
American Association of Museums. *The Official Museum Directory, 1992.* Wilmette, Ill., 1991.
National Historical Publications and Records Commission.*Directory of Archives and Manuscript Repositories in the United States.* 2d ed. Phoenix, Ariz., 1988.
National Park Service, U.S. Department of the Interior. *The National Parks: Index 1985.* Washington, D.C., 1985.

GUY R. SWANSON

MUSIC

The music of the Confederacy was in part a distinct cultural flowering and in part a reflection of the national musical trends of the 1860s. It included songs and tunes actually performed by soldiers in the field, military and marching music, concert music that entertained the troops, sentimental parlor songs popular on the home front, and rousing patriotic songs designed to rally support for the cause. Some songs dealt with specific topics from the war, but far more dealt with the ageless and universal subjects of love, death, family, and separation.

Sheet Music

The primary medium for popular songs during the war was, for both North and South, sheet music. Well before the war, the music publishing industry had become surprisingly sophisticated in marketing and promoting hit songs, and though it was still centered in New York, dozens of independent publishers had sprung up in smaller cities around the country. This meant that the South had in place a network of publishers on the eve of the war, and that throughout the four years of the conflict a steady stream of Confederate imprints flowed forth. Over 650 different pieces of sheet music have been identified as items published by Confederate presses from venues not under Federal occupation. Most of the pieces came from New Orleans (167), Augusta (137), Richmond (91), Macon-Savannah (73), and Macon (60), though cities like Charleston, Nashville, Columbia, Danville, Memphis, Mobile, and Wilmington also boasted some publications.

Not all these songs were originals written by Confederate composers; many were Southern editions of songs that had nationwide popularity. Blackmar and Brother, for instance, issued a series called "The Exotics: Flowers of Song Transplanted to Southern Soil," which included Northern favorites like "What Is Home without a Mother" and "Cottage by the Sea." John Schreiner and Son of Macon had a similar series called "The Southern Musical Bouquet" that included "Her Bright Smile Haunts Me Still" and Mrs. Norton's "Juanita." As the war dragged on, many of these publishers found it hard to get quality paper, and this led to a downsizing of the sheet music and, later, publication on inferior paper that quickly deteriorated.

The two most prolific New Orleans publishers were the firms of P. P. Werlein and Halsey, and the brothers Armand Edward and Henry Clay Blackmar. Werlein, the city's leading firm since 1854, had established a cadre of his own engravers and printers. A. E. Blackmar, originally from Vermont, was a graduate of Western Reserve College in Cleveland who had taught music in Huntsville, Alabama, and at Centenary College in Jackson, Louisiana. He and his brother opened a music store and publishing business in New Orleans in 1860. One of their most spectacular successes was a song that would become, next to the wellknown "Dixie," the best remembered of all the Confederate songs: "The Bonnie Blue Flag." From 1861 to 1864 the Blackmars published no fewer than six different editions of the song. The title came from a flag used by South Carolina after the state's secession in 1860; it was a plain blue flag with a single white star in its center, and it became the temporary banner for the seceding states. Different verses of the song, in fact, listed the states of the Confederacy, with new verses added as new states joined the cause.

The words to the song were written by Harry Macarthy, a singer who was born in England in 1834 and came to America when he was fifteen. Described by a contemporary as "a good vocalist as well as protean actor," Macarthy was noted for his "impersonation concerts," which featured songs in dialect and in which he billed himself (for obscure reasons) as "The Arkansas Comedian." In September he grafted his words to an old melody called "The Irish Jaunting Car" and premiered the song in New Orleans before an audience of soldiers on their way to the Virginia front. It was an immediate success, and Macarthy's friend A. E. Blackmar arranged not only to publish it but to help Macarthy further popularize it. Soon the singer was the most popular entertainer in the South; his fellow songwriter Will S. Hays dedicated "The Drummer Boy of Shiloh" to him. The song was so potent that when New Orleans was captured by Northern forces in April 1862, Union commander Gen. Benjamin F. Butler tried to suppress the song by destroying all copies of the sheet music, fining Blackmar, and threatening a fine of twenty-four dollars for anyone caught singing or even whistling the song.

With the fall of New Orleans, the center for Confederate music publishing moved to Georgia. The Blackmars relocated in Augusta, where they continued to sell their hit songs like "Bonnie Blue Flag," Macarthy's "The Volunteer," "The Confederate Flag," and "Maryland, My Maryland." Also located in Georgia was the firm of Herman L. Schreiner, a German immigrant who arrived in the United States in 1849, settling in Macon and doing business as John Schreiner and Sons. After the fall of New Orleans, he made his way north, purchased a font of music type, and smuggled it back through Union lines to Georgia. This gave the firm a major advantage in the Confederate publishing scene—some historians have said that for a time it was the only publishing house active in the Confederacy—and its headquarters in Macon and Savannah produced over seventy pieces. Schreiner himself often gave concerts for hospitals and relief societies, and did musical scores for songs like "The Mother of the Soldier Boy."

Schreiner often worked with John Hill Hewitt, a dramatist, poet, historian, publisher, and songwriter par excellence. Before the war, Hewitt had won a national reputation as a writer of what many consider to be America's first native ballad, "The Minstrel's Return from the War" (1827). A student at West Point, an acquaintance of Edgar Allan Poe, and a magazine editor and playright active in the upper South through the 1850s, Hewitt spent the first part of the war managing a theater in Richmond and then moved to Augusta. He continued to write musical plays and operettas, but won most fame with songs like "All Quiet along the Potomac Tonight" (1862), "Rock Me to Sleep, Mother" (1862), and "Somebody's Darling" (1864).

In addition to Macarthy and Hewitt, the third major Confederate songwriter was a colorful Louisville newspaperman and riverboat captain named William Shakespeare Hays. Hays would eventually publish over three hundred songs, some of them among the best-selling sheet music editions in history. Hays appears not to have had strong sympathies with either side in the war—he wrote a campaign song for George B. McClellan—but many of his songs, such as "The Old Sergeant," have a distinct pro-South tone. "The Drummer Boy of Shiloh" (1862), Hays's memorable account of a dying drummer boy on "Shiloh's dark and bloody ground," was published repeatedly throughout the war and inspired a flood of imitative pieces. When Blackmar issued later editions of the song, the music credit was given to "the First Tennessee Concert troupe."

Some songs were so popular that their fame transcended any association with publisher or even composer. One of these, of course, was "Dixie." Another, only slightly less popular, was "Maryland, My Maryland," written by James Ryder Randall in April 1861 at Poydras College in Pointe Coupee, Louisiana. Randall was a native of Baltimore who wrote the song after hearing about a clash between the city's residents and the Sixth Massachusetts Regiment; a Baltimore musician named Charles Ellerbrock later grafted to it an arrangement of the tune to the German Christmas song "Tannenbaum, O Tannenbaum." The South's favorite marching song became "The Yellow Rose of Texas," a minstrel song from the decade before the war. "Stonewall Jackson's Way" was first published in Baltimore in 1862 (before Jackson's death) and was banned by Union occupation troops; the song made its way South and enjoyed renewed popularity after its subject's death.

Probably the best loved of all sentimental songs was "Lorena," written by a Massachusetts minister named H. D. L. Webster in 1857. It was published by several publishers in both Northern and Southern cities and was sung, according to Brander Matthews, "until the last musket was fired and the last camp fire grew cold." The song remained indelibly etched in the public image of the Confederacy for decades after—even to the point of being used in both the novel and the film of *Gone with the Wind.*

Since very few Confederate music business records survived, it is hard to know what songs were most popular during the war or which ones the soldiers sang the most. The best attempt to ascertain the latter is found in historian Bell Irwin Wiley's *The Life of Johnny Reb,* in which he surveyed hundreds of soldiers' letters and diaries and compiled a list of the songs most frequently mentioned. In addition to well-known songs like "Home Sweet Home," "Lorena," "Just Before the Battle, Mother," and "All Quiet along the Potomac Tonight," the list was composed almost entirely of songs from Northern sources that were popular before the war. These included "Annie Laurie" (an 1838 song popularized by British soldiers during the Crimean War); "Lily Dale" (a morose 1852 ballad popularized by the Continental Vocalists, a rival to New England's famed Hutchinson Family singing group); "Bell Brandon" (an 1854 song by T. Elwood Garrett and Francis Woolcott); and "Listen to the Mocking Bird" (an 1855 tune by veteran songsmith Septimus Winner, writing under the name "Alice Hawthorne"; this song was a favorite of Abraham Lincoln's).

Two of the songs on Wiley's list were published during the war: "Annie of the Vale," an 1861 song by New Yorker H. S. Thompson, composer of "Woodman, Spare That Tree," and "Her Bright Smile Haunts Me Still," a sailor's song that originated in England and bore composer credits of J. E. Carpenter and W. T. Wrighton. Two of the songs, "Sweet Evelina" and "The Girl I Left behind Me," probably came from folk tradition; the latter song was a special favorite with brass bands and fiddlers alike and appears to have derived from an English tune called "Brighton Camp" dating from the 1770s. Wiley's list shows the extent to which Confederate and Union troops shared a common heritage of popular songs, and the extent to which soldiers in the field favored older, sentimental songs that reminded them of happier times before the war.

Slave Spirituals and Folk Music

One musical genre from the war that was to have a profound impact on later American music was the slave spiritual. Though these unique songs had been part of plantation life for decades, it was only after the war started that missionaries, educators, and aid society workers began to collect and publish them and introduce them to the rest of the nation. Not long after the firing on Fort Sumter, refugee slaves began streaming into the Union's Fortress Monroe in Virginia; here the commander, General Butler, declared them "contraband of war" so he would have a legal reason for not returning them to their owners. Newspapers picked up the phrase, and soon "contraband" became a new Northern synonym for "slave." As more and more ex-slaves arrived at the Chesapeake Bay fort, and Butler's resources were stretched to the breaking point, Northern churches and missionary societies began to organize relief drives and sent representatives down to assess the situation.

On September 3, 1861, the Reverend Lewis C. Lockwood arrived at the fort from the New York YMCA; that night, from the piazza of his hotel, he heard a strange new music coming from "a long building just outside the entrance of the Fortress" where a number of "colored people" had assembled for a prayer meeting. Lockwood listened to a song he later learned was "Go Down, Moses," a spiritual that had been sung for "at least fifteen or twenty years in Virginia and Maryland, and perhaps in all the slave states, though stealthily, for fear of the lash." Lockwood eventually copied the words to the song and sent them to the *New York Tribune,* where they caused a stir when published there in December

> *. . . soldiers in the field favored older, sentimental songs that reminded them of happier times before the war.*

1861. Two weeks later a piece of sheet music entitled "The Song of the Contrabands: O Let My People Go" was published by the Horace Waters Company on Broadway, with a note that read, "words and music obtained through the Rev. L. C. Lockwood, Chaplain of the Contrabands at Fortress Monroe." Soon the song—apparently the first published spiritual—was being sung at antislavery meetings and even at the first White House emancipation signing in 1863. It has remained popular ever since, enjoying renewed popularity during the civil rights movement of the 1960s.

The first real description of African American spiritual singing came from a woman named Lucy McKim, the nineteen-year-old daughter of a noted abolitionist; she had spent three weeks collecting songs on the Sea Islands off the South Carolina coast. A formally trained musician, she understood the musical content of what she heard; in a famous letter to Dwight's *Journal of Music* (November 8, 1862), she called attention to the unique qualities of the spirituals, admitting that the classical European musical notation system had no way to accommodate the "odd turns" and "irregular intervals" of the songs. She planned a series of sheet music editions of eight of the songs she collected, but apparently only two of these came out. As "Songs of the Freedmen of Port Royal," two titles, "Roll Jordan Roll" and "Poor Rosy, Poor Gal," were issued in November 1862, probably more accurate with transcriptions of words and music than those of Lockwood.

In the meantime, Charles Pickard Ware, a Harvard graduate, began working on the Sea Islands for the Educational Commission, and he too became interested in the songs he

> **The war was also the subject of a rich variety of other types of folk music, from ballads to fiddle and banjo tunes. . . . folk ballads of the South often dealt with specific battles.**

found there. He soon had "175 pages of Negro melodies" and by 1865 had joined forces with his cousin William Allen, a trained historian and accomplished musician who had spent two years in Arkansas collecting songs. At the instigation of Wendell Phillips Garrison, editor of the *Nation* magazine, the cousins pooled their collections, added songs from Lucy McKim, and produced one of the most important cultural documents to come out of the war, *Slave Songs of the United States* (1867). This volume contained both words and music to some 136 songs and became the first serious collection of African American folk culture.

Throughout the war, and in the months after it, various magazine letters and journal entries continued to describe the music of the freed slaves, and evidence emerged that such spirituals had played a significant role in the war. Songs like "Go in the Wilderness" became favorite marching songs of black regiments. Thomas Wentworth Higginson, the Unitarian clergyman who commanded one of the Union's first black regiments, described this as "their best marching song." After the war, African American groups like the Fisk Jubilee Singers took the spirituals across the nation and, indeed, around the world.

The war was also the subject of a rich variety of other types of folk music, from ballads to fiddle and banjo tunes. Though they have been much more sparsely documented— there has never been a major collection of them—folk ballads of the South often dealt with specific battles. Ballads have been collected about Sharpsburg (Antietam), Shiloh,

Manassas (Bull Run), the Battle of the Wilderness, Wilson's Creek, Murfreesboro (Stones River), and the *Cumberland-Virginia* encounter; others tell of how "Booth Killed Lincoln," how Sherman marched to the sea, or the monotony of eating "Goober Peas." Most of these songs circulated by word of mouth and were kept alive for generations before they were collected or published. Other songs came from cheap pocket "songsters"—tiny books sold and passed around that contained words, but no music. *The Stonewall Songbook* (Richmond, 1864) was one of the most popular of these; others bore titles like *The Gen. Lee Songster* (1865), *The Dixie Land Songster* (1863), and *Hopkins' New Orleans 5 Cent Song-Book* (1861).

Most instrumental music was the province of the fiddle and banjo—the guitar was still a rare instrument in the South, and cheap, mass-produced harmonicas were just starting to filter into the country. Even more than ballad singers, fiddlers both North and South shared a common repertory of tunes often borrowed from Scotch and Irish sources. Tunes mentioned as favorites among Confederate soldiers included not only predictable fare such as "Dixie" and "My Old Kentucky Home" but also numbers like "Hell Broke Loose in Georgia" (which is still played by Georgia fiddlers today), "Billy in the Low Ground," "Natchez under the Hill," "The Goose Hangs High," "Oh Lord Gals One Friday," and "Arkansas Traveler." Many tunes were fiddled unaccompanied, as they had been for decades in the rural South, but occasionally a camp would boast of a string band that might include one or more fiddles accompanied by a banjo, or somebody "beating straws" on the fiddle bridge to accompany the fiddler's bowing.

Military Music

In the two decades before the war, the mass production of rotary valve instruments had created a national boom in the popularity of the community brass band. Even small towns often boasted an amateur brass band, and when fighting began, some of these bands enlisted en masse; other individual musicians found their way to newly formed regimental bands. Bands played at the train stations as recruits left town for the front; later they played for ceremonies, during the interminable inspections of camp life, at funerals and some church services, and even during battles. Many of them featured a selection of instruments seldom heard today: E-flat cornets and alto horns, ophicleides, and keyed bugles. Since instrument makers had not yet agreed on a standard pitch for the basic "concert A" note, keeping in tune was always a problem. Confederate bands were generally smaller than their Union counterparts; some of them would have as few as ten or twelve members, whereas the Union bands often boasted of twenty or more.

Most of the bands had their own "band books," which contained their basic repertoires: sixty to eighty selections drawn from the full range of nineteenth-century sources. These included patriotic airs and marches such as "Colonel Kirkland's March," "Garry Owen," and "La Marseillaise"; pieces adapted from current or recent popular songs, such as "Juanita," "My Old Kentucky Home," "Lorena," and "Come Dearest, the Daylight Is Gone"; quicksteps and dance tunes like "Mockingbird Quickstep," "Slumber Polka," "Jenny Lynd Polka," "Hurrah Storm Galop," and "Martha Quickstep"; waltzes, used both for dances and for long inspections on the parade grounds; religious music used for funerals and solemn occasions; and adaptations of both light and serious classics, such as "Anvil Chorus" (which was played during the burning of Atlanta), "Schubert's Serenade," and "In Happy Moments" from the opera *Maritana*.

The other major type of military music was that of the fife and drum corps. Though the war generated one of the most famous bugle pieces, "Taps," most of the day-to-day functions of a camp were regulated by the sound of the fife and drum. These calls and tunes were codified in books like *The Drummers and Fifers Guide,* compiled by George B. Bruce and "Dixie" composer Dan Emmett; it contained the music for the camp duty, as well as a selection of marches and quicksteps and "side-beats."

Many fifers and drummers—often the youngest men in a company—had to learn the bulk of the pieces by heart. Each call had a specific function in camp routine: "drummer's call," often played at 5:45 A.M., signaled the other musicians to assemble; a "second call," by drummers alone, told the troops to fall out and form up. After roll call and announcements came "Reveille," not a single call but a series of six pieces with names like "Three Camps," "Slow Scotch," "Austrian," and "The Dutch." Then, around 6:15, came "pioneer's call" or "fatigue call" to summon work parties and invite any camp followers to leave. "Surgeon's call" was sounded for the sick or lame to report to the hospital, and finally, at around 7:00, a tune called "Peas on a Trencher" was often sounded as breakfast call. Similar calls were heard throughout the day, marking the various stages of camp duty. Fifers were used also on special occasions; men who had been found guilty of desertion or any misdemeanor were often drummed out of a unit to the playing of the "Rogue's March."

Drummers especially were often used in actual battles, and more than a few were killed or captured. Thomas J. ("Stonewall") Jackson used a young drummer boy to "beat the rally" at Fredericksburg. Another well-known story involves Pvt. David Scantlon, a drummer with the Fourth Virginia Regiment of the same Stonewall Brigade, who beat the rally at the height of the Battle of First Manassas by turning his back to the enemy so they could not shoot a hole in his drum. Such stories doubtless inspired comments like that of Gen. Robert E. Lee, who said, "I don't believe we can have an army without music."

[*See also* Discography; Dixie; Folk Naratives.]

BIBLIOGRAPHY

Allen, Francis William, Charles Pickard Ware, and Lucy McKim Garrison, eds. *Slave Songs of the United States.* New York, 1867. Reprint, with new introduction by William K. McNeil, Baltimore, 1992.

Crawford, Richard, ed. *The Civil War Songbook.* New York, 1977.

Emurian, Earnest K. *Stories of Civil War Songs.* Natick, Mass., n.d.

Epstein, Dena J. *Sinful Tunes and Spirituals: Black Folk Music to the Civil War.* Urbana, Ill., 1977.

Glass, Paul, and Louis G. Singer. *Singing Soldiers: The Spirit of the Sixties.* New York, 1968.

Harwell, Richard B. *Confederate Music.* Chapel Hill, N.C., 1950.

Hoogerwerf, Frank W. *Confederate Sheet-Music Imprints.* Brooklyn, N.Y., n.d.

Olson, Kenneth. *Music and Muskets: Bands and Bandsmen of the American Civil War.* Westport, Conn., 1981.

Our War Songs, North and South. Cleveland, Ohio, 1887.

Silber, Irwin. *Songs of the Civil War.* New York, 1960.

Songs of Dixie: A Collection of Camp Songs, Home Songs, Marching Songs, Plantation Songs. New York, 1890.

Wellman, Manly Wade. *The Rebel Songster: Songs the Confederates Sang.* Chapel Hill, N.C., 1959.

Wiley, Bell Irwin. *The Life of Johnny Reb.* New York, 1943.

CHARLES K. WOLFE

NASHVILLE, TENNESSEE

When Tennessee voted on June 8, 1861, to leave the Union, Nashville was its capital city with a population of approximately thirty thousand. There were about twenty-four thousand whites, one thousand free blacks, and five thousand slaves in the city and its suburbs. The vast majority of the whites were immigrants or descendants of immigrants from England, Scotland, and Ireland.

Located on the banks of the Cumberland River, the Tennessee capital was one of the largest and most important American cities south of the Ohio River. A busy user of river transportation since its settlement in 1780, Nashville had expanded its commerce in the 1850s through the construction of five railroads that connected to most of the major markets in the South and East.

The principal economic activity was the importation and wholesale distribution of goods. From their location at the center of several neighboring towns, wholesalers distributed groceries, liquors and wines, boots and shoes, dry goods, hardware, and other farm and home supplies. Commission merchants shipped agricultural produce of the region to Southern and Midwestern markets.

Manufacturing was important to the city, with $1,520,000 invested in 73 factories that employed 1,318 workers. Notable manufactures were lumber and wood products, leather goods, stoves, carriages, rail cars, castings, farm implements, and tobacco products.

The intellectual life of Nashville was nurtured by three outstanding educational institutions with a combined enrollment of approximately 1,150 students: the Shelby Medical College, the University of Nashville and its medical college, and the Nashville Female Academy. There were more students enrolled in the two Nashville medical colleges than in the medical schools of any other city in the United States with the exception of Philadelphia.

The religious preference of the citizens was overwhelmingly Protestant Christian. There were two Catholic churches, two Jewish congregations, and numerous churches of the various Protestant denominations, including four for blacks. The Methodists and Baptists published tracts, periodicals, and books in Nashville and distributed them throughout the Southeast.

Nashville was headquarters for all the branches of the state government. Most offices were in the new capitol, completed only a short time before war broke out. The state maintained a school for the blind, an asylum for the insane, and a penitentiary in the city.

Before Union occupation, Nashville was a major supply center for the Southern army. Local plants produced cannons, muskets, ball and shot, percussion caps, friction primers, swords, saddles, harnesses, carriages, and gray uniform cloth.

To protect Nashville, the Confederate army depended on a defensive line across southern Kentucky and two forts on the Cumberland River. Forts Henry and Donelson, overlooking the river about sixty-five miles northwest of Nashville, guarded against invasion of the city by water. Seemingly secure behind these defenses, Nashvillians were stunned on February 16, 1862, by the unexpected surrender of the forts on the third day of siege by Union forces. Southern troops simultaneously abandoned the defense line in Kentucky, and by nightfall many of those troops had passed through Nashville toward Murfreesboro. The capital city was no longer defended.

Terror gripped the populace. Many fled south by train to Alabama and Georgia and some took to the country, but

> **Nashvillians were stunned . . . by the unexpected surrender of the forts on the third day of siege by Union forces.**

most remained behind. From February 16 until February 25, a bizarre period known locally as "the great panic," Nashville was engulfed by rumors and false reports that Federal gunboats were about to level the city. Convinced they were facing starvation, fearful mobs pillaged Confederate army supplies even as they were being loaded on trains for shipment to the South. After a few days of chaos, order was restored by the arrival of Col. Nathan Bedford Forrest's regiment, which had escaped capture at Fort Donelson.

On February 25, 1862, Nashville became the first Confederate state capital to fall. The mayor surrendered the city to Gen. Don Carlos Buell, and Union troops began a military occupation that lasted until after the war. It was the longest uninterrupted wartime occupation experienced by any Confederate city.

Nashville quickly became the principal supply center for the western operations of the Union army, and to protect it, army engineers erected forts and other defenses along its southern perimeters. Within the city, the quartermaster seized schools, churches, and public and private buildings for use as offices, hospitals, barracks, and warehouses.

Immediately after occupation, Nashville received the war's first military governor. President Abraham Lincoln sent Andrew Johnson, governor of Tennessee from 1853 to 1857 and staunch Unionist U.S. senator when the war erupted. Although popular during his earlier term as governor, Military Governor Johnson found most of his old friends hostile to him and the Union.

At once the governor undertook the task of reconstructing the state into a viable member of the Union. Finding that loyalists were a small minority, Johnson implored the majority to return their allegiance to the Union. Responses to his pleas were so negative that he arrested three prominent Confederate sympathizers and dispatched them to prison in northern Michigan as an example. Although the citizens were neither intimidated nor persuaded, Johnson continued to threaten, arrest, and imprison leading Confederate supporters.

The city's white population was slow to recommit its loyalty because they believed they would be liberated by the Southern army. Confederate raiding parties frequently threatened the city, and letters home from Nashville soldiers in gray promised that the Northerners would soon be driven out. Citizens feared, in that event, of being accused of having collaborated with the enemy.

Slaves in the city were thoroughly confused. When the Union army came in, many left their owners, thinking they were free, only to discover they were not. Later when the first Emancipation Proclamation was issued, most believed they had been freed by the president but then learned that, at Governor Johnson's behest, Tennessee had been excluded from the provisions of the proclamation.

Upon its arrival, the Union army established several hospitals, many of them in schools and churches. Soon afterward, their successful treatment of the heavy casualties from the battles of Murfreesboro and Shiloh prepared the way for Nashville to become the major hospital center for the Union army in the West.

Pioneering in the wartime use of railroads to move men and matèriel, the Union command built extensive machine shops to maintain and repair rolling stock. The government brought in additional locomotives and freight cars and rushed the completion of the Nashville and Northwestern Railroad to Johnsonville, a military port established on the Tennessee River. The connection provided a route into the city for mili-

tary supplies when navigation on the Cumberland was halted by low water. Gunboats regularly patrolled the Cumberland River and often escorted cargo and troop carriers up and down its waters. To maintain the various river craft, the U.S. Navy set up a navy yard just downstream from the Nashville public square on the opposite bank of the river.

The Union quartermaster found the many wholesale distribution warehouses made to order for storage of military supplies. His department operated shops to manufacture and repair harnesses, carts, wagons, and other carriages, and to repair weapons.

By the middle of 1864, approximately ten thousand persons were employed by the government to assist the army at Nashville, and nearly all of them had been imported from the North. Several local whites and free blacks were among their numbers, however. Frequently, the occupying army impressed slaves to work on construction projects. Hundreds of slaves built Fort Negley, the city's largest bastion. Other blacks who had walked away from slavery worked as laborers, servants, cooks, and maids in hospitals and camps. Their numbers were constantly augmented by the arrival of refugees from the surrounding countryside.

The appearance of the city was militaristic in the extreme. Fort Negley dominated the skyline south of the capitol and other forts were under construction. Even the proud new capitol was fortified. Heavy military traffic clogged the streets. Uniformed men were everywhere as fresh troops arrived from the North and those they were to replace returned from duty in the South. Army tent cities appeared and disappeared on all sides.

The soldiers and the sizable corps of male government employees provided a ready clientele for prostitutes. These

> **The city's white population . . . believed they would be liberated by the Southern army.**

women flowed into the city, and venereal disease became rampant, especially among the soldiers. Recognizing prostitution as a major problem, civil and military authorities tried to exile the women. In 1863, they sent many of them northward on riverboats destined for Louisville or Cincinnati, but these cities would not accept them and they were returned to Nashville. Army medical officers then attempted to control the problem by permitting women to practice prostitution but only with a license that required an initial physical examination and periodic reexaminations. The army maintained a hospital for the diseased prostitutes, and the licensing procedure was continued during the remaining years of the war.

The occupying army dominated the city's economy. The quartermaster purchased large quantities of locally produced goods. Logs and lumber were in great demand, but the largest purchases were of farm produce, especially foodstuffs and forage. Hotels, boardinghouses, restaurants, theaters, and saloons thrived. Although several local merchants closed their stores rather than sign a loyalty oath, new retailers appeared often among people arriving from the North.

The presence of the Union army left no aspect of life in the city untouched. At various times most houses of worship were in the hands of the army, and congregations gathered in private homes or wherever space could be found. The large public and private schools were closed during much of the occupation, their facilities in use by the army. Only the medical school of the University of Nashville was able to continue without major interruption, though on a much reduced scale.

At first most white citizens were hostile to Union soldiers, but their attitude gradually mellowed. While they retained their bitterness toward the military governor, significant numbers had declared their loyalty to the Union by the summer of 1864. With national elections scheduled for the autumn, Governor Johnson issued an amnesty oath that was required of all voters. Even many of his Union friends were outraged. Citizens quickly dubbed it "the Damnesty Oath" and vented their wrath on the governor, by then the Republican party's nominee for vice president on the ticket with President Lincoln. Few Nashvillians went to the polls that fall.

By the autumn of 1864, most Nashvillians—old and new—had concluded that the Confederacy could not win the war. Consequently, the city was shocked when news was received in the latter part of October that Gen. John Bell Hood had disengaged his army from operations near Atlanta and was sweeping northward toward middle Tennessee. Thirty days later, it was clear that he was moving on Nashville.

Although Hood took staggering losses at the Battle of Franklin on November 30, the Union army also suffered heavily and fell back to Nashville twenty-five miles away. The Confederates followed, but stopped about three miles south of the city. Unable to build up his forces, Hood remained immobile for two severely cold weeks while Union Gen. George H. Thomas accumulated a force twice the size of Hood's.

The Battle of Nashville was swift and decisive. On December 15, Union forces drove the Confederates out of their dug-in positions, and by nightfall of the second day, the Southerners were in full retreat. General Thomas pursued them for about one hundred miles before breaking off contact. By that time the shattered enemy had divided into several small detachments, making their ways eastward to join other forces still in the field. The Union victory at Nashville eliminated the last vestiges of a Confederate army in the area between the Appalachians and the Mississippi River. The battle destroyed the last hope the Confederates had for

sending a strike force into the undefended midwestern states. Had such a maneuver been successful, it could have led to a negotiated settlement of the war.

On February 24 Andrew Johnson left Nashville to be inaugurated vice president of the United States. Before leaving, he had set the stage for a tightly controlled election in which the only candidate, William G. Brownlow, Knoxville Methodist preacher, editor, and abolitionist, would be elected governor on March 4, 1865. The Confederacy capitulated April 9 at Appomattox, Lincoln was assassinated on April 14, and Andrew Johnson succeeded to the presidency on April 15.

In Nashville military installations were speedily dismantled, and soldiers and most civilian employees of the army soon departed. Yet converting to a peacetime economy was difficult for those left behind, especially for former slaves who were now free and adrift. Like the slaves, most whites were unsure of their roles in the postwar era. Only the Nashville planters and businessmen who had become reluctant partners with the Union and had prospered during the latter years of the conflict found the adjustment to peace relatively easy.

[*For further discussion of the fall of Forts Henry and Donelson, see* Henry and Donelson Campaign. *See also* Franklin and Nashville Campaign.]

BIBLIOGRAPHY

Crabb, Alfred Leland. "The Twilight of the Nashville Gods." *Tennessee Historical Quarterly* 15 (December 1956).

Durham, Walter T. *Nashville, the Occupied City.* Nashville, Tenn., 1985.

Durham, Walter T. *Reluctant Partners—Nashville and the Union.* Nashville, Tenn., 1987.

Fitch, John. *Annals of the Army of the Cumberland.* Philadelphia, 1864.

Graf, Leroy P., and Ralph W. Haskins, eds. *The Papers of Andrew Johnson.* 9 vols. to date. Knoxville, Tenn., 1967–1991.

Horn, Stanley F. *The Decisive Battle of Nashville.* Knoxville, Tenn., 1968.

Maslowski, Peter. *Treason Must Be Made Odious.* Millwood, N.Y., 1978.

WALTER T. DURHAM

NATIONALISM

The discussion of nationalism and the Confederacy can be divided usefully into two parts: a discussion of the Old South, Southern nationalism, and secession, and a discussion of Confederate nationalism. Inevitably, questions about the existence of Southern nationalism also become questions about the coming of the Civil War. If the South was so distinct and distinctive from the North as to be its own nation, then secession can be easily explained, if not the war itself. (Indeed, then the question becomes, if the South was so different, why did the rest of the country fight to keep it?) If the South was more a region than a nation, what did provoke secession and the ensuing war?

Historian David M. Potter, who long considered the question of Southern nationalism, wrote that

> students of the theory of nationalism generally agree that while nationalism itself is a subjective, psychological phenomenon—a matter of sentiment, will, feeling, loyalty—and not an objective phenomenon, capable of being measured by given ingredients, it is nevertheless true that a certain core of cultural conditions is conducive to the development of nationalism, and that among these conditions are "common descent, language, territory, political entity, customs and tradition, and religions."

Antebellum Nationalism

Many have argued—at the time and later—that the antebellum South did possess the "core of cultural conditions" necessary to maintain a sense of separate nationhood. If this was the case, then Southern secession was primarily the product of Southern nationalism. If not, then Southern secession might be explained in various other ways, such as a breakdown of the political system, hysteria over real or perceived threats to slavery, or even as a ruse intended to gain the South more advantages within the Union. Those who believe in antebellum Southern nationalism point to the Old South's ethnic and religious homogeneity, its agrarian society, its economic system, and its aristocracy as factors in cre-

> **. . . Southern secession might be explained in various other ways, such as a breakdown of the political system. . . .**

ating a viable nationalism. Others argue that the existence of antebellum differences has been exaggerated.

Ethnically—if one ignores the obvious presence of a sizable African American minority and focuses on the political community—the South was more homogeneous than the North. Most Southern white people were of British descent. Some have seen the Old South as more unified than the North religiously. Most Southerners were orthodox Protestants. Presbyterians and Episcopalians dominated the upper classes, while the bulk of the population—white and black—were Methodist and Baptist. Thus religion contributed to the homogeneity of the Old South.

Southern nationalists also manufactured imaginary ethnic differences. White Southerners were told that they were descended from Cavaliers, English gentlemen who had fought for Charles I. Northerners, on the other hand, were held to be the descendants of Roundheads, Puritan supporters of Oliver Cromwell who were not gentlemen at all. The Cavalier-Roundhead myth invoked both ethnicity and class to postulate a hereditary Southern distinctiveness. This myth—which had very little in the way of hard evidence behind it—proved remarkably durable, perhaps because it succeeded in flattering the self-images of both Northerners and Southerners.

The ethnic thesis has reemerged in recent years, although in very different form. One interpretation advanced for Southern distinctiveness is the so-called Celtic thesis. This postulates that most Southern white people were of Celtic stock—Irish or Scottish or Scotch-Irish—and those that were not had been Celticized by intimate contact with Southern Celts.

The most obvious ethnic difference between the North and South was one that Southern nationalists could not exploit. The North was fundamentally European American; the South was European African American. If the presence of slavery set the South apart legally and economically, the presence of a large African population set it apart ethnically. And although the laws of Southern states defined them as black, many Southerners had both European and African ancestry. Nobody, however, proposed that this crucial ethnic difference justified the creation of a Southern nation. (Abolitionist John Brown, however, did envision a revolutionary government of freed slaves fortified in the Appalachian Mountains, and in the twentieth century, the Communist party advocated the creation of a black socialist soviet republic in the Deep South.)

Ignoring the black presence in the Old South, though difficult, was probably reassuring to the not overwhelming white majority. That Southern nationalists left black Southerners—but not the enormous fact of slavery—out of their calculations is also understandable. But for anyone since then seeking to understand the nature of Southern distinctiveness, ignoring the black presence would be blind folly. Surely one of the things that set the Old South apart from the rest of the nation was its African American community. Southern culture itself is a product of the interaction between African Americans and European Americans. Just as significant for the course of events that led to the Civil War and its conclusion, only the South, among all American regions, based its political, social, and political order on the systematic denial of rights to large numbers of people defined as racially distinct. The white South lived in constant fear of insurrection on the part of the black South. Its response was oppression. This oppression, being at the heart of Southern society, really did make the Old South different.

There is also the question of the relationship of the Old South to capitalism. Some have boldly argued that the Old

South's planter class was precapitalistic and even anticapitalistic. Others have seen the planters as a historic anomaly—slaveholding capitalists, as much bent on maximizing profits as any Northerner. Whether or not planters should be viewed as capitalist, what is undeniable is that the Southern slave economy emerged within the context of a capitalist Atlantic economy.

Slavery increasingly set off the South not only from the North but from the rest of the world. The fact that slavery was globally a dying institution by the mid-nineteenth century made Southern defensiveness all the greater. Yet if slavery set off the South, the products of slavery linked it thoroughly to the capitalist world. The plantation may have seemed to be a little world of its own, one in which the owner was master not only of his slaves but of his fate, but in fact the plantation depended on the world market. Both the North and Britain purchased Southern cotton. Yet Southerners, proclaiming that Cotton was King, reversed the dependency. They argued that the rest of the world depended on them for its raw material. These economic interdependencies argued neither for a separate Southern nation nor against it. Economic forces routinely cross national boundaries. An independent South probably would have been as dependent on trade with the North and the rest of the world as it had been as a region of the United States.

Proponents of Southern nationalism also argue that the South's agrarian economy was key to its identity. They contrast an industrial North with an agrarian South. Southern reliance on agriculture created a separate set of economic interests. It also, they argue, created a Southern way of life. Oddly enough, this argument is most frequently evoked not by those who ground Southern distinctiveness in slavery and the production of staple crops but by those who seek an alternative to slavery to explain why the Old South was different.

Another common conception is that the Old South was "aristocratic" in comparison with a "democratic North." This view generally is sustained by ignoring the actual politics of the Old South and focusing on the pretensions of Southern planters. It is also sustained by a failure to consider the nature of a real aristocracy on the European model, whose power was maintained by an elaborate system of legal privilege. Instead, what is too frequently offered is a description of a cosmetic aristocracy—people living in big houses with lots of servants and lots of leisure. More sophisticated analysis suggests that the dominance of the planter image in the Old South helped organize the aspirations of Southern white men so that ambition was channeled into replicating the existing social structure rather than transforming society, and that within a democratic political structure, the planters exerted a disproportionate political power. Of course, the same might be said of rich capitalists in the Northeast. It is, however, undeniable that the Old South was led by a planter

class, which, if not an aristocracy, had no counterpart in the rest of the United States.

The problem is that most of the things that united Southern white people were shared by most other Americans, too. If most white Southerners were of British origins, so were most white native-born Americans. Both North and South were predominantly Protestant. Immigrants and their children, to be sure, were often Irish or German and frequently Catholic. But the antebellum North hardly welcomed these new Americans with open arms. As for the contrasting images of the agrarian South and the industrial North, these too have been exaggerated. The antebellum North was industrializing, not industrialized. The South, while by no means as industrial as the North or Great Britain, had more factories than most existing nations—although a large percentage of them were in Virginia, where agriculture had become less profitable. North and South shared common political institutions. Suffrage for white men—and white men only—characterized both sections of the country. The political subdivisions of town, county, and state organized government North and South, and the regions shared a similar system of legislature, governor, and courts. Both revered the U.S. Constitution, even while reading it in different ways.

Even the greatest unifying force the white South possessed—racism, with its devotion to white supremacy—was something they shared with the North. Some historians have pointed to the prevalence of racism to explain why white nonslaveholders supported slavery, arguing that the white South was a "herrenvolk democracy," in which all white people acquired status from the simple fact that they were white. Ulrich B. Phillips went so far as to identify white supremacy as the unifying theme in Southern history. Other white Americans shared the racism. They did not, however, share Southern white fears that "the white man's country" might become "the black man's country." Other white Americans also had become less convinced that what they too perceived as black inferiority required or justified the institution of slavery.

Southern Nationalists

Whether or not there was a distinct Southern nation, there were certainly Southern nationalists in the Old South. These were Southerners whose political and cultural goal was to create a widespread belief in a separate Southern destiny and then to encourage the establishment of a separate Southern nation. As historian John McCardell points out, several movements in the Old South contributed to a belief in separate Southern identity. Southern nationalism is sometimes traced to the doctrine of nullification, as espoused by John C. Calhoun in the 1830s. Calhoun and many of his supporters saw nullification as a means to preserve the Union, not break it up. But there was a tiny group of South Carolina nullifiers, led by Thomas Cooper, the president of South

Carolina College, who looked to the eventual creation of a Southern nation. Both nullification and Southern nationalist thinking was inevitably linked with proslavery thought. It was slavery that set the South apart from the rest of the nation. Slavery was the interest that Southern politicians most wished to defend, and it was the basis of the distinctive Southern society that nationalists wanted to incorporate as an independent nation. Initially, however, proslavery thought was reactive; it appeared in response to the heightened abolitionist attacks on slavery in the 1830s. Yet the desire to maintain slavery did not require the desire for an independent Southern nation. Many slavery advocates believed that the institution would best be protected within the Union—and events proved them right. As John McCardell observed, "To support slavery, then, did not alone make a man a Southern nationalist."

The antebellum South also witnessed a series of commercial conventions dedicated to eliminating the section's economic dependence on the North. Northern merchants marketed the Southern cotton crop; Northern and British factories bought the crop; and Northern and British factories provided the South with its manufactured goods. These conventions called upon Southerners to invest not just in land and slaves but in banks, steamships and railroads, and factories. Although advocates of Southern nationalism welcomed the call for Southern economic independence, one question troubled them. Was economic diversification compatible with the distinctiveness that other antebellum nationalists claimed for the South? The worry was theoretical: the principal product of the commercial conventions was rhetoric. In the 1850s, Southerners continued to put the bulk of their capital into the production of cotton. They did so less because of a commitment to Southern distinctiveness than of a commitment to high profits.

For slavery expansionists, the key issue for Southern nationalism was not so much a Southern civilization as a Southern government. The U.S. government was increasingly reluctant to admit new slave states. This threatened to decrease the Southern side of the sectional balance of power and to prevent the spread of slavery. Slavery expansionists looked not just to the territories already owned by the United States but to the Caribbean and Latin American nations as well. Presumably, a Southern government would at the most aid and encourage the territorial expansion of slavery and at the least not hinder it. In October 1860, a pro-secession Mississippi newspaper claimed that "the acquisition of Mexico, Central America, Cuba, Santo Domingo, and other West India Islands would follow as a direct and necessary result" of the establishment of a Southern nation.

For much of the antebellum period, most Southern white people seem to have regarded the vocal Southern nationalists as quasi lunatics. But if they were fools, they were licensed fools. Some were persuaded of their ideas by argu-

ment and others by reiteration. However the nationalists themselves were viewed—and they would not obtain high office within the Confederacy—they put their ideas into circulation; their rhetoric became part of the common political discourse. They made secession and Southern independence thinkable.

Sectionalism

Arguably more important than the movement for Southern nationalism was the rise of political sectionalism in the antebellum era. Sectionalists were those concerned with maintaining the region's balance of power within the United States. They viewed the South as having interests distinct from the rest of the country, although they often hoped to make common cause with the West against the Northeast. One such interest, the most important one, was slavery. Its expansion, the return of fugitive slaves, the possibility of reopening the international slave trade, even its very existence—all might be determined by national policy. But there

> ... most Southern white people seem to have regarded the vocal Southern nationalists as quasi lunatics.

were other political interests that sectionalists believed the South must protect. As a staple-producing region, for example, the South preferred free trade; the tariff was a source of constant grievance to most Southern farmers.

As the nineteenth century wore on, Southern politicians were increasingly aware that the South was becoming a minority section within the United States as a whole. Its control over first the House of Representatives and then the presidency and the Senate diminished. Sectionalists desperately wanted to halt this trend, and they had hopes to reverse it. Both proslavery ideologues and practical sectionalists could agree that extending slavery into the territories was crucial. For apologists, a national prohibition on slavery in the territories would indicate a condemnation of an institution they believed righteous. For sectionalists, the failure of slavery to reach the West meant the South's accepting a minority status within the Union—and within Congress. Thus the struggle between North and South developed first over the status of the West.

As a political solution, secession had its drawbacks. Although it opened the possibility that the new Confederacy might expand southward, it would not gain slaveholders access to the disputed western territories. Why should the remaining still-united states let foreigners bring slaves into U.S. territories? Nor would any future treaty provisions really make the return of fugitive slaves to the South any more likely. Many of the irritants of the sectional conflict would have remained in place even had peaceable secession occurred.

What would secession accomplish? It would allow the Confederacy to try to colonize Latin America. It would permit the Confederacy to become a free-trade zone. If successful, it would prevent the U.S. government from abolishing slavery within the Southern states.

In 1860, many advocates of secession viewed it as a last resort. The withdrawal of the Southern states and the establishment of an independent Confederacy was a refuge to which they felt driven, not a national destiny that they eagerly embraced. Southern nationalists had succeeded in making secession an acceptable recourse in the Southern mind; they had generally failed in creating a regionwide desire for a Southern nation. For many, secession would be not the beginnings of a glorious national destiny but a defensive move in an increasingly hostile world.

Confederate Nationalism

Nationalism—or its failure—has been invoked to explain the causes, the course, and the conclusion of the Civil War. There are two distinct lines of thought about the relationship of nationalism to the Confederate experience. Some invoke nationalism to explain how the Confederacy fought as long and as hard as it did; others to explain why the Confederacy was defeated—or, as they would have it, why the Confederate people gave up.

Historian Emory Thomas has been one of the leaders in finding within the Confederacy a nationalism so strong that it was willing to embrace revolutionary means to achieve independence. He points to the fact that the Confederacy centralized its government, subjected its economy to government control, sponsored industrialization, instituted the first national draft in America, and finally agreed to recruit slaves into its army. All of this unprecedented innovation, he argues, constituted a revolution—not one intended by Southern nationalists but one into which Confederate nationalists were forced. For Thomas, their willingness to advocate and implement these measures, however falteringly, proves the existence of a strong nationalism— although he admits that for many white Southerners, black enlistment was going too far.

For other historians, Confederate defeat itself undermines the notion of thoroughgoing Confederate nationalism. They argue that in April 1865 the Confederacy still had the means to continue the fight against the Union forces. If Confederates chose surrender over struggle, then their desire for independence was insufficient. For them, nationalism implies a will to achieve and maintain nationhood on the part of a majority of citizens so great that they would accept death more readily than the end of national identity.

Of course, if this standard is applied, there are probably few nations. The South endured a great deal in its fight for independence—social dislocation followed by social revolu-

tion, a death toll on the order of France's in the First World War. Another viewpoint might be offered by the military historian. Nationalism in military history is usually associated with the French Revolution and the Napoleonic Wars. In that context, nationalism implies citizen armies, the levee en masse, and patriotically motivated soldiers. If this definition of nationalism is employed, there can be no question that the Confederacy was nationalistic. It raised mass armies— approximately four of every five white men of military age served—its government took unprecedented control of the economy to shift it to war production, its popular press supported the war passionately, its soldiers, initially, were volunteers. If the French Revolution and the Napoleonic Wars had created new rules of patriotism and nationalism for warfare, the Confederacy played by them.

But a military historian would never assume that the presence of nationalism would be decisive on the battlefield. The nineteenth and twentieth centuries have been periods of nationalistic wars, where two or more nation-states battled with one another. Nobody suggests that the France that lost the Franco-Prussian War was not a nation; it clearly was, but it was a nation defeated by a more militarily adept nation. Nations routinely make war against one another and lose. Nationalism is not a magic potion that conveys invulnerability on those who drink it.

Southern nationalists presented the new Confederacy with a contradictory agenda. The Confederacy was to become a "nation among nations"—a powerful, respected force in world politics. As such, it would have to industrialize, raise armies and navies, establish a vigorous government. But the Confederacy was established to resist what Southerners viewed as potential tyrannies of the Federal government; it was established in rebellion against a vigorous government and against an industrializing region. From that point of view, the Confederacy should celebrate diversity, strong state governments and a weak central government, and an agrarian, not an industrial, way of life. The problem with this vision of the new nation was that it seemed inadequate for establishing the Confederacy's very existence.

Another part of Southern political culture said to set it off from the rest of the United States was its devotion to the concept of state rights. But zeal in defense of state rights, though a potent motive for secession, was hardly a desirable passion for nation-building. If the South's state rights ideology helped create the Confederacy, it also helped destroy it. Indeed, Frank Oswley suggested that "Died of States Rights" was the most appropriate epitaph for the Confederacy. Yet it must also be acknowledged that in many ways the Confederacy went further overturning state rights than did its opponent to the north.

One thing was clear: if the Confederacy failed to defeat the Union, Confederate nationalism would be meaningless. Even if antebellum Southern nationalism had been widespread and deeply felt, even if the Confederacy embodied white Southerners' sincere desire for an independent nation, its existence depended on practical success, both military and political. A genuine nationalism can be suppressed by force. The Union planned to crush the rebellion. If the Confederacy did not win, Southern nationalism would have produced, most notably, dead Southerners. So the cause of Confederate nationalism became one with the cause of the Confederate army.

At the time, the relationship between military events and Confederate nationalism raised the issue of what it sometimes called national strategy. How the Confederacy should fight its war could not be divorced from the question of its war aims and national identity. Was the ultimate aim of the South a Confederate nation, or was the Confederate nation itself primarily a means to some other end—such as the preservation of slavery? If the latter was the case, what would happen to support for the new nation if it failed to serve its ends?

The Confederacy had to do more than simply defeat the Union armies. It had to persuade Southerners that the new nation and its government served them well enough to justify the demands it placed on them. It had to do this because without ongoing popular support, Confederate victory was unlikely. Historian Drew Gilpin Faust observes that "the ideological foundations of nationalism required popular consent; nationalism, not to mention total war, necessarily involved and thus empowered the people at large." But here the diversity that underlay the South's vaunted homogeneity made the political problems extremely difficult. Policies that pleased slaveholders might not please nonslaveholders, nor would they necessarily please the slaves themselves.

> ... as suffering became commonplace throughout the South, the enthusiasm dwindled.

How successful was the Confederacy in building a national consensus? That depends on at what point in the Confederacy's brief existence the question is asked. Among the white population, perhaps 10 percent were still Unionist after secession took place and the war began. The other 90 percent of new Confederates seemed to be wildly enthusiastic in their support of the war for independence. As Union armies penetrated the South, as demands made by the war became more extreme, as Confederate victory became less likely, and as suffering became commonplace throughout the South, the enthusiasm dwindled. Disaffection with the Confederacy was hardly limited to any single group in society. Women wanted their sons and husbands home. Both planters and yeomen grew disillusioned. Even the army was not immune: by 1865, desertion was crippling the war effort.

Perhaps the most significant Confederate failure is one that was predestined: the Confederacy could not persuade slaves that the creation of a nation based on their continued slavery was desirable. Confederate nationalism could not be a cause backed by the South's substantial black minority. Black Southerners were instinctive Unionists. During the war, they slowed the pace of their labor and sabotaged much of the war effort, they fled Confederate areas of the South to enter the lines of the Union army and so gain their freedom, and they enlisted in that army to fight for freedom and for Union. If black Southerners had accepted their enslavement, the Confederacy probably would have established its independence.

One problem with most approaches to Southern nationalism is that they treat nationalism as a thing, as an inherent quality, indeed as a measurable quality. It is almost as though historians have tried to count how many "nationalism units" the Confederacy had. This approach to nationalism stems from the nineteenth century, the era in which the notion of nationalism itself was invented. The initial theorists of nationalism—not surprisingly, nationalists themselves—saw it as something inherent among peoples, a force, sometimes latent, that existed in the souls of a people. If a people were a nation, it gave legitimacy to that people's aspirations to be free. Needless to say, this way of thinking is troublesome when applied to the Confederacy, as it suggests that the South had a moral right to independence, which in turn seems to deny any right of nationhood to black Southerners.

The question of Southern nationalism is, for many, really a moral question. "Was the South a nation?" is often a cover for the question "Did the South deserve to be a nation?" As its nineteenth-century theorists desired, nationalism is still seen as giving moral legitimacy. In this regard, the question of Southern nationalism is linked to the question of Confederate defeat; as Drew Gilpin Faust has pointed out, "Confederate defeat became for many southerners an expression of the region's moral inadequacies."

It might be better to think of nationalism as not a thing but a process. If we do think of nationalism as a process, how successful was Confederate nationalism? The instinctive answer is, not very—there is no Confederate nation. But that is the result of military defeat. Military defeat is not the same as a failure of the nationalistic process.

If the Confederacy had succeeded, would the new political reality of an independent state have created a sense of nation among at least white Southerners? And if Confederate independence had been established by a war of secession, would the war itself have helped create that sense of nation? Any answer is speculative. Mine is "probably."

What is clear is that the Confederate experience itself created "the South" as nothing had done before it. Now white Southerners had a new set of heroes, a new series of grievances and griefs, a new history that united them at the same time it set them apart from the rest of the nation. If nationalism is primarily an emotional response, it was one deeply felt after 1865 as Southerners created the mythology of the Lost Cause. One final product of the Civil War, one final product of Confederate nationalism, was loyalty to a dead nation.

[*See also* Civil War, *articles on* Causes of the War, Strategy, *and* Causes of Defeat; Economy; Expansionism in the Antebellum South; Fire-eaters; Honor; Morale; Population; Proslavery; Religion; Slavery.]

BIBLIOGRAPHY

Beringer, Richard E., Herman Hattaway, Archer Jones, and William N. Still, Jr. *Why the South Lost the Civil War.* Athens, Ga., 1986.

Escott, Paul D. *After Secession: Jefferson Davis and the Failure of Confederate Nationalism.* Baton Rouge, La., 1978.

Faust, Drew G. *The Creation of Confederate Nationalism: Ideology and Identity in the Civil War South.* Baton Rouge, La., 1988.

Genovese, Eugene. *The Political Economy of Slavery: Studies in the Economy and Society of the Slave South.* New York, 1965.

McCardell, John. *The Idea of a Southern Nation: Southern Nationalists and Southern Nationalism, 1830–1860.* New York, 1979.

McWhiney, Gray, and Perry D. Jamieson. *Attack and Die: Civil War Military Tactics and the Southern Heritage.* University, Ala., 1982.

Owsley, Frank L. *States Rights in the Confederacy.* Chicago, 1925.

Potter, David M. *The Impending Crisis, 1848–1861.* New York, 1976.

Powell, Lawrence, and Michael Wayne. "Self-Interest and the Decline of Confederate Nationalism." In *The Old South in the Crucible of War.* Edited by Harry Owens and James Cooke. Jackson, Miss., 1983.

Stampp, Kenneth M. "The Southern Road to Appomattox." In *The Imperilled Union: Essays on the Background of the Civil War.* New York, 1980.

Thomas, Emory M. *The Confederate Nation, 1861–1865.* New York, 1979.

REID MITCHELL

NAVAL GUNS

[*This entry is composed of four articles:* Confederate Naval Guns; Captured U.S. Naval Guns; European Naval Guns; *and* Naval Munitions. *See also* Charlotte Navy Yard; Columbus Naval Ironworks; Gosport Navy Yard; Munitions, *article on* Naval Munitions; Selma Naval Ordnance Works; Tredegar Ironworks.]

Confederate Naval Guns

The Confederacy faced serious problems in securing naval ordnance. Its sole prewar source for the manufacture of heavy guns was the Tredegar works (J. R. Anderson and Company) at Richmond. During the conflict Tredegar produced the bulk of ordnance for the Confederacy: between 1,043 and 1,099 pieces of all types, an output equal to the total of 1,050 guns produced by the eleven other Southern firms during the same period. Tredegar, however, was not able to cast heavy guns hollow on the Rodman method, which cooled the gun from the interior by means of water passed through a hollow core. This process produced guns of greater strength. Anderson's refusal to adopt the Rodman method in the years before the war had a profound impact on the Confederate ability to cast heavy guns during the conflict, and no Rodman-method guns were finished in time for actual service on the Confederate side.

In February 1863, the Confederate government purchased a new facility, which became the Selma, Alabama,

> **Confederate naval ordnance production was sufficient to meet the Confederacy's more modest requirements. . . .**

Naval Works. It cast ordnance, chiefly for use against Union ironclads, but as of February 1865, it had produced less than two hundred guns. Other heavy guns were also manufactured at the Bellona Foundry near Richmond.

Despite problems, Confederate naval ordnance production was sufficient to meet the Confederacy's more modest requirements, although the lack of manufacturing facilities and skilled labor led to difficulties in mounting guns and shortages in shells and wrought-iron bolts.

Most Confederate naval ordnance consisted of captured Union pieces, but some excellent pieces were designed by John M. Brooke. A lieutenant in the U.S. Navy, Brooke resigned his commission upon the secession of Virginia. He was in charge of naval ordnance experiments and later was chief of naval ordnance for the Confederacy. Brooke developed shells, fuses, a flat-headed bolt for use against ironclads, and submarine mines, but he is best known for his naval ordnance.

Brooke designed 32-pounder and 10- and 11-inch smoothbores, all based on standard U.S. Navy patterns. An 1863 design for a 10-inch smoothbore gun was double-banded and 158.5 inches in length. Brooke, however, is best known for his rifled guns. The Union navy favored Dahlgren smoothbores in turreted ironclads, but the Confederate navy embraced rifled guns in ironclad, casemated vessels. Brooke's rifles, in 6.4-, 7-, and 8-inch sizes, were the most accurate and powerful guns developed in the Confederacy and quite possibly the best naval weapons on either side in the war. The guns greatly resembled the Union Parrott rifled gun in form, but differed from it in having a second and even third ring of reinforcing bands. Instead of being solid, these bands, approximately six inches wide, were made up of a succession of rings. Brooke's rifled guns weighed more than comparable Union Parrott rifles.

The first Brooke rifle was a 7-inch. It was essentially the 9-inch Dahlgren pattern gun, bored out to only 7 inches and then rifled. From 143 to 147.5 inches long, it weighed 15,000 pounds, was designed for pivot use, and was produced in four patterns. It took shells of 110 pounds and bolts of 120 pounds. Brooke 7-inch rifled guns firing armor-piercing bolts were responsible for much of the damage on Union monitors attacking Charleston in 1863.

The 6.4-inch Brooke rifle, based on the standard U.S. Navy 32-pounder design, was from 141 to 144 inches long, weighed 9,000 pounds, and was intended as a broadside gun only. It was produced in two patterns. It took shells of 65 pounds and bolts of 80 pounds.

Little is known of the 8-inch Brooke, which was produced in only one pattern. Some Brooke rifles were later reamed up to make larger smoothbores: the 6.4-inch rifle, for example, became an 8-inch piece, and the 8-inch rifle a 10-inch smoothbore.

The output of Brooke guns during the Civil War was quite small. Tredegar cast no more than eighty-three rifled guns; most were 7-inch types, and only one was an 8-inch. The same foundry cast sixteen Brooke smoothbores. But these were only a small amount of the total produced by Tredegar.

> **. . . the exteriors of Confederate guns were often the same as when they left the molds.**

At Selma an additional fifty-five Brooke rifles and eighteen smoothbores were cast from January 1864 to March 1865.

A principal difference between Union and Confederate naval guns was that Confederate pieces were not given a smooth exterior finish. "Turning smooth" contributed nothing to the functioning of the gun and was a costly operation; the exteriors of Confederate guns were often the same as when they left the molds.

Tennessee, most powerful of all Confederate ironclads, mounted two 7-inch Brookes in pivot and four 6.4-inch rifled guns in broadside on two-truck Marsilly carriages. The two 7-inch pieces are now at the Washington Navy Yard. Among Confederate vessels mounting Brookes were the ironclads *Virginia* and *Nashville* and gunboats *Gaines, Morgan, Selma, Peedee, Muscogee,* and *Chattahoochee.*

Confederate navy ordnance practices were essentially those of the U.S. Navy, and the 1864 Confederate navy ordnance manual is an almost word-for-word copy of that of the U.S. Navy.

Contrary to what some Union naval officers thought at the start of the conflict, Confederate naval ordnance arrangements were on a par with their own. As Rear Adm. Louis Goldsborough, commander of the Union North Atlantic Blockading Squadron, noted regarding Confederate vessels in early 1862: "His ordnance arrangements take us quite by surprise. They are really excellent, if not admirable. We have captured quite a large number of his guns & fixings, & are mounting some of the former on board our own vessels."

BIBLIOGRAPHY

Tucker, Spencer C. *Arming the Fleet: U.S. Navy Ordnance in the Muzzle-Loading Era.* Annapolis, Md., 1989.
Tucker, Spencer C. "Confederate Naval Ordnance." *Journal of the Confederacy* 4 (1989): 133–152.

SPENCER C. TUCKER

Captured U.S. Naval Guns

The Confederacy was fortunate in that Virginia's secession gave it access to the largest prewar U.S. Navy Yard, that of Gosport, also known as the Norfolk Navy Yard. There the Confederates captured 1,198 heavy guns, ranging from carronades to modern shell guns and including fifty-two 9-inch Dahlgrens. They also took three Dahlgren boat howitzers, as well as large quantities of powder and shell. The frigate *Merrimack* alone yielded 2,200 powder cartridges stored in her magazines in watertight tanks. Within a few months the yard had shipped 533 guns all over the Confederacy. Most went to arm fortifications, but a number saw service afloat. In addition, the Confederacy obtained thirty-three cannon and some ordnance stores at Pensacola.

Throughout the war, the Confederates made excellent use of their captured Union ordnance. For example, two 9-inch Dahlgrens were mounted in pivot on board *Charleston,* along with four Brookes in broadside. *Virginia* mounted six 9-inch Dahlgrens in broadside along with two Brookes in pivot. The Confederacy modified a number of the captured pieces by giving them rifling and banding. Usually these were single-banded, but there were also double-banded pieces.

At the beginning of the war, the U.S. Navy employed a mix of old-system and new Dahlgren-system guns. It is safe to assume that all old-system guns were employed by both sides during the war. The U.S. Navy's Dahlgren pieces had been introduced in the 1850s. They were instantly recognizable by their heavier weight of metal around the breech, leading them to be known as "soda bottles." The mainstay of the Dahlgren system was the 9-inch smoothbore, introduced in 1850, which was designed for both pivot and broadside use. It weighed 9,200 pounds and was 107 inches in length of bore. Both sides used it during the war.

BIBLIOGRAPHY

Tucker, Spencer C. *Arming the Fleet: U.S. Navy Ordnance in the Muzzle-Loading Era.* Annapolis, Md., 1989.
Tucker, Spencer C. "Confederate Naval Ordnance." *Journal of the Confederacy* 4 (1989): 133–152.

SPENCER C. TUCKER

European Naval Guns

Because the Confederacy lacked facilities to manufacture sufficient guns for its needs, the government sought to purchase them abroad. Virtually all ordnance obtained from overseas was of English manufacture, and the most highly prized were rifled guns. Three were successful: the Armstrong, Whitworth, and Blakely. A fourth, the Clay, was a failure.

William G. Armstrong produced his first breech-loading rifled gun in 1855. Armstrongs were built-up guns of wrought-iron tubes from spiral coils; some had a main tube of steel. The breech unscrewed for loading. Armstrongs were also made as muzzleloaders and came in a variety of calibers from 6- to 600-pounders. *Stonewall,* constructed for the Confederacy in France, mounted three: a 300-pounder in a casemate forward and two 70-pounders aft. There may have been attempts to produce Armstrongs at New Orleans and Norfolk during the war.

The Whitworth rifled gun, designed by Joseph Whitworth, was also both a breechloader and a muzzleloader. Its unique feature was a hexagonal spiral bore. Its delicate mechanisms were prone to jam, however, and projectiles sometimes lodged in the bore and could be freed only by heavy blows, with occasional fatal results. The Whitworth was made both of cast iron bored from the solid, and of steel, with wrought-iron rings shrunk on. By 1862, Whitworth guns were of 3-, 12, and 80-pounder sizes and ranged in weight from 208 pounds to 4 tons. The Union navy captured four 5-inchers on the blockade runner *Princess Royal* near Morris Island in January 1863, two of which were part of the Union battery on Morris Island.

The Blakely was constructed on the same built-up principle as the Armstrong and Whitworth, with wrought-iron rings shrunk around a cast-iron core. It appeared only as a muzzleloader. Because Alexander T. Blakely had no manufacturing facilities of his own, his designs were cast by others in a variety of sizes and configurations. *Alabama,* constructed in England under the name *Enrica,* mounted a 7-inch Blakely in pivot, as well as other English-manufactured guns: a 68-pounder pivot gun and six long 32-pounder smoothbores in broadside. (To satisfy Britain's Foreign Enlistment Act, *Enrica,* like other English-made Confederate ships, had to be sent out of the country unarmed. Its armament was sent on another vessel and transferred at the Portuguese island Terceira after the Confederates had taken possession of *Enrica.*) A 7-inch Blakely rifle, mounted in pivot on *Florida,* may be seen at the Washington Navy Yard.

BIBLIOGRAPHY

Ripley, Warren. *Artillery and Ammunition of the Civil War.* New York, 1970.
Tucker, Spencer C. "Confederate Naval Ordnance." *Journal of the Confederacy* 4 (1989): 133–152.

SPENCER C. TUCKER

Naval Munitions

Confederate warships were equipped with a wide variety of artillery projectiles, depending on the type of ordnance carried aboard. Smoothbore cannons were usually supplied with spherical solid shot and explosive shell, grapeshot, and canister. Late in the war, particularly with the advent of the large-caliber Brooke smoothbores, wrought-iron bolts were issued in limited quantities for use against ironclads at close range. Rifled cannons, especially the much-favored Brooke rifles, could be provided with some or all of the following projectile types: cast-iron bolts, chilled-iron bolts, wrought-iron bolts (the latter two for use against ironclads), percussion- and time-fused shell, grape, canister, and shrapnel. In addition, incendiary shell were sometimes furnished in small numbers to both types of cannons.

The navy initially procured projectiles from numerous government and private sources, but by 1864 naval ordnance works at Atlanta, Charlotte, Richmond, and Selma were the principal suppliers. A considerable amount of ordnance was also brought in through the blockade.

To satisfy propellant needs, the navy established a powder mill at Petersburg, Virginia, but removed it to Columbia, South Carolina, in mid-1862. Army and imported powder supplemented the facility's output, even after production was able to meet the navy's demands in 1864.

The Confederate navy's Bureau of Ordnance and Hydrography was progressive and innovative. Under the guidance of Comdr. John Mercer Brooke through most of the war, the bureau developed new types of fuses and projectiles and experimented extensively with others. It was particularly interested in developing projectiles able to penetrate the thick-skinned armor of Union monitors and tested such modern designs as an armor-piercing rifle shell with a delayed action fuse that caused detonation only after penetration was achieved. Although the Confederate navy never gained parity with its foe in the quantity of ordnance produced, the technology it employed was often superior.

BIBLIOGRAPHY

Dickey, Thomas S., and Peter C. George. *Field Artillery Projectiles of the American Civil War.* Atlanta, Ga., 1980.

Kerkis, Sidney C., and Thomas S. Dickey. *Heavy Artillery Projectiles of the Civil War, 1861–1865.* Kennesaw, Ga., 1972.

Ripley, Warren. *Artillery and Ammunition of the Civil War.* 4th ed. rev. Charleston, S.C., 1984.

Still, William N. *Confederate Shipbuilding.* 2d ed. Columbia, S.C., 1987.

Wells, Tom H. *The Confederate Navy: A Study in Organization.* University, Ala., 1971.

A. ROBERT HOLCOMBE, JR.

NAVAL STATIONS

Confederate naval stations were administrative and logistical units occupying specific geographical areas defined by the secretary of the navy. The station commander, often assisted by an ordnance officer, a surgeon, a paymaster, and an engineer, was responsible for recruiting, ordnance works, naval storehouses, hospitals, marine detachments, and sometimes naval construction in his district. He also inspected commissioned vessels in port and reported their conditions to the department, and he received all reports and requisitions from the commanders of vessels within the limits of his station. By regulation he exercised no authority or control over the commanding officer of a navy yard without the express permission or order of the secretary of the navy. In practice, however, the administrative distinction between station and yard was often ambiguous, and many stations and yards within the same area were under the command of a single officer. Prior to the spring of 1863 the station commander had operational control of warships within his territorial limits.

> ... the Confederate navy operated at least fourteen stations during the course of the war.

Afterward, in an effort to have younger, more aggressive officers in control of the naval forces afloat, he was taken out of the operational chain of command and placed in a logistical support role.

Although the imprecise terminology used in contemporary records often makes it difficult to distinguish between various types of naval establishments, the Confederate navy operated at least fourteen stations during the course of the war: Richmond, Virginia; Halifax, Kinston, Charlotte, and Wilmington, North Carolina; Marion Court House and Charleston, South Carolina; Savannah and Columbus,

Georgia; St. Marks, Florida; Mobile, Alabama; Jackson, Mississippi; and New Orleans and Shreveport, Louisiana. Additionally, some sources consider the installations at Little Rock, Arkansas; Selma, Alabama; and Yazoo City, Mississippi, as naval stations.

BIBLIOGRAPHY

C.S. Navy Department. *Regulations for the Navy of the Confederate States, 1862.* Richmond, Va., 1862.

Still, William N. *Confederate Shipbuilding.* 2d ed. Columbia, S.C., 1987.

Wells, Tom H. *The Confederate Navy: A Study in Organization.* University, Ala., 1971.

A. ROBERT HOLCOMBE, JR.

NAVY

[*This entry is composed of four articles:* Confederate Navy, *which overviews the creation and activities of the Confederate Navy;* Navy Department, *which discusses the organization and leadership of the cabinet-level department overseeing the navy;* Manpower, *which discusses the demographic makeup of the navy; and* African Americans in the Confederate Navy, *which examines the role of African Americans in the construction, maintenance, and operations of the navy. For further discussion of naval ordnance, shipbuilding, and ships, see* Arms, Weapons, and Ammunition, *article on* Naval Ordnance; Blockade, *article on* Blockade Runners; Davids; Powder Works; Rams; Shipyards; Submarines. *See also* Anglo-Confederate Purchasing; Marine Corps; Naval Stations; State Navies; Uniforms, *article on Navy and Marines Uniforms;* Waterways.]

Confederate Navy

On February 20, 1861, delegates from the seven Southern states that had proclaimed their secession from the Union passed an act to establish a Navy Department. The act provided for the appointment of a secretary, a chief clerk, and other minor officials. The following day Stephen R. Mallory of Florida was designated secretary of the Confederate States Navy. The organization of the Confederate navy was patterned after that of the U.S. Navy. A congressional act created four bureaus: Ordnance and Hydrography, Orders and Details, Medicine and Surgery, and Provisions and Clothing. The act also established a Marine Corps. Later a chief constructor and chief engineer were added.

Building the Navy. The newly organized navy needed ships and personnel to man them. Some 343 officers, approximately 24 percent of the 1,554 officers who were serving in the U.S. Navy as of December 1, 1860, resigned their Union commissions and joined the Confederate navy. Of this number about a third would in time actually serve. The majority of the remainder accepted appointments with the Confederate army or state military forces or were too old and unfit for active duty. The navy's officer corps would reach a maximum number of 753.

Enlisted personnel were more difficult to acquire. Few left the U.S. Navy for Confederate service. Through volunteering, conscription, and transfer from the army, 3,674 were on active duty by the beginning of 1865.

Confederate Marines numbered 539 officers and men in October 1864. Detachments served on various warships including commerce cruisers, as well as stations and other shore facilities and fortifications.

Ships were equally scarce. The Confederate navy inherited five small vessels from the seceded states. In addition, four revenue cutters, three slavers, two privately owned coastal steamers, and *Fulton,* an old side-wheeler laid up in the Pensacola Navy Yard, were purchased or seized. As a stopgap measure the Navy Department continued purchasing merchant steamers for conversion, but Secretary Mallory determined to initiate a warship construction program at home and abroad.

In May 1861 naval agents were sent to Great Britain and France to obtain vessels that could be used for commerce raiding. Later the department contracted for the construction of armored warships. *Stonewall,* however, was the only one of these ironclads to reach Confederate hands. The South was more successful in obtaining wooden cruisers. Commerce raiding has traditionally been a strategy of nations with weak navies, and the Confederacy, with its limited warship building expertise and facilities, could not create a navy strong enough to challenge Union seapower. Also, Mallory hoped to weaken the blockade by forcing the Union navy to convoy merchant ships and seek out and destroy the raiders in various parts of the world. Finally, commerce raiding might disrupt Union shipping to the point where Abraham Lincoln's government would have to negotiate an end to the conflict in order to prevent economic disaster.

The Confederate government built or purchased at home and abroad more than a dozen raiders including *Alabama, Florida,* and *Shenandoah.* Together they destroyed some 5 percent of the Union merchant fleet and seized or destroyed millions of dollars in cargo. For every vessel the Confederate raiders destroyed or seized, the Union merchant fleet lost eight others as an indirect result. Exorbitant insurance rates caused by war risks resulted in hundreds of vessels remaining in port. In addition nearly a thousand were transferred to other flags, principally British. Altogether, more than 1,616 vessels, with a total tonnage of 774,000 tons, were lost to the American merchant marine during the war. Nevertheless, the Confederate raiders had little of the hoped-for influence on

Union policy; the blockade was not weakened and Lincoln and his advisers gave no thought to a negotiated peace.

In contrast to the raiders, ironclad warships built by the Confederate government played a more useful role in the war. Secretary Mallory emphasized armored vessels in his construction program. On May 9, 1861, he wrote: "I regard the possession of an iron armored ship as a matter of the first necessity . . . inequality of numbers may be compensated by invulnerability; and thus not only does economy but naval

> **. . . ironclad warships built by the Confederate government played a more useful role. . . .**

success dictate the wisdom and expediency of fighting with iron against wood." Initially, the secretary concentrated on obtaining armored warships in Europe but in the summer he ordered the conversion of *Merrimack* into *Virginia* and contracted for the building of two ironclads in New Orleans (*Mississippi* and *Louisiana*), and two in Memphis (*Arkansas* and *Tennessee*). These five ironclads were all unusually large and were designed to operate on the open sea as well as on inland waters. They were intended not only to break the blockade but also, as Secretary Mallory wrote, to "traverse the entire coast of the United States . . . and encounter, with a fair prospect of success, their entire Navy."

By 1862 Mallory abandoned his decision to build large seagoing ironclads within the Confederacy and instead concentrated on small, shallow-draft, harbor-defense armored vessels. Various factors influenced this change in policy: the apparent unseaworthiness of *Virginia* and the ironclads built in New Orleans and Memphis, the belief that the South would be able to obtain powerful seagoing armored ships in Europe, and the pressing need for defensive vessels. Because of the continuing success of the Union's combined operations along the Southern coastline as well as the ineffectiveness of the blockade, Confederate naval strategy emphasized defense. Naval forces were organized to guard ports and rivers and inlets that opened the interior to invasion. The small ironclads were designed to be the nucleus of these naval forces.

Approximately forty were laid down within the Confederacy and half of them completed and placed in operation. The James River Squadron included *Virginia II, Richmond,* and *Fredericksburg;* the Wilmington Squadron, *North Carolina* and *Raleigh;* the Charleston Squadron, *Chicora, Palmetto State, Charleston,* and *Columbia;* the Savannah Squadron, *Atlantic, Georgia,* and *Savannah;* and the Mobile Squadron, *Tennessee* (II), *Nashville, Tuscaloosa,* and *Huntsville.* A number of ironclads were constructed on the rivers: *Albemarle* on the Roanoke, *Neuse* on the Neuse,

Jackson on the Chattahoochee, and *Missouri* on the Red. In cooperation with wooden gunboats, forts, and other land and water defenses, these armored warships played a major role in Confederate defense efforts, and they contributed significantly to the defense of Richmond, Charleston, Savannah, and Mobile. *Albemarle* was instrumental in the recapture of Plymouth, North Carolina, in April 1864.

The Confederate government also contracted for a large number of wooden gunboats, many of which were completed and joined the various squadrons. Several experimental vessels such as the submarine *H. L. Hunley* and the semi-submergible *David* were completed. Both *Hunley* and *David* successfully attacked Union warships. Other vessels similar to *David* were laid down but never became operational.

Gun foundries, machine shops, rolling mills, and other manufacturing facilities needed to outfit warships were established in the Confederacy, but these industries were severely handicapped by the lack of labor. Nevertheless, ordnance works in Richmond and Selma, Alabama, cast hundreds of guns, the majority designed by John Mercer Brooke, chief of the Bureau of Ordnance and Hydrography. Armor plate was rolled by Tredegar in Richmond, the Shelby Iron Works in Alabama, and the Atlanta Rolling Mill. Machinery was manufactured in Columbus, Georgia.

The Naval War. The Confederacy suffered setbacks before the new warships were ready for active service. In November 1861, a combined Union army and naval force captured Port Royal, South Carolina, despite Confederate defenses including a small naval squadron of converted steamers. In the winter and spring of 1862, Federal forces occupied much of coastal North Carolina, defeating a number of small Confederate gunboats in the process. During this period Confederate naval forces were also involved in combat in Virginia waters.

The James River Squadron was established in 1861 and consisted of the small gunboats *Patrick Henry, Jameston, Teaser, Raleigh,* and *Beaufort.* In early March 1862, the ironclad *Virginia* converted from *Merrimack* joined the small naval force. *Virginia* encountered the Union ironclad *Monitor* in an indecisive engagement that lasted nearly four hours. Both vessels, damaged but intact, withdrew. In May with the capture of Norfolk by Union forces, *Virginia* was blown up by its crew, and the remainder of the James River Squadron withdrew up the James.

In the West, the year 1862 was equally disastrous for Confederate naval forces. On April 24 a Union fleet under Flag Officer David Farragut ran past two forts guarding the Mississippi River below New Orleans and engaged more than a dozen Confederate vessels. All were destroyed or surrendered including the ironclad *Manassas. Mississippi* and *Louisiana,* two large ironclads under construction in New Orleans, were also destroyed by the Confederates to prevent their capture.

Although the Confederate government would lay down additional warships in the Yazoo and Red rivers, including the ironclad *Missouri* at Shreveport, Louisiana, none would be combat-tested. By late 1862, however, the first of the harbor defense ironclads were approaching completion. *Palmetto State* in Charleston and *Georgia* in Savannah, were commissioned in the fall. Sixteen additional armored vessels would be added to the fleet in the following two years and would become the nucleus of the various Confederate squadrons. More than a dozen would never be completed because of the lack of iron and the scarcity of workers.

Newly built wooden gunboats were also joining the fleet. *Morgan* and *Gaines* in Mobile and *Hampton* and *Nansemond* in Norfolk, Virginia, were completed and commissioned in the fall of 1862. The latter two were "Maury gunboats," named after Matthew Fontaine Maury, famous oceanographer and father of hydrography in the U.S. Navy, who resigned his commission to join the Confederate navy. One hundred of these small wooden gunboats were planned, but very few were actually finished. *Chattahoochee* was completed on the Chattahoochee River in 1863, and the *Pee Dee* on the Pee Dee in 1864.

By 1863 Union blockading squadrons along the Atlantic and Gulf coasts had increased to more than three hundred ships including several of the recently completed monitors. Confederate military officials in Charleston determined to attack the Federal naval force off the port before it was closed. On the last day of January 1863 two Confederate ironclads, *Chicora* and *Palmetto State,* steamed out of the harbor and forced the surrender of two blockaders, *Mercedita* and *Keystone State.* Efforts to bring other Union warships under fire were unsuccessful, and in fact the two that surrendered took advantage of the confusion to rejoin the retiring Union naval force. The two Confederate ironclads returned to the harbor. For the remainder of the war the Charleston Squadron guarded the channels and cooperated with the forts and batteries in defending the port. The Confederate vessels were destroyed by their crews as Gen. William Tecumseh Sherman's army approached the city.

In the spring of 1862 Federal forces took Fort Pulaski, guarding the river entry to Savannah, Georgia. The combined forces, however, were unable to capture the port. Confederate defenses included a squadron of ironclads and wooden gunboats. The first ironclad in the squadron, *Georgia,* was moored in the Savannah River where it could fire down either channel. Later the ironclad *Savannah* and the wooden gunboats *Isondiga* and *Macon* reinforced *Georgia.* The squadron included a third ironclad, *Atlanta.* It was converted from the blockade runner *Fingal* and when completed was probably the most powerful armored warship in Confederate service. In July 1863 it attempted to evade blockaders off the port but ran aground in the river and surrendered to two monitors. As in Charleston the approach of

Sherman's army resulted in the destruction of the Confederate naval vessels by their crews.

Richmond, Virginia, the capital, was also defended by a Confederate naval squadron. After the fall of Norfolk in May 1862, the James River Squadron retired up the James above obstructions at Drewry's Bluff. There the ships remained throughout the war, venturing below the obstructions only twice. The nucleus of the Confederate naval forces in the James were the ironclads *Virginia II, Richmond,* and *Fredericksburg.* This force exchanged gunfire with Federal land batteries and warships below the obstructions until Richmond was evacuated in April 1865. The decision to evacuate led to the destruction of the ironclads, the wooden gunboats, and the training ship *Patrick Henry* by their crews. They then joined other naval personnel and Marines who had manned batteries along the river and retired from the abandoned capital.

In North Carolina Flag Officer William F. Lynch commanded the naval forces. His force consisted of a small squadron of ironclads and wooden vessels in the Cape Fear River guarding Wilmington and two ironclads constructed on the Neuse and Roanoke rivers. These two warships were built to cooperate in the recapture of eastern North Carolina including the sounds. In April 1864 *Albemarle,* constructed on the Roanoke River, successfully cooperated in a combined attack against Federal forces at Plymouth. The Confederate attempt to enter the sound was repulsed by Union warships. Later *Albemarle* was sunk at its moorings by a Union raiding force in a small boat. In May the ironclad *Raleigh* attacked blockaders off the Cape Fear River. After a futile effort to destroy the Union ships, the Confederate ironclad grounded while attempting to reenter the river. With the exception of *Albemarle,* which was raised and towed to Norfolk by Union personnel, all Confederate naval vessels in North Carolina waters were destroyed by their own crews, the Cape Fear Squadron upon the fall of Fort Fisher in February 1865 and the ironclad *Neuse* in the Neuse River in April.

The Mobile Squadron was commanded by Adm. Franklin Buchanan. In 1864 it consisted of four ironclads and wooden gunboats. On August 5, 1864, units of the squadron engaged a Federal fleet under Adm. David Farragut. Buchanan's force was defeated: the ironclad *Tennessee* and wooden gunboat *Selma* were captured, the gunboat *Gaines* ran aground, and the gunboat *Morgan* escaped. In the months that followed, *Morgan* along with the ironclads *Huntsville, Tuscaloosa,* and *Nashville* defended the river approaches to Mobile in cooperation with land forces. The capture of Mobile on April 12, 1865, resulted in the destruction of these ships by their crews.

Mobile was the last important port in the Confederacy to surrender. In all the ports, except Galveston, naval units contributed to their defense. Nonetheless, the Confederate navy had limited success against Federal warships. Only a half-dozen Union vessels of war were actually sunk in action by Confederate warships. This includes *Underwriter,* destroyed in a small-boat engagement. Torpedoes (mines) proved to be the most successful weapon used against Union ships. More than sixty ships including armored vessels were sunk by

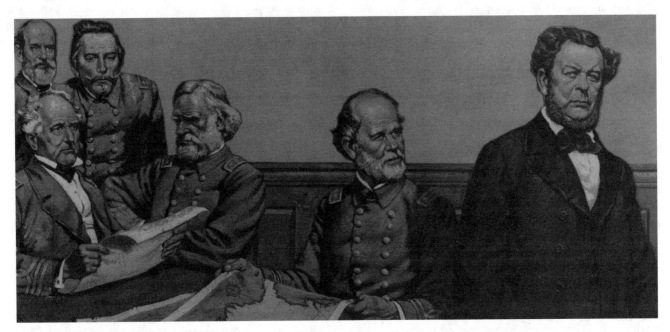

CONFEDERATE NAVAL LEADERS. Seated from left to right are Franklin Buchanan, Josiah Tattnall, and Matthew Fontaine Maury. Standing from left to right are George N. Hollins, Raphael Semmes, and Stephen R. Mallory. Painted by Creative Arts Studio for *Naval History Film,* part 1.

NAVAL HISTORICAL CENTER, WASHINGTON, D.C.

Confederate torpedoes during the war. In the final analysis, however, the Confederate navy had little chance against its more formidable opponent.

[*For further discussion of particular naval squadrons, see* Charleston Squadron; James River Squadrons; Mobile Squadron; River Defense Fleet; Savannah Squadron.]

BIBLIOGRAPHY

Merli, Frank J. *Great Britain and the Confederate Navy.* Bloomington, Ind., 1970.

Perry, Milton F. *Infernal Machines: The Story of Confederate Submarine and Mine Warfare.* Baton Rouge, La., 1965.

Scharf, J. Thomas. *History of the Confederate States Navy.* New York, 1887. Reprint, New York, 1977.

Spencer, Warren F. *The Confederate Navy in Europe.* University, Ala., 1983.

Still, William N., Jr. *Confederate Shipbuilding.* Columbia, S.C., 1987.

Still, William N., Jr. *Iron Afloat: The Story of the Confederate Armorclads.* Columbia, S.C., 1986.

Wells, Tom H. *The Confederate Navy: A Study in Organization.* University, Ala., 1971.

WILLIAM N. STILL, JR.

Navy Department

On February 20, 1861, the Confederate Congress meeting in Montgomery enacted legislation creating the Confederate Navy Department. To head this department President Jefferson Davis turned to Stephen R. Mallory. Born on the island of Jamaica, Mallory moved as an infant to Key West, Florida, a place he would always cherish as home. A successful lawyer, he entered the U.S. Senate in 1851 and served on the Naval Committee, becoming chairman in 1855. Thanks to his position, Mallory was without doubt well informed on naval matters. When Florida left the Union in January 1861, Mallory resigned from the Senate and returned home until summoned by Davis to his new post.

Under the legislation of February 20 the Navy Department's administrative structure consisted of the secretary, two chief clerks, three additional clerks, and a messenger. Initially the department had its offices in Montgomery, but during May and June 1861 it moved with the rest of the Confederate government to Richmond. The Navy Department's offices were located in the Mechanics Institute on Ninth Street between Main and Franklin. Here Mallory and his staff wrestled with the problems of creating and managing a navy.

For the most part matters of policy and strategy were decided by the secretary and his two chief clerks, French Forrest and E. M. Tidball. Forrest was an old navy veteran who had joined the service shortly before the War of 1812. He detested bureaucratic routine, and after importuning the

secretary, he was assigned to more active duty. Tidball was not an officer but a bureaucrat who brought to the office political and managerial skills the secretary would find useful.

Despite the tidal wave of problems the department encountered, its employees were fortunate in one respect: they did not have to contend with constant meddling from the president. As a West Point graduate and former secretary of war, Jefferson Davis felt competent to intrude into matters of Confederate military policy and strategy, a habit that often proved troublesome. Having virtually no background in naval matters, however, he rarely interfered in that department's affairs. On the other hand, although this hands-off policy was generally positive, it did have some negative impact. Davis's lack of appreciation for naval power bordered at times on indifference, a common characteristic among Confederate leaders. As secretary, one of Mallory's chief tasks was simply to make the president and his colleagues aware of the value of the Confederate navy in order to garner support.

Organization

To assist the secretary in formulating and executing policy, four offices were created, all located at the general headquarters on Ninth Street. The organization closely resembled the one Mallory had helped fashion to administer the Federal navy in the antebellum years.

J. K. Mitchell was in charge of the Office of Orders and Detail, which held primary responsibility for matters of personnel, including the recruiting, promotion, and assignment of officers and crews. The office also had logistical responsibilities that included procurement and distribution of coal and operations at the naval ropewalk in Petersburg.

The Office of Ordnance and Hydrography was in the hands of John M. Brooke, an Annapolis graduate. As its name implies, Brooke's department was responsible for obtaining and distributing to the fleet ordnance and munitions. It was also the duty of this office to provide navigational equipment including instruments and charts as well as to oversee the maintenance of docks and yards.

Medicine and Surgery was under the direction of W. A. W. Spotswood and was charged with providing medical service to the navy. The department administered a hospital in Richmond and smaller institutions at various ports. Providing sufficient quantities of drugs was a particular problem: the department was forced to place an inordinate reliance on costly supplies delivered by blockade runners.

The fourth principal office was that of Provisions and Clothing under the command of John De Bree. Acting much like a quartermaster corps, the men under De Bree were responsible for delivering food, clothing, and other such items to the men in the fleet. Key to the functioning of this office were the paymasters and assistant paymasters, who dealt both with officers and enlisted men of the navy and with civilian contractors and suppliers.

Although these four offices handled the bulk of the affairs of the Navy Department, there were other places of power that, because they did not fall neatly under these offices, enjoyed a fair degree of autonomy. Among them were Steam Engineering, Naval Constructor, Torpedo Bureau, and the Marine Corps. In addition there were floating forces under army command, most notably the Mississippi River Defense Force in 1862 and the Texas Marine Department.

Mallory's organization had much to recommend it, but it suffered from two chronic weaknesses of the Confederacy itself: poverty and state rights, or decentralization. Problems arising from an inadequate budget were compounded by the independent attitudes of the Confederate states. Having left the Union in the name of state rights, the members of the Confederacy were reluctant to grant another central government, this one in Richmond, power over them. The result for the navy was a high degree of decentralization that often resulted in poor planning and control.

Outfitting the Navy

Although shortages of nearly everything would greatly hamper the Confederate navy, at the beginning of the war it was ironically a surplus that proved nettlesome. When confronted with the need to decide where their loyalty lay—with the Union or with their home state—many Federal naval officers chose their state. These men who "went south" either wrote to or showed up at the offices on Ninth Street to offer their services. To accommodate these officers, at least on paper, the Confederate Congress in April 1862 authorized the appointment of nine admirals, six commodores, twenty captains, twenty commanders, twenty first lieutenants, sixty-five second lieutenants, and sixty masters.

Finding berths for all these men was impossible, and few of these billets were actually filled. At its height the Confederate navy never had more than forty vessels in service. Most of the officers who volunteered their services either ended up on furlough awaiting orders or were directed to the army where they were often attached to a heavy ordnance unit. Those for whom berths were found, however, generally proved to be able and courageous officers.

Under Mallory's direction, the department focused on three strategic goals: the harassment of Union shipping; protection of the Atlantic and Gulf ports; and defense of the Mississippi and its southern tributaries. Each of these tasks presented special problems, but they shared a common requirement—ships.

From the outset Mallory appreciated that it would never be possible for the Confederacy to outbuild the Union; Southerners had neither the shipyards nor the resources to win a race against the North. Driven by that constraint, Mallory opted to build ironclads, hoping that a superior weapons system would compensate for numbers. His prescience in this matter helped make the Confederate States

Navy far more effective than it might otherwise have been. Despite critical shortages of nearly everything necessary for the construction of modern ironclad warships, the South managed to launch a goodly number, enough at least to keep a vastly superior Union navy busily engaged. Altogether during the war the Confederate Navy Department built at least twenty ironclads.

Some of the ironclads, as well as conventional vessels, were built at private yards in the South. Others, however, were built in facilities under direct Department of the Navy control. During the war the department had in operation at one time or another twenty yards, one powderworks, two shops for constructing marine engines, five ordnance manufactories, and the ropewalk in Petersburg. Given the general lack of shipbuilding resources, the Confederacy did remarkably well to build as many warships as it did.

Because Mallory understood the domestic limitations on construction, he looked abroad for assistance. In May 1861 he dispatched a secret naval agent, James Dunwoody Bulloch, to England to procure suitable war vessels. Over the next four years Bulloch played a central role in the intrigue designed to evade laws of neutrality so that the Confederacy might obtain warships. Although Bulloch did contract for the construction of two ironclad rams with which Mallory hoped to attack Union blockaders, his work for the secretary for the most part was aimed at obtaining fast vessels designed to raid Union commerce. In this he was very successful.

Mallory believed that by sending raiders to sea he could accomplish two tasks—wreak havoc on Union commerce and at the same time force the Federal navy to withdraw vessels from blockade duty to chase down *Alabama, Florida,* and their sister ships. This did not prove to be the case. The

> Southerners had neither the shipyards nor the resources to win a race against the North.

raiders provided an aura of adventure and romance, but the damage they inflicted, although harmful to Union commerce, was nonetheless tolerable. Furthermore, the Union navy had sufficient vessels available to both chase the raiders and maintain the blockade. Eventually, because no European nation was willing to risk the wrath of the Union, they allowed the raiders to remain in their ports only long enough to make essential repairs and to take on enough fuel to reach the next port. Alone and isolated, unable to find safe ports for resupply and refitting, the raiders found themselves hunted down and either captured or destroyed.

Mallory believed that large ironclads were indispensable for defending Southern ports, a conviction that was reinforced in November 1861 when Port Royal, South Carolina, was attacked by a Federal fleet commanded by Samuel Francis DuPont. Confederate Commodore Josiah Tattnall sortied to defend the port with an assortment of ragtag converted wooden gunboats. A few Federal broadsides sent them scurrying. Unless the Confederacy built vessels more substantial than these cockleshells, Tattnall's rout was likely to be repeated at every Confederate port.

Under the secretary's direction, considerable resources were gathered at New Orleans to build ironclads. The money seems not to have been well spent, however, and during the summer of 1861 the Navy Department was being heavily criticized for its wasteful practices by, among others, Louisiana's governor. Mallory dispatched officers to the Crescent City to clear up the mess and get the ironclads built. Adding to the department's woes was the difficulty of securing sufficient funds for construction from the Confederate Treasury Department and a disagreement within the local army command as to responsibilities for the defense of the city.

The fall of New Orleans in April 1862 sparked numerous investigations within the Confederate government. The Navy Department was not spared. For more than six months a congressional committee took testimony in its inquiry into the administration of the department. In the end Mallory was exonerated from any misconduct; nonetheless, it was a humiliating experience and one that damaged his and the department's reputation.

With New Orleans in Union hands, the Confederate Navy Department was deprived of its only significant shipbuilding facility on the Mississippi. Although the department was able to take into service a variety of rivercraft, these were lightly built vessels that would prove no match for the heavily armed and armored Union squadrons. Mallory's greatest success on the rivers was *Arkansas,* an ironclad built at Yazoo City. It came down the Yazoo in July 1862 and blazed its way through the somnolent Union fleet at anchor near Vicksburg. But it later suffered engine problems and had to be scuttled to avoid capture. The Confederate navy had little impact on the war in the West.

The Navy in Action

Mallory's commitment to ironclads could be most clearly seen along the Atlantic coast. The appearance of *Virginia* on March 8, 1862, demonstrated his belief that large ironclads could both aid in defending the ports and on occasion interrupt the Union blockade. Under his authority other ironclads were built to defend Savannah, Charleston, and the North Carolina sound. At each of these ports Mallory's ironclads posed a threat that the Union forces could not ignore. At the same time, however, with the exception of those at Charleston these ironclads remained only a potential force and never succeeded in attacking and inflicting damage on the enemy. Their inactivity was the object of considerable criticism.

At Charleston Mallory endured an uncomfortable relationship with the army commander Gen. P. G. T. Beauregard. Under the Navy Department's direction two ironclads, *Palmetto State* and *Chicora,* had been built at Charleston for the defense of that port. (In 1864 they were joined by a third, *Charleston.*) To the dismay of Mallory and his department, these ironclads in practice came under the operational authority of Beauregard. At the general's orders in January 1863 these two vessels steamed out of the harbor and drove off the blockaders. It was only a temporary victory, however, for soon the Federals were back with a force sufficient to demolish the Confederates should they make a similar attempt again. Despite the danger, Beauregard urged repeatedly that the ironclads sortie. Mallory would not permit it. The same situation existed at Savannah where the ironclads *Atlanta* and *Savannah* were stationed. Mallory's argument was that sending these vessels out to engage a vastly superior Union force was suicide. He was right; however, the fact that the navy's ironclads remained snug in the harbor angered some and presented a sorry picture to the Southern public. *Atlanta* was run aground and then captured by Union forces in Wassaw Sound, while *Albemarle* was destroyed by Union Navy Lt. William Cushing in one of the great tales of the war. All the Confederate ironclads on the Atlantic coast were destroyed or captured.

One of the arguments Beauregard persisted in making was that the Navy Department ignored the value of torpedoes (underwater mines). Under Mallory's direction the department had established a Torpedo Bureau. Although often unreliable, these weapons had been employed with success on the western rivers, but the department was slow to use them to advantage in the East.

It was at Charleston that the Confederate Navy employed *H. L. Hunley,* a submarine built at Mobile but brought to Charleston in the summer of 1863 on the orders of Beauregard. *Hunley* proved exceedingly unreliable. On two dives it failed to return to the surface with a heavy loss of life. Desperate to find some way to drive the blockaders away, the Confederates on the night of February 17, 1864, sent *Hunley* to attack the Union frigate *Housatonic.* It succeeded in its mission but then went down with all hands lost.

On the Gulf coast at Mobile, the Navy Department placed under construction four ironclads for that port's defense. It was an overly ambitious program that went beyond what local resources could sustain. Only one of the ironclads, *Tennessee,* was completed to the point where it could play a role in defending against the Union attack in August 1864 commanded by Adm. David Farragut. The Confederate naval forces under Franklin Buchanan put up a stiff resistance against a much superior Federal force. *Tennessee* steamed bravely into the middle of the fray only to be sent to the bottom. The remaining unfinished ironclads played no role in the fight.

In addition to building and managing fighting ships, the Navy Department also had under its jurisdiction several blockade runners. Many of these were specially built for the trade under the direction of Bulloch operating under various guises. Altogether about twenty of these vessels served the Confederacy, bringing in much needed supplies, particularly munitions and medicines. On the outward voyage they generally carried cotton. The success of the department's blockade runners is attested to by the fact that Bulloch seemed always to have sufficient cash and credit to carry on his business of ship buying and building. His principal source of income was the sale of cotton run out of the South.

As the war dragged to its climax, Mallory watched unhappily as his ships were captured, scuttled, or destroyed. Some of his vessels participated in the defense of Richmond by trying to hold on to the James River. But the situation was hopeless, and on Sunday evening April 2 Mallory joined Jefferson Davis and the remainder of his cabinet on a train out of Richmond. The withdrawal of the Confederate government soon turned into flight. On May 2 Mallory resigned from the government and a few days later was captured. After an imprisonment of less than a year he was released. He returned to Florida and settled in Pensacola where he remained until his death in November 1873.

Given the resources at hand, the Confederate Navy Department accomplished a great deal. Although Mallory may be faulted for too heavy a reliance on large ironclads and high seas raiders, and inattention to torpedoes, overall he and his department were remarkably effective under the circumstances.

BIBLIOGRAPHY

Anderson, Bern. *By Sea and by River: A Naval History of the Civil War.* New York, 1962.

Bulloch, James D. *The Secret Service of the Confederate States.* 2 vols. New York, 1884.

Durkin, Joseph T. *Stephen R. Mallory: Confederate Navy Chief.* Chapel Hill, N.C., 1954.

Fowler, William M. *Under Two Flags: The American Navy in the Civil War.* New York, 1990.

Sharf, J. Thomas. *History of the Confederate States Navy from Its Organization to the Surrender of Its Last Vessel.* New York, 1887. Reprint, New York, 1977.

U.S. War Department. *Official Records of the Union and Confederate Navies in the War of the Rebellion.* 30 vols. Washington: Government Printing Office, 1892–1921.

WILLIAM M. FOWLER, JR.

Manpower

From the very beginning of the Civil War, Southern naval authorities struggled to acquire adequate personnel, for the navy had no pool of trained seamen to augment its enlisted force. Throughout four years of war, and in the face of overwhelming personnel and material shortages, the navy nevertheless amassed an honorable record. By 1864, its strength was almost four thousand officers and men.

President Jefferson Davis in his inaugural address called upon the Provisional Congress to establish a navy to protect the harbors and commerce of the Southern states, and on February 20, 1861, the Confederate States Navy came into being. Stephen R. Mallory of Florida was appointed secretary of the navy and given a clerical force consisting of a chief clerk, a correspondence clerk, and a messenger. The secretary was charged with administering the various bureaus, which included Ordnance and Hydrography, Orders and Details, Medicine and Surgery, and Provisions and Clothing.

On March 16, an act of Congress established manpower limits for the navy and authorized President Davis to create the posts of four captains, four commanders, thirty lieutenants, five surgeons, five assistant surgeons, six paymasters, and two chief engineers. He was also empowered to employ as many as three thousand masters, midshipmen, engineers, naval constructors, boatswains, gunners, carpenters, sailmakers, warrant and petty officers, and seamen. The act made provisions for a marine corps to consist of one major, one quartermaster, one paymaster, one adjutant, one sergeant major, and six companies of marines. In turn, each company was to have a captain, a first and a second lieutenant, four sergeants, four corporals, one hundred men, and ten musicians.

The navy benefited from the 332 officers who resigned from the Federal navy and returned to their native states. Eventually, they transferred from state service to the Confederate States Navy, carrying the same rank they had held in the "old" service. To accommodate this large increase in officers, the Amendatory Act of April 21, 1862, increased the number of officers authorized for the navy.

To train additional officers the navy founded an academy on March 23, 1863, at Drewry's Bluff, Virginia, on the James River. The steamship *Patrick Henry* was the school's ship. Cabins were built on shore for the midshipmen, who were expected to spend half their time ashore and the other half aboard the training ship. The academy did not have sufficient longevity to graduate any cadets; the first class of 1863 contained fifty acting midshipmen.

The experience of naval administrators in obtaining qualified officers was duplicated in their attempts to recruit enlisted men. The South's lack of a seafaring tradition limited opportunities for finding trained seamen. To encourage enlistments, the navy opened rendezvous stations (recruiting stations) in all major Southern cities and towns, a practice long followed by the U.S. Navy. At the rendezvous, the recruit was interviewed and given a physical. Upon passing the tests, the recruit signed shipping articles that corresponded with the descriptive roll used by the army and was assigned to a receiving ship for training.

The navy also followed the U.S. Navy practice of stationing receiving ships at major ports. These ships served as barracks and training areas for the sailors before they shipped off to a regular assignment. Each receiving ship had a small complement of officers and petty officers to act as instructors. Here the new sailor literally "learned the ropes." The basic rank assigned a raw recruit was landsman; after some training he was promoted to ordinary seaman and then to seaman—the same enlisted rank structure used by the Union navy. The initiate received instruction in seamanship, gunnery, naval regulations and discipline, and a seaman's life in general. The Confederate navy had receiving ships, at one time or another, at Wilmington, North Carolina, Mobile, Alabama, Charleston, South Carolina, Savannah, Georgia, New Orleans, Louisiana, and Norfolk, Virginia.

In an effort to increase its strength, the navy frequently requested men from the army, but the army was reluctant to release any. In early 1862, the navy offered a bounty of fifty dollars to any man who enlisted for three years. This offer met with only limited success. One source of manpower overlooked by the navy was the slave population. The Confederate navy did not enlist African Americans in any large numbers, unlike the Federal navy, which recruited nearly nine thousand black sailors.

The Confederate conscription acts of April 1862, October 1862, and May 1863 allowed men with seafaring experience who had enlisted in the army to transfer to the navy. In March 1864 Congress passed the General Conscription Law, which ordered the army to release 1,200 men to the navy; 960 men were transferred. By the end of 1864 the Confederate navy had reached its manpower peak of 3,674 enlisted men, but more were still needed, and convicts were ordered to serve aboard warships.

The one area in which recruitment went well was the oceangoing navy. The raiding cruisers that sailed the high seas interdicting Union shipping had little trouble acquiring personnel. Most of these seamen were of foreign birth and signed on for the prize money.

The navy had started with a dearth of men and ships, but within four years it had made some progress in creating a viable naval force. The officers and men served their cause well and earned the respect of their adversaries.

BIBLIOGRAPHY

Jones, Virgil Carrington. *The Civil War at Sea.* 3 vols. New York, 1960.
Scharf, John Thomas. *History of the Confederate States Navy.* 2 vols. New York, 1887. Reprint, New York, 1977.
Spencer, Warren F. *The Confederate Navy in Europe.* University, Ala., 1983.

Turner, Maxine T. *Navy Gray: The Story of the Confederate Navy on the Chattahoochee and Apalachicola Rivers.* Tuscaloosa, Ala., 1988.

DAVID L. VALUSKA

African Americans in the Confederate Navy

The Confederate navy never adopted a policy comparable to the Federal navy regarding the utilization of blacks in the naval service. From the outset of the war the Union navy employed African Americans aboard ship in an integrated fashion, and approximately 9 percent of the Federal navy was black. These men could be recruited in the ranks of landsman, ordinary seaman, and seaman, and by 1863, they were also receiving pay equal to that of white shipmates. There was no similar program in the Confederate navy, and any blacks brought on board were slaves. It is difficult to find any record of free blacks serving aboard ship.

The Southern navy employed slaves in many different ways within the service: they worked in navy yards and armament factories, constructed naval land batteries, and filled noncombat roles on board ships. In an act passed on February 17, 1863, the Confederate Congress authorized the rental of 20,000 slaves for service in workshops and hospitals run by the military. The Selma Naval Ordnance Works, among other such plants, augmented their work force with rented slaves.

On March 13, 1865, less than a month before Appomattox, President Jefferson Davis signed an act providing for the recruitment of 300,000 slaves into the military. But it was too late for the Confederate navy to benefit from the act.

BIBLIOGRAPHY

Turner, Maxine T. *Navy Gray: A Story of the Confederate Navy on the Chattahoochee and Apalachicola Rivers.* Tuscaloosa, Ala., 1988.
Wells, Tom Henderson. *The Confederate Navy: A Study in Organization.* University, Ala., 1971.

DAVID L. VALUSKA

NEW MADRID AND ISLAND NUMBER 10

An operation at New Madrid and Island Number 10 in March and April 1862 opened to Union forces the Mississippi River up to Fort Pillow, Tennessee. In April 1861, Brig. Gen. Gideon Pillow began fortifying the Tennessee bluffs overlooking the Mississippi River and the eastern side of Island Number 10 to halt Union navigation. Ten miles downriver, at New Madrid, Missouri, Confederate warships supported a substantial redoubt that guarded the western approaches to New Madrid Bend, an elongated, crescent-shaped peninsula that cradled Island Number 10.

When Maj. Gen. Leonidas Polk abandoned Columbus, Kentucky, February 29 through March 2, 1862, he sent John Porter McCown (promoted to major general March 10) with 5,000 men and numerous cannons to reinforce the 2,000 sol-

> While the infantry cut Mackall's only line of retreat . . . Union sailors silenced the river batteries upstream.

diers already garrisoning New Madrid and Island Number 10. A floating battery augmented the defenses, now the uppermost on the Mississippi.

Opposing McCown was Maj. Gen. John Pope's Army of the Mississippi and Flag Officer Andrew H. Foote's six gunboats and eleven mortar boats. On March 3 Pope surrounded New Madrid with 18,000 soldiers, but fifty heavy guns ashore supported by gunboats necessitated a siege. While awaiting the arrival and deployment of siege cannons, the Federals fended off M. Jeff Thompson's troopers in their rear. On March 13 Pope commenced a massive bombardment that quickly convinced Confederate navy Capt. George N. Hollins to withdraw his gunboats. That night McCown ordered the evacuation of New Madrid and transferred his garrison to the peninsula across the river to avoid being trapped on the north shore.

McCown's abandonment of the west bank severed river communication with and supply of Island Number 10 and that, coupled with the virtually impassable swamps east of New Madrid Bend, effectively trapped the garrison on the peninsula and island, from which McCown nevertheless refused to withdraw. Abandonment of New Madrid cost McCown his command on March 31. His successor, Brig. Gen. William W. Mackall, also chose not to withdraw.

Pope's men occupied the deserted New Madrid fortifications on March 14. A few days later Foote's flotilla proved unable to silence the batteries upriver. Pope now determined to isolate the entire Confederate garrison. He set his men to cut a canal through the swamps on the west bank so that shallow-draft steamboats could bypass the Confederate river batteries.

To enable the gunboats to run the gauntlet, forty-five volunteers landed near the uppermost battery. They dispersed

its guard, spiked six guns, and escaped safely. The canal was finished April 4 and that night during a storm *Carondelet* successfully passed the island. At 2:00 A.M. on the seventh, *Pittsburg* ran the batteries. By noon, four steamers were landing four regiments on the east bank. While the infantry cut Mackall's only line of retreat via the road to Tiptonville, Union sailors silenced the river batteries upstream.

Trapped, Mackall on April 8 surrendered some 6,000 men, including over 1,500 sick, with all their equipment and ordnance; the balance of the garrison escaped through the swamps. The combined operations cost the Federals 17 killed, 34 wounded, and 3 captured or missing; the Confederates had 17 killed and 6,976 captured, of whom a few were wounded. This Union success convinced President Abraham Lincoln to select Pope to command the newly formed Army of Virginia.

BIBLIOGRAPHY

Greene, Francis V. *The Mississippi.* Vol. 8 of *Campaigns of the Civil War.* New York, 1885. Reprint, Wilmington, N.C., 1989.

Mullen, Jay C. "Pope's New Madrid and Island Number Ten Campaign." *Missouri Historical Review* 49 (1965): 325–343.

Schutz, Wallace J., and Walter N. Trenerry. *Abandoned by Lincoln: A Military Biography of General John Pope.* Champaign, Ill., 1990.

White, Lonnie J. "Federal Operations at New Madrid and Island Number Ten." *West Tennessee Historical Society Papers* 17 (1963): 47–67.

LAWRENCE L. HEWITT

NEW MARKET, VIRGINIA

The little town of New Market was the site of an important Confederate victory on May 14, 1864, that kept the vital Shenandoah Valley in Southern hands most of the last summer of the war. Federal plans for the spring of 1864 called for a three-pronged operation against Confederate positions in Virginia. While large Union armies moved on the Southerners in southeastern and central Virginia, a third invasion menaced the strategic Shenandoah Valley, an agriculturally important area between the Blue Ridge and Allegheny mountain ranges.

This third thrust into the Old Dominion consisted of two parts. One force would move from West Virginia into the upper (southern) Shenandoah Valley to cut the Virginia and Tennessee Railroad, damage the saltworks at Saltville and the lead mines at Wytheville, and then move on Lynchburg or Staunton. Meanwhile, another column, some 9,000 men under Maj. Gen. Franz Sigel, would march into the lower (northern) part of the valley to distract the Confederates, keep them from sending reinforcements to other points, and perhaps meet the column from the west. Sigel's advance got underway in late April.

The Confederates defending the area were also divided. Brig. Gen. John D. Imboden commanded 2,000 men in the lower Shenandoah Valley; Maj. Gen. John C. Breckinridge with 6,700 men was charged with defending the upper valley. In early May Breckinridge was given authority over all Confederates in the valley. Wisely, the Southerners chose to concentrate the bulk of their available forces against Sigel. His advance menaced the lower and middle valley, and he might turn east, cross the Blue Ridge, and join in the attack on the main Southern army in central Virginia.

Leaving some of his men to guard key areas in southwestern Virginia, Breckinridge hurried to unite with Imboden. As he went, he called out local reserve forces, including the 250 members of the Corps of Cadets from the Virginia Military Institute in Lexington. When he got all his available force together, Breckinridge had about 5,300 men with whom to meet Sigel's column. On the rainy day of May 15 the two forces collided at New Market.

The battle was a simple one, fought in a small area between the North Fork of the Shenandoah River on the west and Smith's Creek to the east. Breckinridge deployed his small army on an east-west line across the southern part of the battlefield. The Federals occupied a parallel line to the north, though not all their units had reached the field.

Breckinridge originally planned to fight a defensive battle. He hoped to lure Sigel into attacking a strong fortified position and trusted that the usual advantage enjoyed by the defense over the offensive would offset the numerical superiority of the Federals. When they refused to take the bait, Breckinridge decided to strengthen the left of his line and attack at the spot where the terrain offered some advantage to his men. At about 11:30 A.M. the Confederate advance lurched forward. By that time Sigel had begun to pull back to a position north of New Market.

In midafternoon, as Breckinridge pushed ahead, his men began to take heavy casualties. A gap opened in his line, and the Southerners feared that Sigel would see it and launch a counthercharge. The only reserve was the Corps of Cadets, and Breckinridge reluctantly threw it into the line. The gap was plugged, and Confederate fire soon halted feeble Federal efforts at a counterblow. Sigel began to withdraw from the field. By 3:00 P.M. momentum had shifted to the Southerners, and they began the final charge of the day. As the Federals withdrew, the Confederates occupied the field.

About 6,300 Union troops had fought at New Market; 96 had been killed, 520 wounded, and 225 captured or missing. Breckinridge had sent about 4,100 men into the fight. Partial reports indicate that he lost at least 43 killed, 474 wounded, and 3 captured.

After the battle Breckinridge transferred most of his little command across the Blue Ridge to reinforce the main

Confederate army then engaged in desperate fighting north of Richmond. By the time the Federals in the Shenandoah Valley managed to get themselves organized for another advance, the situation near Richmond had stabilized, and the Southerners were able to dispatch enough reinforcements to hold the valley through the summer of 1864.

Had New Market been a Federal victory, the Confederates would have lost control of the Shenandoah Valley in the spring of 1864. Deprived of the valley and its agricultural produce, they probably would have been unable to hold out as long as they did. Because it enabled the Southerners to retain possession of the valley, New Market has been called "the biggest little battle of the war."

BIBLIOGRAPHY

Davis, William C. *The Battle of New Market*. New York, 1975.
Davis, William C. *Breckinridge: Statesman, Soldier, Symbol*. Baton Rouge, La., 1974.
Turner, E. Raymond. *The New Market Campaign, May, 1864*. Richmond, Va., 1912.

RICHARD M. MCMURRY

NEW ORLEANS, LOUISIANA

[*This entry includes two articles,* City of New Orleans, *which profiles the city during the Confederacy, and* Capture of New Orleans, *which discusses the Federal capture of the city in 1862.*]

City of New Orleans

The South's largest and most cosmopolitan city, New Orleans had the briefest of stints under Confederate authority. Fifteen months after Louisiana seceded, the Crescent City was back under Union rule after Adm. David G. Farragut dropped anchor outside the levee on April 25, 1862.

Pinched into a shallow clay saucer between Lake Pontchartrain and the Mississippi, New Orleans derives its nickname from the huge crescent bend that the river describes near the French Quarter. Most of the city's 168,000 residents in 1860 hugged the high ground near the river levee, on either side of Canal Street, which historically separates Gallic downtown and Anglo uptown. It was a population of infinite ethnic variety and romantic charm. To the original white creole population (of mixed French and Spanish ancestry) were added, during the antebellum period, heavy infusions of Protestant Americans from both North and South, continuing inputs of foreign French—often refugees from the

French and Haitian revolutions—and a huge influx of German and Irish immigration. Even driblets of Italian settlement had reached the Crescent City prior to the Civil War. Comprising nearly 40 percent of the 1860 population, New Orleans's foreign-born community loomed larger than any other Southern city's at the time. Although only one-sixth the size of the white population, the black population in 1860 was also ethnically diverse. In addition to slaves, New Orleans was home to the most prosperous and sophisticated free black community in the United States, which itself was split between the more numerous Francophone Catholics and a small coterie of Protestant African Americans.

New Orleans's heterogeneity, plus the city's historic trade ties with the upper Mississippi valley, rendered secession difficult. John C. Breckinridge, the Southern rights candidate in 1860, ran third in every district of the city. John Slidell, one of New Orleans's two Democratic U.S. senators, blamed Breckinridge's poor showing on the fact that "here in the city seven-eighths of the vote for [Stephen] Douglas were cast by the Irish and Germans." The Crescent City's business community, a substantial element of which hailed from the Northeast, was also tugged toward Unionism by trade and shipping connections with the free states. But for the hysteria aroused by well-organized Southern nationalist groups— helped by Presbyterian minister Benjamin M. Palmer's fire-breathing Thanksgiving Day sermon—the city's immediate secessionists, in the January 7, 1861, election, might not have won a 52 to 48 percent victory for their delegate slate to the state's secessionist convention. Voter turnout was noticeably lower than it had been in the presidential election two months earlier.

Although divided in secession, New Orleans was momentarily united in war. Some of the contagion of the city's being a troop-mustering center spread to the local population. Uptown New Orleans's famed Washington Artillery, which traced its military tradition back to the Mexican War, entrained for Virginia in May to a citywide send-off. A variety of privately outfitted Zouave units also enlisted in the Confederacy. So did assorted ethnic regiments: the French and creole populations set the pace, but various German and Irish units followed close behind. Polyglot New Orleans also furnished a Garibaldi Legion, a Spanish Legion, a Scandinavian Guard, a Polish Brigade, a Scotch Rifle Guard, a Belgian Guard, two companies of Slavonian Rifles, and a company of Greek citizens wearing the national Albanian uniform. Tracing its military tradition back to the colonial period, the city's Franco-African population also offered its services to the Confederacy, but because the idea of black soldiers contradicted Confederate racial nationalism, their Native Guard was mustered into the state militia only.

As the gateway to the Mississippi valley, the country's second leading port early on felt squeezed by the Union blockade. After May 26, 1861, when the USS *Brooklyn* anchored off the mouth of the Mississippi, ocean vessels ceased docking in the Crescent City, although some coastal shipping slipped into the city through the lake. From the summer onward, trade stagnated, prices soared, and necessities like coal and food grew scarce. The city council tried to fend off destitution by establishing a free market in the new ironworks building at the foot of Canal Street, where foodstuffs supplied by local planters were distributed to poor families. In September the banks, by order of the Confederacy, sus-

> New Orleans's heterogeneity, plus the city's historic trade ties with the upper Mississippi valley, rendered secession difficult.

pended specie payments, drying up the supply of small change and giving rise to a variety of makeshift expedients (like streetcar tickets). Meanwhile, military recruiters siphoned some of the unemployed, mainly the Irish poor, into Confederate armies.

Because the Union brass was determined to split the Confederacy by seizing the Mississippi, it was only a matter of time before a joint army-navy expedition took aim at the Crescent City. The War of 1812 had made local authorities conscious that such an attack was likely, but work on local defenses lagged under Maj. Gen. David Twigg, who was in command of New Orleans and vicinity until October 1861. Twigg's replacement, Mansfield Lovell, who had been a New York City street commissioner only weeks before moving to the South (he was an unpopular choice because favorite sons like P. G. T. Beauregard had been passed over), invigorated the work of military preparedness, creating powder works, helping local foundries convert to armament production, supervising naval shipbuilding, and completing work on exterior entrenchments. The press extolled his "restless activity." One item of local defense that Lovell pushed to conclusion was the cypress log raft, tied together with chains and huge timbers, that reached between opposite banks of the Mississippi, near Fort Jackson and Fort St. Phillip, seventy-five miles downriver from New Orleans.

This manmade invasion barrier proved porous. Proceeding from their staging area at Ship Island (which guarded the approaches to the lake), Union Adm. David G. Farragut's seventeen-ship fleet, together with twenty mortar schooners under Como. David Porter, and a fifteen-thousand-man army recruited in New England by Maj. Gen. Benjamin F. Butler, reached the two forts by mid-April, and, after a five-day mortar bombardment, cut the river chain and ran the gauntlet on April 24. The following day Farragut's naval guns were peering over the levee of a panic-stricken city, many of whose defenders had just been sent to reinforce the collapsing Confederate line in Tennessee and Mississippi.

For a few days Mayor John Monroe defied Farragut's surrender order, galvanizing some of the nativist thugs whose votes and fists had put him into office. "We don't want you here, damn it!" a menacing mob yelled at the first Union officers to come ashore. Farragut threatened to cannonade the city into submission, despite pleas from foreign consuls. In the meantime, General Lovell had evacuated his troops from the city, and drayloads of cotton and sugar, corn and rice, were brought to the riverfront and set afire. Monroe capitulated when word arrived that the downriver forts had surrendered on April 28 (in part because immigrant troops from New Orleans had mutinied). When Ben Butler's troops clambered down the gangplank on May 1, 1862, New Orleans joined New York as one of only two major cities in U.S. history to undergo enemy occupation for an extended period. For the next three years Union-occupied New Orleans served as the nerve center of the newly formed Department of the Gulf.

Because the Crescent City was a command headquarters in a combat zone, military security took first priority, and Ben Butler wasted little time in bringing the turbulent population to heel. He hanged a professional gambler, William Mumford, for lowering the U.S. flag that Farragut had hoisted over the Federal mint. He silenced females who acted insultingly toward Union soldiers by issuing an edict directing that they be treated as streetwalkers—and acquired the nickname "Beast." (The Davis government in retaliation placed a bounty on Butler's head.) He seized newspapers, censored sermons, and made schoolteachers swear allegiance to the Union. He even threatened to confiscate the hotel where he made his headquarters when the proprietor refused to serve him breakfast. And when Mayor Monroe kept up his obstructionism, Butler had him incarcerated for the duration of the war. Thereafter New Orleans's municipal affairs were administered by a succession of military-appointed mayors.

In local legend Butler was also known as "Spoons" for allegedly helping himself to family silver (the corruption charge is probably truer of his brother). But historians better remember Butler, a skillful Massachusetts politician, for sponsoring a new political and social order in the Crescent City. President Lincoln looked on New Orleans as a promising location in which to field-test various emancipation and Reconstruction experiments. Butler galvanized working-class immigrant Unionism by putting destitute Irish and Germans to work cleaning canals and streets, which he financed by taxing wealthy Confederates. He accommodated the slaves' yearning for freedom by ordering that they be paid wages. He accepted the military services of a black creole regiment (the Corps d'Afrique, which was disbanded by Butler's successor), thereby encouraging the city's influential free people of color to follow the lead of its philosophical radicals, men like the Roudanez brothers, Charles and Louis, and Paul Trevigne. By the time Butler was replaced seven months later, the nucleus of an interracial political party called the Free State movement had taken shape in New Orleans.

A Massachusetts politician like his predecessor, Maj. Gen. Nathaniel P. Banks extended and modified Butler's race and Reconstruction policies after taking command of the Department of the Gulf in December 1862. But Banks sought to conciliate upper-class conservative Unionists by clamping down on the black population, both freeborn and slave, and dampening the indigenous drive to extend the vote to creoles of color. When Lincoln's Ten Percent Plan took effect in December 1863—restoring civil government whenever one-tenth of the 1860 voting population resumed their Unionist allegiance—Banks helped ensure that a top-down coalition of white Unionists took control. Although the state was returned to civil rule (albeit under military supervision) in 1864, New Orleans continued to be administered by occupying authorities for the duration of the war.

New Orleans's status as an occupied city officially ended when John Monroe was reelected mayor in March 1866. It was under Monroe's administration that the police massacre known as the New Orleans Riot of 1866 occurred. Many of the policemen were probably the same plug-uglies who had jeered Farragut's officers when they first stepped ashore four years earlier.

[*See also* Butler's Woman Order.]

BIBLIOGRAPHY

Bragg, Jefferson Davis. *Louisiana in the Confederacy.* Baton Rouge, La., 1941.

Capers, Gerald M., Jr. "Confederates and Yankees in Occupied New Orleans, 1862–1865." *Journal of Southern History* 30 (November 1964): 405–426.

Dufour, Charles L. *The Night the War Was Lost.* New York, 1960.

McCrary, Peyton. *Abraham Lincoln and Reconstruction: The Louisiana Experiment.* Princeton, N.J., 1978.

Ripley, C. Peter. *Slaves and Freedmen in Civil War Louisiana.* Baton Rouge, La., 1976.

Winters, John D. *The Civil War in Louisiana.* Baton Rouge, La., 1963.

LAWRENCE N. POWELL

Capture of New Orleans

Despite the strategic and commercial importance of New Orleans, Union authorities did not turn their attention to the Crescent City until November 15, 1861. Although his Southern heritage raised doubts about his loyalty, Capt. David G. Farragut was assigned to command the naval forces; Maj. Gen. Benjamin F. Butler led the army contingent. Union forces first concentrated on Ship Island in the Gulf of

Mexico, which led Confederate officials to conclude that their objective was Mobile or Pensacola, not New Orleans. By early April 1862, when Farragut's ships entered the Mississippi River, troop transfers had reduced the defenses of New Orleans to little more than 4,500 militia scattered among the masonry forts that protected the city.

Two forts, eighty miles downriver, guarded the Mississippi: Jackson on the west bank and St. Philip, eight hundred yards north, on the east bank. A chain floated on barges barricaded the river, although high water had partially destroyed this obstacle in late February and again on April 11. An unusual fleet supported the five hundred men and eighty cannon in the forts: three ironclads (the ram *Manassas,* the underpowered *Louisiana* anchored above St. Philip as a floating battery, and the unfinished *Mississippi*), fire barges, and nine other vessels divided among the Confederate navy, the Louisiana navy, and the river defense fleet.

Just above Head of Passes on April 8 Farragut assembled twenty-four wooden vessels, mounting about two hundred guns, and Commdr. David D. Porter's nineteen mortar schooners, each carrying one 13-inch mortar. On April 18 the mortars began a bombardment that Porter believed would silence the forts, thus permitting Farragut's ships to pass them safely. During an eight-hour period that day, Porter fired 2,997 rounds into Fort Jackson. But Farragut, lacking faith in the mortars, had his vessels open a channel through the barricade during the night of April 20. Although the mortars failed to silence Jackson, at 2:00 A.M. on the twenty-fourth, Farragut's fleet steamed upriver. By dawn, twenty-one of his

> ... Johnson Kelly Duncan's men in the forts mutinied, and he surrendered the same day.

vessels had successfully passed the barricade and the forts. Then, in a free-for-all, Farragut's ships avoided the bull-like charges of *Manassas* and the fire rafts and destroyed the enemy's flotilla. Farragut lost the converted merchantman *Varuna,* and 171 sailors were killed or wounded. The forts' defenders had sustained fewer than 50 casualties.

Leaving two gunboats above the forts to support Butler's troops marching overland from their gulf landing toward the rear of St. Philip, Farragut continued upriver to New Orleans. The city, now undefended since Confederate Maj. Gen. Mansfield Lovell had evacuated it, fell on April 25. Civilian authorities formally surrendered on the twenty-eighth. With the city lost and Union infantry closing in, most of Brig. Gen. Johnson Kelly Duncan's men in the forts mutinied, and he surrendered the same day. Butler occupied New Orleans on May 1. A court of inquiry cleared Lovell on July 9, 1863, of any responsibility for the loss of the city. The onus fell upon

the Richmond government for having stripped the garrison of its troops and having failed to place Lovell in command of all naval forces. In all, the Federals had lost 39 men killed and 171 wounded while taking the city. The Confederates had lost 85 men killed, 113 wounded, and approximately 900 captured.

BIBLIOGRAPHY

Dufour, Charles L. *The Night the War Was Lost.* Garden City, N.Y., 1960.

Heleniak, Roman J., and Lawrence L. Hewitt, eds. *The 1989 Deep Delta Civil War Symposium: Leadership during the Civil War.* Shippensburg, Pa., 1992.

Lewis, Charles L. *David Glasgow Farragut.* 2 vols. Annapolis, Md., 1941–1943.

Mahan, Alfred T. *Admiral Farragut.* Great Commanders Series. New York, 1892.

LAWRENCE L. HEWITT

NEW PLAN

The *New Plan* was the name given to a series of administrative actions and congressional laws whose object was to evade the blockade and put Confederate finances abroad on a cash basis. President Jefferson Davis authorized this program in 1863 and 1864. The indispensable first step was the appointment of an agent to supervise fund-raising abroad. Colin J. McRae, a former Confederate congressman, accepted this appointment and went to Paris. In September 1863, after carefully surveying the situation, he sent President Davis a series of recommendations that became the New Plan.

First, McRae suggested that he be given full authority to allocate scarce Confederate funds abroad among the conflicting claims of the War and Navy departments' procurement offices. In addition, no agents were to sign contracts without securing McRae's approval for the payment terms.

Second, the government should stop making contracts payable in cotton. The Confederacy was spending six hundred dollars in cotton to get one hundred dollars worth of goods. If the contractors could ship cotton out of the country, there was no reason the government could not do so on its own account.

Third, McRae urged that the government employ its powers over foreign commerce to regulate imports and exports. The practice of blockade runners bringing in luxury goods and refusing to take government cotton cargoes had to be stopped.

Fourth, McRae asked that he be appointed a Confederate Depositary at Paris and that as bursar he alone be authorized to make payments for goods purchased by government procurement agents.

McRae's suggestions met with President Davis's approval. Davis then authorized Secretary of State Judah P. Benjamin to arbitrate the differences among the War, Navy, and Treasury departments and to formulate a specific program to implement McRae's recommendations. Meanwhile, in late 1863, the War Department empowered its officers to preempt a third of all outbound cargo space for the export of government cotton.

Secretary Benjamin swiftly carried out his mandate. Acting on the suggestions of John Slidell, the Confederate commissioner to Paris, which largely coincided with McRae's

> The . . . object was to evade the blockade and put Confederate finances abroad on a cash basis.

views, he armed McRae with full powers to supervise other agents, to coordinate their actions, and to control all payments. Benjamin then drafted an agreement and got his cabinet colleagues' assent to coordinate their policies and not to enter into any more agreements with private contractors. It then proved an easy matter to induce a lame-duck Congress to enact other key parts of the government plan.

By one act passed on February 6, 1864, Congress empowered the president to prohibit the exportation of staple produce except under regulations of his own devising. The only exemption (in deference to state rights sentiment) was for state-owned blockade runners. A second act, passed the same day, expressly prohibited the importation of items "not of common necessity and use." This put a stop to the cargoes of brandy, silks, and jewelry that did little to feed or clothe the army or the people.

Finally, President Davis promulgated a whole series of regulations to put the plan into effect. All government cotton became the property of the Treasury Department, and the War Department was empowered to collect Treasury cotton and export it. To finance this effort, $20 million was appropriated, Lt. Col. Thomas L. Bayne was made bureau chief, and half of all incoming and outgoing cargo space was reserved for the government. In addition, McRae was authorized to purchase a fleet of blockade runners.

These measures encountered considerable opposition. Resistance centered on the government's control of cargo space. State rights advocates were alienated because state sovereignty did not protect ships leased by state governments. Blockade-running firms attempted to exempt themselves from the regulations by leasing their ships to the states or by refusing to sail. President Davis, however, remained adamant. Ships not authentically operated under state authority were compelled to follow the new rules, and ultimately the shippers yielded.

Government finances abroad were greatly improved. By December 1864, James Seddon, the secretary of war, reported that over 27,299 bales of cotton had been exported, for $5.3 million of sales. Only 1,272 bales were lost, despite the fact that exports were largely limited to the port of Wilmington. In addition, the government had added fourteen steamers to its fleet.

Given the effectiveness of this program in 1864 and 1865, and the fact that the government had entertained such ideas since early 1862, the question arises as to why the New Plan was so long delayed. One problem was the Confederates' aversion to innovations that would augment the government's power. Another factor was the early hope that, because of foreign intervention, the war would be short. By the time the Confederates realized that they must fight on alone, it was too late to realize the benefits that would have accrued from an earlier implementation of this plan.

BIBLIOGRAPHY

Ball, Douglas B. *Financial Failure and Confederate Defeat.* Urbana, Ill., 1991.
Todd, Richard Cecil. *Confederate Finance.* Athens, Ga., 1954.
Wise, Stephen R. *Life Line of the Confederacy: Blockade Running during the Civil War.* Columbia, S.C., 1988.

DOUGLAS B. BALL

NEWSPAPERS

With the exception of New Orleans, which fell to Union forces in 1862, the South had no major metropolises, and consequently, there were few newspapers with large circulations. Moreover, as the South's fortunes declined, shortages of newsprint, ink, and manpower, as well as reduced advertising revenue, forced many newspapers to cease publication or severely cut back in order to survive. With the advance of Union troops, others became refugees or had to adapt to the regulations of the occupying forces. Nevertheless, Southern newspapers endeavored to serve a public clamoring for military information and news about the government. Aiding in this daunting task was the Confederate Press Association, established in 1863 and eventually serving forty-three papers.

The government attempted to censor battlefield reports and other types of sensitive military information, and most editors voluntarily refused to publish military data that might damage the cause. But there were few other restrictions on news, and editorial freedom of expression was virtually absolute. Approximately eight hundred newspapers, 10 percent of which were dailies, were published in the Confederacy at various times, and in the tradition of nineteenth-century journalism all were unique and mostly concerned with local matters. Within this context, however, the major papers engaged in a serious debate on issues of national concern.

Richmond. Located in the Confederate capital and in close proximity to a major theater of military operations, Richmond newspapers were among the most influential in the South. Five major dailies were published during the war: the *Dispatch, Enquirer, Whig, Examiner,* and *Sentinel.*

The *Dispatch,* edited by James Cowardin and John Hammersley, boasted the largest circulation, which increased during the war from eighteen thousand to thirty thousand. Always patriotic, it usually maintained a moderate editorial policy and remained neutral on most governmental matters. This prompted Henry Hotze, the Confederate agent in London and editor of the *Index,* to describe it as lacking a political creed. Even as disillusion began to spread in late 1863, it spared the administration and instead focused its ire on Northerners and Southern "croakers."

Known as the "Democratic Bible," the *Daily Enquirer* was distinguished for its journalistic quality. Its first editor, O. J. Wise, was the son of former two-time Virginia governor, Henry A. Wise, himself a bold advocate of secession. After the younger Wise died in the Battle of Roanoke Island in February 1862, his editorial successors steadfastly supported the Davis administration throughout the war and usually avoided editorial comment that might threaten the success of the cause.

Another of the South's great newspapers was the *Enquirer'*s traditional rival, the *Whig and Public Advertiser.* Its prewar editor, Robert Ridgway, had supported the Constitutional Union party in 1860 and vigorously opposed secession. His successors, Alexander Mosely (April 1861–March 1863) and James McDonald, supported the cause, but in early 1862 the *Whig* became openly hostile toward the Davis administration. Despite being threatened with suppression by Provost Marshal John H. Winder, the newspaper continued its critical editorial policy for the remainder of the war.

Much more unrelenting and brutal in its criticism of the Davis administration was the *Examiner.* Its editor, John M. Daniel, and his able assistant, Edward A. Pollard, were convinced that ill-advised government policies were responsible for all the South's misfortunes. The *Examiner* focused its most savage attacks on Jefferson Davis himself, charging him with incompetence, lack of energy, and political favoritism. Henry Hotze categorized the *Examiner* as an archenemy of the government and referred to it as the "Ishmael" of the Confederate press because it seemed to be against everybody. During the war the *Examiner* became known as a school for journalists because its contributors included some of the South's most talented young writers: George Bagby, Basil Gildersleeve, and John R. Thompson.

The *Sentinel* began publishing in Richmond in March 1863, having relocated from Alexandria. Hoping to preserve unity by boosting confidence in the government, at times it appeared to be the administration's official mouthpiece—a charge its editor, Richard M. Smith, hastened to deny. Nevertheless, the *Sentinel* defended Davis against his press critics and energetically attacked his enemies such as Governor Joseph E. Brown of Georgia.

North Carolina. With only eight dailies circulating in 1860, few North Carolina towns could boast newspapers of influence during the war. The notable exception was Raleigh where the outspoken antiwar, anti-administration *Standard* engaged its bitter rivals, the prosecessionist, pro-war, pro-administration *Register* and *State Journal,* in near mortal journalistic combat. William W. Holden, editor of the *Standard,* initially opposed secession; but when Governor John W. Ellis issued a call for troops, Holden reversed course and assumed a pro-war position.

In the summer of 1862 Holden again shifted position, justifying his reputation as the "Talleyrand of North Carolina politics," and thereafter his denunciations of the Confederate government became so bitter as to border on treason. He spoke against conscription and suspension of habeas corpus. He attacked taxation-in-kind, arguing that it placed an unfair burden on the small farmer. Never a friend of the slavocracy, he suggested that slave property be taxed instead. He called Davis a tyrant and accused him of wanting to impose military despotism on the South. In the meantime Holden condemned John Spelman of the Democratic *State Journal* for recommending that newspapers be subject to tighter censorship in order to prevent sensitive military information from falling into enemy hands. In the summer of 1863 Holden demanded that the Confederate government seek peace negotiations, and when Davis failed to respond, Holden suggested that the states seek a separate peace on their own initiative.

Holden's peace position drew fire from the pro-administration *Raleigh Register,* which accused him of undermining morale and spreading defeatism. The *Richmond Enquirer* labeled him a traitor. But with the largest circulation of any North Carolina newspaper, the *Standard* might well have represented the views of a significant segment of the state's population. The *Standard'*s peace position provoked some Georgia troops who happened to be in Raleigh to break into the paper's office and wreck it. Holden escaped, and only prompt action by Governor Zebulon Vance averted the complete destruction of the paper's printing equipment. The next day, however, Holden's supporters wrecked the offices of the pro-Confederate *State Journal* and demolished its presses and type. When he ran for governor in 1864, Holden advocated North Carolina's secession from the Confederacy. To counter this position, his opponent, Vance, founded the *Conservative,* which along with the *Raleigh Sentinel* attacked Holden for this dangerous idea.

Such controversy did not characterize the press in the state's chief port of Wilmington. When the war broke out, the city had two dailies, the *Herald* and the *Journal,* both of which supported secession. The *Herald's* editor, A. M. Waddell, although initially critical of South Carolina's precipitate action, soon joined the secessionist cause. When he subsequently enlisted in the military, the *Herald* ceased publication. James Fulton edited the *Journal.* Unquestionably loyal to the Confederacy, he resisted the temptation to publish information that might aid the enemy and urged his fellow editors to do likewise. Moreover, he consistently tried to minimize the significance of Confederate defeats. He occasionally criticized government and military policies, however. He wondered about Joseph E. Johnston's tactics against William Tecumseh Sherman in Georgia and lamented that the South seemed always to be on the defensive. Sharing most of the *Journal's* views on the war but slightly more critical of the government was H. H. Munson, who moved the *Daily North Carolinian* from Fayetteville to Wilmington in December 1864.

Remaining in Fayetteville until the last days of the war was Edward J. Hale, editor of the *Observer.* A longtime Whig, Hale opposed secession but became a staunchly loyal Southerner after Abraham Lincoln issued his call for troops. Both of his sons enlisted in the Confederate army. Hale's pro-Southern sentiments led to reprisals by Sherman's troops, who singled out the *Observer's* plant for destruction and allegedly offered a $10,000 reward for his body.

Tennessee. In neighboring Tennessee, Union military successes in 1862 and 1863 led to the occupation of several major cities. Consequently many Tennessee newspapers had to stop publication, operate under stringent restrictions imposed by Federal authorities, or become refugees. The most prominent and influential of these refugees was the peripatetic *Memphis Appeal.* Its editors, John McClanahan and Benjamin Dill, were early champions of Southern nationalism even though they did not support secession until late 1860. During the night of June 5, 1862, the editors loaded their paper's equipment on a boxcar and fled just before Union forces occupied Memphis. For the remainder of the war the *Appeal* continued to publish, first in Grenada, Mississippi, then in Jackson, and thereafter in Montgomery, Atlanta, and Columbus, where Union troops captured Dill and destroyed some of his equipment. The press, however, had been hidden in Macon, so that in early November 1865 the *Appeal* resumed publication in Memphis.

During its wartime odyssey, the "Moving *Appeal*" remained very much a Memphis newspaper, frequently carrying news about the city and its former residents scattered throughout Dixie. Although priding itself on its coverage of political and military news, it diligently avoided publishing military information that might help the enemy. Editorially it disapproved of any strategy to invade the North and instead advocated a policy of "offensive defense," which stressed expulsion of Union troops from Southern territory. It also emphasized the importance of the western theater and the necessity of controlling the Mississippi. It constantly sought to boost the spirit of resistance and frequently defended the Davis administration from its critics.

> **. . . he resisted the temptation to publish information that might aid the enemy and urged his fellow editors to do likewise.**

Memphis's other newspapers survived under Union occupation. Federal officials seized the *Argus* but returned it to its owners after a month. They also pressured the secessionist *Avalanche,* which had absorbed the *Bulletin* and the *Eagle and Enquirer* in 1861, to assume the name *Bulletin.* The paper was constantly at odds with Union authorities, as when Jeptha Folkes was forced to resign for writing an editorial that offended Ulysses S. Grant.

The *Chattanooga Rebel,* considered the mouthpiece of the Army of Tennessee, was another of the state's peripatetic papers. After moving from Bowling Green the *Rebel's* owners, John Burch and F. M. Paul, hired Henry Watterson as editor. Watterson had left the *Republican Banner* of Nashville after that city fell to Union forces. When a Watterson editorial, highly critical of Braxton Bragg, appeared in the *Rebel,* the outraged general temporarily forbade the circulation of the paper within his command. Watterson then left the *Rebel* and went to Atlanta where he edited the *Southern Confederacy.* Forced to flee from Chattanooga in September 1863, the *Rebel's* editors continued to publish it in various places. They managed to stay ahead of Union troops until April 1865, when they ceased operations in Selma.

Union occupation of Knoxville proved a boon to a refugee of a different sort. William G. ("Parson") Brownlow, who had earlier been run out of Tennessee for publishing treasonous articles in the *Whig,* returned and began publishing again. He called his new paper the *Whig and Rebel Ventilator.*

South Carolina. Unlike Tennessee, South Carolina cities avoided Union attacks and occupation until late in the war. Such was the case with Charleston, which became the focus of lively competition between the fervently anti-administration *Mercury* and the pro-Davis *Courier.* The *Mercury* had the well-justified reputation of being the most acerbic of Davis's critics. Robert Barnwell Rhett, Jr., an ardent state rights advocate edited the paper, but his father, a long-time fire-eater known as the "Father of Secession," penned many of its editorials. The elder Rhett had been spurned for the

Confederate presidency and then overlooked by Davis for a cabinet position. Feeling that those who had initiated the rebellion had been denied the chance to lead it, the Rhetts denounced the government with a fury. They criticized Davis for failing to prosecute the war aggressively, accused him of inept diplomacy, questioned the competence of his political and military appointees, charged him with harboring dictatorial ambitions, and even advocated his impeachment.

William Porcher Miles remarked that the widows and orphans of Confederate dead must have felt especially disheartened when they read in the *Mercury* that their misery was the result of such an inefficient government. The unending torrent of abuse eventually provoked Varina Howell Davis to admit that she hated the younger Rhett more than any Republican. Uncompromising to the end, the *Mercury* rejected any discussion of using blacks in the Confederate army and questioned Davis's commitment to slavery. In early 1865 it branded those seeking peace as the South's bitterest enemies.

The *Courier* served as the ever-faithful champion of the Davis administration and condemned the *Mercury* for undermining confidence in the government. Aaron Willington, a late convert to secession, edited the paper until his death in February 1862. Thereafter Richard Yeardon and Thomas Simons wrote most of its editorials. Always more moderate and restrained than its rival, the *Courier* warned against reckless and irresponsible journalism. In early 1865, however, it found itself in agreement with the *Mercury* when it opposed the use of blacks in the army. Yet even in the darkest days of 1865 it was the only South Carolina paper to support the government consistently.

Georgia. Georgia newspapers seemed especially vulnerable to the vicissitudes of war. Chronic shortages of materials and labor, rising subscription prices, and the depredations of Union troops forced almost half the state's newspapers and magazines to cease publication; many more were discontinued for differing lengths of time. Conventions held in Atlanta, Macon, and Augusta considered ways to improve the supply of paper and ink, but by the end of the war almost all Georgia papers had shrunk to one sheet.

Despite these hardships, the vast majority of Georgia editors, most notably James Gardner of the *Augusta Constitutionalist,* tended to be optimistic about the Confederate cause and supportive of the government until late in the war. When forced to grudgingly concede a Union military victory, they frequently followed it with an editorial note predicting ultimate victory for the South. But it was difficult to ignore reality, and as the Confederacy's fortunes declined, George Adair's *Atlanta Southern Confederacy,* the *Macon Intelligencer,* Joseph Clisby's *Macon Telegraph,* the *Columbus Sun,* and the *Savannah Republican* all became outspoken critics of the government at various times. And in 1863 the *Atlanta Register,* edited by Louis Dupre, published several articles that gave momentum to the incipient peace movement in the state.

In September 1863, anti-administration sentiment assumed an entirely different tone, when Governor Joseph E. Brown helped finance the purchase of the *Augusta Chronicle* by its editor Nathaniel Morse. Brown was determined to destroy President Davis, and Morse, a transplanted Connecticut Yankee, rose to the challenge, attacking the president with a viciousness unmatched by any other editor in the Deep South. Meanwhile, he did his best to promote the growing peace movement and spread defeatism. John Forsyth, editor of the *Mobile Register,* became so outraged by what he considered Morse's disloyalty that he considered challenging him to a duel.

Other Areas. When Union troops occupied New Orleans with its six dailies in early 1862, Forsyth's *Mobile Register* emerged as one of the South's most influential papers. According to Hotze's *Index,* it was among the most often quoted papers in the Confederacy. Hotze, a former associate of Forsyth on the *Register,* praised the paper for its literary excellence, news accuracy, candor, and editorial restraint. Forsyth, however, was unrestrained in his attacks on "croakers," grumblers, and peace advocates.

Alabama's other major paper, the *Montgomery Daily Advertiser,* was less steadfast in its support for Davis. In 1861 and 1862 it heartily endorsed administration policies, but by 1863 it was criticizing the president for favoring incompetent officials, maltreating Joseph E. Johnston and P. G. T. Beauregard, ignoring the western theater, and favoring policies that would subvert state rights. Such a metamorphosis of editorial opinion was typical of many other papers in the Confederacy when faced with the sobering reality of defeat. Elsewhere in the Deep South, urban newspapers had to endure close supervision by Union authorities. Such was the case with the New Orleans dailies: the *Bee, Bulletin, Crescent, Delta, Picayune,* and *True Delta.* Others, like the *Vicksburg Whig,* suffered a worse fate. A fire destroyed its office on May 9, 1863. More typical were papers such as the *Arkansas Gazette,* which continued to publish despite severe shortages of paper and other supplies.

With a few significant exceptions, editorial opinion within the Confederacy on national issues followed a distinct pattern. Initially, there was hearty enthusiasm for the war effort and support for the new Davis administration. Seeking to boost morale, many editors tended to overemphasize the South's early military successes while minimizing those of the Union. But when Confederate military fortunes began to decline and economic hardship spread, many editors became more critical of government policies and military leadership. By 1864 and 1865, though most editors remained loyal to the cause, disillusionment and defeatism began to appear, and a growing minority promoted the peace movement.

[See also Brownlow, William G.; Censorship; Rhett, Robert Barnwell.]

BIBLIOGRAPHY

Andrews, J. Cutler. *The South Reports the Civil War.* Princeton, N. J., 1970.

Baker, Thomas Harrison. *The Memphis Commercial Appeal: The History of a Southern Newspaper.* Baton Rouge, La., 1971.

Brantly, Raburn Lee. *Georgia Journalism of the Civil War Period.* Nashville, Tenn., 1929.

Carter, Hodding. *Their Words Were Bullets: The Southern Press in War, Reconstruction, and Peace.* Athens, Ga., 1969.

Connelly, Thomas L. "Editorial Opinion in South Carolina's Wartime Press." In *South Carolina Journals and Journalists.* Edited by James B. Meriwether. Spartanburg, S.C., 1975.

Griffith, Louis Turner, and John Erwin Talmadge. *Georgia Journalism, 1763–1950.* Athens, Ga., 1951.

Jobe, Nat. "Edward Alfred Pollard: Symbol of Opposition." In *Divided We Fall: Essays on Confederate Nation Building.* Edited by John M. Belohlavek and Lewis N. Wynne. Saint Leo, Fla., 1991.

Trexler, Harrison A. "The Davis Administration and the Richmond Press, 1861–1865." *Journal of Southern History* 16 (May 1950): 177–195.

CHARLES MCARVER

NITER AND MINING BUREAU

At the instigation of Josiah Gorgas, head of the Ordnance Department, the Confederate Congress, on April 11, 1862, passed an act establishing a niter corps as a branch of the Ordnance Department. This corps was to be composed of a superintendent, four assistants, and eight subordinates with the rank, pay, and allowances of majors, captains, and first lieutenants of artillery respectively. The primary responsibility of these officers was to procure niter (saltpeter), a mineral that comprised about 75 percent of gunpowder. To head the corps, Gorgas chose Isaac M. St. John, an able civil engineer who had supervised the construction of defenses in the Yorktown, Virginia, area.

In April 1863 the Congress passed another act that separated the corps from the Ordnance Department and made it an independent bureau, directly responsible to the War Department, under the new name of the Niter and Mining Bureau. In addition to procuring niter, the new bureau was responsible for mining or otherwise collecting and purchasing iron, copper, lead, coal, and zinc for military uses. In order to allow the bureau to perform these tasks more efficiently, the act provided for more officers and increased their rank to one lieutenant colonel, three majors, six captains, and ten lieutenants, with rank and pay equivalent to that of cavalry officers. Finally, in June 1864, a third act allowed a maximum of six chemists and six professional assistants to be attached to the bureau to aid it in the scientific aspects of mineral collection.

The Confederacy was divided into about fourteen niter and mining districts, smaller administrative units supervised by bureau officers who were responsible for the production of minerals in their area. Most of the districts were east of the Mississippi River, but the Trans-Mississippi district did provide a substantial amount of some materials, at least for its own use.

Niter could be procured by four methods. The first was importation, a means quickly jeopardized by the Union blockade, causing the bureau to seek to expand domestic production. Second, niter could be mined from certain caves with particular geologic and climatic characteristics, generally located in the mountains of Tennessee, Arkansas, Virginia, Georgia, and Alabama. Third, it could be gathered from the dirt under old buildings. Finally, niter could be manufactured artificially in carefully tended niter beds containing decomposing vegetable, animal, and human waste products. At least thirteen "nitriaries" were established in the eastern Confederacy near major cities such as Richmond, Virginia, Selma, Alabama, and Augusta, Georgia, but they required months of preparation before the beds produced much niter. Private citizens were encouraged to produce niter, and several instruction pamphlets were published to assist them. Records show that by September 30, 1864, government workers and private contractors, working caves as well as other deposits, had delivered 1,735,531.75 pounds of niter to the bureau, just slightly more than the 1,720,072 pounds that had been imported. Of this total amount, 408,905 pounds were procured in Arkansas and Texas.

Copper, to make percussion caps for firing guns as well as bronze for cannons, was another necessity. This mineral was found in few places in the Confederacy, and the bureau relied on several mines near Ducktown in Polk County, Tennessee. Incomplete reports indicate that these mines produced at least 775,000 pounds of copper before the Confederates lost control of the area in late 1863.

The Union Lead Mines, usually called the Wytheville Mines, in Wythe County, Virginia, were the major domestic source of lead for the Confederate states. Including materials from the Silver Hill Mines in North Carolina and the collection of scrap lead, the Confederates produced at least 2,508,079 pounds and imported about 1,368,125 pounds more by September 30, 1864. The Trans-Mississippi Department contributed 897,815 pounds of lead from Mexico and Arkansas, as well as scrap lead, to these figures.

Iron, critical not only for armaments but also for railroad repair, plating iron-clad ships, making agricultural implements, and numerous other military and civilian uses, was always in very short supply. Alabama and Virginia had the most mines and blast furnaces, but some iron was also manufactured in North Carolina, South Carolina, Tennessee, Georgia, and the Trans-Mississippi West. By September 30, 1864, the bureau had received a total of 25,354.6 tons of iron, which it carefully dispensed to what seemed the most crucial projects.

Sulphur and sulphuric acid (the latter manufactured at Charlotte, North Carolina) were being produced on a small scale of about 4,000 pounds per month by late 1864. By this time the single zinc factory, near Petersburg, Virginia, had been closed because of the proximity of Union forces.

Although all the minerals and metals to be gathered by the bureau also came through the blockade in limited quantities, most blockade runners were reluctant to bring in products such as niter and lead, which consumed considerable space and weight. In case of pursuit, the blockade runner would throw these supplies overboard first to lighten the ship. As the war progressed and greater shortages resulted, the Niter Bureau was authorized to impress raw materials as well as railroad tracks no longer in service and copper tubing from turpentine and apple brandy stills in North Carolina. After the battles around Atlanta, bureau workers scoured the battlefields collecting lead to be recycled into new bullets.

In its various endeavors the bureau employed a great many workers of different types. Exempted from military service, civilians worked as miners, carpenters, and wagon drivers, or contracted to provide livestock, other foodstuffs, or necessary construction materials. A number of the workers were men detailed from the army, in some cases because of useful prewar experience or skills. In March 1864, for example, at least 2,783 men were detailed for bureau jobs. The bureau also hired many slaves from their owners and impressed free blacks to do most of the hard labor. In September 1864, 4,557 blacks were employed at the iron mines and foundries, 1,252 mined niter, and 490, the entire nitriary staff except for superintendents, cared for the niter beds.

In addition, the bureau employed several notable chemists and geologists including John and Joseph LeConte in Columbia, South Carolina, and Nathaniel A. Pratt, the bureau chemist at the laboratory in Augusta, Georgia. These men made geological maps, sought to speed up the formation of niter in nitriaries, produced various chemicals, and inspected niter and other mines and works.

The location of most of the Confederate mines in the mountainous areas of western Virginia, eastern Tennessee, and northern Georgia and Alabama led to several types of problems. Since many of the local residents were outright Unionists or only marginally loyal to the Confederacy, they were often not very reliable workers. Conscripts and detailed men deserted and slaves ran away into the wild hilly areas near the mines. Union troops also raided the mines with increasing frequency as the war progressed, destroying

equipment, capturing workers, and causing many of the installations to cease production. Finally, threats of raids and the general manpower shortage forced bureau workers into active military service, either temporarily or permanently, despite vigorous protests from bureau officers. All of these factors combined to decrease the production of niter and other necessary minerals, but the resources of the bureau were not exhausted before the war ended.

Isaac M. St. John remained in charge of the bureau until February 16, 1865, when he was promoted to brigadier general and replaced Lucius B. Northrop as commissary general. Richard Morton, who succeeded St. John on February 22, had served with St. John as an engineer on the Virginia peninsula and then as second in command of the Niter Bureau, so he was well-prepared to assume his responsibilities, which, however, lasted only a few more weeks.

[*See also* Lead; Mining; Saltpeter.]

BIBLIOGRAPHY

Donnelly, Ralph W. "The Bartow County Confederate Saltpetre Works." *Georgia Historical Quarterly* 54 (1970): 305–319.
Donnelly, Ralph W. "Confederate Copper." *Civil War History* 1 (1955): 355–370.
Donnelly, Ralph W. "The Confederate Lead Mines in Wythe County, Virginia." *Civil War History* 5 (1959): 402–414.
Donnelly, Ralph W. "Scientists of the Confederate Nitre and Mining Bureau." *Civil War History* 2 (1956): 69–92.
Schroeder, Glenna R. "'We Will Support the Govt. to the Bitter End': The Augusta Office of the Confederate Nitre and Mining Bureau." *Georgia Historical Quarterly* 70 (1986): 288–305.
Sheridan, Richard C. "Production of Saltpetre from Alabama Caves." *Alabama Review* 33 (1980): 25–34.
Smith, Marion O. "The Sauta Cave Confederate Niter Works." *Civil War History* 29 (1983): 293–315.
U.S. War Department. *War of the Rebellion: A Compilation of the Official Records of the Union and Confederate Armies.* Washington, D.C., 1880–1901. Ser. 4, vols. 1–3.
Vandiver, Frank E. *Ploughshares into Swords: Josiah Gorgas and Confederate Ordnance.* Austin, Tex., 1952.

GLENNA R. SCHROEDER-LEIN

NORFOLK, VIRGINIA

Situated near the Elizabeth River's confluence with the James River at Hampton Roads, Norfolk proved important militarily in the early stages of the Civil War.

In 1860 Norfolk contained 14,620 people, of whom 3,284 were slaves. Of the free inhabitants, about 10 percent were of African descent and another 7 to 8 percent had been born in states north of Virginia. Natives of North Carolina and Ireland composed about 6 percent each, and a smaller percentage came from Germany. The majority of the population were native Virginians. Directly across the Elizabeth River lay Portsmouth, with 9,496 residents. The population of the two cities rose during the 1850s despite an 1855 epidemic of yellow fever that killed several thousand people.

Although secession sentiment surfaced in the city before the Civil War, support for preserving the Union was dominant until after the fall of Fort Sumter. The existence of the Gosport Shipyard (Norfolk Navy Yard), a Federal facility located just south of Portsmouth on the southern branch of the Elizabeth River, and the presence of the U.S. Navy throughout Hampton Roads, especially in Norfolk's harbor, encouraged the Union sentiment. On the eve of the Civil War, the Navy Yard, the biggest single employer in the district, provided work for about 1,400 local people. Its size and importance were magnified because of the relatively small manufacturing base of the private sector.

In addition, overseas exports and imports in the district totaled barely 100,000 tons in 1860—far less than the amount for the Richmond district. Coastal commerce included cotton from North Carolina, corn from eastern Virginia and North Carolina, oysters from local waters, and a wide variety of truck crops from small farms on the outskirts of the two cities. Norfolk's waterfront contained over forty warehouses and numerous wharves and piers, including stations for steamboats plying Virginia's rivers, the Chesapeake Bay, and the Atlantic Ocean. Near its wharves over seventy wholesalers and retailers conducted business. Two canals connected Norfolk and Portsmouth with northeastern North Carolina. A railroad tapped the Roanoke River at Weldon, North Carolina, and another rail line reached Petersburg, Virginia, just before the Civil War.

In 1860 Norfolk had a public school system, a large private library, three major newspapers, many churches, and several charitable associations such as the Humane Society, the Dorcas Society, and the Howard Association (founded as a result of the 1855 epidemic). With municipal gaslighting and street improvements, the city had countered negative publicity regarding its earlier backwardness.

Early in the war, Confederate troops occupied the Gosport Shipyard, partially destroyed by departing Union forces. After restoring a stone drydock, the Confederates salvaged the Federal ship *Merrimack,* rebuilt it as an ironclad, and renamed it *Virginia.* In March 1862, *Virginia* engaged in an inconclusive duel with the Federal ironclad *Monitor* in Hampton Roads.

In January and February 1862, Federal troops under Gen. Ambrose Burnside threatened the Elizabeth River cities from the south. In May, Federals under Gen. John Wool, along with President Abraham Lincoln and other officials, crossed Hampton Roads from Fort Monroe (which remained in Union hands throughout the war) and landed at Ocean View in the northern part of Norfolk County. Confederate forces then abandoned the forts protecting Norfolk and Portsmouth, severely damaging the shipyard as they departed.

Norfolk's mayor William Lamb and a delegation of city fathers met the Federal entourage outside the city and surrendered it to General Wool. When the civilians refused to take an oath of allegiance to the Union, Wool imposed martial law and placed Gen. Egbert Viele in command. During his tenure, Dr. David Wright, a hero during the yellow fever outbreak, killed a white Union officer who commanded black troops. Tried by a military court, Wright was convicted and, despite numerous appeals, executed.

Civilian government returned in June 1863, composed of those who would take the oath of allegiance. But the Union government of Francis H. Peirpoint, located in Alexandria, claimed jurisdiction over the local civilians, and a year later Gen. Benjamin F. Butler, the new commandant of the district, took over the operations of the civil court and issued a series of orders aimed at controlling the population. Although many Confederate sympathizers complained about the general, Butler restored gaslighting, cleaned the streets, and opened up commerce with the outside world. Under Union occupation freed slaves worked some thirty-five farms owned by Confederates, including one located east of Norfolk, the property of Gen. Henry A. Wise, a former Virginia governor. On that plantation was a school for black children, one of several in the district.

All prewar newspapers stopped publication during the war, and the Federals put out their own, the *New Regime.* African American fraternal associations such as the Freemasons, which had operated clandestinely before the war, appeared openly by the end.

When the fighting ceased in 1865, Norfolk had an expanded population of African Americans and an improving economy. In 1870, the number of whites in the town was slightly less than it had been in 1860, but the number of blacks had more than doubled. John Lonsdale Roper, a Union officer stationed in Norfolk, remained after the war and developed a lumber business in the 1870s and later a major shipbuilding company. Norfolk's residents also began processing peanuts, a local product whose fame had spread during the war. Cotton flowed directly to Europe in considerable quantities as local businessmen erected cotton compresses. With ships becoming ever larger, Norfolk replaced Richmond as the state's major seaport for overseas commerce.

[*See also* Gosport Navy Yard.]

BIBLIOGRAPHY

Dabney, Virginius. *Virginia: The New Dominion.* Garden City, N.Y., 1971.

Wertenbaker, Thomas J. *Norfolk: Historic Southern Port.* 2d ed. Edited by Marvin W. Schlegel. Durham, N.C., 1962.

PETER C. STEWART

NORTH CAROLINA

In 1860 North Carolina's voters gave a narrow majority to John C. Breckinridge, the candidate of the Southern Democrats, but popular sentiment differed sharply from the secessionist mood of the Deep South states. Both Unionism and competitive two-party politics remained strong in North Carolina, and the dominance of nonslaveholding small farmers in the white population posed a potential challenge for the Confederacy. When war came, North Carolinians made exceptional sacrifices for the Southern cause, but unusually strong protests and opposition to the Confederacy also developed. The burdens of the Civil War severely tested Confederate loyalties, and the internal problems that plagued the Confederacy were especially salient in this upper South state.

The Secession Crisis

When the crisis of 1860–1861 arrived, it affected a people whose material circumstances were quite different from those in the Deep South. Of North Carolina's population of 992,622 people, 631,100 were white. There were 331,059 slaves in the Tarheel State, and 30,463 free African Americans. Overwhelmingly rural, North Carolina had few towns or cities of any size—Wilmington was the largest with only 10,000 residents. For decades economic growth had been comparatively slow, and as a result the state had attracted few immigrants. Less than 1 percent of the population was foreign-born, and most of these individuals came from the British Isles. Mixed farming was the rule, even for many of the largest slaveholders, and plantation districts were rare. The influence of the market economy remained

> **Seventy-two percent of the white families in the state owned no slaves. . . .**

weak, although tobacco flourished in a line of counties along the Virginia border, some eastern counties grew substantial amounts of cotton, and rice plantations existed near Wilmington. Seventy-two percent of the white families in the state owned no slaves, and most farms were small, self-sufficient operations encompassing no more than fifty or one hundred acres.

Few leaders of the state shared secessionists' alarm about Southern rights. Charles Manly, former Whig governor, condemned the "fanatics" on both sides and fervently hoped that "the People will save" the nation. Democrat Rufus Lenoir Patterson fumed about the influence of fire-eaters like William Lowndes Yancey of Alabama who were pursuing

"ulterior objects in which the *citizens of N.C.* cannot be interested." The state treasurer, Jonathan Worth, similarly declared that if Abraham Lincoln "should pledge himself to execute the Fugitive Slave Law, and do it, I care nothing about the question as to Squatter Sovereignty."

The vote for Breckinridge was a vote for the candidate of the regular Democratic organization, and most voters, whether supporters of the Democrats or of the (formerly Whig) Opposition party, hoped the Union would be preserved. As the lower South seceded and organized the Confederate States of America, even large slaveholders felt dismay. Paul Cameron, the wealthiest planter in the state, wrote: "I try to keep myself employed, but I find my mind nearly all the time occupied with the State of the Country and it makes me very unhappy. I love the Union."

On February 28, 1861, voters cast ballots on the question of calling a convention to consider secession. Although Governor John W. Ellis favored and was working for secession, the voters refused to hold a convention. The drift of events toward war, however, steadily affected North Carolinians. As one man wrote to future governor Zebulon Vance, "I am a Union man but when they send men South it will change my notions." Vance himself was speaking for the Union and gesturing with upraised hand when word of the firing on Fort Sumter reached him. His hand fell "slowly and sadly by the side of a Secessionist." With war a reality, the North Carolina General Assembly passed a bill for a convention, and on May 20 this body took the state out of the Union and into the Confederacy.

Contributions to the War

Immediately, Tarheel citizens began to make unusually large contributions and sacrifices for the Confederate cause. In fact, the First North Carolina Regiment boarded trains for Virginia on May 11, nine days before the state formally left the Union. The initial excitement and romance of military service faded quickly before the grim tragedies of war, but North Carolina continued, through volunteering and conscription, to furnish a disproportionate number of soldiers to the Confederacy.

Before the war was over the state provided thirty-six generals to the armies, including Theophilus H. Holmes, D. H. Hill, William Dorsey Pender, and Dodson Ramseur. Among the state's naval officers were Capt. James W. Cooke of the ram *Albemarle* and Capt. James Waddell of *Shenandoah,* which destroyed more Union commerce than any ship save *Alabama.* But the greatest contributions were made by the common soldiers and their immediate superiors, who fought and died in substantial numbers in every theater east of the Mississippi.

The heaviest fighting for the state's troops took place on the battlefields of Virginia. George E. Pickett's famous charge on the third day at Gettysburg is identified with his gallant

Virginia troops, but four brigades under Gen. J. Johnston Pettigrew also answered the call to advance "for the honor of the good Old North State." They, too, fell in large numbers before the withering Union fire. Only three of Pettigrew's field officers returned from that charge, and of the 15,301 Confederates killed or wounded at Gettysburg, 4,033 were North Carolinians. Many other battles in the Old Dominion exacted heavy Tarheel casualties.

Although North Carolina contained only about one-ninth of the Confederacy's white population, it supplied nearly one-sixth of the Southern nation's fighting men. Nearly one-fourth of all Southern conscripts, 21,348 men, came from North Carolina. The normal military population of the state (white males between the ages of eighteen and forty-five) has been estimated at 116,000, yet 120,000 North Carolinians served in the Confederate armies before the war was over. Of these, 40,275 died, falling in roughly equal numbers to battle and disease. These statistics represented one-quarter of all Confederate battle deaths and the largest death toll of any Southern state. (Only a few white citizens fought for the North, but 7,000 black Tarheels joined the Union army.)

North Carolina also made unusual efforts to supply and support its Confederate troops. In the first year of the war, as state officials struggled to clothe volunteers, they ordered the entire output of the state's thirty-nine cotton mills and nine woolen mills for manufacture into uniforms. This became a continuing practice, and as time went on the state undertook to clothe all its troops and, after buying up all cloth produced in the state, sent purchasing agents into other Southern states. In the final years of the war, Governor Vance, who was first elected in 1862, used state-chartered blockade runners to exchange cotton for blankets, shoes, and uniforms.

Military Operations in the State

Military operations within North Carolina were comparatively minor through most of the war, although they always aroused anxiety among the population. The first threat came in the form of Federal invasion of the coast, beginning with the capture of Fort Hatteras in August 1861. Next Union forces under the command of Gen. Ambrose Burnside captured Roanoke Island on February 8, a defeat that dismayed many Tarheels. At his post in Richmond, Attorney General Thomas Bragg heard of complaints that "No. Ca. has been neglected, her troops sent to other points, while she is left to the tender mercies of the enemy." General Burnside followed up his victory with raids on Elizabeth City and Edenton and the capture of New Bern on February 14. Morehead City and Beaufort fell in March, and Fort Macon surrendered on April 25, 1862. From this point onward the Union forces controlled most of North Carolina's coastline north of Wilmington.

Occasional Federal raids and Confederate counterstrikes occurred thereafter in the eastern part of the state without a substantial occupation of territory. Unionist sympathizers and "Buffaloes," who were generally poorer whites, often preyed on the property of large planters. The major Federal presence was in New Bern, where large numbers of runaway slaves arrived in search of freedom. Freedmen's Bureau officials later organized their settlement in a community known as James City. Meanwhile, President Lincoln appointed Edward Stanly, an old-line Whig, as the military governor of North Carolina. On May 26 Stanly assumed jurisdiction in New Bern, but he found that a groundswell of pro-Union sentiment was not forthcoming and resigned following issuance of the Emancipation Proclamation.

In 1864 Confederate forces recaptured, and then lost again, the eastern town of Plymouth, and there were some small-scale Union raids in the western mountains. Major military operations, however, did not occur until the closing months of the war. The first of these focused on Wilmington, a favorite base for blockade runners and the last major port open for the Confederacy, and on Fort Fisher, the massive earthwork structure that guarded the approaches to Wilmington.

In December 1864 Union naval and infantry forces under Rear Adm. David D. Porter and Gen. Benjamin F. Butler attacked Fort Fisher without success. Despite a lengthy bombardment by Porter's massive armada, Butler's men were turned back within fifty yards of the fort. In January Porter tried again with troops commanded by Maj. Gen. Alfred H. Terry. This time the fort and its outnumbered defenders, commanded by Col. William Lamb, fell after vicious hand-to-hand combat. Wilmington was captured by the Federals on February 22, 1865.

Early in March 1865 the army of Gen. William Tecumseh Sherman entered the state. After his destructive march through Georgia, Sherman had paused at Savannah and then headed north through Columbia, South Carolina. His objective in North Carolina, besides the continued destruction of Southern resources and spirit, was the town of Goldsboro, where there were important railroad connections to the coast. Sherman's army of sixty thousand men traveled in two columns. Opposing them were no more than thirty thousand Confederates under the command of Gen. Joseph E. Johnston.

The challenge for Sherman was to keep the two wings of his army in close communication, while Johnston sought to fall upon one or the other column separately. On March 15 a sharp engagement took place at Averasboro, which allowed Johnston to slow Sherman's left wing and separate it farther from the other Federal column. Four days later at Bentonville the Confederates attacked Gen. Henry W. Slocum's forces in a day of heavy fighting. But Sherman reinforced Slocum during the next two days, and Johnston had to withdraw. On March 23 Sherman entered Goldsboro.

The next day Maj. Gen. George H. Stoneman left Tennessee and initiated a highly destructive cavalry raid through southwestern Virginia and western North Carolina. Commanding a veteran cavalry division of approximately six thousand men, Stoneman encountered little serious opposition. In North Carolina his forces struck at Boone, Wilkesboro, Elkin, High Point, Salisbury, Statesville, Lincolnton, Morganton, and other places. They cut railroad lines near Greensboro, burned factories anywhere they found them, and in Salisbury destroyed the Confederate prison and a large quantity of food and supplies. After ransacking Asheville on April 26, they left the state.

> **. . . citizens began to experience shortages of both imported luxury items and essentials such as salt.**

Meanwhile, General Johnston had surrendered the last major Confederate army to General Sherman. After resting at Goldsboro, Sherman's men had moved west, rejoicing at news of the fall of Richmond, and occupied Raleigh on April 13. General Johnston, recognizing the futility of further resistance, met Sherman on April 17, 1865, at the farmhouse of James and Lucy Bennett near Durham. Sherman had just learned of President Lincoln's assassination, which he announced that night. On the eighteenth he concluded terms of surrender with Johnston, but his political superiors rejected these as too liberal, for they included recognition of existing state governments and a guarantee of property rights that could be interpreted to include slaves. On April 26, 1865, Sherman and Johnston met again at the Bennett farmhouse and signed a document based on the terms agreed to at Appomattox. By early May minor skirmishes in the mountains had ceased, and the fighting was over.

Burdens on the Home Front

North Carolina's large contributions of fighting men had their counterpart in the heavy burdens borne by citizens on the home front. Shortly after the Union navy imposed its blockade, citizens began to experience shortages of both imported luxury items and essentials such as salt. Inflation and speculation or extortion aroused much concern as ordinary Tarheels wondered how they could pay the skyrocketing prices of goods. The burden felt most widely, however, was the shortage of labor in nonslaveholding families. Because most farms in the state were small, subsistence operations lacking any slave labor, the absence of men in the armies quickly affected the women and children left behind. North Carolina's large contribution of soldiers threw heavy burdens on families that were ill-equipped to carry them.

On numerous occasions Governor Vance pleaded with the War Department to suspend conscription in hard-pressed localities or to allow men to return home for a few weeks to help with the harvest. Officials in Richmond complied with his requests as far as they could, but their attempts to cooperate could not remove the problem. By March of 1863 Vance was protesting that conscription had swept off "a large class whose labor was, I fear, absolutely necessary to the existence of the women and children left behind."

Impressment also deprived citizens of valuable food or supplies, and, as Secretary of War James A. Seddon once admitted, it did so in an unequal manner that was much resented. Governor Vance often protested against impressment, but he reserved his hottest denunciations for the depredations of Confederate cavalry forces. "If God Almighty had yet in store," Vance once thundered, "another plague [for the Egyptians] worse than all others . . . I am sure it must have been a regiment or so of half-armed, half-disciplined Confederate cavalry." Had God turned the Confederate cavalry "loose among Pharaoh's subjects . . . he never would have followed the children of Israel to the Red Sea! No sir; not an inch!"

The geographical position of North Carolina exacerbated these difficulties. As the Confederacy lost territory around its periphery, government officials had to draw more and more heavily upon the regions that remained under their control. Most of North Carolina remained firmly under Confederate authority throughout the war, and to many Tarheel citizens it appeared that the Richmond administration relentlessly increased its demands for men, money, and supplies. Records of the tax-in-kind are incomplete, but surviving statistics suggest that substantial collections of farm produce were made in 1863 and 1864. North Carolina farms, because they were available to government officials, figured prominently in these levies.

The burdens of the home front produced a great deal of human suffering. In the early months of the war, many North Carolinians petitioned the War Department (usually in vain) for the exemption of craftsmen who were needed in rural districts, especially those who could repair farming tools. "We are getting scarce of almost every article of necessity, from a needle to a scythe blade," wrote one citizen in 1862. As prices rose, Zebulon Vance observed that "the cry of distress comes up from the poor wives and children of our soldiers . . . from all parts of the State." Shortage of provisions became the most serious problem, caused not only by bad weather and crop failures but also by the government's policy of "taking too many men from their farms," as one private described it.

Even conservative members of the political elite, who for decades had controlled local government from appointive, rather than elected, positions, grew alarmed at the deteriorating conditions of life among the common people. As early as June of 1862 Walter Gwynn wrote to former state Supreme Court justice Thomas Ruffin, "I have witnessed great distress, among the lower and poorer classes." He added, "I fear . . . starvation." Kenneth Rayner, a planter from Hertford County, agreed that the "suffering among the poor . . . is dreadful to contemplate." In January 1863 Joseph A. Worth wrote to his brother Jonathan, the state treasurer, that "if more men are called to the field, . . . many *must* starve." A year later he reported that "much suffering among the people exists. . . . In Chatham county one of the best counties in the state for provisions a great many have not had any meat for months. Clothing is very scarce. People known as the poorer class are almost destitute."

Members of "the poorer class" also spoke up about their own plight. Among the hundreds of wives who wrote to Governor Vance was one who explained, in a direct manner, "I want you . . . and Mr. Davis to . . . send home the poor solgers." Another noted that she was one of the many "who have neither brother, husband, nor Father at home . . . and no slave labor to depend on." A soldier let Vance know that "I have received a letter from home yesterday and [my family] are sufering very much for the want of provisions or money to b[u]y with." Another soldier, Private O. Goddin, pointedly asked the governor: "Now Govr. do tell me how we poor soldiers who are fighting for the 'rich man's negro' can support our families at $11 per month? How can the poor live?"

Survival became increasingly difficult for large segments of the population who felt the grip of poverty and hunger. County courts scrambled to find cornmeal and pork for distribution to the hungry. Newly appointed county corn agents traveled far within North Carolina and outside the state trying to buy provisions. Surviving county records give some evidence of the extent of the problem. In Orange County, 19.7 percent of the adult white women and 35 percent of the white children depended on county relief for food. In Randolph County 34.4 percent of the adult white women were on relief; in Duplin County the figure was 32.9 percent, and in Cumberland it was 40.7 percent. Such need often overwhelmed the resources of local government, and although the state appropriated more than $6 million to buy food for the poor, much of this aid was never more than a figure on a piece of paper.

Disaffection and Unionism

Suffering on this scale was bound to strengthen the disaffection that had always been latent in the state. Unionism was real but a comparatively small part of the problem. Class resentments and a sense of injustice motivated many more Tarheels to withdraw their support from the government. As the conditions of life deteriorated and the failure of government to provide the basic necessities for security became manifest, more and more ordinary people turned against the war.

Unionism in the state was real and sometimes ran deep. In the weeks after secession, individuals who loved the Union mounted a small number of scattered protests in every part of the state. As the Confederate government became more unpopular and adopted objectionable policies, some of these people became more outspoken or determined about their feelings of opposition. The Heroes of America, a secret organization also known as the Red Strings (for an identifying red string worn in the lapel), organized in 1861 and sought to aid draft resisters and deserters and oppose the Confederacy. The HOA was especially active in the "Quakerbelt" counties of Randolph, Davidson, Forsyth, and Guilford, but by 1863 its influence had begun to spread beyond the Piedmont. Working actively behind the scenes, the HOA elected some of its members to office and aided peace candidates. According to the closest students of the organization, it "counted perhaps 10,000 members in North Carolina and . . . played an active part not only in resisting the Confederacy but also in wartime and Reconstruction politics in the state."

Nevertheless, the Heroes of America were a minor, and not typical, part of the serious disaffection that grew in North Carolina. It was a combination of suffering and class resentments that usually caused people's discouragement to ripen into disaffection. Private O. Goddin, who had asked Governor Vance how the families of poor soldiers could live, also made an ominous and insightful prediction. "We will have a revolution," Goddin wrote in February 1863, "unless something is done." The potential for revolution, to which Goddin referred, was rooted in class and in perceptions of class favoritism by the government. "The majority of our soldiers," Goddin

> ## As the conditions of life deteriorated . . . ordinary people turned against the war.

explained, "are poor men with families who say they are tired of the rich mans war & poor mans fight."

Goddin enumerated some of the governmental policies that had aroused class resentment. At the top of his list were the army's acceptance of substitutes (which only the rich could afford to hire) and the exemption of overseers. Many nonslaveholding small farmers had volunteered for the cause only to find, Goddin charged, that "the Govt. has made a distinction between the rich man (who had something to fight for) and the poor man who fights for that he never will have. The exemption of the owners of 20 negroes & the allowing of substitutes clearly proves it." In this statement Goddin surely reflected the feeling of thousands of the state's yeoman farmers, for the exemption of overseers detonated such loud protests that the General Assembly felt compelled to pass resolutions criticizing the Confederate law.

Many also shared Goddin's perception that "healthy and active men who have furnished substitutes are grinding the poor by speculation while their substitutes have been discharged after a month's service as being too old or invalids." A woman in the mountains complained that well-to-do, privileged men in the home guards rounded up draftees with alacrity but fled to Tennessee when drafted themselves. Another woman charged that militia officers and magistrates who "remained at home ever since the war commenced" devoted themselves to arresting "old grey headed fathers" and "shooting down without halting them . . . [men] that has served in the army, some of them for 2 or 3 years." Upper-class status did convey benefits in Southern society, and one patriotic planter lamented that too few "young men of wealth . . . are facing danger and enduring privations." Every instance of a wealthy man who evaded service attracted attention and aroused resentment among the hard-pressed nonslaveholders.

As destitution tightened its grip on the state, desertion from the armies grew rapidly. Sharing Private Goddin's belief that "a man's first duty is to provide for his own household," hundreds of North Carolina soldiers left the armies and, if challenged, merely patted their rifles and said, "This is my furlough." By April 1863 General Pender was expressing alarm at the rate of desertion from "the North Carolina regiments of the army." The men were receiving letters from home "urging them to leave," explained Pender, and he feared that "the matter will grow from bad to worse." Pender was right, and desertion received further encouragement when North Carolina Chief Justice Richmond Pearson issued a decision against the Conscription Act.

From 1863 to the end of the war large numbers of deserters gathered in the western and Piedmont sections of North Carolina, despite periodic efforts by the Confederate army to collect them. Soon after deserters arrived home, events took place that drove many from a quiet withdrawal of support from the Confederacy in order to help their families to open opposition to constituted authority. Local officials decided that they could not tolerate the situation and launched efforts to arrest the deserters, who then had to choose a career as outlaws if they were going to remain near home and benefit their loved ones. In this way thousands of Tarheel deserters became "outliers" or "bushwhackers," men who lived in small bands, hiding in the countryside and stealing from the homes and storehouses of the rich in order to feed themselves and their families.

In the final months of the Civil War, disorder spread alarmingly across North Carolina. Bands of deserters often controlled roads, outnumbered the home guards, and overawed the courts. The situation was so far out of hand that some of the county courts attempted to negotiate a truce with the deserters, or recusant conscripts, as they also were called, in order simply to restore some security to property. Local officials often reported that the general population gave "aid and comfort" to the deserters and refused to muster with the home guards to oppose them. A colonel in Wilkes County pronounced himself "satisfied" that militia and home guard officers were "encouraging desertion and have gone under with the disloyal sentiment with at least one-half of the people of the county." By the time the war ended, Confederate authority as a practical matter had been severely undermined in many parts of the state.

Political Protest and Opposition

Because the Civil War brought such severe sacrifice and suffering to a people who had not been eager to leave the Union, it is not surprising that political protests were frequent and that opposition became strong enough to generate the only open and avowed peace movement in the Confederacy. Political discontent sprang from the ranks of the elite as well as the common people and grew steadily. It was fortunate for the Confederacy that in Zebulon Vance North Carolina had a leader who could express public discontent effectively without destroying cooperation with the central government.

Secession had produced some change in the state's political parties. Secessionists promptly organized a "Confederate" party that consisted mostly of former Democrats. In place of the old Opposition party, a "Conservative" party emerged that was composed of former Whigs and Democrats who had clung to the Union as long as possible. The Confederate party remained a viable organization for only about a year.

The tide of public opinion in the state is indicated by the fact that Conservatives soon branded their opponents as the "Destructives," and the name stuck. As the policies of the central government became more demanding, Conservatives condemned the Destructives and blasted their support of the Davis administration as another sign of their recklessness and irresponsibility. In the spring of 1862 a gubernatorial election took place to elect a successor to Henry T. Clark, who had served for about a year after the death of John Ellis. William W. Holden, the powerful editor of the *Raleigh Standard,* attacked Clark's policies on behalf of the Conservatives, charging that Clark wanted to waste "the last man and the last dollar" to fight the war. Holden supported Zebulon Vance, a colonel in the Twenty-sixth North Carolina, against the Destructives' candidate, William J. Johnston, and Vance rolled up a victory margin greater than five to two. Thereafter the spectrum of politics in the state shifted to the left; the Confederate party virtually disappeared, except as a whipping boy, and the Conservative organization of Vance fought out the next gubernatorial election against a growing peace movement.

Some of the earliest protests against the Richmond government came from upper-class North Carolinians. The resolutely nationalist policies of Jefferson Davis were a shock to many Tarheel politicians. Higher taxes, impressment, conscription, and government-ordered destruction of cotton that was threatened by the enemy were just a few of the policies that offended their state rights principles. They protested most bitterly against suspension of the writ of habeas corpus and fulminated against the Davis government as a despotism. Many of North Carolina's traditional leaders also chafed under the minor role they were called upon to play in the new nation. Feeling that they were overlooked and the state unrepresented in the highest councils of the government, they charged that North Carolina had been taken for granted and neglected. This chorus of protests strengthened discontent and placed the governor under the political necessity of appearing always to defend the interests of the state.

Maintaining North Carolina's support for the war effort grew increasingly difficult.

Zebulon Vance had announced before his election that he favored prosecution of the war until independence was achieved. Although he never abandoned his support for independence, he quickly learned that as governor his actions had to reflect the unpopularity in his state of many Confederate policies. In October 1862 he warned Jefferson Davis that "the original advocates of secession no longer hold the ear of the people" and that, despite "all the popularity with which I came into office, it will be exceedingly difficult for me to execute" the conscript law. This statement prefigured Vance's course as governor, for he balanced sensitivity to his constituents with concern for the national cause. Vehemently protesting against many government policies, Vance also attempted to support the war effort.

Frequently the governor interceded with Richmond authorities on behalf of his citizens, and when a native of another state was sent to enforce the Conscription Act, Vance voiced his own state's feeling of neglect. On many occasions he criticized impressment, conscription, the consumption of corn by Confederate distilleries, and other policies, but he usually avoided prolonged confrontations. On one point, however, Vance stood firm. Officials and employees essential to the state government had to be exempted from conscription, he insisted. Acting on this claim, Vance exempted 14,675 men—an unusually large number, but one perceived as justified in a state that was making great sacrifices.

Where the welfare of North Carolinians was directly concerned, Vance had to stand up to Richmond, and this political reality explains a bizarre situation that developed near the end of his term in office. As Lee's tattered and hungry soldiers fell back toward Appomattox, state warehouses bulged with supplies for North Carolina troops. Vance controlled 40,000 blankets, 150,000 pounds of bacon, cloth for 100,000

uniforms, leather for 10,000 pairs of shoes, plus other supplies, and he refused to relinquish them. The Confederacy needed these goods desperately, but it was impolitic in North Carolina to give them up as long as there was a chance they would be needed by Tarheels.

This reality also explains Vance's challenge to the Confederacy's control of international shipping in the closing months of the war. Using a steamer dubbed *Advance,* the governor was running the blockade and importing essential supplies for the soldiers and people of his suffering state. When the central government tightened regulations and tried to take over most cargo space for Confederate purposes, Vance organized a constitutional protest by other governors. Unless he fought for the welfare of his hard-pressed constituents, he could not keep them in the war.

Maintaining North Carolina's support for the war effort grew increasingly difficult. In January 1863 State Treasurer Jonathan Worth reported that "nearly every man I saw . . . is openly for re-construction on the basis of the Constitution of the U.S., if these terms can be obtained." That fall's congressional elections showed how far discontent and peace sentiment had advanced. Eight of the state's ten newly elected congressmen opposed the administration. No original secessionists and only one Democrat triumphed, and five of the victorious candidates ran on a peace platform.

William W. Holden, the influential Raleigh editor, had organized a popular campaign for peace in the summer of 1863. Approximately one hundred public meetings called for a peace convention and an immediate armistice. Holden then announced that he would challenge Vance in the 1864 gubernatorial elections.

Vance believed that honor required him and his state to stay in the war to the end, but he knew that Holden read the popular sentiment correctly. Independence would require more "blood and misery," Vance wrote, "*and our people will not pay this price* . . . I am convinced of it." Nevertheless he fought Holden shrewdly, emphasizing the efforts that he and the Confederate government had made for peace. He also branded Holden as "the *war* candidate," charging that Holden's plans would embroil North Carolina in war with its neighbors, "a bloodier conflict than that you now deplore."

These tactics, plus Vance's immense personal popularity, carried him to victory and kept North Carolina in the war to the bitter end. But the governor's political adroitness could not remove his people's travail. Thus, it was natural that a state that sacrificed and suffered much for the cause also protested greatly.

[*For further discussion of battles fought in North Carolina, see* Burnside's Expedition to North Carolina; Carolinas Campaign of Sherman; Stoneman's Raids. *For further discussion of North Carolina cities, see* Raleigh, North Carolina; Wilmington, North Carolina. *See also* Heroes of America *and biographies of numerous figures mentioned herein.*]

BIBLIOGRAPHY

Auman, William T., and David D. Scarboro. "The Heroes of America in Civil War North Carolina." *North Carolina Historical Review* 58, no. 4 (1981): 327–363.

Barrett, John G. *The Civil War in North Carolina.* Chapel Hill, N.C., 1963.

Durrill, Wayne K. *War of Another Kind.* New York, 1990.

Escott, Paul D. *Many Excellent People: Power and Privilege in North Carolina, 1850–1900.* Chapel Hill, N.C., 1985.

Kruman, Marc W. *Parties and Politics in North Carolina, 1836–1865.* Baton Rouge, La., 1983.

Mobley, Joe A. *James City: A Black Community in North Carolina, 1863–1900.* Raleigh, N.C., 1981.

Paludan, Phillip Shaw. *Victims.* Knoxville, Tenn., 1981.

Yearns, W. Buck, and John G. Barrett. *North Carolina Civil War Documentary.* Chapel Hill, N.C., 1978.

PAUL D. ESCOTT.

NORTHERNERS

One would not expect to find a significant number of Northerners in either the antebellum or the Confederate South. Yet the census of 1860 indicates that there were approximately 360,000 Northerners residing in the Old South; some estimates place that number as high as 500,000. Many Northerners, of course, found an inhospitable environment in the South and returned to their native states. But a surprising number of Northerners remained in the South and made their life's work there.

Northerners living in the South spanned the entire socioeconomic spectrum. Some were farmers, planters, or overseers; others were common laborers or skilled artisans; many became merchants, shippers, bankers, industrialists, or railroad magnates. A number of Northerners found a rewarding professional life in the South as tutors, college professors or presidents, lawyers, doctors, ministers, and scientists; still others became journalists, politicians, and diplomats.

Some fifty Northern-born men rose to the rank of general in the Confederate army, and many others filled the muster rolls at lesser ranks. Indeed, some of the most vituperative comments directed at Northerners were a consequence of their successful status in the Confederacy. For example, a Richmond editor charged in 1862 that "all the officials, who constitute the very pivot on which the whole war hinges are either Yankees, or foreigners, or Jews."

Several months later, that same editor spoke for many of his fellow Southerners when he became more specific in his vitriol. Judah P. Benjamin, a man who would occupy three cabinet-level positions (in the War, State, and Justice departments) was a "foreigner and a Jew"; Adj. Gen. Samuel Cooper was a "New Yorker"; Secretary of the Navy Stephen R. Mallory was "born in the West Indies of Yankee parents, and educated in Connecticut"; Quartermaster General Abraham C. Meyers was a "Pennsylvanian and a Jew"; and Chief of Ordnance Josiah Gorgas was "a Northern man of an unknown state."

Although they had resided in the South for quite some time, the most prominent native Northerners to become generals in the Confederate army were Gorgas, Cooper, Mansfield Lovell, John C. Pemberton, Daniel Ruggles, and Samuel G. French. Antipathy toward important Northerners in the Confederacy was exacerbated when Lovell and Pemberton, commanding the defenses of New Orleans and Vicksburg, respectively, were forced to surrender to the Federals.

In this regard, President Jefferson Davis became a focal point for criticism of southernized Northerners by appointing them to office and command. Davis and others, however, defended the contributions of the Northerners to the Confederate war effort. "Casting imputations of disloyalty upon those of Northern and Foreign birth because of that fact alone," wrote the editor of the *Macon Telegraph*, "is a poor way of displaying zeal in behalf of the Southern Confederacy." The editor went on to remind his Southern brethren that there had "been as many traitors to our cause of Southern birth as of Northern birth."

In short, Northerners in the Confederacy exerted an influence on Confederate life far more than hitherto believed and certainly disproportionate to their numbers.

BIBLIOGRAPHY

Coulter, E. Merton. *The Confederate States of America, 1861–1865.* A History of the South, vol. 7. Baton Rouge, La., 1950.

Green, Fletcher M. *The Role of the Yankee in the Old South.* Athens, Ga., 1972.

Thomas, Emory M. *The Confederate Nation, 1861–1865.* New York, 1979.

JASON H. SILVERMAN

NORTHWESTERN CONSPIRACY

Even before the Civil War reached the halfway mark, Governor Oliver P. Morton of Indiana expressed fears that Democrats dissenting from the war effort were planning to revolutionize the upper Midwest. He claimed that certain groups intended to free Confederate prisoners held in Camp Morton near Indianapolis and establish a Northwest confederacy allied with the South. In the fall of 1864 a Morton protègè raided the quarters of Harrison H. Dodd and seized papers that enabled him to concoct an exposè of the Sons of Liberty and publicize Morton's conspiracy theory. Dodd, a printer and Democratic activist, had founded the Sons of Liberty as a secret order to promote conservative measures and win elections.

Just prior to the November 1864 elections soldiers seized some revolvers shipped to Dodd's printing plant from New York and made a round of arrests, including Dodd and Joseph J. Bingham, editor of the Democratic-oriented *Indianapolis State Sentinel.* Governor Morton parlayed the arrests into "a gigantic Northwestern conspiracy." Later Dodd and four others were tried by a military commission in the

> **Morton's molehill-to-mountain plot consisted of a few facts and much conjecture—there was no overt act.**

Indianapolis treason trials. Actually, Morton's molehill-to-mountain plot consisted of a few facts and much conjecture—there was no overt act.

In Illinois, too, on the eve of the 1864 elections, an editor of the *Chicago Tribune* and the commandant at Camp Douglas (a compound holding eleven thousand Confederate prisoners) claimed that secret society members and Copperheads intended to free the prisoners, burn Chicago, take over the polls, and establish a Northwestern confederacy. Authorities made a number of arrests and the "Camp Douglas conspiracy," or "Chicago conspiracy," received national publicity. A military commission conducted a treason trial in Cincinnati the next year.

A few Confederate officials at the time convinced themselves that there was a possibility of dissenters establishing a separate confederacy in the upper Midwest. But some present-day historians have debunked the Chicago and Indianapolis conspiracies, contending they were little more than fantasies devised to discredit Democrats and influence the 1864 elections.

[*See also* Copperheads.]

BIBLIOGRAPHY

Klement, Frank L. *Dark Lanterns: Secret Political Societies, Conspiracies, and Treason Trials in the Civil War.* Baton Rouge, La., 1984.

Milton, George Fort. *Abraham Lincoln and the Fifth Column.* New York, 1942.

Tredway, Gilbert R. *Democratic Opposition to the Lincoln Administration in Indiana.* Indianapolis, 1973.

FRANK L. KLEMENT

NULLIFICATION CONTROVERSY

During the late fall and winter of 1832 and 1833, the nullification controversy, the most important constitutional crisis between the adoption of the Constitution and the secession of the South, took place.

The controversy had its origins in the passage of the highly protective Tariff of Abominations in 1828, which many in South Carolina believed to be unconstitutional. Over the next several years, radicals led by James Hamilton and Robert Barnwell Rhett, Sr., effectively organized and enlarged their following. When President Andrew Jackson refused to push very hard for a reduction of the tariff and in 1832 signed into law a new measure that only partially reduced duties and did not abandon the principle of protection, South Carolina proceeded to implement the doctrine of nullification as it had been developed by John C. Calhoun in his "South Carolina Exposition and Protest" (1828) and in several important speeches.

Governor Hamilton convened a special session of the state legislature on October 22, 1832, which immediately called a convention to meet at Columbia on November 19. This convention adopted an ordinance declaring the tariffs of 1828 and 1832 unconstitutional and prohibited the collection of Federal duties within the state beginning on February 1, 1833. It also prescribed a test oath for all military and civil officers of the state, except members of the legislature, and forbade any appeal to the U.S. Supreme Court in cases arising under the ordinance. The convention also warned that any attempt by the Federal government to use force would be cause for South Carolina to secede from the Union. The legislature immediately adopted laws to enforce the ordinance, which included the establishment of a military force and the distribution of weapons.

As these events unfolded, President Jackson's rage mounted. Throughout his first term in office he had made clear his dislike of nullification: it was an illegitimate form of state rights, an assault on the doctrine of majority rule, and a threat to the continued existence of the Union. On December 10 he issued his "Proclamation to the People of South Carolina" making clear his intention to uphold the supremacy of the Federal government even if it meant the shedding of blood. Jackson then ordered a variety of military activities and on January 16, 1833, sent a special message to Congress asking for a Force Bill authorizing him to use the military to collect the Federal revenues.

Most people believed South Carolina had acted rashly. No other state formally endorsed the doctrine of nullification and many condemned it. But there was also, especially in the South, widespread opposition to Jackson's desire to use force and to hang the nullifiers for treason, and a number of states rejected the nationalist principles contained in the president's nullification proclamation. Fearful of civil war, Congress, under the leadership of Henry Clay, formulated a compromise: a new tariff that provided for a gradual reduction of duties over the next decade and that abandoned the principle of protection. As a sop to the president the Force Bill was also adopted. Jackson signed both into law on March 2, 1833.

Upon learning that a compromise was likely, South Carolina suspended its ordinance on January 21. Shortly after the adoption of the congressional compromise, the state reconvened its convention and rescinded its ordinance, but in a final act of defiance it nullified the Force Act. Both sides claimed victory. The most important result of the controversy was that over the next three decades the idea of secession became increasingly enmeshed with the doctrine of state rights and the South's defense of slavery.

BIBLIOGRAPHY

Ellis, Richard E. *The Union at Risk: Jacksonian Democracy, States' Rights and the Nullification Crisis.* New York, 1987.
Freehling, William W. *Prelude to Civil War: The Nullification Controversy in South Carolina, 1811–1836.* New York, 1965.

RICHARD E. ELLIS

NURSING

At the outbreak of the Civil War, the only professional nurses in the South were Roman Catholic nuns of the Sisters of Mercy and the Sisters of Charity. Few other nineteenth-century women ventured into medicine except in the field of midwifery. Nursing took place in the home and was the duty of women in the family. Public nursing practice was viewed as too arduous and unfeminine. One Confederate soldier summed up many soldiers' feelings when he wrote to his wife and cautioned her, "Do not think of coming here as a nurse. It is no place for a young and inexperienced lady. . . . .You cannot imagine the labor you would have to undergo, and disgusting much of it is."

But in early June 1861, Mary Boykin Chesnut commented in her diary that "every woman in the house is ready to rush into the Florence Nightingale business." As men answered the call to arms, women expressed their patriotism by establishing hospitals and tending wounded soldiers. Many nursed the injured in their own homes with their personal physicians in attendance.

As wounded from the Battle of First Manassas flooded into Richmond, it became evident that the government's medical facilities were extremely inadequate and that private resources needed to be pressed into service. Sally L. Tompkins took the lead in establishing and supervising the highly successful Robertson Hospital in Richmond. Operating throughout the war, it served 1,333 patients with only 73 deaths. Juliet Ann Opie Hopkins traveled from Alabama to organize and operate hospitals for her state's wounded soldiers. Using donations from home and $500,000 of her personal funds, she founded the First, Second, and Third Alabama Hospitals. Taking her medical knowledge onto the battlefield, Hopkins was wounded twice at the Battle of Seven Pines, and her injuries left her lame for life. In Williamsburg, Letitia Tyler Semple organized that city's first hospital, staffed in part with visiting North Carolina women as volunteer nurses.

Throughout the South, other women rallied to the cause. Over one thousand women, assigned to duty or as volunteers, served alongside thousands of their male counterparts. Felicia Grundy Porter headed the Women's Relief Society of the Confederate States. This Tennessee native started in her home state and expanded her hospitals throughout the Confederacy. She also sought funds to purchase artificial limbs for the poor. Mrs. Frank Newsone, a doctor's widow, continued his work by administering his hospitals. Others renowned for their dedication were Betsy Sullivan, the "Mother of the First Tennessee Regiment"; Betsy T. Philips, the "Mother of the Orphan Brigade"; and Ella K. Trader, the "Florence Nightingale of the South."

Women first entered hospitals to visit friends and relatives, and remained as volunteers. Their presence was regarded as a mixed blessing. Occasionally, an overly zealous volunteer would try to feed a heavy meal to a patient recovering from surgery. Once a volunteer confused the prescriptions that a surgeon had allowed her to administer. Sometimes volunteers played favorites. In the case of Mary Chesnut, she was reprimanded by Tompkins when she tried to provide special treats to the South Carolina wounded in Robertson Hospital. Young, handsome patients received more attention than older, less attractive men. The nurses in one Georgia hospital were chagrined to discover that the handsome, precariously ill soldier they had watched over so diligently was a Northerner.

Six months after First Manassas, a committee in the Confederate Congress examined the overall state of hospitals in the Confederacy. They found mismanagement, lack of supplies, materials of inferior quality, unsanitary conditions, and unqualified surgeons. Because of a high turnover in wounded soldiers detailed to act as nurses, the committee recommended that females be hired to serve in field and general hospitals as nurses. They authorized each hospital to employ a staff of two matrons in chief, two assistant matrons, and two matrons for each ward. They were to receive food and lodging and monthly stipends of $40, $34, and $30, respectively.

The matrons' duties were limited. They did not give medications, assist in the operating room, or provide routine medical attention, although these restrictions were lifted in the face of emergencies. Matrons then assisted in surgery, administered chloroform, and dressed wounds. Under the law, the domain of the matrons was to oversee the hospital's use of money for quality food and the proper preparation of patients' diets.

As chief matron of Division No. 2 of Chimborazo Hospital in Richmond, Phoebe Yates Pember focused on arranging the daily diet list, making sure that no ward was treated differently from another. Surgeons' as well as her own special instructions helped tailor diets to individual needs. She described the daily fare as "chicken soup for twenty— beef tea for forty—tea and toast for fifty." As food grew short in the course of the war, patients subsisted on salt pork, corn meal,

> **Matrons worked hard to be accepted, to introduce new ideas in patient care, and to bring order.**

and dried peas. At Chimborazo, the men finally rebelled when the menu consisted of pea soup, cold peas, fried peas, and baked peas on a rotating basis. An important duty of the matron was controlling the whiskey supply and restricting it to medical usage.

Matrons worked hard to be accepted, to introduce new ideas in patient care, and to bring order. But visitors to the hospital wards disrupted the daily routine. In one instance, a well-intentioned visitor loosened the compression bandage on an amputated arm, and the patient bled to death. In another case, a Mrs. Daniells from West Virginia visited her hospitalized husband. She displaced her husband in his bed in order to give birth to their daughter, placing Pember in the awkward position of caring for mother and child. Trouble followed when the mother returned home and left little "Phoebe" with Pember. A furlough had to be arranged for the father to take the child home.

According to Kate Cumming, a matron with the Army of Tennessee, a typical nurse's day started at 4:00 A.M. and continued until midnight. Breakfast was eaten with the staff or in their rooms. In addition to their regular assignments, performing personal tasks for patients such as mending, and writing or reading letters, wore the women down. Little respite was found at the day's end. If fortunate, the matron retired to an area of the ward where a bed, table, and chest were her private accommodations.

Matrons, over the objections of surgeons, introduced home remedies, airing of the wards, and simple cleanliness. They became the link between hospital and home for their patients. It was through their persistence and dedication that many a soldier survived his wounds and lived to see his family again.

[*See also* Health and Medicine, *article on* Hospitals; Medical Department; *and biographies of numerous figures mentioned herein.*]

BIBLIOGRAPHY

Buck, A. T. "Founder of the First Confederate Hospital." *Confederate Veteran* 2 (May 1894): 141. Reprint, Wilmington, N.C., 1985.

Cumming, Kate. *A Journal of Hospital Life in the Confederate Army of Tennessee.* Louisville, Ky., 1866.

Cunningham, Horace H. "Confederate General Hospitals: Establishment and Organization." *Journal of Southern History* 20 (1954): 376–394.

Hall, Courtney R. *Medical Life.* New York, 1935.

Harwell, Richard B., ed. *Kate: The Journal of a Confederate Nurse.* Baton Rouge, La., 1959.

Pember, Phoebe Yates. *A Southern Woman's Story: Life in Confederate Richmond.* Edited by Bell I. Wiley. New York, 1959.

Simkins, P. B., and J. W. Patton. *The Women of the Confederacy.* Richmond, Va., 1936.

Sterky, H. E. *Some Notable Alabama Women during the Civil War.* Montgomery, Ala., 1962.

SANDRA V. PARKER

OATH OF ALLEGIANCE

One of the primary problems facing the Federal government when the Civil War began was ensuring that its employees and military men were loyal. Over three hundred U.S. officers resigned to join the Confederacy, as did numerous government clerks and officials. Fearful of disloyalty among those who remained, President Abraham Lincoln on April 30, 1861, ordered all military personnel to retake an oath of allegiance. And Congress, on August 6, 1861, passed legislation requiring civil servants also to take or retake an oath of allegiance.

Even though these regulations were rigidly enforced, fears of disloyalty remained, and numerous ad hoc oaths of allegiance were used as a means of testing and ensuring loyalty. By the summer of 1862, most of the oaths, civil and military, were combined under one oath, the Ironclad Test Oath of Loyalty. The Ironclad Oath was so named because it required the oath taker to swear that "I have never voluntarily borne arms against the United States." In addition, the person had to forsake any allegiance to state authority and swear to "support and defend the Constitution of the United States against all enemies foreign and domestic; . . . bear true faith and allegiance to the same."

An oath of allegiance rapidly became a test of loyalty for common citizens. Maj. Gen. Benjamin F. Butler as military governor of New Orleans required that after October 12, 1861, anyone who wanted to do business in the city or with the U.S. government had to take an oath of allegiance to the United States. As stated by Butler, "It enables the recipient to say, 'I am an American citizen,' the highest title known."

Butler's practice became commonplace as the war progressed, and the Ironclad Oath or a variant thereof was required of thousands of Federals and Southerners. People who wanted to do business with the government, Confederate prisoners of war who wanted parole, Southerners who wanted to be reimbursed for goods taken by foraging Federal troops, and Union sympathizers in the South who wanted to govern themselves—all took the oath. Some took it numerous times: the record might have been set by Robert J. Breckinridge who took the oath nine times between June and December 1865.

After the war the oath presented an immediate problem for both the North and the South. Since its provisions remained in effect, no former Confederate soldier or any Southern citizen who had assisted in the South's war effort could hold a Federal, state, or local office or serve in the military. To evade the "ironclad" portion of the oath concerning bearing arms against the United States, former Confederates had to petition the president of the United States for a pardon, and the presidents immediately after the war approved many such requests.

In 1884 Congress removed all the iron from the Ironclad Oath when it passed into law a new Oath of Allegiance. The 1884 oath removed all the restrictive portions of the older oaths and left it in its current form—an oath to support and defend the Constitution.

BIBLIOGRAPHY

Hyman, Harold M. *Era of the Oath.* Philadelphia, 1954.
Nevins, Allen. *Ordeal of the Union: The Emergence of Lincoln.* Vol. 2. New York, 1950.
Statutes at Large of the United States of America, 1789–1873. Washington, D.C., 1850–1873. Vol. 12, pp. 326–327, 502–503; vol. 23, pp. 21–22.
Tarhane, A. C. "Robert J. Breckinridge." *Confederate Veteran* 23 (May 1915): 215. Reprint, Wilmington, N.C., 1985.
U.S. War Department. *War of the Rebellion: A Compilation of the Official Records of the Union and Confederate Armies.* Washington, D.C., 1880–1901. Ser. 1, vol. 15, p. 483; ser. 3, vol. 2, p. 227.

P. NEAL MEIER

OLUSTEE, FLORIDA

Thirteen miles east of Lake City, Florida, on the Florida Atlantic and Gulf Central Railroad, Olustee was the site of the February 20, 1864, battle that was a decisive victory for Confederate Gen. Joseph Finegan. It was decisive in that the interior of Florida remained in Confederate hands for the duration of the conflict, enabling shipments of foodstuffs from Florida, largely cattle and hogs, to continue to feed Confederate armies. It cost the Confederates 946 men dead, wounded, or missing; the Federals suffered a total of 1,861 casualties.

The Federals made no serious effort to invade and occupy the interior of Florida until February 1864. An abrupt reversal of this policy came that month when 5,000 Federal troops from lower South Carolina and upper Georgia embarked aboard transports for an invasion of northeast Florida. A major invasion objective was political. President Abraham Lincoln doubted that he would be the Republican nominee to succeed himself in 1864. Salmon P. Chase, secretary of the treasury in Lincoln's cabinet, was his major challenger. Lyman P. Stickney, Chase-appointed tax collector, had served in Union-occupied sections of eastern Florida since 1862. He advised Chase that many Union supporters would assist Federal troops in restoring Florida to the Union and would provide a Chase delegation to the Republican National Convention. Lincoln, aware of these activities, sent his personal secretary, John Hay, to Florida, and he reported that the Unionists were friendlier to Lincoln than to Chase. Thus, Lincoln approved of the Federal invasion of February 1864 as a measure to restore Florida to the Union. His advisers were confident that the invasion would encounter little resistance, Floridians would accept Lincoln's generous plan for reconstruction, and the reconstructed state would send a Lincoln delegation to the Republican National Convention.

A second, and more obvious, reason for the invasion was to halt the movement of cattle, hogs, salt, and sugar from Florida that supplied Confederate armies to the north. The capture of Vicksburg by Union forces in 1863 had cut off the supplies of foodstuffs from Texas; the Confederacy needed Florida cattle and hogs to continue the war. A third objective was to free the slaves and enlist them as soldiers in the Union armies.

The Federal forces, commanded by Gen. Truman A. Seymour, reached Jacksonville on February 7, 1864. They moved westward following the route of the Florida Atlantic and Gulf Central Railroad in the direction of Lake City. Finegan, commander of the East Florida Military District, was ordered to halt the invaders and engage them in battle. Despite critical needs for troops elsewhere, Gen. Robert E. Lee ordered reinforcements from Georgia to join Finegan's command. Finegan withdrew his forces ahead of the Union advance in search of a better defensive position and to await the reinforcements. Confederate and Union commanders both overestimated the other's strength. Finegan's reinforced units numbered 5,000. After Seymour enlisted about 500 freed slaves for combat duty, his forces numbered about 5,500. Finegan called his withdrawal to a halt thirteen miles east of Lake City and found a defensive position near the village of Olustee—a rail embankment about a mile and a half long facing an open field. The embankment extended from Ocean Pond on the north to a large cyprus swamp on the south.

About noon on February 20, Union forces approached the Confederate defenses. The Southerners, aware that the Union men were tired from their long march and that many Federals had not yet reached the battle scene, ventured out of their prepared defenses and attacked the vanguard of the

Union forces in an open field. When the Confederate cavalry and infantry attack was repulsed and driven back to the defenses, Seymour ordered the Federals to attack. Artillery prepared the way. Infantry and cavalry fired at a close range of about a hundred yards and then lunged forward. The defenders responded with a curtain of fire that turned back three Federal offensives.

A little after six in the evening, Seymour, responding to extremely high casualties and the stubborn resistance, ordered his units to retreat. He left behind some of the 1,861 dead and wounded. The Confederates, who captured 5 cannons, 1,600 small arms, and 130,000 rounds of ammunition, lost 93 killed, 847 wounded, and 6 missing. Though the battle at Olustee was minor in regard to the number of men engaged, both Confederate and Union forces suffered the highest percentage of casualties of any battle in the Civil War: the Union, about 37 percent and the Confederates, almost 20 percent.

The heavy Confederate casualties persuaded Finegan to halt the pursuit of retreating Federals about twelve miles west of Jacksonville. In April the Union strategy called for withdrawal of military forces from Florida to strengthen attacks to the north.

Olustee was a decisive victory for the Confederacy, and Finegan received a vote of thanks from Congress. Seymour was bitterly criticized by his own troops and by the Northern press. The supply lines to the Confederate armies remained open. Historian Rembert Patrick estimates that these foodstuffs enabled Lee to continue the war for another year. Tallahassee was the only Confederate capital in Confederate hands when the war ended. It was victories elsewhere, not a victory at Olustee, that renominated Abraham Lincoln for the presidency.

BIBLIOGRAPHY

Baltzell, George F. "The Battle of Olustee (Ocean Pond), Florida." *Florida Historical Quarterly* 9 (1930–1931): 199–223.
Johns, John E. *Florida during the Civil War.* Gainesville, Fla., 1963.
Tebeau, Charlton. *A History of Florida.* Coral Gables, Fla., 1980.

MERLIN G. COX

ORAL HISTORY

Oral history is a term used to refer to both a topic of study and the methodology used to record the information studied. An example of this technique are the seven interviews collected by Kate Cashman Conway from survivors of the Civil War and published in the *Vicksburg Evening Post* in 1906. All those who lived in the South during the Civil War are long dead, of course, but in most instances, their families still exist and are one of the prime conduits through which historical traditions concerning the war have survived to the present.

There are several reasons oral history is valuable for researchers interested in the Confederacy. Chief among these is that oral historical traditions preserve information not available in written sources. For example, the activities of Beanie Short, a guerrilla active in the Cumberland region of northern Tennessee and southern Kentucky, would be unknown today if it weren't for oral tradition. No newspapers in the area recounted his exploits, and there is no mention of him in court records, because few guerrillas stood trial for

> **Information gleaned from oral history interviews often humanizes the Civil War.**

their crimes during the war. Oral historical narratives also often preserve what is psychologically true, and that can be as important as what is factually true. A South Carolina family still tells a story about two ancestors that explains why they left the Confederate forces to join the Union side. The brothers were part of a band of Confederates traveling through Virginia during the first half of the war. Although they were starving, they were given strict orders by their commanding officer not to steal apples from a nearby orchard. One of the brothers disobeyed, and the commander shot him in the arm. As a result the brothers left and joined the opposing side. Whether or not such an incident ever occurred is less important than the fact that the family today thinks it did. The story enables family members to regard their ancestors in a positive light rather than think of them as merely deserters.

Information gleaned from oral history interviews often humanizes the Civil War. One may read accounts of noted generals and battles without understanding what life during the conflict was like for most people. Orally preserved accounts of families living for weeks on roasted cottonseed or killing their only mule for food make the difficulty of the times more vivid.

Oral histories also often provide a source for popular beliefs and attitudes. A legend common in the southern Appalachians maintains that Abraham Lincoln was the illegitimate son of a Southerner—in some accounts of John C. Calhoun, in others of an unheralded North Carolina mountaineer named Abraham Enloe. Although those who keep such traditions alive take them seriously, they are probably dismissed by most professional historians. They remain alive mainly because of the mountaineers' pride in having Lincoln as one of their own. Another traditional account preserved in some areas is that Lincoln and Jefferson Davis were half-brothers, which can be seen as symbolizing the healing of

political divisions among the American people. Moreover, for some people Lincoln's illegitimacy explains his presumed persistent melancholy.

Other positive features of oral history include the possibility of verifying incidents and the provision of information concerning minority groups who, during the war, were more dependent on the spoken than on the written word. Yet, despite its advantages, oral history and the related field of folklore have not been used to their fullest potential by historians studying the Confederacy.

[*See also* Folk Narratives.]

BIBLIOGRAPHY

Alley, Judge Felix E. *Random Thoughts and the Musings of a Mountaineer.* Salisbury, N.C., 1941.

Cotton, Gordon A. *Yankee Bullets, Rebel Rations.* Vicksburg, Mississippi, 1989.

Deering, Mary Jo, and Barbara Pomeroy. *Transcribing Without Tears: A Guide to Transcribing and Editing Oral History Interviews.* Washington, D.C., 1976.

Dorson, Richard M. *American Folklore and the Historian.* Chicago, 1971.

Hoopes, James. *Oral History: An Introduction for Students.* Chapel Hill, N.C., 1979.

W.K. MCNEIL

ORDNANCE BUREAU

The Ordnance Bureau of the Confederate army functioned as a subsection of the Artillery Corps, but achieved status as one of the most important and successful supply agencies in the Confederacy. The tasks facing the bureau were formidable. All war munitions would have to be provided as state and Confederate forces came into being, but each state worked to provide for its own troops, so that the bureau encountered proprietary and patchwork efforts across the country.

Fortunately for the bureau, Maj. (later Brig. Gen.) Josiah Gorgas, a Pennsylvanian turned Southerner, became its chief on April 8, 1861. A sober, quiet man, Gorgas after graduating from West Point had distinguished himself in the U.S. ordnance service for his ability, although he chafed at his subordinate role. While serving at Mount Vernon Arsenal in Alabama, he met his future wife, Amelia Gayle, daughter of a former Alabama governor, and became converted to the Southern way of life.

With characteristic energy, Gorgas surveyed his bureau and his new country. On May 7, 1861, he reported to Congress that the South had 164,010 small arms ranging from U.S. rifled muskets to .69-caliber muskets, new and altered percussion and flint muskets, Harpers Ferry rifles, Colt rifles, Hall rifles, varied carbines, and Colt and percussion pistols. He discovered some 3.2 million small arms cartridges, along with 168,000 pounds of musket and rifle powder—enough for another one and a half million cartridges. Cannon powder was located at permanent fortifications. Percussion caps, a vital ingredient in modern weaponry, numbered about 2 million, with "a good many at the arsenals and bundled with the cartridges." Georgia was rumored to have 150 tons of saltpeter, with sulphur enough to make another 200 tons of powder. The question was, would fervent state rights Governor Joseph E. Brown contribute these ingredients to the Confederacy?

Gorgas knew many of the arsenals in the South well, and he worked quickly to revamp and modernize several. Charleston's arsenal received steam power; Montgomery's shops were upgraded to repair small arms and manufacture leather goods. Small works were established at Knoxville, Tennessee, Jackson, Mississippi, and Dublin, Lynchburg, and Danville, Virginia. Nashville had extensive shops already, and they became a mainstay for forces assembling under Gen. Albert Sidney Johnston.

From the beginning, the Ordnance Bureau faced serious procurement, collection, and distribution problems. Gorgas decided early to try to centralize manufacturing in Georgia and use the Atlanta rail hub as well as river arteries to distribute the products. Major manufacturing plants were established at Augusta and Macon. The Augusta Powder Works became one of the best in the world, and the Macon Arsenal and Armory ranked among the most efficient installations, along with that town's Confederate States Central Laboratory.

The success of these plants derived from Gorgas's leadership. Because he himself did not work well under authority, he understood the need for freedom in others. And as high responsibility soothed his own abrasiveness, he cherished independence in his subordinates. Careful searching found the right men. From the start he knew that a gifted scientist was needed in the bureau, and he found John W. Mallet, an Englishman serving on the field staff of Brig. Gen. Robert Rodes. Mallet, a member of Great Britain's Royal Society, had been chemist to the Alabama Geological Survey when the war started. His appointment filled a vital niche in the ordnance technological staff. Assigned as chief of the Central Laboratories, Mallet brought standardization to the maze of calibers in small arm ammunition production, invented new and impressive weapons (the "polygonal shell" broke into a predetermined number of pieces), and worked to institutionalize quality in ammunition production.

James H. Burton, who became superintendent of armories, possessed a complete set of English Enfield rifle plans and put them to good use in making a passable Confederate copy. But George Washington Rains stands out as the most successful of Gorgas's stellar subordinates. On April 10, 1862, his Augusta Powder Works began operations. Rains had found the site, secured the Confederate title, and supervised construction of a plant to rival the famous Waltham Abbey Works in England. The Augusta facility, plus others directed by Rains, provided sufficient powder for the war.

Niter was an essential ingredient in powder manufacture, but neither Gorgas nor Rains could devote time to locating sources of the component. Gorgas pushed for a separate Niter and Mining Bureau, attached to the Ordnance Bureau, to find this necessity. Maj. Isaac M. St. John took charge of this bureau in April 1862, and it grew into an indispensable agency. St. John used human urine to leach niter beds across the South.

Ordnance officers became involved in all kinds of activities. Since they served the artillery, leather harnesses, traces, and caissons were among their concerns. Moreover, supplies for ordnance workers increasingly had to come from ordnance establishments. So the bureau became a small "vertical combine," supplying its workers with food, clothing, shoes, medical services, and other needs.

From the outset ordnance officers counted on three sources for arms and munitions: battlefield captures, home manufacturing, and blockade running. Captures provided early supplies; manufacturing, heavily pressed, took time and resources to reach production; and though organization of blockade running also took time and resources, the Ordnance Bureau—chiefly because of Gorgas's personal attention—quickly assumed a key role in importing supplies from abroad. Relying as always on talent, Gorgas sent Maj. Caleb Huse to Europe, charged with the purchase and shipment of arms and munitions. Energetic, sometimes recklessly eager, Huse did admirable work—his astronomical debts were the best proof of his ability.

Funds were always a problem in foreign purchasing, and Gorgas, working with the quartermaster general and the surgeon general, sought innovative ways to provide money. The best system proved to be the exportation of Confederate cotton for exchange in England or other European countries. Various private firms were involved as cotton brokers. Among the most important were Saul Isaac, Campbell and Co.; Collie, Crenshaw, and Co.; and Fraser, Trenholm, and Co. These and other firms not only traded cotton for funds, but many bought and ran blockade runners to and from the embattled South. Gorgas and other supply chiefs tried various schemes for exporting government bales: space on runners was usually purchased on a bale-for-bale basis—that is, one government bale transported along with one bale paid for the privilege.

Complaints of high costs abroad, even of fraud in the blockade-running business, were hardly unexpected. So profitable a business (a successful run might well pay for a private vessel twice over) and so vital a venture for the Confederacy could not escape some excesses. But gradually Gorgas and other bureau chiefs managed the effort efficiently. A new system went into effect in 1863 when Colin J.

McRae, an Alabama businessman, went abroad to take charge of foreign purchasing under proceeds of the $15 million Erlanger loan. Although not as helpful as hoped, the loan nonetheless did finance the purchase of blockade runners as well as myriad supplies.

Once purchased, supplies had to reach the South. Freighters could not elude the Federal blockade, so they took their cargoes to transshipment harbors in Nassau, Bermuda, and Cuba. From those ports swift, light-draft blockade runners took the cargo on to the Confederacy. These vessels were always at high risk. The derring-do of blockade runners fills some of the most exciting pages of Civil War history. The Ordnance Bureau shared some five runners with the Quartermaster and Medical Departments.

As private vessels entered the trade, Gorgas took charge of managing the government's program. He shifted the duty to Maj. Thomas L. Bayne, head of the Bureau of Foreign Supplies in 1862, but kept pushing foreign operations. He achieved a complete change in government blockade running early in 1864 with the passage of two important laws that partly nationalized space on outgoing and incoming vessels and limited importation of luxury goods.

Blockade running proved highly successful, despite increased captures. In the course of the war the Ordnance Bureau imported no less than 330,000 arms, mostly Enfield rifles (state and private ventures brought in at least 270,000 more) and from December 1863 to December 1864, 1,933,000 pounds of saltpeter and 1,507,000 pounds of lead.

Domestic production grew apace but suffered the vagaries of poor transportation, enemy incursions, and dwindling supplies of lead, powder, copper, and saltpeter. By the end of 1862 monthly small arms ammunition production from eight important arsenals totaled 170,000 rounds. But as the war continued, shortages increased. Copper became so scarce that whiskey stills in mountain country were confiscated, and when lead ran short, window weights were taken from buildings in major cities.

As conscription tightened across the South, skilled ordnance workers often were called up for general service or for local defense. Gorgas pointed out the damage done by the loss of one barrel straightener at the Richmond armory—production dropped 360 rifles per month! Ordnance workers were national resources and the bureau chief strenuously fought to keep them at work.

The various makeshifts did the job. The Ordnance Bureau continued providing munitions to Confederate forces until the end of the war. No other Southern supply bureau achieved so much with so few resources. Gorgas ranks as a logistical genius and a management wizard who picked the right men for the field armies and for production, distribution, and foreign operations.

On April 8, 1864, Gorgas wrote in his diary an assessment of his bureau:

It is three years ago today since I took charge of the Ordnance Department. . . . I have succeeded beyond my utmost expectations. From being the worst supplied of the Bureaus of the War Department it is now the best. Large arsenals have been organized at Richmond, Fayetteville, Augusta, Charleston, Columbus, Macon, Atlanta and Selma, and smaller ones at Danville, Lynchburgh, and Montgomery, besides other establishments. A superb powder mill has been built at Augusta. . . . Lead smelting works were established . . . at Petersburgh. . . . A cannon foundry established at Macon for heavy guns, and bronze foundries at Macon, Columbus, Ga., and Augusta; a foundry for shot and shell at Salisbury, N.C.; a large shop for leather work at Clarksville, Va.; besides the Armories here [Richmond] and at Fayetteville, a manufactory of carbines has been built up here; a rifle factory at Ashville (transferred to Columbia, S.C.); a new and very large armory at Macon, including a pistol factory, built up under contract here and sent to Atlanta, and thence transferred under purchase to Macon; a second pistol factory at Columbus, Ga.;—All of these . . . have borne such fruit as relieves the country from fear of want in these respects.

Gorgas was right. When Robert E. Lee took his army toward Appomattox Courthouse in April 1865, he stuck to a rail line looking for a ration train. No ration train came, but an ammunition train did.

[See also Artillery; Edged Weapons; Niter and Mining Bureau; Powder Works; Small Arms.]

BIBLIOGRAPHY

Broun, W. LeRoy. "The Red Artillery." *Southern Historical Society Papers* 26 (1898): 365–376. Reprint, Wilmington, N.C., 1991.
Goff, Richard D. *Confederate Supply.* Durham, N.C., 1969.
Gorgas, Josiah. *The Civil War Diary of General Josiah Gorgas.* Edited by F. E. Vandiver. University, Ala., 1947.
Gorgas, Josiah. "Ordnance of the Confederacy, I, II." *Southern Historical Society Papers* 12 (1884): 67–94. Reprint, Wilmington, N.C., 1990.
Huse, Caleb. *The Supplies for the Confederate Army, How They Were Obtained in Europe and How Paid For. Personal Reminiscences and Unpublished History.* Boston, 1904.
Thompson, Samuel B. *Confederate Purchasing Operations Abroad.* Chapel Hill, N.C., 1935.
Vandiver, Frank E. *Ploughshares into Swords: Josiah Gorgas and Confederate Ordnance.* Austin, Tex., 1952.

FRANK E. VANDIVER

ORPHAN BRIGADE

Officially designated the First Kentucky Brigade, this most famous of Confederate organizations from the Bluegrass

State had its origins in the pro-secessionist prewar state guard. In the spring and summer of 1861, while Kentucky remained neutral, secessionist sympathizers gathered across the line at Camp Boone, Tennessee, to enlist with the Confederacy. The Second Kentucky Infantry organized on July 13, followed by the Third Infantry a few days later. The Fourth Infantry followed on September 1, along with Edward Byrne's battery of artillery. That fall, through an administrative confusion, two Fifth Kentucky Infantries were organized, one later being designated the Ninth. On November 19, 1861, the Sixth Infantry organized, and two more batteries, H. B. Lyon's and Rice E. Graves's, were added. For a time the First Kentucky Cavalry and a squadron of horsemen led by John Hunt Morgan were also a part of the brigade, making it more of a "legion" in the then-current definition. During the course of the war there would be several cases of tampering with the brigade's organization, but eventually it came down to the Second, Fourth, Fifth, Sixth, and Ninth Infantries, and Robert Cobb's and Graves's batteries.

Simon Bolivar Buckner briefly commanded the brigade as it was forming, but John C. Breckinridge soon superseded him, commencing a long association with the Kentuckians. In turn, he yielded command to Col. Roger W. Hanson, who was captured along with the Second Kentucky in the fall of Fort Donelson. Thus Col. Robert P. Trabue led the men in their first battle at Shiloh, where they distinguished themselves in the taking of the Hornet's Nest. After covering the Confederate retreat from Shiloh, the Kentuckians went on to serve at Vicksburg that summer and then participated in the August 5, 1862, attack on Baton Rouge.

They probably acquired their nickname in the carnage of the abortive January 2, 1863, assault on the Federal left at Murfreesboro. Breckinridge, now division commander, opposed the attack, as did Hanson, who had been exchanged and was back in command of the brigade. Hanson took a mortal wound, and the brigade suffered more than 25 percent casualties. Breckinridge wept, crying "My poor Orphans! My poor Orphan Brigade!" He was presumably referring to the fact that Kentucky never left the Union, leaving its Confederate soldiers cut off from succor and support, material and moral, from home. The nickname stuck, acquiring limited use during the war and universal adoption by the 1880s.

Following Murfreesboro, the brigade returned to Mississippi in the failed attempt to relieve Vicksburg and then fought with the Army of Tennessee at Chickamauga, where commander Ben Hardin Helm fell and Col. Joseph Lewis took command for the balance of the war. The Orphans served through the Atlanta campaign until heavy losses at Jonesboro on September 1, 1864, practically destroyed the brigade. Some of those left were given horses to finish out the war as mounted infantry, operating with Confederate cavalry in Georgia and South Carolina. Of the four thousand who

had enlisted in 1861, barely six hundred were left to give their parole at Washington, Georgia, on May 7, 1865.

Joseph E. Johnston, William J. Hardee, and other leading generals pronounced the Orphans the finest brigade in the Army of Tennessee. Even allowing for hyperbole, the Kentuckians remain one of the most colorful, hard-fighting, and dedicated units of the Confederate service.

BIBLIOGRAPHY

Davis, William C. *The Orphan Brigade.* New York, 1980.
Jackman, John S. *Memoirs of a Confederate Soldier: Soldiering with the Orphan Brigade.* Edited by William C. Davis. Columbia, S.C., 1990.
Thompson, Ed Porter. *History of the First Kentucky Brigade.* Cincinnati, 1868.

WILLIAM C. DAVIS

ORR, JAMES L.

ORR, JAMES L. (1822–1873), South Carolina congressman and postwar governor, and U.S. diplomat. Born in Craytonville, Pendleton District, in up-country South Carolina on May 12, 1822, Orr sprang from an Irish family that had settled first in Pennsylvania and then moved eventually to northwestern South Carolina in the 1790s. His father, who owned twenty-five slaves, moved to the village of Anderson in 1830 where he operated a hotel and a store. Orr entered the University of Virginia in 1839 to study law. After two years he returned home, read law, and in 1843 was admitted to the bar. He became editor of the *Anderson Gazette* and a farmer and slaveholder.

In 1844 Orr was elected to the state legislature as a follower of his neighbor John C. Calhoun and served two terms. He supported efforts to make the state government more democratic. In 1847 Orr narrowly defeated Unionist Benjamin F. Perry for Congress and entered the House in 1849 as the sectional crisis deepened. He denounced the Compromise of 1850, but he opposed the movement for single state secession in South Carolina in 1851.

The following year Orr became convinced that the South could remain safely in the Union. From 1852 to 1860 he was the leader of the National Democrats in South Carolina. He was elected a delegate to the Democratic National Convention in 1856, although he did not attend because of illness. It was the first national party convention to which South Carolina sent a delegation. When Congress assembled in December, Orr was elected Speaker of the House. Because of ill health, he retired from Congress in 1859 and returned to Anderson.

Orr was not a delegate to the Democratic National Convention in Charleston, but he opposed the candidacy of

Stephen A. Douglas. In July he publicly opposed single-state secession, but he saw joint secession as the only alternative to Lincoln's election. He was elected to the secession convention, was an unsuccessful candidate for president of the convention, and served on the committee to draft the ordinance. He was named one of three state commissioners to treat with James Buchanan on the matter of Federal property and was a commissioner to the state of Georgia.

After the firing on Fort Sumter in April 1861, volunteer companies were organized all over South Carolina. Orr organized the South Carolina First Regiment, known as Orr's Rifles. It was mustered into Confederate service and was assigned to protect Charleston. Meanwhile Orr continued to serve in the state convention, which met periodically. It created the Executive Council to govern the state, and when the council became unpopular, Orr signed the request to reconvene the convention to abolish it.

While he was stationed in Charleston, Orr became a contender for a seat first in the Provisional Congress and then in the Confederate Senate. It was a three-way contest for two seats. Orr was opposed by two former U.S. senators, Robert W. Barnwell and James Chesnut. Orr's supporters joined forces with those of Barnwell, and together they carried the election. The "Hotspur State" was represented in the Senate by two former moderates.

Orr took his seat on February 17, 1862, the last day the Provisional Congress was in session, and served until the end of the war. In the Senate he headed the Foreign Affairs Committee and also served at times on the Commerce, Finance, and Printing committees. Unlike Barnwell, who supported Jefferson Davis, Orr became one of the president's bitterest critics.

In the Senate Orr supported individual and state rights, sometimes with rancor. When the Senate was considering a bill to give members of Congress certificates to allow them to travel without annoyance, Orr complained that he and another senator on their way to Richmond were almost ejected from a train carrying soldiers. He bitterly denounced the abuse of military power, but Louis T. Wigfall of Texas called the incident an oversight.

Orr defended the traditional system of having soldiers in the ranks elect their officers. In September 1862, the Senate was debating a bill allowing the president to fill a vacancy when the next in line for promotion was incompetent. James Phelan of Mississippi stated that many units elected the least competent men as officers. Orr responded that he hoped such instances were rare, but that any group that elected a fool or a thief knew better than an examining board or the president.

Orr was one of five senators to vote against the Conscription Law of 1862. He suggested a requisition system for the states, but his proposal was defeated. He opposed the seizure of persons who evaded conscription as well as those whose substitutes had deserted. But when the Senate failed to exempt those who had hired substitutes, Orr was one of two dissenters. He always supported liberal exemptions from the draft. When the Exemption Law of 1862 passed, Orr supported it because it exempted state officers except those specified by the state as subject to militia duty. When the law was criticized because it favored plantation owners or overseers that supervised at least twenty slaves or plantations that required a white man's presence by state law, Orr denounced the notion of class favoritism. Had it been intended, he said on February 12, 1863, the law "would never have received a vote in the Senate."

Orr opposed Confederate regulation of transportation. When the Senate approved partial Confederate operation of

> **Orr defended the traditional system of having soldiers in the ranks elect their officers.**

the railroads in an emergency in April 1863, Orr attacked the plan. He maintained that private management was more effective. On November 15, 1864, Orr introduced a bill to exempt vessels owned by the states from national restrictions on imports and exports. On December 2, he widened the prohibition to include any vessel in which a state had an interest. The Senate never acted on his bill.

In matters of Confederate law, Orr consistently supported state rights. Early in 1863 he backed the creation of a supreme court, but he voted with the majority to deny the court appellate jurisdiction over state courts. He unfailingly voted against suspending the writ of habeas corpus and punishing conspiracy against the Confederacy.

Generally Orr supported the power of the legislative branch over the executive. In March 1863 he favored giving seats in the Senate to cabinet members. Questioning by Congress would make the cabinet more accountable, Orr believed. On June 6, 1864, he opposed providing forage, fuel, and lights for the president on constitutional grounds. The Constitution, he said, provided that the chief executive's salary could not be raised during his term of office. In February 1865 Orr opposed allowing the War Department to employ a solicitor on the ground that the measure would grant too much power to the secretary of war.

On military matters, Orr usually opposed Jefferson Davis. Along with Representatives William Porcher Miles and W. W. Boyce of South Carolina, Orr warmly supported Gen. P. G. T. Beauregard with whom Davis disagreed. When the general asked for additional artillery to defend the Carolina coast, Orr introduced a bill to grant the request and increase the size of South Carolina infantry and artillery units on February 6, 1863. Davis vetoed the bill on the ground that such reorganization was within executive jurisdiction. Orr frequently attacked Gen. Braxton Bragg whom Davis liked. He also supported Gen. Joseph E. Johnston and criticized Davis for removing him.

As debate on the use of blacks in the Confederate cause grew more heated, Orr supported the use of free black laborers in the army, but not black troops, slave or free. As the military situation deteriorated, he backed an impressment act in March 1863 and on January 30, 1864, introduced a bill to use free blacks. But in February 1865 he suggested a ceiling be placed on the number of such laborers and said that the use of black troops and their resulting emancipation would ruin the Confederacy. When the Senate finally approved arming the slaves by one vote, Orr voted in the negative.

As chairman of the Foreign Affairs Committee, Orr constantly asked Davis to inform the Senate on foreign policy, but Davis almost never honored his requests. Orr joined the peace movement when it seemed that Davis's policies were leading to disaster. In early 1864 in private correspondence, he denounced "a weak incompetent President and an imbecile cabinet . . . [and] a truculent and indecisive Congress."

On March 18, 1865, when the Senate adjourned, Orr returned home. He fell ill with typhoid fever as the war was ending, and his home was ransacked by Union troops. After Robert E. Lee's surrender, Orr urged renewed loyalty to the United States.

When Andrew Johnson appointed Benjamin F. Perry provisional governor of South Carolina on June 30, 1865, Orr accompanied Perry to Washington. Orr was subsequently elected a member of the 1865 state constitutional convention, and Johnson granted him a pardon. When former Confederate general Wade Hampton refused to run for governor, Orr was narrowly elected. He took a paternalistic attitude toward African Americans and signed the Black Code into law. He opposed the Fourteenth Amendment but supported limited black suffrage. A new state constitution was adopted under Congressional Reconstruction, and in July 1868 Orr's term ended.

Orr was elected a state circuit judge by the legislature and soon joined the Republican party. He was associated with the "railroad ring" that took control of the Greenville and Columbia Railroad, but by 1872 he had joined the reform Republicans. When they were defeated, Orr accepted President Ulysses S. Grant's appointment as minister to Russia. On May 6, 1873, he died in St. Petersburg, and his body was returned to Anderson for burial.

BIBLIOGRAPHY

Breeze, Donald H. "James L. Orr, Calhoun, and the Cooperationist Tradition in South Carolina." *South Carolina Historical Magazine* 80 (1981): 273–285.

Cauthen, Charles E. *South Carolina Goes to War, 1860–65.* Chapel Hill, N.C., 1950.

Cyclopedia of Eminent and Representative Men of the Carolinas. Madison, Wis., 1982.

Leemhuis, Roger P. *James L. Orr and the Sectional Conflict.* Washington, D.C., 1979.

Warner, Ezra J., and W. Buck Yearns. *Biographical Register of the Confederate Congress.* Baton Rouge, La., 1975.

A.V. HUFF, JR.

ORR, JEHU AMAZIAH

ORR, JEHU AMAZIAH (1828–1921), colonel and congressman from Mississippi. Orr was born in South Carolina and attended Erskine College there before graduating from what is now Princeton University. Orr then set up a law practice in Houston, Mississippi. In 1850 he was named secretary of the state senate and two years later was elected to the state house of representatives. From 1854 to 1855 he was a U.S. district attorney and the next year served as a presidential elector for James Buchanan.

Although opposed to secession and a supporter of Stephen A. Douglas in the Democratic National Convention of 1860, he eventually came to view secession as inevitable and voted for it in the Mississippi secession convention in 1861.

Orr succeeded William Sydney Wilson as a member of the Provisional Congress and served until 1862 when he became commander of the Thirty-first Mississippi Regiment. In that role he participated in many battles—among them, Coffeeville, Baton Rouge, Vicksburg, and Jackson. At the Battle of Harrisburg, he served as the volunteer aide to Gens. Nathan Bedford Forrest and Stephen D. Lee.

Orr lost the election for the First Congress at Richmond. He was defeated by J. W. Clapp, the man whom he in turn defeated two years later for a seat in the Second Congress. While in Congress, Orr opposed most of the powers and policies of Jefferson Davis, working to help the economy of the Southern states and to promote an end to the war through negotiation. As a member of the Committee on Foreign Affairs, he was appointed to report to the Congress on resolutions that sought "to see if the matters in controversy" could be "adjusted by negotiation, without further effusion of blood." His committee suggested that three people be selected to meet with Abraham Lincoln to negotiate for peace. After Orr reported the resolution, the Hampton Roads Conference subsequently took place, but the negotiations failed because of language calling for recognition of the independence of the Confederacy. Orr blamed the failure of the conference on Jefferson Davis's inflexibility.

After the war Orr sought to mend sectional fences and to facilitate Southern recovery. From 1870 to 1876, he served as circuit judge and continued working to rescue the state from the disorder brought on by the war and Reconstruction. Orr lived to the age of ninety-three and actively practiced law until he died.

BIBLIOGRAPHY

Alexander, Thomas B., and Richard E. Beringer. *The Anatomy of the Confederate Congress: A Study of the Influences of Member Characteristics on Legislative Voting Behavior, 1861–1865.* Nashville, Tenn., 1972.
Warner, Ezra J., and W. Buck Yearns. *Biographical Register of the Confederate Congress.* Baton Rouge, La., 1975.

RAY SKATES

OURY, GRANVILLE H.

OURY, GRANVILLE H. (1825–1891), congressional delegate from Arizona Territory. Born March 12, 1825, in Abingdon, Virginia, Oury moved to Missouri in 1836. Here, in 1848, he passed the bar. The following year, on his brother's advice, Oury went to Texas. After arriving in San Antonio, the adventurous lawyer joined a party of California gold seekers. After several years on the Pacific coast, Oury abandoned the gold fields in 1856 and moved to Tucson.

In 1857, Oury supported Henry Crabb's disastrous filibustering expedition into Sonora. He subsequently became active in Tucson politics, advocating a separate territory called Arizona to be created out of the Gadsden Purchase. With the arrival of the secession crisis in 1860, Oury and the citizens of Arizona sided with the Confederacy. On March 23, 1861, a convention of sixty-eight voters in Tucson endorsed secession and elected Oury to represent the new territory in Richmond.

Oury made the difficult trip to Virginia and took office as a nonvoting delegate in January 1862. Political infighting soon led the temperamental governor of Arizona, John Robert Baylor, to replace Oury with Marcus (or Malcolm) Macwillie. Before Macwillie could arrive, Arizona was overrun by Union troops from California and New Mexico Territory. Oury returned to Texas, where he served as a volunteer aide-de-camp in the Confederate army.

After the war, Oury returned to his Tucson law practice and politics. He served in various territorial posts, including attorney general, as well as serving two terms in the U.S. House of Representatives. He died on January 11, 1891.

BIBLIOGRAPHY

Ganaway, Loomis Morton. *New Mexico and the Sectional Controversy, 1846–1861.* Albuquerque, N.M., 1944.
Smith, Cornelius C., Jr. *William Sanders Oury: History-Maker of the Southwest.* Tucson, Ariz., 1967.

Stout, Joseph Allen, Jr. *The Liberators: Filibustering Expeditions into Mexico, 1848–1862, and the Last Thrust of Manifest Destiny.* Los Angeles, 1973.

DONALD S. FRAZIER

OVERSEERS

Employed on virtually all rice and sugar plantations, on most cotton plantations with twenty or more adult field hands, and on many smaller units in the tobacco and grain regions, overseers were essential functionaries in managing Southern plantations and controlling the slave population. The overseer, usually a white man of yeoman farmer antecedents, was the link in the managerial chain between the plantation owner or his agent and the black slave drivers. Chiefly responsible for slave welfare and discipline as well as crop production, he assigned gangs to work, apportioned tasks, supervised field labor, administered punishment, enforced curfews, distributed food and clothing, periodically inspected slave cabins, treated minor medical ailments, and maintained various record and account books. In areas of the plantation South where blacks heavily outnumbered whites—most notably along the rice coast of South Carolina and Georgia and in the Yazoo, Mississippi, delta—overseers provided the sparse white population with its principal security against slave misconduct and possible insurrection.

With the continuing expansion of the plantation system into the Southwest along with a concomitant trend toward consolidation of existing units, the number of overseers doubled during the decade of the 1850s, reaching a total of nearly 38,000 on the eve of the Civil War. Of that number, more than two-thirds were located in the leading plantation states of Alabama, Georgia, Louisiana, Mississippi, North and South Carolina, and Virginia. Although the incidence of overseer utilization was highest on the vast sugar and rice estates of Louisiana and South Carolina, respectively, the majority of plantation superintendents were employed on cotton plantations from southern Virginia to eastern Texas. The ratio of overseers to total slave population within different staple regions ranged from a low of one overseer for every seventy-five to one hundred slaves in the cotton, grain, and tobacco counties to a high of one manager for more than three hundred slaves in the heavily black rice districts between Charleston and Savannah. Clearly, the presence of white overseers in such areas as the latter became more crucial than ever following the outbreak of the Civil War.

When hostilities erupted in April 1861, the relative youth and physical hardiness of overseers made them prime candidates for military service. Although many plantation managers responded enthusiastically to the call of their nascent country, their employers manifested almost universal reluctance to dispense with their services. Indeed, efforts by Confederate authorities to enroll overseers in the military provoked a veritable storm of protest from members of the planter class, who, ironically, had previously berated their subordinates for a variety of alleged shortcomings and transgressions. Now they were suddenly considered indispensable—not only to individual proprietors but to the entire white community. Praising "the Overseer system as the best civil police system that can be invented," South Carolina rice magnate James Barnwell Heyward pleaded for the exemption of overseers in his district both to police the slave population and to render the plantations more effective in furnishing "supplies for the army." Such appeals, with similar reasoning, became general throughout the South.

The exemption of plantation managers proved to be one of the most controversial domestic issues during the war, spawning bitterness and disaffection among small farmers and nonslaveholders. Surprisingly, overseers were not among

> ... youth and physical hardiness of overseers made them prime candidates for military service.

the occupational groups initially exempted from military service under legislation enacted by the Confederate Congress pursuant to the Conscription Act of April 1862. But in October of that year, in order "to secure the proper police of the country," Congress provided for the exemption of "one person, either as agent, owner or overseer" on each plantation with twenty or more slaves. Subsequent revisions of this statute in May 1863 and in February 1864 substantially reduced the number of overseer exemptions. Thus, by the end of 1863 the number of overseers exempted by authority of Congress had dwindled to approximately three hundred in South Carolina and a mere two hundred each in Georgia and Virginia. It should be noted, however, that regulations governing the exemption of overseers varied considerably from state to state, and additional exemptions were granted by governors and local military commanders as circumstances dictated.

Despite efforts by both Confederate and state officials to respond to planters' concern for the security of their chattel, a severe shortage of overseers developed during the war. Various expedients were devised to combat this shortage. Perhaps the most obvious was that of simply getting along without an overseer, a viable option for many smaller planters. On other units women assumed the unaccustomed role of superintending planting operations, frequently with inauspicious results. In some localities proprietors joined forces and entrusted a single overseer with the oversight of multiple properties. Other planters hired novice overseers

from other occupational groups or retained in their employ mediocre managers who, in normal times, would have been summarily discharged. As the war continued, the deficiency in experienced plantation managers became more acute, and Southern agricultural production suffered accordingly.

Malingering as well as more serious violations of plantation regulations became more common in the absence of an overseer, who had enforced discipline primarily through close surveillance of the slave force and by administering corporal punishment to offenders within parameters specified by his employer. Although violent acts of insubordination were rare, at least before Federal troops arrived in their immediate vicinity, slaves took advantage of relaxed supervision to work at a more leisurely pace, to demand additional privileges, and to augment their food supply with more frequent raids upon their owners' larders.

Even for those planters able to secure competent overseers, the war exacerbated long-standing animosities and rendered more difficult the control of the slave population. Always ready to exploit to their own advantage the inherent conflict between the interests of owner and overseer, the slaves found wartime conditions particularly congenial to such efforts to ameliorate their situation. Moreover, relations between overseers and slaves, at best tenuous in normal times, were further inflamed during the war. The problems became most critical in those portions of the plantation South—especially Virginia and Louisiana—that were subjected to repeated Federal incursions. The presence of Union troops frequently engendered disruptive conduct by overseers and slaves alike, thereby resulting in a total failure of agricultural operations in the occupied area.

It seems fair to conclude that Southern agriculture was severely impaired during the war by a scarcity of able plantation managers, by the unsatisfactory performance of their substitutes, and by the resulting insubordination of the laboring force. This failure to solve the problem of controlling slaves had a demoralizing impact on the home front and was therefore a significant factor in the demise of the Confederacy.

[See also Conscription; Slave Drivers.]

BIBLIOGRAPHY

Easterby, James H., ed. The South Carolina Rice Plantation as Revealed in the Papers of Robert F. W. Allston. Chicago, 1945.

Roark, James L. Masters without Slaves: Southern Planters in the Civil War and Reconstruction. New York, 1977.

Roland, Charles P. Louisiana Sugar Plantations during the American Civil War. Leiden, 1957.

Scarborough, William K. The Overseer: Plantation Management in the Old South. Baton Rouge, La., 1966. Reprint, Athens, Ga., 1984.

Wiley, Bell I. Southern Negroes, 1861–1865. New Haven, 1938.

WILLIAM S. SCARBOROUGH

PADUCAH, KENTUCKY

This town, located on the Ohio River at the mouth of the Tennessee River, was the site of a Confederate raid by Gen. Nathan Bedford Forrest on March 25, 1864. It cost the Confederates twenty-five men killed or wounded; the Union forces reported casualties of fourteen killed and forty-six wounded.

Because of its strategic location, Gen. Ulysses S. Grant had occupied the town of Paducah on September 6, 1861. Since the loyalty of the town was in question, military rule was established under successive Union Gens. E. A. Paine, Charles F. Smith, Lew Wallace, and Sol Meredith, and Col. Stephen G. Hicks. The town was defended by Federal gunboats and an earthwork fort surrounded by deep ditches. Fort Anderson was defended by some 665 men from the 122d Illinois Infantry, the 16th Kentucky Cavalry, and the 1st Kentucky Artillery, and the 8th U.S. Heavy Artillery. The latter was a black regiment that was unpopular with the townspeople.

On March 25, 1864, with about 2,700 troops (Forrest's three regiments of 700 men and Gen. Abram Buford's two brigades of 2,000 men), Forrest advanced toward Paducah from Mayfield, Kentucky. When he arrived around two o'clock in the afternoon, Colonel Hicks immediately withdrew into the fort and ordered the Federal gunboats, *Poesta* and *Paw Paw,* to open fire upon the invaders. When Forrest requested the surrender of the fort, Hicks refused, whereupon Forrest gave the order to advance. Led by Col. Albert P. Thompson, the Confederates charged but they were driven back and Thompson was killed. Using nearby residences, Confederate sharpshooters opened fire upon the Union soldiers. Because Hicks's troops were running short of ammunition, he ordered them to fix bayonets, expecting Forrest to charge. After three attempts to reduce the fort, Forrest ordered his troops to cease firing.

The Confederate forces remained in the town until near midnight, seizing Union stores, military supplies, and some 400 horses and mules. According to Forrest, they burned 60 bales of cotton, the steamer *Dacotah,* and a dry dock, and took 50 prisoners. With the withdrawal of the Confederates, Hicks ordered the burning of some 60 houses they had used to fire upon the fort, which aroused the anger of the resi-dents. On the morning of March 26, under a flag of truce, Forrest offered a prisoner exchange, which Hicks refused since he lacked the authority.

When Hicks reported that the Confederates had stolen private property rather than the well-hidden Union mules and horses, Confederate General Buford, with 800 men, returned to Paducah on April 14 and, despite the fire from Federal gunboats, drove the Union forces back into the fort and seized Union stores and supplies together with a large number of horses and mules (Forrest claimed to have taken 140 horses, Hicks, 411). The Confederates remained in Kentucky and Tennessee for more than a month, recruiting and sequestering supplies.

As a result of these raids, there was a change of Union military command, martial law was proclaimed, and the writ of habeas corpus was suspended in Kentucky.

BIBLIOGRAPHY

Harrison, Lowell H. *The Civil War in Kentucky.* Lexington, Ky., 1975.
Jordan, Thomas, and J. P. Pryon. *The Campaigns of Lieut.-General Forrest, and of Forrest's Cavalry, with Portraits, Maps, and Illustrations.* New Orleans, La., 1868.
Neuman, Fred G. *The Story of Paducah (Kentucky).* Paducah, Ky., 1927.
Robertson, John E. L. *Paducah 1830–1980.* Paducah, Ky., 1980.

ROSS A. WEBB

PAGE, RICHARD L.

PAGE, RICHARD L. (1807–1901), naval officer and brigadier general. Page was ordnance officer at the Norfolk navy yard when he resigned from the U.S. Navy in 1860. Joining the Virginia navy first, he helped plan the defenses of the James River. In June 1861, he joined the Confederate navy and once more served as ordnance officer at the Norfolk navy yard. When Norfolk was evacuated in May 1862, Page supervised the movement of machinery and workers to Charlotte, North Carolina. During his two-year administration, Charlotte became a major production center. In the course of these years, Page also joined Como. Josiah Tattnall aboard *Savannah* in defense of Port Royal. He was second in command of the squadron under Tattnall, and during the battle he commanded *Savannah's* forward gun.

In 1864 Page was sent to Mobile to command that port's outer defenses. In line with his new duties, he was transferred to the Confederate army and appointed brigadier general. He was given command of Fort Morgan because of his expertise in ordnance. Page augmented the defenses in Mobile Bay, making it one of the best fortified points in the Confederacy. After the Union navy defeated Confederate forces in the bay in August 1864, Page was cut off from resupply and had no choice but to surrender Fort Morgan. He had held his position as long as he could. Taken prisoner, he was not released until September 1865.

Page spent his later years in Norfolk, where he served in several positions including that of superintendent of the city's public schools.

BIBLIOGRAPHY

Civil War Naval Chronology. 6 vols. Washington, D.C., 1961–1966.
Jones, Virgil C. *The Civil War at Sea.* 3 vols. New York, 1961–1962.
Register of Officers of the Confederate States Navy, 1861–1865. Washington, D.C., 1931.
Scharf, John Thomas. *History of the Confederate States Navy from Its Organization to the Surrender of Its Last Vessel.* New York, 1887. Reprint, New York, 1977.

FRANK LAWRENCE OWSLEY

PALMETTO ARMORY

The Militia Act of 1808 authorized distribution of arms by the Federal government to state militias on an annual basis, but South Carolina, after the nullification movement began in 1832, desired to acquire or build its own arms with which to defend state interests. Stimulated by the secession crisis, William Glaze and Thomas W. Radcliffe, both of Columbia, South Carolina, approached state politicians proposing arms procurement. A Board of Ordnance was established in 1850, and $350,000 was authorized by the General Assembly for purchases. Glaze, selected as agent, procured arms during this period from various sources outside the state, including a firm headed by Benjamin Flagg in Millbury, Massachusetts.

Glaze earlier had entered into a partnership with James Boatwright of Columbia, and about 1850, Glaze, Boatwright, and Flagg founded the Palmetto Armory, with Flagg moving his gun-making machinery to Columbia.

The act of 1850 to build up the South Carolina militia set the stage for the Palmetto Armory's greatest success. The initial contract called for 6,000 muskets with bayonets (.69 caliber smoothbore) at $14.50 each; 1,000 rifles (.54 caliber rifled) at $15.50; 1,000 pair of pistols (.54 caliber smooth-

bore) at $14.50 per pair; 1,000 cavalry sabers with scabbards at $6.50 each; and 1,000 light artillery sabers with scabbards at $6.50 each. All were to be totally manufactured within the state, but problems arose and some component parts were purchased out of state and the contract altered to permit modifications. In addition, the armory received a contract to alter the state's obsolete flintlock arms to the new percussion system. The arms manufactured in 1852 and 1853 are readily identified. The firearms are marked on the lockplate "Palmetto Armory SC" in a circle surrounding a palmetto tree and on the breech of the barrel either "Wm. Glaze & Co." or "W. G. & Co." The edged weapons are usually marked "Wm. Glaze & Co." on the reverse ricasso and "Columbia, S.C." on the obverse. As martial arms these are some of the most pleasing to the eye with their brass mounts. There have been numerous modern efforts to copy them. Specimens of these arms, which were issued primarily to South Carolina state troops, have been excavated at Civil War battle sites.

With no further arms contracts in sight, the Palmetto Armory became the Palmetto Iron Works manufacturing a variety of engines, boilers, iron and brass castings, ornamental iron, farm machinery, and sugar mills. By 1860 Glaze was a wealthy man owning substantial acreage and a successful business.

As soon as the Civil War began, Glaze again offered his state the benefits of his firearms manufacturing expertise. Two of his initial proposals were rejected, but in January 1861, the firm received a contract to produce 10-inch shells and 24-pound shot, which was completed April 8, 1861. Glaze also received a contract to rifle some of the brass-mounted .69 caliber smoothbore muskets that he had manufactured in 1852 and 1853, and he seems to have altered 3,720 of these rare arms. The company also produced bayonets, some of which the state accepted and others of which were sold to Georgia for its state forces. Subsequent efforts to obtain state arms contracts were unsuccessful. In late 1862 Glaze was involved in producing a prototype of the George revolving cannon, which, though marginally effective, never reached production.

When William Tecumseh Sherman occupied Columbia on February 17, 1865, the Palmetto Iron Works, with its vast arms-making potential, was among the first structures burned to the ground. Glaze tried to rebuild after the war, but in April 1868 he went bankrupt and all his property including the ironworks was sold.

BIBLIOGRAPHY

Albaugh, William A., III, and Edward N. Simmons. *Confederate Arms.* Harrisburg, Pa., 1957.
Fuller, Claud E., and Richard D. Steuart. *Firearms of the Confederacy.* Huntington, W.Va., 1944.
Meyer, Jack Allen. *William Glaze and the Palmetto Armory.* Columbia, S.C., 1982.

Reilly, Robert M. *United States Military Small Arms, 1816–1865.* Baton Rouge, La., 1970.

Steuart, Richard D. "A Pair of Navy Sixes." *Confederate Veteran* 33 (1925): 92–95. Reprint, Wilmington, N.C., 1985.

RUSS A. PRITCHARD

PEACE MOVEMENTS

Movements for peace began in the Confederacy soon after hostilities began. They were led by diehard antisecession Unionists, usually old-line Whigs who, unable to accept secession, went underground and formed secret societies dedicated to the overthrow of the Confederacy and the return of the states to the Federal Union. Such societies appeared throughout the Confederacy, but most notably in central North Carolina (the Heroes of America), eastern Tennessee (the Heroes of America and the Peace Society), northern Alabama (the Peace Society), and north-central Arkansas (the Peace and Constitutional Society). Members of these peace societies constantly urged that the fighting end and a peace be made with the North.

In March 1862, the first overt political demonstrations for peace in the Confederacy occurred in central North Carolina. Protesting a state draft of one-third of the militia, some fifty members of the Randolph County militia marched under a white flag and prayed for peace. In neighboring Davidson County, a "Union meeting" was held in which leaders denounced the Confederacy and advocated reunion. Three hundred troops (who were later reinforced by a regiment) were rushed into the central counties to arrest draft resisters and disloyalists.

Bryan Tyson, one of the reunionists, published two works in September 1862—a book entitled *A Ray of Light* and a one-page circular—that influenced the peace movement that would emerge in the Tarheel State in 1863. Tyson argued that a Confederate defeat was inevitable. To avoid that as well as emancipation of the slaves, Southerners should declare an armistice and offer to return to the Union on the basis suggested by the Northern Democrats—with all their rights protected, including a constitutional guarantee of slavery.

In January 1863, a peace movement was launched in the U.S. Congress by Northern Democrats. Led by Clement L. Vallandigham of Ohio, the Democrats demanded that Abraham Lincoln stop the bloodletting by arranging an armistice and working out a compromise that would bring the South back into the Union.

The Northern peace movement precipitated a Southern peace movement, especially in North Carolina, where strong peace sentiment already existed. In May 1863, James T. Leach, a planter and owner of 150 slaves, wrote a letter to the *Weekly Standard* (Raleigh) in which he suggested that the South consider returning to the Union on the basis offered by the Northern Democrats. That fall, Leach was elected as a peace candidate to the Confederate House where, until war's end, he remained the most outspoken advocate of peace in the Congress.

Leach's letter marked the beginning of the peace movement that swept North Carolina in the summer of 1863. Across the state over a hundred peace party political rallies were held in which speakers expressed their discontent with Confederate rule and advocated various proposals for peace. The U.S. flag was hoisted by ardent reunionists at a few of these meetings. Many wanted the authorities in Richmond to arrange a peace. Others blatantly called for reunion on the basis offered by the Northern Democrats. The most prominent among these was Lewis Hanes, a farmer who published a lengthy justification for reunion in the *Standard* on July 31, 1863. The movement inspired an insurrection among deserters, draft dodgers, and militant Unionists in the central counties. It took hundreds of Confederate troops five months to quell the uprising. In September they destroyed the press of William W. Holden, editor of the *North Carolina Standard* and leader of the peace faction in the state. Thus did the 1863 peace movement in North Carolina end in military repression.

Holden's movement influenced the development of peace factions in other Confederate states, especially in Alabama and Georgia. In the fall of 1863, several candidates advocating an honorable peace were elected to Congress, most of them from North Carolina and Georgia. They exerted con-

> ### Democrats demanded that Abraham Lincoln stop the bloodletting. . . .

stant pressure on Jefferson Davis and other congressmen to open negotiations for peace with the North.

At the instigation of Holden and Leach, a new series of peace meetings was held in North Carolina in the early months of 1864. Advocates urged that separate state conventions or a convention of all the Southern states treat for peace with Northern officials or possibly with a convention of Northern states. This would bypass congressional and presidential authorities who, restrained by Davis's intransigence, refused to negotiate for peace on terms that did not include Confederate independence. Intimidated by Davis's suspension of the writ of habeas corpus in February, Holden's convention movement, and his subsequent bid for the governorship in the August gubernatorial election, failed.

In March 1864, a peace movement emerged in Georgia led by Governor Joseph E. Brown, Confederate Vice

President Alexander H. Stephens, and Stephens's half-brother, Linton. The trio introduced peace resolutions into the legislature, calling for Davis to initiate peace negotiations with the North after every Southern military victory. In the fall, they endorsed the call by Northern Democrats for a convention of all the states, North and South, to discuss peace.

In September, the peace faction in Congress, led by W. W. Boyce of South Carolina, proposed that an armistice be arranged and a convention of all the states hammer out a permanent peace. Encouraged by Robert E. Lee's victories from the Wilderness to Cold Harbor and by the peace initiatives proposed by the Northern Democrats at their convention in Chicago, Boyce's supporters tried to force Davis to start peace negotiations or step aside and let someone else do so. Their efforts, however, were to no avail.

Francis Blair, prominent journalist and political confidant to Lincoln, traveled from Washington to Richmond in December 1864 and spoke to congressional peace leaders. He urged them to try to return the seceded states to the Union based on a plan of gradual emancipation. To satisfy those who responded to Blair's proposal, Davis agreed to send delegates to the Hampton Roads conference in January 1865. Alexander Stephens and two congressmen met with Lincoln and Secretary of State William H. Seward. The meeting failed because Lincoln insisted on reunion, and the Southerners, faithful to Davis's instructions, demanded Confederate independence. Thus ended the last major effort by Confederate officials to make peace prior to military defeat.

By this point, however, the peace movement had already seriously compromised morale and encouraged defeatism, reunionism, and desertion. Consequently, those who spoke out in favor of peace were usually denounced in the press and by political leaders as disloyal or traitors. In spite of its negative image, the peace movement continued to grow in popularity during the last two years of the war, especially among those who saw reunion on the Democratic basis as preferable to defeat and emancipation. By late 1864, a substantial minority of Southerners favored peace, even if it were based upon reunion; but by then, the question had become moot.

[*See also* Hampton Roads Conference; Heroes of America; *and biographies of numerous figures mentioned herein.*]

BIBLIOGRAPHY

Brumgardt, John R. "Alexander H. Stephens and the State Convention Movement in Georgia: A Reappraisal." *Georgia Historical Quarterly* 59 (1975): 38–49.

Coulter, E. Merton. *The Confederate States of America, 1861–1865.* A History of the South, vol. 7. Baton Rouge, La., 1950.

Reid, Richard. "William W. Holden and 'Disloyalty' in the Civil War." *Canadian Journal of History.* 20 (1985): 23–44.

Tatum, Georgia Lee. *Disloyalty in the Confederacy.* Chapel Hill, N.C., 1934.

Yearns, Wilfred B. "The Peace Movement in the Confederate Congress." *Georgia Historical Quarterly* 41 (1957): 1–18.

WILLIAM THOMAS AUMAN

PEGRAM, JOHN

PEGRAM, JOHN (1832–1865), brigadier general. Pegram was born in Petersburg, Virginia, on January 24, 1832. After graduating from West Point in 1854, he saw frontier duty in California and Kansas, where he was commissioned second lieutenant of Dragoons.

Pegram resigned from the U.S. Army on May 10, 1861, and accepted a commission as lieutenant colonel of the Twentieth Virginia. His unit took part in the Rich Mountain campaign that summer, serving under Gen. Richard S. Garnett. Forced to retreat from Rich Mountain by an attack from Gen. William. S. Rosecran's troops, he surrendered his command at Beverly on July 13.

Upon his return to the army after being paroled, Pegram was promoted to colonel in July 1862 and assigned to Braxton Bragg's staff at Tupelo, Mississippi, as chief of engi-

JOHN PEGRAM. NATIONAL ARCHIVES

neers. Later he became chief of staff for Gen. E. Kirby Smith, with whom he participated in the invasion of Kentucky.

Appointed brigadier general to rank from November 7, 1862, Pegram was assigned to lead a cavalry brigade in Nathan Bedford Forrest's corps, and with him he fought at Murfreesboro and Chickamauga. Pegram was then transferred to the Army of Northern Virginia and was assigned an infantry brigade in Jubal Early's division of the Second Corps. At the Battle of the Wilderness, he was seriously wounded in the leg, but participated later in the Shenandoah Valley campaign. After the death of Gen. Richard Rodes at Winchester, he was assigned to command his division. Pegram returned to Petersburg in December 1864. In the battle of Hatcher's Run, February 6, 1865, he was killed near Dabney's Sawmill.

He was buried at Hollywood Cemetery in Richmond, Virginia.

BIBLIOGRAPHY

Freeman, Douglas S. *Lee's Lieutenants: A Study in Command.* Vol. 3. New York, 1944. Reprint, New York, 1986.

Griggs, Walter S. "Until Death Us Do Part." *Blue & Gray Magazine* 7 (April 1990): 40–41.

Hotchkiss, Jed. *Virginia.* Vol. 3 of *Confederate Military History.* Edited by Clement A. Evans. Atlanta, 1899. Vol. 4 of extended ed. Wilmington, N.C., 1987.

Warner, Ezra J. *Generals in Gray: Lives of the Confederate Commanders.* Baton Rouge, La., 1959.

CHRIS CALKINS

PEIRPOINT, FRANCIS H.

PEIRPOINT, FRANCIS H. (1814–1899), Unionist governor of Virginia. A lawyer and businessman of Fairmont in northwestern Virginia, Francis Harrison Peirpoint became active in Whig politics as early as 1840. Ardently opposed to slavery but unsympathetic to abolitionism, Peirpoint found inspiration in Henry Ruffner's 1847 *Address to the People of West Virginia,* which proposed the division of Virginia and the gradual emancipation of slaves. His marriage in 1854 to Julia Augusta Robinson, a New Yorker of abolitionist background, probably influenced his increasingly sharp attacks on slavery, although he never became an abolitionist.

During the 1850s as the Whig party almost disappeared in Virginia, Peirpoint and the Whigs of northwestern Virginia found themselves with little political influence or hope. Although the governing Democrats made occasional concessions to the western part of the state, Peirpoint believed the eastern-dominated General Assembly too concerned with defending slavery to give appropriate attention to the interests of northwestern Virginia. His outspokenness on the issues of sectionalism and slavery propelled Peirpoint to leadership among the Opposition, a group that carried on a campaign, largely through the small independent newspapers of northwestern Virginia, alleging the dominance of the "slave power" over Virginia.

Although Peirpoint did not condone John Brown's raid on Harpers Ferry, he was incensed by what he believed was the demagoguery in Richmond in the aftermath of the incident. Peirpoint rejoiced that John Bell and the Constitutional Union party won a plurality of Virginia's votes in the presidential election of 1860, but he believed that the disruption in the Democratic party made civil war inevitable.

After the Virginia convention adopted an ordinance of secession on April 17, 1861, mass meetings throughout northwestern Virginia expressed opposition. Peirpoint was among the 436 delegates representing twenty-seven counties who met in Wheeling on May 13 to determine what action northwestern Virginia should take. Members at the meeting, known as the First Wheeling Convention, tabled a new state proposal, as Peirpoint urged, and agreed to campaign against approval of the secession ordinance, scheduled for a popular vote on May 23. They also agreed that if the ordinance passed, they would elect delegates to a second Wheeling convention. In the interim, a central committee, including Peirpoint as one of its nine members, served as a temporary authority in northwestern Virginia.

The popular vote having approved the secession ordinance (although voters in western counties voted nearly two to one against it), the Second Wheeling Convention convened on June 11, 1861, and adopted Peirpoint's proposal to set up a loyal government to be called the Restored Government of Virginia. The convention elected Peirpoint governor to serve until "an election can be properly held."

Peirpoint took the job of governor seriously, establishing headquarters in Wheeling, raising money and troops, and cooperating with military authorities in establishing Union control of northwestern Virginia. Both President Abraham Lincoln and Congress recognized the Restored Government of Virginia, accepting its military appointments and the senators elected by the Restored General Assembly to replace the expelled senators of Virginia's Confederate government.

In spite of the successful establishment of a Unionist alternative to the Confederate state government, the idea of creating a separate state in western Virginia continued to grow. The Second Wheeling Convention reconvened in August 1861 and moved quickly to establish a new state. Because Peirpoint cooperated with the statehood movement by securing the consent of the Restored General Assembly of Virginia and by actively lobbying both president and Congress for its success, he has been called "the Father of West Virginia." But though he was offered leadership in the new state, he chose to remain the governor of Restored Virginia.

With the creation of the new state, Peirpoint's government moved to Alexandria, where he and other officials of his government struggled to be taken seriously. Though still claiming to represent loyal Virginia, the Peirpoint government controlled only Alexandria and a few nearby counties, the eastern shore, and areas under Union military control around Norfolk. Congress would seat neither representatives nor senators of the Alexandria administration, and Peirpoint no longer enjoyed the close cooperation of military officials as he had in Wheeling.

In May 1865, under the authority of an order by President Andrew Johnson, Peirpoint and his restored government moved to Richmond, but his hopes for a quick and painless reconstruction proved naive. He assumed that the main issues—the preservation of the Union and the end of slavery—had been settled and that the former Confederates would now cooperate in building a new order based on free labor. In June 1865, with Peirpoint's urging, the Restored General Assembly restored voting and officeholding privileges to former Confederates. When elections were held in October, they won with ease, embittering Unionists and Republicans and alerting moderate Republicans in Congress to the need for strong congressional guidance in Reconstruction.

When the new General Assembly ignored Peirpoint and passed many reactionary measures, he found himself without significant support. Former Confederates could not forgive his wartime role, and he had alienated strong Unionists and Republicans with his lenient policy toward former Confederates. The coming of Congressional Reconstruction in March 1867 left him in office but powerless as martial law was imposed. He continued his efforts to build a moderate political base, but few rallied to his cause. The Union general in charge of Reconstruction, John M. Schofield, dismissed Peirpoint on April 4, 1868.

Peirpoint returned to Fairmont, West Virginia, in 1868. He served one term in the West Virginia House of Delegates, but after 1869 he concentrated on his business and legal activities in Fairmont.

Believing that he was correcting errors that had crept into the spelling of his family name, he changed the spelling from "Peirpoint" to "Pierpont" in 1881. This is the spelling that historians and biographers have generally followed since.

BIBLIOGRAPHY

Ambler, Charles H. *Francis H. Pierpont: Union War Governor of Virginia and Father of West Virginia.* Chapel Hill, N.C., 1937.

Lowe, Richard G. "Francis Harrison Pierpont: Wartime Unionist, Reconstruction Moderate." In *The Governors of Virginia, 1860–1978.* Edited by Edward Younger and James Tice Moore. Charlottesville, Va., 1982.

JERRY BRUCE THOMAS

PEMBERTON, JOHN C.

PEMBERTON, JOHN C. (1814–1881), lieutenant general. Born August 10, 1814, in Philadelphia, Pennsylvania, John Clifford Pemberton's marriage to a Virginia woman influenced him to fight for the South. By war's end, he had become one of the Confederacy's most controversial generals.

An 1837 graduate of the U.S. Military Academy, Pemberton saw action in the Second Seminole War and was decorated for bravery in the Mexican War. In peacetime, he proved to be an effective administrative officer. Though his defenders would later claim that Pemberton frequently exhibited antebellum pro-Southern sentiments, there is much evidence to the contrary. When war broke out in 1861, he agonized for weeks before coming to Virginia to fight for his wife's native land.

Pemberton's first significant duty came in March 1862, when he was promoted to major general and took command of the Department of South Carolina and Georgia. Always adept at military politics, he had moved rapidly upward in rank despite a lack of accomplishments.

The new commander soon was embroiled in controversy. Many South Carolinians feared that the Northern-born general was not dedicated to an all-out defense of the department. Pemberton added to their fears by declaring that, if he had to make a choice, he would abandon the area rather than risk losing his outnumbered army. When state officials complained to Robert E. Lee, Pemberton's predecessor and now adviser to Confederate President Jefferson Davis, Lee told Pemberton that he must defend the department at all cost. Pemberton was eventually relieved from command, but he had learned a fateful lesson from Lee.

Despite Pemberton's preference for administrative duties and his problems in South Carolina, Davis promoted him to lieutenant general and gave him arguably the most difficult command in the Confederacy. Pemberton was to defend Vicksburg, a Mississippi city standing on high bluffs above the Mississippi River. Its defenses were the last major river obstacle to Union shipping.

Taking command of the Department of Mississippi and East Louisiana on October 14, 1862, Pemberton immediately set to work solving supply problems and improving troop morale. For several months he enjoyed remarkable success, defeating attempts by Union Gen. Ulysses S. Grant to take Vicksburg in the winter of 1862–1863.

In the spring, however, Grant confused Pemberton with a series of diversions and crossed the Mississippi below Vicksburg practically unnoticed. Grant was free to maneuver because Pemberton had remembered Lee's admonishment and had fought to hold Vicksburg at all cost. Jefferson Davis reinforced Pemberton's thinking with an order not to give up

JOHN C. PEMBERTON.

the river city "for a single day." Now that Grant had successfully crossed the Mississippi, Pemberton determined to stay close to Vicksburg. Davis complicated matters by sending Gen. Joseph E. Johnston to Mississippi to try to reverse declining Confederate fortunes. Johnston ordered Pemberton to unite his forces and attack Grant, if practicable, even if that meant abandoning the defense of Vicksburg.

Torn by conflicting orders, Pemberton marked time while Grant swept inland scoring a series of quick victories at Port Gibson, Raymond, and Jackson. Pemberton finally tried to please both Davis and Johnston. He moved his army east from Edwards Station, all the while maintaining close contact with Vicksburg. A new order from Johnston forced Pemberton to reverse his course and unite with Johnston's forces that had been defeated at Jackson. Before the order could be carried out, Pemberton's army bumped into Grant's forces at Champion's Hill and suffered a major defeat. Pemberton retreated to the Big Black River where he suffered more heavy losses. Remembering Lee's and Davis's orders, Pemberton chose to ignore another order from Johnston to evacuate Vicksburg. He would try to save the city even if that meant risking the loss of his army. He retreated into the city where he and his men endured a forty-seven day siege before surrendering on July 4, 1863. Pemberton became a

pariah in the South and was accused by his immediate superior, General Johnston, of causing the Confederate disaster by disobeying orders.

John Pemberton might have made a positive contribution to the Confederate war effort had his talents been properly used. An able administrator, he was uncomfortable in combat. He had demonstrated his weaknesses in South Carolina, yet Davis had sent him to Mississippi anyway. A few months after Vicksburg, Pemberton displayed his loyalty to the Confederate cause by requesting a reduction in rank. He served the remainder of the war as a lieutenant colonel of artillery in Virginia and South Carolina.

After the war, Pemberton lived in Virginia and Pennsylvania. He died August 14, 1881, and is buried in Laurel Hill Cemetery in Philadelphia.

BIBLIOGRAPHY

Ballard, Michael B. *Pemberton: A Biography.* Jackson, Miss., 1991.
Bearss, Edwin Cole. *The Campaign for Vicksburg.* 3 vols. Dayton, Ohio, 1985–1986.
Pemberton, John C. [III]. *Pemberton: Defender of Vicksburg.* Chapel Hill, N.C., 1942. Reprint, Wilmington, N.C., 1987.

MICHAEL B. BALLARD

PENDER, WILLIAM DORSEY

PENDER, WILLIAM DORSEY (1834–1863), major general. Pender was born February 6, 1834, in North Carolina and was educated at the U.S. Military Academy. He graduated nineteenth in the class of 1854. As a lieutenant of artillery and then of dragoons, Pender served on frontier duty in New Mexico and on the west coast. He saw enough fighting to be able to report with pride having been "mentioned three times [in reports] for conduct in Indian engagements."

Lieutenant Pender resigned from the U.S. Army in March 1861 and immediately received a Confederate commission as captain of artillery. Two months later Pender was elected colonel of the Third (later the Thirteenth) North Carolina Infantry. He assumed command of the Sixth North Carolina in August 1861 and led that regiment with such èlan at Seven Pines the following spring that President Jefferson Davis commended him on the field and promoted him to brigadier general to date from June 3, 1862. General Pender took command of a brigade of North Carolina regiments, including his old Thirteenth, in A. P. Hill's division. He led the brigade through the heaviest fighting during the Seven Days' Battles with notable success and suffered in the process the first of a series of slight wounds incurred in battles. Pender and his men also fought at the heart of the battles of Second Manassas and Ox Hill and participated in the Maryland campaign. At Fredericksburg his North Carolinians stood on the far left of Hill's division.

Pender earned a reputation for stern, even brutal, discipline as a result of his ardent efforts to reduce the desertion rate that bedeviled North Carolina units. According to J. R. Boyles, a Confederate soldier at the time, troops of adjacent brigades "had a perfect horror" of Pender "as being such a strict disciplinarian." Although Pender was of very slight build (about 135 pounds), a member of J. E. B. Stuart's staff declared that the North Carolinian was one of the two "most splendid looking soldiers of the war." His ability to hold his troops to their duty appealed strongly both to units that served near them and to the army high command. Late in 1862 Hill commended Pender as "one of the very best officers I know" and in January 1863 again recommended promotion for him. In the reorganization after Chancellorsville, where he had again performed brilliantly, Pender won promotion to major general.

Pender's new division included the best troops of Hill's old command. The men who had feared him soon discovered Pender to be "quite humane, [he] treated us kindly," as long as no one deserted. Major General Pender's only day in combat was July 1, 1863, when he pushed his command through bitterly contested ground just west of Gettysburg and onto Seminary Ridge at the climax of that day's fighting. The next day a piece of shell wounded Pender in the thigh, though not in a fashion to prompt concern for his recovery. A sudden hemorrhage, however, led to amputation of the leg on July 18, and the general died a few hours later. Pender's solid contributions to the Army of Northern Virginia as one of its most able brigadiers are a matter of clear record. His further potential seemed large, as attested by several wistful comments by both Hill and Lee after Pender's death.

BIBLIOGRAPHY

Hassler, William W., ed. *The General to His Lady.* Chapel Hill, N.C., 1965.
Montgomery, Walter A. *Life and Character of Major-General W. D. Pender.* Raleigh, N.C., 1894.

ROBERT K. KRICK

PENDLETON, WILLIAM N.

PENDLETON, WILLIAM N. (1809–1883), brigadier general. The future father of Col. Alexander ("Sandie") Pendleton and father-in-law of Brig. Gen. Edwin G. Lee was born in Richmond, Virginia, December 26, 1809. He graduated from the U.S. Military Academy in 1830, ranking fifth in a class of forty-two that also included John B. Magruder. Pendleton

resigned from the army after three years to accept a college professorship in Pennsylvania. He then became principal of Episcopal high schools in Alexandria and Baltimore before accepting the rectorship of, first, All Saints Church, Frederick, Maryland, and in 1853, of Grace Church, Lexington, Virginia.

When the Civil War broke out, Pendleton was elected captain of the Rockbridge Artillery, which was attached to the brigade of Thomas J. ("Stonewall") Jackson. The battery consisted of four guns that were christened "Mathew," "Mark," "Luke," and "John" in tribute to the clergyman-commander. At First Manassas, by which time Pendleton had been promoted to colonel, the battery figured prominently in the repulse of the Federal attack on the left of the Confederate line.

> **Pendleton suffered his most humiliating embarrassment on the retreat from Sharpsburg.**

Pendleton also served as chief of artillery on the staff of Joseph E. Johnston. He was appointed brigadier on March 26, 1862.

Pendleton continued as artillery chief under Robert E. Lee, always mingling his military and ecclesiastical fervor. Once, while directing artillery fire against the enemy, he shouted, "Lord have mercy on their souls!"

Pendleton suffered his most humiliating embarrassment on the retreat from Sharpsburg. Commanding the army's rear guard to dispute the enemy's crossing of the Potomac, he mismanaged his task so egregiously that, he reported to Lee, he had lost his 44 guns. The next day, however, he escaped a possible court martial when Jackson recaptured all but four of the field pieces.

Dissatisfaction over Pendleton's performances mounted, and for the last two years of the war his duties were chiefly administrative. In March 1864, Adjutant General Samuel Cooper ordered Pendleton to Dalton, Georgia, to inspect Johnston's artillery. When Pendleton dallied, a second order was issued a month later. By November, strained relations existed between Cooper and the brigadier. Pendleton complained about the "exclusive & extremely invidious obstruction placed at the door of your Dept." for field officers wishing to see the adjutant.

Paroled at Appomattox, Pendleton resumed his rectorship in Lexington, where he died January 15, 1883. He was buried in the town cemetery.

BIBLIOGRAPHY

Bean, William G. *Stonewall's Man, Sandie Pendleton.* Chapel Hill, N.C., 1959. Reprint, Wilmington, N.C., 1987.

Compiled Military Service Records. William Nelson Pendleton. Microcopy M331, Roll 196. Record Group 109. National Archives, Washington, D.C.

Hotchkiss, Jed. *Virginia.* Vol. 3 of *Confederate Military History.* Edited by Clement A. Evans. Atlanta, 1899. Vol. 4 of extended ed. Wilmington, N.C., 1987.

Lee, Susan P. *Memoirs of William Nelson Pendleton.* Philadelphia, 1893.

Warner, Ezra J. *Generals in Gray: Lives of the Confederate Commanders.* Baton Rouge, La., 1959.

LOWELL REIDENBAUGH

PENINSULAR CAMPAIGN

The Peninsular campaign lasted nearly four months, from March to July 1862, and stretched across the southeastern Virginia Peninsula from the Chesapeake Bay to the suburbs of Richmond. Union Maj. Gen. George B. McClellan had planned to advance his Army of the Potomac triumphantly up the stretch of land between the York and James rivers and capture Richmond. With the Confederate capital taken, the Federal government hoped to bring the year-old Civil War to a swift and decisive end. Throughout the spring and early summer months of 1862 approximately 60,000 Confederates doggedly fought nearly double that number of Federals. After several weeks of mud-drenched marches and siege warfare, several bloody battles ensued, which cost the Union army over 15,000 soldiers; the defending Confederates lost 20,000 men killed, wounded, and missing. Richmond was free from capture, the Union suffered another embarrassing setback, and the war dragged on for three more years.

Two divisions from McClellan's army landed at Federally held Fort Monroe at the tip of the peninsula in mid-March. As scores of bluecoats debarked from vessels onto Southern soil, Maj. Gen. John B. Magruder, commander of the Confederate defenses at Yorktown, readied his scanty force of 10,000 men for combat. Magruder's Army of the Peninsula lay directly in McClellan's path up the peninsula. Luckily for the Confederates, McClellan severely overestimated Confederate strength—he thought it to be nearly ten times as strong as it was. Magruder added to the Federals' confusion by marching his men through clearings in circles to give the impression of many more troops. Instead of attacking frontally, which would have crumbled Magruder's meager force, McClellan began to amass artillery to pound Yorktown into submission. All through April, McClellan pressed his siege of Yorktown.

Meanwhile, Joseph E. Johnston and his Army of Northern Virginia had lain idle following the Confederate victory at the Battle of Manassas in July 1861. Johnston did not wish to engage McClellan's formidable forces head on and remained content waiting for the enemy's attack. But on April 14, Confederate President Jefferson Davis held a special council of war to determine Johnston's next move. For fourteen hours, Johnston, Maj. Gen. James Longstreet, Secretary of War George Wythe Randolph, Maj. Gen. Gustavus W. Smith, and Davis's military adviser, Gen. Robert E. Lee, discussed how to deal with the growing Union threat at Yorktown. Johnston suggested that his army move inland and await McClellan's approach to Richmond before fighting. Lee, fearful to allow this undetermined force of Federals to move so close to the capital, argued that the peninsula offered numerous defensive positions from which the Confederates could derive advantage. At 1:00 A.M. on April 15, President Davis came to a decision. He ordered Johnston to move his army to Yorktown to reinforce Magruder and fight back the enemy on the peninsula. Johnston abandoned central Virginia to the Union and grudgingly joined Magruder at Yorktown. His men settled into the flooded trenches, unsure how long they would have to remain.

On May 4, McClellan deemed himself ready to do battle. But on that same day, Johnston left, intending to follow his original plan to fight outside of Richmond. On May 5, 1862, the rear guard of Johnston's retreating army turned to fight pursuing Federals near the old colonial capitol of Williamsburg. Six brigades of James Longstreet's division fought to gain needed time for the fleeing Confederates. The Battle of Williamsburg yielded 2,239 Federal casualties and 1,603 Confederate. Many more would soon follow.

Johnston's movement up the peninsula required the abandonment of the seaport town of Norfolk, Virginia. The famed Southern ironclad CSS *Virginia* would be without a port. Rather than leave the ship to the enemy, Confederates burned the vessel. Soon Union troops moved in and spread to nearby Suffolk. Seven miles of the James River below Richmond were now open to Federal forces. A Union fleet attempted to move up the James, but on May 15, Confederates fired on the Federal ships at Drewry's Bluff. The orphaned crew of *Virginia,* a detachment of infantry, and a slew of heavy artillery guns mustered enough resistance to spoil the enemy's plans.

Outside of Richmond, three corps of McClellan's large force positioned themselves south of the swollen Chickahominy River; the other two were on the northern side. When word reached Johnston that McClellan might soon receive reinforcements from Maj. Gen. Irvin McDowell's corps, he concluded that quick, decisive action was in order. On May 31 incessant rains washed away bridges connecting McClellan's corps, leaving two isolated and vulnerable corps north of the Chickahominy. The Battle of Seven Pines was an embarrassing Confederate failure. Johnston's officers bungled orders and moved sluggishly. When fighting finally began, it was heavy but the Southerners failed to gain any ground. Johnston fell severely wounded and Gustavus W.

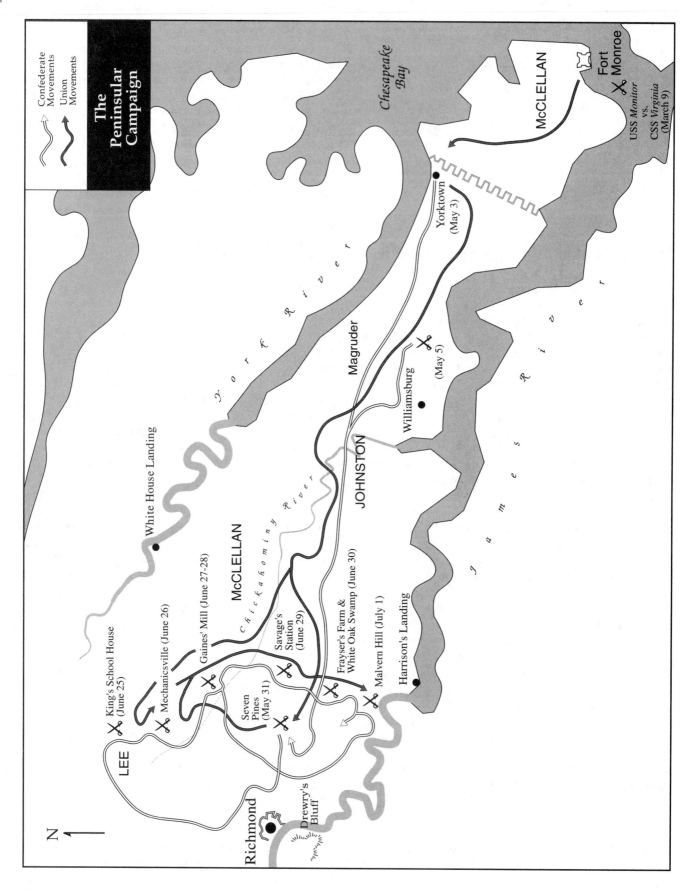

The Peninsular Campaign

Confederate Movements
Union Movements

Chesapeake Bay

McCLELLAN

Fort Monroe

USS *Monitor*
vs.
CSS *Virginia*
(March 9)

Yorktown
(May 3)

York River

Magruder

(May 5)

Williamsburg

JOHNSTON

James River

White House Landing

McCLELLAN

Chickahominy River

King's School House
(June 25)

Mechanicsville (June 26)

Gaines' Mill (June 27–28)

Savage's
Station
(June 29)

Frayser's Farm &
White Oak Swamp (June 30)

Malvern Hill (July 1)

Harrison's Landing

Seven
Pines
(May 31)

LEE

Richmond

Drewry's
Bluff

N

Smith briefly took command. The next day a renewed offensive by the Confederates again failed. By afternoon Robert E. Lee had arrived on the field to take command and order a withdrawal. The Confederate failure cost over 6,000 casualties; the Federals suffered over 5,000. During the next three weeks both armies waited and watched for new bloodletting.

Lee's first concern as commander was to bolster Richmond's defenses. He soon had his men digging field fortifications outside the city. On June 12, Lee sent Maj. Gen. J. E. B. Stuart on a reconnaissance mission into Union lines to determine enemy strength. Stuart rode entirely around McClellan's army in a dramatic cavalry sweep. In the process his troopers discovered that the right flank of McClellan's army stood vulnerable to attack. Upon receiving this information, Lee quickly laid plans to strike at McClellan's weakness. But the Federals were not unaware; Stuart's ride prompted McClellan to execute a "change of base" southward from his vulnerable position on the York to the James River.

Lee hurried to attack. Leaving a mere 25,000 men between Richmond and the Federal army, Lee moved his remaining 47,000 soldiers to assault the Union flank. With the aid of Maj. Gen. Thomas J. ("Stonewall") Jackson's Army of the Valley, Lee planned to surprise the exposed Federals. The subsequent battles at Mechanicsville on June 26 and Gaines' Mill on June 27 were indecisive. Unfulfilled was Lee's primary objective of destroying the isolated corps and seriously damaging McClellan's strength. Stonewall Jackson's poor performance was especially disappointing. At both of these engagements his delay undeniably contributed to the Confederate failures. But Lee was undaunted. The next day he continued in bold pursuit while McClellan, stunned by the Confederates' continued aggressiveness, retreated. He was now even more convinced that his men faced superior numbers.

Beginning with a brief engagement at King's School House on June 25, the Seven Days' Battles consisted largely of Lee's dogged attempts to corner and destroy pieces of McClellan's army. Mechanicsville and Gaines' Mill were followed by Savage's Station on June 29, Frayser's Farm on June 30, and finally Malvern Hill on July 1. Similar to Johnston's mishap at Seven Pines, Lee's ambitious plans went awry owing to failed coordination between units, misunderstood orders, and poor staff performance. Savage's Station yielded 626 Confederate casualties and 1,590 Federals; Frayser's Farm cost 2,853 Federal casualties and 3,615 Confederate. At Malvern Hill, Lee suffered a severe defeat when he ordered his troops to charge the enemy's nearly impregnable position atop the hill. When Union artillery unmercifully poured into the infantrymen attempting to charge forward, 5,355 Confederates were lost; Federal casualties numbered 3,214. Confederate Maj. Gen. D. H. Hill later remarked that Malvern Hill was "not war—it was murder."

With this Union victory, McClellan completed his retreat to Harrison's Landing on the James River. He soon turned north to Washington, and the threat to Richmond had passed.

General Lee did not write his report of the Peninsular campaign for two years. Citing a lack of maps and information, he admitted his failure to destroy or even weaken the Union army. But Lee had successfully managed to take advantage of McClellan's overcautiousness and halt the enemy movement toward Richmond. For two full years the Federals would not attempt such an operation again. The Peninsular campaign also cemented Lee's reputation as an aggressive and stubborn fighter. For the next two years of war, Lee showed this ability again and again in the face of Union commanders more talented than McClellan.

[See also Drewry's Bluff, Virginia; Seven Days' Battles; Stuart's Raids; Williamsburg, Virginia; Yorktown, Virginia.]

BIBLIOGRAPHY

Cullen, Joseph P. The Peninsular Campaign. Harrisburg, Penn., 1973.
Dowdey, Clifford. The Seven Days: The Emergence of Lee. Boston, 1964.
Freeman, Douglas S. Lee's Lieutenants: A Study in Command. Vol. 1. New York, 1942. Reprint, New York, 1986.
Sears, Stephen W. The Peninsula Campaign. New York, 1993.
Thomas, Emory M. "The Peninsular Campaign: Parts I-II."Civil War Times Illustrated 17, no. 10 (February 1979): 4–9; 18, no. 1 (April 1979): 28–35; 18, no. 2 (May 1979): 12–18; 18, no. 3 (June 1979): 10–17; 18, no. 4 (July 1979): 14–24.

LESLEY JILL GORDON-BURR

PERRYVILLE, KENTUCKY

On October 8, 1862, the town of Perryville was the site of an indecisive battle that marked the turning point in Gen. Braxton Bragg's ill-starred Kentucky campaign. After taking most of the state and inaugurating a Confederate state government, Bragg faced a perilous strategic situation. Arrayed against his 48,776 men was a Union army of over 80,000 troops centered at Louisville and another 45,000 at Cincinnati. To complicate matters, Bragg's divisions were scattered in garrisons across central Kentucky.

In the first week of October 1862, Union Gen. Don Carlos Buell and 61,000 men moved away from the Ohio River in four corps on separate roads a day's march apart. Confederate cavalrymen under Col. Joseph Wheeler reported Federal troops moving toward Versailles and Perryville, threatening Confederate depots. Bragg reacted by dispatching troops to both points. On October 7, near the hamlet of Perryville, Southern horsemen skirmished with the advance elements of Buell's army along the Springfield and Mackville pikes. Confederate infantry under Maj. Gen. William J. Hardee hurried forward, forming a battle line east of town.

Hardee soon ascertained that the main Union blow would fall against him. He called for his divisional commander, Simon Bolivar Buckner, to bring his men up. Bragg, too, left Lexington for Perryville, ordering Maj. Gen. Leonidas Polk, commander of the Confederate troops in the vicinity, to "attack the enemy immediately," defeat him, and then join Maj. Gen. E. Kirby Smith.

In early morning darkness the following day, Union skirmishers, who were desperate for water, moved toward Doctor's Creek and ran into Confederate pickets at Peter's Hill. Both sides called for reinforcements. The Union brigade of Brig. Gen. Philip Sheridan pushed the Southerners down the Springfield Pike, but by daybreak the fighting had lulled and the Federal advance stalled.

The Confederates responded, though Polk hesitated despite General Bragg's orders for an attack at dawn. As additional Federals arrived, the Southerners deployed their 16,000 men in three divisions along the banks of Doctor's Creek in a battle line facing west. Maj. Gen. B. Franklin Cheatham's men occupied the Confederate right, anchored on Walker's Bend of the Chaplin River. In the center was Buckner's division, with Brig. Gen. James Patton Anderson's troops on its left. On the Confederate extreme right rode the cavalry of Col. John Austin Wharton, searching for the enemy flank, while Wheeler's troopers covered the left. By midday, Confederate cavalry reported the Union left flank to be farther north than expected. Accordingly, Cheatham ordered his men across the Chaplin River and into Walker's Bend to gain more room to launch an assault.

At 2:00 P.M. on October 8, the Confederate troops finally splashed across the stream and directly into the front of Union Maj. Gen. Alexander McCook's First Corps of the Army of the Ohio. Having missed the flank, Cheatham's infantry fought desperately while Buckner and Anderson added their troops to the fight, advancing obliquely to the right. With increasing pressure upon their front and left, McCook's men gave ground. Two Union brigadier generals, James S. Jackson and William R. Terrill, fell dead as the battle intensified.

On Buckner's front, the Confederate brigade of Brig. Gen. Bushrod Rust Johnson ran into heavy fire near the H. P. Bottom house on Doctor's Creek, forcing the Southerners to take cover behind a stone fence. Reinforcing brigades under Patrick Cleburne and Daniel Adams pushed beyond the stalled Confederate line and advanced up the slopes overlooking the creek, driving the Federals before them along the Mackville Pike. The Confederate push continued as Bragg's generals concentrated the major portion of his army against McCook's corps. One by one the Northern brigades broke and retreated before the onslaught. To the south, the Union troops of Maj. Gen. Charles C. Gilbert's corps nervously watched the disaster to their left—Buell had issued orders for

no other troops to engage. By 4:00 P.M., however, the Confederate advance slowed as McCook's men formed a tattered but intact line.

The fighting now shifted to the Confederate left as Col. Samuel Powell's advancing brigade collided with Gilbert's untested corps. After a severe exchange, the outnumbered Southerners gave way, pursued down the Springfield Pike by Sheridan's Federals. Soon the fighting moved into the streets of Perryville. As the Confederates gave ground, Sheridan grew uneasy about his exposed position and ordered a withdrawal back to his original lines. This ended the fighting for the day.

Bragg had committed all of his available troops at Perryville. Almost 3,100 men had been killed, wounded, or captured—nearly 20 percent of the Confederates involved. Buell, however, had used only half of his men. About 25,000 of his 61,000 troops fought at Perryville, of which nearly 3,700 became casualties. The untested portion of the Federal army appeared ready to continue the fight the following morning.

That evening, as additional Union divisions moved into place, Bragg ordered a withdrawal. Badly outnumbered, the Southern leader hastened to concentrate his troops with the balance of the Confederate army under Kirby Smith at Harrodsburg. The battle had had a potential for disaster, as unsupported elements of the Confederate army had met the bulk of Buell's force; only the lack of decisive Union leadership and aggressive pursuit had spared the Confederates.

Tactically, the Battle of Perryville was a draw. McCook's corps had been roughly treated and had given ground but still managed to hold off the repeated Confederate attacks. Elsewhere on the battlefield, however, the outcome had been different. Nightfall and lack of adequate support were all that kept Sheridan from inflicting a disaster on the Confederate left.

The Battle of Perryville ended Bragg's campaign in Kentucky. The concentration of Federal forces against him, plus his lackluster reception by the citizens of the state, compelled him to withdraw. After combining with Kirby Smith's forces, the Confederate army marched through Cumberland Gap into Tennessee, leaving Kentucky behind.

BIBLIOGRAPHY

Connelly, Thomas L. *Army of the Heartland: The Army of Tennessee, 1861–1862.* Baton Rouge, La., 1967.

Coulter, E. Merton. *The Civil War and Readjustment in Kentucky.* Chapel Hill, N.C., 1926.

Gilbert, Charles C. "On the Field of Perryville." In *Battles and Leaders of the Civil War.* Edited by Robert U. Johnson and C. C. Buel. Vol. 2. New York, 1888. Reprint, Secaucus, N.J., 1982.

Hawke, Paul. "Perryville Kentucky." In *The Civil War Battlefield Guide.* Edited by Francis H. Kennedy. Boston, 1990.

McWhiney, Grady. *Braxton Bragg and Confederate Defeat.* Vol. 1. New York, 1968. Reprint, Tuscaloosa, Ala., 1991.

Wheeler, Joseph. "Bragg's Invasion of Kentucky." In *Battles and Leaders of the Civil War.* Edited by Robert U. Johnson and C. C. Buel. Vol. 2. New York, 1888. Reprint, Secaucus, N.J., 1982.

DONALD S. FRAZIER

PETERSBURG CAMPAIGN

For ten grinding months—from June 15, 1864, to April 3, 1865—Confederate forces under Gen. Robert E. Lee conducted the longest sustained defensive operation of the war in the works surrounding Petersburg, Virginia. All but one of the railroads that connected Richmond to remaining Confederate supplies passed first through Petersburg. Both Lee and Lt. Gen. Ulysses S. Grant, commander of all Federal armies, recognized that Union possession of the city would force the evacuation of Richmond and shorten the war.

By early June, Grant's strategy had failed to capture Lee's army northeast of Richmond. Maj. Gen. Benjamin Butler's Army of the James was ignominiously bottled up by Confederate forces near Bermuda Hundred, unable to threaten either Richmond or Petersburg. Maj. Gen. George G. Meade's Army of the Potomac incurred huge casualties in the Overland campaign, leaving the Army of Northern Virginia damaged but not destroyed. In an effort to break the stalemate near Cold Harbor, Grant looked south to Petersburg. If he could sever Confederate supply lines, Lee's army would have to leave entrenchments for open combat.

On June 12 Grant's army slipped away from Cold Harbor and began an audacious turning movement. Maj. Gen. William Smith's Eighteenth Corps went by ship to Bermuda Hundred while the Army of the Potomac marched through fifty miles of enemy territory to the James River. Transports and the 2,100-foot-long James River pontoon bridge, a marvel of combat engineering, placed Federal units a day's march from Petersburg.

Through rapid movement and a convincing feint against Richmond, Grant had frozen Lee north of the James. In Petersburg, Brig. Gen. Henry A. Wise's patchwork force of 2,200 Confederates faced the arrival of Smith's 12,500 men. Despite delays and command mistakes, Union attackers quickly overwhelmed three and one-half miles of the imposing Dimmock Line that surrounded the city. As darkness fell on June 15 and Maj. Gen. Winfield S. Hancock's Second Corps arrived, Smith exercised caution and stopped his advance within sight of Petersburg's spires. Confederate Gen. P. G. T. Beauregard took advantage of this delay to reinforce Petersburg with units from the Bermuda Hundred lines. By June 16 Beauregard had marshaled 14,000 men to face Federal troops that would number between 63,000 and 80,000 men on June 17.

On June 16, 17, and 18, Federal forces continued pouring into the Petersburg area. Each day witnessed piecemeal Union attacks against strongly entrenched Confederate lines. Petersburg might have fallen on June 17 when Confederate lines were twice shattered, but heroic Confederate counterattacks by Maj. Gen. Bushrod Rust Johnson's division closed the gaps when Union reinforcements failed to arrive.

Beauregard fought his finest battle at Petersburg, while the Union army suffered from a combination of poor leadership and extreme combat exhaustion. After four days of fighting, Federal losses totaled 10,586 compared to an estimated 4,000 Confederate casualties. With the arrival of Lee's forces on June 18, Grant halted frontal attacks and chose instead "to use the spade."

On June 19 Lee and Grant found themselves in a position neither wanted. For Grant, siege tactics meant slow progress and dwindling morale, something Abraham Lincoln's party could ill-afford in an election year. Lee likewise recognized that the offensive skills of his smaller army would mean little in a campaign of attrition. By late June, Lee's 50,000 men

> **Grant began a two-pronged strategy designed to encircle Petersburg while cutting Lee's supply lines.**

had covered a twenty-six-mile line from Richmond to Petersburg and faced a Federal host that hovered around 112,000 troops.

Drawing upon his Vicksburg experience, Grant began a two-pronged strategy designed to encircle Petersburg while cutting Lee's supply lines. On June 22 through 24, the Second and Sixth Corps challenged Maj. Gen. A. P. Hill's corps for possession of the Weldon Railroad. Hill, however, exploited a gap that developed between the two corps and inflicted 2,962 casualties while maintaining control of the railroad. The Battle of Jerusalem Plank Road (or Weldon Railroad) foreshadowed the coming nine months of action. With each Federal movement westward, Lee launched increasingly desperate counterattacks to prevent the extension of earthworks while preserving connections with Southern supplies.

In late July, Grant hesitantly moved the focus of his strategy from the left flank to an attack in the center of the Confederate line opposite Maj. Gen. Ambrose Burnside's Ninth Corps. Coal miners from the Forty-eighth Pennsylvania tunneled 511 feet to the Confederate line and packed eight thousand pounds of black powder into a gallery under Brig. Gen. Stephen Elliot's salient. Brig. Gen. Edward Ferrero's large, fresh division of black soldiers had been carefully trained to spearhead the attack through the breach made by

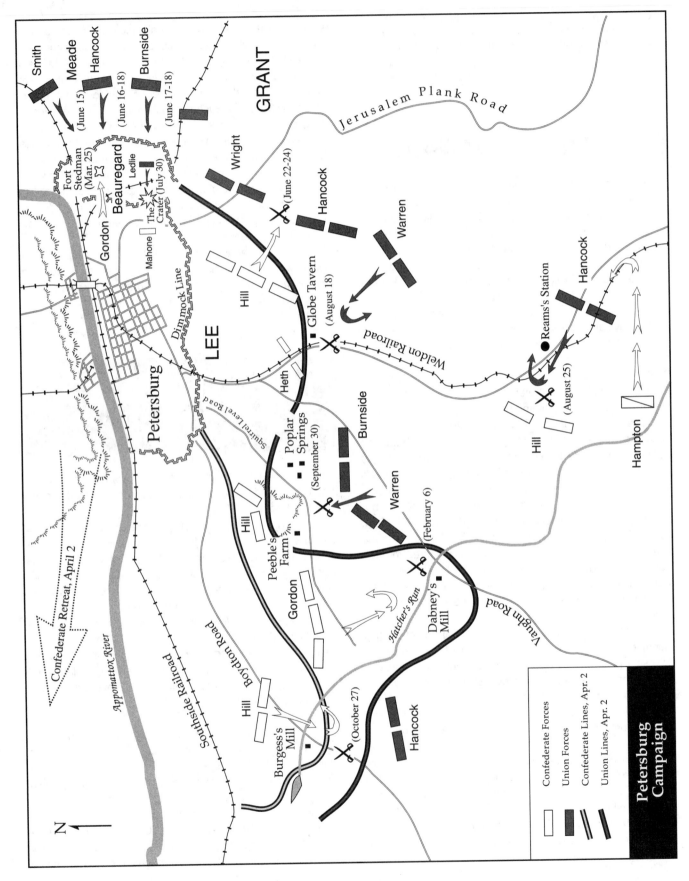

Smith

Meade

Hancock
(June 16-18)

Burnside
(June 17-18)

(June 15)

GRANT

Jerusalem Plank Road

Wright

Fort
Stedman
(Mar. 25)

Beauregard

Ledlie

Hancock
(June 22-24)

Gordon

Mahone

The
Crater (July 30)

Hancock

Warren

Dimmock Line

Hill

Hancock

Globe Tavern
(August 18)

Petersburg

LEE

Reams's Station

Heth

Weldon Railroad

Squirrel Level Road

Burnside

Poplar
Springs
(September 30)

Hill

(August 25)

Confederate Retreat, April 2

Peeble's Farm

Hill

Warren

Hampton

Appomattox River

Gordon

(February 6)

Hatcher's Run

Dabney's
Mill

Boydton Road

Southside Railroad

Vaughn Road

Hill

(October 27)

Hancock

Burgess's
Mill

N

**Petersburg
Campaign**

☐	Confederate Forces
▰	Union Forces
╱	Confederate Lines, Apr. 2
═	Union Lines, Apr. 2

"springing the mine." Meade, however, had reservations about the black division's inexperience and about potential political fallout should heavy casualties lead to charges that the army deliberately sacrificed black soldiers. With Grant's approval, Meade ordered an enraged Burnside to choose a new lead division only one day before the assault. The job fell by lot to the division of Brig. Gen. James Ledlie, an incompetent officer who was to spend the attack hiding in a bombproof.

At 4:40 A.M. on July 30 a spectacular explosion blasted a hole 170 feet long, 60 feet wide, and 30 feet deep in the Confederate line. Defenders were thrown into disarray, and despite a late start more than 15,000 troops from the Ninth Corps rushed into the Crater and adjacent works. Lacking leadership, the men milled about in the captured line and failed to gain the high ground just beyond.

Confederate counterattacks, led by Brig. Gen. William Mahone's division, drove Federal troops from the captured works and slaughtered those trapped in the Crater. By 1:00 P.M. the attack was over. The Union army lost an estimated 4,000 men against just 1,500 for the Confederates in a fiasco that prompted a congressional investigation and a military court of inquiry. Grant called the Battle of the Crater "the saddest affair" of the war and resigned himself to a strategy of exhaustion.

In mid-August Federal forces moved again to extend their lines westward. On August 18, as the Union Second and Tenth Corps attacked north of the James near Fussell's Mill, Maj. Gen. Gouverneur Warren's Fifth Corps struck the Weldon Railroad near Globe Tavern, about four miles south of Petersburg. Warren's soldiers moved north from the tavern for a mile, ripping up track as they marched. Two Confederate brigades under Maj. Gen. Henry Heth responded promptly to contest the railroad's destruction. The next day Hill's corps joined the fight and captured more than 2,500 prisoners while driving the Federal line south. Warren's corps regrouped and dug in around Globe Tavern, and on August 21 Hill's men attacked but failed to carry the Union line. Lee then arrived on the field from north of the James and called a halt to assaults against the Union position. Federal losses in the Battle of Globe Tavern (or Weldon Railroad) totaled 4,455, well in excess of the Confederate's estimated 1,600 casualties, but the railroad was cut. Confederate teamsters now had to supply Petersburg by wagon from Stony Creek Depot, twenty miles south of Petersburg. In December a Federal raid at Hicksford destroyed another sixteen miles of the Weldon Railroad and forced an even longer wagon supply route.

Confederate forces did enjoy some success in late summer. On August 25 Hancock's Second Corps was five miles south of Globe Tavern, destroying track at Reams's Station, when a vigorous attack by Hill's corps stampeded raw Union recruits and crumpled Hancock's left. Confederate forces captured 9 guns, 12 flags, and more than 2,150 men. And between September 11 and 17, Maj. Gen. Wade Hampton's horsemen rode into the rear of the Union army and captured about 300 men and 2,400 head of cattle. Reams's Station and the Beefsteak Raid improved Confederate morale, but the Federal army missed neither the men nor the meals.

Grant's inexorable strategy continued in late September. As part of a major thrust north of the James at Fort Harrison, elements of the Fifth and Ninth Corps near the Weldon Railroad staged a reconnaissance in force north and west toward the Southside Railroad. On September 30 Union forces captured trenches and a Confederate redoubt at Peeble's Farm near Squirrel Level Road. With characteristic combativeness, Hill attacked the Union position with two divisions and temporarily drove the Federals south. Union counterattacks reestablished the line near Peeble's Farm, and by October 2 Federal troops had extended their line more than a mile west of Globe Tavern. The Battle of Peeble's Farm (or Poplar Springs Church) cost Grant another 2,889 casualties, but it forced Lee to match the extended line or risk envelopment.

In a final attempt to capture the Southside Railroad before winter, Grant employed elements of three corps and on October 27 gained control of the Boydton Road near Burgess's Mill. Hill responded immediately. Confederate infantry on the left flank and cavalry on the right drove back Hancock's Second Corps. Hill's men were driven back themselves by a Union counterattack, but when difficult terrain, slashing, and strong earthworks stopped the Fifth and Ninth Corps from joining the Second Corps, Grant ordered Hancock's men withdrawn. As a result, the road remained in Confederate hands. Federal losses in the Battle of Hatcher's Run (also called Boydton Plank Road and Burgess's Mill) totaled 1,758; Confederate casualties were not reported.

By December 1864 the well-supplied Federal army totaled about 110,000 men. Lee counted 66,000 gaunt and poorly equipped men to protect a thirty-five-mile line from Richmond to Hatcher's Run, southwest of Petersburg. Desertion, disease, sniping, unreliable supply, and sinking morale further weakened Lee's army throughout the winter, and every extension west threatened to cause the collapse of the Richmond-Petersburg line.

On February 5 through 7, 1865, in the middle of what had become a miserable winter, Grant launched the Second and Fifth Corps, elements of the Sixth Corps, and a cavalry division to secure the Boydton Plank Road, one of the last remaining Confederate supply routes into Petersburg. On February 6, Maj. Gen. John B. Gordon's corps struck the Fifth Corps near Dabney's Mill, driving Warren's men away from the road. Union forces halted Gordon's attack, but only after Warren had lost more than 1,300 men. Federal leaders suspended the effort to secure the road when Union cavalry determined that the Confederates were no longer using it as a supply route. After the Battle of Hatcher's Run (or Dabney's Mill), Federal soldiers extended their works to the Vaughn Road crossing over Hatcher's Run. Confederate forces matched the line with their own, which now reached about thirty-seven miles.

By March 1865, Lee recognized that the Richmond-Petersburg line could not be held once Union armies under Maj. Gens. William Tecumseh Sherman and Philip Sheridan, then in North Carolina and the Shenandoah Valley, respectively, arrived to join Grant. Consequently, Lee decided upon a preemptive strike and ordered Gordon to plan an attack on Union lines. If it was successful, Grant might shorten his Petersburg lines, allowing Lee to reinforce Gen. Joseph E. Johnston for an attack on Sherman in North Carolina. If the attack failed, Lee would retreat and join Johnston for a final stand.

Gordon selected Fort Stedman, only 125 yards from the Confederate lines, as the site of Lee's last offensive. Although the March 25 predawn attack was well conducted and met with early success, Union troops soon rallied and recaptured Fort Stedman and adjacent works that Gordon briefly held. The Battle of Fort Stedman cost Lee between 4,400 and 5,000 casualties and made clear his only remaining option: retreat.

Lee awaited only supplies and dry roads before marching to join Johnston. His plans for an April 10 move were upset by the arrival of Sheridan's forces. Augmented by the Fifth and Second Corps, Sheridan concentrated on the Confederate right near Dinwiddie Court House and Five Forks. Lee gave Maj. Gen. George E. Pickett command of 19,000 infantry and cavalry and charged him with protection of the Southside Railroad, Petersburg's single remaining rail link with the south. On March 31, Federal forces were driven back in the Battle of Dinwiddie Court House, but this minor Confederate victory did not change strategic dispositions.

Late on March 31, Pickett withdrew to Five Forks, which Lee ordered him to hold "at all hazards." Sheridan's attack at Five Forks was delayed until 4:00 P.M. on April 1, but before dusk Pickett's left flank had collapsed under the weight of Fifth Corps attacks as his right was enveloped by cavalry. At least 4,500 Confederate troops became casualties including 3,200 captured. Federal losses numbered under 1,000. The Battle of Five Forks convinced Grant to launch an all-out effort to capture Petersburg.

At 4:40 A.M. on April 2, a Union gun signaled the final assault on Petersburg. Federal troops met with stout resistance, but Maj. Gen. Horatio Wright's Sixth Corps broke through on the Confederate right and drove southwest along the line. Much of Lee's right withdrew in a fighting retreat toward the city. By midday, Federal troops had reached the Appomattox River west of Petersburg, and most of the outer line south and west of the city was in Union hands. Lee informed President Jefferson Davis that he would hold

Petersburg until nightfall to allow for Richmond's evacuation. Confederate forces fought delaying actions and launched counterattacks that stopped Federal forces short of city streets. By 8:00 P.M. the Confederate retreat toward Amelia Courthouse had begun. The Petersburg final assault had cost Grant between 3,300 and 4,100 men; Confederate losses are not known but included A. P. Hill, who had served the Confederacy so well at Petersburg and was killed in its defense.

The next day, April 3, 1865, Federal forces entered the city unchallenged. Several hours later Richmond fell; within a week Grant forced Lee's surrender at Appomattox Courthouse. The end of the Confederacy had come at a frightful cost though; from June 15, 1864, to April 3, 1865, the Petersburg campaign claimed an estimated 42,000 Federal casualties. Confederate losses—irreplaceable owing to the South's limited manpower—totaled at least 28,000.

The Petersburg campaign heralded more than the Confederacy's death; it also marked the birth of a new type of warfare. Both sides used complex trench systems replete with abatis, fraise, covered ways, bombproofs, and second lines. The United States Military Railroad snaked just behind Federal lines and provided rapid resupply from the massive City Point supply depot on the James River. Grant continually extended and strengthened his lines, knowing that superior numbers and the debilitating effects of attrition, desertion, and starvation would eventually destroy Lee's army. Most important, Grant held the Confederacy's most powerful army and its masterful commander in a static position while his subordinates devastated the South's ability to make war and destroyed its remaining armies piecemeal. Grant at Petersburg demonstrated the keys to success in modern war: superb organization and a genius for doing the obvious.

Lee adjusted to his defensive role with equal skill, marshaling forces to meet threats both north and south of the James, ordering attacks to prevent line extension and the capture of supply lines, and aiding those forces outside Petersburg when practicable and possible. In the end, however, Petersburg was about matèriel and men, and Lee was, at last, drained of both.

[See also Beefsteak Raid.]

BIBLIOGRAPHY

Cavanaugh, Michael, and William Marvel. *The Petersburg Campaign: The Battle of the Crater—"The Horrid Pit," June 25–August 6, 1864.* Lynchburg, Va., 1989.

Davis, William C. *Death in the Trenches: Grant at Petersburg.* Alexandria, Va., 1986.

Freeman, Douglas S. *R. E. Lee: A Biography.* Vols. 3 and 4. New York, 1935.

Howe, Thomas J. *The Petersburg Campaign: Wasted Valor, June 15–18, 1864.* Lynchburg, Va., 1988.

Humphreys, Andrew A. *The Virginia Campaign of '64 and '65.* New York, 1883. Reprint, Wilmington, N.C., 1989.

Lykes, Richard Wayne. *Campaign for Petersburg.* National Park Service Handbook 134. Washington, D.C., 1985.

Sommers, Richard T. *Richmond Redeemed: The Siege at Petersburg.* Garden City, N.Y., 1981.

Trudeau, Noah André. *The Last Citadel: Petersburg, Virginia, June 1864–April 1865.* Boston, 1991.

THOMAS J. HOWE

PETTIGREW, J. JOHNSTON

PETTIGREW, J. JOHNSTON (1828–1863), brigadier general. Johnston Pettigrew is best known for his role in the first and third days' battles at Gettysburg and his death two weeks later after an insignificant action on the retreat. Douglas Southall Freeman wrote, "for none who fought so briefly in the Army of Northern Virginia was there more praise while living or more laments when dead."

Born in Tyrrell County, North Carolina, on July 4, 1828, Pettigrew graduated first in the class of 1847 at the University of North Carolina. He later moved to South Carolina, where he practiced law, served in the legislature, and was an officer in the militia.

After serving as military adviser to the governor and colonel of a state regiment from South Carolina's secession to the fall of Fort Sumter, Pettigrew became colonel of the Twenty-second North Carolina Infantry in July 1861. He was promoted to brigadier general in February 1862. At Seven Pines, on May 31, 1862, Pettigrew was severely wounded and captured in his first battle.

When he returned to duty Pettigrew commanded a newly formed brigade which saw service on the North Carolina and Virginia coasts and joined the Army of Northern Virginia for the Gettysburg campaign. On July 1, 1863, his brigade suffered heavy casualties but fought brilliantly. Pettigrew, in temporary command of the division on July 3, led it and was wounded in the assault popularly known as Pickett's Charge. On July 14, during the retreat through Maryland, Pettigrew was mortally wounded at Falling Waters; he died July 18, 1863.

He was one of the best educated and most intellectual Southern generals. Lee called him "an officer of great promise" and observed, "his loss will be deeply felt by the country and the army."

BIBLIOGRAPHY

Freeman, Douglas S. *Lee's Lieutenants: A Study in Command.* 3 vols. New York, 1942–1944. Reprint, New York, 1986.

U.S. War Department. *War of the Rebellion: A Compilation of the Official Records of the Union and Confederate Armies.* Washington, D.C., 1880-1901. Ser. 1, vol. 11, pts. 1–2.

Wilson, Clyde N. *Carolina Cavalier: The Life and Mind of James Johnston Pettigrew.* Athens, Ga., 1990.

J. TRACY POWER

PETTUS, J. J.

PETTUS, J. J. (1813–1867), governor of Mississippi. John Jones Pettus moved to Mississippi from Tennessee as a youth and became a lawyer and cotton planter in Kemper County. Throughout his life, Pettus never lost his identification with his roots and his frontier simplicity. From 1846 to 1848, Pettus served in the state house of representatives, and from 1848 to 1858, in the senate. For five days in 1854 he served as acting governor, when Governor Henry S. Foote resigned in a feud with Senator Jefferson Davis. In 1859, he was elected governor, beating his opponent 34,559 to 10,308 on the issue of taking decisive action to protect the rights of slave-owning states if a Republican was elected president. He pledged he would ask the legislature "to fill the arsenal with arms that the state might be prepared for the worst."

Soon after Pettus took office John Brown raided the arsenal at Harpers Ferry, and Pettus's views became more extreme. He envisioned a South united under the motto "Superiority and Supremacy of the White Race" and believed that whites in the North would seek union with the South. He began to arm the state as early as 1860, using a legislative appropriation of $150,000 to purchase several thousand rifles with bayonets. He also encouraged the organization of many volunteer companies.

Mississippi at this time was split between the cooperationists and the secessionists. Although agreeing with the secessionists that the South had grievances against the Northern states, the cooperationists wanted to fight for their rights within the Union. The extreme secessionists, of course, favored immediate separation, and Pettus was a member of this group. (At one point, a short play was staged in which Pettus was portrayed as an inmate of a "lunatic asylum"; he was described as sensible on many subjects, but if anyone said to him the word *abolition*, "you will see his knees tremble, the color leave his cheeks, his eye-balls start, his whole countenance become distorted with fear.")

After Abraham Lincoln's election, Pettus called a special session of the Mississippi legislature to debate the best course for the state. The legislature ordered elections to a state convention, and on January 9, 1861, the members voted 84 to 15 to pass an ordinance of secession. In a message to the legislature on January 18, Pettus reported that the state had sent seven companies to assist in the Fort Pickens siege at Pensacola and predicted the likely approach of "open war."

Pettus was optimistic when the war began. In a special session of the legislature soon after the Confederate victory at Manassas, he announced that the revolution was "prosperous and successful." Financial problems, however, immediately surfaced, and Pettus had to suspend all payments of state debts, call for private donations to the military, and request increased taxes.

In October 1861, Pettus was reelected governor with little opposition. Problems intensified, and early in 1862, the war reached Mississippi. The governor called for all males to enroll in the militia, and after the Confederate defeats at Corinth, Memphis, and New Orleans, he decided to use the state troops to defend Vicksburg. This action was criticized as a feeble resistance that could backfire, and the militia in 1863 got restive in camp. But Pettus refused to disband the militia or place it under Confederate control. Newspapers attacked him as "Pettus the Firm."

During the remainder of his term, Pettus struggled with the lack of adequate provisions, with inflation, with conscription, with finances, and with the impossibility of holding back the invading forces. As Ulysses S. Grant closed in on Vicksburg, Pettus, in desperation, proclaimed to the people of Mississippi that the state battle flag could not be "dragged to the dust by barbarian hordes on her own soil." At the same time he was calling the state to action, he was preparing to flee the capital. After battles at Raymond and Jackson, the state government was moved to Enterprise and later to Macon. In October 1863, in the regular biennial elections, Gen. Charles Clark won the governorship. Under the state constitution Pettus was ineligible for another term.

After the fall of the Confederacy, Pettus's political career was over. He was even rumored to have had some part in Lincoln's assassination. According to one account, he fled to the swamps to hide until he escaped to Arkansas, traveling under a pseudonym. There he died in 1867.

BIBLIOGRAPHY

Dubay, Robert W. *John Jones Pettus, Mississippi Fire-Eater: His Life and Times, 1813–1867.* Oxford, Miss., 1975.
Yearns, W. Buck, ed. *The Confederate Governors.* Athens, Ga., 1985.

RAY SKATES

PHOTOGRAPHY

When the Civil War commenced, there were in the United States more than 3,100 ambrotypists, daguerreotypists, calotypists, melainotypists, and others, all of whom were, by one process or another, photographers. Of their number, only a fraction practiced their trade in the seceded states. New York City alone boasted more artists than almost the entire Confederacy. Arkansas, by contrast, had a mere nineteen. Moreover, while the number of photographers grew in the North during the war, it shriveled in the South, where demands for manpower took many artists into the armies and the ever-increasing shortage of chemicals, paper, and other necessaries simply put others out of business.

Still the Confederate photographers did create and leave behind an indelible record of several aspects of their side of the conflict. Indeed, the first war photographer was a

> **The Confederate photographers did create and leave behind an indelible record of several aspects of their side of the conflict.**

Confederate, J. D. Edwards. A thirty-year-old New Hampshire native, he was working in New Orleans when the secession crisis erupted. Perhaps as early as January 1861 he was taking images of local volunteers, including excellent outdoor group portraits of members of New Orleans' colorful Washington Artillery (local artist J. W. Petty would also do a series on this unit). Then in April he took his camera to Pensacola, Florida, to produce what still remains the finest body of outdoor work by any Southern photographer. He made at least sixty-nine images of Fort Pickens, Fort Barrancas, Fort McRee, the navy yard, and the dozens of volunteer units there mustered. Many have since been lost, but about fifty are known to survive, constituting nearly half of the extant body of Confederate outdoor views.

Edwards, like all other artists at the war's outset, viewed his work as a commercial enterprise, not a historical record. He advertised his prints in the New Orleans press and sold copies, as did other artists as long as their supplies held out. While Edwards worked in large format, the South's other war artists took another direction. Just three days after the fall of Fort Sumter, the business team of James M. Osborn and F. W. Durbec of King Street, Charleston, took a camera and portable darkroom inside the still smoldering ruins of the fort to make over forty images of it and the Confederate batteries that forced it to submit. Theirs is still the most complete contemporaneous record of any Civil War event, North or South.

Edwards worked in the wet plate process, making a negative in emulsion on glass. Osborn and Durbec made stereo views, nearly duplicate images placed side by side that, when viewed in a stereo viewer, gave a three-dimensional effect. They were probably the only Confederate photographers to do so. Virtually all the rest used the wet plate process, or else made tintypes on sensitized iron plates. None was successful in marketing this work extensively. The real demand in the Confederacy was for soldier portraits, and consequently, the photographers husbanded their precious raw materials for this more lucrative trade. By comparison with barely more than 100 outdoor views of scenes and soldiers in the field that are known to have been taken, probably 100,000 or more studio portraits were made of individual Confederates.

The Confederates rarely attempted to put the camera to military use. A. D. Lytle of Baton Rouge has long been believed to have made images of Federal troops to send to Confederate leaders, but there is nothing in his surviving images that would have any military value. Richmond's David Rees did make a few 1863 images of the infamous Libby Prison, and on August 17, 1864, Georgia photographer A. J. Riddle made a series of photos of Camp Sumter at Andersonville. None of this work appears to have been inspired by anything more than commercial motivation or curiosity.

George Cook, who lived in Charleston at the beginning of the war, eventually moved to Richmond, but not before making a memorable series of prints of the interior of Fort Sumter on September 8, 1863, while the Northern fleet bombarded the garrison. He caught the only known image of a shell bursting and soon afterward made an image of three Union ironclads as they were firing. They are the only action images of the war, North or South.

By the last months of the war, most photographers were out of materials and out of business. Those who continued to operate were located in areas occupied by the Federals. With a free flow of supplies to these areas, such artists could resume their craft, and many made a lucrative business from their one-time enemies, especially in New Orleans, Baton Rouge, Nashville, Memphis, and other larger cities. Ironically, then, the largest remaining output from the Confederate photographers as a whole is pictures of Union soldiers and officers. Some of their work even found its way into the North's illustrated press via woodcuts. The Confederacy's one such newspaper, the *Southern Illustrated News,* died early and made little use of Confederate photographers' work.

Unfortunately, after the war hundreds—maybe thousands—of Confederate images disappeared, lost or destroyed as baleful reminders of defeat and devastation.

BIBLIOGRAPHY

Davis, William C., ed. *The Image of War.* 6 vols. New York, 1981–1984.
Roberts, Bobby, and Carl Moneyhon. *Portraits of Conflict.* Fayetteville, Ark., 1987.

WILLIAM C. DAVIS

PICKENS, FRANCIS W.

PICKENS, FRANCIS W. (1807–1869), U.S. congressman, diplomat, and governor of South Carolina. Born on April 7, 1807, in St. Paul's Parish, near Charleston, Pickens was the grandson of Revolutionary Gen. Andrew Pickens and son of Governor Andrew Pickens, Jr., and Susan Wilkinson. He grew up near Pendleton until his family moved to Edgefield and to Alabama. He attended South Carolina College and then practiced law and managed six plantations with 417 slaves.

In 1832 Pickens was elected to the state legislature and was prominent in the nullification crisis. In 1834 he went to Congress and was John C. Calhoun's spokesman. He urged his state to reject the Compromise of 1850 and secede, but in 1852 he supported cooperation with other states. In 1858, he became minister to Russia.

In 1860, Pickens returned home, still a cooperationist. But in November he urged secession at a rally in Edgefield. A few days later, before the legislature, he "appeal[ed] to the god of battles—if need be [to] cover the state with ruin, conflagration and blood rather than submit." Mary Boykin Chesnut called him "a fire-eater down to the ground." On December 12, he was elected governor. Aloof and overbearing, Pickens was not popular. He was elected because he had not been involved in the disputes of the past two years. Pickens wrote, "I believe it my destiny to be disliked by all who know me well."

After secession, the convention assumed extraordinary powers. It ordered Pickens to prevent the garrisoning of Federal forts in Charleston. Despite his efforts, Maj. Robert Anderson occupied Fort Sumter, and on December 30, the governor ordered the occupation of Federal property. The convention created a five-member Executive Council as a cabinet for Pickens as the head of state. It was advisory, but served as a check on the governor.

Meanwhile Pickens refused to move against Sumter. Not until the Confederacy decided to act did he demand the fort be taken. When Pickens authorized volunteers to leave the state without council approval, he was severely criticized. The council ceased to function after April 1861.

In his address to the legislature on November 5, 1861, Pickens only revived the glories of secession. When a Federal force occupied Beaufort two days later, there was a chorus of criticism regarding his lack of preparation. The convention reconvened on December 27 and ordered improvement of the state's defenses and the creation of a new Executive Council. This time the council became a plural executive, with the governor casting one vote. Pickens was furious.

The council ruled dictatorially, conscripted troops, and impressed slaves. It became increasingly unpopular, although Mary Chesnut blamed its reputation on "Pickens' miserable jealousy." In addressing the legislature in November 1862, the governor attacked the council, and it was abolished. In the closing weeks of his term, Pickens's popularity increased. He returned to Edgefield on December 18 and resumed planting.

By 1864 Pickens was "patiently waiting the catastrophe," as he wrote to Governor Andrew G. Magrath. He served as a delegate to the state constitutional convention of 1865 and died without a pardon in Edgefield on January 25, 1869.

BIBLIOGRAPHY

Edmunds, John B., Jr. *Francis W. Pickens and the Politics of Destruction.* Chapel Hill, N.C., 1986.
Yearns, W. Buck, ed. *The Confederate Governors.* Athens, Ga., 1985.

A. V. HUFF, JR.

PICKETT, GEORGE E.

PICKETT, GEORGE E. (1825–1875), major general. George Edward Pickett was born into the Virginia aristocracy on January 28, 1825, and grew up on the family plantation on the James River. He attended Richmond Academy and in 1824 received an appointment to West Point. Four unhappy years later, he graduated at the bottom of his class but fought the Mexican War with the Eighth Infantry Regiment and received two brevets for bravery. From 1849 through 1861 he served on frontier duty, first in Texas and then in Washington Territory, where in 1859 he helped provoke a near-war with the British over the possession of San Juan Island.

When the Civil War started, Pickett resigned his commission in the U.S. Army and returned to Virginia. His first commission in Confederate service was as a captain of infantry in the Provisional Army. He was quickly promoted to colonel and posted on the Rappahannock front under Theophilus H. Holmes. Although he was the most junior of all the colonels in his district, he was promoted to brigadier general in 1862, reflecting more the need for experienced officers than a high regard for his services.

The spring of 1862 found him on the peninsula as part of Joseph E. Johnston's army, James Longstreet's division. Pickett led his brigade ably at Seven Pines and (after Robert E. Lee took over) during the Seven Days' Battles, where he reported "quite severe" losses. In the Battle of Gaines' Mill, Pickett suffered his first wound, a severe shoulder injury that put him out of combat for three months. When he returned in October 1862, he became a major general in Longstreet's First Corps. His division was in reserve at the Battle of

Fredericksburg. In the spring of 1863 when two of Longstreet's divisions were detached for service in the Suffolk campaign in southeastern Virginia, Pickett went along but spent more time courting LaSalle Corbell than fighting Yankees.

Pickett did not reach the battlefield at Gettysburg until late on the second day. The next afternoon he led his division forward as part of the assault that bears his name. Three-fourths of his command became casualties in less than an hour, although Pickett himself emerged unscathed, raising questions about his whereabouts at the height of the charge. His moment of glory had come and gone.

After the army returned to Virginia he was assigned to garrison duty south of Richmond during the early part of 1864. He organized an unsuccessful attack on New Bern, North Carolina, in February 1864, which led to charges of murder of Carolina Unionists. Twenty-two prisoners from the Second U.S. North Carolina Volunteers were accused of being deserters from Confederate service and were hanged under Pickett's orders. After the war when the U.S. secretary of war and the judge advocate recommended filing formal charges against Pickett, only Ulysses S. Grant's personal intervention prevented any action from being taken.

In May 1864 Pickett distinguished himself for the last time in the war by helping "bottle up" Gen. Benjamin Butler at Bermuda Hundred. After stopping Butler, he seems to have suffered a mental breakdown in May 1864, for he took to his bed for a week or more and was relieved of duty. He returned to his command in June, after the siege of Petersburg had already started, but little was heard of him until March 1865 when Gen. Robert E. Lee sent him to hold the strategic junction at Five Forks. On April 1 his division was destroyed while he was enjoying himself at an impromptu shad-bake with Gens. Fitzhugh Lee and Thomas Lafayette Rosser two miles behind the lines. In the confusion of the retreat to Appomattox he remained with the army, although Gen. Robert E. Lee pointedly dismissed him just one day before the surrender.

After the war he fled to Canada to escape prosecution for war crimes. He returned to Virginia in 1866, sold life insurance, and participated in veterans' activities. He died suddenly on July 30, 1875, in Norfolk, Virginia, a prematurely old and embittered man. He is remembered as a giant of Confederate history, but that mythic reputation rests on the events of one afternoon, July 3, 1863. His career up to that date had been unremarkable, and afterwards it was marred by disasters and doubts.

BIBLIOGRAPHY

Freeman, Douglas S. *Lee's Lieutenants: A Study In Command.* 3 vols. New York, 1942–1944. Reprint, New York, 1986.
Harrison, Walter. *Pickett's Men: A Fragment of War History.* New York, 1870. Reprint, Gaithersburg, Md., 1984.

Hotchkiss, Jed. *Virginia.* Vol. 3 of *Confederate Military History.* Edited by Clement A. Evans. Atlanta, 1899. Vol. 4 of extended ed. Wilmington, N.C., 1987.

Pickett, LaSalle Corbell. *Pickett and His Men.* Atlanta, 1899.

Stewart, George R. *Pickett's Charge: A Microhistory of the Final Attack at Gettysburg, July 3, 1863.* Boston, 1959.

RICHARD SELCER

PLAIN FOLK

Plain folk formed the core of the South's rural middle class. Neither rich nor very poor, they were the self-sufficient farming and herding families that defined Southern agriculture. Their social and economic condition ranged from tenant farmers to middling landowners who might own as many as two hundred acres. Few plain folk owned or rented slaves, and those who did generally kept fewer than six.

Most plain folk inhabited three distinct parts of the South: the upper South, where they benefited from agricultural diversification; Piedmont regions of the lower South, where they did not have to compete directly against low-country planters; and the backwoods, areas particularly suited to open-range herding and subsistence farming. Everywhere they lived in log or plank dwellings, sparsely furnished and largely unkempt. Most houses contained only one or two rooms, although a few ambitious people had as many as seven or eight. A farmer in the latter group might even own a clock, a half dozen books, or a piano. Most plain folk achieved only an elementary ability to read and write. Their schools operated on a subscription basis, tuition often payable in farm products. The school year lasted only a few months during the winter, when it would not interfere with planting and harvesting. Socially, plain folk exhibited a cordiality and friendliness that bade all welcome to bed and board, whether strangers or neighbors. Dancing (to fiddles and banjos), drinking, gambling, and storytelling constituted their favorite social activities.

Depending on whether they relied more heavily on crops or livestock for a living, some plain folk enjoyed more leisure than others, but none seemed to labor very hard. Plain folk—and to some degree all Southerners—prized their freedom and leisure time. Most were not acquisitive, and they worked only enough to secure life's necessities. Those dependent largely on livestock let their hogs and cattle run free most of the year while they devoted minimal energy to their crops. Corn reigned as the universal crop, but, where geography allowed, tobacco or cotton also served personal and market needs. Only those plain folk who lived in regions dominated by planters had very strong ties to a market economy. Nearly all plain folk tended small vegetable patches in addition to their tilled fields, and they spent a good deal of time hunting and fishing. Some farmers achieved this balance between leisure and survival by owning or hiring slaves. Others planted only enough land to meet their needs and secure some ready cash. Even at that, much rural trade utilized barter rather than money.

Political and social tensions existed between planters and plain folk, but they were not intense or terribly divisive. The strong kinship bonds that defined Southern society preempted much potential class tension. Also, Southern families frequently ran the gamut from nonslaveholder to planter, a circumstance that produced some degree of sympathy and understanding between social classes. Equally important was the communal power of rural society. In mixed planter-plain folk neighborhoods, landholdings and wealth varied widely, and ties of mutual political and economic dependency generally outweighed class resentment. Most rural Southerners, particularly in up-country and backwoods neighborhoods, remained geographically isolated from regions dominated by the plantation economy. The resulting sense of independence and liberty defused tensions and minimized the threat of planter dominance.

White Southerners also enjoyed a common ethnic heritage and a number of shared cultural traits, including heightened sense of honor, the Protestant religion, and an interest in black slavery. Slaveholders prized the latter institution for its economic benefits, but even nonslaveholders viewed slavery as a means of controlling a potentially dangerous portion of the South's population. As abolitionist attacks increased after 1830, and as political reform provided nearly all white adult males with the vote by the 1850s, most white Southerners could rally together in a common cause.

Plain folk played a pivotal role in the history of the Confederacy, beginning with the secession crisis. Plain folk divided on that heart-wrenching issue, as did planters, poor whites, merchants, and craftsmen. Allegiance to class or vocation became less important than kinship, age, economic interests, political affiliation, and a community's racial composition when deciding whether to support or resist disunion. For instance, in those parts of the South where railroads, a market economy, and industry had gained a foothold, many plain folk endorsed secession because they believed Northern economic imperialism threatened their independence. On the other hand, the strongest resistance to secession came in the upper South, where plain folk did not believe that Abraham Lincoln's election posed an immediate threat to local autonomy and security. They became alarmed only when Lincoln, following the attack on Fort Sumter, declared the South to be in rebellion. Upper South plain folk then cursed Lincoln for embarking on "a war of conquest" and forcing them to choose between the Union and the South. Interestingly, 52 percent of the Confederacy's white population, and the majority of its plain folk, resided in the upper South states of Arkansas, North Carolina, Tennessee, and

Virginia, the last four states to secede. It is thus conceivable that war could have been avoided, or vastly shortened, had not those key states been driven out of the Union.

Plain folk initially flocked to the Stars and Bars, but their loyalty became severely tested. Young men spoke excitedly about maintaining Southern honor, defending their homes, and preserving the Southern way of life. Their enthusiasm stemmed, in part, from a romantic image of war, but they also believed that the war would be short and hugely successful. As the war bogged down and as common soldiers witnessed

> **Plain folk initially flocked to the Stars and Bars, but their loyalty became severely tested.**

the slaughter and suffering of the battlefield, they lost much of their zeal. Once experiencing the exhaustion, discomfort, and sickness of campaigning and camp life, some men declined to reenlist and drifted home.

Others received pitiful pleas from their families, begging them to return. Southern women spun cloth, tended crops, and did all they could to further the war effort, but their resilience had limits. "Unless you come home," warned one hard-pressed soldier's wife, "we must die. Last night I was aroused by little Eddie's crying . . . 'O mamma! I am so hungry!'" Such laments naturally affected soldiers. One Confederate wrote in 1863, "Our men have stayed here till they are very anxious to go home and anxious for the war to end a heap of them says there famileys is out of provisions."

Regions of the South first scorched by the flames of war—Tennessee and northern Virginia in particular—suffered much destruction, confiscation, and social upheaval. Black and white refugees flooded the South as slaves fled their masters and whites fled contesting armies. Whether staying or fleeing, plain folk lost much of their property. "In every direction there appeared a frightful scene of devastation," confessed a Union cavalryman as he surveyed the wreck of one Virginia farming community. "Furniture" was mutilated and defaced; beds were defiled and cut to pieces" windows were broken, doors torn from their hinges, houses and barns burned down." Federal forces "plundered" another farmer "of all he had, his corn, wheat, and pork, killed his hogs, drove off his beef cattle and even his milch cows." As a Northern policy of "total war" emerged after mid-1862, Southern civilians suffered increasingly greater deprivation over an ever-broadening area.

The growing centralization of the Confederate government also sapped confidence. By 1863, military conscription, suspension of habeus corpus, increased taxes, impressment of farm products and livestock, and a passport system for travel seemed to make a mockery of the doctrine of state

rights. Likewise, local communities, jealous of their autonomy, believed the authority of state government far exceeded prescribed bounds. Conscription became a particular sore point as plain folk saw many professional people, skilled urban workers, and planters exempted from military service. Cries were heard of a "rich man's war and a poor man's fight."

Making matters worse was a belief that government sought greater power while shirking its responsibility. Neither state nor national government seemed to concern itself with the suffering and privation of civilians. Complaints about hunger, labor shortages, and insufficient military defenses seemed to draw little sympathy from the governments the plain folk supported with their blood and toil. As more areas of the South fell under Federal control, discontent, caused by physical suffering and hardship, produced widespread grumbling. Politicians seemed unable or unwilling to shore up the Confederacy's flagging economy. Rampant inflation, price gouging, and illegal hoarding wreaked havoc on plain folk.

Some parts of the Confederacy populated largely by plain folk became notorious Unionist strongholds. Northwestern Arkansas, eastern Tennessee, western Virginia, and the upcountry of North Carolina, Georgia, and Alabama opposed Confederate rule throughout the war. Many communities in those places offered havens to deserters, conscripts, and tax evaders. West Virginia rejoined the Union, and vocal peace organizations thrived in Arkansas and North Carolina.

Yet, despite the steadily declining fortunes of the Confederate nation and the increased suffering of families and soldiers, most plain folk supported the Confederacy to the bitter end. The explanations are several. First, plain folk became not so much disloyal as disillusioned and discouraged, not so much anti-Confederacy as anti-authoritarian. Thousands of men deserted the Confederate army, particularly after 1863, and, insofar as plain folk comprised most of the army, it is safe to say that they supplied most of the deserters. They left the army in response to pleas from their families, and because they were worn out and discouraged. "I have a very large family of whites consisting of a wife and 10 children," wrote a Virginian seeking exemption from further military service. "I feel that I am willing to bear my full part in this struggle but having served 16 mos . . . I feel that I am worth more to the government at home to raise meat and bread." The principal complaint of this man and many like him was the power of the government to interfere in his life and challenge his independence.

Plain folk also remained loyal advocates of slavery, the existence of which was starkly challenged after 1862. Plain folk became increasingly resentful of slaveholders as the war progressed, yet they seldom renounced slavery or advocated its abolition. They supported slavery for the same reasons they had always supported it; it was part of the Southern way of life, and plain folk were not social revolutionaries. They feared that should the Confederacy fail, over 3 million freed blacks would lead the South to chaos and ruin.

Thus plain folk played a critical role in the life and death of the Confederacy. Without their consent, secession would have failed. Without their presence in army ranks, the Confederacy would have collapsed far sooner. A sense of class resentment emerged as the war dragged on, a more visible and divisive variety than anything that had preceded the war, but this was not the ultimate reason that plain folk loyalty wavered. Their will to fight faded only after they and their families had been battered into submission by hunger and a stronger military force, and after their own government had initiated policies that left little to choose between the Confederate States and the United States.

[See also Class Conflicts; Desertion; Farming; Honor; Morale; Poverty; Unionism.]

BIBLIOGRAPHY

Escott, Paul D. *After Secession: Jefferson Davis and the Failure of Confederate Nationalism.* Baton Rouge, La., 1978.

Genovese, Eugene D. "Yeomen Farmers in a Slaveholders' Democracy." *Agricultural History.* 49 (1975): 331–342.

Harris, J. William. *Plain Folk and Gentry in a Slave Society: White Liberty and Black Slavery in Augusta's Hinterlands.* Middleton, Conn., 1985.

McWhiney, Grady. *Cracker Culture: Celtic Ways in the Old South.* Tuscaloosa, Ala., 1988.

Owsley, Frank L. *Plain Folk of the Old South.* Baton Rouge, La., 1949.

Thomas, Emory M. *The Confederate Nation: 1861–1865.* New York, 1979.

Watson, Harry L. "Conflict and Collaboration: Yeomen, Slaveholders, and Politics in the Antebellum South." *Social History* 10 (1985): 273–298.

Wiley, Bell I. *The Plain Folk of the Confederacy.* Baton Rouge, La., 1944. Reprint, Gloucester, Mass., 1971.

DANIEL E. SUTHERLAND

PLANTATION

A large plantation was not just cotton fields and a stately mansion approached along an oak-lined drive. A plantation included many other buildings: the smokehouse where meat was preserved, the henhouse where poultry was raised, stables where thoroughbreds were tended, the barn where dairy cows and work animals were housed, and sheds and silos for tools, grain, and other farm necessities. In workshops scattered near the barnyard, slave artisans might craft barrels, horseshoes, furniture, and cloth for use on the plantation. Gardens were cultivated to supply herbs and vegetables. Larger plantations might also maintain a schoolhouse for white children. Some planters built chapels for family wor-

ship, and some allowed religious services for slaves as well. More commonly, large plantations included slave infirmaries and nursery facilities where older slave women tended the children of women who worked in the fields. As a safety precaution, almost all plantations had kitchen structures separate from the "big house," the main mansion that housed the planter family.

The big house, usually a two or three-storied mansion, was a visible symbol of the planter's wealth. Coming in from the front porch, a wide entrance hall might lead into a dining room, a parlor, a library, and one or more sitting rooms. In these rooms a planter could display his wealth with European furnishings and imported artwork. On the upper floors, bedrooms for family members and guests were maintained with the most comfortable and luxurious decor available. Nurseries for planters' children were located on the uppermost floors and could be reached by the servants' stairs at the back of the house.

The big house, the centerpiece of the entire plantation, might have formal flower gardens, like the famed plantings at Middleton Place outside Charleston, which took nearly ten years to complete. A separate office for the planter or overseer might be attached to the main house. Slave cabins were often built not far from the big house. Overseers sometimes lived on the plantation, in which case their modest homes might also be found not far from the slave cabins, especially in the case of absentee planters. But economic studies indicate that fewer than 30 percent of planters employed white supervisors for their slave labor. Although not all plantations contained every element listed above, the crucial components were the master's home and the slaves' domiciles, reflecting the difference in status between the black and white worlds on the plantation.

Plantations in Antebellum Society. These large plantations were not the average, but the model to which the majority of white Southerners—owners of small slaveholdings and yeomen farmers—might aspire. On the eve of the Civil War, approximately 400,000 masters owned slaves, but only 50,000 boasted plantations—farms with 20 slaves or more—and only 2,300 planters owned holdings of over 100 slaves. Yet almost all slave owners followed the planters' lead and subscribed to the cash crop system, devoting a majority of arable land to a single crop to be sold at market. And in the case of the Confederate South, cotton was king. In the border states as well as Virginia, tobacco cultivation still employed slave labor. In Missouri and Kentucky hemp growers also supplied an eager market, but these crops involved only a small proportion of slave labor. More commonly, coastal planters in the Deep South might plow and irrigate rice fields to harvest their profitable crop, and Louisiana planters could and did put slaves to use in the backbreaking cane field to produce sugar. In all areas, corn was grown to supplement these cash crops and to feed the slave work force.

Because slaves were considered property, the per capita wealth of Southern whites was nearly double that of Northern whites in 1860. With only 30 percent of the nation's free population, the South boasted 60 percent of the nation's wealthiest men. Income levels were lower for Southern whites than for Northern whites, however, and many economists continue to wrangle over the figures and their meaning.

Plantations Mobilize for War. From Abraham Lincoln's election onward, secession fever propelled the South into war. Once South Carolina broke with the Union and the rest of the Southern states fell like dominoes in the early part of 1861, war appeared inevitable. Mary Boykin Chesnut saw the handwriting on the wall: "These foolish, rash, harebrained southern lads . . . are thrilling with fiery ardor. The red-hot Southern martial spirit is in the air," she wrote in her diary.

Southern gentlemen, especially the young, knew their choices and, buoyed by secessionist bravado, enlisted when the war broke out. Confederate manhood ironically required husbands and fathers to leave the very home and loved ones they were pledging to protect. Slave-owning patriarchs had to abandon their beloved plantations. Loyal Confederate plantation mistresses had to hammer home the necessity of fighting, in case men might falter in their duty. The press and private correspondence overflowed with parables of strident patriotic females: the belle who broke an engagement because her fiancè did not enlist before the proposed wedding day, the sweethearts who sent skirts and female undergarments to shirkers.

The formation of many Confederate units demonstrated the resolve of the planter class to serve. In Selma, Alabama, the Magnolia Cadets assembled, manned entirely by local gentry. In Georgia, the Savannah Rifles, the Blue Caps, the Rattlesnakes, and many other colorful groups closed ranks against the charge that the battle would be a "rich man's war and a poor man's fight."

Class solidarity was built on the bedrock of white superiority to which most white Southerners subscribed. As contemporary Southerner William Cabell Rives proclaimed, "It is not a question of slavery at all; it is a question of race." Therefore planters necessarily blurred class lines for whites by engaging in cooperative ventures during wartime. Parthenia Hague described the way in which Alabamians forged alliances during war: "We were drawn together in a closer union, a tenderer feeling of humanity linking us all together, both rich and poor; from the princely planter, who could scarce get off his wide domains in a day's ride, and who could count his slaves by the thousand, down to the humble tenants of the log cabin on rented or leased land."

The blockade, of course, threw all within the Confederacy's borders back on their own resources. Plantations were not the hardest hit, but they did have to modify long-established patterns of production and consumption. Most significantly, the Confederate government wanted planters to switch voluntarily from the cash crop system to a more diversified subsistence strategy, which would include the planting of crops that could feed the army and civilian populations. A slogan that appeared in the press captured Confederate philosophy: "Plant Corn and Be Free, or plant cotton and be whipped."

Many planters in the Deep South, which was more dependent upon food imports than the upper South border states, adopted the "corn and bread" ideology early on. Cotton production was severely curtailed, dramatically so in the first year of the war. The South's output, 4.5 million bales in 1861, was cut to 1.5 million in 1862. Some states complied more than others; indeed, Georgia reduced its cotton output by nine-tenths from 1861 to 1862. In the coastal regions, especially Louisiana, sugar planters responded to the call, with a decline from 459 million pounds in 1861 to 87 million in 1862.

Many planters were concerned about this move and wondered how they could keep their slaves occupied and afford their upkeep under such conditions. The more conservative decided to reverse the traditional proportion of cash crops to foodstuffs; instead of the usual 600 acres of cotton to 200 acres of corn, they planted 200 acres of cotton to 600 acres of corn. A high rate of cotton production was nevertheless maintained by a minority of planters who refused to toe the patriotic line. As private speculators sought out cotton to store for future sale, a number of planters were happy to supply them, viewing war as an opportunity for profit. Indeed, many smuggled their cotton to Europe through Texas and Mexico, ignoring the government proscription. A handful of planters, oblivious to the charge of treason that could be brought against them, sought out Northern buyers. They hid their bales in remote warehouses or buried the cotton on their plantations until safe passage might be secured.

One such manipulator, James Alcorn, whose plantation was in the fertile Mississippi Delta, owned a hundred slaves and property worth nearly $250,000. When war broke out, Alcorn sent his family to Alabama and continued his prosperous trade in cotton, hiding and selling it, and avoiding both armies. In 1862 he reported that he had sold over a hundred bales, with another ninety ready to ship. Greed was his motive: "I wish to fill my pockets," he said, and boasted, "I can in five years make a larger fortune than ever. I know how to do it and will do it." At war's end, however, Alcorn decided to cater to loyalist dictates rather than side with the enemies with whom he had collaborated in matters of business. Although he had traded with Northerners, after the surrender at Appomattox he refused to take the oath of allegiance to the Union and was credited with being a great Southern patriot, much to the mystification of his former slaves.

Planters and Conscription. Planters were divided on the subject of cotton policy and many other issues, but the question that seemed to dominate the Cotton Planters Convention in Memphis during their meeting in February 1862 was not agriculture but politics. And many expressed doubt that their revolution, Confederate independence, would succeed. The intertwining of economics and politics was too tied to the fortunes of war.

When in September 1862 the Confederate Congress raised the upper age limit of conscription from thirty-five to forty-five, heads of many poor families were for the first time subject to the draft. This legislation appeared just at a time when that summer's drought had ruined most harvests. Compounding the difficulties, the Confederate Congress in October passed an even more unpopular statute that

> ## Members of the planter class already could afford to buy substitutes. . . .

became known as the Twenty-Slave Law, which exempted from army service any white man who could demonstrate that he was in a managerial role on a plantation with twenty slaves or more; both owners and overseers qualified. This law was intended ostensibly both to control the slave population and to keep the Confederacy fed. But the argument that the law would benefit all whites stuck in the craw of most white Southerners. Even when in May 1863 exempted slaveholders were taxed $500 (to fund the distribution of food for soldiers' families), civilians and especially soldiers were not mollified.

Throughout the war, only 4,000 to 5,000 men received exemptions under this law; indeed, only 3 percent of those men who claimed exemptions took them on the basis of the Twenty-Slave Law. On 85 percent of those plantations that qualified for exemptions, none was taken. Nevertheless, the perception of favoritism rankled. Members of the planter class already could afford to buy substitutes, and now any choice to sit out the war was ratified by government legitimation. Attitudes may have been regionalized: within the Deep South more planters perhaps took advantage of the system, sparking more resentment. There were 1,500 exemptions issued in Alabama alone and of the nineteen categories of exemption, only medical disability was employed more often than the Twenty-Slave Law. Thus, the law was a public relations disaster, to say the least. Mississippian James Phelan wrote a warning to Jefferson Davis: "It has aroused a spirit of rebellion in some places, I am informed, and bodies of men have banded together to resist; whilst in the army it is said it only needs some daring men to raise the standard to develop a revolt."

White women, too, voiced their alarm over conscription. Many left behind in parishes and counties without adequate male assistance appealed to their government. Late in the

war a group of women in South Carolina sent a plaintive letter to the governor:

> We are personally acquainted with Erwin Midlen for over three years and do no that he is a sickly and feeble man and we do Believe that he is not able for service in the field. We are informed that he is in the 56th year of his age. And we do further sware that he has done all our hawling for the last three years and attended to all our domestic business as we could not Procure any other man to do—see to our hawling and other business as our Husbands are all in the army and some of them killed and some died in service.

The seventeen women who signed begged that Midlen be spared military service. The governor's ruling on the matter remains unknown.

The Decline of Plantation Agriculture and Planter Morale. Even more disheartening to both the Confederate government and the Southern farmer was the fact that all agricultural indicators in the South spelled decline, while prosperity reigned in the fertile regions of the Midwest. Although over 75,000 farm boys left Iowa for Union service and over 90,000 came from Wisconsin, Northern agriculture did not suffer. Iowa and Wisconsin both reported improved acreage and grain production as well as a rise in farm income during the war.

The South's declining agriculture created a dilemma. The army needed fresh troops, but the home front required care as well. President Davis, among others, harped on the dangers of deserted or unproductive plantations; these Cassandras were unpopular yet prophetic. One advised: "We are today in greater danger of whipping our selves than being whipped by our enemy." Sinking morale and declining food supplies contributed to gloomy predictions of further degradation. The crippling of cotton production undermined the ruling elite's sense of mastery and helped pave the way for defeat. There were countless examples of reduced fortunes: by 1864 James Heyward of South Carolina planted only 330 acres in rice and 90 in provisions; a mere one-tenth of his land holdings were under cultivation.

Heyward at least was able to continue planting. Many slave owners were driven off their plantations, losing homes and livelihoods in one fell swoop. Some former mistresses, hoping to elude Federal troops, were reduced to living in cabins in the woods. In the first few months of the war, Confederates feared the unknown threat of a Union army, but by 1862 too many Southerners knew firsthand the toll such an invasion extracted. In December 1863 the Confederate Congress railed against the enemy:

> Houses are pillaged and burned, churches are defaced, towns are ransacked, clothing of women and infants is stripped from their persons, jewelry and momentoes of the

dead are stolen, mills and implements of agriculture are destroyed, private salt works are broken up, the introduction of medicines is forbidden.

Indeed, plantation mistresses turned to the woods as "nature's drugstore" and for other necessities of life. One woman reported that after the enemy left her home she was "forced to go out into the woods nearby and with my two little boys pick up fagots to cook the scanty food left to me." The scorched-earth policy of William Tecumseh Sherman and other Union generals reduced many plantations to ashes and permanently impaired the planters' ability to recover.

Morale was at a low ebb and hopes were being steadily dashed against the shoals of wartime reality. Those planters who stockpiled their cotton crop were in as much danger of losing it to the Confederate cause as to invading Northerners. It was the policy of the Confederate army to burn cotton whenever Federals moved within striking distance. This was an unpopular measure, to say the least, especially at a time when planters were pressing the government to buy their unsold crops. To have their hopes go up in smoke at the hands of soldiers in gray rather than the hated Federals created conflicting loyalties.

Some of these policies alienated planters to the point of political disaffection. In the 1870s the Southern Claims Commission was empowered to rule on the petitions of planters who declared both their pro-Union sympathies during wartime and the destruction of property by Union troops. Of the 700 claims filed to obtain damages of over $10,000, only 191 were successful, and a mere 224 of the 800 and more who complained of property losses of less than $10,000 were granted.

Perhaps no more than 5 percent of the planter class were Union loyalists during wartime. But many more simply resisted the entreaties of the Confederate government to perform patriotically. As many as 25 percent of the slaveholders in Virginia refused to comply with the government's requisition of their property—slaves—in 1864. Both the loss of labor and the strong resistance combined to weaken the Confederacy's ability to win its war for independence.

The End of Slavery and the Plantation System. The dangers within arose not only from recalcitrant planters but from the omnipresent threat of slave resistance. John Edwin Fripp of Saint Helena Island off the coast of South Carolina was able to write: "I am happy to say my negroes have acted orderly and well all the time, none going off excepting one or two Boys who accompanied the yanks for plunder but have returned home and appear quite willing to work." Nevertheless, Fripp's experience was the exception rather than the rule. The majority of planters made careful notations in their logs about African Americans deserting plantations. Whenever Union troops moved into a region, slaves fled behind enemy lines. Many, if not most planters, felt wounded

when their slaves abandoned the plantation for "Lincoln land." They were especially angered by those African Americans who led Federal troops to storehouses of food and buried treasure—the family silver and other heirlooms. Even after the issuance of the Emancipation Proclamation in January 1863, slave owners mistakenly placed their faith in paternalism. As one woman complained bitterly, "Those we loved best, and who loved us best—as we thought—were the first to leave us."

Planters who feared insurrection, however, were pleasantly surprised, in contrast to those whose cherished notions of slave loyalty were disappointed. Historian James Roark has suggested: "Slavery did not explode; it disintegrated . . . eroded plantation by plantation, often slave by slave, like slabs of earth slipping into a Southern stream." Some planters responded by moving their slaves away from approaching Federal troops, but as the war dragged on, there was nowhere left to hide and hundreds of thousands of African Americans made their way to freedom.

During the fall of 1863 over 20,000 slaves were recruited for service in the Union army in the Mississippi valley alone. Jane Pickett, a plantation mistress and a refugee, recounted the planters' predicament: "The negroes in most instances refused to leave with their masters, and in some cases have left the plantations in a perfect stampede. Mississippi is almost depopulated of its black population." By the winter of 1864–1865, slave owners were reduced to a lengthy process of negotiation with those African Americans who remained. Emma LeConte of Berkeley County, South Carolina, lamented: "The field negroes are in a dreadful state; they will not work, but either roam the country, or sit in their houses. . . . I do not see how we are to live in this country without any rule or regulation. We are afraid now to walk outside of the gate."

The fall, then, came from within, as historian Armstead Robinson has argued, as well as from without. The plantation South simply crumbled, unable to withstand African American challenges to slavery as well as the burdens of blockades, wartime production, and invading armies. The superhuman task of retaining the illusion of white superiority in the face of black resistance, African American independence, and the final blow—the full-blown glory of black manhood in the form of African American Union soldiers—combined to destroy Confederate dreams. Economic ruin further eroded the fragile leadership of the struggling nation. Confederate wealth (excluding slave property) declined nearly 45 percent during the war.

In February 1864 the Confederate Congress authorized impressment of free blacks and slaves for noncombatant military roles, and by November 1864 President Davis was advocating gradual emancipation and military use of African Americans. Davis wrongly assumed that Southerners would choose to give up slavery rather than go down to defeat. But slaveholders stuck to their guns. The Confederacy had been founded because of the perceived threat that Northern Republicans presented to the institution of slavery, and proslavery stalwarts stayed the course: "We want no confederate Government without our institutions." These and other sentiments have prompted historian David Herbert Donald to suggest that the Confederacy might ironically have "died from democracy." Whatever the cause, the plantation system, with its fortunes so tied to black labor, died along with slavery.

The surrender at Appomattox triggered a long, slow process of recovery, but planters never actually recovered. Rather, they devoted their time and energies to promoting romantic legends of the Lost Cause—seeking historical justification rather than economic recovery. Planters' devotion to an imagined past was embodied in Margaret Mitchell's mythic re-creation of Tara and Twelve Oaks, perhaps the most famous plantations of all, in her 1936 novel, *Gone with the Wind*. Despite such fictional exaggerations, most plantations were scarred visibly by the war. And even those not damaged by wartime destruction indisputably suffered a permanent stain—the psychic blight of Confederate defeat.

[*See also* Class Conflict; Conscription; Cotton; Impressment; Planters; Rice; Slavery; Sugar; Tobacco.]

BIBLIOGRAPHY

Clinton, Catherine. *Tara Revisited: Women, War, and the Plantation Legend*. New York, forthcoming.

Durden, Robert. *The Gray and the Black: The Confederate Debate on Emancipation*. Baton Rouge, La., 1972.

Massey, Mary Elizabeth. *Refugee Life in the Confederacy*. Baton Rouge, La., 1964.

Mohr, Clarence. *On the Threshold of Freedom: Masters and Slaves in Civil War Georgia*. Athens, Ga., 1986.

Roark, James L. *Masters without Slaves: Southern Planters in the Civil War and Reconstruction*. New York, 1977.

CATHERINE CLINTON

PLANTERS

Although plantation slavery never dominated the entire South, the plantation belt contained the region's best farmland, the major portion of its wealth, and the majority of its slaves. It gave rise to a planter class that, though less than 5 percent of the white population, dominated local and state governments and shaped regional institutions in its own interests. The sprawling plantation South was vast enough to encompass a variety of planter types and personalities. Whether old money or new, paternalist or pure capitalist, planters (owners of twenty or more slaves) formed a distinctive and self-conscious elite that was united in its commit-

ment to preserving slavery as the basis of its power, wealth, and identity. From the moment of secession to the end of the Civil War, plantation slavery remained the touchstone of planters' existence.

During the secession crisis of 1860 and 1861, planters divided on whether the defense of slavery required the destruction of one national government and the creation of another. Those who resisted Southern independence showed no less dedication to slavery. They argued that slavery was safer—for the moment, at least—within the Union than out of it. Still, there was a strong correlation between

> ## Large slaveholders suffered less than plain folk, but they yelled louder.

slavery and support for secession. In general, the greater the density of slaves and slaveholders in a state's population, the greater the support for Southern independence. By spring 1861, planters had led eleven states out of the Union. The Confederate States of America became home to some 43,000 planters (plus those in Arkansas, for which the census returns are incomplete), and no more than a tiny fraction, perhaps one in twenty, remained loyal to the United States.

Planters greeted war with a burst of Confederate patriotism. They rushed to buy Confederate bonds and marched off at the head of regiments they organized and often outfitted with their own money. They eagerly assumed prominent positions in their new nation's government. Confident that cotton was king, they looked forward to bringing the North to its knees and cotton-importing Europe to their side. Victory would secure both the preservation of slavery and Southern independence. To planters, it was obvious that slavery and Southern nationhood went hand in hand.

But mobilization for war required that the government in Richmond build armies and regiment the home front. Government, which traditionally had borne lightly on the people, reached more and more deeply into civilian life, restricted personal freedom, imposed unprecedented burdens, and demanded unimaginable sacrifices. As the war lengthened, Richmond grew increasingly single-minded in its commitment to political independence and more and more willing to subordinate all other interests to that goal. Confederate action forced planters to reveal that they assigned different values to independence and slavery.

At first, Richmond was sensitive to the interests of the planter class, which had brought the new nation into being. A raft of class legislation favored the elite. The Conscription Act of 1861 provided for hiring substitutes, but the cost put the option beyond the reach of most nonslaveholders. The Twenty-Slave Law exempted one able-bodied white male from military service for every twenty slaves on a plantation. Nonslaveholders were quick to point out that the provision allowed many overseers and planters' sons to escape the fighting. The gentry defended the government's favoritism, arguing that without white men to supervise slaves, they would refuse to work, run off, and threaten white women. Only well-ordered plantations could provide the Confederacy with the food and fiber necessary for victory.

In time, however, the elite experienced the rigors of war and the sting of intrusive Confederate policy. Large slaveholders suffered less than plain folk, but they yelled louder. At first, privation meant no more than learning to live without luxuries, but in time necessities such as salt and medicines grew scarce. Planters tolerated privation better than the growing government intervention into plantation affairs. Before the war, as the daughter of a Mississippi planter put it, "each plantation was a law unto itself." Laws had existed to regulate slaves, rarely planters. But as Richmond centralized power in order to fight efficiently, it increasingly ran roughshod over prewar notions of the proper relationship between government and citizens. Jealous of their prerogatives, large slaveholders fought fiercely to maintain their authority, even against their own government, the cornerstone of which, Vice President Alexander H. Stephens had said, was slavery.

Early in the war, state governments and public opinion demanded that planters cease growing cotton, perceived as a selfish act, and start growing corn, vital to the Confederate war effort. Some complied voluntarily, but others resisted. Later, when the Federal blockade choked cotton exports, planters had little choice but to switch to food production. With most white men away at war, responsibility for supervising the transformation often fell to white women. Female planters were not unknown before the war—thousands of women legally owned plantations—but few actually managed their estates. Planters kept up a heavy correspondence with their wives, and plantation women successfully oversaw the formidable adjustment from staples to food crops. But without cotton, planters' incomes shriveled.

With every passing month, Richmond became more entangled in plantation affairs. Confederate officials told planters what and with whom they could trade and took or burned the cotton or sugar crops when they deemed it prudent. Officials dragged white men away from the plantation and impressed food, livestock, tools, animals, and wagons, paying whatever prices they saw fit in notes. The government created currency and tax systems that planters perceived as discriminatory, even though Richmond never taxed slaves. Confederate troops raided plantations, picking them as clean as Federal soldiers did. Hatred of the North soared, but with few Southern military victories or diplomatic successes, love of the Confederacy did not blossom correspondingly. Instead, planter support for Richmond faded.

Planters found Confederate impressment of slaves particularly troubling. Although slaves were barred from combat, they were theoretically available for military labor. But slaveholders resisted giving up their bondsmen to build fortifications, standing on principle—they felt a man had a right to control his slave property—and complaining that the military mistreated slaves and returned them in poor health and recalcitrant. Planters believed they had enough difficulty maintaining control without the government adding to their troubles. When the war began, they made every effort to tighten controls over slaves and those who came into contact with them. They buttressed slave patrols and canceled exemptions from duty. They called home slaves who were on hire in cities and voided their passes to travel and visit families. But nothing they could do restored the stable order upon which slavery depended.

When the war reached the plantations, it sent slavery into a spiral of disintegration. As traditional routines crumbled, planters complained that slaves were "demoralized," a generic term that referred to every sort of misbehavior from rudeness to outright rebellion. Accustomed to respect and obedience from servants they had convinced themselves were loyal and loving, planters were beset by insolence, disobedience, theft, and malingering. Moreover, whenever proximity to Union soldiers made escape possible, the slaves ran away. As their owners' power eroded, they claimed their freedom bit by bit. On many estates, effective control shifted from the "big house" to the slave quarters. Before the war ended, the master-slave relationship was in tatters.

Slavery died for many reasons, but planters pointed the finger of blame at Richmond almost as often as at Washington. On January 1, 1863, Abraham Lincoln issued the Emancipation Proclamation, which planters denounced as an invitation to slaves to rise up in bloody "servile insurrection." Less than two years later, Jefferson Davis, in an equally revolutionary move, proposed that the Confederacy itself arm and free its slaves. The government had concluded that only by sacrificing slavery could the South win its independence. Planters branded Richmond's plan an outrageous betrayal. A partial version of the plan became law on March 13, 1865, but planters gave up their slaves only when Union soldiers appeared at their gates.

In parts of the Confederacy, however, Federal troops arrived long before the war ended, freeing the slaves in each area they occupied. Planters often fled before their arrival, taking their slaves with them to refuge elsewhere. But in the lower Mississippi valley, many stayed and participated in federally sponsored wartime experiments with free black labor. Union officials sought to resurrect the devastated sugar and cotton economies and to restore the link between planter self-interest and political loyalty. Because the system of contract labor they initiated resembled the South's prewar labor system, some planters found reason for hope. But Federal efforts to maintain control of blacks and to stabilize agriculture did not revive planters' material fortunes. Most plantation owners saw little value in free black labor and no reason to pledge allegiance to a government that had made black freedom a war aim.

On the other hand, planters no longer sympathized with Richmond either. They were unwilling to defend a government that, for whatever reason, did not defend them. Indeed, complying with government policy meant collaborating in their own destruction. Yeomen also felt alienated from their government, but they believed that Richmond favored the wealthy and failed to make them carry their fair share of the burden. Planters judged the matter of sacrifice differently. No longer loyal to Richmond and unable to transfer loyalty to Washington, they withdrew to their plantations and did what they could to help themselves. They grew increasingly ready to evade conscription, desert from the army, plant cotton rather than corn, and engage in cotton trading with whomever would buy. In the end, they chose the homestead over the homeland.

By the time of the surrender at Appomattox, the planters' world lay in shambles. The North had triumphed over the South, free labor had triumphed over slave labor, and industrial capitalism had triumphed over the political economy of slavery. Because of remarkable miscalculation, the South's planters went from being one of the strongest agrarian classes in the western world to being the weakest. War had destroyed the very institution that secession was intended to secure. Armies had turned plantations into battlefields, hospitals, barracks, feed and fuel centers, and labor pools. Large slaveholders had been devastated physically, economically, and psychologically. Thousands had died; thousands more had lost their sons, their slaves, their life savings. A few planters weathered the storm—those who had extensive Northern investments, those who had hidden away cotton and could reap dollar-a-pound prices, those who could attract rich Northerners to lease their plantations. But war had impoverished the overwhelming majority. Stripped of slaves, wealth, and power, hundreds fled the region, although most saw no choice but to remain.

Planters understood that defeat and emancipation meant a revolution in their lives. They were painfully aware of what Jefferson Davis called a "break in time." The old order was gone, but the new had not yet emerged. Proslavery doctrine had predicted that emancipation would lead to racial warfare, social anarchy, and economic collapse, and, indeed, planters found themselves surrounded by devastation. Northern radicals demanded even more: confiscation and perhaps banishment to stamp out the South's aristocratic "traitors." Planters welcomed peace, but they found little reason for optimism. In their minds, defeat had not invalidated the basic assumptions that had undergirded their belief in slavery: that blacks were inherently and immutably lazy, that without total

subordination they were dangerous and destructive, and that without coercion they would not work. "Nothing could overcome this rooted idea," a visiting newspaper man noted in 1865, "that the negro was worthless, except under the lash." Unwilling to admit that they had been wrong about slavery or about the nature of the Union, planters had little choice but to give up their dream of an independent slaveholders' republic and to go on farming in a slaveless South.

[*See also* Class Conflict; Conscription; Cotton; Currency, *overview article;* Impressment; Plantation; Rice; Slavery; Sugar; Taxation; Tobacco.]

BIBLIOGRAPHY

Ash, Stephen W. *Middle Tennessee Society Transformed, 1860–1870: War and Peace in the Upper South.* Baton Rouge, La., 1988.

Escott, Paul D. *After Secession: Jefferson Davis and the Failure of Confederate Nationalism.* Baton Rouge, La., 1978.

Foner, Eric. *Reconstruction: America's Unfinished Revolution, 1863–1877.* New York, 1988.

McPherson, James M. *Battle Cry of Freedom: The Civil War Era.* New York, 1988.

Owens, Harry P., and James J. Cooke, eds. *The Old South in the Crucible of War.* Jackson, Miss., 1983.

Potter, David M. "The Historian's Use of Nationalism and Vice Versa." In *The South and the Sectional Conflict.* Baton Rouge, La., 1968.

Roark, James L. *Masters without Slaves: Southern Planters in the Civil War and Reconstruction.* New York, 1977.

Thomas, Emory M. *The Confederate Nation, 1861–1865.* New York, 1979.

Wayne, Michael. *The Reshaping of Plantation Society: The Natchez District, 1860–1880.* Baton Rouge, La., 1983.

JAMES L. ROARK

POINT LOOKOUT PRISON

After the Battle of Gettysburg, the United States provided for the sudden increase of prisoners by opening a depot on Point Lookout, Maryland, the peninsula formed where the Potomac River joins Chesapeake Bay. The land was flat, mostly sandy with some marsh, and barely above the water. Because of the Point's proximity to the eastern battlefields, the government had already found it convenient to lease this prewar resort locale for a hospital that was subsequently used, in part, for wounded Confederates.

In late July 1863, quartermaster officers opened a camp for 10,000 men to be housed in old tents. Though the War Department rejected later proposals for barracks, there were wooden cookhouses. The camp consisted of two pens surrounded by fourteen-foot high fences, one for enlisted men of about twenty-three acres and a smaller one for the officers infrequently and temporarily held at the prison. With 14,489 inmates in July 1864 and an exceptionally large population of 19,786 during the exchange of prisoners in May 1865, this was the largest Union prison and with its overall total of some 52,000 was probably the largest prison of either side. Officially called Camp Hoffman after Commissary General of Prisoners William Hoffman, the prison was usually referred to by the name of its location.

Point Lookout's first commander was Brig. Gen. Gilman Marston. There were complaints, even from Union inspectors, about physical conditions under his and his successors' management. In July 1864, Brig. Gen. James Barnes, a Massachusetts-born West Pointer, took command, and he and his provost marshall, Maj. Allen G. Brady, made some improvements. The guard force at first consisted of troops drawn from the field, but these were rapidly succeeded by white semidisabled troops from the Veteran Reserve Corps and newly recruited blacks, often recent slaves. To the latter the Confederates usually reacted contemptuously and hostilely, feelings frequently returned by the black soldiers. With occasional exceptions, relations between the races were unfriendly. Partly because of the prisoners' unhappiness, the Federal authorities were able to recruit over a thousand of them who became "galvanized Yankees" to fight the western Indians.

Far more prisoners continued to endure the hardships of a pen unshaded in summer and frigid in winter. The wood needed to heat the tents was limited in quantity as were blankets and clothing. The United States attempted simply to prevent nakedness and often discouraged outsiders from sending such items. The official ration of food was also limited, and prisoners caught crabs and made jewelry, fans, and even pictures of the prison to trade for additional food. A particular grievance concerned the quality of the water. Some was shipped in, but much came from shallow wells that rapidly became polluted by sewage from the camp's surface. This contributed to diseases, which, along with less common causes like shootings by guards, accounted for 3,584 deaths, according to Federal records, or in the opinion of a recent historian, over 4,000. Such mortality and the hunger and cold experienced by the prisoners left a postwar legacy of bitterness.

Inevitably some prisoners attempted escape. Prior to the completion of the fence it was possible with luck to run the sentry line at night and get away with help from the strongly pro-Southern inhabitants of the vicinity. After the prisoners were surrounded by boards, the river offered an alternative for those willing to risk swimming with the help of some form of flotation device. From the beginning, Federal authorities stationed naval vessels in the river to forestall any attempt to use boats for escape or rescue.

The accessibility of the equivalent of a small army of reinforcements tempted the Confederates to try to recover the captives. In the winter of 1863–1864, Robert E. Lee formu-

lated a scheme to throw across the Potomac a force of Marylanders drawn from his army to free the prisoners. In July 1864, he added the release of the prisoners to the mission of Jubal Early's Maryland raid. But the partial failure of Early's raid caused the abandonment of the plan. The alarmed Federals immediately built earthworks mounting cannons and a stockade to cut off either attack from the mainland or an uprising from within the prison. They also reduced the temptation for a rescue by moving half of the prison population farther north.

The prison camp continued to operate on a reduced scale until February 1865, when exchange resumed. Union authorities wished to send troops from western states to be exchanged in the East (believing that these would be least likely to retake the field for the Confederates) and hence began to accumulate such troops at Point Lookout. When the fall of Richmond disrupted exchange, the Union retained additional prisoners at Lookout, crowding the prison to its utmost. But the end of the war produced a speedy exodus of prisoners who took the oath of allegiance. By July 1865, the last were gone and the prison was abandoned.

The government preserved the camp's graves, which were moved several times to a nearby national cemetery containing both U.S. and Maryland monuments. The prison site reverted to recreational purposes with considerable portions vanishing through erosion. The remainder is today a Maryland state park.

[*See also* Early's Washington Raid.]

BIBLIOGRAPHY

Beitzell, Edwin W. *Point Lookout Prison Camp for Confederates.* Abell, Md., 1972.

Byrne, Frank. "Prison Pens of Suffering." In *Fighting for Time.* Edited by William C. Davis. Vol. 4 of *The Image of War, 1861–1865.* Garden City, N.Y., 1983.

Hesseltine, William B. *Civil War Prisons: A Study in War Psychology,* Columbus, Ohio, 1930. Reprint, New York, 1964.

Maryland State Park Foundation, Inc. *Sketches from Prison: A Confederate Artist's Record of Life at the Point Lookout Prisoner-of-War Camp.* Baltimore, Md., 1990.

FRANK L. BYRNE

POLITICS

Like most aspects of life in the South, politics underwent profound changes during the Civil War. The predominant issues of the prewar period, secession and union, were supplanted by war-related controversies. Parties disappeared, replaced by a wartime unity that only barely masked a continuation of antebellum partisan hostility. Elections changed as well, as politicians adopted new standards of campaigning that seemed more appropriate for a nation at war. The electorate, of course, remained the same, as did most of the prominent personalities involved in politics. But even these groups would be permanently altered by the War between the States.

Political Issues

The greatest political changes in the South during the Civil War concerned issues debated by politicians and voters. In the 1840s and 1850s, a variety of national and local issues determined the tenor of Southern political discourse. Most Southerners in the antebellum period believed that state rights were paramount, that the right to hold slaves in the territories could not be abridged by Congress, and that tariff rates ought to be lower. They disagreed, however, about issues such as temperance, government subsidies for railroads, and whether secession was the best way to guarantee the South's rights.

The creation of the Confederacy rendered these issues either moot or insignificant. At first, there were no questions of importance to fill this void. Believing it necessary to present a united front to the enemy, candidates in the elections for the First Confederate Congress conducted virtually no campaigns. Office seekers often placed notices in the local press informing the public of their candidacy, but these announcements rarely differed from one aspirant to another. They uniformly proclaimed themselves to be ardent supporters of Southern independence, proponents of a vigorous prosecution of the war, and so forth.

After the Confederate war effort began to falter, differences concerning the conduct of the war became the focus of political contention. One of the most hotly debated issues concerned the Confederate government's conscription system. Sensing their constituents' displeasure with this "horror of conscription," many candidates running for seats in the Second Congress condemned the policy. Some did so on the grounds that it detracted from state and local defense efforts, while others argued that it placed too much power in the hands of President Jefferson Davis. Even more controversial was the provision added to the law in September 1862 that exempted from military duty one white man on every plantation containing twenty or more slaves. Administration defenders insisted that the clause was necessary in order to maintain agricultural production as well as to prevent disciplinary problems with slaves. Nonetheless, by pointing out that the exemption provisions of the conscription law "made a broad and degrading line of distinction between . . . the silken son of pleasure and the hardy son of the soil," many candidates for the Second Congress were able to defeat incumbents who supported the administration's conscription policy.

Another issue that sparked controversy was the suspension of habeas corpus. Local judges were enabling army deserters to avoid prosecution by issuing writs for those held

under Confederate authority. Congress attempted to eliminate this practice by granting Davis the power to suspend the writ and declare martial law as well if necessary, and it was primarily a perception of the overzealous use of this latter proviso that brought about the preponderance of disaffection. As with the conscription issue, most of the outcry against suspending habeas corpus came from radical state rights advocates. Among the most vociferous critics of the suspension were Georgia Governor Joseph E. Brown, North Carolina Governor Zebulon Vance, and Vice President Alexander H. Stephens. "Away with the idea of getting independence first, and looking for liberty afterwards," Stephens declared. "Our liberties, once lost, may be lost forever." Davis, however, suspended the writ for only sixteen months in all, and his abridgments of civil liberties were never as frequent or severe as those carried out by his counterpart in Washington.

The government's taxation policies also caused political divisions. Runaway inflation had by the spring of 1863 forced Congress to find alternative means of financing the war. Although a variety of taxes was imposed, the one that gen-

> **One of the most hotly debated issues concerned the Confederate government's conscription system.**

erated the most discontent was the 10 percent tax-in-kind levied on agricultural products. Poor yeoman farmers complained that it was unfair for the government to take 10 percent of their meager surpluses, while city dwellers such as clerks and teachers paid only 2 percent of their income. Moreover, the legislation left the principal possession of the wealthy—slaves—untaxed. The administration's advocates argued that slaves could not be taxed without a census, something that could not be undertaken during a war, but this provided little comfort to the impoverished farmer whose produce was hauled away while his rich neighbor's slaves escaped taxation. The army's impressment policy, by which it purchased whatever supplies it wanted from nearby farmers in exchange for worthless promissory notes, also bred resentment toward the Richmond government. Many Southerners harboring political ambitions used opposition to the tax-in-kind and impressment policies to unseat incumbents in the 1863 elections.

As the war grew longer and hopes of victory became increasingly remote, peace became the overriding political issue in the Confederacy. At first, peace proponents sought to win independence simply by negotiating with the U.S. government. They asserted that Davis was stubbornly continuing the fighting even though the South might gain its sovereignty at the negotiating table. The president argued, however, that a peace overture would be fruitless and would irreparably damage public morale as well. Later on, and especially after the defeats at Gettysburg and Vicksburg, the peace movement became a haven for a wide variety of politicians. Some, such as W. W. Boyce of South Carolina, merely believed that a well-defined peace policy would bring about Southern independence more quickly by making it easier for Peace Democrats in the North to oust Abraham Lincoln. Others, such as William W. Holden of North Carolina, seemed to favor peace even if Southern independence had to be sacrificed, and he proposed that North Carolina initiate its own negotiations if Davis refused to do so. "We would prefer our independence, if that were possible," one of Holden's followers stated, "but let us prefer *reconstruction* infinitely to *subjugation.*" Campaigning primarily on this issue and holding election rallies that administration supporters characterized as treasonous (the Stars and Stripes were supposedly flown at some of these gatherings), Holden's "Conservative party" won widespread support, especially in western North Carolina, and captured at least five, and perhaps as many as eight, of the state's ten seats in the 1863 congressional elections. In Georgia and Alabama, as well as the more isolated up-country regions of other states, candidates for the Second Congress managed to defeat incumbents by stressing the peace issue.

Disappearance of Parties

Ordinarily, political parties would have served as the conduit through which voters would express their opinions on these issues. In the Confederacy, however, there were no formal parties. This resulted in part from the belief that a political process unencumbered by partisan squabbling would best aid the war effort. Yet while the same belief pervaded the North, partisanship there subsided only temporarily, and the parties themselves never ceased operations. Why, then, did parties so abruptly disappear in the Confederacy?

The answer lies primarily in the decline of the two-party system in the South during the 1850s. After the demise of the Whig party in 1854 and 1855, Southerners who opposed the "Democracy" sought alternative affiliations. At first, it appeared as if the anti-immigrant Know-Nothing movement, which eventually became known as the American party, might win the loyalty of former Whigs, but the dismal performance in 1856 of its presidential candidate, Millard Fillmore, doomed that party to extinction. The Constitutional Union party captured a respectable 39 percent of the Southern vote in the presidential election of 1860, but because that organization had opposed secession as a means to guarantee the South's rights, it too disintegrated soon after the canvass. Recognizing no further reason to continue operations and believing that the energy previously exerted on its behalf would better serve the war effort, the Democratic party ceased functioning soon after the completion of the secession process.

Southerners were proud of the fact that their nation contained no political parties. Like those who had started the previous American revolution, most Southerners believed that in an ideal society there would be no parties, because more often than not these organizations degenerated into self-serving associations that placed the perpetuation of their own power ahead of the public good. Thus, the president pro tem of the First Confederate Congress congratulated legislators that "the spirit of party has never shown itself for an instant in your deliberations." Parties were not merely absent

> **. . . a political process unencumbered by partisan squabbling would best aid the war effort.**

from the floors of Confederate legislative bodies. Party offices closed and officials found new work. In addition, no caucuses were held, no fund-raising took place, no propaganda was distributed, and no party committees directed communications from the electorate to the officeholders and back.

Although Southerners were proud that their nation lacked partisan political organizations, there were drawbacks to this state of affairs that became clear only in retrospect. For example, the lack of parties created a major impediment to the smooth and successful implementation of Davis's legislative agenda. In the North, Republican congressmen and governors understood that publicly opposing Lincoln's policies would make them pariahs within the Republican party and doom their political careers, convincing most of them that they should support the president even if they privately harbored doubts about his proposals. For the same reasons, party members were obligated to support their organization's policies after the legislation was implemented. In the South, however, obstructionist governors such as Brown and Vance were able to paralyze the war effort because, as historian James M. McPherson has noted, "the centrifugal tendencies of state's rights were not restrained by the centripetal force of party."

The lack of organized parties created other difficulties as well. For example, without the existence of a unified opposition party, Davis could not convincingly argue that his policies were superior to the program of his opponents, because he could not focus on a single opposition agenda with which to compare his own. In addition, the absence of parties created frustration for voters, because they could not identify those responsible for the government's program and register approval or disapproval on election day by voting a party's ticket. Finally, without parties to oversee the distribution of patronage, these appointees could no longer be used as a means to mobilize support for either the administration's policies or friends.

Despite the absence of formal political parties, historians have noted an "unconscious spirit of party" in the national and state governments of the Confederacy. Each of Davis's original cabinet nominees, for example, had been Democrats before the war. Furthermore, many states made deliberate decisions to send one ex-Democrat and one ex-Whig to the Confederate Senate. Nonetheless, statistical studies of the Confederate Congress have demonstrated that an office-holder's stance on secession and the proximity of his district to the war zones tended to play a larger role than prior party affiliation in determining the representative's stance on the measures before him. Yet even these factors were far from reliable predictors of congressional voting behavior. To a much greater extent than perhaps at any previous time in American history, congressmen seem to have genuinely voted according to their consciences on most issues before the Confederate Congress, and as a result no single consistently identifiable opposition grouping ever emerged.

Nonetheless, the public noticed the formation of a number of small opposition factions in Congress. One, which concentrated its attention on the peace issue, coalesced around the leadership of Boyce. The bulk of the Second Congress's North Carolina delegation, which seemed to oppose virtually everything proposed by the administration, was another such faction. The single individual most commonly identified as the leader of the opposition in Congress, however, Senator Louis T. Wigfall of Texas, belonged to neither of these groups. Formerly a fire-eating Democrat, Wigfall had initially supported Davis's most controversial proposals. It seems to have been a perceived insult concerning Wigfall's advice on a cabinet selection, combined with his admiration for another emerging foe of Davis, Gen. Joseph E. Johnston (under whom Wigfall had served during the first year of the war), that pushed the Texan into the opposition camp. Outside of Congress, many of Davis's opponents took their cues from a triumvirate of Georgians: Stephens, Brown, and ex-general and Confederate secretary of state Robert Toombs, who did everything in their power to embarrass the president and discredit his policies. These groupings, however, never assumed the official trappings of prewar political organizations; they more closely resembled the cliques and factions of the pre-Jacksonian era.

These opposition groups always constituted a small minority in the Confederate Congress. The administration's supporters, like the Southern Democratic party that had preceded them, were dominated by the same prominent personalities and families that had taken the lead in politics before the war. Robert M. T. Hunter of Virginia and Robert Barnwell Rhett, Sr., of South Carolina, as well as Stephens and Toombs, continued to play leading roles as they had

before secession. These personalities remained in the forefront of Southern politics in part because ambitious young men who would ordinarily have entered politics instead chose to make their names in the military. Consequently, newspapers complained throughout the war that the state legislatures were filled with amateurs and incompetents, and although this resulted to some extent from the press's dissatisfaction with the legislators' inability to remedy the problems caused by the war, such comments also reflected a very real vacuum of experience and talent in state and local politics.

Other Political Voices

Although prominent politicians and families continued to dominate national political life in the Confederacy as they had in the antebellum period, the war did provide some unique opportunities for poor whites to exert political influence. For example, the belief that the conflict represented a "rich man's war and a poor man's fight" prompted many poor whites to funnel their energy into electing representatives who better reflected their socioeconomic outlook. In addition, poor yeoman farmers dominated the Unionist organizations that began proliferating in the up-country in late 1863. These associations, such as the Heroes of America in western North Carolina and eastern Tennessee, the Peace Society in northern Georgia and northern Alabama, and the Peace and Constitution Society in Arkansas, served as incubators for the Southern Republican party, in which poor whites would exert far more influence than they had in the South's prewar parties. Poor whites did not necessarily have to wait until after the war to wield this political power. The eventual Union occupation of areas such as West Virginia, eastern Tennessee, the Sea Islands of South Carolina, and Louisiana enabled poorer politicians such as Andrew Johnson to gain significant political clout in these regions well before the war had ended. With the reconstruction of each state government in the South, poor whites gained power that had been unattainable under a political system previously weighted in favor of slaveholders.

Like the South's poor white inhabitants, women also enjoyed increased political power during the Civil War. The most common method by which women made their influence felt in politics was still, as it had been before the war, through their politically active husbands. The diary of Mary Boykin Chesnut documents the efforts of these "female politicians" to have their concerns addressed by their male counterparts. Yet these well-to-do women were not the only ones whose voices were heard in political circles during the war. The correspondence of wartime governors contains an unprecedented number of letters from women, especially those running family farms while their husbands served in the army, concerning political issues. These women often explained in their letters that although they preferred to avoid politics, conditions in the countryside had become so unbearable (usually because of the tax-in-kind or impressment policies) that they felt obligated to inform government officials of the situation and seek redress.

Women may have exercised the most political clout during the Civil War through their participation in civil unrest. On April 2, 1863, for example, several hundred women in Richmond marched to the state capitol to complain that the price and supply of bread had reached intolerable levels. When Governor John Letcher told the protesters that he was incapable of remedying the situation, the crowd took matters into its own hands. Pulling knives, hatchets, and a few pistols from their skirts and pocketbooks, the women proceeded to loot the commercial district of whatever bread and other food items they could find. The events in Richmond were far from unique, as bread riots instigated wholly or in part by women also broke out in Atlanta, Macon, Augusta, Mobile, and a half-dozen other towns. Although the bread riots accomplished little in terms of increasing the supply of food in urban areas, they served as a warning that even without the vote, women were determined to make politicians act upon their concerns.

> **. . . the bread riots accomplished little in terms of increasing the supply of food in urban areas. . . .**

As the unprecedented role of women in the civil unrest in Richmond demonstrates, politics underwent significant change during the Civil War. Issues were transformed, parties disappeared, and many constituencies learned to wield unprecedented political power. Although it might be argued that the political revolution wrought by Reconstruction would prove even more profound, it was during the Civil War that Southern politicians abandoned the two-party system of politics, and this innovation laid the groundwork for the one-party system that would characterize the region's politics for the succeeding century.

[*See also* American Party; Bread Riots; Class Conflict; Congress; Conscription; Constitutional Union Party; Democratic Party; Election of 1863; Habeas Corpus; Judicial System; Peace Movements; Presidency; Public Finance; State Rights; Unionism; *and biographies of numerous figures mentioned herein.*]

BIBLIOGRAPHY

Alexander, Thomas B. "Persistent Whiggery in the Confederate South, 1860–1877." *Journal of Southern History* 27 (1961): 305–329.

Alexander, Thomas B., and Richard E. Beringer. *The Anatomy of the Confederate Congress: A Study of the Influences of Member Characteristics on Legislative Voting Behavior, 1861–1865.* Nashville, Tenn., 1972.

Beringer, Richard E. "The Unconscious 'Spirit of Party' in the Confederate Congress." *Civil War History* 18 (1972): 312–333.

McKitrick, Eric L. "Party Politics and the Union and Confederate War Efforts." In *The American Party Systems: Stages of Political Development.* Edited by William N. Chambers and Walter D. Burnham. New York, 1967.

McPherson, James M. *Battle Cry of Freedom: The Civil War Era.* New York, 1988.

Ringold, May. *The Role of State Legislatures in the Confederacy.* Athens, Ga., 1966.

Yearns, Wilfred B. *The Confederate Congress.* Athens, Ga., 1960.

Yearns, W. Buck, ed. *The Confederate Governors.* Athens, Ga., 1985.

TYLER ANBINDER

POLK, LEONIDAS

POLK, LEONIDAS (1806–1864), lieutenant general. Born April 10, 1806, at Raleigh into a prominent North Carolina family, Polk was educated by private tutors before entering the University of North Carolina in 1821. He wanted to be a soldier, however, and in 1823 he received an appointment to the U.S. Military Academy.

Polk did well in his West Point studies and at his 1827 graduation stood a respectable eighth in a thirty-eight-man class. While at the academy he formed two friendships that were to be of great importance to his Confederate career— one with Albert Sidney Johnston (class of 1826); the other with Jefferson Davis (class of 1828).

Around 1826 Polk underwent a religious experience that convinced him to enter into the ministry. On December 1, 1827, therefore, he resigned his artillery lieutenant's commission and began studies for the Episcopal ministry. In April 1830 he was ordained a deacon and in 1838 missionary bishop of the Southwest (then Louisiana, Arkansas, Texas, Mississippi, and Alabama). In 1841 Polk was chosen bishop of Louisiana.

Meanwhile, he married Frances Anne Devereux and through his wife and her family acquired land and slaves in Tennessee. In 1841 he purchased a sugar plantation in Louisiana and in 1847 sold his Tennessee property. In 1854 he moved to New Orleans. He was also a leader in the movement to create a university of the South where Southern boys could be educated without the "contaminating" influence of Yankee ideas.

When disunion came in 1861, Polk hastened to offer his services to the Confederacy. President Jefferson Davis commissioned Polk major general and sent him to command Department No. 2, consisting of western Tennessee and eastern Arkansas.

Establishing his headquarters in Memphis, Polk quickly fell under the influence of locals who believed that the major threat to the South would come from a Federal thrust down the Mississippi River. They thought that the Confederates should build up their defenses in the Mississippi Valley at the expense of less important areas. Polk, thoroughly under their sway, tended to neglect all but the Mississippi River route into the Confederacy.

In early September Polk—acting without the approval or knowledge of the government—sent troops to occupy Columbus, Kentucky, on the Mississippi a few miles north of the Tennessee-Kentucky border. Since Polk did not push on to seize Paducah, Kentucky, at the mouth of the Tennessee River, occupation of Columbus was of no benefit to the South. (Whoever held Paducah controlled the Tennessee River; whoever controlled that river could easily outflank Columbus and force its evacuation.) Historian Steven Woodworth has called Polk's action "one of the most decisive catastrophes the Confederacy ever suffered" and notes that "Polk's presence in Kentucky was a political disaster" for the South because it drove the state—which had been trying to remain neutral—into the arms of the Federal government.

In early 1862 the Northerners moved up the Tennessee River and forced the Confederates to evacuate Columbus along with most of western Tennessee. Polk and his troops joined the force Gen. Albert Sidney Johnston was organizing at Corinth, Mississippi, that eventually became the Army of Tennessee. When that army was divided into corps, Polk was given command of the First Corps, which he led at the Battle of Shiloh.

In the summer of the same year the army was informally organized into wings, and Polk commanded one of them. In October he was promoted to the newly created grade of lieutenant general and assigned to command a corps.

During those same months, Polk became embroiled in numerous petty quarrels. He developed a consuming hatred for his commander, Braxton Bragg, and quickly became the leader of what amounted to an anti-Bragg clique within the army. For more than a year Polk waged a more or less open campaign to discredit Bragg and have him removed from command. Polk bombarded the government with criticism of Bragg, and on several occasions he and other anti-Bragg officers simply refused to obey that general's orders. Bragg, meanwhile, distrusted Polk's ability and tried to replace him with some better general. Polk's high rank, his close friendship with Davis, and what historian Thomas Connelly called his "remarkable ability to evade the blame for situations that were the result of . . . flaws in his character" all combined to nullify Bragg's efforts.

Polk remained in command of his corps until after the Battle of Chickamauga. Then Bragg, angered because several officers had again disobeyed orders, brought matters to a head by relieving Polk from command. He charged Polk himself with disobeying orders on September 20, 1863, and sent him away from the army. Bragg's action forced Davis to try to deal with the command crisis in the Army of Tennessee. As part of his "solution" to the problem, Davis transferred Polk to take charge of the Department of Alabama, Mississippi, and East Louisiana.

Polk remained in Mississippi until May 1864 when he was ordered to North Georgia to reinforce the Army of Tennessee, then under Gen. Joseph E. Johnston. The troops who accompanied Polk to Georgia, although technically an independent army, became in effect a corps in the Army of Tennessee. They and Polk took part in the early battles of the Atlanta campaign.

In June the Confederates occupied a position above Marietta, Georgia, some twenty-five miles north of Atlanta. On the fourteenth Polk went with a group of officers to Pine Mountain to observe the area. The group attracted the attention of Federal troops, and a Northern artillery battery opened fire. One of the shells hit Polk, killing him instantly. He was buried in Augusta, Georgia, but in 1945 his remains were removed to Christ Church Cathederal in New Orleans.

Polk had some popular appeal, but his military ability was very limited. His 1861 seizure of Columbus was a geopolitical mistake of the first magnitude, and his vendetta against Bragg weakened the Army of Tennessee. It is certain that President Davis's unwillingness to remove Polk or to curb his insubordination greatly damaged the Confederate cause.

BIBLIOGRAPHY

Connelly, Thomas L. *Army of the Heartland: The Army of Tennessee, 1861–1862*. Baton Rouge, La., 1967.

Connelly, Thomas L. *Autumn of Glory: The Army of Tennessee, 1862–1865*. Baton Rouge, La., 1971.

Parks, Joseph H. *General Leonidas Polk, CSA: The Fighting Bishop*. Baton Rouge, La., 1962.

Polk, William Mecklenburg. *Leonidas Polk: Bishop and General*. 2 vols. Rev. ed. New York, 1915.

Woodworth, Steven E. *Jefferson Davis and His Generals: The Failure of Confederate Command in the West*. Lawrence, Kans., 1990.

RICHARD M. MCMURRY

POLLARD, EDWARD A.

POLLARD, EDWARD A. (1832–1872), journalist and contemporary historian of the Confederacy. Pollard, a descendant of the Rives family, grew up on its Oakridge estate in Nelson County, Virginia. Educated at Hampden-Sydney College and the University of Virginia, he was expelled from law school at the College of William and Mary for misconduct. In the early 1850s he prospected for gold in California, became a journalist in San Francisco, and traveled in eastern Asia. Returning to the eastern states in 1856, he became a publicist for Southern rights causes, including William Walker's projects in Nicaragua and reopening of the African slave trade. In *Black Diamonds* (1859), he combined such arguments with sketches of plantation life and master-slave relations.

The attempt to resupply Fort Sumter in 1861 impelled Pollard (then living in Washington) to join the Southern Confederacy. After a brief advocacy of secession in Maryland, he and his brother H. Rives Pollard joined the staff of the *Richmond Examiner.* Many have had the mistaken impression that Pollard was its wartime editor. He was acting editor only in the summer of 1862 during the absence of editor John Moncure Daniel. He and others contributed draft editorials, but Daniel thoroughly rewrote them before publication. Pollard shared the *Examiner's* extreme Southern-rights views and its animus against Jefferson Davis's administration.

Pollard resolved in 1861 to be the contemporary historian of the war for Confederate independence. He published *The First Year of the War* in 1862 and followed it with annual volumes thereafter. In 1864 the Federal navy captured him trying to travel through the blockade to Europe. He was imprisoned in Boston, then paroled in Brooklyn and exchanged from Fortress Monroe in January 1865. Back in Richmond, he exhorted Confederates to fight on until victory.

After the surrender, Pollard continued his laudatory histories of the Confederacy. He completed his annual series and published it as *Southern History of the War* (1865) and followed it with his most famous work, *The Lost Cause* (1866), and *Lee and His Lieutenants* (1867). Those works embroiled him in historical controversy with D. H. Hill and other Confederate generals and with admirers of Jefferson Davis about those leaders' wartime performance.

In 1868 Pollard, who had hoped for a renewed Confederate struggle, became reconciled to the national conservative politics of President Andrew Johnson and the Northern Democrats. In *The Lost Cause Regained,* he interpreted their effort for white supremacy and state rights as the substance of what Southerners had sought in the Confederacy. That winter he returned to Richmond to seek judicial vengeance for the murder of Rives Pollard there. In 1869 he wrote his hostile *Life of Jefferson Davis, and Secret History of the Southern Confederacy.*

After that Pollard settled with relatives in Lynchburg and (except for a travel guide) directed his writing to articles. He continued to discuss Confederate history but became a "reconstructed" Southern conservative, urging national reconciliation, economic development, and benevolence toward blacks. He died in 1872, but his writings continued to influence Southern thought about the Lost Cause.

BIBLIOGRAPHY

Davidson, James Wood. "Edward A. Pollard." In *The Living Writers of the South.* New York, 1869.

Maddex, Jack P., Jr. *The Reconstruction of Edward A. Pollard: A Rebel's Conversion to Postbellum Unionism.* Chapel Hill, N.C., 1974.

Wilson, James Southall. "Edward Alfred Pollard." In *Library of Southern Literature.* Edited by Edward A. Alderman, Joel Chandler Harris, and Charles W. Kent. New Orleans, 1907.

JACK P. MADDEX, JR.

POOR RELIEF

The unexpected and unprecedented poverty that afflicted the Confederacy provoked innovative but inadequate responses. In a region that had never employed extensive means of poor relief, substantial new initiatives came from individuals and from local and state governments. Ultimately, however, the scope of the war effort required Confederate involvement if aid to the poor was to be effective. Despite some relief activities by the Richmond administration, the problems of poverty and hunger remained unsolved and severely eroded support for the government among the common people.

Poor relief had been a modest affair before the war. The states employed a variety of means to assist the poor, but all were on a small scale. A stigma attached to the recipients of aid; healthy children usually were apprenticed rather than supported as paupers. Government-sponsored poor farms or poorhouses sheltered many of the destitute, and local authorities entrusted others (often elderly persons) to the care of some responsible person who agreed to maintain them for a modest fee. The counties of North Carolina, for example, practiced all these methods and levied taxes at varying levels to defray costs. In Southern cities charitable organizations had developed to give some aid to the destitute. In the words of one writer, poverty was "associated in public opinion with illness and petty crime." An antebellum North Carolinian observed that "the poor will suffer almost any privations before" accepting public relief.

The war forced enormous changes in these practices and public attitudes, but the experience of poverty remained physically harsh and psychologically painful for thousands of yeoman families. In the early days of the conflict there was a widespread recognition that soldiers and their families might need—and deserved—support. Governor Joseph E. Brown of Georgia appealed in May 1861 for contributions to aid soldiers' families and offered prizes to recognize those citizens who did the most to contribute. Artisans, such as tanners or millers, offered their services free to soldiers' families, and some merchants invited local troops to select the goods they needed. Many companies and factories contributed money or donated some of their products. As the war went on, "free markets" came into being in the cities. Tickets were distributed to the poor in New Orleans, Mobile, Charleston, and Richmond; ticket holders then could visit the market to obtain free supplies. Macon, Atlanta, Savannah, Shreveport, and other cities had stores that sold goods to the needy at cost. In Richmond the Union Benevolent Society received aid from the city government and fed 4,500 people by the end of the war.

As the size of the conflict became apparent, local and state governments became more heavily involved. Most states passed laws early in the war to suspend the collection of debts ("stay laws") or exempt soldiers' families from certain taxes. Between November 1861 and March 1862, seven states formulated relief laws, which typically gave county governments responsibility for using the funds raised by a special tax. With hunger spreading, a corps of county officials came into being who scoured their region, or even distant areas, seeking to buy foodstuffs and distribute them to the poor. To assist the county officials, state lawmakers appropriated as much as $6 million at one time for poor relief, in addition to buying and distributing items such as salt, medicines, cloth, and cotton and wool cards. In 1863 the Georgia legislature bought 97,500 bushels of corn for the poor in sixteen suffering counties of that state.

These impressive efforts did not solve the problem, however. Many of the larger state appropriations never existed except on paper, and county purchasing agents increasingly came into competition with the Confederacy's efforts to supply the armies. Only the Confederate government was large enough to cope with the problem of hunger. What, then, did the Confederacy do?

Occasionally the Confederate government cooperated with private charities by exempting their goods from impressment or encouraging the railroads to arrange transportation. In especially deserving cases, under the Exemption Act of May 1, 1863, the Davis administration allowed individual soldiers to return home to their families. Under the Exemption Act of February 17, 1864, Congress required planters who wished to retain their overseers to promise under bond to raise stated amounts of meat and food for the government. These foodstuffs were sometimes sold to soldiers' families at below-market prices. In August 1864, the War Department instructed its commissaries to leave one-half of the surplus raised by bonded planters for "persons who purchase on behalf of the families of soldiers." Records of bonded farmers also show that a small proportion of them were small farmers exempted for "Care of Private Necessity."

The greatest potential for relieving hunger, however, lay with the Confederate tax-in-kind. In 1863, as the central government began to collect large quantities of crops in depots, county relief agents sought help, asking to buy back the crops from poverty-stricken counties at the low prices set by local boards under the Impressment Act. Records show that for a year the Confederacy extended some aid in this way, but the military's needs soon precluded assistance to civilians.

Thus the problem of poverty in the Confederacy remained unsolved. It brought physical and mental suffering to proud, independent yeoman families that had never before needed aid. In 1862 some nonslaveholding citizens of Smith and Scott counties, Mississippi, had petitioned Congress for a law to aid the poor. Although they expressed a willingness to defend slave property, these petitioners warned that they were "not willing to sacry fize our wives and childron and leave them to starve for bread and clothing." As poverty spread and poor relief proved inadequate, discontent, disaffection, and desertion grew. Commanders recognized that despairing letters from home caused many men to leave the armies. Poverty influenced many others to turn against the cause. The inadequacy of poor relief, and the fact that it had become necessary, did great damage to the Confederacy.

[See also Free Markets; Poverty; State Socialism; Tax-in-Kind.]

BIBLIOGRAPHY

Coulter, E. Merton. The Confederate States of America, 1861–1865. A History of the South, vol. 7. Baton Rouge, La., 1950.

Escott, Paul D. After Secession: The Failure of Confederate Nationalism. Baton Rouge, La., 1978.

Escott, Paul D. "'The Cry of the Sufferers': The Problem of Welfare in the Confederacy." Civil War History 23, no. 3 (September 1977): 228–240.

Escott, Paul D. "Poverty and Governmental Aid for the Poor in Confederate North Carolina." North Carolina Historical Review 61, no. 4 (October 1984): 462–480.

Massey, Mary Elizabeth. Ersatz in the Confederacy. Columbia, S.C., 1952.

Thomas, Emory M. The Confederate State of Richmond: A Biography of the Capital. Austin, Tex., 1971.

PAUL D. ESCOTT

POPULAR CULTURE

In September 1861 the Southern Literary Messenger pointed with excitement to the "splendid opening which the impending Revolution secures to every Southern enterprize," not the least of which was the evolution of a Confederate popular culture. Not necessarily distinct from that of the antebellum South's, it at least "should occupy, in some respects," as an 1864 broadside remarked, "a different sphere of usefulness." Thus traditional pastimes, fetes, and other entertainments were adapted to wartime civilian and military society, particularly so "for the benefit of the soldiers" and "their wives and children."

Enormously popular, for example, were cartes de visite, small photographic images mounted on heavy card stock usually measuring two and a half by four inches. Easily carried in a pocket or haversack and cheap to produce—created from a negative from which any number of reproductions could be made—they provided accessible and affordable mementos or keepsakes for soldiers and their families. Despite paper shortages, photo studios such as Minnis and Cowell in Richmond and the Metropolitan Gallery in

> **[Cartes de visite] provided accessible and affordable mementos or keepsakes for soldiers and their families.**

Nashville did a brisk business in marketing carte de visite likenesses of famous individuals as well. Period scrapbooks thus abound with pictures of family members alongside images of Robert E. Lee, Jefferson Davis, and other Confederate leaders. Somewhat more expensive were daguerreotype, ambrotype, and ferrotype images. An ambrotype, for example, cost from one dollar for a small image to several dollars for a larger one. Whereas the cards could be copied in any number, the more elaborate likenesses were one-of-a-kind positive images, often hand-tinted, mounted under plush velvet in elaborate decorative frames, and available in a variety of sizes.

Prints and engravings proved far more difficult to produce. With the fall of New Orleans, the South lost much of its printing expertise. And whereas Northern printers produced several Confederate scenes—a Baltimore firm, for example, published a series of pro-Confederate etchings by Adalbert J. Volck in 1863 and 1864—such pictures remained largely unseen in the South until after the war. Plagued also by shortages of skilled craftsmen, inadequate paper supplies, and a more pressing need for stamps and currency, graphic art thus remained rare in the Confederacy. There were exceptions, though. In 1861 both Pessou and Simon, of New Orleans, and R. H. Howell, of Savannah, issued handsome lithographs of early Confederate scenes; Tucker and Perkins of Augusta, Georgia, that same year published a finely rendered print of Jefferson Davis, copied from a prewar Mathew Brady photograph; and Ernest Crehen in Richmond as late as 1863 published a striking portrait of J. E. B. Stuart. By and large, however, popular prints were infrequent and poorly produced. Hoyer and Ludwig's highly fanciful 1861 lithograph of an oddly uniformed Jefferson Davis is far more representative. Cartoons were somewhat more forgiving of style and quality. The four lithographed *Dissolving Views of Richmond,*

published by Blanton Duncan in Columbia in 1862, ridiculed George B. McClellan's Peninsula campaign, and Richmond's George Dunn and Company issued a biting series of caricatures aimed at shirkers, hoarders, and doomsayers.

Painters, too, suffered from scant supplies. With no canvas available, artist John R. Key, nephew of Francis Scott Key, resorted to using burlap for his painting of Fort Sumter. Such topical work was nevertheless eagerly awaited. In Richmond, William D. Washington attracted considerable attention with his masterwork, *The Burial of Latanè,* depicting Southern women and their slaves mourning the death of the sole Confederate casualty of Stuart's 1862 ride around McClellan's army. In 1865, soldiers and civilians crowded through the Virginia capitol to view Edward Caledon Bruce's monumental portrait of Lee, since disappeared. Bruce, deaf since the age of fourteen and thus unable to enlist, was unique. Louis M. Montgomery, of the famed Washington Artillery, completed nearly two hundred sketches of military life, but like most other Southern artists—Conrad Wise Chapman, John Elder, Alan Christian Redwood, and William Ludwell Sheppard, for example—he was unable to exhibit much work while actively serving in the army.

Confederate theaters offered artwork of a sort. One Richmond playhouse featured the "Southern Moving Dioramic Panorama," a canvas eight feet high and seventy-five feet long filled with historical scenes. The nearby Metropolitan Theater presented a massive "scenic and automatic spectacle" of wartime illustrations, accompanied by animated "miniature moving, life like figures" and an explanatory lecture. Usually the plays alone were enough to bring in large audiences. Theater provided a vibrant source of entertainment in each of the Confederacy's major cities, although, after the fall of New Orleans in 1862, Charleston's Hibernian Hall and Richmond's Metropolitan, New Richmond, and Varieties theaters remained the most active. Besides Charles Morton, the "most versatile and popular Comedian and Vocalist in the Confederacy," and Ella Wrenn, the "accomplished Tragedienne and Prima Donna," other popular actors included E. R. Dalton, Walter Keeble, D'Orsay Ogden, Harry Macarthy, Mary Partington, Jennie Powell, and Ida Vernon. Easily the most famous of the many traveling companies was the W. H. Crisp troupe, its male members all honorably discharged Confederate veterans.

In the press of wartime, however, performances often degenerated into rowdy brawls. Soldiers on leave, civilian workers, and drunken troublemakers all eager for a good time filled the cheaper seats, often firing pistols and otherwise disturbing the more cultured theatergoers in the lower tiers. So bad did the situation become that the gentler sort regularly urged theater owners to close down their saloons and upper tiers—hardly a likely prospect in the face of an overwhelming demand from all quarters for entertainment. Theaters presented an array of productions, from traditional operas such as *Il Trovatore* and Shakespearean plays to the melodramatic *Corsican Brothers* and *The Marble Heart.*

Many more dramas—such as *The Ticket-of-Leave Man, The Capture of Courtland, Alabama,* and *Miscegenation; or, A Virginia Negro in Washington*—reflected the times. In 1864, the New Richmond Theater introduced *The Ghost of Dismal Swamp; or, Marteau, the Guerrilla* with special effects so realistic that critics called it "the great Spectral wonder of the nineteenth century." Most of the productions were abysmally written but were at least presented with unflagging enthusiasm; actors often perceived of themselves as charged with a patriotic duty to bolster morale. Minstrels such as Tom Morris, "the renowned negro delineator," and his Iron-Clad Ethiopian Troupe were especially popular, although keeping any acting company intact was always difficult. Morris and his minstrels were drafted in 1864.

Like theater, music attracted the broadest possible audience. In the first year of the war alone the public could buy the eighteen-page *New-Orleans 5 Cent Song-Book,* the sixteen-page *Original Songs of the Atlanta Amateurs* ("containing more truth than poetry"), or, the next year, the massive two-hundred-page *War Songs of the South.* Until 1865, despite the shortages that so plagued every printer, song sheets and collections remained available. A Charleston publisher as late as 1864 issued a monthly pocket-size *Taylor's Southern Songster.* As expected, many of the titles honored the ordinary Confederate soldier, various generals, or Southern sentiments. There were nearly fifty musical selections published on Stonewall Jackson's death alone. Popular music titles included "Dear Mother, I'll Come Home Again," "Boys, Keep Your Powder Dry," "The Murmur of the Shell," and "Adieu to the Star Spangled Banner Forever."

> **. . . many of the [song] titles honored the ordinary Confederate soldier, various generals, or Southern sentiments.**

Although attracting a smaller segment of the Confederate public, magazines were also part of wartime popular culture. But of the approximately one hundred Southern periodicals in business in 1861, only a few survived the war. The *Southern Literary Messenger* lasted until 1864, as did the *Southern Literary Companion* and *Southern Field and Fireside,* both published in Georgia; *De Bow's Review,* except for a single issue, suspended publication in 1862 until after the surrender. The *Southern Monthly,* with hopes of becoming a Confederate *Harper's,* lasted only for several issues. Richmond's *Southern Punch,* Mobile's *Confederate Spirit and Knapsack of Fun,* and Atlanta's *Hard Tack* were game attempts at Confederate, especially military, humor.

Two new periodicals published in Richmond, the *Southern Illustrated News* and *Magnolia,* a literary magazine, by 1863 were forced to charge twenty dollars for a year's subscription; neither lasted out the war. One that did, the *Countryman,* published in Eatonton, Georgia, employed a young typesetter and writer named Joel Chandler Harris. For children, there were the *Portfolio,* published in Charleston and later Columbia, and the *Child's Index,* printed in Macon.

Popular fiction fared little better than the magazine. Printers issued barely more than a hundred literary titles during the war years. In 1861 Strother and Marcom in Raleigh published a collection of poetry, Hunter Hill's *Hesper;* a Charleston printer that same year issued Claudian B. Northrop's *Southern Odes.* West and Johnston in Richmond and Goetzel and Company in Mobile produced nine literary titles each, the most of any single printer. Both issued editions of two of the war's most popular titles, Victor Hugo's *Les Misèrables* (1863–1864) and Augusta Evans Wilson's stilted romance, *Macaria* (1864). Sigmund Goetzel's firm also published two stories by Charles Dickens, George Eliot's *Silas Marner,* and Julian Fane's *Tannhauser.* It was Goetzel too who, faced with the shortage of paper, resorted to printing book covers on sample sheets of wallpaper. Some Confederate fiction, such as Sallie Rochester Ford's *Raids and Romance of Morgan and His Men,* proved popular enough to be pirated in the North. Other works—such as W. D. Herrington's *The Captain's Bride* or Braxton Craven's *Mary Barker*—were but cheap novelettes, worthy of only a moment's attention.

The same might be said of many Confederate broadsides, posters, newspaper notices, and other forms of advertising. While educational, religious, and civic organizations usually struck a serious tone, many merchants and other entrepreneurs were seldom timid in touting their products. A grocery in Cold Springs, Texas, for example, boasted of its "largest and best" inventory, adding that "If you want the worth of your money, call and see us!" In Greensboro, North Carolina, the locally produced Tarpley Rifle was "the best . . .introduced in the country." Some notices were practical: a New Orleans company in late 1861 finally bowed to the inevitable and agreed to accept Confederate currency in order "to facilitate the efforts of our customers."

That some vestiges of Confederate popular culture were less than ideal was not significant, however. As the editor of a leading Southern newspaper put it, for many citizens it was equally important that the South "along with her political independence" achieve an "independence in thought and education, and in all . . .forms of mental improvement," whether they were extraordinary or mundane.

[*See also* Literature, *article on* Literature in the Confederacy; Lost Cause, *article on* Iconography of the Lost Cause; Music; Newspapers; Photography.]

BIBLIOGRAPHY

Albaugh, William A., III. *Confederate Faces: A Pictorial Review of the Individuals in the Confederate Armed Forces.* Solana Beach, Calif., 1970.

Harwell, Richard B. *Brief Candle: The Confederate Theatre.* Worcester, Mass., 1971.

Harwell, Richard B. *Confederate Belles-Lettres: A Bibliography and a Finding List of the Fiction, Poetry, Drama, Songsters, and Miscellaneous Literature Published in the Confederate States of America.* Hattiesburg, Miss., 1941.

Harwell, Richard B. *Confederate Music.* Chapel Hill, N.C., 1950.

Kennerly, Sarah Law. "Confederate Juvenile Imprints: Children's Books and Periodicals Published in the Confederate States of America, 1861–1865." Ph.D. diss., University of Michigan, 1956.

Neely, Mark E., Jr., Harold Holzer, and Gabor S. Boritt. *The Confederate Image: Prints of the Lost Cause.* Chapel Hill, N.C., 1987.

Parrish, T. Michael, and Robert M. Willingham, Jr., comps. *Confederate Imprints: A Bibliography of Southern Publications from Secession to Surrender.* Austin, Tex., and Katonah, N.Y., 1987.

EDWARD D. C. CAMPBELL, JR.

POPULATION

The eighth census of the United States reported that, as of June 30, 1860, the total population of the United States of America was 31.18 million people. Just over 9 million of these people lived in the states that formed the Confederate States of America in the spring of 1861, and another 3.1 million, many of them sympathetic to the Confederate cause, lived in the border states of Delaware, Kentucky, Maryland, and Missouri. The census numbers confirmed that the slaveholding states of the Union were a distinct minority of the total population of the United States. Not counting slaves, the free population of the Confederacy represented only about one-fourth of all free Americans.

This had not always been the case. In 1790, the population—including slaves—of the Southern states approximately equaled that of the North. But while the population of the North had increased by a factor of about five between 1790 and 1860, that of the South had only doubled. This growing demographic imbalance posed a major dilemma for the political leaders of the South in 1860. On the one hand, the realignment of congressional seats in the House of Representatives following the 1860 census would further increase the power of Northern interests in the Federal government, and the election of Abraham Lincoln—who was not even on the ballot in the Deep South—underscored the fact that Southerners could no longer block the choice of a president opposed to their interests. In this respect, the demographic imbalance supported a political argument favoring

secession. On the other hand, the population figures meant that, should the North contest secession, the South would find itself at a considerable disadvantage in terms of military manpower. In this respect, demographic considerations urged caution.

The manpower disadvantage became evident once war broke out. Since slaves were not allowed to fight, the primary pool of manpower for the Confederate army was the 1.1 million white males aged fifteen to thirty-nine who lived in the eleven states of the Confederacy. This pool was augmented by volunteers from the slaveholding border states who joined the South's cause and by enlistment of younger and older men as the war continued. A maximum estimate of men available to serve in the Confederate army would be 1.75 million men. By comparison, the Union army could draw upon a pool of over 6 million men. Thus, the Confederacy began the war with a disadvantage of more than three to one in terms of military manpower.

Numbers alone do not tell the full story. An examination of the reasons for the divergent patterns of regional population growth reveals the fundamental differences in economic and social structure of the Northern and the Southern societies. In the states that formed the Confederacy, population growth before 1860 was largely the result of a high birthrate among both the native population of free whites and black slaves. One consequence of this pattern of natural increase was that, despite the settlement of a vast territory of western lands and the emergence of cotton to replace tobacco and rice as the major staple crops of Southern agriculture, the social and demographic contours of Southern society remained essentially unchanged.

> **The Confederacy began the war with a disadvantage of more than three to one. . . .**

On the eve of the Civil War, most Southerners farmed their land much as their grandfathers had seventy years earlier. Indeed, a visitor from 1790 would have felt quite at home in the South of 1860. Slave owners cultivated cash crops with slave labor on their plantations. Most other whites lived on family farms, where they produced a modest surplus of staple crops for the market. Slaves toiled under the control of their owners as they had in colonial times.

A visitor from 1790 to the Northern states, on the other hand, would have noticed enormous changes in the everyday life of people. Population growth in the free states reflected not only a high birthrate among the native population but also the effects of immigration. In the three decades before the Civil War, nearly 5 million people emigrated from Europe to the United States. Most of these newcomers stayed north of the Ohio River, claiming land to farm or settling in the growing urban centers of the North. As a consequence of this immigration, one out of six persons living in the free states in 1860 was foreign-born, and an equal fraction was composed of first-generation Americans whose parents had immigrated to the United States.

By contrast, only one in thirty individuals living in the Confederacy was born outside the United States. (Since very few black slaves were brought into the United States after the closure of the Atlantic slave trade in 1809, by the time of the Civil War almost all slaves were native-born.) The presence of foreign-born residents in rural areas of the South was particularly rare. Compared to the North, where ethnic diversity was an important influence in virtually every sphere of life, Southerners lived in a world where values and institutional arrangements—especially their peculiar institution of slavery—reflected a uniquely *American* experience.

The influx of European immigrants was not the only change in the Northern states that would have struck a visitor from 1790. Equally evident would be the growth of urban centers. Only one city in the Confederacy—New Orleans—had a population over 175,000 in 1860, and two others—Richmond, Virginia, and Charleston, South Carolina—had populations approaching 50,000. In all, only nine cities in the Confederacy had populations in excess of 10,000 people. The presence of many times that number of urban areas in the North reflected the greater role of commerce and manufacturing. In 1860 more than a million men and women were employed in Northern factories. Barely one-tenth that number were factory workers in the Confederacy. Only Virginia, which accounted for one-third of all manufacturing employment in the Confederacy, could boast of a city—Richmond—with any significant industrial employment.

Equally striking was the absence of smaller towns in the South. Southern families lived on self-sufficient farms and sent their cash crops directly to the cotton brokers located along the major rivers or on the seacoast. They had little need for the commercial services provided by small towns that were an essential part of agriculture in the North and West. Thus, whereas villages and towns dotted the landscape of New England, the Mid-Atlantic states and the Old Northwest Territory, visitors to the South consistently complained of the long distances traveled without encountering any towns.

The Confederacy, in short, was a rural society of 9.1 million people scattered over a vast territory that stretched from the Atlantic Ocean to the Gulf of Mexico. It was a class society where economic and social power rested primarily on the ownership of two assets—land and slaves. There were basically three classes of people in the Confederacy: slaveholders, nonslaveholding whites, and black slaves.

The most powerful class comprised the 300,000 slave owners. Together with their family members, this group numbered some 1.7 million individuals, or about 30 percent of the total free population. The basis of these people's power stemmed from the enormous wealth represented by the land and slaves they owned. The average slaveholder in the Confederacy owned eleven slaves and farmed more than ten thousand acres of land. These statistics do not reveal the enormous range in the size of slaveholdings. In areas such as the alluvial regions of the Mississippi River or the rice regions of South Carolina or Louisiana, planters often owned several hundred slaves. The wealth of these families rivaled that of anyone in the United States. Yet 30 percent of all slaveholders owned only one or two slaves and operated modest-sized farms. Though they could hardly claim to be "planters," this group of farmers was very well off by contemporary standards. In 1860 a single male slave field hand was worth between $1,500 and $2,000, a sum nearly equal to the total value of a farm reported to the census by the average family in the Old Northwest.

Slaveholders were instrumental in the formation of the Confederate States of America, and they dominated the politics of the new nation from its birth until its collapse in 1865. The planter-aristocrats of the South felt that breaking away from the Union in 1860 was the best way to protect the system of slavery. But they also had the most to lose should the Confederacy be defeated. The emancipation of slaves in 1865 brought huge financial losses to those who owned large numbers of slaves. Their financial woes did not, however, mean total ruin. Thanks to their vast holdings of land, many of the prominent families retained their dominant social and economic position in the postbellum period despite the impact of the war.

At the other end of the economic and social spectrum in the Confederacy were the 3.5 million black slaves. By law, these people were the personal property of their owners. Despite the fact that almost one-half of all slaveholdings were of five or less slaves, nine out of ten slaves lived on farms or plantations with five or more slaves. Few were skilled. Apart from a small fraction of overseers, craftsmen, and house servants, slaves—men, women, and children—worked in the fields. Slaves clearly had the most to gain from a Confederate defeat—their freedom. As the war progressed, thousands of blacks responded to the promise of freedom by leaving their plantation to seek refuge behind the Union lines. When Union victory became more certain and the Confederate government's control weakened, an increasing number of blacks left their owner's plantation to search for family, friends, and a better life. This migration, which swelled to very large numbers of people near the end of the war, created considerable stress on cities, which offered refuge for blacks who were seeking a new start under freedom.

The largest single class of people in the Confederacy were the 3.9 million whites who owned no slaves at all.

Most of these people operated farms that relied entirely on family labor. They devoted their attention primarily to the production of the corn, poultry, and pork that ensured food for the family and farm animals. They grew cotton or tobacco to earn cash for the modest supplies they had to purchase.

A substantial majority of these people probably supported the idea of secession from the Union in 1861. They were, however, much less enthusiastic about the war that followed. In the western regions of Virginia and the Carolinas, or the hills of northern Georgia, Alabama, and Mississippi, many people were at best ambivalent about the war. There were few slaves in these areas, and as the cost of the war mounted in both human and economic terms, opposition to the war effort became more pronounced. But their opposition to the war did not mean they embraced the Union cause. Although most of these people had only a limited interest in the protection of slavery, they were not eager to see blacks freed through emancipation, and they deeply resented the invasion of their territory and the deprivations brought by the Federal army. If forced to choose between the invading Northerners or the Confederate cause, these people tended to side with the South. It was men from this class throughout the South who formed the backbone of the Confederate armies in Virginia and Tennessee.

The Civil War brought vast changes to Southern society with the emancipation of slaves. Yet it did not produce major changes in the demographic patterns of the Southern population. The birthrate remained high, which helped to offset the loss of a quarter of a million young men as casualties in the war. Plantations disappeared, but blacks remained in the cotton belt as sharecroppers and tenant farmers. Immigrants continued to flow into the United States, but they still settled mostly in the North and West. Perhaps the most significant impact of the war was the impetus it gave to growth of the larger urban centers in the South. The war stimulated economic activity in such cities as Richmond, Atlanta, Augusta, and Selma. Though these cities suffered considerable destruction toward the end of the war, the economic stimulus for growth remained. A second source of urban growth was the flight of refugees—whites as well as freed blacks—to cities. Most of the urban centers of the South experienced significant population growth after the war.

Still, the South remained essentially a rural, agrarian society. The destruction of slavery had momentarily altered the political balance of power in the South, but there remained three basic classes of people: white planters (now using tenant or wage labor); white farmers (many now tenants), and free blacks (who at least had gained freedom).

[*See also* African Americans in the Confederacy; Army, *article on* Manpower; Civil War, *article on* Losses and Numbers; Foreigners; Navy, *article on* Manpower; Urbanization; Women.]

BIBLIOGRAPHY

Cooper, William J., Jr., and Thomas E. Terrill. *The American South: A History.* 2 vols. New York, 1991.

Gray, Lewis Cecil. *History of Agriculture in the Southern United States to 1860.* 2 vols. Pittsburgh, 1933. Reprint, Gloucester, Mass., 1958.

Olmsted, Frederick Law. *The Cotton Kingdom.* Edited by Lawrence Powell and Arthur M. Schlesinger, Sr. New York, 1983.

Ransom, Roger L. *Conflict and Compromise: The Political Economy of Slavery, Emancipation, and the American Civil War.* New York, 1989.

Stampp, Kenneth. *The Peculiar Institution: Slavery in the Antebellum South.* New York, 1956.

ROGER L. RANSOM

PORT GIBSON, MISSISSIPPI

Nestled along the south bank of Little Bayou Pierre, thirty-five miles south of Vicksburg, the town of Port Gibson witnessed the horrors of war on May 1, 1863, as opposing armies battled for control of the fortress city on the Mississippi River. At stake was the "Gibraltar of the Confederacy," Vicksburg, one of the last Confederate strongholds on the Mississippi River and the connecting link between the eastern and western parts of the Southern nation. Its defense was seen as vital.

The final campaign for Vicksburg began to unfold in the spring of 1863 as Maj. Gen. Ulysses S. Grant launched his Army of the Tennessee on a march down the west side of the Mississippi River from Milliken's Bend to Hard Times, Louisiana. It was Grant's intention to force a crossing of the river at Grand Gulf and move on "Fortress Vicksburg" from the south. The battle-tested division of Confederate Brig. Gen. John S. Bowen, however, was poised at Grand Gulf to meet such an invasion attempt.

When the combined Union land and naval force appeared opposite the Grand Gulf defenses on April 28, Bowen sent an urgent plea requesting "that every man and gun that can be spared from other points be sent here." Lt. Gen. John C. Pemberton immediately ordered two brigades, those of Brig. Gens. Edward Dorr Tracy and William Edwin Baldwin, dispatched from the Vicksburg defenses.

As the soldiers headed south from Vicksburg, the Union fleet bombarded the fortifications at Grand Gulf in an attempt to silence the Confederate guns and clear the way for a landing by Grant's troops. For five hours on April 29, Bowen's gunners stood at their posts and fired their guns, inflicting heavy damage on the fleet. Having successfully thwarted a landing at Grand Gulf, however, the

Confederates could only watch helplessly as the enemy fleet passed their batteries and headed south toward a rendezvous with Grant.

Bowen moved quickly to redeploy his men as Grant's army stormed ashore at Bruinsburg on April 30. He moved two brigades into the woods west of Port Gibson and deployed Brig. Gen. Martin E. Green's brigade of Missourians and Arkansans astride the Rodney Road. Tracy's brigade assumed position athwart the Bruinsburg Road. The two wings were widely separated by the densely wooded valley of Centers Creek, but terrain favored the defenders.

Elements of the Union army pushed inland and took possession of the bluffs, thereby securing the landing area. By late afternoon, April 30, seventeen thousand men were

> **"We have been engaged in a furious battle since daylight; losses very heavy—The men act nobly, but the odds are overpowering."**

ashore and the march inland began. Instead of taking the Bruinsburg Road, which was the direct road from the landing area to Port Gibson, Grant's columns swung into the Rodney Road and marched through the night. Shortly after midnight Green's outpost near the A. K. Shaifer house opened fire. A spirited skirmish ensued that lasted until 3:00 A.M. The Confederates, however, held their ground. For the next several hours an uneasy calm settled over the woods and scattered fields. Throughout the night the Federals gathered their forces in hand, and both sides prepared for the battle that was to come at sunrise.

Green watched at dawn as Union troops deployed in battle formation and moved in force along the Rodney Road toward Magnolia Church. One Union division was sent along a connecting plantation road toward the Bruinsburg Road and the Confederate right flank. With skirmishers well in advance, the Federals began a slow and deliberate advance around 5:30 A.M. On both fronts the Confederates contested the advance, and the battle began in earnest.

Most of the Union forces moved along the Rodney Road toward the Confederate left held by Green's brigade. Heavily outnumbered and hard-pressed, Green's men gave way shortly after 10:00 A.M., falling back a mile and a half. Here the infantrymen of Baldwin's and Col. Francis M. Cockrell's brigades, recent arrivals on the field, established a new line between the White and Irwin branches of Willow Creek, and reestablished the Confederate left flank. Exhausted and badly shaken, Green's brigade was ordered to re-form on the march and move to support the Confederate right along the Bruinsburg Road.

The morning hours witnessed Green's brigade driven from its position by the principal Federal attack. Ed Tracy's Alabama Brigade, astride the Bruinsburg Road, also experienced hard fighting. Tracy watched with anxiety as the Federal line crept toward his position. Sgt. Francis G. Obenchain of the Botetourt (Virginia) Artillery recalled that while speaking to the general, "a ball struck him on back of the neck passing through. He fell with great force on his face and in falling cried 'O Lord!' He was dead when I stooped to him."

Although Tracy was killed early in the action, his brigade managed to hold its tenuous line. It was clear, however, that unless the Confederates received heavy reinforcements they would lose the day. Bowen wired his superiors: "We have been engaged in a furious battle since daylight; losses very heavy—The men act nobly, but the odds are overpowering."

Early afternoon found the Alabamians, now under the command of Col. Isham Garrott, slowly giving ground. Green's weary soldiers arrived to bolster the line on the Bruinsburg Road. Even so, late in the afternoon, the Federals advanced all along the line in superior numbers. As Union pressure built, Cockrell's Missourians unleashed a counterattack near the Rodney Road, which began to roll up the blue line. The Sixth Missouri also counterattacked, hitting the Federals near the Bruinsburg Road. But all this was to no avail. On both fronts the Confederates were checked and driven back.

At 5:30 P.M., as the Confederates began to retire from the field, Pemberton notified the authorities in Richmond of the day's events. He implored them, "Large reenforcements should be sent me from other departments. Enemy's movement threatens Jackson, and, if successful, cuts off Vicksburg and Port Hudson from the east." The inland campaign for Vicksburg had begun.

In the Battle of Port Gibson, the Southerners inflicted 131 killed, 719 wounded, and 25 missing on Grant's force of 23,000 men. Bowen's command suffered 60 killed, 340 wounded, and 387 missing out of 8,000 men engaged. In addition, four guns of the Botetourt Artillery were lost. The action at Port Gibson underscored Confederate inability to defend the line of the Mississippi River and to respond to amphibious operations. The defeat not only secured Grant's position on Mississippi soil but opened the road to Raymond, Jackson, Champion Hill, Big Black River Bridge, and, ultimately, Vicksburg.

BIBLIOGRAPHY

Bearss, Edwin C. *Grant Strikes a Fatal Blow.* Vol. 2 of *The Vicksburg Campaign.* Dayton, Ohio, 1986.

Johnson, Robert U., and C. C. Buel, eds. *Battles and Leaders of the Civil War.* 4 vols. New York, 1887–1888. Reprint, Secaucus, N.J., 1982.

TERRENCE J. WINSCHEL

PORT HUDSON, LOUISIANA

Located 25 miles up the Mississippi River from Baton Rouge, Port Hudson was the site of the longest true siege in American military history. Some 7,500 Confederates resisted more than 40,000 Union soldiers for nearly two months. Confederate casualties included 750 killed and wounded, 250 dead of disease, and 6,500 captured. The Federals lost nearly 10,000, almost evenly divided between battle casualties and disease.

Control of the Mississippi River was a key objective of Union strategists at the outset of the Civil War. Aware of this, the Confederacy, in August 1862, had its forces under Maj. Gen. John C. Breckinridge begin erecting earthworks at Port Hudson. Within six months the bastion was as formidable as Vicksburg.

In March 1863 Union Rear Adm. David G. Farragut attempted to force the Confederates to evacuate Port Hudson by cutting off their provisions from the Trans-Mississippi. Seven Union vessels tried to steam past Port Hudson on March 14. But only two succeeded, and they proved insufficient to enforce an effective blockade of the Red River. Later that month, Union Maj. Gen. Nathaniel P. Banks advanced west of the Mississippi to achieve Farragut's objective by land. Although he severed Port Hudson's Trans-Mississippi supply line, the Confederate garrison refused to capitulate.

In mid-May Banks finally moved against the bastion. While three divisions came down the Red River to assail Port Hudson from the north, two others advanced from Baton Rouge and New Orleans to strike from the east and south. By May 22, 30,000 Union soldiers, assisted by Farragut's fleet, had isolated 7,500 Confederates behind 4½ miles of earthen fortifications.

On May 26 Banks issued orders for a simultaneous attack all along the Confederate perimeter the following morning. But the vagueness of the orders, uncooperative subordinates, and the terrain rendered a coordinated effort impossible. First assailed was the Confederate left wing, which guarded the northern approaches. Timely reinforcements from the Confederate center enabled the defenders to repulse several assaults. Except for sporadic sharpshooting and artillery fire, the fighting in this sector ended before Banks's remaining two divisions advanced against the Confederate center. This delay enabled the Confederates to virtually abandon their center and replace those departing from the center with men from the right. When the Federals finally advanced across Slaughter's Field toward the Confederate center, they were easily repulsed. Approximately 2,000 Union soldiers had been killed or wounded;

Confederate casualties were less than 500. That evening, both sides were amazed that the Confederate lines remained unbreached.

Union casualties included 600 African Americans of the First and Third Louisiana Native Guards who had advanced across the flooded batture (the land between the river and the levee) against the extreme left of the Confederate line, where the Thirty-ninth Mississippi was deployed along the edge of a sixty-foot bluff and supported by several cannon. Wealthy, well-educated, free blacks from New Orleans composed a majority of the First Louisiana Native Guards, including the line officers. Former slaves commanded by white officers composed the Third Louisiana Native Guards, which had been organized in late 1862.

A free black from New Orleans, Capt. Andrew Cailloux, shouted his orders in both English and French until a shell struck him dead. A few of the assailants managed to reach the fortifications before they were killed. Although quickly repulsed, the black soldiers had demonstrated both their willingness and their ability to fight.

Unwilling to withdraw, Banks brought up additional troops and cannon and commenced siege operations. Finally, on June 13, he believed he could breach the fortifications. After terrorizing the Confederates with a one-hour artillery bombardment, Banks demanded that they surrender. Northern-born and Southern-wed Maj. Gen. Franklin Gardner declined. Banks resumed the bombardment and deployed for an assault the next day.

> **Both sides were amazed that the Confederate lines remained unbreached.**

Brig. Gen. Halbert E. Paine's division then spearheaded the main assault against the Confederate center on June 14. Diversionary attacks were made against the extreme Confederate right by Brig. Gen. William Dwight's division and, just west of Paine, by the division of Brig. Gen. Godfrey Weitzel. Paine's assault, supported by Weitzel, began at 4:00 A.M., with Dwight contributing little assistance. The few Federals who managed to breach the fortifications quickly surrendered and by 10:00 A.M. the assault had failed. The Union had suffered 1,805 casualties; the Confederates less than 200.

Banks resumed siege warfare, devoting the remainder of June and early July to digging approach saps and advancing his artillery. Although reduced to eating rats and mules, the Confederates held out until Gardner learned of the surrender of Vicksburg. Without its upriver counterpart, Port Hudson lacked strategic significance. The Confederate garrison surrendered on July 9.

BIBLIOGRAPHY

Hewitt, Lawrence Lee. *Port Hudson, Confederate Bastion on the Mississippi.* Baton Rouge, La., 1987.

Wright, Howard G. *Port Hudson: Its History from an Interior Point of View, as Sketched from the Diary of an Officer, Howard G. Wright, 1863.* Baton Rouge, La., 1961.

LAWRENCE L. HEWITT

POST OFFICE DEPARTMENT

Created on February 21, 1861, the Post Office Department of the Confederacy became one of Jefferson Davis's triumphs. Davis benefited by the seventy-year-old in-place system constructed by the Federal government. Even after the firing on Fort Sumter, the U.S. Post Office continued to provide uninterrupted service in the South, and Southerners still attached U.S. stamps to their local, intra-Confederacy, and foreign letters. On June 1, 1861, the postal system ceased to be Federal and became Confederate.

Creation of the Post Office Department. Davis insisted that the new post office be self-sufficient, unlike the old system, which had never paid for itself since its establishment in 1789. In 1860, mail service in the eleven states that would form the Confederacy cost $2,897,530.77, with receipts of $938,105.34, leaving a deficit of nearly $2 million. In February 1861, the Confederate Congress passed an act calling for a balanced operation by March 1, 1863, and raised the postage rate from three cents to five cents on a half-ounce letter for the first five hundred miles, with double rates thereafter. One year later, when that increase failed to cover costs, Congress doubled the standard rate to ten cents to be effective on July 1, 1862. Newspaper and book rates were set by the number of papers and weight to be sent. Further, the congressional Committee for Postal Affairs called upon the still-to-be-named postmaster general to discontinue unprofitable routes, to eliminate duplicate routes, and to replace daily with triweekly service in most areas.

On March 6, 1861, Davis asked forty-three-year-old John H. Reagan to head the Confederate Post Office. Reagan, who had represented Texas in the U.S. Congress (1857–1861) and in the Provisional Government of the Confederacy, was Davis's third choice after fellow Mississippians Henry T. Ellet and William Wirt Adams declined the position. Reagan himself twice turned down the job before deciding it was his patriotic duty to accept. Reagan feared the enormity of the job and worried that in its frustration, the public would criticize the department and focus its contempt on the postmaster general.

The day he took the office, Reagan sent a friend to Washington, D.C., to persuade Southern sympathizers in the U.S. Post Office to abandon their jobs and accept new posts with the Confederacy. Reagan wrote a letter to each of these men and asked them to bring reports, route maps of the Southern states, forms, and other useful administrative materials when they relocated to the South. Within a fortnight, Reagan had an experienced staff and the requisite materials to organize his charge. The U.S. postmaster general's appointment book gave Reagan the name of every postmaster in the South. To house the department, he rented a three-story building on Bibb Street in downtown Montgomery and oversaw the training of new employees at an evening school in the building. By April 2, Reagan was advertising for company bids to provide stamps and postal supplies such as mail bags, forms, paper, and wax.

From the beginning, Reagan tried to keep costs low so that he could comply with the administrative and legislative mandates for a balanced budget. He expeditiously cut weight and volume by inducing Congress to eliminate the franking privilege—marking letters with official signatures of officeholders so that mail goes postage-free—except for postal business. He cut the number of employees by one-half and implemented the recommendations of Congress concerning superfluous, unprofitable routes. Of course, he did not have to deal with the costs of modern mail delivery to private houses or corner boxes because everyone deposited and inquired for mail at the central post office, which occupied either its own building or, more commonly, a corner of the local general store.

The biggest costs, comprising two-thirds of antebellum postal expenses, were transportation charges. On April 16, 1861, Reagan sent a circular letter to railroad executives and asked them to meet him in Montgomery on April 26 to discuss hauling rates. Thirty-five managers came to the meeting. Reagan appealed to their patriotism to help the new country through its emergency. He suggested one daily haul instead of two, and he got the executives to agree to cut their rates in half by promising that once the war was won, they could again ask for premium prices. Later, as the conflict dragged on, as inflation devoured profits, and as war damage brought increased costs, many felt less patriotic and pressed for higher rates.

Postal Service in the Confederacy. By April 29, Reagan had organized the Confederate Post Office and was ready to inaugurate service. After the government relocated to Richmond, the Post Office Department established itself in Goddin Hall near the capitol. On May 13, Reagan issued orders to Southern postmasters to continue to work under the U.S. government until June 1, when they would come under control of the Confederacy. He instructed his men to close accounts on May 31 and to forward moneys, stamps, and stamped envelopes to Washington. Lincoln's Postmaster

General Montgomery Blair issued similar orders to cease U.S. service to the Confederacy on the same date.

On June 1, postmasters found themselves without Confederate stamps. In response to his advertisement for bids, Reagan gave the contract to supply stamps to the Richmond firm Hoyer & Ludwig Printers, the only Southern firm to bid among the many Northern bidders. Later, printers Archer & Daly of Richmond also secured a contract from Reagan. For the moment, however, no stamps were available. In this period of nearly twenty weeks, postmasters produced provisional issues or used handstamps to fill the void.

The first Confederate stamp, a green five-center with the likeness of Jefferson Davis, was sold in Richmond on October 16, 1861. One month later it was being used throughout the South. This and later Confederate issues were inconsistent in quality and had varying shades of color owing to shortages of pigments and paper. In addition, the

> **Few people entrusted letters of value or envelopes containing money to the post office, for it provided no insurance.**

supply of stamps never kept pace with demand and postmasters often reverted to emergency provisionals. In an attempt to make up for the shortages, Reagan ordered stamps and plates from the London firm of Thomas de la Rue & Company. The first order was dumped overboard from the blockade runner *Bermuda* just before its capture by USS *Mercidita*. A reorder for 12 million five-centers and new plates reached Richmond safely and cost $1,007.88 in gold—Confederate currency and bonds being unacceptable to foreign firms. These lithographed English stamps were of a fine quality unattainable by Confederate printers, who lacked the materials, tools, and expertise to turn out high-resolution stamps.

The general issues of Confederate stamps bore images of Jefferson Davis, Thomas Jefferson, Andrew Jackson, and John C. Calhoun. There is no evidence of counterfeit stamps being made or used during the war. Few people entrusted letters of value or envelopes containing money to the post office, for it provided no insurance. Instead, these letters were sent via the Southern Express Company, which provided faster and safer transportation.

Although Southerners praised Reagan's efforts, they were never satisfied with the efficiency of the postal service. Frequent delays, lost letters, and high postal rates brought much criticism of the department. In the year after First Manassas, citizens' complaints steadily increased, although after mid-1862, these declined dramatically. Newspaper editors, on the other hand, never halted their criticism of high

rates and late service. Blaming false economy and lack of clerks to handle the great increase in mail, some editors claimed that two of every three letters were lost. Disenchantment over late or lost mails even led several congressmen to support a motion to abolish the post office and turn the mail service over to the Southern Express Company. This motion was defeated on February 5, 1862, as most people realized the difficulties imposed by the transition, the economy, and the war.

Certainly the war itself led to delays and poor service, as few trains met schedules and troop transport took priority over letter delivery. Union raids and armies increasingly pushed south, destroying trainloads of mail, setting fire to postal facilities, and tearing up tracks and roads, so that mail had to be rerouted. In addition, the depletion in the ranks of qualified postal workers, who dropped the mail to pick up guns, left inexperienced replacements to learn the business. Most editorial attacks on the postal service were in response to Reagan's elimination of wasteful offices and superfluous routes, and his bare-bones budget. Wartime service never matched antebellum delivery in the North or the South.

In late 1862, with expenses outnumbering receipts, Reagan asked for higher rates. The hike was deemed unnecessary because it failed to allow for evaluation of the July rate hike, which had doubled existing rates. And as the Confederacy ran short of coins, Southerners bought postage stamps for use as petty cash and thereby helped Reagan balance his budget. Congress augmented the income of the Post Office Department by establishing an express mail service for government correspondence at a rate of one dollar for a half-ounce letter traveling over five hundred miles. After December 8, 1863, the department met congressional demands; Reagan reported expenses for the fiscal year ending in June 1863 to be $2,662,804.67 and receipts, $3,337,853.01, for a profit of $675,048.34. The surplus continued to grow, and the department operated at an overall profit for the entire period of its existence.

Low postal worker salaries, low hauling charges, and high postage rates in a time of enormous inflation helped produce the profit that probably could not have been achieved in other than wartime. Certainly, Reagan mismanaged the department in that he did not use the profits to improve service. The express mail service payment for government letters was taken from the Treasury to pay the post office—thereby hiding the true costs on Reagan's balance sheet. Economy was valued over service at a time when war casualties and grief begged that service come first. But Congress had pushed for economy and Reagan followed its demands as well as he could.

Some politicians, however, felt that service should come first and proposed allowing soldiers to send and receive letters and newspapers free of postage. In various votes, these measures were defeated in the House or Senate, or vetoed by Davis as too costly. In a compromise, soldiers were permitted to send letters postage due to the recipient. Not until January 28, 1865, did Congress override a presidential veto and allow newspapers to be sent to the front postage-free.

Mail transport from outside the Confederacy was fraught with complications. With the Union navy blockading Southern ports, the Confederacy had difficulty receiving and shipping foreign mail. Blockade runners carried the shipments past the naval cordon to Cuba, Bermuda, Nassau, Canada, and Mexico where English and French vessels took on or off-loaded the cargo. Confederate stamps were not recognized by foreign countries—to accept its stamps would imply recognition of the Confederacy—so ship captains arranged to take the mail and have suitable postage affixed at the port of entry. Mail delivery with the United States was handled by private express companies, primarily through the Adams–Southern Express connections that ebbed and flowed in response to the changing fronts.

After Vicksburg fell to Ulysses S. Grant and the Confederacy was cut in two, Reagan had Congress establish a Trans-Mississippi office at Marshall, Texas, under the direction of James H. Starr, former secretary of the treasury for the state of Texas. Reagan and Starr sent mail east and west in rowboats that crossed the Mississippi at night to avoid Federal patrols.

On August 20, 1863, four months after local bread riots, Richmond postal employees went on strike for higher wages. They made as little as sixty dollars a month and inflation had advanced prices over 500 percent. The *Richmond Examiner* railed against the workers and said they should be forced back to work or conscripted into the army. Reagan settled the matter by admitting that the grievances were real. After he promised to support their demand for better salaries, the employees returned to work on August 23. When the department showed a profit in 1863, Congress raised salaries for postal employees.

Reagan's efforts to deliver the mail brought him into conflict with other cabinet officers. A three-month squabble with Secretary of the Treasury Christopher G. Memminger was the most acrimonious. Reagan needed gold coin to pay English suppliers, but Memminger insisted that he could release only Confederate scrip. Reagan argued that his department had put at least fifty thousand in specie into the Treasury and that it must have coin to maintain routes. Davis finally let the attorney general settle the dispute in Reagan's favor.

Reagan also had a four-year struggle with the secretary of war over the military seizure of trains, the takeover of post office property, and the drafting of postal employees. Congress did exempt postal workers from military service, but after passage of the 1862 Conscription Act, only those employees nominated by the president and confirmed by the Senate were exempt. Davis supported Reagan's demands for high-quality personnel, and Congress extended the postal exemptions, but with many exceptions. After Secretary of War James A. Seddon accused Reagan of accepting low bids from those who could not give good service but simply wanted exemptions, Reagan countered that he often refused contracts if he believed the bid was only an effort to avoid conscription. Reagan insisted that the War Department granted as many exemptions to able-bodied men as did his department, which had less than five hundred men so exempted. Furthermore, he pointed out, mail was important to morale and must have strong men to deliver it. In 1864, Robert E. Lee, looking for all available men, complained that exemption of postal employees helped to drain his army. As the Confederacy crumbled, Reagan dropped the controversy and did the best he could with an increasingly limited staff.

Overall, Davis trusted Reagan implicitly and did not interfere with his programs. In return he got a devoted friend who believed strongly in Davis's administration of civilian and military policies. Along with Secretary of the Navy Stephen R. Mallory, Reagan was one of only two cabinet members to serve for the full war. He was with the president when Davis was taken prisoner on May 10, 1865, near Irwinville, Georgia. Reagan had been stable and sensible in his counsel, and he made the post office one of the major successes of the Confederate nation.

[*See also* Newspapers; Reagan, John H.; Southern Express Company; Stamps.]

BIBLIOGRAPHY

Crown, Francis J., Jr., ed. *Confederate Postal History.* Lawrence, Mass., 1976.

Deitz, August. *The Postal Service of the Confederate States of America.* Richmond, Va., 1929.

Garrison, L. R. "Administrative Problems of the Confederate Post Office Department." *Southwestern Historical Quarterly* 19 (1915–1916): 111–142, 232–251.

Patrick, Rembert. *Jefferson Davis and His Cabinet.* Baton Rouge, La., 1944.

Post Office Department of the Confederate States of America. Record of Letters and Other Communications from March 7, 1861, to October 12, 1863, and Reports of the Postmaster General. Manuscripts Division, Library of Congress, Washington, D.C.

Procter, Ben H. *Not without Honor: The Life of John H. Reagan.* Austin, Tex., 1962.

Reagan, John H. "An Account of the Organization and Operations of the Post Office Department of the Confederate States of America, 1861–1865." *Publications of the Southern Historical Association* 6 (1902): 314–327.

Reagan, John H. *Memoirs: With Special Reference to Secession and the Civil War.* New York, 1906.

RUSSELL DUNCAN

POVERTY

Poverty became a serious problem in the Confederacy and ultimately deprived the struggling Southern nation of the active allegiance of many individuals. Though initially unexpected, poverty was so widespread by 1862 that thousands of private persons and officials of state and local government labored to alleviate it. Eventually even the Confederate government became involved in relief efforts. Yet the scope of the problem was so great that it overwhelmed relief activities. Poverty exacerbated class resentments, and hunger caused many Southerners to put the welfare of their families above loyalty to the cause.

A variety of factors contributed to the poverty that descended on the Confederacy. The South had always depended on the North or foreign suppliers for manufactured goods. As the war and blockade disrupted trade, shortages developed in diverse commodities such as iron rails and sewing needles, nails and scythe blades, glass and medi-

> *... poverty stimulated desertion and caused many frustrated and suffering people to withdraw their cooperation. ...*

cines, cloth and coffee. Salt, an essential preservative, became scarce and remained so, despite large-scale Confederate efforts to acquire it.

Shortages grew worse as a result of hoarding. Merchants and panicky citizens often bought large quantities of potentially scarce items. The *Richmond Enquirer* reported that one man purchased seven hundred barrels of flour, and another planter carted in wagon loads of supplies until his "lawn and paths looked like a wharf covered with a ship's loads." Early in the war speculators hoarded salt, bacon, and leather, and six men gained control of the Confederacy's two nail factories. Newspapers and citizens hotly denounced known instances of speculation and extortion, but deficiencies in the Southern transportation network also hampered distribution of those commodities that were available. As a result, Confederates had to develop an ersatz economy, employing their ingenuity to substitute for many items.

Most Southerners assumed that food would not be a problem for their agricultural nation. Why, then, were shortages of food the primary cause of poverty and suffering? Some food rotted in depots, never reaching soldiers or urban markets. Civilians also lost food to the government through policies such as the tax-in-kind and impressment. Secretary of War James A. Seddon called impressment "a harsh, unequal, and odious mode of supply," yet the War

Department depended upon it to supply the armies. Impressment aroused intense anger among the people, as did unauthorized foraging by soldiers, especially troops of cavalry. The *Richmond Enquirer* reported in August 1862 that people were saying, "The *Yankees cannot do us any more harm than our own soldiers have done.*" Drought and crop failures also affected crops in some sections of the Confederacy. But the greatest cause of food shortages was also the most general: the presence in the army of hundreds of thousands of yeoman farmers.

Slave owners could keep their unfree labor force at work while they fought, but non-slave-owning soldiers had to rely on their wives and children or other relatives to cultivate the fields. For many families this burden proved too great, especially as the war dragged on. In a typical plea to the War Department, a Georgia woman wrote, "I can't manage a farm well enough to make a surporte," and an elderly man in Virginia said of his son, "if you dount send him home I am bound to louse my crop and cum to suffer." Zebulon Vance, governor of North Carolina, informed President Jefferson Davis in 1863 that conscription had carried away "a large class whose labor was, I fear, absolutely necessary to the existence of the women and children left behind." Similarly, Governor Milledge L. Bonham of South Carolina opposed a call-up of troops in 1864 on the grounds that it would cause "great suffering next year, and possible starvation." The absence of key artisans, such as blacksmiths who could repair farming tools, aggravated the labor shortage, and the files of the War Department contain hundreds of letters appealing for the detail or exemption of blacksmiths and other artisans.

By the fall of 1862 alarming cries of hunger were being heard in the South. "Want and starvation are staring thousands in the face," declared the *Atlanta Daily Intelligencer.* "What shall we do for something to eat?" asked a paper in the hill country of Georgia in 1863. Tens, even hundreds of thousands of yeoman families, who had always prided themselves on their independence, fell into poverty and suffering. The dimensions of the problem are indicated by the governor of Alabama's admission at the end of the war that more than one-quarter of the white citizens in his state were on relief. A study of surviving records from several counties in North Carolina found that from one-fifth to two-fifths of the white population depended on government relief efforts for cornmeal and pork.

The South's response to this unprecedented social problem was significant but ultimately inadequate. In the Confederacy's straitened circumstances, not enough food, clothing, and other necessary items were available to serve the armies and the civilian population. The resulting poverty had significant effects. An anonymous Virginian wrote to the War Department in 1863 and asked a critical question: "What man is there that would stay in the armey and no that his family is sufring at home?" Later that year W. S. Keen, a provost marshal in Allegheny County, Virginia, answered the question in a letter to the secretary of war. "When our brave and true men, shall hear that their wives and little ones are actually suffering for bread," he warned, "they will naturally become restless and dissatisfied, and mutiny in our army will result, as naturally and as certainly as gravitation."

Provost Marshall Keen's prediction proved to be correct, as poverty stimulated desertion and caused many frustrated and suffering people to withdraw their cooperation or their allegiance from the government. Thus the problem of poverty was a crucial internal problem for the Confederacy.

[See also Bread Riots; Class Conflict; Conscription; Desertion; Extortion; Free Markets; Impressment; Inflation; Labor; Morale; Poor Relief; Salt; Speculation; State Socialism; Substitutes; Tax-in-Kind; Transportation.]

BIBLIOGRAPHY

Escott, Paul D. *After Secession: The Failure of Confederate Nationalism.* Baton Rouge, La., 1978.

Escott, Paul D. "'The Cry of the Sufferers': The Problem of Welfare in the Confederacy." *Civil War History* 23, no. 3 (September 1977): 228–240.

Escott, Paul D. "Poverty and Governmental Aid for the Poor in Confederate North Carolina." *North Carolina Historical Review* 61, no. 4 (October 1984): 462–480.

Massey, Mary Elizabeth. *Ersatz in the Confederacy.* Columbia, S.C., 1952.

Ringold, May Spencer. *The Role of the State Legislatures in the Confederacy.* Athens, Ga., 1966.

Thomas, Emory M. *The Confederate State of Richmond: A Biography of the Capital.* Austin, Tex., 1971.

PAUL D. ESCOTT

POWDER WORKS

To supply gunpowder to their growing armies and coastal defenses, both the Confederate and state governments contracted in the war's first months with small, private powder mills in Tennessee, Virginia, the Carolinas, and Louisiana.

But Chief of Ordnance Col. Josiah Gorgas saw that a large, permanent national gunpowder work would be required. He assigned Maj. George W. Rains to select a site and design, build, and manage the work. Rains proved an excellent choice. A West Point graduate, he had construction and manufacturing experience, expertise in chemistry, and exceptional management ability.

Rains chose Augusta, Georgia, as his factory location, impressed with its combination of temperate climate, good water and rail transportation, and security from attack. Along a two-mile stretch of the Augusta canal he designed and built a world-class gunpowder factory. His complex of brick, granite, glass, and wood structures was architecturally attractive and designed for efficiency, quality, and volume in production. The array of buildings (situated on both sides of the canal) included a laboratory, charcoal kiln, preparation facilities, incorporating mills, and drying and granulating houses and magazines, as well as offices, blacksmith and carpentry shops, repair facilities, forges, and a cannon range for testing grades of powder.

Production began with raw materials: potassium nitrate, sulphur, and charcoal, all purified to Rains's exacting quality standards. These were ground and sized, then steamed for safety and mixed in massive rolling mills. The incorporating mills, each with two five-ton rollers running in circular iron beds, were built by foundries in Atlanta, Chattanooga, and Richmond. They were housed in a dozen bays, each with three massive brick walls, light roofs, and a fourth wall of wood and glass, designed to direct accidental blasts out and up with as little peripheral damage as possible. A large steam engine turned a subterranean power shaft that ran the length of the factory grounds, providing most of the motive power to the complex.

The mill first ran on April 10, 1862, production starting in doorless, windowless—even roofless—shells of buildings still under construction. Production continued uninterrupted until April 18, 1865. In those three years the plant, capable of running twenty-four hours a day, manufactured 2,750,000 pounds of top-quality gunpowder. While prepared ammunition might sometimes run short in the front lines, at no time after April 1862 did the Confederate arsenals suffer a shortage of gunpowder.

In 1863 the Confederate navy opened its own gunpowder mill in Columbia, South Carolina, under a civilian manager, P. Baudery Garésche. Similar in operation to Rains's work, but much smaller, the mill had the capacity to produce 20,000 pounds per month. It ran until the fall of Columbia in March 1865.

[See also Niter and Mining Bureau; Saltpeter.]

BIBLIOGRAPHY

Goff, Richard D. *Confederate Supply.* Durham, N.C., 1969.

Melton, Maurice. "'A Grand Assemblage': George W. Rains and the Augusta Powder Works." *Civil War Times Illustrated* 11 (1973): 28–37.

Milgram, Joseph P., and Norman P. Gentieu. *George Washington Rains: Gunpowdermaker to the Confederacy.* Philadelphia, 1961.

Rains, George W. *History of the Confederate Powder Works.* Augusta, Ga., 1882.

Vandiver, Frank E. *Ploughshares into Swords: Josiah Gorgas and Confederate Ordnance.* Austin, Tex., 1952.

MAURICE K. MELTON

PRESIDENCY

The office of the chief executive officer of the Confederacy derived its powers from the Provisional and Permanent Constitutions. Both documents prescribed an office almost exactly like the presidency of the United States, though they gave the Confederate president the item veto in appropriation bills. The Permanent Constitution gave him direct removal power over department heads and diplomats.

Since the Confederacy was at war, the powers of the presidency were used mainly to sustain military activities. President Jefferson Davis noted impending martial problems in his inaugural address, and in shaping his administration turned his attention first toward creating armies and a navy. Civil functions were not neglected, but were harnessed finally to sustaining a besieged nation.

As "commander-in-chief of the army and navy . . . and of the militia or the several States, when called into the actual service of the Confederate States," Davis found his responsibilities growing with the conflict. His concerns extended from raising and supporting armies and navies to providing supplies, providing commanders for soldiers and sailors, commissioning all Confederate officers, and devising a national strategy for victory. Fortunately for the Confederacy, the president had considerable military experience and knew how to begin.

He picked a cabinet with care, and it was part of the presidency. For war secretary Davis selected Alabamian Leroy P. Walker, whose apparent incapacity led to a long line of succeeding secretaries—but Davis really served as his own war

> Finally a tough value-added tax came, along with an income tax, an excise tax, and taxes on virtually everything. But it was too late. . . .

minister. For secretary of the navy Davis picked Floridian Stephen R. Mallory and left most sea operations in his highly capable hands. Christopher G. Memminger took the treasury portfolio.

Judah P. Benjamin, regarded as the brilliant man of the cabinet, had an uncanny ability to get along with an increasingly besieged president. Benjamin cruised through several departments—Justice, War, finally State—and his management of secondary diplomacy (blockade running, foreign purchasing, diplomatic negotiations for increased belligerency) was sound. The Treasury Department, late in the war, came under George A. Trenholm, a South Carolina banker possessed of toughness and acumen.

While organizing military departments, the president considered strategy in a state rights context: governors were jealous of state territory and authority, and any national strategy had to be shaped around that reality. Davis adopted the "offensive-defensive" as the Confederacy's war plan. Weaker Southern forces would stand on the defensive when necessary to husband resources; when the right chance came, they would concentrate against smaller or isolated enemy forces. A look at Confederate operations from First Manassas to the end of the war will show the president's adherence to his strategy. There were those who argued for a more defensive posture—Braxton Bragg, Joseph E. Johnston, and P. G. T. Beauregard, for instance. And clearly the idea of standing on the defensive and receiving attack had an important precedent in American revolutionary history. But it is doubtful that such a strategy would have been better, given the growing strength of Union forces. Davis's plan probably best fitted the Southern situation.

Davis recognized that power came to his office from the Constitution, and he used the supreme law of the land to centralize war government—to secure Confederate assumption of all military operations (taking them out of state hands), to create a strong national army (the best prop for federal authority over the states), and to frame a national tax structure to underwrite the war.

Taxation proved the most difficult problem for the presidency. Secretary Memminger had hard-money penchants in a soft-money environment. And a laissez-faire Congress could never quite face up to the harsh decisions war demanded. Land, cotton, and slaves were the Confederacy's wealth resources, and the president urged their taxation. Congress dodged that necessity for a time with bond issues, loans, and some fairly innovative measures such as the tax-in-kind, the produce loan, and other levies. Finally a tough value-added tax came, along with an income tax, an excise tax, and taxes on virtually everything. But it was too late; expenses ran away with the currency. By early 1864 the Treasury Department did not know how many notes were circulating.

As Confederate money lost value, so did the foreign credibility of the cause. The president sponsored the important loan through Emile Erlanger and Co. in 1863 for $15 million. Discounted almost from the outset, the loan actually produced somewhere between $6 million and $10 million. More would have been lent by the Erlangers, but a conscientious, if whimsical, Congress did not want to encumber future generations.

A recent scholar, Douglas Ball, in *Financial Failure and Confederate Defeat* (1991), echoes a lingering theme in showing that financial chaos might have been avoided and lays the blame for failing to come to a modern financial system on the executive branch. Davis and Memminger, he says, had every reason to know better. That is probably true, but blame needs softening with sympathy. These men were caught up in the daily rigors of war; they were pushing an agrarian system into modern times and trying to shove a reluctant Congress the same way. That anything was done to sustain the currency is a triumph for the presidency and its branches.

Davis embodied the presidency. He is flayed often for aloofness, for petty defense of incompetent friends—General Bragg, Commissary Gen. Lucius B. Northrop, Gen. John Pemberton—and, like most presidents, he did rely on cronies. But he deserves much credit for changing himself from a private to something of a public man. Though he thought politicking distasteful, and surely unnecessary in a warring nation, he took several "swings around the Confederacy" to speak about the war, to sustain public morale. He lacked Abraham Lincoln's language in persuasion, but he had a zealot's fiery eloquence at times when he talked of the cause he tried to win.

War powers expanded from the moment the war began. The role of the commander in chief enlarged by necessity as Davis pushed military organization, recruiting, strategy, and logistics. Davis did not, despite later accusations, overcommand his forces. Some field commanders received special direction if the chief executive thought they needed it, but trusted ones like Lee, Albert Sidney Johnston, Bragg, and E. Kirby Smith enjoyed wide discretionary powers. Presidential attention went to strategical and logistical support of major campaigns (Albert Sidney Johnston's operations in Tennessee in 1862, for instance), but tactics were left to battle commanders.

Confederate affairs increasingly involved the presidency in state affairs. State rights supporters frayed Confederate nationalism and President Davis conducted wide correspondence with various governors in an effort to prop up their commitment to the war. Governors Joseph E. Brown of Georgia and Zebulon Vance of North Carolina worked almost openly against the cause, and Davis fought them with letters, speeches, and proclamations. State rights governors hampered a national strategy by forcing the president to fragment concentration of forces in defense of particular states. As the executive branch grew in power, it confronted these governors with increasing zeal but uneven results. Important legislation aimed at increasing national power (conscription, impressment, partial commandeering of space on blockade runners, heavy taxation) received presidential support before a fractious and reluctant congress.

Acutely aware of the need for centralized national power, the president fought for a strong war program. He expanded war powers by giving authority to the military departments and supported patriotic governors with such aid as a beleaguered executive could give. Congress followed the executive lead in much war legislation. But it balked at suspending habeas corpus by fiat and grudgingly moved toward a federalism that seemed too much like Abraham Lincoln's Union.

The presidency intruded into almost every phase of Confederate life as regulations abounded to manage the draft, impressment, taxation, manufacturing, transportation, even state legislative matters affecting the war. A presidential hand increasingly touched logistics. Influenced by such able logisticians as Gen. Josiah Gorgas, the chief of ordnance, the president worked to improve roads and railroads and to break or elude the blockade.

That the war lasted for four years is largely the result of Davis's expansion of the powers of his office. Presidential zeal transformed a fragmented feudalism into a small, modern martial nation. Because that happened, the Confederate executive is worth examining as an important facet of the American presidency.

[See also Cabinet; Davis, Jefferson.]

BIBLIOGRAPHY

Commager, Henry Steele, ed. Documents of American History. 5th ed. New York, 1949.

Coulter, E. Merton. The Confederate States of America, 1861–1865. A History of the South, vol. 7. Baton Rouge, La., 1950.

Davis, William C. Jefferson Davis: The Man and His Hour. New York, 1991.

Journal of the Congress of the Confederate States of America, 1861–1865. 7 vols. Washington, D.C., 1904–1905.

Matthews, James M., ed. Statutes at Large of the Provisional Government of the Confederate States of America. Richmond, Va., 1864.

Patrick, Rembert W. Jefferson Davis and His Cabinet. Baton Rouge, La., 1944.

Yearns, Wilfred B. The Confederate Congress. Athens, Ga., 1960.

FRANK E. VANDIVER

PRICE, STERLING

PRICE, STERLING (1809–1867), U.S. congressman, antebellum governor of Missouri, and major general. Born in Virginia to a wealthy, slave-owning family, Price moved with them to Missouri in 1830. Elected to Congress in 1844, he left his seat to lead a regiment in the Mexican War, during which he received promotion to brigadier general and became military governor of Chihuahua. After he had served one term as governor of Missouri, his popularity and moderate Unionist stance earned him election as president of the 1861 state convention charged with deciding the issue of secession; the convention voted against it. But Price became angered by radical Unionists in St. Louis, in particular Congressman Frank P. Blair and Federal army captain Nathaniel Lyon, who were working to forestall secessionist

STERLING PRICE.   LIBRARY OF CONGRESS

efforts in the state. As a result, Price offered his services to secessionist Governor Claiborne F. Jackson as commander of state militia forces.

In an effort to prevent war in Missouri, Price signed an agreement with Federal Western Department commander William S. Harney that both sides would maintain neutrality. Blair and Lyon promptly abrogated the agreement by persuading President Abraham Lincoln to remove Harney from command. After a famous conference with Union leaders on June 11 at St. Louis's Planters' House Hotel, Price mobilized his state troops to oppose the Federal force Lyon was leading toward the state capital. Defeated at Boonville (Price was not present), the state troops retreated with Price to the southwestern corner of the state, where he collected and trained nearly 10,000 state guard recruits. While there, Price traveled to Arkansas and persuaded Confederate commander Ben McCulloch to enter neutral Missouri and join forces to attack Lyon, encamped at Springfield. On August 10, at Oak Hills, the Southern forces defeated Lyon's Federal troops in a battle that resulted in Lyon's death and a Union withdrawal. Buoyed by his ensuing popularity, Price in September marched northward, besieging and capturing 3,000 Federal troops and supplies at Lexington. Pressed by troops under John C. Frèmont, he then retreated into Arkansas.

In March 1862, Price (called "Old Pap" by his men) again joined forces with McCulloch in the newly formed Army of the West, under overall command of Earl Van Dorn, to drive

Federal forces from northern Arkansas. After being defeated at Elkhorn Tavern, he and his troops officially joined the Confederate army, and Price was commissioned a major general. Against the Missourian's wishes, Van Dorn transferred the army to northern Mississippi to assist Confederate defensive operations in the area against Federal forces under Ulysses S. Grant. Angered by this apparent abandonment of the Trans-Mississippi theater, Price twice traveled to Richmond and confronted President Jefferson Davis, engendering poor relations between the two. Davis called Price the vainest man he had ever met.

Price led forces in successive defeats at Iuka and Corinth before receiving transfer again to Arkansas in the spring of 1863. After leading a mismanaged attack on Helena, Price wintered his troops at Camden. The following spring he and E. Kirby Smith took part at Jenkins' Ferry in successful defensive operations against Union forces under Frederick Steele in the Red River campaign. In an effort to liberate his home state and raise recruits, Price invaded Missouri in the fall of 1864 with a force of 12,000, mostly cavalry. While advancing on St. Louis in September, Price fought a bloody engagement at Pilot Knob and then headed west along the Missouri River pursued by a large Union force. After being defeated in a battle at Westport, he retreated in late October with his troops as far as Texas before turning back to Arkansas.

After the war, rather than surrender, Price escaped to Mexico, where he founded Carlota, a colony of ex-Confederates. When Maximilian's Mexican empire collapsed, Price returned to Missouri in early 1867, where he died suddenly less than a year later.

BIBLIOGRAPHY

Castel, Albert. *General Sterling Price and the Civil War in the West.* Baton Rouge, La., 1968.

Monaghan, Jay. *Civil War on the Western Border, 1854–1865.* Lincoln, Nebr., 1955.

Phillips, Christopher. *Damned Yankee: The Life of General Nathaniel Lyon.* Columbia, Mo., 1990.

Rea, Ralph. *Sterling Price: The Lee of the West.* Little Rock, Ark., 1959.

Shalhope, Robert E. *Sterling Price: Portrait of a Southerner.* Columbia, Mo., 1971.

CHRISTOPHER PHILLIPS

PRICE'S MISSOURI RAID

This grand though ultimately unsuccessful cavalry raid in September and October 1864 was conducted by Sterling Price, major general and commander of the District of

Arkansas and Missouri, and E. Kirby Smith, commander of the Trans-Mississippi Department. They planned to capture St. Louis and recover Missouri, controlled by Union troops since the fall of 1861, for the Confederacy. In July 1864, when transfer of two Union corps to Mississippi weakened Federal strength in Louisiana, exiled Missouri Governor Thomas C. Reynolds wrote Price proposing a cavalry raid into Missouri. Eager to lead an expedition into his home state, Price met with Smith at Shreveport, Louisiana, in early August. Price had become convinced by members of the Order of American Knights, a secret organization loyal to the Confederacy, that such an invasion would cause thousands of recruits to swarm into the Southern ranks. Moreover, Price believed that a successful raid would exacerbate Northern dissatisfaction with the war and contribute to Abraham Lincoln's defeat in the upcoming presidential election. Then Lincoln's Peace Democrat successor, George B. McClellan, would recognize the Confederacy and sue for peace.

On August 4, 1864, Price received orders to make arrangements to invade Missouri, providing him with command of all cavalry west of the Mississippi. Three weeks later, he turned over command of his district to Maj. Gen. John B. Magruder and ordered Brig. Gen. Joseph O. Shelby to attack DeVall's Bluff, Arkansas, located on the White River, to divert the attention of Federal forces at nearby Helena. On August 28, Price left Camden, Arkansas, assuming command of cavalry divisions under Maj. Gens. John Sappington Marmaduke and James F. Fagan the next day. Proceeding to the Arkansas River, the column crossed on September 6 at Dardanelle. On September 12, the force made its way over the White River and the next day rendezvoused with Shelby's force at Pocahontas. While there, Price organized the Army of Missouri into three divisions under Marmaduke, Fagan, and Shelby, totaling 12,000 men and fourteen guns. Over 4,000 of his troops were unarmed, since Shelby had only recently conscripted them from northeastern Arkansas. Price hoped to obtain supplies and arms in Missouri.

Traveling in three parallel columns in order to gather forage and provisions, the force entered Missouri on September 19 and arrived at Fredericktown five days later. There Price received word that 1,500 Federals under Brig. Gen. Thomas Ewing lay poised at Ironton, twenty miles west. Moreover, he learned that a Union infantry corps under Maj. Gen. A. J. Smith had been diverted from Mississippi and was now encamped south of St. Louis. Price dispatched Shelby's division to Mineral Point to wreck railroad bridges between Ironton and St. Louis in order to prevent Smith from reinforcing Ewing. Price himself advanced toward Ironton on September 26. His force encountered slight resistance at Arcadia and quickly pushed Federal troops into Fort Davidson, a hexagonal earthen structure at nearby Pilot Knob.

The fort was armed with sixteen cannon and protected by nearly 900 yards of open meadow. But rather than position artillery on the mountains surrounding it and shelling it into submission, Price unwisely ordered a frontal assault at 2:00 P.M. Within twenty minutes, the Southern troops suffered more than 1,000 casualties, many from Price's most experienced brigades who had advanced several times to the very walls of the fort. Dismayed, he canceled further assaults, opting to use artillery from the heights. During the night, Ewing blew up the powder magazine and escaped with his command to Potosi, 25 miles distant, leaving the fort, cannons, and supplies to the Confederates. In all, the Federals had suffered less than 100 casualties. Discovering the following morning that Ewing had escaped, Price sent Shelby and Marmaduke in pursuit. When they learned that 4,500 Federal cavalry under Brig. Gen. Alfred Pleasonton were advancing from St. Louis to reinforce Ewing, both units withdrew.

The decimation of his best troops at Pilot Knob and the arrival of Smith's 8,000-strong veteran corps at St. Louis convinced Price that any hope of capturing the city had passed. Yet, despite the obvious setback, Price believed that the continued presence of a large, supplied army would not only entice volunteers but might yet stir public opinion and affect the outcome of the November election. On September 30, after sending Shelby's cavalry as a feint toward St. Louis, Price began a slow march westward along the south bank of the Missouri River, hoping to gain recruits and foraging for supplies. As they moved toward the state capital, Jefferson City, the columns destroyed bridges and miles of the Pacific Railroad's track, avoiding all conflict other than minor skirmishes. Despite the supreme commander of the Order of American Knights' calling on members to enlist in Price's Army of Missouri, recruits proved sparse and many of those taken were unwilling to be disciplined. Moreover, Price's languid pace allowed nearly 7,000 Federal militia and regular troops to fortify the capital, rendering its capture difficult. On October 5, Price occupied Hermann, but shaken by the debacle at Pilot Knob and harassed by Pleasonton's cavalry, he bypassed Jefferson City and proceeded toward Boonville, which he occupied four days later.

At Boonville, Price added some 2,000 recruits, bringing his total force to 15,000, though many were unarmed and untrained. Moreover, looters and pillagers, including seasoned guerrillas and bushwhackers, abounded among new recruits. Their exploits had become so notorious that Governor Reynolds wrote Price in disgust, claiming that his troops' ravaging of the river counties would make it difficult to supplant the state's provisional Unionist government. Desperate for arms, Price on October 14 sent Shelby with a brigade to Glasgow, where locals reported that Federals had stored a large cache of weapons. Though Shelby captured more than 500 troops, the Union soldiers were able to destroy the arms before surrendering. Meanwhile, the rest of the army took up the march westward, with a detachment under Confederate partisan leader M. Jeff Thompson raiding

Sedalia and capturing the militia there. Throughout, Union elements skirmished with Price's rear guard, which was protecting his cumbersome five-hundred-wagon supply train loaded with booty.

As Price plodded through the center of the state, Maj. Gen. William Rosecrans, commander of the Department of Missouri, mobilized forces to trap and destroy the invading army. In addition to instructing Pleasonton to dog Price in an effort to slow him, Rosecrans sent A. J. Smith's infantry to Sedalia in pursuit of the Confederate column and ordered 4,500 veterans under Maj. Gen. Joseph A. Mower to move from Arkansas to assist. Finally, he tried to communicate with Maj. Gen. Samuel Curtis, commander of the Department of Kansas, and have him send troops to trap Price between the converging Federal forces. Though ignorant of Rosecrans's plan, Curtis was well aware of Price's whereabouts and massed more than 15,000 militiamen and regulars near the border. On October 15, he ordered forward three brigades under Maj. Gen. James G. Blunt to Lexington, Missouri. Because most of Blunt's force were militia and would go no farther than the Big Blue River, six miles east of Kansas City, only 2,000 regulars reached Lexington.

Price's army reached Waverly, Missouri, on October 18 and the next day moved toward Lexington. Shelby encountered Blunt's lead units and pushed them back easily. Now aware that separate Union forces numbering more than twice his own were encircling him, Price moved quickly both to prevent Smith and Blunt from effecting a juncture and to leave himself an avenue of escape. He turned southward, planning to position his men between the two Union forces and defeat each in turn, and then to confront Curtis. On October 21, at the Little Blue River, Price encountered 400 dismounted horsemen with two howitzers, a token contingent of Blunt's troops. Blunt's main force had fallen back on the Big Blue, where Curtis's militia was entrenched on the steep west bank of the river. After a sharp skirmish, Price's men forced the small group of Federals to retreat to the hills behind the river. But as the Confederates continued their assault, Blunt returned with the rest of his infantry and artillery, most of whom were armed with repeating rifles and breechloaders. The Federals' superior firepower pushed back the advancing Confederates briefly, but Price's superior numbers soon threatened to turn both of Blunt's flanks, forcing the Union troops to retreat. That night, Blunt rejoined Curtis at the Big Blue.

On October 22, Price sent Marmaduke's division to the east to keep Pleasonton at bay and sent one brigade of Shelby's division to feint against Curtis at the main crossing ford of the Big Blue. Price's major thrust, made by brigades under Thompson and Sidney D. Jackman, came at Byram's Ford, the next upstream crossing, but in three hours of hard fighting, they were unable to prevail. Late in the afternoon, Alonzo Slayback's regiment found an uncontested crossing farther upriver. Taking that route, they fell upon the exposed

right of Curtis's line. As the Union line withdrew, Shelby pushed his entire division across and drove the Federals toward Westport. With nightfall, the Confederates were forced to break off the attack before they could complete the victory, allowing Curtis to re-form his line just south of Westport.

While Price successfully forced a crossing of the Big Blue, Marmaduke in the rear experienced defeat. Pleasonton crossed the Little Blue and mauled William L. Cabell's brigade, taking nearly 400 prisoners and two cannons. Fighting through Independence, Pleasonton's cavalry pushed Marmaduke's division almost to the Big Blue. Marmaduke fell back to the west side of the river at nightfall

> Marmaduke's troops had spent all their ammunition, and they broke into a rout across the prairie, with Federal horsemen thundering after. . . .

and sent word to Price that the army was in danger of being trapped and destroyed. Fearing the loss of his men and his valuable wagon train, Price made preparations for a fighting withdrawal to the south.

At daybreak on October 23, Price sent Shelby's division, supported by two of Fagan's brigades, to attack the Federals at Westport. During two brutal hours of fighting, the opposing lines of horsemen charged and countercharged in the rolling woodlands along Brush Creek. Meanwhile, Pleasonton hurled a savage assault against Marmaduke at Byram's Ford, both sides taking heavy losses. By noon, Marmaduke's troops had spent all their ammunition, and they broke into a rout across the prairie, with Federal horsemen thundering after and capturing hundreds of them. Simultaneously, Blunt launched an attack on Shelby's line, nearly breaking the Confederate right. Learning of the collapse of Marmaduke's division, Price ordered all troops to retreat southward while Shelby fought for time. As Marmaduke and Fagan streamed toward Little Santa Fe, only Shelby's dogged withdrawal saved Price's army from complete destruction. The Battle of Westport proved to be Price's high-water mark, the last major action to take place in the Trans-Mississippi region. The exact number of casualties is unavailable, but Shelby estimated he had left at least eight hundred dead and wounded on the field. Price fled southward with a disorganized mass of horsemen, cattle, refugees, wagons, and unarmed men.

Curtis failed to order a pursuit for twelve hours, enabling Price to escape the Union pincers and secure his wagon train. Ultimately Price would regret this decision, for the ponderously slow wagons retarded his mounted forces' retreat, allowing the Federals to overtake them just one day later at the Marais des Cygnes River, sixty miles south. While

Marmaduke and Fagan held off the advancing Federals, Shelby returned with his command from a foray to Fort Scott, Kansas, surprising Pleasonton and allowing Price to cross the river. In the fray, Marmaduke was captured. That night, Price burned nearly a third of his wagons. Skirmishing continued the entire next day and night, and on the afternoon of October 28, Blunt (now leading the pursuit) caught up with Price's retreating column near Newtonia, Missouri. Again, Shelby managed to drive off the advancing Federals before assistance could arrive. On October 29, Rosecrans recalled all troops belonging to the Department of Missouri, leaving Curtis with just 3,500 cavalry to continue the chase.

Before the situation could be rectified, Price had crossed the Arkansas River and dispersed his forces, marching into Indian Territory. On November 23, they arrived at Bonham, Texas. When the column returned to Laynesport, Arkansas, on December 2, 1864, Price's army had marched an incredible 1,488 miles. Though it had destroyed miles of railroad in Missouri and had diverted a corps of Federal infantry destined for William Tecumseh Sherman in Georgia, Price's raid had failed largely to achieve any of its objectives, and his army had lost an estimated 4,000 casualties, mostly to desertion.

BIBLIOGRAPHY

Britton, Wiley. *The Civil War on the Border*. New York, 1890.
Buresh, Lumir F. *October 25th and the Battle of Mine Creek*. Edited by Dan L. Smith. Kansas City, Mo., 1977.
Castel, Albert. *General Sterling Price and the Civil War in the West*. Baton Rouge, La., 1968.
Hinton, Richard J. *Rebel Invasion of Missouri and Kansas, and the Campaign of the Army of the Border, against General Sterling Price, in October and November, 1864*. Chicago, 1865.
Jenkins, Paul. *The Battle of Westport*. Kansas City, Mo., 1906.
Monaghan, Jay. *Civil War on the Western Border, 1854–1865*. Lincoln, Nebr., 1955.
Peterson, Cyrus A., and Joseph M. Hanson. *Pilot Knob: The Thermopylae of the West*. New York, 1914. Reprint, Cape Girardeau, Mo., 1964.
Shalhope, Robert E. *Sterling Price: Portrait of a Southerner*. Columbia, Mo., 1971.

CHRISTOPHER PHILLIPS

PRISONERS OF WAR

Since neither the Confederacy nor the Union expected a long war, both sides failed to plan for the enemy soldiers they would capture. There were in existence U.S. Army regulations known to both combatants, which placed upon the quartermaster general the duty of taking charge of prisoners and provided for a commissary general of prisoners to carry out responsibilities for them. Such an officer had served dur-

ing the War of 1812, providing a precedent familiar to North and South. But people on both sides also knew that the War of 1812 and the Revolutionary War had been characterized by charges of atrocious treatment of American captives. Confederates and Federals therefore were suspicious from the start of how their foe would treat prisoners.

Before the outbreak of fighting, the two sides released most potential enemies whom they took into custody. The Confederates, though they held enlisted men as prisoners, paroled U.S. Army officers captured in Texas upon their promise not to serve against the South. The Union similarly paroled captured Missouri militia.

Once fighting began both the Confederacy and the Union improvised arrangements for prisoners. The United States was the first to create a formal system, naming in 1861 Lt. Col. William H. Hoffman as commissary general of prisoners. Hoffman, who was one of the paroled prisoners from Texas, was a veteran army officer with experience only in managing the limited number of men in the peacetime army as economically as possible. Like his Confederate counterpart, John H. Winder, who during most of the war was the officer principally responsible for prisoners, Hoffman was preoccupied with preventing prisoners from escaping. To hold his captives, Hoffman began by leasing Johnson's Island on Lake Erie near Sandusky, Ohio. Though Hoffman originally intended it to be the main depot for Confederate prisoners, the rapid expansion of the war outstripped the capacity of the barracks, and it came to be used mainly to hold officers.

Hoffman then pressed into service Union training camps at Camp Randall (Madison, Wisconsin), Camp Douglas (Chicago), Camp Butler (Springfield, Illinois), Camp Morton (Indianapolis), and Camp Chase (Columbus, Ohio). Existing barracks were fenced in and new ones hastily constructed. The Union also used vacant buildings in St. Louis and seacoast forts such as Delaware on that river and Warren in Boston Harbor. Meanwhile the Confederates commandeered empty warehouses and similar structures for prisons. Both sides selected sites in considerable part because of proximity to transportation facilities, including rivers, bays, and especially railroads.

Prisoner Exchanges

As prisoners accumulated, they and their relatives pressed for their release on parole and exchange. An impediment was the insistence of the United States that it would take no action that recognized the legitimacy of secession or the legality of the Confederate States government. The Federals tolerated the generals in the field making exchanges with their opponents, and they permitted an informal system under which captured officers went on parole to the opposing capital and sought to arrange special exchanges for particular (often influential) captives.

But the Union declined to recognize the authority of the Confederates to license privateering by their people, and it proceeded in 1861 to bring captured privateers to trial as pirates. The Confederates, however, had captured at First Manassas over a thousand Union prisoners, putting the South in a position to retaliate if the privateers were executed. In November 1861, General Winder selected by lot high-ranking prisoners to undergo the same fate as the privateers. Although the Federal authorities concluded that exchanging privateers for hostages would not be equivalent to recognizing the Confederate government, and the Confederates for their part wanted even the limited recognition implicit in a plan for general exchange, the respective army commanders were unwilling to make this special exchange.

Since both sides had an incentive to end the controversy and be relieved of the growing burden of providing for prisoners, they agreed on July 22, 1862, to a cartel modeled on that between the United States and the British in the War of 1812. Gen. D. H. Hill on behalf of the South and Gen. John A. Dix on behalf of the North made an arrangement whereby all prisoners were to be paroled within ten days and sent to their own lines; a formal exchange would take place as soon as equivalent numbers had reached the lines. Agents for both sides were to administer the cartel, keeping records for an elaborate system under which men who could not be exchanged for enemies of equal rank would be matched according to a sliding scale of equivalents. (For example, a general commanding in chief or admiral equaled sixty privates or common seamen.) The cartel stated that it would continue during the war regardless of which side held the most prisoners and that no "misunderstanding" would interrupt the release of prisoners on parole. After the exchange began, both sides closed all but a few transient prisons.

But the belligerents discovered that they would have to create parole camps to house their men awaiting formal exchange, and sometimes they adapted facilities previously used for enemy prisoners. Both sides had difficulty in maintaining discipline among these idle men, who were prohibited from doing military duty, and they feared the likelihood that some of their soldiers in the field would readily surrender in order to obtain a vacation from combat. Moreover, a system resting on mutual trust was difficult to carry out between combatants who had gone to war partly because of their mistrust. Almost from the start, Robert Ould, the Confederate agent of exchange, was embroiled in a controversy with his Union counterparts characterized by interminable bickering letters.

One issue that arose in these disputes involved a Confederate protest against Gen. Benjamin F. Butler's execution of William B. Mumford for hauling down the U.S. flag at New Orleans. Believing that the threat of retaliation had forced the United States to back down in such episodes as that of the imprisoned privateers, Ould's superior, President Jefferson Davis, made a major tactical blunder. On December 24, 1862, he issued a proclamation declaring Butler to be an outlaw and ordering that no captured U.S. commissioned officer should be released on parole until Butler had been caught and hanged. At the same time he ordered that black troops when captured should be turned over to the authorities of the state in which they were taken. He and the Confederate Congress subsequently resolved that captured white officers of black units were to be tried and put to death. The Confederates thus had taken actions that effectively ended the release of officers under the cartel, after May 25, 1863. Moreover, Confederate threats to retaliate against captured Union officers for the execution of two Confederates captured while recruiting, allegedly behind the Union lines, proved ineffective. Although the Confederates held another lottery among their prisoners, they found that the Federals by capturing Brig. Gen. William Henry Fitzhugh Lee, son of Robert E. Lee, had obtained a hostage that could not be topped in the game of threatened retaliation.

Meanwhile the exchange of noncommissioned officers and privates had continued. But the belligerents' exchange agents became involved in controversy over the legality of paroles of prisoners associated with the great battles of the summer of 1863, and in July the United States decided to cease further deliveries of prisoners. Butler, despite his status as an outlaw imposed by President Davis, claimed that he could break the deadlock over exchange, and in early 1864 the Union authorities permitted him to try. He succeeded only in exchanging two experimental boatloads of prisoners. In March 1864, he and Ould came to a final parting of the ways over the status of black soldiers. Ould agreed that those blacks who had been free before the war would be treated as prisoners of war but refused to grant such status to those who had been slaves. Inconsistent with this declaration, however, the two navy departments exchanged several naval prisoners without raising questions of race or slave status.

Indeed, though the new Federal general in chief, Ulysses S. Grant, urged Butler to insist on equal treatment for black troops, he privately raised several objections to exchanges. He indicated that ceasing exchanges would have the effect of discouraging easy surrenders and desertions to the enemy. He also pointed out that the Confederate conscription system permitted them to put into the field anyone released by the United States. "If we commence a system of exchange, which liberates all prisoners taken," he argued, "we will have to fight on until the whole South is exterminated." Instead of openly acknowledging this brutally realistic argument, Butler and Grant repeatedly demanded that the Confederates agree that their proposals for a man-for-man exchange include ex-slaves as well as other prisoners. Regular exchanges were not resumed during the 1864 campaign season.

Prison Conditions

As the unexchanged prisoners accumulated, both sides crowded more men into existing prisons and built new ones. The Union opened camps at Rock Island, Illinois, and Point Lookout, Maryland (the latter being the only Federal facility to use tents exclusively), and in July 1864, began to move prisoners into a fenced camp at Elmira, New York, which quickly became one of the more overcrowded and deadly Union prisons. Meanwhile, the Confederates had built a stockade at Andersonville, Georgia, which grew into the largest and most notorious Civil War prison. The overflow was sent to several smaller prisons. By the end of 1864, the incidence of deaths at one of these, the camp at Salisbury, North Carolina, began to rival that at Andersonville.

Officers. The inmates of both sides' prisons, new and old, henceforth experienced for a prolonged period conditions that previously had been mostly temporary. A prisoner's treatment was strongly affected by whether or not he was a commissioned officer. Both sides tried to house officers separately from enlisted men and usually in different prisons. One reason was the military tradition that officers had every interest in upholding—they were to be treated as gentlemen. Moreover, segregation of imprisoned officers from enlisted men had the practical effect of disrupting enemy military organization and discipline, facilitating control of the prisoners. (Indeed, the relatively few instances in which officers and men were temporarily held close to one another resulted in their increased plotting to escape, which convinced authorities of the importance of separation according to rank.)

Since officers were less numerous than enlisted men, their prisons were always smaller, which made for better sanitation. Moreover, because officers usually came from above average economic backgrounds and were better paid, they could buy additional food and comforts, and during most of the war both sides permitted them to do so. Thus, though mortality was high among officers on Civil War battlefields, it was relatively low in the prisons. Nonetheless, highly literate officers, resentful of their captivity, often wrote complaints about their treatment, which added to the notoriety of the Confederates' Libby Prison and the Union's Johnson's Island.

> A prisoner's treatment was strongly affected by whether or not he was a commissioned officer.

One of the few areas in which officers might suffer more than enlisted men was in that of retaliation. As mentioned above, their status made them obvious targets when either side wished to put pressure on the other. The most notorious instance of their literally becoming targets occurred in the summer of 1864. The Confederate commander at Charleston proposed to discourage the Union bombardment of the city from Morris Island by confining in it fifty high-ranking Union prisoners. With the approval of President Davis, the men were taken into the city. When the local Union commander learned of this and requested that fifty Confederate hostages be sent to him for the same purpose, the Confederates disingenuously denied that they had intended to place captives under fire and agreed to a special exchange of the two groups. Grant, upon learning of this violation of his suspension of exchanges, forbade its repetition.

Thus the Confederates did not succeed in an attempt to reopen exchanges by sending six hundred more captured officers to Charleston. Instead, Union officers, believing that the Confederates intended to place these prisoners under fire, ordered six hundred Confederate officers to be confined after September 7 in a hastily built stockade near the batteries on Morris Island. Housed in crowded tents on short rations, they were guarded by those men of the black Fifty-fourth Massachusetts who had survived the previous year's assault on Battery Wagner. Though most of the Confederates here and elsewhere resented and reacted hostilely to black guards, a few got along better with their keepers than their fellows liked. In October, the Federal authorities had the hostages transferred to Fort Pulaski, Georgia. For many years, this group of ex-Confederate officers recalled their sufferings as the objects of retaliation and proclaimed themselves "The Immortal Six Hundred."

Security Problems. Like the Confederate officers on Morris Island, prisoners of both sides and of all ranks often complained about their guards and the arrangements for security. As might be anticipated in a war involving strong popular emotion, the prisoners were often the focus of animus. As they were marched through enemy cities, civilians mocked and insulted them. In the prisons, officers and guards often treated them as despised enemies. Yet, though clearly some prison personnel acted the part of brutes and sadists, there is abundant evidence that many on both sides behaved with perhaps surprising kindness toward the men under their control. In several instances, clergymen, nuns, and members of the Masonic Order ministered to prisoners.

The problems of prison security that proved so controversial on both sides stemmed less from sadism than from the prison authorities' lack of confidence in their ability to maintain control. Neither side was willing to use first-class officers or men to run prisons. By 1864 when the prisons were especially crowded, they were guarded in the Confederacy mostly by reserves composed of boys and old men, and in the United States by men on short-term enlistments or unfit for field service. Commanders on both sides complained of their guards' lack of training and discipline. These outnumbered, mediocre guards were expected to keep throngs of prisoners within often flimsy fences and stockades. Should any number of prisoners break out, it was unlikely that guards armed with single-shot muskets could intimidate them. To discourage outbreaks, several prisons directed artillery pieces at their inmates, and Johnson's Island issued revolvers to its guards. But the most common security precaution was to lay out "deadlines" along the fences, which prisoners were forbidden to cross. Considering the quality of many of the guards, it was probably inevitable that some shot on almost any pretext at prisoners near the deadline. Neither side made any serious effort to enforce discipline in such cases.

Like prisoners in all times, those of the Civil War thought much about and often attempted escapes. The largest and best known was the exodus of 109 Union officers from Libby through a tunnel on February 9, 1864. Inmates of other prisons, Southern and Northern, also dug tunnels, sometimes successfully. Given the inadequacies of the guards, some prisoners found it possible to pass out in various disguises. At the unfenced camp at Columbia, South Carolina, some 373 prisoners simply ran the guard lines. Once out, prisoners on both sides often received help from sympathetic civilians, with Union escapees receiving assistance from mountain whites and slaves. Organized uprisings were less common, but a large one occurred on November 25, 1864, at Salisbury. Most prisoners simply endured prison life.

Prisoners' Lives. Their physical setting contributed to the captives' misery. The Union usually housed its prisoners in flimsily built, scantily heated barracks. The Confederates used some warehouses and similar buildings but far more camps, with tents for only a minority of the prisoners. Large numbers were forced to burrow into the earth with little or no shelter from the weather. When critics of the Confederacy asked why the prisoners could not have been permitted to cut timber to build their own huts, a partial explanation was the inability to guard working parties. A further problem at all of the larger prisons was the lack of facilities for disposing of human waste if the prison was not located along a large stream (as at Salisbury) or authorities were unwilling to spend money to build sewers (as at Chicago and Elmira). Inadequate shelter and sanitation contributed to the diseases that filled the insufficient hospitals.

Lack of clothing made conditions worse. Confederates often reached Northern prisons in garments badly worn and unsuited to winter weather. Federal commanders issued limited amounts of substandard clothing and sometimes permitted prisoners to receive clothing from relatives and friends. Confederate prison keepers, on the other hand, supplied no clothing to their captives whose distress mounted as their uniforms wore out. Neither side provided prisoners with more than a limited number of blankets, and the plight of Northern prisoners was worsened by the Confederates' policy of systematically stripping newly captured men of bedding and other equipment. The typical prisoner was ragged and cold.

The most controversial aspect of the treatment of prisoners was the matter of food. Both the Confederacy and the Union claimed that they provided their prisoners with the same rations issued to their own troops; yet their captives claimed to be hungry and in many cases demonstrably lost weight. These contentions were less contradictory than they might seem. Although controversialists would later argue in precise terms about the ounces issued of various foods, the wartime records make it clear that the actual amounts were approximations. Moreover, both sides deducted a portion of the ration to create a so-called camp or hospital fund, theoretically for the prisoners' benefit. The keepers diverted additional rations to those captives willing to work around the prison. Thus no individual prisoner could count on receiving the officially announced quantity. And when the food available for the army as a whole was insufficient, as in the Confederacy, the needs of the guards were met first.

Ultimately, however, quantity was only part of the food problem. The basic ration of both sides consisted mainly of bread and meat. Unless supplemented with vegetables, the diet resulted in nutritional deficiencies and such diseases as scurvy. Guards could supplement from several sources; prisoners had only severely limited opportunities to buy vegetables. The Confederates issued none; the Union mainly did so only when scurvy actually appeared. As the cornbread issued by the Confederates was very rough and caused diarrhea, it is not surprising that their captives sickened and that many died.

Despite their hardships, most prisoners had an overabundance of leisure. Neither side attempted to compel them to work. The men read, participated in classes and religious

> **The most controversial aspect of the treatment of prisoners was the matter of food.**

meetings, and wrote diaries and letters. Many made jewelry or other small items as souvenirs for relatives or for sale to their captors. A significant minority seeking better treatment gave their paroles not to escape and agreed to do physical or clerical work for the prison keepers. Both sides thereby reduced the cost of running their prisons.

The prison life of blacks was very different. As the Confederacy declined to recognize them as legitimate soldiers, they often did not survive to reach the prisons; in several well-documented cases Confederate soldiers refused to give them quarter. But hundreds of black soldiers and civilian employees of the United States did reach the Confederate prisons where they were required to perform the more menial tasks. Others were sent to labor in niter works or to construct fortifications. Some were advertised in the newspapers in an effort to return them to slavery.

Prisoners as Manpower

White as well as black prisoners seemed to offer a source of manpower to both belligerents in the desperate year of 1864. The numerically inferior Confederates could gain particular advantage because their more rigorous conscription made it likely that they could return to the field a higher proportion of any exchanged prisoners. Hence the Confederates permitted prisoners in their hands to publicize their sufferings in Southern prisons and petition their government for an exchange. Grant and the Union leadership, however, believed that this would play into the hands of the South. Privately the Union commander admitted, "It is hard on our men held in Southern prisons not to exchange them, but it is humanity to those left in the ranks to fight our battles. Every man we hold, when released . . . becomes an active soldier against us. . . . If we hold those caught they amount to no more than dead men." He persistently asked the Confederates whether their proposed man-for-man exchange included equal treatment for black prisoners. As the Confederates were unwilling to agree to this, they were unable to obtain reinforcements through exchange.

The Confederates then concocted schemes to recapture their soldiers in Northern prisons. Rebel agents in Canada with the aid of Northern sympathizers devoted considerable time and money to plots to release prisoners in Camps Douglas and Morton. All their plans proved abortive, including an attempt to capture a Federal warship and then release the Confederate officers imprisoned on Johnson's Island. Also futile were hopes of conducting a naval expedition against Point Lookout and an attempt as part of Jubal Early's 1864 raid on Washington to continue to that prison.

Unable to retrieve their own men, the Confederates in desperation attempted to recruit soldiers from the Union prisoners in their camps. The War Department authorized recruiting foreign-born soldiers whose loyalty to the United States was presumed to be relatively low. In the summer and fall of 1864, Confederate recruiters visited the Eastern prison camps for enlisted men, told the inmates their government had abandoned them, and offered extra rations and pay if they joined the Confederate army. They were able to persuade about 4,500 men, not all foreign-born, to join several battalion-sized units led by Confederate officers. The Southerners hoped to use these men behind the lines and for peripheral military operations. Unsurprisingly, their record was mixed and sometimes disastrous, though some did labor effectively as engineers for the Confederacy.

It was as workers rather than soldiers that the prisoners supplied the Confederates with additional manpower. As mentioned above, the South, like the Union, used parolees to help run their prisons. Without such aid the Confederate system could not have functioned. General Winder estimated that the services of some eight hundred captive workers at Andersonville alone saved the Confederacy a million dollars

yearly. And the Confederates recruited skilled men for a variety of enterprises besides prison-related work. They attempted to run shoemaking shops at several prisons. At Richmond over one hundred prisoners worked in the quartermaster shops, making shoes, clothing, and other equipment for the Confederates. Others worked for public and private manufacturers of a wide variety of war-related goods.

Although the Union with its abundance of skilled labor made little attempt to use its prisoners thus, it recruited even more Confederate prisoners for combat duty. Confronted with an outbreak of Indian warfare on the Great Plains, the Federals met part of their need for troops by enlisting prisoners to fight there rather than against their fellow Confederates. Organized into six regiments under Northern officers, the United States recruited about six thousand men, including several hundred recaptured Union prisoners who had previously joined the Confederates. Both sides tended to refer to their prisoner recruits as "Galvanized Yankees," verbal evidence of the suspicion that their new loyalty represented a thin coating. But those who fought for the United States for over a year after the war's end often rendered effective service.

The Effects of Politics

As unexchanged prisoners accumulated on both sides, the belligerents exploited their treatment for political purposes. In 1864 both the U.S. Congress's Committee on the Conduct of the War and a committee of the U.S. Sanitary Commission interviewed returned Union prisoners about conditions in Southern prisons. In addition to their verbal descriptions of horrors, both committees' reports included ghastly pictures of individual returnees.

The Lincoln administration used charges of mistreatment of prisoners to arouse bitter feeling against the South. Arguing that Confederate prisoners should be subject to the same treatment, the War Department reduced rations and forbade the sending of parcels from friends. Meanwhile Democrats and other opponents of the administration blamed Abraham Lincoln and Secretary of War Edwin M. Stanton for the lack of exchange and sought to use the prisoners' suffering as an issue in the 1864 presidential election.

The Confederates attempted to rebut Union propaganda and counterattacked with their own. To remind the world that Confederates also were spending long months in prison, President and Mrs. Davis proudly displayed in their White House objects made by time-killing prisoners. In October 1864, English sympathizers held a Southern Bazaar at Liverpool to publicize the sufferings of Confederate prisoners and raise money for their relief. In March 1865, a joint congressional committee denounced the Union reports of prisoner mistreatment as mere sensationalism. It claimed that the reports' illustrations showing almost skeletal men were not typical of the prisoners, and though not furnishing pictures of returned Confederates, the committee asserted that many of them were in as bad or worse condition as the Federals.

The Confederates denied any deliberate mistreatment of their prisoners and attributed any shortages of supplies to the uncivilized nature of the warfare being waged by the United States against the Confederate economy, citing such operations as Gen. Philip Sheridan's devastation of the Shenandoah Valley. Moreover, they sought to attribute the sufferings on both sides to the Union's refusal to exchange prisoners. The Confederates' belated reply to Northern charges, however, received only limited circulation before or after the war's end.

Meanwhile, the warring powers had agreed upon measures to mitigate the prisoners' condition. To reduce political pressure for a general exchange, the Union authorities agreed to release the sick. In September 1864, General Butler proposed the exchange of men believed to be unfit for field service within sixty days. Reports of the bad condition of the several thousand men released under this arrangement built pressure to relieve the remaining prisoners. Confederate exchange agent Ould suggested and Grant agreed to an arrangement whereby each side would be allowed to forward food and clothing to be distributed by paroled officers to its own prisoners. To make this possible for the Confederates, they were permitted to send through the blockade a shipload of cotton for sale in the North. One load was sent and both sides distributed large amounts of goods early in 1865.

At almost the same time, general exchange resumed. Beginning the process in January 1865, Grant accepted a previous Confederate proposal to exchange all prisoners being held in close confinement under various attempts at retaliation. The Confederates—so unable to care for their prisoners that General Winder had unsuccessfully suggested paroling them and simply sending them across the lines— now again attempted to reopen exchange. On February 11, Ould proposed to Grant the delivery of "all the Federal prisoners now in our custody" if the Union would deliver an equal number of Confederates. Grant quickly agreed and both sides notified their overjoyed captives that they would be released.

Why was the Union now willing to exchange? With the administration under increasing attack in and out of Congress for the failure to exchange, Grant had been given personal public responsibility for the controversial matter. He knew that the resumption of active campaigning was still weeks away and that the approach of William Tecumseh Sherman who was about to capture Columbia, South Carolina, made reinforcements for the collapsing Confederate armies a less critical concern. But what of the black prisoners whose plight the Federals had used to explain the earlier refusal to exchange anyone? Did the Confederate offer to free all prisoners include ex-slaves?

Previously the Federal authorities had pressed the Confederates to be specific regarding the fate of former slaves. In 1865, the Union did not raise the question, and though the Confederates exchanged several hundred blacks, they never acknowledged returning one who had been a slave before the war. Lincoln's reelection and the anticipated end of the war had reduced the immediate political significance of the status of imprisoned former slaves.

Even as the war entered its final days, both sides continued to manipulate the prisoners for maximum advantage. Grant, correctly believing that his opponents were putting released prisoners into their ranks as quickly as possible, ordered that when possible physically unfit men should be sent first and that prisoners whose homes were in the West should be sent to the East. The Confederates, while too disorganized and harried to discriminate effectively, sought to send Union men who were sick or whose enlistments had expired. Like the Union, the dying Confederacy anticipated taking new prisoners and improvised facilities to hold them. As the surrender of Robert E. Lee marked the beginning of the end, however, the bulk of the remaining Confederate armies were paroled in the field without being held as prisoners of war.

Postwar Issues

It fell to the United States to provide for the repatriation of the prisoners on both sides. Federal prisoners released in the South were fed, reclothed, and returned either to their units or to their home states to be mustered out. As for the imprisoned Confederates, the Union authorities on May 8 ordered the release of all below the rank of colonel who were willing to take the amnesty oath of future allegiance to the United States, a privilege subsequently extended to all prisoners. Out of practical necessity, the Federals paid for their transportation home. The abandoned facilities that had held prisoners on both sides mostly disappeared except for the graves for which the United States ultimately assumed responsibility.

The Federal authorities also took charge of investigating alleged mistreatment of Union soldiers while in Confederate hands and of attempting to punish those responsible. The principal official in charge was Brig. Gen. Joseph Holt, judge advocate general. This Kentucky Unionist, moved by a passionate animus against the Confederates, ordered the arrest of a number of prison keepers and through his Bureau of Military Justice collected evidence and supervised trials by military commission. The flight from the country of several of the accused and the difficulty of finding witnesses after the demobilization of the Union army limited Holt's success. The best-known outcome of his efforts was the trial of Andersonville commandant Capt. Henry Wirz. After a military trial at Washington whose outcome was all but predetermined, Wirz was convicted of conspiring with "others unknown"—presumably the Confederate leadership—to mistreat Union prisoners and was hanged. More fortunate was the commander of Salisbury Prison, Major John H. Gee. After trial in the field, he was acquitted.

The trials came quickly to an end, but the government continued to make its case in the forum of public opinion. In the published records of the Wirz trial and other proceedings such as the trial of the Lincoln assassins, high Confederate officials from Jefferson Davis on down were linked with prison atrocities. In 1869 under Republican auspices, a committee of the House of Representatives investigated conditions in the former Confederate prisons, seeking evidence of

> **In memoirs, Jefferson Davis and others sought to show that they had tried to care for the prisoners.**

Southern "barbarism" stemming from slavery. After hearing some three thousand witnesses, the committee produced a voluminous and highly negative report.

Ex-prisoners often drew upon these government documents to supplement their own recollections and diaries as they wrote memoirs of their prison days. Though a minority believed that their keepers had done their best, most were convinced that they had been the victims of a deliberate plot to destroy the prisoners. Some of them reflected the political partisanship of Reconstruction; others tried to make a case for pensioning the ex-prisoners.

Apologists for the Confederacy struggled against the tide. In memoirs, Jefferson Davis and others sought to show that they had tried to care for the prisoners. Minimizing their own roles in the attempts at retaliation, they blamed the Federal officials for the breakdown of exchange and the resultant suffering of prisoners of both sides. Former Confederates imprisoned in the North also wrote complaints about how they had been treated. No Northern prison, however, could equal the unique horror of Andersonville; moreover, fewer of the nation's publishers and readers of books were in the South. Thus the Confederacy's defenders were never able effectively to answer the Northern prisoners' charges.

The Confederacy's case fared somewhat better in the hands of professional historians. The Ohioan James Ford Rhodes, while doing research for his history of the Civil War, sought from the U.S. adjutant general statistics on the mortality rates in the prisons. He was told by Gen. Fred C. Ainsworth in 1903 that according to the best information obtainable, 211,411 Union soldiers were captured in the Civil War, of whom 16,668 were paroled in the field and 30,218 died in captivity; on the other hand, 462,634 Confederates were captured, of whom 247,769 were paroled and 25,976

died in prison. Rhodes concluded that the prison mortality rate was a bit over 12 percent in the North and 15.5 percent in the South, a difference less than he had expected. Though these percentages rested on admittedly incomplete records, they have been repeated by scholars ever since. Thus historians, including William B. Hesseltine, author of an old but still useful history of Civil War prisons, have not judged harshly the Confederacy's treatment of its captives.

Such has not been true of the popular literature. Even after the deaths of the prisoners, their memoirs and diaries have continued to appear in print to heap shame on their captors. After World War II, MacKinlay Kantor's widely circulated novel *Andersonville* (1955), based on the familiar charges against the Confederacy, suggested a contrived comparison with the horrors of the Nazi death camps and the culpability of their keepers. Interest in the treatment of American prisoners in later wars has helped keep alive the memory of those of the Civil War, ensuring that this topic will remain one of the more controversial aspects of the Confederacy.

[*See also* African American Troops in the Union Army; Andersonville Prison; Belle Isle Prison; Castle Thunder Prison; *Enchantress* Affair; Fort Delaware Prison; Galvanized Yankees; Johnson's Island Prison; Libby Prison; Northwestern Conspiracy; Point Lookout Prison; Prisons; Privateers; Provost Marshal; Winder, John H.; Wirz, Henry.]

BIBLIOGRAPHY

Blakey, Arch Frederic. *General John H. Winder, C.S.A.* Gainesville, Fla., 1990.

Brown, Louis A. *The Salisbury Prison: A Case Study of Confederate Military Prisons, 1861–1865.* Wendell, N.C., 1980.

Bryant, William O. *Cahaba Prison and the Sultana Disaster.* Tuscaloosa, Ala., and London, 1990.

Byrne, Frank L. "Prison Pens of Suffering." In *Fighting for Time.* Vol. 4 of *The Image of War, 1861–1865.* Edited by William C. Davis. Garden City, N.Y., 1983.

Futch, Ovid L. *History of Andersonville Prison.* Gainesville, Fla., 1968.

Hesseltine, William B. *Civil War Prisons: A Study in War Psychology.* Columbus, Ohio, 1930. Reprint, New York, 1964.

Hesseltine, William B. "The Propaganda Literature of Confederate Prisons." *Journal of Southern History* 1 (1935): 56–66.

Hesseltine, William B., ed. *Civil War Prisons.* Kent, Ohio, 1962.

Shriver, Philip R., and Donald J. Breen. *Ohio's Civil War Prisons in the Civil War.* Columbus, Ohio, 1964.

FRANK L. BYRNE

PRISONS

The Confederate prisons began and ended more as a series of improvisations than as a systematic organization. Even before the outbreak of fighting, the Confederates held in temporary camps enlisted men of the U.S. Army taken prisoner in Texas. After the war began, the Confederates captured over a thousand Unionists at their victory at First Manassas and shipped them to Richmond. These they housed in Ligon's Warehouse and Tobacco Factory and in several similar structures. The officer responsible for these captives as well as for the Confederate soldiers and civilians held in other Richmond prisons was the city's provost marshal, Brig. Gen. John H. Winder. Winder had attended West Point and served in the U.S. Army. Because of his age (he was sixty-one when the war started) and probably because he had been lieutenant governor of Vera Cruz during the Mexican War, Winder received his behind-the-lines assignment and quickly became commander of the District of Henrico which surrounded the capital. Stern and unsympathetic, his attempts to regulate civilian life soon made him an object of hatred. Although at first some prisoners found him acceptable, his concern for security combined with the hardships of prolonged captivity in time caused the Union captives to blame him for their woes.

To reduce crowding, the Confederates almost immediately began to disperse their prisoners. They had acquired a cotton factory building in Salisbury, North Carolina, which they put into use. They housed others at Castle Pinckney in Charleston Harbor and at jails there and in Columbia, South Carolina. Seeking yet more space, the Confederates also used an abandoned paper mill at Tuscaloosa, Alabama, and the parish prison at New Orleans. Winder remained generally responsible for all these men, although on a rather vague basis. Unlike the Union, the Confederacy did not then have an office of commissary general of prisoners.

In 1862, Winder expanded his Richmond prisons. He took possession of the brick storehouse of Libby and Son, which became notorious as Libby Prison. Besides housing prisoners, it provided office space for Winder's subordinates who

> ## To reduce crowding, the Confederates almost immediately began to disperse their prisoners.

managed the local prisons. By midsummer, Winder had found additional space on Belle Isle in the James River on which he opened a rapidly growing camp. Besides the facilities for Union captives, Winder controlled Castle Thunder, a group of tobacco factories used to confine Confederate deserters, civilians, and political prisoners.

Feeding and providing for all these prisoners presented problems the Confederates very much wanted to eliminate. Hence on July 16, 1862, they agreed with the Union army authorities on a cartel providing for prompt paroling and

exchange. They rapidly released the inmates of their prisons and closed or abandoned many of them. For some months, Winder was able to make do with a few temporary holding places (notably Libby) while retaining Castle Thunder and Salisbury as prisons for limited numbers of Confederate offenders. But by 1863, quarrels over the execution of the cartel had led to a breakdown of the exchange, and captives were again accumulating. The Confederates still did not appoint a central authority, and Winder continued to improvise prisons.

Because so many prisoners were in or near Richmond when exchange ceased, the Confederate capital became increasingly crowded. Winder converted Libby into a prison mainly for Union officers. To hold enlisted men, he impressed additional warehouses and enlarged the camp on Belle Isle. The presence of thousands of prisoners added to the war-swollen population of Richmond and made it difficult to provide food for all. By the winter of 1863–1864, soldiers and prisoners alike complained of hunger, and the prison authorities worried whether they could control their embittered charges. Moreover, they realized that so many enemies within the capital created a security problem, the gravity of which was underscored by a cavalry raid on February 28 to March 4, 1864, which reached the city's outskirts. To reduce the prison population, the Confederates removed hundreds to six tobacco warehouses in Danville, Virginia.

Seeking a more substantial solution, Winder sent several officers to Georgia to locate sites for additional prisons. He hoped to reduce the difficulty in obtaining food and simultaneously to move the prisoners as far as possible from Union forces who could free them. Andersonville was chosen for a stockade (officially named Camp Sumter for its county) that became the most heavily populated and notorious Confederate prison for enlisted men. In February 1864, the authorities at Richmond began shipping trainloads of prisoners to the still unfinished stockade. In May, they moved the imprisoned officers from Richmond to a camp at Macon, Georgia. Enclosed by a high board fence, the camp had only one small building, which was used as a hospital and as housing for generals; the rest improvised as best they could. Some fifteen hundred officers were at Macon in the summer of 1864.

To control the new prisons, the Confederacy sent General Winder who had been relieved of his Richmond command. Setting his headquarters at Andersonville, he showed some concern over the wretched conditions of the pen and its inmates but devoted most of his attention to worry over its security, fearing breakouts, treachery by local residents, and Union rescue attempts. In July 1864, he was placed in command of all prisons in Georgia and Alabama, including an unfinished cotton warehouse surrounded by a fence on the Alabama River at Cahaba. Set up in 1863 as a temporary holding facility, the Cahaba Prison, which prisoners often informally called "Castle Morgan," held at one time over two thousand enlisted men. Though its prisoners were transferred several times, the Alabama facility remained in use until the war's end. It was less well known than others in the postwar period because of its smaller size and because a large number of its released inmates were killed in the destruction of the Mississippi steamboat *Sultana*.

At the same time Winder took charge of the Deep South prisons, Gen. W. M. Gardner was put in command of prisons in the other states east of the Mississippi. A Georgian who earlier had been wounded, Gardner, from headquarters at Richmond, supervised prisons in Virginia and North Carolina, which continued to be used largely for transients. When the Confederate War Department ordered the suspension of shipments to overcrowded Andersonville, the prisons farther north again began to overflow. Considering the deteriorating conditions, it is not inappropriate to compare the prisons to ill-constructed, partially blocked sewers.

Meanwhile conditions were slightly better in the Trans-Mississippi region of the Confederacy where prisons, like every other aspect of life, were run independently of the Richmond authorities after 1863. The Confederates selected as sites for prisons training camps in Texas, which offered a supply of guards. One was Camp Groce at Hempstead; another and more important one was Camp Ford at Tyler. Its stockade enclosed five acres and was later enlarged to ten. As at Andersonville, the prisoners had to improvise their own shelter and received no clothing from their captors. They were issued rations of cornmeal and beef. Unlike most prisons, Camp Ford confined both army officers and enlisted men, as well as navy men and enemy civilians. At maximum it held over 4,500 prisoners at one time, but because of its abundant water, only 286 died out of a total of 6,000.

Meanwhile, General Winder struggled to create new prisons and to shift captives to more remote locations. In August 1864, at a site near the railroad at Millen, Georgia, he ordered work to begin on a stockade enclosing forty-two acres, which he called Camp Lawton after the Confederate quartermaster general, Alexander R. Lawton, a Georgian. With a strange pride, Winder remarked, "I presume it is the largest prison in the world." Although the interior was laid out in a more orderly fashion than was Andersonville (from which most of its inmates were transferred), the prisoners again were left to

LIBBY PRISON, RICHMOND, VIRGINIA. May 1865.

improvise shelter. By November 8, 1864, some 10,299 prisoners had been incarcerated there under the command of Capt. D. W. Vowles. But a week later the approach of Gen. William Tecumseh Sherman's raiding troops forced the hasty abandonment of Millen. Winder had some of the prisoners shifted to temporary camps at Blackshear and Thomasville in southern Georgia and then returned some to Andersonville, where the Confederates belatedly erected a few sheds to shelter a minority of the inmates.

When the Confederates had sent some Andersonville prisoners to Millen, they had dispersed others to Savannah where they were held in a fenced camp. Still others were transported to a similar encampment at the fairgrounds in Charleston, with some crowding into the yard of the city jail. Earlier in the summer, the Confederates had moved the imprisoned officers at Macon to the same two cities. At Charleston the officers gave their paroles not to escape and were lodged comfortably in the Roper Hospital. Southern commanders at the besieged seaports objected to the accumulation of prisoners and moved quickly to rid themselves of them.

These movements of prisoners were decided upon by local commanders rather than by the man who on November 21, 1864, was placed in charge of all prisoners. The Confederate adjutant general issued an order putting General Winder in command of all guard personnel and inmates in prisons east of the Mississippi. Officers were warned not to interfere with his charges. At last the Confederacy had a commissary general of prisoners, but it was too late to do much good. The South's diminishing resources and Sherman's armies made it all but impossible to provide adequately for the prisoners or indeed to move them to places safe from recapture. Nonetheless the elderly general established headquarters at Augusta, Georgia, and set about his job.

The commander at Charleston, Gen. Samuel Jones, had begun in September 1864 to send off prisoners to the interior rail junction at Florence. There thousands were held in an open field while the local military built a stockade surrounded by an earthwork from which guards could keep watch. As at Andersonville and Millen, a stream ran through it, around which developed a swamp occupying six out of twenty-six acres. The men received rations so limited that by late January 1865, the commandant pronounced them near starvation. Of a total of 12,000 men at Florence, 2,802 died. While enlisted men suffered at Florence, their officers were only a little better off at Columbia, South Carolina. There in an open field they were directed to build huts before winter. When syrup was substituted for the meat ration, the prisoners called it "Camp Sorghum." Because so many escaped, the South Carolina state authorities consented to the transfer of the officers to a more secure location on the grounds of a local institution for the insane, which became known as Camp Asylum.

Meanwhile the government at Richmond decided on desperate action to free their capital of imprisoned officers and enlisted men. To eliminate the drain on the food supply of the besieged city before the winter of 1864–1865, they sent the officers to the tobacco warehouses at Danville where 2,400 prisoners of all ranks were crowded. Early in October they emptied the camp of enlisted men on Belle Isle, sending about 7,500 to Salisbury. Given the 800 military and political

> **At last the Confederacy had a commissary general of prisoners, but it was too late to do much good.**

prisoners already there, the prison was instantly overcrowded. It was rather like someone trying to pour a gallon of water into a quart bottle. General Winder reported in December that conditions at Salisbury were worse than at Florence (indeed, both resembled Andersonville on a smaller scale).

Winder's solution was to build another prison. He sought property on the railroad fourteen miles above Columbia, and there at Killian's Mills began to construct a new stockade, which he hoped would, with Andersonville and Millen, house all his captives. Hence he moved his headquarters to Columbia. But unable either to supply his prisoners or to move them to safety from recapture by Sherman's troops advancing through the Carolinas, he suggested paroling the prisoners and sending them home without exchange. On February 6, 1865, just before the resumption of exchange, Winder died suddenly of a massive heart attack while inspecting the prison at Florence.

The prisoners rejoiced at the death of Winder, whom they viewed as the chief villain responsible for their sufferings. They circulated a rumor that his last words were "Cut off the molasses, boys." On February 14, the Confederates replaced him with Brig. Gen. Gideon Pillow, who had been largely inactive since being discredited by his involvement in the surrender of Fort Donelson. On March 20, he in turn was replaced by the invalided W. M. Gardner, superseded four days later by the more vigorous Gen. Daniel Ruggles. Under the supervision of these men, the prisoners in the Carolinas were moved up to a temporary holding site at Charlotte. Union forces subsequently seized the prisons at Columbia and Salisbury.

Meanwhile exchanges were occurring at Wilmington, North Carolina; City Point, Virginia; Vicksburg; and the mouth of the Red River. The Richmond prisons, including Libby and Castle Thunder, continued to hold mostly transient inmates until the city's fall. Even then, General Ruggles continued construction of the new prison at Killian's Mills and expected to house at Danville prisoners captured by Robert E. Lee.

With Lee's surrender and the collapse of the Confederacy, the prison system was abandoned. The last to close was Camp Ford, evacuated on May 17. Later the Federal authorities arrested a number of the prison officials. Though they were blamed then and later for the terrible conditions, far more responsibility lay with their superiors. They had delayed until too late the systematizing of the prisons and, like their Union counterparts, never gave enough attention to the welfare of the helpless pawns with which they were playing.

[*For further discussion of Confederate prisons, see* Andersonville Prison; Belle Isle Prison; Castle Thunder Prison; Libby Prison; Salisbury Prison. *For discussion of Federal prisons, see* Fort Delaware Prison; Johnson's Island Prison; Point Lookout Prison. *See also* Enchantress Affair; Prisoners of War; Provost Marshal; Winder, John H.]

BIBLIOGRAPHY

Blakey, Arch Frederic. *General John H. Winder, C.S.A.* Gainesville, Fla., 1990.

Brown, Louis A. *The Salisbury Prison: A Case Study of Confederate Military Prisons, 1861–1865.* Wendell, N.C., 1980.

Bryant, William O. *Cahaba Prison and the Sultana Disaster.* Tuscaloosa, Ala., and London, 1990.

Byrne, Frank L. "Prison Pens of Suffering." In *Fighting for Time.* Vol. 4 of *The Image of War, 1861–1865.* Edited by William C. Davis. Garden City, N.Y., 1983.

Futch, Ovid L. *History of Andersonville Prison.* Gainesville, Fla., 1968.

Hesseltine, William B. *Civil War Prisons: A Study in War Psychology.* Columbus, Ohio, 1930. Reprint, New York, 1964.

Lawrence, F. Lee, and Robert W. Glover. *Camp Ford, C.S.A.: The Story of Union Prisoners in Texas.* Austin, Tex., 1964.

Parker, Sandra V. *Richmond's Civil War Prisons.* Lynchburg, Va., 1990.

FRANK L. BYRNE

PRODUCE LOAN

A series of produce loans contributed to financing the Confederate war effort. The concept had its origin when many people became aware that the Confederacy had to acquire supplies for the military; that it had to secure funds sooner than it could establish a tax system; and that it had to pay for those supplies when possible with bonds instead of Treasury notes in order to limit the currency and thus forestall inflation. Commodities, still in the hands of their producers, might be exchanged for twenty-year, 8 percent bonds. The produce loan was designed to persuade farmers and planters to lend to the Confederacy a portion of the proceeds from the sale of such staples as cotton, tobacco, and sugar; it might secure military provisions, too. The Confederate Treasury could employ the anticipated receipts as the basis for establishing credit in Europe and across the South.

The Confederate Congress inaugurated the plan in a measure approved May 16, 1861, and expanded its terms to $100 million from $50 million on August 19. Additional acts of April 21, 1862, February 20, 1863, and April 30, 1863, expanded it further. Many planters proved enthusiastic about the plan, though smaller farmers typically had greater need for cash for their crops. In any case, the produce loan had as its premise a sale of commodities, and the Federal blockade rendered the export of cotton problematic. In addition, volunteer personnel failed to canvass some parts of the Deep South, and with much of the upper South the scene of military action, tobacco remained only marginal to the plan's operation. Finally, conditions for many producers had changed mightily between the time in the summer of 1861 when they pledged a loan and the time that fall when the crops came in.

Like so much of Confederate finance, the produce loan was flawed in both conception and implementation. That the 1861 acts generated only $34 million, one-third the stipulated amount (and 1.1 percent of the $3 billion in aggregate Confederate revenue), points to the limited success of the program. To a degree, however, the plan achieved its objectives. The produce loan operated to restrain the issue of Treasury notes and thus postponed destabilization of the currency, and the cotton thus obtained helped secure the Erlanger loan.

[*See also* Erlanger Loan.]

BIBLIOGRAPHY

Ball, Douglas, B. *Financial Failure and Confederate Defeat.* Urbana, Ill., 1991.

Schwab, John Christopher. *The Confederate States of America, 1861–1865: A Financial and Industrial History of the South during the Civil War.* New York, 1901. Reprint, New York, 1968.

Todd, Richard Cecil. *Confederate Finance.* Athens, Ga., 1954.

PETER WALLENSTEIN

PROPAGANDA

The South chose correctly to focus its propaganda effort on Great Britain because, as the world's greatest power, that nation's action or inaction could not only decide the outcome of the American war but also influence the position of France and other European states. Yet, despite its obvious importance, the Southern campaign to obtain British intervention was delayed until 1862 owing to the understandable but mistaken belief that Britain's dependence upon Southern raw cotton would force its hand. Confederate complacency was also strengthened by the knowledge that most of the English press, a majority of the Parliament, and the ministerial leaders were either anti-Northern or pro-Southern. Although Confederate leaders knew that many of the English hated slavery, President Abraham Lincoln had weakened that barrier to favorable relations by declaring that his objective was to save the Union, not destroy slavery.

Organized propaganda began inauspiciously when twenty-seven-year-old Henry Hotze, a naturalized Swiss journalist from Mobile, returned to Richmond from Europe late in 1861 and persuaded a skeptical Robert M. T. Hunter, secretary of state, to send him to England to educate British writers about the South. Arriving in January 1862 Hotze quickly succeeded in obtaining the help of several English journalists. He either wrote articles for them or assisted them in their preparation while permitting them to collect the customary fee. Soon there was a marked increase in pro-Southern materials in leading London newspapers. Hotze also boldly helped Southern sympathizers in Parliament prepare their speeches and supplied them with timely and accurate information.

Much encouraged, the opportunistic young Swiss decided to publish a weekly newspaper called the *Index*. While providing employment, money, and education for the English writers, it also served as a much needed repository for collecting and controlling Southern news. Given this monopoly, Hotze designed the *Index* to reach not the mass public but a select readership of the most influential groups in Great Britain such as the cabinet, Parliament, business leaders, and the print media. To instill confidence in the *Index*, he made the paper thoroughly English in style and appearance and moderate in its content.

Hotze faced some serious problems, however. Inadequate government funding forced him to depend on uncertain private contributions. Some impatient Southerners and English friends withheld support because they disliked the paper's temperate tone or doubted its effectiveness. It was also difficult to obtain timely and accurate information. But Hotze persevered. He published the *Index* until August 1865 and succeeded in making it the centerpiece of the Confederate propaganda program.

Meanwhile, a South Carolinian, Edwin de Leon, while in Europe had also observed a need for propaganda. Returning to Richmond, he persuaded President Jefferson Davis, an old friend, to appoint him chief Confederate propagandist overseas. His large contingency fund and instructions left no doubt that much was expected of him. At the time, President Davis, Judah P. Benjamin (recently appointed secretary of state), and de Leon were unaware of Hotze's success.

Arriving in London in late June 1862, de Leon observed Hotze's thriving operation and quickly moved on to France. There he incurred the wrath of John Slidell, Confederate commissioner to France, by delivering to him dispatches from Richmond with broken seals. But undaunted and confident of President Davis's friendship and support, de Leon pushed ahead. He hired French writers, thereby substantially increasing the flow of pro-Southern articles in French papers. He prepared a brochure called *La vèritè sur les Etats Confèdèrès d'Amèrique,* which served as source material for French journalists. Taking a cue from Hotze, de Leon subsidized Felix Aucaigne, editor of the *Paris Patrie,* making that journal a Confederate paper.

He ventured across the English Channel, inserted articles in English newspapers and magazines, countered Federal attacks on the Southern cotton loan, and supported Hotze in the distribution of an important piece entitled *An Address of the Southern Clergy to Christians.*

De Leon's mission ended abruptly late in 1863 when the Federals intercepted a dispatch of his to Richmond in which he criticized Slidell and denounced the French press as mercenary. After publication in the *New York Daily Tribune,* it created such a stir that Davis was forced to remove de Leon, much to the delight of Slidell and the relief of Hotze.

Benjamin, by now a strong supporter of Hotze, promptly asked him to extend operations to the Continent. In France he reversed de Leon's practice of hiring French writers and canceled the subsidy to Aucaigne's *Patrie.* He persuaded Auguste Havas, director of the Havas Agency, which enjoyed a monopoly in supplying foreign news to French editors, to accept pro-Southern articles previously published in England. He thus succeeded in expanding the dissemination of the Southern version of the conflict at little cost. Late in 1864 in the German states Hotze attempted to thwart the sale of Union bonds but with little success.

The efforts of Hotze and de Leon were bolstered by a contingent of English propagandists. Among the more prominent and effective of them were Alexander James Beresford Hope, who published two influential pieces: *A Popular View of the American War* and *The American Disruption;* F. W. Tremblett, an Anglican minister, who organized the Society for Cessation of Hostilities in America; and James Spence, by far the most important, who published in 1861 *The American Union* in which he vindicated the South but upset Southerners by suggesting that an independent Confederacy would abandon slavery. The book quickly went through four editions and became the most influential propaganda tract produced during the war. Spence also wrote many letters to the London *Times,* organized numerous Southern Clubs, staged proSouthern rallies, and vigorously supported Tremblett's peace movement.

Still another aspect of Confederate propaganda involved efforts in 1863 and 1864 to counter Federal recruiting of Irishmen and Germans to relieve labor shortages and replenish the ranks of Northern armies. The alert Hotze hired private detectives to shadow Federal recruiters in Ireland to obtain evidence of violations of the British Foreign Enlistment Act (which forbade recruitment for foreign armies). But he found that Northern agents recruited Irishmen as laborers and did not offer them enlistment in the army until after they had left Ireland. In response to urgent pleas from James Mason, Confederate commissioner to Great Britain, and A. Dudley Mann, Confederate envoy to Belgium, Benjamin sent several agents to Ireland to operate under Hotze's supervision. Among them were Father John Bannon, a Confederate army chaplain, and Bishop P. N. Lynch from Charleston who worked directly with Irish priests to discourage parishioners from leaving. No agents were sent to the German states, but Mann himself undertook several small projects there, and at Benjamin's request he successfully petitioned Pope Pius IX

> **. . . Lincoln's obstinacy produced instead a backlash that exacerbated the peace movement.**

to appeal directly to Irishmen and Germans not to emigrate. These measures may have slowed emigration, but harsh living conditions in the Old World coupled with the lure of Northern job opportunities and enlistment bounties were simply too great to overcome.

In the meantime, on both sides of the Atlantic, Confederate supporters by 1864 were noting with growing interest and anticipation the unrest and clamor for peace in the North, especially in the Old Northwest. The reports of disaffection gained increased credibility when Republicans, fearing Lincoln's defeat in the upcoming presidential election, charged vociferously that peacemongers and opponents of the war were traitors to the Union cause.

The swelling uproar convinced Southern leaders that with encouragement war-weary northwesterners, joined in a tenuous alliance with the East, might revolt and perhaps establish a separate government. Failing that, they could provide sufficient votes, in combination with those of dissident easterners, to defeat Lincoln and install in the White House a peace Democrat who would negotiate a settlement on Southern terms.

Consequently efforts toward this end were launched both in Great Britain and in the South. Hotze called the attention of *Index* readers to Northern disenchantment and the emerging peace movement, and Spence and Tremblett gathered several hundred thousand signatures for a peace petition. In Richmond, Davis commissioned Jacob Thompson of Mississippi and Clement C. Clay of Alabama to set up a base in Canada. There they were in touch with many Northerners including the notorious copperhead Clement L. Vallandigham; Benjamin Wood, owner and editor of the *New York Daily News,* vigorously pro-Southern and a contributor

of news and articles to Hotze's *Index;* and Horace Greeley, the eccentric editor of the *New York Tribune.* Greeley succeeded with the help of the Southern commissioners in inducing Lincoln to discuss peace negotiations. The president was politically afraid to refuse peace overtures outright and was lured by the possibility that peace talks could weaken Peace Democrat opposition while strengthening his support among moderate Republicans. But when he insisted that reunion and abolition must be preconditions for negotiations, Lincoln's obstinacy produced instead a backlash that exacerbated the peace movement.

Thompson and Clay also helped plan and finance plots to promote an insurrection in the Old Northwest to liberate Confederate prisoners in Northern prison camps, to create a financial panic by buying gold and shipping it to Europe, to burn New York City, and to raid towns along the Canadian border. But their plots came to nothing. Although operational plans were well conceived, there were frequent communication breakdowns, and close surveillance by Union and Canadian authorities constantly plagued the conspirators. Above all else Confederate operations backfired because, as Thompson and Clay discovered time and again, agitated Northerners, Republican allegations to the contrary, were not prepared to take the bold leap from political rhetoric to insurrection and disunion.

After Gen. George B. McClellan, the Democratic nominee for president, openly repudiated the peace plank in the party's platform and Federal military fortunes improved dramatically in the fall of 1864, any hope for a Northern insurrection or peace negotiations evaporated, Lincoln's reelection was assured, and the fate of the Confederacy sealed.

In retrospect, the Southern propaganda program, though belated, was accurately focused and, despite the ineptness of de Leon and the failure of the Thompson and Clay mission, surprisingly well coordinated, owing chiefly to the spirited, imaginative, and tireless efforts of Henry Hotze and James Spence.

[*See also* Clay, Clement C.; Northwestern Conspiracy; Thompson, Jacob.]

BIBLIOGRAPHY

Cullop, Charles P. *Confederate Propaganda in Europe, 1861–1865.* Coral Gables, Fla., 1969.

Jenkins, Brian. *Britain and the War for the Union.* 2 vols. Montreal, 1980.

Kinchen, Oscar A. *Confederate Operations in Canada and the North.* North Quincy, Mass., 1970.

Nelson, Lawrence. *Bullets, Ballots, and Rhetoric.* University, Ala., 1980.

Owsley, Frank L. *King Cotton Diplomacy: Foreign Relations of the Confederate States of America.* 2d ed. Revised by Harriet C. Owsley. Chicago, 1959.

CHARLES P. CULLOP

PROSLAVERY

The term *proslavery,* as used by antebellum abolitionists and proponents of slavery, and by historians, encompasses two historical phenomena: first, the attitude of favoring slavery (particularly black slavery) and its continuance and of opposing any interference with it, and second, the emergence in the United States from the 1830s through the Civil War of a literature vigorously arguing that the institution of slavery was beneficial for both slaves and society. The term has also been used incorrectly and inconsistently to describe certain writings that denigrate the role of African Americans, Hispanics, Asiatics, and other ethnic groups in the United States.

Once believed to be peculiar to the Old South and the Confederacy, proslavery literature, recent studies have shown, appeared wherever slavery existed; in the United States proslavery books, tracts, and pamphlets were produced prior to the Civil War by a great variety of individuals in both the North and the South. Particularly important in the early articulation of America's proslavery outlook, for example, were individuals who were born or educated in New England and Northern states, well educated (especially at such institutions as Yale and Princeton), professional (clergy, lawyers, journalists), and among the nation's most eminent nonpolitical leaders. As time passed, however, America's proslavery writers more frequently tended to be individuals native to and educated in the South. Many were members of the intellectual and cultural elite of the period.

A number of the more important pieces of proslavery literature appeared in the 1830s and 1840s. Although some historians have cited an 1832 essay by Thomas R. Dew, *Review of the Debate in the Virginia Legislature of 1831 and 1832,* as the launching pad for the aggressive Southern defense of slavery, it was actually an argument against African colonization as a permanent solution to what were seen as the dual problems of slavery and a large African population in the United States. William Harper's *Anniversary Oration* (1836) is often noted as one of the next major articulations of a proslavery perspective. James H. Hammond's *Two Letters on Slavery in the United States, Addressed to Thomas Clarkson, esq.* (1845) expressed the widely held position in the South that not only was slavery not evil; it was a positive benefit to society.

Other studies of the arguments that slavery was a positive good have noted that they also appeared in contexts other than the Old South, including the British West Indies and Great Britain itself. As early as the 1790s, in the course of parliamentary debates on the African slave trade and the future of slavery in the West Indies, numerous British writers held that slavery was not only a benefit to the West Indian plantation economy. They also held that it was a benefit to Africans who were thereby saved from the "savagery" of their native lands to live in peace within the Christian religion under the guidance of enlightened Englishmen. Even at this early period of the Industrial Revolution, these writers argued that the lot of the slave was superior to that of factory workers and their families.

Some of the most widely distributed and frequently cited proslavery publications during and just before the Civil War were the following:

From the North: Nehemiah Adams (Congregational clergyman, Boston), *A South-side View of Slavery* (1854); Charles Hodge (professor, Princeton Theological Seminary), *The Bible Argument on Slavery* (1857); John Henry Hopkins (Episcopal bishop of Vermont), *Bible View of Slavery* (1861) and *Scriptural, Ecclesiastical, and Historical View of Slavery* (1864); Charles Jared Ingersoll (lawyer and congressman, Philadelphia), *African Slavery in America* (1856); Nathan Lord (president of Dartmouth College), *A Letter of Inquiry to Ministers of the Gospel of all Denominations on Slavery* (1860) and *A True Picture of Abolition* (1863); Samuel F. B. Morse (inventor, artist, and manufacturer, New York), *Present Attempt to Dissolve the American Union* (1862); Nathan L. Rice (editor and college professor, Chicago), *Lectures on Slavery* (1860); Stuart Robinson (editor and clergyman, Louisville, Kentucky), *Slavery as Recognized in the Mosaic Civil Law* (1856) (1865); Samuel Seabury (Episcopal clergyman and college professor, New York City), *American Slavery Distinguished from the Slavery of English Theorists and Justified by the Law of Nature* (1861); and Hubbard Winslow (editor and author, Brooklyn), *Elements of Moral Philosophy* (1856).

From the South: E. N. Elliott (lawyer and college president, Mississippi), *Cotton Is King, and Pro-Slavery Arguments* (1860); George Dodd Armstrong (Presbyterian clergyman, Norfolk, Virginia), *The Christian Doctrine of Slavery* (1857); Albert Taylor Bledsoe (college professor at the University of Virginia), *Essay on Liberty and Slavery* (1856); George Fitzhugh (lawyer and author, Virginia), *Sociology for the South* (1854) and *Cannibals All!* (1859); James Henry Hammond (planter, governor, and U.S. senator), *Speech at Barnwell Courthouse, Oct. 29, 1858* (1858) and *Speech on the Admission of Kansas* (1858); Josiah Nott (physician, Mobile, Alabama), *Types of Mankind* (1854); Frederick A. Ross (manufacturer, clergyman, Alabama), *Slavery Ordained of God* (1857); Edmund Ruffin (planter, agronomist, Virginia), *The Political Economy of Slavery* (1857); William A. Smith (clergyman, president of Randolph-Macon College), *Lectures on the Philosophy & Practice of Slavery* (1856); Thornton Stringfellow (clergyman, planter), *Scriptural and Statistical Views in Favor of Slavery* (1856); and James H. Thornwell (clergyman, president of South Carolina College), *The Rights and Duties of Masters* (1850).

Wherever proslavery literature appeared, virtually identical arguments were used to justify the perpetuation of the institution. Because most American slaves were African Americans, many arguments related to their African past. Proslavery authors generally maintained that Africans historically had lived in uncivilized, barbaric, and degraded conditions, that many had always been held in slavery, and that therefore they did not find slavery an unusual or irksome condition. Many also held that Africans were racially inferior and were incapable of being civilized or of functioning well in situations where they would have to compete with European Americans. In their view, Africans would always require supervision and control. Indeed, some argued, Africans were happier in an enslaved than in a free condition.

Other proslavery authors maintained that slavery was the most perfect labor and welfare system ever devised: because slaves were property—a capital investment—slaveholders had a direct interest in treating them kindly. To preserve their investment, slaveholders would provide housing, food, and clothing and guard their chattels' health and welfare. No other form of labor—especially "wage slavery"—provided such protection.

The institution, it was argued, also benefited society at large. Because slaves were controlled by laws and occupied a dependent condition, societies with slavery were ensured against radical and revolutionary movements. Whereas capitalism tended to abandon the indigent and the ill, ran the reasoning, slavery provided a place and a caretaker for every individual.

Its advocates also held that American slavery was qualitatively different from other slave systems in history. Given the enlightened, religious, and freedom-loving character of Americans, they argued that slavery in the United States was the mildest and most benevolent form of slavery that had ever existed. The American system tended to civilize and Christianize barbaric Africans. The writers asserted that slaveholders, guided by the examples of slavery in the Bible, by Christian teachings, and by principles of the American Revolution, looked upon slavery as a "divine trust" practiced as God would have it for all ages.

Slavery, they further argued, was clearly a moral institution. This they supported by reference to the Bible. God had sanctioned slavery by placing his curse on Ham, by issuing laws for the governance of slavery among the patriarchs and the people of Israel, and by countenancing the practice in both the Old and the New Testaments. Not only did Christ and his apostles not condemn the practice of slavery; they admonished slaves to obey their masters and decreed that fugitive slaves should be returned to their owners.

Whereas many in America held with Thomas Jefferson and other framers of the Declaration of Independence that all men have the right to life, liberty, and the pursuit of happiness, proslavery writers insisted that such a right did not extend to the enslaved. Since, in these men's minds, slavery was a humane institution that provided for the comfort and care of those enslaved, it followed that it was a reasonable and fair practice, not inconsistent with the laws of nature. Essay after essay contended that the Founding Fathers never intended to argue that the enslavement of a servile race was inconsistent with the laws of nature.

Nor, they argued, was it theologically incorrect. God would not decree sin into existence. Indeed, it seemed to them that God specifically brought slavery into existence as a tool to save the "heathen." The master-slave relationship seemed just as divinely ordained as that of husband and wife or father and child; it would end only with the millennium or the end of time.

Most proslavery writers went beyond the mere justification of slavery as a moral and viable institution. They also held that in the master-slave relationship certain duties and responsibilities fell to the master. Whatever legal authority he had, the master was also morally responsible to provide the comforts of life to slaves, to give them just and fair treatment, to protect their families, and to provide religious instruction. When all was said and done, proslavery writers contended, masters were answerable to God for carrying out their divinely ordained roles.

Within the broad field of proslavery history there developed an American school of ethnology that—through pseudoscientific methods and theories—found the Negro to be a separate species from Caucasian whites. Dr. Samuel George Morton published *Crania Americana* in 1839 documenting his measurements and analyses of human skulls from all parts of the world. George R. Glidden, America's premier

> Whatever legal authority he had, the master was also morally responsible to provide the comforts of life to slaves, to give them just and fair treatment. . . .

Egyptologist; Louis Agassiz, Swiss-born Harvard biologist; and many others added endless data intended to confirm the theory of separate species among humankind.

Although these ethnological treatises suggested separate origins for various races and thereby flew in the face of the biblical account of a single creation, the burgeoning field of scientific studies attracted clergymen who attempted to resolve the disparities among theology, science, and racial theory. Moses Ashley Curtis in North Carolina and John Bachman and Thomas Smyth in Charleston—all Northern-born and educated clergy—wrote profusely on the subject in religious as well as scientific publications.

Others made use of this pseudoscience either to defend slavery or to argue for the expulsion of blacks from America. Dr. Josiah C. Nott, a physician in Mobile, Alabama, and Dr.

John H. Van Evrie, a physician in New York City, were among the most prolific popularizers of the theory. But the numbers of disciples were legion and included Sidney George Fisher of Philadelphia, Thomas Ewbank of Washington (U.S. commissioner of patents), and even Boston's Charles Eliot Norton, a conservative intellectual at Harvard.

Despite the abundance of arguments in the proslavery arsenal and the emergence of popular theory about racial disparities, typical proslavery literature wasted little space in recounting arguments that were largely part and parcel of the Western heritage. Most proslavery writers were concerned with other issues relating to the world of slaveholding. Many felt that those who opposed slavery were in actuality "jacobins," "infidels," and revolutionaries who wanted to upend not only slavery but also American society and government. Some were fearful that if slavery were abolished, America would forever harbor an alien population that might rise against whites or descend into "bestiality" and sap the energy and financial resources of the nation. Others looked with disfavor at the effects of laissez-faire capitalism on the nation's work force, wishing to avert what they saw as a sys-

> **... slavery and the future of blacks in America were such divisive issues that they would lead to the Union's disruption.**

tem of wage slavery in the United States. Still others argued that slavery and the future of blacks in America were such divisive issues that they would lead to the Union's disruption.

Moreover, most proslavery literature in America not specifically intended to argue issues of race, ethnology, scripture, theology, or the economy contained a specific worldview that was conservative socially and philosophically, that was reformist and positive in purpose, and that promoted order and responsibility in society. It was not allied with any political party or movement; rather, it was an outgrowth of reactions to disruptive and revolutionary forces in the Western world. Fearful of the chaos they associated particularly with the French and Haitian revolutions, most proslavery writers excoriated abolitionists as irresponsible revolutionaries bent on destroying the American republic. To avoid such disruption, they espoused the reform of slavery, urging masters to exercise their proper duties and responsibilities to slaves and to bring their slaves into religious institutions.

Eventually the problems of slavery and Union became so intertwined that they could no longer be avoided. The election of Abraham Lincoln as president in 1860 brought the issues to a head. Immediately following his election, hundreds of orators and clergymen throughout the nation addressed the future of slavery and the Union in furious speeches and ser-

mons. In the South, such men as Benjamin Morgan Palmer of New Orleans called for the Southern states to leave the Union and protect the "divine trust" of slavery. In the North, other voices concurred, including such prominent clergy as Henry J. Van Dyke of the First Presbyterian Church of Brooklyn and Rabbi Morris Jacob Raphall at B'nai Jeshurum in New York City.

As the nation's political institutions faltered, Southerners thought the time at hand when the South could pursue the practice of slavery without interference from outside forces. Proslavery ideas and arguments fused with religious images, as speakers envisioned the Confederacy building the Kingdom of God on earth complete with a perfected form of slavery. The new nation would become a harmonious organic unity with places for masters and slaves, capital and labor, merchants and craftsmen. Some men, such as Leonidas Spratt of Charleston, a proponent for the reopening of the African slave trade, thought that the time was at hand to augment the South's work force with fresh hands from Africa. Others, such as Henry Hughes of Mississippi, called the South's perfected form of slavery "warranteeism"; slaveholders, he said, owned not the person but his productive labor.

Alexander H. Stephens, Confederate vice president, took a contrary point of view in 1861 in what came to be known as the "cornerstone speech." Believing the popular literature classifying whites and blacks as separate species, Stephens asserted that the Confederacy provided an opportunity to enforce the laws of nature: "Our system commits no . . . violation of nature's laws. With us, all the white race, however high or low, rich or poor, are equal in the eyes of the law. Not so with the Negro. Subordination is his place. He, by nature, or by the curse against Canaan, is fitted for that condition which he occupies in our system."

Euphoria surrounding the creation of the Confederacy complete with slavery continued despite the onset of the war. In dozens of fast days and thanksgiving days proclaimed by President Jefferson Davis to celebrate military victories or contemplate the meaning of defeats, the barrage of proslavery pronouncements continued apace. Among the thousands of Confederate imprints still in existence—pamphlets, books, sermons, broadsides, and the like—half or more are reiterations of the centrality of slavery in Southern life and the appropriateness of the institution in the Confederacy.

Nor did the opening of a war for Southern independence halt the publication of proslavery literature throughout the North. After the election of Lincoln, Samuel F. B. Morse gathered like-minded individuals in first the American Society for Promoting National Unity (1861) and later the Society for the Diffusion of Political Knowledge (1863) to issue tracts in support of slavery and the right of the South to secede from the Union. He and his colleagues continued to defend slavery as a moral institution throughout the Civil War period.

And even with the end of the war and the abolition of slavery, some continued to argue the issue. In the South, disgruntled souls such as Robert L. Dubney, clergyman and former aide to Thomas J. ("Stonewall") Jackson, carried on the debate. His *Defense of Virginia (and through Her of the South) in Recent and Pending Contests* (1867) was an angry digest of virtually every proslavery argument. Dr. John H. Van Evrie of New York presented the racist perspective on slavery as he had for many years in a new book entitled *White Supremacy and Negro Subordination* (1868). Evidence of the tenacity of the issue in America is further indicated by the fact that as late as 1868 Norwegian Lutherans meeting in convention in Chicago attempted—unsuccessfully—to rescind a church tenet originally adopted in 1861 declaring the practice of slavery both moral and consistent with scripture.

[*See also* Cornerstone Speech.]

BIBLIOGRAPHY

Elliott, E. N., ed. *Cotton Is King, and Pro-Slavery Arguments.* Augusta, Ga., 1860.

Farmer, James Oscar, Jr. *The Metaphysical Confederacy.* Macon, Ga., 1986.

Faust, Drew Gilpin. *Confederate Nationalism: Ideology and Identity in the Civil War South.* Baton Rouge, La., 1988.

Faust, Drew Gilpin, ed. *The Ideology of Slavery: Proslavery Thought in the Antebellum South, 1830–1860.* Baton Rouge, La., 1981.

Fredrickson, George M. *The Black Image in the White Mind: The Debate on Afro-American Character and Destiny, 1817–1914.* New York, 1971.

Jenkins, William Sumner. *Pro-slavery Thought in the Old South.* Chapel Hill, N.C., 1935.

Takaki, Ronald T. *A Pro-slavery Crusade: The Agitation to Reopen the African Slave Trade.* New York, 1971.

Tise, Larry E. *Proslavery: A History of the Defense of Slavery in America, 1701–1840.* Athens, Ga., 1987.

LARRY E. TISE

PROSTITUTION

The Civil War created a climate that contributed to the widespread growth of brothels and prostitution, especially in the Confederate states. The large number of unattached men gathered into regiments at camps were targeted by the professional class of women who sold sexual favors, while the length of the war and its devastating effects upon the South led to the displacement of thousands of women, many of whom were forced into prostitution for economic survival.

By June 1863 Maj. W. J. Mims, stationed in eastern Tennessee, complained to his wife that "female virtue if it ever existed in this Country seems now almost a perfect wreck. Prostitutes are thickly crowded through mountain & valley, in hamlet & city." Mims was able to concede that "the influence of the armies has largely contributed to this state of things, as soldiers do not seem to feel the same restraints away from home, which at home regulated their intercourse with the gentler sex." A less charitable Northern hospital steward commented, "The lower class (both black & white in the south) seem to be totally ignorant of the meaning of the word 'Virtue' & both officers & men appear to have cast off all the restraints of home & indulge their passions to the fullest extent."

These relationships fueled vice and disease. Washington, D.C., boasted 450 bordellos by 1862, and over 7,000 prostitutes worked in the district. Richmond, the Confederate capital, was equally a mecca for sin, although it could not match the numbers attributed to D.C. By 1864 the Virginia city's mayor was forced to confess, "Never was a place more changed than Richmond. Go on the Capital Square any afternoon, and you may see these women promenading up and down the shady walks jostling respectable ladies into the gutters."

Many citizens were horrified and the *Richmond Enquirer* was full of complaints—one protester advocated horsewhipping to reduce this activity—but the paper argued that prostitutes, like buzzards and vultures, were simply a part of the army's entourage. Nevertheless, the YMCA hospital superintendent was able to mobilize against a madam who opened her bawdy house directly across from his hospital and encouraged her prostitutes to expose themselves in the windows to lure potential customers out of their hospital beds.

Evidence as to the extent and particulars of prostitution is difficult to determine. Historian Bell Wiley complained of the "veil of reticence" that shrouded the subject, quoting a veteran who confided, "Confederate soldiers were too much gentlemen to stoop to such things." Most material on the topic can be culled only from court records and newspaper accounts rather than private correspondence, which many family members and descendants were likely to censor.

Rare glimpses do emerge despite censorship. A journalist traveling with Confederate Gen. Albert Sidney Johnston reported, "It is really curious to observe how well and how strictly the three classes of women in camp keep aloof from each other." He goes on to distinguish wives and daughters of officers from the cooks and washers, and then concludes:

The third and last class is happily the smallest; here and there a female of elegant appearance and unexceptionable manners; truly wife-like in their tented seclusion, but lacking that great and only voucher of respectability for females in camp—the marriage tie.

Increasingly, precautions were taken to rid the army of these camp followers. Army regulations restricted the number of laundresses per company and required them to furnish documentation of their good character. Further, in September 1862 near Vicksburg, an order was issued that provided that "company laundresses who do not actually wash for the men must be discharged." This kind of camp cleaning appears irregularly in the military records. In the spring of 1864 General Johnston demanded that the surrounding countryside in Tennessee be searched and all women who were unable to provide "proof of respectability" be shipped outside the reach of his soldiers.

Many prostitutes served the troops as seamstresses, washerwomen, and nurses, and some were female sutlers, like a woman described by Mary Chesnut: "She was dressed in the uniform of her regiment, but wore Turkish pantaloons. She frisked about in her hat and feathers. . . .She was followed at every step by a mob of admiring soldiers and boys." Although they may have been celebrated by the ranks, many met less favorable fates confronted by the brass. Mary and Mollie Bell posed as Confederate soldiers, assuming the aliases of Tom Parker and Bob Morgan, and worked the ranks for two years before they were charged with "aiding in the demoralization of General Early's veterans." The two women were put on trial, found guilty, and sentenced to terms in military prison.

Without comprehensive statistics, the scope of the problem of venereal disease arising from prostitution can only be guessed from irregular reports filed by regimental surgeons. In July 1861 nearly 11,500 men in 12 regiments reported 204 new cases of gonorrhea and 44 new cases of syphilis. By December of 1861, 43 regiments with nearly 35,000 men reported only 36 new cases of gonorrhea and 40 of syphilis. In September 1862 only 8 regiments with 6,200 men reported 36 new cases of gonorrhea and 10 of syphilis. After reviewing these and other compilations, Bell Wiley concluded that the high rate in the summer of 1861 was due to the concentration of troops in Richmond. In December 1862 the *Richmond Examiner* editorialized:

> If the Mayor of Richmond lacks any incentive to stimulate . . . breaking up the resorts of ill-fame in the city, let him visit the military hospitals where sick and disabled soldiers are received for treatment, and look upon the human forms lying there, wrecked upon the treacherous shoals of vice and passion which encounters the soldier at the corner of every street, lane and alley of the city.

For example, after a single month, the Tenth Alabama, while stationed in Richmond, reported 68 new cases of venereal disease.

Wiley believed that increased outbreaks in sexually transmitted diseases could be traced directly to proximity to towns with brothels, as when the North Carolina Fifty-fifth moved to Petersburg in October 1862. The town of Petersburg was legendary, and in the fall of 1863 a North Carolinian reported:

"about two weeks ago there was a woman come from petersburg and stoped about 200 yards from our camp several of the boys went up and had lots of fun with her. it was about drill time and one of the boys missed drill and they put him on double duty."

Nashville was another town with a deservedly lewd reputation. In July 1863 Union Gen. William Rosecrans, desperate to stem the tide of disease, commandeered a boat, rounded up 111 prostitutes (there were over 450 licensed prostitutes in the city), forced them onto the cruiser, and shipped them to Louisville (where they were refused permission to disembark). By October 1864, Nashville supported both a hospital for prostitutes and another for syphilitic soldiers.

As for the lives of the prostitutes themselves, we have no testimony and few insights—only observations from unsympathetic commentators, such as the Alabama private Orville Bumpass who wrote to his wife about local "whoredom" who were "the ugliest, sallowfaced, shaggy headed, bare footed dirty wretches you ever saw." When W. C. McClellan wrote to his sister about a male burlesque show among the troops at Fredericksburg, he insisted that the prostitutes in the audience "ware dresses [but there is about them] not much of the Lady."

Although prostitution was remarkably common, we know very little about the economics of the sex trade within the Confederacy. Further, although gonorrhea and syphilis contributed to the debilitation of troops on both sides through frequent contact with these women who sold sexual favors, the immediate impact and subsequent consequences of this behavior remain unexplored in historical literature. For a society so obsessed with the purity of its women, the sullying effects of wartime might have rewrought the complex web of virtue and reputation that kept white Southern women on the pedestal. The history of prostitutes could contribute significantly to our appreciation of the war's impact on postwar society as a whole, but especially on the lives of Southern women.

BIBLIOGRAPHY

Massey, Mary. *Bonnet Brigades: American Women and the Civil War.* New York, 1966.

Wiley, Bell. *The Life of Johnny Reb: The Common Soldier of the Confederacy.* Indianapolis, 1943.

CATHERINE CLINTON

PROVOST MARSHAL

Provost marshals commanded military police in camps or on active service within the Confederacy and in occupied territories. They and their provost guards, collectively called "provost," served as the Confederate version of the Union Provost Marshal General's Department.

Military courts and provost marshals, as authorized by the Articles of War in March 1861, accompanied some armies even before First Manassas. Eventually, to help improve discipline, commanders established provost at every level from brigade to army and at each level within the military departments. Unlike the Union, however, the Confederacy did not immediately appoint a provost marshal general. Brig. Gen. Daniel Ruggles was so appointed in February 1865, and held the appointment until the end of the war in April.

Before that, Brig. Gen. John H. Winder functioned as de facto provost marshal general, in addition to being provost marshal of Richmond in 1861 and 1862 and afterward commissary-general for prisons. Winder, widely regarded as a martinet, was said to have been the most hated man in the Confederacy, a description based, no doubt, on his personal traits—belligerence, irascibility, abrasiveness, and arrogance—and his overzealous, high-handed execution of his duties, which, by their very nature, were difficult, contentious, and thankless. While he was roundly criticized and generally scorned by the public, many of his military contemporaries praised him as energetic, upright, and efficient. His operation of the passport system was commendable, resulting in thorough control of civilian and military movement. It is debatable, however, how effective the system was in achieving another of its chief aims, the apprehension of the spies, subversives, and traitors that were assumed to have infested Richmond. While Winder had some success in coping with crime in Richmond, and his police did reduce, for a time, the level of violence, he was unable to impose consistent or permanent law and order. Overall, Winder deserves credit for his devotion to duty and for his energetic performance as provost marshal. It is difficult to see, in view of the paucity of resources, how another officer could have done better. The task assigned him was probably beyond the capacity and talents of any officer.

A separate provost corps did not exist; rather, officers and men and units were detailed to provost duty, most units only temporarily, although a few served more or less permanently. The Twenty-fifth Georgia Battalion (Atlanta Provost Battalion) was one such unit, as were the First North Carolina, the Fifth Alabama, and the First Virginia Battalions—respectively, the provost guards of the Second Corps, the Third Corps, and the headquarters of the Army of Northern Virginia.

The absence of comprehensive provost strength records and the often ad hoc and transitory nature of such employment prevents definitive compilation of provost strength. The evidence does show that provost duty was manpower-intensive: in 1864 there were 1,200 men on provost duty in Richmond and some 2,200 in the Department of Alabama,

Mississippi, and East Louisiana. Two years earlier, provost strength in the Army of Northern Virginia had been about 2,000. Assuming similar manpower allocations in other armies and departments, several thousand or more men experienced provost service.

The primary provost duty—to assist commanders in maintaining good order and discipline—eventually incorporated responsibility for arrest of offenders against military law (and often their custody); apprehension and return to their units of stragglers and deserters (perhaps the most important duty once the armies were in the field); operation on the railroads and throughout the nation of the passport system that was instituted to help the provost identify and capture stragglers, deserters, spies, and subversives; administration of martial

> **Passports, for example, were seen as an intolerable oppression.**

law; initial custody of prisoners of war; and enforcement of conscription.

Performance of such intrusive duties, often with excessive zeal, made the provost odious to soldiers and civilians alike. Passports, for example, were seen as an intolerable oppression. Enforcement of martial law, which entailed such unpopular measures as prohibitions on liquor, caused more public outrage. Enforcement of conscription similarly tarnished the provost image. One particularly explosive issue was military arrest of civilians, which, although less common than in the United States, stood condemned as interference with state rights.

Other provost tasks included mobilizing and controlling black laborers; taking custody of captured black soldiers and Union deserters to the Confederacy; guarding hospitals and other vital installations and captured equipment and matériel pending salvage for Confederate use; stopping unauthorized departure from Confederate ports; and preventing valuable commodities like cotton or tobacco reaching the enemy through illicit trade or by seizure.

The provost frequently participated in operations, too, acting as advance and rear guards, reconnoitering the enemy, controlling the activities of scouts and spies, and, when necessary, joining in hard fighting, as they did in the Wilderness in May 1864.

After the Conscription Act of 1862, and more frequently after the 1864 act, many regular soldiers employed as provost returned to the various fronts, leaving disabled men, reserves, and over- and underage men to fill their place. This posed an insoluble dilemma: using the less able as provost would degrade Confederate ability to keep order and maintain front-line strength; on the other hand, using able-bodied regulars would maintain provost effectiveness at the cost of reducing front-line fighting strength.

Notwithstanding insufficient manpower and the use of incompetent men; sometimes bad or indifferent leadership; abuses of power, which created controversy and dissension; and the inconsistencies of the military judicial system, the provost made a significant contribution to the war effort. Despite their mixed record, they were an important element in the maintenance of Confederate strength.

The enormous vituperation directed at the provost was, in effect, a backhand tribute to them. Although the public often regarded provost as useless, their vigorous execution of their duties also won them a reputation as efficient and ubiquitous. In any case, they became a pervasive feature of life in a beleaguered Confederate States of America.

[*See also* File Closers; Habeas Corpus; Military Justice; Winder, John H.]

BIBLIOGRAPHY

Blakey, Arch Fredric. *General John H. Winder, C.S.A.* Gainesville, Fla., 1990.
Radley, Kenneth. *Rebel Watchdog: The Confederate States Army Provost Guard.* Baton Rouge, La., 1989.

KENNETH RADLEY

PUBLIC FINANCE

The Confederate era involved many innovations in public finance, for the Civil War was not just the end of the slavery era. It was also a transitional period characterized by a partial retrogression to past practices and simultaneously by innovative new procedures that looked forward to the Reconstruction epoch.

Money in Circulation

When the U.S. Constitution was debated and written in 1787, James Madison's proposal to allow the Federal government to issue its own currency (then styled "bills of credit") was voted down by a large majority. So too was a section prohibiting such issues. Simultaneously, the states were prohibited from issuing their notes as a currency, and this prohibition was thought to extend to any local government erected under their authority. (Because of these prohibitions, paper currency at this time consisted largely of notes emitted by state-chartered private banks.)

Despite these legal impediments, the United States during the War of 1812 did put out a few circulating notes. From 1837 to 1861, interest-bearing notes, originally intended to be closely held as an investment, were retained after their interest ceased to accumulate in order that they might be used as internal bills of exchange to make remittances to New York.

State governments, from 1789 to 1860, particularly in the South, issued small amounts of currency. North Carolina was the most serious offender, but Alabama, Kentucky, Mississippi, Florida, and Texas also circulated their own notes. Florida, as a territory, did so apparently with Congress's approval. Texas put out quite a few notes, presumably in its capacity as an independent republic. Practically all the other Southern states, except Virginia and Texas, chartered wholly owned state banks. The bills of these institutions were made tax receivable and their payment was guaranteed by the states. Chief Justice John Marshall declared, in *Craig v. Missouri,* that state notes were bills of credit within the meaning of the Constitution. He died, however, before a decision could be reached on state bank notes, and his successors upheld the validity of such issues.

Various counties and municipalities issued due bills in fractional parts of a dollar during the 1814–1821 and 1837–1842 depressions. This action was in part necessitated by the need to provide the public with a currency under the denomination of five dollars. The banks, for the most part, were prohibited from issuing such notes, and the hoarding of gold and silver coins meant that without local government note issues, there would not have been any currency between the copper cent pieces and the bank five-dollar notes. In light of this, they were urgently required for the needs of commerce.

These experiences played an important role in influencing the Southern people's currency policies from 1861 to 1865. Moreover, when it is remembered that John C. Calhoun, the intellectual father of the secession, had advocated a central government currency in 1837 as a cure for a crash and depression, it is not surprising that the Confederate, state, and local governments all issued their own currency.

Confederate Currency. The Confederate government, in a reprise of events during the American Revolution, proceeded to issue a large quantity of paper currency, which depreciated heavily. To begin with, however, the South copied the antebellum practices of the United States by issuing interest-bearing Treasury notes. But on May 16, 1861, the Confederate Congress, contrary to the recommendations of Secretary of the Treasury Christopher G. Memminger, inaugurated a policy of issuing non-interest-bearing notes in denominations as low as five dollars. Such bills were clearly intended to serve as currency.

Subsequently, in 1862, Congress again took the initiative by ordering the issue of one-dollar and two-dollar notes. Only in 1863 was a fifty-cent note authorized. No lower-denomination note was ever issued because by that time the purchasing power of the Confederate currency had fallen to the point where anything under fifty cents would have been practically worthless.

Congress was encouraged in this policy by three considerations. First, it was recognized that taxes were unpopular and that in any case there would be delays before even a well-digested and comprehensive fiscal program could be put into effect. Thus, at a minimum, the issue of Treasury notes was necessary to provide mobilization funds.

Second, there was also pressure to issue such notes because, unlike those emitted by the state banks, the states, or the local governments, Confederate Treasury notes were receivable throughout the country at their face value without being made subject to bank and note broker collection charges.

Finally, the popularity of such notes with the financial community and the public differed markedly from the bitter opposition to them in the United States. The Northern banks did not want a more popular rival currency in opposition to their own notes. And in any event, prior to the end of 1861, the Northern banks were still exchanging coin for their notes. The Federal demand notes, by drawing coin from their vaults, threatened them with an ultimate suspension of gold payments on their notes and deposits.

On the other hand, the Southern banks had suspended the payment of gold and silver coin on their obligations (with the notable exception of New Orleans) by the end of 1860. Everyone by mid-1861 was used to an exclusively paper money currency and wanted to have the best available. A currency put out by the central government clearly fell into that category, and so the Confederacy, unlike the United States, never had to pass a legal tender law compelling creditors to receive its notes.

Once started down the slippery path of currency issues, the Congress passed act after act, steadily enlarging the amount authorized. It was hoped that the right of the note holders to purchase bonds paying 8 percent interest in coin would prevent the currency from becoming redundant. But as neither Congress nor Secretary Memminger took any positive steps to assure long-term coin payments, this protective device ceased to function after July 1, 1862, when specie payments on the debt ceased.

Under these circumstances, the prewar circulation, which had had a face value in coin of approximately $150 million, soon underwent a rapid expansion. The Confederate-issued currency amounted to $96 million by February 1862. Act followed act until October 13, 1862, when Congress ceased to put any limits on the amount of currency to be issued. By the act of March 23, 1863, the secretary was allowed to emit $50 million a month. Under these circumstances, it was not surprising that the total amount of such notes in circulation had reached nearly $800 million on April 1, 1864.

Since there was no effective tax legislation passed until April 1863, and few collections were made before the begin-

ning of 1864, efforts to prevent a redundant currency were limited solely to making such notes voluntarily exchangeable for bonds. Despite efforts in 1863 to compel the purchase of bonds with notes by a reduction in interest rates, the currency continued to grow. Then by the act of February 17, 1864, Congress required the note holders to exchange all of their currency for 4 percent registered bonds. Despite the large sums taken in, the issue of a further $460 million of notes dated February 17, 1864, kept the Confederate Treasury

> Once started down the slippery path of currency issues, the Congress passed act after act. . . .

notes outstanding in excess of $800 million up to the collapse of the government in April 1865.

It must also be noted that, despite the large sums emitted, the Confederate government as the years passed fell ever further behind in its efforts to meet its obligations. Such arrears were $26 million in early 1862, rising by the war's end to $350 million.

Most of this deficit arose from the Treasury's inability to procure the necessary notes from the Confederate security printers and from the department's inefficiency in distributing its funds to the paymasters. The failure to pay soldiers and contractors in a timely manner promoted supply shortages and massive desertion.

State Government Currency Issues. The state governments were at first limited in their note emissions because the Confederate Provisional Constitution carried over the Federal prohibition against such issues. Most states, with the exception of those who styled their issues as "Treasury warrants," contented themselves with selling a few high-denomination interest-bearing notes in 1861. But after February 18, 1862, the states passed act after act authorizing the emission of non-interest-bearing notes. Military mobilization requirements, the demands of the public for small-denomination notes to replace hoarded gold and silver coins, and the necessity of providing aid to the families of soldiers all furnished a plausible pretext or solid grounds to justify such issues.

State notes were issued in denominations of five cents up to $500, with Georgia exchanging some $5,000, $10,000, and $20,000 certificates for smaller bills. Some states, such as Virginia and Arkansas, abstained from issuing notes under the denomination of $1, leaving that function to their local governments.

Most authorizing laws appeared between 1861 and 1863. Thereafter, such legislation became rare because the legislatures feared the inflationary effect of such acts and were concerned about the public perception that state issues were excessive.

The use of Treasury notes was also to some degree dictated by a state's credit rating and its ability to borrow through the issue of bonds. The absence of state currency issues in Tennessee and South Carolina simply reflected the ability of those states to sell bonds and to order the state-owned Bank of Tennessee and the Bank of the State of South Carolina to issue the desired small notes in denominations from five cents up to two dollars. Georgia authorized the Western and Atlantic Railroad, which it owned, to issue notes in fractional parts of a dollar before undertaking this business directly on its own account.

The financial community, particularly in the East, entertained a higher opinion of the value of the state notes than those put out by the Confederacy. This was particularly true as the tide of battle shifted against the Richmond regime. Consequently, the high-denomination notes of many states, especially those bearing interest, were hoarded by the bankers and were seldom seen in circulation.

Since some states copied the Confederate government by making their notes exchangeable for bonds, a modest quantity of notes was absorbed by this means. Thus by the end of the war, when all such issues were repudiated, the states had issued directly or indirectly over $100 million of treasury notes. With the funding of notes and some tax collections, probably about a total of $65 million was still outstanding in 1865.

Local Government Notes. Issues by county and municipal governments also flourished during this period. Faced with the same demands as those made on the states, coupled with the widespread suspension of local tax collections, many municipal and county governments felt obliged to emit large quantities of notes, mostly in amounts of less than a dollar.

The prevalence of such notes varied greatly from state to state. South Carolina flatly prohibited them, with a special exemption for fire-devastated Charleston. Others, such as Virginia, Louisiana, and Texas, were marked by state authorizations of such issues and widespread abuses. Virginia was especially notorious in this regard: the capital, Richmond, issued nearly $500,000 worth. Some were used for local defense works and to buy the White House of the Confederacy for the use of Jefferson Davis. Others were issued to cover routine expenses and to help make change.

In addition to the issues in those three states, over one hundred cities and counties in eight other states issued their own money. Such issues, coming to a total of nearly $18 million, of which over $12 million was outstanding at the end of the war, further added to an already redundant currency.

Public Debt

The Confederate government, unlike the Union, started the war without a substantial debt. But the rapid expansion of public expenditures for military operations, the payments made for the civil establishment, and the discharge of the interest on the government's bonds led to the creation of a large debt consisting of interest-bearing and circulating Treasury notes, together with interest-bearing bonds and call certificates (an obligation convertible on demand into cash for both principal and interest).

The funded indebtedness commenced on February 28, 1861, with a modest $15 million loan and ended in 1865 with over $825 million outstanding. The interest rates on this debt varied from 8 percent in 1861 down to 4 percent in 1864. Nearly $600 million of this indebtedness was the result of more or less compulsory exchanges of Treasury notes for bonds with a view to reducing the high levels of inflation.

To meet the demands of those who were prepared to make only short-term loans, the Confederacy also authorized various issues of call certificates. Nearly $300 million worth of these were sold between 1861 and 1865, at rates starting at 8 percent and 6 percent in 1861 and dwindling to 5 percent in 1863 and 4 percent thereafter. The total amount outstanding in 1865 was probably less than $75 million.

State Debt. In addition to their prewar debts and their issues of Treasury notes, the states of the Confederacy accumulated substantial funded debts of their own. To begin with, many states copied the Confederate government by providing that holders of their Treasury notes might exchange them for bonds. A few states, such as Georgia, merely allowed such an exchange after the war with a view to diminishing current interest charges. Interest rates, as befitted the public's greater confidence in the states' credit, were typically 6 percent when the Confederacy was paying 8 percent, but less creditworthy western states such as Mississippi and Texas paid up to 10 percent on their bonds. The total amount of these issues came to slightly in excess of $50 million.

County and Municipal Debts. Local governments also accumulated debts above and beyond their note issues. Most of these came through the sale of registered bonds whose proceeds were typically employed for recruiting and equipping local military units. Because of the ease with which such governments could issue circulating bills, probably only $3 million or so was raised by these means, primarily for military and other public purposes.

Taxation

An important element in public finance, particularly as it related to the issue of circulating Treasury notes and interest-bearing bonds, could be found in the tax-levying and collecting policies of the Confederate, state, and local governments. The less the public authorities taxed, the more they had to borrow. And the more they borrowed, particularly in the form of circulating notes, the more public expenses were unnecessarily multiplied by price inflation.

Confederate Taxation. Confederate fiscal policies directly reflected the South's immediate past experience under the

Federal government. No Federal levy on real estate or personal property had been made since 1815, a direct result of the War of 1812. Federal revenues were practically limited to the collection of customs dues and the sales of public lands.

The Confederate government, prior to the outbreak of hostilities, did little to depart from this pattern. There was some tinkering with the tariff rates. In a retrogression to the pattern of the colonial era, allowed by the abolition of the Federal constitutional prohibition against taxes on exports, the Confederate Provisional Congress laid a duty of ⅛ cent per pound on all cotton shipped out of the Confederacy.

> **The estimated revenue from this tax was less than that needed for its announced purpose.**

Typically, the estimated revenue from this tax was less than that needed for its announced purpose: to pay the interest and principal of the $15 million loan of February 28, 1861.

After the engagement at Fort Sumter, Secretary Memminger asked Congress for a direct tax on real estate, slaves, livestock, securities, and other forms of personal property. After bitter debate, this proposed $25 million levy was reluctantly agreed to. It proved a distinct disappointment in practice since it produced only $15 million in revenue, and 10 percent of the revenue was lost and the benefits of a tax forfeited when the states issued bonds and assumed the tax on behalf of their citizens. This was retrogression to Revolutionary War practices, copied by the Federal government from 1813 to 1815.

Still worse, no provision was made to continue this tax or to get around the prohibition in the Permanent Constitution that blocked similar levies in the absence of a census. Moreover, no serious effort was made by the executive branch to pressure Congress into passing tax legislation of any kind before January 1, 1863. And when Congress did finally pass a tax act on April 23, 1863, it was a complicated grab bag of income and license taxes amalgamated with a tax-in-kind on agricultural produce that was riddled with exemptions.

Nor were matters much improved by the act of February 17, 1864, insofar as it pertained to taxes. Taxes in one area were made dependent upon the complicated calculation of the taxpayer's obligations in regard to some other tax. As a result, the difficulty in administering the internal revenue system was greatly complicated.

The planters, whose property interest in slaves the country was fighting to defend, especially after Abraham Lincoln's Emancipation Proclamation, fought bitterly to exempt themselves from contributing to the cause. Thus the anomalous spectacle was created of those holding roughly 40 percent of the South's property values (slaves) refusing to make any contribution to the cause that was protecting their interests.

Tax revenues by October 1, 1864, were seriously inadequate. Customs and export duties, despite optimistic predictions, came to a paltry $3 million. The war tax produced less than $15 million and the 1863 and 1864 taxes yielded only $123.5 million. In the end, only 8.2 percent of the Confederacy's income was derived from taxes, as compared with 20.1 percent of the Union's.

State Taxation. At the time the Federal Constitution was adopted in 1787, the American states secured most of their income from customs dues. The transfer of this revenue source to the Federal government meant that the states had to find a new way of paying their expenses.

In the years up to 1860, the Southern states had largely depended upon real estate taxes as their primary source of income. State bond sales made for the purpose of providing capital for banks, canals, turnpikes, and railroads, combined with demands for better police protection, aid to public education, and other public expenditures, soon created a growing deficit. Not only did the regular revenues not keep up with the demands on the public Treasury, but many companies in which the states invested went bankrupt or proved less remunerative than had been anticipated. This put pressure on the legislature to increase tax rates or find new sources of revenue.

Tax rates even by 1860 were low, averaging but $\frac{1}{10}$ of 1 percent on the assessed value of property and up $\frac{4}{10}$ of 1 percent in states such as Virginia where the public debt was heavy. Bitter debate revolved around how property should be appraised and how often. Moreover, should rates simply be laid on a flat basis at so much per acre of woodland or agricultural land, or should a real assessment be made? Debates on this point reached such a pitch that South Carolina was unable to conduct a new assessment after 1840.

One of the most contentious points and one that was never satisfactorily handled before the war or during the brief existence of the Confederacy was the question of how slaves should be assessed at the state level and what tax rate was appropriate for a species of property that represented anywhere from 30 to 60 percent of estimated property values in each state. The large slaveholders, anticipating their attitudes during the war, wanted to keep assessment levels low and if possible to avoid assessments altogether. Instead, they argued in favor of a low fixed tax per slave as a means of reducing assessment costs and tax avoidance.

Those who owned only a few slaves or none favored a full assessment of slaves and the same rate of tax on that type of property as on any other. Despite a vigorous rearguard action, the large slaveholders by 1861 had had to compromise. The use of a fixed tax per slave was still largely the rule, but in more and more states the tax began to approximate, as a percentage of value, that levied on land. It should not be thought, however, that state slave tax revenues constituted a small proportion of state revenues. Georgia and Alabama derived nearly half of their tax revenues from slave levies, and South Carolina derived over 60 percent.

The states experimented with other revenue sources. Luxury taxes were laid on "pleasure carriages," gold and silver plate, watches, pistols, pianos, and jewelry. Some states tried taxing the profits and dividends of corporations, then predominantly railroads or banks. Others had a crude income tax for individuals.

In many states the sheriffs were delinquent in their accounts. In some cases, taxes had not been collected but it had not been politically expedient to seize the debtor's property for a tax sale. In other cases, the sheriffs had collected the taxes but had diverted the money for their own use. The unreliability of the tax collectors before the war presaged what would happen during the war.

These trends were accentuated during the years of the Confederacy. The states, faced with large military expenses for which the Confederate Treasury did not reimburse them and confronted by the need to pay the interest on the newly issued notes and bonds, had to increase their revenues. And since there was neither time nor the manpower available for property reassessments, this invariably meant tax rate increases.

Yet there were contradictory trends. On the one hand, many state governments authorized tax surcharges on existing rates particularly for the benefit of soldiers' families. On the other hand, while doing this, Mississippi suspended the collection of the levee taxes. Many states in 1864 canceled or suspended their taxes for the duration of the war on the ground that the inadequate Confederate government taxes were so heavy a burden that the states should not add to it. And given the initial popularity of state issues of Treasury notes, the need for heavy taxes was not immediately apparent.

Contradictorily, however, many states did increase their taxes rates between 1861 and 1864. Alabama increased its income tax rate from 1 percent to 5 percent. Mississippi ordered a 30 percent surcharge on its real estate taxes. South Carolina increased rates on the assessed value of land from slightly over 1 percent in 1861 to 6 percent in 1865. South Carolina also took the assessment books for the Confederate war tax in 1861 and proceeded to collect the amounts due from its own citizens.

Georgia increased its property levy to 1 percent from its prewar level of $\frac{1}{10}$ of 1 percent. Also, its tax structure became more progressive, with an income tax and an ad valorem tax on other property, particularly cotton held by speculators.

Similar energy was displayed in North Carolina where the tax on land rose from $\frac{1}{5}$ of 1 percent to 1 percent in 1864.

Virginia, on the other hand, raised rates from $\frac{4}{10}$ of 1 percent to 1 percent in 1861. It then repealed the increases and lowered rates in 1864. Other states, although prepared to levy heavy but unenforceable taxes against speculators and profiteers, allowed many of their taxes to remain uncollected. This behavior was justified by the incursions of the enemy, the general decline of the economy, and the poverty of the public.

Moreover, it must not be forgotten that though there were rate increases and an apparent increase in nominal total revenues, such proceeds when converted into gold dollars showed an actual decline in real revenue. This anomaly can be attributed to the fact that the state tax rates did not keep

> ... there was neither time nor the manpower available for property reassessments. ...

pace with inflation. To do even that, by early 1864, taxes would have had to be twenty times what they were in 1861. The states, like the Confederate Congress, were seldom willing to put public sentiment to the test of real tax increases. Nonetheless, higher Confederate-era taxes proved a transition between the low antebellum rates and the comparatively high levies of the Reconstruction period.

Local Government Taxes. Local governments also came under pressure to increase their revenues to cover their expenses in raising military units and looking after the families of soldiers. In many instances, the state governments encouraged this trend. For example, Mississippi permitted the counties to levy a tax up to the amount secured by the prewar state real estate tax to aid soldiers' families. Virginia required that any local government issuing notes had to retire them in equal installments from 1864 to 1866. Any benefit from this act in the form of a reduction in the bloated currency was dissipated when the redemption date was deferred for up to six years.

Local government tax collections in militarily contested areas practically ceased, particularly when rival pro-Union and pro-Confederate governments competed for the loyalty of the citizenry. Many state and local government functions were abandoned during the war, and these bodies copied the state and the Confederate governments in their reluctance to tax their constituents.

Inflation

Given the fact that the Confederate government alone issued currency in excess of five times the prewar circulation, and taking further into account that state and local governments issued over $112 million of notes and that banks, railroads, other corporations, and private citizens also circulated their due bills, it is not surprising that the Confederacy was afflicted by severe inflation. This inflation was exacerbated by the absence of effective internal revenue systems at any level of government, by the blockade that greatly raised the prices of all imported goods or local goods made with foreign components, and by the breakdown of the transportation system, which made it increasingly difficult to move surplus goods from one part of the Confederacy to another.

Inflation had a devastating effect on the South's public finances. War required that the Confederate and state governments vastly increase their employment of soldiers and sailors, and those civilians needed to pay, clothe, house, equip, and feed them. It also increased the cost of goods purchased by any government, regardless of whether they were made at home or abroad. Inflation, broadly speaking, grew at an accelerating level from year to year. Inflation ran at 20 percent in 1861, 200 percent by the end of 1862, 2,000 percent by the end of 1863, and 5,000 percent in January 1865.

This in turn had a deadly circular effect on the governments' finances. The more that was spent, the more Treasury notes and near-monetary instruments like interest-bearing notes and coupon bonds had to be issued. And with no effective means to curtail the growth of the money supply, each gain in the size of the currency ensured a further expansion of inflation. This process was exacerbated by Confederate defeats that resulted in more desertions and more defeats. These in turn curtailed the area under Confederate control and reduced the number of people and the size of the economy in which Confederate currency could circulate, thus further raising prices.

State Socialism

The Confederate, state, and local governments did make various efforts to check inflation by exerting their powers over the economy and by taking upon themselves new responsibilities for the welfare of their people.

Confederate Government Actions. In the years between 1789 and 1829, in keeping with Alexander Hamilton's view that the government should create an identity of interest between itself and its wealthier citizens, the Federal government chartered two Federal banks, sponsored the construction of canals, built post roads, and took other steps to encourage the economic development of the United States.

After President Andrew Jackson entered the White House in 1829, these activities more or less ceased. The Democrats adopted the doctrine of laissez-faire, which opposed government intervention. This, combined with the South's growing fear of Northern economic power exercised through the Washington regime, and with the popular doctrine of state rights, led many Southerners to adopt the view that economic development or regulation was beyond the proper scope of the central government's powers.

These attitudes found their reflection in both Confederate Constitutions. The general welfare clause present in the Federal Constitution was deleted and provisions inserted against what were then styled "internal improvements." These put a crimp on what the Confederate government might legitimately do either for itself or for its citizens.

Nonetheless, the Davis administration did take a number of actions that had far-reaching effects on the national economy and war efforts. Belatedly, in 1863 and 1864, the government asserted its control over interstate and foreign commerce by prohibiting the import of foreign luxury goods and by commandeering for government use both the incoming and the outgoing cargo space of blockade-running ships. This program, known as the "New Plan," effected a great improvement in governmental supply operations and finances, but it was adopted so late that most ports had been effectively closed before it could be put into operation.

At home, the administration undertook a variety of actions in keeping with the suggestions made by John C. Calhoun in 1816. Without waiting for private enterprise to deal with its various problems, the War Department created powder mills, nitrate beds, and a variety of manufacturing plants to provide the armed forces with weapons, munitions, clothing, shoes, and other equipment. The quantities furnished were never adequate, outside of munitions, but the army could hardly have endured its unequal contest with the Union forces without them.

In another departure from previous practice, the War Department also assumed increasing control over the South's ill-assorted railroad system. Companies were required, where possible, to share equipment, spare parts, and rolling stock. Railroad schedules were regulated. The government also built three important connecting lines. One provided a third route south from Richmond to North Carolina, and another from Georgia tied up with Florida's railroads and cattle supply. The third involved an attempt to complete the line between Montgomery, Alabama, and Jackson, Mississippi.

Despite widespread public clamor for a government advance on the cotton crop, all efforts to enact such a program were opposed by Secretary Memminger. As a result, the so-called 1861 Produce Loan (a scheme whereby the planters lent the government money secured by a pledge of the proceeds of the sale of their crops) produced a paltry $20 million. Only on April 14, 1862, did Congress enact and Jefferson Davis approve a law allowing the government to buy $35 million of produce with bonds. This action was too limited and too late to be of much benefit to either the Confederacy or the planters.

For the most part, the central government confined its activities to the military sphere and did little for the civilian sector of the economy. The government might have done more and done it earlier, but public suspicion of and state government opposition to any display of activism by the central regime go far to explain its apparent passivity. By 1863, the Richmond regime was seen as a necessitous body, always making demands on the people and giving nothing in exchange.

State and Local Government Activities. Although the Confederate government had to work carefully to placate or get around local sentiment and opposition to the exercise of governmental powers even in wartime, the state and local governments faced fewer obstacles in their efforts to intervene in the economy. Prior to the war, the states had lent money or their credit to banks, bridge and turnpike companies, railroads, and even manufacturing facilities. State leadership in economic development was taken for granted, and local governments supported the building of transportation facilities. Thus, when hostilities broke out, Southerners looked instinctively to their governors and state legislatures for relief.

In addition to their contribution to mobilizing the South's manpower for war, state governments undertook a variety of other activities. State and local governments were active in many cases in furnishing cash and food supplies to the impoverished families of soldiers. Without such programs, spotty and inadequate as many of them were, desertion among the Confederate troops would have been far worse than it was.

Southern state governments also manufactured, secured, and distributed scarce salt with which people preserved their meat supplies. Wool cards were made available in order that families might weave their own woolen cloth. State governments also attempted to regulate the distribution of scarce goods and to make contracts with manufacturers in order to prevent speculators from cornering supplies. A well-intended but crude effort was also made in some states to impose for the duration of the war a form of prohibition, but without much success. Mississippi was the only state that attempted to assist the blockaded planters by advancing them $5 million in Treasury notes secured by the pledge of cotton.

Nor did the more active states, particularly North Carolina and Georgia, neglect actions intended to maintain the morale of their citizens serving with the Confederate army. They purchased or leased vessels to ship state-owned cotton abroad. They sent supplies to the states' troops, an action necessitated by the fact that, because of the inefficiency of Confederate quartermaster and commissary authorities, troops were frequently left without uniforms, shoes, blankets, or food.

State agents also purchased and ran through the blockade supplies needed by the civilian population. These were in many cases distributed practically at cost. Significantly, these actions were undertaken within a year or so after hostilities broke out and a year and a half before President Davis promulgated the New Plan, which was the Confederate government's equivalent of the states's actions.

The management of the South's public finances exhibited wide-ranging errors of omission and commission. Many important opportunities were allowed to slip away, particularly in regulating trade and in enacting and enforcing effective tax legislation. The central government, more concerned with legalistic considerations than practical realities, did very little to help the South's planters or to smuggle goods in through the blockade.

The state governments, albeit with fewer resources and larger initial debts, did more, and they encountered fewer objections from the public regarding their interventionist policies. Whether they could have accomplished more had the Confederate government reimbursed them for their military expenditures is a moot point. The fact was that the two levels of government went pretty much their own way and failed to coordinate their efforts. The result was a declining economy riddled with inflation, suffering from a shortage of foreign goods, and unable to move goods internally. It was a classical prescription for the collapse of civilian morale, desertion from the army, and military defeat.

[*See also* Bonds; Currency, *overview article;* Debt; Erlanger Loan; Inflation; New Plan; Produce Loan; State Socialism; Taxation.]

BIBLIOGRAPHY

Ball, Douglas B. *Financial Failure and Confederate Defeat.* Urbana, Ill., 1991.

Ballagh, James Curtis. *The South in the Building of the Nation.* Vol. 5 of *Southern Economic History.* Richmond, Va., 1909.

Black, Robert C., III. *The Railroads of the Confederacy.* Chapel Hill, N.C., 1952.

Coulter, E. Merton. *The Confederate States of America, 1861–1865.* A History of the South, vol. 7. Baton Rouge, La., 1950.

Easton, Clement. *A History of the Southern Confederacy.* New York, 1954.

Hawk, Emory Q. *Economic History of the South.* New York, 1934.

Hill, Louise B. *State Socialism in the Confederate States of America.* Charlottesville, Va., 1936.

Schwab, John Christopher. *The Confederate States of America, 1861–1865: A Financial and Industrial History of the South during the Civil War.* New York, 1901.

Thorton, Mills. "Fiscal Policy and the Failure of Radical Reconstruction." In *Region, Race, and Reconstruction: Essay in Honor of C. Vann Woodward.* Edited by J. Morgan Kousser and James M. McPherson. New York, 1982.

Todd, Richard Cecil. *Confederate Finance.* Athens, Ga., 1954.

Wallenstein, Peter. "Rich Man's War, Rich Man's Fight." *Journal of Southern History* 50, no. 1 (February 1964): 15–42.

Woolfolk, George Ruble. "Taxes and Slavery in the Antebellum South." *Journal of Southern History* 26, no. 2 (May 1960): 180–200.

DOUGLAS A. BALL

QUANTRILL, WILLIAM CLARKE

QUANTRILL, WILLIAM CLARKE (1835-1865), pro-Confederate Missouri guerrilla. At age sixteen, following the death of his father, an Ohio school principal, Quantrill drifted west, teaching school in Illinois, Indiana, and finally, in 1857, in Tuscarora Lake, Kansas, a settlement of Ohio migrants. Expelled from Tuscarora Lake as a thief, Quantrill joined an army expedition to Utah as a teamster, from where, late in 1858, he joined a gold party headed for Pikes Peak. Twelve of the nineteen men in the party died of exposure in the Rocky Mountains, and Quantrill's survival led him to believe that he was a man of destiny. Back in Kansas in 1859, Quantrill became something of a double agent, consorting with political bandits of both antislavery Kansans and proslavery Missourians, before finally throwing in his lot with the proslavery camp.

When the war began, the area around Independence, Missouri, went up in flames. Kansas Jayhawkers (antislavery Unionists, some enrolled in the militia, some freebooters) crossed the Missouri River to burn and plunder. In retaliation, many young Missourians took to the bush and spontaneously organized guerrilla bands. Quantrill, a bit older than most of these boys, a fine horseman and dead shot, and with a little military experience and a lot of self-confidence, led one of the most active gangs in attacking Union troops and raiding Kansas border towns. Such bands had the support of many local citizens, a difficult terrain in which to hide, and a cunning ability to attack the enemy at his weak spots, and then to scatter and melt back into the countryside.

In the summer of 1863, Union authorities began expelling or imprisoning suspected guerrilla sympathizers. On August 13, a rickety Kansas City prison collapsed, killing five young female kin of the Quantrill band. In retaliation, Quantrill gathered about 450 guerrillas and, on the morning of August 21, burst into Lawrence, Kansas, burning, looting, and killing about 150 unarmed men and boys, a raid that gained him national notoriety.

When his men sojourned in Texas that winter, Confederate authorities could neither enroll them nor control them. Quantrill's cohort disintegrated into smaller groups, led by younger and even more reckless men, notably George Todd and "Bloody" Bill Anderson, who carried on in 1864 in Missouri as before, while Quantrill sat out the summer in hiding. In October, Todd and Anderson were both killed, and Quantrill reassembled about thirty of his old band for an expedition into Kentucky. On May 10, 1865, Quantrill, surprised while sleeping in a barn, was shot, paralyzed, and captured. He was taken to a military prison hospital in nearby Louisville where, following his conversion to Roman Catholicism, he died on June 6.

> **Quantrill's fighters had been the James and Younger brothers. . . .**

Quantrill's fighters had been the James and Younger brothers; as their reputations rose during their postwar careers, so did his. Noble guerrillas had become noble outlaws, fighting those dreaded outsiders—bankers and railroad men—particularly in the historical fiction of the alcoholic newspaperman, John N. Edwards. By 1888, mythically rehabilitated Quantrill veterans were organizing annual reunions, at which they would have their pictures taken, always holding up a portrait of their fallen captain, Quantrill. In the twentieth century, Hollywood would utilize this romance in films about the Old West. Finally, some of his bones were buried with full Confederate military honors on October 24, 1992, in Higginsville, Missouri, by a rather macabre group of historical romanticists.

BIBLIOGRAPHY

Brownlee, Richard S. *Gray Ghosts of the Confederacy: Guerrilla Warfare in the West, 1861–1865*. Baton Rouge, La., 1958.

Castel, Albert. *William Clarke Quantrill: His Life and Times*. New York, 1962.

Connelley, William Elsey. *Quantrill and the Border Wars*. Cedar Rapids, Iowa, 1909. Reprint, New York, 1956.

Edwards, John N. *Noted Guerrillas, or the Warfare on the Border*. St. Louis, 1877.

Fellman, Michael. *Inside War: The Guerrilla Conflict in Missouri during the American Civil War*. New York, 1989.

MICHAEL FELLMAN

QUARTERMASTER BUREAU

Established February 26, 1861, the Quartermaster Bureau was responsible for providing the Confederate armies with nonfood and nonordnance items, as well as transportation functions. Thus, the production of uniforms, shoes, shirts, hats, tents, saddles, and wagons and their transportation were quartermaster functions, as was the transportation of the armies themselves. The bureau was headed first by Col. Abraham C. Myers of South Carolina (March 25, 1861–August 10, 1863) and then by Brig. Gen. Alexander R. Lawton of Georgia (August 10, 1863, to the end of the war).

An act establishing the department stipulated that it be manned by a colonel as quartermaster general, six majors as quartermasters, and as many lieutenants (subalterns) as assistant quartermasters as were necessary. All the quartermasters were authorized to act as paymasters.

The department was organized in the same manner as its prewar Federal counterpart. It was to run a simple senior office. The subordinate officers were to oversee functional areas such as shoes or uniforms for the major Confederate armies. Each of the major armies usually had a staff officer assigned to handle quartermaster functions, thus relieving the commanding general of what most officers considered an onerous task. Custom dictated that each division, brigade, and regimental commander assign quartermaster duties to an officer. Those assigned were rarely professional or experienced in supply matters, and those who were often faced the conflict of dual allegiance to their commander in the field and their superior, the quartermaster general, in Richmond. Consequently, supply problems related to the internal functioning of the quartermasters grew as the war progressed. At the company level, quartermaster functions, such as the actual distribution of uniforms to individual soldiers, were handled by a designated sergeant, who was often overseen by an officer.

What appeared to be the simple task of supplying soldiers in the field rapidly became extremely complicated as the number of soldiers and the distance over which they served increased. The quartermasters' problems were exacerbated by a number of factors: declining means of transportation, lack of coordination, spiraling wartime inflation, corruption, divisive politics, shortage of manpower, and the lack of glamour associated with nonbattle staff duties.

Following in the tradition of the Federal army, the Quartermaster Bureau was the senior department and the quartermaster general the ranking staff officer after the adjutant general. Because of seniority, he and his subordinates could and did usurp the assets of other staff departments, particularly in the functional area of transportation. This practice led to friction, rivalry, and an intense competition for limited assets that continued to the war's end. The combat efficiency of the Confederate armies was often affected by departments that rerouted scheduled trains, only to have the rerouted trains rescheduled by a local quartermaster. The lack of clear direction and coordination by the president and secretary of war accentuated this deadly problem.

Wartime inflation was another factor in the failure of the bureau to carry out its mission. The well-known tales of Confederate civilians having to pay incredible prices for goods and services also reflected the situation of the quartermasters, but they had a partial remedy—impressment. Using constitutional powers delegated by the secretary of war, they could commandeer private property, be it cloth for tents and uniforms or leather for shoes and saddles. Necessary goods could be impressed as long as the quartermaster provided just compensation. But given the rapidly spiraling inflation of the Confederacy, quartermasters often paid only half of an item's true market value. Civilians complained vehemently to the Congress, which eventually enacted legislation to curtail and regulate the process. The practice of impressment did nothing to enhance the quartermasters' reputation and stimulated charges of corruption.

> The practice of impressment did nothing to enhance the quartermasters' reputation and stimulated charges of corruption.

Starting in the summer of 1862 and continuing until the end of the war, the Quartermaster Bureau was under almost continual investigation by Congress. Anger about quartermaster practices and in particular corruption led to the introduction of numerous resolutions and acts regarding their activities. One of the most telling was an Act to Protect the Confederate States against Frauds, Etc. The Senate debated the act on December 31, 1864, and the comments of Senator George N. Lester of Georgia reveal the deep-seated anger the Confederacy felt for the quartermasters. Lester admitted that there were some honest men in the bureau but asserted that the rest had been "engaged in plundering the government from the beginning of the war till now."

This sentiment led to legislation that was designed to destroy the department. An act submitted to President Jefferson Davis in March 1865 would have sent all able-bodied quartermasters under the age of forty-five to field positions. Davis vetoed the bill because it would have been a disaster for the already faltering war effort and would have added only two hundred men to the army.

Divisive politics was another factor in the quartermasters' failure. Almost as soon as the war began, state governors withheld vital supplies for their own states' use. Quartermaster General Lawton recognized the problem as soon as he took the job. He wrote two letters in 1864 to the secretary of war complaining that the governors controlled assets, like cotton and woolen factories, that the bureau needed:

> We draw not a single yard of any kind of material. . . . It would be better for the State authorities to allow this department to control factory production so far as they may be needed for military purposes. . . .The necessities of the people and the objects of charity must be postponed to the wants of the Army.

In the state rights–oriented Confederacy many governors would continue to control necessary supplies even to the detriment of the war effort.

Another problem for the bureau was manpower. In February 1865, it reported that it needed 2,299 white males, 3,451 blacks full time, and 5,000 women for part-time or piecework. Many important people thought that the department controlled too many skilled white males who in the manpower-short Confederacy were needed on the battlefront. President Davis, however, usually disagreed.

The last factor affecting the performance of the quartermasters was the lack of respect for their specialty. Often not the highest caliber officers, they had a poor reputation. In fact, Lawton, a former brigadier and division commander under Thomas J. ("Stonewall") Jackson, complained at length when he was assigned to his new billet. The comments of Gen. Richard S. Ewell at the Battle of Cedar Mountain reflected the feeling of most Confederate officers regarding quartermasters. When Ewell saw a well-dressed officer on the battlefield, he asked, "I do say, young man with the fine clothes on! Who are you and where do you belong?" Being informed that he was a quartermaster with a Virginia regiment, Ewell exploded: "Great Heavens! A Quartermaster on the battle-field; who ever heard of such a thing before?"

Nevertheless, given the difficulties they faced, it is amazing that the quartermasters accomplished as much as they did. Both Myers and Lawton struggled against impossible odds. Myers did a creditable job and Lawton's work bordered on superb.

BIBLIOGRAPHY

Coulter, Merton E. *The Confederate States of America, 1861–1865.* A History of the South, vol. 7. Baton Rouge, La., 1950.

Davis, Jefferson. *Jefferson Davis, Constitutionalist: His Letters, Papers and Speeches.* Jackson, Miss., 1923.

Eaton, Clement. *A History of the Southern Confederacy.* New York, 1954.

Goff, Richard D. *Confederate Supply.* Durham, N.C., 1969.

U.S. War Department. *War of the Rebellion: A Compilation of the Official Records of the Union and Confederate Armies.* Washington, 1880–1901. Ser. 4, vol. 3, pp. 556–557.

Vandiver, Frank E. *Rebel Brass: The Confederate Command System.* Baton Rouge, La., 1956.

Weinert, Richard P. *The Confederate Regular Army.* Shippensburg, Pa., 1991.

P. NEAL MEIER

RAILROADS

The decade of the 1850s was one of the most important periods in the history of American railroads. What had been at the beginning of the decade a scattering of short lines from Maine to Georgia had become by 1860 an iron network serving all the states east of the Mississippi. New construction in the ten years resulted in a growth from 9,021 to 30,626 miles. The mileage in 1850 was concentrated in a network stretching from Portland, Maine, and Buffalo, New York, south to Richmond, Virginia, and Wilmington, North Carolina. A separate 900-mile system served the major cities in South Carolina and Georgia. West of the mountains the only states with 100 miles or more of line were Michigan, Ohio, Indiana, Illinois, and Alabama.

Antebellum Sectional Differences. In the early 1830s railroad mileage in the Southern states (those south of the Potomac and Ohio rivers) had nearly matched that of the North, but by 1850 the North had 5,612 miles of line and the South only 2,133 miles. Clearly the industrial states in the North felt a greater need for the new mode of transport than did the more agrarian South. But in the 1850s the South did much to catch up. Arkansas and Texas laid their first track and the South (the future Confederate states plus Kentucky) built 7,402 miles of railroad, climbing to a total of 9,535 miles, or an increase of 347 percent.

Probably more significant was the new construction in the West. During the 1850s mileage in the eight Western states (the Old Northwest plus Iowa, Missouri, and California) increased from 1,276 to 11,078 miles. And by the end of the Civil War the network from western Pennsylvania to the Mississippi River seemed complete. Most of the new mileage ran east and west and connected with one or more major trunk lines.

For a generation prior to mid-century steamboats had had a monopoly on commerce and transportation in the Mississippi-Ohio basin, but the major railroad construction in the Old Northwest soon resulted in a new east-west trade axis that replaced the earlier north-south traffic of the Ohio and Mississippi River steamboats. The economic shift is noted by William and Bruce Catton in their *Two Roads to Sumter:* "Southerners who dreamed that the Northwest might be neutral or even an ally in the event of a civil conflict should have looked more closely at the endless parade of freight trains clattering across the mountains between the ocean and the lakes."

Certainly there was no lack of enthusiasm for railroads in the South. On the eve of the Civil War over a hundred companies shared the 9,000 miles of line in the Confederacy. The average length was 85 miles, with a third over 100 miles in length, and nine over 200 miles. Most of the Confederate lines represented a single state, with all their mileage within the state. In 1860 the average investment per mile of road was about $27,000 in the South, $36,000 in the West, and $48,000 in the Northeast. Southern railroads cost less for several reasons: cheaper slave labor, lighter and often inferior rails, easier terrain along the coastal plains of the South, and smaller amounts of rolling stock per mile of road. Financial support for the construction in the decade had come from some cities and counties and a few states, especially Virginia, North Carolina, and Tennessee, but most lines were chiefly financed by the private sector. A Federal land grant pushed through Congress by William R. King, senator from Alabama, and his colleague, Stephen A. Douglas of Illinois, had provided aid for the Mobile and Ohio and the Illinois Central in Illinois.

Construction of the 7,000 miles of new line in the eleven Southern states in the fifties was rather even during the ten years, but more than half of the new track was put down in the four years 1857 through 1860. This was in contrast to the pattern north of the Ohio River where nearly three-quarters

> **The Civil War was the first major conflict in which railroads played an important role.**

was laid between 1852 and 1856. Southern lines, like those in the rest of the nation, were built in a variety of track gauges. The 5-foot gauge was dominant, but three states, with modest mileage, favored the 5-foot 6-inch gauge, and two states favored the 4-foot 8 1/2-inch gauge, which was fairly standard in the North.

The Civil War was the first major conflict in which railroads played an important role. In 1861 the Union and Confederate rail systems were in some ways a study in contrast. The eleven Southern states with their 9,000 miles of line had nearly a third of the nation's rail mileage, but employed less than a fifth of the country's railroad work force. Many workers from the North were employed on Southern lines in 1861, probably because of the Southerners' traditional dislike for mechanical pursuits. When war came, many Northerners returned home, and those who remained were often viewed with suspicion, sometimes rightly so.

The South was also at a disadvantage in motive power, rolling stock, and track materials. The entire Confederacy had hardly as many locomotives as those found on the combined motive power rosters of the New York Central, the Pennsylvania, and the Erie. The states north of the Potomac had a dozen locomotive factories for every one located in the South. The few locomotive factories in the South, such as the Tredegar Iron Works at Richmond, were pressed by the Davis government into the production of ordnance. The states of Virginia, South Carolina, and Tennessee had produced a fair number of railroad cars, but Pennsylvania produced twice as many as the entire Confederacy. Obtaining replacement rail and spikes was also soon a problem. Before the war Southern railroad presidents preferred English to Northern rails, claiming the English to be superior and cheaper. The South produced some rail, but its production of 26,000 tons in 1860 was about a ninth of the Northern output. The Union blockade of Southern ports, plus the Confederate priority given to ordnance production, soon had Southern track maintenance officials hoarding their iron.

While the Confederate railways lagged well behind Northern roads in the quantity and maintenance of equipment, the types of engines and cars used by the rivals varied only slightly. Both North and South relied heavily on the American-type locomotive (a swiveled four-wheel truck in front plus four drivers) with its functional cowcatcher, balloon stack, and large headlight. This kind of engine (4-4-0) had a name rather than a number, weighed from fifteen to twenty-five tons, cost $8,000 to $10,000 new, used wood or coal for fuel, and was the pride and joy of the engine crew to whom it was assigned. Northern lines shifted to coal for fuel far faster than the Southern roads; nearly all Confederate railroads depended on cord wood. A few Northern railroads owned some engines with six rather than four drivers, but such locomotives were rare in the South.

The typical freight car, either Northern or Southern, had two four-wheel trucks, was from twenty-four to thirty-four feet in length, and had a load capacity of eight to twelve tons. First-class boxcars rarely cost more than $400 to $500 per car and often were built in company shops for much less. Passenger cars on the eve of the war normally came equipped with corner toilet, water tank, a wood-burning stove, and inadequate lighting. In 1860 first-class cars were about fifty feet in length, could hold fifty passengers, and were stopped with hand brakes. New cars cost from $1,500 to $3,000 each. Dining cars had not yet been introduced, and sleeping cars were almost unknown on Southern lines.

The principal railroad centers in the Confederacy were Richmond, Chattanooga, and Atlanta. Richmond was served by five roads, whereas the Union capital, a hundred miles to the north, depended upon a single branch line of the Baltimore and Ohio. Chattanooga and Atlanta both were served by three roads, but each was a vital line serving much of the region. At the start of the war, Richmond had two major routes to the south. An eastern coastal line, formed of six railroads, reached Wilmington, Charleston, and Savannah, the major Confederate eastern seaports. A second transmountain route via Petersburg, Lynchburg, Bristol, and Knoxville reached Chattanooga in the southeastern corner of Tennessee. Late in the war Richmond was served by a third line via Danville and Greensboro, which became a vital supply route for Robert E. Lee. West of Chattanooga the 296-mile Memphis and Charleston ran to Corinth and Memphis with connections serving Tennessee, Alabama, Mississippi, Louisiana, and New Orleans. South of Chattanooga the Georgia state-owned 138-mile Western and Atlantic reached Atlanta and several lines serving the Carolinas, Georgia, and Florida. The Western and Atlantic later would be a bone of contention between Joseph E. Brown, state rights governor of Georgia, and Jefferson Davis. These three junction cities were in states that had the greatest rail mileage in the Confederacy.

War's Effect on Southern Lines. In the spring of 1861 the *American Railroad Journal* predicted that the majority of the railroads would be unaffected by the Civil War, a mistaken prophecy, indeed. Southern lines leading toward the Virginia and Tennessee fronts soon were overwhelmed with a flood of excited soldiers and ancient ordnance moving north. South of Richmond the Petersburg Railroad doubled its gross revenue by 1862 and in that year had a record low operating ratio under 28 percent. Between 1861 and 1863 the Georgia Railroad lowered its operating ratio from 57 to 42 percent. The Wilmington and Weldon paid a 31 percent dividend in 1863, and between 1860–1861 and 1862–1863 total receipts on the North Carolina Railroad increased nearly fourfold. The operating ratio dropped to 38 percent, and dividends doubled. Of course, the lower operating ratios and higher dividends resulted in part from the scarcity of labor and replacement parts.

In these years military personnel made up well over a third of the passenger traffic. But freight traffic was declining on many Confederate lines in the early war months, especially in the cotton-producing states where the rail movement of cotton was reduced by the effective Union blockade of the Southern coastline. Also the early indications of rail prosperity must be discounted because the growing receipts and dividends were expressed in Confederate dollars, which were rapidly declining in real value.

Railroad Construction in the South during the 1850s

STATE	MILEAGE IN 1850	MILEAGE IN 1860	INCREASE IN DECADE	INVESTMENT PER MILE	DOMINANT GAUGE
Virginia	481	1,731	1,250	$36,679	4′8½″
North Carolina	283	937	654	18,796	4′8½″
South Carolina	289	973	684	22,675	5′0″*
Georgia	643	1,420	777	20,696	5′0″*
Florida	21	402	381	21,356	5′0″*
Tennessee	—	1,253	1,253	24,677	5′0″*
Alabama	183	743	560	25,022	5′0″
Mississippi	75	862	787	27,982	5′0″
Louisiana	80	335	255	35,988	5′6″
Arkansas	—	38	38	30,394	5′6″*
Texas	—	307	307	36,706	5′6″
Total	2,055	9,001	6,946		

*Only gauge in the state

Certainly much of the seeming prosperity was false, given the persistent inflation. The costs of railway operation generally rose faster than did the freight rates and passenger fares. In the first two or three years of war, mechanics' wages climbed from $2.50 to $20.00 a day, nails from 4 cents to $4.00 a pound, shovels from $10.50 to $300.00 per dozen, coal from 12 cents to $2.00 per bushel, and lubricating oil from $1.00 to $50.00 a gallon. Railroad officials found it hard to raise rates fast enough to match these rising costs. John P. King, the president of the 232-mile Georgia Railroad, long a prosperous line, complained in 1864 that because of inflation his road had been losing money for two years. He wrote of his railroad: "The more business it does, the more money it loses, and the greatest favor that could be conferred upon it—if public wants permitted—would be the privilege of quitting business until the end of the war!"

Early in the war major problems faced two railroads in border states—the Louisville and Nashville in Kentucky and Tennessee, and the Baltimore and Ohio in Maryland and Virginia. Both lines had major mileage in the Confederacy—the L & N in Tennessee on its way to Nashville, and the B & O in northern and western Virginia. As the war came to Kentucky in the spring of 1861, the L & N was enjoying prosperity, with merchants and public officials in Tennessee and points farther south ordering vast amounts of Northern goods. James Guthrie, its president, found his road so clogged with south-bound freight that he imposed a ten-day embargo late in April to clear his tracks. Through the summer of 1861 the cagey Guthrie tried to serve two masters at once. But by the end of the summer, he was forced to choose, and he broke with the Confederacy. Parts of his lines were in Confederate hands, but before too long northern Tennessee was again under Union control. Guthrie fully supported the Union, and he may have received higher than normal rates for his Federal business.

In a way the first violence of the Civil War had come to the B & O eighteen months before the capture of Fort Sumter, when John Brown made his raid on Harpers Ferry in 1859. In Baltimore John W. Garrett, president of the line, wired the Secretary of War, who sent Col. Robert E. Lee with a detachment of U.S. Marines to subdue Brown. All of Garrett's 379-mile railroad was located in slave states, and the majority of the line was in Virginia, a state soon to secede. Garrett had long considered the B & O to be a Southern railroad, but he knew that the future of his road lay with the North and the Union rather than the South. Western flour and Cumberland coal, both headed north, not the tobacco and cotton from Southern plantations, had made Baltimore and the B & O prosperous. In the troubled days of late April and early May 1861, Garrett and the B & O were regarded suspiciously and pressured by both the Union and the Confederacy.

Col. Thomas J. ("Stonewall") Jackson and his Confederate forces started to occupy the Harpers Ferry area in May 1861. Soon he was in effective control of forty-four miles of B & O track west of Harpers Ferry. On May 23, 1861, he captured fifty-six B & O engines and three hundred freight cars. Many of the locomotives were put to the torch, but a few were dragged on wagons behind dozens of horses to other Virginia lines to serve the Confederate war effort. Jackson also destroyed dozens of bridges and other B & O equipment west of Harpers Ferry. The B & O was not able to restore service in the region fully until March 1862. It is not surprising that during the spring months of 1861 Garrett's language describing the Confederacy shifted from "our southern friends" to "misguided friends" and finally to "damned rebels."

Confederate Administration. During the entire conflict the Confederate government's control of the railroads was far from effective. The widespread belief that the war would be short, the early failure to recognize the importance of the railroads in the war effort, and the reluctance of the Davis administration to override state authority contributed to the lack of effective regulation. Late in April 1861, thirty-three railroad presidents met in Montgomery and agreed to a uniform fare of two cents a mile for troops, and half the normal freight rate for the shipping of war munitions and provisions. They also agreed to accept Confederate bonds at par in payment for military transportation. A second convention of presidents at Chattanooga in October 1861 modified the Montgomery agreement, and the new rate structure was approved by Quartermaster General Abraham C. Myers. As the currency depreciated, steadily higher fares and rates were approved. The government never tried to control railroad charges for the general public.

On the eve of First Manassas, President Jefferson Davis believed rail congestion so severe that he commissioned as a major and assistant quartermaster William S. Ashe, former president of the Wilmington and Weldon. Ashe was placed in charge of military rail transportation in Virginia, especially the lines serving Richmond. Major Ashe quickly set up his Richmond office, but Myers retained real control of railroad traffic, employing Ashe only as a subordinate. Confederate rail traffic problems were little improved, and in December 1862, Secretary of War George Wythe Randolph assigned Col. William M. Wadley to the supervision of "all the railroads in the Confederate States." But Wadley's appointment was never approved, and a third man, Capt. Frederick W. Sims,

> **. . . few railroad officials would permit their cars to be used on a foreign road.**

replaced him in May 1863. Sims had no greater success than his predecessors, however.

Some problems, such as changes of gauge at transfer points, were incapable of solution. At such cities as Richmond, Petersburg, and Lynchburg in Virginia; Wilmington and Charlotte in North Carolina; Columbus in Georgia; and Montgomery in Alabama, the connecting lines were of different gauges: 5 feet or 4 feet 8 ½ inches. At these points the shifting of freight from one car to another could not be avoided. Even when connecting lines were in the same gauge, few railroad officials would permit their cars to be used on a foreign road. In many cities, such as Petersburg, Bristol, Knoxville, Chattanooga, Savannah, and Augusta, the

terminating lines did not actually connect, and freight had to be hauled by wagon from one station to another. In June 1861, General Lee had urged that connecting track be laid in Petersburg. Many lines had earlier sought such tracks but had been stopped by strong transfer and hotel interests. During the war rail connections were achieved in some cities, but delays in the movement of troops and supplies persisted.

Early in the war both Davis and Lee were aware of several major gaps in the rail system. The 300-mile system in Texas was not tied to the Confederate rail network, and only a weak connecting line on the Georgia border eventually gave service to the 400 miles of railroad in Florida. Far more serious were smaller gaps—one along the Virginia–North Carolina border and a second in Alabama. In November 1861, Davis strongly urged the construction of a 48-mile connecting line between Danville, the southern terminal of the 143-mile Richmond and Danville, and Greensboro, located on the North Carolina Railroad. The building of such a link would give Richmond a third rail route with the states to the south, located between the exposed Weldon-Wilmington coastal line and the mountain route through eastern Tennessee. The Confederate Congress, in February 1862, appropriated $1 million to aid a private company, the Piedmont Railroad, to build such a line. But prominent leaders like Robert Barnwell Rhett, Sr., and Robert Toombs strongly protested the action. North Carolina planters along the route would not permit their slaves to work on the line, and North Carolina Governor Zebulon Vance, a firm advocate of state rights, also opposed it. As a result the project lagged and was finished only in the spring of 1864. The completion was timely since the Weldon-Wilmington coastal route was broken by Union troops later in the year. In the last year of the war a major portion of Lee's supplies moved north over the Piedmont Railroad.

The other major gap closed was between Selma, Alabama, and Meridian, Mississippi, a distance of under a hundred miles. Upon the recommendation of Davis the Confederate Congress on February 15, 1862, provided $150,000 to finish the partially built road between the two cities. The completion of this link late in 1862 provided both a shorter rail route from Vicksburg to Richmond and rail transportation well removed from the vulnerable Gulf coast. But during the war the Confederacy built no more than 200 miles of new line while over 3,000 miles were constructed in the United States.

The most pressing problem facing Confederate railroad officials was simply keeping their lines operating. Proper maintenance grew more difficult with every passing month. Rail, ties, fuel, replacement parts, and labor became more scarce as the war progressed. With all sources for new iron rail exhausted early in the war, managers were desperate to find iron. Though the Southern lines should have had about 4,000 tons of replacement rail each month, not a single new rail was produced in the Confederacy between 1862 and 1865.

The Western and Atlantic stumbled upon 1,100 tons of rail in Savannah and quickly bought it for $50 a ton, giving the line enough for about 15 miles of track. Late in 1861 Stonewall Jackson removed much of the rail from 19 miles of B&O double track between Harpers Ferry and Martinsburg and sent it south for the hard-pressed Confederate roads. In 1862 it was said there were 1,200 broken rails on the line from Nashville to Chattanooga, and many roads were so hard up for replacements they took up rail from side tracks, and later even branch lines, to repair their main stems.

Even the Confederate navy sought railroad iron. In June 1862, the Navy Department, headed by Stephen R. Mallory, impressed 1,100 tons of rail belonging to the 109-mile Atlantic and Gulf Railroad in Georgia to be used for the manufacture of ship's armor. In January 1863, the Iron Commission was created to determine what railroad iron could "best be dispensed with." Soon whole railroads were being taken over so their rail could be used on more important routes. Short lines were seized in North Carolina, Georgia, Florida, and Texas, but this only created new problems: as short or branch lines were dismantled, supplies for the army correspondingly declined.

By the middle years of the war, wood for cross ties and fuel grew scarce because of a shortage of labor to cut the wood. Often train crews made frequent stops on their routes to gather wood. In 1863 the North Carolina Railroad found cordwood so scarce it purchased wooded acres to ensure a steady supply and for a while demanded that half of any wood it hauled had to be sold to it.

The care and repair of locomotives and cars was another problem. Longer trains, the shortage of replacement parts, and the lack of skilled labor combined to make engines deteriorate more rapidly. By 1863 and 1864 a quarter of the locomotives of many lines needed repairs, and at least fifty engines were laid up because of the lack of tires for their drivers. The quality of passenger service also declined. By midwar many passenger cars were operating with broken windows, no water for the passengers, and no firewood for the coach's stove. Army use of passenger cars was often cited as the cause of missing seats, stoves, lamps, and water barrels when the coaches were finally returned to the owning road. The vast numbers of soldiers being moved by rail made it frequently necessary to use boxcars fitted with plank seats. In winter weather the troops often built fires on the floors of freight cars and left them burning when they debarked. When Gen. James Longstreet's men rode the rails to Chickamauga in September 1863, the soldiers pried boards from the side walls of the boxcars to improve the ventilation and the view. Passenger trains that had traveled 15 to 20 miles an hour in 1860 had dropped to 6 miles an hour by the end of the war.

The shortage of labor that started in 1861 when Northerners returned home grew worse when wages in munition plants outstripped the pay scales of most railroads. Eventually railroads raised wages but still lagged well behind the growing inflation rate. Several Confederate generals aggravated the shortage of skilled mechanics by keeping such men in uniform when they would have been more useful in railroad work. The Conscription Act of 1862 treated rail workers generously, exempting some six thousand. But the 1864 act was stiffer; it raised the draft age to fifty, and permitted no railroad to have more employees than miles of road.

Though there are no firm figures for the number of railroad employees, it seems probable that the number of employees early in the war was much larger than the number of miles of

> **By midwar many passenger cars were operating with broken windows, no water for the passengers, and no firewood for the coach's stove.**

line (5,500–6,000) in operation in 1864. Of course, slaves made up an important portion of all railroad workers. Usually performing the less skilled jobs, they were either owned by the railroad or rented from slaveholders. Certainly all railroad workers at the end of the war were paid far less in real dollars than they were receiving in 1861. Thomas Webb, president of the North Carolina Railroad, made $6,000 a year in 1864, a figure worth no more at that point than $300 in gold. Before the war locomotive firemen were paid $300 a year, and the president received $2,500 a year.

But even with all their problems, rail lines on several occasions moved large bodies of Confederate troops long distances. When George B. McClellan's Union army threatened Richmond in early June 1862, Lee felt secure enough to send two brigades (nearly 10,000 men) by rail west to Charlottesville to strengthen Stonewall Jackson in the Shenandoah Valley. Later Jackson's enlarged forces returned by rail to face McClellan's left flank and pushed the Union army away from Richmond in the Seven Days' Battles. The entire operation lasted just over three weeks, with the troops moving more than 250 miles over seven or eight railroads.

Two massive troop movements were carried out later near Chattanooga. By the summer of 1862 Corinth and a large portion of the Memphis and Charleston line were in Union hands. In the last days of June, Braxton Bragg decided to move his army of about 25,000 men from northeastern Mississippi to Chattanooga, which was threatened by Union forces under Don Carlos Buell. The distance from Tupelo to Chattanooga is a little over 200 miles as the crow flies.

Bragg's route by railroad covered 775 miles via the Mobile and Ohio to Mobile and then northeast over five short Alabama and Georgia lines to Atlanta and Chattanooga. The entire operation took a little more than a week. A year later, in mid-September, Bragg was reinforced during the Battle of Chickamauga when James Longstreet's First Corps of the Army of Virginia arrived from Richmond. The 12,000 Confederate troops had moved south about 900 miles in ten days using a dozen railroads in Virginia, the Carolinas, and Georgia. Confederate railroads were still in reasonable shape in the fall of 1863.

Union Capture and Destruction. During the four years of the war Union forces slowly but steadily encroached upon the northern and western frontiers of the Confederacy. During 1861 the Union armies reclaimed the northwestern counties of Virginia. In 1862 the South lost more of what would become West Virginia, half of Arkansas, the western half of Tennessee, a portion of Mississippi, and the area around New Orleans. The loss of the Mississippi River cut the Confederacy in two, and most of Arkansas and Tennessee plus large portions of Mississippi and Louisiana came under Union control. These Union gains were accompanied by the destruction of hundreds of miles of Confederate railways. The more important of the lines were rebuilt by the U.S. Military Railroad, an agency of the War Department created in 1862, under the supervision of Gen. Daniel C. McCallum.

One of the first railroad raids—colorful but totally ineffective—was the Andrews Raid of April 1862, in which a band of disguised Union soldiers stole the locomotive General and tried to wreck the Western and Atlantic Railroad. Two years later, in spring 1864, William Tecumseh Sherman with a strong Union army left Chattanooga and headed for Atlanta, following the track of the Western and Atlantic. For several months the normal daily flow of supplies to the 100,000 men and 35,000 animals in Sherman's army consisted of sixteen trains, each composed of ten cars (10-ton capacity). This daily total of 1,600 tons was in marked contrast to the pitiful rations reaching Lee's army defending Richmond in 1864 and 1865. In the last months of the war Lee's supply trains were often delayed and his army was frequently reduced to two or three days of rations.

After taking Atlanta late in the summer of 1864 Sherman destroyed the rail line back to Chattanooga and set out for Savannah. On his march to the sea he left the railroads in central Georgia in tatters. He destroyed hundreds of miles of line, especially hitting the 191-mile Central of Georgia and the 102-mile Macon and Western. After leaving Savannah early in 1865, Sherman wreaked equal havoc on the rail system of South Carolina, including the railroads serving Columbia, the state capital.

By 1865 the U.S. Military Railroad controlled 2,100 miles of line, most of it former Confederate railroads. Hundreds of miles of railroads were out of operation by March and April.

When Union forces cut the South Side Railroad near Richmond early in April, the end of the long conflict was near. As Lee's exhausted army moved toward Appomattox, the railroads were as crippled and defeated as the Southern armies they had vainly sought to support.

The long war had broken or destroyed the great majority of the Southern railroads, leaving twisted rails, burnt ties, gutted shops and depots, ruined bridges, and dilapidated or lost rolling stock. In May 1865, Chief Justice Salmon P. Chase visited North Carolina. The judge was provided with a train described by the correspondent Whitelaw Reid as "a wheezy little locomotive and an old mail agent's car, with all the windows smashed out and half the seats gone." Some lines were out of operation for many months. But a rehabilitation program aided by the Federal government resulted in both the fast return of the Southern roads General McCallum had rebuilt and the sale of government-owned cars and equipment to private parties. Most Southern roads were offering some kind of service by Christmas, 1865.

The inability of the Southern railways to support the Confederacy adequately resulted from several factors. In 1861 Confederate railroads were generally weak and inferior to Northern lines. Shortages of materials and labor made proper maintenance more difficult with each passing year. But a fundamental factor was the Southern belief in state rights. Since most railroads represented a single state, the individual lines subscribed to this doctrine with the same vigor as the governors and cabinet members who quarreled with Jefferson Davis. As a result the Richmond government was never able to provide a strong centralized supervision of the railroads and failed to support them when they were in peril.

[*See also entries on numerous battles and campaigns mentioned herein, particularly* Andrews Raid.]

BIBLIOGRAPHY

Black, Robert C., III. *The Railroads of the Confederacy.* Chapel Hill, N.C., 1952.

Coulter, E. Merton. *The Confederate States of America, 1861–1865.* A History of the South, vol. 7. Baton Rouge, La., 1950.

Johnston, Angus James, II. *Virginia Railroads in the Civil War.* Chapel Hill, N.C., 1961.

Ramsdell, C. W. "The Confederate Government and the Railroads." *American Historical Review* 22 (1916–17): 494–810.

Stover, John F. *Iron Road to the West: American Railroads in the 1850s.* New York, 1978.

Stover, John F. *The Railroads of the South, 1865–1900: A Study in Finance and Control.* Chapel Hill, N.C., 1955.

Trelease, Allen W. *The North Carolina Railroad, 1849–1871, and the Modernization of North Carolina.* Chapel Hill, N.C., 1991.

Turner, George Edgar. *Victory Rode the Rails.* Indianapolis, 1953.

Lash, Jeffrey N. *Destroyer of the Iron Horse: General Joseph E. Johnston and Confederate Rail Transport.* Kent, Ohio, 1991.

JOHN F. STOVER

military value and were not immoral. Rains reasoned that each new weapon was declared "barbarous" when first introduced, but eventually "each took its place according to its efficacy in human slaughter." On May 25, he began supervising the defense of a number of harbors—namely, Mobile, Charleston, and Savannah. For his efforts, Rains was assigned the superintendency of the Torpedo Bureau on June 17, 1864. His innovative development of an explosive sub terra shell demonstrated the future potential of mines.

After the war, Rains worked as a chemist in Augusta, Georgia. He died on August 6, 1881, and was buried in Aiken, South Carolina.

BIBLIOGRAPHY

Hill, D. H., Jr. *North Carolina*. Vol. 4 of *Confederate Military History*. Edited by Clement A. Evans. Atlanta, 1899. Vol. 5 of extended ed. Wilmington, N.C., 1987.

Perry, Milton F. *Infernal Machines*. Baton Rouge, La., 1965.

Rain, G. J. "Torpedoes." *Southern Historical Society Papers* 3 (1887): 255–260. Reprint, Wilmington, N.C., 1990.

Vandiver, Frank E. *Ploughshares into Swords: Josiah Gorgas and Confederate Ordnance*. Austin, Tex., 1952.

PETER S. CARMICHAEL

GABRIEL J. RAINS.

LIBRARY OF CONGRESS

RAINS, GABRIEL

RAINS, GABRIEL J. (1803–1881), brigadier general. A native of Craven County, North Carolina, Rains graduated from West Point in 1827. He distinguished himself in the Seminole War (1839–1842, 1849–1850) and the Mexican War. Resigning from the U.S. Army with a rank of lieutenant colonel on July 1, 1861, Rains began his Confederate service as a colonel of infantry in the army. On September 23, 1861, he received a brigadier general's commission and a brigade on the Virginia Peninsula. He saw action at Yorktown (April 4–May 3), Williamsburg (May 4–5), and Seven Pines (May 31–June 1). During the retreat from Williamsburg and Yorktown, Rains planted shells with percussion caps in the road, which caused considerable destruction as the Federals advanced. Controversy surrounded his booby traps in the North and the South, and Gen. James Longstreet prohibited him from further engaging in such questionable means of warfare.

Shortly after Seven Pines, George Wythe Randolph, the secretary of war, placed Rains under the War Department so that he could experiment with explosives. Commanding Richmond's Bureau of Conscription during the winter of 1862–1863, Rains convinced Jefferson Davis that mines had

RALEIGH, NORTH CAROLINA

The capital of North Carolina was authorized by the General Assembly in 1792 and laid out on a wooded tract near the center of the state. An early example of a planned town, it had wide streets in a regular grid. A new state capitol completed in 1840 replaced the first one that burned in 1831; a handsome granite structure in the Doric style, it is located on a six-acre plot at the center of the city. Union soldiers arriving in the spring of 1865 commented on the white houses, picket fences, and gardens that appeared "real Northern-like."

Even after ten years the new town had a population of only 669 and little more than government offices and modest trade to attract newcomers. By 1860 its population had grown to 4,780 of whom 1,624 were slaves. Merchants, grocers, clerks, printers, and carpenters were major occupations. The town was a center of rail transportation, and a number of engineers, conductors, clerks, and other employees lived there. It was also the headquarters of the State Bank of North Carolina and supported branches of the Bank of New Bern and the Bank of Cape Fear. The capital was visited by those who had business with state officials, and hotels (one of which had a rare shower bath) provided accommodations for them. Members of the General Assembly took rooms in the hotels or stayed in private homes and ate at some of the numerous boardinghouses. At least two express companies did business in the town, and telegraph service had been available since 1848.

Perhaps the quality of life for some of the residents who could afford their services or goods is indicated by the presence of occupation lists of gardeners, governesses, mantua-makers, tailors, milliners, jewelers, and confectioners, as well as an artist, an architect, a music teacher, a bookseller, a man who made daguerreotypes, and two men who installed gas fixtures—a luxury only recently available. A large number

> **With Richmond under siege, Mrs. Jefferson Davis and her children moved to Raleigh. . . .**

of clergymen and almost as many lawyers, together with five druggists, four doctors, and three dentists, practiced their professions.

In addition to two public schools for boys and one for girls, there were several private academies and seminaries as well as others operated by the Baptist, Methodist, Presbyterian, and Episcopal churches. A college for young women operated by Episcopalians opened in 1842, and when the war began one supported by Presbyterians was under construction; although this college did not open until 1872, its building was used as a Confederate hospital.

Between 1861 and 1865 eleven newspapers appeared. Editors received news by telegraph, and with rival editors holding different points of view, readers were well informed. Nine periodicals pertaining to agriculture, religion, education, and other subjects were also published. A mill on the outskirts of town provided paper for the town's presses.

Despite its small size and lack of a varied economic base, the town undoubtedly had a metropolitan air. Among its residents were natives of eight foreign countries. There were no citizens from other Southern states except South Carolina, but people born in Vermont, Massachusetts, Connecticut, New York, Delaware, Pennsylvania, Maryland, and Tennessee lived in Raleigh.

North Carolina was largely Unionist in sentiment until Abraham Lincoln's call for volunteer troops. Afterward Southern sympathies prevailed. A convention in Raleigh took the state out of the Union on May 20, 1861, and adopted the state's first flag. At least half a dozen training camps were established along the railroad in and around the city; troops were also accommodated in the parks in town or in buildings cleared for their use. A powder mill and a bayonet factory opened, and the paper mill turned to production for the government. Raleigh became a hub of activity as officials prepared the state for war. They set up warehouses for supplies,

and equipment soon was being shipped to troops in training and in the field. When the need arose, a large hospital was established on the state fairgrounds, and in time other buildings were put to the same use.

Zebulon Vance was governor from 1862 until the end of the war. In his relations with the Confederate government he upheld the principle of state rights and resisted directives from President Jefferson Davis and the Congress that he considered improper. This feud, it was widely asserted, denied promotion to military leaders from the state. A Raleigh newspaper editor, William W. Holden, opposed secession, called for the election of Vance, and even during the war advocated personal liberty. By 1863, however, he supported the peace movement and was quickly denounced as a traitor. Georgia troops passing through Raleigh in September 1863 burned his office. The next day about two hundred of Holden's followers retaliated by destroying the office of the rival conservative newspaper.

The hardships of war affected Raleigh as they did the rest of the South. Shortages of food and clothing, inflation, and news from the battlefront of illness, wounds, and death took their toll on civilian morale. Although some Union prisoners were confined in the city, the enemy posed no serious military threat until the spring of 1865. With Richmond under siege, Mrs. Jefferson Davis and her children moved to Raleigh, as did other refugees from Richmond and eastern North Carolina. It was even rumored that the Confederate capital might be moved to Raleigh.

Following the Battle of Bentonville from March 19 through 21, Union troops began to move toward Raleigh. State officials hastily shipped state records and other valuables by train to the west. Governor Vance permitted three emissaries to go by locomotive to intercept and confer with Gen. William Tecumseh Sherman; they secured a "suspension of hostilities" and his pledge not to damage Raleigh if his troops met no resistance. Sherman arrived in Raleigh on April 13, 1865, and set up headquarters in the governor's mansion. Nearly 100,000 Federal troops occupied the city and surrounding countryside. There was a single act of defiance when a Lieutenant Walsh from Texas fired on approaching Union troops. He was seized and hanged within ten minutes. Surplus horses, mules, and wagons from the Union army were released for the use of farmers in the area in readying their land for planting.

Raleigh, unlike the capitals of the four surrounding states, suffered virtually no damage during the war. Life quickly returned to normal as rail lines were repaired, shops were freshly stocked, newspapers resumed publication, schools and churches continued to operate, and doctors and other professional people returned home from the war. State records, which had been sent out of town as federal troops approached, were returned and the government began operating again.

BIBLIOGRAPHY

Carroll, Grady Lee Ernest. *The City of Raleigh, North Carolina, and the Civil War Experience.* [Raleigh, N.C.], 1979.

Harris, William C. *William Woods Holden: Firebrand of North Carolina Politics.* Baton Rouge, La., 1987.

Murray, Elizabeth Reid. *Wake, Capital County of North Carolina.* Raleigh, N.C., 1983.

Writers' Program, Work Projects Administration. *Raleigh, Capital of North Carolina.* Raleigh, N.C., 1942.

WILLIAM S. POWELL

RAMS

The ship-killing ram of the ancient Mediterranean was given new life during the Civil War: steam power replaced the human muscles of the rowed galleys of antiquity, and iron armor protected rams from enemy gunfire. Southern leaders recognized that they would be unable to equal the North in numbers of warships, so they sought to build a fleet that was qualitatively superior. Armored rams provided an equalizing weapon. Existing vessels and power plants (propulsion machineries) were reinforced for ramming and rebuilt with iron armor. In addition, new vessels were built with rams and armored casemates; most had simplified hull forms designed to be built by carpenters unfamiliar with ship construction. Steam propulsion was universal, but rams built for service on the coast used screw propellers; those on the western rivers usually used paddle wheels in armored housings.

The first armored ram to see service was the propeller tugboat *Enoch Train,* which was rebuilt by private parties in New Orleans to become the privateer *Manassas.* It was seized by the Confederate navy and led the Confederate fleet in the Battle of the Mississippi, below New Orleans. *Manassas* rammed two Union warships but ran aground and was destroyed by its crew to prevent capture.

The most famous and influential ram was CSS *Virginia,* rebuilt from the burned steam frigate *Merrimack. Virginia* enjoyed a single day of success in Hampton Roads, Virginia, sinking two powerful Union vessels before meeting the Union ironclad *Monitor,* which had been built particularly to counter the threat posed by *Virginia. Monitor* and the turreted ironclads that followed it were designed with a projecting knuckle or "raft" to protect against Confederate rams. The two ironclads, the ram and the antiram, stalemated each other for over two months before Norfolk was captured, forcing the destruction of *Virginia.*

Rams were built on the shores of all the major navigable rivers of the Confederacy. They were intended to protect the rivers as interior lines of communication and to prevent the North from dividing the country by taking the rivers. Ironclads were built on the James River; on the North Carolina sounds; at Wilmington, Charleston, Savannah, and Mobile; and on the Mississippi and Red rivers. They were feared by Federal sailors, inducing in many the fearful condition derisively known as "ram fever."

Many vessels on the Western Rivers—the Mississippi, Missouri, Ohio, Red, Yellow, Yazoo, and their tributaries—were heavily reinforced and rebuilt with projecting ram bows. These river rams were usually paddle-wheel river steamers, with fragile hulls and superstructures. Lightly armed because their light hulls could not support the shock of firing heavy guns, they were protected with whatever materials were available: many Southern riverboats were covered with compressed bales of cotton, becoming cottonclads. Both sides also added heavy wood walls (woodclads) or sheets of half- to one-inch iron plates (tinclads). All depended on the ram as their main weapon.

Most Confederate rams were built with a strong armored beak ram on the bow, an armored knuckle protecting the waterline, and a sloping armored casemate to protect a small number of heavy guns. The ram was intended to be the main offensive weapon. The fatal flaw of most Southern rams was their low speed and poor maneuverability. Few foundries were capable of producing marine engines, and those that could were already producing at capacity. Confederate naval engineers adapted engines from other vessels, but few rams could steam over five knots.

Five powerful oceangoing steam rams were built abroad for the Confederate navy. James Dunwoody Bulloch ordered two rams from the shipyards of England and two from France. The first two, to be named *North Carolina* and *Mississippi,* were built by the shipyard of John Laird and Sons, Birkenhead, England. Their destination became known before delivery, however, leading to a lengthy court case and seizure by the British government to prevent the violation of neutrality. Bulloch, at the urging of John Slidell, also ordered a pair of ironclad rams from the shipyard of Lucien Arman of France. The rams were given the cover names *Sphinx* and *Cheops,* but they were prevented from sailing when their destination became known. Through a complicated arrangement, one ram was sold to Denmark, resold to the Confederacy, and delivered at sea. This ram was armed, commissioned CSS *Stonewall,* and taken to Havana, where it was delivered to the Spanish authorities at the end of the war. The fifth and largest ram was ordered by James H. North from the shipyard of James and George Thomson, of Govan, Glasgow, Scotland. It was built using the cover name *No. 61,* but proved too expensive and grand for Confederate needs. The ship was sold and became *Danmark* in the Danish navy. The Thomsons also proposed building a double-turret armored ram that was not ordered.

Only one Confederate ironclad ram was sunk in action by the enemy: *Albemarle,* defending Plymouth, North Carolina, and much of the interior of the state, was sunk by a small boat expedition using a spar torpedo. Two were captured in action: the rams *Atlanta,* near Savannah, and *Tennessee,* in Mobile Bay, were taken after they were rammed repeatedly and heavily shelled by Union vessels.

Many Confederate rams were destroyed to prevent capture. *Virginia* was blown up when Norfolk was abandoned. The large rams *Louisiana* and *Mississippi* were destroyed near New Orleans after the forts and city surrendered. *Arkansas* was set afire when it lost power and capture appeared imminent. Retreating forces destroyed four ironclad rams of the James River Fleet, two on Mobile Bay, two in Charleston Harbor, and one each on the Chattahoochee,

> They were feared by Federal sailors, inducing in many the fearful condition derisively known as "ram fever."

Savannah, and Neuse rivers. Other, incomplete ironclad rams were destroyed across the South before advancing Union ground forces could take possession.

Confederate rams were the capital ships of the navy: fleets were built around the armored juggernauts that could convey naval force anywhere on the rivers. Rams offered the only possible counter to Union seapower and were successful in defending many areas of the South. Despite the small amount of action they saw, the Confederate ironclad rams *Chicora* and *Palmetto State* at Charleston; *Virginia II, Richmond, Fredericksburg,* and *Texas* in the James River Fleet; and *Huntsville, Tuscaloosa, Tennessee, Nashville,* and *Phoenix* in Mobile Bay all protected large seaboard cities for most of the war. Ironclad rams were an integral part of Confederate coastal defense plans. Those defenses allowed the South to retain control of important seaport cities, prevented the enemy from using the easy routes inland along the rivers, and kept seaports open for trade with other areas.

[*See also entry on the ship* Virginia.]

BIBLIOGRAPHY

Baxter, James P., III. *The Introduction of the Ironclad Warship.* Cambridge, Mass., 1933. Reprint, New York, 1968.

Crandall, W. D., and I. D. Newell. *History of the Ram Fleet and the Mississippi Marine Brigade.* St. Louis, 1907.

Gosnell, A. Allen. *Guns on the Western Waters: The Story of River Gunboats in the Civil War.* Baton Rouge, La., 1949.

Mahan, Alfred T. *The Navy in the Civil War: The Gulf and Inland Waters.* New York, 1883.

Still, William N., Jr. *Iron Afloat: The Story of the Confederate Armorclads.* Columbia, S.C., 1985.

KEVIN J. FOSTER

RANDOLPH, GEORGE WYTHE

RANDOLPH, GEORGE WYTHE (1818–1867), brigadier general and secretary of war. Randolph was the most successful of Thomas Jefferson's grandsons. Educated at home, in Boston, and in Washington, he entered the U.S. Navy as a midshipman at the age of thirteen. He became a charismatic leader, toured the ports of the Mediterranean and Caribbean, and attended David Farragut's school at Norfolk. On the USS *Constitution* he contracted tuberculosis, followed by a long period of remission. After qualifying as a passed midshipman, he attended the University of Virginia, where in 1841 he took one of its first law degrees and studied engineering and science. For a decade he practiced law at Charlottesville before moving to Richmond. Randolph was an officer of the Virginia Historical Society, a founder of the Richmond Mechanics Institute, and a leading criminal and admiralty lawyer.

Alarmed by John Brown's raid at Harpers Ferry, Randolph in 1859 organized the Richmond Howitzers, which he took to Charles Town in present-day West Virginia to act as guards until Brown was hanged. In 1860 Randolph served as a Virginia commissioner to contract for armaments in the North. Predicting Abraham Lincoln's election and arguing that neutrality was impossible, he urged that Virginia join in a Southern republic. He was a member of the Virginia convention of 1861, which sent him, William Ballard Preston, and A. H. H. Stuart to confer with President Lincoln. On April 12, Lincoln told them that he would meet force with force. After his call for troops, Virginia seceded.

Colonel Randolph then oversaw the enlargement of the Richmond Howitzers, which he led in winning the Battle of Big Bethel on June 10, 1861. As Gen. John B. Magruder's chief of ordnance, he helped design and arm fortifications at Yorktown. He was promoted to brigadier general and given a command in southeastern Virginia.

Randolph made three major contributions to the Confederacy. The first was his drafting of Virginia's conscription law, based on European models. It, in turn, became the model for Confederate conscription. His second was his work as secretary of war, a post he assumed in March 1862. At the outset of the Peninsular campaign, he and Robert E. Lee advised against Joseph E. Johnston's proposal for a hasty abandonment of Yorktown and retreat toward Richmond. Randolph delayed execution of Johnston's order to evacuate Norfolk until war matèriel could be removed.

In organizing the War Office, Randolph named his nephew-in-law Garlick Kean chief of the Bureau of War and Josiah Gorgas chief of the Bureau of Ordnance. To solve problems of procuring war matèriel and foodstuffs, he recruit-

GEORGE WYTHE RANDOLPH.

ed specialists in foreign trade, agriculture, and railroads, as well as a number of lawyers who were alumni of the University of Virginia and Yale. These technocrats administered centralized planning and control from Richmond. Randolph increased the importation of war goods, including tinned bully-beef and Enfield rifles, by offering foreign suppliers and blockade runners greater profits for essential goods. To encourage manufacturers to convert to war goods, he assigned low priorities on the railroads for shipping civilian goods.

Randolph believed that Confederate armies were under strength not because governors hoarded troops but because lenient officers condoned absenteeism. His proposed remedy was to send missions authorized to investigate and punish offenders. When he became convinced that he could not provide enough food for the Confederate armies, he tried to persuade President Davis to permit the exchange of Confederate cotton for Union bacon. Although Randolph was secretary only nine months, his organization of the War Office endured for the life of the Confederacy.

Randolph's third contribution was his advising Davis to devote more attention to the West. Relying on information from his New Orleans recruits, he devised a scheme to liberate that city in the summer of 1862 through a combination of conventional means and a fifth-column uprising. Military events in Tennessee and Virginia occupied the Southern troops, however. From the outset of his secretaryship, he had

declared that, unless there were radical changes in policy, he would be unable to provision adequately the Army of Northern Virginia, much less the other military units or the civilian population. Denying this, Davis procrastinated in authorizing Randolph's plans to recover New Orleans, the South's greatest port, and to import foodstuffs from Europe and the U.S. The secretary and the president did not make a good team. Davis's indecisiveness wore Randolph down, and he finally seized on a procedural pretext to resign in November 1862, leaving no possibility of reconsideration.

No longer in the Confederate army, Randolph assumed command of volunteers to defend Richmond from a threatened Union raid in May 1863. As a member of the city council at the time of the bread riots, he encouraged workers to demand increased wages to meet inflation. In November 1864 his health had so deteriorated that he and his wife ran the blockade and sailed for Europe. He consulted doctors in London, conferred with manufacturers, and wintered in southern France. Randolph delayed his return to the United States until September 1866 when he received a pardon. He died in April 1867 in Albemarle County, Virginia.

BIBLIOGRAPHY

Kean, Robert Garlick Hill. *Inside the Confederate Government.* Edited by Edward Younger. New York, 1957.
Patrick, Rembert W. *Jefferson Davis and His Cabinet.* Baton Rouge, La., 1944.
Shackelford, George Green. *George Wythe Randolph and the Confederate Elite.* Athens, Ga., 1988.

GEORGE GREEN SHACKELFORD

RANSOM, MATT WHITAKER

RANSOM, MATT WHITAKER (1826–1904), brigadier general, U.S. senator and diplomat. Though several pairs of brothers became Confederate generals— Robert E. Lee's sons are probably the best known—it was rare for one brother to be the other's immediate superior. When Matt Whitaker Ransom succeeded to the command of a North Carolina brigade, his predecessor and new division commander was his younger brother Robert.

The elder Ransom was born in Warren County, North Carolina, on October 8, 1826. He graduated from the University of North Carolina, practiced law, was state attorney general, and served in the state legislature before the war. Ransom was appointed lieutenant colonel of the First North Carolina Infantry in June 1861 and then colonel of the Thirty-fifth North Carolina Infantry in the spring of 1862.

Though severely wounded at Malvern Hill during the Seven Days' Battles, Ransom returned to his regiment for the Battle of Sharpsburg. At Fredericksburg, in December 1862, he commanded a brigade in his brother's division. Ransom was transferred to the Department of North Carolina and Southern Virginia in the spring of 1863 and succeeded to permanent command of his brother's old brigade, with the rank of brigadier general, on June 15, 1863. His service for the rest of 1863 was primarily in North Carolina, but Ransom's brigade spent most of 1864 in Virginia in the trenches at Petersburg. He was wounded at Drewry's Bluff in May of that year, commanded a division for several months in the fall and winter of 1864–1865, and surrendered at Appomattox.

Ransom resumed his public career after the war, serving many years as a U.S. senator and briefly as minister to Mexico. Ransom died near Garysburg, North Carolina, on October 8, 1904.

BIBLIOGRAPHY

Compiled Military Service Records. Matt Whitaker Ransom. Microcopy M331, Roll 207. Record Group 109. National Archives, Washington, D.C.

Hill, D. H., Jr. *North Carolina*. Vol. 4 of *Confederate Military History*. Edited by Clement A. Evans. Atlanta, 1899. Vol. 5 of extended ed. Wilmington, N.C., 1987.

J. TRACY POWER

REAGAN, JOHN H.

REAGAN, JOHN H. (1818–1905), congressman from Texas and postmaster general. John Henninger Reagan, a native of Tennessee, was born October 8, 1818, and moved to Texas in 1839. He had a farm in Kaufman County and was an attorney, judge, and Democratic politician in the prewar years. He served two terms in the U.S. House of Representatives, 1857 to 1861. Although an advocate of Southern rights, he was not a radical Southerner in Congress and opposed such controversial issues as reopening the African slave trade and the acquisition of territory in Cuba, Mexico, and Central America. His experiences in the Thirty-fifth and Thirty-sixth Congresses convinced him, however, that the Republican majority would not look after the interests of his state or the South.

Reagan returned to the national capital following the election of Abraham Lincoln as president with some hope that the Union could be preserved, but that optimism quickly dissolved as he observed the efforts in Washington to reach a compromise. On December 14, 1860, he and twenty-nine other Southern congressmen composed a joint letter to their constituents. The group concluded that compromise with the Republican majority was impossible and that separation from the Union was necessary. Convinced that he could do nothing more to help achieve a solution to the sectional conflict, Reagan returned to Texas in January 1861.

On the way home Reagan learned that he had been elected to the Texas secession convention. He went directly to Austin but did not arrive there until January 30, two days after the convention began. Reagan nevertheless played a critical role in the proceedings. Believing that Governor Sam Houston, who remained loyal to the Union, might cause trouble for the secessionists, Reagan met with the governor on the day he arrived and tried to persuade him not to obstruct the proceedings of the convention. Houston informed Reagan that he would not oppose the will of the people and that he would meet with a delegation from the convention. Reagan headed the committee sent the next day to confer with the governor. Houston provided a formal announcement that he recognized the results of the election of delegates and the legitimacy of the convention. This paved the way for the passage of an ordinance of secession on February 1.

The convention elected Reagan as a member of the Provisional Congress at Montgomery. Personal business required him to remain in Texas until that March, however; thus he missed the establishment of the Confederacy and the election of Jefferson Davis as provisional president. He arrived in Montgomery on March 1 and took his seat in Congress the next day. There he earned the admiration of President Davis and a reputation for bluntness. Reagan told the newly elected president that he would not have voted for him had he been present. Reagan explained that his decision was not based on any question concerning Davis's fitness for the office; rather, he would have preferred that Davis head the army.

Reagan's encounter with the president may have helped the executive make his decision to appoint the congressman as postmaster general. The cabinet post was a critical one for the new government. Good mail service was essential for the dissemination of information, particularly the distribution of newspapers. The mails were also a potentially important factor in the event of war; letters between soldiers in the field and their families at home could help morale.

The task faced by the postmaster general, however, would be extremely difficult for two reasons: the constitutional provision that the Post Office Department must pay its own expenses out of revenue after March 1, 1863, and the strain a war would place on the system. When the president's first two choices turned the job down, Davis turned to Reagan, who had been a member of the Postal Committee in the U.S. House of Representatives and had been recommended by the Texas delegation. On March 6, Davis asked Reagan to accept the post. Reagan initially turned it down but finally accepted, despite his reluctance to take on such a difficult

JOHN H. REAGAN.

job. His nomination was immediately confirmed by the Congress.

The new postmaster general began building his system by raiding the Washington offices of the U.S. Post Office for men with knowledge of that system's operations. His department heads brought with them the annual reports of the postmaster general, blank forms, and postal maps and modeled their post office on that of the United States. As much as possible those connected with the Federal post offices in the South were integrated into the Confederate department, although some individuals and contractors refused to remain with it.

From the beginning the constitutional provision requiring the post office to be self-supporting was a major concern for Reagan. Figures showing the cost of mail service in the South during the last full year of peace indicated the extent of his problem. In 1860 the Post Office Department had spent nearly $3 million while producing revenues of less than $1 million. Reagan would not be able to continue that system, but would have to both cut costs and increase revenues. He kept his own office staff at a minimum, closed some post offices, reduced the number of mail routes, discontinued duplicate service, and cut service on some routes from daily to triweekly delivery. He also negotiated a 50 percent reduction in the rates railroads charged to deliver the mail and cut mail service on the roads. In addition, he raised postage rates with the approval of Congress.

The U.S. postal system continued to operate in the South until Reagan ordered the inauguration of Confederate mail service on June 1, 1861, and provided for a final accounting and the return of all Federal property to the U.S. Post Office Department. From the beginning of its operations Reagan's system elicited complaints. It could not duplicate the service that Southerners had been used to receiving. Inadequate staffing, elimination of routes, reduction of the number of post offices, plus problems associated with creating a new system—contractors could not be found to deliver the mail in Texas and Arkansas, for example—produced a decline in service. Delays in delivery, loss of mail, thefts, lack of stamps and mail supplies, and high postal rates plagued the Confederate post office.

By the autumn of 1861 the press was filled with complaints. Even members of the cabinet expressed concern about the service. Burdened by the illness of his wife and upset by the criticism, Reagan submitted his resignation in 1862. President Davis persuaded him to remain in the cabinet, however, arguing that if he left, the public might see it as an expression of dissatisfaction with the administration. Reagan continued in office, but though he earned a reputation for hard work and personal integrity, the postmaster general was never able to satisfy the system's numerous critics.

Producing satisfactory service and adhering to the constitutional provision of self-sufficiency became even more difficult as the war progressed. The destruction of railroads and the cutting of communication lines by the movement of the armies inevitably disrupted service. Many materials necessary for postal operations, ranging from stamps to mail bags, were difficult to obtain. Confederate conscription policy, however, proved to be one of the post office's most onerous burdens. This problem developed as the result of a supplemental Confederate conscription law passed in October 1862. The initial law, passed in April 1862, had provided extensive exemptions from conscription, including postal employees, but the October legislation exempted only those postmasters and contractors nominated for their positions by the president and confirmed by the Senate. Reagan reported that the number of individuals available to deliver the mails was thus reduced by some seven-eighths. He lobbied Congress for legislation that ultimately restored many of the exemptions for post office personnel, but as the Confederate army faced growing manpower shortages, conscript officers continued to impress employees. The postmaster general finally became involved in a virtual war with the military, encouraging his men to resist conscription by securing writs of habeas corpus and then suing the conscript officers for false arrest. The fight between Reagan and Secretary of War James A. Seddon over the conscription of post office personnel continued into the autumn of 1864 and ended only when Reagan decided that conditions in the Confederacy were so bad there was no point in pursuing the issue further.

The struggle between the post office and the military did have one favorable result. Reagan was able to obtain staff who would work for low wages and who bid low for mail delivery contracts so long as postal workers were exempt from military service. Mail service may have been inefficient, but the cost was low. This, combined with Reagan's early reduction in the overall size of the system, meant that the postmaster general was able to make the post office self-sustaining in the time allotted to him. By the end of 1863, his report indicated, the department was operating at a surplus.

Despite the criticism leveled at the postal service, many observers from the beginning considered Reagan to be one

> **He was one of the men Davis turned to for advice on the general problems facing the Confederacy.**

of the most capable of Davis's cabinet appointees. Even while accusing him of inefficiency, no critic ever considered Reagan to be anything other than of the most upstanding character. Considering the overwhelming problems of creating the new system, Reagan accomplished much, and the Confederacy never experienced within his department the same problems that developed in other government offices.

Reagan's duties as a cabinet officer went beyond his official role as postmaster general. He was one of the men Davis turned to for advice on the general problems facing the Confederacy. Despite his personal loyalty to the president, Reagan was forthright in his opposition to administration policies with which he disagreed. In 1863, the postmaster general found himself consistently in the minority on military matters. In particular, he opposed Robert E. Lee's invasion of Pennsylvania in the summer of that year and argued instead for moving more forces west in order to destroy Ulysses S. Grant's army, which was maneuvering to capture Vicksburg and cut the Confederacy in two. The differences between Reagan and other cabinet officials reached a point where Reagan offered to resign for a second time. But President Davis held his services to be too valuable and dissuaded him from this course.

On April 2, 1865, Postmaster General Reagan abandoned Richmond with President Davis in the hope of establishing the seat of government farther in the Confederate interior—a plan that went awry when Lee surrendered his army in northern Virginia. Another course was taken when Gen. Joseph E. Johnston began negotiating the surrender of his army. Reagan and Secretary of War John C. Breckinridge were sent to assist in the talks, where they offered a total Confederate surrender if the United States preserved the existing state governments, respected the political and property rights of Confederate citizens, and promised to impose

no penalties on participants or to persecute them. After presenting this proposal, Reagan rejoined the president at Charlotte, North Carolina. When William Tecumseh Sherman ultimately offered only the terms Grant gave to Lee at Appomattox, the remaining cabinet members and the president resumed their flight, recommending that Johnston simply disband so that the army could reorganize elsewhere. Johnston chose to accept Sherman's terms.

At this point they hoped to reach Texas, where E. Kirby Smith's army remained intact. Other cabinet members resigned and returned home as the South's ultimate fate became obvious, but Reagan remained with the president. He was captured with the president's party on the evening of May 10, 1865, near Irwinville, Georgia.

Reagan was imprisoned until December 1865 at Fort Warren, where he wrote two important letters. The first, on May 28, urged President Andrew Johnson to adopt a lenient policy toward the defeated South, warning that a more radical approach would end in evil. A more controversial letter, on August 11, advised Texans to accept the results of the war, including the end of slavery and the guarantee of civil rights and suffrage—restricted with educational and property qualifications—for blacks. The second letter was condemned by his constituents, but Reagan believed that such a course was necessary to avoid military rule and unqualified black suffrage.

After his release, Reagan returned to Texas and practiced law. He was also active in Democratic politics. He served in the Texas constitutional convention in 1875 and was a U.S. congressman (1875–1877) and senator (1887–1891). He died at Palestine, Texas, March 6, 1905.

BIBLIOGRAPHY

McCaleb, Walter Flavius. "John H. Reagan." *Texas Historical Association Quarterly* 5 (July 1905): 41–50.

Patrick, Rembert W. *Jefferson Davis and His Cabinet.* Baton Rouge, La., 1944.

Proctor, Ben H. *Not without Honor: The Life of John H. Reagan.* Austin, Tex., 1962.

Reagan, John H. *Memoirs with Special Reference to Secession and the Civil War.* New York, 1906.

CARL H. MONEYHON

RED RIVER CAMPAIGNS

Two ill-fated Union campaigns along central Louisiana's Red River, a natural invasion route into Texas, were fought for political, economic, ideological, and diplomatic reasons rather than for purely military objectives. The liberation of Texas by the Union would placate Northern antislavery forces who considered Texas's 1845 admission as a slave state the culmination of a conspiracy led by Southern slave owners. Once freed, Texas, it was believed, would provide free-labor-grown cotton, which would simultaneously demonstrate the inferiority of slave labor and keep Northern mills running. This in turn would cement political support for the Republican party. Moreover, the occupation of Texas would eliminate Mexico's role in breaking the blockade and lessen the likelihood of French interference in Mexico. Last, the Red River valley itself contained large supplies of cotton, the capture of which offered huge financial and political incentives to the invading forces.

In the course of the campaigns, the Union lost 5,200 men and the Confederates, 4,200. Most important, these campaigns forced Gen. Ulysses S. Grant to delay his planned attack on Mobile, Alabama, for ten months and denied Gen. William Tecumseh Sherman 10,000 veterans when he marched against Gen. Joseph E. Johnston in Georgia. The campaigns ended in great controversy in both the North and the South.

The 1863 campaign was a sideline to the Union effort to capture Port Hudson, Louisiana, on the Mississippi River. In December 1862 Maj. Gen. Nathaniel P. Banks took command of the Department of the Gulf. He had been sent ostensibly to occupy any part of Texas in order to show the U.S. flag to the French in Mexico. But the more pressing matter of controlling the Mississippi claimed his attention. From April through July 1863 Banks cooperated with army and navy forces under Grant and Rear Adm. David G. Farragut operating against Port Hudson. Determined to clear all Confederate opposition to his west before moving on Port Hudson, Banks advanced up the Atchafalaya River and Bayou Teche as he headed for Alexandria, Louisiana. He defeated a small force under Maj. Gen. Richard Taylor at the Battles of Irish Bend and Fort Bisland on April 12 through 14. Banks then moved unopposed into Alexandria. At this point, Union General in Chief Henry W. Halleck reminded Banks of his orders. As a result Banks's planned move up the Red River to collect cotton and livestock ceased. In late May he left the Red River and moved against Port Hudson, which fell July 9.

With the Mississippi cleared, Banks was free to move against Texas; instead he and Grant wanted to attack Mobile. Halleck, however, now insisted on the campaign against Texas via the Red River, and with President Abraham Lincoln's strong backing, he ordered the campaign. The plan called for Banks with his 17,000 troops to be joined by 10,000 of Sherman's men commanded by Brig. Gen. Andrew Jackson Smith, Brig. Gen. Frederick Steele's force of 15,000 from the Department of Arkansas, and a naval flotilla that included thirteen ironclads under Rear Adm. David D. Porter. Banks was to move north up Bayou Teche, Smith and Porter to steam up the Red River, and Steele to move south from Little Rock. The first two groups were to meet at Alexandria

and advance on Shreveport, the ultimate goal of the campaign, where they would join Steele. In opposition, Gen. E. Kirby Smith could concentrate between 25,000 and 30,000 men taken from his commands in Texas, Louisiana, and Arkansas. Smith instructed Taylor, commanding in Louisiana, to decline any offer for a general engagement until all the reinforcements arrived.

The Union plan fell apart from the outset. Banks and A. J. Smith were to meet at Alexandria by March 17, 1864. Timing was crucial for two reasons: first, Porter's vessels required the high water brought by the spring rains to navigate the river; second, Grant released Sherman's men only with the promise that they would be returned no later than April 10. Porter entered the Red River on March 12 and moved upstream. Smith's corps, landed at Simsport by Porter, marched on and captured Fort DeRussy on March 14 after a brief engagement. Porter then steamed unopposed to Alexandria, arriving on the fifteenth, Smith's men joining them the next day. In the meantime, Banks was detained in New Orleans supervising elections to install a new free state government, and he did not arrive until the twenty-fourth; his men were not present until the twenty-sixth.

While the Union forces were assembling in Alexandria, Kirby Smith had ordered all but 2,300 men of Maj. Gen. John B. Magruder's Texas force to join Taylor and also instructed Maj. Gen. Sterling Price's entire Arkansas command of 14,000 to move to Shreveport. Taylor offered only token resistance as he waited for the promised help.

Banks advanced despite the late date. After reaching Grand Encore, he made the key mistake of the campaign. Rather than advancing along the Red River in concert with

> ## Taylor, despite Kirby Smith's orders to avoid a pitched battle, attacked.

Porter's powerful fleet, he ordered the bulk of his army to move inland, which gave Porter the opportunity to scour the surrounding countryside for contraband. The two armies skirmished continually through the end of March and into early April as Taylor ordered his forces back, first to Natchitoches, then to Pleasant Hill, and finally to Mansfield.

At Mansfield, Taylor established a strong defensive position with his own men and the recently arrived reinforcements. On the morning of April 8 Banks's advance force encountered Taylor's cavalry under Gen. Tom Green, just in from Texas. Green offered stiff resistance as he fell back to the main defensive line. Banks, thinking his opponent would retreat as he had for the past two weeks, pressed on. Taylor, despite Kirby Smith's orders to avoid a pitched battle, attacked. Gen. Alfred Mouton's division led the Confederate charge that routed Banks's army. Union losses at Mansfield numbered almost 2,900, while Confederate casualties totaled 1,000. During the night Banks fell back to Pleasant Hill. On the afternoon of the ninth, Taylor again attacked, but the Union lines held. Union losses at Pleasant Hill numbered almost 1,400, Confederate losses, nearly 1,500.

Each side considered Pleasant Hill a defeat, and both Banks and Kirby Smith—recently arrived on the battlefield—ordered a withdrawal. When Smith learned that Banks was retreating, he ordered all of Taylor's force except Brig. Gen. Camille J. Polignac's infantry division (for merly under Mouton, who was killed at Mansfield) and Brig. Gen. John Austin Wharton's cavalry to join Price so that he could "dispose of Steele." Taylor pleaded to keep the force together and to pursue Banks, but to no avail.

The Battles of Mansfield and Pleasant Hill marked Banks's farthest advance. The two defeats, the rapidly falling river, the overdue date for A. J. Smith's departure, and the inability to link up with Steele convinced Banks that he had to withdraw. Taylor continued to attack—at Blair's Landing (April 12), and Cane River Crossing (April 23)—but his remaining force was too small to stop Banks. Porter's fleet, meanwhile, faced the dual problems of low water and Confederate attacks. Only the engineering feats of Col. Joseph Bailey, who constructed a series of dams near Alexandria, saved the fleet. Taylor's and Banks's forces skirmished until May 13, the day the fleet finally floated by the rapids in Alexandria. The final engagement of the campaign was at Yellow Bayou on May 18. The next day an improvised bridge of ships allowed Banks's men and wagons to cross the Atchafalaya River. The campaign was over; it was time for the controversy.

In the South, Richard Taylor asked to be and was relieved of his command because of his dispute with Kirby Smith over the latter's deployment of Confederate forces. In the North, Banks, for his failures, was replaced, and the congressional Joint Committee on the Conduct of the War investigated the campaign, infamous for its cotton speculation as well as its military shortcomings.

[*See also* Arkansas Campaign of 1864.]

BIBLIOGRAPHY

Harrington, Fred H. *Fighting Politician: Major General N. P. Banks.* Philadelphia, 1948.

Johnson, Ludwell H. *Red River Campaign: Politics and Cotton in the Civil War.* Baltimore, 1958.

Johnson, Robert U., and C. C. Buel, eds. *Battles and Leaders of the Civil War.* 4 vols. New York, 1887–1888. Reprint, Secaucus, N.J., 1982.

Taylor, Richard. *Destruction and Reconstruction: Personal Experiences of the Late War in the United States.* New York, 1879. Reprint, Philadelphia, 1955.

Winters, John S. *The Civil War in Louisiana.* Baton Rouge, La., 1963.

THOMAS J. LEGG

REENACTMENTS

In the heat and humidity of midsummer Virginia, hundreds of Union soldiers mill down a dusty road past the bodies of men lying along the sides. Behind the exhausted troops the crash of musketry and the roar of cannons can be heard. Suddenly a horse-drawn battery gallops toward the men with artillerists shouting to them to clear the road; the Northerners scatter in every direction. On the battlefront Union and Confederate officers desperately try to maintain the integrity of their lines amid clouds of gunsmoke and the dust of a dry July. Just out of range of artillery sit civilian picnickers out for a summer's day of excitement. As the defeated Federals stream word-lessly by the civilians look on incredulously: how could their army be beaten so handily? Then the gunfire dies away, the battle smoke clears, and the rival armies march back to camp and head for their automobiles.

The time was 1986; the soldiers, reenactors; the occasion, the 125th anniversary of First Manassas. Tens of thousands of people from all over the world volunteered to wear an army uniform or civilian costume from the Civil War. Australian Confederates fought Federals from Germany; Californians shared hardtack with soldiers from Maine. Each year hundreds of such reenactments and living history demonstrations take place throughout the United States.

Reenactments started almost immediately after Robert E. Lee surrendered at Appomattox. Veterans of the Grand Army of the Republic and the United Confederate Veterans often donned their uniforms for reunions and were photographed reliving the battles they had fought. As these men died, they were succeeded by the next generation of organizations, the Sons of Union Veterans and the Sons of Confederate Veterans, who continued to honor their fathers with ceremonies and reenactments. In the 1990s hundreds of organizations with memberships of as few as five to as many as three thousand carried on the tradition.

The reenactors themselves are responsible for the creation of what is called an "impression"—the look the reenactor chooses to portray to the public. Meticulously researched, the impression can range from that of a civilian child to a particular general. All the clothing and equipment, privately purchased and custom-made, are careful reproductions of the originals. An average infantry soldier's impression includes a rifled musket, cartridge box and sling, cap box and waist belt, canteen, haversack, knapsack or blanket roll, brogans, cotton shirt, and woolen trousers, coat, and cap. Most reenactors also collect smaller items such as a pocket Bible, a comb, a "housewife" (sewing kit), and hardtack to provide the details for a well-rounded impression needed to re-create an individual from the past. The desire to honor and understand the Civil War from the perspective of the participants is the primary motivation for reenactors. They also wish to bring

REFUGEE FAMILY.

history to life, to make vivid the courage and sacrifice of the participants in an ugly war.

Re-creating a Civil War battle is a difficult, time-consuming, labor-intensive operation. In late June 1988, for example, over 12,000 reenactors participated in the largest re-creation of a battle ever staged on the 125th anniversary of the Battle of Gettysburg. The week-long event featured five scripted battles, authentic soldier and civilian camps, field hospital programs, seminars on nineteenth-century life, filming for a motion picture and a documentary, courses for college credit, and the assembling of two armies of soldiers not seen since 1865.

The phenomenon of reenacting has continued to grow, finding new avenues of expression. In the 1990s, over 30,000 people were engaged in bringing to life America's past to ensure that it would not die.

BIBLIOGRAPHY

Camp Chase Gazette. Lancaster, Ohio, 1964–.
The Civil War News. Arlington, Mass., 1979–.

DALE FETZER, JR.

REFUGEEING

Beginning with northern Virginia families in the spring of 1861, perhaps as many as 200,000 Southerners became refugees during the Civil War. As the Confederacy shrank, people left Kentucky, Tennessee, New Orleans, the Virginia peninsula, the Shenandoah Valley, and other areas to avoid the Northern invaders. Later on, many more fled from William Tecumseh Sherman's advancing army in Georgia and the Carolinas. Raids, skirmishes, and larger military campaigns all sent Southerners into short-term or long-term exile.

Simple fear of the enemy was the most powerful impetus: newspapers carried frightening tales of depredations and assaults on civilians. But food shortages and widespread suffering also forced families to move, even though some debated, planned, and hesitated for months before finally departing.

Refugees constituted a rough cross section of Southern society, and as the war dragged on, the planter class increasingly joined the exodus. Officers' families, state political leaders, and many professional men added a certain sophistication to this bedraggled group. Cities naturally attracted the most refugees, though yeoman and poor white families generally moved only short distances.

Packing (for those lucky enough to have sufficient warning of approaching Federals) became a major chore and a psychological ordeal as families tried to pile all their worldly possessions onto wagons or boxcars. Sifting through possessions accumulated during a lifetime could add to the distress, but if the refugees tried to take too much with them, they often had to leave surplus baggage along the roads. Given the scarcity and expense of transportation, Southerners traveled by any available means including train, wagon, horse, or on foot. Hazardous river crossings and washed-out roads made for tortuous journeys. Along the way, filthy rooms and poor food were standard, and the more aristocratic resented hobnobbing with their social inferiors.

Cities, towns, and rural areas lacked the housing and even the food necessary to accommodate the flood of newcomers. "Shew me a safe point and I'll go tomorrow," South Carolinian Jane Pringle wrote, "but no such happy valley exists in the Confederacy." Richmond's population doubled during the war's first year, and displaced persons continued to arrive for the next three years. Other families chose surrounding towns and rural areas, making Virginia the state with the largest refugee population. Those fleeing the Carolina coast flocked to Raleigh, North Carolina, and Columbia, South Carolina. Georgia—especially Atlanta—attracted refugees from Kentucky, Tennessee, and the Deep South. Texas offered a spacious and relatively secure haven for families in the Trans-Mississippi Confederacy.

Refugees who managed to find a new home complained of spartan conditions and extortionate rents. By any standards their housing was uncomfortable, but a simple frame house must have looked magnificent to the poor souls who slept on church pews or in stables, carriage houses, tents, caves and even abandoned boxcars. Landlords seldom provided board and often raised rents, driving families to seek more affordable accommodations. With families often forced to cook in their rooms, speculators soon raised prices for all kinds of provisions. Grits, bacon, and cornbread became staples of the refugee diet, but the more destitute sometimes lived on berries, tomatoes, or fish. Bedding, clothing, and firewood were in equally short supply. The desperately poor finally had to rely on handouts from tight-fisted natives.

Often the social adjustment was even more difficult. Loneliness and despair dogged the lives of normally optimistic people. Families regularly welcomed kinfolk from distant places, but these new living arrangements caused considerable tension. Blood ties were often not strong enough to withstand the strain. Especially for women used to running their own households, living with relatives, much less strangers, could be frustrating. Natives begrudged sharing scarce housing and food with newcomers, particularly those from other states. Newspaper editors sympathized with the refugees' plight but often criticized their behavior. Even churches sometimes shunned them. A social cold war erupted, especially when displaced plantation families tried to lord it over their poorer neighbors. Provincialism and suspicion on both sides reinforced this hostility. So too boredom and homesickness made some refugees into chronic malcontents. "Everyone speaks of the high spirits and cheerfulness of the refugees," wrote Louisianian Sidney Harding, "They little know of how many sad hours we have."

Refugees who idled away their time sparked resentment, but doctors, lawyers, bankers, and artisans tried to establish their old professions in their new homes. Ministers set up new churches; refugee newspaper editors kept changing their mastheads; in desperation, displaced housewives turned to teaching, though most found their new profession neither profitable nor satisfying. Governors had to move state capitals to more secure locations. Although the Confederate government hired some refugees in the various departments, many had to settle for work as farm or day laborers. Women had few opportunities other than sewing or domestic service but still donated their mite to relief funds and labored long for charitable associations.

Regardless of these problems, refugees did manage to have a social life, notably in the towns and cities. Shared suffering could build a sense of community and even provide opportunity for pleasant diversions. Reading, writing letters, keeping a diary, and going to church filled in the times between special events. Among the fashionable set, parties, dances, and amateur theatricals, including the popular tableaux vivants (staged, motionless representations of famous scenes), helped the lonely and disheartened wile away the hours. Food was scarce and decorations limited, but weddings and holidays offered some relief from the drab lives led by most refugees. Christmas became the occasion for recalling happier times and perhaps momentarily forgetting the war, but makeshift gifts and disappointed children also served as painful reminders of the Confederacy's desperate straits.

Although refugees sometimes became revelers, such pleasures were transitory. Families who thought they had found safety and security were threatened again by the invaders or banished by Federal commanders. Under the best circumstances, crossing enemy lines entailed passes, oaths of allegiance, bureaucratic hassles, and some danger. For both Union and Confederate armies, dealing with refugees created logistical and security headaches.

With their property at the Federals' mercy and their lives disrupted, refugees sought public relief. Although indigent soldiers' families received some help, state and local governments discriminated against refugee families. Many disheartened Confederates returned to their homes before the end of the war even if they had to live under military occupation. Others had to wait weeks or even months after

Appomattox to begin rebuilding lives that had been shattered by the war.

[*See also* Poor Relief; Poverty.]

BIBLIOGRAPHY

Andrews, Matthew Page. *The Women of the South in War Times.* Baltimore, 1920.

Massey, Mary Elizabeth. *Refugee Life in the Confederacy.* Baton Rouge, La., 1964.

Rable, George C. *Civil Wars: Women and the Crisis of Southern Nationalism.* Urbana, Ill., 1989.

GEORGE C. RABLE

RELIGION

Antebellum Southern Protestants—by 1860 approximately two million strong—generally agreed on an evangelical theology of individual personal salvation, divine justification for all actions, opposition to secular activities, a literal reading of the Scriptures, and a just and benevolent Providence overseeing a chosen people. A number of clergy, however, advocated missionary reform, which included opposition to alcohol, religious instruction for slaves, and admonitions to masters to treat their slaves decently.

Slavery also divided the Northern and Southern branches of the Protestant churches, and by 1845 the two largest denominations, the Methodist Episcopal Church South and the Southern Baptist Convention, had been organized after separation from their Northern brethren. When the Civil War began, the other major denominations, Presbyterians, Lutherans, and Episcopalians, also formed separate Southern churches. While the Roman Catholic church avoided a split during the Civil War, Catholic clergy in the South firmly supported the Confederate cause. Despite the belief that churches should keep out of secular politics, the evangelical clergy supported Southern rights during the sectional crisis, while a number led in the movement to secede.

During the Civil War most Southern Protestant and Roman Catholic clergy called for civilian and military sacrifices for unity of purpose, and many held out to the very end for Confederate victory. Many clergy preached and wrote on the idea of a new nation, while some of them advocated a Christian Confederate nation. Churches supported the civil leaders' proclamations of fast days of abstinence and contrition, and clergy conducted services during the fasts. Churches assigned ministers to preach to and care for the souls of their soldiers. Chaplains in the front lines led prayer groups, held rousing evangelical revivals, and carried out mass baptisms, which at times turned the Confederate armies into religious crusaders. A religious revival swept through the Confederate armies in 1863. Church-owned presses published religious tracts, hymn books, and Bibles to distribute among the troops. Printed sermons often stirred the soldiers to regard the Northerners as infidels. Individual preachers used their multiple talents in military service. Presbyterian theologian Robert L. Dabney served on Gen. Thomas J. ("Stonewall") Jackson's staff, from which he helped to bring young college men into the army. Dr. Charles T. Quintard, later Episcopal bishop of Tennessee, gained fame as a chaplain and surgeon in the First Tennessee Regiment. Roman Catholic chaplain Abraham Ryan ministered to the religious needs of the Catholic soldiers and preached continued resistance against the invading Yankees.

Behind the lines women and clergy held rallies in churches, where they urged enlistees to sacrifice all to protect faith, honor, and home. Women worked in local churches, making clothing, blankets, and bandages for the soldiers. They organized Home Missionary Societies to care for slaves, to feed the poor, and to provide education for children of deceased veterans. Women also helped found church-related hospitals and served as nurses and aides near the front lines. A few women even preached to the troops.

The Civil War also produced divisions among the Southern churches and religious leaders over support for the Confederate cause. Tennessee Methodist William G. Brownlow and Kentucky Presbyterian Robert J. Breckinridge remained loyal to the Union and preached against Confederate victory. In middle Tennessee, David Lipscomb of the Disciples of Christ believed in Christian pacifism and opposed all war. Southerners as well as Northerners accused the Jewish people of war profiteering, and despite the fact that some ten thousand Southern Jews fought in Confederate ranks, clergy quoted New Testament admonitions against them, which unleashed waves of anti-Semitic activities. German Catholic Unionists in central Texas faced hostile nativists and had to fight or flee for their lives. Some clergy seized the moment to advocate decent treatment of the slaves, with a few even calling for eventual abolition of slavery. Black churches confronted wartime restrictions and hardships by advocating mutual support among slaves. Black clergy preached self-discipline and resisted white control by demanding the right to travel freely to serve their people.

As the fighting wore on, disruptions in the Southern churches abounded: property was lost, membership declined, and the war's devastation made clergy and laity alike question the central evangelical belief in a providential God. Border and upper South churchgoers often had to flee before approaching armies. Northern troops used churches as stables, staff headquarters, and hospitals. Both by mistake and deliberately, advancing Union armies pillaged and burned churches, church schools, and church orphanages. Lasting wounds were created as Northern Methodist clergy came south to take over abandoned churches, preach to the slaves, and proselytize among the worried citizenry. In West Virginia, Northern Methodist ministers at the state constitutional convention of 1863 led the movement to abolish slavery. Church schools and colleges lost students and were forced to close down; a number shut their doors permanently. Clergy and the faithful alike believed that defeat in battle meant that the Lord had deserted his chosen people. Many came to doubt the justice of their cause. Chaplains, too, noticed that their influence had declined among the soldiers. The resultant loss of religious faith no doubt undermined Confederate civilian and military morale.

At war's end, church leaders had to confront the demise of slavery. Some clergy deserted the South to settle with parishioners in such places as Brazil where slavery was still legal. Others sought to control the religious life of the ex-slaves. But the churches made little effort to assist the black people and soon segregated them in the rear of churches. The freed people founded their own churches. Northern black clergy came south to organize the African Methodist Episcopal church. In 1867 Georgia black clergy formed a separate Presbyterian church, and black Baptists founded Atlanta Baptist College (later Morehouse College) to train black preachers. Before the end of Reconstruction, the Southern Methodist and Baptist churches had lost most of their black members to separate denominations.

Church leaders attempted to ease the postwar guilt over defeat and to stem the loss of faith in a benevolent deity. For them, defeat in the war meant only that the Southern people had been tested to see whether they would remain true to their faith and heritage. Mainstream preachers joined ex-military leaders to advance the theme of a glorious Lost Cause, a past worthy of sacrifice. The concept of the Lost Cause soon prevailed among Protestants, as churches became centers for the rituals of Confederate heroics and the perpetuation of Old South religious values. Those who sought reform and the growth of a New South seemed lost in that atmosphere, which turned defeat into a victory for nostalgia. This marriage of reaction and piety resulted in the deepening of fundamentalism, proliferation of sectarianism, rapid growth in evangelical church membership, and continued separation of major northern and southern Protestant churches.

[*See also* Baptist Church; Fast Days; Lost Cause, *overview article;* Sermons.]

BIBLIOGRAPHY

Beringer, Richard E., et al. *Why the South Lost the Civil War.* Athens, Ga., 1986.
Clebsch, William A. *Christian Interpretations of the Civil War.* Philadelphia, 1969.
Connelly, Thomas L., and Barbara L. Bellows. *God and General Longstreet: The Lost Cause in the Southern Mind.* Baton Rouge, La., 1982.
Faust, Drew Gilpin. *The Creation of Confederate Nationalism.* Baton Rouge, La., 1988.
Hill, Samuel S., Jr., ed. *Religion in the Southern States: A Historical Study.* Macon, Ga., 1983.
Mohr, Clarence L. *On the Threshold of Freedom: Masters and Slaves in Civil War Georgia.* Athens, Ga., 1986.

JON L. WAKELYN

REPUBLICAN PARTY

At its birth, the Republican party was an avowedly sectional party. Arising out of the Northern protest over the Kansas-Nebraska Act (1854), the party opposed the expansion of slavery and called on Congress to exclude the institution from all the territories. Although Republicans denied any intention to interfere with slavery in the Southern states, the party had little strength in the South before 1865.

In the 1856 presidential election, the Republican party polled about one thousand votes in the border states and Virginia, but it had no viable organization below the Mason-Dixon Line. During the next four years, some Republican leaders sought to deflect the issue of sectionalism by building up the party in the South, and the party attracted a few notable Southern adherents, including Francis P. Blair, Jr., in Missouri, his brother Montgomery in Maryland, Cassius Clay in Kentucky, and Archibald Campbell in Virginia. Southern Republicans generally emphasized slavery's adverse effects on Southern whites and disavowed any concern for the welfare of blacks. Yet the party made little headway in the region. In 1860 Abraham Lincoln polled a mere twenty-six thousand votes in the slave states; his Southern support was confined to the border states and the western counties of Virginia.

During the war, the Unionist coalitions that took power in the border states eventually fragmented. Calling for immediate emancipation, the use of black troops, and stringent penalties against Confederates, radical organizations emerged led by such men as Henry Winter Davis in Maryland and Benjamin Gratz Brown in Missouri. Aided by military officials and federal patronage, the radicals won control of Maryland and Missouri and abolished slavery. They provided the nucleus of the full-fledged Republican parties that formed in the border states after the war. In the 1864 presidential election, Lincoln carried Maryland, West Virginia, and Missouri.

In the Confederacy the Republican movement was closely tied to the advance of the Union army. Shadow Republican parties, made up of a handful of die-hard Unionists and propped up by military support, had developed by 1864 in the occupied areas of Virginia, Arkansas, and Tennessee. The most serious attempt to establish the foundation for a postwar Republican party in a Confederate state occurred in

Louisiana under the direction of Nathaniel P. Banks, the Union military commander. Wishing to create a white-only party, Banks backed the moderate faction led by Michael Hahn, who was elected governor of the reconstructed government. The moderates wrote a new state constitution that abolished slavery but rejected black suffrage. Prominent state leaders held aloof from the Union party, however, and it attracted support primarily from urban groups in the Union-controlled region around New Orleans.

The Republican party confronted major difficulties in establishing a Southern wing before 1865. Intimidation and violence, Southern whites' hostility to the party's program, the race issue, and factional squabbles all limited the Republican party's strength in the South. When the war ended, the party lacked any organization in most of the former Confederate states, and where it did exist in some guise, it represented only a very small minority of the white population.

[*See also* Kansas-Nebraska Act.]

BIBLIOGRAPHY

Abbott, Richard H. *The Republican Party and the South, 1855–1877.* Chapel Hill, N.C., 1986.
McCrary, Peyton. *Abraham Lincoln and Reconstruction: The Louisiana Experiment.* Princeton, N.J., 1978.

WILLIAM E. GIENAPP

RHETT, ROBERT BARNWELL, SR.

RHETT, ROBERT BARNWELL, SR. (1800–1876), congressman from South Carolina and editor. Born in Beaufort, South Carolina, on December 21, 1800, Robert Barnwell Rhett was a classic Southern fire-eater whose uncompromising devotion to Southern independence earned him the title of "the father of secession." Although Rhett could claim a distinguished Carolina lineage, his father failed as a planter, and the young Rhett had to make his own fortune and carve out his own career. He chose the traditional path of law and politics. He was admitted to the South Carolina bar in 1821 and soon established a thriving legal business, but his real love was politics. As a member of the South Carolina legislature from 1826 to 1832, he quickly stamped himself as a bold and self-assured leader when he championed the cause of nullification. From the very start of his public career, he was identified as a firebrand eager to challenge established authority.

In 1837, the same year that he went along with the wishes of his brothers and changed the family name from Smith to Rhett in recognition of a distinguished ancestor, Rhett entered Congress as a state rights Democrat. Until 1844 he served as John C. Calhoun's lieutenant in Congress and tried to work through the national Democratic organization in an effort to control it in the interests of the South. When Calhoun's bid for the presidency faltered in 1844, and the old issues of the tariff and abolitionism flared up once again, Rhett reverted to the intransigence that had first characterized his political reputation. He led the ultraradicals of the Carolina low country in the Bluffton movement, a political protest that threatened nullification and even secession if the demands of South Carolina for a lower tariff and an end to abolitionist agitation were not met. The Bluffton movement soon faded, but Rhett's call for separate state action to protect Southern interests became the rallying cry of South Carolina secessionists in the prolonged crisis from 1849 to 1852 that was touched off by Southern demands for equal access to the territories recently won in the Mexican War.

In the midst of this crisis Rhett realized his long cherished goal of reaching the U.S. Senate. In 1851 the South Carolina legislature elected him to fill the seat vacated by Calhoun's death. By this time Rhett was a confirmed secessionist committed to a permanent Southern confederacy. This goal eluded him, however, when his stand on separate state secession in opposition to the Compromise of 1850 was rejected in South Carolina. True to his state rights principles, Rhett then resigned from the Senate in 1852 after his state had repudiated his policies. With his leadership and his party defeated, he retired from politics. When he reemerged in 1857 with all his old radicalism, he worked closely with William Lowndes Yancey of Alabama and Edmund Ruffin of Virginia to fire the Southern imagination in favor of secession. He now owned the *Charleston Mercury* and, with a son as the editor, he used the paper as a pulpit for his secessionist views.

Rhett's unrelenting radicalism finally came to fruition in the fall of 1860. Abraham Lincoln's election triggered a successful secession movement in South Carolina and throughout the lower South, and, as Rhett had long preached that they must, the radicals pursued a strategy of separate state secession. Southern unity in favor of independence, Rhett had concluded as early as the Bluffton movement, could be achieved only if one state took the lead in secession and pulled the others along in its wake.

Rhett played a major role at the South Carolina secession convention. He wrote the *Address to the Slave-Holding States,* a formal statement of South Carolina's justification for secession. Rhett stressed the inalienable right of Southern whites to self-government, a right they must now seize to free themselves from the centralizing despotism of a Federal government dominated by a hostile Northern majority. Slavery, he reasoned, could not long survive a Union controlled by Lincoln's Republican party. On December 26 Rhett also proposed the calling of a Southern convention of the slaveholding states at the earliest possible date. Now that South Carolina had seceded and other states apparently were soon to follow, Rhett's great fear was that an independent South would be stillborn, the victim of scheming politicians who would use secession as leverage to exact concessions from the North with the aim of reconstructing the Union on a basis more favorable to the South. Thus, for Rhett, it was imperative that a new and permanent Southern confederacy be formed as soon as possible. Moreover, such a government had to be irrevocably wedded to the interests of that slave civilization to which Rhett had given his undying devotion.

Rhett headed the South Carolina delegation to the convention that met at Montgomery, Alabama, in early February 1861 to form a provisional government for the Confederate States of America. He went to Montgomery determined to shape the new Confederacy in the image of his beloved Carolina low country. Complete security for the slave society of his Beaufort district required not only separation from the threatening North but the political reshaping of the South into a homogeneous slave society approximating what Rhett knew at home. In pursuit of this goal he pushed a four-pronged program designed to safeguard the revolution of 1860 that he had been so instrumental in fomenting. He wanted a constitutional provision prohibiting the admission of any nonslave state, an opening of the African slave trade when desired by the planters, and full political representation of all slaves as a substitute for the old three-fifths clause in the U.S. Constitution. Since the profits from slave-produced staples were to be the engine of economic growth for the Confederacy, he insisted on a policy of free trade with the outside world so as to maximize the market for Southern exports. Free trade, Rhett believed, would quickly lead to an alliance with Britain, ever eager to guarantee its chief supply of raw cotton. Such an alliance would eliminate any talk of reconstructing the old Union and provide British military protection for Southern independence.

Perhaps more than any other delegate at the Montgomery convention, Rhett had a vision of what he wanted the new Southern republic to be. As he feared, however, his vision was rejected. At the urging of the Mississippi and Georgia delegations, Jefferson Davis of Mississippi, a late convert to secession and a reconstructionist in Rhett's view, was chosen as president. When he organized his administration, Davis pointedly did not offer Rhett either of the two posts he most wanted, that of secretary of state or commissioner to England. Rhett distrusted Davis, and the feeling was mutual. Despite serving on the committees for Foreign Affairs, Financial Independence, and a Permanent Constitution, Rhett was unable to implement the fundamental changes he felt were essential for the success of the Confederacy. The U.S. Constitution was adopted virtually without change by the Confederacy. The three-fifths clause for slave representation, the prohibition on the African slave trade, and the Federal tar-

iff of 1857 were all retained. Most galling of all for Rhett was his defeat on the issue of admitting only slave states to the Confederacy. About all that Rhett could claim as victories were constitutional prohibitions against protective tariffs and Confederate expenditures for internal improvements.

Honored in Charleston as a prophet in the heady days of secession, Rhett was spurned in Montgomery as a spokesman for the Confederacy. Unlike Rhett, Davis expected a war with the North, and he rejected Rhett's program at Montgomery in part because he did not want a radically proslavery Confederacy to scare off the states of the upper South that had not yet left the Union. The economic and military resources of the upper South would be essential for any

> **Rhett had a vision of what he wanted the new Southern republic to be. . . .**

successful defense of the Confederacy against Northern armies. The war came in April 1861 with the firing on Fort Sumter, and five states in the upper South joined the original seven states of the Confederacy. Although heartened by the apparent Southern unity that accompanied the outbreak of war, Rhett remained deeply suspicious of Davis, and he set out as a congressman in the Provisional Congress to shape the policy of the Davis administration.

Rhett first tried to seize the initiative on foreign policy. He introduced resolutions calling for a diplomacy offering favorable and long-term trading ties to Europe in return for Confederate recognition. Unwilling to tie Davis's hands in foreign relations, Congress rejected the resolutions. In June, after Congress had adjourned, Rhett began a campaign through the *Charleston Mercury* to formulate war policy for the Confederacy. The *Mercury* attacked Davis for indecision and delay in waging the war. Frustrated by Union successes in Maryland, Missouri, and Kentucky, and concerned by the ominous signs of extensive war preparations in the North, Rhett called for a rapid and massive Confederate offensive. The war must be carried to the Yankees, proclaimed the *Mercury*. Any delay would favor the North by giving it time to mobilize its superior manpower and industrial resources. Once launched, a Confederate offensive would capitalize on the enthusiasm and innate fighting skills of Southern troops and smash Northern armies before they were disciplined into effective fighting units.

The Confederate victory at First Manassas on July 12, 1861, confirmed Rhett's belief in an offensive policy. Despite the success of Southern armies in the first major test of the war, Rhett stepped up his criticisms of the administration. The *Mercury* charged that a great opportunity for an advance on Washington after First Manassas had been lost because of Davis's timid generalship and inability to adequately supply Gen. P. G. T. Beauregard's troops. Rhett also returned to his claim that Davis was a reconstructionist at heart. The Northern rout at Manassas led to rumors that Northern commercial interests, especially those in the lower Midwest, were eager for an economic alliance with the Confederacy. Fearful that any commercial reunion would be but the first step toward eventual political reunion, Rhett lashed out at Davis for allegedly restraining Confederate armies in the hopes of a reconciliation with the North. As confirmation of his view, Rhett cited the blockage by the administration in Congress of his July resolutions imposing additional duties on Northern goods and banning trade in any European goods imported through the North.

Foreign policy continued to be a divisive issue between Rhett and Davis. Rhett was both angered and surprised by Britain's refusal to recognize Confederate independence. With his initial policy of diplomatic conciliation rejected by the Davis administration, Rhett switched to a policy of coercion in the summer of 1861. His resolutions in Congress called for an embargo of trade with all nations that did not recognize the Confederacy. Britain, he argued, must be forced to choose sides, and he was confident that the power of King Cotton would force the British to align with the Confederacy. Once again, Rhett met defeat. Most congressmen, as well as the Davis administration, wavered between conciliation and coercion. The result was a voluntary embargo, a withholding of cotton from the seaports by the planters. A compromise that reflected divided sentiment within the South, this policy was favored by the administration because it put economic pressure on Britain without being specifically identified with a hard-line policy by the Confederate government.

By the fall of 1861, the time of the elections for the First Congress, Rhett's unrelenting criticism of Davis was beginning to backfire. In the absence of a formal opposition party to serve as an institutional outlet for attacks on the administration's handling of the war, Rhett's opposition came to be seen as a personal vendetta and a drain on Confederate morale. Public opinion in his own state of South Carolina turned against him. Rhett had no interest in running for the Confederate House. His eyes were on the Senate, but he failed to secure either of the two Senate seats chosen by the legislature. On top of this political defeat, his plantation and hometown of Beaufort fell to the Federals in November 1861, when an amphibious invasion occupied much of the Carolina low country.

Chastened but hardly bowed, Rhett returned to Richmond in December for the last session of the Provisional Congress. Consistent with his earlier record, he assailed the administration but was unable to gain passage of the changes he favored. His navigation bill concerning direct trade with Europe, which would have restricted foreign trade to ships built in the Confederacy or by the countries that were sup-

plying imports, was rejected by Congress. He failed to carry a new naturalization bill that would have made it more difficult for Northerners to become Confederate citizens, a measure prompted by Rhett's constant dread of reconstruction. Over Rhett's constitutional objections, the administration won passage of an act permitting the Confederate government to construct connecting lines for railroads in the name of national defense. The constitutional issue of centralization versus state rights involved in the railroad bill also dominated debate over legislation to raise fresh troops for the army now that the enlistments of the original twelve-month volunteers were about to expire. Rhett supported a bill introduced by Robert Toombs of Georgia, which, though requiring the states to raise fresh troops, left the appointment of the new officers for these troops up to the states. The administration blocked the Toombs bill and subsequently pushed through national conscription in April 1862.

The end of the Provisional Congress in the winter of 1861–1862 severed Rhett's only official link with the Confederacy. For all his sharp criticism of Davis, Rhett had never wavered in his commitment to Southern independence. Indeed, on crucial financial and military matters, he was a surprisingly strong supporter of the administration. Despite the obvious challenge to state rights in the Conscription Act of 1862, Rhett backed the measure as essential for military victory. By now he had teamed with his son, Barnwell, Jr., in running the *Charleston Mercury.* For the remainder of the war, the two Rhetts mounted a propaganda offensive in a desperate attempt to effect fundamental changes in the Confederate government and its prosecution of the war.

Their editorials were especially vitriolic in early 1862 after the Confederacy had been staggered by a series of military reverses that opened up Tennessee and the lower Mississippi valley to Union forces. After leading the call for a congressional investigation of the military losses, the Rhetts were bitterly disappointed when Davis vetoed a bill creating the office of commander in chief. The successful defense of Richmond in the Peninsular campaign in the spring of 1862 did little to change their opinion that Davis was utterly unfit to be setting military policy.

As the war reached its midpoint in 1863, Rhett was still confident of Southern victory. Indeed, he worried more about a reconciliation with the North and the subsequent loss of the opportunity to establish a thoroughly slave-based society than he did about the possibility of a vanquished South. When his confidence in victory was badly shaken by the twin Confederate disasters at Gettysburg and Vicksburg in July 1863, he turned on Davis with a renewed vehemence and accused him of criminal incompetence. Rhett now argued that only the South's best men, leaders such as Toombs and himself who had heretofore played but minor roles in the Confederate government, could save the South. Consequently, he ran for Congress in the fall elections of 1863. The result was the most stunning defeat of his political career. Contrary to his expectations, the incumbent in Rhett's Third Congressional District, Lewis M. Ayer, refused to step aside. Ayer won reelection by depicting Rhett as a divisive, if not disloyal, opponent of Davis and the war effort.

Gloom and demoralization permeated South Carolina in the last year and a half of the war. Although he welcomed any actions directed against the administration, Rhett viewed with alarm the peace movements that swelled in neighboring North Carolina and Georgia and gave signs of stirring even in South Carolina. Once Lincoln's reelection in November 1864 apparently ended once and for all the threat of reconciliation, Rhett called on his fellow South Carolinians to rely on their own resources in a last-ditch bid to achieve their independence. Davis and his government, Rhett believed, were now nearly as much to be feared as Lincoln's invading armies. Rhett was aghast when he heard of the plans coming out of Richmond to arm the slaves as Confederate soldiers. In what was to be the last public act of his career, he

> ...to the end of his life he remained as proud, obstinate, and self-righteous as he had been while fighting for the cause.

published a letter in November 1864 damning Davis for destroying the constitutional liberties and institution of slavery that Southerners had gone to war to protect. He hoped against hope that Congress and the states could still bring Davis to his senses and force him to wage the war within the confines of the Confederate Constitution.

At the end of the war all of Rhett's hopes had turned to ashes, but to the end of his life he remained as proud, obstinate, and self-righteous as he had been while fighting for the cause of Southern independence first as an American and then as a Confederate citizen. Many of his last years were spent in writing an unpublished history of the Confederacy, his final testament to the correctness of his views and the failures of Davis. Too proud to seek a pardon from the U.S. government after the war, he retired from public life. He moved to Louisiana in the early 1870s and lived at the plantation of a son-in-law in St. James Parish. He died on September 14, 1876, in the centennial year of the republic whose liberties he had always professed to celebrate.

BIBLIOGRAPHY

Cauthen, Charles Edward. *South Carolina Goes to War, 1861–1865.* Chapel Hill, N.C., 1950.
Escott, Paul D. *After Secession: Jefferson Davis and the Failure of Confederate Nationalism.* Baton Rouge, La., 1978.
Schultz, Harold S. *Nationalism and Sectionalism in South Carolina, 1852–1860.* Durham, N.C., 1950.
White, Laura A. *Robert Barnwell Rhett: Father of Secession.* New York, 1931.
Yearns, Wilfred B. *The Confederate Congress.* Athens, Ga., 1960.

WILLIAM L. BARNEY

RICE

Although never king of Southern agricultural staples, rice has been of central importance to the region's economy since the early eighteenth century. Moreover, it has retained its place in the royal retinue long after cotton's departure from the throne. Prior to the Civil War, furthermore, the major rice-producing area in the South—the low country of South Carolina and Georgia—was perhaps the wealthiest and most heavily commercialized plantation district in North America.

Domestication of the cereal *Oryza sativa* began in Southeast Asia seven millennia ago, whence it spread to other parts of Asia, the Middle East, Africa, and, much later, Mediterranean Europe. The cereal was transferred to the Western Hemisphere during the early modern period as part of the so-called Columbian exchange of biogens.

Some rice may have been grown in Spanish Florida in the sixteenth century, and the English experimented with the crop in Virginia in the early seventeenth century. It was not until the last decade of the latter century, however, that rice became firmly established in the American South, and it did so neither in Florida nor in Virginia, but in the youthful English settlement of Carolina.

From the time of initial settlement in 1670, the white colonists in the precociously commercialized Carolina colony searched hard for a viable export commodity. After more than two decades of experiments, failures, and false starts with a variety of minerals, raw materials, and plant and animal products, they began to have some success with rice. The precise origins of rice cultivation in the southern part of the colony (Carolina did not split into two separate entities, North Carolina and South Carolina, until 1729) are controversial, but relatively unimportant. Whether one believes that rice cultivation initially owed more to Europeans or to Africans ultimately matters little. The cereal was well known throughout the Old World by the late seventeenth century, and small quantities had already been grown successfully in the New. Whichever foundation myth one prefers, it was not until the mid-1690s that the colony possessed sufficient stocks of labor, capital, and local knowledge to begin cultivating, processing, and marketing successfully a staple agricultural commodity such as rice.

For a short period of time, apparently, rice was grown in Carolina without irrigation on dry and relatively high ground in the low country, that is, the easternmost third of what is now South Carolina. By the 1720s, production had shifted almost entirely to freshwater swamps in the area, where rudimentary irrigation works could be employed. Cultivation remained centered in these inland swamps in the low country of South Carolina and, after roughly 1750, Georgia until the last quarter of the eighteenth century, when the locus of activity shifted again, this time to swampland on or adjacent to the area's principal tidal rivers. Indeed, rice production in South Carolina and Georgia, and, to a lesser extent, in the Cape Fear region of North Carolina and parts of northeastern Florida, became increasingly concentrated geographically in the narrow zone on each of this area's major tidal rivers, close enough to the coast to be affected significantly by tidal action, but far enough inland to run with fresh water. It was along such rivers—six major ones in South Carolina and five in Georgia—that American rice production would be concentrated until the late nineteenth century when production shifted increasingly to the Old Southwest.

Rice cultivation in South Carolina and Georgia was arduous in nature—the crop demanded a great deal of hoeing and weeding—and was characterized by tight labor controls and considerable coercion throughout its history. No area in the entire South, in fact, was so thoroughly dominated by the institution of slavery as the low country under the rice regime and in no area were the role of African Americans and the influence of African American culture so profound.

To say this is not to suggest, as some have, that African Americans were alone responsible for the technical evolution of the low-country rice industry. If some slaves were from rice countries in West Africa and some technology—fanner baskets, for example—was clearly of African origin, much of the technology employed was generic in nature, and, thus, familiar to cereal producers throughout the world. The origins of even the task system, the distinguishing feature of labor organization in the low country, are open to question. Under this system, which evolved gradually after the mid-eighteenth century, a slave was responsible for completing a specified amount of work daily, a certain number of specified tasks as it were, upon the completion of which he or she was free to do what he or she so chose. This system most likely grew out of an ongoing process of informal negotiations between laborers bargaining for greater autonomy, and managers hoping to raise productivity and to lessen labor unrest by injecting the incentive of free time into the labor equation. However uncertain the origins of the system, its results are clear: over time, slaves used the relative freedom gained through the task system to work for themselves or to sell their free time to others. In so doing, they were often able to accumulate considerable amounts of personal property, which was, of course, only one of many ironies under slavery.

In any case, with the shift in the early eighteenth century to irrigation, rice production technology became increasingly elaborate and costly. In combination with the geographical limits imposed by nature, such technological considerations helped create an agricultural complex dominated by a relatively small number of capital-intensive plantations, which utilized sizable numbers of dependent laborers to produce rice and, at times, other staples for distant, largely foreign, markets.

The main markets for rice produced in the Southeast were never local. Until the late antebellum period, they usually were not even domestic, for most of the crop produced each year was destined for shipment abroad, particularly to the grain markets of northern Europe. In these markets, rice was viewed as a cheap commodity with numerous uses. It was sold as a dietary supplement or complement, for example, and as an animal feed. It was used in distilling and, by the mid-nineteenth century, in brewing and found employment in the starch, paper, and paste industries. Its most common use, however, was as a source of cheap, bulk calories for the poor and for soldiers, sailors, inmates, and schoolchildren in the absence of, or instead of, more desirable but often more expensive foodstuffs.

Prior to the entrance of American rice in European markets, most of the Continent's supply came from the Italian states of Lombardy and Piedmont, or from the Levant. By the mid-eighteenth century, though, rice from South Carolina and, later, Georgia had supplanted other suppliers in the principal European markets, and American rice maintained this position until the 1830s, when exports from the United States were surpassed by those from India and Southeast Asia.

Given the character of European demand, it is not surprising that Southeast Asia, the lowest-cost supplier in the market, could outcompete other supply sources. As a result of this penetration of its major markets, U.S. producers shifted their attention in the late antebellum period to the domestic market and others in the Western Hemisphere. Despite some success with this strategy, the rice industry of the South Atlantic states was clearly mature well before the Civil War: the rate of growth in output was slowing down, soil fertility was declining, costs (particularly for labor) were rising, and profit possibilities in the industry were diminishing—all of this before the disruption of four years of civil war.

Until recently, historians believed that the problems of the South Atlantic rice industry began in 1861 and that the industry's demise was a direct outgrowth of the Civil War and emancipation. It is now clear, however, that its problems were both structural and long-term in nature, having as much to do with the expansion and elaboration of capitalism and with shifts in international comparative advantage as with Federal occupation, wartime destruction of production facilities, and postwar shortages of capital and changes in labor relations.

To be sure, the latter short-term factors impeded the South Atlantic rice industry. Production in the four South Atlantic states of North Carolina, South Carolina, Georgia, and Florida fell from an all-time high of 179.4 million pounds of clean rice in 1859 (95.9 percent of the U.S. total) to 57 million pounds in 1869. But production in the area rose by nearly 48 percent between 1869 and 1879, and even as late as 1899 almost 69 million pounds of clean rice were produced in the South Atlantic region. By that time, however, Southeast Asian competition had not only knocked U.S. rice out of Europe but had penetrated the domestic market as well. The United States, in fact, was a major importer of rice for a half century after the Civil War.

One important long-term result of such competition was the gradual migration of the U.S. rice industry to Louisiana, Texas, and Arkansas. Here, highly mechanized production technology was employed, particularly after the so-called rice revolution of the mid-1880s, which raised productivity and minimized the problems posed by scarce or restive labor. Although rice *could* still be grown in the South Atlantic region at the turn of the century, highly mechanized production technology was not introduced on the reconstituted plantations, tenant plots, and yeoman freeholdings in the area. Consequently, production no longer meant profits, and the low country of South Carolina and Georgia lapsed into generations of stagnation and decline. In the last analysis, however, the evolution of the U.S. rice industry owed as much to European imperialism and to developments in Calcutta, Batavia, and Rangoon, as to more familiar events closer to home.

BIBLIOGRAPHY

Coclanis, Peter A. *The Shadow of a Dream: Economic Life and Death in the South Carolina Low Country, 1670–1920.* New York, 1989.

Dethloff, Henry C. *A History of the American Rice Industry, 1685–1985.* College Station, Tex., 1988.

Joyner, Charles W. *Down by the Riverside: A South Carolina Slave Community.* Urbana, Ill., 1984.

Smith, Julia Floyd. *Slavery and Rice Culture in Low Country Georgia, 1750–1860.* Knoxville, Tenn., 1985.

PETER A. COCLANIS

RICHMOND, VIRGINIA

In 1860, Richmond was the twenty-fifth largest American city, with a population of 37,910. Its manufactures ranked thirteenth in value, far above those of Charleston, which it soon surpassed in size, and even those of New Orleans, a much larger city. Its industry, and its status since the Revolution as the seat of Virginia's government, impelled the leaders of the infant Confederacy to suggest that Richmond become the permanent capital if the Old Dominion seceded.

The Confederacy's move from Montgomery, the first capital city, in May 1861 was appropriate for a conservative revolution, for Richmond had long been a bastion of Whigs "who knew each other by the instincts of gentlemen." They so dominated antebellum politics that the city's few Democrats were called "the Spartan band." Know-Nothings triumphed in the 1855–1856 elections because of national Whiggery's disintegration and conservative fears of the city's growing ethnic and religious mix, noted by contemporary observer Frederick Law Olmsted. In the 1860 presidential election, the Constitutional Union ticket won 20 percent more of the 6,555 votes cast than the two Democratic slates combined.

Richmond's population was 62 percent white, over a fifth of which was foreign-born, chiefly Irish Catholics, and Germans, many of whom were Lutherans. Catholics had three churches, including a cathedral. Wealthy Methodists, Presbyterians, and Baptists dominated, with Episcopalians at the pinnacle of prestige. There was also a significant Jewish minority with three synagogues.

African Americans, 18 percent of whom were free, had declined from 45 percent of the 1850 population. Corporations owned more slaves and in larger concentrations than did white families, two-thirds of whom owned none. Slaves and free blacks were essential to the city's major industries, where many held skilled jobs. Others worked in the trades and service occupations. There were active charitable and fraternal associations, large churches, and distinct gradations in black society as in white.

Richmond rivaled Baltimore as a milling center, with annual sales of $3 million from its twelve flour and meal mills, including the Gallego, largest in the world. Highly regarded for its quality, city flour was shipped to Australia and South America. Return cargoes of Brazilian coffee made Richmond the leading importer in 1860. In its tobacco market, the world's largest, sixty factories and related firms processed tobacco worth $5 million, making it the city's most profitable sector. Joseph R. Anderson's Tredegar Iron Works, the second largest foundry in the United States, was half of a substantial industry that employed one-fifth of the labor force and included dozens of firms with total sales of over $2 million. Profits from the city's slave trade, described by Charles Dickens and other visitors, probably exceeded those derived from milling or metal working. Only New Orleans was a larger slave mart. To this business and industrial complex, which was already diversifying, the war added powder mills, armories, laboratories, government offices, and huge troop encampments.

Richmond, Virginia's largest port, was a transportation hub. There were overnight steamship connections to Washington and Baltimore down the James River. Ocean and coasting vessels crowded Rocketts, the city's harbor. Five railroads terminated here, bringing passengers and freight from all directions. The Richmond and York River Railroad ran east to West Point, another deep-water port. The Richmond, Fredericksburg, and Potomac went north to Aquia Creek, with steamship connections to Washington and Baltimore via the Potomac. The Virginia Central also ran north to Gordonsville below Manassas Junction, continuing south and west to Charlottesville and Staunton. The Richmond and Petersburg connected to Wilmington via Weldon. The Richmond and Danville was the city's main direct link with the Deep South, although this line also crossed the Virginia and Tennessee,

> **Richmond's location made it inevitable that Virginia would become the main battleground. Richmond was the goal of the Army of the Potomac. . . .**

which ran through Bristol. The James River and Kanawha Canal extended west beyond Lynchburg more than two hundred miles from the Richmond docks. As late as 1859 the canal brought more freight tonnage into Richmond than all the railroads combined.

Edgar Allan Poe had lived here and edited the *Southern Literary Messenger,* which continued until 1864. George W. Bagby, George Fitzhugh, Edmund Ruffin, John R. Thompson, and Nathaniel Beverly Tucker all published in Richmond. The city boasted four major dailies, with total circulation of almost 84,000, including the *Whig, Enquirer, Examiner,* and *Dispatch,* and a German daily, *Taglicher Anzeiger.* It added a sixth, the *Sentinel,* during the war, as well as Confederate journals like the *Southern Illustrated News, Magnolia Weekly,* and *Southern Punch.* The city had several theaters and public halls but no library.

Richmond was the social center for Virginia east of the mountains and for much of the Mid-Atlantic seaboard. Genteel antebellum society became rougher in wartime. Entertainment included elegant receptions at the presidential mansion; "starvation parties" for young soldiers and beautiful belles, at which only water was served; and saloons, brothels, and gambling dens or "tigers," all of which ranged from the posh to the squalid. Writers as diverse as Mary Boykin Chesnut, Thomas C. DeLeon, J. B. Jones, and Sallie Brock Putnam described the Confederate citadel.

Schools included the Medical College of Virginia; Richmond College, a Baptist institution; the Richmond Female Institute; and the Virginia Mechanics Institute. All were taken over for military use. There were dozens of private academies, but no true public school system.

The state arsenal, armory, and penitentiary were here, and Richmond became the prison and hospital center of the South. The city held thirteen thousand prisoners in November 1863. Libby Prison, for Union officers, was locat-ed in a Maine ship chandler and slave trader's warehouse. Belle Isle, for enlisted men, was on a low island in the middle of the James. There were smaller prisons like Castle Thunder and Castle Lightning for spies, deserters, rowdies, political prisoners, and women.

Camp Winder, west of the city, was the largest hospital, and Phoebe Yates Pember's Chimborazo, on an eastern hill, was the most famous. There were at least sixty smaller military hospitals, run by the Confederate government, states, private individuals, and churches and other institutions.

The influx of politicians, clerks, office seekers, soldiers, and camp followers from all over the Confederacy, along with Southern refugees from the North, tripled or quadrupled the 1860 population, straining municipal services, including the markets, water and gas works, and police and fire protection. City employees were subject to conscription.

Tension between Richmonders and Confederate officials can be seen in the early furor over Provost Marshal John Winder's enforcement of martial law and resentment of his feared detectives or "plug-uglies," in John M. Daniel's bitter criticism of the Davis administration in his *Examiner,* and in the minutes of the city council.

Rampant inflation caused severe suffering for those on fixed incomes, and even regular increases in government salaries failed to keep pace, resulting in such ironies as a free black cobbler earning more than Confederate congress-men. The April 1863 bread riot was the most serious of the Southern food protests over shortages and high prices.

Organized resistance to the Confederacy by a Union underground included the spy Elizabeth Van Lew and Richmond, Fredericksburg, and Potomac Railroad Superintendent Samuel Ruth, who delayed beef shipments to Robert E. Lee's army. Unionists helped slaves and Federal prisoners to escape, committed arson and other sabotage, and chalked pro-Northern slogans on walls.

More than 7,300 men from the area served in the Confederate army, furnishing over forty companies of infantry, artillery, and cavalry, including two regiments, the First and Fifteenth Virginia infantries. Confederate dead filled the city's cemeteries, Shockoe, Oakwood, and Hollywood; the latter, the most famous after the war, is the burial site of J. E. B. Stuart, George E. Pickett and his men, and eventual-ly Jefferson Davis and his family.

Although it may have been a strategic error for Confederate leaders to move their capital so close to the North, a decision still argued by Civil War historians, Richmond's location made it inevitable that Virginia would become the main battleground. Richmond was the goal of the Army of the Potomac for four years. After Irvin McDowell's drive ended at First Manassas in July 1861, George B. McClellan's Peninsular campaign threatened Richmond in 1862. Lee's Army of Northern Virginia pushed the front lines back in 1862 and 1863 in the Seven Days' Battles and at

Second Manassas, Fredericksburg, and Chancellorsville. A series of star forts and three concentric lines of trenches encircled Richmond. There were never enough troops to man these earthworks fully, but they were used against major campaigns and raids, notably Stoneman's in May 1863 and Kilpatrick-Dahlgren's in March 1864.

The city was again threatened by Ulysses S. Grant's massive offensive that same spring. He was unable to take Richmond after the Wilderness, Spotsylvania, and Cold Harbor, but his siege of Petersburg eventually cut the city's direct rail link with Wilmington. Forced to evacuate after his lines were finally broken at Five Forks on April 1, 1865, Lee notified Jefferson Davis that Richmond must be abandoned. His army did not survive the loss of its capital for even a week.

The Confederate government evacuated the night of April 2, 1865. The Southerners blew up ironclads in the James and munitions in the city, including its powder magazine. The explosions caused more than a dozen fatalities. Custis Lee's rear guard burned Mayo's Bridge, the only vehicular and pedestrian link, as well as the two railroad viaducts. Fires set to destroy supplies of tobacco and cotton, despite the objections of city officials, were spread by high winds. Hindered by penitentiary inmates who cut their hoses, Richmond's few firemen were unable to control the flames. A mob of thousands of hungry civilians, as well as Confederate stragglers and deserters and Union prisoners, swarmed through the streets ahead of the blaze, looting stores and warehouses.

The evacuation fire consumed much of Richmond's industrial and business district, including all of the banks and most of the food suppliers. Property loss estimates ranged as high as $30 million. Residential neighborhoods were largely spared, but more than eight hundred buildings burned in four dozen blocks, and the downtown area was a smoking wasteland when Union forces entered the city early on April 3, restoring order and putting out fires that were still burning.

Reconstruction in Richmond was moderate, despite legends to the contrary, but the impact of war and defeat was enormous. Rebuilding of the burned district began almost immediately after the Union occupation (largely financed by Northern backers who remain mostly unidentified), although ruins from the evacuation fire could still be seen in the 1870s. Economic recovery was slower and only partially successful. Panics in 1873 and 1893, lack of capital and access to raw materials, failure to adopt new technology, continued reliance on erratic water power from the James, the shift of the wheat belt farther west, and corporate consolidations all had their effect. The Tredegar Iron Works never recovered its antebellum stature. The city's mills declined after 1883, although the last lingered until 1932. Richmond's once-dominant industry was taken over in 1890 by James B. Duke's trust, the American Tobacco Company. Efforts to deepen the river channel failed, and Norfolk had surpassed the port of Richmond by 1881. Canal owners struggled to repair war

damage but were stymied by floods, the 1873 depression, and rail competition. The towpath became a railroad right-of-way. The railroads fell under the control of outside interests or built extensions so that the city ceased to be a terminus.

No longer a major industrial center or transport hub, Richmond remained Virginia's capital and became the mausoleum of the Lost Cause, with thousands of Confederate graves, monuments to Southern heroes, and shrines like the White House of the Confederacy, the Lee House, the soldiers' homes, the Southern Historical Society at Battle Abbey (now the Virginia Historical Society), the Home for Confederate Women, and the headquarters of the United Daughters of the Confederacy. Battlefields and other historic sites, most administered by the National Park Service, still ring the capital, and trenches greet the visitor leaving the airport. Richmond's population in the last half of the twentieth century has been roughly one-half black, and African Americans have often controlled the government and elected mayors in Virginia's "Holy City," the capital of a vanished nation.

[*See also* Belle Isle Prison; Bread Riots; Castle Thunder Prison; Libby Prison.]

BIBLIOGRAPHY

Bill, Alfred H. *The Beleaguered City: Richmond, 1861–1865.* New York, 1946.

Chesson, Michael B. *Richmond after the War, 1865–1890.* Richmond, Va., 1981.

Jones, Katherine M., ed. *Ladies of Richmond, Confederate Capital.* Indianapolis, 1962.

Jones, Virgil Carrington. *Eight Hours before Richmond.* New York, 1957.

Manarin, Louis H., ed. *Richmond at War: The Minutes of the City Council, 1861–1865.* Chapel Hill, N.C., 1966.

Manarin, Louis H., and Lee A. Wallace, Jr., eds. *Richmond Volunteers: The Volunteer Companies of the City of Richmond and Henrico County, Virginia, 1861–1865.* Richmond, Va., 1969.

Patrick, Rembert. *The Fall of Richmond.* Baton Rouge, La., 1960.

Thomas, Emory M. *The Confederate State of Richmond: A Biography of the Capital.* Austin, Tex., 1971.

MICHAEL B. CHESSON

RIVER DEFENSE FLEET

To defend the Mississippi south of New Orleans and to the north as far as Memphis, Confederates assembled fourteen river steamers, pilot boats, and tugs under the appellation the River Defense Fleet.

The large, well-armed Union force that threatened the entire Mississippi in 1861 set state legislators in Missouri and Mississippi clamoring for protection. Kentucky boatmen

James Edward Montgomery and James H. Townsend originated the idea for the fleet, and Secretary of War Judah P. Benjamin engineered a million-dollar appropriation by late 1861.

In the loosely structured Confederate command system, naval officers assigned to the Mississippi had little or no part in plans or operations for the fleet. In January 1862, orders to purchase the boats went to Maj. Gen. Mansfield Lovell. Gen. M. Jeff Thompson of the Missouri State Guard later added his daring temperament to the enterprise.

The ships were first rechristened for Confederate army leaders. Armed with one 24- or 32-pounder mounted astern, they were not designed to engage the enemy as gunboats. Instead, reinforcing the prow of each boat with iron created a ram that could damage and sink a Union ship in a collision. "Cottonclad" came into the vocabulary of the Civil War when cotton was stuffed inside the hulls; this was done so that a cannonball that pierced the hull would bury itself in the matted fibers.

Six of the boats stood below New Orleans to meet the Union's April 24, 1862, assault on Forts Jackson and St. Philip. Five were run aground and abandoned by their untrained crews: *Defiance, General Breckenridge, General Lovell, Resolute,* and *Warrior. Stonewall Jackson* rammed and sank the Union *Varuna* before being burned by its fleeing crew.

The eight boats upriver saw more action. On May 10, *General Bragg, General Price, General Sumter, General Van Dorn,* and *Little Rebel* engaged the Union fleet at Plum Point, Tennessee, ramming and damaging U.S. ships *Cincinnati* and *Mound City.*

On June 5 and 6, other boats of the fleet joined in the Battle of Memphis. Of the veterans of the May 10 encounter, all were captured except *Van Dorn,* which was later destroyed at its mooring up the Yazoo River. Of the remaining four, *Colonel Lovell* was sunk with great loss of life; *General Thompson* exploded; *General Beauregard* was badly damaged when it and *Price* missed USS *Monarch* and rammed each other.

Thus ended the story of the River Defense Fleet—like so many Confederate naval efforts, better conceived than constructed and operated with a certain raffish optimism in the face of a much superior Union force.

BIBLIOGRAPHY

Civil War Naval Chronology, 1861–1865. 6 vols. Washington, D.C., 1961–1965.
Gillespie, Michael L. "The Novel Experiment: Cottonclads and Steamboatmen." *Civil War Times Illustrated* 22 (December 1983): 34–39.
Pratt, Fletcher. *Guns on the Western Waters.* New York, 1956.

MAXINE TURNER

RIVES, WILLIAM C.

RIVES, WILLIAM C. (1793–1868), U.S. diplomat, representative to the Washington peace conference, and congressman from Virginia. William Cabell Rives was born May 4, 1793, at Union Hill in Amherst County, Virginia. He was educated at Hampden-Sydney College and the College of William and Mary. After his graduation from the latter in 1809, he studied law under Thomas Jefferson and became an intimate of James Madison. During the War of 1812 he served as aide-de-camp to John H. Cocke on the Chickahominy River. In 1817 Rives was elected to the first of several terms in Virginia's House of Delegates, where he served on the Courts and Justice, Executive Expenditures, and Finance committees.

Rives married Judith Page Walker on March 24, 1819. As heiress to the Castle Hill estate in Albemarle County, she brought Rives a four-thousand-acre plantation and almost a hundred slaves. After moving to Castle Hill, Rives served an additional year in the House of Delegates as a representative of Albemarle County before being elected to Congress in 1823. During the next six years, he ardently supported the cause of Andrew Jackson. The president rewarded Rives's loyalty by naming him minister to France in 1829.

During his time in Paris, Rives witnessed the deposing of Charles X in favor of Louis Philippe at the head of a new constitutional monarchy, scenes he would replay many times in his mind during the secession winter of 1860–1861. Under the Berlin and Milan decrees, the American minister negotiated a settlement of spoliation claims under which the French agreed to pay a $5 million indemnity and the Americans, in turn, agreed to reduce the duty on French wine imported into the United States.

On his return to America in 1832, Rives was elected to the U.S. Senate. His support for the Force Bill angered a number of members of the state legislature. On January 17, 1834, he rose to support Jackson's removal of Federal deposits from the Second Bank of the United States. Virginia's General Assembly instructed its congressional delegation to vote for censuring the president for his actions. Refusing to bow to pressure, Rives chose to resign his seat.

In 1835 Rives campaigned behind the scenes to win the vice presidential nomination on the Democratic ticket. Jackson, however, backed Richard M. Johnson of Kentucky for the office. Thwarted in his ambitions, Rives sought to return to the Senate. He lobbied the General Assembly to instruct the state's congressional delegation to vote for Thomas Hart Benton's resolution asking that the censure of Jackson for removing deposits be expunged. Senator John Tyler refused to do as instructed and resigned his seat, to which Rives was then elected.

Soon after his return to Washington in 1836, Rives found himself at loggerheads with President Martin Van Buren over what to do about the country's fiscal situation. Rives favored placing the Federal surplus in state banks and vehemently opposed both Jackson's specie circular and Van Buren's sub-treasury system. A group calling itself the Conservative Democrats began to coalesce around Rives's leadership and in the 1838 elections won control of the Virginia General Assembly.

In 1839 Rives came up for reelection and was nominated by the Conservative Democrats. He faced former senator John Tyler, nominated by the Whigs, and John Young Mason, the regular Democratic nominee. Henry Clay, the national leader of the Whigs, wanted the support of the Conservative

> ## Calling for "dignity and coolness," he enumerated the legal means of self-protection and defense. . . .

Democrats in 1840, so he offered Tyler a deal: if Tyler would withdraw from the race in favor of Rives, then Clay would see that Tyler received the Whig vice presidential nomination the next year. Tyler refused. None of the three candidates could win a majority, so the election was postponed until the next session. As a result, Virginia had but one senator until 1841, when Rives finally won reelection after Tyler became vice president.

Once in Washington, Rives consistently supported former rival Tyler against Clay until the question of the annexation of Texas came up. Rives maintained that Texas was a foreign nation and that as such, it was unconstitutional to admit it to the Union. By the end of Tyler's term, Rives had aligned himself with the Whig party, and he gave his support to Clay's candidacy in the presidential election of 1844.

When his senatorial term expired in 1845, Rives retired to Castle Hill and private life. Several works from his pen were published in Richmond, including *Discourse on the Character and Services of John Hampden* (1845) and *Discourse on the Uses and Importance of History* (1847). During this time he served a second stint as a member of the board of visitors of the University of Virginia. His first appointment to the board in 1828 had ended with his departure for France in 1829. His second term, begun in 1834, lasted until 1849, when he again stepped down upon receiving another appointment as minister to France, this one from President Zachary Taylor.

For the second time Rives went to turbulent Paris. Louis Philippe, whose relationship with Rives had been so cordial that his queen had consented to act as godmother to Rives's elder daughter, had been forced to abdicate in February 1848 after a series of revolts. In June a bloody uprising of Parisian workers marred the unstable peace of the newly

proclaimed Second Republic. All around him Rives witnessed the aftermath of the bloody nationalist uprisings that erupted in Europe in 1848. He watched as the French moved into Italy to quell Garibaldi's risorgimento. He carried the memories with him when the United States stood on the brink of its own crisis a dozen years later.

Rives returned to Castle Hill in 1853 and again resumed the life of a private citizen. John Brown's raid on Harpers Ferry in October 1859 and Brown's subsequent canonization by radical elements in the North alarmed Rives about the safety of the Union. Fearing what would happen if the Republicans won the White House in 1860, Rives was instrumental in organizing the Constitutional Union party and was mentioned as a possible nominee for president. The party eventually selected as its candidate John Bell, whom Rives supported but did not actively campaign for because of feeble health. After Abraham Lincoln's victory, Rives issued a public *Letter from the Hon. William C. Rives to a Friend, on the Important Questions of the Day* (Richmond, 1860). He condemned the Northern reaction to what he termed "the bloody and revolting tragedy at Harper's Ferry" but believed it was the temporary triumph of a vociferous and radical minority. Calling for "dignity and coolness," he enumerated the legal means of self-protection and defense accorded the states under the Constitution. He called for Virginia to reorganize its militia, form volunteer units, procure arms for its state guard, and encourage domestic manufacture to reduce dependence on the North. He advocated an end to sectionally based parties, both North and South, and the removal of the slavery issue from agitation on the national political level. Finally, he pointed to the lack of feasibility of creating a nation out of the states in which slavery was legal. The differences between the economies of the lower South and the upper South and the ties of the border states to the Old Northwest would, in his opinion, be impossible to overcome.

On December 8 Rives called for a national peace conference to halt the secession crisis in its tracks. In mid-January he traveled to the nation's capital at the urging of several Virginia Unionists, including Winfield Scott, to lobby for such a national convention. During five days of social calls and dinners, Rives capitalized on his position as an elder statesman of the defunct Whig party and as a former intimate of Jefferson and Madison to meet informally with leaders of the Republican party, including Secretary of State-designate William H. Seward. On January 17, Rives advised Unionist Alexander H. H. Stuart to push the resolution calling for a national peace convention through the Virginia General Assembly. Two days later, the state legislature passed the resolution in the wording suggested by Rives and chose the former diplomat and senator as one of the Old Dominion's five delegates. At the same time, however, the General Assembly voted to summon a state convention to consider secession. Rives agreed to stand for election to this convention from Albemarle County and campaigned as well for Unionist Valentine W. Southall. Although Rives was not selected to attend the Richmond convention, he rejoiced at the enormous majority Unionist delegates held.

Rives returned to Washington on February 4 for the opening of the peace conference. He was unhappy with the composition of Virginia's delegation. He and George W. Summers were Unionists; John Tyler and John White Brockenbrough were moderate conditional Unionists but fast moving toward the secessionist position; and James A. Seddon was a fire-eater. To Rives's distress, Tyler was elected president of the convention on February 5, and Tyler, Brockenbrough, and Seddon finagled the selection of Seddon as Virginia's single representative to the Guthrie committee, which was assigned the task of drawing up compromise resolutions to keep the peace and reconcile the sections. To counteract any damage that Seddon might do, Rives began a series of private meetings with members of the Guthrie committee. Although most of the Republicans believed that a second constitutional convention was the only viable solution to the disagreements between the Union and the seceded states, Rives argued that immediate concessions were necessary to halt the spread of secession and to defuse the crisis.

Most of Rives's lobbying was carried on behind the scenes. He made only two major speeches in the course of the peace conference. The first, on February 13, was a eulogy of delegate John C. Wright of Ohio, with whom Rives had served in Congress in the 1820s. The second, on February 19, was a plea for concessions. Secession, he believed, was illegal, but it was a fait accompli. To keep Virginia, the upper South, and the border states in the Union would require only a guarantee of the rights of the slaveholding states. He painted for the conference delegates vivid pictures of what civil war looked like. "I have seen," he reminded them, "the pavements of Paris covered, and her gutters running with fraternal blood: God forbid that I should see this horrid picture repeated in my own country."

With other delegates from the conference, Rives called on Lincoln at the Willard Hotel on February 23. The former senator left the meeting convinced that the president-elect's views had been misrepresented in the Southern press but also that Lincoln did not understand the gravity of the situation facing his administration.

Three days after the delegates' interview with Lincoln, the conference voted on the Guthrie report. Although Rives and Summers supported the resolution calling for a constitutional amendment to extend the Missouri Compromise line to the Pacific Ocean, they were outvoted by the other three members of the Virginia delegation. After the resolution went down in defeat, eight states to eleven, a reconsideration was moved and carried. The conference then adjourned for the day. When the delegates reconvened on February 27,

Virginia still voted in the negative, but the resolution passed, nine states to eight. The other proposals of the Guthrie committee also carried, though in most instances the votes of Tyler, Brockenbrough, and Seddon put Virginia in opposition. The convention then rose.

That afternoon Rives received an invitation to call on Lincoln with Alexander Doniphan of Missouri and Charles Morehead and James Guthrie of Kentucky. The president-elect promised he had no intentions to attack slavery in the states in which it already existed and that he would enforce the Fugitive Slave Laws. He would not, however, heed Morehead's pleas for concessions to the border states. Rives warned that if Lincoln did not abandon Fort Sumter, war was inevitable and that if violence broke out, Virginia would secede. Rives stated that if Virginia left the Union, "in that event I go, with all my heart and soul." Lincoln responded that he would withdraw Federal troops from Fort Sumter if Virginia would vote to remain in the Union. Rives said that he could not speak for his state and could make no promises, though he would work to prevent the secession of the Old Dominion.

Worn out by his exertions, Rives slept for twenty hours and then headed not for home but for Richmond, where the secession convention was then sitting. In a two-hour oration at Metropolitan Hall on March 8, he pleaded the cause of Union. He urged the approval of the resolutions of the peace conference as a just and equitable settlement to the sectional crisis. Rives met privately with convention president Robert Young Conrad and other delegates and returned, exhausted, to Albemarle County.

After the attack on Fort Sumter and Virginia's secession, Rives was selected as one of the commonwealth's delegates to the Provisional Confederate Congress, in which he sat until February 1862. In May 1864 he took a seat in the Second Congress. Because of his experience as minister to France, he served on the Committee on Foreign Relations and succeeded Henry S. Foote of Tennessee as chairman. Rives also sat on the Flag and Seal Committee. His activity was limited by poor health, but he generally supported the policies of the Davis administration.

His only major speech during his second term was a two-hour argument on May 20 opposing Foote's resolution to repeal the suspension of habeas corpus. Rives maintained that the Magna Carta, the Constitution, and the Bill of Rights all allowed the suspension of the writ in wartime. Those who protested the suspension as "a dangerous inroad" on personal liberty and free speech, he declaimed, were ignoring the larger crisis of "an exterminating war of the most tremendous magnitude, waged by a ruthless foe, governed by no rules of humanity, obeying no laws of war." The congressman in fact attributed Richmond's deliverance from the most recent Union assaults at the Wilderness, Spotsylvania, and Yellow Tavern to the suspension of habeas corpus.

On November 21 Rives voted yea on a unanimous resolution reaffirming that the Confederacy would accept no peace terms that did not recognize its independence. The next month, he unsuccessfully opposed a bill to increase the salaries of members of the House by 50 percent. As the year closed, he endorsed a measure for the reduction and redemption of the currency and another for sequestering the property of men fleeing the Confederacy to escape military service. His support was critical in the adoption of a bill authorizing generals commanding departments to consolidate companies, battalions, and regiments; the bill passed by only one vote on January 9, 1865. The next day, he voted to kill the motion to reconsider the measure and return it to the Military Committee. In one of his final official acts, he reported on sundry resolutions on peace negotiations from the Committee on Foreign Relations. Rives was granted a leave of absence on January 28 and resigned his seat on March 2, 1865, citing failing health.

Three days after his resignation, Rives met in Richmond with Robert E. Lee to review a survey of the military situation drawn up by Assistant Secretary of War John A. Campbell. According to Rives, Lee maintained that the only hope for the Confederacy was to come to terms with the United States. The Confederate States could then marshal their resources and await more favorable circumstances to resume the fight for independence. With Lee's assessment in mind, Rives drew up a resolution for the Senate stating that prosecution of the war had become "impracticable" and advising Jefferson Davis to propose, through Lee, "an armistice preliminary to the re-establishment of peace & union." Rives, no longer part of Congress, intended that Senators William A. Graham of North Carolina, James L. Orr of South Carolina, and Robert M. T. Hunter of Virginia should shepherd the resolution through their chamber. The senators considered the resolution but decided in the end that pushing it through Congress would change nothing. Rives returned, for the last time, to Castle Hill and private life.

In the course of his duties as the third president of the Virginia Historical Society (an office he held from 1847 until his death), Rives had been persuaded to undertake a multi-volume biography of his old friend James Madison, the Father of the Constitution. The first volume of the *History of the Life and Times of James Madison* had appeared in 1859. The Civil War delayed the composition and publication of volume two until 1866; volume three, which brought Madison up to 1797, made its appearance in 1868. Rives did not live to complete the fourth volume of the work Henry Cabot Lodge called "one of the most solemn, learned and respectable biographies ever penned by the hand of man." He died April 25, 1868, at Castle Hill and was buried in the family cemetery there. His four-volume edition of *Letters and Other Writings of James Madison* was completed by Philip R. Fendall and appeared in 1884.

BIBLIOGRAPHY

Brown, Alexander. *The Cabells and Their Kin: A Memorial Volume of History, Biography, and Genealogy.* Boston and New York, 1895.

Gunderson, Robert G. "William C. Rives and the 'Old Gentlemen's Convention.'" *Journal of Southern History* 22 (1956): 459–476.

Moore, John Hammond. "The Rives Peace Resolution—March, 1865." *West Virginia History* 26 (1964–1965): 153–160.

Rives, William Cabell. *Letter from the Hon. William C. Rives to a Friend, on the Important Questions of the Day.* Richmond, Va., 1860.

Rives, William Cabell. *Speech of Hon. William C. Rives on the Proceedings of the Peace Conference and the State of the Union, Delivered in Richmond, Virginia, March 8, 1861.* Richmond, Va., 1861.

Sowle, Patrick. "The Trials of a Virginia Unionist: William Cabell Rives and the Secession Crisis, 1860–1861." *Virginia Magazine of History and Biography* 80 (1972): 3–20.

Wingfield, Russell Stewart. "William Cabell Rives: A Biography." *Richmond College Historical Papers* 1 (1915): 57–72.

SARA B. BEARSS

ROBERTSON, BEVERLY HOLCOMBE

ROBERTSON, BEVERLY HOLCOMBE (1826–1910), brigadier general. Robertson was born in Amelia County, Virginia, on June 5, 1826. He graduated twenty-fifth in the class of 1849 at West Point and then served on the frontier with the Second Dragoons.

After the capture of Fort Sumter, Robertson returned to Virginia. In the fall he was named colonel of the Fourth Virginia Cavalry and commanded the regiment until the spring of 1862. During a reorganization, he lost the election for commander and was replaced because the troopers disliked his stern discipline and propensity for drill and military bearing. On June 9 Robertson was promoted to brigadier general and given command of the Laurel Brigade in order to bring some discipline to the troopers. With this command, Robertson participated at Cedar Mountain, Second Manassas, and the Maryland campaign. He was relieved of his command on September 5 and ordered to North Carolina to organize and instruct the cavalry in that department. It seems that Robertson was considered a good organizer and disciplinarian at drill, but unpredictable and lax in battle. During Brandy Station, as Stuart's entire cavalry engaged the Federals, Robertson's force did not engage the enemy at all. He missed the biggest cavalry battle of the war. A historian later noted that Robertson then "lost all self possession and [became] perfectly unreliable."

By February 1863 Robertson had fallen into disfavor with Maj. Gen. D. H. Hill, who wanted Robertson transferred back to Virginia. Hill described his cavalry as "the wonderfully inefficient brigade of Robertson." Lt. Gen. James Longstreet held a similar view of the man: he said that Robertson was "not . . . a very efficient officer in the field" and added that the cavalry could be better used "in proper hands." In May, Robertson was transferred to Virginia, as his cavalry had been parceled out by Hill to the different commands in Carolina. Once again in Virginia, Robertson led a brigade, but in early August he was relieved of this command, too. On October 15 Robertson was given command of the Second Military District of South Carolina, Georgia, and Florida, which he commanded until the end of the war. He had led his troops north and joined up with Joseph E. Johnston's army in North Carolina before surrendering there.

After the war Robertson moved to Washington and worked in insurance until his death on November 12, 1910.

BIBLIOGRAPHY

Eliot, Ellsworth, Jr. *West Point in the Confederacy.* New York, 1941.

Faust, Patricia L., ed. *Historical Times Illustrated Encyclopedia of the Civil War.* New York, 1986.

Thomas, Emory M. *Bold Dragon: The Life of J. E. B. Stuart.* New York, 1986.

Warner, Ezra J. *Generals in Gray: Lives of the Confederate Commanders.* Baton Rouge, La., 1959

KENNETH L. STILES

ROSSER, THOMAS LAFAYETTE

ROSSER, THOMAS LAFAYETTE (1836–1910), major general. Rosser, who was born October 15, 1836, near Lynchburg, Virginia, stood within a few weeks of graduating from the U.S. Military Academy when his adopted state of Texas seceded. He served the Confederacy as a lieutenant and then as a captain in the Washington Artillery of New Orleans for more than a year before being elected colonel of the Fifth Virginia Cavalry on June 24, 1862. The young officer caught J. E. B. Stuart's eye and prospered under the cavalry chief's steady support and recommendations—though grumbling the entire time that Stuart was not pressing his case firmly enough. Stuart's constant applause for Rosser resulted finally in a commission as brigadier general to date from September 28, 1863.

Rosser's subordinates invariably attested to the general's bravery, but with almost as much unanimity they complained of his incompetence, particularly when he assumed division command in 1864. Rosser "knows no more about putting a command into a fight than a school boy," wrote one field-grade officer who also openly admired the general's valor. During Jubal Early's 1864 campaign in the Shenandoah Valley, Rosser undertook the unenviable task of controlling the undisciplined Confederate cavalry in that theater. At Tom's Brook on October 9, 1864, Rosser suffered the most thorough thrashing any large Confederate cavalry force endured in Virginia during the war. Despite that reverse and others, late in October Robert E. Lee, calling Rosser "gallant & zealous," promoted him to major general to date from November 1, 1864. Rosser remained in the valley until March 1865 and then escaped from Appomattox just before Lee's surrender.

After the war Rosser spent some time in the West, where he was closely associated with George Armstrong Custer. He died March 29, 1910, in Charlottesville, Virginia.

BIBLIOGRAPHY

Beane, Thomas O. "Thomas Lafayette Rosser." *Magazine of Albemarle County History* 16 (1957–1958): 25–46.

McDonald, William N. *A History of the Laurel Brigade.* Baltimore, 1907. Reprint, Gaithersburg, Md., 1988.

Rosser, Thomas L. Papers. University of Virginia, Charlottesville.

ROBERT K. KRICK

RUFFIN, EDMUND

RUFFIN, EDMUND (1794–1865), agricultural reformer, proslavery ideologue, and Southern nationalist. Born into a prominent Tidewater Virginia planter family, Ruffin earned wide acclaim during the first half of the nineteenth century as the preeminent agricultural reformer in the Old South.

When his inherited lands on the James River proved unresponsive to traditional ameliorative practices, Ruffin, in 1818, inaugurated a series of experiments with marl, a shell-like deposit containing calcium carbonate which neutralized soil acidity and enabled sterile soils to become once again productive. When the results proved efficacious, he published his findings, first in *An Essay on Calcareous Manures* (1832) and then in his celebrated agricultural journal, the *Farmers' Register* (1833–1842). After conducting an agricultural survey of South Carolina at the request of Governor James H. Hammond, Ruffin acquired a new tract of land on the Pamunkey River, naming it appropriately Marlbourne, and proceeded to transform it into a model estate. Subsequently, he was instrumental in reviving the Virginia State Agricultural Society and was four times elected president of that body.

Upon retiring from the management of his agricultural enterprises in the mid-1850s, Ruffin turned his attention to politics. Strongly opinionated, little disposed to compromise, and sharply critical of democracy, Ruffin had eschewed

EDMUND RUFFIN. HARPER'S PICTORIAL HISTORY OF THE GREAT REBELLION

active participation in politics, serving only an abbreviated term as state senator in the 1820s. By mid-century, however, he, like many others in his class, had become alarmed by the increasingly intemperate attacks upon Southern institutions by the abolitionists and their political allies in the North. Sufficiently moderate in 1831 to have interceded on behalf of a black wrongfully accused of complicity in the Nat Turner revolt, Ruffin later assumed an inflexible proslavery posture. Convinced that slavery was the very cornerstone of Southern society and that its future could not be guaranteed within the existing Union, Ruffin became an outspoken secessionist.

Although he had adopted a secessionist stance at least as early as 1850, it was during the last four years of the antebellum period that Ruffin's crusade for disunion became most intense. Lacking the oratorical skills of fellow fire-eater William Lowndes Yancey or the political influence of Robert Barnwell Rhett, Sr., Ruffin resorted instead to personal conversation and the power of his written prose to influence the course of events. Just as he had earlier propagated the gospel of marl so now he proselytized for his dream of Southern independence. In hotel lobbies from Washington to Charleston, at Virginia summer resorts, at the Southern Commercial Convention in Montgomery, on trains and steamboats—everywhere he traveled—Ruffin was indefatigable in his effort to persuade Southerners that their only salvation lay in separate nationhood. Even more significant were his voluminous writings. In addition to numerous articles and editorials prepared for newspapers in Richmond and Charleston, these included three lengthy pamphlets and two major articles, one of them serialized in *De Bow's Review*, as well as a 426-page political novel, *Anticipations of the Future*, which had been inspired by John Brown's raid on Harpers Ferry.

Despite such herculean efforts, Ruffin appears to have had only minimal influence in effecting secession. Certainly he had little in his home state of Virginia, as he later bitterly lamented. His writings, prolific as they were, seem to have attracted little notice from the public, and his attempt in 1858, in concert with Yancey, to mobilize public opinion behind the secessionist cause through a League of United Southerners proved ineffectual. Still, he remained active and highly visible. Excited by the events at Harpers Ferry, he enlisted in the Corps of Cadets of the Virginia Military Institute for one day in order to witness the execution of Brown. Subsequently, he dispatched pikes seized from the conspirators to the governors of all slaveholding states with the injunction that they be displayed as a "sample of the favors designed for us by our Northern Brethren."

It was only after the sectional crisis reached a climax in 1860 and 1861 that Ruffin finally received the public adulation so long denied him. Although he began to receive compliments and honors wherever he traveled outside of Virginia, it was in South Carolina that he was most appreciated. When that state became the first to secede he was there to participate in the celebration, and, on the eve of Abraham Lincoln's inauguration, he again departed for Charleston, vowing never to return to his native state until it joined the Confederacy. With his destiny now bound inextricably to that of his adopted state, it was altogether fitting that the venerable Ruffin was accorded the honor of firing the first artillery shot against Fort Sumter—a distinction that, though still controversial, was recognized generally by his contemporaries on both sides.

The notoriety engendered by Ruffin's role in the Sumter engagement elevated him to the status of a popular hero in the South. Rejoining his South Carolina unit, the Palmetto Guard, in time for the Manassas campaign, the aging fire-eater once again performed symbolic military service for his beloved Confederacy, firing several artillery rounds at the fleeing Federals as they retreated over the suspension bridge at Cub Run. Plagued, however, by physical infirmities and wartime tribulations, he was soon reduced to the role of a passive observer of the momentous conflict he had helped to instigate. Family properties were pillaged during the successive Federal campaigns against Richmond, and Ruffin was compelled to seek refuge as an exile, settling eventually at Redmoor, a small farm situated about thirty-five miles west of the capital. Despite the deteriorating military situation, the increasingly embittered Ruffin remained steadfast in his commitment to the cause of Southern independence until that dream was shattered at nearby Appomattox.

With the demise of the Confederacy, Ruffin no longer had any reason to live. Despondent over the deaths of family members and his own declining health, reduced to virtual destitution by enemy depredations during the war, and fearful lest he become both a political and a pecuniary burden to his eldest son, Ruffin had long contemplated suicide. After the fall of Richmond his resolve became fixed, and for more than two months he planned methodically for the act of self-destruction, which he carried out shortly after noon on June 17, 1865. Thus did Ruffin, despite numerous reverses and disappointments, once again assume command of his own destiny. Contrary to popular belief, Ruffin did not wrap himself in a Confederate flag before firing the shot that ended his life.

BIBLIOGRAPHY

Allmendinger, David F., Jr. *Ruffin: Family and Reform in the Old South*. New York, 1990.

Allmendinger, David F., Jr., and William K. Scarborough. "The Day Ruffin Died." *Virginia Magazine of History and Biography* 97 (1989): 75–96.

Craven, Avery O. *Edmund Ruffin, Southerner: A Study in Secession*. New York, 1932. Reprint, Baton Rouge, La., 1966.

Mitchell, Betty L. *Edmund Ruffin: A Biography*. Bloomington, Ind., 1981.

Scarborough, William K., ed. *The Diary of Edmund Ruffin*. 3 vols. Baton Rouge, La., 1972–1989.

Walther, Eric H. *The Fire-Eaters*. Baton Rouge, La., 1992.

WILLIAM K. SCARBOROUGH

RULES OF WAR

Even after a full year of fighting, few officers on either side of the Civil War had more than a functional understanding of the customary principles of war and the rights of combatants and noncombatants. In April 1863, Abraham Lincoln approved General Orders No. 100 (the Lieber Code) establishing guidelines for field commanders and soldiers of the Union army, but Confederate Secretary of War James A. Seddon rejected them out of hand in June, saying they encouraged unrestricted warfare. Thereafter, although both sides continued to stake out severely conflicting theoretical interpretations of the rules of war, they in fact worked toward the middle and treated each other with a remarkable degree of civility until the summer of 1864.

The war began taking an ugly turn for the South then, but only several months after Ulysses S. Grant had changed his predecessors' strategy from attacking at various weak points to a cordon offensive that attacked along the entire southern perimeter. The Confederates, who had been so good at drawing Union forces into set piece battles at places of their choosing, were now forced onto the defensive because manpower shortages left them unable to respond effectively to broad Northern thrusts. In addition, the extensive use of rifled bores, repeating rifles, machine guns, and even flamethrowers had been exacting especially heavy tolls on Confederate formations, which were still practicing massed assaults. When this change in the North's strategic doctrine and its deployment of increasingly destructive weapons were coupled with the South's own use of land mines and guerrillas, the reasonably humane war conducted up to that point could legitimately be described as having become a total war.

Nowhere was this more evident than during Philip H. Sheridan's Shenandoah campaign in 1864, when John S. Mosby's raids so ravaged Union supply columns that Sheridan destroyed everything in his path on his way out of the valley. A few months later in November, this scorched-earth policy was repeated on the roads to Atlanta, Savannah, and Columbia (which was truly savaged) after William Tecumseh Sherman concluded—correctly, as it turned out—that subjecting Southern civilians to the psychological stresses of military action would break their will. The South had been holding on until then in the vain hope that Lincoln would be upset in November, but with his reelection, based largely on the results of Sheridan's and Sherman's campaigns, vanished what little hope remained in Richmond for reaching some accommodation with peace advocates in the North.

In effect, while total war for the North in late 1864 meant utilizing every offensive means possible, it forced the South into an almost exclusively defensive strategy that came to rely on units like Mosby's—one of the few innovative tools still left at Robert E. Lee's disposal. At this point, Confederate regiments were so depleted that strategic retaliation on a small scale was the only form of offense showing any positive returns. That many professional soldiers on either side looked with great disfavor upon the activities of Confederate and pro-Confederate guerrillas did little to inhibit these scattered, but well-led and highly imaginative groups from holding down tens of thousands of Union troops in guard duty—several thousand in Missouri alone after 1862. Since this form of combat could be so brutal, however, the South felt a certain moral obligation not to employ it in an unrestricted manner, and its generally restrained use of this alternative may well have been one reason it lost the war.

It was also during the summer campaigns of 1864 that the North hardened its view on total war after learning of the treatment of its prisoners. Few had been taken by either side in the first year of conflict, so opposing field commanders often were able to work out paroles and exchanges immediately after skirmishes that included the wounded, their chaplains, and medical personnel; but after 1862, large battles accounted for such enormous numbers of captives that more permanent structures had to be hastily built. Although conditions at Libby (Richmond, Virginia) were slightly better than average, life in Confederate prisons like Andersonville (Georgia) and Belle Isle (North Carolina) was extremely harsh at best; overcrowding and inadequate supplies of food, water, clothing, medicine, trained guards, and competent administrators led to a 15.5 percent mortality rate. Confederate prisoners, though generally better off than their Union counterparts, still lost about 12 percent of their men in camps like Elvira (New York) and Point Lookout (Maryland).

Unknown to Northern troops, however, the South could barely treat its own wounded by late 1864 because of inadequate hospital facilities. This once led Union Gen. George B. McClellan to offer medical supplies for his wounded being held by Lee. Black Union captives fared the worst, though. Confederate policy in late 1862 denying them and their white officers prisoner-of-war status led initially to their occasional summary execution in the field and to a subsequent suspension of exchanges by the Union in May 1863; but well-publicized retaliations against Confederate prisoners compelled the South, by January 1865, to offer the unrestricted exchange of all prisoners. In fact, the use of cartels for formal exchanges thrived from 1862 until Grant became general in chief in the spring of 1864 and decided that he needed his prisoners back much less than Lee needed his. Ending the cartel was a tough decision to make, but in this attempt to shorten the war, Grant may inadvertently have helped create the very conditions that led to prisons like Andersonville and Fort Delaware.

Maritime law was infinitely more formalized than the corpus of agreements dictating military conduct on land. Lincoln announced a blockade of Southern ports a week after the war began, thus ignoring the advice of U.S. Secretary of the Navy Gideon Welles, who insisted that in doing so, the president had inadvertently conferred the status of belligerency upon the Confederacy. A municipal closure of the ports to commerce would have been preferable, Welles felt, because a blockade was legal only in a time of war, and technically, this was nothing more than a domestic insurrection.

Lincoln, though, realized that a policy of port closure—or "paper blockade" in the words of British Foreign Secretary John Russell—was unenforceable and would serve only to antagonize Great Britain by completely destroying its trade with the South, while coincidentally not legally obligating the British, as neutrals, to honor the act.

Neutral crew members serving aboard neutral blockade runners that had been captured by Union ships were seldom even detained, and the penalty was confined solely to the ship and its cargo. Both were sold after a prize court determined the legitimacy of their capture, and the proceeds were divided among Union crew members. Consequently, even Confederate blockade runners were seldom harmed—and

then only if they resisted—making this form of war far less risky than what was happening on the fields of Franklin, Cold Harbor, and the Wilderness.

Following the Crimean War, the Declaration of Paris (April 1856) had established four rules that defined a blockade, abolished privateering, protected enemy goods on neutral carriers, and protected neutral goods on enemy carriers. But because it had failed to exempt from capture by privateer the private property of citizens of belligerent nations, Washington withheld its formal acceptance. After all, the United States could (and, of course, would) attain belligerent status sometime in the future and did not want the property of its subjects confiscated at sea. When Confederate privateers began terrorizing Union shipping in 1861, the Federal government debated hanging their crews as pirates, but reconsidered when faced with the certainty of reprisals by the South. Thereafter, the prosecution of privateers as civilian criminals was abandoned and they were afforded prisoner-of-war status with the same rights of parole and exchange as their landlubber colleagues.

[*See also* Blockade, *overview article;* Guerrilla Warfare; Prisoners of War; Torpedoes and Mines.]

BIBLIOGRAPHY

Beringer, Richard E., et al. *Why the South Lost the Civil War.* Athens, Ga., 1986.

Hoffman, Michael H. "The Customary Law of Non-international Armed Conflict: Evidence from the United States Civil War." *International Review of the Red Cross* 277 (July–August 1990): 322–344.

Johnson, Ludwell H. "The Confederacy: What Was It? A View from the Courts." *Civil War History* 32 (1986): 5–13.

Jones, Archer. *Civil War Command and Strategy.* New York, 1992.

McPherson, James C. *Battle Cry of Freedom.* New York, 1988.

Royster, Charles. *The Destructive War: William Tecumseh Sherman, Stonewall Jackson, and the Americans.* New York, 1991.

U.S. War Department. *War of the Rebellion: A Compilation of the Official Records of the Union and Confederate Armies.* Washington, D.C., 1880–1901. Ser. 2, vols. 3, 4, and 6.

JOHN R. CRONIN

RUST, ALBERT

RUST, ALBERT (1818–1870), congressman from Arkansas and brigadier general. Born in Virginia, Rust moved to Arkansas in 1837 and became a prominent planter, attorney, and politician in El Dorado, Union County. He was a Democrat and represented his district in the U.S. Congress for two terms (1855–1857 and 1859–1861). In 1860 he supported Stephen A. Douglas for president and urged compromise in the secession crisis. In March 1861, he resigned from

Congress and returned home. After the firing on Fort Sumter, Rust shifted his position to favor secession and joined the Confederacy.

The Arkansas secession convention adopted an ordinance of secession in its second session but selected a delegation to the Provisional Congress composed almost totally of men who had originally opposed secession. Rust, one of those chosen, went to Montgomery immediately. As a congressman, Rust was instrumental in having two companies of volunteers that had been raised in Ashley County accepted for Confederate service. He did little more in Congress before he returned to Arkansas to raise eight more companies to join the first two in July 1861, forming the Third Arkansas Infantry. Rust was elected colonel of the regiment. He participated in the Cheat Mountain campaign in the autumn and commanded the left wing of Gen. Henry Rootes Jackson's force in the Battle of Greenbrier River on October 3.

Rust left his regiment in November 1861 to attend a session of Congress at Richmond. When he returned in January 1862, Rust found his men outraged by orders to shift their winter quarters from an established camp to a new one at Romney, Virginia. Rust returned to Richmond to protest the matter to Jefferson Davis, showing a tendency to ignore the chain of command that recurred throughout his military career. Told to use proper channels, Rust resigned, but Davis appealed to him to withdraw his resignation. The president had already decided that he wanted Rust back in Arkansas to lead a brigade composed of several new regiments being raised there. Rust acceded to the president's wishes, and rather than being out of the army he found himself promoted to the rank of brigadier general.

Rust was appointed to the Army of the West and went to DeValls Bluff, Arkansas, where he assumed command of his new brigade, consisting of the Eighteenth, Nineteenth, and Twenty-second Infantry Regiments plus three battalions. He took his brigade to Corinth but then returned to Arkansas to help defend the state against an invading Federal army. Gen. Thomas C. Hindman assigned Rust to command his cavalry and sent them into the northeastern part of the state with orders to devastate the countryside and keep Gen. Samuel Curtis's column from being reinforced. In the Battle of the Cache, July 7, 1862, the Federals, moving toward the Mississippi River to secure their line of supplies, easily pushed Rust's force aside in a battle in which the Confederate units broke and ran. Hindman held Rust responsible for the poor performance of his men and also for Curtis's escape. Hindman complained in his report that General Rust had failed to carry out his assignment of destroying the countryside so that Curtis could not live off of it.

In September 1862, Rust was sent back to his old brigade, now a part of the division of Maj. Gen. John C. Breckinridge. He was with the brigade in the Battle of Corinth in October 1862 but demonstrated no particular skills as a commander. He was popular among his men, however. When a vacancy at the head of the division opened up in January 1863, the officers of his brigade petitioned President Davis for his appointment as a major general and commander of their division. But his failure at the Cache, his unexceptional leadership of his brigade, and his reputation for not getting

> **Rust acceded to the president's wishes, and rather than being out of the army he found himself promoted. . . .**

along with his senior officers ensured that he did not receive the promotion. These problems apparently limited his military career.

In March 1863, Rust seemed to have a new opportunity for promotion and a senior command when Gen. Sterling Price requested that he be reassigned to Little Rock to lead the Arkansas troops in Price's command. Price asked for Rust because he considered it important to name officers who enjoyed the confidence of the army and who would inspire hope among the people of the state. He believed Rust was such a man. In April 1863, Rust was sent to Arkansas and ordered to report to Price. Gen. E. Kirby Smith, however, wanted nothing to do with Rust. His reasons are not clear, but Smith told Theophilus H. Holmes that unless otherwise ordered by Richmond, Holmes should send Rust back to his command in Mississippi. Rust nevertheless remained in Arkansas, but he never received a command in the Trans-Mississippi Department.

In January 1864, he was sent to Texas, and Gen. John B. Magruder was asked to give him an assignment if Magruder wanted him. Once in Texas, Rust again found there was no command for him to assume. At the end of the war Rust still was listed as a part of E. Kirby Smith's force, but he was unassigned. In June 1865, Rust surrendered and was paroled at Galveston, Texas.

After the war Rust returned to Arkansas and settled at Little Rock. For a time he was active in state Republican politics. He died in Little Rock on April 3, 1870.

BIBLIOGRAPHY

Kerby, Robert L. *Kirby Smith's Confederacy: The Trans-Mississippi South, 1863–1865.* New York, 1972.

Morrow, John P., Jr. "Confederate Generals from Arkansas." *Arkansas Historical Quarterly* 21 (Autumn 1962): 240–241.

Obituary. *Arkansas Gazette* (Little Rock), April 7, 1870.

CARL H. MONEYHON

SABINE PASS, TEXAS

The pass, an outlet for both the Sabine and the Neches rivers between Jefferson County, Texas, and Cameron Parish, Louisiana, provided a suitable route for a Federal expedition planning to cut the railroad between Houston and Beaumont. On September 8, 1863, a small group of Confederates overpowered a superior Union force in its attempt to invade the Texas coast, prompting President Jefferson Davis to call the battle "one of the most brilliant and most heroic achievements in the history of warfare."

This was not the first Union assault at Sabine Pass; in September 1862 Federal troops had forced the Confederates to abandon the position, but early in 1863 Texans drove Union gunboats away, reoccupied the pass, and constructed crude earthworks. After Vicksburg and Port Hudson fell, Federal authorities decided once more to "raise the flag in Texas." The attempt was to be a combined land and sea operation under Maj. Gen. Nathaniel P. Banks and Rear Adm. David G. Farragut. At New Orleans the Federals readied four gunboats, *Sachem, Clifton, Arizona,* and *Granite City,* and ordered some five thousand men of the Nineteenth Army Corps to board navy transports. In immediate command of the expedition was Maj. Gen. William B. Franklin.

To defend the pass the Confederates had forty-two men of the First Texas Heavy Artillery at Fort Griffin, an unfinished earthwork located about two miles above the entrance to the pass. The defenders, known as the Davis Guard, were mostly Irishmen from Houston, under the command of twenty-five-year-old Lt. Richard W. ("Dick") Dowling, a successful Houston saloon keeper born in Ireland.

On the night of September 7, the Union expedition arrived off the pass; the gunboats planned to silence the fort the next day in preparation for the landing of troops. During the afternoon on September 8, *Clifton* and *Sachem* moved up the channel, but a hit from one of the six Confederate cannons disabled *Sachem;* another shell struck the boiler, causing it to explode. *Clifton* was similarly disabled, and both vessels quickly surrendered. When an officer aboard *Granite City* mistakenly reported that Southern reinforcements were arriving, Franklin ordered a general withdrawal. The fighting lasted less than an hour, but the Federal losses included two gunboats, 19 men killed, 9 wounded, 37 missing, and 315

taken prisoner. The Confederates, who fired their artillery pieces over a hundred times, sustained no injuries.

This was the most significant battle in Texas during the war, and Dowling became a hero. The stunning Southern victory caused a temporary drop in the stock prices in New York City, and the *New York Herald* credited Dowling's victory, combined with the Federal defeat at Chickamauga, with drastically lowering the nation's credit. Franklin, who headed the expedition, was ridiculed as "the first American general . . . who managed to lose a fleet in contest with land batteries alone." As a result, Banks diverted his attack to southern Texas along the Rio Grande, and Sabine Pass was not used again as a route to invade Texas.

BIBLIOGRAPHY

Barr, Alwyn. "Sabine Pass, September 1863." *Texas Military History* 2 (1962): 17–22.
Barr, Alwyn. "Texas Coastal Defense, 1861–1865." *Southwestern Historical Quarterly* 65 (July 1962): 1–31.
Drummond, John A. "The Battle of Sabine Pass." *Confederate Veteran* 25 (August 1917): 364–365. Reprint, Wilmington, N.C., 1985.
McCormack, John. "Sabine Pass." *Civil War Times Illustrated* 12 (1973): 4–9, 34–37.
Muir, Andrew Forest. "Dick Dowling and Sabine Pass." *Civil War History* 4 (December 1958): 399–428.
Tolbert, Frank X. *Dick Dowling at Sabine Pass.* New York, 1962.
Young, Jo. "The Battle of Sabine Pass." *Southwestern Historical Quarterly* 52 (1948): 398–410.

ANNE J. BAILEY

SAILORS

The introduction of steam in 1802 had caused sweeping changes in the sea services, and with the introduction of ironclad warships, navies changed forever. Sailors no longer needed to be seamen. Engineers and coal heavers were beginning to replace sailing masters. Sailmakers and boatswains, the men responsible for ships' sails and rigging, found little to do in a vessel without sails. Confederate sailors, while facing these many changes, faced others equally deadly. In vessels primarily restricted to the rivers and bays of the

South, they contended with malaria, typhus, yellow fever, and extremes of weather. Yet they still performed their duty.

From 1861 to 1865 the Confederate States Navy enlisted approximately six thousand seamen. Of these, only a small percentage were actually trained sailors. Seamen and marines were recruited at naval rendezvous and military and conscription camps throughout the South. Competition with the army deprived the navy of much-needed manpower. A fifty-dollar bounty, better pay, and better conditions prompted many to try to join the navy rather than the army, but army officers frequently refused to allow transfers to proceed.

Sailors inducted into the navy were first sent to a receiving ship, usually at the station they would serve. After being examined by a surgeon to determine their health and receiving a set of clothing, they were trained in the basic skills

> **Aboard a ship of war, regulations pertaining to the behavior of sailors . . . were strict.**

needed to run a ship of war. This was followed by a short, usually inadequate introduction to naval life, and then the men were transferred to the vessel that would be their home.

Once aboard ship the sailors were separated into two watch divisions: port and starboard. These divisions were again divided into two or three watch sections, each capable of keeping guard while in port. No more than one-sixth of the crew was allowed on liberty at any given time. Sailors were assigned berthing spaces and grouped into messes of eight to fourteen men. All unessential gear was stowed below, and the new sailors began their daily duties.

The sailor's day was separated into seven watches and regulated by the ship's bell. Following the morning watch (4:00 A.M. to 8:00 A.M.) was the forenoon watch (8:00 A.M. to 12:00 P.M.), the afternoon watch (12:00 P.M. to 4:00 P.M.), the first dogwatch (4:00 P.M. to 6:00 P.M.), the second dogwatch (6:00 P.M. to 8:00 P.M.), the evening watch (8:00 P.M. to 12:00 A.M.), and the night watch (12:00 A.M. to 4:00 A.M.). Sailors were expected to be on duty every other four hours. To ensure that the men would not stand the same watch each day, the dogwatches, each two hours in length, were used. The time for each watch was kept by the ship's bell with the first bell of the watch being struck at the end of the first half-hour and a bell added for each half-hour after that until eight bells in all were struck and the four-hour watch ended.

Reveille aboard ship was 7:00 A.M. (six bells of the morning watch). All hands were called to scrub and clean the ship, pump out the bilges, wash clothes, clean and dry the decks, polish the ship's brass, wipe down the guns, and clear the ship for inspection. Breakfast, usually two ship's biscuits (hardtack) and water, was served at 8:00 A.M. Inspection was

at 9:30 every day. Division officers examined the men for sickness, clothing deficiencies, and cleanliness and reported their findings to the executive officer. Any inadequacy was noted, and the men were required to make up their deficiency from the ship's paymaster in the case of clothing, or by seeing the ship's surgeon at sick call at 11:00 A.M.

At sick call the surgeon would examine the sailor, give him a "sick ticket," and place him on a sick list, which excused him from duty until he recovered. Chronically ill sailors were usually discharged quickly and sent home. Those wounded in the service could expect to receive the best medical attention available. All the naval surgeons and most of the assistant surgeons had to fulfill vigorous requirements and testing designed to screen out the incompetent. Most of the surgeons were from the old navy. Disabled seamen and those who recovered from a chronic illness were enlisted in the Naval Invalid Corps and given shore duty and half pay.

Deficiencies in clothing resulted in the sailor being issued new garments, with his pay account debited to reflect the purchase. Clothing prices could range from fifteen dollars to as little as fifty cents. A landsman's pay was sixteen dollars a month. Because the initial uniform purchase could cost as much as ninety-seven dollars, it took a new sailor a little over six months to pay for his uniform. After deducting their clothing issue from their pay, many sailors were left with no money, sometimes for the entire war. Pay for sailors was infrequent and usually inadequate. They could have an allotment sent home, but they were expected to keep six dollars for themselves to pay any debts incurred. A seaman could commute his unused spirit ration of four cents per day to supplement his pay, but it was seldom enough. Families of seamen often had insufficient funds and were faced with much hardship. In order to supplement their income, some sailors sold parts of their uniforms to civilians, a practice so rampant by 1864 that the Navy Department instructed officers to forbid it.

Shoes were of great importance in a navy powered by steam. Men on sailing vessels, who climbed rigging and worked sails, could go barefoot, but standing watch on ironclads and steamships required shoes. Fire and engine rooms and the decks adjacent to them became very hot, and conversely, in winter the iron armor was often covered by a thin layer of ice. The navy never solved the problem of shoes and clothing. By November 1864 the men of the James River Squadron were standing watch on freezing decks without shoes, coats, or blankets. And in December when Savannah fell, the seamen of the Savannah Squadron had to leave their belongings on the ships, which were scuttled. The Navy Department could not replace their lost clothing, and the men suffered much hardship on their march to Drewry's Bluff and the Appomattox campaign.

Formal duties aboard ship began at 11:00 A.M. with the crew, excluding those on watch, drilling on the use of heavy artillery, small arms, light artillery, or cutlasses and pistols. The division on watch worked the vessel and did a visual inspection of every line, sheet, sail, and seam to ensure that the ship was in operating condition. Lookouts were posted to watch for enemy warships, signals from the squadron's commander, and approaching vessels. All guns and gun carriages were inspected for any defects and repaired if necessary. In port or on a river defense vessel, sailors spent a great deal of time coaling the ship, loading firewood and provisions, transporting officers to the commander of the fleet in the ship's launch, and, especially during the summer months and to the sailors' consternation, taking visitors on trips in the ship's small boats.

Most jobs aboard ship were performed by gangs. Each warrant officer had a gang of men working for him. The carpenter's gang repaired the wooden parts of the vessel, including masts and spars. The gunner's gang inspected the ship's cannons, powder, cartridges, small arms ammunition, and signaling flares to ensure their serviceability. The boatswain's gang saw to the maintenance of the ropes, lines, sheets, and rigging. The sailmaker's gang repaired and maintained the ship's sails and awnings. The armorer's gang inspected the ship's small arms, rifles, pistols, revolvers, cutlasses, pikes, and swords and kept them in good condition.

Each petty officer was assigned a specific area or task to perform. To aid them, a "quarter-bill," or watch bill, was posted telling each sailor where to report to work. Some petty officers also had gangs. The master-at-arms, the ship's policeman, and his gang supervised the sailors being punished, kept discipline, and enforced the Articles of War. The captain-of-the-hold, a seaman, and his gang saw to the proper storage of supplies and the rotation of empty casks and containers. Improper storage could reduce the ship's speed, increase the ship's draft, or cause the vessel to handle poorly. The captain-of-the-tops, another seaman, and his gang inspected the topmasts of the vessel and made any repairs that were needed. Some duties could require the whole crew. If a gun carriage was found defective or the ship had to be coaled, the entire crew could be called to work under the direction of an officer until the job was completed.

At noon the crew was called to dinner, the largest meal of the day and the only one served hot. It usually consisted of meat, rice, beans, and bread. Sailors on the river squadrons could expect fresh meat and vegetables three times a week; those at sea got fresh meat and vegetables only while in port or from captured prizes. Although the acquisition of provisions at sea was precarious, men on the cruisers seemed to eat better than their counterparts at home. The portions of the meals as established by the Navy Department were much larger than those of soldiers. Each sailor was to receive $1/2$ pound of meat, $1/2$ cup of rice, $1/2$ cup of beans, a $1/4$ pound of bread a day. These rations were supplemented by fresh vegetables, fowl, oysters, fish, molasses, spirits, and condi-

ments. By pooling the men's rations, messes could provide a rather large meal. Monies specified for the mess but not used could purchase pepper, salt, mustard, and other spices and small stores from the paymaster. Menus were decided by the commanding officer, and the ship's cook drew rations from the steward. In 1864 the Navy Department cut the daily rations because, it was thought, the sailors were growing too fat. For the sake of morale it was decided that the navy's rations should be more in line with those of the army. The navy was then placed under the army's Commissary Department for provisions.

Afternoons were spent drilling, maintaining the ship, and finishing work begun in the morning. The only free time allowed the men was after the 6:00 P.M. roll call and supper. This was traditionally the time when sailors could freely talk, smoke, sing, or otherwise entertain themselves. Ships in port or on rivers usually allowed those not on duty to go ashore on a four-hour liberty. Sailors at Savannah, Charleston, and Richmond visited playhouses, taverns, and other centers of entertainment. Those who had not returned to their vessels by 11:00 P.M. could be punished for being late. All lights were ordered out by 8:00 P.M. (9:00 P.M. in the summer), signaling the end of the workday.

Sailors kept the evening and night watches on picket boats and in remote areas along rivers and streams, leaving the ship at nightfall and returning at daybreak. Naval pickets listened for Federal gunboats, launches, or infantry movements, working in conjunction with the army and supplementing the land forces performing the same duty. Because of the close proximity to Federal troops, many desertions occurred among those on picket duty.

Aboard a ship of war, regulations pertaining to the behavior of sailors and marines were strict. Unauthorized talking was not permitted, nor were sailors allowed to stand on the quarterdeck or bridge unless on watch or performing a specific duty. Officers' country, usually the stern of the vessel, was prohibited to enlisted men. Sailors of high rank, petty officers and warrant officers, were accorded some privileges. They ate separately from the rest of the crew, and their quarters were forward of the main mast or the forecastle. Sailors of lower rank were quartered aft of the main mast and were allowed only hammocks. Rules and regulations were posted and read weekly to the crew. Infractions were punished by anything from simple fines to courts-martial. Serious offenses, such as striking an officer or desertion, were punishable by death, although most sentences of this type were commuted by President Jefferson Davis.

Crews serving aboard ironclad warships and the Torpedo Battery Service had to brave the elements as well as work in temperatures that could reach 140 degrees. Ironclads were dark, damp, leaky, and poorly ventilated vessels that caused more deaths in the naval services than did combat. Because of the crowded conditions, men were prone to pulmonary diseases as well as other maladies. Disease in these ships was difficult to control, and sailors often were quartered ashore in warehouses where they could breathe fresh air. Those in the Torpedo Service spent most of their time in small boats or on shore. The task of building and placing torpedoes required constant attention, and sailors performing this service were usually detached from other duty.

Battle aboard the Confederate warship was much like that in the Federal navy. Sailors were detailed to specific duties at the guns and also assigned to "trimming" parties for operating the sails, boarding parties, fire parties, and powder divisions. The call to battle was sounded by the beat of a drum followed by two rolls. Rapid ringing of the ship's bell signaled a fire. Orders were passed verbally by the petty officers and boatswain. Marines were stationed at strategic places on the heavy guns and on the bridge to direct rifle fire at enemy officers. Aboard ironclads, the only personnel exposed to the enemy were the pilot and the captain; all others were protected by the heavy armor. With the advent of ironclads and rifled cannon, the importance of boarding parties decreased. Any need to board an enemy ship was far outweighed by the danger, for the common practice to repel boarders was for every ship in the fleet to fire on the boarded vessel. Boarders were used a few times, however, with positive results. The Confederate cutting-out expedition to board and capture USS *Waterwitch* in Ossabaw Sound, Georgia, in 1864 ended in the capture of a Federal warship; it was one of two successful attempts at boarding an enemy vessel during the war.

Confederate sailors and marines served with distinction for four years. Their lives were no less hard than those of their comrades in the army. Although they were few in number, their role was vital to the war effort. By keeping the ports open for much-needed supplies, the sailors of the Confederate navy enabled the army to fight as long as it did.

[*See also* Marine Corps; Navy, *particularly articles on* Confederate Navy *and* Manpower; Uniforms, *articles on* Navy *and* Marine Uniforms.]

BIBLIOGRAPHY

Chapelle, Howard I. *The History of the American Sailing Navy: The Ships and their Development.* New York, 1949.

Confederate States Navy Department. *Regulations for the Navy of the Confederate States of America.* Richmond, Va., 1862.

Donnelly, Ralph W. *The Confederate States Marine Corps: The Rebel Leathernecks.* Shippingham, Pa., 1989.

Durkin, Joseph T. S. J. *Confederate Navy Chief Stephen R. Mallory.* Columbia, S.C., 1954.

Scales, Dabney, Midshipman, C.S.N. Unpublished Diary, 1863. Savannah River Squadron Papers. Emory University Manuscript Collection, Atlanta, Ga.

Upton, Commander U. P. *Manual of Internal Rules and Regulations for Men of War.* New York, 1862.

Watson, Thomas, Seaman. Unpublished diary, 1864–1865. Collections of the Coastal Heritage Society. Savannah, Ga.

Wells, Thomas H. *The Confederate Navy: A Study in Organization.* Tuscaloosa, Ala., 1971.

JOHN W. KENNINGTON, JR.

SALT

This mineral was vital to the civilian population as well as the military forces of the Confederacy. In an era with no reliable method of refrigeration, salt was the primary means of preserving meat. In addition, salt was used to pack cheese and eggs and preserve hides during leather making, as well as being employed in numerous chemical processes, various medications, and livestock dietary supplements.

Prior to the war, the Southern states had bought much of their salt from the North or imported it from Europe. Once the war started, the Confederacy had to develop internal sources for its requirements. The primary areas for salt production were Great Kanawha River near Charleston, West Virginia; Goose Creek near Manchester, Kentucky; southwest Alabama; Avery Island, Louisiana; and southwest Virginia. Salt was also produced along the Confederate seacoast. The largest industry to develop in Florida, during the war, was salt making.

Several of these locations (in West Virginia, Kentucky, and Louisiana) were captured early in the war. By 1863, most of the Confederacy's salt, especially for those states east of the Mississippi, was being produced at the Stuart, Buchanan & Co. saltworks in Saltville, Virginia. In 1864, thirty-eight furnaces containing over 2,600 kettles were producing about 4 million bushels of salt per year at just this one saltworks.

There were three methods of producing salt in the 1860s: extracting it from brine wells, extracting it from seawater or inland salt ponds, and mining deposits of rock salt. The process for extracting salt from seawater and brine wells was the same—evaporation. At Saltville, the brine was pumped from a well by steam engine and transported to furnaces through wooden pipes. After the water had evaporated, the crystallized salt was placed in split baskets to dry and then stored in bulk.

Federal forces did not allow salt manufacturing to continue unchallenged. The navy raided coastal salt makers, especially along the Florida coast, and the army made a point of destroying all saltworks in its path.

In the fall of 1864, Federal cavalry made two raids against the Saltville saltworks. In October, the Federals were unsuccessful, and following the battle over one hundred captured black troops were killed by Confederate soldiers. This was one of the war's worst massacres. In December, the Federals were able to capture and temporarily put the saltworks out of operation.

Each Confederate state had its own salt commissioner or agent, who acquired salt from the available sources and then passed it along to local agents for public distribution. Although resources were sufficient to provide all the salt needed, there were shortages throughout the war, especially for civilians. Causes for these shortages included the blockade, speculation and corruption, and inadequate transportation. These shortages, however, were never severe enough to cause serious problems for the army. Lucius B. Northrop, commissary-general, stated on January 25, 1865, that "the supply of salt has always been sufficient and the Virginia works were able to meet the demand for the army."

BIBLIOGRAPHY

Johns, John E. *Florida during the Civil War.* Gainesville, Fla., 1963.
Lonn, Ella. *Salt as a Factor in the Confederacy.* University, Ala., 1965.
Rachal, William M. E. "Salt the South Could Not Savor." *Virginia Cavalcade,* Autumn 1953.

MICHAEL E. HOLMES

SALTPETER

Known to the Confederates as niter, this mineral, potassium nitrate (KNO_3), was crucial to the Confederate war effort because it comprised about 75 percent of the gunpowder used. (The other ingredients were about 12.5 percent sulphur and 12.5 percent charcoal.) Although some saltpeter had been mined in the United States for local use since before the War of 1812, most was imported. The Union blockade forced the Confederacy to consider other sources of the mineral, although substantial importation, both by sea and from Mexico, continued throughout the war.

Three possible domestic saltpeter sources were available to the Confederates: limestone caves, residue under old buildings, and artificial niter beds. Caves with appropriate mineral and climatic conditions for the natural production of saltpeter could be found primarily in the foothills of Tennessee, Georgia, Arkansas, Virginia, and Alabama, areas that tended to be occupied by Union troops fairly early in the war. The Sauta Cave in Jackson County, Alabama, and a cave near Kingston in Bartow County, Georgia, were among the most famous and productive of the sites.

The dirt under old buildings, tobacco barns, stables, outhouses, and manure piles could also bear saltpeter, but mining these sources required the cooperation of private citizens. A potentially more reliable source of the mineral was the artificial manufacture of saltpeter in niter beds. These beds were composed of heaps of earth, manure, rotted vegetable matter, and other waste products, which were careful-

ly tended, moistened with urine, and turned over for a considerable period of time to produce a coating of the mineral. Although the Confederates were able to procure some saltpeter by this method, most of the niter beds, established in "nitriaries" near the major cities, were not mature enough by the time the war ended to produce to their full capacity. In all cases of mining and manufacturing, the raw product was still primarily dirt and had to go through a leaching and refining process before the saltpeter could be used in gunpowder.

The Confederate Niter and Mining Bureau, headed by Isaac M. St. John, supervised the collection and production of saltpeter, sponsoring a number of mining ventures and the thirteen or more nitriaries. But the government also encouraged private citizens to manufacture saltpeter and published pamphlets by George W. Rains and Joseph LeConte to instruct the novice in the proper procedures.

Although complete records for the bureau do not exist, those available indicate that private and government manufacturing had produced 1,735,531.75 pounds of saltpeter and that 1,720,072 pounds had been imported by September 30, 1864.

[*See also* Niter and Mining Bureau.]

BIBLIOGRAPHY

Donnelly, Ralph W. "The Bartow County Confederate Saltpetre Works." *Georgia Historical Quarterly* 54 (1970): 305–319.
LeConte, Joseph. *Instructions for the Manufacture of Saltpetre.* Columbia, S.C., 1862.
Rains, George W. *Notes on Making Saltpetre from the Earth of Caves.* Augusta, Ga., 1861.
Schroeder, Glenna R. "'We Will Support the Govt. to the Bitter End': The Augusta Office of the Confederate Nitre and Mining Bureau." *Georgia Historical Quarterly* 70 (1986): 288–305.
Smith, Marion O. "The Sauta Cave Confederate Niter Works." *Civil War History* 29 (1983): 293–315.

GLENNA R. SCHROEDER-LEIN

SAVANNAH, GEORGIA

[*This entry includes two articles,* City of Savannah, *which profiles the city during the Confederacy, and* Savannah Campaign, *which discusses the capture of the city in 1864. See also* Fort Pulaski, Georgia; Savannah Squadron.]

City of Savannah

Many of the commercial interests of antebellum Georgia revolved around Savannah, the state's largest city, which enjoyed the benefits of a commercial and demographic boom in the years prior to 1860. Its population in 1860 totaled nearly 23,000, having doubled during these preceding two decades. The city attracted rural Georgians and South Carolinians, ambitious Northerners, and a growing number of foreign-born. The 1860 census counted 4,696 foreign-born individuals among a white population of 13,875; three in every four of these came from Ireland. The ethnic mix also included 705 free blacks and 7,712 slaves.

Commercial expansion drew most of these people to Savannah. Railroad connections between the port and the Georgia interior, completed in 1843, directed the state's growing output of cotton and lumber through the port at Savannah to customers throughout Europe and the northern United States. The value of Savannah's exports leapt from $6 million in 1840 to $18 million in 1860. In the last year of the Union, half a million bales of cotton and 40 million board feet

> ... in December, citizens broke out "secession cockades" made from Palmetto leaves.

of lumber left the state by way of Savannah. Slave labor produced these commodities, giving the city a powerful economic as well as social stake in the preservation of slavery. But worry over the safety of its trade connections figured along with the security of slavery in shaping Savannah's reactions to the crisis of 1860.

On November 8 of that year, over 3,000 citizens gathered at the Masonic Hall to the accompaniment of brass bands, fireworks, and bonfires. They heard speakers denounce the election of Abraham Lincoln and approved the formation of a vigilance committee to enforce public support for Southern resistance to the Republican regime in Washington. Julian Hartridge, their representative in the Georgia Assembly, offered resolutions condemning the election results and calling for steps "to alleviate any unusual embarrassment of the commercial interest of the state consequent upon the present political emergency."

When the news of South Carolina's secession reached the city in December, citizens broke out "secession cockades" made from palmetto leaves; they wore them to almost nightly public meetings throughout the Christmas season in the downtown public squares. The people raised a platform in front of the statue of Revolutionary hero Nathaniel Greene, in Johnson Square, and decorated it with placards depicting rattlesnakes with the legend, "Don't tread on me!" The trio of local notables who represented Savannah at the state secession convention in January 1861 had plenty of evidence of the public's opinion on the question.

A few merchants saw the municipal situation differently. Secession meant war, they believed, and war meant the disruption of trade. By diverting capital and labor resources, armed conflict would, at the least, diminish the supply of export commodities upon which the city's prosperity rested. Even before the firing on Fort Sumter, local merchants remarked on the decline of business activity as customers at home and abroad waited to see what would happen. The leaders of Savannah, as war approached, sought ways to balance their patriotic duty to the South with personal and municipal well-being—objectives that, in the course of the conflict, grew increasingly incompatible.

At first the priorities were clear enough. Even before secession, the city worried about its defense needs. The city council voted immediately after the presidential election to buy ammunition for the city's nine volunteer militia companies. The public, believing Savannah a primary target in any military showdown, badgered authorities for troops, weapons, and funds for its defense. The state government responded even before secession became official. On January 3, 1861, local militia authorized by Governor Joseph E. Brown seized nearby Fort Pulaski, which commanded the river passage from Savannah to the Atlantic. (In this action they overpowered and captured a garrison consisting of one elderly Federal sergeant.) By the end of the month local forces had also taken over the Oglethorpe Barracks and Fort Jackson. Fort Pulaski was garrisoned with 400 troops, Fort Jackson with 120. State and local militia used both facilities to acclimate new recruits to military discipline and camp life.

Georgia seceded from the Union on January 16, 1861, and in the following month joined the Confederacy. Savannah's citizens elected Francis S. Bartow to represent them in the First Congress, but he resigned on May 1 to join the Oglethorpe Light Infantry in Virginia. Governor Brown attacked Bartow for leaving the state without authorization, a charge Bartow dismissed with contempt, denying that he needed the state's permission to defend his country. Bartow was killed at Manassas on July 21, 1861, becoming Savannah's first war hero. His clash with Brown presaged the tug of war over troops and materials between the state of Georgia and the Confederacy that would last throughout the war.

Savannah for the most part took the more cosmopolitan view of the Confederacy in this matter. The city's nine volunteer militia companies went to Virginia as the First Volunteer Regiment of Georgia, despite efforts to persuade them to stay home. In April 1861, the War Department appointed Alexander R. Lawton brigadier general and commander at Savannah, charged with the defense of the city and the coastal region. Lawson oversaw the garrisoning of the forts along the coast and the construction of works in the rivers that cut through the district. Meanwhile, Brown tried to prevent the departure of the Georgia Hussars for the Virginia front by declaring their equipment state property and forbidding them to take it out of Georgia. In order to leave for the front without interference from the governor, the Hussars spent $25,000 of their own money on horses and weapons.

In November 1861, the public's fears for the safety of Savannah suddenly took on a new urgency. Federal forces captured Port Royal at the beginning of the month and by November 25 moved onto Tybee Island as well. Union troops threatened the mouth of the Savannah River from these positions, and artillery they installed on Tybee jeopardized local defensive installations. Robert E. Lee, commander of the Department of South Carolina, Georgia, and Florida since November 1861, responded by designing a network of defenses around the city's exterior perimeter to be built by squads of soldiers and slaves. Lee left for Virginia in March 1862 before the new works were finished. Within a few weeks, Fort Pulaski fell to the rifled cannon of Tybee Island. Its commander, Col. Charles Olmstead, surrendered the fort on April 11, 1862, after a bombardment that rattled windows in downtown Savannah and rendered Pulaski indefensible. His decision, taken on humanitarian as well as practical grounds, was extremely unpopular in the city. After the fall of Fort Pulaski, Savannah was cut off from its conventional outlet to the Atlantic. Civilian authorities debated the wisdom of abandoning the city, and in May, Gen. John C. Pemberton seriously recommended that the city council evacuate women and children, declare martial law, and demolish the buildings along the forty-foot bluff that raises Savannah above the banks of the river so that heavy artillery could be installed to defend the position. The Georgia Assembly contributed to the deliberations a call for house-to-house resistance, if necessary.

In fact, by May 1862, the issue of whether and how to defend Savannah was moot. With the fall of Fort Pulaski the city was too vulnerable to serve as a base for blockade running, shipbuilding, or any other strategically significant enterprises. The Confederate government recognized this and moved its Savannah arsenal to Macon in May. An effective Federal naval blockade rendered any direct attack on the city superfluous. Union Gen. David Hunter thought 30,000 troops held Savannah (the accurate figure as of June was 13,000) and elected not to challenge them. Fort McAllister, at the mouth of the Ogeechee River south of town, came under sporadic shelling during that tense summer, but it, and the city, stayed in Southern hands until William Tecumseh Sherman arrived two years later.

The blockade and the immediacy of the Federal threat certainly damaged the local economy. At the beginning of the war Governor Brown prohibited cotton exports, on the theory that the resulting cotton famine would hasten European intervention on behalf of the Confederacy. By 1863, when that prospect had faded, Brown switched to a policy promoting exports to raise needed money and goods, but by then the blockade had minimized the profits in trade. During the first half of 1862 no export fees were collected at Savannah, and import duties totaled only $112.92. The export trade did not rebound until after the war ended.

Other business activity also fell off sharply during the war. Industrial enterprise in support of the war effort was never extensive. Henry F. Willink operated one of the Confederacy's largest shipyards during the first year of fighting, and the Central Railroad's shops were used to manufacture gun carriages and rifled cannon for state and Confederate forces. But after spring 1862, neither the state nor the Confederacy permitted any essential production to continue, since Federal troops were so near.

By 1862 the most pressing economic concerns in Savannah revolved around the problems of inflation and scarcity. Disruption of the import trade, the region's loss of personnel to the armed forces, and the military's demand combined to create commodity shortages that hit the population especially hard. Fresh vegetables, wheat, beef, and dairy products, together with imports like coffee and sugar, practically vanished from local groceries. By 1862 clothing, shoes, and salt had become all but impossible to buy. The scarcity drove prices to unthinkable levels. In October 1863, consumers paid $1.50 for a dozen eggs, $5.00 to $6.00 for a pound of butter, and up to $100 for eight bushels of sweet potatoes. Rumors about hoarding accompanied the rising prices. George Mercer, son of Confederate Gen. Hugh Weedon Mercer, was one of many who blamed it on "sordid speculators, composed chiefly of German Jews, of aliens, of Yankees." In 1863 the city council set up a municipal store to combat inflation, promising to keep prices reasonable. But the scarcities driving prices up were real, not the result of conspiracy.

These pressures highlighted two critical social problems. The business collapse and induction of thousands of wage earners into the military left families all over the city with diminished income or none at all. The city government recognized the problem almost immediately. On May 27, 1861, a public meeting organized a system to gather donations and distribute them to needy military dependents, but by the following February, this fund was exhausted. During 1862 the city spent almost $23,000 on food and fuel for the destitute, and the following March, six banks lent the city $55,000 without interest to help the poor. Sometimes aid took other forms. The city council threatened to publish the names of landlords who evicted soldiers' families for delinquent rent in 1863. Apparently the prospect of publicity had the desired effect. But the problems of food and fuel, complicated by inflation and dwindling municipal resources, persisted.

The other problem exacerbated by wartime conditions was ethnic antagonism among whites. Some conflicts predated the outbreak of war. Irish and German workers had spearheaded a campaign in the 1850s to exclude slaves and free blacks from the skilled crafts. In January 1861, while most citizens were talking secession and war, the city's master bootmakers resolved "that we will not contract to employ, hire, or learn any Negro the boot-making business from this date." Similar disputes left relations between immigrant craftspeople and slaveholding interests strained. When the war began, trouble developed over the reluctance of many European-born men to be drafted into the military. When the first Conscription Act passed in 1862, hundreds of aliens in Savannah signed affadavits denying they had ever had any intention of becoming citizens; as aliens, of course, they were exempt from the draft. While Charleston was under Federal attack in July 1863, Mayor Thomas Holcombe refused to issue passes to 30 foreigners desiring to leave town. That December, another 120 aliens forswore any plans to become citizens. Other residents reacted bitterly to what seemed, to many, no more than a combination of cowardice and avarice. In fact, when the war started, hundreds of immigrants enlisted either individually or through such ethnically based militia units as the Irish Jasper Greens. But the public's perception held that immigrants, along with Northern business types, represented Savannah's worst "internal security problem." Another vigilance committee appeared late in the war to enforce loyalty and encourage enrollments in the military.

In the long run, the effect of the war on slavery represented a far more serious threat to the status quo. The military challenged the principle of owners' control over slave property by trying repeatedly to draft slaves for work on the defensive fortifications. Slave owners fought such efforts, claiming their slaves were irreplaceable and risked injury when they worked for the army. Hazards notwithstanding, the slaveholders' were really supporting the autonomy of private property when they refused to let slaves help defend slavery. Slave discipline broke down as the war continued. Between 1862 and 1864, the number of mayor's court cases involving slave defendants increased by 400 percent. The number of slaves jailed, despite owners' protests on their behalf, grew

> **The public's perception held that immigrants, along with Northern business types, represented Savannah's worst "internal security problem."**

by 50 percent. To replace these hands became a more expensive proposition as inflation affected the purchase price and hire rates of slaves along with the costs of commodities. And slaves did not necessarily feel any need to stand by their troubled owners. In 1863, a boatload of slaves trying to escape to Fort Pulaski drowned when their boat capsized in the Savannah River. Others, as persistent complaints indicated, were more successful.

The war ended for Savannah when Sherman arrived on December 21, 1864, but its consequences continued to be felt. Military action had eroded the property that citizens had

fought to protect. Now Union soldiers reported mobs of looters in the streets. Federal soldiers promptly dispersed these and set up a military government that earned the citizens' respect for its fairness and commitment to order. Civilians, relieved that the city had been spared bombardment, cooperated with Sherman's program to appropriate privately held provisions for the relief of the needy. Federal soldiers observed that black citizens regularly sought interviews with the Union commander to pledge their loyalty and offer their assistance to the occupying force. George Mercer was not the only resident to view this and other "social changes that progress[ed] with the revolution" uneasily. Still, if the people went into the war with enthusiasm, they came out with a sense of relief. Sherman offered the city a chance to recover, and by the end of 1864, Savannah was glad to have it.

BIBLIOGRAPHY

Gamble, Thomas, Jr., comp. *A History of the City Government of Savannah, Ga., from 1790 to 1901.* Savannah, Ga., 1900.
Griffin, J. David. "Benevolence and Malevolence in Confederate Savannah." *Georgia Historical Quarterly* 49 (1965): 347–368.
Harden, William. *A History of Savannah and South Georgia.* 2 vols. Chicago, 1913.
Jones, Charles C., O. F. Vedder, and Frank Weldon. *History of Savannah, Ga.* Syracuse, N.Y., 1890.
Lawrence, Alexander A. *A Present for Mr. Lincoln: The Story of Savannah from Secession to Sherman.* Macon, Ga., 1961.
Mohr, Clarence L. *On the Threshold of Freedom, Masters and Slaves in Civil War Georgia.* Athens, Ga., 1986.
Myers, Robert Manson, ed. *The Children of Pride: A True Story of Georgia and the Civil War.* New Haven, 1972.
Nichols, George Ward. *The Story of the Great March, From the Diary of a Staff Officer.* New York, 1865.

EDWARD M. SHOEMAKER

Savannah Campaign

Gen. William Tecumseh Sherman with an army of some 60,000 veterans departed Atlanta for Savannah with twenty days of rations on November 15, 1864. The right wing was commanded by Gen. O. O. Howard and the left by Gen. Henry W. Slocum; two cavalry brigades were commanded by Gen. Hugh H. Kilpatrick. Violating standard military procedure by operating without a line of communications and supply, the army had to forage across the state, and supplies were running low when Sherman arrived at Savannah on December 10.

Upon Sherman's approach, Gen. William J. Hardee, commanding 10,000 troops at Savannah, skillfully took advantage of the terrain to concentrate his primary defenses two and a half miles west of the city on a peninsula about thirteen miles wide, which was flanked on the north by the Savannah

River and on the south by the Little Ogeechee River. Hardee ordered his men to construct earthen redoubts and emplace heavy artillery along this line; then they flooded the rice fields to the front. The right of the line was commanded by Maj. Gen. Gustavus W. Smith, the center by Maj. Gen. Lafayette McLaws, and the left by Maj. Gen. Ambrose Ransom Wright. Hardee relied on Confederate gunboats on the Savannah River to protect northern Savannah and his army. Gen. P. G. T. Beauregard had ordered him to evacuate the city, if necessary.

The only major fortification not linked directly with Savannah's defenses was Fort McAllister at the mouth of the Ogeechee River, about sixteen miles south of the city. It was here that Sherman decided to attack to open a sea route for the resupply of his army.

General Sherman ordered Brig. Gen. William B. Hazen's division of the Fifteenth Corps to take Fort McAllister. Maj. George W. Anderson, Jr., commanding 250 Confederates in the sand and timber fortification, had planted abatis and mines around the fort. On December 13, they were surprised by an attack from the landside by 4,300 troops under Hazen's command. The defenders fought hand to hand until they were overwhelmed by superior numbers. Twenty-four Union officers and men were killed and 110 wounded. The Confederates had 1 officer and 15 men killed, and 54 wounded; 17 officers and 178 enlisted men were taken prisoner.

General Hardee now decided to evacuate the city. Confederate engineers began building a pontoon bridge across the Savannah River to Hutchinson Island, a distance of about one thousand feet; next the engineers laid temporary spans across the Middle and Back Rivers to the shore of South Carolina. Joseph Wheeler and his cavalry kept open the line of retreat, which was threatened by Federal forces.

On December 17 Sherman formally demanded the surrender of the city. When Hardee refused, Sherman ordered an attack to begin in three days. But after dark on December 20 Confederate forces around the city spiked their guns and began withdrawing over the pontoon bridges. By the following morning Hardee's army had safely crossed into South Carolina.

Although disappointed that the army had escaped, Sherman was pleased that his troops had captured over two hundred artillery pieces, large quantities of ammunition, and thirty thousand bales of cotton with minimal loss of personnel. He had also ended his March to the Sea and established a supply base. General Sherman presented Savannah to President Abraham Lincoln as a Christmas present.

BIBLIOGRAPHY

Durham, Roger S. "Savannah: Mr. Lincoln's Christmas Present." *Blue and Gray Magazine*, February 1991.
Hughes, Nathaniel C., Jr. *General William J. Hardee: Old Reliable.* Baton Rouge, La., 1965.
Lawrence, Alexander A. *A Present for Mr. Lincoln: The Story of Savannah from Secession to Sherman.* Macon, Ga., 1961.

WALTER J. FRASER, JR.

SAVANNAH SQUADRON

In March 1861 three small wooden gunboats, *Savannah, Sampson,* and *Resolute,* armed with one 32-pounder smoothbore each, were turned over to the Confederate government by the state of Georgia. The vessels had composed the Georgia State Navy created shortly after Georgia seceded. In the Confederate navy they were designated the Savannah Squadron with Capt. Josiah Tattnall as flag officer. The squadron was concentrated on the Savannah River until the fall of 1861 when a powerful Union amphibious force threatened Port Royal, South Carolina. Tattnall shifted his small force, reinforced by the gunboat *Lady Davis* from Charleston, through the sounds and waterways to Port Royal, but his efforts were futile. The small Confederate squadron was forced to retire hastily by the fleet of Flag Officer Samuel DuPont. Port Royal was captured by the Federal force.

The threat to Savannah persuaded the Confederate Navy Department to reinforce the Savannah Squadron. In November 1861 two 150-foot wooden gunboats were laid down on the Savannah River; four months later three additional vessels 112 feet in length were contracted for. Only one of the larger class, *Macon,* and one of the smaller class, *Isondiga,* were completed. The others were unfinished primarily because of the navy's decision to concentrate on building ironclads. In March 1862 the large armored vessel *Georgia* was laid down; the 250-foot warship armed with ten naval guns was completed in the fall of 1862. Because her motive power was incapable of moving the vessel, she was moored in the river to guard the channel approaches to the port.

Shortly after *Georgia* joined the squadron, a second ironclad was completed. *Atlanta* was converted from the iron-hulled blockade runner *Fingal.* In July 1863 *Atlanta* attempted to leave the river and attack Union blockaders in the sounds. Steaming down river, she ran aground, came under fire from two monitors, and surrendered.

In the summer of 1863 a third ironclad, the 150-foot *Savannah,* joined the squadron. Two additional ironclads were laid down in Savannah but never completed.

The Savannah Squadron cooperated with the land fortifications in defending the river approaches to Savannah. In December 1864, however, the city was captured by Gen. William Tecumseh Sherman's army from the west. The ships in the squadron were destroyed by their crews after covering the withdrawal of Confederate troops to South Carolina.

[*See also* Savannah, Georgia.]

BIBLIOGRAPHY

Scharf, J. Thomas. *History of the Confederate States Navy.* New York, 1887. Reprint, New York, 1977.
Still, William N., Jr. *Savannah Squadron.* Savannah, Ga., 1989.

WILLIAM N. STILL, JR.

SECESSION

The formal withdrawal of individual states from the Federal Union created at the Constitutional Convention of 1787 occurred in two distinct phases of separate state actions. The first took the seven states of the lower South out of the Union by February 1, 1861. This phase, triggered by Abraham Lincoln's election in November 1860, started when South Carolina withdrew on December 20, 1860. When Lincoln responded to the Confederate firing on Fort Sumter in April 1861 by calling upon the states to furnish seventy-five thousand militia to put down the Southern "insurrection," four additional states from the upper South left in the second phase of secession. These states—Virginia, North Carolina, Tennessee, and Arkansas—rounded out the political dimensions of the new Southern Confederacy. The other four slave states of Missouri, Kentucky, Maryland, and Delaware in the border South remained within the Union (the Confederacy claimed Missouri and Kentucky as member states, and both were represented in the Confederate Congress).

Secession rested on the constitutional doctrine of state sovereignty. According to this state rights position, the Union of 1787 was a confederation of sovereign states. The Federal government was simply the agent of the states entrusted with certain specified and limited powers. The individual states retained ultimate sovereign power, and they could leave the Union the same way they had entered it by calling a special state convention. Contrary to this view, most Northerners believed by 1860 that the Union was sovereign and perpetual. The states had surrendered their individual sovereignty when they joined the Union, and the legal right of secession did not exist. Far from residing within the Constitution, secession was a revolutionary act of defiance directed against the Constitution and the Union it had created.

The debate over the legal nature of the Union was as old as the Union itself. Both sides could turn to the Constitution for confirmation of their respective views because of its studied ambiguity over the ultimate locus of sovereign power in the Union. Such ambiguity was necessary in order to provide for a middle constitutional position that could blur the sharp differences between nationalists and state righters at the Philadelphia Convention. The Founding Fathers were able to secure the ratification of the Constitution only by agreeing to set up a Federal system in which power was divided and shared between the central government and the state governments.

Early Sectional Crises

The looseness of the Federal system left plenty of room for Jeffersonian Republicans and Hamiltonian Federalists to jockey for power in the early Republic. Although the Hamiltonians were associated with a broad construction of the Constitution and the Jeffersonians with a strict one, the slaveholding Virginia presidents during the era of Democratic-Republican dominance from 1802 to 1824 by no means sought to crimp Federal power. Indeed, their control of the Federal government, combined with an aggressive policy of territorial expansion and the imposition of economic sanctions and a declaration of war against Britain in 1812, placed New England in the position of a beleaguered sectional minority chafing under Federal dominance. New Englanders, not Southerners, muttered the first cries of secession.

Missouri Crisis. The Missouri crisis of 1819–1820 marked the first major sectional confrontation in which the South turned to the doctrine of state rights in the defense of slavery. Down to 1819 Congress had routinely admitted new slave states into the Union. Southerners were thus surprised when Representative James Tallmadge of New York, in February 1819, attached a resolution to the Missouri statehood bill banning the future introduction of slaves and providing for the emancipation at the age of twenty-five of all slaves born in Missouri after its admission as a state. Passed in the Northern-dominated House by nearly unanimous Northern votes, the Tallmadge proviso was blocked in the Senate where the slave and free states were in even balance.

Congress finally reached a compromise in March 1820. Missouri, part of the original Louisiana Purchase territory, was admitted as a slave state with no restrictions placed upon slavery, and Maine was admitted as a free state, thereby maintaining sectional parity in the Senate. Slavery was prohibited from the remainder of the Louisiana Purchase territory north of latitude 36° 30′, the southern boundary of Missouri. Only the threat of Southern disunion forced the Northern concessions that made possible the Missouri Compromise. Cries of secession became for the first time a weapon in the Southern arsenal of proslavery defenses. Few Southern whites, however, seriously contemplated secession in 1820. They remained confident of their ability to protect slavery by clinging more tightly to the strict constructionist doctrines of the original Jeffersonians.

Nullification Crisis. Despite Southern control of the Jacksonian Democratic party that captured the presidency in

1828, South Carolina planters precipitated another sectional crisis in the early 1830s. These planters insisted that high protective tariffs were sacrificing the export economy of the slave South in the interests of Northern manufacturing capital. Their resistance to Federal authority produced the nullification crisis of 1832 and 1833.

Extending the arguments put forth by James Madison and Thomas Jefferson in the Virginia and Kentucky Resolutions of 1798, John C. Calhoun of South Carolina developed an elaborate constitutional theory by which a state could legally nullify Federal legislation that it determined violated its interests. The most delicate of those interests in the South involved slavery. For all the economic opposition to the tariff, the underlying issue ran much deeper. The tariff was only symptomatic of the far greater threat of centralizing Federal

> They remained confident of their ability to protect slavery by clinging more tightly to the strict constructionist doctrines. . . .

power encroaching upon the prerogatives of slave owners and the perceived personal safety of Southern whites.

After the tariff of 1832 failed to reduce duties as much as the nullifiers demanded, a special South Carolina convention met in the fall of 1832 and nullified the tariffs of 1828 and 1832. The result was a major constitutional crisis that produced, for the first time, a firm case in the North for a perpetual Union. Although a compromise tariff in 1833 satisfied the nullifiers, their defiance of Federal authority had sharpened the ideological lines in the sectional conflict. Secessionist doctrines now began to attract a popular following in the South.

The Crisis of Slavery in the Territories

In the midst of the nullification controversy, abolitionism burst upon the national scene. It was a product both of evangelical Christianity and the radical idea in a racist society that equality of opportunity and the right of self-betterment should be color-blind. The abolitionists had an impact far greater than their numbers alone. Never more than a very small minority of Northern whites (Northern blacks, of course, were far more likely to be abolitionists), the abolitionists used every conceivable means to spread their message that slavery was a moral abomination. Most particularly, they targeted slaveholders as moral pariahs who were a disgrace to Christianity and the Republic's ideals of human rights as expressed in the Declaration of Independence.

Slaveholders, many of whom were evangelicals themselves, were stung to the quick. They lashed back at their accusers by using their political power to deny the abolition-

ists a hearing. Mails were censored in the South to keep out abolitionist literature, and Congress passed a series of gag rules that automatically tabled antislavery petitions. By enacting such measures, Southern politicians unwittingly strengthened the cause of antislavery. The image of the "Slave Power," a conspiratorial force of tyrannical slaveholders running roughshod over the civil liberties and constitutional rights of Northern whites, began to take root in the popular consciousness of the North.

The demands of Southern Democrats in the early 1840s for the annexation of Texas, an independent slaveholding republic since 1836, fed Northern fears of a Southern plot to spread slavery. The push for Texas ultimately led to the Mexican War of 1846 through 1848. In that war American armies added California and most of the present-day Southwest to the Union and secured American claims to Texas as far south as the Rio Grande. The price of these territorial gains was the nation's worst sectional crisis since the flare-up over the admission of Missouri.

In the early stages of the Mexican War, David Wilmot, a congressman from Pennsylvania, introduced a proviso that prohibited slavery from any territory acquired as a result of the war. A Northern antislavery majority immediately formed in the House in support of the proviso. In response, Southern congressmen, almost to a man, rose up in defense of their right to expand slavery into Federal territories. Although Southern votes in the Senate were sufficient to defeat the Wilmot Proviso, the issues it raised continued to fester until the passage of a series of measures known collectively as the Compromise of 1850.

Compromise of 1850. Congress, against a backdrop of secessionist activity in the lower South and a call for a Southern convention to meet in Nashville, Tennessee, hammered out a compromise in the late summer of 1850. Concessions by the Northern antislavery majority in the House made possible the compromise. To be sure, California was admitted as a free state, the slave trade in Washington, D.C., was abolished, and the slave state of Texas yielded its claim on New Mexico (the eastern half bordered by the Rio Grande) in return for a Federal buyout of its debt. But the principle of the Wilmot Proviso was abandoned. The remaining lands in the Mexican Cession were organized into the territories of New Mexico and Utah with no mention of slavery. Even more damaging to the cause of antislavery was Northern acquiescence to a strengthened Fugitive Slave Act. This legislation put the full weight of the Federal government behind the efforts of slaveholders to recover their escaped slaves.

The Compromise of 1850 neutralized the Nashville Convention, and the secessionists were checkmated. Their strongholds were in South Carolina and Mississippi, but the refusal of Georgia, politically the bellwether in the lower South, to go along made Unionism respectable and politically profitable once again in the South. Nonetheless, the case for secession was significantly advanced. Even most Southern Unionists were forced to acknowledge that secession was a legal right. In the lower South the Unionism that triumphed was of a decidedly conditional variety. As the Georgia legislature made explicit, Southern states reserved the right to weigh the value of the Union against the safety of the institution of slavery.

Kansas-Nebraska Act. Hopes in both sections that the Compromise of 1850 would be the final word on the sectional controversy shattered in 1854 with the passage of the Kansas-Nebraska Act. In order to gain Southern votes necessary for the passage of his bill organizing the Louisiana Purchase territory north of 36° 30′, Senator Stephen A. Douglas of Illinois had to write into the Kansas-Nebraska Act a repeal of the Missouri Compromise restriction on slavery. Northerners widely interpreted this repeal as confirmation of a plot by the "Slave Power" to monopolize the territories for slavery at the expense of free labor.

The Northern storm of protest over the Kansas-Nebraska Act led to the formation of a sectionalized Republican party committed to preventing the spread of slavery into the territories. By 1856 the Republicans were the strongest party in the North. The Democrats were still a national party, but they were increasingly dominated by their Southern wing. In 1856, and with nearly solid support from the South, James Buchanan of Pennsylvania was elected as the last of the antebellum Democratic presidents.

The Buchanan presidency was a disaster for what remained of national unity. The Supreme Court ruled in the *Dred Scott* case of 1857 that Congress had no constitutional authority to prohibit slavery in the territories. The decision enraged Northerners and lent further credence to the notion of a "Slave Power" controlling the highest councils of government. A year later Democratic unity collapsed when Buchanan attempted to bring Kansas into the Union as a slave state. Convinced that the Free Soil majority in Kansas had been denied a fair opportunity to express its wishes on slavery, Douglas led a party revolt against Buchanan and his Southern supporters. Although few Southerners felt that slavery could thrive on the plains of Kansas, they were determined to establish the principle that a slave state could still be added to the Union. Largely because of the Douglas-led revolt, a slave Kansas was kept out of the Union. Southern Democrats never again trusted Douglas, and they would wreck the party before they would submit to his presidential nomination in 1860.

Election of 1860. John Brown's raid against the Harpers Ferry arsenal in October 1859 heightened sectional tensions as the election of 1860 approached. Brown, the epitome of the fiery abolitionist, failed in his attempt to incite a slave uprising and was executed in early December. Most Northerners, including the Republicans, denounced Brown as a wild-eyed fanatic. But, the fact that Brown had mounted a frontal attack upon slavery and then was elevated to martyrdom by a handful of New England reformers sent paroxysms of fear and anger throughout the South. Rumors of conspiracies and slave uprisings were rampant during the winter of 1859–1860, and Southerners were convinced that the Republican party was dominated by abolitionists and was plotting with them to unleash a bloodbath in the slave states.

The presidential election of 1860 was a four-way race. After the Southern Democrats bolted the party's national convention in Charleston, South Carolina, over the refusal of the Douglas Democrats to support a congressional slave code for the protection of slavery in the territories, the separate wings of the party nominated their own candidates for the presidency—Douglas for the North and John C. Breckinridge of Kentucky for the South. The Republicans ran Abraham Lincoln of Illinois, the favorite son of a state in the lower North that was crucial to Republican hopes for victory in 1860. The fourth candidate was John Bell of Tennessee

> **Lincoln's election was the signal the secessionists had been waiting for.**

who was backed by members of the now defunct Whig party in the upper South.

As expected, Lincoln was elected on November 6, 1860. With the exception of New Jersey, whose electoral vote was split, he swept the free states and commanded a clear majority in the electoral college though securing only 40 percent of the total popular vote. Breckinridge carried eleven of the fifteen slave states, including the entire lower South. Bell took Virginia, Kentucky, and Tennessee. Douglas, whose popular vote was second to Lincoln's, won only Missouri.

Lincoln's election was the signal the secessionists had been waiting for. Southerners had anticipated with dread the election of 1860, and on November 6 their worst fears were confirmed. Southern political power had shrunk to the point where an antislavery minority party with no pretense of support in the South could capture the presidency. It would be hard to imagine a greater insult to Southern honor than this demonstration of the South's political impotency in the face of a growing Northern majority. Here then was the first great advantage of the secessionists. Regardless of party affiliation or political beliefs, Southerners felt tremendously wronged. For more than a generation they had cast themselves as the aggrieved innocents in an unequal sectional struggle that unleashed more and more Northern aggressions on Southern rights. They believed they had been denied their fair share of the Federal territories and unfairly taxed through high tariffs to subsidize Northern industrial might. They were infuriated by the personal liberty laws passed by many Northern states that made it more difficult to recover fugitive slaves. Above all, they had been branded as moral monsters for upholding the institution of slavery. Their self-respect demanded that a stand be taken against the latest Northern outrage, the election of a Republican president.

Secession Looms

Young, slaveholding lawyers and planters spearheaded secession. They came to political maturity in the 1850s at a time of intensifying sectional hostilities, and they turned to the Breckinridge movement for vindication of their rights and status against the onslaughts of the antislavery North. The Breckinridge demand for Federal protection of slavery in the territories was their answer to the Republican commitment to free soil. Their recently acquired wealth in land and slaves rested on a rickety structure of credit that required rising slave prices to keep from collapsing. Economic self-interest, as well as wounded pride, drove them to secession once Lincoln's election threatened to limit Southern growth by ending the expansion of slavery.

The Fire-eaters. The most prominent secessionists were known as the fire-eaters. In particular, William Lowndes Yancey of Alabama, Edmund Ruffin of Virginia, and Robert Barnwell Rhett, Sr., of South Carolina had earned this label for their long and uncompromising devotion to the cause of Southern independence. Outside the inner circle of Southern political power at the national level, and hence free of the need to fashion a middle position to hold together a bisectional party coalition, the fire-eaters consistently had taken a hard line on Southern rights. They pushed sectional issues to their logical extreme and applauded the breakup of the national Democratic party in 1860. Aided immeasurably by the fears provoked by John Brown's raid, they popularized the right of secession among the Southern masses.

As veterans of sectional agitation, the fire-eaters had learned an invaluable lesson: a united South was a myth. South Carolina had stood alone during the nullification crisis, and Calhoun had called in vain for a monolithic South to rise up and demand its rights from the Yankee aggressors. In the crisis of 1850 and 1851, the secessionists were left isolated in South Carolina and Mississippi. Unity was impossible because of statewide and regional divisions that broke along lines of geography and social development. Virtually every slave state was rife with tensions between the yeoman-dominated backcountry and the planter-dominated black belts and lowcountry. A very broad division ran along a line from South Carolina westward to the Mississippi that differentiated the lower South from the slave states above it. In the upper South slaveholdings and percentages of slave owners were relatively smaller, fears of losing racial control less intense, and integration into the free-labor economies of the North tighter. Following the leadership of Virginia, the states

of the upper South counseled moderation in the sectional confrontations of the 1850s.

Now that a Republican victory had fired the Southern resolve to resist, the radicals of the lower South were determined not to repeat their mistakes of the past by waiting for the upper South to act. They rejected any plan of prior cooperation among the slave states and launched secession on their own. They pursued a strategy of separate state action and confidently predicted that wavering states would be forced to join those that had already gone out. Separate state action was indeed the key to secession. It enabled the secessionists to lead from strength and create an irreversible momentum.

"Resistance or submission" was the rallying cry of the secessionists. The former, Southerners were told, was an honorable act of self-defense demanded by a love of liberty and equality. The latter was the slavish servility of a dishonorable coward. Frightened white males, often spurred on by white women, responded by rushing to join vigilance committees, military companies, and associations of "Minute Men." All these paramilitary groups pledged to defend the South against widely feared incursions of abolitionists incited by Lincoln's success. Southern communities were thrown into an emotional frenzy as they mobilized on an emergency footing.

The Republican Threat. For all the popular hysteria they were instrumental in whipping up, the secessionists quite rationally assessed the nature of the Republican threat. The Republican stand against the expansion of slavery struck at the vital interests of the slave South. Economically, it threatened to choke off the profits of plantation agriculture by denying it access to fresh, arable lands. As a consequence, Southerners told themselves, whites would flee the slave states, and to save themselves, the dwindling numbers of whites would have to wage a preemptive war of extermination against the growing black majority. Politically, as free states were carved out of the territories, Southern power in Congress would be reduced to the point where slavery in the states could be dismantled by the ever larger political majority in the North. Most degrading of all from the Southern perspective was the humiliation implicit in submitting to the rule of an antislavery party. To do so would be an admission to Northerners and the outside world that the Southern way of life was morally suspect. Only slaves, the secessionists insisted, acted in such a servile fashion.

The secessionists did not expect the Republicans to make an immediate and direct move against slavery. They were well aware that the Republicans did not control Congress or the Supreme Court. As a new and still untested party, the Republicans would have to cooperate with Southern and Democratic politicians. But, reasoned the secessionists, such a demonstration that the slave South could, in the short run, survive under a Republican administration, would establish the fatal precedent of submitting to Republican rule and blunt the spirit of Southern resistance. In the meantime, the Republicans could use what power they had to begin the slow dismantling of slavery. The whole purpose of the Republican determination to prohibit the expansion of slavery was to put it on the road to extinction in the states where it existed.

In addition to all the perceived horrors of encirclement by a swelling majority of free states, the secessionists warned of changes in the sectional balance that the Republicans could potentially implement. They could move against slavery in Washington, D.C., and in Federal forts and installations. They could force the introduction of antislavery literature into the South by banning censorship of the Federal mails and simultaneously position the Supreme Court to overturn the *Dred Scott* ruling. They could weaken or repeal the Fugitive Slave Act and prohibit the interstate slave trade, a key link in the profitability of slavery to the South as a whole. Most alarming of all from the standpoint of the secessionists was the possibility that the Republicans would use Federal patronage and appointments to build a free labor party in the South. Senator Robert Toombs of Georgia echoed the concerns of many secessionists when he predicted in 1860 that Republican control of Federal jobs would create an "abolition party" within a year in Maryland, within two years in Kentucky, Missouri, and Virginia, and throughout the South by the end of four years.

Southern Divisions over Slavery. The Toombs prediction went to the heart of secessionists' fears over the commitment to slavery *within* the South. To be sure, very few Southern whites by 1860 favored an immediate end to slavery. Most such whites had left the South in the preceding generation, either voluntarily or in response to community pressures forcing them out. Nonetheless, deep divisions existed over the future of slavery and the direction of Southern society itself.

The Jeffersonian dream of a gradual withering away of slavery persisted in the upper South. Many whites could contemplate and even accept the eventual end of the institution as long as there was no outside interference in the process of disentanglement. In this region, as the proportion of slaves in the total population steadily declined in the late antebellum decades, slavery was increasingly becoming a matter of expediency, not of necessity. The secessionists had every reason to believe that a Republican administration would encourage the emancipationist sentiment that had already emerged among the white working classes in such slave cities as St. Louis, Baltimore, and Richmond.

In the lower South the secessionists doubted the loyalty to slavery of the yeomanry, a class of nonslaveholding farmers who composed the largest single bloc in the electorate. Although tied to the planters by a mutual commitment to white supremacy and often by bonds of kinship, these farmers occupied an ambivalent position in Southern society. They fervently valued their economic independence and political liberties, and hence they resented the spread of the plantation economy and the planters' pretensions to speak for them. But as long as the yeomen were able to practice their subsistence-oriented agriculture and the more ambitious ones saw a reasonable chance of someday buying a few slaves, this resentment fell far short of class conflict. In the 1850s, however, both these safety valves were being closed off. The proportion of families owning slaves fell from 31 to 25 percent. Sharply rising slave prices prevented more and more whites from purchasing slaves. At the same time, railroads spread the reach of a plantation agriculture geared

The Process of Secession

	SECESSION ORDINANCE	POPULAR RATIFICATION	JOINED THE CONFEDERACY*
South Carolina	Dec. 20, 1860	None	Apr. 3, 1861
Mississippi	Jan. 9, 1860	None	Mar. 29, 1861
Florida	Jan. 10, 1861	None	Feb. 26, 1861
Alabama	Jan. 11, 1861	None	Mar. 13, 1861
Georgia	Jan. 19, 1861	None	Mar. 16, 1861
Louisiana	Jan. 26, 1861	None	Mar. 21, 1861
Texas	Feb. 1, 1861	Feb. 23, 1861	Mar. 23, 1861
Virginia	Apr. 17, 1861	May 23, 1861	Apr. 27, 1861
Arkansas	May 6, 1861	None	May 10, 1861
Tennessee	May 6, 1861	June 8, 1861	May 7, 1861
North Carolina	May 20, 1861	None	May 20, 1861

*With the exceptions of Tennessee and Virginia, these are the dates that the secession conventions ratified the Confederate Constitution. On April 27, the Virginia convention invited the Confederate government to shift its capital to Richmond, and on May 7 Governor Isham Harris of Tennessee committed his state to a military alliance with the Confederacy.

to market production. Rates of farm tenancy rose in the older black belts, and the yeomen's traditional way of life was under increasing pressure.

Distrustful of the upper South as a region and the yeomanry as a class, the secessionists pushed for immediate as well as separate state secession. By moving quickly, they hoped to prevent divisions within the South from coalescing into a paralyzing debate over the best means of resisting Republican rule. Since most of the rabid secessionists were Breckinridge Democrats, the party that controlled nearly all the governorships and state legislatures in the lower South, the secessionists were able to set their own timetable for disunion.

The South Secedes

South Carolina was in the perfect position to launch secession. Its governor, William H. Gist, was on record as favoring a special state convention in the event of a Republican victory, and the legislature, the only one in the Union that still cast its state's electoral votes, was in session when news of Lincoln's election first reached the state. Aware of South Carolina's reputation for rash, precipitate action and leery of the state's being isolated, Gist would have preferred that another state take the lead in secession. But having been rebuffed a month earlier in his attempt to convince other Southern governors to seize the initiative, he was now prepared to take the first overt step. The South Carolina legislature almost immediately approved a bill setting January 8 as the election day for a state convention to meet on January 15.

Secession might well have been stillborn had the original convention dates set by the South Carolina legislature held. A two-month delay, especially in the likely event that no Southern state other than South Carolina would dare to go out alone, would have allowed time for passions to subside and lines of communication to be opened with the incoming Republican administration. But on November 10 a momentous shift occurred in the timing of South Carolina's convention. Reports of large secession meetings in Jackson, Mississippi, and Montgomery, Alabama, and reports that Georgia's governor, Joseph E. Brown, had recommended the calling of a convention in his state emboldened the South Carolina secessionists to accelerate their own timetable. They successfully pressured the South Carolina legislature to move up the dates of the state's convention to December 6 for choosing delegates and December 17 for the meeting.

Secession in the Lower South. The speedy call for an early South Carolina convention triggered similar steps toward secession by governors and legislatures throughout the lower South. On November 14 Governors Andrew B. Moore of Alabama and J. J. Pettus of Mississippi issued calls for state conventions, both of which were to be elected on December 24 and meet on January 7. Moore had prior leg-

islative approval for calling a convention, and Pettus was given his mandate on November 26. Once the Georgia legislature voted its approval on November 18, Governor Brown set January 2 for the election of Georgia's convention and January 16 for its convening. The Florida legislature in late November and the Louisiana legislature in early December likewise authorized their governors to set in motion the electoral machinery for January meetings of their conventions. Texas was a temporary exception to the united front developing in the lower South for secession. Its governor, Sam Houston, was a staunch Unionist who refused to call his leg-

> **Within three weeks of Lincoln's election the secessionists had generated a strong momentum for the breakup of the Union.**

islature into special session. As a result, Texas secessionists resorted to the irregular, if not illegal, expedient of issuing their own call for a January convention.

Within three weeks of Lincoln's election the secessionists had generated a strong momentum for the breakup of the Union by moving quickly and decisively. In contrast, Congress, acting slowly and hesitantly, did nothing to derail the snowballing movement.

Congress convened on December 3, and the House appointed a Committee of Thirty-three (one representative from each state) to consider compromise measures. The committee, however, waited a week before calling its first meeting, and the creation of a similar committee in the Senate was temporarily blocked by bitter debates between Republicans and Southerners. When the House committee did meet on December 14, its Republican members failed (by a vote of eight to eight) to endorse a resolution calling for additional guarantees of Southern rights. Choosing to interpret this Republican stand as proof that Congress could accomplish nothing, thirty congressmen from the lower South then issued an address to their constituents declaring their support for an independent Southern confederacy. A week later, on December 20, South Carolina became the first state to leave the Union when its convention unanimously approved an ordinance of secession.

South Carolina provided the impetus, but the ultimate fate of secession in the lower South rested on the outcome of the convention elections held in late December and early January in the six other cotton states. The opponents of immediate secession in these states were generally known as cooperationists. Arguing that in unity there was strength, the cooperationists wanted to delay secession until a given number of states had agreed to go out as a bloc. Many of the cooperationists were merely cautious secessionists in need of greater assurances before taking their states out. But an indeterminate number of others clung to the hope that the Union could still be saved if the South as a whole forced concessions from the Republicans and created a reconstructed Union embodying safeguards for slavery.

Any delay, however, was anathema to the immediate secessionists. They countered the cooperationists' fears of war by asserting that the North would accept secession rather than risk cutting off its supply of Southern cotton. The secessionists also neutralized the cooperationist call for unanimity of action by appointing secession commissioners to each of the states considering secession. The commissioners acted as the ambassadors of secession by establishing links of communication between the individual states and stressing the need for a speedy withdrawal. In a brilliant tactical move, the South Carolina convention authorized its commissioners on December 31 to issue a call for a Southern convention to launch a provisional government for the Confederate States of America. Even before another state had joined South Carolina in seceding, the call went out on January 3 for a convention to meet in Montgomery, Alabama, on February 4, 1861.

The secessionists won the convention elections in the lower South, but their margins of victory were far narrower than in South Carolina. The cooperationists polled about 40 percent of the overall vote, and in Alabama, Georgia, and Louisiana they ran in a virtual dead heat with the straight-out secessionists. Somewhat surprisingly, given the issues involved and the high pitch of popular excitement, voter turnout fell by more than one-third from the levels in the November presidential election. The short time allotted for campaigning and the uncontested nature of many of the local races held down the vote. In addition, many conservatives boycotted the elections out of fear of reprisals if they publicly opposed secession. The key to the victory of the secessionists was their strength in the plantation districts. They carried four out of five counties in which the slaves comprised a majority of the population and ran weakest in counties with the fewest slaves. The yeomen, especially in the Alabama and Georgia mountains, were against immediate secession. Characteristically, they opposed a policy they associated with the black belt planters.

Mississippi, Florida, Alabama, Georgia, and Louisiana successively seceded in their January conventions. They were joined by Texas on February 1, 1861. Like falling dominoes, the secession of one state made it easier for the next to follow. In each convention the secessionists fought back efforts for a cooperative approach or last-ditch calls for a Southern conference to make final demands on the Republicans. They also defeated attempts by cooperationists to submit the secession ordinances to a popular referendum. Only in Texas, where the secessionists were sensitive to the dubious legality by which they had forced the calling of a con-

vention, was the decision on secession referred to the voters for their approval. In the end the secession ordinances passed by overwhelming majorities in all the conventions. This apparent unanimity, however, belied the fact that in no state had the immediate secessionists carried enough votes to have made up a majority in the earlier presidential election. Once the decision for secession was inevitable, the cooperationists voted for the ordinances in a conscious attempt to impress the Republicans with Southern resolve and unity.

Delegates from the seven seceded states met in Montgomery, Alabama, in February. Here, on the seventh, they adopted a Provisional Constitution (one closely modeled on the U.S. Constitution) for an independent Southern government and, on the ninth, elected Jefferson Davis of Mississippi as president. Thus, nearly a month before Lincoln's inauguration on March 4, the secessionists had achieved one of their major goals. They had a functioning government in place before the Republicans had even assumed formal control of the Federal government.

The Northern Response. Buchanan, the lame-duck president, did nothing to stem the tide of disunion. He officially held the reins of power in the four-month period between the presidential election in early November and Lincoln's inauguration in early March, but he had lost any popular mandate to govern. The secessionists had anticipated his indecision and cited it as confirmation of their argument that secession would be peaceable. Buchanan—reasoning that just as secession was unconstitutional so was any attempt by the Federal government to resist it by force—preferred to leave the problem for the Republicans to settle. He thought they were chiefly responsible for the crisis, and he said as much in his last annual message of December 3, 1860. His policy was a negative one of doing nothing to provoke an armed conflict with the seceding states.

The Republicans initially denied the existence of any real crisis. They were acutely aware of the pattern of Southern bluster and Northern concessions that had characterized former sectional confrontations, and they were not about to surrender their integrity as an antislavery party by yielding to Southern demands. At Lincoln's urging they drew the line at sanctioning the territorial expansion of slavery. Such a sanction was the crucial feature of the Crittenden Compromise, a package of six proposed constitutional amendments that came out of a Senate committee led by John J. Crittenden of Kentucky in mid-December. Under Crittenden's plan, slavery would be recognized south of 36° 30′ in all present territories, as well as those "hereafter acquired." To a man, congressional Republicans rejected what they interpreted as a blank check for the future expansion of slavery into Mexico and the Caribbean.

Secession in the Upper South. The collapse of the Crittenden Compromise in late December eliminated the already slim possibility that the drive toward secession might end with the withdrawal of South Carolina. Still, when Lincoln took office on March 4, the Republicans had reason to believe that the worst of the crisis was over. February elections in the Upper South had resulted in Unionist victories. In January the legislatures of five states—Arkansas, Virginia, Missouri, Tennessee, and North Carolina—had issued calls for conventions. The secessionists suffered a sharp setback in all the elections.

On February 4, Virginia voters chose to send moderates of various stripes to their convention by about a three-to-one margin. In yet another defeat for the secessionists, who opposed the measure, they also overwhelmingly approved a popular referendum on any decision reached by the convention. On February 9, Tennessee voted against holding a convention. Had one been approved, the Unionists elected would have composed an 80-percent majority. Arkansas and Missouri voted on February 18, and both elected Unionist

> In a region that lacked the passionate commitment of the lower South to defending slavery, they were able to mobilize large Unionist majorities. . . .

majorities. On February 28, North Carolinians repeated the Tennessee pattern. They rejected the calling of a convention, which, in any event, would have been dominated by Unionists.

By the end of February secession apparently had burnt itself out in the upper South. It was defeated either by a popular vote or, as in the case of the slave states of Kentucky, Delaware, and Missouri, by the inability of the secessionists to pressure the legislatures or governors to issue a call for a convention. Despite fiery speeches and persistent lobbying by secession commissioners appointed by the Confederate government, the antisecessionists held their ground. In a region that lacked the passionate commitment of the lower South to defending slavery, they were able to mobilize large Unionist majorities of nonslaveholders. In particular, they succeeded in detaching large numbers of the Democratic yeomanry from the secessionist, slaveholding wing of their party. The yeomanry responded to the fears invoked by the Unionists of being caught in the crossfire of a civil war, and nonslaveholders in general questioned how well their interests would be served in a planter-dominated Confederacy.

A final factor accounting for the Unionist victories in the upper South was the meeting in Washington of the so-called Peace Convention called by the Virginia legislature. The delegates spent most of February debating various proposals

for additional guarantees for slave property in an effort to find some basis for a voluntary reconstruction of the Union. Although boycotted by some of the Northern states and all of the states that had already seceded, the convention raised hopes of a national reconciliation and thereby strengthened the hand of the Unionists in the upper South. In the end, however, the convention was an exercise in futility. All it could come up with was a modified version of the Crittenden Compromise. Just before Lincoln's inauguration, Republican votes in the Senate killed the proposal.

Pressures for Action Mount. Throughout March and early April the Union remained in a state of quiescence that no one expected to last indefinitely. Both of the new governments, Lincoln's and Davis's, were under tremendous pressure to break the suspense by taking decisive action. Davis was criticized for not moving aggressively enough to bring the upper South into the Confederacy. Without that region and especially Virginia, it was argued, the Confederacy was but a cipher of a nation. It had negligible manufacturing capacity and only one-third of the South's free population. It desperately needed additional slave states to have a viable chance for survival. Just as desperately, Lincoln's government needed to make good on its claim that the Union was indivisible. Buchanan had been mocked for his indecisiveness, and Lincoln knew that he had to take a stand on enforcing Federal authority.

The upper South now became a pawn in a power struggle between Lincoln and Davis. However much moderates in the upper South wanted to avoid a confrontation that would ignite a war, they were publicly committed to coming to the assistance of any Southern state that the Republicans attempted to coerce back into the Union. In short, Unionism in the upper South was always highly conditional in nature. This in turn made the region hostage to events beyond its control and gave the Confederacy the leverage it needed to pull in additional states.

The only major Federal installations in the Confederacy still under Federal control when Lincoln became president were Fort Pickens in Pensacola Harbor and Fort Sumter in Charleston Harbor. The retention of these forts thereby became a test of the credibility of the Republicans as the defenders of the Union. By the same token, the acquisition of these forts was essential if the Confederacy were to lay claim to the full rights of a sovereign nation.

On March 5, Lincoln learned from Maj. Robert Anderson, the commander at Fort Sumter, that dwindling food supplies would force an evacuation of the fort within four to six weeks. Lincoln decided against any immediate attempt to save the fort. On March 12, however, he issued orders for the reinforcement of Fort Pickens. More accessible to the Federal navy because of its location outside Pensacola Harbor beyond the range of Confederate artillery, Fort Pickens had the additional advantage of being overshadowed in the public consciousness by Fort Sumter, a highly charged symbol of Federal resolve in the state that had started secession. Presumably, it could be reinforced with less risk of precipitating a war than could Fort Sumter.

Lincoln's initial decision not to act on Fort Sumter was also a concession to William H. Seward, his secretary of state. Seward was the chief spokesman for what was called the policy of "masterly inactivity." He believed that Unionists in the upper South were on the verge of leading a process of voluntary reunion. If the upper South were not stampeded into joining the Confederacy by a coercive act by the Republicans, Seward argued, an isolated Confederacy would soon have no choice but to bargain to rejoin the Union. Everything depended, of course, on a conciliatory Republican policy.

In pursuing this strategy, Lincoln temporarily considered a withdrawal from Fort Sumter in exchange for a binding commitment from the upper South not to leave the Union. Seward then made the mistake of assuming that evacuation was a foregone conclusion. He was conducting informal negotiations with three Confederate commissioners who were in Washington seeking a transfer of Fort Pickens and Fort Sumter. On March 15 he informed them through an intermediary to expect a speedy evacuation of Fort Sumter. When no such evacuation was forthcoming, Confederate leaders felt betrayed, and they vowed never again to trust the word of the Lincoln administration.

Mounting demands in the North to take a stand at Fort Sumter, combined with Lincoln's growing disillusionment over Southern Unionism, convinced the president that he would have to challenge the Confederacy over the issue of Fort Sumter. On March 29 he told his cabinet that he was preparing a relief expedition. He delayed informing Major Anderson of that decision until after a meeting on April 4 with John Baldwin, a Virginia Unionist. Although no firsthand account of this meeting exists, the discussion apparently confirmed Lincoln's belief that the upper South could not broker a voluntary reunion on terms acceptable to the Republican party. The final orders for the relief expedition were issued on April 6, the day that Lincoln learned that Fort Pickens had not yet been reinforced because of a mix-up in the chain of command.

News of Lincoln's decision to reinforce Fort Sumter "with provisions only" reached Montgomery, the Confederate capital, on April 8. The next day Davis ordered Gen. P. G. T. Beauregard, the Confederate commander at Charleston, to demand an immediate surrender of the fort. If Major Anderson refused, Beauregard was to attack the fort. Davis always felt that war was inevitable, and for months the most radical of the secessionists had been insisting that a military confrontation would be necessary to force the upper South into secession. Davis was convinced that he had no alternative but to counter Lincoln's move with a show of force.

Confederate batteries opened fire on Fort Sumter on April 12, and the fort surrendered two days later. On April 15 Lincoln issued a call for seventy-five thousand state militia to put down what he described as an insurrection against lawful authority. It was this call for troops, and not just the armed clash at Fort Sumter, that specifically triggered secession in the upper South. The Unionist majorities there suddenly dissolved once the choice shifted from supporting the Union or the Confederacy to fighting for or against fellow Southerners.

The Virginia convention, which had remained in session after rejecting immediate secession on April 4, passed a secession ordinance on April 17. Its decision was overwhelmingly ratified on May 23 in a popular referendum. Three other states quickly followed. A reconvened Arkansas convention voted to go out on May 6. The Tennessee legislature, in a move later ratified in a popular referendum, also approved secession on May 6. A hastily called North Carolina convention, elected on May 13, took the Tarheel State out on May 20.

By the late spring of 1861 the stage was set for the bloodiest war in American history. The popular reaction to the firing on Fort Sumter and Lincoln's call for troops unified the North behind a crusade to preserve the Union and solidified, at least temporarily, a divided South behind the cause of Southern independence.

[*See also* Compromise of 1850; Constitutional Union Party; Cooperationists; Crittenden Compromise; Declaration of Immediate Causes; Democratic Party; Dred Scott Decision; Election of 1860; Fire-eaters; Fort Sumter, South Carolina; Fugitive Slave Law; Harpers Ferry, West Virginia, *article on* John Brown's Raid; Kansas-Nebraska Act; Missouri Compromise; Montgomery Convention; Nullification Controversy; Republican Party; State Rights; Unionism; Washington Peace Conference; Wilmot Proviso; and *entries on particular states and biographies of numerous figures mentioned herein.*]

BIBLIOGRAPHY

Barney, William L. *The Road to Secession.* New York, 1972.
Channing, Steven A. *Crisis of Fear: Secession in South Carolina.* New York, 1970.
Craven, Avery O. *The Growth of Southern Nationalism, 1848–1861.* Baton Rouge, La., 1953.
Crofts, Daniel W. *Reluctant Confederates: Upper South Unionists in the Secession Crisis.* Chapel Hill, N.C., 1989.
Fehrenbacher, Don E. *The South and Three Sectional Crises.* Baton Rouge, La., 1980.
Ford, Lacy K., Jr. *Origins of Southern Radicalism: The South Carolina Upcountry, 1800–1860.* New York, 1988.
Freehling, William W. *The Road to Disunion: Secessionists at Bay, 1776–1854.* New York, 1990.
Genovese, Eugene D. *The Political Economy of Slavery.* New York, 1965.
Johnson, Michael P. *Toward a Patriarchal Republic: The Secession of Georgia.* Baton Rouge, La., 1977.

McCardell, John. *The Idea of a Southern Nation: Southern Nationalists and Southern Nationalism, 1830–1860.* New York, 1979.

Oakes, James. *The Ruling Race: A History of American Slaveholders.* New York, 1982.

Potter, David M. *The Impending Crisis, 1848–1861.* New York, 1976.

Stampp, Kenneth M. *And the War Came: The North and the Secession Crisis.* Baton Rouge, La., 1950.

Thornton, J. Mills, III. *Politics and Power in a Slave Society: Alabama, 1800–1860.* Baton Rouge, La., 1978.

Wooster, Ralph A. *The Secession Conventions of the South.* Princeton, N.J., 1962.

WILLIAM L. BARNEY

SEDDON, JAMES A.

SEDDON, JAMES A. (1815–1880), Congressman from Virginia and secretary of war. Seddon was descended from English immigrants who arrived in Virginia in the eighteenth century and settled near Fredericksburg. Here they built Snowden, later destroyed by Union soldiers during the Civil War. Seddon was born in the town on July 13, 1815. He graduated from the University of Virginia law school with honors in 1835. Soon afterward, he opened a law office in Richmond and became active in the Calhoun wing of the Democratic party. In 1845 he married Sarah Bruce, daughter of a renowned Virginia family, and settled into the Clay Street mansion that later became the White House of the Confederacy. The couple quickly joined the social elite of the city. Shortly before, he had been elected to the U.S. House of Representatives.

Seddon served in Congress from 1845 to 1847, and again from 1849 to 1851. An ardent disciple of Calhoun, he adopted the state rights stance on most national issues in his first term. He supported the admission of Texas, the acquisition of Oregon, free trade over protectionism, and the necessity and value of slavery to the Southern way of life. He declined reelection in 1847 because of poor health. By 1849, when he returned to Congress, he had become a Southern expansionist, sharing the dream of a large slave-based empire embracing the Caribbean. He had despaired of securing Southern rights in the Union and secretly favored secession and the formation of a Southern republic. In all measures of the Compromise of 1850, he affirmed ultra-Southern demands, siding with such extremist leaders as Robert Barnwell Rhett, Sr., and Jefferson Davis (with whom he had earlier become acquainted).

After leaving Congress in 1851, Seddon led the life of a planter in outlying Goochland County, where he acquired land, slaves, and a new twenty-six room home, Sabot Hill. He was infrequently in the public eye in the 1850s. Yet behind the scenes he corresponded, politicked, and championed the ambitions of friends, notably Robert M. T. Hunter (his closest political associate); gave strong support to opponents in the state against the Know-Nothings; and continued to be a power in the politics of the South. In 1856 he was a delegate to the Democratic National Convention at Cincinnati and was nominated for vice president on the Buchanan ticket, which he refused. In 1858 he spoke at a dinner in Richmond honoring Nicaragua filibusterer William Walker, whom Seddon praised as an evangel of progress and civilization. His own views on slavery and Southern nationalism deepened as he read the latest Southern theorists and promoted the distribution of their proslavery literature throughout the South.

He saw the election of Abraham Lincoln in 1860 as the death knell of the territorial ambitions of the South. Immediately he counseled resistance to expected Northern aggression and advised friends to prepare for the disruption of the Union. In January 1861 he was chosen as a delegate to the Washington peace conference. As a member of its committee on resolutions, he defended the right of secession (and the legitimacy of the new Southern Confederacy) and submitted a minority report seeking a constitutional amendment protecting the permanence of slavery in the Union. In

JAMES A. SEDDON.

the end, together with the majority of the Virginia delegation, he voted against the compromise proposals of the body. Throughout the debates he was a vigorous defender of Southern interests. To some he recalled one of his own heroes, John Randolph of Roanoke, while to others he was a firebrand secessionist. Two days before adjournment, a reception was given for the newly arrived President-elect Lincoln. Seddon was among those with questions for the Republican leader, and a heated exchange of views followed, especially regarding abolitionists, their objectives, and the "incendiary" press of the Northern states. Lincoln's response and humorous wit defused the debate.

Seddon returned to Richmond with ex-President John Tyler, also a delegate and old acquaintance, to urge their

> ... Seddon himself would have donned a uniform but for his health and feeble constitution.

state to secede and join the Southern Confederacy. Nothing, they felt, of compromise or guarantees would be granted by the Republican-controlled Union. The Seddon-Tyler report to Governor John Letcher concluded that the conference had been a failure and "independent state action" was the only alternative to certain Northern coercion. In several speeches, Seddon urged crowds of frenzied Richmonders to prepare for the worst. He also implored the Virginia state convention, then sitting in the city, to act. On April 16, 1861, following the firing on Fort Sumter and Lincoln's call for troops, Seddon spoke before the "Spontaneous Peoples' Convention," demanding immediate secession. The following day, Virginia responded and left the Union. As Seddon observed to Charles Bruce, his brother-in-law, "The whole State is [now] in movement and the difficulty is rather to restrain any men at home than to fire them to the War." He was elated—the South had at long last been delivered from "Yankee Thralldom," and his dreams for an independent nation had finally been realized.

From April to early summer of 1861, the peace of the Virginia countryside was shattered by the bustle of military preparations. Many of Seddon's relatives responded to the call, and Seddon himself would have donned a uniform but for his health and feeble constitution. Soon after President Davis's arrival in Richmond and transfer of the Confederate capital to Virginia, he met several times with his old friend, perhaps to discuss Hunter's or Seddon's availability for the post of secretary of state. The question was on the lips of many of his friends. In June, he was chosen by Virginia for the Provisional Confederate Congress.

Seddon's eight months in Congress proved helpful to the new Davis administration and to his own political fortunes. In

this critical time the unicameral body was setting up the government, recruiting and provisioning armies, and financing the war. Seddon gave special attention to the latter—the revision of the Produce Loan of 1861 to double its bond and currency issue to $100 million; passage of a law to make Treasury notes legal tender for all debts; and issuance of bonds to underwrite the currency and overall deficit spending. He also helped shape the Sequestration Act, in reprisal for similar Federal legislation; a strict embargo on cotton export; subsidies to arms manufacturers; impressment laws for military needs; railroad legislation to consolidate the lines and close major gaps in their routes; prisoner of war exchange and establishment of prison camps; and numerous military bills. As congressman, he had introduced ten bills, most enacted into law. He met not infrequently with the president and lobbied with colleagues to support the administration and a vigorous prosecution of the war. He saw the conflict in large terms and tried to imbue others with his own perception. He thus emerged as a strong Confederate nationalist rather than a narrow state rights advocate on most major issues.

In the summer of 1862, Seddon was approached through a lengthy correspondence by oceanographer Capt. Matthew Fontaine Maury with various schemes for promoting innovations in naval warfare, use of metal ships and torpedo weaponry, and government use, if not control, of blockade runners for the strategic needs of the South. Some of these ideas would later be enacted once Seddon was in charge of the War Department.

In mid-November, when Secretary of War George Wythe Randolph resigned, Davis prevailed upon Seddon to fill the office. The choice was a personal one for Davis: he wanted a solid friend in this difficult post and also another Virginian in his cabinet. Others did as well, including critically outspoken foes of the president. They applauded Seddon's appointment on November 20. He would hold his post almost to the end of the war, longer than the combined tenure of the three previous occupants. The choice proved an excellent one. Seddon brought to his task not only dedication and intelligence but also independence of thought and tact. A good judge of men, he impressed diarist Mary Boykin Chesnut as a warm and caring man and a fascinating conversationalist. Usually diplomatic, he was best as a sympathetic listener and convincing advocate. Seddon's cadaverous appearance was deceptive, for he was a tireless worker. Save for Robert E. Lee, he became Davis's most influential military adviser and devised much of the South's offensive strategy of concentration and total war. Together with Stephen R. Mallory and Judah P. Benjamin, he was one of the ablest of Davis's cabinet heads.

Unlike his predecessor, Seddon lacked military experience and at first relied heavily on the president, Assistant Secretary of War John A. Campbell, and Inspector General Samuel Cooper. Later he took upon himself the burdens of responsibility. One month after his appointment, he observed to Charles Bruce:

> The life is one rather of close confinement and incessant worry than of severe labor, and so far I have not suffered tho' giving daily from 9 a m to 9 or 10 p m to my duties. Indeed few persons are so well prepared by previous habits for [such] a sedatory life. . . . I trust to do reasonably well, as soon as I get a little more trained to the routine and versed in the military knowledge of the place.

Davis gave most of his cabinet members wide latitude in running their offices. He sought their advice and tolerated opinions contrary to his own. But having been a secretary of war himself and as an experienced military man, Davis naturally took a strong personal interest in the War Department and to a degree regarded it as his own domain. He carefully scrutinized the activities of this office and kept a tighter rein on its head than on other cabinet officers. As armies, strategy, and war itself were the chief concern of the Confederacy's leaders, the secretary and president had to work closely together.

Seddon found Davis not an impossible taskmaster at first, though often a difficult one. In working with him, he had to act by suggestion rather than command, relying on tact in his relations with the egocentric president. In lesser matters Seddon was seldom overruled, but when he was, he bowed to the will of his chief. An unselfish man without political ambition, Seddon did not seek power; rather, he was simply devoted to the Southern cause. He was in no way obsequious; he was much too proud to serve as a mere figurehead. He valued his appointment as an expression of Davis's respect and remained in the cabinet only as long as he shared the esteem of the president and the confidence of the people.

By November 1862 the enemy was again on the move in Virginia. Ambrose Burnside was advancing on the capital by way of Fredericksburg. Lee maneuvered to counter him. At the same time Charleston and Wilmington to the south feared imminent assault; but in the West there were even graver fears that the Union would soon seize the Mississippi and sever the Confederacy in two. Seddon was not long in responding to this impending crisis. With confidence in Lee in Virginia and while giving assurances of support to P. G. T. Beauregard and the Atlantic defenses, he focused major attention on the western theater. He believed that the decisive contest in the war at this time was to be waged there. His deep concern for this theater and the planning he put forth serve as a good index of the kind of strategist he could have been, had Davis given him greater latitude. His fears of a major debacle in the Trans-Mississippi and his recognition of the need for a reorientation of Confederate strategy there had in large measure been shared by his predecessor. But

where Randolph had failed, Seddon succeeded. He not only won Davis's support for a newly organized Department of the West and persuaded him to visit the region (the following month) but got him to name Joseph E. Johnston to its command. It was a good solution to a large dilemma but depended for success upon the audacity and imagination of the chosen commander. Johnston failed to rise to the occasion. Seddon repeatedly pleaded with him to assert his authority over the entire area and to assume command of the scattered forces of Braxton Bragg, John C. Pemberton, and lesser units, but to no avail. Disappointment followed disappointment until Pemberton's large army was pent up in Vicksburg by the summer of 1863.

December 1862 had seen Lee again victorious, at Fredericksburg. It was a costly but timely victory. Virginia was freed of the invader until spring, and the capital yet secure. Another lesser triumph came on January 1, 1863, when John B. Magruder retook the vital Gulf port of Galveston. Seddon, in the meantime, "borrowed" troops and taxed the resources of lesser points to brace Beauregard's command at Charleston. On April 7 an ironclad fleet appeared before the city and, after a brisk battle, was turned back.

The year 1863 started out as the high watermark in the life of the Confederacy, but with the loss of Vicksburg and the Mississippi River and the simultaneous repulse at Gettysburg, the Confederates were thereafter on the defensive. Seddon had favored sending a part of Lee's army to the West, but after lengthy debate in the cabinet and with Lee, he abandoned his plan and gave support to a second invasion of the North. Years later he would declare in a letter that the "disaster of Vicksburg . . . was the fatal turning point of the war."

Seddon once again sought to snatch victory in the West. In the fall of 1863 he persuaded Davis and Lee to send James Longstreet from Virginia to Tennessee, where his timely arrival and generalship helped win the Battle of Chickamauga. But no one could single-handedly win the war, least of all the secretary. Only by mustering its resources

> . . . Seddon did not seek power; rather, he was simply devoted to the Southern cause.

could the South hope to drive off the invaders, and only through teamwork, which he sought to promote, was victory possible. Incompetents and malcontents had to be removed, and those with ability, experience, and a will to win be empowered to lead the fight. Pemberton, for instance, found no admirer in the secretary; numerous complaints had poured into Richmond questioning his competency and retention in command. Most tragic to Seddon was the prolonged retention of Bragg in the West. He tried repeatedly for

Bragg's recall, but Johnston and later Davis himself blocked him. Only after the disastrous defeat at Chattanooga in November 1863 was Bragg finally removed. William J. Hardee, his most promising subordinate, refused his place. Seddon and a majority of the cabinet favored a second chance for Johnston, and he was returned to the Army of Tennessee. Barely a year later, he would be removed, this time before the defenses of Atlanta. Seddon, in general, supported the "fighting" generals—Lee, Longstreet, later John Bell Hood, and, despite Davis's disdain, Beauregard. One prime fighter that all overlooked was Nathan Bedford Forrest, whose recognition came too late for the West.

By 1864 the South was fighting a holding action. Two-thirds of its territory was gone, and a third of its armies was absent without leave (as Seddon admitted to the president in his annual report). The day for offensives was over. Seddon was now preoccupied with keeping the two major armies alive despite eroding morale, mass desertions, and widespread disaffection and starvation on the home front. He fought with Governors Joseph E. Brown of Georgia and Zebulon Vance of North Carolina over conscription, impressment, and martial law. He struggled to save worn-out railroads, which he commandeered for the government. He sequestered space on blockade runners and sent forth the department's own vessels to bring in vital supplies. He broke the rules and allowed cotton to be traded with the enemy for meat and other food for the army. And he assisted secret service and espionage ventures behind Northern lines to promote disaffection, peace movements, and the defeat of Lincoln's reelection—all this, and much more, during the last months of the war.

The cause was crumbling, yet Seddon could not admit it. There was talk of resignation, but friends urged him to hold on. He did, as he continued to live with only a single body servant, bearing alone the anguish of a lost child and the death from combat wounds of his brother, Maj. John Seddon. Even the threat to his own life, implicit with the Dahlgren raid on Richmond and its plot to kill Davis and his cabinet, he discounted. In February 1865, he saw his old Democrat friend Francis P. Blair, who came to the Confederate capital to promote peace. This and the subsequent Hampton Roads conference were the latest expressions of the reality of ultimate defeat. Nor was he able at this late date to think his way beyond Hunter and Cobb on the issue of black soldiers. (Earlier, in 1863, he had agreed with Davis to suppress Patrick Cleburne's proposal to arm the slaves.) Only when Lee urged the measure because of his desperate need for more men did Seddon reconsider—but it was too late.

Finally, when the Virginia congressional delegation, in anger over conditions generally and in hopes of restoring public confidence, requested the president to reorganize his cabinet, Seddon was piqued and immediately resigned. He had mistaken the motives of this body, who did not seek his ouster. But perhaps it was time for him to step aside and return to his family. Despite Davis's reassurances (and the lengthy correspondence that ensued), his resignation became final. On February 5, 1865, he quit his office and returned to Sabot Hill.

With his retirement, some now realized the breadth of the services he had rendered. Although his name had become a household word throughout the South, his popularity, like that of other politicians in this military-conscious society, never approached that of the fighting generals. But many recognized him as a man of dedication, will, and strength. Perhaps he was not the ideal man for the position, in view of his lack of military background and inexperience as an administrator, but he was the best the South had to offer. "His critics were numerous," wrote Douglas S. Freeman, "but a student will search the list vainly to find the name of one who could have done better than Seddon."

Out of office, he could do little more than witness the last acts of the struggle. He had little hope that Richmond would not fall, he told his sister in March. A week later, in a letter to Davis, he thought better of the cause, which he now believed would prevail; "the Liberties and Independence of your Country" will be achieved, he asserted. When the end finally came, he "was completely crushed . . . and considered his life to have been a complete failure" (as he told his son).

On May 20, Seddon took the oath of amnesty, but three days later he was suddenly arrested and confined in Libby Prison with Hunter and Campbell. On June 5, the three arrived at Fort Pulaski, Georgia, where they were joined by eight other former leaders. After Seddon's release in December, he returned to Sabot Hill. He was able largely to restore his fortunes through his law practice and his plantations in Virginia and Louisiana. He never wrote his memoirs, having destroyed most of his papers out of fear of their seizure by the Radical Republicans. Seddon died on August 19, 1880, and was buried in Hollywood Cemetery, Richmond.

BIBLIOGRAPHY

Curry, Roy Watson. "James A. Seddon: A Southern Prototype." *Virginia Magazine of History and Biography* 63 (1955): 123–150.

Dowdey, Clifford. *Experiment in Rebellion.* New York, 1946.

Escott, Paul D. *After Secession: Jefferson Davis and the Failure of Confederate Nationalism.* Baton Rouge, La., 1978.

Jones, J. B. *A Rebel War Clerk's Diary at the Confederate States Capital.* 2 vols. Philadelphia, 1866. Reprint, New York, 1958.

O'Brien, G. F. J. "James A. Seddon: Statesman of the Old South." Ph.D. diss., University of Maryland, 1963.

Patrick, Rembert W. *Jefferson Davis and His Cabinet.* Baton Rouge, La., 1944.

Strode, Hudson. *Jefferson Davis.* 3 vols. New York, 1955–1964.

Younger, Edward, ed. *Inside the Confederate Government: The Diary of Robert Garlick Hill Kean.* New York, 1957.

JOHN O'BRIEN

SELMA, ALABAMA

[*This entry includes three articles,* City of Selma, *which profiles the city during the Confederacy,* Selma Naval Ordnance Works, *which discusses the establishment and operations of the ordnance works, and* Wilson's Raid on Selma, *which discusses the Federal raid of 1865.*]

City of Selma

Founded in 1820 on a high bluff overlooking the Alabama River, Selma, Alabama, served as the seat of government for Dallas County during the Civil War. Before the conflict, the city was the focal point of trade, industry, education, and social life for local black belt planters. The cotton producers' African American labor force dominated the population of the surrounding county. By 1860, Dallas County's population numbered 30,197 people, consisting of 7,785 whites and 22,412 blacks; the city was populated by 1,132 whites and 2,516 blacks. As Selma's war industries grew, its population increased. At the end of the conflict, the city's factories and foundries employed at least 10,000 men who, as war industry employees, were exempt from conscription.

Social and cultural life for Selma's whites revolved around the city's schools and churches. Before the war, the Dallas Male and Female academies attracted over a hundred students each. The Male Academy folded at the outbreak of the war, but the women's school remained open until forced to close for financial reasons in 1864. Religion centered on Selma's six Protestant churches and one Roman Catholic institution.

The war made Selma an industrial center. Two railroads—the Alabama and Tennessee River and the Alabama and Mississippi lines—connected the city to northern Alabama's coal and iron reserves and the plantation regions of neighboring Mississippi. The Alabama River linked Selma to Montgomery, Mobile, and the Gulf of Mexico to the south. With easy access to iron-making resources and an efficient transportation network, the city quickly became the site of numerous war industries.

The Confederate arsenal was moved from Mount Vernon, Alabama, to Selma in 1862 for security reasons. Lt. Col. James L. White commanded the twenty-four-building facility that, toward the end of the war, became a major supply depot for the Confederate army. When Union troops seized the facility in 1865, they found fifteen siege guns, ten heavy carriages, ten field pieces, sixty field carriages, ten caissons, sixty thousand rounds of artillery ammunition, and a million rounds of small arms ammunition.

The Confederate government also established the Selma Naval Foundry in the city. Managed by Capt. Catesby Jones and employing over three thousand men, the foundry produced heavy artillery, siege guns, and gunboats. Selma workers built four Confederate ships—*Tennessee, Selma, Morgan,* and *Gaines.* The ships' armor plating came from the Selma Iron Works, which produced thirty tons of iron a day. Additional firms, such as the Nitre Works, the Powder Mill and Magazine, and at least ten other ironworks and foundries, boosted the importance of Selma as an industrial center. Historians have estimated that during the last two years of the war approximately one-half of the Confederate army's cannons and two-thirds of its ammunition came from Selma.

The city was also a center for light manufacturing, locomotive repair and production, and food distribution. Local industries generated guns, bayonets, swords, shovels, knapsacks, and clothing. When Selma fell to Union soldiers, the troops found five locomotives and ninety-two railroad cars in the city's two railroad production centers. Throughout the war, the Confederate Subsistence Department used Selma's

> **. . . approximately one-half of the Confederate army's cannons and two-thirds of its ammunition came from Selma.**

excellent railroad connections and location on the Alabama River to direct the flow of foodstuffs from the surrounding countryside to the Southern armies.

Although Selma's remote position from the fighting protected it from attack during the first four years of the war, the city's isolation ended in April 1865. At that time, Union Maj. Gen. James H. Wilson led over thirteen thousand cavalrymen on what one historian has described as a "Yankee Blitzkrieg" through central Mississippi, Alabama, and Georgia. Wilson's objective, like that of Gen. William Tecumseh Sherman, was to destroy the Confederacy's remaining production centers and to crush the Deep South's will to resist. His cavalry smashed into Selma on April 2, 1865, meeting a Confederate force led by Gen. Nathan Bedford Forrest. By nightfall, Wilson had routed Forrest's forces, capturing 2,700 men and wounding or killing an unknown number of others. Forty-six Union men were dead and 300 had been wounded. Before the attack, Selma residents had destroyed as much property as possible to keep it from falling into enemy hands.

Selma lay burned and its industries destroyed following Wilson's raid. As the war ended, the black belt slaveholders lost their human chattel and, as a result, much of their wealth. The freedmen received the franchise during the next ten years of Reconstruction and participated in local politics. But when the white elites returned to political power in 1874, white supremacy reappeared. Selma emerged from the Confederacy a poor farm town dominated by segregation and reactionary politics until the civil rights revolution in the 1960s.

BIBLIOGRAPHY

Fleming, Walter L. *Civil War and Reconstruction in Alabama.* New York, 1905.

Hardy, John. *Selma: Her Institutions and Her Men.* Selma, Ala., 1879. Reprint, Spartanburg, S.C., 1978.

Jackson, Walter M. *The Story of Selma.* Birmingham, Ala., 1954.

Jones, James P. *Yankee Blitzkrieg: Wilson's Raid through Alabama and Georgia.* Athens, Ga., 1976.

McMillan, Malcolm C. *The Alabama Confederate Reader.* Tuscaloosa, Ala., 1963.

RIC A. KABAT

Selma Naval Ordnance Works

Selma, on the Alabama River in south central Alabama, became a manufacturing center for the Confederacy early in the war. Access by water, rail, and stage (far from the early active theaters of combat) and nearby iron furnaces made Selma an attractive site. The overall complex included a shipyard, a niter facility, a foundry, and a machine shop.

The foundry and machine shop eventually became the Selma Naval Ordnance Works. Originally the Selma Manufacturing Company, the facilities were not well built and had failed financially. Colin J. McRae, a member of the Provisional Congress, undertook early in the war with other investors to sell the firm to the Confederate government. McRae intended to continue as manager and to use the new capital to construct a rolling mill and otherwise expand the facility. The Confederate government twice declined. McRae and his colleagues then purchased the works and used McRae's position to obtain contracts. In the fall of 1862, McRae was forced to cut back construction of expanded facilities for lack of skilled workers. Iron molders struck for higher wages, and McRae was able to retain only seven of eighteen needed molders.

The Confederate government bought McRae and his colleagues out in February 1863. Col. George W. Raines assumed command of the facility "in behalf of the Army and Navy." Raines personally disapproved of the facility and urged that it be turned over to the navy. On June 1, 1863, the navy took over sole operation.

The new commander was Catesby Jones, former executive officer of the ironclad *Virginia.* Jones, with the assistance of an experienced foundryman, George Peacock, completed renovation of the works by the end of January 1864, with the exception of the rolling mill.

The rolling mill never became a reality, and its machinery was leased to the nearby Shelby Iron Company. Once in production, the Selma works became the South's second major producer (after the Tredegar Iron Works in Richmond) of large rifled Brooke naval guns and cannon. The Brooke guns were made in two sizes: 6.4 inches weighing 10,000 pounds and 7 inches weighing 14,000 pounds. Over 100 were produced.

Secretary of the Navy Stephen R. Mallory in early 1865 estimated the capacity of the facility to be seven heavy guns and five fieldpieces per week with projectiles. Shortages of iron and skilled labor, however, reduced production to one or two heavy guns and one fieldpiece per week.

This output required day-and-night operations every day of the week except Sunday. By 1865 the facility employed over four hundred men, of whom three hundred were blacks. The Selma works shared the general problem of retaining skilled labor. When skilled white workers entered the army, the army controlled them. Requests from the navy to the army to have these men detailed back to navy facilities were slow in being answered and required renewal every two months.

The Selma facilities were raided by Maj. Gen. James H. Wilson's cavalry corps on April 3, 1865, and effectively destroyed.

BIBLIOGRAPHY

Layton, Edwin. "Colin J. McRae and the Selma Arsenal." *Alabama Review* 18 (1966): 125–136.

Still, William N., Jr. "Selma and the Confederate States Navy." *Alabama Review* 14 (1962): 19–37.

ROBERT H. MCKENZIE

Wilson's Raid on Selma

The 1865 raid on Selma by Union Brig. Gen. James Harrison Wilson resulted in the defeat of Confederate Lt. Gen. Nathan Bedford Forrest's cavalry and the capture of the city.

On January 24, Lt. Gen. Richard Taylor named Forrest commander of the cavalry in the Department of Alabama, Mississippi, and East Louisiana, and in February he was promoted to lieutenant general. He then reorganized his command and attempted to instill confidence and discipline in his men.

In the meantime, Wilson gathered a vast array of cavalry in two camps along the north bank of the Tennessee River, at Waterloo and Gravelly Springs, Alabama, and set about preparing for his campaign. He sent an officer to meet with Forrest under the guise of discussing a prisoner exchange, but for the main purpose of gathering intelligence on his adversary. Finally, on March 22, following two months of preparations, Wilson started south. The Union command of just under 14,000 troopers constituted the largest mounted force assembled during the war and was particularly well-armed and equipped.

From the start, Wilson enjoyed good fortune. A threatened Union movement from Pensacola, Florida, briefly diverted Forrest's attention and delayed the convergence of his scattered forces. Even so, Forrest hoped to concentrate his men near the vital industrial center of Selma.

By March 30, Wilson was in Elyton (Birmingham). He dispatched 1,100 men under Brig. Gen. John Croxton to march to Tuscaloosa, where they were to burn anything of supposed military value, including the University of Alabama. This expedition took Croxton's men out of the remainder of the Selma campaign.

Forrest attempted to throw various forces in the path of the Union column to delay its advance, but Wilson's men, under Brig. Gen. Emory Upton, brushed the Confederates aside near Montevallo. Only a timely counterthrust by Forrest, his 75-man escort, and some 200 troopers enabled the Southerners to stop their opponents temporarily. In the fighting, Col. Edward Crossland's Confederate brigade lost 100 men killed, wounded, and captured, or about one-sixth of the brigade's strength.

At some point on March 31 or April 1, Wilson's men captured a Confederate courier shuttling messages between Forrest and his subordinates. The captured dispatches revealed Forrest's plans and dispositions and gave Wilson a distinct advantage at a pivotal point in the campaign. He acted immediately on what he had learned by dispatching a force to destroy a critical bridge at Centerville, over which Forrest hoped to bring a substantial part of his scattered command. Brig. Gen. Edward M. McCook's troopers seized and destroyed the bridge, preventing Brig. Gen. William H. Jackson and his 3,000 veterans from uniting with Forrest in time to halt Wilson short of Selma. The Union commander could now concentrate his efforts upon defeating the Confederates in front of him and pushing on to Selma.

Forrest made a final stand in a strong position at Bogler's Creek, near Ebenezer Church. Here, following a brief but sharp fight, Union cavalry under Upton and Brig. Gen. Eli Long forced Forrest to retreat to Selma, when the Alabama State Militia broke under the weight of the combined Union assault. The Battle of Ebenezer Church cost Wilson 12 killed and 40 wounded, but cost Forrest 300 or more, mostly captured, and three artillery pieces. The Confederate commander himself suffered painful wounds when a Union captain slashed at him with his saber before Forrest got his pistol free and killed his assailant.

By 2:00 P.M. on April 2, the first of Wilson's men had arrived before Selma. Here, the Union commander received a last piece of good fortune when his men captured one of the designers of the city's defenses, which the prisoner willingly drew for his captors. At 5:00 P.M., Wilson sent Long and Upton against the Confederate defenses. Although the

Southern fire was heavier and more effective than expected, the Federals soon drove their opponents out of their first line of works and into a second. A renewed assault shattered this line when the Southern militia broke for the final time. For Forrest and the rest of his men, the battle degenerated into hundreds of individual combats as the Confederates struggled to escape or gave in and surrendered.

By the end of the day, Wilson securely held the industrial center as well as some 2,700 Confederate prisoners, at a cost of 46 killed, 300 wounded, and 13 missing. Forrest had one final fight in which he killed his thirtieth man in personal combat before successfully evading capture and escaping from Selma.

BIBLIOGRAPHY

Jones, James Pickett. *Yankee Blitzkrieg: Wilson's Raid through Alabama and Georgia.* Athens, Ga., 1976.

Longacre, Edward G. *From Union Stars to Top Hat: A Biography of the Extraordinary General James Harrison Wilson.* Harrisonburg, Pa., 1972.

Wills, Brian Steel. *A Battle from the Start: The Life of Nathan Bedford Forrest.* New York, 1992.

Wilson, James Harrison. *Under the Old Flag: Recollections of Military Operations in the War for the Union, the Spanish War, the Boxer Rebellion, etc.* New York, 1912.

BRIAN S. WILLS

SEMMES, RAPHAEL

SEMMES, RAPHAEL (1809–1877), rear admiral. Semmes was captain of CSS *Sumter* and CSS *Alabama* and admiral of the James River Squadron. His duty on the two ships was to prey upon enemy merchant vessels, and he did that job better than any other naval captain in naval history, burning sixty-four U.S. registered merchant vessels and bonding thirteen others. On *Sumter* he was the first to show the Confederate flag on the high seas and in neutral ports; on *Alabama* he sank USS *Hatteras*, a new U.S. Navy ironclad side-wheeler.

The experiences of his youth foreshadowed the introspective and self-reliant captain of *Sumter* and *Alabama*. Born in Maryland and orphaned at age nine, Raphael and his younger brother moved to Georgetown, D.C., to live with two of their uncles. Raphael, influenced by a merchant shipping uncle, was drawn first to sea life and second to law. A third uncle, a Maryland politician and future congressman, secured an appointment for him as a midshipman in the U.S. Navy, dated April 1, 1826. Raphael was sixteen.

A second career was necessary in the old navy because officers frequently received long enforced leaves without pay.

RAPHAEL SEMMES. Civil War–period engraving.
NAVAL HISTORICAL CENTER, WASHINGTON, D.C.

Thus, after Semmes spent five years as a trainee officer, he was promoted to passed midshipman and placed on extended leave. He seized the opportunity to read law, passed the bar exam in 1833, and established a law office in Cincinnati, Ohio.

When recalled to duty, now Lieutenant Semmes was assigned to the Pensacola, Florida, Navy Yard. He moved his family to nearby Alabama and from that moment considered himself a citizen of that state. To help his wife with their growing family, he purchased three household slaves. His conversion to the Southern way of life was complete.

Semmes's experiences in the U.S. Navy prepared him for his role in the Civil War. On various ships he sailed the Gulf coasts on survey duty, was lighthouse inspector on the Gulf and Atlantic coasts, and performed blockade duty off Vera Cruz during the Mexican War. He commanded four U.S. Navy vessels.

From the end of the Mexican War until 1855 he remained on leave, practicing law in Mobile and writing *Service Afloat and Ashore during the War with Mexico,* a best-seller in the early 1850s. He was promoted to the rank of commander (1855), assigned as inspector of the Eighth Lighthouse District, and then transferred to Washington as secretary of the Lighthouse Board (1858) and later as member of the board (February 1861). By then his survey and lighthouse assignments had provided him with a thorough knowledge of Gulf, Caribbean, and North Atlantic shorelines, tides, and winds.

When Alabama seceded from the Union, Semmes resigned from the U.S. Navy to offer his services to the Confederacy. In 1861 his appearance commanded respect. Slightly below medium height with an erect bearing, he wore his hair long over his ears, had a large waxed mustache and small goatee, and had piercing black eyes. Highly intelligent and a voracious reader, he based the decision to follow his adopted state out of the Union on the constitutional ground that the Federal government had no right to impose its will on the several Southern states.

While traveling by train to Montgomery, Alabama, where Jefferson Davis had established the Provisional Government, he rode through a pine-forest fire. The flames prompted him to muse that "civil war is a terrible crucible through which to pass character."

He arrived in Montgomery in February 1861, met with President Davis, and left a day later to shop for arms and munitions in Northern states. In Montgomery, on April 4, Secretary of the Navy Stephen R. Mallory appointed Semmes commander in the Confederate navy and chief of the Lighthouse Bureau.

The firing on Fort Sumter led Semmes to realize that "it was time to leave the things of peace to the future." He asked Mallory for a ship suitable for commerce raiding, and Mallory showed him a file on a ship in New Orleans, already examined and condemned. "Give me that ship," Semmes said. On the newly converted *Sumter,* Semmes cleverly eluded USS *Brooklyn* and sailed into the Gulf of Mexico on June 30, 1861.

President Abraham Lincoln's proclamation of a blockade of Southern ports and Davis's statement of intent to issue letters of marque forced Great Britain and France to proclaim their neutrality, which effectively recognized the Confederacy as de facto belligerent with the same international rights and limitations as held by the United States.

Semmes's objective was to draw U.S. warships from blockade duty by sinking U.S. merchant ships. His success against merchantmen led merchants worldwide to refuse to ship under the U.S. flag. (In Singapore, Semmes found seventeen U.S. merchantmen lying without cargoes for over three months.) Still, the United States would not weaken the blockade, and its merchant fleet has never recovered its prewar second position in world commercial shipping.

The *Sumter* cruise was a learning experience for Semmes. The blockade of Southern ports and limitations imposed by neutral countries prevented him from taking a prize into any port for adjudication. He regretfully burned his first victim, *Golden Rocket,* and then vainly attempted to force the weak Caribbean neutrals to accept his captures for adjudication. Afterward, constituting himself a maritime court and carefully following international law, he condemned, bonded, or released his prizes (except for two) according to their flag or registration and ownership of their cargo (neutral ownership protected the ship). On *Alabama* he converted one prize into CSS *Tuscaloosa* (June 1863) and sold another in August 1863.

Sumter was small, slowed when under sail by the drag of her propeller, and could ship only an eight-day supply of coal. Yet in six months Semmes captured eighteen ships, seven of which he destroyed. He hunted along the currents and winds that merchant ships traveled. Only the vessel's limitations hampered his success. He was blockaded at St. Pierre, Martinique, by USS *Iroquois,* but drawing upon his experiences as a blockader he eluded the more powerful ship. Semmes then headed for Cadiz, Spain, to effect needed repairs. Frustrated by Spanish delays, he sailed to Gibraltar, making his last capture within sight of the rock. Unable to repair *Sumter's* boilers and blockaded by three Union vessels, he abandoned the ship and with 1st Lt. John McIntosh Kell went to London.

In England he met Commdr. James Dunwoody Bulloch who had designed a ship (*#290*) being built in the Laird Shipyards on the Mersey River, Liverpool. Semmes admired the ship as being perfect for a commerce cruiser. Assuming Bulloch would command her, Semmes sailed for home. In

> **From then on, Semmes referred to the ship as if she were his living partner in a great endeavor.**

Nassau on June 8, 1862, he learned of his promotion to captain and assignment to command (*#290*). He returned to England.

Bulloch meanwhile had sent (*#290*), unarmed, to the Azores Islands. Semmes and Bulloch with supplies, arms, officers, and sailors rendezvoused just off the islands in international waters. Semmes's first glimpse of (*#290*) afloat with her "perfect symmetry" and "lifting device to prevent drag when under sail" excited him. From then on, Semmes referred to the ship as if she were his living partner in a great endeavor. The partnership would last for twenty-three months. Together they would set a record of merchant ship captures that still stands. On August 24, 1862, in neutral waters, Semmes commissioned *Alabama* as a regular warship of the Confederate navy.

Alabama's crew, an international mix, required a firm discipline tempered with mercy. Semmes rarely appeared on deck except to take readings of the ship's position and give orders of the day to 1st Lieutenant Kell, who controlled the crew. Most of the officers had served on *Sumter.*

Semmes began the cruise on nearby waters where Northern whalers were at work. His first victim, heavy with whale oil, was the first of 54 ships he would capture and of

447 he would speak or board. When hailing a ship he would fly the U.S. flag and, if answered by the same, raise the Confederate standard and command the ship to halt. Should she attempt to flee, he would fire a shot and send aboard an armed party whose officer would escort the victim's captain and papers to Semmes's cabin. Should the papers show the cargo to be neutral-owned, Semmes would bond the ship and allow it to continue its voyage; if enemy-owned, the boarding party would take off the victim's crew and passengers, if any, plus whatever *Alabama* could use—food, clothing, rigging, coal—and then set the ship afire. Semmes would cruise one area until he felt Northern warships might learn of his location and then seek other hunting grounds.

Semmes moved southward to the Caribbean Sea and the Gulf of Mexico. He resented the reputation Northern newspapers bestowed upon him: "He never fights, just plunders." Learning of a Union fleet off the Texas coast, he decided to disrupt it. Approaching it, he lured USS *Hatteras* from the fleet and sank her in a close exchange.

Later, Semmes, heading for the East Indies, crossed the South Atlantic for South Africa and in Simon's Town refurbished the ship and refreshed the men. En route he noted in his ship's journal that his time afloat "had produced a constant tension of the nervous system and a wear and tear of body . . . . I am supremely disgusted with the sea and all its belongings." After a stormy voyage to the East Indies, he sank three merchant ships, futilely sought combat with USS *Wyoming,* and sailed to Singapore for rest.

Despite disheartening news from America, on the return voyage his spirits were momentarily raised by his last capture. In the eastern Atlantic Ocean, *Alabama* chased a victim all night. "When the day dawned we were within a couple of miles of him. It was the old spectacle of the panting breathless fawn, and the inexorable staghound." But as Semmes read the latest newspapers taken from the victim and learned of the Northern victories—it was late May 1864—he saw himself, in the third person, as one on whose shoulders the stress and strain of three years had laid "a load of a dozen years." Now *Alabama* was only a "wearied foxhound." And above his visions of man and ship, he saw "shadows of a sorrowful future."

On June 11, 1864, Semmes and *Alabama* limped into the harbor of Cherbourg, France, seeking refuge in the imperial docks. Immediately, Semmes wrote to Comm. Samuel Barron in Paris: "My health has suffered so much from a constant and harassing service of three years almost continuously at sea, that I shall have to ask for relief [from command of *Alabama*]." But fate in the form of Capt. John A. Winslow and USS *Kearsarge* intervened. *Alabama* now faced a possible blockade. Semmes decided that the ship should fight rather than rot in a French port. So he sent a message to

Winslow, a former shipmate: "If you will give me time to recoal, I will come out and give you battle."

On June 19, 1864, *Alabama,* her sailors and officers in full dress uniform, sailed out of the harbor before cheering crowds. About seven miles into the English Channel, the two ships began firing; after sixty-five minutes *Alabama* was foundering. As she sank stern first, Semmes threw his sword into the sea, and then he and Kell jumped from the ship and swam to a boat from the English yacht *Deerhound.* "We fought her until she could no longer swim," Semmes later wrote, "and then gave her to the waves."

In Southampton, Semmes wrote his report to Mallory. Devastated by defeat and slightly wounded, he tried to explain the loss of his ship. Noting that *Alabama*'s shells did little damage to the side of the *Kearsarge,* he later blamed the loss on *Kearsarge*'s chain-covered sides. He was entertained by pro-Confederate groups, presented with a new sword, and traveled on the Continent. Refreshed, he began a strenuous seven-and-one-half-week trip to his home in Mobile, arriving on December 19, 1864.

He left Mobile on January 2, 1865, for Richmond, where President Davis and Congress honored him, promoted him to rear admiral, and assigned him to command the James River Squadron. When Ulysses S. Grant turned Robert E. Lee's right flank, Semmes was ordered to destroy his fleet and join Davis in Danville, Virginia. There the president appointed him a brigadier general of artillery. Ordered to join Joseph E. Johnston's forces in North Carolina, Semmes received the generous pardon granted by William Tecumseh Sherman to Johnston at Guilford Courthouse.

Semmes returned to his home in Mobile, but on December 15, 1865, he was arrested and imprisoned in Washington, D.C., charged by Secretary of the Navy Gideon Welles with having fled from the *Kearsarge-Alabama* battle after having surrendered by showing a white flag and, later, "without having been exchanged as a prisoner engaged in hostilities against the United States." After four months of imprisonment, he was released for lack of proper evidence.

Semmes returned to Mobile and, forbidden to hold public office, attempted to make a living by teaching in the Louisiana Military Institute, editing a newspaper in Memphis, Tennessee, and lecturing for small fees. Finally, he practiced law in Mobile, specializing in maritime law. In 1869 he published the 833-page *Memoirs of Service Afloat during the War between the States.* He died in 1877 at his summer cottage on Point Clear, across the bay from Mobile, from food poisoning.

BIBLIOGRAPHY

Case, Lynn M., and Warren F. Spencer. *The United States and France: Civil War Diplomacy.* Philadelphia, 1970.

Humphreys, Anderson, and Curt Guenther. *Semmes America.* Memphis, Tenn., 1989.

Kell, John McIntosh. *Recollections of a Navy Life Including the Cruises of the Confederate States Steamers "Sumter" and "Alabama."* Washington, D.C., 1900.

Newman, Harry Wright. *The Maryland Semmes and Kindred Families.* Baltimore, 1936.

Roberts, W. Adolfe. *Semmes of the Alabama.* New York, 1938.

Summersell, Charles Grayson. *The Cruise of the C.S.S. Sumter.* Tuscaloosa, Ala., 1965.

Summersell, Charles Grayson. *CSS Alabama: Builder, Captain, and Plans.* University, Ala., 1985.

WARREN F. SPENCER

SEMMES, THOMAS

SEMMES, THOMAS (1824–1899), congressman from Louisiana. For the last fifty years of the nineteenth century, Thomas Jenkins Semmes was a prominent New Orleans lawyer, Democratic politician, and senior statesmen. Although seldom associated with any single piece of significant legislation, Semmes as a Confederate senator helped shape policy in the areas of martial law, conscription, retaliation, and finances.

Semmes, first cousin and foster brother of Confederate Adm. Raphael Semmes, was born and raised in Washington, D.C. His father, a prominent merchant, came from a wealthy, Catholic landholding family from Maryland's Western Shore. His mother had been on personal terms with every U.S. president from James Monroe to Abraham Lincoln. While in the White House, Martin Van Buren used to visit the family, playing games with young Thomas and his playmates. Semmes enrolled in Georgetown College at age eleven, finishing at the top of his class six years later. In 1845 he graduated from Harvard Law School, where his classmates included President John Tyler's nephew, Henry Semple, and future Republican president Rutherford B. Hayes. Semmes was well positioned to launch his own career in law and politics.

One of two defining moments in Semmes's early political career occurred while he was studying at Harvard. He chanced to read proslavery theorist and Virginia jurist Abel P. Upshur's *Brief Enquiry into the True Nature and Character of our Federal Government* (1840), arguably one of the strongest historical cases for state sovereignty ever written. Upshur's treatise was an extended attack upon the constitutional nationalism embedded in Harvard Professor and U.S. Supreme Court Justice Joseph Story's widely influential *Commentaries on the Constitution of the United States.* Impressed with Upshur's logic, Semmes abandoned his family's staunch allegiance to the Whig party and became a Democrat—presumably of the extreme state rights persuasion. Like many young Southern intellectuals coming of age just prior to the Civil War, Semmes was swept along by the growing popularity of Southern nationalism.

The other defining moment in Semmes's early political career occurred five years after he relocated to New Orleans. From 1850 to 1855 Semmes had built up a moderately successful commercial practice as an attorney to cotton factors and brokers, and he had moved his family into a fashionable uptown section of the city, upriver from the Catholic French Quarter and the mixed immigrant wards. New Orleans had just emerged from four decades of rancorous American-Creole rivalry when a heavy influx of potato-famine Irish immigrants triggered an explosion of nativist political violence that divided New Orleans into armed camps. As Whigs, most of Semmes's clients and neighbors had joined the anti-immigrant American, or Know-Nothing, party, but in 1855 Semmes delivered an impassioned antinativist speech that ended his law partnership with a former Harvard classmate. The address caught the attention of the city's and state's Democratic leadership, who doubtless recognized that Semmes combined political and social characteristics that were unusual for antebellum New Orleans. He was an Anglo-American transplant, yet a Catholic; an uptown lawyer, yet a Democrat. And he had excellent national connections. The Democratic sachems immediately tapped him for the State Central Committee. A short time later Semmes was elected to the Louisiana legislature that met in 1856 and 1857.

Thereafter Semmes's political star rose quickly. In 1858 Democratic President James Buchanan appointed him U.S. attorney for the Eastern District of New Orleans—a position that gave him the duty of prosecuting ex–New Orleanian William Walker for filibustering in Nicaragua (Semmes persuaded Buchanan to drop the charges). The following year Semmes was elected by a comfortable margin to be state attorney general. He was only thirty-five years old.

From secession through Appomattox, Semmes figured prominently in the politics of the short-lived Confederate nation. A member of the New Orleans Southern Rights Association, which helped tip a divided city toward disunion during the 1860–1861 secession winter, Semmes was elected as an "immediate secessionist"—that is, a believer in separate state action—to the Louisiana secession convention of 1861. As a member of the convention's important Committee of Fifteen, he helped draft the ordinance that severed the Pelican State's ties to the old Union. His action was almost predictable in light of his youthful Southern nationalism. Semmes's first Confederate service was as a district judge, advising President Jefferson Davis about the legality of suspending bank specie payments in New Orleans. To conserve scarce bullion and facilitate the circulation of Confederate currency, the central government ordered banks to cease paying drafts in gold and silver.

After several close ballots, the Louisiana legislature in November 1861 elected Semmes to the Confederate Senate. He took his seat in February 1862. As Semmes was the fifth youngest senator in a group whose average age was nearly ten years older than his own, his role in that body was as an auxiliary, not a principal. He served on the important Finance and Judiciary committees but did not chair a major committee until picked to head Judiciary late in the war. His most well-known (and apparently lengthiest) speech was one he delivered as chairman of the Committee on the Flag and the Seal, when he argued for a Latin word change on the Confederate seal, partly on the ground that the word choice for *God* was too "pagan."

Notwithstanding his junior status, Semmes played an active part in shaping important legislation. His contribution was as a conservative, which stemmed naturally from his upper-class background, Catholic fundamentalism, and experience as a lawyer serving the interests of the rich and powerful. He thus worked closely with Virginia's Robert M. T. Hunter, chairman of the Senate Finance Committee, in drafting the regressive tax-in-kind bill—the unpopular tithing law that generated the bulk of the Richmond government's tax revenues after 1863. He also assisted the effort by Louisiana's senior senator, Edward Sparrow, a fabulously wealthy slave-owning planter from the state's cotton delta, in getting overseers exempted from the wartime draft. Semmes's amendment to the 1862 Conscription Law was the chief impetus for the hated Twenty-Slave Law that subsequently fueled the "rich man's war, poor man's fight" backlash.

Semmes also played a pivotal role in shaping Confederate policy on retaliation. The running congressional debates as to how to respond to "Yankee atrocities" boiled over after Lincoln's Emancipation Proclamation took effect and the Union began systematically enlisting black soldiers. Believing the Lincoln administration was trying to foment slave insurrections, Jefferson Davis made known his intention to hand over to state prosecutors captured white officers of black troops. The Senate Judiciary Committee, however, issued an adverse report on Davis's plan. Declaring retaliation was a belligerent right that could be exercised only by the central government, Semmes introduced and secured passage of a joint resolution assigning such cases to military tribunals rather than state courts. The Lincoln administration's threat to retaliate against retaliation, however, discouraged the Confederate government from carrying out its threat to execute white officers.

Although one study of the Confederate Congress places Semmes with the proadministration faction, the fact is the junior senator from Louisiana was consistently opposed to Davis on most issues where there was room for disagreement. The only important issue on which they apparently concurred was the establishment of a supreme court, which Davis favored and Semmes unsuccessfully tried to create by means of legislation. Otherwise, the two men were at policy loggerheads—on martial law, the military role of P. G. T. Beauregard, and cabinet term limitations. Given the Confederate president's tendency to personalize conflict, his relationship with Semmes doubtless became strained as early as August 1862, when the New Orleanian asked the Judiciary Committee to report a bill prohibiting military officers from usurping civilian authority. Semmes was acting at the behest of Vice President Alexander H. Stephens, who, along with such other anti-administration stalwarts as Sparrow and Arkansas Senator Augustus Hill Garland, boarded at Semmes's rented mansion across the street from Davis's official Richmond residence. The martial law controversy had first blown up when the president asked Congress to suspend indefinitely the writ of habeas corpus, in effect making martial law part of "the permanent war effort." Like most western senators, especially from states where Union armies had established a beachhead, Semmes felt strong constituent pressure to keep Confederate generals from seizing authority to fix prices and muzzle the press. Trying to finesse the argument, the Senate Judiciary Committee let its House counterpart conduct a thorough study of the points at issue. In the end Semmes's martial law limitation bill was narrowly defeated because of congressional reluctance to enact laws that would likely be disregarded under emergency conditions.

If the martial law debates did not completely strain Semmes's and Davis's relationship, the controversy over Davis's treatment of New Orleans Gen. P. G. T. Beauregard produced an open break between senator and president. The disagreement flared up after Davis, still trading recriminations with Beauregard over the aftermath of First Manassas, let the Creole general languish as commander of the inconsequential Department of South Carolina and Georgia rather than reassign him to the Army of the West, which he had commanded for a short spell after Albert Sidney Johnston's death at Shiloh. By agreement with their congressional colleagues, in September 1862 while the martial law controversy was simmering, Semmes and Sparrow personally presented Davis with a petition signed by sixty senators and representatives appealing for Beauregard's restoration to the western command. Davis gave the senators a cool reception. Reading the petition aloud, including all sixty names, and interweaving his interpretive disagreements into the running commentary, Davis ended the interview by declaring he would not turn over the western army to Beauregard even if *"the whole world united in the petition."* Semmes and Sparrow came away from the meeting obviously miffed.

By January 1864, Semmes had become closely identified with the loosely organized anti-administration faction's effort to circumscribe Davis's power and authority. The previous December the Senate Judiciary Committee had taken up a bill introduced by Senator Waldo Johnson of Missouri that would limit cabinet terms to two years; in effect, the president would have to secure Senate reconfirmation of his bureau heads at the beginning of each new Congress. Partly a reflection of fears that a British cabinet form of government was evolving from the practice of some cabinet officers serving concurrently in Congress, the bill sought to assert the rights of the states over those of the central government. Semmes wrote the Judiciary Committee's favorable report sending the legislation onto the floor, arguing that the bill was constitutionally necessary to brake the executive's propensity for retaining in high office "individuals obnoxious to the States, as represented in the Senate." The Confederate War Department clerk John B. Jones said the measure was a declaration of war between Davis and the Congress. Confederate diarist Mary Boykin Chesnut recorded that Davis would have resigned had the bill become law—which it failed to do.

It also fell to Senator Semmes to fire Congress's parting shot at the disgruntled president. In March 1865, Davis aroused congressional ire by scolding lawmakers for their grudging approval of his plan to enlist black soldiers and grant them freedom. His brief message rehearsing old arguments about congressional obstructionism provoked the Senate to set up a secret Committee of Five to answer Davis's charges. Semmes drafted a report that canvassed every area of disagreement between Congress and the executive—impressment, exemptions, martial law, taxes—and concluded by rebuking Davis for transmitting a message "calculated to excite discord and dissension." A short while later, the Confederate Congress adjourned—sine die as military events would soon dictate.

For all his important behind-the-scenes committee and legislative floor work, Semmes's sociability made the most lasting impression on many of his contemporaries. At the time of his Richmond sojourn, Semmes was not a wealthy man by the standards of the Confederate Senate; he lost the wealth he had accumulated in New Orleans when Union authorities confiscated and sold his house and all his belongings shortly after occupying the city. But Semmes had married well. His wife, Myra Knox, was the daughter of a wealthy banker-planter from Montgomery, Alabama. Her father sent the hampers of food (and possibly the costly rent payments) that made Semmes's mansion in Richmond such an affordably popular boardinghouse for Confederate influentials. Myra furnished the hospitality and grace that made social occasions at the mansion the stuff of wartime legend—as well as the target of wrathful barbs from the Richmond press. Mary Chesnut's famous diary alludes frequently to the couple's charade-filled parties and soirees attended by the brass and class of Confederate Richmond. Of medium height and middle-class girth, the balding and mustachioed Semmes used to perform upper-class renditions of slave heel-and-toe hoedowns as parlor audiences in his home cried out "The Honorable Senator from Louisiana has the floor."

Indeed, Semmes's wartime memories were more vivid regarding Confederate social life than congressional legislation. Those days were, as he recalled in the 1890s, "the last chapter in the history of that olden life." More than thirty years later, Semmes and his wife could still remember the price they paid for the 1864 New Year's turkey banquet—"one of the last big dinners that we had at our house," Myra Semmes told a New Orleans reporter.

In October 1865, Semmes joined the stream of pardon-seekers appealing for amnesty from President Andrew Johnson. It required only a five-minute interview for Semmes to secure his pardon and Johnson's good wishes. With a hundred-dollar loan, Semmes returned to his private law practice and financial well-being by landing such lucrative clients as the notorious Louisiana Lottery Company whose case he argued before the U.S. Supreme Court in 1891. Semmes rose quickly to the head of the state bar. From 1873 to 1879 he served as professor of civil law at the University of Louisiana (now Tulane). Called "the incarnation of logic" by local lawyers who admired his grasp of Greek and Latin, Semmes was counsel on almost every leading case that came before the civil courts in the postbellum era. In 1887 Semmes was elected president of the American Bar Association, and in 1890 he was invited to address the centennial celebration of the founding of the U.S. Supreme Court. Semmes was also in contention for the Supreme Court seat eventually filled by Mississippian L. Q. C. Lamar.

The couple's social life after the Civil War also resumed its busy pace. Well into the twentieth century, New Orleans's society still remembered Myra Semmes's masked balls and strict social conventions; getting on her exclusive party call list was a clear sign one had arrived. Thomas Semmes also perched atop the carnival and social hierarchy of uptown New Orleans. His national connections (he entertained President Grover Cleveland when he visited the Crescent City) added to a social cachet already impeccable by virtue of his Confederate pedigree. Among his other social honors, Semmes served as president of New Orleans's exclusive Boston Club. While consolidating his authority in New Orleans's society, Semmes was also deepening his involvement with organized Catholicism, becoming active in the Jesuit Alumni Association, lending his legal expertise to the church, and befriending several of the city's archbishops. Semmes's Anglo-Catholicism helped bridge the ethnocultural divisions that had split the New Orleans upper class during the first five decades of the nineteenth century.

As for postwar politics, Semmes played the role of senior statesman. He served prominently in both state constitutional conventions of 1879 and 1898. In the earlier convention he was instrumental in defeating agrarian efforts to repudiate the Reconstruction bonded debt and thus damage state credit. As chairman of the 1898 convention's Judiciary Committee, Semmes helped enact Louisiana's sweeping dis-franchisement provision—which by the early 1900s had resulted in purging nearly all blacks and a substantial number of illiterate poor whites from the voting lists. His conservatism was also felt on New Orleans's school board, to which Semmes had been appointed in 1877 by Governor Francis T. Nicholls. As board president, Semmes was in the forefront of the effort to end New Orleans's successful experiment with integrated public schools and to slash expenditures to the bone. As an upper-class, extremely conservative Catholic, Semmes believed, as he put it at the 1874 law school graduation, that "compulsory education ignores moral and religious culture, [and] sacrifices heart and soul on the altar of material science."

By the time of Jefferson Davis's death in 1889, the scars of wartime politics had not completely healed. Deliberately excluded from the carriages escorting the ex–Confederate president's funeral cortege, Semmes paid tribute to Davis by marching with the procession of Confederate veterans from New Orleans to Metairie Cemetery. When Semmes died ten years later, he, too, as the last surviving Confederate senator, was given full military rites. According to a contemporary, his funeral was "one of the largest and most imposing" ever witnessed in New Orleans.

BIBLIOGRAPHY

Alexander, Thomas B., and Richard E. Beringer. *The Anatomy of the Confederate Congress: A Study of the Influences of Member Characteristics on Legislative Voting Behavior, 1861–1865.* Nashville, Tenn., 1972.

Biographical and Historical Memoirs of Louisiana. Vol. 2. Chicago, 1892.

Chesnut, Mary Boykin. *Mary Chesnut's Civil War.* Edited by C. Vann Woodward. New Haven, Conn., 1981.

"Hon. Thomas J. Semmes: An Evening with the Venerable Statesman and Jurist." *Southern Historical Society Papers* 25 (1897): 317–333. Reprint, Wilmington, N.C., 1991.

Humphreys, Anderson, and Curt Guenther. *Semmes America.* Memphis, Tenn., 1989.

"University of Louisiana, Law Department. Address of Hon. Thos. J. Semmes." *New Orleans Picayune,* April 28, 1874.

"When Mrs. Thomas J. Semmes Was Hostess." *New Orleans Item-Tribune,* March 24, 1929.

Yearns, Wilfred B. *The Confederate Congress.* Athens, Ga., 1960.

LAWRENCE N. POWELL

SERMONS

Prior to the summer and fall of 1860 the sermons of Southern clergymen, generally, were apolitical in content; they were evangelical and emphasized the theological importance of religious experience for the salvation of the individual. In this respect the sermons of Southern clergymen were similar to those of clergymen throughout the country. As sectional tensions increased and secession drew closer, however, the sermons of some Southern clergymen increasingly began to reflect the tensions polarizing the nation and to espouse the views, values, and opinions of their environment.

Political issues became the subject of many sermons during this period. Some espoused secession from the Union, whereas others urged a more moderate or cautious approach to the political situation. The sermons of two prominent Presbyterian clergymen illustrate this reflection of Southern sentiment. Robert Lewis Dabney, moderator of the Synod of Virginia, preached a fast-day sermon on the first Sunday in November 1860. He denounced the passionate men whom he said were agitating the country and advised his listeners to pray for peace, vote for virtuous men, and be calm in language and manner. About the same time, James H. Thornwell, the most influential person in Southern Presbyterianism and a professor of theology at the denomination's seminary in Columbia, South Carolina, preached a thanksgiving sermon in which he declared that the Federal Union had become intolerable and was synonymous with tyranny, oppression, and falsehood. He denounced the Federal government as corrupt and declared that it was no longer possible to live with self-respect in a Union with a Republican chief executive. He recommended that the state of South Carolina secede from the Union at once.

Prior to the firing on Fort Sumter in April 1861, sentiments similar to those of Dabney and Thornwell were expressed by Baptist, Episcopal, Lutheran, Methodist, and other clergy in the South. But once war erupted and Abraham Lincoln called for volunteers to subdue rebellion, most clergymen, including moderates like Dabney, espoused the cause of the South.

Sermons justifying secession were based on three arguments. One was the state sovereignty doctrine enunciated forcefully by John C. Calhoun and other politicians since the 1830s. A second was the alleviation of unjust economic exploitation. Basil Manly and James C. Furman, Baptist clergymen in Alabama and South Carolina, respectively, argued that the South, for years, had been unjustly treated by Federal tariff laws. A final argument offered to justify secession was based upon Holy Scripture. The creation of the Confederacy was described as the working of the hand of God in history in a manner not unlike his creation of the Kingdom of Israel under David. It was asserted that the prosperity, atheism, and materialism of the North had prompted the Almighty to move against the United States, to divide it and to set apart a righteous remnant in the South to preserve his truth, justice, and honor.

The clergy's arguments defending secession and the Confederacy and placing the blame for the breakup of the Union on the North reflected the opinions many Southern politicians had been expressing for decades. The sermons of

the vast majority of churchmen were in harmony with their intellectual environment, indicating that the clergymen were more followers than leaders of events and opinion at this time in Southern history.

It should be noted, however, that even after the war began not all Southern clergymen were apologists for the Confederacy and its values and institutions. Scattered throughout the region were some clergy, found in all denominations, who opposed the course of the South, viewed it as a road to destruction, and remained pro-Union in their sympathies. This sentiment was greatest in the areas of southwestern Virginia, eastern Tennessee, and western North Carolina, but it could be heard in every Southern state. Perhaps the most prominent clergymen of this persuasion were the Methodist William G. Brownlow of Tennessee, the Presbyterian James A. Lyon of Columbus, Mississippi, and Protestant Episcopal Bishop Alexander Gregg of Texas.

Among the overwhelming majority of clergymen supporting the Confederacy, religion became practically synonymous with patriotism during the war. The struggle was portrayed from numerous pulpits as a just or holy cause against a tyrannical aggressor. Southern men were urged to defend their homes and were told that they could enter into the war without compunction and with the faith that, though the battles might be bloody and rugged, the God of Hosts would be with them. Some clergymen, in their sermons, urged men to volunteer for the army. A prominent Presbyterian clergyman, Benjamin Morgan Palmer, composed a sermon based on *Psalms* 144:1, "Blessed be the Lord, my strength, which teacheth my hands to war and my fingers to fight," which he preached on numerous occasions to arouse the people and stimulate men to join the army. Mary B. Chesnut once attended a fast-day service and confessed that the sermon "stirred my blood, my flesh crept and tingled. A red hot glow of patriotism passed over me. There was . . . .exhortation to fight and die." Other clergymen such as David Sullins and Bishop George F. Pierce, both Methodists, would occasionally accompany recruiters and address gatherings, urging the people to keep the faith and young men to volunteer for the army.

It was customary for sermons to explain the role of Almighty God in every victory and defeat of Confederate forces. Defeats were usually portrayed as necessary preparations for peace and prosperity; they were God's means of testing and building character. Southerners were reminded that God always chastises those whom he loves the most. The people were implored to remain firm in the faith and were assured that God would grant them the ultimate victory and independence. On the other hand, Confederate victory in battle was considered a gift of God and the evidence of his good pleasure toward the South. When George B. McClellan was forced to withdraw from the vicinity of Richmond in the summer of 1862, clergymen from Virginia to Texas proclaimed to their congregations that God had delivered the South from the oppressor and that it was evident that he was on the side of the South.

Clergymen of all denominations participated in numerous days of fasting and thanksgiving. These days were usually designated by secular authorities, and at such times businesses were closed and worship services were held. These fast-day sermons might thank the Almighty for some victory; urge citizens to greater efforts for independence; implore the people to keep the faith; and assure their listeners of God's continual care, even in the face of a military defeat.

Although the churches in the South had been engaged in missions to convert the slaves prior to 1861, denominational leaders were not pleased with the success of their efforts. During the war church spokesmen urged their constituency not to neglect the religious instruction of their servants. Some churchmen in the South speculated that the war was partially God's wrath for their failure to devote sufficient time and resources to converting the blacks. During the war the conscience of Protestantism was stirred by certain aspects of slavery which it was believed were not in keeping with Biblical teachings. For example, in a fast-day sermon in 1863 Methodist Bishop George F. Pierce declared that slave owners should recognize the legality and sacredness of slave marriages. Various Baptist and Presbyterian spokesmen in the South echoed Pierce's sentiments. Other reforms requested by churchmen included removing the ban on teaching slaves to read and write, and repealing the laws prohibiting blacks from preaching the gospel. Before the end of the war a few churchmen expressed sympathy for emancipation, especially for those slaves who might serve in the Confederate military forces.

Sermons by prominent clergymen were published in denominational weekly newspapers and journals, and by tract organizations such as the Evangelical Tract Society of Petersburg, Virginia, and the General Tract Agency of Raleigh, North Carolina. Some sermons were also printed and distributed by denominational agencies such as the Sunday School and Bible Board of the Baptist General Association of Virginia or the Presbyterian Committee of Publications in Richmond, Virginia. An indeterminate number of sermons were published in the South during the war. Some sources list approximately one hundred; probably as many more were printed in religious newspapers and journals during the same period.

During the course of the war, ecumenical organizations printed and distributed to soldiers more than one hundred tracts totaling over 60,000,000 pages. These tracts, consisting of four to sixteen pages, contained sermons, devotionals, instructions for Christian conduct, and exegesis on various items of Christian doctrine. Some denominations also published religious newspapers intended specifically for the men in the armed forces. Two of these papers, *The Soldiers'*

Paper and the *Army and Navy Herald,* claimed a monthly circulation of 40,000 copies in 1862.

When the Confederacy collapsed in the spring of 1865 the sermons did not reflect bitterness and despair. Clergymen explained that the outcome of the war was still the will of God. The people of the South were counseled to accept the surrender of their armies as a part of the inscrutable plan of Providence and to endeavor to be loyal and obedient to the powers that be. Perhaps James B. Taylor, a respected Baptist clergyman in Virginia, exemplified most clergymen at the end of the war. He had argued that secession and the war were just and that the Almighty would bless the South with victory and independence. Yet in the spring and summer of 1865 he accepted the verdict of arms as being the decision of God, and he counseled his fellow Southerners and Baptists to accept the collapse of the Confederacy.

[*See also* Fast Days.]

BIBLIOGRAPHY

Chesebrough, David B., ed. *God Ordained This War: Sermons on the Sectional Crisis, 1830–1865.* Columbia, S.C., 1991.

Daniel, W. Harrison. *Southern Protestantism in the Confederacy.* Bedford, Va., 1989.

Faust, Drew G. *The Creation of Confederate Nationalism: Ideology and Identity in the Civil War South.* Baton Rouge, La., 1988.

Romero, Sidney J. *Religion in the Rebel Ranks.* Lanham, Md., 1983.

Shattuck, Gardiner Humphrey, Jr. *A Shield and Hiding Place: The Religious Life of the Civil War Armies.* Macon, Ga., 1987.

Silver, James W. *Confederate Morale and Church Propaganda.* Tuscaloosa, Ala., 1957.

W. HARRISON DANIEL

SEVEN DAYS' BATTLES

The battles that took place from June 25 to July 1, 1862, on the Virginia Peninsula were the culmination of Union Maj. Gen. George B. McClellan's Peninsular campaign, which had carried his Army of the Potomac to within seven miles of Richmond.

While McClellan positioned his 100,000-man army just outside the Confederate capital, Gen. Robert E. Lee, who had replaced wounded Gen. Joseph E. Johnston as commander of the newly designated Army of Northern Virginia, shored up the city's defenses and sought an opportunity to seize the initiative. That opportunity came when Brig. Gen. J. E. B. Stuart, following a cavalry reconnaissance that took him completely around McClellan's forces, reported that the Union right flank was unsecured and vulnerable to attack. The Chickahominy River separated Maj. Gen. Fitz John Porter's 30,000 men from the remainder of the Union army.

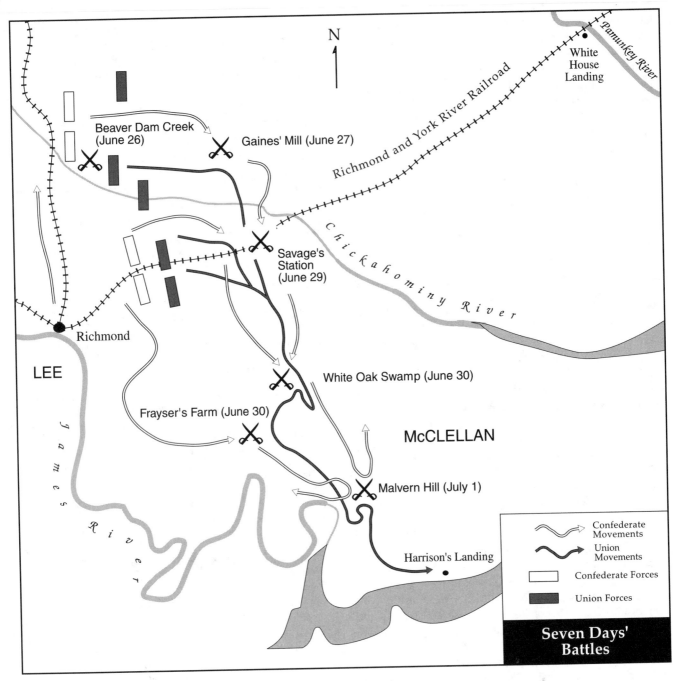

N

Beaver Dam Creek
(June 26)

Gaines' Mill (June 27)

Richmond and York River Railroad

White
House
Landing

Pamunkey River

Chickahominy River

Savage's
Station
(June 29)

Richmond

LEE

James River

White Oak Swamp (June 30)

Frayser's Farm (June 30)

McCLELLAN

Malvern Hill (July 1)

Harrison's Landing

Confederate
Movements

Union
Movements

Confederate Forces

Union Forces

**Seven Days'
Battles**

Lee decided to launch his attack before McClellan realized the flaw in his troop dispositions. Lee divided his smaller army in the face of the enemy, leaving a fraction of his forces to confront McClellan while sending the bulk of his troops to attack Porter. In addition to his own men, Lee would have the services of Maj. Gen. Thomas J. ("Stonewall") Jackson's veterans from the Shenandoah Valley.

The opposing forces clashed briefly at Oak Grove on June 25, the day before Lee planned to open his offensive. Despite this action, he still hoped to surprise Porter with attacks from three divisions under Maj. Gens. A. P. Hill, James Longstreet, and D. H. Hill, in cooperation with Jackson's troops. Uncharacteristically, Jackson failed to arrive, and an impatient A. P. Hill started the attack prematurely. Porter's men, well entrenched in prepared positions along Beaver Dam Creek, near Mechanicsville, easily repulsed the repeated Confederate assaults. The bold but bloody attacks cost the Southerners 1,484 casualties to the Federals' 361.

On the following day, June 27, Lee's Confederates attacked the Federals in their new positions near Gaines' Mill.

Again the Southerners suffered heavy losses in brutal assaults on the Union lines. Lee continued to press McClellan, hoping to annihilate his army in one battle. McClellan, now anxious about his army's survival, ordered a change of base from the York River to the James and steadily retreated.

The opposing forces clashed again at Savage's Station on June 29, Frayser's Farm on June 30, and finally at Malvern Hill on July 1. Although Lee had failed to execute his complicated plans to destroy McClellan's army, he had forced the Federals farther from the gates of Richmond. By the time the Seven Days' Battles ended, the Army of the Potomac was thirty miles from the city. Lee had driven his enemy from position to position, but at a tremendous cost to the Southerners: 3,286 killed, 15,909 wounded, and 946 missing; the Federals lost 1,734 killed, 8,062 wounded, and 6,053 missing.

Robert E. Lee had saved Richmond from capture in 1862. In the process, he established a reputation for boldness and innovation and shook off the derogatory references to "Granny Lee" and the "King of Spades" (the latter for his use of defensive earthworks). McClellan remained at his base on the James River, assessing the campaign and placing blame on anyone other than himself.

[*See also* Gaines' Mill, Virginia; Malvern Hill, Virginia; Mechanicsville, Virginia.]

BIBLIOGRAPHY

Cullen, Joseph P. *The Peninsula Campaign, 1862: McClellan and Lee Struggle for Richmond.* Harrisburg, Pa., 1973.

Freeman, Douglas S. *Lee's Lieutenants: A Study in Command.* 3 vols. New York, 1942–1944. Reprint, New York, 1986.

Johnson, Robert U., and C. C. Buel, eds. *Battles and Leaders of the Civil War.* 4 vols. New York, 1887–1888. Reprint, Secaucus, N.J., 1982.

McPherson, James M. *Battle Cry of Freedom: The Civil War Era.* New York, 1988.

Sears, Stephen W. *George B. McClellan: The Young Napoleon.* New York, 1988.

Sears, Stephen W. *To the Gates of Richmond: The Peninsula Campaign.* New York, 1992.

BRIAN S. WILLS

SEVEN PINES, VIRGINIA

On May 31 and June 1, 1862, Confederate forces attempted to halt the advance of Gen. George B. McClellan's Army of the Potomac against the Southern capital. The battle, called either Seven Pines or Fair Oaks (from small villages some ten miles east of Richmond), illustrates the command-related difficulties inherent in Civil War combat, where armies occupied miles of space but information usually moved no faster than the speed of a horse. On the Confederate side, poor staff work, misunderstandings, and faulty execution robbed Gen. Joseph E. Johnston's well-designed plans of success.

Although McClellan had been delayed at Yorktown and bloodied at Williamsburg, by mid-May his slow, methodical Peninsula campaign seemed near success. Having advanced inland from Fortress Monroe, his flanks guarded by the York and James rivers, McClellan's 105,000-man army stood poised on the outskirts of Richmond, awaiting reinforcements under Gen. Irvin McDowell, who was scheduled to march overland from Washington. Although Johnston had barely 60,000 men, McClellan believed himself outnumbered.

As McClellan neared Richmond, the terrain necessitated that his large force straddle the rain-swollen Chickahominy River. Johnston realized that this split the Union army into two virtually isolated wings, and he seized the opportunity to strike McClellan's men north of the Chickahominy before McDowell joined them. The attack was slated for May 29. But when he learned that Thomas J. ("Stonewall") Jackson's campaign in the Shenandoah Valley had diverted McDowell, Johnston canceled his plans. He formulated instead an attack on the smaller, weaker portion of McClellan's army south of the river. This consisted of two corps, under Gens. Erasmus D. Keyes and Samuel P. Heintzelman, with Keyes's men occupying positions nearest the Confederates.

After a lengthy meeting on May 30, Johnston gave verbal instructions for the commander of his right wing, Gen. James Longstreet, to assault the center and flanks of Keyes's corps. The left wing under Gen. Gustavus W. Smith was to lend assistance if needed and prevent any Federal units from crossing the Chickahominy to support Keyes and Heintzelman.

Longstreet, however, advanced part of his troops over the wrong road. The confusion this caused combined with rain and a dispute over seniority with Gen. Benjamin Huger (who had not been notified that he was under Longstreet's command) to delay the attack until afternoon. Once the battle began, Longstreet's troop dispositions were so poor that only six of his thirteen brigades were effectively engaged.

Johnston realized quite early in the morning that coordination had broken down but could do little to restore it. The dispositions he had made, though typical of nineteenth-century attempts to control combat, actually added to his problems. Johnston had ordered some units to advance when Huger's division, marching from the rear, reached them. Others were to attack when they heard artillery fire. The delay caused by Longstreet's argument with Huger therefore pinned some brigades in place, while freakish acoustics prevented others from hearing the opening guns. Moreover, with only the small staff typical of Civil War commanders,

Johnston could neither effectively ascertain nor correct Longstreet's errors. He shifted some of Smith's men to support Longstreet's attack, but Confederate divisions fought piecemeal. Although the Federals were mauled, the opportunity for a crushing blow was lost. Johnston was severely wounded late in the day, and command passed by seniority to Smith.

On the Federal side, McClellan, who was quite ill, exercised minimal control over the course of the battle. He knew that his advancing army was temporarily vulnerable as it straddled the Chickahominy, but in the unlikely event of a Confederate attack he expected his right wing, not his left, to be the target. When the sound of firing from the south reached his headquarters at New Bridge, on the north bank of the river, he did no more than alert Gen. Edward Sumner to ready his nearby command for action.

The Confederate attack, which began around 1:00 P.M., initially struck Keyes's men, who occupied the ground between Fair Oaks and Seven Pines. For much of the day they fought alone, as Keyes's messages to Heintzelman, who commanded the left wing, went astray. It was 2:30 P.M. or later before Heintzelman realized a major battle was underway. He then ordered his own corps to Keyes's support and around 3:00 P.M. telegraphed McClellan for help. Ironically, it was easier for Heintzelman to communicate with his commander across the river than with his subordinates at the front. McClellan promptly ordered Sumner's men to the south bank. Unimpeded by Smith, they crossed the swirling river on two rickety bridges and joined the battle in time to halt the Confederate advance.

The battle continued the next day, June 1, but events proved anticlimactic and did little but lengthen the casualty lists. Smith lacked both the physical and mental stamina needed to command an army. Although historians credit him too little for assuming command of a disorganized force and leading it into battle only a few hours later, he wasted Confederate strength in a series of uncoordinated assaults. McClellan had consulted carefully with Heintzelman during the night, and the Federals fought well. By the time McClellan reached the field in late morning, the Confederates had withdrawn and the battle was over. Federal losses for the two-day conflict were around 5,000, a full 1,100 fewer than those the Confederates suffered.

Most of the Federal army was never engaged, but the swollen Chickahominy prevented any immediate counterblow. Regardless, McClellan considered Seven Pines a Union victory. In its wake, he asked for and received reinforcements. His subsequent delay allowed the Confederates to recoup and reinforce as well. When the campaign for Richmond continued, McClellan faced a new opponent. Broken by the strain of command, Smith had asked to be relieved. As his successor Jefferson Davis chose Robert E. Lee.

BIBLIOGRAPHY

Freeman, Douglas S. *Lee's Lieutenants: A Study in Command.* 3 vols. New York, 1942–1944. Reprint, New York, 1986.

Govan, Gilbert G., and James W. Livingood. *A Different Valor: The Story of General Joseph E. Johnston.* Westport, Conn., 1973.

Johnston, Joseph E. *Narrative of Military Operations Directed during the late War between the States.* New York, 1872. Reprint, New York, 1969.

McClellan, George B. *McClellan's Own Story.* Edited by William C. Prime. New York, 1887.

Sears, Stephen W. *George B. McClellan: The Young Napoleon.* New York, 1988.

WILLIAM GARRETT PISTON

SHARPSBURG CAMPAIGN

Robert E. Lee's withdrawal from the passes of South Mountain on the night of September 14–15, 1862, signaled the end of a frustrating week of campaigning in Maryland. Following his day-long engagement with George B. McClellan at Fox's and Turner's gaps, Lee informed his subordinates, "The day has gone against us, and this army will go by way of Sharpsburg and cross the [Potomac] river." Lee thus canceled further continuation of his first invasion of the North.

Nothing had gone well for the Confederate army since it had entered the Old Line State during the first week of September. Western Marylanders greeted Lee with a cool reception rather than shouts of liberation. The Federals had not abandoned Harpers Ferry as expected, thus blocking critical supply and communication lines into the Shenandoah Valley. Thomas J. ("Stonewall") Jackson's subsequent operations against the Ferry had fallen behind schedule, and Lee's army remained dangerously divided into five parts as McClellan moved toward Frederick. McClellan's fortunate discovery of Special Order 191 on September 13 provided him with "all the plans of the Rebels," and his drive toward South Mountain on the fourteenth was intended to "cut the enemy in two and beat him in detail." Stubborn Confederate resistance at the mountain passes foiled McClellan's plans, but Lee realized that further resistance on the fifteenth would prove futile. No choice remained but retreat from Maryland.

Yet during the withdrawal from South Mountain toward Sharpsburg, Lee received a message from Jackson. "I believe Harpers Ferry and its garrison will be surrendered on the morrow," Jackson reported. The commanding general, boosted by this possible good fortune, halted the retreat at Sharpsburg; and when word arrived of Stonewall's success late on the morning of the fifteenth, Lee gazed over the Antietam Creek and announced, "We will make our stand on these hills."

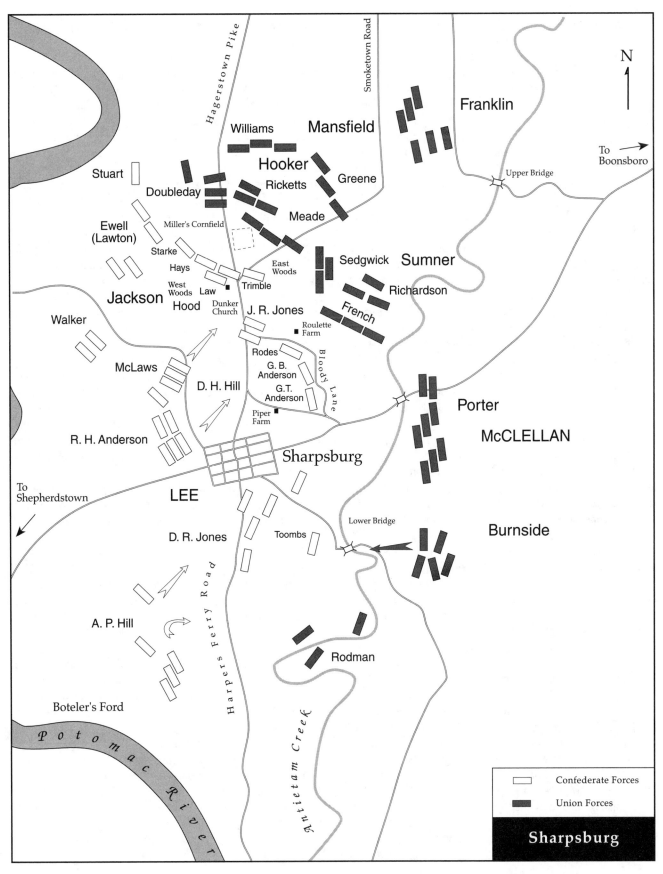

N

To Boonsboro

Hagerstown Pike

Smoketown Road

Williams

Mansfield

Franklin

Stuart

Hooker

Doubleday

Ricketts

Greene

Upper Bridge

Ewell
(Lawton)

Miller's Cornfield

Meade

Starke

East
Woods

Sedgwick

Sumner

Hays

Trimble

Richardson

West
Woods

Law

French

Jackson

Hood

Dunker
Church

J. R. Jones

Roulette
Farm

Walker

Rodes

McLaws

G. B.
Anderson

Bloody Lane

G.T.
Anderson

Porter

D. H. Hill

Piper
Farm

McCLELLAN

R. H. Anderson

Sharpsburg

To
Shepherdstown

LEE

Lower Bridge

Burnside

D. R. Jones

Toombs

A. P. Hill

Harpers Ferry Road

Rodman

Boteler's Ford

Antietam Creek

Potomac River

☐ Confederate Forces

◼ Union Forces

Sharpsburg

Lee's decision to stand at Sharpsburg was influenced by several factors. To begin with, the Southerners needed time to remove the large booty captured at Harpers Ferry. In addition, Boteler's (also known as Blackford's) Ford provided good access across the Potomac for Jackson's force of 23,000 marching seventeen miles north from Harpers Ferry. Lee also realized a stand in Maryland would gain time for the gathering of the fall harvest in the Shenandoah Valley. Foremost, however, was the opportunity to engage McClellan on Northern soil. A Confederate victory would embarrass the Republicans in an election year and perhaps provide the peace Democrats with an upper hand in Congress. The possibility of European diplomatic recognition for the South also loomed on the horizon.

Lee's determination to stand at Sharpsburg also carried great risks. If McClellan attacked before Lee's Harpers Ferry contingent arrived, the Federals would outnumber the Confederate commander five to one. In addition, with the Potomac River to his back and only one practicable crossing available at Boteler's Ford, Lee could be trapped along the Antietam if McClellan turned either flank. Lee's experience with and intuitive understanding of McClellan compelled him to gamble. Lee felt the Union general would not attack until the Confederates had reunited, and McClellan's cautious tendencies would forestall aggressive challenges to the Southern flanks.

Lee's belief that McClellan would not immediately attack proved correct. Although the Union commander pursued the Confederates to the east bank of the Antietam on the fifteenth, McClellan spent the sixteenth reconnoitering the terrain and deploying his 87,000 men. In the meantime, Jackson arrived on the afternoon of the sixteenth with his own division, and the divisions of Richard S. Ewell, and John G. Walker soon followed. The 8,000 men of Lafayette McLaws and Richard Heron Anderson were expected early on the morning of the seventeenth, and A. P. Hill's division, left behind at Harpers Ferry to arrange for the disposition of prisoners and booty, was half a day's march from Sharpsburg.

By the morning of September 17, with the exception of Hill's division, Lee's army of 35,000 sprawled over a four-mile line, anchored two miles north of Sharpsburg on the Potomac and stretching two miles south of the town to the lower bridge crossing of the Antietam. J. E. B. Stuart's horse artillery guarded the extreme left, while the infantry of Jackson's, Ewell's, and Hood's divisions covered the Confederate left in the cornfield and pastures of D. R. Miller and in the West Woods around a small Dunker church. D. H. Hill's division protected the middle, manning a sunken farm lane between the Roulette and Piper farms. D. R. Jones's and Walker's divisions initially defended the Confederate right on the high bluffs overlooking the Antietam. The Hagerstown Pike provided Lee with interior communications north of Sharpsburg, and the road leading west to Boteler's Ford, four miles from

Lee's position, gave the Confederates their only avenue of escape.

McClellan, recognizing Lee's vulnerability with his back to the Potomac and with only one option for escape, devised an initial battle plan that primarily focused on the destruction of Lee's left flank. On the sixteenth, McClellan instructed Joseph Hooker's First Corps and the Twelfth Corps of Joseph Mansfield to cross the Antietam at the upper bridge and to swing north of Lee's line, and then return south at dawn on the seventeenth to smash Jackson and the left flank. Although the column of 20,000 made the flank march without detection, Hooker telegraphed the punch on the evening of the sixteenth when he pushed his advance too far south. Warned by this unexpected appearance of Federals on his left, Lee shifted Walker from his right to his left, and he poised the divisions of McLaws and Anderson, arriving on the seventeenth from Harpers Ferry at 3:00 A.M., toward the left.

At 5:30 A.M., Hooker's advance began. Although the Confederate left was outnumbered three to one, Hooker directed his three divisions badly, sending them forward piecemeal, thus negating his numerical superiority. The brigades of Hays, Laws, and Trimble smashed Hooker's first attack by James Ricketts's division in D. R. Miller's cornfield. Jackson's division crushed the assault by Abner Doubleday's division along the Hagerstown Pike. Hood's Texans drove the Pennsylvanians of George Meade's division backward through the cornfield and into the East Woods. With Hooker's corps demolished, Mansfield's Twelfth Corps began its advance. Piecemeal attacks by its two divisions again enabled the Confederates to stand their ground. To stop the attack of Alpheus Williams's division, Lee transferred three brigades from D. H. Hill's division north from the Confederate center. Then the Federal assault of George Greene's division stalled before the Dunker church.

Five Union divisions had failed to break Lee's left, but the Confederate carnage had been terrible. Almost half of Ewell's division had been slaughtered, and all but two of its regimental commanders had fallen. Brig. Gen. William E. Starke had been killed. Jackson's division suffered such extreme losses that a colonel now commanded a division. Hood's First Texas incurred 82 percent casualties during its assault. All totaled, 5,500 dead and wounded Union and Confederate soldiers lay in the cornfield and its environs after three hours of ferocious fighting.

Yet McClellan had not finished with the Confederate left. About 9:20 A.M., marching from the east toward the West Woods, came the three divisions of the Union Second Corps. At first, Southern resistance proved sporadic and light; but as John Sedgwick's division entered the West Woods in line formation, suddenly from its left and center was unleashed the fury of Lafayette McLaws's 4,000 Confederates. Lee had ordered McLaws up from the rear just in time to rout

Sedgwick's advance, and the Confederate fire proved deadly—Sedgwick suffered 2,200 casualties in twenty minutes in the West Woods.

The morning phase of the Battle of Sharpsburg had ended. Lee's left remained intact, although tenuous, and attention now shifted south from the cornfield and the West Woods toward the sunken road defining the Confederate center. The 2,000 men in the brigades of George B. Anderson and Robert Rodes, reinforced by Richard Anderson's 4,000, defended the road against 8,000 men in two divisions of the Second Corps. William French's Union division struck first at 10:00 A.M. but, after repeated assaults, failed to dent the Confederate line. Israel Richardson's division followed and also failed to dislodge the stubborn Southerners. Finally at 1:00 P.M., after the death of G. B. Anderson and the wounding of Rodes, confusion developed in the Southern command, and the Confederates abandoned the lane owing to a misinterpreted order. The Federals quickly occupied the center of General Lee's line, and as one Southerner noted, "the end of the Confederacy was in sight." But McClellan refused to follow up on this breakthrough, and the battle for the Bloody Lane ended.

Attention now focused on the Confederate right. Defending the high bluffs overlooking the lower bridge across the Antietam were 500 Georgians of Robert Toombs's brigade. Facing Toombs were 12,000 men in the Ninth Corps, commanded by Ambrose Burnside. Fortunately for the Georgians, the bridge they defended was located in a narrow defile, making it impossible for Burnside to launch a large-scale frontal assault. For three hours, Toombs's men held off brigade-level attacks ordered by Burnside. At 1:00 P.M., however, a concerted charge by the Fifty-first New York and Fifty-first Pennsylvania finally established a bridgehead on the west bank of the Antietam. When Toombs discovered his right flank had been turned as well by I. P. Rodman's division, he abandoned his position, and the lower bridge belonged to Burnside.

For the next two hours, Burnside shuttled men, supplies, and food across the Antietam in preparation for a final assault against the Confederate right, now positioned along the Harpers Ferry Road just south of Sharpsburg. About 3:00 P.M., Burnside's corps began its advance, soon engaging D. R. Jones's thin division. The situation was desperate for General Lee. He could not maneuver Confederates from other parts of his line, and he had no reserves north of the Potomac. Suddenly, from the south, as Burnside methodically pressed forward, A. P. Hill and his Light Division arrived from Harpers Ferry, following a seventeen-mile forced march in seven hours. Lee ordered Hill to attack, and when his brigades smashed into Burnside's left flank, the stunned Federals retired toward the Antietam, ending the battle about dusk. Confederate Brig. Gen. Lawrence O'Bryan Branch was mortally wounded during Hill's assault.

It was the twelve bloodiest hours in American military history. In one day, almost 23,000 Union and Confederate casualties had fallen along the Antietam Creek. More than twice as many Americans lost their lives in one day at Sharpsburg as fell in the War of 1812, the Mexican War, and the Spanish-American War *combined.* Total casualties for the Federals included 12,410 (2,108 killed, 9,549 wounded, 753 missing). Confederate losses equaled 10,318 (1,546 killed, 7,754 wounded, 1,018 missing).

Despite the dangerous weakening of his army, Lee remained on the battlefield on the eighteenth, challenging McClellan to attack. The Union commander refused to reinitiate battle, however, and that night, the Army of Northern Virginia retired across Boteler's Ford and returned to Virginia.

Sharpsburg often is considered a turning point of the war. The Confederate military wave was at its peak in the fall of 1862, but with Braxton Bragg's failure in Kentucky and Lee's disappointing campaign in Maryland, hopes for diplomatic recognition and gains by the peace Democrats soon faded. In addition, Abraham Lincoln used McClellan's victory at Sharpsburg to announce his preliminary Emancipation Proclamation.

[*See also* Harpers Ferry, West Virginia.]

BIBLIOGRAPHY

Cox, Jacob D. "The Battle of Antietam." In *Battles and Leaders of the Civil War.* Vol. 2. Edited by Robert U. Johnson and C. C. Buel. New York, 1888. Reprint, Secaucus, N.J., 1982.

Longstreet, James. "The Invasion of Maryland." In *Battles and Leaders of the Civil War.* Vol. 2. Edited by Robert U. Johnson and C. C. Buel. New York, 1888. Reprint, Secaucus, N.J., 1982.

Murfin, James V. *The Gleam of Bayonets.* New York, 1965.

Palfry, Francis. *The Antietam and Fredericksburg.* New York, 1881. Reprint, Wilmington, N.C., 1984.

Sears, Stephen. *Landscape Turned Red.* New York, 1983.

DENNIS E. FRYE

SHELBY IRON COMPANY

Among the oldest and most prominent of the pioneer iron enterprises in Alabama, the Shelby Iron Company was located near the geographical center of the state some thirty miles southeast of present-day Birmingham. Founded in 1846 by Horace Ware, who soon took on a partner, it was incorporated by the state of Alabama in 1858. With the onset of the Civil War, Ware sold six-sevenths of his interest to local investors to raise capital for expansion.

The improved furnaces had a capacity of approximately 250 tons per week. The firm provided iron to both army and navy facilities in Selma, Mobile, Griswoldville (Georgia),

Yazoo City (Mississippi), and Atlanta. Until January 1865, when a spur railroad was completed, all manufactured iron had to be shipped by wagon to the Alabama and Tennessee Rivers Railroad at Columbiana for reshipment.

Shelby experienced difficulty in getting a rolling mill in operation to produce two-inch armor plate for the navy and did not begin production for that purpose until March 1863. Shelby's iron, however, was in demand for producing guns, and most was used for that purpose.

Shelby employed 450 to 550 workers. Skilled white labor was recruited from throughout the South, and details from the army produced 40 to 75 men. Approximately three-fourths of the work force were hired slaves. One hundred or so skilled slave laborers were rented from industrial sites in Virginia, North Carolina, Tennessee, Georgia, and Mississippi, and unskilled slaves came from nearby sources.

The works were raided by forces of Maj. Gen. James H. Wilson's cavalry brigade on March 31, 1865.

BIBLIOGRAPHY

Armes, Ethel. *The Story of Coal and Iron in Alabama.* Birmingham, Ala., 1910. Reprint, Birmingham, Ala., 1972.

Vandiver, Frank E. "The Shelby Iron Company in the Civil War: A Study of a Confederate Industry." *Alabama Review* 1 (1948): 12–26, 111–127, 203–217.

ROBERT H. MCKENZIE

CSS SHENANDOAH. Flying the Confederate flag at the Williamstown dockyard in Melbourne, Australia, February 1865.

NAVAL HISTORICAL CENTER, WASHINGTON, D.C.

SHENANDOAH

The steam-auxiliary cruiser *Shenandoah* was built as the china clipper *Sea King* in 1863. It was designed by noted London naval architect William Rennie and built by Alexander Stephen and Sons, Linthouse, Glasgow, Scotland, for Robertson & Company, London. It measured 2,190 tons, 220 feet long, 32.5 feet in breadth, and 20.5 feet in depth. *Sea King* made one trip to New Zealand before Confederate naval agent James Dunwoody Bulloch bought it for the Confederacy. The steamer *Laurel,* at Funchal, Madeira, provided crew, supplies, and armament (four 8-inch cannon, two Whitworth 32-pounder rifles, and two 12-pounders).

James Waddell commissioned CSS *Shenandoah* on October 20, 1864. The ship captured eleven prizes on the way to Melbourne, Australia. Refitted, it sailed for northern Pacific whaling grounds on February 19, 1865. The ship bonded four vessels and burned twenty-two, mostly whalers, on a continued voyage through the Caroline Islands, the seas of Japan and Okhotsk, and into the Bering Sea. There, on August 2, 1865, Waddell learned that the war had ended. He struck the armament down into the hold, dismantled *Shenandoah* as a warship, and sailed for England.

The cruiser arrived in Liverpool on November 6, 1865, flying the Confederate flag, the last Southern military unit in service. Waddell paid the crew and turned the ship over to the British government. The U.S. consul in Liverpool brought suit, won ownership of the vessel, and sold it at auction to the sultan of Zanzibar. The ship led an adventurous life before its bottom was torn out on a reef near the island of Socotra in the northern Indian Ocean in 1879.

BIBLIOGRAPHY

Dalzell, George W. *The Flight from the Flag: The Continuing Effect of the Civil War upon the American Carrying Trade.* Chapel Hill, N.C., 1940.

Horan, James D., ed. *C.S.S. Shenandoah: The Memoirs of Lieutenant Commander James I. Waddell.* New York, 1960.

Hunt, Cornelius E. *The Shenandoah; or, The Last Confederate Cruiser.* New York, 1866.

Maffitt, Emma Martin. *The Life and Services of John Newland Maffitt.* New York, 1906.

KEVIN J. FOSTER

SHENANDOAH VALLEY

[*This entry includes three articles:* An Overview; Shenandoah Valley Campaign of Jackson, *which discusses the campaign of 1862; and* Shenandoah Valley Campaign of Sheridan, *which discusses the campaign of 1864. For further discussion of military action in the Shenandoah Valley, see* Cedar Creek, Virginia; Cross Keys and Port Republic, Virginia; Early's Washington Raid; Front Royal, Virginia; Lynchburg, Virginia; New Market, Virginia; Winchester, Virginia.]

An Overview

During the Civil War the Shenandoah Valley of Virginia was vital to the Confederacy for both military and economic reasons. Militarily, the region had a considerable influence on the campaigns in Virginia. The Shenandoah Valley was like a shield, protecting the Confederate capital. A Federal army could not advance against Richmond by the way of the valley because as it marched south it would be moving farther and farther away from its objective. Conversely, the valley was an asset for any Confederate army marching through it, for the army became an immediate threat to Washington, D.C., Baltimore, and other Northern cities. Nor did the Confederates have to maintain possession of the area to retain its advantages. In order to deny the Confederates the use of the valley, the Federals had to gain control of the entire region, which was beyond their capabilities.

Economically, the Shenandoah Valley was a major source of subsistence for the Confederacy. In the early stages of the war the farmers of the valley were called upon for large quantities of supplies, which they gave heartily. But as the war dragged on, their support faltered for several reasons, including adverse weather conditions and the valley's strategic location. It was the scene of continuous military operations; from the start of the war until October 1864, major portions were repeatedly fought over, marched through, or occupied.

Once the war started, the Confederate Subsistence Department began to accumulate the vast quantities of foodstuffs that would be required to sustain the armies in the field. In Virginia, the valley was one of the first regions they turned to for supplies. Its railroad lines were in constant use, so much so that the Virginia Central Railroad was limited at times exclusively to the transportation of supplies.

In the spring of 1862 the Shenandoah Valley was the scene of one of the major campaigns of the war— Confederate Maj. Gen. Thomas J. ("Stonewall") Jackson's famous Valley campaign. In a series of brilliant maneuvers from March 23 to June 9, Jackson's forces defeated three Federal armies in five battles. Jackson's exploits electrified the Southern populace and, more important, completely dismantled the Federal plan of operation in Virginia. Owing to the perceived threat to Washington, D.C., troops scheduled to be sent to Maj. Gen. George B. McClellan on the peninsula were diverted to the valley in an attempt to defeat Jackson. In the end, Jackson eluded his potential captors, united with Gen. Robert E. Lee outside of Richmond, and helped drive the Union forces back from the Confederate capital, while the troops slated to reinforce McClellan floundered in northern Virginia.

Although the valley was one of the major theaters of the war in Virginia in 1862, no major fighting occurred in the region the next year. For the most part, military operations were limited to Federal cavalry raids and scouting expeditions. The only time large bodies of troops were in the valley was during the Gettysburg campaign, when Lee used it as an avenue to invade Pennsylvania. Although the military operations in the valley had no major effect on the direction of the war in Virginia, they did have an adverse impact on agricultural production. Federal raiders destroyed crops, confiscated livestock and farm animals, and demoralized the civilian population.

Several other factors intervened now to reduce the valley's importance as a primary source of subsistence for the Confederacy. One was the weather. In 1862 a severe drought had diminished the year's harvest, and in 1863 there was excessive rain. Severe flooding destroyed most of the wheat crop in Virginia and negated any chance of accumulating a reserve for the army. Virginia experienced a 50- to 75-percent decline in crop production between 1862 and 1864. A second factor was the war's drain on manpower, as men of military age either joined the army or were later drafted. In many instances women and young children were the only ones left to work the farms. Yet another factor was the military situation. By 1863 a major portion of the valley was under the control of the Federal army. Military exigencies had compelled the Confederacy to abandon the entire lower valley to the enemy. And this loss was not temporary—throughout the rest of the war the lower valley remained in the hands of the Federals. As a result the resources of Berkeley, Clarke, Frederick, and Jefferson counties were lost to the Confederates.

With the commencement of active military operations in May 1864, the Shenandoah Valley once again became one of the major battlegrounds of the war. From May through October the valley was the scene of continuous military action. The Federal strategic plan called for simultaneous attacks against Confederate forces in Virginia from three directions. In one part of the operation, an army under the command of Maj. Gen. Franz Sigel was to march up the valley and destroy the Virginia Central Railroad. Sigel's march went smoothly until he reached the town of New Market on May 15, 1864. There outnumbered Confederate troops routed his army, forcing it to retreat back down the valley.

Lt. Gen. Ulysses S. Grant then replaced Sigel with Maj. Gen. David Hunter and directed him to carry out the previous orders. At first Hunter was successful in his advance. He had reached the outskirts of Lynchburg by June 15, destroying homes and crops as he went. His campaign, however, ended up even more of a disaster than Sigel's. To prevent

Lynchburg from being captured and to reclaim the valley, Lee, on June 12, 1864, pulled the Second Corps of his army out of the trenches at Petersburg and sent it west under the command of Maj. Gen. Jubal Early. The reinforcements arrived at Lynchburg five days later. After making several attacks against the Confederate defenses on June 18, Hunter realized he was outnumbered and made a hasty retreat. But instead of retiring back down the valley, he retreated into West Virginia. This action took his command out of the war for several weeks and left the valley to the Confederates.

Early wasted no time in capitalizing on Hunter's error. After giving his army a day's rest he proceeded to advance down the valley. By the end of the first week in July, Early had traversed the entire valley, crossed over the Potomac River into Maryland, and begun to march on Washington, D.C. The Confederate army reached the outskirts of the city on July 11, but the Confederate commander knew he did not have the strength to capture it. So he began an orderly withdrawal back to Virginia and the valley the next day. By threatening Washington once more, Lee was hoping the Federals would be forced to lessen their hold on the Confederate capital. This time, however, the Confederate tactics were not successful, for Grant never relinquished his grip on Richmond.

Still, Early's continued presence in the valley had become a considerable annoyance to Grant in his efforts to defeat the Army of Northern Virginia. The Confederate advance on Washington had forced him to transfer two full army corps from the Petersburg front to quell the fears of the Lincoln administration. Determined to remove Early as a threat to the Northern capital and to close off the valley as an avenue of invasion and a source of supply, Grant placed Maj. Gen. Philip H. Sheridan in command of all military forces in northern Virginia.

Sheridan assumed command of the Army of the Shenandoah on the night of August 6, 1864, and began to make preparations to engage the enemy. In a series of battles between September 19 and October 19, 1864, the Federal army totally defeated the Confederate forces, routing them so completely that they were never again an effective fighting force. But the most dramatic aspect of Sheridan's campaign was the destruction of the valley's resources. Federal troops burned everything of value between Staunton and Winchester, leaving the valley a barren wasteland. This devastation, however, was not the loss it once would have been. For the last two years of the war the Confederacy had supported its military forces in Virginia with subsistence transported from the Deep South, not the valley.

By 1865 the Shenandoah Valley had become a reflection of the Confederacy itself. Before the war the valley had been one of the most fertile regions in Virginia, but in the course of the conflict its productivity vanished under the onslaught of modern armies. Four years of warfare had converted a fruitful countryside into one of charred homes and desolate farms.

BIBLIOGRAPHY

Catton, Bruce. *Terrible Swift Sword.* Garden City, N.Y., 1963.

Freeman, Douglas S. *Lee's Lieutenants: A Study in Command.* New York, 1942–1944. Reprint, New York, 1986.

McPherson, James M. *Ordeal by Fire: The Civil War and Reconstruction.* New York, 1982.

Vandiver, Frank E., ed. *The Civil War Diary of Josiah Gorgas.* Tuscaloosa, Ala., 1947.

Wert, Jeffry D. *From Winchester to Cedar Creek: The Shenandoah Campaign of 1864.* Carlisle, Pa., 1987.

MICHAEL G. MAHON

Shenandoah Valley Campaign of Jackson

Few areas in the Civil War had more strategic value for both sides than did the Shenandoah Valley of Virginia. The valley lies between the two most eastern ranges of the Allegheny Mountains. The eastern boundary of the valley is marked by the famed Blue Ridge Mountains, with the Alleghenies proper to the west. The valley stretches 165 miles from Lexington to Harpers Ferry and averages 30 miles in width. At the southern terminus the mountains on both sides press close upon Lexington. The ranges diverge at the other end around Harpers Ferry. There the Shenandoah River merges with the Potomac; there too the Baltimore and Ohio Railroad—then the main line of transportation between Washington and the West—crossed the Potomac. The Shenandoah loses altitude running south to north. Hence, and contrary to usual terminology, one travels northward down and southward up the valley.

Two factors gave the region important military value. The Shenandoah was a veritable breadbasket for the Confederacy. Grain, orchards, and livestock were in great abundance. The Army of Northern Virginia came to be all but totally dependent upon the produce of the area. Geographically the valley was a natural avenue into the heart of the North and the center of the Deep South. Any army that advanced into either Virginia or Maryland had to have control of the valley to protect its western flank against attack. With only eleven passes through the Blue Ridge, the Shenandoah was a long, natural fortress. It became the key to military movements, and military supremacy, in the eastern theater.

In the spring of 1862 the valley was the scene of one of the most brilliant campaigns in history. It was a campaign that made Confederate Gen. Thomas J. ("Stonewall") Jackson the hero of the South and a legend in his own time.

Jackson had returned to the Shenandoah in November 1861 to take charge of its defenses. His headquarters were at Winchester, twenty-six miles southwest of Harpers Ferry. Winchester guarded all the mountain passes in the lower Shenandoah and was a commercial center as well. Jackson's force at that time consisted of 3,600 infantry, 600 cavalry, and twenty-seven guns. Most of his soldiers were Virginians and familiar with the valley.

Late in February 1862, a Federal army slowly moved into the Shenandoah. It numbered 38,000 men, mostly hardy farmboys from the Midwest. Commanding the army was Maj. Gen. Nathaniel P. Banks, a Massachusetts political general with limited military capacities.

The small Confederate force in the valley seemed no threat to Banks's invaders. Yet Jackson was always a man who took responsibility very seriously. His instructions from the beginning had been to protect the left flank of the main

> **"If this valley is lost,"**
> **[Jackson] stated to a friend,**
> **"Virginia is lost."**

Confederate force at Manassas, to guard the valley against all Federal intrusions, and to expect no reinforcements in the process. Determination outweighed concern by Jackson that he was outnumbered by ten-to-one odds. "If this valley is lost," he stated to a friend, "Virginia is lost."

With the Federal army slowly forming an arc around his small force, Jackson on March 11 abandoned Winchester. He retired slowly up the valley to Mount Jackson and encamped. Four Federal regiments of Gen. James Shields's division pursued cautiously at a distance. On a sleety March 21, those Federal units started back to Winchester. Jackson deduced that Shields was consolidating his troops with Banks's main command preparatory to uniting with Gen. George B. McClellan's massive army for a grand offensive against Richmond. He promptly put his brigades into motion heading north.

The Confederates covered forty-one miles in two days. A third of Jackson's men fell out along the way from exhaustion and sickness. On the afternoon of March 23, Jackson and barely two thousand soldiers reached the hamlet of Kernstown, two miles from Winchester. A crushing blow on Shields would stop Banks's withdrawal from the valley and possibly blunt McClellan's offensive as well.

Jackson quickly deployed his fatigued troops and attacked what he thought was only a segment of Shields's command. All too soon, owing to faulty intelligence reports, Jackson found himself locked in combat with a full Union division. Three hours of fighting brought his advance to a halt. After nightfall the Confederates retired up the valley. Yet Jackson's

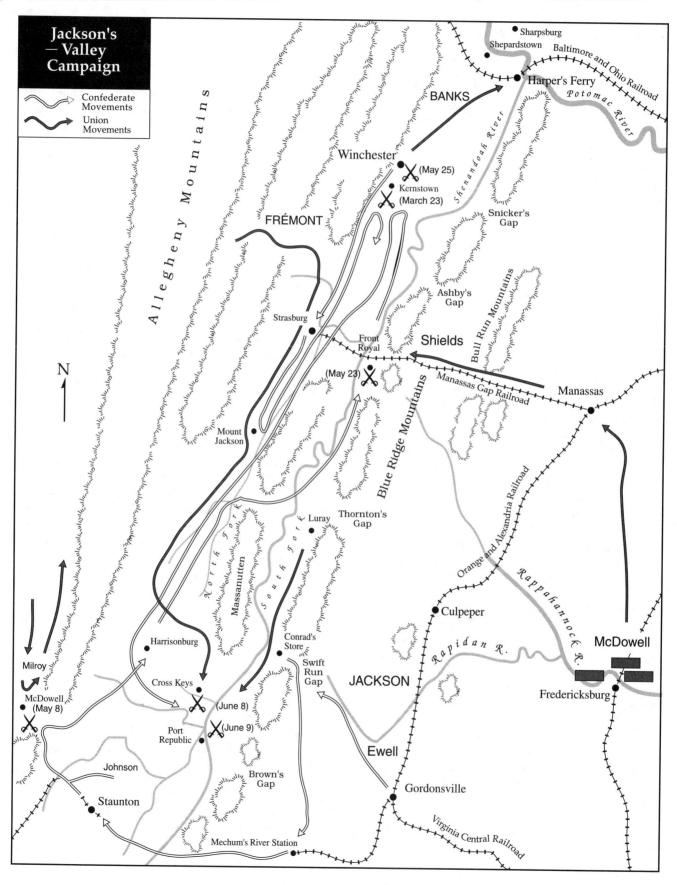

Jackson's Valley Campaign

Confederate Movements

Union Movements

N

Sharpsburg

Shepardstown

Baltimore and Ohio Railroad

Harper's Ferry

Potomac River

BANKS

Winchester (May 25)

Kernstown (March 23)

FRÉMONT

Snicker's Gap

Shenandoah River

Ashby's Gap

Strasburg

Front Royal

Shields

(May 23)

Manassas Gap Railroad

Bull Run Mountains

Manassas

Mount Jackson

Luray

Thornton's Gap

Blue Ridge Mountains

Allegheny Mountains

North Fork

South Fork

Massanutten

Orange and Alexandria Railroad

Rappahannock R.

Culpeper

Rapidan R.

Harrisonburg

Conrad's Store

Swift Run Gap

JACKSON

McDowell

Cross Keys

(June 8)

Milroy

McDowell (May 8)

Port Republic

(June 9)

Fredericksburg

Johnson

Brown's Gap

Ewell

Staunton

Gordonsville

Mechum's River Station

Virginia Central Railroad

tactical failure proved a strategic success. Even though Shields's men moved on to Fredericksburg, Banks received orders to remain in the valley. This heretofore buffer zone now became a major theater of operations.

Grim resolution marked every step of Jackson's march as he led his forces to Conrad's Store, seventeen miles east of Harrisonburg. That point, at the base of Swift Run Gap, offered the Southern general a number of options. He could attack Banks's army if it sought to pass up the Valley Turnpike to the railroad town of Staunton; he could wage a strong defense if assailed at Conrad's Store; the mountain pass afforded a safe escape if needed. Banks halted at Harrisonburg and then backtracked forty-five miles to Strasburg so as to shorten his line of communication. The Federal general was convinced that Jackson was now a mere nuisance.

For most of April, as Confederate ranks filled and hardened into a tight military force, Jackson developed a master plan. He knew that a second Federal force of 15,000 soldiers under Gen. John C. Frémont was two ranges over in the Alleghenies. Another 40,000 bluecoats of Gen. Irvin McDowell's command were at Fredericksburg and poised to move easily toward Richmond or the valley. What Jackson first hoped to accomplish was to keep Banks and Frémont west of the Blue Ridge and isolated one from the other. At the same time, Jackson did not want McDowell leaving Fredericksburg. If Confederates in the valley could pin down Frémont, Banks, and McDowell, attack and defeat each, one by one, all other Southern defenders in Virginia could concentrate at Richmond and confront McClellan's 120,000 Federals.

The chances of this plan succeeding were slim. Yet "Old Jack" felt that deception, rapid marches, and unexpected attacks would accomplish his goals. As for the overwhelming numerical superiority of the enemy, Jackson would trust God to handle that problem.

Gen. Robert E. Lee, President Jefferson Davis's chief military adviser, was himself a gambler. He not only endorsed Jackson's proposal but sent badly needed reinforcements: 8,000 troops under eccentric, crusty, but highly dependable Gen. Richard S. Ewell. Another 2,000 Southerners, with gruff and profane Gen. Edward Johnson at their head, were in the mountains guarding the western approaches to Staunton. They were added to Jackson's command. By the end of April, Jackson was ready to go into action.

He ordered Ewell's division into the Conrad's Store encampment to keep an eye on Banks's movements. "Old Jack" then disappeared to the south with his own 6,000-man force. The men trudged three days through pouring rain and heavy mud. They finally reached Mechum's River Station on the Virginia Central Railroad and boarded trains with the belief that they were heading east to Richmond. Instead, the trains lumbered west. Confederates disembarked at Staunton to the surprise of townspeople answering the bells for Sunday church services. Jackson sealed the town to mask his presence. Meanwhile, Banks was reassuring officials in Washington that Jackson's "greatly demoralized and broken" army was fleeing toward the safety of Richmond.

On May 6, Jackson led his still-jaded troops in a hard thirty-five-mile march over rugged mountains to McDowell. His objective was Gen. Robert H. Milroy's 4,000 Federals comprising the vanguard of Frémont's army. At 4:00 P. M. on the eighth, from a commanding hilltop, the Confederates fired point-blank volleys of musketry into the advancing columns. The battle lasted until sundown. Though Federals inflicted twice their own losses, they could not pierce Jackson's lines. Milroy retreated. Jackson pursued for a distance. Confederate engineers closed the mountain passes, thus protecting Jackson's left flank in the upper valley. Now the stern and taciturn Southern commander was ready to clear the valley of Federal intruders.

Thanks in great part to his mapmaker, Maj. Jedediah Hotchkiss, Jackson could discuss valley terrain as easily as he could quote Scripture. He knew that it was eighty miles on the macadamized Valley Turnpike from Staunton to Winchester. East of that main thoroughfare, inside the valley from Harrisonburg to Strasburg, lay a dark ridge called Massanutten Mountain. To the east of it was a parallel and almost hidden road. It snaked through the narrow Luray Valley to Front Royal and beyond. More important, in that forty-mile stretch was only one point where the Massanutten could be crossed: the pass connecting the towns of New Market and Luray.

The next stage of Jackson's strategy was to unite his forces, sneak through and secure that pass, use the Massanutten as a screen, and head north. By hard marching he intended to strike unsuspecting advance positions at Front Royal and Strasburg; then he hoped to shatter Banks's army as he drove to the main Federal supply base at Winchester. Jackson swiftly merged the units of Ewell's and Johnson's forces into an army of 17,000 soldiers. That gave him an almost two-to-one superiority over Banks. Jackson drove his troops down the valley and disappeared across the Massanutten. The first Federal inkling that anything was amiss came on May 23, when a Confederate tidal wave appeared from nowhere and crushed the Union garrison at Front Royal.

Jackson spent the following day urging his near-exhausted soldiers to get between rapidly retreating Federals and Winchester. Confederates struck several times at the long and disjointed Union column but could not break it. Abandoned wagons loaded with goods littered the road for miles. Large numbers of the half-starved Southerners could not resist the temptation to pause for food.

On the morning of May 25, Jackson launched a full-scale assault at Winchester and by noon had Banks's entire army fleeing for the safety of the Potomac River. The three days of fighting had cost Jackson but 400 men. His army had seized 3,030 prisoners, 9,300 small arms, 2 rifled cannon, and such a wealth of quartermaster stores that Confederates scornfully referred thereafter to their Union opponent as "Commissary Banks."

Smashing victories by Jackson had now disrupted the entire Federal offensive in Virginia. With Banks cowering on the north bank of the Potomac and Jackson's army poised like a dagger at the north end of the Shenandoah, Union officials in Washington reacted sharply. McDowell's huge force at Fredericksburg, about to join McClellan, was to remain there as protection for the Northern capital. Shields's 20,000-man division, which had just reached Fredericksburg, was ordered to return to the valley. Frémont received instructions to advance with all haste into the Shenandoah. With Shields moving west and Frémont advancing east, both toward Strasburg, Jackson seemingly would be caught in the jaws of a massive vise.

The counterstrategy failed because of a combination of Federal vacillation and incredible marching by Jackson's "foot cavalry." In less than a day, Confederate units covered thirty-five to fifty miles and escaped the trap. Jackson retired to Harrisonburg and then to a point southeast of town where the North and South rivers came together to form the South Fork of the Shenandoah. Frémont was giving chase on the Valley Turnpike; Shields was advancing up the Luray Valley road.

On June 8, Ewell's division easily beat back feeble stabs by Frémont at Cross Keys. Jackson waited patiently three miles away at Port Republic. The next day he assailed Shields's force. Severe fighting occurred before the Federals broke off the engagement and headed northward. The great campaign was over; the Shenandoah Valley was still in Confederate hands.

Jackson and 17,000 men had totally thwarted the plans of 64,000 Federals in three different forces sent to destroy him. In forty-eight days his soldiers had marched 676 miles and fought four battles, six skirmishes, and a dozen delaying actions. Confederates had inflicted seven thousand casualties at a loss of half that number. Immense quantities of Union weapons and stores were in Confederate hands. The Federal military machine in Virginia was sputtering badly. Southerners everywhere took new faith in the success of the Confederate cause. Jackson would accept no accolades for his strategic masterpiece. He summarized the Valley campaign in a short note to his wife: "God has been our shield, and to His name be all the glory."

BIBLIOGRAPHY

Allan, William. *History of the Campaign of Gen. T. J. (Stonewall) Jackson in the Shenandoah Valley of Virginia*. Dayton, Ohio, 1987.
Henderson, G. F. R. *Stonewall Jackson and the American Civil War*. 2 vols. London, 1898. Reprint, Gloucester, Mass., 1968.

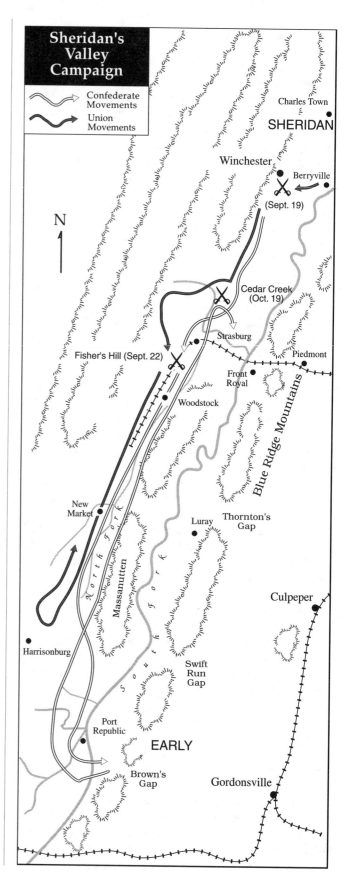

Sheridan's Valley Campaign

Hotchkiss, Jedediah. *Make Me a Map of the Valley.* Dallas, Tex., 1973.

Robertson, James I., Jr. *The Stonewall Brigade.* Baton Rouge, La., 1963.

Tanner, Robert G. *Stonewall in the Valley.* New York, 1976.

JAMES I. ROBERTSON, JR.

Shenandoah Valley Campaign of Sheridan

This Federal campaign, which took place from August to October 1864, effectively ended the Confederate presence in the Shenandoah Valley.

Following the near capture of Washington, D.C., by Lt. Gen. Jubal Early in mid-July 1864, and Early's subsequent burning of Chambersburg, Pennsylvania, on July 30, Gen. Ulysses S. Grant assigned Maj. Gen. Philip H. Sheridan to the Shenandoah Valley with instructions to "put himself south of the enemy and follow him to the death."

The thirty-three-year-old Irish-born Sheridan had been commanding Grant's cavalry, and although President Abraham Lincoln, Secretary of War Edwin M. Stanton, and Chief of Staff Henry W. Halleck all considered Sheridan too young and inexperienced for the Shenandoah position, Grant's opinion prevailed. Sheridan subsequently arrived at Harpers Ferry on August 6 to take command of the Army of the Shenandoah, composed of 35,000 infantry and artillery and 8,000 cavalry. The army's infantry consisted of three corps under Maj. Gen. Horatio G. Wright (Sixth Corps), Maj. Gen. George Crook (Eighth Corps), and Maj. Gen. William H. Emory (Nineteenth Corps). Brig. Gen. Alfred T. A. Torbert commanded the three divisions of cavalry.

Sheridan outnumbered Early three to one. Old Jube's Army of the Valley included 10,000 veterans from the Second Corps and 4,000 poorly equipped and ill-disciplined cavalrymen. Recognizing this disparity, Robert E. Lee on August 6 dispatched from the Richmond-Petersburg line the 3,500-man division of Maj. Gen. Joseph B. Kershaw, the artillery battalion of Maj. Wilfred E. Cutshaw, and the cavalry division of Maj. Gen. Fitzhugh Lee. When this additional force arrived at Front Royal on August 14, Sheridan, who had advanced fifty miles from Harpers Ferry to Cedar Creek, ordered a withdrawal north to Halltown, where he entrenched on a commanding ridge four miles west of Harpers Ferry.

From August 22 to September 18, Sheridan and Early marched and countermarched across the lower valley, conducting a "mimic war" that avoided major confrontation. Politics tempered Sheridan's usual aggressiveness; Secretary of War Stanton had informed him that the administration could not withstand one battlefield defeat. "I deemed it necessary to be very cautious," Sheridan wrote in his memoirs. "The fact that the Presidential election was impending made me doubly so . . . .[since] the defeat of my army might be followed by the overthrow of the party in power." Sheridan's political sensitivity led Jubal Early to underestimate badly his dangerous opponent. Concluding that Sheridan "possessed an excessive caution which amounted to timidity," Early agreed to return to Petersburg the reinforcements he had received from Lee in mid-August.

When Sheridan on September 15 learned of this departure, he planned his strike. With Early's army scattered toward the Potomac on a raid to destroy the Baltimore and Ohio Railroad, Sheridan intended to smash Early's rear guard at Winchester and cut off the Confederate line of retreat south via the Valley Pike. Sheridan outlined this plan to Grant at Charles Town on September 17, and the commanding general responded, "Go in."

At 1:00 A.M. on September 19, Sheridan's army roused from its bivouac near Berryville and began marching west toward Winchester. Union cavalry seized the Opequon Creek crossing with little opposition, and Federal infantry soon splashed across the Opequon into the two-mile Berryville Canyon—a narrow defile through which passed the turnpike connecting Winchester and Berryville. Fortunately for Early, Sheridan's army became entangled in the canyon by the slow-moving wagons of the Sixth Corps. This delay robbed Sheridan of his tactical surprise and enabled Early to reconcentrate his army at Winchester.

Sheridan's infantry assault finally commenced at 11:40 A.M. with a blow against Maj. Gen. Dodson Ramseur's division on the Confederate right. A spirited Southern counterattack by Maj. Gen. Robert Rodes's division drove a wedge between the Sixth and Nineteenth Corps and nearly cost

> **. . . Early's outnumbered and outflanked army cracked and went "whirling through Winchester" in headlong flight.**

Sheridan the battle, but a stand by Maj. Gen. David Russell's division stalled the Confederate offensive. During this bloody action, Rodes lost his life, and General Russell died conducting the Union defense. Meeting failure on the Confederate right and center, Sheridan deployed Crook's Eighth Corps and two divisions of cavalry against the Confederate left flank. When the 10,000-man charge commenced at 4:00 P.M., Early's outnumbered and outflanked army cracked and went "whirling through Winchester" in headlong flight south on the Valley Pike. Early's defeat at the Third Battle of Winchester (known as the Battle of Opequon in the North) cost him 199 killed, 1,508 wounded, and 1,818 missing. Sheridan suffered 697 killed, 3,983 wounded, and 338 missing. For the first time in its history, the Second

Corps, formerly commanded by Stonewall Jackson, had been driven from a field it defended.

During the night of September 19, Early retreated twenty miles south from Winchester to Fisher's Hill, a line of dominating ridges running perpendicular to the valley and anchored on the east by the North Fork of the Shenandoah River and to the west by North Mountain. Some considered it a Confederate "Gibraltar," but Early did not have enough men to hold the four-mile line. On September 21 and 22, while Sheridan feinted attack against the Confederate front, the 5,500 men of the Union's Eighth Corps under Crook secretly marched to North Mountain to attain a position behind Early's left flank. At 4:00 P.M. on the twenty-second, Crook's men smashed into the Confederate left held by Lunsford Lindsay Lomax's cavalry division. The panicked horsemen scattered in disarray, and with its left now exposed, Early's army fled from Fisher's Hill in a rout. Although Early's casualties were relatively light (30 killed, 210 wounded, 995 missing), he lost 14 guns to the Federals. He also lost his chief of staff, Lt. Col. William N. Pendleton, who was killed while attempting to rally his routed comrades. Sheridan accomplished his second victory in three days at a cost of 36 killed, 414 wounded, and 6 missing.

Following his September 22 defeat at Fisher's Hill, Early retreated 60 miles south and east to Brown's Gap in the Blue Ridge, where he awaited reinforcement from Kershaw's division and Cutshaw's battalion of artillery. Sheridan followed to Harrisonburg, arriving there on September 25. Concluding that Early's army was finished, Sheridan commenced burning the upper valley in accordance with Grant's orders to make the Shenandoah Valley a "barren waste." By October 7, as Sheridan's army moved north to Woodstock, his cavalry had systematically destroyed 2,000 barns filled with wheat, hay, and farming implements and over 70 mills filled with flour and wheat. In addition, 3,000 sheep had been slaughtered and 4,000 cattle driven north. Sheridan notified Grant that the destruction was so thorough that the 92 miles from Winchester to Staunton "will have but little in it for man or beast."

As Sheridan retired north, Confederate Brig. Gen. Thomas Lafayette Rosser and his Laurel Brigade arrived in the valley and began menacing Sheridan's rear guard. At Tom's Brook, Sheridan tired of the harassment and ordered his cavalry to "whip the Rebel cavalry or get whipped." Subsequently, on October 9, Maj. Gen. George Armstrong Custer, in his first fight as a division commander, flanked Rosser's left while Maj. Gen. Wesley Merritt smashed Rosser's right, sending the Confederates reeling in a 26-mile chase known as the "Woodstock Races." Sheridan's horsemen captured 330 prisoners, 11 guns, and the headquarters wagons of four Confederate cavalry generals. The Federals lost 9 killed and 48 wounded.

Following the victory at Tom's Brook, Sheridan encamped north of Cedar Creek on October 10. Since he considered

Early "disposed of," Sheridan began making plans to transfer his army back to Grant. To confer on future operations, Sheridan started for Washington on October 15, leaving the army in temporary command of General Wright. Meanwhile, Early had advanced north following his reinforcement at Brown's Gap. On October 17, Maj. Gen. John B. Gordon surveyed the Union army from Three Top Mountain and convinced Early that a surprise attack against the Union left flank at Cedar Creek was possible. Following an all-night march by the Second Corps along the base of Massanutten Mountain, Gordon's and Kershaw's 8,000 Confederates routed Crook's unsuspecting Eighth Corps at dawn on the nineteenth and then drove the Nineteenth Corps and Sixth Corps three miles north of their Cedar Creek camps. Early had seized twenty enemy cannon and 1,500 prisoners in the morning victory, but fatigue and rampant plundering stalled the Confederate offensive at about 11:00 A.M.

Meanwhile, Sheridan, who had returned by late morning, rallied his army and redeployed the cavalry on his flanks. At 4:00 P.M., the rejuvenated Federal army advanced. When Custer's cavalry division overran the Confederate left, Early's panicked line broke and a rout began. In one of the most remarkable one-day turnarounds in military history, Sheridan had snatched victory from defeat. As Early lamented, "The Yankees got whipped and we got scared."

Confederate losses in the Cedar Creek disaster included 320 killed, 1,540 wounded, and 1,050 missing; General Ramseur was mortally wounded. In addition, Early lost 43 cannon and at least 300 wagons and ambulances. Union casualties were 644 killed, 3,430 wounded, and 1,591 missing.

Early had faced Sheridan's overwhelming numbers and suffered four defeats in thirty days. With the Confederates routed and the valley breadbasket burned, Sheridan transferred much of his army to Grant, while Lee ordered all of Early's remaining infantry, with the exception of one division, to return to Petersburg.

BIBLIOGRAPHY

DuPont, Henry A. *The Campaign of 1864 in the Valley of Virginia and the Expedition to Lynchburg.* New York, 1925.

Early, Jubal A. *Autobiographical Sketch and Narrative of the War between the States.* Philadelphia, 1912. Reprint, Wilmington, N.C., 1989.

Gallagher, Gary W. *Struggle for the Shenandoah: Essays on the Valley Campaign of 1864.* Kent, Ohio, 1991.

Sheridan, Philip H. *Personal Memoirs of P. H. Sheridan.* New York, 1888.

Taylor, James E. *The James E. Taylor Sketchbook: With Sheridan in the Shenandoah in 1864.* Dayton, Ohio, 1989.

Wert, Jeffrey D. *From Winchester to Cedar Creek: The Shenandoah Campaign of 1864.* Carlisle, Pa., 1987.

DENNIS E. FRYE

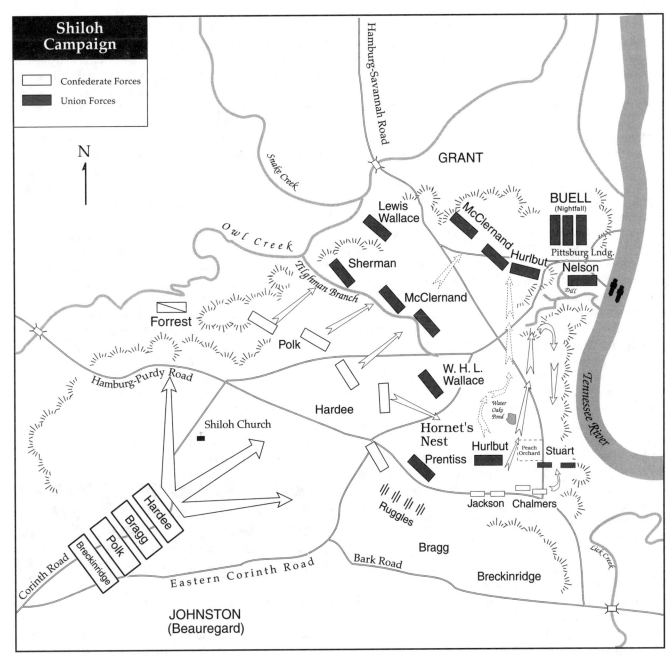

SHILOH CAMPAIGN

A small Methodist church gave its name to the first major land battle in the West on April 6 and 7, 1862. In February 1862, Gen. Ulysses S. Grant moved south against Confederate Forts Henry and Donelson guarding the Tennessee and Cumberland rivers. He had captured them by the sixteenth. Their loss forced the evacuation of parts of middle and western Tennessee by the Confederate army commanded by Gen. Albert Sidney Johnston. When

Johnston abandoned Nashville, Gen. Don Carlos Buell's Army of the Ohio occupied the city. West of the Tennessee River, Gen. P. G. T. Beauregard, Johnston's deputy commander, withdrew the Southern forces from Columbus, Kentucky. He established a new line stretching from Island Number 10 on the Mississippi River to Corinth, Mississippi, and concentrated the bulk of his forces there.

After the surrender of the forts, the gunboats of the Union navy effectively controlled the Tennessee from its mouth to Muscle Shoals, Alabama. The Federals massed at Pittsburg Landing, the closest all-weather landing to Corinth, which, as a major rail junction, was the next Union target. Gen. Henry W. Halleck, now in command of Union forces west of the Appalachian Mountains, ordered Buell to march the Army of the Ohio west from Nashville and join the forces at Pittsburg Landing.

Johnston and Beauregard, to regain the initiative, decided to concentrate a large force at Corinth and attack Grant. Johnston ordered over 44,000 men to the town. These troops, however, were insufficiently trained on the division level. Johnston divided his army into four corps under the command of Gens. Leonidas Polk, Braxton Bragg, William J. Hardee, and John C. Breckinridge. The Reserve Corps, Breckinridge's unit, was no more than a large division.

While the Confederates concentrated at Corinth, four Union divisions were training at Pittsburg Landing. Another division, the Third, commanded by Gen. Lew Wallace, was stationed at Crump Landing seven miles to the north, and the Sixth Division under Gen. Joseph Prentiss was being assembled as new units arrived. Grant, confident that the battle at Corinth would be the last in the West and that he would win it, did not take the necessary steps to keep informed of what was going on in his front.

On the evening of April 2, Beauregard received word from Bethel Springs that a portion of the Union army was moving out of its camps around Shiloh Church. He sent his chief of staff, Col. Thomas Jordan, to Johnston to recommend immediate attack. Johnston conferred with Bragg, who also advised attack, and sent Jordan back to Beauregard's headquarters, where he drafted Special Orders No. 8, the Confederate order of battle. On the morning of the third, Jordan presented this order to all corps commanders except Breckinridge. It called for marching that day and attacking on the fourth. Hardee's corps was to form one long line of battle and then press forward. A thousand yards behind it would be Bragg's corps also in the line of battle. Polk's and Breckinridge's corps would serve as reserves.

Owing to muddy roads and poor discipline during their march, the Confederates were not ready to attack on the fourth or on the fifth. That evening, Beauregard recommended calling the attack off, but Johnston refused. The attack would go on.

In the Union camps, Col. Everett Peabody, commander of the First Brigade, Sixth Division, was not happy with the developments in his front. He sent out a patrol before dawn on the sixth to learn the true strength of the Southerners. These men, at 5:45 A.M., collided with the Third Mississippi Battalion serving as pickets under the command of Maj. Aaron Hardcastle. The patrol sent back word that it had met a major Confederate force and asked for reinforcements. Peabody sent out the Twenty-first Missouri, but before they arrived, the Southerners advanced, pushing the patrol back. Col. David Moore, commander of the Twenty-first, ordered the patrol to stand and fight. Further reinforced by elements

of the Sixteenth Wisconsin, the patrol delayed the Confederates for about thirty minutes.

Meanwhile, Prentiss called his Sixth Division into the line of battle and prepared to meet the Confederates. The two forces met just south of the division camps. This was the first battle for most of these men, Northern or Southern. Prentiss's men held for a short while, but then Confederate brigades under John K. Jackson and James R. Chalmers got around their left flank. S. A. M. Woods's brigade found a hole to the left of their Fifth Division, forcing Prentiss to fall back. The Sixth held for a short time in their camps and then fell back again. Prentiss and about 3,000 men dug in at what came to be called the Hornet's Nest.

While the North's Sixth Division was under attack, its Fifth Division, to the right, was also meeting the enemy. First, Patrick Cleburne's brigade slammed into the brigades of Jessie Hildebrand and Ralph Buckland. Cleburne's right pushed back the Fifty-third Ohio, but was stopped cold by Buckland on the Southern left. S. A. M. Woods supported Cleburne on the right. Units from Bragg's and Polk's corps coming up to continue the drive forced Buckland and Hildebrand back.

By late morning, Confederate attacks had pushed the Union right back almost a mile to the Hamburg-Purdy Road. Here the North's First Division joined the line to protect the left of the Fifth. One brigade of the Fourth Division joined the left of the First. This concentration, however, had drawn the bulk of the Confederate troops. By 11:00 A.M., all but two

> . . . regiments of Hildebrand's and Buckland's brigades were scattered and ceased to exist as organized units.

brigades of the Southerners were massed against this line. It broke and was forced back about a half mile. John McDowell's brigade of the Fifth Division was cut off and had to fight its way back to the main force. Due to the shock of the Southern attack, the regiments of Hildebrand's and Buckland's brigades were scattered and ceased to exist as organized units.

On the Union left, Col. David Stuart's brigade of the Fifth Division guarded the eastern approaches to the battlefield. Stuart saw Confederate flags moving in Prentiss's camps and deployed his brigade to meet the expected attacks. Gen. Stephen D. Hurlbut brought his Fourth Division up to support Stuart. Gen. John McArthur's Brigade of the Second Division filled the gap between Stuart and Hurlbut. Behind Hurlbut, Prentiss was rallying the remains of his division, and at 11:00 A.M. they took up a position on Hurlbut's right. Gen. W. H. L. Wallace brought up the Second Division to extend the Union right toward the First Division's left. The First was commaned by Gen. John McClernand.

The first Confederate attacks against the Union left were made by Chalmers's and Jackson's brigades. Stuart's line stopped them at about 10:00 A.M. By using a heavy skirmish line and detaching troops to cover his left, Stuart led the Confederates to believe they were attacking a division. Johnston moved to the Southern right with Jackson's and Chalmers's brigades. There he took personal command of the eastern sector. All along the Confederate line, the various corps became hopelessly intermingled. As a result, the corps commanders split the line into sectors. Polk took the left, Hardee the center left, and Bragg the center right. Breckinridge assisted Johnston on the right.

Johnston began a series of probing attacks looking for the Union left flank. His intention was to turn this flank and force the Northerners to the west and away from Pittsburg Landing. But he was not able to bring enough strength to bear until about 2:00 P.M. Then he advanced five brigades. Aided by Stuart's running out of ammunition, Johnston forced the Union troops out of the Peach Orchard area, and they withdrew toward Pittsburg Landing. Unfortunately, Johnston was hit in the leg by a stray round and bled to death before his aides were able to find the wound.

On the Union right, McClernand and Gen. William Tecumseh Sherman (commanding the Union's Fifth Division) had fallen back to Jones Field. Here they organized a counterattack that forced the Southerners back, but they were unable to sustain the drive and had to withdraw. With Stuart withdrawing, McArthur was forced to fall back. This exposed Hurlbut's left to the attacks of Jackson's and Chalmers's brigades, as well as three other Confederate brigades. Hurlbut sent word to Prentiss that he would have to fall straight back for Pittsburg Landing. Prentiss realized this would leave his left in the air, but his orders from Grant were to hold the Hornet's Nest area at all costs.

Grant arrived on the battlefield in the middle of the morning. Earlier he had sent orders to Buell to march his lead division up the east bank of the river. He planned to ferry the men across to Pittsburg Landing. Grant also stopped at Crump Landing long enough to tell Lew Wallace to prepare his division for a quick move and then await orders. Once he arrived, Grant made a tour of the field and then sent orders to Wallace to move to Shiloh.

Polk and Hardee kept up the pressure against Sherman and McClernand, forcing them to fall back. Their left connected with Wallace's division in the Hornet's Nest. Their right guarded the River Road by which they expected Lew Wallace to arrive. As the pressure mounted, Sherman and McClernand fell back, breaking contact with Wallace on their left, which opened up a hole in the Union line. The Confederates poured through it and met their right flank brigades. The movement surrounded the Hornet's Nest.

In the Confederate center, Bragg threw attack after attack against Prentiss's and Wallace's divisions. They were all forced back until Gen. Daniel Ruggles took over the sector. A gun line established under his command pinned the Union troops down. This prevented many of them from withdrawing while the Confederates closed the purse on the Hornet's Nest.

With Prentiss's surrender, the Southerners regrouped for a final attack on Pittsburg Landing. Grant, however, had managed to establish a gun line of fifty-four cannons. This line, supported by those soldiers who were able to fall back, stopped the final Confederate attacks of the day. At dusk, Beauregard, who did not realize that Buell was arriving, called off the fighting. With Buell's arrival, along with that of Wallace, the Union losses of the day were more than made good.

On April 7 Grant went over to the offensive. Buell's fresh troops were on the left; the elements of the army that fought on the sixth were in the center; and Lew Wallace's Third Division was on the right. Beauregard tried to stop their advance, but with no fresh troops at hand, he didn't have a chance. Local counterattacks were successful (the most notable one was at Water Oaks Pond), but they did not stop the Union drive. At 2:30 Beauregard realized that the Confederates could not regain the offensive, and he ordered a withdrawal back to Corinth. Breckinridge took command of the rear guard. The Battle of Shiloh ended.

On the morning of the eighth, Grant sent out Sherman with some of his troops to discover how far the Confederates had withdrawn. At Fallen Timbers, just west of the battlefield, he ran into the rear guard under Col. Nathan Bedford Forrest. Forrest forced Sherman back. There was no further pursuit because Grant had lost the bulk of his ammunition and equipment. Buell's reserves were still downriver in Savannah awaiting shipment to Pittsburg Landing.

As a result of the battle, the Confederates' losses were 1,727 men killed, 8,012 wounded, and 959 missing for a total of 10,698 casualties. The Union losses were 1,254 killed, 8,408 wounded, and 2,885 missing for a total of 12,547 casualties. The Union did not relax its pressure on Corinth and on June 1, took the city. As a result, the Confederates lost Memphis and the rest of western Tennessee.

BIBLIOGRAPHY

Frank, Joseph A., and George A. Reaves. *Seeing the Elephant.* New York, 1989.

Johnson, Robert U., and C. C. Buel, eds. *Battles and Leaders of the Civil War.* 4 vols. New York, 1887–1888. Reprint, Secaucus, N.J., 1982.

McDonough, James L. *Shiloh: In Hell before Night.* Knoxville, Tenn., 1977.

Sword, Wiley. *Shiloh: Bloody April.* New York, 1974.

GEORGE A. REAVES III

SHINPLASTERS

A generic term applied at various times to paper money, especially small-change notes, *shinplasters* also went by the names *shingles, stump tails, red dogs,* and *wildcat* currency. Any term so indiscriminately used probably defies an accurate definition: usually, shinplasters referred to low-value paper money issued by state banks during the free banking era (1837–1863), to virtually all small-change bills, and, during the war in the Confederacy, to any paper money (except of Confederate notes) that circulated at a high rate of depreciation to gold or silver (specie).

Such money, however, was not unusual prior to the free banking era. The scarcity of circulating coin meant that, despite state laws against small-change notes, they circulated widely. Many antebellum Southern cities circulated notes

> *. . . shinplasters also went by the names shingles, stump tails, red dogs, and wildcat currency.*

of all types during emergencies, with lottery and railcar tickets also passing as a medium of exchange. In the most general sense, they too constituted shinplasters. During panic times, when banks suspended all specie payments, local businesses and governments issued change scrip in order to continue daily commerce.

Specifically, in the Confederacy, the currency of a number of state banks lost credibility as Federal forces closed in and as the bank specie reserves—already turned over to the Confederate government as backing for bonds or hidden from the government as its policies grew increasingly confiscatory—dwindled. Thus the value of many of those notes dropped to nearly nothing.

One other factor accounted for the depreciation of various notes into shinplasters. After the Emancipation Proclamation, Southerners knew that Federal forces would free slaves as soon as the Union armies occupied an area. To banks, that meant that the collateral for many of their loans had disappeared, thus eroding whatever assets the Southern banks still had.

To alleviate the problem that caused some types of shinplasters, the Confederate Senate, in September 1862, passed a bill to authorize Confederate Secretary of the Treasury Christopher G. Memminger to coin copper tokens of one, five, ten, and twenty-five cents. The Confederate House tabled the measure, and no other small-change law was enacted. Before the war, of course, many individual states had laws prohibiting small notes, but those proved ineffectual even in peacetime.

Neither version of shinplasters—small-change notes or depreciated money—developed owing to any inherent instability in the banking system (North or South). Instead, depreciation of such notes resulted from depreciating bond prices. The shinplaster experience reflected both the confiscatory Confederate policy toward banks and the public's reaction to battlefield events as well as the sudden change in the property status of slaves.

BIBLIOGRAPHY

Hummel, Jeffrey. "Confederate Finance." In *The Encyclopedia of American Business History and Biography: Banking and Finance to 1913.* Edited by Larry Schweikart. Columbia, S.C., 1990.

Pecquet, Gary. "The Tug of War over Southern Banks." In *Durrell Foundation Proceedings.* Berryville, Va., 1992.

Rockhoff, Hugh. *The Free Banking Era: A Reexamination.* New York, 1975.

Rolnick, Arthur J., and Warren E. Weber. "Free Banking, Wildcat Banking, and Shinplasters." *Federal Reserve Bank of Minneapolis Quarterly Review,* Fall 1982, 10–19.

Schweikart, Larry. *Banking in the American South from the Age of Jackson to Reconstruction.* Baton Rouge, La., 1987.

LARRY SCHWEIKART

SHIPYARDS

At war's outbreak the Confederacy seized two U.S. Navy shipyards, Gosport Navy Yard at Norfolk, Virginia, and Pensacola Navy Yard on Florida's Gulf coast.

The Gosport yard converted the frigate *Merrimack* to the ironclad *Virginia,* which battled *Monitor* in Hampton Roads (March 9, 1862). Then advancing Union troops forced Norfolk's abandonment. A similar fate befell Pensacola, and both government yards were lost. The navy established a new yard at Rocketts in Richmond, a site described by one officer as "a shed with 200 or 300 carpenters." Rocketts was active throughout the war, building three ironclads— *Richmond, Fredericksburg,* and *Virginia II*—and maintaining the other ships of the James River Squadron.

Whenever possible, the Navy Department sought to use private industry for wartime manufacturing, including shipbuilding. In the first months of the war both the Confederate and state governments bought commercial steamers and had them converted to warships by private shipyards in Nashville, Savannah, Mobile, and New Orleans. Gunboat contracts were signed with individuals in Mars Bluff and Charleston, South Carolina; Washington and Elizabeth City, North Carolina; Jacksonville and Pensacola, Florida; and Savannah, Saffold, and Early County, Georgia.

When the Navy Department's focus shifted to ironclads, the government continued to rely on independent contractors to build most of the new-style fighting ships. Usually, contractors were forced to create a building site for their project, in effect building their shipyard and then building their ship. Charleston foundry owner James Eason built *Chicora* in a vacant lot behind the post office. To build *Mississippi* at New Orleans, contractors Nelson and Asa Tift first tried to rent the Hughes shipyard at Algiers and then to subcontract the hull to the Harrem and Company or Hyde and Mackey yards. Failing in these efforts, they acquired four acres on the river, installed a sawmill, and opened their own yard. Contractor E. C. Murray rented a lot adjoining that of the Tifts and, in the same way, began building the ironclad *Louisiana*.

Neither New Orleans ironclad survived the capture of the city. Nelson Tift went to Savannah and contracted to convert a blockade runner to the armored *Atlanta* at Henry F. Willink's shipyard. Willink's, one of the few professional shipbuilding facilities left in Confederate control after the spring of 1862, also turned out the ironclads *Savannah* and *Milledgeville* and serviced the rest of the Savannah River Squadron.

By the summer of 1862, with most of the coast and both ends of the Mississippi lost to the South, most Confederate shipbuilding had moved to locations on inland rivers. John Shirley began two ironclads at a steamboat landing below Memphis. When Memphis fell, he burned one and had the other—*Arkansas*—towed up the Yazoo River, where a shipyard was created at the Yazoo City cotton wharf. Gilbert Elliott built the ironclad *Albemarle* in a cornfield at Edwards Ferry, North Carolina. Swampy land at Oven Bluff, Alabama, on the Tombigbee River served as the construction site for three hulls (which were towed to Mobile and never completed).

That contractors had to create their building sites was not a peculiarity of the war. Of the 145 Southern shipyards listed in the 1850 census, the great majority were created for the construction of a single river-going commercial steamer. The wartime experience of shipyards springing up along river banks was just the peacetime practice of Southern shipbuilding gone to war.

Once a yard like Yazoo City or Edwards Ferry was established, other ships were often laid down but rarely completed. Initial construction usually went quickly, as timber was plentiful. But when armor plate and machinery were needed, the work would halt for lack of materials. The ships sat incomplete until advancing Union troops forced the destruction of the vessels and the abandonment of the yard. The Confederate navy contracted for—and saw begun—nearly four times as many ships as were commissioned.

[*See also* Charlotte Navy Yard; Gosport Navy Yard.]

BIBLIOGRAPHY

Melton, Maurice. *The Confederate Ironclads.* South Brunswick, N.J., 1968.

Scharf, J. Thomas. *History of the Confederate States Navy.* New York, 1887. Reprint, New York, 1977.

Still, William N., Jr. *Confederate Shipbuilding.* Athens, Ga., 1969.

Still, William N., Jr. "Facilities for the Construction of War Vessels in the Confederacy." *Journal of Southern History* 31 (1965):285–304.

MAURICE K. MELTON

SHORTER, JOHN G.

SHORTER, JOHN G. (1818–1872), Alabama congressman and governor. Born in Monticello, Georgia, John Gill Shorter graduated from Franklin College (the University of Georgia) in 1837 and then settled in Eufaula, Alabama, where he practiced law and invested heavily in land and slaves. He served briefly in both houses of the Alabama legislature before being elected circuit judge of the Eufaula District in 1852, a position he held until the outbreak of war. Shorter represented Alabama at the Nashville convention in 1850, where he took an early stand in favor of secession. His support of that position grew stronger throughout the 1850s.

When Alabama seceded on January 11, 1861, Shorter was appointed the state's commissioner to the Georgia secession convention. While there he received word that he had been elected to the Confederate Provisional Congress; during his service in Congress, he gave strong support to Jefferson Davis's program. With Governor Andrew B. Moore constitutionally barred from serving a third term, Shorter ran for the office and won easily that fall over Thomas H. Watts.

Little did Shorter realize the magnitude of his prophecy when he warned Alabamians in his inaugural address on December 2, 1861, that they faced "unaccustomed burdens." Within five months Federal troops occupied the state's northern section beyond the Tennessee River, following the Confederate defeat at Shiloh. Shorter had done what he could to support Albert Sidney Johnston, sending him two regiments and a battalion together with five hundred slaves for fortification work. Now one of the areas where he had received his strongest support a year earlier turned bitter as it faced the terrible destruction of war. Caught off guard by the invasion, Shorter delayed two weeks before dispatching four cavalry units to harass the Union forces. When he had to cut short a tour of the region in early 1863 because of pressing business in Montgomery, the people there were further alienated.

Meanwhile Shorter faced a similar threat at the other end of the state. In March 1862 word came that the Confederacy planned to abandon Pensacola. Because Shorter considered it vital to Alabama's coastal defense, he persuaded the Confederacy to postpone the evacuation until May. This gave him time to salvage several cannon and considerable military supplies for use in the defense of Mobile, which appeared threatened following the landing of Federal troops on nearby

Ship Island. He also rushed reinforcements to that area, but the Federals moved instead against New Orleans.

Shorter's biggest problem at this time was not lack of manpower but a critical shortage of arms and ammunition. His complaints to the secretary of war went unheeded, so he sought permission from the legislature to impress arms from the citizenry. When this request was turned down, he sent agents throughout the state to bring in militia muskets and buy other arms. Shorter also contracted with local foundries for weapons, but eighteen months later none had made any deliveries.

> **Shorter's biggest problem at this time was . . . a critical shortage of arms and ammunition.**

As problems mounted throughout 1862, securing enlistments became more difficult. Although initially opposed to conscription, Shorter finally accepted it but counseled Confederate officials to postpone its enforcement until after the harvest season, especially in northern Alabama, a rich agricultural region and increasingly a hotbed of dissatisfaction. Armed resistance did indeed break out that fall, forcing Confederate cavalry to move in and restore order. But the problems of resistance and desertion continued to plague the northern hill country and the southeastern corner of the state. When the legislature in October refused Shorter's request that he be allowed to reorganize the state militia with all those from age sixteen to sixty not subject to the draft, the governor turned to volunteers; but the response was disappointing. The legislature finally passed a compromise bill in August 1863 organizing "County Reserves," but this proved generally ineffective.

The legislature was more amenable to Shorter's pleas for assistance for the indigent families of Alabama troops. Many of them were in dire straits, and their condition encouraged desertion by soldiers who felt they were needed at home. The legislature appropriated $2 million for relief in October 1862 to be distributed through county officials who were also encouraged to supplement it through their own efforts. As conditions on the home front worsened, Shorter in November 1863 secured legislative approval for the state to purchase and distribute relief supplies directly. As food shortages mounted and salt became scarce, the governor banned the distillation of alcohol and placed restrictions on cotton production in favor of grain. He established a state salt works and threatened private salt works with confiscation if they overcharged. Exacerbating the situation was a deteriorating railroad system, which handicapped distribution.

Another manpower problem confronting Shorter involved the need for slave labor to work on fortifications and defens-

es. He had no difficulty in securing 500 slaves in early 1862 to help with Fort Henry; but by October the planters of west central Alabama had become reluctant to let their slaves work on railroad construction because of reports of their neglect and abuse. The governor then persuaded the legislature to give him the power to make requisitions upon the request of military commanders, with the Confederacy reimbursing the owners. With this authorization, he impressed 2,100 slaves to place obstructions on the state's rivers in anticipation of a new invasion. An additional 9,000 were requisitioned in 1863 to work on Mobile's defenses. But reports of abuses mounted in spite of Shorter's protests to the military. When Congress approved the Confederate Impressment Act of March 26, 1863, the governor thought seriously of removing the state from the process but felt honor-bound to continue his cooperation.

Shorter considered this issue, together with his continued strong support of the Davis administration, as the biggest detriment to his reelection. With the state beleaguered on many fronts, Alabamians went to the polls in the fall of 1863 and turned Shorter out of office in favor of his 1861 opponent, Watts, by a margin of three to one. Expressing little bitterness, he retired to his plantation and law practice in Eufaula, appearing only briefly at conservative Reconstruction meetings in Montgomery until his death from tuberculosis in 1872.

BIBLIOGRAPHY

Fleming, Walter L. *Civil War and Reconstruction in Alabama.* New York, 1905. Reprint, Spartanburg, S.C., 1978.

Garrett, William. *Reminiscences of Public Men in Alabama for Thirty Years.* Atlanta, 1872.

Martin, Bessie. *Desertion of Alabama Troops.* New York, 1932.

McMillan, Malcolm C. "Alabama." In *The Confederate Governors.* Edited by W. Buck Yearns. Athens, Ga., 1985.

McMillan, Malcolm C. *The Disintegration of a Confederate State: Three Governors and Alabama's Wartime Home Front, 1861–1865.* Macon, Ga., 1986.

McMillan, Malcolm C., ed. *The Alabama Confederate Reader.* University, Ala., 1963.

WILLIAM E. PARRISH

SIBLEY, HENRY HOPKINS

SIBLEY, HENRY HOPKINS (1816–1886), brigadier general. Sibley was born at Natchitoches, Louisiana, May 25, 1816. He attended West Point and graduated thirty-first in a class of forty-five in 1838. Commissioned a second lieutenant in the Second Dragoons, he saw action in Florida against the Seminoles and fought in Mexico where he was breveted for heroism near Vera Cruz. He spent five years on the Texas frontier, served in Bleeding Kansas, and participated in the 1857–1858 expedition against the Mormons in Utah. Sent to New Mexico Territory, Sibley was with Maj. E. R. S. Canby during the 1860 Navajo campaign.

After resigning from the Federal army in May 1861, Sibley went to Richmond where he convinced President Jefferson Davis of the practicality of seizing New Mexico Territory as a prelude to a Confederate conquest of Colorado and eventually California. Returning to Texas, Sibley assembled a brigade of Texans at San Antonio and set out for Fort Bliss. Pushing up the Rio Grande, Sibley was victorious at Valverde on February 21, 1862, but was turned back at Glorieta Pass near Santa Fe in March and was forced to evacuate the territory. Largely because of his heavy drinking and lack of leadership ability, Sibley was widely blamed for the failure of the campaign. He was sent to Louisiana where he was court-martialed in 1863 following the Battle of Bisland. Although acquitted, he was without a command for the remainder of the war.

After the war, he was recruited into the Egyptian army as a general but was expelled in 1873 for drunkenness. Although well known at one time for his Sibley Tent and Stove Company, he died largely forgotten at Fredericksburg, Virginia, on August 23, 1886.

BIBLIOGRAPHY

Hall, Martin H. *The Confederate Army of New Mexico.* Austin, Tex., 1978.
Hall, Martin H. *Sibley's New Mexico Campaign.* Austin, Tex., 1960.
Thompson, Jerry. *Henry Hopkins Sibley: Confederate General of the West.* Natchitoches, La., 1987.

JERRY THOMPSON

SIGNAL CORPS

The Confederate Signal Corps was, in effect, the creation of a single officer, Edward Porter Alexander, who, while an instructor at West Point, had assisted army surgeon Albert J. Myer in the perfection of his "wig-wag" system of military signaling. After going South in 1861, Alexander was at once put to work organizing, training, and equipping a Signal Corps. Thanks to his skill and energy, the Confederates had a functioning signal service with their forces at First Manassas (July 21, 1861), several months before the confused U.S. War Department could put an effective organization into the field with the Federal armies.

Alexander formed his first signal unit by requesting the detail of some twenty intelligent young privates who could be commissioned if they proved competent. In April 1862 the Confederate government officially established the Signal Service as a branch of its Adjutant General's Department, to consist of one major, ten captains, ten first lieutenants, ten second lieutenants, and twenty sergeants. These men were assigned in small teams to the headquarters of the Confederacy's various field armies, which furnished any needed additional personnel. In 1865 its total strength was approximately 1,500. Its missions were to include signaling, telegraphy, and secret service work.

The Confederate Signal Corps had no distinctive uniform or insignia. Signaling equipment was the same as that used by the Federal Signal Corps, though probably not as complete. The basic items were the signal flags (in the Federal signal service, these were in three sizes—six feet, four feet, and two feet square) and a sixteen-foot staff, made up of four 4-foot sections. The flag commonly used was white, with a red central square, but under some conditions a red flag with a white central square might have greater visibility. A black flag with a white center was used when the ground was snow-covered.

For night signaling, flags were replaced by torches—hollow copper cylinders filled with turpentine or other liquid fuel. Members of the signal detail would carry extra fuel in large round canteens. Torches could be supplemented by a variety of pyrotechnics, such as rockets, flares, and star shells. There were also a variety of improvised methods of communication—fires, signal cannon, and contraptions like the four black-cloth balls that Alexander used for signaling from the Confederacy's one short-lived observation balloon. A Signal Corps officer's most important item of equipment was a powerful telescope or field glasses, essential for reading signals from other stations and observing enemy movements.

The Signal Corps established chains of signal stations, each manned by one or two officers and several enlisted men, from their army's outposts back to its headquarters. These were placed on commanding heights so that each station had a clear line of sight to the stations on either side of it. Where such hills were lacking, tall buildings or specially built signal towers (shaped much like oil derricks) were utilized. The distance between stations depended on the terrain.

Since these stations frequently provided excellent views of the opposing army, the Signal Corps detachments manning them thus had the dual mission of transmitting messages and observing and reporting enemy activities. They also could often observe and copy the messages from the enemy's signal stations. Though all important messages were sent in some type of code, Confederate skills in this art were decidedly inferior to the Federals', who periodically broke Confederate codes and so gained valuable military intelligence. In contrast, the Confederates never were able to read Federal messages, though they occasionally deceived their opponents by sending false information they knew would be intercepted.

One unusual communications function of the Confederate Signal Corps was service aboard blockade runners. Exchanging signals with the Confederate shore defenses, they could obtain the location of close-in Federal warships blockading the seaport and of the safest channels for their ship to use. In 1864 numerous blockade runners reportedly were forced to wait idly in the Bahamas until signal officers could be run out through the blockade to help pilot them in.

The Signal Corps' role in telegraphic communications is not too well recorded. The Confederacy had only limited commercial telegraph service in 1861; there was no unified network to connect Richmond with the various battle fronts and armies. Also, there were relatively few skilled telegraph operators, and telegraph wire was in short supply. The weaknesses of the existing system were aggravated by the damage done to it by Federal raiders—damage that was increasingly difficult to repair as supplies of materials dwindled. (On at least one occasion in 1864 considerable quantities of telegraph wire were stolen by Southern planters for use in baling their cotton.) Though the Signal Corps utilized the existing Southern telegraph systems with their civilian employees and may have somewhat improved and extended them, they never achieved either a nationwide system (such as the North possessed) or a military telegraph service (such as the North had from 1864) to accompany Confederate armies into the field.

The Signal Corps' involvement in "secret service" (a phrase covering what now would be called military intelligence operations) probably grew out of its efforts during the period after First Manassas, when the Confederate outposts were within sight of Washington, D.C., to set up a signal station within that city itself. It was to be managed by a daring spy to whom Confederate sympathizers (including the famous Rose O'Neal Greenhow) would furnish information on Federal forces in the Washington area. This effort failed because the outposts had to be withdrawn, but the Signal Corps continued to be involved in espionage of one sort or another for the duration of the war. It did not have a monopoly on this activity; the Confederate State Department maintained its own intelligence network and practically every Confederate commander utilized his personal contingent of scouts, agents, and spies. (Also there was practically a surplus of enthusiastic amateur spies of both sexes.) This whole business was under no sort of central coordination and control; records of its workings are very incomplete and those available generally exaggerated.

The Signal Corps' one special function in all this seems to have been wire tapping—cutting into Federal telegraph lines and reading the messages being transmitted or inserting their own messages containing false information. Skilled telegraph operators rode with J. E. B. Stuart and John Hunt Morgan on their famous raids; on one occasion Stuart had his operator, a soldier named Sheppard, send the quarter-master general of the U.S. Army a taunting dispatch concerning the poor quality of the mules he had just captured. Other operators infiltrated Federal-occupied territory, tapped wires in some secluded area, and remained there quietly for days recording all messages, as did C. A. Gaston, who was Gen. Robert E. Lee's confidential operator in 1864. Since all important Federal messages were encoded, the amount of valuable information gained from such exploits was minor. But a good many operational messages—such as those directing forces attempting to trap Confederate raiders—were sent "in the clear," and their interception could be highly valuable to the raiders.

Organized hurriedly from scratch, always hampered by shortages of equipment, the Confederate Signal Corps nevertheless rapidly became an effective force. Unfortunately, its services have received little recognition.

[*See also* Alexander, Edward Porter; Balloon; Espionage; Telegraph.]

BIBLIOGRAPHY

Alexander, Edward P. *Fighting for the Confederacy.* Chapel Hill, N.C., 1989.
Coggins, Jack. *Arms and Equipment of the Civil War.* Garden City, N.Y., 1962.
Miller, Francis T. *The Photographic History of the Civil War.* Vol. 8. New York, 1912.
Todd, Frederick P., ed. *American Military Equipage, 1851–1872,* Vol. 2. Providence, R.I., 1977.

JOHN R. ELTING

SLAVE DRIVERS

Drivers were slaves responsible for plantation field production and labor discipline. By the 1830s they were widely employed in the Tidewater rice- and Sea Island cotton-growing areas, the Delta region, and Louisiana sugar parishes, where large agricultural units required close management; many small cotton planters also relied on drivers. On large plantations drivers worked directly under white (and sometimes black) overseers meting out daily work tasks, leading and disciplining work gangs, and managing crop production. On small plantations drivers served as foremen-overseers who reported directly to the master. The staple-crop economy of the plantation South, with its emphasis on regimentation and discipline, meant that the drivers' principal role was to "drive" the slaves by coaxing or coercion. But masters also expected drivers to maintain order in the quarters and to relate the masters' interests to the slaves. Masters rewarded drivers with extra rations, money, access to the local market, and other privileges. Slaves, in turn, suffered drivers so long as they did not abuse their power, kept the masters out of their lives in the quarters, and respected the slaves' community norms. Drivers thus occupied a precarious middle ground between master and slave.

The Civil War fundamentally altered the master-slave relationship, even before emancipation. With the menfolk away, plantation management often was left to planters' wives and "trustworthy" slave drivers. The situation expanded the driver's responsibilities, while paradoxically eroding the structure of bondage on which his power rested. Where drivers had ruled by undue force, embittered slaves retaliated for past abuses by beating and even murdering overseers and drivers, violent acts that were especially widespread in the sugar parishes in 1863 during the Union army advance. Mostly, the unraveling of planter authority forced drivers increasingly to accommodate the slaves' interests to main-

> . . . even as drivers lightened slavery's burdens, they tried to maintain minimum levels of production and upkeep.

tain their own authority. Meanwhile, whites at home complained of driver complicity in raiding plantation storehouses (to which drivers often held the keys), aiding runaways, and slowing work, yet planters continued to entrust daily farm management to black drivers and overseers. The trust was not wholly misplaced, for even as drivers lightened slavery's burdens, they tried to maintain minimum levels of production and upkeep. Perhaps more than any other slave, the driver understood that the slaves' physical well-being, and even avoidance of sale, depended on their producing enough foodstuffs and cash crops to keep slaves fed and masters solvent.

Southern whites' postwar accounts of faithful slaves, especially drivers and house servants, protecting the farms and hiding the master's silver from Northern bummers exaggerated the loyalty of slaves but revealed what had bound such "privileged bondsmen" as drivers to the plantations—namely, that they claimed a vested, proprietary interest in the goods and farmsteads they had planted and built. This was most graphically demonstrated on the South Carolina Sea Islands in 1861 when the masters fled their plantations during the Union landing at Port Royal. Before the abolitionists arrived to begin their famous "Port Royal experiment," the drivers already had kept the slaves growing food crops and prevented destruction of farm equipment and buildings.

Immediately after the war some drivers functioned as straw bosses on plantations where owners sought to bind former slaves to long-term contracts in gang-labor systems, but virtually everywhere by the late 1860s sharecropping and tenancy arrangements left no place for drivers. Many former drivers, especially in the Sea Island and Delta areas, parlayed their planting and marketing experience and personal relationships with former masters into access to credit and local markets few other freedmen could command. Their conservative mediating behavior during slavery inclined former drivers toward personal profit and away from politics. Few former drivers held office during Reconstruction. Their public lives had ended with slavery.

BIBLIOGRAPHY

Miller, Randall M. "The Man in the Middle: The Black Slave Driver." *American Heritage* 30 (1979): 40–49.

Mohr, Clarence L. *On the Threshold of Freedom: Masters and Slaves in Civil War Georgia.* Athens, Ga., 1986.

Rose, Willie Lee. *Rehearsal for Reconstruction: The Port Royal Experiment.* New York, 1964.

Thomas, Emory M. *The Confederate Nation: 1861–1865.* New York, 1979.

Van Deburg, William L. *The Slave Drivers: Black Agricultural Labor Supervisors in the Antebellum South.* Westport, Conn., 1979.

RANDALL M. MILLER

SLAVERY

[*This entry is composed of three articles:* Antebellum Slavery *and* Slavery during the Civil War, *which discuss the institution of slavery before and during the war, and* Slave Life, *which discusses the daily lives of slaves and their society and culture. See also* African Americans in the Confederacy; Antislavery; Cotton; Labor; Plantation; Proslavery; Slave Drivers; Slave Traders; Sugar; Tobacco.]

Antebellum Slavery

The enslavement of African Americans in what became the United States formally began during the 1630s and 1640s. At that time colonial courts and legislatures made clear that Africans—unlike white indentured servants—served their masters for life and that their slave status would be inherited by their children. Slavery in the United States ended in the mid-1860s. Abraham Lincoln's Emancipation Proclamation of January 1863 was a masterful propaganda tactic, but in truth, it proclaimed free only those slaves outside the control of the Federal government—that is, only those in areas still controlled by the Confederacy. The legal end to slavery in the nation came in December 1865 when the Thirteenth Amendment was ratified. It declared: "Neither slavery nor involuntary servitude, except as a punishment for crime whereof the party shall have been duly convicted, shall exist within the United States, or any place subject to their jurisdiction."

Development of American Slavery

The history of African American slavery in the United States can be divided into two periods: the first coincided with the colonial years, about 1650 to 1790; the second lasted from American independence through the Civil War, 1790 to 1865. Prior to independence, slavery existed in all the American colonies and therefore was not an issue of sectional debate. With the arrival of independence, however, the new Northern states—those of New England along with New York, Pennsylvania, and New Jersey—came to see slavery as contradictory to the ideals of the Revolution and instituted programs of gradual emancipation. By 1820 there were only about 3,000 slaves in the North, almost all of them working on large farms in New Jersey. Slavery could be abolished more easily in the North because there were far fewer slaves in those states, and they were not a vital part of Northern economies. There were plenty of free white men to do the sort of labor slaves performed. In fact, the main demand for abolition of slavery came not from those who found it morally wrong but from white working-class men who did not want slaves as rivals for their jobs.

Circumstances in the newly formed Southern states were quite different. The African American population, both slave and free, was much larger. In Virginia and South Carolina in 1790 nearly half of the population was of African descent. (Historians have traditionally assumed that South Carolina had a black majority population throughout its pre–Civil War history. But census figures for 1790 to 1810 show that the state possessed a majority of whites.) Other Southern states also had large black minorities.

Because of their ingrained racial prejudice and ignorance about the sophisticated cultures in Africa from which many of their slaves came, Southern whites were convinced that free blacks would be savages—a threat to white survival. So Southerners believed that slavery was necessary as a means of race control.

Of equal importance in the Southern states was the economic role that slaves played. These states were much more dependent on the agricultural sector of their economies than were Northern ones. Much of the wealth of Delaware, Maryland, Virginia, the Carolinas, and Georgia came from the cash crops that slaves grew. Indeed, many white Southerners did not believe white men could (or should) do the backbreaking labor required to produce tobacco, cotton, rice, and indigo, which were the region's chief cash crops.

As a consequence of these factors, the Southern states were determined to retain slavery after the Revolution. Thus began the fatal division between "free states" and "slave states" that led to sectionalism and, ultimately, to civil war.

Some historians have proposed that the evolution of slavery in most New World societies can be divided (roughly, and with some risk of overgeneralization) into three stages: developmental, high-profit, and decadent. In the developmental stage, slaves cleared virgin forests for planting and built the dikes, dams, roads, and buildings necessary for plantations. In the second, high-profit stage, slave owners earned enormous income from the cash crop they grew for export. In these first two phases, slavery was always very brutal.

During the developmental phase, slaves worked in unknown, often dangerous territory, beset by disease and sometimes hostile inhabitants. Clearing land and performing heavy construction jobs without modern machinery was extremely hard labor, especially in the hot, humid climate of the South.

During the high-profit phase, slaves were driven mercilessly to plant, cultivate, and harvest the crops for market. A failed crop meant the planter could lose his initial investment in land and slaves and possibly suffer bankruptcy. A successful crop could earn such high returns that the slaves were often worked beyond human endurance. Plantation masters argued callously that it was "cheaper to buy than to breed"—it was cheaper to work the slaves to death and then buy new ones than it was to allow them to live long enough and under sufficiently healthy conditions that they could bear children to increase their numbers. During this phase, on some of the sugar plantations in Louisiana and the Caribbean, the life span of a slave from initial purchase to death was only seven years.

The final, decadent phase of slavery was reached when the land upon which the cash crops were grown had become exhausted—the nutrients in the soil needed to produce large harvests were depleted. When that happened, the slave regime typically became more relaxed and less laborintensive. Plantation owners turned to growing grain crops like wheat, barley, corn, and vegetables. Masters needed fewer slaves, and those slaves were not forced to work as hard because the cultivation of these crops required less labor.

This model is useful in analyzing the evolution of Southern slavery between independence and the Civil War. The process, however, varied considerably from state to state. Those of the upper South—Delaware, Maryland, and Virginia—essentially passed through the developmental and high-profit stages *before* American independence. By 1790, Maryland and Virginia planters could no longer produce the bumper harvests of tobacco that had made them rich in the earlier eighteenth century, because their soil was depleted. So they turned to less labor-intensive and less profitable crops such as grains, fruits, and vegetables. This in turn meant they had a surplus of slaves.

One result was that Virginia planters began to free many of their slaves in the decade after the Revolution. Some did so because they believed in the principles of human liberty.

(After all, Virginian slave owners wrote some of the chief documents defining American freedom like the Declaration of Independence, the Constitution, and much of the Bill of Rights.) Others, however, did so for a much more cynical reason. Their surplus slaves had become a burden to house and feed. In response, they emancipated those who were too old or feeble to be of much use on the plantation. Ironically, one of the first laws in Virginia restricting the rights of masters to free their slaves was passed for the protection of the slaves. It denied slave owners the right to free valueless slaves, thus throwing them on public charity for survival. Many upper South slave owners around 1800 believed that slavery would gradually die out because there was no longer enough work for the slaves to do, and without masters to care for them, the ex-slaves would die out as well.

> By 1860 ten of the richest men in America lived . . . in the Natchez district of Mississippi.

Two initially unrelated events solved the upper South's problem of a surplus slave population, caused slavery to become entrenched in the Southern states, and created what we know as the antebellum South. They were the invention of the cotton gin by Eli Whitney of Connecticut in 1793 and the closing of the international slave trade in 1808.

The cotton gin is a relatively simple machine. Its horizontally crossing combs extract tightly entwined seeds from the bolls of short-staple cotton. Prior to the invention of the gin, only long-staple cotton, which has long soft strands, could be grown for profit. Its soft fibers allowed easy removal of its seeds. But this strain of cotton grew in America only along the coast and Sea Islands of South Carolina and Georgia. In contrast, short-staple cotton could grow in almost any non-mountainous region of the South below Virginia. Before the invention of the cotton gin, it took a slave many hours to de-seed a single pound of "lint," or short-staple cotton. With the gin, as many as one hundred pounds of cotton could be de-seeded per hour.

The invention of the cotton gin permitted short-staple cotton to be grown profitably throughout the lower South. Vast new plantations were created from the virgin lands of the territories that became the states of Kentucky, Tennessee, Alabama, Mississippi, and Arkansas. (Louisiana experienced similar growth in both cotton and sugar agriculture.) In 1810, the South produced 85,000 pounds of cotton; by 1860, it was producing well over 2 billion pounds a year.

There was an equally enormous demand for the cotton these plantations produced. It was so profitable that by 1860 ten of the richest men in America lived not just in the South but in the Natchez district of Mississippi alone. In 1810, the

cotton crop had been worth $12,495,000; by 1860, it was valued at $248,757,000.

Along with this expansion in cotton growing came a restriction on the supply of slaves needed to grow it. The transatlantic slave trade was one of the most savage and inhumane practices in which people of European descent have ever engaged. The writers of the Constitution had recognized its evil, but to accommodate the demands of slave owners in the lower South, they had agreed to permit the transatlantic slave trade to continue for twenty years after the Constitution was ratified. Thus, it was not until 1808 that Congress passed legislation ending the transatlantic trade.

These two circumstances—the discovery of a means of making the cultivation of short-staple cotton profitable throughout the lower South and territories and the restriction on the supply of slaves needed to produce it—created the unique antebellum slave system of the South. It made at least some Southerners very rich and it also made slaves much more valuable. One consequence was that some American slaves were perhaps better treated than those elsewhere in the New World, not because American slave owners were kinder, but because American slaves were in short supply and expensive to replace. The price of slaves increased steadily from 1802 to 1860. In 1810, the price of a "prime field hand" was $900; by 1860, that price had doubled to $1,800.

The Slave System in the Nineteenth Century

Slavery in the antebellum South was not a monolithic system; its nature varied widely across the region. At one extreme one white family in thirty owned slaves in Delaware; in contrast, half of all white families in South Carolina did so. Overall, 26 percent of Southern white families owned slaves.

In 1860, families owning more than fifty slaves numbered less than 10,000; those owning more than a hundred numbered less than 3,000 in the whole South. The typical Southern slave owner possessed one or two slaves, and the typical white Southern male owned none. He was an artisan, mechanic, or more frequently, a small farmer. This reality is vital in understanding why white Southerners went to war to defend slavery in 1861. Most of them did not have a direct financial investment in the system. Their willingness to fight in its defense was more complicated and subtle than simple fear of monetary loss. They deeply believed in the Southern way of life, of which slavery was an inextricable part. They also were convinced that Northern threats to undermine slavery would unleash the pent-up hostilities of 4 million African American slaves who had been subjugated for centuries.

Regulating Slavery. One half of all Southerners in 1860 were either slaves themselves or members of slaveholding families. These elite families shaped the mores and political stance of the South, which reflected their common concerns. Foremost among these were controlling slaves and assuring an adequate supply of slave labor. The legislatures of the Southern states passed laws designed to protect the masters' right to their human chattel. Central to these laws were "slave codes," which in their way were grudging admissions that slaves were, in fact, human beings, not simply property like so many cattle or pigs. They attempted to regulate the system so as to minimize the possibility of slave resistance or rebellion. In all states the codes made it illegal for slaves to read and write, to attend church services without the presence of a white person, or to testify in court against a white person. Slaves were forbidden to leave their home plantation without a written pass from their masters. Additional laws tried to secure slavery by restricting the possibility of manumission (the freeing of one's slaves). Between 1810 and 1860, all Southern states passed laws severely restricting the right of slave owners to free their slaves, even in a will. Free blacks were dangerous, for they might inspire slaves to rebel. As a consequence, most Southern states required that any slaves who were freed by their masters leave the state within thirty days.

To enforce the slave codes, authorities established "slave patrols." These were usually locally organized bands of young white men, both slave owners and yeomen farmers, who rode about at night checking that slaves were securely in their quarters. Although some planters felt that the slave patrolmen abused slaves who had been given permission to travel, the slave patrols nevertheless reinforced the sense of white solidarity between slave owners and those who owned none. They shared a desire to keep the nonwhite population in check. (These antebellum slave patrols are seen by many historians as antecedents of the Reconstruction era Ku Klux Klan, which similarly tried to discipline the freed blacks. The Klan helped reinforce white solidarity in a time when the class lines between ex–slave owners and white yeomen were collapsing because of slavery's end.)

The Internal Slave Trade. The factor that made the antebellum system viable was the internal slave trade. White Southerners were embarrassed by the trade, and there is little documentation about how it operated. Slave traders were considered the least reputable of white men. Nevertheless, the genteel aristocrats of the upper South and the aggressive new planters of the lower South both needed slave traders to keep their economic system working. The economy could prosper only because of the transfer of surplus slaves from the upper South to the labor-short, high-profit plantations of the cotton-growing lower South.

The slave trade operated in two forms. The first form of transfer occurred through endowment of heirs. Because states of the upper South still had laws of primogeniture (the eldest son inherited all his father's property), fathers often purchased land for their younger sons in the developing lower South and gave them a number of slaves to work the new land. This meant that some of the caravans of slaves

seen by Northern observers traveling southward were, in fact, plantation units composed of intact families being transferred to new locations.

Most historians agree, however, that the second form of slave trade—commercial sale—was by far the most dominant means of transferring slave property from the upper to the lower South. Hundreds of thousands of slaves were sold as individuals, separated from their loved ones through the internal slave trade. Husbands were separated from their wives; children, from their parents. Two million slaves were transferred from one region to the other between 1790 and 1860.

The extent of the interstate slave trade is revealed by figures showing the distribution of the black population between 1790 and 1860. The number of slaves in the upper South grew by 175,000, whereas the number in the lower South increased from 237,000 in 1790 to over 3 million in 1860. Basically, the entire natural increase in the slave population of the upper South was exported to the lower South cotton plantations between 1820 and 1860. Very few slaves born in the upper South grew up there. The antebellum Southern slave economy survived because the upper South—in which fewer slaves were needed because the soil was exhausted—sold its excess slaves to the burgeoning cotton plantations of the lower South.

Slave Labor in the Upper South. If there was a "least bad" place to be a slave in the antebellum South, it was in the towns and on the smaller farms of Virginia and Maryland. When those states turned from growing high-yield crops like tobacco to cultivating crops like grains and vegetables, the change carried some benefits for slaves. The new crops required less intensive labor and permitted some slaves to work under the "task system." Slaves were assigned chores individually or in small groups. They were permitted to work at their own pace, often without direct white supervision. They would be assigned another task upon completion of the first.

The decline in the profitability of slavery appears to have led to a more relaxed and open regime for some slaves in the upper South. Since fewer slaves were needed on plantations, many were allowed by their master to live in town and "hire their own time"—find their own work—paying their masters a portion of their wages, usually two-thirds to three-quarters. This benefited the masters by enabling them to make a profit on an otherwise surplus slave. It was attractive to the slaves because it gave them more independence. Many hoped to save enough from their wages to buy their freedom from their owners.

This more relaxed system extended to other aspects of slave life in the upper South. It appears that most slaves in Virginia and Maryland were allowed to marry and have families, although these families had no legal standing. They existed only through permission of the master. In addition, laws against literacy and holding church services without a white person present were widely ignored or unenforced.

Of course, Virginia slaves were still the property of white masters, to be used as the masters saw fit. To put it bluntly, the chief cash crop of Virginia slave owners after 1807 was the slaves themselves. Historians have been unable to find plantations that openly "bred" slaves for sale, but this does not change the central appalling fact—the number of slaves born in Virginia between 1807 and 1860 was the same number as those sold farther South. So if conditions for slaves *were* better in Virginia, few of those born there grew up to enjoy them there. Indeed, the standard and most effective way to discipline a slave was to threaten to sell him or a loved one to the Deep South.

Slave Labor in the Lower South. The possibility of being "sold south" was no empty threat. Slaves in the lower South were often ill housed, ill fed, and ill cared for. It was more profitable to keep them at work on cotton than allow them time to build decent shelter. It was more profitable to plant every inch of land in cotton than to allot space for growing foodstuffs. Even the little garden plots allowed slaves in the upper South were usually absent in Mississippi. That state, with some of the richest soil in America, was actually a net importer of foodstuffs before the Civil War.

Life on the Deep South plantations was also characterized by the impersonality of master-slave relationships. Owners were often absent, and overseers were paid by how much cotton they produced, not by the condition of the slaves they supervised.

On lower South plantations, like those of the upper South, both men and women slaves were expected to toil in the fields from "first light" to "full dark." Because men were stronger and able to work harder, the plantations often had a much larger number of male slaves than female. This made the possibility of marriage problematic for the slave men. Moreover, women were sometimes seen as liabilities because "female problems" such as the menstrual cycle and pregnancy periodically incapacitated them for hard labor. In the cotton and sugar South, slaves were usually worked in gangs supervised by black drivers and white overseers with whips. The pace for plowing, hoeing, weeding, or picking was set by the overseers, and if a worker fell behind, he or she felt the sting of the lash.

Impact of Slavery on the Southern Economy

As the preceding discussion makes clear, slavery in the antebellum South was overwhelmingly a rural phenomenon. This was, in part, because most slave owners believed that slavery would not work well in an urban industrialized environment. Slaves were thought to be too stupid to understand machinery and too careless to be trusted with complex tools.

In fact, however, slaves *were* used successfully in factories such as the Tredegar Iron Works in Richmond. They also

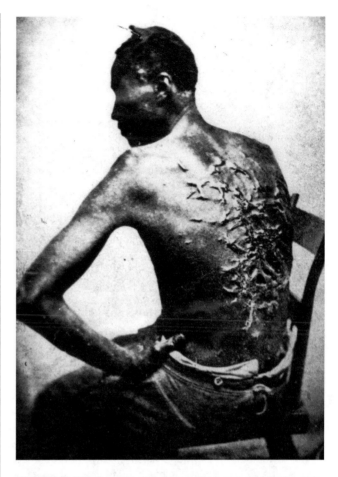

WHIPPED SLAVE. Peter, the slave pictured above, gave the following explanation of his scars when posing for this photograph on April 2, 1863, in Baton Rouge, Louisiana: "Overseer Artayou Carrier whipped me. I was two months in bed sore from the whipping. My master come after I was whipped; he discharged the overseer." NATIONAL ARCHIVES

labored in the salt mines and turpentine plants of North Carolina, the coal mines of western Virginia, and the sugar mills of Louisiana. Moreover, when, during the Civil War, Southerners confronted a manpower shortage and the need for rapid industrialization, they quickly overcame their prejudices against using slaves in factories.

Objections to Urban Slavery. A major reason for slavery being confined mostly to rural areas in the South concerned its dual purpose for the white population. It was both a means of labor exploitation and a means of race control. It was this second aspect that made the institution problematic in urban areas. Simply put, slaves in cities were much more difficult to supervise.

It was the custom of factory owners to hire slaves from masters rather than purchase them outright. In the upper South, where urban slaves were more common, this allowed slave owners to profit from their excess slaves without having to sell them South. The problem was that industrialists preferred to avoid the burden of overseeing their slave employees outside of the factory, and they tended to give them stipends to pay for their own housing and board. This enabled urban slaves to live in a varied community that included free blacks, slaves who hired their own time, and white people— some of whom might oppose slavery.

As white Southerners saw it, the urban environment exposed slaves to dangerous ideas about freedom. Most Southern cities were ports that provided access to the outside world where slavery was generally outlawed. Free black sailors and sympathetic white ship captains were known to help slaves escape aboard their vessels.

Cities, therefore, were considered antithetical to effective slave control. White Southerners well remembered that the two largest slave conspiracies (those of Gabriel Prosser in Richmond in 1800 and Denmark Vesey in Charleston in 1822) were urban phenomena. Moreover, both men were free blacks who had persuaded urban slaves to join them in their plots.

Yet another factor militating against urban slavery was the attitudes of workers in antebellum America. Southern white men felt demeaned if they were required to perform the same sort of job as a slave. Moreover, slaves, who received no wages, could do the same labor more cheaply than free white men. White workers—like the caulkers in Baltimore who beat up Frederick Douglass when his master sent him to work in the dockyards—often refused to labor alongside slaves.

So, to maintain better supervision of slaves and assure white solidarity and the status of white laborers, urban slavery in the antebellum South was minimal. The numbers of urban slaves actually declined between 1830 and 1860.

Negative Effects of Rural Slavery. The rural nature of antebellum slavery had unintended negative effects on the Southern economy. The investment of so much capital in land and slaves discouraged the growth of cities and diverted funds from factories. This meant that the South lacked the industrial base it needed to counter the North when the Civil War began. Indeed, in 1860, the South had approximately the same number of industrial *workers* (110,000), as the North had industrial *plants.*

Other detrimental effects arose from the South's devotion to rural slavery. Wealthy planters liked to claim they were living out the Jeffersonian ideal of an agrarian democracy. In truth, the South was agrarian because slave owners found that the best way to maintain their wealth and contain their slaves. Moreover, its "democracy" was very limited because the planters had enormous influence over how white yeomen cast their votes. Except in remote areas of the South with few slaves or plantations, it was the needs and beliefs of the planter class that shaped Southern politics on the local, state, and national levels.

The consequences of this planter dominance was seen in many aspects of the society. The South failed to develop a varied economy even within the agricultural realm. All the most fertile land in the South was owned by slaveholders who chose to grow high-profit staple crops—cotton, tobacco, sugar. That left only marginal land for the vast majority of white farmers. This problem was compounded by the dominance of the planter's image as the social ideal. Alternative means of advancement were unavailable, so yeomen farmers aspired to become planters themselves. They used some of their land to grow food for their family's consumption and devoted the rest to cash crops like cotton. Their hope was to produce enough to save, buy a few slaves, produce yet more, and, ultimately, accumulate the wealth that would elevate them to planter status. For most, this was a futile dream, but they remained committed to it, thereby neglecting other possible avenues for economic advancement.

One reason for the yeomen farmers' lack of aspirations was ignorance. The antebellum South neglected to provide for the education of its people. Planters controlled the governmental revenues that could have financed public education, but they saw no need to do so. Their slaves were forbidden to learn; their own children were educated by private tutors or in exclusive and expensive private academies. As a result, most white yeomen were left without access to education. A few lucky ones near towns or cities could sometimes send their children to fee schools or charity schools, but many were too poor or too proud to use either option.

In a similar vein, the dominating slaveholding class saw no need to create the means to produce inexpensive consumer goods for ordinary whites or to build an infrastructure by which such goods could be moved from production sites to markets in the countryside. Wealthy planters acquired what they wanted by importing expensive European or Northern goods. Thus poor whites were left to their own minimal resources and were deprived of goods they might have bought, had they been available.

This lack of consumer production and markets also retarded the growth of Southern transportation. Highways, canals, and railroads were constructed to move crops to ports and bring in luxury items for the planter class. The need of yeomen farmers to transport their crops to local markets was ignored. As a consequence, it was usually cheaper for plantation owners to import food from the North or upper South than to purchase it from white farmers in the same region. This deficiency in the Southern transportation system proved a serious liability for the Confederacy during the Civil War.

Slavery in the antebellum South, then, made a minority of white Southerners—owners of large slaveholdings—enormously wealthy. At the same time, it demeaned and exploited Southerners of African descent, left the majority of white Southerners impoverished and uneducated, and retarded the overall economic, cultural, and social growth of the region. Slavery was the institution by which the South defined itself when it chose to secede from the Union. But it was the existence of slavery, with its negative impact on politics, economics, and social relations, that fatally crippled the South in its bid for independence.

[*See also* Expansionism in the Antebellum South; Urbanization.]

BIBLIOGRAPHY

Blassingame, John. *The Slave Community.* New York, 1979.

Davis, David Brion. *The Problem of Slavery in Western Culture.* New York, 1966.

Fox-Genovese, Elizabeth. *Within the Plantation Household: Black and White Women in the Old South.* New York, 1988.

Genovese, Eugene. *Roll, Jordan, Roll.* New York, 1974.

Higginbotham, A. Leon. *In the Matter of Color.* New York, 1978.

Morgan, Edmund. *American Slavery, American Freedom.* New York, 1975.

Oakes, James. *The Ruling Race: A History of America's Slaveholders.* New York, 1982.

Rawick, George. *From Sundown to Sunup.* Westport, Conn., 1972.

Scarborough, William K. *The Overseer: Plantation Management in the Old South.* Athens, Ga., 1966.

Stampp, Kenneth. *The Peculiar Institution.* New York, 1956.

Wade, Richard. *Slavery in the Cities.* Oxford, 1964.

ROBERT FRANCIS ENGS

Slavery during the Civil War

Although slavery was at the heart of the sectional impasse between North and South in 1860, it was not the *singular* cause of the Civil War. Rather, it was the multitude of differences arising from the slavery issue that impelled the Southern states to secede.

The presidential election of 1860 had resulted in the selection of a Republican, Abraham Lincoln of Illinois, as president of the United States. Lincoln won because of an overwhelming electoral college vote from the Northern states. Not a single Southern slave state voted for him. Lincoln and his Republican party were pledged only to stop the expansion of slavery. Although they promised to protect slavery where it existed, white Southerners were not persuaded. The election results demonstrated that the South was increasingly a minority region within the nation. Soon Northerners and slavery's opponents might accumulate the voting power to overturn the institution, no matter what white Southerners might desire.

Indeed, many Southern radicals, or fire-eaters, openly hoped for a Republican victory as the only way to force Southern independence. South Carolina had declared it would secede from the Union if Lincoln was elected, and it did so in December 1861. It was followed shortly by the other lower South states of Alabama, Mississippi, Louisiana,

Georgia, Florida, and Texas. In February 1861, a month before Lincoln was inaugurated, these states formed a new nation, the Confederate States of America. After the firing on Fort Sumter and Lincoln's call for volunteers to suppress the rebellion, the other slave states of Virginia, North Carolina, Tennessee, and Arkansas joined the Confederacy. The border slave states of Delaware, Maryland, Kentucky, and Missouri remained—not entirely voluntarily—in the Union.

The new republic claimed its justification to be the protection of state rights. In truth, close reading of the states' secession proclamations and of the new Confederate Constitution reveals that it was primarily *one* state right that impelled their separation: the right to preserve African American slavery within their borders. But the white South's decision to secede proved to be the worst possible choice it could have made in order to preserve that right.

There was enormous antislavery sentiment in the North, but such sentiment was also strongly anti-Negro. White Northerners did not wish slavery to expand into new areas of the nation, which they believed should be preserved for white nonslaveholding settlers. This was, in part, why Republicans pledged to protect slavery where it existed. They and their constituencies did not want an influx of ex-slaves into their exclusively white territories, should slavery end abruptly.

Some historians argue that, had the South remained within the Union, its representatives could have prevented any radical Northern plan for emancipation. By leaving the Union, white Southerners gave up their voice in national councils. Moreover, by seceding, the South compelled the North to realize the extent of its allegiance to a united American

> **But the white South's decision to secede proved to be the worst possible choice. . . .**

nation. Thus, the North went to war to preserve the Union, and the white South went to war for independence so that it might protect slavery. Most participants on both sides did not initially realize that the African American slaves might view the conflict as an occasion that they could turn to their own advantage.

Slaves' Efforts to Undermine the South. In 1861, as the Civil War began, there were four open questions among Northerners and Southerners with regard to the slaves: First, would they rebel? Second, did they want their freedom? Third, would they fight for their freedom? And, finally, would they know what to do with their freedom if they got it? The answer to each question was yes, but in a manner that reflected the peculiar experience of blacks in white America.

First was the question of whether bondsmen would rebel or remain passive. The fear of slave rebellion preoccupied both the Southern slaveholder and the Northern invader. Strikingly, Northerners were as uneasy about the possibility as were Southerners. Initially the Northern goal in the war was the speedy restoration of the Union under the Constitution and the laws of 1861, all of which recognized the legitimacy of slavery. Interfering with slavery would make reunion more difficult. Thus, Union generals like George B. McClellan in Virginia and Henry W. Halleck in the West were ordered not only to defeat the Southern armies but also to prevent slave insurrections. In the first months of the war, slaves who escaped to Union lines were returned to their masters in conformity with the Fugitive Slave Act of 1850.

Concern about outright slave insurrections proved unfounded, however. Slaves were not fools, nor were they suicidal. Mary Boykin Chesnut, the famed Southern diarist and one of the South's most perceptive observers of slavery, understood the slaves' strategy. She wrote from her plantation: "Dick, the butler here, reminds me that when we were children, I taught him to read as soon as I could read myself. . . . But he won't look at me now. He looks over my head. He scents freedom in the air."

Slaves like Dick knew the war was about their freedom, but they were both shrewd and cautious. To rebel on their own was hopeless; the whites were too powerful. But now the Southern whites had an equally powerful outside enemy, and the odds had changed. The slaves, like successful rebels everywhere, bided their time until a revolt could succeed.

Meanwhile, through desertion and noncooperation, they did much to undermine the South long before Union armies triumphed. When the war began, some Confederates claimed that the disparity in white manpower between North and South (6 million potential soldiers for the North versus only 2 million for the South) was irrelevant. The South, Confederates claimed, could put a far higher proportion of their men in the field because they had slaves to do the labor at home.

The South, however, quickly learned that it had what would now be called a "fifth column" in its midst, providing aid and comfort to the enemy. At the beginning of the war, Southern officers took their body servants with them to the front to do their cooking and laundry. A unit of two thousand white soldiers would sometimes depart with as many as a thousand slaves in tow. The custom did not last beyond the first summer of the conflict. The servants deserted at the first opportunity and provided excellent intelligence to Union forces about Southern troop deployments.

In one incident during the early months of the war, Union soldiers on the Virginia Peninsula, stationed at Fort Monroe, repeatedly set out to capture the nearby city of Newport News, but without success. Their inaccurate maps showed the town to be *southwest* of Fort Monroe. Each would-be attack concluded with the troops mired in the swampy land bordering Hampton Roads (the bay between the Virginia

Peninsula and Norfolk on the "Southside"). In fact, Newport News was slightly *northwest* of Fort Monroe, and Union forces were unable to find it until an escaped body servant led them there.

Slave Labor with the Confederate Military. Despite such subversion by the slaves, the Confederacy nevertheless successfully used them to advance its war effort. White Southerners, though convinced of the African Americans' inherent inferiority, were far less reluctant about putting the slaves to work militarily than were white Northerners. The Confederate government never used them as soldiers, but it did press them into labor brigades to build fortifications, dig latrines, and haul supplies. Tens of thousands of slaves toiled for the Confederacy in a service both the bondsmen and their owners disliked. For the slave impressed into labor on the frontline, the work frequently was not only harder than that on the plantation but also dangerous. Because of the possibility of escape through Union lines, slaves at the front were much more closely supervised than on their home farms. Moreover, those sent to work with the Confederate army were usually men in their prime, between eighteen and forty. Service with the army denied them their accustomed time with their wife and family.

The slave owners, for their part, were reluctant to send their bondsmen to the front for two reasons. First, they risked the loss of their most valuable property, and, second, because the men were usually overworked and mistreated, they frequently returned to their homes in very poor physical condition. Thus, the owners often contrived to send only their most unmanageable and therefore least marketable slaves to the army. During the war, threatening to send a slave to the front became the disciplinary equivalent of threatening to sell a slave farther South in antebellum days. Ironically, as the South's cause became more desperate, masters were increasingly reluctant to send their slaves to the military. Slavery was dying, yet those with the most to lose hung on tenaciously to their human property, thereby withholding the one remaining resource that might have saved their nation—and them.

The exigencies of war also finally settled the decades-old debate as to whether slaves could be used safely and efficiently in industry. The shortage of white manpower left the South with no other choice than to put slaves to work in its factories and mines. In the Tredegar Iron Works of Richmond alone, thousands of slaves were employed. The Augusta munitions plants of Georgia likewise were primarily staffed by bondsmen. Thousands of others labored in the ultimately futile effort to keep Southern rail lines operating. As with service on the front lines, this labor—especially in extractive industries like the coal mines and salt factories—was harsher than life on the plantation, and slaves resisted it if they could. Many made the long-delayed decision to run away when faced with such dire prospects.

Although their service was extracted involuntarily, slaves in industry and on the battlefield enabled the South to fight on longer than would been possible otherwise. In the final desperate days of the war, the Confederacy even considered using blacks as soldiers, offering emancipation as a reward. The Union had struck that bargain two years earlier. The Southern proposal was made in February 1865 and approved, in part, on March 13 of that year. By then Southerners of both races knew the Confederacy was doomed. Richmond fell less than thirty days later. The provision was never implemented and no slaves officially served as soldiers in the Confederate military.

> ### As the war continued to go badly, . . . slave owners moved their bondsmen across the Mississippi.

The Wartime Slave Economy. Just as it did all other aspects of Southern life, the war severely disrupted the slave economy and the market for slaves. The chaos of the period makes an accurate account of change very difficult. Three conclusions, however, can be made about the war years. First, masters tried desperately to protect their investment in slave property to the very end of the war. Second, the slave trade and the antebellum trend of a slave population movement toward the Southwest continued during the war. Third, the prices of slaves rose astronomically (although in inflated currency) during the war even as the security of that form of property became increasingly doubtful.

Slaveholders had seceded and gone to war in the first place to protect their property in human beings, and they adopted various protective measures in the course of that war. Besides resisting the use of their slaves in the Confederate military, they developed another strategy: they transferred their slaves to more secure regions of the Confederacy. Thus, early in the war, thousands of slaves were moved from areas of active conflict or potential invasion—such as Tidewater Virginia and coastal areas along the Atlantic seaboard—to seemingly more secure inland regions. As the war continued to go badly and Northern armies penetrated more deeply into the Confederacy, slave owners moved their bondsmen across the Mississippi to areas in the West, especially Texas.

Their attempt to secure their investment in slave property also resulted in a continuation of the internal slave trade during the war. Owners of healthy young males or of females who were potentially "good breeders" tried to sell them to buyers from more secure regions of the South or simply to those willing to risk their money on Confederate victory. As Union forces triumphed, however, the trade was much dis-

rupted, and it became impossible to move large bands of slaves through areas of possible conflict. The largest slave-trading city, New Orleans, was captured by the North in April 1862. By war's end, only Charleston in the East had an active slave market, although slaves were reportedly still being traded in Richmond on the eve of its fall.

Prices of slaves increased exponentially during the war. A "prime field hand" valued at a thousand dollars in 1860 could fetch ten thousand dollars in 1865. The increased price, however, reflected the inflated Confederate currency. It is impossible to estimate the *volume* of the slave trade during the war. The corresponding value of these prices in gold—from one thousand dollars in 1861 to one hundred dollars in 1865—is evidence of a dramatic price collapse. The inflation of slave prices and the growing insecurity of slave property both grew out of and reinforced the general disintegration of the Southern economy. In the end, it appears that many masters had more faith in the survival of slavery than in Confederate money or bonds. They tried to hold onto their human property until forced to surrender it because of Union victory.

Slave Resistance on the Plantations. When given the option, slaves made it very clear that they wanted *freedom.* The vast majority of slaves, however, remained on their plantations in the countryside. Nevertheless, even these slaves in the Southern interior found ways to demonstrate their desire for freedom. Their behavior could be described as the first massive labor slowdown in American history. They did not cease to work, but they contrived to do considerably less than they had before the war.

Part of the reason for the drop in their industriousness was the South's ill-advised self-imposed cotton embargo. Although this was never official policy, many Southerners believed they could provoke European intervention in the war by refusing to grow or export cotton. This decision changed the nature of Southern agriculture. The region began to emphasize food production, a less intensive form of agricultural labor. But this change did not necessarily reduce the burden on slave laborers. The war cut off many of the South's antebellum sources of food and other goods in the North and abroad. These shortages had to be replaced by what the slaves could produce at home. Their inability to make up the shortfall meant that they, their masters, the soldiers in the field, and the general population all suffered from increasing deprivation as the war went on. Especially problematic were shortages of wool, leather, and salt for the curing of meat, since most of these were diverted for military use. One consequence was the rapid escalation of prices for such necessities. Frugal planters cut back on these supplies for their slaves. Bondsmen did not receive their prewar rations of clothes and shoes, and they had less meat and vegetables in their diet. Even those slaves well removed from the front lines throughout the war recalled it later as a time of great privation.

In addition to the change in the kinds of crops grown and the increasing scarcity of necessities, the quality of management on the plantations changed. Once the war intensified in 1862, there were not enough white men left on the farms and plantations to provide adequate supervision of slave laborers. The Confederacy had attempted to defuse this potential problem through the Ten-Slave Law (later, the Twenty-Slave Law), whereby a percentage of white men were exempted from military service in proportion to the number of slaves in a county or on a plantation. The law clearly favored slaveholders and drew a storm of protest from white yeomen who owned no slaves yet were called upon to defend the Southern cause.

As the war progressed, Southern manpower shortages became acute. In some parts of Georgia, it was reported that there was only one able-bodied white man in a ten-square-mile area. As a result, management of agriculture increasingly fell to white women and their youngest children, elderly fathers, and black slave drivers. All proved less effective taskmasters than the earlier overseers, and the efficiency of Southern farm production declined markedly.

Slaves quickly took advantage of the situation, reducing the pace of their labor, disobeying orders, leaving their farms to visit with friends and relatives. Their perceived "impudence" and "laziness" caused enormous frustration for the white women left to oversee them. Although these women had often been most resourceful managers of household economies in the prewar South, they had never been trained or given experience in day-to-day supervision of farming operations. Many were unequal to the burden and resentful that they were being forced to shoulder it.

One important consequence of this management crisis was the disappearance of even the veneer of paternalism in the master-slave relationship. White women and the few white men left in the countryside viewed the increasingly recalcitrant slaves as a threat, especially the young males. Slave patrols composed of the remaining white men became more energetic and violent in "disciplining" slaves. Those accused or suspected of "misconduct" were brutally punished and sometimes murdered.

Despite these draconian efforts, slaves in the South's interior stepped up their resistance and increasingly worked at a much slower pace. More disturbing yet to the whites around them was their outright refusal to obey orders when they could get away with it. Slaves ran off with greater frequency; they stole food and violated curfew with impunity. They began to hold religious services more openly and even created schools for their children in violation of state laws.

Escaping from Slavery. The second of the four questions preoccupying European Americans, North and South, was: Did the slaves want freedom? Of course they did, as long as they could attain it without losing their lives in the process. The unrest on the plantations clearly indicated their longing for freedom. Even more demonstrable evidence was offered by slaves living on the borders of the Confederacy. Beginning in 1861, and continuing throughout the war, whenever the proximity of Union troops made successful escape likely, slaves abandoned their plantations by the hundreds, even the thousands.

The process of successful slave escapes began in Virginia, in Union-held territory across the Potomac from Washington and around Fort Monroe at the tip of the Virginia Peninsula in Hampton Roads. In May 1861, three slaves fled to the fort and claimed sanctuary because their masters were about to take them South to work on Confederate fortifications. The Union commander there was Gen. Benjamin Butler, a War Democrat from Massachusetts and a perennial thorn in Lincoln's side. Thinking more about the political advantage to be gained among Northern antislavery advocates than about the needs of the fugitives, Butler declared the blacks to be "contraband of war"—enemy property that could be used against the Union. This designation neatly avoided the question of whether or not the escapees were free and turned the Southerners' argument that slaves were property against them. Lincoln reluctantly approved the rul-

> **The process of successful slave escapes began in Virginia, in Union-held territory. . . .**

ing, and as a consequence, escaped slaves throughout the war were referred to by Northerners as "contrabands."

This legal hairsplitting was of no concern to Virginia slaves. All they knew was that fugitives had gone to Fort Monroe and found sanctuary. Within a month, over 900 had joined those first three. By war's end, there were over 25,000 escaped slaves in and around Fort Monroe. Many of them served in the Union army.

A more massive instance of slaves' defecting occurred the following spring in the Sea Islands off South Carolina. The Union navy landed troops on the islands and the whites fled. Despite efforts by masters—some told the slaves that the Yankees were cannibals—the slaves refused to join their owners and fled to the woods until the Southern whites had left. As a consequence, the Union army suddenly had several thousand contrabands to care for. Interestingly, the first task of the Union commanders on the Sea Islands was to stop the ex-slaves from looting and burning their masters' mansions.

With the fall of New Orleans, also in the spring of 1862, the informal emancipation process expanded into the lower Mississippi valley. It never reached much of the Trans-Mississippi South until war's end because Union forces did not penetrate deeply there.

Throughout the South, the first slaves to escape were typically house servants and skilled craftsmen. They were the people who had the most access to information about Union troop movements (acquired primarily by overhearing their masters' indiscreet conversations around them) and those who had the greatest knowledge of the outside world. Usually the first ones to escape were men. Once they found they would be protected behind Union lines, they returned for their friends and relatives.

The North had not anticipated massive slave escapes. It had no plans about how to care for these black refugees. As a consequence, many escapees found themselves in worse physical conditions than they had known on the plantations. They were herded into camps and given tents and rations in exchange for work. The blacks were put to work in much the way Southern troops were using them, building fortifications, digging latrines, and cleaning the camps. Blacks frequently complained that their Union supervisors treated them worse than their former masters and overseers. In truth, many Union soldiers resented having to serve in the war, especially those who were draftees, and they blamed the blacks for their predicament.

The black refugees in the Union camps usually received no actual income. Most of the money they earned was withheld to pay for their food and clothing, and any remainder was reserved to pay for indigent or crippled escapees who could not work. This was administered by the Quartermaster's Department, a notoriously unreliable branch of any army throughout history. Blacks were defrauded at every turn. Often their rations and clothing were sold on the black market—sometimes to the Southerners—by greedy supply officers.

Hearing of the plight of the contrabands in the camps, Northern benevolent organizations, such as the Freedmen's Aid Societies, and religious groups, such as the American Missionary Association, sent hundreds of missionaries and teachers to the South to aid the blacks. They provided much of the food and clothing that enabled the refugees to survive. They also created the first schools and churches most blacks had ever attended.

It was the blacks themselves, however, who were primarily responsible for their survival in these harsh circumstances. The more enterprising of them earned cash through private work with officers of the camps. Those who fared best struck out from the encampments and squatted on lands abandoned by fleeing Confederates. Frequently they were able to make the land far more productive than it had ever been during slavery.

Lincoln and the Emancipation Proclamation. The extent of slave escapes in the South and the burden it placed upon the Union presented a major dilemma for President Lincoln. From the moment the conflict began at Fort Sumter, Lincoln's foremost goals had been to preserve the Union, to

bring the war to an end with a minimum of bloodshed, and to avoid lingering animosity between Northern and Southern whites. If that could best be achieved by preserving slavery, he said, he would do so; if it could be achieved by freeing every slave, he would do that instead. Lincoln despised slavery, but he, like Thomas Jefferson and many others before him, doubted that blacks and whites could ever live in America in a condition of equality.

The spring and summer of 1862 aggravated Lincoln's problem. The slaves, by running away in massive numbers, were freeing themselves. The border slave states of Delaware, Maryland, Kentucky, and Missouri were resisting all of Lincoln's proposals for gradual compensated emancipation. His own schemes to find somewhere outside of the United States where the freed black population could be colonized failed completely.

At the same time, Lincoln was confronted at home by abolitionists who insisted that the war should be one for emancipation. Abroad, he was faced with growing skepticism about Northern war aims. If the Union goal was simply to reunite the country and preserve slavery, then the North was undertaking a war of aggression. The South's claim that it was fighting for its independence, just as the United States had done during the Revolution, was therefore valid, and foreign powers had the right to intervene as the French had done in 1778. All these pressures forced Lincoln to conclude that emancipation would have to become a Union war goal.

The critics of Lincoln and the Emancipation Proclamation are technically correct in observing that the proclamation in January 1863 did not *legally* free a single slave. Slavery's end required a constitutional amendment, which Lincoln advocated and which was ratified as the Thirteenth Amendment in 1865. The *symbolic* importance of the Emancipation Proclamation should not, however, be underestimated. Lincoln thereby silenced his abolitionist critics in the North, defused interventionist sentiment abroad, and energized black slave resisters to continue their efforts in the South.

Lincoln advised his cabinet of his plan in the early summer of 1862. Because the Union cause was not faring well on the battlefield, he delayed its issuance until a Union victory could be attained. He claimed the bloody Battle of Sharpsburg (Antietam), during which Robert E. Lee's first invasion of the North was repulsed, as an appropriate occasion. Slaves in states or territories still in rebellion against the United States on January 1, 1863, would be freed. He hoped, probably only halfheartedly, that this threat would energize Southern moderates and influence them to persuade their leaders to lay down their arms. That was not to be the case.

On January 1, 1863, throughout the Union-occupied areas of the South, contrabands, their Northern white allies, and some Union soldiers gathered to pray, to sing hymns, and to celebrate slavery's demise. (The fact that none of those contrabands had been *legally* freed was irrelevant.) Moreover, the proclamation welcomed all escaping slaves into Union lines and held out the prospect that ex-slaves could volunteer for service in the Union military. African American slaves had tried to make the Civil War one of black liberation. In the Emancipation Proclamation, Abraham Lincoln and the Union appeared to have embraced their cause.

Certainly this was the belief of Southern slave owners. They wrote that both "misbehavior" on the plantations and escape attempts increased significantly after the issuance of the proclamation. Only in the Trans-Mississippi regions of Arkansas, Louisiana, and Texas was the impact of the proclamation minimal. One reminder of that difference is that blacks in that area and their descendants in the Midwest celebrate emancipation not on January 1 but on "Juneteenth," that period in mid-June after the surrender of the last Confederate armies in the West under E. Kirby Smith. Union officers, many now also superintendents of the newly formed Freedmen's Bureau, rode around those western states announcing Lincoln's Emancipation Proclamation to slaves and their masters.

In the eastern half of the Confederacy, slavery had collapsed long before those final western Union victories, in part because of the efforts of former slaves as Union soldiers.

Ex-Slaves in the Union Army. The third of the four questions preoccupying white Americans during the Civil War was whether blacks would be willing to fight for their freedom. Once again the answer was yes. The fury of the white South when the North decided to make escaped slaves into soldiers is not surprising. What may be more so is the horror with which much of the white North regarded the idea.

Some Northerners, including the editorial board of the *New York Times,* claimed that using black troops would sully the purity of the North's cause. "Better lose the War," it cried, "than use the Negro to win it." A more representative statement was made by a Northern soldier who reflected, "I reckon if I have to fight and die for the nigger's freedom, he can fight and die for it along with me." That was really the point. The Union needed more men, and its efforts to enlist them were encountering increasing resistance among Northern white men. Why not let the black man fight for his own freedom?

In the fall of 1862, with Union victory still doubtful and the Preliminary Emancipation Proclamation already announced, Lincoln yielded to pressure and authorized the formation of the first black army units. African Americans were offered a step toward freedom not because the white North especially wanted them but because the North needed them so much.

The fashion in which black troops were treated was illustrative of Northern white attitudes toward the whole enterprise. At first, black soldiers were confined to service units and not allowed to fight—until white Union casualties became so high that blacks, though often untrained for combat, were simply thrown into the battle. Moreover, until just before the war's end, African American soldiers received unequal pay for the same duty and were denied the enlistment bonuses given to white troops.

The record of one of the most famous black Union regiments illustrates the contributions of ex-slave soldiers in the Confederacy's defeat. The First South Carolina Volunteers was the darling of Northern imagination. It was the first regiment composed entirely of fugitive slaves, organized, as Northerners loved to say, "in the birthplace of treason."

It was at first unclear that the North was entirely serious about this regiment. The unit was supposed to be made up of volunteers, but the first soldiers were acquired by sending white troops on raiding parties into the refugee camps and hauling back any able-bodied black men they could find. Their uniforms were made up of a bright blue jacket, brighter red pantaloons, and a red fez, making them ideal targets for sharpshooters. Nevertheless, the First South Carolina ran up a credible record in Union service. They were, for example, the first known military unit to consistently return from battle with more soldiers than those which with they entered. Slaves on outlying plantations, seeing them in uniform, simply laid down their hoes, picked up discarded guns, and followed the troops back to their camp.

The soldiers of the First South Carolina were only the first of tens of thousands of former slaves who fought for the Union cause. Despite discrimination throughout the war, African American troops distinguished themselves and were instrumental in the North's victory. Overall, about 180,000 blacks served in the Union army, and another 20,000 in the Union navy. Together, they made up about 15 percent of all Northern forces in the war. Of all the Union troops, the African American soldier was fighting for the most tangible of causes—freedom for himself and his people.

The Final Question. The determination with which blacks seized freedom shocked whites, both North and South. In an unanticipated and unplanned war, the African Americans' behavior may have been the element for which both sides were least prepared. In the end, black slaves played a major role in bringing down the Confederacy. They had demonstrated that they wanted freedom and were prepared to fight for its realization.

The fourth question that whites had posed about the slaves—"Would they know what to do with their freedom if they got it?"—would be more candidly phrased—"Would white America let blacks truly exercise their freedom?" That question remains unresolved at the end of the twentieth century. But the limitations that crippled black freedom after Reconstruction did not discourage many African Americans who had been slaves. As one black Union veteran said after the war, "In slavery, I had no worriment. . . . In freedom I'se got a family and a little farm. All that causes me worriment. . . . But I takes the FREEDOM!"

[*See also* African American Forgeworkers; African American Troops in the Union Army, *article on* African Americans in the Confederate Army; Contraband; Emancipation Proclamation; Navy, *article on* African Americans in the Confederate Navy; Thirteenth Amendment.]

BIBLIOGRAPHY

Brewer, James. *The Confederate Negro: Virginia's Craftsmen and Military Laborers, 1861–1865.* Durham, N.C., 1969.

Chesnut, Mary Boykin. *Mary Chesnut's Civil War.* Edited by C. Vann Woodward. New Haven, 1981.

Cornish, Dudley Taylor. *The Sable Arm.* New York, 1966.

Foner, Eric. *Reconstruction: America's Unfinished Revolution.* New York, 1987.

Glatthaar, Joseph. *Forged in Battle: The Civil War Alliance of Black Soldiers and White Officers.* New York, 1990.

McPherson, James. *Abraham Lincoln and the Second American Revolution.* New York, 1991.

McPherson, James. *Battle Cry of Freedom: The Civil War Era.* New York, 1988.

Mohr, Clarence L. *On the Threshold of Freedom.* Athens, Ga., 1986.

Quarles, Benjamin. *The Negro in the Civil War.* New York, 1953. Reprint, New York, 1989.

Taylor, Susie King. *A Black Woman's Civil War Memoirs.* New York, 1988.

Wiley, Bell Irwin. *The Southern Negro, 1861–1865.* New Haven, 1966.

ROBERT FRANCIS ENGS

Slave Life

The African American slave society in the antebellum South (1807–1860) was unique among New World slave systems. In the United States, the slave population not only sustained itself; it expanded exponentially. In other New World nations, slave populations were maintained by continuous importation from Africa. In the American South, however, the slave population grew through natural increase—that is, slave mothers had children who also became slaves. As a result, the vast majority of African Americans in slavery in the United States after 1810 were not African captives but native-born Americans, some of whose ancestors had been in this country nearly as long as the oldest white families.

This longevity of residence in America did not mean that slaves lost all their rich heritage from their African origins. White slave owners, however, were frightened by African customs and behaviors they could not understand. They forced their slaves to give up African means of communication such as their own languages and their drums (a widely used means of "talking" across great distances in West Africa). Indeed, slaves were denied even their original African names and made to accept whatever names their master imposed upon them.

In these circumstances, Southern slaves were forced into syncretism—the process of mixing divergent cultural elements together to create an entirely new culture. They had to combine what they could retain of their African culture with the new European and Native American cultures imposed upon them by their masters. The result was the first genuinely United States culture. It was part African, part European, and part Native American, but refined and developed in a land new to all but one of these groups.

> . . . on most plantations, blacks far outnumbered whites. They could not all be kept under constant white supervision.

American slaves were able to carve out a unique culture of their own because of the way in which Southern slavery was structured. Most white Southerners did not own slaves. In 1860 only ten thousand Southern white families owned more than twenty slaves, and only three thousand owned more than fifty slaves. Nevertheless, most slaves lived in units of twenty or more. This meant that, on most plantations, blacks far outnumbered whites. They could not all be kept under constant white supervision.

Masters had to evolve a system of rewards and punishments to maintain control over their more numerous slaves. As in any brutal system of unpaid labor, punishment was used more often than reward. As historian Kenneth Stampp has written, the slave owners' strategy in handling their slaves was "to make them stand in fear!" A plantation, however, was not an extermination camp; it was a profit-making enterprise, and blacks had to be given certain rights and privileges to maximize their productivity. They were also valuable pieces of "property." To abuse them too harshly would diminish their value. Slaves seized upon this necessity to create a culture of their own possessing the values that shaped family life, religion, education, and attitudes toward work.

Slave Family Life. The black family in slavery had no legal standing. Slaves and their children were the property of their masters. Slavery was hereditary through the status of the mother; therefore, even children conceived through the rape of a slave woman by a white man (sometimes the woman's master) were still legally slaves. Husbands and wives and their children could be sold apart from one another whenever the desires or economic needs of the master required such sales. Indeed, probably 2 million slaves were sold from the upper South (Virginia, Maryland, and Delaware) to the Deep South between 1800 and 1860. Many of these sales involved the breakup of families.

In the face of the constant threat of separation from loved ones, a strong family system developed. Most slave families in the South were structured like other American families. They were nuclear—that is, they consisted of a father, mother, and their children. The realities of slavery, however, forced the additional creation of an extended family that incorporated all the other slaves on a plantation. This informal family helped protect children (and adults) when a family member was sold away. Thus, every slave child had many honorary aunts, uncles, and cousins who were not biologically related, but who were prepared to assume family roles, should a child be orphaned by the workings of the slave trade.

In the upper South, it was the custom among many slave owners to encourage slave families. The offspring of such unions brought high prices in the lower South's slave markets. In addition, it was an excellent means of slave control. Those slaves most likely to run away were young males between sixteen and thirty. A wife and family might make them more content. Moreover, since successful escape in groups, especially ones including children, was almost impossible, a husband and father was less likely to run away and leave his family behind.

In the lower South, however, cotton profits were so high that some slavemasters had no regard for slave family life. Pregnant women could not pick as much cotton as other field hands. Birth incapacitated mothers for days, and infants or little children were of no use in the fields. Some planters of the lower South thought it cheaper to work their slaves to death and buy more slaves rather than encourage families.

For the slaves, like all other Americans, their families were central to the definition of who they were. Evidence of this truth was demonstrated when the Civil War started and slaves began to desert their plantations in the upper South. To the surprise of whites, both North and South, these escapees often fled *south* rather than to the so-called Freedom Land in the North. They were going in search of loved ones sold through the interstate slave trade.

Religion. Religion was one of the main buttresses that supported the slave family. African American slaves were denied the right to practice the religion of their ancestors. Some African slaves were Muslims; most believed in a variety of forms of ancestor worship that was more similar to Christianity than Europeans understood. Slave owners viewed African religion as a combination of witchcraft and superstition, and they banned its practice, in part, for fear that slaves might use it to put spells or curses on them.

Most slave owners believed that Christianizing their slaves would make them more passive. They also pointed to Christianization as a justification for slavery; they claimed to be uplifting the slaves from their barbarous past. Although the slave owner extracted unpaid labor from his slaves in this life, he ensured their salvation in the next by making them Christians.

Of course, the Christianity taught to slaves by their masters was very different from that which the masters practiced themselves. Omitted were the implicit and explicit messages in the New Testament about individual freedom and responsibility. Instead, slave owners used the Bible selectively. They argued that Africans were the descendants of Ham, who, in the Old Testament, were cursed by Noah to be "servants of servants." From the New Testament, slave owners cited Christ's admonition to "render unto Caesar that which is Caesar's" to justify their right to demand obedience from their slaves. In part to ensure that slaves could not learn all of the other, contrary messages about freedom to be found in the Bible, slavemasters outlawed the teaching of reading and writing to slaves.

Slaves, however, once again combined what they could remember from their old religions with what their masters told them about Christianity and what they learned about Christianity from literate blacks and antislavery whites. From this information they evolved their own form of Christianity, which was a religion of hope and liberation.

In the slaves' version of Christianity, Christ and Moses played almost equal roles as heroes who had led their people to freedom. Black religion was very much anchored in the real world rather than in life after death. Slaves learned to phrase the words of their prayers and spirituals to speak of salvation and freedom in heaven, but, in truth, they were praying and singing about deliverance from slavery in this world, not the next. Thus, a black woman like Harriet Tubman who led dozens of slaves to freedom, used spirituals like "Steal Away to Jesus" to signal plans for escape. She became known, as a result, as "The Moses of Her People."

The burdens of slavery led African Americans to different definitions of God, sin, and even the devil. Slaves did not conceive of God as the stern taskmaster envisioned by their white owners. Rather, they thought of God as an all-forgiving Father who understood the tribulations that his people were suffering and who was planning a better world for them. This vision of the Almighty led, among other things, to a very different style of worship among slaves. As one ex-bondsman tried to explain: "White folks pray powerful *sad*. Black folks pray powerful *glad*!"

Slave religion even resulted in a different understanding of sin. It was, for example, a sin to steal from a fellow slave who, like yourself, had nothing. But it was not necessarily a sin to steal food or clothing from the master. He had "aplenty," as the slaves would say, while their children were hungry and naked. God would understand your necessity and forgive you your small transgression.

It was in their conception of the devil that the slaves' remembrance of their African religion was most evident. To white Protestant slave owners, the devil was the Antichrist, the embodiment of evil. To the slaves, however, the devil was just another powerful spirit, albeit a malevolent one. African

Always the practitioner, never the ideologue, Slidell figured hardly at all in the great political debates of the 1850s. But he consistently tried to dampen what he considered the excesses of Southern radicalism, fearing destruction of the national system he was determined to dominate. Aided by family connections to the banker August Belmont, and with the help of fellow senators James Bayard and John Bright, he moved closer to that objective by masterminding James Buchanan's election to the presidency in 1856. Viewed by contemporaries as the power behind Buchanan's throne, he soon saw his plans for continued national influence threatened by a reopening of the debate over the expansion of slavery into the territories, a push to disruption he now identified as coming not from Southern extremists but from party dissidents like Stephen A. Douglas.

The 1860 presidential campaign, therefore, found him a convert to the radical Southern position he had resisted. Bolting the Democratic convention in Charleston and rejecting Douglas's nomination at Baltimore, he joined the forces backing John C. Breckinridge, convinced that a Republican victory would so change the nation that the South must then indeed secede. Characteristically, he still favored cautious restraint, arguing in November 1860 that withdrawal from the Union might best be effected by joint action of the Southern states. When events took a different course, he unhesitatingly withdrew from the Senate and vigorously supported the independent secession of Louisiana.

He is most widely identified in American history along with James M. Mason as one of the Confederate commissioners seized off the Bahamas from the British mail packet *Trent* by Captain Charles Wilkes of the Union sloop *San Jacinto* in November 1861. Confederate hopes that the incident would result in a diplomatic breach or even war between the United States and England crumbled when President Abraham Lincoln yielded and Slidell was freed to proceed to his post in France. There he enjoyed at first an intimate relationship with Louis Napoleon and Empress Eugènie, as well as with a large coterie of highly placed figures at court and in private circles. But these associations brought little success on the diplomatic front. A small number of commerce raiders built for the Confederacy in French shipyards through his efforts remained blocked in port by diplomatic pressure from the United States, and a Confederate loan based on a European bond issue engineered by him through the French banking house of Erlanger raised only a meager $2,599,000 on a cotton collateral of $45,000,000. Most critical of all, Confederate designs to win French recognition through the promise of cotton exports came to naught because of inability to get shipments through to Europe. Napoleon refused to countenance any French challenge to the United States without backing from the British, and Lord John Russell's opposition to recognition of the Confederacy or any attempt to break the Union blockade of Southern ports never wavered. When it finally became clear as well that Louis Napoleon's hopes of Confederate protection for his protègè Maximilian in Mexico had no basis, Slidell's diplomatic mission collapsed.

Defeat of the Confederacy left Slidell bitter and unreconcilable. He refused to appeal for pardon or restoration of U.S. citizenship and lived out the remainder of his years in Europe, dying in Cowes on the Isle of Wight.

[*See also* Erlanger Loan; Trent Affair.]

BIBLIOGRAPHY

Hendrick, Burton J. *Statesmen of the Lost Cause.* Boston, 1939.
Nichols, Roy F. *The Disruption of American Democracy.* New York, 1948.
Owsley, Frank L. *King Cotton Diplomacy.* Chicago, 1931. Reprint, Chicago, 1959.
Tregle, Joseph G., Jr. "The Political Apprenticeship of John Slidell." *Journal of Southern History* 26 (1960): 57–70.
Willson, Beckles. *John Slidell and the Confederates in Paris (1862–1865).* New York, 1932. Reprint, New York, 1970.

JOSEPH G. TREGLE, JR.

SMALL ARMS

[*This entry contains nine articles that discuss in detail the diverse types of firearms and munitions used in the Confederate army and navy. For definitions of small arms terminology and a more general discussion of the impact on military tactics of developments in small arms technology, see* Arms, Weapons, and Ammunition. *For a discussion of the swords, bayonettes, and sabers used by Confederate forces, see* Edged Weapons.]

Confederate Long Arms

Over the course of its four-year existence, the Confederacy would produce at most 75,000 long arms for its armies. Considering that the South put 900,000 men into the field during the course of the war, it is easy to see that the bulk of its guns were acquired by other means (primarily from the import of European guns and secondarily from the seizure, capture, and prewar purchase of Federal arms). The quality of the Confederate-produced arms was also below that of arms made in Europe and the North because the South lacked the necessary skilled labor and raw materials. Often inferior materials were substituted (brass for iron) because they were easier to work. With the exceptions of those guns made on the captured Federal machinery at Fayetteville, North Carolina, and Richmond, Virginia, Confederate guns were all practically hand-made, with very little interchangeability of parts.

The fortuitous seizure of the U.S. Arsenal at Harpers Ferry, Virginia, by elements of Virginia state troops the evening of April 18, 1861, provided the tools, machinery, and stock to establish the Virginia Armory in Richmond, later known as the Richmond Armory, and the Fayetteville Armory at Fayetteville, North Carolina. Anticipating just such action, Lt. Roger Jones, commander of Federal forces at Harpers Ferry, set fire to the establishment but was unsuccessful in his efforts to destroy all arms and machinery. The acquisition of this material was the impetus for the most successful Confederate small arms manufactories.

Virginia forces began immediately to salvage material at the arsenal and transport it to Richmond. After initial setup in a tobacco warehouse, the machinery was installed in the empty Virginia Manufactory site and was soon in use to repair damaged arms. The Virginia Armory, as a result of negotiations between the central government and the commonwealth of Virginia, came under the control of the Confederate Ordnance Department on August 23, 1861, for the duration of the war. Thereafter, it was known as the Richmond Armory and arms manufacture began in earnest.

The first arms produced under state auspices were assembled from seized parts and were conventional U.S. models. Subsequently, a modified .58-caliber rifle-musket based on the U.S. model 1855 arm evolved with the same basic configuration and 40-inch barrel. After the central gov-

> ## Virginia forces began immediately to salvage material . . . and transport it to Richmond.

ernment assumed control, the lockplates were marked "CS" indicating government ownership. The Richmond Armory manufactured long arms from the fall of 1861 until early 1865, when the machinery was sent south. The armory buildings were subsequently destroyed by fire during the evacuation of Richmond on April 3, 1865.

The Armory produced four distinct long arms during its period of operation. These were the model 1855–based rifle-musket, a rifle with 33-inch barrel, a musketoon with 30-inch barrel, and a carbine with 25-inch barrel. All were rifled and .58 caliber with the exception of the musketoon, which was smoothbore and .60 caliber. The rifle-musket, dated 1861 through 1864, is the most commonly encountered. Dates of the others include rifles, 1864; musketoons, 1862 and 1863; and carbines, 1863 and 1864. The musketoon and rifle are quite rare today. The armory managed to produce some 1,500 arms per month once operations got under way, but it never approached its potential because of material shortages. The Richmond Armory manufactured about 45 percent of the long arms produced in the Confederacy during the war,

nearly the combined output of all private contractors. Total production is estimated to have been about 35,000 arms of all types.

The carbine factory of S. C. Robinson was adjacent to the Richmond Armory. Robinson contracted to make for the government a breech-loading carbine like that produced by Christian Sharps in the North. Although enthusiastic about the project, he ran into problems because of his inexperience. Nevertheless, the company built the machinery and fabricated about 1,900 carbines bearing the Robinson name from December 1862 until March 1, 1863, when the central government took over the operation. Some 3,500 unmarked Sharps carbines were produced under government supervision until the spring of 1864, when the machinery was removed to Tallassee, Alabama, where it was used to make a muzzle-loading carbine. Total production of the Richmond Sharps by Robinson and the government was about 5,400 arms.

Farther south in Virginia was the ordnance complex at Danville that included the establishments of Bilharz, Hall, and Company; Keen, Walker, and Company; Read and Watson; and probably the unknown maker of the Getty brass-framed Sharps carbine.

Bilharz, Hall, and Company early in the war was an established firm, having delivered 100 breech-loading carbines to the Ordnance Department by September 1862. These .54-caliber rising-breech carbines are well made and entirely hand-fitted (they were called rising-breech because the breech literally rose when opened for loading). Later the company produced a copy of the U.S. model 1855 muzzle-loading carbine, .58 caliber. Judging from the surviving serial numbers, it would appear that about 700 of these arms were made. The breech-loading arm is especially rare today. The firm also provided stocks for the Richmond carbine and Richmond Sharps carbine.

Keen, Walker, and Company manufactured brass-framed breech-loading carbines of .54 caliber, which were all delivered at Danville in 1862. Invoices indicate that total production was 282 arms. The company then became involved as a subcontractor with the Read and Watson firm.

Read and Watson made rifles and carbines for the state of Virginia in 1862 and some Virginia state troops in 1863. These are unusual in that components of breech-loading arms were altered to manufacture a muzzle-loading weapon. Two types of alteration have been noted. The first, seen on rifles and carbines, consists of a small brass breechpiece fitted to the barrel with an iron breechplug with cone. The second type of alteration used a much larger brass breechpiece with the iron breechplug and cone. (The breechplug closes the breech of the gun; into it fits the breechpiece, which holds the cone, a nipple on which the hammer falls to strike the percussion cap and ignite the charge.) This method is more substantial and is found only on rifles. The few carbines extant appear to have been manufactured from Hall model 1833 carbines. Rifles were made using parts from both Harpers Ferry and model 1819 contract Hall rifles. The firm's total production is estimated to have been 900 arms of all types.

There is strong circumstantial evidence that the intriguing .52-caliber Getty brass-framed Sharps carbine was also made at or near Danville. This arm utilizes Hall parts in much the same fashion as those of Read and Watson, and it has a brass breechpiece similar to the products of Read and Watson and Keen, Walker, and Company. All three use Roman numeral assembly numbers. Production was very limited, probably less than 100 arms.

The machinery and parts captured at Harpers Ferry were used not only for the Richmond Armory but also for the Fayetteville Arsenal. In early 1862 the machinery for making the U.S. model 1855 rifle, .58 caliber, with 33-inch barrel, was sent to Fayetteville. The shipment included the essential cutting and milling machines together with necessary dies, gauges, and belting with which to run the machines. The material was installed in the old North Carolina Arsenal, and production of a brass-mounted two-band .58-caliber rifle began in January and February 1862. The lack of raw materials continually hampered production, so that the projected output was never achieved. The rifles made at Fayetteville were excellent, however, and production reached about 7,500 arms before the machinery was moved to avoid the advance of William Tecumseh Sherman's army. The vacant arsenal was destroyed on March 14, 1865.

The ordnance complex around Greensboro, North Carolina, was another source primarily for the state. Several companies in the area collaborated in varying degrees to produce a limited number of weapons for North Carolina. All were more or less copies of the U.S. model 1841 rifle, with the exception of a carbine of unique design patented in the Confederacy by Jere H. Tarpley.

Clapp, Gates, and Company near Gibsonville manufactured a relatively crude iron-mounted two-band rifle from 1862 to 1864. Extant specimens are quite scarce, with a total production of probably no more than 200 rifles. Clapp, Gates also furnished components and fittings for other firms. Gillam and Miller at High Point made a very small number of brass-mounted rifles, probably no more than 50. The firm name is stamped in the wood of the stock on one surviving specimen and the arm shows signs of much hand finishing. H. C. Lamb and Company in Jamestown produced good copies of the model 1841 rifle without patchbox (a recessed area in the stock where gun tools are kept). The arms, while handmade and fitted, were substantially built. Production of this .58-caliber rifle was probably about 700 pieces; it is one of the more frequently seen North Carolina contract rifles. Mendenhall, Jones, and Company (Mendenhall, Jones, and Gardner) in Jamestown also made a good brass-mounted copy of the model 1841 rifle. This company was active from late 1861 until the partnership was dissolved in December 1864. During this time they produced some 2,000 serviceable rifles for the state. Searcy and Moore of Greensboro produced about 50 rifles, few of which are extant today. Those that do survive indicate much hand fitting.

A breech-loading brass-frame Tarpley carbine made by J. and F. and E. T. Garrett and Company of Greensboro was sold both commercially and to the state. Between April and September 1863 the state bought some 200 of these .52-caliber arms. One specimen is known to be serial number 421, indicative of a figure near total production. The Tarpley carbine is today one of the Confederate arms most sought after by collectors.

The Asheville Armory produced an excellent .58-caliber copy of the model 1841 rifle. This brass-mounted rifle was fabricated during 1862 and 1863, and some 300 were made before the machinery was shipped to Columbia, South Carolina, during the fall of 1863. The few specimens that survive show good craftsmanship.

George W. Morse produced the most advanced-design long arm used by Southern forces at the State Military Works at Greenville, South Carolina. This brass-frame breech-loading carbine used self-primed, reloadable .50-caliber metallic cartridges. The state ordered 1,000 carbines, which were produced with three variations. The survival rate of these arms is relatively high, indicating the state probably kept them and they were not much used in the field. At the same time Morse developed a simple internal lock that could be adapted for use in any percussion arm. Examples of a .52-caliber rifled carbine and .69-caliber smoothbore musket are known to exist. Utilization must have been very limited with less than 200 arms produced.

The most successful private manufacturer of arms for the Confederacy was the firm of Cook and Brother founded by two Englishmen, Ferdinand W. Cook and his brother, Francis, in New Orleans in June 1861. The firm produced arms of three basic configurations based on current English patterns—the pattern 1856 short rifle, pattern 1853 artillery musketoon, and pattern 1856 cavalry carbine. All were brass-mounted and .58 caliber with barrel lengths of 33 inches, 24 inches, and 21 inches, respectively. Production, which began in New Orleans, was initially for the state of Alabama. Some 1,000 arms were manufactured before the company had to flee the city ahead of Federal occupation forces. The Cooks managed to save their machinery and unfinished arms and set up shop in Selma, Alabama, where more arms were assembled. The firm relocated to Athens, Georgia, in 1863 and manufactured another 6,500 arms. Total production was about 8,500 arms of all types, the rifle being the most common. Production probably ceased during the summer of 1864 for lack of payment. Maj. Ferdinand Cook was killed in action that year in South Carolina, and after the war, Francis Cook sold the plant to the Athens Manufacturing Company.

The firm of Greenwood and Gray of Columbus, Georgia, manufactured rifles, carbines, and musketoons for both the central government and the state of Alabama. The master armorer was an Englishman named J. P. Murray, whose name appears on many of the locks of arms made by this firm. The company received a contract in 1862 to build 200 rifles and 1,000 carbines of the model 1841 pattern in .58 caliber. Later, the delivery of 262 Mississippi-type rifles and 73 carbines is noted. Total production was less than 1,500 arms of all types. Apparently, not all the carbines were delivered, judging from the number of surviving specimens.

The Georgia Armory at Milledgeville produced a brass-mounted copy of the model 1841 rifle in .58 caliber. Production proceeded from 1862 until November 1864, when the facility was burned by Federal forces. The very few surviving specimens indicate a small operation with total production of less than 100 rifles.

The manufactory of Davis and Bozeman located in Equality, Alabama, built another copy of the model 1841 rifle and a carbine under contract to the state of Alabama. These were well-made .58-caliber arms with brass mountings. Alabama records indicate receipt of 749 rifles and 89 carbines during the period October 1, 1863, to November 1, 1864. State markings on the barrels are identical to those found on the arms of Greenwood and Gray (J. P. Murray) and Dickson, Nelson, and Company.

The Shakanoosa Arms Company (Dickson, Nelson, and Company) was established by Dickson, Nelson, and Sadler at Dickson, Alabama, to manufacture yet another copy of the model 1841 rifle under contract to the state. Fortunes of war forced the firm to move first to Rome, Georgia, then to Adairsville, and finally to Dawson in March 1864. These well-made brass-mounted .58-caliber rifles are marked on the lockplate "Dickson, Nelson & Co." and include the date, either 1864 or 1865. Some 645 rifles were delivered prior to November 1, 1864, under a contract for 5,000 arms. Their carbines are very rare with probably less than 100 completed, but carbine stock blanks found at the armory site after the war indicate there were plans, interrupted when the war ended, to produce a considerable number. Total production was about 750 arms of all types.

The Tallassee carbine was made at Tallassee, Alabama, with machinery sent from the carbine factory in Richmond, formerly the S. C. Robinson Company. These arms were made for the central government rather than a state. The carbine was based on the current English pattern 1856 carbine and was built in .58 caliber. What little evidence survives indicates that 500 carbines were manufactured from June 1864 until April 1865 and that all were still in storage at the arsenal on April 3, 1865. What happened to them after the war is a mystery.

The Pulaski Gun Factory in Pulaski, Tennessee, was in operation during 1861 and 1862 and was the only state armory known to build new arms. These were copies, more or less, of the model 1841 rifle and utilized some sporting arms components. The few surviving specimens are brass-mounted and .54 caliber. Production may have totaled 500 arms.

The only identified major long-arm maker in the TransMississippi theater was the Confederate States Ordnance Works at Tyler, Texas. This facility seems to have produced several different models of iron-mounted rifles and some shorter arms of musketoon length. Calibers varied, .54 and .577 being noted. There was also considerable variation of lock markings. The different models may have been dictated by the availability of used parts and barrels. What few specimens are extant are of consistently poor quality. Total production from October 1, 1863, through March 31, 1865, was about 2,000 arms of all types.

There were other small manufacturers whose arms have not been recognized, but their output was insignificant. A number of entrepreneurs advanced funds for manufacturing but never produced a single firearm. The efforts of the central government and the states to build an ordnance system were sometimes counterproductive and in the end proved to be ineffectual. The Confederate Ordnance Department was unable to influence the outcome of the war.

BIBLIOGRAPHY

Albaugh, William A., III, and Edward N. Simmons. *Confederate Arms.* Harrisburg, Pa., 1957.

Cromwell, Giles. "The Alteration of Virginia Manufactory Weapons, 1818–1863." *Bulletin of the American Society of Arms Collectors,* no. 52 (1985): 25–45.

Flayderman, Norman E. *Flayderman's Guide to Antique American Arms.* 5th ed. Northbrook, Ill., 1990.

Floyd, William B. "The Asheville Armory and Rifle." *Bulletin of the American Society of Arms Collectors,* no. 44 (1981): 21–26.

Fuller, Claud E., and Richard D. Steuart. *Firearms of the Confederacy.* Huntington, W.V., 1944.

Jones, Douglas E. "The Dickson, Nelson Company: Alabama Civil War Gunmakers." *Bulletin of the American Society of Arms Collectors,* no. 60 (1989): 29–37.

Madaus, Howard Michael. "North Carolina Rifle Contracts of the Civil War." *Bulletin of the American Society of Arms Collectors,* no. 54 (1986): 46–53.

Michel, Benjamin P. "The Richmond Armory." *Bulletin of the American Society of Arms Collectors,* no. 33 (1976): 65–74.

Murphy, John M. *Confederate Carbines and Musketoons.* Dallas, Tex., 1986.

RUSS A. PRITCHARD

Confederate Handguns

Handguns were issued to mounted personnel and to officers of all branches of service. Because of their small caliber, limited range, and questionable accuracy, they were considered defensive weapons, with the exception of offensive use by cavalry. In general, the handgun was carried by military personnel who had their hands full performing their primary duties but needed a convenient, accessible weapon in an emergency situation. Weapons of this type had little impact on the conduct of the war.

The great majority of handguns used by the Confederates were in fact various models of the Colt and Remington revolvers captured from Federal forces or seized at Federal installations. A considerable number of weapons were also imported from England, with a lesser number from France. The preponderance of handguns actually manufactured in the South for Confederate forces were the product of only a few concerns: Leech and Rigdon; Rigdon, Ansley, and Company; Spiller and Burr; and Griswold and Gunnison. Their combined production was less than 8,000 firearms. Even if one adds those manufactured by smaller firms, the total production was only about 9,000 pieces at best, thereby accounting for the extreme rarity of these weapons today.

The most prolific manufacturer was the firm operated by Samuel Griswold and A. W. Gunnison. Griswold, a Connecticut native, moved south in 1832 to establish a manufacturing facility at what became Griswoldville, Georgia, about ten miles south of Macon. Gunnison was in New Orleans at the beginning of the war and became engaged in revolver manufacture. He escaped Federal occupation troops with his machinery in April 1862 and moved to Macon, joining with Griswold shortly thereafter. Their revolver is a brass-framed copy of the Colt navy revolver, model 1851, .36 caliber, with minor modifications. Deliveries began in October 1862. The earlier revolver has a round barrel housing, which was changed to part octagon around the serial number 1500, probably during July 1863. All Griswold revolvers are remarkably standard, given their hand-finishing by semiskilled slaves. Production ceased in November 1864 when the factory and most of the surrounding structures were demolished by elements of the Tenth Ohio and Third Union Kentucky Cavalry Regiments, part of William Tecumseh Sherman's army on its March to the Sea. Total production was some 3,700 revolvers.

Thomas Leech and Charles H. Rigdon formed a business partnership in Memphis, Tennessee, just before the Civil War, resulting in the firm of Leech and Rigdon, which was closely allied with another enterprise, the Memphis Novelty Works, manufacturers of edged weapons, spurs, musical instruments, and accoutrements. In anticipation of the Federal occupation of the city, the firm moved to Columbus, Mississippi, where a contract for 1,500 revolvers was secured and limited production began. Again moving to avoid Federal interference, the firm settled in Greensboro, Georgia, in March 1863. Focusing on revolver production, the company ceased edged-weapon fabrication, but the partnership

was dissolved in December 1863 after production of about 1,000 revolvers. Upon the partnership's dissolution, Rigdon moved the machinery and workers to Augusta, Georgia, site of existing ordnance installations, and continued production under the name of Rigdon, Ansley, and Company, completing the remaining 500 revolvers of the original contract.

This revolver was an iron-framed copy of the Colt navy revolver, model 1851, but with a part-octagon barrel housing like the later Griswold revolvers. The top flat of this barrel housing bears the name "Leech & Rigdon" and the letters "CSA." Revolvers produced by Leech and Rigdon and the successor company are almost identical, since both were made with the same machinery. Minor variations in details exist, however, and the firm name changes as the new company evolves. Markings on arms above serial number 1500 indicate the move to Augusta. Later production revolvers are marked only "CSA" on the barrel flat. Rigdon, Ansley production is identifiable by their twelve-stop cylinder; some 900 were made. Total production of both companies was about 2,500 revolvers.

The next most important manufacturer was the firm founded by Edward N. Spiller of Baltimore and David J. Burr of Richmond, principals, with Lt. Col. James H. Burton, former

> **The great majority of handguns used by the Confederates were . . . seized at Federal installations.**

master armorer at the U.S. Arsenal at Harpers Ferry, then assigned to the Confederate Bureau of Ordnance. The firm secured a contract for 15,000 Colt-style navy revolvers but subsequently bought the Robinson Revolver Factory, which was already tooled to produce a Whitney-style navy revolver. Burton was transferred south to Atlanta in May 1862, and Spiller and Burr left Richmond with him. The trio began delivery of the brass-framed Whitney-type revolver, .36 caliber, at Atlanta in December 1862. Early production had a light Whitney frame prone to fracture. Later revolvers had a heavier frame, but problems continued to plague the company.

The Confederate government, after having received about 840 revolvers, bought the firm in January 1864 and moved the operation to Macon, where an additional 400 revolvers were made. Early specimens are often marked with the firm name on the barrel and the letters "CS" on the left or right side of the brass frame. The firm name was dropped after the government took control. Total production was about 1,250 pieces. These revolvers are very rare, most having been issued to the western armies. (Confederate weapons in the East were often taken into New England after the war by former Union soldiers and preserved as souvenirs. Guns in the

West often saw additional action on the frontier, and thus their survival rate was lower.)

The next largest handgun producer of the Confederacy was the firm of J. H. Dance and Bros., also known as Dance and Park, located first in Columbia, Texas, and later in Anderson. The firm was unique in that it furnished both .36- and .44-caliber weapons. The frame configuration of these revolvers was quite different from that of other manufacturers, with the omission of the recoil shield on the frame giving it a somewhat flat, slab-sided appearance. The .36-caliber navy revolver is slightly smaller than the Colt model 1851, and the .44-caliber handgun is actually about dragoon size. Both types are unmarked except for the serial numbers on all major parts. From these numbers it would appear that at least 350 army revolvers and about 135 navy revolvers were produced, no more than a total of 500. Almost all were delivered to the Ordnance Department for issue to Texas mounted units. Many fakes, particularly of the navy model, exist and, like genuine Confederate arms, are very collectible.

The products of the Augusta Machine Works, Augusta, Georgia, constitute an enigma. It is known from several sources that there was a central government–owned revolver factory in the ordnance complex there, but positive identification of its products has never been made. There exists in very limited numbers a well-made iron-framed revolver, a copy of the Colt navy revolver, model 1851, .36 caliber, that has been generally accepted as the product of this establishment, even though none is known to be marked with the firm name. Initial production has a six-stop cylinder like Colt products. Later production appears with a twelve-stop cylinder, a safety feature much like that of the Rigdon, Ansley, and Company revolver. Most specimens extant have letters rather than serial numbers, although there are a few that have single-digit numbers, again indicative of rather limited production. No records exist to determine the start or termination of production. Surviving specimens suggest that over a hundred were produced, and since some are in very good condition, it may be supposed that they were made near the end of the war and did not see sustained combat use. These weapons are particularly well made for Confederate arms and are very scarce and desired by collectors.

The ordnance complex at Columbus, Georgia, was the source of a wide variety of arms and equipment fabricated for the Confederate cause. One of the primary contractors was the firm of Louis Haiman & Bros. Active in the manufacture of edged weapons, Louis and Elias Haiman purchased the Muscogee Foundry and Machinery Company in August 1862 and shortly thereafter set up the Columbus Fire Arms Manufacturing Company. They obtained a contract to furnish 10,000 navy revolvers, copies of the Colt model 1851, .36-caliber arm. Production began slowly, and it is estimated that possibly a hundred revolvers were delivered before the government purchased the factory during the spring of 1864 and

integrated it into the Confederate States Armory there. Revolver production was never resumed. These extremely rare handguns are usually marked with the full firm name "Columbus Fire Arms Manuf. Co., Columbus, Ga." on the cylinder and the full firm name or just "Columbus, Ga." on the top flat of the barrel housing. Probably no more than six authentic specimens exist today. So-called unmarked examples are of questionable authenticity.

Besides revolvers made under government contract for military issue, others were made by two more firms—Thomas W. Cofer of Portsmouth, Virginia, and Schneider and Glassick of Memphis, Tennessee. They produced a very small number of weapons for the Southern market, some of which are known to have seen military use.

Cofer patented and produced a unique series of brass-framed, spur-trigger .36-caliber revolvers. All are marked with the Cofer name, patent date, and place of manufacture. There is considerable variation in these handmade revolvers, but there appear to be three major types. The first two require a special cartridge with integral nipple that is reloadable. The first has a two-piece cylinder to facilitate reloading; the second has a one-piece cylinder with an ejector attached to the frame to push fired cartridges out of the cylinder. A third type, possibly the production model, has a conventional percussion cylinder. Less than fifteen of these revolvers survive today. Only double-digit serial numbers have been noted, indicating that less than a hundred were manufactured. These arms are extremely rare.

Firearms production by Schneider and Glassick of Memphis probably began during the fall of 1861 and terminated in March 1862 with the Federal occupation of the city. There are only three known authentic specimens extant. The revolver is a copy of the Colt navy revolver, model 1851, .36 caliber, and has a brass frame similar to that of the Griswold and Gunnison. All are marked with the full firm name on top of the barrel, and serial numbers appear on all major parts. Total production is unknown but certainly very limited.

In addition to these revolvers, a number of obsolete single-shot pistols were manufactured in an effort to arm hard-pressed Confederate units, particularly in the early stages of the conflict. All these weapons were stopgap at best and were manufactured in limited numbers.

One such weapon was the so-called Fayetteville pistol-carbine made of parts captured when Virginia troops occupied the Federal arsenal at Harpers Ferry, Virginia. This was no more than the U.S. model 1855 pistol-carbine, .58 caliber, with the Maynard tape primer system deleted to simplify production. Only those parts captured were assembled into firearms; few if any parts were fabricated. The very few specimens that survive indicate manufacture in 1862.

The other single-shot pistol has tentatively been identified as the product of J. and F. Garrett, Greensboro, North Carolina, also maker of the rare Tarpley carbine. These brass-framed pistols are .54 caliber and utilize at least some surplus parts of the U.S. model 1842 pistol, specifically the barrel, hammer, trigger, and trigger guard. The brass frame follows no known U.S. pattern. Serial numbers extant indicate production of probably 500 pistols.

Although production of single-shot pistols was not seriously undertaken, ordnance records of ammunition delivered during the war would indicate that a substantial number of these arms of .54 and .69 caliber, obviously captured obsolete U.S. models, were pressed into service throughout the war.

Italian-made replicas of some Confederate revolvers began appearing during the centennial in the 1960s, and numerous fakes have been produced over the years. Confederate handguns are in greater demand than ever, and values have increased substantially in recent years.

BIBLIOGRAPHY

Albaugh, William A., III. *The Confederate Brass-Framed Colt and Whitney.* Published privately, 1955.
Albaugh, William A., III, and Edward N. Simmons. *Confederate Arms.* Harrisburg, Pa., 1957.
Albaugh, William A., III, Hugh Benet, Jr., and Edward N. Simmons.*Confederate Handguns.* Philadelphia, 1963.
Albaugh, William A., III, and Richard D. Steuart. *The Original Confederate Colt.* New York, 1953.
Fuller, Claud E., and Richard D. Steuart. *Firearms of the Confederacy.* Huntington, W.Va., 1944.
Gary, William A. *Confederate Revolvers.* Dallas, Tex., 1987.
Wiggins, Gary. *Dance and Brothers: Texas Gunmakers of the Confederacy.* Orange, Va., 1986.

RUSS A. PRITCHARD

Captured and Purchased U.S. Small Arms

At the commencement of hostilities, there was not a single private small arms manufactory in operation in the Southern states. The various state militia units were equipped with mostly obsolete arms. Limited numbers of sporting arms and self-protection handguns were privately owned, as were souvenirs of prior conflicts. There were also thousands of mostly second-class arms (muskets altered from a flintlock to a percussion firing system) in storage at Federal arsenals and other facilities scattered throughout the South.

The organized militias rallied to the new Confederate flag with antiquated flintlocks of various models, smoothbore percussion alterations and muskets, and a number of U.S. model 1841 and 1855 rifles and U.S. model 1855 rifle-muskets. Other men carried sporting arms, double- and single-barrel shotguns, and hunting rifles, which were brought from home or hastily purchased from private sources, all mostly inadequate for their purpose.

The Confederates early in the war seized U.S. arsenals and installations in Southern states at Baton Rouge and New Orleans, Louisiana; Fayetteville, North Carolina; Charleston, South Carolina; Augusta and Macon, Georgia; Mount Vernon, Alabama; Apalachicola, Florida; Little Rock, Arkansas; and San Antonio, Texas. These seizures resulted in the acquisition of about 150,000 arms, primarily obsolete altered flintlocks, and possibly 15,000 rifles of current pat-

> The various state militia units were equipped with mostly obsolete arms.

tern. Together with arms already in state hands, Confederate forces began the war with at least 220,000 small arms, most of questionable effectiveness.

Early battles until the summer of 1863 were primarily Southern victories. With the battlefields under Southern control, ordnance personnel could gather dropped, surrendered, and damaged weapons of their Federal opponents. This source proved most productive. Over 150,000 small arms of all types were acquired as a result of the Battles of First and Second Manassas, the Seven Days' Battles around Richmond, and Fredericksburg, Chancellorsville, and Chickamauga.

Captured Federal weapons, early seizures, and battlefield recoveries amounted overall to over 300,000 arms, second only in importance to imported weapons. By September 1862 Confederate Ordnance could report the manufacture of less than 15,000 arms in recently established Southern arms manufactories.

Arms acquired from Federal repositories varied from nonfunctional or obsolete flintlock muskets to modern breech-loading rifles and multishot revolvers. Ordnance authorities endeavored to alter to a percussion firing system the flintlocks on hand by methods similar to those already used with some success by Federal facilities. But they were never able to develop the expertise to manufacture metallic cartridges used in the more advanced magazine arms and thus were totally dependent on captured ammunition.

The diverse inventory of captured arms included flintlock and altered flintlock muskets and rifles, percussion muskets, rifle-muskets and rifles, a variety of patent breech-loading carbines, and a bewildering array of flintlock, altered flintlock, and percussion single-shot pistols of varying calibers. In all, they were an ordnance department nightmare.

Flintlock muskets were primarily the model 1822 made by various contractors that had not already been percussioned by Federal authorities, and smaller numbers of earlier flintlock arms still in government stores. These antiquated .69-caliber smoothbore arms used a flint and steel ignition system developed in the seventeenth century. The way they were tactically employed acknowledged the inherent inaccuracy of smoothbores: whole regiments of 800 to 1,000 men would fire volleys at opposing formations of a similar size, so that individual accuracy was irrelevant.

Understanding the advantages of rifled and, to a lesser extent, breech-loading arms for special units, U.S. Ordnance began the manufacture of rifles with the model 1803. Subsequent models 1814 and 1817 were produced in limited numbers. The Hall model 1819 breech-loading rifle was purchased by Federal authorities. Rendered obsolete by improved arms, thousands of these, especially Hall models, were stored in Southern repositories.

The Federal ordnance officials also understood the advantages of the percussion system of ignition and adopted the model 1841 rifle and model 1842 musket. The latter retained all the obsolete features of earlier flintlocks with the exception of the ignition system, which made the arm more reliable. Otherwise, it was still the same inaccurate .69-caliber smoothbore arm. The model 1841 rifle, in .54 caliber, was very favorably received and set the stage for acceptance of reduced-bore rifled arms with greater effective range over a decade later. Many thousands of these model 1842 muskets and a lesser number of model 1841 rifles were in Southern hands or seized at the beginning of the war. Confederate forces in April 1861 were armed primarily with these .69-caliber arms, which were already obsolete by U.S. standards.

The U.S. model 1855 rifle-musket, rifle, and carbine were adopted during Jefferson Davis's tenure as U.S. secretary of war. The caliber was reduced from .69 to .58. The rifling of arms increased their effective range from 100 yards to 300 yards. The Maynard tape priming device integral to the rifle and rifle musket proved in humid or inclement weather to be more of a problem than an improvement and was omitted in subsequent models 1861, 1863, and 1864.

With the general acceptance of the percussion system, all obsolete flintlock arms in government stores were categorized in four grades, with first-class serviceable arms to be altered to the percussion system. All model 1816 arms and subsequent models deemed Class I were percussioned, using one of three primary methods. The cone-in-barrel method simply removed the flintlock components from the lock, sealed the vent in the barrel, added a percussion hammer, and placed a percussion cone in a hole drilled on the upper surface of the barrel. This method was both efficient and inexpensive. The patent-breech method was somewhat more elaborate. The breech of the barrel was removed and a new forged bolster with cone was screwed onto the barrel; flintlock components of the lock were removed and replaced by a new percussion hammer. The drum-in-barrel alteration required that a drum with cone be screwed into the side of the barrel over the old vent; the flintlock components were removed from the lock and were replaced by a percussion

hammer. Regardless of the method used, the service life of the firearm was extended by these simple, cost-effective modifications, all of which were reasonably satisfactory. A small number of these arms were also rifled and sighted at the time of alteration in a further effort to upgrade their performance. Some few model 1795 and 1808 arms were also altered by the individual states under private contract. The majority of this work took place during the period 1848 to 1852. Thus, thousands of altered muskets and a considerable number of flintlock muskets were stored in Southern Federal repositories when hostilities erupted.

> ## The early battles were the source of most of the current models acquired. . . .

The Militia Act of 1808 had authorized the annual transfer and distribution of Federal arms to the organized military forces of the states. This system had been in effect for decades before the war. Some 115,000 arms in varying condition were sent to Southern Federal arsenals in the year 1860 alone, in accordance with established procedure. These were the arms that were seized so quickly when war began.

In the months immediately preceding hostilities, Southern agents scoured Northern arsenals and supplies held by entrepreneurs, purchasing significant quantities of arms from sources who had no qualms concerning the sale of arms and munitions to a potential belligerent. Numbers of current model Colt, Maynard, Sharps, and Whitney arms were acquired in this manner and shipped to Southern states. Whitney even purchased condemned parts from U.S. armories and other sources to put together weapons to sell to eager agents of both Northern and Southern states. Such commerce continued into the spring of 1861 even after the first shots had been fired.

The early battles were the source of most of the current models acquired by Confederate forces. Frequent captures of the model 1841 and model 1855 rifles and model 1855 rifle-musket greatly added to the limited number of effective arms in the Confederate arsenal. During 1861 and 1862 captures of the Springfield model 1861 and various 1861 contract rifle-muskets were a great boon.

A variety of breech-loading rifles and carbines found their way into Confederate service. It is virtually impossible to calculate the actual numbers seized or captured, but so many of the various models of Colt, Maynard, Merrill, and Sharps arms were in service that Confederate laboratories manufactured specific ammunition for them. Thousands of Burnside and Spencer arms were captured, but again because the Confederates could not manufacture their special metallic cartridges, these arms were relegated to storage arsenals after captured ammunition was expended. Several models of the Hall carbine, the model 1847 carbine, and Musketoon, Cosmopolitan, Jenks, Joslyn, Merrill, and Starr carbines saw service. Calibers ranged from .35 to .72 with almost no ammunition interchangeable.

The vast array of handguns in Confederate service was just as diverse as the long arms with calibers .31, .34, .36, .41, .44, .54, and .69 being used throughout the war. These handguns included current metallic cartridge revolvers of the latest design, such as the Smith and Wesson number 2 army revolver, a popular private-purchase arm, with the other extreme being the obsolete model 1816 and model 1836 single-shot flintlock pistols in .54 caliber, respectively. By far the most common were various Colt and Remington models in .36 and .44 caliber, supplemented by substantial numbers of altered single-shot pistols of .54 caliber and imported revolvers. These percussioned single-shot pistols were received by the states under the 1808 act and were pathetically outdated when compared to the latest revolver of Colt or Remington manufacture. Nevertheless, they were used by Confederate forces, as the manufacture of tens of thousands of rounds of ammunition for them indicates.

The Colt models most commonly encountered were the model 1848 dragoon revolver, .44 caliber; model 1849 pocket revolver, .31 caliber; model 1851 navy revolver, .36 caliber; model 1860 army revolver, .44 caliber; model 1861 navy revolver, .36 caliber; and model 1862 police revolver, .36 caliber. Remington models were primarily the Beals army and navy, .44 and .36 caliber, respectively, and the model 1861 (old model) army and navy revolvers, also .44 and .36 caliber, respectively.

Handguns manufactured by the Massachusetts Arms Company, Allen and Wheelock, Pettengill, Savage Starr, and Whitney in .36 and .44 calibers were obtained by seizure, capture, or private purchase in lesser quantities.

It is easy to see that Confederate forces used just about every American firearm made up to 1861. Regrettably few, if any, of these weapons bear legitimate markings to indicate Confederate use, although there are numerous spurious examples extant. That the Confederate States of America managed to keep nearly a million men of several armies separated by hundreds of miles in the field armed and equipped to conduct war for four years was something of a major accomplishment.

BIBLIOGRAPHY

Cromwell, Giles. *The Virginia Manufactory of Arms*. Charlottesville, Va., 1975.

Edwards, William B. *Civil War Guns*. Harrisburg, Pa., 1962.

The Field Manual for the Use of the Officers on Ordnance Duty. Richmond, Va., 1862. Reprint, edited by Howard Michael Madaus. Arendtsville, Pa., 1984.

Flayderman, Norman E. *Flayderman's Guide to Antique American Arms*. 5th ed. Northbrook, Ill., 1990.

Fuller, Claud E., and Richard D. Steuart. *Firearms of the Confederacy*. Huntington, W.V., 1944.

Lewis, Berkeley R. *Small Arms and Ammunition in the United States, 1776–1865*. Washington, D.C., 1956.

Madaus, Howard Michael. "The Maynard Rifle and Carbine in the Confederate Service." *Bulletin of the American Society of Arms Collectors*, no. 52 (1985): 66–79.

RUSS A. PRITCHARD

Altered U.S. Small Arms

Under the terms of the Militia Act of 1808, a proportionate amount of ordnance was available to the states on an annual basis for arming their militias. Most of the states, both North and South, took advantage of these provisions to obtain field artillery and small arms for issue to the volunteer militia companies. Until 1850, the small arms received were invariably flintlock muskets, either of the muzzle-loading U.S. model 1795 or of the model 1822 pattern; flintlock rifles, either of the muzzle-loading U.S. model 1817 pattern or of the Hall breech-loading model 1819 pattern; or single-shot flintlock pistols, either of the U.S. model 1819 or of the model 1836 pattern.

Between 1820 and 1855, the eleven states that would secede from the Union in 1860 and 1861 received under the 1808 act no fewer than 98,844 smoothbore muskets, 14,954 muzzle-loading rifles (as well as 3,138 of Hall's pattern), 28,935 single-shot pistols, and 17,999 sabers and swords. In addition to those flintlocks supplied by the U.S. government, the Commonwealth of Virginia had manufactured at its state-owned facility in Richmond between 1800 and 1821 a total of 58,400 flintlock muskets, 2,100 flintlock rifles, and 4,200 flintlock pistols. Although many of these arms would be lost to the Southern states owing to general wear and mistreatment by the militia companies, several states retained a significant portion of these obsolete weapons in store at their state arsenals.

At the beginning of 1860, the state arsenals in Virginia stored 51,370 flintlock muskets and 1,020 flintlock rifles. Similarly, Tennessee reported 8,480 flintlock muskets and 350 Hall rifles on hand at its state arsenal in January of 1861. Moreover, when the eight Federal arsenals in the South were seized by the seceding states, they were found to still hold more than 14,500 flintlock muskets, 7,170 flintlock rifles (nearly 7,000 of which were Hall's design), and almost 400 flintlock pistols. Technically obsolete with the introduction of the percussion system, many of these flintlocks were, nevertheless, issued in the South during the arms crisis of mid-1861. Eventually, most of these were recalled and altered to percussion locks during the winter of 1861–1862.

The Confederate states also inherited a large number of U.S. model 1822 muskets already altered from flintlock to percussion at U.S. arsenals and armories. During the twelve years preceding the war, an estimated 7,739 percussion muskets had been transferred to Southern states under the 1808 Militia Act. These were primarily U.S. model 1822 muskets altered from flintlock to percussion. Another 40,000 of these same type muskets (together with 65,000 U.S. model 1842 smoothbore percussion muskets and 10,000 U.S. model 1841 percussion rifles) had been transferred to Southern arsenals in 1860 under orders from Secretary of War (and former Virginia governor) John B. Floyd. Between February and December of 1860, Southern states or their agents purchased no fewer than 11,000 of the altered flintlocks from Southern Federal arsenals, and another 19,050 from Northern Federal arsenals.

These 77,789 muskets had been altered by closing the old vent, crudely cold-forging a cone seat near the breech of the barrel, threading in a percussion nipple, and substituting a percussion hammer for the old flintlock battery. The method was inexpensive but lacked strength. Although at least one contractor in Virginia and another in Alabama copied this system in 1861, most alterations effected in the South instead relied upon a separate bolster for the nipple, either brazed to the side of the breech over the old vent or screwed into an enlarged vent hole. Attaching a percussion hammer in place of the flintlock battery completed the operation.

Of these two systems, the former had been pioneered in South Carolina by William Glaze & Co. in 1852, when Glaze altered 5,960 state-owned flintlocks to percussion; it was championed by Virginia contractors, both for their state and the Confederacy. North Carolina contractors copied Virginia's method of percussioning flintlocks. In the western Confederacy, the use of the drum bolster screwed into the old vent at first predominated; it was found inadequate for muskets but sufficient for old flintlock sporting rifles that were pressed into Confederate service.

Although the Confederacy was able to expand its quantity of usable muskets significantly by altering obsolete flintlocks to percussion, little effort was made to upgrade these smoothbore muskets by rifling and sighting them for long range. Although the flintlock alterations, particularly those altered by the old Federal arsenal method, were generally not suitable for rifling, the smoothbore U.S. model 1842 musket was. In 1861, South Carolina contractor William Glaze rifled and sighted 3,720 of the model 1842 brass-mounted muskets he had made for that state in 1852 and 1853, but the demand for arms in the field, the lack of sights, and limited rifling machinery prevented any mass effort at rifling smoothbore muskets by the South.

The same factors prevented the numerous U.S. model 1841 percussion rifles in the South from being upgraded to "long-range" rifles, although some were at least adapted to accept saber bayonets. The large number of flintlock Hall breech-loading rifles in the South, however, led to numerous attempts to make effective arms of them. Many were percussioned by replacing the flintlock battery with a simple hammer and threading a nipple into the tilting breechblock. Others, notably those in North Carolina, were altered to percussion and then shortened and remodeled into carbines. Perhaps the most interesting attempt to make effective weapons from the Hall breechloaders took place in Virginia, where the firm of Read & Watson salvaged the barrels, some of the furniture, and parts of the stocks from the state's 1808 Militia Act Halls and made between 900 and 1,200 muzzle-loading rifles from them.

BIBLIOGRAPHY

Madaus, Howard Michael. *Warners Collectors Guide to American Longarms.* New York, 1981.
Virginia. *Annual Reports of the Adjutant-General.* Richmond, Va., 1920–1960.

HOWARD MICHAEL MADAUS

Imported English Small Arms

As a result of John Brown's 1859 raid upon the Harpers Ferry Armory, Virginia began in 1860 to seek the means to rebuild the old "Virginia Manufactory of Arms" into a modern factory for the production of a copy of the English pattern 1853 rifle-musket. That plan was altered when the state seized the machinery for the U.S. model 1855 rifle-musket at Harpers Ferry in April of 1861. Prior to this, however, Virginia had arranged through R. H. Maury of Petersburg to import 2,500 of the English rifle-muskets. Payments to Maury in early 1861 indicate that at least some of these were delivered.

In addition to Virginia, four other states made significant purchases of the English pattern 1853 rifle-musket. Between December of 1860 and the end of 1862, South Carolina purchased a minimum of 4,170 (exclusive of the number imported by Charleston speculators, estimated at at least 3,000); Georgia bought at least 5,000; Louisiana acquired about 7,000; and North Carolina imported 2,000 (with another 2,000 following in 1863). Many of these imported English long arms were confiscated by Confederate Ordnance Bureau officers upon their arrival at Southern ports, to the great consternation of the governors of the states that had purchased them from state funds. Although these importations were significant, they were overshadowed by purchases made directly by the agents of the Confederate central government, Capt. Caleb Huse and Maj. Edward C. Anderson.

The Confederacy's prime agent for obtaining ordnance abroad was transplanted New Englander Caleb Huse, who departed for England via Portland, Maine, and Canada, in late April 1861. Initially he would be frustrated in his attempts to acquire small arms. Northern agents from New York and New England arrived in England before him and emptied the market of existing pattern 1853 rifle-muskets. His efforts were further hampered by inadequate and delayed finances, which limited his ability to contract for newly made weapons. With the arrival of Maj. Edward C. Anderson in June, the situation improved dramatically. Together they arranged for the shipment of 10,620 rifle-muskets on the steamer *Fingal,* which arrived in Savannah with Anderson aboard in early November 1861.

Although this first Confederate shipment did little to satiate the demand for small arms (then approaching crisis proportions in the Confederacy), Huse's continued efforts resulted in a dramatic increase in armaments by mid-1862. After several losses to the Union blockade, the Confederate War Department determined not to risk large shipments directly into Southern ports. Instead, shipments from England were diverted to Nassau in the Bahamas. From there the cargoes were transshipped to the Florida coast. The first transshipment of 6,000 rifle-muskets landed there in February of 1862; an equal number arrived the following month. From the end of April until the beginning of August 1862, no fewer than 48,500 English small arms eluded the Union blockade and landed at the ports of Savannah, Georgia; Charleston, South Carolina; and Wilmington, North Carolina. By February 1863, the total importations of English long arms had risen to more than 104,000; 71,000 of these were the latest pattern rifle-muskets and another 9,700 were short rifles. From the end of September 1862 to October 1863, the Confederacy imported another 113,500 small arms, of which 56,800 were of English manufacture. Most of these were received prior to the summer of 1863: from July to October, only 8,200 rifle-muskets and 1,140 carbines of English make were received in Wilmington (the principal blockade-running port from 1863 until December 1864, when it was closed). Another 19,800 English long arms arrived in Wilmington between October 1863 and January 1864, and English imports for 1864 through that city amounted to nearly 26,000 rifle-muskets and 5,900 carbines.

Although gaps in the record (principally in 1862) leave the total number of English arms imported into the South during the war open to some question, it is evident that no fewer than 250,000 and more likely 300,000 long arms of English manufacture entered the Confederate service. These arms principally followed the patterns established for English military service and consisted of eight basic types. The pattern 1853 rifle-musket, in its four variations, was the principal infantry arm of the British service. Its 39-inch-long rifled barrel had a .577-caliber bore and mounted a triangular socket bayonet. The pattern 1851 rifle-musket was the first rifle-musket adopted by the British service, but was quickly supplanted by the pattern 1853. Its 39-inch-long rifled barrel had a .71-caliber bore and mounted a triangular socket bayonet. The five variations of the patterns 1856, 1857 (naval), 1858, 1860, and 1861 rifles had a 33-inch-long rifled barrel, .577-caliber bore, and mounted a saber bayonet with yatagan blade. The pattern 1856 sergeant's rifled fusil had a 33.5-inchlong rifled barrel, a .577-caliber rifled bore, and mounted a triangular socket bayonet. All known examples bear Georgia ownership marks. Up to 500 may have been imported.

> ... the Confederate War Department determined not to risk large shipments directly into Southern ports.

The three variations of the patterns 1853, 1858, and 1860 artillery carbines had a 24-inch-long rifled barrel, .577-caliber bore, and mounted the same bayonet as the rifles. A minimum of 1,040 of these were imported by the Confederacy in 1863 and 1864. The patterns 1856 and 1860 carbine were the principal shoulder arms issued to mounted units of the English army. Their 21-inch-long rifled barrel had a .577-caliber bore and took no bayonet. At least 6,040 of these weapons were imported in 1863 and 1864 alone, and another 350 purchased prior to 1863.

The pattern 1842 musket (and rifle-musket) and pattern 1839 musket were the percussion replacements for flintlock muskets of the Napoleonic era. Their 39-inch-long barrels had .75-caliber bores and mounted triangular socket bayonets. The pattern 1842 deviated from the pattern 1838 only in minor differences at the percussion bolster, as the latter had originally been intended to take a flintlock mechanism. More than 21,000 pattern 1851 rifle-muskets, 1842 rifle-muskets or smoothbore muskets, and 1839 muskets were imported into the Confederacy by February of 1863; the majority of these were sent to the western theater.

The pattern 1837 "Brunswick" rifle was considered obsolete by 1860. Its 36-inch-long barrel had a .70-caliber bore rifled with only two grooves for its peculiar belted projectile. A sword bayonet was affixed to two lugs on the right side of the barrel. Only 2,200 of these rifles had reached the Confederacy by February of 1863; many more were captured aboard blockade runners.

Although the prime small arms acquired by the Confederacy in England were muskets and rifles, a number of English-made handguns were also secured. The handgun of choice was the percussion revolver. Three basic types entered the Confederacy.

As a result of long-standing commercial ties between the South and English manufacturers, numerous examples of English-patent belt and pocket revolvers were imported into the South from 1859 until 1861. Nearly all were "double acting": it was not necessary to cock the hammer as a separate action before squeezing the trigger; pulling the trigger both cocked the hammer and in succession discharged the pistol. The most common English double-action revolvers imported prior to hostilities were those made under Adams's, Bently's, Tranter's, and Webley's patents. Unlike the contemporary Colt products, these revolvers exhibited a solid frame with a top strap. This top strap or the barrel were occasionally marked with the name of the Southern agency importing the revolver, particularly on Tranter models.

Although imports of the various English models of revolvers continued into 1861, usually through Charleston, efforts directed by the Confederate Ordnance Bureau and Navy Department concentrated on the acquisition of the Kerr revolver, a product of the London Armory Company, of which James Kerr was superintendent. The Kerr was purchased in quantity through the auspices of Sinclair, Hamilton, & Co. An estimated nine thousand revolvers in .44-caliber (54-bore) were imported into the Confederacy, the final nine hundred arriving on October 31, 1864.

BIBLIOGRAPHY

Anderson, Edward C. *Confederate Foreign Agent: The European Diary of Major Edward C. Anderson.* University, Ala., 1976.

Bailey, D. W. *British Military Longarms.* Harrisburg, Pa., 1972.

Gaidis, Henry L. "The Confederate Kerr Revolver." *Gun Report* 24, no. 8 (January 1979): 14–21.

Huse, Caleb. *The Supplies of the Confederate Army.* Boston, 1904.

Roads, C. H. *The British Soldier's Firearm, 1850–1864: From Smooth Bore to Small Bore.* London, 1964.

Sword, Wiley. *Firepower from Abroad.* Providence, R.I., 1986.

Vandiver, Frank E., ed. *Confederate Blockade Running through Bermuda, 1861–1865: Letters and Cargo Manifests.* Austin, Tex., 1972.

C. A. HUEY and HOWARD MICHAEL MADAUS

Imported English Long-Range Rifles

A full regiment of sharpshooters was authorized by the Confederate Congress in January 1862, but there was no viable source in the Confederacy for a thousand sharpshooter rifles. In fact, the Ordnance Bureau was hard pressed to keep up with the demand for standard rifled percussion muskets. Importation seemed the natural answer. The largest numbers were purchased from Joseph Whitworth of Manchester, England, a world-famous mechanical engineer who perfected his patented hexagonally bored .451-caliber rifle between 1854 and 1858. In highly publicized trials at Hythe, England, in 1857 and 1858, Whitworth's new rifle was shown to be dramatically more accurate than the standard Enfield rifle of .577 caliber.

Confederate Maj. Edward Anderson in July 1861 visited Whitworth's works in Manchester, where he purchased two Whitworth military match rifles. They were dispatched at once to Josiah Gorgas at Richmond and shown to President Jefferson Davis. Agents from the various states also purchased additional Whitworths in 1861. For example, the Eighth North Carolina Infantry was armed with Whitworths at the siege of Charleston. They were very expensive—£25 ($120 in 1860 dollars), cased complete, compared to a standard British rifle-musket at a bit over £3.

After receiving approval in Richmond, Anderson and Maj. Caleb Huse placed an order with Whitworth in September or October 1861 for arms for the Confederacy's sharpshooter service. The gun was to be a less expensive version of the standard Whitworth military match rifle. Savings were made by specifying a musket lock without sliding safety, two standard barrel bands, open elevator rear sight, elimination of the patch box, and a block front sight rather than a globe with screw adjustment. Many of these rifles, however, were equipped with the Davison telescopic sight mounted opposite the lock parallel to the barrel. These weapons, known as the Confederate-contract, second-quality, military-match rifles, were produced from the end of 1861 until late summer of 1862.

The exact number ordered is not known, but it is estimated that the South intended to acquire some fifty cases of twenty rifles each, for a total of one thousand arms. (The serial numbers fall between B500 and C750, a spread of 1,250.) Owing to the limited number of surviving examples, one must conclude that many were never delivered to the Confederacy, having been lost in running the blockade, or that the survival rate was extremely low.

Confederate agents were close to the London Armory Company and its superintendent, James Kerr, who also designed a small-bore rifle with a rifling system similar to Whitworth's but not as acclaimed. Kerr rifles were referred to as Enfield .44s, because their exterior dimensions were the same as a standard .577 musket. Kerr's rifling was a six-groove ratchet form. They had 37-inch barrels, full-sized stocks, three barrel bands, and open long-range sighting, although some had globe front sights, and adjustable wrist-mounted peep sights were available.

Best estimates put Whitworth's at 70 percent of the imported Confederate sharpshooter weapons, Kerr's at 20 percent, and 10 percent other small-bore arms. The majority of the latter were by Thomas Turner of Birmingham and Alexander Henry of Edinburgh, Scotland. Turner's were of .451-caliber five-groove rifling, making one turn in 20 inches. Henry's were of .451-caliber seven-groove rifling, making one turn in 30 inches. Small numbers of Calisher and Terry breech-loading rifles were used, but in much smaller quantities than their carbine. A few J. Rigby rifles of .451-caliber octagonal rifling, making one turn in 18 inches, were reportedly used. Given that at least fifteen types of small-bore Enfields were produced, the Confederates were very selective in keeping the great percentage of their imports to two varieties—Whitworths and Kerrs. All small-bores utilized the standard .442-diameter conical projectiles, which simplified ammunition procurement.

The importation of the English long-range rifles was significant in the Confederate struggle for several reasons. The only combat use of the famous Whitworth weapons occurred during the Civil War. All Whitworth rifles and all but four Whitworth cannons were used by Confederates. Whitworth rifles were capable of striking targets with power at up to 2,000 yards. Numerous mounted officers were hit at ranges of 1,200 to 1,800 yards, a distance considered safe unless Confederate snipers were at work. The morale of the always hard-pressed Confederate army and navy was surely raised by their sharpshooters' use of the finely tooled Whitworths. They had the most accurate long-range rifle in the war. Many a Confederate letter home began proudly, "We have a wonderful new rifle in our army."

BIBLIOGRAPHY

Albaugh, William A., III, and Edward N. Simmons. *Confederate Arms.* Harrisburg, Pa., 1957.

Burton, E. Milby. *The Siege of Charleston, 1861–1865.* Columbia, S.C., 1970.

Edwards, William B. *Civil War Guns.* Harrisburg, Pa., 1962.

Fuller, Claude E., and Richard D. Steuart. *Firearms of the Confederacy.* Lawrence, Mass., 1944.

Hoole, Stanley W. *Confederate Foreign Agent: The European Diary of Major Edward C. Anderson.* Tuscaloosa, Ala., 1976.

Sword, Wiley. *Firepower from Abroad.* Lincoln, R.I., 1986.

Vandiver, Frank E. *Confederate Blockade Running through Bermuda, 1861–1865.* Austin, Tex., 1947.

C. A. HUEY

Imported Austrian, Belgian, and French Small Arms

Although the bulk of the small arms imported to the Confederacy between 1861 and 1865 originated in England, significant quantities were also purchased on the Continent. These arms were principally of Imported Austian, Belgian, and French Small ArmsAustrian and Belgian manufacture, the former conforming to the most recent Austrian government model and the latter primarily Liège-made copies or adaptations of French models.

In early 1862, the Confederacy's main European purchasing agent, Caleb Huse, obtained a significant number of Austrian field cannons, paying for them with money borrowed in England. By February of 1863, he had also managed to purchase and deliver to the Confederacy 27,000 Austrian rifles and had another 30,000 in Vienna awaiting payment. Not only were these 30,000 arms eventually secured, but additional arms of the same type were also purchased, allowing the Confederacy to import 56,600 Austrian rifles through Wilmington between July and December of 1863. An additional 4,740 came through the same port in 1864.

All of these nearly 90,000 small arms were of the most recent pattern adopted by Austria in 1854 and known from its designer as the Lorenz. All were rifle-muskets having a 37 1/2-inch-long barrel with a .54-caliber rifled bore and taking a quadrangular socket bayonet. The rifle-musket came with two types of rear sight. Since the greatest number of these arms arrived in 1863, they played a significant role in the rearming of the Army of Tennessee during the winter of 1863–1864.

Although Liège, Belgium, was initially rejected by Huse as a source for small arms in 1861, the evidence is overwhelming that the city served as the South's third most important source of foreign armament during the war. Liège's contacts with the South had begun in 1860 when commercial relations were established with the city during Georgia's industrial fair. As a result of these contacts, efforts were made in 1861 to import Liège-made rifles through New Orleans for the South. These efforts were only partly successful, although at least 820 *rifles à tige* (pillar breech rifles) of Belgian make found their way up the Mississippi to arm a brigade of Confederate Kentuckians. These are believed to have been Liège-made copies of the French model 1846 rifle, whose 34 1/4-inch-long barrel had a rifled bore of .70 caliber and which accepted a long yatagan saber bayonet on a lug and guide on its right side.

Other purchases of Liège-made small arms trickled through the blockade in 1862. In June, 700 Liège-made rifles were brought through the blockade into Charleston aboard the steamer *Memphis.* Although exact details of the type imported are speculative, these were probably .58-caliber variants of the French model 1859 rifle. Transfer records from the Fayetteville, Richmond, Atlanta, and Montgomery arsenals indicate shipments and issuance of Belgian rifles (and at least 160 smoothbore muskets) from the late summer of 1862 through the spring of 1864. These shipments included at least 218 described as having double-set triggers, which in fact may have been German model 1835 "yager" rifles, tentatively part of a shipment of German rifles that entered Charleston in September 1861 aboard the steamer *Bermuda.* Other shipments of Belgian copies of French arms were less successful in reaching their destinations. The prize court records of the steamers *Ella Warley* (captured in April 1862) and *Columbia* (captured in August 1862) indicate that the former bore at least 280 rifle-muskets of probable Liège manufacture for Louisiana, and the latter 540 Belgian-made .69-caliber rifle-muskets copying the French model 1822 (rifled and altered from flintlocks to percussion ignition) and the French model 1853 (rifled). Clearly Belgian imports were significant, though exact figures remain nebulous.

The Ordnance Bureau also imported in quantity from France a revolver of American design. Jean A. F. LeMat designed and patented a revolver in the United States whose main feature was a hollow cylinder pin that, in conjunction with an adjustment on the hammer, permitted the pistol to serve as a small shotgun or as a revolver at the will of its owner. With the outbreak of the Civil War, LeMat, armed with contracts for his patented revolver, went to Paris to arrange for their manufacture in association with Charles Girard. After production of approximately five hundred revolvers had begun, operations were shifted to England, where another two thousand of the larger .42-caliber–.63-caliber combination revolver-shotguns were made for the army, and about six hundred smaller .32-caliber–.41-caliber revolver-shotguns for the navy.

BIBLIOGRAPHY

Bailey, D. W. *Percussion Guns and Rifles.* Harrisburg, Pa., 1972.
Balace, Francis. *L'Armurerie liègeoise et la guerre de sècession, 1861–1865.* Liège, Belgium, 1978.
Edwards, William B. *Civil War Guns.* Harrisburg, Pa., 1962.

HOWARD MICHAEL MADAUS

Naval Small Arms

Ordnance instructions for the Confederate navy specified a variety of small arms to be carried aboard ship: battle-axes, muskets with bayonets, carbines with bayonets, revolvers, pistols, pikes, and cutlasses, all equipped with appropriate accoutrements. In practice, smoothbore muskets, rifles, and carbines were issued but rarely in combination with one another, and revolvers were often used exclusively in lieu of single-shot, muzzle-loading pistols. The marine guard was usually equipped with weapons apart from those issued the general crew.

Small arms were distributed in combinations based on the crew's duty assignments. Cutlasses were most often issued with pistols or revolvers, and shoulder arms with pikes or battle-axes. Weapons could also be used in other mixtures or alone.

Southern warships were generally well equipped with weapons acquired by early-war seizure of Federal stocks, by capture, by local production, and by import. British-made Enfield muzzle-loading rifles and Kerr revolvers, along with French-made LeMat revolvers, were special favorites in the Confederate navy. Union-made Maynard breech-loading carbines were popular on some ironclads, where cramped space made cumbersome muzzleloaders difficult to handle.

[*See also* Edged Weapons, *article on* Edged Weapons in the Navy.]

BIBLIOGRAPHY

Albaugh, William A., III. *Confederate Edged Weapons.* New York, 1960.
Albaugh, William A., III, and Edward A. Simmons. *Confederate Arms.* Harrisburg, Pa., 1957.
Confederate Navy Department. *Ordnance Instructions for the Confederate States Navy.* 3d ed. London, 1864.
Edwards, William B. *Civil War Guns.* Harrisburg, Pa., 1962.
Sword, Wiley. *Firepower from Abroad: The Confederate Enfield LeMat Revolver.* Lincoln, R.I., 1986.

A. ROBERT HOLCOMBE, JR.

Munitions

The first step toward provisions for ordnance needs was taken by the Confederate government while it was still at Montgomery, when Josiah Gorgas was commissioned as chief of the Ordnance Bureau. Although a number of Federal ordnance facilities would fall into Confederate hands (at Little Rock, Baton Rouge, Mount Vernon, Appalachicola, Augusta, Charleston, Fayetteville, and San Antonio), Gorgas was to find that

> there was little ammunition of any kind, or powder, at the arsenals in the South, and that little relics of the Mexican war, stored principally at Baton Rouge and Mount Vernon arsenals. I doubt whether there were a million rounds of small-arms cartridges in the Confederacy. Lead there was none in store. Of powder the chief supply was that captured at Norfolk, though there was a small quantity at each of the Southern arsenals, say 60,000 pounds in all, chiefly old cannon powder. The stock of percussion caps could not have exceeded one-quarter of a million.

Immediate steps were taken by the central government and the states to fabricate and procure small arms ammunition. Before the commencement of hostilities, some proprietary rounds for carbines and revolvers were purchased in the North; however, a great reliance was placed on importation from abroad, chiefly from Great Britain (although never with official English sanction).

The Confederacy established nine primary sites for the production of small arms ammunition: Atlanta, Columbus, Macon, and Augusta, Georgia; Charleston, South Carolina; Fayetteville, North Carolina; Lynchburg and Richmond, Virginia; and Selma, Alabama. Other facilities at Columbus and Jackson, Mississippi; Little Rock, Arkansas; Nashville, Tennessee; New Orleans and Baton Rouge, Louisiana; San

Antonio and Marshall, Texas; and Savannah, Georgia, had far lower production during the war or were abandoned after operating only briefly.

Gorgas estimated that during the war these manufactories produced 150 million small arms cartridges; half of that number was produced at Richmond alone. Once the facilities were established, the South had ample ordnance workers (mostly women and children for cartridges), but a major continuing concern was the lack of raw materials: lead, paper, gunpowder (niter, sulfur, and charcoal), and copper and mercury for percussion caps.

It was not uncommon for small arms ammunition production to be halted at a laboratory for a month or more for a want of lead for bullets. Gorgas calculated that it required 10 million pounds of lead to produce 150 million cartridges (see accompanying table).

About a dozen small paper mills supplied cartridge paper to the Ordnance Department. By May 1863, and after the accidental burning of the Bath Paper Mills in Augusta, a critical shortage of manila fibers developed and led to curtailed production of ammunition. A heavier reliance was placed on imported English "white-fine" paper for Enfield cartridges.

In 1861, there were in the South two small private powder mills in Tennessee, two in South Carolina, one in North Carolina, and a little stamping mill in New Orleans. Large orders for powder were sent to the North and, according to Gorgas, "were being rapidly filled at the date of the attack on Fort Sumter." Early on, Jefferson Davis pressed for the erection of a large government powder mill. Under the direction of Col. George W. Rains, the Augusta Powder Works from 1862 to 1865 turned out 2,750,000 pounds of gunpowder. Charcoal was made from cottonwood from the banks of the Savannah River. Several hundred tons of sulfur were found at New Orleans intended for sugar making. Niter from saltpeter was the chief concern. Much was "mined" in bat guano–enriched caves, but most had to be imported. Artificial beds were established throughout the South, but were not fully mature until the war ended.

Percussion cap machinery built in the South was put in operation at Richmond, Atlanta, Augusta, and for a time Columbus, Mississippi. Gorgas also imported English caps. The Union forces' closure of the Ducktown, Tennessee, mines jeopardized the supply of copper, and the casting of bronze field cannons was immediately suspended. An officer was given authority to purchase or impress all copper stills for making turpentine and apple brandy. The commander of the Richmond Arsenal estimated that during the last twelve months of the war all caps there were manufactured from the copper stills of North Carolina. Mercury for the fulminate of mercury explosive in percussion caps came principally from Mexico, although other substitutes also came into use.

Gorgas did not perform these labors alone. In May 1862, John W. Mallet was commissioned superintendent of laboratories to, in his words, "bring order out of the confusion," and also to prepare plans for a Central Ordnance Laboratory to be built at Macon. Here would be produced all the Confederacy's ammunition. Although it was never completed, Mallet performed admirably, overseeing construction, ordering machinery, developing suppliers, and visiting other small arms ammunition sites to maintain quality products. When the visits became too time-consuming, he ordered the facilities to send him monthly samples, which he inspected and reported on to Gorgas and the commanders. He revived an abandoned U.S. Ordnance procedure requiring the quantity, kind, and place and date of manufacture of ammunition to be marked on all packages. This made it easier to track down the source of complaints and make necessary corrections.

The most distinctive Confederate bullet used during the war was the invention of Frederick J. Gardner of Hillsboro, North Carolina. On Mallet's first tour of inspection, he found at the Richmond Laboratory "the simple and effective little machine invented by Mr. Gardner." His patented process saved paper and time. Mallet initially recommended the machine for other laboratories, but complaints from the field about poorly made cartridges led him, in 1863, to work for its elimination from service.

Confederate laboratories and arsenals produced small arms ammunition for all the types of weapons in their service: smoothbore muskets, rifles, rifled muskets, carbines, revolvers, and shotguns. But ordnance officers had to cope with inadequate transportation and severe shortages of raw materials. Nevertheless, William LeRoy Broun, commander of the Richmond Arsenal, was justly proud of his department, stating, "Never was an order received from General Lee's army for ammunition that it was not immediately supplied, even to the last order of sending a train-load of ammunition to Petersburg after the order was received for the evacuation of Richmond."

[See also Niter and Mining Bureau; Ordnance Bureau.]

BIBLIOGRAPHY

Confederate Ordnance Bureau. *The Confederate Field Manual.* Richmond, Va., 1862. Reprint, Gettysburg, Pa., 1984.
Thomas, Dean S. *Ready . . . Aim . . . Fire! Small Arms Ammunition in the Battle of Gettysburg.* Gettysburg, Pa., 1981.

DEAN S. THOMAS

SMITH, E. KIRBY

SMITH, E. KIRBY (1824–1893), general. Edmund Kirby Smith was born at St. Augustine, Florida, on May 16, 1824. Two years before his birth his New England parents moved

E. KIRBY SMITH. Pictured as a lieutenant general.
CIVIL WAR LIBRARY AND MUSEUM, PHILADELPHIA

to the Florida Territory where his father served as a Federal judge. As a young man Smith attended school in Alexandria, Virginia, before entering West Point where he graduated in 1845, twenty-fifth in a class of forty-one. He fought in the Mexican War under both Zachary Taylor and Winfield Scott and then went on to a career in the U.S. Army. When Abraham Lincoln was elected, Smith was on duty in Texas as part of the Second U.S. Cavalry—the regiment known as Jeff Davis's own, which produced half of the full generals for the Confederate States.

As a young man Smith had gone by the name Ted or Ned, and his elder brother Ephraim Kirby Smith had used E. Kirby Smith. But sometime after the elder Smith died in the Mexican War, the younger brother began signing his name as E. Kirby Smith, and in 1861 this was how he endorsed all official correspondence.

When Texas seceded, Smith was in charge of Camp Colorado in West Texas but evacuated his command on February 26 after surrendering the post to Col. Henry Eustace McCulloch. Smith was in line for promotion when he resigned his commission to join the Confederacy. Upon hearing this Earl Van Dorn wrote the Confederate secretary of

war: "Major Smith has always been considered by the Army as one of its leading spirits . . . .He is so well known to the President, however, that it would be superfluous to say anything to call his attention to his merits as an officer."

Although Van Dorn requested that his friend be assigned to him in Texas, Smith was placed in command at Lynchburg, Virginia. But he was soon assigned to Joseph E. Johnston at Harpers Ferry and became the general's adjutant. On June 17, 1861, while at Winchester, Smith was promoted to brigadier general and accompanied Johnston to Manassas. He was slightly wounded in the battle, a bullet striking him near his collarbone, and while recovering from his wound at Lynchburg, he married Cassie Selden. Smith was promoted to major general on October 11 and assigned a division in P. G. T. Beauregard's Potomac District. During the winter Smith was ordered to report to Richmond, and in March he took command of the Department of East Tennessee at Knoxville.

In the summer of 1862 Smith was part of the Confederate plan for a far-reaching offensive in the West. One army under Braxton Bragg would move north toward Kentucky while Smith marched from Knoxville. By September both armies had reached Kentucky where they had a chance to cut the supply line for Don Carlos Buell's army in Tennessee. Over Smith's objections, the two armies met at Frankfort to inaugurate a Confederate governor, but the approach of Federal troops broke up the ceremony. Although the early offenses were successful, the campaign failed because of a lack of cooperation etween the two armies. After the Battle of Perryville on October 8 the Southern armies withdrew to Tennessee, and Smith returned to Knoxville on October 24. Depressed over the recent failures, Smith thought about resigning and entering the ministry, a move he had contemplated before, but on October 26 he learned of his promotion to lieutenant general.

Although still at his post in Knoxville in late December, Smith, early in January 1863, was called to Richmond where he was reassigned to duty west of the Mississippi River. This apparently came as a result of a combination of reasons; the relationship between Smith and Bragg was strained, and President Jefferson Davis needed to appoint a competent commander west of the Mississippi. Robert E. Lee had recently written Davis: "I need not remind you of the merits of General E. K. Smith whom I consider one of our best officers." On January 14, 1863, Smith was ordered to take command of the Southwestern Army, but on February 9, while on his way to Alexandria, Louisiana, he received a second communication that read "The command of Lieut. Gen. E. Kirby Smith is extended so as to embrace the Trans-Mississippi Department." He replaced the unpopular Theophilus H. Holmes and thus entered a new phase of his career.

After the surrender of Vicksburg and Port Hudson in the summer of 1863 the Trans-Mississippi region was virtually isolated from the rest of the Confederacy; operating independently, the area became known as "Kirby Smithdom." Not all the commanders in the region were pleased with Smith's measures. Most important, he had several disagreements about strategy with the influential Maj. Gen. Richard Taylor, who commanded in Louisiana. But President Davis gave Smith a wide range of powers and backed them up by promoting him to the permanent rank of general in the Provisional Army on February 19, 1864.

The greatest threat to Smith's department came in the spring of 1864 when two Federal armies moved toward Shreveport, Louisiana. Nathaniel P. Banks pushed his army up the Red River, being stopped at Mansfield and Pleasant Hill in April, while Frederick Steele marched his army south out of Little Rock toward the same objective. Neither succeeded, but the results of the campaign magnified the differences between Smith and Taylor, and the outcome of this was Taylor's transfer out of the department. Another controversial act was Smith's independent appointment of several Confederate generals, many of whom were later rejected by Richmond.

As the war drew to an end, Smith moved his headquarters from Shreveport to Houston. On June 2 he officially signed a surrender agreement aboard a Federal steamer in Galveston Harbor, but fearing that he might be arrested, he fled to Mexico. He returned to the United States several months later and signed an amnesty oath on November 14 at Lynchburg.

After the war Smith held various positions. Two companies he was associated with, the Accident Insurance Company and the Atlantic and Pacific Telegraph Company, failed. He also served as president of the University of Nashville before moving to Sewanee, Tennessee, in 1875 where he taught at the University of the South. He was the last survivor of the eight full Confederate generals, dying on March 28, 1893. Smith was buried in Sewanee Cemetery.

BIBLIOGRAPHY

Blackwood, Emma Jerome, ed. *To Mexico with Scott: Letters of Captain E. Kirby Smith to His Wife.* Cambridge, Mass., 1917.

Kerby, Robert L. *Kirby Smith's Confederacy: The Trans-Mississippi South, 1863–1865.* New York, 1972.

Johnson, Ludwell H. *Red River Campaign: Politics and Cotton in the Civil War.* Baltimore, 1958.

Parks, Joseph Howard. *General Edmund Kirby Smith, C.S.A.* Baton Rouge, La., 1954.

ANNE J. BAILEY

Smith, Gustavus W.

SMITH, GUSTAVUS W. (1821–1896), major general and ad interim secretary of war. During the early months of the Civil War, Smith seemed one of the most capable officers the nearly formed Confederate nation could call its own. Forty years old in 1861, he was tall, burly, and unashamedly smug. He had graduated from the U.S. Military Academy near the top of his class in 1842. In the Mexican War, Smith served with distinction and earned a reputation as a talented engineer. He later taught engineering at West Point before leaving the army to pursue a prosperous career in civil engineering. In 1858 Smith became street commissioner of New York City. He still held this position when civil war came to the United States.

From New York, Smith watched the events leading to war closely, sensitive to which side his native state of Kentucky would join. Then circumstances made his choice for him. In April 1861, just before the firing on Fort Sumter, Smith suffered an attack of paralysis. In September his doctor recommended that he go south to Hot Springs, Arkansas, for relief. En route, Smith discovered that the U.S. government, deeming his leaving the North traitorous, had posted a warrant for his arrest. This clinched Smith's decision to join the South. As soon as he was able, he traveled to Richmond and promptly received a commission as major general.

During the next nine months, nothing but praise seemed to surround the name of G. W. Smith. In a letter to President Jefferson Davis, Gen. Joseph E. Johnston referred to Smith as a "man of high ability, fit to command in chief." It seemed great things might come of the tall and confident Kentuckian. The chance for distinction came on May 31, 1862, at the Battle of Seven Pines. Johnston fell severely wounded, and Smith took chief command of the army. But mysteriously, his paralysis again overcame him the next day and made him unfit for duty. Smith's hour of greatness had passed.

When Robert E. Lee became commander of the newly named Army of Northern Virginia, he seemed not to trust Smith's reliability on the field. Lee reassigned Smith to the right wing of the army, which included military responsibility for southeastern Virginia and coastal North Carolina. But uneasiness over Smith's abilities mounted. It was not very long until native North Carolinian Brig. Gen. Robert Ransom, Jr., confided to Lee that he thought Smith was lacking in energy and purpose, and was unfit for his position.

Soon there was overt evidence of the high command's doubts about him. In the fall of 1862 Smith learned that six officers junior to him had received promotion to lieutenant general. He was incensed. Smith believed that the Confederacy had wronged him by failing to appreciate his services and talents. He drafted a letter of resignation and threatened to send it, but was dissuaded temporarily by Secretary of War George Wythe Randolph. He later wrote the secretary, "I would rather have been shot dead than to have had my usefulness in so important a command impaired, if not destroyed, by the recent wholesale overslaughing to which I have been subjected." Smith continued in his post until November 1862, when he briefly acted as secretary of war between the tenures of Randolph and James A. Seddon.

In February 1863 Smith finally resigned in disgust, gave up his commission as major general, and left Virginia. Seeking out those who would appreciate him, he went first to his old army friend Gen. P. G. T. Beauregard to aid in the defense of Charleston, South Carolina. Next, he journeyed farther south to Georgia and assumed the presidency of Etowah Manufacturing and Mining Company. By 1864, Georgia Governor Joseph E. Brown had appointed Smith his aide-de-camp and made him responsible for fortification construction for the defense of the state. When Gen. William Tecumseh Sherman wrought his path of destruction through the heart of Georgia, Smith shuttled state militia forces about in stubborn defiance of Sherman's veterans.

It is ironic that Smith proved himself an able leader in Georgia, most notably during the heated action along the Chattahoochie River before Atlanta and later in defense of Savannah. Although the days of the Confederacy were numbered, Smith's efforts offered some of the strongest resistance Sherman met during the long campaign. On April 20, 1865, Smith surrendered his remaining troops to the victorious Federals in Macon, Georgia.

Smith's commendable performance in Georgia in face of an overwhelming enemy did not expunge his memories of the early war. Through the postwar years, his bitterness lingered. He eventually moved back to New York City and became heavily involved in the fledgling insurance industry. In his spare hours he found time to write numerous articles and books about the war and the part he had played in it. In his *Confederate War Papers,* published in 1883, Smith devoted an appendix of the book to refuting accusations that he had conspired against the United States while serving as a New York City commissioner. He also rehashed the old matter concerning the promotion of the six officers junior to him and included copies of the biting letters exchanged between himself and President Jefferson Davis. He added a section full of favorable appraisals by friends and fellow officers. To the end, Smith remained convinced that he had been unappreciated and misunderstood.

BIBLIOGRAPHY

Evans, Clement A. *Confederate History.* Vol. 1 of *Confederate Military History.* Edited by Clement A. Evans. Atlanta, 1899. Vol. 1 of extended ed. Wilmington, N.C., 1987.

Freeman, Douglas S. *Lee's Lieutenants: A Study in Command.* 3 vols. New York, 1942–1944. Reprint, New York, 1986.

Smith, Gustavus Woodson. *The Battle of Seven Pines.* New York, 1891. Reprint, Dayton, Ohio, 1974.

Smith, Gustavus Woodson. *Confederate War Papers.* New York, 1884.

LESLEY JILL GORDON-BURR

SMITH, ROBERT HARDY

SMITH, ROBERT HARDY (1813–1878), congressman from Alabama and colonel. Smith was born on March 21, 1813, at Edenton in Camden County, North Carolina. He was appointed to the class of 1835 at the U.S. Military Academy at West Point; however, his father's financial reverses forced him to withdraw before graduation. Smith taught school in Virginia before moving to Dallas County, Alabama, in 1834. He continued to teach, studied medicine briefly, and then read law. He was admitted to the Alabama bar in 1837 and opened a practice in Livingston, eventually forming a partnership with William M. Inge.

As a Whig, Smith supported William Henry Harrison for president in 1840 and Henry Clay in 1844. In 1849, he was elected to the Alabama House of Representatives and quickly became one of the leading Whigs in the state. During the 1849 session of the Alabama General Assembly, Smith gave offense to John J. Seibles, who challenged him to a duel. Accepting the challenge, Smith was on his way to meet Seibles when friends intervened and submitted the matter to a board of honor, which settled the dispute to their mutual satisfaction. In 1851 he campaigned for the Alabama Senate, advocating support for the Compromise of 1850 and opposing both the Nashville Convention and state rights Democrats. He was defeated by a single vote.

In 1853 Smith moved to Mobile, Alabama, continued to practice law, and became an active opponent of William Lowndes Yancey and the secession movement. In the 1860 presidential election, Smith actively supported the Constitutional Union party's nominee, John Bell, and worked to ally Bell's supporters with those of Democratic candidate Stephen H. Douglas to defuse the secession movement. Also in 1860 Smith and Isham Warren Garrott were appointed the state's commissioners to confer with North Carolina officials about coordinating the actions of Southern states and forming a confederation should the Southern states secede. Once the sectional crisis destroyed the Whig party, Smith became a Democrat.

Smith's efforts to prevent Alabama's withdrawal from the Union failed, and the state convention voted to secede on January 11, 1861. Once the decision for secession was made, Smith declared his loyalty to Alabama and the South. In January 1861 he was elected as one of two deputies-at-large to represent Alabama in the Provisional Congress meeting in Montgomery, where he was named to the Judiciary Committee and the Committee on Naval Affairs. He also worked with a former law partner, Representative William B. Ochiltree of Texas, to prepare several military options to protect the South from an invasion by Northern troops. The plan was rejected because the Confederacy did not have the resources to implement it.

Smith's most important work was as a member of the committee that drafted the Constitution of the Confederate States of America. He worked diligently on its preparation, stressing the need for a strong national government, a viewpoint that was not shared by his fellow delegates from Alabama. He was determined that the Confederate Constitution be as clear and simple as possible and spent many hours working to clarify and define vague wording. It was Smith who suggested that the terms of office for the provisional government be limited to one year. Afterward he published *An Address to the Citizens of Alabama on the Constitution and Laws of the Confederate States of America* to inform the citizenry of their new form of government and stress his support for the Confederacy.

> **Smith's most important work was as a member of the committee that drafted the [Confederate] Constitution. . . .**

After the firing on Fort Sumter, Smith proposed that the Confederacy raise a force of independent volunteers that would form the nucleus of a national army to thwart any attack by Federal troops. He broke with President Jefferson Davis, however, over the question of a produce loan to finance the war effort, believing that the measure placed too large a burden on the planter class.

At the end of his first term, Smith declined to seek reelection and raised the Thirty-sixth Alabama Infantry Regiment in the spring of 1862. Although he was elected the regiment's colonel, Smith was forced to resign his commission because of health problems in April 1862. He remained active in the Southern military organization, however, and was appointed president of the military court of Brig. Gen. John Horace Forney's command of South Alabama and West Florida.

After the Civil War, Smith reopened his law practice in Mobile, specializing in constitutional law. He became a well-known litigator, arguing against the validity of a Reconstruction-inspired oath required of attorneys and playing a key role in the impeachment of Richard Busteed, the U.S. District judge for the Southern District of Alabama. Smith's arguments were so convincing that Busteed resigned. Smith also prosecuted the million-dollar case of *Alabama v. The Stanton, Alabama and Chattanooga Railroad*. He died in Mobile on March 13, 1878.

BIBLIOGRAPHY

Brewer, W. *Alabama: Her History, Resources, War Record, and Public Men from 1540 to 1872.* Montgomery, Ala., 1872.
Evans, Clement A., ed. *Confederate Military History.* 12 vols. Atlanta, 1899. Extended ed. in 19 vols. Wilmington, N.C., 1987–1989.
Garrett, William. *Reminiscences of Public Men in Alabama.* Atlanta, 1872.
Owen, Thomas M. *History of Alabama and Dictionary of Alabama Biography.* 4 vols. Chicago, 1921.
Smith, Robert H. *An Address to the Citizens of Alabama on the Constitution and Laws of the Confederate States of America.* Montgomery, Ala., 1861.
Warner, Ezra J., and W. Buck Yearns. *Biographical Register of the Confederate Congress.* Baton Rouge, La., 1975.

PAUL F. LAMBERT

SMITH, WILLIAM "EXTRA BILLY"

SMITH, WILLIAM "EXTRA BILLY" (1797– 1887), major general, Virginia congressman and governor. Smith grew up in a well-to-do, middle-class plantation family near Fredericksburg. He received a sound education at private academies, clerked in several law offices, and in 1818 became a practicing attorney in the upper Piedmont, first at Culpeper and then at Warrenton. He married and started a large family. He did some farming with slave labor and ran a successful mail and coach service that wangled so many extra fees from the post office that he won the enduring nickname "Extra Billy."

An ardent Jacksonian Democrat, he soon became primarily a politician. From 1836 to 1841 he served in the state senate and from 1841 to 1843 in the U.S. House of Representatives. Then the state legislature elected him governor. He served from January 1, 1846, to December 31, 1848, enthusiastically and effectively supporting the war against Mexico. He was especially successful in mobilizing Virginia troops for combat. As soon as his term was over, Smith moved alone to California to recoup his finances, and he prospered by practicing law and speculating in land. In 1853 he returned to his family in Virginia and almost immediately won election again to the U.S. House of Representatives where he served until 1861.

When war erupted the sixty-three-year-old Smith volunteered to serve his state in combat, and Governor John Letcher appointed him colonel of the Forty-ninth Virginia Infantry Regiment. Brave but inexperienced, Colonel Smith was a barely adequate military leader, though he saw much action and was wounded in the Peninsular campaign and more seriously at Sharpsburg in September 1862. Eight months later Brigadier General Smith returned to active duty in time for the Battle of Chancellorsville, but a poor performance at Gettysburg led to his removal from combat command and reassignment to recruiting duties where his gubernatorial experience during the Mexican War proved useful.

During the first two years of the war Smith had also been a member of the Confederate Congress. Since he participated only while on leave from the army, he played a minor role, concentrating on financial and military affairs and generally supporting President Jefferson Davis and the Confederate central government. Then Smith returned to full-time politics by winning a second term as governor of the state. Virginians were distracted by the war, but Major General Smith won a large majority of the army vote, and on January 1, 1864, he began his new administration.

The new governor was elected to serve four years, but the massive Union war machine had already gained a clear advantage over the battered Southern armies. In reality Smith would hold office only a little over fifteen months within the doomed Confederacy.

At first he occasionally bogged down in routine matters, but generally he performed efficiently. Like his predecessor, John Letcher, he followed the practical policy of broadly cooperating with the Confederate government, and, again like Letcher, he urged Virginians to put away for the duration of the war their traditional devotion to state rights, individual freedoms, and strict legalism and to strive even harder for victory. And just like Letcher, he clashed frequently with the increasingly disaffected legislature.

Concerned about Virginia's growing vulnerability, Governor Smith tried to marshal new home defense forces, but the steadily expanding Confederate draft soon drained away manpower from this program. Smith yielded to the draft and called out his few remaining state troops whenever the Confederates made such a request. He also supported Confederate efforts to reduce the number of draft-exempt state and local officials, a scam all over the South, and he especially opposed exempting such officials who had refugeed from enemy-held parts of Virginia, though he did occasionally yield to local protests. He cooperated, too, with Confederate impressment, including the seizure of slave laborers, always an especially sensitive issue. He even ordered state officials to seize uncooperative saltworks in southwestern Virginia, something his predecessor could never quite bring himself to do. And finally Governor Smith acceded to rapidly expanding Confederate control of Virginia's manufacturing facilities and transportation systems. Inevitably these emergency wartime policies led to rising protests that were soon concentrated in the restive legislature, but the pragmatic governor knew that extraordinary, even desperate measures had to be taken if the South was to have any real hope of victory.

A combat veteran, Smith was fully aware of the desperate manpower shortage in the Confederate armed forces. The South still had one great untapped manpower pool—slaves, black Southerners by the hundreds of thousands. Early in 1862 invading Union armies had begun to recruit Southern blacks, and after the Emancipation Proclamation this policy accelerated, so that by the end of the war the Union armed forces had enlisted almost 200,000 blacks, mostly Southerners. Yet even as the war dragged on and Southern casualties soared, the Confederates hesitated to take this final step.

Then in September 1864 Louisiana governor Henry W. Allen's secret call for the use of black troops surfaced. The next month the governors of Virginia, Alabama, Georgia, Mississippi, and the Carolinas met in Augusta, Georgia, and Smith prodded them into issuing a resolution obliquely calling for the use of black troops. Finally, very late in the war, the Davis administration itself moved toward this position.

With Atlanta lost and Abraham Lincoln reelected, Governor Smith in December appealed to the hostile legislature to begin recruiting slaves as soldiers. Conservative Virginia wavered, but when Robert E. Lee called for black

> ## Smith was fully aware of the desperate manpower shortage in the . . . armed forces.

troops in January 1865, Smith renewed his appeals, and finally early in March the legislators approved furnishing black Virginians to the Confederate army. In the middle of March the Confederate Congress passed similar legislation, and, thanks in part to continued agitation by Governor Smith, the War Department's new regulations for slave soldiers promised freedom for honorable service. Never in his career had Smith challenged slavery or the assumption of black inferiority upon which it was based, but he saw the desperate need for new manpower and placed contemporary crisis ahead of old dogma. A dramatic, indeed radical change in recruitment finally came, but Virginia and the Confederacy had waited far too long; the war was already lost.

The governor also pushed other sweeping changes during his administration. He early advocated action to control inflation, but the legislature delayed, and the Confederates also failed to restrain the soaring prices that were undermining the Southern economy. After the legislature rejected one of his specific appropriations, the governor tapped his own contingency funds and borrowed more money from a Richmond bank to finance the operation of his state supply system to ease some extreme shortages. A few scarce items began to come in from abroad and from the Deep South, but again it was too little too late as the economy continued to disintegrate.

Early in his administration Governor Smith did gain one large appropriation from the legislature to combat the clothing shortage. He set up a new bureaucracy to obtain cotton and cotton cards to sell to the people at reasonable prices, and he even talked the Confederates into handing over a mill where cotton cloth could be cheaply manufactured. But such stopgap measures could not halt the accelerating decline of Virginia and the Confederacy.

Throughout his administration of slightly more than fifteen months, Governor Smith's best efforts made much sense. He selflessly cooperated with the Confederate central government, convinced that this was the only possible way to win the war against the huge Federal military forces that threatened Virginia on several fronts. But the tide had turned too powerfully against the South. Like Davis and Lee, Smith might delay defeat, but he could not gain victory.

In the last year of the war Union armies knifed deeper and deeper into Virginia's vitals, and finally on April 1, 1865, troops under Ulysses S. Grant overran Lee's massive defenses at Petersburg. On April 3 Smith fled from Richmond just one step ahead of Federal troops. He and a pathetic remnant of the state government fled to Lynchburg and then farther west to Danville. Smith thought about fighting on after Lee surrendered on April 9. He unsuccessfully tried to take command of all remaining Confederate forces in the state and even considered guerrilla warfare. But he soon saw that his people had had enough, and on June 8 he surrendered to Federal officials in Richmond. Five days later he went home to Warrenton and the following month received a pardon from President Andrew Johnson.

Still healthy at sixty-seven, Smith farmed for a living. He remained active in politics and in the mid-1870s served again in the state legislature. On May 18, 1887, he died at home just short of his ninetieth birthday.

BIBLIOGRAPHY

Bell, John W. *Memoirs of Governor William Smith of Virginia: His Political, Military and Personal History.* New York, 1891.

Boney, F. N. "Virginia." In *The Confederate Governors.* Edited by W. Buck Yearns. Athens, Ga., 1985.

Fahrner, Alvin A. "The Public Career of William 'Extra Billy' Smith." Ph.D. diss., University of North Carolina, 1953.

Fahrner, Alvin A. "William ('Extra Billy') Smith: Governor in Two Wars." In *The Governors of Virginia, 1860–1978.* Edited by Edward Younger and James Tice Moore. Charlottesville, Va., 1982.

Fahrner, Alvin A. "William 'Extra Billy' Smith, Governor of Virginia, 1864–1865: A Pillar of the Confederacy." *Virginia Magazine of History and Biography* 74 (1966): 68–87.

F. N. BONEY

SMITH, WILLIAM RUSSELL

SMITH, WILLIAM RUSSELL (1815–1896), colonel and congressman from Alabama. Smith was born in Russellville, Logan County, Kentucky, on March 27, 1815. After his father died in 1817, his mother moved the family to Alabama. When she too died in 1823, Smith, his sister, and his brother were distributed among several Tuscaloosa families to be reared, but Smith soon ran away to be with his brother. After his sister married, he went to work in his brother-in-law's tailor shop.

While still a young man, Smith attracted the attention of George W. Crabb, a prominent citizen. Realizing that Smith was above average in ability, Crabb loaned him money to attend preparatory schools. Smith studied at the University of Alabama from 1831 until 1834, when he ran short of funds and withdrew to read law in Crabb's law office. A year later he was admitted to the Alabama bar and in 1835 opened a practice at Greensboro, Alabama. He became popular in Alabama society, often dressing like a Spanish cavalier, complete with cloak.

When the Creek War broke out in Alabama in 1836, Smith raised a company of mounted infantry, which he commanded as a captain. Smith's Alabama volunteers arrived in the Creek territory too late to take part in the fighting. When he heard of the death of his brother, who had been fighting for the independence of Texas, Smith persuaded his men to follow him to Texas and join the fight. Smith learned of the Texan victory at San Jacinto before his men could reach Texas, however, and the troops disbanded at Mobile.

Smith remained in Mobile for about six months in 1836 and 1837 to edit *The Bachelor's Button: A Monthly Museum of Southern Literature.* Although the periodical was unsuccessful, it marked the beginning of Smith's career as a prolific writer. He published many volumes of poetry, plays, essays, and legal studies over the years. Proud of his literary accomplishments, he was the only member of the Confederate Congress to list his vocation as "writer."

After returning to Tuscaloosa in 1838, Smith resumed his law practice and became active in Alabama Whig politics. He was elected mayor of Tuscaloosa in 1839 and won a seat in the Alabama General Assembly in 1841 and 1842. He fell out with the Whig leadership over policy and left the party in 1843.

Smith then moved to Fayette County, where in 1850 he was elected judge of the Seventh Circuit and a general of militia. He returned to Tuscaloosa that same year and was elected to the U.S. House of Representatives. He resigned his judgeship to assume his seat in Congress.

Smith was reelected in 1852 on a Union Democrat ticket. As a Unionist, he denied the constitutional right of secession but refused to comment on it as a "sovereign" right. In 1854, he joined the American (Know-Nothing) party, and voters returned him to Congress a third time. Later, he became disenchanted with the Know-Nothing party's anti-Catholic and nativist sentiments and split with its leaders.

As a congressman in the 1850s, Smith was opposed to Southern secession and in 1856 declared that "the union of the states is a political indestructibility." His viewpoint was so well received that there was talk of nominating him for vice president in the 1856 election. He lost his bid for a fourth congressional term that same year, however.

During the 1860 presidential election, Smith campaigned for John Bell and the Constitutional Union party. Afterward he was chosen as a delegate to the Alabama secession convention which convened in Montgomery on January 4, 1861. There he espoused Unionism and was characterized as a cooperationist who sought to secure state rights within the Union, and failing that, to maintain them outside the Union. To Smith, allegiance to the state was paramount. Although he refused to sign the ordinance of secession, once it was approved he declared his loyalty to Alabama. Smith's book *History and Debates of the Convention of the People of Alabama . . .,* which was published in 1861, is a principal source for the events that occurred during the Alabama secession convention.

After secession, Smith helped raise the Sixth Alabama Infantry Regiment at Tuscombia in May, and when it was redesignated the Twenty-sixth Alabama, he was elected its colonel. He accompanied the troops to the training camp, but resigned his commission after being elected to the Confederate House of Representatives. Upon taking his seat, Smith was assigned to the Printing Committee, the Flag and Seal Committee, the Foreign Relations Committee, and several special committees. As a member of the Committee on Foreign Relations, Smith opposed reopening the African slave trade, arguing that there were sufficient slaves in the South to fill current needs and that reopening the trade would give credibility to those who said that that had been the main reason for secession.

While in Congress, Smith often found himself at odds with the policies of President Jefferson Davis. He opposed numerous executive appointments as well as many of the administration's tax, commerce, and international relations programs. He supported a ban on hiring slaves to work for the Confederate army and opposed any effort to curtail free trade. He bitterly fought legislation first enacted on February 27, 1862, empowering the president to suspend the writ of habeas corpus and to declare martial law. He also opposed the enactment of conscription legislation.

Smith was reelected to Congress in 1863, but because of his opposition to Davis's administration and his earlier Unionist views, he was not well received by his fellow congressmen. As a result he did not regularly attend sessions. In February 1865 he stopped going altogether when the House of Representatives refused to pass a resolution condemning the *Richmond Sentinel's* editorial calling any movement for a negotiated peace "treason."

After the war, Smith practiced law in Fayette County and reentered politics, unsuccessfully running for governor in November 1865. In 1870 he was chosen to be the president

of the University of Alabama by the Radical Republicans controlling the state government. The university had ceased operations during the war, and when classes resumed in 1865, only one student applied for admission. In the next three years efforts were made to rejuvenate the institution, rebuild its facilities, and replace its equipment. The university reopened in 1868, but because its faculty and president were carpetbaggers, few Southern students entered. The Radical Republicans thus turned to Smith in 1870 in the hope of generating support for the school among Alabama citizens. As a Unionist before the war, but a supporter of the Confederacy after secession, he appeared to be the ideal compromise candidate. In addition, his literary background qualified him as an educator. Unfortunately, Smith faced intractable problems in revitalizing the university, including a continued paucity of students. During his tenure as president only ten students enrolled, and four of them were sons of professors. In addition the Ku Klux Klan became active on campus, and by the time Smith resigned as president in July 1871 there were no students remaining in class.

Smith made one final attempt to reenter politics, seeking election to the U.S. House of Representatives in 1878, but was defeated. He continued to practice law in Tuscaloosa until 1879 when he moved his practice to Washington, D.C. He died there on February 26, 1896, and was buried in Tuscaloosa.

BIBLIOGRAPHY

Brewer, W. *Alabama: Her History, Resources, War Record, and Public Men from 1540 to 1872.* Montgomery, Ala., 1872.

Easley-Smith, Mildred. *William Russell Smith of Alabama: His Life and Works Including the Entire Text of "The Uses of Solitude."* Philadelphia, 1931.

Fleming, Walter L. *Civil War and Reconstruction in Alabama.* New York, 1905.

Garrett, William. *Reminiscences of Public Men in Alabama.* Atlanta, 1872.

Moore, Albert Burton. *History of Alabama and Her People.* New York, 1927.

Pickett, Albert J. *History of Alabama and Incidentally of Georgia and Mississippi from the Earliest Period.* Birmingham, Ala., 1900.

Smith, William Russell. *History and Debates of the Convention of the People of Alabama, Begun and Held in the City of Montgomery, on the Seventh Day of January, 1861; in Which Is Preserved the Speeches of the Secret Sessions and Many Valuable State Papers, 1861.* Montgomery and Atlanta, 1861.

PAUL F. LAMBERT

SOCIETY

Tales of military drama dominate the historiography of the Civil War. Only recently have historians shifted their perspective away from the sacrifices on the battlefield and toward the effects of the war on society.

To evaluate Confederate society, one has to question whether it existed as a viable society at all. Many see it as essentially antebellum Southern society in crisis and, thus, a society that was really only changed by the processes of conquest and Reconstruction. Yet the Confederacy itself changed social relations in the South as it geared to fight a war of survival. The desire to preserve a way of life that precluded change was strong enough to wage war over, but paradoxically the war itself forced change upon that way of life.

Early in the Confederacy, white social unity generally prevailed, but as the war continued many white Southernors came to feel that their society had failed them. The societal changes on the home front are fundamental to an understanding of the nature of Confederate society. In the midst of wartime dislocation, the contrasting lifestyles of the planter-lawyer "aristocrats" and the common folks were at the heart of the divisions in the society. Furthermore, black and white relationships changed radically once the war began.

Although the antebellum South is usually considered a homogeneous region, an increasing number of regional and local studies suggest significant differences within the South. Moreover, themes discussed in this essay—planters and aristocracy, poor whites, yeomen, and plain folk, the business and professional classes, slaves and free blacks, and the impact of the war on class unity and class conflict—may or may not be peculiar to the South. How one views these issues depends largely on the interpretation one has of antebellum Southern society.

A young up-country white South Carolinian precisely defined the ramifications of what his society meant to him as he marched off to war: "I go first for Greenville, then for Greenville District, then for the up-country, then for South Carolina, then for the South, then for the United States, and after that I don't go for anything." First and foremost, Southerners understood the unfolding drama through the lens of their own local society. But those societies varied enormously. The aggregate of communities that came together to form the Confederacy were far from a monolith.

Demographics

In 1860, 60 percent of all Southerners were free, but significant deviations existed among the eleven states that would form the Confederacy. In South Carolina 57.2 percent of its population was composed of slaves and in Mississippi, 55.2 percent. Border states had much lower percentages of slave populations; in Arkansas, only a fourth of its population was composed of slaves. Free blacks lived mostly in the northern border regions of the Confederacy, with two-thirds of them in Virginia and North Carolina. Most of the free blacks in Louisiana, the other state with a significant free African

American population (18,647), were located in New Orleans (10,689).

The Confederacy was overwhelmingly rural, with only one large city of over 50,000—New Orleans. Cities contained proportionately fewer African Americans than did the Confederacy at large. The black population (free and slave) was disproportionately female in the urban areas. In the Confederacy in general, as in most settled areas, the male-to-female ratio was roughly equal among both black and white. Indicative of a lack of urban industrial centers, relatively few people (37,303) lived in single-member households. Since much of the agricultural labor was provided by slaves, a single white farm laborer had fewer job opportuni-

> ... many white Southernors came to feel that their society had failed them.

ties in the South. The average free household size of 5.6 members was consistent for most states, North and South, and included boarders.

If household and family size was consistent across the Confederacy, the size of farms was not. Overall, the distribution of farm sizes was fairly wide (see table 1). Half of the farms in the Confederate states, 54.4 percent, fell into the small-farm category of twenty to one hundred acres. Less than 1 percent (4,275) of farms fell in the largest category of a thousand or more acres. The census designations for farms of three acres or more do not distinguish between people who owned farms and those who were tenant farm operators, but some evidence suggests that the number of white tenant farmers and landless laborers was increasing in certain areas of the South on the eve of the Civil War. Moreover, many wealthy white Southerners owned several farms or plantations, each of which would be listed individually. In some cases, people in the same households were operating separate farms. Thus, the proportion of householders who were farming three or more acres was overestimated, but it could not have been more than 48 percent. While some of these were town and urban dwellers (professionals and artisans), many Southern whites were landless in a society where land and slaves defined social status.

The distribution of slaveholders by the number of slaves owned (see table 2) correlates with the size of farms. Approximately 25 percent of Southern free families were slaveholders; probably more than three-fourths of all white Southerners lived in nonslaveholding households. Of some 306,300 slaveholders, more than 45 percent held less than five slaves and 85 percent held less than twenty, the number usually considered enough for the owner to be categorized as a planter. "Planter" and "slave owner" were by no means synonymous. Moreover, as with the size of farms, great deviations existed among the Confederate states and within each state. Most slaveholders in Tennessee, Texas, and Arkansas had very few slaves; Alabama (17.9 percent), Mississippi (18.6 percent), and South Carolina (19.9 percent) had the largest share of owners of more than twenty slaves.

These regional differences in slave ownership and size of slaveholdings assumed class overtones with secession. Opposition to secession was strongest in nonslaveholding areas; only after the firing on Fort Sumter did many of these regions take the remarkable step of leaving the Union. Some areas never did, and some Southern whites took an even more extreme position: 100,000 whites from the Confederate states fought for the Union. When one combines that figure with the number of African Americans from the Confederate states who fought for the Union, the term *Civil War* takes on added significance. It was indeed a war between fellow citizens of a nation.

Slavery and Free Blacks in the South

Some historians view secession as a rational act on the part of capitalists to protect their investments; some argue that secession was an act of people determined to preserve their nonbourgeois way of life; others contend that Southern whites were attempting to preserve their republican values as they understood them; and still others assert that extremists whipped citizens into a racist terror. All major historians agree, however, that the Confederacy left the Union between 1860 and 1865 to preserve slavery. "Slavery informs all our modes of life, all our habits of thought, lies at the basis of our social existence, and of our political faith," explained an important South Carolina politico and planter. No less an authority on the war than Robert E. Lee understood that the South was fighting for its society and that slavery was its fundamental underpinning. In 1859, Robert M. T. Hunter argued in Congress that the United States was like an arch "and the very keystone of this arch consists of the black marble cap of African slavery; knock that out, and the mighty fabric, with all that it upholds, topples and tumbles to its fall." Alexander H. Stephens, soon after his inauguration as vice president of the Confederacy, explained that slavery "was the immediate cause of the late rupture and present revolution." Stephens said that "slavery, subordination to the superior race, is his [the African American's] natural and moral condition." Northerners had rejected slavery and now "the stone which was rejected by the first builders is become the chief stone of the corner." Slavery was the cornerstone of the Confederacy.

Table 3 ranks the slave states in the order of their date of secession from the Union and includes the proportion of the population that was slave and African American. A nearly perfect correlation exists between the proportion of blacks and the date of leaving the Union. The six states with more than 44 percent of their population black left in the first wave

of secession between December 20, 1860, and January 26, 1861. The next five states with an average black population of about 31 percent seceded between February 1 and May 11, 1861. The four slave states with less than a quarter of their population black never seceded. It is apparent what a large part slavery and race played in a state's decision to leave the Union.

Slavery shaped the nature of Southern society; even its few cities and industries were structurally influenced by plantation slavery. White Southerners' liberty and the institution of slavery were linked in their cultural understanding. White Confederates initially believed that slavery would allow more white men to enter the army, for slaves would cultivate the crops and man the industries on the home front. Slaves would also release white soldiers for fighting. Impressed into the army as laborers, they would build fortifications and perform other menial tasks, including cooking and cleaning.

But not all blacks in the South were slaves; a small proportion of them was composed of free African Americans. Some were the descendants of slaves who had gained their freedom during the colonial era. Others had been freed during a brief period of liberalization inspired by the American Revolution. In addition, many light-skinned "free people of color" immigrated to the United States despite bans on what were called "French Negroes." And some antebellum free African Americans derived from the manumission of mulatto children, usually the result of unions between masters and their slave mistresses.

In 1860 about 4.5 million people in the United States were African Americans; 11 percent of them were free blacks, of whom half lived in the North and half in the South. Most free blacks lived in urban areas. They formed associations, such as the Brown Fellowship Society of Charleston, founded urban black churches, and published their own newspapers. Free black artisans lived both in the city and in rural areas. Prosperous free blacks provided a model for former slaves building new lives after emancipation. Of those who lived in rural areas, the more economically secure they were, the more likely they resided among white men and women of equal economic status. Some antebellum African Americans owned land and even slaves. A few were antebellum tenant farmers, but most rural free blacks were farm laborers living in poverty.

In certain locales, census takers classified a person as black, mulatto, or white depending on skin color. Some evidence exists that light-skinned African Americans had some choice in whether they integrated into the white world or were part of the black community. In some rural areas, free black men were as likely to marry white women as free black women. Some may have married slaves, which would not have been recorded.

The story of free blacks in the Civil War is complicated, particularly because free African Americans fought on or helped both sides in the conflict. Their loyalties often depended upon their positions within the local society. Before the war free blacks composed a small minority that was often allowed some leeway by a white society unafraid of their privileges. But during the war the situation was especially bad for free African Americans, for the crisis brought them under close scrutiny. The majority concentrated simply on surviving; indeed, black independent farmers and artisans persevered despite white suspicions.

Some Southern states did not allow antebellum free blacks to enter military service at all, and though early in the war some permitted "colored men" to muster into local or state militia units, no Southern state allowed African Americans to serve as regular soldiers. Yet some light-

> ## Yet some light-skinned free blacks became "honorary white men". . . .

skinned free blacks became "honorary white men" and actually enlisted and fought for the Confederacy. Free blacks in cities like New Orleans, Mobile, Savannah, Richmond, and Charleston joined such services as fire companies or were impressed into labor battalions (as were the slaves) to dig ditches and perform other manual labor. Their families, however, generally were not eligible for even the meager aid furnished to whites by state and local governments.

The war changed the nature of race relations, and even slavery itself changed. As white men left communities to go off with the army, the racial balance of power shifted dramatically in rural areas and on plantations. Fear of slave insurrections pervaded white Confederate society, although in many areas slaves were able to negotiate more freedom and autonomy for themselves and their families as the war continued.

The extent of the changed nature of race relations and slavery can be seen in the last desperate acts of Jefferson Davis. He offered to emancipate slaves in order to obtain recognition and aid from France and England. With the support of Robert E. Lee, Davis also persuaded Congress to arm slaves as Confederate soldiers. Ultimately, of course, the Civil War ended slavery, which constituted the greatest change in Southern society.

Gender Roles in the South

The antebellum South was a society founded upon patriarchy, hierarchy, and tradition. Rich and poor shared these values. A man was patriarch of his home, his family, and his slaves if he had any, and this might be complemented by his dominant position in the local community, the county, the state, or the nation. Patriarchy was pervasive throughout Southern society from the smallest unit, the family, to the largest, the nation. Male domination was cemented by tradition and most of all by community, by familial and organic bonds between rich and poor whites, all knitted together by the racial fears of the consequences of white disunity.

Patriarchy was by definition reciprocal: white men enjoyed the privileges of domination, but they also had the duty to protect slaves, wives, children, kin, and community. Thus the Civil War was about the defense of all that was dear—family, home town, plantation, community, and society.

The role of white women in Southern society cut across class lines. Whether charwoman or chatelaine, the woman was first of all mother, homemaker, and partner in the family economy. Women of all social classes usually bore many children. When a woman was not confined to bed in pregnancy or childbirth, she was responsible for all domestic chores. Of course, her social standing dictated her day-to-day routines. Most women were active partners in the running of plantation, farm, or business. They were administrators and supervisors of complex and busy households. Occasionally a woman was able to show business ability in a man's world, and there are success stories of women paying off their husband's debts and bringing their family through tough financial times.

Prior to the Civil War, white women had no official role in Southern society outside of the family. Within church structures, for instance, they held no leadership positions; they were, however, a powerful force in ensuring the participation of their families, both immediate and extended. Except for church functions, quilting parties, and the like, however, women had few opportunities to gather in rural antebellum society.

This changed during the life of the Confederacy. Whereas white women had expected that in return for wifely devotion and subservience they would receive from the men protection for their families, now they had to fend for themselves, trying to obtain food and supplies and making family decisions. Slaveholding women were fortunate in that they still had slaves for manual labor, but there was now the additional responsibility of controlling and disciplining them, a task that had always been men's work. Southern women had supported patriarchal society before the war, and they blamed the men now for the failure to defend the home against invaders or to provide necessities for the family. Even upper-class Southern women felt betrayed by their husbands, who had abandoned them to unfamiliar plantation duties. They felt that they had upheld their role in the patriarchal social system, but the men had not.

The war necessarily changed the role of women and therefore had a significant impact upon society itself. During the war, women met to sew uniforms, knit socks, pack supplies, and roll bandages. Soldiers' Relief Associations throughout the South included some on boards of directors.

With so many men away at war, the number of women relative to the number of men increased, and so did their influence. They found that the exigencies of the war enabled them to make a more substantial contribution to family and community life than they had previously had the opportunity to make. Women ran their farms, businesses, and communities with increasing confidence as the war progressed.

In both North and South women formed a spate of aid associations to raise funds for their local militias. A lasting legacy of these societies was the continued church and community clubs such as the Woman's Christian Temperance Union, missionary societies, library associations, and other voluntary groups. The war increased women's interest in politics as well as their political acumen. At this time some white women envisioned a broader, more active position for themselves in social and political life. But though private diaries demonstrate that women often took pride in their newfound abilities and assertiveness, society as a whole expected women in the postbellum years to return to their old roles in the social order.

The teaching profession did not revert to the prewar situation, offering increased opportunity for women. During the Confederacy women's schools and seminaries were able to stay open, although by 1862 most colleges were closed. Nevertheless, some teaching positions remained, and as men went to war, educated women filled those vacancies. An ideology that the female teacher was a surrogate mother who eased the transition of the child from the home to the community developed and solidified during the war.

The Civil War also opened vocational opportunities in nursing, government agencies, and industry, as women took over traditional male jobs. Prior to the war, only young, unmarried women worked in Southern textile mills, but now adult women joined them, adding to the family income. Thus, to a certain extent, the Confederacy undermined patriarchy.

But after the war the patriarchal system rapidly returned, and most of the new vocational opportunities vanished. Only teaching remained, but the number of applications for teaching was much greater than the number of positions, and the pay was inadequate. The activities of Southern women focused on survival and delayed the reordering of gender roles that was occurring in the North.

Class in the South

Relations among the various classes in the South changed dramatically during the Civil War. Historians have tended to agree that underlying class frictions were kept in check in antebellum Southern society, but that those frictions surfaced when subjected to the pressures of the war. Scholars have never accepted the popular myth of an easy-to-categorize "solid" South. Its society was complex and varied with the region. For the most part, the culture was not dictated by planters, nor was it determined by harmonious communities of yeomen. Unlike New England settlements, Southern locales never had an overarching ideology that defined society. The meaning of each community developed from its everyday behavior, social rituals, and shared experiences. Nevertheless, Southern society exhibited some intriguing similarities among rich and poor whites, free African Americans and slaves. Without exception, the society revered the family, maintaining kinship networks and promoting religious beliefs that glorified domestic life. Both rich and poor connected family values with a sense of personal and regional honor.

Social relationships shaped Southern culture by ordered divisions of domination and subordination: white over black, male over female, wealthy over poor, respected lineage over obscure ancestry, women perceived as "virtuous" over those perceived as "loose," education over illiteracy, age over youth. All whites—men and women—had a societal claim for respect from blacks and from each other. Although wealthy men were at the top of the social ladder, they were expected not to look down on a poorer white man but to play a friendly, paternalistic role. The South's famed diarist Mary Boykin Chesnut provides a delightful vignette of Southern aristocrats paying homage to a muddied, barefoot well-digger.

Face-to-face interactions formed the style of Southern exchange. The poor, the yeoman middle class, and the rich were tied to one another in a multifaceted social network of obligations, trade, and exchanges of labor and services. In agrarian areas people knew and trusted one another; one's word was one's bond. Although in the very few Southern cities, one could find segregation by ethnicity and wealth, in rural towns and the country, whites were not segregated by occupation or income. The landless lived next door to landowning elites and had reciprocal community obligations. The poor often worked for the rich, and small farmers frequently depended upon the help of large planters in getting cotton ginned and to market. Across class lines, families and

> **Face-to-face interactions formed the style of Southern exchange.**

neighbors got together for cornshuckings, birthday parties, fairs, fish fries, revivals, and prayer meetings. Funerals also brought the community together. Whether in a grand mansion, a log house, or a slave cabin, kin, friends, neighbors, and church members supported one another in times of grief and reinforced the bonds of society.

Kinship ties influenced all segments of the society. Not only did relatives help one another, but people kept close track of each other even when separated by considerable distances, as when family members or acquaintances moved away. Mississippians subscribed to the newspaper of the community from which they had migrated, and letters and visits reinforced ties. Migration patterns often reflected kinship and community. The concept of community extending beyond geographical boundaries was not limited to any one class.

Since nearly everyone farmed, rich and poor alike shared similar concerns about the weather, crop prices, and so on. Neighbors belonged to the same kin networks and the same churches. Because so much of the power in the South was exercised on the plantation, governmental power and social services were limited; the great planters were generally content to let their poorer neighbors live their own lives and manage their own economic and political affairs. The overwhelmingly agricultural plantation South fostered an extremely decentralized system. Thus, instead of the conflicting economic and social interests that developed in Northern society, most social conflict in the South occurred in terms of personal ambitions and personality.

White Southerners' ideas of liberty, linked closely to race and slavery, also diluted class conflict in the South. Freedom depended on personal independence and the wherewithal to take care of one's family. Tragically, even nonslaveholding whites believed that freedom depended on the subjugation of African Americans, and almost all whites were united in racism toward blacks. In 1848 John C. Calhoun characterized the lack of class conflict this way: "With us the two great divisions of society are not the rich and the poor, but white and black; and all the former, the poor as well as the rich, belong to the upper class, and are respected and treated as equals." Slavery was a powerful symbol of degradation, which white yeomen contrasted with their own independence. A society where no one could voice disapproval of slavery demanded community consensus.

Poor Whites. Although groups were not precisely demarcated, white social classes in Confederate society fell into roughly three categories with varying dimensions within each. The line between the poor and the yeomen, for instance, was never very distinct. The poor were landless in an agrarian society that honored landowners. Landless whites accounted for between 25 and 40 percent of the white population. The dividing line between destitution and "respectable" poverty was drawn by different people at different levels. Although some members of white Southern society prejudicially conceived of the white poor as 'ignorant and lazy,' the poor actually shared the values of the larger white society. Some white poor were related to yeomen, and a few to the wealthy. Some actually moved up the social ladder into the ranks of the more prosperous, and some of the more affluent slid from prosperity into the ranks of the poor.

The poor could work as laborers on someone else's farm or could be overseers of someone else's slaves. A small Southern proletariat worked in the few urban areas. Some were employed in antebellum textile mills and lived in segregated mill villages. Fathers usually received all the wages that wives and children made working at the mill. Mill families, like the country people from whom they came, looked to religion as a way of life. As the Civil War progressed, both urban areas and the size of the working class grew. Workers toiled as railroad laborers, sawmill hands, or factory operatives.

Among the very poorest were the inhabitants of poorhouses. These included the blind, deformed, afflicted, epileptic, crippled, and mentally disabled. Southern society did not do much for these people, but they were housed and fed.

The Middle Class and Yeomen. "Middle class" usually connotes merchants and professionals or the bourgeoisie in urban areas. Confederate society had an urban middle class, but it was small. While Northern society industrialized, most people in the South continued to farm. In 1860, less than 10 percent of Southerners lived in urban areas, compared to 25 percent of Northerners. Although within the agrarian South were some commercial-mercantile centers such as Charleston and Richmond, the white labor force remained 80 percent agricultural in the first half of the 1800s. (In the North the labor force changed from 70 percent agricultural to 40 percent.) The South had 15,000 factories with 0.1 million industrial workers. Without cities, Southern society lacked a dynamic urban middle class. The South had no need for the middle-class insurance salesmen, financial agents, and corporate executives whom the North needed for industrialization. The South required only cotton factors to represent the interests of the slaveholding planters.

Although most professional opportunities were in short supply in the agrarian South, attorneys abounded. The legal profession was one of those avenues in the three to four decades preceding the Civil War that white Southern men used for upward mobility. In 1824, noted South Carolinian William Preston had explained, "The object of a Southern man's life is politics and to this end we all practice law." Doctors also pursued their profession as a springboard into the elite.

The middle class also included schoolteachers and preachers. The latter expanded their roles in Confederate society. Using moral positions to support "the cause," the clergy became vitally important in forging a nationalistic perspective in the Confederacy. At this time Southern preachers also became more professionalized.

For the most part, the middle class was not part of an urban class, but consisted of yeoman farmers. Historian Frank Owsley has called the yeomen the plain folk of the South. Unlike the large planters, nonslaveholding yeomen were more interested in self-sufficiency than in profit. They were staunch believers in family honor, which included patriotism and religion; they tended to be more evangelical than the elite. In contrast to historical stereotypes, the Southern yeoman considered hard work a point of honor. Yeomen were for the most part nonslaveholders. Yet slavery permitted the yeomen a certain degree of independence, as each white male presided over his household and farm.

The Civil War had a major impact on the development of the middle class. As Southern industry expanded to meet the demand for war goods and city populations swelled, business responded. A need for housing stimulated construction, and companies earned huge profits in textiles and the iron industry. Thus, the formation of the Confederacy and the war encouraged the growth of an urban middle class.

The Elite. Ultimately, success in Confederate society meant membership in the landholding elite with wealth invested in slaves. Some have argued that slavery made possible an aristocracy that dominated society and its values and condemned the South to backwardness. The elite is as difficult to define in Confederate society as it is today. It was a continuum rather than a category, and one felt rather than articulated its meaning. It was a recruited aristocracy, and its status was based more on wealth than on kinship and breeding, although the latter two factors played a role. It was not a unified community, but comprised varying economic levels and old- and new-rich factions. Its ranks included planters and those who had worked themselves up from the professions: attorneys, doctors, newspaper editors, political officeholders. Patriciate clans of interlocking kin networks formed political alliances, and the elite controlled newspapers. Military service was another route into the elite, and when war broke out, the ambitious rushed to join the army and take advantage of the opportunity for glory and advancement.

Owners of large slaveholdings composed a unique class that was reared to command and manage large agricultural enterprises. They were inculcated from birth with notions of honor, duty, manliness, and paternalism; duels were part of their way of life.

Social Mobility. Although upward mobility was possible in antebellum society, it was more difficult to become a great planter in the South than to become a great merchant in the North. In the South, one needed both land and slaves. By the time of the American Revolution, only a tenth of Virginia's great planters were self-made men, whereas a third of all Boston merchants were self-made, and that increased to 60 or 70 percent after the Revolution. The South's society was much more unequal than the North's. In the rural South the population was never dense enough or the economy complex enough to require innovative leadership. Democratic forms or institutions might be introduced into government, but community leaders continued to come from slaveholding classes.

Education was a means of social advancement, but in the rural South, where reliable literate workers were rarely in demand, public education was a low priority. The planter elite hired private tutors for their own children and enrolled them in the best academies and colleges (some in the North).

Wealthy sons and daughters continued their private education throughout the Civil War. The elite, however, either ignored the campaigns of poorer whites for public schools or actively opposed them, fearing that education would only promote new yearnings for upward mobility and blur the distinction between themselves and the masses. In the South, about 58 percent of the population was literate. Among whites and free blacks, the figure was 83 percent; among slaves, about 10 percent.

Social mobility was not easy in antebellum society, but it was possible. Free blacks could not move up or down the social ladder in the larger community, but they could within their own communities.

Class Conflict during the War

Why class tensions did not convulse antebellum white society is a subject of much historiographical debate. Although the economy and the social structure helped mute class conflict, discrepancies in wealth among whites pointed to the existence of class interests. The conduct of the Civil War brought these interests to the fore.

Even within the white consensus, class conflicts occasionally occurred, however, and antagonisms erupted during political campaigns. Yeomen tended to be suspicious of people who did not work by the sweat of their brow, lawyers in particular. The antebellum temperance movement focused on the habits of the poor. The middle class and yeomen resented the fact that education was a prerogative of the rich.

Yet with the first call to support a war for Southern independence, white people interpreted the meaning of the conflict from the perspective of their own families, friends, and local society. For most, the war was being fought not simply to secure slavery or protect the planters' way of life; it was a matter of honor—a fight to protect community values. Initially, many white Southerners saw the Civil War as a test of manhood; a high percentage of young men from the professions enlisted, as did yeomen who had no slaves and little or no wealth. All, however, had a stake in the community and went to war to preserve it. Men who led in the local community were likely to lead on the battlefield, too; they were considered the natural leaders. Thus, the war initially strengthened society's bonds among Confederate men.

In a society founded upon the notion of patriarchy, the absence of large numbers of men created a vacuum of power that would prove problematic. Local communities complained about the scarcity of doctors and, even more, about the lack of skilled craftsmen, such as blacksmiths, tanners, wheelwrights, and carpenters. Food shortages developed quickly, with men not home to plant crops.

At first, the society responded in traditional ways to the needs of families whose menfolk were away at the front. As in the past, kin helped kin in times of want, and the richer helped the poorer. Slaveholding families who retained their labor force of slaves could afford to be generous. But gradually the Confederacy put new demands upon richer citizens. Taxes were increased, slaves were impressed into government service, and the administration sequestered planters' cotton. Many of the rich could no longer provide for the community as they had before, and other wealthy families chose not to.

This breakdown of noblesse oblige led to increasing resentment between classes. Elite women resented queuing in food lines alongside poorer women and tired of the constant stream to their homes of beggars whom they could no longer help. The problem had more serious repercussions for the yeoman class. Poverty became a reality for many for the first time. Yeomen lost their self-sufficiency and with it their social autonomy. They blamed the war, the Confederate government, and, increasingly, their richer neighbors.

Yeomen noticed how easily the rich got exemptions from fighting or acquired safe army jobs behind the lines. Planters justified their exemptions in patriotic terms, proclaiming the importance of aiding the Southern economy. But many of them were growing cotton, not food, and to yeomen and poor whites it appeared that the elite were reneging on their responsibilities of leadership. In turn, these poorer men questioned their previous deference to the elite and began to doubt their reasons for fighting.

Class conflict exploded when the Confederate government failed to provide adequate relief for its citizens and thus to retain their support when it was needed most. For the common people the key element in their discontent was increased economic hardship. Soldiers' income was inadequate, and often they were not paid for months on end. Although prices were initially lowered, they soon became exorbitant. Compounding the difficulties for the South were its comparatively few resources, the fact that most of the fighting took place on its soil, and the increasing effectiveness of the Union blockade. Almost from the beginning there were shortages of foodstuffs, clothing, footwear, medicines, and other necessary items. People resorted to a barter system rather than using the inflated currency. After the destruction of its railroads, the Confederacy increasingly was unable to distribute farm products. The situation was hardest on urban dwellers and the yeomen but, typically, the poorest suffered the worst.

Two hundred fifty thousand Southern refugees compounded the dislocations. Refugees formed a cross-section of society with members of the elite joining the migrations. Most of the aristocrats resented hobnobbing with what they considered to be their social inferiors, and yeoman hosts resented these snobbish guests. Most refugees fled to cities, and Richmond, for one, doubled in size the first year of the Confederacy and, during the remainder of the war, tripled in population. This enormous movement of people necessarily shook society. The flow of refugees produced a new mix of people, altering local societies and making them more cosmopolitan.

But in the midst of want, not everyone suffered. Blockade runners accumulated huge personal fortunes and sometimes even became heroes. Yet, at a time when people were desperate for food, clothes, guns, and ammunition, blockade runners brought in cargoes of needles and pins, buttons and bows. Graft, corruption, and extortion were common in both the North and the South. Some amassed fortunes through speculation, particularly in land. A very few wealthy planters even made money during the war by investing in Northern railroads and other enterprises. Shortages encouraged hoarding and greed. On an individual level, blockade runners, speculators, and merchants were depicted as pariahs and often condemned as outsiders. Yet there was an ambivalent attitude toward such individuals, and many ordinary people were pleased to associate with them as they never would have in the stable prewar social order.

Popular discontent was evident as early as 1861. From Georgia a citizen wrote an open letter:

Is it right that the poor man should be taxed for the support of the war, when the war was brought about on the slave question, and the slave at home accumulating for the benefit of this master, and the poor man's farm left uncultivated, and a chance for his wife to be a widow, and his children orphans?

The Twenty-Slave Law passed in October 1862 ripped the fabric of white Confederate society. This law allowed the exemption from military service of one white man for every twenty slaves. The law affected only a small number of people, but it was a powerful symbol for the common folk that the war benefited the rich at the expense of the poor. The Twenty-Slave Law was enacted in response to the perceived dangers of slave insurrection in the light of Lincoln's Emancipation Proclamation, but common soldiers and their families saw only that "we poor soldiers . . . are fighting for the 'rich man's negro.'" Southern men resisted conscription at rates that increased dramatically until by 1865 desertion had become epidemic. A hundred thousand Confederates—one out of seven who were inducted into the army—went AWOL at one time or another.

When the war came home to society, some Confederates were more dedicated than others. In local communities, where the war caused a lower standard of living for all, folks noticed who sacrificed the most. Some of the wealthy continued to live well; for them, sacrifice meant giving up some luxuries. For yeomen and the poor, sacrifice meant doing without necessities, and they were galled by the disparity.

The war also intensified class conflict by reserving certain special perquisites for members of the planter class. In North and South huge resentment resulted when the wealthy used the legal and political processes to their own advantage.

Yeomen believed conscription was unfair, a burden that fell most heavily on nonslaveholders since they had to work their own farms without the help of slaves. The rich man's ability to hire a paid substitute if he was drafted aroused great popular discontent. Upper-class women who needed jobs used their connections to obtain positions as scribes and clerks in the Confederate government. Taxes to support the war were not equitable, and initially slaves, although considered property, were not taxed.

Inflation and shortages hit the poor much harder than planters, but measures to fight inflation and price gouging were unsuccessful. Provisions to take care of the wives of soldiers were not adequate. When the noblesse oblige of the planter class failed to support them, yeoman women begged for government relief. Desperate letters to the Confederate government spoke of hunger, high prices, and shortages. By mid-1862, survival outranked patriotism as a motivating factor in the South. Some women took revolutionary action and broke into stores demanding food at fair prices in bread riots in Richmond, Augusta, and other cities.

In the midst of hard times, any revelry, a banquet, or the purchase of a fashionable Parisian gown to lift upper-class spirits bordered on treason from the yeoman perspective. On April 4, 1865, as the Confederacy neared its final days, Robert Collins, the son of a wealthy Mississippi cotton planter, married Kate Watts, daughter of the governor of Alabama. Matching bay horses with silver-plated harnesses carried the newlyweds in a luxurious carriage. The bride wore a satin gown that had been brought through the blockade at the expense of food, clothing, weapons, or medicine—this at a time when ordinary Alabamians were desperate. Thousands faced starvation, and near-anarchy reigned. Class antagonism reached a point where large numbers of Southern women came subtly or overtly to war against the war and encouraged their menfolk to desert.

In Alabama internecine warfare broke out between conscription enforcers and people resisting conscription. In parts of Mississippi chaos prevailed. Border areas like Arkansas witnessed merciless bushwhacking and repeated revenge and retaliation. Social order completely collapsed in some areas; in others order was strained but not broken. Late in the war Northern bummers, Union raiders, and Confederate deserters alike roamed the countryside for food, sometimes just destroying wantonly.

A breakdown of civil order followed class lines in Washington County, North Carolina, and social unity declined rapidly as yeoman farmers disagreed with the way planters led recruitment and draft efforts. In June 1862, yeomen with Unionist sympathies combined with tenant farmers and white laborers to confiscate the property of planters who had moved up-country to avoid the Union invasion of the region. Guerrilla war ensued when planters tried to reassert their antebellum level of control. In this area of North Carolina the planter aristocracy had never managed to dominate in either numbers or influence because of geographic and climatic factors that inhibited large-scale plantation farming, and yeoman influence had always remained strong. Now these two groups, who had been united since the 1832 nullification crisis, bitterly split.

In other border states an internal war also threatened to break Confederate control. Dominated by yeoman farmers and poor whites with Union sympathies, guerrilla groups, such as the Heroes of America, were organized. In Piedmont North Carolina, several counties closed their borders against

> **Inflation and shortages hit the poor much harder than planters. . . .**

Confederate recruiting agents. Farmers barricaded themselves into hollows in the mountains. Tennessee, Arkansas, and Alabama had organized guerrilla bands. Even the Deep South suffered a crisis of loyalty. Many Southern communities contained disaffected yeoman families who hid male relatives by day and fed and comforted them by night. In what some scholars have interpreted as episodes of class warfare among whites, some areas of the South broke out in guerrilla fighting. One Confederate judge in South Carolina confessed his joy when the Union army of occupation arrived, thereby ending "the civil war" between Confederate deserters and South Carolina militia.

Open Questions about the Confederacy

How much the Confederacy altered Southern society remains unanswered but speaks to gender, class, and race, as well as to both the Old and the New South. Alone among slaveholders of the world, Southern planters thought their system was worth fighting a war. Although only a small minority of the white population was composed of slaveholders, they were able to persuade ordinary Southerners that they had a stake in keeping black people in bondage. For that the majority paid a heavy price because they supplied most of the troops who died for the Confederacy, and their families bore most of the suffering.

Scholars have yet to establish conclusively the specifics on who sacrificed what, who stayed the entire four years, who fought, who deserted, who managed through political connections to serve in the relatively safe state home guards. Scholars still need to separate out those things that persevered, such as family and landownership, and those that changed, such as black and white Southerners' worldviews. If one sees the New South as *different* from the Old in terms of leadership, ideals, and community, Confederate society may be considered the start of this process of change. If, however, one stresses the *continuity* between the Old South and the New, Confederate society appears an aberration, which is the way it probably seemed to the majority of Southerners at the time. The answer will come as more studies of Confederate society focus on long-term continuity and change. Nevertheless, most scholars would agree that the Civil War certainly unleashed pent-up white class conflict in Southern society and that these tensions remained in postbellum society.

[*See also* African Americans in the Confederacy; Civil War, *articles on* Causes of the War, Causes of Defeat, *and* Losses and Numbers; Class Conflicts; Community Life; Desertion; Education; Family Life; Foreigners; Honor; Indians; Nationalism; Peace Movements; Plain Folk; Planters; Popular Culture; Population; Poverty; Religion; Slavery; Soldiers' Aid Societies; Urbanization; Women.]

BIBLIOGRAPHY

Ash, Stephen A. *Middle Tennessee Society Transformed, 1860–1870: War and Peace in the Upper South.* Baton Rouge, La., 1988.

Auman, William Thomas. "Neighbor against Neighbor: The Inner Civil War in the Central Counties of Confederate North Carolina." Ph.D. diss., University of North Carolina, 1988.

Burton, Orville Vernon. *In My Father's House Are Many Mansions: Family and Community in Edgefield, South Carolina.* Chapel Hill, N.C., 1985.

Campbell, Randolph B. *A Southern Community in Crisis: Harrison County, Texas, 1850–1880.* Austin, Tex., 1983.

Durrill, Wayne K. *War of Another Kind: A Southern Community in the Great Rebellion.* New York, 1990.

Escott, Paul D. *Many Excellent People: Power and Privilege in North Carolina, 1850–1900.* Chapel Hill, N.C., 1985.

Harris, J. William. *Plain Folk and Gentry in a Slave Society: White Liberty and Black Slavery in Augusta's Hinterlands.* Middletown, Conn., 1985.

Kenzer, Robert C. *Kinship and Neighborhood in a Southern Community: Orange County North Carolina, 1849–1881.* Knoxville, Tenn., 1987.

Krug, Donna Rebecca D. "The Folks Back Home: The Confederate Homefront during the Civil War." Ph.D. diss., University of California, Irvine, 1990.

Massey, Mary Elizabeth. *Refugee Life in the Confederacy.* Baton Rouge, La., 1964.

Palaudan, Philip Shaw. *Victims: A True Story of the Civil War.* Knoxville, Tenn., 1981.

Rable, George C. *Civil Wars: Women and the Crisis of Southern Nationalism.* Urbana, Ill., 1989.

Ramsdell, Charles W. *Behind the Lines in the Southern Confederacy.* Baton Rouge, La., 1944.

Siegel, Frederick F. *The Roots of Southern Distinctiveness: Tobacco and Society in Danville, Virginia, 1780–1865.* Chapel Hill, N.C., 1987.

Wiley, Bell I. *The Plain People of the Confederacy.* Baton Rouge, La., 1944.

ORVILLE VERNON BURTON

SOLDIERS

Ordinary men made the Civil War an extraordinary struggle. That war from first to last was a conflict of the plain people. Statesmen and diplomats did their best to plot the struggle; generals did their best to conduct its campaigns; yet the real load of serving, fighting, suffering, and dying was borne by the soldiers in the ranks. Historian Bell I. Wiley summarized them by observing:

> For the most part they were earthy people, in whose natures the fear of God was rivaled by the attraction of the world, the flesh, and the Devil. Among those who donned the uniform, evil, or at least that which was adjudged evil by Americans of a century ago, flourished more freely than righteousness.

Like their Union counterparts, Confederates were volunteer soldiers—civilians in arms who, in many ways, never fully adapted to military life. Fighting they did, to a heroic degree; but at the same time Johnny Rebs tended to be independent, proud, and happy-go-lucky fellows who scoffed at discipline, criticized (often with justification) all facets of army life, fended for themselves much of the time, and displayed the full gauntlet of diversity inherent in the lower classes from which the predominant majority of them sprung.

Southern males became soldiers because they had been caught up in the heated atmosphere and angry words of the day, or they had been moved by fiery oratory, inspiring music, a patriotic call to arms, or the sight of a flag waving defiantly. Products of an unsophisticated age, they went off to combat with dreamy enthusiasm and youthful innocence. The greatest anxiety for many of them was that peace would come before they could get a shot at the enemy or win their "red badge of courage" (a battle wound).

Physical examinations of recruits in the early stages of the war were a sham. The basic if not sole requirement of a potential soldier was whether he possessed all four limbs and most of his sensory organs. A man's performing adequately in any civilian job was proof to most recruiting agents that he was fit for military service. Ease of enlistments and the poor health of many volunteers accepted into the armies were among the primary reasons for the high incidence of sickness and disability among the first waves of men who answered the Confederacy's call.

Following enlistment and muster into an official unit, recruits underwent about two weeks of training at a rendezvous camp. There they faced the awkward process of learning the rudiments of camp life, drill, marches, and discipline. The climax of this basic training period usually came when a delegation—dominated largely by ladies—bestowed an ornate flag upon the new regiment. An officer would accept the flag and pledge in glowing terms that his soldiers would never disgrace the sacred banner.

Foul-ups occasionally turned this solemn ceremony into a comedy. The ladies of Fayetteville, North Carolina, presented a lovingly sewn flag to the Forty-third North Carolina. None of them was willing to make the presentation speech, so they invited a local orator of some reputation to do the honors. The man, quite nervous at his starring role, fortified himself with liquor just before the ceremony. He somehow stumbled through the address; then, in a stupor, he proceeded to give the same speech again. At the end the gentleman sat down and cried—to the mortification of the ladies and the amusement of the soldiers.

The Men's Characteristics. Foreign-born elements composed only 5 percent of the Confederate fighting force since the plantation-dominated antebellum South did not attract immigrants in great numbers. Johnny Rebs were a relatively homogeneous group. A majority of them were rural, Protestant, and single. Less than a fourth of the Southern soldiers possessed slaves or were from slaveholding families.

Four of every five Confederates were between eighteen and thirty years old, but the age spectrum was wide. Charles C. Hay joined an Alabama regiment at the age of eleven. Texas soldier John M. Sloan lost a leg in battle at thirteen. Fifteen-year-old John Roberts of Tennessee fought in the two-day struggle at Shiloh. Roberts's colonel reported that the lad was twice struck by spent bullets and had his musket blown from his hands, but that he continued to display throughout the contest "the coolness and courage of a veteran." At the same time, a Virginia artilleryman recalled seeing a half-dozen soldiers "over sixty years who volunteered, and served in the ranks, during the war." David Scantlon was almost fifty-two when he became "drummer boy" of the Fourth Virginia. The chaplain of another regiment kept a protective eye on his son, a lieutenant in the unit. In 1862 a substitute named E. Pollard joined a North Carolina detachment. Although he is listed as sixty-two, indications exist that Pollard was over seventy years of age.

Many of the Southern rank and file were men of excellent education, refined and well-read. Outnumbering them at the opposite end, however, were soldiers who were at best semiliterate. Typical of this class was a Tarheel boy who stated in a June 1862 letter: "Mother when you wright to me get somebody to wright that can wright a Plain hand . . . . I cold not read your letter to make sence of it it [was] wrote so bad. I have lurnd to do my one wrading and writing and it is a grate help to me."

Confederates were not as diverse in occupation as Federal troops. Still, more than 100 different occupations are listed on Southern muster rolls. A case in point was the Nineteenth Virginia. Of its original 749 members, 302 were farmers, 80 were laborers, and 56 were machinists. Among the remainder were 10 lawyers, 14 teachers, 24 students, 3 blacksmiths, 2 artists, a distiller, a well-digger, a dentist, and 4 men who classified themselves as "Gentleman."

The advent of Confederate conscription in 1862 brought a different class of men into the army. Volunteers tended to view them, and treat them, with open contempt. "Conscripts" were so often suspect in loyalty and behavior that officers entrusted with getting the draftees to the armies sometimes transported them as if they were prisoners of war. When a group of conscripted recruits arrived at the Army of Northern Virginia in 1864, a veteran snorted: "Some of them looked like they had been resurrected from the grave, after laying therein for twenty years or more."

Supplies. Official manuals described the gray Confederate uniform, but few soldiers had one. What they wore when they left home composed their military dress. A number of soldiers learned to take captured Federal blue uniforms and dye them in a solution of walnut hulls and lye. The result were coats and trousers of a beige color that gave rise to the nickname "Butternuts" for Confederate troops. For those unable to acquire any kind of military attire, raggedness was their lot. Some men complained; others made light of their condition. A Texan wrote from the trenches of Atlanta in 1864: "In this army one hole in the seat of the breeches indicates a captain, two holes a lieutenant and the seat of the pants all out indicates that the individual is a private."

Although Johnny Rebs were supposed to receive eleven dollars monthly, appearances in camp by paymasters were rare. Making matters worse was the galloping inflation in the wartime South, which rendered money of steadily decreasing value. By 1863, for instance, it required six months' pay just to purchase a pair of boots.

The aspect of camp life that produced the most condemnation by soldiers were army rations. One might expect an agricultural South to have had an abundance of foodstuffs, but its major antebellum crops were cotton and tobacco. Even though the Confederacy did produce large amounts of food crops, transportational breakdowns, hoarding, and black marketeering kept much of it from reaching the front. As a result, hunger was a constant companion of the armies. Many men in gray, especially in the last half of the war, went for days without food save for a few grains of corn picked up from the places where the horses fed, stolen apples and peaches, sassafras roots, and the like.

When available, meat and bread were the standard fare of Southern troops. Quality left a great deal to be desired. Army beef was either fresh or salt-pickled. If chewable, the fresh meat was often eaten raw because it seemed to taste just as good that way as cooked. Preserved meat—"salted horse," the troops called it—was often so tough that a meal of it produced sore teeth. The beef issued to the Confederacy's western army in the war's first year was petrified to the extent that a Louisiana officer threatened to requisition files so that his men could hone their teeth before eating. Later in the war an Alabama soldier complained of his beef being "too old for the conscript law," and a Georgia compatriot described the cows assigned to his regiment for beef as so feeble that "it takes two hands to hold up one beef to shoot it."

Rations became progressively worse as the war continued. From the Petersburg trenches early in 1865 a South Carolinian noted: "We get corn bread now in place of wheat bread. . . . It looks like a pile of cow dung Baked in the sun. I could nock down a cow with a pone of it."

Homesickness and Loneliness. Most men in the Confederate armies were away from home for the first time in their lives. The novelty of army life was short-lived. In its place came homesickness and an overpowering desire to be with loved ones. The plain folk of that era had deep devotion to home and family. Long absence in service produced more anguish than any other aspect of the war. Homesickness crippled morale and filled army hospitals with illnesses baffling to the surgeons.

"I am almost down with histericks to hear from home," an Alabama infantryman wrote in 1863, and his feelings echoed those of thousands of Confederates. A member of the Sixth Mississippi once confided to his wife:

I have been studying about you and the children all day. oh how I wish I was at home with you this day. it seems as if there is nothing else in this world would please me better than to be with my family.

A number of soldiers tried to mask their loneliness through teasing a loved one at home. In the spring of 1863 a Georgia private "reassured" his wife by stating:

If I did not write and receive letters from you I believe that [I] would forgit that I was marrid. I don't feel much like a maryed man but I never furgit it sofar as to court enny other lady but if I should you must forgive me as I am so forgitful.

Far more prevalent in the lonely letters of soldiers were such sentiments as those expressed in a May 1863 letter from Alabama cavalryman John Cotton:

I want to come home as bad as any body can . . . but I shant run away. . . . I dont want it throwed up to my children after I am dead and gone that I was a deserter . . . I don't want to do anything if I no it will leave a stain on my posterity hereafter.

Accentuating the loneliness was a sentimentality both deep and characteristic of that age. The Civil War brought those two emotions together and created a degree of love not customarily found in the whirlpool that marks life in the late twentieth century. For Confederates in the field, romance became one of life's real treasures. The longer soldiers went

without even a glimpse of a woman, the stronger became the yearning. A Virginia private once informed his cousin: "I have not seen a gal in so long a time that I would not know what to do with myself if I were to meet up with one, though I reckon I would learn before I left her."

In love letters, soldiers were temperate in language. Few references were made to the physical aspects of romance. The primary concern of the men in gray was to convey expressions of devotion and hope to receive many like sentiments in return. Quite often they used poetry to enhance their prose. The most frequently used couplets were: "When this you see remember me / Though many miles apart we be," and "My pen is poor my ink is pale / My love for you shall never fail." Georgia soldier William Stillwell wrote many verses to his wife. One closed with the expression: "When silence reigns o'er lawn or lea / Then dearest love I watch for thee."

> Long absence in service produced more anguish than any other aspect of the war.

Camp Life. Every Confederate with the ability to write had something to say about camp life. It was generally negative. A Louisiana soldier told his wife: "Dont never come here as long as you can ceep away, for you will smell hell here." A young Alabama recruit asked his brother to visit him in camp, but to bring a shotgun with him for his own protection.

Much about camp life made it the subject of widespread criticism. Oppressive, stifling heat and constant movements prevailed during the months of activity. With their winter quarters located in tents, drafty log huts, or makeshift shanties, the men spent the cold months trying merely to survive. Any army camp had an overbearing stench. A lack of knowledge about hygienic practices, plus inattention given to latrine procedures and garbage pits, created an always-unhealthy environment. In 1862 a Virginia soldier confided in his diary: "On rolling up my bed this morning I found I had been lying in—I won't say what—something that didn't smell like milk and peaches." The presence of swarms of insects was a natural by-product and additional unpleasantness.

Commanders sought to minimize the stagnation of camp life, and at the same time produce better soldiers, by keeping the men as busy as possible. This meant drill, drill, and more drill, particularly in the first months. Since many officers and men were starting out as complete novices, drill was often akin to the ignorant leading the uneducated. A Virginia recruit observed:

Maneuvers of the most utterly impossible sort were taught to the men. Every amateur officer had his own system of tactics, and the effect of the incongruous teachings, when brought out in battalion drill, closely resembled that of the music at Mr. Bob Sawyer's party, where each guest sang the chorus to the tune he knew best.

Green officers trying to give correct instructions while scores of men were attempting to maintain lines and proper cadence during these drills could be a nerve-wracking experience. One day a captain was marching his new company when it rapidly approached a fence. The captain suddenly could not think of the command to give. The closer the column got to the fence, the less his thinking processes functioned. Finally, he frantically called the men to a halt. "Gentlemen!" he then shouted. "We will now take a recess of ten minutes. And when you fall in, please re-form on the other side of the fence!"

The discipline of camp life was irritating to a great many. Disrespect for authority was the most prevalent offense committed by Civil War soldiers. Confederates who had joined the army were products of a new nation dedicated to the ideal that one white man was as good as another. When many of the officers showed themselves to be either as green as the men they were supposed to be leading or know-it-all martinets, troops in the ranks freely displayed or voiced their disgust.

> They were in a strange world they wanted to share with family and friends, so they wrote letters. . . .

Courts-martial were a daily part of camp life. Usually, insubordination involved verbal attacks. Writings by soldiers reveal such uncomplimentary references to officers as "a vain, stuck-up, illiterate ass," "whore-house pimp," "horse's ass," and the time-honored "son of a bitch." One Johnny Reb classified his colonel as "an ignoramus fit for nothing higher than the cultivation of corn." Similarly, a Florida soldier thought all of his superiors "not fit to tote guts to a Bear."

It was during the two-thirds or three-fourths of each year when Johnny Rebs were in camp that a constant search prevailed for diversions to overcome the tedium and monotony of army routine. Radio, movies, and television, of course, were technologies of the future. There were no army service agencies, post exchanges, lounges, libraries, or camp newspapers. Few entertainment groups visited the troops. Soldiers were left to themselves to provide for their own pastimes. Fortunately for them, their needs and tastes were simple.

The most popular occupation of soldiers was letter-writing. This was the only contact with a loved one back home. Further, the Civil War was the first time in the nation's histo-

ry when so large a percentage of the male population was pulled away from farms, schools, factories, and shops. As soldiers, they were seeing new things and living an unusual life. They were in a strange world they wanted to share with family and friends, so they wrote letters—untold thousands of letters.

Thoughts poured forth on paper with little attention to continuity or grammar. They described army life, marches, battles, the merits of commanding officers, and prospects for the future. Interspersed throughout the rambling epistles would be questions about conditions at home. Usually a soldier ran out of paper before he exhausted everything he wanted to write. Many Johnny Rebs developed a sensitivity to gossip or criticism emanating from the home front. In June 1864, a young Confederate responded to muttering from his neighbors about his lack of battle experience by writing to his wife: "The people there that speaks slack of me may kiss my ass. Mollie, excuse the vulgar language if you will."

More than American fighting men of any other time, troops of the 1860s were singing soldiers. Music, next to sending and receiving letters, was the most popular diversion for Johnny Rebs. The Civil War gave rise to more than two thousand new songs. Among the favorite camp tunes were "Home Sweet Home," "Dixie," "Annie Laurie," "Lorena," "Bonnie Blue Flag," "The Girl I Left Behind Me," "Her Bright Eyes Haunt Me Still," "Maryland, My Maryland," "When Johnny Comes Marching Home Again," and dozens of familiar hymns.

Cherished melodies were many, but regimental bands were few. This may have been a blessing. The scarcity of instruments, limited talent among band members, and weariness from campaigning led to inferior renditions on too many occasions. In any sizable group of soldiers, on the other hand, could generally be found someone reasonably proficient with banjo, fiddle, or jew's-harp. That was enough to keep men entertained with such foot-stomping airs as "Arkansas Traveler," "Billy in the Low Ground," "The Yellow Rose of Texas," and "Hell Broke Loose in Georgia."

Physical contests were an integral part of camp life. Boxing, broad-jumping, wrestling, footraces, hurdles, and an occasional free-for-all were common recreations. A new game called baseball was becoming popular. At that time a player had to hit the base runner with a thrown or batted ball to put him out. When the Texas Rangers achieved early championship status in baseball, teams began refusing to play them until a private named Frank Ezell was disqualified. An observer explained that Ezell, a burly Texan, "could throw harder and straighter than any other man. . . . He came very near knocking the stuffing out of three or four of the boys."

Alcohol triggered the most misbehavior in Civil War camps. It is understandable that the men drank, but they also had a tendency to do so excessively. Most of the whiskey smuggled into the armies could be classified as "mean" in those days, "vile" by modern standards. The potency of the liquor is evident from some of the nicknames given to it by Confederates: "Old Red Eye," "Rifle Knock-Knee," "How Come You So," and "Help Me to Sleep, Mother." Whatever the quality of the whiskey, it almost inevitably produced disorder among the imbibers.

The primitive conditions under which the soldiers lived, their lack of immunity to diseases, and insufficient medical treatment combined to make sickness the worst enemy that Confederates faced. More than twice as many men perished from illness and infection as fell in battle. Recruits invariably encountered two onslaughts of sickness. Because so many came from isolated farms, they had been unexposed to childhood diseases when they entered service. Chicken pox, measles, mumps, and whooping cough circulated through camps in epidemic proportions. Next came camp illnesses triggered by impure water, poor food, exposure, insects, and general filth. Such conditions produced the principal killers of the war: diarrhea, dysentery, typhoid fever, pneumonia, and malaria. The smallest abrasion literally opened the door for bacterial infection. With little resistance because of general debilitation, Southern soldiers died daily in camp or in primitive hospitals.

Religious Beliefs. Faith in God became the greatest institution in the maintenance of morale in Confederate as well as Union armies. Because a Louisiana sergeant did not believe "a bullet can go through a prayer," he considered his allegiance to the Almighty a "much better shield than . . . steel armor." Religion also was a connecting link between camp and home. Most devout Johnny Rebs practiced an evangelical faith that was active and expressive. When a soldier prayed or sang a hymn on Sunday, his thoughts could not help but wander far behind the lines to the church where his family was gathering. At such times, a member of the Sixteenth Tennessee confessed, he "had not much hope of ever meeting again the loved ones at home . . . I thought of earthly home sweet home & cried."

The horrors of war often strained soldiers' beliefs in a merciful God. Some men became embittered from the hell of battle and the loss of friends and compatriots. For the majority, however, war and its uncertainties led to a strengthening of religion. Countless Johnny Rebs would have agreed with the observation by President Abraham Lincoln: "I have often been driven to my knees by the realization that I had nowhere else to go."

Army chaplains were few in number and variable in ability. The good ones were indefatigable in their labors to keep God's love in front of man's evil. Yet for most soldiers faith was an individual matter. Each man worshiped as he saw fit, and the degree of his religion was no one else's business. One Confederate wrote his brother in May 1862: "the greatest pleasure that I have is when I am reading my Bible and praying to my Creator my Heavenly Father for in his car a lon

do I feel safe. I som time tak my Bible on the Sabath and go to some grove where I have no on in my way." When a Virginia infantryman was asked to give a testimonial at a prayer service, he succinctly responded: "My brethren, I'se got nothin' agin nobody, and I hope nobody's got nothin' agin me."

Praying in public was difficult for many men of limited education and simple faith. Nevertheless, they usually managed to convey their thoughts. During one trying period, a North Carolinian intoned: "Oh Lord, we have a mighty big fight down here, and a sight of trouble; and we hope, Lord, that you will take the proper view of the matter, and give us the victory." A fellow soldier, obviously not as devout, once offered this supplication on the eve of battle: "Lord, if you ain't with us, don't be against us. Just step aside and watch the damndest fight you are ever likely to see!"

Motivation and Conduct in Battle. An acute sense of duty was notable among Confederate soldiers. The words *duty* and *honor* appear regularly in their letters. Duty to cause and country were major motivations of most Rebs. They interpreted patriotic duty to be defending their section and their people against Northern invaders who would deny them the inherent right of self-determination, and whose aim was to destroy the South's cherished way of life.

Sergeant John Hagan of a Georgia regiment was one of innumerable Confederates who viewed the Civil War as a struggle parallel to that of the colonists in the 1770s. Hagan stated at one point in 1863:

I & every Southern Soldier should be like the rebbil blume which plumed more & shinned briter the more it was trampled on. I believe . . . we will have to fight like Washington did, but I hope our people will never be reduced to destress & poverty as the people of that day was, but if nothing elce will give us liberties I am willing for the time to come.

Hagan survived the war. Another Georgia soldier, Robert McGill, told his wife after his first engagement: "I [had] rather die and you be free than live and be slaves. . . . I know that we will be victorious." Gill was killed in an 1864 battle.

The ultimate test of a soldier is battle. All else in warfare is incidental to two armies closing in combat. The Civil War required more raw courage than most conflicts in history. Enormous numbers of men were engaged, yet troops still massed in battle formation with a minimum of support and protection. They charged across open ground against entrenched positions. The advent of the rifle and major improvements in artillery pieces swung the advantage of war from the offense to the defense. Whereas in the old days an attacking column could approach to a hundred yards or less without taking heavy losses, Civil War weapons made it deadly to approach within a quarter-mile of a fixed position. Commanders on both sides nevertheless continued to make massive frontal assaults to the end of the war. Casualties exceeded anything in American history.

Although the men in gray may have left a good deal to be desired in camp and on the march, they more than compensated for those deficiencies by their overall performance on the battlefield. The most prevalent fear among a Civil War soldier was not of being wounded or captured but of "showing the white feather": displaying cowardice that would bring humiliation to himself and his family. Untested soldiers did not know what to expect in their baptism into combat. Battle scenes, they were told, were enough to try men's souls.

> ... "our men were turablely Shocked but all acted the part of a Soldier."

Most soldiers were shocked by the noise and trauma. An Arkansas soldier wrote after his first engagement at Murfreesboro, Tennessee: "I cannot use language to Express the nois of this Battle. The Earth seemed to be in perfect commotion as if a heavy Earth Quake was on." Confederate soldier E. D. Patterson wrote in his diary that when he and his comrades assaulted Union works at Gaines' Mill, they met such a concentrated fire "that the whole brigade literally staggered backward several paces as though pushed back by a tornado."

A teenage soldier from Alabama also had deep anxieties over what to expect in combat. Then his regiment was called into its first battle. He responded in the same way as did his fellow soldiers. "My heart beat quick and my lips became dry," he wrote afterward. "My legs felt weak and a prayer rose to my lips. We had barely entered the woods when pandemonium broke loose. The artillery redoubled its fury, the musketry of both sides began to roar like a storm, and I knew I was into it now. Strange to say, the fear passed away, and I no longer realized the danger amid the excitement, and I could face the bullets with perfect indifference." In like vein, a Georgia private proudly told his wife after his first engagement: "our men were turablely Shocked but all acted the part of a Soldier."

Such comments are truly commendable; for in marked contrast to Currier and Ives paintings and other orderly depictions of the Civil War, combat was not clean or easily seen at all. Chaos reigned everywhere. Thick, acrid smoke settled over the field; and in the crash of musketry, the explosions of cannon fire, the shouts and screams of men fighting with clubbed muskets, bayonets, fists, stones, and anything else at hand, a soldier saw only what was directly in front of him. The mass heroism displayed by these citizen-soldiers inspired Winston Churchill to salute them years later with the words: "With them, extraordinary valor became a common virtue."

Maj. James Waddell, in the official report of his Georgia regiment's conduct at Second Manassas, stated that he "carried into the fight over 100 men who were barefoot, many of whom left bloody foot-prints among the thorns and briars through which they rushed, with Spartan courage and jubilant impetuosity, upon the ranks of the foe."

When in an assault and receiving concentrated musketry, soldiers were known to lean forward as if they were moving into the face of a strong wind. Calling for volunteers to perform dangerous tasks would bring a shout of responses. Repeatedly, soldiers jumped atop parapets to yell defiance at the enemy; they begged for the privilege of carrying the colors in front of the ranks; they took command without being told when all the officers were disabled; many refused to leave the field although seriously wounded.

Countless numbers of those men demonstrated fully that they loved their country more than they loved their lives. Before a battle, it became a common practice for soldiers to write their names and addresses on pieces of paper and pin them to their shirts so that burial details afterward could make easy identification. A Louisiana lieutenant was directing the fire of his guns when a Federal shell tore off his left arm at the shoulder. The man grabbed the reins of his horse with his right hand, swung the animal around in an attempt to hide his injury, and shouted: "Keep it up, boys! I'll be back in a moment!" He started riding down a hill and then pitched forward dead.

John Moseley was the youngest member of the Third Alabama. On July 4, 1863, from Gettysburg, he wrote his mother:

> I am here a prisoner of war & mortally wounded. I can live but a few hours more at farthest—I was shot fifty yards [from] the enemy's lines . . . I have no doubts of the final results of this battle and I hope I may live long enough to hear the shouts of victory yet, before I die. I am very weak . . . Farewell to you all.

When Gen. William B. Bate concluded his report of the 1863 Battle of Chickamauga, he unknowingly paid a tribute to all troops in every Confederate army when he wrote:

> The private soldier . . . [vied] with the officer in deeds of high daring and distinguished courage. While the "River of Death" shall float its sluggish current . . . and the night wind chant its solemn dirges over their soldier graves, their names, enshrined in the hearts of their countrymen, will be held in grateful remembrance.

Their record of endurance in the nation's darkest hour stands as an eternal monument to their greatness.

[See also Artillery, *overview article;* Brothers of War; Cavalry; Civil War, *article on* Losses and Numbers; Conscription; Desertion; Engineer Bureau; File Closers;

Food; Health and Medicine, *particularly articles on* Sickness and Disease *and* Battle Injuries; Infantry; Military Justice; Military Training; Morale; Music; Prisoners of War; Prostitution; Signal Corps; Substitutes; Uniforms, *article on* Army Uniforms.]

BIBLIOGRAPHY

Barton, Michael. *Goodmen: The Character of Civil War Soldiers.*
Daniel, Larry J. *Soldiering in the Army of Tennessee.* Chapel Hill, N.C., 1991. University Park, Pa., 1981.
Linderman, Gerald. *Embattled Courage: The Experience of Combat in the American Civil War.* New York, 1987.
Mitchell, Reid. *Civil War Soldiers.* New York, 1988.
Robertson, James I., Jr. *Soldiers Blue and Gray.* Columbia, S.C., 1988.
Wiley, Bell Irwin. *The Life of Johnny Reb.* Baton Rouge, La., 1971.
Womack, Bob. *Call Forth the Mighty Men.* Bessemer, Ala., 1987.

JAMES I. ROBERTSON, JR.

SOLDIERS' HOMES

Throughout the Civil War various residences scattered across the South served as makeshift convalescent homes for wounded veterans of Southern armies. But these "soldiers' homes" were relatively small-scale endeavors supported wholly by private means, and they ceased operating soon after the war ended. The previous year, in February 1864, President Jefferson Davis vetoed a bill that would have established a national Confederate soldiers' home with a board of managers appointed by the governors of the then-existing Confederate states. Although recognizing that disabled ex-Confederate soldiers and sailors were "peculiar objects of governmental benevolence," Davis objected to the act on constitutional grounds, arguing that control and management of the institution properly belonged to the central government in Richmond.

The first state-supported Confederate soldiers' home, chartered in Louisiana in March 1866, was soon abandoned after a Radical Republican–dominated legislature cut off funding. Seventeen years later, however, two strong Confederate veterans' benevolent societies headquartered in New Orleans cosponsored the establishment of what would later become the Camp [Francis T.] Nicholls Confederate Soldiers' Home of Louisiana. Also among the first homes founded by and for Confederate veterans was the R. E. Lee Camp Soldiers' Home of Virginia, established in 1884. Inspired by the success of these two examples in Louisiana and Virginia, Confederate veterans' groups in several other states joined the soldiers' home movement. Numerous ex-Confederate generals— including Joseph E. Johnston, E. Kirby Smith, James Longstreet, Clement A. Evans, Fitzhugh Lee, Bradley Tyler Johnson, John B. Gordon, Lawrence Sullivan Ross, and Joseph Wheeler, as well as the wives and daughters of Gens. Robert E. Lee, Thomas J. ("Stonewall") Jackson, and A. P. Hill, among others—participated in and gave their pledges and influence to the benevolence activity. By 1929, sixteen homes were founded, one in each of the eleven states that had composed the Confederacy, plus Maryland, Kentucky, Oklahoma, Missouri, and even California.

Originally, only honorably discharged and poor Confederate veterans (and in some cases veterans' wives, but only when accompanied by their husbands) were admitted as inmates to Confederate soldiers' homes. Funding for the homes came from private contributions and, predominantly, state revenues, but never from the Federal government; and unlike their national counterparts, Confederate soldiers' homes from the outset excluded veterans of other wars. In all, an estimated twenty thousand indigent and disabled Confederate veterans resided in the sixteen homes, where they were given food, medical care, and shelter. Some of the men died at the homes and were buried in nearby cemeteries. But a majority resided temporarily, in many cases for less than a year, before leaving. Initiated during a period of rampant ex-Confederate activity, the soldiers' homes also served the larger public; there, Southerners of all ages could congregate on special occasions to help celebrate and relive the achievements of the Lost Cause with the men who had fought during the war.

Most of the Confederate soldiers' homes remained open until the 1930s, when the last veteran died, and the surviving widows and daughters were transferred to other institutions. But a few of the homes continued operating until the mid- to late 1950s. Today, several of the original buildings of the Virginia home in Richmond are extant, the Alabama home site located near Montgomery is open to the public, and the Jefferson Davis Memorial Home for Confederate Soldiers and Sailors at Biloxi, Mississippi—built on the grounds of the ex-president's beloved estate, Beauvoir—continues to attract thousands of tourists each year.

[*See also* Beauvoir.]

BIBLIOGRAPHY

Lashley, Tommy G. "Oklahoma's Confederate Veterans Home." *Chronicles of Oklahoma* 55 (1977): 34–45.
Poole, Herbert. "Final Encampment: The North Carolina Soldiers' Home." *Confederate Veteran* 26 (1987): 10–17.
Rosenburg, R. B. "Living Monuments: Confederate Soldiers' Homes in the New South." Ph.D. diss., University of Tennessee, 1989.
Williams, Emily J. "'A Home . . . for the Old Boys': The Robert E. Lee Camp Confederate Soldiers' Home." *Virginia Cavalcade* 28 (1979): 40–47.

R. B. ROSENBURG

SORREL, GILBERT MOXLEY

SORREL, GILBERT MOXLEY (1838–1901), brigadier general. Sorrel was the grandson of a colonel of engineers in the French army and brother-in-law of Gen. W. W. Mackall. He was born February 23, 1838, in Savannah, Georgia, where he worked before the war as a clerk in the banking department of the Georgia Central Railroad.

When the war broke out, Sorrel saw service at Fort Pulaski and Skidway Island as a member of the Georgia Hussars. Thereafter, however, he grew impatient over the delay of the Hussars' acceptance into Confederate service and went to Virginia where he was a volunteer aide to James Longstreet at First Manassas. In time he became adjutant of Longstreet's division and ultimately chief of staff of the First Corps. Promotions came quickly for Sorrel: he was commissioned captain, September 11, 1861; major, May 5, 1862; and lieutenant colonel, June 18, 1863.

Sorrel was instrumental in healing the breach between Longstreet and A. P. Hill in early 1862. He helped with the guns at Sharpsburg (where he was severely wounded) and performed admirably in the Wilderness. In the 1864 engagement, Sorrel led three brigades in a successful flanking attack against Winfield Scott Hancock, a movement that drew Longstreet's praise for his "skill, promptness and address." Longstreet also recommended Sorrel's promotion to brigadier general. With similar endorsements by Richard Anderson and Robert E. Lee, Sorrel received his wreathed three stars, October 27, 1864. He also was given command of Ambrose Ransom Wright's old brigade in William Mahone's division.

In the closing months of the war Sorrel was wounded in the leg near Petersburg and shot through the lung at Hatcher's Run. The Federals were so confident that the second wound was mortal that his obituary was published in the *New York Herald.* Sorrel recovered, but Lee surrendered before he could rejoin his command.

Described by a fellow officer as "bad tempered and inclined to be overbearing," Sorrel was depicted by historian John Warwick Daniel as "tall, slender and graceful with a keen, dark eye, a trim military figure and an engaging countenance."

After receiving his parole at Lynchburg, May 20, 1865, Sorrel returned to Savannah, where he became manager successively of the Ocean Steamship Company and of the Georgia Export and Import Company. He also served on the city council and was vice president of the Georgia Historical Society for twelve years. Sorrel died August 10, 1901, at the home of his brother, Dr. Francis Sorrel, near Roanoke, Virginia. He was buried in Savannah.

BIBLIOGRAPHY

Dawson, Francis W. *Reminiscences of Confederate Service, 1861–1865.* Charleston, S.C., 1882.

Goree, Thomas Jewett. *The Civil War Correspondence of Thomas Jewett Goree.* Vol. 1. Bryan, Tex., 1981.

Obituary. *Atlanta Journal,* August 17, 1901.

Sorrel, Gilbert Moxley. *Recollections of a Confederate Staff Officer.* Jackson, Tenn., 1958.

Warner, Ezra J. *Generals in Gray: Lives of the Confederate Commanders.* Baton Rouge, La., 1959.

LOWELL REIDENBAUGH

GILBERT MOXLEY SORREL. Late or post-Civil War photograph.
NAVAL HISTORICAL CENTER, WASHINGTON, D.C.

SOULÈ, PIERRE

SOULÈ, PIERRE (1801–1870), U.S. diplomat and provost marshal of New Orleans. Born in the French Pyrenees, Soulè fled to America in 1825 to avoid imprisonment for antimonarchical activities. He prospered in New Orleans and defeated John Slidell for a U.S. Senate seat in 1848, becoming a leader of the state rights Democrats after the death of John C. Calhoun.

A flamboyant character, Soulè was involved in controversial episodes throughout his life. His principal historical notoriety stems from his role as U.S. minister to Spain from 1853 to 1855, when his eagerness to annex Cuba provoked international confrontations in the *Black Warrior* and Ostend Manifesto affairs. He also injured the French ambassador in a duel. Repudiated, he resigned, returned to law practice, defended Nicaraguan filibusterer William Walker, and played a hand in the projected Central American isthmian canal.

Although initially opposed to secession, Soulè joined the government of New Orleans as provost marshal and confidant of Mayor John T. Monroe. After Union troops captured the city, he clashed with Gen. Benjamin F. Butler and was arrested on April 28, 1862, for "plotting treason" and for writing "insolent letters" to David Farragut. Imprisoned at Fort Lafayette, New York, until November 1862, he was paroled in Boston but fled back to the Confederacy by way of the Bahamas and Cuba.

He served as an honorary brigadier general on the staff of P. G. T. Beauregard in the defense of Charleston and also attempted to recruit troops abroad, but Jefferson Davis refused to confirm his rank or give him an active command. After the war, he dabbled in an abortive plan to settle Confederate veterans in the Mexican province of Sonora under French protection. He died in New Orleans on March 26, 1870.

BIBLIOGRAPHY

Malone, Dumas, ed. *Dictionary of American Biography.* New York, 1935.
Moore, J. Preston. "Pierre Soulè: Southern Expansionist and Promoter." *Journal of Southern History* 21 (May 1955): 203–223.

JAMES J. HORGAN

SOUTH CAROLINA

In 1860 the population of South Carolina was 703,708. About 30 percent was concentrated in the coastal region, or low country, and some 70 percent in the rest of the state, or the up-country. South Carolina ranked as the tenth most populous state in the South and eighteenth in the nation. There were 291,300 whites, 402,406 African American slaves, and 10,002 free nonwhites. Slaves comprised 57.2 percent and free blacks 1.4 percent of the population, or together 58.6 percent. This black majority represented the highest proportion of African Americans to whites of any state in the nation.

The slaves were employed in the agricultural economy of South Carolina, producing its two main cash crops, cotton and rice. More than one-third of the slaves were located in the state's coastal region—its low country and Sea Islands—from Georgetown to the Savannah River where they cultivated rice and long-staple or Sea Island cotton. Black majorities predominated in the low-country districts in 1860 with the percentage of slaves ranging from a low of 77 percent of the population in Colleton, to 81 percent in Beaufort, to a high of 85 percent in Georgetown.

Over 440 planters using slave labor each raised more than 20,000 pounds of rice annually in the coastal region, while in Georgia, the second most productive rice state, only 88 planters cultivated the crop. South Carolina's Sea Islands in 1859 also produced 43 percent of the long-staple cotton grown in the United States.

Charleston was the social and cultural center of the low country, the state's manufacturing center, and its principal and most cosmopolitan city. With a population of some 40,522 in 1860, it was the second largest city after New Orleans in those states that subsequently left the Union, and it was the twenty-second largest urban center in the nation. Charleston's annual industrial output was exceeded only by Mobile and New Orleans in the South. It ranked eighty-fifth nationwide. An excellent railroad system linked Charleston with the up-country. According to the eighth Federal census, Charleston contained 5.8 percent of the state's population in 1860.

The African American population of Charleston was 17,146 and constituted approximately 42 percent of the city's population. Of these, 34 percent or 13,909 were slaves, and 3,237 free persons of color made up 8 percent of the city's population in 1860; about 75 percent of the latter were mulattoes. The city's free blacks accounted for about one-third of South Carolina's entire free African American population. Approximately 3 percent of Charleston's free people of color constituted a mulatto aristocracy. Some were slaveholders themselves. Their position locally was unequaled in numbers and status elsewhere in the state.

In other ways Charleston was an anomaly in South Carolina and the nation. The inequality in the distribution of wealth in the city was enormous by comparison to Northern cities. About 10 percent of the 4,644 free heads-of-households owned 77 percent of the city's wealth; the top 3 percent owned approximately half of the assets in Charleston and were at the top of the pyramid of wealth in the city, state, and nation.

Most Charlestonians owned neither land nor slaves. Some of the poorest whites in the city were recent immigrants. Two-fifths of the laboring class were white people and about 60 percent foreign-born in 1860. The well-to-do were concerned that these propertyless classes represented a threat to their society and institutions. Charleston's middle class included small merchants, teachers, and craftsmen, but visitors to the city reported they saw only two classes: rich and poor. Poor white farmers across the low country produced some grain, hogs, and cattle on the least desirable land.

The production of short-staple cotton grown in South Carolina's up-country increased enormously during the first half of the nineteenth century. This cotton boom opened opportunities for small farmers to become slave owners, and by 1860 there were black majorities in about half of the up-country districts of South Carolina. The numbers of middle-class farmers multiplied. About 80 percent of these rural whites and more than 45 percent of all slaves came to live on small or medium-sized farms. Indeed, counting slave assets the per capita wealth of South Carolina in 1860 was $864, the third highest in the nation and behind only Mississippi and Louisiana. By this date the wealth production of the low country and up-country was approximately equal.

There were, however, vast imbalances in the geographic distribution of wealth throughout the state. For instance, the ten wealthiest districts had black majorities, whereas the ten districts with white majorities ranked among the poorest in the state. The per capita wealth was approximately $1,000 in the plantation districts of the state's lower cotton belt and was sharply less in the districts with white majorities in the upper Piedmont, sandhills, and pine barrens. Wealth, then, was unevenly distributed in the up-country and skewed especially toward the wealthiest one-fifth of households, but approached the existing inequalities elsewhere in the nation. Indeed, the widespread ownership of property tended to mitigate any popular concerns over the uneven distribution of wealth in the Carolina up-country.

The Move Toward Secession

The vast inequalities in wealth in South Carolina did not appear to give rise to any class-based opposition to the movement for secession. Although the well-planned attack by the antislavery extremist John Brown on the Federal arsenal at Harpers Ferry in October 1859 failed, it shocked whites of all classes. Brown's abortive raid played into the hands of radical secessionists who had long advocated separate state action like Robert Barnwell Rhett, Sr., the Charleston lawyer, planter, politician, and owner of the disunionist paper, the *Mercury*.

Meanwhile, Charleston's Christopher G. Memminger, leader of South Carolina's cooperationists (those who sought a united secession movement among the other Southern states) visited Virginia in December to urge a joint call for disunion, but Virginia preferred to wait; subsequently, South Carolina's Governor William H. Gist urged governors of the Deep South to secede together.

In April 1860 the Democratic National Convention met in Charleston, but in a few days the convention divided into Northern and Southern wings and disbanded. Later, in Baltimore, the Northern Democrats nominated Stephen A. Douglas and the Southerners, meeting in Richmond, put forward John C. Breckinridge. When the national Republican party nominated Abraham Lincoln for president, Charleston disunionists formed the "1860 Association," which became the South's leading publisher of pamphlets calling for secession. Disunion sentiment spread rapidly across South Carolina. The sectional split in the Democratic party facilitated Lincoln's election in November.

With Lincoln's victory, the movement for secession peaked, uniting planters and plain folk alike in South Carolina. One interpretation is that the remarkable unity and enthusiasm for such revolutionary, separate state action was precipitated by a crisis of fear of slave insurrections and abolitionism; secession was deemed necessary for race control. Another interpretation is that both yeoman farmers and planters rose together since they believed that only secession could protect their liberty and economic independence from powerful external forces. White unity was founded on the old "country-republican" ideal of personal independence, which was reinforced by the use of black slaves as the mudsill class.

In sum, despite the occasional incidents of class conflict and the historic hostility of up-country toward low country, South Carolina was more of one mind than ever before and more so than any other Southern state in 1860. Within a deferential society plain folk and planters nevertheless were bound together by ties of ethnicity, culture, personal relationships, self-interest, and racism. They were convinced that their property and way of life were threatened, and Lincoln's election provided the catalyst for the revolutionary act of secession.

When news of Lincoln's victory arrived, the legislature issued a call for elections to a secession convention. Now cooperationists like Memminger and Gist joined advocates of separate state action like the radical secessionist Rhett. Within days Rhett lost a bid for the governorship when the state legislature picked the more moderate candidate, Francis W. Pickens. Still there were few who dissented from the movement for secession. The old up-country Unionist Benjamin F. Perry was defeated in his bid for election to the convention; in Charleston, Unionist James L. Petigru, who did not actively oppose secession, wrote Perry: "why should one put himself to the pains of speaking to the insane if he has not the power of commanding a strait jacket for them?"

Following an outbreak of smallpox in Columbia, the secession convention reconvened in Charleston on December 20. The 169 delegates, mostly a wealthy, middle-aged, native-born, slaveholding elite of planters and lawyers, unanimously adopted an ordinance of secession, which dissolved South Carolina's union with the United States. The Palmetto Republic now stood alone.

The secession convention also adopted a set of resolutions written by the fire-eater Rhett proposing a convention of seceded states to meet in Montgomery, Alabama, in early February 1861 to adopt a constitution for a Southern confederacy. Commissioners were dispatched to alert all slaveholding states to the meeting. In touch with radicals throughout the South, Rhett planned for the rapid creation of a Southern nation and a concerted program that would appeal to cooperationists. Rhett has been called the "father of disunion."

Fort Sumter

While the secession convention met in Charleston, Maj. Robert Anderson, commanding the U.S. garrison at Fort Moultrie on nearby Sullivan's Island, quietly moved his eighty-two soldiers to Fort Sumter, a more defensible site in Charleston Harbor. Though the fort was still unfinished, its guns could command the shipping channel and fire on the city.

Governor Francis W. Pickens immediately began raising troops and ordered the occupation of federal properties in and around Charleston. The few Federal soldiers holding Fort Moultrie, Castle Pinckney, and the U.S. Arsenal offered no resistance when, in the first military encounter of the war, South Carolina troops quickly seized all three. They hauled down the Stars and Stripes and hoisted a flag with a new moon and a palmetto tree—the South Carolina flag.

As tensions increased, Charleston's mulatto aristocracy was harassed and threatened. Some left the city at great personal loss, but others volunteered to assist in its defense.

In January 1861 President James Buchanan sent a merchant vessel, *Star of the West,* to reinforce Major Anderson in Fort Sumter. On January 9 it was fired on from Morris

> **On March 7 Lincoln . . . promised to "hold, occupy, and possess the property and places belonging to the government."**

Island and, following orders, turned back. Major Anderson had not returned the fire from the shore batteries because he was awaiting orders from Washington.

Governor Pickens, regarding the Federal occupation of Fort Sumter as a threat to South Carolina, asked Buchanan to cede it to the state. Sentiment was rising to storm the fort and criticism of Pickens mounted, but he refused to be stampeded by firebrands. Meanwhile, the legislature passed an act creating a regular army for the Palmetto Republic.

When the Montgomery convention opened in February, the South Carolina delegation included Memminger and Rhett, who was disappointed when he was not elected president of the new Confederate States of America established

there. Memminger chaired the committee that drafted the Provisional Constitution and subsequently was appointed secretary of the treasury.

The Palmetto delegation demanded that the assembly either accept the Fort Sumter problem as a common one or allow South Carolina forces to attack the fort. The new Congress accepted the responsibility, and in March Gen. P. G. T. Beauregard was sent to take command of all Southern military forces in the Charleston area. He redeployed the troops there and rearranged the growing ring of batteries around the harbor.

On March 7 Lincoln took the oath of office in Washington as president and promised to "hold, occupy, and possess the property and places belonging to the government." South Carolinians knew this meant Fort Sumter.

On April 7 a naval expedition sailed for Charleston to reprovision the fort. The following day a representative of the U.S. State Department delivered a message to Governor Pickens informing him of the expedition. The governor passed the information to General Beauregard, who asked for instructions from Jefferson Davis, president of the Confederacy. Davis thought war was inevitable, but he had hoped to avoid firing the first shot. Now he saw no alternative.

On April 10 Beauregard was instructed by telegraph to demand the surrender of Fort Sumter or to reduce it. When Major Anderson refused to surrender, Beauregard ordered the bombardment of the fort on April 12. After a fierce shelling from Confederate shore batteries and with food and ammunition running low, Anderson surrendered the following day. Celebrations erupted in Charleston as Confederate soldiers occupied Fort Sumter and its Federal garrison departed for the North.

The final catalyst for war had come in Charleston Harbor. President Lincoln now called for 75,000 volunteers from the loyal states and a blockade of Southern ports. States in the upper South that had initially hesitated now joined the Confederacy.

South Carolina in the War

The Confederate government requested Pickens to dispatch troops to Virginia, as the South Carolinians were better prepared than similar units in other Southern states. When he sent these volunteer units to fight at First Manassas, he was roundly criticized. He also became unpopular for requisitioning slaves as laborers, and foodstuffs and medicines for South Carolina troops.

Gen. Robert E. Lee arrived in Charleston on November 6 to take command of the Military Department of South Carolina, Georgia, and Florida. The following day Hilton Head Island, Port Royal, and Beaufort fell to a force of 12,000 Union soldiers who planned to use the area as a base for military operations and headquarters of the blockading fleet. Here the first South Carolina slaves were mustered into the

Union army. Eventually, 5,462 black South Carolinians entered Federal service.

The invasion struck panic in white citizens, and they blamed Pickens for inadequate coastal defenses. South Carolina's secession convention was reconvened. Action was taken to improve the defenses around Charleston and a new Executive Council was created. The governor was furious since the council assumed almost unlimited powers. But when the new body began requisitioning slaves, declaring martial law, and recruiting troops for the Confederate government, its popularity waned among the independent-minded South Carolinians. Now the council was branded as dictatorial.

After the initial rush to the colors, recruitment of troops for both home defense and Confederate quotas proved difficult. In March 1862 the council passed a conscription plan for white males between the ages of eighteen and forty-five. The Confederate Congress enacted a similar law to enlist men between eighteen and thirty-five. South Carolina then organized two militia corps of men over thirty-five for home defense, and the council gave to Confederate draft officials the rolls that were to be used by the state for conscription. In September 1862, when the Confederate government passed

> ## When Beauregard refused, Gillmore ordered the bombardment of Charleston. It would continue for the next 587 days.

a law to draft all men between eighteen and forty-five, South Carolina's plans for defending the state were disrupted. The state now was forced to enact a law calling up all men between the ages of sixteen and sixty-five. That same month the legislature abolished the Executive Council and nullified its acts.

During most of 1862 thousands of South Carolina troops were rushed into fierce fighting in Virginia, Maryland, Mississippi, Kentucky, and Tennessee. The following year they were in the thick of the battles at Chancellorsville, Gettysburg, and Chickamauga. They suffered heavy losses.

When Pickens's term as governor ended in December 1862, a joint session of the legislature elected Milledge L. Bonham as the state's new chief executive. Bonham, a former brigadier general in the Confederate army, had been serving as a representative from South Carolina in the Confederate Congress. He pledged to continue the policy of supporting the Confederacy but soon faced the same problems that had plagued his predecessor.

General Beauregard, who now commanded the Department of South Carolina and Georgia, believed that a minimum of 30,000 troops were needed for the defense of South Carolina alone. But in January 1863 there were only 10,000 Confederate soldiers available in the entire state.

Union strategists were determined to seize Charleston, "the cradle of secession," to stop the daily manufacture of cartridges in the former U.S. arsenal there and the building of ironclad vessels, and to stem the flow of vast amounts of military supplies and luxury goods brought in by blockade runners. Anticipating an attack, Beauregard ordered all noncombatants out of Charleston in February and appealed to Bonham for armed forces. Reluctantly, Bonham ordered all white males sixteen to eighteen and forty-five to fifty years of age to be called up for the defense of Charleston. Three regiments were mustered, but arming and supplying them was problematic since the state had turned over most of its supplies to the Confederacy. Nevertheless, by April, Beauregard had under his command a poorly equipped force of 22,648 men thinly stretched from Charleston to the Savannah River, with 12,856 occupying the fortifications in the city and on the nearby islands.

The first attack came in June when 6,000 Union troops landed southeast of the city and a fierce firefight took place on James Island. Casualties were heavy on both sides and the Union forces retreated. On April 7 Federal ironclads under the command of Commo. Samuel L. Du Pont attempted to destroy Fort Sumter. They were forced to withdraw, however, owing to Confederate fire and the threat of mines or submarine torpedoes, a naval weapon developed by the Confederate Torpedo Bureau that inaugurated a new era in naval warfare. The third attack, a joint army-navy operation, began in July.

Six thousand Federal troops under Gen. Quincy A. Gillmore quickly occupied most of Morris Island. But heroic and costly assaults by African American troops failed to overrun the Confederate strong point, Fort Wagner, which withstood fifty-eight days of fierce bombardment. This prevented the navy from executing its role in the operation, since the batteries around the harbor and the well-placed torpedoes remained formidable obstacles. Gillmore dug in on Morris Island and trained his long-range rifled guns on Fort Sumter, which was soon reduced to rubble though it remained garrisoned. One 200-pounder Parrott rifled gun was aimed at Charleston some four miles away. On August 21 Gillmore demanded that Beauregard evacuate Fort Sumter and Morris Island. When Beauregard refused, Gillmore ordered the bombardment of Charleston. It would continue for the next 587 days. Charlestonians were angry and frightened. Those in the city who could afford the fare took the next train or carriage to safer communities.

The Union occupation of Morris Island and the increased surveillance by the Union navy severely curtailed blockade running while Federal land forces inched closer to the city. In Charleston and across the state, Confederate money depreciated and the costs of goods and services soared. A few speculators in foodstuffs made huge profits, but destitution was widespread.

By mid-1863 war-weariness had grown to alarming proportions in South Carolina. Rhett's newspaper, *Mercury,* attacked President Davis's ability to wage war successfully. Among the poor, resentment flared against speculators and Confederate and state conscription laws that permitted the well-to-do to evade the draft. Some embittered soldiers took up the cry, "It's a rich man's war and a poor man's fight." Deserters swarmed through the western regions of the state terrorizing the citizenry. Governor Bonham called on the Confederate War Department to provide protection against deserters as well as the new threat in early 1864 posed by Union cavalry in the region. But Bonham lost this argument and another with the Confederate secretary of war when Beauregard was ordered to release most of his cavalry for duty in Virginia in March 1864.

By late 1864 Gen. William Tecumseh Sherman with 60,000 battle-hardened veterans had marched across Georgia and now posed a threat to South Carolina. In the entire state there was a mere 22,000 regular and irregular troops to oppose the Union forces. Bonham recommended that the state assume more responsibility for its defense and urged the new legislature to pass a conscription law to be carried out by state officials rather than Confederate authorities. Bonham had cooperated with the Confederacy until near the end of his term when he believed that his state faced a crisis. After his term ended in late 1864, the legislature once more became a champion of state rights and nullified most important Confederate laws. This anti-Confederate attitude was also that of the new governor, Andrew G. Magrath, a Charlestonian and former Confederate district judge.

The legislature passed acts permitting Magrath to exempt from Confederate service whomever he wished and restricting the Confederacy's authority to impress slaves in South Carolina. At the same time Magrath repeatedly asked the Richmond government for assistance, but to little avail.

Magrath concluded that the state could no longer depend on the Confederacy and that the only way to save it was to convince North Carolina and Georgia to cooperate militarily. Any such plan collapsed in early February 1865 when Sherman invaded South Carolina, which his army referred to as "the Hellhole of Secession."

After a feint toward Charleston and Augusta, Sherman's army continued its strategy of total war and cut a wide swath of destruction across the state. Sherman's real destination was Columbia, the state capital. The army lived off the land and plundered the countryside; within three weeks planters' homes, churches, and a dozen villages went up in flames. Governor Magrath called on South Carolinians to destroy or carry away anything that might be of value to the enemy.

With his supply lines cut and Union troops closing in, Gen. William J. Hardee, the commanding officer at Charleston, decided that the city was no longer defensible. On the evening of February 17–18 he ordered military equipment and supplies set afire, and the city's 10,000 defenders left the city, retreating northward across the Santee River. As the Union forces entered Charleston, one citizen observed, "Total ruin is staring us in the face."

Governor Magrath fled Columbia when Sherman's army reached the state capital. As they had done in other towns, Sherman's soldiers set it afire, although one Ohio lieutenant claimed that "*whiskey done it* and *not the* soldiers." About one-third of Columbia was destroyed. When the army marched away from the city and toward North Carolina, Sherman's soldiers burned and pillaged portions of Camden, Winnsboro, Lancaster, Chesterfield, and Cheraw.

Meanwhile, the governor's office was a rolling entourage moving from one town to another. In April Magrath met with a few members of the legislature in Greenville and apprised them of the near anarchy in the state. Several days later he fled to Columbia when Union cavalry seized Greenville. By late May the government of the state had collapsed, Magrath had been captured and imprisoned, and Union forces were in control of South Carolina.

South Carolina's battlefield casualties were among the highest of any state in the Confederacy. Approximately 75,000 white, male South Carolinians entered the field as regulars and another 10,000 served in the home guard. Of these some 40,000 were killed or gravely wounded, which was a rate of loss sharply higher than the average of about 10 percent for other states in the Confederacy. This high casualty rate resulted from the fact that South Carolina units were among the best prepared for combat and therefore were rushed into some of the early, bloodiest battles of the war.

South Carolina's countryside was devastated, its villages and cities were in ruins. The economic, labor, and social system of the state was no more. Once enslaved African Americans were now free and they exuberantly embraced their new freedom. Many left their farms and plantations and streamed into the cities. But in these urban centers and the countryside there was starvation among blacks and whites alike. One member of the South Carolina white elite observed, "The war has ruined us." Most whites who had survived were demoralized and dispirited.

A Northern reporter who toured Charleston a few months after the war ended described it as "a city of ruins, of desolation, of vacant homes, of widowed women, . . . of weed-wild gardens, . . . of grass-grown streets." He could have been describing many South Carolina cities in 1865.

[*For further discussion of South Carolina cities and battles, see* Carolinas Campaign of Sherman; Charleston, South Carolina; Columbia, South Carolina; Port Royal, South

Carolina. *See also* Fort Sumter, South Carolina, *biographies of numerous figures mentioned herein]*

BIBLIOGRAPHY

Cauthen, Charles Edward. *South Carolina Goes to War, 1860–1865.* Chapel Hill, N.C., 1950.

Channing, Steven A. *Crisis of Fear: Secession in South Carolina.* New York, 1970.

Coclanis, Peter A., and Lacy K. Ford. "The South Carolina Economy Reconstructed and Reconsidered: Structure, Output, and Performance, 1670–1985." In *Developing Dixie: Modernization in a Traditional Society.* Edited by Winfred B. Moore, Jr., Joseph F. Tripp, and Lyon G. Tyler, Jr. New York, 1988.

Doyle, Don. *New Men, New Cities, New South: Atlanta, Nashville, Charleston, Mobile, 1860–1910.* Chapel Hill, N.C., 1990.

Edmunds, John B., Jr. "South Carolina." In *The Confederate Governors.* Edited by W. Buck Yearns. Athens, Ga., 1985.

Ford, Lacy K., Jr. *Origins of Southern Radicalism: The South Carolina Upcountry, 1800–1860.* New York, 1988.

Fraser, Walter J., Jr. *Charleston! Charleston!: The History of a Southern City.* Columbia, S.C., 1989.

Glatthaar, Joseph T. *The March to the Sea and Beyond: Sherman's Troops in the Savannah and Carolinas Campaigns.* New York, 1985.

Johnson, Michael P., and James L. Roark, eds. *No Chariot Let Down: Charleston's Free People of Color on the Eve of the Civil War.* Chapel Hill, N.C., 1984.

Thomas, Emory M. *The Confederate Nation: 1861–1865.* New York, 1979.

Wallace, David Duncan. *A Short History of South Carolina, 1520–1948.* Chapel Hill, N.C., 1951.

WALTER J. FRASER

SOUTHERN EXPRESS COMPANY

Privately owned companies that hauled freight and delivered mail expanded their businesses during the Civil War. Many small shippers, some with a single wagon and team of horses, carried goods locally and over short intercity distances. Before the war, five companies monopolized the interstate trade, but only one of these, the Adams Express Company, with origins in 1840 and consolidations in 1854, stretched into the South.

With the onset of war, the Confederate government threatened to confiscate the assets of Northern businesses within its borders. To protect itself, the Adams Express transferred its Southern branches to company superintendent Henry B. Plant. Plant, a Connecticut man who had expanded the company into the South in 1854, felt the need to "prove" his allegiance to the Confederacy in order to conduct business. He reorganized the company under a group of Southern stock-holders and renamed it the Southern Express Company. On May 1, 1861, Plant petitioned the Georgia legislature for a charter, which was granted on July 5. Plant met with Jefferson Davis, swore his loyalty to the Confederacy, and negotiated to become an adjunct to the Confederate Quartermaster Corps. Plant's express was the largest private company to transport supplies for Southern armies and collect tariffs for the government. Secretary of the Treasury Christopher G. Memminger exempted express workers from military service because of their critical duties as civilian contractors. Often, commanders detailed soldiers for temporary service with the company.

Headquartered at Augusta, Georgia, the Southern Express Company continued its established weekly routes to New Orleans, Richmond, Nashville, Vicksburg, Charleston, and other major cities from the eastern seaboard to Texas. It made large profits shipping payrolls, munitions, and supplies, transporting millions of packages to soldiers in hospitals, prisons, or camps, and delivering letters to widely located rural homes. For most of the war, the company carried soldiers' mail free of charge. It provided an alternative to the Confederate Post Office, which handled mostly letters, and it helped sustain the morale of Confederate soldiers by bringing them packages from home and conveying battlefield souvenirs and pay to their families.

The company carried happy packages from home as well as the saddest of all shipments—coffins with dead soldiers. There are no figures on the costs of transporting a body. Generally, it cost twenty-five cents to send a letter within the South and fifty cents to mail it north. Many packages cost one dollar per pound, but as Confederate money lost value, company agents refused script in favor of barter items, including chickens, pigs, corn, and other commodities.

The Southern Express never really severed itself from the Adams Express Company; its name change and charter were chimerical political moves to divert criticism and maintain profits. As rival armies moved along the battlefront, the Southern Express cooperated with Adams at various points to keep packages flowing across the lines. When Confederate armies advanced, the Southern occupied Adams's offices and freely used its wagons and supplies. Confederate retreats brought Adams's employees back to their old stations. Since the U.S. Post Office refused to deliver mail to and from the Confederate states, the two express companies filled the void.

Many Southerners questioned the patriotism of Plant and the company. Although some editors challenged the company's motives, insisting it had not broken from Adams and charging it with treason, most agreed with an Augusta editor that the Southern Express was "a powerful auxiliary to the Government and of incalculable benefit to the soldiers in the field, and to commerce generally." Nevertheless, the company operated first for profits and second to help the Confederacy.

BIBLIOGRAPHY

Confederate Papers Relating to Citizens or Business Firms. Microcopy M346. Record Group 109. National Archives, Washington, D.C.

Harlow, Alvin F. *Old Waybills: The Romance of the Express Companies.* New York, 1934.

Martin, S. Walter. "Henry Bradley Plant." In *Georgians in Profile: Historical Essays in Honor of Ellis Merton Coulter.* Edited by Horace Montgomery. Athens, Ga., 1958.

Smyth, G. Hutchinson. *The Life of Henry B. Plant: Founder and President of the Plant System of Railroads and Steamships and also of the Southern Express Company.* New York, 1898.

Wells, Henry. *Sketch of the Rise, Progress, and Present Condition of the Express System.* Albany, N.Y., 1864.

RUSSELL DUNCAN

SOUTHERN HISTORICAL SOCIETY

Devoted to the preservation of Confederate history, the Southern Historical Society was organized in New Orleans in 1869. Led by former officers and supporters of the Confederacy, the society sought to mobilize Southerners to preserve a "true history" of the Civil War, one that established the honor and nobility of the Confederate cause. The society met with very little response, however; probably no more than a hundred people joined. In hopes of increasing interest, the society in 1873 met at White Sulphur Springs, West Virginia. There a group of Virginians, led by former Confederate general Jubal Early, took control of the organization. The society then moved its headquarters to Richmond and in 1876 began to publish the *Southern Historical Society Papers.*

Under the leadership of Early, an irascible fellow never reconciled to the Confederacy's defeat, and J. William Jones, a Baptist minister with similar attitudes who served as editor of the *Papers,* the Southern bias of the SHS became even more pronounced. At times, its partisans appeared to be refighting the war (Early once referred to an article as a bomb delivered against the enemy) and clearly hoped to revive the culture of the Old South and the Confederacy. To rally the South to this cause, the SHS dispatched agents and sought to establish auxiliary societies in other states. A few short-lived auxiliary groups formed, but for the most part the SHS never boasted a large following in the South. The *Papers* had only a little over fifteen hundred subscribers and encountered repeated financial problems. Publication, which had initially been monthly, became annual with the 1885 volume.

The *Papers* nevertheless became the most important legacy of the SHS. These volumes not only preserved reports, reminiscences, and other historical material about the Confederacy but helped develop interpretations that became central to the Lost Cause mythology and to the modern historiography of the Civil War. Articles published in the *Papers* provided evidence to support a growing Southern conviction that the Confederacy had succumbed only to the North's overwhelming numbers and resources. Others celebrated the military genius of Robert E. Lee, helping establish him as the South's premier hero, and accused Gen. James Longstreet of tardiness during the second day at Gettysburg, implying that his failure there had lost the war.

Much of this contribution had been made by 1887, when Jones resigned and financial difficulties overtook the SHS. R. A. Brock, another Virginia veteran and secretary of the Virginia Historical Society, became the new editor of the *Papers.* The originality of contributions declined, and after 1910, with Brock ill, Confederate veterans dying off, and the SHS all but defunct, volumes appeared only sporadically. In 1926, Douglas Southall Freeman, the distinguished Lee biographer, and a few of his friends in Richmond took over the SHS and saw through to publication additional volumes of the *Papers,* which printed the proceedings of the Confederate Congress. After Freeman's death in 1953, the Virginia Historical Society received all of the society's assets and completed the publication of the proceedings. The final volume of the *Papers,* the fifty-second, appeared in 1959.

[*See also* Lost Cause, *overview article.*]

BIBLIOGRAPHY

Connelly, Thomas L. *The Marble Man: Robert E. Lee and His Image in American Society.* New York, 1977.

Coulter, E. Merton. "What the South Has Done about Its History." *Journal of Southern History* 2 (February 1936): 3–28.

Foster, Gaines M. *Ghosts of the Confederacy: Defeat, the Lost Cause, and the Emergence of the New South, 1865 to 1913.* New York, 1987.

Piston, William Garrett. *Lee's Tarnished Lieutenant: James Longstreet and His Place in Southern History.* Athens, Ga., 1987.

Wilson, Charles Reagan. *Baptized in Blood: The Religion of the Lost Cause, 1865–1920.* Athens, Ga., 1980.

GAINES M. FOSTER

SOUTH MOUNTAIN, MARYLAND

This slope, two miles east of Harpers Ferry, was the site of a battle, fought on September 14, 1862, as a result of the Federals' inadvertent discovery of Gen. Robert E. Lee's campaign plans (Special Order 191) on September 13.

In the order, issued September 9 at Frederick, Maryland, the unorthodox Lee divided his forces, directing three columns to attack and capture the Federal garrison at Harpers Ferry, while the remainder of the army awaited reunion of the detached forces west of South Mountain near Boonsboro, Maryland. Although outnumbered two to one, Lee considered Army of the Potomac commander George B. McClellan a minimal threat since the Union army remained in a defensive stance protecting the approaches to Washington and Baltimore.

But when McClellan arrived at Frederick on September 13, two Indiana soldiers discovered Special Order 191 wrapped around three cigars in an abandoned Confederate camp east of Frederick. The "lost order" arrived at McClellan's headquarters before noon on the thirteenth, and the ecstatic Federal commander wired President Lincoln: "I think Lee has made a gross mistake. I have all the plans of the rebels and will catch them in their own trap." McClellan subsequently ordered an advance against South Mountain on the fourteenth "to cut the enemy in two and beat him in detail."

South Mountain commences at the Potomac River two miles east of Harpers Ferry, and it runs north into Pennsylvania. Its precipitous, wooded slopes range from eight hundred to nearly two thousand feet, and with the exception of three gaps near its southern end, South Mountain presents a formidable barrier.

McClellan's strategy drove three wedges into South Mountain. At Crampton's Gap, six miles northeast of Harpers Ferry, McClellan ordered Maj. Gen. William B. Franklin and his twelve-thousand-man corps to relieve the besieged Harpers Ferry garrison and entrap seven thousand isolated Southerners in Pleasant Valley. Six miles north of Crampton's, McClellan directed Maj. Gen. Jesse L. Reno's corps to strike at Fox's Gap. One mile farther north at Turner's Gap, the corps of Maj. Gen. Joseph Hooker was to advance. By smashing through Fox's and Turner's Gaps, McClellan expected to slice the retreat routes of Lee and the remaining Confederates in Maryland—James Longstreet's and John Bell Hood's divisions at Hagerstown and D. H. Hill's division near Boonsboro.

McClellan failed to accomplish any of his objectives. Delays in marching and deployment, extravagant Federal exaggerations about the number of Confederate defenders, and the rugged mountain terrain all conspired in General Lee's favor. At Crampton's Gap, five hundred Southerners behind a stone wall near Burkittsville at the eastern base of the mountain held off Franklin's corps for three hours. Crampton's Gap finally was seized at dark, but too late to rescue the Harpers Ferry garrison, which surrendered on the morning of the fifteenth, thus allowing the Confederates in Pleasant Valley to escape south of the Potomac. At Fox's Gap, Samuel Garland, Jr.'s, brigade of a thousand North Carolinians bruised the head of a Federal corps and held the gap long enough to allow reinforcements to arrive from Hill

and Hood. North of Turner's Gap, Robert Rodes's Alabama brigade of eleven hundred stalled Hooker's corps, and the one thousand Georgians of Alfred H. Colquitt's brigade stopped the Union Iron Brigade advance along the National Pike. About 10:00 P.M. on the night of the fourteenth, Lee ordered a withdrawal from Fox's and Turner's Gaps toward Sharpsburg, but he had gained the extra time needed to force Harpers Ferry's surrender and to reunite his army along the Antietam Creek.

Federal casualties in the battle include 1,821 wounded, 87 missing, and 438 killed; Maj. Gen. Jesse L. Reno was mortally wounded at Fox's Gap. The Confederates lost 1,768 wounded, 1,279 missing, and 387 killed (including Brig. Gen. Samuel Garland, Jr.).

BIBLIOGRAPHY

Cox, Jacob D. "Forcing Fox's Gap and Turner's Gap." In *Battles and Leaders of the Civil War*. Edited by Robert U. Johnson and C. C. Buel. Vol. 2. New York, 1888. Reprint, Secaucus, N.J., 1982.

Hill, Daniel Harvey. "The Battle of South Mountain or Boonsboro." In *Battles and Leaders of the Civil War*. Edited by Robert U. Johnson and C. C. Buel. Vol. 2. New York, 1888. Reprint, Secaucus, N.J., 1982.

Murfin, James V. *The Gleam of Bayonets*. New York, 1964.

Priest, John Michael. *Before Antietam: The Battle for South Mountain*. Shippensburg, Pa., 1992.

Sears, Stephen. *Landscape Turned Red*. New York, 1985.

U.S. War Department. *War of the Rebellion: A Compilation of the Official Records of the Union and Confederate Armies*. Ser. 1, vol. 19, pts. 1–2. Washington, D.C., 1888.

DENNIS E. FRYE

SPECIAL UNITS

Confederate elite units were many in number, spanning both the western and eastern theaters of operations, as well as the inland water navy, the high seas navy, and coastal defense units.

In the western theater of operations the infantry division of Maj. Gen. Patrick Cleburne stands out as such a unit, as do the First Missouri Brigade and the Kentucky Orphan Brigade. Nathan Bedford Forrest's cavalry and his artillery under the command of Capt. John Morton were outstanding in every respect. An elite Confederate western artillery unit was the Fifth Company, Washington Artillery of New Orleans, also known as Slocum's Battery. Other units included John Hunt Morgan's cavalry, and Capt. John Dickinson's guerrillas who operated in Florida. Another special unit, the Davis Guards, received medals (the only ones awarded by the Confederacy) for their heroic stand at Sabine Pass, Texas, in 1863.

The eastern theater of operations saw an abundance of elite ground forces. Foremost were the Stonewall Brigade and John Bell Hood's Texas Brigade, both of which were models of courage, discipline, and esprit de corps. In addition, A. P. Hill's Light Division and the Louisiana Tiger Brigade

> **The eastern theater of operations saw an abundance of elite ground forces.**

were exceptionally fine units, as was Wade Hampton's Legion, formed early in the war. The First Virginia Infantry Regiment, which traced its origin to George Washington in the French and Indian War, spearheaded George E. Pickett's charge at Gettysburg. Composing an elite unit that was not a regular part of the Army of Northern Virginia were the Virginia Military Institute cadets who gained immortality at the Battle of New Market in 1864. The Army of Northern Virginia included the famed Washington Artillery of New Orleans, the Rockbridge Artillery of the Stonewall Brigade, the Richmond Howitzers, and John Pegram's and William T. Pougue's Artillery Battalions.

Like the western theater, the Confederate cavalry in the eastern theater contained many elite units. Their names ring across the years: Turner Ashby's cavalry, John S. Mosby's Rangers, the Laurel Brigade, and J. E. B. Stuart's Cavalry Corps. Accompanying the latter was the elite Stuart Horse Artillery under John Pelham.

On the high seas the Confederacy was equally well served. Such vessels as *Alabama* and *Shenandoah* were renowned. In the inland water navy, elite units manned *Virginia* and *Tennessee*. The volunteer crew of *Hunley,* the first submarine that sank a warship, manned an experimental vessel whose previous crews had drowned during test voyages. Such courage could be found only among the finest of fighting units.

[*See also entries on the numerous biographical figures, military units, and ships mentioned herein.*]

BIBLIOGRAPHY

Connolly, Thomas L. *Army of the Heartland: The Army of Tennessee, 1861–1862.* Baton Rouge, La., 1967.

Connolly, Thomas L. *Autumn of Glory: The Army of Tennessee, 1862–1865.* Baton Rouge, La., 1971.

Freeman, Douglas S. *Lee's Lieutenants: A Study in Command.* 3 vols. New York, 1942–1944. Reprint, New York, 1986.

Jones, Virgil Carrington. *The Civil War at Sea.* 3 vols. New York, 1960–1962. Reprint, Wilmington, N.C., 1990.

Roth, David. "The Battle of Sabine Pass, Texas." *Blue and Gray Magazine* 4, no. 1 (August–September 1986): 7–24.

KIM BERNARD HOLIEN

SPECULATION

Both real and imagined, speculation hit all Southerners at one point or another during the war and created bitterness and anger toward the perpetrators. Moreover, it precipitated a decline in living standards and thus affected morale.

From the beginning of its existence, the Confederacy faced the problem of how to pay for the war effort. Secretary of the Treasury Christopher G. Memminger tried a number of plans, but by the midpoint of the war, his office was forced to rely upon the printing press and loans to pay for the war. The increased circulation of paper currency produced inflation. At first, the general commodity price index stood at antebellum levels, but by 1863 it had skyrocketed to levels twenty-eight times higher than those of 1861.

The increased cost of manufactured goods and agricultural products hit people hard, especially those living in the urban centers. Residents of Richmond and Atlanta, for example, saw the cost of foodstuffs grow prohibitive: in 1864, flour was sold for $250 a barrel—when it could be had; sweet potatoes garnered $16 a bushel; and meat commanded over $2 a pound. Discontent increased in proportion to the rise in prices, and most Southerners began to seek a cause for the exorbitant cost of necessities. Initially, they blamed the Commissary Department for buying up goods for the army and thus creating shortages on the home front which led to higher prices. Soon, manufacturers were also targeted: editorials and diarists argued that the factories charged higher prices on goods for the public in order to compensate for the loss they took producing for the government at lower fixed prices. Before long, merchants and traders were also pilloried in the press and in private. Such accusations often became anti-Semitic in tone, as Confederates began equating all traders with Jews and all Jews with Shylock-like practices.

Some Southerners, mostly women, refused to accept inflation and speculators without protest. The year 1863 witnessed a number of food riots throughout the urban Confederacy. Women, beaten down by high prices, took matters into their own hands in Richmond, Atlanta, Salisbury and High Point, North Carolina, and other places and demanded relief. These outbursts of violence can be interpreted as manifestations of unrest motivated by the perception and reality that speculation and speculators caused inflation and shortages, and hence deprivation.

The extent of real speculation in the Confederate South is difficult to assess. Basically, anyone who bought food, clothing, or other goods and held them for a period of time could expect to make a profit as money became increasingly cheaper. Still, some did not realize as great a profit as critics alleged. Though a merchant or manufacturer might hold an item off the shelves for a while to realize a profit, that profit was gained in inflated currency and was probably less than the original price of the good.

Speculators did exist in the Confederacy from the very beginning. Their practices were time-honored: buy a commodity in bulk to corner the market, float rumors of shortages, and then raise prices and sell at a profit. Most speculators dealt in such goods as cotton, salt, and meat; others dealt in necessities like shoes and clothing.

Confederate state governments could not ignore the problem of speculation—public outrage as inflation grew made some type of action imperative. Governors Andrew B. Moore of Alabama and Zebulon Vance of North Carolina published denunciations of speculators and extortioners (the words were usually used synonymously) and threatened to take drastic action. But Governor Joseph E. Brown of Georgia admitted laws against speculation were largely meaningless because speculators would find a way to evade them by continuing to withhold goods from the market or by refusing to sell goods to military authorities. Brown's comments to the General Assembly of Georgia in April 1863 epitomize the kind of language used to describe speculators: They are "a class . . . who remain at home preying upon the vitals of society, determined to make money at every hazard, who turn a deaf ear to the cries of the soldiers' families and are prepared to immolate even our armies and sacrifice our liberties upon the altar of mammon." Brown saw to it that Georgia taxed those speculating in needed commodities, but like other legislation aimed at speculators, it had little effect.

Although it is true that many did seek private gain at public expense, the real reasons for inflated prices and shortages of goods lay elsewhere. Many farmers found that government policies of impressment and the tax-in-kind hurt them; consequently, they withheld food from the market or planted less, which added to the inflationary spiral. Other farmers who did produce for both the people and the army had to cope with a transportation system that was woefully inadequate: often food would rot at depots awaiting transportation to markets or the front. Finally, the Union blockade stopped the flow of European goods, adding to the shortages and inflated prices. The net effect of all these factors—poor transportation facilities, the blockade, government policies, and the unscrupulous efforts of some who sought to reap profits during wartime—created inflated prices and led to charges of speculation and extortion.

There is no doubt that speculation—real and imagined—had a tremendous impact on the Confederate nation. Diaries, newspaper editorials, and public pronouncements against speculation demonstrate that Southerners detested the problem and the culprits. Disgust with unsavory practices and the inability to obtain needed goods for survival caused many Confederates to lose faith in a government that seemed ill equipped and unprepared to deal with the problem. The net

result of inflation and speculation was a noticeable decline in support for the Confederate cause.

[See also Bread Riots; Extortion; Inflation.]

BIBLIOGRAPHY

Escott, Paul D. After Secession: Jefferson Davis and the Failure of Confederate Nationalism. Baton Rouge, La., 1978.

Escott, Paul D. Many Excellent People: Power and Privilege in North Carolina, 1850–1900. Chapel Hill, N.C., 1985.

Lerner, Eugene. "Inflation in the Confederacy." In Studies in the Quantity Theory of Money. Edited by Milton Friedman. Chicago, 1956.

Thomas, Emory. The Confederate Nation, 1861–1865. New York, 1979.

Todd, Richard Cecil. Confederate Finance. Athens, Ga., 1954.

MARY A. DECREDICO

SPOTSYLVANIA CAMPAIGN

Spotsylvania Court House, Virginia, a county seat approximately nine miles southwest of Fredericksburg, became for a two-week period in May 1864 the focus of a series of engagements between the Army of Northern Virginia and the Army of the Potomac commanded respectively by Gens. Robert E. Lee and George G. Meade. When the opposing armies began to depart the area on the evening of May 20, the Confederates had sustained between 9,000 and 10,000 casualties here and the Federals more than 18,000.

Following two days of fighting in the Wilderness on May 5 and 6, Union General in Chief Ulysses S. Grant, who accompanied Meade's army in this summer campaign, ordered the army commander to move his force southeast twelve miles to the vicinity of Spotsylvania Court House. The movement began after dark on May 7. Lee also decided to move his First Corps to the same location during the night. The Confederates arrived just before the Federals, and the opposing advanced forces collided one and a half miles northwest of the village on the morning of May 8. Throughout the remainder of the day additional units from each army arrived and became engaged, with the Confederates maintaining their original position.

During the campaign Lee was operating at a disadvantage concerning two of his key subordinates. His ablest corps commander, Lt. Gen. James Longstreet, had been seriously wounded by friendly troops in the Wilderness fighting. Lee selected Maj. Gen. Richard Heron Anderson to command his First Corps until "Old Pete" returned. On the morning of May 8 Third Corps commander Maj. Gen. A. P. Hill was too ill to

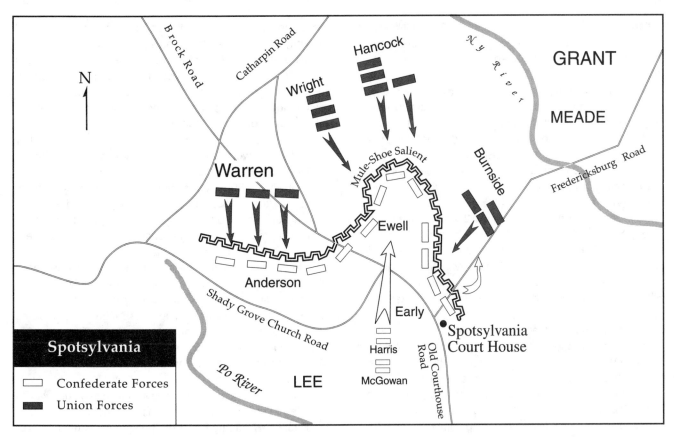

mount his horse. Maj. Gen. Jubal Early, a division commander in Maj. Gen. Richard S. Ewell's Second Corps, was chosen to replace Hill.

On May 9 the Union Ninth Corps, commanded by Maj. Gen. Ambrose E. Burnside, advanced south from the area of Chancellorsville and assumed position east of the courthouse with its left lying on the Fredericksburg-Spotsylvania Court House Road. As a result, when Early's Third Corps arrived, Lee placed it opposite Burnside's troops immediately east of the village. In the morning a Confederate sharpshooter killed the commander of the Union Sixth Corps, Maj. Gen. John Sedgwick. On this day, the Union's chief of cavalry, Maj. Gen. Philip Sheridan, led most of the Federal cavalry corps from the area on a raid south toward Richmond. Lee dispatched his chief of cavalry, Maj. Gen. J. E. B. Stuart, with Maj. Gen. Fitzhugh Lee's division to pursue the Federal horsemen. Two days later Stuart was mortally wounded in an engagement at Yellow Tavern, immediately north of Richmond. This was a crippling loss to the Confederacy.

At Spotsylvania the Confederate battle line consisted of Anderson's First Corps on the left and Ewell's Second in the center; both of these units faced north. Early's Third Corps manned the right of the line facing east. The center of the line occupied by Ewell's troops bulged forward to the north in the form of a salient, or "mule-shoe."

On May 10 the Federals executed attacks all along the line but were unable to coordinate them. Union Maj. Gen. Winfield S. Hancock's Second Corps advanced beyond Anderson's left flank, but darkness fell before the Northerners were prepared to assault that vulnerable flank. Late in the afternoon twelve Union regiments commanded by Col. Emory Upton succeeded in penetrating a segment of Ewell's line along the western face of the salient and captured nearly a thousand Confederates. The Unionists were not supported, however, and were pushed back by Confederate reserve forces. Upton's temporary success gave Grant an idea. The twelve regiments had been massed compactly and had penetrated the Southern position with relative ease. Grant ordered Meade to move Hancock's entire Second Corps from the right of the Union line to the center opposite Ewell and with it attack the tip or apex of the Confederate salient at first light on May 12.

On May 11 General Lee, evaluating certain Union activities behind their lines such as reconnaissance missions and the repositioning of supply wagons, erroneously concluded that the Federals were preparing to break contact that night and move east to Fredericksburg and thence south toward Richmond. If this occurred, the Southern commander was determined to attack the Federals in transit. He ordered his artillery corps commanders to move rearward after dark any batteries that would be difficult to relocate rapidly once a movement by the army had been determined. Thus, many of the guns positioned along the apex of the salient were withdrawn.

As Hancock's troops moved into position for the attack, they were heard by Ewell's pickets who immediately reported these sounds. Ewell was eventually persuaded by one of his division commanders, Maj. Gen. Edward ("Allegheny") Johnson, whose division was positioned along the apex of the salient, to recall the artillery pieces that had been withdrawn. The recall order did not reach the artillerymen in the rear until 3:40 A.M.

Visibility on the morning of May 12 was reduced to fifty yards by ground fog. Hancock's troops began their advance at 4:35 A.M. Their number totaled 19,000 with the two leading divisions consisting of 11,000. "Allegheny" Johnson's division of 4,000 infantrymen would bear the brunt of this onslaught with little artillery support. Some Confederate pickets were captured. Others fired a hasty round and took to their heels. They warned their comrades manning the main line of the mass of Federals approaching, but the troops could only wait until the Bluecoats became visible about a hundred yards in front. At this time the orders to fire were given. Rain had fallen intermittently during the night, and much of the Southern powder was damp and did not ignite. The Northerners poured over the works in overwhelming numbers. The returning artillery pieces arrived at this time and were overrun and captured. A few gun crews were able to fire a round or two before surrendering.

Many of the Federals continued to advance southward inside of the salient in disorganized groups. These were stopped and driven back to the outside of the works by Confederate reserves. Approximately 3,000 Southerners including "Allegheny" Johnson were captured in the attack along with twenty pieces of artillery.

With most of Johnson's division gone, a considerable segment of the line was unoccupied on the inside by any Confederate troops. To correct this, Lee forwarded two brigades from the Third Corps during the morning. These were Brig. Gen. Nathaniel H. Harris's Mississippi Brigade and the South Carolinians of Brig. Gen. Samuel McGowan's brigade who arrived on the scene at 7:30 A.M. and 9:30 A.M., respectively. These troops upon arrival drove the Federals away from the outside of the works and reoccupied a portion of the trench line formerly held by Johnson's troops. McGowan was wounded in the advance to the front line and was superseded in command by Col. Joseph N. Brown. By noon the entire Federal Sixth Corps, now commanded by Brig. Gen. Horatio G. Wright, had been moved opposite Harris's and McGowan's positions.

These opposing forces—Harris's and Brown's brigades inside the works, and the Union Sixth Corps and portions of Hancock's Second outside—retained their relative positions along the northern face of the salient front and maintained continuous fire of varying intensity until 4:00 the following morning. At times the antagonists were only twenty yards apart. Occasionally an impulsive surge forward by a hundred or so Northerners would carry over the works and be immediately hurled back in bloody hand-to-hand fighting. Rain fell intermittently during the afternoon.

While this desperate fighting occurred, other Confederates were constructing a new defensive line of works across the base of the salient nearly one mile to the rear. Finally, at 4:00 A.M., Harris's, Brown's, and the remaining Confederate troops in position along the sides of the salient were permitted to retire to the new line. Thus ended what was probably the most intense twenty-three-hour period of land warfare in a confined area up to that time.

The operations conducted during the remaining ten days of the campaign were anticlimactic. The Army of the Potomac joined the Ninth Corps east of the village where its line lay in a north-south direction facing west. The Confederates changed their relative alignment accordingly. The opposing forces departed the vicinity of Spotsylvania Court House on May 21 and May 22. They would meet again at the North Anna River.

Assuming that Lee's objective in the campaign was to keep the enemy out of central Virginia by holding the line of the Rapidan River, the Battle of Spotsylvania can be considered a strategic defeat. After the Wilderness fighting on May 7 and again on May 21, Lee was unable to prevent the Federals from moving their forces in the direction they desired. This had not happened before in northern Virginia during the war.

The Army of Northern Virginia had once again inflicted severe casualties upon its old antagonist, but its own losses were in some respects more damaging. On May 12 alone Lee lost the services of one major general and seven brigadier generals. During the two weeks of Spotsylvania, 4,600 troops from Ewell's Second Corps became prisoners. Lee could not readily replace these losses.

Spotsylvania was only one of the many series of battles that swept across Virginia in May and early June of 1864. It took a heavy toll of experienced officers and invaluable enlisted men from the Army of Northern Virginia. These losses contributed significantly to the weakening of the Confederacy's military capabilities.

[*See also* Yellow Tavern, Virginia.]

BIBLIOGRAPHY

Brown, Varina D. *A Colonel at Gettysburg and Spotsylvania.* Columbia, S.C., 1931.

Freeman, Douglas S. *Lee's Lieutenants: A Study in Command.* 3 vols. New York, 1942–1944. Reprint, New York, 1986.

Humphreys, Andrew A. *The Virginia Campaign of '64 and '65.* New York, 1883.

Johnson, Robert U., and C. C. Buel, eds. *Battles and Leaders of the Civil War.* 4 vols. New York, 1887–1888. Reprint, Secaucus, N.J., 1982.

Matter, William D. *If It Takes All Summer: The Battle of Spotsylvania.* Chapel Hill, N.C., 1988.

U.S. War Department. *War of the Rebellion: A Compilation of the Official Records of the Union and Confederate Armies.* Washington, D.C., 1880–1901. Ser. 1, vol. 36, pts. 1–3; ser. 1, vol. 51, pts. 1–2.

The Wilderness Campaign, May–June, 1964. Papers of the Military Historical Society of Massachusetts, no. 4. Boston, 1905. Reprint, Wilmington, N.C., 1989.

WILLIAM D. MATTER

STAMPS

The Confederate government was continually frustrated in its attempts to supply citizens with postage stamps—either in the quantity or of the quality to which they had become accustomed under Federal postal jurisdiction. Making use of experienced specialists in stamp design and production would have answered this need, but these printers were located in the North, and any hope of contracting with Union publishers to produce Confederate stamps ended when the war began. On occasion, the Confederacy would try importing its stamps, but the blockade eventually choked off such trade. As for homemade products—when there were enough artists available to design them and sufficient ink and paper to print them—they were invariably inferior to anything available in the North or abroad. What one period observer remarked about the new nation's currency might as easily have been said of its postage stamps: "Neither in material nor in execution would they have reflected credit on a village printing-office."

Southern-born heroes like George Washington had long adorned Federal postage stamps, and with the establishment of the Confederate Post Office Department in 1861, officials determined to maintain this tradition. The government awarded the first contract to produce stamps to Hoyer & Ludwig, Richmond-based publishers best known for their parlor prints and songsheet covers. (The awarding of such priority contracts all but ended the production of decorative prints for the remainder of the war; firms like Hoyer & Ludwig were virtually ordered to focus on what one journalist called "needed articles," and it was not unusual for the government to transfer artists from other firms, or from the army, to assist with official orders.)

By April 1861 Hoyer & Ludwig had supplied John H. Reagan, postmaster general of the Confederacy, with their first "samples of postal stamps," explaining: "The ten-cent stamps represent the C. S. Flag, which we have engraved. The two- and five-cent stamps we only made the drawings of,

which we intend to make if the order should be given to us. The twenty we would like to make with President Davis's portrait, in which case you would have to furnish us with a good likeness, if you should favor us with the contract for making the stamps." Hoyer & Ludwig still found it necessary to add their hope that they would receive "preference" over "Northern houses."

By the time their designs were under review, Fort Sumter had been taken and the war was underway; "Northern houses" were no longer competing. But the problems facing the Richmond publisher were obvious from their first letter: they did not even have on hand a likeness of the new president on which to model a portrait.

Hoyer & Ludwig got their contract, but not for engraved stamps, which were too expensive to produce. Instead they issued lithographed five-cent stamps in sheets of one hundred each. These first stamps were not perforated; users had to cut them apart themselves. A portrait of Jefferson Davis was evidently obtained and copied, for the new stamps featured a blurry, if familiar prewar likeness of the president. The stamps were on sale by October 1861, when the *Richmond Daily Dispatch* generously praised the "very excellent bust of President Davis," adding of the stamps: "Their introduction supplies a want which has heretofore seriously taxed the public endurance." Prior to the issue of these first stamps, local postmasters had been left to their own initiative. They had marked postal rate, town, and cancellation by hand or had used provisional hand stamps. Some postmasters had even prepared their own postage stamps for local sale and use.

> **"Neither in material nor in execution would they have reflected credit on a village printing-office."**

Hoyer & Ludwig continued to manufacture stamps for the Confederacy for the duration of the war. One artist remembered that the firm's twelve presses were on line "most of the time," usually for the production of stamps and currency. "At first my output was 200 sheets per day," he added, shedding light on the human side of stamp production in the Confederacy. "But I soon got it up to a ream—480 sheets. You see, I was getting $5.00 a week in Confederate money, with a bonus for all over 200 sheets pulled per day."

The very month the Hoyer & Ludwig stamps first appeared, Postmaster General Reagan was already searching for an alternative to the homemade products. He authorized a government agent traveling to England in search of arms imports to arrange also for the creation of higher-quality stamps. A contract was signed with Thomas

De La Rue & Co. of London, which commissioned an artist named Jean Ferdinand Joubert de la Ferte to engrave a Davis likeness for a new stamp, a vast improvement over the Richmond models. In February 1862 De La Rue exported the finished plates, along with 2 million stamps, to the Confederacy. But even this huge supply was quickly depleted, and the blockade made it difficult to continue relying on such imports.

That year, Reagan contracted with another Richmond firm, Archer & Daly, to make their own stamps directly from the De La Rue plates. Native paper and ink, however, proved inferior to the British variety, and so did native skill with the presses. The results from Archer & Daly were wildly inconsistent, and one infamous run proved so flawed it made President Davis appear to be wearing a long white tie. The "white cravat" Davis stamp eventually became one of the most coveted among postwar collectors.

On July 1, 1862, the Confederacy doubled its basic postal rate to ten cents, requiring new issues. The De La Rue company was hired to make new plates, but apparently did little more than burnish out the "five cents" inscription on the old plates, replacing it with the new rate. These stamps were issued in a rose-colored hue, supplanting the "five cent blues" that had become familiar to Confederates, flaws notwithstanding. De La Rue also supplied some 400,000 copies of a one-cent stamp depicting John C. Calhoun and intended for less expensive mailings, such as circulars and newspapers. By the time these stamps arrived, the circular rate had increased to two cents; as a result, the stamps were never released for sale or use. The Confederacy also managed to issue a ten-cent stamp (from Hoyer & Ludwig) depicting Thomas Jefferson, and a two-cent "green" featuring a horribly smudged portrait of Andrew Jackson. It was not unusual for the colors of these issues to vary as markedly as the quality of their portrait likenesses.

Whatever their shortcomings, Confederate postage stamps after the war became highly desirable collectibles, not only in unused states, but affixed to patriotic envelopes or even canceled on everyday mail. The rage inspired its share of bogus reissues from surviving plates and stones, as well as out-and-out fakes, including a clever Stonewall Jackson ten-cent issue that in all likelihood originated no earlier than 1867. One scholar of the Confederate postal service and its stamp issues has estimated that nearly a quarter of the examples he has inspected have been forgeries.

BIBLIOGRAPHY

Dietz, August, Sr. *The Postal Service of the Confederate States of America.* Richmond, Va., 1929.

Green, Brian M. *The Confederate States Five-Cent Blue Lithograph.* New York, 1978.

Green, Brian M. *The Confederate States Ten-Cent Rose Lithograph.* New York, 1978.

Green, Brian M. *The Confederate States Two-Cent Green Lithograph.* New York, 1977.

Green, Brian M. *The Typographs of the Confederate States of America: Postal Stamps and Postal History.* New York, 1981.

Neely, Mark E., Jr., Harold Holzer, and Gabor S. Boritt. *The Confederate Image: Prints of the Lost Cause.* Chapel Hill, N.C., 1977.

HAROLD HOLZER

STANLEY, HENRY MORTON

STANLEY, HENRY MORTON (1841–1904), Confederate private, Union artillerist and sailor, journalist, and explorer. Born in Wales, John Rowlands immigrated to the United States in 1859. He found employment in New Orleans with a cotton broker, Henry Morton Stanley, whose name he took.

In 1861, swept along by the emotion and enthusiasm of the moment, he enlisted with the Sixth Arkansas Infantry (Dixie Grays), a decision he later considered a "grave blunder." His *Autobiography* contains a highly critical account of the hardships endured by the Grays during their "seasoning" and a compelling and graphic description of the fighting at Shiloh where Stanley was made a prisoner.

Confined at Camp Douglas, near Chicago, Stanley was unable to endure the privations of prison life. Thus, after two months, he enrolled in the U.S. Artillery Service, motivated not by conversion to the Northern cause but by "a fear of being incarcerated for years." When he arrived at Harpers Ferry, dysentery and fever overcame him and led to his discharge on June 22, 1862. In August 1864 he joined the U.S. Navy. He served as a ship's writer and witnessed the attacks on Fort Fisher, North Carolina, in January 1865. Northern newspapers welcomed his vivid accounts of the action, and this launched him on a journalistic career.

After the war, Stanley distinguished himself as a correspondent for the *New York Herald* and achieved international fame for finding missionary David Livingstone in central Africa. Subsequently he returned to Britain and became a member of Parliament.

BIBLIOGRAPHY

Hohenberg, John. *Foreign Correspondence: The Great Reporters and Their Times.* New York, 1964.

Stanley, Henry Morton. *The Autobiography of Sir Henry Morton Stanley.* Edited by Dorothy Stanley. New York, 1937.

Stanley, Henry Morton. *My Early Travels and Adventures in America and Asia.* 2 vols. London, 1895.

CHARLES MCARVER

STAR OF THE WEST

After Maj. Robert Anderson moved his garrison from Fort Moultrie to Fort Sumter in Charleston Harbor on December 26, 1861, he continued to face the threat of attack from hostile South Carolinians. President James Buchanan considered sending a warship to relieve Anderson, but Gen. Winfield Scott persuaded Buchanan instead to send a merchant vessel with concealed troops and armament so as to assure secrecy and avoid the appearance of coercion. Accordingly, the administration chartered for $1,500 a day the side-wheeler *Star of the West,* which left New York ostensibly for New Orleans on January 5, 1861. Buchanan's secretary of the interior, the North Carolinian Jacob Thompson, surreptitiously telegraphed warnings to Charleston, but Buchanan neglected to notify Anderson.

When *Star of the West* approached the entrance to Charleston Harbor early on the morning of January 9, the battery on Morris Island opened a cannonade, scoring a couple of hits but causing no serious damage. Major Anderson withheld his fire. He had orders to remain "strictly on the defensive," and in any case the Morris Island battery was

> Pickens replied that Anderson himself had committed a warlike act when he recently transferred his garrison from Fort Moultrie to Fort Sumter. . . .

beyond the reach of the Sumter guns. Receiving no support, the captain of the *Star* decided to steam away.

Anderson then dispatched a messenger to inquire of South Carolina Governor Francis W. Pickens whether he had authorized the firing and to notify him that unless he "disclaimed" it Anderson would "regard it as an act of war." Pickens replied that Anderson himself had committed a warlike act when he recently transferred his garrison from Fort Moultrie to Fort Sumter and that Buchanan must have known that his attempt to reinforce Sumter would be viewed as another such act. Pickens insisted that the firing was "perfectly justified."

While depressing morale in the North, the incident buoyed the confidence of the Southerners. The South Carolina governor called upon his military experts to get ready to "reduce that fortress," and they began to construct additional batteries to surround Sumter and command the approaches to it. Authorities in other seceding states, having been encouraged to believe they could do so with impunity, hastened to seize the forts and other Federal properties within the respective state boundaries.

BIBLIOGRAPHY

Stern, Philip Van Doren. *Prologue to Sumter.* Bloomington, Ind., 1961.

Swanberg, W. A. *First Blood: The Story of Fort Sumter.* New York, 1957.

RICHARD N. CURRENT

STATE DEPARTMENT

Diplomacy could not ensure the Confederacy's independence, but it could open channels of communication to the major powers of Europe and encourage the assertion of foreign interests that favored the Southern cause. With the formation of the Confederate State Department on February 21, 1861, Jefferson Davis selected Robert Toombs, a leading Georgia Whig and recent member of the U.S. Senate, as secretary. Toombs's detailed instructions of March 16, 1861, to the Confederate commissioners—William Lowndes Yancey, Pierre A. Rost, and A. Dudley Mann—inaugurated the Confederate quest for European recognition. To aid the commissioners Toombs provided a full rationale for Southern secession and delineated all the political and moral reasons why the Confederacy merited membership in the family of nations.

While the commissioners made their way to London, Toombs lost interest in the department. His staff was small, and except for writing occasional instructions, he found little to occupy his time. He once refused to accept additional assistants, explaining, in the words of the *Daily Richmond Examiner,* that he "carried the business of the State Department around in his hat." In May 1861 the Confederate government moved from Montgomery to Richmond. There the State Department acquired offices, as did the president, on the upper floor of a spacious granite building known as the Federal Customs House. In July, Toombs, long preferring a military career, sought and obtained an appointment as brigadier general. He fought at Manassas and Sharpsburg in 1862, resigned, and returned to Georgia in 1863.

President Davis named Robert M. T. Hunter of Virginia as Toombs's successor. During his long political career Hunter had remained a Democrat and a strong defender of slavery and its expansion. In 1861 he was, like Toombs, a member of the U.S. Senate. Hunter was far more learned and methodical than Toombs, however, and had a better grasp of public affairs. His elaborate instructions to James M. Mason and John Slidell, commissioned to London and Paris, respectively, in September 1861, embodied the grand policy of the Confederacy toward the European powers. Hunter argued again that the Confederacy was not a coalition of rebellious states but a country presenting itself to the world "through a

Government competent to discharge its civil functions, and strong enough to be responsible for its actions to the other nations of the earth." He emphasized the ineffectiveness of the Federal blockade and its contravention of the Treaty of Paris (1856), which declared that blockades, to be legal, had also to be effective.

Hunter saw the immense danger to Confederate interests in Europe's refusal to challenge the blockade; it permitted the North, with a minimum of naval power, to seriously curtail the Southern war effort. Despite his determination to enlist European support, Hunter was powerless to capitalize on the South's victory at Manassas in July 1861 and the *Trent* affair of November and December. The decision of Union naval captain Charles Wilkes to remove two Confederate leaders from the British mail-steamer *Trent* unleashed a seething anger in Britain and, for expectant Southerners, the specter of war and a British-Confederate alliance. But Lincoln and Secretary of State William H. Seward acknowledged Wilkes's error, freed the Confederates, and quickly terminated the crisis. Hunter left the State Department in March 1862 to become a senator from Virginia, a position he held until the end of the war. Beyond Europe's acknowledgment of Confederate belligerency in May 1861, Confederate diplomacy had achieved nothing.

During March, as the Confederacy's permanent government went into effect, President Davis faced the task of reconstituting his generally unpopular cabinet. Among its least popular members was Judah P. Benjamin, then temporary secretary of war. Benjamin, who had the appearance of a stocky, prosperous shopkeeper, was renowned for his wit and intelligence, his strong yet ingratiating personality, and a fatalism that attributed importance only to the present. A New Orleans lawyer of major repute, he had won election to the U.S. Senate in 1852 and, like Toombs and Hunter, was a member of that body in 1861. Benjamin had entered the cabinet in February 1861 as attorney general, a position too confining for his energy and ambition. His open criticism of the Southern war effort led him to the War Department, where Secretary Leroy P. Walker had found the challenge of organizing and directing the Confederate army beyond his capabilities. Upon Walker's resignation in September, the president appointed Benjamin acting secretary of war. Benjamin brought order to the department, but made mistakes and carried the blame for the army's reverses after Manassas. Nevertheless Davis appointed him secretary of state in the permanent cabinet.

Benjamin inherited from Hunter his assistant secretary, William M. Browne, a former Washington newspaperman. Browne, a man of considerable talent and totally acceptable to Benjamin, resigned in April to become a member of President Davis's personal staff. Benjamin did not fill Browne's position but relied rather on the department's chief clerk, Lucius Quinton Washington, formerly an editorial writer for the *Richmond Examiner.* Washington, who had entered the department in November 1861, remained at his post until April 1865. The other members of the State Department staff consisted of three clerks, a messenger, and a laborer—Philip Green, a hired slave. A Northern visitor described Benjamin's office in 1864 as unattractive, with maps and battle plans on the walls, a tier of shelves loaded with books in one corner, and a green-baize-covered desk, littered with papers, in the middle of the room.

Years later Washington recalled Benjamin's high competence as secretary of state:

> He was a man of wonderful and varied gifts, rare eloquence and accomplishments, a great lawyer, senator, and man of affairs. He could despatch readily and speedily a very large amount of business. I have known him to compose a most important State paper of twenty pages or more at a single sitting in a clear, neat chirography, and hardly a single word interlined or erased. His style was a model of ease and perspicuity.

President Davis set great value on Benjamin's services and friendship. Their offices were separated by only a hundred feet, permitting Benjamin to visit the president almost every day to discuss the problems confronting the Confederacy.

Benjamin was determined to succeed where his predecessors had failed. In letters to Mason and Slidell on April 8, 1862, he launched an attack on the legitimacy of the blockade by listing over a hundred vessels that had passed between Southern and foreign ports during November, December, and January. Seven European nations including the five great powers had, in the Treaty of Paris, adopted the principle that blockades "to be binding, must be effective— that is to say, maintained by a force sufficient really to prevent access to the coast of the enemy." The Confederation had accepted that principle.

Then on February 11, 1862, British foreign minister Earl Russell explained to Lord Lyons in Washington:

> Her Majesty's government . . . are of opinion that, assuming that the blockade was duly notified and also that a number of ships is stationed and remains at the entrance of a port sufficient really to prevent access to it, *or to create an evident danger of entering it or leaving it,* and that these ships do not voluntarily permit ingress or egress, the fact that various ships may have successfully escaped through it . . . will not of itself prevent the blockade from being an effectual one by international law.

Benjamin observed that the underscored words in Russell's statement did not appear in the Treaty of Paris and seemed to be an abandonment of its principles. He noted additionally that Russell's defense of the British decision hinged on the premise that the ships stationed at the entrance of a port were sufficient to prevent access or at least to render it dangerous. The fact that vessels moved freely through the blockade challenged the validity of the British assumption. "The absurdity of pretending that 2,500 miles of seacoast are guarded by the United States 'by a force sufficient really to prevent access,'" he wrote, "is too glaring to require comment; yet it is for this extravagant assumption that the United States claim and neutral powers accord respect." By Russell's definition, Benjamin added, any blockade could be rendered effective if, by common consent, no nation chose to challenge it.

Benjamin simultaneously assaulted Europe's refusal to recognize the Confederacy as a separate nation. Nonrecognition, he reminded Mason, merely sustained an unnecessary war by perpetuating the notion that conquest of the South was possible. But recognition, as the verdict of an impartial jury, Benjamin predicted, would lead to "the immediate organization of a large and influential party in the Northern States favorable to putting an end to the war." Thus Britain, with little effort or detriment to its interests, could end the desolating struggle in America.

Benjamin's special appeal for French recognition focused on material considerations. He offered that country a Southern commercial dependency by instructing Slidell to propose a treaty under which the South would accept French products free of duty for a specified period of time in exchange for France's abandonment of its policies regarding recognition and the blockade. Benjamin suggested that the Confederacy supply French merchant vessels in designated ports 100,000 bales of cotton, worth enough to "maintain afloat a considerable fleet for a length of time quite sufficient to open the Atlantic and Gulf ports to the commerce of France." Benjamin wanted the French, like the British, to understand that the continuance of the war was "attributable in no small degree to the attitude of the European powers in abstaining from the acknowledgement of our independent existence as a nation of the earth."

Emboldened by the Confederate military successes of June and July 1862, especially in Virginia, Benjamin framed a new approach to break Europe's neutrality. During July Mason and Slidell, on their own, agreed to demand recognition as a matter of right, but concluded that such a course, without the leverage of additional Confederate victories, would produce only further European alienation. On August 14, however, Benjamin advised A. Dudley Mann, assigned to Brussels in September 1861 with the appointments of Mason and Slidell, that further communications with foreign governments would presume the unquestioned justice of the Confederate cause. Earlier Confederate efforts to explain the South's right to secede may have been proper, Benjamin conceded, but when common sense had failed to elicit any response but a timid neutrality, he concluded, "we prefer

speaking in other tones and insisting that an admission into the family of nations is a right which we have conquered by the sword." In November Benjamin instructed L. Q. C. Lamar, commissioner to Russia, that he should not maintain the Southern right of secession unless the czar's government should inquire about it, but rather insist that the Confederacy had won its right to recognition in war.

In August 1863, convinced that Britain would never grant recognition or modify its attitude toward the blockade, Benjamin ordered Mason to conclude his mission and withdraw from London unless the British cabinet revealed a changed attitude. After receiving Benjamin's instructions on September 21 and conferring with Slidell, Mason departed for Paris. For more than a year Benjamin had argued that breaking the blockade would enhance British commerce and that recognition would bring peace, but he failed to convince the British ministry.

In September 1863 Benjamin turned to France, reminding the emperor of the damage that Europe's recognition of the Federal blockade had imposed on the South. He instructed Slidell to urge the French government to stop giving countenance "either to the validity of the pretended blockade, . . . tor to the innovations and modifications which the Government of Great Britain has attempted to engraft on the declaration of Paris in derogation . . . of the rights of all other parties." In November the French minister, èdouard Drouyn de Lhuys, declared that France was not responsible for Europe's decision on the blockade and that the vulnerability of French interests in Europe and Mexico ruled out any policy that might antagonize the governments in London and

> **. . . any blockade could be rendered effective if, by common consent, no nation chose to challenge it.**

Washington. In the end Benjamin revealed only contempt for French behavior, troubled by the contrast between the emperor's perennial professions of sympathy for the Southern cause and his persistent subservience to the anti-Confederate policies of Britain and the United States.

In a dispatch to Slidell on December 27, 1864, Benjamin lamented the contribution that the neutral powers had made to the Union cause. Why, he wondered, had the Europeans refused to recognize the Confederacy? He concluded that the elusive element had been the South's failure to offer a program of emancipation. He dispatched Duncan F. Kenner, congressman from Louisiana, to convey such a proposal to Mason and Slidell in Paris. In March 1865 the French emperor assured Slidell that the offer of emancipation would not have influenced his decision regarding recognition; in

London Prime Minister Lord Palmerston offered the same response to Mason.

Before Benjamin could receive the assurance that slavery had not damaged the Southern cause in Europe, the Confederacy no longer existed. The secretary had acknowledged often enough that the experience on the battlefield would determine the success of Southern diplomacy no less than the future of the Confederacy itself. His quest for recognition and foreign cooperation failed because he could never convince Europe's leaders that Confederate arms would triumph. With the fall of Richmond, Benjamin, in a variety of disguises, fled to the Florida coast and made his way to Europe. Throughout the war his wife and family had resided in Paris. Benjamin chose, however, to move to England where he became a distinguished member of the English bar, leaving behind the trials of his Confederate years as if they had never occurred.

[See also Blockade, overview article; France; Great Britain; Mexico; Trent Affair; and biographies of numerous figures mentioned herein.]

BIBLIOGRAPHY

Evans, Eli N. Judah P. Benjamin: The Jewish Confederate. New York, 1988.

Hendrick, Burton J. Statesmen of the Lost Cause. Boston, 1939.

Meade, Robert Douthat. Judah P. Benjamin: Confederate Statesman. New York, 1943.

Owsley, Frank Lawrence. King Cotton Diplomacy: Foreign Relations of the Confederate States of America. Revised by Harriet Chappell Owsley. Chicago, 1959.

Patrick, Rembert W. Jefferson Davis and His Cabinet. Baton Rouge, La., 1961.

Phillips, Ulrich Bonnell. The Life of Robert Toombs. New York, 1913.

Washington, L. Q. "Confederate States State Department." Southern Historical Society Papers 29 (1901): 341–349. Reprint, Wilmington, N.C., 1991.

NORMAN A. GRAEBNER

STATE NAVIES

Seven Southern states—South Carolina, Georgia, Florida, North Carolina, Louisiana, Alabama, and Texas—established state navies following secession and prior to joining the Confederacy. Each state had a different conception of its navy's function. Georgia floated the Naval Coast Guard; Florida called its service the Marine Police; and North Carolina operated a force of small steamers dubbed the Mosquito Fleet.

Although each state gave its navy a different name, all had similar characteristics. They were makeshift forces comprising former Federal vessels and merchant steamers. The ships flew the state flag, performing coastal patrols. They served as much for peace of mind as for action against the enemy. Officers were commissioned in state service at the rank held in the U.S. Navy or Revenue Cutter Service.

South Carolina was the first state to create a navy; it also commissioned the largest fleet. It seized vessels and armed them, making them serviceable. On December 30, 1860, ten days after declaring secession, South Carolina took over the revenue schooner William Aiken at Charleston. In the following weeks a lighthouse tender schooner, a coastal passenger side-wheeler, and two coast survey schooners were added to the South Carolina State Navy. The state purchased the iron propeller tug James Gray at Charleston, armed it, and renamed it Lady Davis. The large coastal passenger side-wheeler Marion was seized and armed.

The Georgia State Navy arose from a resolution of the Georgia state convention on January 25, 1861, six days after secession, authorizing the navy to procure three steamers to defend the state. The first officer appointed was Lt. John McIntosh Kell of Darien. On February 25, Kell purchased the side-wheel steamer Everglade, which was armed and renamed Savannah. Three days later, Capt. Josiah Tattnall became senior flag officer. Savannah reported ready for service March 7. The 500-ton sidewheel steamer Huntress was bought at New York by a "Mr. Hall" and armed. The U.S. steamer Ida was seized by the state. The Georgia navy was absorbed into the Confederate States Navy in mid-April 1861. Savannah and Ida were both taken into the navy under the same names. They operated in the Naval Coast Guard squadron primarily on the Georgia coast. Huntress later became the blockade runner Tropic.

Florida seized the coast survey schooner F. W. Dana, used it briefly, and released it. The state also seized the U.S. war steamer Fulton under repair at the Pensacola Navy Yard. The state employed the schooner Judah as a vessel of the Florida Marine Police.

North Carolina's Mosquito Fleet acquired the 207-ton passenger steamer J. E. Coffee, armed it, and renamed it Winslow. Four river tugs rounded out the fleet. Winslow captured sixteen prizes while operating out of Hatteras Inlet. It was lost while attempting to rescue a shipwrecked crew. When North Carolina joined the Confederacy, the entire flotilla entered the navy. It fought in several battles in the sounds of North Carolina.

The state of Louisiana likewise seized revenue service vessels: the schooner Robert McClelland and the brig Washington at New Orleans on January 26. The state also seized the armament of the cutter Lewis Cass, using it to arm other vessels.

Alabama seized two Federal vessels for the state. The revenue cutter service schooner Lewis Cass, and the lighthouse tender schooner Alert were taken on January 30, 1861, at Mobile. Lewis Cass was later transferred to the Confederate States Navy.

The commander of the decrepit revenue service schooner *Henry Dodge,* armed with one pivot gun, turned it over to the state of Texas on March 2, 1862, at Galveston. Texas operated a Marine Department throughout the war as an adjunct of the Confederate forces. The department was instrumental in the recapture of Galveston in 1864, seizing seven vessels in the process.

State leaders appear to have expected that the state navies would be subsumed into the national service. As anticipated, all were taken into the Confederate States Navy and served as regional coastal forces. The state navies served a valuable purpose—as an interim force until a Confederate navy could be created.

[*See also entries on particular states.*]

BIBLIOGRAPHY

d'Antignac, Munroe. *Georgia's Navy.* Griffin, Ga., 1944.
Brown, Alexander Crosby. *Juniper Waterway: A History of the Albemarle and Chesapeake Canal.* Charlottesville, Va., 1981.
Scharf, J. Thomas. *History of the Confederate States Navy.* New York, 1887. Reprint, New York, 1977.

KEVIN J. FOSTER

STATE RIGHTS

Secession was based on the idea of state rights (or "states' rights," a variant that came into use after the Civil War). This exalted the powers of the individual states as opposed to those of the Federal government. It generally rested on the theory of state sovereignty—that in the United States the ultimate source of political authority lay in the separate states. Associated with the principle of state rights was a sense of state loyalty that could prevail over a feeling of national patriotism. Before the war, the principle found expression in different ways at different times, in the North as well as in the South. During the war it reappeared in the Confederacy.

From Colonies to Constitution. The idea of state rights antedated the U.S. Constitution. During the colonial period the people of each colony showed an attachment to their own and often an antagonism toward other colonies. Intercolonial jealousies prevented union when, in 1754, Benjamin Franklin proposed the Albany Plan for combining to meet a threat from the French and their Indian allies. The same sentiments hampered intercolonial cooperation during the ensuing French and Indian War. Traveling through the middle settlements in 1759 and 1760, the Englishman Andrew Burnaby was struck by the disparities he observed: "Fire and water are not more heterogeneous than the different colonies in North America. Nothing can exceed the jealousy and emulation which they possess in regard to each other." Burnaby

thought the colonies differed so much in culture and in economic interests that "were they left to themselves, there would even be a civil war."

Their shared hostility to the British government enabled the colonies to join in the Continental Congress and, as states from 1776 on, to win the Revolutionary War. Their rivalries continued, however, and delayed the adoption of the Articles of Confederation until 1781. The second of the Articles affirmed: "Each state retains its sovereignty, freedom and independence, and every Power, Jurisdiction and right, which is not by this confederation expressly delegated to the United States, in Congress assembled." The separate states retained, among other powers, the exclusive power to tax. All had to approve before the Articles could be amended. When New York refused to approve an amendment giving Congress the power to levy customs duties, it failed to be adopted.

Alexander Hamilton and other "nationalists" desired a stronger government, and since they could not amend the Articles, they undertook to replace them. At the Philadelphia Convention of 1787, delegates from the various states drew up a new plan of government, which its "father" James Madison said was "in structure, neither a national nor a federal Constitution, but a composition of both." Indeed, it was the result of compromises between nationalists and state-rightists, and it evaded a number of issues that might have prevented any agreement. Still, the new Constitution gave much greater power to the central government than the Articles of Confederation had given.

The Constitution was to be ratified by separate state conventions and was to go into effect among the ratifying states when nine of them had acted. Antinationalists, who called themselves "Antifederalists," opposed ratification. To reassure them, Madison wrote in one of the Federalist Papers (later gathered in *The Federalist*) that the document was to be ratified "by the people, not as individuals composing one nation; but as composing the distinct and independent States to which they respectively belong." Before the end of 1788 eleven states had ratified, but some had done so only on the understanding that certain amendments would soon be added. Two others (North Carolina and Rhode Island) still held out, waiting to see what would happen.

All were satisfied by the ten amendments proposed by the new Congress at its first session. These amendments further limited the powers of the central government, and the tenth provided: "The powers not delegated to the United States by the Constitution, nor prohibited by it to the States, are reserved to the States respectively, or to the people." Thus amended, the Constitution was more nearly balanced between national and state rights tendencies—and was more ambiguous.

Hamiltonians and Jeffersonians. The Constitution could be interpreted in opposite ways. In its clause giving Congress all powers "necessary and proper" for carrying the specified powers into effect, Alexander Hamilton as secretary of the treasury found ample authorization for his financial program, including a national bank. In the Tenth Amendment, however, Thomas Jefferson as secretary of state discovered a bar to congressional legislation of that kind: no power to establish a bank having been delegated to Congress, that power must have been reserved to the states. As president, George Washington sided with Hamilton and signed the bills that Congress passed to enact Hamilton's plan. Eventually Jefferson withdrew from the Washington administration and, with Madison, organized an opposition to it. Thus, in the 1790s, originated the two parties, Federalist and Republican, the one willing to exploit the "implied powers" of the Constitution, the other demanding a "strict construction" of the document.

The Republicans, already convinced that much of the Federalist legislation was unconstitutional, were further outraged when, in 1798, Congress passed the Alien and Sedition Acts. The Sedition Act—providing for the fining and imprisoning of those who uttered anything "false, scandalous, and malicious" against the government, the Congress, or the president—seemed flagrantly to violate the First Amendment, which stated that Congress should pass no law abridging freedom of speech or of the press.

What agency should decide the question of constitutionality? The Constitution did not, in so many words, give the Supreme Court the power to decide, and the Republicans denied that the Court could rightfully assume the power. Their leaders, Jefferson and Madison, arguing that the state legislatures should decide, ably expounded their views in two sets of resolutions, one written (anonymously) by Jefferson and adopted by the Kentucky legislature (1798–1799) and the other drafted by Madison and approved by the Virginia legislature (1798).

These Kentucky and Virginia Resolutions asserted the following propositions: The Federal government had been formed by a "compact" or contract among the states. It was a limited government, possessing only specific delegated powers. Whenever it attempted to exercise any additional, undelegated powers, its acts were "unauthoritative, void, and of no force." The parties to the contract, the states, must decide for themselves when and whether the central government exceeded its powers. The state legislatures must serve as "sentinels" to watch out for unconstitutional acts. And "nullification" by the states was the "rightful remedy" whenever the general government went too far. The resolutions urged all the states to join in declaring the Alien and Sedition Acts null and void and in demanding their repeal at the next session of Congress, but none of the other states went along with Virginia and Kentucky.

State rights and strict construction were usually the arguments of the party out of power (and so they were to be throughout American history). As long as the Republicans were outsiders, they remained strict constructionists, but once they had become insiders, with Jefferson as president, they used the full powers of the Federal government to further the agrarian interests they represented. Indeed, they used much more than the rightful and constitutional powers, according to the Federalists, who now adopted the state rights point of view.

The Jefferson administration bought Louisiana from France in 1803 even though the Constitution gave Congress no explicit power to acquire new territory. On the constitutionality of the purchase Jefferson himself had serious doubts but managed to overcome them. The administration also imposed an embargo in 1807 forbidding American ships to leave American ports, though the Constitution allowed Congress only to regulate interstate and foreign commerce, not to prohibit it. In anger against the Louisiana Purchase, a few extreme Federalists, the Essex Junto, conspired to bring about the secession of New England. In condemning the embargo, a much larger number resorted to the doctrine of state rights. The young New Hampshire Federalist Daniel Webster, for one, paraphrased the Virginia and Kentucky Resolutions: "The Government of the United States is a delegated, *limited* Government."

During the presidency of Jefferson's friend and successor James Madison, the New England state rights men gained their largest following in opposition to the War of 1812. In Congress, Webster attacked and helped defeat a conscription bill. "The operation of measures thus unconstitutional and illegal ought to be prevented by a resort to other measures which are both constitutional and legal," he declared, hinting at nullification by New Hampshire. "It will be the solemn duty of the state governments to protect their own authority over their own militia and to interpose between their citizens and arbitrary power." In fact, some of the New England states, by refusing to support the war, virtually nullified the war effort of the Federal government. New England state-rightism and sectionalism reached a climax in the Hartford Convention (1814–1815), which demanded changes in the Constitution and threatened secession if they were not made.

Some of Jefferson's followers had turned against him when, as they saw it, he departed from his own principles. His distant cousin and (before 1804) House leader John Randolph of Roanoke organized within the Republican party a state rights faction known as the Quids. Randolph remained a fanatical defender of Virginia rights. John Taylor of Caroline, an equally consistent but more original thinker than Randolph, led the Virginia School, which included St. George Tucker and Spencer Roane. These men rationalized resistance to the centralizing trend, especially to the work of the Supreme Court under Virginian John Marshall. Jefferson, after his retirement from the presidency, joined in opposing the Federalist-minded judges as "sappers and miners" who were undermining the Constitution. The Georgia state rights men, whose leader was William H. Crawford, had their own quarrel with Marshall, who ruled against them when the state undertook to evict its Indians from their tribal lands.

Calhoun's Contribution. John C. Calhoun was a latecomer to the state rights cause, but he developed the theory more fully than anyone else. In Congress he had favored the War of 1812 and had advocated protective tariffs, internal improvements at Federal expense, and a national bank. By 1828 he was convinced that a protective tariff was not only harmful to his state, South Carolina, but was also contrary to the Constitution. He then began to work out his system for state resistance to unconstitutional laws.

Calhoun refined and elaborated the doctrine of sentinelship that Madison and Jefferson had presented in the Virginia and Kentucky Resolutions. He based his theory on the assumption that the people (not the government) in each state were sovereign and, in their sovereign capacity, had ratified and thus given validity to both the state constitution and the U.S. Constitution. They had done so, he argued, through their delegates in specially elected conventions. In this ratification process he discovered the procedure for dealing with questions of constitutionality. A state convention—not the state legislature as in Madison's and Jefferson's proposal—could nullify a Federal law. That law would remain null and void within the state until three-fourths of all the states had ratified a constitutional amendment specifically giving Congress the power in question. If they should ever do so, the nullifying state would still have a recourse—secession. Just as a state could "*accede*" to the Union by ratifying the Constitution, it could "*secede*" by repealing its ordinance of ratification.

South Carolina put nullification to the test in 1832, when a state convention declared all protective tariffs, particularly those of 1828 and 1832, to be null and void within the state. Calhoun having resigned the vice presidency, the nullifiers sent him to the Senate to present their case. Debating him was Daniel Webster, now a senator from Massachusetts, who had switched from a state rights position to a nationalist one while Calhoun was doing the reverse. "The truth is," Webster contended, "and no ingenuity of argument, no subtlety of distinction, can evade it, that, as to certain purposes, the people of the United States are one people." According to the new Webster, a state might secede from the Union, but only on the basis of the right of revolution, not on the basis of any constitutional right. While remaining in the Union, however, a state could not nullify congressional acts, for nullification was no right at all, he maintained.

President Andrew Jackson, agreeing with Webster, denounced nullification as treason and asked Congress for authority to use the army and the navy to enforce the laws. Though the nullificationists had sympathizers in other Southern states, not one of those states officially endorsed the South Carolina stand. Calhoun claimed a victory for nullification when Congress passed and Jackson signed a compromise bill for gradually lowering the tariff. But nullification had not really worked the way Calhoun had intended. It had not been generally accepted as a legitimate and constitutional procedure. Calhoun came to realize that a single state, unaided, was powerless to interpose against Federal authority. So he set about cultivating a spirit of unity among all the slave states.

> **"The truth is,"** Webster contended, **". . . the people of the United States are one people."**

Slavery, according to Calhoun, occupied a special place in the Constitution, and certainly it occupied a special place in his theory of state rights. It was, he insisted, the only kind of property that the Constitution specifically recognized (though, in fact, the document did not mention slaves or slavery by name; it referred only to "free Persons" and "all other Persons" and to a "Person held to Service or Labour"). Therefore, nullification could be used to defend or strengthen slavery but not to attack or weaken it. Calhoun strenuously objected when, after 1842, several free states tried their own brand of nullification by adopting "personal liberty" laws that forbade state authorities to assist in the enforcement of the Federal Fugitive Slave Act of 1793.

Calhoun was further outraged when the House, though not the Senate, passed the Wilmot Proviso in 1848, which aimed to exclude slavery from all territories to be acquired in consequence of the Mexican War. Then, when the Compromise of 1850 proposed to admit California as a free state and thus to upset the balance of free and slave states, he thought the time had come for the slave states to resort to their ultimate redress, secession.

Taney and the Territories. During the 1850s the doctrine of state rights became a dogma of state powers—powers that extended beyond the boundaries of the states themselves. The development of this dogma was occasioned by the question of slavery in the territories.

Many Northerners held that Congress could exclude slavery, as it had done with respect to the Northwest Territory in the Northwest Ordinance (1787, 1789) and with respect to part of the Louisiana Purchase in the Missouri Compromise (1820–1821). Some advocated "popular sovereignty," or "squatter sovereignty," which would allow the settlers themselves to decide whether to permit slavery in a particular territory, and this principle was embodied in the Kansas-Nebraska Act of 1854. But proslavery Southerners insisted that any prohibition of slavery in a territory, whether by Congress or by the local people, was unconstitutional.

From the proslavery point of view, the sovereign states had delegated to Congress only the power to make routine "rules and regulations" for the territories, not the power to make basic policies for them. When dealing with the subject, the Federal government must act merely as a trustee for the states and must give effect to their laws, particularly the laws respecting slavery. State rights was no longer just a defense of local self-determination; it had become a means of imposing a state's laws on people outside the state.

The theory now called for an enlargement rather than a reduction of Federal authority, at least in regard to the territories, though this authority could be exercised only to protect slavery. As President Franklin Pierce said in 1855, the Federal government was "forbidden to touch this matter in the sense of attack or offense" and could do so only "in the sense of defense." Proslavery advocates looked to the Supreme Court for an endorsement of their new theory of state sovereignty. The Court obliged in the *Dred Scott* case (1857) with an obiter dictum declaring unconstitutional the Missouri Compromise prohibition of slavery in part of the Louisiana Purchase. Chief Justice Roger B. Taney said: "The Government of the United States had no right to interfere for any other purpose but that of protecting the rights of the [slave] owner."

For the time being, the strongest assertion of state rights in defiance of Federal authority came not from any Southern state but from Wisconsin, which invoked the doctrine to oppose slavery rather than to support it. When a Federal court convicted Sherman Booth of violating the Fugitive Slave Act of 1850, the Wisconsin Supreme Court repeatedly (1854–1855) issued writs of habeas corpus to release him on the ground that the act was unconstitutional. Booth and fellow antislavery radicals made state rights a test of orthodoxy in the newly formed Republican party; they demanded that the party's candidates endorse the principles of the Virginia and Kentucky Resolutions of 1798 and 1799. In the case of *Ableman* v. *Booth* (1859) Taney and the Supreme Court again upheld the Southern as opposed to the Northern state rights position. They overruled the supreme court of Wisconsin.

The Wisconsin governor then reasserted the sovereignty of his state. As commander in chief of the state militia, he challenged the president as commander in chief of the U.S. Army and Navy. "It is reported," a Wisconsin official notified the captain of one of the militia companies, " . . . that you have stated that, in the possible contingency of a conflict between the U.S. authorities and those of this State, you . . . would obey a call for your company to turn out, made by the U.S. authorities, but would *not* obey a call by your superior officials under the State laws." When the captain replied that he would consider it treason to disobey a presidential order, the governor dismissed him and disbanded his company. That was in 1860, only months before South Carolina began the secession of the Southern states.

Secession and the Confederate Constitution. Some advocates of secession justified it as a revolutionary right, but most of them based it on constitutional grounds. The 1860 South Carolina Declaration of the Causes of Secession quoted the state's 1852 declaration, which said that "the frequent violations of the Constitution of the United States by the Federal Government, and its encroachments upon the reserved rights of the States," would justify the state in withdrawing from the Union. The South Carolina secession ordinance, following the procedure that Calhoun had prescribed, simply repealed the state's ratification of the Constitution and subsequent amendments. The secession ordinances of other states did the same.

The Confederate Constitution proved to be somewhat inconsistent in regard to state rights. It contained no provision for secession, though its preamble averred that each Confederate state was "acting in its sovereign and independent character." One article (like the Tenth Amendment of the U.S. Constitution) affirmed that the "powers not delegated" were "reserved to the States." The states, however, were limited in important ways. For example, they could not (just as the states of the Union could not) pass any law "impairing the obligation of contracts." They could not get rid of slavery, for the citizens of each state were to "have the right of transit and sojourn in any State . . . with their slaves."

Congress was forbidden to impose duties or taxes "to promote or foster any branch of industry" but in some ways was given even greater powers than the U.S. Congress. The ambiguity regarding territories and slavery was removed. The Confederacy could "acquire new territory," and Congress could "legislate" (not merely make "rules and regulations") for the territories. In all of them "the institution of negro slavery" was to be "recognized and protected by Congress and by the territorial government." Congress could make all laws "necessary and proper" for carrying out its specified powers. If this or any other clause should lead to a dispute over the constitutionality of a law, the Confederate courts (rather than state legislatures or conventions) would presumably decide the issue. This was implied by the following provision: "The judicial power shall extend to all cases arising under the Constitution."

In sum, the new Constitution was more *national* than the old one with regard to slavery, which it guaranteed as a nationwide institution. The document provided no more basis for nullification or secession than its predecessor had done—despite the preamble's reference to the member states as "sovereign" and "independent." Nevertheless, there remained room for the reassertion of state rights in the Confederacy.

State Rights in the Confederacy. To win its independence, the Confederacy needed a government strong enough to make the most of all the available human and material resources, but some of the state leaders were no more willing to concede power to the Confederate government than they had been to the Federal government. Appealing to the principle of state rights, they resisted the efforts of the Jefferson Davis administration to control blockade running and manufacturing, to impress slaves and other property, and even to raise troops. Georgia was the locus of the greatest recalcitrance, Joseph E. Brown the most obstreperous of the governors, and Vice President Alexander H. Stephens the busiest fomenter and philosopher of resistance. North Carolina, under Governor Zebulon Vance, was the next most important center of obstructionism, but practically all the states had some occasion for expressing opposition to Confederate measures.

The most serious question was the constitutionality of the conscription acts (April/September 1862, and February 1864). Davis justified the legislation on the basis of the con-

> Stephens declared: "The citizen of the State owes no allegiance to the Confederate States...."

stitutional clause giving Congress the power to raise and support armies. But Brown and Stephens argued that the Confederate government could raise troops only by making requisitions upon the states, which alone, they said, had the constitutional power to impose a draft. Stephens declared: "The citizen of the State owes no allegiance to the Confederate States Government . . . and can owe no 'military service' to it except as required by his own State." Brown protested to Davis that conscription was a "bold and dangerous usurpation by Congress of the reserved rights of the States."

To enforce conscription, Congress authorized the president to suspend the privilege of the writ of habeas corpus. To Stephens, this seemed as bad as conscription itself. He denounced the suspension in resolutions which the Georgia legislature passed and which, along with speeches by Brown and Stephens's half-brother Linton Stephens, were printed and widely circulated. The legislatures of North Carolina and Mississippi adopted similar resolutions.

The question of constitutionality could not be referred to a Confederate supreme court, for there was none. In 1861 the Provisional Congress provided for such a court, with the power of judicial review, but the permanent Congress established only a system of lower tribunals. When Congress considered adding a supreme court in 1863, opponents objected to the potential subordination of the state supreme courts.

These consequently were left to go on deciding the constitutionality of both state and Confederate laws. The supreme court in Georgia and in every other state except North Carolina upheld the Confederate conscription acts. "When Congress calls for the military service of the citizen," the Texas judges ruled, " . . . the right of the State government must cease or yield to the paramount demand of Congress."

Despite the pro-Confederate decisions of state courts, conflicts between the Confederate government and the state governments persisted. Texas objected to giving up control of state troops, as did Alabama, Mississippi, and all the Gulf states except Florida. A Florida judge, however, issued an injunction against Confederate officers who were ordered to take up some of the track of the Florida Railroad—and who disregarded the injunction.

More serious obstruction came from North Carolina, where Governor Vance took pains to "preserve the rights and honor of the State." He said it was "mortifying" to see North Carolinians "commanded by strangers"—that is, by men from other states—and he demanded that their officers be North Carolinians. Operating a state-owned blockade runner, *Advance,* he objected to the Confederacy's claim to half of the cargo space. He warehoused uniforms, shoes, and blankets for the exclusive use of North Carolina troops at a time when Robert E. Lee's army in Virginia was suffering from the want of such supplies. State officials being exempt from the draft, he appointed thousands of men to state jobs to keep them out of the Confederate army.

Governor Brown of Georgia went even further in making unnecessary state appointments. Then, after enrolling ten thousand militiamen, he refused to allow them to enter the Confederate service even when in 1864 Davis attempted to requisition them—as Brown had previously said the president had a right to do. Brown now insisted he was protecting his state against both "external assaults and internal usurpations." The Confederate secretary of war compared him to the New England governors who had resisted the war effort during the War of 1812. Brown rejected the Richmond authorities' references to "refractory Governors" and "loyal States." Such remarks were "utterly at variance with the principles upon which we entered into this contest in 1861," he said. The Confederate government was "the agent or creature of the States," and its officers had no business "discussing the loyalty and disloyalty of the sovereign States to their central agent—the loyalty of the creator to the creature."

The right of secession followed logically from such Calhounian doctrine. Vance, however, would not hear of it when disaffected North Carolinians talked of calling a secession convention in 1863. Brown and Stephens declined when, after taking Atlanta, Gen. William Tecumseh Sherman proposed a meeting to discuss Georgia's leaving the Confederacy and making a separate peace. But Stephens wrote privately: "Should any State at any time become satisfied that the war is not waged for purposes securing her best interests . . . she has a perfect right to withdraw." By early 1865, at least one Georgia planter had come to suspect that Stephens and his associates were plotting to "withdraw if possible this and two other States from the Confed. and set up for themselves."

In fact, none of the states ever came close to seceding from the Confederacy, and most of them avoided an extreme state rights position all along. Nevertheless, Davis had ample cause for complaint. In a private letter of December 15, 1864, he wrote that his difficulties had been "materially increased by the persistent interference of some of the State Authorities, Legislative, Executive, and Judicial, hindering the action of the Government, obstructing the execution of its laws, denouncing its necessary policy, impairing its hold upon the confidence of the people, and dealing with it rather as if it were the public enemy than the Government which they themselves had established for the common defense, and which was the only hope of safety from the untold horrors of Yankee despotism."

Historians have differed about the importance of state rights as a cause of Confederate defeat. One writer has gone so far as to suggest that the following words should be engraved on the Confederacy's tombstone: "Died of State Rights." Others minimize its effects, pointing out that it was a symbol of more fundamental grievances (as, indeed, it had been throughout American history). Some have even argued that it was an asset rather than a liability to the Confederate cause, since, they say, it served as a safety valve for possibly disruptive discontent.

The doctrine may have influenced the outcome through its effect on Davis personally and directly. He prided himself on being a state-rightist and a strict constructionist, and though his state rights opponents accused him of dictatorship, he was generally careful to confine himself to the letter of the Confederate Constitution. The *Times* of London said in 1865 that one reason for the defeat of the Confederacy was his reluctance to "assume at any risk the dictatorial powers" that were "alone adapted to the successful management of revolutions."

Afterward Davis agreed with Stephens about the basic issue of the war. In *A Constitutional View of the Late War between the States* (1868–1870) Stephens maintained: "It was a strife between the principles of Federation, on the one side, and Centralism, or Consolidation, on the other." In *The Rise and Fall of the Confederate Government* (1881) Davis held that the Confederates had "fought for the maintenance of their State governments in all their reserved rights and powers." Both men forgot that the preservation of slavery had been the object of state sovereignty, state rights, secession, and the formation of the Confederacy.

[*See also* Civil War, *article on* Causes of the War; Compromise of 1850; Conscription; Constitution; Dred Scott Decision; Fugitive Slave Law; Habeas Corpus; Judiciary; Kansas-Nebraska Act; Nullification Controversy; Secession; Wilmot Proviso; *and entries on particular states and biographies of numerous figures mentioned herein.*]

BIBLIOGRAPHY

Bestor, Arthur. "State Sovereignty and Slavery: A Reinterpretation of Proslavery Constitutional Doctrine, 1846–1860." *Journal of the Illinois State Historical Society* 54 (1961): 147–178.

Current, Richard N. *John C. Calhoun.* New York, 1963.

Escott, Paul D. *After Secession: Jefferson Davis and the Failure of Confederate Nationalism.* Baton Rouge, La., 1978.

Freehling, William W. *Prelude to Civil War: The Nullification Controversy in South Carolina.* New York, 1966.

Merriam, Charles E. *A History of American Political Theories.* New York, 1926.

Moore, Albert B. *Conscription and Conflict in the Confederacy.* New York, 1924.

Owsley, Frank L. *State Rights in the Confederacy.* Chicago, 1925.

Schlesinger, Arthur M. "The State Rights Fetish." In *New Viewpoints in American History.* New York, 1922.

RICHARD N. CURRENT

STATE SOCIALISM

The Confederacy was founded on the premise of state rights, but during the course of the war, this ideology underwent many changes. Indeed, one of the most obvious ways in which state rights and limited government were abandoned was in the economic sphere. The government took an increased role in the economic life of the nation, an action that led to government control of shipping and war industry. These endeavors are reflective of the Confederacy's embrace of state socialism, a system approximating the central government's control of the economy at the expense of state sovereignty.

The need for armaments, ammunition, and other accoutrements of war was great in 1861. Initially, the Ordnance Bureau under the direction of Josiah Gorgas relied upon war matèriel stockpiled in Federal arsenals that was seized once the Southern states seceded. This was obviously not enough, so Gorgas also endeavored to purchase goods from abroad. Soon he deemed this source too risky because of the Union naval blockade of Southern ports. Undaunted, he set out to tap domestic sources. Gorgas contracted with private factories and established government works in virtually every Confederate state. The results were impressive: Gorgas estimated that, by 1863, the Confederacy was self-sufficient in war matèriel.

In the process of negotiating contracts, and as the war's scope grew ever larger, Gorgas, with government approval, had to exert increased control over private enterprises. In essence, all firms with government contracts were forced to sell their full output to War Department agents. In some instances (and the Tredegar Iron Works of Richmond is the most famous case), key factories were taken over by government agents.

The government's seizure or impressment of factories with war contracts was not limited to firms producing arms and ammunition. Similar actions took place in the textile manufacturing sector. There, quartermaster agents saw to it that all firms with government contracts for uniforms, blankets, tents, and the like produced almost solely on government account if they were not to lose their sources of raw materials and labor.

The other area in which the government assumed a role approximating state socialism was in shipping. After President Jefferson Davis realized that the self-imposed embargo on cotton was not going to produce European intervention, he changed the policy and encouraged private shipping companies and individuals to run the Union blockade. This policy served to enrich the blockade runners, both Southern and European, because they found that lucrative profits could be made from the importation of luxuries. At Davis's request, Congress passed a law in 1863 that radically altered the private enterprise aspect of blockade running: beginning in that year, all vessels running the blockade had to carry one-third to one-half of their inbound and outbound cargoes on government account. In other words, those ships had to carry government cotton out and bring war supplies in. Congress enacted a supplemental law in 1864 that outlawed the importation of luxuries and the exportation of cotton, tobacco, military supplies, and other goods.

Many individuals—state governors who were also running the blockade on state accounts, and private citizens— protested these measures, but Davis stood firm. With the government involved in shipping, the rate of success running the blockade was very high. The cotton that reached Europe played a crucial role in boosting Confederate credit abroad. It is not too much to say that had the government taken control of shipping sooner, the military outcome of the war might have been different.

Historians have debated the extent to which the Confederacy truly became a "socialistic" nation. The earliest treatment of state socialism, Louise B. Hill's monograph, noted that there is no conclusive evidence that Southern leaders consciously embraced the economic theories of European socialists. Rather, these individuals pushed for and oversaw the centralization of the Southern economy because it seemed the most efficacious way to mobilize and fight the war. For Hill, the embrace of state socialism by men untrained and implicitly uninterested in socialist economic theory demonstrates that exigencies developed talent and the desire to innovate in the economic realm in order to win the war.

Other scholars have echoed this assessment, though several have pushed the interpretation one step further. Most agree that the Confederacy created a "quasi-nationalized" economy, but they differ as to the reason the Confederacy embraced such a position. For some historians, the Confederacy's state-managed economy was a logical reaction to the need for raw materials and manufactured goods; for others, centralization or state socialism was necessary because "there was too little time for a class of industrial entrepreneurs to . . . flower 'naturally.'"

There is no doubt that the Confederacy did, by 1863, direct the production and distribution of war materials. Nor is there any doubt that legislation directing impressment and shipping regulations led to increased government involvement in the economy. Still, the Richmond government stopped short of totally directing the economic affairs of the nation. It did not, for example, nationalize the Southern railroad system in the manner it did Confederate shipping. This failure was probably one of the most disastrous: the South depended on its rail network for supply and troop deployments, but railroad managers resisted any attempts to regulate rates, schedules, or routes, and the Confederate government allowed them to have their way. Consequently, railroad affairs remained in the hands of the managers who pursued policies more beneficial to their companies. This situation remained unchanged until the very end of the war, and it undoubtedly contributed to Confederate defeat.

In the final analysis, the Confederacy's control of the economy, though not total, was, indeed, the nearest thing to a socialistic system that existed in the nineteenth century. The South's regulation of most sectors of the wartime economy indicates once again the way in which Southerners compromised or dispensed with the ideology of laissez-faire and limited government when events demanded it. Confronted with the need to fight a war and supply the troops, the Confederate government adopted a number of expedients that would have been considered anathema in 1860.

[See also Naval Ordnance Works; New Plan; Ordnance Bureau; Quartermaster Bureau; Railroads; State Rights; Textile Industry; Tredegar Iron Works.]

BIBLIOGRAPHY

Hill, Louise B. *State Socialism in the Confederate States of America.* Charlottesville, Va., 1936.

Luraghi, Raimondo. "The Civil War and the Modernization of American Society: Social Structure and Industrial Revolution in the Old South before and during the War." *Civil War History* 18 (September 1972): 230–250.

Owsley, Frank L. *State Rights in the Confederacy.* Chicago, 1925.

Thomas, Emory M. *The Confederate Nation, 1861–1865.* New York, 1979.

MARY A. DECREDICO

STEPHENS, ALEXANDER H.

STEPHENS, ALEXANDER H. (1812–1883), vice president, and postwar Georgia congressman and governor. The son of a yeoman farmer of modest fortune, Alexander Stephens, sickly from birth to death and cursed with a freakish, spectral appearance, never weighed more than ninety pounds. His myriad physical ailments and the early death of his father doubtless contributed to a crippling melancholy that plagued Stephens for most of his life. Despite these handicaps in a society that put a premium on physical prowess, he parlayed driving ambition, substantial intelligence, spellbinding oratorical talents, and prodigious capacity for work into one of the antebellum South's most illustrious political careers.

After a short, unhappy stint as a teacher upon graduation from Franklin College at Athens, Georgia, in 1832, Stephens took up the practice of law in his hometown of Crawfordville, Georgia. His success as a lawyer led him, in 1836, into politics, his first and last love. He never married, but throughout his life he maintained an extraordinarily close relationship with his half-brother Linton.

Elected to the U.S. Congress in 1843 as a Whig, he soon assumed a position of leadership in the party. When the Whigs foundered on the shoals of the Compromise of 1850—which he vigorously supported—Stephens pursued an independent course until 1855, when he became a Democrat rather than espouse Know-Nothingism. The year before, he had played a pivotal role in the passage of the Kansas-Nebraska Act in the House. Although he served as a key administration operative in the unsuccessful attempt to gain acceptance of the proslavery Lecompton constitution for the admission of Kansas, he did not break with Stephen A. Douglas and the Northern Democrats on the issue. Worn out and disgusted, he retired from the House in 1859. Deploring the split of the Democratic party in 1860, he supported Douglas in the election. After Abraham Lincoln's election, he opposed secession as a hasty and ill-advised movement undertaken without sufficient provocation. Nonetheless, he bowed to the wishes of his state when it seceded.

The Georgia secession convention then selected him as a delegate to the Montgomery convention. There he played a leading role in the shaping of the Confederate Constitution, especially the provision allowing the future admission of free states. As the most prominent opponent of secession in the South, Stephens was a logical choice for executive office in the new Confederate government. Impelled by a desire to balance competing factions in the South, to appeal to the border states, and to present a united front to the world, the convention elected Jefferson Davis, a moderate secessionist and old Democrat, provisional president and Stephens,

cooperationist and old Whig, as provisional vice president of the Confederacy on February 9, 1861. (They were elected, without opposition, to their permanent positions in national elections on November 6, 1861.)

Although the working relations between these two proud men began amicably enough, they were deteriorating even before the war started. Davis regarded Stephens's extolling of slavery as the "cornerstone" of the Confederacy in a widely reported speech at Savannah as heedless of the paramount issue at stake between the Federal and Confederate governments: state versus national sovereignty. Ironically, the future split between Davis and Stephens turned on this issue within the Confederacy itself.

Stephens grew increasingly disenchanted with his office. In Montgomery, the president had consulted with him frequently, had dispatched him as commissioner to Virginia before that state seceded, and had offered other important assignments. In early summer, the vice president diligently undertook an extensive speaking tour on behalf of the produce loan to raise money for the government, and he faithfully attended to his official duties. But things had changed by early 1862. For months Stephens had been systematically ignored by Davis and the cabinet. For a man of ability once secure in his power and influence, this inactivity was a bitter pill. With little to do but preside over the Senate where he could neither speak nor vote, Stephens saw no point in spending much time in the capital. He began staying at home for long periods of time.

After months of frustration, Stephens moved to more overt opposition against the government with passage of the first Confederate Conscription Act in April 1862. He regarded conscription as a dangerous and unconstitutional centralization of power, counter to the whole reason the Confederacy existed: to be a bastion of both state sovereignty and personal liberty. Accordingly, he approved of Georgia Governor Joseph E. Brown's long public argument with Davis on the subject and under a pseudonym in September 1862 denounced the draft himself in a public letter. Shortly thereafter, in another public letter, he denied that martial law even existed under the Constitution.

Contrary to his detractors, who contended that he was at heart a Unionist, Stephens remained devoted to the cause of Southern independence. But he differed sharply with the administration over the means to achieve the end. For example, from the beginning and throughout the war he was one of the few to espouse stiff taxation in lieu of issuance of Treasury notes to finance the war. For this reason, Confederate financial policy, which rested on the highly inflationary expedient of printing money to finance its debts, never met his approval. He had similarly urged, to no avail, that the government use cotton as credit to back its bonds and finance the purchase of war matèriel abroad. And although not theoretically averse to impressment—indeed, he sanctioned a broad reading of the Constitution to reach the taxable property of the wealthy—he deplored the capricious way in which the law operated.

Far more than Davis, Stephens heeded political currents in the North and was willing to court them to achieve independence. The best time to extend peace feelers, he thought, was during times of relative quiescence on the battlefields. Accordingly, in June 1863, following Robert E. Lee's great victory at Chancellorsville and with the North discontented over the passage of conscription there, he placed a proposal before Davis. He would undertake a mission to the North to reestablish the cartel for the exchange of prisoners that had broken down amid bitter threats of mutual retaliation on innocent prisoners after the Emancipation Proclamation in January. Such a conference, Stephens hinted, might afford him the opportunity to address the larger issue of a general settlement. Davis, who knew as Stephens did not that Lee was invading the North, accepted the offer.

Upon his arrival in Richmond, Stephens discovered to his horror that the president wanted him to accompany Lee's army north. The president thought this would improve Stephens's chances of being received. Stephens emphatically disagreed, but at the urging of cabinet and president, he consented to undertake the mission. According to his instructions, its purpose was "humanitarian" with "no political aspect." Rainy weather, which made roads impassable, dictated that Stephens travel to Washington by steamer. As he had anticipated, the venture came to naught. Stephens arrived at Newport News, Virginia, at noon on July 4, 1863. After keeping the Confederate envoy waiting for two days, the Lincoln government, buoyed by the victories at Gettysburg and the fall of Vicksburg, refused to let him proceed. Disgusted that his advice had once again been disregarded, Stephens returned to Georgia.

Except for a few speeches trying to encourage his countrymen in the wake of the midsummer disasters, Stephens kept his peace for the balance of 1863. But he had not retreated an inch from his convictions about the course the Confederacy should take. He could barely find words to express his abhorrence of the notion in some quarters that the South appoint a dictator to rule the country during the war. The only way to preserve "constitutional liberty," his umbrella term for individual and state rights, was to preserve constitutional limits on authority. Preserving the purity of that document was the war's chief object; even independence was secondary. "Nothing could be more unwise than for a free people," he told Howell Cobb, "at any time, under any circumstances, to give up their rights under the vain hope and miserable delusion that they might thereby be enabled to defend them."

Stephens dallied over returning to Richmond for the opening of the congressional session in November 1863; first one thing and then another delayed his leaving Georgia.

Meanwhile, Governor Brown was seriously considering calling the Georgia legislature into special session to formally protest government policies as well as broach the subject of peace negotiations with the Federal government. Stephens dissuaded Brown from doing so until Congress had acted on some of the vexatious issues. And from his sickbed, he penned a long letter to the president warning that it would be impolitic to suspend again the writ of habeas corpus and to extend conscription; he also reasserted the evils of the present impressment machinery, to no avail. In mid-February, the Congress authorized another six-month suspension of the writ and extended conscription.

The events in Richmond spurred Brown to go ahead with his plans: he called the Georgia Assembly into special session on March 10, 1864. The vice president and his brother

> **What he wanted was to keep the present revolution on the right track.**

Linton, a member of the legislature, both advised Brown about how the protest should be handled. In accordance with these plans, Brown delivered a scalding message on Confederate policy on the heels of which Linton Stephens offered two sets of resolutions. The first condemned the suspension of the writ; the second proposed that the South proffer peace negotiations to the North after every victory it won in the field. Although he had not intended to become publicly identified with the protest for obvious reasons of propriety, the vice president yielded to the entreaties of his brother to come to Milledgeville, the capital, when it appeared that the resolutions might fail.

There, on the night of March 16, Stephens delivered an impassioned address in support of the resolutions. He branded both conscription and suspension of the writ as unconstitutional and unwise. The latter act also presented a grave danger to public liberty: the legislature should request its immediate repeal and its constitutionality should be tested in the courts. Stephens dismissed the notion that Davis would be circumspect about using the power. Abuses would inevitably arise from the military authorities who would enforce the law. Stephens took pains to deny that he desired a counterrevolution. What he wanted was to keep the present revolution on the right track. The best way to prevent a counterrevolution was for the state to speak out. The truest supporters of the government and the troops in the field upheld the fundamental law.

After a fierce struggle, the Georgia Assembly passed the resolutions two days later but accompanied them with another expressing undiminished confidence in Davis. Stephens had long since lost such confidence, but with palpable self-delusion, he also denied any personal antipathy to the president. In fact, he had always considered Davis unfit for the presidency, and although he professed in March 1864 to believe Davis "a man of good intentions," their ensuing relations would prove just how corrosive Stephens's suspicions of him had become.

As the war dragged on into the summer of 1864, an increasing number of prominent Confederates both in and outside of Congress began broaching various plans for peace. Stephens, too, was vitally interested in the subject. One of his enduring beliefs from the beginning of the war was that the political, economic, and cultural ties between the South and the Old Northwest could be used to further the cause of the Confederacy. Consequently, he believed that the Confederacy should do all it could to influence Northern elections, should offer to negotiate on the basis of state sovereignty, and, if need be, should accept an offer to negotiate on the basis of reunion. With a friendly government in place, the South could obtain an armistice through negotiation, which, in Stephens's opinion, would inevitably lead to its independence.

Davis, though he sanctioned covert aid to anti-Lincoln elements in the North, did not believe the Confederacy should be involved with foreign elections. Nor should it court negoti-

> **[This] . . . led to the final breach between the Confederacy's two top executives.**

ation with the enemy save only on one unalterable basis: Confederate independence. The surest way of securing independence in his view was to demonstrate the futility of subduing the South by force. This fundamental difference of opinion led to the final breach between the Confederacy's two top executives.

Davis had already publicly misrepresented Stephens's futile 1863 mission as an illustration of the North's intractability on the peace issue. This enraged the vice president, who was even more upset when in a speech at Columbia, South Carolina, in October 1864 the president repeated the charge and barely alluded to the Northern elections. Stephens found it incomprehensible that the Confederate government did not respond favorably to the peace plank in the platform of the Northern Democrats in 1864, which demanded a cessation of hostilities so that "at the earliest moment peace may be restored on the basis of the Federal Union." Contrary to what many thought, the vice president did not favor any scheme for separate state action for peace—indeed, for any course of action that bypassed the Richmond government. As the fortunes of the Confederacy became increasingly desperate, many in the South, including Governor Brown and Linton Stephens, came to favor this course. Stephens opposed

them all, arguing that under the Constitution only the central government was empowered to conclude treaties. Even a general convention of the states would have to be acceded to by Richmond and Washington.

Partly to further legitimate peace initiatives and partly to oppose additional draconian war measures being proposed by the government, Stephens returned to Richmond in December 1864. Almost immediately he engaged in an acrimonious exchange of letters with Davis over the latter's remarks in Columbia. Shortly thereafter, his considerable dignity wounded when the Senate refused to allow him to speak on the habeas corpus issue, Stephens decided to resign his office. Only the importuning of the president pro tem of the Senate, Robert M. T. Hunter, dissuaded him.

To Stephens's surprise, however, on January 6, 1865, the Senate invited him to address it after adjournment. He spoke for two hours, urging a complete revision of policy to reanimate the people: an end to conscription and impressment, friendship toward the Northern Democrats (i.e., agreement to a general convention of the states), and a revamped military policy. Although typically unrealistic, it had not been a gloomy speech. Stephens gave up his idea of returning home for the moment and continued to aid those in Congress who were trying to force the president's hand on peace negotiations. Several resolutions to do this (a couple framed by Stephens) had been introduced in the Congress.

It was largely to forestall these plans that Jefferson Davis entertained a proposal that had been carried down from Washington, with Lincoln's blessing, by Francis P. Blair. Blair suggested that the two sides cease fighting and join forces against the French in Mexico. Lincoln did not subscribe to this idea, but he was willing to talk "informally" to secure peace "to the people of our common country." Davis, for political reasons of his own, seized the opportunity. Not only was peace sentiment strong and increasing among congressmen, press, and people, but several states, including Georgia, threatened separate state action for peace. By responding favorably to Blair's initiative, Davis, who knew Lincoln's terms but felt fairly sure that a Confederate delegation would be received and fail, saw the chance to silence his critics and rally the populace to the government again.

At the urging of Georgia Senator Benjamin H. Hill, Davis appointed Stephens (along with Hunter and John A. Campbell) to the Confederate delegation. Unknown to Davis, Hill had struck a deal with Stephens: the support of Georgia's delegation for peace resolutions in Congress in exchange for the vice president's help in restraining Brown from initiating separate state action for peace in Georgia. Fearful of being hamstrung by his instructions, Stephens tried to avoid serving on the commission, but he could not. As he had feared, the object of the mission spelled out in the official commission was "an informal conference . . . for . . . securing peace to the two countries."

The three Confederate commissioners met with Lincoln and U.S. Secretary of State William Seward on board a steamer at Hampton Roads, Virginia, on February 3, 1865. Although Stephens tried to steer discussion to the Blair proposal, Lincoln would have none of it and insisted on reunion and an end to the rebellion. After four hours, the conference ended. All that had been decided was that the war would continue, although Stephens did secure Lincoln's promise to release his nephew from a Federal prisoner of war camp.

Stephens returned to the capital and stayed only long enough to write his report of the conference. The result at Hampton Roads, besides engendering a final upsurge of warlike resistance in the South, had effectively silenced Davis's congressional critics. In his last interview with Davis, Stephens said he would return home and say nothing further. On May 11, 1865, Stephens was arrested by Union troops and two weeks later was incarcerated at Fort Warren in Boston Harbor. He was released on parole in early October.

Elected to the U.S. Senate by the Georgia legislature in 1866, Stephens, like many other ex-Confederates, was prevented from taking his seat. Thus barred by the provisions of Reconstruction and extremely poor health from participation in public life in the immediate postwar period, Stephens devoted his time to writing. His ponderous two-volume work, *A Constitutional View of the Late War between the States,* published from 1868 through 1870, presented a detailed justification of secession and the antebellum Southern interpretation of the Union. It has been judged the ablest defense of the Southern position ever made.

With his political disabilities removed, Stephens in 1873 assumed his familiar position as representative of Georgia's Eighth District in the U.S. House. He remained there until 1882 when he was elected governor of Georgia. Stephens died in office the next year, barely one hundred days into his term.

Less understood than labeled, Alexander Stephens has not been treated kindly by most historians. Although guilty of many of the sins they have accused him of—naivetè, pettiness, narrowness, rashness—Stephens does not deserve the reputation of either a closet Unionist or traitor to the Confederate cause. His critics often overlook or excuse the obstinate refusal of Davis to countenance criticism from any source and his political ineptness in dealing with a host of other antagonists. Stephens represented a widespread segment of Southern opinion. He was hardly alone in his passionate concern for individual liberties and state rights against what was widely perceived as encroachments by a powerful central government. But at no time during the conflict did Stephens ever counsel resistance to government authority except through lawful, constitutional means: the courts and Congress.

Stephens's critics also ignore clear evidence of the vice president's commitment to Confederate independence. It never wavered throughout the war. Whether the remedies to the Confederacy's ills that Stephens proposed would have worked is not the question. A better question might be whether anyone who opposes a government's policy in the midst of war is likely to get a fair hearing—then or later.

[*See also* Cornerstone Speech; Hampton Roads Conference.]

BIBLIOGRAPHY

Avary, Myrta Lockett, ed. *Recollections of Alexander H. Stephens: His Diary Kept When a Prisoner at Fort Warren, Boston Harbor, 1865; Giving Incidents and Reflections of His Prison Life and Some Letters and Reminiscences.* New York, 1910.

Cleveland, Henry. *Alexander H. Stephens in Public and Private: With Letters and Speeches, before, during, and since the War.* Philadelphia, 1886.

Escott, Paul D. *After Secession: Jefferson Davis and the Failure of Confederate Nationalism.* Baton Rouge, La., 1978.

Johnston, Richard Malcolm, and William Hande Browne. *Life of Alexander H. Stephens.* Philadelphia, 1878.

Schott, Thomas E. *Alexander H. Stephens of Georgia: A Biography.* Baton Rouge, La., 1988.

Stephens, Alexander H. *A Constitutional View of the Late War between the States: Its Causes, Character, Conduct and Results, Presented in a Series of Colloquies at Liberty Hall.* 2 vols. Philadelphia, 1868–1870.

Von Abele, Rudolph. *Alexander H. Stephens: A Biography.* New York, 1946.

THOMAS E. SCHOTT

STEVENSON, CARTER

STEVENSON, CARTER (1817–1888), major general. Carter Littlepage Stevenson was born September 21, 1817, in Fredericksburg, Virginia. In 1838 he graduated from the U.S. Military Academy—a lowly forty-second in a forty-five-man class—and was commissioned into the Fifth Infantry. In 1861, when he "went south," he was a captain.

Stevenson was commissioned into the Confederate army and served briefly as colonel of the Fifty-third Virginia Regiment and as assistant adjutant general of the Army of the Northwest. On March 6, 1862, he was appointed brigadier general and sent to the Department of East Tennessee. In the fall of that year, he served with the East Tennessee army of Maj. Gen. E. Kirby Smith during the Kentucky campaign.

In October 1862, Stevenson was promoted to major general and assigned to command a division that was soon sent to Mississippi. Captured at Vicksburg in July 1863, he was paroled and put in command of a camp of paroled prisoners of war at Demopolis, Alabama. That fall, after his exchange, he resumed command of his division.

Sent to Georgia in 1864, Stevenson and his division joined the Army of Tennessee and fought with that army through the Atlanta, Franklin and Nashville, and Carolinas campaigns. On May 1, 1865, after the surrender of the Army of Tennessee, Stevenson was paroled at Greensboro, North Carolina.

After the war Stevenson worked as a civil and mining engineer. He died August 15, 1888, and was buried in the Fredericksburg city cemetery.

BIBLIOGRAPHY

Hewitt, Lawrence L. "Carter Littlepage Stevenson." In *The Confederate General.* Edited by William C. Davis. Vol. 6. Harrisburg, Pa., 1991.

Warner, Ezra J. *Generals in Gray: Lives of the Confederate Commanders.* Baton Rouge, La., 1959.

RICHARD M. MCMURRY

STONEMAN'S RAIDS

Union Maj. Gen. George Stoneman, Jr., campaigned in both the eastern and the western theaters of the war. As chief of cavalry of the Army of the Potomac, his first foray behind Confederate lines began on April 12, 1863, when Maj. Gen. Joseph Hooker ordered him across the Rappahannock River to flank Gen. Robert E. Lee's Army of Northern Virginia, cut the supply lines south to Richmond, and block Lee's anticipated retreat.

Stoneman was slow getting started and a spring freshet soon made the Rappahannock unfordable. It was April 29 before the river subsided enough for him to cross at Kelly's Ford. Orders from Hooker diverted half his column westward to engage Confederate cavalry stationed at Culpeper Court House, while Stoneman continued south with 3,500 men and six pieces of artillery.

Crossing the Rapidan River at Raccoon Ford, he struck the Virginia Central Railroad at Louisa Court House, wrecking eighteen miles of track. Meeting only feeble opposition, he closed to within a few miles of Richmond, damaging sections of the Richmond, Fredericksburg, and Potomac Railroad and destroying several wagon bridges across the North and South Anna rivers, the Chickahominy, and the James. The raid caused considerable consternation in the Confederate capital, but the trains were running again by the time Stoneman recrossed the Rappahannock on May 8.

Stoneman suffered only 200 casualties, but his absence deprived Hooker of the cavalry to screen his flanks and scout his advance. Lee deliberately kept his own cavalry close at hand and these troopers discovered Hooker's exposed right flank, enabling Lee to win a stunning victory at the Battle of Chancellorsville (May 2–3, 1863). Stoneman was made a scapegoat and relieved.

Reassigned to the western theater as chief of cavalry of the Army of the Ohio, he commanded a division during Union Maj. Gen. William Tecumseh Sherman's Atlanta campaign. On July 25, 1864, Sherman outlined plans to cut the last railroad supplying the city's beleaguered defenders. Stoneman was to lead his division and one commanded by Brig. Gen. Kenner Dudley Garrard around the east side of the city; Brig. Gen. Edward Moody McCook would bring two others around from the west. The two columns, 9,400 strong, were to meet at Lovejoy's Station, twenty-five miles south of Atlanta, and tear up the Macon and Western Railroad while Sherman's Fifteenth, Sixteenth, and Seventeenth Corps moved in a shorter arc around the west side of the city to capture the railroad junction at East Point.

The day before the raid was scheduled to begin, Stoneman asked Sherman for permission to make a dash southward after cutting the railroad to liberate 32,000 Union prisoners of war held at Macon and Andersonville. Sherman admitted there was something "captivating" about the idea and gave the scheme his blessing, telling Stoneman it would be "an achievement that will entitle you and the men of your command to the love and admiration of the whole country."

Stoneman marched at dawn on July 27, 1864. Leaving Garrard's division at Flat Rock to keep Maj. Gen. Joseph Wheeler's Confederate cavalry at bay, he crossed the headwaters of the Ocmulgee River with 2,200 men and two pieces of artillery and moved down the east bank. Unable or unwilling to recross the Ocmulgee, Stoneman failed to keep his rendezvous with McCook and marched straight to Macon, where he confronted 2,000 Georgia militia and Confederate convalescents commanded by Maj. Gen. Howell Cobb on July 30. Unable to breech the city's defenses, Stoneman retraced his steps northward.

By this time, Wheeler had turned back Garrard, overtaken McCook, and dispatched Brig. Gen. Alfred Iverson, Jr., after Stoneman. Iverson's three small brigades intercepted the Federal column nineteen miles northeast of Macon and, after a day-long struggle at Sunshine Church on July 31, forced Stoneman and 500 of his men to surrender. The abortive raid, combined with Wheeler's defeat of McCook at the Battle of Newnan, Georgia, on July 30, cost Sherman almost a third of his cavalry and prolonged the outcome of the campaign.

Exchanged in October 1864, Stoneman returned to duty as second in command of the Army of the Ohio, over the strident objections of Secretary of War Edwin M. Stanton, who characterized him as "one of the most worthless officers in the service." Eager to salvage his reputation, Stoneman proposed to destroy the railroad and saltworks in southwest Virginia.

Leaving Knoxville, Tennessee, on December 10, 1864, he led a mounted column of 5,500 men and four guns across the Holston River at Kingsport and into Virginia. Following the line of the East Tennessee and Virginia Railroad, his troopers drove forces led by Brig. Gen. Basil W. Duke and John C. Vaughn through Bristol, Abington, Marion, and Mount Airy, Virginia, burning the trestles, rolling stock, and depots from Bristol to ten miles beyond Wytheville. After sending a detachment to destroy the lead mines near Wytheville, Stoneman doubled back toward Marion, defeating 1,000 Confederates led by Maj. Gen. John C. Breckinridge on December 17 and 18. He captured the saltworks at Saltville on December 20 and destroyed the Confederacy's most important source of this valuable commodity before returning to Knoxville on December 29.

His reputation restored, Stoneman was given command of the District of East Tennessee in February 1865. Acting on orders from Lt. Gen. Ulysses S. Grant, on March 21 he mounted a raid across the Blue Ridge, feinting toward Salisbury, North Carolina, and then turning north into Virginia to pick up where he had left off in December. By April 5, his 3,000 troopers had wrecked the East Tennessee and Virginia Railroad from Wytheville to Lynchburg. Turning south, Stoneman's columns cut the Richmond and Danville Railroad and rampaged unchecked through western North Carolina, destroying the railroads from Greensboro to Salisbury and west to the Catawba River. The raid ended any hope of a junction between the armies of Robert E. Lee and Joseph E. Johnston and hastened the end of the war.

BIBLIOGRAPHY

Mathews, Byron H., Jr. *The McCook-Stoneman Raid*. Philadelphia, 1976.

Starr, Stephen Z. *The Union Cavalry in the Civil War*. 3 vols. Baton Rouge, La., 1979–1985.

Van Noppen, Ina Woestemeyer. *Stoneman's Last Raid*. Raleigh, N.C., 1961.

DAVID EVANS

STONEWALL BRIGADE

One of the most famous battle units in American history, the Stonewall Brigade achieved a record for marching, fighting, and sacrifice rarely equaled in the annals of war. Writers over the years have likened it to Caesar's Tenth Legion, Charlemagne's Paladins, and Napoleon's Old Guard. The brigade's original members were in the initial wave of volunteers who answered Virginia's call to arms. All the soldiers in the unit were from the Shenandoah Valley and adjacent areas.

In the spring of 1861, the Second, Fourth, Fifth, Twenty-seventh, and Thirty-third Virginia Infantry Regiments, plus the Rockbridge Artillery Battery, were organized into a brigade. Their commander was Gen. Thomas J. Jackson. The unit was Virginia's First Brigade until July 21, 1861, when, at the Battle of First Manassas, it and its general received the nickname "Stonewall." Jackson left his regiments in the autumn for higher command, but the Stonewall Brigade remained under him, was always his favorite unit, and became the brigade on whom he called as a pacesetter both on the march and in combat.

The brigade's mobility in the 1862 Shenandoah Valley campaign (particularly a fifty-seven-mile march in fifty-one hours) earned it the title "Jackson's foot cavalry." It, along with

> **The brigade's mobility . . . earned it the title "Jackson's foot cavalry."**

Jackson's forces, joined the Army of Northern Virginia on the eve of the Seven Days' Battles. Thereafter, from Mechanicsville to Appomattox, the brigade participated in every major battle in the East. It took especially heavy losses at First Manassas, Kernstown, Cedar Mountain, Groveton, Second Manassas, Chancellorsville, Gettysburg, and Spotsylvania. On May 30, 1863, following Jackson's death, the Confederate War Department officially designated the unit as the Stonewall Brigade. It was the only large command in the Southern armies to have a sanctioned nickname.

After vicious 1864 combat at Spotsylvania's Bloody Angle, so few troops remained in the brigade that it ceased to exist as a separate command. Its survivors, along with those of other equally decimated units, were reorganized into a loose brigade. Over 6,000 men served in the Stonewall Brigade during the course of the Civil War. At Appomattox, after thirty-nine engagements, only 210 ragged and footsore soldiers were left—none above the rank of captain.

Jackson's successors as brigade commander were Gens. Richard B. Garnett and Charles S. Winder, Col. William S. H. Baylor, Gens. Elisha Franklin Paxton, James Alexander Walker, and William Terry. Not one of those six officers lived, or escaped serious wounds long enough, to be promoted to higher command.

The original Stonewall Brigade had a makeup and personality unique among Confederate units. Two of every three of its members were farmers, blacksmiths, masons, or machinists. An unusually high percentage of non-English, foreign-born men were in the ranks; Irish and Scotch-Irish were the largest ethnic groups. Few slaveholders were members of the brigade. In addition, the five regiments were typically a family affair, with numerous companies consisting of fathers, sons, brothers, uncles, and cousins.

The brigade came to possess a combination of Jackson's iron discipline and a feeling of confidence gained from repeated successes. It was always an independent-minded unit: a brigade that was outstanding and knew it.

BIBLIOGRAPHY

Frye, Dennis E. *Second Virginia Infantry.* Lynchburg, Va., 1984.

Reidenbaugh, Lowell. *Thirty-third Virginia Infantry.* Lynchburg, Va., 1987.

Robertson, James I., Jr. *Fourth Virginia Infantry.* Lynchburg, Va., 1982.

Robertson, James I., Jr. *The Stonewall Brigade.* Baton Rouge, La., 1963.

Wallace, Lee A., Jr. *Fifth Virginia Infantry.* Lynchburg, Va., 1988.

JAMES I. ROBERTSON, JR.

STUART, J. E. B.

STUART, J. E. B. (1833–1864), major general. Born February 6, 1833, at Laurel Hill in Patrick County, Virginia, James Ewell Brown ("Jeb") Stuart spent his youth in a large family possessed of political and social influence, but lacking comfortable wealth. At age twelve Stuart took an oath at his mother's knee that he would never drink alcohol—very likely a commentary upon Elizabeth Letcher Pannill Stuart's rectitude and Archibald Stuart's fondness for creature comforts. Young Stuart attended Emory and Henry College and then secured an appointment to West Point, where he became "Beauty" Stuart because his classmates considered him anything but.

Despite a penchant for fistfights, Stuart enjoyed success at West Point. His pattern of attaching himself to successful people began now, and he counted such disparate cadets as Custis Lee, son of academy Superintendent Robert E. Lee, and Oliver Otis Howard, at the time a stereotypical Yankee prig, among his friends. In 1854 Stuart graduated thirteenth in his class of forty-six and secured a commission in the cavalry. By this time he was committed to a career as a "bold dragoon."

Following a short tour of duty in western Texas, Stuart joined the First Cavalry at Fort Leavenworth, Kansas. There he met and married (November 14, 1855) Flora Cooke, daughter of the post commander, Phillip St. George Cooke. The couple named their firstborn son Phillip St. George Cooke Stuart.

Stuart saw action against Cheyenne warriors in Kansas and once survived a pistol ball fired at him at point-blank range. Fortunately for Stuart, the powder charge was too small, and he suffered only a flesh wound. While on the frontier Stuart served at Forts Leavenworth and Riley in Kansas

J. E. B. STUART. NAVAL HISTORICAL CENTER, WASHINGTON, D.C.

and at Fort Wise, Colorado. In 1856, while involved in a peacekeeping force attempting to staunch civil unrest in Bleeding Kansas, Stuart encountered radical abolitionist John Brown, an incident that later rendered Stuart the only person at Harpers Ferry able to identify the insurgent "Mr. Smith" as Brown.

Alert to ways of improving his fortune, Stuart spent time during the winter months on the plains tinkering with inventions. He developed something he called "Stuart's Lightening Horse Hitcher" and in the fall of 1859 secured leave to go to Washington to try to sell the War Department a device designed to assist cavalrymen to mount and dismount while armed with sabers.

By coincidence Stuart was at the War Office when the first reports of trouble at Harpers Ferry arrived. He volunteered to help quell the disturbance and served as aide to Robert E. Lee, who commanded the marines sent to Harpers Ferry. Very early on the morning of October 18, 1859, Stuart delivered Lee's demand for surrender to the raiders, who were barricaded in a fire engine house with thirteen hostages. When the engine house door opened a crack, Stuart recognized John Brown pointing a carbine at him. Brown tried to bargain—hostages for freedom—but Stuart in accord with Lee's orders gave a signal to the storming party of marines, and they soon overwhelmed Brown and his followers. Stuart acquired Brown's Bowie knife and some local notice from the event.

As the secession crisis deepened during 1860 and 1861, Stuart vowed to "go with Virginia" but otherwise remained essentially apolitical. When Virginia seceded, Stuart resigned his U.S. commission and secured first a Virginia, later a Confederate, commission as colonel of cavalry. He commanded the First Virginia Cavalry at Harpers Ferry initially under the command of Thomas J. ("Stonewall") Jackson and then in the army of Joseph E. Johnston.

Soon Stuart emerged as a master teacher of cavalry tactics, and he trained his regiment by toying with the then less competent Union horsemen. Stuart grasped the essentials of the mission of mounted troops in the mid-nineteenth century. He had intuited that cavalry charges against massed infantry were doomed relics of Napoleon's day, and although he once said that he wanted to die at the head of a cavalry charge, he never led a charge against an enemy prepared to receive such an assault. Cavalry, Stuart realized, had to dominate the ground between major armies, discern the enemy strength, disposition, and intentions, and deny such information about friendly forces to the enemy. Cavalry could raid, wreck, and disrupt enemy supply and communications; but the first function of horsemen in this conflict was reconnaissance, and to this purpose Stuart schooled his soldiers.

In the campaign that produced the first major battle of the war, Stuart and his three hundred men were appropriately active. He screened the movement of Johnston's army from the Shenandoah Valley to Manassas Junction and then rejoined Johnston for the battle on Bull Run. The First Virginia did charge some disorganized New Yorkers during fighting on July 21, 1861, but for the most part Stuart directed artillery and guided troop units during the conflict. It was Stuart who led Jubal Early and his brigade to the position on the Federal flank at the critical moment in the battle. Early's appearance provoked the Federal withdrawal and the Confederate rush that won the day for the Southerners.

Promoted to brigadier general on September 24, 1861, Stuart commanded the cavalry attached to the Confederacy's primary eastern army. A massed mounted command gave Stuart the advantage over Federal cavalry, which then operated in smaller units dispersed throughout the Union army. Stuart rode in strength, confident of his capacity to overwhelm his adversaries, and so he continued his control of the space between field armies in Virginia. He cultivated his reputation as a "jolly centaur," recruited musicians for his retinue, and seemed to have wonderful fun playing at war.

In June of 1862 Stuart expanded his fame and became known throughout the United States and the Confederacy. Union Gen. George B. McClellan and his huge army threatened Richmond from the suburbs of the Confederate capital. Stuart's West Point superintendent and Harpers Ferry supe-

rior Robert E. Lee assumed command of the Army of Northern Virginia and, intending to attack the Federal right flank and rear, dispatched Stuart upon the crucial mission of reconnaissance beyond the Confederate left. On June 12, 1862, Stuart roused his staff at 2:00 A.M. with the proclamation, "Gentlemen, in ten minutes every man must be in his saddle!" and led 1,200 troopers behind the Federal right flank to discover what Lee needed to know. Then he continued his ride completely around the Union army, covering one hundred miles in three days and causing considerable destruction of enemy property and frustrated embarrassment for the Federals—all at the cost of only one Confederate casualty.

Stuart's only regret regarding his Ride around McClellan, or Pamunkey raid, was not encountering his father-in-law in combat. Most of Stuart's in-laws in some way served the Confederacy; Flora Cooke Stuart's cousin John Esten Cooke, for example, served periodically on Stuart's staff. But Phillip St. George Cooke remained with the U.S. Army. "He will regret it [his decision] but once," Stuart remarked, "and that will be continuously." Stuart also directed that his son no longer bear the name of this loyal traitor; Phillip St. George Cooke Stuart became James Ewell Brown Stuart, Jr. During the Ride around McClellan, Cooke commanded the Union cavalry reserve, but he was too slow and cautious to intercept Stuart's horsemen.

Stuart's success enhanced his legendary fame. But the jingling spurs, plumed hat, and fiddle music were in a sense a façade concealing hard work and meticulous planning. Stuart had dispatched John S. Mosby to scout this region days before his ride, and Stuart had consulted with his spies before he ever left camp. He knew what he would find on his reconnaissance before he made his scout. And he carefully placed in his ranks men familiar with the ground over which he would ride and brought them forward as guides at the appropriate times. Stuart was indeed a calculating cavalier.

Lee's army made good use of Stuart's intelligence in the Seven Days' campaign and drove McClellan from Richmond. In the aftermath of victory Stuart became a major general (July 25, 1862), and his cavalry played important roles in the series of victories subsequently achieved by the Army of Northern Virginia. In addition Stuart led a raid on Catlett's Station (August 22, 1862), purloining Union Gen. John Pope's uniform and dispatch book, and he seized 1,200 horses during the Chambersburg raid (October 10–12, 1862). With each new adventure Stuart's fame expanded, giving rise to stories, songs, and poems about him.

In the spring of 1863 Stuart discovered the exposed flank of Joseph Hooker's Union army near Chancellorsville and guided Stonewall Jackson's corps on the flank march to launch the Southern assault. Stuart was at hand when Jackson suffered his mortal wound, and thereafter Stuart took command of Jackson's infantry corps. Stuart handled his sudden assignment quite well and managed the crucial reconnecting with Lee's lines at the same time that he pounded Hooker's with massed artillery. Once more Lee won a significant victory, with Stuart playing an important part.

By June 1863, Stuart commanded almost 10,000 horsemen as Lee's army concentrated for a thrust into Pennsylvania. On June 9, however, Union Gen. Alfred Pleasonton sent an equal number of Federal troopers, plus infantry, against the unsuspecting Stuart at Brandy Station. The Federals achieved surprise and compelled the Confederates to fight for their lives. Brandy Station was the largest, exclusively cavalry battle of the war—indeed, the largest ever in North America—and Stuart held his own only with immense difficulty. His enemies had served notice that they could fight him on equal terms. Still, Stuart claimed victory, although most Southerners knew otherwise.

As Lee persisted with his campaign into Pennsylvania, Stuart dutifully screened the army's march. Then, however, he determined again to ride around another Union army and began his own march north by circling east of the Federal force. En route Stuart captured 150 supply wagons, and this baggage impeded his capacity to move and scout. Thus, on the eve of the Gettysburg campaign, Stuart somehow lost contact with two huge armies, friend and foe, and failed in his vital obligation of reconnaissance.

"Well, General Stuart, you are here at last," were Lee's reported words when Stuart finally joined the army at Gettysburg on the second day of the battle. Stuart's tardiness left Lee uninformed about the strength of his enemy, but he knew the location of George G. Meade's Federals by this time; on the third and climactic day of Gettysburg he sent a massive infantry charge at the center of Union lines on Cemetery Ridge. As George Pickett led the assault that bears his name, Stuart mounted his own charge against Federal cavalry a mile or two from the infantry action. Both Stuart's and Pickett's charges failed; had they succeeded, Stuart would certainly have shared the glory of having slashed Meade's army into fragments. As he had done after Brandy Station, Stuart attempted to compensate for his errors in the field with a bombastic report of his actions. Unfortunately, he confused fantasy and reality, in much the same way he confused fame with greatness, because he lacked the depth and maturity to know the difference.

Stuart nevertheless was a great cavalry commander, arguably the best in the war. He had proved capable of leading a large mounted force, of cooperating and contributing within a major field army, and of carrying out raids and reconnaissance with equal facility.

By 1864, though, his horsemen were outnumbered and outmounted. He served Lee well in the Wilderness campaign, but then had to confront a thrust against Richmond by Union Gen. Philip Sheridan. The Federal commander planned to lure Stuart away from Lee's army and destroy him. On May 11, at Yellow Tavern, only six miles from Richmond, Stuart confronted Sheridan's 10,000 men with a force less than a third its size. In the battle Stuart suffered a wound that proved mortal. Carried to Richmond, he lay in pain as well-wishers, including Jefferson Davis, visited him. At 7:38 P.M. on May 12 Stuart died; his legend, though, still lives.

[*See also* Stuart's Raids.]

BIBLIOGRAPHY

Blackford, W. W. *War Years with Jeb Stuart.* New York, 1945.
Davis, Burke. *Jeb Stuart: The Last Cavalier.* New York, 1957.
Freeman, Douglas S. *Lee's Lieutenants: A Study in Command.* 3 vols. New York, 1942–1944. Reprint, New York, 1986.
McClellan, H. B. *The Life and Campaigns of Major-General J. E. B. Stuart.* Boston and New York, 1885.
Thomas, Emory M. *Bold Dragoon: The Life of J. E. B. Stuart.* New York, 1986.
Thomason, John W., Jr. *Jeb Stuart.* New York, 1930.

EMORY M. THOMAS

STUART'S RAIDS

James Ewell Brown ("Jeb") Stuart and his cavalry disrupted Union supply lines and gathered significant intelligence for Robert E. Lee in support of operations of the Army of Northern Virginia throughout 1862.

Stuart's most spectacular expedition occurred on June 12 through 15 in the Peninsular campaign. As a prelude to his plan to relieve Northern pressure upon Richmond, Lee instructed the twenty-nine-year-old Stuart to "make a secret movement to the rear of the enemy" to determine the practicability of striking the Federal army's right wing north of the Chickahominy River. Subsequently at 2:00 A.M. on the twelfth, Stuart ordered 1,200 troopers from four Virginia regiments into the saddle, and the half-mile-long column began moving northwest toward Hanover Court House.

Breaking bivouac early on the thirteenth, Stuart shifted his direction from north to east, heading for Old Church Crossroads. With the exception of a brief encounter with a Fifth U.S. Cavalry detachment, in which Capt. William Latanè of the Ninth Virginia Cavalry was killed, Stuart met with no opposition. (The *Burial of Latanè,* an 1864 oil painting by William Washington, idealized Southern womanhood and soldierly valor and became a central icon of the postwar Lost Cause movement.)

Arriving at Old Church on the afternoon of the thirteenth, Stuart's semicircular route had carried him thirty-five miles from Richmond and behind George B. McClellan's army. He had discovered McClellan's right was vulnerable, but the Confederate cavalier now became concerned about his own rear. Reasoning that the Federals would intercept his return, Stuart decided upon "the quintessence of prudence," turning his mounts south in an attempt to ride completely around McClellan's army. "There was something of the sublime in the implicit confidence and unquestioning trust of the rank and file," Stuart later informed Lee, "in a leader guiding them straight . . . into the very jaws of the enemy."

Nine miles south at Tunstall's Station, on the York River Railroad, Stuart seized and burned supply wagons and near-

> **Lee also asked Stuart to arrest "citizens of Pennsylvania holding State or government office . . . [so] that they may be used as hostages. . . ."**

ly captured a train. By midnight of the fourteenth, the column reached the Chickahominy, but its rain-swollen swamps prevented easy passage. Stuart ordered a bridge constructed, and his troopers crossed the river just ahead of pursuing Federals, commanded by Stuart's father-in-law, Brig. Gen. Philip St. George Cooke. Stuart then headed for the James River, returning to Richmond on June 15 after nearly a hundred miles of riding. He had captured 165 prisoners and 260 mules and horses during his journey around 105,000 Union soldiers, and he had learned that McClellan's right flank was "in the air." McClellan likewise observed this vulnerability, and he began moving his base of supplies and his army south toward the James.

Following the Seven Days' campaign and the Union decision to withdraw McClellan from the Virginia Peninsula, Lee turned north to encounter John Pope. On August 22, while sparring with Pope along the Rappahannock, Stuart received approval to strike the enemy's rear. With 1,500 men and two guns, Stuart crossed the Rappahannock at Waterloo Bridge and proceeded toward Catlett's Station on the Orange and Alexandria Railroad. Reaching Catlett's after dark on the twenty-second, Stuart surprised Pope's headquarters camp and seized Pope's uniform and dispatch book. The Confederates failed to sever Pope's supply line, however, as the railroad bridge across Cedar Run had become saturated during a terrific thunderstorm. In addition to Pope's personal baggage, Stuart captured over three hundred prisoners during this one-day raid.

Three weeks after the conclusion of the Sharpsburg campaign, Lee and McClellan remained stationary about sixty miles northwest of Washington. On October 8, in an effort to determine the Federals' "position, force, and probable intention," Lee ordered Stuart to embark on an expedition into western Maryland and southern Pennsylvania. Lee specifically instructed Stuart to slice McClellan's main supply line

by destroying the Conococheague bridge of the Cumberland Valley Railroad near Chambersburg. Lee also asked Stuart to arrest "citizens of Pennsylvania holding State or government office . . . [so] that they may be used as hostages, or the means of exchange." Lee also granted Stuart permission to round up horses from Maryland and Pennsylvania farmers.

Execution of Stuart's Pennsylvania raid commenced during the night of October 9–10 when a force of 1,800 cavalry and four guns left Darkesville near Opequon Creek. When the Confederate crossing of the Potomac began about 3:00 A.M. at McCoy's Ferry, Union cavalry detected the movement and quickly spread the word. Meanwhile, Stuart rode swiftly north, arriving at Chambersburg at dark. The Confederates had ridden forty miles without opposition.

While at Chambersburg, Stuart's men failed to destroy the iron trestle of the Conococheague bridge, but the Southerners did torch the railroad's extensive machine shops and depot buildings. In addition, about five thousand muskets were destroyed, and 280 wounded Federals paroled.

As Stuart headed east toward Gettysburg on the eleventh, Union authorities plotted to seal off his escape routes. "Not a man should be permitted to return to Virginia," insisted General in Chief H. W. Halleck. McClellan responded by sending infantry divisions north and west of the Potomac and cavalry to the east. As McClellan declared, "I hope we may be able to teach them a lesson they will not soon forget."

Stuart, anticipating the Union clamp, kept the Federal chasers off guard with deceptive cross-country maneuvers. Finally he recrossed the Potomac at White's Ford near Poolesville late in the morning on the twelfth.

In three days, Stuart's command had traveled 180 miles, 80 in the last twenty-four hours of the raid. The Confederates captured over 1,200 horses and suffered no men killed and only one wounded. In addition to detecting the position of the enemy and causing a political fallout for the Lincoln administration, Stuart concluded that "the consternation among property holders in Pennsylvania beggars description."

Stuart's final behind-the-enemy raid of 1862 occurred following the Confederate victory at Fredericksburg in mid-December. On Christmas Day, Stuart led 1,800 men and four guns across the Rappahannock at Kelly's Ford and then in the direction of Dumfries and the Occoquan River. His purpose was to seize the Telegraph Road and destroy any trains supplying Ambrose Burnside's Army of the Potomac.

Stuart discovered Dumfries too well defended by Federal infantry and little traffic on the Telegraph Road. His command did capture nearly a hundred prisoners at Greenwood Church near the Occoquan before moving northwest toward the Orange and Alexandria Railroad. At Burke's Station, Stuart seized the telegraph and wired the quartermaster general of the United States to complain about the poor quality of the Federal mules he had lately captured. His command then destroyed the railroad bridge over the Accotink River before proceeding north and west toward Fairfax Court House and Loudoun County. Stuart returned to Fredericksburg on New Year's Day with more than two hundred prisoners and twenty-five wagons, with a loss of only one killed and six wounded.

[*See also* Brandy Station; Gettysburg Campaign.]

BIBLIOGRAPHY

Blackford, W. W. *War Years with Jeb Stuart.* New York, 1945.
Davis, Burke. *Jeb Stuart: The Last Cavalier.* New York, 1957.
McClellan, H. B. *The Life and Campaigns of Maj. Gen. J. E. B. Stuart.* Richmond, Va., 1985.
Thomas, Emory M. *Bold Dragoon: The Life of J. E. B. Stuart.* New York, 1988.

DENNIS E. FRYE

SUBMARINES

The Union blockade of Southern ports forced Confederates to develop a variety of weapons to counter it: the ironclad, the rifled cannon, the torpedo, the semisubmersible torpedo boat, and, most remarkably innovative, the submarine.

Experiments with submarines had been made as early as the American Revolution; Robert Fulton was among the first inventors. The Civil War concentrated and accelerated efforts that had previously been merely speculative.

By the late summer of 1861, submarine development got underway at Tredegar Iron Works in Richmond and along the James River. The major effect was psychological, for the Union fleet at Hampton Roads was unnerved by rumors and false sightings of what later came to be known as an "infernal machine." A strong possibility exists that the Confederacy also built other submarines for which no conclusive evidence exists. Federal reports placed submarines in the James River, Virginia, at Houston, Texas, and Shreveport, Louisiana.

The dreaded threat of a submarine strike did not become reality until February 17, 1864, when USS *Housatonic* became the first ship sunk in battle by a submarine—*H. L. Hunley* in Charleston Harbor. That single triumph had been hard bought by a New Orleans group composed of inventor J. R. McClintock and investors H. L. Hunley, R. F. Barrow, Henry L. Leovy, Baxter Watson, and J. K. Scott.

The men first constructed *Pioneer* at Leeds Foundry in a civilian for-profit operation. *Pioneer* was commissioned as a privateer, and the group applied for a letter of marque to attack Union shipping. The risks were great, but so were the potential returns on their investment.

Pioneer served as a prototype for the more famous *Hunley.* The cigar-shaped craft was thirty-four feet long, with a cabin four feet by four feet by ten feet. The crew could sight through circular windows on the sides, and a manhole on the conning tower above provided access to the vessel. This earliest design of a submarine carried a crew of two, one to man a hand crank that turned the propeller and the other to steer the sub beneath a ship and screw a clock torpedo (mine) to the hull. Tests conducted in Lake Pontchartrain were successful, but New Orleans fell to Adm. David Farragut's fleet before *Pioneer* could inflict any damage on Union vessels. It was destroyed to avoid capture. (The submarine currently preserved at the Louisiana State Museum in New Orleans is believed not to be *Pioneer*, but some other, unknown vessel.)

Hunley, Watson, and McClintock moved their operation to Parks and Lyon's Foundry in Mobile, where they constructed *American Diver,* with dimensions thirty-six feet long by three feet wide by four feet deep. Because the cylindrical ends of *Pioneer* had created steering problems, twelve feet of hull on each end were tapered. An expensive effort to develop an electromagnetic engine was abandoned in favor of four crewmen cranking the propeller shaft. Foul weather prevented *American Diver* from attacking the Mobile blockaders, but Hunley's group, now joined by army engineers Lts. W. A. Alexander and G. E. Dixon, was deterred to launch a fully operational submarine.

H. L. Hunley was a larger, nine-man version of previous ships at 40 feet long by 3½ feet wide by 4 feet deep. Ballast tanks at either end of the hull could be flooded for submersion and pumped out to ascend. A heavy iron keel plate supplied ballast, but could be released by loosening bolts inside the hull should an emergency ascent be necessary. Eight men cranked the propeller. In addition to the manhole in the conning tower and the round windows, this sub had more sophisticated equipment: two hollow pipes with stop cocks that extended above the surface as a kind of snorkle, a mercury depth gauge, and a compass. A candle served the dual purpose of providing light and warning of dangerously low oxygen.

The original design called for *Hunley* to pass under a ship with a cylinder torpedo in tow. Once the sub had cleared the hull, the torpedo would detonate on contact. Because this tactic would not work against a ship in shallow water, this design was replaced by a spar torpedo.

Reports of *Hunley* distressed the Union blockaders but so impressed Gen. P. G. T. Beauregard that he ordered it transferred from Mobile Harbor to Charleston, where the need for such a weapon was more critical. In August 1863, the submarine was raised and sent with priority scheduling through the rail system to Charleston. Test runs immediately got underway with the help of veteran pilots who knew the slightest variations of wind and tide in the harbor. Even so, a navy crew promptly sank the "New Fangled boat," which was beginning to earn another name: "peripatetic coffin."

Hunley was summoned from Mobile, with Dixon, Alexander, and Thomas Parks, to train a crew and manage the sub. On October 15, Hunley, Parks, and six crewmen were lost when they were unable to raise the ship in an emergency. Partially turned bolts on the keel plate, a cock inadvertently left open, and the death agonies apparent in the bodies of the crew were painful evidence of the risks of the new technology.

Despite Beauregard's refusal to allow further risk of life, Dixon assembled a crew and soon was conducting further training, including submersion for increasingly longer periods. Once, when they remained submerged for more than an hour, anxious observers mistakenly gave them up for dead and left the wharf.

Sinking *Housatonic* after more than two years of labor became, then, an immense achievement for the Confederacy. The event was all *Hunley*'s inventors and crew might have imagined. Just after 8:00 P.M., the officer of the deck glimpsed what appeared to be a log floating toward his

> ... the giant ship was lifted out of the water by an exploding torpedo.

ship; he shouted a warning, the drummer beat to quarters, and in another moment the giant ship was lifted out of the water by an exploding torpedo.

At dawn, Union rescue boats found many crewmen perched in the ship's rigging, for it had settled into the relatively shallow harbor. *Hunley,* however, was nowhere to be found. The effect of the threat remained, for Union blockaders thought it had been concealed or even returned to Mobile. Alexander, Beauregard, and the rest knew better. Dixon, his crew, and *Hunley* had vanished. Years later, a diver found the little craft, which apparently had been trapped beneath the hull of the sinking *Housatonic.*

The Confederacy had repeated a familiar chapter in its naval history: inventive, persistent, heroic, and ultimately futile—except in this sense: future navies would successfully adapt the technology that claimed the lives and fortunes of history's first submariners.

BIBLIOGRAPHY

Civil War Naval Chronology, 1861–1865. 6 vols. Washington, D.C., 1961–1965.

Kloppel, James E. *Danger beneath the Waves.* College Park, Ga., 1987.

Perry, Milton F. *Infernal Machines: The Story of Confederate Submarine and Mine Warfare.* Baton Rouge, La., 1965.

Robinson, William H., Jr. *The Confederate Privateers.* New Haven, 1928.

MAXINE TURNER

SUBSTITUTES

[*This entry discusses the use by Confederate citizens and soldiers of substitutes for previously available goods that became unavailable as the Civil War progressed. For discussion of the hiring of military substitutes to avoid conscription into the Confederate army, see* Conscription.]

The establishment of the Confederate nation produced many changes in the daily life of the average Southerner. Very early in the conflict Southerners discovered that the common things they had taken for granted in the past had become scarce or nonexistent. The increased effectiveness of the Union blockade and the South's shortage of essential—and nonessential—raw materials and finished goods forced Southerners to develop substitutes. In this realm, they proved to be resourceful and ingenious.

One of the most common complaints was the lack of certain foods and beverages, especially coffee. Southerners became adept at creating substitutes for that favorite drink. Many women submitted recipes to local newspapers calling for such ingredients as chicory, okra, crushed acorns, or rye. Confederate soldiers, too, argued the merits of various nut and fruit concoctions that produced a dark liquid reminiscent of coffee—at least in color. Sugar for that coffee or for baking was also in short supply. Southerners turned to sorghum or honey or boiled down fresh fruits to make a thick, sweet syrup.

Clothing shortages affected everyone. The South's textile base was virtually monopolized by the demands of the Quartermaster Bureau. Consequently, civilians were often forced to make do with old clothes. People recycled old material to create everyday clothing. Many women pulled spinning wheels out of the attic and began to manufacture homespun, or they utilized their sewing skills to convert draperies, carpets, and bed sheets into usable clothing for their families. The loss of wool supplies from areas overrun by Federal troops produced severe shortages of that commodity. In its place, Southerners combined cotton with rabbit or raccoon fur to make warmer garments. In order to render these homemade pieces more attractive, people turned to nature for dyes: berries, bark, and the like produced colors that helped hide the makeshift nature or origin of the piece. Shoes, however, were the scarcest item, and it took every bit of ingenuity to devise usable substitutes. Generally, families recycled old bits of leather, but some used wood and heavy canvas duck to create shoes.

On both the battle front and the home front the shortage of medicine had potentially dire consequences. In this realm, the blockade had a far-reaching effect, as did the cessation of trade with the Northern states. Shortages of quinine, morphine, and other necessary drugs were common. Home remedies enjoyed some popularity, but for many ailments, there was no adequate substitution. Substitutes for quinine were tried and found to be effective—cottonseed tea and dog fennel, for example. But for other drugs, such as chloroform or morphine, no makeshift sufficed, so Southerners were forced to rely upon the contraband trade in drugs.

Although most shortages affected mainly the civilian population behind the lines, other people, more directly related to the war effort, also encountered difficulties. For example, many war contractors found that shortages of raw materials hampered their production for the government. These entrepreneurs tried myriad experiments with substitute items. When supplies of oil for engines and lubrication ran short, railroad engineers discovered that lard oil, peanut oil, and castor oil worked just as well. Those manufacturing artillery or cavalry harnesses substituted oak or hickory wood splints for leather. People made ropes for battlefield or farm use by weaving moss, grasses, cotton, or okra stalks into twine.

It is safe to say that shortages of goods affected all Confederates at one time or another, and the dearth of everyday items probably took a toll after a while. Wax for good-quality candles was lacking; paper and ink for letters and newspapers disappeared; lost buttons became irreplaceable. Through it all, Southerners adapted. But as ingenious as they were, they never fully solved the problem. Shortages, and the adoption of substitutes, testifies to how dependent the region was upon foreign and domestic importations for the most common goods.

[See also Clothing; Food; Health and Medicine, article on Medical Treatments; Sugar; Uniforms.]

BIBLIOGRAPHY

Coulter, E. Merton. The Confederate States of America, 1861–1865. A History of the South, vol. 7. Baton Rouge, La., 1951.
Massey, Mary Elizabeth. Ersatz in the Confederacy. Columbia, S.C., 1952.
Thomas, Emory M. The Confederate Nation, 1861–1865. New York, 1979.

MARY A. DECREDICO

SUGAR

The sugar industry of the antebellum South was largely concentrated in south Louisiana (95 percent) with some small production in Texas, coastal South Carolina and Georgia, and south Florida. In the 1850s the annual crop averaged about 150,000 tons (300,000 hogsheads of 1,000 pounds). Sugar planters shipped their product to the southern Mississippi valley and to eastern cities where it was consumed largely as raw sugar rather than refined. Southern sugar production supplied one-third to one-half of total U.S.

consumption. The remainder was imported from the West Indies.

Ideal conditions for the growth of sugar cane include a temperature averaging 75°F year-round with no freezes, an annual rainfall of sixty inches well distributed, and a fertile soil that drains rapidly and thoroughly. The Southern sugar region possessed most of these characteristics, but it was subject to cold weather and freezes, which threatened the crops.

> **Southern sugar production supplied one-third to one-half of total U.S. consumption. The remainder was imported. . . .**

Sugar cane is planted from seed cane taken from the preceding year's crop. Southern cane planters took only three crops from a field before replanting, in contrast to the many years cane was allowed to ratoon (sprout from the roots) in tropical areas. Cane, planted in rows of five to seven feet in width, was cultivated mainly by mule-driven plows by the 1850s, although hoe cultivation was still used from time to time.

The large farm or plantation was the dominant agricultural unit in the Southern cane region; farms of fewer than a hundred acres were neither numerous nor important in the output of sugar. The working force included planter-owners, overseers, sugar makers, and from time to time hired skilled laborers. But the major part of the labor force was made up of slaves, who by 1860 composed 60 percent of the population of the Louisiana sugar region.

The harvesting season began in mid- or late October when the slaves, working with huge knives, began the cutting, which was completed in late December or early January. Once the juice was crushed from the cane with steam-driven rollers, the process of making sugar began. Most common was the open-kettle process utilizing a set of six cast iron kettles. The heated juice was ladled from one to another as impurities were removed, water evaporated, and the juice clarified. When the juice reached the last kettle, the temperature was extremely hot and the syrup was ready for granulation; after the crystals had formed, the sugar was packed into hogsheads and the remaining syrup allowed to drain.

Southern sugar houses produced raw sugar of varying quality that was usually consumed in that form. By the 1850s, greatly improved apparatus for sugar making had been developed by Norbert Rillieux, a distinguished black creole of Louisiana who had studied physics and mechanics in France and was familiar with developments in the manufacture of beet sugar. The advanced equipment utilized vacuum pan evaporators, which produced a sugar that was of more uniform consistency and whiter and dryer than open-kettle sugar.

The Texas and Florida sugar areas escaped the ravages of war, but the Louisiana area was not so fortunate. Life in that region experienced abrupt changes when Federal troops arrived in 1862. As the troops extended their control, great numbers of blacks left the plantations in order to join the Northerners. Both planters and newly freed blacks attempted to adjust to the altered situation in 1862 and 1863, but neither group was satisfied with the new relationship. In order to ensure an adequately disciplined labor force, especially during the harvesting season, planters sought to regulate both the working and nonworking hours of the cane cutters. Many of the blacks viewed their efforts as tantamount to a reimposition of slavery.

In January 1863 Gen. Nathaniel P. Banks, commander of the Department of the Gulf, issued orders dealing with the operation of plantations. Planters were to provide "food, clothes, proper treatment, and just compensation" for the blacks. Workers were to receive one-twentieth of the proceeds of the crop at the end of the year or a fixed monthly compensation of two dollars for field hands and three dollars for mechanics and sugar hands.

Early in 1864 General Banks, attempting to respond to dissatisfaction by both planters and sugar cane workers, issued new orders, which increased wages, regulated the workday, and guaranteed just treatment, healthy rations, clothing, quarters, medical attention, and education for children. Workers could choose their employers, but contracts were to remain in force for one year. In order to ensure completion of the year, one-half of a worker's wages could be withheld until the end of the year. Contracts based on these stipulations were entered into throughout the sugar region in 1864 and 1865.

After the Confederates lost control of the Mississippi River and the sugar region of south Louisiana in 1862, the sugar supply almost entirely disappeared from Mississippi to Virginia. Only the small amounts arriving by blockade-runners and that cultivated in Florida and Georgia were available. Substitute sweeteners such as honey, maple syrup, and especially sorghum cane syrup were used instead.

Under the disordered conditions of the war years, it was impossible to grow, harvest, manufacture, and market the sugar crop successfully. From a record 460,000 hogsheads (230,000 tons) of sugar valued at $25 million, the crop declined steadily until the cumulative effect of an inadequate labor force and widespread destruction of capital equipment resulted in an 1864 crop of only 10,000 hogsheads valued at less than $2 million. Although more than 1,200 plantations in twenty-four parishes had produced sugar in 1861, in 1864 only 175 plantations in sixteen parishes were still making sugar.

The collapse of the industry can be seen in its capital losses. In 1861 the total capital invested in the industry was estimated at $194 million of which $100 million was in slave property, $25 million in land, and $69 million in capital equipment and rolling stock. With the investment in slave property wiped out, capital equipment largely destroyed, and a drastic decline in the value of sugar lands, the industry was worth only $25 million in 1865.

With the end of the Civil War, sugar planters and workers alike had to adjust to a new order of society, which demanded abandonment of old habits, convictions, and prejudices.

BIBLIOGRAPHY

Heitmann, John. *Modernization of the Louisiana Sugar Industry, 1830–1910*. Baton Rouge, La., 1987.

Prichard, Walter. "The Effects of the Civil War on the Louisiana Sugar Industry." *Journal of Southern History* 5 (1939): 315–332.

Roland, Charles P. *Louisiana Sugar Plantations during the American Civil War*. Leiden, Holland, 1957.

Sitterson, J. Carlyle. *Sugar Country: The Cane Sugar Industry in the South, 1753–1950*. Lexington, Ky., 1953.

Sitterson, J. Carlyle. "The Transition from Slave to Free Economy on the William J. Minor Plantations." *Agricultural History* 17 (1943): 216–224.

J. CARLYLE SITTERSON

SUMNER, CANING OF

On May 22, 1856, Preston Brooks, a congressman from South Carolina, entered the chambers of the upper house and beat Senator Charles Sumner of Massachusetts senseless with a cane. This event, which came at a time when the struggle over slavery in Kansas was creating powerful tensions between the North and the South, further polarized the sections, contributed to the rapid rise of the Republican party, and was an important landmark on the road to the Civil War.

Sumner had been elected to the Senate in 1851; by that date he was already well known in Massachusetts as a leading critic of slavery. In 1855 he had helped organize the Republican party, which was pledged to stop the expansion of slavery into the western territories. On May 19 and 20, 1856, he delivered a carefully prepared speech in the Senate on "The Crime against Kansas" in which he lashed out at slavery and the South. Sumner launched scathing attacks on individual Southerners, including his fellow senator Andrew P. Butler of South Carolina, who was absent at the time Sumner spoke. Butler, Sumner charged, had taken "the harlot, Slavery" as "his mistress to whom he has made his vows," and Sumner contended that if the whole history of South Carolina were blotted out of existence "civilization might lose . . . little." Most who heard the speech were appalled at

Sumner's language, and Congressman Brooks, who was a cousin of Butler's, was outraged. Two days after Sumner had concluded his remarks, Brooks assaulted him.

News of Sumner's caning rapidly swept the nation. In the North, even conservatives who were critical of Sumner's antislavery views and vituperative speeches were infuriated by Brooks's assault. Their anger mounted as it became evident that Southerners, rather than condemning Brooks, revered him for defending the honor not only of his relative but of the whole section. Constituents showered him with new canes; merchants of South Carolina sent him one inscribed with the words "hit him again." Southern votes prevented the House from expelling Brooks, who resigned anyway but was triumphantly reelected by his constituents. A fine of three hundred dollars levied by a Washington court proved to be his only punishment.

At the very time news of Sumner's caning reached the North, word came from Kansas that a proslavery mob had attacked the homes, shops, and newspapers of free-state advocates in Lawrence. Republicans, whose party had just been formed and whose future seemed uncertain, were quick to exploit Northern anger at both these actions, char-

> **Sumner's caning . . . provided the Republicans with their most effective image of Southern arrogance.**

acterizing them as proof of Southern willingness to assault free institutions in order to defend slavery. This contention proved popular with many Northerners who were not particularly concerned about the issue of slavery but were worried about defending freedom of speech and press from Southern attack.

Sumner's caning, rather than the sack of Lawrence, provided the Republicans with their most effective image of Southern arrogance. Widespread indignation at the deed led many moderates and conservatives who had previously joined the newly formed American, or Know-Nothing, party to join them instead, and in the 1856 presidential election the Republicans almost defeated the Democratic candidate.

Sumner did not return to the Senate until December 1859, and his empty seat was a constant reminder to the North of Brooks's deed. His critics argued that the senator was feigning illness, but his injuries, complicated by posttraumatic syndrome, had truly disabled him. In 1860 the Republicans took the White House, thereby precipitating the secession of the lower South. Sumner's caning, by arousing the North and helping to make the Republican party a major political force, had proved to be a long step toward war.

[*See also* Bleeding Kansas.]

BIBLIOGRAPHY

Donald, David. *Charles Sumner and the Coming of the Civil War.* New York, 1960.

Gienapp, William. "The Crime against Sumner: The Caning of Charles Sumner and the Rise of the Republican Party." *Civil War History* 25 (1979): 218–245.

RICHARD H. ABBOTT

T

TALIAFERRO, WILLIAM BOOTH

TALIAFERRO, WILLIAM BOOTH (1822–1898), major general. Born into the Tidewater aristocracy in Gloucester County, Virginia, Taliaferro graduated from William and Mary in 1841, attended Harvard Law School, and fought as a captain in the Eleventh and as a major in the Ninth U.S. Infantry during the Mexican War. From 1850 to 1853, Taliaferro represented Gloucester County in the Virginia legislature. In November 1859, he commanded the state's militia at Harpers Ferry in the aftermath of John Brown's raid.

WILLIAM BOOTH TALIAFERRO.

Commissioned a colonel on May 1, 1861, Taliaferro participated that day in the engagement at Gloucester Point. Two months later he fought at Carrick's Ford. He was a strict disciplinarian and his manner alienated many of his men, one of whom physically assaulted him. Serving under Thomas J. ("Stonewall") Jackson in 1862, Taliaferro rankled Jackson by appealing to his political friends in Richmond to support W. W. Loring's protest over Jackson's tactics and winter quarters. Jackson resigned, reconsidered, and protested Taliaferro's promotion to brigadier general in March 1862, but he still had confidence in the military abilities of his mutinous subordinate.

Taliaferro proved himself during the Shenandoah Valley campaign of 1862 and took command of the Stonewall Division after the death of Gen. Charles S. Winder at Cedar Mountain on August 9, 1862. Wounded at Groveton, Taliaferro recovered in time to help repulse the Union attack at Fredericksburg.

In February 1863 Taliaferro was in charge of the military district of Savannah before being assigned to command Fort Wagner on Morris Island, where on July 18 he repulsed the charge of the Fifty-fourth Massachusetts Infantry and other Federal units. Subsequently, Taliaferro served on James Island, in Florida, and at Savannah. Promoted to major general on January 1, 1865, Taliaferro surrendered with Joseph E. Johnston on April 26.

He returned to Virginia, where he served as county judge and state legislator until his death in 1898.

BIBLIOGRAPHY

Krick, Robert K. *Stonewall Jackson at Cedar Mountain.* Chapel Hill, N.C., 1990.

Taliaferro, William B. "Jackson's Raid around Pope." In *Battles and Leaders of the Civil War.* Vol. 2. Edited by Robert U. Johnson and C. C. Buel. New York, 1888. Reprint, Secaucus, N.J., 1982.

Tanner, Robert G. *Stonewall in the Valley.* Garden City, N.Y., 1976.

RUSSELL DUNCAN

TALLAHASSEE, FLORIDA

The small town of Tallahassee was the only Confederate capital east of the Mississippi not captured and occupied by

Union forces during the entire war. Located halfway between St. Augustine and Pensacola, it was twenty miles north of its cotton port of St. Marks on the Gulf of Mexico. Throughout the war Tallahassee was isolated from much of the state and the rest of the Confederacy by inadequate roads, bridges, and ferries and an incomplete railroad system, although a good railroad and parallel plank road joined the capital to Port St. Marks. One east-west railroad, the Pensacola and Georgia, had its western terminus 40 miles west on the Apalachicola River but 160 miles from the vital port of Pensacola. Eastward the railroad passed through Tallahassee to join, in late 1861, the Florida Atlantic and Gulf Coast at Lake City, giving the capital rail access to the Atlantic port of Jacksonville. There was no track north of Jacksonville into Georgia. Thus Florida's thousands of

> ## Tallahassee had less strategic value than many other Southern cities.

troops, if they were not coming from the vicinity of Pensacola, had to leave the state on foot to reach the rest of the Confederacy. Regular transportation north from Tallahassee was by stagecoach.

This frontier capital's streets were unpaved and unnumbered, with very little public lighting. The public water supply consisted of three open wells in the center of town. Human waste removal was not a responsibility of the village, nor did it have a police force. Two years before the war the town got its first telegraph line.

In 1861 the capital had a population of 1,932 individuals equally divided by race—997 whites, 889 slaves, and 46 free persons of color. Of the town's 241 heads of households, 143, or 60 percent, owned slaves. The ethnic and cultural background of the free population was predominantly native-born white, Anglo-Saxon, and Protestant. The small foreign-born element was made up of Scottish, Irish, English, German, and French immigrants.

Wartime Tallahassee had no industrial capacity. The town's chief business before and during the war was supplying the wealthiest plantations in the state with the necessities of a cotton-growing region. At the beginning of the war fifty thousand bales of cotton were being shipped out annually from St. Marks until the Union navy's blockade closed both St. Marks and Jacksonville in 1862. The town had six churches within its city limits—two Methodist (one for blacks and one for whites), one Presbyterian, one Episcopal, one Baptist, and one Catholic. There were two newspapers. The larger, the Democratic-oriented *Floridian and Journal,* was owned by Charles Dykes and James Carlisle. Edwin Hart owned the smaller Whig-oriented *Florida Sentinel,* which

ceased operation in December 1863 owing to wartime shortages. The higher education center of the state of Florida was Tallahassee's West Florida Seminary and Female Academy (forerunner of Florida State University), which granted B.A. degrees.

Because of its isolation, lack of industrial capacity, and the blockade of its only gulf port, Tallahassee had less strategic value than many other Southern cities. But the efficient wartime governor John Milton and his Tallahassee legislature made up for much of the shortfall by organizing the provision, throughout the war, of a constant supply of Florida beef to the Confederacy. The Tallahassee legislature also raised more troops, over 13,000, than were registered voters in the entire state of Florida. Among them was Brig. Gen. Theodore W. Brevard, the last general officer appointed by Jefferson Davis at the end of the war. The city also supplied eleven colonels and twenty-three captains as well as six army surgeons. All of Florida's infantrymen in the east were brigaded together in the Army of Northern Virginia and called, successively, the Florida, Perry, and Finegan Brigade. Tallahassee's most notable casualty of the war was planter Col. George T. Ward, who died leading the Florida Brigade at the Battle of Williamsburg, May 5, 1862.

No serious Union attempt was ever made to capture the capital. In February 1864 a Union army of about 5,000 men led by Brig. Gen. Truman Seymour marched west out of Jacksonville along the Florida Atlantic and Gulf Coast Railroad toward Tallahassee. Their objective, however, was not the capital but the Suwanee River where they hoped to cut Florida's supply links with Confederate forces farther north. The Union troops were defeated February 20 at the Battle of Olustee, or Ocean Pond, near Lake City, by an equal number of mostly Georgia regulars under Gen. Joseph Finegan and Gen. Alfred H. Colquitt. For the Union this was the third bloodiest battle of the war in terms of percentage of losses per unit.

A year later Tallahasseans braced themselves for what they thought was to be an assault on their capital. In February 1865 around 1,000 troops, led by Maj. Gen. John Newton, disembarked near the St. Marks lighthouse and marched northward along the St. Marks River toward Newport so as to flank the target of the expedition, Port St. Marks. The Tallahassee militia hastily built a large square earthwork, Fort Houston, on the southern edge of town, at the juncture of the plank road from Newport, to repel the Union men. On February 28 over 2,000 Confederate regular and militia troops under Maj. Gen. Samuel Jones met and defeated 893 black troops at the Battle of Natural Bridge ten miles southeast of the capital. Sixty cadets from West Florida Seminary, led by Col. George W. Scott, participated in the battle.

On April 1, 1865, Governor Milton, despondent over Confederate reverses elsewhere, left Tallahassee and killed himself near his home in Marianna, Florida. On May 10, the Union cavalry general Brig. Edward M. McCook, riding in advance of 500 troops, entered the capital to receive its surrender from Major General Jones. On May 20, with acting Governor Abraham K. Allison presiding, the Union flag was raised over the old capitol building. The only military fortification of the Civil War today in Tallahassee is a remnant of Fort Houston.

[*See also* Olustee, Florida.]

BIBLIOGRAPHY

Groene, Bertram. *Antebellum Tallahassee*. Tallahassee, Fla., 1981.
Keen, Mary W. "Some Phases of Life in Leon County during the Civil War." *Tallahassee Historical Society Annual* 4 (1939): 20–47.
Robertson, Fredric L. *Soldiers of Florida in the Seminole Indian, Civil and Spanish-American Wars*. Live Oak, Fla., 1909. Reprint, Macclenny, Fla., 1983.
Rogers, William. "A Great Stirring in the Land and Leon County in 1860." *Florida Historical Quarterly* 64 (1985): 148–160.

BERTRAM HAWTHORNE GROENE

TAXATION

Taxation supplied only a fraction of all government revenues, state and Confederate, in the Civil War South. Throughout the war, the Confederate government issued Treasury notes, from which it derived half of all its revenue (in current dollars), and sold bonds, which generated another one-fourth of the total. In addition, it impressed, or seized, vast quantities of supplies and thus obtained 17 percent of its aggregate purchasing power. That left only 7 percent of all Confederate national revenue secured through taxation. That increment of taxation permitted the Confederacy to purchase some supplies on the open market, while also offering a means of absorbing a minor portion of the Confederacy's redundant currency.

Only gradually did the Confederacy adopt direct taxes. At first, members of the new national government anticipated either no war or only a short one. Moreover, given the pervasive unpopularity of direct taxes, the Provisional Congress enacted only import and export duties. But the war came, expenditures grew, and the Federal blockade curtailed revenues from duties. Therefore, in August 1861, the Congress imposed direct taxes payable in Treasury notes. The new tax, at one-half of 1 percent of assessed property valuation, relied on the fiscal machinery of the state governments and ultimately generated $17.4 million. Reflecting the structure of the tax base across the South, the new tax derived 35 percent of that amount from slaves and another 33 percent from real estate. Most states took advantage of a provision that

permitted a state to pay its citizens' share of the tax by April 1, 1862, at a 10 percent discount. Similarly, most states borrowed to obtain that money and then failed to tax their citizens to retrieve the amount paid over to the Confederacy. Thus the national tax took the form of state debt.

Only in April 1863 did the Confederacy enact a comprehensive tax law. It levied taxes on occupations, income, and produce as well as on property. Like the 1861 act, which had exempted any head of family whose taxable property was valued at less than $500, the new law was designed to secure purchasing power, on a graduated (or at least proportional) basis, only from those families who likely had some surplus to contribute. The statute placed license taxes ranging from $50 to $500 on many occupations, levied a graduated tax on annual incomes of more than $500, taxed at 8 percent all naval stores, money, and agricultural products "not necessary for family consumption," and imposed a tax-in-kind of 10 percent of annual agricultural productions beyond an allowance for subsistence. Subsequent measures in February 1864, June 1864, and March 1865 raised these rates.

The Confederate system of direct taxes, such as it was, carried several unmanageable burdens. For one, though reliance on taxation became greater in the second half of the war, the aggregate value of supplies seized through impressment dwarfed the revenue achieved through taxation, and nothing guaranteed anything remotely resembling fiscal fairness in the activities of the impressment agents. Heedless of local needs or of producers' ability to pay, those agents gathered supplies, instead, according to local availability and government need. For another, the issue of Treasury notes generated seven times the purchasing power that taxation did, three times the amount raised through impressment, and twice the combined total of impressment and taxation. The tax system simply failed to absorb a sufficient quantity of the Treasury notes from circulation. Inflation raced ahead of revenues.

With four years of war, state and local governments, too, faced huge demands. Their revenue systems, however, were already in place and fully functional in 1861, though the war forced major adjustments in their operations. The states varied widely in particulars of their wartime fiscal behavior, yet they tended to share a number of general features. They typically resorted at first to huge bond issues and then moved primarily to the issue of Treasury notes. They maintained the core of their prewar tax systems throughout the war, but rates on traditional objects of taxation climbed, and new measures tapped new objects.

Though taxation supplied only a small fraction of each state's wartime revenue, taxation provided an even smaller share of the Confederate government's total income. In contrast to both Confederate and state governments, counties generated little long-term debt, as they typically paid for large portions of their expenditures by issuing certificates of indebtedness, which they then called back in by means of taxes payable in those certificates. The larger political units mostly ignored calls that they do likewise. Nobody thought that wartime taxes should fully match public expenditures, whether by the states or the Confederate governments, but, though bonds offered a means of making long-term loans, many Southerners argued that a larger fraction of Treasury notes should be called in for taxes than was the case.

Georgia offers one model of fiscal change in the Confederate South. On the eve of the war, its state tax system relied on a general property tax that, with low (and even declining) rates, supplied all the tax revenue that expenditures required. A poll tax more or less offset a standard deduction against the property tax. The state poll tax stayed unchanged through the war, while state property taxes multiplied by almost sixteen between 1860 and 1864. That increase was greater than any other state displayed, but virtually every state substantially hiked its rates on property.

Georgia also illustrates another major facet of the Confederate South's fiscal experience. On the tax side of the state budget, Georgia favored its less wealthy citizens. Across the South, public authorities sought to cushion the smaller farmers and other less wealthy white families from the full force of the tax rate increases. Exemptions from the property tax grew for Confederate soldiers' families who held property of only modest valuation. Thus new exemptions characterized Southern tax systems at the same time that much higher general property tax rates did. Moreover, Georgia left its poll tax rates unchanged throughout the war, and by 1863 it suspended even those rates for all soldiers with only small holdings.

On the spending side, too, Georgia proved a representative state in offering benefits to small farmers that it denied the more wealthy. State and local authorities recognized early on that winning the war depended on retaining in the army the tens of thousands of soldiers from farm families who had little economic cushion. As one Mississippi soldier wrote his governor, "we are poor men and are willing to defend our country but our families first and then our count[r]y." Soldiers would, and did, desert the battlefront to head back home when they believed their loved ones to be suffering from inadequate supplies of food and other necessities.

Authorities therefore made commitments to allocate enormous sums for the support of soldiers' families. At first, the counties acted, particularly when it became clear that calls for voluntary contributions drew uneven—and thus unequal and insufficient—amounts of aid. Counties responded by resorting to the coercion of the tax system to obtain the funds (or the provisions) that they needed. But then it became clear that the counties most in need often had the least resources, and thus the state stepped in. Georgia's state government,

matching its own direct military expenditures almost dollar for dollar through the war, supplied huge sums for the support of soldiers' families. Throughout much of the South, state and local authorities alike allocated large, even major, portions of their budgets to the distribution of cash or such commodities as salt, corn, and bacon.

In these ways, the Georgia experience demonstrates how Southern state and local governments became more progressive during the war, and how authority and responsibility grew more centralized. The tax system became more progressive as rates on the wealthy rose at the same time that the less wealthy gained exemptions. And, on the spending side, the state government taxed planters in the black belt to generate funds with which to acquire food to supply soldiers' families in the nonplantation counties. The huge increases in state tax rates midway through the war reflected, in part, an assumption by the state of responsibilities that the counties had undertaken in the first two years of the war.

In these various ways, state and local authorities demonstrated that they acted with one eye on the home front and one eye on the battlefront. And they supplied tangible benefits to constituents whose support was essential if the war was to be prosecuted with much chance of success. As part of a wartime agenda, the higher taxes—first at the county level, then at the state—could be seen to be purchasing real goods for real constituents. Governments at the state and local levels revealed themselves as in the business of caring for civilians as much as they were covering the costs of rifles, tents, and boots for the troops. Such could not be said for Confederate national spending policies. These facets of state and local operations may help explain why the men who set state and local taxes felt that they could demand escalating taxes—why they may have detected less resistance to higher and higher taxes than their national counterparts seemed to perceive.

> **The Confederate system of direct taxes . . . carried several unmanageable burdens.**

Yet all such considerations highlight, too, the differences, by class and by region within each state, that separated the larger slaveholders from their less prosperous fellow citizens. The differences were real, and they emerged in struggles over tax policy. Indeed, a central issue in parts of the South related to the taxes on planters' slaves. In North Carolina, for example, perhaps the leading issue in state politics in the 1850s had been whether slave property should carry a larger share of the state tax burden. On the eve of the war, small farmers had finally achieved success, they thought, in demanding that planters carry a larger share, but their victory proved illusory, even in the crucible of war. In Virginia in 1861, by contrast, planters from the eastern half of the state offered the small farmers of the west a major concession—higher taxes on slaves—in hopes of cementing their support for the Confederacy. Though the concession was real, much of that support evaporated, as West Virginia went its separate political, military, and fiscal way.

By late 1864 and early 1865, the Confederacy's war effort was winding down, and for more reasons than a shortage of military manpower in a war of attrition. Real shortages and runaway inflation each help explain why the Confederacy lost. Tax rates climbed much higher than ever before, yet they played only a minor role in the Confederate government's efforts to finance its operations, and they proved too low to absorb enough of the endless supply of state and Confederate Treasury notes. Though state and local governments clearly treated their citizens on the bases of ability to pay and nature of need, the Confederacy's heavy reliance on impressment could operate to vitiate those policies. In any case, the logistical problems of distributing aid to civilians proved as great as the logistical problems of moving battalions of troops. The Confederacy ran too low on food and clothing, on the means of purchasing them, and on the means of distributing them. The fiscal system failed. And the war ended.

[See also Currency, overview article; Impressment; State Socialism; Tax-in-Kind.]

BIBLIOGRAPHY

Ball, Douglas B. *Financial Failure and Confederate Defeat.* Urbana, Ill., 1991.

Bettersworth, John K. *Confederate Mississippi: The People and Policies of a Cotton State in Wartime.* Baton Rouge, La., 1943. Reprint, Philadelphia, Pa., 1978.

Butts, Donald C. "A Challenge to Planter Rule: The Controversy over Ad Valorem Taxation of Slaves in North Carolina, 1858–1862." Ph.D. diss., Duke University, 1978.

Ramsdell, Charles W. *Behind the Lines in the Southern Confederacy.* Baton Rouge, La., 1944. Reprint, New York, 1969.

Ringold, May Spencer. *The Role of the State Legislatures in the Confederacy.* Athens, Ga., 1966.

Todd, Richard Cecil. *Confederate Finance.* Athens, Ga., 1954.

Wallenstein, Peter. *From Slave South to New South: Public Policy in Nineteenth-Century Georgia.* Chapel Hill, N.C., 1987.

PETER WALLENSTEIN

TAX-IN-KIND

The Confederate States of America tried from its inception to develop a system to provide revenue for its treasury. Resistant to enacting an income tax, Confederate Treasury Secretary Christopher G. Memminger and the Congress proposed and passed into law other initiatives. One of the most unpopular was the tax-in-kind, enacted in April 1863.

Secretary Memminger designed the tax-in-kind to serve as an alternative to the impressment of agricultural products. The Treasury and War departments, the chief administrators of the tax-in-kind, enumerated items that agents, or "T.I.K. men," would collect in each locality. The list of goods included wheat, oats, corn, rice, potatoes, fodder, sugar, cotton, wool, tobacco, and rye. Each farmer was to retain for his or her own use fifty bushels of sweet potatoes, either one hundred bushels of corn or fifty bushels of wheat, and twenty

> **The tax-in-kind proved to be one of the most, if not *the* most, unpopular acts . . . ever passed.**

bushels of peas or beans; from what remained, the farmer was required to donate 10 percent to government agents. Southern agriculturalists were also required to pay in kind on bacon and pork, based upon a 10 percent tax on all hogs slaughtered during 1863. The agents would assess the value of the farms' products and notify the farmers of the amount they were required to tithe. If the assessor's estimate varied greatly from the farmer's, a mediator would make the final determination of the value of the goods. Farmers who failed to pay their tithe were subject to a stiff penalty. The agents collected the goods and funneled them to local and district-level quartermasters who were supposed to ensure that the items reached the armies in the field.

The tax-in-kind proved to be one of the most, if not *the* most, unpopular acts the Confederate Congress ever passed. Farmers resisted the quotas, especially since they were based on the gross value of crops, not on profits, and they loathed the T.I.K. men who pressed them for payment. A serious problem with the tax lay in its collection and distribution: often crops would rot at depots before quartermasters could transport them to the army. The program was also plagued by phony agents who swindled farmers out of their produce.

It is difficult to determine how much the Treasury gained from the tax-in-kind. Confederate agents estimated that about $6 million in produce was collected by the end of 1863; by late winter of 1864, the figure stood at $40 million. Public outcry against the tax led to its amendment. In December 1863, Congress allowed the tax on sweet potatoes to be paid in cash. By February 1864, Congress was extending exemptions on the collection of the tax-in-kind for soldiers' families and small farmers; by 1865, the act barely resembled its 1863 version: individuals could substitute cash payments for payments in farm produce.

The criticisms of and alterations to the tax-in-kind indicate that Congress was not oblivious to the flaws of the original act. Despite the chorus of protest, however, the tax-in-kind did help supply and feed the Confederate armies during the final two years of the war.

BIBLIOGRAPHY

Ball, Douglas B. *Financial Failure and Confederate Defeat.* Urbana, Ill., 1991.
Coulter, E. Merton. *The Confederate States of America, 1861–1865.* A History of the South, vol. 7. Baton Rouge, La., 1951.
Goff, Richard. *Confederate Supply.* Durham, N.C., 1969.
Todd, Richard Cecil. *Confederate Finance.* Athens, Ga., 1954.

MARY A. DECREDICO

TAYLOR, RICHARD

TAYLOR, RICHARD (1826–1879), lieutenant general. A Confederate general with no formal military education, Taylor served with distinction and in 1865 surrendered the last organized Confederate force east of the Mississippi.

Born in Kentucky, the son of President Zachary Taylor, Richard studied at Harvard, Edinburgh, and Yale, before becoming a Louisiana sugar planter. Elected colonel of the Ninth Louisiana Infantry at the war's outset, he and his regiment reached Virginia too late for the First Battle of Manassas. Taylor was a brother-in-law of President Jefferson Davis, and rumor had it that in the fall of 1861 he was offered the post of quartermaster general of the Confederate army. If so, he declined it, but from time to time throughout the war he continued to be the beneficiary of Davis's favoritism. In October he was promoted to brigadier general and given command of a Louisiana brigade that became part of Richard S. Ewell's division.

Taylor served with distinction in the Shenandoah Valley campaign during the spring of 1862 but was kept out of the Seven Days' Battles by rheumatoid arthritis. Recovering within a few weeks, he was promoted to major general and was assigned to command of the District of Western Louisiana in August 1862. Although dreaming of retaking New Orleans, he generally found himself falling back before Federal forays such as Maj. Gen. Nathaniel P. Banks's April 1863 Bayou Teche expedition. At the urging of Trans-Mississippi commander E. Kirby Smith, who was himself under pressure from Richmond, Taylor moved against Ulysses S. Grant's supply lines on the west bank of the Mississippi opposite Vicksburg. The attempt was a failure, and Grant's campaign culminated in the capture of that key Confederate stronghold.

Taylor was forced to fall back before Banks's Red River expedition in the spring of 1864 but defeated Banks at the Battle of Mansfield, Louisiana, south of Shreveport, on April 8, 1864. Outnumbered twelve thousand to nine thousand in troops engaged, Taylor inflicted double his own casualties and captured twenty cannons and two hundred supply wagons. Although defeated the next day at Pleasant Hill and ordered by Smith to fall back temporarily on Shreveport, he had succeeded in forcing the withdrawal of Banks's ill-fated expedition.

Rewarded with a promotion to lieutenant general, Taylor was nevertheless bitter toward Smith, blaming him for Banks's escape. He thus welcomed orders to take his troops across the Mississippi for service in the East. Finding the river too heavily patrolled by the U.S. Navy, he had to remain in the Trans-Mississippi until August 22, 1864, when he was ordered to go east personally to take command of the Department of Alabama, Mississippi, and Eastern Louisiana.

On January 23, 1865, Taylor was named as successor to John Bell Hood as commander of the remnants of the Army of Tennessee, which Hood had wrecked at Franklin and Nashville. As such, Taylor's prime role was shipping his units off to the Carolinas to oppose William Tecumseh Sherman. On May 4, 1865, he surrendered to Gen. E. R. S. Canby at Citronelle, Alabama.

After the war, Taylor was active in Democratic party politics in Louisiana, opposing the Reconstruction regime. In 1879, the year of his death, he published his reminiscences of the war, *Destruction and Reconstruction,* one of the best of the memoirs of the conflict's participants.

BIBLIOGRAPHY

Parrish, T. Michael. *Richard Taylor: Soldier Prince of Dixie.* Chapel Hill, N.C., 1992.
Taylor, Richard. *Destruction and Reconstruction.* New York, 1879. Reprint, edited by Charles P. Roland. Waltham, Mass., 1968.

STEVEN E. WOODWORTH

TELEGRAPH

The Civil War was the first war in which the electric telegraph played a major role. It was used by both sides at both the tactical and strategic levels, though much more effectively by the Union. Indeed, it can be said with some justification that the way that Union forces used telegraph communications was a major factor in determining the outcome of the war.

The simple and rugged American telegraph design was well suited to battlefield use. For transmitting, the operator used a "key" to make and break electrical contact and to send short and long pulses of current from a battery over the wire (only a single wire was needed; connections were made to the ground at each end, and the ground performed the function of a second wire to complete the circuit.) At the receiver the current activated an electromagnet, which pulled against a lever to make short and long clicking noises—"dots" and "dashes" that in combinations represented letters and numbers.

Samuel F. B. Morse, a portrait painter, had invented this form of telegraphy in the 1830s. With money from Congress and practical assistance from Alfred Vail, he constructed a successful demonstration line between Baltimore and Washington in 1844. When no further interest was shown by the government, he licensed private individuals to develop the system. The result was a rapid expansion over the next decade and a half (including competition from non-Morse systems), culminating in a transcontinental line that was completed in the fall of 1861. A transatlantic cable was momentarily successful in 1858, but it failed before it could be placed in commercial operation and was not replaced until 1866.

On the eve of the war there thus existed an infrastructure of tens of thousands of miles of wire, about 10 percent of it in the states of the Confederacy. These latter lines lay along two major routes reaching to New Orleans: in the east, from Washington through Richmond, Petersburg, Raleigh, Columbia, Augusta, Macon, Montgomery, and Mobile (with side links to Charleston, Savannah, and Atlanta); in the west, along two competing lines from Nashville, one by way of Vicksburg and Natchez, the other through Florence and Jackson. Along with the advantage in miles of wire, the Union had a comparable advantage in numbers of trained operators. The North also, apparently, had a better sense of the value of this form of communications. The Union established a military telegraph service, which constructed and operated fifteen thousand miles of lines during the war; individual Confederate forces established a total of one thousand miles. Furthermore, Union forces used codes to protect their messages; the Confederates, in general, did not.

The significance of these communications systems had thus far been told only in anecdotal form. At the Battle of First Manassas, for instance, P. G. T. Beauregard used the telegraph to call for reinforcements; Theophilus H. Holmes arrived in time to be a decisive factor in the outcome. Another account tells that C. A. Gaston, Robert E. Lee's confidential operator, was able to wiretap Ulysses S. Grant's line for six weeks during the siege of Richmond and Petersburg. Among the unciphered messages was one telling of the impending arrival of 2,536 head of beef at Coggins' Point. A timely raid captured the entire herd. On another front, John H. Morgan's success has been attributed in considerable part to the skill of his operator in intercepting messages and in sending false and misleading messages. Similar stories have been told about virtually every major battle of the war.

Use of the telegraph dramatically altered the manner in which commanders exercised their authority. No longer did they have to be close to the battlefield, and they could be aware of all aspects of a conflict, no matter how large. Thus, during the Wilderness and Atlanta campaigns both Grant and Lee were in almost hourly contact with the various elements of their troops. During the period before and during the battle at Gettysburg, Abraham Lincoln followed the action closely from the War Department office in Washington, where he spent much of his time. By telegraph before the conflict he relieved Joseph Hooker of command and replaced him with George G. Meade. In the aftermath he unsuccessfully urged Meade to pursue Lee to prevent him from escaping across the Potomac River.

The significance of the telegraph in the American Civil War (during which 6.5 million messages are estimated to have been sent by the Union side alone) was not lost on military planners elsewhere. Every regular army in Europe soon had its telegraph corps, and every war fought since then has depended on electrical communications for command and control systems.

BIBLIOGRAPHY

Beringer, Richard E., et al. *Why the South Lost the Civil War.* Athens, Ga., 1986.
Harlow, Alvin F. *Old Wires and New Waves.* New York, 1936.
Plum, William R. *The Military Telegraph during the Civil War in the United States.* Chicago, 1882. Reprint, New York, 1974.
Scheips, Paul J., ed. *Military Signal Communications.* New York, 1980.
Thompson, Robert L. *Wiring a Continent.* Princeton, N.J., 1947. Reprint, New York, 1972.

BERNARD S. FINN

TENNESSEE

One of only three states to cast its electoral ballots for Constitutional Unionist John Bell in the 1860 presidential election, Tennessee resisted secession until after the fall of Fort Sumter and did not officially leave the Union until June 8, 1861. With a population of 1,109,801 (of whom 275,719 were slaves and 7,300 were free blacks), the state provided 140,000 men to the Confederate army. Internal divisions and Federal military occupation, however, limited Tennessee's contributions to the Confederate cause and encouraged at least 51,000 other Tennesseans, white and black, to join the Union army.

From beginning to end, Tennessee's experience was unique among the Confederate states. The last state to secede, it was also the only one to leave the Union by means of a legislative "declaration of independence" rather than a secession ordinance adopted by a special convention, the only one to experience large-scale *Confederate* military occupation and martial law, the only one wholly exempted from the Emancipation Proclamation, the only one fully under Federal control before the war ended, the only one with a reconstructed state government with uncontested political authority operating before the end of the war, and the only one that freed its own slaves.

Geography profoundly influenced the course of events in Tennessee from 1860 to 1865. The state's three "grand divisions" are physically distinct, and in the antebellum decades they diverged socially and economically. In eastern Tennessee, a relatively isolated region of hills and mountains, there evolved a yeoman-dominated society marked by small, self-sufficient farms and little reliance on slavery; in 1860 only 9 percent of eastern Tennessee's 301,056 inhabitants were slaves. Western Tennessee, a flat alluvial plain, developed an economy resembling the staple-producing plantation system of the Deep South; over 33 percent of its 304,311 inhabitants were slaves. Middle Tennessee, a lush basin surrounded by highlands, produced corn and livestock on commercial farms of middling size; 29 percent of its 504,434 inhabitants were slaves. Though the state was overwhelmingly rural, each grand division boasted an important urban center: Memphis in the west, Nashville in the middle, and Knoxville in the east. Three major rivers—the Mississippi, Tennessee, and Cumberland—provided access to western and middle Tennessee and would assume great importance in Civil War military strategy.

Secession Crisis in Tennessee

Two-party politics persisted in Tennessee even after the collapse of the national Whig party in the 1850s. A strong opposition party, composed mostly of former Whigs, provided a solid base for Unionism in the state—in contrast to the Deep South, where Democratic hegemony fostered secessionism. In 1860 Tennessee oppositionists endorsed middle Tennessean John Bell, a strong Unionist, for president. Bell quickly attracted a national following among voters who rejected the sectionalism embodied by the three other presidential contenders (Stephen A. Douglas, the Northern Democratic candidate; John C. Breckinridge, representing Southern Democrats, especially the fervent state rights advocates; and the Republican Abraham Lincoln, representing antislavery Northerners). In the November election Bell won Tennessee with 69,710 votes, a plurality of 48 percent. Breckinridge (65,053 votes) and Douglas (11,394) split the Democratic vote (Lincoln was not on the ballot in Tennessee). The election was not a clear-cut referendum on secession in Tennessee: for one thing, the voting closely mimicked the traditional Whig-Democratic pattern of the antebellum years; and, too, many devoutly Unionist Democrats—including Andrew Johnson of eastern Tennessee—supported Breckinridge. Nevertheless, the com-

bined Bell-Douglas total suggests that a solid majority of Tennessee voters favored a conservative approach to the sectional issue.

That conservatism was reaffirmed in the months that followed. The election of Lincoln provoked the secession of South Carolina in December and gave Tennessee's secessionist minority, led by Governor Isham G. Harris, hope that Tennessee might follow South Carolina's lead. Harris called the legislature into session on January 7, 1861, and asked it to authorize a secession convention. The legislature approved a referendum to be held February 9, in which Tennessee voters would decide whether a convention should be held and would also elect delegates.

By February 9 the Deep South states had all seceded, but in Tennessee, Unionism was triumphant that day. The call for a convention was defeated by 69,675 to 57,798, figures that understate the Unionist majority, because many Unionists voted for a convention in the hope that it would decisively reject secession. In fact, the votes amassed by declared Unionist candidates for delegate exceeded those of secessionist candidates by nearly four to one. Nevertheless, the election results indicated an incipient political realignment in the state. Western Tennesseans voted 74 to 26 percent in favor of a convention, eastern Tennesseans 81 to 19 percent against, and middle Tennesseans 51 to 49 percent against, a pattern reflecting a stronger correlation between slaveholding and secessionism than in the November election.

Secession had thus been rejected in Tennessee, but events were to show that (except in the eastern section) Tennessee Unionism was contingent on a conciliatory policy toward the South on the part of the incoming administration. When Lincoln called for troops to suppress the rebellion following the bombardment of Fort Sumter on April 12, Unionism in middle and western Tennessee evaporated. Forced now to take sides in a civil war, most citizens outside eastern Tennessee chose to join the Deep South. John Bell himself, who since November had urged support of Lincoln, now reluctantly renounced his Unionism.

Again Governor Harris put himself at the head of the secession movement and this time led it to victory. Having informed the Lincoln administration that "Tennessee will not furnish a single man for purposes of coercion but 50,000 if necessary for the defence of our rights and those of our Southern brothers," Harris called the legislature into session. When it met on April 25, the governor asked for a declaration of independence based on the right of revolution. The legislature obliged, by a vote of twenty to four in the Senate and forty-six to twenty-one in the House, stipulating that the declaration be submitted to a popular vote on June 8.

By that time traditional party lines had broken down almost completely, and regionalism had emerged as the most important voting determinant. Eastern Tennessee held fast to the Union even as the other two sections went over to secession. (Of the twenty-five legislators who voted against the declaration of independence, all but seven were eastern Tennesseans.) As old-line Whigs and Democrats jumped on the secession bandwagon in middle and western Tennessee, those in eastern Tennessee joined hands to resist the secessionist onslaught. Several hundred Unionists held a convention in Knoxville on May 30 and 31, where they heard speeches by longtime political foes T. A. R. Nelson and Andrew Johnson and then adopted resolutions denouncing secession.

In the June 8 referendum, which officially took the state out of the Union by a vote of 104,913 to 47,238, eastern Tennesseans voted 69 to 31 percent against secession, whereas western Tennesseans voted 83 to 17 percent in

> ## Confederate military reverses in middle and western Tennessee had resulted in the dissolution of the state government.

favor and middle Tennesseans 88 to 12 percent in favor. On July 22 Tennessee formally joined the Confederate States of America.

Even before the June 8 referendum, however, Governor Harris had taken steps to prepare the state for war and ally it with the Confederacy. On April 20 he dispatched an official envoy to the Confederate government. On May 7 he endorsed a military pact with the Confederacy, which the state legislature immediately ratified. He also granted the Confederacy permission to build a defensive work at Memphis and began raising and arming troops. Before the legislators adjourned on May 9 they and Harris had approved legislation creating a 55,000-man state military force, which was turned over to the Confederacy in July and formed the nucleus of the Army of Tennessee. In these and subsequent actions Harris proved himself an ardent Confederate and a tireless administrator who cooperated wholeheartedly with the Confederate government.

Most eastern Tennesseans refused to acquiesce in the state's secession even after the June 8 referendum. The Unionist convention that had met in Knoxville reassembled in Greeneville from June 17 through 20 and approved a resolution asking the legislature to grant separate statehood to eastern Tennessee. (The legislature declined to act on the matter.) Governor Harris initially adopted a conciliatory policy toward the restive eastern Tennessee Unionists, hoping to win them over. Confederate military authorities (who stationed troops in eastern Tennessee to guard the strategic Cumberland Gap and the vital railroad linking Virginia and the Deep South) likewise treated the citizens with kid gloves.

They even permitted the prominent Knoxville newspaper editor William G. Brownlow to continue his vehemently pro-Union editorializing unmolested.

Eventually, however, the stiff-necked defiance of the eastern Tennessee Unionists wore down the patience of Harris and the Confederates. The results of the August 1861 state elections particularly perturbed Harris. Though he swept middle and western Tennessee and easily won another two-year term as governor over his opponent, William H. Polk, Harris lost eastern Tennessee by a considerable margin. Moreover, Unionists there nominated and elected *Federal* congressmen in every congressional district in the region.

Thereafter, state and Confederate authorities tightened the screws. For example, they forced Brownlow to shut down his newspaper and flee Knoxville; later he was jailed and eventually exiled to the North. Resistance persisted, however. A Unionist leader traveled secretly to Washington and obtained official approval of a plot to burn the railroad bridges in eastern Tennessee. The deed was supposed to be carried out in conjunction with a Federal military invasion of the region and a mass uprising of Unionists. On the night of November 8, 1861, Unionists burned five bridges. But the promised Federal invasion failed to materialize, the uprising fizzled, and most of the bridge burners were arrested; several were hanged.

Subsequently, Confederate authorities adopted an even harsher policy in eastern Tennessee, including martial law, mass arrests, forced loyalty oaths, and confiscation of Unionist property. By the spring of 1862, ten thousand Confederate troops were posted in the region as a virtual army of occupation. Thousands of eastern Tennesseans fled to Kentucky, where many joined the Union army. Others who stayed at home took up arms as guerrillas against the Confederacy.

In the meantime, however, Confederate military reverses in middle and western Tennessee had resulted in the dissolution of the state government. The legislature met in the summer of 1861 and again from October to December. When next it met, in January 1862, Union armies were threatening the state. When the Cumberland River defenses fell in February, the legislators fled Nashville and reassembled in Memphis. A short session there in March 1862 proved to be the legislature's last.

With Federal forces occupying middle and western Tennessee and the state government defunct, Governor Harris attached himself to the Army of Tennessee as a staff officer, though he continued to exercise what few official gubernatorial functions remained. He even insisted on carrying out another state election in August 1863. Harris himself declined to run again for office, however, and the vote was miniscule. Because the state legislature could not meet, the winning gubernatorial candidate, Robert Looney Caruthers, was never inaugurated.

Military Action in Tennessee

Tennessee's strategic location made it the focus of military operations in the western theater for much of the war. Among the states, only Virginia was the scene of more battles and skirmishes than Tennessee. All three of Tennessee's grand divisions were prime targets of the Federal armies, and all three were in Federal hands well before the war's end.

Control of the Mississippi River, a major Union objective, was impossible without possession of western Tennessee. Middle Tennessee and lower eastern Tennessee had to be held to allow Union armies to invade the Confederate heartland by way of the Nashville-Chattanooga-Atlanta corridor, the second major Federal objective in the West. Furthermore, middle Tennessee was a rich food-producing region; Nashville was an important Confederate manufacturing center and military supply depot; the Cumberland-Tennessee River region near the Kentucky border boasted some of the South's largest ironworks; and the mines of eastern Tennessee produced lead, copper, and saltpeter. Moreover, eastern Tennessee had vast human resources—the loyal Unionists—that the North hoped to pry from the Confederacy's grip.

The campaigns and battles in Tennessee were, with few exceptions, disappointments or disasters for the Confederacy. When Gen. Albert Sidney Johnston assumed command of Confederate forces defending Tennessee in September 1861, he faced an overwhelming task. In the preceding months Confederate authorities had concentrated on the Mississippi River defenses, neglecting the Tennessee and Cumberland. The works defending the latter two rivers, Forts Henry and Donelson, were still unfinished when Union Gen. Ulysses S. Grant led army and naval forces against them early in 1862. Fort Henry fell on February 6, leaving the Tennessee River open to Federal penetration. Fort Donelson surrendered on February 16, leaving middle Tennessee unprotected. Nashville was captured February 25 by a second Union army under Don Carlos Buell.

Johnston retreated into northern Mississippi, whence he launched an attack on Grant, who had moved up the Tennessee River to Pittsburg Landing, just north of the Mississippi state line. The attack precipitated the bloody Battle of Shiloh (April 6–7, 1862), which turned in Grant's favor after reinforcements from Buell arrived. Meanwhile a third Union army advanced down the Mississippi River, capturing the Confederate fort at Island Number 10 on April 7 and thus endangering Memphis, which fell to Union forces in June.

Johnston was killed at Shiloh. His successor, Braxton Bragg, led the Army of Tennessee on an abortive invasion of Kentucky in the fall of 1862, in which he was joined by the Confederate troops defending eastern Tennessee, commanded by E. Kirby Smith. This offensive forced Buell's army to evacuate middle Tennessee temporarily, though a strong garrison retained control of Nashville. Bragg soon retreated into middle Tennessee, where at year's end he attacked the Federals (now commanded by Buell's successor, William S. Rosecrans). In the ensuing Battle of Murfreesboro or Stones River (December 31, 1862–January 2, 1863), success again eluded the Confederates. Bragg then withdrew into the southeastern corner of middle Tennessee.

Thus, by early 1863 all of western Tennessee and most of middle Tennessee were in Union hands. The exploits of the brilliant Confederate cavalry commanders Nathan Bedford Forrest and John Hunt Morgan, who roamed the state destroying isolated Union detachments and disrupting enemy communications, were the only bright spots in the generally dismal Confederate military record in Tennessee up to that time.

The year 1863 brought more Confederate failures. Rosecrans's Tullahoma campaign that summer maneuvered Bragg out of middle Tennessee without a fight. Bragg retreated into northern Georgia, where he finally bested Rosecrans in September at the Battle of Chickamauga with the aid of troops under James Longstreet sent from the Virginia front. Rosecrans withdrew northward to Chattanooga; Bragg followed and laid siege. Grant then arrived to take command of the Federal forces and in the Battles of Lookout Mountain (November 24, 1863) and Missionary Ridge (November 25) drove Bragg back into Georgia.

Meanwhile Longstreet had marched northeastward to oppose a Federal army under Ambrose Burnside that had invaded eastern Tennessee in August 1863 and had occupied Knoxville in September. In the Battle of Fort Sanders (November 29, 1863) Longstreet failed to crack Knoxville's defenses. He then withdrew his troops toward the northeast and in the spring of 1864 returned to Virginia, leaving Union forces in undisputed control of the entire state of Tennessee. Late in 1864 the Army of Tennessee, now under John Bell Hood, made a last desperate attempt to recapture the state. Hood marched into middle Tennessee from Georgia, where he had recently lost Atlanta to William Tecumseh Sherman's Union army. Sherman dispatched troops to Gen. George H. Thomas in Tennessee to stop Hood. At the Battles of Franklin (November 30, 1864) and Nashville (December 15–16) Thomas's forces dealt crushing blows that destroyed the Army of Tennessee as an effective fighting force and ended the Confederate hope of redeeming Tennessee.

Union Occupation

Soon after Fort Donelson fell, Abraham Lincoln had appointed Andrew Johnson military governor of Tennessee. Johnson, a stalwart Unionist and the only senator from a seceding state who had stayed at his post in Washington, arrived in Nashville in March 1862. His position was somewhat anomalous. He was expected to oversee the reestablishment of a loyal civil government in the state, but he was also given military rank as a brigadier general and was granted broad powers, including suspension of habeas corpus. Moreover, he was initially cut off from his natural constituency—the eastern Tennessee Unionists, who remained under Confederate domination until the autumn of 1863. Thus, for the first year and a half of his administration, Johnson's only allies were the Unionists of middle and western Tennessee, a tiny minority of the populace and (being mostly former Whigs) longtime political adversaries of Johnson's. Furthermore, the fact that his military governorship functioned side by side with the Federal army command in Tennessee inevitably provoked conflicts of authority.

At the time he assumed his duties, Johnson shared Lincoln's belief that the majority of the South's citizens were really Unionists at heart who had been duped or browbeaten by secessionist demagogues. He also shared Lincoln's desire to restore the South to the Union quickly and without revolutionary social or economic upheaval. Consequently, Johnson adopted a policy of suppressing the hard-core secessionist leaders while encouraging the "erring and misguided" masses to renounce secession and take a hand in the speedy political reconstruction of the state.

In Nashville Johnson summarily arrested or banished a number of prominent secessionists, including the mayor and city councilmen and certain newspaper editors, wealthy planters, and clergymen. But he received a shock in his first attempt to get the reconstruction process underway. In an election for circuit judge in middle Tennessee in May 1862, the voters defiantly rejected the Unionist candidate and elected a secessionist. Johnson permitted the winner to take office but then had him arrested.

That incident, along with other evidence of persistent secessionism and rabid antipathy to Johnson in middle and western Tennessee, forced the military governor to rethink his policy. He concluded that only original Unionists, not oath-taking ex-Confederates, could be relied on to help rebuild the state government. Furthermore, by 1863 Johnson (like Lincoln) adopted a more radical, punitive approach toward the rebellious South.

Johnson's conversion to radicalism split the Tennessee Unionists, many of whom continued to favor a mild reconstruction policy that would restore the status quo ante bellum. The conservative Unionists were especially alarmed by emancipation, which Johnson eventually advocated, even though Lincoln exempted Tennessee from the Emancipation Proclamation. The division in the Unionist ranks became very evident in August 1863, when conservative Unionists insisted on holding a gubernatorial election despite the refusal of Johnson, who wanted to wait until eastern Tennesseans could participate. The conservatives elected their candidate, William B. Campbell, only to have Lincoln reject the election. The president deplored the Unionist factionalism in Tennessee, but in this and other instances he consistently supported Johnson and the radical wing.

Lincoln's Proclamation of Amnesty and Reconstruction in December 1863 gave Johnson a method by which to bring Tennessee back into the Union; but he considered it too lenient, for it granted political rights to any citizen who took a simple oath of allegiance. As a prerequisite to participating in the county elections he planned for March 1864, Johnson devised his own oath, which required voters "to ardently desire" and "heartily aid" the defeat of the Confederacy. This effectively disfranchised not only most of the former secessionists who had taken Lincoln's amnesty oath but also some conservative Unionists, who protested loudly but unavailingly. The turnout in the county elections was, not surprisingly, quite meager.

Another controversy arose as the November 1864 presidential election neared. Conservative Unionists supported the Democratic nominee, but Johnson was determined that

> **Johnson permitted the winner to take office but then had him arrested.**

the state's electoral ballots would go to the Lincoln ticket, on which he himself was the vice-presidential candidate. Consequently he demanded from each voter an oath opposing any negotiated peace with the Confederacy—which was a key plank of the Democratic platform. Naturally the Lincoln-Johnson ticket won in Tennessee; Congress, however, rejected the Tennessee vote.

The reconstruction of the state's civil government finally got underway in January 1865, when some five hundred Unionists, mostly radicals, gathered in convention in Nashville. Ignoring objections that the convention was unrepresentative and its proceedings irregular under Tennessee law, the delegates approved a state constitutional amendment abolishing slavery and a series of resolutions that repudiated Tennessee's declaration of independence, voided all acts of the Confederate state government, and called for state elections. These actions received Johnson's endorsement and then were ratified by popular referendum on February 22, 1865. On March 4 the voters elected a governor and state legislature. The new governor was William G. Brownlow, who had returned to Knoxville after its capture by Federal troops. The March turnout was small (about 25,000 votes), but it was large enough to satisfy the Ten Percent Clause of Lincoln's December 1863 proclamation. Thus the reconstructed Tennessee state government was acceptable in Washington. The new legislature met in Nashville and inaugurated Brownlow on April 5, 1865, ten days before Johnson succeeded Lincoln as president.

The abolition of slavery by state constitutional amendment merely gave legal imprimatur to an accomplished fact.

Ironically, slaves in Tennessee—the only Confederate state wholly exempted from the Emancipation Proclamation—found more opportunities to free themselves from bondage than did slaves in any other Confederate state. The early Federal military conquest of Tennessee was of course the key factor.

No sooner did Union troops invade the state than slaves began running off to the army camps seeking refuge. Despite the initial conservatism of the Federal commanders, the army soon began welcoming runaways as laborers and rebuffing the attempts of masters to reclaim them. Eventually the army became an active agent of emancipation and established "contraband camps" across the state to care for fugitive slaves. After military recruitment of blacks became Federal policy in 1863, over twenty thousand Tennessee blacks volunteered as Union soldiers. In addition to freedom and military service, blacks in Tennessee seized other opportunities during the war that blacks in most other parts of the South would not have until the postwar Reconstruction period, including contract labor, education, and political activity.

To be sure, black Tennesseans also experienced hardships and mistreatment during the war at the hands of Northern soldiers as well as Southern slaveholders, but they could at least revel in their newfound freedom. Most white Tennesseans, on the other hand, found nothing at all to celebrate about their wartime experience. Whether they lived in towns or with the great majority in the countryside, they suffered severely, for military invasion brought in its wake immense property destruction, harsh military rule, and violence and privation on a previously unimaginable scale.

Tennessee's three major cities and many of its towns were held by large Union garrison forces during much of the war, even after the main field armies moved on to Georgia. These occupation troops seized buildings for their own use, dug mountains of fortifications, and enforced strict army and Treasury Department edicts governing disloyalty, travel, and trade. Moreover, the huge influx of soldiers, runaway slaves, white refugees, Northern speculators and humanitarians, and others into the occupied cities and towns led to overcrowding, unemployment, inflation, food and fuel shortages, and disease.

Rural Tennesseans were less often directly under the thumb of the Federal occupiers than urbanites were, but they nonetheless encountered extreme hardship. The Union army depended on Tennessee's farms for supplies of all sorts and thus ruthlessly seized crops, stored food, livestock, and fencing, not to mention slaves. Military impressment and pillaging were so frequent and so devastating in some sections of the state that many farmers abandoned their homesteads and fled to the Deep South or to the occupied towns. Those who stayed at home had to endure not only privation but also anarchy and violence. With local government suspended by the Federal invasion, and battles, skirmishes, and guerrilla

warfare ravaging the countryside, communal institutions disintegrated and law and order collapsed. Banditry was widespread by 1864, and the rural areas remained places of danger and disorder until peace was restored in the spring and summer of 1865.

The enormous destruction and suffering, combined with the incontrovertible Federal control of the state, withered Confederate morale in Tennessee. Well before the war's end, the great majority of Tennessee's Confederates resigned themselves to defeat and emancipation. They did not, however, resign themselves to Unionist political predominance nor to equal rights for the freedmen. Thus, the stage was set for Tennessee's postwar Reconstruction era, which would prove to be quite as unique as its Confederate experience.

[For further discussion of battles and campaigns fought in Tennessee, see Chattanooga, Tennessee, article on Chattanooga Campaign; Chickamauga Campaign; Forrest's Raids; Franklin and Nashville Campaign; Henry and Donelson Campaign; Knoxville Campaign; Morgan's Raids; Murfreesboro, Tennessee; New Madrid and Island Number 10; Shiloh Campaign; Wheeler's Raids. For further discussion of Tennessee cities, see Chattanooga, Tennessee, article on City of Chattanooga; Memphis, Tennessee; Nashville, Tennessee. See also Knoxville and Greeneville Conventions and biographies of numerous figures mentioned therein.]

BIBLIOGRAPHY

Alexander, Thomas B. Political Reconstruction in Tennessee. Nashville, Tenn., 1950.

Ash, Stephen V. Middle Tennessee Society Transformed, 1860–1870: War and Peace in the Upper South. Baton Rouge, La., 1988.

Bryan, Charles F., Jr. "A Gathering of Tories: The East Tennessee Convention of 1861." Tennessee Historical Quarterly 39 (1980): 27–48.

Bryan, Charles F., Jr. "'Tories' Amidst Rebels: Confederate Occupation of East Tennessee, 1861–63." East Tennessee Historical Society's Publications 60 (1988): 3–22.

Cimprich, John. Slavery's End in Tennessee, 1861–1865. University, Ala., 1985.

Connelly, Thomas L. Civil War Tennessee: Battles and Leaders. Knoxville, Tenn., 1979.

Crofts, Daniel W. Reluctant Confederates: Upper South Unionists in the Secession Crisis. Chapel Hill, N.C., 1989.

Hall, Kermit L. "Tennessee." In The Confederate Governors. Edited by W. Buck Yearns. Athens, Ga., 1985.

Maslowski, Peter. Treason Must Be Made Odious: Military Occupation and Wartime Reconstruction in Nashville, Tennessee. Millwood, N.Y., 1978.

Parks, Joseph H. "Memphis under Military Rule, 1862 to 1865." East Tennessee Historical Society's Publications 14 (1942): 31–58.

Patton, James Welch. Unionism and Reconstruction in Tennessee, 1860–1869. Chapel Hill, N.C., 1934.

STEPHEN V. ASH

TEXAS

In the election of 1860 Texas favored Southern Democrat John C. Breckinridge with 75 percent of its votes over Constitutional Unionist John Bell and then moved to secede on February 1, 1861. From a population of 604,215 (420,891 white and 182,921 black), the Lone Star State sent perhaps 90,000 troops to serve in the Confederate military.

On the eve of the Civil War, Texas ranked ninth among future Confederate states in population. Within the white population, settlers from the upper South provided a majority in North and Central Texas counties, and migrants from the lower South formed a majority in East Texas counties. German immigrant families, concentrated mostly in Central Texas and in larger towns, represented over 7 percent of free Texans; Hispanics in South Texas formed between 3 and 5 percent. The 182,566 slaves, primarily on East Texas farms and plantations, composed 30 percent of the total population. There were only 355 free blacks, since state laws had limited their number. Settlement in 1860 had advanced one or two counties beyond San Antonio, Austin, and Fort Worth, with the exception of El Paso in the Trans-Pecos region. Native Americans, primarily Apaches and Comanches, controlled much of West Texas.

Cotton formed the major export crop with 431,000 bales in 1860, and some grain crops and over 3 million cattle were raised primarily for subsistence. Trade flowed through Galveston, the major port with a population of 7,307, slightly smaller than San Antonio. The state contained only 3,449 workers in industry, 306 miles of railroads, and a few banks.

As Texans approached the election of 1860, the Unionist sentiment that had carried Sam Houston to the governorship in 1859 weakened, and passions rose as many Texans attributed fires in the summer of 1860 to slaves and abolitionists.

> **Three Texas infantry regiments developed a tough combat reputation as Hood's Brigade. . . .**

Houston, a national Democrat, received some consideration as a nominee for president by the Constitutional Union party, but he failed to gain enough support. Texans cast 47,548 votes for the state rights Democrat Breckinridge and 15,438 votes for Constitutional Unionist Bell. With the election of Republican Abraham Lincoln, several leading Democrats in Texas, fearing Northern dominance and slave unrest, urged separation. Despite opposition from Houston, a convention met and on February 1, 1861, easily passed a secession ordinance, which received ratification later that month with 46,153 in favor and 14,747 opposed. Several counties in

North and Central Texas and one in East Texas produced majorities against secession.

The secession convention also established a Committee of Public Safety for the purpose of assuming control over the Federal forts in Texas. To accomplish that goal the committee called for volunteer troops. Ben McCulloch led 500 men who captured the department commander, David Twiggs, and 160 U.S. soldiers at his headquarters in San Antonio on February 16, 1861. John S. ("Rip") Ford directed another force that seized Fort Brown near the entrance to the Rio Grande, while Henry Eustace McCulloch and a third group occupied frontier posts. The Texans captured extensive supplies, weapons, and ammunition as well as 2,700 Federal troops. Most of the soldiers were allowed to depart by ship, but 600 who remained after the firing on Fort Sumter became prisoners of war at Camp Verde.

Texans on the War Front

To counter Lincoln's call for troops, Texas joined the other Confederate states in recruiting soldiers. Early enthusiasm led 25,000 men to enlist during 1861. By 1865 the number of men enrolled in Confederate units from Texas had grown to possibly 90,000. The first troops left amid fiery speeches after receiving flags sewn by ladies of their communities. Their weapons ranged widely from rifles to shotguns and other types of firearms. Because of a strong volunteer military tradition based on service in the Texas Revolution, the war with Mexico, and frontier ranger companies, two out of three among the almost ninety regiments enlisted as cavalry, a reversal of the pattern in other states. The need for greater numbers of infantry led to the dismounting of fifteen Texas cavalry regiments, which at least temporarily hurt morale in each unit. Texans also raised forty-three batteries of artillery. The strong frontier military tradition meant that about half of the thirty-seven Texas generals had volunteer experience, but only about one-fourth had been professional soldiers, also the reverse of patterns in most states. The Confederacy with its small population introduced military conscription in 1862, which stimulated volunteering in Texas as in other states.

Many of the first regiments from Texas hurried across the Mississippi River to join the major Confederate armies defending against Union attacks in Virginia and Tennessee. Three Texas infantry regiments developed a tough combat reputation as Hood's Brigade in the Army of Northern Virginia. They participated in almost every major battle in the East from the Seven Days' Battles in 1862 to Appomattox in 1865. Among the 4,350 men of the regiments 62 percent were wounded, killed, or captured.

Greater numbers of Texans served in the Army of Tennessee defending the region from the Appalachian Mountains to the Mississippi River. Albert Sidney Johnston, a former officer in the armies of the Republic of Texas and of the United States, became a full general and the Confederate commander in Tennessee. His effort to surprise and defeat Ulysses S. Grant at Shiloh in April 1862 ended when Johnston died in the battle. The Eighth Texas Cavalry, called Terry's Rangers, fought with Johnston's army and later with Joseph Wheeler's cavalry corps over a span of four years. Four Texas cavalry regiments, some with early combat experience, crossed the Mississippi River in 1862 and became known as Ross's Brigade in Mississippi and later in the Atlanta and Nashville campaigns of 1864.

The Army of Tennessee also included several Texas infantry units. The Second Texas Infantry Regiment saw action at Shiloh in Tennessee and Corinth in Mississippi during 1862 before being captured, along with Thomas Neville Waul's Texas Legion, after defending Vicksburg for several weeks in 1863. Four dismounted cavalry regiments fought at Murfreesboro, Chickamauga, Atlanta, Nashville, and Mobile as Ector's Brigade. Other Texas infantry and dismounted cavalry regiments were consolidated after they had been captured at Arkansas Post and exchanged. They became best known as Granbury's Brigade during service in the Chattanooga, Atlanta, and Nashville campaigns. John Bell Hood, former commander of the Texas Brigade in Virginia, led the Army of Tennessee in the Atlanta and Nashville campaigns without success.

Many Texans protected their state in fighting around its borders. In 1861 the Eleventh Texas Cavalry occupied Federal forts above the Red River in the Indian Territory (now Oklahoma). The Forty-sixth Texas Cavalry held the posts on the western fringe of Texas settlement, though Comanche Indian raids drove back the frontier in many areas. At Dove Creek in 1865 a band of Kickapoo Indians drove off a Confederate attack in the largest frontier engagement of the war. From Texas a cavalry brigade under Henry H. Sibley advanced toward New Mexico and Arizona in the winter of 1861–1862. After a victory at Valverde in February 1862, Sibley occupied Albuquerque and then Santa Fe. A defeat at Glorieta Pass in March forced a retreat into Texas with heavy losses by summer.

To defend the coast, district commanders of Texas, first Earl Van Dorn and then Paul O. Hébert, formed artillery units and began to entrench Galveston and other ports in 1861. After raiding Corpus Christi and Sabine Pass, the Federal blockading fleet occupied Galveston in October 1862. A new district commander, John B. Magruder, planned a successful counterattack to retake the port with cottonclad river steamers as well as army troops on January 1, 1863. At Sabine Pass a small artillery battery under Dick Dowling drove off a Union attempt to land troops on September 8, 1863. Federal troops under Nathaniel P. Banks did occupy Brownsville and the coast from the Rio Grande to Matagorda Bay in the fall and winter of 1863. John S. Ford led a Confederate recapture of the Rio Grande Valley in 1864. Because they captured

Union soldiers along the coast, Confederates built two military prisons, Camp Ford at Tyler and Camp Groce near Houston.

Union advances into Arkansas, the Indian Territory, and Louisiana also appeared threatening to Texans. Ben McCulloch led Confederate troops including some Texans who defeated a Federal force at Wilson's Creek in Missouri during 1861. While directing one wing of the Confederate army at Elkhorn Tavern, Arkansas, early in 1862, McCulloch died in action. After helping recapture Galveston, Sibley's cavalry regiments marched into Louisiana where they became known as Green's Brigade while holding back Union forces with the help of Major's Brigade of Texas cavalry in 1863. Several Texas cavalry regiments, usually called Parsons' Brigade, defended Arkansas during 1862 and 1863. Gano's Brigade of Texas cavalry helped protect against Union movements into the Indian Territory. Walker's Division, three brigades of Texas infantry, served in Arkansas during 1862 and in Louisiana during 1863. Additional infantry, best known as Polignac's Brigade, also defended Louisiana in 1863. The commander of the Trans-Mississippi Department, E. Kirby Smith, brought these units together in early 1864 to turn back the Union Red River expedition. Further support came from Bee's Division, two Texas cavalry brigades drawn from the Gulf coast. Thomas Green, the most successful of the Texas cavalry officers and commander of all mounted units in the Red River campaign, died in the fighting that spring. Little combat occurred in or near Texas during the final months of the war, though small units skirmished at Palmito Ranch in the Rio Grande Valley on May 13, 1865, shortly before the surrender of the Trans-Mississippi Department on June 2.

The Home Front

Not all the conflict took place on the battlefield. Once the war began, those who had opposed secession faced difficult decisions. Some like James Throckmorton served the Confederacy but urged restraint in the use of government power. Others who were old enough to avoid military service, such as former governors Sam Houston and Elisha M. Pease, left the field of politics. But when the Confederacy adopted a military draft in 1862, the option of neutrality disappeared for younger men. Many German immigrants on the edge of settlement in Central Texas had tried to serve only for frontier defense. Confederate authorities created a military court in San Antonio to hear charges of disloyalty and imprisoned or exiled those who were convicted. When a company of German Unionists left home for Mexico to avoid harassment, Confederate cavalry intercepted them at the Nueces River in August 1862, killing wounded prisoners, though others escaped. Confederate troops entered Mexico to capture and hang Unionist William Montgomery. Edmund J. Davis and Andrew Jackson Hamilton successfully departed from

Texas to become Union generals. They recruited two Federal cavalry regiments, half of whom were German immigrants and Tejano troops.

Unionists in North Texas began to meet privately to consider alternatives to conscription. Their actions stirred fears among Confederates who seized numerous suspects in the fall of 1862. An unofficial jury in Cooke County, under mob pressure, offered none of the normal opportunities for a legal defense before ordering the execution of forty-seven men. Of the several men arrested in Wise, Denton, and Grayson counties only six were executed, as the authorities there exercised more restraint. Unionists killed two prominent Confederates in retaliation.

Both the Confederate and Texas governments sought to support the war effort, but the state rights and limited-government views of 1861 increasingly came into conflict with wartime exigencies. Confederate Senator Louis T. Wigfall had

> **Slavery retained more stability in Texas than in most states of the Confederacy because of the limited Union movements into the state.**

strongly supported state rights before the war, but now became a proponent of the military draft. John H. Reagan represented Texas in the Confederate cabinet as postmaster general. Political parties dissolved in Texas as in other Confederate states, though factions and individuals struggled over power and position. When Houston refused to accept secession, Lieutenant Governor Edward Clark completed his term. Francis R. Lubbock then led the state from 1861 to 1863 and cooperated well with Confederate authorities.

When better known political leaders joined the army, Pendleton Murrah won the election for governor in 1863 and served until Confederate surrender in 1865. He soon clashed with Magruder, the district commander, on two issues. Murrah wanted to retain control over 6,000 state troops, though many fell within the draft ages set by the Confederate government. In a compromise he agreed the army could assume command of the units in a military crisis, such as the Red River campaign of 1864, though cooperation even then proved less than perfect.

The governor and the general confronted each other again over government roles in the cotton trade. The Texas State Military Board, created in 1862, found it could not compete well with private speculators for cotton to pay for military supplies. The Confederate army and Treasury Department sought to regulate the trade with little success, which led E. Kirby Smith to create a Cotton Bureau in 1863 for impressment of cotton. The Confederate and state governments continued to clash over the trade until Murrah and Smith reached an agreement favoring the Confederacy in 1864.

During the war Texans at various levels of government also entered into new areas of activity. The Confederate government created its own shops and arsenals in Texas and elsewhere to produce weapons and supplies. Texas used its prison to manufacture cloth. Counties limited liquor production to save grain for food. City and county governments aided disabled soldiers and war widows.

Although the Texas government faced some economic problems during the conflict, the state's economy fared better than those of most Confederate states. Foreign trade continued on a more elaborate scale in Texas because most commerce shifted to flow south by wagon across the Rio Grande into Mexico, where shippers at Matamoros sent a significant amount on to Europe or even to the Union states. Through that pattern of trade over 300,000 bales of cotton left the state, about two-thirds being shipped to England and the rest to New York. Because of the civil war in Mexico, shifts in political control of the border could alter or slow the flow of goods. Benito Juàrez and the republicans favored the Union, while Maximilian, the French-supported emperor, preferred the Confederates. Santiago Vidaurri, who governed Nuevo Leòn and Coahuila during 1862 and 1863, also traded with the Confederates. Rio Grande Valley merchants profited enough from the trade to develop major landholdings such as the great ranch of Richard King.

Lesser amounts of goods came and went via blockade runners at Galveston and other Gulf ports. Federal warships in the Gulf tightened their watch on the coast but captured only about two hundred ships during some fifteen hundred attempts to run the blockade. But it was small sailing ships carrying no more than forty bales of cotton on each voyage that conducted most of the risky commerce. Thus the total trade through the blockade amounted to only twenty-five thousand to fifty thousand bales during the war.

Given the reduction in the exchange of cotton for manufactured goods, the Texas government sought to encourage industry. The number of manufacturers chartered by the state increased from six in 1861–1862 to thirty-three in 1863–1864; nevertheless, they remained too few to meet the variety of needs.

Because of the Mexican outlet for cotton and the limited Union invasions of Texas, agriculture suffered less disruption than in most Confederate states. Planters and slaveholding farmers lost part of their wealth, however, as a result of emancipation in 1865. Texans who committed themselves to Confederate currency also felt the pinch of reduced capital after the Confederates' defeat.

Conflict brought change to Texas society as it did in the economy. Shortages of various products resulted in makeshift substitutions. Inflation pushed the prices of food and other necessities to three or four times their prewar levels. Civilian frustrations led to food riots at San Antonio in 1862 and at Galveston in 1864. As the Union army advanced through Arkansas and Louisiana refugees from those states flooded into East Texas. Citizens of Galveston moved to Houston seeking escape from bombardment or occupation. Some stayed with friends or relatives, and others received aid from churches. Growing bands of deserters dominated some rural areas in spite of efforts by local law officers and the Confederate army to apprehend them.

To meet problems created by the war, churches sent chaplains to the army where they aided wounded and disabled soldiers as well as the families of those who died. With so many men leaving home for military service, their mothers, wives, and daughters assumed new roles. Some took over farms and businesses, others raised money or sewed uniforms, and still others nursed the wounded or taught in schools for the first time.

Slavery retained more stability in Texas than in most states of the Confederacy because of the limited Union movements into the state. The slave population continued to grow rapidly because some refugees from nearby states brought their slaves with them. By 1865 probably 250,000 slaves labored in Texas. The army's need for laborers, especially to dig entrenchments along the coast, led to the impressment of several hundred slaves. Some bondsmen continued to escape to Mexico, and others sought freedom with the Federal forces in the Indian Territory or on the coast. White fears of revolt resulted in arrests and executions of slaves. In 1864 some Texas officers and political figures favored freeing individual slaves if they agreed to fight for the Confederacy, but opposition from other government leaders and several editors delayed any serious effort. Confederate defeat brought freedom for all slaves when the Union army landed at Galveston on June 19, 1865, which became the date of Texas emancipation celebrations in following years.

Texans felt the impact of the Civil War in every aspect of society. Military campaigns resulted in thousands of men killed or disabled and some destruction in coastal areas. To conduct the war, every level of government expanded its activities, which led to numerous conflicts. Lingering differences over secession added further tensions. Some economic dislocations and inflation left the state poorer, but more diverse in its range of economic activities. Deaths, shortages, and refugee problems created social disorder. On the other hand, the expanded roles for women and emancipation for slaves represented positive steps amid the tragedy of war.

[*For further discussion of battles and campaigns fought in Texas, see* Andrews Raid; Brownsville, Texas, *article on* Battle of Brownsville; Galveston, Texas, *article on* Battle of Galveston. *For further discussion of Texas cities, see* Austin, Texas; Brownsville, Texas, *article on* City of Brownsville; Galveston, Texas, *article on* City of Galveston. *See also* Hood's Texas Brigade *and biographies of numerous figures mentioned herein.*]

BIBLIOGRAPHY

Ashcraft, Allan C. *Texas in the Civil War: A Rèsumè History.* Austin, Tex., 1962.

Betts, Vicki. *Smith County, Texas, in the Civil War.* Tyler, Tex., 1978.

Buenger, Walter L. *Secession and the Union in Texas.* Austin, Tex., 1984.

Campbell, Randolph B. *An Empire for Slavery: The Peculiar Institution in Texas.* Baton Rouge, La., 1989.

Marten, James. *Texas Divided: Loyalty and Dissent in the Lone Star State, 1856–1874.* Lexington, Ky., 1990.

Oates, Stephen B. "Texas under the Secessionists." *Southwestern Historical Quarterly* 67 (1963): 167–212.

Winsor, Bill. *Texas in the Confederacy: Military Installations, Economy, and People.* Hillsboro, Tex., 1978.

Wright, Marcus J. *Texas in the War, 1861–1865.* Hillsboro, Tex., 1965.

ALWYN BARR

TEXTILE INDUSTRY

The South's cotton textile industry was called upon to play an active role in the Confederacy's war mobilization. Although the states of the Confederacy did not build any new mills, many of those that existed at the outbreak of hostilities expanded production dramatically in order to meet the demand for war matèriel.

When the Southern states seceded in 1860 and 1861, they contained 143 "cotton goods establishments." These mills represented 164,840 spindles and 4,013 looms. The vast majority of textile establishments were located in Georgia, North Carolina, South Carolina, and Alabama, and they relied upon water for their motive power. These mills became the primary suppliers for the Confederate Quartermaster Bureau.

For many Southern mill owners, the outbreak of war was a godsend: it meant that they would receive lucrative war contracts that would allow them to expand the Southern industrial base. They also hoped that the need for manufactures would encourage those uninterested in manufacturing to support such endeavors. Mill entrepreneurs eagerly sought government contracts for the production of uniforms, tents, blankets, and other cotton goods. Most mills produced only the cloth: material such as kerseys or osnaburgs. This material would then be farmed out to private or government-sponsored shops where a mixed work force of men and women would fashion the cloth into uniforms or blankets. In many ways, the Confederacy's wartime textile industry resembled a preindustrial cottage system: some factories could produce finished goods, and others were dependent on outside workers.

Textile managers found that the government was a voracious consumer of cotton and woolen goods. Initially, textile owners realized huge profits: government profit ceilings stood at 75 percent. But the government changed these generous terms in 1862: profit ceilings were lowered to 33 percent and draft exemptions for workers were made contingent upon the factory's furnishing the government with a minimum of two-thirds of its output. These stringent controls enabled the Confederate government to attain a virtual monopoly on all textile products produced in the South.

Most of the Confederacy's textile factories were destroyed by retreating Southerners or invading Northerners. Only the establishments in the Augusta, Georgia, area remained relatively untouched, but many of them had deteriorated as a result of increased wartime demands. Nonetheless, those who had been the leaders in wartime textile manufacturing would reorganize and refurbish their companies. They would survive the unsettled financial conditions of the postwar South and would lay the groundwork for the expansion of the region's textile industry in the late 1870s and 1880s.

[See also Uniforms.]

BIBLIOGRAPHY

Coulter, E. Merton. The Confederate States of America, 1861–1865. A History of the South, vol. 7. Baton Rouge, La., 1951.

DeCredico, Mary A. Patriotism for Profit: Georgia's Urban Entrepreneurs and the Confederate War Effort. Chapel Hill, N.C., 1990.

Goff, Richard. Confederate Supply. Durham, N.C., 1969.

MARY A. DECREDICO

THIRTEENTH AMENDMENT

Drawing on the antislavery belief that slavery destroyed an inherent right to self-ownership, Republican members of Congress, in late 1863 and early 1864, introduced several bills to abolish slavery by constitutional amendment. The precise wording of those bills elicited an intense and protracted debate. Some argued that the amendment should specify only that slaves be freed from physical restraint; others said it should vest blacks with certain rights, including the right to own property, testify in court, and sign marriage contracts. Charles Sumner declared that the amendment should state that "all persons are equal before the law." In the end, after intense lobbying by President Abraham Lincoln, a final version passed the House of Representatives on January 31, 1865, by a vote of 119 to 56, two votes more than the necessary two-thirds. The proposed amendment read simply:

"Neither slavery nor involuntary servitude, except as a punishment for crime whereof the party shall have been duly convicted, shall exist within the United States, or any place subject to their jurisdiction." Section 2 said that "Congress shall have power to enforce this article by appropriate legislation."

During the final months of the Civil War, most white Southerners recognized that slavery was doomed. Nevertheless, after the war, when the amendment was submitted for ratification to Southern states now under President Andrew Johnson's newly formed governments, some former Confederates worked to defeat the article. The question, they argued, was not whether chattel slavery was dead but whether Congress should be granted the power to intrude into the "domestic affairs" of a state. When the Mississippi legislature rejected the amendment by a vote of 45–25 in the fall of 1865, a writer for the Jackson Clarion, reflecting the

> Nevertheless, Article 13 was the first amendment designed to accomplish a national reform. . . .

views of other whites in the lower South, proclaimed that to adopt the amendment would be tantamount to surrendering "all of our rights as a State to the Federal Congress." He and others refused "to sharpen the sword" that would "sever the arteries of our political life." The Alabama legislature ratified the amendment, but only after declaring that its approval did not extend to the second section.

President Johnson, however, pressed the former Confederate states to ratify the amendment as one precondition for restoration to the Union, assuring them that an end to slavery meant essentially that freedmen and women should be at liberty to work and enjoy the fruits of their labor. With such assurances and the backing of the president, the amendment was ratified by three-fourths of the states on December 18, 1865.

In proposing the amendment, neither Congress nor the framers envisioned a radical change in the relationship between the states and the Federal government; nor did they seek to endow newly freed slaves with citizenship rights. Nevertheless, Article 13 was the first amendment designed to accomplish a national reform, the first to grant Congress power of execution, and the first of the Reconstruction era. During the next few years Congress passed several civil rights laws and the nation ratified two additional constitutional amendments—the Fourteenth Amendment (1868) granting citizenship rights to former slaves, and the Fifteenth Amendment (1870) extending the franchise to freedmen. Thus, the passage of the amendment ending slavery began a process that would fundamentally alter the legal position of blacks in the United States and increasingly shift the responsibility for the protection of former slaves to the Federal government.

BIBLIOGRAPHY

Belz, Herman. "The Constitution and Reconstruction." In *The Facts of Reconstruction: Essays in Honor of John Hope Franklin.* Edited by Eric Anderson and Alfred A. Moss, Jr. Baton Rouge, La., 1991.

Belz, Herman. *Emancipation and Equal Rights: Politics and Constitutionalism in the Civil War Era.* New York, 1978.

Berry, Mary Frances. *Military Necessity and Civil Rights Policy: Black Citizenship and the Constitution, 1861–1868.* Port Washington, N.Y., 1977.

Buchanan, G. Sidney. *The Quest for Freedom: A Legal History of the Thirteenth Amendment.* Houston, Tex., 1976.

Harris, William C. *Presidential Reconstruction in Mississippi.* Baton Rouge, La., 1967.

Malz, Earl M. *Civil Rights, the Constitution, and Congress, 1863–1869.* Lawrence, Kans., 1990.

LOREN SCHWENINGER

THOMAS, EDWARD LLOYD

THOMAS, EDWARD LLOYD (1825–1898), brigadier general. Born in Clarke County, Georgia, March 23, 1825, Thomas graduated from Emory College in 1846 and enlisted as a private in a Georgia cavalry regiment for the Mexican War. In the Battle of Huemaretta, he captured the son of the ex-emperor who was a member of Santa Anna's staff. In recognition of the feat, the Georgia legislature adopted resolutions in 1848 commending Thomas for his gallantry. At the close of hostilities, Thomas was offered a commission in the regular army, which he declined. While in Mexico, Thomas also captured a sword that led to bitter feelings between Thomas and his immediate superior, Capt. George Thomas ("Tige") Anderson. On their return to Georgia, Anderson apparently represented the sword as his personal trophy of war. Intense acrimony resulted and a duel was threatened before mature judgment intervened. The pair subsequently became close friends.

At the start of the Civil War, Thomas recruited a regiment, which became the Thirty-fifth Georgia Infantry, with Thomas as its colonel. When the regiment marched onto the field at Seven Pines, it was, according to historian Joseph T. Derry, "armed with the old remodeled flint-lock guns, the very best that the majority of the Southern soldiers could procure; but when it came out it was provided with the very best arms of the enemy."

Thomas opened the Battle of Mechanicsville as a part of A. P. Hill's division. Though wounded in the engagement, he took part in the remaining battles of the Seven Days' campaign. When brigade commander Joseph R. Anderson was knocked unconscious by a blow to the forehead at Frayser's Farm, Thomas, as senior colonel, assumed command of the brigade.

He also participated in all the subsequent battles fought by the Army of Northern Virginia with the exception of Sharpsburg. During that engagement Thomas was on detached duty at Harpers Ferry supervising the removal of captured property. On November 1, 1862, he received his brigadier's commission, which was confirmed April 22, 1863.

Paroled at Appomattox, Thomas returned to his plantation where he lived quietly for twenty years. He returned to public life in 1885 when President Grover Cleveland appointed him to an office in the Land Department. In Cleveland's second administration Thomas was named agent to the Sac and Fox in the Oklahoma Territory, a post he resigned when William McKinley became president. Thereafter Thomas participated actively in veteran affairs until his death, March 8, 1898, at South McAlester in present-day Oklahoma. He was buried in Kiowa, Oklahoma.

BIBLIOGRAPHY

Compiled Military Service Records. Edward Lloyd Thomas. Microcopy M331, Roll 245. Record Group 109. National Archives, Washington, D.C.

Derry, Joseph T. *Georgia.* Vol. 6 of *Confederate Military History.* Edited by Clement A. Evans. Atlanta, 1899. Vol. 7 of extended ed. Wilmington, N.C., 1987.

"Gen. Edward L. Thomas." *Confederate Veteran* 6 (1989): 191. Reprint, Wilmington, N.C., 1985.

Jed Hotchkiss Papers. Library of Congress, Washington, D.C.

Warner, Ezra J. *Generals in Gray: Lives of the Confederate Commanders.* Baton Rouge, La., 1959.

LOWELL REIDENBAUGH

THOMPSON, JACOB

THOMPSON, JACOB (1810–1885), U.S. congressman, U.S. secretary of the interior, Confederate colonel, and agent for the Confederacy. Born and raised in North Carolina, Jacob Thompson graduated from the University of North Carolina in 1831 and was admitted to the bar in 1835. He moved to Mississippi where he married well, practiced law, became a planter, and was politically active. A Democrat, he served six terms (1839–1851) in the U.S. House of Representatives but lost a bid to become U.S. senator from Mississippi in 1855. Active in national party politics, Thompson supported Franklin Pierce in 1852 and worked for the nomination and election of James Buchanan in 1856. Buchanan made Thompson secretary of the interior, and he was an energetic department head.

With regard to the intensifying sectional controversy, Thompson insisted that Southern grievances were legitimate. The central issue in his view was Northern unwillingness to vouchsafe "the rights of Southern men in their slave property." Although defending secession as an inherent right of the states, he was not eager to see the South withdraw from the Union and took a cooperationist stance on the matter. Following Abraham Lincoln's election in November 1860, Thompson hoped that the Buchanan administration could preserve the peace in the crucial months before Lincoln's inauguration and thereby provide an opportunity for the success of compromise efforts that were underway within and without Congress. During cabinet sessions, Thompson counseled restraint in dealing with the secessionists and, if necessary, acceptance of disunion. While still a member of the cabinet and with the acquiescence of the president, Thompson visited the legislature of North Carolina as a formal representative of Mississippi to discuss a cooperationist strategy in the event of drastic provocation on the part of the Federal government. Upon learning of the presidential decision that dispatched *Star of the West* with reinforcements and supplies for Fort Sumter, Thompson resigned his cabinet post.

During the early years of the war, Thompson served with the Confederate army in Tennessee and Mississippi and was also a member of the Mississippi legislature. He accepted an assignment from Jefferson Davis in the spring of 1864 to head a mission to Canada for the purpose of exploiting and encouraging discontent and peace sentiment throughout the North. To finance the undertaking, Davis authorized Thompson to spend as much as $1 million at his own discretion. Clement C. Clay of Alabama agreed to serve with Thompson, and they traveled to Wilmington, North Carolina, where they slipped through the blockade to Bermuda and took passage to Halifax, Nova Scotia. Thompson's usual base of operations while in Canada was Toronto, and Clay operated from St. Catharines, Ontario. Thompson coordinated activities with Clay and had the services of agents sent from the Confederacy. Thompson also enlisted the cooperation of Confederate soldiers who had escaped from Northern prisons, Southerners residing in Canada, and sympathetic Northerners.

He invested considerable time and money in efforts to wreak havoc in the North. He joined with leaders of the Order of the Sons of Liberty during the summer of 1864 in plotting armed uprisings timed to coincide with the return of Clement L. Vallandigham to Ohio from exile and with the Democratic National Convention at Chicago. These plots collapsed amid the hesitation, indecision, and disorganization of the Sons of Liberty. In another scheme, Thompson helped lay plans for

armed insurrections in Chicago and New York City on election day, November 8, 1864. The work of spies brought the arrest of key leaders in Chicago, and rumors of trouble in New York prompted the Federal government to send ten thousand soldiers to patrol the city during the canvass. After the troops withdrew, the conspirators, with Thompson's sanction, undertook a plan to burn the city by simultaneously setting fires in several buildings. The resulting blazes created panic but produced little property damage. Various schemes forcibly to release Confederate soldiers held as prisoners of war at Camp Douglas and Johnson's Island also came to naught.

Not all the plans Thompson laid involved violence. He contributed money to the political campaign of the Democratic candidate for governor of Illinois. He gave financial backing to a feeble effort to undermine the Federal currency by converting greenbacks to gold and shipping the gold to England where it was converted to sterling bills of exchange with which to purchase more U.S. gold for export to England. Through repeating the process, the conspirators managed to send $2 million in gold out of the country before ending the operation out of fear of detection and arrest. Thompson also worked to obtain the release of fellow conspirators in the custody of either Canadian or U.S. authorities.

As the mission to Canada drew to a close, Thompson recognized that his efforts had been largely unsuccessful. He attributed his failures to the frustration of his plans by Federal spies who managed to obtain crucial information and to arrest important leaders. He also cited the presence of large numbers of Federal troops who made organization of disaffected citizens impossible. Thompson did not realize that his failures were also due to a misreading of Northern public opinion. Contrary to his assumptions, Northerners who were weary of the war and unhappy with the Lincoln administration were not necessarily Confederate sympathizers or willing to aid in the dismemberment of the Union. On the other hand, Thompson rightly contended that his mission successfully brought consternation and fear in the North.

The assignment ended when Edwin Gray Lee reached Canada early in 1865 at the behest of the Confederate government to relieve Thompson. As instructed, Thompson gave some of the funds entrusted to him to Lee and deposited about $400,000 to the credit of the Confederacy in a British financial institution. Prior to departing Canada for Europe, he learned of President Andrew Johnson's proclamation of May 2, 1865, naming Thompson as one of the conspirators in the assassination of Lincoln. The charge was utterly false, as Thompson declared in a public letter sent to a New York newspaper. He remained out of the United States until 1869 when he returned only to find his property in northern Mississippi devastated. Shunning politics, he went into business in Memphis, Tennessee, and was residing there at the time of his death.

BIBLIOGRAPHY

Kinchen, Oscar A. *Confederate Operations in Canada and the North.* North Quincy, Mass., 1970.

Nelson, Larry E. *Bullets, Ballots, and Rhetoric: Confederate Policy for the Presidential Election of 1864.* University, Ala., 1980.

Robbins, Peggy. "The Greatest Scoundrel." *Civil War Times Illustrated* 31, no. 5 (November–December 1992): 54–59, 89–90.

LARRY E. NELSON

TOBACCO

Native Americans cultivated tobacco in North America before the first English settlers arrived in Jamestown in 1607. The Indians believed that native tobacco had both religious and medicinal importance. Its use, for example, had great ritual significance for the Indians in the Chesapeake region. Native Americans often smoked tobacco in a pipe to cement a peace accord.

Colonists at Jamestown were the first Europeans on the North American mainland to cultivate tobacco. As early as 1610 John Rolfe shipped a cargo to England for sale. But the naturally occurring tobacco plant in the Chesapeake region (*Nicotiana rustica*) was considered too bitter and harsh, and in 1611 Rolfe obtained seeds of the milder *Nicotiana tabacum* from the Spanish West Indies, Venezuela, and Trinidad for the Jamestown colonists. Thereafter, tobacco production increased rapidly in the Chesapeake Bay area, soon spreading to Maryland. Production continued to increase throughout the colonial period and by the middle of the eighteenth century, Maryland and Virginia were shipping nearly 70 million pounds of tobacco a year to Britain.

Some colonial aristocrats in both Britain and the American colonies believed that tobacco smoking was evil and hazardous to the health. This had little effect in halting the spread of the practice. By the eve of the Revolutionary War, tobacco had become the leading cash crop produced by all the colonies, North and South. Exports rose to over 100 million pounds a year, constituting half of all colonial export trade with Britain.

The methods used for cultivating and curing tobacco have changed over time and varied from region to region. Initially, planters in the Chesapeake region cured tobacco by gathering the plant on the ground and letting the sun dry the leaves, but sun-curing was soon given up in favor of a technique known as air-curing. Tobacco workers gathered leaves in parcels called "hands" and placed them over polls five feet in length. Then the hands were hung inside an open barn to complete the curing process. When fully dried, the tobacco was packed into large containers called hogsheads for shipping. Air-curing, popular in the Piedmont and tidewater regions until the early nineteenth century, resulted in a milder-tasting leaf.

Methods of curing tobacco by heat were known in the 1700s, but the process did not become popular until the early nineteenth century. In the 1820s the bright tobacco leaves of North Carolina and eastern Virginia, and later Kentucky and middle Tennessee, were cured by using enclosed smoking-sawdust fires to dry the tobacco hung in small barns. Although the modern method of flu-curing tobacco using charcoal heat was invented in 1839 in North Carolina, this method was not widely used until after the Civil War.

Both tobacco cultivation and manufacturing are labor-intensive activities. Initially, the Virginia Company of London used white indentured servants to harvest the crop, but they were soon replaced by African slaves. The presence of a large slave population engaged in the cultivation and curing of tobacco tied the growth of slavery to the rise of the plantation system. By 1860, 350,000 slaves were cultivating tobacco. It was, however, an exploitive crop that quickly exhausted the soil, requiring constant clearing of new land. The system also worked against the establishment of urban industrial centers in the colonial and antebellum South.

Throughout the colonial period commercial production of tobacco had centered in Northern port cities, but by the antebellum period, as a result of a surplus of slave labor and the great supply of raw material, commercial manufacturing shifted to the tobacco-growing regions in the South. Virginia dominated the industry with factories located at Richmond, Petersburg, Lynchburg, and Danville, and the border states of Kentucky, Tennessee, and Missouri also became tobacco-manufacturing centers.

The differing ways of consuming tobacco have often mirrored larger cultural trends. Tobacco has been smoked in pipes, cigars, and cigarettes, and also chewed and taken as snuff. Pipe smoking was the most prevalent form of tobacco consumption in the colonial period, although in the late 1700s taking snuff became popular among the elite who were emulating the European aristocracies. Chewing was distinctly American and became popular on the expanding frontier. After the Mexican War cigar smoking became the fad, but during the Civil War people returned to pipes and began rolling cigarettes for the first time.

As in so many other areas of Southern life, the Civil War seriously disrupted the South's tobacco growing and manufacturing. The tobacco-rich states of Virginia, North Carolina, and Tennessee sided with the Confederacy; the success of their crop rose and fell with that of the rebel nation. The tobacco-producing border states of Missouri, Kentucky, and Maryland fell early to Union control. Under the pressure of war, tobacco manufacturing, located in the South throughout the antebellum period, shifted quickly to the North. New York city became the North's tobacco-manufacturing center, servicing the area once dominated by Virginia tobacco planters.

Like New York, Louisville also profited by the war's disruption of Southern market towns, becoming the center of tobacco trade in the West.

Confederate policy and military campaigns in the heartland of the South's tobacco regions devastated Southern tobacco planting and manufacturing. In an attempt to encourage the planting of foodstuffs, the Confederate Congress in March 1862 passed a joint resolution recommending that Confederate states refrain from planting tobacco. Planters often ignored Congress's suggestions, however. The Virginia Assembly also attempted to limit tobacco growing with a law passed in March 1863, and renewed planting restrictions again in February 1864. Other tobacco-growing states passed similar legislation during the war. In addition, local newspapers such as the *Edgefield Advertiser* of South Carolina also exhorted their readers to switch from the planting of tobacco to desperately needed foodstuffs.

Union control of the Mississippi from mid-1863, combined with the naval blockade, restricted the export and manufacturing of tobacco products, as did the shift of factories to manufacturing war matèriel. In Richmond, after the First Battle of Manassas, several tobacco warehouses were converted into prisons for Union soldiers. The tobacco-rich county of Louisa, Virginia, saw the kind of physical destruction typical of regions exposed to intense military activity. Intermittent Union raids into the county and one of the war's largest cavalry battles at Trevillian's Depot destroyed not only the crops and livestock but also the county's infrastructure. Every Confederate and border state saw a decline in tobacco production in the 1860s.

The tobacco town of Danville, Virginia, however, took advantage of the vicissitudes of war. In the late 1850s its tobacco industry was in decline, and the community was reluctant to answer the call to arms in 1861. Nevertheless, Danville prospered during the war. Located safely behind enemy lines along a major railroad to Richmond, Danville became a lucrative place for the activities of merchants and manufacturers. Through their investments, the town and the surrounding county saw a revival in the tobacco industry. As a result of its returning prosperity, Danville citizens opposed attempts by Confederate soldiers to destroy the rail connection with Richmond in order to stop the Union advance. Local businessmen also looked favorable upon the Union takeover on the ground that it would bring peace and stability to the region.

While the war made it difficult for the public to obtain tobacco, both Confederate and Union soldiers found it plentiful. Since much of the fighting took place in the tobacco-rich regions of the South, soldiers often helped themselves. For years the U.S. Navy had supplied its sailors with tobacco rations. In February 1864 the Confederate government followed suit and included tobacco as part of the army's rations. Often, in the quiet moments between battle, Confederate and Union soldiers would exchange goods. The traditional swap was Northern coffee for Southern tobacco. Tobacco habits also revealed class distinctions in the South. Confederate officers did not receive the tobacco rations granted to soldiers. Nevertheless, Confederate officers favored the more fashionable smoking of cigars.

Tobacco had a profound influence on the history of the South. Early cultivation brought prosperity and helped ensure the economic survival of the colonies. The development of the tobacco plantation system, however, helped establish slavery in the South to a degree not found in the North. Because tobacco cultivation quickly wore out the soil, planters were constantly clearing new land, leading to the expansion of slavery and tobacco growing. The slave plantation system also worked to slow urban industrial development in the South. Moreover, the early opponents of tobacco use have been proven correct in their argument that it is hazardous to one's health. Thus, at best, tobacco has been a mixed blessing for the South.

BIBLIOGRAPHY

Gates, Paul. *Agriculture and the Civil War.* New York, 1965.
Gray, Lewis Cecil. *History of Agriculture in the United States to 1860.* 2 vols. New York, 1941.
Hilliard, Sam Bowers. *Atlas of Antebellum Southern Agriculture.* Baton Rouge, La., 1984.
Kulikoff, Allen. *Tobacco and Slaves: The Development of Southern Cultures in the Chesapeake, 1680–1800.* Chapel Hill, N.C., 1986.
Rachleff, Peter J. *Black Labor in the South: Richmond, Virginia, 1865–1890.* Philadelphia, 1984.
Robert, John C. *The Story of Tobacco in America.* Chapel Hill, N.C., 1967.
Seigel, Frederick F. *The Roots of Southern Distinctiveness: Tobacco and Society in Danville, Virginia, 1780–1865.* Knoxville, Tenn., 1982.
Shifflett, Crandall A. *Patronage and Poverty in the Tobacco South: Louisa County, Virginia, 1860–1890.* Knoxville, Tenn., 1982.

ORVILLE VERNON BURTON and HENRY KAMERLING

TOMPKINS, SALLY L.

TOMPKINS, SALLY L. (1833–1916), captain and nurse. On November 9, 1833, Sally Tompkins was born at Poplar Grove in Matthews County, Virginia, and lived in Richmond from the age of five. When troops from the Battle of First Manassas overwhelmed the city's medical facilities, President Jefferson Davis appealed to the citizens to establish private hospitals.

Responding to his call, Tompkins received permission from Judge John Robertson to utilize his home on Third and Main streets as a hospital. Established on July 31, 1861, the Robertson Hospital opened under her supervision. Within weeks, it was evident that too many patients lingered in Richmond well past their recovery, and Davis ordered all private hospitals to be placed under military personnel. With the help of Judge W. W. Crump, assistant secretary of the treasury, Tompkins met with Davis in an attempt to retain control of Robertson Hospital. To circumvent the military order rule, the president commissioned Tompkins a captain of cavalry (unassigned) in charge of her hospital. When signing her commission, Tompkins noted underneath her name that she "would not allow my name to be placed upon the pay roll of the army."

Tompkins operated Robertson Hospital until June 13, 1865, using her family's money and government rations. Among the 1,333 patients who passed through her hospital, only 73 died. It primarily served the most seriously wounded and earned the distinction of having the highest rate of soldiers returning to action.

In postwar Richmond, the woman described by her contemporaries as "not over 5 feet, hardly a Southern beauty, with a splendid face, her dark eyes [shining] out under smooth hair parted squarely in the middle," continued to be active in charity work and religious activities. Affectionately referred to as "Captain Sally," she regularly attended Daughters of the Confederacy and veterans' meetings. In 1905, she retired to the Confederate Women's Home in Richmond, where having exhausted her resources, she remained as a guest until her death on July 25, 1916.

As an honorary member of the R. E. Lee Camp of the Confederate Veterans, she was buried with full military honors in Matthews County. In the Confederate Women's Home, her room became a hospital ward. Four chapters of the United Daughters of the Confederacy are named in her honor. On September 10, 1961, a stained glass window depicting her many works was dedicated at the church she attended, St. James's Episcopal in Richmond.

BIBLIOGRAPHY

Dabney, Virginius. *Richmond: The Story of a City.* New York, 1976.
Richmond News Leader, July 26, 1916; January 29, 1959; September 9, 1961; July 21, 1966.
Richmond Times Dispatch, July 26-27, 1916; October 4, 1942.
Tompkins, Sally. Papers. Museum of the Confederacy, Richmond, Virginia.
Tompkins, Sally. Papers. The Valentine Museum, Richmond, Virginia.

SANDRA V. PARKER

TOOMBS, ROBERT

TOOMBS, ROBERT (1810–1885), U.S. congressman, Confederate secretary of state, and brigadier general. Wilkes County, Georgia, was the first and last home of Robert Toombs, who was born there in comfortable economic circumstances on July 2, 1810. Toombs seemed to enjoy a tempestuous youth that presaged his mercurial life and career. He attended Franklin College (which became the University of Georgia) but suffered expulsion on the eve of his graduation in 1828. Legend has it that Toombs appeared at the ceremony anyway, stood beside an oak tree outside of the college chapel, and delivered his own graduation oration. He did graduate from Union College in Schenectady, New York, and then studied law for a year at the University of Virginia. He returned to Georgia in 1830, married Julia Ann Dubose, and gained admittance to the Georgia bar.

> ## When the Confederacy collapsed, Toombs fled to Europe and lived in Paris until 1867.

Toombs, a large man, lived on an equally large scale. He was six feet tall and weighed over two hundred pounds. A brilliant courtroom lawyer, he was famous for his speeches to juries. He possessed inherited wealth and augmented his inheritance with the profits from his law practice and speculations in land and slaves. Toombs lived in a Greek Revival mansion in Washington, Georgia, and at various times owned plantations in Stewart County, Georgia; Desha County, Arkansas; and Tarrant County, Texas.

Elected to the Georgia House of Representatives six times (1837–1843), Toombs then won election to the U.S. Congress for four consecutive terms (1844–1851). He became a Whig in Georgia and national politics and voted for the tariff and against war with Mexico. Agitation over slavery alarmed Toombs, however, and in the course of supporting the Compromise of 1850, he helped form the Constitutional Union party as a haven for dissident Whigs. In 1855 Toombs became a Democrat and thereafter counted himself a strong Southern rights advocate, if not a fire-eater. By this time Toombs was in the Senate (1852–1861), where he was one of the leading Southern radicals.

Although he had serious second thoughts about secession following the election of Abraham Lincoln to the presidency, Republican rejection of the Crittenden Compromise drove Toombs into the front ranks of the immediate secessionists. And when delegates from seceded states convened in Montgomery to form the Confederacy, Toombs was a serious candidate for president of the new republic.

Toombs, however, seemed too radical to many of the delegates, and according to fellow Georgian Alexander H. Stephens, he sealed his fate with his fondness for the grape in Montgomery. Stephens wrote that Toombs was "tight every day at dinner" and on one evening shortly before the election became "*tighter* than I ever saw him." Whatever the reason, Toombs lost to Jefferson Davis and did not much like it. He did accept Davis's offer to name him secretary of state, though, and began his Confederate career in what was supposed to be an exalted post.

Toombs wrote out the instructions for the Confederacy's unofficial foreign ministers before they left to try to secure recognition in Europe. But then he had nothing left to do. He was secretary of state in a nation with no foreign relations, and he chafed at his inactivity and at what he perceived to be a lack of influence in the Davis administration. When pressed by a would-be bureaucrat for a job in his department, Toombs removed his hat and informed the supplicant that his entire department was inside. He resigned his position in July 1861, used his influence to secure an appointment as a brigadier general, and tried to contribute to the war effort.

General Toombs was a poor soldier made worse because he was entirely unaware of how unsuited he was for the military. He resented professional officers and carried on his own campaign against "West Pointers" in the Southern army. He derided the defensive strategy to which the Davis government resorted out of necessity. After the Seven Days' campaign (June 25–July 1, 1862), Toombs challenged D. H. Hill, his immediate superior, to a duel; Hill declined and pointed out that they might better spend their energy killing the enemy. At Sharpsburg on September 17, Toombs and his brigade fought well and Toombs himself was wounded. For this service he demanded a promotion; when it was not forthcoming, he resigned his commission.

Back home in Georgia, Toombs devoted most of the remainder of his Confederate career to criticizing Davis and the Richmond government. In his enterprise he joined Georgia Governor Joseph E. Brown and Vice President Alexander H. Stephens. Brown in 1864 made Toombs a colonel of Georgia troops and gave him a cavalry regiment in the effort to thwart Gen. William Tecumseh Sherman's invasion. Like everyone else, Toombs was ineffective.

When the Confederacy collapsed, Toombs fled to Europe and lived in Paris until 1867. He then returned home, resumed his practice of law in Washington, Georgia, and regained much of his antebellum influence in state politics. He never asked for a pardon—"Pardon for what? I haven't pardoned you all yet!" he supposedly said—and so was never able to hold national office again. Nevertheless he furthered the efforts of white conservatives for "home rule" and also supported some protopopulist causes such as state regulation of railroads and other corporations.

Toombs's health declined rapidly during the 1880s, and he died December 15, 1885. He remained very much unreconstructed to the end. Local lore in Wilkes County has Toombs at the telegraph office in town during the Great Chicago Fire of 1870. When he emerged, a crowd gathered to hear the news, and Toombs described the heroic efforts of the many fire companies to stem the spread of the flames. Firemen and volunteers from miles around Chicago were doing their best. "But the wind," Toombs added, "is in our favor."

BIBLIOGRAPHY

Freeman, Douglas S. *Lee's Lieutenants: A Study in Command.* 3 vols. New York, 1942–1944. Reprint, New York, 1986.
Patrick, Rembert W. *Jefferson Davis and His Cabinet.* Baton Rouge, La., 1944.
Phillips, Ulrich B. *The Life of Robert Toombs.* New York, 1913.
Phillips, Ulrich B., ed. "The Correspondence of Robert Toombs, Alexander H. Stephens, and Howell Cobb." In *Annual Report of the American Historical Association.* Vol. 2. Washington, D.C., 1911.
Thompson, William Y. *Robert Toombs of Georgia.* Baton Rouge, La., 1966.

EMORY M. THOMAS

TORPEDOES AND MINES

Torpedo is a generic term for a variety of naval and land mines employed mainly by the Confederacy. The word derived from the Latin name for an electric ray fish whose sting numbs its prey; it was first used to describe a weapon in 1776. Disapproved on moral grounds because targets were struck without warning, the torpedo satisfied the Confederacy's urgent need to make technology compensate for its inferior strength of arms.

Torpedoes destroyed more Union vessels than all other actions: forty-three were sunk or damaged, according to the best estimate. The psychological effect in naval and military action is incalculable. Yet only one Confederate vessel fell victim to a Union torpedo: the ironclad *Albemarle* in Lt. William B. Cushing's famous raid.

As early as June 1861, Matthew Fontaine Maury initiated experiments to design and test torpedoes in the James River. Working with him were Lt. Hunter Davidson and Lt. William L. Maury. As with other naval technologies that the Confederacy refined, primitive torpedos had been used as early as the Revolution and the Crimean War.

Maury, who was past fifty and crippled by old injuries from a carriage accident, continually placed himself at risk in experimental attempts to torpedo ships in the James. Partly because of these circumstances, the Confederate authorities sent him to England in 1862 to procure supplies and test his designs under safer conditions. Davidson succeeded Maury as commander of the newly formed Naval Submarine Battery Service, a unit of the Bureau of Ordnance and Hydrography. From the James, use of torpedoes quickly spread southward, not only in large harbors like Charleston and Mobile, but on the inland waters of rivers like the St. Johns and Tennessee.

In addition to major factories such as Tredegar in Richmond and the Augusta Powder Works, many small facilities around the South were engaged in manufacturing torpedoes. In Atlanta, wives of naval personnel at the Atlanta Naval Arsenal were employed in this work. An array of moorings, floats, kegs, boilers, springs, triggers, and levers was utilized in various torpedo manufactures. Each type presented three basic design problems—how to deliver the torpedo to the target, how to keep the powder dry, and how to detonate the charge—problems that were addressed in a variety of ways.

> **Some torpedoes were set adrift in a river current or on a rising tide to strike a ship's hull in random collisions.**

Some torpedoes were set adrift in a river current or on a rising tide to strike a ship's hull in random collisions. Others were anchored by grapnels or on weights to float just beneath the surface. In more shallow waters in slower currents, stationary frames held "plantations" of torpedoes. On one such frame, the torpedoes were set at a 45-degree angle facing downstream. This arrangement gave Confederate vessels unobstructed passage over the frame, but Union ships traveling upstream would trigger explosions on contact.

The most daring means of delivering a torpedo to its target was the spar torpedo. This device was fixed at the end of a movable spar attached to the prow of a small, semisubmersible ship, which approached the target ship at such close range that a ten- or twenty-foot spar could reach the ship's hull below the waterline. When these small armored Davids were not available, open canoes fitted with a boom and spar carried out the same mission.

Very large barrels floating just beneath the surface or large boilers resting on a riverbed and loaded with many hundreds of pounds of powder were formidable—if the powder was kept dry. Thus, watertight casing was essential. Wooden kegs and demijohns were available, as were ships' boilers and lengths of pipe. Tin was frequently used to fabricate cones, cylinders, or lantern-shaped casings.

The crux of torpedo design was the triggering device. Some were detonated mechanically by means of a percussion fuse or a trigger pulled on a lanyard. Detonating a torpedo on a thirty-fathom lanyard or a ten-foot spar involved considerable danger. Setting torpedoes adrift or planting an unmanned stand of torpedoes involved a considerable element of chance. A ship might not collide with the weapon or might "sweep" and destroy them. Powder and fuses deteriorated swiftly in the water, or live torpedoes created a peril for Confederates.

If precise, reliable electrical firing devices could be designed, a very large torpedo in a channel could be linked to a station on shore by insulated wire and then fired by an operator at the moment a Union ship was over the torpedo. Developing the technology to do that obsessed Maury. And even when he could address the problem in principle, supplies were scarce. Galvanic batteries were inefficient if they were available at all. A Wallaston battery used in the earliest trials consisted of eighteen pairs of ten-by-twelve-inch zinc plates in thirty-six-gallon vats of sulfuric acid. Acid was requisitioned in the small lots kept in pharmacies and soon cost twenty-five dollars per gallon. In one operation, twenty-one batteries were networked in sheds along the James River.

Only a few miles of insulated wire were available in the Confederacy and only a few feet of fine platinum wire needed for fuses. These fuses combined both modern and ancient supplies. Electricity passed through the insulated copper wire to a short length of platinum wire run through the center of a short quill. The quill formed a little vial filled with fulminate of mercury, sealed with beeswax, and enclosed in a cartridge pouch of rifle powder. The electric current melted the platinum wire and set off a chain reaction, which ignited the charge.

Torpedoes were to take many configurations, for their production was limited only by ingenuity and available supplies. The term was applied not just to floating mines studded with percussion fuses; the "coal torpedo," for instance, could probably be classified as a booby trap, for it was a bomb disguised as a lump of coal and hidden in coal bunkers. Shoveled into a Union ship's boiler, it had a devastating effect. A "clock torpedo" smuggled aboard a ship at City Point on the James functioned like a time bomb to create one of the most spectacular and costly explosions of the war.

CONFEDERATE TORPEDO. Wooden torpedo recovered from Light House Inlet, Charleston, South Carolina. Photographed at the U.S. Military Academy Museum, Highland Falls, New York, 1950. NATIONAL ARCHIVES

Ships, military and naval personnel, and civilians were imperiled by stray torpedoes after the war. But by 1865 they had become an established and accepted mode of warfare.

[*See also* Davids.]

BIBLIOGRAPHY

Perry, Milton F. *Infernal Machines: The Story of Confederate Submarine and Mine Warfare.* Baton Rouge, La., 1965.

Scharf, J. Thomas. *History of the Confederate States Navy from Its Organization to the Surrender of Its Last Vessel.* New York, 1887. Reprint, New York, 1977.

Stern, Philip Van Doren. *Secret Missions of the Civil War.* New York, 1990.

MAXINE TURNER

TRANS-MISSISSIPPI DEPARTMENT

The Trans-Mississippi region included Texas, Arkansas, Missouri, Indian Territory, that part of Louisiana west of the Mississippi River, and the Arizona Territory (about two-fifths of the modern states of New Mexico and Arizona). Although there were numerous minor campaigns and battles in this area, none affected the war's outcome. The Trans-Mississippi was made a separate department in May 1862, but because President Jefferson Davis's primary concern was Virginia and Tennessee, he relegated the region to secondary importance. The surrender of Vicksburg assured the area's virtual isolation, and for all practical purposes the department was out of the war after 1863. Nevertheless, the Trans-Mississippi contributed significant numbers of men to the armies serving east of the river, and provided the Confederacy with a considerable quantity of food and supplies. Moreover, the small Army of the Trans-Mississippi forced the Union to retain a military presence in the region, thus tying up Federal soldiers that could have been used elsewhere.

Although the Trans-Mississippi was not part of the main war effort, the area west of the river comprised a notable portion of the total land mass of the Confederate states. From the Mississippi River to the California border and from Iowa to the Gulf of Mexico, the region covered around 600,000 square miles, but realistically Texas, Arkansas, and West Louisiana (thirty-one complete parishes and parts of six others) became the nucleus of the western limits of the Confederate nation. In 1860 the population of these three states included about 908,000 whites, around 5,500 free blacks, about 543,000 slaves, and 600 Indians. In addition, the Indian Territory reported about 58,000 Indians, whites, and free blacks and over 7,000 slaves. That Missouri did not secede and join the Confederacy was significant because, with 1 million white citizens, it was the second-largest slave state, ranking only behind Virginia.

The area was the fastest growing in the South and rich in many commodities. The inhabitants raised a variety of agricultural products, including cotton in the river valleys of Louisiana and Texas. Missourians produced more corn than in any other Southern state and harvested impressive quantities of wheat and oats. Missouri also counted more swine than any other slave state and ranked only behind Kentucky in the number of horses. Texas led the nation in the production of beef: the census reported over 3.5 million cattle in the state. The Trans-Mississippi's geographic location, too, offered advantages. Texas was the only Confederate state to border on a neutral foreign nation, Mexico, and an international waterway, the Rio Grande; thus it gave the South a link to the outside after the Union blockade became effective along the coastline. The region was also the gateway to any dreams of a Confederate empire in the Far West.

The states that composed the Trans-Mississippi had the same problems that plagued other agrarian areas in wartime. The population was widely scattered; there were few towns of any size, and even these were very small. Some of the largest population centers were San Antonio with 8,235, Galveston with 7,307, Little Rock with 3,727, and Shreveport with 2,190. The department had few railroads, almost no industrial facilities, and inadequate telegraph lines. Moreover, it was the only part of the Confederacy that had an Indian problem; the region had some 50,000 to 60,000 "hostile" Indians. The frontier in Texas retreated east after the able-bodied men joined the army, and the dangerous situation in West Texas added to the troubles facing the state authorities.

Early Military Operations

When the war began there was neither an overall military plan for the area nor an intention to make it into one department. In 1861 Louisiana belonged to Department No. 1 and parts of Arkansas belonged to Department No. 2. A separate Department of Texas was created on April 21 and placed under Col. Earl Van Dorn, who soon after capturing *Star of the West* at Galveston was promoted to brigadier general. Van Dorn left the state in September, briefly transferring command to Col. Henry Eustace McCulloch, but on September 18 Brig. Gen. Paul O. Hèbert assumed command. In theory, Confederate commanders worked with state officials to organize and equip the army. Each state raised troops, and each seized Federal arsenals and forts within its boundaries. This arrangement obviously led to difficulties between state and Confederate authorities, and in Missouri it provoked armed conflict.

Missouri was the only state in the department that never officially seceded, and throughout the war it had two rival governments. In May 1861 pro-Confederate Governor

Claiborne F. Jackson tried to lead the state out of the Union, but in St. Louis this effort had been thwarted by Union Capt. Nathaniel Lyon, who organized a force and seized the state militia at Camp Jackson. The ensuing riot had left many civilians dead and persuaded the popular Unionist Sterling Price to throw his support to the South. This led to an armed conflict between the pro-Southern forces of Jackson and Price, on one hand, and the pro-Union army of Lyon, on the other. When the two sides met at Wilson's Creek, Missouri, on August 10, 1861, Lyon was killed. Price tried to take advantage of the victory by moving into Missouri, but Union soldiers forced him back into southwestern Missouri and finally into northwestern Arkansas. Missouri, in effect, had two governors. The pro-Union legislature replaced Jackson with Hamilton R. Gamble and voted to remain within the Union. Jackson, ignoring this, joined the Confederacy and moved his headquarters south.

There were also plans to establish a Confederate empire in the West. In June 1861 Col. John R. Baylor led Confederate troops up the Rio Grande into the New Mexico Territory. In August he claimed Arizona and made himself governor of the territory. Brig. Gen. Henry Hopkins Sibley also moved into the region and early in 1862 defeated Federal forces at Valverde before taking Albuquerque and Santa Fe. After a loss at Glorieta Pass in March, however, Sibley retreated to San Antonio, and the dreams of a Confederate empire in the West vanished.

The first major clash in the Trans-Mississippi came along the Missouri-Arkansas border. In December 1861 Brig. Gen. Samuel R. Curtis took command of the Union Army of the Southwest and early in 1862 advanced toward Springfield, Missouri. The friction between Sterling Price, commanding the Missouri State Guard, and Brig. Gen. Ben McCulloch, commanding Confederate troops, was rectified on January 10, 1862, with the creation of the Trans-Mississippi District of Department No. 2. This district contained the Indian Territory, that portion of Louisiana north of the Red River, and all of the counties of Missouri and Arkansas except those located between the St. Francis and Mississippi rivers. Maj. Gen. Earl Van Dorn was placed in command; he arrived late in January and led the Confederate Army of the West at Elkhorn Tavern, Arkansas, in March. Van Dorn planned to stop Curtis's move south, and the two armies met in the Boston Mountains near Fayetteville. Although the Federals were outnumbered, around 11,000 to Van Dorn's almost 17,000, Van Dorn's plan to split his army and attack from two directions failed. During the fighting on March 7 McCulloch and Brig. Gen. James McIntosh were killed, leaving no one in charge of one wing of the assault. On the second day of the battle, Curtis's men were able to drive the Confederates from the field. Van Dorn moved south toward the Arkansas River and then received orders to join the Confederate army under Gen. Albert Sidney Johnston in Mississippi. Although he did not reach his destination in time to take part in the Battle of Shiloh, he left Arkansas virtually defenseless.

Elkhorn Tavern was the first major battle in which Indians from the Five Civilized Tribes participated. The early fighting in the Indian Territory had consisted mainly of skirmishes between pro-Confederate and pro-Union Indians. When the war began Confederate representatives had negotiated alliances with the five tribes—the Chickasaws, Creeks, Cherokees, Choctaws, and Seminoles. Eventually, the pro-Union Indians retreated to Kansas and left the region briefly under Confederate control. The Indians who fought at Elkhorn Tavern returned to the Indian Territory when Van Dorn crossed the Mississippi River, and by 1863 many had become disillusioned with the Confederacy; both Creeks and Choctaws talked of resuming relations with the United States. Cherokee Stand Watie, who commanded an Indian cavalry brigade in the Army of the Trans-Mississippi, was the only Indian to attain the rank of brigadier general in the Confederate army, and the last general officer to surrender at the end of the war, June 23, 1865.

Creation of the Trans-Mississippi Department

After the disaster at Elkhorn Tavern the Confederate government recognized that something drastic had to be done. Faced with the serious situation of having Curtis's army positioned in northwestern Arkansas and with no way to defend the region, the Confederate government finally created a separate territorial organization, the Trans-Mississippi Department on May 26, 1862. General Order No. 39 stated that the department would embrace the states of Missouri and Arkansas, including the Indian Territory, that part of Louisiana west of the Mississippi River, and the state of Texas. On May 31 Maj. Gen. Thomas C. Hindman was appointed commander, and he did an excellent job of organizing an army and defending Little Rock. Hindman, however, argued with Albert Pike in the Indian Territory. Partly because of this argument (Pike was a friend of Jefferson Davis) and partly because Hindman's draconian measures to instill discipline and order in the army were unpopular, Hindman was replaced by Maj. Gen. Theophilus H. Holmes, another of Davis's personal friends. On July 16, 1862, Holmes was ordered to Little Rock, and he assumed command on July 30. On August 20 the department was divided into districts: the District of Texas was composed of the state of Texas and the territory of Arizona and remained under Hébert; the District of West Louisiana was under the command of Maj. Gen. Richard Taylor; and the District of Arkansas, which included the states of Arkansas and Missouri and the Indian Territory, was under Hindman.

But as overall department commander Holmes was a poor choice; he was difficult to get along with and was sometimes excessively rude. Holmes thought in terms of what best served his own department rather than what might be best for the Confederate nation. When asked to send reinforcements to Vicksburg, he delayed and used his personal friendship with Davis to frustrate the movement of troops out of his department. Not only did he keep his soldiers in the Trans-Mississippi, never providing any real assistance to Vicksburg, but he never satisfactorily defended his own borders. In December, Hindman in northwestern Arkansas was defeated by Federal Brig. Gens. James Blunt and Francis Herron at Prairie Grove, and in early January 1863 Arkansas Post in the southeast surrendered to a superior Union force.

Certainly there were serious problems in the Trans-Mississippi when Holmes took over, but his actions did nothing to improve the situation. Citizens living in the Trans-Mississippi felt abandoned, which created perilous morale problems throughout the department. Holmes, as early as October 1862, had asked Richmond to relieve him. In January 1863 the government was ready to agree. Secretary of War James A. Seddon reported in March that "the most deplorable accounts reached Richmond of the disorder, confusion, and demoralization everywhere prevalent, both with the armies and people of that State." Holmes, he claimed, had "lost the confidence and attachment of all," and the result was "fearful."

The Trans-Mississippi under E. Kirby Smith

On January 14, 1863, Lt. Gen. E. Kirby Smith was assigned to the command of the Southwestern Army, "embracing the Departments of West Louisiana and Texas." The order made it clear that the geographical limits of this "new department" would be separate and distinct from the Trans-Mississippi Department. But Holmes wanted out and urged his friend Davis to find a replacement for him. On February 9 Smith took command of all Confederate forces west of the Mississippi River and made Alexandria, Louisiana, headquarters of the Trans-Mississippi Department. On March 18, Holmes was officially relieved, although he remained in charge at Little Rock.

At the time of Smith's arrival the department still comprised several districts, although some of the commanders had changed since the summer. Holmes took over the District of Arkansas and held this position until he resigned on March 16, 1864. Taylor continued in the District of Western Louisiana and, though he and Smith frequently disagreed, remained in command until late 1864. Brig. Gen. William Steele headed the District of the Indian Territory until replaced by Brig. Gen. Samuel Bell Maxey; and Maj. Gen. John B. Magruder commanded Texas, New Mexico, and Arizona. Magruder had arrived in Texas in October 1862 and promptly recaptured Galveston from the Union forces on January 1, 1863. Magruder, known as "Prince John," would remain in this position until transferred to Arkansas near the war's end. Texas was divided into three subdistricts: Brig. Gen. James E. Slaughter headed the Eastern Sub-District;

Brig. Gen. Hamilton P. Bee, the Western Sub-District; and Brig. Gen. Henry McCulloch, the Northern Sub-District. Upon his arrival, Smith complained, "There was no general system, no common head; each district was acting independently."

The department also encountered problems keeping its men fit and in camp. Sickness took a heavy toll, and it was difficult to procure medicine. Desertion was another serious problem, with men going home and returning to the army at will. The extent of the problem is indicated by the figures reported after an inspection of the department in February 1864. In the District of Arkansas there were 10,354 troops present for duty, 25,623 aggregate present and absent; in the

> **The department also encountered problems keeping its men fit and in camp.**

District of Western Louisiana, 10,657 troops present, 21,808 aggregate present and absent; in the District of Texas, 7,574 troops present, 12,992 aggregate present and absent; among state troops, 1,529 present, 3,960 aggregate present and absent; and in the District of the Indian Territory, 1,666 troops present, 8,885 aggregate present and absent. Overall, counting various other commands, it was reported the total present for duty in the department was 31,780, aggregate present and absent, 73,268.

Supplying these troops was a formidable task. It was imperative, Smith thought, to begin "general systematizing and development of the departmental resources." When Smith arrived, the Quartermaster's Bureau, recently established, reported on hand almost $17 million, but only $12,350 was in money. The remainder was in drafts, which the chief quartermaster complained he could not cash. "The want of funds to meet the necessities of the army embarrasses to a great degree the efficiency of my department," he noted. Moreover, the head of the Clothing Bureau clamored for funds to outfit his men. Hats and shoes were manufactured at several locations, and the Huntsville penitentiary turned out cloth, cotton jeans, woolen plaids, and woolen jeans. But money was needed to meet other pressing demands: many soldiers had not been paid for months.

Kirby Smithdom. The Trans-Mississippi was isolated, with the U.S. Navy making it difficult for troops and supplies to cross the Mississippi River. With Smith in charge, the region became known as "Kirby Smithdom." Powerful Texans believed the Confederate government had abandoned their state by surrendering it to Smith's control. Even Richard Taylor complained that Smith worried too much about "the recovery of his lost empire, to the detriment of the portion yet in his possession," and Taylor believed that "the substance of Louisiana and Texas was staked against the shadow of

Missouri and Northern Arkansas." Smith, in fact, assumed exceptional power, but Jefferson Davis supported him, declaring that his "confidence in the discretion and ability of General Smith assures me that I shall have no difficulty in sustaining any assumption of authority which may be necessary."

Governors and state officials met in the late summer of 1863 and agreed that the department must become self-sustaining. They called for public support and closed with a vote of confidence in Smith. Soon after, Smith organized the Cotton Bureau for the purchase, collection, and disposition of government-owned cotton. Bureaucrats hoped that cotton taken to Mexico could be exchanged for weapons and supplies desperately needed by the South. Although the plan did supply many essential goods, the work of the bureau was hampered by private speculators, currency problems, and an inability to convince Texans of the need to cooperate. Illicit commerce flourished, particularly along the Red River, as Southern cotton made its way to New England factories with the knowledge and support of government officials on both sides. But by mid-1864 most of the available cotton was gone, and Smith, who had come to depend upon this source of revenue, realized his department was in danger of financial collapse. Therefore, without official sanction from Richmond, he ordered the bureau to buy or impress one-half of all cotton grown, thus keeping the trade going until the war's end.

The Trans-Mississippi was unique in the Confederacy in that a Union attack was not the only danger it faced. In the summer of 1863 a serious threat to the region came from the Indians. Comanches and Kiowas began to raid closer to large settlements—at one point just west of Fort Worth. Many families left their homes, moved in together, and built small forts. Confederate soldiers, receiving letters from home, became alarmed; many deserted to check on their families, although most returned when assured that their homes were safe. Texas's governors, first Francis R. Lubbock and then Pendleton Murrah, did their best to control the situation. Henry McCulloch, in command of the Northern Sub-District with headquarters at Bonham, had to deal with Indian war parties roaming along the frontier.

In addition, the frontier was alive with deserters, outlaws, and Unionists. Even the notorious Confederate William Quantrill plagued Texans when he moved south out of Missouri. McCulloch never had enough men to deal with all the problems, and in 1864 the authorities finally closed the frontier in an effort to protect the citizens.

Yet another burden was the sizable number of refugees that flooded Texas. Many Southerners with friends or relatives in the Trans-Mississippi fled other states to escape Federal armies. It is impossible to estimate accurately the number of people who relocated in Confederate-held regions. Women and children often brought slaves with them in order to avoid confiscation of their property, and as many as 200,000 blacks may have entered Texas during the last years of the war. The drain on the department created by these exiles placed a severe strain on Smith's resources, and contributed to the war-weariness that pervaded the region after 1863.

Military Operations of 1863. While Smith wrestled with domestic matters, he had also to cope with the military situation. Davis and the War Department had directed him to give top priority to defending Confederate-held territory along the Mississippi River. Throughout the spring and early summer of 1863, he tried to furnish aid to both Port Hudson and Vicksburg. In an attempt to draw Federal troops away from Vicksburg, Smith authorized an invasion of Missouri in April. Confederates under Brig. Gen. John Sappington Marmaduke tried unsuccessfully to take Cape Girardeau on the Mississippi River and quickly retreated into Arkansas. This strategy to assist Vicksburg failed, and Ulysses S. Grant continued his movement south. Although Holmes had resisted any efforts to send troops from the Trans-Mississippi to Vicksburg while he was department commander, Smith did order Confederates from Arkansas to reinforce Richard Taylor in Louisiana. Also as a diversion to help the Vicksburg defenders, Holmes authorized an attack on the Federal stronghold of Helena, Arkansas, on July 4. But in a mismanaged affair the Confederates were quickly repulsed with heavy losses on their side. Moreover, all attempts to aid Vicksburg from the west side of the river failed, and the town surrendered on July 4, 1863. Port Hudson fell five days later, and with the Union taking control of the river, the Confederacy was split in two.

On July 17, Federal troops decisively defeated the Confederates at the Battle of Honey Springs (or Elk Creek), the largest single engagement of the Civil War in the Indian

> **While Banks unsuccessfully struck at Texas, the Federals were victorious in Arkansas.**

Territory. Late in August Federal forces headed toward Little Rock, and in southern Louisiana Taylor made preparations for an attack. Texans, especially in the Rio Grande valley, feared an invasion. The situation in Mexico provided diplomatic reasons to control Texas; Napoleon III, the French ruler who was openly pro-Southern, had taken advantage of the weakened U.S. government and backed a puppet monarchy in Mexico. Moreover, Abraham Lincoln was not unaware of the interest that New Englanders had in Texas cotton. And yet the important decision of where the assault should be made along the Texas coast was left to the incompetent political general Nathaniel P. Banks.

Banks decided to strike at the mouth of the Sabine River, the boundary between Louisiana and Texas. A surprise assault at Sabine Pass would give access to the port of Beaumont. Moreover, the Confederates manning the pass were not adequately armed and made an easy target for the Union fleet. A combined force under Banks and Adm. David Farragut left New Orleans and sailed for Sabine Pass. On September 8, 1863, they faced the guns of Lt. Dick Dowling and forty-two men of the Davis Guard, a rowdy group composed primarily of Irishmen from Houston. The determined Confederates, members of the First Texas Heavy Artillery Regiment, turned their cannons on the naval force under Maj. Gen. William B. Franklin. About 4:00 P.M. *Sachem* was struck in the boilers and *Clifton* was grounded; both ships soon surrendered. The attack lasted less than an hour, and Federal losses were substantial, including the two gunboats. Dowling and his men, who fired their artillery over a hundred times, were unscathed. As a result of this impressive Confederate victory, Lincoln watched Northern morale fall and the stock market temporarily drop. Davis called it "the greatest military victory in the world," and Franklin took his place in American military history as the first general to lose part of his fleet to land batteries alone.

While Banks unsuccessfully struck at Texas, the Federals were victorious in Arkansas. On September 10, 1863, Little Rock fell to Union forces under Maj. Gen. Frederick Steele, and the Confederates fled the city. As Little Rock became the headquarters of the Union Department of Arkansas, another Union expedition under Brig. Gen. James G. Blunt drove Brig. Gen. William Steele from Fort Smith into the Indian Territory. On September 1, the Federals moved into Fort Smith, and Arkansas was divided in half on an east-west line that ran from Helena on the Mississippi to Little Rock and across to Fort Smith. Even Pine Bluff fell to the Union advance, and the Confederates controlled only a strip of land in the southern part of Arkansas. Moreover, except for scattered skirmishes, the Indian Territory was virtually out of the war.

Lincoln, however, still wanted to capture locations on the Texas coast. A new force invaded the Rio Grande valley in November and occupied Brownsville, forcing the Confederates to reroute the cotton crop heading for Mexico. The Union troops continued to move up the coast, and Magruder had to work hard to quell rumors that he had abandoned South Texas. In December, when a threat to Galveston developed, he asked that the Texas cavalry in Louisiana under Brig. Gens. Thomas Green and James Patrick Major be returned to the coast. But the Union released its grip, except at the Rio Grande, when the authorities realized it was impossible to hold the entire shoreline. Washington now turned to strategy for the 1864 spring campaign.

Union Offensive of 1864. As the new year opened, Union authorities plotted a major offensive in the Trans-

Mississippi. As spring approached Lincoln's government planned to invade Arkansas and Louisiana in an effort to move into the rich cotton land of East Texas. Banks was to march up the Red River from Alexandria and meet Steele's advance from Little Rock at Shreveport. Neither army would have to march very far to reach Smith's headquarters. Once they had taken this Red River port, it would be easy to move into Texas. Moreover, victories in this part of the Confederacy could eliminate Arkansas and Louisiana from the war. Perhaps more important, Lincoln needed a meaningful military victory, for the fall election was only months away.

The two-pronged invasion began in March. Banks's force, increased by 10,000 men on loan from William Tecumseh Sherman's army and assisted by Porter's fleet, numbered around 22,000. He easily took Fort DeRussy on the Red River and headed for Shreveport. Smith and Taylor disagreed on how to respond to the columns moving north. Taylor started the campaign with around 6,000 men, and reinforcements from Texas and Arkansas increased the number to about 12,000. With this disparity in numbers, Smith urged caution, but Taylor was eager to strike quickly. On April 8 Taylor hit the strung-out Federal army near the little town of Mansfield. Banks's advance force fell back on their long wagon train, and a complete rout would have occurred if reinforcements had not arrived in time. The next day the Confederates hit Banks's army at Pleasant Hill. Although Taylor did not defeat Banks, the Federal army pulled back to Grand Ecore. Taylor then asked Smith for permission to pursue the disorganized Union army, but Smith refused; he had to shift some of Taylor's troops north to prevent the Federals from succeeding in Arkansas.

The second prong of the Federal advance started in a more promising fashion. Sterling Price had around 8,000 men in Arkansas, along with some recently arrived cavalry from the Indian Territory, to oppose Frederick Steele's 10,000 to 12,000 troops. While Banks pushed up the Red River, Steele advanced south toward Washington, Arkansas. He occupied the town of Camden by the time that Smith had shifted troops back to Arkansas. In late April Confederate forces captured a supply train coming from Pine Bluff. The Battle of Poison Spring was notable because the loss of the supply train was a major factor in Steele's decision to retreat, but it was also a controversial battle in which many black soldiers died. Both sides claimed victory, but Steele withdrew to Little Rock.

The Confederate Trans-Mississippi Department had survived. As Steele fell back to Little Rock, Banks retreated to Alexandria. The politician-turned-general had to use all of his ingenuity to save the army, and Porter was fortunate to maneuver his fleet down the falling river. A Wisconsin soldier suggested that the navy build a dam to raise the water level; the river, having fallen to three feet in some places, was too shallow for the passage of the gunboats. When Banks escaped, Smith and Taylor had another serious disagreement, and Taylor was replaced in Louisiana by Maj. Gen. John G. Walker.

Final Confederate Operations. In August Taylor took command of the Department of East Louisiana, Mississippi, and Alabama, and crossed the river. In fact, Jefferson Davis told Kirby Smith to send any units he could spare to help at Mobile, and Smith received specific orders to have several Trans-Mississippi brigades join the campaigns in the East. He protested that the loss of troops would seriously damage the morale of the department, and when the men learned of the proposed plans they threatened to mutiny rather than fight. As the plan bogged down in controversy, it was dropped. Taylor maintained this was because too many gunboats had arrived at the crossing point to allow such an operation to succeed, but Davis later claimed he had never really planned to cross huge numbers. In fact, Taylor revealed that many men had decided to desert rather than comply. Smith hotly denied this, charging that because of his disagreements with Taylor, the Louisiana general was trying to discredit him. For whatever reason, the scheme to shift Trans-Mississippi troops across the Mississippi failed.

While all of this was occurring in Louisiana, Kirby Smith and Sterling Price were planning a raid into Missouri—the last major campaign in the Trans-Mississippi. Price, who had succeeded Holmes in command of the District of Arkansas, had been a politician before the war, and he was aware of the advantage to be gained by successfully invading his home state before the November presidential election. He personally hoped to take control of regions of the state long enough to elect a new governor and legislature. By taking command of the expedition, however, Price was forced to relinquish command of the District of Arkansas, and he was replaced by Maj. Gen. John B. Magruder. Price headed for Missouri with only cavalry from Arkansas organized into three divisions under Maj. Gen. James Fleming Fagan and Brig. Gens. Joseph O. Shelby and John S. Marmaduke. Price and his 12,000 men entered Missouri in September; he hoped to gain recruits and supplies as he went along. The raid, which covered over 1,500 miles and took three months, turned into a disaster; Price and his badly beaten army returned to Arkansas in early December.

In the winter of 1864–1865 morale plummeted throughout the department. Smith was always fearful that Richmond might order his troops to fight in the East, and he could ill-afford a drain on his manpower; the army was already badly depleted by desertion as many men on leave failed to return. Trade with Mexico was at a wartime low, and much of the gunpowder coming in from that country was of such poor quality it would not fire. Although the states in the department suffered less from shortages than other Southern states, inflation hit hard by winter. Moreover, the Texas frontier was rife with rumors of Indian raids, and large bands of deserters

and bushwhackers tried to take over areas where the military had little control.

When Lee surrendered in April 1865, Kirby Smith, along with military and civil authorities, issued calls for the people of the Southwest to continue the fight. The last battle of the war occurred in the Trans-Mississippi deep in South Texas where Col. John S. ("Rip") Ford and the Second Texas had not learned that the end was near. Three hundred Federal troops from the island of Brazos Santiago under Col. T. H. Barrett landed on the mainland and headed toward Confederate-held Fort Brown. Barrett, whose command was mostly black soldiers, met a detachment of Ford's regiment at Palmito Ranch near Brownsville, but after a brief skirmish both sides withdrew. The following day, May 13, Ford struck at the Union soldiers; 113 surrendered and 30 were killed or wounded. The Texans learned from their prisoners that Lee and Johnston had surrendered in April.

In May military units in the department began to disband, and by the end of the month Smith had only a few scattered troops left in Texas and Louisiana. Lt. Gen. Simon Bolivar Buckner, acting Brig. Gen. Joseph L. Brent, and Maj. Gen. Sterling Price headed for New Orleans to negotiate terms, and on May 25 the military and naval forces of the Trans-Mississippi surrendered to Maj. Gen. E. R. S. Canby. The next day Buckner signed the official terms of surrender, which paroled the Trans-Mississippi soldiers and allowed them to return home unmolested. Kirby Smith, who decided to transfer his headquarters from Shreveport to Houston, arrived there on May 27 only to find he was a general without an army. On June 2 he boarded a Federal steamer in Galveston Harbor and placed his signature on the completed agreement, officially surrendering the Trans-Mississippi Department.

[*See also* Brownsville, Texas; Elkhorn Tavern, Arkansas; Galveston, Texas; Glorieta Pass, New Mexico; Port Hudson, Louisiana; Price's Missouri Raid; Red River Campaigns; Sabine Pass, Texas; Wilson's Creek Campaign; *and biographies of numerous figures mentioned herein.*]

BIBLIOGRAPHY

Bragg, Jefferson Davis. *Louisiana in the Confederacy.* Chapel Hill, N.C., 1952.

Johnson, Ludwell H. *Red River Campaign: Politics and Cotton in the Civil War.* Baltimore, 1958.

Josephy, Alvin M., Jr. *The Civil War in the American West.* New York, 1991.

Kerby, Robert L. *Kirby Smith's Confederacy: The Trans-Mississippi South, 1863–1865.* New York, 1972.

Nichols, James L. *The Confederate Quartermaster in the Trans-Mississippi.* Austin, Tex., 1964.

Oates, Stephen B. *Confederate Cavalry West of the River.* Austin, Tex., 1961.

Parks, Joseph Howard. *General Edmund Kirby Smith, C.S.A.* Baton Rouge, La., 1954.

Thomas, David Y. *Arkansas in War and Reconstruction, 1861–1874.* Little Rock, Ark., 1926.

Wooten, Dudley G., ed. *A Comprehensive History of Texas, 1865 to 1897.* 2 vols. Dallas, Tex., 1898.

ANNE J. BAILEY

TRANSPORTATION

Transportation routes in the antebellum South developed mainly to get cash crops out to the seaports, to bring in manufactured goods from the Northeast, and to bring in grain from the Middle West. Transportation was geared more toward providing access to local markets than toward binding sections of the country together or facilitating rapid transport of military forces, as the great highways of the Roman Empire had done.

In the early days drovers would move herds of cattle and hogs along trails and primitive roads over the mountains to eastern markets, negotiating with farmers along the way to allow the animals to feed in their cornfields. Later the railroads took over most of this business. But the greatest stimulus to railroad building in the South came from the competition of seaport cities whose merchants were anxious to improve their trade.

Major rivers carried products from the hinterlands to the sea, and roads and railroads tended to supplement that movement without major redirections of the flow of traffic. Few major interstate highways were to be found. The South for the most part resisted the canal-building craze that spread across the North. It participated to an extent in the great railroad building of the 1850s, but only on a small fraction of the scale and still with few long-distance lines.

In 1850 if a man wanted to travel from Richmond to New Orleans, for instance, he could go by a series of railroads from Richmond to Wilmington, North Carolina, in twenty-one hours for $8.40. From Wilmington he would take a steamboat for a sixteen-hour voyage to Charleston at a fare of $6.00. Thence he would take a railroad train to Atlanta, with a change in Augusta. There he would have to take a stagecoach for twenty-four hours to the town of Chehaw on the Alabama border and then a railroad again to Montgomery. Now came a long leg of 200 miles that took thirty-six hours by stagecoach to reach Mobile. He would make the final leg of 175 miles to New Orleans by steamboat. The whole trip of about 1,460 miles would take seven days at a cost of about $56.00.

In 1861 it was possible to go by rail all the way from Richmond to New Orleans by way of Abingdon, Knoxville, Chattanooga, Decatur, Alabama, and Corinth and Jackson, Mississippi. But there still was no rail connection between Texas and the Mississippi, and none for Arkansas except a short line from Madison.

Similar obstacles blocked travel by highways and waterways, although in 1850 one could travel by main roads and turnpikes from Washington to New Orleans or from Nashville to Augusta. Improvements of the waterways went little beyond clearing snags from the rivers.

The attitude in the South was one of hostility toward internal improvements at the expense of the general government. In 1856, when Congress passed an internal improvements bill that included $100,000 for clearing impediments to navigation on the Mississippi, and another $50,000 for the Tennessee, it was over the strong opposition of Southern leaders who insisted that the locales and the users should pay for their own improvements.

Indeed the Confederate Constitution forbade appropriations for internal improvements. It stated: "Neither this, nor any other clause contained in the Constitution, shall ever be construed to delegate the power to Congress to appropriate money for any internal improvement intended to facilitate commerce." The only exceptions were for lights and buoys on the coasts, the improvement of harbors, and the removal of obstructions in the rivers, but in all cases the users were to be taxed to pay the costs.

When war came in 1861, the whole Southern transportation system suffered and then broke under the strain. The advance of Federal armies and river flotillas gained control of the Cumberland and Tennessee rivers and then of the Mississippi for its entire length. In his campaign to Atlanta and then the marches to Savannah and to Goldsboro, William Tecumseh Sherman wrought havoc with the railroads in his path. Cotton could not be moved out to market, and many farmers planted corn instead. But much of what did not fall to the enemy remained in the granaries for want of horses and wagons and railroads and boats. Local roads fell into such disrepair as to be almost impassable for wagons, but most of the wagons and horses were with the armies anyway.

Railroads deteriorated further with each month of war. There was no iron to repair the tracks. There were no new cars or locomotives to replace worn rolling stock. The army itself was hard pressed to keep up supplies of food, ammunition, and replacement weapons with the altogether insufficient means of transportation in the country to support it.

The U.S. Congress in 1862 passed an act that authorized the president to take possession of the railroads whenever he considered that the situation demanded it. The Confederates were reluctant to do this. Not until February 28, 1865, did the Confederate Congress approve such a measure, and then it was a broad one. Although coming at a time when it could have little practical effect, it gave the secretary of war power to put navigation and railroad companies under military officers and to provide assistance to secure their efficiency.

[*See also* Horses and Mules; Railroads; Waterways.]

BIBLIOGRAPHY

The American Heritage Pictorial Atlas of United States History. New York, 1966.

Black, C. F. *The Railroads of the Confederacy.* Chapel Hill, N.C., 1952.

Dunbar, Seymour. *A History of Travel in America.* Indianapolis, 1915.

Hunter, Louis C. *Steamboats on the Western Rivers.* Cambridge, Mass., 1969.

Parsons, Lewis B. *Rail and River Army Transportation in the Civil War.* St. Louis, Mo., 1899.

Randall, J. G., and David Donald. *The Civil War and Reconstruction.* Boston, 1961.

Turner, George Edgar. *Victory Rode the Rails.* Indianapolis, 1953.

JAMES A. HUSTON

TREASURY DEPARTMENT

The Confederate Treasury Department was created by the Provisional Congress on February 21, 1861, at Montgomery, Alabama. The department then moved to Richmond, Virginia. Its operations in Richmond were hindered because, from 1863 on, all the able-bodied men were frequently called out for military duty. At such times, the dispatch of business slowed to a crawl. The department ceased to exist after the evacuation of Richmond on April 2, 1865.

Next to the War Department, the Treasury was the most important arm of the government. It not only collected and dispersed all the government's funds, but its payment or non-payment of the War Department's bills meant the difference between success and defeat.

The department was a copy of that existing in Washington. It comprised the secretary, the assistant secretary, the chief clerk, the treasurer, the register, the comptroller, an auditor, and their staffs. This force totaled roughly one hundred persons at the seat of government and seven hundred more at the ports and mints. Many of these persons had Washington experience, and some brought with them sets of the Federal Treasury forms. Thus, within a few weeks, the Confederate Treasury was organized with an invaluable continuity of bureaucratic procedure and experience. By 1864, the Treasury had one thousand employees in Richmond and two thousand in the field offices.

The key figure in the department was the secretary, an office occupied by Christopher G. Memminger from February 21, 1861, until June 15, 1864, when he was succeeded by George Trenholm. The secretary was responsible for his department's efficient operation, and he had to prepare for Congress the government's recommendations for financial legislation.

The assistant secretary was the department's special projects officer and the acting secretary in the absence of his chief. This post was filled in February 1861 by Philip Clayton, who had been Howell Cobb's assistant secretary. His unbusinesslike practices forfeited the confidence of his chief, and he was dismissed in 1863. He was replaced by William W. Crump, who served until 1865.

The Office of the Treasurer was headed by Edward C. Ellmore from March 1861 until October 1, 1864, when he was succeeded by John N. Hendren. The treasurer received, held, and dispersed Confederate government funds, signed all but the post office warrants, and kept records of all receipts and disbursements. He signed, together with the register, the first Confederate notes.

The treasurer also supervised the Treasury Note Bureau. This bureau was headed by Thompson Allen until it was split into two parts in May 1862; one division, which printed the notes, moved to Columbia, South Carolina. The other, which signed, numbered, clipped, packed, and shipped the notes, remained in Richmond. The Columbia bureau was headed by Joseph Daniel Pope until April 1863, when he was succeeded by Charles F. Hanckel. The Richmond bureau was headed by Sanders G. Jamison until September 1864, when the two parts were reunited in Columbia and Jamison resumed sole control. The bureau broke up with the fall of Columbia in February 1865.

The printers required close supervision because they were short of men and supplies and were far more interested in their profits than in the proper execution of their contracts. In addition, there were obstructions to getting treasury

> ## Next to the War Department, the Treasury was the most important arm of the government.

notes and securities to Richmond because of a shortage of trains and couriers. This delayed the preparation and distribution of the treasury notes, which in turn prevented the government from making urgently needed military payments.

The Treasury Note Bureau in Richmond had to number and sign twice over eighty million notes, requiring a staff of nearly three hundred clerks. Because of the manpower shortage, Secretary Memminger hired women to perform these tasks.

A related bureau was the Office of the Register, headed by Alexander B. Clitherall in early 1861 and subsequently by Robert Charles Tyler, from August 13, 1861, on. The register was responsible for appointing individuals to countersign the treasury notes and to keep registers of those emitted and canceled. The register's staff had to number every Confederate bond and to sign the coupons on each of over

800,000 bonds. In 1864 the register's signature was printed on each coupon. The register was also required to sign all warrants, transfer drafts, coupon bonds, registered bonds, and call certificates. This paperwork load resulted in the designation of Charles T. Jones, Tyler's chief clerk (another Washington veteran), as acting register and the appointment of two assistant registers in early 1863.

The duty to audit claims and accounts devolved upon the comptroller. This office was occupied throughout the war by Louis Cruger, who had held a similar position in Washington. In performing his duties, Cruger was required to adjust and preserve the public accounts, to examine all accounts and certify the balances to the register, to countersign all the warrants drawn by the secretary, to report the collection of the customs and export duties to the secretary, and to provide for the payment of all moneys collected. Finally, he was to sue delinquent officers or debtors and to rule on all claims made against the Confederacy. To perform these tasks, Cruger was furnished with twenty clerks and one messenger. His work force had increased to thirty-two clerks by 1864, in five sections: those covering civil expenses, the War Department, canceled treasury notes, deceased soldiers' claims, and the bookkeepers.

The first auditor of the treasury, Bolling Baker, who had held that post in Washington, was initially responsible for auditing all the government's accounts. By 1864 he had fifty-three employees who were assigned to six divisions covering the customs service, the navy, the interest on the public debt, taxes, funding, and a miscellaneous section.

To reduce Baker's work load, the office of second auditor was created on March 16, 1861, and Walter H. S. Taylor, a former U.S. Treasury clerk, was appointed to the post. He was responsible solely for the War Department's accounts. To perform this duty, he was assigned 40 clerks, which by 1864 had become 158 persons working in seven divisions—bookkeeping, claims, pay, ordinance, engineer and medical, quartermaster, and subsistence expenses.

In 1864, the position of third auditor was created. That officer dealt exclusively with the voluminous post office accounts.

The Lighthouse Bureau was a small office carried over from the Federal government. It supervised the operation of lighthouses in twenty-nine districts from Tappahannock, Virginia, to Padre Island, Texas. The outbreak of hostilities and the suppression of most of the lighthouses left this bureau largely dormant.

There were two bureaus created after the war began. The first of these was the Produce Loan Bureau. The Produce Loan Bureau was supervised during the provisional government by James D. B. De Bow. The register then took over until May 1, 1863, when Archibald Roane became Produce Loan Bureau manager. He supervised produce loan agents in each state and insured that all government cotton was safe-guarded and all food products were handed over to the army commissary department.

The office of the commissioner of taxes was created in 1863. This position was filled by Thompson Allen, another man with Washington experience. In addition to supervising his staff both in Richmond and the field offices, he issued regulations, advised the secretary in tax matters and furnished the Congress with reports and recommendations.

In addition to the officials located at Richmond, there were officials located throughout the Confederacy. The Treasury was fortunate that the personnel at the mints and customs houses stayed at their posts after secession. The secretary therefore did not have to train employees to perform routine government functions. The field offices were located at three sites: the lighthouses, the customs houses, and the mints.

The customs houses were mostly located along the coast and the Mexican border. This service was divided into twenty-five districts, employing approximately six hundred officials. With the proclamation of the blockade and the loss of several ports, there were considerable reductions in this work force. At the same time, because of the increase of trade with Mexico, more officials were posted to that frontier. The remaining officials found it difficult to regulate trade or collect a revenue from it. For example, the export duty on cotton was collected on only a fifth of the bales that left the ports or went overland to Mexico.

A large prewar force was employed by the mints at New Orleans, Dahlonega, and Charlotte. The Confederacy did not have a Bureau of the Mint to coordinate mint activities, and the shortage of supplies needed for minting operations resulted in Charlotte and Dahlonega being reduced to the status of assay offices. The mint in New Orleans was captured on April 25, 1862.

If the previously existing field offices atrophied, new branches burgeoned. The receipt and payment of vast sums for taxes, loans, and government expenses necessitated an expansion of the treasurer's offices. Anthony J. Guirot, formerly the treasurer of the New Orleans mint, was made assistant treasurer on May 11, 1861. Forced to flee from New Orleans in 1862, he was driven from one city to another, ending up at Mobile.

A second assistant treasurer's office was created in Charleston. Later, because of the siege, it relocated to Columbia.

In addition to the two assistant treasurers, there were depositories located throughout the Confederacy. Although there was usually only one office per city, multiple offices existed in Richmond, Wilmington, Charleston, Mobile, and Jackson. There were two kinds of depositories: those that paid out funds ("pay depositories" of which there were usually only two or three per state), and those used only to fund notes ("funding depositories").

Secretary Memminger was slow to establish depositories prior to 1863. The 1864 funding records suggest that had a comprehensive system of depositories been set up in 1861, a considerably larger amount of currency would have been funded at an earlier date.

Most of the depositaries were bank officers, but in Florida, Arkansas, Mississippi, and Texas, the Treasury hired local financiers. There were approximately two hundred depositories, and the Confederate government's ability to supervise their operations or furnish them with standardized forms was limited. For example, after the loss of the Mississippi Valley, the secretary of the treasury was cut off from the Trans-Mississippi Department. As a result, in November 1864, the Treasury was largely ignorant of the names and locations of its agents in that area.

In 1861, when the produce loan idea was first broached, large numbers of citizens volunteered to serve as agents. But there were no agents west of the Mississippi River, and the government put this volunteer effort on a more professional basis in early 1862. Agents were given formal appointments and commissions on subscriptions allowed.

When the Confederate Congress authorized the secretary to purchase cotton with bonds under the act of April 14, 1862, the government created the Produce Loan Bureau, appointing one full-time agent with a staff for each state. These agents collected and safeguarded the produce subscribed, donated, or later collected as part of the tithe tax. These duties proved increasingly onerous as Federal armies captured or compelled the destruction of the government's cotton. The absence of proper bagging and the collapse of the transportation system resulted in much waste.

The last group of field offices were those of the Confederate tax collectors. Under the war tax of August 19, 1861, the secretary was authorized to appoint a chief collec-

> **Most of the depositaries were bank officers, but in Florida, Arkansas, Mississippi, and Texas, the Treasury hired local financiers.**

tor for each state, who in turn appointed a collector and one or more assessors for each county. These persons were to secure appraisals or declarations on all property and then forward a consolidated local report to the chief collector, who furnished a statewide valuation to the Treasury.

The tax machinery created in 1861–1862 then lapsed, and a new tax collection system had to be created for the act of April 24, 1863. Under that law, collectors were appointed for each congressional district, with a collector having one or more assistants. This tax force came to less than five hundred persons.

Taken as a whole, the Treasury Department proved reasonably efficient. The deficiencies of Secretary Memminger, however, particularly in fiscal policy formulation, his governance of the Treasury printers, his mismanagement of the Produce Loan Bureau, and his refusal to collect a specie reserve, reduced the department's effectiveness.

[*See also overview article on* Currency; Produce Loan; Taxation; *biographies of Christopher G. Memminger and George Trenholm.*]

BIBLIOGRAPHY

Capers, Henry D. *The Life and Times of C. G. Memminger.* Richmond, 1893.

Ryan, Carmelita S., comp. *Preliminary Inventory of the Treasury Department Collection of Confederate Records.* Washington, D.C., 1967.

Todd, Richard C. *Confederate Finance.* Atlanta, 1954.

DOUGLAS B. BALL

TREDEGAR IRON WORKS

The Tredegar Iron Works in Richmond, Virginia, the largest industrial base in the South at the beginning of the Civil War, was the only facility capable of producing major ordnance, iron plate, and iron products in 1861. During the war, other ironworks were developed in the lower South, but Tredegar remained the leading ordnance producer and served as a model for further Southern industrialization.

Francis B. Deane, a Richmond businessman, with a group of partners combined a forge, rolling mill, and foundry in the mid-1830s, initiating the Tredegar operations. The company was officially incorporated by the Virginia legislature on February 27, 1837. (Its name derives from ironworks in Tredegar, Wales.) In 1841, sluggish sales and indebtedness induced company directors to accept a proposal by Joseph Reid Anderson that he become the company's commercial agent. Anderson, a West Point graduate and a state engineer for turnpike construction, brought in new investments and provided favorable sales management. He became a leaseholder of the entire company in 1843, and after five years he purchased the company outright from stockholders for $125,000.

In the 1850s the Tredegar Iron Works increased in capacity, and Anderson maintained high quality in order to secure U.S. government contracts for its products. The company diversified its output and used varied partnerships for its different operations in an attempt to promote good management and increase expertise. By 1859, Anderson had merged with an adjacent munitions works run by his in-laws, bought off some old partners, and consolidated remaining ones as Joseph R. Anderson and Company. By this time also, the Tredegar Works was attracting wider markets in the South and was recognized as the largest industrial complex south of the Potomac River.

When the Confederacy was established, Anderson and his partners supported it wholeheartedly. The company severed all trade and sales in the North and concentrated on supplying orders from seceding states for ordnance and munitions. By the end of 1861 Tredegar's work force had grown from 350 free and slave laborers in 1853 to nearly 1,000 men, of whom 10 percent were slaves.

Labor problems in the company had existed since its early days. Anderson in the 1840s increased the firm's use of slave labor, which in 1847 precipitated a strike of white workers who sought to eliminate their black competition. Their demands were overridden by Anderson, and the black labor force—some free, some slave—continued to increase with Tredegar's expansion. But since slaves had to be fed, clothed, and housed on the premises, their use failed to reduce production costs significantly. Nevertheless, black labor proved more and more essential as some Northern and foreign workers departed the company at war's start, and by early 1863, with more skilled labor drawn away for military duty, blacks constituted one-half of Tredegar's 2,000 workers.

As the war got underway, longer-term contracts between the Tredegar Iron Works and the Confederacy's War and Navy departments took the place of orders from individual states, although those from the private railroad system continued. The Confederacy never took over railroads, but very early it moved to centralize and coordinate the securing of war supplies. Steady orders from the government prompted the expansion of Tredegar's rolling mill and ordnance facilities and was further encouraged by the Confederacy's promise of annual financial backing. What the government could not do was live up to its promise to supply all the pig iron and coal that Tredegar's operations needed. In April 1862 the Confederate Congress allowed the War and Navy departments to provide loans to Tredegar to expand the company's pig iron and fuel sources, and new blast furnaces were opened up. Further assistance proved to be very limited, however, and despite Tredegar's wartime growth, its operations remained at only one-third its full capacity throughout the war.

By the years 1863 and 1864 new ironworks at Selma, Alabama, and elsewhere in the lower South, as well as facilities set up by Confederate bureaus, created further difficulties for Tredegar by competing for scarce resources. The Confederacy's industrial thrust, as expansive as it seemed, was slowed by the lack of raw materials. This disadvantage, coupled with the poor distribution service of its rail system, was an ominous portent for the government's survival.

At the outset of the war Joseph Anderson had offered to turn the Tredegar Works over to the Confederate government for lease or purchase, which was rejected in favor of sustaining private business. Increasingly, Anderson and his partners, whose commitment to Southern independence never faltered, complained that the government's control over the prices it would pay for war supplies left Tredegar with no profit margin. The situation worsened in the last year of the war as government payments fell short. In April 1865, the government still owed almost $1 million to the Tredegar Iron Works.

The company had in the early years fulfilled much of its industrial potential, supplying the big guns for the Confederacy before 1863, as well as iron plate for ironclads (e.g., *Merrimac*'s conversion to *Virginia*), munitions, and other war products. It had even participated in experimental developments of submarines and torpedoes and the modernization of naval weapons and machine guns. But by war's end, the insurmountable problems of skilled labor shortages, the depletion of basic raw materials, and the failure to obtain adequate provisions for Tredegar workers had drastically hampered the firm's high-quality productivity.

Near the end of the war Anderson once again offered the Tredegar Works for lease to the government, but it was too late. The Tredegar Battalion, a militia of employees established in 1861, guarded the company's physical plant against rampage when the Confederacy collapsed in April 1865. With the fall of Richmond the Tredegar Iron Works remained intact, though occupied by Union troops for a short while. The company partners feared confiscation of the firm's property under Federal law, and Anderson immediately sought a way to resume operations, underscoring Tredegar's readiness for production and employment. Private meetings with President Andrew Johnson resulted in personal pardons for Anderson and his partners in September 1865. The company reorganized in 1867 with Anderson continuing as president.

Anderson earlier had hedged against future loss or collapse by engaging in blockade running for consumer goods from Europe. Profit from those sales had provided him with the means to maintain a separate London bank account. The London sterling deposits plus additional investments, including some from Northern financiers, enabled the Tredegar Works to move from the leading wartime producer of ordnance for the Confederacy to peacetime operations assisting in the renewal of the South's commerce and industry.

But Tredegar's heyday as the South's major industrial complex was over. Financial ties with a failing New York railroad operation during the panic of 1873 forced the company into receivership, with Joseph Anderson serving as receiver until 1879. Moreover, iron production was rapidly giving way to steel production, and Tredegar could not afford to shift operations to steel. What had once been a great model for Southern industrialization had receded to a more modest operation, which was carried on at the site until 1958.

BIBLIOGRAPHY

Beringer, Richard E., Herman Hattaway, Archer Jones, and William N. Still, Jr. *Why the South Lost the Civil War.* Athens, Ga., 1986.

Bruce, Kathleen. *Virginia Iron Manufacture in the Slave Era.* New York, 1931.

Daniels, Larry J. "Manufacturing Cannon in the Confederacy." *Civil War Times Illustrated* 12 (November 1973): 4–10, 40–46.

Dew, Charles B. *Ironmaker to the Confederacy: Joseph R. Anderson and the Tredegar Iron Works.* New Haven, Conn., 1966.

Tredegar Company Records. Virginia State Library, Richmond, Virginia.

FREDERICK SCHULT

TRENHOLM, GEORGE

TRENHOLM, GEORGE 1807–1876), merchant and secretary of the treasury. George Alfred Trenholm was born on February 25, 1807, at Charleston, South Carolina. After his father's death in 1822, he went to work for John Fraser and Company, a firm engaged in shipping and factoring Sea Island cotton. Trenholm's progress was rapid. In 1836, he succeeded his employer as a director of the Bank of Charleston, the largest bank in South Carolina. He was elected to the legislature (1852–1856), and by 1860 he was a rich man. His personal assets, and those of his firm, consisted of plantations, slaves, warehouses, wharves, ships, and substantial investments. The company had branches in New York (Trenholm Brothers) and Liverpool (Fraser, Trenholm). Trenholm's reputation for integrity assured him of almost unlimited credit.

In a private capacity, Trenholm faithfully served the Confederacy. He built and donated to South Carolina the gunboat *Chicora*. In addition, he worked on the Board of Commissioners fortifying Charleston. He also expanded his fleet until by 1864, his firm either owned or held under charter fifty ships. He used these not to import high-priced luxury goods for profit but to bring in urgently needed military supplies and items for the Confederate civilian market. When James M. Mason and John Slidell, the Confederate commissioners, were unable to get out of Charleston because of the blockade, Trenholm personally leased a ship at half price to convey the two diplomats to Havana.

Nor did his services end there. A personal friend of Secretary of the Treasury Christopher G. Memminger, he provided both practical aid and sound advice in the management of the Confederacy's financial affairs. Starting in April 1861, the firm of Fraser, Trenholm became the government's financial agent in Europe. That office furnished cash advances to the Confederate procurement agents, who otherwise would have been seriously delayed in securing supplies for the army. This relationship was formalized by an act dated November 26, 1861.

Recognizing the importance of furnishing the government with the means for exporting its own produce and importing urgently needed supplies, Trenholm sent his son William to Montgomery in May 1861 to propose the purchase by the government of one or both of two available British shipping lines. The cabinet and President Jefferson Davis rejected this idea, thereby doing serious injury to the Confederate cause.

Trenholm was frustrated on other blockade-related issues. He strongly urged the government to stop the Committees of Safety from inhibiting cotton exports. The government, however, refused to confront the committees, preferring instead to deal with the situation one problem at a time. Trenholm also tried to lease ships on the government's behalf, but his efforts to promote exports of Treasury-owned cotton failed because Memminger blocked the procurement of the requisite cotton.

Trenholm also advised Memminger that it was vital to make treasury notes the South's currency. With that aim in view, Trenholm organized and attended a bankers' convention in June 1861. The meeting was adjourned to Richmond from July 24 to 26, 1861, when the banks agreed to receive and pay out Confederate treasury notes, thereby ensuring a nationwide demand for them.

Moreover, Trenholm was also behind the series of laws passed in February 1864 that provided for stringent controls over imports and exports, the acquisition of government ships, and the preemption of cargo space on the government's account to export cotton and import supplies needed by the army. Had this program been enacted in 1861, as Trenholm had originally proposed, the Treasury would have been strengthened, the army better supplied, and the Confederacy's economic deterioration mitigated.

Disgusted by the uncooperative attitude of the Confederate Congress and its mismanagement of the economy, Trenholm urged Memminger to resign, which he did on June 15, 1864. Much to Trenholm's surprise, President Davis then offered to appoint him secretary of the treasury. Trenholm reluctantly accepted this position on July 18, 1864.

At the time he took office, Trenholm confronted a bankrupt Treasury. He tried to educate the public and win the respect of the congressmen. But he was unable to induce them to pass better legislation, and this soon led to disaster. In November 1864, Trenholm found that the Treasury was over $360 million in arrears in its payments for the army. These arrears undermined the troops' morale and resulted in mass desertions. Trenholm did his best to prevent this by selling off government coin and cotton and even donated $200,000 himself.

Evacuating Richmond on April 2, 1865, Trenholm fled south. By April 27, however, he was so ill he had to resign his post. Accompanied by his son William, Trenholm rejoined his family in Columbia. There he remained under house arrest until June 21, when he was instructed to report to the provost marshal at Charleston.

Arriving with a valise containing the assets of his firm, which he planned to give to its trustees, Trenholm and William were arrested and escorted to jail. There he was told he was to be imprisoned and his assets sequestered. Ordered to leave, William calmly walked out with the bag containing the John Fraser assets. The elder Trenholm went to Fort Pulaski, from which, on October 11, 1865, he was released on parole.

The remaining eleven years of Trenholm's life were devoted to salvaging his personal affairs. The U.S. government sued Fraser, Trenholm for the former Confederate assets the firm had used to offset its claims against the Confederacy. Defeated in the British courts and assessed costs, the Federal government then filed immense claims against Trenholm and his firm in Charleston, seeking penalties and interest for nonpayment of customs dues. As a result of this and bad cotton crops, Trenholm's firms went bankrupt. Nonetheless, by 1874, he was once more a wealthy man. As a token of respect, Charlestonians lowered their flags to half-mast following his death on December 10, 1876.

BIBLIOGRAPHY

Patrick, Rembert W. *Jefferson Davis and His Cabinet.* New York, 1961.
Todd, Richard Cecil. *Confederate Finance.* Atlanta, 1954.

DOUGLAS B. BALL

TRENT AFFAIR

On October 12, 1861, newly appointed Confederate commissioners James Mason and John Slidell boarded the steamer CSS *Theodora* in Charleston, South Carolina. Their mission was to secure recognition for the Confederate States of America in both England and France and find military supplies and negotiate commercial trading agreements that would support the newly declared country. *Theodora* carried Mason and Slidell safely through the Union blockading squadron off Charleston and then to Nassau in the Bahamas. Unable to find immediate passage to Europe from Nassau, the Confederate commissioners were taken on to Cuba aboard *Theodora.* After several weeks of socializing and being entertained by the governor of Cuba, Mason and Slidell booked passage to England on the royal mail steamship *Trent* on November 8, 1861. Both men assumed their voyage on *Trent* would be protected by international laws that guaranteed the sovereignty of every nation's ves-

sels. As a consequence they made no effort to conceal their plans.

When word of their voyage reached Capt. Charles Wilkes aboard USS *San Jacinto* at Cienfuegos, he decided to intervene. After a serious examination of the potential consequences and consultation with the U.S. consul general, Wilkes decided to intercept *Trent* and capture Mason and Slidell. On November 8, Captain Wilkes discovered the British steamer 240 miles east of Havana. Against legal council Wilkes fired a shell across *Trent*'s bow, forcing the ship to stop, and brought *San Jacinto* alongside. Over the

> **Wilkes decided to intercept *Trent* and capture Mason and Slidell.**

protests of Capt. James Moir, an armed crew from *San Jacinto* forcibly removed Mason and Slidell. As *Trent* steamed on to St. Thomas, Captain Wilkes headed for Hampton Roads, Virginia. There he took on coal and telegraphed the secretary of the navy of his intent to sail for Boston. Upon arrival there Wilkes received orders from Secretary of State William H. Seward to take the prisoners to Fort Warren in Boston Harbor for detention.

News of Wilkes's seizure of the Confederate commissioners was greeted with enthusiasm throughout the Union. At a time when the fortunes of war appeared to favor the Confederacy, the event was perceived as something of a military victory over the South if not also Great Britain. Northern newspapers generally reflected the public opinion. With the exception of newspapers in some northeastern cities that would be vulnerable in the event of hostilities with Great Britain, most viewed the incident as Wilkes's victory and glossed over or denied the impact of potential political repercussions. Regardless of international consequences, the press expressed a consensus that the captives should not be surrendered. Many editorialized that Captain Wilkes had not done anything more serious than the British had on numerous occasions. The *Philadelphia Sunday Dispatch* commented that Britain could hardly protest "a good old English practice" of search and seizure. Union leaders, however, were divided in their feelings. Seward was reported to be "elated," but Abraham Lincoln was concerned that the British reaction would provide political support for the Confederacy. It was clear that the Union was in no position to risk angering the European community. At the same time Lincoln did not want to dampen much-needed enthusiasm in the North. Instead of adopting an antagonistic position, he waited for Britain to officially react to the incident.

In the Confederacy Wilkes's forcible removal of Mason and Slidell was received with both indignation and satisfaction. Southerners were outraged by the United States's blatant disregard for the sovereignty of a British vessel and the seizing of duly appointed commissioners of the Confederate States of America. At the same time they appear to have been as elated about the incident as Northern supporters of Wilkes. Many felt that the affair would advance the South's cause by generating support for British recognition of the Confederacy. Southern newspapers were as vocal on the issue as those of the North. The *Richmond Enquirer* stated that Great Britain would find it impossible to accept the "disgrace," and the *Atlanta Southern Confederacy* called the *Trent* affair "one of the most fortunate things for our cause." Secretary of War Judah P. Benjamin agreed with the *Southern Confederacy.* Many officials felt the crisis would lead Great Britain into a war with the United States and thus assist the Confederate bid for independence.

Relations between Great Britain and the United States had frequently been strained prior to the Civil War. The rebellion in Canada; disputed boundaries between Maine, Oregon, and Canada; the acquisition of Texas and California; competing interests in Central America; and American reaction to British recruiting in the United States during the Crimean War all contributed to the impression that Americans were a disagreeable sort at best. Lincoln's selection of William H. Seward to head the State Department had reinforced British apprehension, as Seward was on occasion highly antagonistic toward Great Britain. The situation did not improve when Queen Victoria issued a proclamation of neutrality in May 1861. The seizure of Mason and Slidell appeared to bring many festering issues to a head. Though British newspapers admitted that "the honor of England" was "tarnished" and the injustice should be resolved, some were willing to admit that the United States had done nothing more than Great Britain had on previous occasions.

Richard B. Pemell, the second Lord Lyons and Her Majesty's minister to the United States, suggested possible courses of action. The first was to clearly establish that Britain would not condone violations of its sovereignty. Lord Lyons also suggested that the threat of war warranted the reinforcement of Canada and the strengthening of naval squadrons in the Atlantic, Pacific, and West Indies. He was of the opinion that Britain should act in concert with France in responding to the affair and to resist offering aid to the South but not reject their envoys. The French minister of foreign affairs, Antoine Edouard Thouvenel, confirmed that though France was not directly involved, the government viewed the incident as a breach of international law.

The gravity of the *Trent* affair was evident in the creation of a War Committee in the British cabinet. The committee members considered their options and, after determining that Wilkes's act was illegal, contemplated preparing for war with the United States. At the same time they approved a dispatch drafted by Lord John Russell to be delivered in Washington by Lord Lyons. Great Britain was willing to concede that Wilkes may have acted on his own or had misunderstood his orders, but the prisoners had to be released and a public apology issued. For Britain the matter was one of national honor. Lord Lyons was to give Lincoln and his government seven days to respond to the communication. If a satisfactory answer was not received within that time, Lyons was to break off relations with the United States and return with his staff to England.

President Lincoln's initial reaction to the British note was immediate rejection. News of it set off waves of public protest and heated debate in Congress. In spite of intense popular opinion and congressional pressure, Lincoln eventually yielded to Seward's argument that the United States could not risk war with Great Britain at a time when suppression of the rebellion and major financial problems were paramount. After lengthy consideration of the matter, Lincoln and his cabinet agreed that the prisoners must be released and a satisfactory apology issued to Great Britain. Seward drafted a complex and rambling document that affirmed that Wilkes had indeed acted without orders and that by "voluntarily" intercepting *Trent* he had committed an illegal act for which Britain justifiably deserved reparations. On January 1, 1862, amid public protests, Slidell and Mason were released and transported aboard HMS *Rinaldo* to Bermuda, where they boarded the vessel *La Plata* and continued their voyage to Britain. The *Trent* crisis had been resolved after an intense two months of negotiations and compromise. In Great Britain and France, Mason and Slidell served the Confederate States of America until the end of the war, but failed to secure official recognition of the new government.

The *Trent* affair was the most serious crisis of diplomacy faced by the United States during the Civil War. Although resolved to the mutual satisfaction of the United States and Great Britain, the issues associated with the affair complicated diplomacy well into the twentieth century. The problems of neutral and belligerent rights, search and seizure at sea, the nature of contraband and government dispatches, the legal status of mail ships, transport of military and civilian belligerents, and diplomatic privileges and immunities demanded international consideration but defied immediate and concise definition.

[*See also* Mason, James M.; Slidell, John.]

BIBLIOGRAPHY

Adams, Ephram Douglass. *Great Britain and the Civil War.* 2 vols. New York, 1958.

Callahan, James Morton. *Diplomatic History of the Southern Confederacy.* Springfield, Mass., 1957.

Cullop, Charles P. *Confederate Propaganda in Europe, 1861–1865.* Coral Gables, Fla., 1969.

Ferris, Norman B. *Desperate Diplomacy: William H. Seward's Foreign Policy, 1861.* Knoxville, Tenn., 1976.

Ferris, Norman B. *The Trent Affair: A Diplomatic Crisis.* Knoxville, Tenn., 1977.

Jenkins, Brian. *Britain and the War for the Union.* 2 vols. Montreal, Canada, 1974, 1980.

Owsley, Frank Lawrence. *King Cotton Diplomacy: Foreign Relations of the Confederate States of America.* 2d ed. Chicago, 1959.

Warren, Gordon H. *Fountain of Discontent: The* Trent *Affair and Freedom of the Seas.* Boston, 1981.

GORDON WATTS

TRIMBLE, ISAAC

TRIMBLE, ISAAC (1802–1888), major general. Regarded as the most prominent soldier contributed by Maryland to the Southern cause, Isaac Ridgeway Trimble was born May 15, 1802, in Culpeper, Virginia. He graduated from West Point in 1822 and spent ten years as an artillery officer. Trimble then left the army and devoted almost three decades to railroad construction, much of it in his adopted state of Maryland.

In April 1861, as commander of Baltimore defenses, Trimble burned a number of bridges north of the city to impede passage of Federal troops en route to Washington. The next month he accepted a colonelcy of engineers in Virginia forces and helped in the construction of Norfolk's

ISAAC TRIMBLE.   LIBRARY OF CONGRESS

defensive works. Following his appointment on August 9, 1861, as a Confederate brigadier general, Trimble took command of a brigade in Richard S. Ewell's division. He was, a fellow officer stated, "a veteran in years but with the fire and aggressiveness of youth."

Dependable service in Jackson's Shenandoah Valley and the Seven Days' campaigns ended momentarily at Second Manassas when a Federal bullet shattered Trimble's left knee. On January 17, 1863, while still recuperating from his wound, Trimble received advancement to major general. He returned to duty, but on July 3, 1863, while leading two North Carolina brigades in the Pickett-Pettigrew charge, Trimble again was shot in the left leg. Dr. Hunter McGuire amputated the limb the next day. Unable to travel, Trimble surrendered to Union authorities. He endured imprisonment at Johnson's Island and Fort Warren before his February 1865 release.

After the war, and equipped with an artificial leg, Trimble resumed his engineering work. He resided in Baltimore, where he died January 2, 1888. He is one of five Confederate generals buried in that city's Green Mount Cemetery.

BIBLIOGRAPHY

Grace, William M. "Isaac Ridgeway Trimble: The Indefatigable and Courageous." M.A. thesis, Virginia Polytechnic Institute and State University, 1984.

Manakee, Harold R. *Maryland in the Civil War.* Baltimore, Md., 1961.

Trimble, Isaac R. "The Civil War Diary of General Isaac Ridgeway Trimble." *Maryland Historical Magazine* 18 (1922): 1–20.

JAMES I. ROBERTSON, JR.

TUBMAN, HARRIET

TUBMAN, HARRIET (1820 or 1821–1913), Union spy and abolitionist. Tubman was born on a plantation in Dorchester County, Maryland. One of the eleven children born to her slave parents, Harriet Green and Benjamin Ross, she was given the name Araminta. The young slave girl suffered whippings and beatings and sustained a life-threatening head injury in her teens. At the age of twenty-three she married a free black, John Tubman.

In 1849 when her owner died, she escaped into freedom (leaving her husband behind when he refused to accompany her), took the name Harriet Tubman, and found work in Philadelphia. Within a year, she was involved in rescue attempts to free other family members and became an invaluable asset to the movement organized to assist slaves escaping to freedom. Braving the dangers, Tubman became one of the most intrepid conductors on the Underground Railroad. She moved to Canada in 1852, having made a total of eleven trips in three years, rescuing several dozen slaves.

Given the title "General Tubman" by abolitionist John Brown, Tubman became even more active when the Civil War broke out. For this reason, slave owners put a steep price on her head, and she was perhaps the most wanted woman in the Confederacy. Despite this threat, Tubman made nineteen more trips, leading nearly three hundred runaways out of the South. She worked out of Fortress Monroe, Virginia, before being sent to Beaufort, South Carolina, by the governor of Massachusetts. Under the command of Maj. Gen. David Hunter, Tubman was a scout and spy. During the summer of 1863 she assisted Col. James Montgomery in military campaigns designed to terrorize civilians and stir slaves into rebellion along the Combahee River. They were able to liberate nearly eight hundred slaves and effectively undermine Confederate morale in the South Carolina low country.

Tubman remained relatively impoverished, receiving only three hundred dollars for her three years of service to the Union. After the war she retired to Auburn, New York, and opened a Home for Indigent and Aged Negroes. She died in 1913 in relative obscurity, unheralded as a war hero until the modern era.

BIBLIOGRAPHY

Conrad, Earl. *Harriet Tubman*. Washington, D.C., 1990.
Sterling, Dorothy, ed. *We Are Your Sisters: Black Women in the Nineteenth Century.* New York, 1984.

CATHERINE CLINTON

TUPELO, MISSISSIPPI

In the spring of 1864, Gen. William Tecumseh Sherman was pushing his forces toward Atlanta and was concerned about his supply line, which ran through middle Tennessee. The supplies for his 100,000 men traveled over the Nashville and Chattanooga Railroad; its security had to be preserved. His primary fear was Gen. Nathan Bedford Forrest and his successful cavalry, then operating in Mississippi under the command of Gen. Stephen D. Lee. Forrest had a reputation for raiding and defeating formidable forces with limited resources.

Sherman respected Forrest's skill and in May deployed Gen. Samuel D. Sturgis from Memphis to seek out Forrest. Sturgis returned to Memphis when he could not locate the general, who was replenishing his forces in Tupelo, Mississippi, a town in the northeast part of the state. Forrest, under orders from Lee, soon left Tupelo to attack Sherman's supply lines. He did not get far before Sherman again ordered Sturgis to find and destroy him. This time, on June 10, Sturgis's cavalry commander, Gen. Benjamin H.

Grierson, met Forrest at Brice's Cross Roads, about thirty miles north of Tupelo. By noon, Forrest's outnumbered cavalry, armed with six-shot Colt revolvers, had defeated Grierson decisively, and the Federal troops fled, abandoning their supplies.

Now Sherman became even more determined to keep Forrest from interfering with his plans. This time he sent Gen. A. J. Smith, who happened to be in the same area as Forrest. Smith's orders were to "bring Forrest to bay and whip him if possible." Smith collected a force of 14,000 men, made up of

> ### Smith had plans to secure Tupelo and gain possession of the Mobile and Ohio Railroad. . . .

two infantry divisions, Grierson's cavalry, and a brigade of African American troops. They moved south July 5 on two parallel roads. Two days later the force was intercepted by troops sent out by Forrest. This time, the Southerners fled, and Smith moved toward Pontotoc, a town about twenty miles directly west of Tupelo.

The Confederate commanders, Generals Lee and Forrest, with a combined force of 8,000 men (about half the number commanded by Smith), hoped to choose the site for a battle while slowing the march of Smith's column with skirmishes. At Okolona, south of Pontotoc and Tupelo, the Confederates had deployed on a hill behind a swamp that was further obstructed by fallen trees. One of their brigades, under James Roland Chalmers, attacked the Federal forces east of Pontotoc. Because Lee and Forrest felt secure in Okolona, they wanted Smith to continue to move south. Smith hesitated after the attack. The Confederates thought he was starting a retreat and abandoned their secured location to pursue him. Smith, however, surprised them on July 13 by turning east toward Tupelo rather than continuing south toward Okolona. Actually, Smith had plans to secure Tupelo and gain possession of the Mobile and Ohio Railroad, which had been completed just before the war.

Forrest, with Hinchie P. Mabry's Mississippi Brigade, attacked Smith's rear on the Tupelo road. Lee, with Chalmers's and Abraham Buford's divisions, moved parallel to, but south of, Smith's troops. Twice on July 13, Lee attacked Smith's flank. The Confederate attacks were not well coordinated; Smith's brigade of African American troops, acting as a rear guard, successfully deflected Forrest's attempts, and Lee's flank attacks were ineffectual. Smith was able to position his troops for battle in Tupelo.

On the fourteenth, Lee ordered an assault. His troops attacked from the front while Forrest moved on the Union left and rear. Forrest later commented that Smith's fortifications were "almost impregnable." The Confederates made little progress against the enormous firepower of the Union forces. Soldiers repeatedly charged the fortifications only to meet bayonets and volleys at close range. The Mississippi summer heat also took a heavy toll. Yet Lee's forces continued to fall back, rally, and attack again and again, "yelling and howling like Comanches," according to Smith. About 1:00 Lee ordered the Confederates to fall back. They then withdrew and built a fortified position out of rails, logs, and bales of cotton. In the fighting many were killed or wounded. Forrest reported 210 killed, 1,116 wounded; in Mabry's Mississippi Brigade, all the commanders were killed or wounded. Smith suffered fewer casualties—77 killed, 559 wounded, and 38 missing. The Confederates would not give up; they attempted a rear attack and a late night attack at 11:00 P.M. Nothing was successful. Smith's forces remained in position.

Despite his success, Smith did not take the initiative. Forrest was able to rally his troops, and Smith began withdrawing toward Memphis because of a shortage of supplies. Forrest's men pursued and attacked at Old Town Creek. His cavalry outfought Grierson's, but the Confederates could do little against Smith's infantry. In the fighting Forrest received a "painful wound" and had to withdraw. Smith continued his retreat to Memphis, pursued by Confederate soldiers.

The Confederate forces suffered enormous losses; in Forrest's words, the battle would "furnish the historian a bloody record." He consoled himself, however, with the belief that Lee's forces had spared northeastern Mississippi an enormous amount of destruction that Smith would have inflicted had he been able to remain in the area. Also, Forrest was still capable of harassing the Union men.

The battle nevertheless was a costly draw. The Confederates suffered heavy casualties, but Smith failed to destroy Lee's and Forrest's army.

When Gen. Ulysses S. Grant heard of Smith's retreat and the Confederate loss, he wrote Sherman that the Union forces must "keep a close watch on Forrest, and not permit him to gather strength and move into Middle Tennessee." General Sherman was on his way to Atlanta when he got word of the results. Disappointed that Forrest was still capable of fighting and could still attack his supply line, he commanded Smith to "keep after Forrest."

BIBLIOGRAPHY

Bearss, Edwin C. *The Tupelo Campaign, June 22–July 23, 1864: A Documented Narrative and Troop Movement Maps.* Washington, D.C., 1969.
Lee, Stephen D. "The Battle of Tupelo." *Publications of the Mississippi Historical Society* 6 (1902): 38–52.
U.S. War Department. *War of the Rebellion: A Compilation of the Official Records of the Union and Confederate Armies.* Ser. 1, vol. 39, pts. 1–2. Washington, D.C., 1892.

RAY SKATES

TWIGGS, DAVID E.

TWIGGS, DAVID E. (1790–1862), major general. Born in 1790 in Richmond County, Georgia, David Emanuel Twiggs had a distinguished career in the regular army; he fought in the War of 1812 and in the Black Hawk and Seminole wars. When the Mexican War began, he was colonel of the Second Dragoons, was promoted to brigadier general, and earned a brevet to major general at Monterey. Twiggs was not a West Pointer and was not popular with his officers and men. In 1858 he was court-martialed for a breach of military discipline and briefly relieved of his command of the Department of Texas. He was back in charge, however, when the secession crisis began.

Twiggs wrote Winfield Scott in December 1860 and again in January 1861 asking what he should do in the event of the state's secession. Col. C. A. Waite was ordered to relieve him, but before he could do so, Ben McCulloch, a future Confederate brigadier general, raised a force of 500 volunteers and marched on Twigg's headquarters at San Antonio. Twiggs, with only 160 troops, surrendered February 18, 1861, without a shot being fired. For this action, he was dismissed by President James Buchanan "for treachery to the flag of his country" on March 1, 1861. On May 22 he was appointed a major general in the Confederate army and assigned to command the District of Louisiana. He was, however, unable to perform his duties very long. He returned to Georgia where he died July 15, 1862.

Twiggs is buried at the family home near Augusta. His daughter was married to the first Confederate quartermaster general, Col. Abraham C. Myers.

BIBLIOGRAPHY

"An Episode in the Texas Career of General David E. Twiggs." *Southwestern Historical Quarterly* 41 (1937): 167–173.
Brown, Russell K. "An Old Woman with a Broomstick: General David E. Twiggs and the U.S. Surrender in Texas, 1861." *Military Affairs* (1984): 57–61.
Brown, Russell K. "David Emanuel Twiggs." *Richmond County History* (1983): 12–26.
Brown, Russell K. "The Twiggs Swords." *Richmond County History* (1982): 22–31.

ANNE J. BAILEY

TYLER, JOHN

TYLER, JOHN (1790–1862), governor of Virginia, U.S. president, president of the 1861 Washington peace conference, and congressman from Virginia. The only former U.S. president to serve in the Confederate Congress, Tyler was born March 29, 1790, at Greenway, Charles City County, Virginia, the sixth child of John and Mary Marot (Armistead) Tyler. The younger John Tyler entered the College of William and Mary at age twelve and graduated five years later. After reading law with his father, he was admitted to the Virginia bar in 1809. In 1811 he was elected to the Virginia House of Delegates as a representative from Charles City County; he held this seat for five years until his elevation to the Virginia Council. During the War of 1812 he served as a captain of volunteers protecting the state capital. On March 29, 1813, he married Letitia Christian of New Kent County.

In 1816 Tyler was elected to the U.S. House of Representatives, where he showed himself a strict constructionist and opposed the Missouri Compromise. Poor health, which plagued him much of his life, forced him to resign in 1821. Two years later the citizens of Charles City County again sent him to the House of Delegates. In 1825 and 1826 he served one-year terms as governor. Following the completion of Tyler's second term, anti-Jackson forces in the General Assembly elected him to the U.S. Senate, where he remained until he was forced to resign in February 1836 after a dispute over legislative instructions. He retired briefly to Williamsburg to practice law. During the election of 1836 he was nominated for the vice-presidential slot on two of the four regional Whig tickets as the running mate of both William Henry Harrison and Hugh L. White, but he did no campaigning. He returned to the Virginia House of Delegates in the April 1838 election.

An attempt to regain his seat in the U.S. Senate in 1839 was abortive, but Tyler was named as the running mate of William Henry Harrison of Ohio at the Whig National Convention in December. The "log cabin and hard cider" campaign of 1840 swept the Harrison-Tyler ticket into office. When the sixty-eight-year-old Harrison died one month after

> ... Tyler faced a hostile Whig Congress that delighted in passing bills that the president routinely vetoed. ...

his inauguration, Tyler settled the question of the status of a vice president who assumes executive duties on the death of the president. Instead of becoming acting president, Tyler became president in his own right and thus established the precedent for future generations.

Tyler's strict constructionism had always made his association with the Whigs an uneasy one, and his accession to the presidency ruptured his alliance with Henry Clay. Tyler's effort to sustain the delicate balance of factions by not immediately introducing a program allowed Clay, who was seeking to

secure absolute control of the Whig party and to ensure his own election to the White House in 1844, to seize the initiative. Tyler had made it clear that he would support repeal of Martin Van Buren's Independent Treasury but left it to the special session of Congress that had been called by his predecessor to propose a new banking plan, though he reserved the right of veto.

When it became clear that Clay intended to revive the Bank of the United States, Tyler indicated his preference for a district bank. Clay maneuvered several amendments to the presidential plan that rendered it unacceptable to Tyler, who vetoed it on August 16. Unable to override the presidential veto, Clay tried vainly to introduce an amendment to the Constitution that would allow presidential vetoes to be overturned by a simple majority vote. On September 9 Tyler vetoed a second bank bill. In a move engineered by Clay in hopes of forcing Tyler to step down, the entire cabinet, with the exception of Secretary of State Daniel Webster, resigned on September 11. Two days later, Tyler was publicly read out of the Whig party.

For the next two years of his administration, Tyler faced a hostile Whig Congress that delighted in passing bills that the president routinely vetoed as unconstitutional. Several House committees recommended at various times that he be impeached for impeding the operation of government. Of necessity, low-key domestic policy characterized the last years of the administration. Tyler's most lasting contribution—aside from the precedent set by his accession to power—was the annexation of Texas.

Seeking an issue on which to found a third major political party centered on himself, Tyler settled as early as October 1841 on adding Texas to the Union. Downplaying the issue of the expansion of slavery, a specter that raised its head each time talk of Texas was introduced, Tyler and his secretary of state, Abel P. Upshur of Virginia, entered into secret negotiations with Sam Houston, the president of Texas. Midterm elections in 1842 had returned a Democratic majority to the House and reduced the Whig dominance in the Senate, so by the time the finishing touches were being put on the treaty of annexation in February 1844, Tyler was confident of winning congressional approval.

On February 28, however, Secretary of State Upshur and seven others were killed when a bow cannon called the "Peacemaker" exploded on the frigate *Princeton* while on a pleasure cruise on the Potomac. Tyler intimate Henry A. Wise of Virginia made a public pronouncement that Tyler would name John C. Calhoun to succeed Upshur. Backed into a corner, Tyler turned the delicate negotiations over to Calhoun. When the annexation treaty went to the Senate, Calhoun sent along copies of two official letters he had written to the British minister in Washington, stating that annexation was imperative to protect Southern slaveholders and the national security of the United States from the danger of

British abolitionists working to eradicate the peculiar institution in the independent Texas nation. By resurrecting the slavery issue, Calhoun took the treaty down to defeat.

In the meantime, Tyler used his nascent third party to great advantage. On the same day that the Democratic convention met in Baltimore to nominate its presidential candidate for the 1844 election, Tyler followers convened in the same city to nominate their incumbent with the rallying cry "Tyler and Texas." Apprehensive of the potential pulling power of Tyler's state rights, strict constructionist stand and manipulated by Calhoun loyalists, the Democratic convention ignored front-runner Martin Van Buren, who was on record as opposed to annexation, and gave the nod to dark-horse candidate James K. Polk on a platform that included a call for the annexation of Texas. In August Tyler endorsed Polk rather than Clay, the Whig nominee. When Polk won the White House in the November election, Tyler announced that the Democratic victory had been a mandate on the annexation issue. Because a two-thirds majority in the Senate favoring ratification of the treaty was unlikely, Congress passed a joint resolution calling for the annexation of Texas, which Tyler signed into law on March 1, 1845, three days before his term expired.

Tyler retired to Sherwood Forest, a plantation near his birthplace in Charles City County that he had purchased during his presidency, and settled down to the life of a gentleman planter. His wife, Letitia, long partially paralyzed from a stroke, had died on September 10, 1842, while Tyler was in the White House. During his last year in office, on June 26, 1844, the president had married New York belle Julia Gardiner. (He was the first president to marry while in office.) Her father, David, had been one of those killed on board *Princeton;* indeed, both she and Tyler had been present on the fatal Potomac cruise.

Tyler's annexation of Texas exacerbated sectional tensions. Bitter debates over the expansion of slavery into the territories won during the Mexican War seized the national stage. From the peace of Sherwood Forest, Tyler commented on the Compromise of 1850, the Kansas-Nebraska Act, and the *Dred Scott* decision and was even occasionally mentioned as a presidential candidate.

Fearing slave rebellion in Charles City County in the wake of John Brown's raid on Harpers Ferry, Tyler collected firearms at Sherwood Forest and became captain of the Silver Greys, a cavalry unit that would serve as the second line of defense in the event of an uprising.

In the spring of 1859 he supported Henry Wise and his own son, Robert Tyler, for the 1860 Democratic presidential nomination, but by July he was being prodded by moderates such as James D. B. De Bow of *De Bow's Review* to make himself available as a compromise candidate at the upcoming Democratic convention. Tyler believed that the worst mistake the party could make would be to adopt a platform of any sort and criticized the withdrawal of some of the Southern delegates at Charleston as a strategic blunder. During the ensuing campaign he backed Southern Democrat John C. Breckinridge, although he hoped that the election would in fact give none of the candidates a majority in the electoral college and that the election would be thrown to the House of Representatives, where he was sure that Joseph Lane of Oregon would win approval as president.

The peace conference unanimously chose Tyler president on February 5.

When sectional tensions mounted after the election of Abraham Lincoln, Tyler called on December 14, four days before South Carolina seceded, for a peace convention of the twelve border states. The Virginia General Assembly responded the next month by proposing a convention of all the states, a move Tyler considered abortive because it would involve both abolitionist and fire-eater extremists. Tyler won appointment as one of the five representatives the Old Dominion sent to the Washington peace conference. Simultaneously, he was also named as Virginia's special commissioner to James Buchanan with instructions to persuade the lame-duck president to take no action against the seceded states until the peace conference had convened on February 4. Three days later, Tyler was elected to represent Charles City, James City, and New Kent counties in the emergency Virginia convention that was to assemble in Richmond on February 13.

The peace conference unanimously chose Tyler president on February 5. As he had feared, because of the secession of the lower South, there were twice as many free states represented at the conference as there were slave states. Tyler divided his time between chairing the conference and beseeching Buchanan to abandon Fort Sumter and thus avoid a showdown with the hotheads in South Carolina. During the critical period between the convening of the peace conference and the reporting by the resolutions committee chaired by James Guthrie of Kentucky, Tyler abandoned his moderate Unionist stand. Previously he had been a conditional Unionist—one who supported the preservation of the Union but not at the cost of emancipation, even a compensated one. By February 15, Tyler no longer believed that a political solution to the sectional crisis was possible. Instead, he believed that Virginia should leave the Union. The Old Dominion's secession would force the withdrawal of the border states, Pennsylvania, New York, and New Jersey, thus crippling the North, which would not be able to retaliate militarily. In Tyler's view, Virginia's secession would allow the South to battle to a stalemate without a shot being fired.

Tyler's change in view, and his despondency after he and several other commissioners to the peace conference met with Lincoln on February 23, led him to support James A. Seddon's minority report to the peace conference, which reiterated the right of any state to secede from the Union and which would have guaranteed the South control of executive appointments below the old Missouri Compromise line. He consistently voted against the Guthrie resolutions but passed them along to Congress as instructed after they carried by narrow margins.

On the last day of February, Tyler returned to Richmond, condemned the results of the peace conference, and advocated the immediate secession of Virginia. Taking his seat in the state convention, he rose on March 13 and 14 to deliver a set piece calling for secession if Lincoln did not abandon the Federal forts, recognize the Confederate States of America, and begin treaty negotiations with the new nation. In the roll calls on April 3, 15, and 17, he cast his vote for secession.

After the firing on Fort Sumter and Virginia's decision to leave the Union, Tyler served on the Virginia commission that negotiated joining the Confederacy and drafted the resolution placing the commonwealth's military forces under the command of Jefferson Davis. Citing poor health, he declined nomination to the Provisional Confederate Congress while it met in Montgomery but accepted his unanimous election by the Virginia state convention once the Confederate government relocated to Richmond.

In the Confederate House of Representatives elections of November 1861, Tyler handily defeated William H. Macfarland and James Lyons in Virginia's Third Congressional District but had little opportunity to serve his constituents. He died January 18, 1862, at the Exchange Hotel in Richmond after a brief illness. His express wish that he be buried simply at Sherwood Forest was ignored. Tyler's body lay in state in the Confederate Congress on January 20. After an elaborate service the next day at St. Paul's Episcopal Church, he was interred in Hollywood Cemetery near the grave of former president James Monroe.

On May 7, 1864, black troops under the command of Brig. Gen. Edward A. Wild occupied Sherwood Forest. A month later Wild turned possession of the house over to two of the Tyler family slaves. The plantation was looted and the ground floor turned into a school. Although furniture was destroyed, a death mask of Tyler smashed, and outbuildings and fences burned, the former president's papers and most of the family silver and portraits were saved, all having been removed to Richmond for safekeeping in April (ironically, most of the papers were destroyed during the evacuation fire in 1865). In spite of Tyler's position as the only former U.S. president to have advocated secession and served in the Confederate government, his widow successfully lobbied Congress in 1881 for an annual Federal pension of $1,200, an amount increased to $5,000 in March 1882 after the assassination of President James A. Garfield.

BIBLIOGRAPHY

Gunderson, Robert G. *Old Gentlemen's Convention: The Washington Peace Convention of 1861.* Madison, Wis., 1961.

Morgan, Robert J. *A Whig Embattled: The Presidency under John Tyler.* Lincoln, Nebr., 1954.

Peterson, Norma Lois. *The Presidencies of William Henry Harrison and John Tyler.* American Presidency Series. Lawrence, Kans., 1989.

Seager, Robert, II. *and Tyler too: A Biography of John & Julia Gardiner Tyler.* New York, 1963.

Tyler, Lyon Gardiner. *The Letters and Times of the Tylers.* 3 vols. Richmond, Va., 1884–1896.

SARA B. BEARS

UNIFORMS

[*This entry is composed of two articles that discuss the design, production, and distribution of uniforms for the Confederate armed services:* Army Uniforms *and* Navy and Marine Uniforms. *For further discussion of the uniforms of particular branches of the Confederate armed services, see* Artillery, *overview article;* Infantry; Marine Corps; Medical Department; *and* Signal Corps. *See also* Medals and Decorations.]

Army Uniforms

Within the Confederate army, from beginning to end, simply clothing the troops consistently took precedence over achieving uniformity. This fact is central to an understanding of both the variety and the uniformity of Confederate clothing. Also crucial is a grasp of the two main systems the Confederate government employed to get clothing to the troops, the commutation system and the issue system.

The commutation system, decreed by the Confederate Congress at the beginning of the war, was intended to save precious government resources by requiring the 100,000 volunteers of the Provisional Army to clothe themselves. They were to be paid fifty dollars a year per man in commutation money for the use of the clothing. Although the money sometimes was paid to the states, a few of which provided clothing according to state uniform regulations, most went to the captains of companies or the men themselves. With no uniform regulations to follow, the clothing the volunteers obtained was as varied as the hundreds of companies in Confederate service.

The uniform regulations issued by the Confederate government in May 1861 were intended only for the Confederate Regular Army, an organization of about 6,000 men. These regulations were inspired by Austrian Jager and French officers' uniforms and for both officers and enlisted men consisted of cadet gray double-breasted frock coats trimmed in a color indicating the wearer's branch of service, sky blue trousers (dark blue for field and general officers), and branch-color kepis. Only the quality of the uniforms and the insignia distinguished officers from enlisted men. Very few of the enlisted uniforms were actually made, but eventually most officers of both the Regular and Provisional armies adopted versions of the Regular Army uniform.

Confederate insignia was one of the few areas where the Regular Army regulations took a firm hold, in part because it was based on the old U.S. Army system. Branch colors were as follows: infantry, sky blue; artillery, red; cavalry, yellow; medical, black; and staff, buff. These colors were used to trim collars, cuffs, and the fronts of coats and were also the body color of the kepi. Noncommissioned-officer rank insignia was based on chevrons on each sleeve in the branch color, worn points down, two for corporals and three for sergeants. First sergeants wore a lozenge within the angle of the chevrons, ordnance sergeants a star, quartermaster sergeants a tie, and sergeants major an arc. Their trousers were trimmed with branch-color stripes in widths based on rank. Privates wore no insignia, but did wear branch trim on their coats.

Officers' rank insignia was based on the Austrian system of stars or bars worn on the collar, and the French sleeve braid system known as "galons." Line officers—second lieutenants, first lieutenants, and captains—wore one, two, or three bars, respectively, on each side of the collar, with lieutenants wearing one strand of sleeve braid and captains two. Field officers—majors, lieutenant colonels, and colonels—wore one, two, or three stars, respectively, and three strands of sleeve braid. General officers wore three stars surrounded by a wreath and four strands of sleeve braid. The number of sleeve braids was repeated on the kepi. There was also a system of trouser stripes of different widths of gold braid based on rank. Buttons were of brass, sometimes gilt, with a spread eagle for staff officers, a German *E* for engineer officers, and a block *A, I,* or *C* for artillery, infantry, and cavalry.

Waistbelt plates were not specifically uniform items, but rather parts of ordnance-supplied accoutrements. Although regulations specified that the device would be the "Arms of the Confederate States," such arms were never designed. This, plus the fact that officers procured their own sword belts, resulted in a wide variety of plates being worn, some with "CS" or "CSA" on the face, others plain brass, and still others in a buckle form; state seal plates also saw wide use. The most common forms actually used were probably the brass frame buckle, iron roller buckles, or captured U.S. belt plates.

Although the commutation system was intended to avoid both the stockpiling of uniforms and the need for making them, as early as the summer of 1861 there were reports of ragged Confederate troops in the field. The Confederate Quartermaster's Department discovered that much of the clothing the volunteers had purchased was of inferior quality. Far from home, these men now had no way to replenish their supply. As a result, the department sought and obtained congressional sanction to issue clothing. By the fall of 1861 the department had established clothing manufactories in several Southern cities and began to issue clothing to troops in need. This system was considered successful enough by October 1862 that it officially replaced the commutation system, although the changeover took some time to accomplish.

The issue system resulted in large quantities of simple jackets, trousers, shirts, drawers, shoes, and socks being issued, and lesser quantities of hats, caps, overcoats, and blankets. Each depot produced its own patterns and developed its own sources of supply, usually utilizing materials such as gray woolen jeans produced by local mills and supplemented, particularly later in the war, by large quantities of imported English cadet gray cloth. Thus, though each depot's product had some uniformity of its own, there was pattern variation between the depots. The quantity was usually sufficient for overall issue, but the quality of the clothing sometimes left much to be desired. Moreover, baths and the washing of clothing in the field was infrequent or nonexistent, which resulted in an accelerated wearing out of what should have been a sufficient supply. Often the issue clothing was supplemented by contributions from home or by captured Federal items. Occasionally, this captured clothing was dyed to conceal the blue color. When combined with the Confederate soldier's propensity to affect an individual look, these varied sources and styles resulted in a lack of uniformity in the Confederate ranks.

BIBLIOGRAPHY

Hill, Tucker, ed. *Catalogue of Uniforms, the Musuem of the Confederacy.* Richmond, Va., 1987.
Jensen, Leslie D. "A Survey of Confederate Central Government Quartermaster Issue Jackets." *Military Collector & Historian* 41, nos. 3–4 (1989).
Todd, Frederick P. *American Military Equipage, 1851–1872.* Vol. 2. Providence, R.I., 1977.

LES JENSEN

Navy and Marine Uniforms

Both the Confederate navy and the Marine Corps were small organizations, and although they faced shortages like the army, their size often allowed them to achieve a degree of uniformity in clothing that the army lacked.

Unlike the army, the Confederate navy issued clothing to its sailors from the beginning of the war. The initial supply came from captured U.S. Navy uniforms obtained from the Gosport Navy Yard in Norfolk, Virginia; soon after, this supply was supplemented by clothing purchased in England. In both cases, the uniforms were largely dark blue, and most of the navy wore this color through at least 1862. Confederate naval officers also wore dark blue uniforms, often old U.S. Navy clothing with the insignia changed.

Sometime in 1862, the Navy Department issued uniform regulations changing the basic color to gray. The change was not universally liked, many officers objecting on the basis that

> **. . . the Confederate navy issued clothing to its sailors from the beginning of the war.**

no navy in the world wore gray. By 1863, however, the changeover had largely been accepted.

The regulations seem to have been based mainly on the U.S. Navy's 1852 regulations, with the exceptions that there were no dress uniforms and a considerably different and complicated system of rank insignia was adopted. Officers wore double-breasted frock coats of steel gray cloth with rolling collars, gray trousers, and gray visored caps; enlisted ranks wore gray jackets or gray frocks with white duck collars, gray pants, and black or gray visorless caps in winter and white duck frocks with blue collars and cuffs, white pants, and gray or white visorless caps in summer. Officers wore rank insignia on the sleeves and shoulder straps; seamen wore it on their sleeves.

The Confederate Marine Corps was never officially allowed more than ten companies, and only six were recruited during the war. These companies never served together as a unit, instead operating as small detachments on board ship or at naval stations. No Marine Corps uniform regulations are known to exist, and it is probable, given the small size of the corps, that none were issued. Marine uniforms were therefore subject to variations based on local supply situations; yet some elements seem to have been common to most, if not all uniforms. Marine officers appear to have worn navy gray frock coats, double-breasted and cut in either the rolling collar navy style or the standing collar army style. Rank insignia was often the army sleeve braid, although distinctive marine shoulder knots were also sometimes worn.

Enlisted uniforms were probably based on the U.S. Marine Corps 1859 regulations. Enlisted men probably wore double-breasted gray frock coats or single-breasted jackets like the army's. At least in 1862, the style was distinctive and different from the Army's. Rank chevrons were probably worn points up rather than down as in the army. But the fact that there are no known photographs of Confederate enlisted marines, no known surviving enlisted uniforms, and no known regulations make specifics very difficult to establish.

BIBLIOGRAPHY

Donnelly, Ralph W. *The History of the Confederate States Marine Corps.* Washington, D.C., 1976.
Todd, Frederick P. *American Military Equipage, 1851–1872.* Vol. 2. Providence, R.I., 1977.

LES JENSEN

UNIONISM

In simplest terms Unionism describes the attitude of those white Southerners who opposed the Confederacy because they favored the Union. That simple definition, however, does not do justice to the diversity of Unionist sentiments and the changes in its meaning over time. Southern Unionism, after all, has a history older than the Confederacy. Decades before secession took place, Southerners and Northerners were denominating certain white Southerners as Unionists. In those earlier times it usually meant opposition to state rights, as during the nullification crisis, or, later, opposition to the advocacy of secession.

The term is also complicated in that among the states of the United States, only Southern states seceded. That singularity meant that only white Southerners were confronted with the necessity of calculating their degree of commitment to the United States. We will never know, as we do about white Southerners, the depth or intensity of Unionism among Northerners; they were never asked to make a choice between region and nation. Indeed, simply because eleven Southern states seceded and formed the Confederacy, it is often assumed that the existence of Southern Unionism needs to be explained. In fact, it is secession that requires explanation since it was accomplished in a region that during the era of the great Virginian presidents—Jefferson, Madison, and Monroe—was probably the most Unionist section in the nation. And when South Carolina in 1832 challenged the national authority over the tariff issue, it was a Southern-born president, Andrew Jackson, who forced the state to rescind its act of nullification. Significantly, too, no Southern states offered support to South Carolina's position and some fiercely denounced the idea of nullification. Even as late as 1850 and 1851, Southern candidates who supported the Unionist Compromise of 1850 won election across the region. Southern Unionism during the Confederacy, in short, had deep roots in the Southern past. As a result, Unionism helped shape the way secession itself took place.

Unionism during the Election of 1860. The measure of the strength of Unionist sentiment during the election campaign of 1860 was the almost instantaneous creation of the Constitutional Union party. Although national in aims and intention, the party was really a Southern organization, which sought to escape the conflict over slavery by simply asserting the value of keeping the Union intact. Its presidential candidate, John Bell of Tennessee, a large slaveholder and prominent Whig politician, was a well-known and fervent opponent of secession. (He had been Unionist enough to vote against the Kansas-Nebraska Act.) Although many of the South's leading politicians threatened to support secession if Abraham Lincoln were elected in November, both Bell and his new party made no such threats. The election statistics measured how close the Constitutional Union party had come to reflecting the sentiments of the voters of the South. When the Confederacy went to war in April 1861, 49 percent of its voting population less than six months before had supported candidates (Bell, with 40.3 percent, and Stephen A. Douglas, with 8.6 percent) who opposed secession and the formation of the Confederacy. Even John C. Breckinridge, the Southern Democratic candidate, did not advocate secession; he merely was prepared to accept it.

The objection to secession during the election of 1860 was clearly an outgrowth of Southern history, particularly the two-party politics of the antebellum years, and the geographical distribution of slaveholding. Both help account as well for the persistence of Southern Unionism during the Confederate years. Although the Whig party was officially dead throughout the nation by 1860, among Southerners the nationalist or Unionist sentiments that had been the hallmark of the party over the years persisted. Statistical analyses of voting patterns reveal a high correlation between those counties in the South that had voted Whig in the 1840s and those that supported Bell and Douglas in 1860. Surprisingly, many of those counties were in the plantation areas of the Deep South, which had long been Whig. The ballots may have been cast against secession, but the motive was not necessarily enduringly Unionist, as the reaction of these areas showed, once Lincoln won the election.

Unionism during the Secession Crisis. The first real test of the South's commitment to Unionism came soon after the election of Lincoln in November. Within three months seven states of the Deep South had seceded, an alacrity that some historians later thought measured the secessionists' fear that once the excitement of the election had faded Southern Unionist sentiment would revive and stop secession in its tracks. And it is true that, of those seven, only Texas, the last Deep South state to secede, permitted a popular vote on the issue of secession. (Other states voted on the issue, but they were in the upper South.) In any case, even if in fact a majority of white Southerners in the seven states did endorse secession, most historians agree that the margin of those supporting secession was at most only paper-thin. Even in South Carolina prominent figures resisted the call for secession, openly declaring their wish to remain with the Union. Among them were James L. Petigru and Benjamin Perry, both of whom had proclaimed their Unionism during the nullification crisis almost thirty years before. Neither Petigru nor Perry, it is worth noting, left the South once the Confederacy was established. Indeed, Perry worked to recruit soldiers for the Confederate army during the war.

More vocal and powerful opposition to secession was voiced in the conventions of Georgia, Florida, Alabama, and Louisiana, but it would be a mistake to see that as a sign of the strength of Unionism in the Deep South, where slave-holdings were concentrated. The great majority of the delegates to the conventions in the Deep South who fought against secession were really cooperationists—that is, men who wanted their individual states to secede only in conjunction with other states. As one Alabama cooperationist newspaper wrote, "Before Lincoln's election we were against disunion . . . but now the die is cast, the last feather has been placed on the camel's back, and our only salvation is in secession." In sum, the cooperationists' Unionism did not deny the right of secession, merely the practicality of it.

A stronger Unionism was apparent in the four states of the upper South that joined the Confederacy later: Arkansas, North Carolina, Tennessee, and Virginia. They seceded neither with the election of Lincoln nor with the creation of the Confederacy in February 1861. Instead, that same month, the people of North Carolina and Tennessee voted down calls for conventions to decide on secession. In Tennessee the vote was 68,000 against, 59,000 for. In Arkansas and Virginia conventions were convened, but their delegates were strongly opposed to secession. Indeed, the Arkansas convention soon voted against secession (39–35) and adjourned just three weeks before Fort Sumter was fired on. Virginia's convention, on the other hand, stayed in session until it became clear that the Lincoln administration intended to use force against those states that had seceded. It was only then that the decision was taken to secede. Lincoln's call for state troops to suppress the rebellion also tested and found wanting the Unionist majority in Arkansas, North Carolina, and Tennessee, all of which then joined the Confederacy. For many Unionists, like former Whig politician Jonathan Worth of North Carolina, the choice was difficult. Worth as a state senator had led the fight against his state's secession, working to have the decision submitted to the people, but to no avail. His private remarks on the eve of North Carolina's vote to secede captured the inner conflict felt by many Unionists as the fighting began. "I think the annals of the world furnish no instance of so groundless a war," he wrote, "but as our nation will have it—if no peace can be made—let us fight like men for our own firesides."

Unionism in the Confederacy. Generally speaking, the more enduring Unionism of the upper Southern states can be related to their lesser dependence on slavery than the states of the Deep South. Nowhere does this connection become more telling than in the creation in 1863 of the state of West Virginia out of the mountainous region of western Virginia. There slavery was almost nonexistent, and dissatisfaction with the slaveholders' long domination of the state's politics had frequently been heard. Of the fifty-five members of the Virginia convention who had voted against secession, half came from the part of the state that became West Virginia.

Mountainous eastern Tennessee, which like western Virginia counted few slaves, had also resisted the movement toward secession. When a popular vote was taken in the state on dissolving Tennessee's connection with the Union, the people in the eastern part voted to stay with the United States by a majority of two thousand. This was also the area within the South in which unconditional Unionism during the Confederacy reached its height in numbers and intensity. Although that region, unlike the rest of the state, counted few slaveholders, its Unionism was rooted in opposition not to slavery but to the wealth that slaves represented and to the Democratic politics of their owners. The small farmers of East Tennessee had long been staunch Whigs. One native historian of the region has described the hostility of the Unionists toward the Tennessee Confederates as exhibiting signs of a "class struggle as well as a political and military contest." One measure of the threat the Unionists posed to the Southern war effort was the often brutal reprisals that the Confederate authorities mounted against Unionists whose destruction of bridges was especially damaging to the military effort. Dozens of Unionist sympathizers were executed and their bodies left hanging in public as a warning to others. Nevertheless, in 1862, Confederate conscription in eastern Tennessee was brought to a halt by the Unionist resistance. Significantly, the best known Unionist leaders of the state came from both parties. Perhaps the most notorious was William G. Brownlow, a former Whig newspaper editor whose slashing Unionist propaganda caused him to flee the state until U.S. military force could protect him. The leading Democratic Unionist was Andrew Johnson, the only U.S. senator from a seceding state to refuse to abandon his seat in Washington. Later he became the military governor of Tennessee after U.S. troops had conquered portions of the state. His committed Unionism earned him the post of running mate with Abraham Lincoln in 1864.

Wherever slavery was weakly established, as in the mountainous counties of northern Alabama, northwestern Arkansas, and western North Carolina, there, too, Unionist sentiment and overt resistance to the Confederate war effort persisted throughout the life of the Confederacy. Thirty-three members of the Alabama secession convention refused to sign the secession ordinance; by the fall of 1862 the first U.S. regiment of white Alabama troops had been organized, reaching a complement of two thousand men by war's end. The unit even served with William Tecumseh Sherman in his drive across Georgia. Counties in the Ozark Mountains of Arkansas also displayed a continuing resistance to the Confederacy, usually in the form of peace societies, which the Confederate authorities took pains to suppress. By 1863 Union officials were easily recruiting hundreds of Arkansans into the Federal army. The mountain Unionists of North Carolina organized a secret society, the Heroes of America, to sabotage and undermine the Confederate war effort. At the height of the war, in 1863, the Heroes' guerrilla attacks compelled the Confederacy to send six army companies into western North Carolina in an attempt to suppress the society, the membership of which one historian has estimated may have reached ten thousand.

The willingness of white Southerners to fight against their fellow Southerners was undoubtedly the ultimate test of the depth of Unionist conviction. Thousands of white Southerners from eight states passed that test. As one might anticipate, eastern Tennessee supplied more men by far to the Union army than any other Confederate state. More than 31,000 men, organized in 33 regiments, fought for the Union from Tennessee. All told, more than 86,000 white Southerners served in the invading forces, among which were more than a hundred officers of general or admiral rank who had been born in what became the Confederate States of America. (This figure of 86,000 is a minimum; it is known that several thousand white Southerners are uncounted because they served in Northern regiments.) More white men from Tennessee, Florida, Arkansas, and Alabama served in the armed forces of the United States than blacks from those states.

Although the most extensive areas of Unionist sentiment were located in the mountain regions, substantial numbers of individual Union sympathizers were active in the plantation areas, among them some of the wealthiest slaveholders. The counties along the Mississippi River in Mississippi had been conspicuous in their resistance to secession and in their support of cooperation when the state was considering its response to Lincoln's election. Once the Union forces arrived in that region, some of the wealthiest planters gave voice to their Unionist sentiment by freely supplying the invading armies. Especially notable was John Minor of Mississippi who contributed $64,000 worth of supplies to the U.S. military during the war. Another planter of the same state, implacable old Whig William Sharkey, immediately took the oath of allegiance to the United States in 1863 when Federal troops occupied Natchez. After the war he was recompensed some $2,000 for his contributions to the Union military cause.

Former Whig planters of substance in Louisiana also contributed heavily to the Federal army. Conspicuous among them was William Bailey, one of the wealthiest men in the state and the owner of scores of slaves. James Madison Wells, another Louisiana planter of considerable wealth—he owned ninety-six slaves in 1860—denounced secession in 1861 and, once the war began, became a guerrilla leader and highly successful recruiter of troops for the Union army.

Although a number of individual slaveholding or wealthy supporters of the United States in the course of the war can be identified, the significance of this class of Unionists depends upon how numerous they were. Fortunately, thanks to the records of the Southern Claims Commission which Congress set up after the war, some measure, albeit imperfect, of the extent of wealthy, usually slaveholding Unionists in the South can be gained. Because of the stringent criteria Congress specified to substantiate a claim, the number of

> ... some of the wealthiest planters gave voice to their Unionist sentiment by freely supplying the invading armies.

Southerners who finally received compensation from the U.S. government for their contributions to the Union military victory probably represented only a fraction of the actual number. As it was, almost 7,000 claimants received recompense; 22,000 persons had submitted claims. Those who were reimbursed received a total of $4.6 million. These Unionists differed markedly from those of the mountain regions, besides their being considerably less numerous: these were men of property, which was primarily what they contributed to the Union cause.

Since the claims of these wealthy Unionists were broken down into classes of amounts, it is possible to obtain some idea of the extent to which planters supported the Union during the war. At a time when $5,000 was a substantial amount of money (the annual salary of the chief justice of the United States was $6,000), 1,500 white Southerners asserted that they had contributed $5,000 or more to the Federal war effort. Of those 1,500, almost half filed claims of $10,000 or more. About 80 percent of these claimants were large slaveholders; each of them owned, on the average, fifty-four slaves. (In 1860 only about 68,000 people in the whole South owned as many as fifteen or more slaves.) And despite the especially stringent requirements for substantiating a claim of $10,000, almost 200 of the claimants received recompense. Of the 786 claims for amounts between $5,000 and $10,000, 224 obtained reimbursement. In sum, literally hundreds of the planters in the South, many of whom had been Whigs and cooperationists in 1860 and 1861, had persisted in their Unionism throughout a war that was supposed to be defending slavery, the source of their wealth.

Some slaveholders opposed secession simply because they thought it would hasten the end of slavery, as in fact it did. By staying in the Union, these men reasoned, the Southern slaveholders would have at least the Federal government behind them inasmuch as the Constitution upheld slavery. Outside the Union the South would be at the mercy of a world increasingly opposed to slavery.

For many wealthy Unionists, the operative point was that secession was a radical step, as people at the time frequently remarked. One North Carolinian Whig remembered in 1868, "I never was in favor of anything that was radical. I was opposed to abolition because it was radical. I was opposed to secession because it was radical." It is not accidental that students of the secession conventions have found that the younger delegates tended to favor secession and that delegates of an older generation tended to oppose withdrawal from the Union. By its nature, Unionism, like the Union itself, was traditional, the creation of the Founding Fathers; it was the established way of thinking. The natural tendency of men and women of wealth was to keep things as they were. To change them was to threaten the existing order and the success and comfort it had brought these people. In contrast, the nonslaveholders, the former Whigs, men of the backcountry and mountain regions, also favored the traditional Union but because it was threatened by their old enemies, secession-minded planters who dominated the Democratic party.

Southern Unionism needs to be seen not only as varying in degrees as the differences between the sections deepened but also as an underground sentiment that resurfaced as the war progressed and the likelihood of defeat for the Confederacy mounted. The most notable example of this phenomenon was the growth of peace societies, the one in North Carolina under the leadership of William Holden being the most prominent and successful. Holden himself offers special insight into the ambiguities inherent in Unionism. Before 1860, the *North Carolina Standard,* of which Holden was editor, had been a strong advocate of secession, but once the war began Holden and the *Standard* increasingly called for peace and a return to the Union. His opposition to the war in the name of peace became sufficiently strong in 1863 to provoke a sacking of the *Standard's* offices in Raleigh; Holden himself fled into the countryside for a spell. After the war he became the first Republican governor of North Carolina. As the fortunes of the Confederacy waned in 1864 and 1865, peace movements that were thin disguises for a reviving Unionism emerged in other states as well.

The persistence of Unionism not only serves to document once again the diversity within the South and therefore within the Confederacy; it also exposes a significant source of social and political division that persisted long after the Confederacy died at Appomattox. Many of those white Southerners who had been Unionists during the war became the scalawag leaders and rank-and-file supporters of Reconstruction.

[*See also* Compromise of 1850; Constitutional Union Party; Cooperationists; Election of 1860; Heroes of America; Kansas-Nebraska Act; Missouri Compromise; Nullification Controversy; Peace Movements; Whig Party; *and entries on particular states.*]

BIBLIOGRAPHY

Auman, William T., and David D. Scarboro. "The Heroes of America in Civil War North Carolina." *North Carolina Historical Review* 58 (October 1981): 327–363.

Crofts, Daniel W. *Reluctant Confederates: Upper South Unionists in the Secession Crisis.* Chapel Hill, N.C., 1989.

Degler, Carl N. *The Other South: Southern Dissenters in the Nineteenth Century.* New York, 1974.

Harris, William C. *William Woods Holden: Firebrand of North Carolina Politics.* Baton Rouge, La., 1987.

Klingberg, Frank W. *The Southern Claims Commission.* Berkeley, Calif., 1955.

Patton, James Welch. *Unionism and Reconstruction in Tennessee, 1860–1869.* Chapel Hill, N.C., 1934.

Tatum, Georgia Lee. *Disloyalty in the Confederacy.* Chapel Hill, N.C., 1934.

CARL N. DEGLER

UNION OCCUPATION

[*This entry serves only as an introduction to the Union occupation of Confederate territory. For a more detailed examination of specific areas under occupation, see entries on particular states and cities. See also* Contraband.] Large sections of the Confederacy, including a number of important cities, fell under Union control during the Civil War. By mid-1862 the following areas were in Federal hands: northern, southeastern, and western Virginia, including Alexandria and Norfolk; middle and western Tennessee, including Nashville and Memphis; southeastern Louisiana, including New Orleans and Baton Rouge; and several points along the coasts of North and South Carolina and northeastern Florida. By the end of 1863 more territory had been conquered: the remaining cities along the Mississippi River, including Natchez and Vicksburg; the section of Alabama north of the Tennessee River; the northern half of Arkansas; and eastern Tennessee. The final year of the war saw the capture of Atlanta, Savannah, Charleston, and Wilmington.

Military occupation of the South confronted the Union army and government with vast and unprecedented military, political, economic, and social problems. Holding towns and protecting communication lines in the midst of a mostly hostile population required tens of thousands of troops and constant vigilance. Spying, smuggling, guerrilla attacks, and other forms of civilian resistance plagued the occupiers.

Federal commanders imposed martial law in the occupied regions and endeavored not only to subdue resistance but also to assume the functions of municipal government. Moreover, in four states—Tennessee, Louisiana, North Carolina, and Arkansas—President Lincoln appointed military governors to oversee occupation and political reconstruction. Before the war's end, civil governments controlled by native Unionists were established in Tennessee, Louisiana, Arkansas, and Virginia. The military governors and state officials had frequent conflicts of authority with

> **Well before Appomattox, most resigned themselves to defeat and grudgingly accepted black emancipation.**

army commanders and with Treasury Department agents who supervised wartime trade.

Foremost among the transformations wrought by Union occupation was the dissolution of slavery. Wherever Federal forces invaded the South, slaves flocked to their lines. Most military commanders initially declined to tamper with the institution of slavery, but eventually they welcomed runaways as laborers. As the Union government's slavery policy moved from conservative to radical, the army became an active agent of emancipation. Military officials established "contraband camps" to shelter black fugitives, oversaw contracts between black laborers and white employers, and enlisted black recruits. Northern humanitarians went south to organize schools for the freedmen.

Federal actions against slavery were just one aspect of the revolutionary upheaval precipitated by Union occupation. To a far greater extent than in the regions held by the Confederacy, society in the occupied South fractured along its fault lines. Slaves by the hundreds of thousands defied their masters, liberated themselves, and took control of their own lives, even where military authorities were conservative or where the Emancipation Proclamation did not apply. Poor whites likewise seized opportunities to challenge the hegemony of the South's ruling elite. Southern Unionists struck back at the secessionist majority who had tyrannized them. This social turmoil was aggravated by widespread devastation, privation, and institutional disruption.

Facing extreme hardship and unchallengeable Federal power, Confederate sympathizers in the occupied regions soon forsook their cause. Well before Appomattox, most resigned themselves to defeat and grudgingly accepted black emancipation.

BIBLIOGRAPHY

Belz, Herman. *Reconstructing the Union: Theory and Policy during the Civil War.* Ithaca, N.Y., 1969.
Capers, Gerald M. *Occupied City: New Orleans under the Federals, 1862–1865.* Lexington, Ky., 1965.
Durrill, Wayne K. *War of Another Kind: A Southern Community in the Great Rebellion.* New York, 1990.
Futrell, Robert J. "Federal Military Government in the South, 1861–1865." *Military Affairs* 15 (1951): 181–191.
Gerteis, Louis S. *From Contraband to Freedman: Federal Policy toward Southern Blacks, 1861–1865.* Westport, Conn., 1973.

STEPHEN V. ASH

URBANIZATION

The role of cities in the antebellum and Confederate South exhibited a paradox. On the one hand, the cities of the future Confederacy were crucial to the existence of the plantation economy, linking it to the international markets that had created it and the flow of capital and supplies that sustained its growth. In the Confederacy, cities became even more vital as administrative centers, supply depots, and manufacturing points. Yet at the same time cities were marginal to the antebellum South, seriously constricted in their range of functions and in their vitality. In an age when American cities outside the region were developing integrated networks of cities and towns and launching on a process of self-sustaining and mutually reinforcing growth, the urban centers of the future Confederacy remained largely tethered to their hinterlands, on the one hand, and to the great centers of international commerce and credit, on the other. Their inadequacies, like those of other components of Southern society, would be glaringly revealed in the harsh light of war.

Urbanization in the Antebellum South

That the process of urbanization in the future Confederate states lagged behind that of the future Union states is apparent from the summary statistics. In 1790 less than 2 percent of Southerners lived in incorporated places of at least 2,500 people, the current census definition of an "urban place." To be sure, the difference from the North was not striking; the young Republic north of the Potomac was at that time only 7 percent urban. By the time of secession, however, nearly a quarter of the Union's population counted as city people; less than 7 percent of the Confederacy's population did. Of the 102 American cities of over 10,000 people in 1860, the Confederacy, with 29 percent of the old Union's total population, contained only 11. If a more sophisticated measure, the index of relative urbanization, is used to trace Southern urbanization over time, it reveals that the region, while generally less than half as urban as the nation as a whole, urbanized at a slightly faster rate than the larger nation until 1840 and then dramatically lost ground in the late antebellum period.

The summary statistics mask enormous variation, for there was no single kind of "Southern city," nor was there a coherent urban hierarchy in the region before secession. Looming large in the summary statistics was New Orleans . Entering the Union through the Louisiana Purchase in 1803, it was immediately the fifth largest American city, maintaining that rank throughout the antebellum period. The development of the western river steamer after the War of 1812 allowed the city to burgeon as the great entrepôt (intermediary center of trade and transshipment) of the Mississippi valley as well as the leading cotton and sugar port, so that by 1840 it contained nearly 40 percent of the total urban population of the future Confederacy. Its growth slowed dramatically after 1840, though, as the canals and railroads of the later transportation revolution increasingly directed the trade of the Old Northwest toward the Northeast.

Another anomalous case was the state of Virginia. Relatively nonurban in 1790, the Old Dominion (here not including the future West Virginia) by 1840 was, after Louisiana, the South's most urban state, containing eight of the region's twenty-three cities, including the third largest, Richmond, and over a quarter of its urban population. A complex of factors contributed to Virginia's relatively rapid urbanization. The agricultural shift from tobacco to wheat encouraged a vigorous grain trade, increasingly supplemented by the manufacture and export of flour. Changes in tobacco marketing concentrated the trade in Richmond, Petersburg, and Lynchburg and fed their burgeoning tobacco factories. Norfolk and Portsmouth became entrepôts for both Virginia and nearby North Carolina, while Richmond and Petersburg became the South's only true manufacturing cities. After 1840, though, as the pace of urbanization picked up in the North, Virginia lost relative ground, and in 1860 it was less than half as urban as the nation as a whole; except for Richmond, its cities grew slowly, and only one new center, the Shenandoah Valley town of Staunton, appeared in the late antebellum period.

With minor exceptions, notably the western outfitting and provisioning center of Nashville, virtually every other significant Southern city was at least in part the product of the cotton trade, and cotton largely defined the Southern urban character. Dominating the lower South as far north as Tennessee and North Carolina were the cotton ports, which in addition to New Orleans included Charleston, Savannah, Mobile, and Memphis. These cities performed variably during the years before 1860. Charleston, the major city of the South in 1790, stagnated but remained the second city in 1860. As the cotton belt pushed westward, Mobile and, later, Memphis arose, first as outfitting centers for settlers and then as outlets for their staple production. To the interior of these

centers there developed a string of much smaller towns, usually on rivers at or near the fall line. In late antebellum times interior points proliferated; the number of incorporated towns in the region tripled between 1840 and 1860. Generally, though, cotton belt urbanization lagged badly; outside of Virginia and Louisiana only 4.4 percent of the region's people lived in cities.

Behind these and other indicators of antebellum urban underdevelopment lay the failure of most Southern cities to transcend their original roles as entrepôts for the plantation staple economies of their hinterlands. All U.S. cities originated as colonial outposts, funneling settlers and supplies to expanding frontiers and exporting primary products abroad. In the nineteenth century, however, cities outside the future

> **The agricultural shift from tobacco to wheat encouraged a vigorous grain trade. . . .**

Confederacy launched on a path of self-sustaining and mutually reinforcing growth while at the same time drawing strength from relatively densely populated hinterlands generating strong and diverse demand. Southern cities, though, traded little with each other and engaged in little innovative growth; dealing chiefly in one major staple, cotton, these centers did not have much to offer each other. Accordingly, no Southern *system* of cities developed; major centers with their hinterlands developed independently of each other, maintaining their principal trading links with the rising metropolises of western Europe and the American Northeast. Like their colonial forebears they served the undemanding needs of the plantations and the narrowly focused desires of a distant metropolitan core, with profound and deleterious consequences for their development.

The most striking structural feature of Southern urban systems, especially in the cotton belt, was their *primate* character—that is, relative to the North, local centers in the hinterlands of cotton ports were few and underdeveloped, so that the central city largely monopolized both population and urban services. Charleston comprised 83 percent of South Carolina's urban population in 1860, and Mobile 60 percent of Alabama's; New Orleans (with its suburbs) and Memphis together contained 87 percent of the urban dwellers in Louisiana, Mississippi, Arkansas, and western Tennessee. Because cotton and other plantations oriented their production toward outside markets, and because modern means of transportation and communication were slow to develop in the region, planters needed to move their crops to a seaport or one of the larger river towns. Lacking adequate marketing information, they needed the services of agents in those few points enjoying adequate contact with the outside world.

Accordingly, the staple trade, and the factors, buyers, and bankers who controlled it, concentrated at very few points, chiefly on the edge of the region, where shipping facilities could be located and where fast, reliable information was most readily available.

The central figures in antebellum Southern urban commerce were commission merchants called *factors.* Specializing in a specific staple, factors served planters as sales agents, offering their strategic locations and specialized knowledge to interior producers seeking advantageous prices. The same advantages encouraged factors to become all-purpose commercial intermediaries for their clients, purchasing and shipping supplies, providing short- and long-term loans, and vouching for credit. Primarily serving the needs of factors, Southern banks were few in number, relatively large in scale, and highly concentrated in location; in 1860 nine of the eighteen banks in South Carolina were located in Charleston. Buyers similarly clustered around factorage centers, as did merchants catering to the planting trade. Because of the slow pace of these urban outposts, and because factors' businesses relied heavily on personal relationships with their clients, the tone of business life was unhurried and social; Charleston, in particular, had a reputation for being almost as much a resort as a business center. Factors typically forged close alliances with their planter clients, and probably a majority were native Southerners. There was a significant non-Southern presence in the trade, however, especially among buyers and agents for northeastern or English houses; Scotch-Irish merchants became powerful in early nineteenth-century Charleston, and in the newer southwestern ports New Yorkers and Englishmen, often part-time residents, played major commercial roles.

Whatever the origins of urban merchants, they worked within a system that left them dependent for markets, capital, and services on cities outside the region. Although Southern banks became increasingly prominent in late antebellum times, many financial services were obtained from the banks, insurance companies, merchants, and shippers of England and the great northeastern ports. Of the latter, New York became increasingly dominant, in large part because of its success in organizing the international cotton trade. Most shipping was controlled by outside interests; moreover, the pattern of shipping that developed enhanced dependence. Southern ports were typically heavy exporters but light importers; accordingly, to minimize backhaul unit costs on the westbound Atlantic voyage, New York shippers established a triangular trade, carrying cotton directly to England, manufactured goods and immigrants to New York, and manufactured goods south. Although Southern urban spokesmen complained loudly of the tribute they thus had to pay the Northerners, no Southern city save New Orleans could sustain direct European trade on its own, and attempts, notably through the commercial convention movement, to foster a cooperative effort at establishing direct Southern ties to Europe ran chronically afoul of urban rivalries within the region.

The low level of imports through Southern cities was, in turn, primarily a product of the low density of demand in their outlying areas. The very lack of a significant urban population with its characteristic abandonment of rural habits of domestic production was part of the problem, as was the large proportion of poor, thinly populated mountain and pine barren land in the region. The most critical inhibitor of demand for goods, though, was the plantation system itself. Its large units helped reduce population density in the Southern countryside relative to that in the North. More important, the economic logic of the slave plantation system led it to minimize outside consumption. Slaves were underutilized in staple crop production, but as "fixed capital" they were available year-round to perform a variety of provisioning and domestic manufacturing operations at little marginal cost. Because they were slaves, it was to the interest of their masters to keep their consumption, especially of high-value goods, to a minimum. Since planters served as purchasing agents for their slaves and dealt chiefly with factors in the nearest major city, plantations provided little stimulus to the development of smaller commercial centers, reinforcing the primate character of the urban system. To be sure, between two-thirds and three-quarters of the white Southern rural population lived in nonslaveholding households, but the plain folk lived plainly. Fearing the risks of commercial agriculture, they involved themselves little in staple production and either produced for themselves or obtained what they needed through local trade. In any case, they lived disproportionately in up-country regions well away from the predominantly coastal major centers, regions made accessible only near the very end of the antebellum period. Whether planter, slave, or yeoman, then, rural Southerners were generally poor customers for urban importers.

Likewise, they were poor customers for urban manufacturers. Although American cities generally were mercantile in character as late as 1840, manufacturing became increasingly associated with cities over the next twenty years—but not in the South. In 1860, the eleven future Confederate cities with populations of over ten thousand employed proportionately less than half as many workers in manufacturing as did their non-Southern counterparts. Of the 102 American cities for which the statistics were reported, Charleston and Mobile had the lowest proportions, 2.1 percent and 2.3 percent, of the nonsuburban incorporated places; with Norfolk, Savannah, and New Orleans, they composed half of the bottom ten, and Memphis followed three ranks further down.

A yet greater deficiency for the long term was the structure of Southern urban manufacturing. Most Southern industry was designed to process raw materials for shipment (tobacco, lumber), supply commercial services (printing and publishing), or provide cheap slave cloth (cotton textiles). On the other hand, in contrast to the factories and shops of cities in the contemporary West, Southern cities developed few of the varied consumers' and producers' goods industries that would lay the groundwork for the subsequent rise of smoke-stack America. Not only was consumer demand inhibited, but the crude techniques of plantation agriculture and the ability of planters to extend their operations simply by adding more slaves (contrasting with the limited labor available to family farmers in the free states) smothered the development of a large-scale agricultural implement industry. With thin demand in the countryside and poorly developed trading links between cities within the region, few Southern cities could reach the threshold of demand required to sustain urban industrial production.

Finally, Southern cities were handicapped by a dearth of cheap energy sources; usually neither fossil fuels nor water power was available in the coastal zones where Southern cities arose. Petersburg and Richmond, the major exceptions to this rule among cities of over ten thousand in 1860, were likewise the only ones specializing in manufacturing, 17.0 percent and 19.7 percent of their populations being so employed. The two Virginia cities were at or near tidewater, but were endowed with ample water power by virtue of their location on the fall line and had access to nearby deposits of coal. The two cities became leading centers of tobacco manufacture; Petersburg developed extensive cotton mills, and Richmond milled flour and tapped supplies of pig iron that had been floated down the James River and Kanawha Canal from the Great valley to develop a sizable ironworking industry, epitomized by the famous Tredegar Iron Works. Other manufacturing developed at smaller interior points, chiefly along the fall line; the cities of Fayetteville, North Carolina, and Augusta and Columbus, Georgia, became important textile centers, and Lynchburg, up the James River from Richmond, flourished as a tobacco center. Generally, though, the urban manufacturing sector was poorly developed and poorly balanced, and moreover operated under severe handicaps; Tredegar, the flagship iron maker, suffered from high costs, inadequate supplies of pig iron, and poor markets, depending heavily (and, for the Confederacy, fortunately) on Federal ordnance contracts for much of its prewar sustenance.

Southern cities, then, even in relatively favored Virginia, were handicapped in their development by a host of structural disabilities, most of them imposed by the constricted role assigned them by the plantation slave economy. Although the dynamic impulse in antebellum Southern urbanization was weak by comparison with that further north, it was by no means absent. Cities were almost always dominated by a commercial-civic elite, a core of merchants and their commercial allies that commanded not only the central economic institutions of the city but also its press and its government.

As with booster elites elsewhere in the country, Southern urban leaders identified their own aspirations with those of the town, and vice versa. To facilitate their common business they organized banks and insurance companies and developed port facilities. Through franchised private companies and municipally owned enterprises they worked to extend city services such as water, gas, paved streets, police and fire protection, and public amenities such as markets and parks; undertaken to enhance the city's attractions as a business location and improve the quality of life for the elite, these services were unevenly distributed, being concentrated in the business district and the better residential neighborhoods.

Most important, Southern urban boosters sought to extend and consolidate their trade through transportation projects. Economic and geographic expansion in the nineteenth century sparked increasing rivalry among American cities generally, and Southern cities were no exceptions, ardently seeking ways to exploit new opportunities and protect themselves from their competitors. A brief canal boom in the 1820s brought few lasting benefits outside Virginia, but new opportunities appeared with the advent of the railroad. Worried about the constriction of its hinterland by its rival Savannah, Charleston capitalists completed the South Carolina Railroad to Hamburg, opposite Augusta, in 1833; 136 miles in length, it was at the time the longest railroad in the world. In later years other major cities, notably those of Virginia and Georgia, took up the challenge. But Southern railroads suffered from the same lack of hinterland demand and unbalanced traffic flows afflicting their terminal cities, and expansion was slow until the 1850s, when a major building boom tripled Southern mileage.

Financed by combinations of private, municipal, state, and outside investment, Southern railroads were planned and operated in accordance with what one historian has termed a developmental strategy; each city's system served to define and extend its hinterland, encourage market production, and channel shipments down the line to the primate city. Accordingly, railroad systems long remained isolated from each other, maintaining separate terminals, refusing connections, and using different gauges. Even as late as 1860, interconnections between city systems were rare and roundabout; with numerous unfilled gaps and dead ends, the Southern rail network was far less articulated than its Northern counterpart (no model of organization itself). Designed to serve the restricted needs of a staple-producing periphery, Southern railroads were thus poorly equipped to support the Confederacy in its struggle for existence.

Some moves toward articulation, though, began to appear late in the antebellum period. Several major cities nursed regional, and even interregional, aspirations; though none successfully met the competition of northeastern ports for the western trade, these larger ambitions began to create embryonic long-haul systems by the 1850s, drawing over-land shipments from the Deep South and Southwest into South Atlantic ports. Of major future consequence for Southern urbanization was the resulting rise of a new kind of urban place, the interior railroad city. Most of them were still small in 1860; Atlanta, the future regional rail hub, had fewer than ten thousand inhabitants, despite mushroomlike growth since its incorporation in 1843. But the appearance on the scene of cities such as Atlanta and Chattanooga, and the rail-induced expansion of older centers such as Nashville, portended a revolution in the character and spatial distribution of Southern cities. Improved transportation and tele-graphic communication not only encouraged interior eco-nomic development but undercut the economic monopoly of the factorage system, on which rested the primacy of the cot-ton ports, and created new centers with vested interests in breaking free of coastal domination. Interior merchants had long sought to dispense with the factor's expensive services, and direct, ready access to the centers of international mar-kets and finance offered opportunities they were eager to exploit. As a result, the Southern urban landscape would look quite different in 1900 than it did in 1860.

Demographics

However commercial they were, Southern cities were hardly mere nodes of merchants, and the great bulk of their inhabitants were of far humbler status than the commercial-civic elites. Inevitably in a slave society, a large number of city dwellers were slaves; the proportion ranged widely, though only rarely exceeding 50 percent. Some slaves were in town as personal servants of their owners; most worked in the commercial economy, chiefly in unskilled work but in numer-ous skilled trades as well. Slaves provided the principal work force for the tobacco factories, flour mills, and ironworks of Virginia. In contrast to the countryside, slave hiring was com-mon in the cities, especially in manufacturing centers, where the majority were hired. Despite legal restrictions, many of these hired slaves managed their own employment, paying their owners for the privilege. A minority, again larger in man-ufacturing centers and again despite legal prohibitions, were allowed to live apart from either owner or user. As this evi-dence suggests, slavery could be easily adapted to the needs of an urban society, and city growth does not appear to have been inhibited by the institution's inflexibility. Nonetheless, slavery was less important in cities, where there were alternative sources of labor, than it was on the plantation, where the advantages of forced labor were much clearer. Accordingly, urban slave populations tended to drop proportionately over time and in the cotton boom of the 1850s frequently dropped absolutely. Because it encouraged planters to use their chattels in relatively lucrative rural pur-suits, plantation slavery thus imparted a structural anti urban bias to the population distribution of the Old South.

Free blacks constituted a small group in Southern cities (usually less than 10 percent of the population), but they were far more urban in their residence than either native whites or slaves; in the upper South one-third of free blacks, and in the lower South a majority, were urbanites, dispropor-tionately concentrated in larger cities. In Virginia, where they constituted 10 percent of all blacks, urban free blacks engaged largely in unskilled pursuits; farther south, where they were fewer in number, they were more likely to be skilled. Typically, skilled workers tended to be of mixed blood and to be heavily concentrated in personal-service occupa-tions catering to whites, such as barbering. The most suc-cessful of these artisans were able to establish themselves

> **Of major future consequence for Southern urbanization was . . . the interior railroad city.**

as a "colored aristocracy." Other free blacks engaged in petty retailing and other services to fellow blacks, free and slave, and over the course of the antebellum period developed insti-tutions, notably the black church, that would lay the founda-tion for racial consciousness and solidarity after emancipa-tion.

A majority of residents in most cities, as in the region gen-erally, were white, but white urbanites differed in striking respects from those in the countryside. A great many prop-ertyless white poor congregated in the cities, producing greater extremes of wealth and poverty than existed even in the plantation districts; in particular, single or widowed females sought employment in the factories of cities such as Petersburg. Native white males tended to concentrate in white-collar occupations and in skilled pursuits such as print-ing. The most unusual characteristic of the Southern white urban population, though, was its large foreign-born compo-nent. Although few antebellum immigrants chose to settle in the South, most who did moved to the larger cities; sizable minorities of city populations were foreign-born, and non-natives not uncommonly dominated the white male working class. Many of these immigrants, the Irish in particular, were relegated to unskilled work, often substituting for slaves; many more, though, especially among the Germans, provid-ed a number of essential skills and developed vigorous petty entrepreneurial communities. With immigrant people came immigrant culture; Judaism and (outside Louisiana) Roman Catholicism established their principal beachheads in the major cities, ethnic social and mutual-aid institutions became important to urban life and commerce, and the Irish in places like New Orleans left an enduring imprint on local accents. Finally, it was in cities that class consciousness and class conflict were most likely to arise. These took the usual forms (labor unions and strikes) appearing in other American cities, but the presence of slave and free black workers, along with an official ideology of white supremacy, added peculiar twists and complexities to class relationships among whites, leading in particular to increased pressure on vulnerable free black communities in the 1850s.

In contrast to the countryside, cities were crowded, and social relations were characterized by relative anonymity and fluidity, enhancing the concerns of the elite over their ability to control social turmoil. As was underscored by the abortive slave uprising planned by Denmark Vesey and others in Charleston, urban black populations could not be constrained as easily as rural ones. Accordingly, municipalities assumed much of the task of domination handled on plantations by the individual slave owner, and inevitably in the name of the white race rather than the slaveholding class. Thus many of the institutions associated with postwar segregation appeared in antebellum times, although racial separation was explicitly harsher on both slaves and free blacks. The white working class could not be treated so bluntly; nonetheless, the influx of immigrants, in particular, heightened elite concerns over social control, and the visibility of the white urban poor stirred consciences among an elite wedded both to white supremacy and to Whiggish notions of moral stewardship. Cities thus became centers of social benevolence, creating orphanages, hospitals, public and private relief agencies, and, toward the end of the antebellum period, the first genuine public schools in the South. In many of these endeavors the lead was taken by societies of middle-class women assuming roles as "civic housekeepers," in the process beginning a redefinition of their constricted sphere that would prove of long-term significance.

Cities during Secession and the Confederacy

As the antebellum period progressed, especially into the 1850s, the sectional conflict increasingly brought a variety of pressures on cities, and they in turn played a significant role of their own in the events leading up to secession. Engaged as they were in commerce, the Southern commercial-civic elites valued stability and maintained close business and personal ties with their northeastern correspondents. Moreover, their desires for commercial and industrial development, frequently with government aid, had traditionally clashed with the free-trade proclivities of rural Southerners. They had traditionally been inclined to Whiggery, regretted the rise of radicalism in both North and South, and thus in the 1860 election tended to support Constitutional Union party candidate John Bell. Moreover, immigrant workers, in particular, were questionable loyalists to the cause of Southern rights; in 1860, in large part because of their vote, Democratic Stephen A. Douglas, otherwise scarcely a factor in the South, scored heavily in cities such as Memphis, Mobile, and New Orleans.

On the other hand, Southern cities were intellectual centers for the ideology of Southern rights; the leading fire-eaters tended to be young, ambitious urbanites of the sort that generally take the lead in developing nationalist movements, and cities such as Charleston became hotbeds of secessionist sentiment. Moreover, the close ties binding Southern cities to the northeastern metropolises generated frustration over their continued dependency and fears that a Federal government in the hands of the North would distribute internal improvement aid inequitably. Industrialists such

> Cities thus became centers of social benevolence, creating orphanages, hospitals, public and private relief agencies. . . .

as Tredegar's Joseph R. Anderson dreamed that an independent South would provide them a huge protected market. Finally, white Southern urbanites were, above all, white Southerners; when the stark choice was posed between secession and "submission" to a "tyrannical" Federal government, secession won easily.

For many cities the Confederate period was brief, as their strategic importance made them early targets of Union advances. Alexandria, Virginia, nominally the tenth largest Confederate city, was under Federal control from the beginning; within little more than a year after the firing on Fort Sumter, Memphis, Nashville, Norfolk, Portsmouth, and the major urban prize of New Orleans had passed behind enemy lines, spending the remainder of the war chafing under hostile occupation but prospering from the military supply trade and from illicit commerce between the two sides.

For the remaining cities, however, war brought unprecedented importance. Although the expanding Union blockade effectively shut down some ports, notably Savannah, others, such as Charleston (until the summer of 1863), Wilmington, and to a lesser extent Mobile, became major centers of blockade running, thanks not only to their harbors but to their financial and entrepreneurial communities. Richmond, the Confederate capital, swelled to 128,000, over three times its prewar size, with the burgeoning of the Confederate wartime bureaucracy. Manufacturing and supply operations doubled the populations of cities in interior Georgia. Industrial demands brought a flood of new entrepreneurs into manufacturing, along with the Confederate government itself, which established important facilities at, among other locations, Augusta, Georgia, and Selma, Alabama. Military authorities developed urban infrastructure, such as sewers, in the interest of preserving the health of their troops; the Confederate government filled in critical gaps in the rail network, notably between Greensboro, North Carolina, and

Danville, Virginia, an action that would have a major impact on future Southern urban patterns.

In the end, though, the war lent little enduring impetus to urbanization. The operations of critical manufacturing firms such as Tredegar were hampered by supply bottlenecks, and the monopolization of scarce industrial capacity by military production left little opportunity for city building; indeed, the Southern infrastructure deteriorated in the course of the conflict. War-induced growth was hothouse growth, and enterprises begun to satisfy a single tolerant customer were ill equipped to satisfy many demanding ones. Indeed, all told, the war's significance to Confederate cities lay less in its benefits than in the intense strains it placed on them. Cities became bloated with workers and refugees. The deurbanization of slavery was reversed, as numbers of slaves were impressed for military work, brought to town by refugee owners, or simply abandoned by hard-pressed masters and mistresses. Municipal efforts to counter increased slave independence were largely dead letters, and the institution showed clear signs of decay well before formal emancipation. The swelling numbers of propertyless employees, especially women whose men were in military service, were peculiarly vulnerable to the rampant inflation tearing through the Confederate economic fabric; it has been estimated that real wages dropped by 60 percent in the course of the war. Blockade-running ports such as Charleston and Wilmington enjoyed a diseased prosperity, as runners and merchants profited from trade in military supplies and luxuries that clogged supply lines and sent the cost of living soaring. Despite efforts at expanding poor relief, inflation, impressment, and the inadequacies of the Confederate distribution system left poorer urbanites in an increasingly serious plight and generated enormous social tensions, usually directed against speculators. These tensions culminated in a number of bread riots, frequently led by women, the greatest number of which occurred in the spring of 1863.

Confederate cities generally managed to withstand social tensions, but the powerful Union offensives beginning in the summer of 1864 began to tear the urban system apart. Cities, notably Richmond, had long been important Union objectives; by the end of the summer the capital and nearby Petersburg were under siege, and in early 1865 the last major ports east of Texas, Mobile and Wilmington, were sealed by the Union navy. Moreover, beginning in 1864 the deliberate destruction of cities and the transportation links tying them together became integral to a policy of crippling the Confederate war-making capacity. After capitulating in the summer, Atlanta was burned by Gen. William Tecumseh Sherman in November as he embarked on his March to the Sea and the capture of Savannah; in February 1865 Columbia shared Atlanta's fate, although Sherman's culpability in the burning of the South Carolina capital remains in dispute. Gen. James H. Wilson's cavalry, on its sweep through the Deep South in the spring of 1865, destroyed the war-industry centers of Selma and Columbus, aided in the looting of the Georgia city by slaves and women workers. Other cities, such as Charleston, Richmond, and Petersburg, suffered severe damage incidental to military action in the course of the war.

Above all, the end of the war brought the end of the system of plantation slavery that had shaped the character of Southern cities. To be sure, its legacy would continue to influence Southern urban development in profound ways, some still discernible today. Nonetheless, the destruction of the slave regime would fundamentally alter the course of urbanization in the region. From the ashes of the Confederacy would arise a different and more dynamic Southern urban order.

[*See also* Bread Riots; Foreigners; Free People of Color; Inflation; Poor Relief; Poverty; Railroads; Textile Industry; and entries on the numerous cities mentioned herein.]

BIBLIOGRAPHY

Amos, Harriet E. *Cotton City: Urban Development in Antebellum Mobile.* University, Ala., 1985.

Coclanis, Peter A. *The Shadow of a Dream: Economic Life and Death in the South Carolina Low Country, 1670–1920.* New York, 1989.

DeCredico, Mary A. *Patriotism for Profit: Georgia's Urban Entrepreneurs and the Confederate War Effort.* Chapel Hill, N.C., 1990.

Goldfield, David R. *Cotton Fields and Skyscrapers: Southern City and Region, 1607–1980.* Baton Rouge, La., 1982.

Goldfield, David R. *Urban Growth in the Age of Sectionalism: Virginia, 1847–1861.* Baton Rouge, La., 1977.

Goldfield, David R., and Blaine A. Brownell, eds. *The City in Southern History: The Growth of Urban Civilization in the South.* Port Washington, N.Y., 1977.

Goldin, Claudia Dale. *Urban Slavery in the American South, 1820–1860.* Chicago, 1976.

Gutman, Herbert G., and Ira Berlin. "Natives and Immigrants, Free Men and Slaves: Urban Workingmen in the Antebellum American South." *American Historical Review* 88 (1983): 1175–1200.

Meyer, David R. "The Industrial Retardation of Southern Cities, 1860–1880." *Explorations in Economic History* 25 (1988): 366–386.

Wade, Richard C. *Slavery in the Cities: The South, 1820–1860.* New York, 1964.

Woodman, Harold D. *King Cotton and His Retainers: Financing and Marketing the Cotton Crop of the South, 1800–1925.* Lexington, Ky., 1968

DAVID L. CARLTON

VANCE, ZEBULON

VANCE, ZEBULON (1830–1894), colonel, governor of North Carolina, and U.S. senator. Zebulon Baird Vance was born on May 13, 1830, in the Reems Creek community of Buncombe County, North Carolina. A comfortable childhood ended in 1844 when his father died and the family farm and slaves had to be sold. This ended Vance's formal education until 1851 when he studied law at the University of North Carolina. In 1852, he passed the bar examination and was elected solicitor of the Buncombe County court.

In 1854, he was elected to the state legislature as a Whig and soon after became an editor of the *Asheville Spectator*. When the Whig party collapsed, Vance joined the Know-Nothings. He won a special election for the U.S. Congress in 1858 and was reelected the next year. Vance's success was largely due to his popular speaking style, which combined skilled partisan rhetoric with bawdy good humor.

Although Vance was a firm advocate of slavery, he was a strong defender of the Union during the secession crisis. He campaigned for the John Bell presidential ticket during the election of 1860, and in Congress he supported many compromise proposals to end the crisis. During February 1861,

> ## Vance's military career ended in 1862 when he reentered politics.

Vance campaigned as a Union supporter in the secession referendum held in North Carolina. His stand was vindicated when a large majority of the state's voters rejected the call for secession. Because Vance had been assured by William H. Seward that Abraham Lincoln would withdraw the troops from Fort Sumter, he felt betrayed by the attempt to resupply the fort and Lincoln's call for troops.

Vance's career as a Confederate officer was not distinguished. He helped organize the "Rough and Ready Guards" of Buncombe County and was elected company captain. Before the unit saw action, however, he was elected colonel of the Twenty-sixth North Carolina Volunteer Regiment. Vance was poor at organizing a military unit, and only the

presence of Henry King Burgwyn, Jr., as second in command ensured that the regiment learned elemental military tactics. During the Battle of New Bern on March 14, 1862, Vance's regiment was placed on the extreme right of a weak Confederate line. An attack by General Ambrose Burnside's much larger army shattered the Confederate line and forced Vance and his men into rapid retreat. The regiment joined the Army of Northern Virginia and took part in the Seven Days' Battles around Richmond. Vance and his regiment participated in the final and unsuccessful assault on Malvern Hill on July 1, 1862.

Vance's military career ended in 1862 when he reentered politics. On June 15, he became the Conservative party's gubernatorial nominee. That party was formed by the Whig party leadership and William W. Holden, a former leader of North Carolina Democrats. Vance's opponent was William Johnston, the candidate of the original secessionists who now called themselves Confederates. Vance won the August election overwhelmingly by gaining the support of those who opposed the war and those who thought that the Confederate party was responsible for the inadequate defense of the state. Since Vance was the candidate of the dissatisfied, many observers expected him to challenge the Confederacy. Starting with his inaugural address in September 1862, however, he proclaimed his allegiance to the Southern nation.

Although Vance never repudiated his support of the Confederacy, he was more than willing to defend his state and challenge Confederate policies. When North Carolina Supreme Court justice Richmond Pearson ruled that the state militia could not enforce conscription and that men who had hired substitutes could not be subsequently conscripted, Vance refused to override these rulings despite frequent requests from Confederate authorities to do so. Vance defended Pearson despite his personal disagreement with Pearson's findings. Vance's commitment to North Carolina's welfare had many other manifestations. He initiated a very successful state blockade-running plan that predated that of the Richmond government. In addition, he pushed a state program to clothe North Carolina troops, a salt procurement program, and a series of measures to provide more food for the poor.

During this same period, Vance frequently clashed with James A. Seddon and Jefferson Davis. Among his most common complaints were that North Carolina officers were not being promoted as rapidly as those from other states, that Confederate troops were abusing North Carolina civilians, and that the Confederate government was trying to conscript state officials. The correspondence was often heated, and at one point, Davis attempted to break off further communication with Vance. Despite the rather sharp rhetoric in the letters, Vance rarely impeded the war effort and publicly defended conscription and unpopular Confederate tax policies. As late as October 1864, Vance was a moving force in the Confederate governor's conference held in Augusta, Georgia, that reaffirmed the allegiance of the states to the Confederacy.

A significant minority of North Carolinians opposed Vance and the Confederacy. From the beginning of the war, Unionists in all parts of the state resisted Confederate conscription. Despite the use of force in such disparate areas as Washington County, Randolph County, and the Shelton Laurel community, Vance's Home Guards and the Confederate army were unable to eliminate this persistent opposition. By the summer of 1864, there were an estimated ten thousand Unionists enrolled in the Heroes of America. Many other North Carolinians also began to withdraw their commitment to the Confederacy. As early as 1862, yeoman farmers were outraged that those who owned twenty slaves were exempted from conscription. After Confederate defeats at Gettysburg and Vicksburg, Vance's political ally William W. Holden issued a call for peace meetings throughout the state to bring an end to the fighting.

The North Carolina peace movement was the most vocal in the Confederacy. During July and August 1863, about a hundred public meetings were held urging a peaceful end to the war. Vance reluctantly broke with Holden and issued a proclamation on September 7, 1863, that ended the public demonstrations. In the congressional elections of 1863, the peace candidates were successful in a majority of districts. Following up on this victory, Holden urged peace advocates to demand a state convention where delegates could negotiate a truce with Northern political leaders. Vance challenged Holden's program when he opened his reelection campaign in February 1864. After Holden announced his candidacy, Vance stumped the state attacking him and claiming that the peace program would involve North Carolina in a war with the Confederacy. Vance also attacked Davis's use of the writ of habeas corpus. The strategy was successful, and Vance was reelected by an overwhelming majority in August.

Vance tried unsuccessfully to prevent the collapse of the Confederacy in North Carolina after his election. He sought to collect supplies for the Confederate army and to return deserters to Robert E. Lee's army; he rushed the state militia to Wilmington to assist in the defense of Fort Fisher. A month later, Vance refused to take part in an attempted coup against Jefferson Davis engineered by William A. Graham

and other members of Congress. When William Tecumseh Sherman's large army entered North Carolina in April 1865, Vance arranged for the surrender of Raleigh before attending one last meeting with the fleeing Davis. On May 13, 1865, Vance was arrested in Statesville, North Carolina, and transported to Washington where he was placed in the old Capitol prison. On July 6, he was paroled to his home in North Carolina.

During Reconstruction, Vance resumed the practice of law and moved to Charlotte. In 1870, he was elected to the U.S. Senate, but the Republican majority refused to remove his political disabilities and Vance had to relinquish his seat. The Democrats nominated Vance as their gubernatorial candidate in 1876. The outstanding rhetorical abilities of Vance and his Republican opponent, Thomas Settle, and their debates across the state made this the most famous campaign in North Carolina's history. Vance's narrow victory over Settle ended Republican Reconstruction in North Carolina. Vance was elected to the U.S. Senate in January 1879, but his Senate career was frustrating and largely unproductive.

Starting in 1889, Vance suffered from failing health, and he died in Washington on April 14, 1894. His death prompted a massive outpouring of grief in North Carolina where scores of memorial services honored the state's war governor. He is still regarded as the most popular public figure in North Carolina history.

BIBLIOGRAPHY

Barrett, John G. *The Civil War in North Carolina.* Chapel Hill, N.C., 1963.
Davis, Archie K. *Boy Colonel of the Confederacy: The Life and Times of Henry King Burgwyn, Jr.* Chapel Hill, N.C., 1985.
Dowd, Clement. *The Life of Zebulon Vance.* Charlotte, N.C., 1897.
Johnston, Frontis K., ed. *The Letters of Zebulon Baird Vance.* Vol. 1. Raleigh, N.C., 1963.
Kruman, Marc W. *Parties and Politics in North Carolina, 1836–1865.* Baton Rouge, La., 1983.
McKinney, Gordon B., and Richard M. McMurry, eds. *The Papers of Zebulon Vance.* Frederick, Md., 1987.
Tucker, Glenn. *Zeb Vance: Champion of Personal Freedom.* Indianapolis, 1966.
Yates, Richard E. *The Confederacy and Zeb Vance.* Tuscaloosa, Ala., 1958.

GORDON B. MCKINNEY

VAN DORN, EARL

VAN DORN, EARL (1820–1863), major general. Van Dorn was born September 20, 1820, near Port Gibson, Mississippi, the son of a local magistrate and great-nephew of Andrew Jackson. After almost being dismissed from West Point for excessive demerits, Van Dorn graduated fifty-second out of fifty-six. Van Dorn, whose friends called him "Buck," served on the frontier and was seriously wounded in a battle with the Comanches. In Mexico he was wounded again and won two brevets for gallantry. In the mid-1850s he joined the Second U.S. Cavalry and served in Texas.

Van Dorn resigned from the Federal army on January 31, 1861, and offered his services to his home state. He was made a brigadier general of the Mississippi state troops, second only to Maj. Gen. Jefferson Davis. The two were good friends, and Van Dorn eventually succeeded Davis in command. On March 26, 1861, Van Dorn joined the Confederacy as a colonel and took over the forts below New Orleans. On April 11 he was made commander of the Department of Texas and on June 5 was promoted to brigadier general. He was elevated to major general on September 19 and transferred to Virginia where he led a division.

When a disagreement in the West between Sterling Price, commander of the Missourians, and Brig. Gen. Ben McCulloch made coordination almost impossible there, Van Dorn was ordered to the District of the Trans-Mississippi, Department No. 2. He assumed command over the disputatious men and led the Confederates in his first battle as an army commander. At Elkhorn Tavern, Arkansas, poor planning and inadequate management turned the battle into a series of disasters. After this loss Van Dorn took his Army of the West across the Mississippi River but was too late to participate in the Battle of Shiloh. In March 1862 he was appointed district commander and in late June took over the defense of Vicksburg. When Van Dorn attacked William S. Rosecrans at Corinth on October 3 through 4, 1862, he was defeated. Mississippians had already become disenchanted with Van Dorn, partly because of his scandalous private life and partly because of his unpopular decision to implement martial law. Following the loss at Corinth, President Davis had John C. Pemberton promoted to lieutenant general over Van Dorn, and he assumed command of the cavalry. Van Dorn is best remembered for his destruction of Ulysses S. Grant's supply depot at Holly Springs, Mississippi, in December 1862, which halted the Union move on Vicksburg.

Van Dorn might have become a first-class cavalry leader, but he was murdered in his headquarters at Spring Hill, Tennessee, on May 7, 1863. A jealous husband, Dr. George B. Peters, claimed that Van Dorn had "violated the sanctity" of his home, although Van Dorn's numerous friends denied the validity of this charge. Van Dorn had the reputation of being a "horrible rake." He was described as a "small, elegant figure," whom women found attractive. One soldier observed that Van Dorn looked "more like a dandy than a general of an army." Jefferson Davis's brother observed that "when Van Dorn was made a general, it spoiled a good captain." He is buried at Port Gibson, Mississippi.

BIBLIOGRAPHY

Ferguson, John L. *Arkansas and the Civil War.* Little Rock, Ark., 1964.

Hartje, Robert G. *Van Dorn: The Life and Times of a Confederate General.* Nashville, Tenn., 1967.

ANNE J. BAILEY

VAN LEW, ELIZABETH

VAN LEW, ELIZABETH (1818–1900), Union spy. An outspoken opponent of slavery, Van Lew ran a Union spy ring in her hometown of Richmond, Virginia, during the war. At Van Lew's behest, Mary Elizabeth Bowser, a former servant of the Van Lews, gained employment as a domestic in the Confederate White House. There Bowser gathered military information and passed it on to Van Lew, who in turn transmitted it to Union forces.

Van Lew frequently visited Federal prisoners in Libby Prison in Richmond to bring them food, books, and clothing; she is rumored to have helped some escape. In April 1864 she arranged for the clandestine reburial of Union hero Col. Ulric Dahlgren, whose body was mutilated and secretly buried by Confederate forces after he was killed leading a surprise raid on Richmond in March.

Although Van Lew was under close surveillance by Confederate agents during the war, she was never caught at espionage work; her bizarre dress and behavior, which earned her the name "Crazy Bet," was her ploy to divert suspicion. During the last year of the war, her intelligence operations included a network of five relay stations from Richmond to Federal headquarters downriver. When Union forces occupied her native city in 1865, Van Lew raised the first American flag to be seen there since 1861.

After the war President Ulysses S. Grant appointed Van Lew postmistress of Richmond, an office she held until 1877. In her last years she became an advocate of women's suffrage, paying her taxes under protest. In 1900, after enduring years of social ostracism from ex-Confederates, she died and was buried in Richmond.

BIBLIOGRAPHY

Bailey, James H. "Crazy Bet, Union Spy." *Virginia Cavalcade* 1 (1952): 14–17.

Kane, Harnett T. *Spies for the Blue and Gray.* Garden City, N.Y., 1954.

Turney, Catherine. "Crazy Betty." *Mankind: the Magazine of Popular History* 3 (1971): 58–64.

ELIZABETH R. VARON

VENABLE, ABRAHAM WATKINS

VENABLE, ABRAHAM WATKINS (1799–1876), congressman from North Carolina. Venable was born in Prince Edward County, Virginia. He attended both Hampton-Sidney College and Princeton College, graduating in 1816 and 1819, respectively. Forsaking an initial interest in medicine, Venable studied law and was admitted to the Virginia bar in 1821. Practicing first in his native state, he moved to North Carolina, settling in Granville County in 1829.

As a respected lawyer, Venable ventured into the world of politics and was chosen to be an elector on the Democratic tickets in 1832 and 1836. He was elected to the U.S. Congress in 1846 and served in the House of Representatives for three terms. There he spoke out in opposition to the admission of California to the Union and the desire by some to annex Cuba—arguing in both cases that

> **Venable moved unsuccessfully to remove the death penalty for convicted counterfeiters and substitute a . . . prison term.**

each would be detrimental to Southern interests. Losing a bid for reelection in 1852, Venable returned to North Carolina and resumed his law practice.

Never far from the political scene, Venable became an active secessionist and served as an elector on the Democratic ticket of Breckinridge and Lane in 1860. Following North Carolina's secession from the Union, the former congressman was elected to the House of Representatives of the Provisional Confederate Congress. He was appointed to serve on both the Committee on Naval Affairs and the Committee on Foreign Affairs, but was excused from the latter at his own request. Venable generally voted to support the policies of the administration. During the debate over the bill to authorize the issuance of Treasury notes and to provide a war tax for their redemption, Venable moved unsuccessfully to remove the death penalty for convicted counterfeiters and substitute a ten- to fifteen-year prison term. He lost his bid for election to the First Congress and returned to North Carolina. He died in Oxford.

BIBLIOGRAPHY

Biographical Directory of the American Congress, 1774–1971. Washington, D.C., 1971.
Journal of the Congress of the Confederate States of America, 1861–1865. 7 vols. Washington, D.C., 1904–1905.
Wakelyn, Jon L. Biographical Dictionary of the Confederacy. Edited by Frank E. Vandiver. Westport, Conn., 1977.
Warner, Ezra J., and W. Buck Yearns. Biographical Register of the Confederate Congress. Baton Rouge, La., 1975.

ALAN C. DOWNS

VICKSBURG CAMPAIGN

The city of Vicksburg, Mississippi, located on the east bank of the Mississippi River midway between Memphis and New Orleans, was the site of a key Confederate river defense and the focal point of Maj. Gen. Ulysses S. Grant's operations in the West from October 1862 to July 1863. The surrender of its fortifications and a garrison of 29,500 men on July 4, 1863, was a severe psychological blow to the Confederacy and, combined with the simultaneous defeat of the Army of Northern Virginia at Gettysburg, loss of manpower that the South could ill afford.

In 1861, Vicksburg's population of nearly five thousand was the second largest in the state. Its economy was prospering, thanks to the city's status as a commercial center and transportation hub for Mississippi and Louisiana planters. To the east, the Southern Railroad of Mississippi linked Vicksburg and Jackson and connected the former to other lines including the northward-running Mississippi Central Railroad. To the west, the Vicksburg, Shreveport and Texas Railroad went as far as Monroe, Louisiana, giving planters in the bottomlands access to the river and New Orleans. Riverboats of all shapes and sizes docked at the city's wharves and took cargoes of cotton and passengers south to the Crescent City.

When the war began, Vicksburg took on an even greater significance. It became one of the key links between the eastern Confederacy and the Trans-Mississippi South, serving as a transit point for troops and as a port of entry for Louisiana salt, sugar, and molasses, the latter two frequently exchanged for meat for the armies. Efforts to safeguard the city became crucial in the spring of 1862 when Memphis and New Orleans fell to Federal forces. Vicksburg remained the only railhead on the east bank of the river and as such provided the last direct link between the two "halves" of the Confederacy. Its maintenance also effectively blocked Federal waterborne communications down the river.

In May 1862, three thousand troops, evacuated from New Orleans, arrived in Vicksburg along with their commander, Brig. Gen. Martin Luther Smith. They were joined by companies from Mississippi and Louisiana, turning the city into a garrison. Smith concentrated on fortifying the city's river approaches, where he was aided by the natural features of the area. Vicksburg sat in a cluster of hills two hundred feet above the river opposite De Soto Peninsula—ideal defensive terrain. Seven batteries were erected on the bluffs just in time for the arrival of USS *Oneida,* which on May 20 fired upon the city, commencing the thirteen-month-long campaign for Vicksburg.

Early Federal Moves against Vicksburg. Throughout the rest of May and into June, ships from Flag Officer David Farragut's deepwater fleet multiplied in the river south of Vicksburg, reinforced by mortar schooners under Commdr. David D. Porter. On June 27, work began on a plan to bypass the Confederate river defenses by using troops and impressed slaves to dig a canal across the base of the penin- sula created by the river's bend. The following day, Farragut's fleet conducted an early morning run past Vicksburg's gaunt- let of batteries and linked up with Flag Officer Charles H. Davis's gunboat flotilla north of the river's bend out of range of Confederate guns. But the Federal navy was unable to develop a plan to force the city's capitulation and reverted to bombarding Vicksburg while continuing construction on the canal.

Farragut's fortunes took a turn for the worse in July when Porter was transferred east, the subsiding waters of the Mississippi threatened to leave his oceangoing fleet strand- ed upriver for the remainder of the year, and the Confederate ram *Arkansas* created havoc by sailing into the Federal fleet on July 15. Unable to destroy *Arkansas,* Farragut took his ships out to sea on July 25 while Davis steamed north to Helena, Arkansas. It was clear that the U.S. Army would play the predominant role in subduing Vicksburg, and Major General Smith, aware of this, focused on building up the city's fortifications.

On June 28, Maj. Gen. Earl Van Dorn had arrived in the city to assume command. Van Dorn continued to strengthen the defenses of Vicksburg and of the stretch of river south of the city by fortifying Port Hudson. With the departure of the Federal fleet, Van Dorn turned his attention to enemy troops in northern Mississippi and western Tennessee under the command of Grant. The resulting fiasco at Corinth cost Van Dorn five thousand troops and left Vicksburg exposed. Grant now suggested to Maj. Gen. Henry Halleck that he be allowed to conduct "a forward movement against Vicksburg."

While Van Dorn was engaging Federal troops at Corinth, the Confederate War Department appointed Maj. Gen. John C. Pemberton to head a military district comprising the state of Mississippi and that part of Louisiana east of the Mississippi River. Pemberton assumed command on October 14, establishing his headquarters in Jackson. His assignment was part of a large-scale administrative change that placed all Confederate forces west of the Alleghenies and east of the Mississippi River under Gen. Joseph E. Johnston. Johnston, lukewarm about his new assignment, argued that the ambiguities inherent in President Jefferson Davis's new command arrangements made his role purely "nominal" and

that he possessed little authority but great responsibility. Although he established his headquarters at Chattanooga, however, Johnston did not ignore Vicksburg.

Grant Takes Command. Grant's campaign to capture the city officially began on November 2 when he assembled an army of thirty thousand at Grand Junction, Tennessee, and began moving in three columns down the line of the Mississippi Central Railroad toward Holly Springs, twenty miles south. Pemberton's initial response was to fortify the south bank of the Tallahatchie River. But turning movements on both flanks threatened the Confederate rear and forced Pemberton to withdraw to the south bank of the Yalobusha River at Grenada.

Grant, with Halleck's approval, now detached Maj. Gen. William Tecumseh Sherman to lead a waterborne operation. His plan called for simultaneous advances south by his army and Sherman's, forcing Pemberton to divide his resources and fight on two fronts.

Although well conceived, Grant's operation fell victim to Confederate cavalry attacks against the vulnerable Federal lines of communication. Brig. Gen. Nathan Bedford Forrest's destruction of sixty miles of rail lines in western Tennessee caught Grant by surprise. Most damaging of all was a December 20 strike by Van Dorn (now commanding Pemberton's cavalry) against the Federal supply depot at Holly Springs. Grant lost the supplies necessary to continue his half of the two-pronged operation and, thanks to Forrest, could not replace them. By the time Sherman heard of Grant's withdrawal northward he was already committed to proceeding with his own attack. On December 26 and 27, Sherman's expeditionary force of 32,000 men disembarked from transports near Chickasaw Bayou on the Yazoo River and assaulted the city's northernmost defenders under Brig. Gen. Stephen D. Lee. The three-day battle proved to be a Federal disaster, and Sherman withdrew on January 2.

By the end of January, Grant's new objective was to iso- late the city by severing its rail link to Jackson. To accomplish this, he planned to execute a turning movement from the north and east. Realizing that movement along the railroad would leave him vulnerable to attack, he chose to forgo land communications and use the Mississippi as his main line of operations. The Mississippi route was secure from enemy attacks thanks to the return of Union gunboats now under the command of Porter, but lacked sufficient dry ground for offen- sive operations. The ideal terrain for Grant's army was south of the city, but getting vulnerable transport ships south past the batteries would be difficult at best.

Grant's efforts to get his army on dry ground south and east of the city led to several unorthodox maneuvers. Initially, he considered using the transpeninsula canal begun the pre- vious year, but it was turning into a quagmire. He then thought of creating a southerly route to the river south of the city by using a combination of lakes, bayous, and streams west of the Mississippi, including Lake Providence, a six-mile-long body of water that was once part of the river. Grant, however, grew disenchanted with the project after a February 4 inspection trip to the lake and looked for yet another solution.

An alternative was already materializing on the east bank of the river. Grant was notified that by destroying a levee at Yazoo Pass, fifty miles below Memphis, vessels could pass through an old channel to the Coldwater River, enter the Tallahatchie, and steam down the Yazoo River to the rear of Vicksburg. Pemberton quickly caught on to Grant's scheme after the levee was opened on February 2 and responded by sending two thousand troops under Maj. Gen. W. W. Loring to block the movement. Loring constructed a stronghold called Fort Pemberton out of cotton bales and sand, and armed it with thirteen guns, including a 6.5-inch rifled cannon. Between March 11 and 16, a Federal expedition led by Lt. Commdr. Watson Smith and Brig. Gen. Leonard Fulton to reduce the fort was foiled by the ineffectiveness of the gunboats, the accuracy of the Confederate's rifled cannon, and the fort's inaccessibility from land. An operation begun on March 14 by Porter and Sherman up Steele's Bayou in an effort to enter the Yazoo below Fort Pemberton was transformed by Grant into another would-be solution to his problem. Instead of moving to help Smith and Fulton, Porter was ordered to operate against Vicksburg itself with the goal of deploying Sherman's troops northeast of the city. After battling obstructions and sharpshooters, Porter abandoned the operation on March 20 and returned to the Mississippi. On April 4, Grant recalled the Yazoo Pass expedition and prepared to try something else.

Grant's new plan originated out of his earlier designs for Lake Providence and the success in February of two vessels in running past the Vicksburg batteries. His idea was to move the majority of his army down the west side of the Mississippi River below Vicksburg and then run Porter's gunboats and empty transports southward past the Confederate defenses to Hard Times, where they would rendezvous with the awaiting army. The vessels could then ferry the army across the river, allowing Grant to begin his campaign against the city and the rail line. Sherman's corps would initially stay behind to conduct demonstrations near Vicksburg. Col. Benjamin H. Grierson's 1,700 cavalrymen would undertake an extensive raid into Mississippi to disrupt Confederate communications and draw attention away from Grant's operation.

Federal troops began moving south on March 31, and twenty-eight days later two corps had reached Hard Times. On April 16, eleven out of the twelve boats (including two transports) assigned by Porter completed a midnight run past the Vicksburg batteries and proceeded south to join Grant. The next day, Grierson's troopers left their camp in southwest Tennessee and headed south toward the railroads, supply depots, and plantations of eastern Mississippi.

On April 22, five more transports and six barges successfully ran the gauntlet. By April 29, Grant was prepared to ferry his army across the river. From April 30 through May 1, while Sherman conducted his diversion north of Vicksburg, 23,000 Federal troops disembarked at Bruinsburg on the east bank of the Mississippi. Grant was now on dry soil, and the final phase of the campaign for Vicksburg was about to begin.

For Pemberton, the flurry of Federal activity across the river in early April was indicative of a withdrawal. After assuring Davis and Johnston that Grant was abandoning his operations against Vicksburg, Pemberton went so far as to prepare to send reinforcements to Gen. Braxton Bragg's Army of Tennessee, the next logical target of a Federal western offensive. But on April 17, Johnston and Adj. Gen. Samuel Cooper learned from Pemberton that Grant's army was not leaving after all. Nevertheless, Pemberton chose to focus his attention upon Grierson's raid rather than on determining Grant's intentions, deploying an infantry division to try and trap Grierson's cavalry. Johnston, a proponent of maneuverability, informed Pemberton from Tennessee that he should unite his whole force to beat Grant, remarking "Success will give back what was abandoned to win it." Davis, on the other hand, sent Pemberton instructions to hold both Vicksburg and Port Hudson—evacuation ran counter to the president's strategic principles. Thus Pemberton, who had never commanded an army in combat, received conflicting instructions and chose to comply with the president's and his own preference for holding fortifications.

The Confederate indecision and confusion allowed Grant to pursue his strategy at will. After landing at Bruinsburg, he moved quickly against Brig. Gen. John Stevens Bowen's small and divided force at Port Gibson and Grand Gulf, forcing the latter's evacuation on May 3. The line of march chosen by Grant out of now Federally controlled Grand Gulf was in part dictated by the general's original plan to move on Vicksburg from the east after first securing the Southern Railroad of Mississippi. A second factor was the 100-mile-long Big Black River that ran from the center of the state above Jackson southwestwardly to Grand Gulf. Crossing the river and moving directly north toward Vicksburg could be risky if his force was challenged, and the broken terrain between the Big Black and the city favored Pemberton. Therefore, Grant chose to move north and east, threatening both Vicksburg and Jackson. His army advanced in three columns: Maj. Gen. John McClernand's corps on the left, with instructions to "hug the river [the Big Black]," the recently arrived Sherman in the center, and Maj. Gen. James McPherson on the right.

The first major Confederate resistance to the march occurred on May 12 near Raymond, fourteen miles southwest of Jackson. Brig. Gen. John Gregg brought his brigade out of the capital and struck the vanguard of McPherson's corps, led by Maj. Gen. John A. Logan. The Confederates held for six hours before being forced to retire. Grant now knew that Southern troops might be concentrating in Jackson. He decided therefore to take advantage of his central position between two Confederate forces, sending McPherson northeast to Clinton where he was to destroy the railroad and move east to the capital. Sherman was to move his corps through Raymond toward Jackson. McClernand was ordered to be in position to reinforce either of the other two corps and to watch for an advance by Pemberton from the west.

On the same day that Grant issued these orders, Johnston arrived in Jackson to assume command of Confederate forces in Mississippi and learned the full magnitude of the situation: Grant was between Jackson and Vicksburg and Pemberton had not concentrated his forces. Johnston was too late to execute the speedy concentration of force that he had hoped to use against Grant. The railroad and telegraph lines were cut and any union of Pemberton's army and Johnston's gathering reinforcements would have to be coordinated from a distance using unreliable communications. For his part, Pemberton and 17,500 troops ventured out of the Vicksburg defenses on May 12 and advanced as far as Edwards Station, a railroad town east of the Big Black and halfway to Jackson. Aware of Pemberton's general location and seeing an opportunity to strike Grant while his army was divided, Johnston sent word via three couriers for Pemberton to strike the rear of the Federal force on the railroad at Clinton.

On May 14, with only 6,000 troops available in Jackson and inadequate earthworks to use as protection, Johnston evacuated the capital and moved north toward Calhoun. Dispatches were sent east and south to inform incoming reinforcements of the situation. By midafternoon, Federal troops had successfully fought their way through the Confederate rear guard and entered Jackson where they remained until May 16. Pemberton meanwhile pondered Johnston's instructions and held a council of war with his subordinates. Although the majority of his officers favored compliance with Johnston's directive, the council nevertheless decided to move southeast to cut Grant's supply line to the Mississippi. Thus Pemberton decided essentially to send his army away from rather than toward a unification with Johnston's. When the latter was informed of this development, he quickly sent another message urging conformity to his original instructions. By that time it was too late. Grant, learning Johnston's intentions from a Northern sympathizer who happened to be one of the Confederate general's original three couriers, was rapidly moving westward to confront Pemberton.

The two forces clashed on May 16 at Champion's Hill, eighteen miles east of Vicksburg. In an all-day fight, Pemberton displayed little tactical skill and was eventually defeated. In his report to Johnston, Pemberton stated that his current position was too vulnerable, and he felt compelled to withdraw back to the safety of Vicksburg. Consequently, after attempting to slow the Federal advance across the Big Black River on May 17 and losing Loring's division when it was separated from the main body of the army, the majority of Pemberton's troops returned to the city with Grant's entire army in pursuit.

Johnston sent word to Pemberton instructing him to evacuate Vicksburg and march to the northeast. For the commanding general, the object of the campaign was the defeat of Grant's army, not the retention of a geographic point. By now, the strategic significance of Vicksburg was at best questionable. The value of the Mississippi River to the Confederacy had been drastically reduced ever since the capture of New Orleans and Memphis and the resulting loss of two of the three most important rail termini on the river.

> **"I still conceive it to be the most important point in the Confederacy."**

After Porter's gunboats successfully ran past the batteries in April, steamboats could no longer safely reach the railhead at Vicksburg, thus severing the Trans-Mississippi supply line. The only remaining significance of Vicksburg was political and psychological. Davis had promised his fellow Mississippians that Vicksburg would not fall. Moreover, from his point of view, he could ill afford to lose this symbol of Confederate control on the Mississippi.

In response to Johnston's request for an evacuation, Pemberton held a second council of war and this time received, according to his own account, unanimous support for remaining in the city. He wrote Johnston that "I still conceive it to be the most important point in the Confederacy." The decision made, he prepared to turn away the approaching Federals.

The Siege of Vicksburg. Grant, eager to take Vicksburg and avoid a protracted siege, attacked the city's defenses on May 19 and again three days later. Both assaults were repulsed with heavy casualties. He was now forced to resort to a siege and instructed his engineers to begin encircling the nine miles of Confederate entrenchments. Once completed, the twelve-mile-long Federal line paralleled the Confederate earthworks at an average distance of six hundred yards and was anchored at both ends on the Mississippi River. By the end of May, 50,000 men surrounded the city; two weeks later 27,000 more were on hand.

Through May and into June, Johnston, focusing on raising an army sufficient to lift the siege or at least open a hole long enough for Pemberton to escape, wrote repeatedly to the War Department requesting troops from all available sources. On June 1, Johnston reported he had 24,053 effectives and needed more. He, along with Lt. Gen. James Longstreet and Gen. P. G. T. Beauregard, suggested to the War Department that an operation in middle Tennessee might draw Federal troops away from Pemberton. Longstreet and Beauregard also suggested that reinforcements from Virginia be used to aid Bragg in a strike against Maj. Gen. William Rosecrans, followed by an advance to the Ohio valley, but Gen. Robert E. Lee's aversion to reinforcing the West undermined the plan. Little help would be coming from the Trans-Mississippi either, as Maj. Gen. John G. Walker's division attempted too late to destroy Grant's supply base at Milliken's Bend. Consequently, on June 15, Johnston informed the War Department that saving Vicksburg was "hopeless."

Grant, however, was conscious of Johnston's potential ability to disrupt Federal operations if allowed to go unchecked, so he took measures to ensure his army's safety. He had already destroyed the railroads around Jackson, so that Johnston would have to rely upon an insufficient number of wagons to move his army. Likewise, the Federal army thoroughly foraged the countryside, making it difficult for Johnston's troops to sustain themselves within striking distance of Grant's army without an adequate supply line. Most important, Grant was concerned about his central position between two Confederate forces and posted Sherman and 34,000 men on a defensive line fifteen miles east of Vicksburg to protect his rear.

Although often the subject of historical debate, Johnston's military options were very limited. Ideally, he could cooperate with Pemberton in a simultaneous assault against Grant and Sherman. In this scenario, neither Federal army would easily be able to reinforce the other, and the Confederates could hope for a blunder that might open a window of opportunity for success. In order for this plan to work, however, timing, organization, and numerical superiority were critical. With the uncertainty and delays necessarily associated with the courier system, neither general could depend upon timing or be certain about organization. Moreover, both Pemberton and Johnston would have to launch assaults against a numerically superior, entrenched army. Johnston therefore chose another option. By June 28, he had pieced together over 31,000 troops and sent a courier to Pemberton informing him of one last hope—he would make a diversionary attack on July 7 designed to allow the Vicksburg garrison to cut its way out. (Pemberton had earlier informed him that he could hold the city until July 10.) Johnston's message never arrived.

The situation within the city was rapidly deteriorating. Citizens sought shelter from daily bombardments by hiding in basements or digging caves into the hillsides. Water became scarce and the meat supply dwindled. By the end of June mule meat was substituted for bacon and bread rations were

reduced. After questioning his senior officers on the status of their men, Pemberton decided that his garrison was too weakened by the forty-six-day siege to undertake the rigors of the field. Accordingly, on July 3, Pemberton met Grant between the lines and arranged to surrender the following day. All told, he surrendered 2,166 officers, 27,230 enlisted men, 115 civilian employees, 172 cannons, and 60,000 long arms. The symbolic bastion on the Mississippi was now in Federal hands. Port Hudson surrendered five days later, freeing the river of all major Confederate resistance. "The Father of Waters," President Abraham Lincoln observed, "again goes unvexed to the sea."

Johnston heard the news of Vicksburg's surrender on July 5 and, after a brief skirmish with Sherman, fell back from his position on the east bank of the Big Black to Jackson. Eleven days later, the general evacuated the capital city and headed east, first to Brandon and then to Morton, Mississippi. For Grant, the capture of the river fortress vaulted him into national prominence; his martial abilities were confirmed five months later at Chattanooga. For the Confederacy, the first week of July 1863 proved to be a major turning point in the war. The defeats at Gettysburg and Vicksburg did not guarantee ultimate Federal victory, but many Southerners now realized that the Confederacy was running out of manpower and time.

[See also Corinth, Mississippi; Holly Springs, Mississippi; Jackson, Mississippi, article on Port Gibson, Mississippi; Port Hudson, Louisiana.]

BIBLIOGRAPHY

Bearss, Edwin C. The Vicksburg Campaign. 3 Vols. Dayton, Ohio, 1985–1986.

Ballard, Michael B. Pemberton: A Biography. Jackson, Miss., 1991.

Carter, Samuel, III. The Final Fortress: The Campaign for Vicksburg, 1862–1863. New York, 1980.

Govan, Gilbert E, and James W. Livingood. A Different Valor: The Story of General Joseph E. Johnston, C. S. A. New York, 1956.

McFeely, Mary D., and William S. McFeely, eds. Memoirs and Selected Letters: Ulysses S. Grant. New York, 1990.

Miers, Earl Schenck. The Web of Victory: Grant at Vicksburg. New York, 1955. Reprint, Baton Rouge, La., 1984.

Walker, Peter F. Vicksburg: A People at War, 1860–1865. Chapel Hill, N.C., 1960.

Woodworth, Steven E. Jefferson Davis and His Generals: The Failure of Confederate Command in the West. Lawrence, Kans., 1990.

VIRGINIA

In the second year of the Civil War, a Southern newspaperman editorialized: "If the Confederacy loses Virginia it loses the backbone and right arm of the war." Noted historian Bruce Catton later asserted: "The new Southern nation that was struggling to be born [in 1861] needed Virginia as a man needs the breath of life."

These were not exaggerations. Without Virginia, the young Confederacy could not hope to win its fight for independence. With Virginia, the Southern attempt had a chance. Few events in American history were more momentous than the secession of the Old Dominion, for it turned the simple suppression of a rebellion into a four-year upheaval that shook the nation to the depths of its being.

> Few events in American history were more momentous than the secession of the Old Dominion. . . .

That Virginia was among the last states to secede was evidence of its strong ties with the Union. The Old Dominion had been the mother state of the nation. Its sons played many leading roles in the birth and formative years of the Republic. Eight of the first eleven presidents were Virginians. In addition to such Founding Fathers as George Washington, Thomas Jefferson, James Madison, and James Monroe, far-visioned men like Patrick Henry, Richard Henry Lee, George Mason, and John Marshall had plotted the course of democracy in the New World. Other native sons had made marks elsewhere: Stephen F. Austin, founder of Texas, and Sam Houston, its first president; statesmen Henry Clay of Kentucky and William H. Crawford of Georgia; Ephraim McDowell, a pioneer in abdominal surgery; Cyrus McCormick, inventor of the mechanical reaper; plus nine governors of states and twelve governors of territories. It is inconceivable to think of the creation of the United States of America without Virginians participating.

Debate over Secession. By the first months of 1861, however, the state found itself literally in the middle of approaching hostilities between North and South. The issue of the day was slavery, yet three-fourths of all white Virginians were nonslaveholders. For most citizens of the Old Dominion, the *Richmond Examiner* asserted, "the cause . . . the whole cause, on our part, is the maintenance of the sovereign independence of these States."

Both sides looked anxiously to Virginia for support. Sharply divided sentiment existed inside the Old Dominion. Governor John Letcher was a moderate; his predecessor, Henry A. Wise, was an outspoken fire-eater. Secession sentiment was concentrated in the Tidewater and Piedmont regions, with their slave-based economies of tobacco and other crops. Most residents of the mountainous western third of the state felt a closer attachment to the Washington government.

Although Unionist voices were strong throughout the state, their expressions ran counter to Unionist feeling elsewhere. Virginia conservatives opposed the secession of their state, not secession itself. They preferred to work for a solution to the national dilemma from within the national framework; secession was a last-resort measure. But at the same time Virginia Unionists were of one voice in their opposition to coercion of seceded states by the Federal government.

Sharply divided feelings led Governor Letcher in January 1861 to ask the state legislature to convene a secession convention of 152 delegates in order to gauge public opinion. The convention met and quickly voted against Virginia leaving the Union. Debate grew more heated. One conservative explained his position by declaring that "the desire of some for change, the greed of many for excitement . . . seems to have unthroned the reason of men, and left them at the mercy of passion." A Richmond newspaper labeled such spokesmen "old fogies" and "conceited old ghosts who crawled from a hundred damp graves to manacle their state and deliver her up as a husbandman to the hideous chimpanzee from Illinois [Abraham Lincoln]."

In the face of sharply divided opinion and seven states already out of the Union, Virginia moderates continued to work for peace. The Virginia General Assembly invited delegates from twenty-one Northern and Southern states to meet early in February in a concerted effort to avoid a major catastrophe. Venerable ex-president John Tyler presided over the Peace Convention. It drew up a conciliatory plan that basically would have restored the Missouri Compromise line to the Pacific Ocean, thus protecting slavery in the lower half of the nation. Extremists on both sides opposed the plan, victorious Republicans would give it no support, and the measure died in the U.S. Congress.

On April 4, the Virginia convention by an almost 2–1 vote again rejected secession. The delegates, however, agreed to remain in session to await further developments. Letcher dispatched a Virginia delegation to Washington on April 13 in a last-minute effort to avert war. Fort Sumter surrendered that day after a heavy Confederate bombardment. Virginian Edmund Ruffin, a grim, humorless old fire-eater, had fired one of the first cannon shots at Sumter.

War and Secession. Lincoln then issued a call on all Union states for troops to force the belligerent Confederates back into the Union. The Union president, a Richmond editor angrily retorted, "demands a quota of cutthroats to desolate Southern firesides." Virginia could no longer remain neutral. Its people had watched and waited, with the thin hope that the North and Deep South might somehow find a solution for the crisis. The thin hope was now dead. Stronger ties with Southern sister-states, decades of abolitionist denunciations of the region, repeated Northern assaults on state sovereignty in the face of Virginia's deep-rooted belief in local self-government, an 1859 invasion of Virginia by the abolitionist John Brown, and now Lincoln's call for force to coerce the South—all propelled Virginia to the decision it had to make.

"The war is not a civil war," a Virginia newspaper stated. "It is a war of two countries divided by geographical lines and interests. It is a quarrel of patriotism and not of opinion." For the majority of Virginians, jubilation greeted the news that warfare had begun. Crowds in Richmond filled the downtown. Everyone "seemed to be perfectly frantic with delight," a participant declared. "I never in all my life witnessed such excitement."

The day after Lincoln called on Virginia to furnish eight thousand troops as its quota in the confrontation, Letcher responded with a bitterly worded telegram. "Your object is to subjugate the Southern States," the governor stated, "and a requisition made upon me [for troops] for such an object . . . will not be complied with. You have chosen to inaugurate civil war."

In an atmosphere of frenzied emotion, the Virginia convention met on April 17 and took its third vote on the question of secession. The result was eighty-eight for, fifty-five against. Of the affirmative votes, fifty-five came from east of the mountains, ten from the central and northern part of the Shenandoah Valley, eighteen from the southwest peninsula, and five from the northwest mountainous region. The convention adjourned after solemnly resolving that "all acts of

> **During April 18 through 21, state militia seized the arsenal at Harpers Ferry and the navy yard at Norfolk.**

the General Assembly of this State ratifying, or adopting amendments to [the U.S. Constitution] are hereby repealed and abrogated; [and] the union between the State of Virginia and other States under the Constitution is hereby dissolved." For all practical purposes, Virginia joined the Confederacy with that pronouncement. The state had been driven against its will to seek independence.

"The great event of our lives has at last come to pass," one Virginia newspaper intoned. "A war of gigantic proportions . . . is on us, and will affect the interests and happiness of every man, woman, or child, lofty or humble, in this country called Virginia . . . . The hour for action is on us."

Events occurred with lightning speed thereafter. During April 18 through 21, state militia seized the arsenal at Harpers Ferry and the navy yard at Norfolk. Robert E. Lee, whom Army General in Chief Winfield Scott called "the very best soldier I ever saw in the field," arrived in Richmond on April 22 to take command of all state military forces. Lee had cast his lot with his native state because he could not "raise my hand against my relatives, my children, my home."

At an April 25 meeting in Richmond, Letcher and the Virginia convention concluded an alliance with Confederate officials that permitted Southern troops to enter the state and placed Virginia regiments under Confederate authority. Southern leaders expressed appreciation two days later by naming Richmond as the new capital of the Confederacy. Virginia's secession was also a powerful influence in the departure from the Union of three more states: Tennessee, Arkansas, and North Carolina. Late in May, in a fait accompli, Virginians went to the polls and approved the ordinance of secession by a 4–1 margin.

West Virginia formed. The Old Dominion's withdrawal from the Union proved doubly traumatic, for it became the only state to lose territory as a direct result of civil war. In 1861 Virginia was the size of New England. Population west of the Blue Ridge Mountains was ninety thousand greater than in the Piedmont and Tidewater. The western counties, however, had been at odds with the eastern section for decades. When Virginia left the Union, westerners began to talk about leaving Virginia—a threat that came as no real surprise to Richmond officials.

In the summer of 1861, a small Federal force entered the mountainous area and, without great difficulty, defeated the ragtag Confederate defenders. The presence of Union soldiers there afforded the necessary protection to enable mountain Unionists to organize their own state of West Virginia. On June 20, 1863, it received recognition from the Northern government. This secession from a seceded state reduced Virginia's size by a third.

Contributions to the Confederacy. From the moment of its 1861 alignment with the Confederate States, Virginia held the pivotal position. It was the most northern, and most exposed, of all the Southern states. Only the Potomac River divided it from the Federal capital at Washington; on three of its four sides lay enemy territory. The very shape of the state was like a spear thrusting itself toward the heart of the Union.

Additionally, Virginia's heritage and immense prestige were unrivaled. The state was the largest, richest, and most populous of the seceded states. It had more white inhabitants (1,105,000), more slaves (496,000), and more military-age whites (196,500) than any state at war with the North. Virginia's 5,400 manufacturing establishments were nearly as great as those of the seven original Confederate states combined. A third of the South's nonagricultural goods came from Virginia. The iron yield of the Old Dominion was three times greater than that of the next Southern state. Twenty percent of the Confederacy's nine thousand miles of railroads lay in Virginia. The longest of these lines—the only thing in the South akin to a trunk system—ran from Richmond to Lynchburg, Bristol, and on to Chattanooga, Corinth, Jackson, and New Orleans. This railroad provided an unbroken connection between the Confederate capital and the Mississippi River.

Virginia possessed other assets critical to Southern war efforts. The Shenandoah Valley became the "Breadbasket of the Confederacy" because of its abundance of grain fields, livestock herds, and fruit orchards. Most of the South's coal, salt, and lead came from mines in the isolated southwestern part of the state. The southern region was the nation's major producer of tobacco. Northern Virginia enjoyed a world-famous reputation for its horses. Norfolk was a principal sea-port as well as the site of the largest navy yard in the Confederacy.

Richmond was not merely the capital of a state and a country; it was the closest thing to a manufacturing center existing in the lower half of America. The city could boast of business firms that included fourteen iron foundries, six rolling mills, fifty metal works, fifty-two tobacco companies, and eight flour mills (among which was the world's largest). In addition to being an international seaport and the eastern terminus of a two-hundred-mile canal connecting it with the valley of Virginia, Richmond was also the converging point for five railroads. Had the metropolis itself been a Confederate state, it would have ranked in the upper half of the states in production.

Gen. Robert E. Lee faced an ominous task in the first weeks of war. He had to create a fighting machine from little or nothing. A Richmond newspaper voiced the truth in assert-ing: "The state's public means of resistance is simply nil. Virginia has a few serviceable arms and scarcely any pow-der." Weapons and gunpowder came with the seizures of Harpers Ferry and the Gosport Navy Yard. As for manpower, Lee demonstrated within three months his great creative abil-ities. He displayed the hard work and proficiency that had made him famous and organized Virginia units totaling forty thousand soldiers. Absorbed into Confederate forces, these troops enabled the South to have a major army in the field when the first offensive against Richmond began that sum-mer.

The Old Dominion's contributions to Southern leadership were unmatched. Robert M. T. Hunter, Alexander H. H. Stuart, and William Preston Ballard were powerful figures in the political arenas of the Confederacy. Both George Wythe Randolph and James A. Seddon served as secretary of war. Matthew Fontaine Maury, the "Father of Oceanography," superintended the river defenses that protected Richmond for the entirety of the war.

A fourth of the 425 Confederate generals were Virginians. Included in the number were Robert E. Lee, Joseph E. Johnston, Thomas J. ("Stonewall") Jackson, A. P. Hill, J. E. B. Stuart, Jubal Early, Turner Ashby, Edward Johnson, James Lawson Kemper, James Lane, William Mahone, John McCausland, and Robert Rodes. (Seventeen Virginia offi-cers, Winfield Scott and George H. Thomas among them, became Federal generals.) Other native sons such as Archibald B. Fairfax, French Forrest, Sidney Smith Lee, William F. Lynch, Arthur Sinclair, and William C. Whittle made indelible marks in Confederate naval history.

Virginians by the tens of thousands flocked to answer their state's 1861 call to arms. From the mountains to the flatland, from cities, counties, and colleges, they came forward to defend their home. All of them felt a patriotism expressed by one of the recruits: "Noble, grand old state! I love her dearer in her days of tribulation than in her prosperity, and while life is spared me I will fight in [Virginia's] behalf so long as a foe is on her soil."

Fully a fourth of the Army of Northern Virginia, the Confederacy's premier fighting machine, consisted of sons of the Old Dominion. The state came in time to boast of a host of outstanding units: the Stonewall Brigade, Old First Regiment, Pickett's Division, Stuart's Horse Artillery, Richmond Howitzers, Mosby's Rangers, Pegram's Artillery Battalion, to name but a few. In all, Virginia contributed to its defense 104 batteries of artillery, 27 regiments and 22 bat-talions of cavalry, 62 regiments and 11 battalions of infantry, plus local defense troops, state rangers, home guards, reserves, and militia.

Virginia as a Battleground. Every man was needed. For four years the state in general and Richmond in particular were principal targets of Union military might. Virginia felt the brutal hand of war as no other region of America ever has. Irony and tragedy both exist in the fact that one of the last states to join the Confederacy became the principal battle-field in its struggle with the Union.

The major reasons for this were military thinking and geography. European strategists had long taught that the capture of the enemy's capital brought checkmate-victory in the chess game of war. The early stages of the American struggle therefore became "a tale of two cities." Richmond and Washington were barely a hundred miles apart. To the Federals, who necessarily were on the offensive, Richmond was an inviting objective.

> **For four years the state in general and Richmond in particular were principal targets of Union military might.**

Confederate officials were aware that a mere four-day march could bring Federal forces to the outskirts of Richmond. Such a march, however, would be extremely cost-ly for an invader. If shore guns or naval batteries could keep Union warships out of Virginia's large rivers while land troops controlled the mountain passes no more than 150 miles to the west, any Federal army would have to advance south through a relatively narrow corridor. Dense forests, open expanses, swampy areas, and a half-dozen major streams running west to east, would impede any advance on Richmond from the north.

The distance and terrain between the two river capitals lay with the defense. A resourceful Southern general could almost choose his battleground and strike back at the enemy at his pleasure. As long as the opposing armies bore any relation to one another in size, the Northern battle cry "On to Richmond!" was in essence a siren's song—a lullaby of death—for Union soldiers. The capture of Richmond and the neutralization of rich resources at Virginia's perimeters became the overriding Northern war goals.

Vying for control of the state's far western area brought 1861 clashes at Philippi, Rich Mountain, Carnifex Ferry, and Cheat Mountain. Confederates proved more successful on the other end of Virginia by routing a Federal probe at Big Bethel. The North's opening drive on Richmond produced at Manassas the first major land battle of the Civil War. Another Southern victory came in the autumn at Ball's Bluff on the upper Potomac.

War struck Virginia in 1862 with staggering force. The first engagement between ironclad ships occurred in March at Hampton Roads. It was a prelude to the Union's second attempt to capture the Confederate capital. The resultant Peninsular campaign of Gen. George B. McClellan brought heavy fighting at Williamsburg, Drewry's Bluff, Seven Pines, Mechanicsville, Gaines' Mill, Savage's Station, Frayser's Farm, and Malvern Hill. Commensurate with the start of that series of battles east of Richmond, Stonewall Jackson started a separate campaign in the Shenandoah Valley that resulted in defeat for three Union armies. Major actions were at Kernstown, McDowell, Front Royal, Winchester, Cross Keys, and Port Republic.

A summer invasion of north-central Virginia by Gen. John Pope's Federal army resulted in major engagements at Cedar Mountain, Groveton, Second Manassas, and Ox Hill. The Union garrison at Harpers Ferry was bombarded into surrender. Lee closed the 1862 fighting with a lopsided victory at Fredericksburg.

Despite successes in the field, Confederate morale declined slowly as war sapped the resources of the South. More than 30 percent of the Confederate soldiers were absent without leave during the winter of 1862–1863. Many men left the armies because of families starving and freezing at home.

The following year saw army contests at Chancellorsville, Second Fredericksburg, Salem Church, Second Winchester, Stephenson's Depot, Bristoe Station, Rappahannock Station, and Mine Run. Cavalry engagements of a major nature took place at Kelly's Ford, Brandy Station, Aldie, Upperville, and Leesburg. Union efforts to secure southwestern Virginia failed after sharp actions at Wytheville and Bristol.

Virginia was badly battered as the 1864 onslaughts produced the worst pounding of the war. Union horsemen slashed through southwestern Virginia again in an effort to neutralize the Virginia and Tennessee Railroad and the rich salt and lead mines of that area. Confederates put up stiff but ultimately futile resistance at Cloyds Mountain, Wytheville, New River Bridge, Saltville, Abingdon, and Bristol. Gen. Ulysses S. Grant, with the huge Army of the Potomac, began a southbound campaign that produced heavy fighting at the Wilderness, Spotsylvania, North Anna River, Cold Harbor, and the eastern outskirts of Petersburg. Simultaneously, Federal Gen. Benjamin F. Butler's army advanced westward up the James River before it was stopped less than twenty miles from Richmond after bitter clashes around Drewry's Bluff and Bermuda Hundred.

Grant then began a ten-month siege of Richmond and Petersburg. That triggered battles at Jerusalem Plank Road, Weldon Railroad, the Crater, Globe Tavern, Reams's Station, Peeble's Farm, Fort Harrison, Burgess's Mill, and Stony Creek Station. Meanwhile, after mounted fighting at Yellow Tavern and Trevilian Station, Union cavalry destroyed much of the agricultural productivity in the country north and west of Richmond. The summer and autumn of 1864 saw three

> . . . over two hundred engagements had taken place within the state. A half-million men had been killed, wounded, or captured on Virginia soil.

Federal generals in succession trying to end Confederate resistance in the Shenandoah Valley. Combat ensued at New Market, Second Kernstown, Piedmont, Lexington, Lynchburg, Hanging Rock, Opequon Creek, Tom's Brook, Fisher's Hill, and Cedar Creek. At the end of October, Union Gen. Philip H. Sheridan wired Grant: "The whole country from the Blue Ridge to the North Mountains has been made untenable." The great valley was a veritable wasteland, its citizens at the mercy of Federal occupation forces.

The winter of 1864–1865 found Lee's dwindling army facing every adversity in the trenches at Petersburg. Federal Gen. Butler would later state with unconcealed admiration: "The fact is incontestable that a soldier of our army would have quite easily starved on the rations . . . served out to the Confederate soldiers before Petersburg."

Fighting in front of Petersburg continued in 1865 with engagements at Hatcher's Run, Fort Stedman, White Oak Road, Dinwiddie Court House, and Five Forks. On the Confederate retreat westward, fighting occurred at High Bridge and Sayler's Creek that cost Lee a third of what was left of his army. Palm Sunday at Appomattox saw the end of Confederate resistance in the Old Dominion. By then, over two hundred engagements had taken place within the state. A half-million men had been killed, wounded, or captured on

Virginia soil. The state had stood firm and defiant in the Civil War until little else remained. The Southern Confederacy experienced defeat when Virginia experienced destruction.

Prisons and Hospitals. In addition to being the major battleground of the Civil War, Virginia also had two other sad claims of distinction. It contained the largest concentration of prisoner-of-war compounds and the greatest number of soldier-hospitals of any state in that conflict.

Richmond's military prisons became notorious in the first half of the war for their terrible conditions. At one time, four thousand Federal officers were crammed into a warehouse known as Libby Prison. Over ten thousand enlisted men fought exposure, hunger, and sickness on Belle Isle directly in front of downtown Richmond. Hundreds of other captured soldiers huddled in smaller compounds such as Castle Thunder.

When Grant's army began pushing hard against the capital in 1864, many of the Federal prisoners there were transferred to six tobacco warehouses in Danville. Their crowded conditions, shortages of food and clothing, and an epidemic of smallpox only heightened the incidence of death. Smaller prisoner-of-war camps were located at Petersburg, Lynchburg, and several other cities around the state.

What to do with tens of thousands of sick and wounded soldiers was a problem that the hard-pressed Confederacy never adequately solved. In the course of the war, improvised military hospitals were established at every major city at or near a railroad. Danville, Charlottesville, Gordonsville, Staunton, Petersburg, Culpeper, Warrenton, Winchester, and Fredericksburg were among forty Virginia towns with at least one large soldier hospital. Lynchburg became a virtual hospital city with at least two dozen first-aid stations. Yet Richmond quickly became the major medical complex of the Confederacy.

Trainloads of wounded men arrived at the capital beginning with the aftermath of the Battle of First Manassas. Some sixteen thousand Confederate soldiers in bloody bandages poured into the capital by wagon, carriage, and on foot following the 1862 Battle of Seven Pines. The flood rarely lessened thereafter. Accommodations were swamped; businesses, warehouses, churches, and private homes became makeshift hospitals. Richmond eventually contained twenty-eight soldier hospitals, including Winder and Chimborazo, the two largest ever constructed. Three of every five ill Confederate soldiers passed through one of Richmond's medical facilities at some point in the war. Wagons and hearses bearing lifeless soldiers made daily trips to Oakwood and Hollywood cemeteries. The mournful strains of the "Dead March" seemed so prolonged that a local matron said, "It comes and it comes, until I feel inclined to close my eyes and scream."

The Home Front. One of the great myths in American history is the idea that the Confederacy was a patriotic medley of magnolias, mint juleps, and muskets. In reality, and especially in Virginia, the epic of the Southern nation was the story of disorganization and destitution, shortsightedness and sickness, anxiety and misery.

The Davis administration sought throughout the war to centralize the national government as a means of strengthening Southern unity. Such a move, however, ran counter to the state rights principle underlying the existence of the Confederacy. Bitterness between Confederate authorities and state governments quickly developed. Many state officials throughout the South complained that Virginia had more generals in the field and received more partial treatment from the Confederate government than did other members of the Southern nation. Moreover, critics sneered, Virginians never missed an opportunity to remind everyone of their superior status. Overlooked, of course, was the fact that the alleged favoritism of Confederate officials toward Virginia made the state the principal battlefield of the Civil War.

Although Virginia's John Letcher was the governor with whom Davis enjoyed the closest friendship and cooperation, Letcher was unable to join Davis in any nationalistic effort. He and the Virginia legislature were mutually distrustful. Their inability to work together during the war years left Virginia citizens to fend for themselves most of the time. Government instability became the order of the day. So did social chaos as a result.

Civilian populations increasingly became hungry and ill-clad. Hoarding, black marketeering, price-fixing, and speculation became rampant. In January 1863, an angry Governor Letcher told the General Assembly that "a reckless spirit of money making seems to have entire possession of the public mind. . . . avarice has become a ruling passion. . . . patriotism is second to love of 'the almighty dollar.'"

Inflation zoomed as food, clothing, firewood, soap, cloth, metal goods, and other necessary items became scarce. Transportational facilities deteriorated steadily. Life inside Confederate Virginia, especially among the lower classes, slowly devolved into an ordeal of survival. Many families lived in one room because they could not afford coal or wood to heat their entire home. A Richmond matron told of taking her money to the market in a basket and bringing home the purchases in her pocketbook. War Department clerk J. B. Jones wrote in his diary during the winter of 1863–1864 that "we are in a half-starving condition." A few months later, he added, "We are a shabby looking people now—gaunt and many in rags."

As battles raged over the countryside and enemy soldiers occupied communities, destruction was a by-product. In Norfolk, for example, all trade by 1863 had ceased, schools were closed, newspapers nonexistent, streets filled with potholes, filth everywhere. Richmond's population swelled to three times its 1860 figure. No town in the path of war bore any resemblance to its antebellum tranquillity.

Virginia's large black population, both slave and free, pursued two different courses in the war years. Many blacks continued to serve the Confederacy. They labored on fortifications at Richmond and elsewhere; they were employees in ordnance, quartermaster, and commissary departments; they served as teamsters, blacksmiths, carpenters, and cooks; they mined coal, manned riverboats, maintained railroads, and ministered to sick soldiers in hospitals.

Other blacks took the first opportunity to flee into Union lines. "In many cases," one historian has stated, "the flow was so great that it carried away the bulk of the male slave population." Shirley Plantation below Richmond suffered such a fate. By war's end, 5,700 Virginia blacks were soldiers in the Union armies.

Lawlessness was prevalent throughout the war years in every sector of Virginia. Federal occupation forces were rarely known for good behavior. Guerrilla bands roamed the countryside and preyed indiscriminately on the innocent. It was dangerous to walk the crowded streets of a city even in daytime. Because there was no gas or lamp oil for streetlights, those who ventured forth after dark risked their lives.

In that environment, needy citizens often took matters into their own hands. A half-dozen bread riots occurred in the wartime South. By far the worst came on April 2, 1863, when a predominantly female mob of a thousand people poured through Richmond's streets in quest of food and ransacked stores for any items of value.

By April 1865, Virginians looked out at devastation. Countless homes and businesses had been destroyed, fields ruined, farms put to the torch, crops and livestock confiscated, streams contaminated, bridges wrecked, railroads decimated. The Shenandoah Valley would never regain its prewar productivity. A Northern visitor that spring described the region from Alexandria to Manassas as showing "no sign of human industry, save here and there a sickly, half-cultivated corn field. . . . the country for the most part consisted of fenceless fields abandoned to weeds, stump lots and undergrowth."

Virginia's urban areas lay in shambles. All of Fredericksburg, much of Lexington, and the center of Richmond were in ashes; Petersburg was gutted from months of Federal bombardment; Norfolk was an abandoned ghost town; Manassas, Bristol, Wytheville, Saltville, Dublin, Winchester, and scores of small towns bore the scars of war. A half-dozen college campuses appeared beyond repair. Warrenton, Culpeper, Lynchburg, Danville, and many other communities had a general air of neglect and filth. Worst of all, of the 170,000 Virginians who had served in the Confederate armies, over 15,000 were dead and an enormous number crippled or impaired. The state was bankrupt, its governmental agencies all but nonexistent, its constitutional powers suspended. Military occupation would be its lot for years to come. A bleak future loomed for the proud old commonwealth.

John Esten Cooke, a Virginian who had been among the foremost of Confederate writers, begged the victorious Federals to allow Virginians to keep their memories. "Leave us that, at least," Cooke implored. "Leave us the poor consolation of recalling the grand figures and bright hours of the past!"

Virginia has remembered. Preserved battlefields and scores of monuments, museums, and roadside markers exist to a degree found in no other state. The Old Dominion has become the New Dominion, industrialized and progressive. Virginia moves forward with optimism; it looks back with pride.

Colonel G. F. R. Henderson of the British army studied the American conflict in depth. He concluded:

> Far and wide between the mountains and the sea stretches the fair land of Virginia, for which Lee and Jackson and their soldiers, one equal temper of heroic hearts, fought so well and unavailingly. Yet [Virginia's] brows are bound with glory, the legacy of lost children; and her spotless name, uplifted by their victories and manhood, is high among the nations. Surely she must rest content, knowing that so long as men turn to the records of history will their deeds live, giving to all time one of the noblest examples of unyielding courage and devotion the world has known.

[*For further discussion of battles and campaigns fought in Virginia, see* Appomattox Campaign; Ball's Bluff, Virginia; Beefsteak Raid; Big Bethel, Virginia; Bristoe Station, Virginia; Buckland Mills, Virginia; Cedar Mountain, Virginia; Chancellorsville Campaign; Cold Harbor, Virginia; Early's Washington Raid; Fredericksburg Campaign; Gettysburg Campaign; Kelly's Ford, Virginia; Kilpatrick-Dahlgren Raid; Lynchburg, Virginia; Manassas, First; Manassas, Second; Mine Run Campaign; New Market, Virginia; Peninsular Campaign; Petersburg Campaign; Seven Days' Battles; Shenandoah Valley; Spotsylvania Campaign; West Virginia Operations; Wilderness Campaign. *For further discussion of Virginia cities, see* Danville, Virginia; Norfolk, Virginia; Richmond, Virginia. *See also* Bread Riots; Hospitals; Prisons; Virginia Military Institute; West Virginia; *and biographies of numerous figures mentioned herein.*]

BIBLIOGRAPHY

Dabney, Virginius. *Virginia, The New Dominion.* Garden City, N.Y., 1971.

Hotchkiss, Jed. *Virginia.* Vol. 3 of *Confederate Military History.* Edited by Clement A. Evans. Atlanta, 1899. Vol. 4 of extended ed. Wilmington, N.C., 1987.

Robertson, James I., Jr. *Civil War Sites in Virginia: A Tour Guide.* Charlottesville, Va., 1982.

Robertson, James I., Jr. *Civil War Virginia.* Charlottesville, Va., 1991.

Wallace, Lee A., Jr. *A Guide to Virginia Military Organizations, 1861–1865.* Lynchburg, Va., 1986.

JAMES I. ROBERTSON, JR.

VIRGINIA

Built on the hull of the ex-Union steam frigate *Merrimack,* the ironclad ram *Virginia* measured 262 feet in length, 51 feet in width, and 22 feet in draft of water. Its 195-foot-long casemate, angled on sides and ends at thirty-five degrees to better deflect projectiles, carried four inches of iron plate backed with two feet of wood. Within the casemate were ten guns: six 9-inch Dahlgren smoothbores and two 6.4-inch Brooke rifles in broadside, and a 7-inch Brooke rifle pivot-mounted at each end. A crew of 320 was required to operate *Virginia.*

Faced with insurmountable odds in the form of an established and rapidly expanding U.S. Navy, Confederate Navy Secretary Stephen R. Mallory early recognized the potential of armorclad warships in offsetting the numerical disadvantage under which the South labored.

After first attempting to purchase an ironclad in Europe, Mallory decided to construct an armored vessel in the Confederacy. On June 22, 1861, following consultations with Lt. John M. Brooke, Naval Constructor John L. Porter, and Chief Engineer William P. Williamson, the secretary accepted a plan submitted by Brooke and directed that suitable machinery be found with which to power it. Three days later, finding no acceptable engines and boilers and determining that the time entailed in constructing them would be too great, the three officers, on the recommendation of Williamson, suggested that instead the remains of USS *Merrimack* be altered into the desired armor-plated warship.

Mallory agreed and immediately ordered Porter to produce plans based on the previously accepted design and supervise the conversion. Williamson was to refurbish the steam machinery, and Brooke was to arrange the armor and ordnance. Accordingly, *Merrimack,* which had been burned at Gosport Navy Yard in Norfolk, Virginia, the previous April by retreating Union sailors, was raised and placed into dry dock, and on July 11, Mallory ordered the conversion to proceed with all possible dispatch. These orders not only produced one of the most celebrated warships in naval history but launched an acrimonious debate among the officers involved, particularly Brooke and Porter, over who should receive credit for *Virginia*'s design. Although this controversy has been carried over into modern times by devotees of each, the evidence indicates that Brooke, Porter, and Williamson each made significant contributions to the vessel's plan.

In a race to finish the conversion of *Merrimack* before the completion of the Union turreted ironclad *Monitor,* known by the Confederates to be under construction at New York, the huge ironclad was floated in dry dock February 17, 1862, and commissioned *Virginia.* Under the command of Commo. Franklin Buchanan, with Lt. Catesby Jones as ordnance and executive officer, *Virginia* sortied March 8, 1862, from the

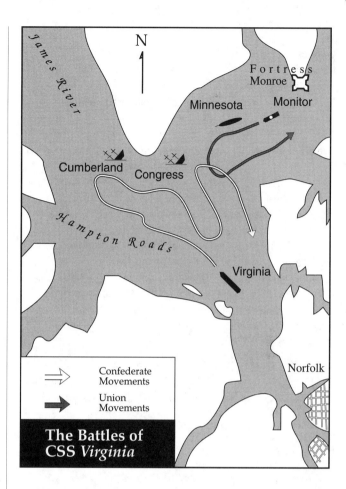

The Battles of CSS *Virginia*

navy yard into Hampton Roads to assault the Union fleet. Fearing its rifled cannon, Buchanan first attacked the sloop-of-war *Cumberland.* After exchanging broadsides, *Virginia* rammed and sank the Union warship but lost its cast-iron prow in the process. Turning to *Congress, Virginia* pounded the helpless frigate into submission with gunfire and then set it afire with hot shot. During the course of this action Buchanan was wounded by musket fire from shore, and command of *Virginia* passed to Jones. Darkness brought an end to the first day's fighting with the steam frigate *Minnesota* aground in shallow water just out of reach of the Confederates' guns.

Intending to renew combat with *Minnesota* and other Federal warships the following morning, Jones was confronted instead by *Monitor,* which had arrived dramatically the night before by the glow of the burning *Congress.* The ensuing four-hour combat between the two armor-plated antagonists was furious but inconclusive. Finally, a well-placed shot by *Virginia*'s stern rifle hit *Monitor*'s pilot house, temporarily blinding its captain and causing the ironclad to veer off. Low on ammunition and faced with a falling tide, *Virginia* returned to the navy yard. Although neither vessel inflicted serious damage on the other, the remainder of the Federal fleet in

Hampton Roads was saved and the blockade was preserved.

Placed under the command of Capt. Josiah Tattnall, *Virginia* was repaired and continued to operate as a threat to Union forces in the area. The Confederate evacuation of Norfolk resulted in the destruction of *Virginia* by its crew on May 11, 1862, when its excessive draft prevented removal up the James River. In 1867 and again from 1874 through 1876, portions of the shattered *Virginia* were recovered and scrapped. A drive shaft and an anchor with chain, currently at the Museum of the Confederacy in Richmond, and a few other relics scattered in museums around the country are all that remain of the once-mighty ironclad.

Virginia's actions in Hampton Roads had worldwide implications. The destruction of *Cumberland* and *Congress* symbolically ended the centuries-long reign of the wooden, sail-powered warship, and its battle with *Monitor* presaged the modern era, adding impetus to a technological revolution in naval warfare already underway.

BIBLIOGRAPHY

Baxter, James P., III. *The Introduction of the Ironclad Warship.* Cambridge, Mass., 1933. Reprint, Cambridge, Mass., 1968.

Brooke, George M., Jr. *John Mercer Brooke: Naval Scientist and Educator.* Charlottesville, Va., 1980.

Daly, R. W. *How the Merrimac Won: The Strategic Story of the C.S.S. Virginia.* New York, 1957.

Davis, William C. *Duel between the First Ironclads.* New York, 1975.

Flanders, Alan B. *The Merrimac: The Story of the Conversion of the U.S.S. Merrimac into the Confederate Ironclad Warship, C.S.S. Virginia.* Portsmouth, Va., 1982.

A. ROBERT HOLCOMBE, JR.

VIRGINIA MILITARY INSTITUTE

After the War of 1812, the Commonwealth of Virginia had a quantity of arms and munitions that needed to be protected and maintained. As a result, the legislature authorized in 1816 the creation of three arsenals, one of which was to be located west of the Blue Ridge Mountains. The site chosen, originally a tract of slightly less than eight acres, was located in Lexington, Virginia, a beautifully situated village in the upper end of Virginia's famed Shenandoah Valley. The arsenal property was to be garrisoned by twenty militiamen and a captain. Because of disturbances and several incidents created by the soldiers at the arsenal, the Virginia state government created the Virginia Military Institute to replace the soldiers with young men whose education was to be combined with military training and guard duty at the arsenal.

Patterned after the Ecole Polytechnique of France and the U.S. Military Academy at West Point, VMI was organized several months before it officially opened on November 11, 1839, when the first cadet sentinel, John B. Strange, mounted the guard at the old arsenal. Largely the brainchild of John Thomas Lewis Preston, a Lexington lawyer and graduate of neighboring Washington College (later Washington and Lee),

> **. . . the Corps of Cadets was called out to help repel the invasion of the Shenandoah Valley by Federal [soldiers]. . . .**

VMI was brought into being by an organizing board but governed by a board of visitors with a superintendent to oversee the daily operations. The first president of the board was Col. Claudius Crozet, a graduate of the Ecole Polytechnique, former artillery officer under Napoleon and professor of engineering at West Point, and state engineer of Virginia. Professor (later Maj. Gen.) Francis Henney Smith, distinguished graduate of West Point, was named the first superintendent.

Smith found the arsenal to be thoroughly inadequate for the new institute. He worked for nearly a decade formulating plans for a new barracks, parade ground, mess hall, and residences. New York architect Alexander Jackson Davis was employed to carry out Smith's plans. Davis, who was to become one of the foremost American architects of the nineteenth century, designed the first of the institute's buildings in the Gothic revival style, a style which influenced every other building on the VMI Post. The first of the new buildings was opened in September 1851. The other buildings of the pre-Civil War period were completed during the 1850s.

Unlike West Point, which had as its educational goal the training of cadets to be professional officers in the American military, VMI focused first on leadership in civil life, but also trained its cadets for service as citizen-soldiers in time of war or national emergency. VMI, from the beginning, has maintained that the best way to achieve its educational goal is within a military framework and a system of individual discipline and guidance based on an honor system.

At the outbreak of the Civil War nearly 300 of the 348-man Corps of Cadets were sent to Richmond to help drill and instruct the thousands of recruits who were daily pouring into the Confederate capital. Estimates vary, but it has been suggested that the recruits drilled by the cadets ranged in number from 25,000 to 50,000. At the beginning of the war there had been 1,217 matriculates at the institute, and another 813 enrolled during the war, bringing the total to 2,030. Of these,

1,902 were living at the commencement of hostilities, and 1,796 (94 percent) went into Confederate service. Of this total, 259 (14.5 percent) died, either killed outright or by wounds or disease. Small wonder, then, that VMI has been referred to as the "West Point of the South" or that Superintendent Francis H. Smith was prompted to say in 1877 that the Institute "left more of its alumni on the battlefield among the slain in the civil war of 1861–65 than West Point in all the wars of the United States since 1802, when the United States Military Academy was established."

The institute gave to the Confederacy 3 major generals, 17 brigadier generals, 92 colonels, 64 lieutenant colonels, 107 majors, 306 captains, and 221 lieutenants. Nor were the casualties or volunteers confined to the ranks filled by cadets or former cadets. The VMI faculty contributed its share. Among these were Lt. Gen. Thomas J. ("Stonewall") Jackson, Maj. Gen. Robert Rodes, Col. Stapleton Crutchfield, Brig. Gen. John McCausland, Lt. Scott Shipp, and more than a dozen others.

Probably the most dramatic moment in VMI history came in May of 1864 when the Corps of Cadets was called out to help repel the invasion of the Shenandoah Valley by Federal Gen. Franz Sigel. The cadets, some 241 in number under the command of Scott Shipp, joined Confederate Gen. John C. Breckinridge's command near New Market, Virginia, in time to participate in the rout of the Union army. The charge of the cadets across a muddy field in the face of determined musketry and artillery fire brought undying fame to the institute; in the course of that brief action ten cadets were killed or mortally wounded and another forty-five wounded. Today, six of the slain, known as New Market Cadets, lie buried on the VMI grounds beside Moses Ezekiel's statue "Virginia Mourning Her Dead." (Ezekiel himself was a New Market Cadet, class of 1866.)

VMI was shelled, needlessly sacked, and burned on June 12, 1864, by Federal Gen. David Hunter. The library was scattered across the grounds and put to the torch along with other property, and many items that belonged to cadets or townspeople, including a replica of Houdon's statue of Washington, were carted off as souvenirs. Had it not been for the tireless efforts of Gen. Francis H. Smith and other members of the faculty, the VMI might never have reopened its doors as it did on October 17, 1865. In 1916 the U.S. government awarded it $100,000 for damages sustained during the war, part of the claim VMI had pressed as a result of property loss during Hunter's raid.

Superintendent Smith continued to lead the institute during the postwar years until his resignation and death in 1890, whereupon Scott Shipp became VMI's second superintendent. Counted among its faculty or the Corps of Cadets during the latter part of the nineteenth century were Matthew Fontaine Maury, Gen. George C. Marshall, Gen. John A. Lejeune, Richard Evelyn Byrd, Jr., and Charles E. Kilbourne.

Two national fraternities were founded by or at VMI—Alpha Tau Omega (1865) and Sigma Nu (1869). In the time-honored tradition, VMI continues to educate citizen-soldiers who serve their state and country.

BIBLIOGRAPHY

Couper, William. *One Hundred Years at Virginia Military Institute.* Richmond, Va., 1939.

Couper, William. *The V.M.I. New Market Cadets.* Charlottesville, Va., 1933.

Smith, Francis H. *History of the Virginia Military Institute.* Lynchburg, Va., 1912.

Wise, Henry. *Drawing Out the Man: The V.M.I. Story.* Charlottesville, Va., 1980.

Wise, Jennings Cropper. *The Military History of the Virginia Military Institute, 1839–1865.* Lynchburg, Va., 1915.

TERRENCE V. MURPHY

VOLCK, ADALBERT

VOLCK, ADALBERT (1828–1912), artist. His only biographer claimed that "what Thomas Nast . . . was to do for the North, Volck . . . did for the South." In truth, this gifted artist was all but unknown to Confederate audiences because during the war his works could not be shipped through the lines into the South. After peace was restored, however, Volck had an enormous impact on the culture of the Lost Cause through the circulation of his brilliantly conceived and crafted etchings.

Born in Bavaria, Volck learned to draw at artists' colonies near Nuremberg. After the Revolutions of 1848 he fled to America, settling in Baltimore and there earning a degree in dental surgery in 1852. Six years later he joined the Allston Association, a devoutly pro-Southern art league.

When war broke out and Baltimore was occupied, Volck was inspired to produce a series of incisive etchings variously vilifying the North and lauding Southern virtues. His first collection, *Ye Exploits of Ye Distinguished Attorney and General B. F. B. (Bombastes Furioso Buncombe)* assailed Union Gen. Benjamin F. Butler. His *Comedians and Tragedians of the North* viciously lampooned such Union leaders as Henry Ward Beecher, whom Volck portrayed as a black man.

Volck's greatest work was his *Sketches from the Civil War in North America,* first published in 1863 under the thinly veiled pseudonym "V. Blada" (the first five letters of his given name spelled backward). Although it bore a London imprint, like his previous works it was published secretly in Baltimore and distributed to only two hundred fellow Confederate sympathizers there.

In several editions of the portfolio, Volck expanded his vitriolic pictorial assault on Northern policies and leaders, particularly Abraham Lincoln, and portrayed Union generals as Hun-like plunderers. By contrast, the artist celebrated Southern life by depicting bathetic but inspiring scenes, which fellow artists overlooked. His *Making Clothes for the Boys in the Army* and *Cave Life in Vicksburg,* for example, poignantly celebrated brave and selfless Southern women. *Slaves Concealing Their Master from a Searching Party* illumined the myth of the eternally loyal slave. And both *Offering of Church Bells to be Cast into Cannon* and *[Prayer] Scene in Stonewall Jackson's Camp* suggested a holy aspect to the Confederate struggle.

After the war, Volck's etchings at last were circulated in the South, where they became immensely popular and helped define the myth of the Lost Cause. Volck himself stayed active, producing several canvases of Robert E. Lee for adaptation into chromolithographs, but he never again approached the brilliance he displayed as an underground artist in wartime.

Although Volck never recanted his pro-Confederate sympathies, he did confess regret at directing "ridicule at that great and good Lincoln." Otherwise, he insisted that his works had shown Civil War events "as truthfully as my close connections with the South enabled me to get at them.'

BIBLIOGRAPHY

Anderson, George McCullough. *The Works of Adalbert Johann Volck, 1828–1912.* Baltimore, 1970.

Foley, Gardner P. H. "Adalbert Volck, Dentist and Artist."*Journal of the American College of Dentists* 16 (March 1949): 60–66.

Halstead, Murat. "Historic Illustrations of the Confederacy." *Cosmopolitan* (August 1890): 496–507.

Neely, Mark E., Jr., Harold Holzer, and Gabor S. Boritt. *The Confederate Image: Prints of the Lost Cause.* Chapel Hill, N.C., 1987.

HAROLD HOLZER

WADDELL, JAMES

WADDELL, JAMES (1824–1886), naval officer. Waddell was born in Pittsboro, North Carolina. Appointed a midshipman in the U.S. Navy in 1841, he was wounded in a duel with another midshipman the same year. Waddell served in the Mexican War, both afloat and ashore, and later on ships worldwide. He resigned from the U.S. Navy in November 1862 while at St. Helena Island, but returned with his ship to New York, where his resignation was accepted.

Waddell traveled to Richmond and obtained a commission as lieutenant in the Confederate navy, March 27, 1862. He served briefly on the ironclad CSS *Mississippi,* scuttling the ship to prevent its capture during the withdrawal from New Orleans. He next served as ordnance officer at the battle between the Union fleet and Confederates at Drewry's Bluff on the James River, Virginia. He later commanded special defenses at the port of Charleston. Waddell was ordered to Great Britain in March 1863, probably to officer one of the Laird rams. When the British government seized the rams, the officers who were intended for them took up other duties.

Waddell's most important service came when he was placed in command of a commerce raiding voyage against the Union whaling fleet in the northern Pacific Ocean. Matthew Fontaine Maury, who had charted the sailing routes used by whalers, assisted Waddell in planning the cruise. Waddell left Liverpool, with other Confederate naval officers and men, on October 8, 1864, aboard the Confederate supply steamer *Laurel.* They met the auxiliary steamer *Sea King* at Funchal, Madeira, in the Azores and transshipped *Laurel's* cargo of arms and supplies to that vessel. On October 20, 1864, Waddell commissioned his new raider CSS *Shenandoah,* shipped a crew, and mounted the guns. He sailed for Melbourne, Australia, taking eight prizes on the way.

In Melbourne, the Union consul petitioned government representatives to prevent *Shenandoah* from making repairs, but Waddell successfully argued his case. The ship repaired mechanical defects on a private slip and took on supplies. Waddell also illegally augmented his crew with a number of stowaways before heading north toward the Pacific whaling grounds. After further successes against the whaling fleet,

and while headed for a raid against San Francisco, Waddell learned of the war's end from a British ship. He ordered *Shenandoah*'s armament dismantled and stored in the hold, and headed back around Cape Horn for England. *Shenandoah* entered Liverpool on November 6, 1865, flying the Confederate flag, the last military unit to do so.

Because he was abroad during the surrender of other Confederate military units, Waddell was not covered by any surrender terms and stayed abroad until 1875. In that year he returned and commanded the large new Pacific Mail Company liner *San Francisco* briefly until the ship was lost on an uncharted Mexican reef. In the early 1880s, Waddell moved to Annapolis, Maryland, where he commanded the state regulatory oyster navy. He died in Annapolis on March 15, 1886.

BIBLIOGRAPHY

Bulloch, James Dunwoody. *The Secret Service of the Confederate States in Europe; or, How the Confederate Cruisers Were Equipped.* 2 vols. New York, 1884. Reprint, New York, 1959.
Horan, James D., ed. *C.S.S. Shenandoah: The Memoirs of Lieutenant Commanding James I. Waddell.* New York, 1960.
Hunt, Cornelius E. *The Shenandoah; or, The Last Confederate Cruiser.* New York, 1866.

ROBERT E.L. KRICK

WALKER, LEROY P.

WALKER, LEROY P. (1817–1884), secretary of war and brigadier general. Leroy Pope Walker was born in Huntsville, Alabama, the son of U.S. Senator John Williams Walker. He attended the universities of Alabama and Virginia in preparation for a career in law. After his admission to the bar in 1837, he practiced law in several Alabama towns before settling in Huntsville in 1850. In 1843 Walker was elected to the Alabama House of Representatives where, as a Democrat, he subsequently played an important role in the formulation of the extremely proslavery Alabama Platform protesting the Wilmot Proviso and threatening secession. His efforts in defense of Southern rights and slavery led to his election in 1847 as Speaker of the Alabama House of Representatives and his reelection in 1849. During the 1850s he became one of the leading attorneys in the state.

In 1860 Walker served as William Lowndes Yancey's chief lieutenant in the Alabama legislature in reaffirming the state's commitment to a strong Southern rights position. He chaired the state's Democratic delegation that bolted the national convention at Charleston, and during the campaign he canvassed northern Alabama for Southern Democratic candidate John C. Breckinridge. When Abraham Lincoln won the election, he called for the immediate secession of the state. During the winter of 1860–1861 Walker served as a state commissioner to secure Tennessee's support for secession.

After the Confederacy was formed, President Jefferson Davis, desiring to have every state represented in his cabinet, looked to Alabama for his secretary of war. Both Clement C. Clay and Yancey, the state's most prominent political leaders, declined the appointment and instead recommended Walker for the position. Although Davis did not know Walker personally, he selected him for the War Department. Despite the fact that the new secretary had no military or even administrative experience, the Southern press, which, like Davis, actually knew little about Walker, applauded the appointment. Astute observers, however, privately predicted that Walker would be only a man of straw for President Davis who would exercise his well-known love for military affairs and control the War Department. They were largely correct.

Walker's term as Confederate secretary of war, extending from February 21 to September 16, 1861, was a brief and troubled one. Beginning with the Fort Sumter crisis, it was clear that Walker would not have an important role in the formulation of policy. Although he participated in the cabinet meetings on Fort Sumter, he did little more than dispatch Davis's messages to Gen. P. G. T. Beauregard at Charleston. It was Walker who wired the fateful order of April 10 for Beauregard to demand the evacuation of Fort Sumter, "and if this is refused proceed, in such manner as you may determine, to reduce it." After the bombardment and surrender of the Federal garrison, Walker gained notoriety in the North when he predicted that "in a few months more the flag of the Confederate States would wave over the capitol at Washington." This rash statement outraged Northerners and helped rally Union support for the war.

Although Davis gave Walker little authority over the planning and conduct of military operations, he did delegate to his secretary the main responsibility for raising the armies and providing the means for them to fight. This task would have taxed the ingenuity and energy of the ablest administrator. Nevertheless, Walker and his subordinates in the War Department managed by September to raise a force of 200,000 men. Although one of the Confederate armies won a stunning victory at Manassas in July, Walker's inability to provide sufficient arms, ammunition, and equipment for Southern forces made him a convenient target for critics.

Walker also received more than his share of blame for the continued vulnerability of coastal defenses. When Fort Hatteras fell to a Federal assault in August, shocking Confederates everywhere, he was severely criticized. His lack of a military background increasingly hurt him among those who wanted a professional army officer in charge of the War Department. Jealous of his prerogative and realizing the necessity for a unified command, Walker became embroiled with state rights–obsessed governors like Joseph E. Brown of Georgia in a conflict over the recruitment and control of troops. His failure to grant commissions to friends of governors created further opposition from powerful politicians.

For a variety of reasons, Davis by the late summer of 1861 had lost confidence in Walker. The president, who had a fetish for administrative detail, became upset when Walker did not maintain a similarly high standard of administration. Walker's periodic absences from the War Office contributed to Davis's concern that the secretary was not doing his job. In early September a conflict over military policy occurred between the two men. The president became irritated when Walker directed Gen. Leonidas Polk to withdraw from Columbus, Kentucky. Although the occupation of Columbus violated Kentucky's neutrality, Davis countermanded the order and indicated his general displeasure with Walker. On September 10, Walker submitted his resignation and asked the president for a military command in Alabama. Davis appointed him a brigadier general and placed him in charge of three regiments of Alabama troops, none of which was properly armed or equipped. Failure was certain, and on January 27, 1862, Gen. Braxton Bragg, an old nemesis, removed Walker from command.

Returning to his law practice in Huntsville, Walker defended Unionists accused of treason against the Confederate government. Although he had reached the conclusion by 1863 that the Confederate cause was hopeless, he accepted an appointment as presiding judge of the Military Court of North Alabama, a position he held until the surrender.

During Reconstruction Walker was one of the Democratic leaders in the overthrow of Republican rule in Alabama, and in 1875 he served as president of the state convention that reversed important and, on the whole, progressive provisions of the so-called Radical Constitution of 1867. He died in Huntsville on August 23, 1884.

BIBLIOGRAPHY

Eaton, Clement. *Jefferson Davis*. New York, 1977.

Harris, William C. *Leroy Pope Walker: Confederate Secretary of War.* Tuscaloosa, Ala., 1962.

Patrick, Rembert W. *Jefferson Davis and His Cabinet.* Baton Rouge, La., 1944.

WILLIAM C. HARRIS

WALKER, REUBEN LINDSAY

WALKER, REUBEN LINDSAY (1827–1890), brigadier general. Born May 29, 1827, in Albemarle County, Virginia, Walker graduated from the Virginia Military Institute in 1845, but made no immediate use of his military education. He worked as an engineer and farmed before the war. Walker received an artillery commission in 1861 and led the Purcell Artillery for a few months. His superiors recognized Walker's aptitude for artillery, and he advanced slowly but steadily through the ranks, becoming brigadier general of artillery on February 18, 1865. His duties from 1862 onward, however, had been commensurate with those of a higher rank.

"Old Rube" Walker served with A. P. Hill throughout the war, working for months as Hill's chief of artillery for the division and then advancing to supervision of the Third Corps artillery. He was a model of consistency. Rarely did he deserve criticism and he was usually present for duty, in part because he escaped the war without being wounded.

Although Hill and others found little fault with Walker, he inspired colorfully insulting descriptions from at least two subordinates. One thought him a "perfect nincompoop"; another found "Old Rube" to be a man of "sloth and uxoriousness." In contrast, Gen. William N. Pendleton lauded him as "zealous, bold, and vigorous."

Walker surrendered with his guns at Appomattox and resumed his prewar occupations. He lived in several states after the war, including Texas where he supervised construction of the state capitol building in Austin. Walker died in Virginia on June 7, 1890, and is buried at Richmond's Hollywood Cemetery.

BIBLIOGRAPHY

Compiled Military Service Records. Reuben Lindsay Walker. Microcopy M331, Roll 257. Record Group 109. National Archives, Washington, D.C.

Evans, Clement A., ed. *Confederate Military History.* 12 vols. Atlanta, 1899. Extended ed. in 19 vols. Wilmington, N.C., 1987–1989.

Freeman, Douglas S. *Lee's Lieutenants: A Study In Command.* 3 vols. New York, 1942–1944. Reprint, New York, 1986.

ROBERT E. L. KRICK

WAR DEPARTMENT

The largest and most important department of the Confederate government, the War Department, was founded with the creation of the Confederacy. Established by an act of Congress on February 21, 1861, it was given charge of all matters pertaining to the army (and Indian tribes), subject to the general direction of the president. Its offices were located in an abandoned warehouse, known as Government House, which shared space with other departments in Montgomery, Alabama, then the capital. Here the military establishment of the South was born, as hundreds of office-seekers appeared and thousands of army commissions and officers' assignments were issued. After Virginia joined the Confederacy in late May, the capital was moved to Richmond, a city of forty thousand people.

The War Department was served by five secretaries and one ad interim appointee during the life of the Confederacy: Leroy Pope Walker (February 21 to September 16, 1861); Judah P. Benjamin (acting secretary starting September 17, official secretary from November 21, 1861, to March 17, 1862); George Wythe Randolph (March 18 to November 15, 1862); Gustavus Woodson Smith (ad interim secretary, November 17 to 20, 1862); James A. Seddon (November 21, 1862, to February 5, 1865); John C. Breckinridge (February 6 to May 3, 1865).

Organization of the War Department

The mission of the department was to raise and arm men for the defense of the South. On March 6, Congress authorized recruitment of 100,000 men, twelve-month volunteers, for a provisional army. State militia and volunteers were mustered into national service, despite a critical deficiency in weapons, uniforms, and equipment. In April, following the opening of hostilities at Fort Sumter, tens of thousands of enthusiastic volunteers thronged Southern towns and cities, only to find the government unable to equip them. Early efforts to purchase war matériel in the North (the Raphael Semmes mission) were terminated with the outbreak of war; similar missions to Europe (those of Maj. Caleb Huse and Capt. James D. Bulloch) were not productive until November 1861 when the blockade runner *Fingal* arrived, carrying ten thousand Enfield rifles from England. Seizure of Federal arms stored in the South, plus the limited resources of state authorities and privately held weapons, provided most of the means for the first battles.

Walker, the new secretary of war, undaunted, requested authorization from Congress in July of 560 regiments, and the following month was granted power to enlist up to 400,000 men, again for only twelve months' service. By September, the department had armies in the field totaling 200,000 men.

The War Department in Richmond was located in an old brick building at Ninth and Franklin streets, which once had housed the Mechanics Institute. All other government departments also occupied this building except the Treasury and State departments. To reach the secretary's office, a visitor had to climb a gas-lighted stairway and traverse a long, gloomy corridor. In the outer room one found clericals pouring over the details of administration (among these, the *Rebel War Clerk* diarist J. B. Jones). Off in one corner (by October 1862) was the assistant secretary, former U.S. Supreme Court justice John A. Campbell, conferring with war leaders. At other desks, paymasters explained arrears in pay to some field officer, while soldiers plied officials for furloughs, and couriers, often mud-splattered, occasionally rushed in and were immediately brought before the secretary. Other callers waited, talking, chewing, speculating (as a foreign visitor noted in mid-1862). The appointments blackboard seldom seemed empty, owing to the department's genial, personal way of doing business. When finally shown into the secretary's presence, a visitor would find a room that breathed austerity. The walls bore no paint or decoration; the floor was without covering. Here, six hours daily, and often late into the night, the secretary waded through the routine of appointments, correspondence, consultation, planning, for-

> ... the War Department, was founded with the creation of the Confederacy.

warding telegrams, signing commissions, and advising on the myriad details of running a war.

By the time of the first secretary's resignation in the fall of 1861, the department had become a going concern. Although the leaders of the Confederacy had originally contemplated a small military organization, by the fall of 1862 a comprehensive system of bureaus staffed by military officers had come into being. In addition to an assistant secretary there was an adjutant and inspector general, the Confederacy's ranking officer Samuel Cooper. A professional soldier and intimate of Jefferson Davis, Cooper was responsible for departmental orders, army records, and the inspection of army personnel. But his purview of power broadened as he became the essential tie between commanders in the field and the civilian administration. His name routinely appeared on all general orders emanating from the department to the armies throughout the South and often on many specific orders to key generals at the front.

Within the War Department were nine bureaus, including Cooper's office. These were staffed by some of the ablest and one or two of the most mediocre officers in the South. Col. Abraham C. Myers was quartermaster general and Col. Lucius B. Northrop, commissary general of subsistence. These two were responsible for furnishing the armies with food, clothing, and all other supplies except munitions. In time, perhaps more from the nature of their task than their personal conduct, they were subjected to increasingly harsh criticism. Myers, victimized by a personal quarrel with the

president, was replaced by Gen. Alexander R. Lawton in August 1863. Northrop, because he was a personal friend of Davis's, remained in office until almost the end of the war. To most he seemed hopelessly incompetent and, in the estimation of most historians, the least qualified man for the critical position he held.

Munitions was the responsibility of the Confederacy's ordnance genius, Col. Josiah Gorgas, who at first headed both the Engineer and the Ordnance bureaus. Later, Capt. Alfred L. Rives and Col. Jeremy P. Gilmer alternately served as chief engineer. Gorgas was the outstanding bureau chief of the department. Thanks to his singular drive and pertinacity, by 1862 the armies of the agricultural South were never without arms or powder.

Related to the Ordnance Bureau was the Niter and Mining Bureau, headed by Isaac M. St. John. Its chief was one of the minor figures in the Confederate hierarchy whose invaluable services made possible its well-equipped armies. In February 1865 his talents were recognized when he was promoted to brigadier and commissary general, to succeed the hapless Northrop.

The Medical Department was first headed by Surgeon General David Camden De Leon, previously a surgeon in the U.S. Army. He served briefly from May 6 to July 12, 1861, then resigned to serve in the field for the remainder of the conflict. On July 30 Samuel Preston Moore, a surgeon before the war, was appointed in De Leon's place. Described as a "venerable, dandyish old fellow," Moore was competent and resolute, with the harrying task of providing medical supplies and overseeing maintenance of military hospitals. His whole medical corps had 3,237 medical officers (23 of whom served with the navy), or less than 4 doctors for every thousand men. There were 6 medical officers on duty in the surgeon general's office.

Two other bureaus completed the original organization of the department, that of Indian Affairs and the Bureau of War, which was the coordinating office of the department. After Seddon's appointment, two additional bureaus were created—the Signal Corps and the Conscription Bureau. The latter was headed successively by two generals, Gabriel J. Raines (until May 1863) and John S. Preston. The secretary worked diligently with them, and with the many conscript officers stationed throughout the South, on the problems of manpower procurement. The Signal Corps, headed by Maj. William Norris, was given authority to supervise the operations of the Confederacy's military communications and the Southern Telegraph Company, a privately owned system. In 1864 this resourceful officer worked intimately with the secretary in the shadowy realm of espionage and secret service activities behind Northern lines.

The War Department bureaus were organized in such a way that each was independent in its own sphere, and the secretary gave the respective heads a wide latitude of authority. Requisitions for special services or for ordnance or quartermaster supplies passed directly from the field commanders to the bureau concerned, and only when the system broke down or specific criticisms were raised did the secretary of war intervene. With the exceptions of criticisms of Northrop and conscription and impressment officers in the field, few complaints were lodged against War Department officials by Confederate commanders or the press. The most important bureaus were, of course, those directly concerned with the maintenance of the armies—the Commissary, Quartermaster, Ordnance, and Conscription bureaus. Each was subjected to excessive demands and responsibilities, which only Gorgas was able to fulfill completely in his own sphere.

Subordinate to the secretary in the daily routine was the collection of clerks and messengers who constituted the Bureau of War. It was headed by a young Virginia captain, Robert Garlick Hill Kean. Although a strong Randolph partisan who disliked Davis, Kean came to view Seddon and Assistant Secretary Campbell with admiration and respect. He worked closely with the latter in coordinating the administrative functions of the department and was directly concerned with keeping the overall operations of his office functioning smoothly. As supervisor of a large clerical staff, Kean was responsible for directing the vast flow of correspondence in the bureaucratic empire. He observed much policy-making at first hand and was a good judge of his superiors and colleagues. He was in a key position to sympathize with the plight of the grossly overworked department and its chiefs, much of which he recorded in his valuable diary (which is often more reliable and perceptive than the more quoted diary of J. B. Jones).

The Department in Action

The first secretary of war, Leroy P. Walker, an Alabama aristocrat, planter, and politician, was selected by Davis to represent his state in the seven-member cabinet. He was "a pure civilian," as Thomas Cooper DeLeon characterized him, "a shrewd lawyer, of great quickness of perception, high cultivation, and grasp of mind." In his initial months, he worked successfully with military and civilian leaders (despite state rights problems with several governors), although he was slow to perceive the dimensions and length of the war. His relations with Davis were harmonious. When Walker left office to seek service in the field, the military establishment of the Confederacy was a fait accompli, even if on delicate foundations. Its armies had won victories east and west, and some part of the credit for these achievements must rest with this civilian leader.

The second secretary of war, Judah P. Benjamin, held office for a brief stormy period. A brilliant lawyer and solid friend of Davis and his wife, he possessed a keen intellect and qualities of statesmanship that earned him the soubri-

quet "the brains of the Confederacy." But he was often lacking in patience with stiff military protocol and at times was insensitive of the egos and ambitions of army men. Too often he sided, uncritically, with Davis. His efforts to obtain from the Congress long-term enlistment laws for the armies failed, though his measures to encourage manufacturing in the South were fruitful. Much of his usefulness was overshadowed by public clashes with several generals. Blame for military reverses (Forts Henry and Donelson, Roanoke Island) he took upon his own shoulders, thus shielding Davis from his critics and, more important, concealing the internal military weakness of the Confederacy. Benjamin was a dedicated public servant but a failure as war secretary.

His successor, George Wythe Randolph, was popular with military leaders, and they expected much of him. But his term was too brief for him to accomplish much. His greatest service was the achievement of the first military draft in America, in April 1862, when the Conscription Act was adopted to meet the Confederacy's manpower needs. Randolph also had a try at grand strategy. By mid-1862 he saw that the weak point in the South's defenses was in the West, and he proposed a strong autonomous Department of the West, with a commander who could coordinate the disparate forces within the region. Differences with Davis over implementation of the plan worsened relations between the two, and Randolph resigned in November after eight months in office. His successor, James A. Seddon, was a vigorous man, a clear thinker, and a tough-minded, dedicated worker. He was also a Southern zealot respected by similar men and much of the press of the South, yet above all a man possessed of tact and diplomacy, and a close friend of the hypersensitive president.

The new secretary's initial months in office saw his efforts to invigorate the Confederate cause by an active prosecution of the war in Virginia, increased support for the Atlantic coastal defenses, and new strategic considerations for the western theater (with the appointment of Joseph E. Johnston to its supreme command). He persuaded Davis to travel to the West, conciliate the commanders there, and rally the people and soldiers against the invaders. He urged the use of internal lines for supply and troop reinforcement, favoring the shifting of men from one theater to another as needs or opportunity suggested. He kept a close eye on unfolding developments, down to the double crisis of Gettysburg and Vicksburg in midsummer 1863. While his concern centered on the two major fronts, the daily activities of the department were focused upon food needs of the armies, the shortage of horses for the cavalry, the deteriorating railroads, the need for regulation of the overall transport system, and better use of blockade runners for supplies from abroad (a small fleet of ships was soon hired by the department, at Seddon's insistence). Another problem was financial. Desperate measures were necessary to replace depreciated currency, and the department began to use cotton as a medium of exchange. The staple was shipped through the blockade almost daily, and a steady stream of war matèriel, uniforms, and rations soon poured into the Confederacy. In 1864 authorization was granted to exchange cotton for meat and other foodstuffs with the Federals in the Trans-Mississippi theater. The starvation that had stalked areas of the South since the second year of the war—the armies were on half-rations—justified such measures.

Manpower needs were reaching a crisis by 1863. In the remaining months of that year, the department had to deal with declining manpower resources, large-scale desertions, and obstructions from the governors of Georgia and North Carolina in matters of conscription and impressment. Defeatism, by early 1864, was rampant in many parts of the South.

Deficiency in military strength was matched by the lack of workers in industry and government bureaus. The low salary scale did not attract employees unless they also received exemption from military duty. After passage of the Third Conscription Act, a system of detail from field duty was put into effect by which soldiers were assigned to service in offices or as industrial or railroad workers. This system succeeded in obtaining laborers at low costs, but military leaders complained that it stripped their commands of fighting men. The War Department was directly involved in the development and operation of munitions and arms works, mining establishments, and clothing factories. Instead of turning to private industries for most of its needs, the government had created its own war enterprise. During Seddon's tenure, attempts were made to expand almost every segment of the military-industrial organization. It was in the scope and magnitude of these government-owned industries that the civil administration of the South differed most from that of the North. Almost all industries in the Union remained in private hands.

Of 70,000 civil employees in the service of the Confederate government, 57,124 were employed by the War Department. The Engineer Bureau and Niter and Mining Bureau alone employed 17,000 persons, which included many blacks (both free and impressed slaves), women, and some children. At the close of 1863, Gorgas reported that the Ordnance Bureau was operating seventeen arsenals, armories, foundries, depots, and powder mills. In Richmond, the department controlled and supervised ordnance shops, munitions plants, foundries, medical laboratories, and uniform and shoe factories.

The department's staff continued to grow as the war progressed. There were, in 1864, twelve major officials (four of them civilians) and 265 clerks and messengers. But unlike the U.S. government, there was no chief of staff, only a military adviser to the president, Gen. Braxton Bragg, and instead of three assistant secretaries such as Edwin M.

Stanton had at his service, Seddon had only one, the invaluable Campbell. Lacking these important posts, the War Department suffered much unnecessary inefficiency. The most unsuccessful bureau, Conscription, was dissolved in February 1865 and its duties delegated to the generals of reserve forces in the individual states. The overall governmental machinery at Richmond was frequently inadequate, yet somehow many of the needs of the fighting South were provided by this overworked and pathetically small bureaucracy.

Foreign imports continued to provide the mainstay needs of the department from 1864 until the end of the war. A special agent, Colin J. McRae, sent by Seddon to England to supervise purchasing operations there, was working near-miracles. A thoroughgoing businessman, he is to be credited with the astute use of funds (especially from the Erlanger cotton loan). In March, Col. Thomas L. Bayne of the Ordnance Bureau was made head of the newly created Bureau of Foreign Supplies and was granted control of the importation of all war matèriel that was to be paid for with exported cotton. All vessels operated by the department were now transferred to his control. Working both sides of the Atlantic, McRae and Bayne supervised the blockade traffic for the remainder of the war. The reports of the secretary and of various bureau heads, as well as letters and dispatches from Fraser, Trenholm, and Company of Liverpool and foreign service correspondence in the Library of Congress, testify to large returns from the department's system. Millions of pounds of meat, coffee, lead, and saltpeter, more than 500,000 pairs of shoes, 316,000 blankets, 2,600 packages of medicines, 69,000 rifles, 43 cannons, and large amounts of other articles came into the Confederacy between October 26, 1864, and January 2, 1865. Vast quantities of cotton shipped out of Southern ports, together with funds on deposit or being created in Europe, completed this bold enterprise.

The last great issue before the department and its leaders and the Southern people in late 1864 was the question of arming the slaves. As the number of troops was drastically reduced by deaths and desertions (Seddon had admitted earlier that one-third of Confederate armies were AWOL in November 1863), it was clear to many that the last great untapped manpower resource of the South must be used. Some military and civil leaders had advocated such a radical policy at different turns in the war, and in November 1864 a conference of Southern governors went on record favoring it. The War Department had long used blacks (free and slave) in menial roles, especially as workmen on coastal defenses; in earthworks about Charleston, Atlanta, and Richmond; and in various parts of the western theater. Blacks had also been in service in all Confederate armies since the beginning of the war as teamsters, cooks, and body servants to officers. Seddon, strongly influenced by his friend Robert M. T. Hunter, held back. Gorgas, Campbell, and others in the war office, however, were in support. Finally when Robert E. Lee, Benjamin, and Davis came out publicly in favor, Congress acted early in February 1865. The department's mission was to implement the policy. Orders quickly were passed down the line, as recruiting officers began to receive volunteers. Two companies of Confederate blacks soon appeared in Richmond—too late to effect the outcome of the struggle.

Early in 1865, as a sense of gloom overshadowed much of the Confederacy, Congress recommended that Davis restructure his cabinet in the hope of restoring public confidence in the cause. Seddon took personal umbrage at this motion and abruptly resigned. The president failed to per-

> He immediately took stock of its health . . . and urged the president to seek peace.

suade him to withdraw his resignation, and a popular successor was sought. In John C. Breckinridge, former U.S. vice president and Confederate general, the fifth secretary of war was found. He presided over the department for less than four months—largely, it seems, to terminate its life preparatory to ending the war. He immediately took stock of its health (results mostly negative) and urged the president to seek peace. In this he was strongly supported by Campbell. Both men felt that the only course was an honorable surrender. Breckinridge organized the government's evacuation of the capital on April 2 and accompanied the president and cabinet on its flight to Danville, Virginia. Here efforts were made *not* to surrender but to restructure the administration. Two weeks later, the "government on wheels" was in further flight south—to Charlotte, North Carolina, and finally Washington, Georgia, where the last official cabinet meeting was held. Here the final disintegration occurred. The War Department ceased to exist as the secretary and other cabinet heads fled. Cooper, who had taken charge of its physical remains, namely its archives, surrendered these valued records to the Federal authorities.

The history of the Confederate War Department is yet to be written. It is contained in the tens of thousands of documents in the "Rebel War Archives" of the National Archives and in related papers in the Library of Congress. Mastery of these materials may reveal the unromantic, yet herculean labors of this body of bureaucrats who helped form the backbone and substance of the Confederate army. When these records are searched, and the odds against which its employees struggled are weighed, the resulting annals will show that the Confederate War Department worked marvels with meager means.

[*See also* Army; Commissary Bureau; Conscription; Engineer Bureau; Espionage, *article on* Confederate Secret Service; Impressment; Medical Department; New Plan; Ordnance Bureau; Quartermaster Bureau; Signal Corps; *and biographies of numerous figures mentioned herein.*]

BIBLIOGRAPHY

DeLeon, Thomas Cooper. *Four Years in Rebel Capitals.* Mobile, Ala., 1892.

Evans, Eli N. *Judah P. Benjamin: The Jewish Confederate.* New York, 1988.

Harris, William C. *Leroy Pope Walker: Confederate Secretary of War.* Tuscaloosa, Ala., 1962.

Jones, J. B. *A Rebel War Clerk's Diary at the Confederate States Capital.* 2 vols. Philadelphia, 1866. Reprint, edited by Earl Schenck Miers. New York, 1958.

O'Brien, G. F. J. "James A. Seddon: Statesman of the Old South." Ph.D. diss., University of Maryland, 1963.

Patrick, Rembert W. *Jefferson Davis and His Cabinet.* Baton Rouge, La., 1944.

Shackelford, George Green. *George Wythe Randolph and the Confederate Elite.* Athens, Ga., 1988.

Younger, Edward, ed. *Inside the Confederate Government: The Diary of Robert Garlick Hill Kean.* New York, 1957.

JOHN O'BRIEN

WASHINGTON PEACE CONFERENCE

In response to a call of the Virginia General Assembly, the Washington Peace Conference met February 4–27, 1861, in the Willard Hotel's Dancing Hall in Washington, D.C. The purpose of the meeting was to seek constitutional guarantees that might hold the border slave states in the Union and ease tensions between the states that had seceded and those dominated by the Republican party whose candidate was soon to occupy the presidential office. Virginia had suggested that the proposals introduced in the Senate by John J. Crittenden of Kentucky in December 1860, though they had been rejected in committee, could be the basis for a resolution of the controversy between slave and free states.

Former president John Tyler, one of Virginia's five commissioners to the conference, had wanted to invite only the border states. Knowing that the Deep South states would not attend, he feared that Northerners would control the meeting. But the General Assembly opted to invite all the states. Eventually 133 commissioners from twenty-one of the existing thirty-four states attended, though only 60 men from eleven states had arrived by the opening day.

In spite of Virginia's plea to all concerned to avoid acts that might lead to war, representatives of six Deep South states met in Montgomery, Alabama, to organize a Southern government on the same day the Peace Conference convened. Those states, as well as one other that had seceded, sent no delegates, nor did Arkansas, Minnesota, Michigan, Wisconsin, California, or Oregon.

Dubbed the "Old Gentlemen's Convention" of "political fossils" by Horace Greeley's *New York Tribune,* the assemblage nevertheless included the "best and the brightest" their states could offer. The delegates selected John Tyler as president of the conference and decided that each state would have one vote and that the proceedings would be kept secret.

Moderates had high hopes of resolving the issue, but the opposing sides made success seem unlikely. Most Republicans had no intention of budging from the Chicago platform that called for a ban on any further extension of slavery in the territories. Southern radicals, for their part, sought extreme measures that had no chance of acceptance. The legislatures of Ohio and Indiana had instructed their commissioners to seek adjournment of the conference at least until after the inauguration of the new president. Ohio had also instructed its delegates that no concessions to the South were necessary. Indiana's governor appointed as delegates only those persons who had convinced him by their answers to a written questionnaire that they likewise would make no concessions.

The Resolutions Committee submitted its report on February 15 after several postponements because of the late arrival of many delegations. Confused debate then ensued over the committee's report and several minority reports. Some delegates defended slavery; others attacked it. All impugned each other's motives. On February 22 the conference agreed to limit debate to ten minutes for each person and got down to business.

The Resolutions Committee had reported seven provisions as a proposed amendment to the Constitution. The first would extend the Crittenden Compromise line of 36° 30` to the Pacific, with involuntary servitude permitted below the line and prohibited above it during territorial status. States subsequently would be admitted on either side of the line as their constitutions directed. The chief argument concerned Virginia's demand that slavery in any territories acquired in the future should be protected, but the conference adopted a substitute resolution that limited the protection of slavery to present territory.

Other sections of the final report provided that major acquisitions of new territory would have to be approved by a majority of all senators from both the free and the slave states and that Congress would have no control over slavery in the District of Columbia without the owners' and Maryland's (but not Virginia's) consent. The slave trade would continue to be prohibited in the District of Columbia and the interstate slave trade protected, at least to a degree. Congress was to prohibit the importation of slaves and of Chinese laborers forever. Congress would compensate an owner when authorities were prevented from recovering a fugitive slave, but the person would lose ownership of the slave by accepting compensation. Key provisions of the proposals and of the existing U.S. Constitution could never be amended or abolished in the future without the agreement of all the states.

Virginia delegates had sought to prohibit blacks from voting and to gain the right to acquire territory for colonization of blacks. They had also hoped to secure condemnation of personal liberty laws, the strengthening of the Fugitive Slave Law, and a declaration of the constitutionality of secession.

The final package, which was not voted on as a whole, satisfied almost no one. William C. Rives had declared that "Virginia steps in to arrest the country on its road to ruin"—

> **Southern radicals, for their part, sought extreme measures that had no chance of acceptance.**

but Virginia voted against the key section (which carried by only one vote) and three others. Two states opposed all seven propositions adopted by the conference, one state opposed six, and four states opposed five. New York deadlocked on every vote and Kansas on all but one, though four Northern states and four border states were on the winning side every time. Had Michigan, Wisconsin, and Minnesota participated, the Peace Conference would have no doubt been totally paralyzed.

Tyler submitted the report as a proposed thirteenth amendment to the Constitution, but with a lukewarm endorsement, and departed for Virginia, where he soon urged his state's secession. It was February 27, less than a week before Lincoln's inauguration and the scheduled adjournment of Congress. Many Southern congressmen had returned to their states, and the remaining representatives were probably less interested in compromise than they had been two months before. The Senate voted against the proposals, 28–7. The House refused to suspend its rules to receive them. The Peace Conference had failed. Once South Carolina had seceded, it was probably too late to arrest the march to war, for Southern secessionists and Northern Republicans had fixed on a collision course.

BIBLIOGRAPHY

Crittenden, Lucius E. *Report of the Debates and Proceedings of the Peace Convention Held at Washington, D.C., 1861.* New York, 1864. Reprint, New York, 1971.

Gunderson, Robert G. "The Old Gentlemen's Convention." *Civil War History* 7 (1961): 5–12.

Gunderson, Robert G. *Old Gentlemen's Convention: The Washington Peace Conference of 1861.* Madison, Wis., 1961.

Keene, Jesse L. *The Peace Convention of 1871.* Confederate Centennial Studies no. 18. Tuscaloosa, Ala., 1961.

Morrison, Samuel E. "The Peace Convention of February, 1861." *Proceedings of the Massachusetts Historical Society* 73 (1961): 58–80.

LYON G. TYLER

WATERWAYS

The Southern states were surrounded by navigable waterways, indeed by protected waterways where small craft could carry the commerce and the forces of the Confederacy. On the northeast was the Chesapeake Bay and the Potomac River; then on the north the great Ohio, and on the west the mighty Mississippi with its tributaries, the Arkansas and the Red River, connecting it with Arkansas and Texas. All along the Atlantic coast, from Virginia to Florida, with some interruptions, a protected waterway, hospitable to shallow-draft steamboats and smaller vessels, ran between the mainland and strings of offshore islands; it continued for most of the way along the Gulf coast, around Florida to Pensacola and on to New Orleans, and then for much of the way along the Texas coast.

There were no great rivers flowing in an east-west direction that could have connected the Confederacy at its heart. But in all the states major rivers drained a rich hinterland to the sea and provided a means of getting crops to seacoast markets and of getting manufactured goods into the interior: the James River gave an outlet from Lynchburg and Richmond to Hampton Roads and Norfolk; the Roanoke from central Virginia to the Carolina coast; the Cape Fear from Fayetteville to Wilmington, North Carolina; the Pee Dee River and the Santee from central South Carolina to Charleston; the Savannah from Augusta to Savannah; the Chattahoochee and the Flint from Atlanta to the Gulf of Mexico; the Alabama from Montgomery to Mobile; in Mississippi the Pearl River from Jackson to the approaches to New Orleans; in the north, the New River connecting the Great Appalachian Valley from western Virginia to the Ohio; the Tennessee connecting the Great Valley, around Knoxville, with Chattanooga and northern Alabama thence across western Tennessee and Kentucky to the Ohio; and the Cumberland connecting northern Tennessee with the Ohio. And the beltway of coastal waterways and major rivers connected them all. It was like a great geopolitical wheel, with the spokes, radiating from the interior, joined by the rim of coastal waterways and peripheral rivers.

Control of this water beltway surely was a key to the solvency of the Southern states and even to the Confederacy's success in the war. But from the outset Federal forces began slowly but inexorably to constrict it. Seizure of Harpers Ferry by Federal forces assured Northern control of the upper Potomac, and George B. McClellan's first action, a relatively minor campaign in western Virginia in July 1861, assured Northern control of the upper Ohio. Before the year was out U.S. forces captured Hatteras Inlet, North Carolina; Port Royal Sound, commanding the waterway between Charleston and Savannah; Tybee Island on the Georgia coast; and Biloxi, Mississippi, on the Gulf of Mexico.

In February 1862, Ulysses S. Grant, with the support of a flotilla of river gunboats under David Farragut, captured Fort Henry on the Tennessee and Fort Donelson on the Cumberland River, and other U.S. forces captured Roanoke Island, North Carolina. Succeeding weeks saw the occupation of Jacksonville, Florida; the neutralization of the ironclad *Virginia* by the *Monitor* in Hampton Roads; the fall of New Orleans on April 25; the loss of Norfolk, Virginia, and Pensacola, Florida, and, on June 6, the loss of Memphis on the Mississippi. The great belt waterway, the rim of the wheel, was being broken all along its course. Surely the fall of Vicksburg on the Mississippi in July 1863 was as much a turning point of the war as was the Battle of Gettysburg going on at the same time in Pennsylvania.

The waterways could have been of utmost advantage to the South in carrying commerce and supporting military forces if all or most of its segments could have been controlled. Commerce-raiding cruisers, such as *Alabama, Shenandoah,* and *Georgia,* were a nuisance and a menace to Northern shipping, but they could have no influence on the outcome of the war. On the other hand, if the Confederate States somehow could have gained and maintained command of the rivers, particularly the Ohio and Mississippi, and the adjacent seas of the Atlantic and the Gulf of Mexico, their success at arms scarcely could have been denied. Great flotillas of gunboats would have been more valuable than great armies without adequate means of support, and a high-seas fleet plus shallow-draft gunboats capable of breaking the Northern blockade would have been more valuable than scores of commerce raiders. It may not be without symbolic significance that the Federals named their armies (with some exceptions) for the rivers—the Army of the Potomac, the Army of the James, the Army of the Ohio, the Army of the Cumberland, the Army of the Tennessee—whereas the Confederates (with a few exceptions) named theirs for states or regions—the Army of Northern Virginia, the Army of Tennessee.

During the first half of the nineteenth century watercraft of many kinds had appeared on the interior rivers. A common one for downstream trips was the flatboat, about twenty feet long and ten feet wide, with a hull rising three feet or so above the water, a little house or shelter in the middle, and a sweep or long oar at the stern to guide it. Rivermen would transport cargoes of grain, salted meat, or other products, then sell the boat as well as the cargo and walk or find wagons or stages back for another boat. Families sometimes would move with all their belongings downstream on a flatboat and then use the boat for lumber at their destination. Pirogues were large, flat-bottom boats with oars and poles to enable them to move upstream. Scows were large flatboats, sometimes referred to as arks. Broadhorns were like scows, but with sweeps both on bow and stern for steering downstream. Similar to the scows were the batteaux, especially significant on the James River. The skiff was a small flat-bottom boat used for local traffic and sometimes carried in tow by larger boats for side trips to the shore. Keel boats were built with heavy timber keels down the center; these had the advantage of being able to absorb the shock of collisions with obstacles in the rivers. Barges were bigger boats, thirty to seventy feet long, equipped with a passenger cabin and oars and sails to move upstream as well as down on the big rivers. Packet boats were larger barges.

A canal-building boom in the Northern states between 1820 and 1850 did not extend into the South. The major exceptions were in Virginia. The Chesapeake and Ohio Canal, a cooperative effort of Virginia, Maryland, and the Federal government, after many years of effort was completed in 1850 between Alexandria, Virginia, and Cumberland, Maryland. When war came this was beyond the reach of the Confederacy, however. More important for its purposes was the James River canal that was completed from the fall line at Richmond 146 miles to Lynchburg in 1840 and to Buchanan in 1856. Plans to extend it to Covington were interrupted by the war. A canal of twenty-three miles connected Deep Creek and Joyce's Creek and the Dismal Swamp area.

Except for one major obstacle the Tennessee River was navigable for large boats for the full 650 miles from Knoxville to Paducah, Kentucky. The obstacle was a series of rapids known as Muscle Shoals in northern Alabama. Attempts to bypass the shoals by a canal ended in failure. Connection of the upper and lower Tennessee valley had to depend on the Tuscumbia and Decatur Railroad, completed in 1834. There were some short connecting canals in Georgia and the Carolinas, but they were in large part abandoned before the war.

The decade preceding the Civil War saw the apogee of the steamboat on the rivers. That also was the decade of great expansion of the railroads that would lead to the steamboat's decline. The first steamboat on the western rivers was *New Orleans,* built at Pittsburgh in 1811. It descended to New Orleans, but never made it back from that city. Others, appearing in subsequent years, were bigger and more powerful; *Eclipse,* built in 1852, reached a length of 363 feet, a width of 76 feet, and carried a crew of 121 men (the smallest steamers might have a crew of only 4 or 5). Most of the early steamboats were driven by sidewheels, but later sternwheelers came to be favored. Many carried passengers above and

freight below, although sometimes bales of cotton were piled so high on the deck that it was necessary to light candles or lamps in the cabins. Most of the boat building for the Mississippi valley was on the upper Ohio; the one boat-building center within the South was at Nashville on the Cumberland.

In 1845 there were 332 steamboat arrivals and departures at Nashville and 580 in 1860. Steamboat arrivals at New Orleans numbered 3,024 in 1847 and 3,566 in 1860. The 1,600 steamboats that plied the Mississippi before the war represented an investment of perhaps $60 million.

Coastal shipping still depended to a considerable extent on wooden sailing vessels, although paddlewheel steamers were coming into use. River-type boats could be used on the inner coastal waterways.

During the war rivers were not subject to sabotage and destruction to the extent that railroads were. The Federal forces, however, gained control of key points or entire segments of the peripheral waterways, and without the rim, the spokes were of little use—and beyond that, in many places, the spokes too were broken. The waterways could have been critical for Confederate success; the foresight and resources were not there to take advantage of them.

BIBLIOGRAPHY

The American Heritage Pictorial Atlas of United States History. New York, 1966.

Dunbar, Seymour. *A History of Travel in America.* Indianapolis, 1915.

Hunter, Louis C. *Steamboats on the Western Rivers.* Cambridge, Mass., 1969.

Meyer, B. H. *A History of Transportation in the United States before 1860.* Washington, D.C., 1917.

Nevins, Allan. *The War for Union.* 4 vols. New York, 1959–1960.

Parsons, Lewis B. *Rail and River Army Transportation in the Civil War.* St. Louis, Mo., 1899.

Randall, J. G., and David Donald. *The Civil War and Reconstruction.* Boston, 1961.

Semple, Ellen Churchill. *American History and its Geographic Conditions.* Boston, 1903.

JAMES A. HUSTON

WATIE, STAND

WATIE, STAND (1806–1871), brigadier general and principal chief of the Confederate Cherokees. Born at Oothcaloga in the Cherokee Nation, Georgia, on December 12, 1806, Stand Watie's Cherokee name was De-ga-ta-ga, or "he stands." He also was known as Isaac S. Watie. He attended Moravian Mission School at Springplace, Georgia, and served as a clerk of the Cherokee Supreme Court and Speaker of the Cherokee National Council prior to removal.

As a member of the Ridge-Watie-Boudinot faction of the Cherokee Nation, Watie supported removal to the Cherokee Nation, West, and signed the Treaty of New Echota in 1835, in defiance of Principal Chief John Ross and the majority of the Cherokees. Watie moved to the Cherokee Nation, West (present-day Oklahoma), in 1837 and settled at Honey Creek. Following the murders of his uncle Major Ridge, cousin John Ridge, and brother Elias Boudinot (Buck Watie) in 1839, and his brother Thomas Watie in 1845, Stand Watie assumed the leadership of the Ridge-Watie-Boudinot faction and was involved in a long-running blood feud with the followers of John Ross. He also was a leader of the Knights of the Golden Circle, which bitterly opposed abolitionism.

At the outbreak of the Civil War, Watie quickly joined the Southern cause. He was commissioned a colonel on July 12, 1861, and raised a regiment of Cherokees for service with the Confederate army. Later, when Chief John Ross signed an alliance with the South, Watie's men were organized as the Cherokee Regiment of Mounted Rifles. After Ross fled Indian Territory, Watie was elected principal chief of the Confederate Cherokees in August 1862.

A portion of Watie's command saw action at Oak Hills (August 10, 1861) in a battle that assured the South's hold on Indian Territory and made Watie a Confederate military hero. Afterward, Watie helped drive the pro-Northern Indians out of Indian Territory, and following the Battle of Chustenahlah (December 26, 1861) he commanded the pursuit of the fleeing Federals, led by Opothleyahola, and drove them into exile in Kansas. Although Watie's men were exempt from service outside Indian Territory, he led his troops into Arkansas in the spring of 1861 to stem a Federal invasion of the region. Joining with Maj. Gen. Earl Van Dorn's command, Watie took part in the Battle of Elkhorn Tavern (March 5–6, 1861). On the first day of fighting, the Southern Cherokees, which were on the left flank of the Confederate line, captured a battery of Union artillery before being forced to abandon it. Following the Federal victory, Watie's command screened the Southern withdrawal.

Watie, or troops in his command, participated in eighteen battles and major skirmishes with Federal troops during the Civil War, including Cowskin Prairie (April 1862), Old Fort Wayne (October 1862), Webbers Falls (April 1863), Fort Gibson (May 1863), Cabin Creek (July 1863), and Gunter's Prairie (August 1864). In addition, his men were engaged in a multitude of smaller skirmishes and meeting engagements in Indian Territory and neighboring states. Because of his wide-ranging raids behind Union lines, Watie tied down thousands of Federal troops that were badly needed in the East.

Watie's two greatest victories were the capture of the federal steamboat *J. R. Williams* on June 15, 1864, and the seizure of $1.5 million worth of supplies in a Federal wagon supply train at the Second Battle of Cabin Creek on

STAND WATIE. LIBRARY OF CONGRESS

September 19, 1864. Watie was promoted to brigadier general on May 6, 1864, and given command of the First Indian Brigade. He was the only Indian to achieve the rank of general in the Civil War. Watie surrendered on June 23, 1865, the last Confederate general to lay down his arms.

After the war, Watie served as a member of the Southern Cherokee delegation during the negotiation of the Cherokee Reconstruction Treaty of 1866. He then abandoned public life and returned to his old home along Honey Creek. He died on September 9, 1871.

BIBLIOGRAPHY

Abel, Annie H. *The American Indian as a Participant in the Civil War.* Cleveland, Ohio, 1919.

Franks, Kenny A. *Stand Watie and the Agony of the Cherokee Nation.* Memphis, Tenn., 1979.

Knight, Wilfred. *Red Fox: Stand Watie's Civil War Years in Indian Territory.* Glendale, Calif., 1988.

KENNY A. FRANKS

WEST VIRGINIA

For Virginians who lived in what became West Virginia the Civil War was a painful experience. Many of them had strong ties to Virginia, but most of the 357,678 white residents, who were chiefly of English, Scotch-Irish, and German extraction, had an even deeper attachment to the Union. In 1860 the 16,401 slaves made up slightly more than 4 percent of the population, and the 2,742 free blacks constituted less than 1 percent. For political, economic, and psychological reasons, both the Union and the Confederacy strove to control this borderland, where communities and even families were divided and brother often fought against brother.

On the eve of the Civil War a spirit of moderation prevailed in western Virginia. In 1860 Virginia gave its electoral vote to John Bell, the Constitutional Unionist, and Southern Democrat John C. Breckinridge was second in popular votes. But in the western part of the state Breckinridge led with 21,961 votes, followed by Bell with 21,175. Stephen A. Douglas, the Northern Democrat, trailed with 5,112, and Abraham Lincoln won about 1,200. With the support of the party organization, press, and leaders, Breckinridge carried the normally Democratic counties of Virginia, including present-day West Virginia, where party loyalty apparently remained intact. Moreover, many voters evidently believed that neither Douglas nor Bell could win the election and that Breckinridge offered the best assurance of defeating Lincoln and preserving the Union.

During the crisis that followed the secession of South Carolina and other states, most western Virginians opposed any hasty action by their state. A large gathering at Parkersburg declared that national well-being and prosperity depended upon preservation of the Union and that the election of Lincoln was no reason to abandon "the best Government ever yet devised by the wisdom and patriotism of men." A Union meeting at Lick Creek, in Greenbrier County, considered it "unwise, impolitic, and unpatriotic not to give Mr. Lincoln a fair trial before we either secede from the Union or condemn his administration."

Following the firing upon Fort Sumter and Lincoln's call for troops, forces of moderation lost ground. On April 17, 1861, the Virginia convention adopted an ordinance of secession by a vote of eighty-eight to fifty-five. Of the forty-seven delegates from present-day West Virginia, thirty-two voted against secession, eleven voted for it, and four did not vote. (Two of those opposing secession and two who did not vote later signed the ordinance.) A popular referendum on the matter was set for May 13.

Western delegates opposed to secession hastened home to organize resistance movements. A mass meeting at Clarksburg, assembled on April 22 by John S. Carlile, initiated steps that led to the First Wheeling Convention on May 13

through 15. The Wheeling gathering, also essentially a mass meeting, had 436 irregularly chosen or self-appointed participants from twenty-seven counties. All but one county became part of West Virginia, and all but four were located west of the Alleghenies and north of the Kanawha River. Carlile favored an immediate proclamation of separate statehood. Waitman T. Willey, John J. Jackson, and others urged another convention, to meet in June after the results of the referendum were known. In the referendum, popular support for secession in eastern Virginia was strong, but almost 65 percent of the voters in present-day West Virginia opposed it.

The Second Wheeling Convention, which met in regular session on June 11, 1861, had 105 delegates from thirty-eight counties, two of which never became part of West Virginia. Fifteen trans-Allegheny counties, later included in the state, sent no delegates. The convention declared all state offices vacant and set up a Reorganized Government of Virginia at Wheeling, on the basis of loyalty to the Union. It chose Francis H. Peirpoint governor, arranged for a complement of state officials, and filled the U.S. Senate and congressional seats vacated by Virginia Confederates. The Senate seats of Robert M. T. Hunter and James M. Mason went to Willey and Carlile.

Meanwhile, twenty-one men represented West Virginia counties or delegate districts in the Richmond legislature, and eight represented senatorial districts embracing forty-six West Virginia counties. Allen T. Caperton of Monroe County became a member of the Confederate Senate. Alexander R. Boteler of Shepherdstown, Albert Gallatin Jenkins of Cabell County, Robert Johnston of Clarksburg, Samuel Augustine Miller of Charleston, and Charles Wells Russell of Wheeling served in the Confederate House of Representatives.

The number of West Virginians who fought for the Confederacy and the Union has not been ascertained. Older histories give figures ranging from 28,000 to 36,000 Union troops and 9,000 to 12,000 Confederate troops. But a recent challenge to these statistics substantially reduces the number of Union troops and increases that of Confederates.

Military Actions in the Region. At the outset of the war the military picture in western Virginia was confused, with Union and Confederate volunteers drilling in many of the same towns. The U.S. secretary of war added the part of the region north of the Kanawha to the Department of Ohio, under Gen. George B. McClellan. Col. George A. Porterfield, the Confederate commander in the Monongahela valley, occupied Grafton, a key junction on the Baltimore and Ohio Railroad, and ordered bridges destroyed between that point and Wheeling. At McClellan's direction, Col. Benjamin F. Kelley occupied Fairmont, forced Porterfield to withdraw from Grafton to Philippi, and on June 3, 1861, routed the Confederates from Philippi in what has sometimes been called the first land battle of the Civil War. McClellan then forced Brig. Gen. Robert S. Garnett, who replaced

Porterfield, from defensive positions at Rich Mountain Pass near Beverly and Laurel Hill near Belington, which were within striking distance of the Baltimore and Ohio, and into battle at Corricks Ford, where Garnett lost his life. The Confederates were left with no important positions in the Monongahela valley.

The Confederate hold upon the Kanawha valley, where Gen. Henry A. Wise had 2,700 men, seemed more secure. In July 1861, however, Gen. Jacob D. Cox, with Federal troops from Ohio, advanced up the Kanawha and engaged the Confederates in an indecisive battle at Scary Creek, about fifteen miles west of Charleston. Believing that Cox was receiving reinforcements, Wise abandoned Tyler Mountain

The most spectacular Confederate actions in West Virginia in 1863 were daring raids.

and Charleston and withdrew by way of the James River and Kanawha Turnpike to White Sulphur Springs. Cox pursued the Confederates and occupied Gauley Bridge at the junction of the New and Gauley rivers.

Confederate authorities directed Gen. John B. Floyd to reoccupy the Kanawha valley, a plan that threatened Cox at Gauley Bridge and Gen. William S. Rosecrans, who had succeeded McClellan in the Monongahela Valley. Failure of Floyd and Wise to cooperate, however, wrecked the plan, and Federal forces defeated the Confederates in the Battle of Carnifex Ferry. With northwestern Virginia under Federal control, the Reorganized Government at Wheeling could continue its work unmolested and the West Virginia statehood movement could proceed.

Keenly aware of the importance of his crumbling mountain front, Gen. Robert E. Lee undertook "a tour of inspection and consultation." He found the Confederates "too wet and too hungry" to dislodge Union forces from Cheat Mountain and their camp at Elkwater, but on December 13 they beat back an attack on their own position at Allegheny Mountain. Meanwhile, angered by the feud between Floyd and Wise, President Jefferson Davis ordered Wise to turn over his command to Floyd, who was instructed to move via the Coal River to the Kanawha and cut Cox's communications with Ohio. Gen. W. W. Loring was directed to push Rosecrans back toward Clarksburg. Wise's men proved too demoralized to provide assistance, and the initiative passed to Rosecrans.

In the eastern panhandle much of the military activity centered around the Baltimore and Ohio Railroad, with Romney as its focal point. In 1861 Thomas J. ("Stonewall") Jackson, West Virginia's most distinguished Confederate officer, harassed Federal troops and destroyed tracks between Harpers Ferry and Martinsburg, appropriating the rails to

Southern use. Jackson also urged a vigorous defense of Harpers Ferry, with its armory and arsenal, but Gen. Joseph E. Johnston regarded it as indefensible.

Jackson then proposed to sweep across the Alleghenies, complete the destruction of the Baltimore and Ohio, and recover northwestern Virginia. He forced Kelley out of Romney, which he placed under Loring before going into winter quarters at Winchester. Chafing under his assignment, Loring engaged in machinations that induced Secretary of War Judah P. Benjamin to direct Jackson to give up Romney and move Loring to Winchester. The distraught Jackson sent a letter of resignation to Governor John Letcher but was persuaded, with great reluctance, to withdraw it.

In order to stop Jackson's devastations in the valley of Virginia and the Potomac valley, Lincoln in 1862 placed John C. Frémont in charge of the newly created Mountain Department, with headquarters at Wheeling. Frémont's plans failed, and Jackson dealt him such a defeat that he resigned his command. Meanwhile, Confederate Gen. Henry Heth, in expectation of an attack upon the Virginia and Tennessee Railroad, dispatched troops to Flat Top Mountain and to Muddy Creek, near Lewisburg, on the James River and Kanawha Turnpike. After indecisive action around Princeton, the Confederates fell back toward Lewisburg, which Gen. George Crook attacked on May 12. Fearing that he himself might be cut off, Crook withdrew to Meadow Bluff, and Cox declined to attack the Virginia and Tennessee line. By then, it was said, "the long shadow of Stonewall Jackson reached even to the banks of the New and Greenbrier rivers."

The Confederates achieved other successes in 1862. Preparatory to an invasion of the Kanawha valley, Brig. Gen. Albert Gallatin Jenkins made a sweeping raid with about six hundred cavalry through the southeastern and central parts of West Virginia. Loring then moved from Fayetteville into the Kanawha valley, forcing Gen. Joseph A. J. Lightburn to give up Gauley Bridge and Charleston and to withdraw toward the Ohio River. Loring, however, disobeyed orders to use the Kanawha valley as a base and attack the Cheat Bridge with part of his troops. In doing so, he threw away Confederate gains, allowing the Federals under Cox to regain control of the Kanawha valley.

The most spectacular Confederate actions in West Virginia in 1863 were daring raids. The Jones-Imboden raid, which covered much of north-central West Virginia, resulted in the destruction of twenty-one railroad bridges and a tunnel, turnpike bridges, oil and oil field equipment, and military installations and supplies; the taking of about five thousand cattle and two thousand horses; and recruitment of about four hundred men for Confederate service. Federal forces under Gen. William W. Averill, however, defeated the Confederates under Gen. John Echols at Droop Mountain and extended the area under Federal control to roughly the eastern boundaries of West Virginia.

Confederate raids also punctuated the fighting in 1864. Gen. John McCausland, a West Virginian, dashed into Pennsylvania and burned the town of Chambersburg. Federal counterstrikes included a raid on Dublin and the Battle of Cloyds Mountain in Virginia. In February 1865 Capt. John McNeill of Hardy County and his son Jesse struck into Maryland and captured Union generals Crook and Kelley in their hotel rooms in Cumberland.

The Creation of West Virginia. Federal military dominance of the trans-Allegheny region allowed the creation of West Virginia, toward which the first steps had been taken at the adjourned session of the Second Wheeling Convention in August 1861, to proceed without serious interruption. A constitutional convention, which met from November 26, 1861, until February 18, 1862, drew up a framework of government and defined boundaries approximating those of the present state. Slavery hung like a shadow over the convention. Gordon Battelle, a Methodist minister and educator, introduced resolutions forbidding the entry of additional slaves into the proposed state and providing for gradual emancipation of those already there. Failing in that, he introduced other resolutions, one of which, calling for a popular referendum on gradual emancipation, failed by a single vote. A compromise provided that no free person of color should be brought into the state for permanent residence.

To comply with a requirement of the U.S. Constitution that a new state must have the approval of the state from which it is carved, the makers of West Virginia turned to the Reorganized Government of Virginia at Wheeling, already known to be friendly to the idea. Since a popular referendum on the question had already resulted in 18,862 votes in favor of statehood and only 514 votes against it, the Virginia General Assembly readily gave its approval on May 13, 1863, and Governor Peirpoint signed the measure.

The West Virginia statehood bill encountered unexpected opposition in the U.S. Senate when Carlile, an original champion of statehood and a member of the Senate Committee on Territories to which the statehood question was referred, drafted a bill calling for the addition of fifteen counties, a new constitutional convention of sixty-three counties (many of them known to be opposed to statehood), and the gradual abolition of slavery. With statehood teetering on the brink of failure, Senator Willey, with help from Senator Benjamin F. Wade of Ohio, saved the bill with an amendment whereby slaves under twenty-one years of age on July 4, 1863, would become free upon attaining that age. Carlile made yet another vain effort to kill the statehood bill by requiring popular ratification of gradual emancipation by a majority of the registered voters in the proposed state; in the end he refused to vote in favor of the new state. President Lincoln, after much consideration, signed the statehood bill, and on June 20, 1863, West Virginia entered the Union as the thirty-fifth state. The Reorganized

Government of Virginia, which was still recognized by Lincoln and the U.S. Congress as the government of Virginia, thereupon moved to Alexandria. At the close of the war, when the Confederate government of the state fell, it moved to Richmond. Wartime animosities gradually receded, and questions regarding the constitutionality of the methods by which West Virginia achieved statehood became academic. For its people, the new state, won at such a frightful cost in human and material resources, stood as the central achievement of the war and as an assurance that they would share in the new economic and social order presaged by the victorious Union.

[*For further discussion of battles and campaigns fought in West Virginia, see* Early's Washington Raid; Gettysburg Campaign; Sharpsburg Campaign; Shenandoah Valley, *articles on the campaigns of Jackson and Sheridan;* West Virginia Operations. *See also* Chambersburg, Pennsylvania; Harpers Ferry, West Virginia; Loring-Jackson Incident; Virginia;*and biographies of numerous figures mentioned herein.*]

BIBLIOGRAPHY

Ambler, Charles H., and Festus P. Summers. *West Virginia, The Mountain State.* 2d ed. Englewood Cliffs, N.J., 1958.

Curry, Richard Orr. *A House Divided: Statehood Politics and the Copperhead Movement in West Virginia.* Pittsburgh, 1964.

McGregor, James C. *The Disruption of Virginia.* New York, 1922.

Moore, George E. *A Banner in the Hills: West Virginia's Statehood.* New York, 1963.

Rice, Otis K. *West Virginia: A History.* Lexington, Ky., 1985.

Summers, Festus P. *The Baltimore and Ohio in the Civil War.* New York, 1939.

Williams, John Alexander. *West Virginia: A Bicentennial History.* New York and Nashville, 1976.

OTIS K. RICE

WEST VIRGINIA OPERATIONS

[*This entry is composed of two articles,* Operations of 1861 *and* Operations of 1862 and 1863.]

Operations of 1861

When the Civil War began on April 12, 1861, after the Confederate bombardment of Fort Sumter in Charleston, South Carolina, many Southerners loyal to the U.S. government were unwilling to side with the secessionist cause. This was particularly true in border states, as well as areas such as eastern Tennessee and western Virginia.

The Commonwealth of Virginia seceded from the Union on April 17, 1861, but the citizens of the state were radically divided on the issue. In the trans-Allegheny region, the majority of the mostly nonslaveholding, small-farm Virginians were extremely pro-Union, their culture and economy long tied more to that of Ohio and Pennsylvania to their north, while the generally politically powerful landed slaveholding class in the Tidewater and Piedmont sections of the state was, by and large, vehemently pro-Confederacy. Western Virginians felt they were very much underrepresented in the legislature and severely overtaxed, receiving little public assistance from the state; to add insult to injury, they felt looked upon as inferior mountain dirt farmers by the well-heeled eastern planter elite. With the state split in two and the population of one section adamantly opposed to the politics of the other, it is not surprising that the outcome was the formal parting of western Virginia from the eastern region of the state.

Upon learning of Virginia's ordinance of secession, the citizenry of the trans-Alleghenies began holding mass pro-Union meetings stating their refusal to secede from the Federal government and, in some cases, raising armed militia for the Union. And with Virginia's separation from the Federal government, the people of the western counties of the state reacted violently and bitterly against any of their fellow citizens—and there were a sizable number of them—who advocated Confederate secession. (This rancor and viciousness would last throughout the war and, in some cases, for generations to come.)

For Washington, the western part of Virginia was of vital strategic importance because of the long stretch of the Ohio River on its border and the Baltimore and Ohio Railroad. The latter tied East Coast cities to western destinations such as Louisville, Indianapolis, and St. Louis, enabling Federal troops and supplies to be shuffled quickly to where they were most needed. The Alleghenies protected Ohio and Pennsylvania, as well as western approaches to the Shenandoah Valley. The mountains also covered eastern Tennessee. One other advantage in holding this area for the Union lay in the fact that many men who might enter the Confederate army would now be available to fight for the North.

Twenty thousand Northern troops from the Department of the Ohio under the command of Gen. George B. McClellan soon came to the aid of the western Virginians, routing a small party of Confederate bridge burners at Philippi on June 3, one of the first actual field combats of the Civil War. Meanwhile, Southern troops from eastern Virginia and Georgia were moving into the mountains. These men were under the command of Gen. Robert S. Garnett, and Garnett had entrenched his troops on Laurel Hill and nearby Rich Mountain in June. On July 6, 1861, McClellan advanced his soldiers, who began skirmishing with Garnett's Confederates

on July 7. Then on July 11, after four days of parrying, McClellan's Ohio troops assaulted and defeated the Confederate forces on Laurel Hill.

Meanwhile, on the same day, a Federal brigade commanded by Gen. William Rosecrans attacked up the steep slopes of Rich Mountain in a rainstorm, swiftly overpowering the weak 1,300-man force and four fieldpieces—under the command of Lt. Col. John Pegram—left there by Garnett to defend that mountain. These victories secured for the Union an important crossroads of the Parkersburg-Staunton Turnpike at Beverly in the Tygart River valley, fifty miles west of the Shenandoah Valley. Holding this road and these two mountains assured the Union victors of the ability to control access to northwestern Virginia. At his disposal for these two relatively minor actions, McClellan had about 15,000 soldiers—not all of whom actually fought—while Garnett could field only some 4,500 men.

After the small battles at Laurel Hill and Rich Mountain, Garnett retreated across Cheat Mountain into the Cheat River valley, while Indiana and Ohio troops in Gen. Thomas A. Morris's brigade pursued over difficult roads and in a driving rain. On July 13, at midday, Morris's men overtook Garnett's Confederates at Carrick's Ford and opened fire, chasing them back to another ford a couple of miles distant. There, fighting resumed until the Confederates were defeated and routed. During this action, while directing his skirmishers, Garnett was killed by Federal gunfire. Total casualties were very light on both sides, however.

With such decisive—but greatly exaggerated—victories in quick succession, George McClellan became a national hero in the North and was called to Washington to assume greater responsibilities. Two weeks later, Gen. Robert E. Lee would come to the Alleghenies in a futile bid to control these western counties.

Politically, meanwhile, the people of the area had been taking every step to become independent from eastern Virginia. On June 11, 1861, delegates from thirty-four northwestern counties—representing four-fifths of the population in the mountainous area—convened in Wheeling and demanded to remain in the Union. The intention of the convention was not to secede from the state of Virginia, but rather to proclaim itself the legitimate government of the commonwealth and to declare the secession of the state illegal.

The plans espoused by this convention were hardly practical, however, and two months later ordinances were adopted by the delegates that effectively made West Virginia—initially called Kanawha—a separate state, with Francis H. Peirpoint its governor. In November, a convention was held to draft a new state constitution, and it was ratified by citizens loyal to the Union on April 2, 1862. On May 13, the West Virginia legislature petitioned the U.S. government for admission to the Union, and after much political wrangling, and an agreement by Wheeling for the eventual abolition of what little slavery existed there, West Virginia became a state on June 20, 1863.

BIBLIOGRAPHY

Cohen, Stan. *The Civil War in West Virginia: A Pictorial History.* Missoula, Mont., 1976.
Moore, George E. *A Banner in the Hills.* New York, 1963.
Smith, Edward Conrad. *The Borderland in the Civil War.* New York, 1927.
Stutler, Boyd B. *West Virginia in the Civil War.* Charleston, W.Va., 1963.

WARREN WILKINSON

Operations of 1862 and 1863

Military activity in West Virginia in 1862 and 1863 centered in the upper Potomac valley and along the Allegheny front, which extended from Flat Top Mountain northward to Cheat Mountain. The upper Potomac front was one of great fluidity. Confederate objectives there included control of its section of the Baltimore and Ohio Railroad and of the lower part of the Shenandoah Valley, which was commonly regarded as the gateway into Virginia and the Confederacy. Towns along the railroad changed hands frequently. Romney, for instance, passed back and forth fifty-six times during the war.

In order to achieve its goals, the Confederacy created its Shenandoah District and placed Thomas J. ("Stonewall") Jackson in command of the 8,500 troops in the region. Jackson immediately undertook to drive Union forces out of his district and to destroy the Baltimore and Ohio Railroad between Harpers Ferry and Martinsburg. Later he organized his winter march against Romney, which he considered one of the most important towns on the railroad. He also believed that if the Confederacy were to move against northwestern Virginia, it must do so in the winter of 1861–1862.

Although he was confident that Federal officers in Romney would not expect an attack in midwinter, Jackson did not march directly from his Winchester headquarters to Romney. Instead, he made use of a feint by marching north to Berkeley Springs and from there into Maryland. Jackson encountered some resistance, but on January 17, 1862, he captured Romney with only minimal difficulty.

Jackson's success in the Shenandoah Valley, especially his deftness in striking and then eluding forces under Nathaniel Banks, influenced Abraham Lincoln's decision to create the overarching Mountain Department in March 1862. He ordered Gen. John C. Frèmont, the commander, who had 35,000 troops at Wheeling, to destroy the Virginia and Tennessee Railroad, but before Frèmont could do so, Lincoln sent him to assist in efforts to trap Jackson in the Shenandoah Valley.

Union strength in the Kanawha valley was also reduced when Brig. Gen. Jacob D. Cox, with headquarters at Gauley Bridge, was ordered to the defense of Washington, D.C. The defense of the Kanawha valley then fell to Brig. Gen. Joseph A. J. Lightburn, who was at Gauley Bridge with six regiments of infantry, one of cavalry, and some local organizations left him by Cox. Aware of Union vulnerability in the Kanawha valley, Confederates believed that the time was propitious for an offensive against northwestern Virginia. They hoped to destroy western sections of the Baltimore and Ohio Railroad, harass the Unionist government of Restored Virginia, obstruct the West Virginia statehood movement, and recruit for the Confederate army.

Fearing that any escape down the Kanawha might be cut off, Lightburn moved his headquarters to Charleston and later to Ohio. W. W. Loring followed him down the Kanawha, but he prepared for any confrontation by sending Gen. Albert Gallatin Jenkins on a wide-ranging raid into territory north and south of the Kanawha River. Their movements dealt Union forces their most severe setback in West Virginia up to that time.

By 1863 the Confederates, as well as the Federals, had reassessed their military objectives and strategies. Confederates thereafter placed less emphasis on moving armies across mountains than in well-executed raids and strikes, as well as moves against Unionist Restored Virginia. The most spectacular and effective military move in 1863 was the William E. Jones–John D. Imboden raids, which covered a vast area of north-central West Virginia. They

> . . . the Shenandoah Valley . . .
> was commonly regarded as
> the gateway into Virginia and
> the Confederacy.

destroyed large segments of the Baltimore and Ohio Railroad, netted the Confederacy large numbers of cattle and horses, resulted in recruitment of men for the Confederate service, wrecked oil production on the Little Kanawha, and spread panic across the state. Such successes helped to mitigate disasters on other fronts.

By the end of 1863 Confederate military and political objectives in West Virginia were no longer attainable. West Virginia had become a state, and Union armies occupied most of the territory within its boundaries. Confederate forces were decimated by deserters, large numbers of whom joined guerrilla bands or became bushwhackers. Although many of these irregulars continued to profess Confederate sympathies, they were no longer a reliable fighting force and constituted no threat to Union supremacy. Prospects for Confederate success had, in fact, vanished forever.

BIBLIOGRAPHY

McKinney, Tim. *Robert E. Lee at Sewell Mountain: The West Virginia Campaign.* Charleston, W.Va., 1990.
Moore, George Ellis. *A Banner in the Hills: West Virginia's Statehood.* New York, 1963.
Rice, Otis K., and Stephen W. Brown. *West Virginia: A History.* 2d ed. Lexington, Ky., 1993.
Stutler, Boyd B. *West Virginia in the Civil War.* Charleston, W.Va., 1963.

OTIS K. RICE

WHEELER, JOSEPH

WHEELER, JOSEPH (1836–1906), major general and U.S. congressman. Born September 10, 1836, in Augusta, Georgia, Wheeler spent much of his childhood in Connecticut. In 1859, he graduated from West Point and received the rank of second lieutenant in the regiment of mounted rifles stationed at Fort Craig, New Mexico Territory. On April 22, 1861, Wheeler resigned his commission to join the Confederate army as a first lieutenant of artillery.

By 1862, West Point officers were in great demand in the South, and Wheeler received a quick promotion to colonel, leading the Nineteenth Alabama Infantry into combat at Shiloh. Afterward, he transferred to the cavalry. Gen. Braxton Bragg, now in command of the Army of Mississippi, named Wheeler his cavalry chief. In this capacity he led the mounted arm of the Confederate armies of Mississippi and later Tennessee throughout the rest of the war.

During Bragg's invasion of Kentucky, Wheeler was notable for his daring leadership of the Southern horsemen, earning promotion to brigadier general on October 30, 1862. He received the rank of major general on January 30, 1863, and later was recommended for, but not confirmed as lieutenant general. Wheeler ably commanded Bragg's cavalry in the Murfreesboro, Tullahoma, and Chattanooga campaigns. By May 1864, he was the ranking Confederate cavalry leader.

During the Atlanta campaign, Wheeler gained additional notoriety by raiding Union Gen. William Tecumseh Sherman's supply and communications lines. After the fall of Atlanta, Wheeler's troopers were the only organized opposition to Sherman's march through Georgia, and the Confederate cavalrymen fared badly. By the end of the year, the corps had earned a reputation for lack of discipline. Wheeler continued to lead the cavalry in the Carolina campaigns until superseded by Lt. Gen. Wade Hampton.

During the course of the war, Wheeler fought in 127 battles; he was wounded three times, had sixteen horses shot out from under him, and had thirty-six staff officers fall by his side. His active style of fighting led to his sobriquet "Fighting Joe." Though he was somewhat disappointing as an independent commander, his true genius was displayed when his cavalry covered the movements of the main army. In 1863, he published *Cavalry Tactics,* a manual for use by the mounted arm.

Wheeler was captured by Federal troops in May 1865 and imprisoned temporarily at Fort Delaware. After his release, he moved first to New Orleans and then in 1868 to Wheeler Station, Alabama, where he started a law practice and a plantation. In 1881, he entered politics, serving eight terms in the U.S. House of Representatives. During the Spanish-American War, Wheeler joined the U.S. Army, serving with the rank of major general of volunteers. He led a division of troops at the Battles of El Caney and Kettle Hill, Cuba, and later served in the Philippines. He retired from the service on September 10, 1900, with the rank of brigadier general of regulars. Wheeler died on January 25, 1906, in Brooklyn, New York.

[*See also* Wheeler's Raids.]

BIBLIOGRAPHY

Dyer, John Percy. *"Fightin' Joe" Wheeler.* Baton Rouge, La., 1941.
Dyer, John Percy. *From Shiloh to San Juan.* Baton Rouge, La., 1961.
Lawson, Lewis A. *Wheeler's Last Raid.* Greenwood, Fla., 1986.

DONALD S. FRAZIER

WHEELER'S RAIDS

As commander of the cavalry corps of the Army of Tennessee, Joseph Wheeler, Jr., enjoyed only limited success as a raider. His first expedition, reminiscent of J. E. B. Stuart's famous ride around McClellan, came during the Battle of Murfreesboro, December 31, 1862 to January 2, 1863. With 1,100 men, Wheeler rode around the opposing Army of the Cumberland, not once, but two and a half times, destroying a thousand wagons and capturing hundreds of horses, mules, and prisoners.

A week later, he captured five transports and a gunboat on the Cumberland River, northwest of Nashville. Some of his men also swam the icy river and burned an enormous supply depot at Ashland, Tennessee, on January 12, 1863, which, combined with the losses at Murfreesboro, virtually immobilized the Army of the Cumberland for the next six months.

The exploit earned Wheeler a promotion to major general and a vote of thanks from the Confederate Congress. It also roused the ire of older, more experienced subordinates, such as Nathan Bedford Forrest, John Hunt Morgan, and John Austin Wharton, who resented taking orders from "that boy."

After the Confederate victory at the Battle of Chickamauga left the Army of the Cumberland besieged in Chattanooga, Wheeler led 3,700 men across the Tennessee River forty miles east of the city on September 29, 1863. Sweeping over Walden's Ridge, he intercepted a heavily laden supply train in the Sequatchie Valley on October 2, destroying an estimated eight hundred to one thousand wagons, but Federal horsemen hounded him so closely he was unable to inflict any lasting damage on the vital railroad linking Chattanooga and Nashville. Blue-coated cavalry overtook him near Farmington, Tennessee, and drove him across the Tennessee River at Muscle Shoals, Alabama, on October 9 with the loss of 2,000 men.

During the Atlanta campaign, Confederate newspapers and politicians were sharply critical of Wheeler for failing to cut the Western and Atlantic Railroad, the sole source of supply for Union Maj. Gen. William Tecumseh Sherman's advancing armies. Wheeler was eager to try, but the Army of Tennessee was so badly outnumbered his cavalry was compelled to fight on foot alongside the infantry.

Not until the army reached Atlanta and withdrew inside the city's formidable defenses was Wheeler given free rein. Between July 27 and 31, 1864, he pursued, caught, and defeated three raiding columns bent on wrecking the Macon and Western Railroad, putting Sherman's cavalry corps out of action for almost a month.

This enabled Wheeler to leave Covington, Georgia on August 10, 1864, with 4,000 men and the long-awaited orders to cut Sherman's supply line. He tore up a few sections of track between Atlanta and Chattanooga and captured a herd of beefs, but when high water kept him from crossing the rain-swollen Tennessee River near Chattanooga, he wandered into the strategically barren highlands of eastern Tennessee. Eventually he swung west, cutting the railroads south of Nashville before being chased across the Tennessee River at Florence, Alabama, on September 9. The damage was quickly repaired, and despite his glowing reports, Wheeler's last raid did little more than deprive the Army of Tennessee of half its cavalry during a critical stage of the Atlanta campaign.

BIBLIOGRAPHY

Dodson, William C. *Campaigns of Wheeler and His Cavalry, 1862–1865.* Atlanta, 1899.

Dubose, John W. *General Joseph Wheeler and the Army of Tennessee.* New York, 1912.

Dyer, John P. *"Fightin' Joe" Wheeler.* Baton Rouge, La., 1941.

Lawson, Lewis A. *Wheeler's Last Raid.* Greenwood, Fla., 1986.

DAVID EVANS

WHIG PARTY

Disturbed by Andrew Jackson's increasing executive power and his opposition to governmental economic activism, opponents organized a coalition of National Republicans, conservative Democrats, and Anti-Masons. Jackson's opponents eventually adopted the name "Whig" as a symbol of resistance to tyranny, since they believed Old Hickory far too powerful an executive who consulted too frequently with personal friends rather than with cabinet members confirmed by Congress. Originally derived from Whiggamore, a Scot who marched on Edinburgh in 1648 to oppose the court party, and applied by extension to those who opposed the royal prerogative in Britain, the name Whig had been adopted by American revolutionaries during the war for independence before its use in the 1830s.

Until the controversy over the expansion of slavery into the territories tore the Whig party apart in the 1850s, the Democratic and Whig parties remained quite evenly balanced in the South. The Whigs dominated in North Carolina, Kentucky, and Tennessee, holding at the same time competitive strength in Virginia and Georgia. The competition offered by the Whigs promoted voter participation and broadened the scope of politics.

Strong party leadership developed in the Southern states. Notable among the Whig luminaries were Alexander H. Stephens and John M. Barrien of Georgia, John Bell and Ephraim Foster of Tennessee, and Henry Clay and John J. Crittenden of Kentucky.

Countering Jackson's general opposition to Federal promotion of economic development, Clay proposed the American System. The Kentuckian offered a protective tariff, distribution of money from sale of Federal lands, construction of roads and canals, and the rechartering of the Second Bank of the United States. As conservatives, the Whigs expected to avoid economic leveling through growth and increased opportunity.

Clay's program did not prove uniformly attractive to Southerners. Proposals for public roads and canals attracted certain well-placed commercial interests. Some, however, opposed internal improvements because they feared the Federal government would fund such projects through revenue from the protective tariff, which bore most heavily on the South. The southeastern Whigs generally opposed the construction of a national road, but many in the Southwest supported it.

At the same time, Whig principles appealed to many evangelical Protestants. Profoundly influenced by the Second Great Awakening, the Southern Whigs proudly stood for religion, morality, paternalism, and duty. Accusations of adultery against Jackson and Secretary of War John Eaton drew denunciations of the two men from moralistic Whigs. Whigs promoted public education, prison and mental hospital reform, and social justice. Even Southern frontiersman Davy Crockett opposed the theft of Cherokee lands.

In practice, the Whigs remained viable competitors until the 1850s. They did well in congressional elections during the 1840s, controlling the House from 1841 through 1842 and from 1847 through 1850. They lost the presidential elections of 1832 and 1836, but succeeded in electing two Virginia-born war heroes—William Henry Harrison (then of Ohio) in 1840 and Zachary Taylor (who grew up in Kentucky but lived in Louisiana) in 1848.

After Whig presidential candidate Winfield Scott's decisive 1852 defeat, the demoralized party failed to mend the growing rift over slavery between its two great sectional wings. Northern Whigs generally opposed slavery and its expansion into the territories, whereas Southerners defended it as a positive good. As the division over slavery deepened, many Southern Whigs like Stephens swallowed their pride and moved into the Democratic party.

When Southern states began to secede, many old Whigs like Stephens opposed the breakup of the Union. As businessmen, professionals, and planters tied to a national market, they had little to gain from disruption or war. Nevertheless, loyal to their section, they went along when their states seceded.

As a ticket-balancing measure, Stephens was elected vice president of the Confederacy to complement Mississippi Democrat Jefferson Davis. The Confederacy repudiated some Whig principles by prohibiting protective tariffs and

> ... the demoralized party failed to mend the growing rift over slavery between its two great sectional wings.

appropriations for internal improvements. The Confederate Constitution offered a sop by proposing congressional seats for cabinet members, but the Congress failed to approve implementing legislation. Although organized political parties failed to emerge in the Confederacy, ex-Whigs tended to show less enthusiasm for military and executive power than did ex-Democrats. Whigs enjoyed a resurgence in some Southern states during the war because of their defense of constitutionalism and compromise. In the Georgia legislature, for instance, Stephens's brother Linton secured the passage of resolutions calling for an armistice followed by plebiscites on joining the Union or Confederacy. The party did not reemerge after the Civil War, and though some former Southern Whigs joined the Republican party, most became Democrats.

BIBLIOGRAPHY

Alexander, Thomas B. *Sectional Stress and Party Strength: A Study of Roll-Call Voting Patterns in the United States House of Representatives, 1836–1860.* Nashville, Tenn., 1967.

Brown, Thomas. *Politics and Statesmanship: Essays on the American Whig Party.* New York, 1985.

Howe, Daniel Walker. *The Political Culture of the American Whigs.* Chicago, 1979.

McCormick, Richard P. *The Second American Party System: Party Formation in the Jacksonian Era.* Chapel Hill, N.C., 1966.

Sellers, Charles Grier, Jr. "Who Were the Southern Whigs?" *American Historical Review* 59 (January 1954): 335–346.

G. ALEXANDER and TRACY L. ALEXANDER

WICKHAM, WILLIAMS CARTER

WICKHAM, WILLIAMS CARTER (1820–1888), brigadier general and congressman from Virginia. Wickham was born in Richmond September 21, 1820. After attending the University of Virginia, he practiced law in his home county of Hanover. Prior to the war he was a member of the Virginia House of Delegates (1849) and Senate (1859) and was a justice in Hanover County. In November 1859 he formed the Hanover Light Dragoons, a mounted militia company. Wickham was elected by Hanover County to attend the Virginia state convention on secession. He was a Unionist initially, but when the convention's outcome was clear, he went along with his colleagues and offered the services of his militia company.

At First Manassas, the Hanover Dragoons pursued the Federals as they retreated across Bull Run to Centreville. On September 18, 1861, Wickham was appointed lieutenant colonel of the Fourth Virginia Cavalry, and when it was reorganized in April 1862, he was elected colonel. On May 4, 1862, during the Battle of Williamsburg, Wickham was sabered in the side, but remained saddled until the battle was over and the open field before Fort Magruder was secured. While recuperating from his wound at his home in Ashland, Wickham was captured by Federal troops on May 29. He was paroled on the spot, promising not to bear arms until his exchange. Though he was ready to rejoin his regiment in a month, he had to wait until August when he was exchanged for his wife's kinsman, Lt. Col. Thomas Kane of Pennsylvania.

Throughout 1862, Wickham and the Fourth Virginia Cavalry participated in all the major campaigns undertaken by Robert E. Lee's Army of Northern Virginia. During J. E. B. Stuart's raid on Catlett's Station (August 22–23), Wickham was praised for being "energetic and thorough-going" by the general. Wickham's regiment was one of the first units to occupy Manassas Junction on August 26, and the men "supplied themselves with all they could carry away." As they had a year earlier at Manassas, Wickham's men pursued the fleeing Federals after the Second Battle of Manassas was fought on August 30. From September 5 until September 19, Wickham's regiment was continually engaged with Federal troops during the Sharpsburg campaign. The 259-man regiment also rode with Stuart on October 10 on his raid into Chambersburg, Pennsylvania. When the Army of Northern Virginia moved back to the Rapidan-Rappahannock River line late in October, Wickham commanded the brigade for the disabled Fitzhugh Lee. On November 3, while protecting A. P. Hill's troops as they moved by Ashby's Gap, the Fourth Virginia engaged Federal cavalry forces at Upperville. The regiment, fighting dismounted, slowly withdrew before the Union forces. The pike was contested all the way to the gap, where the Fourth held the Federals at bay until all the infantry had passed. During this fight, Wickham was wounded in the neck and was praised by Stuart for "great zeal, ability, and bravery."

In April 1863, Wickham ran for and won a seat in the House of Representatives, but he would delay taking his seat until November 1864. During the Chancellorsville campaign, Wickham and the Fourth Virginia were actively engaged covering the army's flanks, capturing some 250 prisoners from April 28 until May 5. At Kelly's Ford, on June 9, the Fourth experienced its worst defeat. Coming up to support the Second South Carolina Cavalry near Stevensburg, the Fourth was overrun, suffering 43 casualties, despite Wickham's efforts to rally his men. Wickham thought the affair so disgraceful he kept his report short, not trying to explain the matter, but leaving it to Stuart to decide if an inquiry should be undertaken. After this humiliation, Wickham and the Fourth redeemed themselves during the Battle of Aldie on June 17 when they held back a much larger Federal force. Wickham commanded his regiment throughout the Gettysburg campaign when it accompanied Stuart. On September 1, with the reorganization of Stuart's cavalry, Wickham was promoted to brigadier general and given command of four cavalry regiments of Fitz Lee's division. The promotion may have been an effort to keep him from leaving the army for Congress—he was apparently promoted over Thomas Munford of the Second Virginia Cavalry. Lee wrote on September 4, "Genl. Wickham still continues in the service, but I fear is getting tired of it."

In February 1864 Wickham's brigade helped counter the Federal raid into Albemarle County, and during the spring and summer, it played a major role in all the battles around Richmond. During the pursuit of Philip Sheridan from Spotsylvania Court House to Yellow Tavern, the brigade led the harassment of the Federal's rear guard. At one point Wickham led his old regiment, the Fourth Virginia, in a headlong charge into the Union ranks, shouting "Give them hell, boys! Damn 'em, give them hell!" In August Wickham's brigade was ordered to the Shenandoah Valley to support Gen. Jubal Early. At Winchester, after Wickham took command of the division for the wounded Fitz Lee, his brigade covered Early's rear during the withdrawal up the valley, pushing back the Federal pursuers along the Luray Pike and preventing Early from being outflanked. When Sheridan began withdrawing down the valley in late September, Wickham's brigade led the Confederate pursuit, engaging in battles at Bridgewater, Mt. Crawford, Brock's Gap, Tom's Brook, and Cedar Creek.

On November 9, 1864, Wickham resigned his commission in the Army of Northern Virginia and took his seat in Congress. He had run his 1863 campaign on a platform of seeking peace, and when he won by a large margin, his election was seen as a "rebuke of the administration," as a Richmond paper put it. He was appointed to the Military Affairs Committee and generally opposed the Davis administration. He saw little hope for victory by late 1864 and wanted to end the suffering and sacrifice of the war. He was against extensions of emergency laws and giving the president additional powers. He worked to settle citizens' claims against the Confederate government, to relieve the hardships of areas under Federal occupation, to exchange prisoners, to exempt men from military service, and to improve the lot of the common soldier. In February 1865 his Bill to Increase the Efficiency of the Cavalry was passed by Congress. This bill required the government to supply horses to cavalry units operating outside of their home states; when cavalrymen lost their horses, good soldiers were to receive remounts and the

> **"Genl. Wickham still continues in the service, but I fear is getting tired of it."**

"unfit" were to be reassigned. In January Wickham wrote, "The house of cards maintained by Davis and Company [is] crumbl[ing]." His actions culminated in his support for the Hampton Roads peace conference of February 3, 1865.

After the war, Wickham joined the Republican party, alienating many of his comrades, and became president of the Virginia Central Railroad. In 1883 he was elected to the Virginia Senate, where he served until his death on July 23, 1888. In 1891, a statue of General Wickham was dedicated in Monroe Park, Richmond. Wickham wrote to a friend after the war in a letter reflecting his early Unionist sentiments, "I have often said to those with whom I was on terms of friendship that I never saw the United States flag, even when approaching it in battle, that I did not feel arising those emotions of regard for it that had been wont to inspire. I have in like manner said that one of the most painful sights I had ever seen was on the night of the first battle of Manassas, when I saw an officer trailing the flag in the dust before a regiment of the line."

BIBLIOGRAPHY

Dowdey, Clifford, and Louis H. Manarin, eds. *The Wartime Papers of R. E. Lee.* New York, 1961.

Hotchkiss, Jed. *Virginia.* Vol. 3 of *Confederate Military History.* Edited by Clement A. Evans. Atlanta, 1899. Vol. 4 of extended ed. Wilmington, N.C., 1987.

Warner, Ezra J. *Generals in Gray: Lives of the Confederate Commanders.* Baton Rouge, La., 1959.

Wright, Marcus Joseph. *General Officers of the Confederate Army.* New York, 1911.

KENNETH L. STILES

WIGFALL, LOUIS T.

WIGFALL, LOUIS T. (1816–1874), brigadier general and congressman from Texas. Louis Trezevant Wigfall was born April 21, 1816, to Levi Durand and Eliza (Thomson) Wigfall, in Edgefield, a frontier district of South Carolina. Both his parents' families had been among the first to arrive in South Carolina and were socially prominent. As a boy and a student at a private military academy, the University of Virginia, and South Carolina College, Wigfall came to believe in a society led by the planter class and based on black slavery and the chivalric code. Politically, he became an avid spokesman for state rights and secession, drawing on his classical education in oratory, history, literature, and Latin.

Wigfall's brief experiences in military school and in the Seminole War helped him get an appointment as a South Carolina militia colonel. He became known for pistol marksmanship, reckless courage, and a thin-skinned sense of honor. He also earned a reputation for drinking, gambling, and financial carelessness while neglecting the law practice his brother had left to him.

In the 1840 South Carolina gubernatorial campaign that pitted two aristocratic cliques against each other, Wigfall supported John P. Richardson out of dislike for the Brooks family, who supported James H. Hammond, Richardson's principal rival. Wigfall's contribution to the campaign was to take over covert editorship of the *Edgefield Advertiser,* turning the newspaper's support from Hammond to Richardson. In well-reasoned editorials, Wigfall helped win the state for Richardson.

When it became known that Wigfall had written the editorials, some of the Brooks family attacked him personally. Over the next five months, Wigfall was involved in a fistfight, three near-duels, two actual duels, and a shooting with the

LOUIS T. WIGFALL. LIBRARY OF CONGRESS

Brooks family—all of which left one man dead and two, including Wigfall, wounded. In the shooting incident, Wigfall fired upon and killed a young man who had shot at him first. In one of the duels, Wigfall and another Brooks family member missed on their first shots and were persuaded to accept an arbitrated settlement favorable to Wigfall. In the last duel, both men were wounded, Wigfall in the thigh and Preston Brooks in the hip. (This wound may have been the reason Brooks carried the cane he later used to beat Senator Charles Sumner of Massachusetts on the floor of the Senate.)

Although Wigfall remained a firm believer in the dueling, this was his last duel. His reputation for violence persisted, however, and he did nothing to discourage false stories about his dueling exploits. Rather, he capitalized on his purported willingness to shoot people who disagreed with him, intimidating political opponents who were fearful of triggering his temper.

Governor Richardson appointed Wigfall aide-de-camp for his services in the 1840 election campaign, but his first foray into politics and newspaper editing had been costly. Although a grand jury failed to bring in an indictment for the killing of the young man and murder charges were dropped, many people in the community still blamed Wigfall. His neglected law practice dwindled further, and despite his marriage to his respected second cousin, Charlotte Cross, Wigfall was nearly ruined socially, professionally, and financially. Their first son's serious illness became an additional drain on their finances.

But even as his son lay dying and his debts mounted, Wigfall became more interested than ever in politics. As a delegate to the state Democratic convention, he helped draw up resolutions for the 1844 campaign. At the convention, Wigfall spoke in favor of the annexation of Texas in order to maintain the right of slavery, and against protective tarriffs, seeing them as a threat to Southern civilization. John C. Calhoun argued only for nullification to oppose the tariffs, but Wigfall, sixteen years ahead of most South Carolinians, said the state should secede, alone if necessary.

Unable to rebuild his standing in South Carolina, Wigfall moved Charlotte and their three children to Texas in 1846, a

> . . . Wigfall asserted that the Federal government was a creation of the states, not of the people, and that each state had the right to leave the Union. . . .

year after it joined the Union. He opened a law office in Marshall, Texas, building a practice and a reputation as a lawyer. Nevertheless, his first concern was still politics, and he was never financially solvent for more than a few weeks at a time.

Wigfall headed a committee that formulated resolutions reiterating the state rights argument and condemning the Wilmot Proviso and the concept of "squatter sovereignty" to prevent expansion of slavery into territories. Speaking for the resolutions, Wigfall asserted that the Federal government was a creation of the states, not of the people, and that each state had the right to leave the Union if it acted "unconstitutionally." Although the resolutions passed, Wigfall expressed sorrow that Texas would not take the lead in seceding.

Named in 1850 to the Texas House of Representatives, Wigfall attacked Sam Houston, then a U.S. senator and strongly pro-Union, as a recreant to Texas and the South and denounced him for voting for the Compromise of 1850. Wigfall played a major role in organizing Texas Democrats to oppose Houston and the Know-Nothings in 1855 and 1856. He led a successful fight in the Texas legislature to pass a resolution censuring Houston for his opposition to the Kansas-Nebraska Act and was widely credited with Houston's defeat for the governorship in 1857, which put an end to Houston's influence in the U.S. Senate. Now recognized in Texas as the leader of the radical state rights Democrats, Wigfall was elected to the Texas Senate in 1857 and had a strong voice in the 1858 state Democratic convention, which adopted a state rights platform.

With the breakup of the Know-Nothings, however, many moderates moved back into the Democratic party, and it appeared that Wigfall's radicalism was repudiated. He chose this time, however, to push two of his ultraradical proposals: the revival of the foreign slave trade and filibustering in Cuba, Mexico, and farther south for more slave territory. When these proposals split Texas Democrats, Wigfall had to abandon them. Nevertheless, he was elected to the U.S. Senate in 1859, with the inadvertent help of John Brown. By capitalizing on the fear engendered by Brown's Harpers Ferry raid, Wigfall defeated more moderate candidates.

Wigfall was the most pugnacious of the radical members of the Thirty-sixth Congress, who were intensifying the sectionalism that was leading to war. As a freshman senator, Wigfall was in the forefront of the Southern fire-eaters, earning a reputation for eloquence, witty but bitter debate, acerbic taunts, and a readiness for personal encounters. And his debates did not end on the Senate floor; he frequented bars and gaming rooms, always seeking out adversaries. In opposing the Homestead Act, partly on the ground that 160 acres was too small for a plantation with slaves, Wigfall lampooned it as a bill that would provide land for the landless and homes for the homeless, but not "niggers for the niggerless," as he put it. It is not surprising that he failed to obtain Federal funds for Texas to defend its frontiers against Indian attacks and to build the Southern Pacific Railroad into the state. He assured his fellow senators that the South would never accept a Black Republican as president. Let war come, he declared, "and if we do not get into Boston . . . . before you get into Texas, you may shoot me."

In the campaign of 1860, Wigfall helped discredit Stephen A. Douglas and split the Democratic party. After Abraham Lincoln was elected president, Wigfall coauthored the Southern Manifesto, declaring that any hope for relief within the Union was gone and that the honor, safety, and independence of the Southern people required the organization of a Southern confederacy. The manifesto was widely quoted in the Deep South, and even Southern moderates seemed to give up any idea of remaining in the Union.

Wigfall contributed greatly to thwarting compromises to save the Union. Although he occasionally expressed hope that separation would be peaceful, most of the time he equated it with war, avowing that the concluding treaty would be signed in Boston's Faneuil Hall. Wigfall stayed in the U.S. Senate even after Texas left the Union. He spied for the South, baited Northern senators, raised and trained troops in Maryland and sent them to South Carolina, and bought revolvers and rifles for Texas Confederates through July 1861, when he was finally expelled from the Senate well after the war started.

Typically, Wigfall had made his presence felt when the Civil War began at Fort Sumter in April, rowing under fire to the fort and dictating unauthorized surrender terms to the

Federal commander. Many Southern newspapers hailed the recklessness and gallantry of Senator Wigfall, calling him the Confederate man of the hour. He refused an offer of the Texas governorship and became instead an aide to President Jefferson Davis, a Texas colonel, a Confederate colonel, and a member of the Confederate Provisional Congress, for a time concurrently while he was still a U.S. senator.

Wigfall initially was a friend and supporter of Davis and helped him become president. Most fire-eaters had wanted Barnwell Rhett, but Wigfall helped persuade Rhett to support Davis. Wigfall was influential with Davis, prevailing upon him to select Leroy P. Walker as the Confederacy's first secretary of war. The Davises and Wigfalls were together a great deal during May and June 1861. And in early July, Gen. P. G. T. Beauregard, in command of the Confederate troops at Manassas, wrote to Wigfall, seeking his assistance in presenting his grievances to Davis.

In early July, Wigfall became commander of the Texas troops, now a battalion, near Richmond. Since the command was not a large one, his appointment carried only a lieutenant colonelcy. Wigfall had hoped to be named a general, but the battalion was being mustered into Confederate service, and more troops from Texas were slow in coming.

Because Wigfall's battalion was in a train wreck on the way to the First Battle of Manassas, it did not arrive until the morning after the fighting. Nevertheless, Wigfall criticized the Confederates' failure to march on to Washington after the victory. Gen. Joseph E. Johnston said his army had been unable to press the attack because of a shortage of food supplies— a shortage he attributed to the failure of Davis's commissary general, Lucius B. Northrop, to deliver them. Wigfall sided with his friend Johnston, and apparently Davis considered criticism of Northrop to be criticism of himself.

Wigfall also took Johnston's side in the controversy over his rank, agreeing with his friend that he should be the highest ranking Confederate general because he was the highest to leave the U.S. Army. The controversy began when Robert E. Lee, then Davis's military adviser, ordered a new adjutant general into Johnston's headquarters. Johnston, certain he outranked Lee, protested repeatedly to the War Department. Even Lee was uncertain of his rank and position. But instead of clarifying their positions, Davis simply marked Johnston's letters "Insubordinate."

Wigfall soon had his own disagreement with Davis over rank. Prominent Texas friends recommended that Wigfall be moved up two steps to brigadier general. But Davis in August nominated him to move up only one step, to colonel, and Congress confirmed it immediately. The number of Texas troops was increasing to brigade level, however, and Davis nominated Wigfall for a brigadier generalcy in November. Wigfall was then still devoting part of his time to serving as

Texas senator in the Permanent Congress. About the time Congress confirmed his generalcy in December, Wigfall resigned it to devote full time to Congress in order to press for military legislation.

During the optimistic period of February 1862 until May 1863, Congress debated many important military topics but took little action on them. During these months, Wigfall was a pro-administration militarist if not a nationalist. He backed almost all legislation that Davis favored and introduced several administration bills, including a proposal for the first conscription system in American history. One of the few staunch state rights advocates to support the measure, Wigfall argued that there should be only Confederate armies under Confederate generals, a stance that put him at loggerheads with other Texas delegates, who wanted to retain soldiers in their own state to protect its borders. Texas colleague W. P. Ballinger said that some of his friends thought Wigfall was a ruthless man.

During the Peninsular campaign, Wigfall blamed Gen. George B. McClellan's threat to Richmond on Davis's failure to order an invasion of Maryland. To a friend, Wigfall confided that he regretted ever having tried to move such a "dish of skimmed milk" to honorable action. Davis for his part said he lost confidence in Wigfall because of his drunkenness and his antipresident speeches in hotels. In the Peninsular campaign's Battle of Seven Pines, Wigfall cared for the wounded and became an aide to Gen. James Longstreet and a good friend of his and Lee's. They and other Confederate generals considered him their champion in pleading their needs to Congress and Davis.

Both Davis and Wigfall considered themselves expert military strategists, and this was the focus of many of their quarrels. Nevertheless, they agreed on the need for widespread conscription to defend the Confederacy. This issue brought Wigfall into conflict with many of his colleagues in Congress. By 1863 when others were coming to agree with him, Wigfall was still ahead of them, proposing extending the original age limits of eighteen through thirty-five to sixteen through sixty. Both houses accepted his basic bill, though lowering the upper age to fifty. And yet Wigfall seemed surprised when his own sixteen-year-old son Halsey ignored advice to stick to his schoolbooks and instead volunteered and saw extensive action as a member of J. E. B. Stuart's cavalry.

Wigfall used the argument of military necessity to pass a bill he had tried to get through the U.S. Senate, calling for the construction of a railroad through Texas. This would connect Richmond with key positions in the West and South. Texas would have played a greater role in the war effort had it not been so remote and cut off by the Federal sea blockade. Ten days after the bill was enacted, however, New Orleans fell to Union troops and Texas was effectively separated from the rest of the Confederacy. Wigfall led the legislative struggle that established the government's power to impress private railroads and finally, in February 1865, to take control of all railroads in the Confederacy.

Although Wigfall was consistent with his earlier state rights arguments in insisting that Confederate courts had no right to override the decisions of state courts, he generally worked to provide the central government with enough powers to sustain itself. Concerned that state rights were hampering the military, Wigfall introduced a resolution in May 1864, seeking to define Confederate and state jurisdiction over civil rights. Wigfall defined a federal rather than a confederate system of government and even introduced a successful bill providing for military impressment of private property as needed to sustain the army.

When many conscripts defied the draft law and were protected by state judges who readily released them by issuing writs of habeas corpus, Wigfall responded to another Davis plea. He introduced and helped pass a bill in Congress to authorize the president to suspend the writ when necessary to ensure viable Confederate armies.

In arguing for suspension of the writ of habeas corpus, Wigfall assured his colleagues that Davis could be trusted to use the power wisely. Nevertheless, Wigfall did not trust the president to appoint army staff. In October 1862, he persuaded both houses to pass a bill limiting Davis's power of appointment and providing generals with staffs of their own choosing. The president vetoed the bill. Nor did Wigfall trust the president to appoint heads of armies. Wigfall's covert efforts forced Davis to replace Gen. Braxton Bragg with Joseph Johnston as head of the Army of Tennessee, but Wigfall could not induce Davis to provide Johnston with adequate support. Announcing his loss of trust in Johnston, the president replaced him with John Bell Hood, with ruinous results. Wigfall admired Hood's bravery and probably encouraged the close relationship that developed in his home between his fifteen-year-old daughter and the Texas general while he recuperated there from serious battle wounds. But the senator predicted Hood's fiasco at Atlanta.

Having lost all faith in Davis, Wigfall decided that the Confederacy's only hope lay in leadership by Senate hegemony. During the last two years of the war, Wigfall waged a four-pronged public and conspiratorial campaign against the president's power and popularity in an effort to bend him to the Senate's will: the Senate rejected his unwise appointments; Wigfall fixed responsibility for military losses on Davis, where he thought they belonged; Congress tried to force the president to observe the Constitution and hemmed him in with restrictions; and Wigfall and others belittled Davis in public to destroy the people's confidence in him. A positive relationship between Wigfall and Davis might have made it possible for the executive and legislative branches to collaborate, extending the life of the Confederacy. But neither the president nor the senator was willing to compromise, even as the Confederacy was facing destruction.

Probably Wigfall's policies were more sound than Davis's, and it is not surprising that several of the best generals looked to Wigfall for legislation and to plead their cases. But he rejected their pleas to strengthen their armies by arming slaves. Wigfall was willing to lose the war rather than admit that African Americans were worthy of being soldiers.

After the fall of the Confederacy, Wigfall fled to England where he tried to foment war between Britain and the United States, hoping to give the South an opportunity to rise again. He returned to Texas in 1872, died in Galveston in 1874, and was buried there in the Episcopal Cemetery.

BIBLIOGRAPHY

Chesnut, Mary Boykin. *Mary Chesnut's Civil War.* Edited by C. Vann Woodward. New Haven, Conn., 1981.

Clay-Clopton, Virginia. *A Belle of the Fifties.* New York, 1904.

Eaton, Clement. *Mind of the Old South.* Baton Rouge, La., 1964.

Hofstadter, Richard. *Paranoid Style in American Politics.* New York, 1965.

King, Alvy L. *Louis T. Wigfall: Southern Fire-Eater.* Baton Rouge, La., 1970.

Ledbetter, Billy D. "The Election of Louis T. Wigfall to the United States Senate, 1859: A Reevaluation." *Southwestern Historical Quarterly* 77 (1973): 241–254.

Russell, William H. *My Diary North and South: The Civil War in America.* London, 1863. Reprint, New York, 1954.

Wright, Louise Wigfall. *A Southern Girl in '61.* New York, 1905.

ALVY L. KING

WILDERNESS CAMPAIGN

The Wilderness, a region in Orange and Spotsylvania counties in northern Virginia, gave its name to a major battle fought in its tangled thickets on May 5 and 6, 1864. The battle pitted Robert E. Lee against Ulysses S. Grant in the opening stage of the overland campaign that eventually led to the siege of Richmond and Petersburg. Lee had wintered his Army of Northern Virginia in Orange County, west of the Wilderness, while the Federal Army of the Potomac camped across the Rapidan River in Culpeper County. Grant, newly appointed commander in chief of all Federal armies, took his headquarters into the field with the Army of the Potomac in March. Gen. George G. Meade remained in nominal command of that army for the rest of the war, but Grant exerted his authority over all substantive decisions. During the Wilderness, for instance, Meade had no control over one of the army's four corps, Burnside's Ninth.

The Army of the Potomac began its move south over the Rapidan early on May 4, crossing primarily at Germanna Ford, with nearly 120,000 men in the ranks. That number seemed to Grant to be operationally appropriate to begin the

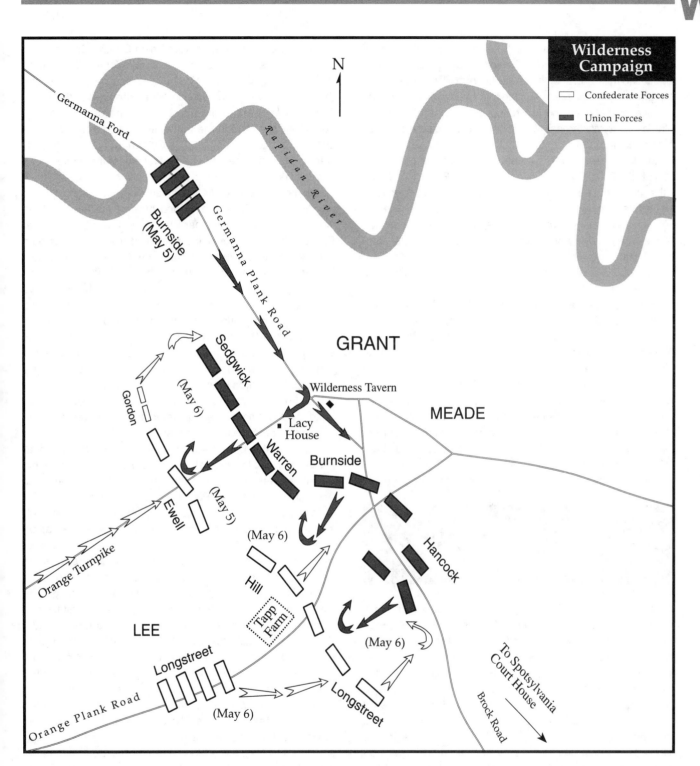

campaign. He also could draw on virtually limitless replacements. Lee's army counted about 65,000 troops, with only limited reserves in prospect, and those available only at the cost of stripping other threatened points. Grant and Meade hoped to march straight through the Wilderness in the direction of Spotsylvania Court House without hindrance, moving past Lee's right flank before he could respond effectively and thus interposing between the Confederate army and Richmond.

Lee responded to the threat by moving swiftly eastward toward the Wilderness, camping on the night of May 4 within easy striking distance of the roads Grant had to use on his projected southward march. The Confederate army moved on two roads that ran through the Wilderness on roughly parallel courses and that eventually joined east of the ground that became the battlefield. The old Orange Turnpike was about two miles north of the newer Orange Plank Road at the longitude of the heaviest fighting. No means of ready communication between the two roads existed. As a result the Battle of the Wilderness was fought in two discrete halves that remained remarkably isolated from each other. Richard S. Ewell's Second Corps marched east on the turnpike while A. P. Hill's Third Corps paralleled it on the Plank Road. The other corps of Lee's army, the First under James Longstreet, began its march unfortunately far to the southwest in the vicinity of Boswell's Tavern in Louisa County. Lee's incaution in leaving so large a force so far from his other units, combined with a slow and confused march to action by the First Corps, would have a major impact on the conduct of the battle.

Fighting broke out first on the turnpike on the morning of May 5. The advance brigades of Ewell's force clashed with Federals marching south past the vicinity of Wilderness Tavern. Union Gen. G. K. Warren's Fifth Corps turned west onto the turnpike to face Ewell's men. Northern troops rolled over the first opposition they met and Confederate Brig. Gen. John M. Jones was shot from his horse. Elements of the division commanded by Robert Rodes restored order for the Confederates, who took up a line perpendicular to the turnpike in woods at the western edge of a large clearing straddling the pike known as Saunders Field. Fighting in this northern sector of the Wilderness on both days of the battle

> They had been fought to a frazzle, however, and lay haphazardly in the thickets. . . .

centered on the turnpike and especially on Saunders Field. Grant and Meade established their headquarters on a knoll just north of the pike and a mile east of the field. Warren made his headquarters just across the road from his two superiors at the Lacy house, Ellwood, which is the only building on the battlefield that survives today. Fighting ebbed and flowed around Saunders Field during May 5 as the rest of Ewell's Second Corps arrived and the Federal Fifth Corps, supported by most of the Sixth, deployed to face it. The Confederates lost Brig. Gen. Leroy A. Stafford, who was mortally wounded in one fierce localized attack by the Sixth Corps.

Meanwhile the Confederate column on the Plank Road had approached its intersection with the north-south Brock Road, on which Grant was moving south, and fighting broke out in that zone. Confederate control of the intersection would break Grant's attenuated army into two pieces and leave it susceptible to destruction in detail. During May 5 Hill came

up against stout resistance from Union Gen. W. S. Hancock's Second Corps, supported by one division of the Sixth Corps under George W. Getty. Most of the fighting raged in the thickly overgrown woodland on either shoulder of the Plank Road not far west of the intersection. The only clearing of note along the road in the battle area was the meager subsistence farm of a widow named Catharine Tapp, and that lay west of the front lines during the first day of the battle.

As darkness closed the fighting on May 5, the Southern position near the turnpike remained along the western edge of Saunders Field and extended beyond the field on both sides in a straight line, particularly northward, to counter Federal threats. All over the battlefield the soldiers of both sides energetically threw up earthworks reinforced with logs; the era of major entrenchments had arrived to stay and would reach unprecedented levels during the next two weeks. On the Plank Road front, Hill's brigades maintained a tenuous grip on ground fairly close to the crucial intersection with the Brock Road. They had been fought to a frazzle, however, and lay haphazardly in the thickets without adequate connection between units. Hill's subordinates desperately petitioned the corps commander to fall back and regroup. He refused on the premise that Longstreet's men would be on hand by morning as reinforcements and insisted that the weary soldiers be allowed to rest.

Early on May 6 a massive assault arranged by the capable Hancock rolled irresistibly over Hill's tattered remnants and threatened to destroy the Army of Northern Virginia. According to Edward Porter Alexander and James Fitz Caldwell, Lee rode among his fleeing troops, asking one veteran brigade why it was "fleeing like wild geese" and atypically expressing himself "rather roughly." At this critical moment, probably the most desperate in the army's career to date, the first units of Longstreet's First Corps finally began arriving on the field. Hancock had smashed through the woods to the Widow Tapp's clearing, where a battalion of Confederate artillery had been parked. The artillery of both armies accomplished little during the battle because of dense ground cover that rendered cannon less important here than in any other major action in the Virginia theater. These reserve guns suddenly became Lee's last line of defense, however, while Longstreet's men deployed. When the veteran Texas Brigade (three Texas and one Arkansas regiments) moved past the guns and into the breach, Lee attempted to lead them forward in an episode that became instantly famous and eventually grew larger than life in later years. Fearing for Lee's safety, the men of the brigade turned him back and then rushed forward in an attack that left half of them casualties.

Longstreet's reinforcements gradually stabilized the front along the Plank Road. The tide turned when a broadly mixed Confederate task force—four brigades from four divisions—moved secretly through the woods south of the road to an unfinished railroad bed that provided them with a corridor to use in creeping past the far left Federal flank. When the flanking column spread out into line and then dashed north, it routed the Union troops who had been flushed with success, rolling up the line "like a wet blanket," in Hancock's phrase. As the victorious Confederate attackers dashed northward toward the Plank Road, Longstreet and his subordinates led their men east on that road to exploit Hancock's collapse. But some of the Confederates in the woods, apparently of William Mahone's Virginia Brigade, fired at the group of horsemen along the road and with that volley ruined their army's chance for a great success. The volley killed Gen. Micah Jenkins and severely wounded Longstreet. In the shocked aftermath, the movement lost its momentum. Later in the day, Lee directed a renewal of the attack toward the intersection, but it resulted in a costly repulse after surging close to its goal.

May 6 on the Orange Turnpike front featured more fighting over and around Saunders Field. The exposed Federal right north of the field offered a tempting target, but corps commander Ewell timidly refused suggestions to exploit the opening. Finally, near dusk, Georgian John B. Gordon led a column that smashed the Federal right, just as Longstreet had destroyed the Federal left earlier in the day. Gordon captured hundreds of prisoners, including two brigadier generals, and pushed the Union right back through an arc of nearly ninety degrees in the gathering darkness.

The two armies faced each other from behind steadily deepening earthworks on May 7. Then Grant moved south in a race for the next crucial crossroads, a race that resulted in a two-week battle around Spotsylvania Court House. The Wilderness battlefield meeting between Lee and Grant had cost the Federal army about eighteen thousand casualties. Lee's losses, which cannot be computed precisely for this stage of the war, totaled at least eight thousand and probably reached near ten thousand. Lee's tactical skill had thwarted the intentions of an army twice the size of his own. Grant had quickly discovered the difference between fighting Lee and toying with Braxton Bragg. At the Wilderness Grant's army earned the distinction of having both of its exposed flanks abruptly turned and crumpled, the only such result in any of the war's battles in the Virginia theater. Nonetheless he pushed steadily on from the Wilderness toward Richmond. The war had turned its final corner in the Wilderness, and now it would grind inexorably by means of attrition through eleven months of steady fighting to Appomattox.

BIBLIOGRAPHY

Dowdey, Clifford. *Lee's Last Campaign.* Boston, 1960.
Kelley, Dayton. *General Lee and Hood's Texas Brigade at the Battle of the Wilderness.* Hillsboro, Tex., 1969.
Schaff, Morris. *The Battle of the Wilderness.* Boston, 1910.
Steere, Edward. *The Wilderness Campaign.* Harrisburg, Pa., 1960.
Trudeau, Noah Andrè. *Bloody Roads South.* Boston, 1989.

ROBERT K. KRICK

WILMINGTON, NORTH CAROLINA

Situated on the Cape Fear River twenty-eight miles from the river's mouth, Wilmington in 1860 was North Carolina's largest city. Its population was 9,542, which was made up of 2,722 white males, 2,480 white females, 244 free black males, 329 free black females, 1,882 male slaves, and 1,895 female slaves. A deep-water port, the city was known for its beautiful churches and impressive homes, and it boasted a theater in the town hall run by a local Thalian Association.

At the start of the war most of Wilmington was not considered a major port; however, it did have excellent internal communications through three railroad lines: the Wilmington and Manchester, which connected the port to Charleston and Columbia, South Carolina; the Wilmington and Weldon, which ran north to Virginia; and the unfinished Wilmington, Charlotte, and Rutherford, which extended into North Carolina's interior. The city also had daily steamboat service up the Cape Fear River to Fayetteville and was connected by steamships to Charleston and New York. Wilmington's main exports were turpentine, resin, tar, lumber, rice, corn, and flour.

Wilmington could be reached through two channels that connected the Cape Fear River to the Atlantic. The main channel, which led out to the southwest, was called Old Inlet. It had a treacherous, shifting bar that varied in depth from ten to fifteen feet. The second entrance, called New Inlet, had been formed in 1761, when a hurricane cut a northeast channel through Federal Point Peninsula. The new pass was more shallow than the main channel but was quite navigable for small and medium-sized vessels.

From 1860 until the end of the war, Wilmington's mayor was John Dawson, a local businessman. At the start of the secession crisis, citizens of Wilmington formed the Cape Fear Minutemen and on January 10, 1861, seized Forts Caswell and Johnston at the mouth of the Cape Fear River; since North Carolina had not yet seceded, however, the governor ordered the forts returned the next day. Three months later, on April 13, 1861, militia with proper authorization recaptured the forts.

Considered to be a secondary port by the Federal navy, Wilmington was not blockaded until July 21, 1861, nearly two months after blockades were set up off Charleston and

Savannah. For the first few months of the war, Wilmington's shipping trade stagnated and the city's economy entered into a depression. Some businessmen made profits from the production of salt, which soon became a major wartime industry. A few owners of schooners and brigs continued a small coastal trade, and some sailing ships undertook the 570-mile voyage to Nassau or the 674-mile trip to Bermuda in search of profits.

At the beginning of the war, only a few steam blockade runners used Wilmington. One of these, *Kate,* brought with it yellow fever. From early September until November 11, 1862, the town suffered 1,500 cases and 700 deaths, 15 percent of the town's population. After the epidemic, city and military authorities undertook an extensive quarantine program to keep such a severe outbreak from occurring again.

In the fall of 1862, the head of the Confederate Ordnance Bureau, Josiah Gorgas, chose Wilmington as the port of entry for his bureau's line of blockade runners. The steamers, operating out of St. George, Bermuda, some 674 miles away, brought immense amounts of military supplies to Wilmington and carried away government cotton. In charge of the Ordnance Bureau's operations at Wilmington was James M. Sexias. The Ordnance Bureau's runners were soon joined by private runners who also saw the advantages of using Wilmington, and in July 1863, after the Federal attack on Charleston effectively closed down blockade running there, Wilmington became the South's primary port.

Like other ports, Wilmington gained little from the supplies being unloaded at its docks; most went inland. As a result, goods grew scarce and prices went up. Conditions quickly became bad, and soon the prewar society was forced out by the influx of speculators, sailors, and other individuals associated with blockade running. Prostitution became rampant, and other citizens were reduced to begging. Some civic groups and individuals, such as the Ladies Relief Society operated by Miss Mary Ann Buie, tried to help those in need, but their activity was often lost among the fast-living blockade runners who came to dominate the town. As one commentator reported, Wilmington was the meanest place in the Confederacy. The presence of sailors, speculators, businessmen, and the other elements of a wartime port was a necessary evil, however, for after July 1863, Wilmington became the most important element in the Confederate supply system. Before the war ended, blockade runners made over three hundred round trips to Wilmington—more than all the other Confederate ports combined.

Because of its vital importance to the Confederacy, Wilmington was guarded by a number of fortifications. An outer ring guarded New and Old Inlets while other forts lined the Cape Fear River, and the city was encircled by a line of trenches. Its major fortifications were Fort Caswell at Old Inlet and Fort Fisher at New Inlet. Since most blockade runners preferred New Inlet, Fort Fisher, under the command of

Col. William Lamb, became the most important and largest fort in Wilmington's defenses.

For most of the war Wilmington's commander was Brig. Gen. W. H. C. Whiting, who worked to make Wilmington one of the best defended cities in the Confederacy. Besides coordinating the area's defenses, Whiting controlled blockade running through the issuance of strict regulations. No vessel could leave the port without permission from the army. Curfews were established in Wilmington, and the army assigned the blockade runners with their signalmen and pilots. All vessels were inspected, and captains were required to keep an accurate list of their vessel's cargo, crew, and passengers. In March 1864, after a disastrous fire burned nearly one thousand bales of cotton worth $691,000, Whiting ordered that all runners had to be towed into the river before firing their engines. To help enforce these regulations, the army purchased the former blockade runner *Flora,* which they renamed *Cape Fear,* to use as an armed transport.

Whiting's tight regulations often caused friction with Wilmington's naval commander, Flag Officer William F. Lynch, who commanded a small squadron of wooden gunboats. On one occasion, in February 1864, the army and navy nearly came to blows over a cargo of naval cotton. The matter was settled in Richmond, and Lt. John Wilkinson was sent to Wilmington to assist blockade running and secure harmony between the military authorities.

During the war the casemated ironclads *Raleigh* and *North Carolina* were completed at Wilmington. *North Carolina* was plagued with mechanical problems and spent most of its career moored off Smithville near the mouth of the Cape Fear River where it eventually sank owing to a worm-eaten bottom. *Raleigh* made a foray from New Inlet against the Federal blockaders on the evening of May 6, 1864, but the next morning ran aground off Smithville and became a total loss. A double-ended, twin-tower ironclad called *Wilmington* was started late in the war, but was unfinished at the war's end.

In July 1864, the Confederate navy purchased the twin-screw-propeller blockade runner *Atalanta* and renamed it *Tallahassee;* in September another twin-screw runner, *Edith,* was purchased, and in October, under the name *Chickamauga,* it joined the *Tallahassee,* now called *Olustee.*

Though these raiders carried out various missions and returned safely, many government officials feared their use as commerce raiders would result in a tightened blockade and lead to an attack on Wilmington. Their complaints stopped further raids, and none of the ships ever again ventured out as warships, except *Olustee,* which later went out as a blockade runner under the name *Chameleon.*

During the war Wilmington served as the port not only for the Ordnance Bureau vessels but for all east-coast blockade runners operating under contracts with the Confederacy. It was also used by the vessels owned by the states of North

Carolina, Virginia, and Georgia, as well as private companies. During the war numerous Confederate agents passed through Wilmington on their missions, including Rose O'Neal Greenhow, who drowned when her blockade runner, *Condor*, ran aground near New Inlet on September 30, 1864. She was later buried in Wilmington with full military honors.

During 1864, the blockade-running trade at Wilmington greatly increased as the South's demand for overseas goods grew. Though luxury items continued to arrive, the Confederacy placed tighter restrictions on the blockade runners, which resulted in the importation of vast amounts of military goods. Besides munitions, Wilmington was also the receiving point for the Army of Northern Virginia's meat rations. Gen. Robert E. Lee, knowing the reliance of his army on the supplies coming into Wilmington, reported that should the port fall, he would be unable to maintain his troops.

Throughout the war the North attempted to keep Wilmington under a tight blockade, but the port's widely spaced entrances forced the Union navy to split its warships into two squadrons that could not support each other. This division of strength coupled with the power of the Confederate forts stymied any effective blockade. Though active operations against Wilmington had been considered as early as the summer of 1862, the North was unable to put together a combined army and navy expedition against Fort Fisher until December 1864. Two assaults were made against the fort, and it, along with Whiting and Lamb, was captured on January 15, 1865.

The fall of Fort Fisher ended Wilmington's role as a blockade-running port and effectively cut the Confederacy's lifeline to Europe. Though the Confederates, under Gen. Braxton Bragg, continued to resist Northern advances against Wilmington for another month, the city's fate as well as that of the Confederacy was sealed, and on February 22, 1865, while a rear guard destroyed government property and records, Bragg evacuated Wilmington. On March 14, in order to show Wilmington's new loyalty and encourage business, Mayor Dawson organized a mass celebration called the Grand Rally, which celebrated the return of Wilmington to Federal control.

[*See also* Fort Fisher, North Carolina.]

BIBLIOGRAPHY

Johns, John. "Wilmington during the Blockade." *Harper's New Monthly Magazine* 33 (September 1866): 497–503.
Sprunt, James. *Tales and Traditions of the Lower Cape Fear, 1661–1898.* Raleigh, N.C., 1916.
Watson, Alan D. *Wilmington: Port of North Carolina.* Columbia, S.C., 1991.
Wood, Richard E. "Port Town at War: Wilmington, North Carolina, 1860–1865." Ph.D. diss., Florida State University, 1976.

STEPHEN R. WISE

WILMOT PROVISO

During an 1846 debate over a $2 million appropriation for the acquisition of California and New Mexico, Pennsylvania Congressman David Wilmot proposed a prohibition on slavery in any territory acquired in the Mexican-American War that was then underway. Wilmot's motivations for offering the proposal were mixed. As a Northern Democrat he supported the war effort and Manifest Destiny but opposed the expansion of slavery and the settlement of free blacks in the territories. He told the Congress that the proviso would create territories where "my own race and own color can live without the disgrace" of "association with negro slavery." By offering the proviso, Wilmot hoped to finesse the issue—coming out both for the war and against the expansion of slavery. This would allow Northern Democrats to resist Whig attacks on them as doughfaces who always appeased the South.

The House adopted Wilmot's proviso by a vote of 83 to 64 in the face of almost unanimous Southern opposition, but the Senate adjourned before taking action on the appropriations bill to which it was attached. In 1847 the House attached the proviso to a $3 million appropriation despite unanimous Southern opposition in that body. In the Senate a few Northerners joined their unanimous Southern colleagues to defeat the proviso. Southern members of Congress unanimously rejected both the goal of the proviso—to prohibit slavery in the new territories—and its implication that Southern institutions (and thus Southerners) were too immoral to enter

> . . . the Southern territories were open to slavery and the Northern ones were not.

the new territories. The debate over the proviso revealed the danger to the South posed by a Congress increasingly polarized over slavery. The change of one vote in the Senate could prevent slaveholders from taking their slaves into Mexican Cession territory.

The proviso was a radical departure from American politics before the Mexican War. From the Northwest Ordinance (1787) until 1846, American politics had institutionalized the notion that the Southern territories were open to slavery and the Northern ones were not. The proviso threatened this balance, and in the process put the South on the defense in a new and dramatic way. A resolution of the Virginia legislature, adopted in February 1850, illustrates how the proposal of the proviso helped shape Southern thought and served as a prelude to secession. After asserting that Virginia's "loyalty to the Union . . . is stamped upon every page of her history," the legislature declared, "in the event of the passage of the Wilmot proviso . . .Virginia will be prepared to unite with her sister slaveholding states, in convention or otherwise" to consider "measures . . .tfor their mutual defence."

While the proviso inspired Southern fears and secessionist stirrings, it inspired an entire political party in the North, the Free-Soil party. The new party was a coalition of forces, including political abolitionists and former Liberty Party members, antislavery (conscience) Whigs, and antislavery Democratic negrophobes who were fed up with Southern domination of their party. The main platform of the party was the proviso and a demand for keeping slavery (and blacks) out of the territories. Although the party did poorly in 1848, the idea behind the proviso remained strong and reemerged as part of the main slogan of the Republican party in 1856, "Free Soil, Free Labor, Free Speech, Free Men."

[See also Compromise of 1850; Kansas-Nebraska Act; Missouri Compromise; Republican Party.]

BIBLIOGRAPHY

Bestor, Arthur. "State Sovereignty and Slavery: A Reinterpretation of Proslavery Constitutional Doctrine, 1846–1860." *Journal of the Illinois State Historical Society* 54 (1961): 117–180.
Freehling, William W. *The Road to Disunion: Sectionalism at Bay, 1776–1854.* New York, 1990.
Morrison, Chaplin. *Democratic Politics and Sectionalism: The Wilmot Proviso Controversy.* Chapel Hill, N.C., 1967.

PAUL FINKELMAN

WILSON'S CREEK CAMPAIGN

The Planter's House conference had failed. The meeting between Unionists Brig. Gen. Nathaniel Lyon and Congressman Frank Blair and secessionists Governor Claiborne F. Jackson and Maj. Gen. Sterling Price had represented the last chance to quell the unrest growing in Missouri. On June 11, 1861, after hours of fruitless discussion, Lyon terminated the meeting by declaring war on the state of Missouri. The campaign that culminated in the Battle of Oak Hills (or Wilson's Creek) began two days later.

Lyon left St. Louis, marching with one column of Union troops up the Missouri River to capture Jefferson City, the state capital. Aware that Confederate troops were organizing in northern Arkansas, a logical rendezvous point for the pro-Confederate Missouri State Guard and Confederate troops, he directed Brig. Gen. of Missouri Volunteers Thomas Sweeny to lead a column to southwestern Missouri.

On June 15, as Lyon neared Jefferson City, Jackson abandoned the capital and moved up river to Boonville. The Federals secured the capital, pursued Jackson, and defeated him in a skirmish on the seventeenth. Jackson and his troops retreated southwest, while Lyon concentrated his efforts on establishing Union control of the vital Missouri River. Meanwhile, Sweeny's column easily secured the route from St. Louis to Springfield.

While Jackson marched south with elements of the state guard, Price moved to the southwestern corner of the state and selected Cowskin Prairie as the rendezvous point for the state guard. Camped just across the state line, in Arkansas, were the troops of Gens. Ben McCulloch and N. Bart Pearce. On July 1, a portion of Sweeny's column led by Col. Franz Sigel marched west from Springfield in an attempt to block Jackson and Price from joining forces. As Jackson's column moved south, however, thousands of Missourians joined him. Sigel was outnumbered four to one, and his command of a thousand men was defeated in the Battle of Carthage on July 5. The Federals retreated to Springfield, while Jackson continued south and joined forces with Price.

Lyon, having secured the Missouri River, began marching south. On July 7, his command was reinforced by Maj. Samuel Sturgis's troops from Fort Leavenworth, Kansas. Two days later, Lyon received word of Sigel's defeat at Carthage, and he ordered an immediate forced march to Springfield. After four grueling days during which the Federals marched over a hundred miles and crossed three major rivers and numerous streams, they arrived in Springfield on the thirteenth.

Although Lyon's force now numbered about seven thousand effectives, the Army of the West faced numerous problems. The men were in need of food and supplies, and still more worrisome were three Southern forces camped to the southwest. If they united and moved against Lyon, he would be outnumbered almost two to one. Nevertheless, Gen. John C. Frèmont in St. Louis repeatedly denied Lyon's requests for reinforcements. In addition, most of Lyon's army was composed of ninety-day enlistees whose terms of service were coming to an end. By mid-August, the army would be reduced to a skeleton force facing a growing Southern army.

On July 31, Lyon's fears became a reality. At the town of Cassville, about fifty miles southwest of Springfield, McCulloch, Price, and Pearce rendezvoused. Their twelve-thousand-man force began its march up Telegraph Road toward the enemy on the first of August. Lyon learned of the advance, but mistakenly thought the Southerners were moving in three separate columns and would unite near Springfield. He knew that once united, the larger Southern army could defeat his command and force him to abandon the region's pro-Union population. To avert this, Lyon led a column of more than 5,800 down Telegraph Road, planning to engage each column separately.

The next day, when advance elements of both armies fought a brief skirmish at Dug Springs, the victorious

Federals learned that the Confederates were now united. Lyon ordered his men back to Springfield. The Southern army followed and went into camp where Telegraph Road crossed Wilson's Creek, only ten miles from the city.

By August 9, both armies had decided on similar plans of action. The Confederates planned to advance up Telegraph Road and strike the Federals at dawn on the tenth. But a light rainfall and the threat of a downpour canceled the operation. The majority of Southerners were without cartridge boxes, and heavy rain would disarm them. Lyon planned to leave a small force in Springfield, while he led 4,200 men out to attack the Confederate encampment from the north. At the same time Sigel, with 1,200 soldiers, would attack from the

> **As the cavalry closed on the enemy's line, musket volleys and artillery broke the charge, turning it back.**

south. The element of surprise would be critical to the success of the operation.

To Lyon's great fortune, the Southern pickets had not returned to their posts after the night march was canceled, and the dawn attack was a success. The Federals overran several camps and drove the enemy south. The Union column advanced about one mile, reaching a ridge crest later called "Bloody Hill." From the east and across Wilson's Creek, a Confederate battery opened fire and stalled the advance. Price seized the opportunity to organize elements of the state guard into line of battle and ordered them up the hill's south slope to repulse the Federals.

As the Federals advanced down the west side of Wilson's Creek, Lyon, realizing his left flank was vulnerable to any force on the east side of the stream, ordered Capt. Joseph Plummer across the creek with a small force to advance in conjunction with the main column and guard the flank. After crossing the creek, Plummer observed the Confederate artillery's effect on the Federals on Bloody Hill and immediately moved against the battery. But two Confederate regiments blocked Plummer in John Ray's cornfield. In a brief, violent fight the Federals were routed and retreated across the stream. Plummer's defeat secured this section of the battlefield for the Southerners.

About a mile and a half south of Bloody Hill, Sigel had heard Lyon's attack and ordered his artillery to open fire on the main Southern cavalry camp. The Confederates abandoned their camp and retreated to the protection of nearby woods, leaving the way unopposed for Sigel's Federals to cross to the west side of Wilson's Creek, advance north, and take a position on a hill where they overlooked the cavalry camp and blocked Telegraph Road. Despite the strength of

this position, Sigel was attacked and routed by Southern infantry led by McCulloch. The rear of the Confederate army was now secure, and all its efforts could be concentrated on Bloody Hill.

By 6:30 A.M. the battle lines had been drawn on Bloody Hill. The Federals held the crest and Price's Missourians the south slope. Between 7:30 and 10:00 A.M., the state guard assaulted the Union line twice, failing in each attempt. During the second attack Lyon was wounded but continued to direct his command. Around 9:30 Lyon ordered the Second Kansas and First Iowa Infantry regiments forward to reinforce the line, and the Southern attack stalled. But while leading the Second Kansas into position Lyon was killed by a musket ball.

As Price's attack lost its momentum, Confederate cavalry launched an assault on the Union right and rear. This diversion of the Federals' attention permitted Price to disengage his troops and fall back down the hill. As the cavalry closed on the enemy's line, musket volleys and artillery broke the charge, turning it back.

After Lyon's death, Sturgis, as senior officer, assumed command of the Union forces. Realizing that Price was organizing for a third assault, Sturgis reinforced his line to meet the attack. Around 10:30, some five to six thousand Confederates surged up the hill, and the fighting raged unabated for thirty minutes. At one point Southern infantry closed to within twenty paces of the Union-held crest, and battle smoke from both lines formed one huge cloud on the south slope. The Federal line was hammered along its entire length, but it did not break. By 11:00 Price realized the attack had failed and withdrew to the base of the hill.

During this lull Sturgis learned that Sigel had been routed and that the troops on Bloody Hill were dangerously low on ammunition. Deciding he could not withstand a fourth assault, Sturgis began withdrawing his forces, and by 11:30 the Federals had abandoned Bloody Hill. Unaware of Sturgis's move, the Southerners launched a fourth assault. Upon reaching the crest, they observed the Union rear guard and main column retreating to Springfield. Exhausted by almost five hours of combat, low on ammunition, lacking in experience, and misled by rumors of Federal reinforcements approaching Springfield, the Confederates chose not to pursue their adversaries.

The Battle of Oak Hills was over. Of the 5,400 Federals on the field, 1,317 were casualties with 258 killed, 873 wounded, and 186 missing. The Southerners suffered 1,222 losses, with 277 dead and 945 wounded out of 10,125 effectives. Losses totaled 24.5 percent for the Federals and 12 percent for the Confederates.

The campaign marked the beginning of the war in Missouri and the Trans-Mississippi. Afterward the Federal army withdrew to Rolla, Missouri, leaving the Southerners in possession of most of the southwestern region of the state.

McCulloch and Pearce returned to Arkansas, and Price and the Missouri State Guard advanced north toward Lexington, where, on September 20, they captured the Union garrison. With victories at Wilson's Creek and Lexington, Confederate hopes in the state reached new heights. In October, Governor Jackson led his exiled state government out of the Union, and Missouri became the twelfth Confederate state. Meanwhile, pro-Union Missourians organized a loyal government in Jefferson City. Throughout the remainder of the war, Missouri never politically reunited.

BIBLIOGRAPHY

Adamson, Hans Christian. *Rebellion in Missouri: 1861.* Philadelphia, 1961.

Bearss, Edwin C. *The Battle of Wilson's Creek.* 3d ed. Bozeman, Mont., 1988.

Brown, Dee Alexander. "Wilson's Creek." *Civil War Times Illustrated* 11, no. 1 (April 1972): 8–18.

Holcombe, Return I., and W. S. Adams. *An Account of the Battle of Wilson's Creek, or Oak Hills, Fought between the Union Troops, Commanded by Gen. N. Lyon, and the Southern, or Confederate Troops, under Command of Gens. McCulloch and Price, on Saturday, August 10, 1861, in Greene County, Missouri.* Springfield, Mo., 1883. Reprint, Springfield, Mo., 1985.

Monaghan, Jay. *Civil War on the Western Border, 1854–1865.* Boston, 1955.

Phillips, Christopher. *Damned Yankee: The Life of General Nathaniel Lyon.* Edited by William E. Foley. Columbia, Mo., 1990.

Snead, Thomas L. *The Fight for Missouri: from the Election of Lincoln to the Death of Lyon.* New York, 1886.

Ware, Eugene F. *The Lyon Campaign in Missouri. Being a History of the First Iowa Infantry and of the Causes which Led up to Its Organization, and How It Earned the Thanks of Congress, which It Got. Together with a Birdseye View of the Conditions in Iowa Preceding the Great Civil War of 1861.* Topeka, Kans., 1907.

RICHARD W. HATCHER III

WINCHESTER, VIRGINIA

Located at the northern, or lower, end of the Shenandoah Valley, Winchester played a vital role in three campaigns—Thomas J. ("Stonewall") Jackson's Valley campaign of 1862, the Gettysburg campaign of 1863, and Philip Sheridan's Valley campaign against Jubal Early in 1864. The first two battles (May 25, 1862, and June 14–15, 1863) resulted in Southern victories, but the final one (September 19, 1864) proved the beginning of the end of Confederate control of its eastern granary.

Founded in 1743, Winchester sat at an important juncture of roads and rail. The Valley Turnpike, a macadamized road that ran from Staunton to Martinsburg, split the town. The Winchester and Potomac rail line connected with the Baltimore and Ohio Railroad at Harpers Ferry, thirty-two miles away. The town lay on the invasion route the South or North would choose as a flanking movement around Washington or Richmond. Control of Winchester allowed the South to threaten Washington and some of the Union's logistical communications with the West. And the town provided an entry into the Shenandoah Valley, one of the most productive agricultural regions in the Confederacy. Winchester and the lower valley consequently saw numerous small engagements, as well as battles of larger proportion and meaning on three occasions.

Battle of 1862. The first came on May 25, 1862, when 17,000 Confederates under Maj. Gen. Thomas J. ("Stonewall") Jackson overwhelmed between 7,000 and 8,000 Union soldiers under Maj. Gen. Nathaniel P. Banks. The First Battle of Winchester came at the end of a three-day running fight that had begun on May 23 when the Confederates defeated a thousand-man force at Front Royal. Jackson forced his men on long marches to chase the retreating Federals and captured a number of wagons and supplies at Newtown on May 24. His men made a particularly exhausting march to bring them to the vicinity of Winchester, with Jackson distributing his troops in two groups—one along the Front Royal road to the southeast and the main attack column on the Valley Turnpike to the southwest.

Jackson wanted his men to take high ground to the west of the Valley Turnpike to dislodge Union troops who had formed on Bowers Hill. Because every second counted, the strictly religious Jackson laid aside his usual reservations about fighting on a Sunday and pressed his troops to take hills about four hundred yards from the Union forces. Federal artillery pummeled the Confederates, causing Jackson to order Louisianans under Brig. Gen. Richard Taylor to flank the enemy's left by marching northwest along Abraham's Creek. While a brigade held Union attention on the Front Royal Road, Taylor's men marched under fire across a plain and swept the Union forces from the high ground.

Poor leadership—particularly on the part of Brig. Gen. George Hume Steuart—kept the cavalry far from the action, botching the chance to inflict even more damage on Banks's men as they abandoned the town and retreated across the Potomac at sundown. As it was, the Union sustained the loss of nearly half its force, with 3,030 captured along with 9,300 small arms, 2 field guns, and supplies valued by Jackson at $125,185. This came at a cost of only 400 Confederates over the three days. More important, the action halted the advance of 40,000 Union troops from Fredericksburg to the peninsula where Maj. Gen. George B. McClellan threatened Richmond.

Battle of 1863. The Second Battle of Winchester, like the first, also occurred on the Sabbath. The action on June 14, 1863, pitted the Army of Northern Virginia's Second Corps under Lt. Gen. Richard Ewell against 6,900 Union soldiers of the Second Division, Eighth Corps, led by Maj. Gen. Robert H. Milroy. Ewell's men led the advance of the army under Gen. Robert E. Lee that began in early June and culminated in the Battle of Gettysburg (July 1–3, 1863). The garrison at Winchester blocked the Southern advance and threatened Lee's communications. Intelligence had warned the Union commander about the Southern threat, but Milroy discounted the information and also failed to withdraw on the night of the thirteenth after brushing with the vanguard of the Southern army as it moved into position for an attack.

Winchester was protected on the north and northwest by three unfinished earthworks. Confederates focused on the one farthest west called West Fort. Ewell wanted a division under Maj. Gen. Edward Johnson to demonstrate on the road to Front Royal from the southeast while Maj. Gen. Jubal Early led his division on a flank march to Little North Mountain west of town. Early left a brigade under Brig. Gen. John B. Gordon to hold the crest of Bowers Hill to the southwest and by 4:00

> **Perhaps more important to the Confederates was the sting of defeat—for the first time, the Second Corps of Lee's army retreated from ground it had held.**

P.M. on June 14 had three brigades on Little North Mountain. Shortly after 6:00 P.M., Confederate artillerists wheeled out twenty guns and opened a crushing fire on West Fort. Forty-five minutes later, Hays's Louisianans led the successful assault on the fort. A counterattack failed. Milroy decided to evacuate the town at 1:00 A.M. on June 15, but Johnson's force cut him off near Stephenson's Depot, four miles from Winchester on the way to Martinsburg.

The Union commander escaped with a small force but lost nearly 3,500 men, most of them captured. He was later exonerated of blame by a board of inquiry. Confederates sustained light casualties, totaling 269. The attack cleared the path for the rest of the army to advance and alerted Northerners that the Southern army had eluded the Army of the Potomac.

Battle of 1864. The Third Battle of Winchester, September 19, 1864, became the first of three losses that cost the South control of the Shenandoah Valley. Operating in the valley since mid-June, Jubal Early had managed to save Lynchburg, threaten Washington, D.C., and force Union commander Ulysses S. Grant to divert troops from the siege against Lee at Petersburg. And since August 10, Early had made a nuisance of himself in the lower valley.

Grant visited the theater and approved of Union Maj. Gen. Philip Sheridan's plans to attack Early's army at Winchester.

Federals consistently estimated the Confederate force at around 20,000, but Early had at best 12,500 men as opposed to Sheridan's 35,000 infantry and artillery, plus 8,000 cavalry. Unfortunately for Early, he had weakened his force shortly before Sheridan's attack by returning an infantry brigade under Maj. Gen. Joseph B. Kershaw to Lee at Petersburg. Unlike the prior two battles, most of the fighting at Third Winchester took place to the east and northeast of town.

Preliminary maneuvers featured mistakes by both sides. On September 18, Old Jube sent a cavalry brigade and divisions under Maj. Gen. Robert Rodes and Maj. Gen. John B. Gordon to Martinsburg to check rumors of work crews on the Baltimore and Ohio Railroad. Another division under Maj. Gen. Dodson Ramseur guarded the Berryville Pike. Early's best defensive position was miles to the south of Winchester, but his scattered divisions forced him to reconcentrate his army near town or face piecemeal destruction. Sheridan blundered by launching his attack through Berryville Canyon, a narrow, two-mile-long gorge east of Winchester that became clogged with 20,000 infantrymen and bought the Confederate army precious time in which to position itself.

When the attack began at 11:40 A.M., Ramseur's division bore the brunt of the fighting until Rodes and Gordon returned and launched two major counterattacks. Gordon's division nearly smashed the Nineteenth Corps. And as the Sixth Corps advanced, a gap occurred in the Union lines when soldiers followed the Berryville Pike, which slanted southward away from the main line of advance. Rodes's men struck at the gap and nearly split the Union forces in two. Rodes was killed during the assault, which Union veterans finally managed to stop. Late in the day, a final surge by Brig. Gen. George Crook's Eighth Corps, supported by cavalry, broke the Confederate left. Early's men retreated through town and headed south.

The Confederates had fought stubbornly all day, but they were outnumbered three to one and they lost 1,707 killed and wounded and another 1,800 missing. Sheridan's Army of the Shenandoah sustained just over 5,000 total casualties. Perhaps more important to the Confederates was the sting of defeat—for the first time, the Second Corps of Lee's army retreated from ground it had held.

Sheridan followed his victory with another success on September 22, 1864, at Fisher's Hill near Strasburg, twenty-some miles south of Winchester. The battles left Winchester in Union hands for the remainder of the war and opened much of the Shenandoah Valley to the Federals, allowing Sheridan to begin the massive destruction of crops that residents referred to as "The Burning." The victories, along with others at Atlanta and Mobile, Alabama, helped turn the tide for Northern morale and ensure the reelection of Abraham Lincoln.

BIBLIOGRAPHY

Freeman, Douglas S. *Lee's Lieutenants: A Study in Command.* 3 vols. New York, 1942–1944. Reprint, New York, 1986.

Gallagher, Gary W., ed. *Struggle for the Shenandoah: Essays on the 1864 Valley Campaign.* Kent, Ohio, 1991.

Nye, Wilbur Sturtevant. *Here Come the Rebels!* Baton Rouge, La., 1965.

Tanner, Robert G. *Stonewall in the Valley: Thomas J. "Stonewall" Jackson's Shenandoah Valley Campaign, Spring 1862.* New York, 1966.

Wert, Jeffry D. *From Winchester to Cedar Creek: The Shenandoah Campaign of 1864.* Carlisle, Pa., 1987.

WILLIAM ALAN BLAIR

WINDER, JOHN H.

WINDER, JOHN H. (1800–1865), provost marshal general of Richmond and Confederate commissary general of prisons. Winder was born February 21, 1800, at the family plantation, Rewston, in Somerset County, Maryland. Admitted to West Point in 1814, he arrived there just as his father, Gen. William Henry Winder, was being routed at the Battle of Bladensburg, August 24, 1814. Determined to redeem the family reputation, Winder graduated in 1820 and served with distinction in the old army (he was twice brevetted during the Mexican War, finishing as lieutenant colonel), but he was not satisfied with his military rank or status in 1861 and resigned to join the Confederacy.

Too old for field command, Brigadier General Winder served from 1862 to 1864 as provost marshal general of Richmond, where he was much resented because of his strict enforcement of martial law. Simultaneously, he was placed in control of Union prisoners (1861–1865) and finished his career as commissary general of prisons, a position that blackened his reputation ineradicably. Criticized as a tyrant in the Southern press and vilified as the "inhuman fiend of Andersonville prison" in the North, he was damned no matter what he did. Had he not died of a heart attack on February 6, 1865, he might have suffered the same fate as his subordinate, Henry Wirz, who was tried and executed for war crimes.

Winder was not the cruel villain long portrayed in the history books. He performed thankless tasks as ably as he could, and the ultimate tragedy is that no one in the Confederacy could have done any better.

BIBLIOGRAPHY

Blakey, Arch Fredric. *General John H. Winder, C.S.A.* Gainesville, Fla., 1990.

Thomas, Emory M. *The Confederate State of Richmond: A Biography of the Capital.* Austin, Tex., 1971.

ARCH FREDRIC BLAKEY

WIRZ, HENRY

WIRZ, HENRY (1823–1865), commandant of Andersonville Prison. Wirz was born Heinrich Hermann Wirz in Zurich, Switzerland, on November 25, 1823, the son of a tailor. He received elementary and some secondary schooling. Although he was interested in medicine, his father insisted on mercantile training. He later claimed to be a physician and assisted doctors in America, but he almost certainly had no medical degree. While in Europe, he married and had two children, but legal troubles led to brief imprisonment followed by divorce. Immigrating to America in 1849, he lived in Massachusetts and then Kentucky, where he married a widow. At the start of the Civil War he was living in Milliken's Bend, Louisiana. He enlisted in the Fourth Louisiana Infantry and became a sergeant. At the Battle of Seven Pines, he incurred a wound above his right wrist, which left him partially incapacitated and in pain for the rest of his life.

Wirz was then assigned to the Confederate military prisons at Richmond headed by Gen. John H. Winder. On June 12, 1862, he was promoted to captain and became one of Winder's adjutants. He was then sent to supervise prisoners farther south and for a time headed the prison at Tuscaloosa, Alabama. On December 19, 1862, he was furloughed to go

> When Winder died of a heart attack, Wirz was left to bear the brunt of Northern outrage.

as a representative of President Jefferson Davis on a mission to Paris and Berlin.

Returning to the Confederacy in February 1864, he was ordered on March 27 to Andersonville Prison in Georgia, where he was given command of the prison's interior. Faced with problems largely created by his supervisors, who crammed prisoners into the ill-supplied stockade, Wirz vainly attempted to reorganize the prison. He had only limited authority over most of the personnel, however, and to strengthen his position, he sought promotion. Though supported by superiors and sometimes referred to as "major," he never received that rank. As conditions deteriorated at Andersonville, Wirz was blamed by the prisoners for their suffering. Inmates of earlier prisons had often been amused at his manner, but those at Andersonville described him as a brutal tyrant. Observers commented negatively on his German accent, his frequent use of profanity, and his outbreaks of rage. By war's end, he and General Winder were among the most notorious Confederate prison officials. When Winder died of a heart attack, Wirz was left to bear the brunt of Northern outrage.

Perhaps because of naivetè or lack of understanding of the North's anger over prison conditions, Wirz did not join other prison officers who fled. Instead he stayed on at Andersonville, where he was arrested and taken to Washington, D.C. There, beginning August 23, 1865, he was tried by a military commission on charges of murder and mistreatment of prisoners. The hostile commission permitted Wirz only a limited opportunity to defend himself, and it heard much testimony, often conflicting, against both Wirz and his superiors. The commission found him guilty, and when clemency was denied, he was hanged on November 10 in the yard of the Old Capitol Prison.

The published record of his trial became a leading source for postwar anti-Confederate propaganda. Nonetheless, some former Confederates and even ex-prisoners defended Wirz. In 1909, the Georgia chapter of the United Daughters of the Confederacy unveiled at Andersonville a memorial shaft to the only Confederate executed in the aftermath of the Civil War.

[*See also* Andersonville Prison.]

BIBLIOGRAPHY

Blakey, Arch Fredric. *General John H. Winder, C.S.A.* Gainesville, Fla., 1990.
Futch, Ovid. *History of Andersonville Prison.* Gainesville, Fla., 1968.
Hesseltine, William B. *Civil War Prisons: A Study in War Psychology.* Columbus, Ohio, 1930. Reprint, New York, 1964.
Parker, Sandra V. *Richmond's Civil War Prisons.* Lynchburg, Va., 1990.

FRANK L. BYRNE

WISE, HENRY A.

WISE, HENRY A. (1806–1876), U.S. diplomat, governor of Virginia, and brigadier general. Born on December 3, 1806, and reared in Drummondtown, Virginia, Henry Alexander Wise was graduated with honors in 1825 from Washington and Jefferson College in Washington, Pennsylvania. Admitted to the bar after studying law for two additional years, Wise practiced the legal profession in Virginia and Tennessee. A successful farmer, Jacksonian Democrat, and outspoken champion of slavery and state rights, he was elected to the U.S. House of Representatives in 1835, serving in that body and vehemently espousing the Southern way of life until 1843. In 1844, Wise was named U.S. minister to Brazil. Wise was too candid with his views to ever succeed as a diplomat, however, and in 1847 he resigned his post and returned to Virginia. Elected governor of Virginia in 1855 by the Democrats, he served as chief executive of that state from 1856 until 1860. After John Brown was convicted for his 1859 attempt to seize the U.S. Arsenal at Harpers Ferry, Wise oversaw Brown's hanging, even visiting him before his execution.

After the start of the Civil War, Wise helped engineer the capture of Harpers Ferry in the spring of 1861. On June 5, 1861, Henry Wise, with much political clout but absolutely no military experience, was commissioned a brigadier general in the Confederate army. His first assignment was commanding the Confederate Army of the Kanawha in present-day West Virginia. A failure in all respects, Wise was soon replaced by Gen. John B. Floyd, an equally inept political soldier with whom Wise could not and would not get along. After an unqualified defeat at Carnifix Ferry in September and a disastrous November campaign, Wise and his brigade, known as Wise's Legion, were ordered to North Carolina.

On February 7, Union Gen. Ambrose Burnside made a successful amphibious assault on Roanoke Island, North Carolina, and the following day his troops defeated the Confederate forces there. Wise was in overall command of the island, and his son was killed during the battle. Posted next with Gen. Robert E. Lee's Army of Northern Virginia, he and his men saw action during the Seven Days' fighting as Union Gen. George B. McClellan battled up the Virginia Peninsula in a disastrous attempt to capture Richmond. Remaining in the Richmond defenses for about a year following the Peninsular campaign, Wise was sent to command the Sixth Military District of South Carolina from October 1863 until returning to the Army of Northern Virginia to take part in the Battle of Drewry's Bluff on May 16, 1864. There, the Confederate forces under Gen. P. G. T. Beauregard effectively sealed up the Union army of Gen. Benjamin Butler at Bermuda Hundred.

Commanding a district at Petersburg, Virginia, Wise served with Lee's army during the ten-month-long siege there. When Petersburg fell to the Union forces on April 2, 1865, Wise joined the Confederate retreat to Appomattox, fighting with his troops at the Battle of Sayler's Creek on April 6. Present at Lee's surrender at Appomattox Courthouse three days later, Wise took his parole, but never applied for amnesty for his role in the Confederate service.

Following the war, he resumed his career in law until he died in Richmond on September 12, 1876.

BIBLIOGRAPHY

Patterson, Richard. "Schemes and Treachery: The 1861 Plot to Seize the Arsenal at Harpers Ferry." *Civil War Times Illustrated* 28, no. 2, April, 1989.
Simpson, Craig M. *A Good Southerner: The Life of Henry A. Wise of Virginia.* Chapel Hill, N.C., 1985.
Wise, Barton H. *The Life of Henry A. Wise of Virginia, 1806–1876.* N.p., 1899.
Wise, Henry A. *Seven Decades of the Union.* Philadelphia, 1871.

WARREN WILKINSON

WOMEN

As the secession movement spread across the South, it encompassed nearly three million adult women, white and black, living in many different situations.

White Women in the Confederacy

Those who were most visible to publicists at the time and to historians since composed a minority: daughters and wives of successful planters in the old black belt or the newer cotton and sugar lands to the west and their counterparts in the urban elite. We know a great deal about these women because at least some of them were highly literate and much given to writing letters and journals.

Some were planters in their own right. From early times a not inconsiderable number of Southern women had owned plantations; of the 440 South Carolinians who owned one hundred slaves or more on a single estate, for example, more than 10 percent were women, many of them married. Across the South scores of such women directed planting operations themselves.

In every town and city there were a few "leading families," whose women set the pace for the urban middle class. In places like Charleston, Savannah, Montgomery, and New Orleans, a small but highly visible group, made up of wives of lawyers and politicians, played an informal but vigorous and sometimes influential part in politics themselves. Mary Boykin Chesnut, Virginia Clay, and Varina Howell Davis were among the best known. Public policy and the men who made it were central to their interests.

With the election of Abraham Lincoln in November 1860 more women began to take part in political discussion, as the debate over a response to the election took shape. In

> **Women on plantations, large or small, often had to take over as planters when their husbands were called to serve. . . .**

Alabama women proposed a boycott of Northern goods, modeled on the boycotts of British goods in the 1770s. Many spoke out strongly in defense of slavery and the Southern ideology. Others wrote for their local papers or regional journals such as *DeBow's Review*. When fighting began, a surprising number made a strenuous effort to understand, and record, the military progress of the war.

Though these two elite groups shared economic and social status, their experiences, once war began, were quite different. Women on plantations, large or small, often had to take over as planters when their husbands were called to

serve in the government or the army. Despite the Confederate law that permitted owners of twenty slaves to avoid military service on the grounds that they were indispensable to food production and to keeping the peace, the countryside was gradually drained of white men. Many areas took on the aspect of a matriarchy. Women had to learn or improve their knowledge of agricultural and financial management and struggle with the management of slaves. Some handled these responsibilities very well while keeping up the fiction that they were only following advice from absent spouses. Those who had reliable overseers or trusted slave managers or who had been managers behind the scene all along were lucky. Others found the task too much to bear and complained bitterly of their burdens. The woman who described her state as "anxiety about something to eat, something to wear and anxiety about everything" or the one who wrote her husband "I tell you candidly all this attention to farming is uphill work. . . . I am heartily tired" had plenty of company.

But however much some might complain, there was no one else to do the job. In the end it was largely women who kept the plantations going and managed the difficult but essential shift from cotton to food production. A South Carolina senator's daughter remarked in 1865 upon the strange turn of events that meant that women could not count on men to help them. She added that the men, when asked for advice, were apt to say that since they knew not what to advise, the women must simply do their best and get away from the Yankees if possible.

Somewhere in the middle of the social ladder, and not so visible in the record, were a large number of white women who lived on small farms or small plantations (those with ten slaves or less). For these the demands were even more strenuous than those resting on large planters' wives. Since they were less likely than their more prosperous sisters to keep records, it has been easy to overlook their response to the challenge of the Civil War. But a handful of surviving records indicates that these women functioned much as farmers had for generations: overseeing planting and plowing whether the actual labor was done by slaves or family members, growing gardens, and raising chickens, pigs, and sheep for home use, and selling or bartering the surplus.

The diary of Emily Lyles Harris provides the most detailed picture of a woman's life on this kind of farm. Though carrying on as a highly competent farmer, she was exceedingly self-critical, fretting about her children, worrying as slaves became more restive and, by her lights, impudent, and wondering what wickedness of her own had brought her to such a pass. Emily Harris can stand for thousands of women who filled the evangelical churches on Sundays, went to revival meetings when they could, raised numerous children, and kept the economy going for the four years of war. Few had her skill with a pen, though most shared her profound religious commitment. Her support for the war was lukewarm from the first and diminished each time her husband went off to the army. She thought the Confederate government woefully mismanaged and once wrote that she would as soon get rid of the men who ran it as the Yankees. The isolation and localism of her experience, in the South Carolina Piedmont, emerges vividly in her diary entries and was doubtless characteristic of many people in her situation.

Further down the social scale were families who had barely managed to survive in peacetime and faced the real possibility of starvation when the men went off to war. Some of these fell into that dim category of "poor whites" or "sand hillers" or "crackers"—people for whom a combination of poor land and poor health dictated a marginal existence.

Effects of the War

Women of childbearing age—rich or poor, country or town—whose husbands went off to war enjoyed a welcome reprieve from constant pregnancy; for this reason visits to or from the patriarch were often viewed with mixed emotions. On the other hand, thousands of women—presumably those too old to have little children—risked considerable danger to follow the army. Wives of officers sometimes felt it better to be where they could know what was going on than to stay at home waiting for uncertain mail, so they set up housekeeping as near to army camps as they could. Other women followed the army—as women always have—to earn a living by washing or cooking, and some, of course, by prostitution.

Once the war was actually under way, spirited young women began to wonder, why should men have all the excitement? The most daring dressed as men and enlisted in the army, sometimes serving for years before they were found out. Others found adventure that peacetime seldom provided by undertaking espionage work for the Confederacy. The best known of these spies was Belle Boyd, only seventeen in 1861, who by the following year had become a heroine in the South and a most-wanted character in the North. She served intermittently throughout the war, despite several terms in Northern prisons. Her final mission took her on a ship to England. The ship was captured, and she was exiled to Canada, but she eventually married the captain whose ship had intercepted her. A man of similar exploits would probably have been executed early on.

Next to spying, the most demanding service women could undertake was that of acting as volunteers in army hospitals. Many women, mostly single or widowed, offered their services as nurses and—despite the extreme reluctance of the male doctors to accept them—performed admirably; a number finally took charge of hospitals. An official report to the Confederate Senate contains evidence that mortality rates in hospitals run by women was about half that in those run by men.

Working long hours under uncomfortable conditions, the nurses sometimes allowed themselves the luxury of pouring scorn on their less adventurous sisters. One remarked with heavy sarcasm that a woman who thought her reputation could be ruined by serving her country had obviously not much reputation to lose. Another, listening to a younger woman say she had often wished to volunteer, commented laconically, "I wondered what hindered her." Along with the well-known nurses (Phoebe Pember, Kate Stone, Sally Tompkins, Louisa Cheves McCord, Ella King Newsome) were thousands of nameless women who staffed and supplied wayside hospitals in nearly every community along railroad lines to take care of wounded soldiers trying to get home. These functioned until the very end of the war when supplies ran so short they could no longer carry on.

> The most daring dressed as men and enlisted in the army, sometimes serving for years. . . .

Urban women, more dependent on the market than those in the country, were the first to feel the pinch of shortages, a pinch that would develop into a vise by the end of the war and that in time would encompass much of the countryside as well. Women brought astonishing ingenuity to bear on the problem of shortages: salt was retrieved from smokehouses, old clothes were unraveled and reknitted, carpets were transformed into blankets, herbs and edible plants were gathered, and every family had its coffee substitute, though no satisfactory one was ever devised. By 1865 in many places it was no longer a matter of finding substitutes but of finding any food at all. Black-eyed peas and corn kept people alive, but widespread malnutrition laid the groundwork for postwar epidemics.

Once-pampered women worked all day, seven days a week, as spinning wheels and looms were dragged from attics and goods once routinely bought were made at home. Mistress and slave worked in tandem. We have Mary Chesnut's word for it that she rarely saw a woman without knitting in her hand.

The Confederacy from the first was in dire need of all kinds of supplies for the army, and women turned to supplying soldiers as they had long supplied their families. Every town and hamlet had its soldiers' aid society, and more than a thousand took shape across the South to provide uniforms, medical supplies, tents, sandbags for fortifications, and fresh food (to ward off scurvy) for the Confederate army. Working every day, not excluding Sundays, some of these voluntary associations developed primitive systems of mass production and turned out extraordinary quantities of goods. If it were not for their meticulous record keeping, the amount of materials Southern women transformed into uniforms, shirts, hospital supplies, and the like would defy belief. In addition to supplying the needs of soldiers—most often those from their own communities—women's societies took on responsibility for the indigent families of men in the army and those who had been killed.

While women who could afford to do so supported the war effort with their labor, poorer women, suffering from inflation and extortion, were the major players in urban food riots. In 1863 such riots occurred in several North Carolina, Georgia, and Alabama towns, as wives of soldiers, working-class women, and others who found it impossible to feed their families intimidated merchants and carried away flour, molasses, and salt. In Richmond women who had perhaps read of women in other Southern cities demanding that merchants sell them goods at government-established prices met to consider their own situation. The following day more than two thousand took to the streets, and though they began in good order, anger took over and riot ensued. The women made off with flour, bacon, shoes, brooms, and whatever else they had found too scarce or too expensive to buy. Mayor Joseph Mayo came out to plead with them, and the governor threatened to shoot them all. The women went home, and in due course the city council set up a system of food distribution for soldiers' families.

In addition to the vast amount of volunteer work, many women, usually out of necessity, found paying jobs. Only 7 percent of Southern teachers had been women before the war; by 1865 they constituted 50 percent of the teaching force. Other women went to work as clerks for the government in Richmond (paid half what their male counterparts received) or in state and local governments. Women replaced men in stores, shops, sawmills, and any other place where the need was great.

The war propelled women into public life in other ways. As time went by, an astonishing number from every social class all across the South wrote letters or petitions to various government bodies, proposing improvements in the way the government was doing things or asking that their husbands be promoted or sent home because their families were starving. At one end of the social spectrum was author Augusta Jane Evans who wrote long letters of unsolicited advice on the conduct of the war to J. L. M. Curry; at the other end were the almost illiterate women whose letters of complaint poured into Raleigh or Montgomery.

As these letters and many private ones make clear, women's support for the war diminished steadily as casualties mounted and life at home became one continuous struggle for existence. At the beginning virtually everybody who talked openly exhibited vigorous patriotism; young women, in particular, were famous (or infamous) for insisting that men they knew should enlist. In private, opinion was less unanimous. Surviving diaries and letters show that some women

from the beginning doubted that separation from the Union was possible or that the war would be as short as the leaders seemed to think. One doubter wrote scornfully of men "drunk with passion and women who share their frenzy." But however they felt at the beginning, as the war stretched on, more and more women decided that the price of independence was too high. Women who visited battlefields came home convinced that nothing could justify such carnage. Those who at the start felt confident that God would not allow the Confederacy to be defeated began to realize that they

> ## Women in the path of either army often suffered traumatic experiences.

could not count on divine protection. For some this meant a gradual change in the nature of their religious convictions.

Women in the path of either army often suffered traumatic experiences. The loss of possessions and the shock of discovering the worst side of human nature could be devastating. Neither white hair nor pregnancy provided protection against Sherman's soldiers who, toward the end of his march through Georgia, were often out of control. Deserters and outlaws from the Confederate army were not much better, and even ordinary hungry Southern soldiers had little respect for the goods and crops of wealthy planters.

Those who could get away before invaders arrived became refugees, sometimes for the rest of the life of the Confederacy. Living with friends, relatives, or strangers, sometimes farming on borrowed land, these people usually joined, at least in their minds, the peace party.

Some women, the subject of much comment, could not bear to give up their accustomed luxuries and provided a market for blockade runners who were willing to put profit before patriotism. Mary Chesnut's diary offers plenty of evidence of an "eat, drink, and be merry" spirit in Richmond in the final years. But counterbalancing this image is that of the many others described by a contemporary as women "with coarse, lean and brown hands . . .women with scant, faded cotton gowns and coarse leather shoes . . .who silently and apathetically packed the boxes [for soldiers] looking into them with the intense and sorrowful gaze that one casts into a tomb."

Black Women in the Confederacy

Alongside the white women of the Confederacy were perhaps a million adult black women, most of them slaves. Of all the women who went through the Confederate experience these are the least well recorded from their own perspective. Evidence from their owners is more plentiful, but far from perceptive.

Like white women, slave women did not comprise a homogeneous group. Their individual life experiences were largely shaped by the economic situation and the character of their owners. The range from best to worst was very wide. For slave women life continued to be principally endless hard work, shadowed by the insecurity of family ties, the ever-present danger of being sold away from husband, children, kin, and friends. Some few who were the property of humane planter families—we have no way of knowing how many—had carved out for themselves within the humiliating confines of servitude a life of some comfort and satisfaction. Even the luckiest, however, were always at the mercy of some turn of fate over which they had no control.

The war brought with it a host of rumors, and whenever word spread that the Northern army was near, some slaves seized the opportunity to run away. Few things are more ironic than the dismay of a mistress when a favorite ("pampered" was the word often used) slave woman was one of the first to leave. Such sisterhood as the plantation system had permitted evaporated when the promise of freedom reached the land. Among those who stayed—especially on plantations or farms being run by women—insubordination grew. As little groups of slaves planned ways to take advantage of the new situation, women often turned out to be the leaders.

Slave women did their share of the hard work of supplying the Confederate army, spinning, weaving, and sewing for those who were fighting to keep them in servitude.

When the Union army liberated an area, its black women suddenly found themselves free. In Memphis these newly freed women, working in the existing black churches, moved at once to form their own voluntary associations to provide help for their own people. In the South Carolina Sea Islands, where Northerners came to teach the freed people, women among the thousands of slaves who had been abandoned by their owners flocked to school to learn to read. Similarly, in the Hampton Roads area of Virginia, thousands of slaves seeking freedom with the Union army gathered. A free black woman, Mary Peake, who had conducted illegal classes before the war took the lead in meeting the pressing demand for schooling.

Life after the Confederacy

For women as for men, after the brief failed experiment with independence and four years of bloody warfare, life would never be the same again. For white women who had been adults in 1861 the Civil War became the central event of their lives, shaping their self-images and fantasies ever after. Those who had succeeded in unaccustomed responsibilities were among those whose response to Reconstruction amazed Northern and Southern observers alike. Caroline Merrick, writing in Mississippi, noted that "in these days of awful uncertainties when men's hearts failed them, it was the woman who brought her greater adaptability and elasticity to

control circumstances, and to lay the foundation of a new order." An Alabama woman wrote that "the women, the courageous women, everywhere were busy reorganizing lives, building up new homes out of the wrecks." Northern journalists made similar comments, and in 1891 a native Southerner, writing on the way the war had affected women, said flatly that it was the women who had set the South going again after the war, "filling the stronger sex with utter amazement at the readiness and power with which they began to perform duties to which they had never been used before." (He seemed not to notice any irony in his characterization of men as the stronger sex.) Attitudes, self-images, were changed. An amusing memoir of one South Carolina woman recounts her effort to conceal from her returned soldier-husband all the things she was now able to do for herself, lest his self-esteem be damaged. She was wittier than most, but there is no reason to think her unique.

Years later, Thomas Dabney, a great planter from Mississippi who had lost everything in the war, wrote to one of his daughters: "That you and Ida are quite able to take care of yourselves I entertain no doubt, but still it does me good to find you asserting the fact with so much boldness. Of all the principles developed by the late war, I think the capability of our Southern women to take care of themselves was by no means the least important."

The most dramatic change, of course, came to black women who at last had their freedom, if not much more. For

> ... it was the women who had set the South going again after the war. . . .

them the end of the Confederacy was the first step toward a new life, a life not fully attained even yet.

For white women the long-term consequences were various: women expanded their role in the educational structure; some continued to work for wages in the postwar years; widows struggled to carry on plantations with free labor; younger women faced a generation in which the number of available husbands was very small. It took a generation before the full effect of the changes the war had wrought in the South were manifested in the lives of women. But by the 1890s many perceptive observers had come to realize the import of what Cornelia Phillips Spencer had written in 1870: "with the strongest conservative principles it is impossible to believe that women will continue to move in the same narrow ruts as heretofore." Rebecca Latimer Felton, in 1915, contrasted the postwar world with the prewar years when a woman's only chance lay "in finding herself a good master." By the 1890s the new woman, born in the Confederacy, growing up during Reconstruction, was everywhere appearing in the South.

[*See also* Bread Riots; Civil Service; Diaries, Letters, and Memoirs; Education, *article on* Women's Education; Espionage, *article on* Confederate Military Spies; Family Life; Hospitals; Marriage and Divorce; Nursing; Prostitution; Refugeeing; Soldiers' Aid Societies; *and biographies.*]

BIBLIOGRAPHY

Crabtree, Beth Gilbert, and James W. Patton, eds. *Journal of a Secesh Lady: The Diary of Catherine Ann Devereux Edmonston, 1860–1866.* Raleigh, N.C., 1979.

Cumming, Kate. *Gleanings from the Southland.* Birmingham, Ala., 1895.

Faust, Drew Gilpin. "Altars of Sacrifice: Confederate Women and the Narratives of War." *Journal of American History* 76, no. 4 (1990): 1200–1228.

Friedman, Jean E. *The Enclosed Garden.* Chapel Hill, N.C., 1990.

Harwell, Richard Barksdale, ed. *Kate: The Journal of a Confederate Nurse.* Baton Rouge, La., 1959.

Lebsock, Suzanne. *Virginia Women, 1600–1945.* Richmond, 1987.

Patton, James, and Francis Butler Simkins. *The Women of the Confederacy.* Richmond, 1936.

Pember, Phoebe Yates. *A Southern Woman's Story.* New York, 1879.

Perdue, Charles L., Jr., Thomas E. Barden, and Robert K. Phillips, eds. *Weevils in the Wheat: Interviews with Virginia Ex-Slaves.* Charlottesville, Va., 1976.

Rable, George. *Civil Wars: Women and the Crisis of Southern Nationalism.* Urbana, Ill., 1989.

Racine, Philip N., ed. *Piedmont Farmer: The Journals of David Golightly Harris, 1855–1870.* Knoxville, Tenn., 1990.

Scott, Anne Firor. *The Southern Lady: From Pedestal to Politics.* Chicago, 1970.

White, Deborah Gray. *Ar'n't I a Woman? Female Slaves in the Plantation South.* New York, 1985.

Woodward, C. Vann, ed. *Mary Chesnut's Civil War.* New Haven, 1981.

ANNE FIROR SCOTT

YANCEY, WILLIAM LOWNDES

YANCEY, WILLIAM LOWNDES (1814–1863), diplomat and congressman from Alabama. Renowned in his lifetime as the most fiery and eloquent orator for Southern independence, Yancey was born in Warren County, Georgia, in 1814. His father died of yellow fever a year later, and in 1821 his mother married the Reverend Nathan Beman, the headmaster of a Presbyterian academy in Georgia, which the young Yancey attended. After selling his wife's slaves, Beman, a native New Englander, moved his family to Troy, New York, in 1823 and soon took up the cause of abolitionism. Beman's relations with Carolina, Yancey's mother, were stormy, and the adolescent Yancey bitterly resented what he saw as the hypocritical and cruel self-righteousness of his abolitionist stepfather. Indeed, throughout his public career Yancey would attack the abolitionists in much the same terms as he had denounced the values of his stepfather.

In 1833 Yancey returned to the society and culture his stepfather had rejected. He left Williams College in Massachusetts before graduating and moved to South Carolina. He read law in Greenville under Benjamin Perry, the leader of the up-country Unionists during the nullification

> **He had a beautifully clear speaking voice that could hold an audience enraptured. . . .**

crisis, and, like his mentor, defended the Union against the Calhounite state rights enthusiasts. Marriage in 1835 to Sarah Caroline Earle, the daughter of a wealthy slave owner, brought with it thirty-five slaves and instant elevation to planter status. Yancey abandoned his law practice and moved in 1836 to Dallas County in the Alabama black belt where he rented a plantation. In 1838, while on a return trip to Greenville, Yancey killed his wife's uncle, Dr. Robinson Earle, in a brawl that stemmed from an exchange of personal insults. Although convicted of manslaughter, Yancey exulted in the affair as a vindication of his honor. Far more dam-

aging to his career than any notoriety in the wake of the killing of Earle, however, was the economic loss occasioned by accidental poisoning of his slaves in 1839. Already suffering financially from low cotton prices after the panic of 1837, Yancey was now forced to return to law for the funds needed to rebuild his estate.

Yancey entered politics for a second time in 1840, and, in a marked reversal of his earlier attitudes, he returned as a committed state righter. He edited a newspaper and backed Martin Van Buren for the presidency in 1840. After serving in the Alabama house in 1841 and 1843, he was elected to fill a vacant seat in Congress in 1844 and was reelected in 1845. But Yancey had neither the taste nor the talent for the compromising posture that was necessary for effective party politics at the congressional level, and he resigned his seat in 1846. Before he did so, he fought a duel (ending in a harmless exchange of shots) with Congressman Thomas Lanier Clingman of North Carolina, a future Confederate general. Clingman challenged Yancey in response to a congressional speech that Clingman believed had sullied his honor.

Yancey held no other political office before the outbreak of the Civil War. His fame and influence rested on his oratory. He had a beautifully clear speaking voice that could hold an audience enraptured while he espoused the cause of Southern rights. Yancey first became identified in the public mind as the champion of the South against the antislavery North as the result of the Alabama Platform of 1848, a set of resolutions passed by the Alabama legislature denying the right of Congress to prevent slavery from expanding into the Federal territories. Reveling in the role of a sectional agitator in the 1850s, he spread the message of secession as a legal right of individual Southern states in hundreds of speeches. He helped make secession possible by first making it conceivable. In a famous publicized letter of 1858 to James S. Slaughter, a letter that Yancey insisted was meant to be private, he called for committees of safety to "fire the Southern heart" in defense of liberties allegedly being trampled by a hostile North.

His oratory won him a reputation as the "prince of the fire-eaters," and it was only fitting that he led the Southern delegates who bolted the National Democratic Convention at Charleston in 1860 over the party's refusal to endorse the old Alabama Platform of 1848 with its demand for the right of slavery to expand into the territories. Yancey went on a

WILLIAM LOWNDES YANCEY.　　　　LIBRARY OF CONGRESS

Northern speaking tour in support of John C. Breckinridge, the nominee of the Southern state rights Democrats in 1860. When the election resulted in Abraham Lincoln's victory, Yancey capped his career as a fire-eater by leading the secessionist forces in the state convention of January 1861 that took Alabama out of the Union.

Yancey's reputation and career peaked in the flush of enthusiasm over the success of secession. Yet neither he nor the other leading fire-eaters were to be entrusted with positions of power in the new Confederate government. He received scant support for the presidency of the Confederacy from the delegates assembled at Montgomery, Alabama, in February 1861. Indeed, Yancey himself was not even chosen as a delegate. The founders of the Confederacy wanted to project an image of careful moderation, and Yancey was considered far too radical and headstrong for such politically delicate tasks as persuading the upper South, especially Virginia, to join the lower South in leaving the Union.

Yancey's oratorical skills as an agitator and his influence in Alabama politics, however, made him a potential disruptive threat to the fledgling Davis administration, were he denied any position or office. Jefferson Davis moved to counteract

the threat by offering Yancey his choice of either the relatively minor cabinet post of attorney general or leadership of a three-man diplomatic mission to Europe. Against the advice of his fellow radical, Robert Barnwell Rhett, Sr., of South Carolina, Yancey accepted the diplomatic assignment in March 1861 and sailed for England in early April with the other commissioners, Pierre A. Rost of Louisiana and A. Dudley Mann of Georgia.

Yancey's diplomatic mission was a failure, but it is hard to see how it could have succeeded in its goal of securing official recognition of the Confederacy. One problem was Yancey himself. His quick temper, impatience with temporizing, and rhetorical outbursts were precisely those personality traits most ill-suited to effective diplomacy. Moreover, and as Rhett had forewarned him, he brought very little leverage to his discussions with the British and French. Contrary to Rhett's urgings, Davis did not empower Yancey to offer long-term commercial treaties in exchange for diplomatic recognition. Without this power, Yancey could not make any direct appeal to the economic self-interest of his European adversaries. All he could do was argue for the legitimacy of the Confederate cause and hint at a cotton embargo in the event of European nonrecognition.

Lord John Russell, the British foreign secretary, coldly distanced himself from Yancey's diplomatic team. He did grant a brief interview on May 3 and an even shorter one on May 9, but he refused to commit himself. In response to Lincoln's proclamation of a Union blockade of the Southern coast, the British issued a proclamation of neutrality in mid-May conferring on the Confederacy the rights of a belligerent, but they withheld official diplomatic recognition. Meanwhile, Napoleon III of France, although professing sympathy for the Confederate cause, made it clear that he would not move unless Britain took the first step toward recognition. By the late summer, after Lord Russell had cut off personal interviews with the Confederate commissioners and limited contact with them to formal, written statements, Yancey was ready to leave for home. Requested to stay until the arrival of James Mason of Virginia, the newly appointed Confederate commissioner to England, Yancey was still in London when news of the *Trent* affair reached England in late November. This Union seizure of two Confederate diplomats from a British mail packet ignited a crisis in Anglo-American affairs that gave Yancey one last chance to make his case for British assistance to the Confederacy.

In a letter of November 30 Yancey repeated his argument that the British were not bound by international law to recognize a Union blockade that was both ineffective and harmful to European commercial interests. He declared that the Confederacy would never be subdued by the blockade and urged the British to reopen their access to the cheap, abundant cotton supplies of the South. Lord Russell was unmoved and on December 7 informed Yancey, Rost, and Mann that "he must decline to enter into official communication with them." This was the final insult for Yancey, and he sailed for home once Mason arrived in January.

Yancey was chastened and angry when he returned to the South in February 1862. Shortly after disembarking in New Orleans, he told a crowd of well-wishers that the Confederacy could count on no friends abroad. He blamed the prevalence of antislavery public opinion in England for the failure of his diplomatic mission and confessed that it was naive to believe that the power of King Cotton could force European recognition of the Confederacy. The South's salvation, he concluded, could be achieved only through military victories that subjugated the Northern enemy.

Yancey had passed on word from England that he would gladly consent to serve as a senator in the First Regular Confederate Congress. So elected in his absence by the Alabama legislature, Yancey took his seat in Congress in April 1862. He soon became entangled in a contest of wills with Davis. Now believing, as Rhett had from the very beginning, that Davis had played him for the fool on the abortive European mission, Yancey was quick to find fault with Davis's handling of the war effort.

Having been forced to borrow funds in London to pay for his passage home, Yancey knew from personal experience that Confederate diplomats and foreign agents suffered from a lack of timely financial assistance. In a thinly veiled criticism of the administration's conduct of its foreign affairs, he wrote Davis in early April outlining missed opportunities for arms purchases by Confederate agents in Europe. Davis's reply was cool but tactful. He was stung more deeply by a letter of April 21 written by Yancey and his Alabama colleague in the Senate, Clement C. Clay. The senators lodged an official protest over Davis's appointment policy for generals. They cited figures showing that Alabama had forty regiments in the field but only five brigadier generals. After hinting that Davis was guilty of political favoritism in his appointments, they submitted the names of five regimental commanders of Alabama troops for promotion to brigadier general. Offended by what he viewed as a blatant challenge to his constitutional prerogatives, Davis indignantly responded that the charges were unfair and unworthy of any further consideration.

Yancey's early clashes with Davis were symptomatic of the ideological rift that soon developed in the Confederacy between the Davis administration and the more radical secessionists, men such as Yancey, Rhett, and Louis T. Wigfall of Texas. Yancey, like his fellow fire-eaters, was willing enough to support essential war measures. For example, he voted for the first Conscription Act in April 1862. He set aside his constitutional misgivings over granting such a power to the national government in consideration of the overriding military necessity of retaining in the field the original twelve-month volunteers raised through the action of the individual states. By the same token, he generally backed the economic measures of the increasingly unpopular Treasury Department. For Yancey and other radicals, however, the Confederate bid for independence rested above all else on the individual rights and liberties of the Southern (white) people. He was thus quick to see in the broadening powers of Davis and Confederate officials a pattern of executive tyranny that endangered the very liberties he believed the Confederacy had been created to protect.

Consistent with the prewar stand that had won him fame as a fire-eater, Yancey the senator repudiated party ties and institutional loyalties for the role of agitator. He used his position in the Senate as a forum to warn fellow Confederates of the despotic threats of a distant, centralizing government controlled by President Davis. He granted the military need for such government programs as the impressment of private goods to supply Confederate armies but argued in vain that such seizures should be pegged to the market value of the impressed property in order to be fair and equitable. Despite his early rebuff by Davis on the issue of appointing generals, Yancey continued to accuse Davis of damaging army morale through a policy that slighted the pride and valor of state troops in its selection of brigadier generals. In particular, Yancey still believed that Davis was ignoring the rightful claims of Alabamians to top commands. In September 1862, at a time when Virginia had twenty-four brigadier generals

> **. . . it was a form of despotism that he feared "more than a million Yankee bayonets."**

and Alabama but four, he introduced a bill setting up a quota system for the nomination and appointment of brigadier generals based upon the number of troops furnished by each state. The bill was defeated, in part because many senators felt that Yancey was engaging in a personal vendetta against Davis.

One of the clearest expressions of Yancey's conceptions of the Confederate experience came during a debate over an amendment offered by Senator William T. Dortch of North Carolina to the Conscription Act in the late summer of 1862. Dortch proposed that the Confederate government be authorized to draft justices of the peace. Benjamin H. Hill of Georgia, a leading spokesman for the Davis administration in the Senate, supported Dortch's amendment by claiming that the war-making powers of Congress extended to the conscription of civil officials. For Yancey, this claim smacked of the heretical nationalism of the hated Lincoln government. He feared that such a nationalist belief, what he called the fallacy of a "national life," would supersede and submerge individual and state liberties and thus negate the constitutional freedoms Southern armies were fighting to uphold. "The province of this government, its sole province," he insisted, "is to defend Constitutional government–the Constitutional liberties of States and of the people of States. There is no National life to defend." The unwarranted power of the national government to draft civil officials, he warned, was the power to destroy state governments, and it was a form of despotism that he feared "more than a million Yankee bayonets."

In his unsuccessful attempts to liberalize the access of the press to Senate debates and to loosen the rules by which the Senate often sat in secret sessions, Yancey continued to portray himself as the champion of the Southern people against a national government that shrank from full public accountability for its actions. His last major battle for what he construed as endangered Southern liberties culminated in the most celebrated episode of his Senate career when Benjamin Hill hurled two glass inkstands at him on February 4, 1863. Hill hit Yancey flush on the right cheekbone with the first inkstand. The two men had been exchanging personal insults for days. Before a bleeding Yancey could attack the Georgian, fellow senators restrained the combatants. Yancey, but not Hill, was officially censured by the Senate for his part in the affair.

The Yancey-Hill clash erupted in the context of a debate over Hill's bill to establish a Confederate supreme court with appellate jurisdiction over state supreme courts. Yancey led the floor fight against the bill, and his state rights arguments were by now familiar to his colleagues: "When we decide that the state courts are of inferior dignity to this Court, we have sapped the main pillar of this Confederacy." He conceded to supporters of the bill that the First Congress of the United States under the venerable George Washington had established a supreme court in 1789, but, in a remarkable statement, given the near deification of Washington's generation in Southern political rhetoric, he claimed that "we are wiser than the men of those days." The Founding Fathers, he noted, could only speculate as to the impact of their legislation. The founders of the new Southern republic, however, should have known from bitter experience how the implied centralizing powers of a federal government could be used to sap individual liberties.

Yancey may have been bloodied by Hill, but he won the court battle. The Confederacy never did have a supreme court. In addition to Yancey's success in arousing fears of centralization, the Davis administration decided there was no pressing need for such a court in light of the generally favorable treatment of Confederate legislation by the existing state courts.

Yancey did not live to see the death of the Confederacy that his oratory had been so instrumental in bringing to life. Already plagued by the late 1850s with a severe case of neuralgia, he suffered through increasingly poor health during his years of Confederate service. Bladder and kidney ailments reduced him to a bedridden invalid by the summer of 1863, and he died at his farmhouse near Montgomery on July 27. In a final tribute to the prince of the fire-eaters, a magnificent funeral procession accompanied the body from the Presbyterian church to its interment in the city cemetery.

BIBLIOGRAPHY

Denman, Clarence P. *The Secession Movements in Alabama.* Montgomery, Ala., 1933.
Draughon, Ralph B. "The Young Manhood of William L. Yancey." *Alabama Review* 19 (1966): 28–37.
DuBose, John Witherspoon. *The Life and Times of William Lowndes Yancey.* 2 vols. Birmingham, Ala., 1892. Reprint, New York, 1942.
Thornton, J. Mills, III. *Politics and Power in a Slave Society: Alabama, 1800–1860.* Baton Rouge, La., 1978.
Walther, Eric H. *The Fire-Eaters.* Baton Rouge, La., 1992.

WILLIAM L. BARNEY

YELLOW TAVERN, VIRGINIA

Six miles outside Richmond, J. E. B. Stuart's Confederate cavalry corps met Philip Sheridan's force on May 11, 1864. The fierce battle took its toll on both armies, but the Southerners suffered an irreplaceable loss—the death of J. E. B. Stuart.

At the beginning of May, the Army of the Potomac crossed the Rapidan and began thrusting southward. From the densely covered terrain of the Wilderness to the crossroads at Spotsylvania Court House, the Federals engaged the Army of Northern Virginia in desperate and bitter fighting while inching ever closer to the Confederate capital.

Philip Sheridan, the commander of the Federal cavalry corps, had brashly told Gen. George Meade that, given the chance, he could beat J. E. B. Stuart. Meade conferred with Ulysses S. Grant, and on May 8 Sheridan received orders to move southward, "engage Stuart, and clean him out." Sheridan hoped to find Stuart in an isolated position, cut off from Robert E. Lee's infantry.

Early on the morning of May 9, Sheridan set out with seven brigades, totaling nearly ten thousand troopers, to meet Stuart. That same day, Stuart received the news that Sheridan and his force were moving down Telegraph Road in the direction of Richmond. The Confederate general mobilized his three brigades to pursue the Union cavalry.

Sheridan veered his men southwest from Telegraph Road until they reached Beaver Dam, a Confederate supply base. There the Union troops destroyed precious rations and medical supplies and liberated over three hundred prisoners before continuing toward Richmond.

Arriving at Beaver Dam the next morning, Stuart surveyed the damage and tried to anticipate Sheridan's next move. He had information that Sheridan was traveling with an enormous number of soldiers; hence Stuart supposed that he planned to take Richmond. Yet Sheridan also might strike the Richmond, Fredericksburg, and Potomac Railroad. To ascertain Sheridan's real objective, Stuart sent one brigade to follow the Union troops while he took his remaining two

> **Stuart's corps continued to repulse Sheridan's division until dark as an ambulance carried Stuart to his brother-in-law's home in Richmond.**

brigades to rush toward Richmond in an attempt to place himself between the Confederate capital and the enemy.

That night, following on the heels of the Federal troops, Stuart and his men reached Hanover Junction where they briefly stopped to rest. At 1:00 A.M., they began moving again in the direction of Ashland, which they found in a shambles. During the night Sheridan's cavalry had torn up six miles of the railroad, destroyed several railroad cars, and burned Confederate storehouses.

Stuart forged ahead, and at 8:00 A.M. on May 11 he reached Yellow Tavern ahead of the Federal troops. Yellow Tavern sat at the junction of Mountain Brook Road from Louisa, Telegraph Road from Fredericksburg, and Brook Turnpike, which led into Richmond. There Stuart chose to wait for the Federals.

In the hours before Sheridan arrived, Stuart planned his strategy. He pondered whether to confront Sheridan's corps outright or rely on help from Braxton Bragg, the commanding officer in Richmond, and attempt to flank the Federals. Stuart sent a messenger to Bragg to ask him if he could hold Richmond, manned only by local troops.

At 11:00, before Bragg had time to answer Stuart's inquiry, Sheridan's troops began positioning themselves in front of the Confederate lines. Stuart chose to place his men, unmounted, along Mountain Road and hope for the best from Richmond. The Confederates held off the waves of Federal attacks through the afternoon. At 2:00 P.M. the messenger returned with Bragg's answer; he felt he could defend the capital with his four thousand local men. Stuart breathed easier.

After a lull in the fighting in the late afternoon, the Federals launched a coordinated attack at 4:00. They simultaneously struck both the center and the left of Stuart's line. On the extreme left, George Armstrong Custer's troops hit

Lunsford Lindsay Lomax's brigade particularly hard. Stuart rode to the left to lend encouragement to Lomax's men. Another wave of Federals advanced on the Confederates. In the ensuing melee the Southerners rallied and beat Custer's men back behind the Union lines.

Though the Confederates had managed to repel the latest Northern attack, a retreating Federal shot Stuart in his right side; the ball pierced his abdomen and lodged in his body. Stuart's corps continued to repulse Sheridan's division until dark as an ambulance carried Stuart to his brother-in-law's home in Richmond. He died the next day.

At Yellow Tavern, Stuart's cavalry succeeded in resisting the Federal move on the Confederate capital. Sheridan abandoned his position around Richmond and then moved east and down the Chickahominy River. He later stated that he chose not to enter Richmond because he would have lost five hundred to six hundred soldiers in the process, and he did not have sufficient strength to hold the city. Besides, he had already accomplished what he set out to do—beat J. E. B. Stuart.

BIBLIOGRAPHY

Freeman, Douglas. *Lee's Lieutenants: A Study in Command.* 3 vols. New York, 1942–1944. Reprint, New York, 1986.
Thomas, Emory M. *Bold Dragoon: The Life of J. E. B. Stuart.* New York, 1986.

JENNIFER LUND

YORK, ZEBULON

YORK, ZEBULON (1819–1890), brigadier general. Born on October 10, 1819, in Avon, Maine, York moved to Louisiana and became one of the state's wealthiest planters. When the war began he raised a company of infantry and was elected major of the Fourteenth Louisiana Volunteers. He later was promoted to lieutenant colonel and fought well at the Battle of Winchester, Virginia, where he was wounded.

Widely known as a very brave but profane officer, York became colonel of the regiment in August 1862 and was wounded again at Second Manassas. After serving at Sharpsburg and Fredericksburg, he spent much of 1863 in Louisiana recruiting and drilling conscripts. During the Wilderness campaign the First and Second Louisiana Brigades were consolidated under the overall command of Gen. Harry Thompson Hays. York was given command of the Second Brigade but apparently was absent at the Battle of Spotsylvania. When Hays was wounded at Spotsylvania, York was promoted to brigadier general on June 2, 1864, (to date from May 31) and given command of the consolidated brigade. He was the only Polish-American to become a Confederate general.

York's brigade participated in Jubal Early's raid on Washington and played a major role in his victory at Monocacy, where York's casualties ran at almost 50 percent. At the Third Battle of Winchester, York again was in the thick of the fighting and received a wound that led to the amputation of his arm. He ended his military career in Salisbury, North Carolina, trying unsuccessfully to gather recruits from the disillusioned German and Irish Union prisoners held there.

After the war, York moved to Natchez, Mississippi. Financially ruined by the war, he operated the York House until his death on August 5, 1890.

BIBLIOGRAPHY

Jones, Terry L. *Lee's Tigers: The Louisiana Infantry in the Army of Northern Virginia*. Baton Rouge, La., 1987.
Uminski, Sigmund H. "Poles and the Confederacy." *Polish-American Studies* 22 (1965): 99–106.

TERRY L. JONES

YORKTOWN, VIRGINIA

Throughout most of the month of April and early May 1862, Confederates under Maj. Gen. John B. Magruder held a much larger Federal army under Maj. Gen. George B. McClellan at bay along defensive lines established near Yorktown, Virginia. McClellan had landed at Fortress Monroe in March, planning to sweep up the Virginia Peninsula and threaten Richmond. Magruder had less than fifteen thousand men on the Yorktown line to oppose him, but Federal intelligence reports, offered in part by Allan Pinkerton, exaggerated that number.

Advance elements of the Union army reported the presence of the Confederate line of fortifications early on April 5. Rather than aggressively testing the strength of these defenses, McClellan chose to move cautiously. Marshy ground, muddy roads, and rainy conditions further compounded the Union general's problems.

Under these circumstances and lacking the cooperation he expected from the navy, McClellan decided to undertake siege operations. This was the type of military operation with which he was familiar, having participated in the Crimean War at the siege of Sevastopol as an observer from the United States. McClellan believed that this style of fighting was the surest way to prevent the heavy loss of life he had witnessed in frontal assaults against well-entrenched opponents. Early in the siege, he clearly expressed his desire to avoid "the faults of the Allies at Sebastopol."

Shortly after beginning the siege of Yorktown, McClellan received word that President Abraham Lincoln had decided to retain Maj. Gen. Irvin McDowell's corps in northern Virginia. The Union commander was outraged, seeing this as a sign of the lengths to which his political enemies would go to discredit him. McClellan was convinced that, should he fail to deliver a victory for the Union cause, the blame would lie with the president who he thought had sabotaged his campaign from the start.

Actually, Lincoln spent most of his time encouraging McClellan to act or attempting to bolster his confidence. He carefully stroked the general's ego, but added on one occasion, "you must act." Finally, on May 1, an exasperated President Lincoln inquired, "Is anything to be done?"

Magruder was responsible for some of McClellan's indecision and caution. He shrewdly deceived the Union commander by moving his minimal forces from point to point to magnify their numbers. At the same time, he desperately hoped that Gen. Joseph E. Johnston would arrive with the rest of the Confederate forces before McClellan found his nerve. Johnston shifted his forces and arrived himself at Yorktown late in April. He immediately determined that he would not be able to hold the Yorktown line against McClellan's larger army.

On May 3, the twenty-ninth day of the siege, McClellan sounded a depressed note to his wife, noting that he expected to be relieved of duty at any time. For weeks his men had dug entrenchments and dragged siege weapons into place through the mud. McClellan planned to unleash the full force of over one hundred heavy guns and mortars, but Johnston denied him the opportunity by pulling his 56,000 men out of their positions on the night of May 3–4. By midday on May 5, McClellan accepted the fact that his adversary had withdrawn and set his army in motion in pursuit.

BIBLIOGRAPHY

Cullen, Joseph P. *The Peninsula Campaign, 1862: McClellan & Lee Struggle for Richmond*. Harrisburg, Pa., 1973.
Marks, J. J. *The Peninsular Campaign in Virginia; or, Incidents and Scenes on the Battlefields and in Richmond*. Philadelphia, 1864.
Sears, Stephen W. *George B. McClellan: The Young Napoleon*. New York, 1988.
Sears, Stephen W. *To the Gates of Richmond: The Peninsula Campaign*. New York, 1992.

BRIAN S. WILLS

Z

ZOLLICOFFER, FELIX K.

ZOLLICOFFER, FELIX K. (1812–1862), U.S. congressman and brigadier general. Zollicoffer went down in Southern history as an early martyr to the cause. Of Swiss descent, he was born in Tennessee May 19, 1812, into the planter class and attended college for a year. As a newspaper editor, he rose in state political circles. In 1835 he was named state printer and served in the Second Seminole War. In the 1840s Zollicoffer edited the *Nashville Republican Banner,* the major Whig journal, which made him a political king-maker in the state. He served in the state senate and helped elect a governor and carry Tennessee for Winfield Scott in the 1852 presidential contest. He won a seat the same year in the U.S. House of Representatives, which he held for three terms. In 1860 he supported John Bell for president and later became a Unionist delegate to the Washington peace conference of 1861.

Abraham Lincoln's call for troops in April created a crisis of loyalties for this political moderate. Zollicoffer (nicknamed "Zollie") stood by his state and accepted a general's com-

> This brave leader, like so many others, was cut down at the outset of a promising military career and became one of the might-have-beens of history.

mission from Governor Isham G. Harris. In July he became a Confederate brigadier and was ordered to eastern Tennessee, where it was hoped his name would rally Unionists to the support of the state. Here his great opportunity came—and ended tragically.

In November he moved his small command to the Cumberland and then crossed the river into Kentucky. There he was encamped, the river at his rear, when Maj. Gen. George B. Crittenden, his immediate superior, arrived. With Union forces advancing on January 19, 1862, the two Confederates rushed to attack at Mill Springs. In the lead of his men, Zollicoffer was instantly killed by a Union volley. Had he ridden impulsively directly into enemy fire? This brave leader, like so many others, was cut down at the outset of a promising military career and became one of the might-have-beens of history. His body, graciously, was sent across the lines by his opponent, Gen. George H. Thomas. His name subsequently became the subject of much verse and memorialization in the wartime South: "A name in song and story 'He died on the field of glory.'"

BIBLIOGRAPHY

Connelly, Thomas L. *Army of the Heartland: The Army of Tennessee, 1861–1862.* Baton Rouge, La., 1967.

Horn, Stanley F. *The Army of Tennessee.* Indianapolis, 1941.

Myers, Raymond E. *The Zollie Tree.* Louisville, Ky., 1964.

Woodworth, Steven E. *Jefferson Davis and His Generals: The Failure of Confederate Command in the West.* Lawrence, Kans., 1990.

JOHN O'BRIEN

Index